GET INTO YOUR

HANDS-ON BIBLE!

Discover why the Hands-On Bible is the book you can't put down.

INTRODUCTIONS

tell you about things you won't want to miss in each book of the Bible.

These quick, funny overviews are written in a style you can relate to.

GENESIS
The Book of Beginnings

Look for 4 hidden messages in Genesis!

Genesis is all about beginnings. There's too much to tell here, so you'll just have to read the book yourself. IT'S AWESOME!

FAMOUS FIRSTS IN GENESIS

- CREATION OF THE WORLD
- FIRST MAN
- FIRST WOMAN
- FIRST MARRIAGE
- FIRST SIN
- FIRST RESULTS OF SIN
- FIRST KIDS
- FIRST MURDER
- FIRST TIME GOD POINTED OUT HIS PLAN TO SAVE PEOPLE FROM THEIR SIN

Trouble in Paradise

Adam and Eve, the first people God created, got busted. After eating the forbidden fruit, God questioned them, and the finger-pointing began.

"She made me do it," said Adam.

"The snake made me do it," said Eve.

The snake could not be reached for comment. **Read Genesis 3:14-24 to see God's reply.**

Sends you straight into the BIBLE!

Starting From Scratch

In a shocking move, God created the whole universe by just speaking. God said, "Let there be light." And there was light. It was the same way with the land, the animals—everything! All God had to say was "Let there be..."—and there was.

Not bad! In fact, according to God, it was all good. **For details, see Genesis 1:1–2:3.**

It's All Good!

Weather News

Rain, rain, and more rain

Noah's weather report from God was rain—and plenty of it. Forty days of rain, in fact. Enough rain to flood the whole earth. But God had a plan. **Read all about it in Genesis 6–8.**

COOL facts!

Colorful covenant... God said the rainbow would be the sign of his promise to never destroy the earth by flood again. Remember *that* the next time you see a rainbow!

How big?... The ark was four stories high. Go outside and look at your house. How many stories (floors) does it have? Imagine a boat four stories high!

Valuable INFO!

What Else?

Every introduction includes a **TIMELINE** to show you when the action took place. Dates from world history add to the fun!

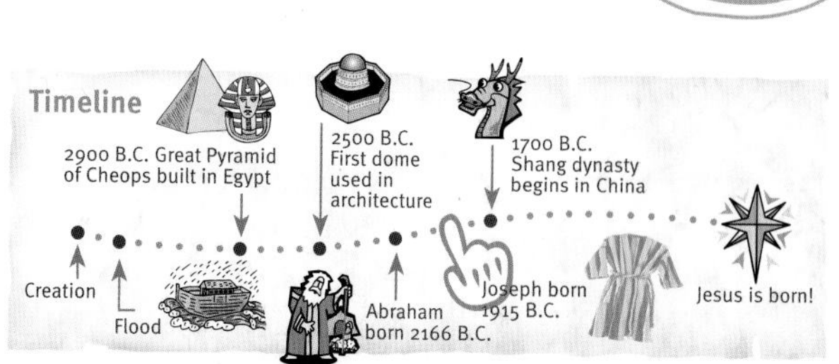

HANDS-ON BIBLE EXPERIENCES

This Bible will excite, ignite, and invite you to experience the Bible as you read it. **Science experiments, crafts, journals, snacks**—you'll *do* the Bible. And that means you'll *remember* the Bible!

Learn it!
Do it!
Share it!

Live it!

Can you find the secret message in this activity?

That's why we've included **SECRET MESSAGES** throughout the Bible that send you searching for *other* places in the Bible. Think of it as a Bible treasure hunt! You'll explore the Bible like never before and discover that God's Word is an amazing whole, not just disconnected books under one cover.

Did someone say
"hospital"?
No, the word is *hospitality*. And that's what Abraham showed his three visitors when he fed them a meal. **Read Genesis 18:1-15.** *Hospitality* means sharing your home and food. Make this snack to show hospitality the next time your friends come over.
Read Hebrews 13:2. Is this what happened to Abraham?
1
Cut a round pita bread in half. (A tortilla would work, too.)
2
Stuff with slices of cheese and lunchmeat.
3
Invite a few friends, and chow down!
I warmed my sandwich in the microwave!
You're on your way!
To practicing hospitality, that is. What other ways can you show hospitality to your friends this week?

BONUS
Free family devos, music, and more at
MyHandsOnBible.com

REAL BIBLE HEROES AND LOTS MORE

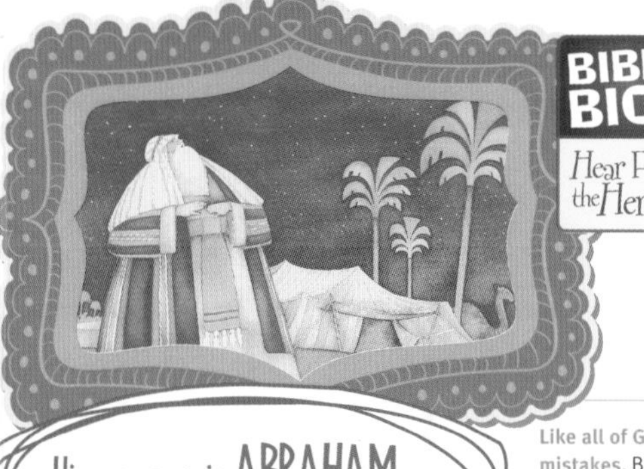

BIBLE BIOS
Hear From the Heroes

BIBLE HERO BIOGRAPHIES

talk straight to you, heart-to-heart. These heroes admit mistakes, joke around, confess when they're scared, and marvel at how God used them. Real people. Real heroes. Real Bible learning. And every biography gives you something to do.

Hi, my name is ABRAHAM
(shepherd, parent of a nation)

Like all of God's heroes (except Jesus), I made some whopper mistakes. But I know I did at least one thing right. When the Lord told me to leave my house and friends, I obeyed. God just said "go" and promised that my children would become a strong nation. But many years went by, and my wife, Sarah, and I almost gave up on God's promise. We still had no children, and we were old! Imagine your grandma and grandpa, or even your great-grandparents, having a baby. Well, that's exactly what happened to us. I was 100 years old and Sarah was 90 when we had Isaac—my wife just couldn't stop laughing! In fact, we picked a name for our son that showed our joy. Isaac means "laughter." That's no joke!

When Isaac grew into his teens, I had the worst day of my life. Read Genesis 22:1-18 to find out what happened. During that frightening day, I obeyed God, and God took care of my son and me. You'll probably make a few mistakes in your life, but whatever you do, obey God. If you follow God's lead, he'll take you to the right place.

Want to see a couple of them? Check out Genesis 12:10-20 and Genesis 20:1-7.

Around this time, God changed Abraham's name. If you want to know what it was before, check out Genesis 17:1-8.

And More

"In the beginning God created the heavens and the earth" (**GENESIS 1:1**).

Look at a sheet of dark construction paper. What do you see? Nothing, right? That's all there was—nothing!—until God set about creating the universe.

Look at GENESIS 1:2.

Read **GENESIS 1:1** out loud. Then take a sheet of light paper and get creative! Draw and color things God made: trees, birds, stars, the ocean, your family, **your dog**. Fill the page, just like God filled the heavens and earth!

Noah had to build a *big* boat to hold the animals. (**See what Noah was up to in GENESIS 6:9-22.**) The ark was as long as one and one-half football fields, as tall as a four-story building, and as wide as a city block.

If God had asked Noah to fill the ark with popcorn, he would have had to pop about 6 million bags. GOOD THING NOAH DIDN'T HAVE A MICROWAVE! Pop up a bag of popcorn to celebrate what God did to save the world.

Lots of FUN FACTS

How big was Noah's ark? How many steps did Abram's journey take? Lots of Fun Facts help you understand Bible-times culture, Bible story details, and key biblical concepts. Each Fun Fact helps you see the Bible as true and amazing.

The facts are fun, true, and—yup—hands-on!

Plus

52 KEY VERSE ACTIVITIES

help you learn, understand, and remember important Bible verses. That's one a week for a year! Plus, 52 more great verses are highlighted!

GET TO KNOW GOD BETTER WITH YOUR

HANDS-ON BIBLE

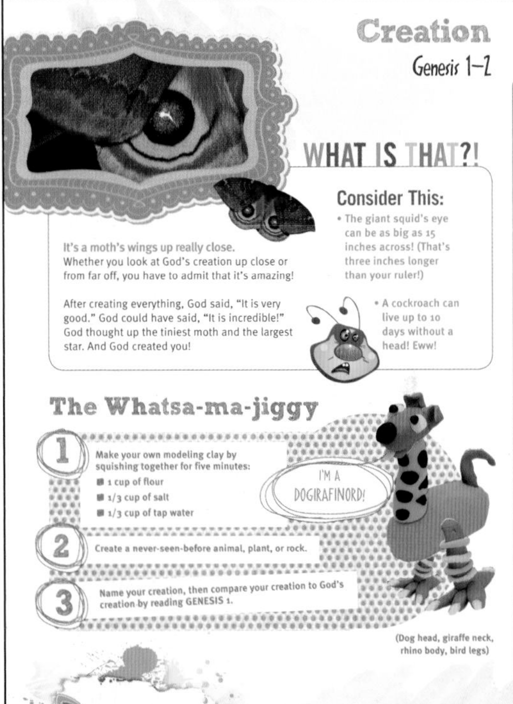

Creation

Genesis 1–2

WHAT IS THAT?!

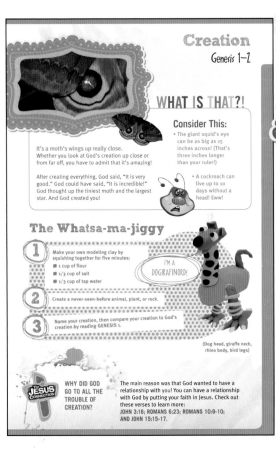

It's a moth's wings up really close.
Whether you look at God's creation up close or from far off, you have to admit that it's amazing!

After creating everything, God said, "It is very good." God could have said, "It is incredible!" God thought up the tiniest moth and the largest star. And God created you!

Consider This:

- The giant squid's eye can be as big as 15 inches across! (That's three inches longer than your ruler!)
- A cockroach can live up to 10 days without a head! Eww!

The Whatsa-ma-jiggy

1. Make your own modeling clay by squishing together for five minutes:
   - 1 cup of flour
   - 1/3 cup of salt
   - 1/3 cup of tap water
2. Create a never-seen-before animal, plant, or rock.
3. Name your creation, then compare your creation to God's creation by reading GENESIS 1.

I'M A DOGIRAFINORD!

(Dog head, giraffe neck, rhino body, bird legs)

The JESUS CONNECTION

WHY DID GOD GO TO ALL THE TROUBLE OF CREATION?

The main reason was that God wanted to have a relationship with you! You can have a relationship with God by putting your faith in Jesus. Check out these verses to learn more: JOHN 3:16; ROMANS 6:23; ROMANS 10:9-10; AND JOHN 15:15-17.

The BIGGEST stories you absolutely have to know.

FROM CREATION TO HEAVEN—

these full-color extravaganzas will wow you as you discover that *you* are part of God's BIG plan.

THE JESUS CONNECTION

God wants you to grow in your friendship with Jesus. Read THE JESUS CONNECTION in every book introduction and on every Bible Bonanza page. Discover how the focus of the Bible is Jesus!

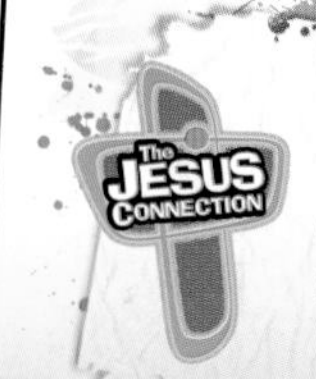

The JESUS CONNECTION

WHY DID GOD GO TO ALL THE TROUBLE OF CREATION?

The main reason was that God wanted to have a relationship with you! You can have a relationship with God by putting your faith in Jesus. Check out these verses to learn more: JOHN 3:16; ROMANS 6:23; ROMANS 10:9-10; AND JOHN 15:15-17.

HANDS-ON BIBLE®

UPDATED EDITION

Visit Group's exciting Web sites at www.MyHandsOnBible.com and www.group.com.

Visit Tyndale online at www.newlivingtranslation.com and www.tyndale.com.

ISBN 978-1-4143-3768-5 Hardcover
ISBN 978-1-4143-3769-2 Softcover
ISBN 978-1-4143-6827-6 LeatherLike Electric Blue
ISBN 978-1-4143-6828-3 LeatherLike Sugar Plum
ISBN 978-0-8423-3247-7 Royal Family Kids Camp edition

Printed in China

18 17 16 15 14
10 9 8 7 6

Tyndale House Publishers and Wycliffe Bible Translators share the vision for an understandable, accurate translation of the Bible for every person in the world. Each sale of the *Holy Bible,* New Living Translation, benefits Wycliffe Bible Translators. Wycliffe is working with partners around the world to accomplish Vision 2025—an initiative to start a Bible translation program in every language group that needs it by the year 2025.

Contents

THE OLD TESTAMENT

THE NEW TESTAMENT

FULL-COLOR BIBLE BONANZA EXPERIENCES

LOOKING FOR THE LOST . . . CAN YOU FIND THIS PAGE? --->

BIBLE HERO BIOS

OTHER COOL STUFF

Alphabetical Listing of Bible Books

How to Use This Bible

You've got the world's coolest Bible in your hands, so where do you start? Anywhere! Any page you open to in this Bible will be a good place to start. God's Word is great, from the first page to the last. Every word is true, inspired by God, and written for you!

If you've opened this Bible, you've probably noticed all the fun activities inside. Good! Here are a few tips about them.

Before you start any activity in this Bible, always check with a parent or teacher first. Here's why:

- **Some activities require adult help or supervision. An adult may know some safety precautions you haven't thought of.**
- **Sometimes it'll be easier to have an adult get the supplies you need.**
- **Some people have food allergies that can be dangerous. So before you do a snack activity, an adult can help you carefully read food labels to check for hidden ingredients that can cause allergy-related problems.**

So, are you ready to get started? Good for you! Remember, this is *your* Bible.

Read it.
Remember it.
Write in it.
Share it.
Measure it.
Treasure it.
Live it!

There's only one last rule—have FUN with it!

How to Find Your Way around the Bible

Finding your way around the Bible is easy!

The first thing is finding the book you want. Just go to the "Contents" page at the beginning of this Bible and look for the name of the book. That'll tell you what page to turn to. (If you already know the order of the books, look it up that way. If not, you can look up the name in the "Alphabetical Listing of Bible Books.")

Next, you'll want to find a certain chapter in that book. Each book of the Bible is divided into chapters and verses, and each chapter and verse has a number. The bigger numbers on the pages are the chapter numbers. You can also find the chapter numbers at the top of every page. The smaller numbers are the verse numbers.

Here's how a Bible verse is usually written. Let's say you want to find the first verse in the Bible. It would be written like this: Genesis 1:1. Here's what that means:

GENESIS 1:1

Here's the Book . . . the Chapter . . . the Verse.

See? It's the book of Genesis, chapter 1, verse 1. It's kind of like each verse has its own address. Let's try another one! Let's look up a verse about when Jesus was born.

LUKE 2:7

1

OK, first you find the BOOK OF LUKE.

Remember how? You got it! Look it up on the Contents page. (The more you read your Bible, the more you'll get to know the books. Pretty soon you won't even have to look at the list. Really!)

2

Next you need to find CHAPTER 2.

Just look for the bigger numbers.

3

Finally, look in CHAPTER 2 for the little number 7—that's VERSE 7.

Now read it! See? You just found a verse that tells a very important part of the history of the world. Way to go!

Now that you have the hang of it, try looking these up on your own! After you read each verse, write it out in your own words. Here's a list to start with: **JOHN 3:16; DEUTERONOMY 6:5; 1 CORINTHIANS 13:13; JEREMIAH 29:11.**

Here's another one that's a little tricky: **MATTHEW 28:5-7.** See the short line between the verse numbers? It means to read more than one verse. So here it means: Read verses 5 through 7.

Why Are There So Many Hard Words in the Bible?

What do you mean? Don't tell me you find Maher-shalal-hash-baz (Isaiah 8:1) hard to pronounce. Or what about Tahtim-hodshi (2 Samuel 24:6)? Piece of cake, right? (OK, just kidding.)

Sure, many words in the Bible are hard to pronounce and understand, especially names of people and places. That's because the Bible was written a long time ago in faraway places. (Even today, people from other countries have different-sounding names for people, places, and things, don't they? Try Heilongjiang, the name of a province in China!)

There are other words in the Bible that might not be as difficult to pronounce, but they're still not familiar to us. We don't use the word *tabernacle* too much in everyday talk, but it's an important word in the Bible—it's the tent where God originally lived among the Israelites (see Exodus 25:8-9).

Some other words seem strange to us because they come from other languages. The fifth book of the Bible, for instance, is called Deuteronomy. What does that mean? Actually, it's Greek for "second" (*deuter*) "law" (*nomos*). It's called that because in Deuteronomy Moses repeats much of the Law God gave him earlier on Mount Sinai.

Other words have big meanings that are hard to understand. For example, Jesus is called our "Mediator" in 1 Timothy 2:5. A mediator is someone who comes between two people who have a disagreement and works out a solution. God is deeply offended by sin, but Jesus took away our sin. He comes between God and us so we can have a friendly relationship again.

Even though you may stumble over the words once in a while, don't stop reading the Bible! Every time you open it, God is speaking to you.

Why Are There So Many Different Bible Versions?

The Bible wasn't originally written in English. In fact, different parts were written in different languages. Most of the Old Testament was written in ancient Hebrew. Small portions of the Old Testament were written in ancient Aramaic. The New Testament was originally written in ancient Greek. See a pattern?

God wants everyone in the world to read, understand, and believe the Bible. To meet this goal, people throughout the ages have translated the Bible into lots of different languages—English, Spanish, Chinese, French, Russian, and Arabic, to name a few. The list goes on and on. In some languages, the Bible has been translated more than once. That's because languages change over time. People don't speak and write English today the same way they did a hundred years ago, right? (Heard anyone say "Four score and seven years ago" lately?)

Bible translators have a special calling to make sure the Bible speaks clearly to as many people as possible. That's the main reason there are so many different versions of the Bible.

A Note to Readers

The *Holy Bible*, New Living Translation, was first published in 1996. It quickly became one of the most popular Bible translations in the English-speaking world. While the NLT's influence was rapidly growing, the Bible Translation Committee determined that an additional investment in scholarly review and text refinement could make it even better. So shortly after its initial publication, the committee began an eight-year process with the purpose of increasing the level of the NLT's precision without sacrificing its easy-to-understand quality. This second-generation text was completed in 2004, with minor changes subsequently introduced in 2007 and 2013.

The goal of any Bible translation is to convey the meaning and content of the ancient Hebrew, Aramaic, and Greek texts as accurately as possible to contemporary readers. The challenge for our translators was to create a text that would communicate as clearly and powerfully to today's readers as the original texts did to readers and listeners in the ancient biblical world. The resulting translation is easy to read and understand, while also accurately communicating the meaning and content of the original biblical texts. The NLT is a general-purpose text especially good for study, devotional reading, and reading aloud in worship services.

We believe that the New Living Translation—which combines the latest biblical scholarship with a clear, dynamic writing style—will communicate God's word powerfully to all who read it. We publish it with the prayer that God will use it to speak his timeless truth to the church and the world in a fresh, new way.

The Publishers
January 2013

Acknowledgments

The following people contributed to the *Hands-On Bible*:

Group Publishing, Inc., editorial team:
Joani Schultz, Sue Geiman, Karl Leuthauser, Jan Kershner, Lyndsay E. Gerwing, Alison Imbriaco, Zach Carlson, Becki Manni

Tyndale House Publishers, Inc., publishing team:
Douglas R. Knox, Blaine A. Smith, Kevin O'Brien, Kim Johnson, Tim Willms, Betty Free Swanberg, Pat LaCosse, Mark Norton, Leanne Rolland, Anisa Baker, Gwen Elliott

Writers:
Linda Anderson, Gwyn Borcherding, Teryl Cartwright, Nancy Wendland Feehrer, Jane Fries, Jennifer Hooks, Allison Hummel, Mikal Keefer, Scott M. Kinner, Gina Leuthauser, Carolyn Luengen, Nappaland Communications, Beth Robinson, Larry Shallenberger, Amy Simpson, Bonnie Temple, Helen Turnbull, Paul Woods

Designers and artists:
Sharon Anderson, Nancy Serbus, Allen Tefft, Stephen Beer, Jeff Spencer, Jacqueline L. Nuñez, Daniel Farrell, Joey Vining, Kate Elvin, Holly Voget, Rebecca Parrott, Toolbox Creative

Other artists include Mitch Mortimer, Joe Stites, Vlasta van Kampen, and Matt Wood

OLD TESTAMENT

GENESIS The Book of Beginnings

Look for 4 hidden messages in Genesis!

Genesis is all about beginnings. There's too much to tell here, so you'll just have to read the book yourself. **IT'S AWESOME!**

- **CREATION OF THE WORLD**
- **FIRST MAN**
- **FIRST WOMAN**
- **FIRST MARRIAGE**
- **FIRST SIN**
- **FIRST RESULTS OF SIN**
- **FIRST KIDS**
- **FIRST MURDER**
- **FIRST TIME GOD POINTED OUT HIS PLAN TO SAVE PEOPLE FROM THEIR SIN**

Starting From Scratch

In a shocking move, God created the whole universe by just speaking. God said, "Let there be light." And there was light. It was the same way with the land, the animals—everything! All God had to say was "Let there be..."—and there was.

Not bad! In fact, according to God, it was all good. **For details, see Genesis 1:1–2:3.**

It's All Good!

Trouble in Paradise

Adam and Eve, the first people God created, got busted. After eating the forbidden fruit, God questioned them, and the finger-pointing began.

"She made me do it," said Adam.

"The snake made me do it," said Eve.

The snake could not be reached for comment. **Read Genesis 3:14-24 to see God's reply.**

Garden of Eden Police Dept. #00002

Weather News

Rain, rain, and more rain

Noah's weather report from God was rain—and plenty of it. Forty days of rain, in fact. Enough rain to flood the whole earth. But God had a plan. **Read all about it in Genesis 6–8.**

Colorful covenant... God said the rainbow would be the sign of his promise to never destroy the earth by flood again. Remember *that* the next time you see a rainbow!

***How* big?...** The ark was four stories high. Go outside and look at your house. How many stories (floors) does it have? Imagine a boat four stories high!

The Birth of Israel

God told Abraham to leave his home and go to a new land far away. He obeyed God (unlike some *other* people in Genesis). God promised to give Abraham many children. God gave Abraham a son (Isaac). Isaac had kids, who had their own kids, who had kids—you get the picture. That's why Abraham is called the father of God's people. **Read the family history in Genesis 12–15.**

Real Estate News

Abraham

Lot

Abraham and Lot split land...
Abraham and his nephew Lot were involved in a real estate deal that made history. When God told Abraham to leave his home and travel, Abraham obeyed. He took all his stuff and family, including his nephew named Lot. Finally, they settled down, and that's when the trouble started. **See Genesis 13 for details.**

Dear Blabby

Tricky situation...

Q: My brother Jacob pulled a mean trick on me. Here's what happened. It all started one day when I was really hungry. **A: Find the answer in Genesis 25:19-34.**

Missing Person

Coat as clue?
Joseph, age 17, was last seen wearing a coat of many colors, a gift from his father. He disappeared while visiting his brothers, who were tending flocks away from home. **For the complete story, turn to Genesis 37:12-36.**

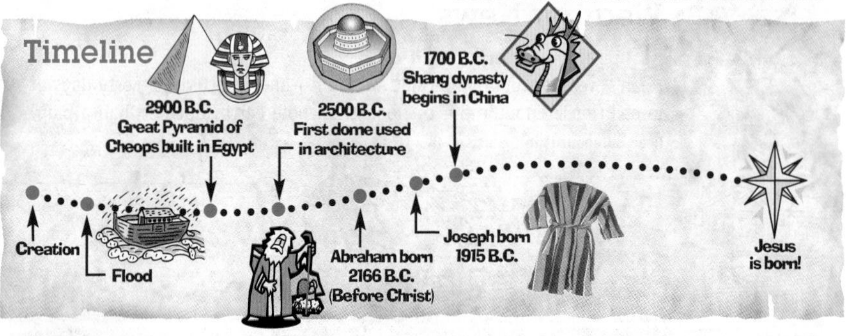

God wanted to be with Adam and Eve, but their sin broke the relationship. But even back then, God had a way planned to take away people's sin. That way is Jesus.

God gave a hint about Jesus in Genesis 3:15. "You will strike his heel" means that Satan tried to make Jesus sin during his time on earth. (It didn't work.) "He will strike your head" means that Jesus defeated Satan. (It *did* work!) **Check out 1 John 3:8 for proof.**

CHAPTER 1

The Account of Creation

**In the beginning God created the
heavens and the earth.** 2The earth was
formless and empty, and darkness covered the
deep waters. And the Spirit of God was hovering
over the surface of the waters.

3Then God said, "Let there be light," and there
was light. 4And God saw that the light was
good. Then he separated the light from the
darkness. 5God called the light "day" and
the darkness "night."

And evening passed and morning came,
marking the first day.

6Then God said, "Let there be a space between
the waters, to separate the waters of the
heavens from the waters of the earth." 7And
that is what happened. God made this space
to separate the waters of the earth from the
waters of the heavens. 8God called the space
"sky."

And evening passed and morning came,
marking the second day.

9Then God said, "Let the waters beneath the sky
flow together into one place, so dry ground
may appear." And that is what happened.
10God called the dry ground "land" and the
waters "seas." And God saw that it was good.
11Then God said, "Let the land sprout with
vegetation—every sort of seed-bearing plant,
and trees that grow seed-bearing fruit. These
seeds will then produce the kinds of plants
and trees from which they came." And that
is what happened. 12The land produced
vegetation—all sorts of seed-bearing plants,
and trees with seed-bearing fruit. Their
seeds produced plants and trees of the same
kind. And God saw that it was good.

13And evening passed and morning came,
marking the third day.

14Then God said, "Let lights appear in the
sky to separate the day from the night. Let
them be signs to mark the seasons, days,
and years. 15Let these lights in the sky
shine down on the earth." And that is what
happened. 16God made two great lights—the
larger one to govern the day, and the smaller
one to govern the night. He also made the
stars. 17God set these lights in the sky to light
the earth, 18to govern the day and night, and
to separate the light from the darkness. And
God saw that it was good.

19And evening passed and morning came,
marking the fourth day.

20Then God said, "Let the waters swarm with
fish and other life. Let the skies be filled
with birds of every kind." 21So God created
great sea creatures and every living thing
that scurries and swarms in the water, and
every sort of bird—each producing offspring
of the same kind. And God saw that it was
good. 22Then God blessed them, saying,
"Be fruitful and multiply. Let the fish fill the
seas, and let the birds multiply on the earth."

23And evening passed and morning came,
marking the fifth day.

24Then God said, "Let the earth produce every
sort of animal, each producing offspring of
the same kind—livestock, small animals that
scurry along the ground, and wild animals."
And that is what happened. 25God made all
sorts of wild animals, livestock, and small
animals, each able to produce offspring of
the same kind. And God saw that it was
good.

26Then God said, "Let us make human
beings in our image, to be like us. They will

before & after

"In the beginning God created the heavens and the earth" (**GENESIS 1:1**).

Look at a sheet of dark construction paper. What do you see? Nothing, right? That's all there was—nothing!—until God set about creating the universe.

Look at GENESIS 1:2.

Read **GENESIS 1:1** out loud. Then take a sheet of light paper and get creative! Draw and color things God made: trees, birds, stars, the ocean, your family, **your dog**. Fill the page, just like God filled the heavens and earth!

reign over the fish in the sea, the birds in the
sky, the livestock, all the wild animals on the
earth, and the small animals that scurry
along the ground."

27 So God created human beings in his own
image.
In the image of God he created them;
male and female he created them.

28Then God blessed them and said, "Be
fruitful and multiply. Fill the earth and
govern it. Reign over the fish in the sea, the
birds in the sky, and all the animals that
scurry along the ground."
29Then God said, "Look! I have given you
every seed-bearing plant throughout the
earth and all the fruit trees for your food.
30And I have given every green plant as food
for all the wild animals, the birds in the sky,
and the small animals that scurry along the
ground—everything that has life." And that
is what happened.
31Then God looked over all he had made,
and he saw that it was very good!
And evening passed and morning came,
marking the sixth day.

CHAPTER 2

So the creation of the heavens and the earth
and everything in them was completed.
2On the seventh day God had finished his
work of creation, so he rested from all his
work. 3And God blessed the seventh day and
declared it holy, because it was the day when
he rested from all his work of creation.

4This is the account of the creation of the heavens
and the earth.

The Man and Woman in Eden

When the LORD God made the earth and the
heavens, 5neither wild plants nor grains were
growing on the earth. For the LORD God had not
yet sent rain to water the earth, and there were no
people to cultivate the soil. 6Instead, springs
came up from the ground and watered all the
land. 7Then the LORD God formed the man from
the dust of the ground. He breathed the breath of
life into the man's nostrils, and the man became a
living person.
8Then the LORD God planted a garden in Eden
in the east, and there he placed the man he had
made. 9The LORD God made all sorts of trees
grow up from the ground—trees that were beautiful and that produced delicious fruit. In the
middle of the garden he placed the tree of life
and the tree of the knowledge of good and evil.
10A river flowed from the land of Eden, watering the garden and then dividing into four
branches. 11The first branch, called the Pishon,
flowed around the entire land of Havilah, where
gold is found. 12The gold of that land is excep-
tionally pure; aromatic resin and onyx stone are
also found there. 13The second branch, called the
Gihon, flowed around the entire land of Cush.
14The third branch, called the Tigris, flowed east
of the land of Asshur. The fourth branch is called
the Euphrates.
15The LORD God placed the man in the Garden
of Eden to tend and watch over it. 16But the LORD
God warned him, "You may freely eat the fruit of
every tree in the garden—17except the tree of the
knowledge of good and evil. If you eat its fruit,
you are sure to die."
18Then the LORD God said, "It is not good for
the man to be alone. I will make a helper who is
just right for him." 19So the LORD God formed
from the ground all the wild animals and all the
birds of the sky. He brought them to the man to
see what he would call them, and the man chose a
name for each one. 20He gave names to all the
livestock, all the birds of the sky, and all the wild
animals. But still there was no helper just right for
him.
21So the LORD God caused the man to fall into
a deep sleep. While the man slept, the LORD God
took out one of the man's ribs and closed up the
opening. 22Then the LORD God made a woman
from the rib, and he brought her to the man.
23"At last!" the man exclaimed.

"This one is bone from my bone,
and flesh from my flesh!
She will be called 'woman,'
because she was taken from 'man.'"

24This explains why a man leaves his father
and mother and is joined to his wife, and the two
are united into one.
25Now the man and his wife were both naked,
but they felt no shame.

CHAPTER 3

The Man and Woman Sin

The serpent was the shrewdest of all the wild animals the LORD God had made. One day he asked
the woman, "Did God really say you must not eat
the fruit from any of the trees in the garden?"
2"Of course we may eat fruit from the trees in
the garden," the woman replied. 3"It's only the
fruit from the tree in the middle of the garden

"Thumb-thing" to Think About

Read Genesis 3. Adam and Eve messed up big time by disobeying. Then they tried to hide from God. Duh!

1 **Use a washable marker to scribble on the bottom of your thumb.**

2 **Press your thumb on a clean piece of paper.**

STOP! You see your thumbprint. But did you know your fingerprints are on everything you touch? You can't see them, but they're there.

God didn't need fingerprints to bust Adam and Eve. **GOD SEES EVERYTHING.** But God *wants* to forgive us—that's why he sent Jesus. When we believe in Jesus and tell God we're sorry, he'll wash away our sins!

that we are not allowed to eat. God said, 'You must
not eat it or even touch it; if you do, you will die.'"
4"You won't die!" the serpent replied to the
woman. 5"God knows that your eyes will be
opened as soon as you eat it, and you will be like
God, knowing both good and evil."
6The woman was convinced. She saw that the
tree was beautiful and its fruit looked delicious,
and she wanted the wisdom it would give her. So
she took some of the fruit and ate it. Then she
gave some to her husband, who was with her, and
he ate it, too. 7At that moment their eyes were
opened, and they suddenly felt shame at their
nakedness. So they sewed fig leaves together to
cover themselves.
8When the cool evening breezes were blowing, the man and his wife heard the LORD God
walking about in the garden. So they hid from
the LORD God among the trees. 9Then the LORD
God called to the man, "Where are you?"
10He replied, "I heard you walking in the garden, so I hid. I was afraid because I was naked."
11"Who told you that you were naked?" the
LORD God asked. "Have you eaten from the tree
whose fruit I commanded you not to eat?"
12The man replied, "It was the woman you gave
me who gave me the fruit, and I ate it."
13Then the LORD God asked the woman, "What
have you done?"
"The serpent deceived me," she replied.
"That's why I ate it."
14Then the LORD God said to the serpent,

"Because you have done this, you are cursed
more than all animals, domestic and wild.
You will crawl on your belly,
groveling in the dust as long as you live.
15 And I will cause hostility between you and
the woman,
and between your offspring and her
offspring.
He will strike your head,
and you will strike his heel."

16Then he said to the woman,

"I will sharpen the pain of your pregnancy,
and in pain you will give birth.
And you will desire to control your husband,
but he will rule over you."

17And to the man he said,

"Since you listened to your wife and ate from
the tree
whose fruit I commanded you not to eat,
the ground is cursed because of you.
All your life you will struggle to scratch
a living from it.
18 It will grow thorns and thistles for you,
though you will eat of its grains.
19 By the sweat of your brow
will you have food to eat
until you return to the ground
from which you were made.
For you were made from dust,
and to dust you will return."

Paradise Lost: God's Judgment

20Then the man—Adam—named his wife Eve,
because she would be the mother of all who live.
21And the LORD God made clothing from animal
skins for Adam and his wife.
22Then the LORD God said, "Look, the human
beings have become like us, knowing both good
and evil. What if they reach out, take fruit from
the tree of life, and eat it? Then they will live forever!" 23So the LORD God banished them from the
Garden of Eden, and he sent Adam out to cultivate
the ground from which he had been made.
24After sending them out, the LORD God stationed
mighty cherubim to the east of the Garden of
Eden. And he placed a flaming sword that flashed
back and forth to guard the way to the tree of life.

CHAPTER 4

Cain and Abel

Now Adam had sexual relations with his wife,
Eve, and she became pregnant. When she gave
birth to Cain, she said, "With the LORD's help, I
have produced a man!" 2Later she gave birth to
his brother and named him Abel.

When they grew up, Abel became a shepherd,
while Cain cultivated the ground. 3When it was
time for the harvest, Cain presented some of his
crops as a gift to the LORD. 4Abel also brought a
gift—the best portions of the firstborn lambs
from his flock. The LORD accepted Abel and his
gift, 5but he did not accept Cain and his gift. This
made Cain very angry, and he looked dejected.

6"Why are you so angry?" the LORD asked
Cain. "Why do you look so dejected? 7You will be
accepted if you do what is right. But if you refuse
to do what is right, then watch out! Sin is crouching at the door, eager to control you. But you
must subdue it and be its master."

8One day Cain suggested to his brother, "Let's
go out into the fields." And while they were in the
field, Cain attacked his brother, Abel, and killed
him.

9Afterward the LORD asked Cain, "Where is
your brother? Where is Abel?"

"I don't know," Cain responded. "Am I my
brother's guardian?"

10But the LORD said, "What have you done?
Listen! Your brother's blood cries out to me from
the ground! 11Now you are cursed and banished
from the ground, which has swallowed your
brother's blood. 12No longer will the ground
yield good crops for you, no matter how hard you
work! From now on you will be a homeless wanderer on the earth."

13Cain replied to the LORD, "My punishment is
too great for me to bear! 14You have banished me
from the land and from your presence; you have
made me a homeless wanderer. Anyone who
finds me will kill me!"

15The LORD replied, "No, for I will give a sevenfold punishment to anyone who kills you." Then
the LORD put a mark on Cain to warn anyone who
might try to kill him. 16So Cain left the LORD's
presence and settled in the land of Nod, east of
Eden.

The Descendants of Cain

17Cain had sexual relations with his wife, and she
became pregnant and gave birth to Enoch. Then
Cain founded a city, which he named Enoch, after his son. 18Enoch had a son named Irad. Irad
became the father of Mehujael. Mehujael became the father of Methushael. Methushael
became the father of Lamech.

19Lamech married two women. The first was
named Adah, and the second was Zillah. 20Adah
gave birth to Jabal, who was the first of those who
raise livestock and live in tents. 21His brother's
name was Jubal, the first of all who play the harp
and flute. 22Lamech's other wife, Zillah, gave
birth to a son named Tubal-cain. He became an
expert in forging tools of bronze and iron. Tubal-
cain had a sister named Naamah. 23One day
Lamech said to his wives,

"Adah and Zillah, hear my voice;
  listen to me, you wives of Lamech.
I have killed a man who attacked me,
  a young man who wounded me.
24 If someone who kills Cain is punished
    seven times,
  then the one who kills me will be
    punished seventy-seven times!"

The Birth of Seth

25Adam had sexual relations with his wife again,
and she gave birth to another son. She named
him Seth, for she said, "God has granted me another son in place of Abel, whom Cain killed."
26When Seth grew up, he had a son and named
him Enosh. At that time people first began to
worship the LORD by name.

CHAPTER 5

The Descendants of Adam

This is the written account of the descendants of
Adam. When God created human beings, he
made them to be like himself. 2He created them
male and female, and he blessed them and called
them "human."

3When Adam was 130 years old, he became the
father of a son who was just like him—in his
very image. He named his son Seth. 4After the
birth of Seth, Adam lived another 800 years,
and he had other sons and daughters. 5Adam
lived 930 years, and then he died.

6When Seth was 105 years old, he became the
father of Enosh. 7After the birth of Enosh,
Seth lived another 807 years, and he had
other sons and daughters. 8Seth lived 912
years, and then he died.

9When Enosh was 90 years old, he became the
father of Kenan. 10After the birth of Kenan,
Enosh lived another 815 years, and he had
other sons and daughters. 11Enosh lived
905 years, and then he died.

12When Kenan was 70 years old, he became

the father of Mahalalel. 13After the birth of
Mahalalel, Kenan lived another 840 years,
and he had other sons and daughters.
14Kenan lived 910 years, and then he died.
15When Mahalalel was 65 years old, he became
the father of Jared. 16After the birth of Jared,
Mahalalel lived another 830 years, and he
had other sons and daughters. 17Mahalalel
lived 895 years, and then he died.
18When Jared was 162 years old, he became the
father of Enoch. 19After the birth of Enoch,
Jared lived another 800 years, and he had
other sons and daughters. 20Jared lived 962
years, and then he died.
21When Enoch was 65 years old, he became the
father of Methuselah. 22After the birth of
Methuselah, Enoch lived in close fellowship
with God for another 300 years, and he had
other sons and daughters. 23Enoch lived
365 years, 24walking in close fellowship with
God. Then one day he disappeared, because
God took him.
25When Methuselah was 187 years old, he
became the father of Lamech. 26After the
birth of Lamech, Methuselah lived another
782 years, and he had other sons and
daughters. 27Methuselah lived 969 years,
and then he died.
28When Lamech was 182 years old, he became
the father of a son. 29Lamech named his son
Noah, for he said, "May he bring us relief
from our work and the painful labor of
farming this ground that the LORD has
cursed." 30After the birth of Noah, Lamech
lived another 595 years, and he had other
sons and daughters. 31Lamech lived
777 years, and then he died.
32After Noah was 500 years old, he became the
father of Shem, Ham, and Japheth.

CHAPTER 6
A World Gone Wrong

Then the people began to multiply on the earth,
and daughters were born to them. 2The sons of
God saw the beautiful women and took any they
wanted as their wives. 3Then the LORD said, "My
Spirit will not put up with humans for such a long
time, for they are only mortal flesh. In the future,
their normal lifespan will be no more than
120 years."

4In those days, and for some time after, giant
Nephilites lived on the earth, for whenever the
sons of God had intercourse with women, they
gave birth to children who became the heroes
and famous warriors of ancient times.

5The LORD observed the extent of human
wickedness on the earth, and he saw that everything they thought or imagined was consistently
and totally evil. 6So the LORD was sorry he had
ever made them and put them on the earth. It
broke his heart. 7And the LORD said, "I will wipe
this human race I have created from the face of
the earth. Yes, and I will destroy every living
thing—all the people, the large animals, the small
animals that scurry along the ground, and even
the birds of the sky. I am sorry I ever made them."
8But Noah found favor with the LORD.

The Story of Noah

9This is the account of Noah and his family.
Noah was a righteous man, the only blameless
person living on earth at the time, and he walked
in close fellowship with God. 10Noah was the father of three sons: Shem, Ham, and Japheth.

11Now God saw that the earth had become
corrupt and was filled with violence. 12God observed all this corruption in the world, for everyone on earth was corrupt. 13So God said to Noah,
"I have decided to destroy all living creatures, for
they have filled the earth with violence. Yes, I will
wipe them all out along with the earth!

14"Build a large boat from cypress wood and
waterproof it with tar, inside and out. Then construct decks and stalls throughout its interior.
15Make the boat 450 feet long, 75 feet wide, and
45 feet high. 16Leave an 18-inch opening below
the roof all the way around the boat. Put the door
on the side, and build three decks inside the
boat—lower, middle, and upper.

17"Look! I am about to cover the earth with a
flood that will destroy every living thing that
breathes. Everything on earth will die. 18But I will
confirm my covenant with you. So enter the
boat—you and your wife and your sons and their
wives. 19Bring a pair of every kind of animal—a
male and a female—into the boat with you to
keep them alive during the flood. 20Pairs of every
kind of bird, and every kind of animal, and every
kind of small animal that scurries along the
ground, will come to you to be kept alive. 21And
be sure to take on board enough food for your
family and for all the animals."

22So Noah did everything exactly as God had
commanded him.

CHAPTER 7
The Flood Covers the Earth

When everything was ready, the LORD said to
Noah, "Go into the boat with all your family, for
among all the people of the earth, I can see that

you alone are righteous. 2Take with you seven pairs—male and female—of each animal I have approved for eating and for sacrifice, and take one pair of each of the others. 3Also take seven pairs of every kind of bird. There must be a male and a female in each pair to ensure that all life will survive on the earth after the flood. 4Seven days from now I will make the rains pour down on the earth. And it will rain for forty days and forty nights, until I have wiped from the earth all the living things I have created."

5So Noah did everything as the LORD commanded him.

6Noah was 600 years old when the flood covered the earth. 7He went on board the boat to escape the flood—he and his wife and his sons and their wives. 8With them were all the various kinds of animals—those approved for eating and for sacrifice and those that were not—along with all the birds and the small animals that scurry along the ground. 9They entered the boat in pairs, male and female, just as God had commanded Noah. 10After seven days, the waters of the flood came and covered the earth.

11When Noah was 600 years old, on the seventeenth day of the second month, all the underground waters erupted from the earth, and the rain fell in mighty torrents from the sky. 12The rain continued to fall for forty days and forty nights.

13That very day Noah had gone into the boat with his wife and his sons—Shem, Ham, and Japheth—and their wives. 14With them in the boat were pairs of every kind of animal—domestic and wild, large and small—along with birds of every kind. 15Two by two they came into the boat, representing every living thing that breathes. 16A male and female of each kind entered, just as God had commanded Noah. Then the LORD closed the door behind them.

17For forty days the floodwaters grew deeper, covering the ground and lifting the boat high above the earth. 18As the waters rose higher and higher above the ground, the boat floated safely on the surface. 19Finally, the water covered even the highest mountains on the earth, 20rising more than twenty-two feet above the highest peaks. 21All the living things on earth died—birds, domestic animals, wild animals, small animals that scurry along the ground, and all the people. 22Everything that breathed and lived on dry land died. 23God wiped out every living thing on the earth—people, livestock, small animals that scurry along the ground, and the birds of the sky. All were destroyed. The only people who survived were Noah and those with him in the boat. 24And the floodwaters covered the earth for 150 days.

CHAPTER 8

The Flood Recedes

But God remembered Noah and all the wild animals and livestock with him in the boat. He sent a wind to blow across the earth, and the floodwaters began to recede. 2The underground waters stopped flowing, and the torrential rains from the sky were stopped. 3So the floodwaters gradually receded from the earth. After 150 days, 4exactly five months from the time the flood began, the boat came to rest on the mountains of Ararat. 5Two and a half months later, as the waters continued to go down, other mountain peaks became visible.

6After another forty days, Noah opened the window he had made in the boat 7and released a raven. The bird flew back and forth until the floodwaters on the earth had dried up. 8He also released a dove to see if the water had receded and it could find dry ground. 9But the dove could find no place to land because the water still covered the ground. So it returned to the boat, and Noah held out his hand and drew the dove back inside. 10After waiting another seven days, Noah released the dove again. 11This time the dove returned to him in the evening with a fresh olive leaf in its beak. Then Noah knew that the floodwaters were almost gone. 12He waited another seven days and then released the dove again. This time it did not come back.

13Noah was now 601 years old. On the first day of the new year, ten and a half months after the flood began, the floodwaters had almost dried up from the earth. Noah lifted back the covering of the boat and saw that the surface of the ground was drying. 14Two more months went by, and at last the earth was dry!

15Then God said to Noah, 16"Leave the boat, all of you—you and your wife, and your sons and their wives. 17Release all the animals—the birds, the livestock, and the small animals that scurry along the ground—so they can be fruitful and multiply throughout the earth."

18So Noah, his wife, and his sons and their wives left the boat. 19And all of the large and small animals and birds came out of the boat, pair by pair.

20Then Noah built an altar to the LORD, and there he sacrificed as burnt offerings the animals and birds that had been approved for that purpose. 21And the LORD was pleased with the

aroma of the sacrifice and said to himself, "I will
never again curse the ground because of the human race, even though everything they think or
imagine is bent toward evil from childhood. I
will never again destroy all living things. 22As
long as the earth remains, there will be planting
and harvest, cold and heat, summer and winter,
day and night."

CHAPTER 9

God Confirms His Covenant

Then God blessed Noah and his sons and told
them, "Be fruitful and multiply. Fill the earth. 2All
the animals of the earth, all the birds of the sky, all
the small animals that scurry along the ground,
and all the fish in the sea will look on you with fear
and terror. I have placed them in your power. 3I
have given them to you for food, just as I have
given you grain and vegetables. 4But you must
never eat any meat that still has the lifeblood in it.

5"And I will require the blood of anyone who
takes another person's life. If a wild animal kills a
person, it must die. And anyone who murders a
fellow human must die. 6If anyone takes a human life, that person's life will also be taken by
human hands. For God made human beings in
his own image. 7Now be fruitful and multiply,
and repopulate the earth."

8Then God told Noah and his sons, 9"I hereby confirm my covenant with you and your descendants, 10and with all the animals that were
on the boat with you—the birds, the livestock,
and all the wild animals—every living creature
on earth. 11Yes, I am confirming my covenant
with you. Never again will floodwaters kill all
living creatures; never again will a flood destroy
the earth."

12Then God said, "I am giving you a sign of my
covenant with you and with all living creatures, for
all generations to come. 13I have placed my rainbow in the clouds. It is the sign of my covenant
with you and with all the earth. 14When I send
clouds over the earth, the rainbow will appear in
the clouds, 15and I will remember my covenant
with you and with all living creatures. Never again
will the floodwaters destroy all life. 16When I see
the rainbow in the clouds, I will remember the
eternal covenant between God and every living
creature on earth." 17Then God said to Noah, "Yes,
this rainbow is the sign of the covenant I am confirming with all the creatures on earth."

Noah's Sons

18The sons of Noah who came out of the boat
with their father were Shem, Ham, and Japheth.

i promise!
The rainbow was—and is—God's sign of the covenant he made with all life on earth. **Check it out in GENESIS 9:8-17.** How cool that the Creator of the whole universe remembers his promise every time a rainbow appears. Here's something to help you remember to live for God.
A covenant is a promise.
1
Cut a paper plate in half. Color or paint a rainbow on the plate half.
2
be nice to my sister
Cut raindrops from heavy paper. On each raindrop, write a promise to God.
3
Tape lengths of yarn to the raindrops, then tape the yarn to the back of the rainbow.
I won't SAY BAD WORDS
be nice to my sister
Help my Parents
do my chores
Hang your rainbow in a window where you'll see it every day. Remember your promises, just like God remembers his.

Genesis 10 . . . page 12

Noah had to build a *big* boat to hold the animals. **(See what Noah was up to in GENESIS 6:9-22.)** The ark was as long as one and one-half football fields, as tall as a four-story building, and as wide as a city block.

If God had asked Noah to fill the ark with popcorn, he would have had to pop about 6 million bags. GOOD THING NOAH DIDN'T HAVE A MICROWAVE! Pop up a bag of popcorn to celebrate what God did to save the world.

(Ham is the father of Canaan.) 19From these three
sons of Noah came all the people who now popu-
late the earth.

20After the flood, Noah began to cultivate the
ground, and he planted a vineyard. 21One day
he drank some wine he had made, and he became drunk and lay naked inside his tent.
22Ham, the father of Canaan, saw that his father
was naked and went outside and told his brothers. 23Then Shem and Japheth took a robe, held
it over their shoulders, and backed into the tent
to cover their father. As they did this, they
looked the other way so they would not see him
naked.

24When Noah woke up from his stupor, he
learned what Ham, his youngest son, had done.
25Then he cursed Canaan, the son of Ham:

"May Canaan be cursed!
May he be the lowest of servants to his
relatives."

26Then Noah said,

"May the Lord, the God of Shem, be blessed,
and may Canaan be his servant!
27 May God expand the territory of Japheth!
May Japheth share the prosperity of Shem,
and may Canaan be his servant."

28Noah lived another 350 years after the great
flood. 29He lived 950 years, and then he died.

CHAPTER 10

This is the account of the families of Shem, Ham, and Japheth, the three sons of Noah. Many children were born to them after the great flood.

Descendants of Japheth

2The descendants of Japheth were Gomer,
Magog, Madai, Javan, Tubal, Meshech, and
Tiras.
3The descendants of Gomer were Ashkenaz,
Riphath, and Togarmah.
4The descendants of Javan were Elishah,
Tarshish, Kittim, and Rodanim. 5Their
descendants became the seafaring peoples
that spread out to various lands, each
identified by its own language, clan, and
national identity.

Descendants of Ham

6The descendants of Ham were Cush, Mizraim,
Put, and Canaan.
7The descendants of Cush were Seba,
Havilah, Sabtah, Raamah, and Sabteca.
The descendants of Raamah were Sheba
and Dedan.
8Cush was also the ancestor of Nimrod,
who was the first heroic warrior on earth.
9Since he was the greatest hunter in the
world, his name became proverbial. People
would say, "This man is like Nimrod, the
greatest hunter in the world." 10He built his
kingdom in the land of Babylonia, with the
cities of Babylon, Erech, Akkad, and Calneh.
11From there he expanded his territory to
Assyria, building the cities of Nineveh,
Rehoboth-ir, Calah, 12and Resen (the great
city located between Nineveh and Calah).
13Mizraim was the ancestor of the Ludites,
Anamites, Lehabites, Naphtuhites, 14Path-
rusites, Casluhites, and the Caphtorites, from
whom the Philistines came.
15Canaan's oldest son was Sidon, the ancestor of
the Sidonians. Canaan was also the ancestor
of the Hittites, 16Jebusites, Amorites, Girgashites, 17Hivites, Arkites, Sinites, 18Arvadites,
Zemarites, and Hamathites. The Canaanite
clans eventually spread out, 19and the
territory of Canaan extended from Sidon
in the north to Gerar and Gaza in the south,
and east as far as Sodom, Gomorrah, Admah,
and Zeboiim, near Lasha.
20These were the descendants of Ham, identified by clan, language, territory, and national
identity.

Descendants of Shem
21 Sons were also born to Shem, the older
brother of Japheth. Shem was the ancestor
of all the descendants of Eber.
22 The descendants of Shem were Elam, Asshur,
Arphaxad, Lud, and Aram.
23 The descendants of Aram were Uz, Hul,
Gether, and Mash.
24 Arphaxad was the father of Shelah, and
Shelah was the father of Eber.
25 Eber had two sons. The first was named Peleg
(which means "division"), for during his
lifetime the people of the world were divided
into different language groups. His brother's
name was Joktan.
26 Joktan was the ancestor of Almodad,
Sheleph, Hazarmaveth, Jerah, 27 Hadoram,
Uzal, Diklah, 28 Obal, Abimael, Sheba,
29 Ophir, Havilah, and Jobab. All these were
descendants of Joktan. 30 The territory they
occupied extended from Mesha all the way
to Sephar in the eastern mountains.
31 These were the descendants of Shem, identified by clan, language, territory, and national
identity.

Conclusion
32 These are the clans that descended from
Noah's sons, arranged by nation according to
their lines of descent. All the nations of the earth
descended from these clans after the great
flood.

CHAPTER 11
The Tower of Babel
At one time all the people of the world spoke the
same language and used the same words. 2 As the
people migrated to the east, they found a plain in
the land of Babylonia and settled there.

3 They began saying to each other, "Let's make
bricks and harden them with fire." (In this region
bricks were used instead of stone, and tar was
used for mortar.) 4 Then they said, "Come, let's
build a great city for ourselves with a tower that
reaches into the sky. This will make us famous
and keep us from being scattered all over the
world."

5 But the LORD came down to look at the city
and the tower the people were building. 6 "Look!"
he said. "The people are united, and they all
speak the same language. After this, nothing
they set out to do will be impossible for them!
7 Come, let's go down and confuse the people
with different languages. Then they won't be
able to understand each other."

8 In that way, the LORD scattered them all over
the world, and they stopped building the city.
9 That is why the city was called Babel, because
that is where the LORD confused the people with
different languages. In this way he scattered
them all over the world.

The Line of Descent from Shem to Abram
10 This is the account of Shem's family.

Two years after the great flood, when Shem
was 100 years old, he became the father of
Arphaxad. 11 After the birth of Arphaxad,
Shem lived another 500 years and had other
sons and daughters.
12 When Arphaxad was 35 years old, he became
the father of Shelah. 13 After the birth of
Shelah, Arphaxad lived another 403 years
and had other sons and daughters.
14 When Shelah was 30 years old, he became
the father of Eber. 15 After the birth of Eber,
Shelah lived another 403 years and had
other sons and daughters.
16 When Eber was 34 years old, he became the
father of Peleg. 17 After the birth of Peleg,
Eber lived another 430 years and had other
sons and daughters.
18 When Peleg was 30 years old, he became the
father of Reu. 19 After the birth of Reu, Peleg
lived another 209 years and had other sons
and daughters.
20 When Reu was 32 years old, he became the
father of Serug. 21 After the birth of Serug,
Reu lived another 207 years and had other
sons and daughters.
22 When Serug was 30 years old, he became the
father of Nahor. 23 After the birth of Nahor,
Serug lived another 200 years and had other
sons and daughters.
24 When Nahor was 29 years old, he became the
father of Terah. 25 After the birth of Terah,
Nahor lived another 119 years and had other
sons and daughters.
26 After Terah was 70 years old, he became the
father of Abram, Nahor, and Haran.

The Family of Terah
27 This is the account of Terah's family. Terah was
the father of Abram, Nahor, and Haran; and Haran was the father of Lot. 28 But Haran died in Ur
of the Chaldeans, the land of his birth, while his
father, Terah, was still living. 29 Meanwhile,
Abram and Nahor both married. The name of
Abram's wife was Sarai, and the name of Nahor's

wife was Milcah. (Milcah and her sister Iscah were daughters of Nahor's brother Haran.) 30But Sarai was unable to become pregnant and had no children.

31One day Terah took his son Abram, his daughter-in-law Sarai (his son Abram's wife), and his grandson Lot (his son Haran's child) and moved away from Ur of the Chaldeans. He was headed for the land of Canaan, but they stopped at Haran and settled there. 32Terah lived for 205 years and died while still in Haran.

CHAPTER 12

The Call of Abram

The LORD had said to Abram, "Leave your native country, your relatives, and your father's family, and go to the land that I will show you. 2I will make you into a great nation. I will bless you and make you famous, and you will be a blessing to others. 3I will bless those who bless you and curse those who treat you with contempt. All the families on earth will be blessed through you."

4So Abram departed as the LORD had instructed, and Lot went with him. Abram was seventy-five years old when he left Haran. 5He took his wife, Sarai, his nephew Lot, and all his wealth—his livestock and all the people he had taken into his household at Haran—and headed for the land of Canaan. When they arrived in Canaan, 6Abram traveled through the land as far as Shechem. There he set up camp beside the oak of Moreh. At that time, the area was inhabited by Canaanites.

7Then the LORD appeared to Abram and said, "I will give this land to your descendants." And Abram built an altar there and dedicated it to the LORD, who had appeared to him. 8After that, Abram traveled south and set up camp in the hill country, with Bethel to the west and Ai to the east. There he built another altar and dedicated it to the LORD, and he worshiped the LORD. 9Then Abram continued traveling south by stages toward the Negev.

Abram and Sarai in Egypt

10At that time a severe famine struck the land of Canaan, forcing Abram to go down to Egypt, where he lived as a foreigner. 11As he was approaching the border of Egypt, Abram said to his wife, Sarai, "Look, you are a very beautiful woman. 12When the Egyptians see you, they will say, 'This is his wife. Let's kill him; then we can have her!' 13So please tell them you are my sister. Then they will spare my life and treat me well because of their interest in you."

14And sure enough, when Abram arrived in Egypt, everyone noticed Sarai's beauty. 15When the palace officials saw her, they sang her praises to Pharaoh, their king, and Sarai was taken into his palace. 16Then Pharaoh gave Abram many gifts because of her—sheep, goats, cattle, male and female donkeys, male and female servants, and camels.

17But the LORD sent terrible plagues upon Pharaoh and his household because of Sarai, Abram's wife. 18So Pharaoh summoned Abram and accused him sharply. "What have you done to me?" he demanded. "Why didn't you tell me she was your wife? 19Why did you say, 'She is my sister,' and allow me to take her as my wife? Now then, here is your wife. Take her and get out of here!" 20Pharaoh ordered some of his men to escort them, and he sent Abram out of the country, along with his wife and all his possessions.

CHAPTER 13

Abram and Lot Separate

So Abram left Egypt and traveled north into the Negev, along with his wife and Lot and all that they owned. 2(Abram was very rich in livestock, silver, and gold.) 3From the Negev, they continued traveling by stages toward Bethel, and they pitched their tents between Bethel and Ai, where they had camped before. 4This was the same place where Abram had built the altar, and there he worshiped the LORD again.

5Lot, who was traveling with Abram, had also become very wealthy with flocks of sheep and goats, herds of cattle, and many tents. 6But the land could not support both Abram and Lot with all their flocks and herds living so close together. 7So disputes broke out between the herdsmen of Abram and Lot. (At that time Canaanites and Perizzites were also living in the land.)

8Finally Abram said to Lot, "Let's not allow this conflict to come between us or our herdsmen. After all, we are close relatives! 9The whole countryside is open to you. Take your choice of any section of the land you want, and we will separate. If you want the land to the left, then I'll take the land on the right. If you prefer the land on the right, then I'll go to the left."

10Lot took a long look at the fertile plains of the Jordan Valley in the direction of Zoar. The whole area was well watered everywhere, like the garden of the LORD or the beautiful land of Egypt. (This was before the LORD destroyed Sodom and Gomorrah.) 11Lot chose for himself the whole Jordan Valley to the east of them. He went

there with his flocks and servants and parted
company with his uncle Abram. 12So Abram settled in the land of Canaan, and Lot moved his
tents to a place near Sodom and settled among
the cities of the plain. 13But the people of this
area were extremely wicked and constantly
sinned against the LORD.
14After Lot had gone, the LORD said to Abram,
"Look as far as you can see in every direction—
north and south, east and west. 15I am giving all
this land, as far as you can see, to you and your
descendants as a permanent possession. 16And I
will give you so many descendants that, like the
dust of the earth, they cannot be counted! 17Go
and walk through the land in every direction, for
I am giving it to you."
18So Abram moved his camp to Hebron and
settled near the oak grove belonging to Mamre.
There he built another altar to the LORD.

CHAPTER 14

Abram Rescues Lot

About this time war broke out in the region. King
Amraphel of Babylonia, King Arioch of Ellasar,
King Kedorlaomer of Elam, and King Tidal of
Goiim 2fought against King Bera of Sodom, King
Birsha of Gomorrah, King Shinab of Admah,
King Shemeber of Zeboiim, and the king of Bela
(also called Zoar).
3This second group of kings joined forces in
Siddim Valley (that is, the valley of the Dead Sea).
4For twelve years they had been subject to King
Kedorlaomer, but in the thirteenth year they rebelled against him.
5One year later Kedorlaomer and his allies
arrived and defeated the Rephaites at Ashteroth-
karnaim, the Zuzites at Ham, the Emites at
Shaveh-kiriathaim, 6and the Horites at Mount
Seir, as far as El-paran at the edge of the wilderness. 7Then they turned back and came to En-
mishpat (now called Kadesh) and conquered all
the territory of the Amalekites, and also the Amorites living in Hazazon-tamar.
8Then the rebel kings of Sodom, Gomorrah,
Admah, Zeboiim, and Bela (also called Zoar) prepared for battle in the valley of the Dead Sea.
9They fought against King Kedorlaomer of Elam,
King Tidal of Goiim, King Amraphel of Babylonia, and King Arioch of Ellasar—four kings
against five. 10As it happened, the valley of the
Dead Sea was filled with tar pits. And as the army
of the kings of Sodom and Gomorrah fled, some
fell into the tar pits, while the rest escaped into
the mountains. 11The victorious invaders then
plundered Sodom and Gomorrah and headed for

The Better WAY!

Abraham deserved the nicer land, and he could have just taken it. Instead, he chose to give it to his nephew. We can all make choices like that.

Here's a way!

- Find a treat.
- Find a friend.
- Cut the treat into two pieces, one a little bigger than the other.
- Take the smaller piece for yourself and give the bigger piece to your friend.

Don't tell your friend that you chose the smaller piece—just keep it between YOU AND GOD.

A lotta land...

Abraham generously let Lot choose the land he wanted. Lot chose the better land. Then God blessed Abraham. How? **Read Genesis 13:14-18.**

home, taking with them all the spoils of war and
the food supplies. 12They also captured Lot—
Abram's nephew who lived in Sodom—and carried off everything he owned.
13But one of Lot's men escaped and reported
everything to Abram the Hebrew, who was living
near the oak grove belonging to Mamre the
Amorite. Mamre and his relatives, Eshcol and
Aner, were Abram's allies.
14When Abram heard that his nephew Lot
had been captured, he mobilized the 318
trained men who had been born into his household. Then he pursued Kedorlaomer's army
until he caught up with them at Dan. 15There he
divided his men and attacked during the night.
Kedorlaomer's army fled, but Abram chased
them as far as Hobah, north of Damascus.
16Abram recovered all the goods that had been
taken, and he brought back his nephew Lot with
his possessions and all the women and other
captives.

Melchizedek Blesses Abram

17After Abram returned from his victory over
Kedorlaomer and all his allies, the king of Sodom

went out to meet him in the valley of Shaveh (that
is, the King's Valley).
18And Melchizedek, the king of Salem and a
priest of God Most High, brought Abram some
bread and wine. 19Melchizedek blessed Abram
with this blessing:

"Blessed be Abram by God Most High,
Creator of heaven and earth.
20 And blessed be God Most High,
who has defeated your enemies for you."

Then Abram gave Melchizedek a tenth of all the
goods he had recovered.
21The king of Sodom said to Abram, "Give back
my people who were captured. But you may keep
for yourself all the goods you have recovered."
22Abram replied to the king of Sodom, "I solemnly swear to the LORD, God Most High, Creator
of heaven and earth, 23that I will not take so much
as a single thread or sandal thong from what belongs to you. Otherwise you might say, 'I am the
one who made Abram rich.' 24I will accept only
what my young warriors have already eaten, and I
request that you give a fair share of the goods to
my allies—Aner, Eshcol, and Mamre."

CHAPTER 15
The LORD's Covenant Promise to Abram

Some time later, the LORD spoke to Abram in a vision and said to him, "Do not be afraid, Abram,
for I will protect you, and your reward will be
great."
2But Abram replied, "O Sovereign LORD, what
good are all your blessings when I don't even
have a son? Since you've given me no children,
Eliezer of Damascus, a servant in my household,
will inherit all my wealth. 3You have given me no
descendants of my own, so one of my servants
will be my heir."
4Then the LORD said to him, "No, your servant
will not be your heir, for you will have a son of
your own who will be your heir." 5Then the LORD
took Abram outside and said to him, "Look up
into the sky and count the stars if you can. That's
how many descendants you will have!"
6And Abram believed the LORD, and the LORD
counted him as righteous because of his faith.
7Then the LORD told him, "I am the LORD who
brought you out of Ur of the Chaldeans to give
you this land as your possession."
8But Abram replied, "O Sovereign LORD, how
can I be sure that I will actually possess it?"
9The LORD told him, "Bring me a three-year-
old heifer, a three-year-old female goat, a three-
year-old ram, a turtledove, and a young pigeon."
10So Abram presented all these to him and killed
them. Then he cut each animal down the middle
and laid the halves side by side; he did not, however, cut the birds in half. 11Some vultures
swooped down to eat the carcasses, but Abram
chased them away.
12As the sun was going down, Abram fell into
a deep sleep, and a terrifying darkness came
down over him. 13Then the LORD said to Abram,
"You can be sure that your descendants will be
strangers in a foreign land, where they will be
oppressed as slaves for 400 years. 14But I will
punish the nation that enslaves them, and in the
end they will come away with great wealth. 15(As
for you, you will die in peace and be buried at a
ripe old age.) 16After four generations your
descendants will return here to this land, for the
sins of the Amorites do not yet warrant their
destruction."
17After the sun went down and darkness fell,
Abram saw a smoking firepot and a flaming
torch pass between the halves of the carcasses.
18So the LORD made a covenant with Abram that
day and said, "I have given this land to your descendants, all the way from the border of Egypt

FUN-fact
CANAAN
Eight million, nine hundred & ninety-nine thousand, nine hundred & ninety-nine steps to go!

FOOTLOOSE

Abraham's trip from Ur to Canaan was probably around 900 miles. If Abraham walked the whole way, he took around 9.5 million steps to make the journey!

Next time you walk to school or to a store, count how many steps you take. **How long do you think it took Abraham to get to Canaan?**

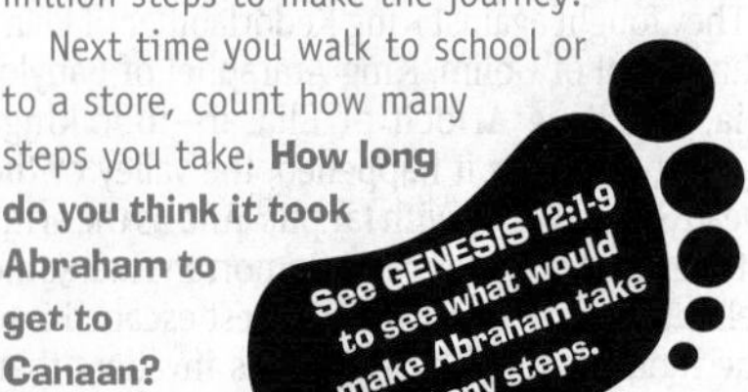
See GENESIS 12:1-9 to see what would make Abraham take so many steps.

to the great Euphrates River—19the land now occupied by the Kenites, Kenizzites, Kadmonites,
20Hittites, Perizzites, Rephaites, 21Amorites,
Canaanites, Girgashites, and Jebusites."

CHAPTER 16

The Birth of Ishmael

Now Sarai, Abram's wife, had not been able to
bear children for him. But she had an Egyptian
servant named Hagar. 2So Sarai said to Abram,
"The LORD has prevented me from having children. Go and sleep with my servant. Perhaps I
can have children through her." And Abram
agreed with Sarai's proposal. 3So Sarai, Abram's
wife, took Hagar the Egyptian servant and gave
her to Abram as a wife. (This happened ten years
after Abram had settled in the land of Canaan.)

4So Abram had sexual relations with Hagar,
and she became pregnant. But when Hagar knew
she was pregnant, she began to treat her mistress, Sarai, with contempt. 5Then Sarai said to
Abram, "This is all your fault! I put my servant
into your arms, but now that she's pregnant she
treats me with contempt. The LORD will show
who's wrong—you or me!"

6Abram replied, "Look, she is your servant, so
deal with her as you see fit." Then Sarai treated
Hagar so harshly that she finally ran away.

7The angel of the LORD found Hagar beside a
spring of water in the wilderness, along the road
to Shur. 8The angel said to her, "Hagar, Sarai's servant, where have you come from, and where are
you going?"

"I'm running away from my mistress, Sarai,"
she replied.

9The angel of the LORD said to her, "Return to
your mistress, and submit to her authority."
10Then he added, "I will give you more descendants than you can count."

11And the angel also said, "You are now pregnant and will give birth to a son. You are to name
him Ishmael (which means 'God hears'), for the
LORD has heard your cry of distress. 12This son of
yours will be a wild man, as untamed as a wild
donkey! He will raise his fist against everyone,
and everyone will be against him. Yes, he will live
in open hostility against all his relatives."

13Thereafter, Hagar used another name to refer to the LORD, who had spoken to her. She said,
"You are the God who sees me." She also said,
"Have I truly seen the One who sees me?" 14So
that well was named Beer-lahai-roi (which
means "well of the Living One who sees me"). It
can still be found between Kadesh and Bered.

15So Hagar gave Abram a son, and Abram
named him Ishmael. 16Abram was eighty-six
years old when Ishmael was born.

CHAPTER 17

Abram Is Named Abraham

When Abram was ninety-nine years old, the LORD
appeared to him and said, "I am El-Shaddai—'God
Almighty.' Serve me faithfully and live a blameless life. 2I will make a covenant with you, by
which I will guarantee to give you countless
descendants."

3At this, Abram fell face down on the ground.
Then God said to him, 4"This is my covenant
with you: I will make you the father of a multitude of nations! 5What's more, I am changing
your name. It will no longer be Abram. Instead,
you will be called Abraham, for you will be the father of many nations. 6I will make you extremely
fruitful. Your descendants will become many
nations, and kings will be among them!

7"I will confirm my covenant with you and
your descendants after you, from generation to
generation. This is the everlasting covenant: I
will always be your God and the God of your descendants after you. 8And I will give the entire
land of Canaan, where you now live as a foreigner, to you and your descendants. It will be
their possession forever, and I will be their
God."

The Mark of the Covenant

9Then God said to Abraham, "Your responsibility is to obey the terms of the covenant. You
and all your descendants have this continual
responsibility. 10This is the covenant that you
and your descendants must keep: Each male
among you must be circumcised. 11You must cut
off the flesh of your foreskin as a sign of the covenant between me and you. 12From generation
to generation, every male child must be circumcised on the eighth day after his birth. This applies not only to members of your family but
also to the servants born in your household and
the foreign-born servants whom you have purchased. 13All must be circumcised. Your bodies
will bear the mark of my everlasting covenant.
14Any male who fails to be circumcised will be
cut off from the covenant family for breaking
the covenant."

Sarai Is Named Sarah

15Then God said to Abraham, "Regarding Sarai,
your wife—her name will no longer be Sarai.
From now on her name will be Sarah. 16And I will
bless her and give you a son from her! Yes, I will

bless her richly, and she will become the mother of many nations. Kings of nations will be among her descendants."

17 Then Abraham bowed down to the ground, but he laughed to himself in disbelief. "How could I become a father at the age of 100?" he thought. "And how can Sarah have a baby when she is ninety years old?" 18 So Abraham said to God, "May Ishmael live under your special blessing!"

19 But God replied, "No—Sarah, your wife, will give birth to a son for you. You will name him Isaac, and I will confirm my covenant with him and his descendants as an everlasting covenant. 20 As for Ishmael, I will bless him also, just as you have asked. I will make him extremely fruitful and multiply his descendants. He will become the father of twelve princes, and I will make him a great nation. 21 But my covenant will be confirmed with Isaac, who will be born to you and Sarah about this time next year." 22 When God had finished speaking, he left Abraham.

23 On that very day Abraham took his son, Ishmael, and every male in his household, including those born there and those he had bought. Then he circumcised them, cutting off their foreskins, just as God had told him. 24 Abraham was ninety-nine years old when he was circumcised, 25 and Ishmael, his son, was thirteen. 26 Both Abraham and his son, Ishmael, were circumcised on that same day, 27 along with all the other men and boys of the household, whether they were born there or bought as servants. All were circumcised with him.

CHAPTER 18

A Son Is Promised to Sarah

The LORD appeared again to Abraham near the oak grove belonging to Mamre. One day Abraham was sitting at the entrance to his tent during the hottest part of the day. 2 He looked up and noticed three men standing nearby. When he saw them, he ran to meet them and welcomed them, bowing low to the ground.

3 "My lord," he said, "if it pleases you, stop here for a while. 4 Rest in the shade of this tree while water is brought to wash your feet. 5 And since you've honored your servant with this visit, let me prepare some food to refresh you before you continue on your journey."

"All right," they said. "Do as you have said."

6 So Abraham ran back to the tent and said to Sarah, "Hurry! Get three large measures of your best flour, knead it into dough, and bake some bread." 7 Then Abraham ran out to the herd and chose a tender calf and gave it to his servant, who quickly prepared it. 8 When the food was ready, Abraham took some yogurt and milk and the roasted meat, and he served it to the men. As they ate, Abraham waited on them in the shade of the trees.

9 "Where is Sarah, your wife?" the visitors asked.

"She's inside the tent," Abraham replied.

10 Then one of them said, "I will return to you about this time next year, and your wife, Sarah, will have a son!"

Sarah was listening to this conversation from the tent. 11 Abraham and Sarah were both very old by this time, and Sarah was long past the age of having children. 12 So she laughed silently to herself and said, "How could a worn-out woman like me enjoy such pleasure, especially when my master—my husband—is also so old?"

13 Then the LORD said to Abraham, "Why did Sarah laugh? Why did she say, 'Can an old woman like me have a baby?' 14 Is anything too hard for the LORD? I will return about this time next year, and Sarah will have a son."

15 Sarah was afraid, so she denied it, saying, "I didn't laugh."

But the LORD said, "No, you did laugh."

Abraham Intercedes for Sodom

16 Then the men got up from their meal and looked out toward Sodom. As they left, Abraham went with them to send them on their way.

17 "Should I hide my plan from Abraham?" the LORD asked. 18 "For Abraham will certainly become a great and mighty nation, and all the nations of the earth will be blessed through him. 19 I have singled him out so that he will direct his sons and their families to keep the way of the LORD by doing what is right and just. Then I will do for Abraham all that I have promised."

20 So the LORD told Abraham, "I have heard a great outcry from Sodom and Gomorrah, because their sin is so flagrant. 21 I am going down to see if their actions are as wicked as I have heard. If not, I want to know."

22 The other men turned and headed toward Sodom, but the LORD remained with Abraham. 23 Abraham approached him and said, "Will you sweep away both the righteous and the wicked? 24 Suppose you find fifty righteous people living there in the city—will you still sweep it away and not spare it for their sakes? 25 Surely you wouldn't do such a thing, destroying the righteous along with the wicked. Why, you would be treating the righteous and the wicked exactly the same!

Surely you wouldn't do that! Should not the Judge
of all the earth do what is right?"
26 And the LORD replied, "If I find fifty righteous people in Sodom, I will spare the entire city
for their sake."
27 Then Abraham spoke again. "Since I have
begun, let me speak further to my Lord, even
though I am but dust and ashes. 28 Suppose there
are only forty-five righteous people rather than
fifty? Will you destroy the whole city for lack of
five?"
And the LORD said, "I will not destroy it if I find
forty-five righteous people there."
29 Then Abraham pressed his request further.
"Suppose there are only forty?"
And the LORD replied, "I will not destroy it for
the sake of the forty."
30 "Please don't be angry, my Lord," Abraham
pleaded. "Let me speak—suppose only thirty
righteous people are found?"
And the LORD replied, "I will not destroy it if I
find thirty."
31 Then Abraham said, "Since I have dared to
speak to the Lord, let me continue—suppose
there are only twenty?"
And the LORD replied, "Then I will not destroy
it for the sake of the twenty."
32 Finally, Abraham said, "Lord, please don't be
angry with me if I speak one more time. Suppose
only ten are found there?"
And the LORD replied, "Then I will not destroy
it for the sake of the ten."
33 When the LORD had finished his conversation with Abraham, he went on his way, and Abraham returned to his tent.

CHAPTER 19

Sodom and Gomorrah Destroyed

That evening the two angels came to the entrance of the city of Sodom. Lot was sitting there,
and when he saw them, he stood up to meet
them. Then he welcomed them and bowed with
his face to the ground. 2 "My lords," he said,
"come to my home to wash your feet, and be my
guests for the night. You may then get up early in
the morning and be on your way again."
"Oh no," they replied. "We'll just spend the
night out here in the city square."
3 But Lot insisted, so at last they went home
with him. Lot prepared a feast for them, complete with fresh bread made without yeast, and
they ate. 4 But before they retired for the night,
all the men of Sodom, young and old, came from
all over the city and surrounded the house.

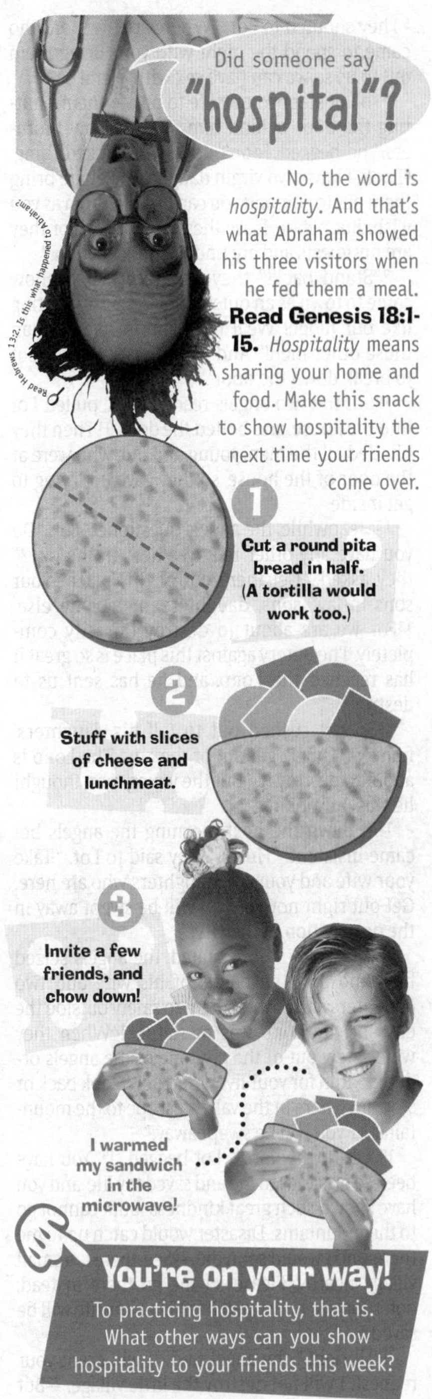

Did someone say
"hospital"?
No, the word is *hospitality*. And that's what Abraham showed his three visitors when he fed them a meal. **Read Genesis 18:1-15.** *Hospitality* means sharing your home and food. Make this snack to show hospitality the next time your friends come over.
Read Hebrews 13:2. Is this what happened to Abraham?
1
Cut a round pita bread in half. (A tortilla would work too.)
2
Stuff with slices of cheese and lunchmeat.
3
Invite a few friends, and chow down!
I warmed my sandwich in the microwave!
You're on your way!
To practicing hospitality, that is. What other ways can you show hospitality to your friends this week?

5They shouted to Lot, "Where are the men who
came to spend the night with you? Bring them
out to us so we can have sex with them!"
6So Lot stepped outside to talk to them, shutting the door behind him. 7"Please, my brothers," he begged, "don't do such a wicked thing.
8Look, I have two virgin daughters. Let me bring
them out to you, and you can do with them as you
wish. But please, leave these men alone, for they
are my guests and are under my protection."
9"Stand back!" they shouted. "This fellow
came to town as an outsider, and now he's acting
like our judge! We'll treat you far worse than
those other men!" And they lunged toward Lot
to break down the door.
10But the two angels reached out, pulled Lot
into the house, and bolted the door. 11Then they
blinded all the men, young and old, who were at
the door of the house, so they gave up trying to
get inside.
12Meanwhile, the angels questioned Lot. "Do
you have any other relatives here in the city?"
they asked. "Get them out of this place—your
sons-in-law, sons, daughters, or anyone else.
13For we are about to destroy this city completely. The outcry against this place is so great it
has reached the LORD, and he has sent us to
destroy it."
14So Lot rushed out to tell his daughters'
fiancés, "Quick, get out of the city! The LORD is
about to destroy it." But the young men thought
he was only joking.
15At dawn the next morning the angels became insistent. "Hurry," they said to Lot. "Take
your wife and your two daughters who are here.
Get out right now, or you will be swept away in
the destruction of the city!"
16When Lot still hesitated, the angels seized
his hand and the hands of his wife and two
daughters and rushed them to safety outside the
city, for the LORD was merciful. 17When they
were safely out of the city, one of the angels ordered, "Run for your lives! And don't look back or
stop anywhere in the valley! Escape to the mountains, or you will be swept away!"
18"Oh no, my lord!" Lot begged. 19"You have
been so gracious to me and saved my life, and you
have shown such great kindness. But I cannot go
to the mountains. Disaster would catch up to me
there, and I would soon die. 20See, there is a small
village nearby. Please let me go there instead;
don't you see how small it is? Then my life will be
saved."
21"All right," the angel said, "I will grant your
request. I will not destroy the little village. 22But
hurry! Escape to it, for I can do nothing until you
arrive there." (This explains why that village was
known as Zoar, which means "little place.")
23Lot reached the village just as the sun was
rising over the horizon. 24Then the LORD rained
down fire and burning sulfur from the sky on
Sodom and Gomorrah. 25He utterly destroyed
them, along with the other cities and villages of
the plain, wiping out all the people and every bit
of vegetation. 26But Lot's wife looked back as she
was following behind him, and she turned into a
pillar of salt.
27Abraham got up early that morning and hurried out to the place where he had stood in the
LORD's presence. 28He looked out across the
plain toward Sodom and Gomorrah and watched
as columns of smoke rose from the cities like
smoke from a furnace.
29But God had listened to Abraham's request
and kept Lot safe, removing him from the disaster that engulfed the cities on the plain.

Lot and His Daughters

30Afterward Lot left Zoar because he was afraid
of the people there, and he went to live in a cave
in the mountains with his two daughters. 31One
day the older daughter said to her sister, "There
are no men left anywhere in this entire area, so
we can't get married like everyone else. And our
father will soon be too old to have children.
32Come, let's get him drunk with wine, and then
we will have sex with him. That way we will preserve our family line through our father."
33So that night they got him drunk with wine,
and the older daughter went in and had intercourse with her father. He was unaware of her lying down or getting up again.
34The next morning the older daughter said
to her younger sister, "I had sex with our father
last night. Let's get him drunk with wine again
tonight, and you go in and have sex with him.
That way we will preserve our family line
through our father." 35So that night they got him
drunk with wine again, and the younger daughter went in and had intercourse with him. As before, he was unaware of her lying down or
getting up again.
36As a result, both of Lot's daughters became
pregnant by their own father. 37When the older
daughter gave birth to a son, she named him
Moab. He became the ancestor of the nation now
known as the Moabites. 38When the younger
daughter gave birth to a son, she named him
Ben-ammi. He became the ancestor of the nation
now known as the Ammonites.

CHAPTER 20
Abraham Deceives Abimelech

Abraham moved south to the Negev and lived for
a while between Kadesh and Shur, and then he
moved on to Gerar. While living there as a foreigner, 2Abraham introduced his wife, Sarah, by
saying, "She is my sister." So King Abimelech of
Gerar sent for Sarah and had her brought to him
at his palace.

3But that night God came to Abimelech in a
dream and told him, "You are a dead man, for
that woman you have taken is already married!"

4But Abimelech had not slept with her yet, so
he said, "Lord, will you destroy an innocent nation? 5Didn't Abraham tell me, 'She is my sister'?
And she herself said, 'Yes, he is my brother.' I
acted in complete innocence! My hands are
clean."

6In the dream God responded, "Yes, I know
you are innocent. That's why I kept you from sinning against me, and why I did not let you touch
her. 7Now return the woman to her husband, and
he will pray for you, for he is a prophet. Then you
will live. But if you don't return her to him, you
can be sure that you and all your people will die."

8Abimelech got up early the next morning
and quickly called all his servants together.
When he told them what had happened, his
men were terrified. 9Then Abimelech called for
Abraham. "What have you done to us?" he demanded. "What crime have I committed that
deserves treatment like this, making me and my
kingdom guilty of this great sin? No one should
ever do what you have done! 10Whatever possessed you to do such a thing?"

11Abraham replied, "I thought, 'This is a godless place. They will want my wife and will kill me
to get her.' 12And she really is my sister, for we
both have the same father, but different mothers.
And I married her. 13When God called me to
leave my father's home and to travel from place to
place, I told her, 'Do me a favor. Wherever we go,
tell the people that I am your brother.'"

14Then Abimelech took some of his sheep
and goats, cattle, and male and female servants,
and he presented them to Abraham. He also returned his wife, Sarah, to him. 15Then Abimelech said, "Look over my land and choose any
place where you would like to live." 16And he
said to Sarah, "Look, I am giving your 'brother'
1,000 pieces of silver in the presence of all these
witnesses. This is to compensate you for any
wrong I may have done to you. This will settle
any claim against me, and your reputation is
cleared."

17Then Abraham prayed to God, and God
healed Abimelech, his wife, and his female servants, so they could have children. 18For the
LORD had caused all the women to be infertile
because of what happened with Abraham's wife,
Sarah.

CHAPTER 21
The Birth of Isaac

The LORD kept his word and did for Sarah exactly what he had promised. 2She became pregnant, and she gave birth to a son for Abraham in
his old age. This happened at just the time God
had said it would. 3And Abraham named their
son Isaac. 4Eight days after Isaac was born, Abraham circumcised him as God had commanded.
5Abraham was 100 years old when Isaac was
born.

6And Sarah declared, "God has brought me
laughter. All who hear about this will laugh with
me. 7Who would have said to Abraham that Sarah would nurse a baby? Yet I have given Abraham
a son in his old age!"

Hagar and Ishmael Are Sent Away

8When Isaac grew up and was about to be
weaned, Abraham prepared a huge feast to celebrate the occasion. 9But Sarah saw Ishmael—
the son of Abraham and her Egyptian servant
Hagar—making fun of her son, Isaac. 10So she
turned to Abraham and demanded, "Get rid of
that slave woman and her son. He is not going to
share the inheritance with my son, Isaac. I won't
have it!"

11This upset Abraham very much because
Ishmael was his son. 12But God told Abraham,
"Do not be upset over the boy and your servant.
Do whatever Sarah tells you, for Isaac is the son
through whom your descendants will be
counted. 13But I will also make a nation of the
descendants of Hagar's son because he is your
son, too."

14So Abraham got up early the next morning,
prepared food and a container of water, and
strapped them on Hagar's shoulders. Then he
sent her away with their son, and she wandered
aimlessly in the wilderness of Beersheba.

15When the water was gone, she put the boy in
the shade of a bush. 16Then she went and sat
down by herself about a hundred yards away. "I
don't want to watch the boy die," she said, as she
burst into tears.

17But God heard the boy crying, and the angel
of God called to Hagar from heaven, "Hagar,

what's wrong? Do not be afraid! God has heard
the boy crying as he lies there. 18 Go to him and
comfort him, for I will make a great nation from
his descendants."

19 Then God opened Hagar's eyes, and she saw
a well full of water. She quickly filled her water
container and gave the boy a drink.

20 And God was with the boy as he grew up in
the wilderness. He became a skillful archer,
21 and he settled in the wilderness of Paran. His
mother arranged for him to marry a woman from
the land of Egypt.

Abraham's Covenant with Abimelech

22 About this time, Abimelech came with Phicol,
his army commander, to visit Abraham. "God is
obviously with you, helping you in everything
you do," Abimelech said. 23 "Swear to me in God's
name that you will never deceive me, my children, or any of my descendants. I have been loyal
to you, so now swear that you will be loyal to me
and to this country where you are living as a foreigner."

24 Abraham replied, "Yes, I swear to it!" 25 Then
Abraham complained to Abimelech about a well
that Abimelech's servants had taken by force
from Abraham's servants.

26 "This is the first I've heard of it," Abimelech
answered. "I have no idea who is responsible.
You have never complained about this before."

27 Abraham then gave some of his sheep,
goats, and cattle to Abimelech, and they made a
treaty. 28 But Abraham also took seven additional
female lambs and set them off by themselves.
29 Abimelech asked, "Why have you set these
seven apart from the others?"

30 Abraham replied, "Please accept these seven
lambs to show your agreement that I dug this
well." 31 Then he named the place Beersheba
(which means "well of the oath"), because that
was where they had sworn the oath.

32 After making their covenant at Beersheba,
Abimelech left with Phicol, the commander of
his army, and they returned home to the land of
the Philistines. 33 Then Abraham planted a tamarisk tree at Beersheba, and there he worshiped
the LORD, the Eternal God. 34 And Abraham lived
as a foreigner in Philistine country for a long
time.

CHAPTER 22

Abraham's Faith Tested

Some time later, God tested Abraham's faith.
"Abraham!" God called.

"Yes," he replied. "Here I am."

2 "Take your son, your only son—yes, Isaac,
whom you love so much—and go to the land of
Moriah. Go and sacrifice him as a burnt offering
on one of the mountains, which I will show you."

3 The next morning Abraham got up early. He
saddled his donkey and took two of his servants
with him, along with his son, Isaac. Then he
chopped wood for a fire for a burnt offering and
set out for the place God had told him about.
4 On the third day of their journey, Abraham
looked up and saw the place in the distance.
5 "Stay here with the donkey," Abraham told the
servants. "The boy and I will travel a little farther.
We will worship there, and then we will come
right back."

6 So Abraham placed the wood for the burnt
offering on Isaac's shoulders, while he himself
carried the fire and the knife. As the two of them
walked on together, 7 Isaac turned to Abraham
and said, "Father?"

"Yes, my son?" Abraham replied.

"We have the fire and the wood," the boy said,
"but where is the sheep for the burnt offering?"

8 "God will provide a sheep for the burnt offering, my son," Abraham answered. And they both
walked on together.

9 When they arrived at the place where God
had told him to go, Abraham built an altar and arranged the wood on it. Then he tied his son,
Isaac, and laid him on the altar on top of the
wood. 10 And Abraham picked up the knife to kill
his son as a sacrifice. 11 At that moment the angel
of the LORD called to him from heaven, "Abraham! Abraham!"

"Yes," Abraham replied. "Here I am!"

12 "Don't lay a hand on the boy!" the angel said.
"Do not hurt him in any way, for now I know that
you truly fear God. You have not withheld from
me even your son, your only son."

13 Then Abraham looked up and saw a ram
caught by its horns in a thicket. So he took the
ram and sacrificed it as a burnt offering in place
of his son. 14 Abraham named the place Yahweh-
Yireh (which means "the LORD will provide").
To this day, people still use that name as a proverb: "On the mountain of the LORD it will be provided."

15 Then the angel of the LORD called again to
Abraham from heaven. 16 "This is what the LORD
says: Because you have obeyed me and have not
withheld even your son, your only son, I swear by
my own name that 17 I will certainly bless you. I
will multiply your descendants beyond number,
like the stars in the sky and the sand on the

seashore. Your descendants will conquer the
cities of their enemies. 18And through your
descendants all the nations of the earth will
be blessed—all because you have obeyed me."
19Then they returned to the servants and traveled back to Beersheba, where Abraham continued to live.
20Soon after this, Abraham heard that Milcah,
his brother Nahor's wife, had borne Nahor eight
sons. 21The oldest was named Uz, the next oldest
was Buz, followed by Kemuel (the ancestor of the
Arameans), 22Kesed, Hazo, Pildash, Jidlaph, and
Bethuel. 23(Bethuel became the father of Rebekah.) In addition to these eight sons from Milcah,
24Nahor had four other children from his concubine Reumah. Their names were Tebah, Gaham,
Tahash, and Maacah.

DO YOU REALLY TRUST ME?
Did Abraham really trust God? God had Abraham build an altar (probably out of stones) to sacrifice his son on. Would he do it? Would God step in at the last minute?
Check out GENESIS 22:1-19 to see what happened.
Even the New Testament talks about Abraham! Check out Hebrews 11:17-19.
Are there times it's hard for you to trust God? Think of a time.
Storms
Storms
1
Find a stone that fits in your pocket.
2
Write or draw something on the stone that reminds you of when it's tough to trust God.
3
Keep the stone in your pocket to remind you to trust God like Abraham did.

CHAPTER 23

The Burial of Sarah

When Sarah was 127 years old, 2she died at
Kiriath-arba (now called Hebron) in the land of
Canaan. There Abraham mourned and wept for
her.
3Then, leaving her body, he said to the Hittite
elders, 4"Here I am, a stranger and a foreigner
among you. Please sell me a piece of land so I can
give my wife a proper burial."
5The Hittites replied to Abraham, 6"Listen,
my lord, you are an honored prince among us.
Choose the finest of our tombs and bury her
there. No one here will refuse to help you in this
way."
7Then Abraham bowed low before the Hittites 8and said, "Since you are willing to help
me in this way, be so kind as to ask Ephron son of
Zohar 9to let me buy his cave at Machpelah,
down at the end of his field. I will pay the full
price in the presence of witnesses, so I will have
a permanent burial place for my family."
10Ephron was sitting there among the others,
and he answered Abraham as the others listened, speaking publicly before all the Hittite elders of the town. 11"No, my lord," he said to
Abraham, "please listen to me. I will give you the
field and the cave. Here in the presence of my
people, I give it to you. Go and bury your dead."
12Abraham again bowed low before the citizens of the land, 13and he replied to Ephron as
everyone listened. "No, listen to me. I will buy it

from you. Let me pay the full price for the field so
I can bury my dead there."
14Ephron answered Abraham, 15"My lord,
please listen to me. The land is worth 400 pieces
of silver, but what is that between friends? Go
ahead and bury your dead."
16So Abraham agreed to Ephron's price and
paid the amount he had suggested—400 pieces
of silver, weighed according to the market standard. The Hittite elders witnessed the transaction.
17So Abraham bought the plot of land belonging to Ephron at Machpelah, near Mamre. This
included the field itself, the cave that was in it,
and all the surrounding trees. 18It was transferred to Abraham as his permanent possession
in the presence of the Hittite elders at the city
gate. 19Then Abraham buried his wife, Sarah,
there in Canaan, in the cave of Machpelah, near
Mamre (also called Hebron). 20So the field and
the cave were transferred from the Hittites to
Abraham for use as a permanent burial place.

CHAPTER 24

A Wife for Isaac

Abraham was now a very old man, and the LORD
had blessed him in every way. 2One day Abraham
said to his oldest servant, the man in charge of
his household, "Take an oath by putting your
hand under my thigh. 3Swear by the LORD, the
God of heaven and earth, that you will not allow
my son to marry one of these local Canaanite
women. 4Go instead to my homeland, to my relatives, and find a wife there for my son Isaac."
5The servant asked, "But what if I can't find a
young woman who is willing to travel so far from
home? Should I then take Isaac there to live
among your relatives in the land you came
from?"
6"No!" Abraham responded. "Be careful never
to take my son there. 7For the LORD, the God of
heaven, who took me from my father's house and
my native land, solemnly promised to give this
land to my descendants. He will send his angel
ahead of you, and he will see to it that you find a
wife there for my son. 8If she is unwilling to
come back with you, then you are free from this
oath of mine. But under no circumstances are
you to take my son there."
9So the servant took an oath by putting his
hand under the thigh of his master, Abraham. He
swore to follow Abraham's instructions. 10Then
he loaded ten of Abraham's camels with all kinds
of expensive gifts from his master, and he traveled to distant Aram-naharaim. There he went to
the town where Abraham's brother Nahor had
settled. 11He made the camels kneel beside a
well just outside the town. It was evening, and
the women were coming out to draw water.
12"O LORD, God of my master, Abraham," he
prayed. "Please give me success today, and show
unfailing love to my master, Abraham. 13See, I
am standing here beside this spring, and the
young women of the town are coming out to
draw water. 14This is my request. I will ask one of
them, 'Please give me a drink from your jug.' If
she says, 'Yes, have a drink, and I will water your
camels, too!'—let her be the one you have selected as Isaac's wife. This is how I will know that
you have shown unfailing love to my master."
15Before he had finished praying, he saw a
young woman named Rebekah coming out with
her water jug on her shoulder. She was the
daughter of Bethuel, who was the son of Abraham's brother Nahor and his wife, Milcah. 16Re-
bekah was very beautiful and old enough to be
married, but she was still a virgin. She went down
to the spring, filled her jug, and came up again.
17Running over to her, the servant said, "Please
give me a little drink of water from your jug."
18"Yes, my lord," she answered, "have a drink."
And she quickly lowered her jug from her shoulder and gave him a drink. 19When she had given
him a drink, she said, "I'll draw water for your
camels, too, until they have had enough to
drink." 20So she quickly emptied her jug into the
watering trough and ran back to the well to draw
water for all his camels.
21The servant watched her in silence, wondering whether or not the LORD had given him success in his mission. 22Then at last, when the
camels had finished drinking, he took out a gold
ring for her nose and two large gold bracelets for
her wrists.
23"Whose daughter are you?" he asked. "And
please tell me, would your father have any room
to put us up for the night?"
24"I am the daughter of Bethuel," she replied.
"My grandparents are Nahor and Milcah. 25Yes,
we have plenty of straw and feed for the camels,
and we have room for guests."
26The man bowed low and worshiped the
LORD. 27"Praise the LORD, the God of my master,
Abraham," he said. "The LORD has shown unfailing love and faithfulness to my master, for he has
led me straight to my master's relatives."
28The young woman ran home to tell her family everything that had happened. 29Now Rebekah
had a brother named Laban, who ran out to meet
the man at the spring. 30He had seen the nose-

ring and the bracelets on his sister's wrists, and
had heard Rebekah tell what the man had said. So
he rushed out to the spring, where the man was
still standing beside his camels. 31Laban said
to him, "Come and stay with us, you who are
blessed by the LORD! Why are you standing here
outside the town when I have a room all ready for
you and a place prepared for the camels?"

32So the man went home with Laban, and Laban unloaded the camels, gave him straw for
their bedding, fed them, and provided water for
the man and the camel drivers to wash their feet.
33Then food was served. But Abraham's servant
said, "I don't want to eat until I have told you why
I have come."

"All right," Laban said, "tell us."

34"I am Abraham's servant," he explained.
35"And the LORD has greatly blessed my master;
he has become a wealthy man. The LORD has
given him flocks of sheep and goats, herds of cattle, a fortune in silver and gold, and many male
and female servants and camels and donkeys.

36"When Sarah, my master's wife, was very
old, she gave birth to my master's son, and my
master has given him everything he owns. 37And
my master made me take an oath. He said, 'Do
not allow my son to marry one of these local
Canaanite women. 38Go instead to my father's
house, to my relatives, and find a wife there for
my son.'

39"But I said to my master, 'What if I can't find
a young woman who is willing to go back with
me?' 40He responded, 'The LORD, in whose presence I have lived, will send his angel with you and
will make your mission successful. Yes, you must
find a wife for my son from among my relatives,
from my father's family. 41Then you will have fulfilled your obligation. But if you go to my relatives and they refuse to let her go with you, you
will be free from my oath.'

42"So today when I came to the spring, I
prayed this prayer: 'O LORD, God of my master,
Abraham, please give me success on this mission. 43See, I am standing here beside this
spring. This is my request. When a young
woman comes to draw water, I will say to her,
"Please give me a little drink of water from your
jug." 44If she says, "Yes, have a drink, and I will
draw water for your camels, too," let her be the
one you have selected to be the wife of my master's son.'

45"Before I had finished praying in my heart, I
saw Rebekah coming out with her water jug on
her shoulder. She went down to the spring and
drew water. So I said to her, 'Please give me a
drink.' 46She quickly lowered her jug from her
shoulder and said, 'Yes, have a drink, and I will
water your camels, too!' So I drank, and then she
watered the camels.

47"Then I asked, 'Whose daughter are you?'
She replied, 'I am the daughter of Bethuel, and
my grandparents are Nahor and Milcah.' So I put
the ring on her nose, and the bracelets on her
wrists.

48"Then I bowed low and worshiped the
LORD. I praised the LORD, the God of my master,
Abraham, because he had led me straight to my
master's niece to be his son's wife. 49So tell me—
will you or won't you show unfailing love and
faithfulness to my master? Please tell me yes or
no, and then I'll know what to do next."

50Then Laban and Bethuel replied, "The LORD
has obviously brought you here, so there is nothing we can say. 51Here is Rebekah; take her and
go. Yes, let her be the wife of your master's son, as
the LORD has directed."

52When Abraham's servant heard their answer, he bowed down to the ground and worshiped the LORD. 53Then he brought out silver
and gold jewelry and clothing and presented
them to Rebekah. He also gave expensive presents to her brother and mother. 54Then they ate
their meal, and the servant and the men with him
stayed there overnight.

But early the next morning, Abraham's servant
said, "Send me back to my master."

55"But we want Rebekah to stay with us at least
ten days," her brother and mother said. "Then
she can go."

56But he said, "Don't delay me. The LORD has
made my mission successful; now send me back
so I can return to my master."

57"Well," they said, "we'll call Rebekah and ask
her what she thinks." 58So they called Rebekah.
"Are you willing to go with this man?" they asked
her.

And she replied, "Yes, I will go."

59So they said good-bye to Rebekah and sent
her away with Abraham's servant and his men.
The woman who had been Rebekah's childhood
nurse went along with her. 60They gave her this
blessing as she parted:

"Our sister, may you become
  the mother of many millions!
May your descendants be strong
  and conquer the cities of their enemies."

61Then Rebekah and her servant girls mounted
the camels and followed the man. So Abraham's
servant took Rebekah and went on his way.

Genesis 25 . . . page 26
Jacob and Esau had other problems, like those found in GENESIS 27. Check out the end of the story in GENESIS 33.
LET'S MAKE A DEAL
Ever make a deal with your brother or sister? Read GENESIS 25:19-34 to see the deal Esau made with his brother. He traded his family blessing for a bowl of stew! Esau didn't treasure his family blessing. Make this box to keep your family treasures in.
1
Get an empty shoe box and some extra favorite family pictures.
2
Cut pictures and words from magazines that show who YOU are!
daughter
Silly
friend
SMART
3
Glue the pictures to the lid (and sides, if you have enough).
silly
daughter
soccer
friend
4
Stash your treasures inside.
friend
FUNNY
Pay attention to the gifts your parents or grandparents pass on to you. ASK THEM TO TELL YOU STORIES ABOUT EACH OF THEM. These things might not seem special now, but someday you'll treasure them.

62Meanwhile, Isaac, whose home was in the
Negev, had returned from Beer-lahai-roi. 63One
evening as he was walking and meditating in the
fields, he looked up and saw the camels coming.
64When Rebekah looked up and saw Isaac, she
quickly dismounted from her camel. 65"Who is
that man walking through the fields to meet us?"
she asked the servant.

And he replied, "It is my master." So Rebekah
covered her face with her veil. 66Then the servant told Isaac everything he had done.

67And Isaac brought Rebekah into his mother
Sarah's tent, and she became his wife. He loved
her deeply, and she was a special comfort to him
after the death of his mother.

CHAPTER 25

The Death of Abraham

Abraham married another wife, whose name was
Keturah. 2She gave birth to Zimran, Jokshan,
Medan, Midian, Ishbak, and Shuah. 3Jokshan was
the father of Sheba and Dedan. Dedan's descendants were the Asshurites, Letushites, and Leum-
mites. 4Midian's sons were Ephah, Epher,
Hanoch, Abida, and Eldaah. These were all descendants of Abraham through Keturah.

5Abraham gave everything he owned to his
son Isaac. 6But before he died, he gave gifts to the
sons of his concubines and sent them off to a
land in the east, away from Isaac.

7Abraham lived for 175 years, 8and he died at a
ripe old age, having lived a long and satisfying life.
He breathed his last and joined his ancestors in
death. 9His sons Isaac and Ishmael buried him in
the cave of Machpelah, near Mamre, in the field of
Ephron son of Zohar the Hittite. 10This was the
field Abraham had purchased from the Hittites
and where he had buried his wife Sarah. 11After
Abraham's death, God blessed his son Isaac, who
settled near Beer-lahai-roi in the Negev.

Ishmael's Descendants

12This is the account of the family of Ishmael,
the son of Abraham through Hagar, Sarah's
Egyptian servant. 13Here is a list, by their names
and clans, of Ishmael's descendants: The oldest
was Nebaioth, followed by Kedar, Adbeel,
Mibsam, 14Mishma, Dumah, Massa, 15Hadad,
Tema, Jetur, Naphish, and Kedemah. 16These
twelve sons of Ishmael became the founders of
twelve tribes named after them, listed according
to the places they settled and camped. 17Ishmael
lived for 137 years. Then he breathed his last
and joined his ancestors in death. 18Ishmael's
descendants occupied the region from Havilah

to Shur, which is east of Egypt in the direction of
Asshur. There they lived in open hostility toward
all their relatives.

The Births of Esau and Jacob

19This is the account of the family of Isaac, the
son of Abraham. 20When Isaac was forty years
old, he married Rebekah, the daughter of Bethuel the Aramean from Paddan-aram and the sister
of Laban the Aramean.
21Isaac pleaded with the LORD on behalf of his
wife, because she was unable to have children.
The LORD answered Isaac's prayer, and Rebekah
became pregnant with twins. 22But the two children struggled with each other in her womb. So
she went to ask the LORD about it. "Why is this
happening to me?" she asked.
23And the LORD told her, "The sons in your
womb will become two nations. From the very
beginning, the two nations will be rivals. One nation will be stronger than the other; and your
older son will serve your younger son."
24And when the time came to give birth, Rebekah discovered that she did indeed have
twins! 25The first one was very red at birth and
covered with thick hair like a fur coat. So they
named him Esau. 26Then the other twin was
born with his hand grasping Esau's heel. So they
named him Jacob. Isaac was sixty years old when
the twins were born.

Esau Sells His Birthright

27As the boys grew up, Esau became a skillful
hunter. He was an outdoorsman, but Jacob had a
quiet temperament, preferring to stay at home.
28Isaac loved Esau because he enjoyed eating the
wild game Esau brought home, but Rebekah
loved Jacob.
29One day when Jacob was cooking some stew,
Esau arrived home from the wilderness exhausted and hungry. 30Esau said to Jacob, "I'm
starved! Give me some of that red stew!" (This is
how Esau got his other name, Edom, which
means "red.")
31"All right," Jacob replied, "but trade me your
rights as the firstborn son."
32"Look, I'm dying of starvation!" said Esau.
"What good is my birthright to me now?"
33But Jacob said, "First you must swear that
your birthright is mine." So Esau swore an oath,
thereby selling all his rights as the firstborn to
his brother, Jacob.
34Then Jacob gave Esau some bread and lentil
stew. Esau ate the meal, then got up and left. He
showed contempt for his rights as the firstborn.

CHAPTER 26

Isaac Deceives Abimelech

A severe famine now struck the land, as had happened before in Abraham's time. So Isaac moved
to Gerar, where Abimelech, king of the Philistines, lived.
2The LORD appeared to Isaac and said, "Do
not go down to Egypt, but do as I tell you. 3Live
here as a foreigner in this land, and I will be with
you and bless you. I hereby confirm that I will
give all these lands to you and your descendants,
just as I solemnly promised Abraham, your father. 4I will cause your descendants to become
as numerous as the stars of the sky, and I will
give them all these lands. And through your descendants all the nations of the earth will be
blessed. 5I will do this because Abraham listened to me and obeyed all my requirements,
commands, decrees, and instructions." 6So
Isaac stayed in Gerar.
7When the men who lived there asked Isaac
about his wife, Rebekah, he said, "She is my sister." He was afraid to say, "She is my wife." He
thought, "They will kill me to get her, because
she is so beautiful." 8But some time later, Abimelech, king of the Philistines, looked out his window and saw Isaac caressing Rebekah.
9Immediately, Abimelech called for Isaac and
exclaimed, "She is obviously your wife! Why did
you say, 'She is my sister'?"
"Because I was afraid someone would kill me
to get her from me," Isaac replied.
10"How could you do this to us?" Abimelech
exclaimed. "One of my people might easily have
taken your wife and slept with her, and you
would have made us guilty of great sin."
11Then Abimelech issued a public proclamation: "Anyone who touches this man or his wife
will be put to death!"

Conflict over Water Rights

12When Isaac planted his crops that year, he harvested a hundred times more grain than he
planted, for the LORD blessed him. 13He became
a very rich man, and his wealth continued to
grow. 14He acquired so many flocks of sheep and
goats, herds of cattle, and servants that the Philistines became jealous of him. 15So the Philistines filled up all of Isaac's wells with dirt. These
were the wells that had been dug by the servants
of his father, Abraham.
16Finally, Abimelech ordered Isaac to leave the
country. "Go somewhere else," he said, "for you
have become too powerful for us."
17So Isaac moved away to the Gerar Valley,

where he set up their tents and settled down. 18He reopened the wells his father had dug, which the Philistines had filled in after Abraham's death. Isaac also restored the names Abraham had given them.

19Isaac's servants also dug in the Gerar Valley and discovered a well of fresh water. 20But then the shepherds from Gerar came and claimed the spring. "This is our water," they said, and they argued over it with Isaac's herdsmen. So Isaac named the well Esek (which means "argument"). 21Isaac's men then dug another well, but again there was a dispute over it. So Isaac named it Sitnah (which means "hostility"). 22Abandoning that one, Isaac moved on and dug another well. This time there was no dispute over it, so Isaac named the place Rehoboth (which means "open space"), for he said, "At last the LORD has created enough space for us to prosper in this land."

23From there Isaac moved to Beersheba, 24where the LORD appeared to him on the night of his arrival. "I am the God of your father, Abraham," he said. "Do not be afraid, for I am with you and will bless you. I will multiply your descendants, and they will become a great nation. I will do this because of my promise to Abraham, my servant." 25Then Isaac built an altar there and worshiped the LORD. He set up his camp at that place, and his servants dug another well.

Isaac's Covenant with Abimelech

26One day King Abimelech came from Gerar with his adviser, Ahuzzath, and also Phicol, his army commander. 27"Why have you come here?" Isaac asked. "You obviously hate me, since you kicked me off your land."

28They replied, "We can plainly see that the LORD is with you. So we want to enter into a sworn treaty with you. Let's make a covenant. 29Swear that you will not harm us, just as we have never troubled you. We have always treated you well, and we sent you away from us in peace. And now look how the LORD has blessed you!"

30So Isaac prepared a covenant feast to celebrate the treaty, and they ate and drank together. 31Early the next morning, they each took a solemn oath not to interfere with each other. Then Isaac sent them home again, and they left him in peace.

32That very day Isaac's servants came and told him about a new well they had dug. "We've found water!" they exclaimed. 33So Isaac named the well Shibah (which means "oath"). And to this day the town that grew up there is called Beersheba (which means "well of the oath").

34At the age of forty, Esau married two Hittite wives: Judith, the daughter of Beeri, and Basemath, the daughter of Elon. 35But Esau's wives made life miserable for Isaac and Rebekah.

CHAPTER 27
Jacob Steals Esau's Blessing

One day when Isaac was old and turning blind, he called for Esau, his older son, and said, "My son."

"Yes, Father?" Esau replied.

2"I am an old man now," Isaac said, "and I don't know when I may die. 3Take your bow and a quiver full of arrows, and go out into the open country to hunt some wild game for me. 4Prepare my favorite dish, and bring it here for me to eat. Then I will pronounce the blessing that belongs to you, my firstborn son, before I die."

5But Rebekah overheard what Isaac had said to his son Esau. So when Esau left to hunt for the wild game, 6she said to her son Jacob, "Listen. I overheard your father say to Esau, 7'Bring me some wild game and prepare me a delicious meal. Then I will bless you in the LORD's presence before I die.' 8Now, my son, listen to me. Do exactly as I tell you. 9Go out to the flocks, and bring me two fine young goats. I'll use them to prepare your father's favorite dish. 10Then take the food to your father so he can eat it and bless you before he dies."

11"But look," Jacob replied to Rebekah, "my brother, Esau, is a hairy man, and my skin is smooth. 12What if my father touches me? He'll see that I'm trying to trick him, and then he'll curse me instead of blessing me."

13But his mother replied, "Then let the curse fall on me, my son! Just do what I tell you. Go out and get the goats for me!"

14So Jacob went out and got the young goats for his mother. Rebekah took them and prepared a delicious meal, just the way Isaac liked it. 15Then she took Esau's favorite clothes, which were there in the house, and gave them to her younger son, Jacob. 16She covered his arms and the smooth part of his neck with the skin of the young goats. 17Then she gave Jacob the delicious meal, including freshly baked bread.

18So Jacob took the food to his father. "My father?" he said.

"Yes, my son," Isaac answered. "Who are you—Esau or Jacob?"

19Jacob replied, "It's Esau, your firstborn son.

I've done as you told me. Here is the wild game.
Now sit up and eat it so you can give me your
blessing."
20Isaac asked, "How did you find it so quickly,
my son?"
"The LORD your God put it in my path!" Jacob
replied.
21Then Isaac said to Jacob, "Come closer so I
can touch you and make sure that you really are
Esau." 22So Jacob went closer to his father, and
Isaac touched him. "The voice is Jacob's, but the
hands are Esau's," Isaac said. 23But he did not
recognize Jacob, because Jacob's hands felt hairy
just like Esau's. So Isaac prepared to bless Jacob.
24"But are you really my son Esau?" he asked.
"Yes, I am," Jacob replied.
25Then Isaac said, "Now, my son, bring me
the wild game. Let me eat it, and then I will give
you my blessing." So Jacob took the food to his
father, and Isaac ate it. He also drank the wine
that Jacob served him. 26Then Isaac said to Jacob, "Please come a little closer and kiss me, my
son."
27So Jacob went over and kissed him. And
when Isaac caught the smell of his clothes, he
was finally convinced, and he blessed his son. He
said, "Ah! The smell of my son is like the smell of
the outdoors, which the LORD has blessed!

28 "From the dew of heaven
and the richness of the earth,
may God always give you abundant harvests
of grain
and bountiful new wine.
29 May many nations become your servants,
and may they bow down to you.
May you be the master over your brothers,
and may your mother's sons bow down
to you.
All who curse you will be cursed,
and all who bless you will be blessed."

30As soon as Isaac had finished blessing Jacob,
and almost before Jacob had left his father, Esau
returned from his hunt. 31Esau prepared a delicious meal and brought it to his father. Then he
said, "Sit up, my father, and eat my wild game so
you can give me your blessing."
32But Isaac asked him, "Who are you?"
Esau replied, "It's your son, your firstborn son,
Esau."
33Isaac began to tremble uncontrollably and
said, "Then who just served me wild game? I
have already eaten it, and I blessed him just before you came. And yes, that blessing must
stand!"
34When Esau heard his father's words, he let
out a loud and bitter cry. "Oh my father, what
about me? Bless me, too!" he begged.
35But Isaac said, "Your brother was here, and
he tricked me. He has taken away your blessing."
36Esau exclaimed, "No wonder his name is Jacob, for now he has cheated me twice. First he
took my rights as the firstborn, and now he has
stolen my blessing. Oh, haven't you saved even
one blessing for me?"
37Isaac said to Esau, "I have made Jacob your
master and have declared that all his brothers
will be his servants. I have guaranteed him an
abundance of grain and wine—what is left for me
to give you, my son?"
38Esau pleaded, "But do you have only one
blessing? Oh my father, bless me, too!" Then Esau
broke down and wept.
39Finally, his father, Isaac, said to him,

"You will live away from the richness of the
earth,
and away from the dew of the heaven
above.
40 You will live by your sword,
and you will serve your brother.
But when you decide to break free,
you will shake his yoke from your neck."

Jacob Flees to Paddan-Aram

41From that time on, Esau hated Jacob because
their father had given Jacob the blessing. And
Esau began to scheme: "I will soon be mourning
my father's death. Then I will kill my brother,
Jacob."
42But Rebekah heard about Esau's plans. So
she sent for Jacob and told him, "Listen, Esau is
consoling himself by plotting to kill you. 43So listen carefully, my son. Get ready and flee to my
brother, Laban, in Haran. 44Stay there with him
until your brother cools off. 45When he calms
down and forgets what you have done to him, I
will send for you to come back. Why should I
lose both of you in one day?"
46Then Rebekah said to Isaac, "I'm sick and
tired of these local Hittite women! I would rather
die than see Jacob marry one of them."

CHAPTER 28

So Isaac called for Jacob, blessed him, and said,
"You must not marry any of these Canaanite
women. 2Instead, go at once to Paddan-aram, to
the house of your grandfather Bethuel, and
marry one of your uncle Laban's daughters.
3May God Almighty bless you and give you many

children. And may your descendants multiply and become many nations! 4May God pass on to you and your descendants the blessings he promised to Abraham. May you own this land where you are now living as a foreigner, for God gave this land to Abraham."

5So Isaac sent Jacob away, and he went to Paddan-aram to stay with his uncle Laban, his mother's brother, the son of Bethuel the Aramean.

6Esau knew that his father, Isaac, had blessed Jacob and sent him to Paddan-aram to find a wife, and that he had warned Jacob, "You must not marry a Canaanite woman." 7He also knew that Jacob had obeyed his parents and gone to Paddan-aram. 8It was now very clear to Esau that his father did not like the local Canaanite women. 9So Esau visited his uncle Ishmael's family and married one of Ishmael's daughters, in addition to the wives he already had. His new wife's name was Mahalath. She was the sister of Nebaioth and the daughter of Ishmael, Abraham's son.

Jacob's Dream at Bethel

10Meanwhile, Jacob left Beersheba and traveled toward Haran. 11At sundown he arrived at a good place to set up camp and stopped there for the night. Jacob found a stone to rest his head against and lay down to sleep. 12As he slept, he dreamed of a stairway that reached from the earth up to heaven. And he saw the angels of God going up and down the stairway.

13At the top of the stairway stood the LORD, and he said, "I am the LORD, the God of your grandfather Abraham, and the God of your father, Isaac. The ground you are lying on belongs to you. I am giving it to you and your descendants. 14Your descendants will be as numerous as the dust of the earth! They will spread out in all directions—to the west and the east, to the north and the south. And all the families of the earth will be blessed through you and your descendants. 15What's more, I am with you, and I will protect you wherever you go. One day I will bring you back to this land. I will not leave you until I have finished giving you everything I have promised you."

16Then Jacob awoke from his sleep and said, "Surely the LORD is in this place, and I wasn't even aware of it!" 17But he was also afraid and said, "What an awesome place this is! It is none other than the house of God, the very gateway to heaven!"

18The next morning Jacob got up very early. He took the stone he had rested his head against, and he set it upright as a memorial pillar. Then he poured olive oil over it. 19He named that place Bethel (which means "house of God"), although it was previously called Luz.

20Then Jacob made this vow: "If God will indeed be with me and protect me on this journey, and if he will provide me with food and clothing, 21and if I return safely to my father's home, then the LORD will certainly be my God. 22And this memorial pillar I have set up will become a place for worshiping God, and I will present to God a tenth of everything he gives me."

CHAPTER 29

Jacob Arrives at Paddan-Aram

Then Jacob hurried on, finally arriving in the land of the east. 2He saw a well in the distance. Three flocks of sheep and goats lay in an open field beside it, waiting to be watered. But a heavy stone covered the mouth of the well.

3It was the custom there to wait for all the flocks to arrive before removing the stone and watering the animals. Afterward the stone would be placed back over the mouth of the well. 4Jacob went over to the shepherds and asked, "Where are you from, my friends?"

"We are from Haran," they answered.

5"Do you know a man there named Laban, the grandson of Nahor?" he asked.

"Yes, we do," they replied.

6"Is he doing well?" Jacob asked.

"Yes, he's well," they answered. "Look, here comes his daughter Rachel with the flock now."

7Jacob said, "Look, it's still broad daylight—too early to round up the animals. Why don't you water the sheep and goats so they can get back out to pasture?"

8"We can't water the animals until all the flocks have arrived," they replied. "Then the shepherds move the stone from the mouth of the well, and we water all the sheep and goats."

9Jacob was still talking with them when Rachel arrived with her father's flock, for she was a shepherd. 10And because Rachel was his cousin—the daughter of Laban, his mother's brother—and because the sheep and goats belonged to his uncle Laban, Jacob went over to the well and moved the stone from its mouth and watered his uncle's flock. 11Then Jacob kissed Rachel, and he wept aloud. 12He explained to Rachel that he was her cousin on her father's side—the son of her aunt Rebekah. So Rachel quickly ran and told her father, Laban.

13As soon as Laban heard that his nephew Jacob had arrived, he ran out to meet him. He embraced and kissed him and brought him home. When Jacob had told him his story, 14Laban exclaimed, "You really are my own flesh and blood!"

Jacob Marries Leah and Rachel

After Jacob had stayed with Laban for about a month, 15Laban said to him, "You shouldn't work for me without pay just because we are relatives. Tell me how much your wages should be."

16Now Laban had two daughters. The older daughter was named Leah, and the younger one was Rachel. 17There was no sparkle in Leah's eyes, but Rachel had a beautiful figure and a lovely face. 18Since Jacob was in love with Rachel, he told her father, "I'll work for you for seven years if you'll give me Rachel, your younger daughter, as my wife."

19"Agreed!" Laban replied. "I'd rather give her to you than to anyone else. Stay and work with me." 20So Jacob worked seven years to pay for Rachel. But his love for her was so strong that it seemed to him but a few days.

21Finally, the time came for him to marry her. "I have fulfilled my agreement," Jacob said to Laban. "Now give me my wife so I can sleep with her."

22So Laban invited everyone in the neighborhood and prepared a wedding feast. 23But that night, when it was dark, Laban took Leah to Jacob, and he slept with her. 24(Laban had given Leah a servant, Zilpah, to be her maid.)

25But when Jacob woke up in the morning—it was Leah! "What have you done to me?" Jacob raged at Laban. "I worked seven years for Rachel! Why have you tricked me?"

26"It's not our custom here to marry off a younger daughter ahead of the firstborn," Laban replied. 27"But wait until the bridal week is over; then we'll give you Rachel, too—provided you promise to work another seven years for me."

28So Jacob agreed to work seven more years. A week after Jacob had married Leah, Laban gave him Rachel, too. 29(Laban gave Rachel a servant, Bilhah, to be her maid.) 30So Jacob slept with Rachel, too, and he loved her much more than Leah. He then stayed and worked for Laban the additional seven years.

Jacob's Many Children

31When the LORD saw that Leah was unloved, he enabled her to have children, but Rachel could not conceive. 32So Leah became pregnant and gave birth to a son. She named him Reuben, for she said, "The LORD has noticed my misery, and now my husband will love me."

33She soon became pregnant again and gave birth to another son. She named him Simeon, for she said, "The LORD heard that I was unloved and has given me another son."

34Then she became pregnant a third time and gave birth to another son. He was named Levi, for she said, "Surely this time my husband will feel affection for me, since I have given him three sons!"

35Once again Leah became pregnant and gave birth to another son. She named him Judah, for she said, "Now I will praise the LORD!" And then she stopped having children.

CHAPTER 30

When Rachel saw that she wasn't having any children for Jacob, she became jealous of her sister. She pleaded with Jacob, "Give me children, or I'll die!"

2Then Jacob became furious with Rachel. "Am I God?" he asked. "He's the one who has kept you from having children!"

3Then Rachel told him, "Take my maid, Bilhah, and sleep with her. She will bear children for me, and through her I can have a family, too." 4So Rachel gave her servant, Bilhah, to Jacob as a wife, and he slept with her. 5Bilhah became pregnant and presented him with a son. 6Rachel named him Dan, for she said, "God has vindicated me! He has heard my request and given me a son." 7Then Bilhah became pregnant again and gave Jacob a second son. 8Rachel named him Naphtali, for she said, "I have struggled hard with my sister, and I'm winning!"

9Meanwhile, Leah realized that she wasn't getting pregnant anymore, so she took her servant, Zilpah, and gave her to Jacob as a wife. 10Soon Zilpah presented him with a son. 11Leah named him Gad, for she said, "How fortunate I am!" 12Then Zilpah gave Jacob a second son. 13And Leah named him Asher, for she said, "What joy is mine! Now the other women will celebrate with me."

14One day during the wheat harvest, Reuben found some mandrakes growing in a field and brought them to his mother, Leah. Rachel begged Leah, "Please give me some of your son's mandrakes."

15But Leah angrily replied, "Wasn't it enough that you stole my husband? Now will you steal my son's mandrakes, too?"

Rachel answered, "I will let Jacob sleep with you tonight if you give me some of the mandrakes."

16So that evening, as Jacob was coming home

from the fields, Leah went out to meet him. "You
must come and sleep with me tonight!" she said.
"I have paid for you with some mandrakes that
my son found." So that night he slept with Leah.
17And God answered Leah's prayers. She became
pregnant again and gave birth to a fifth son for
Jacob. 18She named him Issachar, for she said,
"God has rewarded me for giving my servant to
my husband as a wife." 19Then Leah became
pregnant again and gave birth to a sixth son for
Jacob. 20She named him Zebulun, for she said,
"God has given me a good reward. Now my husband will treat me with respect, for I have given
him six sons." 21Later she gave birth to a daughter and named her Dinah.

22Then God remembered Rachel's plight and
answered her prayers by enabling her to have
children. 23She became pregnant and gave birth
to a son. "God has removed my disgrace," she
said. 24And she named him Joseph, for she said,
"May the LORD add yet another son to my family."

Jacob's Wealth Increases

25Soon after Rachel had given birth to Joseph, Jacob said to Laban, "Please release me so I can go
home to my own country. 26Let me take my wives
and children, for I have earned them by serving
you, and let me be on my way. You certainly know
how hard I have worked for you."

27"Please listen to me," Laban replied. "I have
become wealthy, for the LORD has blessed me because of you. 28Tell me how much I owe you.
Whatever it is, I'll pay it."

29Jacob replied, "You know how hard I've
worked for you, and how your flocks and herds
have grown under my care. 30You had little indeed before I came, but your wealth has increased enormously. The LORD has blessed you
through everything I've done. But now, what
about me? When can I start providing for my
own family?"

31"What wages do you want?" Laban asked
again.

Jacob replied, "Don't give me anything. Just do
this one thing, and I'll continue to tend and
watch over your flocks. 32Let me inspect your
flocks today and remove all the sheep and goats
that are speckled or spotted, along with all the
black sheep. Give these to me as my wages. 33In
the future, when you check on the animals you
have given me as my wages, you'll see that I have
been honest. If you find in my flock any goats
without speckles or spots, or any sheep that are
not black, you will know that I have stolen them
from you."

34"All right," Laban replied. "It will be as you
say." 35But that very day Laban went out and removed the male goats that were streaked and
spotted, all the female goats that were speckled
and spotted or had white patches, and all the
black sheep. He placed them in the care of his
own sons, 36who took them a three-days' journey
from where Jacob was. Meanwhile, Jacob stayed
and cared for the rest of Laban's flock.

37Then Jacob took some fresh branches from
poplar, almond, and plane trees and peeled off
strips of bark, making white streaks on them.
38Then he placed these peeled branches in the
watering troughs where the flocks came to
drink, for that was where they mated. 39And
when they mated in front of the white-streaked
branches, they gave birth to young that were
streaked, speckled, and spotted. 40Jacob separated those lambs from Laban's flock. And at
mating time he turned the flock to face Laban's
animals that were streaked or black. This is how
he built his own flock instead of increasing
Laban's.

41Whenever the stronger females were ready
to mate, Jacob would place the peeled branches
in the watering troughs in front of them. Then
they would mate in front of the branches. 42But
he didn't do this with the weaker ones, so the
weaker lambs belonged to Laban, and the stronger ones were Jacob's. 43As a result, Jacob became very wealthy, with large flocks of sheep and
goats, female and male servants, and many camels and donkeys.

CHAPTER **31**

Jacob Flees from Laban

But Jacob soon learned that Laban's sons were
grumbling about him. "Jacob has robbed our father of everything!" they said. "He has gained all
his wealth at our father's expense." 2And Jacob
began to notice a change in Laban's attitude toward him.

3Then the LORD said to Jacob, "Return to the
land of your father and grandfather and to your
relatives there, and I will be with you."

4So Jacob called Rachel and Leah out to the
field where he was watching his flock. 5He said
to them, "I have noticed that your father's attitude toward me has changed. But the God of my
father has been with me. 6You know how hard I
have worked for your father, 7but he has cheated
me, changing my wages ten times. But God has
not allowed him to do me any harm. 8For if he
said, 'The speckled animals will be your wages,'
the whole flock began to produce speckled

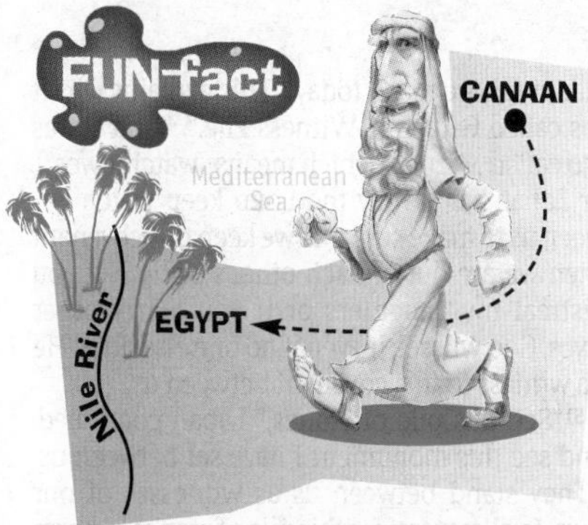

God's chosen people sometimes went
to Egypt for food, help, and safety.
Both Abraham and Joseph went to
Egypt when people couldn't grow food
in Canaan. **Read MATTHEW 2:13-15 to
find out about another important
person who went to
Egypt for
safety.**

**Where do you go
when you need help?**
**Thank someone you know who
helped you when you
needed it.**

young. And when he changed his mind and said,
'The striped animals will be your wages,' then
the whole flock produced striped young. 9In this
way, God has taken your father's animals and
given them to me.
10"One time during the mating season, I had a
dream and saw that the male goats mating with
the females were streaked, speckled, and spotted. 11Then in my dream, the angel of God said to
me, 'Jacob!' And I replied, 'Yes, here I am.'
12"The angel said, 'Look up, and you will see
that only the streaked, speckled, and spotted
males are mating with the females of your flock.
For I have seen how Laban has treated you. 13I
am the God who appeared to you at Bethel, the
place where you anointed the pillar of stone and
made your vow to me. Now get ready and leave
this country and return to the land of your
birth.'"
14Rachel and Leah responded, "That's fine
with us! We won't inherit any of our father's
wealth anyway. 15He has reduced our rights to
those of foreign women. And after he sold us, he
wasted the money you paid him for us. 16All the
wealth God has given you from our father legally
belongs to us and our children. So go ahead and
do whatever God has told you."
17So Jacob put his wives and children on
camels, 18and he drove all his livestock in front
of him. He packed all the belongings he had acquired in Paddan-aram and set out for the land
of Canaan, where his father, Isaac, lived. 19At the
time they left, Laban was some distance away,
shearing his sheep. Rachel stole her father's
household idols and took them with her. 20Jacob
outwitted Laban the Aramean, for they set out
secretly and never told Laban they were leaving.
21So Jacob took all his possessions with him and
crossed the Euphrates River, heading for the hill
country of Gilead.

Laban Pursues Jacob

22Three days later, Laban was told that Jacob had
fled. 23So he gathered a group of his relatives
and set out in hot pursuit. He caught up with Jacob seven days later in the hill country of Gilead.
24But the previous night God had appeared to Laban the Aramean in a dream and told him, "I'm
warning you—leave Jacob alone!"
25Laban caught up with Jacob as he was
camped in the hill country of Gilead, and he set
up his camp not far from Jacob's. 26"What do you
mean by deceiving me like this?" Laban demanded. "How dare you drag my daughters away
like prisoners of war? 27Why did you slip away
secretly? Why did you deceive me? And why
didn't you say you wanted to leave? I would have
given you a farewell feast, with singing and music, accompanied by tambourines and harps.
28Why didn't you let me kiss my daughters and
grandchildren and tell them good-bye? You have
acted very foolishly! 29I could destroy you, but
the God of your father appeared to me last night
and warned me, 'Leave Jacob alone!' 30I can
understand your feeling that you must go, and
your intense longing for your father's home. But
why have you stolen my gods?"
31"I rushed away because I was afraid," Jacob
answered. "I thought you would take your
daughters from me by force. 32But as for your
gods, see if you can find them, and let the person
who has taken them die! And if you find anything
else that belongs to you, identify it before all
these relatives of ours, and I will give it back!" But
Jacob did not know that Rachel had stolen the
household idols.
33Laban went first into Jacob's tent to search
there, then into Leah's, and then the tents of the
two servant wives—but he found nothing. Finally,
he went into Rachel's tent. 34But Rachel had
taken the household idols and hidden them in
her camel saddle, and now she was sitting on
them. When Laban had thoroughly searched her

tent without finding them, 35she said to her father, "Please, sir, forgive me if I don't get up for you. I'm having my monthly period." So Laban continued his search, but he could not find the household idols.

36Then Jacob became very angry, and he challenged Laban. "What's my crime?" he demanded. "What have I done wrong to make you chase after me as though I were a criminal? 37You have rummaged through everything I own. Now show me what you found that belongs to you! Set it out here in front of us, before our relatives, for all to see. Let them judge between us!

38"For twenty years I have been with you, caring for your flocks. In all that time your sheep and goats never miscarried. In all those years I never used a single ram of yours for food. 39If any were attacked and killed by wild animals, I never showed you the carcass and asked you to reduce the count of your flock. No, I took the loss myself! You made me pay for every stolen animal, whether it was taken in broad daylight or in the dark of night.

40"I worked for you through the scorching heat of the day and through cold and sleepless nights. 41Yes, for twenty years I slaved in your house! I worked for fourteen years earning your two daughters, and then six more years for your flock. And you changed my wages ten times! 42In fact, if the God of my father had not been on my side—the God of Abraham and the fearsome God of Isaac—you would have sent me away empty-handed. But God has seen your abuse and my hard work. That is why he appeared to you last night and rebuked you!"

Jacob's Treaty with Laban

43Then Laban replied to Jacob, "These women are my daughters, these children are my grandchildren, and these flocks are my flocks—in fact, everything you see is mine. But what can I do now about my daughters and their children? 44So come, let's make a covenant, you and I, and it will be a witness to our commitment."

45So Jacob took a stone and set it up as a monument. 46Then he told his family members, "Gather some stones." So they gathered stones and piled them in a heap. Then Jacob and Laban sat down beside the pile of stones to eat a covenant meal. 47To commemorate the event, Laban called the place Jegar-sahadutha (which means "witness pile" in Aramaic), and Jacob called it Galeed (which means "witness pile" in Hebrew).

48Then Laban declared, "This pile of stones will stand as a witness to remind us of the covenant we have made today." This explains why it was called Galeed—"Witness Pile." 49But it was also called Mizpah (which means "watchtower"), for Laban said, "May the LORD keep watch between us to make sure that we keep this covenant when we are out of each other's sight. 50If you mistreat my daughters or if you marry other wives, God will see it even if no one else does. He is a witness to this covenant between us.

51"See this pile of stones," Laban continued, "and see this monument I have set between us. 52They stand between us as witnesses of our vows. I will never pass this pile of stones to harm you, and you must never pass these stones or this monument to harm me. 53I call on the God of our ancestors—the God of your grandfather Abraham and the God of my grandfather Nahor—to serve as a judge between us."

So Jacob took an oath before the fearsome God of his father, Isaac, to respect the boundary line. 54Then Jacob offered a sacrifice to God there on the mountain and invited everyone to a covenant feast. After they had eaten, they spent the night on the mountain.

55Laban got up early the next morning, and he kissed his grandchildren and his daughters and blessed them. Then he left and returned home.

CHAPTER 32

As Jacob started on his way again, angels of God came to meet him. 2When Jacob saw them, he exclaimed, "This is God's camp!" So he named the place Mahanaim.

Jacob Sends Gifts to Esau

3Then Jacob sent messengers ahead to his brother, Esau, who was living in the region of Seir in the land of Edom. 4He told them, "Give this message to my master Esau: 'Humble greetings from your servant Jacob. Until now I have been living with Uncle Laban, 5and now I own cattle, donkeys, flocks of sheep and goats, and many servants, both men and women. I have sent these messengers to inform my lord of my coming, hoping that you will be friendly to me.'"

6After delivering the message, the messengers returned to Jacob and reported, "We met your brother, Esau, and he is already on his way to meet you—with an army of 400 men!" 7Jacob was terrified at the news. He divided his household, along with the flocks and herds and camels, into two groups. 8He thought, "If Esau meets one group and attacks it, perhaps the other group can escape."

9Then Jacob prayed, "O God of my grand-

father Abraham, and God of my father, Isaac—
O Lord, you told me, 'Return to your own land
and to your relatives.' And you promised me, 'I
will treat you kindly.' 10 I am not worthy of all the
unfailing love and faithfulness you have shown
to me, your servant. When I left home and
crossed the Jordan River, I owned nothing except a walking stick. Now my household fills two
large camps! 11 O Lord, please rescue me from
the hand of my brother, Esau. I am afraid that he
is coming to attack me, along with my wives and
children. 12 But you promised me, 'I will surely
treat you kindly, and I will multiply your descendants until they become as numerous as the
sands along the seashore—too many to count.'"
13 Jacob stayed where he was for the night.
Then he selected these gifts from his possessions to present to his brother, Esau: 14 200 female goats, 20 male goats, 200 ewes, 20 rams,
15 30 female camels with their young, 40 cows,
10 bulls, 20 female donkeys, and 10 male donkeys. 16 He divided these animals into herds and
assigned each to different servants. Then he told
his servants, "Go ahead of me with the animals,
but keep some distance between the herds."
17 He gave these instructions to the men leading the first group: "When my brother, Esau,
meets you, he will ask, 'Whose servants are you?
Where are you going? Who owns these animals?'
18 You must reply, 'They belong to your servant
Jacob, but they are a gift for his master Esau.
Look, he is coming right behind us.'"
19 Jacob gave the same instructions to the second and third herdsmen and to all who followed
behind the herds: "You must say the same thing
to Esau when you meet him. 20 And be sure to say,
'Look, your servant Jacob is right behind us.'"
Jacob thought, "I will try to appease him by
sending gifts ahead of me. When I see him in
person, perhaps he will be friendly to me." 21 So
the gifts were sent on ahead, while Jacob himself
spent that night in the camp.

Jacob Wrestles with God

22 During the night Jacob got up and took his two
wives, his two servant wives, and his eleven sons
and crossed the Jabbok River with them. 23 After
taking them to the other side, he sent over all his
possessions.
24 This left Jacob all alone in the camp, and a
man came and wrestled with him until the dawn
began to break. 25 When the man saw that he
would not win the match, he touched Jacob's hip
and wrenched it out of its socket. 26 Then the
man said, "Let me go, for the dawn is breaking!"
But Jacob said, "I will not let you go unless you
bless me."
27 "What is your name?" the man asked.
He replied, "Jacob."
28 "Your name will no longer be Jacob," the
man told him. "From now on you will be called
Israel, because you have fought with God and
with men and have won."
29 "Please tell me your name," Jacob said.
"Why do you want to know my name?" the
man replied. Then he blessed Jacob there.
30 Jacob named the place Peniel (which means
"face of God"), for he said, "I have seen God face
to face, yet my life has been spared." 31 The sun
was rising as Jacob left Peniel, and he was limp-
ing because of the injury to his hip. 32 (Even today the people of Israel don't eat the tendon
near the hip socket because of what happened
that night when the man strained the tendon of
Jacob's hip.)

CHAPTER 33
Jacob and Esau Make Peace

Then Jacob looked up and saw Esau coming with
his 400 men. So he divided the children among
Leah, Rachel, and his two servant wives. 2 He put
the servant wives and their children at the front,
Leah and her children next, and Rachel and Joseph last. 3 Then Jacob went on ahead. As he approached his brother, he bowed to the ground
seven times before him. 4 Then Esau ran to meet
him and embraced him, threw his arms around
his neck, and kissed him. And they both wept.
5 Then Esau looked at the women and children
and asked, "Who are these people with you?"
"These are the children God has graciously
given to me, your servant," Jacob replied. 6 Then
the servant wives came forward with their children and bowed before him. 7 Next came Leah
with her children, and they bowed before him.
Finally, Joseph and Rachel came forward and
bowed before him.
8 "And what were all the flocks and herds I met
as I came?" Esau asked.
Jacob replied, "They are a gift, my lord, to ensure your friendship."
9 "My brother, I have plenty," Esau answered.
"Keep what you have for yourself."
10 But Jacob insisted, "No, if I have found favor
with you, please accept this gift from me. And
what a relief to see your friendly smile. It is like
seeing the face of God! 11 Please take this gift I
have brought you, for God has been very gracious
to me. I have more than enough." And because
Jacob insisted, Esau finally accepted the gift.

12“Well,” Esau said, “let’s be going. I will lead
the way.”

13But Jacob replied, “You can see, my lord, that
some of the children are very young, and the
flocks and herds have their young, too. If they are
driven too hard, even for one day, all the animals
could die. 14Please, my lord, go ahead of your servant. We will follow slowly, at a pace that is comfortable for the livestock and the children. I will
meet you at Seir.”

15“All right,” Esau said, “but at least let me assign some of my men to guide and protect you.”

Jacob responded, “That’s not necessary. It’s
enough that you’ve received me warmly, my lord!”

16So Esau turned around and started back to
Seir that same day. 17Jacob, on the other hand,
traveled on to Succoth. There he built himself a
house and made shelters for his livestock. That is
why the place was named Succoth (which means
“shelters”).

18Later, having traveled all the way from
Paddan-aram, Jacob arrived safely at the town of
Shechem, in the land of Canaan. There he set up
camp outside the town. 19Jacob bought the plot
of land where he camped from the family of
Hamor, the father of Shechem, for 100 pieces of
silver. 20And there he built an altar and named it
El-Elohe-Israel.

CHAPTER 34

Revenge against Shechem

One day Dinah, the daughter of Jacob and Leah,
went to visit some of the young women who lived
in the area. 2But when the local prince, Shechem
son of Hamor the Hivite, saw Dinah, he seized
her and raped her. 3But then he fell in love with
her, and he tried to win her affection with tender
words. 4He said to his father, Hamor, “Get me this
young girl. I want to marry her.”

5Soon Jacob heard that Shechem had defiled
his daughter, Dinah. But since his sons were out
in the fields herding his livestock, he said nothing until they returned. 6Hamor, Shechem’s
father, came to discuss the matter with Jacob.
7Meanwhile, Jacob’s sons had come in from the
field as soon as they heard what had happened.
They were shocked and furious that their sister
had been raped. Shechem had done a disgraceful thing against Jacob’s family, something that
should never be done.

8Hamor tried to speak with Jacob and his
sons. “My son Shechem is truly in love with your
daughter,” he said. “Please let him marry her. 9In
fact, let’s arrange other marriages, too. You give
us your daughters for our sons, and we will give
you our daughters for your sons. 10And you may
live among us; the land is open to you! Settle here
and trade with us. And feel free to buy property
in the area.”

11Then Shechem himself spoke to Dinah’s
father and brothers. “Please be kind to me, and
let me marry her,” he begged. “I will give you
whatever you ask. 12No matter what dowry or
gift you demand, I will gladly pay it—just give me
the girl as my wife.”

13But since Shechem had defiled their sister,
Dinah, Jacob’s sons responded deceitfully to
Shechem and his father, Hamor. 14They said to
them, “We couldn’t possibly allow this, because
you’re not circumcised. It would be a disgrace for
our sister to marry a man like you! 15But here is a
solution. If every man among you will be circumcised like we are, 16then we will give you our
daughters, and we’ll take your daughters for ourselves. We will live among you and become one
people. 17But if you don’t agree to be circumcised, we will take her and be on our way.”

18Hamor and his son Shechem agreed to their
proposal. 19Shechem wasted no time in acting
on this request, for he wanted Jacob’s daughter
desperately. Shechem was a highly respected
member of his family, 20and he went with his father, Hamor, to present this proposal to the leaders at the town gate.

21“These men are our friends,” they said.
“Let’s invite them to live here among us and trade
freely. Look, the land is large enough to hold
them. We can take their daughters as wives and
let them marry ours. 22But they will consider
staying here and becoming one people with us
only if all of our men are circumcised, just as they
are. 23But if we do this, all their livestock and
possessions will eventually be ours. Come, let’s
agree to their terms and let them settle here
among us.”

24So all the men in the town council agreed
with Hamor and Shechem, and every male in the
town was circumcised. 25But three days later,
when their wounds were still sore, two of Jacob’s
sons, Simeon and Levi, who were Dinah’s full
brothers, took their swords and entered the
town without opposition. Then they slaughtered
every male there, 26including Hamor and his son
Shechem. They killed them with their swords,
then took Dinah from Shechem’s house and returned to their camp.

27Meanwhile, the rest of Jacob’s sons arrived.
Finding the men slaughtered, they plundered
the town because their sister had been defiled
there. 28They seized all the flocks and herds

and donkeys—everything they could lay their
hands on, both inside the town and outside in
the fields. 29 They looted all their wealth and
plundered their houses. They also took all their
little children and wives and led them away as
captives.

30 Afterward Jacob said to Simeon and Levi,
"You have ruined me! You've made me stink
among all the people of this land—among all the
Canaanites and Perizzites. We are so few that
they will join forces and crush us. I will be ruined,
and my entire household will be wiped out!"

31 "But why should we let him treat our sister
like a prostitute?" they retorted angrily.

CHAPTER 35

Jacob's Return to Bethel

Then God said to Jacob, "Get ready and move to
Bethel and settle there. Build an altar there to the
God who appeared to you when you fled from
your brother, Esau."

2 So Jacob told everyone in his household, "Get
rid of all your pagan idols, purify yourselves, and
put on clean clothing. 3 We are now going to
Bethel, where I will build an altar to the God who
answered my prayers when I was in distress. He
has been with me wherever I have gone."

4 So they gave Jacob all their pagan idols and
earrings, and he buried them under the great
tree near Shechem. 5 As they set out, a terror
from God spread over the people in all the
towns of that area, so no one attacked Jacob's
family.

6 Eventually, Jacob and his household arrived
at Luz (also called Bethel) in Canaan. 7 Jacob built
an altar there and named the place El-bethel
(which means "God of Bethel"), because God had
appeared to him there when he was fleeing from
his brother, Esau.

8 Soon after this, Rebekah's old nurse, Deborah, died. She was buried beneath the oak tree in
the valley below Bethel. Ever since, the tree has
been called Allon-bacuth (which means "oak of
weeping").

9 Now that Jacob had returned from Paddan-
aram, God appeared to him again at Bethel. God
blessed him, 10 saying, "Your name is Jacob, but
you will not be called Jacob any longer. From now
on your name will be Israel." So God renamed
him Israel.

11 Then God said, "I am El-Shaddai—'God Almighty.' Be fruitful and multiply. You will become a great nation, even many nations. Kings
will be among your descendants! 12 And I will
give you the land I once gave to Abraham and
Isaac. Yes, I will give it to you and your descendants after you." 13 Then God went up from the
place where he had spoken to Jacob.

14 Jacob set up a stone pillar to mark the place
where God had spoken to him. Then he poured
wine over it as an offering to God and anointed
the pillar with olive oil. 15 And Jacob named the
place Bethel (which means "house of God"), because God had spoken to him there.

The Deaths of Rachel and Isaac

16 Leaving Bethel, Jacob and his clan moved on
toward Ephrath. But Rachel went into labor
while they were still some distance away. Her
labor pains were intense. 17 After a very hard delivery, the midwife finally exclaimed, "Don't be
afraid—you have another son!" 18 Rachel was
about to die, but with her last breath she named
the baby Ben-oni (which means "son of my sorrow"). The baby's father, however, called him
Benjamin (which means "son of my right hand").
19 So Rachel died and was buried on the way to
Ephrath (that is, Bethlehem). 20 Jacob set up a
stone monument over Rachel's grave, and it can
be seen there to this day.

21 Then Jacob traveled on and camped beyond
Migdal-eder. 22 While he was living there, Reuben had intercourse with Bilhah, his father's concubine, and Jacob soon heard about it.

These are the names of the twelve sons of
Jacob:

23 The sons of Leah were Reuben (Jacob's oldest
son), Simeon, Levi, Judah, Issachar, and
Zebulun.
24 The sons of Rachel were Joseph and
Benjamin.
25 The sons of Bilhah, Rachel's servant, were Dan
and Naphtali.
26 The sons of Zilpah, Leah's servant, were Gad
and Asher.

These are the names of the sons who were born
to Jacob at Paddan-aram.

27 So Jacob returned to his father, Isaac, in
Mamre, which is near Kiriath-arba (now called
Hebron), where Abraham and Isaac had both
lived as foreigners. 28 Isaac lived for 180 years.
29 Then he breathed his last and died at a ripe old
age, joining his ancestors in death. And his sons,
Esau and Jacob, buried him.

CHAPTER 36

Descendants of Esau

This is the account of the descendants of Esau
(also known as Edom). 2 Esau married two young

women from Canaan: Adah, the daughter of Elon
the Hittite; and Oholibamah, the daughter of
Anah and granddaughter of Zibeon the Hivite.
3He also married his cousin Basemath, who was
the daughter of Ishmael and the sister of Nebaioth. 4Adah gave birth to a son named Eliphaz for
Esau. Basemath gave birth to a son named Reuel.
5Oholibamah gave birth to sons named Jeush,
Jalam, and Korah. All these sons were born to
Esau in the land of Canaan.

6Esau took his wives, his children, and his entire household, along with his livestock and cattle—all the wealth he had acquired in the land
of Canaan—and moved away from his brother,
Jacob. 7There was not enough land to support
them both because of all the livestock and possessions they had acquired. 8So Esau (also
known as Edom) settled in the hill country of
Seir.

9This is the account of Esau's descendants,
the Edomites, who lived in the hill country of
Seir.

10These are the names of Esau sons: Eliphaz, the son of Esau's wife Adah; and Reuel, the son of Esau's wife Basemath.
11The descendants of Eliphaz were Teman, Omar, Zepho, Gatam, and Kenaz.
12Timna, the concubine of Esau's son Eliphaz, gave birth to a son named Amalek. These are the descendants of Esau's wife Adah.
13The descendants of Reuel were Nahath, Zerah, Shammah, and Mizzah. These are the descendants of Esau's wife Basemath.
14Esau also had sons through Oholibamah, the daughter of Anah and granddaughter of Zibeon. Their names were Jeush, Jalam, and Korah.

15These are the descendants of Esau who became
the leaders of various clans:

The descendants of Esau's oldest son, Eliphaz, became the leaders of the clans of Teman, Omar, Zepho, Kenaz,
16Korah, Gatam, and Amalek. These are the clan leaders in the land of Edom who descended from Eliphaz. All these were descendants of Esau's wife Adah.
17The descendants of Esau's son Reuel became the leaders of the clans of Nahath, Zerah, Shammah, and Mizzah. These are the clan leaders in the land of Edom who descended from Reuel. All these were descendants of Esau's wife Basemath.
18The descendants of Esau and his wife Oholibamah became the leaders of the clans of Jeush, Jalam, and Korah. These are the clan leaders who descended from Esau's wife Oholibamah, the daughter of Anah.
19These are the clans descended from Esau
(also known as Edom), identified by their clan
leaders.

Original Peoples of Edom

20These are the names of the tribes that descended from Seir the Horite. They lived in the
land of Edom: Lotan, Shobal, Zibeon, Anah,
21Dishon, Ezer, and Dishan. These were the
Horite clan leaders, the descendants of Seir, who
lived in the land of Edom.

22The descendants of Lotan were Hori and Hemam. Lotan's sister was named Timna.
23The descendants of Shobal were Alvan, Manahath, Ebal, Shepho, and Onam.
24The descendants of Zibeon were Aiah and Anah. (This is the Anah who discovered the hot springs in the wilderness while he was grazing his father's donkeys.)
25The descendants of Anah were his son, Dishon, and his daughter, Oholibamah.
26The descendants of Dishon were Hemdan, Eshban, Ithran, and Keran.
27The descendants of Ezer were Bilhan, Zaavan, and Akan.
28The descendants of Dishan were Uz and Aran.
29So these were the leaders of the Horite clans:
Lotan, Shobal, Zibeon, Anah, 30Dishon, Ezer, and
Dishan. The Horite clans are named after their
clan leaders, who lived in the land of Seir.

Rulers of Edom

31These are the kings who ruled in the land of
Edom before any king ruled over the Israelites:

32Bela son of Beor, who ruled in Edom from his city of Dinhabah.
33When Bela died, Jobab son of Zerah from Bozrah became king in his place.
34When Jobab died, Husham from the land of the Temanites became king in his place.
35When Husham died, Hadad son of Bedad became king in his place and ruled from the city of Avith. He was the one who defeated the Midianites in the land of Moab.
36When Hadad died, Samlah from the city of Masrekah became king in his place.
37When Samlah died, Shaul from the city of Rehoboth-on-the-River became king in his place.

[38]When Shaul died, Baal-hanan son of Acbor became king in his place.
[39]When Baal-hanan son of Acbor died, Hadad became king in his place and ruled from the city of Pau. His wife was Mehetabel, the daughter of Matred and granddaughter of Me-zahab.

[40]These are the names of the leaders of the
clans descended from Esau, who lived in the
places named for them: Timna, Alvah, Jetheth,
[41]Oholibamah, Elah, Pinon, [42]Kenaz, Teman,
Mibzar, [43]Magdiel, and Iram. These are the leaders of the clans of Edom, listed according to
their settlements in the land they occupied.
They all descended from Esau, the ancestor of
the Edomites.

CHAPTER 37

Joseph's Dreams

So Jacob settled again in the land of Canaan,
where his father had lived as a foreigner.
[2]This is the account of Jacob and his family.
When Joseph was seventeen years old, he often
tended his father's flocks. He worked for his half
brothers, the sons of his father's wives Bilhah
and Zilpah. But Joseph reported to his father
some of the bad things his brothers were doing.
[3]Jacob loved Joseph more than any of his
other children because Joseph had been born to
him in his old age. So one day Jacob had a special
gift made for Joseph—a beautiful robe. [4]But his
brothers hated Joseph because their father loved
him more than the rest of them. They couldn't
say a kind word to him.
[5]One night Joseph had a dream, and when he
told his brothers about it, they hated him more
than ever. [6]"Listen to this dream," he said. [7]"We
were out in the field, tying up bundles of grain.
Suddenly my bundle stood up, and your bundles
all gathered around and bowed low before
mine!"
[8]His brothers responded, "So you think you
will be our king, do you? Do you actually think
you will reign over us?" And they hated him all
the more because of his dreams and the way he
talked about them.
[9]Soon Joseph had another dream, and again
he told his brothers about it. "Listen, I have had
another dream," he said. "The sun, moon, and
eleven stars bowed low before me!"
[10]This time he told the dream to his father as
well as to his brothers, but his father scolded him.
"What kind of dream is that?" he asked. "Will
your mother and I and your brothers actually

WELL, WELL, WELL!

What happened at the well?

Read GENESIS 37.

Then make this Wacky Well to see how jealousy changes friendships.

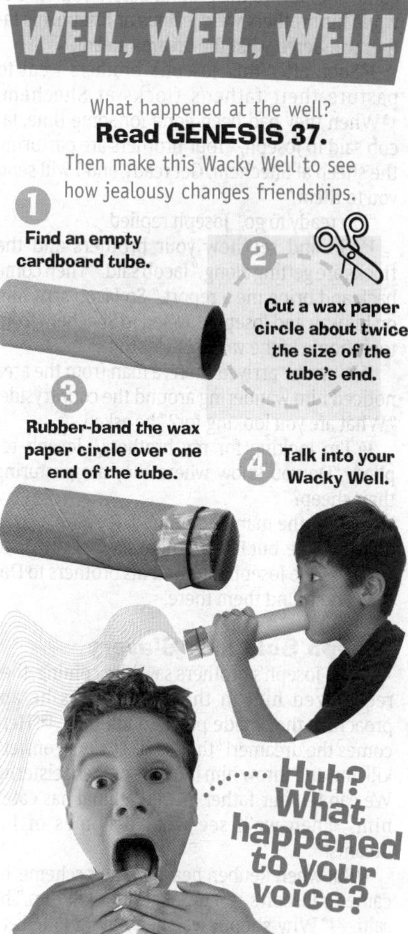

1
Find an empty cardboard tube.
2
Cut a wax paper circle about twice the size of the tube's end.
3
Rubber-band the wax paper circle over one end of the tube.
4
Talk into your Wacky Well.
Huh? What happened to your voice?

The wax paper changed the shape of your sound waves. It messed up your voice so it was hard to understand. Jealousy messed things up between Joseph and his brothers. **When jealousy gets between people, it's hard for them to understand each other and get along.**

If you've let jealousy come between you and a friend, go talk to that person. Explain what happened.

Ask for forgiveness.

You'll feel better—and so will they!

come and bow to the ground before you?" 11But
while his brothers were jealous of Joseph, his father wondered what the dreams meant.

12Soon after this, Joseph's brothers went to
pasture their father's flocks at Shechem.
13When they had been gone for some time, Jacob said to Joseph, "Your brothers are pasturing
the sheep at Shechem. Get ready, and I will send
you to them."

"I'm ready to go," Joseph replied.

14"Go and see how your brothers and the
flocks are getting along," Jacob said. "Then come
back and bring me a report." So Jacob sent him
on his way, and Joseph traveled to Shechem from
their home in the valley of Hebron.

15When he arrived there, a man from the area
noticed him wandering around the countryside.
"What are you looking for?" he asked.

16"I'm looking for my brothers," Joseph replied. "Do you know where they are pasturing
their sheep?"

17"Yes," the man told him. "They have moved
on from here, but I heard them say, 'Let's go on to
Dothan.'" So Joseph followed his brothers to Dothan and found them there.

Joseph Sold into Slavery

18When Joseph's brothers saw him coming, they
recognized him in the distance. As he approached, they made plans to kill him. 19"Here
comes the dreamer!" they said. 20"Come on, let's
kill him and throw him into one of these cisterns.
We can tell our father, 'A wild animal has eaten
him.' Then we'll see what becomes of his
dreams!"

21But when Reuben heard of their scheme, he
came to Joseph's rescue. "Let's not kill him," he
said. 22"Why should we shed any blood? Let's
just throw him into this empty cistern here in the
wilderness. Then he'll die without our laying a
hand on him." Reuben was secretly planning to
rescue Joseph and return him to his father.

23So when Joseph arrived, his brothers ripped
off the beautiful robe he was wearing. 24Then
they grabbed him and threw him into the cistern.
Now the cistern was empty; there was no water in
it. 25Then, just as they were sitting down to eat,
they looked up and saw a caravan of camels in the
distance coming toward them. It was a group of
Ishmaelite traders taking a load of gum, balm,
and aromatic resin from Gilead down to Egypt.

26Judah said to his brothers, "What will we
gain by killing our brother? We'd have to cover
up the crime. 27Instead of hurting him, let's sell
him to those Ishmaelite traders. After all, he is
our brother—our own flesh and blood!" And his
brothers agreed. 28So when the Ishmaelites, who
were Midianite traders, came by, Joseph's brothers pulled him out of the cistern and sold him to
them for twenty pieces of silver. And the traders
took him to Egypt.

29Some time later, Reuben returned to get Joseph out of the cistern. When he discovered that
Joseph was missing, he tore his clothes in grief.
30Then he went back to his brothers and la-
mented, "The boy is gone! What will I do now?"

31Then the brothers killed a young goat and
dipped Joseph's robe in its blood. 32They sent
the beautiful robe to their father with this message: "Look at what we found. Doesn't this robe
belong to your son?"

33Their father recognized it immediately.
"Yes," he said, "it is my son's robe. A wild animal
must have eaten him. Joseph has clearly been
torn to pieces!" 34Then Jacob tore his clothes and
dressed himself in burlap. He mourned deeply
for his son for a long time. 35His family all tried
to comfort him, but he refused to be comforted.
"I will go to my grave mourning for my son," he
would say, and then he would weep.

36Meanwhile, the Midianite traders arrived in
Egypt, where they sold Joseph to Potiphar, an officer of Pharaoh, the king of Egypt. Potiphar was
captain of the palace guard.

CHAPTER 38

Judah and Tamar

About this time, Judah left home and moved to
Adullam, where he stayed with a man named
Hirah. 2There he saw a Canaanite woman, the
daughter of Shua, and he married her. When he
slept with her, 3she became pregnant and gave
birth to a son, and he named the boy Er. 4Then she
became pregnant again and gave birth to another
son, and she named him Onan. 5And when she
gave birth to a third son, she named him Shelah.
At the time of Shelah's birth, they were living at
Kezib.

6In the course of time, Judah arranged for his
firstborn son, Er, to marry a young woman named
Tamar. 7But Er was a wicked man in the LORD's
sight, so the LORD took his life. 8Then Judah said
to Er's brother Onan, "Go and marry Tamar, as our
law requires of the brother of a man who has died.
You must produce an heir for your brother."

9But Onan was not willing to have a child who
would not be his own heir. So whenever he had
intercourse with his brother's wife, he spilled
the semen on the ground. This prevented her
from having a child who would belong to his

brother. 10But the LORD considered it evil for
Onan to deny a child to his dead brother. So the
LORD took Onan's life, too.

11Then Judah said to Tamar, his daughter-in-
law, "Go back to your parents' home and remain a
widow until my son Shelah is old enough to
marry you." (But Judah didn't really intend to do
this because he was afraid Shelah would also die,
like his two brothers.) So Tamar went back to live
in her father's home.

12Some years later Judah's wife died. After the
time of mourning was over, Judah and his friend
Hirah the Adullamite went up to Timnah to supervise the shearing of his sheep. 13Someone
told Tamar, "Look, your father-in-law is going up
to Timnah to shear his sheep."

14Tamar was aware that Shelah had grown up,
but no arrangements had been made for her to
come and marry him. So she changed out of her
widow's clothing and covered herself with a veil
to disguise herself. Then she sat beside the road
at the entrance to the village of Enaim, which is
on the road to Timnah. 15Judah noticed her and
thought she was a prostitute, since she had covered her face. 16So he stopped and propositioned
her. "Let me have sex with you," he said, not realizing that she was his own daughter-in-law.

"How much will you pay to have sex with me?"
Tamar asked.

17"I'll send you a young goat from my flock,"
Judah promised.

"But what will you give me to guarantee that
you will send the goat?" she asked.

18"What kind of guarantee do you want?" he
replied.

She answered, "Leave me your identification
seal and its cord and the walking stick you are
carrying." So Judah gave them to her. Then he
had intercourse with her, and she became pregnant. 19Afterward she went back home, took off
her veil, and put on her widow's clothing as
usual.

20Later Judah asked his friend Hirah the Adullamite to take the young goat to the woman and
to pick up the things he had given her as his
guarantee. But Hirah couldn't find her. 21So he
asked the men who lived there, "Where can I
find the shrine prostitute who was sitting beside
the road at the entrance to Enaim?"

"We've never had a shrine prostitute here,"
they replied.

22So Hirah returned to Judah and told him, "I
couldn't find her anywhere, and the men of the
village claim they've never had a shrine prostitute there."

23"Then let her keep the things I gave her," Judah said. "I sent the young goat as we agreed, but
you couldn't find her. We'd be the laughingstock
of the village if we went back again to look for
her."

24About three months later, Judah was told,
"Tamar, your daughter-in-law, has acted like
a prostitute. And now, because of this, she's
pregnant."

"Bring her out, and let her be burned!" Judah
demanded.

25But as they were taking her out to kill her,
she sent this message to her father-in-law: "The
man who owns these things made me pregnant.
Look closely. Whose seal and cord and walking
stick are these?"

26Judah recognized them immediately and
said, "She is more righteous than I am, because I
didn't arrange for her to marry my son Shelah."
And Judah never slept with Tamar again.

27When the time came for Tamar to give birth,
it was discovered that she was carrying twins.
28While she was in labor, one of the babies
reached out his hand. The midwife grabbed it
and tied a scarlet string around the child's wrist,
announcing, "This one came out first." 29But
then he pulled back his hand, and out came his
brother! "What!" the midwife exclaimed. "How
did you break out first?" So he was named Perez.
30Then the baby with the scarlet string on his
wrist was born, and he was named Zerah.

CHAPTER 39

Joseph in Potiphar's House

When Joseph was taken to Egypt by the Ishmaelite traders, he was purchased by Potiphar, an
Egyptian officer. Potiphar was captain of the
guard for Pharaoh, the king of Egypt.

2The LORD was with Joseph, so he succeeded in
everything he did as he served in the home of his
Egyptian master. 3Potiphar noticed this and realized that the LORD was with Joseph, giving
him success in everything he did. 4This pleased
Potiphar, so he soon made Joseph his personal attendant. He put him in charge of his entire
household and everything he owned. 5From the
day Joseph was put in charge of his master's
household and property, the LORD began to bless
Potiphar's household for Joseph's sake. All his
household affairs ran smoothly, and his crops
and livestock flourished. 6So Potiphar gave Joseph complete administrative responsibility over
everything he owned. With Joseph there, he
didn't worry about a thing—except what kind of
food to eat!

Joseph was a very handsome and well-built young man, 7and Potiphar's wife soon began to look at him lustfully. "Come and sleep with me," she demanded.

8But Joseph refused. "Look," he told her, "my master trusts me with everything in his entire household. 9No one here has more authority than I do. He has held back nothing from me except you, because you are his wife. How could I do such a wicked thing? It would be a great sin against God."

10She kept putting pressure on Joseph day after day, but he refused to sleep with her, and he kept out of her way as much as possible. 11One day, however, no one else was around when he went in to do his work. 12She came and grabbed him by his cloak, demanding, "Come on, sleep with me!" Joseph tore himself away, but he left his cloak in her hand as he ran from the house.

13When she saw that she was holding his cloak and he had fled, 14she called out to her servants. Soon all the men came running. "Look!" she said. "My husband has brought this Hebrew slave here to make fools of us! He came into my room to rape me, but I screamed. 15When he heard me scream, he ran outside and got away, but he left his cloak behind with me."

16She kept the cloak with her until her husband came home. 17Then she told him her story. "That Hebrew slave you've brought into our house tried to come in and fool around with me," she said. 18"But when I screamed, he ran outside, leaving his cloak with me!"

Joseph Put in Prison

19Potiphar was furious when he heard his wife's story about how Joseph had treated her. 20So he took Joseph and threw him into the prison where the king's prisoners were held, and there he remained. 21But the LORD was with Joseph in the prison and showed him his faithful love. And the LORD made Joseph a favorite with the prison warden. 22Before long, the warden put Joseph in charge of all the other prisoners and over everything that happened in the prison. 23The warden had no more worries, because Joseph took care of everything. The LORD was with him and caused everything he did to succeed.

CHAPTER 40

Joseph Interprets Two Dreams

Some time later, Pharaoh's chief cup-bearer and chief baker offended their royal master. 2Pharaoh became angry with these two officials, 3and he put them in the prison where Joseph was, in the palace of the captain of the guard. 4They remained in prison for quite some time, and the captain of the guard assigned them to Joseph, who looked after them.

5While they were in prison, Pharaoh's cup-bearer and baker each had a dream one night, and each dream had its own meaning. 6When Joseph saw them the next morning, he noticed that they both looked upset. 7"Why do you look so worried today?" he asked them.

8And they replied, "We both had dreams last night, but no one can tell us what they mean."

"Interpreting dreams is God's business," Joseph replied. "Go ahead and tell me your dreams."

9So the chief cup-bearer told Joseph his dream first. "In my dream," he said, "I saw a grapevine in front of me. 10The vine had three branches that began to bud and blossom, and soon it produced clusters of ripe grapes. 11I was holding Pharaoh's wine cup in my hand, so I took a cluster of grapes and squeezed the juice into the cup. Then I placed the cup in Pharaoh's hand."

12"This is what the dream means," Joseph said. "The three branches represent three days. 13Within three days Pharaoh will lift you up and restore you to your position as his chief cup-bearer. 14And please remember me and do me a favor when things go well for you. Mention me to Pharaoh, so he might let me out of this place. 15For I was kidnapped from my homeland, the land of the Hebrews, and now I'm here in prison, but I did nothing to deserve it."

16When the chief baker saw that Joseph had given the first dream such a positive interpretation, he said to Joseph, "I had a dream, too. In my dream there were three baskets of white pastries stacked on my head. 17The top basket contained all kinds of pastries for Pharaoh, but the birds came and ate them from the basket on my head."

18"This is what the dream means," Joseph told him. "The three baskets also represent three days. 19Three days from now Pharaoh will lift you up and impale your body on a pole. Then birds will come and peck away at your flesh."

20Pharaoh's birthday came three days later, and he prepared a banquet for all his officials and staff. He summoned his chief cup-bearer and chief baker to join the other officials. 21He then restored the chief cup-bearer to his former position, so he could again hand Pharaoh his cup. 22But Pharaoh impaled the chief baker, just as Joseph had predicted when he interpreted his dream. 23Pharaoh's chief cup-bearer, however, forgot all about Joseph, never giving him another thought.

BIBLE BIOS

Hear From the Heroes

Hi, my name is

ABRAHAM *(shepherd, parent of a nation)*

Like all of God's heroes (except Jesus), I made some whopper mistakes. But I know I did at least one thing right. When the Lord told me to leave my house and friends, I obeyed. God just said "go" and promised that my children would become a strong nation. But many years went by, and my wife, Sarah, and I almost gave up on God's promise. We still had no children, and we were old! Imagine your grandma and grandpa, or even your great-grandparents, having a baby. Well, that's exactly what happened to us. I was 100 years old and Sarah was 90 when we had Isaac—my wife just couldn't stop laughing! In fact, we picked a name for our son that showed our joy. *Isaac* means "laughter." That's no joke!

Want to see a couple of them? Check out GENESIS 12:10-20 and GENESIS 20:1-7.

When Isaac grew into his teens, I had the worst day of my life. Read **GENESIS 22:1-18** to find out what happened. During that frightening day, I obeyed God, and God took care of my son and me. You'll probably make a few mistakes in your life, but whatever you do, obey God. If you follow God's lead, he'll take you to the right place.

Around this time, God changed Abraham's name. If you want to know what it was before, check out GENESIS 17:1-8.

Part of the Family

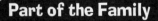

God told Abraham that he'd have as many children as there are stars in the sky—and that's exactly what happened. Abraham's grandson, Jacob (also known as Israel), had a bunch of children. Those children had children who had children. The kids kept coming until, after hundreds of years, there were millions of children who became the nation of Israel.

Everyone who believes in Jesus is a child of God—and part of Abraham's big family. Add a few of the children of God you know (including yourself) to the family of stars. You can squeeze names into the stars or draw faces.

Kyle

BIBLE BIOS

Hear From the Heroes

Hi, my name is

ISAAC *(rancher, shepherd)*

"Stop arguing!" If Rebekah and I told the boys that once, we told them a thousand times. In fact, the twins started getting into it before they were even born—they wrestled in Rebekah's womb! I'm to blame for part of it. Esau was a hunter. He was strong. He was my boy. Don't get me wrong, I loved Jacob, too. He just liked to spend more time at home with Rebekah. They were as different as night and day, and my extra love for Esau just made things worse.

See GENESIS 25:21-26 to see why they fought.

Esau didn't seem to care too much about the birthright until he lost it. Look what Esau did with his birthright in GENESIS 25:27-33.

As the eldest, Esau had the birthright (even though he came just a few minutes before). That meant that when I died, Esau would get twice as much of my riches, and he would take over as the family leader. Well, when it came time to give Esau his birthright, Jacob and Rebekah came up with a sneaky plan. They tricked me into blessing Jacob instead. You can read all about it in **GENESIS 27:1-40.**

Before the birth of the boys, God told Rebekah that Jacob would be the family leader. And that's exactly what happened. My family sure wasn't perfect, but God worked out his plan in us anyway. God is good and God is faithful—no matter what.

Like father, like son. Remember Abraham's mistakes in GENESIS 12:10-20 and GENESIS 20:1-7? Check out Isaac's mistake in GENESIS 26:1-9. Even these two great Bible heroes faced times when their faith was weak!

Pass It On

God gave a blessing to Abraham (read about it in **GENESIS 12:1-3**). Abraham passed that blessing on to Isaac. Isaac gave the blessing to Jacob. Find some old pictures of your parents when they were kids. **Do you have your mom's eyes? your dad's hair?** Ask someone in your family how your personality is like your mom's or dad's personality. What else did your parents pass down to you? How has God passed down blessings through your family?

Write down what you find here:

CHAPTER **41**

Pharaoh's Dreams

Two full years later, Pharaoh dreamed that he was
standing on the bank of the Nile River. 2In his
dream he saw seven fat, healthy cows come up
out of the river and begin grazing in the marsh
grass. 3Then he saw seven more cows come up
behind them from the Nile, but these were
scrawny and thin. These cows stood beside the
fat cows on the riverbank. 4Then the scrawny,
thin cows ate the seven healthy, fat cows! At this
point in the dream, Pharaoh woke up.

5But he fell asleep again and had a second
dream. This time he saw seven heads of grain,
plump and beautiful, growing on a single stalk.
6Then seven more heads of grain appeared, but
these were shriveled and withered by the east
wind. 7And these thin heads swallowed up the
seven plump, well-formed heads! Then Pharaoh
woke up again and realized it was a dream.

8The next morning Pharaoh was very disturbed by the dreams. So he called for all the
magicians and wise men of Egypt. When Pharaoh told them his dreams, not one of them
could tell him what they meant.

9Finally, the king's chief cup-bearer spoke up.
"Today I have been reminded of my failure," he
told Pharaoh. 10"Some time ago, you were angry
with the chief baker and me, and you imprisoned us in the palace of the captain of the guard.
11One night the chief baker and I each had a
dream, and each dream had its own meaning.
12There was a young Hebrew man with us in
the prison who was a slave of the captain of the
guard. We told him our dreams, and he told us
what each of our dreams meant. 13And everything happened just as he had predicted. I was
restored to my position as cup-bearer, and the
chief baker was executed and impaled on a
pole."

14Pharaoh sent for Joseph at once, and he was
quickly brought from the prison. After he shaved
and changed his clothes, he went in and stood before Pharaoh. 15Then Pharaoh said to Joseph, "I
had a dream last night, and no one here can tell
me what it means. But I have heard that when you
hear about a dream you can interpret it."

16"It is beyond my power to do this," Joseph replied. "But God can tell you what it means and set
you at ease."

17So Pharaoh told Joseph his dream. "In my
dream," he said, "I was standing on the bank of
the Nile River, 18and I saw seven fat, healthy cows
come up out of the river and begin grazing in the
marsh grass. 19But then I saw seven sick-looking
cows, scrawny and thin, come up after them. I've
never seen such sorry-looking animals in all the
land of Egypt. 20These thin, scrawny cows ate the
seven fat cows. 21But afterward you wouldn't
have known it, for they were still as thin and
scrawny as before! Then I woke up.

22"In my dream I also saw seven heads of
grain, full and beautiful, growing on a single
stalk. 23Then seven more heads of grain appeared, but these were blighted, shriveled, and
withered by the east wind. 24And the shriveled
heads swallowed the seven healthy heads. I told
these dreams to the magicians, but no one could
tell me what they mean."

25Joseph responded, "Both of Pharaoh's
dreams mean the same thing. God is telling Pharaoh in advance what he is about to do. 26The
seven healthy cows and the seven healthy heads
of grain both represent seven years of prosperity. 27The seven thin, scrawny cows that came
up later and the seven thin heads of grain, withered by the east wind, represent seven years of
famine.

28"This will happen just as I have described it,
for God has revealed to Pharaoh in advance what
he is about to do. 29The next seven years will be a
period of great prosperity throughout the land of
Egypt. 30But afterward there will be seven years
of famine so great that all the prosperity will be
forgotten in Egypt. Famine will destroy the land.
31This famine will be so severe that even the
memory of the good years will be erased. 32As for
having two similar dreams, it means that these
events have been decreed by God, and he will
soon make them happen.

33"Therefore, Pharaoh should find an intelligent and wise man and put him in charge of the
entire land of Egypt. 34Then Pharaoh should appoint supervisors over the land and let them
collect one-fifth of all the crops during the
seven good years. 35Have them gather all the
food produced in the good years that are just
ahead and bring it to Pharaoh's storehouses.
Store it away, and guard it so there will be food
in the cities. 36That way there will be enough to
eat when the seven years of famine come to the
land of Egypt. Otherwise this famine will destroy the land."

Joseph Made Ruler of Egypt

37Joseph's suggestions were well received by
Pharaoh and his officials. 38So Pharaoh asked his
officials, "Can we find anyone else like this man
so obviously filled with the spirit of God?"
39Then Pharaoh said to Joseph, "Since God has

revealed the meaning of the dreams to you,
clearly no one else is as intelligent or wise as you
are. 40You will be in charge of my court, and all
my people will take orders from you. Only I, sitting on my throne, will have a rank higher than
yours."
41Pharaoh said to Joseph, "I hereby put you in
charge of the entire land of Egypt." 42Then Pharaoh removed his signet ring from his hand and
placed it on Joseph's finger. He dressed him in
fine linen clothing and hung a gold chain
around his neck. 43Then he had Joseph ride
in the chariot reserved for his second-in-
command. And wherever Joseph went, the command was shouted, "Kneel down!" So Pharaoh
put Joseph in charge of all Egypt. 44And Pharaoh
said to him, "I am Pharaoh, but no one will lift a
hand or foot in the entire land of Egypt without
your approval."
45Then Pharaoh gave Joseph a new Egyptian
name, Zaphenath-paneah. He also gave him a
wife, whose name was Asenath. She was the
daughter of Potiphera, the priest of On. So Joseph took charge of the entire land of Egypt.
46He was thirty years old when he began serving
in the court of Pharaoh, the king of Egypt. And
when Joseph left Pharaoh's presence, he inspected the entire land of Egypt.
47As predicted, for seven years the land produced bumper crops. 48During those years, Joseph gathered all the crops grown in Egypt and
stored the grain from the surrounding fields in
the cities. 49He piled up huge amounts of grain
like sand on the seashore. Finally, he stopped
keeping records because there was too much to
measure.
50During this time, before the first of the famine years, two sons were born to Joseph and his
wife, Asenath, the daughter of Potiphera, the
priest of On. 51Joseph named his older son Manasseh, for he said, "God has made me forget all
my troubles and everyone in my father's family."
52Joseph named his second son Ephraim, for he
said, "God has made me fruitful in this land of
my grief."
53At last the seven years of bumper crops
throughout the land of Egypt came to an end.
54Then the seven years of famine began, just as
Joseph had predicted. The famine also struck all
the surrounding countries, but throughout
Egypt there was plenty of food. 55Eventually,
however, the famine spread throughout the land
of Egypt as well. And when the people cried out
to Pharaoh for food, he told them, "Go to Joseph,
and do whatever he tells you." 56So with severe
famine everywhere, Joseph opened up the storehouses and distributed grain to the Egyptians,
for the famine was severe throughout the land of
Egypt. 57And people from all around came to
Egypt to buy grain from Joseph because the famine was severe throughout the world.

CHAPTER 42

Joseph's Brothers Go to Egypt

When Jacob heard that grain was available in
Egypt, he said to his sons, "Why are you standing around looking at one another? 2I have
heard there is grain in Egypt. Go down there, and
buy enough grain to keep us alive. Otherwise
we'll die."
3So Joseph's ten older brothers went down to
Egypt to buy grain. 4But Jacob wouldn't let Joseph's younger brother, Benjamin, go with them,
for fear some harm might come to him. 5So Jacob's sons arrived in Egypt along with others to
buy food, for the famine was in Canaan as well.
6Since Joseph was governor of all Egypt and in
charge of selling grain to all the people, it was to
him that his brothers came. When they arrived,
they bowed before him with their faces to the
ground. 7Joseph recognized his brothers instantly, but he pretended to be a stranger and
spoke harshly to them. "Where are you from?"
he demanded.
"From the land of Canaan," they replied. "We
have come to buy food."
8Although Joseph recognized his brothers,
they didn't recognize him. 9And he remembered
the dreams he'd had about them many years
before. He said to them, "You are spies! You have
come to see how vulnerable our land has
become."
10"No, my lord!" they exclaimed. "Your servants have simply come to buy food. 11We are all
brothers—members of the same family. We are
honest men, sir! We are not spies!"
12"Yes, you are!" Joseph insisted. "You have
come to see how vulnerable our land has
become."
13"Sir," they said, "there are actually twelve of
us. We, your servants, are all brothers, sons of a
man living in the land of Canaan. Our youngest
brother is back there with our father right now,
and one of our brothers is no longer with us."
14But Joseph insisted, "As I said, you are spies!
15This is how I will test your story. I swear by the
life of Pharaoh that you will never leave Egypt unless your youngest brother comes here! 16One of
you must go and get your brother. I'll keep the
rest of you here in prison. Then we'll find out

whether or not your story is true. By the life of
Pharaoh, if it turns out that you don't have a
younger brother, then I'll know you are spies."
17So Joseph put them all in prison for three
days. 18On the third day Joseph said to them, "I
am a God-fearing man. If you do as I say, you will
live. 19If you really are honest men, choose one of
your brothers to remain in prison. The rest of
you may go home with grain for your starving
families. 20But you must bring your youngest
brother back to me. This will prove that you are
telling the truth, and you will not die." To this
they agreed.
21Speaking among themselves, they said,
"Clearly we are being punished because of what
we did to Joseph long ago. We saw his anguish
when he pleaded for his life, but we wouldn't listen. That's why we're in this trouble."
22"Didn't I tell you not to sin against the boy?"
Reuben asked. "But you wouldn't listen. And now
we have to answer for his blood!"
23Of course, they didn't know that Joseph
understood them, for he had been speaking to
them through an interpreter. 24Now he turned
away from them and began to weep. When he regained his composure, he spoke to them again.
Then he chose Simeon from among them and
had him tied up right before their eyes.
25Joseph then ordered his servants to fill the
men's sacks with grain, but he also gave secret instructions to return each brother's payment at
the top of his sack. He also gave them supplies
for their journey home. 26So the brothers loaded
their donkeys with the grain and headed for
home.
27But when they stopped for the night and
one of them opened his sack to get grain for his
donkey, he found his money in the top of his
sack. 28"Look!" he exclaimed to his brothers.
"My money has been returned; it's here in my
sack!" Then their hearts sank. Trembling, they
said to each other, "What has God done to us?"
29When the brothers came to their father,
Jacob, in the land of Canaan, they told him everything that had happened to them. 30"The man
who is governor of the land spoke very harshly to
us," they told him. "He accused us of being spies
scouting the land. 31But we said, 'We are honest
men, not spies. 32We are twelve brothers, sons of
one father. One brother is no longer with us, and
the youngest is at home with our father in the
land of Canaan.'
33"Then the man who is governor of the land
told us, 'This is how I will find out if you are honest men. Leave one of your brothers here with
me, and take grain for your starving families and
go on home. 34But you must bring your youngest
brother back to me. Then I will know you are
honest men and not spies. Then I will give you
back your brother, and you may trade freely in
the land.'"
35As they emptied out their sacks, there in
each man's sack was the bag of money he had
paid for the grain! The brothers and their father
were terrified when they saw the bags of money.
36Jacob exclaimed, "You are robbing me of my
children! Joseph is gone! Simeon is gone! And
now you want to take Benjamin, too. Everything
is going against me!"
37Then Reuben said to his father, "You may
kill my two sons if I don't bring Benjamin back to
you. I'll be responsible for him, and I promise to
bring him back."
38But Jacob replied, "My son will not go down
with you. His brother Joseph is dead, and he is all
I have left. If anything should happen to him on
your journey, you would send this grieving,
white-haired man to his grave."

CHAPTER 43

The Brothers Return to Egypt

But the famine continued to ravage the land of
Canaan. 2When the grain they had brought from
Egypt was almost gone, Jacob said to his sons, "Go
back and buy us a little more food."
3But Judah said, "The man was serious when
he warned us, 'You won't see my face again unless your brother is with you.' 4If you send Benjamin with us, we will go down and buy more food.
5But if you don't let Benjamin go, we won't go
either. Remember, the man said, 'You won't see
my face again unless your brother is with you.'"
6"Why were you so cruel to me?" Jacob
moaned. "Why did you tell him you had another
brother?"
7"The man kept asking us questions about
our family," they replied. "He asked, 'Is your father still alive? Do you have another brother?' So
we answered his questions. How could we know
he would say, 'Bring your brother down here'?"
8Judah said to his father, "Send the boy with
me, and we will be on our way. Otherwise we will
all die of starvation—and not only we, but you
and our little ones. 9I personally guarantee his
safety. You may hold me responsible if I don't
bring him back to you. Then let me bear the
blame forever. 10If we hadn't wasted all this
time, we could have gone and returned twice by
now."
11So their father, Jacob, finally said to them,

"If it can't be avoided, then at least do this. Pack
your bags with the best products of this land.
Take them down to the man as gifts—balm,
honey, gum, aromatic resin, pistachio nuts, and
almonds. 12 Also take double the money that was
put back in your sacks, as it was probably someone's mistake. 13 Then take your brother, and go
back to the man. 14 May God Almighty give you
mercy as you go before the man, so that he will
release Simeon and let Benjamin return. But if I
must lose my children, so be it."

15 So the men packed Jacob's gifts and double
the money and headed off with Benjamin. They
finally arrived in Egypt and presented themselves to Joseph. 16 When Joseph saw Benjamin
with them, he said to the manager of his household, "These men will eat with me this noon.
Take them inside the palace. Then go slaughter
an animal, and prepare a big feast." 17 So the man
did as Joseph told him and took them into
Joseph's palace.

18 The brothers were terrified when they saw
that they were being taken into Joseph's house.
"It's because of the money someone put in our
sacks last time we were here," they said. "He
plans to pretend that we stole it. Then he will
seize us, make us slaves, and take our donkeys."

A Feast at Joseph's Palace

19 The brothers approached the manager of Joseph's household and spoke to him at the entrance to the palace. 20 "Sir," they said, "we came
to Egypt once before to buy food. 21 But as we
were returning home, we stopped for the night
and opened our sacks. Then we discovered that
each man's money—the exact amount paid—was
in the top of his sack! Here it is; we have brought
it back with us. 22 We also have additional money
to buy more food. We have no idea who put our
money in our sacks."

23 "Relax. Don't be afraid," the household
manager told them. "Your God, the God of your
father, must have put this treasure into your
sacks. I know I received your payment." Then he
released Simeon and brought him out to them.

24 The manager then led the men into Joseph's
palace. He gave them water to wash their feet
and provided food for their donkeys. 25 They
were told they would be eating there, so they prepared their gifts for Joseph's arrival at noon.

26 When Joseph came home, they gave him the
gifts they had brought him, then bowed low to
the ground before him. 27 After greeting them, he
asked, "How is your father, the old man you
spoke about? Is he still alive?"

28 "Yes," they replied. "Our father, your servant, is alive and well." And they bowed low
again.

29 Then Joseph looked at his brother Benjamin, the son of his own mother. "Is this your
youngest brother, the one you told me about?"
Joseph asked. "May God be gracious to you, my
son." 30 Then Joseph hurried from the room because he was overcome with emotion for his
brother. He went into his private room, where he
broke down and wept. 31 After washing his face,
he came back out, keeping himself under control. Then he ordered, "Bring out the food!"

32 The waiters served Joseph at his own table,
and his brothers were served at a separate table.
The Egyptians who ate with Joseph sat at their
own table, because Egyptians despise Hebrews
and refuse to eat with them. 33 Joseph told each
of his brothers where to sit, and to their amazement, he seated them according to age, from oldest to youngest. 34 And Joseph filled their plates
with food from his own table, giving Benjamin
five times as much as he gave the others. So they
feasted and drank freely with him.

CHAPTER 44

Joseph's Silver Cup

When his brothers were ready to leave, Joseph
gave these instructions to his palace manager:
"Fill each of their sacks with as much grain as
they can carry, and put each man's money back
into his sack. 2 Then put my personal silver cup
at the top of the youngest brother's sack, along
with the money for his grain." So the manager
did as Joseph instructed him.

3 The brothers were up at dawn and were sent
on their journey with their loaded donkeys. 4 But
when they had gone only a short distance and
were barely out of the city, Joseph said to his palace manager, "Chase after them and stop them.
When you catch up with them, ask them, 'Why
have you repaid my kindness with such evil?
5 Why have you stolen my master's silver cup,
which he uses to predict the future? What a
wicked thing you have done!'"

6 When the palace manager caught up with
the men, he spoke to them as he had been
instructed.

7 "What are you talking about?" the brothers
responded. "We are your servants and would
never do such a thing! 8 Didn't we return the
money we found in our sacks? We brought it
back all the way from the land of Canaan. Why
would we steal silver or gold from your master's
house? 9 If you find his cup with any one of us, let

A CLEAN SLATE

Joseph's brothers were really rotten to him. They threw him in a well and sold him into slavery. Years later, Joseph had the power to get even. **Read GENESIS 45:1-15** to see what happened.

1 On a chalkboard, finish this sentence:
It's hard for me to forgive when...

2 Now finish this sentence:
When I don't forgive, I feel...

3 One more to finish:
I need help right now forgiving...

4 Ask God to help you forgive the person in #3. THEN FORGIVE!

Now erase everything you've written so your chalkboard is clean. **That's the way God wipes the slate clean when he forgives *you!***

that man die. And all the rest of us, my lord, will
be your slaves."
10"That's fair," the man replied. "But only the
one who stole the cup will be my slave. The rest
of you may go free."
11They all quickly took their sacks from the
backs of their donkeys and opened them. 12The
palace manager searched the brothers' sacks,
from the oldest to the youngest. And the cup was
found in Benjamin's sack! 13When the brothers
saw this, they tore their clothing in despair. Then
they loaded their donkeys again and returned to
the city.
14Joseph was still in his palace when Judah
and his brothers arrived, and they fell to the
ground before him. 15"What have you done?"
Joseph demanded. "Don't you know that a man
like me can predict the future?"
16Judah answered, "Oh, my lord, what can we
say to you? How can we explain this? How can we
prove our innocence? God is punishing us for
our sins. My lord, we have all returned to be your
slaves—all of us, not just our brother who had
your cup in his sack."
17"No," Joseph said. "I would never do such a
thing! Only the man who stole the cup will be my
slave. The rest of you may go back to your father
in peace."

Judah Speaks for His Brothers

18Then Judah stepped forward and said, "Please,
my lord, let your servant say just one word to you.
Please, do not be angry with me, even though you
are as powerful as Pharaoh himself.
19"My lord, previously you asked us, your servants, 'Do you have a father or a brother?' 20And
we responded, 'Yes, my lord, we have a father
who is an old man, and his youngest son is a child
of his old age. His full brother is dead, and he
alone is left of his mother's children, and his
father loves him very much.'
21"And you said to us, 'Bring him here so I can
see him with my own eyes.' 22But we said to you,
'My lord, the boy cannot leave his father, for his
father would die.' 23But you told us, 'Unless your
youngest brother comes with you, you will never
see my face again.'
24"So we returned to your servant, our father,
and told him what you had said. 25Later, when
he said, 'Go back again and buy us more food,'
26we replied, 'We can't go unless you let our
youngest brother go with us. We'll never get to
see the man's face unless our youngest brother
is with us.'
27"Then my father said to us, 'As you know,

my wife had two sons, 28and one of them went away and never returned. Doubtless he was torn to pieces by some wild animal. I have never seen him since. 29Now if you take his brother away from me, and any harm comes to him, you will send this grieving, white-haired man to his grave.'

30"And now, my lord, I cannot go back to my father without the boy. Our father's life is bound up in the boy's life. 31If he sees that the boy is not with us, our father will die. We, your servants, will indeed be responsible for sending that grieving, white-haired man to his grave. 32My lord, I guaranteed to my father that I would take care of the boy. I told him, 'If I don't bring him back to you, I will bear the blame forever.'

33"So please, my lord, let me stay here as a slave instead of the boy, and let the boy return with his brothers. 34For how can I return to my father if the boy is not with me? I couldn't bear to see the anguish this would cause my father!"

CHAPTER 45
Joseph Reveals His Identity

Joseph could stand it no longer. There were many people in the room, and he said to his attendants, "Out, all of you!" So he was alone with his brothers when he told them who he was. 2Then he broke down and wept. He wept so loudly the Egyptians could hear him, and word of it quickly carried to Pharaoh's palace.

3"I am Joseph!" he said to his brothers. "Is my father still alive?" But his brothers were speechless! They were stunned to realize that Joseph was standing there in front of them. 4"Please, come closer," he said to them. So they came closer. And he said again, "I am Joseph, your brother, whom you sold into slavery in Egypt. 5But don't be upset, and don't be angry with yourselves for selling me to this place. It was God who sent me here ahead of you to preserve your lives. 6This famine that has ravaged the land for two years will last five more years, and there will be neither plowing nor harvesting. 7God has sent me ahead of you to keep you and your families alive and to preserve many survivors. 8So it was God who sent me here, not you! And he is the one who made me an adviser to Pharaoh—the manager of his entire palace and the governor of all Egypt.

9"Now hurry back to my father and tell him, 'This is what your son Joseph says: God has made me master over all the land of Egypt. So come down to me immediately! 10You can live in the region of Goshen, where you can be near me with all your children and grandchildren, your flocks and herds, and everything you own. 11I will take care of you there, for there are still five years of famine ahead of us. Otherwise you, your household, and all your animals will starve.'"

12Then Joseph added, "Look! You can see for yourselves, and so can my brother Benjamin, that I really am Joseph! 13Go tell my father of my honored position here in Egypt. Describe for him everything you have seen, and then bring my father here quickly." 14Weeping with joy, he embraced Benjamin, and Benjamin did the same. 15Then Joseph kissed each of his brothers and wept over them, and after that they began talking freely with him.

Pharaoh Invites Jacob to Egypt

16The news soon reached Pharaoh's palace: "Joseph's brothers have arrived!" Pharaoh and his officials were all delighted to hear this.

17Pharaoh said to Joseph, "Tell your brothers, 'This is what you must do: Load your pack animals, and hurry back to the land of Canaan. 18Then get your father and all of your families, and return here to me. I will give you the very best land in Egypt, and you will eat from the best that the land produces.'"

19Then Pharaoh said to Joseph, "Tell your brothers, 'Take wagons from the land of Egypt to carry your little children and your wives, and bring your father here. 20Don't worry about your personal belongings, for the best of all the land of Egypt is yours.'"

21So the sons of Jacob did as they were told. Joseph provided them with wagons, as Pharaoh had commanded, and he gave them supplies for the journey. 22And he gave each of them new clothes—but to Benjamin he gave five changes of clothes and 300 pieces of silver. 23He also sent his father ten male donkeys loaded with the finest products of Egypt, and ten female donkeys loaded with grain and bread and other supplies he would need on his journey.

24So Joseph sent his brothers off, and as they left, he called after them, "Don't quarrel about all this along the way!" 25And they left Egypt and returned to their father, Jacob, in the land of Canaan.

26"Joseph is still alive!" they told him. "And he is governor of all the land of Egypt!" Jacob was stunned at the news—he couldn't believe it. 27But when they repeated to Jacob everything Joseph had told them, and when he saw the wagons Joseph had sent to carry him, their father's spirits revived.

[28]Then Jacob exclaimed, "It must be true! My son Joseph is alive! I must go and see him before I die."

CHAPTER 46

Jacob's Journey to Egypt

So Jacob set out for Egypt with all his possessions. And when he came to Beersheba, he offered sacrifices to the God of his father, Isaac.
[2]During the night God spoke to him in a vision. "Jacob! Jacob!" he called.

"Here I am," Jacob replied.

[3]"I am God, the God of your father," the voice said. "Do not be afraid to go down to Egypt, for there I will make your family into a great nation.
[4]I will go with you down to Egypt, and I will bring you back again. You will die in Egypt, but Joseph will be with you to close your eyes."

[5]So Jacob left Beersheba, and his sons took him to Egypt. They carried him and their little ones and their wives in the wagons Pharaoh had
provided for them. [6]They also took all their livestock and all the personal belongings they had acquired in the land of Canaan. So Jacob and his
entire family went to Egypt—[7]sons and grandsons, daughters and granddaughters—all his descendants.

[8]These are the names of the descendants of Israel—the sons of Jacob—who went to Egypt:

Reuben was Jacob's oldest son. [9]The sons of Reuben were Hanoch, Pallu, Hezron, and Carmi.

[10]The sons of Simeon were Jemuel, Jamin, Ohad, Jakin, Zohar, and Shaul. (Shaul's mother was a Canaanite woman.)

[11]The sons of Levi were Gershon, Kohath, and Merari.

[12]The sons of Judah were Er, Onan, Shelah, Perez, and Zerah (though Er and Onan had died in the land of Canaan). The sons of Perez were Hezron and Hamul.

[13]The sons of Issachar were Tola, Puah, Jashub, and Shimron.

[14]The sons of Zebulun were Sered, Elon, and Jahleel.

[15]These were the sons of Leah and Jacob who were born in Paddan-aram, in addition to their daughter, Dinah. The number of Jacob's descendants (male and female) through Leah was thirty-three.

[16]The sons of Gad were Zephon, Haggi, Shuni, Ezbon, Eri, Arodi, and Areli.

[17]The sons of Asher were Imnah, Ishvah, Ishvi, and Beriah. Their sister was Serah. Beriah's sons were Heber and Malkiel.

[18]These were the sons of Zilpah, the servant given to Leah by her father, Laban. The number of Jacob's descendants through Zilpah was sixteen.

[19]The sons of Jacob's wife Rachel were Joseph and Benjamin.

[20]Joseph's sons, born in the land of Egypt, were Manasseh and Ephraim. Their mother was Asenath, daughter of Potiphera, the priest of On.

[21]Benjamin's sons were Bela, Beker, Ashbel, Gera, Naaman, Ehi, Rosh, Muppim, Huppim, and Ard.

[22]These were the sons of Rachel and Jacob. The number of Jacob's descendants through Rachel was fourteen.

[23]The son of Dan was Hushim.

[24]The sons of Naphtali were Jahzeel, Guni, Jezer, and Shillem.

[25]These were the sons of Bilhah, the servant given to Rachel by her father, Laban. The number of Jacob's descendants through Bilhah was seven.

[26]The total number of Jacob's direct descendants who went with him to Egypt, not counting
his sons' wives, was sixty-six. [27]In addition, Joseph had two sons who were born in Egypt. So altogether, there were seventy members of Jacob's family in the land of Egypt.

Jacob's Family Arrives in Goshen

[28]As they neared their destination, Jacob sent Judah ahead to meet Joseph and get directions to the region of Goshen. And when they finally arrived there, [29]Joseph prepared his chariot and traveled to Goshen to meet his father, Jacob. When Joseph arrived, he embraced his father
and wept, holding him for a long time. [30]Finally, Jacob said to Joseph, "Now I am ready to die, since I have seen your face again and know you are still alive."

[31]And Joseph said to his brothers and to his father's entire family, "I will go to Pharaoh and tell him, 'My brothers and my father's entire family have come to me from the land of Canaan.
[32]These men are shepherds, and they raise livestock. They have brought with them their flocks and herds and everything they own.'"

[33]Then he said, "When Pharaoh calls for you
and asks you about your occupation, [34]you must
tell him, 'We, your servants, have raised livestock

all our lives, as our ancestors have always done.'
When you tell him this, he will let you live here in
the region of Goshen, for the Egyptians despise
shepherds."

CHAPTER 47

Jacob Blesses Pharaoh

Then Joseph went to see Pharaoh and told him,
"My father and my brothers have arrived from
the land of Canaan. They have come with all their
flocks and herds and possessions, and they are
now in the region of Goshen."
2 Joseph took five of his brothers with him and
presented them to Pharaoh. 3 And Pharaoh asked
the brothers, "What is your occupation?"
They replied, "We, your servants, are shepherds, just like our ancestors. 4 We have come to
live here in Egypt for a while, for there is no pasture for our flocks in Canaan. The famine is very
severe there. So please, we request permission to
live in the region of Goshen."
5 Then Pharaoh said to Joseph, "Now that your
father and brothers have joined you here,
6 choose any place in the entire land of Egypt for
them to live. Give them the best land of Egypt.
Let them live in the region of Goshen. And if any
of them have special skills, put them in charge of
my livestock, too."
7 Then Joseph brought in his father, Jacob, and
presented him to Pharaoh. And Jacob blessed
Pharaoh.
8 "How old are you?" Pharaoh asked him.
9 Jacob replied, "I have traveled this earth for
130 hard years. But my life has been short compared to the lives of my ancestors." 10 Then
Jacob blessed Pharaoh again before leaving his
court.
11 So Joseph assigned the best land of Egypt—
the region of Rameses—to his father and his
brothers, and he settled them there, just as Pharaoh had commanded. 12 And Joseph provided
food for his father and his brothers in amounts
appropriate to the number of their dependents,
including the smallest children.

Joseph's Leadership in the Famine

13 Meanwhile, the famine became so severe that
all the food was used up, and people were starving throughout the lands of Egypt and Canaan.
14 By selling grain to the people, Joseph eventually collected all the money in Egypt and Canaan,
and he put the money in Pharaoh's treasury.
15 When the people of Egypt and Canaan ran out
of money, all the Egyptians came to Joseph. "Our
money is gone!" they cried. "But please give us
food, or we will die before your very eyes!"
16 Joseph replied, "Since your money is gone,
bring me your livestock. I will give you food in
exchange for your livestock." 17 So they brought
their livestock to Joseph in exchange for food. In
exchange for their horses, flocks of sheep and
goats, herds of cattle, and donkeys, Joseph provided them with food for another year.
18 But that year ended, and the next year they
came again and said, "We cannot hide the truth
from you, my lord. Our money is gone, and all our
livestock and cattle are yours. We have nothing
left to give but our bodies and our land. 19 Why
should we die before your very eyes? Buy us and
our land in exchange for food; we offer our land
and ourselves as slaves for Pharaoh. Just give us
grain so we may live and not die, and so the land
does not become empty and desolate."
20 So Joseph bought all the land of Egypt for
Pharaoh. All the Egyptians sold him their fields
because the famine was so severe, and soon all
the land belonged to Pharaoh. 21 As for the people, he made them all slaves, from one end of
Egypt to the other. 22 The only land he did not
buy was the land belonging to the priests. They
received an allotment of food directly from Pharaoh, so they didn't need to sell their land.
23 Then Joseph said to the people, "Look, today I
have bought you and your land for Pharaoh. I will
provide you with seed so you can plant the fields.
24 Then when you harvest it, one-fifth of your crop
will belong to Pharaoh. You may keep the remaining four-fifths as seed for your fields and as food
for you, your households, and your little ones."
25 "You have saved our lives!" they exclaimed.
"May it please you, my lord, to let us be Pharaoh's
servants." 26 Joseph then issued a decree still in
effect in the land of Egypt, that Pharaoh should
receive one-fifth of all the crops grown on his
land. Only the land belonging to the priests was
not given to Pharaoh.
27 Meanwhile, the people of Israel settled in
the region of Goshen in Egypt. There they acquired property, and they were fruitful, and their
population grew rapidly. 28 Jacob lived for seventeen years after his arrival in Egypt, so he lived
147 years in all.
29 As the time of his death drew near, Jacob
called for his son Joseph and said to him, "Please
do me this favor. Put your hand under my thigh
and swear that you will treat me with unfailing
love by honoring this last request: Do not bury
me in Egypt. 30 When I die, please take my body
out of Egypt and bury me with my ancestors."

So Joseph promised, "I will do as you ask."
31"Swear that you will do it," Jacob insisted. So
Joseph gave his oath, and Jacob bowed humbly at
the head of his bed.

CHAPTER 48
Jacob Blesses Manasseh and Ephraim

One day not long after this, word came to Joseph,
"Your father is failing rapidly." So Joseph went to
visit his father, and he took with him his two
sons, Manasseh and Ephraim.
2When Joseph arrived, Jacob was told, "Your
son Joseph has come to see you." So Jacob gathered his strength and sat up in his bed.
3Jacob said to Joseph, "God Almighty appeared
to me at Luz in the land of Canaan and blessed
me. 4He said to me, 'I will make you fruitful, and I
will multiply your descendants. I will make you a
multitude of nations. And I will give this land of
Canaan to your descendants after you as an everlasting possession.'
5"Now I am claiming as my own sons these
two boys of yours, Ephraim and Manasseh, who
were born here in the land of Egypt before I arrived. They will be my sons, just as Reuben and
Simeon are. 6But any children born to you in the
future will be your own, and they will inherit land
within the territories of their brothers Ephraim
and Manasseh.
7"Long ago, as I was returning from Paddan-
aram, Rachel died in the land of Canaan. We were
still on the way, some distance from Ephrath
(that is, Bethlehem). So with great sorrow I buried her there beside the road to Ephrath."
8Then Jacob looked over at the two boys. "Are
these your sons?" he asked.
9"Yes," Joseph told him, "these are the sons
God has given me here in Egypt."
And Jacob said, "Bring them closer to me, so I
can bless them."
10Jacob was half blind because of his age and
could hardly see. So Joseph brought the boys
close to him, and Jacob kissed and embraced
them. 11Then Jacob said to Joseph, "I never
thought I would see your face again, but now God
has let me see your children, too!"
12Joseph moved the boys, who were at their
grandfather's knees, and he bowed with his face
to the ground. 13Then he positioned the boys in
front of Jacob. With his right hand he directed
Ephraim toward Jacob's left hand, and with his
left hand he put Manasseh at Jacob's right hand.
14But Jacob crossed his arms as he reached out to
lay his hands on the boys' heads. He put his right
hand on the head of Ephraim, though he was the
younger boy, and his left hand on the head of Manasseh, though he was the firstborn. 15Then he
blessed Joseph and said,

"May the God before whom my grandfather
Abraham
and my father, Isaac, walked—
the God who has been my shepherd
all my life, to this very day,
16 the Angel who has redeemed me from all
harm—
may he bless these boys.
May they preserve my name
and the names of Abraham and Isaac.
And may their descendants multiply greatly
throughout the earth."

17But Joseph was upset when he saw that his
father placed his right hand on Ephraim's head.
So Joseph lifted it to move it from Ephraim's
head to Manasseh's head. 18"No, my father," he
said. "This one is the firstborn. Put your right
hand on his head."
19But his father refused. "I know, my son; I
know," he replied. "Manasseh will also become a
great people, but his younger brother will become even greater. And his descendants will become a multitude of nations."
20So Jacob blessed the boys that day with this
blessing: "The people of Israel will use your
names when they give a blessing. They will say,
'May God make you as prosperous as Ephraim
and Manasseh.'" In this way, Jacob put Ephraim
ahead of Manasseh.
21Then Jacob said to Joseph, "Look, I am about
to die, but God will be with you and will take you
back to Canaan, the land of your ancestors.
22And beyond what I have given your brothers, I
am giving you an extra portion of the land that
I took from the Amorites with my sword and
bow."

CHAPTER 49
Jacob's Last Words to His Sons

Then Jacob called together all his sons and said,
"Gather around me, and I will tell you what will
happen to each of you in the days to come.

2 "Come and listen, you sons of Jacob;
listen to Israel, your father.

3 "Reuben, you are my firstborn, my strength,
the child of my vigorous youth.
You are first in rank and first in power.
4 But you are as unruly as a flood,
and you will be first no longer.

For you went to bed with my wife;
you defiled my marriage couch.

5 "Simeon and Levi are two of a kind;
their weapons are instruments of
violence.
6 May I never join in their meetings;
may I never be a party to their plans.
For in their anger they murdered men,
and they crippled oxen just for sport.
7 A curse on their anger, for it is fierce;
a curse on their wrath, for it is cruel.
I will scatter them among the descendants
of Jacob;
I will disperse them throughout Israel.

8 "Judah, your brothers will praise you.
You will grasp your enemies by the neck.
All your relatives will bow before you.
9 Judah, my son, is a young lion
that has finished eating its prey.
Like a lion he crouches and lies down;
like a lioness—who dares to rouse him?
10 The scepter will not depart from Judah,
nor the ruler's staff from his
descendants,
until the coming of the one to whom it
belongs,
the one whom all nations will honor.
11 He ties his foal to a grapevine,
the colt of his donkey to a choice vine.
He washes his clothes in wine,
his robes in the blood of grapes.
12 His eyes are darker than wine,
and his teeth are whiter than milk.

13 "Zebulun will settle by the seashore
and will be a harbor for ships;
his borders will extend to Sidon.

14 "Issachar is a sturdy donkey,
resting between two saddlepacks.
15 When he sees how good the countryside
is and how pleasant the land,
he will bend his shoulder to the load
and submit himself to hard labor.

16 "Dan will govern his people,
like any other tribe in Israel.
17 Dan will be a snake beside the road,
a poisonous viper along the path
that bites the horse's hooves
so its rider is thrown off.
18 I trust in you for salvation, O LORD!

19 "Gad will be attacked by marauding bands,
but he will attack them when they
retreat.

20 "Asher will dine on rich foods
and produce food fit for kings.

21 "Naphtali is a doe set free
that bears beautiful fawns.

22 "Joseph is the foal of a wild donkey,
the foal of a wild donkey at a spring—
one of the wild donkeys on the ridge.
23 Archers attacked him savagely;
they shot at him and harassed him.
24 But his bow remained taut,
and his arms were strengthened
by the hands of the Mighty One of Jacob,
by the Shepherd, the Rock of Israel.
25 May the God of your father help you;
may the Almighty bless you
with the blessings of the heavens above,
and blessings of the watery depths
below,
and blessings of the breasts and womb.
26 May my fatherly blessings on you
surpass the blessings of my ancestors,
reaching to the heights of the eternal hills.
May these blessings rest on the head of
Joseph,
who is a prince among his brothers.

27 "Benjamin is a ravenous wolf,
devouring his enemies in the morning
and dividing his plunder in the evening."

28 These are the twelve tribes of Israel, and this
is what their father said as he told his sons good-
bye. He blessed each one with an appropriate
message.

Jacob's Death and Burial

29 Then Jacob instructed them, "Soon I will die
and join my ancestors. Bury me with my father
and grandfather in the cave in the field of Ephron the Hittite. 30 This is the cave in the field of
Machpelah, near Mamre in Canaan, that Abraham bought from Ephron the Hittite as a permanent burial site. 31 There Abraham and his wife
Sarah are buried. There Isaac and his wife, Rebekah, are buried. And there I buried Leah. 32 It is
the plot of land and the cave that my grandfather
Abraham bought from the Hittites."
33 When Jacob had finished this charge to his
sons, he drew his feet into the bed, breathed his
last, and joined his ancestors in death.

CHAPTER 50

Joseph threw himself on his father and wept over
him and kissed him. 2 Then Joseph told the physicians who served him to embalm his father's

body; so Jacob was embalmed. 3The embalming
process took the usual forty days. And the Egyptians mourned his death for seventy days.
4When the period of mourning was over, Joseph approached Pharaoh's advisers and said,
"Please do me this favor and speak to Pharaoh on
my behalf. 5Tell him that my father made me
swear an oath. He said to me, 'Listen, I am about
to die. Take my body back to the land of Canaan,
and bury me in the tomb I prepared for myself.'
So please allow me to go and bury my father.
After his burial, I will return without delay."
6Pharaoh agreed to Joseph's request. "Go and
bury your father, as he made you promise," he
said. 7So Joseph went up to bury his father. He
was accompanied by all of Pharaoh's officials, all
the senior members of Pharaoh's household, and
all the senior officers of Egypt. 8Joseph also took
his entire household and his brothers and their
households. But they left their little children and
flocks and herds in the land of Goshen. 9A great
number of chariots and charioteers accompanied Joseph.
10When they arrived at the threshing floor of
Atad, near the Jordan River, they held a very great
and solemn memorial service, with a seven-day
period of mourning for Joseph's father. 11The local residents, the Canaanites, watched them
mourning at the threshing floor of Atad. Then
they renamed that place (which is near the Jordan) Abel-mizraim, for they said, "This is a place
of deep mourning for these Egyptians."
12So Jacob's sons did as he had commanded
them. 13They carried his body to the land of Canaan and buried him in the cave in the field of
Machpelah, near Mamre. This is the cave that
Abraham had bought as a permanent burial site
from Ephron the Hittite.

Joseph Reassures His Brothers

14After burying Jacob, Joseph returned to Egypt
with his brothers and all who had accompanied
him to his father's burial. 15But now that
their father was dead, Joseph's brothers became
fearful. "Now Joseph will show his anger and pay
us back for all the wrong we did to him," they
said.
16So they sent this message to Joseph: "Before
your father died, he instructed us 17to say to you:
'Please forgive your brothers for the great wrong
they did to you—for their sin in treating you so
cruelly.' So we, the servants of the God of your
father, beg you to forgive our sin." When Joseph
received the message, he broke down and wept.
18Then his brothers came and threw themselves
down before Joseph. "Look, we are your slaves!"
they said.
19But Joseph replied, "Don't be afraid of me.
Am I God, that I can punish you? 20You intended
to harm me, but God intended it all for good. He
brought me to this position so I could save the
lives of many people. 21No, don't be afraid. I will
continue to take care of you and your children."
So he reassured them by speaking kindly to
them.

The Death of Joseph

22So Joseph and his brothers and their families
continued to live in Egypt. Joseph lived to the age
of 110. 23He lived to see three generations of descendants of his son Ephraim, and he lived to see
the birth of the children of Manasseh's son
Makir, whom he claimed as his own.
24"Soon I will die," Joseph told his brothers,
"but God will surely come to help you and lead
you out of this land of Egypt. He will bring you
back to the land he solemnly promised to give to
Abraham, to Isaac, and to Jacob."
25Then Joseph made the sons of Israel swear
an oath, and he said, "When God comes to help
you and lead you back, you must take my bones
with you." 26So Joseph died at the age of 110. The
Egyptians embalmed him, and his body was
placed in a coffin in Egypt.

Creation

Genesis 1–2

Consider This:

- The giant squid's eye can be as big as 15 inches across! (That's three inches longer than your ruler!)

- A cockroach can live up to 10 days without a head! Eww!

It's a moth's wings up really close.
Whether you look at God's creation up close or from far off, you have to admit that it's amazing!

After creating everything, God said, "It is very good." God could have said, "It is incredible!" God thought up the tiniest moth and the largest star. And God created you!

The Whatsa-ma-jiggy

1. Make your own modeling clay by squishing together for five minutes:
   - 1 cup of flour
   - 1/3 cup of salt
   - 1/3 cup of tap water

2. Create a never-seen-before animal, plant, or rock.

3. Name your creation, then compare your creation to God's creation by reading GENESIS 1.

I'M A DOGIRAFINORD!

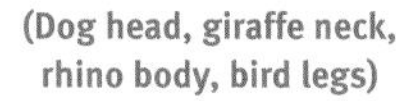

(Dog head, giraffe neck, rhino body, bird legs)

WHY DID GOD GO TO ALL THE TROUBLE OF CREATION?

The main reason was that God wanted to have a relationship with you! You can have a relationship with God by putting your faith in Jesus. Check out these verses to learn more:
JOHN 3:16; ROMANS 6:23; ROMANS 10:9-10; AND JOHN 15:15-17.

The Flood

Genesis 6–9

HEY, WHERE YA GOING?!

Sadly, many animals go extinct every year. (That means we'll never see them again.) But if it hadn't been for God and Noah, *all* of the animals would already be extinct. **Check it out in Genesis 6:13–7:20.**

The Flood covered the whole earth. But God told Noah to build a giant boat for his family and two of every animal. God took care of Noah and the animals. **God takes care of you, too!**

Saving Creation

1. **Make a list of things God created that you really care about. (Like mountains)**
2. **Make a list of all the problems these things face. (Like litter)**
3. **Make a list of all the things you can do to help with or fix one of the problems. (Like take a walk and fill one garbage bag full of litter)**
4. **Talk with an adult about your plan to care for God's creation—THEN DO IT!**

You can!

God wants us to care for creation—especially for other people. Pray for God's help, and ask others to join you in your plan!

GOD LOVES TO SAVE!

God doesn't save money or baseball cards. God loves to save people! God saved Noah's family during the Flood. And God saved us when he sent his Son, Jesus, to die for our sins.

CHECK IT OUT IN ROMANS 5:6-8; TITUS 3:5-6; AND 1 PETER 3:18!

The Ten Commandments

Exodus 20:1-7

If the people you loved were heading for the

EDGE OF A CLIFF,

wouldn't you try to stop them?

Well, that's kind of like what God did when he wrote the Ten Commandments on those stone tablets. God loves us and wants us to be happy and safe. So he wrote down 10 rules to live by. **Read all Ten Commandments in Exodus 20:1-17.** Then make this stone tablet of your own!

1. **Check a narrow cardboard box lid for holes.** (Tape any holes on the back of the lid.)
2. **Cut a strip of poster board, and tape it to the inside of the lid to form a rounded top.**
3. **Coat the inside of the lid with petroleum jelly.**
4. **Mix one cup plaster of Paris and 2/3 cup water in a bowl you can throw away.** DO NOT let any of the mixture go down the drain! Use self-hardening clay instead of plaster if you want.
5. **Pour the mixture in the box lid, and let it harden for an hour. Then carefully tear off the cardboard lid.** Now read Deuteronomy 6:5 and Matthew 22:37-40.

What's the greatest commandment? Write it on your tablet in pencil, then scratch the letters into the plaster. Keep the tablet in your room to remind you how God wants you to live!

Sponge gray tempera paint onto the plaster to make it look like a real stone tablet!

YOU CAN'T EARN YOUR WAY TO HEAVEN. You can't obey the rules enough, do enough good deeds, or go to church enough. Those are all good things to do, but they won't get you into heaven because you're still going to mess up. The only way to get to heaven is by believing in Jesus. He died on the cross to take the punishment for your sins. He rose from the dead to show his victory over sin and death. He wants you to be with him forever in heaven. What do you say?

Jesus and the Ten Commandments

God gave his people the Ten Commandments to teach them how to live in a way that would please him. Jesus says he came not to cancel the laws but to fulfill them (see **Matthew 5:17**). Read this comparison between the Ten Commandments and what Jesus says.

THE TEN COMMANDMENTS SAY...	JESUS SAYS...
Do not worship any other god but me. EXODUS 20:3	You must worship the LORD your God and serve only him. **MATTHEW 4:10**
Do not make idols of any kind, whether in the shape of birds or animals or fish. EXODUS 20:4	No one can serve two masters. **LUKE 16:13**
Do not misuse the name of the LORD your God. The LORD will not let you go unpunished if you misuse his name. EXODUS 20:7	Do not make any vows! Do not say, "By heaven!" because heaven is God's throne. **MATTHEW 5:34**
Remember to observe the Sabbath day by keeping it holy. EXODUS 20:8	The Sabbath was made to benefit people, and not people to benefit the Sabbath. So the Son of Man is Lord, even of the Sabbath! **MARK 2:27-28**
Honor your father and mother. Then you will live a long, full life in the land the LORD your God will give you. EXODUS 20:12	If you love your father or mother more than you love me, you are not worthy of being mine; or if you love your son or daughter more than me, you are not worthy of being mine. **MATTHEW 10:37**
Do not murder. EXODUS 20:13	If you are angry with someone, you are subject to judgment! If you call someone an idiot, you are in danger of being brought before the court. And if you curse someone, you are in danger of the fires of hell. **MATTHEW 5:22**
Do not commit adultery. EXODUS 20:14	Anyone who even looks at a woman with lust has already committed adultery with her in his heart. **MATTHEW 5:28**
Do not steal. EXODUS 20:15	If you are sued in court and your shirt is taken from you, give your coat, too. **MATTHEW 5:40**
Do not testify falsely against your neighbor. EXODUS 20:16	You must give an account on judgment day for every idle word you speak. **MATTHEW 12:36**
Do not covet your neighbor's house. Do not covet your neighbor's wife, male or female servant, ox or donkey, or anything else your neighbor owns. EXODUS 20:17	Guard against every kind of greed. Life is not measured by how much you own. **LUKE 12:15**

Now write your own summary of each commandment.

EXODUS Escape From EGYPT

Look for 3 hidden messages in Exodus!

Read how God rescued his people. Discover the truth about:

- **SLAVE LABOR**
- **THE BIRTH OF MOSES**
- **A BURNING BUSH**
- **A NERVOUS LEADER**
- **GROSS PLAGUES**
- **A GREAT ESCAPE**
- ***LOTS* OF WHINING AND WANDERING**
- **TEN RULES TO LIVE BY**

Plagues Plague Egypt

Frogs. Gnats. Flies. You name it, Egypt got it. How far did God have to go to get Pharaoh's attention? **Skim through Exodus 7–11.**

ACTION NEWS
Things are really hopping here in Egypt.

The Passover

For once, being passed over was a *good* thing. When God struck Egypt with the last—and worst—plague, he spared the Israelites. It was a night for the Israelites to remember—and one the Egyptians wanted to forget. **Find out more in Exodus 12.**

A Great Escape

Turns out the Israelites didn't even need a boat to cross the Red Sea after leaving Egypt. Turns out the Egyptians weren't so lucky. **For all the details, turn to Exodus 14:5-31.**

Birth Announcements

Baby cruise

Pharaoh's daughter found a Hebrew baby boy floating in a basket near the edge of the river. This was one lucky baby! Actually, luck had nothing to do with it. **Find out more in Exodus 1:22–2:10.**

Strange but True

What's behind burning bush?

What—or who—was behind the burning bush Moses reported seeing? **For a full report, go to Exodus 3.**

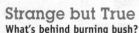

That's right. I saw a burning bush that didn't burn up. But I also *heard* it.

Job News

Slave labor

Because of a shortage of straw, Israelite slaves complained about the number of bricks the Egyptians expected them to make.

"Tough," said Pharaoh.

Will the slaves go on strike? **Read what happens in Exodus 5.**

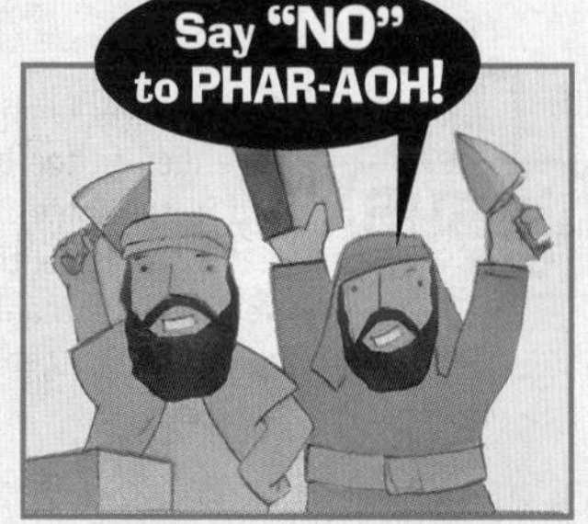

Say "NO" to PHAR-AOH!

Cattle Report

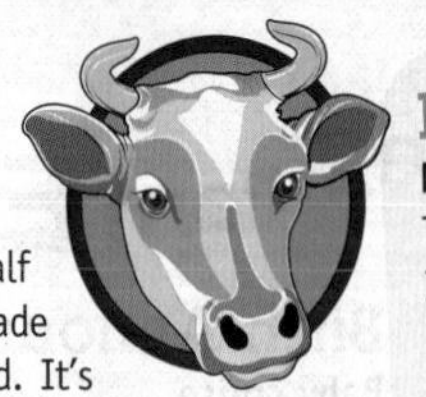

Calf is cooked

The worthless calf the Israelites made of gold is cooked. It's toast. Gone, and good riddance. Find out why the calf got cooked and how God and Moses dealt with the dastardly deed. **Continued in Exodus 32.**

Restaurant Review

Manna in the morning

The Master Chef has done it again. To satisfy the Israelites' hunger, God provided daily portions of manna (bread) and quail (meat). **For the complete menu, go to Exodus 16.**

TASTES LIKE CHICKEN

TOP 10 LIST

From the head office high atop Mount Sinai come the top Ten Commandments:

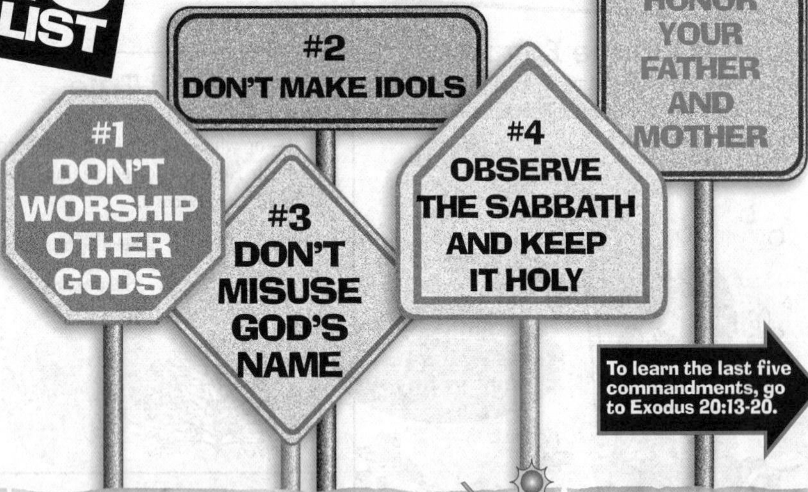

#1 DON'T WORSHIP OTHER GODS

#2 DON'T MAKE IDOLS

#3 DON'T MISUSE GOD'S NAME

#4 OBSERVE THE SABBATH AND KEEP IT HOLY

#5 HONOR YOUR FATHER AND MOTHER

To learn the last five commandments, go to Exodus 20:13-20.

Timeline

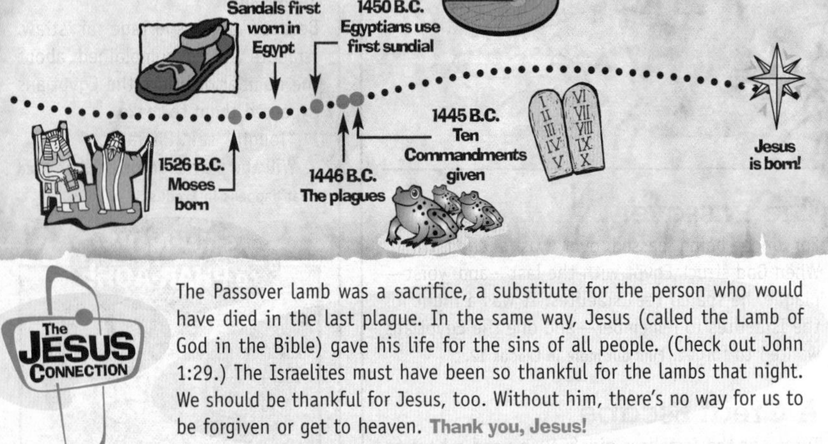

1526 B.C. Moses born

1500 B.C. Sandals first worn in Egypt

1450 B.C. Egyptians use first sundial

1446 B.C. The plagues

1445 B.C. Ten Commandments given

Jesus is born!

The JESUS CONNECTION

The Passover lamb was a sacrifice, a substitute for the person who would have died in the last plague. In the same way, Jesus (called the Lamb of God in the Bible) gave his life for the sins of all people. (Check out John 1:29.) The Israelites must have been so thankful for the lambs that night. We should be thankful for Jesus, too. Without him, there's no way for us to be forgiven or get to heaven. **Thank you, Jesus!**

CHAPTER 1
The Israelites in Egypt

These are the names of the sons of Israel (that is, Jacob) who moved to Egypt with their father, each with his family: 2Reuben, Simeon, Levi, Judah, 3Issachar, Zebulun, Benjamin, 4Dan, Naphtali, Gad, and Asher. 5In all, Jacob had seventy descendants in Egypt, including Joseph, who was already there.

6In time, Joseph and all of his brothers died, ending that entire generation. 7But their descendants, the Israelites, had many children and grandchildren. In fact, they multiplied so greatly that they became extremely powerful and filled the land.

8Eventually, a new king came to power in Egypt who knew nothing about Joseph or what he had done. 9He said to his people, "Look, the people of Israel now outnumber us and are stronger than we are. 10We must make a plan to keep them from growing even more. If we don't, and if war breaks out, they will join our enemies and fight against us. Then they will escape from the country."

11So the Egyptians made the Israelites their slaves. They appointed brutal slave drivers over them, hoping to wear them down with crushing labor. They forced them to build the cities of Pithom and Rameses as supply centers for the king. 12But the more the Egyptians oppressed them, the more the Israelites multiplied and spread, and the more alarmed the Egyptians became. 13So the Egyptians worked the people of Israel without mercy. 14They made their lives bitter, forcing them to mix mortar and make bricks and do all the work in the fields. They were ruthless in all their demands.

15Then Pharaoh, the king of Egypt, gave this order to the Hebrew midwives, Shiphrah and Puah: 16"When you help the Hebrew women as they give birth, watch as they deliver. If the baby is a boy, kill him; if it is a girl, let her live." 17But because the midwives feared God, they refused to obey the king's orders. They allowed the boys to live, too.

18So the king of Egypt called for the midwives. "Why have you done this?" he demanded. "Why have you allowed the boys to live?"

19"The Hebrew women are not like the Egyptian women," the midwives replied. "They are more vigorous and have their babies so quickly that we cannot get there in time."

20So God was good to the midwives, and the Israelites continued to multiply, growing more and more powerful. 21And because the midwives feared God, he gave them families of their own.

22Then Pharaoh gave this order to all his people: "Throw every newborn Hebrew boy into the Nile River. But you may let the girls live."

CHAPTER 2
The Birth of Moses

About this time, a man and woman from the tribe of Levi got married. 2The woman became pregnant and gave birth to a son. She saw that he was a special baby and kept him hidden for three months. 3But when she could no longer hide him, she got a basket made of papyrus reeds and waterproofed it with tar and pitch. She put the baby in the basket and laid it among the reeds along the bank of the Nile River. 4The baby's sister then stood at a distance, watching to see what would happen to him.

5Soon Pharaoh's daughter came down to bathe in the river, and her attendants walked along the riverbank. When the princess saw the basket among the reeds, she sent her maid to get it for her. 6When the princess opened it, she saw the baby. The little boy was crying, and she felt sorry for him. "This must be one of the Hebrew children," she said.

7Then the baby's sister approached the princess. "Should I go and find one of the Hebrew women to nurse the baby for you?" she asked.

8"Yes, do!" the princess replied. So the girl went and called the baby's mother.

9"Take this baby and nurse him for me," the princess told the baby's mother. "I will pay you for your help." So the woman took her baby home and nursed him.

10Later, when the boy was older, his mother brought him back to Pharaoh's daughter, who adopted him as her own son. The princess named him Moses, for she explained, "I lifted him out of the water."

Moses Escapes to Midian

11Many years later, when Moses had grown up, he went out to visit his own people, the Hebrews, and he saw how hard they were forced to work. During his visit, he saw an Egyptian beating one of his fellow Hebrews. 12After looking in all directions to make sure no one was watching, Moses killed the Egyptian and hid the body in the sand.

13The next day, when Moses went out to visit his people again, he saw two Hebrew men fighting. "Why are you beating up your friend?" Moses said to the one who had started the fight.

Baby Moses in
BIG TROUBLE!

Check out why in EXODUS 1:8-22.

His mother had little choice—so she floated baby Moses on the Nile River in a basket. But God held that little basket up with his loving care.

Try this AMAZING FLOATING-EGG TRICK to show a friend what God did for Moses!
1
Fill two glasses with water. Stir a few heaping spoons of salt into one of them.
2
Crack a raw egg and set it on the water. Repeat with the other glass.

Egg-ceptional!

The salt kept the egg afloat. When Moses floated down the Nile like the egg in your glass, God watched out for him and made sure he didn't sink. God watches out for you, and he's holding you up. God loves you sooooo much!

DEAR GOD,

Thank you for holding me up.
I need some help with . . .

14The man replied, "Who appointed you to be
our prince and judge? Are you going to kill me as
you killed that Egyptian yesterday?"
Then Moses was afraid, thinking, "Everyone
knows what I did." 15And sure enough, Pharaoh
heard what had happened, and he tried to kill
Moses. But Moses fled from Pharaoh and went to
live in the land of Midian.
When Moses arrived in Midian, he sat down
beside a well. 16Now the priest of Midian had
seven daughters who came as usual to draw water and fill the water troughs for their father's
flocks. 17But some other shepherds came and
chased them away. So Moses jumped up and rescued the girls from the shepherds. Then he drew
water for their flocks.
18When the girls returned to Reuel, their
father, he asked, "Why are you back so soon
today?"
19"An Egyptian rescued us from the shepherds," they answered. "And then he drew water
for us and watered our flocks."
20"Then where is he?" their father asked.
"Why did you leave him there? Invite him to
come and eat with us."
21Moses accepted the invitation, and he settled there with him. In time, Reuel gave Moses
his daughter Zipporah to be his wife. 22Later she
gave birth to a son, and Moses named him Gershom, for he explained, "I have been a foreigner
in a foreign land."
23Years passed, and the king of Egypt died. But
the Israelites continued to groan under their
burden of slavery. They cried out for help, and
their cry rose up to God. 24God heard their
groaning, and he remembered his covenant
promise to Abraham, Isaac, and Jacob. 25He
looked down on the people of Israel and knew it
was time to act.

CHAPTER **3**

Moses and the Burning Bush

One day Moses was tending the flock of his
father-in-law, Jethro, the priest of Midian. He led
the flock far into the wilderness and came to Sinai, the mountain of God. 2There the angel of the
LORD appeared to him in a blazing fire from the
middle of a bush. Moses stared in amazement.
Though the bush was engulfed in flames, it
didn't burn up. 3"This is amazing," Moses said to
himself. "Why isn't that bush burning up? I must
go see it."
4When the LORD saw Moses coming to take a
closer look, God called to him from the middle of
the bush, "Moses! Moses!"

"Here I am!" Moses replied.
5"Do not come any closer," the LORD warned.
"Take off your sandals, for you are standing on
holy ground. 6I am the God of your father—the
God of Abraham, the God of Isaac, and the God
of Jacob." When Moses heard this, he covered
his face because he was afraid to look at God.
7Then the LORD told him, "I have certainly
seen the oppression of my people in Egypt. I
have heard their cries of distress because of
their harsh slave drivers. Yes, I am aware of their
suffering. 8So I have come down to rescue them
from the power of the Egyptians and lead
them out of Egypt into their own fertile and spacious land. It is a land flowing with milk and
honey—the land where the Canaanites, Hittites,
Amorites, Perizzites, Hivites, and Jebusites now
live. 9Look! The cry of the people of Israel has
reached me, and I have seen how harshly the
Egyptians abuse them. 10Now go, for I am sending you to Pharaoh. You must lead my people Israel out of Egypt."
11But Moses protested to God, "Who am I to
appear before Pharaoh? Who am I to lead the
people of Israel out of Egypt?"
12God answered, "I will be with you. And this
is your sign that I am the one who has sent you:
When you have brought the people out of Egypt,
you will worship God at this very mountain."
13But Moses protested, "If I go to the people
of Israel and tell them, 'The God of your ancestors has sent me to you,' they will ask me, 'What
is his name?' Then what should I tell them?"
14God replied to Moses, "I AM WHO I AM. Say
this to the people of Israel: I AM has sent me to
you." 15God also said to Moses, "Say this to the
people of Israel: Yahweh, the God of your ancestors—the God of Abraham, the God of Isaac, and
the God of Jacob—has sent me to you.

This is my eternal name,
  my name to remember for all generations.

16"Now go and call together all the elders
of Israel. Tell them, 'Yahweh, the God of your
ancestors—the God of Abraham, Isaac, and
Jacob—has appeared to me. He told me, "I have
been watching closely, and I see how the Egyptians are treating you. 17I have promised to rescue you from your oppression in Egypt. I will
lead you to a land flowing with milk and
honey—the land where the Canaanites, Hittites, Amorites, Perizzites, Hivites, and Jebusites now live."'
18"The elders of Israel will accept your message. Then you and the elders must go to the
king of Egypt and tell him, 'The LORD, the God of
the Hebrews, has met with us. So please let us
take a three-day journey into the wilderness to
offer sacrifices to the LORD, our God.'
19"But I know that the king of Egypt will not
let you go unless a mighty hand forces him. 20So
I will raise my hand and strike the Egyptians,
performing all kinds of miracles among them.
Then at last he will let you go. 21And I will cause
the Egyptians to look favorably on you. They will
give you gifts when you go so you will not leave
empty-handed. 22Every Israelite woman will ask
for articles of silver and gold and fine clothing
from her Egyptian neighbors and from the foreign women in their houses. You will dress your
sons and daughters with these, stripping the
Egyptians of their wealth."

CHAPTER 4
Signs of the LORD's Power
But Moses protested again, "What if they won't
believe me or listen to me? What if they say, 'The
LORD never appeared to you'?"
2Then the LORD asked him, "What is that in
your hand?"

Did You See That?
HOW MANY LEGS DO I HAVE?
Does God have a name? See what God told Moses in Exodus 3:13-14.
4? 5? 6? Count them again!

Moses saw something even more amazing than an elephant with lots of legs. He saw a bush that was on fire but didn't burn up! **Check out EXODUS 3:2-12.**

God had a special plan for Moses. God has a special plan for you, too!

Read JEREMIAH 29:11.

"A shepherd's staff," Moses replied.
3 "Throw it down on the ground," the LORD
told him. So Moses threw down the staff, and it
turned into a snake! Moses jumped back.
4 Then the LORD told him, "Reach out and grab
its tail." So Moses reached out and grabbed it,
and it turned back into a shepherd's staff in his
hand.
5 "Perform this sign," the LORD told him.
"Then they will believe that the LORD, the God of
their ancestors—the God of Abraham, the God
of Isaac, and the God of Jacob—really has appeared to you."
6 Then the LORD said to Moses, "Now put your
hand inside your cloak." So Moses put his hand
inside his cloak, and when he took it out again,
his hand was white as snow with a severe skin
disease. 7 "Now put your hand back into your
cloak," the LORD said. So Moses put his hand
back in, and when he took it out again, it was as
healthy as the rest of his body.
8 The LORD said to Moses, "If they do not believe you and are not convinced by the first
miraculous sign, they will be convinced by the
second sign. 9 And if they don't believe you or listen to you even after these two signs, then take
some water from the Nile River and pour it out
on the dry ground. When you do, the water from
the Nile will turn to blood on the ground."
10 But Moses pleaded with the LORD, "O Lord,
I'm not very good with words. I never have been,
and I'm not now, even though you have spoken
to me. I get tongue-tied, and my words get tangled."
11 Then the LORD asked Moses, "Who makes a
person's mouth? Who decides whether people
speak or do not speak, hear or do not hear, see or
do not see? Is it not I, the LORD? 12 Now go! I will
be with you as you speak, and I will instruct you
in what to say."
13 But Moses again pleaded, "Lord, please!
Send anyone else."
14 Then the LORD became angry with Moses.
"All right," he said. "What about your brother,
Aaron the Levite? I know he speaks well. And
look! He is on his way to meet you now. He will
be delighted to see you. 15 Talk to him, and put
the words in his mouth. I will be with both of you
as you speak, and I will instruct you both in what
to do. 16 Aaron will be your spokesman to the
people. He will be your mouthpiece, and you will
stand in the place of God for him, telling him
what to say. 17 And take your shepherd's staff
with you, and use it to perform the miraculous
signs I have shown you."

Moses Returns to Egypt

18 So Moses went back home to Jethro, his father-
in-law. "Please let me return to my relatives in
Egypt," Moses said. "I don't even know if they are
still alive."
"Go in peace," Jethro replied.
19 Before Moses left Midian, the LORD said to
him, "Return to Egypt, for all those who wanted
to kill you have died."
20 So Moses took his wife and sons, put them
on a donkey, and headed back to the land of
Egypt. In his hand he carried the staff of God.
21 And the LORD told Moses, "When you arrive
back in Egypt, go to Pharaoh and perform all the
miracles I have empowered you to do. But I will
harden his heart so he will refuse to let the people go. 22 Then you will tell him, 'This is what the
LORD says: Israel is my firstborn son. 23 I commanded you, "Let my son go, so he can worship
me." But since you have refused, I will now kill
your firstborn son!'"
24 On the way to Egypt, at a place where Moses
and his family had stopped for the night, the
LORD confronted him and was about to kill him.
25 But Moses' wife, Zipporah, took a flint knife
and circumcised her son. She touched his feet
with the foreskin and said, "Now you are a bridegroom of blood to me." 26 (When she said "a
bridegroom of blood," she was referring to the
circumcision.) After that, the LORD left him alone.
27 Now the LORD had said to Aaron, "Go out
into the wilderness to meet Moses." So Aaron
went and met Moses at the mountain of God,
and he embraced him. 28 Moses then told
Aaron everything the LORD had commanded
him to say. And he told him about the miraculous signs the LORD had commanded him to
perform.
29 Then Moses and Aaron returned to Egypt
and called all the elders of Israel together.
30 Aaron told them everything the LORD had told
Moses, and Moses performed the miraculous
signs as they watched. 31 Then the people of
Israel were convinced that the LORD had sent
Moses and Aaron. When they heard that the
LORD was concerned about them and had
seen their misery, they bowed down and worshiped.

CHAPTER 5

Moses and Aaron Speak to Pharaoh

After this presentation to Israel's leaders, Moses
and Aaron went and spoke to Pharaoh. They told
him, "This is what the LORD, the God of Israel,

says: Let my people go so they may hold a festival
in my honor in the wilderness."
2"Is that so?" retorted Pharaoh. "And who is
the LORD? Why should I listen to him and let Israel go? I don't know the LORD, and I will not let
Israel go."
3But Aaron and Moses persisted. "The God of
the Hebrews has met with us," they declared. "So
let us take a three-day journey into the wilderness so we can offer sacrifices to the LORD our
God. If we don't, he will kill us with a plague or
with the sword."
4Pharaoh replied, "Moses and Aaron, why are
you distracting the people from their tasks? Get
back to work! 5Look, there are many of your people in the land, and you are stopping them from
their work."

Making Bricks without Straw

6That same day Pharaoh sent this order to the
Egyptian slave drivers and the Israelite foremen:
7"Do not supply any more straw for making
bricks. Make the people get it themselves! 8But
still require them to make the same number of
bricks as before. Don't reduce the quota. They
are lazy. That's why they are crying out, 'Let us go
and offer sacrifices to our God.' 9Load them
down with more work. Make them sweat! That
will teach them to listen to lies!"
10So the slave drivers and foremen went out
and told the people: "This is what Pharaoh says: I
will not provide any more straw for you. 11Go and
get it yourselves. Find it wherever you can. But
you must produce just as many bricks as before!"
12So the people scattered throughout the land of
Egypt in search of stubble to use as straw.
13Meanwhile, the Egyptian slave drivers continued to push hard. "Meet your daily quota of
bricks, just as you did when we provided you
with straw!" they demanded. 14Then they
whipped the Israelite foremen they had put in
charge of the work crews. "Why haven't you met
your quotas either yesterday or today?" they demanded.
15So the Israelite foremen went to Pharaoh
and pleaded with him. "Please don't treat your
servants like this," they begged. 16"We are given
no straw, but the slave drivers still demand,
'Make bricks!' We are being beaten, but it isn't
our fault! Your own people are to blame!"
17But Pharaoh shouted, "You're just lazy! Lazy!
That's why you're saying, 'Let us go and offer sacrifices to the LORD.' 18Now get back to work! No
straw will be given to you, but you must still produce the full quota of bricks."
19The Israelite foremen could see that they
were in serious trouble when they were told,
"You must not reduce the number of bricks you
make each day." 20As they left Pharaoh's court,
they confronted Moses and Aaron, who were
waiting outside for them. 21The foremen said to
them, "May the LORD judge and punish you for
making us stink before Pharaoh and his officials.
You have put a sword into their hands, an excuse
to kill us!"
22Then Moses went back to the LORD and protested, "Why have you brought all this trouble on
your own people, Lord? Why did you send me?
23Ever since I came to Pharaoh as your spokesman, he has been even more brutal to your people. And you have done nothing to rescue them!"

CHAPTER 6

Promises of Deliverance

Then the LORD told Moses, "Now you will see
what I will do to Pharaoh. When he feels the
force of my strong hand, he will let the people go.
In fact, he will force them to leave his land!"
2And God said to Moses, "I am Yahweh—'the
LORD.' 3I appeared to Abraham, to Isaac, and to
Jacob as El-Shaddai—'God Almighty'—but I did
not reveal my name, Yahweh, to them. 4And I re-
affirmed my covenant with them. Under its
terms, I promised to give them the land of Canaan, where they were living as foreigners. 5You
can be sure that I have heard the groans of the
people of Israel, who are now slaves to the Egyptians. And I am well aware of my covenant with
them.
6"Therefore, say to the people of Israel: 'I am
the LORD. I will free you from your oppression
and will rescue you from your slavery in Egypt. I
will redeem you with a powerful arm and great
acts of judgment. 7I will claim you as my own
people, and I will be your God. Then you will
know that I am the LORD your God who has freed
you from your oppression in Egypt. 8I will bring
you into the land I swore to give to Abraham,
Isaac, and Jacob. I will give it to you as your very
own possession. I am the LORD!'"
9So Moses told the people of Israel what the
LORD had said, but they refused to listen anymore. They had become too discouraged by the
brutality of their slavery.
10Then the LORD said to Moses, 11"Go back to
Pharaoh, the king of Egypt, and tell him to let the
people of Israel leave his country."
12"But LORD!" Moses objected. "My own people won't listen to me anymore. How can I expect
Pharaoh to listen? I'm such a clumsy speaker!"

13 But the LORD spoke to Moses and Aaron and
gave them orders for the Israelites and for Pharaoh, the king of Egypt. The LORD commanded
Moses and Aaron to lead the people of Israel out
of Egypt.

The Ancestors of Moses and Aaron

14 These are the ancestors of some of the clans of
Israel:

The sons of Reuben, Israel's oldest son, were
Hanoch, Pallu, Hezron, and Carmi. Their
descendants became the clans of Reuben.
15 The sons of Simeon were Jemuel, Jamin,
Ohad, Jakin, Zohar, and Shaul. (Shaul's
mother was a Canaanite woman.) Their
descendants became the clans of Simeon.
16 These are the descendants of Levi, as listed
in their family records: The sons of Levi were
Gershon, Kohath, and Merari. (Levi lived to
be 137 years old.)
17 The descendants of Gershon included
Libni and Shimei, each of whom became the
ancestor of a clan.
18 The descendants of Kohath included
Amram, Izhar, Hebron, and Uzziel. (Kohath
lived to be 133 years old.)
19 The descendants of Merari included
Mahli and Mushi.

These are the clans of the Levites, as listed in
their family records.

20 Amram married his father's sister Jochebed,
and she gave birth to his sons, Aaron and
Moses. (Amram lived to be 137 years old.)
21 The sons of Izhar were Korah, Nepheg, and
Zicri.
22 The sons of Uzziel were Mishael, Elzaphan,
and Sithri.
23 Aaron married Elisheba, the daughter of
Amminadab and sister of Nahshon, and she
gave birth to his sons, Nadab, Abihu, Eleazar,
and Ithamar.
24 The sons of Korah were Assir, Elkanah, and
Abiasaph. Their descendants became the
clans of Korah.
25 Eleazar son of Aaron married one of the
daughters of Putiel, and she gave birth to his
son, Phinehas.
These are the ancestors of the Levite families,
listed according to their clans.

26 The Aaron and Moses named in this list are
the same ones to whom the LORD said, "Lead the
people of Israel out of the land of Egypt like an
army." 27 It was Moses and Aaron who spoke to
Pharaoh, the king of Egypt, about leading the
people of Israel out of Egypt.

28 When the LORD spoke to Moses in the land
of Egypt, 29 he said to him, "I am the LORD! Tell
Pharaoh, the king of Egypt, everything I am telling you." 30 But Moses argued with the LORD, saying, "I can't do it! I'm such a clumsy speaker! Why
should Pharaoh listen to me?"

CHAPTER 7

Aaron's Staff Becomes a Serpent

Then the LORD said to Moses, "Pay close attention to this. I will make you seem like God to Pharaoh, and your brother, Aaron, will be your
prophet. 2 Tell Aaron everything I command you,
and Aaron must command Pharaoh to let the
people of Israel leave his country. 3 But I will
make Pharaoh's heart stubborn so I can multiply
my miraculous signs and wonders in the land of
Egypt. 4 Even then Pharaoh will refuse to listen to
you. So I will bring down my fist on Egypt. Then I
will rescue my forces—my people, the Israelites—from the land of Egypt with great acts of
judgment. 5 When I raise my powerful hand and
bring out the Israelites, the Egyptians will know
that I am the LORD."

6 So Moses and Aaron did just as the LORD had
commanded them. 7 Moses was eighty years old,
and Aaron was eighty-three when they made
their demands to Pharaoh.

8 Then the LORD said to Moses and Aaron,
9 "Pharaoh will demand, 'Show me a miracle.'
When he does this, say to Aaron, 'Take your staff
and throw it down in front of Pharaoh, and it will
become a serpent.'"

10 So Moses and Aaron went to Pharaoh and
did what the LORD had commanded them. Aaron
threw down his staff before Pharaoh and his officials, and it became a serpent! 11 Then Pharaoh
called in his own wise men and sorcerers, and
these Egyptian magicians did the same thing
with their magic. 12 They threw down their staffs,
which also became serpents! But then Aaron's
staff swallowed up their staffs. 13 Pharaoh's
heart, however, remained hard. He still refused
to listen, just as the LORD had predicted.

A Plague of Blood

14 Then the LORD said to Moses, "Pharaoh's heart
is stubborn, and he still refuses to let the people
go. 15 So go to Pharaoh in the morning as he goes
down to the river. Stand on the bank of the Nile
and meet him there. Be sure to take along the

LET GO! **Pharaoh refused to let the children of Israel go free from Egypt.** Instead, he wanted the Israelites for his slaves. So God sent 10 plagues to the people of Egypt to help Pharaoh change his mind.

A plague is a disaster that troubles a lot of people. Little brothers or sisters DO NOT count as plagues.

Safe House

Use blankets, chairs, and whatever else you can find to build a fort. Climb inside your fort with a flashlight and read EXODUS 8:20-23. What happened to the Israelites? Now read EXODUS 9:1-4. Do you see a pattern here?

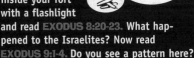

Think or talk about this:

- How has God protected you in the past?
- What do you need God's protection from now?

staff that turned into a snake. 16Then announce
to him, 'The LORD, the God of the Hebrews, has
sent me to tell you, "Let my people go, so they can
worship me in the wilderness." Until now, you
have refused to listen to him. 17So this is what the
LORD says: "I will show you that I am the LORD."
Look! I will strike the water of the Nile with this
staff in my hand, and the river will turn to blood.
18The fish in it will die, and the river will stink.
The Egyptians will not be able to drink any water
from the Nile.'"

19Then the LORD said to Moses: "Tell Aaron,
'Take your staff and raise your hand over the waters of Egypt—all its rivers, canals, ponds, and all the reservoirs. Turn all the water to blood. Everywhere in Egypt the water will turn to blood, even the water stored in wooden bowls and stone pots.'"

20So Moses and Aaron did just as the LORD
commanded them. As Pharaoh and all of his officials watched, Aaron raised his staff and struck the water of the Nile. Suddenly, the whole river
turned to blood! 21The fish in the river died, and
the water became so foul that the Egyptians couldn't drink it. There was blood everywhere throughout the land of Egypt. 22But again the
magicians of Egypt used their magic, and they, too, turned water into blood. So Pharaoh's heart remained hard. He refused to listen to Moses and Aaron, just as the LORD had predicted.
23Pharaoh returned to his palace and put the
whole thing out of his mind. 24Then all the Egyp-
tians dug along the riverbank to find drinking water, for they couldn't drink the water from the Nile.

25Seven days passed from the time the LORD
struck the Nile.

CHAPTER 8

A Plague of Frogs

1Then the LORD said to Moses, "Go back to Pha-
raoh and announce to him, 'This is what the LORD says: Let my people go, so they can worship
me. 2If you refuse to let them go, I will send a
plague of frogs across your entire land. 3The Nile
River will swarm with frogs. They will come up out of the river and into your palace, even into your bedroom and onto your bed! They will enter the houses of your officials and your people. They will even jump into your ovens and your kneading bowls. 4Frogs will jump on you, your
people, and all your officials.'"

5Then the LORD said to Moses, "Tell Aaron,
'Raise the staff in your hand over all the rivers, canals, and ponds of Egypt, and bring up frogs
over all the land.'" 6So Aaron raised his hand
over the waters of Egypt, and frogs came up and
covered the whole land! 7But the magicians were
able to do the same thing with their magic. They, too, caused frogs to come up on the land of Egypt.

8Then Pharaoh summoned Moses and Aaron
and begged, "Plead with the LORD to take the frogs away from me and my people. I will let your people go, so they can offer sacrifices to the LORD."

9"You set the time!" Moses replied. "Tell me
when you want me to pray for you, your officials, and your people. Then you and your houses will be rid of the frogs. They will remain only in the Nile River."

10"Do it tomorrow," Pharaoh said.

"All right," Moses replied, "it will be as you have said. Then you will know that there is no one like
the LORD our God. 11The frogs will leave you and
your houses, your officials, and your people. They will remain only in the Nile River."

12So Moses and Aaron left Pharaoh's palace,
and Moses cried out to the LORD about the frogs
he had inflicted on Pharaoh. 13And the LORD did
just what Moses had predicted. The frogs in the

houses, the courtyards, and the fields all died.
14The Egyptians piled them into great heaps, and
a terrible stench filled the land. 15But when Pharaoh saw that relief had come, he became stubborn. He refused to listen to Moses and Aaron,
just as the LORD had predicted.

A Plague of Gnats

16So the LORD said to Moses, "Tell Aaron, 'Raise
your staff and strike the ground. The dust will
turn into swarms of gnats throughout the land of
Egypt.' " 17So Moses and Aaron did just as the
LORD had commanded them. When Aaron
raised his hand and struck the ground with his
staff, gnats infested the entire land, covering the
Egyptians and their animals. All the dust in the
land of Egypt turned into gnats. 18Pharaoh's magicians tried to do the same thing with their secret arts, but this time they failed. And the gnats
covered everyone, people and animals alike.

19"This is the finger of God!" the magicians exclaimed to Pharaoh. But Pharaoh's heart remained hard. He wouldn't listen to them, just as
the LORD had predicted.

A Plague of Flies

20Then the LORD told Moses, "Get up early in the
morning and stand in Pharaoh's way as he goes
down to the river. Say to him, 'This is what the
LORD says: Let my people go, so they can worship
me. 21If you refuse, then I will send swarms of
flies on you, your officials, your people, and all
the houses. The Egyptian homes will be filled
with flies, and the ground will be covered with
them. 22But this time I will spare the region of
Goshen, where my people live. No flies will be
found there. Then you will know that I am the
LORD and that I am present even in the heart of
your land. 23I will make a clear distinction between my people and your people. This miraculous sign will happen tomorrow.' "

24And the LORD did just as he had said. A thick
swarm of flies filled Pharaoh's palace and the
houses of his officials. The whole land of Egypt
was thrown into chaos by the flies.

25Pharaoh called for Moses and Aaron. "All
right! Go ahead and offer sacrifices to your God,"
he said. "But do it here in this land."

26But Moses replied, "That wouldn't be right.
The Egyptians detest the sacrifices that we offer
to the LORD our God. Look, if we offer our sacrifices here where the Egyptians can see us, they
will stone us. 27We must take a three-day trip
into the wilderness to offer sacrifices to the
LORD our God, just as he has commanded us."

28"All right, go ahead," Pharaoh replied. "I will
let you go into the wilderness to offer sacrifices
to the LORD your God. But don't go too far away.
Now hurry and pray for me."

29Moses answered, "As soon as I leave you, I
will pray to the LORD, and tomorrow the swarms
of flies will disappear from you and your officials
and all your people. But I am warning you, Pharaoh, don't lie to us again and refuse to let the
people go to sacrifice to the LORD."

30So Moses left Pharaoh's palace and pleaded
with the LORD to remove all the flies. 31And the
LORD did as Moses asked and caused the swarms
of flies to disappear from Pharaoh, his officials,
and his people. Not a single fly remained. 32But
Pharaoh again became stubborn and refused to
let the people go.

CHAPTER 9

A Plague against Livestock

"Go back to Pharaoh," the LORD commanded
Moses. "Tell him, 'This is what the LORD, the God
of the Hebrews, says: Let my people go, so they
can worship me. 2If you continue to hold them
and refuse to let them go, 3the hand of the LORD
will strike all your livestock—your horses, donkeys, camels, cattle, sheep, and goats—with a
deadly plague. 4But the LORD will again make a
distinction between the livestock of the Israelites and that of the Egyptians. Not a single one of
Israel's animals will die! 5The LORD has already
set the time for the plague to begin. He has declared that he will strike the land tomorrow.' "

6And the LORD did just as he had said. The next
morning all the livestock of the Egyptians died,
but the Israelites didn't lose a single animal. 7Pha-
raoh sent his officials to investigate, and they discovered that the Israelites had not lost a single
animal! But even so, Pharaoh's heart remained
stubborn, and he still refused to let the people go.

A Plague of Festering Boils

8Then the LORD said to Moses and Aaron, "Take
handfuls of soot from a brick kiln, and have
Moses toss it into the air while Pharaoh watches.
9The ashes will spread like fine dust over the
whole land of Egypt, causing festering boils to
break out on people and animals throughout the
land."

10So they took soot from a brick kiln and went
and stood before Pharaoh. As Pharaoh watched,
Moses threw the soot into the air, and boils
broke out on people and animals alike. 11Even
the magicians were unable to stand before
Moses, because the boils had broken out on

them and all the Egyptians. 12But the LORD hardened Pharaoh's heart, and just as the LORD had
predicted to Moses, Pharaoh refused to listen.

A Plague of Hail

13Then the LORD said to Moses, "Get up early in
the morning and stand before Pharaoh. Tell him,
'This is what the LORD, the God of the Hebrews,
says: Let my people go, so they can worship me.
14If you don't, I will send more plagues on you
and your officials and your people. Then you will
know that there is no one like me in all the earth.
15By now I could have lifted my hand and struck
you and your people with a plague to wipe you
off the face of the earth. 16But I have spared you
for a purpose—to show you my power and to
spread my fame throughout the earth. 17But you
still lord it over my people and refuse to let them
go. 18So tomorrow at this time I will send a hailstorm more devastating than any in all the history of Egypt. 19Quick! Order your livestock and
servants to come in from the fields to find shelter. Any person or animal left outside will die
when the hail falls.'"

20Some of Pharaoh's officials were afraid because of what the LORD had said. They quickly
brought their servants and livestock in from the
fields. 21But those who paid no attention to the
word of the LORD left theirs out in the open.

22Then the LORD said to Moses, "Lift your
hand toward the sky so hail may fall on the people, the livestock, and all the plants throughout
the land of Egypt."

23So Moses lifted his staff toward the sky, and
the LORD sent thunder and hail, and lightning
flashed toward the earth. The LORD sent a tremendous hailstorm against all the land of Egypt.
24Never in all the history of Egypt had there been
a storm like that, with such devastating hail and
continuous lightning. 25It left all of Egypt in ruins. The hail struck down everything in the open
field—people, animals, and plants alike. Even the
trees were destroyed. 26The only place without
hail was the region of Goshen, where the people
of Israel lived.

27Then Pharaoh quickly summoned Moses
and Aaron. "This time I have sinned," he confessed. "The LORD is the righteous one, and my
people and I are wrong. 28Please beg the LORD to
end this terrifying thunder and hail. We've had
enough. I will let you go; you don't need to stay
any longer."

29"All right," Moses replied. "As soon as I leave
the city, I will lift my hands and pray to the LORD.
Then the thunder and hail will stop, and you will
know that the earth belongs to the LORD. 30But I
know that you and your officials still do not fear
the LORD God."

31(All the flax and barley were ruined by the
hail, because the barley had formed heads and
the flax was budding. 32But the wheat and the
emmer wheat were spared, because they had not
yet sprouted from the ground.)

33So Moses left Pharaoh's court and went out
of the city. When he lifted his hands to the LORD,
the thunder and hail stopped, and the downpour
ceased. 34But when Pharaoh saw that the rain,
hail, and thunder had stopped, he and his officials sinned again, and Pharaoh again became
stubborn. 35Because his heart was hard, Pharaoh
refused to let the people leave, just as the LORD
had predicted through Moses.

CHAPTER **10**

A Plague of Locusts

Then the LORD said to Moses, "Return to Pharaoh
and make your demands again. I have made him
and his officials stubborn so I can display my miraculous signs among them. 2I've also done it so
you can tell your children and grandchildren
about how I made a mockery of the Egyptians
and about the signs I displayed among them—
and so you will know that I am the LORD."

3So Moses and Aaron went to Pharaoh and
said, "This is what the LORD, the God of the Hebrews, says: How long will you refuse to submit to
me? Let my people go, so they can worship me. 4If
you refuse, watch out! For tomorrow I will bring a
swarm of locusts on your country. 5They will
cover the land so that you won't be able to see the
ground. They will devour what little is left of your
crops after the hailstorm, including all the trees
growing in the fields. 6They will overrun your
palaces and the homes of your officials and all
the houses in Egypt. Never in the history of Egypt
have your ancestors seen a plague like this one!"
And with that, Moses turned and left Pharaoh.

7Pharaoh's officials now came to Pharaoh and
appealed to him. "How long will you let this man
hold us hostage? Let the men go to worship the
LORD their God! Don't you realize that Egypt lies
in ruins?"

8So Moses and Aaron were brought back to
Pharaoh. "All right," he told them, "go and worship the LORD your God. But who exactly will be
going with you?"

9Moses replied, "We will all go—young and
old, our sons and daughters, and our flocks and
herds. We must all join together in celebrating a
festival to the LORD."

10 Pharaoh retorted, "The LORD will certainly
need to be with you if I let you take your little
ones! I can see through your evil plan. 11 Never!
Only the men may go and worship the LORD,
since that is what you requested." And Pharaoh
threw them out of the palace.
12 Then the LORD said to Moses, "Raise your
hand over the land of Egypt to bring on the locusts. Let them cover the land and devour every
plant that survived the hailstorm."
13 So Moses raised his staff over Egypt, and the
LORD caused an east wind to blow over the land
all that day and through the night. When morning arrived, the east wind had brought the locusts. 14 And the locusts swarmed over the whole
land of Egypt, settling in dense swarms from one
end of the country to the other. It was the worst
locust plague in Egyptian history, and there has
never been another one like it. 15 For the locusts
covered the whole country and darkened the
land. They devoured every plant in the fields and
all the fruit on the trees that had survived the
hailstorm. Not a single leaf was left on the trees
and plants throughout the land of Egypt.
16 Pharaoh quickly summoned Moses and
Aaron. "I have sinned against the LORD your God
and against you," he confessed. 17 "Forgive my
sin, just this once, and plead with the LORD your
God to take away this death from me."
18 So Moses left Pharaoh's court and pleaded
with the LORD. 19 The LORD responded by shifting
the wind, and the strong west wind blew the locusts into the Red Sea. Not a single locust remained in all the land of Egypt. 20 But the LORD
hardened Pharaoh's heart again, so he refused to
let the people go.

A Plague of Darkness

21 Then the LORD said to Moses, "Lift your hand
toward heaven, and the land of Egypt will be
covered with a darkness so thick you can feel it."
22 So Moses lifted his hand to the sky, and a deep
darkness covered the entire land of Egypt for
three days. 23 During all that time the people
could not see each other, and no one moved. But
there was light as usual where the people of Israel lived.
24 Finally, Pharaoh called for Moses. "Go and
worship the LORD," he said. "But leave your flocks
and herds here. You may even take your little
ones with you."
25 "No," Moses said, "you must provide us with
animals for sacrifices and burnt offerings to the
LORD our God. 26 All our livestock must go with
us, too; not a hoof can be left behind. We must
choose our sacrifices for the LORD our God from
among these animals. And we won't know how
we are to worship the LORD until we get there."
27 But the LORD hardened Pharaoh's heart
once more, and he would not let them go. 28 "Get
out of here!" Pharaoh shouted at Moses. "I'm
warning you. Never come back to see me again!
The day you see my face, you will die!"
29 "Very well," Moses replied. "I will never see
your face again."

CHAPTER 11
Death for Egypt's Firstborn

Then the LORD said to Moses, "I will strike Pharaoh and the land of Egypt with one more blow.
After that, Pharaoh will let you leave this country.
In fact, he will be so eager to get rid of you that he
will force you all to leave. 2 Tell all the Israelite
men and women to ask their Egyptian neighbors
for articles of silver and gold." 3 (Now the LORD
had caused the Egyptians to look favorably on
the people of Israel. And Moses was considered a
very great man in the land of Egypt, respected by
Pharaoh's officials and the Egyptian people
alike.)
4 Moses had announced to Pharaoh, "This is
what the LORD says: At midnight tonight I will
pass through the heart of Egypt. 5 All the firstborn sons will die in every family in Egypt, from
the oldest son of Pharaoh, who sits on his throne,
to the oldest son of his lowliest servant girl
who grinds the flour. Even the firstborn of all the
livestock will die. 6 Then a loud wail will rise
throughout the land of Egypt, a wail like no one
has heard before or will ever hear again. 7 But
among the Israelites it will be so peaceful that
not even a dog will bark. Then you will know that
the LORD makes a distinction between the Egyptians and the Israelites. 8 All the officials of Egypt
will run to me and fall to the ground before me.
'Please leave!' they will beg. 'Hurry! And take all
your followers with you.' Only then will I go!"
Then, burning with anger, Moses left Pharaoh.
9 Now the LORD had told Moses earlier, "Pharaoh will not listen to you, but then I will do
even more mighty miracles in the land of Egypt."
10 Moses and Aaron performed these miracles in
Pharaoh's presence, but the LORD hardened Pharaoh's heart, and he wouldn't let the Israelites
leave the country.

CHAPTER 12
The First Passover

While the Israelites were still in the land of
Egypt, the LORD gave the following instruc-

tions to Moses and Aaron: 2"From now on, this
month will be the first month of the year for you.
3Announce to the whole community of Israel
that on the tenth day of this month each family
must choose a lamb or a young goat for a sacrifice, one animal for each household. 4If a family
is too small to eat a whole animal, let them share
with another family in the neighborhood. Divide the animal according to the size of each
family and how much they can eat. 5The animal
you select must be a one-year-old male, either a
sheep or a goat, with no defects.

6"Take special care of this chosen animal until
the evening of the fourteenth day of this first
month. Then the whole assembly of the community of Israel must slaughter their lamb or young
goat at twilight. 7They are to take some of the
blood and smear it on the sides and top of the
doorframes of the houses where they eat the animal. 8That same night they must roast the meat
over a fire and eat it along with bitter salad
greens and bread made without yeast. 9Do not
eat any of the meat raw or boiled in water. The
whole animal—including the head, legs, and internal organs—must be roasted over a fire. 10Do
not leave any of it until the next morning. Burn
whatever is not eaten before morning.

11"These are your instructions for eating this
meal: Be fully dressed, wear your sandals, and
carry your walking stick in your hand. Eat the
meal with urgency, for this is the LORD's Passover. 12On that night I will pass through the
land of Egypt and strike down every firstborn
son and firstborn male animal in the land of
Egypt. I will execute judgment against all the
gods of Egypt, for I am the LORD! 13But the blood
on your doorposts will serve as a sign, marking
the houses where you are staying. When I see
the blood, I will pass over you. This plague of
death will not touch you when I strike the land
of Egypt.

14"This is a day to remember. Each year, from
generation to generation, you must celebrate it
as a special festival to the LORD. This is a law for
all time. 15For seven days the bread you eat
must be made without yeast. On the first day of
the festival, remove every trace of yeast from
your homes. Anyone who eats bread made with
yeast during the seven days of the festival will
be cut off from the community of Israel. 16On
the first day of the festival and again on the seventh day, all the people must observe an official
day for holy assembly. No work of any kind may
be done on these days except in the preparation of food.

17"Celebrate this Festival of Unleavened Bread,
for it will remind you that I brought your forces
out of the land of Egypt on this very day. This festival will be a permanent law for you; celebrate
this day from generation to generation. 18The
bread you eat must be made without yeast from
the evening of the fourteenth day of the first
month until the evening of the twenty-first day
of that month. 19During those seven days, there
must be no trace of yeast in your homes. Anyone
who eats anything made with yeast during this
week will be cut off from the community of Israel. These regulations apply both to the foreigners
living among you and to the native-born Israelites. 20During those days you must not eat anything made with yeast. Wherever you live, eat
only bread made without yeast."

21Then Moses called all the elders of Israel together and said to them, "Go, pick out a lamb or
young goat for each of your families, and slaughter the Passover animal. 22Drain the blood into a
basin. Then take a bundle of hyssop branches
and dip it into the blood. Brush the hyssop across
the top and sides of the doorframes of your
houses. And no one may go out through the door
until morning. 23For the LORD will pass through
the land to strike down the Egyptians. But when
he sees the blood on the top and sides of the
doorframe, the LORD will pass over your home.
He will not permit his death angel to enter your
house and strike you down.

24"Remember, these instructions are a permanent law that you and your descendants must observe forever. 25When you enter the land the
LORD has promised to give you, you will continue
to observe this ceremony. 26Then your children
will ask, 'What does this ceremony mean?' 27And
you will reply, 'It is the Passover sacrifice to the
LORD, for he passed over the houses of the Israelites in Egypt. And though he struck the Egyptians, he spared our families.'" When Moses had
finished speaking, all the people bowed down to
the ground and worshiped.

28So the people of Israel did just as the LORD
had commanded through Moses and Aaron.
29And that night at midnight, the LORD struck
down all the firstborn sons in the land of Egypt,
from the firstborn son of Pharaoh, who sat on his
throne, to the firstborn son of the prisoner in the
dungeon. Even the firstborn of their livestock
were killed. 30Pharaoh and all his officials and all
the people of Egypt woke up during the night,
and loud wailing was heard throughout the land
of Egypt. There was not a single house where
someone had not died.

Exodus 13 . . . page 70

Israel's Exodus from Egypt

31 Pharaoh sent for Moses and Aaron during the
night. "Get out!" he ordered. "Leave my people—
and take the rest of the Israelites with you! Go
and worship the LORD as you have requested.
32 Take your flocks and herds, as you said, and be
gone. Go, but bless me as you leave." 33 All the
Egyptians urged the people of Israel to get out of
the land as quickly as possible, for they thought,
"We will all die!"

34 The Israelites took their bread dough before
yeast was added. They wrapped their kneading
boards in their cloaks and carried them on their
shoulders. 35 And the people of Israel did as
Moses had instructed; they asked the Egyptians
for clothing and articles of silver and gold. 36 The
LORD caused the Egyptians to look favorably on
the Israelites, and they gave the Israelites whatever they asked for. So they stripped the Egyptians of their wealth!

37 That night the people of Israel left Rameses
and started for Succoth. There were about
600,000 men, plus all the women and children.
38 A rabble of non-Israelites went with them,
along with great flocks and herds of livestock.
39 For bread they baked flat cakes from the
dough without yeast they had brought from
Egypt. It was made without yeast because the
people were driven out of Egypt in such a hurry
that they had no time to prepare the bread or
other food.

40 The people of Israel had lived in Egypt for
430 years. 41 In fact, it was on the last day of the
430th year that all the LORD's forces left the land.
42 On this night the LORD kept his promise to
bring his people out of the land of Egypt. So this
night belongs to him, and it must be commemorated every year by all the Israelites, from generation to generation.

Instructions for the Passover

43 Then the LORD said to Moses and Aaron,
"These are the instructions for the festival of
Passover. No outsiders are allowed to eat the
Passover meal. 44 But any slave who has been purchased may eat it if he has been circumcised.
45 Temporary residents and hired servants may
not eat it. 46 Each Passover lamb must be eaten in
one house. Do not carry any of its meat outside,
and do not break any of its bones. 47 The whole
community of Israel must celebrate this Passover festival.

48 "If there are foreigners living among you
who want to celebrate the LORD's Passover, let all
their males be circumcised. Only then may they
celebrate the Passover with you like any native-
born Israelite. But no uncircumcised male may
ever eat the Passover meal. 49 This instruction
applies to everyone, whether a native-born Israelite or a foreigner living among you."

50 So all the people of Israel followed all the
LORD's commands to Moses and Aaron. 51 On that
very day the LORD brought the people of Israel
out of the land of Egypt like an army.

CHAPTER 13

Dedication of the Firstborn

Then the LORD said to Moses, 2 "Dedicate to me
every firstborn among the Israelites. The first
offspring to be born, of both humans and animals, belongs to me."

3 So Moses said to the people, "This is a day to
remember forever—the day you left Egypt, the
place of your slavery. Today the LORD has brought
you out by the power of his mighty hand. (Remember, eat no food containing yeast.) 4 On this
day in early spring, in the month of Abib, you
have been set free. 5 You must celebrate this
event in this month each year after the LORD
brings you into the land of the Canaanites, Hittites, Amorites, Hivites, and Jebusites. (He swore
to your ancestors that he would give you this
land—a land flowing with milk and honey.) 6 For
seven days the bread you eat must be made without yeast. Then on the seventh day, celebrate a
feast to the LORD. 7 Eat bread without yeast during those seven days. In fact, there must be no
yeast bread or any yeast at all found within the
borders of your land during this time.

8 "On the seventh day you must explain to
your children, 'I am celebrating what the LORD
did for me when I left Egypt.' 9 This annual festival will be a visible sign to you, like a mark
branded on your hand or your forehead. Let it
remind you always to recite this teaching of the
LORD: 'With a strong hand, the LORD rescued
you from Egypt.' 10 So observe the decree of this
festival at the appointed time each year.

11 "This is what you must do when the LORD
fulfills the promise he swore to you and to your
ancestors. When he gives you the land where the
Canaanites now live, 12 you must present all firstborn sons and firstborn male animals to the
LORD, for they belong to him. 13 A firstborn donkey may be bought back from the LORD by presenting a lamb or young goat in its place. But if
you do not buy it back, you must break its neck.
However, you must buy back every firstborn son.
14 "And in the future, your children will ask
you, 'What does all this mean?' Then you will

tell them, 'With the power of his mighty hand, the LORD brought us out of Egypt, the place of our slavery. 15 Pharaoh stubbornly refused to let us go, so the LORD killed all the firstborn males throughout the land of Egypt, both people and animals. That is why I now sacrifice all the firstborn males to the LORD—except that the firstborn sons are always bought back.' 16 This ceremony will be like a mark branded on your hand or your forehead. It is a reminder that the power of the LORD's mighty hand brought us out of Egypt."

Israel's Wilderness Detour

17 When Pharaoh finally let the people go, God did not lead them along the main road that runs through Philistine territory, even though that was the shortest route to the Promised Land. God said, "If the people are faced with a battle, they might change their minds and return to Egypt." 18 So God led them in a roundabout way through the wilderness toward the Red Sea. Thus the Israelites left Egypt like an army ready for battle.

19 Moses took the bones of Joseph with him, for Joseph had made the sons of Israel swear to do this. He said, "God will certainly come to help you. When he does, you must take my bones with you from this place."

20 The Israelites left Succoth and camped at Etham on the edge of the wilderness. 21 The LORD went ahead of them. He guided them during the day with a pillar of cloud, and he provided light at night with a pillar of fire. This allowed them to travel by day or by night. 22 And the LORD did not remove the pillar of cloud or pillar of fire from its place in front of the people.

CHAPTER 14

Then the LORD gave these instructions to Moses: 2 "Order the Israelites to turn back and camp by Pi-hahiroth between Migdol and the sea. Camp there along the shore, across from Baal-zephon. 3 Then Pharaoh will think, 'The Israelites are confused. They are trapped in the wilderness!' 4 And once again I will harden Pharaoh's heart, and he will chase after you. I have planned this in order to display my glory through Pharaoh and his whole army. After this the Egyptians will know that I am the LORD!" So the Israelites camped there as they were told.

The Egyptians Pursue Israel

5 When word reached the king of Egypt that the Israelites had fled, Pharaoh and his officials changed their minds. "What have we done, letting all those Israelite slaves get away?" they asked. 6 So Pharaoh harnessed his chariot and called up his troops. 7 He took with him 600 of Egypt's best chariots, along with the rest of the chariots of Egypt, each with its commander. 8 The LORD hardened the heart of Pharaoh, the king of Egypt, so he chased after the people of Israel, who had left with fists raised in defiance. 9 The Egyptians chased after them with all the forces in Pharaoh's army—all his horses and chariots, his charioteers, and his troops. The Egyptians caught up with the people of Israel as they were camped beside the shore near Pi-hahiroth, across from Baal-zephon.

10 As Pharaoh approached, the people of Israel looked up and panicked when they saw the Egyptians overtaking them. They cried out to the LORD, 11 and they said to Moses, "Why did you bring us out here to die in the wilderness? Weren't there enough graves for us in Egypt? What have you done to us? Why did you make us leave Egypt? 12 Didn't we tell you this would happen while we were still in Egypt? We said, 'Leave us alone! Let us be slaves to the Egyptians. It's better to be a slave in Egypt than a corpse in the wilderness!'"

13 But Moses told the people, "Don't be afraid. Just stand still and watch the LORD rescue you today. The Egyptians you see today will never be seen again. 14 The LORD himself will fight for you. Just stay calm."

Escape through the Red Sea

15 Then the LORD said to Moses, "Why are you crying out to me? Tell the people to get moving! 16 Pick up your staff and raise your hand over the sea. Divide the water so the Israelites can walk through the middle of the sea on dry ground. 17 And I will harden the hearts of the Egyptians, and they will charge in after the Israelites. My great glory will be displayed through Pharaoh and his troops, his chariots, and his charioteers. 18 When my glory is displayed through them, all Egypt will see my glory and know that I am the LORD!"

19 Then the angel of God, who had been leading the people of Israel, moved to the rear of the camp. The pillar of cloud also moved from the front and stood behind them. 20 The cloud settled between the Egyptian and Israelite camps. As darkness fell, the cloud turned to fire, lighting up the night. But the Egyptians and Israelites did not approach each other all night.

21 Then Moses raised his hand over the sea, and the LORD opened up a path through the

Exodus 15 . . . page 72

RUN! I MEAN, SWIM!
I MEAN, RUN!

The Egyptian army rode chariots, threw spears, and shot arrows. They closed in on the Israelites who had...sheep...and some gold...and a little bread. It didn't look good. Was it all over? The Israelites felt pinched between the Red Sea and Pharaoh's army. Gulp! **Read EXODUS 14:19-25 to find out what happened next.**

Make your own RED SEA to show someone else what happened.

1 **Fold paper into thirds. Glue sandpaper to the middle section.**

2 **Glue blue tissue paper, paper fish (or fish crackers), and shells (real or paper) to the ocean walls.**

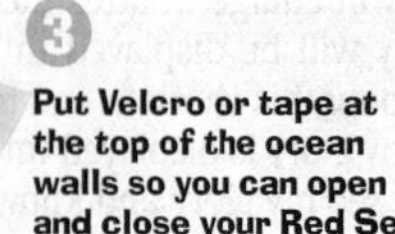

3 **Put Velcro or tape at the top of the ocean walls so you can open and close your Red Sea.**

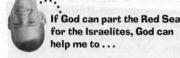

If God can part the Red Sea for the Israelites, God can help me to . . .

water with a strong east wind. The wind blew all
that night, turning the seabed into dry land. 22So
the people of Israel walked through the middle
of the sea on dry ground, with walls of water on
each side!
23Then the Egyptians—all of Pharaoh's horses,
chariots, and charioteers—chased them into the
middle of the sea. 24But just before dawn the
LORD looked down on the Egyptian army from
the pillar of fire and cloud, and he threw their
forces into total confusion. 25He twisted their
chariot wheels, making their chariots difficult to
drive. "Let's get out of here—away from these Israelites!" the Egyptians shouted. "The LORD is
fighting for them against Egypt!"
26When all the Israelites had reached the
other side, the LORD said to Moses, "Raise your
hand over the sea again. Then the waters will
rush back and cover the Egyptians and their
chariots and charioteers." 27So as the sun began
to rise, Moses raised his hand over the sea, and
the water rushed back into its usual place. The
Egyptians tried to escape, but the LORD swept
them into the sea. 28Then the waters returned
and covered all the chariots and charioteers—
the entire army of Pharaoh. Of all the Egyptians
who had chased the Israelites into the sea, not a
single one survived.
29But the people of Israel had walked through
the middle of the sea on dry ground, as the water
stood up like a wall on both sides. 30That is how
the LORD rescued Israel from the hand of the
Egyptians that day. And the Israelites saw the
bodies of the Egyptians washed up on the seashore. 31When the people of Israel saw the
mighty power that the LORD had unleashed
against the Egyptians, they were filled with awe
before him. They put their faith in the LORD and
in his servant Moses.

CHAPTER 15

A Song of Deliverance

Then Moses and the people of Israel sang this song to the LORD:

"I will sing to the LORD,
for he has triumphed gloriously;
he has hurled both horse and rider
into the sea.
2 The LORD is my strength and my song;
he has given me victory.
This is my God, and I will praise him—
my father's God, and I will exalt him!
3 The LORD is a warrior;
Yahweh is his name!

4 Pharaoh's chariots and army
he has hurled into the sea.
The finest of Pharaoh's officers
are drowned in the Red Sea.
5 The deep waters gushed over them;
they sank to the bottom like a stone.

6 "Your right hand, O LORD,
is glorious in power.
Your right hand, O LORD,
smashes the enemy.
7 In the greatness of your majesty,
you overthrow those who rise against you.
You unleash your blazing fury;
it consumes them like straw.
8 At the blast of your breath,
the waters piled up!
The surging waters stood straight like
a wall;
in the heart of the sea the deep waters
became hard.

9 "The enemy boasted, 'I will chase them
and catch up with them.
I will plunder them
and consume them.
I will flash my sword;
my powerful hand will destroy them.'
10 But you blew with your breath,
and the sea covered them.
They sank like lead
in the mighty waters.

11 "Who is like you among the gods,
O LORD—
glorious in holiness,
awesome in splendor,
performing great wonders?
12 You raised your right hand,
and the earth swallowed our enemies.
13 "With your unfailing love you lead
the people you have redeemed.
In your might, you guide them
to your sacred home.
14 The peoples hear and tremble;
anguish grips those who live in Philistia.
15 The leaders of Edom are terrified;
the nobles of Moab tremble.
All who live in Canaan melt away;
16 terror and dread fall upon them.
The power of your arm
makes them lifeless as stone
until your people pass by, O LORD,
until the people you purchased pass by.
17 You will bring them in and plant them on
your own mountain—
the place, O LORD, reserved for your own
dwelling,
the sanctuary, O Lord, that your hands
have established.
18 The LORD will reign forever and ever!"

19 When Pharaoh's horses, chariots, and charioteers rushed into the sea, the LORD brought the
water crashing down on them. But the people of
Israel had walked through the middle of the sea
on dry ground!

20 Then Miriam the prophet, Aaron's sister,
took a tambourine and led all the women as they
played their tambourines and danced. 21 And
Miriam sang this song:

"Sing to the LORD,
for he has triumphed gloriously;
he has hurled both horse and rider
into the sea."

Bitter Water at Marah

22 Then Moses led the people of Israel away from
the Red Sea, and they moved out into the desert
of Shur. They traveled in this desert for three
days without finding any water. 23 When they
came to the oasis of Marah, the water was too bitter to drink. So they called the place Marah
(which means "bitter").

24 Then the people complained and turned
against Moses. "What are we going to drink?"
they demanded. 25 So Moses cried out to the
LORD for help, and the LORD showed him a piece
of wood. Moses threw it into the water, and this
made the water good to drink.

It was there at Marah that the LORD set before
them the following decree as a standard to test
their faithfulness to him. 26 He said, "If you will
listen carefully to the voice of the LORD your God
and do what is right in his sight, obeying his
commands and keeping all his decrees, then I
will not make you suffer any of the diseases I sent
on the Egyptians; for I am the LORD who heals
you."

27 After leaving Marah, the Israelites traveled
on to the oasis of Elim, where they found twelve
springs and seventy palm trees. They camped
there beside the water.

CHAPTER 16

Manna and Quail from Heaven

Then the whole community of Israel set out from
Elim and journeyed into the wilderness of Sin,
between Elim and Mount Sinai. They arrived
there on the fifteenth day of the second month,
one month after leaving the land of Egypt.

2There, too, the whole community of Israel complained about Moses and Aaron.
3"If only the LORD had killed us back in Egypt,"
they moaned. "There we sat around pots filled
with meat and ate all the bread we wanted. But
now you have brought us into this wilderness to
starve us all to death."
4Then the LORD said to Moses, "Look, I'm going to rain down food from heaven for you. Each
day the people can go out and pick up as much
food as they need for that day. I will test them in
this to see whether or not they will follow my instructions. 5On the sixth day they will gather
food, and when they prepare it, there will be
twice as much as usual."
6So Moses and Aaron said to all the people of
Israel, "By evening you will realize it was the
LORD who brought you out of the land of Egypt.
7In the morning you will see the glory of the
LORD, because he has heard your complaints,
which are against him, not against us. What have
we done that you should complain about us?"
8Then Moses added, "The LORD will give you
meat to eat in the evening and bread to satisfy
you in the morning, for he has heard all your
complaints against him. What have we done?
Yes, your complaints are against the LORD, not
against us."
9Then Moses said to Aaron, "Announce this to
the entire community of Israel: 'Present yourselves before the LORD, for he has heard your
complaining.' " 10And as Aaron spoke to the
whole community of Israel, they looked out toward the wilderness. There they could see the
awesome glory of the LORD in the cloud.
11Then the LORD said to Moses, 12"I have
heard the Israelites' complaints. Now tell them,
'In the evening you will have meat to eat, and in
the morning you will have all the bread you want.
Then you will know that I am the LORD your
God.'"
13That evening vast numbers of quail flew in
and covered the camp. And the next morning
the area around the camp was wet with dew.
14When the dew evaporated, a flaky substance
as fine as frost blanketed the ground. 15The Israelites were puzzled when they saw it. "What
is it?" they asked each other. They had no idea
what it was.
And Moses told them, "It is the food the LORD
has given you to eat. 16These are the LORD's instructions: Each household should gather as
much as it needs. Pick up two quarts for each
person in your tent."
17So the people of Israel did as they were told.
Some gathered a lot, some only a little. 18But
when they measured it out, everyone had just
enough. Those who gathered a lot had nothing
left over, and those who gathered only a little
had enough. Each family had just what it
needed.
19Then Moses told them, "Do not keep any of
it until morning." 20But some of them didn't listen and kept some of it until morning. But by
then it was full of maggots and had a terrible
smell. Moses was very angry with them.
21After this the people gathered the food
morning by morning, each family according to
its need. And as the sun became hot, the flakes
they had not picked up melted and disappeared.
22On the sixth day, they gathered twice as much
as usual—four quarts for each person instead of
two. Then all the leaders of the community came
and asked Moses for an explanation. 23He told
them, "This is what the LORD commanded: Tomorrow will be a day of complete rest, a holy Sabbath day set apart for the LORD. So bake or boil as
much as you want today, and set aside what is left
for tomorrow."
24So they put some aside until morning, just as
Moses had commanded. And in the morning the
leftover food was wholesome and good, without
maggots or odor. 25Moses said, "Eat this food today, for today is a Sabbath day dedicated to the
LORD. There will be no food on the ground today.
26You may gather the food for six days, but the
seventh day is the Sabbath. There will be no food
on the ground that day."
27Some of the people went out anyway on the
seventh day, but they found no food. 28The LORD
asked Moses, "How long will these people refuse
to obey my commands and instructions? 29They
must realize that the Sabbath is the LORD's gift to
you. That is why he gives you a two-day supply on
the sixth day, so there will be enough for two
days. On the Sabbath day you must each stay in
your place. Do not go out to pick up food on the
seventh day." 30So the people did not gather any
food on the seventh day.
31The Israelites called the food manna. It was
white like coriander seed, and it tasted like
honey wafers.
32Then Moses said, "This is what the LORD has
commanded: Fill a two-quart container with
manna to preserve it for your descendants. Then
later generations will be able to see the food I
gave you in the wilderness when I set you free
from Egypt."
33Moses said to Aaron, "Get a jar and fill it with
two quarts of manna. Then put it in a sacred

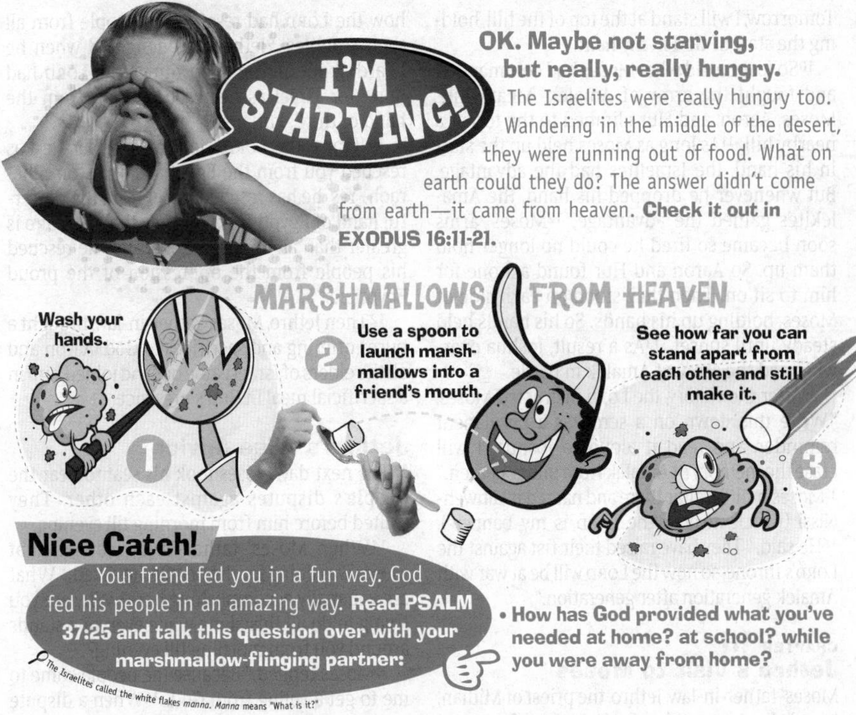

place before the LORD to preserve it for all future
generations." 34Aaron did just as the LORD had
commanded Moses. He eventually placed it in
the Ark of the Covenant—in front of the stone
tablets inscribed with the terms of the covenant.
35So the people of Israel ate manna for forty
years until they arrived at the land where they
would settle. They ate manna until they came to
the border of the land of Canaan.

I'M STARVING!
OK. Maybe not starving, but really, really hungry.
The Israelites were really hungry too. Wandering in the middle of the desert, they were running out of food. What on earth could they do? The answer didn't come from earth—it came from heaven. Check it out in EXODUS 16:11-21.
MARSHMALLOWS FROM HEAVEN
Wash your hands.
1
Use a spoon to launch marsh-mallows into a friend's mouth.
2
See how far you can stand apart from each other and still make it.
3
Nice Catch!
Your friend fed you in a fun way. God fed his people in an amazing way. Read PSALM 37:25 and talk this question over with your marshmallow-flinging partner:
• How has God provided what you've needed at home? at school? while you were away from home?
The Israelites called the white flakes manna. Manna means "What is it?"

36The container used to measure the manna
was an omer, which was one-tenth of an ephah; it
held about two quarts.

CHAPTER 17

Water from the Rock

At the LORD's command, the whole community
of Israel left the wilderness of Sin and moved
from place to place. Eventually they camped at
Rephidim, but there was no water there for the
people to drink. 2So once more the people complained against Moses. "Give us water to drink!"
they demanded.

"Quiet!" Moses replied. "Why are you complaining against me? And why are you testing
the LORD?"

3But tormented by thirst, they continued to
argue with Moses. "Why did you bring us out of
Egypt? Are you trying to kill us, our children,
and our livestock with thirst?"

4Then Moses cried out to the LORD, "What
should I do with these people? They are ready to
stone me!"

5The LORD said to Moses, "Walk out in front
of the people. Take your staff, the one you used
when you struck the water of the Nile, and call
some of the elders of Israel to join you. 6I will
stand before you on the rock at Mount Sinai.
Strike the rock, and water will come gushing
out. Then the people will be able to drink." So
Moses struck the rock as he was told, and water
gushed out as the elders looked on.

7Moses named the place Massah (which
means "test") and Meribah (which means "arguing") because the people of Israel argued with
Moses and tested the LORD by saying, "Is the
LORD here with us or not?"

Israel Defeats the Amalekites

8While the people of Israel were still at Rephidim, the warriors of Amalek attacked them.
9Moses commanded Joshua, "Choose some men
to go out and fight the army of Amalek for us.

Tomorrow, I will stand at the top of the hill, holding the staff of God in my hand."

10 So Joshua did what Moses had commanded and fought the army of Amalek. Meanwhile, Moses, Aaron, and Hur climbed to the top of a nearby hill. 11 As long as Moses held up the staff in his hand, the Israelites had the advantage. But whenever he dropped his hand, the Amalekites gained the advantage. 12 Moses' arms soon became so tired he could no longer hold them up. So Aaron and Hur found a stone for him to sit on. Then they stood on each side of Moses, holding up his hands. So his hands held steady until sunset. 13 As a result, Joshua overwhelmed the army of Amalek in battle.

14 After the victory, the LORD instructed Moses, "Write this down on a scroll as a permanent reminder, and read it aloud to Joshua: I will erase the memory of Amalek from under heaven." 15 Moses built an altar there and named it Yahweh-Nissi (which means "the LORD is my banner"). 16 He said, "They have raised their fist against the LORD's throne, so now the LORD will be at war with Amalek generation after generation."

CHAPTER 18
Jethro's Visit to Moses

Moses' father-in-law, Jethro, the priest of Midian, heard about everything God had done for Moses and his people, the Israelites. He heard especially about how the LORD had rescued them from Egypt.

2 Earlier, Moses had sent his wife, Zipporah, and his two sons back to Jethro, who had taken them in. 3 (Moses' first son was named Gershom, for Moses had said when the boy was born, "I have been a foreigner in a foreign land." 4 His second son was named Eliezer, for Moses had said, "The God of my ancestors was my helper; he rescued me from the sword of Pharaoh.") 5 Jethro, Moses' father-in-law, now came to visit Moses in the wilderness. He brought Moses' wife and two sons with him, and they arrived while Moses and the people were camped near the mountain of God. 6 Jethro had sent a message to Moses, saying, "I, Jethro, your father-in-law, am coming to see you with your wife and your two sons."

7 So Moses went out to meet his father-in-law. He bowed low and kissed him. They asked about each other's welfare and then went into Moses' tent. 8 Moses told his father-in-law everything the LORD had done to Pharaoh and Egypt on behalf of Israel. He also told about all the hardships they had experienced along the way and how the LORD had rescued his people from all their troubles. 9 Jethro was delighted when he heard about all the good things the LORD had done for Israel as he rescued them from the hand of the Egyptians.

10 "Praise the LORD," Jethro said, "for he has rescued you from the Egyptians and from Pharaoh. Yes, he has rescued Israel from the powerful hand of Egypt! 11 I know now that the LORD is greater than all other gods, because he rescued his people from the oppression of the proud Egyptians."

12 Then Jethro, Moses' father-in-law, brought a burnt offering and sacrifices to God. Aaron and all the elders of Israel came out and joined him in a sacrificial meal in God's presence.

Jethro's Wise Advice

13 The next day, Moses took his seat to hear the people's disputes against each other. They waited before him from morning till evening.

14 When Moses' father-in-law saw all that Moses was doing for the people, he asked, "What are you really accomplishing here? Why are you trying to do all this alone while everyone stands around you from morning till evening?"

15 Moses replied, "Because the people come to me to get a ruling from God. 16 When a dispute arises, they come to me, and I am the one who settles the case between the quarreling parties. I inform the people of God's decrees and give them his instructions."

17 "This is not good!" Moses' father-in-law exclaimed. 18 "You're going to wear yourself out—and the people, too. This job is too heavy a burden for you to handle all by yourself. 19 Now listen to me, and let me give you a word of advice, and may God be with you. You should continue to be the people's representative before God, bringing their disputes to him. 20 Teach them God's decrees, and give them his instructions. Show them how to conduct their lives. 21 But select from all the people some capable, honest men who fear God and hate bribes. Appoint them as leaders over groups of one thousand, one hundred, fifty, and ten. 22 They should always be available to solve the people's common disputes, but have them bring the major cases to you. Let the leaders decide the smaller matters themselves. They will help you carry the load, making the task easier for you. 23 If you follow this advice, and if God commands you to do so, then you will be able to endure the pressures, and all these people will go home in peace."

24 Moses listened to his father-in-law's advice

and followed his suggestions. 25He chose capable men from all over Israel and appointed
them as leaders over the people. He put them in
charge of groups of one thousand, one hundred,
fifty, and ten. 26These men were always available to solve the people's common disputes.
They brought the major cases to Moses, but
they took care of the smaller matters themselves.
27Soon after this, Moses said good-bye to his
father-in-law, who returned to his own land.

CHAPTER 19
The LORD Reveals Himself at Sinai

Exactly two months after the Israelites left Egypt,
they arrived in the wilderness of Sinai. 2After
breaking camp at Rephidim, they came to the
wilderness of Sinai and set up camp there at the
base of Mount Sinai.
3Then Moses climbed the mountain to appear
before God. The LORD called to him from the
mountain and said, "Give these instructions to
the family of Jacob; announce it to the descendants of Israel: 4'You have seen what I did to the
Egyptians. You know how I carried you on eagles'
wings and brought you to myself. 5Now if you
will obey me and keep my covenant, you will be
my own special treasure from among all the peoples on earth; for all the earth belongs to me.
6And you will be my kingdom of priests, my holy
nation.' This is the message you must give to the
people of Israel."
7So Moses returned from the mountain and
called together the elders of the people and told
them everything the LORD had commanded him.
8And all the people responded together, "We will
do everything the LORD has commanded." So
Moses brought the people's answer back to the
LORD.
9Then the LORD said to Moses, "I will come to
you in a thick cloud, Moses, so the people themselves can hear me when I speak with you. Then
they will always trust you."
Moses told the LORD what the people had said.
10Then the LORD told Moses, "Go down and prepare the people for my arrival. Consecrate them
today and tomorrow, and have them wash their
clothing. 11Be sure they are ready on the third
day, for on that day the LORD will come down on
Mount Sinai as all the people watch. 12Mark off
a boundary all around the mountain. Warn the
people, 'Be careful! Do not go up on the mountain or even touch its boundaries. Anyone who
touches the mountain will certainly be put to

God is talking. ARE YOU LISTENING?

God spoke to Moses in a powerful voice. **Check it out in EXODUS 19:1-9 and 19:16-25.** But most people would never say they've heard God speaking aloud.

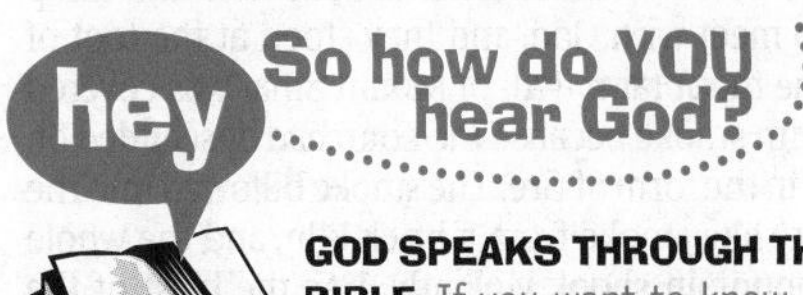

GOD SPEAKS THROUGH THE BIBLE. If you want to know what God is saying, start with the book you're holding right now! **See 2 TIMOTHY 3:16.**

GOD SPEAKS THROUGH OTHER CHRISTIANS. If you have a question, pray and talk about it with someone else. **See PROVERBS 15:22.**

GOD'S SPIRIT SPEAKS TO YOUR HEART. Sometimes God communicates to you through what happens. Sometimes you'll just know what's right. **See JOHN 16:13-15.**

LISTEN UP

Take your Bible to a place where you can be alone. Pray about school, home, a problem—anything! Open your Bible and read. **Ask God to help you hear what he wants to say.**

That's It!

Sometimes God will speak to you loud and clear. Sometimes you won't even know God said anything until later. But God is talking. **JUST KEEP LISTENING!**

death. 13No hand may touch the person or animal that crosses the boundary; instead, stone
them or shoot them with arrows. They must be
put to death.' However, when the ram's horn
sounds a long blast, then the people may go up
on the mountain."

14So Moses went down to the people. He consecrated them for worship, and they washed
their clothes. 15He told them, "Get ready for the
third day, and until then abstain from having
sexual intercourse."

16On the morning of the third day, thunder
roared and lightning flashed, and a dense cloud
came down on the mountain. There was a long,
loud blast from a ram's horn, and all the people
trembled. 17Moses led them out from the camp
to meet with God, and they stood at the foot of
the mountain. 18All of Mount Sinai was covered
with smoke because the LORD had descended on
it in the form of fire. The smoke billowed into the
sky like smoke from a brick kiln, and the whole
mountain shook violently. 19As the blast of the
ram's horn grew louder and louder, Moses spoke,
and God thundered his reply. 20The LORD came
down on the top of Mount Sinai and called
Moses to the top of the mountain. So Moses
climbed the mountain.

21Then the LORD told Moses, "Go back down
and warn the people not to break through the
boundaries to see the LORD, or they will die.
22Even the priests who regularly come near to
the LORD must purify themselves so that the
LORD does not break out and destroy them."

23"But LORD," Moses protested, "the people
cannot come up to Mount Sinai. You already
warned us. You told me, 'Mark off a boundary all
around the mountain to set it apart as holy.'"

24But the LORD said, "Go down and bring
Aaron back up with you. In the meantime, do not
let the priests or the people break through to approach the LORD, or he will break out and destroy
them."

25So Moses went down to the people and told
them what the LORD had said.

CHAPTER 20
Ten Commandments for the Covenant Community

Then God gave the people all these instructions:

2"I am the LORD your God, who rescued you
from the land of Egypt, the place of your
slavery.

3"You must not have any other god but me.

4"You must not make for yourself an idol of
any kind or an image of anything in the
heavens or on the earth or in the sea. 5You
must not bow down to them or worship
them, for I, the LORD your God, am a jealous
God who will not tolerate your affection for
any other gods. I lay the sins of the parents
upon their children; the entire family is
affected—even children in the third and
fourth generations of those who reject me.
6But I lavish unfailing love for a thousand
generations on those who love me and obey
my commands.

7"You must not misuse the name of the LORD
your God. The LORD will not let you go
unpunished if you misuse his name.

8"Remember to observe the Sabbath day by
keeping it holy. 9You have six days each week
for your ordinary work, 10but the seventh day
is a Sabbath day of rest dedicated to the LORD
your God. On that day no one in your
household may do any work. This includes
you, your sons and daughters, your male and
female servants, your livestock, and any
foreigners living among you. 11For in six days
the LORD made the heavens, the earth, the
sea, and everything in them; but on the
seventh day he rested. That is why the LORD
blessed the Sabbath day and set it apart as
holy.

12"Honor your father and mother. Then you will
live a long, full life in the land the LORD your
God is giving you.

13"You must not murder.

14"You must not commit adultery.

15"You must not steal.

16"You must not testify falsely against your
neighbor.

17"You must not covet your neighbor's house.
You must not covet your neighbor's wife,
male or female servant, ox or donkey, or
anything else that belongs to your neighbor."

18When the people heard the thunder and the
loud blast of the ram's horn, and when they saw
the flashes of lightning and the smoke billowing
from the mountain, they stood at a distance,
trembling with fear.

19And they said to Moses, "You speak to us,
and we will listen. But don't let God speak directly to us, or we will die!"

20"Don't be afraid," Moses answered them, "for
God has come in this way to test you, and so that
your fear of him will keep you from sinning!"

21As the people stood in the distance, Moses
approached the dark cloud where God was.

Proper Use of Altars

22And the LORD said to Moses, "Say this to the
people of Israel: You saw for yourselves that I
spoke to you from heaven. 23Remember, you
must not make any idols of silver or gold to rival me.

24"Build for me an altar made of earth, and offer your sacrifices to me—your burnt offerings
and peace offerings, your sheep and goats, and
your cattle. Build my altar wherever I cause my
name to be remembered, and I will come to you
and bless you. 25If you use stones to build my altar, use only natural, uncut stones. Do not shape
the stones with a tool, for that would make the
altar unfit for holy use. 26And do not approach
my altar by going up steps. If you do, someone
might look up under your clothing and see your
nakedness.

CHAPTER 21

Fair Treatment of Slaves

"These are the regulations you must present to
Israel.

2"If you buy a Hebrew slave, he may serve for
no more than six years. Set him free in the seventh year, and he will owe you nothing for his
freedom. 3If he was single when he became your
slave, he shall leave single. But if he was married
before he became a slave, then his wife must be
freed with him.

4"If his master gave him a wife while he was a
slave and they had sons or daughters, then only
the man will be free in the seventh year, but his
wife and children will still belong to his master.
5But the slave may declare, 'I love my master, my
wife, and my children. I don't want to go free.'
6If he does this, his master must present him
before God. Then his master must take him to
the door or doorpost and publicly pierce his ear
with an awl. After that, the slave will serve his
master for life.

7"When a man sells his daughter as a slave,
she will not be freed at the end of six years as the
men are. 8If she does not satisfy her owner, he
must allow her to be bought back again. But he
is not allowed to sell her to foreigners, since he is
the one who broke the contract with her. 9But if
the slave's owner arranges for her to marry his
son, he may no longer treat her as a slave but as
a daughter.

10"If a man who has married a slave wife takes
another wife for himself, he must not neglect the
rights of the first wife to food, clothing, and sexual intimacy. 11If he fails in any of these three
obligations, she may leave as a free woman without making any payment.

Cases of Personal Injury

12"Anyone who assaults and kills another person
must be put to death. 13But if it was simply an accident permitted by God, I will appoint a place of
refuge where the slayer can run for safety.
14However, if someone deliberately kills another
person, then the slayer must be dragged even
from my altar and be put to death.

15"Anyone who strikes father or mother must
be put to death.

16"Kidnappers must be put to death, whether
they are caught in possession of their victims or
have already sold them as slaves.

17"Anyone who dishonors father or mother
must be put to death.

18"Now suppose two men quarrel, and one
hits the other with a stone or fist, and the injured
person does not die but is confined to bed. 19If
he is later able to walk outside again, even with a
crutch, the assailant will not be punished but
must compensate his victim for lost wages and
provide for his full recovery.

20"If a man beats his male or female slave with
a club and the slave dies as a result, the owner
must be punished. 21But if the slave recovers
within a day or two, then the owner shall not be
punished, since the slave is his property.

22"Now suppose two men are fighting, and in
the process they accidentally strike a pregnant
woman so she gives birth prematurely. If no further injury results, the man who struck the
woman must pay the amount of compensation
the woman's husband demands and the judges
approve. 23But if there is further injury, the punishment must match the injury: a life for a life,
24an eye for an eye, a tooth for a tooth, a hand for
a hand, a foot for a foot, 25a burn for a burn, a
wound for a wound, a bruise for a bruise.

26"If a man hits his male or female slave in the
eye and the eye is blinded, he must let the slave
go free to compensate for the eye. 27And if a man
knocks out the tooth of his male or female slave,
he must let the slave go free to compensate for
the tooth.

28"If an ox gores a man or woman to death, the
ox must be stoned, and its flesh may not be
eaten. In such a case, however, the owner will not
be held liable. 29But suppose the ox had a reputation for goring, and the owner had been informed but failed to keep it under control. If the
ox then kills someone, it must be stoned, and
the owner must also be put to death. 30However,

the dead person's relatives may accept payment
to compensate for the loss of life. The owner of
the ox may redeem his life by paying whatever is
demanded.
31"The same regulation applies if the ox gores
a boy or a girl. 32But if the ox gores a slave, either
male or female, the animal's owner must pay the
slave's owner thirty silver coins, and the ox must
be stoned.
33"Suppose someone digs or uncovers a pit
and fails to cover it, and then an ox or a donkey
falls into it. 34The owner of the pit must pay full
compensation to the owner of the animal, but
then he gets to keep the dead animal.
35"If someone's ox injures a neighbor's ox and
the injured ox dies, then the two owners must
sell the live ox and divide the price equally between them. They must also divide the dead animal. 36But if the ox had a reputation for goring,
yet its owner failed to keep it under control, he
must pay full compensation—a live ox for the
dead one—but he may keep the dead ox.

CHAPTER 22

Protection of Property

"If someone steals an ox or sheep and then kills
or sells it, the thief must pay back five oxen for
each ox stolen, and four sheep for each sheep
stolen.
2"If a thief is caught in the act of breaking into
a house and is struck and killed in the process,
the person who killed the thief is not guilty of
murder. 3But if it happens in daylight, the one
who killed the thief is guilty of murder.
"A thief who is caught must pay in full for
everything he stole. If he cannot pay, he must be
sold as a slave to pay for his theft. 4If someone
steals an ox or a donkey or a sheep and it is found
in the thief's possession, then the thief must pay
double the value of the stolen animal.
5"If an animal is grazing in a field or vineyard
and the owner lets it stray into someone else's
field to graze, then the animal's owner must pay
compensation from the best of his own grain or
grapes.
6"If you are burning thornbushes and the fire
gets out of control and spreads into another person's field, destroying the sheaves or the uncut
grain or the whole crop, the one who started the
fire must pay for the lost crop.
7"Suppose someone leaves money or goods
with a neighbor for safekeeping, and they are
stolen from the neighbor's house. If the thief is
caught, the compensation is double the value of
what was stolen. 8But if the thief is not caught,
the neighbor must appear before God, who will
determine if he stole the property.
9"Suppose there is a dispute between two people who both claim to own a particular ox, donkey, sheep, article of clothing, or any lost
property. Both parties must come before God,
and the person whom God declares guilty must
pay double compensation to the other.
10"Now suppose someone leaves a donkey, ox,
sheep, or any other animal with a neighbor for
safekeeping, but it dies or is injured or is taken
away, and no one sees what happened. 11The
neighbor must then take an oath in the presence
of the LORD. If the LORD confirms that the neighbor did not steal the property, the owner must
accept the verdict, and no payment will be required. 12But if the animal was indeed stolen, the
guilty person must pay compensation to the
owner. 13If it was torn to pieces by a wild animal,
the remains of the carcass must be shown as evidence, and no compensation will be required.
14"If someone borrows an animal from a
neighbor and it is injured or dies when the owner
is absent, the person who borrowed it must pay
full compensation. 15But if the owner was present, no compensation is required. And no compensation is required if the animal was rented, for
this loss is covered by the rental fee.

Social Responsibility

16"If a man seduces a virgin who is not engaged
to anyone and has sex with her, he must pay the
customary bride price and marry her. 17But if
her father refuses to let him marry her, the man
must still pay him an amount equal to the bride
price of a virgin.
18"You must not allow a sorceress to live.
19"Anyone who has sexual relations with an
animal must certainly be put to death.
20"Anyone who sacrifices to any god other
than the LORD must be destroyed.
21"You must not mistreat or oppress foreigners in any way. Remember, you yourselves were
once foreigners in the land of Egypt.
22"You must not exploit a widow or an orphan. 23If you exploit them in any way and they
cry out to me, then I will certainly hear their cry.
24My anger will blaze against you, and I will kill
you with the sword. Then your wives will be widows and your children fatherless.
25"If you lend money to any of my people who
are in need, do not charge interest as a money
lender would. 26If you take your neighbor's
cloak as security for a loan, you must return it
before sunset. 27This coat may be the only

Numero Uno, The Big Cheese, The Head Honcho, The Grand Poo-bah.
However you say it, there is only one thing in your life that is the most important thing.
Who or what is #1 in your life?
TOP DOG
TRY THIS
Find the most valuable object in the room.

Think It Over
- Why do you think this object is important?
- Would everyone think it's valuable?

You'd never worship the object you found—because it's just a thing. But the Israelites did something just that crazy. **Read all about it in EXODUS 32:1-8.**

blanket your neighbor has. How can a person sleep without it? If you do not return it and your neighbor cries out to me for help, then I will hear, for I am merciful.

28"You must not dishonor God or curse any of your rulers.

29"You must not hold anything back when you give me offerings from your crops and your wine.

"You must give me your firstborn sons.

30"You must also give me the firstborn of your cattle, sheep, and goats. But leave the newborn animal with its mother for seven days; then give it to me on the eighth day.

31"You must be my holy people. Therefore, do not eat any animal that has been torn up and killed by wild animals. Throw it to the dogs.

CHAPTER 23

A Call for Justice

"You must not pass along false rumors. You must not cooperate with evil people by lying on the witness stand.

2"You must not follow the crowd in doing wrong. When you are called to testify in a dispute, do not be swayed by the crowd to twist justice. 3And do not slant your testimony in favor of a person just because that person is poor.

4"If you come upon your enemy's ox or donkey that has strayed away, take it back to its owner. 5If you see that the donkey of someone who hates you has collapsed under its load, do not walk by. Instead, stop and help.

6"In a lawsuit, you must not deny justice to the poor.

7"Be sure never to charge anyone falsely with evil. Never sentence an innocent or blameless person to death, for I never declare a guilty person to be innocent.

8"Take no bribes, for a bribe makes you ignore something that you clearly see. A bribe makes even a righteous person twist the truth.

9"You must not oppress foreigners. You know what it's like to be a foreigner, for you yourselves were once foreigners in the land of Egypt.

10"Plant and harvest your crops for six years,
11but let the land be renewed and lie uncultivated during the seventh year. Then let the poor among you harvest whatever grows on its own. Leave the rest for wild animals to eat. The same applies to your vineyards and olive groves.

12"You have six days each week for your ordinary work, but on the seventh day you must stop working. This gives your ox and your donkey a chance to rest. It also allows your slaves and the foreigners living among you to be refreshed.

13"Pay close attention to all my instructions. You must not call on the name of any other gods. Do not even speak their names.

Three Annual Festivals

14"Each year you must celebrate three festivals in my honor. 15First, celebrate the Festival of Unleavened Bread. For seven days the bread you eat must be made without yeast, just as I commanded you. Celebrate this festival annually at the appointed time in early spring, in the month of Abib, for that is the anniversary of your departure from Egypt. No one may appear before me without an offering.

16"Second, celebrate the Festival of Harvest, when you bring me the first crops of your harvest.

"Finally, celebrate the Festival of the Final Harvest at the end of the harvest season, when you have harvested all the crops from your fields. 17At these three times each year, every man in Israel must appear before the Sovereign, the LORD.

18"You must not offer the blood of my sacrificial offerings together with any baked goods containing yeast. And do not leave the fat from the festival offerings until the next morning.

19"As you harvest your crops, bring the very best of the first harvest to the house of the LORD your God.

"You must not cook a young goat in its mother's milk.

A Promise of the LORD's Presence

20"See, I am sending an angel before you to protect you on your journey and lead you safely to the place I have prepared for you. 21Pay close attention to him, and obey his instructions. Do not rebel against him, for he is my representative, and he will not forgive your rebellion. 22But if you are careful to obey him, following all my instructions, then I will be an enemy to your enemies, and I will oppose those who oppose you. 23For my angel will go before you and bring you into the land of the Amorites, Hittites, Perizzites, Canaanites, Hivites, and Jebusites, so you may live there. And I will destroy them completely. 24You must not worship the gods of these nations or serve them in any way or imitate their evil practices. Instead, you must utterly destroy them and smash their sacred pillars.

25"You must serve only the LORD your God. If you do, I will bless you with food and water, and I will protect you from illness. 26There will be no miscarriages or infertility in your land, and I will give you long, full lives.

27"I will send my terror ahead of you and create panic among all the people whose lands you invade. I will make all your enemies turn and run. 28I will send terror ahead of you to drive out the Hivites, Canaanites, and Hittites. 29But I will not drive them out in a single year, because the land would become desolate and the wild animals would multiply and threaten you. 30I will drive them out a little at a time until your population has increased enough to take possession of the land. 31And I will fix your boundaries from the Red Sea to the Mediterranean Sea, and from the eastern wilderness to the Euphrates River. I will hand over to you the people now living in the land, and you will drive them out ahead of you.

32"Make no treaties with them or their gods. 33They must not live in your land, or they will cause you to sin against me. If you serve their gods, you will be caught in the trap of idolatry."

CHAPTER 24

Israel Accepts the LORD's Covenant

Then the LORD instructed Moses: "Come up here to me, and bring along Aaron, Nadab, Abihu, and seventy of Israel's elders. All of you must worship from a distance. 2Only Moses is allowed to come near to the LORD. The others must not come near, and none of the other people are allowed to climb up the mountain with him."

3Then Moses went down to the people and repeated all the instructions and regulations the LORD had given him. All the people answered with one voice, "We will do everything the LORD has commanded."

4Then Moses carefully wrote down all the LORD's instructions. Early the next morning Moses got up and built an altar at the foot of the mountain. He also set up twelve pillars, one for each of the twelve tribes of Israel. 5Then he sent some of the young Israelite men to present burnt offerings and to sacrifice bulls as peace offerings to the LORD. 6Moses drained half the blood from these animals into basins. The other half he splattered against the altar.

7Then he took the Book of the Covenant and read it aloud to the people. Again they all responded, "We will do everything the LORD has commanded. We will obey."

8Then Moses took the blood from the basins and splattered it over the people, declaring, "Look, this blood confirms the covenant the LORD has made with you in giving you these instructions."

9Then Moses, Aaron, Nadab, Abihu, and the seventy elders of Israel climbed up the mountain. 10There they saw the God of Israel. Under his feet there seemed to be a surface of brilliant blue lapis lazuli, as clear as the sky itself. 11And though these nobles of Israel gazed upon God, he did not destroy them. In fact, they ate a covenant meal, eating and drinking in his presence!

12Then the LORD said to Moses, "Come up to me on the mountain. Stay there, and I will give you the tablets of stone on which I have inscribed the instructions and commands so you can teach the people." 13So Moses and his assistant Joshua set out, and Moses climbed up the mountain of God.

14Moses told the elders, "Stay here and wait for us until we come back. Aaron and Hur are

here with you. If anyone has a dispute while I am
gone, consult with them."
15Then Moses climbed up the mountain, and
the cloud covered it. 16And the glory of the LORD
settled down on Mount Sinai, and the cloud covered it for six days. On the seventh day the LORD
called to Moses from inside the cloud. 17To the
Israelites at the foot of the mountain, the glory of
the LORD appeared at the summit like a consuming fire. 18Then Moses disappeared into the
cloud as he climbed higher up the mountain. He
remained on the mountain forty days and forty
nights.

CHAPTER 25

Offerings for the Tabernacle

The LORD said to Moses, 2"Tell the people of Israel to bring me their sacred offerings. Accept the
contributions from all whose hearts are moved
to offer them. 3Here is a list of sacred offerings
you may accept from them:

gold, silver, and bronze;
4 blue, purple, and scarlet thread;
fine linen and goat hair for cloth;
5 tanned ram skins and fine goatskin leather;
acacia wood;
6 olive oil for the lamps;
spices for the anointing oil and the fragrant
incense;
7 onyx stones, and other gemstones to be set
in the ephod and the priest's chestpiece.

8"Have the people of Israel build me a holy
sanctuary so I can live among them. 9You must
build this Tabernacle and its furnishings exactly
according to the pattern I will show you.

Plans for the Ark of the Covenant

10"Have the people make an Ark of acacia
wood—a sacred chest 45 inches long, 27 inches
wide, and 27 inches high. 11Overlay it inside
and outside with pure gold, and run a molding of
gold all around it. 12Cast four gold rings and attach them to its four feet, two rings on each side.
13Make poles from acacia wood, and overlay
them with gold. 14Insert the poles into the rings
at the sides of the Ark to carry it. 15These carrying poles must stay inside the rings; never remove them. 16When the Ark is finished, place
inside it the stone tablets inscribed with the
terms of the covenant, which I will give to you.
17"Then make the Ark's cover—the place of
atonement—from pure gold. It must be
45 inches long and 27 inches wide. 18Then make
two cherubim from hammered gold, and place
them on the two ends of the atonement cover.
19Mold the cherubim on each end of the atonement cover, making it all of one piece of gold.
20The cherubim will face each other and look
down on the atonement cover. With their wings
spread above it, they will protect it. 21Place inside
the Ark the stone tablets inscribed with the
terms of the covenant, which I will give to you.
Then put the atonement cover on top of the Ark.
22I will meet with you there and talk to you from
above the atonement cover between the gold
cherubim that hover over the Ark of the Covenant. From there I will give you my commands
for the people of Israel.

Plans for the Table

23"Then make a table of acacia wood, 36 inches
long, 18 inches wide, and 27 inches high.
24Overlay it with pure gold and run a gold molding around the edge. 25Decorate it with a 3-inch
border all around, and run a gold molding along
the border. 26Make four gold rings for the table
and attach them at the four corners next to the
four legs. 27Attach the rings near the border to
hold the poles that are used to carry the table.
28Make these poles from acacia wood, and overlay them with gold. 29Make special containers of
pure gold for the table—bowls, ladles, pitchers,
and jars—to be used in pouring out liquid offerings. 30Place the Bread of the Presence on the
table to remain before me at all times.

Plans for the Lampstand

31"Make a lampstand of pure, hammered gold.
Make the entire lampstand and its decorations
of one piece—the base, center stem, lamp cups,
buds, and petals. 32Make it with six branches going out from the center stem, three on each side.
33Each of the six branches will have three lamp
cups shaped like almond blossoms, complete
with buds and petals. 34Craft the center stem of
the lampstand with four lamp cups shaped like
almond blossoms, complete with buds and petals. 35There will also be an almond bud beneath
each pair of branches where the six branches extend from the center stem. 36The almond buds
and branches must all be of one piece with the
center stem, and they must be hammered from
pure gold. 37Then make the seven lamps for the
lampstand, and set them so they reflect their
light forward. 38The lamp snuffers and trays
must also be made of pure gold. 39You will need
seventy-five pounds of pure gold for the lampstand and its accessories.

If you've ever been to Africa, you may have seen **aardvarks** running around. You may have heard of **Noah's Ark**. And the Bible mentions people called **Arkites**. But have you heard of the **Ark of the Covenant?** God told Moses to build a chest about as big as a toy box and cover it with pure gold. **Boy, it was heavy!** The Ark of the Covenant reminded the Israelites that God was with them. They carried it with them in battle and when they traveled.

Read HEBREWS 9:4-5 to see what the Israelites kept in the Ark of the Covenant. Make a treasure box by decorating a shoe box for your most important treasures.

[40]"Be sure that you make everything according to the pattern I have shown you here on the mountain.

CHAPTER 26
Plans for the Tabernacle

"Make the Tabernacle from ten curtains of finely
woven linen. Decorate the curtains with blue,
purple, and scarlet thread and with skillfully embroidered cherubim. [2]These ten curtains must
all be exactly the same size—42 feet long and
6 feet wide. [3]Join five of these curtains together
to make one long curtain, then join the other five
into a second long curtain. [4]Put loops of blue
yarn along the edge of the last curtain in each set.
[5]The fifty loops along the edge of one curtain are
to match the fifty loops along the edge of the
other curtain. [6]Then make fifty gold clasps and
fasten the long curtains together with the clasps.
In this way, the Tabernacle will be made of one
continuous piece.

[7]"Make eleven curtains of goat-hair cloth to
serve as a tent covering for the Tabernacle.
[8]These eleven curtains must all be exactly the
same size—45 feet long and 6 feet wide. [9]Join
five of these curtains together to make one long
curtain, and join the other six into a second long
curtain. Allow 3 feet of material from the second
set of curtains to hang over the front of the sacred tent. [10]Make fifty loops for one edge of each
large curtain. [11]Then make fifty bronze clasps,
and fasten the loops of the long curtains with the
clasps. In this way, the tent covering will be made
of one continuous piece. [12]The remaining 3 feet
of this tent covering will be left to hang over the
back of the Tabernacle. [13]Allow 18 inches of remaining material to hang down over each side,
so the Tabernacle is completely covered.
[14]Complete the tent covering with a protective
layer of tanned ram skins and a layer of fine goatskin leather.

[15]"For the framework of the Tabernacle, construct frames of acacia wood. [16]Each frame must
be 15 feet high and 27 inches wide, [17]with two
pegs under each frame. Make all the frames
identical. [18]Make twenty of these frames to support the curtains on the south side of the Tabernacle. [19]Also make forty silver bases—two bases
under each frame, with the pegs fitting securely
into the bases. [20]For the north side of the Tabernacle, make another twenty frames, [21]with their
forty silver bases, two bases under each frame.
[22]Make six frames for the rear—the west side of
the Tabernacle—[23]along with two additional
frames to reinforce the rear corners of the Tabernacle. [24]These corner frames will be matched at
the bottom and firmly attached at the top with a
single ring, forming a single corner unit. Make
both of these corner units the same way. [25]So
there will be eight frames at the rear of the Tabernacle, set in sixteen silver bases—two bases
under each frame.

[26]"Make crossbars of acacia wood to link the
frames, five crossbars for the north side of the
Tabernacle [27]and five for the south side. Also
make five crossbars for the rear of the Tabernacle, which will face west. [28]The middle crossbar,
attached halfway up the frames, will run all the
way from one end of the Tabernacle to the other.
[29]Overlay the frames with gold, and make gold
rings to hold the crossbars. Overlay the crossbars
with gold as well.

[30]"Set up this Tabernacle according to the
pattern you were shown on the mountain.

[31]"For the inside of the Tabernacle, make a
special curtain of finely woven linen. Decorate it

with blue, purple, and scarlet thread and with
skillfully embroidered cherubim. 32Hang this
curtain on gold hooks attached to four posts of
acacia wood. Overlay the posts with gold, and set
them in four silver bases. 33Hang the inner curtain from clasps, and put the Ark of the Covenant
in the room behind it. This curtain will separate
the Holy Place from the Most Holy Place.

34"Then put the Ark's cover—the place of
atonement—on top of the Ark of the Covenant
inside the Most Holy Place. 35Place the table outside the inner curtain on the north side of the
Tabernacle, and place the lampstand across the
room on the south side.

36"Make another curtain for the entrance to
the sacred tent. Make it of finely woven linen and
embroider it with exquisite designs, using blue,
purple, and scarlet thread. 37Craft five posts
from acacia wood. Overlay them with gold, and
hang the curtain from them with gold hooks.
Cast five bronze bases for the posts.

CHAPTER 27

Plans for the Altar of Burnt Offering

"Using acacia wood, construct a square altar
7½ feet wide, 7½ feet long, and 4½ feet high.
2Make horns for each of its four corners so that
the horns and altar are all one piece. Overlay the
altar with bronze. 3Make ash buckets, shovels,
basins, meat forks, and firepans, all of bronze.
4Make a bronze grating for it, and attach four
bronze rings at its four corners. 5Install the grating halfway down the side of the altar, under the
ledge. 6For carrying the altar, make poles from
acacia wood, and overlay them with bronze. 7In-
sert the poles through the rings on the two sides
of the altar. 8The altar must be hollow, made
from planks. Build it just as you were shown on
the mountain.

Plans for the Courtyard

9"Then make the courtyard for the Tabernacle,
enclosed with curtains made of finely woven
linen. On the south side, make the curtains
150 feet long. 10They will be held up by twenty
posts set securely in twenty bronze bases. Hang
the curtains with silver hooks and rings. 11Make
the curtains the same on the north side—
150 feet of curtains held up by twenty posts set
securely in bronze bases. Hang the curtains with
silver hooks and rings. 12The curtains on the
west end of the courtyard will be 75 feet long,
supported by ten posts set into ten bases. 13The
east end of the courtyard, the front, will also be
75 feet long. 14The courtyard entrance will be on
the east end, flanked by two curtains. The curtain
on the right side will be 22½ feet long, supported
by three posts set into three bases. 15The curtain
on the left side will also be 22½ feet long, supported by three posts set into three bases.

16"For the entrance to the courtyard, make a
curtain that is 30 feet long. Make it from finely
woven linen, and decorate it with beautiful embroidery in blue, purple, and scarlet thread. Support it with four posts, each securely set in its
own base. 17All the posts around the courtyard
must have silver rings and hooks and bronze
bases. 18So the entire courtyard will be 150 feet
long and 75 feet wide, with curtain walls 7½ feet
high, made from finely woven linen. The bases
for the posts will be made of bronze.

19"All the articles used in the rituals of the Tabernacle, including all the tent pegs used to support the Tabernacle and the courtyard curtains,
must be made of bronze.

Light for the Tabernacle

20"Command the people of Israel to bring you
pure oil of pressed olives for the light, to keep the
lamps burning continually. 21The lampstand will
stand in the Tabernacle, in front of the inner curtain that shields the Ark of the Covenant. Aaron
and his sons must keep the lamps burning in the
LORD's presence all night. This is a permanent law
for the people of Israel, and it must be observed
from generation to generation.

CHAPTER 28

Clothing for the Priests

"Call for your brother, Aaron, and his sons, Nadab, Abihu, Eleazar, and Ithamar. Set them apart
from the rest of the people of Israel so they may
minister to me and be my priests. 2Make sacred
garments for Aaron that are glorious and beautiful. 3Instruct all the skilled craftsmen whom I
have filled with the spirit of wisdom. Have them
make garments for Aaron that will distinguish
him as a priest set apart for my service. 4These
are the garments they are to make: a chestpiece,
an ephod, a robe, a patterned tunic, a turban,
and a sash. They are to make these sacred garments for your brother, Aaron, and his sons to
wear when they serve me as priests. 5So give
them fine linen cloth, gold thread, and blue,
purple, and scarlet thread.

Design of the Ephod

6"The craftsmen must make the ephod of finely
woven linen and skillfully embroider it with gold

and with blue, purple, and scarlet thread. 7It will
consist of two pieces, front and back, joined at
the shoulders with two shoulder-pieces. 8The
decorative sash will be made of the same materials: finely woven linen embroidered with gold
and with blue, purple, and scarlet thread.

9"Take two onyx stones, and engrave on them
the names of the tribes of Israel. 10Six names
will be on each stone, arranged in the order of
the births of the original sons of Israel. 11En-
grave these names on the two stones in the
same way a jeweler engraves a seal. Then mount
the stones in settings of gold filigree. 12Fasten
the two stones on the shoulder-pieces of the
ephod as a reminder that Aaron represents the
people of Israel. Aaron will carry these names
on his shoulders as a constant reminder whenever he goes before the LORD. 13Make the settings of gold filigree, 14then braid two cords of
pure gold and attach them to the filigree settings on the shoulders of the ephod.

Design of the Chestpiece

15"Then, with great skill and care, make a chestpiece to be worn for seeking a decision from
God. Make it to match the ephod, using finely
woven linen embroidered with gold and with
blue, purple, and scarlet thread. 16Make the
chestpiece of a single piece of cloth folded to
form a pouch nine inches square. 17Mount four
rows of gemstones on it. The first row will contain a red carnelian, a pale-green peridot, and an
emerald. 18The second row will contain a turquoise, a blue lapis lazuli, and a white moonstone. 19The third row will contain an orange
jacinth, an agate, and a purple amethyst. 20The
fourth row will contain a blue-green beryl, an
onyx, and a green jasper. All these stones will be
set in gold filigree. 21Each stone will represent
one of the twelve sons of Israel, and the name of
that tribe will be engraved on it like a seal.

22"To attach the chestpiece to the ephod,
make braided cords of pure gold thread.
23Then make two gold rings and attach them to
the top corners of the chestpiece. 24Tie the two
gold cords to the two rings on the chestpiece.
25Tie the other ends of the cords to the gold
settings on the shoulder-pieces of the ephod.
26Then make two more gold rings and attach
them to the inside edges of the chestpiece next
to the ephod. 27And make two more gold rings
and attach them to the front of the ephod, below the shoulder-pieces, just above the knot
where the decorative sash is fastened to the
ephod. 28Then attach the bottom rings of the
chestpiece to the rings on the ephod with blue
cords. This will hold the chestpiece securely to
the ephod above the decorative sash.

29"In this way, Aaron will carry the names of
the tribes of Israel on the sacred chestpiece
over his heart when he goes into the Holy Place.
This will be a continual reminder that he represents the people when he comes before the
LORD. 30Insert the Urim and Thummim into the
sacred chestpiece so they will be carried over
Aaron's heart when he goes into the LORD's
presence. In this way, Aaron will always carry
over his heart the objects used to determine the
LORD's will for his people whenever he goes in
before the LORD.

Additional Clothing for the Priests

31"Make the robe that is worn with the ephod
from a single piece of blue cloth, 32with an
opening for Aaron's head in the middle of it. Reinforce the opening with a woven collar so it will
not tear. 33Make pomegranates out of blue, purple, and scarlet yarn, and attach them to the hem
of the robe, with gold bells between them. 34The
gold bells and pomegranates are to alternate all
around the hem. 35Aaron will wear this robe
whenever he ministers before the LORD, and the
bells will tinkle as he goes in and out of the
LORD's presence in the Holy Place. If he wears it,
he will not die.

36"Next make a medallion of pure gold, and
engrave it like a seal with these words: HOLY TO
THE LORD. 37Attach the medallion with a blue
cord to the front of Aaron's turban, where it
must remain. 38Aaron must wear it on his forehead so he may take on himself any guilt of the
people of Israel when they consecrate their sacred offerings. He must always wear it on his
forehead so the LORD will accept the people.

39"Weave Aaron's patterned tunic from fine
linen cloth. Fashion the turban from this linen
as well. Also make a sash, and decorate it with
colorful embroidery.

40"For Aaron's sons, make tunics, sashes, and
special head coverings that are glorious
and beautiful. 41Clothe your brother, Aaron, and
his sons with these garments, and then anoint
and ordain them. Consecrate them so they can
serve as my priests. 42Also make linen undergarments for them, to be worn next to their bodies, reaching from their hips to their thighs.
43These must be worn whenever Aaron and his
sons enter the Tabernacle or approach the altar
in the Holy Place to perform their priestly du-

ties. Then they will not incur guilt and die. This is
a permanent law for Aaron and all his descendants after him.

CHAPTER 29
Dedication of the Priests

"This is the ceremony you must follow when you
consecrate Aaron and his sons to serve me as
priests: Take a young bull and two rams with no
defects. 2Then, using choice wheat flour and no
yeast, make loaves of bread, thin cakes mixed
with olive oil, and wafers spread with oil. 3Place
them all in a single basket, and present them at
the entrance of the Tabernacle, along with the
young bull and the two rams.
4"Present Aaron and his sons at the entrance
of the Tabernacle, and wash them with water.
5Dress Aaron in his priestly garments—the tunic,
the robe worn with the ephod, the ephod itself,
and the chestpiece. Then wrap the decorative
sash of the ephod around him. 6Place the turban
on his head, and fasten the sacred medallion to
the turban. 7Then anoint him by pouring the
anointing oil over his head. 8Next present his
sons, and dress them in their tunics. 9Wrap the
sashes around the waists of Aaron and his sons,
and put their special head coverings on them.
Then the right to the priesthood will be theirs by
law forever. In this way, you will ordain Aaron and
his sons.
10"Bring the young bull to the entrance of the
Tabernacle, where Aaron and his sons will lay
their hands on its head. 11Then slaughter the bull
in the LORD's presence at the entrance of the Tabernacle. 12Put some of its blood on the horns of
the altar with your finger, and pour out the rest at
the base of the altar. 13Take all the fat around the
internal organs, the long lobe of the liver, and the
two kidneys and the fat around them, and burn it
all on the altar. 14Then take the rest of the bull, including its hide, meat, and dung, and burn it outside the camp as a sin offering.
15"Next Aaron and his sons must lay their
hands on the head of one of the rams. 16Then
slaughter the ram, and splatter its blood against
all sides of the altar. 17Cut the ram into pieces,
and wash off the internal organs and the legs. Set
them alongside the head and the other pieces of
the body, 18then burn the entire animal on the altar. This is a burnt offering to the LORD; it is a
pleasing aroma, a special gift presented to the
LORD.
19"Now take the other ram, and have Aaron
and his sons lay their hands on its head. 20Then
slaughter it, and apply some of its blood to the
right earlobes of Aaron and his sons. Also put it
on the thumbs of their right hands and the big
toes of their right feet. Splatter the rest of the
blood against all sides of the altar. 21Then take
some of the blood from the altar and some of the
anointing oil, and sprinkle it on Aaron and his
sons and on their garments. In this way, they and
their garments will be set apart as holy.
22"Since this is the ram for the ordination of
Aaron and his sons, take the fat of the ram, including the fat of the broad tail, the fat around
the internal organs, the long lobe of the liver, and
the two kidneys and the fat around them, along
with the right thigh. 23Then take one round loaf
of bread, one thin cake mixed with olive oil, and
one wafer from the basket of bread without yeast
that was placed in the LORD's presence. 24Put all
these in the hands of Aaron and his sons to be
lifted up as a special offering to the LORD.
25Afterward take the various breads from their
hands, and burn them on the altar along with the
burnt offering. It is a pleasing aroma to the LORD,
a special gift for him. 26Then take the breast of
Aaron's ordination ram, and lift it up in the
LORD's presence as a special offering to him.
Then keep it as your own portion.
27"Set aside the portions of the ordination
ram that belong to Aaron and his sons. This includes the breast and the thigh that were lifted
up before the LORD as a special offering. 28In the
future, whenever the people of Israel lift up a
peace offering, a portion of it must be set aside
for Aaron and his descendants. This is their permanent right, and it is a sacred offering from the
Israelites to the LORD.

29"Aaron's sacred garments must be preserved
for his descendants who succeed him, and they
will wear them when they are anointed and ordained. 30The descendant who succeeds him as
high priest will wear these clothes for seven days
as he ministers in the Tabernacle and the Holy
Place.
31"Take the ram used in the ordination ceremony, and boil its meat in a sacred place. 32Then
Aaron and his sons will eat this meat, along with
the bread in the basket, at the Tabernacle entrance. 33They alone may eat the meat and bread
used for their purification in the ordination ceremony. No one else may eat them, for these
things are set apart and holy. 34If any of the ordination meat or bread remains until the morning,
it must be burned. It may not be eaten, for it is
holy.
35"This is how you will ordain Aaron and his
sons to their offices, just as I have commanded

you. The ordination ceremony will go on for seven days. 36Each day you must sacrifice a young bull as a sin offering to purify them, making them right with the LORD. Afterward, cleanse the altar by purifying it; make it holy by anointing it with oil. 37Purify the altar, and consecrate it every day for seven days. After that, the altar will be absolutely holy, and whatever touches it will become holy.

38"These are the sacrifices you are to offer regularly on the altar. Each day, offer two lambs that are a year old, 39one in the morning and the other in the evening. 40With one of them, offer two quarts of choice flour mixed with one quart of pure oil of pressed olives; also, offer one quart of wine as a liquid offering. 41Offer the other lamb in the evening, along with the same offerings of flour and wine as in the morning. It will be a pleasing aroma, a special gift presented to the LORD.

42"These burnt offerings are to be made each day from generation to generation. Offer them in the LORD's presence at the Tabernacle entrance; there I will meet with you and speak with you. 43I will meet the people of Israel there, in the place made holy by my glorious presence. 44Yes, I will consecrate the Tabernacle and the altar, and I will consecrate Aaron and his sons to serve me as priests. 45Then I will live among the people of Israel and be their God, 46and they will know that I am the LORD their God. I am the one who brought them out of the land of Egypt so that I could live among them. I am the LORD their God.

CHAPTER 30

Plans for the Incense Altar

"Then make another altar of acacia wood for burning incense. 2Make it 18 inches square and 36 inches high, with horns at the corners carved from the same piece of wood as the altar itself. 3Overlay the top, sides, and horns of the altar with pure gold, and run a gold molding around the entire altar. 4Make two gold rings, and attach them on opposite sides of the altar below the gold molding to hold the carrying poles. 5Make the poles of acacia wood and overlay them with gold. 6Place the incense altar just outside the inner curtain that shields the Ark of the Covenant, in front of the Ark's cover—the place of atonement—that covers the tablets inscribed with the terms of the covenant. I will meet with you there.

7"Every morning when Aaron maintains the lamps, he must burn fragrant incense on the altar. 8And each evening when he lights the lamps, he must again burn incense in the LORD's presence. This must be done from generation to generation. 9Do not offer any unholy incense on this altar, or any burnt offerings, grain offerings, or liquid offerings.

10"Once a year Aaron must purify the altar by smearing its horns with blood from the offering made to purify the people from their sin. This will be a regular, annual event from generation to generation, for this is the LORD's most holy altar."

Money for the Tabernacle

11Then the LORD said to Moses, 12"Whenever you take a census of the people of Israel, each man who is counted must pay a ransom for himself to the LORD. Then no plague will strike the people as you count them. 13Each person who is counted must give a small piece of silver as a sacred offering to the LORD. (This payment is half a shekel, based on the sanctuary shekel, which equals twenty gerahs.) 14All who have reached their twentieth birthday must give this sacred offering to the LORD. 15When this offering is given to the LORD to purify your lives, making you right with him, the rich must not give more than the specified amount, and the poor must not give less. 16Receive this ransom money from the Israelites, and use it for the care of the Tabernacle. It will bring the Israelites to the LORD's attention, and it will purify your lives."

Plans for the Washbasin

17Then the LORD said to Moses, 18"Make a bronze washbasin with a bronze stand. Place it between the Tabernacle and the altar, and fill it with water. 19Aaron and his sons will wash their hands and feet there. 20They must wash with water whenever they go into the Tabernacle to appear before the LORD and when they approach the altar to burn up their special gifts to the LORD—or they will die! 21They must always wash their hands and feet, or they will die. This is a permanent law for Aaron and his descendants, to be observed from generation to generation."

The Anointing Oil

22Then the LORD said to Moses, 23"Collect choice spices—12½ pounds of pure myrrh, 6¼ pounds of fragrant cinnamon, 6¼ pounds of fragrant calamus, 24and 12½ pounds of cassia—as measured by the weight of the sanctuary shekel. Also get one gallon of olive oil. 25Like a skilled incense

maker, blend these ingredients to make a holy
anointing oil. 26Use this sacred oil to anoint the
Tabernacle, the Ark of the Covenant, 27the table
and all its utensils, the lampstand and all its accessories, the incense altar, 28the altar of burnt
offering and all its utensils, and the washbasin
with its stand. 29Consecrate them to make them
absolutely holy. After this, whatever touches
them will also become holy.

30"Anoint Aaron and his sons also, consecrating them to serve me as priests. 31And say to the
people of Israel, 'This holy anointing oil is reserved for me from generation to generation.
32It must never be used to anoint anyone else,
and you must never make any blend like it for
yourselves. It is holy, and you must treat it as holy.
33Anyone who makes a blend like it or anoints
someone other than a priest will be cut off from
the community.'"

The Incense

34Then the LORD said to Moses, "Gather fragrant
spices—resin droplets, mollusk shell, and
galbanum—and mix these fragrant spices with
pure frankincense, weighed out in equal
amounts. 35Using the usual techniques of the incense maker, blend the spices together and
sprinkle them with salt to produce a pure and
holy incense. 36Grind some of the mixture into a
very fine powder and put it in front of the Ark of
the Covenant, where I will meet with you in the
Tabernacle. You must treat this incense as most
holy. 37Never use this formula to make this incense for yourselves. It is reserved for the LORD,
and you must treat it as holy. 38Anyone who
makes incense like this for personal use will be
cut off from the community."

CHAPTER 31

Craftsmen: Bezalel and Oholiab

Then the LORD said to Moses, 2"Look, I have specifically chosen Bezalel son of Uri, grandson of
Hur, of the tribe of Judah. 3I have filled him with
the Spirit of God, giving him great wisdom, ability, and expertise in all kinds of crafts. 4He is a
master craftsman, expert in working with gold,
silver, and bronze. 5He is skilled in engraving and
mounting gemstones and in carving wood. He is
a master at every craft!

6"And I have personally appointed Oholiab
son of Ahisamach, of the tribe of Dan, to be his
assistant. Moreover, I have given special skill to
all the gifted craftsmen so they can make all the
things I have commanded you to make:

7 the Tabernacle;
the Ark of the Covenant;
the Ark's cover—the place of atonement;
all the furnishings of the Tabernacle;
8 the table and its utensils;
the pure gold lampstand with all its
accessories;
the incense altar;
9 the altar of burnt offering with all its utensils;
the washbasin with its stand;
10 the beautifully stitched garments—the
sacred garments for Aaron the priest, and
the garments for his sons to wear as they
minister as priests;
11 the anointing oil;
the fragrant incense for the Holy Place.

The craftsmen must make everything as I have
commanded you."

Instructions for the Sabbath

12The LORD then gave these instructions to
Moses: 13"Tell the people of Israel: 'Be careful to
keep my Sabbath day, for the Sabbath is a sign of
the covenant between me and you from generation to generation. It is given so you may know
that I am the LORD, who makes you holy. 14You
must keep the Sabbath day, for it is a holy day for
you. Anyone who desecrates it must be put to
death; anyone who works on that day will be cut
off from the community. 15You have six days
each week for your ordinary work, but the seventh day must be a Sabbath day of complete rest,
a holy day dedicated to the LORD. Anyone who
works on the Sabbath must be put to death.
16The people of Israel must keep the Sabbath day
by observing it from generation to generation.
This is a covenant obligation for all time. 17It is a
permanent sign of my covenant with the people
of Israel. For in six days the LORD made heaven
and earth, but on the seventh day he stopped
working and was refreshed.'"

18When the LORD finished speaking with
Moses on Mount Sinai, he gave him the two stone
tablets inscribed with the terms of the covenant,
written by the finger of God.

CHAPTER 32

The Gold Calf

When the people saw how long it was taking
Moses to come back down the mountain, they
gathered around Aaron. "Come on," they said,
"make us some gods who can lead us. We don't
know what happened to this fellow Moses, who
brought us here from the land of Egypt."

2So Aaron said, "Take the gold rings from the
ears of your wives and sons and daughters, and
bring them to me."
3All the people took the gold rings from their
ears and brought them to Aaron. 4Then Aaron
took the gold, melted it down, and molded it into
the shape of a calf. When the people saw it, they
exclaimed, "O Israel, these are the gods who
brought you out of the land of Egypt!"
5Aaron saw how excited the people were, so he
built an altar in front of the calf. Then he announced, "Tomorrow will be a festival to the
LORD!"
6The people got up early the next morning to
sacrifice burnt offerings and peace offerings. After this, they celebrated with feasting and drinking, and they indulged in pagan revelry.
7The LORD told Moses, "Quick! Go down the
mountain! Your people whom you brought from
the land of Egypt have corrupted themselves.
8How quickly they have turned away from the
way I commanded them to live! They have melted
down gold and made a calf, and they have bowed
down and sacrificed to it. They are saying, 'These
are your gods, O Israel, who brought you out of
the land of Egypt.'"
9Then the LORD said, "I have seen how stubborn and rebellious these people are. 10Now
leave me alone so my fierce anger can blaze
against them, and I will destroy them. Then I will
make you, Moses, into a great nation."
11But Moses tried to pacify the LORD his God.
"O LORD!" he said. "Why are you so angry with
your own people whom you brought from the
land of Egypt with such great power and such a
strong hand? 12Why let the Egyptians say, 'Their
God rescued them with the evil intention of
slaughtering them in the mountains and wiping
them from the face of the earth'? Turn away
from your fierce anger. Change your mind about
this terrible disaster you have threatened
against your people! 13Remember your servants
Abraham, Isaac, and Jacob. You bound yourself
with an oath to them, saying, 'I will make your
descendants as numerous as the stars of heaven.
And I will give them all of this land that I have
promised to your descendants, and they will
possess it forever.'"
14So the LORD changed his mind about the terrible disaster he had threatened to bring on his
people.
15Then Moses turned and went down the
mountain. He held in his hands the two stone
tablets inscribed with the terms of the covenant.
They were inscribed on both sides, front and
back. 16These tablets were God's work; the words
on them were written by God himself.
17When Joshua heard the boisterous noise of
the people shouting below them, he exclaimed to
Moses, "It sounds like war in the camp!"
18But Moses replied, "No, it's not a shout of victory nor the wailing of defeat. I hear the sound of
a celebration."
19When they came near the camp, Moses saw
the calf and the dancing, and he burned with anger. He threw the stone tablets to the ground,
smashing them at the foot of the mountain. 20He
took the calf they had made and burned it. Then
he ground it into powder, threw it into the water,
and forced the people to drink it.
21Finally, he turned to Aaron and demanded,
"What did these people do to you to make you
bring such terrible sin upon them?"
22"Don't get so upset, my lord," Aaron replied.
"You yourself know how evil these people are.
23They said to me, 'Make us gods who will lead
us. We don't know what happened to this fellow
Moses, who brought us here from the land of
Egypt.' 24So I told them, 'Whoever has gold jewelry, take it off.' When they brought it to me, I
simply threw it into the fire—and out came this
calf!"
25Moses saw that Aaron had let the people get
completely out of control, much to the amuse-
ment of their enemies. 26So he stood at the entrance to the camp and shouted, "All of you who
are on the LORD's side, come here and join me."
And all the Levites gathered around him.
27Moses told them, "This is what the LORD, the
God of Israel, says: Each of you, take your swords
and go back and forth from one end of the camp
to the other. Kill everyone—even your brothers,
friends, and neighbors." 28The Levites obeyed
Moses' command, and about 3,000 people died
that day.
29Then Moses told the Levites, "Today you
have ordained yourselves for the service of the
LORD, for you obeyed him even though it meant
killing your own sons and brothers. Today you
have earned a blessing."

Moses Intercedes for Israel

30The next day Moses said to the people, "You
have committed a terrible sin, but I will go back
up to the LORD on the mountain. Perhaps I will be
able to obtain forgiveness for your sin."
31So Moses returned to the LORD and said,
"Oh, what a terrible sin these people have committed. They have made gods of gold for themselves. 32But now, if you will only forgive their

sin—but if not, erase my name from the record
you have written!"
33But the LORD replied to Moses, "No, I will
erase the name of everyone who has sinned
against me. 34Now go, lead the people to the
place I told you about. Look! My angel will lead
the way before you. And when I come to call the
people to account, I will certainly hold them responsible for their sins."
35Then the LORD sent a great plague upon the
people because they had worshiped the calf
Aaron had made.

CHAPTER 33

The LORD said to Moses, "Get going, you and the
people you brought up from the land of Egypt.
Go up to the land I swore to give to Abraham,
Isaac, and Jacob. I told them, 'I will give this land
to your descendants.' 2And I will send an angel
before you to drive out the Canaanites, Amorites,
Hittites, Perizzites, Hivites, and Jebusites. 3Go up
to this land that flows with milk and honey. But I
will not travel among you, for you are a stubborn
and rebellious people. If I did, I would surely destroy you along the way."
4When the people heard these stern words,
they went into mourning and stopped wearing
their jewelry and fine clothes. 5For the LORD had
told Moses to tell them, "You are a stubborn and
rebellious people. If I were to travel with you for
even a moment, I would destroy you. Remove
your jewelry and fine clothes while I decide what
to do with you." 6So from the time they left
Mount Sinai, the Israelites wore no more jewelry
or fine clothes.
7It was Moses' practice to take the Tent of
Meeting and set it up some distance from the
camp. Everyone who wanted to make a request
of the LORD would go to the Tent of Meeting outside the camp.
8Whenever Moses went out to the Tent of
Meeting, all the people would get up and stand
in the entrances of their own tents. They would
all watch Moses until he disappeared inside. 9As
he went into the tent, the pillar of cloud would
come down and hover at its entrance while the
LORD spoke with Moses. 10When the people saw
the cloud standing at the entrance of the tent,
they would stand and bow down in front of their
own tents. 11Inside the Tent of Meeting, the
LORD would speak to Moses face to face, as one
speaks to a friend. Afterward Moses would return to the camp, but the young man who assisted him, Joshua son of Nun, would remain
behind in the Tent of Meeting.

Moses Sees the LORD's Glory

12One day Moses said to the LORD, "You have
been telling me, 'Take these people up to the
Promised Land.' But you haven't told me whom
you will send with me. You have told me, 'I know
you by name, and I look favorably on you.' 13If it is
true that you look favorably on me, let me know
your ways so I may understand you more fully
and continue to enjoy your favor. And remember
that this nation is your very own people."
14The LORD replied, "I will personally go with
you, Moses, and I will give you rest—everything
will be fine for you."
15Then Moses said, "If you don't personally go
with us, don't make us leave this place. 16How
will anyone know that you look favorably on
me—on me and on your people—if you don't go
with us? For your presence among us sets your
people and me apart from all other people on the
earth."
17The LORD replied to Moses, "I will indeed do
what you have asked, for I look favorably on you,
and I know you by name."
18Moses responded, "Then show me your glorious presence."
19The LORD replied, "I will make all my goodness pass before you, and I will call out my name,
Yahweh, before you. For I will show mercy to anyone I choose, and I will show compassion to anyone I choose. 20But you may not look directly at
my face, for no one may see me and live." 21The
LORD continued, "Look, stand near me on this
rock. 22As my glorious presence passes by, I will
hide you in the crevice of the rock and cover you
with my hand until I have passed by. 23Then I will
remove my hand and let you see me from behind. But my face will not be seen."

CHAPTER 34

A New Copy of the Covenant

Then the LORD told Moses, "Chisel out two stone
tablets like the first ones. I will write on them the
same words that were on the tablets you
smashed. 2Be ready in the morning to climb up
Mount Sinai and present yourself to me on the
top of the mountain. 3No one else may come
with you. In fact, no one is to appear anywhere on
the mountain. Do not even let the flocks or herds
graze near the mountain."
4So Moses chiseled out two tablets of stone
like the first ones. Early in the morning he
climbed Mount Sinai as the LORD had commanded him, and he carried the two stone tablets in his hands.
5Then the LORD came down in a cloud and

stood there with him; and he called out his own
name, Yahweh. 6The LORD passed in front of
Moses, calling out,

"Yahweh! The LORD!
The God of compassion and mercy!
I am slow to anger
and filled with unfailing love and
faithfulness.
7 I lavish unfailing love to a thousand
generations.
I forgive iniquity, rebellion, and sin.
But I do not excuse the guilty.
I lay the sins of the parents upon their
children and grandchildren;
the entire family is affected—
even children in the third and fourth
generations."

8Moses immediately threw himself to the
ground and worshiped. 9And he said, "O Lord, if
it is true that I have found favor with you, then
please travel with us. Yes, this is a stubborn and
rebellious people, but please forgive our iniquity
and our sins. Claim us as your own special possession."

10The LORD replied, "Listen, I am making a
covenant with you in the presence of all your
people. I will perform miracles that have never
been performed anywhere in all the earth or in
any nation. And all the people around you will
see the power of the LORD—the awesome power
I will display for you. 11But listen carefully to
everything I command you today. Then I will go
ahead of you and drive out the Amorites, Canaanites, Hittites, Perizzites, Hivites, and Jebusites.

12"Be very careful never to make a treaty with
the people who live in the land where you are
going. If you do, you will follow their evil ways
and be trapped. 13Instead, you must break
down their pagan altars, smash their sacred pillars, and cut down their Asherah poles. 14You
must worship no other gods, for the LORD,
whose very name is Jealous, is a God who is jealous about his relationship with you.

15"You must not make a treaty of any kind
with the people living in the land. They lust after their gods, offering sacrifices to them. They
will invite you to join them in their sacrificial
meals, and you will go with them. 16Then you
will accept their daughters, who sacrifice to
other gods, as wives for your sons. And they will
seduce your sons to commit adultery against
me by worshiping other gods. 17You must not
make any gods of molten metal for yourselves.

18"You must celebrate the Festival of Unleavened Bread. For seven days the bread you eat
must be made without yeast, just as I commanded you. Celebrate this festival annually at
the appointed time in early spring, in the month
of Abib, for that is the anniversary of your departure from Egypt.

19"The firstborn of every animal belongs to
me, including the firstborn males from your
herds of cattle and your flocks of sheep and
goats. 20A firstborn donkey may be bought back
from the LORD by presenting a lamb or young
goat in its place. But if you do not buy it back,
you must break its neck. However, you must buy
back every firstborn son.

"No one may appear before me without an
offering.

21"You have six days each week for your ordinary work, but on the seventh day you must stop
working, even during the seasons of plowing
and harvest.

22"You must celebrate the Festival of Harvest
with the first crop of the wheat harvest, and celebrate the Festival of the Final Harvest at the
end of the harvest season. 23Three times each
year every man in Israel must appear before the
Sovereign, the LORD, the God of Israel. 24I will

FUN-fact
HERE A GOD,
THERE A GOD,
EVERYWHERE
A GOD, GOD.

Most of the people the Israelites fought believed that there were all sorts of gods. They had a god for just about everything. God showed the Israelites and the people around them that there was only one true God. **Check out EXODUS 7:10-13 and 1 KINGS 18:20-38.**

GOD IS THE CREATOR OF EVERYTHING AND HAS EVERYTHING UNDER CONTROL.

Make a list of things in your life you can't control. When you've finished, give thanks that God has control over everything.

drive out the other nations ahead of you and expand your territory, so no one will covet and
conquer your land while you appear before the
LORD your God three times each year.

25 "You must not offer the blood of my sacrificial offerings together with any baked goods
containing yeast. And none of the meat of the
Passover sacrifice may be kept over until the
next morning.

26 "As you harvest your crops, bring the very
best of the first harvest to the house of the LORD
your God.

"You must not cook a young goat in its
mother's milk."

27 Then the LORD said to Moses, "Write down
all these instructions, for they represent the
terms of the covenant I am making with you and
with Israel."

28 Moses remained there on the mountain
with the LORD forty days and forty nights. In all
that time he ate no bread and drank no water.
And the LORD wrote the terms of the covenant—
the Ten Commandments—on the stone tablets.

29 When Moses came down Mount Sinai carrying the two stone tablets inscribed with the
terms of the covenant, he wasn't aware that his
face had become radiant because he had spoken to the LORD. 30 So when Aaron and the people of Israel saw the radiance of Moses' face,
they were afraid to come near him.

31 But Moses called out to them and asked
Aaron and all the leaders of the community to
come over, and he talked with them. 32 Then all
the people of Israel approached him, and Moses
gave them all the instructions the LORD had
given him on Mount Sinai. 33 When Moses finished speaking with them, he covered his face
with a veil. 34 But whenever he went into the
Tent of Meeting to speak with the LORD, he
would remove the veil until he came out again.
Then he would give the people whatever instructions the LORD had given him, 35 and the
people of Israel would see the radiant glow of
his face. So he would put the veil over his face
until he returned to speak with the LORD.

CHAPTER 35

Instructions for the Sabbath

Then Moses called together the whole community of Israel and told them, "These are the instructions the LORD has commanded you to
follow. 2 You have six days each week for your
ordinary work, but the seventh day must be a
Sabbath day of complete rest, a holy day dedicated to the LORD. Anyone who works on that
day must be put to death. 3 You must not even
light a fire in any of your homes on the Sabbath."

Offerings for the Tabernacle

4 Then Moses said to the whole community of Israel, "This is what the LORD has commanded:
5 Take a sacred offering for the LORD. Let those
with generous hearts present the following gifts
to the LORD:

gold, silver, and bronze;
6 blue, purple, and scarlet thread;
fine linen and goat hair for cloth;
7 tanned ram skins and fine goatskin leather;
acacia wood;
8 olive oil for the lamps;
spices for the anointing oil and the fragrant incense;
9 onyx stones, and other gemstones to be set in the ephod and the priest's chestpiece.

10 "Come, all of you who are gifted craftsmen.
Construct everything that the LORD has commanded:

11 the Tabernacle and its sacred tent, its covering, clasps, frames, crossbars, posts, and bases;
12 the Ark and its carrying poles;
the Ark's cover—the place of atonement;
the inner curtain to shield the Ark;
13 the table, its carrying poles, and all its utensils;
the Bread of the Presence;
14 for light, the lampstand, its accessories, the lamp cups, and the olive oil for lighting;
15 the incense altar and its carrying poles;
the anointing oil and fragrant incense;
the curtain for the entrance of the Tabernacle;
16 the altar of burnt offering;
the bronze grating of the altar and its carrying poles and utensils;
the washbasin with its stand;
17 the curtains for the walls of the courtyard;
the posts and their bases;
the curtain for the entrance to the courtyard;
18 the tent pegs of the Tabernacle and courtyard and their ropes;
19 the beautifully stitched garments for the priests to wear while ministering in the Holy Place—the sacred garments for Aaron the priest, and the garments for his sons to wear as they minister as priests."

Exodus 36 . . . page 94

20So the whole community of Israel left Moses
and returned to their tents. 21All whose hearts
were stirred and whose spirits were moved came
and brought their sacred offerings to the LORD.
They brought all the materials needed for the
Tabernacle, for the performance of its rituals, and
for the sacred garments. 22Both men and women
came, all whose hearts were willing. They
brought to the LORD their offerings of gold—
brooches, earrings, rings from their fingers, and
necklaces. They presented gold objects of every
kind as a special offering to the LORD. 23All those
who owned the following items willingly brought
them: blue, purple, and scarlet thread; fine linen
and goat hair for cloth; and tanned ram skins and
fine goatskin leather. 24And all who had silver
and bronze objects gave them as a sacred offering
to the LORD. And those who had acacia wood
brought it for use in the project.

25All the women who were skilled in sewing
and spinning prepared blue, purple, and scarlet
thread, and fine linen cloth. 26All the women
who were willing used their skills to spin the goat
hair into yarn. 27The leaders brought onyx
stones and the special gemstones to be set in the
ephod and the priest's chestpiece. 28They also
brought spices and olive oil for the light, the
anointing oil, and the fragrant incense. 29So the
people of Israel—every man and woman who
was eager to help in the work the LORD had given
them through Moses—brought their gifts and
gave them freely to the LORD.

30Then Moses told the people of Israel, "The
LORD has specifically chosen Bezalel son of Uri,
grandson of Hur, of the tribe of Judah. 31The
LORD has filled Bezalel with the Spirit of God,
giving him great wisdom, ability, and expertise in
all kinds of crafts. 32He is a master craftsman, expert in working with gold, silver, and bronze.
33He is skilled in engraving and mounting gemstones and in carving wood. He is a master at
every craft. 34And the LORD has given both him
and Oholiab son of Ahisamach, of the tribe of
Dan, the ability to teach their skills to others.
35The LORD has given them special skills as en-
gravers, designers, embroiderers in blue, purple,
and scarlet thread on fine linen cloth, and weavers. They excel as craftsmen and as designers.

CHAPTER 36

"The LORD has gifted Bezalel, Oholiab, and the
other skilled craftsmen with wisdom and ability
to perform any task involved in building the
sanctuary. Let them construct and furnish the
Tabernacle, just as the LORD has commanded."

2So Moses summoned Bezalel and Oholiab
and all the others who were specially gifted by
the LORD and were eager to get to work. 3Moses
gave them the materials donated by the people
of Israel as sacred offerings for the completion
of the sanctuary. But the people continued to
bring additional gifts each morning. 4Finally the
craftsmen who were working on the sanctuary
left their work. 5They went to Moses and reported, "The people have given more than
enough materials to complete the job the LORD
has commanded us to do!"

6So Moses gave the command, and this message was sent throughout the camp: "Men and
women, don't prepare any more gifts for the
sanctuary. We have enough!" So the people
stopped bringing their sacred offerings. 7Their
contributions were more than enough to complete the whole project.

Building the Tabernacle

8The skilled craftsmen made ten curtains of
finely woven linen for the Tabernacle. Then Bezalel decorated the curtains with blue, purple, and
scarlet thread and with skillfully embroidered
cherubim. 9All ten curtains were exactly the
same size—42 feet long and 6 feet wide. 10Five of
these curtains were joined together to make one
long curtain, and the other five were joined to
make a second long curtain. 11He made fifty
loops of blue yarn and put them along the edge
of the last curtain in each set. 12The fifty loops
along the edge of one curtain matched the fifty
loops along the edge of the other curtain. 13Then
he made fifty gold clasps and fastened the long
curtains together with the clasps. In this way, the
Tabernacle was made of one continuous piece.

14He made eleven curtains of goat-hair cloth
to serve as a tent covering for the Tabernacle.
15These eleven curtains were all exactly the same
size—45 feet long and 6 feet wide. 16Bezalel
joined five of these curtains together to make
one long curtain, and the other six were joined to
make a second long curtain. 17He made fifty
loops for the edge of each large curtain. 18He
also made fifty bronze clasps to fasten the long
curtains together. In this way, the tent covering
was made of one continuous piece. 19He completed the tent covering with a layer of tanned
ram skins and a layer of fine goatskin leather.

20For the framework of the Tabernacle, Bezalel
constructed frames of acacia wood. 21Each frame
was 15 feet high and 27 inches wide, 22with two
pegs under each frame. All the frames were identical. 23He made twenty of these frames to

support the curtains on the south side of the Tabernacle. 24He also made forty silver bases—two bases under each frame, with the pegs fitting securely into the bases. 25For the north side of the Tabernacle, he made another twenty frames, 26with their forty silver bases, two bases under each frame. 27He made six frames for the rear—the west side of the Tabernacle—28along with two additional frames to reinforce the rear corners of the Tabernacle. 29These corner frames were matched at the bottom and firmly attached at the top with a single ring, forming a single corner unit. Both of these corner units were made the same way. 30So there were eight frames at the rear of the Tabernacle, set in sixteen silver bases—two bases under each frame.

31Then he made crossbars of acacia wood to link the frames, five crossbars for the north side of the Tabernacle 32and five for the south side. He also made five crossbars for the rear of the Tabernacle, which faced west. 33He made the middle crossbar to attach halfway up the frames; it ran all the way from one end of the Tabernacle to the other. 34He overlaid the frames with gold and made gold rings to hold the crossbars. Then he overlaid the crossbars with gold as well.

35For the inside of the Tabernacle, Bezalel made a special curtain of finely woven linen. He decorated it with blue, purple, and scarlet thread and with skillfully embroidered cherubim. 36For the curtain, he made four posts of acacia wood and four gold hooks. He overlaid the posts with gold and set them in four silver bases.

37Then he made another curtain for the entrance to the sacred tent. He made it of finely woven linen and embroidered it with exquisite designs using blue, purple, and scarlet thread. 38This curtain was hung on gold hooks attached to five posts. The posts with their decorated tops and hooks were overlaid with gold, and the five bases were cast from bronze.

CHAPTER 37

Building the Ark of the Covenant

Next Bezalel made the Ark of acacia wood—a sacred chest 45 inches long, 27 inches wide, and 27 inches high. 2He overlaid it inside and outside with pure gold, and he ran a molding of gold all around it. 3He cast four gold rings and attached them to its four feet, two rings on each side. 4Then he made poles from acacia wood and overlaid them with gold. 5He inserted the poles into the rings at the sides of the Ark to carry it.

6Then he made the Ark's cover—the place of atonement—from pure gold. It was 45 inches long and 27 inches wide. 7He made two cherubim from hammered gold and placed them on the two ends of the atonement cover. 8He molded the cherubim on each end of the atonement cover, making it all of one piece of gold. 9The cherubim faced each other and looked down on the atonement cover. With their wings spread above it, they protected it.

Building the Table

10Then Bezalel made the table of acacia wood, 36 inches long, 18 inches wide, and 27 inches high. 11He overlaid it with pure gold and ran a gold molding around the edge. 12He decorated it with a 3-inch border all around, and he ran a gold molding along the border. 13Then he cast four gold rings for the table and attached them at the four corners next to the four legs. 14The rings were attached near the border to hold the poles that were used to carry the table. 15He made these poles from acacia wood and overlaid them with gold. 16Then he made special containers of pure gold for the table—bowls, ladles, jars, and pitchers—to be used in pouring out liquid offerings.

Building the Lampstand

17Then Bezalel made the lampstand of pure, hammered gold. He made the entire lampstand and its decorations of one piece—the base, center stem, lamp cups, buds, and petals. 18The lampstand had six branches going out from the center stem, three on each side. 19Each of the six branches had three lamp cups shaped like almond blossoms, complete with buds and petals. 20The center stem of the lampstand was crafted with four lamp cups shaped like almond blossoms, complete with buds and petals. 21There was an almond bud beneath each pair of branches where the six branches extended from the center stem, all made of one piece. 22The almond buds and branches were all of one piece with the center stem, and they were hammered from pure gold.

23He also made seven lamps for the lampstand, lamp snuffers, and trays, all of pure gold. 24The entire lampstand, along with its accessories, was made from seventy-five pounds of pure gold.

Building the Incense Altar

25Then Bezalel made the incense altar of acacia wood. It was 18 inches square and 36 inches high, with horns at the corners carved from the same piece of wood as the altar itself. 26He overlaid the top, sides, and horns of the altar with pure gold, and he ran a gold molding around the entire altar. 27He made two gold rings and attached them on opposite sides of the altar below the gold molding to hold the carrying poles. 28He made the poles of acacia wood and overlaid them with gold.

29Then he made the sacred anointing oil and the fragrant incense, using the techniques of a skilled incense maker.

CHAPTER 38

Building the Altar of Burnt Offering

Next Bezalel used acacia wood to construct the square altar of burnt offering. It was 7½ feet wide, 7½ feet long, and 4½ feet high. 2He made horns for each of its four corners so that the horns and altar were all one piece. He overlaid the altar with bronze. 3Then he made all the altar utensils of bronze—the ash buckets, shovels, basins, meat forks, and firepans. 4Next he made a bronze grating and installed it halfway down the side of the altar, under the ledge. 5He cast four rings and attached them to the corners of the bronze grating to hold the carrying poles. 6He made the poles from acacia wood and overlaid them with bronze. 7He inserted the poles through the rings on the sides of the altar. The altar was hollow and was made from planks.

Building the Washbasin

8Bezalel made the bronze washbasin and its bronze stand from bronze mirrors donated by the women who served at the entrance of the Tabernacle.

Building the Courtyard

9Then Bezalel made the courtyard, which was enclosed with curtains made of finely woven linen. On the south side the curtains were 150 feet long. 10They were held up by twenty posts set securely in twenty bronze bases. He hung the curtains with silver hooks and rings. 11He made a similar set of curtains for the north side—150 feet of curtains held up by twenty posts set securely in bronze bases. He hung the curtains with silver hooks and rings. 12The curtains on the west end of the courtyard were 75 feet long, hung with silver hooks and rings and supported by ten posts set into ten bases. 13The east end, the front, was also 75 feet long.

14The courtyard entrance was on the east end, flanked by two curtains. The curtain on the right side was 22½ feet long and was supported by three posts set into three bases. 15The curtain on the left side was also 22½ feet long and was supported by three posts set into three bases. 16All the curtains used in the courtyard were made of finely woven linen. 17Each post had a bronze base, and all the hooks and rings were silver. The tops of the posts of the courtyard were overlaid with silver, and the rings to hold up the curtains were made of silver.

18He made the curtain for the entrance to the courtyard of finely woven linen, and he decorated it with beautiful embroidery in blue, purple, and scarlet thread. It was 30 feet long, and its height was 7½ feet, just like the curtains of the courtyard walls. 19It was supported by four posts, each set securely in its own bronze base. The tops of the posts were overlaid with silver, and the hooks and rings were also made of silver.

20All the tent pegs used in the Tabernacle and courtyard were made of bronze.

Inventory of Materials

21This is an inventory of the materials used in building the Tabernacle of the Covenant. The Levites compiled the figures, as Moses directed, and Ithamar son of Aaron the priest served as recorder. 22Bezalel son of Uri, grandson of Hur, of the tribe of Judah, made everything just as the LORD had commanded Moses. 23He was assisted by Oholiab son of Ahisamach, of the tribe of Dan, a craftsman expert at engraving, designing, and embroidering with blue, purple, and scarlet thread on fine linen cloth.

24The people brought special offerings of gold totaling 2,193 pounds, as measured by the weight of the sanctuary shekel. This gold was used throughout the Tabernacle.

25The whole community of Israel gave 7,545 pounds of silver, as measured by the weight of the sanctuary shekel. 26This silver came from the tax collected from each man registered in the census. (The tax is one beka, which is half a shekel, based on the sanctuary shekel.) The tax was collected from 603,550 men who had reached their twentieth birthday. 27The hundred bases for the frames of the sanctuary walls and for the posts supporting the inner curtain required 7,500 pounds of silver, about 75 pounds for each base. 28The remaining 45 pounds of silver was used to make the hooks and rings and to overlay the tops of the posts.

29The people also brought as special offerings 5,310 pounds of bronze, 30which was used for casting the bases for the posts at the entrance to

the Tabernacle, and for the bronze altar with its
bronze grating and all the altar utensils.
31Bronze was also used to make the bases for the
posts that supported the curtains around the
courtyard, the bases for the curtain at the entrance of the courtyard, and all the tent pegs for
the Tabernacle and the courtyard.

CHAPTER 39
Clothing for the Priests

The craftsmen made beautiful sacred garments
of blue, purple, and scarlet cloth—clothing for
Aaron to wear while ministering in the Holy
Place, just as the LORD had commanded Moses.

Making the Ephod

2Bezalel made the ephod of finely woven linen
and embroidered it with gold and with blue, purple, and scarlet thread. 3He made gold thread by
hammering out thin sheets of gold and cutting it
into fine strands. With great skill and care, he
worked it into the fine linen with the blue, purple, and scarlet thread.

4The ephod consisted of two pieces, front and
back, joined at the shoulders with two shoulder-
pieces. 5The decorative sash was made of the
same materials: finely woven linen embroidered
with gold and with blue, purple, and scarlet thread,
just as the LORD had commanded Moses. 6They
mounted the two onyx stones in settings of gold
filigree. The stones were engraved with the names
of the tribes of Israel, just as a seal is engraved. 7He
fastened these stones on the shoulder-pieces of
the ephod as a reminder that the priest represents
the people of Israel. All this was done just as the
LORD had commanded Moses.

Making the Chestpiece

8Bezalel made the chestpiece with great skill and
care. He made it to match the ephod, using finely
woven linen embroidered with gold and with
blue, purple, and scarlet thread. 9He made the
chestpiece of a single piece of cloth folded to
form a pouch nine inches square. 10They
mounted four rows of gemstones on it. The first
row contained a red carnelian, a pale-green
peridot, and an emerald. 11The second row contained a turquoise, a blue lapis lazuli, and a white
moonstone. 12The third row contained an orange jacinth, an agate, and a purple amethyst.
13The fourth row contained a blue-green beryl,
an onyx, and a green jasper. All these stones were
set in gold filigree. 14Each stone represented one
of the twelve sons of Israel, and the name of that
tribe was engraved on it like a seal.

15To attach the chestpiece to the ephod, they
made braided cords of pure gold thread. 16They
also made two settings of gold filigree and two
gold rings and attached them to the top corners of
the chestpiece. 17They tied the two gold cords to
the rings on the chestpiece. 18They tied the other
ends of the cords to the gold settings on the
shoulder-pieces of the ephod. 19Then they made
two more gold rings and attached them to the inside edges of the chestpiece next to the ephod.
20Then they made two more gold rings and attached them to the front of the ephod, below the
shoulder-pieces, just above the knot where the
decorative sash was fastened to the ephod. 21They
attached the bottom rings of the chestpiece to the
rings on the ephod with blue cords. In this way,
the chestpiece was held securely to the ephod
above the decorative sash. All this was done just as
the LORD had commanded Moses.

Additional Clothing for the Priests

22Bezalel made the robe that is worn with the
ephod from a single piece of blue woven cloth,
23with an opening for Aaron's head in the middle
of it. The opening was reinforced with a woven
collar so it would not tear. 24They made pomegranates of blue, purple, and scarlet yarn, and attached them to the hem of the robe. 25They also
made bells of pure gold and placed them between the pomegranates along the hem of the
robe, 26with bells and pomegranates alternating
all around the hem. This robe was to be worn
whenever the priest ministered before the LORD,
just as the LORD had commanded Moses.

27They made tunics for Aaron and his sons
from fine linen cloth. 28The turban and the special head coverings were made of fine linen, and
the undergarments were also made of finely woven linen. 29The sashes were made of finely woven linen and embroidered with blue, purple,
and scarlet thread, just as the LORD had commanded Moses.

30Finally, they made the sacred medallion—
the badge of holiness—of pure gold. They engraved it like a seal with these words: HOLY TO
THE LORD. 31They attached the medallion with a
blue cord to Aaron's turban, just as the LORD had
commanded Moses.

Moses Inspects the Work

32And so at last the Tabernacle was finished. The
Israelites had done everything just as the LORD
had commanded Moses. 33And they brought the
entire Tabernacle to Moses:

the sacred tent with all its furnishings, clasps,
frames, crossbars, posts, and bases;
34 the tent coverings of tanned ram skins and
fine goatskin leather;
the inner curtain to shield the Ark;
35 the Ark of the Covenant and its carrying
poles;
the Ark's cover—the place of atonement;
36 the table and all its utensils;
the Bread of the Presence;
37 the pure gold lampstand with its symmetrical
lamp cups, all its accessories, and the olive
oil for lighting;
38 the gold altar;
the anointing oil and fragrant incense;
the curtain for the entrance of the sacred
tent;
39 the bronze altar;
the bronze grating and its carrying poles and
utensils;
the washbasin with its stand;
40 the curtains for the walls of the courtyard;
the posts and their bases;
the curtain for the entrance to the courtyard;
the ropes and tent pegs;
all the furnishings to be used in worship at
the Tabernacle;
41 the beautifully stitched garments for the
priests to wear while ministering in the
Holy Place—the sacred garments for
Aaron the priest, and the garments for
his sons to wear as they minister as
priests.

42 So the people of Israel followed all of the
LORD's instructions to Moses. 43 Then Moses inspected all their work. When he found it had
been done just as the LORD had commanded
him, he blessed them.

CHAPTER 40
The Tabernacle Completed

Then the LORD said to Moses, 2 "Set up the Tabernacle on the first day of the new year. 3 Place the
Ark of the Covenant inside, and install the inner
curtain to enclose the Ark within the Most Holy
Place. 4 Then bring in the table, and arrange the
utensils on it. And bring in the lampstand, and
set up the lamps.

5 "Place the gold incense altar in front of the
Ark of the Covenant. Then hang the curtain at
the entrance of the Tabernacle. 6 Place the altar
of burnt offering in front of the Tabernacle entrance. 7 Set the washbasin between the Tabernacle and the altar, and fill it with water. 8 Then
set up the courtyard around the outside of the
tent, and hang the curtain for the courtyard
entrance.

9 "Take the anointing oil and anoint the Tabernacle and all its furnishings to consecrate
them and make them holy. 10 Anoint the altar of
burnt offering and its utensils to consecrate
them. Then the altar will become absolutely
holy. 11 Next anoint the washbasin and its stand
to consecrate them.

12 "Present Aaron and his sons at the entrance
of the Tabernacle, and wash them with water.
13 Dress Aaron with the sacred garments and
anoint him, consecrating him to serve me as a
priest. 14 Then present his sons and dress them
in their tunics. 15 Anoint them as you did their
father, so they may also serve me as priests.
With their anointing, Aaron's descendants are
set apart for the priesthood forever, from generation to generation."

16 Moses proceeded to do everything just as
the LORD had commanded him. 17 So the Tabernacle was set up on the first day of the first
month of the second year. 18 Moses erected the
Tabernacle by setting down its bases, inserting
the frames, attaching the crossbars, and setting
up the posts. 19 Then he spread the coverings
over the Tabernacle framework and put on the
protective layers, just as the LORD had commanded him.

20 He took the stone tablets inscribed with
the terms of the covenant and placed them
inside the Ark. Then he attached the carrying
poles to the Ark, and he set the Ark's cover—
the place of atonement—on top of it. 21 Then he
brought the Ark of the Covenant into the Tabernacle and hung the inner curtain to shield it
from view, just as the LORD had commanded
him.

22 Next Moses placed the table in the Tabernacle, along the north side of the Holy Place,
just outside the inner curtain. 23 And he arranged the Bread of the Presence on the table
before the LORD, just as the LORD had commanded him.

24 He set the lampstand in the Tabernacle
across from the table on the south side of the
Holy Place. 25 Then he lit the lamps in the LORD's
presence, just as the LORD had commanded
him. 26 He also placed the gold incense altar
in the Tabernacle, in the Holy Place in front of
the inner curtain. 27 On it he burned the fragrant incense, just as the LORD had commanded
him.

28 He hung the curtain at the entrance of the

Tabernacle, [29]and he placed the altar of burnt
offering near the Tabernacle entrance. On it he
offered a burnt offering and a grain offering,
just as the LORD had commanded him.

[30]Next Moses placed the washbasin between
the Tabernacle and the altar. He filled it with
water so the priests could wash themselves.
[31]Moses and Aaron and Aaron's sons used water
from it to wash their hands and feet. [32]When-
ever they approached the altar and entered the
Tabernacle, they washed themselves, just as the
LORD had commanded Moses.

[33]Then he hung the curtains forming the
courtyard around the Tabernacle and the altar.
And he set up the curtain at the entrance of the
courtyard. So at last Moses finished the work.

The LORD's Glory Fills the Tabernacle

[34]Then the cloud covered the Tabernacle, and
the glory of the LORD filled the Tabernacle.
[35]Moses could no longer enter the Tabernacle
because the cloud had settled down over it, and
the glory of the LORD filled the Tabernacle.

[36]Now whenever the cloud lifted from the
Tabernacle, the people of Israel would set out on
their journey, following it. [37]But if the cloud did
not rise, they remained where they were until it
lifted. [38]The cloud of the LORD hovered over the
Tabernacle during the day, and at night fire
glowed inside the cloud so the whole family of
Israel could see it. This continued throughout all
their journeys.

LEVITICUS God's Instruction Manual

In the book of Leviticus, God tells the Israelites how to live. It explains how to

- **GET RIGHT WITH GOD**
- **BE HOLY** (not "holey" like the holes in your jeans; "holy" like without sin)
- **BECOME HEALTHY, WEALTHY, AND WISE** (OK, maybe just healthy. And wise.)
- **PARTY!**

Substitute for Sins

In Bible times, animal sacrifice was a big deal. The Israelites had to...well, never mind; it's kind of gross. (If you just *have* to know the details, read Leviticus 1:1-9. But, really, it's gross.)

Today we don't have to make animal sacrifices to God. **Find out why in Hebrews 9:13-14.**

Rules Rule!

God gave the Israelites all kinds of rules. There were rules for what the people should eat, how they should act, and what the priests should do. The rules were like a road map for living. God wasn't trying to make things difficult. He had a reason for each of those rules! **Read all about it in Leviticus 18:1-5. Then compare that to what Romans 12:2 says about how *we* should live.**

NOW I GET IT!

Wholly Holy!

Ever wonder why God expects good behavior from us? He explained it to the Israelites, and it goes for us today too! **Find out why in Leviticus 19:1-2.**

Party Time!

Leviticus isn't *all* about rules. There's plenty of stuff about how God wanted the Israelites to celebrate, too. **Check out Leviticus 23 for all the festival fun!**

Timeline

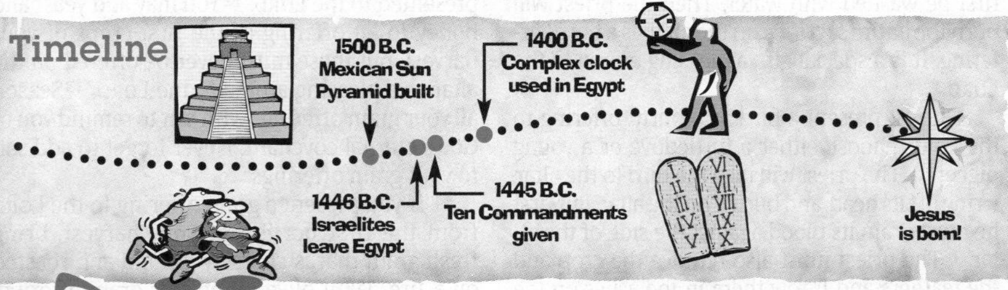

The JESUS CONNECTION

God takes sin seriously. But God also has *lots* of love for sinners. In Leviticus, God told the Israelites how to offer animal sacrifices for their sins. The animals died in place of the people as a picture of what Jesus would one day do for the whole world. In the New Testament, God offered Jesus as the final sacrifice for *our* sins. **See the connection?**

Leviticus 1 . . . page 102

CHAPTER 1
Procedures for the Burnt Offering

The LORD called to Moses from the Tabernacle
and said to him, 2"Give the following instructions
to the people of Israel. When you present an animal as an offering to the LORD, you may take it
from your herd of cattle or your flock of sheep
and goats.

3"If the animal you present as a burnt offering
is from the herd, it must be a male with no defects. Bring it to the entrance of the Tabernacle
so you may be accepted by the LORD. 4Lay your
hand on the animal's head, and the LORD will accept its death in your place to purify you, making
you right with him. 5Then slaughter the young
bull in the LORD's presence, and Aaron's sons, the
priests, will present the animal's blood by splattering it against all sides of the altar that stands at
the entrance to the Tabernacle. 6Then skin the
animal and cut it into pieces. 7The sons of Aaron
the priest will build a wood fire on the altar.
8They will arrange the pieces of the offering, including the head and fat, on the wood burning
on the altar. 9But the internal organs and the legs
must first be washed with water. Then the priest
will burn the entire sacrifice on the altar as a
burnt offering. It is a special gift, a pleasing
aroma to the LORD.

10"If the animal you present as a burnt offering
is from the flock, it may be either a sheep or a goat,
but it must be a male with no defects. 11Slaughter
the animal on the north side of the altar in the
LORD's presence, and Aaron's sons, the priests, will
splatter its blood against all sides of the altar.
12Then cut the animal in pieces, and the priests
will arrange the pieces of the offering, including
the head and fat, on the wood burning on the altar. 13But the internal organs and the legs must
first be washed with water. Then the priest will
burn the entire sacrifice on the altar as a burnt offering. It is a special gift, a pleasing aroma to the
LORD.

14"If you present a bird as a burnt offering to
the LORD, choose either a turtledove or a young
pigeon. 15The priest will take the bird to the altar,
wring off its head, and burn it on the altar. But first
he must drain its blood against the side of the altar. 16The priest must also remove the crop and
the feathers and throw them in the ashes on the
east side of the altar. 17Then, grasping the bird by
its wings, the priest will tear the bird open, but
without tearing it apart. Then he will burn it as a
burnt offering on the wood burning on the altar. It
is a special gift, a pleasing aroma to the LORD.

CHAPTER 2
Procedures for the Grain Offering

"When you present grain as an offering to the
LORD, the offering must consist of choice flour.
You are to pour olive oil on it, sprinkle it with
frankincense, 2and bring it to Aaron's sons, the
priests. The priest will scoop out a handful of
the flour moistened with oil, together with all
the frankincense, and burn this representative
portion on the altar. It is a special gift, a pleasing
aroma to the LORD. 3The rest of the grain offering will then be given to Aaron and his sons. This
offering will be considered a most holy part of
the special gifts presented to the LORD.

4"If your offering is a grain offering baked in
an oven, it must be made of choice flour, but
without any yeast. It may be presented in the
form of thin cakes mixed with olive oil or wafers
spread with olive oil. 5If your grain offering is
cooked on a griddle, it must be made of choice
flour mixed with olive oil but without any yeast.
6Break it in pieces and pour olive oil on it; it is
a grain offering. 7If your grain offering is prepared in a pan, it must be made of choice flour
and olive oil.

8"No matter how a grain offering for the LORD
has been prepared, bring it to the priest, who will
present it at the altar. 9The priest will take a representative portion of the grain offering and
burn it on the altar. It is a special gift, a pleasing
aroma to the LORD. 10The rest of the grain offering will then be given to Aaron and his sons as
their food. This offering will be considered a
most holy part of the special gifts presented to
the LORD.

11"Do not use yeast in preparing any of the
grain offerings you present to the LORD, because
no yeast or honey may be burned as a special gift
presented to the LORD. 12You may add yeast and
honey to an offering of the first crops of your
harvest, but these must never be offered on the
altar as a pleasing aroma to the LORD. 13Season
all your grain offerings with salt to remind you of
God's eternal covenant. Never forget to add salt
to your grain offerings.

14"If you present a grain offering to the LORD
from the first portion of your harvest, bring
fresh grain that is coarsely ground and roasted
on a fire. 15Put olive oil on this grain offering,
and sprinkle it with frankincense. 16The priest
will take a representative portion of the grain
moistened with oil, together with all the frankincense, and burn it as a special gift presented to
the LORD.

CHAPTER 3

Procedures for the Peace Offering

"If you present an animal from the herd as a peace offering to the LORD, it may be a male or a female, but it must have no defects. 2Lay your hand on the animal's head, and slaughter it at the entrance of the Tabernacle. Then Aaron's sons, the priests, will splatter its blood against all sides of the altar. 3The priest must present part of this peace offering as a special gift to the LORD. This includes all the fat around the internal organs, 4the two kidneys and the fat around them near the loins, and the long lobe of the liver. These must be removed with the kidneys, 5and Aaron's sons will burn them on top of the burnt offering on the wood burning on the altar. It is a special gift, a pleasing aroma to the LORD.

6"If you present an animal from the flock as a peace offering to the LORD, it may be a male or a female, but it must have no defects. 7If you present a sheep as your offering, bring it to the LORD, 8lay your hand on its head, and slaughter it in front of the Tabernacle. Aaron's sons will then splatter the sheep's blood against all sides of the altar. 9The priest must present the fat of this peace offering as a special gift to the LORD. This includes the fat of the broad tail cut off near the backbone, all the fat around the internal organs, 10the two kidneys and the fat around them near the loins, and the long lobe of the liver. These must be removed with the kidneys, 11and the priest will burn them on the altar. It is a special gift of food presented to the LORD.

12"If you present a goat as your offering, bring it to the LORD, 13lay your hand on its head, and slaughter it in front of the Tabernacle. Aaron's sons will then splatter the goat's blood against all sides of the altar. 14The priest must present part of this offering as a special gift to the LORD. This includes all the fat around the internal organs, 15the two kidneys and the fat around them near the loins, and the long lobe of the liver. These must be removed with the kidneys, 16and the priest will burn them on the altar. It is a special gift of food, a pleasing aroma to the LORD. All the fat belongs to the LORD.

17"You must never eat any fat or blood. This is a permanent law for you, and it must be observed from generation to generation, wherever you live."

CHAPTER 4

Procedures for the Sin Offering

Then the LORD said to Moses, 2"Give the following instructions to the people of Israel. This is how you are to deal with those who sin unintentionally by doing anything that violates one of the LORD's commands.

3"If the high priest sins, bringing guilt upon the entire community, he must give a sin offering for the sin he has committed. He must present to the LORD a young bull with no defects. 4He must bring the bull to the LORD at the entrance of the Tabernacle, lay his hand on the bull's head, and slaughter it before the LORD. 5The high priest will then take some of the bull's blood into the Tabernacle, 6dip his finger in the blood, and sprinkle it seven times before the LORD in front of the inner curtain of the sanctuary. 7The priest will then put some of the blood on the horns of the altar for fragrant incense that stands in the LORD's presence inside the Tabernacle. He will pour out the rest of the bull's blood at the base of the altar for burnt offerings at the entrance of the Tabernacle. 8Then the priest must remove all the fat of the bull to be offered as a sin offering. This includes all the fat around the internal organs, 9the two kidneys and the fat around them near the loins, and the long lobe of the liver. He must remove these along with the kidneys, 10just as he does with cattle offered as a peace offering, and burn them on the altar of burnt offerings. 11But he must take whatever is left of the bull—its hide, meat, head, legs, internal organs, and dung—12and carry it away to a place outside the camp that is ceremonially clean, the place where the ashes are dumped. There, on the ash heap, he will burn it on a wood fire.

13"If the entire Israelite community sins by violating one of the LORD's commands, but the people don't realize it, they are still guilty. 14When they become aware of their sin, the people must bring a young bull as an offering for their sin and present it before the Tabernacle. 15The elders of the community must then lay their hands on the bull's head and slaughter it before the LORD. 16The high priest will then take some of the bull's blood into the Tabernacle, 17dip his finger in the blood, and sprinkle it seven times before the LORD in front of the inner curtain. 18He will then put some of the blood on the horns of the altar for fragrant incense that stands in the LORD's presence inside the Tabernacle. He will pour out the rest of the blood at the base of the altar for burnt offerings at the entrance of the Tabernacle. 19Then the priest must remove all the animal's fat and burn it on the altar, 20just as he does with the bull offered as a sin offering for the high priest. Through this process, the priest will purify the people, making them right with the LORD, and

they will be forgiven. 21 Then the priest must take
what is left of the bull and carry it outside the
camp and burn it there, just as is done with the
sin offering for the high priest. This offering is
for the sin of the entire congregation of Israel.

22 "If one of Israel's leaders sins by violating
one of the commands of the LORD his God but
doesn't realize it, he is still guilty. 23 When he becomes aware of his sin, he must bring as his offering a male goat with no defects. 24 He must lay his
hand on the goat's head and slaughter it at the
place where burnt offerings are slaughtered before the LORD. This is an offering for his sin.
25 Then the priest will dip his finger in the blood
of the sin offering and put it on the horns of the
altar for burnt offerings. He will pour out the rest
of the blood at the base of the altar. 26 Then he
must burn all the goat's fat on the altar, just as he
does with the peace offering. Through this process, the priest will purify the leader from his sin,
making him right with the LORD, and he will be
forgiven.

27 "If any of the common people sin by violating one of the LORD's commands, but they don't
realize it, they are still guilty. 28 When they become aware of their sin, they must bring as an offering for their sin a female goat with no defects.
29 They must lay a hand on the head of the sin offering and slaughter it at the place where burnt
offerings are slaughtered. 30 Then the priest will
dip his finger in the blood and put it on the horns
of the altar for burnt offerings. He will pour out
the rest of the blood at the base of the altar.
31 Then he must remove all the goat's fat, just as he
does with the fat of the peace offering. He will
burn the fat on the altar, and it will be a pleasing
aroma to the LORD. Through this process, the
priest will purify the people, making them right
with the LORD, and they will be forgiven.

32 "If the people bring a sheep as their sin offering, it must be a female with no defects.
33 They must lay a hand on the head of the sin offering and slaughter it at the place where burnt
offerings are slaughtered. 34 Then the priest will
dip his finger in the blood of the sin offering and
put it on the horns of the altar for burnt offerings. He will pour out the rest of the blood at the
base of the altar. 35 Then he must remove all the
sheep's fat, just as he does with the fat of a sheep
presented as a peace offering. He will burn the
fat on the altar on top of the special gifts presented to the LORD. Through this process, the
priest will purify the people from their sin, making them right with the LORD, and they will be
forgiven.

CHAPTER 5

Sins Requiring a Sin Offering

"If you are called to testify about something you
have seen or that you know about, it is sinful to
refuse to testify, and you will be punished for
your sin.

2 "Or suppose you unknowingly touch something that is ceremonially unclean, such as the
carcass of an unclean animal. When you realize
what you have done, you must admit your defilement and your guilt. This is true whether it is a
wild animal, a domestic animal, or an animal that
scurries along the ground.

3 "Or suppose you unknowingly touch something that makes a person unclean. When you realize what you have done, you must admit your
guilt.

4 "Or suppose you make a foolish vow of any
kind, whether its purpose is for good or for bad.
When you realize its foolishness, you must admit
your guilt.

5 "When you become aware of your guilt in
any of these ways, you must confess your sin.
6 Then you must bring to the LORD as the penalty
for your sin a female from the flock, either a
sheep or a goat. This is a sin offering with which
the priest will purify you from your sin, making
you right with the LORD.

7 "But if you cannot afford to bring a sheep,
you may bring to the LORD two turtledoves or two
young pigeons as the penalty for your sin. One of
the birds will be for a sin offering, and the other
for a burnt offering. 8 You must bring them to the
priest, who will present the first bird as the sin
offering. He will wring its neck but without sev-
ering its head from the body. 9 Then he will
sprinkle some of the blood of the sin offering
against the sides of the altar, and the rest of the
blood will be drained out at the base of the altar.
This is an offering for sin. 10 The priest will then
prepare the second bird as a burnt offering, following all the procedures that have been prescribed. Through this process the priest will
purify you from your sin, making you right with
the LORD, and you will be forgiven.

11 "If you cannot afford to bring two turtledoves or two young pigeons, you may bring two
quarts of choice flour for your sin offering. Since
it is an offering for sin, you must not moisten it
with olive oil or put any frankincense on it.
12 Take the flour to the priest, who will scoop out
a handful as a representative portion. He will
burn it on the altar on top of the special gifts presented to the LORD. It is an offering for sin.
13 Through this process, the priest will purify

those who are guilty of any of these sins, making
them right with the LORD, and they will be forgiven. The rest of the flour will belong to the
priest, just as with the grain offering."

Procedures for the Guilt Offering

14Then the LORD said to Moses, 15"If one of you
commits a sin by unintentionally defiling the
LORD's sacred property, you must bring a guilt offering to the LORD. The offering must be your
own ram with no defects, or you may buy one of
equal value with silver, as measured by the
weight of the sanctuary shekel. 16You must make
restitution for the sacred property you have
harmed by paying for the loss, plus an additional
20 percent. When you give the payment to the
priest, he will purify you with the ram sacrificed
as a guilt offering, making you right with the
LORD, and you will be forgiven.

17"Suppose you sin by violating one of the
LORD's commands. Even if you are unaware of
what you have done, you are guilty and will be
punished for your sin. 18For a guilt offering, you
must bring to the priest your own ram with no
defects, or you may buy one of equal value.
Through this process the priest will purify you
from your unintentional sin, making you right
with the LORD, and you will be forgiven. 19This is
a guilt offering, for you have been guilty of an offense against the LORD."

CHAPTER 6

Sins Requiring a Guilt Offering

Then the LORD said to Moses, 2"Suppose one of
you sins against your associate and is unfaithful
to the LORD. Suppose you cheat in a deal involving a security deposit, or you steal or commit
fraud, 3or you find lost property and lie about it,
or you lie while swearing to tell the truth, or you
commit any other such sin. 4If you have sinned in
any of these ways, you are guilty. You must give
back whatever you stole, or the money you took
by extortion, or the security deposit, or the lost
property you found, 5or anything obtained by
swearing falsely. You must make restitution by
paying the full price plus an additional 20 percent to the person you have harmed. On the same
day you must present a guilt offering. 6As a guilt
offering to the LORD, you must bring to the priest
your own ram with no defects, or you may buy
one of equal value. 7Through this process, the
priest will purify you before the LORD, making
you right with him, and you will be forgiven for
any of these sins you have committed."

Further Instructions for the Burnt Offering

8Then the LORD said to Moses, 9"Give Aaron and
his sons the following instructions regarding
the burnt offering. The burnt offering must be
left on top of the altar until the next morning,
and the fire on the altar must be kept burning all
night. 10In the morning, after the priest on duty
has put on his official linen clothing and linen
undergarments, he must clean out the ashes of
the burnt offering and put them beside the altar.
11Then he must take off these garments, change
back into his regular clothes, and carry the ashes
outside the camp to a place that is ceremonially
clean. 12Meanwhile, the fire on the altar must
be kept burning; it must never go out. Each
morning the priest will add fresh wood to the
fire and arrange the burnt offering on it. He will
then burn the fat of the peace offerings on it.
13Remember, the fire must be kept burning on
the altar at all times. It must never go out.

Further Instructions for the Grain Offering

14"These are the instructions regarding the grain
offering. Aaron's sons must present this offering
to the LORD in front of the altar. 15The priest on
duty will take from the grain offering a handful
of the choice flour moistened with olive oil, together with all the frankincense. He will burn
this representative portion on the altar as a
pleasing aroma to the LORD. 16Aaron and his
sons may eat the rest of the flour, but it must be
baked without yeast and eaten in a sacred place
within the courtyard of the Tabernacle. 17Re-
member, it must never be prepared with yeast. I
have given it to the priests as their share of the
special gifts presented to me. Like the sin offering and the guilt offering, it is most holy. 18Any of
Aaron's male descendants may eat from the special gifts presented to the LORD. This is their permanent right from generation to generation.
Anyone or anything that touches these offerings
will become holy."

Procedures for the Ordination Offering

19Then the LORD said to Moses, 20"On the day
Aaron and his sons are anointed, they must present to the LORD the standard grain offering of
two quarts of choice flour, half to be offered in
the morning and half to be offered in the evening. 21It must be carefully mixed with olive oil
and cooked on a griddle. Then slice this grain offering and present it as a pleasing aroma to the

LORD. 22In each generation, the high priest who
succeeds Aaron must prepare this same offering.
It belongs to the LORD and must be burned up
completely. This is a permanent law. 23All such
grain offerings of a priest must be burned up entirely. None of it may be eaten."

Further Instructions for the Sin Offering

24Then the LORD said to Moses, 25"Give Aaron
and his sons the following instructions regarding the sin offering. The animal given as an offering for sin is a most holy offering, and it must
be slaughtered in the LORD's presence at the
place where the burnt offerings are slaughtered.
26The priest who offers the sacrifice as a sin offering must eat his portion in a sacred place
within the courtyard of the Tabernacle. 27Any-
one or anything that touches the sacrificial meat
will become holy. If any of the sacrificial blood
spatters on a person's clothing, the soiled garment must be washed in a sacred place. 28If a
clay pot is used to boil the sacrificial meat, it
must then be broken. If a bronze pot is used, it
must be scoured and thoroughly rinsed with water. 29Any male from a priest's family may eat
from this offering; it is most holy. 30But the offering for sin may not be eaten if its blood was
brought into the Tabernacle as an offering for
purification in the Holy Place. It must be completely burned with fire.

CHAPTER 7

Further Instructions for the Guilt Offering

"These are the instructions for the guilt offering.
It is most holy. 2The animal sacrificed as a guilt
offering must be slaughtered at the place where
the burnt offerings are slaughtered, and its blood
must be splattered against all sides of the altar.
3The priest will then offer all its fat on the altar,
including the fat of the broad tail, the fat around
the internal organs, 4the two kidneys and the fat
around them near the loins, and the long lobe of
the liver. These are to be removed with the kidneys, 5and the priests will burn them on the altar
as a special gift presented to the LORD. This is the
guilt offering. 6Any male from a priest's family
may eat the meat. It must be eaten in a sacred
place, for it is most holy.

7"The same instructions apply to both the
guilt offering and the sin offering. Both belong
to the priest who uses them to purify someone,
making that person right with the LORD. 8In the
case of the burnt offering, the priest may keep
the hide of the sacrificed animal. 9Any grain offering that has been baked in an oven, prepared
in a pan, or cooked on a griddle belongs to the
priest who presents it. 10All other grain offerings, whether made of dry flour or flour moistened with olive oil, are to be shared equally
among all the priests, the descendants of Aaron.

Further Instructions for the Peace Offering

11"These are the instructions regarding the different kinds of peace offerings that may be presented to the LORD. 12If you present your peace
offering as an expression of thanksgiving, the
usual animal sacrifice must be accompanied by
various kinds of bread made without yeast—thin
cakes mixed with olive oil, wafers spread with oil,
and cakes made of choice flour mixed with olive
oil. 13This peace offering of thanksgiving must
also be accompanied by loaves of bread made
with yeast. 14One of each kind of bread must be
presented as a gift to the LORD. It will then belong to the priest who splatters the blood of the
peace offering against the altar. 15The meat of
the peace offering of thanksgiving must be eaten
on the same day it is offered. None of it may be
saved for the next morning.

16"If you bring an offering to fulfill a vow or as
a voluntary offering, the meat must be eaten on
the same day the sacrifice is offered, but whatever is left over may be eaten on the second day.
17Any meat left over until the third day must be
completely burned up. 18If any of the meat from
the peace offering is eaten on the third day, the
person who presented it will not be accepted by
the LORD. You will receive no credit for offering
it. By then the meat will be contaminated; if you
eat it, you will be punished for your sin.

19"Meat that touches anything ceremonially
unclean may not be eaten; it must be completely
burned up. The rest of the meat may be eaten,
but only by people who are ceremonially clean.
20If you are ceremonially unclean and you eat
meat from a peace offering that was presented to
the LORD, you will be cut off from the community. 21If you touch anything that is unclean
(whether it is human defilement or an unclean
animal or any other unclean, detestable thing)
and then eat meat from a peace offering presented to the LORD, you will be cut off from the
community."

The Forbidden Blood and Fat

22Then the LORD said to Moses, 23"Give the following instructions to the people of Israel. You

BIBLE BIOS

Hear From the Heroes

Hi, my name is JACOB *(rancher, trickster)*

God can change *anyone*. I know because God changed me. As a youngster, I only cared about numero uno—that is, myself. I tricked my brother, Esau, out of his birthright and blessing. My mother and I hatched a clever plan, but it was also selfish and wrong. Esau almost killed me when he found out!

Jacob actually played two crafty tricks. Read about the first one in GENESIS 25:27-34. Look up the second one in GENESIS 27:1-40.

I think the change in my heart started when I ran away from Esau. As I slept one night out in the middle of nowhere, God came to me in a dream. He showed me the most incredible thing I had ever seen. You can read all about it in **GENESIS 28:10-22.** I knew that God was with me and that he loved me—even though I lied and cheated.

Want to see other things that God did to change Jacob's heart? See GENESIS 32:22-30 and GENESIS 33:1-15.

God changed my heart even more when I moved in with my uncle, Laban. We agreed that if I cared for his sheep for seven years, I could marry his daughter Rachel. Laban tricked *me*, the trickster! Look at how he did it in **GENESIS 29:16-28.** I couldn't help but think about how I tricked Esau and my dad, Isaac. No one likes to be lied to.

God changed my name to Israel, and my 12 boys became the fathers of the 12 tribes of Israel. The God of Abraham, Isaac, and Jacob (that's me) made us into a powerful nation. Amazing—especially since we all made so many mistakes along the way. No matter what you have done, you can go to God for help when you need it. God can change anyone. I know because he changed me.

Can you name Israel's 12 sons? They became the 12 tribes of Israel. You can find them listed together in GENESIS 35:23-26.

Time for a Change

Have you ever lied to, cheated, or hurt someone?

Make a card to say you're sorry. Give the card to the person. Better yet, read it to him or her before you give it.

How does God want to change you? Read **HEBREWS 4:16** and ask God to start.

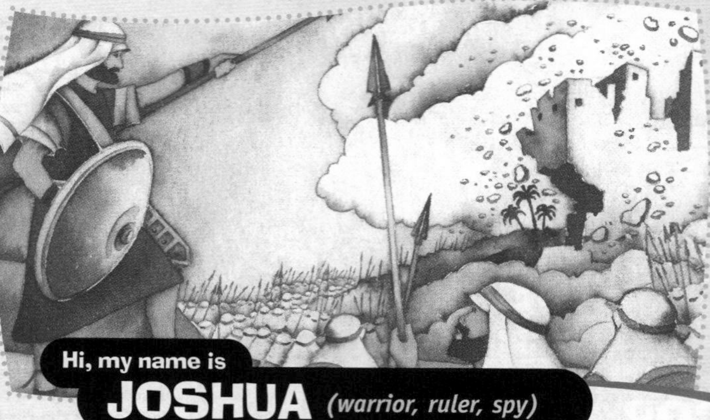

BIBLE BIOS

Hear From the Heroes

Hi, my name is

JOSHUA *(warrior, ruler, spy)*

Imagine that your team made it to the championship game. While the other team comes out to the field to play, your coach tells you he has a new game plan. Your team is going to march around the field without saying a word. At the final second of the game, you'll all turn toward your opponent and yell, "We think—you stink!" as loud as you can.

Well, that's sort of what happened to me. When Moses died, God promoted me to be the leader of Israel. We battled the city of Jericho right when we entered the land God promised to give us. They had humongous walls all around the city. It looked hopeless. God told us to march around the city every day for seven days. On the last day, we were supposed to march around Jericho seven times and then yell. A lot of my men thought I was crazy when I told them the plan. Check out what happened in **JOSHUA 6:15-20**.

Read the famous words in JOSHUA 24:14-15 that Joshua gave to the Israelites just before he died.

Right after Moses died, God said four unforgettable words to me: "Be strong and courageous." We fought some incredible battles and faced a lot of fears. But we held on to the courage God gave us, and we took the land God promised!

During one battle, the sun stood still! Read about it in JOSHUA 10:12-13.

Stronger Than You Think

We can be courageous because God gives us strength!

Here's an easy experiment that reminds us God is supporting us. Try to balance a Bible on the edge of an ordinary piece of paper.

What happens?

Now roll up a single sheet of paper to the size of a toilet paper tube and tape it together. Then try to balance a Bible in the middle of this sheet.

WOW!

- **How are you like the paper? the Bible?**
- **How is God like the tube and the tape?**
- **How do you need God's strength and courage at home? at school?**

must never eat fat, whether from cattle, sheep, or goats. 24 The fat of an animal found dead or torn to pieces by wild animals must never be eaten, though it may be used for any other purpose. 25 Anyone who eats fat from an animal presented as a special gift to the LORD will be cut off from the community. 26 No matter where you live, you must never consume the blood of any bird or animal. 27 Anyone who consumes blood will be cut off from the community."

A Portion for the Priests

28 Then the LORD said to Moses, 29 "Give the following instructions to the people of Israel. When you present a peace offering to the LORD, bring part of it as a gift to the LORD. 30 Present it to the LORD with your own hands as a special gift to the LORD. Bring the fat of the animal, together with the breast, and lift up the breast as a special offering to the LORD. 31 Then the priest will burn the fat on the altar, but the breast will belong to Aaron and his descendants. 32 Give the right thigh of your peace offering to the priest as a gift. 33 The right thigh must always be given to the priest who offers the blood and the fat of the peace offering. 34 For I have reserved the breast of the special offering and the right thigh of the sacred offering for the priests. It is the permanent right of Aaron and his descendants to share in the peace offerings brought by the people of Israel. 35 This is their rightful share. The special gifts presented to the LORD have been reserved for Aaron and his descendants from the time they were set apart to serve the LORD as priests. 36 On the day they were anointed, the LORD commanded the Israelites to give these portions to the priests as their permanent share from generation to generation."

37 These are the instructions for the burnt offering, the grain offering, the sin offering, and the guilt offering, as well as the ordination offering and the peace offering. 38 The LORD gave these instructions to Moses on Mount Sinai when he commanded the Israelites to present their offerings to the LORD in the wilderness of Sinai.

CHAPTER 8

Ordination of the Priests

Then the LORD said to Moses, 2 "Bring Aaron and his sons, along with their sacred garments, the anointing oil, the bull for the sin offering, the two rams, and the basket of bread made without yeast, 3 and call the entire community of Israel together at the entrance of the Tabernacle."

4 So Moses followed the LORD's instructions, and the whole community assembled at the Tabernacle entrance. 5 Moses announced to them, "This is what the LORD has commanded us to do!" 6 Then he presented Aaron and his sons and washed them with water. 7 He put the official tunic on Aaron and tied the sash around his waist. He dressed him in the robe, placed the ephod on him, and attached the ephod securely with its decorative sash. 8 Then Moses placed the chestpiece on Aaron and put the Urim and the Thummim inside it. 9 He placed the turban on Aaron's head and attached the gold medallion—the badge of holiness—to the front of the turban, just as the LORD had commanded him.

10 Then Moses took the anointing oil and anointed the Tabernacle and everything in it, making them holy. 11 He sprinkled the oil on the altar seven times, anointing it and all its utensils, as well as the washbasin and its stand, making them holy. 12 Then he poured some of the anointing oil on Aaron's head, anointing him and making him holy for his work. 13 Next Moses presented Aaron's sons. He clothed them in their tunics, tied their sashes around them, and put their special head coverings on them, just as the LORD had commanded him.

14 Then Moses presented the bull for the sin offering. Aaron and his sons laid their hands on the bull's head, 15 and Moses slaughtered it. Moses took some of the blood, and with his finger he put it on the four horns of the altar to purify it. He poured out the rest of the blood at the base of the altar. Through this process, he made the altar holy by purifying it. 16 Then Moses took all the fat around the internal organs, the long lobe of the liver, and the two kidneys and the fat around them, and he burned it all on the altar. 17 He took the rest of the bull, including its hide, meat, and dung, and burned it on a fire outside the camp, just as the LORD had commanded him.

18 Then Moses presented the ram for the burnt offering. Aaron and his sons laid their hands on the ram's head, 19 and Moses slaughtered it. Then Moses took the ram's blood and splattered it against all sides of the altar. 20 Then he cut the ram into pieces, and he burned the head, some of its pieces, and the fat on the altar. 21 After washing the internal organs and the legs with water, Moses burned the entire ram on the altar as a burnt offering. It was a pleasing aroma, a special gift presented to the LORD, just as the LORD had commanded him.

22 Then Moses presented the other ram,

which was the ram of ordination. Aaron and his sons laid their hands on the ram's head, 23and Moses slaughtered it. Then Moses took some of its blood and applied it to the lobe of Aaron's right ear, the thumb of his right hand, and the big toe of his right foot. 24Next Moses presented Aaron's sons and applied some of the blood to the lobes of their right ears, the thumbs of their right hands, and the big toes of their right feet. He then splattered the rest of the blood against all sides of the altar.

25Next Moses took the fat, including the fat of the broad tail, the fat around the internal organs, the long lobe of the liver, and the two kidneys and the fat around them, along with the right thigh. 26On top of these he placed a thin cake of bread made without yeast, a cake of bread mixed with olive oil, and a wafer spread with olive oil. All these were taken from the basket of bread made without yeast that was placed in the LORD's presence. 27He put all these in the hands of Aaron and his sons, and he lifted these gifts as a special offering to the LORD. 28Moses then took all the offerings back from them and burned them on the altar on top of the burnt offering. This was the ordination offering. It was a pleasing aroma, a special gift presented to the LORD. 29Then Moses took the breast and lifted it up as a special offering to the LORD. This was Moses' portion of the ram of ordination, just as the LORD had commanded him.

30Next Moses took some of the anointing oil and some of the blood that was on the altar, and he sprinkled them on Aaron and his garments and on his sons and their garments. In this way, he made Aaron and his sons and their garments holy.

31Then Moses said to Aaron and his sons, "Boil the remaining meat of the offerings at the Tabernacle entrance, and eat it there, along with the bread that is in the basket of offerings for the ordination, just as I commanded when I said, 'Aaron and his sons will eat it.' 32Any meat or bread that is left over must then be burned up. 33You must not leave the Tabernacle entrance for seven days, for that is when the ordination ceremony will be completed. 34Everything we have done today was commanded by the LORD in order to purify you, making you right with him. 35Now stay at the entrance of the Tabernacle day and night for seven days, and do everything the LORD requires. If you fail to do this, you will die, for this is what the LORD has commanded." 36So Aaron and his sons did everything the LORD had commanded through Moses.

CHAPTER **9**

The Priests Begin Their Work

After the ordination ceremony, on the eighth day, Moses called together Aaron and his sons and the elders of Israel. 2He said to Aaron, "Take a young bull for a sin offering and a ram for a burnt offering, both without defects, and present them to the LORD. 3Then tell the Israelites, 'Take a male goat for a sin offering, and take a calf and a lamb, both a year old and without defects, for a burnt offering. 4Also take a bull and a ram for a peace offering and flour moistened with olive oil for a grain offering. Present all these offerings to the LORD because the LORD will appear to you today.'"

5So the people presented all these things at the entrance of the Tabernacle, just as Moses had commanded. Then the whole community came forward and stood before the LORD. 6And Moses said, "This is what the LORD has commanded you to do so that the glory of the LORD may appear to you."

7Then Moses said to Aaron, "Come to the altar and sacrifice your sin offering and your burnt offering to purify yourself and the people. Then present the offerings of the people to purify them, making them right with the LORD, just as he has commanded."

8So Aaron went to the altar and slaughtered the calf as a sin offering for himself. 9His sons brought him the blood, and he dipped his finger in it and put it on the horns of the altar. He poured out the rest of the blood at the base of the altar. 10Then he burned on the altar the fat, the kidneys, and the long lobe of the liver from the sin offering, just as the LORD had commanded Moses. 11The meat and the hide, however, he burned outside the camp.

12Next Aaron slaughtered the animal for the burnt offering. His sons brought him the blood, and he splattered it against all sides of the altar. 13Then they handed him each piece of the burnt offering, including the head, and he burned them on the altar. 14Then he washed the internal organs and the legs and burned them on the altar along with the rest of the burnt offering.

15Next Aaron presented the offerings of the people. He slaughtered the people's goat and presented it as an offering for their sin, just as he had first done with the offering for his own sin. 16Then he presented the burnt offering and sacrificed it in the prescribed way. 17He also presented the grain offering, burning a handful of the flour mixture on the altar, in addition to the regular burnt offering for the morning.

18Then Aaron slaughtered the bull and the ram for the people's peace offering. His sons brought him the blood, and he splattered it against all sides of the altar. 19Then he took the fat of the bull and the ram—the fat of the broad tail and from around the internal organs—along with the kidneys and the long lobes of the livers. 20He placed these fat portions on top of the breasts of these animals and burned them on the altar. 21Aaron then lifted up the breasts and right thighs as a special offering to the LORD, just as Moses had commanded.

22After that, Aaron raised his hands toward the people and blessed them. Then, after presenting the sin offering, the burnt offering, and the peace offering, he stepped down from the altar. 23Then Moses and Aaron went into the Tabernacle, and when they came back out, they blessed the people again, and the glory of the LORD appeared to the whole community. 24Fire blazed forth from the LORD's presence and consumed the burnt offering and the fat on the altar. When the people saw this, they shouted with joy and fell face down on the ground.

CHAPTER 10

The Sin of Nadab and Abihu

Aaron's sons Nadab and Abihu put coals of fire in their incense burners and sprinkled incense over them. In this way, they disobeyed the LORD by burning before him the wrong kind of fire, different than he had commanded. 2So fire blazed forth from the LORD's presence and burned them up, and they died there before the LORD.

3Then Moses said to Aaron, "This is what the LORD meant when he said,

'I will display my holiness
    through those who come near me.
I will display my glory
    before all the people.'"

And Aaron was silent.

4Then Moses called for Mishael and Elzaphan, Aaron's cousins, the sons of Aaron's uncle Uzziel. He said to them, "Come forward and carry away the bodies of your relatives from in front of the sanctuary to a place outside the camp." 5So they came forward and picked them up by their garments and carried them out of the camp, just as Moses had commanded.

6Then Moses said to Aaron and his sons Eleazar and Ithamar, "Do not show grief by leaving your hair uncombed or by tearing your clothes. If you do, you will die, and the LORD's anger will strike the whole community of Israel. However, the rest of the Israelites, your relatives, may mourn because of the LORD's fiery destruction of Nadab and Abihu. 7But you must not leave the entrance of the Tabernacle or you will die, for you have been anointed with the LORD's anointing oil." So they did as Moses commanded.

Instructions for Priestly Conduct

8Then the LORD said to Aaron, 9"You and your descendants must never drink wine or any other alcoholic drink before going into the Tabernacle. If you do, you will die. This is a permanent law for you, and it must be observed from generation to generation. 10You must distinguish between what is sacred and what is common, between what is ceremonially unclean and what is clean. 11And you must teach the Israelites all the decrees that the LORD has given them through Moses."

12Then Moses said to Aaron and his remaining sons, Eleazar and Ithamar, "Take what is left of the grain offering after a portion has been presented as a special gift to the LORD, and eat it beside the altar. Make sure it contains no yeast, for it is most holy. 13You must eat it in a sacred place, for it has been given to you and your descendants as your portion of the special gifts presented to the LORD. These are the commands I have been given. 14But the breast and thigh that were lifted up as a special offering may be eaten in any place that is ceremonially clean. These parts have been given to you and your descendants as your portion of the peace offerings presented by the people of Israel. 15You must lift up the thigh and breast as a special offering to the LORD, along with the fat of the special gifts. These parts will belong to you and your descendants as your permanent right, just as the LORD has commanded."

16Moses then asked them what had happened to the goat of the sin offering. When he discovered it had been burned up, he became very angry with Eleazar and Ithamar, Aaron's remaining sons. 17"Why didn't you eat the sin offering in the sacred area?" he demanded. "It is a holy offering! The LORD has given it to you to remove the guilt of the community and to purify the people, making them right with the LORD. 18Since the animal's blood was not brought into the Holy Place, you should have eaten the meat in the sacred area as I ordered you."

19Then Aaron answered Moses, "Today my sons presented both their sin offering and their burnt offering to the LORD. And yet this tragedy has happened to me. If I had eaten the people's sin offering on such a tragic day as this, would the LORD have been pleased?" 20And when Moses heard this, he was satisfied.

CHAPTER 11

Ceremonially Clean and Unclean Animals

Then the LORD said to Moses and Aaron, 2"Give the following instructions to the people of Israel.

"Of all the land animals, these are the ones you may use for food. 3You may eat any animal that has completely split hooves and chews the cud. 4You may not, however, eat the following animals that have split hooves or that chew the cud, but not both. The camel chews the cud but does not have split hooves, so it is ceremonially unclean for you. 5The hyrax chews the cud but does not have split hooves, so it is unclean. 6The hare chews the cud but does not have split hooves, so it is unclean. 7The pig has evenly split hooves but does not chew the cud, so it is unclean. 8You may not eat the meat of these animals or even touch their carcasses. They are ceremonially unclean for you.

9"Of all the marine animals, these are ones you may use for food. You may eat anything from the water if it has both fins and scales, whether taken from salt water or from streams. 10But you must never eat animals from the sea or from rivers that do not have both fins and scales. They are detestable to you. This applies both to little creatures that live in shallow water and to all creatures that live in deep water. 11They will always be detestable to you. You must never eat their meat or even touch their dead bodies. 12Any marine animal that does not have both fins and scales is detestable to you.

13"These are the birds that are detestable to you. You must never eat them: the griffon vulture, the bearded vulture, the black vulture, 14the kite, falcons of all kinds, 15ravens of all kinds, 16the eagle owl, the short-eared owl, the seagull, hawks of all kinds, 17the little owl, the cormorant, the great owl, 18the barn owl, the desert owl, the Egyptian vulture, 19the stork, herons of all kinds, the hoopoe, and the bat.

20"You must not eat winged insects that walk along the ground; they are detestable to you. 21You may, however, eat winged insects that walk along the ground and have jointed legs so they can jump. 22The insects you are permitted to eat include all kinds of locusts, bald locusts, crickets, and grasshoppers. 23All other winged insects that walk along the ground are detestable to you.

24"The following creatures will make you ceremonially unclean. If any of you touch their carcasses, you will be defiled until evening. 25If you pick up their carcasses, you must wash your clothes, and you will remain defiled until evening.

26"Any animal that has split hooves that are not evenly divided or that does not chew the cud is unclean for you. If you touch the carcass of such an animal, you will be defiled. 27Of the animals that walk on all fours, those that have paws are unclean. If you touch the carcass of such an animal, you will be defiled until evening. 28If you pick up its carcass, you must wash your clothes, and you will remain defiled until evening. These animals are unclean for you.

29"Of the small animals that scurry along the ground, these are unclean for you: the mole rat, the rat, large lizards of all kinds, 30the gecko, the monitor lizard, the common lizard, the sand lizard, and the chameleon. 31All these small animals are unclean for you. If any of you touch the dead body of such an animal, you will be defiled until evening. 32If such an animal dies and falls on something, that object will be unclean. This is true whether the object is made of wood, cloth, leather, or burlap. Whatever its use, you must dip it in water, and it will remain defiled until evening. After that, it will be ceremonially clean and may be used again.

33"If such an animal falls into a clay pot, everything in the pot will be defiled, and the pot must be smashed. 34If the water from such a container spills on any food, the food will be defiled. And any beverage in such a container will be defiled. 35Any object on which the carcass of such an animal falls will be defiled. If it is an oven or hearth, it must be destroyed, for it is defiled, and you must treat it accordingly.

36"However, if the carcass of such an animal falls into a spring or a cistern, the water will still be clean. But anyone who touches the carcass will be defiled. 37If the carcass falls on seed grain to be planted in the field, the seed will still be considered clean. 38But if the seed is wet when the carcass falls on it, the seed will be defiled.

39"If an animal you are permitted to eat dies and you touch its carcass, you will be defiled until evening. 40If you eat any of its meat or carry away its carcass, you must wash your clothes, and you will remain defiled until evening.

41"All small animals that scurry along the

because I am holy.
46 "These are the instructions regarding land
animals, birds, marine creatures, and animals
that scurry along the ground. 47 By these instructions you will know what is unclean and clean,
and which animals may be eaten and which may
not be eaten."

CHAPTER 12

Purification after Childbirth

The LORD said to Moses, 2 "Give the following instructions to the people of Israel. If a woman becomes pregnant and gives birth to a son, she will
be ceremonially unclean for seven days, just as
she is unclean during her menstrual period. 3 On
the eighth day the boy's foreskin must be circumcised. 4 After waiting thirty-three days, she
will be purified from the bleeding of childbirth.
During this time of purification, she must not
touch anything that is set apart as holy. And she
must not enter the sanctuary until her time of
purification is over. 5 If a woman gives birth to a
daughter, she will be ceremonially unclean for
two weeks, just as she is unclean during her menstrual period. After waiting sixty-six days, she
will be purified from the bleeding of childbirth.
6 "When the time of purification is completed
for either a son or a daughter, the woman must
bring a one-year-old lamb for a burnt offering
and a young pigeon or turtledove for a purification offering. She must bring her offerings to the
priest at the entrance of the Tabernacle. 7 The
priest will then present them to the LORD to purify her. Then she will be ceremonially clean
again after her bleeding at childbirth. These are
the instructions for a woman after the birth of a
son or a daughter.
8 "If a woman cannot afford to bring a lamb,
she must bring two turtledoves or two young pigeons. One will be for the burnt offering and the

nounce the person ceremonially unclean.
4 "But if the affected area of the skin is only a
white discoloration and does not appear to be
more than skin-deep, and if the hair on the spot
has not turned white, the priest will quarantine
the person for seven days. 5 On the seventh day
the priest will make another examination. If he
finds the affected area has not changed and the
problem has not spread on the skin, the priest
will quarantine the person for seven more days.
6 On the seventh day the priest will make another
examination. If he finds the affected area has
faded and has not spread, the priest will pronounce the person ceremonially clean. It was
only a rash. The person's clothing must be
washed, and the person will be ceremonially
clean. 7 But if the rash continues to spread after
the person has been examined by the priest and
has been pronounced clean, the infected person
must return to be examined again. 8 If the priest
finds that the rash has spread, he must pronounce the person ceremonially unclean, for it
is indeed a skin disease.
9 "Anyone who develops a serious skin disease
must go to the priest for an examination. 10 If the
priest finds a white swelling on the skin, and
some hair on the spot has turned white, and
there is an open sore in the affected area, 11 it is a
chronic skin disease, and the priest must pronounce the person ceremonially unclean. In
such cases the person need not be quarantined,
for it is obvious that the skin is defiled by the
disease.
12 "Now suppose the disease has spread all
over the person's skin, covering the body from
head to foot. 13 When the priest examines the
infected person and finds that the disease covers the entire body, he will pronounce the person ceremonially clean. Since the skin has
turned completely white, the person is clean.

If anyone has suffered a burn on the skin
and the burned area changes color, becoming
either reddish white or shiny white, 25the priest
must examine it. If he finds that the hair in the
affected area has turned white and the problem
appears to be more than skin-deep, a skin disease has broken out in the burn. The priest
must then pronounce the person ceremonially
unclean, for it is clearly a serious skin disease.
26But if the priest finds no white hair on the affected area and the problem appears to be no
more than skin-deep and has faded, the priest
must quarantine the infected person for seven
days. 27On the seventh day the priest must examine the person again. If the affected area has
spread on the skin, the priest must pronounce
that person ceremonially unclean, for it is
clearly a serious skin disease. 28But if the affected area has not changed or spread on the
skin and has faded, it is simply a swelling from
the burn. The priest will then pronounce the
person ceremonially clean, for it is only the scar
from the burn.

29"If anyone, either a man or woman, has a

must examine the affected area. If he finds that
the shiny patches are only pale white, this is a
harmless skin rash, and the person is ceremonially clean.

40"If a man loses his hair and his head becomes bald, he is still ceremonially clean. 41And
if he loses hair on his forehead, he simply has a
bald forehead; he is still clean. 42However, if a
reddish white sore appears on the bald area on
top of his head or on his forehead, this is a skin
disease. 43The priest must examine him, and if
he finds swelling around the reddish white sore
anywhere on the man's head and it looks like a
skin disease, 44the man is indeed infected with
a skin disease and is unclean. The priest must
pronounce him ceremonially unclean because
of the sore on his head.

45"Those who suffer from a serious skin disease must tear their clothing and leave their
hair uncombed. They must cover their mouth
and call out, 'Unclean! Unclean!' 46As long as the
serious disease lasts, they will be ceremonially
unclean. They must live in isolation in their
place outside the camp.

Treatment of Contaminated Clothing

47"Now suppose mildew contaminates some woolen or linen clothing, 48woolen or linen fabric, the hide of an animal, or anything made of leather. 49If the contaminated area in the clothing, the animal hide, the fabric, or the leather article has turned greenish or reddish, it is contaminated with mildew and must be shown to the priest. 50After examining the affected spot, the priest will put the article in quarantine for seven days. 51On the seventh day the priest must inspect it again. If the contaminated area has spread, the clothing or fabric or leather is clearly contaminated by a serious mildew and is ceremonially unclean. 52The priest must burn the item—the clothing, the woolen or linen fabric, or piece of leather—for it has been contaminated by a serious mildew. It must be completely destroyed by fire.

53"But if the priest examines it and finds that the contaminated area has not spread in the clothing, the fabric, or the leather, 54the priest will order the object to be washed and then quarantined for seven more days. 55Then the priest must examine the object again. If he finds that the contaminated area has not changed color after being washed, even if it did not spread, the object is defiled. It must be completely burned up, whether the contaminated spot is on the inside or outside. 56But if the priest examines it and finds that the contaminated area has faded after being washed, he must cut the spot from the clothing, the fabric, or the leather. 57If the spot later reappears on the clothing, the fabric, or the leather article, the mildew is clearly spreading, and the contaminated object must be burned up. 58But if the spot disappears from the clothing, the fabric, or the leather article after it has been washed, it must be washed again; then it will be ceremonially clean.

59"These are the instructions for dealing with mildew that contaminates woolen or linen clothing or fabric or anything made of leather. This is how the priest will determine whether these items are ceremonially clean or unclean."

CHAPTER 14

Cleansing from Skin Diseases

And the LORD said to Moses, 2"The following instructions are for those seeking ceremonial purification from a skin disease. Those who have been healed must be brought to the priest, 3who will examine them at a place outside the camp. If the priest finds that someone has been healed of a serious skin disease, 4he will perform a purification ceremony, using two live birds that are ceremonially clean, a stick of cedar, some scarlet yarn, and a hyssop branch. 5The priest will order that one bird be slaughtered over a clay pot filled with fresh water. 6He will take the live bird, the cedar stick, the scarlet yarn, and the hyssop branch, and dip them into the blood of the bird that was slaughtered over the fresh water. 7The priest will then sprinkle the blood of the dead bird seven times on the person being purified of the skin disease. When the priest has purified the person, he will release the live bird in the open field to fly away.

8"The persons being purified must then wash their clothes, shave off all their hair, and bathe themselves in water. Then they will be ceremonially clean and may return to the camp. However, they must remain outside their tents for seven days. 9On the seventh day they must again shave all the hair from their heads, including the hair of the beard and eyebrows. They must also wash their clothes and bathe themselves in water. Then they will be ceremonially clean.

10"On the eighth day each person being purified must bring two male lambs and a one-year-old female lamb, all with no defects, along with a grain offering of six quarts of choice flour moistened with olive oil, and a cup of olive oil. 11Then the officiating priest will present that person for purification, along with the offerings, before the LORD at the entrance of the Tabernacle. 12The priest will take one of the male lambs and the olive oil and present them as a guilt offering, lifting them up as a special offering before the LORD. 13He will then slaughter the male lamb in the sacred area where sin offerings and burnt offerings are slaughtered. As with the sin offering, the guilt offering belongs to the priest. It is a most holy offering. 14The priest will then take some of the blood of the guilt offering and apply it to the lobe of the right ear, the thumb of the right hand, and the big toe of the right foot of the person being purified.

15"Then the priest will pour some of the olive oil into the palm of his own left hand. 16He will dip his right finger into the oil in his palm and sprinkle some of it with his finger seven times before the LORD. 17The priest will then apply some of the oil in his palm over the blood from the guilt offering that is on the lobe of the right ear, the thumb of the right hand, and the big toe of the right foot of the person being purified. 18The priest will apply the oil remaining in his hand to the head of the person being purified.

Through this process, the priest will purify the
person before the LORD.
19"Then the priest must present the sin offering to purify the person who was cured of the
skin disease. After that, the priest will slaughter
the burnt offering 20and offer it on the altar
along with the grain offering. Through this process, the priest will purify the person who was
healed, and the person will be ceremonially
clean.

21"But anyone who is too poor and cannot afford these offerings may bring one male lamb
for a guilt offering, to be lifted up as a special offering for purification. The person must also
bring two quarts of choice flour moistened with
olive oil for the grain offering and a cup of olive
oil. 22The offering must also include two turtledoves or two young pigeons, whichever the person can afford. One of the pair must be used for
the sin offering and the other for a burnt offering. 23On the eighth day of the purification ceremony, the person being purified must bring the
offerings to the priest in the LORD's presence at
the entrance of the Tabernacle. 24The priest will
take the lamb for the guilt offering, along with
the olive oil, and lift them up as a special offering to the LORD. 25Then the priest will slaughter
the lamb for the guilt offering. He will take some
of its blood and apply it to the lobe of the right
ear, the thumb of the right hand, and the big toe
of the right foot of the person being purified.

26"The priest will also pour some of the olive
oil into the palm of his own left hand. 27He will
dip his right finger into the oil in his palm and
sprinkle some of it seven times before the LORD.
28The priest will then apply some of the oil in
his palm over the blood from the guilt offering
that is on the lobe of the right ear, the thumb of
the right hand, and the big toe of the right foot
of the person being purified. 29The priest will
apply the oil remaining in his hand to the head
of the person being purified. Through this process, the priest will purify the person before the
LORD.

30"Then the priest will offer the two turtledoves or the two young pigeons, whichever the
person can afford. 31One of them is for a sin offering and the other for a burnt offering, to be
presented along with the grain offering.
Through this process, the priest will purify the
person before the LORD. 32These are the instructions for purification for those who have recovered from a serious skin disease but who cannot
afford to bring the offerings normally required
for the ceremony of purification."

Treatment of Contaminated Houses

33Then the LORD said to Moses and Aaron,
34"When you arrive in Canaan, the land I am giving you as your own possession, I may contaminate some of the houses in your land with
mildew. 35The owner of such a house must then
go to the priest and say, 'It appears that my house
has some kind of mildew.' 36Before the priest
goes in to inspect the house, he must have
the house emptied so nothing inside will be pronounced ceremonially unclean. 37Then the
priest will go in and examine the mildew on the
walls. If he finds greenish or reddish streaks and
the contamination appears to go deeper than the
wall's surface, 38the priest will step outside the
door and put the house in quarantine for seven
days. 39On the seventh day the priest must return
for another inspection. If he finds that the mildew on the walls of the house has spread, 40the
priest must order that the stones from those areas be removed. The contaminated material will
then be taken outside the town to an area designated as ceremonially unclean. 41Next the inside
walls of the entire house must be scraped thoroughly and the scrapings dumped in the unclean
place outside the town. 42Other stones will be
brought in to replace the ones that were removed, and the walls will be replastered.

43"But if the mildew reappears after all the
stones have been replaced and the house has
been scraped and replastered, 44the priest must
return and inspect the house again. If he finds
that the mildew has spread, the walls are clearly
contaminated with a serious mildew, and the
house is defiled. 45It must be torn down, and all
its stones, timbers, and plaster must be carried
out of town to the place designated as ceremonially unclean. 46Those who enter the house during the period of quarantine will be ceremonially
unclean until evening, 47and all who sleep or eat
in the house must wash their clothing.

48"But if the priest returns for his inspection
and finds that the mildew has not reappeared in
the house after the fresh plastering, he will pronounce it clean because the mildew is clearly
gone. 49To purify the house the priest must take
two birds, a stick of cedar, some scarlet yarn, and
a hyssop branch. 50He will slaughter one of the
birds over a clay pot filled with fresh water. 51He
will take the cedar stick, the hyssop branch, the
scarlet yarn, and the live bird, and dip them into
the blood of the slaughtered bird and into the
fresh water. Then he will sprinkle the house
seven times. 52When the priest has purified the

house in exactly this way, 53he will release the
live bird in the open fields outside the town.
Through this process, the priest will purify the
house, and it will be ceremonially clean.

54"These are the instructions for dealing with
serious skin diseases, including scabby sores;
55and mildew, whether on clothing or in a house;
56and a swelling on the skin, a rash, or discolored
skin. 57This procedure will determine whether
a person or object is ceremonially clean or unclean.

"These are the instructions regarding skin diseases and mildew."

CHAPTER 15

Bodily Discharges

The LORD said to Moses and Aaron, 2"Give the
following instructions to the people of Israel.

"Any man who has a bodily discharge is ceremonially unclean. 3This defilement is caused by
his discharge, whether the discharge continues
or stops. In either case the man is unclean. 4Any
bed on which the man with the discharge lies
and anything on which he sits will be ceremonially unclean. 5So if you touch the man's bed, you
must wash your clothes and bathe yourself in
water, and you will remain unclean until evening. 6If you sit where the man with the discharge has sat, you must wash your clothes and
bathe yourself in water, and you will remain unclean until evening. 7If you touch the man with
the discharge, you must wash your clothes and
bathe yourself in water, and you will remain unclean until evening. 8If the man spits on you, you
must wash your clothes and bathe yourself in
water, and you will remain unclean until evening. 9Any saddle blanket on which the man
rides will be ceremonially unclean. 10If you
touch anything that was under the man, you will
be unclean until evening. You must wash your
clothes and bathe yourself in water, and you will
remain unclean until evening. 11If the man
touches you without first rinsing his hands, you
must wash your clothes and bathe yourself in
water, and you will remain unclean until evening. 12Any clay pot the man touches must be
broken, and any wooden utensil he touches
must be rinsed with water.

13"When the man with the discharge is
healed, he must count off seven days for the period of purification. Then he must wash his
clothes and bathe himself in fresh water, and he
will be ceremonially clean. 14On the eighth day
he must get two turtledoves or two young pigeons and come before the LORD at the entrance
of the Tabernacle and give his offerings to the
priest. 15The priest will offer one bird for a sin
offering and the other for a burnt offering.
Through this process, the priest will purify the
man before the LORD for his discharge.

16"Whenever a man has an emission of semen, he must bathe his entire body in water, and
he will remain ceremonially unclean until the
next evening. 17Any clothing or leather with semen on it must be washed in water, and it will remain unclean until evening. 18After a man and a
woman have sexual intercourse, they must each
bathe in water, and they will remain unclean until the next evening.

19"Whenever a woman has her menstrual period, she will be ceremonially unclean for seven
days. Anyone who touches her during that time
will be unclean until evening. 20Anything on
which the woman lies or sits during the time of
her period will be unclean. 21If any of you touch
her bed, you must wash your clothes and bathe
yourself in water, and you will remain unclean
until evening. 22If you touch any object she has
sat on, you must wash your clothes and bathe
yourself in water, and you will remain unclean
until evening. 23This includes her bed or any
other object she has sat on; you will be unclean
until evening if you touch it. 24If a man has sexual intercourse with her and her blood touches
him, her menstrual impurity will be transmitted
to him. He will remain unclean for seven days,
and any bed on which he lies will be unclean.

25"If a woman has a flow of blood for many
days that is unrelated to her menstrual period, or
if the blood continues beyond the normal period, she is ceremonially unclean. As during her
menstrual period, the woman will be unclean as
long as the discharge continues. 26Any bed she
lies on and any object she sits on during that
time will be unclean, just as during her normal
menstrual period. 27If any of you touch these
things, you will be ceremonially unclean. You
must wash your clothes and bathe yourself in
water, and you will remain unclean until evening.

28"When the woman's bleeding stops, she
must count off seven days. Then she will be ceremonially clean. 29On the eighth day she must
bring two turtledoves or two young pigeons and
present them to the priest at the entrance of the
Tabernacle. 30The priest will offer one for a sin
offering and the other for a burnt offering.
Through this process, the priest will purify her
before the LORD for the ceremonial impurity
caused by her bleeding.

31"This is how you will guard the people of

Israel from ceremonial uncleanness. Otherwise they would die, for their impurity would defile my Tabernacle that stands among them. 32These are the instructions for dealing with anyone who has a bodily discharge—a man who is unclean because of an emission of semen 33or a woman during her menstrual period. It applies to any man or woman who has a bodily discharge, and to a man who has sexual intercourse with a woman who is ceremonially unclean."

CHAPTER 16

The Day of Atonement

The LORD spoke to Moses after the death of Aaron's two sons, who died after they entered the LORD's presence and burned the wrong kind of fire before him. 2The LORD said to Moses, "Warn your brother, Aaron, not to enter the Most Holy Place behind the inner curtain whenever he chooses; if he does, he will die. For the Ark's cover—the place of atonement—is there, and I myself am present in the cloud above the atonement cover.

3"When Aaron enters the sanctuary area, he must follow these instructions fully. He must bring a young bull for a sin offering and a ram for a burnt offering. 4He must put on his linen tunic and the linen undergarments worn next to his body. He must tie the linen sash around his waist and put the linen turban on his head. These are sacred garments, so he must bathe himself in water before he puts them on. 5Aaron must take from the community of Israel two male goats for a sin offering and a ram for a burnt offering.

6"Aaron will present his own bull as a sin offering to purify himself and his family, making them right with the LORD. 7Then he must take the two male goats and present them to the LORD at the entrance of the Tabernacle. 8He is to cast sacred lots to determine which goat will be reserved as an offering to the LORD and which will carry the sins of the people to the wilderness of Azazel. 9Aaron will then present as a sin offering the goat chosen by lot for the LORD. 10The other goat, the scapegoat chosen by lot to be sent away, will be kept alive, standing before the LORD. When it is sent away to Azazel in the wilderness, the people will be purified and made right with the LORD.

11"Aaron will present his own bull as a sin offering to purify himself and his family, making them right with the LORD. After he has slaughtered the bull as a sin offering, 12he will fill an incense burner with burning coals from the altar that stands before the LORD. Then he will take two handfuls of fragrant powdered incense and will carry the burner and the incense behind the inner curtain. 13There in the LORD's presence he will put the incense on the burning coals so that a cloud of incense will rise over the Ark's cover—the place of atonement—that rests on the Ark of the Covenant. If he follows these instructions, he will not die. 14Then he must take some of the blood of the bull, dip his finger in it, and sprinkle it on the east side of the atonement cover. He must sprinkle blood seven times with his finger in front of the atonement cover.

15"Then Aaron must slaughter the first goat as a sin offering for the people and carry its blood behind the inner curtain. There he will sprinkle the goat's blood over the atonement cover and in front of it, just as he did with the bull's blood. 16Through this process, he will purify the Most Holy Place, and he will do the same for the entire Tabernacle, because of the defiling sin and rebellion of the Israelites. 17No one else is allowed inside the Tabernacle when Aaron enters it for the purification ceremony in the Most Holy Place. No one may enter until he comes out again after purifying himself, his family, and all the congregation of Israel, making them right with the LORD.

18"Then Aaron will come out to purify the altar that stands before the LORD. He will do this by taking some of the blood from the bull and the goat and putting it on each of the horns of the altar. 19Then he must sprinkle the blood with his finger seven times over the altar. In this way, he will cleanse it from Israel's defilement and make it holy.

20"When Aaron has finished purifying the Most Holy Place and the Tabernacle and the altar, he must present the live goat. 21He will lay both of his hands on the goat's head and confess over it all the wickedness, rebellion, and sins of the people of Israel. In this way, he will transfer the people's sins to the head of the goat. Then a man specially chosen for the task will drive the goat into the wilderness. 22As the goat goes into the wilderness, it will carry all the people's sins upon itself into a desolate land.

23"When Aaron goes back into the Tabernacle, he must take off the linen garments he was wearing when he entered the Most Holy Place, and he must leave the garments there. 24Then he must bathe himself with water in a sacred place, put on his regular garments, and go out to sacrifice a burnt offering for himself and a burnt offering for the people. Through this process, he will purify himself and the people, mak-

ing them right with the LORD. 25He must then
burn all the fat of the sin offering on the altar.
26"The man chosen to drive the scapegoat
into the wilderness of Azazel must wash his
clothes and bathe himself in water. Then he may
return to the camp.
27"The bull and the goat presented as sin offerings, whose blood Aaron takes into the Most
Holy Place for the purification ceremony, will be
carried outside the camp. The animals' hides, internal organs, and dung are all to be burned.
28The man who burns them must wash his
clothes and bathe himself in water before returning to the camp.
29"On the tenth day of the appointed month in
early autumn, you must deny yourselves. Neither
native-born Israelites nor foreigners living
among you may do any kind of work. This is a
permanent law for you. 30On that day offerings
of purification will be made for you, and you will
be purified in the LORD's presence from all your
sins. 31It will be a Sabbath day of complete rest
for you, and you must deny yourselves. This is a
permanent law for you. 32In future generations,
the purification ceremony will be performed by
the priest who has been anointed and ordained
to serve as high priest in place of his ancestor
Aaron. He will put on the holy linen garments
33and purify the Most Holy Place, the Tabernacle,
the altar, the priests, and the entire congregation.
34This is a permanent law for you, to purify the
people of Israel from their sins, making them
right with the LORD once each year."

Moses followed all these instructions exactly as the LORD had commanded him.

CHAPTER 17

Prohibitions against Eating Blood

Then the LORD said to Moses, 2"Give the following instructions to Aaron and his sons and all the
people of Israel. This is what the LORD has commanded.
3"If any native Israelite sacrifices a bull or a
lamb or a goat anywhere inside or outside the
camp 4instead of bringing it to the entrance of
the Tabernacle to present it as an offering to the
LORD, that person will be as guilty as a murderer.
Such a person has shed blood and will be cut off
from the community. 5The purpose of this rule
is to stop the Israelites from sacrificing animals
in the open fields. It will ensure that they bring
their sacrifices to the priest at the entrance of
the Tabernacle, so he can present them to the
LORD as peace offerings. 6Then the priest will be

FUN-fact
Has the Herd Heard?

The Bible says the penalty for sin is death. So the Israelites sacrificed animals in their place when they sinned.

THEIR HERDS MUST HAVE FELT PRETTY NERVOUS!

TAKE THIS TEST . . .

- ☐ **Have you ever lied?**
- ☐ **Hit your brother or sister?**
- ☐ **Disobeyed your parents?**

If you have, you've sinned. The Bible says everyone sins. But there's good news: **You don't have to sacrifice an animal or anything else for your sin.** When Jesus died on the cross, his sacrifice took care of our sins completely. If you believe in Jesus, you will live forever with him in heaven.

HAVE YOU HEARD? Ask an adult Christian what it means to be a Christian. Here's a suggested prayer that will help you: ***Lord Jesus, thank you for dying on the cross for my sins. I believe in you and receive you as my Savior and Lord. Thank you for forgiving my sins and giving me eternal life. Amen.***

able to splatter the blood against the LORD's altar at the entrance of the Tabernacle, and he will burn the fat as a pleasing aroma to the LORD. 7The people must no longer be unfaithful to the LORD by offering sacrifices to the goat idols. This is a permanent law for them, to be observed from generation to generation.

8"Give them this command as well. If any native Israelite or foreigner living among you offers a burnt offering or a sacrifice 9but does not bring it to the entrance of the Tabernacle to offer it to the LORD, that person will be cut off from the community.

10"And if any native Israelite or foreigner living among you eats or drinks blood in any form, I will turn against that person and cut him off from the community of your people, 11for the life of the body is in its blood. I have given you the blood on the altar to purify you, making you right with the LORD. It is the blood, given in exchange for a life, that makes purification possible. 12That is why I have said to the people of Israel, 'You must never eat or drink blood—neither you nor the foreigners living among you.'

13"And if any native Israelite or foreigner living among you goes hunting and kills an animal or bird that is approved for eating, he must drain its blood and cover it with earth. 14The life of every creature is in its blood. That is why I have said to the people of Israel, 'You must never eat or drink blood, for the life of any creature is in its blood.' So whoever consumes blood will be cut off from the community.

15"And if any native-born Israelites or foreigners eat the meat of an animal that died naturally or was torn up by wild animals, they must wash their clothes and bathe themselves in water. They will remain ceremonially unclean until evening, but then they will be clean. 16But if they do not wash their clothes and bathe themselves, they will be punished for their sin."

CHAPTER 18

Forbidden Sexual Practices

Then the LORD said to Moses, 2"Give the following instructions to the people of Israel. I am the LORD your God. 3So do not act like the people in Egypt, where you used to live, or like the people of Canaan, where I am taking you. You must not imitate their way of life. 4You must obey all my regulations and be careful to obey my decrees, for I am the LORD your God. 5If you obey my decrees and my regulations, you will find life through them. I am the LORD.

6"You must never have sexual relations with a close relative, for I am the LORD.

7"Do not violate your father by having sexual relations with your mother. She is your mother; you must not have sexual relations with her.

8"Do not have sexual relations with any of your father's wives, for this would violate your father.

9"Do not have sexual relations with your sister or half sister, whether she is your father's daughter or your mother's daughter, whether she was born into your household or someone else's.

10"Do not have sexual relations with your granddaughter, whether she is your son's daughter or your daughter's daughter, for this would violate yourself.

11"Do not have sexual relations with your stepsister, the daughter of any of your father's wives, for she is your sister.

12"Do not have sexual relations with your father's sister, for she is your father's close relative.

13"Do not have sexual relations with your mother's sister, for she is your mother's close relative.

14"Do not violate your uncle, your father's brother, by having sexual relations with his wife, for she is your aunt.

15"Do not have sexual relations with your daughter-in-law; she is your son's wife, so you must not have sexual relations with her.

16"Do not have sexual relations with your brother's wife, for this would violate your brother.

17"Do not have sexual relations with both a woman and her daughter. And do not take her granddaughter, whether her son's daughter or her daughter's daughter, and have sexual relations with her. They are close relatives, and this would be a wicked act.

18"While your wife is living, do not marry her sister and have sexual relations with her, for they would be rivals.

19"Do not have sexual relations with a woman during her period of menstrual impurity.

20"Do not defile yourself by having sexual intercourse with your neighbor's wife.

21"Do not permit any of your children to be offered as a sacrifice to Molech, for you must not bring shame on the name of your God. I am the LORD.

22"Do not practice homosexuality, having sex with another man as with a woman. It is a detestable sin.

23"A man must not defile himself by having sex with an animal. And a woman must not offer

herself to a male animal to have intercourse with
it. This is a perverse act.
24"Do not defile yourselves in any of these
ways, for the people I am driving out before you
have defiled themselves in all these ways. 25Be-
cause the entire land has become defiled, I am
punishing the people who live there. I will cause
the land to vomit them out. 26You must obey all
my decrees and regulations. You must not commit any of these detestable sins. This applies
both to native-born Israelites and to the foreigners living among you.
27"All these detestable activities are practiced
by the people of the land where I am taking you,
and this is how the land has become defiled. 28So
do not defile the land and give it a reason to
vomit you out, as it will vomit out the people who
live there now. 29Whoever commits any of these
detestable sins will be cut off from the community of Israel. 30So obey my instructions, and do
not defile yourselves by committing any of these
detestable practices that were committed by the
people who lived in the land before you. I am the
LORD your God."

CHAPTER 19
Holiness in Personal Conduct

The LORD also said to Moses, 2"Give the following
instructions to the entire community of Israel.
You must be holy because I, the LORD your God,
am holy.
3"Each of you must show great respect for
your mother and father, and you must always
observe my Sabbath days of rest. I am the LORD
your God.
4"Do not put your trust in idols or make metal
images of gods for yourselves. I am the LORD
your God.
5"When you sacrifice a peace offering to the
LORD, offer it properly so you will be accepted by
God. 6The sacrifice must be eaten on the same
day you offer it or on the next day. Whatever is
left over until the third day must be completely
burned up. 7If any of the sacrifice is eaten on the
third day, it will be contaminated, and I will not
accept it. 8Anyone who eats it on the third day
will be punished for defiling what is holy to the
LORD and will be cut off from the community.
9"When you harvest the crops of your land, do
not harvest the grain along the edges of your
fields, and do not pick up what the harvesters
drop. 10It is the same with your grape crop—do
not strip every last bunch of grapes from the
vines, and do not pick up the grapes that fall to
the ground. Leave them for the poor and the foreigners living among you. I am the LORD your
God.
11"Do not steal.
"Do not deceive or cheat one another.
12"Do not bring shame on the name of your
God by using it to swear falsely. I am the LORD.
13"Do not defraud or rob your neighbor.
"Do not make your hired workers wait until
the next day to receive their pay.
14"Do not insult the deaf or cause the blind to
stumble. You must fear your God; I am the LORD.
15"Do not twist justice in legal matters by favoring the poor or being partial to the rich and
powerful. Always judge people fairly.
16"Do not spread slanderous gossip among
your people.
"Do not stand idly by when your neighbor's
life is threatened. I am the LORD.
17"Do not nurse hatred in your heart for any of
your relatives. Confront people directly so you
will not be held guilty for their sin.
18"Do not seek revenge or bear a grudge
against a fellow Israelite, but love your neighbor
as yourself. I am the LORD.
19"You must obey all my decrees.
"Do not mate two different kinds of animals.
Do not plant your field with two different kinds
of seed. Do not wear clothing woven from two
different kinds of thread.
20"If a man has sex with a slave girl whose
freedom has never been purchased but who is
committed to become another man's wife, he
must pay full compensation to her master. But
since she is not a free woman, neither the man
nor the woman will be put to death. 21The man,
however, must bring a ram as a guilt offering and
present it to the LORD at the entrance of the Tabernacle. 22The priest will then purify him before
the LORD with the ram of the guilt offering, and
the man's sin will be forgiven.
23"When you enter the land and plant fruit
trees, leave the fruit unharvested for the first
three years and consider it forbidden. Do not eat
it. 24In the fourth year the entire crop must be
consecrated to the LORD as a celebration of
praise. 25Finally, in the fifth year you may eat the
fruit. If you follow this pattern, your harvest will
increase. I am the LORD your God.
26"Do not eat meat that has not been drained
of its blood.
"Do not practice fortune-telling or witchcraft.
27"Do not trim off the hair on your temples or
trim your beards.
28"Do not cut your bodies for the dead, and do
not mark your skin with tattoos. I am the LORD.

29"Do not defile your daughter by making her a prostitute, or the land will be filled with prostitution and wickedness.

30"Keep my Sabbath days of rest, and show reverence toward my sanctuary. I am the LORD.

31"Do not defile yourselves by turning to mediums or to those who consult the spirits of the dead. I am the LORD your God.

32"Stand up in the presence of the elderly, and show respect for the aged. Fear your God. I am the LORD.

33"Do not take advantage of foreigners who live among you in your land. 34Treat them like native-born Israelites, and love them as you love yourself. Remember that you were once foreigners living in the land of Egypt. I am the LORD your God.

35"Do not use dishonest standards when measuring length, weight, or volume. 36Your scales and weights must be accurate. Your containers for measuring dry materials or liquids must be accurate. I am the LORD your God who brought you out of the land of Egypt.

37"You must be careful to keep all of my decrees and regulations by putting them into practice. I am the LORD."

CHAPTER 20

Punishments for Disobedience

The LORD said to Moses, 2"Give the people of Israel these instructions, which apply both to native Israelites and to the foreigners living in Israel.

"If any of them offer their children as a sacrifice to Molech, they must be put to death. The people of the community must stone them to death. 3I myself will turn against them and cut them off from the community, because they have defiled my sanctuary and brought shame on my holy name by offering their children to Molech. 4And if the people of the community ignore those who offer their children to Molech and refuse to execute them, 5I myself will turn against them and their families and will cut them off from the community. This will happen to all who commit spiritual prostitution by worshiping Molech.

6"I will also turn against those who commit spiritual prostitution by putting their trust in mediums or in those who consult the spirits of the dead. I will cut them off from the community. 7So set yourselves apart to be holy, for I am the LORD your God. 8Keep all my decrees by putting them into practice, for I am the LORD who makes you holy.

9"Anyone who dishonors father or mother must be put to death. Such a person is guilty of a capital offense.

10"If a man commits adultery with his neighbor's wife, both the man and the woman who have committed adultery must be put to death.

11"If a man violates his father by having sex with one of his father's wives, both the man and the woman must be put to death, for they are guilty of a capital offense.

12"If a man has sex with his daughter-in-law, both must be put to death. They have committed a perverse act and are guilty of a capital offense.

13"If a man practices homosexuality, having sex with another man as with a woman, both men have committed a detestable act. They must both be put to death, for they are guilty of a capital offense.

14"If a man marries both a woman and her mother, he has committed a wicked act. The man and both women must be burned to death to wipe out such wickedness from among you.

15"If a man has sex with an animal, he must be put to death, and the animal must be killed.

16"If a woman presents herself to a male animal to have intercourse with it, she and the animal must both be put to death. You must kill both, for they are guilty of a capital offense.

17"If a man marries his sister, the daughter of either his father or his mother, and they have sexual relations, it is a shameful disgrace. They must be publicly cut off from the community. Since the man has violated his sister, he will be punished for his sin.

18"If a man has sexual relations with a woman during her menstrual period, both of them must be cut off from the community, for together they have exposed the source of her blood flow.

19"Do not have sexual relations with your aunt, whether your mother's sister or your father's sister. This would dishonor a close relative. Both parties are guilty and will be punished for their sin.

20"If a man has sex with his uncle's wife, he has violated his uncle. Both the man and woman will be punished for their sin, and they will die childless.

21"If a man marries his brother's wife, it is an act of impurity. He has violated his brother, and the guilty couple will remain childless.

22"You must keep all my decrees and regulations by putting them into practice; otherwise the land to which I am bringing you as your new home will vomit you out. 23Do not live according to the customs of the people I am driving out before you. It is because they do these shameful things that I detest them. 24But I have promised you, 'You will possess their land because I will give it to you as your possession—a land flowing with milk and honey.' I am the LORD your God, who has set you apart from all other people.

25"You must therefore make a distinction between ceremonially clean and unclean animals, and between clean and unclean birds. You must not defile yourselves by eating any unclean animal or bird or creature that scurries along the ground. I have identified them as being unclean for you. 26You must be holy because I, the LORD, am holy. I have set you apart from all other people to be my very own.

27"Men and women among you who act as mediums or who consult the spirits of the dead must be put to death by stoning. They are guilty of a capital offense."

CHAPTER 21
Instructions for the Priests

The LORD said to Moses, "Give the following instructions to the priests, the descendants of Aaron.

"A priest must not make himself ceremonially unclean by touching the dead body of a relative. 2The only exceptions are his closest relatives—his mother or father, son or daughter, brother, 3or his virgin sister who depends on him because she has no husband. 4But a priest must not defile himself and make himself unclean for someone who is related to him only by marriage.

5"The priests must not shave their heads or trim their beards or cut their bodies. 6They must be set apart as holy to their God and must never bring shame on the name of God. They must be holy, for they are the ones who present the special gifts to the LORD, gifts of food for their God.

7"Priests may not marry a woman defiled by prostitution, and they may not marry a woman who is divorced from her husband, for the priests are set apart as holy to their God. 8You must treat them as holy because they offer up food to your God. You must consider them holy because I, the LORD, am holy, and I make you holy.

9"If a priest's daughter defiles herself by becoming a prostitute, she also defiles her father's holiness, and she must be burned to death.

10"The high priest has the highest rank of all the priests. The anointing oil has been poured on his head, and he has been ordained to wear the priestly garments. He must never leave his hair uncombed or tear his clothing. 11He must not defile himself by going near a dead body. He may not make himself ceremonially unclean even for his father or mother. 12He must not defile the sanctuary of his God by leaving it to attend to a dead person, for he has been made holy by the anointing oil of his God. I am the LORD.

13"The high priest may marry only a virgin. 14He may not marry a widow, a woman who is divorced, or a woman who has defiled herself by prostitution. She must be a virgin from his own clan, 15so that he will not dishonor his descendants among his clan, for I am the LORD who makes him holy."

16Then the LORD said to Moses, 17"Give the following instructions to Aaron: In all future generations, none of your descendants who has any defect will qualify to offer food to his God. 18No one who has a defect qualifies, whether he is blind, lame, disfigured, deformed, 19or has a broken foot or arm, 20or is hunchbacked or dwarfed, or has a defective eye, or skin sores or scabs, or damaged testicles. 21No descendant of Aaron who has a defect may approach the altar to present special gifts to the LORD. Since he has a defect, he may not approach the altar to offer food to his God. 22However, he may eat from the food offered to God, including the holy offerings and the most holy offerings. 23Yet because of his physical defect, he may not enter the room behind the inner curtain or approach the altar, for this would defile my holy places. I am the LORD who makes them holy."

24So Moses gave these instructions to Aaron and his sons and to all the Israelites.

CHAPTER 22

The LORD said to Moses, 2"Tell Aaron and his sons to be very careful with the sacred gifts that the Israelites set apart for me, so they do not bring shame on my holy name. I am the LORD. 3Give them the following instructions.

"In all future generations, if any of your descendants is ceremonially unclean when he approaches the sacred offerings that the people of Israel consecrate to the LORD, he must be cut off from my presence. I am the LORD.

4"If any of Aaron's descendants has a skin disease or any kind of discharge that makes him ceremonially unclean, he may not eat from the sacred offerings until he has been pronounced clean. He also becomes unclean by touching a corpse, or by having an emission of semen, 5or by touching a small animal that is unclean, or by touching someone who is ceremonially unclean for any reason. 6The man who is defiled in any of these ways will remain unclean until evening. He may not eat from the sacred offerings until he has bathed himself in water. 7When the sun goes down, he will be ceremonially clean again and may eat from the sacred offerings, for this is his food. 8He may not eat an animal that has died a natural death or has been torn apart by wild animals, for this would defile him. I am the LORD.

9"The priests must follow my instructions carefully. Otherwise they will be punished for their sin and will die for violating my instructions. I am the LORD who makes them holy.

10"No one outside a priest's family may eat the sacred offerings. Even guests and hired workers in a priest's home are not allowed to eat them. 11However, if the priest buys a slave for himself, the slave may eat from the sacred offerings. And if his slaves have children, they also may share his food. 12If a priest's daughter marries someone outside the priestly family, she may no longer eat the sacred offerings. 13But if she becomes a widow or is divorced and has no children to support her, and she returns to live in her father's home as in her youth, she may eat her father's food again. Otherwise, no one outside a priest's family may eat the sacred offerings.

14"Any such person who eats the sacred offerings without realizing it must pay the priest for the amount eaten, plus an additional 20 percent. 15The priests must not let the Israelites defile the sacred offerings brought to the LORD 16by allowing unauthorized people to eat them. This would bring guilt upon them and require them to pay compensation. I am the LORD who makes them holy."

Worthy and Unworthy Offerings

17And the LORD said to Moses, 18"Give Aaron and his sons and all the Israelites these instructions, which apply both to native Israelites and to the foreigners living among you.

"If you present a gift as a burnt offering to the LORD, whether it is to fulfill a vow or is a voluntary offering, 19you will be accepted only if your offering is a male animal with no defects. It may be a bull, a ram, or a male goat. 20Do not present an animal with defects, because the LORD will not accept it on your behalf.

21"If you present a peace offering to the LORD from the herd or the flock, whether it is to fulfill a vow or is a voluntary offering, you must offer a perfect animal. It may have no defect of any kind. 22You must not offer an animal that is blind, crippled, or injured, or that has a wart, a skin sore, or scabs. Such animals must never be offered on the altar as special gifts to the LORD. 23If a bull or lamb has a leg that is too long or too short, it may be offered as a voluntary offering, but it may not be offered to fulfill a vow. 24If an animal has damaged testicles or is castrated, you may not offer it to the LORD. You must never do this in your own land, 25and you must not accept such an animal from foreigners and then offer it as a sacrifice to your God. Such animals will not be accepted on your behalf, for they are mutilated or defective."

26And the LORD said to Moses, 27"When a calf or lamb or goat is born, it must be left with its mother for seven days. From the eighth day on, it will be acceptable as a special gift to the LORD. 28But you must not slaughter a mother animal and her offspring on the same day, whether from the herd or the flock. 29When you bring a thanksgiving offering to the LORD, sacrifice it properly so you will be accepted. 30Eat the entire sacrificial animal on the day it is presented. Do not leave any of it until the next morning. I am the LORD.

31"You must faithfully keep all my commands by putting them into practice, for I am the LORD. 32Do not bring shame on my holy name, for I will display my holiness among the people of Israel. I am the LORD who makes you holy. 33It was I who rescued you from the land of Egypt, that I might be your God. I am the LORD."

CHAPTER 23

The Appointed Festivals

The LORD said to Moses, 2"Give the following instructions to the people of Israel. These are the LORD's appointed festivals, which you are to proclaim as official days for holy assembly.

3"You have six days each week for your ordinary work, but the seventh day is a Sabbath day of complete rest, an official day for holy assembly. It is the LORD's Sabbath day, and it must be observed wherever you live.

4"In addition to the Sabbath, these are the LORD's appointed festivals, the official days for holy assembly that are to be celebrated at their proper times each year.

Passover and the Festival of Unleavened Bread

5"The LORD's Passover begins at sundown on the fourteenth day of the first month. 6On the next day, the fifteenth day of the month, you must begin celebrating the Festival of Unleavened Bread. This festival to the LORD continues for seven days, and during that time the bread you

BIBLE BIOS

Hear From the Heroes

Hi, my name is

GIDEON *(farmer, warrior, judge)*

I sure didn't feel like a mighty hero.

I was just about the least important guy in all of Israel. In fact, I was *hiding* from our enemies, the Midianites, when the angel appeared and said, "Mighty hero, the Lord is with you." I just wanted to say, "Whatever. Don't you see that I'm hiding?" Instead, I asked God to give me a sign. God clearly showed me that he wanted me to lead the people of Israel against the Midianites.

HEBREWS 11:32-34 may give us a clue about why God chose Gideon. What do you think?

Gideon asked for all sorts of signs and proof that God wanted him to lead the people in battle. Read all about them in JUDGES 6:15-21; 6:36-40; and 7:9-15.

Even though God told me to fight, I still felt pretty nervous. We had 32,000 men, and there were about 135,000 of our enemies. I think my jaw fell all the way to the ground when God told me to send home everyone except 300 men! Imagine that you were playing a game of soccer. Your team had 11 people. The other team was really grumpy, they really didn't like you, and they had 4,950 players—all on the field at the same time! Winning might seem impossible—unless God's on your side.

Read JUDGES 7:2-8 to learn about the cool ways God showed Gideon which men would stay.

And God was on our side. All 300 of us sneaked around the Midianite camp really early in the morning. We held up our torches and yelled out. Check out what happened in **JUDGES 7:19-24.** I can't really say that I'm a courageous person, and I still don't really feel like a mighty hero. But with God on my side, that's exactly what I am. I mean, if God is for us, who can ever be against us?

World's Strongest Kid

Find an old phone book.

Ask a really strong person you know to try to rip the phone book in half. Tell Sergeant Strength to hand the book back over to you. Show him or her how you can rip the phone book in half. Just start ripping it a few pages at a time. Before your volunteer leaves (or squishes you), tell him or her about how God helped Gideon do the impossible.

BIBLE BIOS

Hear From the Heroes

Hi, my name is

DAVID *(shepherd, musician, warrior, king)*

God has done some big things through me. With a sling and a stone, I beat Goliath, the great Philistine giant. Some people say I was the greatest king Israel ever had. God promised that the Messiah would come from my family. God even used me to write part of the Bible! I'm thankful for all of that, but all that stuff doesn't really matter that much to me.

The Messiah was the ruler God promised would come to bring freedom to God's people. Jesus was the promised Messiah.

David wrote a lot of the book of Psalms. Check out what he wrote in PSALM 27!

If there's one thing that I always wanted, it was just to be with God. In good and bad times, God stayed near to me. And God was the only one who really made me happy. After God chose me to be the future king of Israel, King Saul tried to kill me and chased me all over the place. One time, I acted completely crazy to get away! Even then I knew God was with me. After I sinned and made mistakes, God was still with me. When I was crowned king over all of Israel, God was with me.

Want to know more of David's story? Read 1 SAMUEL 21:10-15.

I've experienced some amazing things, and people call me a great hero of Israel. But nothing is better or more important than just being with God. I hope you learn to make your relationship with God the most important thing in your life. Start right now by asking God to help you know him more.

Write It!

Read what David wrote to God in PSALM 27:4.

If you could ask any one thing of God, what would you ask? Find a notebook and start a prayer journal. Write down the questions that you have for God, the reasons you love God, and your prayers about what you and others need.

Remember to look back in your journal from time to time to see how God answered.

eat must be made without yeast. 7On the first day of the festival, all the people must stop their ordinary work and observe an official day for holy assembly. 8For seven days you must present special gifts to the LORD. On the seventh day the people must again stop all their ordinary work to observe an official day for holy assembly."

Celebration of First Harvest

9Then the LORD said to Moses, 10"Give the following instructions to the people of Israel. When you enter the land I am giving you and you harvest its first crops, bring the priest a bundle of grain from the first cutting of your grain harvest. 11On the day after the Sabbath, the priest will lift it up before the LORD so it may be accepted on your behalf. 12On that same day you must sacrifice a one-year-old male lamb with no defects as a burnt offering to the LORD. 13With it you must present a grain offering consisting of four quarts of choice flour moistened with olive oil. It will be a special gift, a pleasing aroma to the LORD. You must also offer one quart of wine as a liquid offering. 14Do not eat any bread or roasted grain or fresh kernels on that day until you bring this offering to your God. This is a permanent law for you, and it must be observed from generation to generation wherever you live.

The Festival of Harvest

15"From the day after the Sabbath—the day you bring the bundle of grain to be lifted up as a special offering—count off seven full weeks. 16Keep counting until the day after the seventh Sabbath, fifty days later. Then present an offering of new grain to the LORD. 17From wherever you live, bring two loaves of bread to be lifted up before the LORD as a special offering. Make these loaves from four quarts of choice flour, and bake them with yeast. They will be an offering to the LORD from the first of your crops. 18Along with the bread, present seven one-year-old male lambs with no defects, one young bull, and two rams as burnt offerings to the LORD. These burnt offerings, together with the grain offerings and liquid offerings, will be a special gift, a pleasing aroma to the LORD. 19Then you must offer one male goat as a sin offering and two one-year-old male lambs as a peace offering.

20"The priest will lift up the two lambs as a special offering to the LORD, together with the loaves representing the first of your crops. These offerings, which are holy to the LORD, belong to the priests. 21That same day will be proclaimed an official day for holy assembly, a day on which you do no ordinary work. This is a permanent law for you, and it must be observed from generation to generation wherever you live.

22"When you harvest the crops of your land, do not harvest the grain along the edges of your fields, and do not pick up what the harvesters drop. Leave it for the poor and the foreigners living among you. I am the LORD your God."

The Festival of Trumpets

23The LORD said to Moses, 24"Give the following instructions to the people of Israel. On the first day of the appointed month in early autumn, you are to observe a day of complete rest. It will be an official day for holy assembly, a day commemorated with loud blasts of a trumpet. 25You must do no ordinary work on that day. Instead, you are to present special gifts to the LORD."

The Day of Atonement

26Then the LORD said to Moses, 27"Be careful to celebrate the Day of Atonement on the tenth day of that same month—nine days after the Festival of Trumpets. You must observe it as an official day for holy assembly, a day to deny yourselves and present special gifts to the LORD. 28Do no work during that entire day because it is the Day of Atonement, when offerings of purification are made for you, making you right with the LORD your God. 29All who do not deny themselves that day will be cut off from God's people. 30And I will destroy anyone among you who does any work on that day. 31You must not do any work at all! This is a permanent law for you, and it must be observed from generation to generation wherever you live. 32This will be a Sabbath day of complete rest for you, and on that day you must deny yourselves. This day of rest will begin at sundown on the ninth day of the month and extend until sundown on the tenth day."

The Festival of Shelters

33And the LORD said to Moses, 34"Give the following instructions to the people of Israel. Begin celebrating the Festival of Shelters on the fifteenth day of the appointed month—five days after the Day of Atonement. This festival to the LORD will last for seven days. 35On the first day of the festival you must proclaim an official day for holy assembly, when you do no ordinary work. 36For seven days you must present special gifts to the LORD. The eighth day is another holy day on which you present your special gifts to the LORD. This will be a solemn occasion, and no ordinary work may be done that day.

37("These are the LORD's appointed festivals. Celebrate them each year as official days for holy assembly by presenting special gifts to the LORD—burnt offerings, grain offerings, sacrifices, and liquid offerings—each on its proper day. 38These festivals must be observed in addition to the LORD's regular Sabbath days, and the offerings are in addition to your personal gifts, the offerings you give to fulfill your vows, and the voluntary offerings you present to the LORD.)

39"Remember that this seven-day festival to the LORD—the Festival of Shelters—begins on the fifteenth day of the appointed month, after you have harvested all the produce of the land. The first day and the eighth day of the festival will be days of complete rest. 40On the first day gather branches from magnificent trees—palm fronds, boughs from leafy trees, and willows that grow by the streams. Then celebrate with joy before the LORD your God for seven days. 41You must observe this festival to the LORD for seven days every year. This is a permanent law for you, and it must be observed in the appointed month from generation to generation. 42For seven days you must live outside in little shelters. All native-born Israelites must live in shelters. 43This will remind each new generation of Israelites that I made their ancestors live in shelters when I rescued them from the land of Egypt. I am the LORD your God."

44So Moses gave the Israelites these instructions regarding the annual festivals of the LORD.

CHAPTER 24

Pure Oil and Holy Bread

The LORD said to Moses, 2"Command the people of Israel to bring you pure oil of pressed olives for the light, to keep the lamps burning continually. 3This is the lampstand that stands in the Tabernacle, in front of the inner curtain that shields the Ark of the Covenant. Aaron must keep the lamps burning in the LORD's presence all night. This is a permanent law for you, and it must be observed from generation to generation. 4Aaron and the priests must tend the lamps on the pure gold lampstand continually in the LORD's presence.

5"You must bake twelve flat loaves of bread from choice flour, using four quarts of flour for each loaf. 6Place the bread before the LORD on the pure gold table, and arrange the loaves in two stacks, with six loaves in each stack. 7Put some pure frankincense near each stack to serve as a representative offering, a special gift presented to the LORD. 8Every Sabbath day this bread must be laid out before the LORD as a gift from the Israelites; it is an ongoing expression of the eternal covenant. 9The loaves of bread will belong to Aaron and his descendants, who must eat them in a sacred place, for they are most holy. It is the permanent right of the priests to claim this portion of the special gifts presented to the LORD."

An Example of Just Punishment

10One day a man who had an Israelite mother and an Egyptian father came out of his tent and got into a fight with one of the Israelite men. 11During the fight, this son of an Israelite woman blasphemed the Name of the LORD with a curse. So the man was brought to Moses for judgment. His mother was Shelomith, the daughter of Dibri of the tribe of Dan. 12They kept the man in custody until the LORD's will in the matter should become clear to them.

13Then the LORD said to Moses, 14"Take the blasphemer outside the camp, and tell all those who heard the curse to lay their hands on his head. Then let the entire community stone him to death. 15Say to the people of Israel: Those who curse their God will be punished for their sin. 16Anyone who blasphemes the Name of the LORD must be stoned to death by the whole community of Israel. Any native-born Israelite or foreigner among you who blasphemes the Name of the LORD must be put to death.

17"Anyone who takes another person's life must be put to death.

18"Anyone who kills another person's animal must pay for it in full—a live animal for the animal that was killed.

19"Anyone who injures another person must be dealt with according to the injury inflicted—20a fracture for a fracture, an eye for an eye, a tooth for a tooth. Whatever anyone does to injure another person must be paid back in kind.

21"Whoever kills an animal must pay for it in full, but whoever kills another person must be put to death.

22"This same standard applies both to native-born Israelites and to the foreigners living among you. I am the LORD your God."

23After Moses gave all these instructions to the Israelites, they took the blasphemer outside the camp and stoned him to death. The Israelites did just as the LORD had commanded Moses.

CHAPTER 25

The Sabbath Year

While Moses was on Mount Sinai, the LORD said to him, 2"Give the following instructions to the

people of Israel. When you have entered the land
I am giving you, the land itself must observe a
Sabbath rest before the LORD every seventh year.
[3]For six years you may plant your fields and
prune your vineyards and harvest your crops,
[4]but during the seventh year the land must have
a Sabbath year of complete rest. It is the LORD's
Sabbath. Do not plant your fields or prune your
vineyards during that year. [5]And don't store away
the crops that grow on their own or gather the
grapes from your unpruned vines. The land must
have a year of complete rest. [6]But you may eat
whatever the land produces on its own during its
Sabbath. This applies to you, your male and female servants, your hired workers, and the temporary residents who live with you. [7]Your
livestock and the wild animals in your land will
also be allowed to eat what the land produces.

The Year of Jubilee

[8]"In addition, you must count off seven Sabbath
years, seven sets of seven years, adding up to
forty-nine years in all. [9]Then on the Day of
Atonement in the fiftieth year, blow the ram's
horn loud and long throughout the land. [10]Set
this year apart as holy, a time to proclaim freedom throughout the land for all who live there. It
will be a jubilee year for you, when each of you
may return to the land that belonged to your ancestors and return to your own clan. [11]This fiftieth year will be a jubilee for you. During that year
you must not plant your fields or store away any
of the crops that grow on their own, and don't
gather the grapes from your unpruned vines. [12]It
will be a jubilee year for you, and you must keep it
holy. But you may eat whatever the land produces
on its own. [13]In the Year of Jubilee each of you
may return to the land that belonged to your ancestors.

[14]"When you make an agreement with your
neighbor to buy or sell property, you must not
take advantage of each other. [15]When you buy
land from your neighbor, the price you pay must
be based on the number of years since the last jubilee. The seller must set the price by taking into
account the number of years remaining until
the next Year of Jubilee. [16]The more years until
the next jubilee, the higher the price; the fewer
years, the lower the price. After all, the person
selling the land is actually selling you a certain
number of harvests. [17]Show your fear of God by
not taking advantage of each other. I am the
LORD your God.

[18]"If you want to live securely in the land, follow my decrees and obey my regulations. [19]Then
the land will yield large crops, and you will eat
your fill and live securely in it. [20]But you might
ask, 'What will we eat during the seventh year,
since we are not allowed to plant or harvest crops
that year?' [21]Be assured that I will send my blessing for you in the sixth year, so the land will produce a crop large enough for three years.
[22]When you plant your fields in the eighth year,
you will still be eating from the large crop of the
sixth year. In fact, you will still be eating from
that large crop when the new crop is harvested in
the ninth year.

Redemption of Property

[23]"The land must never be sold on a permanent
basis, for the land belongs to me. You are only
foreigners and tenant farmers working for me.

[24]"With every purchase of land you must
grant the seller the right to buy it back. [25]If one
of your fellow Israelites falls into poverty and is
forced to sell some family land, then a close relative should buy it back for him. [26]If there is no
close relative to buy the land, but the person who
sold it gets enough money to buy it back, [27]he
then has the right to redeem it from the one
who bought it. The price of the land will be dis-
counted according to the number of years until
the next Year of Jubilee. In this way the original owner can then return to the land. [28]But if
the original owner cannot afford to buy back the
land, it will remain with the new owner until the
next Year of Jubilee. In the jubilee year, the land
must be returned to the original owners so they
can return to their family land.

[29]"Anyone who sells a house inside a walled
town has the right to buy it back for a full year after its sale. During that year, the seller retains the
right to buy it back. [30]But if it is not bought back
within a year, the sale of the house within the
walled town cannot be reversed. It will become
the permanent property of the buyer. It will not
be returned to the original owner in the Year of
Jubilee. [31]But a house in a village—a settlement
without fortified walls—will be treated like property in the countryside. Such a house may be
bought back at any time, and it must be returned
to the original owner in the Year of Jubilee.

[32]"The Levites always have the right to buy
back a house they have sold within the towns allotted to them. [33]And any property that is sold by
the Levites—all houses within the Levitical
towns—must be returned in the Year of Jubilee.
After all, the houses in the towns reserved for the
Levites are the only property they own in all Israel. [34]The open pastureland around the Levitical

towns may never be sold. It is their permanent possession.

Redemption of the Poor and Enslaved

35"If one of your fellow Israelites falls into poverty and cannot support himself, support him as you would a foreigner or a temporary resident and allow him to live with you. 36Do not charge interest or make a profit at his expense. Instead, show your fear of God by letting him live with you as your relative. 37Remember, do not charge interest on money you lend him or make a profit on food you sell him. 38I am the LORD your God, who brought you out of the land of Egypt to give you the land of Canaan and to be your God.

39"If one of your fellow Israelites falls into poverty and is forced to sell himself to you, do not treat him as a slave. 40Treat him instead as a hired worker or as a temporary resident who lives with you, and he will serve you only until the Year of Jubilee. 41At that time he and his children will no longer be obligated to you, and they will return to their clans and go back to the land originally allotted to their ancestors. 42The people of Israel are my servants, whom I brought out of the land of Egypt, so they must never be sold as slaves. 43Show your fear of God by not treating them harshly.

44"However, you may purchase male and female slaves from among the nations around you. 45You may also purchase the children of temporary residents who live among you, including those who have been born in your land. You may treat them as your property, 46passing them on to your children as a permanent inheritance. You may treat them as slaves, but you must never treat your fellow Israelites this way.

47"Suppose a foreigner or temporary resident becomes rich while living among you. If any of your fellow Israelites fall into poverty and are forced to sell themselves to such a foreigner or to a member of his family, 48they still retain the right to be bought back, even after they have been purchased. They may be bought back by a brother, 49an uncle, or a cousin. In fact, anyone from the extended family may buy them back. They may also redeem themselves if they have prospered. 50They will negotiate the price of their freedom with the person who bought them. The price will be based on the number of years from the time they were sold until the next Year of Jubilee—whatever it would cost to hire a worker for that period of time. 51If many years still remain until the jubilee, they will repay the proper proportion of what they received when they sold themselves. 52If only a few years remain until the Year of Jubilee, they will repay a small amount for their redemption. 53The foreigner must treat them as workers hired on a yearly basis. You must not allow a foreigner to treat any of your fellow Israelites harshly. 54If any Israelites have not been bought back by the time the Year of Jubilee arrives, they and their children must be set free at that time. 55For the people of Israel belong to me. They are my servants, whom I brought out of the land of Egypt. I am the LORD your God.

CHAPTER 26

Blessings for Obedience

"Do not make idols or set up carved images, or sacred pillars, or sculptured stones in your land so you may worship them. I am the LORD your God. 2You must keep my Sabbath days of rest and show reverence for my sanctuary. I am the LORD.

3"If you follow my decrees and are careful to obey my commands, 4I will send you the seasonal rains. The land will then yield its crops, and the trees of the field will produce their fruit. 5Your threshing season will overlap with the grape harvest, and your grape harvest will overlap with the season of planting grain. You will eat your fill and live securely in your own land.

6"I will give you peace in the land, and you will be able to sleep with no cause for fear. I will rid the land of wild animals and keep your enemies out of your land. 7In fact, you will chase down your enemies and slaughter them with your swords. 8Five of you will chase a hundred, and a hundred of you will chase ten thousand! All your enemies will fall beneath your sword.

9"I will look favorably upon you, making you fertile and multiplying your people. And I will fulfill my covenant with you. 10You will have such a surplus of crops that you will need to clear out the old grain to make room for the new harvest! 11I will live among you, and I will not despise you. 12I will walk among you; I will be your God, and you will be my people. 13I am the LORD your God, who brought you out of the land of Egypt so you would no longer be their slaves. I broke the yoke of slavery from your neck so you can walk with your heads held high.

Punishments for Disobedience

14"However, if you do not listen to me or obey all these commands, 15and if you break my covenant by rejecting my decrees, treating my regu-

lations with contempt, and refusing to obey my
commands, 16I will punish you. I will bring sudden terrors upon you—wasting diseases and
burning fevers that will cause your eyes to fail
and your life to ebb away. You will plant your
crops in vain because your enemies will eat
them. 17I will turn against you, and you will be
defeated by your enemies. Those who hate you
will rule over you, and you will run even when no
one is chasing you!

18"And if, in spite of all this, you still disobey
me, I will punish you seven times over for your
sins. 19I will break your proud spirit by making
the skies as unyielding as iron and the earth as
hard as bronze. 20All your work will be for nothing, for your land will yield no crops, and your
trees will bear no fruit.

21"If even then you remain hostile toward me
and refuse to obey me, I will inflict disaster on
you seven times over for your sins. 22I will send
wild animals that will rob you of your children
and destroy your livestock. Your numbers will
dwindle, and your roads will be deserted.

23"And if you fail to learn the lesson and continue your hostility toward me, 24then I myself
will be hostile toward you. I will personally strike
you with calamity seven times over for your sins.
25I will send armies against you to carry out the
curse of the covenant you have broken. When
you run to your towns for safety, I will send a
plague to destroy you there, and you will be
handed over to your enemies. 26I will destroy
your food supply, so that ten women will need
only one oven to bake bread for their families.
They will ration your food by weight, and though
you have food to eat, you will not be satisfied.

27"If in spite of all this you still refuse to listen
and still remain hostile toward me, 28then I will
give full vent to my hostility. I myself will punish
you seven times over for your sins. 29Then you
will eat the flesh of your own sons and daughters. 30I will destroy your pagan shrines and
knock down your places of worship. I will leave
your lifeless corpses piled on top of your lifeless
idols, and I will despise you. 31I will make your
cities desolate and destroy your places of pagan
worship. I will take no pleasure in your offerings
that should be a pleasing aroma to me. 32Yes, I
myself will devastate your land, and your enemies who come to occupy it will be appalled at
what they see. 33I will scatter you among the
nations and bring out my sword against you.
Your land will become desolate, and your cities
will lie in ruins. 34Then at last the land will enjoy
its neglected Sabbath years as it lies desolate
while you are in exile in the land of your enemies.
Then the land will finally rest and enjoy the Sabbaths it missed. 35As long as the land lies in ruins,
it will enjoy the rest you never allowed it to take
every seventh year while you lived in it.

36"And for those of you who survive, I will de-
moralize you in the land of your enemies. You
will live in such fear that the sound of a leaf
driven by the wind will send you fleeing. You will
run as though fleeing from a sword, and you will
fall even when no one pursues you. 37Though no
one is chasing you, you will stumble over each
other as though fleeing from a sword. You will
have no power to stand up against your enemies.
38You will die among the foreign nations and be
devoured in the land of your enemies. 39Those of
you who survive will waste away in your enemies'
lands because of their sins and the sins of their
ancestors.

40"But at last my people will confess their sins
and the sins of their ancestors for betraying me
and being hostile toward me. 41When I have
turned their hostility back on them and brought
them to the land of their enemies, then at last
their stubborn hearts will be humbled, and they
will pay for their sins. 42Then I will remember
my covenant with Jacob and my covenant with
Isaac and my covenant with Abraham, and I will
remember the land. 43For the land must be abandoned to enjoy its years of Sabbath rest as it lies
deserted. At last the people will pay for their sins,
for they have continually rejected my regulations
and despised my decrees.

44"But despite all this, I will not utterly reject
or despise them while they are in exile in the
land of their enemies. I will not cancel my covenant with them by wiping them out, for I am the
LORD their God. 45For their sakes I will remember my ancient covenant with their ancestors,
whom I brought out of the land of Egypt in the
sight of all the nations, that I might be their God.
I am the LORD."

46These are the decrees, regulations, and instructions that the LORD gave through Moses on
Mount Sinai as evidence of the relationship between himself and the Israelites.

CHAPTER 27

Redemption of Gifts Offered to the LORD

The LORD said to Moses, 2"Give the following
instructions to the people of Israel. If anyone
makes a special vow to dedicate someone to the
LORD by paying the value of that person, 3here is
the scale of values to be used. A man between the

ages of twenty and sixty is valued at fifty shekels of silver, as measured by the sanctuary shekel. 4A woman of that age is valued at thirty shekels of silver. 5A boy between the ages of five and twenty is valued at twenty shekels of silver; a girl of that age is valued at ten shekels of silver. 6A boy between the ages of one month and five years is valued at five shekels of silver; a girl of that age is valued at three shekels of silver. 7A man older than sixty is valued at fifteen shekels of silver; a woman of that age is valued at ten shekels of silver. 8If you desire to make such a vow but cannot afford to pay the required amount, take the person to the priest. He will determine the amount for you to pay based on what you can afford.

9"If your vow involves giving an animal that is acceptable as an offering to the LORD, any gift to the LORD will be considered holy. 10You may not exchange or substitute it for another animal—neither a good animal for a bad one nor a bad animal for a good one. But if you do exchange one animal for another, then both the original animal and its substitute will be considered holy. 11If your vow involves an unclean animal—one that is not acceptable as an offering to the LORD—then you must bring the animal to the priest. 12He will assess its value, and his assessment will be final, whether high or low. 13If you want to buy back the animal, you must pay the value set by the priest, plus 20 percent.

14"If someone dedicates a house to the LORD, the priest will come to assess its value. The priest's assessment will be final, whether high or low. 15If the person who dedicated the house wants to buy it back, he must pay the value set by the priest, plus 20 percent. Then the house will again be his.

16"If someone dedicates to the LORD a piece of his family property, its value will be assessed according to the amount of seed required to plant it—fifty shekels of silver for a field planted with five bushels of barley seed. 17If the field is dedicated to the LORD in the Year of Jubilee, then the entire assessment will apply. 18But if the field is dedicated after the Year of Jubilee, the priest will assess the land's value in proportion to the number of years left until the next Year of Jubilee. Its assessed value is reduced each year. 19If the person who dedicated the field wants to buy it back, he must pay the value set by the priest, plus 20 percent. Then the field will again be legally his. 20But if he does not want to buy it back, and it is sold to someone else, the field can no longer be bought back. 21When the field is released in the Year of Jubilee, it will be holy, a field specially set apart for the LORD. It will become the property of the priests.

22"If someone dedicates to the LORD a field he has purchased but which is not part of his family property, 23the priest will assess its value based on the number of years left until the next Year of Jubilee. On that day he must give the assessed value of the land as a sacred donation to the LORD. 24In the Year of Jubilee the field must be returned to the person from whom he purchased it, the one who inherited it as family property. 25(All the payments must be measured by the weight of the sanctuary shekel, which equals twenty gerahs.)

26"You may not dedicate a firstborn animal to the LORD, for the firstborn of your cattle, sheep, and goats already belong to him. 27However, you may buy back the firstborn of a ceremonially unclean animal by paying the priest's assessment of its worth, plus 20 percent. If you do not buy it back, the priest will sell it at its assessed value.

28"However, anything specially set apart for the LORD—whether a person, an animal, or family property—must never be sold or bought back. Anything devoted in this way has been set apart as holy, and it belongs to the LORD. 29No person specially set apart for destruction may be bought back. Such a person must be put to death.

30"One-tenth of the produce of the land, whether grain from the fields or fruit from the trees, belongs to the LORD and must be set apart to him as holy. 31If you want to buy back the LORD's tenth of the grain or fruit, you must pay its value, plus 20 percent. 32Count off every tenth animal from your herds and flocks and set them apart for the LORD as holy. 33You may not pick and choose between good and bad animals, and you may not substitute one for another. But if you do exchange one animal for another, then both the original animal and its substitute will be considered holy and cannot be bought back."

34These are the commands that the LORD gave through Moses on Mount Sinai for the Israelites.

NUMBERS

Look for 1 hidden message in Numbers!

Numbers tells about the Israelites getting ready to enter the Promised Land. It includes

- COUNTING PEOPLE
- A PILLAR OF CLOUD AND FIRE
- SPIES AND CHICKENS
- WANDERING IN THE DESERT
- LOTS MORE WHINING
- A TALKING DONKEY
- WHAT GOD THINKS ABOUT NOT TRUSTING HIM

One Potato, Two Potato

OK, the Israelites weren't really counting potatoes. They were counting people. They wanted to see how many Israelites there were and how many could fight in the army. Actually, they took the census twice, once in the beginning of the book and once near the end. **Check out the numbers in Numbers 1 and 26.**

Let's Go!

Red Light, Green Light

Remember the game Red Light, Green Light? That's kind of how it was as God led the Israelites toward the Promised Land, except it wasn't a game. The tent of the Tabernacle (where the Ark of the Covenant was kept) was set up, and a cloud covered it. At night the cloud looked like fire. During the day, the cloud lifted and led the people through the desert.

When they saw the cloud of fire, the Israelites knew to stop and camp. When the cloud lifted, the people knew it was time to move on. **For complete travel news, go to Numbers 9:15-22.**

Mission Impossible?

Honey, they blew up the grapes!

When they got close to the Promised Land, Moses sent spies to check out the land and people. All but two of the spies came back sounding like big chickens. **To see what they were scared of, read Numbers 13.**

Dear Blabby

Q: My Israelite friends and I are sick of Moses, and we're scared of the people in the Promised Land, and we want to go back to Egypt! I guess God's pretty mad at us for all our whining, though it looks like Moses is over there asking God to forgive us. What do you think God will do?

A: Find out for yourself in Numbers 14:20-25.

UH-OH...
Oops!

So after 37 years of wandering in the desert, the Israelites were right back where they started. Camped where Moses had sent out the spies, they were doing their usual whining. This time it was about water.

Moses asked God what to do, and God told him. But then Moses made a *big* mistake. **Find out what he did wrong in Numbers 20:1-12.**

Timeout!

Can we come out now?

Have you ever been punished by being given a timeout? That's sort of what happened to the Israelites. March. Camp. March. Camp. Finally the Israelites camped just across the river from the Promised Land. But then the complaining started again. They just didn't trust God.

So God punished them. With a *big* timeout. Imagine being sent to your room for 40 years! OK, the Israelites weren't sent to their room, but they *were* sent into the wilderness for 40 years. **Read more about it in Numbers 14:34.**

WHAT'S YOUR PROBLEM?

Say What?

He wasn't Dr. Dolittle, but he *did* hear a talking donkey. Get the story right from the horse's...I mean donkey's...mouth in Numbers 22:21-35!

Timeline

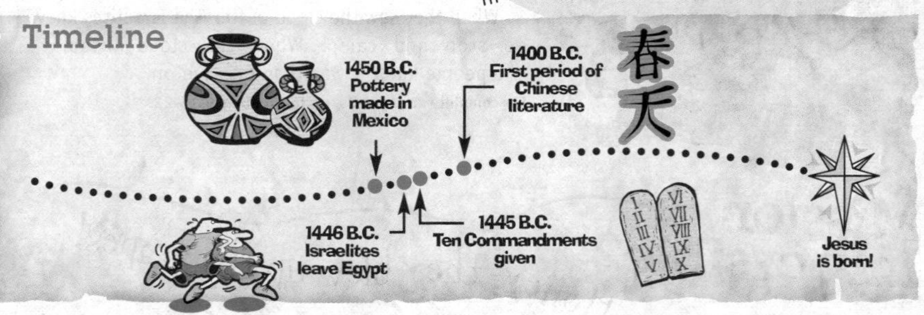

1450 B.C. Pottery made in Mexico
1400 B.C. First period of Chinese literature
春
天
1446 B.C. Israelites leave Egypt
1445 B.C. Ten Commandments given
I II III IV V
VI VII VIII IX X
Jesus is born!

The JESUS CONNECTION

The Israelites didn't trust God. Even after witnessing one miracle after another, they complained and disobeyed. In 1 Corinthians 10:1-12, Paul warns us not to be like the Israelites. We can trust God because he's faithful. He loves us. He sent his Son to take the punishment we deserve. **What more do we need? (Nothing!)**

CHAPTER 1

Registration of Israel's Troops

A year after Israel's departure from Egypt, the
LORD spoke to Moses in the Tabernacle in the
wilderness of Sinai. On the first day of the second month of that year he said, 2"From the whole
community of Israel, record the names of all the
warriors by their clans and families. List all the
men 3twenty years old or older who are able to go
to war. You and Aaron must register the troops,
4and you will be assisted by one family leader
from each tribe.

5"These are the tribes and the names of the
leaders who will assist you:

Tribe	*Leader*
Reuben	Elizur son of Shedeur
6 Simeon	Shelumiel son of Zurishaddai
7 Judah	Nahshon son of Amminadab
8 Issachar	Nethanel son of Zuar
9 Zebulun	Eliab son of Helon
10 Ephraim son of Joseph	Elishama son of Ammihud
Manasseh son of Joseph	Gamaliel son of Pedahzur
11 Benjamin	Abidan son of Gideoni
12 Dan	Ahiezer son of Ammishaddai
13 Asher	Pagiel son of Ocran
14 Gad	Eliasaph son of Deuel
15 Naphtali	Ahira son of Enan

16These are the chosen leaders of the community, the leaders of their ancestral tribes, the
heads of the clans of Israel."

17So Moses and Aaron called together these
chosen leaders, 18and they assembled the whole
community of Israel on that very day. All the people were registered according to their ancestry
by their clans and families. The men of Israel
who were twenty years old or older were listed
one by one, 19just as the LORD had commanded
Moses. So Moses recorded their names in the
wilderness of Sinai.

20-21This is the number of men twenty years
old or older who were able to go to war, as their
names were listed in the records of their clans
and families:

Tribe	*Number*
Reuben (Jacob's oldest son)	46,500
22-23 Simeon	59,300
24-25 Gad	45,650
26-27 Judah	74,600
28-29 Issachar	54,400
30-31 Zebulun	57,400
32-33 Ephraim son of Joseph	40,500
34-35 Manasseh son of Joseph	32,200
36-37 Benjamin	35,400
38-39 Dan	62,700
40-41 Asher	41,500
42-43 Naphtali	53,400

44These were the men registered by Moses and
Aaron and the twelve leaders of Israel, all listed
according to their ancestral descent. 45They
were registered by families—all the men of Israel
who were twenty years old or older and able to go
to war. 46The total number was 603,550.

47But this total did not include the Levites.
48For the LORD had said to Moses, 49"Do not include the tribe of Levi in the registration; do not
count them with the rest of the Israelites. 50Put
the Levites in charge of the Tabernacle of the
Covenant, along with all its furnishings and
equipment. They must carry the Tabernacle and
all its furnishings as you travel, and they must
take care of it and camp around it. 51Whenever it
is time for the Tabernacle to move, the Levites
will take it down. And when it is time to stop, they
will set it up again. But any unauthorized person
who goes too near the Tabernacle must be put to
death. 52Each tribe of Israel will camp in a designated area with its own family banner. 53But the
Levites will camp around the Tabernacle of the
Covenant to protect the community of Israel
from the LORD's anger. The Levites are responsible to stand guard around the Tabernacle."

54So the Israelites did everything just as the
LORD had commanded Moses.

CHAPTER 2

Organization for Israel's Camp

Then the LORD gave these instructions to Moses
and Aaron: 2"When the Israelites set up camp,
each tribe will be assigned its own area. The
tribal divisions will camp beneath their family
banners on all four sides of the Tabernacle, but at
some distance from it.

3-4"The divisions of Judah, Issachar, and Zebulun are to camp toward the sunrise on the east
side of the Tabernacle, beneath their family banners. These are the names of the tribes, their leaders, and the numbers of their registered troops:

Tribe	*Leader*	*Number*
Judah	Nahshon son of Amminadab	74,600
5-6 Issachar	Nethanel son of Zuar	54,400
7-8 Zebulun	Eliab son of Helon	57,400

9So the total of all the troops on Judah's side of
the camp is 186,400. These three tribes are to
lead the way whenever the Israelites travel to a
new campsite.

10-11"The divisions of Reuben, Simeon, and

Gad are to camp on the south side of the Tabernacle, beneath their family banners. These are
the names of the tribes, their leaders, and the
numbers of their registered troops:

Tribe	*Leader*	*Number*
Reuben	Elizur son of Shedeur	46,500
12-13Simeon	Shelumiel son of Zurishaddai	59,300
14-15Gad	Eliasaph son of Deuel	45,650

16So the total of all the troops on Reuben's side of
the camp is 151,450. These three tribes will be
second in line whenever the Israelites travel.
17"Then the Tabernacle, carried by the Levites,
will set out from the middle of the camp. All the
tribes are to travel in the same order that they
camp, each in position under the appropriate
family banner.
18-19"The divisions of Ephraim, Manasseh,
and Benjamin are to camp on the west side of the
Tabernacle, beneath their family banners. These
are the names of the tribes, their leaders, and the
numbers of their registered troops:

Tribe	*Leader*	*Number*
Ephraim	Elishama son of Ammihud	40,500
20-21Manasseh	Gamaliel son of Pedahzur	32,200
22-23Benjamin	Abidan son of Gideoni	35,400

24So the total of all the troops on Ephraim's side
of the camp is 108,100. These three tribes will
be third in line whenever the Israelites travel.
25-26"The divisions of Dan, Asher, and Naphtali are to camp on the north side of the Tabernacle, beneath their family banners. These are the
names of the tribes, their leaders, and the numbers of their registered troops:

Tribe	*Leader*	*Number*
Dan	Ahiezer son of Ammishaddai	62,700
27-28Asher	Pagiel son of Ocran	41,500
29-30Naphtali	Ahira son of Enan	53,400

31So the total of all the troops on Dan's side of the
camp is 157,600. These three tribes will be last,
marching under their banners whenever the Israelites travel."
32In summary, the troops of Israel listed by
their families totaled 603,550. 33But as the LORD
had commanded, the Levites were not included
in this registration. 34So the people of Israel did
everything as the LORD had commanded Moses.
Each clan and family set up camp and marched
under their banners exactly as the LORD had instructed them.

CHAPTER 3

Levites Appointed for Service

This is the family line of Aaron and Moses as it
was recorded when the LORD spoke to Moses on
Mount Sinai: 2The names of Aaron's sons were
Nadab (the oldest), Abihu, Eleazar, and Ithamar.
3These sons of Aaron were anointed and ordained to minister as priests. 4But Nadab and
Abihu died in the LORD's presence in the wilderness of Sinai when they burned before the LORD
the wrong kind of fire, different than he had
commanded. Since they had no sons, this left
only Eleazar and Ithamar to serve as priests with
their father, Aaron.
5Then the LORD said to Moses, 6"Call forward
the tribe of Levi, and present them to Aaron the
priest to serve as his assistants. 7They will serve
Aaron and the whole community, performing
their sacred duties in and around the Tabernacle. 8They will also maintain all the furnishings
of the sacred tent, serving in the Tabernacle on
behalf of all the Israelites. 9Assign the Levites to
Aaron and his sons. They have been given from
among all the people of Israel to serve as their assistants. 10Appoint Aaron and his sons to carry
out the duties of the priesthood. But any unauthorized person who goes too near the sanctuary
must be put to death."
11And the LORD said to Moses, 12"Look, I have
chosen the Levites from among the Israelites to
serve as substitutes for all the firstborn sons of
the people of Israel. The Levites belong to me,
13for all the firstborn males are mine. On the day
I struck down all the firstborn sons of the Egyptians, I set apart for myself all the firstborn in
Israel, both of people and of animals. They are
mine; I am the LORD."

Registration of the Levites

14The LORD spoke again to Moses in the wilderness of Sinai. He said, 15"Record the names of the
members of the tribe of Levi by their families
and clans. List every male who is one month old
or older." 16So Moses listed them, just as the
LORD had commanded.

17Levi had three sons, whose names were
Gershon, Kohath, and Merari.
18The clans descended from Gershon were
named after two of his descendants, Libni
and Shimei.
19The clans descended from Kohath were
named after four of his descendants, Amram,
Izhar, Hebron, and Uzziel.
20The clans descended from Merari were

table where the Bread of the Presence is displayed, and on the cloth they will place the bowls, ladles, jars, pitchers, and the special bread. 8They must spread a scarlet cloth over all of this, and finally a covering of fine goatskin leather on top of the scarlet cloth. Then they must insert the carrying poles into the table.

9"Next they must cover the lampstand with a blue cloth, along with its lamps, lamp snuffers, trays, and special jars of olive oil. 10Then they must cover the lampstand and its accessories with fine goatskin leather and place the bundle on a carrying frame.

11"Next they must spread a blue cloth over the gold incense altar and cover this cloth with fine goatskin leather. Then they must attach the carrying poles to the altar. 12They must take all the remaining furnishings of the sanctuary and wrap them in a blue cloth, cover them with fine goatskin leather, and place them on the carrying frame.

13"They must remove the ashes from the altar for sacrifices and cover the altar with a purple cloth. 14All the altar utensils—the firepans, meat forks, shovels, basins, and all the containers—must be placed on the cloth, and a covering of fine goatskin leather must be spread over them. Finally, they must put the carrying poles in place. 15The camp will be ready to move when Aaron and his sons have finished covering the sanctuary and all the sacred articles. The Kohathites will come and carry these things to the next destination. But they must not touch the sacred objects, or they will die. So these are the things from the Tabernacle that the Kohathites must carry.

16"Eleazar son of Aaron the priest will be responsible for the oil of the lampstand, the fragrant incense, the daily grain offering, and the anointing oil. In fact, Eleazar will be responsible for the entire Tabernacle and everything in it, including the sanctuary and its furnishings."

17Then the LORD said to Moses and Aaron, 18"Do not let the Kohathite clans be destroyed from among the Levites! 19This is what you must do so they will live and not die when they approach the most sacred objects. Aaron and his sons must always go in with them and assign a specific duty or load to each person. 20The Kohathites must never enter the sanctuary to look at the sacred objects for even a moment, or they will die."

Duties of the Gershonite Clan

21And the LORD said to Moses, 22"Record the names of the members of the clans and families of the Gershonite division of the tribe of Levi. 23List all the men between the ages of thirty and fifty who are eligible to serve in the Tabernacle.

24"These Gershonite clans will be responsible for general service and carrying loads. 25They must carry the curtains of the Tabernacle, the Tabernacle itself with its coverings, the outer covering of fine goatskin leather, and the curtain for the Tabernacle entrance. 26They are also to carry the curtains for the courtyard walls that surround the Tabernacle and altar, the curtain across the courtyard entrance, the ropes, and all the equipment related to their use. The Gershonites are responsible for all these items. 27Aaron and his sons will direct the Gershonites regarding all their duties, whether it involves moving the equipment or doing other work. They must assign the Gershonites responsibility for the loads they are to carry. 28So these are the duties assigned to the Gershonite clans at the Tabernacle. They will be directly responsible to Ithamar son of Aaron the priest.

Duties of the Merarite Clan

29"Now record the names of the members of the clans and families of the Merarite division of the tribe of Levi. 30List all the men between the ages of thirty and fifty who are eligible to serve in the Tabernacle.

31"Their only duty at the Tabernacle will be to carry loads. They will carry the frames of the Tabernacle, the crossbars, the posts, and the bases; 32also the posts for the courtyard walls with their bases, pegs, and ropes; and all the accessories and everything else related to their use. Assign the various loads to each man by name. 33So these are the duties of the Merarite clans at the Tabernacle. They are directly responsible to Ithamar son of Aaron the priest."

Summary of the Registration

34So Moses, Aaron, and the other leaders of the community listed the members of the Kohathite division by their clans and families. 35The list included all the men between thirty and fifty years of age who were eligible for service in the Tabernacle, 36and the total number came to 2,750. 37So this was the total of all those from the Kohathite clans who were eligible to serve at the Tabernacle. Moses and Aaron listed them, just as the LORD had commanded through Moses.

38The Gershonite division was also listed by its clans and families. 39The list included all the men between thirty and fifty years of age who were eligible for service in the Tabernacle, 40and

named after two of his descendants, Mahli
and Mushi.
These were the Levite clans, listed according to
their family groups.

21 The descendants of Gershon were composed of the clans descended from Libni and
Shimei. 22 There were 7,500 males one month
old or older among these Gershonite clans.
23 They were assigned the area to the west of the
Tabernacle for their camp. 24 The leader of the
Gershonite clans was Eliasaph son of Lael.
25 These two clans were responsible to care for
the Tabernacle, including the sacred tent with its
layers of coverings, the curtain at its entrance,
26 the curtains of the courtyard that surrounded
the Tabernacle and altar, the curtain at the courtyard entrance, the ropes, and all the equipment
related to their use.

27 The descendants of Kohath were composed
of the clans descended from Amram, Izhar, Hebron, and Uzziel. 28 There were 8,600 males one
month old or older among these Kohathite clans.
They were responsible for the care of the sanctuary, 29 and they were assigned the area south of
the Tabernacle for their camp. 30 The leader of
the Kohathite clans was Elizaphan son of Uzziel.
31 These four clans were responsible for the care
of the Ark, the table, the lampstand, the altars,
the various articles used in the sanctuary, the inner curtain, and all the equipment related to
their use. 32 Eleazar, son of Aaron the priest, was
the chief administrator over all the Levites, with
special responsibility for the oversight of the
sanctuary.

33 The descendants of Merari were composed
of the clans descended from Mahli and Mushi.
34 There were 6,200 males one month old or
older among these Merarite clans. 35 They were
assigned the area north of the Tabernacle for
their camp. The leader of the Merarite clans was
Zuriel son of Abihail. 36 These two clans were responsible for the care of the frames supporting
the Tabernacle, the crossbars, the pillars, the
bases, and all the equipment related to their use.
37 They were also responsible for the posts of the
courtyard and all their bases, pegs, and ropes.

38 The area in front of the Tabernacle, in the
east toward the sunrise, was reserved for the
tents of Moses and of Aaron and his sons, who
had the final responsibility for the sanctuary on
behalf of the people of Israel. Anyone other than
a priest or Levite who went too near the sanctuary was to be put to death.

39 When Moses and Aaron counted the Levite
clans at the LORD's command, the total number
was 22,000 males one month old or older.

Redeeming the Firstborn Sons

40 Then the LORD said to Moses, "Now count all
the firstborn sons in Israel who are one month
old or older, and make a list of their names. 41 The
Levites must be reserved for me as substitutes
for the firstborn sons of Israel; I am the LORD.
And the Levites' livestock must be reserved for
me as substitutes for the firstborn livestock of
the whole nation of Israel."

42 So Moses counted the firstborn sons of the
people of Israel, just as the LORD had commanded. 43 The number of firstborn sons who
were one month old or older was 22,273.

44 Then the LORD said to Moses, 45 "Take the Levites as substitutes for the firstborn sons of the
people of Israel. And take the livestock of the Levites as substitutes for the firstborn livestock of
the people of Israel. The Levites belong to me; I
am the LORD. 46 There are 273 more firstborn
sons of Israel than there are Levites. To redeem
these extra firstborn sons, 47 collect five pieces of
silver for each of them (each piece weighing the
same as the sanctuary shekel, which equals
twenty gerahs). 48 Give the silver to Aaron and his
sons as the redemption price for the extra firstborn sons."

49 So Moses collected the silver for redeeming
the firstborn sons of Israel who exceeded the
number of Levites. 50 He collected 1,365 pieces
of silver on behalf of these firstborn sons of Israel
(each piece weighing the same as the sanctuary
shekel). 51 And Moses gave the silver for the redemption to Aaron and his sons, just as the LORD
had commanded.

CHAPTER 4

Duties of the Kohathite Clan

Then the LORD said to Moses and Aaron, 2 "Record
the names of the members of the clans and families of the Kohathite division of the tribe of Levi.
3 List all the men between the ages of thirty and
fifty who are eligible to serve in the Tabernacle.

4 "The duties of the Kohathites at the Tabernacle will relate to the most sacred objects. 5 When
the camp moves, Aaron and his sons must enter
the Tabernacle first to take down the inner curtain and cover the Ark of the Covenant with it.
6 Then they must cover the inner curtain with
fine goatskin leather and spread over that a single piece of blue cloth. Finally, they must put the
carrying poles of the Ark in place.

7 "Next they must spread a blue cloth over the

the total number came to 2,630. 41So this was the total of all those from the Gershonite clans who were eligible to serve at the Tabernacle. Moses and Aaron listed them, just as the LORD had commanded.

42The Merarite division was also listed by its clans and families. 43The list included all the men between thirty and fifty years of age who were eligible for service in the Tabernacle, 44and the total number came to 3,200. 45So this was the total of all those from the Merarite clans who were eligible for service. Moses and Aaron listed them, just as the LORD had commanded through Moses.

46So Moses, Aaron, and the leaders of Israel listed all the Levites by their clans and families. 47All the men between thirty and fifty years of age who were eligible for service in the Tabernacle and for its transportation 48numbered 8,580. 49When their names were recorded, as the LORD had commanded through Moses, each man was assigned his task and told what to carry.

And so the registration was completed, just as the LORD had commanded Moses.

CHAPTER 5

Purity in Israel's Camp

The LORD gave these instructions to Moses: 2"Command the people of Israel to remove from the camp anyone who has a skin disease or a discharge, or who has become ceremonially unclean by touching a dead person. 3This command applies to men and women alike. Remove them so they will not defile the camp in which I live among them." 4So the Israelites did as the LORD had commanded Moses and removed such people from the camp.

5Then the LORD said to Moses, 6"Give the following instructions to the people of Israel: If any of the people—men or women—betray the LORD by doing wrong to another person, they are guilty. 7They must confess their sin and make full restitution for what they have done, adding an additional 20 percent and returning it to the person who was wronged. 8But if the person who was wronged is dead, and there are no near relatives to whom restitution can be made, the payment belongs to the LORD and must be given to the priest. Those who are guilty must also bring a ram as a sacrifice, and they will be purified and made right with the LORD. 9All the sacred offerings that the Israelites bring to a priest will belong to him. 10Each priest may keep all the sacred donations that he receives."

Protecting Marital Faithfulness

11And the LORD said to Moses, 12"Give the following instructions to the people of Israel.

"Suppose a man's wife goes astray, and she is unfaithful to her husband 13and has sex with another man, but neither her husband nor anyone else knows about it. She has defiled herself, even though there was no witness and she was not caught in the act. 14If her husband becomes jealous and is suspicious of his wife and needs to know whether or not she has defiled herself, 15the husband must bring his wife to the priest. He must also bring an offering of two quarts of barley flour to be presented on her behalf. Do not mix it with olive oil or frankincense, for it is a jealousy offering—an offering to prove whether or not she is guilty.

16"The priest will then present her to stand trial before the LORD. 17He must take some holy water in a clay jar and pour into it dust he has taken from the Tabernacle floor. 18When the priest has presented the woman before the LORD, he must unbind her hair and place in her hands the offering of proof—the jealousy offering to determine whether her husband's suspicions are justified. The priest will stand before her, holding the jar of bitter water that brings a curse to those who are guilty. 19The priest will then put the woman under oath and say to her, 'If no other man has had sex with you, and you have not gone astray and defiled yourself while under your husband's authority, may you be immune from the effects of this bitter water that brings on the curse. 20But if you have gone astray by being unfaithful to your husband, and have defiled yourself by having sex with another man—'

21"At this point the priest must put the woman under oath by saying, 'May the people know that the LORD's curse is upon you when he makes you infertile, causing your womb to shrivel and your abdomen to swell. 22Now may this water that brings the curse enter your body and cause your abdomen to swell and your womb to shrivel.' And the woman will be required to say, 'Yes, let it be so.' 23And the priest will write these curses on a piece of leather and wash them off into the bitter water. 24He will make the woman drink the bitter water that brings on the curse. When the water enters her body, it will cause bitter suffering if she is guilty.

25"The priest will take the jealousy offering from the woman's hand, lift it up before the LORD, and carry it to the altar. 26He will take a handful of the flour as a token portion and burn it on the altar, and he will require the woman to

drink the water. 27If she has defiled herself by
being unfaithful to her husband, the water that
brings on the curse will cause bitter suffering.
Her abdomen will swell and her womb will
shrink, and her name will become a curse
among her people. 28But if she has not defiled
herself and is pure, then she will be unharmed
and will still be able to have children.

29"This is the ritual law for dealing with sus-
picion. If a woman goes astray and defiles herself while under her husband's authority, 30or if
a man becomes jealous and is suspicious that
his wife has been unfaithful, the husband must
present his wife before the LORD, and the priest
will apply this entire ritual law to her. 31The
husband will be innocent of any guilt in this
matter, but his wife will be held accountable for
her sin."

CHAPTER 6

Nazirite Laws

Then the LORD said to Moses, 2"Give the following instructions to the people of Israel.

"If any of the people, either men or women,
take the special vow of a Nazirite, setting themselves apart to the LORD in a special way, 3they
must give up wine and other alcoholic drinks.
They must not use vinegar made from wine or
from other alcoholic drinks, they must not drink
fresh grape juice, and they must not eat grapes or
raisins. 4As long as they are bound by their Nazirite vow, they are not allowed to eat or drink anything that comes from a grapevine—not even the
grape seeds or skins.

5"They must never cut their hair throughout
the time of their vow, for they are holy and set
apart to the LORD. Until the time of their vow has
been fulfilled, they must let their hair grow long.
6And they must not go near a dead body during
the entire period of their vow to the LORD. 7Even
if the dead person is their own father, mother,
brother, or sister, they must not defile themselves, for the hair on their head is the symbol of
their separation to God. 8This requirement applies as long as they are set apart to the LORD.

9"If someone falls dead beside them, the hair
they have dedicated will be defiled. They must
wait for seven days and then shave their heads.
Then they will be cleansed from their defilement. 10On the eighth day they must bring two
turtledoves or two young pigeons to the priest at
the entrance of the Tabernacle. 11The priest will
offer one of the birds for a sin offering and the
other for a burnt offering. In this way, he will purify them from the guilt they incurred through
contact with the dead body. Then they must reaffirm their commitment and let their hair begin
to grow again. 12The days of their vow that were
completed before their defilement no longer
count. They must rededicate themselves to the
LORD as a Nazirite for the full term of their vow,
and each must bring a one-year-old male lamb
for a guilt offering.

13"This is the ritual law for Nazirites. At the
conclusion of their time of separation as Nazirites, they must each go to the entrance of the
Tabernacle 14and offer their sacrifices to the
LORD: a one-year-old male lamb without defect
for a burnt offering, a one-year-old female lamb
without defect for a sin offering, a ram without
defect for a peace offering, 15a basket of bread
made without yeast—cakes of choice flour
mixed with olive oil and wafers spread with olive
oil—along with their prescribed grain offerings
and liquid offerings. 16The priest will present
these offerings before the LORD: first the sin offering and the burnt offering; 17then the ram for
a peace offering, along with the basket of bread
made without yeast. The priest must also present
the prescribed grain offering and liquid offering
to the LORD.

18"Then the Nazirites will shave their heads at
the entrance of the Tabernacle. They will take
the hair that had been dedicated and place it on
the fire beneath the peace-offering sacrifice.
19After the Nazirite's head has been shaved, the
priest will take for each of them the boiled shoulder of the ram, and he will take from the basket a
cake and a wafer made without yeast. He will put
them all into the Nazirite's hands. 20Then the
priest will lift them up as a special offering before the LORD. These are holy portions for the
priest, along with the breast of the special offering and the thigh of the sacred offering that are
lifted up before the LORD. After this ceremony
the Nazirites may again drink wine.

21"This is the ritual law of the Nazirites, who
vow to bring these offerings to the LORD. They
may also bring additional offerings if they can
afford it. And they must be careful to do whatever they vowed when they set themselves apart
as Nazirites."

The Priestly Blessing

22Then the LORD said to Moses, 23"Tell Aaron
and his sons to bless the people of Israel with
this special blessing:

24 'May the LORD bless you
and protect you.

[25] May the LORD smile on you
and be gracious to you.
[26] May the LORD show you his favor
and give you his peace.'

[27] Whenever Aaron and his sons bless the people
of Israel in my name, I myself will bless them."

CHAPTER 7
Offerings of Dedication

On the day Moses set up the Tabernacle, he
anointed it and set it apart as holy. He also
anointed and set apart all its furnishings and the
altar with its utensils. [2] Then the leaders of Israel—the tribal leaders who had registered the
troops—came and brought their offerings. [3] Together they brought six large wagons and twelve
oxen. There was a wagon for every two leaders
and an ox for each leader. They presented these
to the LORD in front of the Tabernacle.

[4] Then the LORD said to Moses, [5] "Receive
their gifts, and use these oxen and wagons for
transporting the Tabernacle. Distribute them
among the Levites according to the work they
have to do." [6] So Moses took the wagons and
oxen and presented them to the Levites. [7] He
gave two wagons and four oxen to the Gershonite division for their work, [8] and he gave four
wagons and eight oxen to the Merarite division
for their work. All their work was done under
the leadership of Ithamar son of Aaron the
priest. [9] But he gave none of the wagons or oxen
to the Kohathite division, since they were required to carry the sacred objects of the Tabernacle on their shoulders.

[10] The leaders also presented dedication gifts
for the altar at the time it was anointed. They
each placed their gifts before the altar. [11] The
LORD said to Moses, "Let one leader bring his gift
each day for the dedication of the altar."

[12] On the first day Nahshon son of Amminadab,
leader of the tribe of Judah, presented his offering.

[13] His offering consisted of a silver platter
weighing 3¼ pounds and a silver basin
weighing 1¾ pounds (as measured by
the weight of the sanctuary shekel). These
were both filled with grain offerings of
choice flour moistened with olive oil. [14] He
also brought a gold container weighing four
ounces, which was filled with incense. [15] He
brought a young bull, a ram, and a one-year-
old male lamb for a burnt offering, [16] and a
male goat for a sin offering. [17] For a peace
offering he brought two bulls, five rams,
five male goats, and five one-year-old male
lambs. This was the offering brought by
Nahshon son of Amminadab.

[18] On the second day Nethanel son of Zuar,
leader of the tribe of Issachar, presented his
offering.

[19] His offering consisted of a silver platter
weighing 3¼ pounds and a silver basin
weighing 1¾ pounds (as measured by
the weight of the sanctuary shekel). These
were both filled with grain offerings of
choice flour moistened with olive oil. [20] He
also brought a gold container weighing four
ounces, which was filled with incense. [21] He
brought a young bull, a ram, and a one-year-
old male lamb for a burnt offering, [22] and a
male goat for a sin offering. [23] For a peace
offering he brought two bulls, five rams,
five male goats, and five one-year-old male
lambs. This was the offering brought by
Nethanel son of Zuar.

[24] On the third day Eliab son of Helon, leader
of the tribe of Zebulun, presented his offering.

[25] His offering consisted of a silver platter
weighing 3¼ pounds and a silver basin
weighing 1¾ pounds (as measured by
the weight of the sanctuary shekel). These

FUN-fact
Gene-what-ogy?

GENEALOGY! That's a fancy way to say a record of your family history.

As you read the Bible, you'll find all sorts of lists of relatives.

Way before Jesus' birth, God promised that the Messiah would come from King David's family. **Check out Jesus' genealogy in LUKE 3:23-38.** It showed that Jesus came from David's family!

You Try It!
Fill in your genealogy. Use a sheet of paper and keep going back! Ask your parents or grandparents for help!

were both filled with grain offerings of
choice flour moistened with olive oil. 26He
also brought a gold container weighing four
ounces, which was filled with incense. 27He
brought a young bull, a ram, and a one-year-
old male lamb for a burnt offering, 28and a
male goat for a sin offering. 29For a peace
offering he brought two bulls, five rams,
five male goats, and five one-year-old male
lambs. This was the offering brought by Eliab
son of Helon.

30On the fourth day Elizur son of Shedeur, leader
of the tribe of Reuben, presented his offering.
31His offering consisted of a silver platter
weighing 3¼ pounds and a silver basin
weighing 1¾ pounds (as measured by
the weight of the sanctuary shekel). These
were both filled with grain offerings of
choice flour moistened with olive oil. 32He
also brought a gold container weighing four
ounces, which was filled with incense. 33He
brought a young bull, a ram, and a one-year-
old male lamb for a burnt offering, 34and a
male goat for a sin offering. 35For a peace
offering he brought two bulls, five rams,
five male goats, and five one-year-old male
lambs. This was the offering brought by
Elizur son of Shedeur.

36On the fifth day Shelumiel son of Zurishaddai,
leader of the tribe of Simeon, presented his offering.
37His offering consisted of a silver platter
weighing 3¼ pounds and a silver basin
weighing 1¾ pounds (as measured by
the weight of the sanctuary shekel). These
were both filled with grain offerings of
choice flour moistened with olive oil. 38He
also brought a gold container weighing four
ounces, which was filled with incense. 39He
brought a young bull, a ram, and a one-year-
old male lamb for a burnt offering, 40and a
male goat for a sin offering. 41For a peace
offering he brought two bulls, five rams,
five male goats, and five one-year-old male
lambs. This was the offering brought by
Shelumiel son of Zurishaddai.

42On the sixth day Eliasaph son of Deuel, leader
of the tribe of Gad, presented his offering.
43His offering consisted of a silver platter
weighing 3¼ pounds and a silver basin
weighing 1¾ pounds (as measured by
the weight of the sanctuary shekel). These
were both filled with grain offerings of
choice flour moistened with olive oil. 44He
also brought a gold container weighing four
ounces, which was filled with incense. 45He
brought a young bull, a ram, and a one-year-
old male lamb for a burnt offering, 46and a
male goat for a sin offering. 47For a peace
offering he brought two bulls, five rams,
five male goats, and five one-year-old male
lambs. This was the offering brought by
Eliasaph son of Deuel.

48On the seventh day Elishama son of Ammihud,
leader of the tribe of Ephraim, presented his
offering.
49His offering consisted of a silver platter
weighing 3¼ pounds and a silver basin
weighing 1¾ pounds (as measured by
the weight of the sanctuary shekel). These
were both filled with grain offerings of
choice flour moistened with olive oil. 50He
also brought a gold container weighing four
ounces, which was filled with incense. 51He
brought a young bull, a ram, and a one-year-
old male lamb for a burnt offering, 52and a
male goat for a sin offering. 53For a peace
offering he brought two bulls, five rams,
five male goats, and five one-year-old male
lambs. This was the offering brought by
Elishama son of Ammihud.

54On the eighth day Gamaliel son of Pedahzur,
leader of the tribe of Manasseh, presented his offering.
55His offering consisted of a silver platter
weighing 3¼ pounds and a silver basin
weighing 1¾ pounds (as measured by
the weight of the sanctuary shekel). These
were both filled with grain offerings of
choice flour moistened with olive oil. 56He
also brought a gold container weighing four
ounces, which was filled with incense. 57He
brought a young bull, a ram, and a one-year-
old male lamb for a burnt offering, 58and a
male goat for a sin offering. 59For a peace
offering he brought two bulls, five rams,
five male goats, and five one-year-old male
lambs. This was the offering brought by
Gamaliel son of Pedahzur.

60On the ninth day Abidan son of Gideoni, leader
of the tribe of Benjamin, presented his offering.
61His offering consisted of a silver platter
weighing 3¼ pounds and a silver basin
weighing 1¾ pounds (as measured by
the weight of the sanctuary shekel). These
were both filled with grain offerings of

choice flour moistened with olive oil. 62He
also brought a gold container weighing four
ounces, which was filled with incense. 63He
brought a young bull, a ram, and a one-year-
old male lamb for a burnt offering, 64and a
male goat for a sin offering. 65For a peace
offering he brought two bulls, five rams,
five male goats, and five one-year-old male
lambs. This was the offering brought by
Abidan son of Gideoni.

66On the tenth day Ahiezer son of Ammishaddai, leader of the tribe of Dan, presented his offering.

67His offering consisted of a silver platter
weighing 3¼ pounds and a silver basin
weighing 1¾ pounds (as measured by
the weight of the sanctuary shekel). These
were both filled with grain offerings of
choice flour moistened with olive oil. 68He
also brought a gold container weighing four
ounces, which was filled with incense. 69He
brought a young bull, a ram, and a one-year-
old male lamb for a burnt offering, 70and a
male goat for a sin offering. 71For a peace
offering he brought two bulls, five rams,
five male goats, and five one-year-old male
lambs. This was the offering brought by
Ahiezer son of Ammishaddai.

72On the eleventh day Pagiel son of Ocran, leader
of the tribe of Asher, presented his offering.

73His offering consisted of a silver platter
weighing 3¼ pounds and a silver basin
weighing 1¾ pounds (as measured by
the weight of the sanctuary shekel). These
were both filled with grain offerings of
choice flour moistened with olive oil. 74He
also brought a gold container weighing four
ounces, which was filled with incense. 75He
brought a young bull, a ram, and a one-year-
old male lamb for a burnt offering, 76and a
male goat for a sin offering. 77For a peace
offering he brought two bulls, five rams,
five male goats, and five one-year-old male
lambs. This was the offering brought by
Pagiel son of Ocran.

78On the twelfth day Ahira son of Enan, leader of
the tribe of Naphtali, presented his offering.

79His offering consisted of a silver platter
weighing 3¼ pounds and a silver basin
weighing 1¾ pounds (as measured by
the weight of the sanctuary shekel). These
were both filled with grain offerings of
choice flour moistened with olive oil. 80He
also brought a gold container weighing four
ounces, which was filled with incense. 81He
brought a young bull, a ram, and a one-year-
old male lamb for a burnt offering, 82and a
male goat for a sin offering. 83For a peace
offering he brought two bulls, five rams,
five male goats, and five one-year-old male
lambs. This was the offering brought by
Ahira son of Enan.

84So this was the dedication offering brought
by the leaders of Israel at the time the altar was
anointed: twelve silver platters, twelve silver basins, and twelve gold incense containers. 85Each
silver platter weighed 3¼ pounds, and each silver basin weighed 1¾ pounds. The total weight
of the silver was 60 pounds (as measured by the
weight of the sanctuary shekel). 86Each of the
twelve gold containers that was filled with incense weighed four ounces (as measured by the
weight of the sanctuary shekel). The total weight
of the gold was three pounds. 87Twelve young
bulls, twelve rams, and twelve one-year-old male
lambs were donated for the burnt offerings,
along with their prescribed grain offerings.
Twelve male goats were brought for the sin offerings. 88Twenty-four bulls, sixty rams, sixty male
goats, and sixty one-year-old male lambs were
donated for the peace offerings. This was the
dedication offering for the altar after it was
anointed.

89Whenever Moses went into the Tabernacle
to speak with the LORD, he heard the voice speaking to him from between the two cherubim
above the Ark's cover—the place of atonement—
that rests on the Ark of the Covenant. The LORD
spoke to him from there.

CHAPTER 8

Preparing the Lamps

The LORD said to Moses, 2"Give Aaron the following instructions: When you set up the seven
lamps in the lampstand, place them so their light
shines forward in front of the lampstand." 3So
Aaron did this. He set up the seven lamps so they
reflected their light forward, just as the LORD
had commanded Moses. 4The entire lampstand,
from its base to its decorative blossoms, was
made of beaten gold. It was built according to the
exact design the LORD had shown Moses.

The Levites Dedicated

5Then the LORD said to Moses, 6"Now set the Levites apart from the rest of the people of Israel
and make them ceremonially clean. 7Do this by

sprinkling them with the water of purification, and have them shave their entire body and wash their clothing. Then they will be ceremonially clean. [8]Have them bring a young bull and a grain offering of choice flour moistened with olive oil, along with a second young bull for a sin offering. [9]Then assemble the whole community of Israel, and present the Levites at the entrance of the Tabernacle. [10]When you present the Levites before the LORD, the people of Israel must lay their hands on them. [11]Raising his hands, Aaron must then present the Levites to the LORD as a special offering from the people of Israel, thus dedicating them to the LORD's service.

[12]"Next the Levites will lay their hands on the heads of the young bulls. Present one as a sin offering and the other as a burnt offering to the LORD, to purify the Levites and make them right with the LORD. [13]Then have the Levites stand in front of Aaron and his sons, and raise your hands and present them as a special offering to the LORD. [14]In this way, you will set the Levites apart from the rest of the people of Israel, and the Levites will belong to me. [15]After this, they may go into the Tabernacle to do their work, because you have purified them and presented them as a special offering.

[16]"Of all the people of Israel, the Levites are reserved for me. I have claimed them for myself in place of all the firstborn sons of the Israelites; I have taken the Levites as their substitutes. [17]For all the firstborn males among the people of Israel are mine, both of people and of animals. I set them apart for myself on the day I struck down all the firstborn sons of the Egyptians. [18]Yes, I have claimed the Levites in place of all the firstborn sons of Israel. [19]And of all the Israelites, I have assigned the Levites to Aaron and his sons. They will serve in the Tabernacle on behalf of the Israelites and make sacrifices to purify the people so no plague will strike them when they approach the sanctuary."

[20]So Moses, Aaron, and the whole community of Israel dedicated the Levites, carefully following all the LORD's instructions to Moses. [21]The Levites purified themselves from sin and washed their clothes, and Aaron lifted them up and presented them to the LORD as a special offering. He then offered a sacrifice to purify them and make them right with the LORD. [22]After that the Levites went into the Tabernacle to perform their duties, assisting Aaron and his sons. So they carried out all the commands that the LORD gave Moses concerning the Levites.

[23]The LORD also instructed Moses, [24]"This is the rule the Levites must follow: They must begin serving in the Tabernacle at the age of twenty-five, [25]and they must retire at the age of fifty. [26]After retirement they may assist their fellow Levites by serving as guards at the Tabernacle, but they may not officiate in the service. This is how you must assign duties to the Levites."

CHAPTER 9

The Second Passover

A year after Israel's departure from Egypt, the LORD spoke to Moses in the wilderness of Sinai. In the first month of that year he said, [2]"Tell the Israelites to celebrate the Passover at the prescribed time, [3]at twilight on the fourteenth day of the first month. Be sure to follow all my decrees and regulations concerning this celebration."

[4]So Moses told the people to celebrate the Passover [5]in the wilderness of Sinai as twilight fell on the fourteenth day of the month. And they celebrated the festival there, just as the LORD had commanded Moses. [6]But some of the men had been ceremonially defiled by touching a dead body, so they could not celebrate the Passover that day. They came to Moses and Aaron that day [7]and said, "We have become ceremonially unclean by touching a dead body. But why should we be prevented from presenting the LORD's offering at the proper time with the rest of the Israelites?"

[8]Moses answered, "Wait here until I have received instructions for you from the LORD."

[9]This was the LORD's reply to Moses. [10]"Give the following instructions to the people of Israel: If any of the people now or in future generations are ceremonially unclean at Passover time because of touching a dead body, or if they are on a journey and cannot be present at the ceremony, they may still celebrate the LORD's Passover. [11]They must offer the Passover sacrifice one month later, at twilight on the fourteenth day of the second month. They must eat the Passover lamb at that time with bitter salad greens and bread made without yeast. [12]They must not leave any of the lamb until the next morning, and they must not break any of its bones. They must follow all the normal regulations concerning the Passover.

[13]"But those who neglect to celebrate the Passover at the regular time, even though they are ceremonially clean and not away on a trip, will be cut off from the community of Israel. If they fail to present the LORD's offering at the proper time, they will suffer the consequences

of their guilt. 14And if foreigners living among
you want to celebrate the Passover to the LORD,
they must follow these same decrees and regulations. The same laws apply both to native-
born Israelites and to the foreigners living
among you."

The Fiery Cloud

15On the day the Tabernacle was set up, the
cloud covered it. But from evening until morning the cloud over the Tabernacle looked like a
pillar of fire. 16This was the regular pattern—at
night the cloud that covered the Tabernacle had
the appearance of fire. 17Whenever the cloud
lifted from over the sacred tent, the people of Israel would break camp and follow it. And wherever the cloud settled, the people of Israel would
set up camp. 18In this way, they traveled and
camped at the LORD's command wherever he
told them to go. Then they remained in their
camp as long as the cloud stayed over the Tabernacle. 19If the cloud remained over the Tabernacle for a long time, the Israelites stayed and
performed their duty to the LORD. 20Sometimes
the cloud would stay over the Tabernacle for
only a few days, so the people would stay for only
a few days, as the LORD commanded. Then at the
LORD's command they would break camp and
move on. 21Sometimes the cloud stayed only
overnight and lifted the next morning. But
day or night, when the cloud lifted, the people
broke camp and moved on. 22Whether the
cloud stayed above the Tabernacle for two days,
a month, or a year, the people of Israel stayed in
camp and did not move on. But as soon as it
lifted, they broke camp and moved on. 23So they
camped or traveled at the LORD's command, and
they did whatever the LORD told them through
Moses.

CHAPTER 10

The Silver Trumpets

Now the LORD said to Moses, 2"Make two trumpets of hammered silver for calling the community to assemble and for signaling the breaking
of camp. 3When both trumpets are blown, everyone must gather before you at the entrance of the
Tabernacle. 4But if only one trumpet is blown,
then only the leaders—the heads of the clans of
Israel—must present themselves to you.

5"When you sound the signal to move on, the
tribes camped on the east side of the Tabernacle must break camp and move forward. 6When
you sound the signal a second time, the tribes
camped on the south will follow. You must
sound short blasts as the signal for moving on.
7But when you call the people to an assembly,
blow the trumpets with a different signal. 8Only
the priests, Aaron's descendants, are allowed to
blow the trumpets. This is a permanent law for
you, to be observed from generation to generation.

9"When you arrive in your own land and go to
war against your enemies who attack you, sound
the alarm with the trumpets. Then the LORD your
God will remember you and rescue you from
your enemies. 10Blow the trumpets in times of
gladness, too, sounding them at your annual festivals and at the beginning of each month. And
blow the trumpets over your burnt offerings and
peace offerings. The trumpets will remind your
God of his covenant with you. I am the LORD your
God."

The Israelites Leave Sinai

11In the second year after Israel's departure from
Egypt—on the twentieth day of the second
month—the cloud lifted from the Tabernacle of
the Covenant. 12So the Israelites set out from the
wilderness of Sinai and traveled on from place to
place until the cloud stopped in the wilderness
of Paran.

13When the people set out for the first time,
following the instructions the LORD had given
through Moses, 14Judah's troops led the way.
They marched behind their banner, and their
leader was Nahshon son of Amminadab. 15They
were joined by the troops of the tribe of Issachar,
led by Nethanel son of Zuar, 16and the troops of
the tribe of Zebulun, led by Eliab son of Helon.

17Then the Tabernacle was taken down, and
the Gershonite and Merarite divisions of the Levites were next in the line of march, carrying the
Tabernacle with them. 18Reuben's troops went
next, marching behind their banner. Their
leader was Elizur son of Shedeur. 19They were
joined by the troops of the tribe of Simeon, led
by Shelumiel son of Zurishaddai, 20and the
troops of the tribe of Gad, led by Eliasaph son of
Deuel.

21Next came the Kohathite division of the Levites, carrying the sacred objects from the Tabernacle. Before they arrived at the next camp, the
Tabernacle would already be set up at its new location. 22Ephraim's troops went next, marching
behind their banner. Their leader was Elishama
son of Ammihud. 23They were joined by the
troops of the tribe of Manasseh, led by Gamaliel
son of Pedahzur, 24and the troops of the tribe of
Benjamin, led by Abidan son of Gideoni.

25Dan's troops went last, marching behind
their banner and serving as the rear guard for all
the tribal camps. Their leader was Ahiezer son of
Ammishaddai. 26They were joined by the troops
of the tribe of Asher, led by Pagiel son of Ocran,
27and the troops of the tribe of Naphtali, led by
Ahira son of Enan.

28This was the order in which the Israelites
marched, division by division.

29One day Moses said to his brother-in-law,
Hobab son of Reuel the Midianite, "We are on
our way to the place the LORD promised us, for he
said, 'I will give it to you.' Come with us and we
will treat you well, for the LORD has promised
wonderful blessings for Israel!"

30But Hobab replied, "No, I will not go. I must
return to my own land and family."

31"Please don't leave us," Moses pleaded. "You
know the places in the wilderness where we
should camp. Come, be our guide. 32If you do,
we'll share with you all the blessings the LORD
gives us."

33They marched for three days after leaving
the mountain of the LORD, with the Ark of the
LORD's Covenant moving ahead of them to show
them where to stop and rest. 34As they moved on
each day, the cloud of the LORD hovered over
them. 35And whenever the Ark set out, Moses
would shout, "Arise, O LORD, and let your enemies be scattered! Let them flee before you!"
36And when the Ark was set down, he would say,
"Return, O LORD, to the countless thousands of
Israel!"

CHAPTER 11

The People Complain to Moses

Soon the people began to complain about their
hardship, and the LORD heard everything they
said. Then the LORD's anger blazed against them,
and he sent a fire to rage among them, and he destroyed some of the people in the outskirts of the
camp. 2Then the people screamed to Moses for
help, and when he prayed to the LORD, the fire
stopped. 3After that, the area was known as Tabe-
rah (which means "the place of burning"), because fire from the LORD had burned among
them there.

4Then the foreign rabble who were traveling
with the Israelites began to crave the good things
of Egypt. And the people of Israel also began to
complain. "Oh, for some meat!" they exclaimed.
5"We remember the fish we used to eat for free in
Egypt. And we had all the cucumbers, melons,
leeks, onions, and garlic we wanted. 6But now our
appetites are gone. All we ever see is this manna!"

7The manna looked like small coriander
seeds, and it was pale yellow like gum resin. 8The
people would go out and gather it from the
ground. They made flour by grinding it with
hand mills or pounding it in mortars. Then they
boiled it in a pot and made it into flat cakes.
These cakes tasted like pastries baked with olive
oil. 9The manna came down on the camp with
the dew during the night.

10Moses heard all the families standing in the
doorways of their tents whining, and the LORD
became extremely angry. Moses was also very ag-
gravated. 11And Moses said to the LORD, "Why
are you treating me, your servant, so harshly?
Have mercy on me! What did I do to deserve the
burden of all these people? 12Did I give birth to
them? Did I bring them into the world? Why did
you tell me to carry them in my arms like a
mother carries a nursing baby? How can I carry
them to the land you swore to give their ancestors? 13Where am I supposed to get meat for all
these people? They keep whining to me, saying,
'Give us meat to eat!' 14I can't carry all these people by myself! The load is far too heavy! 15If this is
how you intend to treat me, just go ahead and kill
me. Do me a favor and spare me this misery!"

Moses Chooses Seventy Leaders

16Then the LORD said to Moses, "Gather before
me seventy men who are recognized as elders
and leaders of Israel. Bring them to the Tabernacle to stand there with you. 17I will come down
and talk to you there. I will take some of the Spirit
that is upon you, and I will put the Spirit upon
them also. They will bear the burden of the people along with you, so you will not have to carry it
alone.

18"And say to the people, 'Purify yourselves, for
tomorrow you will have meat to eat. You were
whining, and the LORD heard you when you
cried, "Oh, for some meat! We were better off in
Egypt!" Now the LORD will give you meat, and you
will have to eat it. 19And it won't be for just a day
or two, or for five or ten or even twenty. 20You will
eat it for a whole month until you gag and are
sick of it. For you have rejected the LORD, who is
here among you, and you have whined to him,
saying, "Why did we ever leave Egypt?"'"

21But Moses responded to the LORD, "There are
600,000 foot soldiers here with me, and yet you
say, 'I will give them meat for a whole month!'
22Even if we butchered all our flocks and herds,
would that satisfy them? Even if we caught all the
fish in the sea, would that be enough?"

23 Then the LORD said to Moses, "Has my arm
lost its power? Now you will see whether or not
my word comes true!"
24 So Moses went out and reported the LORD's
words to the people. He gathered the seventy elders and stationed them around the Tabernacle.
25 And the LORD came down in the cloud and
spoke to Moses. Then he gave the seventy elders
the same Spirit that was upon Moses. And when
the Spirit rested upon them, they prophesied.
But this never happened again.
26 Two men, Eldad and Medad, had stayed behind in the camp. They were listed among the
elders, but they had not gone out to the Tabernacle. Yet the Spirit rested upon them as well, so
they prophesied there in the camp. 27 A young
man ran and reported to Moses, "Eldad and Medad are prophesying in the camp!"
28 Joshua son of Nun, who had been Moses' assistant since his youth, protested, "Moses, my
master, make them stop!"
29 But Moses replied, "Are you jealous for my
sake? I wish that all the LORD's people were
prophets and that the LORD would put his Spirit
upon them all!" 30 Then Moses returned to the
camp with the elders of Israel.

The LORD Sends Quail

31 Now the LORD sent a wind that brought quail
from the sea and let them fall all around the
camp. For miles in every direction there were
quail flying about three feet above the ground.
32 So the people went out and caught quail all
that day and throughout the night and all the
next day, too. No one gathered less than fifty
bushels! They spread the quail all around the
camp to dry. 33 But while they were gorging themselves on the meat—while it was still in their
mouths—the anger of the LORD blazed against
the people, and he struck them with a severe
plague. 34 So that place was called Kibroth-
hattaavah (which means "graves of gluttony")
because there they buried the people who
had craved meat from Egypt. 35 From Kibroth-
hattaavah the Israelites traveled to Hazeroth,
where they stayed for some time.

CHAPTER 12
The Complaints of Miriam and Aaron

While they were at Hazeroth, Miriam and Aaron
criticized Moses because he had married a
Cushite woman. 2 They said, "Has the LORD spoken only through Moses? Hasn't he spoken
through us, too?" But the LORD heard them.
3 (Now Moses was very humble—more humble
than any other person on earth.)
4 So immediately the LORD called to Moses,
Aaron, and Miriam and said, "Go out to the Tabernacle, all three of you!" So the three of them
went to the Tabernacle. 5 Then the LORD descended in the pillar of cloud and stood at
the entrance of the Tabernacle. "Aaron and Miriam!" he called, and they stepped forward.
6 And the LORD said to them, "Now listen to
what I say:

"If there were prophets among you,
I, the LORD, would reveal myself
in visions.
I would speak to them in dreams.
7 But not with my servant Moses.
Of all my house, he is the one I trust.
8 I speak to him face to face,
clearly, and not in riddles!
He sees the LORD as he is.
So why were you not afraid
to criticize my servant Moses?"

9 The LORD was very angry with them, and he
departed. 10 As the cloud moved from above the
Tabernacle, there stood Miriam, her skin as
white as snow from leprosy. When Aaron saw
what had happened to her, 11 he cried out to
Moses, "Oh, my master! Please don't punish us
for this sin we have so foolishly committed.
12 Don't let her be like a stillborn baby, already decayed at birth."
13 So Moses cried out to the LORD, "O God, I beg
you, please heal her!"
14 But the LORD said to Moses, "If her father
had done nothing more than spit in her face,
wouldn't she be defiled for seven days? So keep
her outside the camp for seven days, and after
that she may be accepted back."
15 So Miriam was kept outside the camp for
seven days, and the people waited until she was
brought back before they traveled again. 16 Then
they left Hazeroth and camped in the wilderness
of Paran.

CHAPTER 13
Twelve Scouts Explore Canaan

The LORD now said to Moses, 2 "Send out men to
explore the land of Canaan, the land I am giving
to the Israelites. Send one leader from each of
the twelve ancestral tribes." 3 So Moses did as the
LORD commanded him. He sent out twelve men,
all tribal leaders of Israel, from their camp in the
wilderness of Paran. 4 These were the tribes and
the names of their leaders:

Numbers 13 . . . page 148

Cross-Eyed

God has made tons of promises to you in his Word. Here are just a few of them: Deuteronomy 31:6; Jeremiah 29:11; John 3:16. What others can you find in the Bible?

When Moses sent spies into the Promised Land, Caleb and Joshua were the only ones who could see past the soldiers to God's promises. **Read all about it in NUMBERS 13:25-14:9.** Try this amazing optical illusion to see things like Caleb and Joshua did!

1 Fold a piece of paper in half. Draw a person just to the left of your fold without drawing on the fold. Draw a field just to the right.

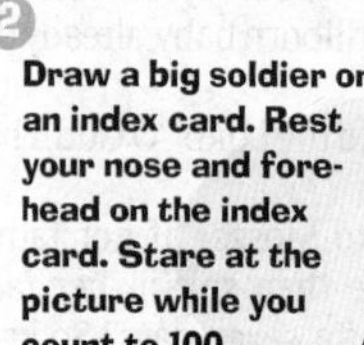

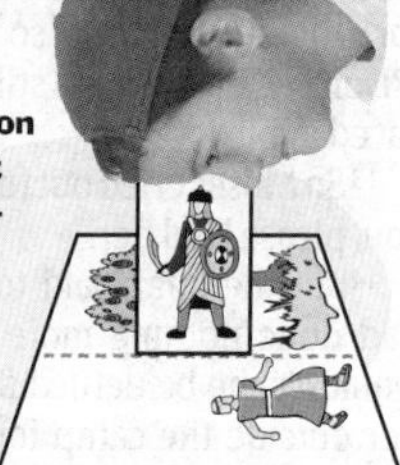

2 Draw a big soldier on an index card. Rest your nose and forehead on the index card. Stare at the picture while you count to 100.

What do you see?

Did you see the Israelite cross over to the Promised Land? Pretty cool, huh? Caleb and Joshua saw past the soldiers, and they remembered God's promises.

When have you had to stand up for what God says is true when others disagreed? What happened?

Tribe	*Leader*
Reuben	Shammua son of Zaccur
5 Simeon	Shaphat son of Hori
6 Judah	Caleb son of Jephunneh
7 Issachar	Igal son of Joseph
8 Ephraim	Hoshea son of Nun
9 Benjamin	Palti son of Raphu
10 Zebulun	Gaddiel son of Sodi
11 Manasseh son of Joseph	Gaddi son of Susi
12 Dan	Ammiel son of Gemalli
13 Asher	Sethur son of Michael
14 Naphtali	Nahbi son of Vophsi
15 Gad	Geuel son of Maki

16These are the names of the men Moses sent out
to explore the land. (Moses called Hoshea son of
Nun by the name Joshua.)
17Moses gave the men these instructions as he
sent them out to explore the land: "Go north
through the Negev into the hill country. 18See
what the land is like, and find out whether the
people living there are strong or weak, few or
many. 19See what kind of land they live in. Is it
good or bad? Do their towns have walls, or are
they unprotected like open camps? 20Is the soil
fertile or poor? Are there many trees? Do your
best to bring back samples of the crops you see."
(It happened to be the season for harvesting the
first ripe grapes.)
21So they went up and explored the land from
the wilderness of Zin as far as Rehob, near Lebo-hamath. 22Going north, they passed through the
Negev and arrived at Hebron, where Ahiman,
Sheshai, and Talmai—all descendants of Anak—
lived. (The ancient town of Hebron was founded
seven years before the Egyptian city of Zoan.)
23When they came to the valley of Eshcol, they
cut down a branch with a single cluster of grapes
so large that it took two of them to carry it on a
pole between them! They also brought back
samples of the pomegranates and figs. 24That
place was called the valley of Eshcol (which
means "cluster"), because of the cluster of grapes
the Israelite men cut there.

The Scouting Report

25After exploring the land for forty days, the men
returned 26to Moses, Aaron, and the whole community of Israel at Kadesh in the wilderness of
Paran. They reported to the whole community
what they had seen and showed them the fruit
they had taken from the land. 27This was their
report to Moses: "We entered the land you sent
us to explore, and it is indeed a bountiful country—a land flowing with milk and honey. Here is

the kind of fruit it produces. 28But the people living there are powerful, and their towns are large
and fortified. We even saw giants there, the descendants of Anak! 29The Amalekites live in the
Negev, and the Hittites, Jebusites, and Amorites
live in the hill country. The Canaanites live along
the coast of the Mediterranean Sea and along the
Jordan Valley."

30But Caleb tried to quiet the people as they
stood before Moses. "Let's go at once to take the
land," he said. "We can certainly conquer it!"

31But the other men who had explored the
land with him disagreed. "We can't go up against
them! They are stronger than we are!" 32So they
spread this bad report about the land among the
Israelites: "The land we traveled through and explored will devour anyone who goes to live there.
All the people we saw were huge. 33We even saw
giants there, the descendants of Anak. Next to
them we felt like grasshoppers, and that's what
they thought, too!"

CHAPTER 14

The People Rebel

Then the whole community began weeping
aloud, and they cried all night. 2Their voices rose
in a great chorus of protest against Moses and
Aaron. "If only we had died in Egypt, or even here
in the wilderness!" they complained. 3"Why is
the LORD taking us to this country only to have us
die in battle? Our wives and our little ones will be
carried off as plunder! Wouldn't it be better for
us to return to Egypt?" 4Then they plotted among
themselves, "Let's choose a new leader and go
back to Egypt!"

5Then Moses and Aaron fell face down on the
ground before the whole community of Israel.
6Two of the men who had explored the land,
Joshua son of Nun and Caleb son of Jephunneh,
tore their clothing. 7They said to all the people of
Israel, "The land we traveled through and explored is a wonderful land! 8And if the LORD is
pleased with us, he will bring us safely into that
land and give it to us. It is a rich land flowing with
milk and honey. 9Do not rebel against the LORD,
and don't be afraid of the people of the land.
They are only helpless prey to us! They have no
protection, but the LORD is with us! Don't be
afraid of them!"

10But the whole community began to talk
about stoning Joshua and Caleb. Then the glorious presence of the LORD appeared to all the Israelites at the Tabernacle. 11And the LORD said to
Moses, "How long will these people treat me with
contempt? Will they never believe me, even after
all the miraculous signs I have done among
them? 12I will disown them and destroy them
with a plague. Then I will make you into a nation
greater and mightier than they are!"

Moses Intercedes for the People

13But Moses objected. "What will the Egyptians
think when they hear about it?" he asked the
LORD. "They know full well the power you displayed in rescuing your people from Egypt.
14Now if you destroy them, the Egyptians will
send a report to the inhabitants of this land, who
have already heard that you live among your
people. They know, LORD, that you have appeared to your people face to face and that your
pillar of cloud hovers over them. They know that
you go before them in the pillar of cloud by day
and the pillar of fire by night. 15Now if you
slaughter all these people with a single blow, the
nations that have heard of your fame will say,
16'The LORD was not able to bring them into the
land he swore to give them, so he killed them in
the wilderness.'

17"Please, Lord, prove that your power is as
great as you have claimed. For you said, 18'The
LORD is slow to anger and filled with unfailing
love, forgiving every kind of sin and rebellion.
But he does not excuse the guilty. He lays the
sins of the parents upon their children; the entire family is affected—even children in the
third and fourth generations.' 19In keeping with
your magnificent, unfailing love, please pardon
the sins of this people, just as you have forgiven
them ever since they left Egypt."

20Then the LORD said, "I will pardon them as
you have requested. 21But as surely as I live, and
as surely as the earth is filled with the LORD's
glory, 22not one of these people will ever enter
that land. They have all seen my glorious presence and the miraculous signs I performed
both in Egypt and in the wilderness, but again
and again they have tested me by refusing to listen to my voice. 23They will never even see the
land I swore to give their ancestors. None of
those who have treated me with contempt will
ever see it. 24But my servant Caleb has a different attitude than the others have. He has remained loyal to me, so I will bring him into the
land he explored. His descendants will possess
their full share of that land. 25Now turn around,
and don't go on toward the land where the Amalekites and Canaanites live. Tomorrow you must
set out for the wilderness in the direction of the
Red Sea."

The LORD Punishes the Israelites

26 Then the LORD said to Moses and Aaron, 27 "How long must I put up with this wicked community and its complaints about me? Yes, I have heard the complaints the Israelites are making against me. 28 Now tell them this: 'As surely as I live, declares the LORD, I will do to you the very things I heard you say. 29 You will all drop dead in this wilderness! Because you complained against me, every one of you who is twenty years old or older and was included in the registration will die. 30 You will not enter and occupy the land I swore to give you. The only exceptions will be Caleb son of Jephunneh and Joshua son of Nun.

31 " 'You said your children would be carried off as plunder. Well, I will bring them safely into the land, and they will enjoy what you have despised. 32 But as for you, you will drop dead in this wilderness. 33 And your children will be like shepherds, wandering in the wilderness for forty years. In this way, they will pay for your faithlessness, until the last of you lies dead in the wilderness.

34 " 'Because your men explored the land for forty days, you must wander in the wilderness for forty years—a year for each day, suffering the consequences of your sins. Then you will discover what it is like to have me for an enemy.' 35 I, the LORD, have spoken! I will certainly do these things to every member of the community who has conspired against me. They will be destroyed here in this wilderness, and here they will die!"

36 The ten men Moses had sent to explore the land—the ones who incited rebellion against the LORD with their bad report—37 were struck dead with a plague before the LORD. 38 Of the twelve who had explored the land, only Joshua and Caleb remained alive.

39 When Moses reported the LORD's words to all the Israelites, the people were filled with grief. 40 Then they got up early the next morning and went to the top of the range of hills. "Let's go," they said. "We realize that we have sinned, but now we are ready to enter the land the LORD has promised us."

41 But Moses said, "Why are you now disobeying the LORD's orders to return to the wilderness? It won't work. 42 Do not go up into the land now. You will only be crushed by your enemies because the LORD is not with you. 43 When you face the Amalekites and Canaanites in battle, you will be slaughtered. The LORD will abandon you because you have abandoned the LORD."

44 But the people defiantly pushed ahead toward the hill country, even though neither Moses nor the Ark of the LORD's Covenant left the camp. 45 Then the Amalekites and the Canaanites who lived in those hills came down and attacked them and chased them back as far as Hormah.

CHAPTER **15**

Laws concerning Offerings

Then the LORD told Moses, 2 "Give the following instructions to the people of Israel.

"When you finally settle in the land I am giving you, 3 you will offer special gifts as a pleasing aroma to the LORD. These gifts may take the form of a burnt offering, a sacrifice to fulfill a vow, a voluntary offering, or an offering at any of your annual festivals, and they may be taken from your herds of cattle or your flocks of sheep and goats. 4 When you present these offerings, you must also give the LORD a grain offering of two quarts of choice flour mixed with one quart of olive oil. 5 For each lamb offered as a burnt offering or a special sacrifice, you must also present one quart of wine as a liquid offering.

6 "If the sacrifice is a ram, give a grain offering of four quarts of choice flour mixed with a third of a gallon of olive oil, 7 and give a third of a gallon of wine as a liquid offering. This will be a pleasing aroma to the LORD.

8 "When you present a young bull as a burnt offering or as a sacrifice to fulfill a vow or as a peace offering to the LORD, 9 you must also give a grain offering of six quarts of choice flour mixed with two quarts of olive oil, 10 and give two quarts of wine as a liquid offering. This will be a special gift, a pleasing aroma to the LORD.

11 "Each sacrifice of a bull, ram, lamb, or young goat should be prepared in this way. 12 Follow these instructions with each offering you present. 13 All of you native-born Israelites must follow these instructions when you offer a special gift as a pleasing aroma to the LORD. 14 And if any foreigners visit you or live among you and want to present a special gift as a pleasing aroma to the LORD, they must follow these same procedures. 15 Native-born Israelites and foreigners are equal before the LORD and are subject to the same decrees. This is a permanent law for you, to be observed from generation to generation. 16 The same instructions and regulations will apply both to you and to the foreigners living among you."

17 Then the LORD said to Moses, 18 "Give the following instructions to the people of Israel.

"When you arrive in the land where I am taking you, 19 and you eat the crops that grow there, you must set some aside as a sacred offering to the LORD. 20 Present a cake from the first of the flour you grind, and set it aside as a sacred offering, as you do with the first grain from the threshing floor. 21 Throughout the generations to come, you are to present a sacred offering to the LORD each year from the first of your ground flour.

22 "But suppose you unintentionally fail to carry out all these commands that the LORD has given you through Moses. 23 And suppose your descendants in the future fail to do everything the LORD has commanded through Moses. 24 If the mistake was made unintentionally, and the community was unaware of it, the whole community must present a young bull for a burnt offering as a pleasing aroma to the LORD. It must be offered along with its prescribed grain offering and liquid offering and with one male goat for a sin offering. 25 With it the priest will purify the whole community of Israel, making them right with the LORD, and they will be forgiven. For it was an unintentional sin, and they have corrected it with their offerings to the LORD—the special gift and the sin offering. 26 The whole community of Israel will be forgiven, including the foreigners living among you, for all the people were involved in the sin.

27 "If one individual commits an unintentional sin, the guilty person must bring a one-year-old female goat for a sin offering. 28 The priest will sacrifice it to purify the guilty person before the LORD, and that person will be forgiven. 29 These same instructions apply both to native-born Israelites and to the foreigners living among you.

30 "But those who brazenly violate the LORD's will, whether native-born Israelites or foreigners, have blasphemed the LORD, and they must be cut off from the community. 31 Since they have treated the LORD's word with contempt and deliberately disobeyed his command, they must be completely cut off and suffer the punishment for their guilt."

Penalty for Breaking the Sabbath

32 One day while the people of Israel were in the wilderness, they discovered a man gathering wood on the Sabbath day. 33 The people who found him doing this took him before Moses, Aaron, and the rest of the community. 34 They held him in custody because they did not know what to do with him. 35 Then the LORD said to Moses, "The man must be put to death! The whole community must stone him outside the camp." 36 So the whole community took the man outside the camp and stoned him to death, just as the LORD had commanded Moses.

Tassels on Clothing

37 Then the LORD said to Moses, 38 "Give the following instructions to the people of Israel: Throughout the generations to come you must make tassels for the hems of your clothing and attach them with a blue cord. 39 When you see the tassels, you will remember and obey all the commands of the LORD instead of following your own desires and defiling yourselves, as you are prone to do. 40 The tassels will help you remember that you must obey all my commands and be holy to your God. 41 I am the LORD your God who brought you out of the land of Egypt that I might be your God. I am the LORD your God!"

CHAPTER 16

Korah's Rebellion

One day Korah son of Izhar, a descendant of Kohath son of Levi, conspired with Dathan and Abiram, the sons of Eliab, and On son of Peleth, from the tribe of Reuben. 2 They incited a rebellion against Moses, along with 250 other leaders of the community, all prominent members of the assembly. 3 They united against Moses and Aaron and said, "You have gone too far! The whole community of Israel has been set apart by the LORD, and he is with all of us. What right do you have to act as though you are greater than the rest of the LORD's people?"

4 When Moses heard what they were saying, he fell face down on the ground. 5 Then he said to Korah and his followers, "Tomorrow morning the LORD will show us who belongs to him and who is holy. The LORD will allow only those whom he selects to enter his own presence. 6 Korah, you and all your followers must prepare your incense burners. 7 Light fires in them tomorrow, and burn incense before the LORD. Then we will see whom the LORD chooses as his holy one. You Levites are the ones who have gone too far!"

8 Then Moses spoke again to Korah: "Now listen, you Levites! 9 Does it seem insignificant to you that the God of Israel has chosen you from among all the community of Israel to be near him so you can serve in the LORD's Tabernacle and stand before the people to minister to them? 10 Korah, he has already given this special ministry to you and your fellow Levites. Are you now demanding the priesthood as well? 11 The LORD is the one you and your followers are really

revolting against! For who is Aaron that you are complaining about him?"

12Then Moses summoned Dathan and Abiram, the sons of Eliab, but they replied, "We refuse to come before you! 13Isn't it enough that you brought us out of Egypt, a land flowing with milk and honey, to kill us here in this wilderness, and that you now treat us like your subjects? 14What's more, you haven't brought us into another land flowing with milk and honey. You haven't given us a new homeland with fields and vineyards. Are you trying to fool these men? We will not come."

15Then Moses became very angry and said to the LORD, "Do not accept their grain offerings! I have not taken so much as a donkey from them, and I have never hurt a single one of them." 16And Moses said to Korah, "You and all your followers must come here tomorrow and present yourselves before the LORD. Aaron will also be here. 17You and each of your 250 followers must prepare an incense burner and put incense on it, so you can all present them before the LORD. Aaron will also bring his incense burner."

18So each of these men prepared an incense burner, lit the fire, and placed incense on it. Then they all stood at the entrance of the Tabernacle with Moses and Aaron. 19Meanwhile, Korah had stirred up the entire community against Moses and Aaron, and they all gathered at the Tabernacle entrance. Then the glorious presence of the LORD appeared to the whole community, 20and the LORD said to Moses and Aaron, 21"Get away from all these people so that I may instantly destroy them!"

22But Moses and Aaron fell face down on the ground. "O God," they pleaded, "you are the God who gives breath to all creatures. Must you be angry with all the people when only one man sins?"

23And the LORD said to Moses, 24"Then tell all the people to get away from the tents of Korah, Dathan, and Abiram."

25So Moses got up and rushed over to the tents of Dathan and Abiram, followed by the elders of Israel. 26"Quick!" he told the people. "Get away from the tents of these wicked men, and don't touch anything that belongs to them. If you do, you will be destroyed for their sins." 27So all the people stood back from the tents of Korah, Dathan, and Abiram. Then Dathan and Abiram came out and stood at the entrances of their tents, together with their wives and children and little ones.

28And Moses said, "This is how you will know that the LORD has sent me to do all these things that I have done—for I have not done them on my own. 29If these men die a natural death, or if nothing unusual happens, then the LORD has not sent me. 30But if the LORD does something entirely new and the ground opens its mouth and swallows them and all their belongings, and they go down alive into the grave, then you will know that these men have shown contempt for the LORD."

31He had hardly finished speaking the words when the ground suddenly split open beneath them. 32The earth opened its mouth and swallowed the men, along with their households and all their followers who were standing with them, and everything they owned. 33So they went down alive into the grave, along with all their belongings. The earth closed over them, and they all vanished from among the people of Israel. 34All the people around them fled when they heard their screams. "The earth will swallow us, too!" they cried. 35Then fire blazed forth from the LORD and burned up the 250 men who were offering incense.

36And the LORD said to Moses, 37"Tell Eleazar son of Aaron the priest to pull all the incense burners from the fire, for they are holy. Also tell him to scatter the burning coals. 38Take the incense burners of these men who have sinned at the cost of their lives, and hammer the metal into a thin sheet to overlay the altar. Since these burners were used in the LORD's presence, they have become holy. Let them serve as a warning to the people of Israel."

39So Eleazar the priest collected the 250 bronze incense burners that had been used by the men who died in the fire, and the bronze was hammered into a thin sheet to overlay the altar. 40This would warn the Israelites that no unauthorized person—no one who was not a descendant of Aaron—should ever enter the LORD's presence to burn incense. If anyone did, the same thing would happen to him as happened to Korah and his followers. So the LORD's instructions to Moses were carried out.

41But the very next morning the whole community of Israel began muttering again against Moses and Aaron, saying, "You have killed the LORD's people!" 42As the community gathered to protest against Moses and Aaron, they turned toward the Tabernacle and saw that the cloud had covered it, and the glorious presence of the LORD appeared.

43Moses and Aaron came and stood in front of the Tabernacle, 44and the LORD said to Moses,

45"Get away from all these people so that I can instantly destroy them!" But Moses and Aaron fell face down on the ground.

46And Moses said to Aaron, "Quick, take an incense burner and place burning coals on it from the altar. Lay incense on it, and carry it out among the people to purify them and make them right with the LORD. The LORD's anger is blazing against them—the plague has already begun."

47Aaron did as Moses told him and ran out among the people. The plague had already begun to strike down the people, but Aaron burned the incense and purified the people. 48He stood between the dead and the living, and the plague stopped. 49But 14,700 people died in that plague, in addition to those who had died in the affair involving Korah. 50Then because the plague had stopped, Aaron returned to Moses at the entrance of the Tabernacle.

CHAPTER 17
The Budding of Aaron's Staff

1Then the LORD said to Moses, 2"Tell the people of Israel to bring you twelve wooden staffs, one from each leader of Israel's ancestral tribes, and inscribe each leader's name on his staff. 3Inscribe Aaron's name on the staff of the tribe of Levi, for there must be one staff for the leader of each ancestral tribe. 4Place these staffs in the Tabernacle in front of the Ark containing the tablets of the Covenant, where I meet with you. 5Buds will sprout on the staff belonging to the man I choose. Then I will finally put an end to the people's murmuring and complaining against you."

6So Moses gave the instructions to the people of Israel, and each of the twelve tribal leaders, including Aaron, brought Moses a staff. 7Moses placed the staffs in the LORD's presence in the Tabernacle of the Covenant. 8When he went into the Tabernacle of the Covenant the next day, he found that Aaron's staff, representing the tribe of Levi, had sprouted, budded, blossomed, and produced ripe almonds!

9When Moses brought all the staffs out from the LORD's presence, he showed them to the people. Each man claimed his own staff. 10And the LORD said to Moses: "Place Aaron's staff permanently before the Ark of the Covenant to serve as a warning to rebels. This should put an end to their complaints against me and prevent any further deaths." 11So Moses did as the LORD commanded him.

12Then the people of Israel said to Moses, "Look, we are doomed! We are dead! We are ruined! 13Everyone who even comes close to the Tabernacle of the LORD dies. Are we all doomed to die?"

CHAPTER 18
Duties of Priests and Levites

Then the LORD said to Aaron: "You, your sons, and your relatives from the tribe of Levi will be held responsible for any offenses related to the sanctuary. But you and your sons alone will be held responsible for violations connected with the priesthood.

2"Bring your relatives of the tribe of Levi—your ancestral tribe—to assist you and your sons as you perform the sacred duties in front of the Tabernacle of the Covenant. 3But as the Levites go about all their assigned duties at the Tabernacle, they must be careful not to go near any of the sacred objects or the altar. If they do, both you and they will die. 4The Levites must join you in fulfilling their responsibilities for the care and maintenance of the Tabernacle, but no unauthorized person may assist you.

5"You yourselves must perform the sacred duties inside the sanctuary and at the altar. If you follow these instructions, the LORD's anger will never again blaze against the people of Israel. 6I myself have chosen your fellow Levites from among the Israelites to be your special assistants. They are a gift to you, dedicated to the LORD for service in the Tabernacle. 7But you and your sons, the priests, must personally handle all the priestly rituals associated with the altar and with everything behind the inner curtain. I am giving you the priesthood as your special privilege of service. Any unauthorized person who comes too near the sanctuary will be put to death."

Support for the Priests and Levites

8The LORD gave these further instructions to Aaron: "I myself have put you in charge of all the holy offerings that are brought to me by the people of Israel. I have given all these consecrated offerings to you and your sons as your permanent share. 9You are allotted the portion of the most holy offerings that is not burned on the fire. This portion of all the most holy offerings—including the grain offerings, sin offerings, and guilt offerings—will be most holy, and it belongs to you and your sons. 10You must eat it as a most holy offering. All the males may eat of it, and you must treat it as most holy.

11"All the sacred offerings and special offerings presented to me when the Israelites lift them up before the altar also belong to you. I have given them to you and to your sons and daughters as your permanent share. Any member of your family who is ceremonially clean may eat of these offerings.

12"I also give you the harvest gifts brought by the people as offerings to the LORD—the best of the olive oil, new wine, and grain. 13All the first crops of their land that the people present to the LORD belong to you. Any member of your family who is ceremonially clean may eat this food.

14"Everything in Israel that is specially set apart for the LORD also belongs to you.

15"The firstborn of every mother, whether human or animal, that is offered to the LORD will be yours. But you must always redeem your firstborn sons and the firstborn of ceremonially unclean animals. 16Redeem them when they are one month old. The redemption price is five pieces of silver (as measured by the weight of the sanctuary shekel, which equals twenty gerahs).

17"However, you may not redeem the firstborn of cattle, sheep, or goats. They are holy and have been set apart for the LORD. Sprinkle their blood on the altar, and burn their fat as a special gift, a pleasing aroma to the LORD. 18The meat of these animals will be yours, just like the breast and right thigh that are presented by lifting them up as a special offering before the altar. 19Yes, I am giving you all these holy offerings that the people of Israel bring to the LORD. They are for you and your sons and daughters, to be eaten as your permanent share. This is an eternal and unbreakable covenant between the LORD and you, and it also applies to your descendants."

20And the LORD said to Aaron, "You priests will receive no allotment of land or share of property among the people of Israel. I am your share and your allotment. 21As for the tribe of Levi, your relatives, I will compensate them for their service in the Tabernacle. Instead of an allotment of land, I will give them the tithes from the entire land of Israel.

22"From now on, no Israelites except priests or Levites may approach the Tabernacle. If they come too near, they will be judged guilty and will die. 23Only the Levites may serve at the Tabernacle, and they will be held responsible for any offenses against it. This is a permanent law for you, to be observed from generation to generation. The Levites will receive no allotment of land among the Israelites, 24because I have given them the Israelites' tithes, which have been presented as sacred offerings to the LORD. This will be the Levites' share. That is why I said they would receive no allotment of land among the Israelites."

25The LORD also told Moses, 26"Give these instructions to the Levites: When you receive from the people of Israel the tithes I have assigned as your allotment, give a tenth of the tithes you receive—a tithe of the tithe—to the LORD as a sacred offering. 27The LORD will consider this offering to be your harvest offering, as though it were the first grain from your own threshing floor or wine from your own winepress. 28You must present one-tenth of the tithe received from the Israelites as a sacred offering to the LORD. This is the LORD's sacred portion, and you must present it to Aaron the priest. 29Be sure to give to the LORD the best portions of the gifts given to you.

30"Also, give these instructions to the Levites: When you present the best part as your offering, it will be considered as though it came from your own threshing floor or winepress. 31You Levites and your families may eat this food anywhere you wish, for it is your compensation for serving in the Tabernacle. 32You will not be considered guilty for accepting the LORD's tithes if you give the best portion to the priests. But be careful not to treat the holy gifts of the people of Israel as though they were common. If you do, you will die."

CHAPTER 19
The Water of Purification

The LORD said to Moses and Aaron, 2"Here is another legal requirement commanded by the LORD: Tell the people of Israel to bring you a red heifer, a perfect animal that has no defects and has never been yoked to a plow. 3Give it to Eleazar the priest, and it will be taken outside the camp and slaughtered in his presence. 4Eleazar will take some of its blood on his finger and sprinkle it seven times toward the front of the Tabernacle. 5As Eleazar watches, the heifer must be burned—its hide, meat, blood, and dung. 6Eleazar the priest must then take a stick of cedar, a hyssop branch, and some scarlet yarn and throw them into the fire where the heifer is burning.

7"Then the priest must wash his clothes and bathe himself in water. Afterward he may return to the camp, though he will remain ceremonially unclean until evening. 8The man who burns the animal must also wash his clothes and bathe himself in water, and he, too, will remain unclean

until evening. 9Then someone who is ceremonially clean will gather up the ashes of the heifer
and deposit them in a purified place outside the
camp. They will be kept there for the community
of Israel to use in the water for the purification
ceremony. This ceremony is performed for the
removal of sin. 10The man who gathers up the
ashes of the heifer must also wash his clothes,
and he will remain ceremonially unclean until
evening. This is a permanent law for the people
of Israel and any foreigners who live among
them.

11"All those who touch a dead human body will
be ceremonially unclean for seven days. 12They
must purify themselves on the third and seventh
days with the water of purification; then they will
be purified. But if they do not do this on the third
and seventh days, they will continue to be unclean even after the seventh day. 13All those who
touch a dead body and do not purify themselves
in the proper way defile the LORD's Tabernacle,
and they will be cut off from the community of
Israel. Since the water of purification was not
sprinkled on them, their defilement continues.

14"This is the ritual law that applies when
someone dies inside a tent: All those who enter
that tent and those who were inside when the
death occurred will be ceremonially unclean for
seven days. 15Any open container in the tent that
was not covered with a lid is also defiled. 16And if
someone in an open field touches the corpse of
someone who was killed with a sword or who
died a natural death, or if someone touches a human bone or a grave, that person will be defiled
for seven days.

17"To remove the defilement, put some of the
ashes from the burnt purification offering in
a jar, and pour fresh water over them. 18Then
someone who is ceremonially clean must take a
hyssop branch and dip it into the water. That
person must sprinkle the water on the tent, on
all the furnishings in the tent, and on the people
who were in the tent; also on the person who
touched a human bone, or touched someone
who was killed or who died naturally, or
touched a grave. 19On the third and seventh
days the person who is ceremonially clean must
sprinkle the water on those who are defiled.
Then on the seventh day the people being
cleansed must wash their clothes and bathe
themselves, and that evening they will be
cleansed of their defilement.

20"But those who become defiled and do not
purify themselves will be cut off from the community, for they have defiled the sanctuary of the
LORD. Since the water of purification has not
been sprinkled on them, they remain defiled.
21This is a permanent law for the people. Those
who sprinkle the water of purification must afterward wash their clothes, and anyone who
then touches the water used for purification will
remain defiled until evening. 22Anything and
anyone that a defiled person touches will be ceremonially unclean until evening."

CHAPTER 20

Moses Strikes the Rock

In the first month of the year, the whole community of Israel arrived in the wilderness of Zin and
camped at Kadesh. While they were there, Miriam died and was buried.

2There was no water for the people to drink at
that place, so they rebelled against Moses and
Aaron. 3The people blamed Moses and said, "If
only we had died in the LORD's presence with our
brothers! 4Why have you brought the congregation of the LORD's people into this wilderness to
die, along with all our livestock? 5Why did you
make us leave Egypt and bring us here to this
terrible place? This land has no grain, no figs,
no grapes, no pomegranates, and no water to
drink!"

6Moses and Aaron turned away from the people and went to the entrance of the Tabernacle,
where they fell face down on the ground. Then
the glorious presence of the LORD appeared to
them, 7and the LORD said to Moses, 8"You and
Aaron must take the staff and assemble the entire community. As the people watch, speak to
the rock over there, and it will pour out its water.
You will provide enough water from the rock to
satisfy the whole community and their livestock."

9So Moses did as he was told. He took the staff
from the place where it was kept before the
LORD. 10Then he and Aaron summoned the people to come and gather at the rock. "Listen, you
rebels!" he shouted. "Must we bring you water
from this rock?" 11Then Moses raised his hand
and struck the rock twice with the staff, and water gushed out. So the entire community and
their livestock drank their fill.

12But the LORD said to Moses and Aaron, "Because you did not trust me enough to demonstrate my holiness to the people of Israel, you will
not lead them into the land I am giving them!"
13This place was known as the waters of Meribah (which means "arguing") because there the
people of Israel argued with the LORD, and there
he demonstrated his holiness among them.

Numbers 21 . . . page 156

Edom Refuses Israel Passage

14While Moses was at Kadesh, he sent ambassadors to the king of Edom with this message:

> "This is what your relatives, the people of
> Israel, say: You know all the hardships we
> have been through. 15Our ancestors went
> down to Egypt, and we lived there a long
> time, and we and our ancestors were brutally
> mistreated by the Egyptians. 16But when we
> cried out to the LORD, he heard us and sent
> an angel who brought us out of Egypt. Now
> we are camped at Kadesh, a town on the
> border of your land. 17Please let us travel
> through your land. We will be careful not
> to go through your fields and vineyards.
> We won't even drink water from your wells.
> We will stay on the king's road and never
> leave it until we have passed through your
> territory."

18But the king of Edom said, "Stay out of my
land, or I will meet you with an army!"

19The Israelites answered, "We will stay on the
main road. If our livestock drink your water, we
will pay for it. Just let us pass through your country. That's all we ask."

20But the king of Edom replied, "Stay out! You
may not pass through our land." With that he
mobilized his army and marched out against
them with an imposing force. 21Because Edom
refused to allow Israel to pass through their
country, Israel was forced to turn around.

The Death of Aaron

22The whole community of Israel left Kadesh
and arrived at Mount Hor. 23There, on the border
of the land of Edom, the LORD said to Moses and
Aaron, 24"The time has come for Aaron to join
his ancestors in death. He will not enter the land
I am giving the people of Israel, because the two
of you rebelled against my instructions concerning the water at Meribah. 25Now take Aaron and
his son Eleazar up Mount Hor. 26There you will
remove Aaron's priestly garments and put them
on Eleazar, his son. Aaron will die there and join
his ancestors."

27So Moses did as the LORD commanded. The
three of them went up Mount Hor together as the
whole community watched. 28At the summit,
Moses removed the priestly garments from
Aaron and put them on Eleazar, Aaron's son.
Then Aaron died there on top of the mountain,
and Moses and Eleazar went back down.
29When the people realized that Aaron had died,
all Israel mourned for him thirty days.

CHAPTER 21

Victory over the Canaanites

The Canaanite king of Arad, who lived in the Negev, heard that the Israelites were approaching
on the road through Atharim. So he attacked the
Israelites and took some of them as prisoners.
2Then the people of Israel made this vow to the
LORD: "If you will hand these people over to us,
we will completely destroy all their towns." 3The
LORD heard the Israelites' request and gave them
victory over the Canaanites. The Israelites completely destroyed them and their towns, and the
place has been called Hormah ever since.

The Bronze Snake

4Then the people of Israel set out from Mount
Hor, taking the road to the Red Sea to go around
the land of Edom. But the people grew impatient
with the long journey, 5and they began to speak
against God and Moses. "Why have you brought
us out of Egypt to die here in the wilderness?"
they complained. "There is nothing to eat here
and nothing to drink. And we hate this horrible
manna!"

6So the LORD sent poisonous snakes among
the people, and many were bitten and died.
7Then the people came to Moses and cried out,
"We have sinned by speaking against the LORD
and against you. Pray that the LORD will take away
the snakes." So Moses prayed for the people.

8Then the LORD told him, "Make a replica of a
poisonous snake and attach it to a pole. All who
are bitten will live if they simply look at it!" 9So
Moses made a snake out of bronze and attached
it to a pole. Then anyone who was bitten by a
snake could look at the bronze snake and be
healed!

Israel's Journey to Moab

10The Israelites traveled next to Oboth and
camped there. 11Then they went on to Iye-
abarim, in the wilderness on the eastern border
of Moab. 12From there they traveled to the valley
of Zered Brook and set up camp. 13Then they
moved out and camped on the far side of
the Arnon River, in the wilderness adjacent to
the territory of the Amorites. The Arnon is the
boundary line between the Moabites and the
Amorites. 14For this reason *The Book of the Wars*
of the LORD speaks of "the town of Waheb in the
area of Suphah, and the ravines of the Arnon
River, 15and the ravines that extend as far as the
settlement of Ar on the border of Moab."

16From there the Israelites traveled to Beer,
which is the well where the LORD said to Moses,

"Assemble the people, and I will give them
water." 17There the Israelites sang this song:

"Spring up, O well!
Yes, sing its praises!
18 Sing of this well,
which princes dug,
which great leaders hollowed out
with their scepters and staffs."

Then the Israelites left the wilderness and
proceeded on through Mattanah, 19Nahaliel, and
Bamoth. 20After that they went to the valley in
Moab where Pisgah Peak overlooks the wasteland.

Victory over Sihon and Og

21The Israelites sent ambassadors to King Sihon
of the Amorites with this message:

22"Let us travel through your land. We will be
careful not to go through your fields and
vineyards. We won't even drink water from
your wells. We will stay on the king's road
until we have passed through your territory."

23But King Sihon refused to let them cross his
territory. Instead, he mobilized his entire army
and attacked Israel in the wilderness, engaging
them in battle at Jahaz. 24But the Israelites
slaughtered them with their swords and occupied their land from the Arnon River to the
Jabbok River. They went only as far as the Ammonite border because the boundary of the Ammonites was fortified.
25So Israel captured all the towns of the Amorites and settled in them, including the city of
Heshbon and its surrounding villages. 26Hesh-
bon had been the capital of King Sihon of the
Amorites. He had defeated a former Moabite
king and seized all his land as far as the Arnon
River. 27Therefore, the ancient poets wrote this
about him:

"Come to Heshbon and let it be rebuilt!
Let the city of Sihon be restored.
28 A fire flamed forth from Heshbon,
a blaze from the city of Sihon.
It burned the city of Ar in Moab;
it destroyed the rulers of the Arnon
heights.
29 What sorrow awaits you, O people of Moab!
You are finished, O worshipers of
Chemosh!
Chemosh has left his sons as refugees,
his daughters as captives of Sihon, the
Amorite king.
30 We have utterly destroyed them,
from Heshbon to Dibon.
We have completely wiped them out
as far away as Nophah and Medeba."

31So the people of Israel occupied the territory
of the Amorites. 32After Moses sent men to explore the Jazer area, they captured all the towns in
the region and drove out the Amorites who lived
there. 33Then they turned and marched up the
road to Bashan, but King Og of Bashan and all his
people attacked them at Edrei. 34The LORD said to
Moses, "Do not be afraid of him, for I have
handed him over to you, along with all his people
and his land. Do the same to him as you did to
King Sihon of the Amorites, who ruled in Heshbon." 35And Israel killed King Og, his sons, and all
his subjects; not a single survivor remained. Then
Israel occupied their land.

CHAPTER 22
Balak Sends for Balaam

Then the people of Israel traveled to the plains of
Moab and camped east of the Jordan River, across
from Jericho. 2Balak son of Zippor, the Moabite
king, had seen everything the Israelites did to the
Amorites. 3And when the people of Moab saw
how many Israelites there were, they were terrified. 4The king of Moab said to the elders of Midian, "This mob will devour everything in sight, like
an ox devours grass in the field!"

So Balak, king of Moab, 5sent messengers to
call Balaam son of Beor, who was living in his native land of Pethor near the Euphrates River. His
message said:

"Look, a vast horde of people has arrived
from Egypt. They cover the face of the earth
and are threatening me. 6Please come and
curse these people for me because they are
too powerful for me. Then perhaps I will be
able to conquer them and drive them from
the land. I know that blessings fall on any
people you bless, and curses fall on people
you curse."

7Balak's messengers, who were elders of
Moab and Midian, set out with money to pay Balaam to place a curse upon Israel. They went to
Balaam and delivered Balak's message to him.
8"Stay here overnight," Balaam said. "In the
morning I will tell you whatever the LORD directs me to say." So the officials from Moab
stayed there with Balaam.
9That night God came to Balaam and asked
him, "Who are these men visiting you?"

10Balaam said to God, "Balak son of Zippor,
king of Moab, has sent me this message: 11'Look,
a vast horde of people has arrived from Egypt,
and they cover the face of the earth. Come and
curse these people for me. Then perhaps I will be
able to stand up to them and drive them from the
land.'"
12But God told Balaam, "Do not go with them.
You are not to curse these people, for they have
been blessed!"
13The next morning Balaam got up and told
Balak's officials, "Go on home! The LORD will not
let me go with you."
14So the Moabite officials returned to King
Balak and reported, "Balaam refused to come
with us." 15Then Balak tried again. This time he
sent a larger number of even more distinguished
officials than those he had sent the first time.
16They went to Balaam and delivered this message to him:

"This is what Balak son of Zippor says: Please
don't let anything stop you from coming to
help me. 17I will pay you very well and do
whatever you tell me. Just come and curse
these people for me!"

18But Balaam responded to Balak's messengers, "Even if Balak were to give me his palace
filled with silver and gold, I would be powerless
to do anything against the will of the LORD my
God. 19But stay here one more night, and I will
see if the LORD has anything else to say to me."
20That night God came to Balaam and told him,
"Since these men have come for you, get up and go
with them. But do only what I tell you to do."

Balaam and His Donkey

21So the next morning Balaam got up, saddled
his donkey, and started off with the Moabite officials. 22But God was angry that Balaam was going, so he sent the angel of the LORD to stand in
the road to block his way. As Balaam and two servants were riding along, 23Balaam's donkey saw
the angel of the LORD standing in the road with a
drawn sword in his hand. The donkey bolted off
the road into a field, but Balaam beat it and
turned it back onto the road. 24Then the angel of
the LORD stood at a place where the road narrowed between two vineyard walls. 25When the
donkey saw the angel of the LORD, it tried to
squeeze by and crushed Balaam's foot against
the wall. So Balaam beat the donkey again.
26Then the angel of the LORD moved farther
down the road and stood in a place too narrow
for the donkey to get by at all. 27This time when
the donkey saw the angel, it lay down under Balaam. In a fit of rage Balaam beat the animal
again with his staff.
28Then the LORD gave the donkey the ability to
speak. "What have I done to you that deserves
your beating me three times?" it asked Balaam.
29"You have made me look like a fool!" Balaam
shouted. "If I had a sword with me, I would kill
you!"
30"But I am the same donkey you have ridden
all your life," the donkey answered. "Have I ever
done anything like this before?"
"No," Balaam admitted.
31Then the LORD opened Balaam's eyes, and
he saw the angel of the LORD standing in the
roadway with a drawn sword in his hand. Balaam
bowed his head and fell face down on the
ground before him.
32"Why did you beat your donkey those three
times?" the angel of the LORD demanded. "Look,
I have come to block your way because you are
stubbornly resisting me. 33Three times the donkey saw me and shied away; otherwise, I would
certainly have killed you by now and spared the
donkey."
34Then Balaam confessed to the angel of the
LORD, "I have sinned. I didn't realize you were
standing in the road to block my way. I will return
home if you are against my going."
35But the angel of the LORD told Balaam, "Go
with these men, but say only what I tell you to
say." So Balaam went on with Balak's officials.
36When King Balak heard that Balaam was on
the way, he went out to meet him at a Moabite
town on the Arnon River at the farthest border of
his land.
37"Didn't I send you an urgent invitation? Why
didn't you come right away?" Balak asked Balaam. "Didn't you believe me when I said I would
reward you richly?"
38Balaam replied, "Look, now I have come, but
I have no power to say whatever I want. I will
speak only the message that God puts in my
mouth." 39Then Balaam accompanied Balak to
Kiriath-huzoth, 40where the king sacrificed cattle and sheep. He sent portions of the meat to Balaam and the officials who were with him. 41The
next morning Balak took Balaam up to Bamoth-
baal. From there he could see some of the people
of Israel spread out below him.

CHAPTER 23

Balaam Blesses Israel

Then Balaam said to King Balak, "Build me seven
altars here, and prepare seven young bulls and

seven rams for me to sacrifice." 2Balak followed
his instructions, and the two of them sacrificed a
young bull and a ram on each altar.
3Then Balaam said to Balak, "Stand here by
your burnt offerings, and I will go to see if the
LORD will respond to me. Then I will tell you
whatever he reveals to me." So Balaam went
alone to the top of a bare hill, 4and God met him
there. Balaam said to him, "I have prepared seven
altars and have sacrificed a young bull and a ram
on each altar."
5The LORD gave Balaam a message for King
Balak. Then he said, "Go back to Balak and give
him my message."
6So Balaam returned and found the king
standing beside his burnt offerings with all the
officials of Moab. 7This was the message Balaam
delivered:

"Balak summoned me to come from Aram;
the king of Moab brought me from the
eastern hills.
'Come,' he said, 'curse Jacob for me!
Come and announce Israel's doom.'
8 But how can I curse those
whom God has not cursed?
How can I condemn those
whom the LORD has not condemned?
9 I see them from the cliff tops;
I watch them from the hills.
I see a people who live by themselves,
set apart from other nations.
10 Who can count Jacob's descendants,
as numerous as dust?
Who can count even a fourth of Israel's
people?
Let me die like the righteous;
let my life end like theirs."

11Then King Balak demanded of Balaam,
"What have you done to me? I brought you to
curse my enemies. Instead, you have blessed
them!"
12But Balaam replied, "I will speak only the
message that the LORD puts in my mouth."

Balaam's Second Message

13Then King Balak told him, "Come with me to
another place. There you will see another part of
the nation of Israel, but not all of them. Curse at
least that many!" 14So Balak took Balaam to the
plateau of Zophim on Pisgah Peak. He built
seven altars there and offered a young bull and a
ram on each altar.
15Then Balaam said to the king, "Stand here by
your burnt offerings while I go over there to
meet the LORD."
16And the LORD met Balaam and gave him a
message. Then he said, "Go back to Balak and
give him my message."
17So Balaam returned and found the king
standing beside his burnt offerings with all the
officials of Moab. "What did the LORD say?"
Balak asked eagerly.
18This was the message Balaam delivered:

"Rise up, Balak, and listen!
Hear me, son of Zippor.
19 God is not a man, so he does not lie.
He is not human, so he does not change
his mind.

Who Said THAT?!

I think it was the donkey. God really wanted to get Balaam's attention, and he used a donkey to do it. **See how in NUMBERS 22:21-38.**

Imagine you had an invisible . . .

talking donkey that rode on your shoulder. Finish some of these sentences from the donkey's point of view:

You did what God wanted you to do last week when you...
I've noticed that when you are at school, you...
I think God would want you to change the way you...

You don't need a donkey to help you do what's right. Everyone who follows Jesus has the Holy Spirit inside him or her all the time. **Find out more about what the Holy Spirit does by reading JOHN 14:15-30.**

Has he ever spoken and failed to act?
Has he ever promised and not carried it through?
20 Listen, I received a command to bless;
God has blessed, and I cannot reverse it!
21 No misfortune is in his plan for Jacob;
no trouble is in store for Israel.
For the LORD their God is with them;
he has been proclaimed their king.
22 God brought them out of Egypt;
for them he is as strong as a wild ox.
23 No curse can touch Jacob;
no magic has any power against Israel.
For now it will be said of Jacob,
'What wonders God has done for Israel!'
24 These people rise up like a lioness,
like a majestic lion rousing itself.
They refuse to rest
until they have feasted on prey,
drinking the blood of the slaughtered!"

25 Then Balak said to Balaam, "Fine, but if you
won't curse them, at least don't bless them!"
26 But Balaam replied to Balak, "Didn't I tell you
that I can do only what the LORD tells me?"

Balaam's Third Message

27 Then King Balak said to Balaam, "Come, I will
take you to one more place. Perhaps it will please
God to let you curse them from there."
28 So Balak took Balaam to the top of Mount
Peor, overlooking the wasteland. 29 Balaam
again told Balak, "Build me seven altars, and
prepare seven young bulls and seven rams for
me to sacrifice." 30 So Balak did as Balaam ordered and offered a young bull and a ram on
each altar.

CHAPTER 24

By now Balaam realized that the LORD was determined to bless Israel, so he did not resort to divination as before. Instead, he turned and looked
out toward the wilderness, 2 where he saw the
people of Israel camped, tribe by tribe. Then the
Spirit of God came upon him, 3 and this is the message he delivered:

"This is the message of Balaam son of Beor,
the message of the man whose eyes see clearly,
4 the message of one who hears the words of God,
who sees a vision from the Almighty,
who bows down with eyes wide open:
5 How beautiful are your tents, O Jacob;
how lovely are your homes, O Israel!
6 They spread before me like palm groves,
like gardens by the riverside.
They are like tall trees planted by the LORD,
like cedars beside the waters.
7 Water will flow from their buckets;
their offspring have all they need.
Their king will be greater than Agag;
their kingdom will be exalted.
8 God brought them out of Egypt;
for them he is as strong as a wild ox.
He devours all the nations that oppose him,
breaking their bones in pieces,
shooting them with arrows.
9 Like a lion, Israel crouches and lies down;
like a lioness, who dares to arouse her?
Blessed is everyone who blesses you, O Israel,
and cursed is everyone who curses you."

10 King Balak flew into a rage against Balaam.
He angrily clapped his hands and shouted, "I
called you to curse my enemies! Instead, you
have blessed them three times. 11 Now get out of
here! Go back home! I promised to reward you
richly, but the LORD has kept you from your reward."
12 Balaam told Balak, "Don't you remember
what I told your messengers? I said, 13 'Even if Balak were to give me his palace filled with silver
and gold, I would be powerless to do anything
against the will of the LORD.' I told you that I
could say only what the LORD says! 14 Now I am returning to my own people. But first let me tell
you what the Israelites will do to your people in
the future."

Balaam's Final Messages

15 This is the message Balaam delivered:

"This is the message of Balaam son of Beor,
the message of the man whose eyes see clearly,
16 the message of one who hears the words of God,
who has knowledge from the Most High,
who sees a vision from the Almighty,
who bows down with eyes wide open:
17 I see him, but not here and now.
I perceive him, but far in the distant future.
A star will rise from Jacob;
a scepter will emerge from Israel.
It will crush the heads of Moab's people,
cracking the skulls of the people of Sheth.
18 Edom will be taken over,
and Seir, its enemy, will be conquered,
while Israel marches on in triumph.

19 A ruler will rise in Jacob
who will destroy the survivors of Ir."
20Then Balaam looked over toward the people of
Amalek and delivered this message:

"Amalek was the greatest of nations,
but its destiny is destruction!"

21Then he looked over toward the Kenites and
delivered this message:

"Your home is secure;
your nest is set in the rocks.
22 But the Kenites will be destroyed
when Assyria takes you captive."

23Balaam concluded his messages by saying:

"Alas, who can survive
unless God has willed it?
24 Ships will come from the coasts of Cyprus;
they will oppress Assyria and afflict Eber,
but they, too, will be utterly destroyed."

25Then Balaam left and returned home, and
Balak also went on his way.

CHAPTER 25

Moab Seduces Israel

While the Israelites were camped at Acacia
Grove, some of the men defiled themselves by
having sexual relations with local Moabite
women. 2These women invited them to attend
sacrifices to their gods, so the Israelites feasted
with them and worshiped the gods of Moab. 3In
this way, Israel joined in the worship of Baal of
Peor, causing the LORD's anger to blaze against
his people.

4The LORD issued the following command to
Moses: "Seize all the ringleaders and execute
them before the LORD in broad daylight, so his
fierce anger will turn away from the people of
Israel."

5So Moses ordered Israel's judges, "Each of
you must put to death the men under your authority who have joined in worshiping Baal of
Peor."

6Just then one of the Israelite men brought a
Midianite woman into his tent, right before the
eyes of Moses and all the people, as everyone was
weeping at the entrance of the Tabernacle.
7When Phinehas son of Eleazar and grandson of
Aaron the priest saw this, he jumped up and left
the assembly. He took a spear 8and rushed after
the man into his tent. Phinehas thrust the spear
all the way through the man's body and into the
woman's stomach. So the plague against the Israelites was stopped, 9but not before 24,000
people had died.

10Then the LORD said to Moses, 11"Phinehas
son of Eleazar and grandson of Aaron the priest
has turned my anger away from the Israelites
by being as zealous among them as I was. So I
stopped destroying all Israel as I had intended to
do in my zealous anger. 12Now tell him that I am
making my special covenant of peace with him.
13In this covenant, I give him and his descendants a permanent right to the priesthood, for in
his zeal for me, his God, he purified the people of
Israel, making them right with me."

14The Israelite man killed with the Midianite
woman was named Zimri son of Salu, the leader
of a family from the tribe of Simeon. 15The
woman's name was Cozbi; she was the daughter
of Zur, the leader of a Midianite clan.

16Then the LORD said to Moses, 17"Attack the
Midianites and destroy them, 18because they as-
saulted you with deceit and tricked you into worshiping Baal of Peor, and because of Cozbi, the
daughter of a Midianite leader, who was killed at
the time of the plague because of what happened
at Peor."

CHAPTER 26

The Second Registration of Israel's Troops

After the plague had ended, the LORD said to
Moses and to Eleazar son of Aaron the priest,
2"From the whole community of Israel, record
the names of all the warriors by their families.
List all the men twenty years old or older who are
able to go to war."

3So there on the plains of Moab beside the Jordan River, across from Jericho, Moses and Eleazar the priest issued these instructions to the
leaders of Israel: 4"List all the men of Israel
twenty years old and older, just as the LORD commanded Moses."

This is the record of all the descendants of
Israel who came out of Egypt.

The Tribe of Reuben

5These were the clans descended from the sons
of Reuben, Jacob's oldest son:
The Hanochite clan, named after their
ancestor Hanoch.
The Palluite clan, named after their ancestor
Pallu.
6 The Hezronite clan, named after their
ancestor Hezron.
The Carmite clan, named after their ancestor
Carmi.

7These were the clans of Reuben. Their registered troops numbered 43,730.
8Pallu was the ancestor of Eliab, 9and Eliab was the father of Nemuel, Dathan, and Abiram. This Dathan and Abiram are the same community leaders who conspired with Korah against Moses and Aaron, rebelling against the LORD.
10But the earth opened up its mouth and swallowed them with Korah, and fire devoured 250 of their followers. This served as a warning to the entire nation of Israel. 11However, the sons of Korah did not die that day.

The Tribe of Simeon

12These were the clans descended from the sons of Simeon:

The Jemuelite clan, named after their ancestor Jemuel.
The Jaminite clan, named after their ancestor Jamin.
The Jakinite clan, named after their ancestor Jakin.
13 The Zoharite clan, named after their ancestor Zohar.
The Shaulite clan, named after their ancestor Shaul.

14These were the clans of Simeon. Their registered troops numbered 22,200.

The Tribe of Gad

15These were the clans descended from the sons of Gad:

The Zephonite clan, named after their ancestor Zephon.
The Haggite clan, named after their ancestor Haggi.
The Shunite clan, named after their ancestor Shuni.
16 The Oznite clan, named after their ancestor Ozni.
The Erite clan, named after their ancestor Eri.
17 The Arodite clan, named after their ancestor Arodi.
The Arelite clan, named after their ancestor Areli.

18These were the clans of Gad. Their registered troops numbered 40,500.

The Tribe of Judah

19Judah had two sons, Er and Onan, who had died in the land of Canaan. 20These were the clans descended from Judah's surviving sons:

The Shelanite clan, named after their ancestor Shelah.
The Perezite clan, named after their ancestor Perez.
The Zerahite clan, named after their ancestor Zerah.

21These were the subclans descended from the Perezites:

The Hezronites, named after their ancestor Hezron.
The Hamulites, named after their ancestor Hamul.

22These were the clans of Judah. Their registered troops numbered 76,500.

The Tribe of Issachar

23These were the clans descended from the sons of Issachar:

The Tolaite clan, named after their ancestor Tola.
The Puite clan, named after their ancestor Puah.
24 The Jashubite clan, named after their ancestor Jashub.
The Shimronite clan, named after their ancestor Shimron.

25These were the clans of Issachar. Their registered troops numbered 64,300.

The Tribe of Zebulun

26These were the clans descended from the sons of Zebulun:

The Seredite clan, named after their ancestor Sered.
The Elonite clan, named after their ancestor Elon.
The Jahleelite clan, named after their ancestor Jahleel.

27These were the clans of Zebulun. Their registered troops numbered 60,500.

The Tribe of Manasseh

28Two clans were descended from Joseph through Manasseh and Ephraim.

29These were the clans descended from Manasseh:

The Makirite clan, named after their ancestor Makir.
The Gileadite clan, named after their ancestor Gilead, Makir's son.

30These were the subclans descended from the Gileadites:

The Iezerites, named after their ancestor Iezer.
The Helekites, named after their ancestor Helek.
31 The Asrielites, named after their ancestor Asriel.
The Shechemites, named after their ancestor Shechem.
32 The Shemidaites, named after their ancestor Shemida.
The Hepherites, named after their ancestor Hepher.
33 (One of Hepher's descendants, Zelophehad, had no sons, but his daughters' names were Mahlah, Noah, Hoglah, Milcah, and Tirzah.)

34 These were the clans of Manasseh. Their registered troops numbered 52,700.

The Tribe of Ephraim

35 These were the clans descended from the sons of Ephraim:
The Shuthelahite clan, named after their ancestor Shuthelah.
The Bekerite clan, named after their ancestor Beker.
The Tahanite clan, named after their ancestor Tahan.

36 This was the subclan descended from the Shuthelahites:
The Eranites, named after their ancestor Eran.

37 These were the clans of Ephraim. Their registered troops numbered 32,500.

These clans of Manasseh and Ephraim were all descendants of Joseph.

The Tribe of Benjamin

38 These were the clans descended from the sons of Benjamin:
The Belaite clan, named after their ancestor Bela.
The Ashbelite clan, named after their ancestor Ashbel.
The Ahiramite clan, named after their ancestor Ahiram.
39 The Shuphamite clan, named after their ancestor Shupham.
The Huphamite clan, named after their ancestor Hupham.

40 These were the subclans descended from the Belaites:
The Ardites, named after their ancestor Ard.
The Naamites, named after their ancestor Naaman.

41 These were the clans of Benjamin. Their registered troops numbered 45,600.

The Tribe of Dan

42 These were the clans descended from the sons of Dan:
The Shuhamite clan, named after their ancestor Shuham.

43 These were the Shuhamite clans of Dan. Their registered troops numbered 64,400.

The Tribe of Asher

44 These were the clans descended from the sons of Asher:
The Imnite clan, named after their ancestor Imnah.
The Ishvite clan, named after their ancestor Ishvi.
The Beriite clan, named after their ancestor Beriah.

45 These were the subclans descended from the Beriites:
The Heberites, named after their ancestor Heber.
The Malkielites, named after their ancestor Malkiel.

46 Asher also had a daughter named Serah.

47 These were the clans of Asher. Their registered troops numbered 53,400.

The Tribe of Naphtali

48 These were the clans descended from the sons of Naphtali:
The Jahzeelite clan, named after their ancestor Jahzeel.
The Gunite clan, named after their ancestor Guni.
49 The Jezerite clan, named after their ancestor Jezer.
The Shillemite clan, named after their ancestor Shillem.

50 These were the clans of Naphtali. Their registered troops numbered 45,400.

Results of the Registration

51 In summary, the registered troops of all Israel numbered 601,730.

52 Then the LORD said to Moses, 53 "Divide the land among the tribes, and distribute the grants

of land in proportion to the tribes' populations,
as indicated by the number of names on the list.
54Give the larger tribes more land and the
smaller tribes less land, each group receiving a
grant in proportion to the size of its population.
55But you must assign the land by lot, and give
land to each ancestral tribe according to the
number of names on the list. 56Each grant of
land must be assigned by lot among the larger
and smaller tribal groups."

The Tribe of Levi

57This is the record of the Levites who were
counted according to their clans:

The Gershonite clan, named after their ancestor Gershon.
The Kohathite clan, named after their ancestor Kohath.
The Merarite clan, named after their ancestor Merari.

58The Libnites, the Hebronites, the Mahlites, the
Mushites, and the Korahites were all subclans of
the Levites.

Now Kohath was the ancestor of Amram,
59and Amram's wife was named Jochebed. She
also was a descendant of Levi, born among the
Levites in the land of Egypt. Amram and Jochebed became the parents of Aaron, Moses, and
their sister, Miriam. 60To Aaron were born Nadab, Abihu, Eleazar, and Ithamar. 61But Nadab
and Abihu died when they burned before the
LORD the wrong kind of fire, different than he
had commanded.

62The men from the Levite clans who were
one month old or older numbered 23,000. But
the Levites were not included in the registration
of the rest of the people of Israel because they
were not given an allotment of land when it was
divided among the Israelites.

63So these are the results of the registration of
the people of Israel as conducted by Moses and
Eleazar the priest on the plains of Moab beside
the Jordan River, across from Jericho. 64Not one
person on this list had been among those listed
in the previous registration taken by Moses and
Aaron in the wilderness of Sinai. 65For the LORD
had said of them, "They will all die in the wilderness." Not one of them survived except Caleb son
of Jephunneh and Joshua son of Nun.

CHAPTER 27

The Daughters of Zelophehad

One day a petition was presented by the daughters of Zelophehad—Mahlah, Noah, Hoglah,
Milcah, and Tirzah. Their father, Zelophehad,
was a descendant of Hepher son of Gilead, son of
Makir, son of Manasseh, son of Joseph. 2These
women stood before Moses, Eleazar the priest,
the tribal leaders, and the entire community at
the entrance of the Tabernacle. 3"Our father
died in the wilderness," they said. "He was not
among Korah's followers, who rebelled against
the LORD; he died because of his own sin. But he
had no sons. 4Why should the name of our father
disappear from his clan just because he had no
sons? Give us property along with the rest of our
relatives."

5So Moses brought their case before the
LORD. 6And the LORD replied to Moses, 7"The
claim of the daughters of Zelophehad is legitimate. You must give them a grant of land along
with their father's relatives. Assign them the
property that would have been given to their
father.

8"And give the following instructions to the
people of Israel: If a man dies and has no son,
then give his inheritance to his daughters. 9And
if he has no daughter either, transfer his inheritance to his brothers. 10If he has no brothers,
give his inheritance to his father's brothers.
11But if his father has no brothers, give his inheritance to the nearest relative in his clan. This is a
legal requirement for the people of Israel, just as
the LORD commanded Moses."

Joshua Chosen to Lead Israel

12One day the LORD said to Moses, "Climb one of
the mountains east of the river, and look out over
the land I have given the people of Israel. 13After
you have seen it, you will die like your brother,
Aaron, 14for you both rebelled against my instructions in the wilderness of Zin. When the
people of Israel rebelled, you failed to demonstrate my holiness to them at the waters." (These
are the waters of Meribah at Kadesh in the wilderness of Zin.)

15Then Moses said to the LORD, 16"O LORD, you
are the God who gives breath to all creatures.
Please appoint a new man as leader for the community. 17Give them someone who will guide
them wherever they go and will lead them into
battle, so the community of the LORD will not be
like sheep without a shepherd."

18The LORD replied, "Take Joshua son of Nun,
who has the Spirit in him, and lay your hands on
him. 19Present him to Eleazar the priest before
the whole community, and publicly commission
him to lead the people. 20Transfer some of your
authority to him so the whole community of

Israel will obey him. 21When direction from the
LORD is needed, Joshua will stand before Eleazar
the priest, who will use the Urim—one of the sacred lots cast before the LORD—to determine his
will. This is how Joshua and the rest of the community of Israel will determine everything they
should do."
22So Moses did as the LORD commanded. He
presented Joshua to Eleazar the priest and the
whole community. 23Moses laid his hands on
him and commissioned him to lead the people,
just as the LORD had commanded through
Moses.

CHAPTER 28

The Daily Offerings

The LORD said to Moses, 2"Give these instructions to the people of Israel: The offerings you
present as special gifts are a pleasing aroma to
me; they are my food. See to it that they are
brought at the appointed times and offered according to my instructions.
3"Say to the people: This is the special gift you
must present to the LORD as your daily burnt offering. You must offer two one-year-old male
lambs with no defects. 4Sacrifice one lamb in
the morning and the other in the evening. 5With
each lamb you must offer a grain offering of two
quarts of choice flour mixed with one quart of
pure oil of pressed olives. 6This is the regular
burnt offering instituted at Mount Sinai as a
special gift, a pleasing aroma to the LORD.
7Along with it you must present the proper liquid offering of one quart of alcoholic drink with
each lamb, poured out in the Holy Place as an
offering to the LORD. 8Offer the second lamb in
the evening with the same grain offering and
liquid offering. It, too, is a special gift, a pleasing
aroma to the LORD.

The Sabbath Offerings

9"On the Sabbath day, sacrifice two one-year-old
male lambs with no defects. They must be accompanied by a grain offering of four quarts of
choice flour moistened with olive oil, and a liquid offering. 10This is the burnt offering to be
presented each Sabbath day, in addition to the
regular burnt offering and its accompanying
liquid offering.

The Monthly Offerings

11"On the first day of each month, present an extra burnt offering to the LORD of two young bulls,
one ram, and seven one-year-old male lambs, all
with no defects. 12These must be accompanied
by grain offerings of choice flour moistened
with olive oil—six quarts with each bull, four
quarts with the ram, 13and two quarts with each
lamb. This burnt offering will be a special gift, a
pleasing aroma to the LORD. 14You must also
present a liquid offering with each sacrifice: two
quarts of wine for each bull, a third of a gallon for
the ram, and one quart for each lamb. Present
this monthly burnt offering on the first day of
each month throughout the year.
15"On the first day of each month, you must
also offer one male goat for a sin offering to the
LORD. This is in addition to the regular burnt offering and its accompanying liquid offering.

Offerings for the Passover

16"On the fourteenth day of the first month, you
must celebrate the LORD's Passover. 17On the
following day—the fifteenth day of the month—
a joyous, seven-day festival will begin, but no
bread made with yeast may be eaten. 18The first
day of the festival will be an official day for holy
assembly, and no ordinary work may be done on
that day. 19As a special gift you must present a
burnt offering to the LORD—two young bulls,
one ram, and seven one-year-old male lambs, all
with no defects. 20These will be accompanied
by grain offerings of choice flour moistened
with olive oil—six quarts with each bull, four
quarts with the ram, 21and two quarts with each
of the seven lambs. 22You must also offer a male
goat as a sin offering to purify yourselves and
make yourselves right with the LORD. 23Present
these offerings in addition to your regular
morning burnt offering. 24On each of the seven
days of the festival, this is how you must prepare
the food offering that is presented as a special
gift, a pleasing aroma to the LORD. These will be
offered in addition to the regular burnt offerings and liquid offerings. 25The seventh day of
the festival will be another official day for holy
assembly, and no ordinary work may be done on
that day.

Offerings for the Festival of Harvest

26"At the Festival of Harvest, when you present
the first of your new grain to the LORD, you must
call an official day for holy assembly, and you
may do no ordinary work on that day. 27Present
a special burnt offering on that day as a pleasing aroma to the LORD. It will consist of two
young bulls, one ram, and seven one-year-old
male lambs. 28These will be accompanied by
grain offerings of choice flour moistened with

olive oil—six quarts with each bull, four quarts with the ram, 29 and two quarts with each of the seven lambs. 30 Also, offer one male goat to purify yourselves and make yourselves right with the LORD. 31 Prepare these special burnt offerings, along with their liquid offerings, in addition to the regular burnt offering and its accompanying grain offering. Be sure that all the animals you sacrifice have no defects.

CHAPTER 29

Offerings for the Festival of Trumpets

"Celebrate the Festival of Trumpets each year on the first day of the appointed month in early autumn. You must call an official day for holy assembly, and you may do no ordinary work. 2 On that day you must present a burnt offering as a pleasing aroma to the LORD. It will consist of one young bull, one ram, and seven one-year-old male lambs, all with no defects. 3 These must be accompanied by grain offerings of choice flour moistened with olive oil—six quarts with the bull, four quarts with the ram, 4 and two quarts with each of the seven lambs. 5 In addition, you must sacrifice a male goat as a sin offering to purify yourselves and make yourselves right with the LORD. 6 These special sacrifices are in addition to your regular monthly and daily burnt offerings, and they must be given with their prescribed grain offerings and liquid offerings. These offerings are given as a special gift to the LORD, a pleasing aroma to him.

Offerings for the Day of Atonement

7 "Ten days later, on the tenth day of the same month, you must call another holy assembly. On that day, the Day of Atonement, the people must go without food and must do no ordinary work. 8 You must present a burnt offering as a pleasing aroma to the LORD. It will consist of one young bull, one ram, and seven one-year-old male lambs, all with no defects. 9 These offerings must be accompanied by the prescribed grain offerings of choice flour moistened with olive oil—six quarts of choice flour with the bull, four quarts of choice flour with the ram, 10 and two quarts of choice flour with each of the seven lambs. 11 You must also sacrifice one male goat for a sin offering. This is in addition to the sin offering of atonement and the regular daily burnt offering with its grain offering, and their accompanying liquid offerings.

Offerings for the Festival of Shelters

12 "Five days later, on the fifteenth day of the same month, you must call another holy assembly of all the people, and you may do no ordinary work on that day. It is the beginning of the Festival of Shelters, a seven-day festival to the LORD. 13 On the first day of the festival, you must present a burnt offering as a special gift, a pleasing aroma to the LORD. It will consist of thirteen young bulls, two rams, and fourteen one-year-old male lambs, all with no defects. 14 Each of these offerings must be accompanied by a grain offering of choice flour moistened with olive oil—six quarts for each of the thirteen bulls, four quarts for each of the two rams, 15 and two quarts for each of the fourteen lambs. 16 You must also sacrifice a male goat as a sin offering, in addition to the regular burnt offering with its accompanying grain offering and liquid offering.

17 "On the second day of this seven-day festival, sacrifice twelve young bulls, two rams, and fourteen one-year-old male lambs, all with no defects. 18 Each of these offerings of bulls, rams, and lambs must be accompanied by its prescribed grain offering and liquid offering. 19 You must also sacrifice a male goat as a sin offering, in addition to the regular burnt offering with its accompanying grain offering and liquid offering.

20 "On the third day of the festival, sacrifice eleven young bulls, two rams, and fourteen one-year-old male lambs, all with no defects. 21 Each of these offerings of bulls, rams, and lambs must be accompanied by its prescribed grain offering and liquid offering. 22 You must also sacrifice a male goat as a sin offering, in addition to the regular burnt offering with its accompanying grain offering and liquid offering.

23 "On the fourth day of the festival, sacrifice ten young bulls, two rams, and fourteen one-year-old male lambs, all with no defects. 24 Each of these offerings of bulls, rams, and lambs must be accompanied by its prescribed grain offering and liquid offering. 25 You must also sacrifice a male goat as a sin offering, in addition to the regular burnt offering with its accompanying grain offering and liquid offering.

26 "On the fifth day of the festival, sacrifice nine young bulls, two rams, and fourteen one-year-old male lambs, all with no defects. 27 Each of these offerings of bulls, rams, and lambs must be accompanied by its prescribed grain offering and liquid offering. 28 You must also sacrifice a male goat as a sin offering, in addition to the reg-

ular burnt offering with its accompanying grain
offering and liquid offering.
29"On the sixth day of the festival, sacrifice
eight young bulls, two rams, and fourteen one-
year-old male lambs, all with no defects. 30Each
of these offerings of bulls, rams, and lambs must
be accompanied by its prescribed grain offering
and liquid offering. 31You must also sacrifice a
male goat as a sin offering, in addition to the regular burnt offering with its accompanying grain
offering and liquid offering.
32"On the seventh day of the festival, sacrifice
seven young bulls, two rams, and fourteen one-
year-old male lambs, all with no defects. 33Each
of these offerings of bulls, rams, and lambs must
be accompanied by its prescribed grain offering
and liquid offering. 34You must also sacrifice
one male goat as a sin offering, in addition to the
regular burnt offering with its accompanying
grain offering and liquid offering.
35"On the eighth day of the festival, proclaim
another holy day. You must do no ordinary work
on that day. 36You must present a burnt offering
as a special gift, a pleasing aroma to the LORD. It
will consist of one young bull, one ram, and seven
one-year-old male lambs, all with no defects.
37Each of these offerings must be accompanied
by its prescribed grain offering and liquid offering. 38You must also sacrifice one male goat as a
sin offering, in addition to the regular burnt offering with its accompanying grain offering and
liquid offering.
39"You must present these offerings to the
LORD at your annual festivals. These are in addition to the sacrifices and offerings you present in
connection with vows, or as voluntary offerings,
burnt offerings, grain offerings, liquid offerings,
or peace offerings."
40So Moses gave all of these instructions to the
people of Israel as the LORD had commanded
him.

CHAPTER 30
Laws concerning Vows

Then Moses summoned the leaders of the tribes
of Israel and told them, "This is what the LORD
has commanded: 2A man who makes a vow to the
LORD or makes a pledge under oath must never
break it. He must do exactly what he said he
would do.
3"If a young woman makes a vow to the LORD
or a pledge under oath while she is still living at
her father's home, 4and her father hears of the
vow or pledge and does not object to it, then all
her vows and pledges will stand. 5But if her
father refuses to let her fulfill the vow or pledge
on the day he hears of it, then all her vows and
pledges will become invalid. The LORD will forgive her because her father would not let her fulfill them.
6"Now suppose a young woman makes a vow
or binds herself with an impulsive pledge and
later marries. 7If her husband learns of her vow
or pledge and does not object on the day he hears
of it, her vows and pledges will stand. 8But if her
husband refuses to accept her vow or impulsive
pledge on the day he hears of it, he nullifies her
commitments, and the LORD will forgive her. 9If,
however, a woman is a widow or is divorced, she
must fulfill all her vows and pledges.
10"But suppose a woman is married and living
in her husband's home when she makes a vow or
binds herself with a pledge. 11If her husband
hears of it and does not object to it, her vow or
pledge will stand. 12But if her husband refuses to
accept it on the day he hears of it, her vow or
pledge will be nullified, and the LORD will forgive
her. 13So her husband may either confirm or
nullify any vows or pledges she makes to deny
herself. 14But if he does not object on the day he
hears of it, then he is agreeing to all her vows and
pledges. 15If he waits more than a day and then
tries to nullify a vow or pledge, he will be punished for her guilt."
16These are the regulations the LORD gave
Moses concerning relationships between a man
and his wife, and between a father and a young
daughter who still lives at home.

CHAPTER 31
Conquest of the Midianites

Then the LORD said to Moses, 2"On behalf of the
people of Israel, take revenge on the Midianites
for leading them into idolatry. After that, you will
die and join your ancestors."
3So Moses said to the people, "Choose some
men, and arm them to fight the LORD's war of revenge against Midian. 4From each tribe of Israel,
send 1,000 men into battle." 5So they chose
1,000 men from each tribe of Israel, a total of
12,000 men armed for battle. 6Then Moses sent
them out, 1,000 men from each tribe, and Phinehas son of Eleazar the priest led them into battle.
They carried along the holy objects of the sanctuary and the trumpets for sounding the charge.
7They attacked Midian as the LORD had commanded Moses, and they killed all the men. 8All
five of the Midianite kings—Evi, Rekem, Zur, Hur,
and Reba—died in the battle. They also killed Balaam son of Beor with the sword.

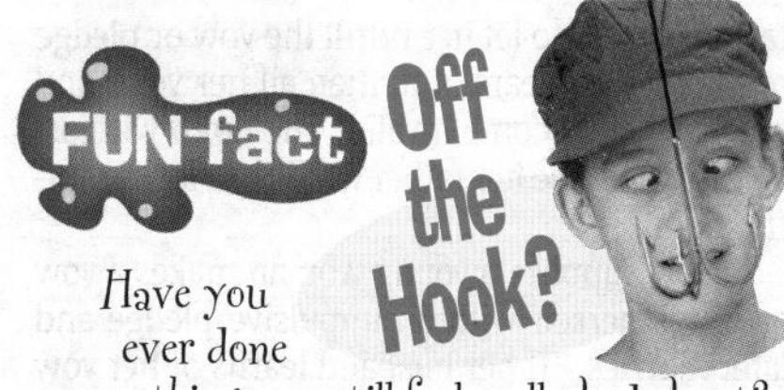

Have you ever done something you still feel really bad about?

The incredible news is that if you believe in Jesus, **GOD FORGIVES YOU!** No matter how wrong it was, Jesus paid for it when he died on the cross.

The Israelites made a lot of mistakes. Even though they were forgiven, they still often faced the consequences or results of their actions.

What are some possible consequences for each of these actions?

LYING

ACTING MEAN

APOLOGIZING

9Then the Israelite army captured the Midianite women and children and seized their cattle
and flocks and all their wealth as plunder. 10They
burned all the towns and villages where the Midianites had lived. 11After they had gathered the
plunder and captives, both people and animals,
12they brought them all to Moses and Eleazar the
priest, and to the whole community of Israel,
which was camped on the plains of Moab beside
the Jordan River, across from Jericho. 13Moses,
Eleazar the priest, and all the leaders of the community went to meet them outside the camp.
14But Moses was furious with all the generals
and captains who had returned from the battle.
15"Why have you let all the women live?" he
demanded. 16"These are the very ones who followed Balaam's advice and caused the people of
Israel to rebel against the LORD at Mount Peor.
They are the ones who caused the plague to
strike the LORD's people. 17So kill all the boys and
all the women who have had intercourse with a
man. 18Only the young girls who are virgins may
live; you may keep them for yourselves. 19And all
of you who have killed anyone or touched a dead
body must stay outside the camp for seven days.
You must purify yourselves and your captives on
the third and seventh days. 20Purify all your
clothing, too, and everything made of leather,
goat hair, or wood."
21Then Eleazar the priest said to the men who
were in the battle, "The LORD has given Moses
this legal requirement: 22Anything made of gold,
silver, bronze, iron, tin, or lead—23that is, all metals that do not burn—must be passed through
fire in order to be made ceremonially pure.
These metal objects must then be further purified with the water of purification. But everything that burns must be purified by the water
alone. 24On the seventh day you must wash your
clothes and be purified. Then you may return to
the camp."

Division of the Plunder

25And the LORD said to Moses, 26"You and Eleazar
the priest and the family leaders of each tribe are
to make a list of all the plunder taken in the battle,
including the people and animals. 27Then divide
the plunder into two parts, and give half to the
men who fought the battle and half to the rest of
the people. 28From the army's portion, first give
the LORD his share of the plunder—one of every
500 of the prisoners and of the cattle, donkeys,
sheep, and goats. 29Give this share of the army's
half to Eleazar the priest as an offering to the
LORD. 30From the half that belongs to the people
of Israel, take one of every fifty of the prisoners
and of the cattle, donkeys, sheep, goats, and other
animals. Give this share to the Levites, who are in
charge of maintaining the LORD's Tabernacle."
31So Moses and Eleazar the priest did as the LORD
commanded Moses.
32The plunder remaining from everything the
fighting men had taken totaled 675,000 sheep
and goats, 3372,000 cattle, 3461,000 donkeys,
35and 32,000 virgin girls.
36Half of the plunder was given to the fighting
men. It totaled 337,500 sheep and goats, 37of
which 675 were the LORD's share; 3836,000 cattle, of which 72 were the LORD's share; 3930,500
donkeys, of which 61 were the LORD's share;
40and 16,000 virgin girls, of whom 32 were the
LORD's share. 41Moses gave all the LORD's share to
Eleazar the priest, just as the LORD had directed
him.
42Half of the plunder belonged to the people
of Israel, and Moses separated it from the half
belonging to the fighting men. 43It totaled
337,500 sheep and goats, 4436,000 cattle,
4530,500 donkeys, 46and 16,000 virgin girls.
47From the half-share given to the people, Moses
took one of every fifty prisoners and animals and
gave them to the Levites, who maintained the

LORD's Tabernacle. All this was done as the LORD
had commanded Moses.

48Then all the generals and captains came to
Moses 49and said, "We, your servants, have accounted for all the men who went out to battle
under our command; not one of us is missing!
50So we are presenting the items of gold we captured as an offering to the LORD from our share
of the plunder—armbands, bracelets, rings, earrings, and necklaces. This will purify our lives
before the LORD and make us right with him."

51So Moses and Eleazar the priest received the
gold from all the military commanders—all
kinds of jewelry and crafted objects. 52In all, the
gold that the generals and captains presented as
a gift to the LORD weighed about 420 pounds.
53All the fighting men had taken some of the
plunder for themselves. 54So Moses and Eleazar
the priest accepted the gifts from the generals
and captains and brought the gold to the Tabernacle as a reminder to the LORD that the people
of Israel belong to him.

CHAPTER 32

The Tribes East of the Jordan

The tribes of Reuben and Gad owned vast numbers of livestock. So when they saw that the lands
of Jazer and Gilead were ideally suited for their
flocks and herds, 2they came to Moses, Eleazar
the priest, and the other leaders of the community. They said, 3"Notice the towns of Ataroth, Dibon, Jazer, Nimrah, Heshbon, Elealeh, Sibmah,
Nebo, and Beon. 4The LORD has conquered this
whole area for the community of Israel, and it is
ideally suited for all our livestock. 5If we have
found favor with you, please let us have this land
as our property instead of giving us land across
the Jordan River."

6"Do you intend to stay here while your brothers go across and do all the fighting?" Moses
asked the men of Gad and Reuben. 7"Why do
you want to discourage the rest of the people of
Israel from going across to the land the LORD has
given them? 8Your ancestors did the same thing
when I sent them from Kadesh-barnea to explore the land. 9After they went up to the valley
of Eshcol and explored the land, they discouraged the people of Israel from entering the land
the LORD was giving them. 10Then the LORD was
very angry with them, and he vowed, 11'Of all
those I rescued from Egypt, no one who is twenty
years old or older will ever see the land I swore to
give to Abraham, Isaac, and Jacob, for they have
not obeyed me wholeheartedly. 12The only exceptions are Caleb son of Jephunneh the Kenizzite and Joshua son of Nun, for they have wholeheartedly followed the LORD.'

13"The LORD was angry with Israel and made
them wander in the wilderness for forty years
until the entire generation that sinned in the
LORD's sight had died. 14But here you are, a brood
of sinners, doing exactly the same thing! You are
making the LORD even angrier with Israel. 15If
you turn away from him like this and he abandons them again in the wilderness, you will be responsible for destroying this entire nation!"

16But they approached Moses and said, "We
simply want to build pens for our livestock and
fortified towns for our wives and children.
17Then we will arm ourselves and lead our fellow
Israelites into battle until we have brought them
safely to their land. Meanwhile, our families will
stay in the fortified towns we build here, so they
will be safe from any attacks by the local people.
18We will not return to our homes until all the
people of Israel have received their portions of
land. 19But we do not claim any of the land on the
other side of the Jordan. We would rather live
here on the east side and accept this as our grant
of land."

20Then Moses said, "If you keep your word and
arm yourselves for the LORD's battles, 21and if
your troops cross the Jordan and keep fighting
until the LORD has driven out his enemies, 22then
you may return when the LORD has conquered
the land. You will have fulfilled your duty to the
LORD and to the rest of the people of Israel. And
the land on the east side of the Jordan will be
your property from the LORD. 23But if you fail to
keep your word, then you will have sinned
against the LORD, and you may be sure that your
sin will find you out. 24Go ahead and build towns
for your families and pens for your flocks, but do
everything you have promised."

25Then the men of Gad and Reuben replied,
"We, your servants, will follow your instructions
exactly. 26Our children, wives, flocks, and cattle
will stay here in the towns of Gilead. 27But all
who are able to bear arms will cross over to fight
for the LORD, just as you have said."

28So Moses gave orders to Eleazar the priest,
Joshua son of Nun, and the leaders of the clans of
Israel. 29He said, "The men of Gad and Reuben
who are armed for battle must cross the Jordan
with you to fight for the LORD. If they do, give
them the land of Gilead as their property when
the land is conquered. 30But if they refuse to arm
themselves and cross over with you, then they
must accept land with the rest of you in the land
of Canaan."

[31]The tribes of Gad and Reuben said again,
"We are your servants, and we will do as the LORD
has commanded! [32]We will cross the Jordan into
Canaan fully armed to fight for the LORD, but our
property will be here on this side of the Jordan."
[33]So Moses assigned land to the tribes of Gad,
Reuben, and half the tribe of Manasseh son of Joseph. He gave them the territory of King Sihon of
the Amorites and the land of King Og of Bashan—the whole land with its cities and surrounding lands.
[34]The descendants of Gad built the towns of
Dibon, Ataroth, Aroer, [35]Atroth-shophan, Jazer,
Jogbehah, [36]Beth-nimrah, and Beth-haran.
These were all fortified towns with pens for their
flocks.
[37]The descendants of Reuben built the towns
of Heshbon, Elealeh, Kiriathaim, [38]Nebo, Baal-
meon, and Sibmah. They changed the names of
some of the towns they conquered and rebuilt.
[39]Then the descendants of Makir of the tribe
of Manasseh went to Gilead and conquered it,
and they drove out the Amorites living there.
[40]So Moses gave Gilead to the Makirites, descendants of Manasseh, and they settled there. [41]The
people of Jair, another clan of the tribe of Manasseh, captured many of the towns in Gilead
and changed the name of that region to the
Towns of Jair. [42]Meanwhile, a man named Nobah captured the town of Kenath and its surrounding villages, and he renamed that area
Nobah after himself.

CHAPTER 33
Remembering Israel's Journey

This is the route the Israelites followed as they
marched out of Egypt under the leadership of
Moses and Aaron. [2]At the LORD's direction,
Moses kept a written record of their progress.
These are the stages of their march, identified by
the different places where they stopped along
the way.
[3]They set out from the city of Rameses in early
spring—on the fifteenth day of the first month—
on the morning after the first Passover celebration. The people of Israel left defiantly, in full
view of all the Egyptians. [4]Meanwhile, the Egyptians were burying all their firstborn sons, whom
the LORD had killed the night before. The LORD
had defeated the gods of Egypt that night with
great acts of judgment!

[5]After leaving Rameses, the Israelites set up camp at Succoth.

[6]Then they left Succoth and camped at Etham on the edge of the wilderness.

[7]They left Etham and turned back toward Pi-hahiroth, opposite Baal-zephon, and camped near Migdol.

[8]They left Pi-hahiroth and crossed the Red Sea into the wilderness beyond. Then they traveled for three days into the Etham wilderness and camped at Marah.

[9]They left Marah and camped at Elim, where there were twelve springs of water and seventy palm trees.

[10]They left Elim and camped beside the Red Sea.

[11]They left the Red Sea and camped in the wilderness of Sin.

[12]They left the wilderness of Sin and camped at Dophkah.

[13]They left Dophkah and camped at Alush.

[14]They left Alush and camped at Rephidim, where there was no water for the people to drink.

[15]They left Rephidim and camped in the wilderness of Sinai.

[16]They left the wilderness of Sinai and camped at Kibroth-hattaavah.

[17]They left Kibroth-hattaavah and camped at Hazeroth.

[18]They left Hazeroth and camped at Rithmah.

[19]They left Rithmah and camped at Rimmon-perez.

[20]They left Rimmon-perez and camped at Libnah.

[21]They left Libnah and camped at Rissah.

[22]They left Rissah and camped at Kehelathah.

[23]They left Kehelathah and camped at Mount Shepher.

[24]They left Mount Shepher and camped at Haradah.

[25]They left Haradah and camped at Makheloth.

[26]They left Makheloth and camped at Tahath.

[27]They left Tahath and camped at Terah.

[28]They left Terah and camped at Mithcah.

[29]They left Mithcah and camped at Hashmonah.

[30]They left Hashmonah and camped at Moseroth.

[31]They left Moseroth and camped at Bene-jaakan.

[32]They left Bene-jaakan and camped at Hor-haggidgad.

[33]They left Hor-haggidgad and camped at Jotbathah.

[34]They left Jotbathah and camped at Abronah.

[35]They left Abronah and camped at Ezion-geber.

36They left Ezion-geber and camped at Kadesh
in the wilderness of Zin.
37They left Kadesh and camped at Mount Hor,
at the border of Edom. 38While they were at
the foot of Mount Hor, Aaron the priest was
directed by the LORD to go up the mountain,
and there he died. This happened in midsummer, on the first day of the fifth month of
the fortieth year after Israel's departure from
Egypt. 39Aaron was 123 years old when he
died there on Mount Hor.
40At that time the Canaanite king of Arad,
who lived in the Negev in the land of Canaan,
heard that the people of Israel were
approaching his land.
41Meanwhile, the Israelites left Mount Hor
and camped at Zalmonah.
42Then they left Zalmonah and camped
at Punon.
43They left Punon and camped at Oboth.
44They left Oboth and camped at Iye-abarim
on the border of Moab.
45They left Iye-abarim and camped at Dibon-
gad.
46They left Dibon-gad and camped at Almon-
diblathaim.
47They left Almon-diblathaim and camped in
the mountains east of the river, near Mount
Nebo.
48They left the mountains east of the river and
camped on the plains of Moab beside the
Jordan River, across from Jericho. 49Along
the Jordan River they camped from Beth-
jeshimoth as far as the meadows of Acacia
on the plains of Moab.

50While they were camped near the Jordan
River on the plains of Moab opposite Jericho, the
LORD said to Moses, 51"Give the following instructions to the people of Israel: When you
cross the Jordan River into the land of Canaan,
52you must drive out all the people living there.
You must destroy all their carved and molten images and demolish all their pagan shrines.
53Take possession of the land and settle in it, because I have given it to you to occupy. 54You must
distribute the land among the clans by sacred lot
and in proportion to their size. A larger portion
of land will be allotted to each of the larger clans,
and a smaller portion will be allotted to each of
the smaller clans. The decision of the sacred lot
is final. In this way, the portions of land will be
divided among your ancestral tribes. 55But if you
fail to drive out the people who live in the land,
those who remain will be like splinters in your
eyes and thorns in your sides. They will harass
you in the land where you live. 56And I will do to
you what I had planned to do to them."

CHAPTER 34

Boundaries of the Land

Then the LORD said to Moses, 2"Give these instructions to the Israelites: When you come into
the land of Canaan, which I am giving you as your
special possession, these will be the boundaries.
3The southern portion of your country will extend from the wilderness of Zin, along the edge of
Edom. The southern boundary will begin on the
east at the Dead Sea. 4It will then run south past
Scorpion Pass in the direction of Zin. Its southern-
most point will be Kadesh-barnea, from which it
will go to Hazar-addar, and on to Azmon. 5From
Azmon the boundary will turn toward the Brook
of Egypt and end at the Mediterranean Sea.

6"Your western boundary will be the coastline
of the Mediterranean Sea.

7"Your northern boundary will begin at the
Mediterranean Sea and run east to Mount Hor,
8then to Lebo-hamath, and on through Zedad
9and Ziphron to Hazar-enan. This will be your
northern boundary.

10"The eastern boundary will start at Hazar-
enan and run south to Shepham, 11then down to
Riblah on the east side of Ain. From there the
boundary will run down along the eastern edge
of the Sea of Galilee, 12and then along the Jordan
River to the Dead Sea. These are the boundaries
of your land."

13Then Moses told the Israelites, "This territory is the homeland you are to divide among
yourselves by sacred lot. The LORD has commanded that the land be divided among the nine
and a half remaining tribes. 14The families of the
tribes of Reuben, Gad, and half the tribe of Manasseh have already received their grants of land
15on the east side of the Jordan River, across from
Jericho toward the sunrise."

Leaders to Divide the Land

16And the LORD said to Moses, 17"Eleazar the
priest and Joshua son of Nun are the men designated to divide the grants of land among the people. 18Enlist one leader from each tribe to help
them with the task. 19These are the tribes and
the names of the leaders:

Tribe	*Leader*
Judah	Caleb son of Jephunneh
20 Simeon	Shemuel son of Ammihud
21 Benjamin	Elidad son of Kislon

22 Dan . . . . Bukki son of Jogli
23 Manasseh son of Joseph. . . . . . Hanniel son of Ephod
24 Ephraim son of Joseph. . . . . Kemuel son of Shiphtan
25 Zebulun. . . . . Elizaphan son of Parnach
26 Issachar . . . . Paltiel son of Azzan
27 Asher . . . . Ahihud son of Shelomi
28 Naphtali. . . . . Pedahel son of Ammihud

29 These are the men the LORD has appointed to
divide the grants of land in Canaan among the
Israelites."

CHAPTER 35
Towns for the Levites
While Israel was camped beside the Jordan on
the plains of Moab across from Jericho, the LORD
said to Moses, 2 "Command the people of Israel
to give to the Levites from their property certain
towns to live in, along with the surrounding
pasturelands. 3 These towns will be for the Levites to live in, and the surrounding lands will
provide pasture for their cattle, flocks, and other
livestock. 4 The pastureland assigned to the Levites around these towns will extend 1,500 feet
from the town walls in every direction. 5 Measure
off 3,000 feet outside the town walls in every direction—east, south, west, north—with the town
at the center. This area will serve as the larger
pastureland for the towns.

6 "Six of the towns you give the Levites will be
cities of refuge, where a person who has accidentally killed someone can flee for safety. In addition, give them forty-two other towns. 7 In all,
forty-eight towns with the surrounding pastureland will be given to the Levites. 8 These towns
will come from the property of the people of Israel. The larger tribes will give more towns to the
Levites, while the smaller tribes will give fewer.
Each tribe will give property in proportion to the
size of its land."

Cities of Refuge
9 The LORD said to Moses, 10 "Give the following
instructions to the people of Israel.

"When you cross the Jordan into the land of
Canaan, 11 designate cities of refuge to which
people can flee if they have killed someone accidentally. 12 These cities will be places of protection from a dead person's relatives who want to
avenge the death. The slayer must not be put to
death before being tried by the community.
13 Designate six cities of refuge for yourselves,
14 three on the east side of the Jordan River and
three on the west in the land of Canaan. 15 These
cities are for the protection of Israelites, foreigners living among you, and traveling merchants.
Anyone who accidentally kills someone may flee
there for safety.

16 "But if someone strikes and kills another
person with a piece of iron, it is murder, and the
murderer must be executed. 17 Or if someone
with a stone in his hand strikes and kills another
person, it is murder, and the murderer must be
put to death. 18 Or if someone strikes and kills another person with a wooden object, it is murder,
and the murderer must be put to death. 19 The
victim's nearest relative is responsible for putting
the murderer to death. When they meet, the
avenger must put the murderer to death. 20 So if
someone hates another person and waits in ambush, then pushes him or throws something at
him and he dies, it is murder. 21 Or if someone
hates another person and hits him with a fist and
he dies, it is murder. In such cases, the avenger
must put the murderer to death when they meet.

22 "But suppose someone pushes another person without having shown previous hostility,
or throws something that unintentionally hits
another person, 23 or accidentally drops a huge
stone on someone, though they were not enemies,
and the person dies. 24 If this should happen, the
community must follow these regulations in making a judgment between the slayer and the
avenger, the victim's nearest relative: 25 The community must protect the slayer from the avenger
and must escort the slayer back to live in the city
of refuge to which he fled. There he must remain
until the death of the high priest, who was
anointed with the sacred oil.

26 "But if the slayer ever leaves the limits of the
city of refuge, 27 and the avenger finds him outside the city and kills him, it will not be considered murder. 28 The slayer should have stayed
inside the city of refuge until the death of the
high priest. But after the death of the high priest,
the slayer may return to his own property.
29 These are legal requirements for you to observe from generation to generation, wherever
you may live.

30 "All murderers must be put to death, but
only if evidence is presented by more than one
witness. No one may be put to death on the testimony of only one witness. 31 Also, you must never
accept a ransom payment for the life of someone
judged guilty of murder and subject to execution; murderers must always be put to death.
32 And never accept a ransom payment from
someone who has fled to a city of refuge, allowing a slayer to return to his property before the
death of the high priest. 33 This will ensure that

the land where you live will not be polluted, for
murder pollutes the land. And no sacrifice except the execution of the murderer can purify
the land from murder. 34You must not defile the
land where you live, for I live there myself. I am
the LORD, who lives among the people of Israel."

CHAPTER 36

Women Who Inherit Property

Then the heads of the clans of Gilead—descendants of Makir, son of Manasseh, son of Joseph—
came to Moses and the family leaders of Israel
with a petition. 2They said, "Sir, the LORD instructed you to divide the land by sacred lot
among the people of Israel. You were told by the
LORD to give the grant of land owned by our
brother Zelophehad to his daughters. 3But if
they marry men from another tribe, their grants
of land will go with them to the tribe into which
they marry. In this way, the total area of our tribal
land will be reduced. 4Then when the Year of Jubilee comes, their portion of land will be added
to that of the new tribe, causing it to be lost forever to our ancestral tribe."

5So Moses gave the Israelites this command
from the LORD: "The claim of the men of the
tribe of Joseph is legitimate. 6This is what the
LORD commands concerning the daughters of
Zelophehad: Let them marry anyone they like, as
long as it is within their own ancestral tribe.
7None of the territorial land may pass from tribe
to tribe, for all the land given to each tribe must
remain within the tribe to which it was first allotted. 8The daughters throughout the tribes of
Israel who are in line to inherit property must
marry within their tribe, so that all the Israelites
will keep their ancestral property. 9No grant of
land may pass from one tribe to another; each
tribe of Israel must keep its allotted portion of
land."

10The daughters of Zelophehad did as the
LORD commanded Moses. 11Mahlah, Tirzah,
Hoglah, Milcah, and Noah all married cousins on
their father's side. 12They married into the clans
of Manasseh son of Joseph. Thus, their inheritance of land remained within their ancestral
tribe.

13These are the commands and regulations that the LORD gave to the people of Israel
through Moses while they were camped on the
plains of Moab beside the Jordan River across
from Jericho.

DEUTERONOMY Moses Says Goodbye

Look for  hidden messages in Deuteronomy!

Deuteronomy is a farewell speech by Moses to the Israelites. He reminded the people

- **OF WILD TIMES IN THE WILDERNESS**
- **OF WAYS TO OBEY**
- **OF BLESSINGS AND CURSES**
- **TO KEEP ON KEEPIN' ON**

Remember When...

Do you ever sit around with your family and talk about places you've been and things you've done? Well, that's kinda like what Moses did with the Israelites while they camped near the Jordan River. **Read all about their memories in Deuteronomy 1–3.**

Are We There Yet?

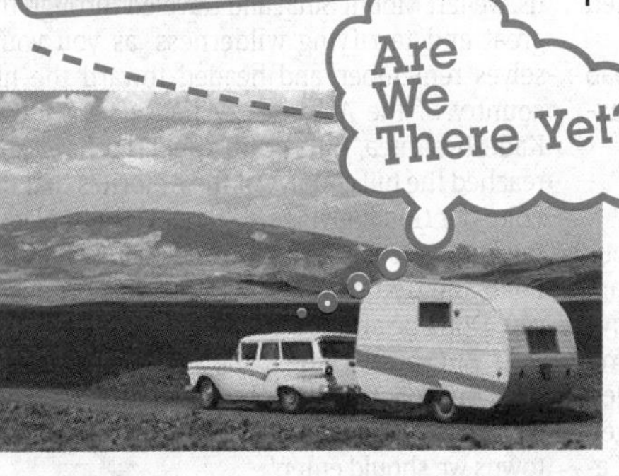

The Israelites were just across the river from the Promised Land. They were almost there! But before they could go in, Moses had some important advice. In fact, most of Deuteronomy is advice about how to live in the Promised Land. **Look for one important piece of advice in Deuteronomy 6:4-9.**

Job News

Moses knew he wasn't allowed to enter the Promised Land. (Remember why? It's in Numbers 20:1-13.) So he chose a new leader to take his place. **Find out who it was in Deuteronomy 31:1-8.**

Timeline

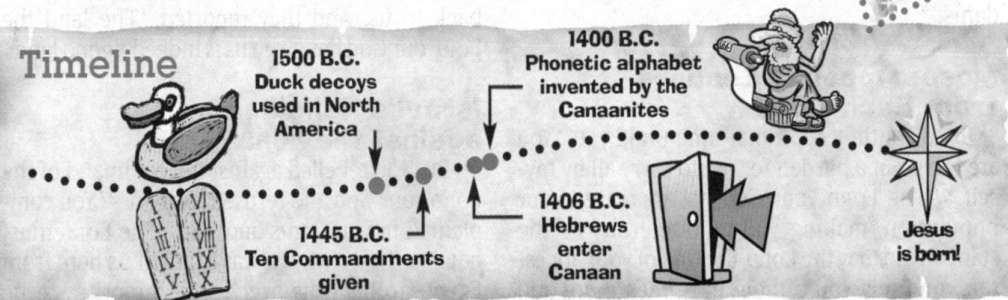

Even though Moses was Israel's greatest prophet and he spoke with God face to face, he still wasn't allowed to go into the Promised Land. "Not fair!" you might think. But Moses had disobeyed God and had to pay the price for that.

There were other powerful prophets during Israel's history, but it would be another thousand years before someone greater than Moses would appear—Jesus! But Jesus never sinned, and he is much more than a prophet. Jesus is God's Son! When Jesus died on the cross, he took the punishment for our sins. **When we believe in Jesus, we can be forgiven and live forever with him in heaven.**

Deuteronomy 1 . . . page 176

CHAPTER 1

Introduction to Moses' First Address

These are the words that Moses spoke to all the people of Israel while they were in the wilderness east of the Jordan River. They were camped in the Jordan Valley near Suph, between Paran on one side and Tophel, Laban, Hazeroth, and Dizahab on the other.

2 Normally it takes only eleven days to travel from Mount Sinai to Kadesh-barnea, going by way of Mount Seir. 3 But forty years after the Israelites left Egypt, on the first day of the eleventh month, Moses addressed the people of Israel, telling them everything the LORD had commanded him to say. 4 This took place after he had defeated King Sihon of the Amorites, who ruled in Heshbon, and at Edrei had defeated King Og of Bashan, who ruled in Ashtaroth.

5 While the Israelites were in the land of Moab east of the Jordan River, Moses carefully explained the LORD's instructions as follows.

The Command to Leave Sinai

6 "When we were at Mount Sinai, the LORD our God said to us, 'You have stayed at this mountain long enough. 7 It is time to break camp and move on. Go to the hill country of the Amorites and to all the neighboring regions—the Jordan Valley, the hill country, the western foothills, the Negev, and the coastal plain. Go to the land of the Canaanites and to Lebanon, and all the way to the great Euphrates River. 8 Look, I am giving all this land to you! Go in and occupy it, for it is the land the LORD swore to give to your ancestors Abraham, Isaac, and Jacob, and to all their descendants.'"

Moses Appoints Leaders from Each Tribe

9 Moses continued, "At that time I told you, 'You are too great a burden for me to carry all by myself. 10 The LORD your God has increased your population, making you as numerous as the stars! 11 And may the LORD, the God of your ancestors, multiply you a thousand times more and bless you as he promised! 12 But you are such a heavy load to carry! How can I deal with all your problems and bickering? 13 Choose some well-respected men from each tribe who are known for their wisdom and understanding, and I will appoint them as your leaders.'

14 "Then you responded, 'Your plan is a good one.' 15 So I took the wise and respected men you had selected from your tribes and appointed them to serve as judges and officials over you. Some were responsible for a thousand people, some for a hundred, some for fifty, and some for ten.

16 "At that time I instructed the judges, 'You must hear the cases of your fellow Israelites and the foreigners living among you. Be perfectly fair in your decisions 17 and impartial in your judgments. Hear the cases of those who are poor as well as those who are rich. Don't be afraid of anyone's anger, for the decision you make is God's decision. Bring me any cases that are too difficult for you, and I will handle them.'

18 "At that time I gave you instructions about everything you were to do.

Scouts Explore the Land

19 "Then, just as the LORD our God commanded us, we left Mount Sinai and traveled through the great and terrifying wilderness, as you yourselves remember, and headed toward the hill country of the Amorites. When we arrived at Kadesh-barnea, 20 I said to you, 'You have now reached the hill country of the Amorites that the LORD our God is giving us. 21 Look! He has placed the land in front of you. Go and occupy it as the LORD, the God of your ancestors, has promised you. Don't be afraid! Don't be discouraged!'

22 "But you all came to me and said, 'First, let's send out scouts to explore the land for us. They will advise us on the best route to take and which towns we should enter.'

23 "This seemed like a good idea to me, so I chose twelve scouts, one from each of your tribes. 24 They headed for the hill country and came to the valley of Eshcol and explored it. 25 They picked some of its fruit and brought it back to us. And they reported, 'The land the LORD our God has given us is indeed a good land.'

Israel's Rebellion against the LORD

26 "But you rebelled against the command of the LORD your God and refused to go in. 27 You complained in your tents and said, 'The LORD must hate us. That's why he has brought us here from Egypt—to hand us over to the Amorites to be slaughtered. 28 Where can we go? Our brothers have demoralized us with their report. They tell us, "The people of the land are taller and more powerful than we are, and their towns are large, with walls rising high into the sky! We even saw giants there—the descendants of Anak!"'

29 "But I said to you, 'Don't be shocked or afraid of them! 30 The LORD your God is going ahead of you. He will fight for you, just as you saw him do in

Egypt. 31And you saw how the LORD your God
cared for you all along the way as you traveled
through the wilderness, just as a father cares for
his child. Now he has brought you to this place.'

32"But even after all he did, you refused to trust
the LORD your God, 33who goes before you looking for the best places to camp, guiding you with a
pillar of fire by night and a pillar of cloud by day.

34"When the LORD heard your complaining, he
became very angry. So he solemnly swore, 35'Not
one of you from this wicked generation will live to
see the good land I swore to give your ancestors,
36except Caleb son of Jephunneh. He will see this
land because he has followed the LORD completely. I will give to him and his descendants
some of the very land he explored during his
scouting mission.'

37"And the LORD was also angry with me because of you. He said to me, 'Moses, not even you
will enter the Promised Land! 38Instead, your
assistant, Joshua son of Nun, will lead the people
into the land. Encourage him, for he will lead
Israel as they take possession of it. 39 I will give the
land to your little ones—your innocent children.
You were afraid they would be captured, but they
will be the ones who occupy it. 40As for you, turn
around now and go on back through the wilderness toward the Red Sea.'

41"Then you confessed, 'We have sinned
against the LORD! We will go into the land
and fight for it, as the LORD our God has commanded us.' So your men strapped on their weapons, thinking it would be easy to attack the hill
country.

42"But the LORD told me to tell you, 'Do not attack, for I am not with you. If you go ahead on your
own, you will be crushed by your enemies.'

43"This is what I told you, but you would not listen. Instead, you again rebelled against the LORD's
command and arrogantly went into the hill country to fight. 44But the Amorites who lived there
came out against you like a swarm of bees. They
chased and battered you all the way from Seir to
Hormah. 45Then you returned and wept before
the LORD, but he refused to listen. 46So you stayed
there at Kadesh for a long time.

CHAPTER 2
Remembering Israel's Wanderings

"Then we turned around and headed back
across the wilderness toward the Red Sea, just as
the LORD had instructed me, and we wandered
around in the region of Mount Seir for a long
time.

2"Then at last the LORD said to me, 3'You have
been wandering around in this hill country long
enough; turn to the north. 4Give these orders to
the people: "You will pass through the country
belonging to your relatives the Edomites, the descendants of Esau, who live in Seir. The Edomites
will feel threatened, so be careful. 5Do not bother
them, for I have given them all the hill country
around Mount Seir as their property, and I will
not give you even one square foot of their land.
6If you need food to eat or water to drink, pay
them for it. 7For the LORD your God has blessed
you in everything you have done. He has watched
your every step through this great wilderness.
During these forty years, the LORD your God has
been with you, and you have lacked nothing."'

8"So we bypassed the territory of our relatives,
the descendants of Esau, who live in Seir. We
avoided the road through the Arabah Valley that
comes up from Elath and Ezion-geber.

"Then as we turned north along the desert
route through Moab, 9the LORD warned us,
'Do not bother the Moabites, the descendants of
Lot, or start a war with them. I have given them Ar
as their property, and I will not give you any of
their land.'"

10(A race of giants called the Emites had once
lived in the area of Ar. They were as strong and
numerous and tall as the Anakites, another race
of giants. 11Both the Emites and the Anakites are
also known as the Rephaites, though the Moabites call them Emites. 12In earlier times the Horites had lived in Seir, but they were driven out
and displaced by the descendants of Esau, just as
Israel drove out the people of Canaan when the
LORD gave Israel their land.)

13Moses continued, "Then the LORD said to
us, 'Get moving. Cross the Zered Brook.' So we
crossed the brook.

14"Thirty-eight years passed from the time we
first left Kadesh-barnea until we finally crossed
the Zered Brook! By then, all the men old enough
to fight in battle had died in the wilderness, as
the LORD had vowed would happen. 15The LORD
struck them down until they had all been elimi-
nated from the community.

16"When all the men of fighting age had died,
17the LORD said to me, 18'Today you will cross the
border of Moab at Ar 19and enter the land of the
Ammonites, the descendants of Lot. But do not
bother them or start a war with them. I have given
the land of Ammon to them as their property, and
I will not give you any of their land.'"

20(That area was once considered the land of
the Rephaites, who had lived there, though the

Deuteronomy 3 . . . page 178

FUN-fact

Out of the BOX

Some Israelites made little boxes called phylacteries (sorta rhymes with *bill factories*) that they strapped to their heads or arms. They wrote parts of God's law and put the writings in the boxes. **Look at DEUTERONOMY 6:4-8 for more!**

Into the Heart!

It's OK to put God's Word on your stuff, juicebox, or notebook as long as you also put it in your heart. Write one key verse on your hand. Think about how the things you say and do all day fit with what your verse says.

Ammonites call them Zamzummites. 21 They
were also as strong and numerous and tall as the
Anakites. But the LORD destroyed them so the
Ammonites could occupy their land. 22 He had
done the same for the descendants of Esau who
lived in Seir, for he destroyed the Horites so they
could settle there in their place. The descendants of Esau live there to this day. 23 A similar
thing happened when the Caphtorites from
Crete invaded and destroyed the Avvites, who
had lived in villages in the area of Gaza.)

24 Moses continued, "Then the LORD said,
'Now get moving! Cross the Arnon Gorge. Look, I
will hand over to you Sihon the Amorite, king of
Heshbon, and I will give you his land. Attack him
and begin to occupy the land. 25 Beginning today
I will make people throughout the earth terrified
because of you. When they hear reports about
you, they will tremble with dread and fear.'"

Victory over Sihon of Heshbon

26 Moses continued, "From the wilderness of
Kedemoth I sent ambassadors to King Sihon of
Heshbon with this proposal of peace:

> 27 'Let us travel through your land. We will
> stay on the main road and won't turn off into
> the fields on either side. 28 Sell us food to eat
> and water to drink, and we will pay for it. All
> we want is permission to pass through your
> land. 29 The descendants of Esau who live in
> Seir allowed us to go through their country,
> and so did the Moabites, who live in Ar. Let
> us pass through until we cross the Jordan
> into the land the LORD our God is giving us.'

30 "But King Sihon of Heshbon refused to allow us to pass through, because the LORD your
God made Sihon stubborn and defiant so he
could help you defeat him, as he has now done.

31 "Then the LORD said to me, 'Look, I have begun to hand King Sihon and his land over to you.
Begin now to conquer and occupy his land.'

32 "Then King Sihon declared war on us and
mobilized his forces at Jahaz. 33 But the LORD our
God handed him over to us, and we crushed him,
his sons, and all his people. 34 We conquered all
his towns and completely destroyed everyone—
men, women, and children. Not a single person
was spared. 35 We took all the livestock as plunder for ourselves, along with anything of value
from the towns we ransacked.

36 "The LORD our God also helped us conquer
Aroer on the edge of the Arnon Gorge, and the
town in the gorge, and the whole area as far as
Gilead. No town had walls too strong for us.
37 However, we avoided the land of the Ammonites all along the Jabbok River and the towns in
the hill country—all the places the LORD our God
had commanded us to leave alone.

CHAPTER 3

Victory over Og of Bashan

"Next we turned and headed for the land of
Bashan, where King Og and his entire army
attacked us at Edrei. 2 But the LORD told me, 'Do
not be afraid of him, for I have given you victory
over Og and his entire army, and I will give you all
his land. Treat him just as you treated King Sihon
of the Amorites, who ruled in Heshbon.'

3 "So the LORD our God handed King Og and all
his people over to us, and we killed them all. Not
a single person survived. 4 We conquered all sixty
of his towns—the entire Argob region in his kingdom of Bashan. Not a single town escaped our
conquest. 5 These towns were all fortified with
high walls and barred gates. We also took many
unwalled villages at the same time. 6 We completely destroyed the kingdom of Bashan, just as
we had destroyed King Sihon of Heshbon. We
destroyed all the people in every town we conquered—men, women, and children alike.

7But we kept all the livestock for ourselves and
took plunder from all the towns.

8"So we took the land of the two Amorite kings
east of the Jordan River—all the way from the
Arnon Gorge to Mount Hermon. 9(Mount Hermon is called Sirion by the Sidonians, and the Amorites call it Senir.) 10We had now conquered all
the cities on the plateau and all Gilead and Bashan, as far as the towns of Salecah and Edrei,
which were part of Og's kingdom in Bashan.
11(King Og of Bashan was the last survivor of the
giant Rephaites. His bed was made of iron and was
more than thirteen feet long and six feet wide. It
can still be seen in the Ammonite city of Rabbah.)

Land Division East of the Jordan

12"When we took possession of this land, I gave
to the tribes of Reuben and Gad the territory beyond Aroer along the Arnon Gorge, plus half of
the hill country of Gilead with its towns. 13Then I
gave the rest of Gilead and all of Bashan—Og's
former kingdom—to the half-tribe of Manasseh.
(This entire Argob region of Bashan used to be
known as the land of the Rephaites. 14Jair, a
leader from the tribe of Manasseh, conquered
the whole Argob region in Bashan, all the way to
the border of the Geshurites and Maacathites.
Jair renamed this region after himself, calling it
the Towns of Jair, as it is still known today.) 15I
gave Gilead to the clan of Makir. 16But I also gave
part of Gilead to the tribes of Reuben and Gad.
The area I gave them extended from the middle
of the Arnon Gorge in the south to the Jabbok
River on the Ammonite frontier. 17They also received the Jordan Valley, all the way from the Sea
of Galilee down to the Dead Sea, with the Jordan
River serving as the western boundary. To the
east were the slopes of Pisgah.

18"At that time I gave this command to the
tribes that would live east of the Jordan: 'Although the LORD your God has given you this
land as your property, all your fighting men must
cross the Jordan ahead of your Israelite relatives,
armed and ready to assist them. 19Your wives,
children, and numerous livestock, however, may
stay behind in the towns I have given you.
20When the LORD has given security to the rest of
the Israelites, as he has to you, and when they occupy the land the LORD your God is giving them
across the Jordan River, then you may all return
here to the land I have given you.'

Moses Forbidden to Enter the Land

21"At that time I gave Joshua this charge: 'You
have seen for yourself everything the LORD your
God has done to these two kings. He will do the
same to all the kingdoms on the west side of the
Jordan. 22Do not be afraid of the nations there,
for the LORD your God will fight for you.'

23"At that time I pleaded with the LORD and
said, 24'O Sovereign LORD, you have only begun
to show your greatness and the strength of your
hand to me, your servant. Is there any god in
heaven or on earth who can perform such great
and mighty deeds as you do? 25Please let me
cross the Jordan to see the wonderful land on the
other side, the beautiful hill country and the Lebanon mountains.'

26"But the LORD was angry with me because of
you, and he would not listen to me. 'That's
enough!' he declared. 'Speak of it no more. 27But
go up to Pisgah Peak, and look over the land in
every direction. Take a good look, but you may
not cross the Jordan River. 28Instead, commission Joshua and encourage and strengthen him,
for he will lead the people across the Jordan. He
will give them all the land you now see before you
as their possession.' 29So we stayed in the valley
near Beth-peor.

CHAPTER 4

Moses Urges Israel to Obey

"And now, Israel, listen carefully to these decrees
and regulations that I am about to teach you.
Obey them so that you may live, so you may enter
and occupy the land that the LORD, the God of
your ancestors, is giving you. 2Do not add to or
subtract from these commands I am giving you.
Just obey the commands of the LORD your God
that I am giving you.

3"You saw for yourself what the LORD did to
you at Baal-peor. There the LORD your God destroyed everyone who had worshiped Baal, the
god of Peor. 4But all of you who were faithful to
the LORD your God are still alive today—every
one of you.

5"Look, I now teach you these decrees and regulations just as the LORD my God commanded
me, so that you may obey them in the land you
are about to enter and occupy. 6Obey them completely, and you will display your wisdom and intelligence among the surrounding nations.
When they hear all these decrees, they will exclaim, 'How wise and prudent are the people of
this great nation!' 7For what great nation has a
god as near to them as the LORD our God is near
to us whenever we call on him? 8And what great
nation has decrees and regulations as righteous
and fair as this body of instructions that I am giving you today?

9"But watch out! Be careful never to forget what you yourself have seen. Do not let these memories escape from your mind as long as you live! And be sure to pass them on to your children and grandchildren. 10Never forget the day when you stood before the LORD your God at Mount Sinai, where he told me, 'Summon the people before me, and I will personally instruct them. Then they will learn to fear me as long as they live, and they will teach their children to fear me also.'

11"You came near and stood at the foot of the mountain, while flames from the mountain shot into the sky. The mountain was shrouded in black clouds and deep darkness. 12And the LORD spoke to you from the heart of the fire. You heard the sound of his words but didn't see his form; there was only a voice. 13He proclaimed his covenant—the Ten Commandments—which he commanded you to keep, and which he wrote on two stone tablets. 14It was at that time that the LORD commanded me to teach you his decrees and regulations so you would obey them in the land you are about to enter and occupy.

A Warning against Idolatry

15"But be very careful! You did not see the LORD's form on the day he spoke to you from the heart of the fire at Mount Sinai. 16So do not corrupt yourselves by making an idol in any form—whether of a man or a woman, 17an animal on the ground, a bird in the sky, 18a small animal that scurries along the ground, or a fish in the deepest sea. 19And when you look up into the sky and see the sun, moon, and stars—all the forces of heaven—don't be seduced into worshiping them. The LORD your God gave them to all the peoples of the earth. 20Remember that the LORD rescued you from the iron-smelting furnace of Egypt in order to make you his very own people and his special possession, which is what you are today.

21"But the LORD was angry with me because of you. He vowed that I would not cross the Jordan River into the good land the LORD your God is giving you as your special possession. 22You will cross the Jordan to occupy the land, but I will not. Instead, I will die here on the east side of the river. 23So be careful not to break the covenant the LORD your God has made with you. Do not make idols of any shape or form, for the LORD your God has forbidden this. 24The LORD your God is a devouring fire; he is a jealous God.

25"In the future, when you have children and grandchildren and have lived in the land a long time, do not corrupt yourselves by making idols of any kind. This is evil in the sight of the LORD your God and will arouse his anger.

26"Today I call on heaven and earth as witnesses against you. If you break my covenant, you will quickly disappear from the land you are crossing the Jordan to occupy. You will live there only a short time; then you will be utterly destroyed. 27For the LORD will scatter you among the nations, where only a few of you will survive. 28There, in a foreign land, you will worship idols made from wood and stone—gods that neither see nor hear nor eat nor smell. 29But from there you will search again for the LORD your God. And if you search for him with all your heart and soul, you will find him.

30"In the distant future, when you are suffering all these things, you will finally return to the LORD your God and listen to what he tells you. 31For the LORD your God is a merciful God; he will not abandon you or destroy you or forget the solemn covenant he made with your ancestors.

There Is Only One God

32"Now search all of history, from the time God created people on the earth until now, and search from one end of the heavens to the other. Has anything as great as this ever been seen or heard before? 33Has any nation ever heard the voice of God speaking from fire—as you did—and survived? 34Has any other god dared to take a nation for himself out of another nation by means of trials, miraculous signs, wonders, war, a strong hand, a powerful arm, and terrifying acts? Yet that is what the LORD your God did for you in Egypt, right before your eyes.

35"He showed you these things so you would know that the LORD is God and there is no other. 36He let you hear his voice from heaven so he could instruct you. He let you see his great fire here on earth so he could speak to you from it. 37Because he loved your ancestors, he chose to bless their descendants, and he personally brought you out of Egypt with a great display of power. 38He drove out nations far greater than you, so he could bring you in and give you their land as your special possession, as it is today.

39"So remember this and keep it firmly in mind: The LORD is God both in heaven and on earth, and there is no other. 40If you obey all the decrees and commands I am giving you today, all will be well with you and your children. I am giving you these instructions so you will enjoy a long life in the land the LORD your God is giving you for all time."

Eastern Cities of Refuge

41 Then Moses set apart three cities of refuge east
of the Jordan River. 42 Anyone who killed another
person unintentionally, without previous hostility, could flee there to live in safety. 43 These were
the cities: Bezer on the wilderness plateau for
the tribe of Reuben; Ramoth in Gilead for the
tribe of Gad; Golan in Bashan for the tribe of Manasseh.

Introduction to Moses' Second Address

44 This is the body of instruction that Moses presented to the Israelites. 45 These are the laws, decrees, and regulations that Moses gave to the
people of Israel when they left Egypt, 46 and as
they camped in the valley near Beth-peor east of
the Jordan River. (This land was formerly occupied by the Amorites under King Sihon, who
ruled from Heshbon. But Moses and the Israelites destroyed him and his people when they
came up from Egypt. 47 Israel took possession of
his land and that of King Og of Bashan—the two
Amorite kings east of the Jordan. 48 So Israel conquered the entire area from Aroer at the edge of
the Arnon Gorge all the way to Mount Sirion, also
called Mount Hermon. 49 And they conquered the
eastern bank of the Jordan River as far south as
the Dead Sea, below the slopes of Pisgah.)

CHAPTER 5

Ten Commandments for the Covenant Community

Moses called all the people of Israel together and
said, "Listen carefully, Israel. Hear the decrees
and regulations I am giving you today, so you may
learn them and obey them!

2 "The LORD our God made a covenant with us
at Mount Sinai. 3 The LORD did not make this
covenant with our ancestors, but with all of us
who are alive today. 4 At the mountain the LORD
spoke to you face to face from the heart of the
fire. 5 I stood as an intermediary between you
and the LORD, for you were afraid of the fire and
did not want to approach the mountain. He
spoke to me, and I passed his words on to you.
This is what he said:

6 "I am the LORD your God, who rescued you
from the land of Egypt, the place of your
slavery.
7 "You must not have any other god but me.
8 "You must not make for yourself an idol of
any kind, or an image of anything in the
heavens or on the earth or in the sea. 9 You
must not bow down to them or worship
them, for I, the LORD your God, am a jealous
God who will not tolerate your affection for
any other gods. I lay the sins of the parents
upon their children; the entire family is
affected—even children in the third and
fourth generations of those who reject me.
10 But I lavish unfailing love for a thousand
generations on those who love me and obey
my commands.
11 "You must not misuse the name of the LORD
your God. The LORD will not let you go
unpunished if you misuse his name.
12 "Observe the Sabbath day by keeping it holy,
as the LORD your God has commanded you.
13 You have six days each week for your
ordinary work, 14 but the seventh day is a
Sabbath day of rest dedicated to the LORD
your God. On that day no one in your household may do any work. This includes you,
your sons and daughters, your male and
female servants, your oxen and donkeys and
other livestock, and any foreigners living
among you. All your male and female
servants must rest as you do. 15 Remember
that you were once slaves in Egypt, but the
LORD your God brought you out with his
strong hand and powerful arm. That is why
the LORD your God has commanded you to
rest on the Sabbath day.
16 "Honor your father and mother, as the LORD
your God commanded you. Then you will live
a long, full life in the land the LORD your God
is giving you.
17 "You must not murder.
18 "You must not commit adultery.
19 "You must not steal.
20 "You must not testify falsely against your
neighbor.
21 "You must not covet your neighbor's wife.
You must not covet your neighbor's house
or land, male or female servant, ox or donkey,
or anything else that belongs to your
neighbor.

22 "The LORD spoke these words to all of
you assembled there at the foot of the mountain.
He spoke with a loud voice from the heart of
the fire, surrounded by clouds and deep darkness. This was all he said at that time, and he
wrote his words on two stone tablets and gave
them to me.

23 "But when you heard the voice from the
heart of the darkness, while the mountain was
blazing with fire, all your tribal leaders and

elders came to me. 24They said, 'Look, the LORD
our God has shown us his glory and greatness,
and we have heard his voice from the heart of the
fire. Today we have seen that God can speak to us
humans, and yet we live! 25But now, why should
we risk death again? If the LORD our God speaks
to us again, we will certainly die and be consumed by this awesome fire. 26Can any living
thing hear the voice of the living God from the
heart of the fire as we did and yet survive? 27Go
yourself and listen to what the LORD our God
says. Then come and tell us everything he tells
you, and we will listen and obey.'

28"The LORD heard the request you made to
me. And he said, 'I have heard what the people
said to you, and they are right. 29Oh, that they
would always have hearts like this, that they
might fear me and obey all my commands! If
they did, they and their descendants would prosper forever. 30Go and tell them, "Return to your
tents." 31But you stand here with me so I can give
you all my commands, decrees, and regulations.
You must teach them to the people so they can
obey them in the land I am giving them as their
possession.'"

32So Moses told the people, "You must be
careful to obey all the commands of the LORD
your God, following his instructions in every detail. 33Stay on the path that the LORD your God
has commanded you to follow. Then you will live
long and prosperous lives in the land you are
about to enter and occupy.

CHAPTER 6
A Call for Wholehearted Commitment

"These are the commands, decrees, and regulations that the LORD your God commanded me to
teach you. You must obey them in the land you are
about to enter and occupy, 2and you and your
children and grandchildren must fear the LORD
your God as long as you live. If you obey all his decrees and commands, you will enjoy a long life.
3Listen closely, Israel, and be careful to obey.
Then all will go well with you, and you will have
many children in the land flowing with milk and
honey, just as the LORD, the God of your ancestors, promised you.

4"Listen, O Israel! The LORD is our God, the
LORD alone. **5And you must love the
LORD your God with all your heart, all
your soul, and all your strength.** 6And
you must commit yourselves wholeheartedly to
these commands that I am giving you today. 7Re-
peat them again and again to your children. Talk
about them when you are at home and when you
are on the road, when you are going to bed and
when you are getting up. 8Tie them to your
hands and wear them on your forehead as reminders. 9Write them on the doorposts of your
house and on your gates.

10"The LORD your God will soon bring you into
the land he swore to give you when he made a vow
to your ancestors Abraham, Isaac, and Jacob. It is
a land with large, prosperous cities that you did
not build. 11The houses will be richly stocked
with goods you did not produce. You will draw
water from cisterns you did not dig, and you will
eat from vineyards and olive trees you did not
plant. When you have eaten your fill in this land,
12be careful not to forget the LORD, who rescued
you from slavery in the land of Egypt. 13You must
fear the LORD your God and serve him. When you
take an oath, you must use only his name.

14"You must not worship any of the gods of
neighboring nations, 15for the LORD your God,
who lives among you, is a jealous God. His anger
will flare up against you, and he will wipe you
from the face of the earth. 16You must not test
the LORD your God as you did when you complained at Massah. 17You must diligently obey
the commands of the LORD your God—all the
laws and decrees he has given you. 18Do what is
right and good in the LORD's sight, so all will go
well with you. Then you will enter and occupy
the good land that the LORD swore to give your
ancestors. 19You will drive out all the enemies
living in the land, just as the LORD said you would.

20"In the future your children will ask you,
'What is the meaning of these laws, decrees, and
regulations that the LORD our God has commanded us to obey?'

21"Then you must tell them, 'We were Pharaoh's slaves in Egypt, but the LORD brought us out
of Egypt with his strong hand. 22The LORD did miraculous signs and wonders before our eyes, dealing terrifying blows against Egypt and Pharaoh
and all his people. 23He brought us out of Egypt so
he could give us this land he had sworn to give our
ancestors. 24And the LORD our God commanded
us to obey all these decrees and to fear him so he
can continue to bless us and preserve our lives, as
he has done to this day. 25For we will be counted
as righteous when we obey all the commands the
LORD our God has given us.'

CHAPTER 7
The Privilege of Holiness

"When the LORD your God brings you into the
land you are about to enter and occupy, he will

clear away many nations ahead of you: the Hittites, Girgashites, Amorites, Canaanites, Perizzites, Hivites, and Jebusites. These seven nations
are greater and more numerous than you.
2When the LORD your God hands these nations
over to you and you conquer them, you must
completely destroy them. Make no treaties with
them and show them no mercy. 3You must not
intermarry with them. Do not let your daughters
and sons marry their sons and daughters, 4for
they will lead your children away from me to
worship other gods. Then the anger of the LORD
will burn against you, and he will quickly destroy
you. 5This is what you must do. You must break
down their pagan altars and shatter their sacred
pillars. Cut down their Asherah poles and burn
their idols. 6For you are a holy people, who belong to the LORD your God. Of all the people on
earth, the LORD your God has chosen you to be
his own special treasure.

7"The LORD did not set his heart on you and
choose you because you were more numerous
than other nations, for you were the smallest of
all nations! 8Rather, it was simply that the LORD
loves you, and he was keeping the oath he had
sworn to your ancestors. That is why the LORD
rescued you with such a strong hand from your
slavery and from the oppressive hand of Pharaoh, king of Egypt. 9Understand, therefore, that
the LORD your God is indeed God. He is the faithful God who keeps his covenant for a thousand
generations and lavishes his unfailing love on
those who love him and obey his commands.
10But he does not hesitate to punish and destroy
those who reject him. 11Therefore, you must
obey all these commands, decrees, and regulations I am giving you today.

12"If you listen to these regulations and faithfully obey them, the LORD your God will keep his
covenant of unfailing love with you, as he promised with an oath to your ancestors. 13He will love
you and bless you, and he will give you many children. He will give fertility to your land and your
animals. When you arrive in the land he swore to
give your ancestors, you will have large harvests
of grain, new wine, and olive oil, and great herds
of cattle, sheep, and goats. 14You will be blessed
above all the nations of the earth. None of your
men or women will be childless, and all your livestock will bear young. 15And the LORD will protect
you from all sickness. He will not let you suffer
from the terrible diseases you knew in Egypt, but
he will inflict them on all your enemies!

16"You must destroy all the nations the LORD
your God hands over to you. Show them no

Key Verse **"Love the LORD your God with all your heart, all your soul, and all your strength."**
—DEUTERONOMY 6:5

I JUST... DON'T...LOVE YOU.

We can kind of like broccoli or put up with a song. But we can't just sort of love God. We need to love God with our whole hearts. That means that we need to think about and live for God when we're at school, home, church, or anywhere! The more we know God, the more we'll love God. So give your whole heart to God and love him in *everything* you do.

Make this heart mobile as a reminder to love God with every little piece of your heart.

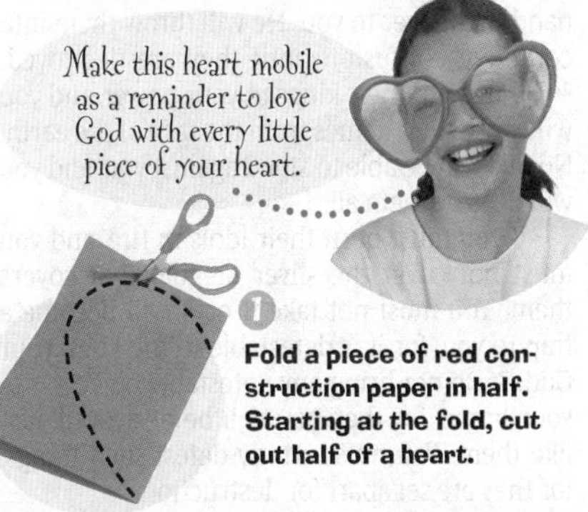

1 **Fold a piece of red construction paper in half. Starting at the fold, cut out half of a heart.**

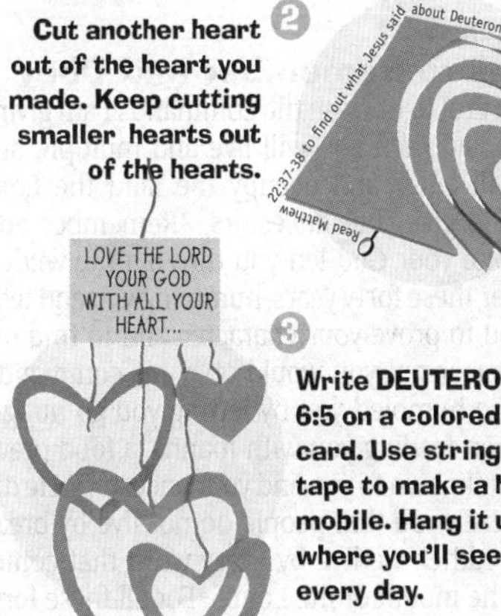

Read Matthew 22:37-38 to find out what Jesus said about Deuteronomy 6:5.
LOVE THE LORD YOUR GOD WITH ALL YOUR HEART...

2 **Cut another heart out of the heart you made. Keep cutting smaller hearts out of the hearts.**

3 **Write DEUTERONOMY 6:5 on a colored index card. Use string and tape to make a heart mobile. Hang it up where you'll see it every day.**

mercy, and do not worship their gods, or they
will trap you. 17 Perhaps you will think to yourselves, 'How can we ever conquer these nations
that are so much more powerful than we are?'
18 But don't be afraid of them! Just remember
what the LORD your God did to Pharaoh and to
all the land of Egypt. 19 Remember the great terrors the LORD your God sent against them. You
saw it all with your own eyes! And remember the
miraculous signs and wonders, and the strong
hand and powerful arm with which he brought
you out of Egypt. The LORD your God will use
this same power against all the people you fear.
20 And then the LORD your God will send terror
to drive out the few survivors still hiding from
you!

21 "No, do not be afraid of those nations, for the
LORD your God is among you, and he is a great
and awesome God. 22 The LORD your God will
drive those nations out ahead of you little by
little. You will not clear them away all at once,
otherwise the wild animals would multiply too
quickly for you. 23 But the LORD your God will
hand them over to you. He will throw them into
complete confusion until they are destroyed.
24 He will put their kings in your power, and you
will erase their names from the face of the earth.
No one will be able to stand against you, and you
will destroy them all.

25 "You must burn their idols in fire, and you
must not covet the silver or gold that covers
them. You must not take it or it will become a
trap to you, for it is detestable to the LORD your
God. 26 Do not bring any detestable objects into
your home, for then you will be destroyed, just
like them. You must utterly detest such things,
for they are set apart for destruction.

CHAPTER 8
A Call to Remember and Obey

"Be careful to obey all the commands I am giving
you today. Then you will live and multiply, and
you will enter and occupy the land the LORD
swore to give your ancestors. 2 Remember how
the LORD your God led you through the wilderness for these forty years, humbling you and testing you to prove your character, and to find out
whether or not you would obey his commands.
3 Yes, he humbled you by letting you go hungry
and then feeding you with manna, a food previously unknown to you and your ancestors. He did
it to teach you that people do not live by bread
alone; rather, we live by every word that comes
from the mouth of the LORD. 4 For all these forty
years your clothes didn't wear out, and your feet
didn't blister or swell. 5 Think about it: Just as a
parent disciplines a child, the LORD your God disciplines you for your own good.

6 "So obey the commands of the LORD your
God by walking in his ways and fearing him. 7 For
the LORD your God is bringing you into a good
land of flowing streams and pools of water, with
fountains and springs that gush out in the valleys
and hills. 8 It is a land of wheat and barley; of
grapevines, fig trees, and pomegranates; of olive
oil and honey. 9 It is a land where food is plentiful
and nothing is lacking. It is a land where iron is
as common as stone, and copper is abundant in
the hills. 10 When you have eaten your fill, be sure
to praise the LORD your God for the good land he
has given you.

11 "But that is the time to be careful! Beware
that in your plenty you do not forget the LORD
your God and disobey his commands, regulations, and decrees that I am giving you today.
12 For when you have become full and prosperous and have built fine homes to live in, 13 and
when your flocks and herds have become very
large and your silver and gold have multiplied
along with everything else, be careful! 14 Do not
become proud at that time and forget the LORD
your God, who rescued you from slavery in the
land of Egypt. 15 Do not forget that he led you
through the great and terrifying wilderness with
its poisonous snakes and scorpions, where it was
so hot and dry. He gave you water from the rock!
16 He fed you with manna in the wilderness, a
food unknown to your ancestors. He did this to
humble you and test you for your own good. 17 He
did all this so you would never say to yourself, 'I
have achieved this wealth with my own strength
and energy.' 18 Remember the LORD your God. He
is the one who gives you power to be successful,
in order to fulfill the covenant he confirmed to
your ancestors with an oath.

19 "But I assure you of this: If you ever forget
the LORD your God and follow other gods, worshiping and bowing down to them, you will certainly be destroyed. 20 Just as the LORD has
destroyed other nations in your path, you also
will be destroyed if you refuse to obey the LORD
your God.

CHAPTER 9
Victory by God's Grace

"Listen, O Israel! Today you are about to cross the
Jordan River to take over the land belonging to
nations much greater and more powerful than
you. They live in cities with walls that reach to the
sky! 2 The people are strong and tall—descen-

dants of the famous Anakite giants. You've heard
the saying, 'Who can stand up to the Anakites?'
3But recognize today that the LORD your God is
the one who will cross over ahead of you like a
devouring fire to destroy them. He will subdue
them so that you will quickly conquer them and
drive them out, just as the LORD has promised.
4 "After the LORD your God has done this for
you, don't say in your hearts, 'The LORD has given
us this land because we are such good people!'
No, it is because of the wickedness of the other
nations that he is pushing them out of your way.
5It is not because you are so good or have such
integrity that you are about to occupy their land.
The LORD your God will drive these nations out
ahead of you only because of their wickedness,
and to fulfill the oath he swore to your ancestors
Abraham, Isaac, and Jacob. 6You must recognize
that the LORD your God is not giving you this
good land because you are good, for you are
not—you are a stubborn people.

Remembering the Gold Calf

7"Remember and never forget how angry you
made the LORD your God out in the wilderness.
From the day you left Egypt until now, you have
been constantly rebelling against him. 8Even at
Mount Sinai you made the LORD so angry he was
ready to destroy you. 9This happened when I was
on the mountain receiving the tablets of stone
inscribed with the words of the covenant that
the LORD had made with you. I was there for forty
days and forty nights, and all that time I ate no
food and drank no water. 10The LORD gave me
the two tablets on which God had written with
his own finger all the words he had spoken to you
from the heart of the fire when you were assembled at the mountain.
11"At the end of the forty days and nights, the
LORD handed me the two stone tablets inscribed
with the words of the covenant. 12Then the LORD
said to me, 'Get up! Go down immediately, for the
people you brought out of Egypt have corrupted
themselves. How quickly they have turned away
from the way I commanded them to live! They
have melted gold and made an idol for themselves!'
13"The LORD also said to me, 'I have seen
how stubborn and rebellious these people are.
14Leave me alone so I may destroy them and
erase their name from under heaven. Then I will
make a mighty nation of your descendants, a nation larger and more powerful than they are.'
15"So while the mountain was blazing with fire
I turned and came down, holding in my hands the
two stone tablets inscribed with the terms of the
covenant. 16There below me I could see that you
had sinned against the LORD your God. You had
melted gold and made a calf idol for yourselves.
How quickly you had turned away from the path
the LORD had commanded you to follow! 17So I
took the stone tablets and threw them to the
ground, smashing them before your eyes.
18"Then, as before, I threw myself down before the LORD for forty days and nights. I ate no
bread and drank no water because of the great
sin you had committed by doing what the LORD
hated, provoking him to anger. 19I feared that the
furious anger of the LORD, which turned him
against you, would drive him to destroy you. But
again he listened to me. 20 The LORD was so angry with Aaron that he wanted to destroy him,
too. But I prayed for Aaron, and the LORD spared
him. 21I took your sin—the calf you had made—
and I melted it down in the fire and ground it
into fine dust. Then I threw the dust into the
stream that flows down the mountain.
22"You also made the LORD angry at Tab-
erah, Massah, and Kibroth-hattaavah. 23And at
Kadesh-barnea the LORD sent you out with this
command: 'Go up and take over the land I have
given you.' But you rebelled against the command of the LORD your God and refused to put
your trust in him or obey him. 24Yes, you have
been rebelling against the LORD as long as I have
known you.
25"That is why I threw myself down before the
LORD for forty days and nights—for the LORD said
he would destroy you. 26I prayed to the LORD and
said, 'O Sovereign LORD, do not destroy them.
They are your own people. They are your special
possession, whom you redeemed from Egypt
by your mighty power and your strong hand.
27Please overlook the stubbornness and the awful sin of these people, and remember instead
your servants Abraham, Isaac, and Jacob. 28If you
destroy these people, the Egyptians will say, "The
Israelites died because the LORD wasn't able to
bring them to the land he had promised to give
them." Or they might say, "He destroyed them because he hated them; he deliberately took them
into the wilderness to slaughter them." 29But
they are your people and your special possession,
whom you brought out of Egypt by your great
strength and powerful arm.'

CHAPTER 10

A New Copy of the Covenant

"At that time the LORD said to me, 'Chisel out
two stone tablets like the first ones. Also make

a wooden Ark—a sacred chest to store them in.
Come up to me on the mountain, 2and I will
write on the tablets the same words that were on
the ones you smashed. Then place the tablets in
the Ark.'
3"So I made an Ark of acacia wood and cut
two stone tablets like the first two. Then I went
up the mountain with the tablets in my hand.
4Once again the LORD wrote the Ten Commandments on the tablets and gave them to me. They
were the same words the LORD had spoken to
you from the heart of the fire on the day you
were assembled at the foot of the mountain.
5Then I turned and came down the mountain
and placed the tablets in the Ark of the Covenant, which I had made, just as the LORD commanded me. And the tablets are still there in the
Ark."
6(The people of Israel set out from the wells of
the people of Jaakan and traveled to Moserah,
where Aaron died and was buried. His son Eleazar ministered as high priest in his place. 7Then
they journeyed to Gudgodah, and from there to
Jotbathah, a land with many brooks and streams.
8At that time the LORD set apart the tribe of Levi
to carry the Ark of the LORD's Covenant, and to
stand before the LORD as his ministers, and to
pronounce blessings in his name. These are their
duties to this day. 9That is why the Levites have
no share of property or possession of land
among the other Israelite tribes. The LORD himself is their special possession, as the LORD your
God told them.)
10"As for me, I stayed on the mountain in the
LORD's presence for forty days and nights, as I
had done the first time. And once again the LORD
listened to my pleas and agreed not to destroy
you. 11Then the LORD said to me, 'Get up and resume the journey, and lead the people to the land
I swore to give to their ancestors, so they may
take possession of it.'

A Call to Love and Obedience

12"And now, Israel, what does the LORD your God
require of you? He requires only that you fear the
LORD your God, and live in a way that pleases him,
and love him and serve him with all your heart
and soul. 13And you must always obey the LORD's
commands and decrees that I am giving you today for your own good.
14"Look, the highest heavens and the earth
and everything in it all belong to the LORD your
God. 15Yet the LORD chose your ancestors as the
objects of his love. And he chose you, their descendants, above all other nations, as is evident
today. 16Therefore, change your hearts and stop
being stubborn.
17"For the LORD your God is the God of gods
and Lord of lords. He is the great God, the mighty
and awesome God, who shows no partiality and
cannot be bribed. 18He ensures that orphans and
widows receive justice. He shows love to the foreigners living among you and gives them food and
clothing. 19So you, too, must show love to foreigners, for you yourselves were once foreigners in the
land of Egypt. 20You must fear the LORD your God
and worship him and cling to him. Your oaths
must be in his name alone. 21He alone is your God,
the only one who is worthy of your praise, the one
who has done these mighty miracles that you have
seen with your own eyes. 22When your ancestors
went down into Egypt, there were only seventy of
them. But now the LORD your God has made you
as numerous as the stars in the sky!

CHAPTER 11

"You must love the LORD your God and always
obey his requirements, decrees, regulations, and
commands. 2Keep in mind that I am not talking
now to your children, who have never experienced the discipline of the LORD your God or seen
his greatness and his strong hand and powerful
arm. 3They didn't see the miraculous signs and
wonders he performed in Egypt against Pharaoh
and all his land. 4They didn't see what the LORD
did to the armies of Egypt and to their horses and
chariots—how he drowned them in the Red Sea
as they were chasing you. He destroyed them, and
they have not recovered to this very day!
5"Your children didn't see how the LORD cared
for you in the wilderness until you arrived here.
6They didn't see what he did to Dathan and Abiram (the sons of Eliab, a descendant of Reuben)
when the earth opened its mouth in the Israelite
camp and swallowed them, along with their
households and tents and every living thing that
belonged to them. 7But you have seen the LORD
perform all these mighty deeds with your own
eyes!

The Blessings of Obedience

8"Therefore, be careful to obey every command
I am giving you today, so you may have strength
to go in and take over the land you are about to
enter. 9If you obey, you will enjoy a long life in
the land the LORD swore to give to your ancestors and to you, their descendants—a land flowing with milk and honey! 10For the land you are
about to enter and take over is not like the land
of Egypt from which you came, where you

BIBLE BIOS

Hear From the Heroes

Hi, my name is

JONATHAN *(prince, warrior)*

If you want a friend, you have to be a friend. And everyone wants friends. I found a true, lifelong friend by *being* a true friend to David. When we met, I promised David that I would always remain his friend. I kept my promise—even when my own father tried to break us apart.

Jonathan gave gifts to David, too. See what he gave in 1 SAMUEL 18:1-4.

Something strange happened with my dad, Saul. I think it started when David defeated Goliath. When David came home, the people sang and shouted out how David fought better than my dad. From that day on, my dad's jealousy caused him to chase David all over Israel, trying to kill him.

See what the people said in 1 SAMUEL 18:6-8.

At first, I couldn't believe my dad would ever hurt David. But when David didn't show up for dinner when he was invited to my father's table, I found out the truth. My dad started screaming that he wanted to kill David and almost killed me when I stuck up for David. I told David what my dad planned to do, and David got away. Even when it was hard, I was a true friend to David. How can you be a true friend? **Write the name of your friend right here.**

____

STUCK ON YOU

Find two small trinkets, and ask a friend to find two items also.

For example, you could bring a shoelace, a picture, or a bracelet.

With your friend, read PROVERBS 18:24.

Glue one of your items to your friend's item to make a symbol of friendship. Repeat with the other two items. Have your friend take home one of the glued symbols of friendship while you take the other one home.

Keep the symbol as a reminder to be a true friend.

BIBLE BIOS

Hear From the Heroes

Hi, my name is

ABIGAIL *(homemaker)*

My husband, Nabal, always had a bad temper. But this time, he just went too far. You see, David and his men had protected our family and workers for some time. When robbers or bullies would come our way, they had to get past David first. But when David asked for help from us, Nabal refused. In fact, he lost his temper and even insulted David!

Imagine spending the whole day mowing your neighbors' lawns and picking their weeds. At the end of the day, when you asked for a cup of water, your neighbors told you to go home and get your own water and then made fun of you and your entire family. That's kind of what it was like for David—but worse!

Well, when I found out, I knew David would be steaming mad and that he might lose *his* temper. It took all my courage to go out right away and apologize for Nabal. I helped David, too. I think he was ready to take revenge against Nabal. But David accepted my apology, and my family was saved. Nothing good ever comes from losing your temper. But being humble and working for peace stops a disaster from happening. Look for ways to bring peace to your family and friends. And try to always keep your temper. Trust me, you'll be glad you did!

Wow! Look at how Abigail apologized in 1 SAMUEL 25:18-35.

Read MATTHEW 5:9 to see what Jesus says about people who work for peace.

This isn't the end of the story for David and Abigail. Read 1 SAMUEL 25:39-42 for more.

Temper, Temper

Work with your family to find a way to deal with out-of-control tempers.

For example, you could agree that when family members lose their tempers, they have to go to the cool-down corner for two minutes.

Or they might have to write down their thoughts and feelings before they're allowed to talk about them.

Think of all sorts of temper-control ideas. Agree as a family about which ideas you'll use and how and when you'll use them.

planted your seed and made irrigation ditches
with your foot as in a vegetable garden. 11Rather,
the land you will soon take over is a land of hills
and valleys with plenty of rain—12a land that
the LORD your God cares for. He watches over it
through each season of the year!

13"If you carefully obey the commands I am
giving you today, and if you love the LORD your
God and serve him with all your heart and soul,
14then he will send the rains in their proper seasons—the early and late rains—so you can bring
in your harvests of grain, new wine, and olive oil.
15He will give you lush pastureland for your livestock, and you yourselves will have all you want
to eat.

16"But be careful. Don't let your heart be deceived so that you turn away from the LORD and
serve and worship other gods. 17If you do, the
LORD's anger will burn against you. He will shut
up the sky and hold back the rain, and the
ground will fail to produce its harvests. Then you
will quickly die in that good land the LORD is giving you.

18"So commit yourselves wholeheartedly to
these words of mine. Tie them to your hands and
wear them on your forehead as reminders.
19Teach them to your children. Talk about them
when you are at home and when you are on the
road, when you are going to bed and when you
are getting up. 20Write them on the doorposts of
your house and on your gates, 21so that as long as
the sky remains above the earth, you and your
children may flourish in the land the LORD swore
to give your ancestors.

22"Be careful to obey all these commands I am
giving you. Show love to the LORD your God by
walking in his ways and holding tightly to him.
23Then the LORD will drive out all the nations
ahead of you, though they are much greater and
stronger than you, and you will take over their
land. 24Wherever you set foot, that land will be
yours. Your frontiers will stretch from the wilderness in the south to Lebanon in the north, and
from the Euphrates River in the east to the Mediterranean Sea in the west. 25No one will be able
to stand against you, for the LORD your God will
cause the people to fear and dread you, as he
promised, wherever you go in the whole land.

26"Look, today I am giving you the choice
between a blessing and a curse! 27You will be
blessed if you obey the commands of the LORD
your God that I am giving you today. 28But you
will be cursed if you reject the commands of the
LORD your God and turn away from him and
worship gods you have not known before.

29"When the LORD your God brings you into
the land and helps you take possession of it,
you must pronounce the blessing at Mount Gerizim and the curse at Mount Ebal. 30(These two
mountains are west of the Jordan River in the
land of the Canaanites who live in the Jordan
Valley, near the town of Gilgal, not far from the
oaks of Moreh.) 31For you are about to cross the
Jordan River to take over the land the LORD your
God is giving you. When you take that land and
are living in it, 32you must be careful to obey
all the decrees and regulations I am giving you
today.

CHAPTER 12

The LORD's Chosen Place for Worship

"These are the decrees and regulations you must
be careful to obey when you live in the land that
the LORD, the God of your ancestors, is giving
you. You must obey them as long as you live.

2"When you drive out the nations that live
there, you must destroy all the places where they
worship their gods—high on the mountains, up
on the hills, and under every green tree. 3Break
down their altars and smash their sacred pillars.
Burn their Asherah poles and cut down their
carved idols. Completely erase the names of
their gods!

4"Do not worship the LORD your God in the
way these pagan peoples worship their gods.
5Rather, you must seek the LORD your God at the
place of worship he himself will choose from
among all the tribes—the place where his name
will be honored. 6There you will bring your
burnt offerings, your sacrifices, your tithes, your
sacred offerings, your offerings to fulfill a vow,
your voluntary offerings, and your offerings of
the firstborn animals of your herds and flocks.
7There you and your families will feast in the
presence of the LORD your God, and you will rejoice in all you have accomplished because the
LORD your God has blessed you.

8"Your pattern of worship will change. Today
all of you are doing as you please, 9because you
have not yet arrived at the place of rest, the land
the LORD your God is giving you as your special
possession. 10But you will soon cross the Jordan
River and live in the land the LORD your God is
giving you. When he gives you rest from all your
enemies and you're living safely in the land,
11you must bring everything I command you—
your burnt offerings, your sacrifices, your tithes,
your sacred offerings, and your offerings to fulfill a vow—to the designated place of worship,

the place the LORD your God chooses for his name to be honored.

12"You must celebrate there in the presence of the LORD your God with your sons and daughters and all your servants. And remember to include the Levites who live in your towns, for they will receive no allotment of land among you. 13Be careful not to sacrifice your burnt offerings just anywhere you like. 14You may do so only at the place the LORD will choose within one of your tribal territories. There you must offer your burnt offerings and do everything I command you.

15"But you may butcher your animals and eat their meat in any town whenever you want. You may freely eat the animals with which the LORD your God blesses you. All of you, whether ceremonially clean or unclean, may eat that meat, just as you now eat gazelle and deer. 16But you must not consume the blood. You must pour it out on the ground like water.

17"But you may not eat your offerings in your hometown—neither the tithe of your grain and new wine and olive oil, nor the firstborn of your flocks and herds, nor any offering to fulfill a vow, nor your voluntary offerings, nor your sacred offerings. 18You must eat these in the presence of the LORD your God at the place he will choose. Eat them there with your children, your servants, and the Levites who live in your towns, celebrating in the presence of the LORD your God in all you do. 19And be very careful never to neglect the Levites as long as you live in your land.

20"When the LORD your God expands your territory as he has promised, and you have the urge to eat meat, you may freely eat meat whenever you want. 21It might happen that the designated place of worship—the place the LORD your God chooses for his name to be honored—is a long way from your home. If so, you may butcher any of the cattle, sheep, or goats the LORD has given you, and you may freely eat the meat in your hometown, as I have commanded you. 22Anyone, whether ceremonially clean or unclean, may eat that meat, just as you do now with gazelle and deer. 23But never consume the blood, for the blood is the life, and you must not consume the lifeblood with the meat. 24Instead, pour out the blood on the ground like water. 25Do not consume the blood, so that all may go well with you and your children after you, because you will be doing what pleases the LORD.

26"Take your sacred gifts and your offerings given to fulfill a vow to the place the LORD chooses. 27You must offer the meat and blood of your burnt offerings on the altar of the LORD your God. The blood of your other sacrifices must be poured out on the altar of the LORD your God, but you may eat the meat. 28Be careful to obey all my commands, so that all will go well with you and your children after you, because you will be doing what is good and pleasing to the LORD your God.

29"When the LORD your God goes ahead of you and destroys the nations and you drive them out and live in their land, 30do not fall into the trap of following their customs and worshiping their gods. Do not inquire about their gods, saying, 'How do these nations worship their gods? I want to follow their example.' 31You must not worship the LORD your God the way the other nations worship their gods, for they perform for their gods every detestable act that the LORD hates. They even burn their sons and daughters as sacrifices to their gods.

32"So be careful to obey all the commands I give you. You must not add anything to them or subtract anything from them.

CHAPTER 13

A Warning against Idolatry

1"Suppose there are prophets among you or those who dream dreams about the future, and they promise you signs or miracles, 2and the predicted signs or miracles occur. If they then say, 'Come, let us worship other gods'—gods you have not known before—3do not listen to them. The LORD your God is testing you to see if you truly love him with all your heart and soul. 4Serve only the LORD your God and fear him alone. Obey his commands, listen to his voice, and cling to him. 5The false prophets or visionaries who try to lead you astray must be put to death, for they encourage rebellion against the LORD your God, who redeemed you from slavery and brought you out of the land of Egypt. Since they try to lead you astray from the way the LORD your God commanded you to live, you must put them to death. In this way you will purge the evil from among you.

6"Suppose someone secretly entices you—even your brother, your son or daughter, your beloved wife, or your closest friend—and says, 'Let us go worship other gods'—gods that neither you nor your ancestors have known. 7They might suggest that you worship the gods of peoples who live nearby or who come from the ends of the earth. 8But do not give in or listen. Have no pity, and do not spare or protect them. 9You must put them to death! Strike the first blow yourself, and then all the people must join in. 10Stone the guilty ones to death because they have tried to draw you away from the LORD your God, who rescued you from the land of Egypt, the place of slavery. [11]Then all Israel will hear about it and be afraid, and no one will act so wickedly again.

[12]"When you begin living in the towns the LORD your God is giving you, you may hear [13]that scoundrels among you are leading their fellow citizens astray by saying, 'Let us go worship other gods'—gods you have not known before. [14]In such cases, you must examine the facts carefully. If you find that the report is true and such a detestable act has been committed among you, [15]you must attack that town and completely destroy all its inhabitants, as well as all the livestock. [16]Then you must pile all the plunder in the middle of the open square and burn it. Burn the entire town as a burnt offering to the LORD your God. That town must remain a ruin forever; it may never be rebuilt. [17]Keep none of the plunder that has been set apart for destruction. Then the LORD will turn from his fierce anger and be merciful to you. He will have compassion on you and make you a large nation, just as he swore to your ancestors.

[18]"The LORD your God will be merciful only if you listen to his voice and keep all his commands that I am giving you today, doing what pleases him.

CHAPTER 14

Ceremonially Clean and Unclean Animals

"Since you are the people of the LORD your God, never cut yourselves or shave the hair above your foreheads in mourning for the dead. [2]You have been set apart as holy to the LORD your God, and he has chosen you from all the nations of the earth to be his own special treasure.

[3]"You must not eat any detestable animals that are ceremonially unclean. [4]These are the animals you may eat: the ox, the sheep, the goat, [5]the deer, the gazelle, the roe deer, the wild goat, the addax, the antelope, and the mountain sheep.

[6]"You may eat any animal that has completely split hooves and chews the cud, [7]but if the animal doesn't have both, it may not be eaten. So you may not eat the camel, the hare, or the hyrax. They chew the cud but do not have split hooves, so they are ceremonially unclean for you. [8]And you may not eat the pig. It has split hooves but does not chew the cud, so it is ceremonially unclean for you. You may not eat the meat of these animals or even touch their carcasses.

[9]"Of all the marine animals, you may eat whatever has both fins and scales. [10]You may not, however, eat marine animals that do not have both fins and scales. They are ceremonially unclean for you.

[11]"You may eat any bird that is ceremonially clean. [12]These are the birds you may not eat: the griffon vulture, the bearded vulture, the black vulture, [13]the kite, the falcon, buzzards of all kinds, [14]ravens of all kinds, [15]the eagle owl, the short-eared owl, the seagull, hawks of all kinds, [16]the little owl, the great owl, the barn owl, [17]the desert owl, the Egyptian vulture, the cormorant, [18]the stork, herons of all kinds, the hoopoe, and the bat.

[19]"All winged insects that walk along the ground are ceremonially unclean for you and may not be eaten. [20]But you may eat any winged bird or insect that is ceremonially clean.

[21]"You must not eat anything that has died a natural death. You may give it to a foreigner living in your town, or you may sell it to a stranger. But do not eat it yourselves, for you are set apart as holy to the LORD your God.

"You must not cook a young goat in its mother's milk.

The Giving of Tithes

[22]"You must set aside a tithe of your crops—one-tenth of all the crops you harvest each year. [23]Bring this tithe to the designated place of worship—the place the LORD your God chooses for his name to be honored—and eat it there in his presence. This applies to your tithes of grain, new wine, olive oil, and the firstborn males of your flocks and herds. Doing this will teach you always to fear the LORD your God.

[24]"Now when the LORD your God blesses you with a good harvest, the place of worship he chooses for his name to be honored might be too far for you to bring the tithe. [25]If so, you may sell the tithe portion of your crops and herds, put the money in a pouch, and go to the place the LORD your God has chosen. [26]When you arrive, you may use the money to buy any kind of food you want—cattle, sheep, goats, wine, or other alcoholic drink. Then feast there in the presence of the LORD your God and celebrate with your household. [27]And do not neglect the Levites in your town, for they will receive no allotment of land among you.

[28]"At the end of every third year, bring the entire tithe of that year's harvest and store it in the nearest town. [29]Give it to the Levites, who will receive no allotment of land among you, as well as to the foreigners living among you, the orphans, and the widows in your towns, so they can eat and be satisfied. Then the LORD your God will bless you in all your work.

CHAPTER **15**
Release for Debtors
"At the end of every seventh year you must cancel
the debts of everyone who owes you money.
2This is how it must be done. Everyone must
cancel the loans they have made to their fellow
Israelites. They must not demand payment from
their neighbors or relatives, for the LORD's time
of release has arrived. 3This release from debt,
however, applies only to your fellow Israelites—
not to the foreigners living among you.

4"There should be no poor among you, for the
LORD your God will greatly bless you in the land he
is giving you as a special possession. 5You will receive this blessing if you are careful to obey all the
commands of the LORD your God that I am giving
you today. 6The LORD your God will bless you as he
has promised. You will lend money to many nations but will never need to borrow. You will rule
many nations, but they will not rule over you.

7"But if there are any poor Israelites in your
towns when you arrive in the land the LORD
your God is giving you, do not be hard-hearted
or tightfisted toward them. 8Instead, be generous and lend them whatever they need. 9Do not
be mean-spirited and refuse someone a loan
because the year for canceling debts is close at
hand. If you refuse to make the loan and the
needy person cries out to the LORD, you will be
considered guilty of sin. 10Give generously to the
poor, not grudgingly, for the LORD your God will
bless you in everything you do. 11There will always be some in the land who are poor. That is
why I am commanding you to share freely with
the poor and with other Israelites in need.

Release for Hebrew Slaves
12"If a fellow Hebrew sells himself or herself to
be your servant and serves you for six years, in
the seventh year you must set that servant free.

13"When you release a male servant, do not
send him away empty-handed. 14Give him a generous farewell gift from your flock, your threshing floor, and your winepress. Share with him
some of the bounty with which the LORD your
God has blessed you. 15Remember that you were
once slaves in the land of Egypt and the LORD
your God redeemed you! That is why I am giving
you this command.

16"But suppose your servant says, 'I will not
leave you,' because he loves you and your family,
and he has done well with you. 17In that case, take
an awl and push it through his earlobe into the
door. After that, he will be your servant for life.
And do the same for your female servants.

18"You must not consider it a hardship when
you release your servants. Remember that for six
years they have given you services worth double
the wages of hired workers, and the LORD your
God will bless you in all you do.

Sacrificing Firstborn Male Animals
19"You must set aside for the LORD your God all
the firstborn males from your flocks and herds.
Do not use the firstborn of your herds to work
your fields, and do not shear the firstborn of
your flocks. 20Instead, you and your family must
eat these animals in the presence of the LORD
your God each year at the place he chooses.
21But if this firstborn animal has any defect, such
as lameness or blindness, or if anything else is
wrong with it, you must not sacrifice it to the
LORD your God. 22Instead, use it for food for your
family in your hometown. Anyone, whether ceremonially clean or unclean, may eat it, just as anyone may eat a gazelle or deer. 23But you must not
consume the blood. You must pour it out on the
ground like water.

CHAPTER **16**
Passover and the Festival of Unleavened Bread
"In honor of the LORD your God, celebrate the
Passover each year in the early spring, in the
month of Abib, for that was the month in which
the LORD your God brought you out of Egypt by
night. 2Your Passover sacrifice may be from either the flock or the herd, and it must be sacrificed to the LORD your God at the designated
place of worship—the place he chooses for his
name to be honored. 3Eat it with bread made
without yeast. For seven days the bread you eat
must be made without yeast, as when you escaped from Egypt in such a hurry. Eat this
bread—the bread of suffering—so that as long as
you live you will remember the day you departed
from Egypt. 4Let no yeast be found in any house
throughout your land for those seven days. And
when you sacrifice the Passover lamb on the evening of the first day, do not let any of the meat remain until the next morning.

5"You may not sacrifice the Passover in just any
of the towns that the LORD your God is giving you.
6You must offer it only at the designated place
of worship—the place the LORD your God chooses
for his name to be honored. Sacrifice it there in
the evening as the sun goes down on the anniversary of your exodus from Egypt. 7Roast the lamb
and eat it in the place the LORD your God chooses.

Then you may go back to your tents the next
morning. 8For the next six days you may not eat
any bread made with yeast. On the seventh day
proclaim another holy day in honor of the LORD
your God, and no work may be done on that day.

The Festival of Harvest

9"Count off seven weeks from when you first begin to cut the grain at the time of harvest. 10 Then
celebrate the Festival of Harvest to honor the
LORD your God. Bring him a voluntary offering in
proportion to the blessings you have received
from him. 11This is a time to celebrate before the
LORD your God at the designated place of worship
he will choose for his name to be honored. Celebrate with your sons and daughters, your male
and female servants, the Levites from your towns,
and the foreigners, orphans, and widows who live
among you. 12Remember that you were once
slaves in Egypt, so be careful to obey all these decrees.

The Festival of Shelters

13"You must observe the Festival of Shelters for
seven days at the end of the harvest season, after
the grain has been threshed and the grapes have
been pressed. 14This festival will be a happy time
of celebrating with your sons and daughters, your
male and female servants, and the Levites, foreigners, orphans, and widows from your towns.
15For seven days you must celebrate this festival to
honor the LORD your God at the place he chooses,
for it is he who blesses you with bountiful harvests and gives you success in all your work. This
festival will be a time of great joy for all.
16"Each year every man in Israel must celebrate these three festivals: the Festival of Unleavened Bread, the Festival of Harvest, and the
Festival of Shelters. On each of these occasions,
all men must appear before the LORD your God at
the place he chooses, but they must not appear
before the LORD without a gift for him. 17All must
give as they are able, according to the blessings
given to them by the LORD your God.

Justice for the People

18"Appoint judges and officials for yourselves
from each of your tribes in all the towns the LORD
your God is giving you. They must judge the people fairly. 19You must never twist justice or show
partiality. Never accept a bribe, for bribes blind
the eyes of the wise and corrupt the decisions of
the godly. 20Let true justice prevail, so you may
live and occupy the land that the LORD your God
is giving you.

CELEBRATE!

Jewish people still celebrate the day God passed over the Israelites' houses as the worst plague fell on the Egyptians. **The Passover celebration is kind of like a Thanksgiving feast.** Jews use it to remember how God freed the Israelites from slavery in Egypt.

Lead your family or friends in this celebration.

1. Read Exodus 12:1-30. Pour grape juice for everyone. Lift up your cup, and say: **"Blessed are you, O Lord our God, King of the universe, who creates fruit of the vine."**

2. Dip parsley (or another veggie) in salt water. Say: **"The salt water reminds us of the tears the Israelites shed in Egypt."**

Check out Isaiah 53:3-12 to see how Passover connects to Jesus.

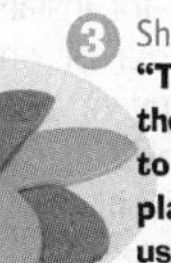

3. Share lunch meat. Say: **"This meat reminds us of the lamb that was sacrificed to spare the people from the plague of death. It reminds us that Jesus was the lamb who died for our sins."**

4. Break apart and share pita bread. Say: **"This flat bread reminds us that the people didn't have time to let their bread rise when they left Egypt."**

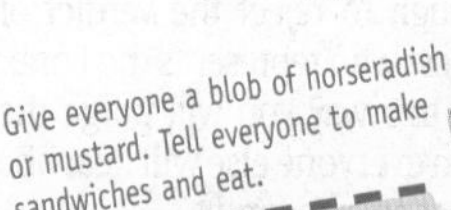

Give everyone a blob of horseradish or mustard. Tell everyone to make sandwiches and eat.

DONE EATING? TALK IT OVER!

- How was your celebration like the Passover celebration God commanded in Deuteronomy 16:1-8?
- How is the lamb in the Passover story like Jesus?
- What do we do to remember and celebrate what Jesus has done for us?

21"You must never set up a wooden Asherah
pole beside the altar you build for the LORD your
God. 22And never set up sacred pillars for worship, for the LORD your God hates them.

CHAPTER 17

"Never sacrifice sick or defective cattle, sheep, or
goats to the LORD your God, for he detests such
gifts.
2"When you begin living in the towns the LORD
your God is giving you, a man or woman among
you might do evil in the sight of the LORD your
God and violate the covenant. 3For instance, they
might serve other gods or worship the sun, the
moon, or any of the stars—the forces of heaven—
which I have strictly forbidden. 4When you hear
about it, investigate the matter thoroughly. If it is
true that this detestable thing has been done in Israel, 5then the man or woman who has committed such an evil act must be taken to the gates of
the town and stoned to death. 6But never put a
person to death on the testimony of only one witness. There must always be two or three witnesses. 7The witnesses must throw the first
stones, and then all the people may join in. In this
way, you will purge the evil from among you.
8"Suppose a case arises in a local court that is
too hard for you to decide—for instance, whether
someone is guilty of murder or only of man-
slaughter, or a difficult lawsuit, or a case involving
different kinds of assault. Take such legal cases to
the place the LORD your God will choose, 9and present them to the Levitical priests or the judge on
duty at that time. They will hear the case and declare
the verdict. 10You must carry out the verdict they announce and the sentence they prescribe at the place
the LORD chooses. You must do exactly what they
say. 11After they have interpreted the law and declared their verdict, the sentence they impose must
be fully executed; do not modify it in any way. 12Any-
one arrogant enough to reject the verdict of the
judge or of the priest who represents the LORD your
God must die. In this way you will purge the evil
from Israel. 13Then everyone else will hear about it
and be afraid to act so arrogantly.

Guidelines for a King

14"You are about to enter the land the LORD your
God is giving you. When you take it over and settle there, you may think, 'We should select a king
to rule over us like the other nations around us.'
15If this happens, be sure to select as king the
man the LORD your God chooses. You must appoint a fellow Israelite; he may not be a foreigner.
16"The king must not build up a large stable
of horses for himself or send his people to Egypt
to buy horses, for the LORD has told you, 'You
must never return to Egypt.' 17The king must not
take many wives for himself, because they will
turn his heart away from the LORD. And he must
not accumulate large amounts of wealth in silver
and gold for himself.
18"When he sits on the throne as king, he
must copy for himself this body of instruction on
a scroll in the presence of the Levitical priests.
19He must always keep that copy with him and
read it daily as long as he lives. That way he will
learn to fear the LORD his God by obeying all the
terms of these instructions and decrees. 20This
regular reading will prevent him from becoming
proud and acting as if he is above his fellow citizens. It will also prevent him from turning away
from these commands in the smallest way. And it
will ensure that he and his descendants will reign
for many generations in Israel.

CHAPTER 18

Gifts for the Priests and Levites

"Remember that the Levitical priests—that is,
the whole of the tribe of Levi—will receive no allotment of land among the other tribes in Israel.
Instead, the priests and Levites will eat from the
special gifts given to the LORD, for that is their
share. 2They will have no land of their own
among the Israelites. The LORD himself is their
special possession, just as he promised them.
3"These are the parts the priests may claim as
their share from the cattle, sheep, and goats that
the people bring as offerings: the shoulder, the
cheeks, and the stomach. 4You must also give to
the priests the first share of the grain, the new
wine, the olive oil, and the wool at shearing time.
5For the LORD your God chose the tribe of Levi
out of all your tribes to minister in the LORD's
name forever.
6"Suppose a Levite chooses to move from his
town in Israel, wherever he is living, to the place
the LORD chooses for worship. 7He may minister
there in the name of the LORD his God, just like all
his fellow Levites who are serving the LORD there.
8He may eat his share of the sacrifices and offerings, even if he also receives support from his
family.

A Call to Holy Living

9"When you enter the land the LORD your God is
giving you, be very careful not to imitate the detestable customs of the nations living there.
10For example, never sacrifice your son or
daughter as a burnt offering. And do not let your

people practice fortune-telling, or use sorcery,
or interpret omens, or engage in witchcraft, 11 or
cast spells, or function as mediums or psychics,
or call forth the spirits of the dead. 12 Anyone
who does these things is detestable to the LORD.
It is because the other nations have done these
detestable things that the LORD your God will
drive them out ahead of you. 13 But you must be
blameless before the LORD your God. 14 The nations you are about to displace consult sorcerers
and fortune-tellers, but the LORD your God for-
bids you to do such things."

True and False Prophets

15 Moses continued, "The LORD your God will
raise up for you a prophet like me from among
your fellow Israelites. You must listen to him.
16 For this is what you yourselves requested of
the LORD your God when you were assembled
at Mount Sinai. You said, 'Don't let us hear the
voice of the LORD our God anymore or see this
blazing fire, for we will die.'

17 "Then the LORD said to me, 'What they have
said is right. 18 I will raise up a prophet like you
from among their fellow Israelites. I will put my
words in his mouth, and he will tell the people
everything I command him. 19 I will personally
deal with anyone who will not listen to the messages the prophet proclaims on my behalf.
20 But any prophet who falsely claims to speak
in my name or who speaks in the name of another god must die.'

21 "But you may wonder, 'How will we know
whether or not a prophecy is from the LORD?'
22 If the prophet speaks in the LORD's name but
his prediction does not happen or come true,
you will know that the LORD did not give that
message. That prophet has spoken without my
authority and need not be feared.

CHAPTER 19

Cities of Refuge

"When the LORD your God destroys the nations
whose land he is giving you, you will take over
their land and settle in their towns and homes.
2 Then you must set apart three cities of refuge
in the land the LORD your God is giving you.
3 Survey the territory, and divide the land the
LORD your God is giving you into three districts,
with one of these cities in each district. Then
anyone who has killed someone can flee to one
of the cities of refuge for safety.

4 "If someone kills another person unintentionally, without previous hostility, the slayer
may flee to any of these cities to live in safety.
5 For example, suppose someone goes into the
forest with a neighbor to cut wood. And suppose
one of them swings an ax to chop down a tree,
and the ax head flies off the handle, killing the
other person. In such cases, the slayer may flee
to one of the cities of refuge to live in safety.

6 "If the distance to the nearest city of refuge
is too far, an enraged avenger might be able to
chase down and kill the person who caused the
death. Then the slayer would die unfairly, since
he had never shown hostility toward the person
who died. 7 That is why I am commanding you
to set aside three cities of refuge.

8 "And if the LORD your God enlarges your territory, as he swore to your ancestors, and gives
you all the land he promised them, 9 you must
designate three additional cities of refuge. (He
will give you this land if you are careful to obey
all the commands I have given you—if you always love the LORD your God and walk in his
ways.) 10 That way you will prevent the death of
innocent people in the land the LORD your God
is giving you as your special possession. You will
not be held responsible for the death of innocent people.

11 "But suppose someone is hostile toward a
neighbor and deliberately ambushes and murders him and then flees to one of the cities of
refuge. 12 In that case, the elders of the murderer's hometown must send agents to the city
of refuge to bring him back and hand him over
to the dead person's avenger to be put to death.
13 Do not feel sorry for that murderer! Purge
from Israel the guilt of murdering innocent
people; then all will go well with you.

Concern for Justice

14 "When you arrive in the land the LORD your
God is giving you as your special possession, you
must never steal anyone's land by moving the
boundary markers your ancestors set up to mark
their property.

15 "You must not convict anyone of a crime on
the testimony of only one witness. The facts of
the case must be established by the testimony of
two or three witnesses.

16 "If a malicious witness comes forward and
accuses someone of a crime, 17 then both the accuser and accused must appear before the LORD
by coming to the priests and judges in office at
that time. 18 The judges must investigate the
case thoroughly. If the accuser has brought
false charges against his fellow Israelite, 19 you
must impose on the accuser the sentence he
intended for the other person. In this way, you

will purge such evil from among you. 20Then the rest of the people will hear about it and be afraid to do such an evil thing. 21You must show no pity for the guilty! Your rule should be life for life, eye for eye, tooth for tooth, hand for hand, foot for foot.

CHAPTER 20

Regulations concerning War

"When you go out to fight your enemies and you face horses and chariots and an army greater than your own, do not be afraid. The LORD your God, who brought you out of the land of Egypt, is with you! 2When you prepare for battle, the priest must come forward to speak to the troops. 3He will say to them, 'Listen to me, all you men of Israel! Do not be afraid as you go out to fight your enemies today! Do not lose heart or panic or tremble before them. 4For the LORD your God is going with you! He will fight for you against your enemies, and he will give you victory!'

5"Then the officers of the army must address the troops and say, 'Has anyone here just built a new house but not yet dedicated it? If so, you may go home! You might be killed in the battle, and someone else would dedicate your house. 6Has anyone here just planted a vineyard but not yet eaten any of its fruit? If so, you may go home! You might die in battle, and someone else would eat the first fruit. 7Has anyone here just become engaged to a woman but not yet married her? Well, you may go home and get married! You might die in the battle, and someone else would marry her.'

8"Then the officers will also say, 'Is anyone here afraid or worried? If you are, you may go home before you frighten anyone else.' 9When the officers have finished speaking to their troops, they will appoint the unit commanders.

10"As you approach a town to attack it, you must first offer its people terms for peace. 11If they accept your terms and open the gates to you, then all the people inside will serve you in forced labor. 12But if they refuse to make peace and prepare to fight, you must attack the town. 13When the LORD your God hands the town over to you, use your swords to kill every man in the town. 14But you may keep for yourselves all the women, children, livestock, and other plunder. You may enjoy the plunder from your enemies that the LORD your God has given you.

15"But these instructions apply only to distant towns, not to the towns of the nations in the land you will enter. 16In those towns that the LORD your God is giving you as a special possession, destroy every living thing. 17You must completely destroy the Hittites, Amorites, Canaanites, Perizzites, Hivites, and Jebusites, just as the LORD your God has commanded you. 18This will prevent the people of the land from teaching you to imitate their detestable customs in the worship of their gods, which would cause you to sin deeply against the LORD your God.

19"When you are attacking a town and the war drags on, you must not cut down the trees with your axes. You may eat the fruit, but do not cut down the trees. Are the trees your enemies, that you should attack them? 20You may only cut down trees that you know are not valuable for food. Use them to make the equipment you need to attack the enemy town until it falls.

CHAPTER 21

Cleansing for Unsolved Murder

"When you are in the land the LORD your God is giving you, someone may be found murdered in a field, and you don't know who committed the murder. 2In such a case, your elders and judges must measure the distance from the site of the crime to the nearby towns. 3When the nearest town has been determined, that town's elders must select from the herd a heifer that has never been trained or yoked to a plow. 4They must lead it down to a valley that has not been plowed or planted and that has a stream running through it. There in the valley they must break the heifer's neck. 5Then the Levitical priests must step forward, for the LORD your God has chosen them to minister before him and to pronounce blessings in the LORD's name. They are to decide all legal and criminal cases.

6"The elders of the town must wash their hands over the heifer whose neck was broken. 7Then they must say, 'Our hands did not shed this person's blood, nor did we see it happen. 8O LORD, forgive your people Israel whom you have redeemed. Do not charge your people with the guilt of murdering an innocent person.' Then they will be absolved of the guilt of this person's blood. 9By following these instructions, you will do what is right in the LORD's sight and will cleanse the guilt of murder from your community.

Marriage to a Captive Woman

10"Suppose you go out to war against your enemies and the LORD your God hands them over to you, and you take some of them as captives. 11And suppose you see among the captives a beautiful woman, and you are attracted to her and want to marry her. 12If this happens, you

may take her to your home, where she must
shave her head, cut her nails, 13 and change the
clothes she was wearing when she was captured.
She will stay in your home, but let her mourn for
her father and mother for a full month. Then you
may marry her, and you will be her husband and
she will be your wife. 14 But if you marry her and
she does not please you, you must let her go free.
You may not sell her or treat her as a slave, for you
have humiliated her.

Rights of the Firstborn

15 "Suppose a man has two wives, but he loves one
and not the other, and both have given him sons.
And suppose the firstborn son is the son of the
wife he does not love. 16 When the man divides
his inheritance, he may not give the larger inheritance to his younger son, the son of the wife he
loves, as if he were the firstborn son. 17 He must
recognize the rights of his oldest son, the son of
the wife he does not love, by giving him a double
portion. He is the first son of his father's virility,
and the rights of the firstborn belong to him.

Dealing with a Rebellious Son

18 "Suppose a man has a stubborn and rebellious
son who will not obey his father or mother, even
though they discipline him. 19 In such a case, the
father and mother must take the son to the elders as they hold court at the town gate. 20 The
parents must say to the elders, 'This son of ours
is stubborn and rebellious and refuses to obey.
He is a glutton and a drunkard.' 21 Then all the
men of his town must stone him to death. In this
way, you will purge this evil from among you, and
all Israel will hear about it and be afraid.

Various Regulations

22 "If someone has committed a crime worthy of
death and is executed and hung on a tree, 23 the
body must not remain hanging from the tree
overnight. You must bury the body that same
day, for anyone who is hung is cursed in the
sight of God. In this way, you will prevent the defilement of the land the LORD your God is giving
you as your special possession.

CHAPTER 22

"If you see your neighbor's ox or sheep or goat
wandering away, don't ignore your responsibility. Take it back to its owner. 2 If its owner
does not live nearby or you don't know who
the owner is, take it to your place and keep it until the owner comes looking for it. Then you
must return it. 3 Do the same if you find your
neighbor's donkey, clothing, or anything else
your neighbor loses. Don't ignore your responsibility.

4 "If you see that your neighbor's donkey or
ox has collapsed on the road, do not look the
other way. Go and help your neighbor get it back
on its feet!

5 "A woman must not put on men's clothing,
and a man must not wear women's clothing. Anyone who does this is detestable in the sight of the
LORD your God.

6 "If you happen to find a bird's nest in a tree
or on the ground, and there are young ones or
eggs in it with the mother sitting in the nest, do
not take the mother with the young. 7 You may
take the young, but let the mother go, so that you
may prosper and enjoy a long life.

8 "When you build a new house, you must
build a railing around the edge of its flat roof.
That way you will not be considered guilty of
murder if someone falls from the roof.

9 "You must not plant any other crop between
the rows of your vineyard. If you do, you are forbidden to use either the grapes from the vineyard or the other crop.

10 "You must not plow with an ox and a donkey
harnessed together.

11 "You must not wear clothing made of wool
and linen woven together.

12 "You must put four tassels on the hem of the
cloak with which you cover yourself—on the
front, back, and sides.

Regulations for Sexual Purity

13 "Suppose a man marries a woman, but after
sleeping with her, he turns against her 14 and publicly accuses her of shameful conduct, saying,
'When I married this woman, I discovered she
was not a virgin.' 15 Then the woman's father and
mother must bring the proof of her virginity to
the elders as they hold court at the town gate.
16 Her father must say to them, 'I gave my daughter to this man to be his wife, and now he has
turned against her. 17 He has accused her of
shameful conduct, saying, "I discovered that
your daughter was not a virgin." But here is the
proof of my daughter's virginity.' Then they must
spread her bed sheet before the elders. 18 The elders must then take the man and punish him.
19 They must also fine him 100 pieces of silver,
which he must pay to the woman's father because he publicly accused a virgin of Israel of
shameful conduct. The woman will then remain
the man's wife, and he may never divorce her.

20 "But suppose the man's accusations are

CHAPTER 25

"Suppose two people take a dispute to court, and
the judges declare that one is right and the other
is wrong. 2If the person in the wrong is sentenced to be flogged, the judge must command
him to lie down and be beaten in his presence
with the number of lashes appropriate to the
crime. 3But never give more than forty lashes;
more than forty lashes would publicly humiliate
your neighbor.

4"You must not muzzle an ox to keep it from
eating as it treads out the grain.

5"If two brothers are living together on the
same property and one of them dies without a
son, his widow may not be married to anyone
from outside the family. Instead, her husband's
brother should marry her and have intercourse
with her to fulfill the duties of a brother-in-law.
6The first son she bears to him will be considered the son of the dead brother, so that his name
will not be forgotten in Israel.

7"But if the man refuses to marry his brother's
widow, she must go to the town gate and say to
the elders assembled there, 'My husband's
brother refuses to preserve his brother's name in
Israel—he refuses to fulfill the duties of a
brother-in-law by marrying me.' 8The elders of
the town will then summon him and talk with
him. If he still refuses and says, 'I don't want to
marry her,' 9the widow must walk over to him in
the presence of the elders, pull his sandal from
his foot, and spit in his face. Then she must
declare, 'This is what happens to a man who
refuses to provide his brother with children.'
10Ever afterward in Israel his family will be referred to as 'the family of the man whose sandal
was pulled off'!

11"If two Israelite men get into a fight and the
wife of one tries to rescue her husband by grab-
bing the testicles of the other man, 12you must
cut off her hand. Show her no pity.

13"You must use accurate scales when you
weigh out merchandise, 14and you must use full
and honest measures. 15Yes, always use honest
weights and measures, so that you may enjoy a
long life in the land the LORD your God is giving
you. 16All who cheat with dishonest weights and
measures are detestable to the LORD your God.

17"Never forget what the Amalekites did to
you as you came from Egypt. 18They attacked
you when you were exhausted and weary, and
they struck down those who were straggling
behind. They had no fear of God. 19Therefore,
when the LORD your God has given you rest from
all your enemies in the land he is giving you as a
special possession, you must destroy the Amalekites and erase their memory from under
heaven. Never forget this!

CHAPTER 26

Harvest Offerings and Tithes

"When you enter the land the LORD your God is
giving you as a special possession and you have
conquered it and settled there, 2put some of the
first produce from each crop you harvest into a
basket and bring it to the designated place of
worship—the place the LORD your God chooses
for his name to be honored. 3Go to the priest in
charge at that time and say to him, 'With this gift
I acknowledge to the LORD your God that I have
entered the land he swore to our ancestors he
would give us.' 4The priest will then take the basket from your hand and set it before the altar of
the LORD your God.

5"You must then say in the presence of the
LORD your God, 'My ancestor Jacob was a wandering Aramean who went to live as a foreigner in
Egypt. His family arrived few in number, but in
Egypt they became a large and mighty nation.
6When the Egyptians oppressed and humiliated
us by making us their slaves, 7we cried out to the
LORD, the God of our ancestors. He heard our
cries and saw our hardship, toil, and oppression.
8So the LORD brought us out of Egypt with a
strong hand and powerful arm, with overwhelming terror, and with miraculous signs and wonders. 9He brought us to this place and gave us
this land flowing with milk and honey! 10And
now, O LORD, I have brought you the first portion
of the harvest you have given me from the
ground.' Then place the produce before the LORD
your God, and bow to the ground in worship before him. 11Afterward you may go and celebrate
because of all the good things the LORD your God
has given to you and your household. Remember
to include the Levites and the foreigners living
among you in the celebration.

12"Every third year you must offer a special
tithe of your crops. In this year of the special tithe
you must give your tithes to the Levites, foreigners, orphans, and widows, so that they will have
enough to eat in your towns. 13Then you must
declare in the presence of the LORD your God, 'I
have taken the sacred gift from my house and
have given it to the Levites, foreigners, orphans,
and widows, just as you commanded me. I have
not violated or forgotten any of your commands.
14I have not eaten any of it while in mourning;
I have not handled it while I was ceremonially unclean; and I have not offered any of it to the dead.

I have obeyed the LORD my God and have done
everything you commanded me. 15Now look
down from your holy dwelling place in heaven
and bless your people Israel and the land you
swore to our ancestors to give us—a land flowing
with milk and honey.'

A Call to Obey the LORD's Commands

16"Today the LORD your God has commanded
you to obey all these decrees and regulations. So
be careful to obey them wholeheartedly. 17You
have declared today that the LORD is your God.
And you have promised to walk in his ways, and
to obey his decrees, commands, and regulations,
and to do everything he tells you. 18The LORD
has declared today that you are his people, his
own special treasure, just as he promised, and
that you must obey all his commands. 19And if
you do, he will set you high above all the other
nations he has made. Then you will receive
praise, honor, and renown. You will be a nation
that is holy to the LORD your God, just as he
promised."

CHAPTER 27

The Altar on Mount Ebal

Then Moses and the leaders of Israel gave this
charge to the people: "Obey all these commands
that I am giving you today. 2When you cross the
Jordan River and enter the land the LORD your
God is giving you, set up some large stones and
coat them with plaster. 3Write this whole body
of instruction on them when you cross the river
to enter the land the LORD your God is giving
you—a land flowing with milk and honey, just as
the LORD, the God of your ancestors, promised
you. 4When you cross the Jordan, set up these
stones at Mount Ebal and coat them with plaster,
as I am commanding you today.

5"Then build an altar there to the LORD your
God, using natural, uncut stones. You must not
shape the stones with an iron tool. 6Build the altar of uncut stones, and use it to offer burnt offerings to the LORD your God. 7Also sacrifice
peace offerings on it, and celebrate by feasting
there before the LORD your God. 8You must
clearly write all these instructions on the stones
coated with plaster."

9Then Moses and the Levitical priests addressed all Israel as follows: "O Israel, be quiet
and listen! Today you have become the people of
the LORD your God. 10So you must obey the LORD
your God by keeping all these commands and decrees that I am giving you today."

Curses from Mount Ebal

11That same day Moses also gave this charge to
the people: 12"When you cross the Jordan River,
the tribes of Simeon, Levi, Judah, Issachar, Joseph, and Benjamin must stand on Mount Gerizim to proclaim a blessing over the people.
13And the tribes of Reuben, Gad, Asher, Zebulun,
Dan, and Naphtali must stand on Mount Ebal to
proclaim a curse.

14"Then the Levites will shout to all the people
of Israel:

15'Cursed is anyone who carves or casts an
idol and secretly sets it up. These idols, the
work of craftsmen, are detestable to the
LORD.'
And all the people will reply, 'Amen.'

16'Cursed is anyone who dishonors father
or mother.'
And all the people will reply, 'Amen.'

17'Cursed is anyone who steals property
from a neighbor by moving a boundary
marker.'
And all the people will reply, 'Amen.'

18'Cursed is anyone who leads a blind person
astray on the road.'
And all the people will reply, 'Amen.'

19'Cursed is anyone who denies justice to
foreigners, orphans, or widows.'
And all the people will reply, 'Amen.'

20'Cursed is anyone who has sexual intercourse
with one of his father's wives, for he has
violated his father.'
And all the people will reply, 'Amen.'

21'Cursed is anyone who has sexual intercourse
with an animal.'
And all the people will reply, 'Amen.'

22'Cursed is anyone who has sexual intercourse
with his sister, whether she is the daughter
of his father or his mother.'
And all the people will reply, 'Amen.'

23'Cursed is anyone who has sexual intercourse
with his mother-in-law.'
And all the people will reply, 'Amen.'

24'Cursed is anyone who attacks a neighbor
in secret.'
And all the people will reply, 'Amen.'

25'Cursed is anyone who accepts payment
to kill an innocent person.'
And all the people will reply, 'Amen.'

26 'Cursed is anyone who does not affirm and
obey the terms of these instructions.'
And all the people will reply, 'Amen.'

CHAPTER 28

Blessings for Obedience

"If you fully obey the LORD your God and carefully keep all his commands that I am giving you
today, the LORD your God will set you high above
all the nations of the world. 2 You will experience
all these blessings if you obey the LORD your
God:

3 Your towns and your fields
will be blessed.
4 Your children and your crops
will be blessed.
The offspring of your herds and flocks
will be blessed.
5 Your fruit baskets and breadboards
will be blessed.
6 Wherever you go and whatever you do,
you will be blessed.

7 "The LORD will conquer your enemies when
they attack you. They will attack you from one direction, but they will scatter from you in seven!
8 "The LORD will guarantee a blessing on
everything you do and will fill your storehouses
with grain. The LORD your God will bless you in
the land he is giving you.
9 "If you obey the commands of the LORD your
God and walk in his ways, the LORD will establish
you as his holy people as he swore he would do.
10 Then all the nations of the world will see that
you are a people claimed by the LORD, and they
will stand in awe of you.
11 "The LORD will give you prosperity in the
land he swore to your ancestors to give you,
blessing you with many children, numerous livestock, and abundant crops. 12 The LORD will send
rain at the proper time from his rich treasury in
the heavens and will bless all the work you do.
You will lend to many nations, but you will never
need to borrow from them. 13 If you listen to
these commands of the LORD your God that I am
giving you today, and if you carefully obey them,
the LORD will make you the head and not the tail,
and you will always be on top and never at the
bottom. 14 You must not turn away from any of
the commands I am giving you today, nor follow
after other gods and worship them.

Curses for Disobedience

15 "But if you refuse to listen to the LORD your God
and do not obey all the commands and decrees I
am giving you today, all these curses will come
and overwhelm you:

16 Your towns and your fields
will be cursed.
17 Your fruit baskets and breadboards
will be cursed.
18 Your children and your crops
will be cursed.
The offspring of your herds and flocks
will be cursed.
19 Wherever you go and whatever you do,
you will be cursed.

20 "The LORD himself will send on you curses,
confusion, and frustration in everything you do,
until at last you are completely destroyed for doing evil and abandoning me. 21 The LORD will afflict you with diseases until none of you are left
in the land you are about to enter and occupy.
22 The LORD will strike you with wasting diseases,
fever, and inflammation, with scorching heat
and drought, and with blight and mildew. These
disasters will pursue you until you die. 23 The
skies above will be as unyielding as bronze, and
the earth beneath will be as hard as iron. 24 The
LORD will change the rain that falls on your land
into powder, and dust will pour down from the
sky until you are destroyed.
25 "The LORD will cause you to be defeated by
your enemies. You will attack your enemies from
one direction, but you will scatter from them in
seven! You will be an object of horror to all the
kingdoms of the earth. 26 Your corpses will be
food for all the scavenging birds and wild animals,
and no one will be there to chase them away.
27 "The LORD will afflict you with the boils of
Egypt and with tumors, scurvy, and the itch, from
which you cannot be cured. 28 The LORD will strike
you with madness, blindness, and panic. 29 You
will grope around in broad daylight like a blind
person groping in the darkness, but you will not
find your way. You will be oppressed and robbed
continually, and no one will come to save you.
30 "You will be engaged to a woman, but another man will sleep with her. You will build a
house, but someone else will live in it. You will
plant a vineyard, but you will never enjoy its fruit.
31 Your ox will be butchered before your eyes,
but you will not eat a single bite of the meat. Your
donkey will be taken from you, never to be returned. Your sheep and goats will be given to your
enemies, and no one will be there to help you.
32 You will watch as your sons and daughters are
taken away as slaves. Your heart will break for
them, but you won't be able to help them. 33 A for-

eign nation you have never heard about will eat
the crops you worked so hard to grow. You will
suffer under constant oppression and harsh
treatment. 34 You will go mad because of all the
tragedy you see around you. 35 The LORD will
cover your knees and legs with incurable boils. In
fact, you will be covered from head to foot.

36 "The LORD will exile you and your king to a
nation unknown to you and your ancestors.
There in exile you will worship gods of wood and
stone! 37 You will become an object of horror, ridicule, and mockery among all the nations to which
the LORD sends you.

38 "You will plant much but harvest little, for locusts will eat your crops. 39 You will plant vineyards and care for them, but you will not drink
the wine or eat the grapes, for worms will destroy
the vines. 40 You will grow olive trees throughout
your land, but you will never use the olive oil, for
the fruit will drop before it ripens. 41 You will have
sons and daughters, but you will lose them, for
they will be led away into captivity. 42 Swarms of
insects will destroy your trees and crops.

43 "The foreigners living among you will become stronger and stronger, while you become
weaker and weaker. 44 They will lend money to
you, but you will not lend to them. They will be
the head, and you will be the tail!

45 "If you refuse to listen to the LORD your God
and to obey the commands and decrees he has
given you, all these curses will pursue and overtake you until you are destroyed. 46 These horrors
will serve as a sign and warning among you and
your descendants forever. 47 If you do not serve
the LORD your God with joy and enthusiasm for
the abundant benefits you have received, 48 you
will serve your enemies whom the LORD will send
against you. You will be left hungry, thirsty, naked,
and lacking in everything. The LORD will put an
iron yoke on your neck, oppressing you harshly
until he has destroyed you.

49 "The LORD will bring a distant nation against
you from the end of the earth, and it will swoop
down on you like a vulture. It is a nation whose
language you do not understand, 50 a fierce and
heartless nation that shows no respect for the old
and no pity for the young. 51 Its armies will devour
your livestock and crops, and you will be destroyed. They will leave you no grain, new wine,
olive oil, calves, or lambs, and you will starve to
death. 52 They will attack your cities until all the
fortified walls in your land—the walls you trusted
to protect you—are knocked down. They will attack all the towns in the land the LORD your God
has given you.

53 "The siege and terrible distress of the enemy's attack will be so severe that you will eat the
flesh of your own sons and daughters, whom
the LORD your God has given you. 54 The most
tenderhearted man among you will have no compassion for his own brother, his beloved wife, and
his surviving children. 55 He will refuse to share
with them the flesh he is devouring—the flesh of
one of his own children—because he has nothing
else to eat during the siege and terrible distress
that your enemy will inflict on all your towns.
56 The most tender and delicate woman among
you—so delicate she would not so much as touch
the ground with her foot—will be selfish toward
the husband she loves and toward her own son or
daughter. 57 She will hide from them the after-
birth and the new baby she has borne, so that she
herself can secretly eat them. She will have nothing else to eat during the siege and terrible distress that your enemy will inflict on all your
towns.

58 "If you refuse to obey all the words of instruction that are written in this book, and if you
do not fear the glorious and awesome name of
the LORD your God, 59 then the LORD will overwhelm you and your children with indescribable
plagues. These plagues will be intense and without relief, making you miserable and unbearably
sick. 60 He will afflict you with all the diseases of
Egypt that you feared so much, and you will have
no relief. 61 The LORD will afflict you with every
sickness and plague there is, even those not mentioned in this Book of Instruction, until you are
destroyed. 62 Though you become as numerous
as the stars in the sky, few of you will be left because you would not listen to the LORD your God.

63 "Just as the LORD has found great pleasure in
causing you to prosper and multiply, the LORD
will find pleasure in destroying you. You will be
torn from the land you are about to enter and occupy. 64 For the LORD will scatter you among all
the nations from one end of the earth to the
other. There you will worship foreign gods that
neither you nor your ancestors have known, gods
made of wood and stone! 65 There among those
nations you will find no peace or place to rest.
And the LORD will cause your heart to tremble,
your eyesight to fail, and your soul to despair.
66 Your life will constantly hang in the balance.
You will live night and day in fear, unsure if you
will survive. 67 In the morning you will say, 'If only
it were night!' And in the evening you will say, 'If
only it were morning!' For you will be terrified by
the awful horrors you see around you. 68 Then the
LORD will send you back to Egypt in ships, to a

destination I promised you would never see
again. There you will offer to sell yourselves to
your enemies as slaves, but no one will buy you."

CHAPTER 29

These are the terms of the covenant the LORD
commanded Moses to make with the Israelites
while they were in the land of Moab, in addition
to the covenant he had made with them at Mount
Sinai.

Moses Reviews the Covenant

2Moses summoned all the Israelites and said to
them, "You have seen with your own eyes everything the LORD did in the land of Egypt to Pharaoh
and to all his servants and to his whole country—
3all the great tests of strength, the miraculous
signs, and the amazing wonders. 4But to this day
the LORD has not given you minds that understand, nor eyes that see, nor ears that hear! 5For
forty years I led you through the wilderness, yet
your clothes and sandals did not wear out. 6You
ate no bread and drank no wine or other alcoholic drink, but he provided for you so you would
know that he is the LORD your God.

7"When we came here, King Sihon of Heshbon
and King Og of Bashan came out to fight against
us, but we defeated them. 8We took their land and
gave it to the tribes of Reuben and Gad and to the
half-tribe of Manasseh as their grant of land.

9"Therefore, obey the terms of this covenant so
that you will prosper in everything you do. 10All of
you—tribal leaders, elders, officers, all the men of
Israel—are standing today in the presence of the
LORD your God. 11Your little ones and your wives
are with you, as well as the foreigners living
among you who chop your wood and carry your
water. 12You are standing here today to enter into
the covenant of the LORD your God. The LORD is
making this covenant, including the curses. 13By
entering into the covenant today, he will establish
you as his people and confirm that he is your God,
just as he promised you and as he swore to your
ancestors Abraham, Isaac, and Jacob.

14"But you are not the only ones with whom I
am making this covenant with its curses. 15I am
making this covenant both with you who stand
here today in the presence of the LORD our God,
and also with the future generations who are not
standing here today.

16"You remember how we lived in the land of
Egypt and how we traveled through the lands of
enemy nations as we left. 17You have seen their
detestable practices and their idols made of
wood, stone, silver, and gold. 18I am making this
covenant with you so that no one among you—no
man, woman, clan, or tribe—will turn away from
the LORD our God to worship these gods of other
nations, and so that no root among you bears bitter and poisonous fruit.

19"Those who hear the warnings of this curse
should not congratulate themselves, thinking, 'I
am safe, even though I am following the desires
of my own stubborn heart.' This would lead to
utter ruin! 20The LORD will never pardon such
people. Instead his anger and jealousy will burn
against them. All the curses written in this book
will come down on them, and the LORD will erase
their names from under heaven. 21The LORD will
separate them from all the tribes of Israel, to
pour out on them all the curses of the covenant
recorded in this Book of Instruction.

22"Then the generations to come, both your
own descendants and the foreigners who come
from distant lands, will see the devastation of
the land and the diseases the LORD inflicts on it.
23They will exclaim, 'The whole land is devastated by sulfur and salt. It is a wasteland with
nothing planted and nothing growing, not even a
blade of grass. It is like the cities of Sodom and
Gomorrah, Admah and Zeboiim, which the LORD
destroyed in his intense anger.'

24"And all the surrounding nations will ask,
'Why has the LORD done this to this land? Why
was he so angry?'

25"And the answer will be, 'This happened because the people of the land abandoned the covenant that the LORD, the God of their ancestors,
made with them when he brought them out of
the land of Egypt. 26Instead, they turned away to
serve and worship gods they had not known before, gods that were not from the LORD. 27That is
why the LORD's anger has burned against this
land, bringing down on it every curse recorded in
this book. 28In great anger and fury the LORD uprooted his people from their land and banished
them to another land, where they still live today!'

29"The LORD our God has secrets known to no
one. We are not accountable for them, but we
and our children are accountable forever for all
that he has revealed to us, so that we may obey all
the terms of these instructions.

CHAPTER 30

A Call to Return to the LORD

"In the future, when you experience all these
blessings and curses I have listed for you, and
when you are living among the nations to which
the LORD your God has exiled you, take to heart
all these instructions. 2If at that time you and

your children return to the LORD your God, and if
you obey with all your heart and all your soul all
the commands I have given you today, 3then the
LORD your God will restore your fortunes. He will
have mercy on you and gather you back from all
the nations where he has scattered you. 4Even
though you are banished to the ends of the earth,
the LORD your God will gather you from there
and bring you back again. 5The LORD your God
will return you to the land that belonged to your
ancestors, and you will possess that land again.
Then he will make you even more prosperous
and numerous than your ancestors!
6"The LORD your God will change your heart
and the hearts of all your descendants, so that
you will love him with all your heart and soul and
so you may live! 7The LORD your God will inflict
all these curses on your enemies and on those
who hate and persecute you. 8Then you will
again obey the LORD and keep all his commands
that I am giving you today.
9"The LORD your God will then make you successful in everything you do. He will give you
many children and numerous livestock, and he
will cause your fields to produce abundant harvests, for the LORD will again delight in being
good to you as he was to your ancestors. 10The
LORD your God will delight in you if you obey his
voice and keep the commands and decrees written in this Book of Instruction, and if you turn to
the LORD your God with all your heart and soul.

The Choice of Life or Death

11"This command I am giving you today is not
too difficult for you, and it is not beyond your
reach. 12It is not kept in heaven, so distant that
you must ask, 'Who will go up to heaven and
bring it down so we can hear it and obey?' 13It is
not kept beyond the sea, so far away that you
must ask, 'Who will cross the sea to bring it to us
so we can hear it and obey?' 14No, the message is
very close at hand; it is on your lips and in your
heart so that you can obey it.
15"Now listen! Today I am giving you a choice
between life and death, between prosperity and
disaster. 16 For I command you this day to love
the LORD your God and to keep his commands,
decrees, and regulations by walking in his ways.
If you do this, you will live and multiply, and the
LORD your God will bless you and the land you are
about to enter and occupy.
17"But if your heart turns away and you refuse
to listen, and if you are drawn away to serve and
worship other gods, 18 then I warn you now that
you will certainly be destroyed. You will not live a

Key Verse

"Today I have given you the choice between life and death... Oh, that you would choose life!"—DEUTERONOMY 30:19

If you want to know where the sins lead to, read James 1:14-15.

Bon Appétit

Have you heard about the old lady who ate a horse? As the story goes, she swallowed the horse to eat a cow.

The whole problem started when she swallowed a fly. I don't know why.

Anyway, that's kind of how sin works. One little sin leads to another sin. Next thing you know, the sin is so big that it's worse than swallowing a horse.

God wants you to choose life!

Map It Out

Imagine that you cheated a little bit on a test. Map out the very worst thing that could happen from that little sin. The first two are done for you.

Cheated
Lied to teacher
"When the teacher asked about it, I lied."
Lied to principal

long, good life in the land you are crossing the
Jordan to occupy.
**19"Today I have given you the
choice between life and death, between blessings and curses. Now I
call on heaven and earth to witness
the choice you make. Oh, that you
would choose life, so that you and
your descendants might live!** 20You can
make this choice by loving the LORD your God,
obeying him, and committing yourself firmly to
him. This is the key to your life. And if you love
and obey the LORD, you will live long in the land
the LORD swore to give your ancestors Abraham,
Isaac, and Jacob."

CHAPTER 31

Joshua Becomes Israel's Leader

When Moses had finished giving these instructions to all the people of Israel, 2he said, "I am
now 120 years old, and I am no longer able to
lead you. The LORD has told me, 'You will not
cross the Jordan River.' 3But the LORD your God
himself will cross over ahead of you. He will destroy the nations living there, and you will take
possession of their land. Joshua will lead you
across the river, just as the LORD promised.
4"The LORD will destroy the nations living in
the land, just as he destroyed Sihon and Og, the
kings of the Amorites. 5The LORD will hand over
to you the people who live there, and you must
deal with them as I have commanded you. 6So be
strong and courageous! Do not be afraid and do
not panic before them. For the LORD your God
will personally go ahead of you. He will neither
fail you nor abandon you."
7Then Moses called for Joshua, and as all Israel watched, he said to him, "Be strong and courageous! For you will lead these people into the
land that the LORD swore to their ancestors he
would give them. You are the one who will divide
it among them as their grants of land. 8Do not be
afraid or discouraged, for the LORD will personally go ahead of you. He will be with you; he will
neither fail you nor abandon you."

Public Reading of the Book of Instruction

9So Moses wrote this entire body of instruction
in a book and gave it to the priests, who carried
the Ark of the LORD's Covenant, and to the elders
of Israel. 10Then Moses gave them this command: "At the end of every seventh year, the Year
of Release, during the Festival of Shelters, 11you
must read this Book of Instruction to all the people of Israel when they assemble before the LORD
your God at the place he chooses. 12Call them all
together—men, women, children, and the foreigners living in your towns—so they may hear
this Book of Instruction and learn to fear the
LORD your God and carefully obey all the terms of
these instructions. 13Do this so that your children who have not known these instructions will
hear them and will learn to fear the LORD your
God. Do this as long as you live in the land you are
crossing the Jordan to occupy."

Israel's Disobedience Predicted

14Then the LORD said to Moses, "The time has
come for you to die. Call Joshua and present yourselves at the Tabernacle, so that I may commission
him there." So Moses and Joshua went and presented themselves at the Tabernacle. 15And the
LORD appeared to them in a pillar of cloud that
stood at the entrance to the sacred tent.
16The LORD said to Moses, "You are about to
die and join your ancestors. After you are gone,
these people will begin to worship foreign gods,
the gods of the land where they are going. They
will abandon me and break my covenant that I
have made with them. 17Then my anger will blaze
forth against them. I will abandon them, hiding
my face from them, and they will be devoured.
Terrible trouble will come down on them, and on
that day they will say, 'These disasters have come
down on us because God is no longer among us!'
18At that time I will hide my face from them on
account of all the evil they commit by worshiping
other gods.
19"So write down the words of this song, and
teach it to the people of Israel. Help them learn it,
so it may serve as a witness for me against them.
20For I will bring them into the land I swore to
give their ancestors—a land flowing with milk
and honey. There they will become prosperous,
eat all the food they want, and become fat. But
they will begin to worship other gods; they will
despise me and break my covenant. 21And when
great disasters come down on them, this song will
stand as evidence against them, for it will never
be forgotten by their descendants. I know the intentions of these people, even now before they
have entered the land I swore to give them."
22So that very day Moses wrote down the
words of the song and taught it to the Israelites.
23Then the LORD commissioned Joshua son of
Nun with these words: "Be strong and courageous,
for you must bring the people of Israel into the
land I swore to give them. I will be with you."

24When Moses had finished writing this entire body of instruction in a book, 25he gave this
command to the Levites who carried the Ark
of the LORD's Covenant: 26"Take this Book of Instruction and place it beside the Ark of the Covenant of the LORD your God, so it may remain
there as a witness against the people of Israel.
27For I know how rebellious and stubborn you
are. Even now, while I am still alive and am here
with you, you have rebelled against the LORD.
How much more rebellious will you be after my
death!

28"Now summon all the elders and officials of
your tribes, so that I can speak to them directly
and call heaven and earth to witness against
them. 29I know that after my death you will become utterly corrupt and will turn from the way I
have commanded you to follow. In the days to
come, disaster will come down on you, for you
will do what is evil in the LORD's sight, making
him very angry with your actions."

The Song of Moses

30So Moses recited this entire song publicly to the
assembly of Israel:

CHAPTER 32

1"Listen, O heavens, and I will speak!
Hear, O earth, the words that I say!
2 Let my teaching fall on you like rain;
let my speech settle like dew.
Let my words fall like rain on tender grass,
like gentle showers on young plants.
3 I will proclaim the name of the LORD;
how glorious is our God!
4 He is the Rock; his deeds are perfect.
Everything he does is just and fair.
He is a faithful God who does no wrong;
how just and upright he is!

5 "But they have acted corruptly toward him;
when they act so perversely,
are they really his children?
They are a deceitful and twisted generation.
6 Is this the way you repay the LORD,
you foolish and senseless people?
Isn't he your Father who created you?
Has he not made you and established you?
7 Remember the days of long ago;
think about the generations past.
Ask your father, and he will inform you.
Inquire of your elders, and they will tell you.
8 When the Most High assigned lands to the nations,
when he divided up the human race,
he established the boundaries of the peoples
according to the number in his heavenly court.

9 "For the people of Israel belong to the LORD;
Jacob is his special possession.
10 He found them in a desert land,
in an empty, howling wasteland.
He surrounded them and watched over them;
he guarded them as he would guard his own eyes.
11 Like an eagle that rouses her chicks
and hovers over her young,
so he spread his wings to take them up
and carried them safely on his pinions.
12 The LORD alone guided them;
they followed no foreign gods.
13 He let them ride over the highlands
and feast on the crops of the fields.
He nourished them with honey from the rock
and olive oil from the stony ground.
14 He fed them yogurt from the herd
and milk from the flock,
together with the fat of lambs.
He gave them choice rams from Bashan,
and goats,
together with the choicest wheat.
You drank the finest wine,
made from the juice of grapes.

15 "But Israel soon became fat and unruly;
the people grew heavy, plump, and stuffed!
Then they abandoned the God who had made them;
they made light of the Rock of their salvation.
16 They stirred up his jealousy by worshiping foreign gods;
they provoked his fury with detestable deeds.
17 They offered sacrifices to demons, which are not God,
to gods they had not known before,
to new gods only recently arrived,
to gods their ancestors had never feared.
18 You neglected the Rock who had fathered you;
you forgot the God who had given you birth.

19 "The LORD saw this and drew back,
provoked to anger by his own sons and daughters.

20 He said, 'I will abandon them;
then see what becomes of them.
For they are a twisted generation,
children without integrity.
21 They have roused my jealousy by worshiping
things that are not God;
they have provoked my anger with their
useless idols.
Now I will rouse their jealousy through
people who are not even a people;
I will provoke their anger through the
foolish Gentiles.
22 For my anger blazes forth like fire
and burns to the depths of the grave.
It devours the earth and all its crops
and ignites the foundations of the
mountains.
23 I will heap disasters upon them
and shoot them down with my arrows.
24 I will weaken them with famine,
burning fever, and deadly disease.
I will send the fangs of wild beasts
and poisonous snakes that glide in the
dust.
25 Outside, the sword will bring death,
and inside, terror will strike
both young men and young women,
both infants and the aged.
26 I would have annihilated them,
wiping out even the memory of them.
27 But I feared the taunt of Israel's enemy,
who might misunderstand and say,
"Our own power has triumphed!
The LORD had nothing to do with this!"'

28 "But Israel is a senseless nation;
the people are foolish, without
understanding.
29 Oh, that they were wise and could
understand this!
Oh, that they might know their fate!
30 How could one person chase a thousand
of them,
and two people put ten thousand to flight,
unless their Rock had sold them,
unless the LORD had given them up?
31 But the rock of our enemies is not like our
Rock,
as even they recognize.
32 Their vine grows from the vine of Sodom,
from the vineyards of Gomorrah.
Their grapes are poison,
and their clusters are bitter.
33 Their wine is the venom of serpents,
the deadly poison of cobras.

34 "The LORD says, 'Am I not storing up these
things,
sealing them away in my treasury?
35 I will take revenge; I will pay them back.
In due time their feet will slip.
Their day of disaster will arrive,
and their destiny will overtake them.'

36 "Indeed, the LORD will give justice to his
people,
and he will change his mind about his
servants,
when he sees their strength is gone
and no one is left, slave or free.
37 Then he will ask, 'Where are their gods,
the rocks they fled to for refuge?
38 Where now are those gods,
who ate the fat of their sacrifices
and drank the wine of their offerings?
Let those gods arise and help you!
Let them provide you with shelter!
39 Look now; I myself am he!
There is no other god but me!
I am the one who kills and gives life;
I am the one who wounds and heals;
no one can be rescued from my powerful
hand!
40 Now I raise my hand to heaven
and declare, "As surely as I live,
41 when I sharpen my flashing sword
and begin to carry out justice,
I will take revenge on my enemies
and repay those who reject me.
42 I will make my arrows drunk with blood,
and my sword will devour flesh—
the blood of the slaughtered and the
captives,
and the heads of the enemy leaders."'

43 "Rejoice with him, you heavens,
and let all of God's angels worship him.
Rejoice with his people, you Gentiles,
and let all the angels be strengthened
in him.
For he will avenge the blood of his children;
he will take revenge against his enemies.
He will repay those who hate him
and cleanse his people's land."

44 So Moses came with Joshua son of Nun and
recited all the words of this song to the people.
45 When Moses had finished reciting all these
words to the people of Israel, 46 he added: "Take
to heart all the words of warning I have given you
today. Pass them on as a command to your children so they will obey every word of these in-

structions. 47These instructions are not empty
words—they are your life! By obeying them you
will enjoy a long life in the land you will occupy
when you cross the Jordan River."

Moses' Death Foretold

48That same day the LORD said to Moses, 49"Go to
Moab, to the mountains east of the river, and
climb Mount Nebo, which is across from Jericho.
Look out across the land of Canaan, the land I am
giving to the people of Israel as their own special
possession. 50Then you will die there on the
mountain. You will join your ancestors, just as
Aaron, your brother, died on Mount Hor and
joined his ancestors. 51For both of you betrayed
me with the Israelites at the waters of Meribah at
Kadesh in the wilderness of Zin. You failed to
demonstrate my holiness to the people of Israel
there. 52So you will see the land from a distance,
but you may not enter the land I am giving to the
people of Israel."

CHAPTER 33

Moses Blesses the People

This is the blessing that Moses, the man of God, gave to the people of Israel before his death:

2 "The LORD came from Mount Sinai
and dawned upon us from Mount Seir;
he shone forth from Mount Paran
and came from Meribah-kadesh
with flaming fire at his right hand.
3 Indeed, he loves his people;
all his holy ones are in his hands.
They follow in his steps
and accept his teaching.
4 Moses gave us the LORD's instruction,
the special possession of the people of Israel.
5 The LORD became king in Israel—
when the leaders of the people assembled,
when the tribes of Israel gathered as one."

6 Moses said this about the tribe of Reuben:

"Let the tribe of Reuben live and not die out,
though they are few in number."

7Moses said this about the tribe of Judah:

"O LORD, hear the cry of Judah
and bring them together as a people.
Give them strength to defend their cause;
help them against their enemies!"

8Moses said this about the tribe of Levi:

"O LORD, you have given your Thummim
and Urim—the sacred lots—
to your faithful servants the Levites.
You put them to the test at Massah
and struggled with them at the waters of Meribah.
9 The Levites obeyed your word
and guarded your covenant.
They were more loyal to you
than to their own parents.
They ignored their relatives
and did not acknowledge their own children.
10 They teach your regulations to Jacob;
they give your instructions to Israel.
They present incense before you
and offer whole burnt offerings on the altar.
11 Bless the ministry of the Levites, O LORD,
and accept all the work of their hands.
Hit their enemies where it hurts the most;
strike down their foes so they never rise again."

12Moses said this about the tribe of Benjamin:

"The people of Benjamin are loved by the LORD
and live in safety beside him.
He surrounds them continuously
and preserves them from every harm."

13Moses said this about the tribes of Joseph:

"May their land be blessed by the LORD
with the precious gift of dew from the heavens
and water from beneath the earth;
14 with the rich fruit that grows in the sun,
and the rich harvest produced each month;
15 with the finest crops of the ancient mountains,
and the abundance from the everlasting hills;
16 with the best gifts of the earth and its bounty,
and the favor of the one who appeared in the burning bush.
May these blessings rest on Joseph's head,
crowning the brow of the prince among his brothers.
17 Joseph has the majesty of a young bull;
he has the horns of a wild ox.

He will gore distant nations,
even to the ends of the earth.
This is my blessing for the multitudes
of Ephraim
and the thousands of Manasseh."

18 Moses said this about the tribes of Zebulun and Issachar:

"May the people of Zebulun prosper in their
travels.
May the people of Issachar prosper
at home in their tents.
19 They summon the people to the mountain
to offer proper sacrifices there.
They benefit from the riches of the sea
and the hidden treasures in the sand."

20 Moses said this about the tribe of Gad:

"Blessed is the one who enlarges Gad's
territory!
Gad is poised there like a lion
to tear off an arm or a head.
21 The people of Gad took the best land for
themselves;
a leader's share was assigned to them.
When the leaders of the people were
assembled,
they carried out the LORD's justice
and obeyed his regulations for Israel."

22 Moses said this about the tribe of Dan:

"Dan is a lion's cub,
leaping out from Bashan."

23 Moses said this about the tribe of Naphtali:

"O Naphtali, you are rich in favor
and full of the LORD's blessings;
may you possess the west and the south."

24 Moses said this about the tribe of Asher:

"May Asher be blessed above other sons;
may he be esteemed by his brothers;
may he bathe his feet in olive oil.
25 May the bolts of your gates be of iron and
bronze;
may you be secure all your days."

26 "There is no one like the God of Israel.
He rides across the heavens to help you,
across the skies in majestic splendor.
27 The eternal God is your refuge,
and his everlasting arms are under you.
He drives out the enemy before you;
he cries out, 'Destroy them!'
28 So Israel will live in safety,
prosperous Jacob in security,
in a land of grain and new wine,
while the heavens drop down dew.
29 How blessed you are, O Israel!
Who else is like you, a people saved
by the LORD?
He is your protecting shield
and your triumphant sword!
Your enemies will cringe before you,
and you will stomp on their backs!"

CHAPTER 34

The Death of Moses

Then Moses went up to Mount Nebo from the
plains of Moab and climbed Pisgah Peak, which
is across from Jericho. And the LORD showed
him the whole land, from Gilead as far as Dan;
2 all the land of Naphtali; the land of Ephraim
and Manasseh; all the land of Judah, extending
to the Mediterranean Sea; 3 the Negev; the Jordan Valley with Jericho—the city of palms—as
far as Zoar. 4 Then the LORD said to Moses, "This
is the land I promised on oath to Abraham,
Isaac, and Jacob when I said, 'I will give it to your
descendants.' I have now allowed you to see it
with your own eyes, but you will not enter the
land."

5 So Moses, the servant of the LORD, died there
in the land of Moab, just as the LORD had said.
6 The LORD buried him in a valley near Beth-peor
in Moab, but to this day no one knows the exact
place. 7 Moses was 120 years old when he died,
yet his eyesight was clear, and he was as strong as
ever. 8 The people of Israel mourned for Moses
on the plains of Moab for thirty days, until the
customary period of mourning was over.

9 Now Joshua son of Nun was full of the spirit
of wisdom, for Moses had laid his hands on him.
So the people of Israel obeyed him, doing just as
the LORD had commanded Moses.

10 There has never been another prophet in
Israel like Moses, whom the LORD knew face
to face. 11 The LORD sent him to perform all
the miraculous signs and wonders in the land
of Egypt against Pharaoh, and all his servants,
and his entire land. 12 With mighty power,
Moses performed terrifying acts in the sight of
all Israel.

JOSHUA A Promise Fulfilled

Look for 2 hidden messages in Joshua!

God promised the land of Canaan to Abraham around 700 years before Joshua led the Israelites into the Promised Land! Read Joshua to find out how God

- **OPENED UP A FLOODING RIVER**
- **KNOCKED DOWN A REALLY BIG WALL WITH TRUMPETS AND SHOUTS**
- **DEFEATED THE ENEMIES OF ISRAEL IN AMAZING WAYS**
- **GAVE THE PROMISED LAND TO THE TRIBES OF ISRAEL.**

New Head Man

In one of his first moves as the head guy of Israel, Joshua pulled a plan from the playbook that was really...different. To fight the humongous fortress of Jericho, Joshua told the Israelites to march around a lot and yell really loud. Sounds like the time to get a new head guy. Except God directed this leader. **Check out what happened in Joshua 6.**

Mysterious Disappearance

Two young Israelite men disappeared from their tribes. More than three days later, they appeared on the outside of camp and were taken directly to Joshua. Rumors about spying, hiding on a roof, and an extreme-adventure basket ride swirled around camp. **Search out the details in Joshua 2.**

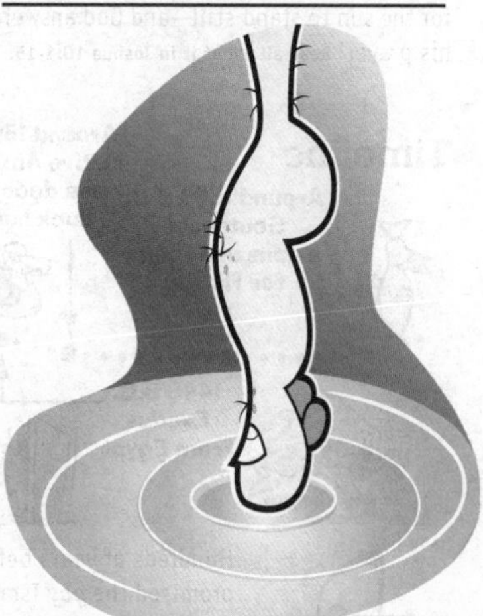

Brrrrr

"My tootsies are cold," remarked the priest as he put his foot in the Jordan River. But just as his feet touched the water, the river stopped flowing! **Find out what happened next in Joshua 3:14–4:11.**

Dear Blabby

Joshin' Joshua

Q: Dear Blabby, they really *looked* like they made a long journey. The Gibeonites came to us in worn-out clothes, carrying moldy bread. So when they asked to make a treaty with us, we agreed without even asking God. What a huge mistake! They tricked us, Blabby! **A: See Joshua 9 to see what happened.**

"Be strong and courageous...For the Lord your God is with you wherever you go." —God (to Joshua just before crossing into the Promised Land)

"Choose today whom you will serve...as for me and my family, we will serve the Lord." —Joshua (to the Israelites after conquering the Promised Land)

Read the book of Joshua to learn about a man who started and ended with God!

A Really Long Day

"Will this day ever end?" an Amorite king complained. The Israelites were crushing the Amorites, but time ran short. Joshua prayed for the sun to stand still—and God answered his prayer! **Read all about it in Joshua 10:1-15.**

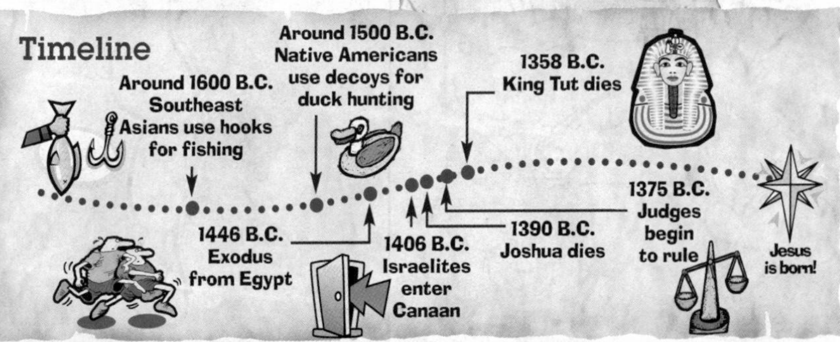
Timeline
Around 1600 B.C. Southeast Asians use hooks for fishing
Around 1500 B.C. Native Americans use decoys for duck hunting
1358 B.C. King Tut dies
1446 B.C. Exodus from Egypt
1406 B.C. Israelites enter Canaan
1390 B.C. Joshua dies
1375 B.C. Judges begin to rule
Jesus is born!

The JESUS CONNECTION

Hundreds of years before the *nation* of Israel took the Promised Land, God promised the *guy* Israel (also known as Jacob) that his descendants would fill up the land and that all the families of earth would be blessed through his children. The first part of God's promise came true when Joshua led the Israelites to take the Promised Land. The second part happened when Jesus was born in Israel 1,400 years after Joshua conquered it! **God was working out his plan for our salvation thousands of years before Jesus completed it!**

CHAPTER 1

The LORD's Charge to Joshua

After the death of Moses the LORD's servant, the
LORD spoke to Joshua son of Nun, Moses' assistant. He said, 2"Moses my servant is dead. Therefore, the time has come for you to lead these
people, the Israelites, across the Jordan River
into the land I am giving them. 3I promise you
what I promised Moses: 'Wherever you set foot,
you will be on land I have given you—4from the
Negev wilderness in the south to the Lebanon
mountains in the north, from the Euphrates
River in the east to the Mediterranean Sea in the
west, including all the land of the Hittites.' 5No
one will be able to stand against you as long as
you live. For I will be with you as I was with
Moses. I will not fail you or abandon you.

6"Be strong and courageous, for you are the
one who will lead these people to possess all the
land I swore to their ancestors I would give
them. 7Be strong and very courageous. Be careful to obey all the instructions Moses gave you.
Do not deviate from them, turning either to the
right or to the left. Then you will be successful
in everything you do. 8Study this Book of Instruction continually. Meditate on it day and
night so you will be sure to obey everything
written in it. Only then will you prosper and
succeed in all you do. 9This is my command—be
strong and courageous! Do not be afraid or discouraged. For the LORD your God is with you
wherever you go."

Joshua's Charge to the Israelites

10Joshua then commanded the officers of Israel,
11"Go through the camp and tell the people to get
their provisions ready. In three days you will
cross the Jordan River and take possession of the
land the LORD your God is giving you."

12Then Joshua called together the tribes of
Reuben, Gad, and the half-tribe of Manasseh. He
told them, 13"Remember what Moses, the servant of the LORD, commanded you: 'The LORD
your God is giving you a place of rest. He has
given you this land.' 14Your wives, children, and
livestock may remain here in the land Moses assigned to you on the east side of the Jordan River.
But your strong warriors, fully armed, must lead
the other tribes across the Jordan to help them
conquer their territory. Stay with them 15until
the LORD gives them rest, as he has given you rest,
and until they, too, possess the land the LORD
your God is giving them. Only then may you return and settle here on the east side of the Jordan
River in the land that Moses, the servant of the
LORD, assigned to you."

16They answered Joshua, "We will do whatever
you command us, and we will go wherever you
send us. 17We will obey you just as we obeyed
Moses. And may the LORD your God be with you
as he was with Moses. 18Anyone who rebels
against your orders and does not obey your
words and everything you command will be put
to death. So be strong and courageous!"

CHAPTER 2

Rahab Protects the Spies

Then Joshua secretly sent out two spies from the
Israelite camp at Acacia Grove. He instructed
them, "Scout out the land on the other side of the
Jordan River, especially around Jericho." So the
two men set out and came to the house of a prostitute named Rahab and stayed there that night.

2But someone told the king of Jericho, "Some
Israelites have come here tonight to spy out
the land." 3So the king of Jericho sent orders to
Rahab: "Bring out the men who have come into
your house, for they have come here to spy out
the whole land."

4Rahab had hidden the two men, but she replied, "Yes, the men were here earlier, but I didn't
know where they were from. 5They left the town
at dusk, as the gates were about to close. I don't
know where they went. If you hurry, you can
probably catch up with them." 6(Actually, she had
taken them up to the roof and hidden them
beneath bundles of flax she had laid out.) 7So the
king's men went looking for the spies along
the road leading to the shallow crossings of the
Jordan River. And as soon as the king's men had
left, the gate of Jericho was shut.

8Before the spies went to sleep that night, Rahab went up on the roof to talk with them. 9"I
know the LORD has given you this land," she told
them. "We are all afraid of you. Everyone in the
land is living in terror. 10For we have heard how
the LORD made a dry path for you through the
Red Sea when you left Egypt. And we know what
you did to Sihon and Og, the two Amorite kings
east of the Jordan River, whose people you completely destroyed. 11No wonder our hearts have
melted in fear! No one has the courage to fight
after hearing such things. For the LORD your God
is the supreme God of the heavens above and the
earth below.

12"Now swear to me by the LORD that you will
be kind to me and my family since I have helped
you. Give me some guarantee that 13when Jericho is conquered, you will let me live, along with

BARBELLS of BRAVERY

Ever face a *really* big, scary job? Be brave! Have courage! **Find out why you can in JOSHUA 1:1-9.**

God promised to be with Joshua every step of the way. He'll be with you, too! Here's something to give your courage a good workout!

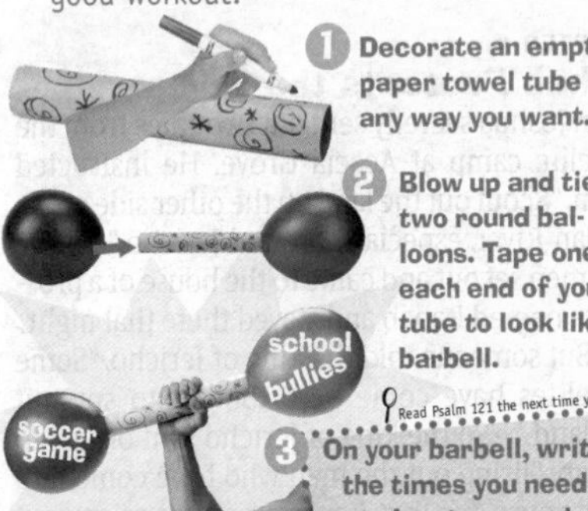

1 Decorate an empty paper towel tube any way you want.

2 Blow up and tie off two round balloons. Tape one to each end of your tube to look like a barbell.

3 On your barbell, write the times you need to be strong and courageous.

Read Psalm 121 the next time you need courage.

When you see the barbell, remember that God is with you wherever you go!

my father and mother, my brothers and sisters,
and all their families."
14"We offer our own lives as a guarantee for
your safety," the men agreed. "If you don't betray
us, we will keep our promise and be kind to you
when the LORD gives us the land."
15Then, since Rahab's house was built into the
town wall, she let them down by a rope through
the window. 16"Escape to the hill country," she
told them. "Hide there for three days from the
men searching for you. Then, when they have returned, you can go on your way."
17Before they left, the men told her, "We will
be bound by the oath we have taken only if you
follow these instructions. 18When we come into
the land, you must leave this scarlet rope hanging
from the window through which you let us
down. And all your family members—your father, mother, brothers, and all your relatives—
must be here inside the house. 19If they go out
into the street and are killed, it will not be our
fault. But if anyone lays a hand on people inside
this house, we will accept the responsibility for
their death. 20If you betray us, however, we are
not bound by this oath in any way."
21"I accept your terms," she replied. And she
sent them on their way, leaving the scarlet rope
hanging from the window.
22The spies went up into the hill country and
stayed there three days. The men who were chasing them searched everywhere along the road,
but they finally returned without success.
23Then the two spies came down from the
hill country, crossed the Jordan River, and reported to Joshua all that had happened to them.
24"The LORD has given us the whole land," they
said, "for all the people in the land are terrified
of us."

CHAPTER **3**

The Israelites Cross the Jordan

Early the next morning Joshua and all the Israelites left Acacia Grove and arrived at the banks of
the Jordan River, where they camped before
crossing. 2Three days later the Israelite officers
went through the camp, 3giving these instructions to the people: "When you see the Levitical
priests carrying the Ark of the Covenant of the
LORD your God, move out from your positions
and follow them. 4Since you have never traveled
this way before, they will guide you. Stay about a
half mile behind them, keeping a clear distance
between you and the Ark. Make sure you don't
come any closer."
5Then Joshua told the people, "Purify yourselves, for tomorrow the LORD will do great wonders among you."
6In the morning Joshua said to the priests,
"Lift up the Ark of the Covenant and lead the
people across the river." And so they started out
and went ahead of the people.
7The LORD told Joshua, "Today I will begin to
make you a great leader in the eyes of all the
Israelites. They will know that I am with you,
just as I was with Moses. 8Give this command
to the priests who carry the Ark of the Covenant: 'When you reach the banks of the Jordan
River, take a few steps into the river and stop
there.'"
9So Joshua told the Israelites, "Come and listen to what the LORD your God says. 10Today you
will know that the living God is among you. He
will surely drive out the Canaanites, Hittites,
Hivites, Perizzites, Girgashites, Amorites, and
Jebusites ahead of you. 11Look, the Ark of the
Covenant, which belongs to the Lord of the
whole earth, will lead you across the Jordan
River! 12Now choose twelve men from the tribes
of Israel, one from each tribe. 13The priests will
carry the Ark of the LORD, the Lord of all the

earth. As soon as their feet touch the water, the flow of water will be cut off upstream, and the river will stand up like a wall."

14So the people left their camp to cross the Jordan, and the priests who were carrying the Ark of the Covenant went ahead of them. 15It was the harvest season, and the Jordan was overflowing its banks. But as soon as the feet of the priests who were carrying the Ark touched the water at the river's edge, 16the water above that point began backing up a great distance away at a town called Adam, which is near Zarethan. And the water below that point flowed on to the Dead Sea until the riverbed was dry. Then all the people crossed over near the town of Jericho.

17Meanwhile, the priests who were carrying the Ark of the LORD's Covenant stood on dry ground in the middle of the riverbed as the people passed by. They waited there until the whole nation of Israel had crossed the Jordan on dry ground.

CHAPTER 4

Memorials to the Jordan Crossing

When all the people had crossed the Jordan, the LORD said to Joshua, 2"Now choose twelve men, one from each tribe. 3Tell them, 'Take twelve stones from the very place where the priests are standing in the middle of the Jordan. Carry them out and pile them up at the place where you will camp tonight.'"

4So Joshua called together the twelve men he had chosen—one from each of the tribes of Israel. 5He told them, "Go into the middle of the Jordan, in front of the Ark of the LORD your God. Each of you must pick up one stone and carry it out on your shoulder—twelve stones in all, one for each of the twelve tribes of Israel. 6We will use these stones to build a memorial. In the future your children will ask you, 'What do these stones mean?' 7Then you can tell them, 'They remind us that the Jordan River stopped flowing when the Ark of the LORD's Covenant went across.' These stones will stand as a memorial among the people of Israel forever."

8So the men did as Joshua had commanded them. They took twelve stones from the middle of the Jordan River, one for each tribe, just as the LORD had told Joshua. They carried them to the place where they camped for the night and constructed the memorial there.

9Joshua also set up another pile of twelve stones in the middle of the Jordan, at the place where the priests who carried the Ark of the Covenant were standing. And they are there to this day.

10The priests who were carrying the Ark stood in the middle of the river until all of the LORD's commands that Moses had given to Joshua were carried out. Meanwhile, the people hurried across the riverbed. 11And when everyone was safely on the other side, the priests crossed over with the Ark of the LORD as the people watched.

12The armed warriors from the tribes of Reuben, Gad, and the half-tribe of Manasseh led the Israelites across the Jordan, just as Moses had directed. 13These armed men—about 40,000 strong—were ready for battle, and the LORD was with them as they crossed over to the plains of Jericho.

14That day the LORD made Joshua a great leader in the eyes of all the Israelites, and for the rest of his life they revered him as much as they had revered Moses.

15The LORD had said to Joshua, 16"Command the priests carrying the Ark of the Covenant to come up out of the riverbed." 17So Joshua gave the command. 18As soon as the priests carrying the Ark of the LORD's Covenant came up out of the riverbed and their feet were on high ground, the water of the Jordan returned and overflowed its banks as before.

19The people crossed the Jordan on the tenth day of the first month. Then they camped at Gilgal, just east of Jericho. 20It was there at Gilgal that Joshua piled up the twelve stones taken from the Jordan River.

21Then Joshua said to the Israelites, "In the future your children will ask, 'What do these stones mean?' 22Then you can tell them, 'This is where the Israelites crossed the Jordan on dry ground.' 23For the LORD your God dried up the river right before your eyes, and he kept it dry until you were all across, just as he did at the Red Sea when he dried it up until we had all crossed over. 24He did this so all the nations of the earth might know that the LORD's hand is powerful, and so you might fear the LORD your God forever."

CHAPTER 5

When all the Amorite kings west of the Jordan and all the Canaanite kings who lived along the Mediterranean coast heard how the LORD had dried up the Jordan River so the people of Israel could cross, they lost heart and were paralyzed with fear because of them.

Joshua 6 . . . page 216

Israel Reestablishes Covenant Ceremonies

2 At that time the LORD told Joshua, "Make flint
knives and circumcise this second generation of
Israelites." 3 So Joshua made flint knives and circumcised the entire male population of Israel at
Gibeath-haaraloth.

4 Joshua had to circumcise them because all
the men who were old enough to fight in battle
when they left Egypt had died in the wilderness.
5 Those who left Egypt had all been circumcised, but none of those born after the Exodus,
during the years in the wilderness, had been circumcised. 6 The Israelites had traveled in the
wilderness for forty years until all the men who
were old enough to fight in battle when they left
Egypt had died. For they had disobeyed the
LORD, and the LORD vowed he would not let
them enter the land he had sworn to give us—a
land flowing with milk and honey. 7 So Joshua
circumcised their sons—those who had grown
up to take their fathers' places—for they had not
been circumcised on the way to the Promised
Land. 8 After all the males had been circumcised, they rested in the camp until they were
healed.

9 Then the LORD said to Joshua, "Today I have
rolled away the shame of your slavery in Egypt."
So that place has been called Gilgal to this day.

10 While the Israelites were camped at Gilgal
on the plains of Jericho, they celebrated Passover on the evening of the fourteenth day of
the first month. 11 The very next day they began
to eat unleavened bread and roasted grain harvested from the land. 12 No manna appeared
on the day they first ate from the crops of the
land, and it was never seen again. So from that
time on the Israelites ate from the crops of
Canaan.

The LORD's Commander Confronts Joshua

13 When Joshua was near the town of Jericho, he
looked up and saw a man standing in front of
him with sword in hand. Joshua went up to him
and demanded, "Are you friend or foe?"

14 "Neither one," he replied. "I am the commander of the LORD's army."

At this, Joshua fell with his face to the ground
in reverence. "I am at your command," Joshua
said. "What do you want your servant to do?"

15 The commander of the LORD's army replied, "Take off your sandals, for the place
where you are standing is holy." And Joshua did
as he was told.

CHAPTER 6

The Fall of Jericho

Now the gates of Jericho were tightly shut because the people were afraid of the Israelites. No
one was allowed to go out or in. 2 But the LORD
said to Joshua, "I have given you Jericho, its king,
and all its strong warriors. 3 You and your fighting men should march around the town once a
day for six days. 4 Seven priests will walk ahead of
the Ark, each carrying a ram's horn. On the seventh day you are to march around the town seven
times, with the priests blowing the horns.
5 When you hear the priests give one long blast
on the rams' horns, have all the people shout as
loud as they can. Then the walls of the town will
collapse, and the people can charge straight into
the town."

6 So Joshua called together the priests and
said, "Take up the Ark of the LORD's Covenant,
and assign seven priests to walk in front of it,
each carrying a ram's horn." 7 Then he gave orders to the people: "March around the town, and
the armed men will lead the way in front of the
Ark of the LORD."

8 After Joshua spoke to the people, the seven
priests with the rams' horns started marching
in the presence of the LORD, blowing the horns
as they marched. And the Ark of the LORD's Covenant followed behind them. 9 Some of the
armed men marched in front of the priests with
the horns and some behind the Ark, with the
priests continually blowing the horns. 10 "Do not
shout; do not even talk," Joshua commanded.
"Not a single word from any of you until I tell you
to shout. Then shout!" 11 So the Ark of the LORD
was carried around the town once that day, and
then everyone returned to spend the night in the
camp.

12 Joshua got up early the next morning, and the
priests again carried the Ark of the LORD. 13 The
seven priests with the rams' horns marched in
front of the Ark of the LORD, blowing their horns.
Again the armed men marched both in front
of the priests with the horns and behind the Ark
of the LORD. All this time the priests were blowing their horns. 14 On the second day they again
marched around the town once and returned
to the camp. They followed this pattern for six
days.

15 On the seventh day the Israelites got up at
dawn and marched around the town as they had
done before. But this time they went around the
town seven times. 16 The seventh time around, as
the priests sounded the long blast on their horns,
Joshua commanded the people, "Shout! For the

LORD has given you the town! 17Jericho and
everything in it must be completely destroyed as
an offering to the LORD. Only Rahab the prostitute and the others in her house will be spared,
for she protected our spies.
18"Do not take any of the things set apart for
destruction, or you yourselves will be completely
destroyed, and you will bring trouble on the
camp of Israel. 19Everything made from silver,
gold, bronze, or iron is sacred to the LORD and
must be brought into his treasury."
20When the people heard the sound of the
rams' horns, they shouted as loud as they could.
Suddenly, the walls of Jericho collapsed, and the
Israelites charged straight into the town and captured it. 21They completely destroyed everything
in it with their swords—men and women, young
and old, cattle, sheep, goats, and donkeys.
22Meanwhile, Joshua said to the two spies,
"Keep your promise. Go to the prostitute's house
and bring her out, along with all her family."
23The men who had been spies went in and
brought out Rahab, her father, mother, brothers,
and all the other relatives who were with her.
They moved her whole family to a safe place near
the camp of Israel.
24Then the Israelites burned the town and
everything in it. Only the things made from silver, gold, bronze, or iron were kept for the treasury of the LORD's house. 25So Joshua spared
Rahab the prostitute and her relatives who were
with her in the house, because she had hidden
the spies Joshua sent to Jericho. And she lives
among the Israelites to this day.
26At that time Joshua invoked this curse:

"May the curse of the LORD fall on anyone
who tries to rebuild the town of Jericho.
At the cost of his firstborn son,
he will lay its foundation.
At the cost of his youngest son,
he will set up its gates."

27So the LORD was with Joshua, and his reputation spread throughout the land.

CHAPTER 7

Ai Defeats the Israelites

But Israel violated the instructions about the
things set apart for the LORD. A man named
Achan had stolen some of these dedicated
things, so the LORD was very angry with the Israelites. Achan was the son of Carmi, a descendant
of Zimri son of Zerah, of the tribe of Judah.
2Joshua sent some of his men from Jericho
to spy out the town of Ai, east of Bethel, near

FALLING WALLS

Read JOSHUA 6:1-20. In this story, the Lord knocks down a huge city wall without force. Sound impossible? Try it!

FIRST!

Break several graham crackers into fourths.

NEXT!

Spread marshmallow creme on one side of each graham cracker section.

BUILD!

Build yourself a mini-wall by stacking the graham crackers on top of each other, using the marshmallow creme like cement. Once you've made a few stacks, line them up next to each other to form your wall.

CRASH TEST!

Now shout at your wall. Play a musical instrument as loud as you can next to it. What happens? That's right—NOTHING!

C'MON, CRASH!

Read about another battle in Judges 7:1-7, 19-25.

THINK ABOUT IT!

It's not easy to bring down a wall with just noise, is it? But God did it! God's awesome! As you eat each section of wall, think of a time you need God's power. Ask God to help you, and he wall—that is, he will!

Beth-aven. 3When they returned, they told Joshua, "There's no need for all of us to go up there;
it won't take more than two or three thousand
men to attack Ai. Since there are so few of them,
don't make all our people struggle to go up
there."

4So approximately 3,000 warriors were sent,
but they were soundly defeated. The men of Ai
5chased the Israelites from the town gate as far
as the quarries, and they killed about thirty-six
who were retreating down the slope. The Israelites were paralyzed with fear at this turn of
events, and their courage melted away.

6Joshua and the elders of Israel tore their clothing in dismay, threw dust on their heads, and
bowed face down to the ground before the Ark of
the LORD until evening. 7Then Joshua cried out,
"Oh, Sovereign LORD, why did you bring us across
the Jordan River if you are going to let the Amorites kill us? If only we had been content to stay on
the other side! 8Lord, what can I say now that Israel has fled from its enemies? 9For when the Canaanites and all the other people living in the land
hear about it, they will surround us and wipe our
name off the face of the earth. And then what will
happen to the honor of your great name?"

10But the LORD said to Joshua, "Get up! Why
are you lying on your face like this? 11Israel has
sinned and broken my covenant! They have stolen some of the things that I commanded must
be set apart for me. And they have not only stolen
them but have lied about it and hidden the
things among their own belongings. 12That is
why the Israelites are running from their enemies in defeat. For now Israel itself has been set
apart for destruction. I will not remain with you
any longer unless you destroy the things among
you that were set apart for destruction.

13"Get up! Command the people to purify
themselves in preparation for tomorrow. For this
is what the LORD, the God of Israel, says: Hidden
among you, O Israel, are things set apart for the
LORD. You will never defeat your enemies until
you remove these things from among you.

14"In the morning you must present yourselves by tribes, and the LORD will point out the
tribe to which the guilty man belongs. That tribe
must come forward with its clans, and the LORD
will point out the guilty clan. That clan will then
come forward, and the LORD will point out the
guilty family. Finally, each member of the guilty
family must come forward one by one. 15The one
who has stolen what was set apart for destruction will himself be burned with fire, along with
everything he has, for he has broken the covenant of the LORD and has done a horrible thing
in Israel."

Achan's Sin

16Early the next morning Joshua brought the
tribes of Israel before the LORD, and the tribe of
Judah was singled out. 17Then the clans of Judah
came forward, and the clan of Zerah was singled
out. Then the families of Zerah came forward,
and the family of Zimri was singled out. 18Every
member of Zimri's family was brought forward
person by person, and Achan was singled out.

19Then Joshua said to Achan, "My son, give
glory to the LORD, the God of Israel, by telling the
truth. Make your confession and tell me what
you have done. Don't hide it from me."

20Achan replied, "It is true! I have sinned
against the LORD, the God of Israel. 21Among the
plunder I saw a beautiful robe from Babylon,
200 silver coins, and a bar of gold weighing
more than a pound. I wanted them so much that
I took them. They are hidden in the ground beneath my tent, with the silver buried deeper
than the rest."

22So Joshua sent some men to make a search.
They ran to the tent and found the stolen goods
hidden there, just as Achan had said, with the
silver buried beneath the rest. 23They took the
things from the tent and brought them to Joshua
and all the Israelites. Then they laid them on the
ground in the presence of the LORD.

24Then Joshua and all the Israelites took
Achan, the silver, the robe, the bar of gold, his
sons, daughters, cattle, donkeys, sheep, goats,
tent, and everything he had, and they brought
them to the valley of Achor. 25Then Joshua said
to Achan, "Why have you brought trouble on us?
The LORD will now bring trouble on you." And all
the Israelites stoned Achan and his family and
burned their bodies. 26They piled a great heap of
stones over Achan, which remains to this day.
That is why the place has been called the Valley
of Trouble ever since. So the LORD was no longer
angry.

CHAPTER 8
The Israelites Defeat Ai

Then the LORD said to Joshua, "Do not be afraid
or discouraged. Take all your fighting men and
attack Ai, for I have given you the king of Ai, his
people, his town, and his land. 2You will destroy
them as you destroyed Jericho and its king. But
this time you may keep the plunder and the livestock for yourselves. Set an ambush behind the
town."

3So Joshua and all the fighting men set out to
attack Ai. Joshua chose 30,000 of his best warriors and sent them out at night 4with these
orders: "Hide in ambush close behind the town
and be ready for action. 5When our main army
attacks, the men of Ai will come out to fight as
they did before, and we will run away from them.
6We will let them chase us until we have drawn
them away from the town. For they will say, 'The
Israelites are running away from us as they did
before.' Then, while we are running from them,
7you will jump up from your ambush and take
possession of the town, for the LORD your God
will give it to you. 8Set the town on fire, as the
LORD has commanded. You have your orders."

9So they left and went to the place of ambush
between Bethel and the west side of Ai. But Joshua remained among the people in the camp that
night. 10Early the next morning Joshua roused
his men and started toward Ai, accompanied by
the elders of Israel. 11All the fighting men who
were with Joshua marched in front of the town
and camped on the north side of Ai, with a valley
between them and the town. 12That night Joshua
sent about 5,000 men to lie in ambush between
Bethel and Ai, on the west side of the town. 13So
they stationed the main army north of the town
and the ambush west of the town. Joshua himself
spent that night in the valley.

14When the king of Ai saw the Israelites
across the valley, he and all his army hurried out
early in the morning and attacked the Israelites
at a place overlooking the Jordan Valley. But he
didn't realize there was an ambush behind the
town. 15Joshua and the Israelite army fled toward the wilderness as though they were badly
beaten. 16Then all the men in the town were
called out to chase after them. In this way, they
were lured away from the town. 17There was not
a man left in Ai or Bethel who did not chase after
the Israelites, and the town was left wide open.

18Then the LORD said to Joshua, "Point the
spear in your hand toward Ai, for I will hand the
town over to you." Joshua did as he was commanded. 19As soon as Joshua gave this signal, all
the men in ambush jumped up from their position and poured into the town. They quickly captured it and set it on fire.

20When the men of Ai looked behind them,
smoke from the town was filling the sky, and they
had nowhere to go. For the Israelites who had
fled in the direction of the wilderness now
turned on their pursuers. 21When Joshua and all
the other Israelites saw that the ambush had succeeded and that smoke was rising from the town,
they turned and attacked the men of Ai. 22Mean-
while, the Israelites who were inside the town
came out and attacked the enemy from the rear.
So the men of Ai were caught in the middle, with
Israelite fighters on both sides. Israel attacked
them, and not a single person survived or escaped. 23Only the king of Ai was taken alive and
brought to Joshua.

24When the Israelite army finished chasing
and killing all the men of Ai in the open fields,
they went back and finished off everyone inside.
25So the entire population of Ai, including men
and women, was wiped out that day—12,000 in
all. 26For Joshua kept holding out his spear until
everyone who had lived in Ai was completely
destroyed. 27Only the livestock and the treasures
of the town were not destroyed, for the Israelites
kept these as plunder for themselves, as the LORD
had commanded Joshua. 28So Joshua burned the
town of Ai, and it became a permanent mound of
ruins, desolate to this very day.

29Joshua impaled the king of Ai on a sharpened pole and left him there until evening. At
sunset the Israelites took down the body, as Joshua commanded, and threw it in front of the town
gate. They piled a great heap of stones over him
that can still be seen today.

The LORD's Covenant Renewed

30Then Joshua built an altar to the LORD, the God
of Israel, on Mount Ebal. 31He followed the commands that Moses the LORD's servant had written
in the Book of Instruction: "Make me an altar
from stones that are uncut and have not been
shaped with iron tools." Then on the altar they
presented burnt offerings and peace offerings to
the LORD. 32And as the Israelites watched, Joshua
copied onto the stones of the altar the instructions Moses had given them.

33Then all the Israelites—foreigners and native-
born alike—along with the elders, officers, and
judges, were divided into two groups. One group
stood in front of Mount Gerizim, the other in
front of Mount Ebal. Each group faced the other,
and between them stood the Levitical priests carrying the Ark of the LORD's Covenant. This was all
done according to the commands that Moses, the
servant of the LORD, had previously given for
blessing the people of Israel.

34Joshua then read to them all the blessings
and curses Moses had written in the Book of Instruction. 35Every word of every command that
Moses had ever given was read to the entire assembly of Israel, including the women and children and the foreigners who lived among them.

CHAPTER 9
The Gibeonites Deceive Israel

Now all the kings west of the Jordan River heard about what had happened. These were the kings of the Hittites, Amorites, Canaanites, Perizzites, Hivites, and Jebusites, who lived in the hill country, in the western foothills, and along the coast of the Mediterranean Sea as far north as the Lebanon mountains. 2These kings combined their armies to fight as one against Joshua and the Israelites.

3But when the people of Gibeon heard what Joshua had done to Jericho and Ai, 4they resorted to deception to save themselves. They sent ambassadors to Joshua, loading their donkeys with weathered saddlebags and old, patched wineskins. 5They put on worn-out, patched sandals and ragged clothes. And the bread they took with them was dry and moldy. 6When they arrived at the camp of Israel at Gilgal, they told Joshua and the men of Israel, "We have come from a distant land to ask you to make a peace treaty with us."

7The Israelites replied to these Hivites, "How do we know you don't live nearby? For if you do, we cannot make a treaty with you."

8They replied, "We are your servants."

"But who are you?" Joshua demanded. "Where do you come from?"

9They answered, "Your servants have come from a very distant country. We have heard of the might of the LORD your God and of all he did in Egypt. 10We have also heard what he did to the two Amorite kings east of the Jordan River—King Sihon of Heshbon and King Og of Bashan (who lived in Ashtaroth). 11So our elders and all our people instructed us, 'Take supplies for a long journey. Go meet with the people of Israel and tell them, "We are your servants; please make a treaty with us."'

12"This bread was hot from the ovens when we left our homes. But now, as you can see, it is dry and moldy. 13These wineskins were new when we filled them, but now they are old and split open. And our clothing and sandals are worn out from our very long journey."

14So the Israelites examined their food, but they did not consult the LORD. 15Then Joshua made a peace treaty with them and guaranteed their safety, and the leaders of the community ratified their agreement with a binding oath.

16Three days after making the treaty, they learned that these people actually lived nearby! 17The Israelites set out at once to investigate and reached their towns in three days. The names of these towns were Gibeon, Kephirah, Beeroth, and Kiriath-jearim. 18But the Israelites did not attack the towns, for the Israelite leaders had made a vow to them in the name of the LORD, the God of Israel.

The people of Israel grumbled against their leaders because of the treaty. 19But the leaders replied, "Since we have sworn an oath in the presence of the LORD, the God of Israel, we cannot touch them. 20This is what we must do. We must let them live, for divine anger would come upon us if we broke our oath. 21Let them live." So they made them woodcutters and water carriers for the entire community, as the Israelite leaders directed.

22Joshua called together the Gibeonites and said, "Why did you lie to us? Why did you say that you live in a distant land when you live right here among us? 23May you be cursed! From now on you will always be servants who cut wood and carry water for the house of my God."

24They replied, "We did it because we—your servants—were clearly told that the LORD your God commanded his servant Moses to give you this entire land and to destroy all the people living in it. So we feared greatly for our lives because of you. That is why we have done this. 25Now we are at your mercy—do to us whatever you think is right."

26So Joshua did not allow the people of Israel to kill them. 27But that day he made the Gibeonites the woodcutters and water carriers for the community of Israel and for the altar of the LORD—wherever the LORD would choose to build it. And that is what they do to this day.

CHAPTER 10
Israel Defeats the Southern Armies

Adoni-zedek, king of Jerusalem, heard that Joshua had captured and completely destroyed Ai and killed its king, just as he had destroyed the town of Jericho and killed its king. He also learned that the Gibeonites had made peace with Israel and were now their allies. 2He and his people became very afraid when they heard all this because Gibeon was a large town—as large as the royal cities and larger than Ai. And the Gibeonite men were strong warriors.

3So King Adoni-zedek of Jerusalem sent messengers to several other kings: Hoham of Hebron, Piram of Jarmuth, Japhia of Lachish, and Debir of Eglon. 4"Come and help me destroy Gibeon," he urged them, "for they have made peace with Joshua and the people of Israel." 5So these five

Amorite kings combined their armies for a united attack. They moved all their troops into place and attacked Gibeon.

6The men of Gibeon quickly sent messengers to Joshua at his camp in Gilgal. "Don't abandon your servants now!" they pleaded. "Come at once! Save us! Help us! For all the Amorite kings who live in the hill country have joined forces to attack us."

7So Joshua and his entire army, including his best warriors, left Gilgal and set out for Gibeon.
8"Do not be afraid of them," the LORD said to Joshua, "for I have given you victory over them. Not a single one of them will be able to stand up to you."

9Joshua traveled all night from Gilgal and took
the Amorite armies by surprise. 10The LORD
threw them into a panic, and the Israelites slaughtered great numbers of them at Gibeon. Then the Israelites chased the enemy along the road to Beth-horon, killing them all along the
way to Azekah and Makkedah. 11As the Amorites
retreated down the road from Beth-horon, the LORD destroyed them with a terrible hailstorm from heaven that continued until they reached Azekah. The hail killed more of the enemy than the Israelites killed with the sword.

12On the day the LORD gave the Israelites victory over the Amorites, Joshua prayed to the LORD in front of all the people of Israel. He said,

"Let the sun stand still over Gibeon,
and the moon over the valley of Aijalon."

13So the sun stood still and the moon stayed in place until the nation of Israel had defeated its enemies.

Is this event not recorded in *The Book of Jashar*? The sun stayed in the middle of the sky,
and it did not set as on a normal day. 14There has
never been a day like this one before or since, when the LORD answered such a prayer. Surely the LORD fought for Israel that day!

15Then Joshua and the Israelite army returned to their camp at Gilgal.

Joshua Kills the Five Southern Kings

16During the battle the five kings escaped and
hid in a cave at Makkedah. 17When Joshua heard
that they had been found, 18he issued this command: "Cover the opening of the cave with large rocks, and place guards at the entrance to keep
the kings inside. 19The rest of you continue chasing the enemy and cut them down from the rear. Don't give them a chance to get back to their towns, for the LORD your God has given you victory over them."

20So Joshua and the Israelite army continued the slaughter and completely crushed the enemy. They totally wiped out the five armies except for a tiny remnant that managed to reach
their fortified towns. 21Then the Israelites returned safely to Joshua in the camp at Makkedah. After that, no one dared to speak even a word against Israel.

22Then Joshua said, "Remove the rocks covering the opening of the cave, and bring the five
kings to me." 23So they brought the five kings out of the cave—the kings of Jerusalem, Hebron,
Jarmuth, Lachish, and Eglon. 24When they
brought them out, Joshua told the commanders of his army, "Come and put your feet on the kings' necks." And they did as they were told.

25"Don't ever be afraid or discouraged," Joshua told his men. "Be strong and courageous, for the LORD is going to do this to all of your enemies." 26Then Joshua killed each of the five
kings and impaled them on five sharpened poles, where they hung until evening.

27As the sun was going down, Joshua gave instructions for the bodies of the kings to be taken down from the poles and thrown into the cave where they had been hiding. Then they covered the opening of the cave with a pile of large rocks, which remains to this very day.

Israel Destroys the Southern Towns

28That same day Joshua captured and destroyed the town of Makkedah. He killed everyone in it, including the king, leaving no survivors. He destroyed them all, and he killed the king of Makkedah as he had killed the king of Jericho.
29Then Joshua and the Israelites went to Libnah
and attacked it. 30There, too, the LORD gave them the town and its king. He killed everyone in it, leaving no survivors. Then Joshua killed the king of Libnah as he had killed the king of Jericho.

31From Libnah, Joshua and the Israelites went
to Lachish and attacked it. 32Here again, the
LORD gave them Lachish. Joshua took it on the second day and killed everyone in it, just as he
had done at Libnah. 33During the attack on
Lachish, King Horam of Gezer arrived with his army to help defend the town. But Joshua's men killed him and his army, leaving no survivors.

34Then Joshua and the Israelite army went on
to Eglon and attacked it. 35They captured it that
day and killed everyone in it. He completely destroyed everyone, just as he had done at Lachish.

Marching bands almost
always include trumpets. But
Bible-times trumpets (**called**
shofars) were made from rams'
horns and blown by leaders to
signal the people or scare their enemies.

You can make your own trumpet:

1. Roll a sheet of paper from one corner to the opposite corner.

2. Pinch one end a little and blow!

Use your shofar to call your family together for important events—like dinner! (**Then tell them what you learned about shofars.**)

36From Eglon, Joshua and the Israelite army went
up to Hebron and attacked it. 37They captured
the town and killed everyone in it, including its
king, leaving no survivors. They did the same
thing to all of its surrounding villages. And just as
he had done at Eglon, he completely destroyed
the entire population.
38Then Joshua and the Israelites turned back
and attacked Debir. 39He captured the town, its
king, and all of its surrounding villages. He completely destroyed everyone in it, leaving no survivors. He did to Debir and its king just what he
had done to Hebron and to Libnah and its king.
40So Joshua conquered the whole region—the
kings and people of the hill country, the Negev,
the western foothills, and the mountain slopes.
He completely destroyed everyone in the land,
leaving no survivors, just as the LORD, the God of
Israel, had commanded. 41Joshua slaughtered
them from Kadesh-barnea to Gaza and from the
region around the town of Goshen up to Gibeon.
42Joshua conquered all these kings and their
land in a single campaign, for the LORD, the God
of Israel, was fighting for his people.
43Then Joshua and the Israelite army returned
to their camp at Gilgal.

CHAPTER 11
Israel Defeats the Northern Armies

When King Jabin of Hazor heard what had happened, he sent messages to the following kings:
King Jobab of Madon; the king of Shimron; the
king of Acshaph; 2all the kings of the northern
hill country; the kings in the Jordan Valley south
of Galilee; the kings in the Galilean foothills; the
kings of Naphoth-dor on the west; 3the kings of
Canaan, both east and west; the kings of the Amorites, the Hittites, the Perizzites, the Jebusites in
the hill country, and the Hivites in the towns on
the slopes of Mount Hermon in the land of
Mizpah.
4All these kings came out to fight. Their combined armies formed a vast horde. And with all
their horses and chariots, they covered the landscape like the sand on the seashore. 5The kings
joined forces and established their camp
around the water near Merom to fight against
Israel.
6Then the LORD said to Joshua, "Do not be
afraid of them. By this time tomorrow I will
hand all of them over to Israel as dead men.
Then you must cripple their horses and burn
their chariots."
7So Joshua and all his fighting men traveled
to the water near Merom and attacked suddenly.
8And the LORD gave them victory over their enemies. The Israelites chased them as far as
Greater Sidon and Misrephoth-maim, and eastward into the valley of Mizpah, until not one
enemy warrior was left alive. 9Then Joshua crippled the horses and burned all the chariots, as
the LORD had instructed.
10Joshua then turned back and captured Hazor and killed its king. (Hazor had at one time
been the capital of all these kingdoms.) 11The Israelites completely destroyed every living thing
in the city, leaving no survivors. Not a single person was spared. And then Joshua burned the city.
12Joshua slaughtered all the other kings and
their people, completely destroying them, just
as Moses, the servant of the LORD, had commanded. 13But the Israelites did not burn any of
the towns built on mounds except Hazor, which
Joshua burned. 14And the Israelites took all the
plunder and livestock of the ravaged towns for
themselves. But they killed all the people, leaving no survivors. 15As the LORD had commanded
his servant Moses, so Moses commanded Joshua. And Joshua did as he was told, carefully
obeying all the commands that the LORD had
given to Moses.
16So Joshua conquered the entire region—the
hill country, the entire Negev, the whole area
around the town of Goshen, the western foothills, the Jordan Valley, the mountains of Israel,
and the Galilean foothills. 17The Israelite territory now extended all the way from Mount
Halak, which leads up to Seir in the south, as far
north as Baal-gad at the foot of Mount Hermon
in the valley of Lebanon. Joshua killed all the

kings of those territories, 18waging war for a
long time to accomplish this. 19No one in this region made peace with the Israelites except the
Hivites of Gibeon. All the others were defeated.
20For the LORD hardened their hearts and caused
them to fight the Israelites. So they were completely destroyed without mercy, as the LORD had
commanded Moses.

21During this period Joshua destroyed all the
descendants of Anak, who lived in the hill country of Hebron, Debir, Anab, and the entire hill
country of Judah and Israel. He killed them all
and completely destroyed their towns. 22None
of the descendants of Anak were left in all the
land of Israel, though some still remained in
Gaza, Gath, and Ashdod.

23So Joshua took control of the entire land,
just as the LORD had instructed Moses. He gave it
to the people of Israel as their special possession, dividing the land among the tribes. So the
land finally had rest from war.

CHAPTER 12

Kings Defeated East of the Jordan

These are the kings east of the Jordan River who
had been killed by the Israelites and whose land
was taken. Their territory extended from the
Arnon Gorge to Mount Hermon and included all
the land east of the Jordan Valley.

2King Sihon of the Amorites, who lived in
Heshbon, was defeated. His kingdom included
Aroer, on the edge of the Arnon Gorge, and
extended from the middle of the Arnon Gorge
to the Jabbok River, which serves as a border
for the Ammonites. This territory included the
southern half of the territory of Gilead. 3Sihon
also controlled the Jordan Valley and regions to
the east—from as far north as the Sea of Galilee
to as far south as the Dead Sea, including the
road to Beth-jeshimoth and southward to the
slopes of Pisgah.

4King Og of Bashan, the last of the Rephaites,
lived at Ashtaroth and Edrei. 5He ruled a territory
stretching from Mount Hermon to Salecah in the
north and to all of Bashan in the east, and westward to the borders of the kingdoms of Geshur
and Maacah. This territory included the northern half of Gilead, as far as the boundary of King
Sihon of Heshbon.

6Moses, the servant of the LORD, and the Israelites had destroyed the people of King Sihon
and King Og. And Moses gave their land as a possession to the tribes of Reuben, Gad, and the half-
tribe of Manasseh.

Kings Defeated West of the Jordan

7The following is a list of the kings that Joshua
and the Israelite armies defeated on the west
side of the Jordan, from Baal-gad in the valley of
Lebanon to Mount Halak, which leads up to Seir.
(Joshua gave this land to the tribes of Israel as
their possession, 8including the hill country, the
western foothills, the Jordan Valley, the mountain slopes, the Judean wilderness, and the Negev. The people who lived in this region were the
Hittites, the Amorites, the Canaanites, the Perizzites, the Hivites, and the Jebusites.) These are
the kings Israel defeated:

9 The king of Jericho
The king of Ai, near Bethel
10 The king of Jerusalem
The king of Hebron
11 The king of Jarmuth
The king of Lachish
12 The king of Eglon
The king of Gezer
13 The king of Debir
The king of Geder
14 The king of Hormah
The king of Arad
15 The king of Libnah
The king of Adullam
16 The king of Makkedah
The king of Bethel
17 The king of Tappuah
The king of Hepher
18 The king of Aphek
The king of Lasharon
19 The king of Madon
The king of Hazor
20 The king of Shimron-meron
The king of Acshaph
21 The king of Taanach
The king of Megiddo
22 The king of Kedesh
The king of Jokneam in Carmel
23 The king of Dor in the town of Naphoth-dor
The king of Goyim in Gilgal
24 The king of Tirzah.

In all, thirty-one kings were defeated.

CHAPTER 13

The Land Yet to Be Conquered

When Joshua was an old man, the LORD said to
him, "You are growing old, and much land remains to be conquered. 2This is the territory that
remains: all the regions of the Philistines and the
Geshurites, 3and the larger territory of the

Canaanites, extending from the stream of Shihor
on the border of Egypt, northward to the boundary of Ekron. It includes the territory of the five
Philistine rulers of Gaza, Ashdod, Ashkelon, Gath,
and Ekron. The land of the Avvites 4in the south
also remains to be conquered. In the north, the
following area has not yet been conquered: all the
land of the Canaanites, including Mearah (which
belongs to the Sidonians), stretching northward
to Aphek on the border of the Amorites; 5the
land of the Gebalites and all of the Lebanon
mountain area to the east, from Baal-gad below
Mount Hermon to Lebo-hamath; 6and all the hill
country from Lebanon to Misrephoth-maim, including all the land of the Sidonians.

"I myself will drive these people out of the
land ahead of the Israelites. So be sure to give
this land to Israel as a special possession, just as I
have commanded you. 7Include all this territory
as Israel's possession when you divide this land
among the nine tribes and the half-tribe of
Manasseh."

The Land Divided East of the Jordan

8Half the tribe of Manasseh and the tribes of
Reuben and Gad had already received their
grants of land on the east side of the Jordan, for
Moses, the servant of the LORD, had previously
assigned this land to them.

9Their territory extended from Aroer on
the edge of the Arnon Gorge (including the
town in the middle of the gorge) to the plain
beyond Medeba, as far as Dibon. 10It also
included all the towns of King Sihon of the
Amorites, who had reigned in Heshbon, and
extended as far as the borders of Ammon.
11It included Gilead, the territory of the kingdoms of Geshur and Maacah, all of Mount
Hermon, all of Bashan as far as Salecah, 12and
all the territory of King Og of Bashan, who
had reigned in Ashtaroth and Edrei. King Og
was the last of the Rephaites, for Moses had
attacked them and driven them out. 13But
the Israelites failed to drive out the people
of Geshur and Maacah, so they continue to
live among the Israelites to this day.

An Allotment for the Tribe of Levi

14Moses did not assign any allotment of land to
thetribe of Levi. Instead, as the LORD had promised
them, their allotment came from the offerings
burned on the altar to the LORD, the God of Israel.

The Land Given to the Tribe of Reuben

15Moses had assigned the following area to the
clans of the tribe of Reuben.

16Their territory extended from Aroer on
the edge of the Arnon Gorge (including the
town in the middle of the gorge) to the plain
beyond Medeba. 17It included Heshbon
and the other towns on the plain—Dibon,
Bamoth-baal, Beth-baal-meon, 18Jahaz,
Kedemoth, Mephaath, 19Kiriathaim, Sibmah,
Zereth-shahar on the hill above the valley,
20Beth-peor, the slopes of Pisgah, and Beth-
jeshimoth.

21The land of Reuben also included all the
towns of the plain and the entire kingdom of
Sihon. Sihon was the Amorite king who had
reigned in Heshbon and was killed by Moses
along with the leaders of Midian—Evi, Rekem,
Zur, Hur, and Reba—princes living in the
region who were allied with Sihon. 22The
Israelites had also killed Balaam son of Beor,
who used magic to tell the future. 23The
Jordan River marked the western boundary
for the tribe of Reuben. The towns and their
surrounding villages in this area were given as
a homeland to the clans of the tribe of Reuben.

The Land Given to the Tribe of Gad

24Moses had assigned the following area to the
clans of the tribe of Gad.

25Their territory included Jazer, all the towns
of Gilead, and half of the land of Ammon, as
far as the town of Aroer just west of Rabbah.
26It extended from Heshbon to Ramath-
mizpeh and Betonim, and from Mahanaim
to the territory of Lo-debar. 27In the valley
were Beth-haram, Beth-nimrah, Succoth,
Zaphon, and the rest of the kingdom of King
Sihon of Heshbon. The western boundary
ran along the Jordan River, extended as far
north as the tip of the Sea of Galilee, and
then turned eastward. 28The towns and their
surrounding villages in this area were given as
a homeland to the clans of the tribe of Gad.

The Land Given to the Half-Tribe of Manasseh

29Moses had assigned the following area to the
clans of the half-tribe of Manasseh.

30Their territory extended from Mahanaim,
including all of Bashan, all the former

kingdom of King Og, and the sixty towns
of Jair in Bashan. 31It also included half of
Gilead and King Og's royal cities of Ashtaroth
and Edrei. All this was given to the clans
of the descendants of Makir, who was
Manasseh's son.

32These are the allotments Moses had made
while he was on the plains of Moab, across the
Jordan River, east of Jericho. 33But Moses gave no
allotment of land to the tribe of Levi, for the
LORD, the God of Israel, had promised that he
himself would be their allotment.

CHAPTER 14
The Land Divided West of the Jordan

The remaining tribes of Israel received land in
Canaan as allotted by Eleazar the priest, Joshua
son of Nun, and the tribal leaders. 2These nine
and a half tribes received their grants of land by
means of sacred lots, in accordance with the
LORD's command through Moses. 3Moses had already given a grant of land to the two and a half
tribes on the east side of the Jordan River, but he
had given the Levites no such allotment. 4The
descendants of Joseph had become two separate
tribes—Manasseh and Ephraim. And the Levites
were given no land at all, only towns to live in
with surrounding pasturelands for their livestock and all their possessions. 5So the land was
distributed in strict accordance with the LORD's
commands to Moses.

Caleb Requests His Land

6A delegation from the tribe of Judah, led by
Caleb son of Jephunneh the Kenizzite, came to
Joshua at Gilgal. Caleb said to Joshua, "Remember what the LORD said to Moses, the man of God,
about you and me when we were at Kadesh-
barnea. 7I was forty years old when Moses, the
servant of the LORD, sent me from Kadesh-
barnea to explore the land of Canaan. I returned
and gave an honest report, 8but my brothers who
went with me frightened the people from entering the Promised Land. For my part, I wholeheartedly followed the LORD my God. 9So that
day Moses solemnly promised me, 'The land of
Canaan on which you were just walking will be
your grant of land and that of your descendants
forever, because you wholeheartedly followed
the LORD my God.'

10"Now, as you can see, the LORD has kept me
alive and well as he promised for all these forty-
five years since Moses made this promise—even
while Israel wandered in the wilderness. Today I
am eighty-five years old. 11I am as strong now as
I was when Moses sent me on that journey, and I
can still travel and fight as well as I could then.
12So give me the hill country that the LORD
promised me. You will remember that as scouts
we found the descendants of Anak living there
in great, walled towns. But if the LORD is with me,
I will drive them out of the land, just as the LORD
said."

13So Joshua blessed Caleb son of Jephunneh
and gave Hebron to him as his portion of land.
14Hebron still belongs to the descendants of
Caleb son of Jephunneh the Kenizzite because
he wholeheartedly followed the LORD, the God
of Israel. 15(Previously Hebron had been called
Kiriath-arba. It had been named after Arba, a
great hero of the descendants of Anak.)

And the land had rest from war.

CHAPTER 15
The Land Given to the Tribe of Judah

The allotment for the clans of the tribe of Judah
reached southward to the border of Edom, as far
south as the wilderness of Zin.

2The southern boundary began at the south
bay of the Dead Sea, 3ran south of Scorpion
Pass into the wilderness of Zin, and then went
south of Kadesh-barnea to Hezron. Then it
went up to Addar, where it turned toward
Karka. 4From there it passed to Azmon until
it finally reached the Brook of Egypt, which it
followed to the Mediterranean Sea. This was
their southern boundary.

5The eastern boundary extended along the
Dead Sea to the mouth of the Jordan River.

The northern boundary began at the bay
where the Jordan River empties into the Dead
Sea, 6went up from there to Beth-hoglah, then
proceeded north of Beth-arabah to the Stone
of Bohan. (Bohan was Reuben's son.) 7From
that point it went through the valley of Achor
to Debir, turning north toward Gilgal, which
is across from the slopes of Adummim on
the south side of the valley. From there the
boundary extended to the springs at En-
shemesh and on to En-rogel. 8The boundary
then passed through the valley of Ben-Hinnom,
along the southern slopes of the Jebusites,
where the city of Jerusalem is located. Then
it went west to the top of the mountain
above the valley of Hinnom, and on up to the
northern end of the valley of Rephaim. 9From

there the boundary extended from the top of
the mountain to the spring at the waters of
Nephtoah, and from there to the towns on
Mount Ephron. Then it turned toward Baalah
(that is, Kiriath-jearim). 10The boundary
circled west of Baalah to Mount Seir, passed
along to the town of Kesalon on the northern
slope of Mount Jearim, and went down to
Beth-shemesh and on to Timnah. 11The
boundary then proceeded to the slope of the
hill north of Ekron, where it turned toward
Shikkeron and Mount Baalah. It passed
Jabneel and ended at the Mediterranean Sea.
12The western boundary was the shoreline
of the Mediterranean Sea.

These are the boundaries for the clans of the tribe of Judah.

The Land Given to Caleb

13The LORD commanded Joshua to assign some
of Judah's territory to Caleb son of Jephunneh.
So Caleb was given the town of Kiriath-arba (that
is, Hebron), which had been named after Anak's
ancestor. 14Caleb drove out the three groups of
Anakites—the descendants of Sheshai, Ahiman,
and Talmai, the sons of Anak.
15From there he went to fight against the people living in the town of Debir (formerly called
Kiriath-sepher). 16Caleb said, "I will give my
daughter Acsah in marriage to the one who attacks and captures Kiriath-sepher." 17Othniel, the
son of Caleb's brother Kenaz, was the one who
conquered it, so Acsah became Othniel's wife.
18When Acsah married Othniel, she urged
him to ask her father for a field. As she got down
off her donkey, Caleb asked her, "What's the matter?"
19She said, "Give me another gift. You have already given me land in the Negev; now please
give me springs of water, too." So Caleb gave her
the upper and lower springs.

The Towns Allotted to Judah

20This was the homeland allocated to the clans
of the tribe of Judah.

21The towns of Judah situated along the
borders of Edom in the extreme south were
Kabzeel, Eder, Jagur, 22Kinah, Dimonah,
Adadah, 23Kedesh, Hazor, Ithnan, 24Ziph,
Telem, Bealoth, 25Hazor-hadattah, Kerioth-
hezron (that is, Hazor), 26Amam, Shema,
Moladah, 27Hazar-gaddah, Heshmon, Beth-
pelet, 28Hazar-shual, Beersheba, Biziothiah,
29Baalah, Iim, Ezem, 30Eltolad, Kesil, Hormah,
31Ziklag, Madmannah, Sansannah, 32Lebaoth,
Shilhim, Ain, and Rimmon—twenty-nine
towns with their surrounding villages.
33The following towns situated in the
western foothills were also given to Judah:
Eshtaol, Zorah, Ashnah, 34Zanoah, En-gannim,
Tappuah, Enam, 35Jarmuth, Adullam, Socoh,
Azekah, 36Shaaraim, Adithaim, Gederah, and
Gederothaim—fourteen towns with their
surrounding villages.
37Also included were Zenan, Hadashah,
Migdal-gad, 38Dilean, Mizpeh, Joktheel,
39Lachish, Bozkath, Eglon, 40Cabbon, Lahmam,
Kitlish, 41Gederoth, Beth-dagon, Naamah,
and Makkedah—sixteen towns with their
surrounding villages.
42Besides these, there were Libnah, Ether,
Ashan, 43Iphtah, Ashnah, Nezib, 44Keilah,
Aczib, and Mareshah—nine towns with their
surrounding villages.
45The territory of the tribe of Judah
also included Ekron and its surrounding
settlements and villages. 46From Ekron the
boundary extended west and included the
towns near Ashdod with their surrounding
villages. 47It also included Ashdod with its
surrounding settlements and villages and
Gaza with its settlements and villages, as
far as the Brook of Egypt and along the coast
of the Mediterranean Sea.
48Judah also received the following towns
in the hill country: Shamir, Jattir, Socoh,
49Dannah, Kiriath-sannah (that is, Debir),
50Anab, Eshtemoh, Anim, 51Goshen, Holon,
and Giloh—eleven towns with their
surrounding villages.
52Also included were the towns of Arab,
Dumah, Eshan, 53Janim, Beth-tappuah,
Aphekah, 54Humtah, Kiriath-arba (that is,
Hebron), and Zior—nine towns with their
surrounding villages.
55Besides these, there were Maon, Carmel,
Ziph, Juttah, 56Jezreel, Jokdeam, Zanoah,
57Kain, Gibeah, and Timnah—ten towns with
their surrounding villages.
58In addition, there were Halhul, Beth-zur,
Gedor, 59Maarath, Beth-anoth, and Eltekon—
six towns with their surrounding villages.
60There were also Kiriath-baal (that is,
Kiriath-jearim) and Rabbah—two towns with
their surrounding villages.
61In the wilderness there were the towns of
Beth-arabah, Middin, Secacah, 62Nibshan,
the City of Salt, and En-gedi—six towns with
their surrounding villages.

63But the tribe of Judah could not drive out
the Jebusites, who lived in the city of Jerusalem,
so the Jebusites live there among the people of
Judah to this day.

CHAPTER 16

The Land Given to Ephraim and West Manasseh

The allotment for the descendants of Joseph
extended from the Jordan River
near Jericho, east of the springs of Jericho,
through the wilderness and into the hill
country of Bethel. 2From Bethel (that is,
Luz) it ran over to Ataroth in the territory
of the Arkites. 3Then it descended westward
to the territory of the Japhletites as far as
Lower Beth-horon, then to Gezer and over
to the Mediterranean Sea.

4This was the homeland allocated to the families
of Joseph's sons, Manasseh and Ephraim.

The Land Given to Ephraim

5The following territory was given to the clans of
the tribe of Ephraim.

The boundary of their homeland began at
Ataroth-addar in the east. From there it
ran to Upper Beth-horon, 6then on to the
Mediterranean Sea. From Micmethath on
the north, the boundary curved eastward
past Taanath-shiloh to the east of Janoah.
7From Janoah it turned southward to Ataroth
and Naarah, touched Jericho, and ended
at the Jordan River. 8From Tappuah the
boundary extended westward, following
the Kanah Ravine to the Mediterranean Sea.
This is the homeland allocated to the clans
of the tribe of Ephraim.

9In addition, some towns with their
surrounding villages in the territory allocated
to the half-tribe of Manasseh were set aside
for the tribe of Ephraim. 10They did not
drive the Canaanites out of Gezer, however,
so the people of Gezer live as slaves among
the people of Ephraim to this day.

CHAPTER 17

The Land Given to West Manasseh

The next allotment of land was given to the half-
tribe of Manasseh, the descendants of Joseph's
older son. Makir, the firstborn son of Manasseh,
was the father of Gilead. Because his descendants were experienced soldiers, the regions of
Gilead and Bashan on the east side of the Jordan
had already been given to them. 2So the allotment on the west side of the Jordan was for the
remaining families within the clans of the tribe
of Manasseh: Abiezer, Helek, Asriel, Shechem,
Hepher, and Shemida. These clans represent the
male descendants of Manasseh son of Joseph.

3However, Zelophehad, a descendant of Hepher son of Gilead, son of Makir, son of Manasseh, had no sons. He had only daughters, whose
names were Mahlah, Noah, Hoglah, Milcah, and
Tirzah. 4These women came to Eleazar the priest,
Joshua son of Nun, and the Israelite leaders and
said, "The LORD commanded Moses to give us a
grant of land along with the men of our tribe."

So Joshua gave them a grant of land along with
their uncles, as the LORD had commanded. 5As a
result, Manasseh's total allocation came to ten
parcels of land, in addition to the land of Gilead
and Bashan across the Jordan River, 6because the
female descendants of Manasseh received a
grant of land along with the male descendants.
(The land of Gilead was given to the rest of the
male descendants of Manasseh.)

7The boundary of the tribe of Manasseh
extended from the border of Asher to
Micmethath, near Shechem. Then the
boundary went south from Micmethath to
the settlement near the spring of Tappuah.
8The land surrounding Tappuah belonged
to Manasseh, but the town of Tappuah
itself, on the border of Manasseh's territory,
belonged to the tribe of Ephraim. 9From
the spring of Tappuah, the boundary of
Manasseh followed the Kanah Ravine to the
Mediterranean Sea. Several towns south of
the ravine were inside Manasseh's territory,
but they actually belonged to the tribe of
Ephraim. 10In general, however, the land
south of the ravine belonged to Ephraim,
and the land north of the ravine belonged to
Manasseh. Manasseh's boundary ran along
the northern side of the ravine and ended at
the Mediterranean Sea. North of Manasseh
was the territory of Asher, and to the east
was the territory of Issachar.

11The following towns within the territory
of Issachar and Asher, however, were given to
Manasseh: Beth-shan, Ibleam, Dor (that is,
Naphoth-dor), Endor, Taanach, and Megiddo,
each with their surrounding settlements.

12But the descendants of Manasseh were unable to occupy these towns because the Canaanites were determined to stay in that region.
13Later, however, when the Israelites became

strong enough, they forced the Canaanites to work as slaves. But they did not drive them out of the land.

14The descendants of Joseph came to Joshua and asked, "Why have you given us only one portion of land as our homeland when the LORD has blessed us with so many people?"

15Joshua replied, "If there are so many of you, and if the hill country of Ephraim is not large enough for you, clear out land for yourselves in the forest where the Perizzites and Rephaites live."

16The descendants of Joseph responded, "It's true that the hill country is not large enough for us. But all the Canaanites in the lowlands have iron chariots, both those in Beth-shan and its surrounding settlements and those in the valley of Jezreel. They are too strong for us."

17Then Joshua said to the tribes of Ephraim and Manasseh, the descendants of Joseph, "Since you are so large and strong, you will be given more than one portion. 18The forests of the hill country will be yours as well. Clear as much of the land as you wish, and take possession of its farthest corners. And you will drive out the Canaanites from the valleys, too, even though they are strong and have iron chariots."

CHAPTER 18

The Allotments of the Remaining Land

Now that the land was under Israelite control, the entire community of Israel gathered at Shiloh and set up the Tabernacle. 2But there remained seven tribes who had not yet been allotted their grants of land.

3Then Joshua asked them, "How long are you going to wait before taking possession of the remaining land the LORD, the God of your ancestors, has given to you? 4Select three men from each tribe, and I will send them out to explore the land and map it out. They will then return to me with a written report of their proposed divisions of their new homeland. 5Let them divide the land into seven sections, excluding Judah's territory in the south and Joseph's territory in the north. 6And when you record the seven divisions of the land and bring them to me, I will cast sacred lots in the presence of the LORD our God to assign land to each tribe.

7"The Levites, however, will not receive any allotment of land. Their role as priests of the LORD is their allotment. And the tribes of Gad, Reuben, and the half-tribe of Manasseh won't receive any more land, for they have already received their grant of land, which Moses, the servant of the LORD, gave them on the east side of the Jordan River."

8As the men started on their way to map out the land, Joshua commanded them, "Go and explore the land and write a description of it. Then return to me, and I will assign the land to the tribes by casting sacred lots here in the presence of the LORD at Shiloh." 9The men did as they were told and mapped the entire territory into seven sections, listing the towns in each section. They made a written record and then returned to Joshua in the camp at Shiloh. 10And there at Shiloh, Joshua cast sacred lots in the presence of the LORD to determine which tribe should have each section.

The Land Given to Benjamin

11The first allotment of land went to the clans of the tribe of Benjamin. It lay between the territory assigned to the tribes of Judah and Joseph.

12The northern boundary of Benjamin's land began at the Jordan River, went north of the slope of Jericho, then west through the hill country and the wilderness of Beth-aven. 13From there the boundary went south to Luz (that is, Bethel) and proceeded down to Ataroth-addar on the hill that lies south of Lower Beth-horon.

14The boundary then made a turn and swung south along the western edge of the hill facing Beth-horon, ending at the village of Kiriath-baal (that is, Kiriath-jearim), a town belonging to the tribe of Judah. This was the western boundary.

15The southern boundary began at the outskirts of Kiriath-jearim. From that western point it ran to the spring at the waters of Nephtoah, 16and down to the base of the mountain beside the valley of Ben-Hinnom, at the northern end of the valley of Rephaim. From there it went down the valley of Hinnom, crossing south of the slope where the Jebusites lived, and continued down to En-rogel. 17From En-rogel the boundary proceeded in a northerly direction and came to En-shemesh and on to Geliloth (which is across from the slopes of Adummim). Then it went down to the Stone of Bohan. (Bohan was Reuben's son.) 18From there it passed along the north side of the slope overlooking the Jordan Valley. The border then went down into the valley, 19ran past the north slope of Beth-hoglah, and ended at the north

(arky-AH-lo-gee)

Archaeologists dig up ancient cities and stuff to see how the people lived. They found the remains of a great tower at the site of Ur in ancient Babylon. (**Go to GENESIS 11:1-9 to read about the Tower of Babel.**) Plus, they found burned timbers and lots of ash that showed there was a fire that burned everything in Jericho. **Check it out in JOSHUA 6.**

Make your own time capsule!

Put a few things in a plastic container that tell what your life is like. (A small toy? Something from church and school? A food wrapper?) Then bury the container outside. Who knows? **Maybe your stuff will be famous someday!**

bay of the Dead Sea, which is the southern
end of the Jordan River. This was the
southern boundary.
20The eastern boundary was the Jordan
River.

These were the boundaries of the homeland allocated to the clans of the tribe of Benjamin.

The Towns Given to Benjamin

21These were the towns given to the clans of the tribe of Benjamin.

Jericho, Beth-hoglah, Emek-keziz, 22Beth-
arabah, Zemaraim, Bethel, 23Avvim, Parah,
Ophrah, 24Kephar-ammoni, Ophni, and
Geba—twelve towns with their surrounding
villages. 25Also Gibeon, Ramah, Beeroth,
26Mizpah, Kephirah, Mozah, 27Rekem,
Irpeel, Taralah, 28Zela, Haeleph, the Jebusite
town (that is, Jerusalem), Gibeah, and Kiriath-
jearim—fourteen towns with their
surrounding villages.

This was the homeland allocated to the clans of the tribe of Benjamin.

CHAPTER 19

The Land Given to Simeon

The second allotment of land went to the clans of the tribe of Simeon. Their homeland was surrounded by Judah's territory.

2Simeon's homeland included Beersheba,
Sheba, Moladah, 3Hazar-shual, Balah, Ezem,
4Eltolad, Bethul, Hormah, 5Ziklag, Beth-
marcaboth, Hazar-susah, 6Beth-lebaoth,
and Sharuhen—thirteen towns with their
surrounding villages. 7It also included Ain,
Rimmon, Ether, and Ashan—four towns with
their villages, 8including all the surrounding
villages as far south as Baalath-beer (also
known as Ramah of the Negev).

This was the homeland allocated to the clans of
the tribe of Simeon. 9Their allocation of land
came from part of what had been given to Judah
because Judah's territory was too large for them.
So the tribe of Simeon received an allocation
within the territory of Judah.

The Land Given to Zebulun

10The third allotment of land went to the clans of the tribe of Zebulun.

The boundary of Zebulun's homeland started
at Sarid. 11From there it went west, going
past Maralah, touching Dabbesheth, and
proceeding to the brook east of Jokneam.
12In the other direction, the boundary went
east from Sarid to the border of Kisloth-
tabor, and from there to Daberath and up
to Japhia. 13Then it continued east to Gath-
hepher, Eth-kazin, and Rimmon and turned
toward Neah. 14The northern boundary of
Zebulun passed Hannathon and ended at
the valley of Iphtah-el. 15The towns in these
areas included Kattath, Nahalal, Shimron,
Idalah, and Bethlehem—twelve towns with
their surrounding villages.

16The homeland allocated to the clans of the tribe of Zebulun included these towns and their surrounding villages.

The Land Given to Issachar

17The fourth allotment of land went to the clans of the tribe of Issachar.

18Its boundaries included the following
towns: Jezreel, Kesulloth, Shunem,
19Hapharaim, Shion, Anaharath, 20Rabbith,
Kishion, Ebez, 21Remeth, En-gannim,
En-haddah, and Beth-pazzez. 22The

boundary also touched Tabor, Shahazumah,
and Beth-shemesh, ending at the Jordan
River—sixteen towns with their surrounding
villages.

23The homeland allocated to the clans of the
tribe of Issachar included these towns and their
surrounding villages.

The Land Given to Asher
24The fifth allotment of land went to the clans of
the tribe of Asher.

25Its boundaries included these towns:
Helkath, Hali, Beten, Acshaph, 26Allamme-
lech, Amad, and Mishal. The boundary on
the west touched Carmel and Shihor-libnath,
27then it turned east toward Beth-dagon,
and ran as far as Zebulun in the valley of
Iphtah-el, going north to Beth-emek and
Neiel. It then continued north to Cabul,
28Abdon, Rehob, Hammon, Kanah, and as
far as Greater Sidon. 29Then the boundary
turned toward Ramah and the fortress of Tyre,
where it turned toward Hosah and came to
the Mediterranean Sea. The territory also
included Mehebel, Aczib, 30Ummah, Aphek,
and Rehob—twenty-two towns with their
surrounding villages.

31The homeland allocated to the clans of the tribe
of Asher included these towns and their surrounding villages.

The Land Given to Naphtali
32The sixth allotment of land went to the clans of
the tribe of Naphtali.

33Its boundary ran from Heleph, from the
oak at Zaanannim, and extended across to
Adami-nekeb, Jabneel, and as far as Lakkum,
ending at the Jordan River. 34The western
boundary ran past Aznoth-tabor, then to
Hukkok, and touched the border of Zebulun
in the south, the border of Asher on the
west, and the Jordan River on the east.
35The fortified towns included in this
territory were Ziddim, Zer, Hammath,
Rakkath, Kinnereth, 36Adamah, Ramah,
Hazor, 37Kedesh, Edrei, En-hazor, 38Yiron,
Migdal-el, Horem, Beth-anath, and Beth-
shemesh—nineteen towns with their
surrounding villages.

39The homeland allocated to the clans of the
tribe of Naphtali included these towns and their
surrounding villages.

The Land Given to Dan
40The seventh allotment of land went to the
clans of the tribe of Dan.

41The land allocated as their homeland
included the following towns: Zorah, Eshtaol,
Ir-shemesh, 42Shaalabbin, Aijalon, Ithlah,
43Elon, Timnah, Ekron, 44Eltekeh, Gibbethon,
Baalath, 45Jehud, Bene-berak, Gath-rimmon,
46Me-jarkon, Rakkon, and the territory across
from Joppa.
47But the tribe of Dan had trouble taking
possession of their land, so they attacked the
town of Laish. They captured it, slaughtered
its people, and settled there. They renamed
the town Dan after their ancestor.

48The homeland allocated to the clans of the tribe
of Dan included these towns and their surrounding villages.

The Land Given to Joshua
49After all the land was divided among the tribes,
the Israelites gave a piece of land to Joshua as his
allocation. 50For the LORD had said he could have
any town he wanted. He chose Timnath-serah in
the hill country of Ephraim. He rebuilt the town
and lived there.

51These are the territories that Eleazar the
priest, Joshua son of Nun, and the tribal leaders
allocated as grants of land to the tribes of Israel
by casting sacred lots in the presence of the LORD
at the entrance of the Tabernacle at Shiloh. So
the division of the land was completed.

CHAPTER 20
The Cities of Refuge
The LORD said to Joshua, 2"Now tell the Israelites
to designate the cities of refuge, as I instructed
Moses. 3Anyone who kills another person accidentally and unintentionally can run to one of
these cities; they will be places of refuge from relatives seeking revenge for the person who was
killed.
4"Upon reaching one of these cities, the one
who caused the death will appear before the elders at the city gate and present his case. They
must allow him to enter the city and give him a
place to live among them. 5If the relatives of the
victim come to avenge the killing, the leaders
must not release the slayer to them, for he killed
the other person unintentionally and without
previous hostility. 6But the slayer must stay in
that city and be tried by the local assembly,
which will render a judgment. And he must continue to live in that city until the death of the

high priest who was in office at the time of the accident. After that, he is free to return to his own home in the town from which he fled."

7 The following cities were designated as cities of refuge: Kedesh of Galilee, in the hill country of Naphtali; Shechem, in the hill country of Ephraim; and Kiriath-arba (that is, Hebron), in the hill country of Judah. 8 On the east side of the Jordan River, across from Jericho, the following cities were designated: Bezer, in the wilderness plain of the tribe of Reuben; Ramoth in Gilead, in the territory of the tribe of Gad; and Golan in Bashan, in the land of the tribe of Manasseh. 9 These cities were set apart for all the Israelites as well as the foreigners living among them. Anyone who accidentally killed another person could take refuge in one of these cities. In this way, they could escape being killed in revenge prior to standing trial before the local assembly.

CHAPTER 21

The Towns Given to the Levites

Then the leaders of the tribe of Levi came to consult with Eleazar the priest, Joshua son of Nun, and the leaders of the other tribes of Israel. 2 They came to them at Shiloh in the land of Canaan and said, "The LORD commanded Moses to give us towns to live in and pasturelands for our livestock." 3 So by the command of the LORD the people of Israel gave the Levites the following towns and pasturelands out of their own grants of land.

4 The descendants of Aaron, who were members of the Kohathite clan within the tribe of Levi, were allotted thirteen towns that were originally assigned to the tribes of Judah, Simeon, and Benjamin. 5 The other families of the Kohathite clan were allotted ten towns from the tribes of Ephraim, Dan, and the half-tribe of Manasseh.

6 The clan of Gershon was allotted thirteen towns from the tribes of Issachar, Asher, Naphtali, and the half-tribe of Manasseh in Bashan.

7 The clan of Merari was allotted twelve towns from the tribes of Reuben, Gad, and Zebulun.

8 So the Israelites obeyed the LORD's command to Moses and assigned these towns and pasturelands to the Levites by casting sacred lots.

9 The Israelites gave the following towns from the tribes of Judah and Simeon 10 to the descendants of Aaron, who were members of the Kohathite clan within the tribe of Levi, since the sacred lot fell to them first: 11 Kiriath-arba (that is, Hebron), in the hill country of Judah, along with its surrounding pasturelands. (Arba was an ancestor of Anak.) 12 But the open fields beyond the town and the surrounding villages were given to Caleb son of Jephunneh as his possession.

13 The following towns with their pasturelands were given to the descendants of Aaron the priest: Hebron (a city of refuge for those who accidentally killed someone), Libnah, 14 Jattir, Eshtemoa, 15 Holon, Debir, 16 Ain, Juttah, and Beth-shemesh—nine towns from these two tribes.

17 From the tribe of Benjamin the priests were given the following towns with their pasturelands: Gibeon, Geba, 18 Anathoth, and Almon—four towns. 19 So in all, thirteen towns with their pasturelands were given to the priests, the descendants of Aaron.

20 The rest of the Kohathite clan from the tribe of Levi was allotted the following towns and pasturelands from the tribe of Ephraim: 21 Shechem in the hill country of Ephraim (a city of refuge for those who accidentally killed someone), Gezer, 22 Kibzaim, and Beth-horon—four towns.

23 The following towns and pasturelands were allotted to the priests from the tribe of Dan: Elteke, Gibbethon, 24 Aijalon, and Gath-rimmon—four towns.

25 The half-tribe of Manasseh allotted the following towns with their pasturelands to the priests: Taanach and Gath-rimmon—two towns. 26 So in all, ten towns with their pasturelands were given to the rest of the Kohathite clan.

27 The descendants of Gershon, another clan within the tribe of Levi, received the following towns with their pasturelands from the half-tribe of Manasseh: Golan in Bashan (a city of refuge for those who accidentally killed someone) and Be-eshterah—two towns.

28 From the tribe of Issachar they received the following towns with their pasturelands: Kishion, Daberath, 29 Jarmuth, and En-gannim—four towns.

30 From the tribe of Asher they received the following towns with their pasturelands: Mishal, Abdon, 31 Helkath, and Rehob—four towns.

32 From the tribe of Naphtali they received the following towns with their pasturelands: Kedesh in Galilee (a city of refuge for those who accidentally killed someone), Hammoth-dor, and Kartan—three towns. 33 So in all, thirteen towns with their pasturelands were allotted to the clan of Gershon.

34 The rest of the Levites—the Merari clan—were given the following towns with their pasturelands from the tribe of Zebulun: Jokneam, Kartah, 35 Dimnah, and Nahalal—four towns.

36From the tribe of Reuben they received the following towns with their pasturelands: Bezer, Jahaz, 37Kedemoth, and Mephaath—four towns.

38From the tribe of Gad they received the following towns with their pasturelands: Ramoth in Gilead (a city of refuge for those who accidentally killed someone), Mahanaim, 39Heshbon, and Jazer—four towns. 40So in all, twelve towns were allotted to the clan of Merari.

41The total number of towns and pasturelands within Israelite territory given to the Levites came to forty-eight. 42Every one of these towns had pasturelands surrounding it.

43So the LORD gave to Israel all the land he had sworn to give their ancestors, and they took possession of it and settled there. 44And the LORD gave them rest on every side, just as he had solemnly promised their ancestors. None of their enemies could stand against them, for the LORD helped them conquer all their enemies. 45Not a single one of all the good promises the LORD had given to the family of Israel was left unfulfilled; everything he had spoken came true.

CHAPTER 22

The Eastern Tribes Return Home

Then Joshua called together the tribes of Reuben, Gad, and the half-tribe of Manasseh. 2He told them, "You have done as Moses, the servant of the LORD, commanded you, and you have obeyed every order I have given you. 3During all this time you have not deserted the other tribes. You have been careful to obey the commands of the LORD your God right up to the present day. 4And now the LORD your God has given the other tribes rest, as he promised them. So go back home to the land that Moses, the servant of the LORD, gave you as your possession on the east side of the Jordan River. 5But be very careful to obey all the commands and the instructions that Moses gave to you. Love the LORD your God, walk in all his ways, obey his commands, hold firmly to him, and serve him with all your heart and all your soul." 6So Joshua blessed them and sent them away, and they went home.

7Moses had given the land of Bashan, east of the Jordan River, to the half-tribe of Manasseh. (The other half of the tribe was given land west of the Jordan.) As Joshua sent them away and blessed them, 8he said to them, "Go back to your homes with the great wealth you have taken from your enemies—the vast herds of livestock, the silver, gold, bronze, and iron, and the large supply of clothing. Share the plunder with your relatives."

9So the men of Reuben, Gad, and the half-tribe of Manasseh left the rest of Israel at Shiloh in the land of Canaan. They started the journey back to their own land of Gilead, the territory that belonged to them according to the LORD's command through Moses.

The Eastern Tribes Build an Altar

10But while they were still in Canaan, and when they came to a place called Geliloth near the Jordan River, the men of Reuben, Gad, and the half-tribe of Manasseh stopped to build a large and imposing altar.

11The rest of Israel heard that the people of Reuben, Gad, and the half-tribe of Manasseh had built an altar at Geliloth at the edge of the land of Canaan, on the west side of the Jordan River. 12So the whole community of Israel gathered at Shiloh and prepared to go to war against them. 13First, however, they sent a delegation led by Phinehas son of Eleazar, the priest, to talk with the tribes of Reuben, Gad, and the half-tribe of Manasseh. 14In this delegation were ten leaders of Israel, one from each of the ten tribes, and each the head of his family within the clans of Israel.

15When they arrived in the land of Gilead, they said to the tribes of Reuben, Gad, and the half-tribe of Manasseh, 16"The whole community of the LORD demands to know why you are betraying the God of Israel. How could you turn away from the LORD and build an altar for yourselves in rebellion against him? 17Was our sin at Peor not enough? To this day we are not fully cleansed of it, even after the plague that struck the entire community of the LORD. 18And yet today you are turning away from following the LORD. If you rebel against the LORD today, he will be angry with all of us tomorrow.

19"If you need the altar because the land you possess is defiled, then join us in the LORD's land, where the Tabernacle of the LORD is situated, and share our land with us. But do not rebel against the LORD or against us by building an altar other than the one true altar of the LORD our God. 20Didn't divine anger fall on the entire community of Israel when Achan, a member of the clan of Zerah, sinned by stealing the things set apart for the LORD? He was not the only one who died because of his sin."

21Then the people of Reuben, Gad, and the half-tribe of Manasseh answered the heads of the clans of Israel: 22"The LORD, the Mighty One, is God! The LORD, the Mighty One, is God!

He knows the truth, and may Israel know it, too!
We have not built the altar in treacherous rebellion against the LORD. If we have done so, do not
spare our lives this day. 23If we have built an
altar for ourselves to turn away from the LORD
or to offer burnt offerings or grain offerings
or peace offerings, may the LORD himself punish us.
24"The truth is, we have built this altar because we fear that in the future your descendants
will say to ours, 'What right do you have to worship the LORD, the God of Israel? 25The LORD has
placed the Jordan River as a barrier between our
people and you people of Reuben and Gad. You
have no claim to the LORD.' So your descendants
may prevent our descendants from worshiping
the LORD.
26"So we decided to build the altar, not for
burnt offerings or sacrifices, 27but as a memorial. It will remind our descendants and your descendants that we, too, have the right to worship
the LORD at his sanctuary with our burnt offerings, sacrifices, and peace offerings. Then your
descendants will not be able to say to ours, 'You
have no claim to the LORD.'
28"If they say this, our descendants can reply,
'Look at this copy of the LORD's altar that our ancestors made. It is not for burnt offerings or sacrifices; it is a reminder of the relationship both of
us have with the LORD.' 29Far be it from us to rebel against the LORD or turn away from him by
building our own altar for burnt offerings, grain
offerings, or sacrifices. Only the altar of the LORD
our God that stands in front of the Tabernacle
may be used for that purpose."
30When Phinehas the priest and the leaders
of the community—the heads of the clans of Israel—heard this from the tribes of Reuben, Gad,
and the half-tribe of Manasseh, they were satisfied. 31Phinehas son of Eleazar, the priest, replied
to them, "Today we know the LORD is among us
because you have not committed this treachery
against the LORD as we thought. Instead, you have
rescued Israel from being destroyed by the hand
of the LORD."
32Then Phinehas son of Eleazar, the priest,
and the other leaders left the tribes of Reuben
and Gad in Gilead and returned to the land of
Canaan to tell the Israelites what had happened.
33And all the Israelites were satisfied and
praised God and spoke no more of war against
Reuben and Gad.
34The people of Reuben and Gad named the
altar "Witness," for they said, "It is a witness between us and them that the LORD is our God, too."

CHAPTER 23

Joshua's Final Words to Israel

The years passed, and the LORD had given the
people of Israel rest from all their enemies.
Joshua, who was now very old, 2called together
all the elders, leaders, judges, and officers of
Israel. He said to them, "I am now a very old
man. 3You have seen everything the LORD your
God has done for you during my lifetime. The
LORD your God has fought for you against your
enemies. 4I have allotted to you as your homeland all the land of the nations yet unconquered, as well as the land of those we have
already conquered—from the Jordan River to
the Mediterranean Sea in the west. 5This land
will be yours, for the LORD your God will himself
drive out all the people living there now. You
will take possession of their land, just as the
LORD your God promised you.
6"So be very careful to follow everything
Moses wrote in the Book of Instruction. Do not
deviate from it, turning either to the right or to
the left. 7Make sure you do not associate with
the other people still remaining in the land. Do
not even mention the names of their gods, much
less swear by them or serve them or worship
them. 8Rather, cling tightly to the LORD your God
as you have done until now.
9"For the LORD has driven out great and powerful nations for you, and no one has yet been
able to defeat you. 10Each one of you will put to
flight a thousand of the enemy, for the LORD your
God fights for you, just as he has promised. 11So
be very careful to love the LORD your God.
12"But if you turn away from him and cling to
the customs of the survivors of these nations remaining among you, and if you intermarry with
them, 13then know for certain that the LORD your
God will no longer drive them out of your land.
Instead, they will be a snare and a trap to you, a
whip for your backs and thorny brambles in your
eyes, and you will vanish from this good land the
LORD your God has given you.
14"Soon I will die, going the way of everything
on earth. Deep in your hearts you know that
every promise of the LORD your God has come
true. Not a single one has failed! 15But as surely as
the LORD your God has given you the good things
he promised, he will also bring disaster on you if
you disobey him. He will completely destroy you
from this good land he has given you. 16If you
break the covenant of the LORD your God by worshiping and serving other gods, his anger will
burn against you, and you will quickly vanish
from the good land he has given you."

CHAPTER 24

The LORD's Covenant Renewed

Then Joshua summoned all the tribes of Israel to
Shechem, including their elders, leaders, judges,
and officers. So they came and presented themselves to God.
2Joshua said to the people, "This is what the
LORD, the God of Israel, says: Long ago your ancestors, including Terah, the father of Abraham
and Nahor, lived beyond the Euphrates River,
and they worshiped other gods. 3But I took your
ancestor Abraham from the land beyond the
Euphrates and led him into the land of Canaan.
I gave him many descendants through his son
Isaac. 4To Isaac I gave Jacob and Esau. To Esau I
gave the mountains of Seir, while Jacob and his
children went down into Egypt.
5"Then I sent Moses and Aaron, and I brought
terrible plagues on Egypt; and afterward I
brought you out as a free people. 6But when your
ancestors arrived at the Red Sea, the Egyptians
chased after you with chariots and charioteers.
7When your ancestors cried out to the LORD, I
put darkness between you and the Egyptians.
I brought the sea crashing down on the Egyptians, drowning them. With your very own eyes
you saw what I did. Then you lived in the wilderness for many years.
8"Finally, I brought you into the land of the
Amorites on the east side of the Jordan. They
fought against you, but I destroyed them before
you. I gave you victory over them, and you took
possession of their land. 9Then Balak son of
Zippor, king of Moab, started a war against Israel. He summoned Balaam son of Beor to curse
you, 10but I would not listen to him. Instead, I
made Balaam bless you, and so I rescued you
from Balak.
11"When you crossed the Jordan River and
came to Jericho, the men of Jericho fought
against you, as did the Amorites, the Perizzites,
the Canaanites, the Hittites, the Girgashites, the
Hivites, and the Jebusites. But I gave you victory
over them. 12And I sent terror ahead of you to
drive out the two kings of the Amorites. It was
not your swords or bows that brought you victory. 13I gave you land you had not worked on,
and I gave you towns you did not build—the
towns where you are now living. I gave you vineyards and olive groves for food, though you did
not plant them.
14"So fear the LORD and serve him wholeheartedly. Put away forever the idols your ancestors
worshiped when they lived beyond the Euphrates River and in Egypt. Serve the LORD alone.
15But if you refuse to serve the LORD, then choose
today whom you will serve. Would you prefer the
gods your ancestors served beyond the Euphrates? Or will it be the gods of the Amorites in
whose land you now live? But as for me and my
family, we will serve the LORD."
16The people replied, "We would never abandon the LORD and serve other gods. 17For the
LORD our God is the one who rescued us and our
ancestors from slavery in the land of Egypt. He
performed mighty miracles before our very eyes.
As we traveled through the wilderness among
our enemies, he preserved us. 18It was the LORD
who drove out the Amorites and the other nations living here in the land. So we, too, will serve
the LORD, for he alone is our God."
19Then Joshua warned the people, "You are
not able to serve the LORD, for he is a holy and
jealous God. He will not forgive your rebellion
and your sins. 20If you abandon the LORD and
serve other gods, he will turn against you and
destroy you, even though he has been so good to
you."
21But the people answered Joshua, "No, we will
serve the LORD!"
22"You are a witness to your own decision,"
Joshua said. "You have chosen to serve the
LORD."
"Yes," they replied, "we are witnesses to what
we have said."
23"All right then," Joshua said, "destroy the
idols among you, and turn your hearts to the
LORD, the God of Israel."
24The people said to Joshua, "We will serve the
LORD our God. We will obey him alone."
25So Joshua made a covenant with the people
that day at Shechem, committing them to follow
the decrees and regulations of the LORD. 26Josh-
ua recorded these things in the Book of God's Instructions. As a reminder of their agreement, he
took a huge stone and rolled it beneath the
terebinth tree beside the Tabernacle of the
LORD.
27Joshua said to all the people, "This stone has
heard everything the LORD said to us. It will be a
witness to testify against you if you go back on
your word to God."
28Then Joshua sent all the people away to their
own homelands.

Leaders Buried in the Promised Land

29After this, Joshua son of Nun, the servant of the
LORD, died at the age of 110. 30They buried him
in the land he had been allocated, at Timnath-

serah in the hill country of Ephraim, north of
Mount Gaash.

31The people of Israel served the LORD
throughout the lifetime of Joshua and of the
elders who outlived him—those who had personally experienced all that the LORD had done
for Israel.

32The bones of Joseph, which the Israelites
had brought along with them when they left
Egypt, were buried at Shechem, in the parcel of
ground Jacob had bought from the sons of
Hamor for 100 pieces of silver. This land was located in the territory allotted to the descendants
of Joseph.

33Eleazar son of Aaron also died. He was buried in the hill country of Ephraim, in the town
of Gibeah, which had been given to his son
Phinehas.

JUDGES Leaders of the People

Look for 2 hidden messages in Judges!

No king ruled over Israel. The Bible says everyone did what they wanted to do. So in the book of Judges, you'll see lots of

- **TURNING AWAY FROM GOD**
- **TURNING BACK TO GOD**
- **TURNING AWAY FROM GOD**
- **TURNING BACK TO GOD**
- **TURNING, TURNING, AND MORE TURNING, AND— OH, YEAH—**
- **A DOZEN JUDGES**

Judges to the Rescue

God sent judges (no, not the courtroom kind) to help the Israelites. Find out what kind of judges they were in (where else?) the book of Judges. **Check out Judges 2:16-19.**

WANTED
A WOMAN JUDGE

Twelve judges. Eleven men. One woman. **Find out who she was in Judges 4.**

RRRRRRR

Cleaning House—Not!

God told the Israelites to get rid of the evil people in the Promised Land. Then God's people wouldn't be tempted by evil ways. But the Israelites didn't do it. **Read Judges 2:10-15 to find out what happened when they disobeyed.**

Manners, Schmanners

God gave Gideon a weird way to pick who would fight in the army. Thirsty for more information? (That's a joke. You'll get it when you read the story.) **Find out more in Judges 7:1-7. (Then go to Judges 7:19-22 to see who won the battle.)**

A Hair-Raising Tale

Talk about a bad hair day! **Go to Judges 16:4-21 for the world's worst haircut.**

Haircuts
Only 5,500 Shekels of Silver

Timeline

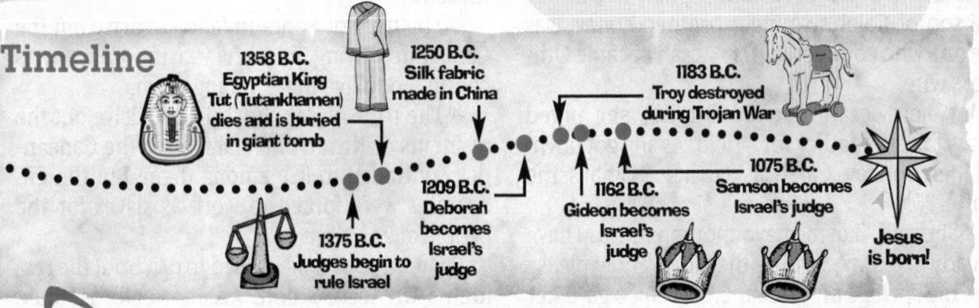
1375 B.C. Judges begin to rule Israel
1358 B.C. Egyptian King Tut (Tutankhamen) dies and is buried in giant tomb
1250 B.C. Silk fabric made in China
1209 B.C. Deborah becomes Israel's judge
1183 B.C. Troy destroyed during Trojan War
1162 B.C. Gideon becomes Israel's judge
1075 B.C. Samson becomes Israel's judge
Jesus is born!

The JESUS CONNECTION

Over and over the Israelites turned away from God, and over and over they got into terrible trouble. Each time, they came crying back to God. And each time, God felt sorry for them and sent a judge to help.

Many, many years later, God sent his Son, Jesus, to rescue all the people of the world from their sins. All we have to do is believe in Jesus, and we can be forgiven and live with him in heaven forever. **Now *that's* God's love at work!**

Judges 1 . . . page 238

CHAPTER 1

Judah and Simeon Conquer the Land

After the death of Joshua, the Israelites asked the
LORD, "Which tribe should go first to attack the
Canaanites?"
2The LORD answered, "Judah, for I have given
them victory over the land."
3The men of Judah said to their relatives from
the tribe of Simeon, "Join with us to fight against
the Canaanites living in the territory allotted to
us. Then we will help you conquer your territory." So the men of Simeon went with Judah.
4When the men of Judah attacked, the LORD
gave them victory over the Canaanites and Perizzites, and they killed 10,000 enemy warriors at
the town of Bezek. 5While at Bezek they encountered King Adoni-bezek and fought against him,
and the Canaanites and Perizzites were defeated.
6Adoni-bezek escaped, but the Israelites soon
captured him and cut off his thumbs and big
toes.
7Adoni-bezek said, "I once had seventy kings
with their thumbs and big toes cut off, eating
scraps from under my table. Now God has paid
me back for what I did to them." They took him
to Jerusalem, and he died there.
8The men of Judah attacked Jerusalem and
captured it, killing all its people and setting the
city on fire. 9Then they went down to fight the
Canaanites living in the hill country, the Negev,
and the western foothills. 10Judah marched
against the Canaanites in Hebron (formerly
called Kiriath-arba), defeating the forces of Sheshai, Ahiman, and Talmai.
11From there they went to fight against the
people living in the town of Debir (formerly
called Kiriath-sepher). 12Caleb said, "I will give
my daughter Acsah in marriage to the one who
attacks and captures Kiriath-sepher." 13Othniel,
the son of Caleb's younger brother, Kenaz, was
the one who conquered it, so Acsah became Othniel's wife.
14When Acsah married Othniel, she urged
him to ask her father for a field. As she got down
off her donkey, Caleb asked her, "What's the
matter?"
15She said, "Let me have another gift. You have
already given me land in the Negev; now please
give me springs of water, too." So Caleb gave her
the upper and lower springs.
16When the tribe of Judah left Jericho—the
city of palms—the Kenites, who were descendants of Moses' father-in-law, traveled with
them into the wilderness of Judah. They settled
among the people there, near the town of Arad
in the Negev.
17Then Judah joined with Simeon to fight
against the Canaanites living in Zephath, and
they completely destroyed the town. So the town
was named Hormah. 18In addition, Judah captured the towns of Gaza, Ashkelon, and Ekron,
along with their surrounding territories.

Israel Fails to Conquer the Land

19The LORD was with the people of Judah, and
they took possession of the hill country. But they
failed to drive out the people living in the plains,
who had iron chariots. 20The town of Hebron
was given to Caleb as Moses had promised. And
Caleb drove out the people living there, who were
descendants of the three sons of Anak.
21The tribe of Benjamin, however, failed to
drive out the Jebusites, who were living in Jerusalem. So to this day the Jebusites live in Jerusalem
among the people of Benjamin.
22The descendants of Joseph attacked the
town of Bethel, and the LORD was with them.
23They sent men to scout out Bethel (formerly
known as Luz). 24They confronted a man coming
out of the town and said to him, "Show us a way
into the town, and we will have mercy on you."
25So he showed them a way in, and they killed
everyone in the town except that man and his
family. 26Later the man moved to the land of the
Hittites, where he built a town. He named it Luz,
which is its name to this day.
27The tribe of Manasseh failed to drive out the
people living in Beth-shan, Taanach, Dor, Ibleam,
Megiddo, and all their surrounding settlements,
because the Canaanites were determined to stay
in that region. 28When the Israelites grew stronger, they forced the Canaanites to work as slaves,
but they never did drive them completely out of
the land.
29The tribe of Ephraim failed to drive out the
Canaanites living in Gezer, so the Canaanites
continued to live there among them.
30The tribe of Zebulun failed to drive out the
residents of Kitron and Nahalol, so the Canaanites continued to live among them. But the Canaanites were forced to work as slaves for the
people of Zebulun.
31The tribe of Asher failed to drive out the residents of Acco, Sidon, Ahlab, Aczib, Helbah,
Aphik, and Rehob. 32Instead, the people of Asher
moved in among the Canaanites, who controlled
the land, for they failed to drive them out.
33Likewise, the tribe of Naphtali failed to
drive out the residents of Beth-shemesh and

Beth-anath. Instead, they moved in among the Canaanites, who controlled the land. Nevertheless, the people of Beth-shemesh and Beth-anath were forced to work as slaves for the people of Naphtali.

34 As for the tribe of Dan, the Amorites forced them back into the hill country and would not let them come down into the plains. 35 The Amorites were determined to stay in Mount Heres, Aijalon, and Shaalbim, but when the descendants of Joseph became stronger, they forced the Amorites to work as slaves. 36 The boundary of the Amorites ran from Scorpion Pass to Sela and continued upward from there.

CHAPTER 2

The LORD's Messenger Comes to Bokim

The angel of the LORD went up from Gilgal to Bokim and said to the Israelites, "I brought you out of Egypt into this land that I swore to give your ancestors, and I said I would never break my covenant with you. 2 For your part, you were not to make any covenants with the people living in this land; instead, you were to destroy their altars. But you disobeyed my command. Why did you do this? 3 So now I declare that I will no longer drive out the people living in your land. They will be thorns in your sides, and their gods will be a constant temptation to you."

4 When the angel of the LORD finished speaking to all the Israelites, the people wept loudly. 5 So they called the place Bokim (which means "weeping"), and they offered sacrifices there to the LORD.

The Death of Joshua

6 After Joshua sent the people away, each of the tribes left to take possession of the land allotted to them. 7 And the Israelites served the LORD throughout the lifetime of Joshua and the leaders who outlived him—those who had seen all the great things the LORD had done for Israel.

8 Joshua son of Nun, the servant of the LORD, died at the age of 110. 9 They buried him in the land he had been allocated, at Timnath-serah in the hill country of Ephraim, north of Mount Gaash.

Israel Disobeys the LORD

10 After that generation died, another generation grew up who did not acknowledge the LORD or remember the mighty things he had done for Israel.

11 The Israelites did evil in the LORD's sight and served the images of Baal. 12 They abandoned the LORD, the God of their ancestors, who had brought them out of Egypt. They went after other gods, worshiping the gods of the people around them. And they angered the LORD. 13 They abandoned the LORD to serve Baal and the images of Ashtoreth. 14 This made the LORD burn with anger against Israel, so he handed them over to raiders who stole their possessions. He turned them over to their enemies all around, and they were no longer able to resist them. 15 Every time Israel went out to battle, the LORD fought against them, causing them to be defeated, just as he had warned. And the people were in great distress.

The LORD Rescues His People

16 Then the LORD raised up judges to rescue the Israelites from their attackers. 17 Yet Israel did not listen to the judges but prostituted themselves by worshiping other gods. How quickly they turned away from the path of their ancestors, who had walked in obedience to the LORD's commands.

18 Whenever the LORD raised up a judge over Israel, he was with that judge and rescued the people from their enemies throughout the judge's lifetime. For the LORD took pity on his people, who were burdened by oppression and suffering. 19 But when the judge died, the people returned to their corrupt ways, behaving worse than those who had lived before them. They went after other gods, serving and worshiping them. And they refused to give up their evil practices and stubborn ways.

20 So the LORD burned with anger against Israel. He said, "Because these people have violated my covenant, which I made with their ancestors, and have ignored my commands, 21 I will no longer drive out the nations that Joshua left unconquered when he died. 22 I did this to test Israel—to see whether or not they would follow the ways of the LORD as their ancestors did." 23 That is why the LORD left those nations in place. He did not quickly drive them out or allow Joshua to conquer them all.

CHAPTER 3

The Nations Left in Canaan

These are the nations that the LORD left in the land to test those Israelites who had not experienced the wars of Canaan. 2 He did this to teach warfare to generations of Israelites who had no experience in battle. 3 These are the nations: the Philistines (those living under the five

Philistine rulers), all the Canaanites, the Sidonians, and the Hivites living in the mountains of Lebanon from Mount Baal-hermon to Lebo-hamath. 4These people were left to test the Israelites—to see whether they would obey the commands the LORD had given to their ancestors through Moses.

5So the people of Israel lived among the Canaanites, Hittites, Amorites, Perizzites, Hivites, and Jebusites, 6and they intermarried with them. Israelite sons married their daughters, and Israelite daughters were given in marriage to their sons. And the Israelites served their gods.

Othniel Becomes Israel's Judge

7The Israelites did evil in the LORD's sight. They forgot about the LORD their God, and they served the images of Baal and the Asherah poles. 8Then the LORD burned with anger against Israel, and he turned them over to King Cushan-rishathaim of Aram-naharaim. And the Israelites served Cushan-rishathaim for eight years.

9But when the people of Israel cried out to the LORD for help, the LORD raised up a rescuer to save them. His name was Othniel, the son of Caleb's younger brother, Kenaz. 10The Spirit of the LORD came upon him, and he became Israel's judge. He went to war against King Cushan-rishathaim of Aram, and the LORD gave Othniel victory over him. 11So there was peace in the land for forty years. Then Othniel son of Kenaz died.

Ehud Becomes Israel's Judge

12Once again the Israelites did evil in the LORD's sight, and the LORD gave King Eglon of Moab control over Israel because of their evil. 13Eglon enlisted the Ammonites and Amalekites as allies, and then he went out and defeated Israel, taking possession of Jericho, the city of palms. 14And the Israelites served Eglon of Moab for eighteen years.

15But when the people of Israel cried out to the LORD for help, the LORD again raised up a rescuer to save them. His name was Ehud son of Gera, a left-handed man of the tribe of Benjamin. The Israelites sent Ehud to deliver their tribute money to King Eglon of Moab. 16So Ehud made a double-edged dagger that was about a foot long, and he strapped it to his right thigh, keeping it hidden under his clothing. 17He brought the tribute money to Eglon, who was very fat.

18After delivering the payment, Ehud started home with those who had helped carry the tribute. 19But when Ehud reached the stone idols near Gilgal, he turned back. He came to Eglon and said, "I have a secret message for you."

So the king commanded his servants, "Be quiet!" and he sent them all out of the room.

20Ehud walked over to Eglon, who was sitting alone in a cool upstairs room. And Ehud said, "I have a message from God for you!" As King Eglon rose from his seat, 21Ehud reached with his left hand, pulled out the dagger strapped to his right thigh, and plunged it into the king's belly. 22The dagger went so deep that the handle disappeared beneath the king's fat. So Ehud did not pull out the dagger, and the king's bowels emptied. 23Then Ehud closed and locked the doors of the room and escaped down the latrine.

24After Ehud was gone, the king's servants returned and found the doors to the upstairs room locked. They thought he might be using the latrine in the room, 25so they waited. But when the king didn't come out after a long delay, they became concerned and got a key. And when they opened the doors, they found their master dead on the floor.

26While the servants were waiting, Ehud escaped, passing the stone idols on his way to Seirah. 27When he arrived in the hill country of Ephraim, Ehud sounded a call to arms. Then he led a band of Israelites down from the hills.

28"Follow me," he said, "for the LORD has given you victory over Moab your enemy." So they followed him. And the Israelites took control of the shallow crossings of the Jordan River across from Moab, preventing anyone from crossing.

29They attacked the Moabites and killed about 10,000 of their strongest and most able-bodied warriors. Not one of them escaped. 30So Moab was conquered by Israel that day, and there was peace in the land for eighty years.

Shamgar Becomes Israel's Judge

31After Ehud, Shamgar son of Anath rescued Israel. He once killed 600 Philistines with an ox goad.

CHAPTER 4

Deborah Becomes Israel's Judge

After Ehud's death, the Israelites again did evil in the LORD's sight. 2So the LORD turned them over to King Jabin of Hazor, a Canaanite king. The commander of his army was Sisera, who lived in Harosheth-haggoyim. 3Sisera, who had 900 iron chariots, ruthlessly oppressed the Israelites for

twenty years. Then the people of Israel cried out
to the LORD for help.

4 Deborah, the wife of Lappidoth, was a prophet
who was judging Israel at that time. 5 She would
sit under the Palm of Deborah, between Ramah
and Bethel in the hill country of Ephraim, and
the Israelites would go to her for judgment. 6 One
day she sent for Barak son of Abinoam, who
lived in Kedesh in the land of Naphtali. She said to
him, "This is what the LORD, the God of Israel,
commands you: Call out 10,000 warriors from
the tribes of Naphtali and Zebulun at Mount
Tabor. 7 And I will call out Sisera, commander of
Jabin's army, along with his chariots and warriors,
to the Kishon River. There I will give you victory
over him."

8 Barak told her, "I will go, but only if you go
with me."

9 "Very well," she replied, "I will go with you.
But you will receive no honor in this venture, for
the LORD's victory over Sisera will be at the hands
of a woman." So Deborah went with Barak to Kedesh. 10 At Kedesh, Barak called together the
tribes of Zebulun and Naphtali, and 10,000 warriors went up with him. Deborah also went with
him.

11 Now Heber the Kenite, a descendant of
Moses' brother-in-law Hobab, had moved away
from the other members of his tribe and pitched
his tent by the oak of Zaanannim near Kedesh.

12 When Sisera was told that Barak son of
Abinoam had gone up to Mount Tabor, 13 he
called for all 900 of his iron chariots and all of his
warriors, and they marched from Harosheth-
haggoyim to the Kishon River.

14 Then Deborah said to Barak, "Get ready!
This is the day the LORD will give you victory over
Sisera, for the LORD is marching ahead of you."
So Barak led his 10,000 warriors down the
slopes of Mount Tabor into battle. 15 When Barak attacked, the LORD threw Sisera and all his
chariots and warriors into a panic. Sisera leaped
down from his chariot and escaped on foot.
16 Then Barak chased the chariots and the enemy army all the way to Harosheth-haggoyim,
killing all of Sisera's warriors. Not a single one
was left alive.

17 Meanwhile, Sisera ran to the tent of Jael, the
wife of Heber the Kenite, because Heber's family
was on friendly terms with King Jabin of Hazor.
18 Jael went out to meet Sisera and said to him,
"Come into my tent, sir. Come in. Don't be
afraid." So he went into her tent, and she covered
him with a blanket.

19 "Please give me some water," he said. "I'm
thirsty." So she gave him some milk from a
leather bag and covered him again.

20 "Stand at the door of the tent," he told her.
"If anybody comes and asks you if there is anyone here, say no."

21 But when Sisera fell asleep from exhaustion,
Jael quietly crept up to him with a hammer and
tent peg in her hand. Then she drove the tent peg
through his temple and into the ground, and so
he died.

22 When Barak came looking for Sisera, Jael
went out to meet him. She said, "Come, and I will
show you the man you are looking for." So he followed her into the tent and found Sisera lying
there dead, with the tent peg through his temple.

23 So on that day Israel saw God defeat Jabin,
the Canaanite king. 24 And from that time on
Israel became stronger and stronger against
King Jabin until they finally destroyed him.

CHAPTER 5
The Song of Deborah

On that day Deborah and Barak son of Abinoam
sang this song:

2 "Israel's leaders took charge,
and the people gladly followed.
Praise the LORD!

3 "Listen, you kings!
Pay attention, you mighty rulers!
For I will sing to the LORD.
I will make music to the LORD, the God
of Israel.

4 "LORD, when you set out from Seir
and marched across the fields of Edom,
the earth trembled,
and the cloudy skies poured down rain.
5 The mountains quaked in the presence
of the LORD,
the God of Mount Sinai—
in the presence of the LORD,
the God of Israel.

6 "In the days of Shamgar son of Anath,
and in the days of Jael,
people avoided the main roads,
and travelers stayed on winding pathways.
7 There were few people left in the villages
of Israel—
until Deborah arose as a mother for
Israel.
8 When Israel chose new gods,
war erupted at the city gates.
Yet not a shield or spear could be seen
among forty thousand warriors in Israel!

9 My heart is with the commanders of Israel,
with those who volunteered for war.
Praise the LORD!

10 "Consider this, you who ride on fine donkeys,
you who sit on fancy saddle blankets,
and you who walk along the road.
11 Listen to the village musicians
gathered at the watering holes.
They recount the righteous victories of the LORD
and the victories of his villagers in Israel.
Then the people of the LORD
marched down to the city gates.

12 "Wake up, Deborah, wake up!
Wake up, wake up, and sing a song!
Arise, Barak!
Lead your captives away, son of Abinoam!

13 "Down from Tabor marched the few against the nobles.
The people of the LORD marched down
against mighty warriors.
14 They came down from Ephraim—
a land that once belonged to the Amalekites;
they followed you, Benjamin, with your troops.
From Makir the commanders marched down;
from Zebulun came those who carry
a commander's staff.
15 The princes of Issachar were with Deborah and Barak.
They followed Barak, rushing into the valley.
But in the tribe of Reuben
there was great indecision.
16 Why did you sit at home among the sheepfolds—
to hear the shepherds whistle for their flocks?
Yes, in the tribe of Reuben
there was great indecision.
17 Gilead remained east of the Jordan.
And why did Dan stay home?
Asher sat unmoved at the seashore,
remaining in his harbors.
18 But Zebulun risked his life,
as did Naphtali, on the heights of the battlefield.

19 "The kings of Canaan came and fought,
at Taanach near Megiddo's springs,
but they carried off no silver treasures.
20 The stars fought from heaven.
The stars in their orbits fought against Sisera.
21 The Kishon River swept them away—
that ancient torrent, the Kishon.
March on with courage, my soul!
22 Then the horses' hooves hammered the ground,
the galloping, galloping of Sisera's mighty steeds.
23 'Let the people of Meroz be cursed,' said the angel of the LORD.
'Let them be utterly cursed,
because they did not come to help the LORD—
to help the LORD against the mighty warriors.'

24 "Most blessed among women is Jael,
the wife of Heber the Kenite.
May she be blessed above all women who live in tents.
25 Sisera asked for water,
and she gave him milk.
In a bowl fit for nobles,
she brought him yogurt.
26 Then with her left hand she reached for a tent peg,
and with her right hand for the workman's hammer.
She struck Sisera with the hammer, crushing his head.
With a shattering blow, she pierced his temples.
27 He sank, he fell,
he lay still at her feet.
And where he sank,
there he died.

28 "From the window Sisera's mother looked out.
Through the window she watched for his return, saying,
'Why is his chariot so long in coming?
Why don't we hear the sound of chariot wheels?'

29 "Her wise women answer,
and she repeats these words to herself:
30 'They must be dividing the captured plunder—
with a woman or two for every man.
There will be colorful robes for Sisera,
and colorful, embroidered robes for me.
Yes, the plunder will include
colorful robes embroidered on both sides.'

31 "LORD, may all your enemies die like Sisera!
But may those who love you rise like the
sun in all its power!"

Then there was peace in the land for forty years.

CHAPTER 6

Gideon Becomes Israel's Judge

The Israelites did evil in the LORD's sight. So the
LORD handed them over to the Midianites for
seven years. 2The Midianites were so cruel that
the Israelites made hiding places for themselves
in the mountains, caves, and strongholds. 3When-
ever the Israelites planted their crops, marauders
from Midian, Amalek, and the people of the east
would attack Israel, 4camping in the land and destroying crops as far away as Gaza. They left the
Israelites with nothing to eat, taking all the sheep,
goats, cattle, and donkeys. 5These enemy hordes,
coming with their livestock and tents, were as
thick as locusts; they arrived on droves of camels
too numerous to count. And they stayed until the
land was stripped bare. 6So Israel was reduced to
starvation by the Midianites. Then the Israelites
cried out to the LORD for help.
7When they cried out to the LORD because of
Midian, 8the LORD sent a prophet to the Israelites. He said, "This is what the LORD, the God of
Israel, says: I brought you up out of slavery in
Egypt. 9I rescued you from the Egyptians and
from all who oppressed you. I drove out your enemies and gave you their land. 10I told you, 'I am
the LORD your God. You must not worship the
gods of the Amorites, in whose land you now
live.' But you have not listened to me."
11Then the angel of the LORD came and sat beneath the great tree at Ophrah, which belonged
to Joash of the clan of Abiezer. Gideon son of
Joash was threshing wheat at the bottom of a
winepress to hide the grain from the Midianites.
12The angel of the LORD appeared to him and
said, "Mighty hero, the LORD is with you!"
13"Sir," Gideon replied, "if the LORD is with us,
why has all this happened to us? And where are
all the miracles our ancestors told us about?
Didn't they say, 'The LORD brought us up out of
Egypt'? But now the LORD has abandoned us and
handed us over to the Midianites."
14Then the LORD turned to him and said, "Go
with the strength you have, and rescue Israel
from the Midianites. I am sending you!"
15"But Lord," Gideon replied, "how can I rescue Israel? My clan is the weakest in the whole
tribe of Manasseh, and I am the least in my entire
family!"

Jars of Protection!
How did God use jars and trumpets to scare a whole army? Read JUDGES 7 to find out. Then come back for some fun!
1
God used jars, torches, and trumpets to win the battle for Gideon. Get an empty jar and some craft paint. Paint a torch and trumpet on your jar. (Leave room at the bottom for words.)
2
The army shouted, "A sword for the Lord and for Gideon!" Around your jar write, "A sword for the Lord and for [your name]."
A sword for the Lord and for Seth.
ZZZZZZZZZZZZ
Read more about God's protection in Psalm 18:1-2.
GRANDMA
Peace
A sword for the Lord and for Seth.
3
Set the jar next to your bed. Write your prayer requests and put them in the jar.
Praise the Lord!
Gideon might have been scared, but he trusted God to help him. God beat a whole army for Gideon. He'll take care of you!

Judges 7 . . . page 244

16 The LORD said to him, "I will be with you.
And you will destroy the Midianites as if you
were fighting against one man."
17 Gideon replied, "If you are truly going to
help me, show me a sign to prove that it is really
the LORD speaking to me. 18 Don't go away until I
come back and bring my offering to you."
He answered, "I will stay here until you return."
19 Gideon hurried home. He cooked a young
goat, and with a basket of flour he baked some
bread without yeast. Then, carrying the meat in a
basket and the broth in a pot, he brought them
out and presented them to the angel, who was
under the great tree.
20 The angel of God said to him, "Place the
meat and the unleavened bread on this rock, and
pour the broth over it." And Gideon did as he was
told. 21 Then the angel of the LORD touched the
meat and bread with the tip of the staff in his
hand, and fire flamed up from the rock and consumed all he had brought. And the angel of the
LORD disappeared.
22 When Gideon realized that it was the angel
of the LORD, he cried out, "Oh, Sovereign LORD,
I'm doomed! I have seen the angel of the LORD
face to face!"
23 "It is all right," the LORD replied. "Do not be
afraid. You will not die." 24 And Gideon built an
altar to the LORD there and named it Yahweh-
Shalom (which means "the LORD is peace"). The
altar remains in Ophrah in the land of the clan of
Abiezer to this day.
25 That night the LORD said to Gideon, "Take
the second bull from your father's herd, the one
that is seven years old. Pull down your father's altar to Baal, and cut down the Asherah pole standing beside it. 26 Then build an altar to the LORD
your God here on this hilltop sanctuary, laying
the stones carefully. Sacrifice the bull as a burnt
offering on the altar, using as fuel the wood of
the Asherah pole you cut down."
27 So Gideon took ten of his servants and did
as the LORD had commanded. But he did it at
night because he was afraid of the other members of his father's household and the people of
the town.
28 Early the next morning, as the people of the
town began to stir, someone discovered that the
altar of Baal had been broken down and that
the Asherah pole beside it had been cut down.
In their place a new altar had been built, and on
it were the remains of the bull that had been
sacrificed. 29 The people said to each other,
"Who did this?" And after asking around and
making a careful search, they learned that it was
Gideon, the son of Joash.
30 "Bring out your son," the men of the town
demanded of Joash. "He must die for destroying
the altar of Baal and for cutting down the Asherah pole."
31 But Joash shouted to the mob that confronted him, "Why are you defending Baal?
Will you argue his case? Whoever pleads his
case will be put to death by morning! If Baal
truly is a god, let him defend himself and destroy the one who broke down his altar!"
32 From then on Gideon was called Jerub-baal,
which means "Let Baal defend himself," because he broke down Baal's altar.

Gideon Asks for a Sign

33 Soon afterward the armies of Midian, Amalek,
and the people of the east formed an alliance
against Israel and crossed the Jordan, camping in
the valley of Jezreel. 34 Then the Spirit of the
LORD clothed Gideon with power. He blew a
ram's horn as a call to arms, and the men of the
clan of Abiezer came to him. 35 He also sent messengers throughout Manasseh, Asher, Zebulun,
and Naphtali, summoning their warriors, and all
of them responded.
36 Then Gideon said to God, "If you are truly
going to use me to rescue Israel as you promised,
37 prove it to me in this way. I will put a wool
fleece on the threshing floor tonight. If the
fleece is wet with dew in the morning but the
ground is dry, then I will know that you are going
to help me rescue Israel as you promised." 38 And
that is just what happened. When Gideon got up
early the next morning, he squeezed the fleece
and wrung out a whole bowlful of water.
39 Then Gideon said to God, "Please don't be
angry with me, but let me make one more request. Let me use the fleece for one more test.
This time let the fleece remain dry while the
ground around it is wet with dew." 40 So that
night God did as Gideon asked. The fleece was
dry in the morning, but the ground was covered
with dew.

CHAPTER 7

Gideon Defeats the Midianites

So Jerub-baal (that is, Gideon) and his army got
up early and went as far as the spring of Harod.
The armies of Midian were camped north of
them in the valley near the hill of Moreh. 2 The
LORD said to Gideon, "You have too many warriors with you. If I let all of you fight the Midianites, the Israelites will boast to me that they saved

themselves by their own strength. 3 Therefore, tell the people, 'Whoever is timid or afraid may leave this mountain and go home.'" So 22,000 of them went home, leaving only 10,000 who were willing to fight.

4 But the LORD told Gideon, "There are still too many! Bring them down to the spring, and I will test them to determine who will go with you and who will not." 5 When Gideon took his warriors down to the water, the LORD told him, "Divide the men into two groups. In one group put all those who cup water in their hands and lap it up with their tongues like dogs. In the other group put all those who kneel down and drink with their mouths in the stream." 6 Only 300 of the men drank from their hands. All the others got down on their knees and drank with their mouths in the stream.

7 The LORD told Gideon, "With these 300 men I will rescue you and give you victory over the Midianites. Send all the others home." 8 So Gideon collected the provisions and rams' horns of the other warriors and sent them home. But he kept the 300 men with him.

The Midianite camp was in the valley just below Gideon. 9 That night the LORD said, "Get up! Go down into the Midianite camp, for I have given you victory over them! 10 But if you are afraid to attack, go down to the camp with your servant Purah. 11 Listen to what the Midianites are saying, and you will be greatly encouraged. Then you will be eager to attack."

So Gideon took Purah and went down to the edge of the enemy camp. 12 The armies of Midian, Amalek, and the people of the east had settled in the valley like a swarm of locusts. Their camels were like grains of sand on the seashore—too many to count! 13 Gideon crept up just as a man was telling his companion about a dream. The man said, "I had this dream, and in my dream a loaf of barley bread came tumbling down into the Midianite camp. It hit a tent, turned it over, and knocked it flat!"

14 His companion answered, "Your dream can mean only one thing—God has given Gideon son of Joash, the Israelite, victory over Midian and all its allies!"

15 When Gideon heard the dream and its interpretation, he bowed in worship before the LORD. Then he returned to the Israelite camp and shouted, "Get up! For the LORD has given you victory over the Midianite hordes!" 16 He divided the 300 men into three groups and gave each man a ram's horn and a clay jar with a torch in it.

17 Then he said to them, "Keep your eyes on me. When I come to the edge of the camp, do just as I do. 18 As soon as I and those with me blow the rams' horns, blow your horns, too, all around the entire camp, and shout, 'For the LORD and for Gideon!'"

19 It was just after midnight, after the changing of the guard, when Gideon and the 100 men with him reached the edge of the Midianite camp. Suddenly, they blew the rams' horns and broke their clay jars. 20 Then all three groups blew their horns and broke their jars. They held the blazing torches in their left hands and the horns in their right hands, and they all shouted, "A sword for the LORD and for Gideon!"

21 Each man stood at his position around the camp and watched as all the Midianites rushed around in a panic, shouting as they ran to escape. 22 When the 300 Israelites blew their rams' horns, the LORD caused the warriors in the camp to fight against each other with their swords. Those who were not killed fled to places as far away as Beth-shittah near Zererah and to the border of Abel-meholah near Tabbath.

23 Then Gideon sent for the warriors of Naphtali, Asher, and Manasseh, who joined in chasing the army of Midian. 24 Gideon also sent messengers throughout the hill country of Ephraim, saying, "Come down to attack the Midianites. Cut them off at the shallow crossings of the Jordan River at Beth-barah."

So all the men of Ephraim did as they were told. 25 They captured Oreb and Zeeb, the two Midianite commanders, killing Oreb at the rock of Oreb, and Zeeb at the winepress of Zeeb. And they continued to chase the Midianites. Afterward the Israelites brought the heads of Oreb and Zeeb to Gideon, who was by the Jordan River.

CHAPTER 8

Gideon Kills Zebah and Zalmunna

Then the people of Ephraim asked Gideon, "Why have you treated us this way? Why didn't you send for us when you first went out to fight the Midianites?" And they argued heatedly with Gideon.

2 But Gideon replied, "What have I accomplished compared to you? Aren't even the leftover grapes of Ephraim's harvest better than the entire crop of my little clan of Abiezer? 3 God gave you victory over Oreb and Zeeb, the commanders of the Midianite army. What have I accomplished compared to that?" When the men

of Ephraim heard Gideon's answer, their anger
subsided.
4Gideon then crossed the Jordan River with
his 300 men, and though exhausted, they continued to chase the enemy. 5When they reached
Succoth, Gideon asked the leaders of the town,
"Please give my warriors some food. They are
very tired. I am chasing Zebah and Zalmunna,
the kings of Midian."
6But the officials of Succoth replied, "Catch
Zebah and Zalmunna first, and then we will feed
your army."
7So Gideon said, "After the LORD gives me victory over Zebah and Zalmunna, I will return and
tear your flesh with the thorns and briers from
the wilderness."
8From there Gideon went up to Peniel and
again asked for food, but he got the same answer.
9So he said to the people of Peniel, "After I return
in victory, I will tear down this tower."
10By this time Zebah and Zalmunna were in
Karkor with about 15,000 warriors—all that remained of the allied armies of the east, for
120,000 had already been killed. 11Gideon circled around by the caravan route east of Nobah
and Jogbehah, taking the Midianite army by surprise. 12Zebah and Zalmunna, the two Midianite
kings, fled, but Gideon chased them down and
captured all their warriors.
13After this, Gideon returned from the battle
by way of Heres Pass. 14There he captured a
young man from Succoth and demanded that he
write down the names of all the seventy-seven
officials and elders in the town. 15Gideon then
returned to Succoth and said to the leaders,
"Here are Zebah and Zalmunna. When we were
here before, you taunted me, saying, 'Catch Zebah and Zalmunna first, and then we will feed
your exhausted army.'" 16Then Gideon took the
elders of the town and taught them a lesson,
punishing them with thorns and briers from the
wilderness. 17He also tore down the tower of
Peniel and killed all the men in the town.
18Then Gideon asked Zebah and Zalmunna,
"The men you killed at Tabor—what were they
like?"
"Like you," they replied. "They all had the look
of a king's son."
19"They were my brothers, the sons of my own
mother!" Gideon exclaimed. "As surely as the
LORD lives, I wouldn't kill you if you hadn't killed
them."
20Turning to Jether, his oldest son, he said,
"Kill them!" But Jether did not draw his sword,
for he was only a boy and was afraid.
21Then Zebah and Zalmunna said to Gideon,
"Be a man! Kill us yourself!" So Gideon killed
them both and took the royal ornaments from
the necks of their camels.

Gideon's Sacred Ephod

22Then the Israelites said to Gideon, "Be our
ruler! You and your son and your grandson will
be our rulers, for you have rescued us from
Midian."
23But Gideon replied, "I will not rule over you,
nor will my son. The LORD will rule over you!
24However, I do have one request—that each of
you give me an earring from the plunder you collected from your fallen enemies." (The enemies,
being Ishmaelites, all wore gold earrings.)
25"Gladly!" they replied. They spread out a
cloak, and each one threw in a gold earring he
had gathered from the plunder. 26The weight of
the gold earrings was forty-three pounds, not including the royal ornaments and pendants, the
purple clothing worn by the kings of Midian, or
the chains around the necks of their camels.
27Gideon made a sacred ephod from the gold
and put it in Ophrah, his hometown. But soon all
the Israelites prostituted themselves by worshiping it, and it became a trap for Gideon and
his family.
28That is the story of how the people of Israel
defeated Midian, which never recovered.
Throughout the rest of Gideon's lifetime—about
forty years—there was peace in the land.
29Then Gideon son of Joash returned home.
30He had seventy sons born to him, for he had
many wives. 31He also had a concubine in Shechem, who gave birth to a son, whom he named
Abimelech. 32Gideon died when he was very old,
and he was buried in the grave of his father, Joash, at Ophrah in the land of the clan of Abiezer.
33As soon as Gideon died, the Israelites prostituted themselves by worshiping the images of
Baal, making Baal-berith their god. 34They forgot
the LORD their God, who had rescued them from
all their enemies surrounding them. 35Nor did
they show any loyalty to the family of Jerub-baal
(that is, Gideon), despite all the good he had done
for Israel.

CHAPTER 9

Abimelech Rules over Shechem

One day Gideon's son Abimelech went to Shechem to visit his uncles—his mother's brothers.
He said to them and to the rest of his mother's
family, 2"Ask the leading citizens of Shechem
whether they want to be ruled by all seventy of

Gideon's sons or by one man. And remember
that I am your own flesh and blood!"
3 So Abimelech's uncles gave his message to all
the citizens of Shechem on his behalf. And after
listening to this proposal, the people of Shechem
decided in favor of Abimelech because he was
their relative. 4 They gave him seventy silver
coins from the temple of Baal-berith, which he
used to hire some reckless troublemakers who
agreed to follow him. 5 He went to his father's
home at Ophrah, and there, on one stone, they
killed all seventy of his half brothers, the sons of
Gideon. But the youngest brother, Jotham, escaped and hid.
6 Then all the leading citizens of Shechem and
Beth-millo called a meeting under the oak beside the pillar at Shechem and made Abimelech
their king.

Jotham's Parable

7 When Jotham heard about this, he climbed to
the top of Mount Gerizim and shouted,

"Listen to me, citizens of Shechem!
Listen to me if you want God to listen
to you!
8 Once upon a time the trees decided to
choose a king.
First they said to the olive tree,
'Be our king!'
9 But the olive tree refused, saying,
'Should I quit producing the olive oil
that blesses both God and people,
just to wave back and forth over the trees?'

10 "Then they said to the fig tree,
'You be our king!'
11 But the fig tree also refused, saying,
'Should I quit producing my sweet fruit
just to wave back and forth over the trees?'

12 "Then they said to the grapevine,
'You be our king!'
13 But the grapevine also refused, saying,
'Should I quit producing the wine
that cheers both God and people,
just to wave back and forth over the
trees?'

14 "Then all the trees finally turned to the
thornbush and said,
'Come, you be our king!'
15 And the thornbush replied to the trees,
'If you truly want to make me your king,
come and take shelter in my shade.
If not, let fire come out from me
and devour the cedars of Lebanon.'"

16 Jotham continued, "Now make sure you
have acted honorably and in good faith by making Abimelech your king, and that you have done
right by Gideon and all of his descendants. Have
you treated him with the honor he deserves for
all he accomplished? 17 For he fought for you and
risked his life when he rescued you from the
Midianites. 18 But today you have revolted
against my father and his descendants, killing
his seventy sons on one stone. And you have chosen his slave woman's son, Abimelech, to be your
king just because he is your relative.
19 "If you have acted honorably and in good
faith toward Gideon and his descendants today,
then may you find joy in Abimelech, and may he
find joy in you. 20 But if you have not acted in
good faith, then may fire come out from Abimelech and devour the leading citizens of Shechem
and Beth-millo; and may fire come out from the
citizens of Shechem and Beth-millo and devour
Abimelech!"
21 Then Jotham escaped and lived in Beer because he was afraid of his brother Abimelech.

Shechem Rebels against Abimelech

22 After Abimelech had ruled over Israel for three
years, 23 God sent a spirit that stirred up trouble
between Abimelech and the leading citizens of
Shechem, and they revolted. 24 God was punishing Abimelech for murdering Gideon's seventy
sons, and the citizens of Shechem for supporting
him in this treachery of murdering his brothers.
25 The citizens of Shechem set an ambush for
Abimelech on the hilltops and robbed everyone
who passed that way. But someone warned
Abimelech about their plot.
26 One day Gaal son of Ebed moved to Shechem with his brothers and gained the confidence of the leading citizens of Shechem.
27 During the annual harvest festival at Shechem,
held in the temple of the local god, the wine
flowed freely, and everyone began cursing Abimelech. 28 "Who is Abimelech?" Gaal shouted.
"He's not a true son of Shechem, so why should
we be his servants? He's merely the son of Gideon, and this Zebul is merely his deputy. Serve the
true sons of Hamor, the founder of Shechem.
Why should we serve Abimelech? 29 If I were in
charge here, I would get rid of Abimelech. I would
say to him, 'Get some soldiers, and come out and
fight!'"
30 But when Zebul, the leader of the city, heard
what Gaal was saying, he was furious. 31 He sent
messengers to Abimelech in Arumah, telling him,

"Gaal son of Ebed and his brothers have come to live in Shechem, and now they are inciting the city to rebel against you. 32Come by night with an army and hide out in the fields. 33In the morning, as soon as it is daylight, attack the city. When Gaal and those who are with him come out against you, you can do with them as you wish."

34So Abimelech and all his men went by night and split into four groups, stationing themselves around Shechem. 35Gaal was standing at the city gates when Abimelech and his army came out of hiding. 36When Gaal saw them, he said to Zebul, "Look, there are people coming down from the hilltops!"

Zebul replied, "It's just the shadows on the hills that look like men."

37But again Gaal said, "No, people are coming down from the hills. And another group is coming down the road past the Diviners' Oak."

38Then Zebul turned on him and asked, "Now where is that big mouth of yours? Wasn't it you that said, 'Who is Abimelech, and why should we be his servants?' The men you mocked are right outside the city! Go out and fight them!"

39So Gaal led the leading citizens of Shechem into battle against Abimelech. 40But Abimelech chased him, and many of Shechem's men were wounded and fell along the road as they retreated to the city gate. 41Abimelech returned to Arumah, and Zebul drove Gaal and his brothers out of Shechem.

42The next day the people of Shechem went out into the fields to battle. When Abimelech heard about it, 43he divided his men into three groups and set an ambush in the fields. When Abimelech saw the people coming out of the city, he and his men jumped up from their hiding places and attacked them. 44Abimelech and his group stormed the city gate to keep the men of Shechem from getting back in, while Abimelech's other two groups cut them down in the fields. 45The battle went on all day before Abimelech finally captured the city. He killed the people, leveled the city, and scattered salt all over the ground.

46When the leading citizens who lived in the tower of Shechem heard what had happened, they ran and hid in the temple of Baal-berith. 47Someone reported to Abimelech that the citizens had gathered in the temple, 48so he led his forces to Mount Zalmon. He took an ax and chopped some branches from a tree, then put them on his shoulder. "Quick, do as I have done!" he told his men. 49So each of them cut down some branches, following Abimelech's example. They piled the branches against the walls of the temple and set them on fire. So all the people who had lived in the tower of Shechem died—about 1,000 men and women.

50Then Abimelech attacked the town of Thebez and captured it. 51But there was a strong tower inside the town, and all the men and women—the entire population—fled to it. They barricaded themselves in and climbed up to the roof of the tower. 52Abimelech followed them to attack the tower. But as he prepared to set fire to the entrance, 53a woman on the roof dropped a millstone that landed on Abimelech's head and crushed his skull.

54He quickly said to his young armor bearer, "Draw your sword and kill me! Don't let it be said that a woman killed Abimelech!" So the young man ran him through with his sword, and he died. 55When Abimelech's men saw that he was dead, they disbanded and returned to their homes.

56In this way, God punished Abimelech for the evil he had done against his father by murdering his seventy brothers. 57God also punished the men of Shechem for all their evil. So the curse of Jotham son of Gideon was fulfilled.

CHAPTER 10

Tola Becomes Israel's Judge

After Abimelech died, Tola son of Puah, son of Dodo, was the next person to rescue Israel. He was from the tribe of Issachar but lived in the town of Shamir in the hill country of Ephraim. 2He judged Israel for twenty-three years. When he died, he was buried in Shamir.

Jair Becomes Israel's Judge

3After Tola died, Jair from Gilead judged Israel for twenty-two years. 4His thirty sons rode around on thirty donkeys, and they owned thirty towns in the land of Gilead, which are still called the Towns of Jair. 5When Jair died, he was buried in Kamon.

The Ammonites Oppress Israel

6Again the Israelites did evil in the Lord's sight. They served the images of Baal and Ashtoreth, and the gods of Aram, Sidon, Moab, Ammon, and Philistia. They abandoned the Lord and no longer served him at all. 7So the Lord burned with anger against Israel, and he turned them over to the Philistines and the Ammonites, 8who began to oppress them that year. For eighteen years they oppressed all the Israelites east of the Jordan River in the land of the Amorites (that is, in Gilead). 9The Ammonites also crossed to the

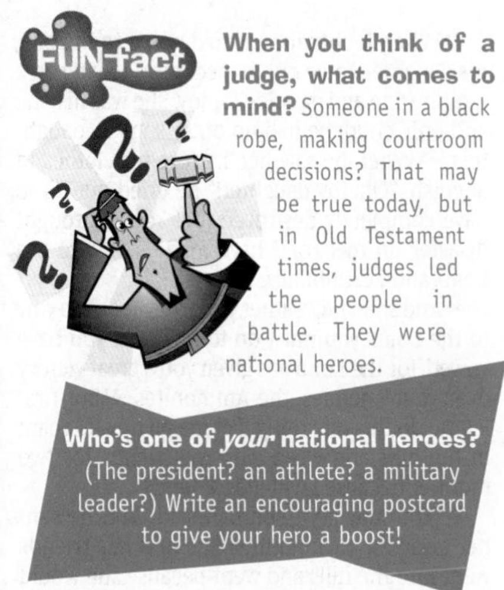

When you think of a judge, what comes to mind? Someone in a black robe, making courtroom decisions? That may be true today, but in Old Testament times, judges led the people in battle. They were national heroes.

Who's one of *your* national heroes? (The president? an athlete? a military leader?) Write an encouraging postcard to give your hero a boost!

west side of the Jordan and attacked Judah, Benjamin, and Ephraim.
The Israelites were in great distress. 10Finally,
they cried out to the LORD for help, saying, "We
have sinned against you because we have abandoned you as our God and have served the images of Baal."
11The LORD replied, "Did I not rescue you from
the Egyptians, the Amorites, the Ammonites, the
Philistines, 12the Sidonians, the Amalekites, and
the Maonites? When they oppressed you, you
cried out to me for help, and I rescued you. 13Yet
you have abandoned me and served other gods.
So I will not rescue you anymore. 14Go and cry
out to the gods you have chosen! Let them rescue
you in your hour of distress!"
15But the Israelites pleaded with the LORD and
said, "We have sinned. Punish us as you see fit,
only rescue us today from our enemies." 16Then
the Israelites put aside their foreign gods and
served the LORD. And he was grieved by their
misery.
17At that time the armies of Ammon had gathered for war and were camped in Gilead, and the
people of Israel assembled and camped at
Mizpah. 18The leaders of Gilead said to each
other, "Whoever attacks the Ammonites first
will become ruler over all the people of Gilead."

CHAPTER 11

Jephthah Becomes Israel's Judge

Now Jephthah of Gilead was a great warrior. He
was the son of Gilead, but his mother was a prostitute. 2Gilead's wife also had several sons, and
when these half brothers grew up, they chased
Jephthah off the land. "You will not get any of
our father's inheritance," they said, "for you are
the son of a prostitute." 3So Jephthah fled from
his brothers and lived in the land of Tob. Soon he
had a band of worthless rebels following him.
4At about this time, the Ammonites began
their war against Israel. 5When the Ammonites
attacked, the elders of Gilead sent for Jephthah in
the land of Tob. 6The elders said, "Come and be
our commander! Help us fight the Ammonites!"
7But Jephthah said to them, "Aren't you the
ones who hated me and drove me from my father's house? Why do you come to me now when
you're in trouble?"
8"Because we need you," the elders replied. "If
you lead us in battle against the Ammonites, we
will make you ruler over all the people of Gilead."
9Jephthah said to the elders, "Let me get this
straight. If I come with you and if the LORD gives
me victory over the Ammonites, will you really
make me ruler over all the people?"
10"The LORD is our witness," the elders replied. "We promise to do whatever you say."
11So Jephthah went with the elders of Gilead,
and the people made him their ruler and commander of the army. At Mizpah, in the presence
of the LORD, Jephthah repeated what he had said
to the elders.
12Then Jephthah sent messengers to the king
of Ammon, asking, "Why have you come out to
fight against my land?"
13The king of Ammon answered Jephthah's
messengers, "When the Israelites came out of
Egypt, they stole my land from the Arnon River to
the Jabbok River and all the way to the Jordan.
Now then, give back the land peaceably."
14Jephthah sent this message back to the
Ammonite king:

> 15"This is what Jephthah says: Israel did
> not steal any land from Moab or Ammon.
> 16When the people of Israel arrived at
> Kadesh on their journey from Egypt after
> crossing the Red Sea, 17they sent messengers
> to the king of Edom asking for permission to
> pass through his land. But their request was
> denied. Then they asked the king of Moab for
> similar permission, but he wouldn't let them
> pass through either. So the people of Israel
> stayed in Kadesh.
> 18"Finally, they went around Edom and
> Moab through the wilderness. They traveled
> along Moab's eastern border and camped on
> the other side of the Arnon River. But they

never once crossed the Arnon River into
Moab, for the Arnon was the border of Moab.
19"Then Israel sent messengers to King
Sihon of the Amorites, who ruled from
Heshbon, asking for permission to cross
through his land to get to their destination.
20But King Sihon didn't trust Israel to pass
through his land. Instead, he mobilized his
army at Jahaz and attacked them. 21But the
LORD, the God of Israel, gave his people
victory over King Sihon. So Israel took
control of all the land of the Amorites, who
lived in that region, 22from the Arnon River
to the Jabbok River, and from the eastern
wilderness to the Jordan.
23"So you see, it was the LORD, the God
of Israel, who took away the land from the
Amorites and gave it to Israel. Why, then,
should we give it back to you? 24You keep
whatever your god Chemosh gives you, and
we will keep whatever the LORD our God
gives us. 25Are you any better than Balak son
of Zippor, king of Moab? Did he try to make a
case against Israel for disputed land? Did he
go to war against them?
26"Israel has been living here for 300 years,
inhabiting Heshbon and its surrounding
settlements, all the way to Aroer and its
settlements, and in all the towns along the
Arnon River. Why have you made no effort
to recover it before now? 27Therefore, I have
not sinned against you. Rather, you have
wronged me by attacking me. Let the LORD,
who is judge, decide today which of us is
right—Israel or Ammon."

28But the king of Ammon paid no attention to
Jephthah's message.

Jephthah's Vow

29At that time the Spirit of the LORD came upon
Jephthah, and he went throughout the land of Gilead and Manasseh, including Mizpah in Gilead,
and from there he led an army against the Ammonites. 30And Jephthah made a vow to the LORD.
He said, "If you give me victory over the Ammonites, 31I will give to the LORD whatever comes out
of my house to meet me when I return in triumph.
I will sacrifice it as a burnt offering."
32So Jephthah led his army against the Ammonites, and the LORD gave him victory. 33He
crushed the Ammonites, devastating about
twenty towns from Aroer to an area near Minnith
and as far away as Abel-keramim. In this way
Israel defeated the Ammonites.

34When Jephthah returned home to Mizpah,
his daughter came out to meet him, playing on a
tambourine and dancing for joy. She was his one
and only child; he had no other sons or daughters. 35When he saw her, he tore his clothes in
anguish. "Oh, my daughter!" he cried out. "You
have completely destroyed me! You've brought
disaster on me! For I have made a vow to the
LORD, and I cannot take it back."
36And she said, "Father, if you have made a vow
to the LORD, you must do to me what you have
vowed, for the LORD has given you a great victory
over your enemies, the Ammonites. 37But first
let me do this one thing: Let me go up and roam
in the hills and weep with my friends for two
months, because I will die a virgin."
38"You may go," Jephthah said. And he sent
her away for two months. She and her friends
went into the hills and wept because she would
never have children. 39When she returned
home, her father kept the vow he had made, and
she died a virgin.
So it has become a custom in Israel 40for
young Israelite women to go away for four days
each year to lament the fate of Jephthah's
daughter.

CHAPTER 12

Ephraim Fights with Jephthah

Then the people of Ephraim mobilized an army
and crossed over the Jordan River to Zaphon.
They sent this message to Jephthah: "Why didn't
you call for us to help you fight against the Ammonites? We are going to burn down your house
with you in it!"
2Jephthah replied, "I summoned you at the
beginning of the dispute, but you refused to
come! You failed to help us in our struggle
against Ammon. 3So when I realized you
weren't coming, I risked my life and went to
battle without you, and the LORD gave me victory over the Ammonites. So why have you now
come to fight me?"
4The people of Ephraim responded, "You men
of Gilead are nothing more than fugitives from
Ephraim and Manasseh." So Jephthah gathered
all the men of Gilead and attacked the men of
Ephraim and defeated them.
5Jephthah captured the shallow crossings of
the Jordan River, and whenever a fugitive from
Ephraim tried to go back across, the men of Gilead would challenge him. "Are you a member of
the tribe of Ephraim?" they would ask. If the man
said, "No, I'm not," 6they would tell him to say
"Shibboleth." If he was from Ephraim, he would

say "Sibboleth," because people from Ephraim
cannot pronounce the word correctly. Then they
would take him and kill him at the shallow crossings of the Jordan. In all, 42,000 Ephraimites
were killed at that time.
7Jephthah judged Israel for six years. When
he died, he was buried in one of the towns of
Gilead.

Ibzan Becomes Israel's Judge

8After Jephthah died, Ibzan from Bethlehem
judged Israel. 9He had thirty sons and thirty
daughters. He sent his daughters to marry men
outside his clan, and he brought in thirty young
women from outside his clan to marry his sons.
Ibzan judged Israel for seven years. 10When he
died, he was buried at Bethlehem.

Elon Becomes Israel's Judge

11After Ibzan died, Elon from the tribe of Zebulun judged Israel for ten years. 12When he died,
he was buried at Aijalon in Zebulun.

Abdon Becomes Israel's Judge

13After Elon died, Abdon son of Hillel, from Pirathon, judged Israel. 14He had forty sons and
thirty grandsons, who rode on seventy donkeys.
He judged Israel for eight years. 15When he died,
he was buried at Pirathon in Ephraim, in the hill
country of the Amalekites.

CHAPTER 13

The Birth of Samson

Again the Israelites did evil in the LORD's sight, so
the LORD handed them over to the Philistines,
who oppressed them for forty years.
2In those days a man named Manoah from the
tribe of Dan lived in the town of Zorah. His wife
was unable to become pregnant, and they had no
children. 3The angel of the LORD appeared to
Manoah's wife and said, "Even though you have
been unable to have children, you will soon become pregnant and give birth to a son. 4So be
careful; you must not drink wine or any other alcoholic drink nor eat any forbidden food. 5You
will become pregnant and give birth to a son, and
his hair must never be cut. For he will be dedicated to God as a Nazirite from birth. He will begin to rescue Israel from the Philistines."
6The woman ran and told her husband, "A
man of God appeared to me! He looked like one
of God's angels, terrifying to see. I didn't ask
where he was from, and he didn't tell me his
name. 7But he told me, 'You will become pregnant and give birth to a son. You must not drink
wine or any other alcoholic drink nor eat any forbidden food. For your son will be dedicated to
God as a Nazirite from the moment of his birth
until the day of his death.'"
8Then Manoah prayed to the LORD, saying,
"Lord, please let the man of God come back to us
again and give us more instructions about this
son who is to be born."
9God answered Manoah's prayer, and the angel of God appeared once again to his wife as she
was sitting in the field. But her husband, Manoah, was not with her. 10So she quickly ran and
told her husband, "The man who appeared to me
the other day is here again!"
11Manoah ran back with his wife and asked,
"Are you the man who spoke to my wife the other
day?"
"Yes," he replied, "I am."
12So Manoah asked him, "When your words
come true, what kind of rules should govern the
boy's life and work?"
13The angel of the LORD replied, "Be sure your
wife follows the instructions I gave her. 14She
must not eat grapes or raisins, drink wine or any
other alcoholic drink, or eat any forbidden
food."
15Then Manoah said to the angel of the LORD,
"Please stay here until we can prepare a young
goat for you to eat."
16"I will stay," the angel of the LORD replied,
"but I will not eat anything. However, you may
prepare a burnt offering as a sacrifice to the
LORD." (Manoah didn't realize it was the angel of
the LORD.)
17Then Manoah asked the angel of the LORD,
"What is your name? For when all this comes
true, we want to honor you."
18"Why do you ask my name?" the angel of
the LORD replied. "It is too wonderful for you to
understand."
19Then Manoah took a young goat and a grain
offering and offered it on a rock as a sacrifice to
the LORD. And as Manoah and his wife watched,
the LORD did an amazing thing. 20As the flames
from the altar shot up toward the sky, the angel
of the LORD ascended in the fire. When Manoah
and his wife saw this, they fell with their faces to
the ground.
21The angel did not appear again to Manoah
and his wife. Manoah finally realized it was the
angel of the LORD, 22and he said to his wife, "We
will certainly die, for we have seen God!"
23But his wife said, "If the LORD were going to
kill us, he wouldn't have accepted our burnt
offering and grain offering. He wouldn't have

appeared to us and told us this wonderful thing
and done these miracles."
24 When her son was born, she named him
Samson. And the LORD blessed him as he grew
up. 25 And the Spirit of the LORD began to stir him
while he lived in Mahaneh-dan, which is located
between the towns of Zorah and Eshtaol.

CHAPTER 14
Samson's Riddle

One day when Samson was in Timnah, one of the
Philistine women caught his eye. 2 When he returned home, he told his father and mother, "A
young Philistine woman in Timnah caught my
eye. I want to marry her. Get her for me."
3 His father and mother objected. "Isn't there
even one woman in our tribe or among all the
Israelites you could marry?" they asked. "Why
must you go to the pagan Philistines to find a
wife?"

But Samson told his father, "Get her for me!
She looks good to me." 4 His father and mother
didn't realize the LORD was at work in this, creating an opportunity to work against the Philistines, who ruled over Israel at that time.
5 As Samson and his parents were going down
to Timnah, a young lion suddenly attacked Samson near the vineyards of Timnah. 6 At that moment the Spirit of the LORD came powerfully
upon him, and he ripped the lion's jaws apart
with his bare hands. He did it as easily as if it
were a young goat. But he didn't tell his father or
mother about it. 7 When Samson arrived in
Timnah, he talked with the woman and was very
pleased with her.
8 Later, when he returned to Timnah for the
wedding, he turned off the path to look at the
carcass of the lion. And he found that a swarm of
bees had made some honey in the carcass. 9 He
scooped some of the honey into his hands and
ate it along the way. He also gave some to his
father and mother, and they ate it. But he didn't
tell them he had taken the honey from the carcass of the lion.
10 As his father was making final arrangements for the marriage, Samson threw a party at
Timnah, as was the custom for elite young men.
11 When the bride's parents saw him, they selected thirty young men from the town to be his
companions.
12 Samson said to them, "Let me tell you a riddle. If you solve my riddle during these seven
days of the celebration, I will give you thirty fine
linen robes and thirty sets of festive clothing.
13 But if you can't solve it, then you must give me
thirty fine linen robes and thirty sets of festive
clothing."

"All right," they agreed, "let's hear your riddle."
14 So he said:

"Out of the one who eats came something to
eat;
out of the strong came something sweet."

Three days later they were still trying to figure
it out. 15 On the fourth day they said to Samson's
wife, "Entice your husband to explain the riddle
for us, or we will burn down your father's house
with you in it. Did you invite us to this party just
to make us poor?"
16 So Samson's wife came to him in tears and
said, "You don't love me; you hate me! You have
given my people a riddle, but you haven't told me
the answer."

"I haven't even given the answer to my father
or mother," he replied. "Why should I tell you?"
17 So she cried whenever she was with him and
kept it up for the rest of the celebration. At last,
on the seventh day he told her the answer because she was tormenting him with her nagging.
Then she explained the riddle to the young men.
18 So before sunset of the seventh day, the
men of the town came to Samson with their
answer:

"What is sweeter than honey?
What is stronger than a lion?"

Samson replied, "If you hadn't plowed with my
heifer, you wouldn't have solved my riddle!"
19 Then the Spirit of the LORD came powerfully
upon him. He went down to the town of Ashkelon, killed thirty men, took their belongings, and
gave their clothing to the men who had solved
his riddle. But Samson was furious about what
had happened, and he went back home to live
with his father and mother. 20 So his wife was
given in marriage to the man who had been Samson's best man at the wedding.

CHAPTER 15
Samson's Vengeance on the Philistines

Later on, during the wheat harvest, Samson took
a young goat as a present to his wife. He said, "I'm
going into my wife's room to sleep with her," but
her father wouldn't let him in.
2 "I truly thought you must hate her," her father explained, "so I gave her in marriage to your
best man. But look, her younger sister is even
more beautiful than she is. Marry her instead."
3 Samson said, "This time I cannot be blamed

for everything I am going to do to you Philistines." 4Then he went out and caught 300 foxes.
He tied their tails together in pairs, and he fastened a torch to each pair of tails. 5Then he lit the
torches and let the foxes run through the grain
fields of the Philistines. He burned all their grain
to the ground, including the sheaves and the uncut grain. He also destroyed their vineyards and
olive groves.

6"Who did this?" the Philistines demanded.

"Samson," was the reply, "because his father-
in-law from Timnah gave Samson's wife to be
married to his best man." So the Philistines went
and got the woman and her father and burned
them to death.

7"Because you did this," Samson vowed, "I
won't rest until I take my revenge on you!" 8So he
attacked the Philistines with great fury and
killed many of them. Then he went to live in a
cave in the rock of Etam.

9The Philistines retaliated by setting up camp
in Judah and spreading out near the town of Lehi.
10The men of Judah asked the Philistines, "Why
are you attacking us?"

The Philistines replied, "We've come to capture Samson. We've come to pay him back for
what he did to us."

11So 3,000 men of Judah went down to get
Samson at the cave in the rock of Etam. They said
to Samson, "Don't you realize the Philistines rule
over us? What are you doing to us?"

But Samson replied, "I only did to them what
they did to me."

12But the men of Judah told him, "We have
come to tie you up and hand you over to the Philistines."

"All right," Samson said. "But promise that you
won't kill me yourselves."

13"We will only tie you up and hand you over
to the Philistines," they replied. "We won't kill
you." So they tied him up with two new ropes and
brought him up from the rock.

14As Samson arrived at Lehi, the Philistines
came shouting in triumph. But the Spirit of the
LORD came powerfully upon Samson, and he
snapped the ropes on his arms as if they were
burnt strands of flax, and they fell from his
wrists. 15Then he found the jawbone of a recently killed donkey. He picked it up and killed
1,000 Philistines with it. 16Then Samson said,

"With the jawbone of a donkey,
    I've piled them in heaps!
With the jawbone of a donkey,
    I've killed a thousand men!"

17When he finished his boasting, he threw away
the jawbone; and the place was named Jawbone
Hill.

18Samson was now very thirsty, and he cried
out to the LORD, "You have accomplished this
great victory by the strength of your servant.
Must I now die of thirst and fall into the hands of
these pagans?" 19So God caused water to gush
out of a hollow in the ground at Lehi, and Samson
was revived as he drank. Then he named that
place "The Spring of the One Who Cried Out,"
and it is still in Lehi to this day.

20Samson judged Israel for twenty years during the period when the Philistines dominated
the land.

CHAPTER 16

Samson Carries Away Gaza's Gates

One day Samson went to the Philistine town of
Gaza and spent the night with a prostitute.
2Word soon spread that Samson was there, so
the men of Gaza gathered together and waited all
night at the town gates. They kept quiet during
the night, saying to themselves, "When the light
of morning comes, we will kill him."

3But Samson stayed in bed only until midnight. Then he got up, took hold of the doors of
the town gate, including the two posts, and lifted
them up, bar and all. He put them on his shoulders and carried them all the way to the top of
the hill across from Hebron.

Samson and Delilah

4Some time later Samson fell in love with a
woman named Delilah, who lived in the valley of
Sorek. 5The rulers of the Philistines went to her
and said, "Entice Samson to tell you what makes
him so strong and how he can be overpowered
and tied up securely. Then each of us will give
you 1,100 pieces of silver."

6So Delilah said to Samson, "Please tell me
what makes you so strong and what it would take
to tie you up securely."

7Samson replied, "If I were tied up with seven
new bowstrings that have not yet been dried, I
would become as weak as anyone else."

8So the Philistine rulers brought Delilah seven
new bowstrings, and she tied Samson up with
them. 9She had hidden some men in one of the
inner rooms of her house, and she cried out,
"Samson! The Philistines have come to capture
you!" But Samson snapped the bowstrings as a
piece of string snaps when it is burned by a fire.
So the secret of his strength was not discovered.

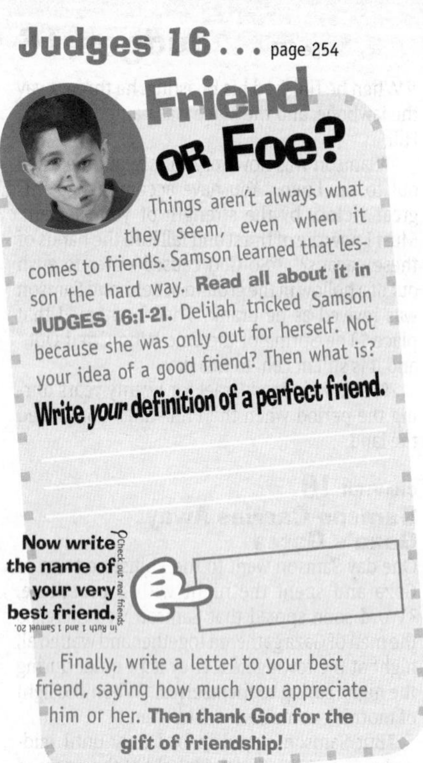

Judges 16 . . . page 254
Friend or Foe?
Things aren't always what they seem, even when it comes to friends. Samson learned that lesson the hard way. Read all about it in JUDGES 16:1-21. Delilah tricked Samson because she was only out for herself. Not your idea of a good friend? Then what is?
Write your definition of a perfect friend.
Now write the name of your very best friend.
Check out real friends in Ruth 1 and 1 Samuel 20.
Finally, write a letter to your best friend, saying how much you appreciate him or her. Then thank God for the gift of friendship!

10 Afterward Delilah said to him, "You've been
making fun of me and telling me lies! Now please
tell me how you can be tied up securely."
11 Samson replied, "If I were tied up with
brand-new ropes that had never been used, I
would become as weak as anyone else."
12 So Delilah took new ropes and tied him up
with them. The men were hiding in the inner
room as before, and again Delilah cried out,
"Samson! The Philistines have come to capture
you!" But again Samson snapped the ropes from
his arms as if they were thread.
13 Then Delilah said, "You've been making fun
of me and telling me lies! Now tell me how you
can be tied up securely."
Samson replied, "If you were to weave the
seven braids of my hair into the fabric on your
loom and tighten it with the loom shuttle, I
would become as weak as anyone else."
So while he slept, Delilah wove the seven
braids of his hair into the fabric. 14 Then she
tightened it with the loom shuttle. Again she
cried out, "Samson! The Philistines have come to
capture you!" But Samson woke up, pulled back
the loom shuttle, and yanked his hair away from
the loom and the fabric.

15 Then Delilah pouted, "How can you tell me,
'I love you,' when you don't share your secrets
with me? You've made fun of me three times
now, and you still haven't told me what makes
you so strong!" 16 She tormented him with her
nagging day after day until he was sick to death
of it.
17 Finally, Samson shared his secret with her.
"My hair has never been cut," he confessed, "for I
was dedicated to God as a Nazirite from birth. If
my head were shaved, my strength would leave
me, and I would become as weak as anyone else."
18 Delilah realized he had finally told her the
truth, so she sent for the Philistine rulers. "Come
back one more time," she said, "for he has finally
told me his secret." So the Philistine rulers returned with the money in their hands. 19 Delilah
lulled Samson to sleep with his head in her lap,
and then she called in a man to shave off the
seven locks of his hair. In this way she began to
bring him down, and his strength left him.
20 Then she cried out, "Samson! The Philistines have come to capture you!"
When he woke up, he thought, "I will do as before and shake myself free." But he didn't realize
the LORD had left him.
21 So the Philistines captured him and gouged
out his eyes. They took him to Gaza, where he
was bound with bronze chains and forced to
grind grain in the prison.
22 But before long, his hair began to grow
back.

Samson's Final Victory

23 The Philistine rulers held a great festival, offering sacrifices and praising their god, Dagon.
They said, "Our god has given us victory over our
enemy Samson!"
24 When the people saw him, they praised
their god, saying, "Our god has delivered our enemy to us! The one who killed so many of us is
now in our power!"
25 Half drunk by now, the people demanded,
"Bring out Samson so he can amuse us!" So he
was brought from the prison to amuse them, and
they had him stand between the pillars supporting the roof.
26 Samson said to the young servant who was
leading him by the hand, "Place my hands
against the pillars that hold up the temple. I want
to rest against them." 27 Now the temple was
completely filled with people. All the Philistine
rulers were there, and there were about 3,000
men and women on the roof who were watching
as Samson amused them.

28 Then Samson prayed to the LORD, "Sovereign LORD, remember me again. O God, please strengthen me just one more time. With one blow let me pay back the Philistines for the loss of my two eyes." 29 Then Samson put his hands on the two center pillars that held up the temple. Pushing against them with both hands, 30 he prayed, "Let me die with the Philistines." And the temple crashed down on the Philistine rulers and all the people. So he killed more people when he died than he had during his entire lifetime.

31 Later his brothers and other relatives went down to get his body. They took him back home and buried him between Zorah and Eshtaol, where his father, Manoah, was buried. Samson had judged Israel for twenty years.

CHAPTER 17

Micah's Idols

There was a man named Micah, who lived in the hill country of Ephraim. 2 One day he said to his mother, "I heard you place a curse on the person who stole 1,100 pieces of silver from you. Well, I have the money. I was the one who took it."

"The LORD bless you for admitting it," his mother replied. 3 He returned the money to her, and she said, "I now dedicate these silver coins to the LORD. In honor of my son, I will have an image carved and an idol cast."

4 So when he returned the money to his mother, she took 200 silver coins and gave them to a silversmith, who made them into an image and an idol. And these were placed in Micah's house. 5 Micah set up a shrine for the idol, and he made a sacred ephod and some household idols. Then he installed one of his sons as his personal priest.

6 In those days Israel had no king; all the people did whatever seemed right in their own eyes.

7 One day a young Levite, who had been living in Bethlehem in Judah, arrived in that area. 8 He had left Bethlehem in search of another place to live, and as he traveled, he came to the hill country of Ephraim. He happened to stop at Micah's house as he was traveling through. 9 "Where are you from?" Micah asked him.

He replied, "I am a Levite from Bethlehem in Judah, and I am looking for a place to live."

10 "Stay here with me," Micah said, "and you can be a father and priest to me. I will give you ten pieces of silver a year, plus a change of clothes and your food." 11 The Levite agreed to this, and the young man became like one of Micah's sons.

12 So Micah installed the Levite as his personal priest, and he lived in Micah's house. 13 "I know the LORD will bless me now," Micah said, "because I have a Levite serving as my priest."

CHAPTER 18

Idolatry in the Tribe of Dan

Now in those days Israel had no king. And the tribe of Dan was trying to find a place where they could settle, for they had not yet moved into the land assigned to them when the land was divided among the tribes of Israel. 2 So the men of Dan chose from their clans five capable warriors from the towns of Zorah and Eshtaol to scout out a land for them to settle in.

When these warriors arrived in the hill country of Ephraim, they came to Micah's house and spent the night there. 3 While at Micah's house, they recognized the young Levite's accent, so they went over and asked him, "Who brought you here, and what are you doing in this place? Why are you here?" 4 He told them about his agreement with Micah and that he had been hired as Micah's personal priest.

5 Then they said, "Ask God whether or not our journey will be successful."

6 "Go in peace," the priest replied. "For the LORD is watching over your journey."

7 So the five men went on to the town of Laish, where they noticed the people living carefree lives, like the Sidonians; they were peaceful and secure. The people were also wealthy because their land was very fertile. And they lived a great distance from Sidon and had no allies nearby.

8 When the men returned to Zorah and Eshtaol, their relatives asked them, "What did you find?"

9 The men replied, "Come on, let's attack them! We have seen the land, and it is very good. What are you waiting for? Don't hesitate to go and take possession of it. 10 When you get there, you will find the people living carefree lives. God has given us a spacious and fertile land, lacking in nothing!"

11 So 600 men from the tribe of Dan, armed with weapons of war, set out from Zorah and Eshtaol. 12 They camped at a place west of Kiriath-jearim in Judah, which is called Mahaneh-dan to this day. 13 Then they went on from there into the hill country of Ephraim and came to the house of Micah.

14 The five men who had scouted out the land around Laish explained to the others, "These buildings contain a sacred ephod, as well as some household idols, a carved image, and a cast

idol. What do you think you should do?" 15 Then
the five men turned off the road and went over to
Micah's house, where the young Levite lived, and
greeted him kindly. 16 As the 600 armed warriors
from the tribe of Dan stood at the entrance of the
gate, 17 the five scouts entered the shrine and removed the carved image, the sacred ephod, the
household idols, and the cast idol. Meanwhile,
the priest was standing at the gate with the
600 armed warriors.

18 When the priest saw the men carrying all
the sacred objects out of Micah's shrine, he said,
"What are you doing?"

19 "Be quiet and come with us," they said. "Be a
father and priest to all of us. Isn't it better to be a
priest for an entire tribe and clan of Israel than
for the household of just one man?"

20 The young priest was quite happy to go with
them, so he took along the sacred ephod, the
household idols, and the carved image. 21 They
turned and started on their way again, placing
their children, livestock, and possessions in
front of them.

22 When the people from the tribe of Dan were
quite a distance from Micah's house, the people
who lived near Micah came chasing after them.
23 They were shouting as they caught up with
them. The men of Dan turned around and said to
Micah, "What's the matter? Why have you called
these men together and chased after us like
this?"

24 "What do you mean, 'What's the matter?'"
Micah replied. "You've taken away all the gods I
have made, and my priest, and I have nothing
left!"

25 The men of Dan said, "Watch what you say!
There are some short-tempered men around
here who might get angry and kill you and your
family." 26 So the men of Dan continued on their
way. When Micah saw that there were too many
of them for him to attack, he turned around and
went home.

27 Then, with Micah's idols and his priest, the
men of Dan came to the town of Laish, whose
people were peaceful and secure. They attacked
with swords and burned the town to the ground.
28 There was no one to rescue the people, for they
lived a great distance from Sidon and had no allies nearby. This happened in the valley near
Beth-rehob.

Then the people of the tribe of Dan rebuilt the
town and lived there. 29 They renamed the town
Dan after their ancestor, Israel's son, but it had
originally been called Laish.

30 Then they set up the carved image, and they
appointed Jonathan son of Gershom, son of
Moses, as their priest. This family continued as
priests for the tribe of Dan until the Exile. 31 So
Micah's carved image was worshiped by the tribe
of Dan as long as the Tabernacle of God remained at Shiloh.

CHAPTER 19
The Levite and His Concubine

Now in those days Israel had no king. There was a
man from the tribe of Levi living in a remote area
of the hill country of Ephraim. One day he
brought home a woman from Bethlehem in Judah to be his concubine. 2 But she became angry
with him and returned to her father's home in
Bethlehem.

After about four months, 3 her husband set out
for Bethlehem to speak personally to her and
persuade her to come back. He took with him a
servant and a pair of donkeys. When he arrived
at her father's house, her father saw him and welcomed him. 4 Her father urged him to stay
awhile, so he stayed three days, eating, drinking,
and sleeping there.

5 On the fourth day the man was up early, ready
to leave, but the woman's father said to his son-
in-law, "Have something to eat before you go."
6 So the two men sat down together and had
something to eat and drink. Then the woman's
father said, "Please stay another night and enjoy
yourself." 7 The man got up to leave, but his
father-in-law kept urging him to stay, so he finally gave in and stayed the night.

8 On the morning of the fifth day he was up
early again, ready to leave, and again the woman's
father said, "Have something to eat; then you can
leave later this afternoon." So they had another
day of feasting. 9 Later, as the man and his concubine and servant were preparing to leave, his
father-in-law said, "Look, it's almost evening. Stay
the night and enjoy yourself. Tomorrow you can
get up early and be on your way."

10 But this time the man was determined to
leave. So he took his two saddled donkeys and
his concubine and headed in the direction of Jebus (that is, Jerusalem). 11 It was late in the day
when they neared Jebus, and the man's servant
said to him, "Let's stop at this Jebusite town and
spend the night there."

12 "No," his master said, "we can't stay in this
foreign town where there are no Israelites. Instead, we will go on to Gibeah. 13 Come on, let's try
to get as far as Gibeah or Ramah, and we'll spend
the night in one of those towns." 14 So they went
on. The sun was setting as they came to Gibeah, a

town in the land of Benjamin, 15so they stopped
there to spend the night. They rested in the town
square, but no one took them in for the night.
16That evening an old man came home from
his work in the fields. He was from the hill country of Ephraim, but he was living in Gibeah,
where the people were from the tribe of Benjamin. 17When he saw the travelers sitting in the
town square, he asked them where they were
from and where they were going.
18"We have been in Bethlehem in Judah," the
man replied. "We are on our way to a remote area
in the hill country of Ephraim, which is my
home. I traveled to Bethlehem, and now I'm returning home. But no one has taken us in for the
night, 19even though we have everything we
need. We have straw and feed for our donkeys
and plenty of bread and wine for ourselves."
20"You are welcome to stay with me," the old
man said. "I will give you anything you might
need. But whatever you do, don't spend the night
in the square." 21So he took them home with him
and fed the donkeys. After they washed their
feet, they ate and drank together.
22While they were enjoying themselves, a
crowd of troublemakers from the town surrounded the house. They began beating at the
door and shouting to the old man, "Bring out the
man who is staying with you so we can have sex
with him."
23The old man stepped outside to talk to
them. "No, my brothers, don't do such an evil
thing. For this man is a guest in my house, and
such a thing would be shameful. 24Here, take my
virgin daughter and this man's concubine. I will
bring them out to you, and you can abuse them
and do whatever you like. But don't do such a
shameful thing to this man."
25But they wouldn't listen to him. So the Levite
took hold of his concubine and pushed her out
the door. The men of the town abused her all
night, taking turns raping her until morning.
Finally, at dawn they let her go. 26At daybreak the
woman returned to the house where her husband was staying. She collapsed at the door of
the house and lay there until it was light.
27When her husband opened the door to
leave, there lay his concubine with her hands on
the threshold. 28He said, "Get up! Let's go!" But
there was no answer. So he put her body on his
donkey and took her home.
29When he got home, he took a knife and cut
his concubine's body into twelve pieces. Then he
sent one piece to each tribe throughout all the
territory of Israel.
30Everyone who saw it said, "Such a horrible
crime has not been committed in all the time
since Israel left Egypt. Think about it! What are
we going to do? Who's going to speak up?"

CHAPTER 20
Israel's War with Benjamin

Then all the Israelites were united as one man,
from Dan in the north to Beersheba in the south,
including those from across the Jordan in the
land of Gilead. The entire community assembled
in the presence of the LORD at Mizpah. 2The
leaders of all the people and all the tribes of Israel—400,000 warriors armed with swords—took
their positions in the assembly of the people of
God. 3(Word soon reached the land of Benjamin
that the other tribes had gone up to Mizpah.) The
Israelites then asked how this terrible crime had
happened.
4The Levite, the husband of the woman who
had been murdered, said, "My concubine and I
came to spend the night in Gibeah, a town that
belongs to the people of Benjamin. 5That night
some of the leading citizens of Gibeah surrounded the house, planning to kill me, and they
raped my concubine until she was dead. 6So I cut
her body into twelve pieces and sent the pieces
throughout the territory assigned to Israel, for
these men have committed a terrible and shameful crime. 7Now then, all of you—the entire community of Israel—must decide here and now
what should be done about this!"
8And all the people rose to their feet in unison
and declared, "None of us will return home! No,
not even one of us! 9Instead, this is what we will
do to Gibeah; we will draw lots to decide who
will attack it. 10One-tenth of the men from each
tribe will be chosen to supply the warriors with
food, and the rest of us will take revenge on Gibeah of Benjamin for this shameful thing they
have done in Israel." 11So all the Israelites were
completely united, and they gathered together
to attack the town.
12The Israelites sent messengers to the tribe
of Benjamin, saying, "What a terrible thing has
been done among you! 13Give up those evil men,
those troublemakers from Gibeah, so we can execute them and purge Israel of this evil."
But the people of Benjamin would not listen.
14Instead, they came from their towns and gathered at Gibeah to fight the Israelites. 15In all,
26,000 of their warriors armed with swords arrived in Gibeah to join the 700 elite troops who
lived there. 16Among Benjamin's elite troops,
700 were left-handed, and each of them could

sling a rock and hit a target within a hairsbreadth without missing. 17 Israel had 400,000 experienced soldiers armed with swords, not counting Benjamin's warriors.

18 Before the battle the Israelites went to Bethel and asked God, "Which tribe should go first to attack the people of Benjamin?"

The LORD answered, "Judah is to go first."

19 So the Israelites left early the next morning and camped near Gibeah. 20 Then they advanced toward Gibeah to attack the men of Benjamin. 21 But Benjamin's warriors, who were defending the town, came out and killed 22,000 Israelites on the battlefield that day.

22 But the Israelites encouraged each other and took their positions again at the same place they had fought the previous day. 23 For they had gone up to Bethel and wept in the presence of the LORD until evening. They had asked the LORD, "Should we fight against our relatives from Benjamin again?"

And the LORD had said, "Go out and fight against them."

24 So the next day they went out again to fight against the men of Benjamin, 25 but the men of Benjamin killed another 18,000 Israelites, all of whom were experienced with the sword.

26 Then all the Israelites went up to Bethel and wept in the presence of the LORD and fasted until evening. They also brought burnt offerings and peace offerings to the LORD. 27 The Israelites went up seeking direction from the LORD. (In those days the Ark of the Covenant of God was in Bethel, 28 and Phinehas son of Eleazar and grandson of Aaron was the priest.) The Israelites asked the LORD, "Should we fight against our relatives from Benjamin again, or should we stop?"

The LORD said, "Go! Tomorrow I will hand them over to you."

29 So the Israelites set an ambush all around Gibeah. 30 They went out on the third day and took their positions at the same place as before. 31 When the men of Benjamin came out to attack, they were drawn away from the town. And as they had done before, they began to kill the Israelites. About thirty Israelites died in the open fields and along the roads, one leading to Bethel and the other leading back to Gibeah.

32 Then the warriors of Benjamin shouted, "We're defeating them as we did before!" But the Israelites had planned in advance to run away so that the men of Benjamin would chase them along the roads and be drawn away from the town.

33 When the main group of Israelite warriors reached Baal-tamar, they turned and took up their positions. Meanwhile, the Israelites hiding in ambush to the west of Gibeah jumped up to fight. 34 There were 10,000 elite Israelite troops who advanced against Gibeah. The fighting was so heavy that Benjamin didn't realize the impending disaster. 35 So the LORD helped Israel defeat Benjamin, and that day the Israelites killed 25,100 of Benjamin's warriors, all of whom were experienced swordsmen. 36 Then the men of Benjamin saw that they were beaten.

The Israelites had retreated from Benjamin's warriors in order to give those hiding in ambush more room to maneuver against Gibeah. 37 Then those who were hiding rushed in from all sides and killed everyone in the town. 38 They had arranged to send up a large cloud of smoke from the town as a signal. 39 When the Israelites saw the smoke, they turned and attacked Benjamin's warriors.

By that time Benjamin's warriors had killed about thirty Israelites, and they shouted, "We're defeating them as we did in the first battle!" 40 But when the warriors of Benjamin looked behind them and saw the smoke rising into the sky from every part of the town, 41 the men of Israel turned and attacked. At this point the men of Benjamin became terrified, because they realized disaster was close at hand. 42 So they turned around and fled before the Israelites toward the wilderness. But they couldn't escape the battle, and the people who came out of the nearby towns were also killed. 43 The Israelites surrounded the men of Benjamin and chased them relentlessly, finally overtaking them east of Gibeah. 44 That day 18,000 of Benjamin's strongest warriors died in battle. 45 The survivors fled into the wilderness toward the rock of Rimmon, but Israel killed 5,000 of them along the road. They continued the chase until they had killed another 2,000 near Gidom.

46 So that day the tribe of Benjamin lost 25,000 strong warriors armed with swords, 47 leaving only 600 men who escaped to the rock of Rimmon, where they lived for four months. 48 And the Israelites returned and slaughtered every living thing in all the towns—the people, the livestock, and everything they found. They also burned down all the towns they came to.

CHAPTER 21

Israel Provides Wives for Benjamin

The Israelites had vowed at Mizpah, "We will never give our daughters in marriage to a man from the tribe of Benjamin." 2 Now the people

went to Bethel and sat in the presence of God
until evening, weeping loudly and bitterly.
3“O LORD, God of Israel,” they cried out, “why has
this happened in Israel? Now one of our tribes is
missing from Israel!”
4Early the next morning the people built an altar and presented their burnt offerings and
peace offerings on it. 5Then they said, “Who
among the tribes of Israel did not join us at
Mizpah when we held our assembly in the presence of the LORD?” At that time they had taken a
solemn oath in the LORD’s presence, vowing that
anyone who refused to come would be put to
death.
6The Israelites felt sorry for their brother
Benjamin and said, “Today one of the tribes of
Israel has been cut off. 7How can we find wives
for the few who remain, since we have sworn
by the LORD not to give them our daughters in
marriage?”
8So they asked, “Who among the tribes of Israel did not join us at Mizpah when we assembled in the presence of the LORD?” And they
discovered that no one from Jabesh-gilead had
attended the assembly. 9For after they counted
all the people, no one from Jabesh-gilead was
present.
10So the assembly sent 12,000 of their best
warriors to Jabesh-gilead with orders to kill
everyone there, including women and children.
11“This is what you are to do,” they said. “Completely destroy all the males and every woman
who is not a virgin.” 12Among the residents of
Jabesh-gilead they found 400 young virgins
who had never slept with a man, and they
brought them to the camp at Shiloh in the land
of Canaan.
13The Israelite assembly sent a peace delegation to the remaining people of Benjamin who
were living at the rock of Rimmon. 14Then the
men of Benjamin returned to their homes, and
the 400 women of Jabesh-gilead who had been
spared were given to them as wives. But there
were not enough women for all of them.
15The people felt sorry for Benjamin because
the LORD had made this gap among the tribes of
Israel. 16So the elders of the assembly asked,
“How can we find wives for the few who remain,
since the women of the tribe of Benjamin are
dead? 17There must be heirs for the survivors so
that an entire tribe of Israel is not wiped out.
18But we cannot give them our own daughters in
marriage because we have sworn with a solemn
oath that anyone who does this will fall under
God’s curse.”
19Then they thought of the annual festival of
the LORD held in Shiloh, south of Lebonah and
north of Bethel, along the east side of the road
that goes from Bethel to Shechem. 20They told
the men of Benjamin who still needed wives, “Go
and hide in the vineyards. 21When you see the
young women of Shiloh come out for their
dances, rush out from the vineyards, and each of
you can take one of them home to the land of
Benjamin to be your wife! 22And when their fathers and brothers come to us in protest, we will
tell them, ‘Please be sympathetic. Let them have
your daughters, for we didn’t find wives for all of
them when we destroyed Jabesh-gilead. And
you are not guilty of breaking the vow since you
did not actually give your daughters to them in
marriage.’”
23So the men of Benjamin did as they were
told. Each man caught one of the women as she
danced in the celebration and carried her off to
be his wife. They returned to their own land, and
they rebuilt their towns and lived in them.
24Then the people of Israel departed by tribes
and families, and they returned to their own
homes.
25In those days Israel had no king; all the people did whatever seemed right in their own eyes.

RUTH A Faithful Woman

Look for 4 hidden messages in Ruth!

The book of Ruth shows that staying true to God and others helps us through tough times. Read Ruth to learn about

- **A FAITHFUL WOMAN WHO WOULDN'T LET GO**
- **TWO WOMEN IN BIG TROUBLE**
- **A REALLY NICE GUY**
- **A REAL-LIFE HAPPY ENDING**

YOU ARE NOT ALONE.

Trail of Tears

Nothing left. Naomi lost her husband and her two sons. She had nowhere to go except back to Bethlehem, her childhood home. She kissed her daughters-in-law goodbye as she started the lonely, tearful journey. But wait! What did Ruth say? Maybe Naomi had hope after all. **Find out in Ruth 1:1-19.**

oops?

The Case of the Fumbly Farmers

The workers kept dropping the barley they worked so hard to harvest. Were they clumsy? sleepy? just really bad farmers? Or was something else going on? **Solve the mysterious case of the Fumbly Farmers and the Falling Food by reading Ruth 2:1-23.**

Dear Blabby

Q: All my dreams are coming true—except for one big problem. I want to marry Ruth, and she wants to marry me. But... there's one person in town who is closer to Ruth than I am. What do I do, Blabby?

A: Find out what Boaz did in Ruth 4:1-12.

The JESUS CONNECTION

You may know that Jesus came from David's family. In fact, David was Jesus' great-great-great-great-great... STOP! We'd have to put 20 more "greats" in before we could finish with grandpa. Did you know that Ruth was David's great-grandma? Before Jesus' birth, God said that the Messiah would come from David's family and that he would be born in Bethlehem. So when God helped Naomi and Ruth move from Moab to Bethlehem, **God was working out the master plan for Jesus' birth.**

Friendship Bracelet

Do you have a best friend? Someone you really like to hang out with? A friend you'd do anything for? The Bible tells about two friends like that. **Read all about them in RUTH 1:1-18.**

NOW MAKE SOMETHING TO GIVE TO *YOUR* BEST FRIEND!

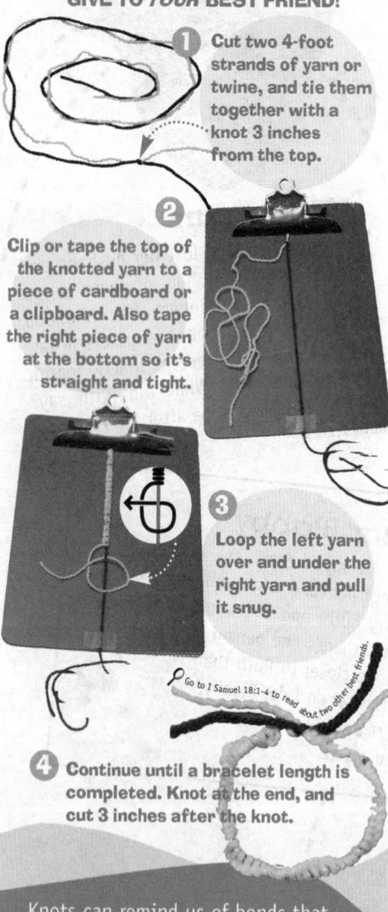

1 Cut two 4-foot strands of yarn or twine, and tie them together with a knot 3 inches from the top.
2 Clip or tape the top of the knotted yarn to a piece of cardboard or a clipboard. Also tape the right piece of yarn at the bottom so it's straight and tight.
3 Loop the left yarn over and under the right yarn and pull it snug.
Go to I Samuel 18:1-4 to read about two other best friends.
4 Continue until a bracelet length is completed. Knot at the end, and cut 3 inches after the knot.

Knots can remind us of bonds that can't be broken, like the bond between Ruth and Naomi. **Give away your bracelet to thank your friend for always being there for you.**

CHAPTER 1

Elimelech Moves His Family to Moab

In the days when the judges ruled in Israel, a severe famine came upon the land. So a man from
Bethlehem in Judah left his home and went to
live in the country of Moab, taking his wife and
two sons with him. 2 The man's name was Elimelech, and his wife was Naomi. Their two sons
were Mahlon and Kilion. They were Ephrathites
from Bethlehem in the land of Judah. And when
they reached Moab, they settled there.
3 Then Elimelech died, and Naomi was left
with her two sons. 4 The two sons married Moabite women. One married a woman named Orpah,
and the other a woman named Ruth. But about
ten years later, 5 both Mahlon and Kilion died.
This left Naomi alone, without her two sons or
her husband.

Naomi and Ruth Return

6 Then Naomi heard in Moab that the LORD had
blessed his people in Judah by giving them good
crops again. So Naomi and her daughters-in-law
got ready to leave Moab to return to her homeland. 7 With her two daughters-in-law she set out
from the place where she had been living, and
they took the road that would lead them back to
Judah.
8 But on the way, Naomi said to her two
daughters-in-law, "Go back to your mothers'
homes. And may the LORD reward you for your
kindness to your husbands and to me. 9 May the
LORD bless you with the security of another marriage." Then she kissed them good-bye, and they
all broke down and wept.
10 "No," they said. "We want to go with you to
your people."
11 But Naomi replied, "Why should you go on
with me? Can I still give birth to other sons who
could grow up to be your husbands? 12 No, my
daughters, return to your parents' homes, for I
am too old to marry again. And even if it were
possible, and I were to get married tonight and
bear sons, then what? 13 Would you wait for them
to grow up and refuse to marry someone else?
No, of course not, my daughters! Things are far
more bitter for me than for you, because the
LORD himself has raised his fist against me."
14 And again they wept together, and Orpah
kissed her mother-in-law good-bye. But Ruth
clung tightly to Naomi. 15 "Look," Naomi said to
her, "your sister-in-law has gone back to her people and to her gods. You should do the same."
16 But Ruth replied, "Don't ask me to leave you

and turn back. Wherever you go, I will go; wherever you live, I will live. Your people will be my
people, and your God will be my God. 17Wher-
ever you die, I will die, and there I will be buried.
May the LORD punish me severely if I allow anything but death to separate us!" 18When Naomi
saw that Ruth was determined to go with her, she
said nothing more.
19So the two of them continued on their journey. When they came to Bethlehem, the entire
town was excited by their arrival. "Is it really Naomi?" the women asked.
20"Don't call me Naomi," she responded. "Instead, call me Mara, for the Almighty has made
life very bitter for me. 21I went away full, but
the LORD has brought me home empty. Why call
me Naomi when the LORD has caused me to suffer and the Almighty has sent such tragedy
upon me?"
22So Naomi returned from Moab, accompanied by her daughter-in-law Ruth, the young Moabite woman. They arrived in Bethlehem in late
spring, at the beginning of the barley harvest.

CHAPTER 2

Ruth Works in Boaz's Field

Now there was a wealthy and influential man in
Bethlehem named Boaz, who was a relative of
Naomi's husband, Elimelech.
2One day Ruth the Moabite said to Naomi,
"Let me go out into the harvest fields to pick up
the stalks of grain left behind by anyone who is
kind enough to let me do it."
Naomi replied, "All right, my daughter, go
ahead." 3So Ruth went out to gather grain
behind the harvesters. And as it happened,
she found herself working in a field that belonged to Boaz, the relative of her father-in-law,
Elimelech.
4While she was there, Boaz arrived from Bethlehem and greeted the harvesters. "The LORD be
with you!" he said.
"The LORD bless you!" the harvesters replied.
5Then Boaz asked his foreman, "Who is that
young woman over there? Who does she belong to?"
6And the foreman replied, "She is the young
woman from Moab who came back with Naomi.
7She asked me this morning if she could gather
grain behind the harvesters. She has been hard
at work ever since, except for a few minutes' rest
in the shelter."
8Boaz went over and said to Ruth, "Listen, my
daughter. Stay right here with us when you
gather grain; don't go to any other fields. Stay
right behind the young women working in my
field. 9See which part of the field they are harvesting, and then follow them. I have warned the
young men not to treat you roughly. And when
you are thirsty, help yourself to the water they
have drawn from the well."
10Ruth fell at his feet and thanked him warmly.
"What have I done to deserve such kindness?"
she asked. "I am only a foreigner."
11"Yes, I know," Boaz replied. "But I also know
about everything you have done for your mother-
in-law since the death of your husband. I have
heard how you left your father and mother and
your own land to live here among complete
strangers. 12May the LORD, the God of Israel,
under whose wings you have come to take refuge,
reward you fully for what you have done."
13"I hope I continue to please you, sir," she replied. "You have comforted me by speaking so
kindly to me, even though I am not one of your
workers."
14At mealtime Boaz called to her, "Come over
here, and help yourself to some food. You can dip
your bread in the sour wine." So she sat with his
harvesters, and Boaz gave her some roasted grain
to eat. She ate all she wanted and still had some
left over.
15When Ruth went back to work again, Boaz
ordered his young men, "Let her gather grain
right among the sheaves without stopping her.
16And pull out some heads of barley from the
bundles and drop them on purpose for her. Let
her pick them up, and don't give her a hard
time!"
17So Ruth gathered barley there all day, and
when she beat out the grain that evening, it filled
an entire basket. 18She carried it back into town
and showed it to her mother-in-law. Ruth also
gave her the roasted grain that was left over from
her meal.
19"Where did you gather all this grain today?"
Naomi asked. "Where did you work? May the
LORD bless the one who helped you!"
So Ruth told her mother-in-law about the man
in whose field she had worked. She said, "The
man I worked with today is named Boaz."
20"May the LORD bless him!" Naomi told her
daughter-in-law. "He is showing his kindness to
us as well as to your dead husband. That man is
one of our closest relatives, one of our family redeemers."
21Then Ruth said, "What's more, Boaz even
told me to come back and stay with his harvesters until the entire harvest is completed."
22"Good!" Naomi exclaimed. "Do as he said, my

Feathered Friends

Boaz took care of Ruth in a special way. **Find out how in RUTH 2:8-12.** Then use grain in your own special way!

Read Luke 12:22-32 to see how God takes care of his flock.
YUM!
If you can't find a pine cone, just scatter birdseed outside on a flat surface instead.

1 Find a pine cone outside or buy one at a craft store. Tie a string to the top so the cone can be hung.

2 Use a spoon to smush softened lard onto the cone.

3 Roll the cone in oatmeal and birdseed.

4 Hang the cone from a tree to help take care of your feathered friends!

BONUS IDEA

Collect unopened bags of barley and rice to give to your local food bank.

daughter. Stay with his young women right
through the whole harvest. You might be harassed
in other fields, but you'll be safe with him."
23So Ruth worked alongside the women in
Boaz's fields and gathered grain with them until
the end of the barley harvest. Then she continued working with them through the wheat harvest in early summer. And all the while she lived
with her mother-in-law.

CHAPTER **3**

Ruth at the Threshing Floor

One day Naomi said to Ruth, "My daughter, it's
time that I found a permanent home for you, so
that you will be provided for. 2Boaz is a close relative of ours, and he's been very kind by letting
you gather grain with his young women. Tonight
he will be winnowing barley at the threshing
floor. 3Now do as I tell you—take a bath and put
on perfume and dress in your nicest clothes.
Then go to the threshing floor, but don't let Boaz
see you until he has finished eating and drinking. 4Be sure to notice where he lies down; then
go and uncover his feet and lie down there. He
will tell you what to do."
5"I will do everything you say," Ruth replied.
6So she went down to the threshing floor that
night and followed the instructions of her
mother-in-law.
7After Boaz had finished eating and drinking
and was in good spirits, he lay down at the far end
of the pile of grain and went to sleep. Then Ruth
came quietly, uncovered his feet, and lay down.
8Around midnight Boaz suddenly woke up and
turned over. He was surprised to find a woman lying at his feet! 9"Who are you?" he asked.

"I am your servant Ruth," she replied. "Spread
the corner of your covering over me, for you are
my family redeemer."
10"The LORD bless you, my daughter!" Boaz exclaimed. "You are showing even more family loyalty now than you did before, for you have not
gone after a younger man, whether rich or poor.
11Now don't worry about a thing, my daughter. I
will do what is necessary, for everyone in town
knows you are a virtuous woman. 12But while it's
true that I am one of your family redeemers, there
is another man who is more closely related to you
than I am. 13Stay here tonight, and in the morning
I will talk to him. If he is willing to redeem you,
very well. Let him marry you. But if he is not willing, then as surely as the LORD lives, I will redeem
you myself! Now lie down here until morning."
14So Ruth lay at Boaz's feet until the morning,
but she got up before it was light enough for people to recognize each other. For Boaz had said,
"No one must know that a woman was here at the
threshing floor." 15Then Boaz said to her, "Bring
your cloak and spread it out." He measured six
scoops of barley into the cloak and placed it on
her back. Then he returned to the town.
16When Ruth went back to her mother-in-law,
Naomi asked, "What happened, my daughter?"

Ruth told Naomi everything Boaz had done for
her, 17and she added, "He gave me these six
scoops of barley and said, 'Don't go back to your
mother-in-law empty-handed.'"
18Then Naomi said to her, "Just be patient, my
daughter, until we hear what happens. The man
won't rest until he has settled things today."

CHAPTER **4**

Boaz Marries Ruth

Boaz went to the town gate and took a seat there.
Just then the family redeemer he had mentioned
came by, so Boaz called out to him, "Come over
here and sit down, friend. I want to talk to
you." So they sat down together. 2Then Boaz
called ten leaders from the town and asked them
to sit as witnesses. 3And Boaz said to the family
redeemer, "You know Naomi, who came back

from Moab. She is selling the land that belonged
to our relative Elimelech. 4I thought I should
speak to you about it so that you can redeem it if
you wish. If you want the land, then buy it here in
the presence of these witnesses. But if you don't
want it, let me know right away, because I am
next in line to redeem it after you."
The man replied, "All right, I'll redeem it."
5Then Boaz told him, "Of course, your purchase of the land from Naomi also requires that
you marry Ruth, the Moabite widow. That way
she can have children who will carry on her husband's name and keep the land in the family."
6"Then I can't redeem it," the family redeemer
replied, "because this might endanger my own
estate. You redeem the land; I cannot do it."
7Now in those days it was the custom in Israel
for anyone transferring a right of purchase to remove his sandal and hand it to the other party.
This publicly validated the transaction. 8So the
other family redeemer drew off his sandal as he
said to Boaz, "You buy the land."
9Then Boaz said to the elders and to the crowd
standing around, "You are witnesses that today I
have bought from Naomi all the property of
Elimelech, Kilion, and Mahlon. 10And with the
land I have acquired Ruth, the Moabite widow of
Mahlon, to be my wife. This way she can have a
son to carry on the family name of her dead husband and to inherit the family property here in
his hometown. You are all witnesses today."
11Then the elders and all the people standing
in the gate replied, "We are witnesses! May the
Lord make this woman who is coming into your
home like Rachel and Leah, from whom all the
nation of Israel descended! May you prosper in
Ephrathah and be famous in Bethlehem. 12And
may the Lord give you descendants by this
young woman who will be like those of our ancestor Perez, the son of Tamar and Judah."

The Descendants of Boaz

13So Boaz took Ruth into his home, and she became his wife. When he slept with her, the Lord
enabled her to become pregnant, and she gave
birth to a son. 14Then the women of the town
said to Naomi, "Praise the Lord, who has now
provided a redeemer for your family! May this
child be famous in Israel. 15May he restore your
youth and care for you in your old age. For he is
the son of your daughter-in-law who loves you
and has been better to you than seven sons!"
16Naomi took the baby and cuddled him to
her breast. And she cared for him as if he were
her own. 17The neighbor women said, "Now at

It was no accident that Ruth and Boaz married and had a baby. It was part of God's plan! **Find out more about their baby in RUTH 4:14-22.**

Get it? Obed became the father of Jesse, who became the father of King David! And guess who became a relative of King David. Jesus! God had a plan for that baby Obed—and he has a plan for all the babies born in your family too—including you!

1. **Fill in as many names as you can on this family tree.**

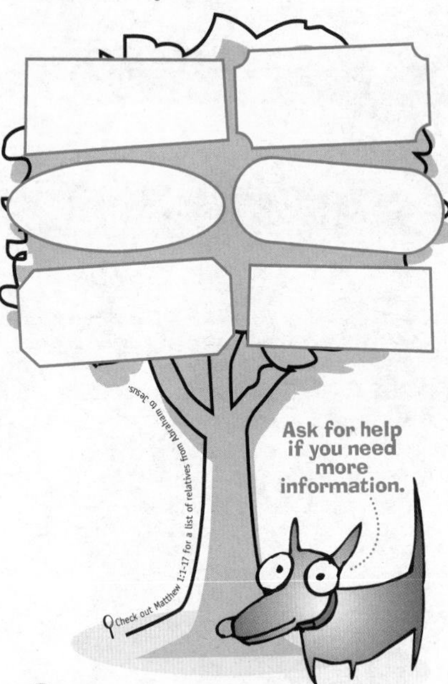

Check out Matthew 1:1-17 for a list of relatives from Abraham to Jesus.
Ask for help if you need more information.

2. **Under each name, write one word to describe that person.**
3. **Your family is a part of God's big plan! Think of what God's plan might be for each person in your family. Write your thoughts near the names.**

Stop right now and pray that your family members will love God and follow his big plan for their lives!

Read Luke 1:32-33 to see what the angel Gabriel said about Jesus and David.

last Naomi has a son again!" And they named him
Obed. He became the father of Jesse and the
grandfather of David.
18 This is the genealogical record of their ancestor Perez:

Perez was the father of Hezron.
19 Hezron was the father of Ram.
Ram was the father of Amminadab.
20 Amminadab was the father of Nahshon.
Nahshon was the father of Salmon.
21 Salmon was the father of Boaz.
Boaz was the father of Obed.
22 Obed was the father of Jesse.
Jesse was the father of David.

1 SAMUEL The First Kings of Israel

Look for 4 hidden messages in 1 Samuel!

Before the Israelites had kings, God led the people and raised up judges to help them. First Samuel tells how kings replaced the judges and names some of the problems that came with the change. Read 1 Samuel to learn about

- **A BOY WHO HEARD GOD'S VOICE**
- **THE JEALOUS FIRST KING**
- **A BIG FIGHT WITH A BIG GUY**
- **AND THE KING WHO LOVED GOD**

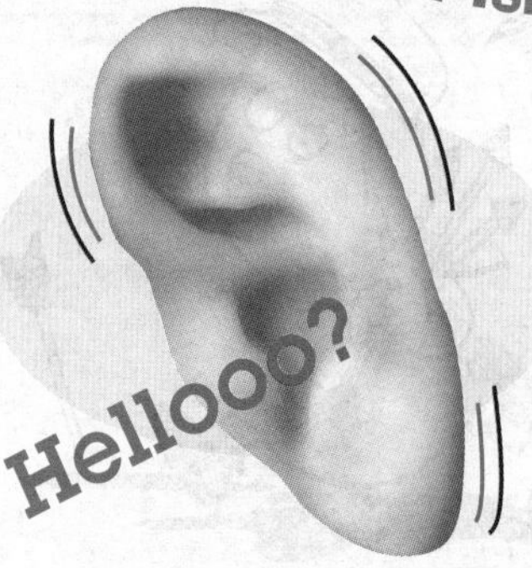

Helloooo?

Did God's new prophet, Samuel, have wax buildup in his ears? Did Eli play a trick on the boy? Did someone make a really bad knock-knock joke? Samuel knew he heard *something*. **Find out what or who in 1 Samuel 3:1-14.**

Where'd He Go?

Saul's big day arrived. All the people of Israel gathered to crown him king. But when the moment came, Saul couldn't be found. Where was the powerful ruler of Israel—the first king over God's people? **Read all about it in 1 Samuel 10:17-26.**

Extra-X-Ray Vision

God has X-ray vision. Actually, better-than-X-ray vision. Sure, God can see bones, teeth, and muscles. But God's X-ray vision goes beyond that. God sees what people think and feel. Samuel knew that God wanted to make one of Jesse's sons the new king of Israel. As each son came to see Samuel, God looked right past his looks or strength. God looked straight at his heart. **Find out in 1 Samuel 16:1-13 which son replaced Saul as king.**

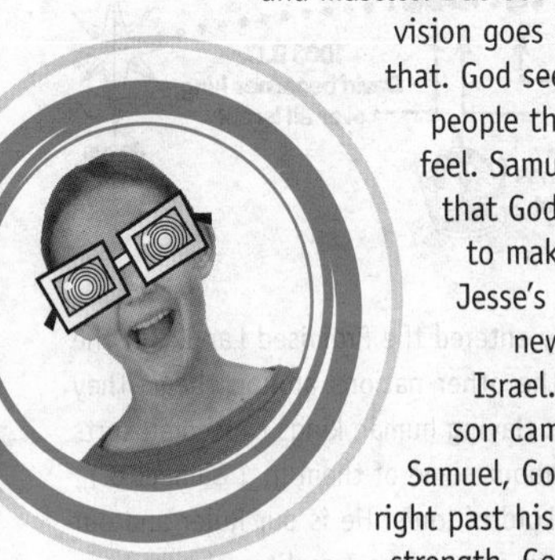

Little Guy... Big Problem

David had a really big, hairy problem. The problem went by the name of Goliath—an angry giant who stood over nine feet tall. David volunteered to take the giant head-on. Did David get smushed like a grape? **Find out in 1 Samuel 17:41-50.**

Dear Blabby

Q: I know it's my job, but I'm just getting tired of it. Jonathan shoots the arrows. I run after them and bring them back. That's it. I can do that. But lately it's been "Hurry up! The arrow is ahead of you!" Jonathan has been making me run all over the place! I know I'm supposed to get the arrows, Blabby. I'm the arrow boy. I'm just sick of running around! What's going on? **A: Read 1 Samuel 20:18-23 to see what Jonathan was up to. Then read 1 Samuel 20:35-42 to find out what happened to the arrow boy.**

The Crime Blotter

King Saul survived a horrible attack. While the great king slept in a cave outside of Israel, the rebel David attempted to murder the king. Well...maybe not murder, exactly. Actually, David just sneaked up to Saul in the cave and took a piece of his robe. Why? **Find out by reading 1 Samuel 24 and 1 Samuel 26.**

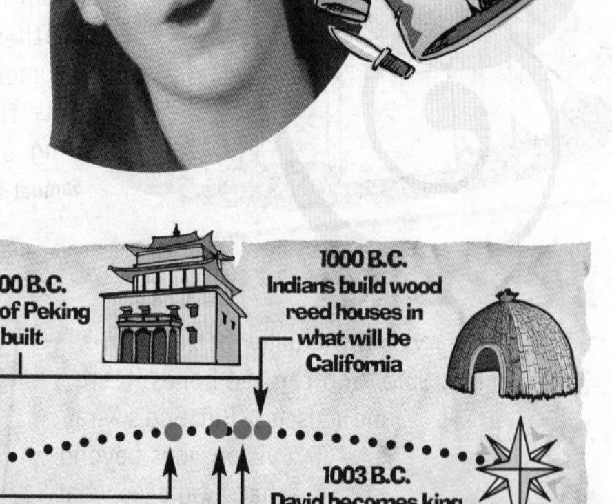

Timeline

1000 B.C. Kite invented in China

1000 B.C. City of Peking built

1000 B.C. Indians build wood reed houses in what will be California

1050 B.C. Saul becomes king

1010 B.C. Saul dies; David becomes king of Judah

1003 B.C. David becomes king over all Israel

Jesus is born!

God led the people of Israel when they entered the Promised Land. But the people wanted a king to be like all the other nations around them. They didn't want to follow God as their king. Having human kings caused all sorts of problems for Israel. (You can read about some of them in 1 Samuel 8.)

Jesus is the King of kings and the Lord of lords. He is our Ruler and our King. We need to follow and serve Jesus just as the Israelites should have followed and served God. **His kingdom will never end!**

CHAPTER 1

Elkanah and His Family

There was a man named Elkanah who lived
in Ramah in the region of Zuph in the hill country of Ephraim. He was the son of Jeroham,
son of Elihu, son of Tohu, son of Zuph, of Ephraim. 2 Elkanah had two wives, Hannah and Peninnah. Peninnah had children, but Hannah
did not.

3 Each year Elkanah would travel to Shiloh to
worship and sacrifice to the LORD of Heaven's
Armies at the Tabernacle. The priests of the
LORD at that time were the two sons of Eli—
Hophni and Phinehas. 4 On the days Elkanah
presented his sacrifice, he would give portions
of the meat to Peninnah and each of her children. 5 And though he loved Hannah, he would
give her only one choice portion because the
LORD had given her no children. 6 So Peninnah
would taunt Hannah and make fun of her
because the LORD had kept her from having children. 7 Year after year it was the same—Peninnah would taunt Hannah as they went to the
Tabernacle. Each time, Hannah would be reduced to tears and would not even eat.

8 "Why are you crying, Hannah?" Elkanah
would ask. "Why aren't you eating? Why be
downhearted just because you have no children? You have me—isn't that better than having
ten sons?"

Hannah's Prayer for a Son

9 Once after a sacrificial meal at Shiloh, Hannah
got up and went to pray. Eli the priest was sitting
at his customary place beside the entrance of
the Tabernacle. 10 Hannah was in deep anguish,
crying bitterly as she prayed to the LORD. 11 And
she made this vow: "O LORD of Heaven's Armies,
if you will look upon my sorrow and answer my
prayer and give me a son, then I will give him
back to you. He will be yours for his entire lifetime, and as a sign that he has been dedicated to
the LORD, his hair will never be cut."

12 As she was praying to the LORD, Eli watched
her. 13 Seeing her lips moving but hearing no
sound, he thought she had been drinking.
14 "Must you come here drunk?" he demanded.
"Throw away your wine!"

15 "Oh no, sir!" she replied. "I haven't been
drinking wine or anything stronger. But I am
very discouraged, and I was pouring out my
heart to the LORD. 16 Don't think I am a wicked
woman! For I have been praying out of great anguish and sorrow."

17 "In that case," Eli said, "go in peace! May the
God of Israel grant the request you have asked of
him."

18 "Oh, thank you, sir!" she exclaimed. Then
she went back and began to eat again, and she
was no longer sad.

Samuel's Birth and Dedication

19 The entire family got up early the next morning
and went to worship the LORD once more. Then
they returned home to Ramah. When Elkanah
slept with Hannah, the LORD remembered her
plea, 20 and in due time she gave birth to a son.
She named him Samuel, for she said, "I asked the
LORD for him."

21 The next year Elkanah and his family went
on their annual trip to offer a sacrifice to the
LORD and to keep his vow. 22 But Hannah did not
go. She told her husband, "Wait until the boy is
weaned. Then I will take him to the Tabernacle
and leave him there with the LORD permanently."

23 "Whatever you think is best," Elkanah
agreed. "Stay here for now, and may the LORD
help you keep your promise." So she stayed
home and nursed the boy until he was weaned.

24 When the child was weaned, Hannah took
him to the Tabernacle in Shiloh. They brought
along a three-year-old bull for the sacrifice and a
basket of flour and some wine. 25 After sacrificing the bull, they brought the boy to Eli. 26 "Sir, do
you remember me?" Hannah asked. "I am the
very woman who stood here several years ago
praying to the LORD. 27 I asked the LORD to give
me this boy, and he has granted my request.
28 Now I am giving him to the LORD, and he will
belong to the LORD his whole life." And they worshiped the LORD there.

CHAPTER 2

Hannah's Prayer of Praise

Then Hannah prayed:

"My heart rejoices in the LORD!
The LORD has made me strong.
Now I have an answer for my enemies;
I rejoice because you rescued me.
2 No one is holy like the LORD!
There is no one besides you;
there is no Rock like our God.

3 "Stop acting so proud and haughty!
Don't speak with such arrogance!
For the LORD is a God who knows what you
have done;
he will judge your actions.
4 The bow of the mighty is now broken,
and those who stumbled are now strong.

1 Samuel 2 . . . page 270

I Neeeeeed It!

Or do you just want it? Hannah *really* wanted a baby, and she prayed for one with all her heart. **Read 1 SAMUEL 1 to find out what happened.**

God answers every prayer request you make with a "yes," "no," or "later." Try this to see if you learn anything about how God answers prayer.

1. **In the space below, make a list of people you know who pray to God.**

2. **Interview them! Have them tell you about times God answered their prayers.**

NEWS!
What does God do with our prayers? Find out by reading John 15:7; James 5:16; and 1 John 5:14-15.

3. **Make up a headline for each of the answers to prayer. For example:**
"GOD HEALS BOY WITH CHICKEN POX."

4. **Now write a headline of how God has answered one of *your* prayers.**

NAME HEADLINE

ME

**God knows what's best for you. God may not give you everything you *want*, but God will give you everything you *need*—
JUST ASK GOD IN PRAYER!**

5 Those who were well fed are now starving,
and those who were starving are now full.
The childless woman now has seven
children,
and the woman with many children
wastes away.
6 The LORD gives both death and life;
he brings some down to the grave but
raises others up.
7 The LORD makes some poor and others rich;
he brings some down and lifts others up.
8 He lifts the poor from the dust
and the needy from the garbage dump.
He sets them among princes,
placing them in seats of honor.
For all the earth is the LORD's,
and he has set the world in order.

9 "He will protect his faithful ones,
but the wicked will disappear in darkness.
No one will succeed by strength alone.
10 Those who fight against the LORD will be
shattered.
He thunders against them from heaven;
the LORD judges throughout the earth.
He gives power to his king;
he increases the strength of his anointed
one."

11 Then Elkanah returned home to Ramah
without Samuel. And the boy served the LORD by
assisting Eli the priest.

Eli's Wicked Sons

12 Now the sons of Eli were scoundrels who had
no respect for the LORD 13 or for their duties as
priests. Whenever anyone offered a sacrifice,
Eli's sons would send over a servant with a three-
pronged fork. While the meat of the sacrificed
animal was still boiling, 14 the servant would stick
the fork into the pot and demand that whatever
it brought up be given to Eli's sons. All the Israelites who came to worship at Shiloh were treated
this way. 15 Sometimes the servant would come
even before the animal's fat had been burned on
the altar. He would demand raw meat before it
had been boiled so that it could be used for
roasting.

16 The man offering the sacrifice might reply,
"Take as much as you want, but the fat must be
burned first." Then the servant would demand,
"No, give it to me now, or I'll take it by force." 17 So
the sin of these young men was very serious in
the LORD's sight, for they treated the LORD's offerings with contempt.

18 But Samuel, though he was only a boy, served

the LORD. He wore a linen garment like that of a priest. 19 Each year his mother made a small coat for him and brought it to him when she came with her husband for the sacrifice. 20 Before they returned home, Eli would bless Elkanah and his wife and say, "May the LORD give you other children to take the place of this one she gave to the LORD." 21 And the LORD blessed Hannah, and she conceived and gave birth to three sons and two daughters. Meanwhile, Samuel grew up in the presence of the LORD.

22 Now Eli was very old, but he was aware of what his sons were doing to the people of Israel. He knew, for instance, that his sons were seducing the young women who assisted at the entrance of the Tabernacle. 23 Eli said to them, "I have been hearing reports from all the people about the wicked things you are doing. Why do you keep sinning? 24 You must stop, my sons! The reports I hear among the LORD's people are not good. 25 If someone sins against another person, God can mediate for the guilty party. But if someone sins against the LORD, who can intercede?" But Eli's sons wouldn't listen to their father, for the LORD was already planning to put them to death.

26 Meanwhile, the boy Samuel grew taller and grew in favor with the LORD and with the people.

A Warning for Eli's Family

27 One day a man of God came to Eli and gave him this message from the LORD: "I revealed myself to your ancestors when they were Pharaoh's slaves in Egypt. 28 I chose your ancestor Aaron from among all the tribes of Israel to be my priest, to offer sacrifices on my altar, to burn incense, and to wear the priestly vest as he served me. And I assigned the sacrificial offerings to you priests. 29 So why do you scorn my sacrifices and offerings? Why do you give your sons more honor than you give me—for you and they have become fat from the best offerings of my people Israel!

30 "Therefore, the LORD, the God of Israel, says: I promised that your branch of the tribe of Levi would always be my priests. But I will honor those who honor me, and I will despise those who think lightly of me. 31 The time is coming when I will put an end to your family, so it will no longer serve as my priests. All the members of your family will die before their time. None will reach old age. 32 You will watch with envy as I pour out prosperity on the people of Israel. But no members of your family will ever live out their days. 33 The few not cut off from serving at my altar will survive, but only so their eyes can go blind and their hearts break, and their children will die a violent death. 34 And to prove that what I have said will come true, I will cause your two sons, Hophni and Phinehas, to die on the same day!

35 "Then I will raise up a faithful priest who will serve me and do what I desire. I will establish his family, and they will be priests to my anointed kings forever. 36 Then all of your surviving family will bow before him, begging for money and food. 'Please,' they will say, 'give us jobs among the priests so we will have enough to eat.'"

CHAPTER 3

The LORD Speaks to Samuel

Meanwhile, the boy Samuel served the LORD by assisting Eli. Now in those days messages from the LORD were very rare, and visions were quite uncommon.

2 One night Eli, who was almost blind by now, had gone to bed. 3 The lamp of God had not yet gone out, and Samuel was sleeping in the Tabernacle near the Ark of God. 4 Suddenly the LORD called out, "Samuel!"

"Yes?" Samuel replied. "What is it?" 5 He got up and ran to Eli. "Here I am. Did you call me?"

"I didn't call you," Eli replied. "Go back to bed." So he did.

6 Then the LORD called out again, "Samuel!"

Again Samuel got up and went to Eli. "Here I am. Did you call me?"

"I didn't call you, my son," Eli said. "Go back to bed."

7 Samuel did not yet know the LORD because he had never had a message from the LORD before. 8 So the LORD called a third time, and once more Samuel got up and went to Eli. "Here I am. Did you call me?"

Then Eli realized it was the LORD who was calling the boy. 9 So he said to Samuel, "Go and lie down again, and if someone calls again, say, 'Speak, LORD, your servant is listening.'" So Samuel went back to bed.

10 And the LORD came and called as before, "Samuel! Samuel!"

And Samuel replied, "Speak, your servant is listening."

11 Then the LORD said to Samuel, "I am about to do a shocking thing in Israel. 12 I am going to carry out all my threats against Eli and his family, from beginning to end. 13 I have warned him that judgment is coming upon his family forever, because his sons are blaspheming God and he hasn't disciplined them. 14 So I have vowed that the sins of Eli and his sons will never be forgiven by sacrifices or offerings."

Samuel Speaks for the LORD
15 Samuel stayed in bed until morning, then got
up and opened the doors of the Tabernacle as
usual. He was afraid to tell Eli what the LORD had
said to him. 16 But Eli called out to him, "Samuel,
my son."
"Here I am," Samuel replied.
17 "What did the LORD say to you? Tell me
everything. And may God strike you and even kill
you if you hide anything from me!" 18 So Samuel
told Eli everything; he didn't hold anything back.
"It is the LORD's will," Eli replied. "Let him do
what he thinks best."
19 As Samuel grew up, the LORD was with him,
and everything Samuel said proved to be reliable. 20 And all Israel, from Dan in the north to
Beersheba in the south, knew that Samuel was
confirmed as a prophet of the LORD. 21 The LORD
continued to appear at Shiloh and gave messages to Samuel there at the Tabernacle. 4:1 And
Samuel's words went out to all the people of
Israel.

CHAPTER 4
The Philistines Capture the Ark
At that time Israel was at war with the Philistines.
The Israelite army was camped near Ebenezer,
and the Philistines were at Aphek. 2 The Philistines attacked and defeated the army of Israel,
killing 4,000 men. 3 After the battle was over, the
troops retreated to their camp, and the elders of
Israel asked, "Why did the LORD allow us to be
defeated by the Philistines?" Then they said,
"Let's bring the Ark of the Covenant of the LORD
from Shiloh. If we carry it into battle with us, it
will save us from our enemies."
4 So they sent men to Shiloh to bring the Ark of
the Covenant of the LORD of Heaven's Armies,
who is enthroned between the cherubim. Hophni and Phinehas, the sons of Eli, were also there
with the Ark of the Covenant of God. 5 When all
the Israelites saw the Ark of the Covenant of the
LORD coming into the camp, their shout of joy
was so loud it made the ground shake!
6 "What's going on?" the Philistines asked.
"What's all the shouting about in the Hebrew
camp?" When they were told it was because the
Ark of the LORD had arrived, 7 they panicked.
"The gods have come into their camp!" they
cried. "This is a disaster! We have never had to
face anything like this before! 8 Help! Who can
save us from these mighty gods of Israel? They
are the same gods who destroyed the Egyptians
with plagues when Israel was in the wilderness.
9 Fight as never before, Philistines! If you don't,
we will become the Hebrews' slaves just as they
have been ours! Stand up like men and fight!"
10 So the Philistines fought desperately, and Israel was defeated again. The slaughter was great;
30,000 Israelite soldiers died that day. The survivors turned and fled to their tents. 11 The Ark of
God was captured, and Hophni and Phinehas,
the two sons of Eli, were killed.

The Death of Eli
12 A man from the tribe of Benjamin ran from the
battlefield and arrived at Shiloh later that same
day. He had torn his clothes and put dust on his
head to show his grief. 13 Eli was waiting beside
the road to hear the news of the battle, for his
heart trembled for the safety of the Ark of God.
When the messenger arrived and told what had
happened, an outcry resounded throughout the
town.
14 "What is all the noise about?" Eli asked.
The messenger rushed over to Eli, 15 who was
ninety-eight years old and blind. 16 He said to Eli,

Um, excuse me...
What does God's voice sound like? Check out 1 Kings 19:11-13 and John 10:27-28.

Is God trying to get your attention? When God spoke, Samuel couldn't figure out who was talking. **Find out if Samuel caught on and what God said in 1 SAMUEL 3.**

Play this game to help you start thinking about God's voice:

1. **Think up a line from a movie or TV show.**
2. **Say the line to a friend or family member, using the same voice the character has.**
3. **See if your friend can guess the movie or character.**
4. **Switch roles and keep playing.**

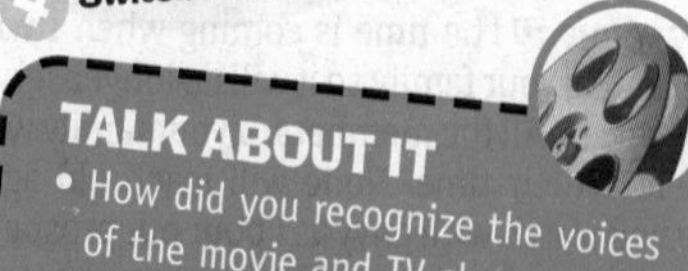

TALK ABOUT IT
- How did you recognize the voices of the movie and TV characters?
- How can we recognize God's voice?
- How does God get our attention?

"I have just come from the battlefield—I was
there this very day."
"What happened, my son?" Eli demanded.
17"Israel has been defeated by the Philistines,"
the messenger replied. "The people have been
slaughtered, and your two sons, Hophni and
Phinehas, were also killed. And the Ark of God
has been captured."
18When the messenger mentioned what had
happened to the Ark of God, Eli fell backward
from his seat beside the gate. He broke his neck
and died, for he was old and overweight. He had
been Israel's judge for forty years.
19Eli's daughter-in-law, the wife of Phinehas,
was pregnant and near her time of delivery.
When she heard that the Ark of God had been
captured and that her father-in-law and husband
were dead, she went into labor and gave birth.
20She died in childbirth, but before she passed
away the midwives tried to encourage her. "Don't
be afraid," they said. "You have a baby boy!" But
she did not answer or pay attention to them.
21She named the child Ichabod (which means
"Where is the glory?"), for she said, "Israel's glory
is gone." She named him this because the Ark of
God had been captured and because her father-
in-law and husband were dead. 22Then she said,
"The glory has departed from Israel, for the Ark
of God has been captured."

CHAPTER 5
The Ark in Philistia

After the Philistines captured the Ark of God,
they took it from the battleground at Ebenezer to
the town of Ashdod. 2They carried the Ark of God
into the temple of Dagon and placed it beside an
idol of Dagon. 3But when the citizens of Ashdod
went to see it the next morning, Dagon had fallen
with his face to the ground in front of the Ark of
the LORD! So they took Dagon and put him in his
place again. 4But the next morning the same
thing happened—Dagon had fallen face down
before the Ark of the LORD again. This time his
head and hands had broken off and were lying in
the doorway. Only the trunk of his body was left
intact. 5That is why to this day neither the priests
of Dagon nor anyone who enters the temple of
Dagon in Ashdod will step on its threshold.
6Then the LORD's heavy hand struck the people
of Ashdod and the nearby villages with a plague of
tumors. 7When the people realized what was
happening, they cried out, "We can't keep the Ark
of the God of Israel here any longer! He is against
us! We will all be destroyed along with Dagon, our
god." 8So they called together the rulers of the
Philistine towns and asked, "What should we do
with the Ark of the God of Israel?"
The rulers discussed it and replied, "Move it to
the town of Gath." So they moved the Ark of the
God of Israel to Gath. 9But when the Ark arrived
at Gath, the LORD's heavy hand fell on its men,
young and old; he struck them with a plague of
tumors, and there was a great panic.
10So they sent the Ark of God to the town of
Ekron, but when the people of Ekron saw it coming they cried out, "They are bringing the Ark of
the God of Israel here to kill us, too!" 11The people summoned the Philistine rulers again and
begged them, "Please send the Ark of the God of
Israel back to its own country, or it will kill us all."
For the deadly plague from God had already begun, and great fear was sweeping across the
town. 12Those who didn't die were afflicted with
tumors; and the cry from the town rose to
heaven.

CHAPTER 6
The Philistines Return the Ark

The Ark of the LORD remained in Philistine territory seven months in all. 2Then the Philistines
called in their priests and diviners and asked
them, "What should we do about the Ark of the
LORD? Tell us how to return it to its own country."
3"Send the Ark of the God of Israel back with a
gift," they were told. "Send a guilt offering so the
plague will stop. Then, if you are healed, you will
know it was his hand that caused the plague."
4"What sort of guilt offering should we
send?" they asked.
And they were told, "Since the plague has
struck both you and your five rulers, make five
gold tumors and five gold rats, just like those
that have ravaged your land. 5Make these things
to show honor to the God of Israel. Perhaps then
he will stop afflicting you, your gods, and your
land. 6Don't be stubborn and rebellious as Pharaoh and the Egyptians were. By the time God
was finished with them, they were eager to let Israel go.
7"Now build a new cart, and find two cows
that have just given birth to calves. Make sure
the cows have never been yoked to a cart. Hitch
the cows to the cart, but shut their calves away
from them in a pen. 8Put the Ark of the LORD on
the cart, and beside it place a chest containing
the gold rats and gold tumors you are sending as
a guilt offering. Then let the cows go wherever
they want. 9If they cross the border of our land
and go to Beth-shemesh, we will know it was the
LORD who brought this great disaster upon us. If

they don't, we will know it was not his hand that
caused the plague. It came simply by chance."
10 So these instructions were carried out. Two
cows were hitched to the cart, and their newborn
calves were shut up in a pen. 11 Then the Ark of
the LORD and the chest containing the gold rats
and gold tumors were placed on the cart. 12 And
sure enough, without veering off in other directions, the cows went straight along the road toward Beth-shemesh, lowing as they went. The
Philistine rulers followed them as far as the border of Beth-shemesh.
13 The people of Beth-shemesh were harvesting wheat in the valley, and when they saw the
Ark, they were overjoyed! 14 The cart came into
the field of a man named Joshua and stopped
beside a large rock. So the people broke up the
wood of the cart for a fire and killed the cows and
sacrificed them to the LORD as a burnt offering.
15 Several men of the tribe of Levi lifted the Ark of
the LORD and the chest containing the gold rats
and gold tumors from the cart and placed them
on the large rock. Many sacrifices and burnt offerings were offered to the LORD that day by the
people of Beth-shemesh. 16 The five Philistine
rulers watched all this and then returned to Ekron that same day.
17 The five gold tumors sent by the Philistines
as a guilt offering to the LORD were gifts from the
rulers of Ashdod, Gaza, Ashkelon, Gath, and Ekron. 18 The five gold rats represented the five Philistine towns and their surrounding villages,
which were controlled by the five rulers. The
large rock at Beth-shemesh, where they set the
Ark of the LORD, still stands in the field of Joshua
as a witness to what happened there.

The Ark Moved to Kiriath-Jearim

19 But the LORD killed seventy men from Beth-
shemesh because they looked into the Ark of the
LORD. And the people mourned greatly because
of what the LORD had done. 20 "Who is able to
stand in the presence of the LORD, this holy
God?" they cried out. "Where can we send the
Ark from here?"
21 So they sent messengers to the people at
Kiriath-jearim and told them, "The Philistines
have returned the Ark of the LORD. Come here
and get it!"

CHAPTER 7

So the men of Kiriath-jearim came to get the Ark
of the LORD. They took it to the hillside home of
Abinadab and ordained Eleazar, his son, to be in
charge of it. 2 The Ark remained in Kiriath-
jearim for a long time—twenty years in all. During that time all Israel mourned because it
seemed the LORD had abandoned them.

Samuel Leads Israel to Victory

3 Then Samuel said to all the people of Israel, "If
you want to return to the LORD with all your
hearts, get rid of your foreign gods and your images of Ashtoreth. Turn your hearts to the LORD
and obey him alone; then he will rescue you from
the Philistines." 4 So the Israelites got rid of their
images of Baal and Ashtoreth and worshiped
only the LORD.
5 Then Samuel told them, "Gather all of Israel
to Mizpah, and I will pray to the LORD for you."
6 So they gathered at Mizpah and, in a great ceremony, drew water from a well and poured it out
before the LORD. They also went without food all
day and confessed that they had sinned against
the LORD. (It was at Mizpah that Samuel became
Israel's judge.)
7 When the Philistine rulers heard that Israel
had gathered at Mizpah, they mobilized their
army and advanced. The Israelites were badly
frightened when they learned that the Philistines were approaching. 8 "Don't stop pleading
with the LORD our God to save us from the Philistines!" they begged Samuel. 9 So Samuel took a
young lamb and offered it to the LORD as a whole
burnt offering. He pleaded with the LORD to help
Israel, and the LORD answered him.
10 Just as Samuel was sacrificing the burnt offering, the Philistines arrived to attack Israel. But
the LORD spoke with a mighty voice of thunder
from heaven that day, and the Philistines were
thrown into such confusion that the Israelites
defeated them. 11 The men of Israel chased them
from Mizpah to a place below Beth-car, slaughtering them all along the way.
12 Samuel then took a large stone and placed it
between the towns of Mizpah and Jeshanah. He
named it Ebenezer (which means "the stone of
help"), for he said, "Up to this point the LORD has
helped us!"
13 So the Philistines were subdued and didn't
invade Israel again for some time. And throughout Samuel's lifetime, the LORD's powerful hand
was raised against the Philistines. 14 The Israelite
villages near Ekron and Gath that the Philistines
had captured were restored to Israel, along with
the rest of the territory that the Philistines had
taken. And there was peace between Israel and
the Amorites in those days.
15 Samuel continued as Israel's judge for the

rest of his life. 16Each year he traveled around, setting up his court first at Bethel, then at Gilgal, and then at Mizpah. He judged the people of Israel at each of these places. 17Then he would return to his home at Ramah, and he would hear cases there, too. And Samuel built an altar to the LORD at Ramah.

CHAPTER 8

Israel Requests a King

As Samuel grew old, he appointed his sons to be judges over Israel. 2Joel and Abijah, his oldest sons, held court in Beersheba. 3But they were not like their father, for they were greedy for money. They accepted bribes and perverted justice.

4Finally, all the elders of Israel met at Ramah to discuss the matter with Samuel. 5"Look," they told him, "you are now old, and your sons are not like you. Give us a king to judge us like all the other nations have."

6Samuel was displeased with their request and went to the LORD for guidance. 7"Do everything they say to you," the LORD replied, "for they are rejecting me, not you. They don't want me to be their king any longer. 8Ever since I brought them from Egypt they have continually abandoned me and followed other gods. And now they are giving you the same treatment. 9Do as they ask, but solemnly warn them about the way a king will reign over them."

Samuel Warns against a Kingdom

10So Samuel passed on the LORD's warning to the people who were asking him for a king. 11"This is how a king will reign over you," Samuel said. "The king will draft your sons and assign them to his chariots and his charioteers, making them run before his chariots. 12Some will be generals and captains in his army, some will be forced to plow in his fields and harvest his crops, and some will make his weapons and chariot equipment. 13The king will take your daughters from you and force them to cook and bake and make perfumes for him. 14He will take away the best of your fields and vineyards and olive groves and give them to his own officials. 15He will take a tenth of your grain and your grape harvest and distribute it among his officers and attendants. 16He will take your male and female slaves and demand the finest of your cattle and donkeys for his own use. 17He will demand a tenth of your flocks, and you will be his slaves. 18When that day comes, you will beg for relief from this king you are demanding, but then the LORD will not help you."

19But the people refused to listen to Samuel's warning. "Even so, we still want a king," they said. 20"We want to be like the nations around us. Our king will judge us and lead us into battle."

21So Samuel repeated to the LORD what the people had said, 22and the LORD replied, "Do as they say, and give them a king." Then Samuel agreed and sent the people home.

CHAPTER 9

Saul Meets Samuel

There was a wealthy, influential man named Kish from the tribe of Benjamin. He was the son of Abiel, son of Zeror, son of Becorath, son of Aphiah, of the tribe of Benjamin. 2His son Saul was the most handsome man in Israel—head and shoulders taller than anyone else in the land.

3One day Kish's donkeys strayed away, and he told Saul, "Take a servant with you, and go look for the donkeys." 4So Saul took one of the servants and traveled through the hill country of Ephraim, the land of Shalishah, the Shaalim area, and the entire land of Benjamin, but they couldn't find the donkeys anywhere.

5Finally, they entered the region of Zuph, and Saul said to his servant, "Let's go home. By now my father will be more worried about us than about the donkeys!"

6But the servant said, "I've just thought of something! There is a man of God who lives here in this town. He is held in high honor by all the people because everything he says comes true. Let's go find him. Perhaps he can tell us which way to go."

7"But we don't have anything to offer him," Saul replied. "Even our food is gone, and we don't have a thing to give him."

8"Well," the servant said, "I have one small silver piece. We can at least offer it to the man of God and see what happens!" 9(In those days if people wanted a message from God, they would say, "Let's go and ask the seer," for prophets used to be called seers.)

10"All right," Saul agreed, "let's try it!" So they started into the town where the man of God lived.

11As they were climbing the hill to the town, they met some young women coming out to draw water. So Saul and his servant asked, "Is the seer here today?"

12"Yes," they replied. "Stay right on this road. He is at the town gates. He has just arrived to take part in a public sacrifice up at the place of worship. 13Hurry and catch him before he goes up there to eat. The guests won't begin eating until he arrives to bless the food."

14So they entered the town, and as they passed
through the gates, Samuel was coming out toward them to go up to the place of worship.
15Now the LORD had told Samuel the previous
day, 16"About this time tomorrow I will send you
a man from the land of Benjamin. Anoint him to
be the leader of my people, Israel. He will rescue
them from the Philistines, for I have looked
down on my people in mercy and have heard
their cry."
17When Samuel saw Saul, the LORD said,
"That's the man I told you about! He will rule my
people."
18Just then Saul approached Samuel at the
gateway and asked, "Can you please tell me where
the seer's house is?"
19"I am the seer!" Samuel replied. "Go up to the
place of worship ahead of me. We will eat there
together, and in the morning I'll tell you what you
want to know and send you on your way. 20And
don't worry about those donkeys that were lost
three days ago, for they have been found. And I
am here to tell you that you and your family are
the focus of all Israel's hopes."
21Saul replied, "But I'm only from the tribe of
Benjamin, the smallest tribe in Israel, and my
family is the least important of all the families of
that tribe! Why are you talking like this to me?"
22Then Samuel brought Saul and his servant
into the hall and placed them at the head of the
table, honoring them above the thirty special
guests. 23Samuel then instructed the cook to
bring Saul the finest cut of meat, the piece that
had been set aside for the guest of honor. 24So
the cook brought in the meat and placed it before Saul. "Go ahead and eat it," Samuel said. "I
was saving it for you even before I invited these
others!" So Saul ate with Samuel that day.
25When they came down from the place of
worship and returned to town, Samuel took Saul
up to the roof of the house and prepared a bed
for him there. 26At daybreak the next morning,
Samuel called to Saul, "Get up! It's time you were
on your way." So Saul got ready, and he and Samuel left the house together. 27When they reached
the edge of town, Samuel told Saul to send his
servant on ahead. After the servant was gone,
Samuel said, "Stay here, for I have received a special message for you from God."

CHAPTER **10**

Samuel Anoints Saul as King

Then Samuel took a flask of olive oil and poured
it over Saul's head. He kissed Saul and said, "I am
doing this because the LORD has appointed you to
be the ruler over Israel, his special possession.
2When you leave me today, you will see two men
beside Rachel's tomb at Zelzah, on the border of
Benjamin. They will tell you that the donkeys
have been found and that your father has stopped
worrying about them and is now worried about
you. He is asking, 'Have you seen my son?'
3"When you get to the oak of Tabor, you will
see three men coming toward you who are on
their way to worship God at Bethel. One will be
bringing three young goats, another will have
three loaves of bread, and the third will be carrying a wineskin full of wine. 4They will greet you
and offer you two of the loaves, which you are to
accept.
5"When you arrive at Gibeah of God, where
the garrison of the Philistines is located, you will
meet a band of prophets coming down from the
place of worship. They will be playing a harp, a
tambourine, a flute, and a lyre, and they will be
prophesying. 6At that time the Spirit of the LORD
will come powerfully upon you, and you will
prophesy with them. You will be changed into a
different person. 7After these signs take place,
do what must be done, for God is with you. 8Then
go down to Gilgal ahead of me. I will join you
there to sacrifice burnt offerings and peace offerings. You must wait for seven days until I arrive and give you further instructions."

Samuel's Signs Are Fulfilled

9As Saul turned and started to leave, God gave him
a new heart, and all Samuel's signs were fulfilled
that day. 10When Saul and his servant arrived at
Gibeah, they saw a group of prophets coming toward them. Then the Spirit of God came powerfully upon Saul, and he, too, began to prophesy.
11When those who knew Saul heard about it, they
exclaimed, "What? Is even Saul a prophet? How
did the son of Kish become a prophet?"
12And one of those standing there said, "Can
anyone become a prophet, no matter who his father is?" So that is the origin of the saying "Is
even Saul a prophet?"
13When Saul had finished prophesying, he
went up to the place of worship. 14"Where have
you been?" Saul's uncle asked him and his servant.
"We were looking for the donkeys," Saul replied, "but we couldn't find them. So we went to
Samuel to ask him where they were."
15"Oh? And what did he say?" his uncle asked.
16"He told us that the donkeys had already
been found," Saul replied. But Saul didn't tell his
uncle what Samuel said about the kingdom.

Saul Is Acclaimed King

17 Later Samuel called all the people of Israel to meet before the LORD at Mizpah. 18 And he said, "This is what the LORD, the God of Israel, has declared: I brought you from Egypt and rescued you from the Egyptians and from all of the nations that were oppressing you. 19 But though I have rescued you from your misery and distress, you have rejected your God today and have said, 'No, we want a king instead!' Now, therefore, present yourselves before the LORD by tribes and clans."

20 So Samuel brought all the tribes of Israel before the LORD, and the tribe of Benjamin was chosen by lot. 21 Then he brought each family of the tribe of Benjamin before the LORD, and the family of the Matrites was chosen. And finally Saul son of Kish was chosen from among them. But when they looked for him, he had disappeared! 22 So they asked the LORD, "Where is he?"

And the LORD replied, "He is hiding among the baggage." 23 So they found him and brought him out, and he stood head and shoulders above anyone else.

24 Then Samuel said to all the people, "This is the man the LORD has chosen as your king. No one in all Israel is like him!"

And all the people shouted, "Long live the king!"

25 Then Samuel told the people what the rights and duties of a king were. He wrote them down on a scroll and placed it before the LORD. Then Samuel sent the people home again.

26 When Saul returned to his home at Gibeah, a group of men whose hearts God had touched went with him. 27 But there were some scoundrels who complained, "How can this man save us?" And they scorned him and refused to bring him gifts. But Saul ignored them.

[Nahash, king of the Ammonites, had been grievously oppressing the people of Gad and Reuben who lived east of the Jordan River. He gouged out the right eye of each of the Israelites living there, and he didn't allow anyone to come and rescue them. In fact, of all the Israelites east of the Jordan, there wasn't a single one whose right eye Nahash had not gouged out. But there were 7,000 men who had escaped from the Ammonites, and they had settled in Jabesh-gilead.]

CHAPTER 11

Saul Defeats the Ammonites

About a month later, King Nahash of Ammon led his army against the Israelite town of Jabesh-gilead. But all the citizens of Jabesh asked for peace. "Make a treaty with us, and we will be your servants," they pleaded.

2 "All right," Nahash said, "but only on one condition. I will gouge out the right eye of every one of you as a disgrace to all Israel!"

3 "Give us seven days to send messengers throughout Israel!" replied the elders of Jabesh. "If no one comes to save us, we will agree to your terms."

4 When the messengers came to Gibeah of Saul and told the people about their plight, everyone broke into tears. 5 Saul had been plowing a field with his oxen, and when he returned to town, he asked, "What's the matter? Why is everyone crying?" So they told him about the message from Jabesh.

6 Then the Spirit of God came powerfully upon Saul, and he became very angry. 7 He took two oxen and cut them into pieces and sent the messengers to carry them throughout Israel with this message: "This is what will happen to the oxen of anyone who refuses to follow Saul and Samuel into battle!" And the LORD made the people afraid of Saul's anger, and all of them came out together as one. 8 When Saul mobilized them at Bezek, he found that there were 300,000 men from Israel and 30,000 men from Judah.

9 So Saul sent the messengers back to Jabesh-gilead to say, "We will rescue you by noontime tomorrow!" There was great joy throughout the town when that message arrived!

10 The men of Jabesh then told their enemies, "Tomorrow we will come out to you, and you can do to us whatever you wish." 11 But before dawn the next morning, Saul arrived, having divided his army into three detachments. He launched a surprise attack against the Ammonites and slaughtered them the whole morning. The remnant of their army was so badly scattered that no two of them were left together.

12 Then the people exclaimed to Samuel, "Now where are those men who said, 'Why should Saul rule over us?' Bring them here, and we will kill them!"

13 But Saul replied, "No one will be executed today, for today the LORD has rescued Israel!"

14 Then Samuel said to the people, "Come, let us all go to Gilgal to renew the kingdom." 15 So they all went to Gilgal, and in a solemn ceremony before the LORD they made Saul king. Then they offered peace offerings to the LORD, and Saul and all the Israelites were filled with joy.

1 Samuel 12 . . . page 278

CHAPTER 12
Samuel's Farewell Address

Then Samuel addressed all Israel: "I have done
as you asked and given you a king. 2 Your king is
now your leader. I stand here before you—an old,
gray-haired man—and my sons serve you. I have
served as your leader from the time I was a boy
to this very day. 3 Now testify against me in the
presence of the LORD and before his anointed
one. Whose ox or donkey have I stolen? Have I
ever cheated any of you? Have I ever oppressed
you? Have I ever taken a bribe and perverted justice? Tell me and I will make right whatever I
have done wrong."

4 "No," they replied, "you have never cheated
or oppressed us, and you have never taken even a
single bribe."

5 "The LORD and his anointed one are my witnesses today," Samuel declared, "that my hands
are clean."

"Yes, he is a witness," they replied.

6 "It was the LORD who appointed Moses and
Aaron," Samuel continued. "He brought your
ancestors out of the land of Egypt. 7 Now stand
here quietly before the LORD as I remind you of
all the great things the LORD has done for you
and your ancestors.

8 "When the Israelites were in Egypt and cried
out to the LORD, he sent Moses and Aaron to rescue them from Egypt and to bring them into this
land. 9 But the people soon forgot about the
LORD their God, so he handed them over to Sisera, the commander of Hazor's army, and also to
the Philistines and to the king of Moab, who
fought against them.

10 "Then they cried to the LORD again and
confessed, 'We have sinned by turning away
from the LORD and worshiping the images of
Baal and Ashtoreth. But we will worship you and
you alone if you will rescue us from our enemies.' 11 Then the LORD sent Gideon, Bedan,
Jephthah, and Samuel to save you, and you lived
in safety.

12 "But when you were afraid of Nahash, the
king of Ammon, you came to me and said that
you wanted a king to reign over you, even though
the LORD your God was already your king. 13 All
right, here is the king you have chosen. You
asked for him, and the LORD has granted your request.

14 "Now if you fear and worship the LORD and
listen to his voice, and if you do not rebel against
the LORD's commands, then both you and your
king will show that you recognize the LORD as
your God. 15 But if you rebel against the LORD's
commands and refuse to listen to him, then his
hand will be as heavy upon you as it was upon
your ancestors.

16 "Now stand here and see the great thing
the LORD is about to do. 17 You know that it does
not rain at this time of the year during the
wheat harvest. I will ask the LORD to send thunder and rain today. Then you will realize how
wicked you have been in asking the LORD for a
king!"

18 So Samuel called to the LORD, and the LORD
sent thunder and rain that day. And all the people were terrified of the LORD and of Samuel.
19 "Pray to the LORD your God for us, or we will
die!" they all said to Samuel. "For now we have
added to our sins by asking for a king."

20 "Don't be afraid," Samuel reassured them.
"You have certainly done wrong, but make sure
now that you worship the LORD with all your
heart, and don't turn your back on him. 21 Don't
go back to worshiping worthless idols that cannot help or rescue you—they are totally useless!
22 The LORD will not abandon his people, because that would dishonor his great name. For it
has pleased the LORD to make you his very own
people.

23 "As for me, I will certainly not sin against the
LORD by ending my prayers for you. And I will
continue to teach you what is good and right.
24 But be sure to fear the LORD and faithfully
serve him. Think of all the wonderful things he
has done for you. 25 But if you continue to sin,
you and your king will be swept away."

CHAPTER 13
Continued War with Philistia

Saul was thirty years old when he became king,
and he reigned for forty-two years.

2 Saul selected 3,000 special troops from the
army of Israel and sent the rest of the men home.
He took 2,000 of the chosen men with him
to Micmash and the hill country of Bethel. The
other 1,000 went with Saul's son Jonathan to
Gibeah in the land of Benjamin.

3 Soon after this, Jonathan attacked and defeated the garrison of Philistines at Geba. The
news spread quickly among the Philistines. So
Saul blew the ram's horn throughout the land,
saying, "Hebrews, hear this! Rise up in revolt!"
4 All Israel heard the news that Saul had destroyed the Philistine garrison at Geba and that
the Philistines now hated the Israelites more
than ever. So the entire Israelite army was summoned to join Saul at Gilgal.

5 The Philistines mustered a mighty army of

3,000 chariots, 6,000 charioteers, and as many
warriors as the grains of sand on the seashore!
They camped at Micmash east of Beth-aven.
6The men of Israel saw what a tight spot they
were in; and because they were hard pressed by
the enemy, they tried to hide in caves, thickets,
rocks, holes, and cisterns. 7Some of them
crossed the Jordan River and escaped into the
land of Gad and Gilead.

FUN fact
The Israelites had a little problem.

Well, a big problem—because it bothered them for hundreds of years. **To get an idea of how long that was, stop right now and count to 100.** How long did it take you? Imagine being bugged by a problem for hundreds of *years*!

The Israelites had some neighbors—the Philistines—who were real pests. When judges like Samson and Samuel led Israel, they fought the Philistines. When Saul and David ruled, they fought the Philistines some more! Finally, David beat most of the Philistines.

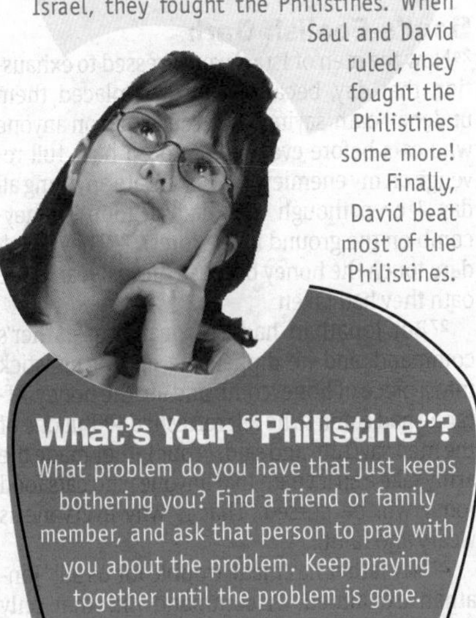

What's Your "Philistine"?

What problem do you have that just keeps bothering you? Find a friend or family member, and ask that person to pray with you about the problem. Keep praying together until the problem is gone.

Saul's Disobedience and Samuel's Rebuke

Meanwhile, Saul stayed at Gilgal, and his men
were trembling with fear. 8Saul waited there
seven days for Samuel, as Samuel had instructed
him earlier, but Samuel still didn't come. Saul realized that his troops were rapidly slipping away.
9So he demanded, "Bring me the burnt offering
and the peace offerings!" And Saul sacrificed the
burnt offering himself.
10Just as Saul was finishing with the burnt offering, Samuel arrived. Saul went out to meet
and welcome him, 11but Samuel said, "What is
this you have done?"

Saul replied, "I saw my men scattering from
me, and you didn't arrive when you said you
would, and the Philistines are at Micmash ready
for battle. 12So I said, 'The Philistines are ready
to march against us at Gilgal, and I haven't even
asked for the LORD's help!' So I felt compelled to
offer the burnt offering myself before you
came."
13"How foolish!" Samuel exclaimed. "You
have not kept the command the LORD your God
gave you. Had you kept it, the LORD would have
established your kingdom over Israel forever.
14But now your kingdom must end, for the LORD
has sought out a man after his own heart. The
LORD has already appointed him to be the leader
of his people, because you have not kept the
LORD's command."

Israel's Military Disadvantage

15Samuel then left Gilgal and went on his way,
but the rest of the troops went with Saul to meet
the army. They went up from Gilgal to Gibeah
in the land of Benjamin. When Saul counted the
men who were still with him, he found only
600 were left! 16Saul and Jonathan and the
troops with them were staying at Geba in the
land of Benjamin. The Philistines set up their
camp at Micmash. 17Three raiding parties soon
left the camp of the Philistines. One went north
toward Ophrah in the land of Shual, 18another
went west to Beth-horon, and the third moved
toward the border above the valley of Zeboim
near the wilderness.
19There were no blacksmiths in the land of Israel in those days. The Philistines wouldn't allow
them for fear they would make swords and
spears for the Hebrews. 20So whenever the Israelites needed to sharpen their plowshares, picks,
axes, or sickles, they had to take them to a Philistine blacksmith. 21The charges were as follows: a
quarter of an ounce of silver for sharpening a

plowshare or a pick, and an eighth of an ounce
for sharpening an ax or making the point of an
ox goad. 22So on the day of the battle none of the
people of Israel had a sword or spear, except for
Saul and Jonathan.

23The pass at Micmash had meanwhile been
secured by a contingent of the Philistine army.

CHAPTER 14

Jonathan's Daring Plan

One day Jonathan said to his armor bearer,
"Come on, let's go over to where the Philistines
have their outpost." But Jonathan did not tell his
father what he was doing.

2Meanwhile, Saul and his 600 men were
camped on the outskirts of Gibeah, around the
pomegranate tree at Migron. 3Among Saul's men
was Ahijah the priest, who was wearing the
ephod, the priestly vest. Ahijah was the son of
Ichabod's brother Ahitub, son of Phinehas, son
of Eli, the priest of the LORD who had served at
Shiloh.

No one realized that Jonathan had left the Israelite camp. 4To reach the Philistine outpost,
Jonathan had to go down between two rocky
cliffs that were called Bozez and Seneh. 5The
cliff on the north was in front of Micmash, and
the one on the south was in front of Geba. 6"Let's
go across to the outpost of those pagans," Jonathan said to his armor bearer. "Perhaps the LORD
will help us, for nothing can hinder the LORD. He
can win a battle whether he has many warriors or
only a few!"

7"Do what you think is best," the armor bearer
replied. "I'm with you completely, whatever you
decide."

8"All right then," Jonathan told him. "We will
cross over and let them see us. 9If they say to us,
'Stay where you are or we'll kill you,' then we will
stop and not go up to them. 10But if they say,
'Come on up and fight,' then we will go up. That
will be the LORD's sign that he will help us defeat
them."

11When the Philistines saw them coming,
they shouted, "Look! The Hebrews are crawling
out of their holes!" 12Then the men from the outpost shouted to Jonathan, "Come on up here, and
we'll teach you a lesson!"

"Come on, climb right behind me," Jonathan
said to his armor bearer, "for the LORD will help
us defeat them!"

13So they climbed up using both hands and
feet, and the Philistines fell before Jonathan, and
his armor bearer killed those who came behind
them. 14They killed some twenty men in all, and
their bodies were scattered over about half an
acre.

15Suddenly, panic broke out in the Philistine
army, both in the camp and in the field, including
even the outposts and raiding parties. And just
then an earthquake struck, and everyone was
terrified.

Israel Defeats the Philistines

16Saul's lookouts in Gibeah of Benjamin saw a
strange sight—the vast army of Philistines began
to melt away in every direction. 17"Call the roll
and find out who's missing," Saul ordered. And
when they checked, they found that Jonathan
and his armor bearer were gone.

18Then Saul shouted to Ahijah, "Bring the
ephod here!" For at that time Ahijah was wearing the ephod in front of the Israelites. 19But
while Saul was talking to the priest, the confusion in the Philistine camp grew louder and
louder. So Saul said to the priest, "Never mind;
let's get going!"

20Then Saul and all his men rushed out to the
battle and found the Philistines killing each
other. There was terrible confusion everywhere.
21Even the Hebrews who had previously gone
over to the Philistine army revolted and joined in
with Saul, Jonathan, and the rest of the Israelites.
22Likewise, the men of Israel who were hiding in
the hill country of Ephraim joined the chase
when they saw the Philistines running away. 23So
the LORD saved Israel that day, and the battle continued to rage even beyond Beth-aven.

Saul's Foolish Oath

24Now the men of Israel were pressed to exhaustion that day, because Saul had placed them
under an oath, saying, "Let a curse fall on anyone
who eats before evening—before I have full revenge on my enemies." So no one ate anything all
day, 25even though they had all found honeycomb on the ground in the forest. 26They didn't
dare touch the honey because they all feared the
oath they had taken.

27But Jonathan had not heard his father's
command, and he dipped the end of his stick
into a piece of honeycomb and ate the honey. After he had eaten it, he felt refreshed. 28But one of
the men saw him and said, "Your father made the
army take a strict oath that anyone who eats food
today will be cursed. That is why everyone is
weary and faint."

29"My father has made trouble for us all!" Jonathan exclaimed. "A command like that only
hurts us. See how refreshed I am now that I have

eaten this little bit of honey. 30 If the men had been allowed to eat freely from the food they found among our enemies, think how many more Philistines we could have killed!"

31 They chased and killed the Philistines all day from Micmash to Aijalon, growing more and more faint. 32 That evening they rushed for the battle plunder and butchered the sheep, goats, cattle, and calves, but they ate them without draining the blood. 33 Someone reported to Saul, "Look, the men are sinning against the LORD by eating meat that still has blood in it."

"That is very wrong," Saul said. "Find a large stone and roll it over here. 34 Then go out among the troops and tell them, 'Bring the cattle, sheep, and goats here to me. Kill them here, and drain the blood before you eat them. Do not sin against the LORD by eating meat with the blood still in it.'"

So that night all the troops brought their animals and slaughtered them there. 35 Then Saul built an altar to the LORD; it was the first of the altars he built to the LORD.

36 Then Saul said, "Let's chase the Philistines all night and plunder them until sunrise. Let's destroy every last one of them."

His men replied, "We'll do whatever you think is best."

But the priest said, "Let's ask God first."

37 So Saul asked God, "Should we go after the Philistines? Will you help us defeat them?" But God made no reply that day.

38 Then Saul said to the leaders, "Something's wrong! I want all my army commanders to come here. We must find out what sin was committed today. 39 I vow by the name of the LORD who rescued Israel that the sinner will surely die, even if it is my own son Jonathan!" But no one would tell him what the trouble was.

40 Then Saul said, "Jonathan and I will stand over here, and all of you stand over there."

And the people responded to Saul, "Whatever you think is best."

41 Then Saul prayed, "O LORD, God of Israel, please show us who is guilty and who is innocent." Then they cast sacred lots, and Jonathan and Saul were chosen as the guilty ones, and the people were declared innocent.

42 Then Saul said, "Now cast lots again and choose between me and Jonathan." And Jonathan was shown to be the guilty one.

43 "Tell me what you have done," Saul demanded of Jonathan.

"I tasted a little honey," Jonathan admitted. "It was only a little bit on the end of my stick. Does that deserve death?"

44 "Yes, Jonathan," Saul said, "you must die! May God strike me and even kill me if you do not die for this."

45 But the people broke in and said to Saul, "Jonathan has won this great victory for Israel. Should he die? Far from it! As surely as the LORD lives, not one hair on his head will be touched, for God helped him do a great deed today." So the people rescued Jonathan, and he was not put to death.

46 Then Saul called back the army from chasing the Philistines, and the Philistines returned home.

Saul's Military Successes

47 Now when Saul had secured his grasp on Israel's throne, he fought against his enemies in every direction—against Moab, Ammon, Edom, the kings of Zobah, and the Philistines. And wherever he turned, he was victorious. 48 He performed great deeds and conquered the Amalekites, saving Israel from all those who had plundered them.

49 Saul's sons included Jonathan, Ishbosheth, and Malkishua. He also had two daughters: Merab, who was older, and Michal. 50 Saul's wife was Ahinoam, the daughter of Ahimaaz. The commander of Saul's army was Abner, the son of Saul's uncle Ner. 51 Saul's father, Kish, and Abner's father, Ner, were both sons of Abiel.

52 The Israelites fought constantly with the Philistines throughout Saul's lifetime. So whenever Saul observed a young man who was brave and strong, he drafted him into his army.

CHAPTER 15

Saul Defeats the Amalekites

One day Samuel said to Saul, "It was the LORD who told me to anoint you as king of his people, Israel. Now listen to this message from the LORD! 2 This is what the LORD of Heaven's Armies has declared: I have decided to settle accounts with the nation of Amalek for opposing Israel when they came from Egypt. 3 Now go and completely destroy the entire Amalekite nation—men, women, children, babies, cattle, sheep, goats, camels, and donkeys."

4 So Saul mobilized his army at Telaim. There were 200,000 soldiers from Israel and 10,000 men from Judah. 5 Then Saul and his army went to a town of the Amalekites and lay in wait in the valley. 6 Saul sent this warning to the Kenites: "Move away from where the Amalekites live, or you will die with them. For you showed kindness to all the people of Israel when they came up from Egypt." So the Kenites packed up and left.

7Then Saul slaughtered the Amalekites from
Havilah all the way to Shur, east of Egypt. 8He
captured Agag, the Amalekite king, but completely destroyed everyone else. 9Saul and his
men spared Agag's life and kept the best of the
sheep and goats, the cattle, the fat calves, and the
lambs—everything, in fact, that appealed to
them. They destroyed only what was worthless
or of poor quality.

The LORD Rejects Saul

10Then the LORD said to Samuel, 11"I am sorry
that I ever made Saul king, for he has not been
loyal to me and has refused to obey my command." Samuel was so deeply moved when he
heard this that he cried out to the LORD all night.
12Early the next morning Samuel went to find
Saul. Someone told him, "Saul went to the town
of Carmel to set up a monument to himself; then
he went on to Gilgal."
13When Samuel finally found him, Saul
greeted him cheerfully. "May the LORD bless you,"
he said. "I have carried out the LORD's command!"
14"Then what is all the bleating of sheep and
goats and the lowing of cattle I hear?" Samuel
demanded.

I Choose

That one—the little one! That's kind of what God did when he had Samuel look for a new king of Israel.
Read 1 SAMUEL 16:8-13 for details.

IN THE BAG

1. **Wrap a nice present in old wrinkly paper without a bow. Wrap a worthless present in shiny paper and a big bow.**
2. **Have your mom or dad choose just one of the presents. Once the first one is opened, open the second.**
3. **Read 1 SAMUEL 16:7 to your parent, then talk about what's important to God.**

15"It's true that the army spared the best of the
sheep, goats, and cattle," Saul admitted. "But they
are going to sacrifice them to the LORD your God.
We have destroyed everything else."
16Then Samuel said to Saul, "Stop! Listen to
what the LORD told me last night!"
"What did he tell you?" Saul asked.
17And Samuel told him, "Although you may
think little of yourself, are you not the leader of
the tribes of Israel? The LORD has anointed you
king of Israel. 18And the LORD sent you on a mission and told you, 'Go and completely destroy the
sinners, the Amalekites, until they are all dead.'
19Why haven't you obeyed the LORD? Why did
you rush for the plunder and do what was evil in
the LORD's sight?"
20"But I did obey the LORD," Saul insisted. "I
carried out the mission he gave me. I brought
back King Agag, but I destroyed everyone else.
21Then my troops brought in the best of the
sheep, goats, cattle, and plunder to sacrifice to
the LORD your God in Gilgal."
22But Samuel replied,

"What is more pleasing to the LORD:
 your burnt offerings and sacrifices
 or your obedience to his voice?
Listen! Obedience is better than sacrifice,
 and submission is better than offering
 the fat of rams.
23 Rebellion is as sinful as witchcraft,
 and stubbornness as bad as worshiping
 idols.
So because you have rejected the command
 of the LORD,
 he has rejected you as king."

Saul Pleads for Forgiveness

24Then Saul admitted to Samuel, "Yes, I have
sinned. I have disobeyed your instructions and
the LORD's command, for I was afraid of the people and did what they demanded. 25But now,
please forgive my sin and come back with me so
that I may worship the LORD."
26But Samuel replied, "I will not go back with
you! Since you have rejected the LORD's command, he has rejected you as king of Israel."
27As Samuel turned to go, Saul tried to hold
him back and tore the hem of his robe. 28And
Samuel said to him, "The LORD has torn the kingdom of Israel from you today and has given it to
someone else—one who is better than you.
29And he who is the Glory of Israel will not lie,
nor will he change his mind, for he is not human
that he should change his mind!"

30 Then Saul pleaded again, "I know I have sinned. But please, at least honor me before the elders of my people and before Israel by coming back with me so that I may worship the LORD your God." 31 So Samuel finally agreed and went back with him, and Saul worshiped the LORD.

Samuel Executes King Agag

32 Then Samuel said, "Bring King Agag to me." Agag arrived full of hope, for he thought, "Surely the worst is over, and I have been spared!" 33 But Samuel said, "As your sword has killed the sons of many mothers, now your mother will be childless." And Samuel cut Agag to pieces before the LORD at Gilgal.

34 Then Samuel went home to Ramah, and Saul returned to his house at Gibeah of Saul. 35 Samuel never went to meet with Saul again, but he mourned constantly for him. And the LORD was sorry he had ever made Saul king of Israel.

CHAPTER 16

Samuel Anoints David as King

Now the LORD said to Samuel, "You have mourned long enough for Saul. I have rejected him as king of Israel, so fill your flask with olive oil and go to Bethlehem. Find a man named Jesse who lives there, for I have selected one of his sons to be my king."

2 But Samuel asked, "How can I do that? If Saul hears about it, he will kill me."

"Take a heifer with you," the LORD replied, "and say that you have come to make a sacrifice to the LORD. 3 Invite Jesse to the sacrifice, and I will show you which of his sons to anoint for me."

4 So Samuel did as the LORD instructed. When he arrived at Bethlehem, the elders of the town came trembling to meet him. "What's wrong?" they asked. "Do you come in peace?"

5 "Yes," Samuel replied. "I have come to sacrifice to the LORD. Purify yourselves and come with me to the sacrifice." Then Samuel performed the purification rite for Jesse and his sons and invited them to the sacrifice, too.

6 When they arrived, Samuel took one look at Eliab and thought, "Surely this is the LORD's anointed!"

7 But the LORD said to Samuel, "Don't judge by his appearance or height, for I have rejected him. The LORD doesn't see things the way you see them. People judge by outward appearance, but the LORD looks at the heart."

8 Then Jesse told his son Abinadab to step forward and walk in front of Samuel. But Samuel said, "This is not the one the LORD has chosen." 9 Next Jesse summoned Shimea, but Samuel said, "Neither is this the one the LORD has chosen." 10 In the same way all seven of Jesse's sons were presented to Samuel. But Samuel said to Jesse, "The LORD has not chosen any of these." 11 Then Samuel asked, "Are these all the sons you have?"

"There is still the youngest," Jesse replied. "But he's out in the fields watching the sheep and goats."

"Send for him at once," Samuel said. "We will not sit down to eat until he arrives."

12 So Jesse sent for him. He was dark and handsome, with beautiful eyes.

And the LORD said, "This is the one; anoint him."

13 So as David stood there among his brothers, Samuel took the flask of olive oil he had brought and anointed David with the oil. And the Spirit of the LORD came powerfully upon David from that day on. Then Samuel returned to Ramah.

David Serves in Saul's Court

14 Now the Spirit of the LORD had left Saul, and the LORD sent a tormenting spirit that filled him with depression and fear.

15 Some of Saul's servants said to him, "A tormenting spirit from God is troubling you. 16 Let us find a good musician to play the harp whenever the tormenting spirit troubles you. He will play soothing music, and you will soon be well again."

17 "All right," Saul said. "Find me someone who plays well, and bring him here."

18 One of the servants said to Saul, "One of Jesse's sons from Bethlehem is a talented harp player. Not only that—he is a brave warrior, a man of war, and has good judgment. He is also a fine-looking young man, and the LORD is with him."

19 So Saul sent messengers to Jesse to say, "Send me your son David, the shepherd." 20 Jesse responded by sending David to Saul, along with a young goat, a donkey loaded with bread, and a wineskin full of wine.

21 So David went to Saul and began serving him. Saul loved David very much, and David became his armor bearer.

22 Then Saul sent word to Jesse asking, "Please let David remain in my service, for I am very pleased with him."

23 And whenever the tormenting spirit from God troubled Saul, David would play the harp. Then Saul would feel better, and the tormenting spirit would go away.

1 Samuel 17 . . . page 284

CHAPTER 17

Goliath Challenges the Israelites

The Philistines now mustered their army for battle and camped between Socoh in Judah and Azekah at Ephes-dammim. 2 Saul countered by gathering his Israelite troops near the valley of Elah. 3 So the Philistines and Israelites faced each other on opposite hills, with the valley between them.

4 Then Goliath, a Philistine champion from Gath, came out of the Philistine ranks to face the forces of Israel. He was over nine feet tall! 5 He wore a bronze helmet, and his bronze coat of mail weighed 125 pounds. 6 He also wore bronze leg armor, and he carried a bronze javelin on his shoulder. 7 The shaft of his spear was as heavy and thick as a weaver's beam, tipped with an iron spearhead that weighed 15 pounds. His armor bearer walked ahead of him carrying a shield.

8 Goliath stood and shouted a taunt across to the Israelites. "Why are you all coming out to fight?" he called. "I am the Philistine champion, but you are only the servants of Saul. Choose one man to come down here and fight me! 9 If he kills me, then we will be your slaves. But if I kill him, you will be our slaves! 10 I defy the armies of Israel today! Send me a man who will fight me!" 11 When Saul and the Israelites heard this, they were terrified and deeply shaken.

Jesse Sends David to Saul's Camp

12 Now David was the son of a man named Jesse, an Ephrathite from Bethlehem in the land of Judah. Jesse was an old man at that time, and he had eight sons. 13 Jesse's three oldest sons—Eliab, Abinadab, and Shimea—had already joined Saul's army to fight the Philistines. 14 David was the youngest son. David's three oldest brothers stayed with Saul's army, 15 but David went back and forth so he could help his father with the sheep in Bethlehem.

16 For forty days, every morning and evening, the Philistine champion strutted in front of the Israelite army.

17 One day Jesse said to David, "Take this basket of roasted grain and these ten loaves of bread, and carry them quickly to your brothers. 18 And give these ten cuts of cheese to their captain. See how your brothers are getting along, and bring back a report on how they are doing." 19 David's brothers were with Saul and the Israelite army at the valley of Elah, fighting against the Philistines.

20 So David left the sheep with another shepherd and set out early the next morning with the gifts, as Jesse had directed him. He arrived at the camp just as the Israelite army was leaving for the battlefield with shouts and battle cries. 21 Soon the Israelite and Philistine forces stood facing each other, army against army. 22 David left his things with the keeper of supplies and hurried out to the ranks to greet his brothers. 23 As he was talking with them, Goliath, the Philistine champion from Gath, came out from the Philistine ranks. Then David heard him shout his usual taunt to the army of Israel.

24 As soon as the Israelite army saw him, they began to run away in fright. 25 "Have you seen the giant?" the men asked. "He comes out each day to defy Israel. The king has offered a huge reward to anyone who kills him. He will give that man one of his daughters for a wife, and the man's entire family will be exempted from paying taxes!"

26 David asked the soldiers standing nearby, "What will a man get for killing this Philistine and ending his defiance of Israel? Who is this pagan Philistine anyway, that he is allowed to defy the armies of the living God?"

27 And these men gave David the same reply. They said, "Yes, that is the reward for killing him."

28 But when David's oldest brother, Eliab, heard David talking to the men, he was angry. "What are you doing around here anyway?" he demanded. "What about those few sheep you're supposed to be taking care of? I know about your pride and deceit. You just want to see the battle!"

29 "What have I done now?" David replied. "I was only asking a question!" 30 He walked over to some others and asked them the same thing and received the same answer. 31 Then David's question was reported to King Saul, and the king sent for him.

David Kills Goliath

32 "Don't worry about this Philistine," David told Saul. "I'll go fight him!"

33 "Don't be ridiculous!" Saul replied. "There's no way you can fight this Philistine and possibly win! You're only a boy, and he's been a man of war since his youth."

34 But David persisted. "I have been taking care of my father's sheep and goats," he said. "When a lion or a bear comes to steal a lamb from the flock, 35 I go after it with a club and rescue the lamb from its mouth. If the animal turns

on me, I catch it by the jaw and club it to death.
36I have done this to both lions and bears, and I'll
do it to this pagan Philistine, too, for he has defied the armies of the living God! 37The LORD
who rescued me from the claws of the lion and
the bear will rescue me from this Philistine!"

Saul finally consented. "All right, go ahead," he
said. "And may the LORD be with you!"

38Then Saul gave David his own armor—a
bronze helmet and a coat of mail. 39David put it
on, strapped the sword over it, and took a step or
two to see what it was like, for he had never worn
such things before.

"I can't go in these," he protested to Saul. "I'm
not used to them." So David took them off again.
40He picked up five smooth stones from a
stream and put them into his shepherd's bag.
Then, armed only with his shepherd's staff and
sling, he started across the valley to fight the Philistine.

41Goliath walked out toward David with his
shield bearer ahead of him, 42sneering in contempt at this ruddy-faced boy. 43"Am I a dog," he
roared at David, "that you come at me with a
stick?" And he cursed David by the names of his
gods. 44"Come over here, and I'll give your flesh
to the birds and wild animals!" Goliath yelled.

45David replied to the Philistine, "You come to
me with sword, spear, and javelin, but I come to
you in the name of the LORD of Heaven's Armies—
the God of the armies of Israel, whom you have
defied. 46Today the LORD will conquer you, and I
will kill you and cut off your head. And then I will
give the dead bodies of your men to the birds and
wild animals, and the whole world will know that
there is a God in Israel! 47And everyone assembled here will know that the LORD rescues his people, but not with sword and spear. This is the
LORD's battle, and he will give you to us!"

48As Goliath moved closer to attack, David
quickly ran out to meet him. 49Reaching into his
shepherd's bag and taking out a stone, he hurled
it with his sling and hit the Philistine in the forehead. The stone sank in, and Goliath stumbled
and fell face down on the ground.

50So David triumphed over the Philistine with
only a sling and a stone, for he had no sword.
51Then David ran over and pulled Goliath's
sword from its sheath. David used it to kill him
and cut off his head.

Israel Routs the Philistines

When the Philistines saw that their champion
was dead, they turned and ran. 52Then the men
of Israel and Judah gave a great shout of triumph and rushed after the Philistines, chasing
them as far as Gath and the gates of Ekron. The
bodies of the dead and wounded Philistines
were strewn all along the road from Shaaraim,
as far as Gath and Ekron. 53Then the Israelite
army returned and plundered the deserted Philistine camp. 54(David took the Philistine's head
to Jerusalem, but he stored the man's armor in
his own tent.)

55As Saul watched David go out to fight the
Philistine, he asked Abner, the commander of his
army, "Abner, whose son is this young man?"

"I really don't know," Abner declared.

56"Well, find out who he is!" the king told him.

57As soon as David returned from killing Goliath, Abner brought him to Saul with the Philistine's head still in his hand. 58"Tell me about
your father, young man," Saul said.

And David replied, "His name is Jesse, and we
live in Bethlehem."

CHAPTER 18

Saul Becomes Jealous of David

After David had finished talking with Saul, he
met Jonathan, the king's son. There was an im-
mediate bond between them, for Jonathan loved
David. 2From that day on Saul kept David with
him and wouldn't let him return home. 3And
Jonathan made a solemn pact with David, because he loved him as he loved himself. 4Jona-
than sealed the pact by taking off his robe and
giving it to David, together with his tunic, sword,
bow, and belt.

5Whatever Saul asked David to do, David did
it successfully. So Saul made him a commander
over the men of war, an appointment that was
welcomed by the people and Saul's officers alike.

6When the victorious Israelite army was returning home after David had killed the Philistine, women from all the towns of Israel came
out to meet King Saul. They sang and danced for
joy with tambourines and cymbals. 7This was
their song:

"Saul has killed his thousands,
and David his ten thousands!"

8This made Saul very angry. "What's this?" he
said. "They credit David with ten thousands and
me with only thousands. Next they'll be making
him their king!" 9So from that time on Saul kept
a jealous eye on David.

10The very next day a tormenting spirit from
God overwhelmed Saul, and he began to rave in
his house like a madman. David was playing the
harp, as he did each day. But Saul had a spear in

his hand, 11and he suddenly hurled it at David, intending to pin him to the wall. But David escaped him twice.

12Saul was then afraid of David, for the LORD was with David and had turned away from Saul. 13Finally, Saul sent him away and appointed him commander over 1,000 men, and David faithfully led his troops into battle.

14David continued to succeed in everything he did, for the LORD was with him. 15When Saul recognized this, he became even more afraid of him. 16But all Israel and Judah loved David because he was so successful at leading his troops into battle.

David Marries Saul's Daughter

17One day Saul said to David, "I am ready to give you my older daughter, Merab, as your wife. But first you must prove yourself to be a real warrior by fighting the LORD's battles." For Saul thought, "I'll send him out against the Philistines and let them kill him rather than doing it myself."

18"Who am I, and what is my family in Israel that I should be the king's son-in-law?" David exclaimed. "My father's family is nothing!" 19So when the time came for Saul to give his daughter Merab in marriage to David, he gave her instead to Adriel, a man from Meholah.

20In the meantime, Saul's daughter Michal had fallen in love with David, and Saul was delighted when he heard about it. 21"Here's another chance to see him killed by the Philistines!" Saul said to himself. But to David he said, "Today you have a second chance to become my son-in-law!"

22Then Saul told his men to say to David, "The king really likes you, and so do we. Why don't you accept the king's offer and become his son-in-law?"

23When Saul's men said these things to David, he replied, "How can a poor man from a humble family afford the bride price for the daughter of a king?"

24When Saul's men reported this back to the king, 25he told them, "Tell David that all I want for the bride price is 100 Philistine foreskins! Vengeance on my enemies is all I really want." But what Saul had in mind was that David would be killed in the fight.

26David was delighted to accept the offer. Before the time limit expired, 27he and his men went out and killed 200 Philistines. Then David fulfilled the king's requirement by presenting all their foreskins to him. So Saul gave his daughter Michal to David to be his wife.

28When Saul realized that the LORD was with David and how much his daughter Michal loved him, 29Saul became even more afraid of him, and he remained David's enemy for the rest of his life.

30Every time the commanders of the Philistines attacked, David was more successful against them than all the rest of Saul's officers. So David's name became very famous.

CHAPTER 19

Saul Tries to Kill David

Saul now urged his servants and his son Jonathan to assassinate David. But Jonathan, because of his strong affection for David, 2told him what his father was planning. "Tomorrow morning," he warned him, "you must find a hiding place out in the fields. 3I'll ask my father to go out there with me, and I'll talk to him about you. Then I'll tell you everything I can find out."

4The next morning Jonathan spoke with his father about David, saying many good things about him. "The king must not sin against his servant David," Jonathan said. "He's never done anything to harm you. He has always helped you in any way he could. 5Have you forgotten about the time he risked his life to kill the Philistine giant and how the LORD brought a great victory to all Israel as a result? You were certainly happy about it then. Why should you murder an innocent man like David? There is no reason for it at all!"

6So Saul listened to Jonathan and vowed, "As surely as the LORD lives, David will not be killed."

7Afterward Jonathan called David and told him what had happened. Then he brought David to Saul, and David served in the court as before.

8War broke out again after that, and David led his troops against the Philistines. He attacked them with such fury that they all ran away.

9But one day when Saul was sitting at home, with spear in hand, the tormenting spirit from the LORD suddenly came upon him again. As David played his harp, 10Saul hurled his spear at David. But David dodged out of the way, and leaving the spear stuck in the wall, he fled and escaped into the night.

Michal Saves David's Life

11Then Saul sent troops to watch David's house. They were told to kill David when he came out the next morning. But Michal, David's wife, warned him, "If you don't escape tonight, you will be dead by morning." 12So she helped him climb out through a window, and he fled and escaped. 13Then she took an idol and put it in his

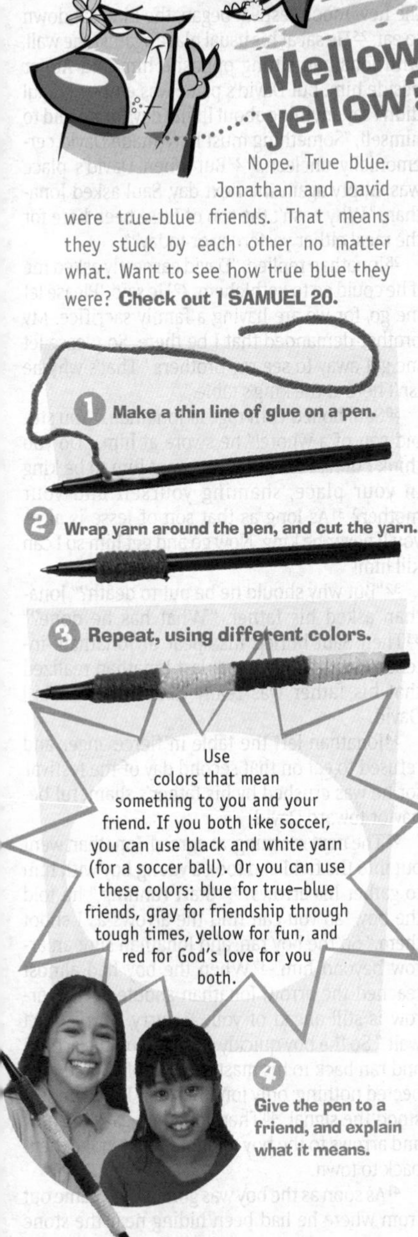
Mean green?
Mellow yellow?
Nope. True blue. Jonathan and David were true-blue friends. That means they stuck by each other no matter what. Want to see how true blue they were? **Check out 1 SAMUEL 20.**
1 Make a thin line of glue on a pen.
2 Wrap yarn around the pen, and cut the yarn.
3 Repeat, using different colors.
Use colors that mean something to you and your friend. If you both like soccer, you can use black and white yarn (for a soccer ball). Or you can use these colors: blue for true-blue friends, gray for friendship through tough times, yellow for fun, and red for God's love for you both.
4 Give the pen to a friend, and explain what it means.

bed, covered it with blankets, and put a cushion
of goat's hair at its head.
14When the troops came to arrest David, she
told them he was sick and couldn't get out of
bed.
15But Saul sent the troops back to get David.
He ordered, "Bring him to me in his bed so I can
kill him!" 16But when they came to carry David
out, they discovered that it was only an idol in the
bed with a cushion of goat's hair at its head.
17"Why have you betrayed me like this and let
my enemy escape?" Saul demanded of Michal.
"I had to," Michal replied. "He threatened to
kill me if I didn't help him."
18So David escaped and went to Ramah to see
Samuel, and he told him all that Saul had done to
him. Then Samuel took David with him to live at
Naioth. 19When the report reached Saul that David was at Naioth in Ramah, 20he sent troops to
capture him. But when they arrived and saw
Samuel leading a group of prophets who were
prophesying, the Spirit of God came upon Saul's
men, and they also began to prophesy. 21When
Saul heard what had happened, he sent other
troops, but they, too, prophesied! The same
thing happened a third time. 22Finally, Saul himself went to Ramah and arrived at the great well
in Secu. "Where are Samuel and David?" he demanded.
"They are at Naioth in Ramah," someone told
him.
23But on the way to Naioth in Ramah the Spirit
of God came even upon Saul, and he, too, began
to prophesy all the way to Naioth! 24He tore off
his clothes and lay naked on the ground all day
and all night, prophesying in the presence of
Samuel. The people who were watching exclaimed, "What? Is even Saul a prophet?"

CHAPTER 20

Jonathan Helps David

David now fled from Naioth in Ramah and found
Jonathan. "What have I done?" he exclaimed.
"What is my crime? How have I offended your
father that he is so determined to kill me?"
2"That's not true!" Jonathan protested.
"You're not going to die. He always tells me
everything he's going to do, even the little things.
I know my father wouldn't hide something like
this from me. It just isn't so!"
3Then David took an oath before Jonathan
and said, "Your father knows perfectly well
about our friendship, so he has said to himself,
'I won't tell Jonathan—why should I hurt him?'
But I swear to you that I am only a step away

from death! I swear it by the LORD and by your
own soul!"
4"Tell me what I can do to help you," Jonathan
exclaimed.
5David replied, "Tomorrow we celebrate the
new moon festival. I've always eaten with the
king on this occasion, but tomorrow I'll hide in
the field and stay there until the evening of the
third day. 6If your father asks where I am, tell him
I asked permission to go home to Bethlehem for
an annual family sacrifice. 7If he says, 'Fine!' you
will know all is well. But if he is angry and loses
his temper, you will know he is determined to kill
me. 8Show me this loyalty as my sworn friend—
for we made a solemn pact before the LORD—or
kill me yourself if I have sinned against your father. But please don't betray me to him!"
9"Never!" Jonathan exclaimed. "You know
that if I had the slightest notion my father was
planning to kill you, I would tell you at once."
10Then David asked, "How will I know whether
or not your father is angry?"
11"Come out to the field with me," Jonathan replied. And they went out there together. 12Then
Jonathan told David, "I promise by the LORD, the
God of Israel, that by this time tomorrow, or the
next day at the latest, I will talk to my father and
let you know at once how he feels about you. If he
speaks favorably about you, I will let you know.
13But if he is angry and wants you killed, may the
LORD strike me and even kill me if I don't warn
you so you can escape and live. May the LORD be
with you as he used to be with my father. 14And
may you treat me with the faithful love of the
LORD as long as I live. But if I die, 15treat my family with this faithful love, even when the LORD destroys all your enemies from the face of the
earth."
16So Jonathan made a solemn pact with David,
saying, "May the LORD destroy all your enemies!"
17And Jonathan made David reaffirm his vow of
friendship again, for Jonathan loved David as he
loved himself.
18Then Jonathan said, "Tomorrow we celebrate the new moon festival. You will be missed
when your place at the table is empty. 19The day
after tomorrow, toward evening, go to the place
where you hid before, and wait there by the stone
pile. 20I will come out and shoot three arrows to
the side of the stone pile as though I were shooting at a target. 21Then I will send a boy to bring
the arrows back. If you hear me tell him, 'They're
on this side,' then you will know, as surely as the
LORD lives, that all is well, and there is no trouble.
22But if I tell him, 'Go farther—the arrows are still
ahead of you,' then it will mean that you must
leave immediately, for the LORD is sending you
away. 23And may the LORD make us keep our
promises to each other, for he has witnessed
them."
24So David hid himself in the field, and when
the new moon festival began, the king sat down
to eat. 25He sat at his usual place against the wall,
with Jonathan sitting opposite him and Abner
beside him. But David's place was empty. 26Saul
didn't say anything about it that day, for he said to
himself, "Something must have made David ceremonially unclean." 27But when David's place
was empty again the next day, Saul asked Jonathan, "Why hasn't the son of Jesse been here for
the meal either yesterday or today?"
28Jonathan replied, "David earnestly asked me
if he could go to Bethlehem. 29He said, 'Please let
me go, for we are having a family sacrifice. My
brother demanded that I be there. So please let
me get away to see my brothers.' That's why he
isn't here at the king's table."
30Saul boiled with rage at Jonathan. "You stupid son of a whore!" he swore at him. "Do you
think I don't know that you want him to be king
in your place, shaming yourself and your
mother? 31As long as that son of Jesse is alive,
you'll never be king. Now go and get him so I can
kill him!"
32"But why should he be put to death?" Jonathan asked his father. "What has he done?"
33Then Saul hurled his spear at Jonathan, intending to kill him. So at last Jonathan realized
that his father was really determined to kill
David.
34Jonathan left the table in fierce anger and
refused to eat on that second day of the festival,
for he was crushed by his father's shameful behavior toward David.
35The next morning, as agreed, Jonathan went
out into the field and took a young boy with him
to gather his arrows. 36"Start running," he told
the boy, "so you can find the arrows as I shoot
them." So the boy ran, and Jonathan shot an arrow beyond him. 37When the boy had almost
reached the arrow, Jonathan shouted, "The arrow is still ahead of you. 38Hurry, hurry, don't
wait." So the boy quickly gathered up the arrows
and ran back to his master. 39He, of course, suspected nothing; only Jonathan and David understood the signal. 40Then Jonathan gave his bow
and arrows to the boy and told him to take them
back to town.
41As soon as the boy was gone, David came out
from where he had been hiding near the stone

pile. Then David bowed three times to Jonathan
with his face to the ground. Both of them were in
tears as they embraced each other and said
good-bye, especially David.
42 At last Jonathan said to David, "Go in peace,
for we have sworn loyalty to each other in the
LORD's name. The LORD is the witness of a bond
between us and our children forever." Then David left, and Jonathan returned to the town.

CHAPTER 21

David Runs from Saul

David went to the town of Nob to see Ahimelech
the priest. Ahimelech trembled when he saw
him. "Why are you alone?" he asked. "Why is no
one with you?"
2 "The king has sent me on a private matter,"
David said. "He told me not to tell anyone why I
am here. I have told my men where to meet me
later. 3 Now, what is there to eat? Give me five
loaves of bread or anything else you have."
4 "We don't have any regular bread," the priest
replied. "But there is the holy bread, which you
can have if your young men have not slept with
any women recently."
5 "Don't worry," David replied. "I never allow
my men to be with women when we are on a
campaign. And since they stay clean even on ordinary trips, how much more on this one!"
6 Since there was no other food available, the
priest gave him the holy bread—the Bread of
the Presence that was placed before the LORD in
the Tabernacle. It had just been replaced that day
with fresh bread.
7 Now Doeg the Edomite, Saul's chief herds-
man, was there that day, having been detained
before the LORD.
8 David asked Ahimelech, "Do you have a spear
or sword? The king's business was so urgent that
I didn't even have time to grab a weapon!"
9 "I only have the sword of Goliath the Philistine, whom you killed in the valley of Elah," the
priest replied. "It is wrapped in a cloth behind
the ephod. Take that if you want it, for there is
nothing else here."
"There is nothing like it!" David replied. "Give
it to me!"
10 So David escaped from Saul and went to
King Achish of Gath. 11 But the officers of Achish
were unhappy about his being there. "Isn't this
David, the king of the land?" they asked. "Isn't he
the one the people honor with dances, singing,

'Saul has killed his thousands,
and David his ten thousands'?"

12 David heard these comments and was very
afraid of what King Achish of Gath might do to
him. 13 So he pretended to be insane, scratching
on doors and drooling down his beard.
14 Finally, King Achish said to his men, "Must
you bring me a madman? 15 We already have
enough of them around here! Why should I let
someone like this be my guest?"

CHAPTER 22

David at the Cave of Adullam

So David left Gath and escaped to the cave of
Adullam. Soon his brothers and all his other relatives joined him there. 2 Then others began coming—men who were in trouble or in debt or who
were just discontented—until David was the captain of about 400 men.
3 Later David went to Mizpeh in Moab, where
he asked the king, "Please allow my father and
mother to live here with you until I know what
God is going to do for me." 4 So David's parents
stayed in Moab with the king during the entire
time David was living in his stronghold.
5 One day the prophet Gad told David, "Leave
the stronghold and return to the land of Judah."
So David went to the forest of Hereth.
6 The news of his arrival in Judah soon reached
Saul. At the time, the king was sitting beneath the
tamarisk tree on the hill at Gibeah, holding his
spear and surrounded by his officers.
7 "Listen here, you men of Benjamin!" Saul
shouted to his officers when he heard the news.
"Has that son of Jesse promised every one of you
fields and vineyards? Has he promised to make
you all generals and captains in his army? 8 Is that
why you have conspired against me? For not one
of you told me when my own son made a solemn
pact with the son of Jesse. You're not even sorry
for me. Think of it! My own son—encouraging
him to kill me, as he is trying to do this very day!"
9 Then Doeg the Edomite, who was standing
there with Saul's men, spoke up. "When I was at
Nob," he said, "I saw the son of Jesse talking to the
priest, Ahimelech son of Ahitub. 10 Ahimelech
consulted the LORD for him. Then he gave him
food and the sword of Goliath the Philistine."

The Slaughter of the Priests

11 King Saul immediately sent for Ahimelech and
all his family, who served as priests at Nob.
12 When they arrived, Saul shouted at him, "Listen to me, you son of Ahitub!"
"What is it, my king?" Ahimelech asked.
13 "Why have you and the son of Jesse conspired against me?" Saul demanded. "Why did

you give him food and a sword? Why have you
consulted God for him? Why have you encouraged him to kill me, as he is trying to do this
very day?"

14"But sir," Ahimelech replied, "is anyone
among all your servants as faithful as David, your
son-in-law? Why, he is the captain of your bodyguard and a highly honored member of your
household! 15This was certainly not the first time
I had consulted God for him! May the king not
accuse me and my family in this matter, for I
knew nothing at all of any plot against you."

16"You will surely die, Ahimelech, along with
your entire family!" the king shouted. 17And he
ordered his bodyguards, "Kill these priests of the
LORD, for they are allies and conspirators with
David! They knew he was running away from me,
but they didn't tell me!" But Saul's men refused to
kill the LORD's priests.

18Then the king said to Doeg, "You do it." So
Doeg the Edomite turned on them and killed
them that day, eighty-five priests in all, still wearing their priestly garments. 19Then he went to
Nob, the town of the priests, and killed the priests'
families—men and women, children and babies—
and all the cattle, donkeys, sheep, and goats.

20Only Abiathar, one of the sons of Ahimelech,
escaped and fled to David. 21When he told David
that Saul had killed the priests of the LORD, 22Da-
vid exclaimed, "I knew it! When I saw Doeg the
Edomite there that day, I knew he was sure to tell
Saul. Now I have caused the death of all your father's family. 23Stay here with me, and don't be
afraid. I will protect you with my own life, for the
same person wants to kill us both."

CHAPTER 23

David Protects the Town of Keilah

One day news came to David that the Philistines
were at Keilah stealing grain from the threshing
floors. 2David asked the LORD, "Should I go and
attack them?"

"Yes, go and save Keilah," the LORD told him.

3But David's men said, "We're afraid even here
in Judah. We certainly don't want to go to Keilah
to fight the whole Philistine army!"

4So David asked the LORD again, and again the
LORD replied, "Go down to Keilah, for I will help
you conquer the Philistines."

5So David and his men went to Keilah. They
slaughtered the Philistines and took all their livestock and rescued the people of Keilah. 6Now
when Abiathar son of Ahimelech fled to David at
Keilah, he brought the ephod with him.

7Saul soon learned that David was at Keilah.
"Good!" he exclaimed. "We've got him now! God
has handed him over to me, for he has trapped
himself in a walled town!" 8So Saul mobilized his
entire army to march to Keilah and besiege David
and his men.

9But David learned of Saul's plan and told Abiathar the priest to bring the ephod and ask the
LORD what he should do. 10Then David prayed,
"O LORD, God of Israel, I have heard that Saul is
planning to come and destroy Keilah because I
am here. 11Will the leaders of Keilah betray me
to him? And will Saul actually come as I have
heard? O LORD, God of Israel, please tell me."

And the LORD said, "He will come."

12Again David asked, "Will the leaders of Keilah betray me and my men to Saul?"

And the LORD replied, "Yes, they will betray
you."

David Hides in the Wilderness

13So David and his men—about 600 of them
now—left Keilah and began roaming the
countryside. Word soon reached Saul that
David had escaped, so he didn't go to Keilah
after all. 14David now stayed in the strongholds
of the wilderness and in the hill country of Ziph.
Saul hunted him day after day, but God didn't let
Saul find him.

15One day near Horesh, David received the
news that Saul was on the way to Ziph to search
for him and kill him. 16Jonathan went to find David and encouraged him to stay strong in his faith
in God. 17"Don't be afraid," Jonathan reassured
him. "My father will never find you! You are going to be the king of Israel, and I will be next to
you, as my father, Saul, is well aware." 18So the
two of them renewed their solemn pact before
the LORD. Then Jonathan returned home, while
David stayed at Horesh.

19But now the men of Ziph went to Saul in Gibeah and betrayed David to him. "We know where
David is hiding," they said. "He is in the strongholds of Horesh on the hill of Hakilah, which is in
the southern part of Jeshimon. 20Come down
whenever you're ready, O king, and we will catch
him and hand him over to you!"

21"The LORD bless you," Saul said. "At last
someone is concerned about me! 22Go and
check again to be sure of where he is staying and
who has seen him there, for I know that he is very
crafty. 23Discover his hiding places, and come
back when you are sure. Then I'll go with you.
And if he is in the area at all, I'll track him down,
even if I have to search every hiding place in Ju-

dah!" 24So the men of Ziph returned home ahead
of Saul.
Meanwhile, David and his men had moved
into the wilderness of Maon in the Arabah Valley
south of Jeshimon. 25When David heard that
Saul and his men were searching for him, he
went even farther into the wilderness to the
great rock, and he remained there in the wilderness of Maon. But Saul kept after him in the wilderness.
26Saul and David were now on opposite sides
of a mountain. Just as Saul and his men began to
close in on David and his men, 27an urgent message reached Saul that the Philistines were raiding Israel again. 28So Saul quit chasing David
and returned to fight the Philistines. Ever since
that time, the place where David was camped
has been called the Rock of Escape. 29David
then went to live in the strongholds of En-gedi.

CHAPTER 24

David Spares Saul's Life

After Saul returned from fighting the Philistines, he was told that David had gone into the
wilderness of En-gedi. 2So Saul chose 3,000
elite troops from all Israel and went to search for
David and his men near the rocks of the wild
goats.
3At the place where the road passes some
sheepfolds, Saul went into a cave to relieve himself. But as it happened, David and his men were
hiding farther back in that very cave!
4"Now's your opportunity!" David's men whispered to him. "Today the LORD is telling you, 'I
will certainly put your enemy into your power, to
do with as you wish.'" So David crept forward and
cut off a piece of the hem of Saul's robe.
5But then David's conscience began bothering
him because he had cut Saul's robe. 6He said to
his men, "The LORD forbid that I should do this
to my lord the king. I shouldn't attack the LORD's
anointed one, for the LORD himself has chosen
him." 7So David restrained his men and did not
let them kill Saul.
After Saul had left the cave and gone on his
way, 8David came out and shouted after him, "My
lord the king!" And when Saul looked around,
David bowed low before him.
9Then he shouted to Saul, "Why do you listen
to the people who say I am trying to harm you?
10This very day you can see with your own eyes it
isn't true. For the LORD placed you at my mercy
back there in the cave. Some of my men told me
to kill you, but I spared you. For I said, 'I will
never harm the king—he is the LORD's anointed
one.' 11Look, my father, at what I have in my
hand. It is a piece of the hem of your robe! I cut it
off, but I didn't kill you. This proves that I am not
trying to harm you and that I have not sinned
against you, even though you have been hunting
for me to kill me.
12"May the LORD judge between us. Perhaps
the LORD will punish you for what you are trying
to do to me, but I will never harm you. 13As that
old proverb says, 'From evil people come evil
deeds.' So you can be sure I will never harm you.
14Who is the king of Israel trying to catch anyway? Should he spend his time chasing one who
is as worthless as a dead dog or a single flea?
15May the LORD therefore judge which of us is
right and punish the guilty one. He is my advocate, and he will rescue me from your power!"
16When David had finished speaking, Saul
called back, "Is that really you, my son David?"
Then he began to cry. 17And he said to David,
"You are a better man than I am, for you have repaid me good for evil. 18Yes, you have been
amazingly kind to me today, for when the LORD
put me in a place where you could have killed
me, you didn't do it. 19Who else would let his enemy get away when he had him in his power?
May the LORD reward you well for the kindness
you have shown me today. 20And now I realize
that you are surely going to be king, and that the
kingdom of Israel will flourish under your rule.
21Now swear to me by the LORD that when that
happens you will not kill my family and destroy
my line of descendants!"
22So David promised this to Saul with an oath.
Then Saul went home, but David and his men
went back to their stronghold.

CHAPTER 25

The Death of Samuel

Now Samuel died, and all Israel gathered for his
funeral. They buried him at his house in Ramah.

Nabal Angers David

Then David moved down to the wilderness of
Maon. 2There was a wealthy man from Maon
who owned property near the town of Carmel.
He had 3,000 sheep and 1,000 goats, and it was
sheep-shearing time. 3This man's name was Nabal, and his wife, Abigail, was a sensible and
beautiful woman. But Nabal, a descendant of
Caleb, was crude and mean in all his dealings.
4When David heard that Nabal was shearing
his sheep, 5he sent ten of his young men to Carmel with this message for Nabal: 6"Peace and

prosperity to you, your family, and everything
you own! 7I am told that it is sheep-shearing
time. While your shepherds stayed among us
near Carmel, we never harmed them, and nothing was ever stolen from them. 8Ask your own
men, and they will tell you this is true. So would
you be kind to us, since we have come at a time
of celebration? Please share any provisions you
might have on hand with us and with your friend
David." 9David's young men gave this message to
Nabal in David's name, and they waited for a
reply.

10"Who is this fellow David?" Nabal sneered
to the young men. "Who does this son of Jesse
think he is? There are lots of servants these days
who run away from their masters. 11Should I
take my bread and my water and my meat that
I've slaughtered for my shearers and give it to a
band of outlaws who come from who knows
where?"

12So David's young men returned and told
him what Nabal had said. 13"Get your swords!"
was David's reply as he strapped on his own.
Then 400 men started off with David, and
200 remained behind to guard their equipment.

14Meanwhile, one of Nabal's servants went to
Abigail and told her, "David sent messengers
from the wilderness to greet our master, but he
screamed insults at them. 15These men have
been very good to us, and we never suffered any
harm from them. Nothing was stolen from us the
whole time they were with us. 16In fact, day and
night they were like a wall of protection to us and
the sheep. 17You need to know this and figure
out what to do, for there is going to be trouble
for our master and his whole family. He's so ill-
tempered that no one can even talk to him!"

18Abigail wasted no time. She quickly gathered 200 loaves of bread, two wineskins full of
wine, five sheep that had been slaughtered,
nearly a bushel of roasted grain, 100 clusters of
raisins, and 200 fig cakes. She packed them on
donkeys 19and said to her servants, "Go on ahead.
I will follow you shortly." But she didn't tell her
husband Nabal what she was doing.

20As she was riding her donkey into a mountain ravine, she saw David and his men coming
toward her. 21David had just been saying, "A lot of
good it did to help this fellow. We protected his
flocks in the wilderness, and nothing he owned
was lost or stolen. But he has repaid me evil for
good. 22May God strike me and kill me if even
one man of his household is still alive tomorrow
morning!"

FIGHTING WON'T SOLVE THE PROBLEM. Nabal and David almost got into a huge fight, but Abigail stepped in just in time. Thank goodness! **Discover why David and Nabal were fighting and what Abigail did by reading 1 SAMUEL 25:2-35.**

1 **Think of someone who hurt you or made you mad.**

2 **Spread a handful of shaving cream in a thin layer on a waterproof surface —like a counter or a bathtub.**

3 **Draw a picture of the problem, then read COLOSSIANS 3:13.**

4 **Ask God to help smooth out the problem. Smooth away the picture of the fight.**

COL. 3:13

The Bible gives all sorts of help on fighting. Check out Matthew 18:15-17; Luke 6:27-31; and Ephesians 4:25-27.

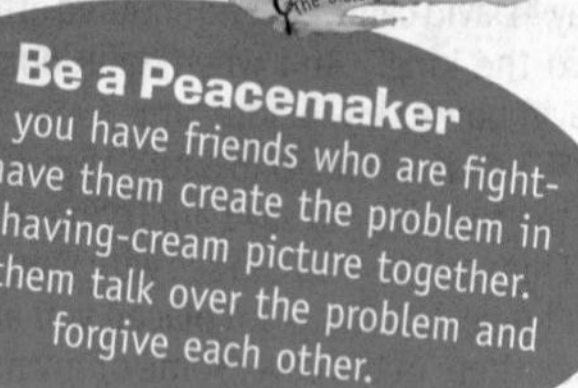

Be a Peacemaker
When you have friends who are fighting, have them create the problem in
the shaving-cream picture together.
Help them talk over the problem and
forgive each other.

Abigail Intercedes for Nabal

23 When Abigail saw David, she quickly got off
her donkey and bowed low before him. 24 She
fell at his feet and said, "I accept all blame in this
matter, my lord. Please listen to what I have to
say. 25 I know Nabal is a wicked and ill-tempered
man; please don't pay any attention to him. He
is a fool, just as his name suggests. But I never
even saw the young men you sent.

26 "Now, my lord, as surely as the LORD lives
and you yourself live, since the LORD has kept
you from murdering and taking vengeance into
your own hands, let all your enemies and those
who try to harm you be as cursed as Nabal is.
27 And here is a present that I, your servant, have
brought to you and your young men. 28 Please
forgive me if I have offended you in any way. The
LORD will surely reward you with a lasting dynasty, for you are fighting the LORD's battles.
And you have not done wrong throughout your
entire life.

29 "Even when you are chased by those who
seek to kill you, your life is safe in the care of the
LORD your God, secure in his treasure pouch!
But the lives of your enemies will disappear like
stones shot from a sling! 30 When the LORD has
done all he promised and has made you leader
of Israel, 31 don't let this be a blemish on your
record. Then your conscience won't have to
bear the staggering burden of needless bloodshed and vengeance. And when the LORD has
done these great things for you, please remember me, your servant!"

32 David replied to Abigail, "Praise the LORD,
the God of Israel, who has sent you to meet me
today! 33 Thank God for your good sense! Bless
you for keeping me from murder and from carrying out vengeance with my own hands. 34 For I
swear by the LORD, the God of Israel, who has
kept me from hurting you, that if you had not
hurried out to meet me, not one of Nabal's men
would still be alive tomorrow morning." 35 Then
David accepted her present and told her, "Return home in peace. I have heard what you said.
We will not kill your husband."

36 When Abigail arrived home, she found that
Nabal was throwing a big party and was celebrating like a king. He was very drunk, so she
didn't tell him anything about her meeting with
David until dawn the next day. 37 In the morning
when Nabal was sober, his wife told him what
had happened. As a result he had a stroke, and
he lay paralyzed on his bed like a stone. 38 About
ten days later, the LORD struck him, and he died.

David Marries Abigail

39 When David heard that Nabal was dead, he
said, "Praise the LORD, who has avenged the insult I received from Nabal and has kept me from
doing it myself. Nabal has received the punishment for his sin." Then David sent messengers to
Abigail to ask her to become his wife.

40 When the messengers arrived at Carmel,
they told Abigail, "David has sent us to take you
back to marry him."

41 She bowed low to the ground and responded, "I, your servant, would be happy to
marry David. I would even be willing to become a
slave, washing the feet of his servants!" 42 Quickly
getting ready, she took along five of her servant
girls as attendants, mounted her donkey, and
went with David's messengers. And so she became his wife. 43 David also married Ahinoam
from Jezreel, making both of them his wives.
44 Saul, meanwhile, had given his daughter Michal, David's wife, to a man from Gallim named
Palti son of Laish.

CHAPTER 26

David Spares Saul Again

Now some men from Ziph came to Saul at Gibeah to tell him, "David is hiding on the hill of Hakilah, which overlooks Jeshimon."

2 So Saul took 3,000 of Israel's elite troops and
went to hunt him down in the wilderness of
Ziph. 3 Saul camped along the road beside the
hill of Hakilah, near Jeshimon, where David was
hiding. When David learned that Saul had come
after him into the wilderness, 4 he sent out spies
to verify the report of Saul's arrival.

5 David slipped over to Saul's camp one night
to look around. Saul and Abner son of Ner, the
commander of his army, were sleeping inside a
ring formed by the slumbering warriors. 6 "Who
will volunteer to go in there with me?" David
asked Ahimelech the Hittite and Abishai son of
Zeruiah, Joab's brother.

"I'll go with you," Abishai replied. 7 So David
and Abishai went right into Saul's camp and
found him asleep, with his spear stuck in the
ground beside his head. Abner and the soldiers
were lying asleep around him.

8 "God has surely handed your enemy over to
you this time!" Abishai whispered to David. "Let
me pin him to the ground with one thrust of the
spear; I won't need to strike twice!"

9 "No!" David said. "Don't kill him. For who
can remain innocent after attacking the LORD's
anointed one? 10 Surely the LORD will strike Saul
down someday, or he will die of old age or in

battle. 11The LORD forbid that I should kill the
one he has anointed! But take his spear and that
jug of water beside his head, and then let's get
out of here!"
12So David took the spear and jug of water
that were near Saul's head. Then he and Abishai
got away without anyone seeing them or even
waking up, because the LORD had put Saul's men
into a deep sleep.
13David climbed the hill opposite the camp
until he was at a safe distance. 14Then he
shouted down to the soldiers and to Abner son
of Ner, "Wake up, Abner!"
"Who is it?" Abner demanded.
15"Well, Abner, you're a great man, aren't you?"
David taunted. "Where in all Israel is there anyone as mighty? So why haven't you guarded your
master the king when someone came to kill him?
16This isn't good at all! I swear by the LORD that
you and your men deserve to die, because you
failed to protect your master, the LORD's
anointed! Look around! Where are the king's
spear and the jug of water that were beside his
head?"
17Saul recognized David's voice and called
out, "Is that you, my son David?"
And David replied, "Yes, my lord the king.
18Why are you chasing me? What have I done?
What is my crime? 19But now let my lord the
king listen to his servant. If the LORD has stirred
you up against me, then let him accept my offering. But if this is simply a human scheme, then
may those involved be cursed by the LORD. For
they have driven me from my home, so I can no
longer live among the LORD's people, and they
have said, 'Go, worship pagan gods.' 20Must I die
on foreign soil, far from the presence of the
LORD? Why has the king of Israel come out to
search for a single flea? Why does he hunt me
down like a partridge on the mountains?"
21Then Saul confessed, "I have sinned. Come
back home, my son, and I will no longer try to
harm you, for you valued my life today. I have
been a fool and very, very wrong."
22"Here is your spear, O king," David replied.
"Let one of your young men come over and get it.
23The LORD gives his own reward for doing good
and for being loyal, and I refused to kill you even
when the LORD placed you in my power, for you
are the LORD's anointed one. 24Now may the
LORD value my life, even as I have valued yours
today. May he rescue me from all my troubles."
25And Saul said to David, "Blessings on you,
my son David. You will do many heroic deeds,
and you will surely succeed." Then David went
away, and Saul returned home.

CHAPTER 27

David among the Philistines

But David kept thinking to himself, "Someday
Saul is going to get me. The best thing I can do is
escape to the Philistines. Then Saul will stop
hunting for me in Israelite territory, and I will finally be safe."
2So David took his 600 men and went over
and joined Achish son of Maoch, the king of
Gath. 3David and his men and their families settled there with Achish at Gath. David brought his
two wives along with him—Ahinoam from Jezreel and Abigail, Nabal's widow from Carmel.
4Word soon reached Saul that David had fled to
Gath, so he stopped hunting for him.
5One day David said to Achish, "If it is all right
with you, we would rather live in one of the country towns instead of here in the royal city."
6So Achish gave him the town of Ziklag (which
still belongs to the kings of Judah to this day),
7and they lived there among the Philistines for a
year and four months.
8David and his men spent their time raiding
the Geshurites, the Girzites, and the Amalekites—people who had lived near Shur, toward the
land of Egypt, since ancient times. 9David did not
leave one person alive in the villages he attacked.
He took the sheep, goats, cattle, donkeys, camels,
and clothing before returning home to see King
Achish.
10"Where did you make your raid today?"
Achish would ask.
And David would reply, "Against the south of
Judah, the Jerahmeelites, and the Kenites."
11No one was left alive to come to Gath and tell
where he had really been. This happened again
and again while he was living among the Philistines. 12Achish believed David and thought to
himself, "By now the people of Israel must hate
him bitterly. Now he will have to stay here and
serve me forever!"

CHAPTER 28

Saul Consults a Medium

About that time the Philistines mustered their
armies for another war with Israel. King Achish
told David, "You and your men will be expected
to join me in battle."
2"Very well!" David agreed. "Now you will see
for yourself what we can do."
Then Achish told David, "I will make you my
personal bodyguard for life."

3Meanwhile, Samuel had died, and all Israel
had mourned for him. He was buried in Ramah,
his hometown. And Saul had banned from the
land of Israel all mediums and those who consult
the spirits of the dead.
4The Philistines set up their camp at Shunem,
and Saul gathered all the army of Israel and
camped at Gilboa. 5When Saul saw the vast Philistine army, he became frantic with fear. 6He
asked the LORD what he should do, but the LORD
refused to answer him, either by dreams or by sacred lots or by the prophets. 7Saul then said to
his advisers, "Find a woman who is a medium, so
I can go and ask her what to do."
His advisers replied, "There is a medium at
Endor."
8So Saul disguised himself by wearing ordinary clothing instead of his royal robes. Then he
went to the woman's home at night, accompanied by two of his men.
"I have to talk to a man who has died," he said.
"Will you call up his spirit for me?"
9"Are you trying to get me killed?" the woman
demanded. "You know that Saul has outlawed all
the mediums and all who consult the spirits of
the dead. Why are you setting a trap for me?"
10But Saul took an oath in the name of the
LORD and promised, "As surely as the LORD lives,
nothing bad will happen to you for doing this."
11Finally, the woman said, "Well, whose spirit
do you want me to call up?"
"Call up Samuel," Saul replied.
12When the woman saw Samuel, she
screamed, "You've deceived me! You are Saul!"
13"Don't be afraid!" the king told her. "What
do you see?"
"I see a god coming up out of the earth," she
said.
14"What does he look like?" Saul asked.
"He is an old man wrapped in a robe," she replied. Saul realized it was Samuel, and he fell to
the ground before him.
15"Why have you disturbed me by calling me
back?" Samuel asked Saul.
"Because I am in deep trouble," Saul replied.
"The Philistines are at war with me, and God has
left me and won't reply by prophets or dreams.
So I have called for you to tell me what to do."
16But Samuel replied, "Why ask me, since the
LORD has left you and has become your enemy?
17The LORD has done just as he said he would. He
has torn the kingdom from you and given it to

David ***coulda*** gotten rid of his enemy, King Saul, for good. See if David did what he ***shoulda*** done in **1 SAMUEL 26.** What ***woulda*** you done? For each situation below, write the things you may want to do or *could* do in the *"coulda"* box. Write what you *should* do in the *"shoulda"* box. Finish by writing what you probably *would* do in the *"woulda"* box.

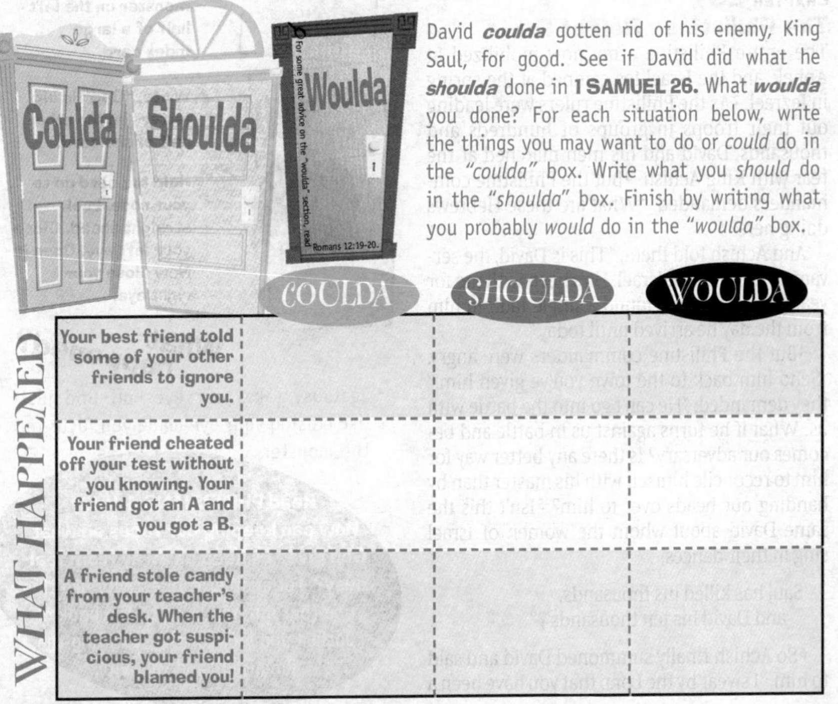

WHAT HAPPENED	COULDA	SHOULDA	WOULDA
Your best friend told some of your other friends to ignore you.			
Your friend cheated off your test without you knowing. Your friend got an A and you got a B.			
A friend stole candy from your teacher's desk. When the teacher got suspicious, your friend blamed you!			

your rival, David. 18The LORD has done this to you
today because you refused to carry out his fierce
anger against the Amalekites. 19What's more, the
LORD will hand you and the army of Israel over to
the Philistines tomorrow, and you and your sons
will be here with me. The LORD will bring down
the entire army of Israel in defeat."

20Saul fell full length on the ground, paralyzed with fright because of Samuel's words. He
was also faint with hunger, for he had eaten
nothing all day and all night.

21When the woman saw how distraught he
was, she said, "Sir, I obeyed your command at the
risk of my life. 22Now do what I say, and let me
give you a little something to eat so you can regain your strength for the trip back."

23But Saul refused to eat anything. Then his
advisers joined the woman in urging him to eat,
so he finally yielded and got up from the ground
and sat on the couch.

24The woman had been fattening a calf, so she
hurried out and killed it. She took some flour,
kneaded it into dough and baked unleavened
bread. 25She brought the meal to Saul and his advisers, and they ate it. Then they went out into
the night.

CHAPTER 29

The Philistines Reject David

The entire Philistine army now mobilized at
Aphek, and the Israelites camped at the spring
in Jezreel. 2As the Philistine rulers were leading
out their troops in groups of hundreds and
thousands, David and his men marched at the
rear with King Achish. 3But the Philistine commanders demanded, "What are these Hebrews
doing here?"

And Achish told them, "This is David, the servant of King Saul of Israel. He's been with me for
years, and I've never found a single fault in him
from the day he arrived until today."

4But the Philistine commanders were angry.
"Send him back to the town you've given him!"
they demanded. "He can't go into the battle with
us. What if he turns against us in battle and becomes our adversary? Is there any better way for
him to reconcile himself with his master than by
handing our heads over to him? 5Isn't this the
same David about whom the women of Israel
sing in their dances,

'Saul has killed his thousands,
and David his ten thousands'?"

6So Achish finally summoned David and said
to him, "I swear by the LORD that you have been a

That's what a lot of people call jealousy. Jealousy is a monster because it takes our eyes off God and it gobbles our joy and peace. The green-eyed monster was really getting to King Saul. **Read all about it in 1 SAMUEL 18:5-16.**

THIS SIMPLE EXPERIMENT KIND OF SHOWS HOW JEALOUSY WORKS.

1. **Draw a green-eyed monster on the left half of a large index card.**
2. **Write, "God" in big letters on the other half of the card.**
3. **Hold the card up to your nose. Look straight ahead. Close your left eye. Open it. Now close your right eye.**

What happened?

Jealousy takes our eyes off God just like closing your eye made you focus on the monster.

Read PHILIPPIANS 4:11-13. How can keeping our focus on what God gives us keep us away from jealousy? For another cool activity like this one (but different!) go to the book of Joshua and look for the "Entering the Promised Land" activity.

trustworthy ally. I think you should go with me
into battle, for I've never found a single flaw in
you from the day you arrived until today. But the
other Philistine rulers won't hear of it. 7Please
don't upset them, but go back quietly."

8"What have I done to deserve this treatment?" David demanded. "What have you ever
found in your servant, that I can't go and fight
the enemies of my lord the king?"

9But Achish insisted, "As far as I'm concerned,
you're as perfect as an angel of God. But the Philistine commanders are afraid to have you with
them in the battle. 10Now get up early in the
morning, and leave with your men as soon as it
gets light."

11So David and his men headed back into the
land of the Philistines, while the Philistine army
went on to Jezreel.

CHAPTER 30

David Destroys the Amalekites

Three days later, when David and his men arrived home at their town of Ziklag, they found
that the Amalekites had made a raid into the Negev and Ziklag; they had crushed Ziklag and
burned it to the ground. 2They had carried off
the women and children and everyone else but
without killing anyone.

3When David and his men saw the ruins and
realized what had happened to their families,
4they wept until they could weep no more. 5Da-
vid's two wives, Ahinoam from Jezreel and Abigail, the widow of Nabal from Carmel, were
among those captured. 6David was now in great
danger because all his men were very bitter
about losing their sons and daughters, and they
began to talk of stoning him. But David found
strength in the LORD his God.

7Then he said to Abiathar the priest, "Bring
me the ephod!" So Abiathar brought it. 8Then
David asked the LORD, "Should I chase after this
band of raiders? Will I catch them?"

And the LORD told him, "Yes, go after them.
You will surely recover everything that was taken
from you!"

9So David and his 600 men set out, and they
came to the brook Besor. 10But 200 of the men
were too exhausted to cross the brook, so David
continued the pursuit with 400 men.

11Along the way they found an Egyptian man
in a field and brought him to David. They gave
him some bread to eat and water to drink.
12They also gave him part of a fig cake and two
clusters of raisins, for he hadn't had anything to
eat or drink for three days and nights. Before
long his strength returned.

13"To whom do you belong, and where do you
come from?" David asked him.

"I am an Egyptian—the slave of an Amalekite,"
he replied. "My master abandoned me three days
ago because I was sick. 14We were on our way
back from raiding the Kerethites in the Negev,
the territory of Judah, and the land of Caleb, and
we had just burned Ziklag."

15"Will you lead me to this band of raiders?"
David asked.

The young man replied, "If you take an oath in
God's name that you will not kill me or give me
back to my master, then I will guide you to them."

16So he led David to them, and they found the
Amalekites spread out across the fields, eating
and drinking and dancing with joy because of
the vast amount of plunder they had taken from
the Philistines and the land of Judah. 17David and
his men rushed in among them and slaughtered
them throughout that night and the entire next
day until evening. None of the Amalekites escaped except 400 young men who fled on camels. 18David got back everything the Amalekites
had taken, and he rescued his two wives. 19Noth-
ing was missing: small or great, son or daughter,
nor anything else that had been taken. David
brought everything back. 20He also recovered all
the flocks and herds, and his men drove them
ahead of the other livestock. "This plunder belongs to David!" they said.

21Then David returned to the brook Besor and
met up with the 200 men who had been left behind because they were too exhausted to go with
him. They went out to meet David and his men,
and David greeted them joyfully. 22But some evil
troublemakers among David's men said, "They
didn't go with us, so they can't have any of the
plunder we recovered. Give them their wives and
children, and tell them to be gone."

23But David said, "No, my brothers! Don't be
selfish with what the LORD has given us. He has
kept us safe and helped us defeat the band of
raiders that attacked us. 24Who will listen when
you talk like this? We share and share alike—
those who go to battle and those who guard the
equipment." 25From then on David made this a
decree and regulation for Israel, and it is still followed today.

26When he arrived at Ziklag, David sent part
of the plunder to the elders of Judah, who were
his friends. "Here is a present for you, taken from
the LORD's enemies," he said.

27The gifts were sent to the people of the

following towns David had visited: Bethel, Ramoth-negev, Jattir, 28 Aroer, Siphmoth, Eshtemoa, 29 Racal, the towns of the Jerahmeelites, the towns of the Kenites, 30 Hormah, Bor-ashan, Athach, 31 Hebron, and all the other places David and his men had visited.

CHAPTER 31

The Death of Saul

Now the Philistines attacked Israel, and the men of Israel fled before them. Many were slaughtered on the slopes of Mount Gilboa. 2 The Philistines closed in on Saul and his sons, and they killed three of his sons—Jonathan, Abinadab, and Malkishua. 3 The fighting grew very fierce around Saul, and the Philistine archers caught up with him and wounded him severely.

4 Saul groaned to his armor bearer, "Take your sword and kill me before these pagan Philistines come to run me through and taunt and torture me."

But his armor bearer was afraid and would not do it. So Saul took his own sword and fell on it. 5 When his armor bearer realized that Saul was dead, he fell on his own sword and died beside the king. 6 So Saul, his three sons, his armor bearer, and his troops all died together that same day.

7 When the Israelites on the other side of the Jezreel Valley and beyond the Jordan saw that the Israelite army had fled and that Saul and his sons were dead, they abandoned their towns and fled. So the Philistines moved in and occupied their towns.

8 The next day, when the Philistines went out to strip the dead, they found the bodies of Saul and his three sons on Mount Gilboa. 9 So they cut off Saul's head and stripped off his armor. Then they proclaimed the good news of Saul's death in their pagan temple and to the people throughout the land of Philistia. 10 They placed his armor in the temple of the Ashtoreths, and they fastened his body to the wall of the city of Beth-shan.

11 But when the people of Jabesh-gilead heard what the Philistines had done to Saul, 12 all their mighty warriors traveled through the night to Beth-shan and took the bodies of Saul and his sons down from the wall. They brought them to Jabesh, where they burned the bodies. 13 Then they took their bones and buried them beneath the tamarisk tree at Jabesh, and they fasted for seven days.

2 SAMUEL

King David: A Man After God's Own Heart

Look for 2 hidden messages in 2 Samuel!

This book is named after the prophet God used to choose David as Israel's future king. In it, you'll discover amazing facts about

- **A KING CROWNED—TWICE**
- **A BUNCH OF BATTLES**
- **MEMORIES OF AN OLD FRIEND**
- **A BIG FATHER-AND-SON MESS**

King Me!

You know how in Checkers you get to say, "King me" when you make it to the other player's side? **Read how David gets "kinged" in 2 Samuel 2:4 and 2 Samuel 5:1-5.**

David's Battle Cry

Here we go again!

Even though he was king, David still had lots of enemies. There were the Philistines, the Moabites, the Edomites, the Ammonites...you get the picture. **Read 2 Samuel 22:47-51 to find out what David said when the fighting was finally over.**

Whose Side Are You On, Anyway?

Every family has problems, right? But David and his son Absalom had *big* problems. *Huge* problems! **Check out 2 Samuel 15:1-10 to find out what Absalom was up to. (Curious how the story ends? Go to 2 Samuel 19:9-10.)**

What's for Dinner?

Remember the story of David and Jonathan? (For a quick refresher, go to 1 Samuel 20.) Years later, David made good on the promise he had made to Jonathan. **Find out how in 2 Samuel 9.**

Timeline

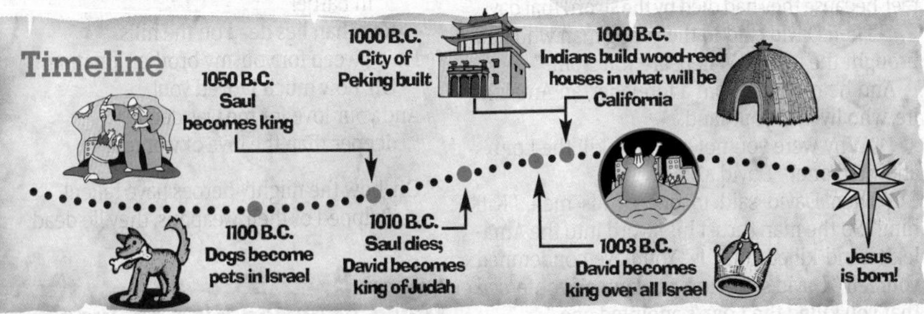
1100 B.C.
Dogs become pets in Israel
1050 B.C.
Saul becomes king
1000 B.C.
City of Peking built
1010 B.C.
Saul dies; David becomes king of Judah
1003 B.C.
David becomes king over all Israel
1000 B.C.
Indians build wood-reed houses in what will be California
Jesus is born!

The JESUS CONNECTION

God made a covenant with David, promising to continue David's family forever. That promise came true when Jesus was born into the house (or family) of David. Jesus, a direct relative of David's, will rule forever!

David also understood God's faithfulness. He knew that even after he sinned, he could cry out to God for forgiveness. (Go to Psalm 51:7-10 for an example of David's repentance.) **When we believe in Jesus, God forgives our sins and makes us pure too.**

2 Samuel 1 . . . page 300

CHAPTER 1

David Learns of Saul's Death

After the death of Saul, David returned from his
victory over the Amalekites and spent two days in
Ziklag. 2On the third day a man arrived from
Saul's army camp. He had torn his clothes and put
dirt on his head to show that he was in mourning.
He fell to the ground before David in deep respect.
3"Where have you come from?" David asked.
"I escaped from the Israelite camp," the man
replied.
4"What happened?" David demanded. "Tell
me how the battle went."
The man replied, "Our entire army fled from
the battle. Many of the men are dead, and Saul
and his son Jonathan are also dead."
5"How do you know Saul and Jonathan are
dead?" David demanded of the young man.
6The man answered, "I happened to be on
Mount Gilboa, and there was Saul leaning on his
spear with the enemy chariots and charioteers
closing in on him. 7When he turned and saw me,
he cried out for me to come to him. 'How can I
help?' I asked him.
8"He responded, 'Who are you?'
"'I am an Amalekite,' I told him.
9"Then he begged me, 'Come over here and put
me out of my misery, for I am in terrible pain and
want to die.'
10"So I killed him," the Amalekite told David,
"for I knew he couldn't live. Then I took his crown
and his armband, and I have brought them here to
you, my lord."
11David and his men tore their clothes in sorrow
when they heard the news. 12They mourned and
wept and fasted all day for Saul and his son Jonathan, and for the LORD's army and the nation of Israel, because they had died by the sword that day.
13Then David said to the young man who had
brought the news, "Where are you from?"
And he replied, "I am a foreigner, an Amalekite, who lives in your land."
14"Why were you not afraid to kill the LORD's
anointed one?" David asked.
15Then David said to one of his men, "Kill
him!" So the man thrust his sword into the Amalekite and killed him. 16"You have condemned
yourself," David said, "for you yourself confessed
that you killed the LORD's anointed one."

David's Song for Saul and Jonathan

17Then David composed a funeral song for Saul
and Jonathan, 18and he commanded that it be
taught to the people of Judah. It is known as the
Song of the Bow, and it is recorded in *The Book of
Jashar.*

19 Your pride and joy, O Israel, lies dead on
the hills!
Oh, how the mighty heroes have fallen!
20 Don't announce the news in Gath,
don't proclaim it in the streets of
Ashkelon,
or the daughters of the Philistines will
rejoice
and the pagans will laugh in triumph.

21 O mountains of Gilboa,
let there be no dew or rain upon you,
nor fruitful fields producing offerings
of grain.
For there the shield of the mighty heroes
was defiled;
the shield of Saul will no longer be
anointed with oil.
22 The bow of Jonathan was powerful,
and the sword of Saul did its mighty
work.
They shed the blood of their enemies
and pierced the bodies of mighty heroes.

23 How beloved and gracious were Saul and
Jonathan!
They were together in life and in death.
They were swifter than eagles,
stronger than lions.
24 O women of Israel, weep for Saul,
for he dressed you in luxurious scarlet
clothing,
in garments decorated with gold.

25 Oh, how the mighty heroes have fallen
in battle!
Jonathan lies dead on the hills.
26 How I weep for you, my brother Jonathan!
Oh, how much I loved you!
And your love for me was deep,
deeper than the love of women!

27 Oh, how the mighty heroes have fallen!
Stripped of their weapons, they lie dead.

CHAPTER 2

David Anointed King of Judah

After this, David asked the LORD, "Should I move
back to one of the towns of Judah?"
"Yes," the LORD replied.
Then David asked, "Which town should I
go to?"

David. As time passed David became stronger and stronger, while Saul's dynasty became weaker and weaker.

David's Sons Born in Hebron

2These are the sons who were born to David in
Hebron:

The oldest was Amnon, whose mother was
Ahinoam from Jezreel.
3 The second was Daniel, whose mother was
Abigail, the widow of Nabal from Carmel.
The third was Absalom, whose mother was
Maacah, the daughter of Talmai, king of
Geshur.
4 The fourth was Adonijah, whose mother
was Haggith.
The fifth was Shephatiah, whose mother
was Abital.
5 The sixth was Ithream, whose mother was
Eglah, David's wife.

These sons were all born to David in Hebron.

Abner Joins Forces with David

6As the war between the house of Saul and the
house of David went on, Abner became a powerful leader among those loyal to Saul. 7One day
Ishbosheth, Saul's son, accused Abner of sleeping with one of his father's concubines, a woman
named Rizpah, daughter of Aiah.
8Abner was furious. "Am I some Judean dog to
be kicked around like this?" he shouted. "After all
I have done for your father, Saul, and his family
and friends by not handing you over to David, is
this my reward—that you find fault with me
about this woman? 9May God strike me and even
kill me if I don't do everything I can to help David
get what the LORD has promised him! 10I'm going to take Saul's kingdom and give it to David. I
will establish the throne of David over Israel as
well as Judah, all the way from Dan in the north to
Beersheba in the south." 11Ishbosheth didn't
dare say another word because he was afraid of
what Abner might do.
12Then Abner sent messengers to David, saying, "Doesn't the entire land belong to you? Make
a solemn pact with me, and I will help turn over
all of Israel to you."
13"All right," David replied, "but I will not negotiate with you unless you bring back my wife
Michal, Saul's daughter, when you come."
14David then sent this message to Ishbosheth,
Saul's son: "Give me back my wife Michal, for I
bought her with the lives of 100 Philistines."
15So Ishbosheth took Michal away from her

FUN-fact
The More the Merrier?

Many Old Testament leaders married more than one wife. They did that so they'd have enough kids to help with the work and to make sure that the family continued. Plus, people looked up to men and women with lots of kids. But having more than one wife wasn't the way God planned things. (**Read GENESIS 2:24 and 1 TIMOTHY 3:2.**)

Find a husband and wife who have been married for a long time. Ask them what the key to a long and happy marriage is. (Write their answer below.)

Tuck the information away—you may need it someday!

husband, Palti son of Laish. 16Palti followed
along behind her as far as Bahurim, weeping as
he went. Then Abner told him, "Go back home!"
So Palti returned.
17Meanwhile, Abner had consulted with the
elders of Israel. "For some time now," he told
them, "you have wanted to make David your king.
18Now is the time! For the LORD has said, 'I have
chosen David to save my people Israel from the
hands of the Philistines and from all their other
enemies.'" 19Abner also spoke with the men of
Benjamin. Then he went to Hebron to tell David
that all the people of Israel and Benjamin had
agreed to support him.

"To Hebron," the Lord answered.
2David's two wives were Ahinoam from Jezreel
and Abigail, the widow of Nabal from Carmel. So
David and his wives 3and his men and their families all moved to Judah, and they settled in the villages near Hebron. 4Then the men of Judah
came to David and anointed him king over the
people of Judah.
When David heard that the men of Jabesh-
gilead had buried Saul, 5he sent them this message: "May the Lord bless you for being so loyal
to your master Saul and giving him a decent
burial. 6May the Lord be loyal to you in return
and reward you with his unfailing love! And I, too,
will reward you for what you have done. 7Now
that Saul is dead, I ask you to be my strong and
loyal subjects like the people of Judah, who have
anointed me as their new king."

Ishbosheth Proclaimed King of Israel

8But Abner son of Ner, the commander of Saul's
army, had already gone to Mahanaim with Saul's
son Ishbosheth. 9There he proclaimed Ishbosheth king over Gilead, Jezreel, Ephraim, Benjamin, the land of the Ashurites, and all the rest of
Israel.
10Ishbosheth, Saul's son, was forty years old
when he became king, and he ruled from Mahanaim for two years. Meanwhile, the people of Judah remained loyal to David. 11David made
Hebron his capital, and he ruled as king of Judah
for seven and a half years.

War between Israel and Judah

12One day Abner led Ishbosheth's troops from
Mahanaim to Gibeon. 13About the same time,
Joab son of Zeruiah led David's troops out and
met them at the pool of Gibeon. The two groups
sat down there, facing each other from opposite
sides of the pool.
14Then Abner suggested to Joab, "Let's have a
few of our warriors fight hand to hand here in
front of us."
"All right," Joab agreed. 15So twelve men were
chosen to fight from each side—twelve men of
Benjamin representing Ishbosheth son of Saul,
and twelve representing David. 16Each one
grabbed his opponent by the hair and thrust his
sword into the other's side so that all of them
died. So this place at Gibeon has been known
ever since as the Field of Swords.
17A fierce battle followed that day, and Abner
and the men of Israel were defeated by the
forces of David.

The Death of Asahel

18Joab, Abishai, and Asahel—the three sons of
Zeruiah—were among David's forces that day. Asahel could run like a gazelle, 19and he began chasing Abner. He pursued him relentlessly, not
stopping for anything. 20When Abner looked
back and saw him coming, he called out, "Is that
you, Asahel?"
"Yes, it is," he replied.
21"Go fight someone else!" Abner warned.
"Take on one of the younger men, and strip him
of his weapons." But Asahel kept right on chasing
Abner.
22Again Abner shouted to him, "Get away from
here! I don't want to kill you. How could I ever
face your brother Joab again?"
23But Asahel refused to turn back, so Abner
thrust the butt end of his spear through Asahel's
stomach, and the spear came out through his
back. He stumbled to the ground and died there.
And everyone who came by that spot stopped
and stood still when they saw Asahel lying there.
24When Joab and Abishai found out what had
happened, they set out after Abner. The sun was
just going down as they arrived at the hill of Am-
mah near Giah, along the road to the wilderness
of Gibeon. 25Abner's troops from the tribe of
Benjamin regrouped there at the top of the hill to
take a stand.
26Abner shouted down to Joab, "Must we always
be killing each other? Don't you realize that bitterness is the only result? When will you call off your
men from chasing their Israelite brothers?"
27Then Joab said, "God only knows what
would have happened if you hadn't spoken, for
we would have chased you all night if necessary."
28So Joab blew the ram's horn, and his men
stopped chasing the troops of Israel.
29All that night Abner and his men retreated
through the Jordan Valley. They crossed the Jordan River, traveling all through the morning,
and didn't stop until they arrived at Mahanaim.
30Meanwhile, Joab and his men also returned
home. When Joab counted his casualties, he discovered that only 19 men were missing in addition to Asahel. 31But 360 of Abner's men had
been killed, all from the tribe of Benjamin. 32Joab
and his men took Asahel's body to Bethlehem
and buried him there in his father's tomb. Then
they traveled all night and reached Hebron at
daybreak.

CHAPTER 3

That was the beginning of a long war between
those who were loyal to Saul and those loyal to

20 When Abner and twenty of his men came to Hebron, David entertained them with a great feast. 21 Then Abner said to David, "Let me go and call an assembly of all Israel to support my lord the king. They will make a covenant with you to make you their king, and you will rule over everything your heart desires." So David sent Abner safely on his way.

Joab Murders Abner

22 But just after David had sent Abner away in safety, Joab and some of David's troops returned from a raid, bringing much plunder with them. 23 When Joab arrived, he was told that Abner had just been there visiting the king and had been sent away in safety.

24 Joab rushed to the king and demanded, "What have you done? What do you mean by letting Abner get away? 25 You know perfectly well that he came to spy on you and find out everything you're doing!"

26 Joab then left David and sent messengers to catch up with Abner, asking him to return. They found him at the well of Sirah and brought him back, though David knew nothing about it. 27 When Abner arrived back at Hebron, Joab took him aside at the gateway as if to speak with him privately. But then he stabbed Abner in the stomach and killed him in revenge for killing his brother Asahel.

28 When David heard about it, he declared, "I vow by the LORD that I and my kingdom are forever innocent of this crime against Abner son of Ner. 29 Joab and his family are the guilty ones. May the family of Joab be cursed in every generation with a man who has open sores or leprosy or who walks on crutches or dies by the sword or begs for food!"

30 So Joab and his brother Abishai killed Abner because Abner had killed their brother Asahel at the battle of Gibeon.

David Mourns Abner's Death

31 Then David said to Joab and all those who were with him, "Tear your clothes and put on burlap. Mourn for Abner." And King David himself walked behind the procession to the grave. 32 They buried Abner in Hebron, and the king and all the people wept at his graveside. 33 Then the king sang this funeral song for Abner:

"Should Abner have died as fools die?
34 Your hands were not bound;
    your feet were not chained.
No, you were murdered—
    the victim of a wicked plot."

All the people wept again for Abner. 35 David had refused to eat anything on the day of the funeral, and now everyone begged him to eat. But David had made a vow, saying, "May God strike me and even kill me if I eat anything before sundown."

36 This pleased the people very much. In fact, everything the king did pleased them! 37 So everyone in Judah and all Israel understood that David was not responsible for Abner's murder.

38 Then King David said to his officials, "Don't you realize that a great commander has fallen today in Israel? 39 And even though I am the anointed king, these two sons of Zeruiah—Joab and Abishai—are too strong for me to control. So may the LORD repay these evil men for their evil deeds."

CHAPTER 4

The Murder of Ishbosheth

When Ishbosheth, Saul's son, heard about Abner's death at Hebron, he lost all courage, and all Israel became paralyzed with fear. 2 Now there were two brothers, Baanah and Recab, who were captains of Ishbosheth's raiding parties. They were sons of Rimmon, a member of the tribe of Benjamin who lived in Beeroth. The town of Beeroth is now part of Benjamin's territory 3 because the original people of Beeroth fled to Gittaim, where they still live as foreigners.

4 (Saul's son Jonathan had a son named Mephibosheth, who was crippled as a child. He was five years old when the report came from Jezreel that Saul and Jonathan had been killed in battle. When the child's nurse heard the news, she picked him up and fled. But as she hurried away, she dropped him, and he became crippled.)

5 One day Recab and Baanah, the sons of Rimmon from Beeroth, went to Ishbosheth's house around noon as he was taking his midday rest. 6 The doorkeeper, who had been sifting wheat, became drowsy and fell asleep. So Recab and Baanah slipped past her. 7 They went into the house and found Ishbosheth sleeping on his bed. They struck and killed him and cut off his head. Then, taking his head with them, they fled across the Jordan Valley through the night. 8 When they arrived at Hebron, they presented Ishbosheth's head to David. "Look!" they exclaimed to the king. "Here is the head of Ishbosheth, the son of your enemy Saul who tried to kill you. Today the LORD has given my lord the king revenge on Saul and his entire family!"

9 But David said to Recab and Baanah, "The LORD, who saves me from all my enemies, is my

witness. 10 Someone once told me, 'Saul is dead,' thinking he was bringing me good news. But I seized him and killed him at Ziklag. That's the reward I gave him for his news! 11 How much more should I reward evil men who have killed an innocent man in his own house and on his own bed? Shouldn't I hold you responsible for his blood and rid the earth of you?"

12 So David ordered his young men to kill them, and they did. They cut off their hands and feet and hung their bodies beside the pool in Hebron. Then they took Ishbosheth's head and buried it in Abner's tomb in Hebron.

CHAPTER 5

David Becomes King of All Israel

Then all the tribes of Israel went to David at Hebron and told him, "We are your own flesh and blood. 2 In the past, when Saul was our king, you were the one who really led the forces of Israel. And the LORD told you, 'You will be the shepherd of my people Israel. You will be Israel's leader.'"

3 So there at Hebron, King David made a covenant before the LORD with all the elders of Israel. And they anointed him king of Israel.

4 David was thirty years old when he began to reign, and he reigned forty years in all. 5 He had reigned over Judah from Hebron for seven years and six months, and from Jerusalem he reigned over all Israel and Judah for thirty-three years.

David Captures Jerusalem

6 David then led his men to Jerusalem to fight against the Jebusites, the original inhabitants of the land who were living there. The Jebusites taunted David, saying, "You'll never get in here! Even the blind and lame could keep you out!" For the Jebusites thought they were safe. 7 But David captured the fortress of Zion, which is now called the City of David.

8 On the day of the attack, David said to his troops, "I hate those 'lame' and 'blind' Jebusites. Whoever attacks them should strike by going into the city through the water tunnel." That is the origin of the saying, "The blind and the lame may not enter the house."

9 So David made the fortress his home, and he called it the City of David. He extended the city, starting at the supporting terraces and working inward. 10 And David became more and more powerful, because the LORD God of Heaven's Armies was with him.

11 Then King Hiram of Tyre sent messengers to David, along with cedar timber and carpenters and stonemasons, and they built David a palace. 12 And David realized that the LORD had confirmed him as king over Israel and had blessed his kingdom for the sake of his people Israel.

13 After moving from Hebron to Jerusalem, David married more concubines and wives, and they had more sons and daughters. 14 These are the names of David's sons who were born in Jerusalem: Shammua, Shobab, Nathan, Solomon, 15 Ibhar, Elishua, Nepheg, Japhia, 16 Elishama, Eliada, and Eliphelet.

David Conquers the Philistines

17 When the Philistines heard that David had been anointed king of Israel, they mobilized all their forces to capture him. But David was told they were coming, so he went into the stronghold. 18 The Philistines arrived and spread out across the valley of Rephaim. 19 So David asked the LORD, "Should I go out to fight the Philistines? Will you hand them over to me?"

The LORD replied to David, "Yes, go ahead. I will certainly hand them over to you."

20 So David went to Baal-perazim and defeated the Philistines there. "The LORD did it!" David exclaimed. "He burst through my enemies like a raging flood!" So he named that place Baal-perazim (which means "the Lord who bursts through"). 21 The Philistines had abandoned their idols there, so David and his men confiscated them.

22 But after a while the Philistines returned and again spread out across the valley of Rephaim. 23 And again David asked the LORD what to do. "Do not attack them straight on," the LORD replied. "Instead, circle around behind and attack them near the poplar trees. 24 When you hear a sound like marching feet in the tops of the poplar trees, be on the alert! That will be the signal that the LORD is moving ahead of you to strike down the Philistine army." 25 So David did what the LORD commanded, and he struck down the Philistines all the way from Gibeon to Gezer.

CHAPTER 6

Moving the Ark to Jerusalem

Then David again gathered all the elite troops in Israel, 30,000 in all. 2 He led them to Baalah of Judah to bring back the Ark of God, which bears the name of the LORD of Heaven's Armies, who is enthroned between the cherubim. 3 They placed the Ark of God on a new cart and brought it from Abinadab's house, which was on a hill. Uzzah and Ahio, Abinadab's sons, were guiding the cart 4 that carried the Ark of God. Ahio walked in front of the Ark. 5 David and all the people of Israel were celebrating before the LORD, singing songs and playing all kinds of musical instruments—lyres, harps, tambourines, castanets, and cymbals.

6 But when they arrived at the threshing floor of Nacon, the oxen stumbled, and Uzzah reached out his hand and steadied the Ark of God. 7 Then the LORD's anger was aroused against Uzzah, and God struck him dead because of this. So Uzzah died right there beside the Ark of God.

8 David was angry because the LORD's anger had burst out against Uzzah. He named that place Perez-uzzah (which means "to burst out against Uzzah"), as it is still called today.

9 David was now afraid of the LORD, and he asked, "How can I ever bring the Ark of the LORD back into my care?" 10 So David decided not to move the Ark of the LORD into the City of David. Instead, he took it to the house of Obed-edom of Gath. 11 The Ark of the LORD remained there in Obed-edom's house for three months, and the LORD blessed Obed-edom and his entire household.

12 Then King David was told, "The LORD has blessed Obed-edom's household and everything he has because of the Ark of God." So David went there and brought the Ark of God from the house of Obed-edom to the City of David with a great celebration. 13 After the men who were carrying the Ark of the LORD had gone six steps, David sacrificed a bull and a fattened calf. 14 And David danced before the LORD with all his might, wearing a priestly garment. 15 So David and all the people of Israel brought up the Ark of the LORD with shouts of joy and the blowing of rams' horns.

Michal's Contempt for David

16 But as the Ark of the LORD entered the City of David, Michal, the daughter of Saul, looked down from her window. When she saw King David leaping and dancing before the LORD, she was filled with contempt for him.

17 They brought the Ark of the LORD and set it in its place inside the special tent David had prepared for it. And David sacrificed burnt offerings and peace offerings to the LORD. 18 When he had finished his sacrifices, David blessed the people in the name of the LORD of Heaven's Armies. 19 Then he gave to every Israelite man and woman in the crowd a loaf of bread, a cake of dates, and a cake of raisins. Then all the people returned to their homes.

20 When David returned home to bless his own family, Michal, the daughter of Saul, came out to meet him. She said in disgust, "How distinguished the king of Israel looked today, shamelessly exposing himself to the servant girls like any vulgar person might do!"

21 David retorted to Michal, "I was dancing before the LORD, who chose me above your father and all his family! He appointed me as the leader of Israel, the people of the LORD, so I celebrate before the LORD. 22 Yes, and I am willing to look even more foolish than this, even to be humiliated in my own eyes! But those servant girls you mentioned will indeed think I am distinguished!" 23 So Michal, the daughter of Saul, remained childless throughout her entire life.

CHAPTER 7

The LORD's Covenant Promise to David

When King David was settled in his palace and the LORD had given him rest from all the surrounding enemies, 2 the king summoned Nathan the prophet. "Look," David said, "I am living in a beautiful cedar palace, but the Ark of God is out there in a tent!"

3 Nathan replied to the king, "Go ahead and do whatever you have in mind, for the LORD is with you."

4 But that same night the LORD said to Nathan,

5 "Go and tell my servant David, 'This is what
the LORD has declared: Are you the one to
build a house for me to live in? 6 I have never
lived in a house, from the day I brought the
Israelites out of Egypt until this very day.
I have always moved from one place to
another with a tent and a Tabernacle as
my dwelling. 7 Yet no matter where I have
gone with the Israelites, I have never once
complained to Israel's tribal leaders, the
shepherds of my people Israel. I have never
asked them, "Why haven't you built me a
beautiful cedar house?"'

8 "Now go and say to my servant David,
'This is what the LORD of Heaven's Armies has
declared: I took you from tending sheep in
the pasture and selected you to be the leader
of my people Israel. 9 I have been with you
wherever you have gone, and I have destroyed
all your enemies before your eyes. Now I will
make your name as famous as anyone who
has ever lived on the earth! 10 And I will
provide a homeland for my people Israel,
planting them in a secure place where they
will never be disturbed. Evil nations won't
oppress them as they've done in the past,

11starting from the time I appointed judges to
rule my people Israel. And I will give you rest
from all your enemies.
"'Furthermore, the LORD declares that
he will make a house for you—a dynasty of
kings! 12For when you die and are buried with
your ancestors, I will raise up one of your
descendants, your own offspring, and I will
make his kingdom strong. 13He is the one
who will build a house—a temple—for my
name. And I will secure his royal throne
forever. 14I will be his father, and he will be
my son. If he sins, I will correct and discipline
him with the rod, like any father would do.
15But my favor will not be taken from him as
I took it from Saul, whom I removed from
your sight. 16Your house and your kingdom
will continue before me for all time, and your
throne will be secure forever.'"

17So Nathan went back to David and told him
everything the LORD had said in this vision.

David's Prayer of Thanks

18Then King David went in and sat before the
LORD and prayed,

"Who am I, O Sovereign LORD, and what is
my family, that you have brought me this
far? 19And now, Sovereign LORD, in addition
to everything else, you speak of giving your
servant a lasting dynasty! Do you deal with
everyone this way, O Sovereign LORD?
20"What more can I say to you? You know
what your servant is really like, Sovereign
LORD. 21Because of your promise and
according to your will, you have done all
these great things and have made them
known to your servant.
22"How great you are, O Sovereign LORD!
There is no one like you. We have never even
heard of another God like you! 23What other
nation on earth is like your people Israel?
What other nation, O God, have you redeemed
from slavery to be your own people? You
made a great name for yourself when you
redeemed your people from Egypt. You performed awesome miracles and drove out the
nations and gods that stood in their way.
24You made Israel your very own people
forever, and you, O LORD, became their God.
25"And now, O LORD God, I am your
servant; do as you have promised concerning
me and my family. Confirm it as a promise
that will last forever. 26And may your name
be honored forever so that everyone will say,
'The LORD of Heaven's Armies is God over
Israel!' And may the house of your servant
David continue before you forever.
27"O LORD of Heaven's Armies, God of
Israel, I have been bold enough to pray this
prayer to you because you have revealed all
this to your servant, saying, 'I will build a
house for you—a dynasty of kings!' 28For you
are God, O Sovereign LORD. Your words are
truth, and you have promised these good
things to your servant. 29And now, may it
please you to bless the house of your servant,
so that it may continue forever before you.
For you have spoken, and when you grant a
blessing to your servant, O Sovereign LORD, it
is an eternal blessing!"

CHAPTER 8

David's Military Victories

After this, David defeated and subdued the Philistines by conquering Gath, their largest town.
2David also conquered the land of Moab. He
made the people lie down on the ground in a row,
and he measured them off in groups with a
length of rope. He measured off two groups to be
executed for every one group to be spared. The
Moabites who were spared became David's
subjects and paid him tribute money.
3David also destroyed the forces of Hadadezer
son of Rehob, king of Zobah, when Hadadezer
marched out to strengthen his control along the
Euphrates River. 4David captured 1,000 chariots, 7,000 charioteers, and 20,000 foot soldiers.
He crippled all the chariot horses except enough
for 100 chariots.
5When Arameans from Damascus arrived to
help King Hadadezer, David killed 22,000 of
them. 6Then he placed several army garrisons in
Damascus, the Aramean capital, and the Arameans became David's subjects and paid him tribute money. So the LORD made David victorious
wherever he went.
7David brought the gold shields of Hadadezer's officers to Jerusalem, 8along with a large
amount of bronze from Hadadezer's towns of
Tebah and Berothai.
9When King Toi of Hamath heard that David
had destroyed the entire army of Hadadezer,
10he sent his son Joram to congratulate King David for his successful compaign. Hadadezer and
Toi had been enemies and were often at war. Joram presented David with many gifts of silver,
gold, and bronze.
11King David dedicated all these gifts to the
LORD, as he did with the silver and gold from the

other nations he had defeated—12from Edom,
Moab, Ammon, Philistia, and Amalek—and from
Hadadezer son of Rehob, king of Zobah.
13So David became even more famous when
he returned from destroying 18,000 Edomites
in the Valley of Salt. 14He placed army garrisons
throughout Edom, and all the Edomites became
David's subjects. In fact, the LORD made David
victorious wherever he went.
15So David reigned over all Israel and did
what was just and right for all his people. 16Joab
son of Zeruiah was commander of the army. Jehoshaphat son of Ahilud was the royal historian.
17Zadok son of Ahitub and Ahimelech son of
Abiathar were the priests. Seraiah was the court
secretary. 18Benaiah son of Jehoiada was captain
of the king's bodyguard. And David's sons served
as priestly leaders.

CHAPTER 9

David's Kindness to Mephibosheth

One day David asked, "Is anyone in Saul's family
still alive—anyone to whom I can show kindness
for Jonathan's sake?" 2He summoned a man
named Ziba, who had been one of Saul's servants. "Are you Ziba?" the king asked.
"Yes sir, I am," Ziba replied.
3The king then asked him, "Is anyone still alive
from Saul's family? If so, I want to show God's
kindness to them."
Ziba replied, "Yes, one of Jonathan's sons is
still alive. He is crippled in both feet."
4"Where is he?" the king asked.
"In Lo-debar," Ziba told him, "at the home of
Makir son of Ammiel."
5So David sent for him and brought him from
Makir's home. 6His name was Mephibosheth;
he was Jonathan's son and Saul's grandson.
When he came to David, he bowed low to the
ground in deep respect. David said, "Greetings,
Mephibosheth."
Mephibosheth replied, "I am your servant."
7"Don't be afraid!" David said. "I intend to show
kindness to you because of my promise to your father, Jonathan. I will give you all the property that
once belonged to your grandfather Saul, and you
will eat here with me at the king's table!"
8Mephibosheth bowed respectfully and exclaimed, "Who is your servant, that you should
show such kindness to a dead dog like me?"
9Then the king summoned Saul's servant Ziba
and said, "I have given your master's grandson
everything that belonged to Saul and his family.
10You and your sons and servants are to farm the

MEPHIBOSHETH
Meph ibosheth became disabled when he was only five years old! Find out what happened in 2 Samuel 4:4.

That's a nifty name! Pronounce it like this: me-FIB-o-sheth.

Kindness Caper

Real kindness means caring for those who need it most!

Read how David showed kindness to Jonathan's son Mephibosheth. **Check out 2 SAMUEL 9.** Then come back for a Kindness Caper!

Read about the promise between two best friends in 1 Samuel 20:13b-15, 42.

Offer *your* friendship, just like David did!

Watch for someone who might feel left out or lonely. Choose him for your partner on a school project. Have a picnic in your backyard and invite her to join you and your friends.

Who might that someone be? Write his or her name in the huddle. Then later, inside the outline, write what you did to show kindness to that person.

land for him to produce food for your master's household. But Mephibosheth, your master's grandson, will eat here at my table." (Ziba had fifteen sons and twenty servants.)

11Ziba replied, "Yes, my lord the king; I am your servant, and I will do all that you have commanded." And from that time on, Mephibosheth ate regularly at David's table, like one of the king's own sons.

12Mephibosheth had a young son named Mica. From then on, all the members of Ziba's household were Mephibosheth's servants. 13And Mephibosheth, who was crippled in both feet, lived in Jerusalem and ate regularly at the king's table.

CHAPTER 10

David Defeats the Ammonites

Some time after this, King Nahash of the Ammonites died, and his son Hanun became king. 2David said, "I am going to show loyalty to Hanun just as his father, Nahash, was always loyal to me." So David sent ambassadors to express sympathy to Hanun about his father's death.

But when David's ambassadors arrived in the land of Ammon, 3the Ammonite commanders said to Hanun, their master, "Do you really think these men are coming here to honor your father? No! David has sent them to spy out the city so they can come in and conquer it!" 4So Hanun seized David's ambassadors and shaved off half of each man's beard, cut off their robes at the buttocks, and sent them back to David in shame.

5When David heard what had happened, he sent messengers to tell the men, "Stay at Jericho until your beards grow out, and then come back." For they felt deep shame because of their appearance.

6When the people of Ammon realized how seriously they had angered David, they sent and hired 20,000 Aramean foot soldiers from the lands of Beth-rehob and Zobah, 1,000 from the king of Maacah, and 12,000 from the land of Tob. 7When David heard about this, he sent Joab and all his warriors to fight them. 8The Ammonite troops came out and drew up their battle lines at the entrance of the city gate, while the Arameans from Zobah and Rehob and the men from Tob and Maacah positioned themselves to fight in the open fields.

9When Joab saw that he would have to fight on both the front and the rear, he chose some of Israel's elite troops and placed them under his personal command to fight the Arameans in the fields. 10He left the rest of the army under the command of his brother Abishai, who was to attack the Ammonites. 11"If the Arameans are too strong for me, then come over and help me," Joab told his brother. "And if the Ammonites are too strong for you, I will come and help you. 12Be courageous! Let us fight bravely for our people and the cities of our God. May the LORD's will be done."

13When Joab and his troops attacked, the Arameans began to run away. 14And when the Ammonites saw the Arameans running, they ran from Abishai and retreated into the city. After the battle was over, Joab returned to Jerusalem.

15The Arameans now realized that they were no match for Israel. So when they regrouped, 16they were joined by additional Aramean troops summoned by Hadadezer from the other side of the Euphrates River. These troops arrived at Helam under the command of Shobach, the commander of Hadadezer's forces.

17When David heard what was happening, he mobilized all Israel, crossed the Jordan River, and led the army to Helam. The Arameans positioned themselves in battle formation and fought against David. 18But again the Arameans fled from the Israelites. This time David's forces killed 700 charioteers and 40,000 foot soldiers, including Shobach, the commander of their army. 19When all the kings allied with Hadadezer saw that they had been defeated by Israel, they surrendered to Israel and became their subjects. After that, the Arameans were afraid to help the Ammonites.

CHAPTER 11

David and Bathsheba

In the spring of the year, when kings normally go out to war, David sent Joab and the Israelite army to fight the Ammonites. They destroyed the Ammonite army and laid siege to the city of Rabbah. However, David stayed behind in Jerusalem.

2Late one afternoon, after his midday rest, David got out of bed and was walking on the roof of the palace. As he looked out over the city, he noticed a woman of unusual beauty taking a bath. 3He sent someone to find out who she was, and he was told, "She is Bathsheba, the daughter of Eliam and the wife of Uriah the Hittite." 4Then David sent messengers to get her; and when she came to the palace, he slept with her. She had just completed the purification rites after having her menstrual period. Then she returned home. 5Later, when Bathsheba discovered that she was pregnant, she sent David a message, saying, "I'm pregnant."

6Then David sent word to Joab: "Send me Uriah the Hittite." So Joab sent him to David. 7When Uriah arrived, David asked him how Joab and the army were getting along and how the war was progressing. 8Then he told Uriah, "Go on home and relax." David even sent a gift to Uriah after he had left the palace. 9But Uriah didn't go home. He slept that night at the palace entrance with the king's palace guard.

10When David heard that Uriah had not gone home, he summoned him and asked, "What's the matter? Why didn't you go home last night after being away for so long?"

11Uriah replied, "The Ark and the armies of Israel and Judah are living in tents, and Joab and my master's men are camping in the open fields. How could I go home to wine and dine and sleep with my wife? I swear that I would never do such a thing."

12"Well, stay here today," David told him, "and tomorrow you may return to the army." So Uriah stayed in Jerusalem that day and the next. 13Then David invited him to dinner and got him drunk. But even then he couldn't get Uriah to go home to his wife. Again he slept at the palace entrance with the king's palace guard.

David Arranges for Uriah's Death

14So the next morning David wrote a letter to Joab and gave it to Uriah to deliver. 15The letter instructed Joab, "Station Uriah on the front lines where the battle is fiercest. Then pull back so that he will be killed." 16So Joab assigned Uriah to a spot close to the city wall where he knew the enemy's strongest men were fighting. 17And when the enemy soldiers came out of the city to fight, Uriah the Hittite was killed along with several other Israelite soldiers.

18Then Joab sent a battle report to David. 19He told his messenger, "Report all the news of the battle to the king. 20But he might get angry and ask, 'Why did the troops go so close to the city? Didn't they know there would be shooting from the walls? 21Wasn't Abimelech son of Gideon killed at Thebez by a woman who threw a millstone down on him from the wall? Why would you get so close to the wall?' Then tell him, 'Uriah the Hittite was killed, too.'"

22So the messenger went to Jerusalem and gave a complete report to David. 23"The enemy came out against us in the open fields," he said. "And as we chased them back to the city gate, 24the archers on the wall shot arrows at us. Some of the king's men were killed, including Uriah the Hittite."

25"Well, tell Joab not to be discouraged," David said. "The sword devours this one today and that one tomorrow! Fight harder next time, and conquer the city!"

26When Uriah's wife heard that her husband was dead, she mourned for him. 27When the period of mourning was over, David sent for her and brought her to the palace, and she became one of his wives. Then she gave birth to a son. But the LORD was displeased with what David had done.

CHAPTER 12

Nathan Rebukes David

So the LORD sent Nathan the prophet to tell David this story: "There were two men in a certain town. One was rich, and one was poor. 2The rich man owned a great many sheep and cattle. 3The poor man owned nothing but one little lamb he had bought. He raised that little lamb, and it grew up with his children. It ate from the man's own plate and drank from his cup. He cuddled it in his arms like a baby daughter. 4One day a guest arrived at the home of the rich man. But instead of killing an animal from his own flock or herd, he took the poor man's lamb and killed it and prepared it for his guest."

5David was furious. "As surely as the LORD lives," he vowed, "any man who would do such a thing deserves to die! 6He must repay four lambs to the poor man for the one he stole and for having no pity."

7Then Nathan said to David, "You are that man! The LORD, the God of Israel, says: I anointed you king of Israel and saved you from the power of Saul. 8I gave you your master's house and his wives and the kingdoms of Israel and Judah. And if that had not been enough, I would have given you much, much more. 9Why, then, have you despised the word of the LORD and done this horrible deed? For you have murdered Uriah the Hittite with the sword of the Ammonites and stolen his wife. 10From this time on, your family will live by the sword because you have despised me by taking Uriah's wife to be your own.

11"This is what the LORD says: Because of what you have done, I will cause your own household to rebel against you. I will give your wives to another man before your very eyes, and he will go to bed with them in public view. 12You did it secretly, but I will make this happen to you openly in the sight of all Israel."

David Confesses His Guilt

13Then David confessed to Nathan, "I have sinned against the LORD."

2 Samuel 13 . . . page 310

Nathan replied, "Yes, but the LORD has forgiven you, and you won't die for this sin. 14 Nevertheless, because you have shown utter contempt for the word of the LORD by doing this, your child will die."

15 After Nathan returned to his home, the LORD sent a deadly illness to the child of David and Uriah's wife. 16 David begged God to spare the child. He went without food and lay all night on the bare ground. 17 The elders of his household pleaded with him to get up and eat with them, but he refused.

18 Then on the seventh day the child died. David's advisers were afraid to tell him. "He wouldn't listen to reason while the child was ill," they said. "What drastic thing will he do when we tell him the child is dead?"

19 When David saw them whispering, he realized what had happened. "Is the child dead?" he asked.

"Yes," they replied, "he is dead."

20 Then David got up from the ground, washed himself, put on lotions, and changed his clothes. He went to the Tabernacle and worshiped the LORD. After that, he returned to the palace and was served food and ate.

21 His advisers were amazed. "We don't understand you," they told him. "While the child was still living, you wept and refused to eat. But now that the child is dead, you have stopped your mourning and are eating again."

22 David replied, "I fasted and wept while the child was alive, for I said, 'Perhaps the LORD will be gracious to me and let the child live.' 23 But why should I fast when he is dead? Can I bring him back again? I will go to him one day, but he cannot return to me."

24 Then David comforted Bathsheba, his wife, and slept with her. She became pregnant and gave birth to a son, and David named him Solomon. The LORD loved the child 25 and sent word through Nathan the prophet that they should name him Jedidiah (which means "beloved of the LORD"), as the LORD had commanded.

David Captures Rabbah

26 Meanwhile, Joab was fighting against Rabbah, the capital of Ammon, and he captured the royal fortifications. 27 Joab sent messengers to tell David, "I have fought against Rabbah and captured its water supply. 28 Now bring the rest of the army and capture the city. Otherwise, I will capture it and get credit for the victory."

29 So David gathered the rest of the army and went to Rabbah, and he fought against it and captured it. 30 David removed the crown from the king's head, and it was placed on his own head. The crown was made of gold and set with gems, and it weighed seventy-five pounds. David took a vast amount of plunder from the city. 31 He also made slaves of the people of Rabbah and forced them to labor with saws, iron picks, and iron axes, and to work in the brick kilns. That is how he dealt with the people of all the Ammonite towns. Then David and all the army returned to Jerusalem.

CHAPTER 13

The Rape of Tamar

Now David's son Absalom had a beautiful sister named Tamar. And Amnon, her half brother, fell desperately in love with her. 2 Amnon became so obsessed with Tamar that he became ill. She was a virgin, and Amnon thought he could never have her.

3 But Amnon had a very crafty friend—his cousin Jonadab. He was the son of David's brother Shimea. 4 One day Jonadab said to Amnon, "What's the trouble? Why should the son of a king look so dejected morning after morning?"

So Amnon told him, "I am in love with Tamar, my brother Absalom's sister."

5 "Well," Jonadab said, "I'll tell you what to do. Go back to bed and pretend you are ill. When your father comes to see you, ask him to let Tamar come and prepare some food for you. Tell him you'll feel better if she prepares it as you watch and feeds you with her own hands."

6 So Amnon lay down and pretended to be sick. And when the king came to see him, Amnon asked him, "Please let my sister Tamar come and cook my favorite dish as I watch. Then I can eat it from her own hands." 7 So David agreed and sent Tamar to Amnon's house to prepare some food for him.

8 When Tamar arrived at Amnon's house, she went to the place where he was lying down so he could watch her mix some dough. Then she baked his favorite dish for him. 9 But when she set the serving tray before him, he refused to eat. "Everyone get out of here," Amnon told his servants. So they all left.

10 Then he said to Tamar, "Now bring the food into my bedroom and feed it to me here." So Tamar took his favorite dish to him. 11 But as she was feeding him, he grabbed her and demanded, "Come to bed with me, my darling sister."

12 "No, my brother!" she cried. "Don't be foolish! Don't do this to me! Such wicked things aren't done in Israel. 13 Where could I go in my shame? And you would be called one of the

greatest fools in Israel. Please, just speak to the
king about it, and he will let you marry me."
14But Amnon wouldn't listen to her, and since
he was stronger than she was, he raped her.
15Then suddenly Amnon's love turned to hate,
and he hated her even more than he had loved
her. "Get out of here!" he snarled at her.
16"No, no!" Tamar cried. "Sending me away
now is worse than what you've already done
to me."

But Amnon wouldn't listen to her. 17He
shouted for his servant and demanded, "Throw
this woman out, and lock the door behind her!"
18So the servant put her out and locked the
door behind her. She was wearing a long, beautiful robe, as was the custom in those days for
the king's virgin daughters. 19But now Tamar
tore her robe and put ashes on her head. And
then, with her face in her hands, she went away
crying.
20Her brother Absalom saw her and asked, "Is
it true that Amnon has been with you? Well, my
sister, keep quiet for now, since he's your brother.
Don't you worry about it." So Tamar lived as a
desolate woman in her brother Absalom's house.
21When King David heard what had happened, he was very angry. 22And though Absalom
never spoke to Amnon about this, he hated Amnon deeply because of what he had done to his
sister.

Absalom's Revenge on Amnon

23Two years later, when Absalom's sheep were
being sheared at Baal-hazor near Ephraim, Absalom invited all the king's sons to come to a
feast. 24He went to the king and said, "My sheep-
shearers are now at work. Would the king and
his servants please come to celebrate the occasion with me?"
25The king replied, "No, my son. If we all came,
we would be too much of a burden on you." Absalom pressed him, but the king would not come,
though he gave Absalom his blessing.
26"Well, then," Absalom said, "if you can't
come, how about sending my brother Amnon
with us?"

"Why Amnon?" the king asked. 27But Absalom kept on pressing the king until he finally
agreed to let all his sons attend, including Amnon. So Absalom prepared a feast fit for a king.
28Absalom told his men, "Wait until Amnon
gets drunk; then at my signal, kill him! Don't be
afraid. I'm the one who has given the command.
Take courage and do it!" 29So at Absalom's signal
they murdered Amnon. Then the other sons of
the king jumped on their mules and fled.
30As they were on the way back to Jerusalem,
this report reached David: "Absalom has killed all
the king's sons; not one is left alive!" 31The king
got up, tore his robe, and threw himself on the
ground. His advisers also tore their clothes in
horror and sorrow.
32But just then Jonadab, the son of David's
brother Shimea, arrived and said, "No, don't believe that all the king's sons have been killed! It
was only Amnon! Absalom has been plotting this
ever since Amnon raped his sister Tamar. 33No,
my lord the king, your sons aren't all dead! It was
only Amnon." 34Meanwhile Absalom escaped.

Then the watchman on the Jerusalem wall saw
a great crowd coming down the hill on the road
from the west. He ran to tell the king, "I see a
crowd of people coming from the Horonaim
road along the side of the hill."
35"Look!" Jonadab told the king. "There they
are now! The king's sons are coming, just as I
said."
36They soon arrived, weeping and sobbing,
and the king and all his servants wept bitterly
with them. 37And David mourned many days for
his son Amnon.

Absalom fled to his grandfather, Talmai son of
Ammihud, the king of Geshur. 38He stayed there
in Geshur for three years. 39And King David, now
reconciled to Amnon's death, longed to be re-
united with his son Absalom.

CHAPTER 14
Joab Arranges for Absalom's Return

Joab realized how much the king longed to see
Absalom. 2So he sent for a woman from Tekoa
who had a reputation for great wisdom. He said
to her, "Pretend you are in mourning; wear
mourning clothes and don't put on lotions. Act
like a woman who has been mourning for the
dead for a long time. 3Then go to the king and
tell him the story I am about to tell you." Then
Joab told her what to say.
4When the woman from Tekoa approached
the king, she bowed with her face to the ground
in deep respect and cried out, "O king! Help me!"
5"What's the trouble?" the king asked.

"Alas, I am a widow!" she replied. "My husband
is dead. 6My two sons had a fight out in the field.
And since no one was there to stop it, one of
them was killed. 7Now the rest of the family is
demanding, 'Let us have your son. We will execute him for murdering his brother. He doesn't

deserve to inherit his family's property.' They want to extinguish the only coal I have left, and my husband's name and family will disappear from the face of the earth."

8"Leave it to me," the king told her. "Go home, and I'll see to it that no one touches him."

9"Oh, thank you, my lord the king," the woman from Tekoa replied. "If you are criticized for helping me, let the blame fall on me and on my father's house, and let the king and his throne be innocent."

10"If anyone objects," the king said, "bring him to me. I can assure you he will never harm you again!"

11Then she said, "Please swear to me by the LORD your God that you won't let anyone take vengeance against my son. I want no more bloodshed."

"As surely as the LORD lives," he replied, "not a hair on your son's head will be disturbed!"

12"Please allow me to ask one more thing of my lord the king," she said.

"Go ahead and speak," he responded.

13She replied, "Why don't you do as much for the people of God as you have promised to do for me? You have convicted yourself in making this decision, because you have refused to bring
home your own banished son. 14All of us must
die eventually. Our lives are like water spilled out on the ground, which cannot be gathered up again. But God does not just sweep life away; instead, he devises ways to bring us back when we have been separated from him.

15"I have come to plead with my lord the king because people have threatened me. I said to myself, 'Perhaps the king will listen to me 16and res-
cue us from those who would cut us off from the
inheritance God has given us. 17Yes, my lord the
king will give us peace of mind again.' I know that you are like an angel of God in discerning good from evil. May the LORD your God be with you."

18"I must know one thing," the king replied, "and tell me the truth."

"Yes, my lord the king," she responded.

19"Did Joab put you up to this?"

And the woman replied, "My lord the king, how can I deny it? Nobody can hide anything from you. Yes, Joab sent me and told me what to
say. 20He did it to place the matter before you in a
different light. But you are as wise as an angel of God, and you understand everything that happens among us!"

21So the king sent for Joab and told him, "All right, go and bring back the young man Absalom."

The Mall at the Wall

Forget the mall! If you needed to shop in Bible times, the city gate was the place to go. Merchants set up their tent-shops near the gate because anyone entering or leaving the city had to pass that way. For the same reason, government leaders met there to make decisions because witnesses were available.

Who makes the decisions in your city?

(Ask your teacher or Mom or Dad.) Take a minute right now to pray for your leaders by name, and ask God to help them make decisions that are pleasing to him.

22Joab bowed with his face to the ground in deep respect and said, "At last I know that I have gained your approval, my lord the king, for you have granted me this request!"

23Then Joab went to Geshur and brought Absalom back to Jerusalem. 24But the king gave this
order: "Absalom may go to his own house, but he must never come into my presence." So Absalom did not see the king.

Absalom Reconciled to David

25Now Absalom was praised as the most handsome man in all Israel. He was flawless from
head to foot. 26He cut his hair only once a year,
and then only because it was so heavy. When he weighed it out, it came to five pounds!
27He had three sons and one daughter. His
daughter's name was Tamar, and she was very beautiful.

28Absalom lived in Jerusalem for two years,
but he never got to see the king. 29Then Absa-
lom sent for Joab to ask him to intercede for him, but Joab refused to come. Absalom sent for him a second time, but again Joab refused to
come. 30So Absalom said to his servants, "Go
and set fire to Joab's barley field, the field next

to mine." So they set his field on fire, as Absalom had commanded.

31 Then Joab came to Absalom at his house and demanded, "Why did your servants set my field on fire?"

32 And Absalom replied, "Because I wanted you to ask the king why he brought me back from Geshur if he didn't intend to see me. I might as well have stayed there. Let me see the king; if he finds me guilty of anything, then let him kill me."

33 So Joab told the king what Absalom had said. Then at last David summoned Absalom, who came and bowed low before the king, and the king kissed him.

CHAPTER **15**

Absalom's Rebellion

After this, Absalom bought a chariot and horses, and he hired fifty bodyguards to run ahead of him. 2 He got up early every morning and went out to the gate of the city. When people brought a case to the king for judgment, Absalom would ask where in Israel they were from, and they would tell him their tribe. 3 Then Absalom would say, "You've really got a strong case here! It's too bad the king doesn't have anyone to hear it. 4 I wish I were the judge. Then everyone could bring their cases to me for judgment, and I would give them justice!"

5 When people tried to bow before him, Absalom wouldn't let them. Instead, he took them by the hand and kissed them. 6 Absalom did this with everyone who came to the king for judgment, and so he stole the hearts of all the people of Israel.

7 After four years, Absalom said to the king, "Let me go to Hebron to offer a sacrifice to the LORD and fulfill a vow I made to him. 8 For while your servant was at Geshur in Aram, I promised to sacrifice to the LORD in Hebron if he would bring me back to Jerusalem."

9 "All right," the king told him. "Go and fulfill your vow."

So Absalom went to Hebron. 10 But while he was there, he sent secret messengers to all the tribes of Israel to stir up a rebellion against the king. "As soon as you hear the ram's horn," his message read, "you are to say, 'Absalom has been crowned king in Hebron.'" 11 He took 200 men from Jerusalem with him as guests, but they knew nothing of his intentions. 12 While Absalom was offering the sacrifices, he sent for Ahithophel, one of David's counselors who lived in Giloh. Soon many others also joined Absalom, and the conspiracy gained momentum.

David Escapes from Jerusalem

13 A messenger soon arrived in Jerusalem to tell David, "All Israel has joined Absalom in a conspiracy against you!"

14 "Then we must flee at once, or it will be too late!" David urged his men. "Hurry! If we get out of the city before Absalom arrives, both we and the city of Jerusalem will be spared from disaster."

15 "We are with you," his advisers replied. "Do what you think is best."

16 So the king and all his household set out at once. He left no one behind except ten of his concubines to look after the palace. 17 The king and all his people set out on foot, pausing at the last house 18 to let all the king's men move past to lead the way. There were 600 men from Gath who had come with David, along with the king's bodyguard.

19 Then the king turned and said to Ittai, a leader of the men from Gath, "Why are you coming with us? Go on back to King Absalom, for you are a guest in Israel, a foreigner in exile. 20 You arrived only recently, and should I force you today to wander with us? I don't even know where we will go. Go on back and take your kinsmen with you, and may the LORD show you his unfailing love and faithfulness."

21 But Ittai said to the king, "I vow by the LORD and by your own life that I will go wherever my lord the king goes, no matter what happens—whether it means life or death."

22 David replied, "All right, come with us." So Ittai and all his men and their families went along.

23 Everyone cried loudly as the king and his followers passed by. They crossed the Kidron Valley and then went out toward the wilderness.

24 Zadok and all the Levites also came along, carrying the Ark of the Covenant of God. They set down the Ark of God, and Abiathar offered sacrifices until everyone had passed out of the city.

25 Then the king instructed Zadok to take the Ark of God back into the city. "If the LORD sees fit," David said, "he will bring me back to see the Ark and the Tabernacle again. 26 But if he is through with me, then let him do what seems best to him."

27 The king also told Zadok the priest, "Look, here is my plan. You and Abiathar should return quietly to the city with your son Ahimaaz and Abiathar's son Jonathan. 28 I will stop at the

shallows of the Jordan River and wait there for a
report from you." 29So Zadok and Abiathar took
the Ark of God back to the city and stayed there.
30David walked up the road to the Mount of
Olives, weeping as he went. His head was covered and his feet were bare as a sign of mourning.
And the people who were with him covered their
heads and wept as they climbed the hill. 31When
someone told David that his adviser Ahithophel
was now backing Absalom, David prayed,
"O LORD, let Ahithophel give Absalom foolish advice!"
32When David reached the summit of the
Mount of Olives where people worshiped God,
Hushai the Arkite was waiting there for him. Hushai had torn his clothing and put dirt on his
head as a sign of mourning. 33But David told
him, "If you go with me, you will only be a burden. 34Return to Jerusalem and tell Absalom, 'I
will now be your adviser, O king, just as I was your
father's adviser in the past.' Then you can frustrate and counter Ahithophel's advice. 35Zadok
and Abiathar, the priests, will be there. Tell them
about the plans being made in the king's palace,
36and they will send their sons Ahimaaz and Jonathan to tell me what is going on."
37So David's friend Hushai returned to Jerusalem, getting there just as Absalom arrived.

CHAPTER 16

David and Ziba

When David had gone a little beyond the summit
of the Mount of Olives, Ziba, the servant of Mephibosheth, was waiting there for him. He had
two donkeys loaded with 200 loaves of bread,
100 clusters of raisins, 100 bunches of summer
fruit, and a wineskin full of wine.
2"What are these for?" the king asked Ziba.

Ziba replied, "The donkeys are for the king's
people to ride on, and the bread and summer
fruit are for the young men to eat. The wine is for
those who become exhausted in the wilderness."
3"And where is Mephibosheth, Saul's grandson?" the king asked him.

"He stayed in Jerusalem," Ziba replied. "He
said, 'Today I will get back the kingdom of my
grandfather Saul.'"
4"In that case," the king told Ziba, "I give you
everything Mephibosheth owns."

"I bow before you," Ziba replied. "May I always
be pleasing to you, my lord the king."

Shimei Curses David

5As King David came to Bahurim, a man came
out of the village cursing them. It was Shimei son
of Gera, from the same clan as Saul's family. 6He
threw stones at the king and the king's officers
and all the mighty warriors who surrounded
him. 7"Get out of here, you murderer, you scoun-
drel!" he shouted at David. 8"The LORD is paying
you back for all the bloodshed in Saul's clan. You
stole his throne, and now the LORD has given it to
your son Absalom. At last you will taste some of
your own medicine, for you are a murderer!"
9"Why should this dead dog curse my lord the
king?" Abishai son of Zeruiah demanded. "Let
me go over and cut off his head!"
10"No!" the king said. "Who asked your opinion, you sons of Zeruiah! If the LORD has told him
to curse me, who are you to stop him?"
11Then David said to Abishai and to all his servants, "My own son is trying to kill me. Doesn't
this relative of Saul have even more reason to do
so? Leave him alone and let him curse, for the
LORD has told him to do it. 12And perhaps the
LORD will see that I am being wronged and will
bless me because of these curses today." 13So
David and his men continued down the road,
and Shimei kept pace with them on a nearby
hillside, cursing and throwing stones and dirt at
David.
14The king and all who were with him grew
weary along the way, so they rested when they
reached the Jordan River.

Ahithophel Advises Absalom

15Meanwhile, Absalom and all the army of Israel
arrived at Jerusalem, accompanied by Ahithophel. 16When David's friend Hushai the Arkite
arrived, he went immediately to see Absalom.
"Long live the king!" he exclaimed. "Long live the
king!"
17"Is this the way you treat your friend David?"
Absalom asked him. "Why aren't you with him?"
18"I'm here because I belong to the man who is
chosen by the LORD and by all the men of Israel,"
Hushai replied. 19"And anyway, why shouldn't I
serve you? Just as I was your father's adviser, now I
will be your adviser!"
20Then Absalom turned to Ahithophel and
asked him, "What should I do next?"
21Ahithophel told him, "Go and sleep with
your father's concubines, for he has left them
here to look after the palace. Then all Israel will
know that you have insulted your father beyond
hope of reconciliation, and they will throw their
support to you." 22So they set up a tent on the
palace roof where everyone could see it, and Absalom went in and had sex with his father's concubines.

23Absalom followed Ahithophel's advice, just
as David had done. For every word Ahithophel
spoke seemed as wise as though it had come directly from the mouth of God.

CHAPTER 17

Now Ahithophel urged Absalom, "Let me choose
12,000 men to start out after David tonight. 2I
will catch up with him while he is weary and discouraged. He and his troops will panic, and
everyone will run away. Then I will kill only the
king, 3and I will bring all the people back to you
as a bride returns to her husband. After all, it is
only one man's life that you seek. Then you will
be at peace with all the people." 4This plan
seemed good to Absalom and to all the elders of
Israel.

Hushai Counters Ahithophel's Advice

5But then Absalom said, "Bring in Hushai the Arkite. Let's see what he thinks about this." 6When
Hushai arrived, Absalom told him what Ahithophel had said. Then he asked, "What is your
opinion? Should we follow Ahithophel's advice?
If not, what do you suggest?"

7"Well," Hushai replied to Absalom, "this time
Ahithophel has made a mistake. 8You know your
father and his men; they are mighty warriors.
Right now they are as enraged as a mother bear
who has been robbed of her cubs. And remember
that your father is an experienced man of war. He
won't be spending the night among the troops.
9He has probably already hidden in some pit or
cave. And when he comes out and attacks and a
few of your men fall, there will be panic among
your troops, and the word will spread that Absalom's men are being slaughtered. 10Then even
the bravest soldiers, though they have the heart of
a lion, will be paralyzed with fear. For all Israel
knows what a mighty warrior your father is and
how courageous his men are.

11"I recommend that you mobilize the entire
army of Israel, bringing them from as far away as
Dan in the north and Beersheba in the south.
That way you will have an army as numerous as
the sand on the seashore. And I advise that you
personally lead the troops. 12When we find David, we'll fall on him like dew that falls on the
ground. Then neither he nor any of his men will
be left alive. 13And if David were to escape into
some town, you will have all Israel there at your
command. Then we can take ropes and drag the
walls of the town into the nearest valley until
every stone is torn down."

14Then Absalom and all the men of Israel said,
"Hushai's advice is better than Ahithophel's."
For the LORD had determined to defeat the
counsel of Ahithophel, which really was the
better plan, so that he could bring disaster on
Absalom!

Hushai Warns David to Escape

15Hushai told Zadok and Abiathar, the priests,
what Ahithophel had said to Absalom and the elders of Israel and what he himself had advised
instead. 16"Quick!" he told them. "Find David
and urge him not to stay at the shallows of the
Jordan River tonight. He must go across at once
into the wilderness beyond. Otherwise he will
die and his entire army with him."

17Jonathan and Ahimaaz had been staying at
En-rogel so as not to be seen entering and leaving
the city. Arrangements had been made for a servant girl to bring them the message they were to
take to King David. 18But a boy spotted them at
En-rogel, and he told Absalom about it. So they
quickly escaped to Bahurim, where a man hid
them down inside a well in his courtyard. 19The
man's wife put a cloth over the top of the well and
scattered grain on it to dry in the sun; so no one
suspected they were there.

20When Absalom's men arrived, they asked
her, "Have you seen Ahimaaz and Jonathan?"

The woman replied, "They were here, but
they crossed over the brook." Absalom's men
looked for them without success and returned
to Jerusalem.

21Then the two men crawled out of the well
and hurried on to King David. "Quick!" they told
him, "cross the Jordan tonight!" And they told
him how Ahithophel had advised that he be captured and killed. 22So David and all the people
with him went across the Jordan River during the
night, and they were all on the other bank before
dawn.

23When Ahithophel realized that his advice
had not been followed, he saddled his donkey,
went to his hometown, set his affairs in order,
and hanged himself. He died there and was buried in the family tomb.

24David soon arrived at Mahanaim. By now,
Absalom had mobilized the entire army of Israel
and was leading his troops across the Jordan
River. 25Absalom had appointed Amasa as commander of his army, replacing Joab, who had been
commander under David. (Amasa was Joab's
cousin. His father was Jether, an Ishmaelite.
His mother, Abigail daughter of Nahash, was
the sister of Joab's mother, Zeruiah.) 26Absalom

and the Israelite army set up camp in the land
of Gilead.
27When David arrived at Mahanaim, he was
warmly greeted by Shobi son of Nahash, who
came from Rabbah of the Ammonites, and by
Makir son of Ammiel from Lo-debar, and by Barzillai of Gilead from Rogelim. 28They brought
sleeping mats, cooking pots, serving bowls,
wheat and barley, flour and roasted grain, beans,
lentils, 29honey, butter, sheep, goats, and cheese
for David and those who were with him. For they
said, "You must all be very hungry and tired and
thirsty after your long march through the wilderness."

CHAPTER **18**

Absalom's Defeat and Death

David now mustered the men who were with him
and appointed generals and captains to lead
them. 2He sent the troops out in three groups,
placing one group under Joab, one under Joab's
brother Abishai son of Zeruiah, and one under
Ittai, the man from Gath. The king told his
troops, "I am going out with you."
3But his men objected strongly. "You must not
go," they urged. "If we have to turn and run—and
even if half of us die—it will make no difference
to Absalom's troops; they will be looking only for
you. You are worth 10,000 of us, and it is better
that you stay here in the town and send help if we
need it."
4"If you think that's the best plan, I'll do it," the
king answered. So he stood alongside the gate of
the town as all the troops marched out in groups
of hundreds and of thousands.
5And the king gave this command to Joab,
Abishai, and Ittai: "For my sake, deal gently with
young Absalom." And all the troops heard the
king give this order to his commanders.
6So the battle began in the forest of Ephraim,
7and the Israelite troops were beaten back by
David's men. There was a great slaughter that
day, and 20,000 men laid down their lives. 8The
battle raged all across the countryside, and more
men died because of the forest than were killed
by the sword.
9During the battle, Absalom happened to
come upon some of David's men. He tried to escape on his mule, but as he rode beneath the
thick branches of a great tree, his hair got caught
in the tree. His mule kept going and left him
dangling in the air. 10One of David's men saw
what had happened and told Joab, "I saw Absalom dangling from a great tree."
11"What?" Joab demanded. "You saw him
there and didn't kill him? I would have rewarded you with ten pieces of silver and a hero's
belt!"
12"I would not kill the king's son for even a
thousand pieces of silver," the man replied to
Joab. "We all heard the king say to you and Abishai and Ittai, 'For my sake, please spare young Absalom.' 13And if I had betrayed the king by killing
his son—and the king would certainly find out
who did it—you yourself would be the first to
abandon me."
14"Enough of this nonsense," Joab said. Then
he took three daggers and plunged them into
Absalom's heart as he dangled, still alive, in the
great tree. 15Ten of Joab's young armor bearers
then surrounded Absalom and killed him.
16Then Joab blew the ram's horn, and his men
returned from chasing the army of Israel. 17They
threw Absalom's body into a deep pit in the forest and piled a great heap of stones over it. And
all Israel fled to their homes.
18During his lifetime, Absalom had built a
monument to himself in the King's Valley, for he
said, "I have no son to carry on my name." He
named the monument after himself, and it is
known as Absalom's Monument to this day.

David Mourns Absalom's Death

19Then Zadok's son Ahimaaz said, "Let me run to
the king with the good news that the LORD has
rescued him from his enemies."
20"No," Joab told him, "it wouldn't be good
news to the king that his son is dead. You can be
my messenger another time, but not today."
21Then Joab said to a man from Ethiopia, "Go
tell the king what you have seen." The man bowed
and ran off.
22But Ahimaaz continued to plead with Joab,
"Whatever happens, please let me go, too."
"Why should you go, my son?" Joab replied.
"There will be no reward for your news."
23"Yes, but let me go anyway," he begged.
Joab finally said, "All right, go ahead." So
Ahimaaz took the less demanding route by way
of the plain and ran to Mahanaim ahead of the
Ethiopian.
24While David was sitting between the inner
and outer gates of the town, the watchman
climbed to the roof of the gateway by the wall. As
he looked, he saw a lone man running toward
them. 25He shouted the news down to David, and
the king replied, "If he is alone, he has news."
As the messenger came closer, 26the watchman saw another man running toward them. He
shouted down, "Here comes another one!"

The king replied, "He also will have news."
27 "The first man runs like Ahimaaz son of Zadok," the watchman said.
"He is a good man and comes with good
news," the king replied.
28 Then Ahimaaz cried out to the king, "Everything is all right!" He bowed before the king with
his face to the ground and said, "Praise to the
LORD your God, who has handed over the rebels
who dared to stand against my lord the king."
29 "What about young Absalom?" the king demanded. "Is he all right?"
Ahimaaz replied, "When Joab told me to
come, there was a lot of commotion. But I didn't
know what was happening."
30 "Wait here," the king told him. So Ahimaaz
stepped aside.
31 Then the man from Ethiopia arrived and
said, "I have good news for my lord the king. Today the LORD has rescued you from all those who
rebelled against you."
32 "What about young Absalom?" the king demanded. "Is he all right?"
And the Ethiopian replied, "May all of your enemies, my lord the king, both now and in the future, share the fate of that young man!"
33 The king was overcome with emotion. He
went up to the room over the gateway and burst
into tears. And as he went, he cried, "O my son
Absalom! My son, my son Absalom! If only I had
died instead of you! O Absalom, my son, my son."

CHAPTER 19

Joab Rebukes the King

Word soon reached Joab that the king was weeping and mourning for Absalom. 2 As all the people heard of the king's deep grief for his son, the
joy of that day's victory was turned into deep sadness. 3 They crept back into the town that day as
though they were ashamed and had deserted in
battle. 4 The king covered his face with his hands
and kept on crying, "O my son Absalom! O Absalom, my son, my son!"
5 Then Joab went to the king's room and said to
him, "We saved your life today and the lives of
your sons, your daughters, and your wives and
concubines. Yet you act like this, making us feel
ashamed of ourselves. 6 You seem to love those
who hate you and hate those who love you. You
have made it clear today that your commanders
and troops mean nothing to you. It seems that if
Absalom had lived and all of us had died, you
would be pleased. 7 Now go out there and congratulate your troops, for I swear by the LORD
that if you don't go out, not a single one of them
will remain here tonight. Then you will be worse
off than ever before."
8 So the king went out and took his seat at the
town gate, and as the news spread throughout
the town that he was there, everyone went to
him.
Meanwhile, the Israelites who had supported
Absalom fled to their homes. 9 And throughout
all the tribes of Israel there was much discussion
and argument going on. The people were saying,
"The king rescued us from our enemies and
saved us from the Philistines, but Absalom
chased him out of the country. 10 Now Absalom,
whom we anointed to rule over us, is dead. Why
not ask David to come back and be our king
again?"
11 Then King David sent Zadok and Abiathar,
the priests, to say to the elders of Judah, "Why
are you the last ones to welcome back the king
into his palace? For I have heard that all Israel is
ready. 12 You are my relatives, my own tribe, my
own flesh and blood! So why are you the last ones
to welcome back the king?" 13 And David told
them to tell Amasa, "Since you are my own flesh
and blood, like Joab, may God strike me and even
kill me if I do not appoint you as commander of
my army in his place."
14 Then Amasa convinced all the men of Judah,
and they responded unanimously. They sent
word to the king, "Return to us, and bring back
all who are with you."

David's Return to Jerusalem

15 So the king started back to Jerusalem. And
when he arrived at the Jordan River, the people of
Judah came to Gilgal to meet him and escort him
across the river. 16 Shimei son of Gera, the man
from Bahurim in Benjamin, hurried across with
the men of Judah to welcome King David. 17 A
thousand other men from the tribe of Benjamin
were with him, including Ziba, the chief servant
of the house of Saul, and Ziba's fifteen sons and
twenty servants. They rushed down to the Jordan
to meet the king. 18 They crossed the shallows of
the Jordan to bring the king's household across
the river, helping him in every way they could.

David's Mercy to Shimei

As the king was about to cross the river, Shimei
fell down before him. 19 "My lord the king, please
forgive me," he pleaded. "Forget the terrible
thing your servant did when you left Jerusalem.
May the king put it out of his mind. 20 I know how
much I sinned. That is why I have come here

today, the very first person in all Israel to greet
my lord the king."
21 Then Abishai son of Zeruiah said, "Shimei
should die, for he cursed the LORD's anointed
king!"
22 "Who asked your opinion, you sons of Zeruiah!" David exclaimed. "Why have you become
my adversary today? This is not a day for execution, for today I am once again the king of Israel!"
23 Then, turning to Shimei, David vowed, "Your
life will be spared."

David's Kindness to Mephibosheth

24 Now Mephibosheth, Saul's grandson, came
down from Jerusalem to meet the king. He had
not cared for his feet, trimmed his beard, or
washed his clothes since the day the king left Jerusalem. 25 "Why didn't you come with me, Mephibosheth?" the king asked him.
26 Mephibosheth replied, "My lord the king,
my servant Ziba deceived me. I told him, 'Saddle
my donkey so I can go with the king.' For as you
know I am crippled. 27 Ziba has slandered me by
saying that I refused to come. But I know that my
lord the king is like an angel of God, so do what
you think is best. 28 All my relatives and I could
expect only death from you, my lord, but instead
you have honored me by allowing me to eat at
your own table! What more can I ask?"
29 "You've said enough," David replied. "I've
decided that you and Ziba will divide your land
equally between you."
30 "Give him all of it," Mephibosheth said. "I
am content just to have you safely back again, my
lord the king!"

David's Kindness to Barzillai

31 Barzillai of Gilead had come down from Rogelim to escort the king across the Jordan. 32 He was
very old—eighty years of age—and very wealthy.
He was the one who had provided food for the
king during his stay in Mahanaim. 33 "Come
across with me and live in Jerusalem," the king
said to Barzillai. "I will take care of you there."
34 "No," he replied, "I am far too old to go with
the king to Jerusalem. 35 I am eighty years old today, and I can no longer enjoy anything. Food
and wine are no longer tasty, and I cannot hear
the singers as they sing. I would only be a burden to my lord the king. 36 Just to go across the
Jordan River with the king is all the honor I
need! 37 Then let me return again to die in my
own town, where my father and mother are buried. But here is your servant, my son Kimham.
Let him go with my lord the king and receive
whatever you want to give him."
38 "Good," the king agreed. "Kimham will go
with me, and I will help him in any way you would
like. And I will do for you anything you want."
39 So all the people crossed the Jordan with the
king. After David had blessed Barzillai and kissed
him, Barzillai returned to his own home.
40 The king then crossed over to Gilgal, taking
Kimham with him. All the troops of Judah and
half the troops of Israel escorted the king on his
way.

An Argument over the King

41 But all the men of Israel complained to the
king, "The men of Judah stole the king and didn't
give us the honor of helping take you, your
household, and all your men across the Jordan."
42 The men of Judah replied, "The king is one
of our own kinsmen. Why should this make you
angry? We haven't eaten any of the king's food or
received any special favors!"
43 "But there are ten tribes in Israel," the others
replied. "So we have ten times as much right to
the king as you do. What right do you have to
treat us with such contempt? Weren't we the first
to speak of bringing him back to be our king
again?" The argument continued back and forth,
and the men of Judah spoke even more harshly
than the men of Israel.

CHAPTER 20

The Revolt of Sheba

There happened to be a troublemaker there
named Sheba son of Bicri, a man from the tribe
of Benjamin. Sheba blew a ram's horn and began
to chant:

"Down with the dynasty of David!
  We have no interest in the son of Jesse.
Come on, you men of Israel,
  back to your homes!"

2 So all the men of Israel deserted David and
followed Sheba son of Bicri. But the men of Judah stayed with their king and escorted him
from the Jordan River to Jerusalem.
3 When David came to his palace in Jerusalem,
he took the ten concubines he had left to look after the palace and placed them in seclusion.
Their needs were provided for, but he no longer
slept with them. So each of them lived like a
widow until she died.
4 Then the king told Amasa, "Mobilize the
army of Judah within three days, and report back
at that time." 5 So Amasa went out to notify Ju-

FUN-fact
The Final Sacrifice
Boy, sacrifices sure have changed!
Whew!

Before Jesus, God told the people to observe a sacrifice called the Day of Atonement. Every year the Israelite people confessed their sins and the high priest sacrificed animals to cover the sins. The sacrifice couldn't take away the sins—it just covered the sins.

Jesus' death on the cross did away with that system forever. Jesus took the punishment for our sins himself.

Want to see a sacrifice? Do your sister's chores or give your brother your allowance. Then think how Jesus took the punishment for everyone's sins! BOY, JESUS MUST REALLY LOVE US!

dah, but it took him longer than the time he had been given.

6Then David said to Abishai, "Sheba son of Bicri is going to hurt us more than Absalom did. Quick, take my troops and chase after him before he gets into a fortified town where we can't reach him."

7So Abishai and Joab, together with the king's bodyguard and all the mighty warriors, set out from Jerusalem to go after Sheba.
8As they arrived at the great stone in Gibeon, Amasa met them. Joab was wearing his military tunic with a dagger strapped to his belt. As he stepped forward to greet Amasa, he slipped the dagger from its sheath.

9"How are you, my cousin?" Joab said and took him by the beard with his right hand as though to kiss him.
10Amasa didn't notice the dagger in his left hand, and Joab stabbed him in the stomach with it so that his insides gushed out onto the ground. Joab did not need to strike again, and Amasa soon died. Joab and his brother Abishai left him lying there and continued after Sheba.

11One of Joab's young men shouted to Amasa's troops, "If you are for Joab and David, come and follow Joab."
12But Amasa lay in his blood in the middle of the road, and Joab's man saw that everyone was stopping to stare at him. So he pulled him off the road into a field and threw a cloak over him.
13With Amasa's body out of the way, everyone went on with Joab to capture Sheba son of Bicri.

14Meanwhile, Sheba traveled through all the tribes of Israel and eventually came to the town of Abel-beth-maacah. All the members of his own clan, the Bicrites, assembled for battle and followed him into the town.
15When Joab's forces arrived, they attacked Abel-beth-maacah. They built a siege ramp against the town's fortifications and began battering down the wall.
16But a wise woman in the town called out to Joab, "Listen to me, Joab. Come over here so I can talk to you."
17As he approached, the woman asked, "Are you Joab?"

"I am," he replied.

So she said, "Listen carefully to your servant."

"I'm listening," he said.

18Then she continued, "There used to be a saying, 'If you want to settle an argument, ask advice at the town of Abel.'
19I am one who is peace loving and faithful in Israel. But you are destroying an important town in Israel. Why do you want to devour what belongs to the LORD?"

20And Joab replied, "Believe me, I don't want to devour or destroy your town!
21That's not my purpose. All I want is a man named Sheba son of Bicri from the hill country of Ephraim, who has revolted against King David. If you hand over this one man to me, I will leave the town in peace."

"All right," the woman replied, "we will throw his head over the wall to you."
22Then the woman went to all the people with her wise advice, and they cut off Sheba's head and threw it out to Joab. So he blew the ram's horn and called his troops back from the attack. They all returned to their homes, and Joab returned to the king at Jerusalem.

23Now Joab was the commander of the army of Israel. Benaiah son of Jehoiada was captain of the king's bodyguard.
24Adoniram was in charge of forced labor. Jehoshaphat son of Ahilud was the royal historian.
25Sheva was the court secretary. Zadok and Abiathar were the priests.
26And Ira, a descendant of Jair, was David's personal priest.

CHAPTER 21

David Avenges the Gibeonites

There was a famine during David's reign that lasted for three years, so David asked the LORD

about it. And the LORD said, "The famine has
come because Saul and his family are guilty of
murdering the Gibeonites."
2 So the king summoned the Gibeonites. They
were not part of Israel but were all that was left of
the nation of the Amorites. The people of Israel
had sworn not to kill them, but Saul, in his zeal
for Israel and Judah, had tried to wipe them out.
3 David asked them, "What can I do for you? How
can I make amends so that you will bless the
LORD's people again?"
4 "Well, money can't settle this matter between us and the family of Saul," the Gibeonites
replied. "Neither can we demand the life of anyone in Israel."
"What can I do then?" David asked. "Just tell
me and I will do it for you."
5 Then they replied, "It was Saul who planned
to destroy us, to keep us from having any place at
all in the territory of Israel. 6 So let seven of Saul's
sons be handed over to us, and we will execute
them before the LORD at Gibeon, on the mountain of the LORD."
"All right," the king said, "I will do it." 7 The
king spared Jonathan's son Mephibosheth who
was Saul's grandson, because of the oath David
and Jonathan had sworn before the LORD. 8 But
he gave them Saul's two sons Armoni and Mephibosheth, whose mother was Rizpah daughter
of Aiah. He also gave them the five sons of Saul's
daughter Merab, the wife of Adriel son of Barzillai from Meholah. 9 The men of Gibeon executed
them on the mountain before the LORD. So all
seven of them died together at the beginning of
the barley harvest.
10 Then Rizpah daughter of Aiah, the mother
of two of the men, spread burlap on a rock and
stayed there the entire harvest season. She prevented the scavenger birds from tearing at their
bodies during the day and stopped wild animals
from eating them at night. 11 When David
learned what Rizpah, Saul's concubine, had
done, 12 he went to the people of Jabesh-gilead
and retrieved the bones of Saul and his son Jonathan. (When the Philistines had killed Saul and
Jonathan on Mount Gilboa, the people of Jabesh-
gilead stole their bodies from the public square
of Beth-shan, where the Philistines had hung
them.) 13 So David obtained the bones of Saul
and Jonathan, as well as the bones of the men the
Gibeonites had executed.
14 Then the king ordered that they bury the
bones in the tomb of Kish, Saul's father, at the
town of Zela in the land of Benjamin. After that,
God ended the famine in the land.

Battles against Philistine Giants

15 Once again the Philistines were at war with Israel. And when David and his men were in the
thick of battle, David became weak and exhausted. 16 Ishbi-benob was a descendant of the
giants; his bronze spearhead weighed more than
seven pounds, and he was armed with a new
sword. He had cornered David and was about to
kill him. 17 But Abishai son of Zeruiah came to
David's rescue and killed the Philistine. Then David's men declared, "You are not going out to battle with us again! Why risk snuffing out the light
of Israel?"
18 After this, there was another battle against
the Philistines at Gob. As they fought, Sibbecai
from Hushah killed Saph, another descendant of
the giants.
19 During another battle at Gob, Elhanan son of
Jair from Bethlehem killed the brother of Goliath
of Gath. The handle of his spear was as thick as a
weaver's beam!
20 In another battle with the Philistines at
Gath, they encountered a huge man with six
fingers on each hand and six toes on each foot,
twenty-four in all, who was also a descendant
of the giants. 21 But when he defied and taunted
Israel, he was killed by Jonathan, the son of
David's brother Shimea.
22 These four Philistines were descendants of
the giants of Gath, but David and his warriors
killed them.

CHAPTER 22

David's Song of Praise

David sang this song to the LORD on the day the
LORD rescued him from all his enemies and from
Saul. 2 He sang:

"The LORD is my rock, my fortress, and my
savior;
3 my God is my rock, in whom I find
protection.
He is my shield, the power that saves me,
and my place of safety.
He is my refuge, my savior,
the one who saves me from violence.
4 I called on the LORD, who is worthy of
praise,
and he saved me from my enemies.

5 "The waves of death overwhelmed me;
floods of destruction swept over me.
6 The grave wrapped its ropes around me;
death laid a trap in my path.
7 But in my distress I cried out to the LORD;
yes, I cried to my God for help.

He heard me from his sanctuary;
my cry reached his ears.

8 "Then the earth quaked and trembled.
The foundations of the heavens shook;
they quaked because of his anger.
9 Smoke poured from his nostrils;
fierce flames leaped from his mouth.
Glowing coals blazed forth from him.
10 He opened the heavens and came down;
dark storm clouds were beneath his feet.
11 Mounted on a mighty angelic being,
he flew,
soaring on the wings of the wind.
12 He shrouded himself in darkness,
veiling his approach with dense rain
clouds.
13 A great brightness shone around him,
and burning coals blazed forth.
14 The LORD thundered from heaven;
the voice of the Most High resounded.
15 He shot arrows and scattered his enemies;
his lightning flashed, and they were
confused.
16 Then at the command of the LORD,
at the blast of his breath,
the bottom of the sea could be seen,
and the foundations of the earth were
laid bare.

17 "He reached down from heaven and
rescued me;
he drew me out of deep waters.
18 He rescued me from my powerful enemies,
from those who hated me and were too
strong for me.
19 They attacked me at a moment when I was
in distress,
but the LORD supported me.
20 He led me to a place of safety;
he rescued me because he delights
in me.
21 The LORD rewarded me for doing right;
he restored me because of my innocence.
22 For I have kept the ways of the LORD;
I have not turned from my God to follow
evil.
23 I have followed all his regulations;
I have never abandoned his decrees.
24 I am blameless before God;
I have kept myself from sin.
25 The LORD rewarded me for doing right.
He has seen my innocence.

26 "To the faithful you show yourself faithful;
to those with integrity you show integrity.
27 To the pure you show yourself pure,
but to the crooked you show yourself
shrewd.
28 You rescue the humble,
but your eyes watch the proud and
humiliate them.
29 O LORD, you are my lamp.
The LORD lights up my darkness.
30 In your strength I can crush an army;
with my God I can scale any wall.

31 "God's way is perfect.
All the LORD's promises prove true.
He is a shield for all who look to him
for protection.
32 For who is God except the LORD?
Who but our God is a solid rock?
33 God is my strong fortress,
and he makes my way perfect.
34 He makes me as surefooted as a deer,
enabling me to stand on mountain
heights.
35 He trains my hands for battle;
he strengthens my arm to draw
a bronze bow.
36 You have given me your shield of victory;
your help has made me great.
37 You have made a wide path for my feet
to keep them from slipping.

38 "I chased my enemies and destroyed them;
I did not stop until they were conquered.
39 I consumed them;
I struck them down so they did not
get up;
they fell beneath my feet.
40 You have armed me with strength for
the battle;
you have subdued my enemies under
my feet.
41 You placed my foot on their necks.
I have destroyed all who hated me.
42 They looked for help, but no one came
to their rescue.
They even cried to the LORD, but he
refused to answer.
43 I ground them as fine as the dust of the
earth;
I trampled them in the gutter like dirt.

44 "You gave me victory over my accusers.
You preserved me as the ruler over
nations;
people I don't even know now serve me.
45 Foreign nations cringe before me;
as soon as they hear of me, they submit.

46 They all lose their courage
and come trembling from their
strongholds.

47 "The LORD lives! Praise to my Rock!
May God, the Rock of my salvation,
be exalted!
48 He is the God who pays back those who
harm me;
he brings down the nations under me
49 and delivers me from my enemies.
You hold me safe beyond the reach of
my enemies;
you save me from violent opponents.
50 For this, O LORD, I will praise you among
the nations;
I will sing praises to your name.
51 You give great victories to your king;
you show unfailing love to your anointed,
to David and all his descendants forever."

CHAPTER 23

David's Last Words

These are the last words of David:

"David, the son of Jesse, speaks—
David, the man who was raised up so high,
David, the man anointed by the God of Jacob,
David, the sweet psalmist of Israel.
2 "The Spirit of the LORD speaks through me;
his words are upon my tongue.
3 The God of Israel spoke.
The Rock of Israel said to me:
'The one who rules righteously,
who rules in the fear of God,
4 is like the light of morning at sunrise,
like a morning without clouds,
like the gleaming of the sun
on new grass after rain.'
5 "Is it not my family God has chosen?
Yes, he has made an everlasting covenant
with me.
His agreement is arranged and guaranteed
in every detail.
He will ensure my safety and success.
6 But the godless are like thorns to be thrown
away,
for they tear the hand that touches them.
7 One must use iron tools to chop them down;
they will be totally consumed by fire."

David's Mightiest Warriors

8 These are the names of David's mightiest warriors. The first was Jashobeam the Hacmonite,
who was leader of the Three—the three mightiest warriors among David's men. He once used
his spear to kill 800 enemy warriors in a single
battle.

9 Next in rank among the Three was Eleazar
son of Dodai, a descendant of Ahoah. Once Eleazar and David stood together against the Philistines when the entire Israelite army had fled.
10 He killed Philistines until his hand was too
tired to lift his sword, and the LORD gave him a
great victory that day. The rest of the army did not
return until it was time to collect the plunder!

11 Next in rank was Shammah son of Agee
from Harar. One time the Philistines gathered at
Lehi and attacked the Israelites in a field full of
lentils. The Israelite army fled, 12 but Shammah
held his ground in the middle of the field and
beat back the Philistines. So the LORD brought
about a great victory.

13 Once during the harvest, when David was at
the cave of Adullam, the Philistine army was
camped in the valley of Rephaim. The Three
(who were among the Thirty—an elite group
among David's fighting men) went down to meet
him there. 14 David was staying in the stronghold
at the time, and a Philistine detachment had occupied the town of Bethlehem.

15 David remarked longingly to his men, "Oh,
how I would love some of that good water from
the well by the gate in Bethlehem." 16 So the
Three broke through the Philistine lines, drew
some water from the well by the gate in Bethlehem, and brought it back to David. But he refused
to drink it. Instead, he poured it out as an offering
to the LORD. 17 "The LORD forbid that I should
drink this!" he exclaimed. "This water is as precious as the blood of these men who risked their
lives to bring it to me." So David did not drink it.
These are examples of the exploits of the Three.

David's Thirty Mighty Men

18 Abishai son of Zeruiah, the brother of Joab,
was the leader of the Thirty. He once used his
spear to kill 300 enemy warriors in a single battle. It was by such feats that he became as famous
as the Three. 19 Abishai was the most famous of
the Thirty and was their commander, though he
was not one of the Three.

20 There was also Benaiah son of Jehoiada, a
valiant warrior from Kabzeel. He did many heroic deeds, which included killing two champions of Moab. Another time, on a snowy day, he
chased a lion down into a pit and killed it.
21 Once, armed only with a club, he killed an
imposing Egyptian warrior who was armed with
a spear. Benaiah wrenched the spear from the

Egyptian's hand and killed him with it. 22Deeds
like these made Benaiah as famous as the Three
mightiest warriors. 23He was more honored than
the other members of the Thirty, though he was
not one of the Three. And David made him captain of his bodyguard.

24Other members of the Thirty included:

Asahel, Joab's brother;
Elhanan son of Dodo from Bethlehem;
25 Shammah from Harod;
Elika from Harod;
26 Helez from Pelon;
Ira son of Ikkesh from Tekoa;
27 Abiezer from Anathoth;
Sibbecai from Hushah;
28 Zalmon from Ahoah;
Maharai from Netophah;
29 Heled son of Baanah from Netophah;
Ithai son of Ribai from Gibeah (in the land
of Benjamin);
30 Benaiah from Pirathon;
Hurai from Nahale-gaash;
31 Abi-albon from Arabah;
Azmaveth from Bahurim;
32 Eliahba from Shaalbon;
the sons of Jashen;
Jonathan 33son of Shagee from Harar;
Ahiam son of Sharar from Harar;
34 Eliphelet son of Ahasbai from Maacah;
Eliam son of Ahithophel from Giloh;
35 Hezro from Carmel;
Paarai from Arba;
36 Igal son of Nathan from Zobah;
Bani from Gad;
37 Zelek from Ammon;
Naharai from Beeroth, the armor bearer of
Joab son of Zeruiah;
38 Ira from Jattir;
Gareb from Jattir;
39 Uriah the Hittite.

There were thirty-seven in all.

CHAPTER 24

David Takes a Census

Once again the anger of the LORD burned against
Israel, and he caused David to harm them by taking a census. "Go and count the people of Israel
and Judah," the LORD told him.

2So the king said to Joab and the commanders
of the army, "Take a census of all the tribes of
Israel—from Dan in the north to Beersheba in
the south—so I may know how many people
there are."

3But Joab replied to the king, "May the LORD
your God let you live to see a hundred times as
many people as there are now! But why, my lord
the king, do you want to do this?"

4But the king insisted that they take the census, so Joab and the commanders of the army
went out to count the people of Israel. 5First they
crossed the Jordan and camped at Aroer, south of
the town in the valley, in the direction of Gad.
Then they went on to Jazer, 6then to Gilead in the
land of Tahtim-hodshi and to Dan-jaan and
around to Sidon. 7Then they came to the fortress
of Tyre, and all the towns of the Hivites and Canaanites. Finally, they went south to Judah as far
as Beersheba.

8Having gone through the entire land for nine
months and twenty days, they returned to Jerusalem. 9Joab reported the number of people to the
king. There were 800,000 capable warriors in Israel who could handle a sword, and 500,000 in
Judah.

Judgment for David's Sin

10But after he had taken the census, David's conscience began to bother him. And he said to the
LORD, "I have sinned greatly by taking this census. Please forgive my guilt, LORD, for doing this
foolish thing."

11The next morning the word of the LORD
came to the prophet Gad, who was David's seer.
This was the message: 12"Go and say to David,
'This is what the LORD says: I will give you three
choices. Choose one of these punishments, and I
will inflict it on you.'"

13So Gad came to David and asked him, "Will
you choose three years of famine throughout
your land, three months of fleeing from your enemies, or three days of severe plague throughout
your land? Think this over and decide what answer I should give the LORD who sent me."

14"I'm in a desperate situation!" David replied
to Gad. "But let us fall into the hands of the LORD,
for his mercy is great. Do not let me fall into human hands."

15So the LORD sent a plague upon Israel that
morning, and it lasted for three days. A total of
70,000 people died throughout the nation, from
Dan in the north to Beersheba in the south. 16But
as the angel was preparing to destroy Jerusalem,
the LORD relented and said to the death angel,
"Stop! That is enough!" At that moment the angel
of the LORD was by the threshing floor of Araunah the Jebusite.

17When David saw the angel, he said to the
LORD, "I am the one who has sinned and done
wrong! But these people are as innocent as

sheep—what have they done? Let your anger fall against me and my family."

David Builds an Altar

18That day Gad came to David and said to him, "Go up and build an altar to the LORD on the threshing floor of Araunah the Jebusite."

19So David went up to do what the LORD had commanded him. 20When Araunah saw the king and his men coming toward him, he came and bowed before the king with his face to the ground. 21"Why have you come, my lord the king?" Araunah asked.

David replied, "I have come to buy your threshing floor and to build an altar to the LORD there, so that he will stop the plague."

22"Take it, my lord the king, and use it as you wish," Araunah said to David. "Here are oxen for the burnt offering, and you can use the threshing boards and ox yokes for wood to build a fire on the altar. 23I will give it all to you, Your Majesty, and may the LORD your God accept your sacrifice."

24But the king replied to Araunah, "No, I insist on buying it, for I will not present burnt offerings to the LORD my God that have cost me nothing." So David paid him fifty pieces of silver for the threshing floor and the oxen.

25David built an altar there to the LORD and sacrificed burnt offerings and peace offerings. And the LORD answered his prayer for the land, and the plague on Israel was stopped.

1 KiNGS Israel's Royal Leaders

Look for 3 hidden messages in 1 Kings!

The book of 1 Kings tells the story of—you guessed it—a bunch of kings. And there were *lots* of kings because Israel split into two kingdoms. Read 1 Kings to discover amazing facts about

- **THE DEATH OF A GOOD GUY**
- **THE REIGN OF A WISE GUY**
- **THE RULE OF SOME BAD GUYS**
- **THE ADVENTURES OF A PROPHET-TYPE GUY**

Famous Last Words

When King David was very old, he knew the time of his death was approaching. **Read some of his last words in 1 Kings 2:1-4.**

Whooo's Wise?

You've heard the saying "wise as an owl," haven't you? Well, this guy was way wiser than any old owl. **Find out whooo it was (and how he got that way) in 1 Kings 3:5-14.**

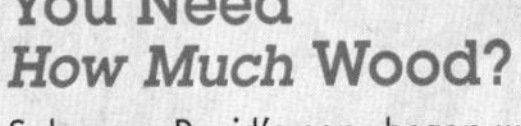

You Need *How Much* Wood?

Solomon, David's son, began work on a Temple for the Lord. He ordered cedar and cypress wood from Lebanon and had stone blocks prepared at the quarry so stonecutters wouldn't make noise at the construction site. **Read more about this amazing seven-year building project in 1 Kings 5:3–6:38.**

Peer Pressure

Even with all his wisdom, Solomon still messed up. He let his wives influence him to turn away from the one true God and worship their fake gods. Want to know how God reacted? **Turn to 1 Kings 11:9-13.**

Twice as Nice? Not Really!

Stay at home, Rehoboam! That's what many Israelites thought. So ten of the tribes of Israel split and formed their own new kingdom of Israel in the north and set up a guy named Jeroboam as their king. Rehoboam ruled the other two tribes in the south, and they called his kingdom Judah. **Read about the big split in 1 Kings 12.**

And the Winner Is...

God sent a prophet named Elijah to talk sense to Israel and to try to turn them back to God. Elijah set up a competition between the one true God and the fake god, Baal. Guess who won! (Easy answer.) **Check out 1 Kings 18 for news on this electrifying contest!**

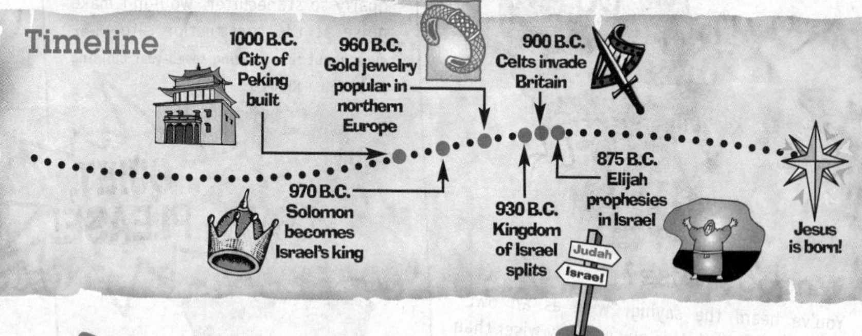
Timeline
1000 B.C. City of Peking built
960 B.C. Gold jewelry popular in northern Europe
900 B.C. Celts invade Britain
970 B.C. Solomon becomes Israel's king
930 B.C. Kingdom of Israel splits
Judah
Israel
875 B.C. Elijah prophesies in Israel
Jesus is born!

The JESUS CONNECTION

The Bible places much emphasis on Solomon's wealth and material possessions. In Old Testament times, wealth was often thought to prove that God approved of a person. But even with all his riches, Solomon still strayed away from God.

We should remember that the most important "treasure" is not on earth—it's heavenly! The greatest treasure of all is free. It's the gift of salvation offered through Jesus. **Hey, that means that if you believe in Jesus, you're richer than Solomon was!**

CHAPTER 1

David in His Old Age

King David was now very old, and no matter how
many blankets covered him, he could not keep
warm. 2So his advisers told him, "Let us find a
young virgin to wait on you and look after you,
my lord. She will lie in your arms and keep you
warm."
3So they searched throughout the land of Israel for a beautiful girl, and they found Abishag
from Shunem and brought her to the king. 4The
girl was very beautiful, and she looked after the
king and took care of him. But the king had no
sexual relations with her.

Adonijah Claims the Throne

5About that time David's son Adonijah, whose
mother was Haggith, began boasting, "I will
make myself king." So he provided himself with
chariots and charioteers and recruited fifty men
to run in front of him. 6Now his father, King David, had never disciplined him at any time, even
by asking, "Why are you doing that?" Adonijah
had been born next after Absalom, and he was
very handsome.
7Adonijah took Joab son of Zeruiah and Abiathar the priest into his confidence, and they
agreed to help him become king. 8But Zadok the
priest, Benaiah son of Jehoiada, Nathan the
prophet, Shimei, Rei, and David's personal bodyguard refused to support Adonijah.
9Adonijah went to the Stone of Zoheleth near
the spring of En-rogel, where he sacrificed sheep,
cattle, and fattened calves. He invited all his
brothers—the other sons of King David—and all
the royal officials of Judah. 10But he did not invite
Nathan the prophet or Benaiah or the king's
bodyguard or his brother Solomon.
11Then Nathan went to Bathsheba, Solomon's
mother, and asked her, "Haven't you heard that
Haggith's son, Adonijah, has made himself king,
and our lord David doesn't even know about it?
12If you want to save your own life and the life
of your son Solomon, follow my advice. 13Go at
once to King David and say to him, 'My lord the
king, didn't you make a vow and say to me, "Your
son Solomon will surely be the next king and
will sit on my throne"? Why then has Adonijah
become king?' 14And while you are still talking
with him, I will come and confirm everything
you have said."
15So Bathsheba went into the king's bedroom.
(He was very old now, and Abishag was taking
care of him.) 16Bathsheba bowed down before
the king.
"What can I do for you?" he asked her.
17She replied, "My lord, you made a vow before
the LORD your God when you said to me, 'Your
son Solomon will surely be the next king and will
sit on my throne.' 18But instead, Adonijah has
made himself king, and my lord the king does not
even know about it. 19He has sacrificed many cattle, fattened calves, and sheep, and he has invited
all the king's sons to attend the celebration. He
also invited Abiathar the priest and Joab, the
commander of the army. But he did not invite
your servant Solomon. 20And now, my lord the
king, all Israel is waiting for you to announce who
will become king after you. 21If you do not act, my
son Solomon and I will be treated as criminals as
soon as my lord the king has died."
22While she was still speaking with the king,
Nathan the prophet arrived. 23The king's officials told him, "Nathan the prophet is here to see
you."
Nathan went in and bowed before the king
with his face to the ground. 24Nathan asked, "My
lord the king, have you decided that Adonijah
will be the next king and that he will sit on your
throne? 25Today he has sacrificed many cattle,
fattened calves, and sheep, and he has invited all
the king's sons to attend the celebration. He also
invited the commanders of the army and Abiathar the priest. They are feasting and drinking
with him and shouting, 'Long live King Adonijah!'
26But he did not invite me or Zadok the priest or
Benaiah or your servant Solomon. 27Has my lord
the king really done this without letting any of his
officials know who should be the next king?"

David Makes Solomon King

28King David responded, "Call Bathsheba!" So
she came back in and stood before the king.
29And the king repeated his vow: "As surely as the
LORD lives, who has rescued me from every danger, 30your son Solomon will be the next king
and will sit on my throne this very day, just as I
vowed to you before the LORD, the God of Israel."
31Then Bathsheba bowed down with her face
to the ground before the king and exclaimed,
"May my lord King David live forever!"
32Then King David ordered, "Call Zadok the
priest, Nathan the prophet, and Benaiah son of
Jehoiada." When they came into the king's presence, 33the king said to them, "Take Solomon
and my officials down to Gihon Spring. Solomon
is to ride on my own mule. 34There Zadok the
priest and Nathan the prophet are to anoint him
king over Israel. Blow the ram's horn and shout,
'Long live King Solomon!' 35Then escort him

back here, and he will sit on my throne. He will
succeed me as king, for I have appointed him to
be ruler over Israel and Judah."
36"Amen!" Benaiah son of Jehoiada replied.
"May the LORD, the God of my lord the king, decree that it happen. 37And may the LORD be with
Solomon as he has been with you, my lord the
king, and may he make Solomon's reign even
greater than yours!"
38So Zadok the priest, Nathan the prophet, Benaiah son of Jehoiada, and the king's bodyguard
took Solomon down to Gihon Spring, with Solomon riding on King David's own mule. 39There
Zadok the priest took the flask of olive oil from
the sacred tent and anointed Solomon with the
oil. Then they sounded the ram's horn and all
the people shouted, "Long live King Solomon!"
40And all the people followed Solomon into Jerusalem, playing flutes and shouting for joy. The
celebration was so joyous and noisy that the
earth shook with the sound.
41Adonijah and his guests heard the celebrating and shouting just as they were finishing their
banquet. When Joab heard the sound of the
ram's horn, he asked, "What's going on? Why is
the city in such an uproar?"
42And while he was still speaking, Jonathan
son of Abiathar the priest arrived. "Come in,"
Adonijah said to him, "for you are a good man.
You must have good news."
43"Not at all!" Jonathan replied. "Our lord King
David has just declared Solomon king! 44The king
sent him down to Gihon Spring with Zadok the
priest, Nathan the prophet, and Benaiah son of
Jehoiada, protected by the king's bodyguard.
They had him ride on the king's own mule, 45and
Zadok and Nathan have anointed him at Gihon
Spring as the new king. They have just returned,
and the whole city is celebrating and rejoicing.
That's what all the noise is about. 46What's more,
Solomon is now sitting on the royal throne as
king. 47And all the royal officials have gone to
King David and congratulated him, saying, 'May
your God make Solomon's fame even greater than
your own, and may Solomon's reign be even
greater than yours!' Then the king bowed his
head in worship as he lay in his bed, 48and he
said, 'Praise the LORD, the God of Israel, who today
has chosen a successor to sit on my throne while I
am still alive to see it.'"
49Then all of Adonijah's guests jumped up in
panic from the banquet table and quickly scattered. 50Adonijah was afraid of Solomon, so he
rushed to the sacred tent and grabbed on to the
horns of the altar. 51Word soon reached Solomon that Adonijah had seized the horns of the
altar in fear, and that he was pleading, "Let King
Solomon swear today that he will not kill me!"
52Solomon replied, "If he proves himself to be
loyal, not a hair on his head will be touched. But
if he makes trouble, he will die." 53So King Solomon summoned Adonijah, and they brought
him down from the altar. He came and bowed respectfully before King Solomon, who dismissed
him, saying, "Go on home."

CHAPTER 2

David's Final Instructions to Solomon

As the time of King David's death approached, he
gave this charge to his son Solomon:
2"I am going where everyone on earth must
someday go. Take courage and be a man. 3Ob-
serve the requirements of the LORD your God,
and follow all his ways. Keep the decrees, commands, regulations, and laws written in the Law
of Moses so that you will be successful in all you
do and wherever you go. 4If you do this, then the
LORD will keep the promise he made to me. He
told me, 'If your descendants live as they should
and follow me faithfully with all their heart and
soul, one of them will always sit on the throne of
Israel.'
5"And there is something else. You know what
Joab son of Zeruiah did to me when he murdered
my two army commanders, Abner son of Ner and
Amasa son of Jether. He pretended that it was an
act of war, but it was done in a time of peace,
staining his belt and sandals with innocent
blood. 6Do with him what you think best, but
don't let him grow old and go to his grave in
peace.
7"Be kind to the sons of Barzillai of Gilead.
Make them permanent guests at your table, for
they took care of me when I fled from your
brother Absalom.
8"And remember Shimei son of Gera, the man
from Bahurim in Benjamin. He cursed me with a
terrible curse as I was fleeing to Mahanaim.
When he came down to meet me at the Jordan
River, I swore by the LORD that I would not kill
him. 9But that oath does not make him innocent.
You are a wise man, and you will know how to
arrange a bloody death for him."
10Then David died and was buried with his ancestors in the City of David. 11David had reigned
over Israel for forty years, seven of them in Hebron and thirty-three in Jerusalem. 12Solomon
became king and sat on the throne of David his
father, and his kingdom was firmly established.

Solomon Establishes His Rule

13 One day Adonijah, whose mother was Haggith,
came to see Bathsheba, Solomon's mother. "Have
you come with peaceful intentions?" she asked
him.

"Yes," he said, "I come in peace. 14 In fact, I
have a favor to ask of you."

"What is it?" she asked.

15 He replied, "As you know, the kingdom was
rightfully mine; all Israel wanted me to be the
next king. But the tables were turned, and the
kingdom went to my brother instead; for that is
the way the LORD wanted it. 16 So now I have just
one favor to ask of you. Please don't turn me
down."

"What is it?" she asked.

17 He replied, "Speak to King Solomon on my
behalf, for I know he will do anything you request. Ask him to let me marry Abishag, the girl
from Shunem."

18 "All right," Bathsheba replied. "I will speak to
the king for you."

19 So Bathsheba went to King Solomon to
speak on Adonijah's behalf. The king rose from
his throne to meet her, and he bowed down before her. When he sat down on his throne again,
the king ordered that a throne be brought for his
mother, and she sat at his right hand.

20 "I have one small request to make of you,"
she said. "I hope you won't turn me down."

"What is it, my mother?" he asked. "You know
I won't refuse you."

21 "Then let your brother Adonijah marry Abishag, the girl from Shunem," she replied.

22 "How can you possibly ask me to give Abishag to Adonijah?" King Solomon demanded.
"You might as well ask me to give him the kingdom! You know that he is my older brother, and
that he has Abiathar the priest and Joab son of
Zeruiah on his side."

23 Then King Solomon made a vow before the
LORD: "May God strike me and even kill me if
Adonijah has not sealed his fate with this request. 24 The LORD has confirmed me and placed
me on the throne of my father, David; he has established my dynasty as he promised. So as
surely as the LORD lives, Adonijah will die this
very day!" 25 So King Solomon ordered Benaiah
son of Jehoiada to execute him, and Adonijah
was put to death.

26 Then the king said to Abiathar the priest,
"Go back to your home in Anathoth. You deserve
to die, but I will not kill you now, because you carried the Ark of the Sovereign LORD for David my
father and you shared all his hardships." 27 So
Solomon deposed Abiathar from his position as
priest of the LORD, thereby fulfilling the prophecy the LORD had given at Shiloh concerning the
descendants of Eli.

28 Joab had not joined Absalom's earlier rebellion, but he had joined Adonijah's rebellion. So
when Joab heard about Adonijah's death, he ran
to the sacred tent of the LORD and grabbed on to
the horns of the altar. 29 When this was reported
to King Solomon, he sent Benaiah son of Jehoiada to execute him.

30 Benaiah went to the sacred tent of the LORD
and said to Joab, "The king orders you to come
out!"

But Joab answered, "No, I will die here."

So Benaiah returned to the king and told him
what Joab had said.

31 "Do as he said," the king replied. "Kill him
there beside the altar and bury him. This will remove the guilt of Joab's senseless murders from
me and from my father's family. 32 The LORD will
repay him for the murders of two men who were
more righteous and better than he. For my father knew nothing about the deaths of Abner
son of Ner, commander of the army of Israel, and
of Amasa son of Jether, commander of the army
of Judah. 33 May their blood be on Joab and his
descendants forever, and may the LORD grant
peace forever to David, his descendants, his dynasty, and his throne."

34 So Benaiah son of Jehoiada returned to the
sacred tent and killed Joab, and he was buried at
his home in the wilderness. 35 Then the king appointed Benaiah to command the army in place
of Joab, and he installed Zadok the priest to take
the place of Abiathar.

36 The king then sent for Shimei and told him,
"Build a house here in Jerusalem and live there.
But don't step outside the city to go anywhere
else. 37 On the day you so much as cross the
Kidron Valley, you will surely die; and your blood
will be on your own head."

38 Shimei replied, "Your sentence is fair; I will
do whatever my lord the king commands." So
Shimei lived in Jerusalem for a long time.

39 But three years later two of Shimei's slaves
ran away to King Achish son of Maacah of Gath.
When Shimei learned where they were, 40 he saddled his donkey and went to Gath to search for
them. When he found them, he brought them
back to Jerusalem.

41 Solomon heard that Shimei had left Jerusalem and had gone to Gath and returned. 42 So the
king sent for Shimei and demanded, "Didn't I
make you swear by the LORD and warn you not to

go anywhere else or you would surely die? And you replied, 'The sentence is fair; I will do as you say.' 43 Then why haven't you kept your oath to the LORD and obeyed my command?"

44 The king also said to Shimei, "You certainly remember all the wicked things you did to my father, David. May the LORD now bring that evil on your own head. 45 But may I, King Solomon, receive the LORD's blessings, and may one of David's descendants always sit on this throne in the presence of the LORD." 46 Then, at the king's command, Benaiah son of Jehoiada took Shimei outside and killed him.

So the kingdom was now firmly in Solomon's grip.

CHAPTER 3

Solomon Asks for Wisdom

Solomon made an alliance with Pharaoh, the king of Egypt, and married one of his daughters. He brought her to live in the City of David until he could finish building his palace and the Temple of the LORD and the wall around the city. 2 At that time the people of Israel sacrificed their offerings at local places of worship, for a temple honoring the name of the LORD had not yet been built.

3 Solomon loved the LORD and followed all the decrees of his father, David, except that Solomon, too, offered sacrifices and burned incense at the local places of worship. 4 The most important of these places of worship was at Gibeon, so the king went there and sacrificed 1,000 burnt offerings. 5 That night the LORD appeared to Solomon in a dream, and God said, "What do you want? Ask, and I will give it to you!"

6 Solomon replied, "You showed great and faithful love to your servant my father, David, because he was honest and true and faithful to you. And you have continued to show this great and faithful love to him today by giving him a son to sit on his throne.

7 "Now, O LORD my God, you have made me king instead of my father, David, but I am like a little child who doesn't know his way around. 8 And here I am in the midst of your own chosen people, a nation so great and numerous they cannot be counted! 9 Give me an understanding heart so that I can govern your people well and know the difference between right and wrong. For who by himself is able to govern this great people of yours?"

10 The Lord was pleased that Solomon had asked for wisdom. 11 So God replied, "Because you have asked for wisdom in governing my people with justice and have not asked for a long life or wealth or the death of your enemies—12 I will give you what you asked for! I will give you a wise and understanding heart such as no one else has had or ever will have! 13 And I will also give you what you did not ask for—riches and fame! No other king in all the world will be compared to you for the rest of your life! 14 And if you follow me and obey my decrees and my commands as your father, David, did, I will give you a long life."

15 Then Solomon woke up and realized it had been a dream. He returned to Jerusalem and stood before the Ark of the Lord's Covenant, where he sacrificed burnt offerings and peace offerings. Then he invited all his officials to a great banquet.

Solomon Judges Wisely

16 Some time later two prostitutes came to the king to have an argument settled. 17 "Please, my lord," one of them began, "this woman and I live in the same house. I gave birth to a baby while she was with me in the house. 18 Three days later this woman also had a baby. We were alone; there were only two of us in the house.

19 "But her baby died during the night when she rolled over on it. 20 Then she got up in the night and took my son from beside me while I was asleep. She laid her dead child in my arms and took mine to sleep beside her. 21 And in the morning when I tried to nurse my son, he was dead! But when I looked more closely in the morning light, I saw that it wasn't my son at all."

22 Then the other woman interrupted, "It certainly was your son, and the living child is mine."

"No," the first woman said, "the living child is mine, and the dead one is yours." And so they argued back and forth before the king.

23 Then the king said, "Let's get the facts straight. Both of you claim the living child is yours, and each says that the dead one belongs to the other. 24 All right, bring me a sword." So a sword was brought to the king.

25 Then he said, "Cut the living child in two, and give half to one woman and half to the other!"

26 Then the woman who was the real mother of the living child, and who loved him very much, cried out, "Oh no, my lord! Give her the child—please do not kill him!"

But the other woman said, "All right, he will be neither yours nor mine; divide him between us!"

27 Then the king said, "Do not kill the child, but give him to the woman who wants him to live, for she is his mother!"

28 When all Israel heard the king's decision,

the people were in awe of the king, for they saw the wisdom God had given him for rendering justice.

CHAPTER 4
Solomon's Officials and Governors

King Solomon now ruled over all Israel, 2and these were his high officials:

Azariah son of Zadok was the priest.
3 Elihoreph and Ahijah, the sons of Shisha, were court secretaries.
Jehoshaphat son of Ahilud was the royal historian.
4 Benaiah son of Jehoiada was commander of the army.
Zadok and Abiathar were priests.
5 Azariah son of Nathan was in charge of the district governors.
Zabud son of Nathan, a priest, was a trusted adviser to the king.
6 Ahishar was manager of the palace property.
Adoniram son of Abda was in charge of forced labor.

7Solomon also had twelve district governors who were over all Israel. They were responsible for providing food for the king's household. Each of them arranged provisions for one month of the year. 8These are the names of the twelve governors:

Ben-hur, in the hill country of Ephraim.
9 Ben-deker, in Makaz, Shaalbim, Beth-shemesh, and Elon-bethhanan.
10 Ben-hesed, in Arubboth, including Socoh and all the land of Hepher.
11 Ben-abinadab, in all of Naphoth-dor. (He was married to Taphath, one of Solomon's daughters.)
12 Baana son of Ahilud, in Taanach and Megiddo, all of Beth-shan near Zarethan below Jezreel, and all the territory from Beth-shan to Abel-meholah and over to Jokmeam.
13 Ben-geber, in Ramoth-gilead, including the Towns of Jair (named for Jair of the tribe of Manasseh) in Gilead, and in the Argob region of Bashan, including sixty large fortified towns with bronze bars on their gates.
14 Ahinadab son of Iddo, in Mahanaim.
15 Ahimaaz, in Naphtali. (He was married to Basemath, another of Solomon's daughters.)

Wise Guy!
God told Solomon to ask for anything he wanted and God would give it to him. Sweet, huh? What would you ask for? You'll be amazed at Solomon's answer.
You can find it in 1 KINGS 3:6-9.
Want to know how wisdom starts? Go to Proverbs 9:10!
NOW SEE HOW WISE YOU ARE!
WHOOO'S WISE?
1 Make a booklet out of folded paper. Put a construction paper cover on it, and staple the folded edge. Make up a "wise" title.
2 Write your own wise sayings in the book. Think of things you could teach your little brother or sister, like
Don't Step on bees!
You can find tons of wise sayings in the book of Proverbs.
3 Now ask friends and family members what wise things they know. Write their sayings in your book.
Feel like you need a little more wisdom? Check out James 1:5.
Don't Step on bees!
Look Out!
4 Draw a picture to go with each saying.
Ask God every day to give you wisdom. Keep your book handy, and add new pages as you learn and grow.

16 Baana son of Hushai, in Asher and in Aloth.
17 Jehoshaphat son of Paruah, in Issachar.
18 Shimei son of Ela, in Benjamin.
19 Geber son of Uri, in the land of Gilead,
including the territories of King Sihon
of the Amorites and King Og of Bashan.
There was also one governor over the land
of Judah.

Solomon's Prosperity and Wisdom

20 The people of Judah and Israel were as numerous as the sand on the seashore. They were very
contented, with plenty to eat and drink. 21 Solomon ruled over all the kingdoms from the Euphrates River in the north to the land of the
Philistines and the border of Egypt in the south.
The conquered peoples of those lands sent tribute money to Solomon and continued to serve
him throughout his lifetime.

22 The daily food requirements for Solomon's
palace were 150 bushels of choice flour and
300 bushels of meal; 23 also 10 oxen from the
fattening pens, 20 pasture-fed cattle, 100 sheep
or goats, as well as deer, gazelles, roe deer, and
choice poultry.

24 Solomon's dominion extended over all the
kingdoms west of the Euphrates River, from
Tiphsah to Gaza. And there was peace on all his
borders. 25 During the lifetime of Solomon, all of
Judah and Israel lived in peace and safety. And
from Dan in the north to Beersheba in the south,
each family had its own home and garden.

26 Solomon had 4,000 stalls for his chariot
horses, and he had 12,000 horses.

27 The district governors faithfully provided
food for King Solomon and his court; each made
sure nothing was lacking during the month assigned to him. 28 They also brought the necessary barley and straw for the royal horses in the
stables.

29 God gave Solomon very great wisdom and
understanding, and knowledge as vast as the
sands of the seashore. 30 In fact, his wisdom exceeded that of all the wise men of the East and
the wise men of Egypt. 31 He was wiser than anyone else, including Ethan the Ezrahite and the
sons of Mahol—Heman, Calcol, and Darda. His
fame spread throughout all the surrounding nations. 32 He composed some 3,000 proverbs and
wrote 1,005 songs. 33 He could speak with authority about all kinds of plants, from the great
cedar of Lebanon to the tiny hyssop that grows
from cracks in a wall. He could also speak about
animals, birds, small creatures, and fish. 34 And
kings from every nation sent their ambassadors
to listen to the wisdom of Solomon.

CHAPTER 5

Preparations for Building the Temple

King Hiram of Tyre had always been a loyal
friend of David. When Hiram learned that David's son Solomon was the new king of Israel, he
sent ambassadors to congratulate him.

2 Then Solomon sent this message back to
Hiram:

3 "You know that my father, David, was not
able to build a Temple to honor the name of
the LORD his God because of the many wars
waged against him by surrounding nations.
He could not build until the LORD gave him
victory over all his enemies. 4 But now the
LORD my God has given me peace on every
side; I have no enemies, and all is well. 5 So
I am planning to build a Temple to honor
the name of the LORD my God, just as he had
instructed my father, David. For the LORD
told him, 'Your son, whom I will place on
your throne, will build the Temple to honor
my name.'

6 "Therefore, please command that cedars
from Lebanon be cut for me. Let my men
work alongside yours, and I will pay your
men whatever wages you ask. As you know,
there is no one among us who can cut timber
like you Sidonians!"

7 When Hiram received Solomon's message,
he was very pleased and said, "Praise the LORD today for giving David a wise son to be king of the
great nation of Israel." 8 Then he sent this reply to
Solomon:

"I have received your message, and I will
supply all the cedar and cypress timber
you need. 9 My servants will bring the
logs from the Lebanon mountains to the
Mediterranean Sea and make them into rafts
and float them along the coast to whatever
place you choose. Then we will break the
rafts apart so you can carry the logs away. You
can pay me by supplying me with food for my
household."

10 So Hiram supplied as much cedar and
cypress timber as Solomon desired. 11 In return,
Solomon sent him an annual payment of
100,000 bushels of wheat for his household
and 110,000 gallons of pure olive oil. 12 So the
LORD gave wisdom to Solomon, just as he had

promised. And Hiram and Solomon made a formal alliance of peace.

13 Then King Solomon conscripted a labor force of 30,000 men from all Israel. 14 He sent them to Lebanon in shifts, 10,000 every month, so that each man would be one month in Lebanon and two months at home. Adoniram was in charge of this labor force. 15 Solomon also had 70,000 common laborers, 80,000 quarry workers in the hill country, 16 and 3,600 foremen to supervise the work. 17 At the king's command, they quarried large blocks of high-quality stone and shaped them to make the foundation of the Temple. 18 Men from the city of Gebal helped Solomon's and Hiram's builders prepare the timber and stone for the Temple.

CHAPTER 6

Solomon Builds the Temple

It was in midspring, in the month of Ziv, during the fourth year of Solomon's reign, that he began to construct the Temple of the LORD. This was 480 years after the people of Israel were rescued from their slavery in the land of Egypt.

2 The Temple that King Solomon built for the LORD was 90 feet long, 30 feet wide, and 45 feet high. 3 The entry room at the front of the Temple was 30 feet wide, running across the entire width of the Temple. It projected outward 15 feet from the front of the Temple. 4 Solomon also made narrow recessed windows throughout the Temple.

5 He built a complex of rooms against the outer walls of the Temple, all the way around the sides and rear of the building. 6 The complex was three stories high, the bottom floor being 7½ feet wide, the second floor 9 feet wide, and the top floor 10½ feet wide. The rooms were connected to the walls of the Temple by beams resting on ledges built out from the wall. So the beams were not inserted into the walls themselves.

7 The stones used in the construction of the Temple were finished at the quarry, so there was no sound of hammer, ax, or any other iron tool at the building site.

8 The entrance to the bottom floor was on the south side of the Temple. There were winding stairs going up to the second floor, and another flight of stairs between the second and third floors. 9 After completing the Temple structure, Solomon put in a ceiling made of cedar beams and planks. 10 As already stated, he built a complex of rooms along the sides of the building, attached to the Temple walls by cedar timbers. Each story of the complex was 7½ feet high.

11 Then the LORD gave this message to Solomon: 12 "Concerning this Temple you are building, if you keep all my decrees and regulations and obey all my commands, I will fulfill through you the promise I made to your father, David. 13 I will live among the Israelites and will never abandon my people Israel."

The Temple's Interior

14 So Solomon finished building the Temple. 15 The entire inside, from floor to ceiling, was paneled with wood. He paneled the walls and ceilings with cedar, and he used planks of cypress for the floors. 16 He partitioned off an inner sanctuary—the Most Holy Place—at the far end of the Temple. It was 30 feet deep and was paneled with cedar from floor to ceiling. 17 The main room of the Temple, outside the Most Holy Place, was 60 feet long. 18 Cedar paneling completely covered the stone walls throughout the Temple, and the paneling was decorated with carvings of gourds and open flowers.

19 He prepared the inner sanctuary at the far end of the Temple, where the Ark of the LORD's Covenant would be placed. 20 This inner sanctuary was 30 feet long, 30 feet wide, and 30 feet high. He overlaid the inside with solid gold. He also overlaid the altar made of cedar. 21 Then Solomon overlaid the rest of the Temple's interior with solid gold, and he made gold chains to protect the entrance to the Most Holy Place. 22 So he finished overlaying the entire Temple with gold, including the altar that belonged to the Most Holy Place.

23 He made two cherubim of wild olive wood, each 15 feet tall, and placed them in the inner sanctuary. 24 The wingspan of each of the cherubim was 15 feet, each wing being 7½ feet long. 25 The two cherubim were identical in shape and size; 26 each was 15 feet tall. 27 He placed them side by side in the inner sanctuary of the Temple. Their outspread wings reached from wall to wall, while their inner wings touched at the center of the room. 28 He overlaid the two cherubim with gold.

29 He decorated all the walls of the inner sanctuary and the main room with carvings of cherubim, palm trees, and open flowers. 30 He overlaid the floor in both rooms with gold.

31 For the entrance to the inner sanctuary, he made double doors of wild olive wood with five-sided doorposts. 32 These double doors were decorated with carvings of cherubim, palm

trees, and open flowers. The doors, including the decorations of cherubim and palm trees, were overlaid with gold.

33Then he made four-sided doorposts of wild olive wood for the entrance to the Temple. 34There were two folding doors of cypress wood, and each door was hinged to fold back upon itself. 35These doors were decorated with carvings of cherubim, palm trees, and open flowers—all overlaid evenly with gold.

36The walls of the inner courtyard were built so that there was one layer of cedar beams between every three layers of finished stone.

37The foundation of the LORD's Temple was laid in midspring, in the month of Ziv, during the fourth year of Solomon's reign. 38The entire building was completed in every detail by midautumn, in the month of Bul, during the eleventh year of his reign. So it took seven years to build the Temple.

CHAPTER 7

Solomon Builds His Palace

Solomon also built a palace for himself, and it took him thirteen years to complete the construction.

2One of Solomon's buildings was called the Palace of the Forest of Lebanon. It was 150 feet long, 75 feet wide, and 45 feet high. There were four rows of cedar pillars, and great cedar beams rested on the pillars. 3The hall had a cedar roof. Above the beams on the pillars were forty-five side rooms, arranged in three tiers of fifteen each. 4On each end of the long hall were three rows of windows facing each other. 5All the doorways and doorposts had rectangular frames and were arranged in sets of three, facing each other.

6Solomon also built the Hall of Pillars, which was 75 feet long and 45 feet wide. There was a porch in front, along with a canopy supported by pillars.

7Solomon also built the throne room, known as the Hall of Justice, where he sat to hear legal matters. It was paneled with cedar from floor to ceiling. 8Solomon's living quarters surrounded a courtyard behind this hall, and they were constructed the same way. He also built similar living quarters for Pharaoh's daughter, whom he had married.

9From foundation to eaves, all these buildings were built from huge blocks of high-quality stone, cut with saws and trimmed to exact measure on all sides. 10Some of the huge foundation stones were 15 feet long, and some were 12 feet long. 11The blocks of high-quality stone used in the walls were also cut to measure, and cedar beams were also used. 12The walls of the great courtyard were built so that there was one layer of cedar beams between every three layers of finished stone, just like the walls of the inner courtyard of the LORD's Temple with its entry room.

Furnishings for the Temple

13King Solomon then asked for a man named Huram to come from Tyre. 14He was half Israelite, since his mother was a widow from the tribe of Naphtali, and his father had been a craftsman in bronze from Tyre. Huram was extremely skillful and talented in any work in bronze, and he came to do all the metal work for King Solomon.

15Huram cast two bronze pillars, each 27 feet tall and 18 feet in circumference. 16For the tops of the pillars he cast bronze capitals, each 7½ feet tall. 17Each capital was decorated with seven sets of latticework and interwoven chains. 18He also encircled the latticework with two rows of pomegranates to decorate the capitals over the pillars. 19The capitals on the columns inside the entry room were shaped like water lilies, and they were six feet tall. 20The capitals on the two pillars had 200 pomegranates in two rows around them, beside the rounded surface next to the latticework. 21Huram set the pillars at the entrance of the Temple, one toward the south and one toward the north. He named the one on the south Jakin, and the one on the north Boaz. 22The capitals on the pillars were shaped like water lilies. And so the work on the pillars was finished.

23Then Huram cast a great round basin, 15 feet across from rim to rim, called the Sea. It was 7½ feet deep and about 45 feet in circumference. 24It was encircled just below its rim by two rows of decorative gourds. There were about six gourds per foot all the way around, and they were cast as part of the basin.

25The Sea was placed on a base of twelve bronze oxen, all facing outward. Three faced north, three faced west, three faced south, and three faced east, and the Sea rested on them. 26The walls of the Sea were about three inches thick, and its rim flared out like a cup and resembled a water lily blossom. It could hold about 11,000 gallons of water.

27Huram also made ten bronze water carts, each 6 feet long, 6 feet wide, and 4½ feet tall. 28They were constructed with side panels braced with crossbars. 29Both the panels and the crossbars were decorated with carved lions, oxen, and

cherubim. Above and below the lions and oxen
were wreath decorations. 30Each of these carts
had four bronze wheels and bronze axles. There
were supporting posts for the bronze basins at the
corners of the carts; these supports were decorated on each side with carvings of wreaths. 31The
top of each cart had a rounded frame for the basin. It projected 1½ feet above the cart's top like a
round pedestal, and its opening was 2¼ feet
across; it was decorated on the outside with carvings of wreaths. The panels of the carts were
square, not round. 32Under the panels were four
wheels that were connected to axles that had
been cast as one unit with the cart. The wheels
were 2¼ feet in diameter 33and were similar to
chariot wheels. The axles, spokes, rims, and hubs
were all cast from molten bronze.

34There were handles at each of the four corners of the carts, and these, too, were cast as one
unit with the cart. 35Around the top of each cart
was a rim nine inches wide. The corner supports
and side panels were cast as one unit with the
cart. 36Carvings of cherubim, lions, and palm
trees decorated the panels and corner supports
wherever there was room, and there were
wreaths all around. 37All ten water carts were the
same size and were made alike, for each was cast
from the same mold.

38Huram also made ten smaller bronze basins, one for each cart. Each basin was six feet
across and could hold 220 gallons of water. 39He
set five water carts on the south side of the Temple and five on the north side. The great bronze
basin called the Sea was placed near the southeast corner of the Temple. 40He also made the
necessary washbasins, shovels, and bowls.

So at last Huram completed everything King
Solomon had assigned him to make for the Temple of the Lord:

41 the two pillars;
the two bowl-shaped capitals on top of
the pillars;
the two networks of interwoven chains that
decorated the capitals;
42 the 400 pomegranates that hung from
the chains on the capitals (two rows
of pomegranates for each of the chain
networks that decorated the capitals
on top of the pillars);
43 the ten water carts holding the ten basins;
44 the Sea and the twelve oxen under it;
45 the ash buckets, the shovels, and the bowls.

Huram made all these things of burnished
bronze for the Temple of the Lord, just as King
Solomon had directed. 46The king had them
cast in clay molds in the Jordan Valley between
Succoth and Zarethan. 47Solomon did not
weigh all these things because there were so
many; the weight of the bronze could not be
measured.

48Solomon also made all the furnishings of
the Temple of the Lord:

the gold altar;
the gold table for the Bread of the Presence;
49 the lampstands of solid gold, five on the
south and five on the north, in front of
the Most Holy Place;
the flower decorations, lamps, and tongs—
all of gold;
50 the small bowls, lamp snuffers, bowls, ladles,
and incense burners—all of solid gold;
the doors for the entrances to the Most Holy
Place and the main room of the Temple,
with their fronts overlaid with gold.

51So King Solomon finished all his work on
the Temple of the Lord. Then he brought all the
gifts his father, David, had dedicated—the silver,
the gold, and the various articles—and he stored
them in the treasuries of the Lord's Temple.

CHAPTER 8

The Ark Brought to the Temple

Solomon then summoned to Jerusalem the elders of Israel and all the heads of the tribes—the
leaders of the ancestral families of the Israelites.
They were to bring the Ark of the Lord's Covenant to the Temple from its location in the City
of David, also known as Zion. 2So all the men of
Israel assembled before King Solomon at the annual Festival of Shelters, which is held in early
autumn in the month of Ethanim.

3When all the elders of Israel arrived, the
priests picked up the Ark. 4The priests and Levites brought up the Ark of the Lord along with
the special tent and all the sacred items that had
been in it. 5There, before the Ark, King Solomon
and the entire community of Israel sacrificed so
many sheep, goats, and cattle that no one could
keep count!

6Then the priests carried the Ark of the
Lord's Covenant into the inner sanctuary of the
Temple—the Most Holy Place—and placed it beneath the wings of the cherubim. 7The cherubim spread their wings over the Ark, forming a
canopy over the Ark and its carrying poles.
8These poles were so long that their ends could
be seen from the Holy Place, which is in front of
the Most Holy Place, but not from the outside.

They are still there to this day. 9Nothing was in
the Ark except the two stone tablets that Moses
had placed in it at Mount Sinai, where the LORD
made a covenant with the people of Israel when
they left the land of Egypt.

10When the priests came out of the Holy Place,
a thick cloud filled the Temple of the LORD. 11The
priests could not continue their service because
of the cloud, for the glorious presence of the
LORD filled the Temple of the LORD.

FUN-fact
Temple Talk
Those soft spots on either side of your head? Temples. But we aren't talking about those kinds of temples. We're talking about a place of worship. King Solomon built the first Temple for the Lord. Solomon's father, King David, wanted to build the Temple, but God said "no." God said that one of David's sons would build the Temple. Instead of getting mad or jealous, David praised God for blessing his family.
Sometimes it's hard when God says "no" to something we want.
Next time that happens, be like David—count your blessings instead! First, write down the thing you wanted. Then list the good things God has given to you and done for you. Look at all the good things compared to the one thing you wanted. The things you want may change, but God's goodness never changes!

Solomon Praises the LORD

12Then Solomon prayed, "O LORD, you have said
that you would live in a thick cloud of darkness.
13Now I have built a glorious Temple for you, a
place where you can live forever!"

14Then the king turned around to the entire
community of Israel standing before him and
gave this blessing: 15"Praise the LORD, the God of
Israel, who has kept the promise he made to my
father, David. For he told my father, 16'From the
day I brought my people Israel out of Egypt, I
have never chosen a city among any of the tribes
of Israel as the place where a Temple should be
built to honor my name. But I have chosen David
to be king over my people Israel.'"

17Then Solomon said, "My father, David,
wanted to build this Temple to honor the name
of the LORD, the God of Israel. 18But the LORD told
him, 'You wanted to build the Temple to honor
my name. Your intention is good, 19but you are
not the one to do it. One of your own sons will
build the Temple to honor me.'

20"And now the LORD has fulfilled the promise he made, for I have become king in my father's place, and now I sit on the throne of Israel,
just as the LORD promised. I have built this Temple to honor the name of the LORD, the God of Israel. 21And I have prepared a place there for the
Ark, which contains the covenant that the LORD
made with our ancestors when he brought them
out of Egypt."

Solomon's Prayer of Dedication

22Then Solomon stood before the altar of the
LORD in front of the entire community of Israel.
He lifted his hands toward heaven, 23and he
prayed,

"O LORD, God of Israel, there is no God like
you in all of heaven above or on the earth
below. You keep your covenant and show
unfailing love to all who walk before you in
wholehearted devotion. 24You have kept
your promise to your servant David, my
father. You made that promise with your
own mouth, and with your own hands you
have fulfilled it today.

25"And now, O LORD, God of Israel, carry
out the additional promise you made to your
servant David, my father. For you said to him,
'If your descendants guard their behavior
and faithfully follow me as you have done,
one of them will always sit on the throne
of Israel.' 26Now, O God of Israel, fulfill this
promise to your servant David, my father.

27"But will God really live on earth? Why,
even the highest heavens cannot contain
you. How much less this Temple I have built!
28Nevertheless, listen to my prayer and my
plea, O LORD my God. Hear the cry and the
prayer that your servant is making to you
today. 29May you watch over this Temple
night and day, this place where you have
said, 'My name will be there.' May you always
hear the prayers I make toward this place.
30May you hear the humble and earnest
requests from me and your people Israel
when we pray toward this place. Yes, hear
us from heaven where you live, and when
you hear, forgive.

31"If someone wrongs another person
and is required to take an oath of innocence
in front of your altar in this Temple, 32then
hear from heaven and judge between your
servants—the accuser and the accused.
Punish the guilty as they deserve. Acquit
the innocent because of their innocence.

33"If your people Israel are defeated by
their enemies because they have sinned
against you, and if they turn to you and
acknowledge your name and pray to you
here in this Temple, 34then hear from
heaven and forgive the sin of your people
Israel and return them to this land you gave
their ancestors.

35"If the skies are shut up and there is no
rain because your people have sinned
against you, and if they pray toward this
Temple and acknowledge your name and
turn from their sins because you have
punished them, 36then hear from heaven
and forgive the sins of your servants, your
people Israel. Teach them to follow the right
path, and send rain on your land that you
have given to your people as their special
possession.

37"If there is a famine in the land or a
plague or crop disease or attacks of locusts
or caterpillars, or if your people's enemies are
in the land besieging their towns—whatever
disaster or disease there is—38and if your
people Israel pray about their troubles, raising
their hands toward this Temple, 39then hear
from heaven where you live, and forgive. Give
your people what their actions deserve, for
you alone know each human heart. 40Then
they will fear you as long as they live in the
land you gave to our ancestors.

41"In the future, foreigners who do not
belong to your people Israel will hear of you.
They will come from distant lands because
of your name, 42for they will hear of your
great name and your strong hand and your
powerful arm. And when they pray toward
this Temple, 43then hear from heaven where
you live, and grant what they ask of you.
In this way, all the people of the earth will
come to know and fear you, just as your own
people Israel do. They, too, will know that this
Temple I have built honors your name.

44"If your people go out where you send
them to fight their enemies, and if they pray
to the LORD by turning toward this city you
have chosen and toward this Temple I have
built to honor your name, 45then hear their
prayers from heaven and uphold their cause.

46"If they sin against you—and who has
never sinned?—you might become angry
with them and let their enemies conquer
them and take them captive to their land
far away or near. 47But in that land of exile,
they might turn to you in repentance and
pray, 'We have sinned, done evil, and acted
wickedly.' 48If they turn to you with their
whole heart and soul in the land of their
enemies and pray toward the land you
gave to their ancestors—toward this city
you have chosen, and toward this Temple
I have built to honor your name—49then
hear their prayers and their petition from
heaven where you live, and uphold their
cause. 50Forgive your people who have
sinned against you. Forgive all the offenses
they have committed against you. Make
their captors merciful to them, 51for they
are your people—your special possession—
whom you brought out of the iron-smelting
furnace of Egypt.

52"May your eyes be open to my requests
and to the requests of your people Israel. May
you hear and answer them whenever they cry
out to you. 53For when you brought our
ancestors out of Egypt, O Sovereign LORD, you
told your servant Moses that you had set
Israel apart from all the nations of the earth
to be your own special possession."

The Dedication of the Temple

54When Solomon finished making these prayers
and petitions to the LORD, he stood up in front of
the altar of the LORD, where he had been kneeling with his hands raised toward heaven. 55He
stood and in a loud voice blessed the entire congregation of Israel:

56"Praise the LORD who has given rest to his

people Israel, just as he promised. Not one word
has failed of all the wonderful promises he gave
through his servant Moses. 57May the LORD our
God be with us as he was with our ancestors; may
he never leave us or abandon us. 58May he give us
the desire to do his will in everything and to obey
all the commands, decrees, and regulations that
he gave our ancestors. 59And may these words
that I have prayed in the presence of the LORD be
before him constantly, day and night, so that the
LORD our God may give justice to me and to his
people Israel, according to each day's needs.
60Then people all over the earth will know that
the LORD alone is God and there is no other. 61And
may you be completely faithful to the LORD our
God. May you always obey his decrees and commands, just as you are doing today."

62Then the king and all Israel with him offered sacrifices to the LORD. 63Solomon offered
to the LORD a peace offering of 22,000 cattle and
120,000 sheep and goats. And so the king and all
the people of Israel dedicated the Temple of the
LORD.

64That same day the king consecrated the central area of the courtyard in front of the LORD's Temple. He offered burnt offerings, grain offerings, and the fat of peace offerings there, because the bronze altar in the LORD's presence was too small to hold all the burnt offerings, grain offerings, and the fat of the peace offerings.

65Then Solomon and all Israel celebrated the
Festival of Shelters in the presence of the LORD
our God. A large congregation had gathered from
as far away as Lebo-hamath in the north and the
Brook of Egypt in the south. The celebration
went on for fourteen days in all—seven days for
the dedication of the altar and seven days for the
Festival of Shelters. 66After the festival was over,
Solomon sent the people home. They blessed
the king and went to their homes joyful and glad
because the LORD had been good to his servant
David and to his people Israel.

CHAPTER 9

The LORD's Response to Solomon

So Solomon finished building the Temple of the
LORD, as well as the royal palace. He completed
everything he had planned to do. 2Then the
LORD appeared to Solomon a second time, as he
had done before at Gibeon. 3The LORD said to
him,

"I have heard your prayer and your petition.
I have set this Temple apart to be holy—this
place you have built where my name will be
honored forever. I will always watch over it,
for it is dear to my heart.

4"As for you, if you will follow me with
integrity and godliness, as David your father
did, obeying all my commands, decrees, and
regulations, 5then I will establish the throne
of your dynasty over Israel forever. For I
made this promise to your father, David: 'One
of your descendants will always sit on the
throne of Israel.'

6"But if you or your descendants abandon
me and disobey the commands and decrees
I have given you, and if you serve and worship other gods, 7then I will uproot Israel
from this land that I have given them. I will
reject this Temple that I have made holy to
honor my name. I will make Israel an object
of mockery and ridicule among the nations.
8And though this Temple is impressive now,
all who pass by will be appalled and will gasp
in horror. They will ask, 'Why did the LORD
do such terrible things to this land and to
this Temple?'

9"And the answer will be, 'Because his
people abandoned the LORD their God, who
brought their ancestors out of Egypt, and
they worshiped other gods instead and
bowed down to them. That is why the LORD
has brought all these disasters on them.'"

Solomon's Agreement with Hiram

10It took Solomon twenty years to build the
LORD's Temple and his own royal palace. At
the end of that time, 11he gave twenty towns in
the land of Galilee to King Hiram of Tyre. (Hiram
had previously provided all the cedar and cypress
timber and gold that Solomon had requested.)
12But when Hiram came from Tyre to see the
towns Solomon had given him, he was not at
all pleased with them. 13"What kind of towns are
these, my brother?" he asked. So Hiram called
that area Cabul (which means "worthless"), as it
is still known today. 14Nevertheless, Hiram paid
Solomon 9,000 pounds of gold.

Solomon's Many Achievements

15This is the account of the forced labor that
King Solomon conscripted to build the LORD's
Temple, the royal palace, the supporting terraces, the wall of Jerusalem, and the cities of
Hazor, Megiddo, and Gezer. 16(Pharaoh, the king
of Egypt, had attacked and captured Gezer, kill-
ing the Canaanite population and burning it

down. He gave the city to his daughter as a wedding gift when she married Solomon. 17 So Solomon rebuilt the city of Gezer.) He also built up the towns of Lower Beth-horon, 18 Baalath, and Tamar in the wilderness within his land. 19 He built towns as supply centers and constructed towns where his chariots and horses could be stationed. He built everything he desired in Jerusalem and Lebanon and throughout his entire realm.

20 There were still some people living in the land who were not Israelites, including Amorites, Hittites, Perizzites, Hivites, and Jebusites. 21 These were descendants of the nations whom the people of Israel had not completely destroyed. So Solomon conscripted them as slaves, and they serve as forced laborers to this day. 22 But Solomon did not conscript any of the Israelites for forced labor. Instead, he assigned them to serve as fighting men, government officials, officers and captains in his army, commanders of his chariots, and charioteers. 23 Solomon appointed 550 of them to supervise the people working on his various projects.

24 Solomon moved his wife, Pharaoh's daughter, from the City of David to the new palace he had built for her. Then he constructed the supporting terraces.

25 Three times each year Solomon presented burnt offerings and peace offerings on the altar he had built for the LORD. He also burned incense to the LORD. And so he finished the work of building the Temple.

26 King Solomon also built a fleet of ships at Ezion-geber, a port near Elath in the land of Edom, along the shore of the Red Sea. 27 Hiram sent experienced crews of sailors to sail the ships with Solomon's men. 28 They sailed to Ophir and brought back to Solomon some sixteen tons of gold.

CHAPTER 10

Visit of the Queen of Sheba

When the queen of Sheba heard of Solomon's fame, which brought honor to the name of the LORD, she came to test him with hard questions. 2 She arrived in Jerusalem with a large group of attendants and a great caravan of camels loaded with spices, large quantities of gold, and precious jewels. When she met with Solomon, she talked with him about everything she had on her mind. 3 Solomon had answers for all her questions; nothing was too hard for the king to explain to her. 4 When the queen of Sheba realized how very wise Solomon was, and when she saw the palace he had built, 5 she was overwhelmed. She was also amazed at the food on his tables, the organization of his officials and their splendid clothing, the cup-bearers, and the burnt offerings Solomon made at the Temple of the LORD.

6 She exclaimed to the king, "Everything I heard in my country about your achievements and wisdom is true! 7 I didn't believe what was said until I arrived here and saw it with my own eyes. In fact, I had not heard the half of it! Your wisdom and prosperity are far beyond what I was told. 8 How happy your people must be! What a privilege for your officials to stand here day after day, listening to your wisdom! 9 Praise the LORD your God, who delights in you and has placed you on the throne of Israel. Because of the LORD's eternal love for Israel, he has made you king so you can rule with justice and righteousness."

10 Then she gave the king a gift of 9,000 pounds of gold, great quantities of spices, and precious jewels. Never again were so many spices brought in as those the queen of Sheba gave to King Solomon.

11 (In addition, Hiram's ships brought gold from Ophir, and they also brought rich cargoes of red sandalwood and precious jewels. 12 The king used the sandalwood to make railings for the Temple of the LORD and the royal palace, and to construct lyres and harps for the musicians. Never before or since has there been such a supply of sandalwood.)

13 King Solomon gave the queen of Sheba whatever she asked for, besides all the customary gifts he had so generously given. Then she and all her attendants returned to their own land.

Solomon's Wealth and Splendor

14 Each year Solomon received about 25 tons of gold. 15 This did not include the additional revenue he received from merchants and traders, all the kings of Arabia, and the governors of the land.

16 King Solomon made 200 large shields of hammered gold, each weighing more than fifteen pounds. 17 He also made 300 smaller shields of hammered gold, each weighing nearly four pounds. The king placed these shields in the Palace of the Forest of Lebanon.

18 Then the king made a huge throne, decorated with ivory and overlaid with fine gold. 19 The throne had six steps and a rounded back. There were armrests on both sides of the seat, and the figure of a lion stood on each side of the

throne. 20 There were also twelve other lions,
one standing on each end of the six steps. No
other throne in all the world could be compared
with it!
21 All of King Solomon's drinking cups were
solid gold, as were all the utensils in the Palace of
the Forest of Lebanon. They were not made of silver, for silver was considered worthless in Solomon's day!
22 The king had a fleet of trading ships of
Tarshish that sailed with Hiram's fleet. Once
every three years the ships returned, loaded with
gold, silver, ivory, apes, and peacocks.
23 So King Solomon became richer and wiser
than any other king on earth. 24 People from
every nation came to consult him and to hear the
wisdom God had given him. 25 Year after year
everyone who visited brought him gifts of silver
and gold, clothing, weapons, spices, horses, and
mules.
26 Solomon built up a huge force of chariots
and horses. He had 1,400 chariots and 12,000
horses. He stationed some of them in the chariot
cities and some near him in Jerusalem. 27 The
king made silver as plentiful in Jerusalem as
stone. And valuable cedar timber was as common as the sycamore-fig trees that grow in the
foothills of Judah. 28 Solomon's horses were imported from Egypt and from Cilicia; the king's
traders acquired them from Cilicia at the standard price. 29 At that time chariots from Egypt
could be purchased for 600 pieces of silver, and
horses for 150 pieces of silver. They were then
exported to the kings of the Hittites and the
kings of Aram.

CHAPTER 11

Solomon's Many Wives

Now King Solomon loved many foreign women.
Besides Pharaoh's daughter, he married women
from Moab, Ammon, Edom, Sidon, and from
among the Hittites. 2 The LORD had clearly instructed the people of Israel, "You must not
marry them, because they will turn your hearts to
their gods." Yet Solomon insisted on loving them
anyway. 3 He had 700 wives of royal birth and
300 concubines. And in fact, they did turn his
heart away from the LORD.
4 In Solomon's old age, they turned his heart to
worship other gods instead of being completely
faithful to the LORD his God, as his father, David,
had been. 5 Solomon worshiped Ashtoreth, the
goddess of the Sidonians, and Molech, the detestable god of the Ammonites. 6 In this way, Solomon did what was evil in the LORD's sight; he
refused to follow the LORD completely, as his father, David, had done.
7 On the Mount of Olives, east of Jerusalem,
he even built a pagan shrine for Chemosh, the
detestable god of Moab, and another for
Molech, the detestable god of the Ammonites.
8 Solomon built such shrines for all his foreign
wives to use for burning incense and sacrificing
to their gods.
9 The LORD was very angry with Solomon, for
his heart had turned away from the LORD, the
God of Israel, who had appeared to him twice.
10 He had warned Solomon specifically about
worshiping other gods, but Solomon did not listen to the LORD's command. 11 So now the LORD
said to him, "Since you have not kept my covenant and have disobeyed my decrees, I will
surely tear the kingdom away from you and give
it to one of your servants. 12 But for the sake of
your father, David, I will not do this while you are
still alive. I will take the kingdom away from your
son. 13 And even so, I will not take away the entire
kingdom; I will let him be king of one tribe, for
the sake of my servant David and for the sake of
Jerusalem, my chosen city."

Solomon's Adversaries

14 Then the LORD raised up Hadad the Edomite, a
member of Edom's royal family, to be Solomon's
adversary. 15 Years before, David had defeated
Edom. Joab, his army commander, had stayed to
bury some of the Israelite soldiers who had died
in battle. While there, they killed every male in
Edom. 16 Joab and the army of Israel had stayed
there for six months, killing them.
17 But Hadad and a few of his father's royal officials escaped and headed for Egypt. (Hadad
was just a boy at the time.) 18 They set out from
Midian and went to Paran, where others joined
them. Then they traveled to Egypt and went to
Pharaoh, who gave them a home, food, and some
land. 19 Pharaoh grew very fond of Hadad, and he
gave him his wife's sister in marriage—the sister
of Queen Tahpenes. 20 She bore him a son named
Genubath. Tahpenes raised him in Pharaoh's palace among Pharaoh's own sons.
21 When the news reached Hadad in Egypt that
David and his commander Joab were both dead,
he said to Pharaoh, "Let me return to my own
country."
22 "Why?" Pharaoh asked him. "What do you
lack here that makes you want to go home?"
"Nothing," he replied. "But even so, please let
me return home."
23 God also raised up Rezon son of Eliada as

Solomon's adversary. Rezon had fled from his
master, King Hadadezer of Zobah, 24 and had become the leader of a gang of rebels. After David
conquered Hadadezer, Rezon and his men fled
to Damascus, where he became king. 25 Rezon
was Israel's bitter adversary for the rest of Solomon's reign, and he made trouble, just as Hadad
did. Rezon hated Israel intensely and continued
to reign in Aram.

Jeroboam Rebels against Solomon

26 Another rebel leader was Jeroboam son of Nebat, one of Solomon's own officials. He came
from the town of Zeredah in Ephraim, and his
mother was Zeruah, a widow.

27 This is the story behind his rebellion. Solomon was rebuilding the supporting terraces and
repairing the walls of the city of his father, David.
28 Jeroboam was a very capable young man, and
when Solomon saw how industrious he was, he
put him in charge of the labor force from the
tribes of Ephraim and Manasseh, the descendants of Joseph.

29 One day as Jeroboam was leaving Jerusalem, the prophet Ahijah from Shiloh met him
along the way. Ahijah was wearing a new cloak.
The two of them were alone in a field, 30 and Ahijah took hold of the new cloak he was wearing
and tore it into twelve pieces. 31 Then he said to
Jeroboam, "Take ten of these pieces, for this is
what the LORD, the God of Israel, says: 'I am
about to tear the kingdom from the hand of Solomon, and I will give ten of the tribes to you!
32 But I will leave him one tribe for the sake of my
servant David and for the sake of Jerusalem,
which I have chosen out of all the tribes of Israel.
33 For Solomon has abandoned me and worshiped Ashtoreth, the goddess of the Sidonians;
Chemosh, the god of Moab; and Molech, the god
of the Ammonites. He has not followed my ways
and done what is pleasing in my sight. He has
not obeyed my decrees and regulations as David
his father did.

34 "'But I will not take the entire kingdom from
Solomon at this time. For the sake of my servant
David, the one whom I chose and who obeyed my
commands and decrees, I will keep Solomon as
leader for the rest of his life. 35 But I will take the
kingdom away from his son and give ten of the
tribes to you. 36 His son will have one tribe so that
the descendants of David my servant will continue to reign, shining like a lamp in Jerusalem,
the city I have chosen to be the place for my
name. 37 And I will place you on the throne of Israel, and you will rule over all that your heart desires. 38 If you listen to what I tell you and follow
my ways and do whatever I consider to be right,
and if you obey my decrees and commands, as
my servant David did, then I will always be with
you. I will establish an enduring dynasty for you
as I did for David, and I will give Israel to you.
39 Because of Solomon's sin I will punish the descendants of David—though not forever.'"

40 Solomon tried to kill Jeroboam, but he fled
to King Shishak of Egypt and stayed there until
Solomon died.

Summary of Solomon's Reign

41 The rest of the events in Solomon's reign, including all his deeds and his wisdom, are recorded in *The Book of the Acts of Solomon.*
42 Solomon ruled in Jerusalem over all Israel for
forty years. 43 When he died, he was buried in the
City of David, named for his father. Then his son
Rehoboam became the next king.

CHAPTER 12

The Northern Tribes Revolt

Rehoboam went to Shechem, where all Israel
had gathered to make him king. 2 When Jeroboam son of Nebat heard of this, he returned
from Egypt, for he had fled to Egypt to escape
from King Solomon. 3 The leaders of Israel summoned him, and Jeroboam and the whole assembly of Israel went to speak with Rehoboam.
4 "Your father was a hard master," they said.
"Lighten the harsh labor demands and heavy
taxes that your father imposed on us. Then we
will be your loyal subjects."

5 Rehoboam replied, "Give me three days to
think this over. Then come back for my answer."
So the people went away.

6 Then King Rehoboam discussed the matter
with the older men who had counseled his father, Solomon. "What is your advice?" he asked.
"How should I answer these people?"

7 The older counselors replied, "If you are willing to be a servant to these people today and give
them a favorable answer, they will always be your
loyal subjects."

8 But Rehoboam rejected the advice of the
older men and instead asked the opinion of the
young men who had grown up with him and
were now his advisers. 9 "What is your advice?"
he asked them. "How should I answer these people who want me to lighten the burdens imposed
by my father?"

10 The young men replied, "This is what you
should tell those complainers who want a lighter

burden: 'My little finger is thicker than my father's waist! 11Yes, my father laid heavy burdens
on you, but I'm going to make them even heavier!
My father beat you with whips, but I will beat you
with scorpions!'"
12Three days later Jeroboam and all the people returned to hear Rehoboam's decision, just
as the king had ordered. 13But Rehoboam spoke
harshly to the people, for he rejected the advice
of the older counselors 14and followed the
counsel of his younger advisers. He told the
people, "My father laid heavy burdens on you,
but I'm going to make them even heavier! My
father beat you with whips, but I will beat you
with scorpions!"
15So the king paid no attention to the people.
This turn of events was the will of the LORD, for it
fulfilled the LORD's message to Jeroboam son of
Nebat through the prophet Ahijah from Shiloh.
16When all Israel realized that the king had
refused to listen to them, they responded,

"Down with the dynasty of David!
We have no interest in the son of Jesse.
Back to your homes, O Israel!
Look out for your own house, O David!"

So the people of Israel returned home. 17But
Rehoboam continued to rule over the Israelites
who lived in the towns of Judah.
18King Rehoboam sent Adoniram, who was in
charge of forced labor, to restore order, but the
people of Israel stoned him to death. When this
news reached King Rehoboam, he quickly
jumped into his chariot and fled to Jerusalem.
19And to this day the northern tribes of Israel
have refused to be ruled by a descendant of
David.
20When the people of Israel learned of Jeroboam's return from Egypt, they called an assembly and made him king over all Israel. So only the
tribe of Judah remained loyal to the family of
David.

Shemaiah's Prophecy

21When Rehoboam arrived at Jerusalem, he mobilized the men of Judah and the tribe of Benjamin—180,000 select troops—to fight against
the men of Israel and to restore the kingdom to
himself.
22But God said to Shemaiah, the man of God,
23"Say to Rehoboam son of Solomon, king of Judah, and to all the people of Judah and Benjamin,
and to the rest of the people, 24'This is what the
LORD says: Do not fight against your relatives, the
Israelites. Go back home, for what has happened
is my doing!'" So they obeyed the message of the
LORD and went home, as the LORD had commanded.

Jeroboam Makes Gold Calves

25Jeroboam then built up the city of Shechem in
the hill country of Ephraim, and it became his
capital. Later he went and built up the town of
Peniel.
26Jeroboam thought to himself, "Unless I am
careful, the kingdom will return to the dynasty of
David. 27When these people go to Jerusalem to
offer sacrifices at the Temple of the LORD, they
will again give their allegiance to King Rehoboam of Judah. They will kill me and make him
their king instead."
28So on the advice of his counselors, the king
made two gold calves. He said to the people, "It is
too much trouble for you to worship in Jerusalem. Look, Israel, these are the gods who brought
you out of Egypt!"

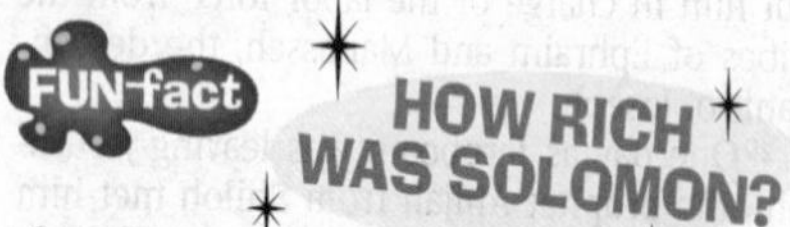

Hey, what would you do with, say, a thousand dollars? King Solomon made way more than that as king of Israel. Every year Solomon received about 25 tons of gold. **YOWZER!** On top of that, he got jewels and other cool stuff.

But all the money in the world didn't do Solomon any good when he forgot to put God first in his life.

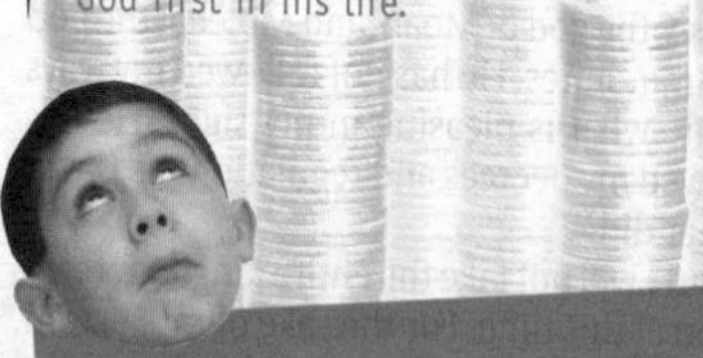

LOOK AROUND YOUR ROOM. Ask yourself how powerful your possessions are. Can your video games help when you're sick? What can your new shoes do? **Now read MATTHEW 6:19-24.** Make a sign that sums up the passage. Read your sign every day to help you remember to put God first!

29He placed these calf idols in Bethel and in
Dan—at either end of his kingdom. 30But this became a great sin, for the people worshiped the
idols, traveling as far north as Dan to worship the
one there.
31Jeroboam also erected buildings at the pagan shrines and ordained priests from the common people—those who were not from the
priestly tribe of Levi. 32And Jeroboam instituted
a religious festival in Bethel, held on the fifteenth day of the eighth month, in imitation of
the annual Festival of Shelters in Judah. There at
Bethel he himself offered sacrifices to the calves
he had made, and he appointed priests for the
pagan shrines he had made. 33So on the fifteenth day of the eighth month, a day that he
himself had designated, Jeroboam offered sacrifices on the altar at Bethel. He instituted a religious festival for Israel, and he went up to the
altar to burn incense.

CHAPTER 13

A Prophet Denounces Jeroboam

At the LORD's command, a man of God from Judah
went to Bethel, arriving there just as Jeroboam was
approaching the altar to burn incense. 2Then at
the LORD's command, he shouted, "O altar, altar!
This is what the LORD says: A child named Josiah
will be born into the dynasty of David. On you he
will sacrifice the priests from the pagan shrines
who come here to burn incense, and human
bones will be burned on you." 3That same day the
man of God gave a sign to prove his message. He
said, "The LORD has promised to give this sign:
This altar will split apart, and its ashes will be
poured out on the ground."
4When King Jeroboam heard the man of God
speaking against the altar at Bethel, he pointed at
him and shouted, "Seize that man!" But instantly
the king's hand became paralyzed in that position, and he couldn't pull it back. 5At the same
time a wide crack appeared in the altar, and the
ashes poured out, just as the man of God had predicted in his message from the LORD.
6The king cried out to the man of God, "Please
ask the LORD your God to restore my hand again!"
So the man of God prayed to the LORD, and the
king's hand was restored and he could move it
again.
7Then the king said to the man of God, "Come
to the palace with me and have something to eat,
and I will give you a gift."
8But the man of God said to the king, "Even if
you gave me half of everything you own, I would
not go with you. I would not eat or drink anything in this place. 9For the LORD gave me this
command: 'You must not eat or drink anything
while you are there, and do not return to Judah by
the same way you came.'" 10So he left Bethel and
went home another way.
11As it happened, there was an old prophet living in Bethel, and his sons came home and told
him what the man of God had done in Bethel that
day. They also told their father what the man had
said to the king. 12The old prophet asked them,
"Which way did he go?" So they showed their father which road the man of God had taken.
13"Quick, saddle the donkey," the old man said.
So they saddled the donkey for him, and he
mounted it.
14Then he rode after the man of God and
found him sitting under a great tree. The old
prophet asked him, "Are you the man of God who
came from Judah?"
"Yes, I am," he replied.
15Then he said to the man of God, "Come
home with me and eat some food."
16"No, I cannot," he replied. "I am not allowed
to eat or drink anything here in this place. 17For
the LORD gave me this command: 'You must not
eat or drink anything while you are there, and do
not return to Judah by the same way you came.'"
18But the old prophet answered, "I am a
prophet, too, just as you are. And an angel gave
me this command from the LORD: 'Bring him
home with you so he can have something to eat
and drink.'" But the old man was lying to him.
19So they went back together, and the man of
God ate and drank at the prophet's home.
20Then while they were sitting at the table, a
command from the LORD came to the old
prophet. 21He cried out to the man of God from
Judah, "This is what the LORD says: You have defied the word of the LORD and have disobeyed
the command the LORD your God gave you. 22You
came back to this place and ate and drank where
he told you not to eat or drink. Because of this,
your body will not be buried in the grave of your
ancestors."
23After the man of God had finished eating
and drinking, the old prophet saddled his own
donkey for him, 24and the man of God started off
again. But as he was traveling along, a lion came
out and killed him. His body lay there on the
road, with the donkey and the lion standing beside it. 25People who passed by saw the body lying in the road and the lion standing beside it,
and they went and reported it in Bethel, where
the old prophet lived.
26When the prophet heard the report, he said,

"It is the man of God who disobeyed the LORD's
command. The LORD has fulfilled his word by
causing the lion to attack and kill him."
27 Then the prophet said to his sons, "Saddle a
donkey for me." So they saddled a donkey, 28 and
he went out and found the body lying in the road.
The donkey and lion were still standing there beside it, for the lion had not eaten the body nor attacked the donkey. 29 So the prophet laid the
body of the man of God on the donkey and took it
back to the town to mourn over him and bury
him. 30 He laid the body in his own grave, crying
out in grief, "Oh, my brother!"
31 Afterward the prophet said to his sons,
"When I die, bury me in the grave where the man
of God is buried. Lay my bones beside his bones.
32 For the message the LORD told him to proclaim
against the altar in Bethel and against the pagan
shrines in the towns of Samaria will certainly
come true."
33 But even after this, Jeroboam did not turn
from his evil ways. He continued to choose
priests from the common people. He appointed
anyone who wanted to become a priest for the
pagan shrines. 34 This became a great sin and resulted in the utter destruction of Jeroboam's dynasty from the face of the earth.

CHAPTER 14

Ahijah's Prophecy against Jeroboam

At that time Jeroboam's son Abijah became very
sick. 2 So Jeroboam told his wife, "Disguise yourself so that no one will recognize you as my wife.
Then go to the prophet Ahijah at Shiloh—the
man who told me I would become king. 3 Take
him a gift of ten loaves of bread, some cakes, and
a jar of honey, and ask him what will happen to
the boy."
4 So Jeroboam's wife went to Ahijah's home at
Shiloh. He was an old man now and could no
longer see. 5 But the LORD had told Ahijah, "Jeroboam's wife will come here, pretending to be
someone else. She will ask you about her son,
for he is very sick. Give her the answer I give
you."
6 So when Ahijah heard her footsteps at the
door, he called out, "Come in, wife of Jeroboam!
Why are you pretending to be someone else?"
Then he told her, "I have bad news for you. 7 Give
your husband, Jeroboam, this message from the
LORD, the God of Israel: 'I promoted you from the
ranks of the common people and made you ruler
over my people Israel. 8 I ripped the kingdom
away from the family of David and gave it to you.
But you have not been like my servant David, who
obeyed my commands and followed me with all
his heart and always did whatever I wanted. 9 You
have done more evil than all who lived before
you. You have made other gods for yourself and
have made me furious with your gold calves. And
since you have turned your back on me, 10 I will
bring disaster on your dynasty and will destroy
every one of your male descendants, slave and
free alike, anywhere in Israel. I will burn up your
royal dynasty as one burns up trash until it is all
gone. 11 The members of Jeroboam's family who
die in the city will be eaten by dogs, and those
who die in the field will be eaten by vultures. I,
the LORD, have spoken.'"
12 Then Ahijah said to Jeroboam's wife, "Go on
home, and when you enter the city, the child will
die. 13 All Israel will mourn for him and bury him.
He is the only member of your family who will
have a proper burial, for this child is the only
good thing that the LORD, the God of Israel, sees
in the entire family of Jeroboam.
14 "In addition, the LORD will raise up a king
over Israel who will destroy the family of Jeroboam. This will happen today, even now! 15 Then
the LORD will shake Israel like a reed whipped
about in a stream. He will uproot the people of
Israel from this good land that he gave their ancestors and will scatter them beyond the Euphrates River, for they have angered the LORD
with the Asherah poles they have set up for worship. 16 He will abandon Israel because Jeroboam
sinned and made Israel sin along with him."
17 So Jeroboam's wife returned to Tirzah, and
the child died just as she walked through the
door of her home. 18 And all Israel buried him
and mourned for him, as the LORD had promised
through the prophet Ahijah.
19 The rest of the events in Jeroboam's reign,
including all his wars and how he ruled, are recorded in *The Book of the History of the Kings of
Israel*. 20 Jeroboam reigned in Israel twenty-two
years. When Jeroboam died, his son Nadab became the next king.

Rehoboam Rules in Judah

21 Meanwhile, Rehoboam son of Solomon was
king in Judah. He was forty-one years old when
he became king, and he reigned seventeen years
in Jerusalem, the city the LORD had chosen from
among all the tribes of Israel as the place to
honor his name. Rehoboam's mother was Naamah, an Ammonite woman.
22 During Rehoboam's reign, the people of Judah did what was evil in the LORD's sight, provok-

ing his anger with their sin, for it was even worse
than that of their ancestors. 23 For they also built
for themselves pagan shrines and set up sacred
pillars and Asherah poles on every high hill and
under every green tree. 24 There were even male
and female shrine prostitutes throughout the
land. The people imitated the detestable practices of the pagan nations the LORD had driven
from the land ahead of the Israelites.

25 In the fifth year of King Rehoboam's reign,
King Shishak of Egypt came up and attacked Jerusalem. 26 He ransacked the treasuries of the
LORD's Temple and the royal palace; he stole
everything, including all the gold shields Solomon had made. 27 King Rehoboam later replaced
them with bronze shields as substitutes, and he
entrusted them to the care of the commanders
of the guard who protected the entrance to the
royal palace. 28 Whenever the king went to the
Temple of the LORD, the guards would also take
the shields and then return them to the guardroom.

29 The rest of the events in Rehoboam's reign
and everything he did are recorded in *The Book
of the History of the Kings of Judah*. 30 There was
constant war between Rehoboam and Jeroboam.
31 When Rehoboam died, he was buried among
his ancestors in the City of David. His mother
was Naamah, an Ammonite woman. Then his
son Abijam became the next king.

CHAPTER 15

Abijam Rules in Judah

Abijam began to rule over Judah in the eighteenth year of Jeroboam's reign in Israel. 2 He
reigned in Jerusalem three years. His mother was
Maacah, the granddaughter of Absalom.

3 He committed the same sins as his father before him, and he was not faithful to the LORD his
God, as his ancestor David had been. 4 But for David's sake, the LORD his God allowed his descendants to continue ruling, shining like a lamp, and
he gave Abijam a son to rule after him in Jerusalem. 5 For David had done what was pleasing in
the LORD's sight and had obeyed the LORD's commands throughout his life, except in the affair
concerning Uriah the Hittite.

6 There was war between Abijam and Jeroboam throughout Abijam's reign. 7 The rest of
the events in Abijam's reign and everything he
did are recorded in *The Book of the History of the
Kings of Judah*. There was constant war between
Abijam and Jeroboam. 8 When Abijam died, he
was buried in the City of David. Then his son Asa
became the next king.

Asa Rules in Judah

9 Asa began to rule over Judah in the twentieth
year of Jeroboam's reign in Israel. 10 He reigned
in Jerusalem forty-one years. His grandmother
was Maacah, the granddaughter of Absalom.

11 Asa did what was pleasing in the LORD's
sight, as his ancestor David had done. 12 He banished the male and female shrine prostitutes
from the land and got rid of all the idols his ancestors had made. 13 He even deposed his grandmother Maacah from her position as queen
mother because she had made an obscene Asherah pole. He cut down her obscene pole and
burned it in the Kidron Valley. 14 Although the
pagan shrines were not removed, Asa's heart remained completely faithful to the LORD throughout his life. 15 He brought into the Temple of the
LORD the silver and gold and the various items
that he and his father had dedicated.

16 There was constant war between King Asa
of Judah and King Baasha of Israel. 17 King Baasha of Israel invaded Judah and fortified Ramah
in order to prevent anyone from entering or leaving King Asa's territory in Judah.

18 Asa responded by removing all the silver
and gold that was left in the treasuries of the
Temple of the LORD and the royal palace. He sent
it with some of his officials to Ben-hadad son of
Tabrimmon, son of Hezion, the king of Aram,
who was ruling in Damascus, along with this
message:

> 19 "Let there be a treaty between you and me
> like the one between your father and my
> father. See, I am sending you a gift of silver
> and gold. Break your treaty with King Baasha
> of Israel so that he will leave me alone."

20 Ben-hadad agreed to King Asa's request and
sent the commanders of his army to attack the
towns of Israel. They conquered the towns of
Ijon, Dan, Abel-beth-maacah, and all Kinnereth,
and all the land of Naphtali. 21 As soon as Baasha
of Israel heard what was happening, he abandoned his project of fortifying Ramah and withdrew to Tirzah. 22 Then King Asa sent an order
throughout Judah, requiring that everyone, without exception, help to carry away the building
stones and timbers that Baasha had been using
to fortify Ramah. Asa used these materials to fortify the town of Geba in Benjamin and the town
of Mizpah.

23 The rest of the events in Asa's reign—the extent of his power, everything he did, and the
names of the cities he built—are recorded in *The
Book of the History of the Kings of Judah*. In his

old age his feet became diseased. 24When Asa died, he was buried with his ancestors in the City of David.

Then Jehoshaphat, Asa's son, became the next king.

Nadab Rules in Israel

25Nadab son of Jeroboam began to rule over Israel in the second year of King Asa's reign in Judah. He reigned in Israel two years. 26But he did what was evil in the LORD's sight and followed the example of his father, continuing the sins that Jeroboam had led Israel to commit.

27Then Baasha son of Ahijah, from the tribe of Issachar, plotted against Nadab and assassinated him while he and the Israelite army were laying siege to the Philistine town of Gibbethon. 28Baasha killed Nadab in the third year of King Asa's reign in Judah, and he became the next king of Israel.

29He immediately slaughtered all the descendants of King Jeroboam, so that not one of the royal family was left, just as the LORD had promised concerning Jeroboam by the prophet Ahijah from Shiloh. 30This was done because Jeroboam had provoked the anger of the LORD, the God of Israel, by the sins he had committed and the sins he had led Israel to commit.

31The rest of the events in Nadab's reign and everything he did are recorded in *The Book of the History of the Kings of Israel.*

Baasha Rules in Israel

32There was constant war between King Asa of Judah and King Baasha of Israel. 33Baasha son of Ahijah began to rule over all Israel in the third year of King Asa's reign in Judah. Baasha reigned in Tirzah twenty-four years. 34But he did what was evil in the LORD's sight and followed the example of Jeroboam, continuing the sins that Jeroboam had led Israel to commit.

CHAPTER 16

This message from the LORD was delivered to King Baasha by the prophet Jehu son of Hanani: 2"I lifted you out of the dust to make you ruler of my people Israel, but you have followed the evil example of Jeroboam. You have provoked my anger by causing my people Israel to sin. 3So now I will destroy you and your family, just as I destroyed the descendants of Jeroboam son of Nebat. 4The members of Baasha's family who die in the city will be eaten by dogs, and those who die in the field will be eaten by vultures."

5The rest of the events in Baasha's reign and the extent of his power are recorded in *The Book of the History of the Kings of Israel.* 6When Baasha died, he was buried in Tirzah. Then his son Elah became the next king.

7The message from the LORD against Baasha and his family came through the prophet Jehu son of Hanani. It was delivered because Baasha had done what was evil in the LORD's sight (just as the family of Jeroboam had done), and also because Baasha had destroyed the family of Jeroboam. The LORD's anger was provoked by Baasha's sins.

Elah Rules in Israel

8Elah son of Baasha began to rule over Israel in the twenty-sixth year of King Asa's reign in Judah. He reigned in the city of Tirzah for two years.

9Then Zimri, who commanded half of the royal chariots, made plans to kill him. One day in Tirzah, Elah was getting drunk at the home of Arza, the supervisor of the palace. 10Zimri walked in and struck him down and killed him. This happened in the twenty-seventh year of King Asa's reign in Judah. Then Zimri became the next king.

11Zimri immediately killed the entire royal family of Baasha, leaving him not even a single male child. He even destroyed distant relatives and friends. 12So Zimri destroyed the dynasty of Baasha as the LORD had promised through the prophet Jehu. 13This happened because of all the sins Baasha and his son Elah had committed, and because of the sins they led Israel to commit. They provoked the anger of the LORD, the God of Israel, with their worthless idols.

14The rest of the events in Elah's reign and everything he did are recorded in *The Book of the History of the Kings of Israel.*

Zimri Rules in Israel

15Zimri began to rule over Israel in the twenty-seventh year of King Asa's reign in Judah, but his reign in Tirzah lasted only seven days. The army of Israel was then attacking the Philistine town of Gibbethon. 16When they heard that Zimri had committed treason and had assassinated the king, that very day they chose Omri, commander of the army, as the new king of Israel. 17So Omri led the entire army of Israel up from Gibbethon to attack Tirzah, Israel's capital. 18When Zimri saw that the city had been taken, he went into the citadel of the palace and burned it down over himself and died in the flames. 19For he, too, had done what was evil in the LORD's sight. He followed the example of

Jeroboam in all the sins he had committed and
led Israel to commit.
20The rest of the events in Zimri's reign and
his conspiracy are recorded in *The Book of the*
History of the Kings of Israel.

Omri Rules in Israel

21But now the people of Israel were split into two
factions. Half the people tried to make Tibni son
of Ginath their king, while the other half supported Omri. 22But Omri's supporters defeated
the supporters of Tibni. So Tibni was killed, and
Omri became the next king.
23Omri began to rule over Israel in the thirty-
first year of King Asa's reign in Judah. He reigned
twelve years in all, six of them in Tirzah. 24Then
Omri bought the hill now known as Samaria from
its owner, Shemer, for 150 pounds of silver. He
built a city on it and called the city Samaria in
honor of Shemer.
25But Omri did what was evil in the LORD's
sight, even more than any of the kings before
him. 26He followed the example of Jeroboam
son of Nebat in all the sins he had committed
and led Israel to commit. The people provoked
the anger of the LORD, the God of Israel, with
their worthless idols.
27The rest of the events in Omri's reign, the
extent of his power, and everything he did are
recorded in *The Book of the History of the Kings*
of Israel. 28When Omri died, he was buried in
Samaria. Then his son Ahab became the next
king.

Ahab Rules in Israel

29Ahab son of Omri began to rule over Israel in
the thirty-eighth year of King Asa's reign in Judah. He reigned in Samaria twenty-two years.
30But Ahab son of Omri did what was evil in the
LORD's sight, even more than any of the kings before him. 31And as though it were not enough to
follow the sinful example of Jeroboam, he married Jezebel, the daughter of King Ethbaal of the
Sidonians, and he began to bow down in worship
of Baal. 32First Ahab built a temple and an altar
for Baal in Samaria. 33Then he set up an Asherah
pole. He did more to provoke the anger of the
LORD, the God of Israel, than any of the other
kings of Israel before him.
34It was during his reign that Hiel, a man from
Bethel, rebuilt Jericho. When he laid its foundations, it cost him the life of his oldest son, Abiram. And when he completed it and set up its
gates, it cost him the life of his youngest son, Segub. This all happened according to the message

JUST A LITTLE BIT

Want to see the saying "A little bit goes a long way" in action? **Read 1 KINGS 17:8-16.** The widow had only a little bit of flour and oil left. But she trusted God to use that little bit to fill her bigger needs. Here's a fun experiment to show how a little bit of something can go a long way.

w a t e r

1 Rinse out a 20-ounce plastic soda bottle, and fill it half full with warm tap water.

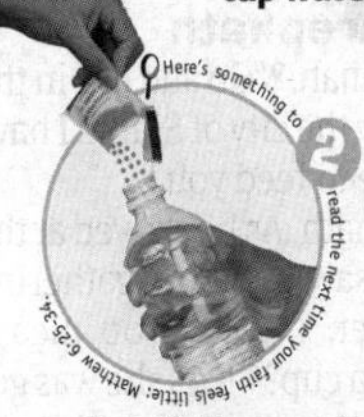

Here's something to read the next time your faith feels little: Matthew 6:25-34

2 Empty a packet of fast-activating bread yeast into the water.

3 Carefully pour 1/3 cup of sugar into the bottle. Place your thumb over the opening of the bottle, and shake the bottle so the ingredients mix.

4 Stretch the opening of a balloon over the top of the bottle.

Now go play, eat, take a bath, or do homework. This is going to take about a half hour.

What happened? The little bit of yeast made so much gas that it filled the balloon. Cool, huh? When times are tough, our faith might seem tiny. **But God is big! He can fill all our needs, no matter what!**

from the LORD concerning Jericho spoken by
Joshua son of Nun.

CHAPTER 17

Elijah Fed by Ravens

Now Elijah, who was from Tishbe in Gilead, told
King Ahab, "As surely as the LORD, the God of
Israel, lives—the God I serve—there will be no
dew or rain during the next few years until I give
the word!"
2Then the LORD said to Elijah, 3"Go to the east
and hide by Kerith Brook, near where it enters
the Jordan River. 4Drink from the brook and eat
what the ravens bring you, for I have commanded them to bring you food."
5So Elijah did as the LORD told him and camped
beside Kerith Brook, east of the Jordan. 6The ravens brought him bread and meat each morning
and evening, and he drank from the brook. 7But
after a while the brook dried up, for there was no
rainfall anywhere in the land.

The Widow at Zarephath

8Then the LORD said to Elijah, 9"Go and live in the
village of Zarephath, near the city of Sidon. I have
instructed a widow there to feed you."
10So he went to Zarephath. As he arrived at the
gates of the village, he saw a widow gathering
sticks, and he asked her, "Would you please
bring me a little water in a cup?" 11As she was going to get it, he called to her, "Bring me a bite of
bread, too."
12But she said, "I swear by the LORD your God
that I don't have a single piece of bread in the
house. And I have only a handful of flour left
in the jar and a little cooking oil in the bottom
of the jug. I was just gathering a few sticks to
cook this last meal, and then my son and I will
die."
13But Elijah said to her, "Don't be afraid! Go
ahead and do just what you've said, but make a little bread for me first. Then use what's left to prepare a meal for yourself and your son. 14For this is
what the LORD, the God of Israel, says: There will
always be flour and olive oil left in your containers until the time when the LORD sends rain and
the crops grow again!"
15So she did as Elijah said, and she and Elijah
and her family continued to eat for many days.
16There was always enough flour and olive oil
left in the containers, just as the LORD had promised through Elijah.
17Some time later the woman's son became
sick. He grew worse and worse, and finally he
died. 18Then she said to Elijah, "O man of God,
what have you done to me? Have you come here
to point out my sins and kill my son?"
19But Elijah replied, "Give me your son." And
he took the child's body from her arms, carried
him up the stairs to the room where he was staying, and laid the body on his bed. 20Then Elijah
cried out to the LORD, "O LORD my God, why have
you brought tragedy to this widow who has
opened her home to me, causing her son to die?"
21And he stretched himself out over the child
three times and cried out to the LORD, "O LORD
my God, please let this child's life return to him."
22The LORD heard Elijah's prayer, and the life of
the child returned, and he revived! 23Then Elijah
brought him down from the upper room and
gave him to his mother. "Look!" he said. "Your
son is alive!"
24Then the woman told Elijah, "Now I know
for sure that you are a man of God, and that the
LORD truly speaks through you."

CHAPTER 18

The Contest on Mount Carmel

Later on, in the third year of the drought, the
LORD said to Elijah, "Go and present yourself to
King Ahab. Tell him that I will soon send rain!"
2So Elijah went to appear before Ahab.
Meanwhile, the famine had become very severe in Samaria. 3So Ahab summoned Obadiah,
who was in charge of the palace. (Obadiah was a
devoted follower of the LORD. 4Once when
Jezebel had tried to kill all the LORD's prophets,
Obadiah had hidden 100 of them in two caves.
He put fifty prophets in each cave and supplied
them with food and water.) 5Ahab said to Obadiah, "We must check every spring and valley in
the land to see if we can find enough grass to save
at least some of my horses and mules." 6So they
divided the land between them. Ahab went one
way by himself, and Obadiah went another way
by himself.
7As Obadiah was walking along, he suddenly
saw Elijah coming toward him. Obadiah recognized him at once and bowed low to the ground
before him. "Is it really you, my lord Elijah?" he
asked.
8"Yes, it is," Elijah replied. "Now go and tell
your master, 'Elijah is here.'"
9"Oh, sir," Obadiah protested, "what harm
have I done to you that you are sending me to my
death at the hands of Ahab? 10For I swear by the
LORD your God that the king has searched every
nation and kingdom on earth from end to end to
find you. And each time he was told, 'Elijah isn't
here,' King Ahab forced the king of that nation to

swear to the truth of his claim. 11And now you
say, 'Go and tell your master, "Elijah is here."'
12But as soon as I leave you, the Spirit of the LORD
will carry you away to who knows where. When
Ahab comes and cannot find you, he will kill me.
Yet I have been a true servant of the LORD all my
life. 13Has no one told you, my lord, about the
time when Jezebel was trying to kill the LORD's
prophets? I hid 100 of them in two caves and
supplied them with food and water. 14And now
you say, 'Go and tell your master, "Elijah is here."'
Sir, if I do that, Ahab will certainly kill me."

15But Elijah said, "I swear by the LORD Almighty,
in whose presence I stand, that I will present myself to Ahab this very day."

16So Obadiah went to tell Ahab that Elijah had
come, and Ahab went out to meet Elijah. 17When
Ahab saw him, he exclaimed, "So, is it really you,
you troublemaker of Israel?"

18"I have made no trouble for Israel," Elijah
replied. "You and your family are the troublemakers, for you have refused to obey the commands of the LORD and have worshiped the
images of Baal instead. 19Now summon all Israel
to join me at Mount Carmel, along with the
450 prophets of Baal and the 400 prophets of
Asherah who are supported by Jezebel."

20So Ahab summoned all the people of Israel
and the prophets to Mount Carmel. 21Then Elijah
stood in front of them and said, "How much longer will you waver, hobbling between two opinions? If the LORD is God, follow him! But if Baal is
God, then follow him!" But the people were completely silent.

22Then Elijah said to them, "I am the only
prophet of the LORD who is left, but Baal has 450
prophets. 23Now bring two bulls. The prophets
of Baal may choose whichever one they wish and
cut it into pieces and lay it on the wood of their
altar, but without setting fire to it. I will prepare
the other bull and lay it on the wood on the altar,
but not set fire to it. 24Then call on the name of
your god, and I will call on the name of the LORD.
The god who answers by setting fire to the wood
is the true God!" And all the people agreed.

25Then Elijah said to the prophets of Baal, "You
go first, for there are many of you. Choose one of
the bulls, and prepare it and call on the name of
your god. But do not set fire to the wood."

26So they prepared one of the bulls and placed
it on the altar. Then they called on the name of
Baal from morning until noontime, shouting,
"O Baal, answer us!" But there was no reply of any
kind. Then they danced, hobbling around the altar they had made.

27About noontime Elijah began mocking
them. "You'll have to shout louder," he scoffed,
"for surely he is a god! Perhaps he is daydream-
ing, or is relieving himself. Or maybe he is away
on a trip, or is asleep and needs to be wakened!"

28So they shouted louder, and following their
normal custom, they cut themselves with knives
and swords until the blood gushed out. 29They
raved all afternoon until the time of the evening
sacrifice, but still there was no sound, no reply,
no response.

30Then Elijah called to the people, "Come over
here!" They all crowded around him as he repaired the altar of the LORD that had been torn
down. 31He took twelve stones, one to represent
each of the tribes of Israel, 32and he used the
stones to rebuild the altar in the name of the
LORD. Then he dug a trench around the altar large
enough to hold about three gallons. 33He piled
wood on the altar, cut the bull into pieces, and
laid the pieces on the wood.

Then he said, "Fill four large jars with water,
and pour the water over the offering and the
wood."

34After they had done this, he said, "Do the
same thing again!" And when they were finished,
he said, "Now do it a third time!" So they did as
he said, 35and the water ran around the altar and
even filled the trench.

36At the usual time for offering the evening
sacrifice, Elijah the prophet walked up to the altar and prayed, "O LORD, God of Abraham, Isaac,
and Jacob, prove today that you are God in Israel
and that I am your servant. Prove that I have done
all this at your command. 37O LORD, answer me!
Answer me so these people will know that you,
O LORD, are God and that you have brought them
back to yourself."

38Immediately the fire of the LORD flashed
down from heaven and burned up the young bull,
the wood, the stones, and the dust. It even licked
up all the water in the trench! 39And when all the
people saw it, they fell face down on the ground
and cried out, "The LORD—he is God! Yes, the
LORD is God!"

40Then Elijah commanded, "Seize all the
prophets of Baal. Don't let a single one escape!" So
the people seized them all, and Elijah took them
down to the Kishon Valley and killed them there.

Elijah Prays for Rain

41Then Elijah said to Ahab, "Go get something to
eat and drink, for I hear a mighty rainstorm
coming!"

42So Ahab went to eat and drink. But Elijah

climbed to the top of Mount Carmel and bowed
low to the ground and prayed with his face
between his knees.
43 Then he said to his servant, "Go and look out
toward the sea."
The servant went and looked, then returned to
Elijah and said, "I didn't see anything."
Seven times Elijah told him to go and look.
44 Finally the seventh time, his servant told him,
"I saw a little cloud about the size of a man's hand
rising from the sea."
Then Elijah shouted, "Hurry to Ahab and tell
him, 'Climb into your chariot and go back home.
If you don't hurry, the rain will stop you!'"
45 And soon the sky was black with clouds. A
heavy wind brought a terrific rainstorm, and
Ahab left quickly for Jezreel. 46 Then the LORD
gave special strength to Elijah. He tucked his
cloak into his belt and ran ahead of Ahab's chariot all the way to the entrance of Jezreel.

CHAPTER 19

Elijah Flees to Sinai

When Ahab got home, he told Jezebel everything
Elijah had done, including the way he had killed
all the prophets of Baal. 2 So Jezebel sent this
message to Elijah: "May the gods strike me and
even kill me if by this time tomorrow I have not
killed you just as you killed them."
3 Elijah was afraid and fled for his life. He went
to Beersheba, a town in Judah, and he left his servant there. 4 Then he went on alone into the wilderness, traveling all day. He sat down under a
solitary broom tree and prayed that he might die.
"I have had enough, LORD," he said. "Take my life,
for I am no better than my ancestors who have already died."
5 Then he lay down and slept under the broom
tree. But as he was sleeping, an angel touched him
and told him, "Get up and eat!" 6 He looked around
and there beside his head was some bread baked
on hot stones and a jar of water! So he ate and
drank and lay down again.
7 Then the angel of the LORD came again and
touched him and said, "Get up and eat some more,
or the journey ahead will be too much for you."
8 So he got up and ate and drank, and the food
gave him enough strength to travel forty days and
forty nights to Mount Sinai, the mountain of God.
9 There he came to a cave, where he spent the
night.

The LORD Speaks to Elijah

But the LORD said to him, "What are you doing
here, Elijah?"

THE BEST BOOK

What's the most popular book in history? What book was written by more than 40 people, yet has only one author? The Bible!

God sent the Holy Spirit to guide people as they wrote the Bible. The words in the Bible are God's words—written to us!

Write the title of your favorite book.

Find out all you can about that book. Who wrote it? When? How many copies have been sold?

Now write what you know about the Bible.

(It had over 40 writers, took about 1,500 years to write, has sold more copies than any other book, and has been translated into more than 2,000 languages!)

NO COMPARISON, HUH? Is it time to make the Bible *your* new favorite book?

10 Elijah replied, "I have zealously served the
LORD God Almighty. But the people of Israel have
broken their covenant with you, torn down your
altars, and killed every one of your prophets. I am
the only one left, and now they are trying to kill
me, too."
11 "Go out and stand before me on the mountain," the LORD told him. And as Elijah stood there,
the LORD passed by, and a mighty windstorm hit
the mountain. It was such a terrible blast that the
rocks were torn loose, but the LORD was not in the
wind. After the wind there was an earthquake, but
the LORD was not in the earthquake. 12 And after
the earthquake there was a fire, but the LORD was
not in the fire. And after the fire there was the
sound of a gentle whisper. 13 When Elijah heard it,
he wrapped his face in his cloak and went out and
stood at the entrance of the cave.
And a voice said, "What are you doing here,
Elijah?"
14 He replied again, "I have zealously served
the LORD God Almighty. But the people of Israel
have broken their covenant with you, torn down
your altars, and killed every one of your prophets. I am the only one left, and now they are trying
to kill me, too."
15 Then the LORD told him, "Go back the same

way you came, and travel to the wilderness of Damascus. When you arrive there, anoint Hazael to
be king of Aram. 16Then anoint Jehu grandson of
Nimshi to be king of Israel, and anoint Elisha son
of Shaphat from the town of Abel-meholah to replace you as my prophet. 17Anyone who escapes
from Hazael will be killed by Jehu, and those who
escape Jehu will be killed by Elisha! 18Yet I will
preserve 7,000 others in Israel who have never
bowed down to Baal or kissed him!"

The Call of Elisha

19So Elijah went and found Elisha son of Shaphat
plowing a field. There were twelve teams of oxen
in the field, and Elisha was plowing with the
twelfth team. Elijah went over to him and threw
his cloak across his shoulders and then walked
away. 20Elisha left the oxen standing there, ran
after Elijah, and said to him, "First let me go and
kiss my father and mother good-bye, and then I
will go with you!"

Elijah replied, "Go on back, but think about
what I have done to you."

21So Elisha returned to his oxen and slaughtered them. He used the wood from the plow to
build a fire to roast their flesh. He passed around
the meat to the townspeople, and they all ate.
Then he went with Elijah as his assistant.

CHAPTER 20

Ben-Hadad Attacks Samaria

About that time King Ben-hadad of Aram mobilized his army, supported by the chariots and
horses of thirty-two allied kings. They went to
besiege Samaria, the capital of Israel, and
launched attacks against it. 2Ben-hadad sent
messengers into the city to relay this message to
King Ahab of Israel: "This is what Ben-hadad
says: 3'Your silver and gold are mine, and so are
your wives and the best of your children!'"

4"All right, my lord the king," Israel's king replied. "All that I have is yours!"

5Soon Ben-hadad's messengers returned
again and said, "This is what Ben-hadad says: 'I
have already demanded that you give me your silver, gold, wives, and children. 6But about this
time tomorrow I will send my officials to search
your palace and the homes of your officials. They
will take away everything you consider valuable!'"

7Then Ahab summoned all the elders of the
land and said to them, "Look how this man is stirring up trouble! I already agreed with his demand that I give him my wives and children and
silver and gold."

8"Don't give in to any more demands," all the
elders and the people advised.

9So Ahab told the messengers from Ben-
hadad, "Say this to my lord the king: 'I will give
you everything you asked for the first time, but I
cannot accept this last demand of yours.'" So the
messengers returned to Ben-hadad with that
response.

10Then Ben-hadad sent this message to Ahab:
"May the gods strike me and even kill me if there
remains enough dust from Samaria to provide
even a handful for each of my soldiers."

11The king of Israel sent back this answer:
"A warrior putting on his sword for battle
should not boast like a warrior who has already
won."

12Ahab's reply reached Ben-hadad and the
other kings as they were drinking in their tents.
"Prepare to attack!" Ben-hadad commanded his
officers. So they prepared to attack the city.

Ahab's Victory over Ben-Hadad

13Then a certain prophet came to see King Ahab
of Israel and told him, "This is what the LORD
says: Do you see all these enemy forces? Today I
will hand them all over to you. Then you will
know that I am the LORD."

14Ahab asked, "How will he do it?"

And the prophet replied, "This is what the
LORD says: The troops of the provincial commanders will do it."

"Should we attack first?" Ahab asked.

"Yes," the prophet answered.

15So Ahab mustered the troops of the 232
provincial commanders. Then he called out the
rest of the army of Israel, some 7,000 men.
16About noontime, as Ben-hadad and the thirty-
two allied kings were still in their tents drinking
themselves into a stupor, 17the troops of the provincial commanders marched out of the city as
the first contingent.

As they approached, Ben-hadad's scouts reported to him, "Some troops are coming from
Samaria."

18"Take them alive," Ben-hadad commanded,
"whether they have come for peace or for war."

19But Ahab's provincial commanders and the
entire army had now come out to fight. 20Each
Israelite soldier killed his Aramean opponent,
and suddenly the entire Aramean army panicked
and fled. The Israelites chased them, but King
Ben-hadad and a few of his charioteers escaped
on horses. 21However, the king of Israel destroyed the other horses and chariots and
slaughtered the Arameans.

22Afterward the prophet said to King Ahab,
"Get ready for another attack. Begin making
plans now, for the king of Aram will come back
next spring."

Ben-Hadad's Second Attack

23After their defeat, Ben-hadad's officers said to
him, "The Israelite gods are gods of the hills; that
is why they won. But we can beat them easily on
the plains. 24Only this time replace the kings
with field commanders! 25Recruit another army
like the one you lost. Give us the same number of
horses, chariots, and men, and we will fight
against them on the plains. There's no doubt that
we will beat them." So King Ben-hadad did as
they suggested.

26The following spring he called up the Aramean army and marched out against Israel, this
time at Aphek. 27Israel then mustered its army,
set up supply lines, and marched out for battle.
But the Israelite army looked like two little flocks
of goats in comparison to the vast Aramean
forces that filled the countryside!

28Then the man of God went to the king of Israel and said, "This is what the LORD says: The Arameans have said, 'The LORD is a god of the hills
and not of the plains.' So I will defeat this vast
army for you. Then you will know that I am the
LORD."

29The two armies camped opposite each
other for seven days, and on the seventh day the
battle began. The Israelites killed 100,000 Aramean foot soldiers in one day. 30The rest fled
into the town of Aphek, but the wall fell on them
and killed another 27,000. Ben-hadad fled into
the town and hid in a secret room.

31Ben-hadad's officers said to him, "Sir, we
have heard that the kings of Israel are merciful.
So let's humble ourselves by wearing burlap
around our waists and putting ropes on our
heads, and surrender to the king of Israel. Then
perhaps he will let you live."

32So they put on burlap and ropes, and they
went to the king of Israel and begged, "Your servant Ben-hadad says, 'Please let me live!'"

The king of Israel responded, "Is he still alive?
He is my brother!"

33The men took this as a good sign and
quickly picked up on his words. "Yes," they said,
"your brother Ben-hadad!"

"Go and get him," the king of Israel told them.
And when Ben-hadad arrived, Ahab invited him
up into his chariot.

34Ben-hadad told him, "I will give back the
towns my father took from your father, and you
may establish places of trade in Damascus, as my
father did in Samaria."

Then Ahab said, "I will release you under these
conditions." So they made a new treaty, and Ben-
hadad was set free.

A Prophet Condemns Ahab

35Meanwhile, the LORD instructed one of the
group of prophets to say to another man, "Hit
me!" But the man refused to hit the prophet.
36Then the prophet told him, "Because you have
not obeyed the voice of the LORD, a lion will kill
you as soon as you leave me." And when he had
gone, a lion did attack and kill him.

37Then the prophet turned to another man
and said, "Hit me!" So he struck the prophet and
wounded him.

38The prophet placed a bandage over his eyes
to disguise himself and then waited beside the
road for the king. 39As the king passed by, the
prophet called out to him, "Sir, I was in the thick
of battle, and suddenly a man brought me a prisoner. He said, 'Guard this man; if for any reason
he gets away, you will either die or pay a fine of
seventy-five pounds of silver!' 40But while I was
busy doing something else, the prisoner disappeared!"

"Well, it's your own fault," the king replied.
"You have brought the judgment on yourself."

41Then the prophet quickly pulled the bandage from his eyes, and the king of Israel recognized him as one of the prophets. 42The prophet
said to him, "This is what the LORD says: Because
you have spared the man I said must be destroyed, now you must die in his place, and your
people will die instead of his people." 43So the
king of Israel went home to Samaria angry and
sullen.

CHAPTER 21

Naboth's Vineyard

Now there was a man named Naboth, from
Jezreel, who owned a vineyard in Jezreel beside
the palace of King Ahab of Samaria. 2One day
Ahab said to Naboth, "Since your vineyard is so
convenient to my palace, I would like to buy it to
use as a vegetable garden. I will give you a better
vineyard in exchange, or if you prefer, I will pay
you for it."

3But Naboth replied, "The LORD forbid that I
should give you the inheritance that was passed
down by my ancestors."

4So Ahab went home angry and sullen because of Naboth's answer. The king went to bed
with his face to the wall and refused to eat!

5"What's the matter?" his wife Jezebel asked him. "What's made you so upset that you're not eating?"

6"I asked Naboth to sell me his vineyard or trade it, but he refused!" Ahab told her.

7"Are you the king of Israel or not?" Jezebel demanded. "Get up and eat something, and don't worry about it. I'll get you Naboth's vineyard!"

8So she wrote letters in Ahab's name, sealed them with his seal, and sent them to the elders and other leaders of the town where Naboth lived. 9In her letters she commanded: "Call the citizens together for a time of fasting, and give Naboth a place of honor. 10And then seat two scoundrels across from him who will accuse him of cursing God and the king. Then take him out and stone him to death."

11So the elders and other town leaders followed the instructions Jezebel had written in the letters. 12They called for a fast and put Naboth at a prominent place before the people. 13Then the two scoundrels came and sat down across from him. And they accused Naboth before all the people, saying, "He cursed God and the king." So he was dragged outside the town and stoned to death. 14The town leaders then sent word to Jezebel, "Naboth has been stoned to death."

15When Jezebel heard the news, she said to Ahab, "You know the vineyard Naboth wouldn't sell you? Well, you can have it now! He's dead!" 16So Ahab immediately went down to the vineyard of Naboth to claim it.

17But the LORD said to Elijah, 18"Go down to meet King Ahab of Israel, who rules in Samaria. He will be at Naboth's vineyard in Jezreel, claiming it for himself. 19Give him this message: 'This is what the LORD says: Wasn't it enough that you killed Naboth? Must you rob him, too? Because you have done this, dogs will lick your blood at the very place where they licked the blood of Naboth!'"

20"So, my enemy, you have found me!" Ahab exclaimed to Elijah.

"Yes," Elijah answered, "I have come because you have sold yourself to what is evil in the LORD's sight. 21So now the LORD says, 'I will bring disaster on you and consume you. I will destroy every one of your male descendants, slave and free alike, anywhere in Israel! 22I am going to destroy your family as I did the family of Jeroboam son of Nebat and the family of Baasha son of Ahijah, for you have made me very angry and have led Israel into sin.'

23"And regarding Jezebel, the LORD says, 'Dogs will eat Jezebel's body at the plot of land in Jezreel.'

24"The members of Ahab's family who die in the city will be eaten by dogs, and those who die in the field will be eaten by vultures."

25(No one else so completely sold himself to what was evil in the LORD's sight as Ahab did under the influence of his wife Jezebel. 26His worst outrage was worshiping idols just as the Amorites had done—the people whom the LORD had driven out from the land ahead of the Israelites.)

27But when Ahab heard this message, he tore his clothing, dressed in burlap, and fasted. He even slept in burlap and went about in deep mourning.

28Then another message from the LORD came to Elijah: 29"Do you see how Ahab has humbled himself before me? Because he has done this, I will not do what I promised during his lifetime. It will happen to his sons; I will destroy his dynasty."

CHAPTER 22

Jehoshaphat and Ahab

For three years there was no war between Aram and Israel. 2Then during the third year, King Jehoshaphat of Judah went to visit King Ahab of Israel. 3During the visit, the king of Israel said to his officials, "Do you realize that the town of Ramoth-gilead belongs to us? And yet we've done nothing to recapture it from the king of Aram!"

4Then he turned to Jehoshaphat and asked, "Will you join me in battle to recover Ramoth-gilead?"

Jehoshaphat replied to the king of Israel, "Why, of course! You and I are as one. My troops are your troops, and my horses are your horses." 5Then Jehoshaphat added, "But first let's find out what the LORD says."

6So the king of Israel summoned the prophets, about 400 of them, and asked them, "Should I go to war against Ramoth-gilead, or should I hold back?"

They all replied, "Yes, go right ahead! The Lord will give the king victory."

7But Jehoshaphat asked, "Is there not also a prophet of the LORD here? We should ask him the same question."

8The king of Israel replied to Jehoshaphat, "There is one more man who could consult the LORD for us, but I hate him. He never prophesies anything but trouble for me! His name is Micaiah son of Imlah."

Jehoshaphat replied, "That's not the way a king should talk! Let's hear what he has to say."

9 So the king of Israel called one of his officials and said, "Quick! Bring Micaiah son of Imlah."

Micaiah Prophesies against Ahab

10 King Ahab of Israel and King Jehoshaphat of Judah, dressed in their royal robes, were sitting on thrones at the threshing floor near the gate of Samaria. All of Ahab's prophets were prophesying there in front of them. 11 One of them, Zedekiah son of Kenaanah, made some iron horns and proclaimed, "This is what the LORD says: With these horns you will gore the Arameans to death!"

12 All the other prophets agreed. "Yes," they said, "go up to Ramoth-gilead and be victorious, for the LORD will give the king victory!"

13 Meanwhile, the messenger who went to get Micaiah said to him, "Look, all the prophets are promising victory for the king. Be sure that you agree with them and promise success."

14 But Micaiah replied, "As surely as the LORD lives, I will say only what the LORD tells me to say."

15 When Micaiah arrived before the king, Ahab asked him, "Micaiah, should we go to war against Ramoth-gilead, or should we hold back?"

Micaiah replied sarcastically, "Yes, go up and be victorious, for the LORD will give the king victory!"

16 But the king replied sharply, "How many times must I demand that you speak only the truth to me when you speak for the LORD?"

17 Then Micaiah told him, "In a vision I saw all Israel scattered on the mountains, like sheep without a shepherd. And the LORD said, 'Their master has been killed. Send them home in peace.'"

18 "Didn't I tell you?" the king of Israel exclaimed to Jehoshaphat. "He never prophesies anything but trouble for me."

19 Then Micaiah continued, "Listen to what the LORD says! I saw the LORD sitting on his throne with all the armies of heaven around him, on his right and on his left. 20 And the LORD said, 'Who can entice Ahab to go into battle against Ramoth-gilead so he can be killed?'

"There were many suggestions, 21 and finally a spirit approached the LORD and said, 'I can do it!'

22 "'How will you do this?' the LORD asked.

"And the spirit replied, 'I will go out and inspire all of Ahab's prophets to speak lies.'

"'You will succeed,' said the LORD. 'Go ahead and do it.'

23 "So you see, the LORD has put a lying spirit in the mouths of all your prophets. For the LORD has pronounced your doom."

24 Then Zedekiah son of Kenaanah walked up to Micaiah and slapped him across the face. "Since when did the Spirit of the LORD leave me to speak to you?" he demanded.

25 And Micaiah replied, "You will find out soon enough when you are trying to hide in some secret room!"

26 "Arrest him!" the king of Israel ordered. "Take him back to Amon, the governor of the city, and to my son Joash. 27 Give them this order from the king: 'Put this man in prison, and feed him nothing but bread and water until I return safely from the battle!'"

28 But Micaiah replied, "If you return safely, it will mean that the LORD has not spoken through me!" Then he added to those standing around, "Everyone mark my words!"

The Death of Ahab

29 So King Ahab of Israel and King Jehoshaphat of Judah led their armies against Ramoth-gilead. 30 The king of Israel said to Jehoshaphat, "As we go into battle, I will disguise myself so no one will recognize me, but you wear your royal robes." So the king of Israel disguised himself, and they went into battle.

31 Meanwhile, the king of Aram had issued these orders to his thirty-two chariot commanders: "Attack only the king of Israel. Don't bother with anyone else!" 32 So when the Aramean chariot commanders saw Jehoshaphat in his royal robes, they went after him. "There is the king of Israel!" they shouted. But when Jehoshaphat called out, 33 the chariot commanders realized he was not the king of Israel, and they stopped chasing him.

34 An Aramean soldier, however, randomly shot an arrow at the Israelite troops and hit the king of Israel between the joints of his armor. "Turn the horses and get me out of here!" Ahab groaned to the driver of his chariot. "I'm badly wounded!"

35 The battle raged all that day, and the king remained propped up in his chariot facing the Arameans. The blood from his wound ran down to the floor of his chariot, and as evening arrived he died. 36 Just as the sun was setting, the cry ran through his troops: "We're done for! Run for your lives!"

37 So the king died, and his body was taken to Samaria and buried there. 38 Then his chariot was washed beside the pool of Samaria, and

dogs came and licked his blood at the place
where the prostitutes bathed, just as the LORD
had promised.
39 The rest of the events in Ahab's reign and
everything he did, including the story of the
ivory palace and the towns he built, are recorded
in *The Book of the History of the Kings of Israel.*
40 So Ahab died, and his son Ahaziah became the
next king.

Jehoshaphat Rules in Judah

41 Jehoshaphat son of Asa began to rule over Judah in the fourth year of King Ahab's reign in Israel. 42 Jehoshaphat was thirty-five years old
when he became king, and he reigned in Jerusalem twenty-five years. His mother was Azubah,
the daughter of Shilhi.
43 Jehoshaphat was a good king, following the
example of his father, Asa. He did what was
pleasing in the LORD's sight. During his reign,
however, he failed to remove all the pagan
shrines, and the people still offered sacrifices
and burned incense there. 44 Jehoshaphat also
made peace with the king of Israel.
45 The rest of the events in Jehoshaphat's
reign, the extent of his power, and the wars he
waged are recorded in *The Book of the History of*
the Kings of Judah. 46 He banished from the land
the rest of the male and female shrine prostitutes, who still continued their practices from
the days of his father, Asa.
47 (There was no king in Edom at that time,
only a deputy.)
48 Jehoshaphat also built a fleet of trading
ships to sail to Ophir for gold. But the ships never
set sail, for they met with disaster in their home
port of Ezion-geber. 49 At one time Ahaziah son
of Ahab had proposed to Jehoshaphat, "Let my
men sail with your men in the ships." But Jehoshaphat refused the request.
50 When Jehoshaphat died, he was buried with
his ancestors in the City of David. Then his son
Jehoram became the next king.

Ahaziah Rules in Israel

51 Ahaziah son of Ahab began to rule over Israel
in the seventeenth year of King Jehoshaphat's
reign in Judah. He reigned in Samaria two years.
52 But he did what was evil in the LORD's sight, following the example of his father and mother and
the example of Jeroboam son of Nebat, who had
led Israel to sin. 53 He served Baal and worshiped
him, provoking the anger of the LORD, the God of
Israel, just as his father had done.

2 KINGS Good Kings, Bad Kings

Look for 2 hidden messages in 2 Kings!

Second Kings shows how Israel and Judah went from being powerful nations to a defeated and scattered people. The people in both kingdoms turned away from God, so God allowed them to be conquered. Read 2 Kings to learn about

- **ELIJAH'S BIG EXIT**
- **HOW GOD DID SOME COOL THINGS THROUGH ELISHA**
- **A BUNCH OF BAD KINGS WHO MADE A LOT OF BAD CHOICES**
- **A BOY KING WHO MADE A BIG DIFFERENCE**
- **THE END OF THE KINGDOMS OF ISRAEL AND JUDAH**

Going Up?

All the prophets knew that the time had come for Elijah to go home to be with God. But they didn't know *how* Elijah would go or who would take his place. **You can read all about Elijah's amazing exit in 2 Kings 2:1-14.**

Jarring

"No one knows where so many of the jars have gone," exclaimed one neighbor. Apparently, a neighborhood in Israel experienced a shortage of jars. "It's gotten so bad that I'm keeping flour in my socks. Won't somebody do something?" cried another. **Find out what happened to the jars by reading 2 Kings 4:1-7.**

More Than Skin Deep

Naaman would do anything to find healing for his skin disease—except take a bath in a dirty Israelite river. Did Naaman swallow his pride and follow God's direction? Did the prophet Elisha ever actually come out and speak with Naaman face to face? **Find out as you read 2 Kings 5:1-19.**

Heavy Metal

Maybe light metal. Maybe heavy water. Or maybe a miracle! The worker lost the ax in the water. How would he ever find it again? **Read 2 Kings 6:1-7 to find out what Elisha did to help!**

THE END?

Enough Is Enough

Yeah, yeah, yeah... Warnings. Prophets. Discipline. Finally, after 300 years, God put an end to the wicked kings of Israel. Read 2 Kings 17:1-23 to see what happened to the people of Israel (in the northern kingdom) and why it happened. Did Judah (in the south) learn anything from the lesson? Nope. **You can read about the sad day for the south in 2 Kings 25:1-6.**

Overachiever

When most kids turn eight, they learn math and get pretty good at reading. When Josiah turned eight, he became king of Israel. And this boy king turned out to be one of the *best* kings. He broke all the idols and did so much more! **Read all about it in 2 Kings 22:1–23:25.**

Timeline

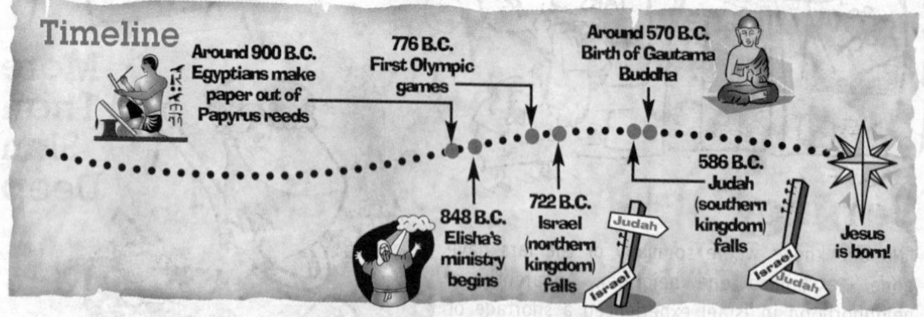

Around 900 B.C. Egyptians make paper out of Papyrus reeds
776 B.C. First Olympic games
Around 570 B.C. Birth of Gautama Buddha
848 B.C. Elisha's ministry begins
722 B.C. Israel (northern kingdom) falls
Judah
Israel
586 B.C. Judah (southern kingdom) falls
Israel
Judah
Jesus is born!

The JESUS CONNECTION

God promised the Israelites that things would work out well for them as long as they worshiped God and kept him first. Sadly, both Israel and Judah turned away from God and worshiped idols. Because of their sin, they were taken away from their homes to serve other nations. If they just would have repented and turned back to God, they would have found forgiveness and healing.

We all sin and do things that are wrong too. If we let our hearts get hard like the Israelites did, our lives will fall apart just like their kingdom did. **But if we repent and turn back to God, we'll find the forgiveness, healing, and help Jesus offers.**

CHAPTER 1
Elijah Confronts King Ahaziah
After King Ahab's death, the land of Moab rebelled against Israel.
2 One day Israel's new king, Ahaziah, fell
through the latticework of an upper room at his
palace in Samaria and was seriously injured.
So he sent messengers to the temple of Baal-
zebub, the god of Ekron, to ask whether he would
recover.
3 But the angel of the LORD told Elijah, who was
from Tishbe, "Go and confront the messengers
of the king of Samaria and ask them, 'Is there no
God in Israel? Why are you going to Baal-zebub,
the god of Ekron, to ask whether the king will
recover? 4 Now, therefore, this is what the LORD
says: You will never leave the bed you are lying
on; you will surely die.'" So Elijah went to deliver
the message.
5 When the messengers returned to the king,
he asked them, "Why have you returned so soon?"
6 They replied, "A man came up to us and told
us to go back to the king and give him this message. 'This is what the LORD says: Is there no
God in Israel? Why are you sending men to Baal-
zebub, the god of Ekron, to ask whether you will
recover? Therefore, because you have done this,
you will never leave the bed you are lying on; you
will surely die.'"
7 "What sort of man was he?" the king demanded. "What did he look like?"
8 They replied, "He was a hairy man, and he
wore a leather belt around his waist."
"Elijah from Tishbe!" the king exclaimed.
9 Then he sent an army captain with fifty soldiers to arrest him. They found him sitting on
top of a hill. The captain said to him, "Man of
God, the king has commanded you to come
down with us."
10 But Elijah replied to the captain, "If I am a
man of God, let fire come down from heaven and
destroy you and your fifty men!" Then fire fell
from heaven and killed them all.
11 So the king sent another captain with fifty
men. The captain said to him, "Man of God, the
king demands that you come down at once."
12 Elijah replied, "If I am a man of God, let fire
come down from heaven and destroy you and
your fifty men!" And again the fire of God fell
from heaven and killed them all.
13 Once more the king sent a third captain
with fifty men. But this time the captain went up
the hill and fell to his knees before Elijah. He
pleaded with him, "O man of God, please spare
my life and the lives of these, your fifty servants.
14 See how the fire from heaven came down and
destroyed the first two groups. But now please
spare my life!"
15 Then the angel of the LORD said to Elijah, "Go
down with him, and don't be afraid of him." So
Elijah got up and went with him to the king.
16 And Elijah said to the king, "This is what the
LORD says: Why did you send messengers to
Baal-zebub, the god of Ekron, to ask whether you
will recover? Is there no God in Israel to answer
your question? Therefore, because you have
done this, you will never leave the bed you are lying on; you will surely die."
17 So Ahaziah died, just as the LORD had promised through Elijah. Since Ahaziah did not have a
son to succeed him, his brother Joram became
the next king. This took place in the second year
of the reign of Jehoram son of Jehoshaphat, king
of Judah.
18 The rest of the events in Ahaziah's reign and
everything he did are recorded in *The Book of the
History of the Kings of Israel.*

CHAPTER 2
Elijah Taken into Heaven
When the LORD was about to take Elijah up to
heaven in a whirlwind, Elijah and Elisha were
traveling from Gilgal. 2 And Elijah said to Elisha,
"Stay here, for the LORD has told me to go to
Bethel."
But Elisha replied, "As surely as the LORD lives
and you yourself live, I will never leave you!" So
they went down together to Bethel.
3 The group of prophets from Bethel came to
Elisha and asked him, "Did you know that the
LORD is going to take your master away from you
today?"
"Of course I know," Elisha answered. "But be
quiet about it."
4 Then Elijah said to Elisha, "Stay here, for the
LORD has told me to go to Jericho."
But Elisha replied again, "As surely as the LORD
lives and you yourself live, I will never leave you."
So they went on together to Jericho.
5 Then the group of prophets from Jericho
came to Elisha and asked him, "Did you know
that the LORD is going to take your master away
from you today?"
"Of course I know," Elisha answered. "But be
quiet about it."
6 Then Elijah said to Elisha, "Stay here, for the
LORD has told me to go to the Jordan River."
But again Elisha replied, "As surely as the LORD
lives and you yourself live, I will never leave you."
So they went on together.

7 Fifty men from the group of prophets also
went and watched from a distance as Elijah and
Elisha stopped beside the Jordan River. 8 Then
Elijah folded his cloak together and struck the
water with it. The river divided, and the two of
them went across on dry ground!

9 When they came to the other side, Elijah said
to Elisha, "Tell me what I can do for you before I
am taken away."

And Elisha replied, "Please let me inherit a
double share of your spirit and become your successor."

10 "You have asked a difficult thing," Elijah replied. "If you see me when I am taken from you,
then you will get your request. But if not, then
you won't."

11 As they were walking along and talking, suddenly a chariot of fire appeared, drawn by horses
of fire. It drove between the two men, separating
them, and Elijah was carried by a whirlwind into
heaven. 12 Elisha saw it and cried out, "My father!
My father! I see the chariots and charioteers
of Israel!" And as they disappeared from sight,
Elisha tore his clothes in distress.

13 Elisha picked up Elijah's cloak, which had
fallen when he was taken up. Then Elisha returned to the bank of the Jordan River. 14 He
struck the water with Elijah's cloak and cried out,
"Where is the LORD, the God of Elijah?" Then the
river divided, and Elisha went across.

15 When the group of prophets from Jericho saw
from a distance what happened, they exclaimed,
"Elijah's spirit rests upon Elisha!" And they went to
meet him and bowed to the ground before him.
16 "Sir," they said, "just say the word and fifty of our
strongest men will search the wilderness for your
master. Perhaps the Spirit of the LORD has left
him on some mountain or in some valley."

"No," Elisha said, "don't send them." 17 But they
kept urging him until they shamed him into
agreeing, and he finally said, "All right, send
them." So fifty men searched for three days but
did not find Elijah. 18 Elisha was still at Jericho
when they returned. "Didn't I tell you not to go?"
he asked.

Elisha's First Miracles

19 One day the leaders of the town of Jericho visited Elisha. "We have a problem, my lord," they
told him. "This town is located in pleasant surroundings, as you can see. But the water is bad,
and the land is unproductive."

20 Elisha said, "Bring me a new bowl with salt
in it." So they brought it to him. 21 Then he went
out to the spring that supplied the town with water and threw the salt into it. And he said, "This is
what the LORD says: I have purified this water. It
will no longer cause death or infertility." 22 And
the water has remained pure ever since, just as
Elisha said.

23 Elisha left Jericho and went up to Bethel. As
he was walking along the road, a group of boys
from the town began mocking and making fun
of him. "Go away, baldy!" they chanted. "Go away,
baldy!" 24 Elisha turned around and looked at
them, and he cursed them in the name of the
LORD. Then two bears came out of the woods and
mauled forty-two of them. 25 From there Elisha
went to Mount Carmel and finally returned to
Samaria.

CHAPTER 3

War between Israel and Moab

Ahab's son Joram began to rule over Israel in the
eighteenth year of King Jehoshaphat's reign in
Judah. He reigned in Samaria twelve years. 2 He
did what was evil in the LORD's sight, but not to
the same extent as his father and mother. He at
least tore down the sacred pillar of Baal that his
father had set up. 3 Nevertheless, he continued in
the sins that Jeroboam son of Nebat had committed and led the people of Israel to commit.

4 King Mesha of Moab was a sheep breeder. He
used to pay the king of Israel an annual tribute of
100,000 lambs and the wool of 100,000 rams.
5 But after Ahab's death, the king of Moab rebelled against the king of Israel. 6 So King Joram
promptly mustered the army of Israel and
marched from Samaria. 7 On the way, he sent this
message to King Jehoshaphat of Judah: "The
king of Moab has rebelled against me. Will you
join me in battle against him?"

And Jehoshaphat replied, "Why, of course!
You and I are as one. My troops are your troops,
and my horses are your horses." 8 Then Jehoshaphat asked, "What route will we take?"

"We will attack from the wilderness of Edom,"
Joram replied.

9 The king of Edom and his troops joined
them, and all three armies traveled along a
roundabout route through the wilderness for
seven days. But there was no water for the men or
their animals.

10 "What should we do?" the king of Israel
cried out. "The LORD has brought the three of us
here to let the king of Moab defeat us."

11 But King Jehoshaphat of Judah asked, "Is
there no prophet of the LORD with us? If there is,
we can ask the LORD what to do through him."

One of King Joram's officers replied, "Elisha

son of Shaphat is here. He used to be Elijah's personal assistant."
12Jehoshaphat said, "Yes, the LORD speaks
through him." So the king of Israel, King Jehoshaphat of Judah, and the king of Edom went to
consult with Elisha.
13"Why are you coming to me?" Elisha asked
the king of Israel. "Go to the pagan prophets of
your father and mother!"

But King Joram of Israel said, "No! For it was
the LORD who called us three kings here—only to
be defeated by the king of Moab!"
14Elisha replied, "As surely as the LORD Almighty lives, whom I serve, I wouldn't even
bother with you except for my respect for King
Jehoshaphat of Judah. 15Now bring me someone
who can play the harp."

While the harp was being played, the power of
the LORD came upon Elisha, 16and he said, "This
is what the LORD says: This dry valley will be
filled with pools of water! 17You will see neither
wind nor rain, says the LORD, but this valley will
be filled with water. You will have plenty for
yourselves and your cattle and other animals.
18But this is only a simple thing for the LORD, for
he will make you victorious over the army of
Moab! 19You will conquer the best of their towns,
even the fortified ones. You will cut down all
their good trees, stop up all their springs, and
ruin all their good land with stones."
20The next day at about the time when the
morning sacrifice was offered, water suddenly
appeared! It was flowing from the direction of
Edom, and soon there was water everywhere.
21Meanwhile, when the people of Moab heard
about the three armies marching against them,
they mobilized every man who was old enough
to strap on a sword, and they stationed themselves along their border. 22But when they got up
the next morning, the sun was shining across
the water, making it appear red to the Moabites—
like blood. 23"It's blood!" the Moabites exclaimed. "The three armies must have attacked
and killed each other! Let's go, men of Moab, and
collect the plunder!"
24But when the Moabites arrived at the Israelite camp, the army of Israel rushed out and attacked them until they turned and ran. The army
of Israel chased them into the land of Moab,
destroying everything as they went. 25They destroyed the towns, covered their good land with
stones, stopped up all the springs, and cut down
all the good trees. Finally, only Kir-hareseth and
its stone walls were left, but men with slings surrounded and attacked it.

Pour It On!
When God blesses people, he heaps it on. **Read 2 KINGS 4:1-7 to see how God helped a poor, starving widow!** The twist? The widow had to *help* to get the blessing!
Check this out. When Elisha asked the woman to gather empty jars from her neighbors, he told her, "Borrow *as many* as you can." **WOW! When God wants to bless us, God really wants to bless us!**
Make this cool oil-art craft to hang in your window. It'll remind you that God wants to bless you big time!
1
Cut a jar shape from a paper bag.
2
Dip a cotton swab in oil. It doesn't take much! Make a cool pattern on the "jar" with the cotton swab.
3
Blot the extra oil with a paper towel.
God says that helping the poor is like giving God a loan! Check it out in Proverbs 19:17.
4
Hang it in a sunny window!
VOILÀ! Instant oil art! Whenever you catch a glimpse of your oil-art masterpiece, stop and thank God for the many blessings in your life.
Thanks, God!

26 When the king of Moab saw that he was losing the battle, he led 700 of his swordsmen in a desperate attempt to break through the enemy lines near the king of Edom, but they failed. 27 Then the king of Moab took his oldest son, who would have been the next king, and sacrificed him as a burnt offering on the wall. So there was great anger against Israel, and the Israelites withdrew and returned to their own land.

CHAPTER 4

Elisha Helps a Poor Widow

One day the widow of a member of the group of prophets came to Elisha and cried out, "My husband who served you is dead, and you know how he feared the LORD. But now a creditor has come, threatening to take my two sons as slaves."

2 "What can I do to help you?" Elisha asked. "Tell me, what do you have in the house?"

"Nothing at all, except a flask of olive oil," she replied.

3 And Elisha said, "Borrow as many empty jars as you can from your friends and neighbors. 4 Then go into your house with your sons and shut the door behind you. Pour olive oil from your flask into the jars, setting each one aside when it is filled."

5 So she did as she was told. Her sons kept bringing jars to her, and she filled one after another. 6 Soon every container was full to the brim!

"Bring me another jar," she said to one of her sons.

"There aren't any more!" he told her. And then the olive oil stopped flowing.

7 When she told the man of God what had happened, he said to her, "Now sell the olive oil and pay your debts, and you and your sons can live on what is left over."

Elisha and the Woman from Shunem

8 One day Elisha went to the town of Shunem. A wealthy woman lived there, and she urged him to come to her home for a meal. After that, whenever he passed that way, he would stop there for something to eat.

9 She said to her husband, "I am sure this man who stops in from time to time is a holy man of God. 10 Let's build a small room for him on the roof and furnish it with a bed, a table, a chair, and a lamp. Then he will have a place to stay whenever he comes by."

11 One day Elisha returned to Shunem, and he went up to this upper room to rest. 12 He said to his servant Gehazi, "Tell the woman from Shunem I want to speak to her." When she appeared, 13 Elisha said to Gehazi, "Tell her, 'We appreciate the kind concern you have shown us. What can we do for you? Can we put in a good word for you to the king or to the commander of the army?'"

"No," she replied, "my family takes good care of me."

14 Later Elisha asked Gehazi, "What can we do for her?"

Gehazi replied, "She doesn't have a son, and her husband is an old man."

15 "Call her back again," Elisha told him. When the woman returned, Elisha said to her as she stood in the doorway, 16 "Next year at this time you will be holding a son in your arms!"

"No, my lord!" she cried. "O man of God, don't deceive me and get my hopes up like that."

17 But sure enough, the woman soon became pregnant. And at that time the following year she had a son, just as Elisha had said.

18 One day when her child was older, he went out to help his father, who was working with the harvesters. 19 Suddenly he cried out, "My head hurts! My head hurts!"

His father said to one of the servants, "Carry him home to his mother."

20 So the servant took him home, and his mother held him on her lap. But around noontime he died. 21 She carried him up and laid him on the bed of the man of God, then shut the door and left him there. 22 She sent a message to her husband: "Send one of the servants and a donkey so that I can hurry to the man of God and come right back."

23 "Why go today?" he asked. "It is neither a new moon festival nor a Sabbath."

But she said, "It will be all right."

24 So she saddled the donkey and said to the servant, "Hurry! Don't slow down unless I tell you to."

25 As she approached the man of God at Mount Carmel, Elisha saw her in the distance. He said to Gehazi, "Look, the woman from Shunem is coming. 26 Run out to meet her and ask her, 'Is everything all right with you, your husband, and your child?'"

"Yes," the woman told Gehazi, "everything is fine."

27 But when she came to the man of God at the mountain, she fell to the ground before him and caught hold of his feet. Gehazi began to push her away, but the man of God said, "Leave her alone. She is deeply troubled, but the LORD has not told me what it is."

28Then she said, "Did I ask you for a son, my
lord? And didn't I say, 'Don't deceive me and get
my hopes up'?"
29Then Elisha said to Gehazi, "Get ready to
travel; take my staff and go! Don't talk to anyone
along the way. Go quickly and lay the staff on the
child's face."
30But the boy's mother said, "As surely as the
LORD lives and you yourself live, I won't go home
unless you go with me." So Elisha returned with
her.
31Gehazi hurried on ahead and laid the staff
on the child's face, but nothing happened. There
was no sign of life. He returned to meet Elisha
and told him, "The child is still dead."
32When Elisha arrived, the child was indeed
dead, lying there on the prophet's bed. 33He went
in alone and shut the door behind him and
prayed to the LORD. 34Then he lay down on the
child's body, placing his mouth on the child's
mouth, his eyes on the child's eyes, and his hands
on the child's hands. And as he stretched out on
him, the child's body began to grow warm again!
35Elisha got up, walked back and forth across the
room once, and then stretched himself out again
on the child. This time the boy sneezed seven
times and opened his eyes!
36Then Elisha summoned Gehazi. "Call the
child's mother!" he said. And when she came in,
Elisha said, "Here, take your son!" 37She fell at his
feet and bowed before him, overwhelmed with
gratitude. Then she took her son in her arms and
carried him downstairs.

Miracles during a Famine

38Elisha now returned to Gilgal, and there was a
famine in the land. One day as the group of
prophets was seated before him, he said to his
servant, "Put a large pot on the fire, and make
some stew for the rest of the group."
39One of the young men went out into the
field to gather herbs and came back with a
pocketful of wild gourds. He shredded them
and put them into the pot without realizing they
were poisonous. 40Some of the stew was served
to the men. But after they had eaten a bite or
two they cried out, "Man of God, there's poison
in this stew!" So they would not eat it.
41Elisha said, "Bring me some flour." Then he
threw it into the pot and said, "Now it's all right;
go ahead and eat." And then it did not harm
them.
42One day a man from Baal-shalishah brought
the man of God a sack of fresh grain and twenty
loaves of barley bread made from the first grain
of his harvest. Elisha said, "Give it to the people
so they can eat."
43"What?" his servant exclaimed. "Feed a
hundred people with only this?"
But Elisha repeated, "Give it to the people so
they can eat, for this is what the LORD says: Everyone will eat, and there will even be some left
over!" 44And when they gave it to the people,
there was plenty for all and some left over, just as
the LORD had promised.

CHAPTER **5**

The Healing of Naaman

The king of Aram had great admiration for Naaman, the commander of his army, because
through him the LORD had given Aram great victories. But though Naaman was a mighty warrior,
he suffered from leprosy.
2At this time Aramean raiders had invaded the
land of Israel, and among their captives was a
young girl who had been given to Naaman's wife
as a maid. 3One day the girl said to her mistress,
"I wish my master would go to see the prophet in
Samaria. He would heal him of his leprosy."
4So Naaman told the king what the young girl
from Israel had said. 5"Go and visit the prophet,"
the king of Aram told him. "I will send a letter of
introduction for you to take to the king of Israel." So Naaman started out, carrying as gifts
750 pounds of silver, 150 pounds of gold, and
ten sets of clothing. 6The letter to the king of Israel said: "With this letter I present my servant
Naaman. I want you to heal him of his leprosy."
7When the king of Israel read the letter, he
tore his clothes in dismay and said, "This man
sends me a leper to heal! Am I God, that I can give
life and take it away? I can see that he's just trying
to pick a fight with me."
8But when Elisha, the man of God, heard that
the king of Israel had torn his clothes in dismay,
he sent this message to him: "Why are you so upset? Send Naaman to me, and he will learn that
there is a true prophet here in Israel."
9So Naaman went with his horses and chariots and waited at the door of Elisha's house.
10But Elisha sent a messenger out to him with
this message: "Go and wash yourself seven times
in the Jordan River. Then your skin will be restored, and you will be healed of your leprosy."
11But Naaman became angry and stalked away.
"I thought he would certainly come out to meet
me!" he said. "I expected him to wave his hand
over the leprosy and call on the name of the LORD
his God and heal me! 12Aren't the rivers of Damascus, the Abana and the Pharpar, better than

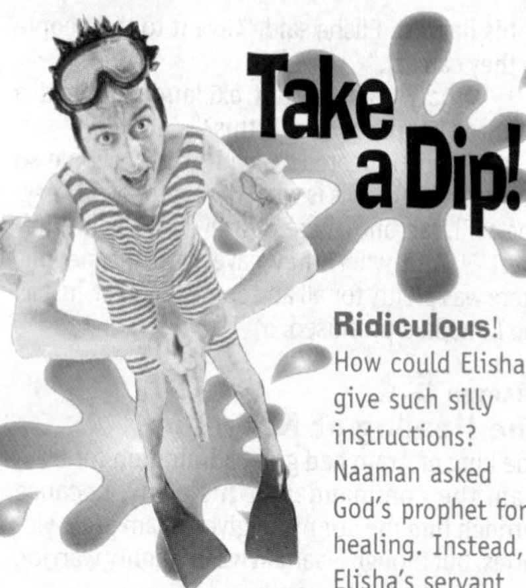

Ridiculous! How could Elisha give such silly instructions? Naaman asked God's prophet for healing. Instead, Elisha's servant told him to take a swim. **Read 2 KINGS 5:1-19 to find what God did.**

Do this experiment to show how God washed away Naaman's leprosy.

1 Fill a bowl with water. Shake some pepper onto the water.

2 Wash, rinse, and dry your hands thoroughly. Stick one finger in the water. Do this six times. Nothing big here.

3 Put a drop of liquid dish detergent on the tip of your finger and dip it into the water. What's happening to the pepper?

Maybe you didn't expect a difference when you put your finger in the water the last time, but there was a big difference. Naaman's stubborn heart almost caused him to miss out on God's healing. **Whenever you see pepper on a table, remember how God wants us to have faith in him!**

any of the rivers of Israel? Why shouldn't I wash
in them and be healed?" So Naaman turned and
went away in a rage.
13But his officers tried to reason with him and
said, "Sir, if the prophet had told you to do something very difficult, wouldn't you have done it?
So you should certainly obey him when he says
simply, 'Go and wash and be cured!' " 14So Naaman went down to the Jordan River and dipped
himself seven times, as the man of God had instructed him. And his skin became as healthy as
the skin of a young child, and he was healed!
15Then Naaman and his entire party went
back to find the man of God. They stood before
him, and Naaman said, "Now I know that there is
no God in all the world except in Israel. So please
accept a gift from your servant."
16But Elisha replied, "As surely as the LORD
lives, whom I serve, I will not accept any gifts."
And though Naaman urged him to take the gift,
Elisha refused.
17Then Naaman said, "All right, but please allow me to load two of my mules with earth from
this place, and I will take it back home with me.
From now on I will never again offer burnt offerings or sacrifices to any other god except the
LORD. 18However, may the LORD pardon me in
this one thing: When my master the king goes
into the temple of the god Rimmon to worship
there and leans on my arm, may the LORD pardon
me when I bow, too."
19"Go in peace," Elisha said. So Naaman
started home again.

The Greed of Gehazi

20But Gehazi, the servant of Elisha, the man of
God, said to himself, "My master should not have
let this Aramean get away without accepting any
of his gifts. As surely as the LORD lives, I will
chase after him and get something from him."
21So Gehazi set off after Naaman.
When Naaman saw Gehazi running after him,
he climbed down from his chariot and went to
meet him. "Is everything all right?" Naaman
asked.
22"Yes," Gehazi said, "but my master has sent
me to tell you that two young prophets from the
hill country of Ephraim have just arrived. He
would like 75 pounds of silver and two sets of
clothing to give to them."
23"By all means, take twice as much silver," Naaman insisted. He gave him two sets of clothing,
tied up the money in two bags, and sent two of
his servants to carry the gifts for Gehazi. 24But
when they arrived at the citadel, Gehazi took the

gifts from the servants and sent the men back.
Then he went and hid the gifts inside the house.
25 When he went in to his master, Elisha asked
him, "Where have you been, Gehazi?"
"I haven't been anywhere," he replied.
26 But Elisha asked him, "Don't you realize that
I was there in spirit when Naaman stepped down
from his chariot to meet you? Is this the time to
receive money and clothing, olive groves and
vineyards, sheep and cattle, and male and female
servants? 27 Because you have done this, you and
your descendants will suffer from Naaman's leprosy forever." When Gehazi left the room, he was
covered with leprosy; his skin was white as snow.

CHAPTER 6

The Floating Ax Head

One day the group of prophets came to Elisha
and told him, "As you can see, this place where we
meet with you is too small. 2 Let's go down to the
Jordan River, where there are plenty of logs.
There we can build a new place for us to meet."
"All right," he told them, "go ahead."
3 "Please come with us," someone suggested.
"I will," he said. 4 So he went with them.
When they arrived at the Jordan, they began
cutting down trees. 5 But as one of them was cutting a tree, his ax head fell into the river. "Oh, sir!"
he cried. "It was a borrowed ax!"
6 "Where did it fall?" the man of God asked.
When he showed him the place, Elisha cut a stick
and threw it into the water at that spot. Then the
ax head floated to the surface. 7 "Grab it," Elisha
said. And the man reached out and grabbed it.

Elisha Traps the Arameans

8 When the king of Aram was at war with Israel,
he would confer with his officers and say, "We
will mobilize our forces at such and such a
place."
9 But immediately Elisha, the man of God,
would warn the king of Israel, "Do not go near
that place, for the Arameans are planning to mobilize their troops there." 10 So the king of Israel
would send word to the place indicated by the
man of God. Time and again Elisha warned the
king, so that he would be on the alert there.
11 The king of Aram became very upset over
this. He called his officers together and demanded, "Which of you is the traitor? Who has
been informing the king of Israel of my plans?"
12 "It's not us, my lord the king," one of the officers replied. "Elisha, the prophet in Israel, tells
the king of Israel even the words you speak in the
privacy of your bedroom!"
13 "Go and find out where he is," the king commanded, "so I can send troops to seize him."
And the report came back: "Elisha is at Dothan." 14 So one night the king of Aram sent a
great army with many chariots and horses to surround the city.
15 When the servant of the man of God got up
early the next morning and went outside, there
were troops, horses, and chariots everywhere.
"Oh, sir, what will we do now?" the young man
cried to Elisha.
16 "Don't be afraid!" Elisha told him. "For there
are more on our side than on theirs!" 17 Then Elisha prayed, "O LORD, open his eyes and let him
see!" The LORD opened the young man's eyes, and
when he looked up, he saw that the hillside
around Elisha was filled with horses and chariots
of fire.
18 As the Aramean army advanced toward him,
Elisha prayed, "O LORD, please make them blind."
So the LORD struck them with blindness as Elisha
had asked.
19 Then Elisha went out and told them, "You
have come the wrong way! This isn't the right
city! Follow me, and I will take you to the man you
are looking for." And he led them to the city of
Samaria.
20 As soon as they had entered Samaria, Elisha
prayed, "O LORD, now open their eyes and let
them see." So the LORD opened their eyes, and
they discovered that they were in the middle of
Samaria.
21 When the king of Israel saw them, he
shouted to Elisha, "My father, should I kill them?
Should I kill them?"
22 "Of course not!" Elisha replied. "Do we kill
prisoners of war? Give them food and drink and
send them home again to their master."
23 So the king made a great feast for them and
then sent them home to their master. After that,
the Aramean raiders stayed away from the land
of Israel.

Ben-Hadad Besieges Samaria

24 Some time later, however, King Ben-hadad of
Aram mustered his entire army and besieged Samaria. 25 As a result, there was a great famine in
the city. The siege lasted so long that a donkey's
head sold for eighty pieces of silver, and a cup of
dove's dung sold for five pieces of silver.
26 One day as the king of Israel was walking
along the wall of the city, a woman called to him,
"Please help me, my lord the king!"
27 He answered, "If the LORD doesn't help you,
what can I do? I have neither food from the

threshing floor nor wine from the press to give
you." 28But then the king asked, "What is the
matter?"
She replied, "This woman said to me: 'Come
on, let's eat your son today, then we will eat my
son tomorrow.' 29So we cooked my son and ate
him. Then the next day I said to her, 'Kill your son
so we can eat him,' but she has hidden her son."
30When the king heard this, he tore his
clothes in despair. And as the king walked along
the wall, the people could see that he was wearing burlap under his robe next to his skin. 31"May
God strike me and even kill me if I don't separate
Elisha's head from his shoulders this very day,"
the king vowed.
32Elisha was sitting in his house with the elders of Israel when the king sent a messenger to
summon him. But before the messenger arrived,
Elisha said to the elders, "A murderer has sent a
man to cut off my head. When he arrives, shut
the door and keep him out. We will soon hear his
master's steps following him."
33While Elisha was still saying this, the messenger arrived. And the king said, "All this misery
is from the LORD! Why should I wait for the LORD
any longer?"

CHAPTER 7

Elisha replied, "Listen to this message from the
LORD! This is what the LORD says: By this time tomorrow in the markets of Samaria, six quarts of
choice flour will cost only one piece of silver, and
twelve quarts of barley grain will cost only one
piece of silver."
2The officer assisting the king said to the man
of God, "That couldn't happen even if the LORD
opened the windows of heaven!"
But Elisha replied, "You will see it happen with
your own eyes, but you won't be able to eat any
of it!"

Lepers Visit the Enemy Camp

3Now there were four men with leprosy sitting at
the entrance of the city gates. "Why should we
sit here waiting to die?" they asked each other.
4"We will starve if we stay here, but with the famine in the city, we will starve if we go back there.
So we might as well go out and surrender to the
Aramean army. If they let us live, so much the
better. But if they kill us, we would have died anyway."
5So at twilight they set out for the camp of the
Arameans. But when they came to the edge of the
camp, no one was there! 6For the Lord had
caused the Aramean army to hear the clatter of
speeding chariots and the galloping of horses
and the sounds of a great army approaching.
"The king of Israel has hired the Hittites and
Egyptians to attack us!" they cried to one another. 7So they panicked and ran into the night,
abandoning their tents, horses, donkeys, and
everything else, as they fled for their lives.
8When the lepers arrived at the edge of the
camp, they went into one tent after another, eating and drinking wine; and they carried off silver
and gold and clothing and hid it. 9Finally, they
said to each other, "This is not right. This is a day
of good news, and we aren't sharing it with anyone! If we wait until morning, some calamity will
certainly fall upon us. Come on, let's go back and
tell the people at the palace."
10So they went back to the city and told the
gatekeepers what had happened. "We went out
to the Aramean camp," they said, "and no one
was there! The horses and donkeys were teth-
ered and the tents were all in order, but there
wasn't a single person around!" 11Then the gatekeepers shouted the news to the people in the
palace.

Israel Plunders the Camp

12The king got out of bed in the middle of the
night and told his officers, "I know what has
happened. The Arameans know we are starving,
so they have left their camp and have hidden in
the fields. They are expecting us to leave the
city, and then they will take us alive and capture
the city."
13One of his officers replied, "We had better
send out scouts to check into this. Let them take
five of the remaining horses. If something happens to them, it will be no worse than if they stay
here and die with the rest of us."
14So two chariots with horses were prepared,
and the king sent scouts to see what had happened to the Aramean army. 15They went all the
way to the Jordan River, following a trail of clothing and equipment that the Arameans had
thrown away in their mad rush to escape. The
scouts returned and told the king about it.
16Then the people of Samaria rushed out and
plundered the Aramean camp. So it was true that
six quarts of choice flour were sold that day for
one piece of silver, and twelve quarts of barley
grain were sold for one piece of silver, just as the
LORD had promised. 17The king appointed his
officer to control the traffic at the gate, but he
was knocked down and trampled to death as the
people rushed out.
So everything happened exactly as the man of

God had predicted when the king came to his house. 18 The man of God had said to the king, "By this time tomorrow in the markets of Samaria, six quarts of choice flour will cost one piece of silver, and twelve quarts of barley grain will cost one piece of silver."

19 The king's officer had replied, "That couldn't happen even if the LORD opened the windows of heaven!" And the man of God had said, "You will see it happen with your own eyes, but you won't be able to eat any of it!" 20 And so it was, for the people trampled him to death at the gate!

CHAPTER 8

The Woman from Shunem Returns Home

Elisha had told the woman whose son he had brought back to life, "Take your family and move to some other place, for the LORD has called for a famine on Israel that will last for seven years." 2 So the woman did as the man of God instructed. She took her family and settled in the land of the Philistines for seven years.

3 After the famine ended she returned from the land of the Philistines, and she went to see the king about getting back her house and land. 4 As she came in, the king was talking with Gehazi, the servant of the man of God. The king had just said, "Tell me some stories about the great things Elisha has done." 5 And Gehazi was telling the king about the time Elisha had brought a boy back to life. At that very moment, the mother of the boy walked in to make her appeal to the king about her house and land.

"Look, my lord the king!" Gehazi exclaimed. "Here is the woman now, and this is her son—the very one Elisha brought back to life!"

6 "Is this true?" the king asked her. And she told him the story. So he directed one of his officials to see that everything she had lost was restored to her, including the value of any crops that had been harvested during her absence.

Hazael Murders Ben-Hadad

7 Elisha went to Damascus, the capital of Aram, where King Ben-hadad lay sick. When someone told the king that the man of God had come, 8 the king said to Hazael, "Take a gift to the man of God. Then tell him to ask the LORD, 'Will I recover from this illness?'"

9 So Hazael loaded down forty camels with the finest products of Damascus as a gift for Elisha. He went to him and said, "Your servant Ben-hadad, the king of Aram, has sent me to ask, 'Will I recover from this illness?'"

10 And Elisha replied, "Go and tell him, 'You will surely recover.' But actually the LORD has shown me that he will surely die!" 11 Elisha stared at Hazael with a fixed gaze until Hazael became uneasy. Then the man of God started weeping.

12 "What's the matter, my lord?" Hazael asked him.

Elisha replied, "I know the terrible things you will do to the people of Israel. You will burn their fortified cities, kill their young men with the sword, dash their little children to the ground, and rip open their pregnant women!"

13 Hazael responded, "How could a nobody like me ever accomplish such great things?"

Elisha answered, "The LORD has shown me that you are going to be the king of Aram."

14 When Hazael left Elisha and went back, the king asked him, "What did Elisha tell you?"

And Hazael replied, "He told me that you will surely recover."

15 But the next day Hazael took a blanket, soaked it in water, and held it over the king's face until he died. Then Hazael became the next king of Aram.

Jehoram Rules in Judah

16 Jehoram son of King Jehoshaphat of Judah began to rule over Judah in the fifth year of the reign of Joram son of Ahab, king of Israel. 17 Jehoram was thirty-two years old when he became king, and he reigned in Jerusalem eight years. 18 But Jehoram followed the example of the kings of Israel and was as wicked as King Ahab, for he had married one of Ahab's daughters. So Jehoram did what was evil in the LORD's sight. 19 But the LORD did not want to destroy Judah, for he had promised his servant David that his descendants would continue to rule, shining like a lamp forever.

20 During Jehoram's reign, the Edomites revolted against Judah and crowned their own king. 21 So Jehoram went with all his chariots to attack the town of Zair. The Edomites surrounded him and his chariot commanders, but he went out at night and attacked them under cover of darkness. But Jehoram's army deserted him and fled to their homes. 22 So Edom has been independent from Judah to this day. The town of Libnah also revolted about that same time.

23 The rest of the events in Jehoram's reign and everything he did are recorded in *The Book of the History of the Kings of Judah*. 24 When Jehoram died, he was buried with his ancestors in the City of David. Then his son Ahaziah became the next king.

Ahaziah Rules in Judah

25 Ahaziah son of Jehoram began to rule over Judah in the twelfth year of the reign of Joram son
of Ahab, king of Israel.
26 Ahaziah was twenty-two years old when he
became king, and he reigned in Jerusalem one
year. His mother was Athaliah, a granddaughter
of King Omri of Israel. 27 Ahaziah followed the
evil example of King Ahab's family. He did what
was evil in the LORD's sight, just as Ahab's family
had done, for he was related by marriage to the
family of Ahab.
28 Ahaziah joined Joram son of Ahab in his war
against King Hazael of Aram at Ramoth-gilead.
When the Arameans wounded King Joram in the
battle, 29 he returned to Jezreel to recover from
the wounds he had received at Ramoth. Because
Joram was wounded, King Ahaziah of Judah went
to Jezreel to visit him.

CHAPTER 9

Jehu Anointed King of Israel

Meanwhile, Elisha the prophet had summoned a
member of the group of prophets. "Get ready to
travel," he told him, "and take this flask of olive
oil with you. Go to Ramoth-gilead, 2 and find Jehu
son of Jehoshaphat, son of Nimshi. Call him into
a private room away from his friends, 3 and pour
the oil over his head. Say to him, 'This is what the
LORD says: I anoint you to be the king over Israel.'
Then open the door and run for your life!"
4 So the young prophet did as he was told and
went to Ramoth-gilead. 5 When he arrived there,
he found Jehu sitting around with the other army
officers. "I have a message for you, Commander,"
he said.
"For which one of us?" Jehu asked.
"For you, Commander," he replied.
6 So Jehu left the others and went into the
house. Then the young prophet poured the oil
over Jehu's head and said, "This is what the LORD,
the God of Israel, says: I anoint you king over the
LORD's people, Israel. 7 You are to destroy the family of Ahab, your master. In this way, I will avenge
the murder of my prophets and all the LORD's servants who were killed by Jezebel. 8 The entire
family of Ahab must be wiped out. I will destroy
every one of his male descendants, slave and free
alike, anywhere in Israel. 9 I will destroy the family
of Ahab as I destroyed the families of Jeroboam
son of Nebat and of Baasha son of Ahijah. 10 Dogs
will eat Ahab's wife Jezebel at the plot of land in
Jezreel, and no one will bury her." Then the young
prophet opened the door and ran.
11 Jehu went back to his fellow officers, and
one of them asked him, "What did that madman
want? Is everything all right?"
"You know how a man like that babbles on,"
Jehu replied.
12 "You're hiding something," they said. "Tell us."
So Jehu told them, "He said to me, 'This is what
the LORD says: I have anointed you to be king
over Israel.'"
13 Then they quickly spread out their cloaks
on the bare steps and blew the ram's horn, shouting, "Jehu is king!"

Jehu Kills Joram and Ahaziah

14 So Jehu son of Jehoshaphat, son of Nimshi, led
a conspiracy against King Joram. (Now Joram
had been with the army at Ramoth-gilead, defending Israel against the forces of King Hazael
of Aram. 15 But King Joram was wounded in the
fighting and returned to Jezreel to recover from
his wounds.) So Jehu told the men with him, "If
you want me to be king, don't let anyone leave
town and go to Jezreel to report what we have
done."
16 Then Jehu got into a chariot and rode to Jezreel to find King Joram, who was lying there
wounded. King Ahaziah of Judah was there, too,
for he had gone to visit him. 17 The watchman on
the tower of Jezreel saw Jehu and his company
approaching, so he shouted to Joram, "I see a
company of troops coming!"
"Send out a rider to ask if they are coming in
peace," King Joram ordered.
18 So a horseman went out to meet Jehu and
said, "The king wants to know if you are coming
in peace."
Jehu replied, "What do you know about
peace? Fall in behind me!"
The watchman called out to the king, "The
messenger has met them, but he's not returning."
19 So the king sent out a second horseman. He
rode up to them and said, "The king wants to
know if you come in peace."
Again Jehu answered, "What do you know
about peace? Fall in behind me!"
20 The watchman exclaimed, "The messenger
has met them, but he isn't returning either! It
must be Jehu son of Nimshi, for he's driving like a
madman."
21 "Quick! Get my chariot ready!" King Joram
commanded.
Then King Joram of Israel and King Ahaziah of
Judah rode out in their chariots to meet Jehu.
They met him at the plot of land that had belonged to Naboth of Jezreel. 22 King Joram demanded, "Do you come in peace, Jehu?"

Jehu replied, "How can there be peace as long
as the idolatry and witchcraft of your mother,
Jezebel, are all around us?"

23 Then King Joram turned the horses around
and fled, shouting to King Ahaziah, "Treason,
Ahaziah!" 24 But Jehu drew his bow and shot Joram between the shoulders. The arrow pierced
his heart, and he sank down dead in his chariot.

25 Jehu said to Bidkar, his officer, "Throw him
into the plot of land that belonged to Naboth of
Jezreel. Do you remember when you and I were
riding along behind his father, Ahab? The LORD
pronounced this message against him: 26 'I solemnly swear that I will repay him here on this plot
of land, says the LORD, for the murder of Naboth
and his sons that I saw yesterday.' So throw him
out on Naboth's property, just as the LORD said."

27 When King Ahaziah of Judah saw what
was happening, he fled along the road to Beth-
haggan. Jehu rode after him, shouting, "Shoot
him, too!" So they shot Ahaziah in his chariot at
the Ascent of Gur, near Ibleam. He was able to go
on as far as Megiddo, but he died there. 28 His
servants took him by chariot to Jerusalem,
where they buried him with his ancestors in the
City of David. 29 Ahaziah had become king over
Judah in the eleventh year of the reign of Joram
son of Ahab.

The Death of Jezebel

30 When Jezebel, the queen mother, heard that
Jehu had come to Jezreel, she painted her eyelids
and fixed her hair and sat at a window. 31 When
Jehu entered the gate of the palace, she shouted
at him, "Have you come in peace, you murderer?
You're just like Zimri, who murdered his master!"

32 Jehu looked up and saw her at the window
and shouted, "Who is on my side?" And two or
three eunuchs looked out at him. 33 "Throw her
down!" Jehu yelled. So they threw her out the
window, and her blood spattered against the wall
and on the horses. And Jehu trampled her body
under his horses' hooves.

34 Then Jehu went into the palace and ate and
drank. Afterward he said, "Someone go and bury
this cursed woman, for she is the daughter of a
king." 35 But when they went out to bury her, they
found only her skull, her feet, and her hands.

36 When they returned and told Jehu, he
stated, "This fulfills the message from the LORD,
which he spoke through his servant Elijah from
Tishbe: 'At the plot of land in Jezreel, dogs will eat
Jezebel's body. 37 Her remains will be scattered
like dung on the plot of land in Jezreel, so that no
one will be able to recognize her.'"

CHAPTER 10

Jehu Kills Ahab's Family

Ahab had seventy sons living in the city of Samaria. So Jehu wrote letters and sent them to
Samaria, to the elders and officials of the city,
and to the guardians of King Ahab's sons. He
said, 2 "The king's sons are with you, and you have
at your disposal chariots, horses, a fortified city,
and weapons. As soon as you receive this letter,
3 select the best qualified of your master's sons to
be your king, and prepare to fight for Ahab's dynasty."

4 But they were paralyzed with fear and said,
"We've seen that two kings couldn't stand
against this man! What can we do?"

5 So the palace and city administrators, together with the elders and the guardians of the
king's sons, sent this message to Jehu: "We are
your servants and will do anything you tell us. We
will not make anyone king; do whatever you
think is best."

6 Jehu responded with a second letter: "If you
are on my side and are going to obey me, bring
the heads of your master's sons to me at Jezreel
by this time tomorrow." Now the seventy sons of
the king were being cared for by the leaders of
Samaria, where they had been raised since childhood. 7 When the letter arrived, the leaders
killed all seventy of the king's sons. They placed
their heads in baskets and presented them to
Jehu at Jezreel.

8 A messenger went to Jehu and said, "They
have brought the heads of the king's sons."

So Jehu ordered, "Pile them in two heaps at the
entrance of the city gate, and leave them there
until morning."

9 In the morning he went out and spoke to the
crowd that had gathered around them. "You are
not to blame," he told them. "I am the one who
conspired against my master and killed him. But
who killed all these? 10 You can be sure that the
message of the LORD that was spoken concerning
Ahab's family will not fail. The LORD declared
through his servant Elijah that this would happen." 11 Then Jehu killed all who were left of
Ahab's relatives living in Jezreel and all his important officials, his personal friends, and his priests.
So Ahab was left without a single survivor.

12 Then Jehu set out for Samaria. Along the
way, while he was at Beth-eked of the Shepherds,
13 he met some relatives of King Ahaziah of Judah. "Who are you?" he asked them.

And they replied, "We are relatives of King
Ahaziah. We are going to visit the sons of King
Ahab and the sons of the queen mother."

14“Take them alive!” Jehu shouted to his men. And they captured all forty-two of them and killed them at the well of Beth-eked. None of them escaped.

15When Jehu left there, he met Jehonadab son of Recab, who was coming to meet him. After they had greeted each other, Jehu said to him, “Are you as loyal to me as I am to you?”

“Yes, I am,” Jehonadab replied.

“If you are,” Jehu said, “then give me your hand.” So Jehonadab put out his hand, and Jehu helped him into the chariot. 16Then Jehu said, “Now come with me, and see how devoted I am to the LORD.” So Jehonadab rode along with him.

17When Jehu arrived in Samaria, he killed everyone who was left there from Ahab’s family, just as the LORD had promised through Elijah.

Jehu Kills the Priests of Baal

18Then Jehu called a meeting of all the people of the city and said to them, “Ahab’s worship of Baal was nothing compared to the way I will worship him! 19Therefore, summon all the prophets and worshipers of Baal, and call together all his priests. See to it that every one of them comes, for I am going to offer a great sacrifice to Baal. Anyone who fails to come will be put to death.” But Jehu’s cunning plan was to destroy all the worshipers of Baal.

20Then Jehu ordered, “Prepare a solemn assembly to worship Baal!” So they did. 21He sent messengers throughout all Israel summoning those who worshiped Baal. They all came—not a single one remained behind—and they filled the temple of Baal from one end to the other. 22And Jehu instructed the keeper of the wardrobe, “Be sure that every worshiper of Baal wears one of these robes.” So robes were given to them.

23Then Jehu went into the temple of Baal with Jehonadab son of Recab. Jehu said to the worshipers of Baal, “Make sure no one who worships the LORD is here—only those who worship Baal.” 24So they were all inside the temple to offer sacrifices and burnt offerings. Now Jehu had stationed eighty of his men outside the building and had warned them, “If you let anyone escape, you will pay for it with your own life.”

25As soon as Jehu had finished sacrificing the burnt offering, he commanded his guards and officers, “Go in and kill all of them. Don’t let a single one escape!” So they killed them all with their swords, and the guards and officers dragged their bodies outside. Then Jehu’s men went into the innermost fortress of the temple of Baal. 26They dragged out the sacred pillar used in the worship of Baal and burned it. 27They smashed the sacred pillar and wrecked the temple of Baal, converting it into a public toilet, as it remains to this day.

28In this way, Jehu destroyed every trace of Baal worship from Israel. 29He did not, however, destroy the gold calves at Bethel and Dan, with which Jeroboam son of Nebat had caused Israel to sin.

30Nonetheless the LORD said to Jehu, “You have done well in following my instructions to destroy the family of Ahab. Therefore, your descendants will be kings of Israel down to the fourth generation.” 31But Jehu did not obey the Law of the LORD, the God of Israel, with all his heart. He refused to turn from the sins that Jeroboam had led Israel to commit.

The Death of Jehu

32At about that time the LORD began to cut down the size of Israel’s territory. King Hazael conquered several sections of the country 33east of the Jordan River, including all of Gilead, Gad, Reuben, and Manasseh. He conquered the area from the town of Aroer by the Arnon Gorge to as far north as Gilead and Bashan.

34The rest of the events in Jehu’s reign—everything he did and all his achievements—are recorded in *The Book of the History of the Kings of Israel.*

35When Jehu died, he was buried in Samaria. Then his son Jehoahaz became the next king. 36In all, Jehu reigned over Israel from Samaria for twenty-eight years.

CHAPTER 11

Queen Athaliah Rules in Judah

When Athaliah, the mother of King Ahaziah of Judah, learned that her son was dead, she began to destroy the rest of the royal family. 2But Ahaziah’s sister Jehosheba, the daughter of King Jehoram, took Ahaziah’s infant son, Joash, and stole him away from among the rest of the king’s children, who were about to be killed. She put Joash and his nurse in a bedroom, and they hid him from Athaliah, so the child was not murdered. 3Joash remained hidden in the Temple of the LORD for six years while Athaliah ruled over the land.

Revolt against Athaliah

4In the seventh year of Athaliah’s reign, Jehoiada the priest summoned the commanders, the Carite mercenaries, and the palace guards to come to the Temple of the LORD. He made a solemn

pact with them and made them swear an oath of
loyalty there in the LORD's Temple; then he
showed them the king's son.
5Jehoiada told them, "This is what you must
do. A third of you who are on duty on the Sabbath are to guard the royal palace itself. 6An-
other third of you are to stand guard at the Sur
Gate. And the final third must stand guard behind the palace guard. These three groups will
all guard the palace. 7The other two units who
are off duty on the Sabbath must stand guard
for the king at the LORD's Temple. 8Form a bodyguard around the king and keep your weapons
in hand. Kill anyone who tries to break through.
Stay with the king wherever he goes."
9So the commanders did everything as Jehoiada the priest ordered. The commanders took
charge of the men reporting for duty that Sabbath, as well as those who were going off duty.
They brought them all to Jehoiada the priest,
10and he supplied them with the spears and
small shields that had once belonged to King
David and were stored in the Temple of the
LORD. 11The palace guards stationed themselves around the king, with their weapons
ready. They formed a line from the south side of
the Temple around to the north side and all
around the altar.
12Then Jehoiada brought out Joash, the
king's son, placed the crown on his head, and
presented him with a copy of God's laws. They
anointed him and proclaimed him king, and
everyone clapped their hands and shouted,
"Long live the king!"

The Death of Athaliah

13When Athaliah heard the noise made by the
palace guards and the people, she hurried to the
LORD's Temple to see what was happening.
14When she arrived, she saw the newly crowned
king standing in his place of authority by the
pillar, as was the custom at times of coronation.
The commanders and trumpeters were surrounding him, and people from all over the land
were rejoicing and blowing trumpets. When
Athaliah saw all this, she tore her clothes in despair and shouted, "Treason! Treason!"
15Then Jehoiada the priest ordered the commanders who were in charge of the troops,
"Take her to the soldiers in front of the Temple,
and kill anyone who tries to rescue her." For the
priest had said, "She must not be killed in the
Temple of the LORD." 16So they seized her and
led her out to the gate where horses enter the
palace grounds, and she was killed there.

Jehoiada's Religious Reforms

17Then Jehoiada made a covenant between the
LORD and the king and the people that they
would be the LORD's people. He also made a covenant between the king and the people. 18And
all the people of the land went over to the temple of Baal and tore it down. They demolished
the altars and smashed the idols to pieces, and
they killed Mattan the priest of Baal in front of
the altars.
Jehoiada the priest stationed guards at the
Temple of the LORD. 19Then the commanders,
the Carite mercenaries, the palace guards, and all
the people of the land escorted the king from the
Temple of the LORD. They went through the gate
of the guards and into the palace, and the king
took his seat on the royal throne. 20So all the
people of the land rejoiced, and the city was
peaceful because Athaliah had been killed at the
king's palace.
21Joash was seven years old when he became
king.

CHAPTER 12

Joash Repairs the Temple

Joash began to rule over Judah in the seventh
year of King Jehu's reign in Israel. He reigned in
Jerusalem forty years. His mother was Zibiah
from Beersheba. 2All his life Joash did what was
pleasing in the LORD's sight because Jehoiada the
priest instructed him. 3Yet even so, he did not
destroy the pagan shrines, and the people still offered sacrifices and burned incense there.
4One day King Joash said to the priests, "Collect all the money brought as a sacred offering to
the LORD's Temple, whether it is a regular assessment, a payment of vows, or a voluntary gift. 5Let
the priests take some of that money to pay for
whatever repairs are needed at the Temple."
6But by the twenty-third year of Joash's reign,
the priests still had not repaired the Temple. 7So
King Joash called for Jehoiada and the other
priests and asked them, "Why haven't you repaired the Temple? Don't use any more money
for your own needs. From now on, it must all be
spent on Temple repairs." 8So the priests agreed
not to accept any more money from the people,
and they also agreed to let others take responsibility for repairing the Temple.
9Then Jehoiada the priest bored a hole in the
lid of a large chest and set it on the right-hand side
of the altar at the entrance of the Temple of the
LORD. The priests guarding the entrance put all of
the people's contributions into the chest. 10When-
ever the chest became full, the court secretary

and the high priest counted the money that had
been brought to the LORD's Temple and put it into
bags. 11 Then they gave the money to the construction supervisors, who used it to pay the people
working on the LORD's Temple—the carpenters,
the builders, 12 the masons, and the stonecutters.
They also used the money to buy the timber and
the finished stone needed for repairing the LORD's
Temple, and they paid any other expenses related
to the Temple's restoration.
13 The money brought to the Temple was not
used for making silver bowls, lamp snuffers, basins, trumpets, or other articles of gold or silver for
the Temple of the LORD. 14 It was paid to the workmen, who used it for the Temple repairs. 15 No accounting of this money was required from the
construction supervisors, because they were honest and trustworthy men. 16 However, the money
that was contributed for guilt offerings and sin offerings was not brought into the LORD's Temple. It
was given to the priests for their own use.

The End of Joash's Reign

17 About this time King Hazael of Aram went to
war against Gath and captured it. Then he turned
to attack Jerusalem. 18 King Joash collected all
the sacred objects that Jehoshaphat, Jehoram,
and Ahaziah, the previous kings of Judah, had
dedicated, along with what he himself had dedicated. He sent them all to Hazael, along with all
the gold in the treasuries of the LORD's Temple
and the royal palace. So Hazael called off his attack on Jerusalem.
19 The rest of the events in Joash's reign and
everything he did are recorded in *The Book of the
History of the Kings of Judah*.
20 Joash's officers plotted against him and assassinated him at Beth-millo on the road to Silla.
21 The assassins were Jozacar son of Shimeath
and Jehozabad son of Shomer—both trusted advisers. Joash was buried with his ancestors in the
City of David. Then his son Amaziah became the
next king.

CHAPTER 13
Jehoahaz Rules in Israel

Jehoahaz son of Jehu began to rule over Israel in
the twenty-third year of King Joash's reign in Judah. He reigned in Samaria seventeen years.
2 But he did what was evil in the LORD's sight. He
followed the example of Jeroboam son of Nebat,
continuing the sins that Jeroboam had led Israel
to commit. 3 So the LORD was very angry with Israel, and he allowed King Hazael of Aram and his
son Ben-hadad to defeat them repeatedly.

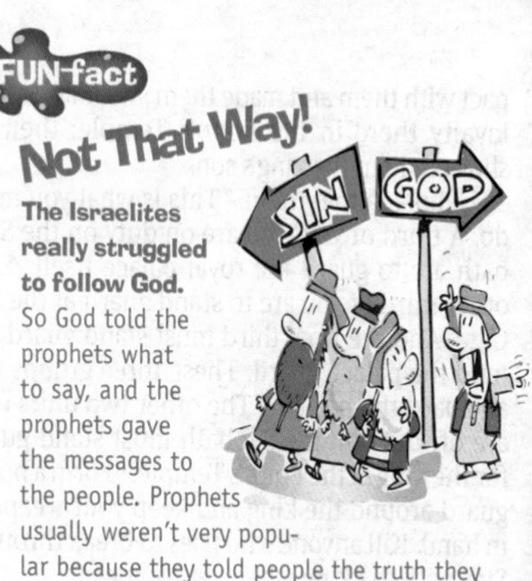

The Israelites really struggled to follow God. So God told the prophets what to say, and the prophets gave the messages to the people. Prophets usually weren't very popular because they told people the truth they didn't want to hear—like "stop sinning." Some really famous prophets include Moses, Isaiah, Elijah, Daniel, and Jeremiah.

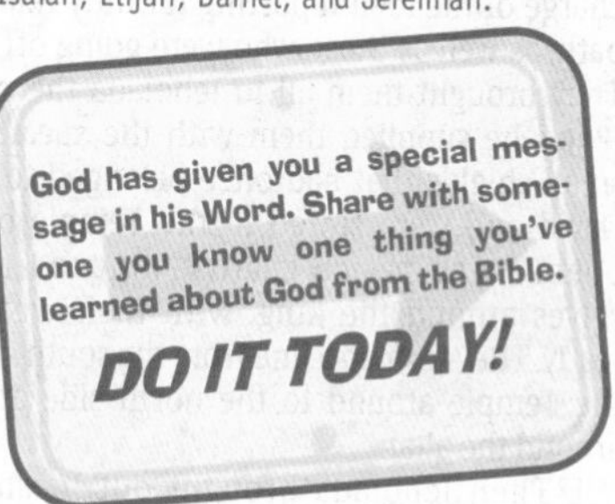

God has given you a special message in his Word. Share with someone you know one thing you've learned about God from the Bible.
DO IT TODAY!

4 Then Jehoahaz prayed for the LORD's help,
and the LORD heard his prayer, for he could see
how severely the king of Aram was oppressing Israel. 5 So the LORD provided someone to rescue
the Israelites from the tyranny of the Arameans.
Then Israel lived in safety again as they had in
former days.
6 But they continued to sin, following the evil
example of Jeroboam. They also allowed the
Asherah pole in Samaria to remain standing.
7 Finally, Jehoahaz's army was reduced to 50
charioteers, 10 chariots, and 10,000 foot soldiers. The king of Aram had killed the others,
trampling them like dust under his feet.
8 The rest of the events in Jehoahaz's reign—
everything he did and the extent of his power—
are recorded in *The Book of the History of the
Kings of Israel*. 9 When Jehoahaz died, he was
buried in Samaria. Then his son Jehoash became
the next king.

Jehoash Rules in Israel

10 Jehoash son of Jehoahaz began to rule over Israel in the thirty-seventh year of King Joash's

reign in Judah. He reigned in Samaria sixteen
years. 11But he did what was evil in the LORD's
sight. He refused to turn from the sins that Jeroboam son of Nebat had led Israel to commit.

12The rest of the events in Jehoash's reign and
everything he did, including the extent of his
power and his war with King Amaziah of Judah,
are recorded in *The Book of the History of the*
Kings of Israel. 13When Jehoash died, he was
buried in Samaria with the kings of Israel. Then
his son Jeroboam II became the next king.

Elisha's Final Prophecy

14When Elisha was in his last illness, King Jehoash of Israel visited him and wept over him. "My
father! My father! I see the chariots and charioteers of Israel!" he cried.

15Elisha told him, "Get a bow and some arrows." And the king did as he was told. 16Elisha
told him, "Put your hand on the bow," and Elisha
laid his own hands on the king's hands.

17Then he commanded, "Open that eastern
window," and he opened it. Then he said,
"Shoot!" So he shot an arrow. Elisha proclaimed,
"This is the LORD's arrow, an arrow of victory over
Aram, for you will completely conquer the Ara-
means at Aphek."

18Then he said, "Now pick up the other arrows and strike them against the ground." So the
king picked them up and struck the ground
three times. 19But the man of God was angry
with him. "You should have struck the ground
five or six times!" he exclaimed. "Then you
would have beaten Aram until it was entirely destroyed. Now you will be victorious only three
times."

20Then Elisha died and was buried.

Groups of Moabite raiders used to invade the
land each spring. 21Once when some Israelites
were burying a man, they spied a band of these
raiders. So they hastily threw the corpse into the
tomb of Elisha and fled. But as soon as the body
touched Elisha's bones, the dead man revived
and jumped to his feet!

22King Hazael of Aram had oppressed Israel
during the entire reign of King Jehoahaz. 23But
the LORD was gracious and merciful to the people of Israel, and they were not totally destroyed.
He pitied them because of his covenant with
Abraham, Isaac, and Jacob. And to this day he still
has not completely destroyed them or banished
them from his presence.

24King Hazael of Aram died, and his son Ben-
hadad became the next king. 25Then Jehoash
son of Jehoahaz recaptured from Ben-hadad son
of Hazael the towns that had been taken from
Jehoash's father, Jehoahaz. Jehoash defeated
Ben-hadad on three occasions, and he recovered
the Israelite towns.

CHAPTER **14**

Amaziah Rules in Judah

Amaziah son of Joash began to rule over Judah in
the second year of the reign of King Jehoash of
Israel. 2Amaziah was twenty-five years old when
he became king, and he reigned in Jerusalem
twenty-nine years. His mother was Jehoaddin
from Jerusalem. 3Amaziah did what was pleasing in the LORD's sight, but not like his ancestor
David. Instead, he followed the example of his father, Joash. 4Amaziah did not destroy the pagan
shrines, and the people still offered sacrifices
and burned incense there.

5When Amaziah was well established as king,
he executed the officials who had assassinated
his father. 6However, he did not kill the children
of the assassins, for he obeyed the command of
the LORD as written by Moses in the Book of the
Law: "Parents must not be put to death for the
sins of their children, nor children for the sins of
their parents. Those deserving to die must be put
to death for their own crimes."

7Amaziah also killed 10,000 Edomites in the
Valley of Salt. He also conquered Sela and
changed its name to Joktheel, as it is called to
this day.

8One day Amaziah sent messengers with this
challenge to Israel's king Jehoash, the son of Jehoahaz and grandson of Jehu: "Come and meet
me in battle!"

9But King Jehoash of Israel replied to King
Amaziah of Judah with this story: "Out in the
Lebanon mountains, a thistle sent a message to a
mighty cedar tree: 'Give your daughter in marriage to my son.' But just then a wild animal of
Lebanon came by and stepped on the thistle,
crushing it!

10"You have indeed defeated Edom, and you
are proud of it. But be content with your victory
and stay at home! Why stir up trouble that will
only bring disaster on you and the people of
Judah?"

11But Amaziah refused to listen, so King Jehoash of Israel mobilized his army against King Amaziah of Judah. The two armies drew up their
battle lines at Beth-shemesh in Judah. 12Judah
was routed by the army of Israel, and its army scattered and fled for home. 13King Jehoash of Israel
captured Judah's king, Amaziah son of Joash and
grandson of Ahaziah, at Beth-shemesh. Then

he marched to Jerusalem, where he demolished
600 feet of Jerusalem's wall, from the Ephraim
Gate to the Corner Gate. 14He carried off all the
gold and silver and all the articles from the Temple of the LORD. He also seized the treasures from
the royal palace, along with hostages, and then returned to Samaria.

15The rest of the events in Jehoash's reign
and everything he did, including the extent of
his power and his war with King Amaziah of
Judah, are recorded in *The Book of the History
of the Kings of Israel.* 16When Jehoash died,
he was buried in Samaria with the kings of Israel. And his son Jeroboam II became the next
king.

17King Amaziah of Judah lived for fifteen
years after the death of King Jehoash of Israel.
18The rest of the events in Amaziah's reign are
recorded in *The Book of the History of the Kings
of Judah.*

19There was a conspiracy against Amaziah's
life in Jerusalem, and he fled to Lachish. But his
enemies sent assassins after him, and they killed
him there. 20They brought his body back to Jerusalem on a horse, and he was buried with his ancestors in the City of David.

21All the people of Judah had crowned Amaziah's sixteen-year-old son, Uzziah, as king in
place of his father, Amaziah. 22After his father's
death, Uzziah rebuilt the town of Elath and restored it to Judah.

Jeroboam II Rules in Israel

23Jeroboam II, the son of Jehoash, began to rule
over Israel in the fifteenth year of King Amaziah's reign in Judah. He reigned in Samaria
forty-one years. 24He did what was evil in the
LORD's sight. He refused to turn from the sins
that Jeroboam son of Nebat had led Israel to
commit. 25Jeroboam II recovered the territories
of Israel between Lebo-hamath and the Dead
Sea, just as the LORD, the God of Israel, had promised through Jonah son of Amittai, the prophet
from Gath-hepher.

26For the LORD saw the bitter suffering of
everyone in Israel, and that there was no one in
Israel, slave or free, to help them. 27And because
the LORD had not said he would blot out the
name of Israel completely, he used Jeroboam II,
the son of Jehoash, to save them.

28The rest of the events in the reign of Jeroboam II and everything he did—including the extent of his power, his wars, and how he recovered
for Israel both Damascus and Hamath, which had
belonged to Judah—are recorded in *The Book of
the History of the Kings of Israel.* 29When Jeroboam II died, he was buried in Samaria with the
kings of Israel. Then his son Zechariah became
the next king.

CHAPTER **15**

Uzziah Rules in Judah

Uzziah son of Amaziah began to rule over Judah
in the twenty-seventh year of the reign of King
Jeroboam II of Israel. 2He was sixteen years old
when he became king, and he reigned in Jerusalem fifty-two years. His mother was Jecoliah
from Jerusalem.

3He did what was pleasing in the LORD's sight,
just as his father, Amaziah, had done. 4But he did
not destroy the pagan shrines, and the people
still offered sacrifices and burned incense there.
5The LORD struck the king with leprosy, which
lasted until the day he died. He lived in isolation
in a separate house. The king's son Jotham was
put in charge of the royal palace, and he governed the people of the land.

6The rest of the events in Uzziah's reign and
everything he did are recorded in *The Book of the
History of the Kings of Judah.* 7When Uzziah
died, he was buried with his ancestors in the City
of David. And his son Jotham became the next
king.

Zechariah Rules in Israel

8Zechariah son of Jeroboam II began to rule over
Israel in the thirty-eighth year of King Uzziah's
reign in Judah. He reigned in Samaria six months.
9Zechariah did what was evil in the LORD's sight,
as his ancestors had done. He refused to turn
from the sins that Jeroboam son of Nebat had led
Israel to commit. 10Then Shallum son of Jabesh
conspired against Zechariah, assassinated him in
public, and became the next king.

11The rest of the events in Zechariah's reign
are recorded in *The Book of the History of the
Kings of Israel.* 12So the LORD's message to Jehu
came true: "Your descendants will be kings of Israel down to the fourth generation."

Shallum Rules in Israel

13Shallum son of Jabesh began to rule over Israel
in the thirty-ninth year of King Uzziah's reign in
Judah. Shallum reigned in Samaria only one
month. 14Then Menahem son of Gadi went to Samaria from Tirzah and assassinated him, and he
became the next king.

15The rest of the events in Shallum's reign, including his conspiracy, are recorded in *The Book
of the History of the Kings of Israel.*

Menahem Rules in Israel

16 At that time Menahem destroyed the town of
Tappuah and all the surrounding countryside as
far as Tirzah, because its citizens refused to surrender the town. He killed the entire population
and ripped open the pregnant women.

17 Menahem son of Gadi began to rule over Israel in the thirty-ninth year of King Uzziah's
reign in Judah. He reigned in Samaria ten years.
18 But Menahem did what was evil in the LORD's
sight. During his entire reign, he refused to turn
from the sins that Jeroboam son of Nebat had led
Israel to commit.

19 Then King Tiglath-pileser of Assyria invaded
the land. But Menahem paid him thirty-seven
tons of silver to gain his support in tightening his
grip on royal power. 20 Menahem extorted the
money from the rich of Israel, demanding that
each of them pay fifty pieces of silver to the king
of Assyria. So the king of Assyria turned from attacking Israel and did not stay in the land.

21 The rest of the events in Menahem's reign
and everything he did are recorded in *The Book of
the History of the Kings of Israel.* 22 When Menahem died, his son Pekahiah became the next
king.

Pekahiah Rules in Israel

23 Pekahiah son of Menahem began to rule over
Israel in the fiftieth year of King Uzziah's reign in
Judah. He reigned in Samaria two years. 24 But
Pekahiah did what was evil in the LORD's sight.
He refused to turn from the sins that Jeroboam
son of Nebat had led Israel to commit.

25 Then Pekah son of Remaliah, the commander of Pekahiah's army, conspired against
him. With fifty men from Gilead, Pekah assassinated the king, along with Argob and Arieh, in
the citadel of the palace at Samaria. And Pekah
reigned in his place.

26 The rest of the events in Pekahiah's reign
and everything he did are recorded in *The Book
of the History of the Kings of Israel.*

Pekah Rules in Israel

27 Pekah son of Remaliah began to rule over Israel in the fifty-second year of King Uzziah's reign
in Judah. He reigned in Samaria twenty years.
28 But Pekah did what was evil in the LORD's sight.
He refused to turn from the sins that Jeroboam
son of Nebat had led Israel to commit.

29 During Pekah's reign, King Tiglath-pileser
of Assyria attacked Israel again, and he captured
the towns of Ijon, Abel-beth-maacah, Janoah, Kedesh, and Hazor. He also conquered the regions
of Gilead, Galilee, and all of Naphtali, and he took
the people to Assyria as captives. 30 Then Hoshea
son of Elah conspired against Pekah and assassinated him. He began to rule over Israel in the
twentieth year of Jotham son of Uzziah.

31 The rest of the events in Pekah's reign and
everything he did are recorded in *The Book of the
History of the Kings of Israel.*

Jotham Rules in Judah

32 Jotham son of Uzziah began to rule over Judah
in the second year of King Pekah's reign in Israel.
33 He was twenty-five years old when he became
king, and he reigned in Jerusalem sixteen years.
His mother was Jerusha, the daughter of Zadok.

34 Jotham did what was pleasing in the LORD's
sight. He did everything his father, Uzziah, had
done. 35 But he did not destroy the pagan shrines,
and the people still offered sacrifices and
burned incense there. He rebuilt the upper gate
of the Temple of the LORD.

36 The rest of the events in Jotham's reign and
everything he did are recorded in *The Book of the
History of the Kings of Judah.* 37 In those days the
LORD began to send King Rezin of Aram and King
Pekah of Israel to attack Judah. 38 When Jotham
died, he was buried with his ancestors in the City
of David. And his son Ahaz became the next
king.

CHAPTER 16

Ahaz Rules in Judah

Ahaz son of Jotham began to rule over Judah in
the seventeenth year of King Pekah's reign in Israel. 2 Ahaz was twenty years old when he became king, and he reigned in Jerusalem sixteen
years. He did not do what was pleasing in the
sight of the LORD his God, as his ancestor David
had done. 3 Instead, he followed the example of
the kings of Israel, even sacrificing his own son
in the fire. In this way, he followed the detestable
practices of the pagan nations the LORD had
driven from the land ahead of the Israelites. 4 He
offered sacrifices and burned incense at the pagan shrines and on the hills and under every
green tree.

5 Then King Rezin of Aram and King Pekah of
Israel came up to attack Jerusalem. They besieged Ahaz but could not conquer him. 6 At that
time the king of Edom recovered the town of
Elath for Edom. He drove out the people of Judah
and sent Edomites to live there, as they do to this
day.

7 King Ahaz sent messengers to King Tiglath-
pileser of Assyria with this message: "I am your

servant and your vassal. Come up and rescue me
from the attacking armies of Aram and Israel."
8Then Ahaz took the silver and gold from the
Temple of the LORD and the palace treasury and
sent it as a payment to the Assyrian king. 9So the
king of Assyria attacked the Aramean capital of
Damascus and led its population away as captives, resettling them in Kir. He also killed King
Rezin.

10King Ahaz then went to Damascus to meet
with King Tiglath-pileser of Assyria. While he
was there, he took special note of the altar. Then
he sent a model of the altar to Uriah the priest,
along with its design in full detail. 11Uriah followed the king's instructions and built an altar
just like it, and it was ready before the king
returned from Damascus. 12When the king returned, he inspected the altar and made offerings on it. 13He presented a burnt offering and a
grain offering, he poured out a liquid offering,
and he sprinkled the blood of peace offerings on
the altar.

14Then King Ahaz removed the old bronze altar from its place in front of the LORD's Temple,
between the entrance and the new altar, and
placed it on the north side of the new altar. 15He
told Uriah the priest, "Use the new altar for the
morning sacrifices of burnt offering, the evening grain offering, the king's burnt offering and
grain offering, and the burnt offerings of all the
people, as well as their grain offerings and liquid
offerings. Sprinkle the blood from all the burnt
offerings and sacrifices on the new altar. The
bronze altar will be for my personal use only."
16Uriah the priest did just as King Ahaz commanded him.

17Then the king removed the side panels and
basins from the portable water carts. He also removed the great bronze basin called the Sea from
the backs of the bronze oxen and placed it on the
stone pavement. 18In deference to the king of Assyria, he also removed the canopy that had been
constructed inside the palace for use on the Sabbath day, as well as the king's outer entrance to
the Temple of the LORD.

19The rest of the events in Ahaz's reign and
everything he did are recorded in *The Book of the
History of the Kings of Judah.* 20When Ahaz died,
he was buried with his ancestors in the City of David. Then his son Hezekiah became the next king.

CHAPTER 17

Hoshea Rules in Israel

Hoshea son of Elah began to rule over Israel in
the twelfth year of King Ahaz's reign in Judah. He
reigned in Samaria nine years. 2He did what was
evil in the LORD's sight, but not to the same extent as the kings of Israel who ruled before him.

3King Shalmaneser of Assyria attacked King
Hoshea, so Hoshea was forced to pay heavy tribute to Assyria. 4But Hoshea stopped paying the
annual tribute and conspired against the king of
Assyria by asking King So of Egypt to help him
shake free of Assyria's power. When the king of
Assyria discovered this treachery, he seized Hoshea and put him in prison.

Samaria Falls to Assyria

5Then the king of Assyria invaded the entire
land, and for three years he besieged the city of
Samaria. 6Finally, in the ninth year of King Hoshea's reign, Samaria fell, and the people of Israel
were exiled to Assyria. They were settled in colonies in Halah, along the banks of the Habor River
in Gozan, and in the cities of the Medes.

7This disaster came upon the people of Israel
because they worshiped other gods. They
sinned against the LORD their God, who had
brought them safely out of Egypt and had rescued them from the power of Pharaoh, the king
of Egypt. 8They had followed the practices of
the pagan nations the LORD had driven from the
land ahead of them, as well as the practices the
kings of Israel had introduced. 9The people of
Israel had also secretly done many things that
were not pleasing to the LORD their God. They
built pagan shrines for themselves in all their
towns, from the smallest outpost to the largest
walled city. 10They set up sacred pillars and
Asherah poles at the top of every hill and under
every green tree. 11They offered sacrifices on all
the hilltops, just like the nations the LORD had
driven from the land ahead of them. So the people of Israel had done many evil things, arousing the LORD's anger. 12Yes, they worshiped
idols, despite the LORD's specific and repeated
warnings.

13Again and again the LORD had sent his
prophets and seers to warn both Israel and Judah: "Turn from all your evil ways. Obey my commands and decrees—the entire law that I
commanded your ancestors to obey, and that I
gave you through my servants the prophets."

14But the Israelites would not listen. They were
as stubborn as their ancestors who had refused
to believe in the LORD their God. 15They rejected
his decrees and the covenant he had made with
their ancestors, and they despised all his warnings. They worshiped worthless idols, so they became worthless themselves. They followed the

God Uses Common People

God uses regular people to do his work—people like you and me! Don't believe it? Just look at these people. Then make a list of ways God might use you!

Person	Known As	Task	Bible Reference
JOSEPH	A SLAVE	To save his family	GENESIS 39–47
MOSES	A SHEPHERD in exile (and a murderer)	To lead Israel out of bondage and into the Promised Land	EXODUS 3
GIDEON	A FARMER	To deliver Israel from Midian	JUDGES 6:11
HANNAH	A HOUSEWIFE	To be the mother of Samuel	1 SAMUEL 1
DAVID	A SHEPHERD BOY and youngest of the family	To be Israel's greatest king	1 SAMUEL 16
ESTHER	AN ORPHAN	To save her people from massacre	ESTHER
MARY	A PEASANT GIRL	To be the mother of Christ	LUKE 1:27-38
MATTHEW	A TAX COLLECTOR	To be an apostle and Gospel writer	MATTHEW 9:9
LUKE	A GREEK DOCTOR	To be a companion of Paul and a Gospel writer	COLOSSIANS 4:14
PETER	A FISHERMAN	To be an apostle, a leader of the church, and a writer of two New Testament letters	MATTHEW 4:18-20

HOW WILL GOD USE YOU?

YOUR NAME	A...	To...	PHILIPPIANS 4:13

About the Old Testament

The first five books of the Bible are called the Pentateuch. (*Pentateuch* means "five books.") These books cover the creation of the world through the start of the nation of Israel. Talk about excitement—the beginning of the universe, a big flood, plagues, a great escape, miraculous food from heaven, the Ten Commandments—you have to read this!

- **Genesis**
- **Exodus**
- **Leviticus**
- **Numbers**
- **Deuteronomy**

These next 12 books tell tons of history about the nation of Israel. (They also tell about some of the most famous women in the Bible!)

- **Joshua**
- **Judges**
- **Ruth**
- **1 and 2 Samuel**
- **1 and 2 Kings**
- **1 and 2 Chronicles**
- **Ezra**
- **Nehemiah**
- **Esther**

These six books are the poetry books of the Bible. (Roses are red; violets are blue...Oh wait, not that kind of poetry!) Hebrew poetry was very different from ours, but it still expressed the writers' deepest emotions. (Just read David's psalms to see how a person can pour out his heart to God, no matter whether he's happy or sad. David knew he could talk to God about anything—and so can you!)

- **Job**
- **Psalms**
- **Proverbs**
- **Ecclesiastes**
- **Song of Songs**
- **Lamentations**

The rest of the books in the Old Testament are called the books of the prophets. There were major and minor prophets, but that had nothing to do with how important they were. It had to do with how long their writings were. God used prophets to pass his messages on to the people of Israel (and to us). These guys were cool—read all about them and their messages from God!

- **Isaiah**
- **Jeremiah**
- **Ezekiel**
- **Daniel**
- **Hosea**
- **Joel**
- **Amos**
- **Obadiah**
- **Jonah**
- **Micah**
- **Nahum**
- **Habakkuk**
- **Zephaniah**
- **Haggai**
- **Zechariah**
- **Malachi**

As you read the Old Testament, keep a list of your favorite people and stories. Then share your list with someone else!

About the New Testament

The first four books of the New Testament are called the Gospels. And here's something you might not know—Gospel means "Good News." Guess what good news the Gospels tell. Did you guess the good news about Jesus? You're right!

All four Gospels tell about the life of Jesus. But that's not all; they tell about his death and resurrection, too! The writers of the Gospels were Matthew, Mark, Luke, and John. Each of the four writers tried to reach a different audience, so each book contains slightly different details. Matthew wrote mostly to the Jews, Mark wrote to the Christians in Rome, Luke tried to reach the Gentile Christians, and John wrote to new Christians. But God inspired all four Gospel writers, and what they wrote long ago was written for us, too!

Acts, the next book in the New Testament, tells the history of the early Christian church. This book is sometimes called the Acts of the Apostles because it tells how the apostles spread the good news about Jesus after his death and resurrection.

The rest of the New Testament (all except for the last book) consists of the epistles, or letters. The apostle Paul wrote thirteen of the letters. Most of Paul's letters were written to give advice and encouragement to new churches. The rest of the letters are more general in nature. But all of the epistles, just like all of the other books in the Bible, are important for us today, too!

The last book of the Bible is the book of Revelation. It's an apocalyptic book of prophecy, meaning it uses powerful images to tell how the whole story ends! And here's how it ends: God wins, and anyone who believes in Jesus will live with him forever in a new heaven and new earth.

As you read the New Testament, mark your favorite parts. You can underline, use stickers—whatever you want!

God Uses Common Objects

God often uses simple, ordinary objects to accomplish his tasks in the world.

They just need to be dedicated to him for his use. Look at these everyday objects from Bible times to see how God used them. Then ask yourself: What do I have that God can use? Anything and everything is a possible "instrument" for him!

OBJECT	REFERENCE	WHO USED IT?	HOW WAS IT USED?
SHEPHERD'S STAFF	EXODUS 4:2-4	**MOSES**	To work miracles before Pharaoh
RAM'S HORN	JOSHUA 6:3-5	**JOSHUA**	To flatten the walls of Jericho
FLEECE	JUDGES 6:36-40	**GIDEON**	To confirm what God wanted Gideon to do
HORNS, JARS, AND TORCHES	JUDGES 7:19-22	**GIDEON**	To defeat the Midianites
JAWBONE	JUDGES 15:15	**SAMSON**	To kill the enemy: 1,000 Philistines
SMALL STONE	1 SAMUEL 17:40	**DAVID**	To kill Goliath
OIL	2 KINGS 4:1-7	**ELISHA**	To show God's power to provide
RIVER	2 KINGS 5:9-14	**ELISHA**	To heal a man of leprosy
POTTERY	JEREMIAH 18:1-10; 19:1-13	**JEREMIAH**	As an object lesson about God the creator
FIVE LOAVES OF BREAD AND TWO FISH	MARK 6:30-44	**JESUS**	To feed a crowd of over 5,000 people

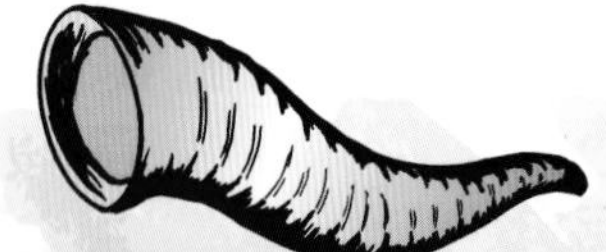

example of the nations around them, disobeying
the LORD's command not to imitate them.
16They rejected all the commands of the LORD
their God and made two calves from metal. They
set up an Asherah pole and worshiped Baal and
all the forces of heaven. 17They even sacrificed
their own sons and daughters in the fire. They
consulted fortune-tellers and practiced sorcery
and sold themselves to evil, arousing the LORD's
anger.
18Because the LORD was very angry with Israel,
he swept them away from his presence. Only the
tribe of Judah remained in the land. 19But even
the people of Judah refused to obey the commands of the LORD their God, for they followed
the evil practices that Israel had introduced.
20The LORD rejected all the descendants of Israel. He punished them by handing them over to
their attackers until he had banished Israel from
his presence.
21For when the LORD tore Israel away from the
kingdom of David, they chose Jeroboam son of
Nebat as their king. But Jeroboam drew Israel
away from following the LORD and made them
commit a great sin. 22And the people of Israel
persisted in all the evil ways of Jeroboam. They
did not turn from these sins 23until the LORD finally swept them away from his presence, just as
all his prophets had warned. So Israel was exiled
from their land to Assyria, where they remain to
this day.

Foreigners Settle in Israel

24The king of Assyria transported groups of people from Babylon, Cuthah, Avva, Hamath, and
Sepharvaim and resettled them in the towns of
Samaria, replacing the people of Israel. They
took possession of Samaria and lived in its
towns. 25But since these foreign settlers did not
worship the LORD when they first arrived, the
LORD sent lions among them, which killed some
of them.
26So a message was sent to the king of Assyria:
"The people you have sent to live in the towns of
Samaria do not know the religious customs of
the God of the land. He has sent lions among
them to destroy them because they have not
worshiped him correctly."
27The king of Assyria then commanded,
"Send one of the exiled priests back to Samaria.
Let him live there and teach the new residents
the religious customs of the God of the land."
28So one of the priests who had been exiled from
Samaria returned to Bethel and taught the new
residents how to worship the LORD.
29But these various groups of foreigners also
continued to worship their own gods. In town after town where they lived, they placed their idols
at the pagan shrines that the people of Samaria
had built. 30Those from Babylon worshiped
idols of their god Succoth-benoth. Those from
Cuthah worshiped their god Nergal. And those
from Hamath worshiped Ashima. 31The Avvites
worshiped their gods Nibhaz and Tartak. And
the people from Sepharvaim even burned their
own children as sacrifices to their gods Adram-
melech and Anammelech.
32These new residents worshiped the LORD,
but they also appointed from among themselves
all sorts of people as priests to offer sacrifices at
their places of worship. 33And though they worshiped the LORD, they continued to follow their
own gods according to the religious customs of
the nations from which they came. 34And this is
still going on today. They continue to follow their
former practices instead of truly worshiping the
LORD and obeying the decrees, regulations, instructions, and commands he gave the descendants of Jacob, whose name he changed to Israel.
35For the LORD had made a covenant with the
descendants of Jacob and commanded them: "Do
not worship any other gods or bow before them or
serve them or offer sacrifices to them. 36But worship only the LORD, who brought you out of Egypt
with great strength and a powerful arm. Bow
down to him alone, and offer sacrifices only to
him. 37Be careful at all times to obey the decrees,
regulations, instructions, and commands that he
wrote for you. You must not worship other gods.
38Do not forget the covenant I made with you, and
do not worship other gods. 39You must worship
only the LORD your God. He is the one who will
rescue you from all your enemies."
40But the people would not listen and continued to follow their former practices. 41So while
these new residents worshiped the LORD, they
also worshiped their idols. And to this day their
descendants do the same.

CHAPTER 18

Hezekiah Rules in Judah

Hezekiah son of Ahaz began to rule over Judah in
the third year of King Hoshea's reign in Israel.
2He was twenty-five years old when he became
king, and he reigned in Jerusalem twenty-nine
years. His mother was Abijah, the daughter of
Zechariah. 3He did what was pleasing in the
LORD's sight, just as his ancestor David had done.
4He removed the pagan shrines, smashed the sacred pillars, and cut down the Asherah poles. He

broke up the bronze serpent that Moses had
made, because the people of Israel had been offering sacrifices to it. The bronze serpent was
called Nehushtan.
5 Hezekiah trusted in the LORD, the God of Israel. There was no one like him among all the
kings of Judah, either before or after his time.
6 He remained faithful to the LORD in everything,
and he carefully obeyed all the commands the
LORD had given Moses. 7 So the LORD was with
him, and Hezekiah was successful in everything
he did. He revolted against the king of Assyria
and refused to pay him tribute. 8 He also conquered the Philistines as far distant as Gaza and
its territory, from their smallest outpost to their
largest walled city.
9 During the fourth year of Hezekiah's reign,
which was the seventh year of King Hoshea's
reign in Israel, King Shalmaneser of Assyria attacked the city of Samaria and began a siege
against it. 10 Three years later, during the sixth
year of King Hezekiah's reign and the ninth year
of King Hoshea's reign in Israel, Samaria fell. 11 At
that time the king of Assyria exiled the Israelites
to Assyria and placed them in colonies in Halah,
along the banks of the Habor River in Gozan, and
in the cities of the Medes. 12 For they refused to
listen to the LORD their God and obey him. Instead, they violated his covenant—all the laws
that Moses the LORD's servant had commanded
them to obey.

Assyria Invades Judah

13 In the fourteenth year of King Hezekiah's
reign, King Sennacherib of Assyria came to attack the fortified towns of Judah and conquered
them. 14 King Hezekiah sent this message to the
king of Assyria at Lachish: "I have done wrong. I
will pay whatever tribute money you demand if
you will only withdraw." The king of Assyria then
demanded a settlement of more than eleven tons
of silver and one ton of gold. 15 To gather this
amount, King Hezekiah used all the silver stored
in the Temple of the LORD and in the palace treasury. 16 Hezekiah even stripped the gold from the
doors of the LORD's Temple and from the
doorposts he had overlaid with gold, and he gave
it all to the Assyrian king.
17 Nevertheless, the king of Assyria sent his
commander in chief, his field commander, and
his chief of staff from Lachish with a huge army
to confront King Hezekiah in Jerusalem. The Assyrians took up a position beside the aqueduct
that feeds water into the upper pool, near the
road leading to the field where cloth is washed.
18 They summoned King Hezekiah, but the king
sent these officials to meet with them: Eliakim
son of Hilkiah, the palace administrator; Shebna
the court secretary; and Joah son of Asaph, the
royal historian.

Sennacherib Threatens Jerusalem

19 Then the Assyrian king's chief of staff told
them to give this message to Hezekiah:

"This is what the great king of Assyria says:
What are you trusting in that makes you so
confident? 20 Do you think that mere words
can substitute for military skill and strength?
Who are you counting on, that you have
rebelled against me? 21 On Egypt? If you lean
on Egypt, it will be like a reed that splinters
beneath your weight and pierces your hand.
Pharaoh, the king of Egypt, is completely
unreliable!
22 "But perhaps you will say to me, 'We are
trusting in the LORD our God!' But isn't he the
one who was insulted by Hezekiah? Didn't
Hezekiah tear down his shrines and altars
and make everyone in Judah and Jerusalem
worship only at the altar here in Jerusalem?
23 "I'll tell you what! Strike a bargain with
my master, the king of Assyria. I will give
you 2,000 horses if you can find that many
men to ride on them! 24 With your tiny army,
how can you think of challenging even the
weakest contingent of my master's troops,
even with the help of Egypt's chariots and
charioteers? 25 What's more, do you think we
have invaded your land without the LORD's
direction? The LORD himself told us, 'Attack
this land and destroy it!'"

26 Then Eliakim son of Hilkiah, Shebna, and
Joah said to the Assyrian chief of staff, "Please
speak to us in Aramaic, for we understand it well.
Don't speak in Hebrew, for the people on the wall
will hear."
27 But Sennacherib's chief of staff replied, "Do
you think my master sent this message only to
you and your master? He wants all the people
to hear it, for when we put this city under siege,
they will suffer along with you. They will be so
hungry and thirsty that they will eat their own
dung and drink their own urine."
28 Then the chief of staff stood and shouted in
Hebrew to the people on the wall, "Listen to this
message from the great king of Assyria! 29 This is
what the king says: Don't let Hezekiah deceive
you. He will never be able to rescue you from my

power. 30Don't let him fool you into trusting in
the LORD by saying, 'The LORD will surely rescue
us. This city will never fall into the hands of the
Assyrian king!'

31"Don't listen to Hezekiah! These are the
terms the king of Assyria is offering: Make peace
with me—open the gates and come out. Then
each of you can continue eating from your own
grapevine and fig tree and drinking from your
own well. 32Then I will arrange to take you to another land like this one—a land of grain and new
wine, bread and vineyards, olive groves and
honey. Choose life instead of death!

"Don't listen to Hezekiah when he tries to mislead you by saying, 'The LORD will rescue us!'
33Have the gods of any other nations ever saved
their people from the king of Assyria? 34What
happened to the gods of Hamath and Arpad?
And what about the gods of Sepharvaim, Hena,
and Ivvah? Did any god rescue Samaria from my
power? 35What god of any nation has ever been
able to save its people from my power? So what
makes you think that the LORD can rescue Jerusalem from me?"

36But the people were silent and did not utter
a word because Hezekiah had commanded
them, "Do not answer him."

37Then Eliakim son of Hilkiah, the palace administrator; Shebna the court secretary; and
Joah son of Asaph, the royal historian, went back
to Hezekiah. They tore their clothes in despair,
and they went in to see the king and told him
what the Assyrian chief of staff had said.

CHAPTER 19

Hezekiah Seeks the LORD's Help

When King Hezekiah heard their report, he tore
his clothes and put on burlap and went into the
Temple of the LORD. 2And he sent Eliakim the
palace administrator, Shebna the court secretary,
and the leading priests, all dressed in burlap, to
the prophet Isaiah son of Amoz. 3They told him,
"This is what King Hezekiah says: Today is a day
of trouble, insults, and disgrace. It is like when a
child is ready to be born, but the mother has no
strength to deliver the baby. 4But perhaps the
LORD your God has heard the Assyrian chief of
staff, sent by the king to defy the living God, and
will punish him for his words. Oh, pray for those
of us who are left!"

5After King Hezekiah's officials delivered the
king's message to Isaiah, 6the prophet replied,
"Say to your master, 'This is what the LORD says:
Do not be disturbed by this blasphemous speech
against me from the Assyrian king's messengers.
7Listen! I myself will move against him, and the
king will receive a message that he is needed at
home. So he will return to his land, where I will
have him killed with a sword.'"

8Meanwhile, the Assyrian chief of staff left Jerusalem and went to consult the king of Assyria,
who had left Lachish and was attacking Libnah.

9Soon afterward King Sennacherib received
word that King Tirhakah of Ethiopia was leading
an army to fight against him. Before leaving to
meet the attack, he sent messengers back to
Hezekiah in Jerusalem with this message:

> 10"This message is for King Hezekiah of
> Judah. Don't let your God, in whom you trust,
> deceive you with promises that Jerusalem will
> not be captured by the king of Assyria. 11You
> know perfectly well what the kings of Assyria
> have done wherever they have gone. They
> have completely destroyed everyone who
> stood in their way! Why should you be any
> different? 12Have the gods of other nations
> rescued them—such nations as Gozan, Haran,
> Rezeph, and the people of Eden who were
> in Tel-assar? My predecessors destroyed them
> all! 13What happened to the king of Hamath
> and the king of Arpad? What happened to
> the kings of Sepharvaim, Hena, and Ivvah?"

14After Hezekiah received the letter from the
messengers and read it, he went up to the LORD's
Temple and spread it out before the LORD. 15And
Hezekiah prayed this prayer before the LORD:
"O LORD, God of Israel, you are enthroned between the mighty cherubim! You alone are God
of all the kingdoms of the earth. You alone created the heavens and the earth. 16Bend down,
O LORD, and listen! Open your eyes, O LORD, and
see! Listen to Sennacherib's words of defiance
against the living God.

17"It is true, LORD, that the kings of Assyria
have destroyed all these nations. 18And they
have thrown the gods of these nations into the
fire and burned them. But of course the Assyrians could destroy them! They were not gods at
all—only idols of wood and stone shaped by human hands. 19Now, O LORD our God, rescue us
from his power; then all the kingdoms of the
earth will know that you alone, O LORD, are God."

Isaiah Predicts Judah's Deliverance

20Then Isaiah son of Amoz sent this message to
Hezekiah: "This is what the LORD, the God of
Israel, says: I have heard your prayer about King

Sennacherib of Assyria. 21 And the LORD has spoken this word against him:

"The virgin daughter of Zion
despises you and laughs at you.
The daughter of Jerusalem
shakes her head in derision as you flee.
22 "Whom have you been defying and
ridiculing?
Against whom did you raise your voice?
At whom did you look with such haughty
eyes?
It was the Holy One of Israel!
23 By your messengers you have defied
the Lord.
You have said, 'With my many chariots
I have conquered the highest mountains—
yes, the remotest peaks of Lebanon.
I have cut down its tallest cedars
and its finest cypress trees.
I have reached its farthest corners
and explored its deepest forests.
24 I have dug wells in many foreign lands
and refreshed myself with their water.
With the sole of my foot
I stopped up all the rivers of Egypt!'
25 "But have you not heard?
I decided this long ago.
Long ago I planned it,
and now I am making it happen.
I planned for you to crush fortified cities
into heaps of rubble.
26 That is why their people have so little power
and are so frightened and confused.
They are as weak as grass,
as easily trampled as tender green shoots.
They are like grass sprouting on a housetop,
scorched before it can grow lush and tall.
27 "But I know you well—
where you stay
and when you come and go.
I know the way you have raged against me.
28 And because of your raging against me
and your arrogance, which I have heard for
myself,
I will put my hook in your nose
and my bit in your mouth.
I will make you return
by the same road on which you came."

29 Then Isaiah said to Hezekiah, "Here is the
proof that what I say is true:

"This year you will eat only what grows up
by itself,
and next year you will eat what springs
up from that.
But in the third year you will plant crops and
harvest them;
you will tend vineyards and eat their fruit.
30 And you who are left in Judah,
who have escaped the ravages of the siege,
will put roots down in your own soil
and will grow up and flourish.
31 For a remnant of my people will spread out
from Jerusalem,
a group of survivors from Mount Zion.
The passionate commitment of the LORD
of Heaven's Armies
will make this happen!

32 "And this is what the LORD says about the king
of Assyria:

"His armies will not enter Jerusalem.
They will not even shoot an arrow at it.
They will not march outside its gates with
their shields
nor build banks of earth against its walls.
33 The king will return to his own country
by the same road on which he came.
He will not enter this city,
says the LORD.
34 For my own honor and for the sake of my
servant David,
I will defend this city and protect it."

35 That night the angel of the LORD went out to
the Assyrian camp and killed 185,000 Assyrian
soldiers. When the surviving Assyrians woke
up the next morning, they found corpses everywhere. 36 Then King Sennacherib of Assyria
broke camp and returned to his own land. He
went home to his capital of Nineveh and stayed
there.

37 One day while he was worshiping in the
temple of his god Nisroch, his sons Adramme-
lech and Sharezer killed him with their swords.
They then escaped to the land of Ararat, and another son, Esarhaddon, became the next king of
Assyria.

CHAPTER 20

Hezekiah's Sickness and Recovery

About that time Hezekiah became deathly ill,
and the prophet Isaiah son of Amoz went to visit
him. He gave the king this message: "This is
what the LORD says: Set your affairs in order, for
you are going to die. You will not recover from
this illness."

God gave the kings of Israel an important job—to lead the people of Israel in God's ways. Most of the kings dropped the ball. Some of the kings ran with it.

Take a quick look at a few of the kings:

GOOD KINGS	BAD KINGS
Asa—1 Kings 15:9-15	**Ahab**—1 Kings 16:29-34
Hezekiah—2 Kings 18:1-8	**Jehoram**—2 Kings 8:16-24
Josiah—2 Kings 22	**Ahaz**—2 Kings 16:1-18

If you're a Christian, you are a prince or a princess—a child of the King of kings! Check it out in John 1:12.

RUN WITH IT! You can lead people to follow God! Make a plan to lead like the good kings led the Israelites:

1. **The good kings stood up for what was right. What is one thing kids in your neighborhood do that is wrong?**

   How can you stand up for what is right?

2. **The good kings told the people about God. Who do you know who doesn't know Jesus?**

   What can you tell that person about Jesus?

3. **The good kings lived for God. What is one thing you do that may lead others away from God? (Maybe something like swearing.)**

   How can you change the way you handle that?

GO FOR THE GOAL!
Power up your plan with prayer—then go and lead like a great king or queen!

2When Hezekiah heard this, he turned his
face to the wall and prayed to the LORD, 3"Remember, O LORD, how I have always been faithful
to you and have served you single-mindedly, always doing what pleases you." Then he broke
down and wept bitterly.
4But before Isaiah had left the middle courtyard, this message came to him from the LORD:
5"Go back to Hezekiah, the leader of my people.
Tell him, 'This is what the LORD, the God of your
ancestor David, says: I have heard your prayer
and seen your tears. I will heal you, and three
days from now you will get out of bed and go to
the Temple of the LORD. 6I will add fifteen years
to your life, and I will rescue you and this city
from the king of Assyria. I will defend this city
for my own honor and for the sake of my servant
David.'"
7Then Isaiah said, "Make an ointment from
figs." So Hezekiah's servants spread the ointment over the boil, and Hezekiah recovered!
8Meanwhile, Hezekiah had said to Isaiah,
"What sign will the LORD give to prove that he
will heal me and that I will go to the Temple of
the LORD three days from now?"
9Isaiah replied, "This is the sign from the
LORD to prove that he will do as he promised.
Would you like the shadow on the sundial to go
forward ten steps or backward ten steps?"
10"The shadow always moves forward," Hezekiah replied, "so that would be easy. Make it go
ten steps backward instead." 11So Isaiah the
prophet asked the LORD to do this, and he caused
the shadow to move ten steps backward on the
sundial of Ahaz!

Envoys from Babylon

12Soon after this, Merodach-baladan son of Baladan, king of Babylon, sent Hezekiah his best
wishes and a gift, for he had heard that Hezekiah
had been very sick. 13Hezekiah received the
Babylonian envoys and showed them everything
in his treasure-houses—the silver, the gold, the
spices, and the aromatic oils. He also took them
to see his armory and showed them everything
in his royal treasuries! There was nothing in his
palace or kingdom that Hezekiah did not show
them.
14Then Isaiah the prophet went to King Hezekiah and asked him, "What did those men want?
Where were they from?"
Hezekiah replied, "They came from the distant land of Babylon."
15"What did they see in your palace?" Isaiah
asked.

"They saw everything," Hezekiah replied. "I showed them everything I own—all my royal treasuries."

16 Then Isaiah said to Hezekiah, "Listen to this message from the LORD: 17 The time is coming when everything in your palace—all the treasures stored up by your ancestors until now—will be carried off to Babylon. Nothing will be left, says the LORD. 18 Some of your very own sons will be taken away into exile. They will become eunuchs who will serve in the palace of Babylon's king."

19 Then Hezekiah said to Isaiah, "This message you have given me from the LORD is good." For the king was thinking, "At least there will be peace and security during my lifetime."

20 The rest of the events in Hezekiah's reign, including the extent of his power and how he built a pool and dug a tunnel to bring water into the city, are recorded in *The Book of the History of the Kings of Judah.* 21 Hezekiah died, and his son Manasseh became the next king.

CHAPTER 21

Manasseh Rules in Judah

Manasseh was twelve years old when he became king, and he reigned in Jerusalem fifty-five years. His mother was Hephzibah. 2 He did what was evil in the LORD's sight, following the detestable practices of the pagan nations that the LORD had driven from the land ahead of the Israelites. 3 He rebuilt the pagan shrines his father, Hezekiah, had destroyed. He constructed altars for Baal and set up an Asherah pole, just as King Ahab of Israel had done. He also bowed before all the powers of the heavens and worshiped them.

4 He built pagan altars in the Temple of the LORD, the place where the LORD had said, "My name will remain in Jerusalem forever." 5 He built these altars for all the powers of the heavens in both courtyards of the LORD's Temple. 6 Manasseh also sacrificed his own son in the fire. He practiced sorcery and divination, and he consulted with mediums and psychics. He did much that was evil in the LORD's sight, arousing his anger.

7 Manasseh even made a carved image of Asherah and set it up in the Temple, the very place where the LORD had told David and his son Solomon: "My name will be honored forever in this Temple and in Jerusalem—the city I have chosen from among all the tribes of Israel. 8 If the Israelites will be careful to obey my commands—all the laws my servant Moses gave them—I will not send them into exile from this land that I gave their ancestors." 9 But the people refused to listen, and Manasseh led them to do even more evil than the pagan nations that the LORD had destroyed when the people of Israel entered the land.

10 Then the LORD said through his servants the prophets: 11 "King Manasseh of Judah has done many detestable things. He is even more wicked than the Amorites, who lived in this land before Israel. He has caused the people of Judah to sin with his idols. 12 So this is what the LORD, the God of Israel, says: I will bring such disaster on Jerusalem and Judah that the ears of those who hear about it will tingle with horror. 13 I will judge Jerusalem by the same standard I used for Samaria and the same measure I used for the family of Ahab. I will wipe away the people of Jerusalem as one wipes a dish and turns it upside down. 14 Then I will reject even the remnant of my own people who are left, and I will hand them over as plunder for their enemies. 15 For they have done great evil in my sight and have angered me ever since their ancestors came out of Egypt."

16 Manasseh also murdered many innocent people until Jerusalem was filled from one end to the other with innocent blood. This was in addition to the sin that he caused the people of Judah to commit, leading them to do evil in the LORD's sight.

17 The rest of the events in Manasseh's reign and everything he did, including the sins he committed, are recorded in *The Book of the History of the Kings of Judah.* 18 When Manasseh died, he was buried in the palace garden, the garden of Uzza. Then his son Amon became the next king.

Amon Rules in Judah

19 Amon was twenty-two years old when he became king, and he reigned in Jerusalem two years. His mother was Meshullemeth, the daughter of Haruz from Jotbah. 20 He did what was evil in the LORD's sight, just as his father, Manasseh, had done. 21 He followed the example of his father, worshiping the same idols his father had worshiped. 22 He abandoned the LORD, the God of his ancestors, and he refused to follow the LORD's ways.

23 Then Amon's own officials conspired against him and assassinated him in his palace. 24 But the people of the land killed all those who had conspired against King Amon, and they made his son Josiah the next king.

25 The rest of the events in Amon's reign and what he did are recorded in *The Book of the History of the Kings of Judah.* 26 He was buried in his

tomb in the garden of Uzza. Then his son Josiah became the next king.

CHAPTER 22
Josiah Rules in Judah

Josiah was eight years old when he became king, and he reigned in Jerusalem thirty-one years. His mother was Jedidah, the daughter of Adaiah from Bozkath. 2He did what was pleasing in the LORD's sight and followed the example of his ancestor David. He did not turn away from doing what was right.

3In the eighteenth year of his reign, King Josiah sent Shaphan son of Azaliah and grandson of Meshullam, the court secretary, to the Temple of the LORD. He told him, 4"Go to Hilkiah the high priest and have him count the money the gatekeepers have collected from the people at the LORD's Temple. 5Entrust this money to the men assigned to supervise the restoration of the LORD's Temple. Then they can use it to pay workers to repair the Temple. 6They will need to hire carpenters, builders, and masons. Also have them buy the timber and the finished stone needed to repair the Temple. 7But don't require the construction supervisors to keep account of the money they receive, for they are honest and trustworthy men."

Hilkiah Discovers God's Law

8Hilkiah the high priest said to Shaphan the court secretary, "I have found the Book of the Law in the LORD's Temple!" Then Hilkiah gave the scroll to Shaphan, and he read it.

9Shaphan went to the king and reported, "Your officials have turned over the money collected at the Temple of the LORD to the workers and supervisors at the Temple." 10Shaphan also told the king, "Hilkiah the priest has given me a scroll." So Shaphan read it to the king.

11When the king heard what was written in the Book of the Law, he tore his clothes in despair. 12Then he gave these orders to Hilkiah the priest, Ahikam son of Shaphan, Acbor son of Micaiah, Shaphan the court secretary, and Asaiah the king's personal adviser: 13"Go to the Temple and speak to the LORD for me and for the people and for all Judah. Inquire about the words written in this scroll that has been found. For the LORD's great anger is burning against us because our ancestors have not obeyed the words in this scroll. We have not been doing everything it says we must do."

14So Hilkiah the priest, Ahikam, Acbor, Shaphan, and Asaiah went to the New Quarter of Jerusalem to consult with the prophet Huldah. She was the wife of Shallum son of Tikvah, son of Harhas, the keeper of the Temple wardrobe.

15She said to them, "The LORD, the God of Israel, has spoken! Go back and tell the man who sent you, 16'This is what the LORD says: I am going to bring disaster on this city and its people. All the words written in the scroll that the king of Judah has read will come true. 17For my people have abandoned me and offered sacrifices to pagan gods, and I am very angry with them for everything they have done. My anger will burn against this place, and it will not be quenched.'

18"But go to the king of Judah who sent you to seek the LORD and tell him: 'This is what the LORD, the God of Israel, says concerning the message you have just heard: 19You were sorry and humbled yourself before the LORD when you heard what I said against this city and its people—that this land would be cursed and become desolate. You tore your clothing in despair and wept before me in repentance. And I have indeed heard you, says the LORD. 20So I will not send the promised disaster until after you have died and been buried in peace. You will not see the disaster I am going to bring on this city.'"

So they took her message back to the king.

CHAPTER 23
Josiah's Religious Reforms

Then the king summoned all the elders of Judah and Jerusalem. 2And the king went up to the Temple of the LORD with all the people of Judah and Jerusalem, along with the priests and the prophets—all the people from the least to the greatest. There the king read to them the entire Book of the Covenant that had been found in the LORD's Temple. 3The king took his place of authority beside the pillar and renewed the covenant in the LORD's presence. He pledged to obey the LORD by keeping all his commands, laws, and decrees with all his heart and soul. In this way, he confirmed all the terms of the covenant that were written in the scroll, and all the people pledged themselves to the covenant.

4Then the king instructed Hilkiah the high priest and the priests of the second rank and the Temple gatekeepers to remove from the LORD's Temple all the articles that were used to worship Baal, Asherah, and all the powers of the heavens. The king had all these things burned outside Jerusalem on the terraces of the Kidron Valley, and he carried the ashes away to Bethel. 5He did away with the idolatrous priests, who had been appointed by the previous kings of Judah, for they had offered sacrifices at the pagan shrines throughout Judah and even in the vicinity of Jerusalem. They had also offered sacrifices to Baal, and to the sun, the moon, the constellations, and to all the powers of the heavens. [6]The king removed the Asherah pole from the LORD's Temple and took it outside Jerusalem to the Kidron Valley, where he burned it. Then he ground the ashes of the pole to dust and threw the dust over the graves of the people. [7]He also tore down the living quarters of the male and female shrine prostitutes that were inside the Temple of the LORD, where the women wove coverings for the Asherah pole.

[8]Josiah brought to Jerusalem all the priests who were living in other towns of Judah. He also defiled the pagan shrines, where they had offered sacrifices—all the way from Geba to Beersheba. He destroyed the shrines at the entrance to the gate of Joshua, the governor of Jerusalem. This gate was located to the left of the city gate as one enters the city. [9]The priests who had served at the pagan shrines were not allowed to serve at the LORD's altar in Jerusalem, but they were allowed to eat unleavened bread with the other priests.

[10]Then the king defiled the altar of Topheth in the valley of Ben-Hinnom, so no one could ever again use it to sacrifice a son or daughter in the fire as an offering to Molech. [11]He removed from the entrance of the LORD's Temple the horse statues that the former kings of Judah had dedicated to the sun. They were near the quarters of Nathan-melech the eunuch, an officer of the court. The king also burned the chariots dedicated to the sun.

[12]Josiah tore down the altars that the kings of Judah had built on the palace roof above the upper room of Ahaz. The king destroyed the altars that Manasseh had built in the two courtyards of the LORD's Temple. He smashed them to bits and scattered the pieces in the Kidron Valley. [13]The king also desecrated the pagan shrines east of Jerusalem, to the south of the Mount of Corruption, where King Solomon of Israel had built shrines for Ashtoreth, the detestable goddess of the Sidonians; and for Chemosh, the detestable god of the Moabites; and for Molech, the vile god of the Ammonites. [14]He smashed the sacred pillars and cut down the Asherah poles. Then he desecrated these places by scattering human bones over them.

[15]The king also tore down the altar at Bethel—the pagan shrine that Jeroboam son of Nebat had made when he caused Israel to sin. He burned down the shrine and ground it to dust, and he burned the Asherah pole. [16]Then Josiah turned around and noticed several tombs in the side of the hill. He ordered that the bones be brought out, and he burned them on the altar at Bethel to desecrate it. (This happened just as the LORD had promised through the man of God when Jeroboam stood beside the altar at the festival.)

Then Josiah turned and looked up at the tomb of the man of God who had predicted these things. [17]"What is that monument over there?" Josiah asked.

And the people of the town told him, "It is the tomb of the man of God who came from Judah and predicted the very things that you have just done to the altar at Bethel!"

[18]Josiah replied, "Leave it alone. Don't disturb his bones." So they did not burn his bones or those of the old prophet from Samaria.

[19]Then Josiah demolished all the buildings at the pagan shrines in the towns of Samaria, just as he had done at Bethel. They had been built by the various kings of Israel and had made the LORD very angry. [20]He executed the priests of the pagan shrines on their own altars, and he burned human bones on the altars to desecrate them. Finally, he returned to Jerusalem.

Josiah Celebrates Passover

[21]King Josiah then issued this order to all the people: "You must celebrate the Passover to the LORD your God, as required in this Book of the Covenant." [22]There had not been a Passover celebration like that since the time when the judges ruled in Israel, nor throughout all the years of the kings of Israel and Judah. [23]But in the eighteenth year of King Josiah's reign, this Passover was celebrated to the LORD in Jerusalem.

[24]Josiah also got rid of the mediums and psychics, the household gods, the idols, and every other kind of detestable practice, both in Jerusalem and throughout the land of Judah. He did this in obedience to the laws written in the scroll that Hilkiah the priest had found in the LORD's Temple. [25]Never before had there been a king like Josiah, who turned to the LORD with all his heart and soul and strength, obeying all the laws of Moses. And there has never been a king like him since.

[26]Even so, the LORD was very angry with Judah because of all the wicked things Manasseh had done to provoke him. [27]For the LORD said, "I will also banish Judah from my presence just as I have banished Israel. And I will reject my chosen city of Jerusalem and the Temple where my name was to be honored."

28 The rest of the events in Josiah's reign and
all his deeds are recorded in *The Book of the History of the Kings of Judah*.
29 While Josiah was king, Pharaoh Neco, king
of Egypt, went to the Euphrates River to help
the king of Assyria. King Josiah and his army
marched out to fight him, but King Neco killed
him when they met at Megiddo. 30 Josiah's officers took his body back in a chariot from Megiddo to Jerusalem and buried him in his own
tomb. Then the people of the land anointed Josiah's son Jehoahaz and made him the next
king.

Jehoahaz Rules in Judah

31 Jehoahaz was twenty-three years old when he
became king, and he reigned in Jerusalem three
months. His mother was Hamutal, the daughter
of Jeremiah from Libnah. 32 He did what was evil
in the LORD's sight, just as his ancestors had
done.
33 Pharaoh Neco put Jehoahaz in prison at Riblah in the land of Hamath to prevent him from
ruling in Jerusalem. He also demanded that Judah pay 7,500 pounds of silver and 75 pounds of
gold as tribute.

Jehoiakim Rules in Judah

34 Pharaoh Neco then installed Eliakim, another
of Josiah's sons, to reign in place of his father, and
he changed Eliakim's name to Jehoiakim. Jehoahaz was taken to Egypt as a prisoner, where he
died.
35 In order to get the silver and gold demanded
as tribute by Pharaoh Neco, Jehoiakim collected
a tax from the people of Judah, requiring them to
pay in proportion to their wealth.
36 Jehoiakim was twenty-five years old when
he became king, and he reigned in Jerusalem
eleven years. His mother was Zebidah, the daughter of Pedaiah from Rumah. 37 He did what was
evil in the LORD's sight, just as his ancestors had
done.

CHAPTER 24

During Jehoiakim's reign, King Nebuchadnezzar
of Babylon invaded the land of Judah. Jehoiakim
surrendered and paid him tribute for three years
but then rebelled. 2 Then the LORD sent bands of
Babylonian, Aramean, Moabite, and Ammonite
raiders against Judah to destroy it, just as the
LORD had promised through his prophets.
3 These disasters happened to Judah because of
the LORD's command. He had decided to banish
Judah from his presence because of the many
sins of Manasseh, 4 who had filled Jerusalem
with innocent blood. The LORD would not forgive this.
5 The rest of the events in Jehoiakim's reign
and all his deeds are recorded in *The Book of the
History of the Kings of Judah*. 6 When Jehoiakim
died, his son Jehoiachin became the next king.
7 The king of Egypt did not venture out of his
country after that, for the king of Babylon captured the entire area formerly claimed by
Egypt—from the Brook of Egypt to the Euphrates
River.

Jehoiachin Rules in Judah

8 Jehoiachin was eighteen years old when he became king, and he reigned in Jerusalem three
months. His mother was Nehushta, the daughter
of Elnathan from Jerusalem. 9 Jehoiachin did
what was evil in the LORD's sight, just as his father
had done.
10 During Jehoiachin's reign, the officers of King
Nebuchadnezzar of Babylon came up against Jerusalem and besieged it. 11 Nebuchadnezzar himself arrived at the city during the siege. 12 Then
King Jehoiachin, along with the queen mother, his
advisers, his commanders, and his officials, surrendered to the Babylonians.
In the eighth year of Nebuchadnezzar's reign,
he took Jehoiachin prisoner. 13 As the LORD had
said beforehand, Nebuchadnezzar carried away
all the treasures from the LORD's Temple and the
royal palace. He stripped away all the gold objects
that King Solomon of Israel had placed in the
Temple. 14 King Nebuchadnezzar took all of Jerusalem captive, including all the commanders and
the best of the soldiers, craftsmen, and artisans—
10,000 in all. Only the poorest people were left in
the land.
15 Nebuchadnezzar led King Jehoiachin away
as a captive to Babylon, along with the queen
mother, his wives and officials, and all Jerusalem's elite. 16 He also exiled 7,000 of the best
troops and 1,000 craftsmen and artisans, all of
whom were strong and fit for war. 17 Then the
king of Babylon installed Mattaniah, Jehoiachin's
uncle, as the next king, and he changed Mattaniah's name to Zedekiah.

Zedekiah Rules in Judah

18 Zedekiah was twenty-one years old when he
became king, and he reigned in Jerusalem eleven
years. His mother was Hamutal, the daughter of
Jeremiah from Libnah. 19 But Zedekiah did what
was evil in the LORD's sight, just as Jehoiakim had
done. 20 These things happened because of the

LORD's anger against the people of Jerusalem and
Judah, until he finally banished them from his
presence and sent them into exile.

The Fall of Jerusalem
Zedekiah rebelled against the king of Babylon.

CHAPTER 25
So on January 15, during the ninth year of Zedekiah's reign, King Nebuchadnezzar of Babylon
led his entire army against Jerusalem. They surrounded the city and built siege ramps against its
walls. 2 Jerusalem was kept under siege until the
eleventh year of King Zedekiah's reign.

3 By July 18 in the eleventh year of Zedekiah's
reign, the famine in the city had become very severe, and the last of the food was entirely gone.
4 Then a section of the city wall was broken
down. Since the city was surrounded by the Babylonians, the soldiers waited for nightfall and escaped through the gate between the two walls
behind the king's garden. Then they headed toward the Jordan Valley.

5 But the Babylonian troops chased the king
and overtook him on the plains of Jericho, for his
men had all deserted him and scattered. 6 They
captured the king and took him to the king of
Babylon at Riblah, where they pronounced judgment upon Zedekiah. 7 They made Zedekiah
watch as they slaughtered his sons. Then they
gouged out Zedekiah's eyes, bound him in
bronze chains, and led him away to Babylon.

The Temple Destroyed
8 On August 14 of that year, which was the nineteenth year of King Nebuchadnezzar's reign,
Nebuzaradan, the captain of the guard and an
official of the Babylonian king, arrived in Jerusalem. 9 He burned down the Temple of the LORD,
the royal palace, and all the houses of Jerusalem.
He destroyed all the important buildings in the
city. 10 Then he supervised the entire Babylonian
army as they tore down the walls of Jerusalem on
every side. 11 Then Nebuzaradan, the captain of
the guard, took as exiles the rest of the people
who remained in the city, the defectors who had
declared their allegiance to the king of Babylon,
and the rest of the population. 12 But the captain
of the guard allowed some of the poorest people
to stay behind to care for the vineyards and
fields.

13 The Babylonians broke up the bronze pillars in front of the LORD's Temple, the bronze
water carts, and the great bronze basin called
the Sea, and they carried all the bronze away to
Babylon. 14 They also took all the ash buckets,
shovels, lamp snuffers, ladles, and all the other
bronze articles used for making sacrifices at the
Temple. 15 The captain of the guard also took the
incense burners and basins, and all the other articles made of pure gold or silver.

16 The weight of the bronze from the two pillars, the Sea, and the water carts was too great to
be measured. These things had been made for
the LORD's Temple in the days of Solomon.
17 Each of the pillars was 27 feet tall. The bronze
capital on top of each pillar was 7½ feet high
and was decorated with a network of bronze
pomegranates all the way around.

18 Nebuzaradan, the captain of the guard,
took with him as prisoners Seraiah the high
priest, Zephaniah the priest of the second rank,
and the three chief gatekeepers. 19 And from
among the people still hiding in the city, he took
an officer who had been in charge of the Judean
army; five of the king's personal advisers; the
army commander's chief secretary, who was in
charge of recruitment; and sixty other citizens.
20 Nebuzaradan, the captain of the guard, took
them all to the king of Babylon at Riblah. 21 And
there at Riblah, in the land of Hamath, the king
of Babylon had them all put to death. So the people of Judah were sent into exile from their land.

Gedaliah Governs in Judah
22 Then King Nebuchadnezzar appointed Gedaliah son of Ahikam and grandson of Shaphan as
governor over the people he had left in Judah.
23 When all the army commanders and their
men learned that the king of Babylon had appointed Gedaliah as governor, they went to see
him at Mizpah. These included Ishmael son of
Nethaniah, Johanan son of Kareah, Seraiah son
of Tanhumeth the Netophathite, Jezaniah son of
the Maacathite, and all their men.

24 Gedaliah vowed to them that the Babylonian
officials meant them no harm. "Don't be afraid of
them. Live in the land and serve the king of Babylon, and all will go well for you," he promised.

25 But in midautumn of that year, Ishmael son
of Nethaniah and grandson of Elishama, who
was a member of the royal family, went to Mizpah with ten men and killed Gedaliah. He also
killed all the Judeans and Babylonians who were
with him at Mizpah.

26 Then all the people of Judah, from the least
to the greatest, as well as the army commanders,
fled in panic to Egypt, for they were afraid of
what the Babylonians would do to them.

Hope for Israel's Royal Line

27In the thirty-seventh year of the exile of King
Jehoiachin of Judah, Evil-merodach ascended to
the Babylonian throne. He was kind to Jehoiachin and released him from prison on April 2 of
that year. 28He spoke kindly to Jehoiachin and
gave him a higher place than all the other exiled
kings in Babylon. 29He supplied Jehoiachin with
new clothes to replace his prison garb and allowed him to dine in the king's presence for the
rest of his life. 30So the king gave him a regular
food allowance as long as he lived.

1 CHRONICLES Family History for God's Children

Look for 2 hidden messages in 1 Chronicles!

First Chronicles reminds us of how God had a plan to build Israel and the holy Temple. Read 1 Chronicles to find

- A *HUGE* FAMILY TREE
- A FOREVER PROMISE TO A FAITHFUL KING
- A LOT OF PEOPLE WITH ALL SORTS OF JOBS
- A BIG PILE OF REALLY EXPENSIVE METALS

Remember When?

The Israelites needed to remember their past. God showed them who they were and where they came from by reminding them of their family history. **Look over the reminder in 1 Chronicles 1–9. It's huge!**

Tough Dudes

With God and tough guys on his side, no wonder David kept winning battles. Want to see how tough they were? **Check out 1 Chronicles 11:10-47.**

Count Me Out!

Maybe David wanted to see just how many people he ruled. Maybe David put his trust in his huge army. We don't know exactly *why* David did it, but we know it was more about David's pride than about following God. **Read 1 Chronicles 21:1-7 to see what David did.**

FOUR... FIVE... SIX... SEVEN...

Umm...We Need Another Offering Plate!

David wanted to help out with the materials needed to build God's Temple. And boy, did he help! **Read 1 Chronicles 28:1–29:20 to read all about what David did!**

Timeline

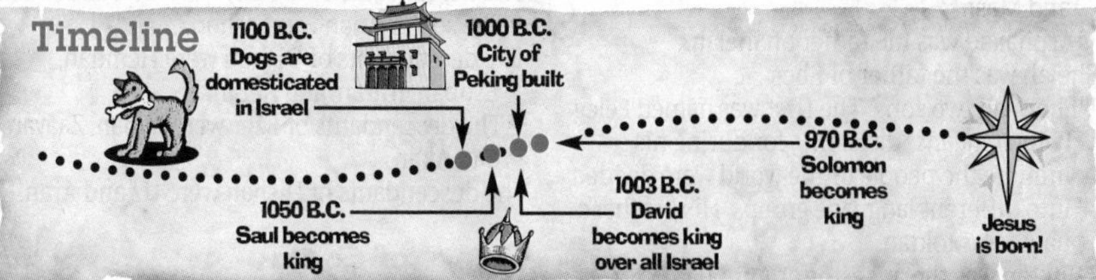
1100 B.C.
Dogs are domesticated in Israel
1000 B.C.
City of Peking built
1050 B.C.
Saul becomes king
1003 B.C.
David becomes king over all Israel
970 B.C.
Solomon becomes king
Jesus is born!

The JESUS CONNECTION

God used the book of 1 Chronicles to help the Israelites remember that they were God's children. If you believe in Jesus, 1 Chronicles offers the same reminder for you. In 1 Chronicles 17:11-14, God promised David that one of his descendants would sit on the throne as king forever. Jesus came from David's family, and he sits on the throne in heaven today as the King of kings. **Jesus' death on the cross made it possible for you to be part of God's family!**

1 Chronicles 1 . . . page 390

CHAPTER 1

From Adam to Noah's Sons

The descendants of Adam were Seth,
Enosh, 2Kenan, Mahalalel, Jared, 3Enoch,
Methuselah, Lamech, 4and Noah.
The sons of Noah were Shem, Ham, and
Japheth.

Descendants of Japheth

5The descendants of Japheth were Gomer,
Magog, Madai, Javan, Tubal, Meshech, and
Tiras.
6The descendants of Gomer were Ashkenaz,
Riphath, and Togarmah.
7The descendants of Javan were Elishah,
Tarshish, Kittim, and Rodanim.

Descendants of Ham

8The descendants of Ham were Cush, Mizraim,
Put, and Canaan.
9The descendants of Cush were Seba,
Havilah, Sabtah, Raamah, and Sabteca.
The descendants of Raamah were Sheba
and Dedan. 10Cush was also the ancestor
of Nimrod, who was the first heroic
warrior on earth.
11Mizraim was the ancestor of the Ludites,
Anamites, Lehabites, Naphtuhites, 12Path-
rusites, Casluhites, and the Caphtorites, from
whom the Philistines came.
13Canaan's oldest son was Sidon, the ancestor of
the Sidonians. Canaan was also the ancestor
of the Hittites, 14Jebusites, Amorites, Girgashites, 15Hivites, Arkites, Sinites, 16Arvadites,
Zemarites, and Hamathites.

Descendants of Shem

17The descendants of Shem were Elam, Asshur,
Arphaxad, Lud, and Aram.
The descendants of Aram were Uz, Hul, Gether,
and Mash.
18Arphaxad was the father of Shelah.
Shelah was the father of Eber.
19Eber had two sons. The first was named Peleg
(which means "division"), for during his
lifetime the people of the world were divided
into different language groups. His brother's
name was Joktan.
20Joktan was the ancestor of Almodad,
Sheleph, Hazarmaveth, Jerah, 21Hadoram,
Uzal, Diklah, 22Obal, Abimael, Sheba,
23Ophir, Havilah, and Jobab. All these were
descendants of Joktan.
24So this is the family line descended from
Shem: Arphaxad, Shelah, 25Eber, Peleg, Reu,
26Serug, Nahor, Terah, 27and Abram, later
known as Abraham.

Descendants of Abraham

28The sons of Abraham were Isaac and Ishmael.
29These are their genealogical records:
The sons of Ishmael were Nebaioth (the oldest),
Kedar, Adbeel, Mibsam, 30Mishma, Dumah,
Massa, Hadad, Tema, 31Jetur, Naphish, and
Kedemah. These were the sons of Ishmael.

32The sons of Keturah, Abraham's concubine,
were Zimran, Jokshan, Medan, Midian,
Ishbak, and Shuah.
The sons of Jokshan were Sheba and Dedan.
33The sons of Midian were Ephah, Epher,
Hanoch, Abida, and Eldaah.
All these were descendants of Abraham through
his concubine Keturah.

Descendants of Isaac

34Abraham was the father of Isaac. The sons
of Isaac were Esau and Israel.

Descendants of Esau

35The sons of Esau were Eliphaz, Reuel, Jeush,
Jalam, and Korah.
36The descendants of Eliphaz were Teman,
Omar, Zepho, Gatam, Kenaz, and Amalek,
who was born to Timna.
37The descendants of Reuel were Nahath,
Zerah, Shammah, and Mizzah.

Original Peoples of Edom

38The descendants of Seir were Lotan, Shobal,
Zibeon, Anah, Dishon, Ezer, and Dishan.
39The descendants of Lotan were Hori and
Hemam. Lotan's sister was named Timna.
40The descendants of Shobal were Alvan,
Manahath, Ebal, Shepho, and Onam.
The descendants of Zibeon were Aiah and Anah.
41The son of Anah was Dishon.
The descendants of Dishon were Hemdan,
Eshban, Ithran, and Keran.
42The descendants of Ezer were Bilhan, Zaavan,
and Akan.
The descendants of Dishan were Uz and Aran.

Rulers of Edom

43These are the kings who ruled in the land of
Edom before any king ruled over the Israelites:

Bela son of Beor, who ruled from his city
of Dinhabah.
44When Bela died, Jobab son of Zerah from
Bozrah became king in his place.

45 When Jobab died, Husham from the land of the Temanites became king in his place.
46 When Husham died, Hadad son of Bedad became king in his place and ruled from the city of Avith. He was the one who destroyed the Midianite army in the land of Moab.
47 When Hadad died, Samlah from the city of Masrekah became king in his place.
48 When Samlah died, Shaul from the city of Rehoboth-on-the-River became king in his place.
49 When Shaul died, Baal-hanan son of Acbor became king in his place.
50 When Baal-hanan died, Hadad became king in his place and ruled from the city of Pau. His wife was Mehetabel, the daughter of Matred and granddaughter of Me-zahab.
51 Then Hadad died.

The clan leaders of Edom were Timna, Alvah,
Jetheth, 52 Oholibamah, Elah, Pinon, 53 Kenaz,
Teman, Mibzar, 54 Magdiel, and Iram. These
are the clan leaders of Edom.

CHAPTER 2

Descendants of Israel

The sons of Israel were Reuben, Simeon,
Levi, Judah, Issachar, Zebulun, 2 Dan, Joseph,
Benjamin, Naphtali, Gad, and Asher.

Descendants of Judah

3 Judah had three sons from Bathshua, a Canaanite woman. Their names were Er, Onan, and Shelah. But the LORD saw that the oldest son, Er, was a wicked man, so he killed him.
4 Later Judah had twin sons from Tamar, his widowed daughter-in-law. Their names were Perez and Zerah. So Judah had five sons in all.
5 The sons of Perez were Hezron and Hamul.
6 The sons of Zerah were Zimri, Ethan, Heman, Calcol, and Darda—five in all.
7 The son of Carmi (a descendant of Zimri) was Achan, who brought disaster on Israel by taking plunder that had been set apart for the LORD.
8 The son of Ethan was Azariah.

From Judah's Grandson Hezron to David

9 The sons of Hezron were Jerahmeel, Ram, and Caleb.
10 Ram was the father of Amminadab.
Amminadab was the father of Nahshon, a leader of Judah.
11 Nahshon was the father of Salmon.
Salmon was the father of Boaz.
12 Boaz was the father of Obed.
Obed was the father of Jesse.
13 Jesse's first son was Eliab, his second was
Abinadab, his third was Shimea, 14 his fourth
was Nethanel, his fifth was Raddai, 15 his
sixth was Ozem, and his seventh was David.
16 Their sisters were named Zeruiah and
Abigail. Zeruiah had three sons named
Abishai, Joab, and Asahel. 17 Abigail married
a man named Jether, an Ishmaelite, and they
had a son named Amasa.

Other Descendants of Hezron

18 Hezron's son Caleb had sons from his wife
Azubah and from Jerioth. Her sons were
named Jesher, Shobab, and Ardon. 19 After
Azubah died, Caleb married Ephrathah, and
they had a son named Hur. 20 Hur was the
father of Uri. Uri was the father of Bezalel.
21 When Hezron was sixty years old, he married
Gilead's sister, the daughter of Makir. They
had a son named Segub. 22 Segub was the
father of Jair, who ruled twenty-three towns
in the land of Gilead. 23 (But Geshur and
Aram captured the Towns of Jair and also
took Kenath and its sixty surrounding
villages.) All these were descendants of
Makir, the father of Gilead.
24 Soon after Hezron died in the town of Caleb-ephrathah, his wife Abijah gave birth to a son named Ashhur (the father of Tekoa).

Descendants of Hezron's Son Jerahmeel

25 The sons of Jerahmeel, the oldest son of
Hezron, were Ram (the firstborn), Bunah,
Oren, Ozem, and Ahijah. 26 Jerahmeel had
a second wife named Atarah. She was the
mother of Onam.
27 The sons of Ram, the oldest son of Jerahmeel, were Maaz, Jamin, and Eker.
28 The sons of Onam were Shammai and Jada.
The sons of Shammai were Nadab and Abishur.
29 The sons of Abishur and his wife Abihail were Ahban and Molid.
30 The sons of Nadab were Seled and Appaim.
Seled died without children, 31 but Appaim
had a son named Ishi. The son of Ishi was
Sheshan. Sheshan had a descendant named
Ahlai.
32 The sons of Jada, Shammai's brother, were
Jether and Jonathan. Jether died without
children, 33 but Jonathan had two sons named
Peleth and Zaza.

These were all descendants of Jerahmeel.
34 Sheshan had no sons, though he did have
daughters. He also had an Egyptian servant
named Jarha. 35 Sheshan gave one of his
daughters to be the wife of Jarha, and they
had a son named Attai.
36 Attai was the father of Nathan.
Nathan was the father of Zabad.
37 Zabad was the father of Ephlal.
Ephlal was the father of Obed.
38 Obed was the father of Jehu.
Jehu was the father of Azariah.
39 Azariah was the father of Helez.
Helez was the father of Eleasah.
40 Eleasah was the father of Sismai.
Sismai was the father of Shallum.
41 Shallum was the father of Jekamiah.
Jekamiah was the father of Elishama.

Descendants of Hezron's Son Caleb

42 The descendants of Caleb, the brother of
Jerahmeel, included Mesha (the firstborn),
who became the father of Ziph. Caleb's
descendants also included the sons of
Mareshah, the father of Hebron.
43 The sons of Hebron were Korah, Tappuah,
Rekem, and Shema. 44 Shema was the father
of Raham. Raham was the father of Jorkeam.
Rekem was the father of Shammai. 45 The son
of Shammai was Maon. Maon was the father
of Beth-zur.
46 Caleb's concubine Ephah gave birth to Haran,
Moza, and Gazez. Haran was the father of
Gazez.
47 The sons of Jahdai were Regem, Jotham,
Geshan, Pelet, Ephah, and Shaaph.
48 Another of Caleb's concubines, Maacah,
gave birth to Sheber and Tirhanah. 49 She
also gave birth to Shaaph (the father of
Madmannah) and Sheva (the father of
Macbenah and Gibea). Caleb also had
a daughter named Acsah.
50 These were all descendants of Caleb.

Descendants of Caleb's Son Hur

The sons of Hur, the oldest son of Caleb's wife
Ephrathah, were Shobal (the founder of
Kiriath-jearim), 51 Salma (the founder
of Bethlehem), and Hareph (the founder
of Beth-gader).
52 The descendants of Shobal (the founder
of Kiriath-jearim) were Haroeh, half the
Manahathites, 53 and the families of Kiriath-
jearim—the Ithrites, Puthites, Shumathites,
and Mishraites, from whom came the people
of Zorah and Eshtaol.
54 The descendants of Salma were the people of
Bethlehem, the Netophathites, Atroth-beth-
joab, the other half of the Manahathites, the
Zorites, 55 and the families of scribes living
at Jabez—the Tirathites, Shimeathites, and
Sucathites. All these were Kenites who
descended from Hammath, the father of
the family of Recab.

CHAPTER 3

Descendants of David

These are the sons of David who were born in
Hebron:

The oldest was Amnon, whose mother was
Ahinoam from Jezreel.
The second was Daniel, whose mother was
Abigail from Carmel.
2 The third was Absalom, whose mother was
Maacah, the daughter of Talmai, king
of Geshur.
The fourth was Adonijah, whose mother
was Haggith.
3 The fifth was Shephatiah, whose mother
was Abital.
The sixth was Ithream, whose mother was
Eglah, David's wife.
4 These six sons were born to David in Hebron,
where he reigned seven and a half years.

Then David reigned another thirty-three years
in Jerusalem. 5 The sons born to David in Jerusalem included Shammua, Shobab, Nathan, and
Solomon. Their mother was Bathsheba, the
daughter of Ammiel. 6 David also had nine other
sons: Ibhar, Elishua, Elpelet, 7 Nogah, Nepheg,
Japhia, 8 Elishama, Eliada, and Eliphelet.
9 These were the sons of David, not including
his sons born to his concubines. Their sister was
named Tamar.

Descendants of Solomon

10 The descendants of Solomon were
Rehoboam, Abijah, Asa, Jehoshaphat,
11 Jehoram, Ahaziah, Joash, 12 Amaziah,
Uzziah, Jotham, 13 Ahaz, Hezekiah, Manasseh,
14 Amon, and Josiah.
15 The sons of Josiah were Johanan (the oldest),
Jehoiakim (the second), Zedekiah (the third),
and Jehoahaz (the fourth).
16 The successors of Jehoiakim were his son
Jehoiachin and his brother Zedekiah.

Descendants of Jehoiachin

17The sons of Jehoiachin, who was taken prisoner by the Babylonians, were Shealtiel,
18Malkiram, Pedaiah, Shenazzar, Jekamiah, Hoshama, and Nedabiah.
19The sons of Pedaiah were Zerubbabel and Shimei.
The sons of Zerubbabel were Meshullam and Hananiah. (Their sister was Shelomith.)
20His five other sons were Hashubah, Ohel, Berekiah, Hasadiah, and Jushab-hesed.
21The sons of Hananiah were Pelatiah and Jeshaiah. Jeshaiah's son was Rephaiah. Rephaiah's son was Arnan. Arnan's son was Obadiah. Obadiah's son was Shecaniah.
22The descendants of Shecaniah were Shemaiah and his sons, Hattush, Igal, Bariah, Neariah, and Shaphat—six in all.
23The sons of Neariah were Elioenai, Hizkiah, and Azrikam—three in all.
24The sons of Elioenai were Hodaviah, Eliashib, Pelaiah, Akkub, Johanan, Delaiah, and Anani—seven in all.

CHAPTER 4

Other Descendants of Judah

The descendants of Judah were Perez, Hezron, Carmi, Hur, and Shobal.
2Shobal's son Reaiah was the father of Jahath. Jahath was the father of Ahumai and Lahad. These were the families of the Zorathites.
3The descendants of Etam were Jezreel, Ishma,
Idbash, their sister Hazzelelponi, 4Penuel
(the father of Gedor), and Ezer (the father of Hushah). These were the descendants of Hur (the firstborn of Ephrathah), the ancestor of Bethlehem.
5Ashhur (the father of Tekoa) had two wives,
named Helah and Naarah. 6Naarah gave birth
to Ahuzzam, Hepher, Temeni, and
Haahashtari. 7Helah gave birth to Zereth,
Izhar, Ethnan, 8and Koz, who became the
ancestor of Anub, Zobebah, and all the families of Aharhel son of Harum.
9There was a man named Jabez who was more honorable than any of his brothers. His mother named him Jabez because his birth
had been so painful. 10He was the one who
prayed to the God of Israel, "Oh, that you would bless me and expand my territory! Please be with me in all that I do, and keep me from all trouble and pain!" And God granted him his request.
11Kelub (the brother of Shuhah) was the father of Mehir. Mehir was the father of Eshton.
12Eshton was the father of Beth-rapha, Paseah, and Tehinnah. Tehinnah was the father of Ir-nahash. These were the descendants of Recah.
13The sons of Kenaz were Othniel and Seraiah. Othniel's sons were Hathath and Meonothai.
14Meonothai was the father of Ophrah. Seraiah was the father of Joab, the founder of the Valley of Craftsmen, so called because they were craftsmen.
15The sons of Caleb son of Jephunneh were Iru, Elah, and Naam. The son of Elah was Kenaz.
16The sons of Jehallelel were Ziph, Ziphah, Tiria, and Asarel.
17The sons of Ezrah were Jether, Mered, Epher, and Jalon. One of Mered's wives became the mother of Miriam, Shammai, and Ishbah
(the father of Eshtemoa). 18He married a
woman from Judah, who became the mother of Jered (the father of Gedor), Heber (the father of Soco), and Jekuthiel (the father of Zanoah). Mered also married Bithia, a daughter of Pharaoh, and she bore him children.
19Hodiah's wife was the sister of Naham. One of her sons was the father of Keilah the Garmite, and another was the father of Eshtemoa the Maacathite.
20The sons of Shimon were Amnon, Rinnah, Ben-hanan, and Tilon.
The descendants of Ishi were Zoheth and Ben-zoheth.

Descendants of Judah's Son Shelah

21Shelah was one of Judah's sons. The descendants of Shelah were Er (the father of Lecah); Laadah (the father of Mareshah); the families of linen workers at Beth-ashbea;
22Jokim; the men of Cozeba; and Joash and Saraph, who ruled over Moab and Jashubi-lehem. These names all come from ancient
records. 23They were the pottery makers who lived in Netaim and Gederah. They lived there and worked for the king.

Descendants of Simeon

24The sons of Simeon were Jemuel, Jamin, Jarib, Zohar, and Shaul.
25The descendants of Shaul were Shallum, Mibsam, and Mishma.
26The descendants of Mishma were Hammuel, Zaccur, and Shimei.
27Shimei had sixteen sons and six daughters, but none of his brothers had large families.

So Simeon's tribe never grew as large as the
tribe of Judah.
[28]They lived in Beersheba, Moladah, Hazar-
shual, [29]Bilhah, Ezem, Tolad, [30]Bethuel,
Hormah, Ziklag, [31]Beth-marcaboth, Hazar-
susim, Beth-biri, and Shaaraim. These towns
were under their control until the time of
King David. [32]Their descendants also lived
in Etam, Ain, Rimmon, Token, and Ashan—
five towns [33]and their surrounding villages
as far away as Baalath. This was their
territory, and these names are listed in
their genealogical records.
[34]Other descendants of Simeon included
Meshobab, Jamlech, Joshah son of Amaziah,
[35]Joel, Jehu son of Joshibiah, son of Seraiah,
son of Asiel, [36]Elioenai, Jaakobah, Jeshohaiah,
Asaiah, Adiel, Jesimiel, Benaiah, [37]and Ziza
son of Shiphi, son of Allon, son of Jedaiah,
son of Shimri, son of Shemaiah.

[38]These were the names of some of the leaders
of Simeon's wealthy clans. Their families grew,
[39]and they traveled to the region of Gerar, in the
east part of the valley, seeking pastureland for
their flocks. [40]They found lush pastures there,
and the land was spacious, quiet, and peaceful.

Some of Ham's descendants had been living in
that region. [41]But during the reign of King Hezekiah of Judah, these leaders of Simeon invaded
the region and completely destroyed the homes
of the descendants of Ham and of the Meunites.
No trace of them remains today. They killed
everyone who lived there and took the land for
themselves, because they wanted its good
pastureland for their flocks. [42]Five hundred of
these invaders from the tribe of Simeon went to
Mount Seir, led by Pelatiah, Neariah, Rephaiah,
and Uzziel—all sons of Ishi. [43]They destroyed
the few Amalekites who had survived, and they
have lived there ever since.

CHAPTER 5
Descendants of Reuben

The oldest son of Israel was Reuben. But since he
dishonored his father by sleeping with one of his
father's concubines, his birthright was given to
the sons of his brother Joseph. For this reason,
Reuben is not listed in the genealogical records
as the firstborn son. [2]The descendants of Judah
became the most powerful tribe and provided a
ruler for the nation, but the birthright belonged
to Joseph.

[3]The sons of Reuben, the oldest son of Israel,
were Hanoch, Pallu, Hezron, and Carmi.

[4]The descendants of Joel were Shemaiah, Gog,
Shimei, [5]Micah, Reaiah, Baal, [6]and Beerah.
Beerah was the leader of the Reubenites
when they were taken into captivity by King
Tiglath-pileser of Assyria.
[7]Beerah's relatives are listed in their genealogical records by their clans: Jeiel (the leader),
Zechariah, [8]and Bela son of Azaz, son of
Shema, son of Joel.
The Reubenites lived in the area that stretches
from Aroer to Nebo and Baal-meon. [9]And
since they had so many livestock in the land
of Gilead, they spread east toward the edge of
the desert that stretches to the Euphrates
River.
[10]During the reign of Saul, the Reubenites
defeated the Hagrites in battle. Then they
moved into the Hagrite settlements all along
the eastern edge of Gilead.

Descendants of Gad

[11]Next to the Reubenites, the descendants of
Gad lived in the land of Bashan as far east
as Salecah. [12]Joel was the leader in the land
of Bashan, and Shapham was second-in-
command, followed by Janai and Shaphat.
[13]Their relatives, the leaders of seven other
clans, were Michael, Meshullam, Sheba,
Jorai, Jacan, Zia, and Eber. [14]These were all
descendants of Abihail son of Huri, son of
Jaroah, son of Gilead, son of Michael, son
of Jeshishai, son of Jahdo, son of Buz. [15]Ahi
son of Abdiel, son of Guni, was the leader of
their clans.

[16]The Gadites lived in the land of Gilead, in
Bashan and its villages, and throughout all the
pasturelands of Sharon. [17]All of these were
listed in the genealogical records during the
days of King Jotham of Judah and King Jeroboam of Israel.

The Tribes East of the Jordan

[18]There were 44,760 capable warriors in the armies of Reuben, Gad, and the half-tribe of Manasseh. They were all skilled in combat and
armed with shields, swords, and bows. [19]They
waged war against the Hagrites, the Jeturites, the
Naphishites, and the Nodabites. [20]They cried
out to God during the battle, and he answered
their prayer because they trusted in him. So the
Hagrites and all their allies were defeated. [21]The
plunder taken from the Hagrites included
50,000 camels, 250,000 sheep and goats, 2,000
donkeys, and 100,000 captives. [22]Many of the

Hi, my name is

SOLOMON *(king)*

"Ask for whatever you want." Now it's one thing if your parents say that to you. But Almighty God said those words to me! I could've asked for money, power, or maybe even a hundred more wishes. I could've asked God for anything! I ended up asking God for wisdom. I knew I needed God's help to rule as king over Israel.

What a wise request! Read 2 CHRONICLES 1:1-12 to find out what God said.

God gave me what I asked for—and so much more. God helped me make some really tough decisions, and he gave me wisdom to show others how to make good choices. God also used me to build the holy Temple in Jerusalem! My father, David, wanted to build it, but God told him "no." God wanted me to build the place of worship for our people—the Temple where God himself would live.

Solomon had plenty of wisdom to go around—he wrote most of the book of Proverbs. Check out PROVERBS 12, for a quick look!

Having all the wisdom in the world doesn't help much if you don't use it. I knew what trouble would come from marrying women who worshiped false gods. But I did it anyway. I had over 700 wives! Many of them didn't serve God, and they led me to worship false gods. Things started out so great. The Kingdom of Israel was powerful, rich, and blessed by God. But my sin caused so much trouble in my own life and for the whole nation of Israel.

Read 1 KINGS 11:1-12 to see the pain Solomon's sin caused.

If I could give you one piece of advice, it would be this: Respect God and choose to follow him in everything you do. You'll be much happier if you do!

Use It or Lose It!

It takes practice and patience to learn to juggle. If you try once then quit, you'll never learn. If you keep practicing, you'll become a great juggler.

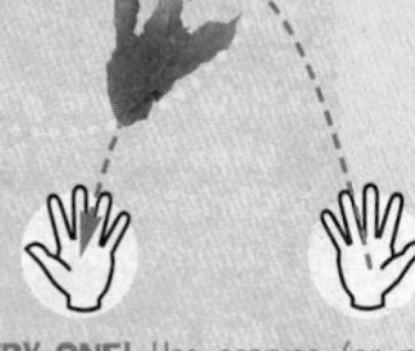

TRY ONE! Use scarves (or plastic grocery bags cut into large squares). Start by throwing one scarf up with your right hand and catching it with your left. You should throw it up in an arc so it goes past your eyes (not straight across).

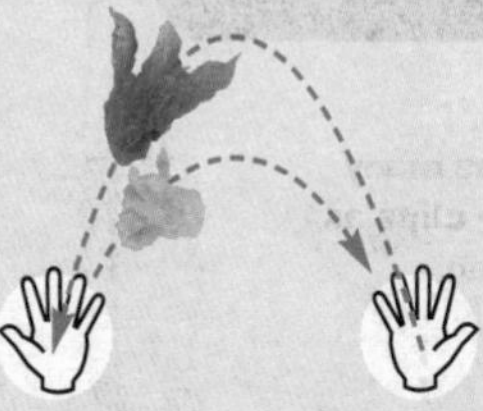

TRY TWO! Toss the scarf in your right hand up toward your left hand. As it starts to come down, toss the scarf in your left hand. Say this little chant as you toss and catch: "Toss. Toss. Catch. Catch." Keep practicing with two scarves!

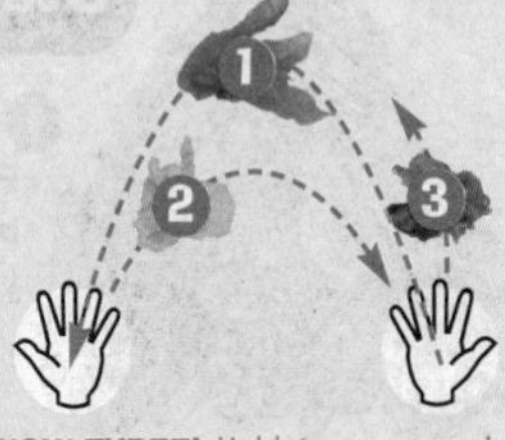

NOW THREE! Hold two scarves in your right hand and one in your left. Toss scarf #1 from your right hand. While it's in the air, toss scarf #2 from your left. Catch scarf #1 with your left hand, then toss scarf #3 from your right hand.

IT TAKES PRACTICE! Solomon knew what was right, but he quit putting it into practice. Whether you practice enough to learn to juggle or not, use the wisdom God has given you to live for him!

Hi, my name is
ELIJAH *(prophet)*

Sometimes things seem worse than they really are. I should've felt brave. I should've been excited. I mean, I saw God bring fire down from heaven to show all the people of Israel that he was really God. After God's show of power, we got rid of all the false prophets who led the people to worship the false god Baal. But when the wicked queen Jezebel found out, she promised to kill me! I ran and ran to get away. I felt so scared and so alone.

Read all about the amazing event in 1 KINGS 18:16-39.

But I really wasn't alone. God was with me. As I watched and waited, God sent a huge windstorm, an earthquake, and a great fire. But God didn't speak to me through any of those powerful displays. Do you know how God spoke to me? God spoke in a gentle whisper. God pointed out that 7,000 people in Israel still served the Living God. God also sent Elisha to help me with my ministry. God's encouragement gave me the strength and courage to keep warning the evil kings of Israel and to keep serving him.

This wasn't the only run Elijah took. Read about another amazing run in 1 KINGS 18:41-46.

No matter how lonely you feel, you are never alone. God is always with you!

Stay Connected

1. **Find as many paper clips as you can.**
2. **Make a really long chain with your paper clips.**
3. **Read ISAIAH 54:10. Now use the paper clip chain to draw a picture of what you read.**

Show and explain your work of art to someone. Then talk it over:

- **How are the paper clips like the other Christians God has put in your life?**
- **How does God keep us connected?**
- **What can you do when you feel alone?**

Hagrites were killed in the battle because God was fighting against them. The people of Reuben, Gad, and Manasseh lived in their land until they were taken into exile.

23 The half-tribe of Manasseh was very large and spread through the land from Bashan to Baal-hermon, Senir, and Mount Hermon.
24 These were the leaders of their clans: Epher, Ishi, Eliel, Azriel, Jeremiah, Hodaviah, and Jahdiel. These men had a great reputation as mighty warriors and leaders of their clans.

25 But these tribes were unfaithful to the God of their ancestors. They worshiped the gods of the nations that God had destroyed.
26 So the God of Israel caused King Pul of Assyria (also known as Tiglath-pileser) to invade the land and take away the people of Reuben, Gad, and the half-tribe of Manasseh as captives. The Assyrians exiled them to Halah, Habor, Hara, and the Gozan River, where they remain to this day.

CHAPTER 6

The Priestly Line

The sons of Levi were Gershon, Kohath, and Merari.
2 The descendants of Kohath included Amram, Izhar, Hebron, and Uzziel.
3 The children of Amram were Aaron, Moses, and Miriam.
The sons of Aaron were Nadab, Abihu, Eleazar, and Ithamar.
4 Eleazar was the father of Phinehas.
Phinehas was the father of Abishua.
5 Abishua was the father of Bukki.
Bukki was the father of Uzzi.
6 Uzzi was the father of Zerahiah.
Zerahiah was the father of Meraioth.
7 Meraioth was the father of Amariah.
Amariah was the father of Ahitub.
8 Ahitub was the father of Zadok.
Zadok was the father of Ahimaaz.
9 Ahimaaz was the father of Azariah.
Azariah was the father of Johanan.
10 Johanan was the father of Azariah, the high priest at the Temple built by Solomon in Jerusalem.
11 Azariah was the father of Amariah.
Amariah was the father of Ahitub.
12 Ahitub was the father of Zadok.
Zadok was the father of Shallum.
13 Shallum was the father of Hilkiah.
Hilkiah was the father of Azariah.
14 Azariah was the father of Seraiah.
Seraiah was the father of Jehozadak,
15 who went into exile when the LORD sent the people of Judah and Jerusalem into captivity under Nebuchadnezzar.

The Levite Clans

16 The sons of Levi were Gershon, Kohath, and Merari.
17 The descendants of Gershon included Libni and Shimei.
18 The descendants of Kohath included Amram, Izhar, Hebron, and Uzziel.
19 The descendants of Merari included Mahli and Mushi.

The following were the Levite clans, listed according to their ancestral descent:
20 The descendants of Gershon included Libni, Jahath, Zimmah,
21 Joah, Iddo, Zerah, and Jeatherai.
22 The descendants of Kohath included Amminadab, Korah, Assir,
23 Elkanah, Abiasaph, Assir,
24 Tahath, Uriel, Uzziah, and Shaul.
25 The descendants of Elkanah included Amasai, Ahimoth,
26 Elkanah, Zophai, Nahath,
27 Eliab, Jeroham, Elkanah, and Samuel.
28 The sons of Samuel were Joel (the older) and Abijah (the second).
29 The descendants of Merari included Mahli, Libni, Shimei, Uzzah,
30 Shimea, Haggiah, and Asaiah.

The Temple Musicians

31 David assigned the following men to lead the music at the house of the LORD after the Ark was placed there.
32 They ministered with music at the Tabernacle until Solomon built the Temple of the LORD in Jerusalem. They carried out their work, following all the regulations handed down to them.
33 These are the men who served, along with their sons:

Heman the musician was from the clan of Kohath. His genealogy was traced back through Joel, Samuel,
34 Elkanah, Jeroham, Eliel, Toah,
35 Zuph, Elkanah, Mahath, Amasai,
36 Elkanah, Joel, Azariah, Zephaniah,
37 Tahath, Assir, Abiasaph, Korah,
38 Izhar, Kohath, Levi, and Israel.
39 Heman's first assistant was Asaph from the clan of Gershon. Asaph's genealogy was traced back through Berekiah, Shimea,
40 Michael, Baaseiah, Malkijah,
41 Ethni, Zerah, Adaiah,
42 Ethan, Zimmah, Shimei,
43 Jahath, Gershon, and Levi.

44Heman's second assistant was Ethan from
the clan of Merari. Ethan's genealogy was
traced back through Kishi, Abdi, Malluch,
45Hashabiah, Amaziah, Hilkiah, 46Amzi, Bani,
Shemer, 47Mahli, Mushi, Merari, and Levi.

48Their fellow Levites were appointed to various
other tasks in the Tabernacle, the house of God.

Aaron's Descendants

49Only Aaron and his descendants served as
priests. They presented the offerings on the altar
of burnt offering and the altar of incense, and
they performed all the other duties related to the
Most Holy Place. They made atonement for Israel by doing everything that Moses, the servant of
God, had commanded them.

50The descendants of Aaron were Eleazar,
Phinehas, Abishua, 51Bukki, Uzzi, Zerahiah,
52Meraioth, Amariah, Ahitub, 53Zadok, and
Ahimaaz.

Territory for the Levites

54This is a record of the towns and territory assigned by means of sacred lots to the descendants of Aaron, who were from the clan of
Kohath. 55This territory included Hebron and its
surrounding pasturelands in Judah, 56but the
fields and outlying areas belonging to the city
were given to Caleb son of Jephunneh. 57So the
descendants of Aaron were given the following
towns, each with its pasturelands: Hebron (a city
of refuge), Libnah, Jattir, Eshtemoa, 58Holon,
Debir, 59Ain, Juttah, and Beth-shemesh. 60And
from the territory of Benjamin they were given
Gibeon, Geba, Alemeth, and Anathoth, each with
its pasturelands. So thirteen towns were given to
the descendants of Aaron. 61The remaining descendants of Kohath received ten towns from
the territory of the half-tribe of Manasseh by
means of sacred lots.

62The descendants of Gershon received by sacred lots thirteen towns from the territories of
Issachar, Asher, Naphtali, and from the Bashan
area of Manasseh, east of the Jordan.

63The descendants of Merari received by sacred lots twelve towns from the territories of
Reuben, Gad, and Zebulun.

64So the people of Israel assigned all these
towns and pasturelands to the Levites. 65The
towns in the territories of Judah, Simeon, and Benjamin, mentioned above, were assigned to them
by means of sacred lots.

66The descendants of Kohath were given the
following towns from the territory of Ephraim,
each with its pasturelands: 67Shechem (a city of
refuge in the hill country of Ephraim), Gezer,
68Jokmeam, Beth-horon, 69Aijalon, and Gath-
rimmon. 70The remaining descendants of
Kohath were assigned the towns of Aner and
Bileam from the territory of the half-tribe of
Manasseh, each with its pasturelands.

71The descendants of Gershon received the
towns of Golan (in Bashan) and Ashtaroth from
the territory of the half-tribe of Manasseh, each
with its pasturelands. 72From the territory of Issachar, they were given Kedesh, Daberath, 73Ra-
moth, and Anem, each with its pasturelands.
74From the territory of Asher, they received Ma-
shal, Abdon, 75Hukok, and Rehob, each with its
pasturelands. 76From the territory of Naphtali,
they were given Kedesh in Galilee, Hammon, and
Kiriathaim, each with its pasturelands.

77The remaining descendants of Merari received the towns of Jokneam, Kartah, Rimmon,
and Tabor from the territory of Zebulun, each
with its pasturelands. 78From the territory of
Reuben, east of the Jordan River opposite Jericho,
they received Bezer (a desert town), Jahaz, 79Ked-
emoth, and Mephaath, each with its pasturelands. 80And from the territory of Gad, they
received Ramoth in Gilead, Mahanaim, 81Hesh-
bon, and Jazer, each with its pasturelands.

CHAPTER 7

Descendants of Issachar

The four sons of Issachar were Tola, Puah,
Jashub, and Shimron.

2The sons of Tola were Uzzi, Rephaiah, Jeriel,
Jahmai, Ibsam, and Shemuel. Each of them
was the leader of an ancestral clan. At the
time of King David, the total number of
mighty warriors listed in the records of these
clans was 22,600.

3The son of Uzzi was Izrahiah. The sons of
Izrahiah were Michael, Obadiah, Joel, and
Isshiah. These five became the leaders of
clans. 4All of them had many wives and many
sons, so the total number of men available
for military service among their descendants
was 36,000.

5The total number of mighty warriors from all
the clans of the tribe of Issachar was 87,000. All
of them were listed in their genealogical records.

Descendants of Benjamin

6Three of Benjamin's sons were Bela, Beker, and
Jediael.

7The five sons of Bela were Ezbon, Uzzi, Uzziel,
Jerimoth, and Iri. Each of them was the

leader of an ancestral clan. The total number
of mighty warriors from these clans was
22,034, as listed in their genealogical
records.
8 The sons of Beker were Zemirah, Joash,
Eliezer, Elioenai, Omri, Jeremoth, Abijah,
Anathoth, and Alemeth. 9 Each of them was
the leader of an ancestral clan. The total
number of mighty warriors and leaders from
these clans was 20,200, as listed in their
genealogical records.
10 The son of Jediael was Bilhan. The sons
of Bilhan were Jeush, Benjamin, Ehud,
Kenaanah, Zethan, Tarshish, and Ahishahar.
11 Each of them was the leader of an ancestral
clan. From these clans the total number of
mighty warriors ready for war was 17,200.
12 The sons of Ir were Shuppim and Huppim.
Hushim was the son of Aher.

Descendants of Naphtali

13 The sons of Naphtali were Jahzeel, Guni, Jezer,
and Shillem. They were all descendants of
Jacob's concubine Bilhah.

Descendants of Manasseh

14 The descendants of Manasseh through his
Aramean concubine included Asriel. She
also bore Makir, the father of Gilead. 15 Makir
found wives for Huppim and Shuppim.
Makir had a sister named Maacah. One of
his descendants was Zelophehad, who had
only daughters.
16 Makir's wife, Maacah, gave birth to a son
whom she named Peresh. His brother's
name was Sheresh. The sons of Peresh were
Ulam and Rakem. 17 The son of Ulam was
Bedan. All these were considered Gileadites,
descendants of Makir son of Manasseh.
18 Makir's sister Hammoleketh gave birth to
Ishhod, Abiezer, and Mahlah.
19 The sons of Shemida were Ahian, Shechem,
Likhi, and Aniam.

Descendants of Ephraim

20 The descendants of Ephraim were Shuthelah,
Bered, Tahath, Eleadah, Tahath, 21 Zabad,
Shuthelah, Ezer, and Elead. These two were
killed trying to steal livestock from the local
farmers near Gath. 22 Their father, Ephraim,
mourned for them a long time, and his
relatives came to comfort him. 23 Afterward
Ephraim slept with his wife, and she became
pregnant and gave birth to a son. Ephraim
named him Beriah because of the tragedy his
family had suffered. 24 He had a daughter
named Sheerah. She built the towns of Lower
and Upper Beth-horon and Uzzen-sheerah.
25 The descendants of Ephraim included
Rephah, Resheph, Telah, Tahan, 26 Ladan,
Ammihud, Elishama, 27 Nun, and Joshua.

28 The descendants of Ephraim lived in the
territory that included Bethel and its surrounding towns to the south, Naaran to the east, Gezer
and its villages to the west, and Shechem and its
surrounding villages to the north as far as Ayyah
and its towns. 29 Along the border of Manasseh
were the towns of Beth-shan, Taanach, Megiddo,
Dor, and their surrounding villages. The descendants of Joseph son of Israel lived in these towns.

Descendants of Asher

30 The sons of Asher were Imnah, Ishvah, Ishvi,
and Beriah. They had a sister named Serah.
31 The sons of Beriah were Heber and Malkiel
(the father of Birzaith).
32 The sons of Heber were Japhlet, Shomer,
and Hotham. They had a sister named Shua.
33 The sons of Japhlet were Pasach, Bimhal, and
Ashvath.
34 The sons of Shomer were Ahi, Rohgah,
Hubbah, and Aram.
35 The sons of his brother Helem were Zophah,
Imna, Shelesh, and Amal.
36 The sons of Zophah were Suah, Harnepher,
Shual, Beri, Imrah, 37 Bezer, Hod, Shamma,
Shilshah, Ithran, and Beera.
38 The sons of Jether were Jephunneh, Pispah,
and Ara.
39 The sons of Ulla were Arah, Hanniel, and
Rizia.
40 Each of these descendants of Asher was the
head of an ancestral clan. They were all select
men—mighty warriors and outstanding leaders.
The total number of men available for military
service was 26,000, as listed in their genealogical records.

CHAPTER 8

Descendants of Benjamin

Benjamin's first son was Bela, the second was
Ashbel, the third was Aharah, 2 the fourth was
Nohah, and the fifth was Rapha.
3 The sons of Bela were Addar, Gera, Abihud,
4 Abishua, Naaman, Ahoah, 5 Gera, Shephu-
phan, and Huram.
6 The sons of Ehud, leaders of the clans living at
Geba, were exiled to Manahath. 7 Ehud's sons
were Naaman, Ahijah, and Gera. Gera, who

led them into exile, was the father of Uzza
and Ahihud.
8 After Shaharaim divorced his wives Hushim
and Baara, he had children in the land of
Moab. 9 His wife Hodesh gave birth to Jobab,
Zibia, Mesha, Malcam, 10 Jeuz, Sakia, and
Mirmah. These sons all became the leaders
of clans.
11 Shaharaim's wife Hushim had already given
birth to Abitub and Elpaal. 12 The sons of
Elpaal were Eber, Misham, Shemed (who built
the towns of Ono and Lod and their nearby
villages), 13 Beriah, and Shema. They were the
leaders of the clans living in Aijalon, and they
drove out the inhabitants of Gath.
14 Ahio, Shashak, Jeremoth, 15 Zebadiah, Arad,
Eder, 16 Michael, Ishpah, and Joha were the
sons of Beriah.
17 Zebadiah, Meshullam, Hizki, Heber,
18 Ishmerai, Izliah, and Jobab were the sons of
Elpaal.
19 Jakim, Zicri, Zabdi, 20 Elienai, Zillethai, Eliel,
21 Adaiah, Beraiah, and Shimrath were the
sons of Shimei.
22 Ishpan, Eber, Eliel, 23 Abdon, Zicri, Hanan,
24 Hananiah, Elam, Anthothijah, 25 Iphdeiah,
and Penuel were the sons of Shashak.
26 Shamsherai, Shehariah, Athaliah,
27 Jaareshiah, Elijah, and Zicri were the sons
of Jeroham.
28 These were the leaders of the ancestral clans;
they were listed in their genealogical records,
and they all lived in Jerusalem.

The Family of Saul

29 Jeiel (the father of Gibeon) lived in the town
of Gibeon. His wife's name was Maacah,
30 and his oldest son was named Abdon.
Jeiel's other sons were Zur, Kish, Baal, Ner,
Nadab, 31 Gedor, Ahio, Zechariah, 32 and
Mikloth, who was the father of Shimeam.
All these families lived near each other in
Jerusalem.
33 Ner was the father of Kish.
Kish was the father of Saul.
Saul was the father of Jonathan, Malkishua,
Abinadab, and Esh-baal.
34 Jonathan was the father of Merib-baal.
Merib-baal was the father of Micah.
35 Micah was the father of Pithon, Melech,
Tahrea, and Ahaz.
36 Ahaz was the father of Jadah.
Jadah was the father of Alemeth, Azmaveth,
and Zimri.
Zimri was the father of Moza.
37 Moza was the father of Binea.
Binea was the father of Rephaiah.
Rephaiah was the father of Eleasah.
Eleasah was the father of Azel.
38 Azel had six sons: Azrikam, Bokeru, Ishmael,
Sheariah, Obadiah, and Hanan. These were
the sons of Azel.
39 Azel's brother Eshek had three sons: the first
was Ulam, the second was Jeush, and the
third was Eliphelet. 40 Ulam's sons were all
mighty warriors and expert archers. They
had many sons and grandsons—150 in all.

All these were descendants of Benjamin.

CHAPTER 9

So all Israel was listed in the genealogical
records in *The Book of the Kings of Israel.*

The Returning Exiles

The people of Judah were exiled to Babylon because they were unfaithful to the LORD. 2 The
first of the exiles to return to their property in
their former towns were priests, Levites, Temple
servants, and other Israelites. 3 Some of the people from the tribes of Judah, Benjamin, Ephraim,
and Manasseh came and settled in Jerusalem.

4 One family that returned was that of Uthai son
of Ammihud, son of Omri, son of Imri, son
of Bani, a descendant of Perez son of Judah.
5 Others returned from the Shilonite clan,
including Asaiah (the oldest) and his sons.
6 From the Zerahite clan, Jeuel returned with
his relatives.
In all, 690 families from the tribe of Judah
returned.

7 From the tribe of Benjamin came Sallu son
of Meshullam, son of Hodaviah, son of
Hassenuah; 8 Ibneiah son of Jeroham; Elah
son of Uzzi, son of Micri; and Meshullam son
of Shephatiah, son of Reuel, son of Ibnijah.
9 These men were all leaders of clans, and they
were listed in their genealogical records. In all, 956
families from the tribe of Benjamin returned.

The Returning Priests

10 Among the priests who returned were
Jedaiah, Jehoiarib, Jakin, 11 Azariah son of
Hilkiah, son of Meshullam, son of Zadok,
son of Meraioth, son of Ahitub. Azariah
was the chief officer of the house of God.
12 Other returning priests were Adaiah son of
Jeroham, son of Pashhur, son of Malkijah,
and Maasai son of Adiel, son of Jahzerah,

son of Meshullam, son of Meshillemith, son
of Immer.
13 In all, 1,760 priests returned. They were heads of clans and very able men. They were responsible for ministering at the house of God.

The Returning Levites

14 The Levites who returned were Shemaiah son
of Hasshub, son of Azrikam, son of Hashabiah, a descendant of Merari; 15 Bakbakkar;
Heresh; Galal; Mattaniah son of Mica, son
of Zicri, son of Asaph; 16 Obadiah son of
Shemaiah, son of Galal, son of Jeduthun; and Berekiah son of Asa, son of Elkanah, who lived in the area of Netophah.
17 The gatekeepers who returned were Shallum, Akkub, Talmon, Ahiman, and their relatives. Shallum was the chief gatekeeper. 18 Prior
to this time, they were responsible for the King's Gate on the east side. These men served as gatekeepers for the camps of the Levites.
19 Shallum was the son of Kore, a descendant of Abiasaph, from the clan of Korah. He and his relatives, the Korahites, were responsible for guarding the entrance to the sanctuary, just as their ancestors had guarded the Tabernacle in the camp of the LORD.
20 Phinehas son of Eleazar had been in charge of the gatekeepers in earlier times, and the LORD had been with him. 21 And
later Zechariah son of Meshelemiah was responsible for guarding the entrance to the Tabernacle.

22 In all, there were 212 gatekeepers in those days, and they were listed according to the genealogies in their villages. David and Samuel the seer had appointed their ancestors because they
were reliable men. 23 These gatekeepers and their descendants, by their divisions, were responsible for guarding the entrance to the house
of the LORD when that house was a tent. 24 The
gatekeepers were stationed on all four sides—east, west, north, and south. 25 Their relatives in the villages came regularly to share their duties for seven-day periods.

26 The four chief gatekeepers, all Levites, were trusted officials, for they were responsible for the rooms and treasuries at the house of God.
27 They would spend the night around the house of God, since it was their duty to guard it and to open the gates every morning.

28 Some of the gatekeepers were assigned to care for the various articles used in worship. They checked them in and out to avoid any loss. 29 Others were responsible for the furnishings, the items in the sanctuary, and the supplies, such as choice flour, wine, olive oil, frankincense, and
spices. 30 But it was the priests who blended the
spices. 31 Mattithiah, a Levite and the oldest son of Shallum the Korahite, was entrusted with baking
the bread used in the offerings. 32 And some members of the clan of Kohath were in charge of preparing the bread to be set on the table each Sabbath day.

33 The musicians, all prominent Levites, lived at the Temple. They were exempt from other responsibilities since they were on duty at all hours.
34 All these men lived in Jerusalem. They were the heads of Levite families and were listed as prominent leaders in their genealogical records.

King Saul's Family Tree

35 Jeiel (the father of Gibeon) lived in the town of
Gibeon. His wife's name was Maacah, 36 and
his oldest son was named Abdon. Jeiel's other
sons were Zur, Kish, Baal, Ner, Nadab, 37 Gedor,
Ahio, Zechariah, and Mikloth. 38 Mikloth was
the father of Shimeam. All these families lived near each other in Jerusalem.
39 Ner was the father of Kish.
Kish was the father of Saul.
Saul was the father of Jonathan, Malkishua, Abinadab, and Esh-baal.
40 Jonathan was the father of Merib-baal.
Merib-baal was the father of Micah.
41 The sons of Micah were Pithon, Melech, Tahrea, and Ahaz.
42 Ahaz was the father of Jadah.
Jadah was the father of Alemeth, Azmaveth, and Zimri.
Zimri was the father of Moza.
43 Moza was the father of Binea.
Binea's son was Rephaiah.
Rephaiah's son was Eleasah.
Eleasah's son was Azel.
44 Azel had six sons, whose names were Azrikam, Bokeru, Ishmael, Sheariah, Obadiah, and Hanan. These were the sons of Azel.

CHAPTER 10

The Death of King Saul

Now the Philistines attacked Israel, and the men of Israel fled before them. Many were slaughtered on the slopes of Mount Gilboa. 2 The Philistines closed in on Saul and his sons, and they killed three of his sons—Jonathan, Abinadab,
and Malkishua. 3 The fighting grew very fierce around Saul, and the Philistine archers caught up with him and wounded him.

4Saul groaned to his armor bearer, "Take your
sword and kill me before these pagan Philistines
come to taunt and torture me."

But his armor bearer was afraid and would not
do it. So Saul took his own sword and fell on it.
5When his armor bearer realized that Saul was
dead, he fell on his own sword and died. 6So Saul
and his three sons died there together, bringing
his dynasty to an end.

7When all the Israelites in the Jezreel Valley
saw that their army had fled and that Saul and his
sons were dead, they abandoned their towns and
fled. So the Philistines moved in and occupied
their towns.

8The next day, when the Philistines went out
to strip the dead, they found the bodies of Saul
and his sons on Mount Gilboa. 9So they stripped
off Saul's armor and cut off his head. Then they
proclaimed the good news of Saul's death before
their idols and to the people throughout the land
of Philistia. 10They placed his armor in the temple of their gods, and they fastened his head to
the temple of Dagon.

11But when everyone in Jabesh-gilead heard
about everything the Philistines had done to
Saul, 12all their mighty warriors brought the
bodies of Saul and his sons back to Jabesh. Then
they buried their bones beneath the great tree at
Jabesh, and they fasted for seven days.

13So Saul died because he was unfaithful to
the LORD. He failed to obey the LORD's command,
and he even consulted a medium 14instead of
asking the LORD for guidance. So the LORD killed
him and turned the kingdom over to David son
of Jesse.

CHAPTER **11**

David Becomes King of All Israel

Then all Israel gathered before David at Hebron
and told him, "We are your own flesh and blood.
2In the past, even when Saul was king, you were
the one who really led the forces of Israel. And
the LORD your God told you, 'You will be the
shepherd of my people Israel. You will be the
leader of my people Israel.'"

3So there at Hebron, David made a covenant
before the LORD with all the elders of Israel. And
they anointed him king of Israel, just as the LORD
had promised through Samuel.

David Captures Jerusalem

4Then David and all Israel went to Jerusalem (or
Jebus, as it used to be called), where the Jebusites,
the original inhabitants of the land, were living.
5The people of Jebus taunted David, saying,
"You'll never get in here!" But David captured the
fortress of Zion, which is now called the City of
David.

6David had said to his troops, "Whoever is first
to attack the Jebusites will become the commander of my armies!" And Joab, the son of David's sister Zeruiah, was first to attack, so he
became the commander of David's armies.

7David made the fortress his home, and that is
why it is called the City of David. 8He extended
the city from the supporting terraces to the surrounding area, while Joab rebuilt the rest of Jerusalem. 9And David became more and more
powerful, because the LORD of Heaven's Armies
was with him.

David's Mightiest Warriors

10These are the leaders of David's mighty warriors. Together with all Israel, they decided to
make David their king, just as the LORD had
promised concerning Israel.

11Here is the record of David's mightiest warriors: The first was Jashobeam the Hacmonite,
who was leader of the Three—the mightiest warriors among David's men. He once used his spear
to kill 300 enemy warriors in a single battle.

12Next in rank among the Three was Eleazar
son of Dodai, a descendant of Ahoah. 13He was
with David when the Philistines gathered for battle
at Pas-dammim and attacked the Israelites in a
field full of barley. The Israelite army fled, 14but
Eleazar and David held their ground in the middle
of the field and beat back the Philistines. So the
LORD saved them by giving them a great victory.

15Once when David was at the rock near the
cave of Adullam, the Philistine army was camped
in the valley of Rephaim. The Three (who were
among the Thirty—an elite group among David's
fighting men) went down to meet him there.
16David was staying in the stronghold at the
time, and a Philistine detachment had occupied
the town of Bethlehem.

17David remarked longingly to his men, "Oh,
how I would love some of that good water from
the well by the gate in Bethlehem." 18So the
Three broke through the Philistine lines, drew
some water from the well by the gate in Bethlehem, and brought it back to David. But David refused to drink it. Instead, he poured it out as an
offering to the LORD. 19"God forbid that I should
drink this!" he exclaimed. "This water is as precious as the blood of these men who risked their
lives to bring it to me." So David did not drink it.
These are examples of the exploits of the Three.

David's Thirty Mighty Men

20 Abishai, the brother of Joab, was the leader of
the Thirty. He once used his spear to kill 300 enemy warriors in a single battle. It was by such
feats that he became as famous as the Three.
21 Abishai was the most famous of the Thirty and
was their commander, though he was not one of
the Three.

22 There was also Benaiah son of Jehoiada, a valiant warrior from Kabzeel. He did many heroic
deeds, which included killing two champions of
Moab. Another time, on a snowy day, he chased a
lion down into a pit and killed it. 23 Once, armed
only with a club, he killed an Egyptian warrior
who was 7½ feet tall and who was armed with a
spear as thick as a weaver's beam. Benaiah
wrenched the spear from the Egyptian's hand and
killed him with it. 24 Deeds like these made Benaiah as famous as the three mightiest warriors.
25 He was more honored than the other members
of the Thirty, though he was not one of the Three.
And David made him captain of his bodyguard.

26 David's mighty warriors also included:

Asahel, Joab's brother;
Elhanan son of Dodo from Bethlehem;
27 Shammah from Harod;
Helez from Pelon;
28 Ira son of Ikkesh from Tekoa;
Abiezer from Anathoth;
29 Sibbecai from Hushah;
Zalmon from Ahoah;
30 Maharai from Netophah;
Heled son of Baanah from Netophah;
31 Ithai son of Ribai from Gibeah (in the land of Benjamin);
Benaiah from Pirathon;
32 Hurai from near Nahale-gaash;
Abi-albon from Arabah;
33 Azmaveth from Bahurim;
Eliahba from Shaalbon;
34 the sons of Jashen from Gizon;
Jonathan son of Shagee from Harar;
35 Ahiam son of Sharar from Harar;
Eliphal son of Ur;
36 Hepher from Mekerah;
Ahijah from Pelon;
37 Hezro from Carmel;
Paarai son of Ezbai;
38 Joel, the brother of Nathan;
Mibhar son of Hagri;
39 Zelek from Ammon;
Naharai from Beeroth, the armor bearer of Joab son of Zeruiah;
40 Ira from Jattir;
Gareb from Jattir;
41 Uriah the Hittite;
Zabad son of Ahlai;
42 Adina son of Shiza, the Reubenite leader who had thirty men with him;
43 Hanan son of Maacah;
Joshaphat from Mithna;
44 Uzzia from Ashtaroth;
Shama and Jeiel, the sons of Hotham, from Aroer;
45 Jediael son of Shimri;
Joha, his brother, from Tiz;
46 Eliel from Mahavah;
Jeribai and Joshaviah, the sons of Elnaam;
Ithmah from Moab;
47 Eliel and Obed;
Jaasiel from Zobah.

FUN-fact

It's all in the details

A lot of what you'll read in 1 and 2 Chronicles is also found in 2 Samuel and 1 Kings. Sometimes one book includes details that another book leaves out. That doesn't make either of the books wrong! It just shows how God led people to write down different important details.

YOU TRY IT!

Watch a movie or listen to a song with a friend or family member. Then talk it over:

- **What was the best part? the worst part?**
- **What do you remember the most?**

Your answers may have been different, but they were still both accurate. How cool that God gave us different details of important events so we could get the whole picture!

CHAPTER 12
Warriors Join David's Army

The following men joined David at Ziklag while
he was hiding from Saul son of Kish. They were
among the warriors who fought beside David in
battle. 2 All of them were expert archers, and they
could shoot arrows or sling stones with their left
hand as well as their right. They were all relatives
of Saul from the tribe of Benjamin. 3 Their leader
was Ahiezer son of Shemaah from Gibeah; his
brother Joash was second-in-command. These
were the other warriors:

Jeziel and Pelet, sons of Azmaveth;
Beracah;
Jehu from Anathoth;
4 Ishmaiah from Gibeon, a famous warrior
and leader among the Thirty;
Jeremiah, Jahaziel, Johanan, and Jozabad
from Gederah;
5 Eluzai, Jerimoth, Bealiah, Shemariah,
and Shephatiah from Haruph;
6 Elkanah, Isshiah, Azarel, Joezer, and
Jashobeam, who were Korahites;
7 Joelah and Zebadiah, sons of Jeroham
from Gedor.

8 Some brave and experienced warriors from
the tribe of Gad also defected to David while he
was at the stronghold in the wilderness. They
were expert with both shield and spear, as fierce
as lions and as swift as deer on the mountains.

9 Ezer was their leader.
Obadiah was second.
Eliab was third.
10 Mishmannah was fourth.
Jeremiah was fifth.
11 Attai was sixth.
Eliel was seventh.
12 Johanan was eighth.
Elzabad was ninth.
13 Jeremiah was tenth.
Macbannai was eleventh.

14 These warriors from Gad were army commanders. The weakest among them could take
on a hundred regular troops, and the strongest
could take on a thousand! 15 These were the men
who crossed the Jordan River during its seasonal
flooding at the beginning of the year and drove
out all the people living in the lowlands on both
the east and west banks.

16 Others from Benjamin and Judah came to
David at the stronghold. 17 David went out to meet
them and said, "If you have come in peace to help
me, we are friends. But if you have come to betray
me to my enemies when I am innocent, then may
the God of our ancestors see it and punish you."

18 Then the Spirit came upon Amasai, the
leader of the Thirty, and he said,

"We are yours, David!
We are on your side, son of Jesse.
Peace and prosperity be with you,
and success to all who help you,
for your God is the one who helps you."

So David let them join him, and he made them
officers over his troops.

19 Some men from Manasseh defected from
the Israelite army and joined David when he set
out with the Philistines to fight against Saul. But
as it turned out, the Philistine rulers refused to let
David and his men go with them. After much discussion, they sent them back, for they said, "It will
cost us our heads if David switches loyalties to
Saul and turns against us."

20 Here is a list of the men from Manasseh who
defected to David as he was returning to Ziklag:
Adnah, Jozabad, Jediael, Michael, Jozabad, Elihu,
and Zillethai. Each commanded 1,000 troops
from the tribe of Manasseh. 21 They helped David
chase down bands of raiders, for they were all
brave and able warriors who became commanders in his army. 22 Day after day more men joined
David until he had a great army, like the army of
God.

23 These are the numbers of armed warriors
who joined David at Hebron. They were all eager
to see David become king instead of Saul, just as
the LORD had promised.

24 From the tribe of Judah, there were 6,800
warriors armed with shields and spears.
25 From the tribe of Simeon, there were 7,100
brave warriors.
26 From the tribe of Levi, there were 4,600
warriors. 27 This included Jehoiada, leader
of the family of Aaron, who had 3,700 under
his command. 28 This also included Zadok,
a brave young warrior, with 22 members
of his family who were all officers.
29 From the tribe of Benjamin, Saul's relatives,
there were 3,000 warriors. Most of the men
from Benjamin had remained loyal to Saul
until this time.
30 From the tribe of Ephraim, there were 20,800
brave warriors, each highly respected in his
own clan.
31 From the half-tribe of Manasseh west of the
Jordan, 18,000 men were designated by
name to help David become king.

32 From the tribe of Issachar, there were 200
leaders of the tribe with their relatives. All
these men understood the signs of the times
and knew the best course for Israel to take.
33 From the tribe of Zebulun, there were 50,000
skilled warriors. They were fully armed and
prepared for battle and completely loyal to
David.
34 From the tribe of Naphtali, there were 1,000
officers and 37,000 warriors armed with
shields and spears.
35 From the tribe of Dan, there were 28,600
warriors, all prepared for battle.
36 From the tribe of Asher, there were 40,000
trained warriors, all prepared for battle.
37 From the east side of the Jordan River—
where the tribes of Reuben and Gad and the
half-tribe of Manasseh lived—there were
120,000 troops armed with every kind of
weapon.

38 All these men came in battle array to Hebron with the single purpose of making David
the king over all Israel. In fact, everyone in Israel
agreed that David should be their king. 39 They
feasted and drank with David for three days, for
preparations had been made by their relatives
for their arrival. 40 And people from as far away
as Issachar, Zebulun, and Naphtali brought food
on donkeys, camels, mules, and oxen. Vast supplies of flour, fig cakes, clusters of raisins, wine,
olive oil, cattle, sheep, and goats were brought to
the celebration. There was great joy throughout
the land of Israel.

CHAPTER 13

David Attempts to Move the Ark

David consulted with all his officials, including
the generals and captains of his army. 2 Then he
addressed the entire assembly of Israel as follows: "If you approve and if it is the will of the
LORD our God, let us send messages to all the Israelites throughout the land, including the
priests and Levites in their towns and pasturelands. Let us invite them to come and join us. 3 It
is time to bring back the Ark of our God, for we
neglected it during the reign of Saul."

4 The whole assembly agreed to this, for the
people could see it was the right thing to do. 5 So
David summoned all Israel, from the Shihor
Brook of Egypt in the south all the way to the
town of Lebo-hamath in the north, to join in
bringing the Ark of God from Kiriath-jearim.
6 Then David and all Israel went to Baalah of Judah (also called Kiriath-jearim) to bring back the
Ark of God, which bears the name of the LORD
who is enthroned between the cherubim. 7 They
placed the Ark of God on a new cart and brought
it from Abinadab's house. Uzzah and Ahio were
guiding the cart. 8 David and all Israel were celebrating before God with all their might, singing
songs and playing all kinds of musical instruments—lyres, harps, tambourines, cymbals, and
trumpets.

9 But when they arrived at the threshing floor
of Nacon, the oxen stumbled, and Uzzah
reached out his hand to steady the Ark. 10 Then
the LORD's anger was aroused against Uzzah,
and he struck him dead because he had laid his
hand on the Ark. So Uzzah died there in the
presence of God.

11 David was angry because the LORD's anger
had burst out against Uzzah. He named that
place Perez-uzzah (which means "to burst out
against Uzzah"), as it is still called today.

12 David was now afraid of God, and he asked,
"How can I ever bring the Ark of God back into
my care?" 13 So David did not move the Ark into
the City of David. Instead, he took it to the house
of Obed-edom of Gath. 14 The Ark of God remained there in Obed-edom's house for three
months, and the LORD blessed the household of
Obed-edom and everything he owned.

CHAPTER 14

David's Palace and Family

Then King Hiram of Tyre sent messengers to David, along with cedar timber, and stonemasons
and carpenters to build him a palace. 2 And David
realized that the LORD had confirmed him as
king over Israel and had greatly blessed his kingdom for the sake of his people Israel.

3 Then David married more wives in Jerusalem, and they had more sons and daughters.
4 These are the names of David's sons who were
born in Jerusalem: Shammua, Shobab, Nathan,
Solomon, 5 Ibhar, Elishua, Elpelet, 6 Nogah, Nepheg, Japhia, 7 Elishama, Eliada, and Eliphelet.

David Conquers the Philistines

8 When the Philistines heard that David had
been anointed king over all Israel, they mobilized all their forces to capture him. But David
was told they were coming, so he marched out to
meet them. 9 The Philistines arrived and made a
raid in the valley of Rephaim. 10 So David asked
God, "Should I go out to fight the Philistines?
Will you hand them over to me?"

The LORD replied, "Yes, go ahead. I will hand
them over to you."

1 Chronicles 15 . . . page 406

11So David and his troops went up to Baal-
perazim and defeated the Philistines there.
"God did it!" David exclaimed. "He used me to
burst through my enemies like a raging flood!"
So they named that place Baal-perazim (which
means "the Lord who bursts through"). 12The
Philistines had abandoned their gods there, so
David gave orders to burn them.

13But after a while the Philistines returned
and raided the valley again. 14And once again David asked God what to do. "Do not attack them
straight on," God replied. "Instead, circle around
behind and attack them near the poplar trees.
15When you hear a sound like marching feet in
the tops of the poplar trees, go out and attack!
That will be the signal that God is moving ahead
of you to strike down the Philistine army." 16So
David did what God commanded, and they
struck down the Philistine army all the way from
Gibeon to Gezer.

17So David's fame spread everywhere, and the
LORD caused all the nations to fear David.

CHAPTER 15

Preparing to Move the Ark

David now built several buildings for himself in
the City of David. He also prepared a place for the
Ark of God and set up a special tent for it. 2Then
he commanded, "No one except the Levites may
carry the Ark of God. The LORD has chosen them
to carry the Ark of the LORD and to serve him forever."

3Then David summoned all Israel to Jerusalem
to bring the Ark of the LORD to the place he had
prepared for it. 4This is the number of the descendants of Aaron (the priests) and the Levites
who were called together:

5From the clan of Kohath, 120, with Uriel as their leader.
6From the clan of Merari, 220, with Asaiah as their leader.
7From the clan of Gershon, 130, with Joel as their leader.
8From the descendants of Elizaphan, 200, with Shemaiah as their leader.
9From the descendants of Hebron, 80, with Eliel as their leader.
10From the descendants of Uzziel, 112, with Amminadab as their leader.

11Then David summoned the priests, Zadok
and Abiathar, and these Levite leaders: Uriel, Asaiah, Joel, Shemaiah, Eliel, and Amminadab. 12He
said to them, "You are the leaders of the Levite
families. You must purify yourselves and all your

Key Verse **"Give thanks to the LORD and proclaim his greatness. Let the whole world know what he has done."—1 CHRONICLES 16:8**

It Ain't Over...

Some of the coolest parts of the Bible were originally songs of praise to God. The Israelites' enemies, the Philistines, took the ark of the covenant away for a while. David sang a song of praise to God after he finally moved it back to Jerusalem. You can read David's song in **1 CHRONICLES 16:8-36.** The singing continues today because God's greatness never stops!

MOVE OVER, BEETHOVEN!

JESUS
MY DAD
MY BIKE
MY DOG
MY SISTER
MY ROOM

Check out Psalm 96 for some great reasons to sing to God!

1 Make a list of all the things you're thankful for.

2 Make a song of thankfulness, using a tune you know like "Row, Row, Row Your Boat" or the theme song to *Arthur*.

Sung to the tune of "Row, Row, Row Your Boat"

"Lord, I thank you for
Moon and sun and stars.
I thank you, Lord, for ice-cream shops
And the planet Mars."

3 Teach your song to a friend, then work together to turn 1 CHRONICLES 16:8-9 into a song.

fellow Levites, so you can bring the Ark of the
LORD, the God of Israel, to the place I have prepared for it. 13 Because you Levites did not carry
the Ark the first time, the anger of the LORD our
God burst out against us. We failed to ask God
how to move it properly." 14 So the priests and the
Levites purified themselves in order to bring the
Ark of the LORD, the God of Israel, to Jerusalem.
15 Then the Levites carried the Ark of God on their
shoulders with its carrying poles, just as the LORD
had instructed Moses.

16 David also ordered the Levite leaders to appoint a choir of Levites who were singers and
musicians to sing joyful songs to the accompaniment of harps, lyres, and cymbals. 17 So the
Levites appointed Heman son of Joel along with
his fellow Levites: Asaph son of Berekiah, and
Ethan son of Kushaiah from the clan of Merari.
18 The following men were chosen as their assistants: Zechariah, Jaaziel, Shemiramoth, Jehiel,
Unni, Eliab, Benaiah, Maaseiah, Mattithiah,
Eliphelehu, Mikneiah, and the gatekeepers—
Obed-edom and Jeiel.

19 The musicians Heman, Asaph, and Ethan
were chosen to sound the bronze cymbals.
20 Zechariah, Aziel, Shemiramoth, Jehiel, Unni,
Eliab, Maaseiah, and Benaiah were chosen to play
the harps. 21 Mattithiah, Eliphelehu, Mikneiah,
Obed-edom, Jeiel, and Azaziah were chosen to
play the lyres. 22 Kenaniah, the head Levite, was
chosen as the choir leader because of his skill.

23 Berekiah and Elkanah were chosen to guard
the Ark. 24 Shebaniah, Joshaphat, Nethanel,
Amasai, Zechariah, Benaiah, and Eliezer—all of
whom were priests—were chosen to blow the
trumpets as they marched in front of the Ark of
God. Obed-edom and Jehiah were chosen to
guard the Ark.

Moving the Ark to Jerusalem

25 Then David and the elders of Israel and the
generals of the army went to the house of Obed-
edom to bring the Ark of the LORD's Covenant up
to Jerusalem with a great celebration. 26 And because God was clearly helping the Levites as they
carried the Ark of the LORD's Covenant, they sacrificed seven bulls and seven rams.

27 David was dressed in a robe of fine linen, as
were all the Levites who carried the Ark, and also
the singers, and Kenaniah the choir leader. David
was also wearing a priestly garment. 28 So all Israel brought up the Ark of the LORD's Covenant
with shouts of joy, the blowing of rams' horns
and trumpets, the crashing of cymbals, and loud
playing on harps and lyres.

29 But as the Ark of the LORD's Covenant entered the City of David, Michal, the daughter of
Saul, looked down from her window. When she
saw King David skipping about and laughing
with joy, she was filled with contempt for him.

CHAPTER 16

They brought the Ark of God and placed it inside
the special tent David had prepared for it. And
they presented burnt offerings and peace offerings to God. 2 When he had finished his sacrifices, David blessed the people in the name of
the LORD. 3 Then he gave to every man and
woman in all Israel a loaf of bread, a cake of dates,
and a cake of raisins.

4 David appointed the following Levites to lead
the people in worship before the Ark of the
LORD—to invoke his blessings, to give thanks,
and to praise the LORD, the God of Israel. 5 Asaph,
the leader of this group, sounded the cymbals.
Second to him was Zechariah, followed by Jeiel,
Shemiramoth, Jehiel, Mattithiah, Eliab, Benaiah,
Obed-edom, and Jeiel. They played the harps and
lyres. 6 The priests, Benaiah and Jahaziel, played
the trumpets regularly before the Ark of God's
Covenant.

David's Song of Praise

7 On that day David gave to Asaph and his fellow
Levites this song of thanksgiving to the LORD:

8 Give thanks to the LORD and
proclaim his greatness.
Let the whole world know what
he has done.
9 Sing to him; yes, sing his praises.
Tell everyone about his
wonderful deeds.

10 Exult in his holy name;
rejoice, you who worship the LORD.
11 Search for the LORD and for his strength;
continually seek him.
12 Remember the wonders he has performed,
his miracles, and the rulings he has
given,
13 you children of his servant Israel,
you descendants of Jacob, his chosen
ones.

14 He is the LORD our God.
His justice is seen throughout the land.
15 Remember his covenant forever—
the commitment he made to a thousand
generations.
16 This is the covenant he made with Abraham
and the oath he swore to Isaac.

17 He confirmed it to Jacob as a decree,
and to the people of Israel as a never-ending covenant:
18 "I will give you the land of Canaan
as your special possession."

19 He said this when you were few in number,
a tiny group of strangers in Canaan.
20 They wandered from nation to nation,
from one kingdom to another.
21 Yet he did not let anyone oppress them.
He warned kings on their behalf:
22 "Do not touch my chosen people,
and do not hurt my prophets."

23 Let the whole earth sing to the LORD!
Each day proclaim the good news that he saves.
24 Publish his glorious deeds among the nations.
Tell everyone about the amazing things he does.
25 Great is the LORD! He is most worthy of praise!
He is to be feared above all gods.
26 The gods of other nations are mere idols,
but the LORD made the heavens!
27 Honor and majesty surround him;
strength and joy fill his dwelling.

28 O nations of the world, recognize the LORD,
recognize that the LORD is glorious and strong.
29 Give to the LORD the glory he deserves!
Bring your offering and come into his presence.
Worship the LORD in all his holy splendor.
30 Let all the earth tremble before him.
The world stands firm and cannot be shaken.

31 Let the heavens be glad, and the earth rejoice!
Tell all the nations, "The LORD reigns!"
32 Let the sea and everything in it shout his praise!
Let the fields and their crops burst out with joy!
33 Let the trees of the forest sing for joy before the LORD,
for he is coming to judge the earth.

34 Give thanks to the LORD, for he is good!
His faithful love endures forever.
35 Cry out, "Save us, O God of our salvation!
Gather and rescue us from among the nations,
so we can thank your holy name
and rejoice and praise you."
36 Praise the LORD, the God of Israel,
who lives from everlasting to everlasting!

And all the people shouted "Amen!" and praised the LORD.

Worship at Jerusalem and Gibeon

37 David arranged for Asaph and his fellow Levites to serve regularly before the Ark of the
LORD's Covenant, doing whatever needed to be
done each day. 38 This group included Obed-
edom (son of Jeduthun), Hosah, and sixty-eight
other Levites as gatekeepers.
39 Meanwhile, David stationed Zadok the
priest and his fellow priests at the Tabernacle of
the LORD at the place of worship in Gibeon,
where they continued to minister before the
LORD. 40 They sacrificed the regular burnt offerings to the LORD each morning and evening on
the altar set aside for that purpose, obeying
everything written in the Law of the LORD, as he
had commanded Israel. 41 David also appointed
Heman, Jeduthun, and the others chosen by
name to give thanks to the LORD, for "his faithful
love endures forever." 42 They used their trumpets, cymbals, and other instruments to accompany their songs of praise to God. And the sons
of Jeduthun were appointed as gatekeepers.
43 Then all the people returned to their homes,
and David turned and went home to bless his
own family.

CHAPTER 17
The LORD's Covenant Promise to David

When David was settled in his palace, he summoned Nathan the prophet. "Look," David said, "I
am living in a beautiful cedar palace, but the Ark
of the LORD's Covenant is out there under a tent!"
2 Nathan replied to David, "Do whatever you
have in mind, for God is with you."
3 But that same night God said to Nathan,

4 "Go and tell my servant David, 'This is what
the LORD has declared: You are not the one to
build a house for me to live in. 5 I have never
lived in a house, from the day I brought the
Israelites out of Egypt until this very day. My
home has always been a tent, moving from
one place to another in a Tabernacle. 6 Yet no
matter where I have gone with the Israelites,
I have never once complained to Israel's
leaders, the shepherds of my people. I have
never asked them, "Why haven't you built
me a beautiful cedar house?"'

7"Now go and say to my servant David,
'This is what the LORD of Heaven's Armies
has declared: I took you from tending sheep
in the pasture and selected you to be the
leader of my people Israel. 8I have been
with you wherever you have gone, and I
have destroyed all your enemies before
your eyes. Now I will make your name as
famous as anyone who has ever lived on the
earth! 9And I will provide a homeland for
my people Israel, planting them in a secure
place where they will never be disturbed.
Evil nations won't oppress them as they've
done in the past, 10starting from the time
I appointed judges to rule my people Israel.
And I will defeat all your enemies.

"'Furthermore, I declare that the LORD will
build a house for you—a dynasty of kings!
11For when you die and join your ancestors,
I will raise up one of your descendants, one
of your sons, and I will make his kingdom
strong. 12He is the one who will build a
house—a temple—for me. And I will secure
his throne forever. 13I will be his father,
and he will be my son. I will never take my
favor from him as I took it from the one who
ruled before you. 14I will confirm him as king
over my house and my kingdom for all time,
and his throne will be secure forever.'"

15So Nathan went back to David and told him
everything the LORD had said in this vision.

David's Prayer of Thanks

16Then King David went in and sat before the
LORD and prayed,

"Who am I, O LORD God, and what is my
family, that you have brought me this far?
17And now, O God, in addition to everything
else, you speak of giving your servant a
lasting dynasty! You speak as though I were
someone very great, O LORD God!

18"What more can I say to you about the
way you have honored me? You know what
your servant is really like. 19For the sake of
your servant, O LORD, and according to your
will, you have done all these great things and
have made them known.

20"O LORD, there is no one like you. We
have never even heard of another God like
you! 21What other nation on earth is like your
people Israel? What other nation, O God,
have you redeemed from slavery to be your
own people? You made a great name for
yourself when you redeemed your people
from Egypt. You performed awesome
miracles and drove out the nations that stood
in their way. 22You chose Israel to be your
very own people forever, and you, O LORD,
became their God.

23"And now, O LORD, I am your servant;
do as you have promised concerning me
and my family. May it be a promise that
will last forever. 24And may your name be
established and honored forever so that
everyone will say, 'The LORD of Heaven's
Armies, the God of Israel, is Israel's God!'
And may the house of your servant David
continue before you forever.

25"O my God, I have been bold enough
to pray to you because you have revealed
to your servant that you will build a house
for him—a dynasty of kings! 26For you are
God, O LORD. And you have promised these
good things to your servant. 27And now, it
has pleased you to bless the house of your
servant, so that it will continue forever
before you. For when you grant a blessing,
O LORD, it is an eternal blessing!"

CHAPTER 18

David's Military Victories

After this, David defeated and subdued the
Philistines by conquering Gath and its surrounding towns. 2David also conquered the
land of Moab, and the Moabites who were
spared became David's subjects and paid him
tribute money.

3David also destroyed the forces of Hadadezer, king of Zobah, as far as Hamath, when Hadadezer marched out to strengthen his control
along the Euphrates River. 4David captured
1,000 chariots, 7,000 charioteers, and 20,000
foot soldiers. He crippled all the chariot horses
except enough for 100 chariots.

5When Arameans from Damascus arrived to
help King Hadadezer, David killed 22,000 of
them. 6Then he placed several army garrisons in
Damascus, the Aramean capital, and the Arameans became David's subjects and paid him tribute money. So the LORD made David victorious
wherever he went.

7David brought the gold shields of Hadadezer's officers to Jerusalem, 8along with a large
amount of bronze from Hadadezer's towns of
Tebah and Cun. Later Solomon melted the
bronze and molded it into the great bronze basin
called the Sea, the pillars, and the various bronze
articles used at the Temple.

9When King Toi of Hamath heard that David

DEMOLITION

It's good to keep our promises. It's even better for people not to make promises at all. Check out James 5:12.

Is there anyone you know who is good at fixing things? Maybe you've had to fix your bike or a favorite toy. But there are some things that can't be fixed after they're broken.

IT'S LIKE THIS!

1 Break an egg into a bowl. Snap a twig or a toothpick. Rip a piece of paper. Peel a piece of fruit.

2 Now work to fix each thing you broke. Try taping or gluing each item back together so it looks and feels like it did before.

COULD YOU FIX ANY OF THEM?

That's how it works with a promise. Once you break a promise, it's almost impossible to unbreak it.

God's Word is full of promises to you. And God *never* breaks a promise. **Check out 1 CHRONICLES 17:1-14 to see a promise God made to David.** God kept that promise when Jesus was born. **See for yourself in LUKE 1:26-38.**

had destroyed the entire army of King Hadadezer of Zobah, 10he sent his son Joram to congratulate King David for his successful campaign.
Hadadezer and Toi had been enemies and were
often at war. Joram presented David with many
gifts of gold, silver, and bronze.
11King David dedicated all these gifts to the
LORD, along with the silver and gold he had taken
from the other nations—from Edom, Moab, Ammon, Philistia, and Amalek.
12Abishai son of Zeruiah destroyed 18,000
Edomites in the Valley of Salt. 13He placed army
garrisons in Edom, and all the Edomites became
David's subjects. In fact, the LORD made David
victorious wherever he went.
14So David reigned over all Israel and did
what was just and right for all his people. 15Joab
son of Zeruiah was commander of the army. Jehoshaphat son of Ahilud was the royal historian.
16Zadok son of Ahitub and Ahimelech son of
Abiathar were the priests. Seraiah was the court
secretary. 17Benaiah son of Jehoiada was captain
of the king's bodyguard. And David's sons served
as the king's chief assistants.

CHAPTER **19**

David Defeats the Ammonites

Some time after this, King Nahash of the Ammonites died, and his son Hanun became king.
2David said, "I am going to show loyalty to Hanun
because his father, Nahash, was always loyal to
me." So David sent messengers to express sympathy to Hanun about his father's death.
But when David's ambassadors arrived in the
land of Ammon, 3the Ammonite commanders
said to Hanun, "Do you really think these men are
coming here to honor your father? No! David has
sent them to spy out the land so they can come in
and conquer it!" 4So Hanun seized David's ambassadors and shaved them, cut off their robes at
the buttocks, and sent them back to David in
shame.
5When David heard what had happened to
the men, he sent messengers to tell them, "Stay at
Jericho until your beards grow out, and then
come back." For they felt deep shame because of
their appearance.
6When the people of Ammon realized how seriously they had angered David, Hanun and the
Ammonites sent 75,000 pounds of silver to hire
chariots and charioteers from Aram-naharaim,
Aram-maacah, and Zobah. 7They also hired
32,000 chariots and secured the support of the
king of Maacah and his army. These forces
camped at Medeba, where they were joined by

the Ammonite troops that Hanun had recruited
from his own towns. 8When David heard about
this, he sent Joab and all his warriors to fight
them. 9The Ammonite troops came out and
drew their battle lines at the entrance of the city,
while the other kings positioned themselves to
fight in the open fields.
10When Joab saw that he would have to fight
on both the front and the rear, he chose some of
Israel's elite troops and placed them under his
personal command to fight the Arameans in the
fields. 11He left the rest of the army under the
command of his brother Abishai, who was to attack the Ammonites. 12"If the Arameans are too
strong for me, then come over and help me," Joab
told his brother. "And if the Ammonites are too
strong for you, I will help you. 13Be courageous!
Let us fight bravely for our people and the cities
of our God. May the LORD's will be done."
14When Joab and his troops attacked, the Arameans began to run away. 15And when the Ammonites saw the Arameans running, they also
ran from Abishai and retreated into the city.
Then Joab returned to Jerusalem.
16The Arameans now realized that they were
no match for Israel, so they sent messengers and
summoned additional Aramean troops from the
other side of the Euphrates River. These troops
were under the command of Shobach, the commander of Hadadezer's forces.
17When David heard what was happening, he
mobilized all Israel, crossed the Jordan River, and
positioned his troops in battle formation. Then
David engaged the Arameans in battle, and they
fought against him. 18But again the Arameans
fled from the Israelites. This time David's forces
killed 7,000 charioteers and 40,000 foot soldiers,
including Shobach, the commander of their army.
19When Hadadezer's allies saw that they had been
defeated by Israel, they surrendered to David and
became his subjects. After that, the Arameans
were no longer willing to help the Ammonites.

CHAPTER 20

David Captures Rabbah

In the spring of the year, when kings normally go
out to war, Joab led the Israelite army in successful attacks against the land of the Ammonites. In
the process he laid siege to the city of Rabbah, attacking and destroying it. However, David stayed
behind in Jerusalem.
2Then David went to Rabbah and removed
the crown from the king's head, and it was placed
on his own head. The crown was made of gold
and set with gems, and he found that it weighed
seventy-five pounds. David took a vast amount of
plunder from the city. 3He also made slaves of
the people of Rabbah and forced them to labor
with saws, iron picks, and iron axes. That is how
David dealt with the people of all the Ammonite
towns. Then David and all the army returned to
Jerusalem.

Battles against Philistine Giants

4After this, war broke out with the Philistines at
Gezer. As they fought, Sibbecai from Hushah
killed Saph, a descendant of the giants, and so
the Philistines were subdued.
5During another battle with the Philistines,
Elhanan son of Jair killed Lahmi, the brother of
Goliath of Gath. The handle of Lahmi's spear
was as thick as a weaver's beam!
6In another battle with the Philistines at Gath,
they encountered a huge man with six fingers on
each hand and six toes on each foot, twenty-four
in all, who was also a descendant of the giants.
7But when he defied and taunted Israel, he was
killed by Jonathan, the son of David's brother
Shimea.
8These Philistines were descendants of the
giants of Gath, but David and his warriors killed
them.

CHAPTER 21

David Takes a Census

Satan rose up against Israel and caused David to
take a census of the people of Israel. 2So David
said to Joab and the commanders of the army, "Take
a census of all the people of Israel—from Beersheba in the south to Dan in the north—and
bring me a report so I may know how many there
are."
3But Joab replied, "May the LORD increase the
number of his people a hundred times over! But
why, my lord the king, do you want to do this? Are
they not all your servants? Why must you cause
Israel to sin?"
4But the king insisted that they take the census, so Joab traveled throughout all Israel to
count the people. Then he returned to Jerusalem
5and reported the number of people to David.
There were 1,100,000 warriors in all Israel who
could handle a sword, and 470,000 in Judah.
6But Joab did not include the tribes of Levi and
Benjamin in the census because he was so distressed at what the king had made him do.

Judgment for David's Sin

7God was very displeased with the census, and
he punished Israel for it. 8Then David said to

God, "I have sinned greatly by taking this census.
Please forgive my guilt for doing this foolish
thing."
9Then the LORD spoke to Gad, David's seer.
This was the message: 10"Go and say to David,
'This is what the LORD says: I will give you three
choices. Choose one of these punishments, and I
will inflict it on you.'"
11So Gad came to David and said, "These are
the choices the LORD has given you. 12You may
choose three years of famine, three months of
destruction by the sword of your enemies, or
three days of severe plague as the angel of the
LORD brings devastation throughout the land of
Israel. Decide what answer I should give the
LORD who sent me."
13"I'm in a desperate situation!" David replied
to Gad. "But let me fall into the hands of the
LORD, for his mercy is very great. Do not let me
fall into human hands."
14So the LORD sent a plague upon Israel, and
70,000 people died as a result. 15And God sent
an angel to destroy Jerusalem. But just as the angel was preparing to destroy it, the LORD relented
and said to the death angel, "Stop! That is
enough!" At that moment the angel of the LORD
was standing by the threshing floor of Araunah
the Jebusite.
16David looked up and saw the angel of the
LORD standing between heaven and earth with
his sword drawn, reaching out over Jerusalem.
So David and the leaders of Israel put on burlap
to show their deep distress and fell face down on
the ground. 17And David said to God, "I am the
one who called for the census! I am the one who
has sinned and done wrong! But these people are
as innocent as sheep—what have they done?
O LORD my God, let your anger fall against me
and my family, but do not destroy your people."

David Builds an Altar

18Then the angel of the LORD told Gad to instruct
David to go up and build an altar to the LORD on
the threshing floor of Araunah the Jebusite. 19So
David went up to do what the LORD had commanded him through Gad. 20Araunah, who was
busy threshing wheat at the time, turned and saw
the angel there. His four sons, who were with
him, ran away and hid. 21When Araunah saw David approaching, he left his threshing floor and
bowed before David with his face to the ground.
22David said to Araunah, "Let me buy this
threshing floor from you at its full price. Then I
will build an altar to the LORD there, so that he
will stop the plague."
23"Take it, my lord the king, and use it as you
wish," Araunah said to David. "I will give the oxen
for the burnt offerings, and the threshing boards
for wood to build a fire on the altar, and the
wheat for the grain offering. I will give it all to
you."
24But King David replied to Araunah, "No, I insist on buying it for the full price. I will not take
what is yours and give it to the LORD. I will not
present burnt offerings that have cost me nothing!" 25So David gave Araunah 600 pieces of gold
in payment for the threshing floor.
26David built an altar there to the LORD and
sacrificed burnt offerings and peace offerings.
And when David prayed, the LORD answered him
by sending fire from heaven to burn up the offering on the altar. 27Then the LORD spoke to the angel, who put the sword back into its sheath.
28When David saw that the LORD had answered his prayer, he offered sacrifices there at
Araunah's threshing floor. 29At that time the
Tabernacle of the LORD and the altar of burnt offering that Moses had made in the wilderness
were located at the place of worship in Gibeon.
30But David was not able to go there to inquire of
God, because he was terrified by the drawn
sword of the angel of the LORD.

CHAPTER 22

Then David said, "This will be the location for
the Temple of the LORD God and the place of the
altar for Israel's burnt offerings!"

Preparations for the Temple

2So David gave orders to call together the foreigners living in Israel, and he assigned them the
task of preparing finished stone for building the
Temple of God. 3David provided large amounts of
iron for the nails that would be needed for the
doors in the gates and for the clamps, and he gave
more bronze than could be weighed. 4He also
provided innumerable cedar logs, for the men of
Tyre and Sidon had brought vast amounts of cedar to David.
5David said, "My son Solomon is still young
and inexperienced. And since the Temple to be
built for the LORD must be a magnificent structure, famous and glorious throughout the world,
I will begin making preparations for it now." So
David collected vast amounts of building materials before his death.
6Then David sent for his son Solomon and instructed him to build a Temple for the LORD, the
God of Israel. 7"My son, I wanted to build a Temple to honor the name of the LORD my God," Da-

vid told him. 8"But the LORD said to me, 'You have killed many men in the battles you have fought. And since you have shed so much blood in my sight, you will not be the one to build a Temple to honor my name. 9But you will have a son who will be a man of peace. I will give him peace with his enemies in all the surrounding lands. His name will be Solomon, and I will give peace and quiet to Israel during his reign. 10He is the one who will build a Temple to honor my name. He will be my son, and I will be his father. And I will secure the throne of his kingdom over Israel forever.'

11"Now, my son, may the LORD be with you and give you success as you follow his directions in building the Temple of the LORD your God. 12And may the LORD give you wisdom and understanding, that you may obey the Law of the LORD your God as you rule over Israel. 13For you will be successful if you carefully obey the decrees and regulations that the LORD gave to Israel through Moses. Be strong and courageous; do not be afraid or lose heart!

14"I have worked hard to provide materials for building the Temple of the LORD—nearly 4,000 tons of gold, 40,000 tons of silver, and so much iron and bronze that it cannot be weighed. I have also gathered timber and stone for the walls, though you may need to add more. 15You have a large number of skilled stonemasons and carpenters and craftsmen of every kind. 16You have expert goldsmiths and silversmiths and workers of bronze and iron. Now begin the work, and may the LORD be with you!"

17Then David ordered all the leaders of Israel to assist Solomon in this project. 18"The LORD your God is with you," he declared. "He has given you peace with the surrounding nations. He has handed them over to me, and they are now subject to the LORD and his people. 19Now seek the LORD your God with all your heart and soul. Build the sanctuary of the LORD God so that you can bring the Ark of the LORD's Covenant and the holy vessels of God into the Temple built to honor the LORD's name."

CHAPTER 23
Duties of the Levites

When David was an old man, he appointed his son Solomon to be king over Israel. 2David summoned all the leaders of Israel, together with the priests and Levites. 3All the Levites who were thirty years old or older were counted, and the total came to 38,000. 4Then David said, "From all the Levites, 24,000 will supervise the work at the Temple of the LORD. Another 6,000 will serve as officials and judges. 5Another 4,000 will work as gatekeepers, and 4,000 will praise the LORD with the musical instruments I have made." 6Then David divided the Levites into divisions named after the clans descended from the three sons of Levi—Gershon, Kohath, and Merari.

The Gershonites

7The Gershonite family units were defined by their lines of descent from Libni and Shimei, the sons of Gershon. 8Three of the descendants of Libni were Jehiel (the family leader), Zetham, and Joel. 9These were the leaders of the family of Libni.

Three of the descendants of Shimei were Shelomoth, Haziel, and Haran. 10Four other descendants of Shimei were Jahath, Ziza, Jeush, and Beriah. 11Jahath was the family leader, and Ziza was next. Jeush and Beriah were counted as a single family because neither had many sons.

The Kohathites

12Four of the descendants of Kohath were Amram, Izhar, Hebron, and Uzziel.

13The sons of Amram were Aaron and Moses. Aaron and his descendants were set apart to dedicate the most holy things, to offer sacrifices in the LORD's presence, to serve the LORD, and to pronounce blessings in his name forever.

14As for Moses, the man of God, his sons were included with the tribe of Levi. 15The sons of Moses were Gershom and Eliezer. 16The descendants of Gershom included Shebuel, the family leader. 17Eliezer had only one son, Rehabiah, the family leader. Rehabiah had numerous descendants.

18The descendants of Izhar included Shelomith, the family leader.

19The descendants of Hebron included Jeriah (the family leader), Amariah (the second), Jahaziel (the third), and Jekameam (the fourth).

20The descendants of Uzziel included Micah (the family leader) and Isshiah (the second).

The Merarites

21The descendants of Merari included Mahli and Mushi.

The sons of Mahli were Eleazar and Kish.

22Eleazar died with no sons, only daughters. His daughters married their cousins, the sons of Kish.

23 Three of the descendants of Mushi were
Mahli, Eder, and Jerimoth.

24 These were the descendants of Levi by clans,
the leaders of their family groups, registered
carefully by name. Each had to be twenty years
old or older to qualify for service in the house of
the LORD. 25 For David said, "The LORD, the God of
Israel, has given us peace, and he will always live
in Jerusalem. 26 Now the Levites will no longer
need to carry the Tabernacle and its furnishings
from place to place." 27 In accordance with David's final instructions, all the Levites twenty
years old or older were registered for service.

28 The work of the Levites was to assist the
priests, the descendants of Aaron, as they served
at the house of the LORD. They also took care of
the courtyards and side rooms, helped perform
the ceremonies of purification, and served in
many other ways in the house of God. 29 They
were in charge of the sacred bread that was set
out on the table, the choice flour for the grain offerings, the wafers made without yeast, the cakes
cooked in olive oil, and the other mixed breads.
They were also responsible to check all the
weights and measures. 30 And each morning and
evening they stood before the LORD to sing songs
of thanks and praise to him. 31 They assisted with
the burnt offerings that were presented to the
LORD on Sabbath days, at new moon celebrations, and at all the appointed festivals. The required number of Levites served in the LORD's
presence at all times, following all the procedures they had been given.

32 And so, under the supervision of the priests,
the Levites watched over the Tabernacle and the
Temple and faithfully carried out their duties of
service at the house of the LORD.

CHAPTER 24

Duties of the Priests

This is how Aaron's descendants, the priests,
were divided into groups for service. The sons of
Aaron were Nadab, Abihu, Eleazar, and Ithamar.
2 But Nadab and Abihu died before their father,
and they had no sons. So only Eleazar and Ithamar were left to carry on as priests.

3 With the help of Zadok, who was a descendant of Eleazar, and of Ahimelech, who was a descendant of Ithamar, David divided Aaron's
descendants into groups according to their various duties. 4 Eleazar's descendants were divided
into sixteen groups and Ithamar's into eight, for
there were more family leaders among the descendants of Eleazar.

5 All tasks were assigned to the various groups
by means of sacred lots so that no preference
would be shown, for there were many qualified
officials serving God in the sanctuary from
among the descendants of both Eleazar and
Ithamar. 6 Shemaiah son of Nethanel, a Levite,
acted as secretary and wrote down the names
and assignments in the presence of the king, the
officials, Zadok the priest, Ahimelech son of
Abiathar, and the family leaders of the priests
and Levites. The descendants of Eleazar and Ithamar took turns casting lots.

7 The first lot fell to Jehoiarib.
The second lot fell to Jedaiah.
8 The third lot fell to Harim.
The fourth lot fell to Seorim.
9 The fifth lot fell to Malkijah.
The sixth lot fell to Mijamin.
10 The seventh lot fell to Hakkoz.
The eighth lot fell to Abijah.
11 The ninth lot fell to Jeshua.
The tenth lot fell to Shecaniah.
12 The eleventh lot fell to Eliashib.
The twelfth lot fell to Jakim.
13 The thirteenth lot fell to Huppah.
The fourteenth lot fell to Jeshebeab.
14 The fifteenth lot fell to Bilgah.
The sixteenth lot fell to Immer.
15 The seventeenth lot fell to Hezir.
The eighteenth lot fell to Happizzez.
16 The nineteenth lot fell to Pethahiah.
The twentieth lot fell to Jehezkel.
17 The twenty-first lot fell to Jakin.
The twenty-second lot fell to Gamul.
18 The twenty-third lot fell to Delaiah.
The twenty-fourth lot fell to Maaziah.

19 Each group carried out its appointed duties
in the house of the LORD according to the procedures established by their ancestor Aaron in
obedience to the commands of the LORD, the
God of Israel.

Family Leaders among the Levites

20 These were the other family leaders descended from Levi:

From the descendants of Amram, the leader
was Shebuel.
From the descendants of Shebuel, the leader
was Jehdeiah.
21 From the descendants of Rehabiah, the
leader was Isshiah.
22 From the descendants of Izhar, the leader
was Shelomith.

From the descendants of Shelomith, the leader was Jahath.
23 From the descendants of Hebron, Jeriah was the leader, Amariah was second, Jahaziel was third, and Jekameam was fourth.
24 From the descendants of Uzziel, the leader was Micah.
From the descendants of Micah, the leader was Shamir,
25 along with Isshiah, the brother of Micah.
From the descendants of Isshiah, the leader was Zechariah.
26 From the descendants of Merari, the leaders were Mahli and Mushi.
From the descendants of Jaaziah, the leader was Beno.
27 From the descendants of Merari through Jaaziah, the leaders were Beno, Shoham, Zaccur, and Ibri.
28 From the descendants of Mahli, the leader was Eleazar, though he had no sons.
29 From the descendants of Kish, the leader was Jerahmeel.
30 From the descendants of Mushi, the leaders were Mahli, Eder, and Jerimoth.

These were the descendants of Levi in their
various families.
31 Like the descendants of
Aaron, they were assigned to their duties by
means of sacred lots, without regard to age or
rank. Lots were drawn in the presence of King
David, Zadok, Ahimelech, and the family leaders
of the priests and the Levites.

CHAPTER 25
Duties of the Musicians

David and the army commanders then appointed men from the families of Asaph, Heman, and Jeduthun to proclaim God's messages to the accompaniment of lyres, harps, and cymbals. Here is a list of their names and their work:

2 From the sons of Asaph, there were Zaccur, Joseph, Nethaniah, and Asarelah. They worked under the direction of their father, Asaph, who proclaimed God's messages by the king's orders.
3 From the sons of Jeduthun, there were Gedaliah, Zeri, Jeshaiah, Shimei, Hashabiah, and Mattithiah, six in all. They worked under the direction of their father, Jeduthun, who proclaimed God's messages to the accompaniment of the lyre, offering thanks and praise to the LORD.
4 From the sons of Heman, there were Bukkiah, Mattaniah, Uzziel, Shubael, Jerimoth, Hananiah, Hanani, Eliathah, Giddalti, Romamti-ezer, Joshbekashah, Mallothi, Hothir, and Mahazioth.
5 All these were the sons of Heman, the king's seer, for God had honored him with fourteen sons and three daughters.

6 All these men were under the direction of
their fathers as they made music at the house of
the LORD. Their responsibilities included the
playing of cymbals, harps, and lyres at the house
of God. Asaph, Jeduthun, and Heman reported
directly to the king.
7 They and their families
were all trained in making music before the
LORD, and each of them—288 in all—was an accomplished musician.
8 The musicians were
appointed to their term of service by means of
sacred lots, without regard to whether they were
young or old, teacher or student.

9 The first lot fell to Joseph of the Asaph clan and twelve of his sons and relatives.
The second lot fell to Gedaliah and twelve of his sons and relatives.
10 The third lot fell to Zaccur and twelve of his sons and relatives.
11 The fourth lot fell to Zeri and twelve of his sons and relatives.

When times were tough for the Israelites, they cried out to God for help, and God helped them. But when things were going peachy, the Israelites forgot God and trusted in their own strength. They forgot that God gave them strength in the first place!

It's easy to ask God for help when you need it—and it's good to do that. But it's just as important to thank God when things go well.

Tell a friend or family member about everything that's going right for you. Point out that God has done those things in your life.

12 The fifth lot fell to Nethaniah and twelve of his sons and relatives.
13 The sixth lot fell to Bukkiah and twelve of his sons and relatives.
14 The seventh lot fell to Asarelah and twelve of his sons and relatives.
15 The eighth lot fell to Jeshaiah and twelve of his sons and relatives.
16 The ninth lot fell to Mattaniah and twelve of his sons and relatives.
17 The tenth lot fell to Shimei and twelve of his sons and relatives.
18 The eleventh lot fell to Uzziel and twelve of his sons and relatives.
19 The twelfth lot fell to Hashabiah and twelve of his sons and relatives.
20 The thirteenth lot fell to Shubael and twelve of his sons and relatives.
21 The fourteenth lot fell to Mattithiah and twelve of his sons and relatives.
22 The fifteenth lot fell to Jerimoth and twelve of his sons and relatives.
23 The sixteenth lot fell to Hananiah and twelve of his sons and relatives.
24 The seventeenth lot fell to Joshbekashah and twelve of his sons and relatives.
25 The eighteenth lot fell to Hanani and twelve of his sons and relatives.
26 The nineteenth lot fell to Mallothi and twelve of his sons and relatives.
27 The twentieth lot fell to Eliathah and twelve of his sons and relatives.
28 The twenty-first lot fell to Hothir and twelve of his sons and relatives.
29 The twenty-second lot fell to Giddalti and twelve of his sons and relatives.
30 The twenty-third lot fell to Mahazioth and twelve of his sons and relatives.
31 The twenty-fourth lot fell to Romamti-ezer and twelve of his sons and relatives.

CHAPTER 26

Duties of the Gatekeepers

These are the divisions of the gatekeepers:

From the Korahites, there was Meshelemiah son
of Kore, of the family of Abiasaph. 2 The sons
of Meshelemiah were Zechariah (the oldest),
Jediael (the second), Zebadiah (the third),
Jathniel (the fourth), 3 Elam (the fifth),
Jehohanan (the sixth), and Eliehoenai (the
seventh).
4 The sons of Obed-edom, also gatekeepers,
were Shemaiah (the oldest), Jehozabad (the
second), Joah (the third), Sacar (the fourth),
Nethanel (the fifth), 5 Ammiel (the sixth),
Issachar (the seventh), and Peullethai (the
eighth). God had richly blessed Obed-edom.
6 Obed-edom's son Shemaiah had sons
with great ability who earned positions of
great authority in the clan. 7 Their names
were Othni, Rephael, Obed, and Elzabad.
Their relatives, Elihu and Semakiah, were
also very capable men.
8 All of these descendants of Obed-edom,
including their sons and grandsons—sixty-
two of them in all—were very capable men,
well qualified for their work.
9 Meshelemiah's eighteen sons and relatives
were also very capable men.

10 Hosah, of the Merari clan, appointed Shimri
as the leader among his sons, though he was
not the oldest. 11 His other sons included
Hilkiah (the second), Tebaliah (the third),
and Zechariah (the fourth). Hosah's sons
and relatives, who served as gatekeepers,
numbered thirteen in all.

12 These divisions of the gatekeepers were
named for their family leaders, and like the
other Levites, they served at the house of the
LORD. 13 They were assigned by families for
guard duty at the various gates, without regard
to age or training, for it was all decided by means
of sacred lots.
14 The responsibility for the east gate went to
Meshelemiah and his group. The north gate was
assigned to his son Zechariah, a man of unusual
wisdom. 15 The south gate went to Obed-edom,
and his sons were put in charge of the storehouse. 16 Shuppim and Hosah were assigned
the west gate and the gateway leading up to the
Temple. Guard duties were divided evenly. 17 Six
Levites were assigned each day to the east gate,
four to the north gate, four to the south gate, and
two pairs at the storehouse. 18 Six were assigned
each day to the west gate, four to the gateway
leading up to the Temple, and two to the courtyard.
19 These were the divisions of the gatekeepers
from the clans of Korah and Merari.

Treasurers and Other Officials

20 Other Levites, led by Ahijah, were in charge of
the treasuries of the house of God and the treasuries of the gifts dedicated to the LORD. 21 From
the family of Libni in the clan of Gershon, Jehiel
was the leader. 22 The sons of Jehiel, Zetham and
his brother Joel, were in charge of the treasuries
of the house of the LORD.

23 These are the leaders that descended from
Amram, Izhar, Hebron, and Uzziel:

24 From the clan of Amram, Shebuel was a
descendant of Gershom son of Moses. He
was the chief officer of the treasuries. 25 His
relatives through Eliezer were Rehabiah,
Jeshaiah, Joram, Zicri, and Shelomoth.
26 Shelomoth and his relatives were in
charge of the treasuries containing the gifts
that King David, the family leaders, and the
generals and captains and other officers of
the army had dedicated to the LORD. 27 These
men dedicated some of the plunder they had
gained in battle to maintain the house of the
LORD. 28 Shelomoth and his relatives also
cared for the gifts dedicated to the LORD by
Samuel the seer, Saul son of Kish, Abner son
of Ner, and Joab son of Zeruiah. All the other
dedicated gifts were in their care, too.

29 From the clan of Izhar came Kenaniah. He
and his sons were given administrative
responsibilities over Israel as officials and
judges.

30 From the clan of Hebron came Hashabiah. He
and his relatives—1,700 capable men—were
put in charge of the Israelite lands west of
the Jordan River. They were responsible for
all matters related to the things of the LORD
and the service of the king in that area.
31 Also from the clan of Hebron came
Jeriah, who was the leader of the Hebronites
according to the genealogical records. (In the
fortieth year of David's reign, a search was
made in the records, and capable men from
the clan of Hebron were found at Jazer in the
land of Gilead.) 32 There were 2,700 capable
men among the relatives of Jeriah. King
David sent them to the east side of the Jordan
River and put them in charge of the tribes
of Reuben and Gad and the half-tribe of
Manasseh. They were responsible for all
matters related to God and to the king.

CHAPTER 27

Military Commanders and Divisions

This is the list of Israelite generals and captains,
and their officers, who served the king by super-
vising the army divisions that were on duty each
month of the year. Each division served for one
month and had 24,000 troops.

2 Jashobeam son of Zabdiel was commander
of the first division of 24,000 troops, which
was on duty during the first month. 3 He was
a descendant of Perez and was in charge of
all the army officers for the first month.

4 Dodai, a descendant of Ahoah, was commander
of the second division of 24,000 troops,
which was on duty during the second month.
Mikloth was his chief officer.

5 Benaiah son of Jehoiada the priest was
commander of the third division of 24,000
troops, which was on duty during the third
month. 6 This was the Benaiah who
commanded David's elite military group
known as the Thirty. His son Ammizabad
was his chief officer.

7 Asahel, the brother of Joab, was commander
of the fourth division of 24,000 troops,
which was on duty during the fourth
month. Asahel was succeeded by his son
Zebadiah.

8 Shammah the Izrahite was commander of the
fifth division of 24,000 troops, which was on
duty during the fifth month.

9 Ira son of Ikkesh from Tekoa was commander
of the sixth division of 24,000 troops, which
was on duty during the sixth month.

10 Helez, a descendant of Ephraim from Pelon,
was commander of the seventh division of
24,000 troops, which was on duty during
the seventh month.

11 Sibbecai, a descendant of Zerah from Hushah,
was commander of the eighth division of
24,000 troops, which was on duty during
the eighth month.

12 Abiezer from Anathoth in the territory of
Benjamin was commander of the ninth
division of 24,000 troops, which was on
duty during the ninth month.

13 Maharai, a descendant of Zerah from
Netophah, was commander of the tenth
division of 24,000 troops, which was on
duty during the tenth month.

14 Benaiah from Pirathon in Ephraim was
commander of the eleventh division of
24,000 troops, which was on duty during
the eleventh month.

15 Heled, a descendant of Othniel from
Netophah, was commander of the twelfth
division of 24,000 troops, which was on
duty during the twelfth month.

Leaders of the Tribes

16 The following were the tribes of Israel and
their leaders:

Tribe	*Leader*
Reuben	Eliezer son of Zicri
Simeon	Shephatiah son of Maacah

17 Levi .... Hashabiah son of Kemuel
Aaron (the priests) .... Zadok
18 Judah .... Elihu (a brother of David)
Issachar .... Omri son of Michael
19 Zebulun .... Ishmaiah son of Obadiah
Naphtali .... Jeremoth son of Azriel
20 Ephraim .... Hoshea son of Azaziah
Manasseh (west) .... Joel son of Pedaiah
21 Manasseh in Gilead (east) .... Iddo son of Zechariah
Benjamin .... Jaasiel son of Abner
22 Dan .... Azarel son of Jeroham

These were the leaders of the tribes of Israel.
23 When David took his census, he did not count
those who were younger than twenty years of age,
because the LORD had promised to make the Israelites as numerous as the stars in heaven. 24 Joab
son of Zeruiah began the census but never finished it because the anger of God fell on Israel.
The total number was never recorded in King David's official records.

Officials of David's Kingdom

25 Azmaveth son of Adiel was in charge of the palace treasuries.

Jonathan son of Uzziah was in charge of the regional treasuries throughout the towns, villages, and fortresses of Israel.

26 Ezri son of Kelub was in charge of the field workers who farmed the king's lands.

27 Shimei from Ramah was in charge of the king's vineyards.

Zabdi from Shepham was responsible for the grapes and the supplies of wine.

28 Baal-hanan from Geder was in charge of the king's olive groves and sycamore-fig trees in the foothills of Judah.

Joash was responsible for the supplies of olive oil.

29 Shitrai from Sharon was in charge of the cattle on the Sharon Plain.

Shaphat son of Adlai was responsible for the cattle in the valleys.

30 Obil the Ishmaelite was in charge of the camels.

Jehdeiah from Meronoth was in charge of the donkeys.

31 Jaziz the Hagrite was in charge of the king's flocks of sheep and goats.

All these officials were overseers of King David's property.

32 Jonathan, David's uncle, was a wise counselor to the king, a man of great insight, and a
scribe. Jehiel the Hacmonite was responsible for
teaching the king's sons. 33 Ahithophel was the
royal adviser. Hushai the Arkite was the king's
friend. 34 Ahithophel was succeeded by Jehoiada
son of Benaiah and by Abiathar. Joab was commander of the king's army.

CHAPTER 28

David's Instructions to Solomon

David summoned all the officials of Israel to
Jerusalem—the leaders of the tribes, the commanders of the army divisions, the other generals and captains, the overseers of the royal
property and livestock, the palace officials, the
mighty men, and all the other brave warriors in
the kingdom. 2 David rose to his feet and said:
"My brothers and my people! It was my desire to
build a Temple where the Ark of the LORD's Covenant, God's footstool, could rest permanently. I
made the necessary preparations for building it,
3 but God said to me, 'You must not build a
Temple to honor my name, for you are a warrior
and have shed much blood.'

4 "Yet the LORD, the God of Israel, has chosen
me from among all my father's family to be king
over Israel forever. For he has chosen the tribe
of Judah to rule, and from among the families of
Judah he chose my father's family. And from
among my father's sons the LORD was pleased to
make me king over all Israel. 5 And from among
my sons—for the LORD has given me many—he
chose Solomon to succeed me on the throne of
Israel and to rule over the LORD's kingdom. 6 He
said to me, 'Your son Solomon will build my
Temple and its courtyards, for I have chosen him
as my son, and I will be his father. 7 And if he continues to obey my commands and regulations as
he does now, I will make his kingdom last forever.'

8 "So now, with God as our witness, and in the
sight of all Israel—the LORD's assembly—I give
you this charge. Be careful to obey all the commands of the LORD your God, so that you may
continue to possess this good land and leave it to
your children as a permanent inheritance.

9 "And Solomon, my son, learn to know the God
of your ancestors intimately. Worship and serve
him with your whole heart and a willing mind.
For the LORD sees every heart and knows every
plan and thought. If you seek him, you will find
him. But if you forsake him, he will reject you forever. 10 So take this seriously. The LORD has chosen you to build a Temple as his sanctuary. Be
strong, and do the work."

11 Then David gave Solomon the plans for the
Temple and its surroundings, including the entry
room, the storerooms, the upstairs rooms, the

inner rooms, and the inner sanctuary—which
was the place of atonement. 12David also gave
Solomon all the plans he had in mind for the
courtyards of the LORD's Temple, the outside
rooms, the treasuries, and the rooms for the gifts
dedicated to the LORD. 13The king also gave Solomon the instructions concerning the work of
the various divisions of priests and Levites in the
Temple of the LORD. And he gave specifications
for the items in the Temple that were to be used
for worship.

14David gave instructions regarding how
much gold and silver should be used to make the
items needed for service. 15He told Solomon the
amount of gold needed for the gold lampstands
and lamps, and the amount of silver for the silver
lampstands and lamps, depending on how each
would be used. 16He designated the amount of
gold for the table on which the Bread of the Presence would be placed and the amount of silver
for other tables.

17David also designated the amount of gold for
the solid gold meat hooks used to handle the sacrificial meat and for the basins, pitchers, and
dishes, as well as the amount of silver for every
dish. 18He designated the amount of refined gold
for the altar of incense. Finally, he gave him a plan
for the LORD's "chariot"—the gold cherubim
whose wings were stretched out over the Ark of
the LORD's Covenant. 19"Every part of this plan,"
David told Solomon, "was given to me in writing
from the hand of the LORD."

20Then David continued, "Be strong and courageous, and do the work. Don't be afraid or discouraged, for the LORD God, my God, is with you.
He will not fail you or forsake you. He will see to
it that all the work related to the Temple of the
LORD is finished correctly. 21The various divisions of priests and Levites will serve in the Temple of God. Others with skills of every kind will
volunteer, and the officials and the entire nation
are at your command."

CHAPTER 29

Gifts for Building the Temple

Then King David turned to the entire assembly
and said, "My son Solomon, whom God has
clearly chosen as the next king of Israel, is still
young and inexperienced. The work ahead of
him is enormous, for the Temple he will build is
not for mere mortals—it is for the LORD God
himself! 2Using every resource at my command,
I have gathered as much as I could for building
the Temple of my God. Now there is enough
gold, silver, bronze, iron, and wood, as well as
great quantities of onyx, other precious stones,
costly jewels, and all kinds of fine stone and
marble.

3"And now, because of my devotion to the
Temple of my God, I am giving all of my own private treasures of gold and silver to help in the
construction. This is in addition to the building
materials I have already collected for his holy
Temple. 4I am donating more than 112 tons of
gold from Ophir and 262 tons of refined silver to
be used for overlaying the walls of the buildings
5and for the other gold and silver work to be
done by the craftsmen. Now then, who will follow my example and give offerings to the LORD
today?"

6Then the family leaders, the leaders of the
tribes of Israel, the generals and captains of the
army, and the king's administrative officers all
gave willingly. 7For the construction of the Temple of God, they gave about 188 tons of gold,
10,000 gold coins, 375 tons of silver, 675 tons
of bronze, and 3,750 tons of iron. 8They also
contributed numerous precious stones, which
were deposited in the treasury of the house of
the LORD under the care of Jehiel, a descendant
of Gershon. 9The people rejoiced over the offerings, for they had given freely and wholeheartedly to the LORD, and King David was filled
with joy.

David's Prayer of Praise

10Then David praised the LORD in the presence
of the whole assembly:

"O LORD, the God of our ancestor Israel, may
you be praised forever and ever! 11Yours,
O LORD, is the greatness, the power, the glory,
the victory, and the majesty. Everything in
the heavens and on earth is yours, O LORD,
and this is your kingdom. We adore you as
the one who is over all things. 12Wealth
and honor come from you alone, for you rule
over everything. Power and might are in
your hand, and at your discretion people
are made great and given strength.

13"O our God, we thank you and praise
your glorious name! 14But who am I, and
who are my people, that we could give
anything to you? Everything we have has
come from you, and we give you only what
you first gave us! 15We are here for only a
moment, visitors and strangers in the land
as our ancestors were before us. Our days
on earth are like a passing shadow, gone so
soon without a trace.

16"O Lord our God, even this material we
have gathered to build a Temple to honor
your holy name comes from you! It all
belongs to you! 17I know, my God, that you
examine our hearts and rejoice when you
find integrity there. You know I have done all
this with good motives, and I have watched
your people offer their gifts willingly and
joyously.

18"O Lord, the God of our ancestors
Abraham, Isaac, and Israel, make your people
always want to obey you. See to it that their
love for you never changes. 19Give my son
Solomon the wholehearted desire to obey all
your commands, laws, and decrees, and to do
everything necessary to build this Temple, for
which I have made these preparations."

20Then David said to the whole assembly,
"Give praise to the Lord your God!" And the entire assembly praised the Lord, the God of their
ancestors, and they bowed low and knelt before
the Lord and the king.

Solomon Named as King

21The next day they brought 1,000 bulls, 1,000
rams, and 1,000 male lambs as burnt offerings
to the Lord. They also brought liquid offerings
and many other sacrifices on behalf of all Israel.
22They feasted and drank in the Lord's presence
with great joy that day.

And again they crowned David's son Solomon
as their new king. They anointed him before the
Lord as their leader, and they anointed Zadok
as priest. 23So Solomon took the throne of the
Lord in place of his father, David, and he succeeded in everything, and all Israel obeyed him.
24All the officials, the warriors, and the sons of
King David pledged their loyalty to King Solomon. 25And the Lord exalted Solomon in the
sight of all Israel, and he gave Solomon greater
royal splendor than any king in Israel before
him.

Summary of David's Reign

26So David son of Jesse reigned over all Israel.
27He reigned over Israel for forty years, seven of
them in Hebron and thirty-three in Jerusalem.
28He died at a ripe old age, having enjoyed long
life, wealth, and honor. Then his son Solomon
ruled in his place.

29All the events of King David's reign, from beginning to end, are written in *The Record of Samuel the Seer*, *The Record of Nathan the Prophet*,
and *The Record of Gad the Seer*. 30These accounts
include the mighty deeds of his reign and everything that happened to him and to Israel and to
all the surrounding kingdoms.

2 CHRONICLES A Time to Remember

Look for 2 hidden messages in 2 Chronicles!

The book of 2 Chronicles tells the history of Judah, the southern kingdom of Israel. Read 2 Chronicles to learn about

- **A FEW GOOD MEN**
- **A WHOLE BUNCH OF BAD MEN**
- **THE DESTRUCTION OF THE TEMPLE**
- **THE DOWNFALL OF A NATION**

OPEN

Open for Business

The very first service held at the Temple of the Lord was a sight to see. **Read 2 Chronicles 5:13-14 to see what made it so special.**

Temple Is Toast

Because the people of Judah ignored God year after year, God finally allowed the Babylonians to conquer Judah. The Babylonians set fire to the Temple and destroyed everything of value. **For more details on the destruction, read 2 Chronicles 36:17-21.**

A String of Kings

Rebellion. Idol worship. War. Murder. These bad kings did it all. The book of 2 Chronicles is *filled* with bad kings. **To read about a few of the worst, turn to 2 Chronicles 28 and 33.**

But not *all* of the kings were bad. **To read about a few of the good guys, check out 2 Chronicles 15 and 19.**

On the Road Again

When the Babylonians conquered Judah, they forced the people of Judah to become their servants. But that wasn't the end of the story. **Check out 2 Chronicles 36:20-23 to find out what finally happened to the people of Judah.**

Timeline

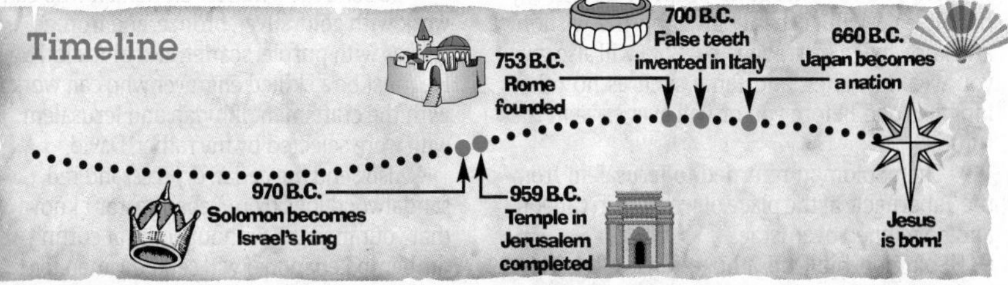
970 B.C.
Solomon becomes Israel's king
959 B.C.
Temple in Jerusalem completed
753 B.C.
Rome founded
700 B.C.
False teeth invented in Italy
660 B.C.
Japan becomes a nation
Jesus is born!

The JESUS CONNECTION

The people of Judah had turned away from God and put their faith in false gods and practices. It's a common theme in the Bible—God's people turning away, then turning back, then turning away again.

You'd think that at some point, God would have just given up on his people. Instead, he did just the opposite. In an act of pure love, God sent his only Son to earth so we could find our way back to God. **When we believe in Jesus, we can live forever with God. Who could ask for more?**

2 Chronicles 1 . . . page 422

CHAPTER 1

Solomon Asks for Wisdom

Solomon son of David took firm control of his
kingdom, for the LORD his God was with him and
made him very powerful.
2Solomon called together all the leaders of Israel—the generals and captains of the army, the
judges, and all the political and clan leaders.
3Then he led the entire assembly to the place of
worship in Gibeon, for God's Tabernacle was located there. (This was the Tabernacle that Moses,
the LORD's servant, had made in the wilderness.)
4David had already moved the Ark of God
from Kiriath-jearim to the tent he had prepared
for it in Jerusalem. 5But the bronze altar made by
Bezalel son of Uri and grandson of Hur was there
at Gibeon in front of the Tabernacle of the LORD.
So Solomon and the people gathered in front of
it to consult the LORD. 6There in front of the Tabernacle, Solomon went up to the bronze altar in
the LORD's presence and sacrificed 1,000 burnt
offerings on it.
7That night God appeared to Solomon and
said, "What do you want? Ask, and I will give it to
you!"
8Solomon replied to God, "You showed great
and faithful love to David, my father, and now
you have made me king in his place. 9O LORD
God, please continue to keep your promise to
David my father, for you have made me king over
a people as numerous as the dust of the earth!
10Give me the wisdom and knowledge to lead
them properly, for who could possibly govern
this great people of yours?"
11God said to Solomon, "Because your greatest
desire is to help your people, and you did not ask
for wealth, riches, fame, or even the death of your
enemies or a long life, but rather you asked for
wisdom and knowledge to properly govern my
people—12I will certainly give you the wisdom
and knowledge you requested. But I will also give
you wealth, riches, and fame such as no other
king has had before you or will ever have in the
future!"
13Then Solomon returned to Jerusalem from
the Tabernacle at the place of worship in Gibeon,
and he reigned over Israel.
14Solomon built up a huge force of chariots
and horses. He had 1,400 chariots and 12,000
horses. He stationed some of them in the chariot
cities and some near him in Jerusalem. 15The
king made silver and gold as plentiful in Jerusalem as stone. And valuable cedar timber was as
common as the sycamore-fig trees that grow in
the foothills of Judah. 16Solomon's horses were
imported from Egypt and from Cilicia; the king's
traders acquired them from Cilicia at the standard price. 17At that time chariots from Egypt
could be purchased for 600 pieces of silver, and
horses for 150 pieces of silver. They were then
exported to the kings of the Hittites and the
kings of Aram.

CHAPTER 2

Preparations for Building the Temple

Solomon decided to build a Temple to honor the
name of the LORD, and also a royal palace for
himself. 2He enlisted a force of 70,000 laborers,
80,000 men to quarry stone in the hill country,
and 3,600 foremen.
3Solomon also sent this message to King
Hiram at Tyre:

"Send me cedar logs as you did for my father,
David, when he was building his palace.
4I am about to build a Temple to honor the
name of the LORD my God. It will be a place
set apart to burn fragrant incense before
him, to display the special sacrificial bread,
and to sacrifice burnt offerings each
morning and evening, on the Sabbaths, at
new moon celebrations, and at the other
appointed festivals of the LORD our God.
He has commanded Israel to do these things
forever.
5"This must be a magnificent Temple
because our God is greater than all other
gods. 6But who can really build him a
worthy home? Not even the highest heavens
can contain him! So who am I to consider
building a Temple for him, except as a place
to burn sacrifices to him?
7"So send me a master craftsman who can
work with gold, silver, bronze, and iron, as
well as with purple, scarlet, and blue cloth.
He must be a skilled engraver who can work
with the craftsmen of Judah and Jerusalem
who were selected by my father, David.
8"Also send me cedar, cypress, and red
sandalwood logs from Lebanon, for I know
that your men are without equal at cutting
timber in Lebanon. I will send my men to
help them. 9An immense amount of timber
will be needed, for the Temple I am going
to build will be very large and magnificent.
10In payment for your woodcutters, I will
send 100,000 bushels of crushed wheat,
100,000 bushels of barley, 110,000 gallons
of wine, and 110,000 gallons of olive oil."

11 King Hiram sent this letter of reply to Solomon:

"It is because the LORD loves his people
that he has made you their king! 12 Praise
the LORD, the God of Israel, who made the
heavens and the earth! He has given King
David a wise son, gifted with skill and
understanding, who will build a Temple
for the LORD and a royal palace for himself.

13 "I am sending you a master craftsman
named Huram-abi, who is extremely talented.
14 His mother is from the tribe of Dan in
Israel, and his father is from Tyre. He is
skillful at making things from gold, silver,
bronze, and iron, and he also works with
stone and wood. He can work with purple,
blue, and scarlet cloth and fine linen. He
is also an engraver and can follow any
design given to him. He will work with your
craftsmen and those appointed by my lord
David, your father.

15 "Send along the wheat, barley, olive oil,
and wine that my lord has mentioned. 16 We
will cut whatever timber you need from the
Lebanon mountains and will float the logs
in rafts down the coast of the Mediterranean
Sea to Joppa. From there you can transport
the logs up to Jerusalem."

17 Solomon took a census of all foreigners in
the land of Israel, like the census his father had
taken, and he counted 153,600. 18 He assigned
70,000 of them as common laborers, 80,000 as
quarry workers in the hill country, and 3,600 as
foremen.

CHAPTER 3
Solomon Builds the Temple

So Solomon began to build the Temple of the
LORD in Jerusalem on Mount Moriah, where
the LORD had appeared to David, his father. The
Temple was built on the threshing floor of Araunah the Jebusite, the site that David had selected.
2 The construction began in midspring, during
the fourth year of Solomon's reign.

3 These are the dimensions Solomon used for
the foundation of the Temple of God (using the
old standard of measurement). It was 90 feet long
and 30 feet wide. 4 The entry room at the front of
the Temple was 30 feet wide, running across the
entire width of the Temple, and 30 feet high. He
overlaid the inside with pure gold.

5 He paneled the main room of the Temple
with cypress wood, overlaid it with fine gold, and
decorated it with carvings of palm trees and
chains. 6 He decorated the walls of the Temple
with beautiful jewels and with gold from the
land of Parvaim. 7 He overlaid the beams, thresh-
olds, walls, and doors throughout the Temple
with gold, and he carved figures of cherubim on
the walls.

8 He made the Most Holy Place 30 feet wide,
corresponding to the width of the Temple, and
30 feet deep. He overlaid its interior with 23
tons of fine gold. 9 The gold nails that were used
weighed 20 ounces each. He also overlaid the
walls of the upper rooms with gold.

10 He made two figures shaped like cherubim,
overlaid them with gold, and placed them in the
Most Holy Place. 11 The total wingspan of the two
cherubim standing side by side was 30 feet. One
wing of the first figure was 7½ feet long, and it
touched the Temple wall. The other wing, also
7½ feet long, touched one of the wings of the
second figure. 12 In the same way, the second figure had one wing 7½ feet long that touched the
opposite wall. The other wing, also 7½ feet long,
touched the wing of the first figure. 13 So the
wingspan of the two cherubim side by side was
30 feet. They stood on their feet and faced out
toward the main room of the Temple.

14 Across the entrance of the Most Holy Place
he hung a curtain made of fine linen, decorated
with blue, purple, and scarlet thread and embroidered with figures of cherubim.

15 For the front of the Temple, he made two pillars that were 27 feet tall, each topped by a capital extending upward another 7½ feet. 16 He
made a network of interwoven chains and used
them to decorate the tops of the pillars. He also
made 100 decorative pomegranates and attached them to the chains. 17 Then he set up the
two pillars at the entrance of the Temple, one to
the south of the entrance and the other to the
north. He named the one on the south Jakin, and
the one on the north Boaz.

CHAPTER 4
Furnishings for the Temple

Solomon also made a bronze altar 30 feet long,
30 feet wide, and 15 feet high. 2 Then he cast a
great round basin, 15 feet across from rim to rim,
called the Sea. It was 7½ feet deep and about
45 feet in circumference. 3 It was encircled just
below its rim by two rows of figures that resembled oxen. There were about six oxen per foot all
the way around, and they were cast as part of the
basin.

4 The Sea was placed on a base of twelve
bronze oxen, all facing outward. Three faced
north, three faced west, three faced south, and

three faced east, and the Sea rested on them.
5 The walls of the Sea were about three inches
thick, and its rim flared out like a cup and resembled a water lily blossom. It could hold about
16,500 gallons of water.

6 He also made ten smaller basins for washing
the utensils for the burnt offerings. He set five
on the south side and five on the north. But the
priests washed themselves in the Sea.

7 He then cast ten gold lampstands according
to the specifications that had been given, and he
put them in the Temple. Five were placed against
the south wall, and five were placed against the
north wall.

8 He also built ten tables and placed them in the
Temple, five along the south wall and five along
the north wall. Then he molded 100 gold basins.

9 He then built a courtyard for the priests, and
also the large outer courtyard. He made doors
for the courtyard entrances and overlaid them
with bronze. 10 The great bronze basin called the
Sea was placed near the southeast corner of the
Temple.

11 Huram-abi also made the necessary washbasins, shovels, and bowls.

So at last Huram-abi completed everything
King Solomon had assigned him to make for the
Temple of God:

12 the two pillars;
the two bowl-shaped capitals on top of the pillars;
the two networks of interwoven chains that decorated the capitals;
13 the 400 pomegranates that hung from the chains on the capitals (two rows of pomegranates for each of the chain networks that decorated the capitals on top of the pillars);
14 the water carts holding the basins;
15 the Sea and the twelve oxen under it;
16 the ash buckets, the shovels, the meat hooks, and all the related articles.

Huram-abi made all these things of burnished
bronze for the Temple of the LORD, just as King
Solomon had directed. 17 The king had them cast
in clay molds in the Jordan Valley between Succoth and Zarethan. 18 Solomon used such great
quantities of bronze that its weight could not be
determined.

19 Solomon also made all the furnishings for
the Temple of God:

the gold altar;
the tables for the Bread of the Presence;
20 the lampstands and their lamps of solid gold, to burn in front of the Most Holy Place as prescribed;
21 the flower decorations, lamps, and tongs—all of the purest gold;
22 the lamp snuffers, bowls, ladles, and incense burners—all of solid gold;
the doors for the entrances to the Most Holy Place and the main room of the Temple, overlaid with gold.

CHAPTER 5

So Solomon finished all his work on the Temple
of the LORD. Then he brought all the gifts his father, David, had dedicated—the silver, the gold,
and the various articles—and he stored them in
the treasuries of the Temple of God.

The Ark Brought to the Temple

2 Solomon then summoned to Jerusalem the elders of Israel and all the heads of tribes—the
leaders of the ancestral families of Israel. They
were to bring the Ark of the LORD's Covenant to
the Temple from its location in the City of David,
also known as Zion. 3 So all the men of Israel assembled before the king at the annual Festival of
Shelters, which is held in early autumn.

4 When all the elders of Israel arrived, the Levites picked up the Ark. 5 The priests and Levites
brought up the Ark along with the special tent
and all the sacred items that had been in it.
6 There, before the Ark, King Solomon and the
entire community of Israel sacrificed so many
sheep, goats, and cattle that no one could keep
count!

7 Then the priests carried the Ark of the
LORD's Covenant into the inner sanctuary of the
Temple—the Most Holy Place—and placed it beneath the wings of the cherubim. 8 The cherubim spread their wings over the Ark, forming
a canopy over the Ark and its carrying poles.
9 These poles were so long that their ends could
be seen from the Holy Place, which is in front of
the Most Holy Place, but not from the outside.
They are still there to this day. 10 Nothing was in
the Ark except the two stone tablets that Moses
had placed in it at Mount Sinai, where the LORD
made a covenant with the people of Israel when
they left Egypt.

11 Then the priests left the Holy Place. All the
priests who were present had purified themselves, whether or not they were on duty that day.
12 And the Levites who were musicians—Asaph,
Heman, Jeduthun, and all their sons and brothers—were dressed in fine linen robes and stood

A Special Reminder

Eleven years after Solomon became king, it was time to party! OK, not really party, but it *was* time to dedicate the finished Temple and place the ark of the covenant inside! **Read all about it in 2 CHRONICLES 5.** Then come back and make something special to help you remember God!

1 Find a box with a lid, and cover the box and the lid separately with aluminum foil.

2 Find a favorite Bible verse that talks about how good God is. (There are a ton of those verses in Psalms!) Write the verse on your card, and decorate the card with markers.

God is our refuge and strength Psalm 46:1a!

3 Read the verse out loud and thank God for being so great. Put the verse inside the box, and put the box in a special place.

The ark of the covenant helped the Israelites remember that God was with them. Just like you put a special verse inside your box, the Israelites put special things inside the ark—like the stone tablets with the Ten Commandments.

Keep your special box, and put things inside it that will remind you that God is with you.

at the east side of the altar playing cymbals, lyres,
and harps. They were joined by 120 priests who
were playing trumpets. 13The trumpeters and
singers performed together in unison to praise
and give thanks to the LORD. Accompanied by
trumpets, cymbals, and other instruments, they
raised their voices and praised the LORD with
these words:

"He is good!
His faithful love endures forever!"

At that moment a thick cloud filled the Temple of the LORD. 14The priests could not continue
their service because of the cloud, for the glorious presence of the LORD filled the Temple of
God.

CHAPTER 6

Solomon Praises the LORD

Then Solomon prayed, "O LORD, you have said
that you would live in a thick cloud of darkness.
2Now I have built a glorious Temple for you, a
place where you can live forever!"

3Then the king turned around to the entire
community of Israel standing before him and
gave this blessing: 4"Praise the LORD, the God of
Israel, who has kept the promise he made to my
father, David. For he told my father, 5'From the
day I brought my people out of the land of Egypt,
I have never chosen a city among any of the
tribes of Israel as the place where a Temple
should be built to honor my name. Nor have I
chosen a king to lead my people Israel. 6But now
I have chosen Jerusalem as the place for my
name to be honored, and I have chosen David to
be king over my people Israel.'"

7Then Solomon said, "My father, David,
wanted to build this Temple to honor the name
of the LORD, the God of Israel. 8But the LORD told
him, 'You wanted to build the Temple to honor
my name. Your intention is good, 9but you are
not the one to do it. One of your own sons will
build the Temple to honor me.'

10"And now the LORD has fulfilled the promise
he made, for I have become king in my father's
place, and now I sit on the throne of Israel, just as
the LORD promised. I have built this Temple to
honor the name of the LORD, the God of Israel.
11There I have placed the Ark, which contains
the covenant that the LORD made with the people
of Israel."

Solomon's Prayer of Dedication

12Then Solomon stood before the altar of the
LORD in front of the entire community of Israel,

and he lifted his hands in prayer. 13Now Solomon had made a bronze platform 7½ feet long,
7½ feet wide, and 4½ feet high and had placed it
at the center of the Temple's outer courtyard. He
stood on the platform, and then he knelt in front
of the entire community of Israel and lifted his
hands toward heaven. 14He prayed,

> "O LORD, God of Israel, there is no God like
> you in all of heaven and earth. You keep your
> covenant and show unfailing love to all who
> walk before you in wholehearted devotion.
> 15You have kept your promise to your servant
> David, my father. You made that promise
> with your own mouth, and with your own
> hands you have fulfilled it today.
>
> 16"And now, O LORD, God of Israel, carry
> out the additional promise you made to your
> servant David, my father. For you said to him,
> 'If your descendants guard their behavior
> and faithfully follow my Law as you have
> done, one of them will always sit on the
> throne of Israel.' 17Now, O LORD, God of
> Israel, fulfill this promise to your servant
> David.
>
> 18"But will God really live on earth among
> people? Why, even the highest heavens
> cannot contain you. How much less this
> Temple I have built! 19Nevertheless, listen
> to my prayer and my plea, O LORD my God.
> Hear the cry and the prayer that your servant
> is making to you. 20May you watch over this
> Temple day and night, this place where you
> have said you would put your name. May
> you always hear the prayers I make toward
> this place. 21May you hear the humble and
> earnest requests from me and your people
> Israel when we pray toward this place. Yes,
> hear us from heaven where you live, and
> when you hear, forgive.
>
> 22"If someone wrongs another person
> and is required to take an oath of innocence
> in front of your altar at this Temple, 23then
> hear from heaven and judge between your
> servants—the accuser and the accused. Pay
> back the guilty as they deserve. Acquit the
> innocent because of their innocence.
>
> 24"If your people Israel are defeated by
> their enemies because they have sinned
> against you, and if they turn back and
> acknowledge your name and pray to you
> here in this Temple, 25then hear from heaven
> and forgive the sin of your people Israel and
> return them to this land you gave to them
> and to their ancestors.
>
> 26"If the skies are shut up and there is no
> rain because your people have sinned against
> you, and if they pray toward this Temple and
> acknowledge your name and turn from their
> sins because you have punished them, 27then
> hear from heaven and forgive the sins of your
> servants, your people Israel. Teach them to
> follow the right path, and send rain on your
> land that you have given to your people as
> their special possession.
>
> 28"If there is a famine in the land or a
> plague or crop disease or attacks of locusts
> or caterpillars, or if your people's enemies
> are in the land besieging their towns—what-
> ever disaster or disease there is—29and if
> your people Israel pray about their troubles
> or sorrow, raising their hands toward this
> Temple, 30then hear from heaven where you
> live, and forgive. Give your people what their
> actions deserve, for you alone know each
> human heart. 31Then they will fear you and
> walk in your ways as long as they live in the
> land you gave to our ancestors.
>
> 32"In the future, foreigners who do not
> belong to your people Israel will hear of you.
> They will come from distant lands when they
> hear of your great name and your strong
> hand and your powerful arm. And when they
> pray toward this Temple, 33then hear from
> heaven where you live, and grant what they
> ask of you. In this way, all the people of the
> earth will come to know and fear you, just as
> your own people Israel do. They, too, will
> know that this Temple I have built honors
> your name.
>
> 34"If your people go out where you send
> them to fight their enemies, and if they pray
> to you by turning toward this city you have
> chosen and toward this Temple I have built
> to honor your name, 35then hear their
> prayers from heaven and uphold their cause.
>
> 36"If they sin against you—and who has
> never sinned?—you might become angry with
> them and let their enemies conquer them and
> take them captive to a foreign land far away or
> near. 37But in that land of exile, they might
> turn to you in repentance and pray, 'We have
> sinned, done evil, and acted wickedly.' 38If
> they turn to you with their whole heart and
> soul in the land of their captivity and pray
> toward the land you gave to their ancestors—
> toward this city you have chosen, and toward
> this Temple I have built to honor your name—
> 39then hear their prayers and their petitions
> from heaven where you live, and uphold their

cause. Forgive your people who have sinned
against you.
40"O my God, may your eyes be open and
your ears attentive to all the prayers made
to you in this place.

41 "And now arise, O LORD God, and enter
your resting place,
along with the Ark, the symbol of
your power.
May your priests, O LORD God, be clothed
with salvation;
may your loyal servants rejoice in your
goodness.
42 O LORD God, do not reject the king you
have anointed.
Remember your unfailing love for your
servant David."

CHAPTER 7

The Dedication of the Temple

When Solomon finished praying, fire flashed
down from heaven and burned up the burnt offerings and sacrifices, and the glorious presence
of the LORD filled the Temple. 2The priests could
not enter the Temple of the LORD because the
glorious presence of the LORD filled it. 3When all
the people of Israel saw the fire coming down
and the glorious presence of the LORD filling the
Temple, they fell face down on the ground and
worshiped and praised the LORD, saying,

"He is good!
His faithful love endures forever!"

4Then the king and all the people offered sacrifices to the LORD. 5King Solomon offered a sacrifice of 22,000 cattle and 120,000 sheep and
goats. And so the king and all the people dedicated the Temple of God. 6The priests took their
assigned positions, and so did the Levites who
were singing, "His faithful love endures forever!"
They accompanied the singing with music from
the instruments King David had made for praising the LORD. Across from the Levites, the priests
blew the trumpets, while all Israel stood.
7Solomon then consecrated the central area
of the courtyard in front of the LORD's Temple.
He offered burnt offerings and the fat of peace
offerings there, because the bronze altar he had
built could not hold all the burnt offerings, grain
offerings, and sacrificial fat.
8For the next seven days Solomon and all Israel celebrated the Festival of Shelters. A large
congregation had gathered from as far away as
Lebo-hamath in the north and the Brook of
Egypt in the south. 9On the eighth day they had a
closing ceremony, for they had celebrated the
dedication of the altar for seven days and the
Festival of Shelters for seven days. 10Then at
the end of the celebration, Solomon sent the
people home. They were all joyful and glad because the LORD had been so good to David and to
Solomon and to his people Israel.

The LORD's Response to Solomon

11So Solomon finished the Temple of the LORD,
as well as the royal palace. He completed everything he had planned to do in the construction of
the Temple and the palace. 12Then one night the
LORD appeared to Solomon and said,

"I have heard your prayer and have chosen this
Temple as the place for making sacrifices.
13At times I might shut up the heavens so that
no rain falls, or command grasshoppers to
devour your crops, or send plagues among
you. **14Then if my people who are
called by my name will humble
themselves and pray and seek my
face and turn from their wicked
ways, I will hear from heaven and
will forgive their sins and restore
their land.** 15My eyes will be open and my
ears attentive to every prayer made in this
place. 16For I have chosen this Temple and set
it apart to be holy—a place where my name
will be honored forever. I will always watch
over it, for it is dear to my heart.
17"As for you, if you faithfully follow me
as David your father did, obeying all my
commands, decrees, and regulations, 18then
I will establish the throne of your dynasty. For
I made this covenant with your father, David,
when I said, 'One of your descendants will
always rule over Israel.'
19"But if you or your descendants abandon
me and disobey the decrees and commands
I have given you, and if you serve and worship
other gods, 20then I will uproot the people
from this land that I have given them. I will
reject this Temple that I have made holy to
honor my name. I will make it an object of
mockery and ridicule among the nations.
21And though this Temple is impressive now,
all who pass by will be appalled. They will ask,
'Why did the LORD do such terrible things to
this land and to this Temple?'
22"And the answer will be, 'Because his
people abandoned the LORD, the God of their

"Then if my people who are called by my name will humble themselves and pray and seek my face and turn from their wicked ways, I will hear from heaven and will forgive their sins and restore their land."—2 CHRONICLES 7:14

Read 2 CHRONICLES 7:14 out loud.
Then make this cross to remind you of what God wants us to do.

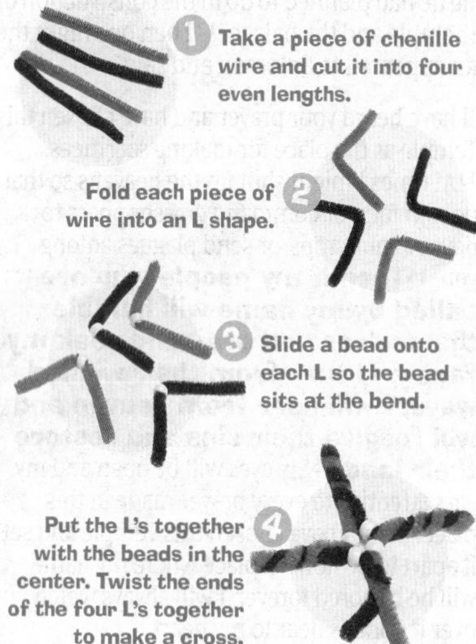

1 Take a piece of chenille wire and cut it into four even lengths.
2 Fold each piece of wire into an L shape.
3 Slide a bead onto each L so the bead sits at the bend.
4 Put the L's together with the beads in the center. Twist the ends of the four L's together to make a cross.

The four beads can remind you of the four things God asks of his people in **2 CHRONICLES 7:14:**

BE HUMBLE,
PRAY,
SEEK GOD, and
BE GOOD.

The next time you wonder what God wants you to do, look at your cross. Remember the four things from this verse and you'll know how to please God!

Do you ever feel like it's too hard to obey God? Read Deuteronomy 30:11-20. Then *choose* to obey!

ancestors, who brought them out of Egypt,
and they worshiped other gods instead and
bowed down to them. That is why he has
brought all these disasters on them.'"

CHAPTER 8
Solomon's Many Achievements

It took Solomon twenty years to build the LORD's
Temple and his own royal palace. At the end of
that time, 2Solomon turned his attention to rebuilding the towns that King Hiram had given
him, and he settled Israelites in them.

3Solomon also fought against the town of
Hamath-zobah and conquered it. 4He rebuilt
Tadmor in the wilderness and built towns in the
region of Hamath as supply centers. 5He fortified the towns of Upper Beth-horon and Lower
Beth-horon, rebuilding their walls and installing
barred gates. 6He also rebuilt Baalath and other
supply centers and constructed towns where his
chariots and horses could be stationed. He built
everything he desired in Jerusalem and Lebanon
and throughout his entire realm.

7There were still some people living in the
land who were not Israelites, including the Hittites, Amorites, Perizzites, Hivites, and Jebusites.
8These were descendants of the nations whom
the people of Israel had not destroyed. So Solomon conscripted them for his labor force, and
they serve as forced laborers to this day. 9But Solomon did not conscript any of the Israelites for
his labor force. Instead, he assigned them to
serve as fighting men, officers in his army, commanders of his chariots, and charioteers. 10King
Solomon appointed 250 of them to supervise
the people.

11Solomon moved his wife, Pharaoh's daughter, from the City of David to the new palace he
had built for her. He said, "My wife must not live
in King David's palace, for the Ark of the LORD
has been there, and it is holy ground."

12Then Solomon presented burnt offerings to
the LORD on the altar he had built for him in front
of the entry room of the Temple. 13He offered
the sacrifices for the Sabbaths, the new moon
festivals, and the three annual festivals—the
Passover celebration, the Festival of Harvest, and
the Festival of Shelters—as Moses had commanded.

14In assigning the priests to their duties, Solomon followed the regulations of his father,
David. He also assigned the Levites to lead the
people in praise and to assist the priests in their
daily duties. And he assigned the gatekeepers to
their gates by their divisions, following the com-

mands of David, the man of God. 15Solomon did not deviate in any way from David's commands concerning the priests and Levites and the treasuries.

16So Solomon made sure that all the work related to building the Temple of the LORD was carried out, from the day its foundation was laid to the day of its completion.

17Later Solomon went to Ezion-geber and Elath, ports along the shore of the Red Sea in the land of Edom. 18Hiram sent him ships commanded by his own officers and manned by experienced crews of sailors. These ships sailed to Ophir with Solomon's men and brought back to Solomon almost seventeen tons of gold.

CHAPTER 9

Visit of the Queen of Sheba

When the queen of Sheba heard of Solomon's fame, she came to Jerusalem to test him with hard questions. She arrived with a large group of attendants and a great caravan of camels loaded with spices, large quantities of gold, and precious jewels. When she met with Solomon, she talked with him about everything she had on her mind. 2Solomon had answers for all her questions; nothing was too hard for him to explain to her. 3When the queen of Sheba realized how wise Solomon was, and when she saw the palace he had built, 4she was overwhelmed. She was also amazed at the food on his tables, the organization of his officials and their splendid clothing, the cup-bearers and their robes, and the burnt offerings Solomon made at the Temple of the LORD.

5She exclaimed to the king, "Everything I heard in my country about your achievements and wisdom is true! 6I didn't believe what was said until I arrived here and saw it with my own eyes. In fact, I had not heard the half of your great wisdom! It is far beyond what I was told. 7How happy your people must be! What a privilege for your officials to stand here day after day, listening to your wisdom! 8Praise the LORD your God, who delights in you and has placed you on the throne as king to rule for him. Because God loves Israel and desires this kingdom to last forever, he has made you king over them so you can rule with justice and righteousness."

9Then she gave the king a gift of 9,000 pounds of gold, great quantities of spices, and precious jewels. Never before had there been spices as fine as those the queen of Sheba gave to King Solomon.

10(In addition, the crews of Hiram and Solomon brought gold from Ophir, and they also brought red sandalwood and precious jewels. 11The king used the sandalwood to make steps for the Temple of the LORD and the royal palace, and to construct lyres and harps for the musicians. Never before had such beautiful things been seen in Judah.)

12King Solomon gave the queen of Sheba whatever she asked for—gifts of greater value than the gifts she had given him. Then she and all her attendants returned to their own land.

Solomon's Wealth and Splendor

13Each year Solomon received about 25 tons of gold. 14This did not include the additional revenue he received from merchants and traders. All the kings of Arabia and the governors of the provinces also brought gold and silver to Solomon.

15King Solomon made 200 large shields of hammered gold, each weighing more than 15 pounds. 16He also made 300 smaller shields of hammered gold, each weighing more than 7½ pounds. The king placed these shields in the Palace of the Forest of Lebanon.

17Then the king made a huge throne, decorated with ivory and overlaid with pure gold. 18The throne had six steps, with a footstool of gold. There were armrests on both sides of the seat, and the figure of a lion stood on each side of the throne. 19There were also twelve other lions, one standing on each end of the six steps. No other throne in all the world could be compared with it!

20All of King Solomon's drinking cups were solid gold, as were all the utensils in the Palace of the Forest of Lebanon. They were not made of silver, for silver was considered worthless in Solomon's day!

21The king had a fleet of trading ships of Tarshish manned by the sailors sent by Hiram. Once every three years the ships returned, loaded with gold, silver, ivory, apes, and peacocks.

22So King Solomon became richer and wiser than any other king on earth. 23Kings from every nation came to consult him and to hear the wisdom God had given him. 24Year after year everyone who visited brought him gifts of silver and gold, clothing, weapons, spices, horses, and mules.

25Solomon had 4,000 stalls for his horses and chariots, and he had 12,000 horses. He stationed some of them in the chariot cities, and some near him in Jerusalem. 26He ruled over all the kings from the Euphrates River in the north

to the land of the Philistines and the border of
Egypt in the south. 27The king made silver as
plentiful in Jerusalem as stone. And valuable cedar timber was as common as the sycamore-fig
trees that grow in the foothills of Judah. 28Solo-
mon's horses were imported from Egypt and
many other countries.

Summary of Solomon's Reign

29The rest of the events of Solomon's reign, from
beginning to end, are recorded in *The Record of
Nathan the Prophet*, and *The Prophecy of Ahijah
from Shiloh*, and also in *The Visions of Iddo the
Seer*, concerning Jeroboam son of Nebat. 30Solo-
mon ruled in Jerusalem over all Israel for forty
years. 31When he died, he was buried in the City
of David, named for his father. Then his son Rehoboam became the next king.

CHAPTER **10**

The Northern Tribes Revolt

Rehoboam went to Shechem, where all Israel
had gathered to make him king. 2When Jeroboam son of Nebat heard of this, he returned from
Egypt, for he had fled to Egypt to escape from
King Solomon. 3The leaders of Israel summoned
him, and Jeroboam and all Israel went to speak
with Rehoboam. 4"Your father was a hard master," they said. "Lighten the harsh labor demands
and heavy taxes that your father imposed on us.
Then we will be your loyal subjects."

5Rehoboam replied, "Come back in three days
for my answer." So the people went away.

6Then King Rehoboam discussed the matter
with the older men who had counseled his father, Solomon. "What is your advice?" he asked.
"How should I answer these people?"

7The older counselors replied, "If you are
good to these people and do your best to please
them and give them a favorable answer, they will
always be your loyal subjects."

8But Rehoboam rejected the advice of the
older men and instead asked the opinion of the
young men who had grown up with him and
were now his advisers. 9"What is your advice?"
he asked them. "How should I answer these people who want me to lighten the burdens imposed
by my father?"

10The young men replied, "This is what you
should tell those complainers who want a lighter
burden: 'My little finger is thicker than my father's waist! 11Yes, my father laid heavy burdens
on you, but I'm going to make them even heavier!
My father beat you with whips, but I will beat you
with scorpions!'"

12Three days later Jeroboam and all the people returned to hear Rehoboam's decision, just
as the king had ordered. 13But Rehoboam
spoke harshly to them, for he rejected the advice of the older counselors 14and followed the
counsel of his younger advisers. He told the
people, "My father laid heavy burdens on you,
but I'm going to make them even heavier! My
father beat you with whips, but I will beat you
with scorpions!"

15So the king paid no attention to the people.
This turn of events was the will of God, for it fulfilled the LORD's message to Jeroboam son of Nebat through the prophet Ahijah from Shiloh.

16When all Israel realized that the king had refused to listen to them, they responded,

"Down with the dynasty of David!
We have no interest in the son of Jesse.
Back to your homes, O Israel!
Look out for your own house, O David!"

So all the people of Israel returned home.
17But Rehoboam continued to rule over the Israelites who lived in the towns of Judah.

18King Rehoboam sent Adoniram, who was
in charge of forced labor, to restore order, but
the people of Israel stoned him to death. When
this news reached King Rehoboam, he quickly
jumped into his chariot and fled to Jerusalem.
19And to this day the northern tribes of Israel
have refused to be ruled by a descendant of
David.

CHAPTER **11**

Shemaiah's Prophecy

When Rehoboam arrived at Jerusalem, he mobilized the men of Judah and Benjamin—180,000
select troops—to fight against Israel and to restore the kingdom to himself.

2But the LORD said to Shemaiah, the man of
God, 3"Say to Rehoboam son of Solomon, king of
Judah, and to all the Israelites in Judah and Benjamin: 4'This is what the LORD says: Do not fight
against your relatives. Go back home, for what
has happened is my doing!'" So they obeyed the
message of the LORD and did not fight against
Jeroboam.

Rehoboam Fortifies Judah

5Rehoboam remained in Jerusalem and fortified various towns for the defense of Judah. 6He
built up Bethlehem, Etam, Tekoa, 7Beth-zur,
Soco, Adullam, 8Gath, Mareshah, Ziph, 9Adora-
im, Lachish, Azekah, 10Zorah, Aijalon, and Hebron.
These became the fortified towns of Judah and

Benjamin. 11Rehoboam strengthened their defenses and stationed commanders in them, and
he stored supplies of food, olive oil, and wine.
12He also put shields and spears in these towns
as a further safety measure. So only Judah and
Benjamin remained under his control.
13But all the priests and Levites living among
the northern tribes of Israel sided with Rehoboam. 14The Levites even abandoned their pasturelands and property and moved to Judah and
Jerusalem, because Jeroboam and his sons
would not allow them to serve the LORD as
priests. 15Jeroboam appointed his own priests
to serve at the pagan shrines, where they worshiped the goat and calf idols he had made.
16From all the tribes of Israel, those who sincerely wanted to worship the LORD, the God of
Israel, followed the Levites to Jerusalem, where
they could offer sacrifices to the LORD, the God
of their ancestors. 17This strengthened the kingdom of Judah, and for three years they supported
Rehoboam son of Solomon, for during those
years they faithfully followed in the footsteps of
David and Solomon.

Rehoboam's Family

18Rehoboam married his cousin Mahalath, the
daughter of David's son Jerimoth and of Abihail,
the daughter of Eliab son of Jesse. 19Mahalath
had three sons—Jeush, Shemariah, and Zaham.
20Later Rehoboam married another cousin,
Maacah, the granddaughter of Absalom. Maacah
gave birth to Abijah, Attai, Ziza, and Shelomith.
21Rehoboam loved Maacah more than any of his
other wives and concubines. In all, he had eighteen wives and sixty concubines, and they gave
birth to twenty-eight sons and sixty daughters.
22Rehoboam appointed Maacah's son Abijah
as leader among the princes, making it clear that
he would be the next king. 23Rehoboam also
wisely gave responsibilities to his other sons and
stationed some of them in the fortified towns
throughout the land of Judah and Benjamin. He
provided them with generous provisions, and he
found many wives for them.

CHAPTER 12

Egypt Invades Judah

But when Rehoboam was firmly established and
strong, he abandoned the Law of the LORD, and
all Israel followed him in this sin. 2Because they
were unfaithful to the LORD, King Shishak of
Egypt came up and attacked Jerusalem in the
fifth year of King Rehoboam's reign. 3He came
with 1,200 chariots, 60,000 horses, and a countless army of foot soldiers, including Libyans,
Sukkites, and Ethiopians. 4Shishak conquered
Judah's fortified towns and then advanced to
attack Jerusalem.
5The prophet Shemaiah then met with Rehoboam and Judah's leaders, who had all fled to
Jerusalem because of Shishak. Shemaiah told
them, "This is what the LORD says: You have abandoned me, so I am abandoning you to Shishak."
6Then the leaders of Israel and the king humbled themselves and said, "The LORD is right in
doing this to us!"
7When the LORD saw their change of heart, he
gave this message to Shemaiah: "Since the people have humbled themselves, I will not completely destroy them and will soon give them
some relief. I will not use Shishak to pour out my
anger on Jerusalem. 8But they will become his
subjects, so they will know the difference between serving me and serving earthly rulers."
9So King Shishak of Egypt came up and attacked Jerusalem. He ransacked the treasuries
of the LORD's Temple and the royal palace; he
stole everything, including all the gold shields
Solomon had made. 10King Rehoboam later replaced them with bronze shields as substitutes,
and he entrusted them to the care of the commanders of the guard who protected the entrance to the royal palace. 11Whenever the king
went to the Temple of the LORD, the guards
would also take the shields and then return
them to the guardroom. 12Because Rehoboam
humbled himself, the LORD's anger was turned
away, and he did not destroy him completely.
There were still some good things in the land of
Judah.

Summary of Rehoboam's Reign

13King Rehoboam firmly established himself in
Jerusalem and continued to rule. He was forty-
one years old when he became king, and he
reigned seventeen years in Jerusalem, the city
the LORD had chosen from among all the tribes
of Israel as the place to honor his name. Rehoboam's mother was Naamah, a woman from Ammon. 14But he was an evil king, for he did not
seek the LORD with all his heart.
15The rest of the events of Rehoboam's reign,
from beginning to end, are recorded in *The
Record of Shemaiah the Prophet* and *The Record of Iddo the Seer,* which are part of the genealogical record. Rehoboam and Jeroboam were
continually at war with each other. 16When Rehoboam died, he was buried in the City of David.
Then his son Abijah became the next king.

CHAPTER 13
Abijah's War with Jeroboam

Abijah began to rule over Judah in the eighteenth
year of Jeroboam's reign in Israel. 2He reigned in
Jerusalem three years. His mother was Maacah,
the daughter of Uriel from Gibeah.

Then war broke out between Abijah and Jeroboam. 3Judah, led by King Abijah, fielded
400,000 select warriors, while Jeroboam mustered 800,000 select troops from Israel.

4When the army of Judah arrived in the hill
country of Ephraim, Abijah stood on Mount Zemaraim and shouted to Jeroboam and all Israel:
"Listen to me! 5Don't you realize that the LORD, the
God of Israel, made a lasting covenant with David,
giving him and his descendants the throne of Israel forever? 6Yet Jeroboam son of Nebat, a mere
servant of David's son Solomon, rebelled against
his master. 7Then a whole gang of scoundrels
joined him, defying Solomon's son Rehoboam
when he was young and inexperienced and could
not stand up to them.

8"Do you really think you can stand against the
kingdom of the LORD that is led by the descendants of David? You may have a vast army, and
you have those gold calves that Jeroboam made
as your gods. 9But you have chased away the
priests of the LORD (the descendants of Aaron)
and the Levites, and you have appointed your
own priests, just like the pagan nations. You let
anyone become a priest these days! Whoever
comes to be dedicated with a young bull and
seven rams can become a priest of these so-
called gods of yours!

10"But as for us, the LORD is our God, and we
have not abandoned him. Only the descendants
of Aaron serve the LORD as priests, and the Levites alone may help them in their work. 11They
present burnt offerings and fragrant incense to
the LORD every morning and evening. They place
the Bread of the Presence on the holy table, and
they light the gold lampstand every evening. We
are following the instructions of the LORD our
God, but you have abandoned him. 12So you see,
God is with us. He is our leader. His priests blow
their trumpets and lead us into battle against
you. O people of Israel, do not fight against the
LORD, the God of your ancestors, for you will not
succeed!"

13Meanwhile, Jeroboam had secretly sent part
of his army around behind the men of Judah to
ambush them. 14When Judah realized that they
were being attacked from the front and the rear,
they cried out to the LORD for help. Then the
priests blew the trumpets, 15and the men of
Judah began to shout. At the sound of their battle
cry, God defeated Jeroboam and all Israel and
routed them before Abijah and the army of
Judah.

16The Israelite army fled from Judah, and God
handed them over to Judah in defeat. 17Abijah
and his army inflicted heavy losses on them;
500,000 of Israel's select troops were killed that
day. 18So Judah defeated Israel on that occasion
because they trusted in the LORD, the God of
their ancestors. 19Abijah and his army pursued
Jeroboam's troops and captured some of his
towns, including Bethel, Jeshanah, and Ephron,
along with their surrounding villages.

20So Jeroboam of Israel never regained his
power during Abijah's lifetime, and finally the
LORD struck him down and he died. 21Meanwhile,
Abijah of Judah grew more and more powerful.
He married fourteen wives and had twenty-two
sons and sixteen daughters.

22The rest of the events of Abijah's reign, including his words and deeds, are recorded in *The
Commentary of Iddo the Prophet*.

CHAPTER 14
Early Years of Asa's Reign

When Abijah died, he was buried in the City of
David. Then his son Asa became the next king.
There was peace in the land for ten years. 2Asa
did what was pleasing and good in the sight of
the LORD his God. 3He removed the foreign altars
and the pagan shrines. He smashed the sacred
pillars and cut down the Asherah poles. 4He
commanded the people of Judah to seek the
LORD, the God of their ancestors, and to obey his
law and his commands. 5Asa also removed the
pagan shrines, as well as the incense altars from
every one of Judah's towns. So Asa's kingdom enjoyed a period of peace. 6During those peaceful
years, he was able to build up the fortified towns
throughout Judah. No one tried to make war
against him at this time, for the LORD was giving
him rest from his enemies.

7Asa told the people of Judah, "Let us build
towns and fortify them with walls, towers, gates,
and bars. The land is still ours because we sought
the LORD our God, and he has given us peace on
every side." So they went ahead with these projects and brought them to completion.

8King Asa had an army of 300,000 warriors
from the tribe of Judah, armed with large shields
and spears. He also had an army of 280,000
warriors from the tribe of Benjamin, armed with
small shields and bows. Both armies were composed of well-trained fighting men.

9Once an Ethiopian named Zerah attacked Judah with an army of 1,000,000 men and
300 chariots. They advanced to the town of Mareshah, 10so Asa deployed his armies for battle in
the valley north of Mareshah. 11Then Asa cried
out to the LORD his God, "O LORD, no one but you
can help the powerless against the mighty! Help
us, O LORD our God, for we trust in you alone. It is
in your name that we have come against this vast
horde. O LORD, you are our God; do not let mere
men prevail against you!"
12So the LORD defeated the Ethiopians in the
presence of Asa and the army of Judah, and the
enemy fled. 13Asa and his army pursued them as
far as Gerar, and so many Ethiopians fell that they
were unable to rally. They were destroyed by the
LORD and his army, and the army of Judah carried
off a vast amount of plunder.
14While they were at Gerar, they attacked all
the towns in that area, and terror from the LORD
came upon the people there. As a result, a vast
amount of plunder was taken from these towns,
too. 15They also attacked the camps of herdsmen
and captured many sheep, goats, and camels before finally returning to Jerusalem.

CHAPTER 15
Asa's Religious Reforms

Then the Spirit of God came upon Azariah son of
Oded, 2and he went out to meet King Asa as he
was returning from the battle. "Listen to me,
Asa!" he shouted. "Listen, all you people of Judah
and Benjamin! The LORD will stay with you as
long as you stay with him! Whenever you seek
him, you will find him. But if you abandon him,
he will abandon you. 3For a long time Israel was
without the true God, without a priest to teach
them, and without the Law to instruct them. 4But
whenever they were in trouble and turned to the
LORD, the God of Israel, and sought him out, they
found him.
5"During those dark times, it was not safe to
travel. Problems troubled the people of every
land. 6Nation fought against nation, and city
against city, for God was troubling them with
every kind of problem. 7But as for you, be
strong and courageous, for your work will be
rewarded."
8When Asa heard this message from Azariah
the prophet, he took courage and removed all the
detestable idols from the land of Judah and Benjamin and in the towns he had captured in the
hill country of Ephraim. And he repaired the altar of the LORD, which stood in front of the entry
room of the LORD's Temple.
9Then Asa called together all the people of Judah and Benjamin, along with the people of
Ephraim, Manasseh, and Simeon who had settled among them. For many from Israel had
moved to Judah during Asa's reign when they
saw that the LORD his God was with him. 10The
people gathered at Jerusalem in late spring,
during the fifteenth year of Asa's reign.
11On that day they sacrificed to the LORD
700 cattle and 7,000 sheep and goats from the
plunder they had taken in the battle. 12Then they
entered into a covenant to seek the LORD, the
God of their ancestors, with all their heart and
soul. 13They agreed that anyone who refused to
seek the LORD, the God of Israel, would be put to
death—whether young or old, man or woman.
14They shouted out their oath of loyalty to the
LORD with trumpets blaring and rams' horns
sounding. 15All in Judah were happy about this
covenant, for they had entered into it with all
their heart. They earnestly sought after God, and
they found him. And the LORD gave them rest
from their enemies on every side.
16King Asa even deposed his grandmother
Maacah from her position as queen mother because she had made an obscene Asherah pole.
He cut down her obscene pole, broke it up,
and burned it in the Kidron Valley. 17Although
the pagan shrines were not removed from Israel, Asa's heart remained completely faithful
throughout his life. 18He brought into the Temple of God the silver and gold and the various
items that he and his father had dedicated.
19So there was no more war until the thirty-
fifth year of Asa's reign.

CHAPTER 16
Final Years of Asa's Reign

In the thirty-sixth year of Asa's reign, King Baasha of Israel invaded Judah and fortified Ramah
in order to prevent anyone from entering or leaving King Asa's territory in Judah.
2Asa responded by removing the silver and
gold from the treasuries of the Temple of the
LORD and the royal palace. He sent it to King Ben-
hadad of Aram, who was ruling in Damascus,
along with this message:

> 3"Let there be a treaty between you and me
> like the one between your father and my
> father. See, I am sending you silver and gold.
> Break your treaty with King Baasha of Israel
> so that he will leave me alone."

4Ben-hadad agreed to King Asa's request and
sent the commanders of his army to attack the

towns of Israel. They conquered the towns of
Ijon, Dan, Abel-beth-maacah, and all the store
cities in Naphtali. 5As soon as Baasha of Israel
heard what was happening, he abandoned his
project of fortifying Ramah and stopped all work
on it. 6Then King Asa called out all the men of
Judah to carry away the building stones and
timbers that Baasha had been using to fortify
Ramah. Asa used these materials to fortify the
towns of Geba and Mizpah.

7At that time Hanani the seer came to King
Asa and told him, "Because you have put your
trust in the king of Aram instead of in the LORD
your God, you missed your chance to destroy the
army of the king of Aram. 8Don't you remember
what happened to the Ethiopians and Libyans
and their vast army, with all of their chariots and
charioteers? At that time you relied on the LORD,
and he handed them over to you. 9The eyes of
the LORD search the whole earth in order to
strengthen those whose hearts are fully committed to him. What a fool you have been! From now
on you will be at war."

10Asa became so angry with Hanani for saying
this that he threw him into prison and put him in
stocks. At that time Asa also began to oppress
some of his people.

Summary of Asa's Reign

11The rest of the events of Asa's reign, from beginning to end, are recorded in *The Book of the
Kings of Judah and Israel.* 12In the thirty-ninth
year of his reign, Asa developed a serious foot
disease. Yet even with the severity of his disease,
he did not seek the LORD's help but turned only
to his physicians. 13So he died in the forty-first
year of his reign. 14He was buried in the tomb he
had carved out for himself in the City of David.
He was laid on a bed perfumed with sweet spices
and fragrant ointments, and the people built a
huge funeral fire in his honor.

CHAPTER 17

Jehoshaphat Rules in Judah

Then Jehoshaphat, Asa's son, became the next
king. He strengthened Judah to stand against
any attack from Israel. 2He stationed troops in
all the fortified towns of Judah, and he assigned
additional garrisons to the land of Judah and to
the towns of Ephraim that his father, Asa, had
captured.

3The LORD was with Jehoshaphat because he
followed the example of his father's early years
and did not worship the images of Baal. 4He
sought his father's God and obeyed his commands instead of following the evil practices of
the kingdom of Israel. 5So the LORD established
Jehoshaphat's control over the kingdom of Judah.
All the people of Judah brought gifts to Jehoshaphat, so he became very wealthy and highly esteemed. 6He was deeply committed to the ways of
the LORD. He removed the pagan shrines and
Asherah poles from Judah.

7In the third year of his reign Jehoshaphat
sent his officials to teach in all the towns of Judah. These officials included Ben-hail, Obadiah,
Zechariah, Nethanel, and Micaiah. 8He sent
Levites along with them, including Shemaiah,
Nethaniah, Zebadiah, Asahel, Shemiramoth, Jehonathan, Adonijah, Tobijah, and Tob-adonijah.
He also sent out the priests Elishama and Jehoram. 9They took copies of the Book of the Law of
the LORD and traveled around through all the
towns of Judah, teaching the people.

10Then the fear of the LORD fell over all the
surrounding kingdoms so that none of them
wanted to declare war on Jehoshaphat. 11Some
of the Philistines brought him gifts and silver as
tribute, and the Arabs brought 7,700 rams and
7,700 male goats.

12So Jehoshaphat became more and more
powerful and built fortresses and storage cities
throughout Judah. 13He stored numerous supplies in Judah's towns and stationed an army of
seasoned troops at Jerusalem. 14His army was
enrolled according to ancestral clans.

From Judah there were 300,000 troops
organized in units of 1,000, under the
command of Adnah. 15Next in command
was Jehohanan, who commanded 280,000
troops. 16Next was Amasiah son of Zicri,
who volunteered for the LORD's service,
with 200,000 troops under his command.
17From Benjamin there were 200,000 troops
equipped with bows and shields. They were
under the command of Eliada, a veteran
soldier. 18Next in command was Jehozabad,
who commanded 180,000 armed men.

19These were the troops stationed in Jerusalem
to serve the king, besides those Jehoshaphat stationed in the fortified towns throughout Judah.

CHAPTER 18

Jehoshaphat and Ahab

Jehoshaphat enjoyed great riches and high esteem, and he made an alliance with Ahab of Israel by having his son marry Ahab's daughter. 2A
few years later he went to Samaria to visit Ahab,
who prepared a great banquet for him and his

BIBLE BIOS

Hear From the Heroes

Hi, my name is

ELISHA *(farmer, prophet of God)*

Yeah, I know. My name sounds like Elijah, the great prophet who came before me. It's easy to get the two names mixed up. You might even get the two prophets mixed up. But remember—I replaced Elijah after God took him to heaven.

It's not unusual for God to take people to heaven. But Elijah wasn't even dead! Read 2 KINGS 2 for more about that amazing day.

Just before God took Elijah, I asked God if I could be Elijah's replacement. It's not that I wanted to be greater than Elijah, or famous, or powerful. I just wanted to be able to serve the Lord. And with God's help, that's just what happened.

God allowed me to do lots of great things, just as he had allowed Elijah. One time God used me to make a little bit of oil go a long, long way. That helped a poor widow keep her sons out of slavery because she was able to sell the oil and pay off her debts. Another time, God helped me raise a boy from the dead.

And one time, God helped me heal an important guy named Naaman.

At first, Naaman thought he was too important to do what Elisha said. But finally he listened. Read all about it in 2 KINGS 5:1-14. After he was healed, Naaman tried to give Elisha presents.

I guess if you asked me the main point of my life, it would be this: I just wanted to serve the Lord. After all, Elijah was a great teacher. Watching God work through Elijah, I learned how great God is and what awesome things he can do! I just wanted to be a part of that. Serving God is the best thing anyone can do. Try it!

Live and Learn

Elisha learned a lot about God by being Elijah's assistant. He watched Elijah at work as he tried to turn the people back to God. And he watched God work *through* Elijah. **Who has taught you a lot about God? Answer these questions to find out!**

1. **Who first told you about God's Son, Jesus?**
2. **Who takes you to church?**
3. **Who prays for you?**

How about giving the person or people whose names you wrote a BIG thank you! After all, they've given you the most precious gift of all—the knowledge that Jesus died for *you*!

BIBLE BIOS
Hear From the Heroes

THE DIVIDED KINGDOM

What? A talking kingdom? A talking *divided* kingdom? Whoever heard of such a thing? You did! So sit back and listen to my story because I have a lot to say!

It all started when the people wanted a human king. God was their leader, but was that good enough for them? Nooo. They had to have a human king like all the other countries. So God gave them what they wanted. Things went OK for a while. But things really started to go sour when Israel's third king, Solomon, started to forget about God. When Solomon died, his son Rehoboam wanted to be king.

Read abou[t the] beginning [and] the end of [the] kingdom [of] Israel i[n] 1 KINGS 11[:]

Solomon had said that Rehoboam should be king, but 10 of the 12 tribes of Israel chose Jeroboam as their leader. Bad news. So the kingdom split in two. The two southern tribes (led by Rehoboam) became known as Judah, or the southern kingdom. The other 10 tribes (led by Jeroboam) kept the name of Israel (sometimes called the northern kingdom).

Let me tell you, it wasn't easy being a kingdom cut in two. Ouch! It was just one bad king after another. And the wars! And don't get me started on the people! So many of them turned away from the one true God and worshiped fake gods. How could they forget all that God had done for them over the years?

Want the ugly details about all those bad kings? Just read through 2 KINGS.

But they did. I guess they thought that God would stand for that kind of sin. No way! The northern kingdom was the first to be punished by God, being invaded and conquered by the Assyrians. Then God punished the southern kingdom by allowing the Babylonians to take Jerusalem. And, sad to say, that was the end of the divided kingdom of Israel.

But that's not the end of the story. Even though God's people weren't faithful, God was. After a time, God allowed the Israelites to return to their land. And God still has plans for his people!

Focus on God

The Israelites just couldn't seem to stay focused on God. And that led to the downfall of the whole kingdom. Don't let that happen to you!

Identify the things that take you away from God, and then turn away from those things instead of turning away from God.

Write the things that take you away from God:

Now write what you can replace those things with. What will help you stay focused on God?

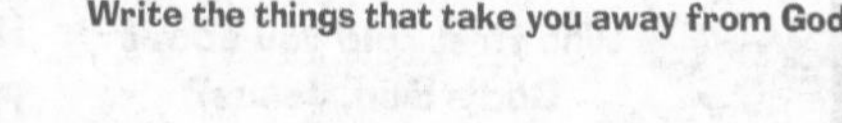

officials. They butchered great numbers of
sheep, goats, and cattle for the feast. Then Ahab
enticed Jehoshaphat to join forces with him to
recover Ramoth-gilead.
3"Will you go with me to Ramoth-gilead?" King
Ahab of Israel asked King Jehoshaphat of Judah.
Jehoshaphat replied, "Why, of course! You and
I are as one, and my troops are your troops. We
will certainly join you in battle." 4Then Jehoshaphat added, "But first let's find out what the LORD
says."
5So the king of Israel summoned the prophets, 400 of them, and asked them, "Should we
go to war against Ramoth-gilead, or should I
hold back?"
They all replied, "Yes, go right ahead! God will
give the king victory."
6But Jehoshaphat asked, "Is there not also a
prophet of the LORD here? We should ask him
the same question."
7The king of Israel replied to Jehoshaphat,
"There is one more man who could consult the
LORD for us, but I hate him. He never prophesies
anything but trouble for me! His name is Micaiah son of Imlah."
Jehoshaphat replied, "That's not the way a
king should talk! Let's hear what he has to say."
8So the king of Israel called one of his officials and said, "Quick! Bring Micaiah son of
Imlah."

Micaiah Prophesies against Ahab

9King Ahab of Israel and King Jehoshaphat of Judah, dressed in their royal robes, were sitting on
thrones at the threshing floor near the gate of Samaria. All of Ahab's prophets were prophesying
there in front of them. 10One of them, Zedekiah
son of Kenaanah, made some iron horns and
proclaimed, "This is what the LORD says: With
these horns you will gore the Arameans to
death!"
11All the other prophets agreed. "Yes," they
said, "go up to Ramoth-gilead and be victorious,
for the LORD will give the king victory!"
12Meanwhile, the messenger who went to get
Micaiah said to him, "Look, all the prophets are
promising victory for the king. Be sure that you
agree with them and promise success."
13But Micaiah replied, "As surely as the LORD
lives, I will say only what my God says."
14When Micaiah arrived before the king,
Ahab asked him, "Micaiah, should we go to war
against Ramoth-gilead, or should I hold back?"
Micaiah replied sarcastically, "Yes, go up and
be victorious, for you will have victory over
them!"
15But the king replied sharply, "How many
times must I demand that you speak only the
truth to me when you speak for the LORD?"
16Then Micaiah told him, "In a vision I saw all
Israel scattered on the mountains, like sheep
without a shepherd. And the LORD said, 'Their
master has been killed. Send them home in
peace.'"
17"Didn't I tell you?" the king of Israel exclaimed to Jehoshaphat. "He never prophesies
anything but trouble for me."
18Then Micaiah continued, "Listen to what the
LORD says! I saw the LORD sitting on his throne
with all the armies of heaven around him, on his
right and on his left. 19And the LORD said, 'Who
can entice King Ahab of Israel to go into battle
against Ramoth-gilead so he can be killed?'
"There were many suggestions, 20and finally a
spirit approached the LORD and said, 'I can do it!'
"'How will you do this?' the LORD asked.
21"And the spirit replied, 'I will go out and inspire all of Ahab's prophets to speak lies.'
"'You will succeed,' said the LORD. 'Go ahead
and do it.'
22"So you see, the LORD has put a lying spirit in
the mouths of your prophets. For the LORD has
pronounced your doom."
23Then Zedekiah son of Kenaanah walked up
to Micaiah and slapped him across the face.
"Since when did the Spirit of the LORD leave me
to speak to you?" he demanded.
24And Micaiah replied, "You will find out soon
enough when you are trying to hide in some secret room!"
25"Arrest him!" the king of Israel ordered.
"Take him back to Amon, the governor of the
city, and to my son Joash. 26Give them this order
from the king: 'Put this man in prison, and feed
him nothing but bread and water until I return
safely from the battle!'"
27But Micaiah replied, "If you return safely, it
will mean that the LORD has not spoken through
me!" Then he added to those standing around,
"Everyone mark my words!"

The Death of Ahab

28So King Ahab of Israel and King Jehoshaphat
of Judah led their armies against Ramoth-gilead.
29The king of Israel said to Jehoshaphat, "As we
go into battle, I will disguise myself so no one will
recognize me, but you wear your royal robes." So
the king of Israel disguised himself, and they
went into battle.

30 Meanwhile, the king of Aram had issued
these orders to his chariot commanders: "Attack
only the king of Israel! Don't bother with anyone
else." 31 So when the Aramean chariot commanders saw Jehoshaphat in his royal robes, they went
after him. "There is the king of Israel!" they
shouted. But Jehoshaphat called out, and the
LORD saved him. God helped him by turning the
attackers away from him. 32 As soon as the chariot commanders realized he was not the king of
Israel, they stopped chasing him.

33 An Aramean soldier, however, randomly
shot an arrow at the Israelite troops and hit the
king of Israel between the joints of his armor.
"Turn the horses and get me out of here!" Ahab
groaned to the driver of the chariot. "I'm badly
wounded!"

34 The battle raged all that day, and the king of
Israel propped himself up in his chariot facing
the Arameans. In the evening, just as the sun was
setting, he died.

CHAPTER 19
Jehoshaphat Appoints Judges

When King Jehoshaphat of Judah arrived safely
home in Jerusalem, 2 Jehu son of Hanani the seer
went out to meet him. "Why should you help the
wicked and love those who hate the LORD?" he
asked the king. "Because of what you have done,
the LORD is very angry with you. 3 Even so, there is
some good in you, for you have removed the
Asherah poles throughout the land, and you have
committed yourself to seeking God."

4 Jehoshaphat lived in Jerusalem, but he went
out among the people, traveling from Beersheba
to the hill country of Ephraim, encouraging the
people to return to the LORD, the God of their ancestors. 5 He appointed judges throughout the
nation in all the fortified towns, 6 and he said to
them, "Always think carefully before pronounc-
ing judgment. Remember that you do not judge
to please people but to please the LORD. He will
be with you when you render the verdict in each
case. 7 Fear the LORD and judge with integrity, for
the LORD our God does not tolerate perverted
justice, partiality, or the taking of bribes."

8 In Jerusalem, Jehoshaphat appointed some
of the Levites and priests and clan leaders in Israel to serve as judges for cases involving the
LORD's regulations and for civil disputes. 9 These
were his instructions to them: "You must always
act in the fear of the LORD, with faithfulness and
an undivided heart. 10 Whenever a case comes to
you from fellow citizens in an outlying town,
whether a murder case or some other violation
of God's laws, commands, decrees, or regulations, you must warn them not to sin against the
LORD, so that he will not be angry with you and
them. Do this and you will not be guilty.

11 "Amariah the high priest will have final say
in all cases involving the LORD. Zebadiah son of
Ishmael, a leader from the tribe of Judah, will
have final say in all civil cases. The Levites will assist you in making sure that justice is served.
Take courage as you fulfill your duties, and may
the LORD be with those who do what is right."

CHAPTER 20
War with Surrounding Nations

After this, the armies of the Moabites, Ammonites, and some of the Meunites declared war on
Jehoshaphat. 2 Messengers came and told Jehoshaphat, "A vast army from Edom is marching
against you from beyond the Dead Sea. They are
already at Hazazon-tamar." (This was another
name for En-gedi.)

3 Jehoshaphat was terrified by this news and
begged the LORD for guidance. He also ordered
everyone in Judah to begin fasting. 4 So people
from all the towns of Judah came to Jerusalem to
seek the LORD's help.

5 Jehoshaphat stood before the community of
Judah and Jerusalem in front of the new courtyard
at the Temple of the LORD. 6 He prayed, "O LORD,
God of our ancestors, you alone are the God who is
in heaven. You are ruler of all the kingdoms of the
earth. You are powerful and mighty; no one can
stand against you! 7 O our God, did you not drive
out those who lived in this land when your people
Israel arrived? And did you not give this land forever to the descendants of your friend Abraham?
8 Your people settled here and built this Temple to
honor your name. 9 They said, 'Whenever we are
faced with any calamity such as war, plague, or
famine, we can come to stand in your presence
before this Temple where your name is honored.
We can cry out to you to save us, and you will hear
us and rescue us.'

10 "And now see what the armies of Ammon,
Moab, and Mount Seir are doing. You would not
let our ancestors invade those nations when Israel left Egypt, so they went around them and did
not destroy them. 11 Now see how they reward us!
For they have come to throw us out of your land,
which you gave us as an inheritance. 12 O our
God, won't you stop them? We are powerless
against this mighty army that is about to attack
us. We do not know what to do, but we are looking to you for help."

13 As all the men of Judah stood before the

Lord with their little ones, wives, and children,
14the Spirit of the Lord came upon one of the
men standing there. His name was Jahaziel son
of Zechariah, son of Benaiah, son of Jeiel, son of
Mattaniah, a Levite who was a descendant of
Asaph.

15He said, "Listen, all you people of Judah and
Jerusalem! Listen, King Jehoshaphat! This is
what the Lord says: Do not be afraid! Don't be
discouraged by this mighty army, for the battle
is not yours, but God's. 16Tomorrow, march out
against them. You will find them coming up
through the ascent of Ziz at the end of the valley
that opens into the wilderness of Jeruel. 17But
you will not even need to fight. Take your positions; then stand still and watch the Lord's victory. He is with you, O people of Judah and
Jerusalem. Do not be afraid or discouraged. Go
out against them tomorrow, for the Lord is with
you!"

18Then King Jehoshaphat bowed low with his
face to the ground. And all the people of Judah
and Jerusalem did the same, worshiping the
Lord. 19Then the Levites from the clans of Kohath and Korah stood to praise the Lord, the God
of Israel, with a very loud shout.

20Early the next morning the army of Judah
went out into the wilderness of Tekoa. On the
way Jehoshaphat stopped and said, "Listen to me,
all you people of Judah and Jerusalem! Believe
in the Lord your God, and you will be able to
stand firm. Believe in his prophets, and you will
succeed."

21After consulting the people, the king appointed singers to walk ahead of the army, singing to the Lord and praising him for his holy
splendor. This is what they sang:

"Give thanks to the Lord;
his faithful love endures forever!"

22At the very moment they began to sing and
give praise, the Lord caused the armies of Ammon, Moab, and Mount Seir to start fighting
among themselves. 23The armies of Moab and
Ammon turned against their allies from Mount
Seir and killed every one of them. After they had
destroyed the army of Seir, they began attacking
each other. 24So when the army of Judah arrived
at the lookout point in the wilderness, all they
saw were dead bodies lying on the ground as far
as they could see. Not a single one of the enemy
had escaped.

25King Jehoshaphat and his men went out to
gather the plunder. They found vast amounts of
equipment, clothing, and other valuables—more
than they could carry. There was so much plunder that it took them three days just to collect it
all! 26On the fourth day they gathered in the Valley of Blessing, which got its name that day because the people praised and thanked the Lord
there. It is still called the Valley of Blessing today.

27Then all the men returned to Jerusalem,
with Jehoshaphat leading them, overjoyed that
the Lord had given them victory over their enemies. 28They marched into Jerusalem to the
music of harps, lyres, and trumpets, and they
proceeded to the Temple of the Lord.

29When all the surrounding kingdoms heard
that the Lord himself had fought against the enemies of Israel, the fear of God came over them.
30So Jehoshaphat's kingdom was at peace, for his
God had given him rest on every side.

Summary of Jehoshaphat's Reign

31So Jehoshaphat ruled over the land of Judah.
He was thirty-five years old when he became
king, and he reigned in Jerusalem twenty-five
years. His mother was Azubah, the daughter of
Shilhi.

32Jehoshaphat was a good king, following the
ways of his father, Asa. He did what was pleasing
in the Lord's sight. 33During his reign, however,
he failed to remove all the pagan shrines, and the
people never fully committed themselves to follow the God of their ancestors.

34The rest of the events of Jehoshaphat's
reign, from beginning to end, are recorded in *The
Record of Jehu Son of Hanani,* which is included
in *The Book of the Kings of Israel.*

35Some time later King Jehoshaphat of Judah
made an alliance with King Ahaziah of Israel,
who was very wicked. 36Together they built a
fleet of trading ships at the port of Ezion-geber.
37Then Eliezer son of Dodavahu from Mareshah
prophesied against Jehoshaphat. He said, "Because you have allied yourself with King Ahaziah,
the Lord will destroy your work." So the ships
met with disaster and never put out to sea.

CHAPTER 21

Jehoram Rules in Judah

When Jehoshaphat died, he was buried with his
ancestors in the City of David. Then his son Jehoram became the next king.

2Jehoram's brothers—the other sons of Jehoshaphat—were Azariah, Jehiel, Zechariah, Az-
ariahu, Michael, and Shephatiah; all these were
the sons of Jehoshaphat king of Judah. 3Their father had given each of them valuable gifts of

silver, gold, and costly items, and also some of Judah's fortified towns. However, he designated Jehoram as the next king because he was the oldest. 4But when Jehoram had become solidly established as king, he killed all his brothers and some of the other leaders of Judah.

5Jehoram was thirty-two years old when he became king, and he reigned in Jerusalem eight years. 6But Jehoram followed the example of the kings of Israel and was as wicked as King Ahab, for he had married one of Ahab's daughters. So Jehoram did what was evil in the LORD's sight. 7But the LORD did not want to destroy David's dynasty, for he had made a covenant with David and promised that his descendants would continue to rule, shining like a lamp forever.

8During Jehoram's reign, the Edomites revolted against Judah and crowned their own king. 9So Jehoram went out with his full army and all his chariots. The Edomites surrounded him and his chariot commanders, but he went out at night and attacked them under cover of darkness. 10Even so, Edom has been independent from Judah to this day. The town of Libnah also revolted about that same time. All this happened because Jehoram had abandoned the LORD, the God of his ancestors. 11He had built pagan shrines in the hill country of Judah and had led the people of Jerusalem and Judah to give themselves to pagan gods and to go astray.

12Then Elijah the prophet wrote Jehoram this letter:

> "This is what the LORD, the God of your ancestor David, says: You have not followed the good example of your father, Jehoshaphat, or your grandfather King Asa of Judah. 13Instead, you have been as evil as the kings of Israel. You have led the people of Jerusalem and Judah to worship idols, just as King Ahab did in Israel. And you have even killed your own brothers, men who were better than you. 14So now the LORD is about to strike you, your people, your children, your wives, and all that is yours with a heavy blow. 15You yourself will suffer with a severe intestinal disease that will get worse each day until your bowels come out."

16Then the LORD stirred up the Philistines and the Arabs, who lived near the Ethiopians, to attack Jehoram. 17They marched against Judah, broke down its defenses, and carried away everything of value in the royal palace, including the king's sons and his wives. Only his youngest son, Ahaziah, was spared.

18After all this, the LORD struck Jehoram with an incurable intestinal disease. 19The disease grew worse and worse, and at the end of two years it caused his bowels to come out, and he died in agony. His people did not build a great funeral fire to honor him as they had done for his ancestors.

20Jehoram was thirty-two years old when he became king, and he reigned in Jerusalem eight years. No one was sorry when he died. They buried him in the City of David, but not in the royal cemetery.

CHAPTER 22

Ahaziah Rules in Judah

Then the people of Jerusalem made Ahaziah, Jehoram's youngest son, their next king, since the marauding bands who came with the Arabs had killed all the older sons. So Ahaziah son of Jehoram reigned as king of Judah.

2Ahaziah was twenty-two years old when he became king, and he reigned in Jerusalem one year. His mother was Athaliah, a granddaughter of King Omri. 3Ahaziah also followed the evil example of King Ahab's family, for his mother encouraged him in doing wrong. 4He did what was evil in the LORD's sight, just as Ahab's family had done. They even became his advisers after the death of his father, and they led him to ruin.

5Following their evil advice, Ahaziah joined Joram, the son of King Ahab of Israel, in his war against King Hazael of Aram at Ramoth-gilead. When the Arameans wounded Joram in the battle, 6he returned to Jezreel to recover from the wounds he had received at Ramoth. Because Joram was wounded, King Ahaziah of Judah went to Jezreel to visit him.

7But God had decided that this visit would be Ahaziah's downfall. While he was there, Ahaziah went out with Joram to meet Jehu grandson of Nimshi, whom the LORD had appointed to destroy the dynasty of Ahab.

8While Jehu was executing judgment against the family of Ahab, he happened to meet some of Judah's officials and Ahaziah's relatives who were traveling with Ahaziah. So Jehu killed them all. 9Then Jehu's men searched for Ahaziah, and they found him hiding in the city of Samaria. They brought him to Jehu, who killed him. Ahaziah was given a decent burial because the people said, "He was the grandson of Jehoshaphat—a man who sought the LORD with all his heart." But none of the surviving members of Ahaziah's family was capable of ruling the kingdom.

Queen Athaliah Rules in Judah

10When Athaliah, the mother of King Ahaziah of Judah, learned that her son was dead, she began to destroy the rest of Judah's royal family. 11But Ahaziah's sister Jehosheba, the daughter of King Jehoram, took Ahaziah's infant son, Joash, and stole him away from among the rest of the king's children, who were about to be killed. She put Joash and his nurse in a bedroom. In this way, Jehosheba, wife of Jehoiada the priest and sister of Ahaziah, hid the child so that Athaliah could not murder him. 12Joash remained hidden in the Temple of God for six years while Athaliah ruled over the land.

CHAPTER 23

Revolt against Athaliah

In the seventh year of Athaliah's reign, Jehoiada the priest decided to act. He summoned his courage and made a pact with five army commanders: Azariah son of Jeroham, Ishmael son of Jehohanan, Azariah son of Obed, Maaseiah son of Adaiah, and Elishaphat son of Zicri. 2These men traveled secretly throughout Judah and summoned the Levites and clan leaders in all the towns to come to Jerusalem. 3They all gathered at the Temple of God, where they made a solemn pact with Joash, the young king.

Jehoiada said to them, "Here is the king's son! The time has come for him to reign! The LORD has promised that a descendant of David will be our king. 4This is what you must do. When you priests and Levites come on duty on the Sabbath, a third of you will serve as gatekeepers. 5Another third will go over to the royal palace, and the final third will be at the Foundation Gate. Everyone else should stay in the courtyards of the LORD's Temple. 6Remember, only the priests and Levites on duty may enter the Temple of the LORD, for they are set apart as holy. The rest of the people must obey the LORD's instructions and stay outside. 7You Levites, form a bodyguard around the king and keep your weapons in hand. Kill anyone who tries to enter the Temple. Stay with the king wherever he goes."

8So the Levites and all the people of Judah did everything as Jehoiada the priest ordered. The commanders took charge of the men reporting for duty that Sabbath, as well as those who were going off duty. Jehoiada the priest did not let anyone go home after their shift ended. 9Then Jehoiada supplied the commanders with the spears and the large and small shields that had once belonged to King David and were stored in the Temple of God. 10He stationed all the people around the king, with their weapons ready. They formed a line from the south side of the Temple around to the north side and all around the altar.

11Then Jehoiada and his sons brought out Joash, the king's son, placed the crown on his head, and presented him with a copy of God's laws. They anointed him and proclaimed him king, and everyone shouted, "Long live the king!"

The Death of Athaliah

12When Athaliah heard the noise of the people running and the shouts of praise to the king, she hurried to the LORDS Temple to see what was happening. 13When she arrived, she saw the newly crowned king standing in his place of authority by the pillar at the Temple entrance. The commanders and trumpeters were surrounding him, and people from all over the land were rejoicing and blowing trumpets. Singers with musical instruments were leading the people in a great celebration. When Athaliah saw all this, she tore her clothes in despair and shouted, "Treason! Treason!"

14Then Jehoiada the priest ordered the commanders who were in charge of the troops, "Take her to the soldiers in front of the Temple, and kill anyone who tries to rescue her." For the priest had said, "She must not be killed in the Temple of the LORD." 15So they seized her and led her out to the entrance of the Horse Gate on the palace grounds, and they killed her there.

Jehoiada's Religious Reforms

16Then Jehoiada made a covenant between himself and the king and the people that they would be the LORD's people. 17And all the people went over to the temple of Baal and tore it down. They demolished the altars and smashed the idols, and they killed Mattan the priest of Baal in front of the altars.

18Jehoiada now put the priests and Levites in charge of the Temple of the LORD, following all the directions given by David. He also commanded them to present burnt offerings to the LORD, as prescribed by the Law of Moses, and to sing and rejoice as David had instructed. 19He also stationed gatekeepers at the gates of the LORD's Temple to keep out those who for any reason were ceremonially unclean.

20Then the commanders, nobles, rulers, and all the people of the land escorted the king from the Temple of the LORD. They went through the upper gate and into the palace, and they seated the king on the royal throne. 21So all the people

of the land rejoiced, and the city was peaceful because Athaliah had been killed.

CHAPTER 24

Joash Repairs the Temple

Joash was seven years old when he became king,
and he reigned in Jerusalem forty years. His
mother was Zibiah from Beersheba. 2Joash did
what was pleasing in the LORD's sight throughout
the lifetime of Jehoiada the priest. 3Jehoiada
chose two wives for Joash, and he had sons and
daughters.

4At one point Joash decided to repair and restore the Temple of the LORD. 5He summoned
the priests and Levites and gave them these instructions: "Go to all the towns of Judah and collect the required annual offerings, so that we can
repair the Temple of your God. Do not delay!" But
the Levites did not act immediately.

6So the king called for Jehoiada the high
priest and asked him, "Why haven't you demanded that the Levites go out and collect the
Temple taxes from the towns of Judah and from
Jerusalem? Moses, the servant of the LORD, levied
this tax on the community of Israel in order to
maintain the Tabernacle of the Covenant."

7Over the years the followers of wicked Athaliah had broken into the Temple of God, and they
had used all the dedicated things from the Temple of the LORD to worship the images of Baal.

8So now the king ordered a chest to be made
and set outside the gate leading to the Temple of
the LORD. 9Then a proclamation was sent
throughout Judah and Jerusalem, telling the people to bring to the LORD the tax that Moses, the
servant of God, had required of the Israelites in
the wilderness. 10This pleased all the leaders
and the people, and they gladly brought their
money and filled the chest with it.

11Whenever the chest became full, the Levites
would carry it to the king's officials. Then the
court secretary and an officer of the high priest
would come and empty the chest and take it back
to the Temple again. This went on day after day,
and a large amount of money was collected.
12The king and Jehoiada gave the money to the
construction supervisors, who hired masons and
carpenters to restore the Temple of the LORD.
They also hired metalworkers, who made articles
of iron and bronze for the LORD's Temple.

13The men in charge of the renovation worked
hard and made steady progress. They restored
the Temple of God according to its original design and strengthened it. 14When all the repairs
were finished, they brought the remaining
money to the king and Jehoiada. It was used to
make various articles for the Temple of the
LORD—articles for worship services and for
burnt offerings, including ladles and other
articles made of gold and silver. And the burnt
offerings were sacrificed continually in the Temple of the LORD during the lifetime of Jehoiada
the priest.

15Jehoiada lived to a very old age, finally dying
at 130. 16He was buried among the kings in the
City of David, because he had done so much
good in Israel for God and his Temple.

Jehoiada's Reforms Reversed

17But after Jehoiada's death, the leaders of Judah
came and bowed before King Joash and persuaded him to listen to their advice. 18They decided to abandon the Temple of the LORD, the
God of their ancestors, and they worshiped
Asherah poles and idols instead! Because of this
sin, divine anger fell on Judah and Jerusalem.
19Yet the LORD sent prophets to bring them back
to him. The prophets warned them, but still the
people would not listen.

20Then the Spirit of God came upon Zechariah
son of Jehoiada the priest. He stood before the
people and said, "This is what God says: Why do
you disobey the LORD's commands and keep yourselves from prospering? You have abandoned the
LORD, and now he has abandoned you!"

21Then the leaders plotted to kill Zechariah,
and King Joash ordered that they stone him to
death in the courtyard of the LORD's Temple.
22That was how King Joash repaid Jehoiada for
his loyalty—by killing his son. Zechariah's last
words as he died were, "May the LORD see what
they are doing and avenge my death!"

The End of Joash's Reign

23In the spring of the year the Aramean army
marched against Joash. They invaded Judah and
Jerusalem and killed all the leaders of the nation.
Then they sent all the plunder back to their king
in Damascus. 24Although the Arameans attacked
with only a small army, the LORD helped them
conquer the much larger army of Judah. The
people of Judah had abandoned the LORD, the
God of their ancestors, so judgment was carried
out against Joash.

25The Arameans withdrew, leaving Joash severely wounded. But his own officials plotted to
kill him for murdering the son of Jehoiada the
priest. They assassinated him as he lay in bed.
Then he was buried in the City of David, but not
in the royal cemetery. 26The assassins were Joza-

car, the son of an Ammonite woman named
Shimeath, and Jehozabad, the son of a Moabite
woman named Shomer.
27The account of the sons of Joash, the prophecies about him, and the record of his restoration
of the Temple of God are written in *The Commentary on the Book of the Kings*. His son Amaziah became the next king.

CHAPTER 25
Amaziah Rules in Judah

Amaziah was twenty-five years old when he became king, and he reigned in Jerusalem twenty-
nine years. His mother was Jehoaddin from Jerusalem. 2Amaziah did what was pleasing in the
LORD's sight, but not wholeheartedly.
3When Amaziah was well established as king,
he executed the officials who had assassinated
his father. 4However, he did not kill the children
of the assassins, for he obeyed the command of
the LORD as written by Moses in the Book of the
Law: "Parents must not be put to death for the
sins of their children, nor children for the sins of
their parents. Those deserving to die must be put
to death for their own crimes."
5Then Amaziah organized the army, assigning
generals and captains for all Judah and Benjamin. He took a census and found that he had an
army of 300,000 select troops, twenty years old
and older, all trained in the use of spear and
shield. 6He also paid about 7,500 pounds of silver to hire 100,000 experienced fighting men
from Israel.
7But a man of God came to him and said,
"Your Majesty, do not hire troops from Israel, for
the LORD is not with Israel. He will not help those
people of Ephraim! 8If you let them go with your
troops into battle, you will be defeated by the enemy no matter how well you fight. God will overthrow you, for he has the power to help you or to
trip you up."
9Amaziah asked the man of God, "But what
about all that silver I paid to hire the army of
Israel?"
The man of God replied, "The LORD is able to
give you much more than this!" 10So Amaziah
discharged the hired troops and sent them back
to Ephraim. This made them very angry with Judah, and they returned home in a great rage.
11Then Amaziah summoned his courage and
led his army to the Valley of Salt, where they
killed 10,000 Edomite troops from Seir. 12They
captured another 10,000 and took them to the
top of a cliff and threw them off, dashing them to
pieces on the rocks below.
13Meanwhile, the hired troops that Amaziah
had sent home raided several of the towns of
Judah between Samaria and Beth-horon. They
killed 3,000 people and carried off great quantities of plunder.
14When King Amaziah returned from slaughtering the Edomites, he brought with him idols
taken from the people of Seir. He set them up as
his own gods, bowed down in front of them, and
offered sacrifices to them! 15This made the LORD
very angry, and he sent a prophet to ask, "Why do
you turn to gods who could not even save their
own people from you?"
16But the king interrupted him and said,
"Since when have I made you the king's counselor? Be quiet now before I have you killed!"
So the prophet stopped with this warning:
"I know that God has determined to destroy you
because you have done this and have refused to
accept my counsel."
17After consulting with his advisers, King Amaziah of Judah sent this challenge to Israel's king
Jehoash, the son of Jehoahaz and grandson of
Jehu: "Come and meet me in battle!"
18But King Jehoash of Israel replied to King
Amaziah of Judah with this story: "Out in the
Lebanon mountains, a thistle sent a message to a
mighty cedar tree: 'Give your daughter in marriage to my son.' But just then a wild animal of
Lebanon came by and stepped on the thistle,
crushing it!
19"You are saying, 'I have defeated Edom,' and
you are very proud of it. But my advice is to stay at
home. Why stir up trouble that will only bring disaster on you and the people of Judah?"
20But Amaziah refused to listen, for God was
determined to destroy him for turning to the
gods of Edom. 21So King Jehoash of Israel mobilized his army against King Amaziah of Judah.
The two armies drew up their battle lines at
Beth-shemesh in Judah. 22Judah was routed by
the army of Israel, and its army scattered and
fled for home. 23King Jehoash of Israel captured
Judah's king, Amaziah son of Joash and grandson of Ahaziah, at Beth-shemesh. Then he
brought him to Jerusalem, where he demolished
600 feet of Jerusalem's wall, from the Ephraim
Gate to the Corner Gate. 24He carried off all the
gold and silver and all the articles from the Temple of God that had been in the care of Obed-
edom. He also seized the treasures of the royal
palace, along with hostages, and then returned
to Samaria.
25King Amaziah of Judah lived for fifteen
years after the death of King Jehoash of Israel.

26 The rest of the events in Amaziah's reign, from
beginning to end, are recorded in *The Book of the
Kings of Judah and Israel.*
27 After Amaziah turned away from the LORD,
there was a conspiracy against his life in Jerusalem, and he fled to Lachish. But his enemies sent
assassins after him, and they killed him there.
28 They brought his body back on a horse, and
he was buried with his ancestors in the City of
David.

CHAPTER 26
Uzziah Rules in Judah

All the people of Judah had crowned Amaziah's
sixteen-year-old son, Uzziah, as king in place of
his father. 2 After his father's death, Uzziah rebuilt the town of Elath and restored it to Judah.
3 Uzziah was sixteen years old when he became king, and he reigned in Jerusalem fifty-two
years. His mother was Jecoliah from Jerusalem.
4 He did what was pleasing in the LORD's sight,
just as his father, Amaziah, had done. 5 Uzziah
sought God during the days of Zechariah, who
taught him to fear God. And as long as the king
sought guidance from the LORD, God gave him
success.
6 Uzziah declared war on the Philistines and
broke down the walls of Gath, Jabneh, and Ashdod. Then he built new towns in the Ashdod area
and in other parts of Philistia. 7 God helped him
in his wars against the Philistines, his battles
with the Arabs of Gur, and his wars with the Meunites. 8 The Meunites paid annual tribute to him,
and his fame spread even to Egypt, for he had become very powerful.
9 Uzziah built fortified towers in Jerusalem at
the Corner Gate, at the Valley Gate, and at the angle in the wall. 10 He also constructed forts in the
wilderness and dug many water cisterns, because he kept great herds of livestock in the foothills of Judah and on the plains. He was also a
man who loved the soil. He had many workers
who cared for his farms and vineyards, both on
the hillsides and in the fertile valleys.
11 Uzziah had an army of well-trained warriors,
ready to march into battle, unit by unit. This army
had been mustered and organized by Jeiel, the
secretary of the army, and his assistant, Maaseiah.
They were under the direction of Hananiah, one
of the king's officials. 12 These regiments of
mighty warriors were commanded by 2,600 clan
leaders. 13 The army consisted of 307,500 men,
all elite troops. They were prepared to assist the
king against any enemy.
14 Uzziah provided the entire army with shields
spears, helmets, coats of mail, bows, and sling
stones. 15 And he built structures on the walls of
Jerusalem, designed by experts to protect those
who shot arrows and hurled large stones from the
towers and the corners of the wall. His fame

Solomon's Temple

Solomon was in charge of building the first Temple of the Lord. Here are some cool facts about the Temple:

- **Solomon built the Temple on the same spot where God stopped Abraham from sacrificing his son Isaac.**
- **It took 80,000 stonecutters to cut the stones for the building.**
- **Timber came on large rafts from the forests of Lebanon.**
- **Water for the Temple was held in huge cisterns or tanks. The water was channeled to the cisterns from the pools of Bethlehem.**

It took a lot of planning to build the Temple! Try this: Take some building blocks, some Lincoln Logs, and a cup of water outside. Place the blocks in one pile, the Lincoln Logs in another pile about five feet away, and the water in another area five feet away. Now make a building! How will you transport the blocks and logs and channel water?

Figuring out how to build the Temple was a tough job, but Solomon did it. Good thing he was so smart!

spread far and wide, for the LORD gave him marvelous help, and he became very powerful.

Uzziah's Sin and Punishment

16But when he had become powerful, he also became proud, which led to his downfall. He
sinned against the LORD his God by entering the
sanctuary of the LORD's Temple and personally
burning incense on the incense altar. 17Azariah
the high priest went in after him with eighty
other priests of the LORD, all brave men. 18They
confronted King Uzziah and said, "It is not for
you, Uzziah, to burn incense to the LORD. That is
the work of the priests alone, the descendants of
Aaron who are set apart for this work. Get out of
the sanctuary, for you have sinned. The LORD God
will not honor you for this!"

19Uzziah, who was holding an incense burner,
became furious. But as he was standing there
raging at the priests before the incense altar in
the LORD's Temple, leprosy suddenly broke out
on his forehead. 20When Azariah the high priest
and all the other priests saw the leprosy, they
rushed him out. And the king himself was eager
to get out because the LORD had struck him. 21So
King Uzziah had leprosy until the day he died.
He lived in isolation in a separate house, for he
was excluded from the Temple of the LORD. His
son Jotham was put in charge of the royal palace,
and he governed the people of the land.

22The rest of the events of Uzziah's reign,
from beginning to end, are recorded by the
prophet Isaiah son of Amoz. 23When Uzziah
died, he was buried with his ancestors; his grave
was in a nearby burial field belonging to the
kings, for the people said, "He had leprosy." And
his son Jotham became the next king.

CHAPTER 27

Jotham Rules in Judah

Jotham was twenty-five years old when he became king, and he reigned in Jerusalem sixteen
years. His mother was Jerusha, the daughter of
Zadok.

2Jotham did what was pleasing in the LORD's
sight. He did everything his father, Uzziah, had
done, except that Jotham did not sin by entering
the Temple of the LORD. But the people continued in their corrupt ways.

3Jotham rebuilt the upper gate of the Temple
of the LORD. He also did extensive rebuilding on
the wall at the hill of Ophel. 4He built towns in
the hill country of Judah and constructed fortresses and towers in the wooded areas. 5Jotham
went to war against the Ammonites and conquered them. Over the next three years he received from them an annual tribute of 7,500
pounds of silver, 50,000 bushels of wheat, and
50,000 bushels of barley.

6King Jotham became powerful because he
was careful to live in obedience to the LORD his
God.

7The rest of the events of Jotham's reign, including all his wars and other activities, are recorded in *The Book of the Kings of Israel and
Judah.* 8He was twenty-five years old when he
became king, and he reigned in Jerusalem sixteen years. 9When Jotham died, he was buried in
the City of David. And his son Ahaz became the
next king.

CHAPTER 28

Ahaz Rules in Judah

Ahaz was twenty years old when he became
king, and he reigned in Jerusalem sixteen years.
He did not do what was pleasing in the sight of
the LORD, as his ancestor David had done. 2In-
stead, he followed the example of the kings of
Israel. He cast metal images for the worship of
Baal. 3He offered sacrifices in the valley of Ben-
Hinnom, even sacrificing his own sons in the
fire. In this way, he followed the detestable
practices of the pagan nations the LORD had
driven from the land ahead of the Israelites.
4He offered sacrifices and burned incense at
the pagan shrines and on the hills and under
every green tree.

5Because of all this, the LORD his God allowed
the king of Aram to defeat Ahaz and to exile
large numbers of his people to Damascus. The
armies of the king of Israel also defeated Ahaz
and inflicted many casualties on his army. 6In a
single day Pekah son of Remaliah, Israel's king,
killed 120,000 of Judah's troops, all of them experienced warriors, because they had abandoned the LORD, the God of their ancestors.
7Then Zicri, a warrior from Ephraim, killed Maaseiah, the king's son; Azrikam, the king's palace
commander; and Elkanah, the king's second-in-
command. 8The armies of Israel captured
200,000 women and children from Judah and
seized tremendous amounts of plunder, which
they took back to Samaria.

9But a prophet of the LORD named Oded was
there in Samaria when the army of Israel returned home. He went out to meet them and
said, "The LORD, the God of your ancestors, was
angry with Judah and let you defeat them. But
you have gone too far, killing them without
mercy, and all heaven is disturbed. 10And now

you are planning to make slaves of these people
from Judah and Jerusalem. What about your own
sins against the LORD your God? 11Listen to me
and return these prisoners you have taken, for
they are your own relatives. Watch out, because
now the LORD's fierce anger has been turned
against you!"

12Then some of the leaders of Israel—Azariah
son of Jehohanan, Berekiah son of Meshillemoth,
Jehizkiah son of Shallum, and Amasa son of
Hadlai—agreed with this and confronted the
men returning from battle. 13"You must not
bring the prisoners here!" they declared. "We
cannot afford to add to our sins and guilt. Our
guilt is already great, and the LORD's fierce anger
is already turned against Israel."

14So the warriors released the prisoners and
handed over the plunder in the sight of the leaders and all the people. 15Then the four men just
mentioned by name came forward and distributed clothes from the plunder to the prisoners
who were naked. They provided clothing and
sandals to wear, gave them enough food and
drink, and dressed their wounds with olive oil.
They put those who were weak on donkeys and
took all the prisoners back to their own people in
Jericho, the city of palms. Then they returned to
Samaria.

Ahaz Closes the Temple

16At that time King Ahaz of Judah asked the king
of Assyria for help. 17The armies of Edom had
again invaded Judah and taken captives. 18And
the Philistines had raided towns located in the
foothills of Judah and in the Negev of Judah.
They had already captured and occupied Beth-
shemesh, Aijalon, Gederoth, Soco with its villages, Timnah with its villages, and Gimzo with
its villages. 19The LORD was humbling Judah because of King Ahaz of Judah, for he had encouraged his people to sin and had been utterly
unfaithful to the LORD.

20So when King Tiglath-pileser of Assyria arrived, he attacked Ahaz instead of helping him.
21Ahaz took valuable items from the LORD's Temple, the royal palace, and from the homes of his
officials and gave them to the king of Assyria as
tribute. But this did not help him.

22Even during this time of trouble, King Ahaz
continued to reject the LORD. 23He offered sacrifices to the gods of Damascus who had defeated
him, for he said, "Since these gods helped the
kings of Aram, they will help me, too, if I sacrifice
to them." But instead, they led to his ruin and the
ruin of all Judah.

24The king took the various articles from the
Temple of God and broke them into pieces. He
shut the doors of the LORD's Temple so that no
one could worship there, and he set up altars to
pagan gods in every corner of Jerusalem. 25He
made pagan shrines in all the towns of Judah for
offering sacrifices to other gods. In this way, he
aroused the anger of the LORD, the God of his ancestors.

26The rest of the events of Ahaz's reign and
everything he did, from beginning to end, are recorded in *The Book of the Kings of Judah and
Israel.* 27When Ahaz died, he was buried in Jerusalem but not in the royal cemetery of the kings
of Judah. Then his son Hezekiah became the
next king.

CHAPTER 29

Hezekiah Rules in Judah

Hezekiah was twenty-five years old when he became the king of Judah, and he reigned in Jerusalem twenty-nine years. His mother was Abijah,
the daughter of Zechariah. 2He did what was
pleasing in the LORD's sight, just as his ancestor
David had done.

Hezekiah Reopens the Temple

3In the very first month of the first year of his
reign, Hezekiah reopened the doors of the Temple of the LORD and repaired them. 4He summoned the priests and Levites to meet him at the
courtyard east of the Temple. 5He said to them,
"Listen to me, you Levites! Purify yourselves, and
purify the Temple of the LORD, the God of your
ancestors. Remove all the defiled things from
the sanctuary. 6Our ancestors were unfaithful
and did what was evil in the sight of the LORD our
God. They abandoned the LORD and his dwelling
place; they turned their backs on him. 7They also
shut the doors to the Temple's entry room, and
they snuffed out the lamps. They stopped burning incense and presenting burnt offerings at the
sanctuary of the God of Israel.

8"That is why the LORD's anger has fallen upon
Judah and Jerusalem. He has made them an object of dread, horror, and ridicule, as you can see
with your own eyes. 9Because of this, our fathers
have been killed in battle, and our sons and
daughters and wives have been captured. 10But
now I will make a covenant with the LORD, the
God of Israel, so that his fierce anger will turn
away from us. 11My sons, do not neglect your duties any longer! The LORD has chosen you to stand
in his presence, to minister to him, and to lead the
people in worship and present offerings to him."

[12]Then these Levites got right to work:

From the clan of Kohath: Mahath son of Amasai and Joel son of Azariah.
From the clan of Merari: Kish son of Abdi and Azariah son of Jehallelel.
From the clan of Gershon: Joah son of Zimmah and Eden son of Joah.
13 From the family of Elizaphan: Shimri and Jeiel.
From the family of Asaph: Zechariah and Mattaniah.
14 From the family of Heman: Jehiel and Shimei.
From the family of Jeduthun: Shemaiah and Uzziel.

[15]These men called together their fellow Levites, and they all purified themselves. Then they began to cleanse the Temple of the LORD, just as the king had commanded. They were careful to follow all the LORD's instructions in their work. [16]The priests went into the sanctuary of the Temple of the LORD to cleanse it, and they took out to the Temple courtyard all the defiled things they found. From there the Levites carted it all out to the Kidron Valley.

[17]They began the work in early spring, on the first day of the new year, and in eight days they had reached the entry room of the LORD's Temple. Then they purified the Temple of the LORD itself, which took another eight days. So the entire task was completed in sixteen days.

The Temple Rededication

[18]Then the Levites went to King Hezekiah and gave him this report: "We have cleansed the entire Temple of the LORD, the altar of burnt offering with all its utensils, and the table of the Bread of the Presence with all its utensils. [19]We have also recovered all the items discarded by King Ahaz when he was unfaithful and closed the Temple. They are now in front of the altar of the LORD, purified and ready for use."

[20]Early the next morning King Hezekiah gathered the city officials and went to the Temple of the LORD. [21]They brought seven bulls, seven rams, and seven male lambs as a burnt offering, together with seven male goats as a sin offering for the kingdom, for the Temple, and for Judah. The king commanded the priests, who were descendants of Aaron, to sacrifice the animals on the altar of the LORD.

[22]So they killed the bulls, and the priests took the blood and sprinkled it on the altar. Next they killed the rams and sprinkled their blood on the altar. And finally, they did the same with the male lambs. [23]The male goats for the sin offering were then brought before the king and the assembly of people, who laid their hands on them. [24]The priests then killed the goats as a sin offering and sprinkled their blood on the altar to make atonement for the sins of all Israel. The king had specifically commanded that this burnt offering and sin offering should be made for all Israel.

[25]King Hezekiah then stationed the Levites at the Temple of the LORD with cymbals, lyres, and harps. He obeyed all the commands that the LORD had given to King David through Gad, the king's seer, and the prophet Nathan. [26]The Levites then took their positions around the Temple with the instruments of David, and the priests took their positions with the trumpets.

[27]Then Hezekiah ordered that the burnt offering be placed on the altar. As the burnt offering was presented, songs of praise to the LORD were begun, accompanied by the trumpets and other instruments of David, the former king of Israel. [28]The entire assembly worshiped the LORD as the singers sang and the trumpets blew, until all the burnt offerings were finished. [29]Then the king and everyone with him bowed down in worship. [30]King Hezekiah and the officials ordered the Levites to praise the LORD with the psalms written by David and by Asaph the seer. So they offered joyous praise and bowed down in worship.

[31]Then Hezekiah declared, "Now that you have consecrated yourselves to the LORD, bring your sacrifices and thanksgiving offerings to the Temple of the LORD." So the people brought their sacrifices and thanksgiving offerings, and all whose hearts were willing brought burnt offerings, too. [32]The people brought to the LORD 70 bulls, 100 rams, and 200 male lambs for burnt offerings. [33]They also brought 600 cattle and 3,000 sheep and goats as sacred offerings.

[34]But there were too few priests to prepare all the burnt offerings. So their relatives the Levites helped them until the work was finished and more priests had been purified, for the Levites had been more conscientious about purifying themselves than the priests had been. [35]There was an abundance of burnt offerings, along with the usual liquid offerings, and a great deal of fat from the many peace offerings.

So the Temple of the LORD was restored to service. [36]And Hezekiah and all the people rejoiced because of what God had done for the people, for everything had been accomplished so quickly.

CHAPTER 30

Preparations for Passover

King Hezekiah now sent word to all Israel and Judah, and he wrote letters of invitation to the people of Ephraim and Manasseh. He asked everyone to come to the Temple of the LORD at Jerusalem to celebrate the Passover of the LORD, the God of Israel. 2The king, his officials, and all the community of Jerusalem decided to celebrate Passover a month later than usual. 3They were unable to celebrate it at the prescribed time because not enough priests could be purified by then, and the people had not yet assembled at Jerusalem.

4This plan for keeping the Passover seemed right to the king and all the people. 5So they sent a proclamation throughout all Israel, from Beersheba in the south to Dan in the north, inviting everyone to come to Jerusalem to celebrate the Passover of the LORD, the God of Israel. The people had not been celebrating it in great numbers as required in the Law.

6At the king's command, runners were sent throughout Israel and Judah. They carried letters that said:

"O people of Israel, return to the LORD, the God of Abraham, Isaac, and Israel, so that he will return to the few of us who have survived the conquest of the Assyrian kings. 7Do not be like your ancestors and relatives who abandoned the LORD, the God of their ancestors, and became an object of derision, as you yourselves can see. 8Do not be stubborn, as they were, but submit yourselves to the LORD. Come to his Temple, which he has set apart as holy forever. Worship the LORD your God so that his fierce anger will turn away from you.

9"For if you return to the LORD, your relatives and your children will be treated mercifully by their captors, and they will be able to return to this land. For the LORD your God is gracious and merciful. If you return to him, he will not continue to turn his face from you."

Celebration of Passover

10The runners went from town to town throughout Ephraim and Manasseh and as far as the territory of Zebulun. But most of the people just laughed at the runners and made fun of them. 11However, some people from Asher, Manasseh, and Zebulun humbled themselves and went to Jerusalem.

12At the same time, God's hand was on the people in the land of Judah, giving them all one heart to obey the orders of the king and his officials, who were following the word of the LORD. 13So a huge crowd assembled at Jerusalem in midspring to celebrate the Festival of Unleavened Bread. 14They set to work and removed the pagan altars from Jerusalem. They took away all the incense altars and threw them into the Kidron Valley.

15On the fourteenth day of the second month, one month later than usual, the people slaughtered the Passover lamb. This shamed the priests and Levites, so they purified themselves and brought burnt offerings to the Temple of the LORD. 16Then they took their places at the Temple as prescribed in the Law of Moses, the man of God. The Levites brought the sacrificial blood to the priests, who then sprinkled it on the altar.

17Since many of the people had not purified themselves, the Levites had to slaughter their Passover lamb for them, to set them apart for the LORD. 18Most of those who came from Ephraim, Manasseh, Issachar, and Zebulun had not purified themselves. But King Hezekiah prayed for them, and they were allowed to eat the Passover meal anyway, even though this was contrary to the requirements of the Law. For Hezekiah said, "May the LORD, who is good, pardon those 19who decide to follow the LORD, the God of their ancestors, even though they are not properly cleansed for the ceremony." 20And the LORD listened to Hezekiah's prayer and healed the people.

21So the people of Israel who were present in Jerusalem joyously celebrated the Festival of Unleavened Bread for seven days. Each day the Levites and priests sang to the LORD, accompanied by loud instruments. 22Hezekiah encouraged all the Levites regarding the skill they displayed as they served the LORD. The celebration continued for seven days. Peace offerings were sacrificed, and the people gave thanks to the LORD, the God of their ancestors.

23The entire assembly then decided to continue the festival another seven days, so they celebrated joyfully for another week. 24King Hezekiah gave the people 1,000 bulls and 7,000 sheep and goats for offerings, and the officials donated 1,000 bulls and 10,000 sheep and goats. Meanwhile, many more priests purified themselves.

25The entire assembly of Judah rejoiced, including the priests, the Levites, all who came from the land of Israel, the foreigners who came to the festival, and all those who lived in Judah.

26There was great joy in the city, for Jerusalem had not seen a celebration like this one since the days of Solomon, King David's son. 27Then the priests and Levites stood and blessed the people, and God heard their prayer from his holy dwelling in heaven.

CHAPTER 31

Hezekiah's Religious Reforms

When the festival ended, the Israelites who attended went to all the towns of Judah, Benjamin, Ephraim, and Manasseh, and they smashed all the sacred pillars, cut down the Asherah poles, and removed the pagan shrines and altars. After this, the Israelites returned to their own towns and homes.

2Hezekiah then organized the priests and Levites into divisions to offer the burnt offerings and peace offerings, and to worship and give thanks and praise to the LORD at the gates of the Temple. 3The king also made a personal contribution of animals for the daily morning and evening burnt offerings, the weekly Sabbath festivals, the monthly new moon festivals, and the annual festivals as prescribed in the Law of the LORD. 4In addition, he required the people in Jerusalem to bring a portion of their goods to the priests and Levites, so they could devote themselves fully to the Law of the LORD.

5When the people of Israel heard these requirements, they responded generously by bringing the first share of their grain, new wine, olive oil, honey, and all the produce of their fields. They brought a large quantity—a tithe of all they produced. 6The people who had moved to Judah from Israel, and the people of Judah themselves, brought in the tithes of their cattle, sheep, and goats and a tithe of the things that had been dedicated to the LORD their God, and they piled them up in great heaps. 7They began piling them up in late spring, and the heaps continued to grow until early autumn. 8When Hezekiah and his officials came and saw these huge piles, they thanked the LORD and his people Israel!

9"Where did all this come from?" Hezekiah asked the priests and Levites.

10And Azariah the high priest, from the family of Zadok, replied, "Since the people began bringing their gifts to the LORD's Temple, we have had enough to eat and plenty to spare. The LORD has blessed his people, and all this is left over."

11Hezekiah ordered that storerooms be prepared in the Temple of the LORD. When this was done, 12the people faithfully brought all the gifts, tithes, and other items dedicated for use in the Temple. Conaniah the Levite was put in charge, assisted by his brother Shimei. 13The supervisors under them were Jehiel, Azaziah, Nahath, Asahel, Jerimoth, Jozabad, Eliel, Ismakiah, Mahath, and Benaiah. These appointments were made by King Hezekiah and Azariah, the chief official in the Temple of God.

14Kore son of Imnah the Levite, who was the gatekeeper at the East Gate, was put in charge of distributing the voluntary offerings given to God, the gifts, and the things that had been dedicated to the LORD. 15His faithful assistants were Eden, Miniamin, Jeshua, Shemaiah, Amariah, and Shecaniah. They distributed the gifts among the families of priests in their towns by their divisions, dividing the gifts fairly among old and young alike. 16They distributed the gifts to all males three years old or older, regardless of their place in the genealogical records. The distribution went to all who would come to the LORD's Temple to perform their daily duties according to their divisions. 17They distributed gifts to the priests who were listed by their families in the genealogical records, and to the Levites twenty years old or older who were listed according to their jobs and their divisions. 18Food allotments were also given to the families of all those listed in the genealogical records, including their little babies, wives, sons, and daughters. For they had all been faithful in purifying themselves.

19As for the priests, the descendants of Aaron, who were living in the open villages around the towns, men were appointed by name to distribute portions to every male among the priests and to all the Levites listed in the genealogical records.

20In this way, King Hezekiah handled the distribution throughout all Judah, doing what was pleasing and good in the sight of the LORD his God. 21In all that he did in the service of the Temple of God and in his efforts to follow God's laws and commands, Hezekiah sought his God wholeheartedly. As a result, he was very successful.

CHAPTER 32

Assyria Invades Judah

After Hezekiah had faithfully carried out this work, King Sennacherib of Assyria invaded Judah. He laid siege to the fortified towns, giving orders for his army to break through their walls. 2When Hezekiah realized that Sennacherib also intended to attack Jerusalem, 3he consulted with his officials and military advisers, and they decided to stop the flow of the springs outside the city. 4They organized a huge work crew to stop the flow of the springs, cutting off the brook that

ran through the fields. For they said, "Why
should the kings of Assyria come here and find
plenty of water?"
5 Then Hezekiah worked hard at repairing all
the broken sections of the wall, erecting towers,
and constructing a second wall outside the first.
He also reinforced the supporting terraces in the
City of David and manufactured large numbers
of weapons and shields. 6 He appointed military
officers over the people and assembled them before him in the square at the city gate. Then Hezekiah encouraged them by saying: 7 "Be strong
and courageous! Don't be afraid or discouraged
because of the king of Assyria or his mighty
army, for there is a power far greater on our side!
8 He may have a great army, but they are merely
men. We have the LORD our God to help us and to
fight our battles for us!" Hezekiah's words
greatly encouraged the people.

Sennacherib Threatens Jerusalem

9 While King Sennacherib of Assyria was still besieging the town of Lachish, he sent his officers
to Jerusalem with this message for Hezekiah and
all the people in the city:

10 "This is what King Sennacherib of Assyria
says: What are you trusting in that makes you
think you can survive my siege of Jerusalem?
11 Hezekiah has said, 'The LORD our God will
rescue us from the king of Assyria.' Surely
Hezekiah is misleading you, sentencing you
to death by famine and thirst! 12 Don't you
realize that Hezekiah is the very person who
destroyed all the LORD's shrines and altars?
He commanded Judah and Jerusalem to
worship only at the altar at the Temple and
to offer sacrifices on it alone.
13 "Surely you must realize what I and the
other kings of Assyria before me have done
to all the people of the earth! Were any of
the gods of those nations able to rescue their
people from my power? 14 Which of their
gods was able to rescue its people from the
destructive power of my predecessors?
What makes you think your God can rescue
you from me? 15 Don't let Hezekiah deceive
you! Don't let him fool you like this! I say it
again—no god of any nation or kingdom has
ever yet been able to rescue his people from
me or my ancestors. How much less will your
God rescue you from my power!"

16 And Sennacherib's officers further mocked
the LORD God and his servant Hezekiah, heaping
insult upon insult. 17 The king also sent letters
scorning the LORD, the God of Israel. He wrote,
"Just as the gods of all the other nations failed to
rescue their people from my power, so the God of
Hezekiah will also fail." 18 The Assyrian officials
who brought the letters shouted this in Hebrew
to the people gathered on the walls of the city,
trying to terrify them so it would be easier to
capture the city. 19 These officers talked about
the God of Jerusalem as though he were one of
the pagan gods, made by human hands.
20 Then King Hezekiah and the prophet Isaiah
son of Amoz cried out in prayer to God in heaven.
21 And the LORD sent an angel who destroyed the
Assyrian army with all its commanders and officers. So Sennacherib was forced to return home
in disgrace to his own land. And when he entered
the temple of his god, some of his own sons killed
him there with a sword.
22 That is how the LORD rescued Hezekiah and
the people of Jerusalem from King Sennacherib
of Assyria and from all the others who threatened them. So there was peace throughout the
land. 23 From then on King Hezekiah became
highly respected among all the surrounding
nations, and many gifts for the LORD arrived at
Jerusalem, with valuable presents for King Hezekiah, too.

Hezekiah's Sickness and Recovery

24 About that time Hezekiah became deathly ill.
He prayed to the LORD, who healed him and gave
him a miraculous sign. 25 But Hezekiah did not
respond appropriately to the kindness shown
him, and he became proud. So the LORD's anger
came against him and against Judah and Jerusalem. 26 Then Hezekiah humbled himself and
repented of his pride, as did the people of Jerusalem. So the LORD's anger did not fall on them
during Hezekiah's lifetime.
27 Hezekiah was very wealthy and highly honored. He built special treasury buildings for his
silver, gold, precious stones, and spices, and for
his shields and other valuable items. 28 He also
constructed many storehouses for his grain, new
wine, and olive oil; and he made many stalls for
his cattle and pens for his flocks of sheep and
goats. 29 He built many towns and acquired vast
flocks and herds, for God had given him great
wealth. 30 He blocked up the upper spring of
Gihon and brought the water down through a
tunnel to the west side of the City of David. And
so he succeeded in everything he did.
31 However, when ambassadors arrived from

Babylon to ask about the remarkable events that
had taken place in the land, God withdrew from
Hezekiah in order to test him and to see what
was really in his heart.

Summary of Hezekiah's Reign

32The rest of the events in Hezekiah's reign and
his acts of devotion are recorded in *The Vision
of the Prophet Isaiah Son of Amoz,* which is included in *The Book of the Kings of Judah and
Israel.* 33When Hezekiah died, he was buried in
the upper area of the royal cemetery, and all
Judah and Jerusalem honored him at his death.
And his son Manasseh became the next king.

CHAPTER 33
Manasseh Rules in Judah

Manasseh was twelve years old when he became
king, and he reigned in Jerusalem fifty-five years.
2He did what was evil in the LORD's sight, following the detestable practices of the pagan nations
that the LORD had driven from the land ahead of
the Israelites. 3He rebuilt the pagan shrines his
father, Hezekiah, had broken down. He constructed altars for the images of Baal and set up
Asherah poles. He also bowed before all the powers of the heavens and worshiped them.

4He built pagan altars in the Temple of the
LORD, the place where the LORD had said, "My
name will remain in Jerusalem forever." 5He built
these altars for all the powers of the heavens in
both courtyards of the LORD's Temple. 6Manas-
seh also sacrificed his own sons in the fire in the
valley of Ben-Hinnom. He practiced sorcery, divination, and witchcraft, and he consulted with
mediums and psychics. He did much that was
evil in the LORD's sight, arousing his anger.

7Manasseh even took a carved idol he had
made and set it up in God's Temple, the very
place where God had told David and his son Solomon: "My name will be honored forever in this
Temple and in Jerusalem—the city I have chosen
from among all the tribes of Israel. 8If the Israelites will be careful to obey my commands—all
the laws, decrees, and regulations given through
Moses—I will not send them into exile from this
land that I set aside for your ancestors." 9But
Manasseh led the people of Judah and Jerusalem
to do even more evil than the pagan nations that
the LORD had destroyed when the people of
Israel entered the land.

10The LORD spoke to Manasseh and his people, but they ignored all his warnings. 11So the
LORD sent the commanders of the Assyrian armies, and they took Manasseh prisoner. They

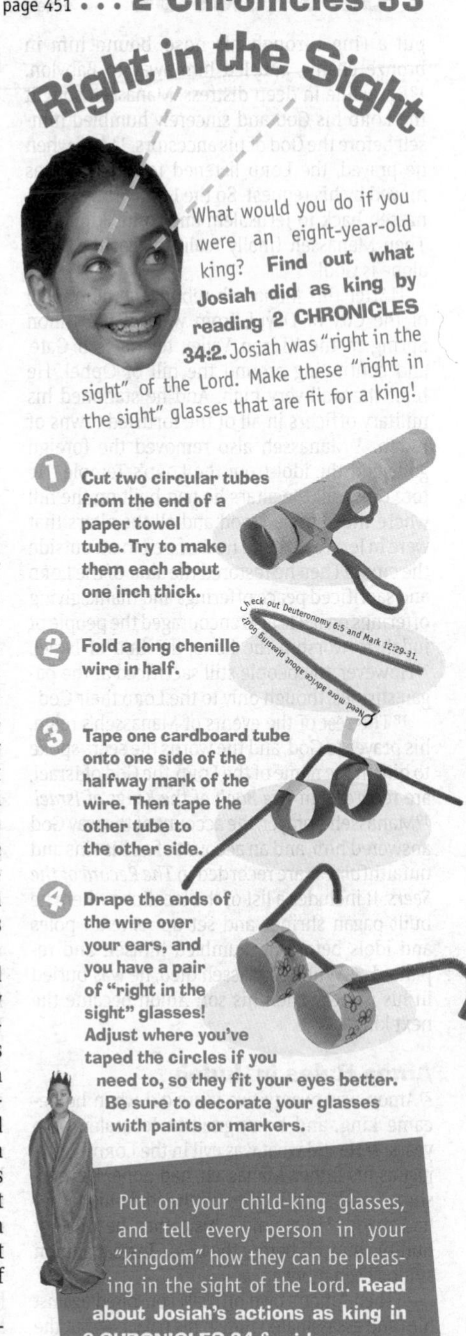
Right in the Sight
What would you do if you were an eight-year-old king? Find out what Josiah did as king by reading 2 CHRONICLES 34:2. Josiah was "right in the sight" of the Lord. Make these "right in the sight" glasses that are fit for a king!
1 Cut two circular tubes from the end of a paper towel tube. Try to make them each about one inch thick.
Check out Deuteronomy 6:5 and Mark 12:29-31.
Need more advice about pleasing God?
2 Fold a long chenille wire in half.
3 Tape one cardboard tube onto one side of the halfway mark of the wire. Then tape the other tube to the other side.
4 Drape the ends of the wire over your ears, and you have a pair of "right in the sight" glasses! Adjust where you've taped the circles if you need to, so they fit your eyes better. Be sure to decorate your glasses with paints or markers.
Put on your child-king glasses, and tell every person in your "kingdom" how they can be pleasing in the sight of the Lord. Read about Josiah's actions as king in 2 CHRONICLES 34 for ideas.

put a ring through his nose, bound him in
bronze chains, and led him away to Babylon.
12But while in deep distress, Manasseh sought
the LORD his God and sincerely humbled himself before the God of his ancestors. 13And when
he prayed, the LORD listened to him and was
moved by his request. So the LORD brought Manasseh back to Jerusalem and to his kingdom.
Then Manasseh finally realized that the LORD
alone is God!

14After this Manasseh rebuilt the outer wall
of the City of David, from west of the Gihon
Spring in the Kidron Valley to the Fish Gate,
and continuing around the hill of Ophel. He
built the wall very high. And he stationed his
military officers in all of the fortified towns of
Judah. 15Manasseh also removed the foreign
gods and the idol from the LORD's Temple. He
tore down all the altars he had built on the hill
where the Temple stood and all the altars that
were in Jerusalem, and he dumped them outside
the city. 16Then he restored the altar of the LORD
and sacrificed peace offerings and thanksgiving
offerings on it. He also encouraged the people of
Judah to worship the LORD, the God of Israel.
17However, the people still sacrificed at the pagan shrines, though only to the LORD their God.

18The rest of the events of Manasseh's reign,
his prayer to God, and the words the seers spoke
to him in the name of the LORD, the God of Israel,
are recorded in *The Book of the Kings of Israel.*
19Manasseh's prayer, the account of the way God
answered him, and an account of all his sins and
unfaithfulness are recorded in *The Record of the
Seers.* It includes a list of the locations where he
built pagan shrines and set up Asherah poles
and idols before he humbled himself and repented. 20When Manasseh died, he was buried
in his palace. Then his son Amon became the
next king.

Amon Rules in Judah

21Amon was twenty-two years old when he became king, and he reigned in Jerusalem two
years. 22He did what was evil in the LORD's sight,
just as his father, Manasseh, had done. He worshiped and sacrificed to all the idols his father
had made. 23But unlike his father, he did not
humble himself before the LORD. Instead, Amon
sinned even more.

24Then Amon's own officials conspired against
him and assassinated him in his palace. 25But the
people of the land killed all those who had conspired against King Amon, and they made his son
Josiah the next king.

CHAPTER 34

Josiah Rules in Judah

Josiah was eight years old when he became
king, and he reigned in Jerusalem thirty-one
years. 2He did what was pleasing in the LORD's
sight and followed the example of his ancestor
David. He did not turn away from doing what
was right.

3During the eighth year of his reign, while he
was still young, Josiah began to seek the God of
his ancestor David. Then in the twelfth year he
began to purify Judah and Jerusalem, destroying
all the pagan shrines, the Asherah poles, and the
carved idols and cast images. 4He ordered that
the altars of Baal be demolished and that the incense altars which stood above them be broken
down. He also made sure that the Asherah poles,
the carved idols, and the cast images were
smashed and scattered over the graves of those
who had sacrificed to them. 5He burned the
bones of the pagan priests on their own altars,
and so he purified Judah and Jerusalem.

6He did the same thing in the towns of
Manasseh, Ephraim, and Simeon, even as far as
Naphtali, and in the regions all around them.
7He destroyed the pagan altars and the Asherah
poles, and he crushed the idols into dust. He cut
down all the incense altars throughout the land
of Israel. Finally, he returned to Jerusalem.

8In the eighteenth year of his reign, after he
had purified the land and the Temple, Josiah appointed Shaphan son of Azaliah, Maaseiah the
governor of Jerusalem, and Joah son of Joahaz,
the royal historian, to repair the Temple of the
LORD his God. 9They gave Hilkiah the high priest
the money that had been collected by the Levites who served as gatekeepers at the Temple of
God. The gifts were brought by people from
Manasseh, Ephraim, and from all the remnant of
Israel, as well as from all Judah, Benjamin, and
the people of Jerusalem.

10He entrusted the money to the men assigned to supervise the restoration of the LORD's
Temple. Then they paid the workers who did the
repairs and renovation of the Temple. 11They
hired carpenters and builders, who purchased
finished stone for the walls and timber for the
rafters and beams. They restored what earlier
kings of Judah had allowed to fall into ruin.

12The workers served faithfully under the
leadership of Jahath and Obadiah, Levites of the
Merarite clan, and Zechariah and Meshullam,
Levites of the Kohathite clan. Other Levites, all
of whom were skilled musicians, 13were put in
charge of the laborers of the various trades. Still

others assisted as secretaries, officials, and gatekeepers.

Hilkiah Discovers God's Law

14While they were bringing out the money collected at the LORD's Temple, Hilkiah the priest
found the Book of the Law of the LORD that was
written by Moses. 15Hilkiah said to Shaphan the
court secretary, "I have found the Book of the
Law in the LORD's Temple!" Then Hilkiah gave
the scroll to Shaphan.

16Shaphan took the scroll to the king and reported, "Your officials are doing everything they
were assigned to do. 17The money that was collected at the Temple of the LORD has been turned
over to the supervisors and workmen." 18Sha-
phan also told the king, "Hilkiah the priest has
given me a scroll." So Shaphan read it to the king.

19When the king heard what was written in
the Law, he tore his clothes in despair. 20Then he
gave these orders to Hilkiah, Ahikam son of Shaphan, Acbor son of Micaiah, Shaphan the court
secretary, and Asaiah the king's personal adviser:
21"Go to the Temple and speak to the LORD for me
and for all the remnant of Israel and Judah. Inquire about the words written in the scroll that
has been found. For the LORD's great anger has
been poured out on us because our ancestors
have not obeyed the word of the LORD. We have
not been doing everything this scroll says we
must do."

22So Hilkiah and the other men went to the
New Quarter of Jerusalem to consult with the
prophet Huldah. She was the wife of Shallum son
of Tikvah, son of Harhas, the keeper of the Temple wardrobe.

23She said to them, "The LORD, the God of
Israel, has spoken! Go back and tell the man
who sent you, 24'This is what the LORD says: I am
going to bring disaster on this city and its people. All the curses written in the scroll that was
read to the king of Judah will come true. 25For
my people have abandoned me and offered sacrifices to pagan gods, and I am very angry with
them for everything they have done. My anger
will be poured out on this place, and it will not
be quenched.'

26"But go to the king of Judah who sent you to
seek the LORD and tell him: 'This is what the
LORD, the God of Israel, says concerning the message you have just heard: 27You were sorry and
humbled yourself before God when you heard
his words against this city and its people. You
humbled yourself and tore your clothing in despair and wept before me in repentance. And I
have indeed heard you, says the LORD. 28So I will
not send the promised disaster until after you
have died and been buried in peace. You yourself
will not see the disaster I am going to bring on
this city and its people.'"

So they took her message back to the king.

Josiah's Religious Reforms

29Then the king summoned all the elders of
Judah and Jerusalem. 30And the king went up to
the Temple of the LORD with all the people of
Judah and Jerusalem, along with the priests and
the Levites—all the people from the greatest to
the least. There the king read to them the entire
Book of the Covenant that had been found in the
LORD's Temple. 31The king took his place of
authority beside the pillar and renewed the covenant in the LORD's presence. He pledged to obey
the LORD by keeping all his commands, laws, and
decrees with all his heart and soul. He promised
to obey all the terms of the covenant that were
written in the scroll. 32And he required everyone
in Jerusalem and the people of Benjamin to make
a similar pledge. The people of Jerusalem did so,
renewing their covenant with God, the God of
their ancestors.

33So Josiah removed all detestable idols from
the entire land of Israel and required everyone to
worship the LORD their God. And throughout the
rest of his lifetime, they did not turn away from
the LORD, the God of their ancestors.

CHAPTER 35

Josiah Celebrates Passover

Then Josiah announced that the Passover of the
LORD would be celebrated in Jerusalem, and so
the Passover lamb was slaughtered on the fourteenth day of the first month. 2Josiah also
assigned the priests to their duties and encouraged them in their work at the Temple of the
LORD. 3He issued this order to the Levites, who
were to teach all Israel and who had been set
apart to serve the LORD: "Put the holy Ark in the
Temple that was built by Solomon son of David,
the king of Israel. You no longer need to carry it
back and forth on your shoulders. Now spend
your time serving the LORD your God and his
people Israel. 4Report for duty according to the
family divisions of your ancestors, following the
directions of King David of Israel and the directions of his son Solomon.

5"Then stand in the sanctuary at the place
appointed for your family division and help the
families assigned to you as they bring their offerings to the Temple. 6Slaughter the Passover

lambs, purify yourselves, and prepare to help
those who come. Follow all the directions that
the LORD gave through Moses."
7Then Josiah provided 30,000 lambs and
young goats for the people's Passover offerings,
along with 3,000 cattle, all from the king's own
flocks and herds. 8The king's officials also made
willing contributions to the people, priests, and
Levites. Hilkiah, Zechariah, and Jehiel, the administrators of God's Temple, gave the priests
2,600 lambs and young goats and 300 cattle as
Passover offerings. 9The Levite leaders—Conaniah and his brothers Shemaiah and Nethanel,
as well as Hashabiah, Jeiel, and Jozabad—gave
5,000 lambs and young goats and 500 cattle to
the Levites for their Passover offerings.
10When everything was ready for the Passover
celebration, the priests and the Levites took their
places, organized by their divisions, as the king
had commanded. 11The Levites then slaughtered
the Passover lambs and presented the blood to
the priests, who sprinkled the blood on the altar
while the Levites prepared the animals. 12They
divided the burnt offerings among the people by
their family groups, so they could offer them to
the LORD as prescribed in the Book of Moses.
They did the same with the cattle. 13Then they
roasted the Passover lambs as prescribed; and
they boiled the holy offerings in pots, kettles, and
pans, and brought them out quickly so the people could eat them.
14Afterward the Levites prepared Passover offerings for themselves and for the priests—the
descendants of Aaron—because the priests had
been busy from morning till night offering the
burnt offerings and the fat portions. The Levites
took responsibility for all these preparations.
15The musicians, descendants of Asaph, were
in their assigned places, following the commands
that had been given by David, Asaph, Heman, and
Jeduthun, the king's seer. The gatekeepers
guarded the gates and did not need to leave their
posts of duty, for their Passover offerings were
prepared for them by their fellow Levites.
16The entire ceremony for the LORD's Passover
was completed that day. All the burnt offerings
were sacrificed on the altar of the LORD, as King
Josiah had commanded. 17All the Israelites present in Jerusalem celebrated Passover and the
Festival of Unleavened Bread for seven days.
18Never since the time of the prophet Samuel
had there been such a Passover. None of the
kings of Israel had ever kept a Passover as Josiah
did, involving all the priests and Levites, all the
people of Jerusalem, and people from all over Judah and Israel. 19This Passover was celebrated in
the eighteenth year of Josiah's reign.

Josiah Dies in Battle

20After Josiah had finished restoring the Temple,
King Neco of Egypt led his army up from Egypt to
do battle at Carchemish on the Euphrates River,
and Josiah and his army marched out to fight
him. 21But King Neco sent messengers to Josiah
with this message:

> "What do you want with me, king of Judah? I
> have no quarrel with you today! I am on my
> way to fight another nation, and God has told
> me to hurry! Do not interfere with God, who
> is with me, or he will destroy you."

22But Josiah refused to listen to Neco, to
whom God had indeed spoken, and he would not
turn back. Instead, he disguised himself and led
his army into battle on the plain of Megiddo.
23But the enemy archers hit King Josiah with
their arrows and wounded him. He cried out to
his men, "Take me from the battle, for I am badly
wounded!"
24So they lifted Josiah out of his chariot and
placed him in another chariot. Then they
brought him back to Jerusalem, where he died.
He was buried there in the royal cemetery. And
all Judah and Jerusalem mourned for him. 25The
prophet Jeremiah composed funeral songs for
Josiah, and to this day choirs still sing these sad
songs about his death. These songs of sorrow
have become a tradition and are recorded in *The
Book of Laments*.
26The rest of the events of Josiah's reign and
his acts of devotion (carried out according to
what was written in the Law of the LORD), 27from
beginning to end—all are recorded in *The Book
of the Kings of Israel and Judah*.

CHAPTER 36

Jehoahaz Rules in Judah

Then the people of the land took Josiah's son
Jehoahaz and made him the next king in Jerusalem.
2Jehoahaz was twenty-three years old when
he became king, and he reigned in Jerusalem
three months.
3Then he was deposed by the king of Egypt,
who demanded that Judah pay 7,500 pounds of
silver and 75 pounds of gold as tribute.

Jehoiakim Rules in Judah

4The king of Egypt then installed Eliakim, the
brother of Jehoahaz, as the next king of Judah

and Jerusalem, and he changed Eliakim's name
to Jehoiakim. Then Neco took Jehoahaz to Egypt
as a prisoner.
5Jehoiakim was twenty-five years old when he
became king, and he reigned in Jerusalem eleven
years. He did what was evil in the sight of the
LORD his God.
6Then King Nebuchadnezzar of Babylon
came to Jerusalem and captured it, and he bound
Jehoiakim in bronze chains and led him away to
Babylon. 7Nebuchadnezzar also took some of
the treasures from the Temple of the LORD, and
he placed them in his palace in Babylon.
8The rest of the events in Jehoiakim's reign, including all the evil things he did and everything
found against him, are recorded in *The Book of
the Kings of Israel and Judah*. Then his son Jehoiachin became the next king.

Jehoiachin Rules in Judah

9Jehoiachin was eighteen years old when he became king, and he reigned in Jerusalem three
months and ten days. Jehoiachin did what was
evil in the LORD's sight.
10In the spring of the year King Nebuchadnezzar took Jehoiachin to Babylon. Many treasures from the Temple of the LORD were also
taken to Babylon at that time. And Nebuchadnezzar installed Jehoiachin's uncle, Zedekiah, as
the next king in Judah and Jerusalem.

Zedekiah Rules in Judah

11Zedekiah was twenty-one years old when he
became king, and he reigned in Jerusalem eleven
years. 12But Zedekiah did what was evil in the
sight of the LORD his God, and he refused to
humble himself when the prophet Jeremiah
spoke to him directly from the LORD. 13He also
rebelled against King Nebuchadnezzar, even
though he had taken an oath of loyalty in God's
name. Zedekiah was a hard and stubborn man,
refusing to turn to the LORD, the God of Israel.
14Likewise, all the leaders of the priests and
the people became more and more unfaithful.
They followed all the pagan practices of the surrounding nations, desecrating the Temple of the
LORD that had been consecrated in Jerusalem.
15The LORD, the God of their ancestors, repeatedly sent his prophets to warn them, for he had
compassion on his people and his Temple. 16But
the people mocked these messengers of God and
despised their words. They scoffed at the prophets until the LORD's anger could no longer be restrained and nothing could be done.

The Fall of Jerusalem

17So the LORD brought the king of Babylon
against them. The Babylonians killed Judah's
young men, even chasing after them into the
Temple. They had no pity on the people, killing
both young men and young women, the old and
the infirm. God handed all of them over to Nebuchadnezzar. 18The king took home to Babylon all
the articles, large and small, used in the Temple
of God, and the treasures from both the LORD's
Temple and from the palace of the king and his
officials. 19Then his army burned the Temple of
God, tore down the walls of Jerusalem, burned all
the palaces, and completely destroyed everything of value. 20The few who survived were
taken as exiles to Babylon, and they became servants to the king and his sons until the kingdom
of Persia came to power.
21So the message of the LORD spoken through
Jeremiah was fulfilled. The land finally enjoyed its Sabbath rest, lying desolate until the
seventy years were fulfilled, just as the prophet
had said.

Cyrus Allows the Exiles to Return

22In the first year of King Cyrus of Persia, the
LORD fulfilled the prophecy he had given
through Jeremiah. He stirred the heart of Cyrus
to put this proclamation in writing and to send it
throughout his kingdom:

> 23"This is what King Cyrus of Persia says:
> "The LORD, the God of heaven, has given
> me all the kingdoms of the earth. He has
> appointed me to build him a Temple at
> Jerusalem, which is in Judah. Any of you
> who are his people may go there for this
> task. And may the LORD your God be
> with you!"

EZRA Rebuilding the Temple

Look for 1 hidden message in Ezra!

The book of Ezra explains how God brought the Israelites from another land, where they had been slaves, back to Jerusalem to rebuild the Temple. Read Ezra to learn about

- **POWERFUL GUYS WHO KEEP WRITING LETTERS**
- **A GROUP OF BACK-STABBING FRIENDS**
- **A LOT OF HARD WORK**
- **PEOPLE TURNING BACK TO GOD**

Pack It Up!

After years of slavery in Babylon, the Israelites finally headed home! They were packing with a purpose. Read Ezra 1:1-4 to see what it was. **Then read Ezra 1:8-11 to see all the goodies the people brought back with them.**

Need a Hand?

Can I Help?

The "friends" of the Israelites came to "help" them rebuild the Temple. When the Israelites passed on the offer, they found out just how helpful these "friends" really were. **Check out Ezra 4:1-23 to find out what these sly guys did.**

What a Mess!

The Israelites cleaned up the burned-down Temple area and built a new Temple for God. Almost 60 years later, Ezra came to help the people clean up their hearts. **Read Ezra 9 to see how the cleanup began.**

Timeline

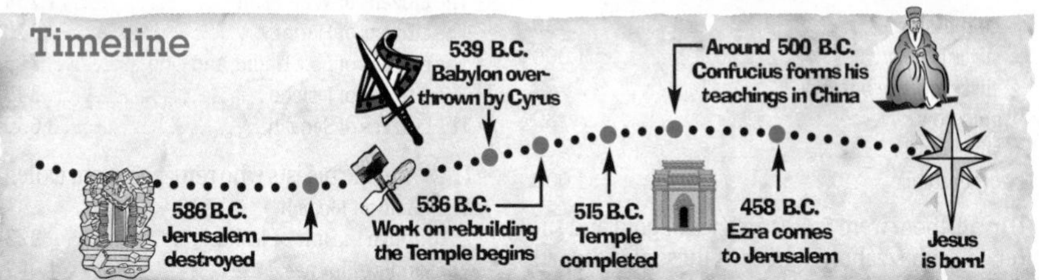
586 B.C. Jerusalem destroyed
539 B.C. Babylon overthrown by Cyrus
536 B.C. Work on rebuilding the Temple begins
515 B.C. Temple completed
Around 500 B.C. Confucius forms his teachings in China
458 B.C. Ezra comes to Jerusalem
Jesus is born!

The JESUS CONNECTION

The Israelites refused to follow God, so he allowed Babylon to take them away and make them slaves. The Israelites were gone but not forgotten by God. Just like God promised (see Jeremiah 29:10), the people came back to Israel and rebuilt the Temple. No matter how bad you've been, you can go to God to find forgiveness. Jesus paid the price for your sins—no matter how big or bad they are! **Believe in Jesus and your sins can be forgiven!**

Ezra 1 . . . page 458

CHAPTER 1
Cyrus Allows the Exiles to Return

In the first year of King Cyrus of Persia, the LORD
fulfilled the prophecy he had given through Jeremiah. He stirred the heart of Cyrus to put this
proclamation in writing and to send it throughout his kingdom:

2"This is what King Cyrus of Persia says:
"The LORD, the God of heaven, has given
me all the kingdoms of the earth. He has
appointed me to build him a Temple at
Jerusalem, which is in Judah. 3Any of you
who are his people may go to Jerusalem in
Judah to rebuild this Temple of the LORD,
the God of Israel, who lives in Jerusalem. And
may your God be with you! 4Wherever this
Jewish remnant is found, let their neighbors
contribute toward their expenses by giving
them silver and gold, supplies for the journey,
and livestock, as well as a voluntary offering
for the Temple of God in Jerusalem."

5Then God stirred the hearts of the priests and
Levites and the leaders of the tribes of Judah and
Benjamin to go to Jerusalem to rebuild the Temple of the LORD. 6And all their neighbors assisted
by giving them articles of silver and gold, supplies
for the journey, and livestock. They gave them
many valuable gifts in addition to all the voluntary offerings.
7King Cyrus himself brought out the articles
that King Nebuchadnezzar had taken from the
LORD's Temple in Jerusalem and had placed in the
temple of his own gods. 8Cyrus directed Mithredath, the treasurer of Persia, to count these items
and present them to Sheshbazzar, the leader of
the exiles returning to Judah. 9This is a list of the
items that were returned:

gold basins 30
silver basins 1,000
silver incense burners 29
10 gold bowls 30
silver bowls 410
other items 1,000

11In all, there were 5,400 articles of gold and silver. Sheshbazzar brought all of these along when
the exiles went from Babylon to Jerusalem.

CHAPTER 2
Exiles Who Returned with Zerubbabel

Here is the list of the Jewish exiles of the provinces who returned from their captivity. King
Nebuchadnezzar had deported them to Babylon,
but now they returned to Jerusalem and the other
towns in Judah where they originally lived. 2Their
leaders were Zerubbabel, Jeshua, Nehemiah, Seraiah, Reelaiah, Mordecai, Bilshan, Mispar, Bigvai,
Rehum, and Baanah.

This is the number of the men of Israel who returned from exile:

3 The family of Parosh 2,172
4 The family of Shephatiah 372
5 The family of Arah 775
6 The family of Pahath-moab
(descendants of Jeshua and Joab) 2,812
7 The family of Elam 1,254
8 The family of Zattu 945
9 The family of Zaccai 760
10 The family of Bani 642
11 The family of Bebai 623
12 The family of Azgad 1,222
13 The family of Adonikam 666
14 The family of Bigvai 2,056
15 The family of Adin 454
16 The family of Ater (descendants of Hezekiah) . . . 98
17 The family of Bezai 323
18 The family of Jorah 112
19 The family of Hashum 223
20 The family of Gibbar 95
21 The people of Bethlehem 123
22 The people of Netophah 56
23 The people of Anathoth 128
24 The people of Beth-azmaveth 42
25 The people of Kiriath-jearim,
Kephirah, and Beeroth 743
26 The people of Ramah and Geba 621
27 The people of Micmash 122
28 The people of Bethel and Ai 223
29 The citizens of Nebo 52
30 The citizens of Magbish 156
31 The citizens of West Elam 1,254
32 The citizens of Harim 320
33 The citizens of Lod, Hadid, and Ono 725
34 The citizens of Jericho 345
35 The citizens of Senaah 3,630

36These are the priests who returned from exile:
The family of Jedaiah
(through the line of Jeshua) 973
37 The family of Immer 1,052
38 The family of Pashhur 1,247
39 The family of Harim 1,017

40These are the Levites who returned from exile:
The families of Jeshua and Kadmiel
(descendants of Hodaviah) 74
41 The singers of the family of Asaph 128

42 The gatekeepers of the families of Shallum,
Ater, Talmon, Akkub, Hatita, and Shobai 139

43 The descendants of the following Temple servants returned from exile:
Ziha, Hasupha, Tabbaoth,
44 Keros, Siaha, Padon,
45 Lebanah, Hagabah, Akkub,
46 Hagab, Shalmai, Hanan,
47 Giddel, Gahar, Reaiah,
48 Rezin, Nekoda, Gazzam,
49 Uzza, Paseah, Besai,
50 Asnah, Meunim, Nephusim,
51 Bakbuk, Hakupha, Harhur,
52 Bazluth, Mehida, Harsha,
53 Barkos, Sisera, Temah,
54 Neziah, and Hatipha.

55 The descendants of these servants of King
Solomon returned from exile:
Sotai, Hassophereth, Peruda,
56 Jaalah, Darkon, Giddel,
57 Shephatiah, Hattil, Pokereth-hazzebaim,
and Ami.

58 In all, the Temple servants and the descendants of Solomon's servants numbered 392.

59 Another group returned at this time from the
towns of Tel-melah, Tel-harsha, Kerub, Addan,
and Immer. However, they could not prove that
they or their families were descendants of Israel.
60 This group included the families of Delaiah,
Tobiah, and Nekoda—a total of 652 people.

61 Three families of priests—Hobaiah, Hakkoz,
and Barzillai—also returned. (This Barzillai had
married a woman who was a descendant of Barzillai of Gilead, and he had taken her family
name.) 62 They searched for their names in the
genealogical records, but they were not found, so
they were disqualified from serving as priests.
63 The governor told them not to eat the priests'
share of food from the sacrifices until a priest
could consult the LORD about the matter by using
the Urim and Thummim—the sacred lots.

64 So a total of 42,360 people returned to Judah, 65 in addition to 7,337 servants and 200
singers, both men and women. 66 They took with
them 736 horses, 245 mules, 67 435 camels, and
6,720 donkeys.

68 When they arrived at the Temple of the
LORD in Jerusalem, some of the family leaders
made voluntary offerings toward the rebuilding
of God's Temple on its original site, 69 and each
leader gave as much as he could. The total of
their gifts came to 61,000 gold coins, 6,250
pounds of silver, and 100 robes for the priests.

70 So the priests, the Levites, the singers, the
gatekeepers, the Temple servants, and some of
the common people settled in villages near Jerusalem. The rest of the people returned to their
own towns throughout Israel.

CHAPTER 3

The Altar Is Rebuilt

In early autumn, when the Israelites had settled
in their towns, all the people assembled in Jerusalem with a unified purpose. 2 Then Jeshua son of
Jehozadak joined his fellow priests and Zerubbabel son of Shealtiel with his family in rebuilding
the altar of the God of Israel. They wanted to sacrifice burnt offerings on it, as instructed in the
Law of Moses, the man of God. 3 Even though the
people were afraid of the local residents, they
rebuilt the altar at its old site. Then they began to
sacrifice burnt offerings on the altar to the LORD
each morning and evening.

4 They celebrated the Festival of Shelters as
prescribed in the Law, sacrificing the number of
burnt offerings specified for each day of the festival. 5 They also offered the regular burnt offerings and the offerings required for the new
moon celebrations and the annual festivals as
prescribed by the LORD. The people also gave
voluntary offerings to the LORD. 6 Fifteen days
before the Festival of Shelters began, the priests
had begun to sacrifice burnt offerings to the
LORD. This was even before they had started to
lay the foundation of the LORD's Temple.

The People Begin to Rebuild the Temple

7 Then the people hired masons and carpenters
and bought cedar logs from the people of Tyre
and Sidon, paying them with food, wine, and olive oil. The logs were brought down from the
Lebanon mountains and floated along the coast
of the Mediterranean Sea to Joppa, for King
Cyrus had given permission for this.

8 The construction of the Temple of God began in midspring, during the second year after
they arrived in Jerusalem. The work force was
made up of everyone who had returned from exile, including Zerubbabel son of Shealtiel, Jeshua
son of Jehozadak and his fellow priests, and all
the Levites. The Levites who were twenty years
old or older were put in charge of rebuilding the
LORD's Temple. 9 The workers at the Temple of
God were supervised by Jeshua with his sons and
relatives, and Kadmiel and his sons, all descendants of Hodaviah. They were helped in this task
by the Levites of the family of Henadad.

10 When the builders completed the foundation of the LORD's Temple, the priests put on their
robes and took their places to blow their trumpets. And the Levites, descendants of Asaph,
clashed their cymbals to praise the LORD, just as
King David had prescribed. 11 With praise and
thanks, they sang this song to the LORD:

"He is so good!
His faithful love for Israel endures
forever!"

Then all the people gave a great shout, praising
the LORD because the foundation of the LORD's
Temple had been laid.
12 But many of the older priests, Levites, and
other leaders who had seen the first Temple
wept aloud when they saw the new Temple's
foundation. The others, however, were shouting
for joy. 13 The joyful shouting and weeping mingled together in a loud noise that could be heard
far in the distance.

CHAPTER 4

Enemies Oppose the Rebuilding

The enemies of Judah and Benjamin heard
that the exiles were rebuilding a Temple to the
LORD, the God of Israel. 2 So they approached
Zerubbabel and the other leaders and said, "Let
us build with you, for we worship your God just
as you do. We have sacrificed to him ever since
King Esarhaddon of Assyria brought us here."
3 But Zerubbabel, Jeshua, and the other leaders of Israel replied, "You may have no part in this
work. We alone will build the Temple for the
LORD, the God of Israel, just as King Cyrus of Persia commanded us."
4 Then the local residents tried to discourage
and frighten the people of Judah to keep them
from their work. 5 They bribed agents to work
against them and to frustrate their plans. This
went on during the entire reign of King Cyrus of
Persia and lasted until King Darius of Persia took
the throne.

Later Opposition under Xerxes and Artaxerxes

6 Years later when Xerxes began his reign, the enemies of Judah wrote a letter of accusation
against the people of Judah and Jerusalem.
7 Even later, during the reign of King Artaxerxes of Persia, the enemies of Judah, led by Bish-
lam, Mithredath, and Tabeel, sent a letter to
Artaxerxes in the Aramaic language, and it was
translated for the king.
8 Rehum the governor and Shimshai the court
secretary wrote the letter, telling King Artaxerxes
about the situation in Jerusalem. 9 They greeted
the king for all their colleagues—the judges and
local leaders, the people of Tarpel, the Persians,
the Babylonians, and the people of Erech and
Susa (that is, Elam). 10 They also sent greetings
from the rest of the people whom the great and
noble Ashurbanipal had deported and relocated
in Samaria and throughout the neighboring
lands of the province west of the Euphrates
River. 11 This is a copy of their letter:

"To King Artaxerxes, from your loyal subjects
in the province west of the Euphrates River.
12 "The king should know that the Jews
who came here to Jerusalem from Babylon
are rebuilding this rebellious and evil city.
They have already laid the foundation and
will soon finish its walls. 13 And the king
should know that if this city is rebuilt and its
walls are completed, it will be much to your
disadvantage, for the Jews will then refuse to
pay their tribute, customs, and tolls to you.
14 "Since we are your loyal subjects and do
not want to see the king dishonored in this
way, we have sent the king this information.
15 We suggest that a search be made in your
ancestors' records, where you will discover
what a rebellious city this has been in the
past. In fact, it was destroyed because of
its long and troublesome history of revolt
against the kings and countries who controlled
it. 16 We declare to the king that if this city
is rebuilt and its walls are completed, the
province west of the Euphrates River will be
lost to you."

17 Then King Artaxerxes sent this reply:

"To Rehum the governor, Shimshai the
court secretary, and their colleagues living
in Samaria and throughout the province
west of the Euphrates River. Greetings.
18 "The letter you sent has been translated
and read to me. 19 I ordered a search of the
records and have found that Jerusalem has
indeed been a hotbed of insurrection against
many kings. In fact, rebellion and revolt are
normal there! 20 Powerful kings have ruled
over Jerusalem and the entire province west
of the Euphrates River, receiving tribute,
customs, and tolls. 21 Therefore, issue orders
to have these men stop their work. That city
must not be rebuilt except at my express
command. 22 Be diligent, and don't neglect

this matter, for we must not permit the situation to harm the king's interests."

23When this letter from King Artaxerxes was read to Rehum, Shimshai, and their colleagues, they hurried to Jerusalem. Then, with a show of strength, they forced the Jews to stop building.

The Rebuilding Resumes

24So the work on the Temple of God in Jerusalem had stopped, and it remained at a standstill until the second year of the reign of King Darius of Persia.

CHAPTER 5

At that time the prophets Haggai and Zechariah
son of Iddo prophesied to the Jews in Judah and
Jerusalem. They prophesied in the name of the
God of Israel who was over them. 2Zerubbabel
son of Shealtiel and Jeshua son of Jehozadak responded by starting again to rebuild the Temple
of God in Jerusalem. And the prophets of God
were with them and helped them.
3But Tattenai, governor of the province west
of the Euphrates River, and Shethar-bozenai and
their colleagues soon arrived in Jerusalem and
asked, "Who gave you permission to rebuild this
Temple and restore this structure?" 4They also
asked for the names of all the men working on
the Temple. 5But because their God was watching over them, the leaders of the Jews were not
prevented from building until a report was sent
to Darius and he returned his decision.

Tattenai's Letter to King Darius

6This is a copy of the letter that Tattenai the governor, Shethar-bozenai, and the other officials of
the province west of the Euphrates River sent to
King Darius:

7"To King Darius. Greetings.
8"The king should know that we went to
the construction site of the Temple of the
great God in the province of Judah. It is being
rebuilt with specially prepared stones, and
timber is being laid in its walls. The work is
going forward with great energy and success.
9"We asked the leaders, 'Who gave you
permission to rebuild this Temple and
restore this structure?' 10And we demanded
their names so that we could tell you who
the leaders were.
11"This was their answer: 'We are the
servants of the God of heaven and earth, and
we are rebuilding the Temple that was built
here many years ago by a great king of Israel.

That's a Pigsty!

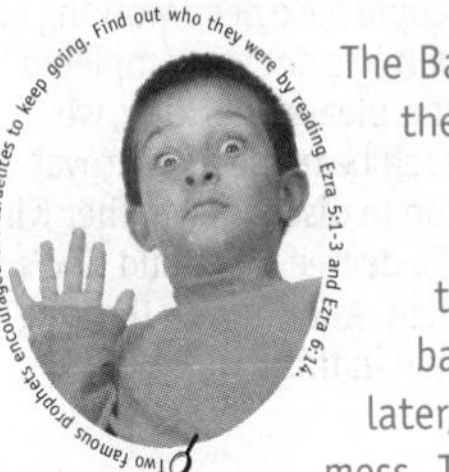

Two famous prophets encouraged the Israelites to keep going. Find out who they were by reading Ezra 5:1-3 and Ezra 6:14.

The Babylonians burned the Temple and took the Israelites as slaves. When the Israelites went back home 70 years later, they found a big mess. The people started rebuilding the Temple, but their enemies kept slowing things down. **Just read EZRA 4!** Good thing God kept things going. **You can see how by reading EZRA 6:6-18.**

Serve God right now with your hard work!
1 Find a really messy part of your house or church.
2 Work really hard to clean it up! Don't stop until the job's done right!
3 Sit back and enjoy the result of your hard work.

12But because our ancestors angered the
God of heaven, he abandoned them to King
Nebuchadnezzar of Babylon, who destroyed
this Temple and exiled the people to
Babylonia. 13However, King Cyrus of Babylon,
during the first year of his reign, issued a
decree that the Temple of God should be
rebuilt. 14King Cyrus returned the gold and
silver cups that Nebuchadnezzar had taken
from the Temple of God in Jerusalem and had
placed in the temple of Babylon. These cups
were taken from that temple and presented
to a man named Sheshbazzar, whom King
Cyrus appointed as governor of Judah. 15The
king instructed him to return the cups to
their place in Jerusalem and to rebuild the

Temple of God there on its original site.
16So this Sheshbazzar came and laid the foundations of the Temple of God in Jerusalem. The people have been working on it ever since, though it is not yet completed.'

17"Therefore, if it pleases the king, we request that a search be made in the royal archives of Babylon to discover whether King Cyrus ever issued a decree to rebuild God's Temple in Jerusalem. And then let the king send us his decision in this matter."

CHAPTER 6

Darius Approves the Rebuilding

So King Darius issued orders that a search be made in the Babylonian archives, which were stored in the treasury. 2But it was at the fortress at Ecbatana in the province of Media that a scroll was found. This is what it said:

"Memorandum:

3"In the first year of King Cyrus's reign, a decree was sent out concerning the Temple of God at Jerusalem.

"Let the Temple be rebuilt on the site where Jews used to offer their sacrifices, using the original foundations. Its height will be ninety feet, and its width will be ninety feet. 4Every three layers of specially prepared stones will be topped by a layer of timber. All expenses will be paid by the royal treasury.
5Furthermore, the gold and silver cups, which were taken to Babylon by Nebuchadnezzar from the Temple of God in Jerusalem, must be returned to Jerusalem and put back where they belong. Let them be taken back to the Temple of God."

6So King Darius sent this message:

"Now therefore, Tattenai, governor of the province west of the Euphrates River, and Shethar-bozenai, and your colleagues and other officials west of the Euphrates River—stay away from there! 7Do not disturb the construction of the Temple of God. Let it be rebuilt on its original site, and do not hinder the governor of Judah and the elders of the Jews in their work.

8"Moreover, I hereby decree that you are to help these elders of the Jews as they rebuild this Temple of God. You must pay the full construction costs, without delay, from my taxes collected in the province west of the Euphrates River so that the work will not be interrupted.

9"Give the priests in Jerusalem whatever is needed in the way of young bulls, rams, and male lambs for the burnt offerings presented to the God of heaven. And without fail, provide them with as much wheat, salt, wine, and olive oil as they need each day.
10Then they will be able to offer acceptable sacrifices to the God of heaven and pray for the welfare of the king and his sons.

11"Those who violate this decree in any way will have a beam pulled from their house. Then they will be lifted up and impaled on it, and their house will be reduced to a pile of rubble.
12May the God who has chosen the city of Jerusalem as the place to honor his name destroy any king or nation that violates this command and destroys this Temple.

"I, Darius, have issued this decree. Let it be obeyed with all diligence."

The Temple's Dedication

13Tattenai, governor of the province west of the Euphrates River, and Shethar-bozenai and their colleagues complied at once with the command
of King Darius. 14So the Jewish elders continued their work, and they were greatly encouraged by the preaching of the prophets Haggai and Zechariah son of Iddo. The Temple was finally finished, as had been commanded by the God of Israel and decreed by Cyrus, Darius, and Artaxerxes, the kings of Persia.
15The Temple was completed on March 12, during the sixth year of King Darius's reign.

16The Temple of God was then dedicated with great joy by the people of Israel, the priests, the Levites, and the rest of the people who had
returned from exile.
17During the dedication ceremony for the Temple of God, 100 young bulls, 200 rams, and 400 male lambs were sacrificed. And 12 male goats were presented as a sin
offering for the twelve tribes of Israel.
18Then the priests and Levites were divided into their various divisions to serve at the Temple of God in Jerusalem, as prescribed in the Book of Moses.

Celebration of Passover

19On April 21 the returned exiles celebrated
Passover.
20The priests and Levites had purified themselves and were ceremonially clean. So they slaughtered the Passover lamb for all the returned exiles, for their fellow priests, and for
themselves.
21The Passover meal was eaten by the people of Israel who had returned from exile and by the others in the land who had turned

from their immoral customs to worship the LORD, the God of Israel. 22 Then they celebrated the Festival of Unleavened Bread for seven days. There was great joy throughout the land because the LORD had caused the king of Assyria to be favorable to them, so that he helped them to rebuild the Temple of God, the God of Israel.

CHAPTER 7

Ezra Arrives in Jerusalem

Many years later, during the reign of King Artaxerxes of Persia, there was a man named Ezra. He was the son of Seraiah, son of Azariah, son of Hilkiah, 2 son of Shallum, son of Zadok, son of Ahitub, 3 son of Amariah, son of Azariah, son of Meraioth, 4 son of Zerahiah, son of Uzzi, son of Bukki, 5 son of Abishua, son of Phinehas, son of Eleazar, son of Aaron the high priest. 6 This Ezra was a scribe who was well versed in the Law of Moses, which the LORD, the God of Israel, had given to the people of Israel. He came up to Jerusalem from Babylon, and the king gave him everything he asked for, because the gracious hand of the LORD his God was on him. 7 Some of the people of Israel, as well as some of the priests, Levites, singers, gatekeepers, and Temple servants, traveled up to Jerusalem with him in the seventh year of King Artaxerxes' reign.

8 Ezra arrived in Jerusalem in August of that year. 9 He had arranged to leave Babylon on April 8, the first day of the new year, and he arrived at Jerusalem on August 4, for the gracious hand of his God was on him. 10 This was because Ezra had determined to study and obey the Law of the LORD and to teach those decrees and regulations to the people of Israel.

Artaxerxes' Letter to Ezra

11 King Artaxerxes had given a copy of the following letter to Ezra, the priest and scribe who studied and taught the commands and decrees of the LORD to Israel:

> 12 "From Artaxerxes, the king of kings, to Ezra the priest, the teacher of the law of the God of heaven. Greetings.
>
> 13 "I decree that any of the people of Israel in my kingdom, including the priests and Levites, may volunteer to return to Jerusalem with you. 14 I and my council of seven hereby instruct you to conduct an inquiry into the situation in Judah and Jerusalem, based on your God's law, which is in your hand. 15 We also commission you to take with you silver and gold, which we are freely presenting as an offering to the God of Israel who lives in Jerusalem.
>
> 16 "Furthermore, you are to take any silver and gold that you may obtain from the province of Babylon, as well as the voluntary offerings of the people and the priests that are presented for the Temple of their God in Jerusalem. 17 These donations are to be used specifically for the purchase of bulls, rams, male lambs, and the appropriate grain offerings and liquid offerings, all of which will be offered on the altar of the Temple of your God in Jerusalem. 18 Any silver and gold that is left over may be used in whatever way you and your colleagues feel is the will of your God.
>
> 19 "But as for the cups we are entrusting to you for the service of the Temple of your God, deliver them all to the God of Jerusalem. 20 If you need anything else for your God's Temple or for any similar needs, you may take it from the royal treasury.
>
> 21 "I, Artaxerxes the king, hereby send this decree to all the treasurers in the province west of the Euphrates River: 'You are to give Ezra, the priest and teacher of the law of the God of heaven, whatever he requests of you. 22 You are to give him up to 7,500 pounds of silver, 500 bushels of wheat, 550 gallons of wine, 550 gallons of olive oil, and an unlimited supply of salt. 23 Be careful to provide whatever the God of heaven demands for his Temple, for why should we risk bringing God's anger against the realm of the king and his sons? 24 I also decree that no priest, Levite, singer, gatekeeper, Temple servant, or other worker in this Temple of God will be required to pay tribute, customs, or tolls of any kind.'
>
> 25 "And you, Ezra, are to use the wisdom your God has given you to appoint magistrates and judges who know your God's laws to govern all the people in the province west of the Euphrates River. Teach the law to anyone who does not know it. 26 Anyone who refuses to obey the law of your God and the law of the king will be punished immediately, either by death, banishment, confiscation of goods, or imprisonment."

Ezra Praises the LORD

27 Praise the LORD, the God of our ancestors, who made the king want to beautify the Temple of the LORD in Jerusalem! 28 And praise him for

demonstrating such unfailing love to me by honoring me before the king, his council, and all his mighty nobles! I felt encouraged because the gracious hand of the LORD my God was on me. And I gathered some of the leaders of Israel to return with me to Jerusalem.

CHAPTER **8**

Exiles Who Returned with Ezra

Here is a list of the family leaders and the genealogies of those who came with me from Babylon during the reign of King Artaxerxes:

2 From the family of Phinehas: Gershom.
From the family of Ithamar: Daniel.
From the family of David: Hattush,
3 a descendant of Shecaniah.
From the family of Parosh: Zechariah and 150 other men were registered.
4 From the family of Pahath-moab: Eliehoenai son of Zerahiah and 200 other men.
5 From the family of Zattu: Shecaniah son of Jahaziel and 300 other men.
6 From the family of Adin: Ebed son of Jonathan and 50 other men.
7 From the family of Elam: Jeshaiah son of Athaliah and 70 other men.
8 From the family of Shephatiah: Zebadiah son of Michael and 80 other men.
9 From the family of Joab: Obadiah son of Jehiel and 218 other men.
10 From the family of Bani: Shelomith son of Josiphiah and 160 other men.
11 From the family of Bebai: Zechariah son of Bebai and 28 other men.
12 From the family of Azgad: Johanan son of Hakkatan and 110 other men.
13 From the family of Adonikam, who came later: Eliphelet, Jeuel, Shemaiah, and 60 other men.
14 From the family of Bigvai: Uthai, Zaccur, and 70 other men.

Ezra's Journey to Jerusalem

15I assembled the exiles at the Ahava Canal, and
we camped there for three days while I went over
the lists of the people and the priests who had arrived. I found that not one Levite had volunteered to come along. 16So I sent for Eliezer,
Ariel, Shemaiah, Elnathan, Jarib, Elnathan, Nathan, Zechariah, and Meshullam, who were leaders of the people. I also sent for Joiarib and
Elnathan, who were men of discernment. 17I sent
them to Iddo, the leader of the Levites at Casiph-
ia, to ask him and his relatives and the Temple
servants to send us ministers for the Temple of
God at Jerusalem.

18Since the gracious hand of our God was on
us, they sent us a man named Sherebiah, along
with eighteen of his sons and brothers. He was a
very astute man and a descendant of Mahli, who
was a descendant of Levi son of Israel. 19They
also sent Hashabiah, together with Jeshaiah
from the descendants of Merari, and twenty of
his sons and brothers, 20and 220 Temple servants. The Temple servants were assistants to the
Levites—a group of Temple workers first instituted by King David and his officials. They were
all listed by name.

21And there by the Ahava Canal, I gave orders
for all of us to fast and humble ourselves before
our God. We prayed that he would give us a safe
journey and protect us, our children, and our
goods as we traveled. 22For I was ashamed to ask
the king for soldiers and horsemen to accompany us and protect us from enemies along the
way. After all, we had told the king, "Our God's

It's All Greek to Me

Most of the Bible was first written in Greek or Hebrew. Parts of Ezra and Daniel were written in Aramaic. Many of the Jews (including Jesus) spoke Aramaic!

Try saying these Aramaic words:

ABBA (rhymes with "job uh" and means "Father")

RABBI (rhymes with "lab eye" and means "teacher")

ELOI (rhymes with "ay glowy" and means "My God")

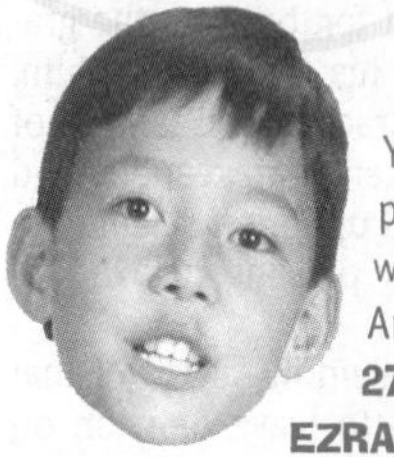

You can read some parts of the Bible that were written first in Aramaic: **MATTHEW 27:46; DANIEL 2:4-7; EZRA 7:12-26.**

hand of protection is on all who worship him,
but his fierce anger rages against those who
abandon him." 23 So we fasted and earnestly
prayed that our God would take care of us, and he
heard our prayer.

24 I appointed twelve leaders of the priests—
Sherebiah, Hashabiah, and ten other priests—
25 to be in charge of transporting the silver, the
gold, the gold bowls, and the other items that the
king, his council, his officials, and all the people
of Israel had presented for the Temple of God.
26 I weighed the treasure as I gave it to them and
found the totals to be as follows:

24 tons of silver,
7,500 pounds of silver articles,
7,500 pounds of gold,
27 20 gold bowls, equal in value to 1,000 gold coins,
2 fine articles of polished bronze, as precious as gold.

28 And I said to these priests, "You and these
treasures have been set apart as holy to the LORD.
This silver and gold is a voluntary offering to the
LORD, the God of our ancestors. 29 Guard these
treasures well until you present them to the leading priests, the Levites, and the leaders of Israel,
who will weigh them at the storerooms of the
LORD's Temple in Jerusalem." 30 So the priests
and the Levites accepted the task of transporting
these treasures of silver and gold to the Temple
of our God in Jerusalem.

31 We broke camp at the Ahava Canal on
April 19 and started off to Jerusalem. And the
gracious hand of our God protected us and saved
us from enemies and bandits along the way. 32 So
we arrived safely in Jerusalem, where we rested
for three days.

33 On the fourth day after our arrival, the silver, gold, and other valuables were weighed at
the Temple of our God and entrusted to Meremoth son of Uriah the priest and to Eleazar son
of Phinehas, along with Jozabad son of Jeshua
and Noadiah son of Binnui—both of whom were
Levites. 34 Everything was accounted for by
number and weight, and the total weight was
officially recorded.

35 Then the exiles who had come out of captivity sacrificed burnt offerings to the God of Israel.
They presented twelve bulls for all the people of
Israel, as well as ninety-six rams and seventy-
seven male lambs. They also offered twelve male
goats as a sin offering. All this was given as a
burnt offering to the LORD. 36 The king's decrees
were delivered to his highest officers and the
governors of the province west of the Euphrates
River, who then cooperated by supporting the
people and the Temple of God.

CHAPTER 9

Ezra's Prayer concerning Intermarriage

When these things had been done, the Jewish
leaders came to me and said, "Many of the people
of Israel, and even some of the priests and Levites, have not kept themselves separate from the
other peoples living in the land. They have taken
up the detestable practices of the Canaanites,
Hittites, Perizzites, Jebusites, Ammonites, Moabites, Egyptians, and Amorites. 2 For the men of Israel have married women from these people and
have taken them as wives for their sons. So the
holy race has become polluted by these mixed
marriages. Worse yet, the leaders and officials
have led the way in this outrage."

3 When I heard this, I tore my cloak and my
shirt, pulled hair from my head and beard, and
sat down utterly shocked. 4 Then all who trembled at the words of the God of Israel came and
sat with me because of this outrage committed
by the returned exiles. And I sat there utterly appalled until the time of the evening sacrifice.

5 At the time of the sacrifice, I stood up from
where I had sat in mourning with my clothes
torn. I fell to my knees and lifted my hands to the
LORD my God. 6 I prayed,

"O my God, I am utterly ashamed; I blush to
lift up my face to you. For our sins are piled
higher than our heads, and our guilt has
reached to the heavens. 7 From the days of
our ancestors until now, we have been
steeped in sin. That is why we and our kings
and our priests have been at the mercy of
the pagan kings of the land. We have been
killed, captured, robbed, and disgraced, just
as we are today.

8 "But now we have been given a brief
moment of grace, for the LORD our God has
allowed a few of us to survive as a remnant.
He has given us security in this holy place.
Our God has brightened our eyes and granted
us some relief from our slavery. 9 For we
were slaves, but in his unfailing love our God
did not abandon us in our slavery. Instead,
he caused the kings of Persia to treat us
favorably. He revived us so we could rebuild
the Temple of our God and repair its ruins. He
has given us a protective wall in Judah and
Jerusalem.

[10]"And now, O our God, what can we say after all of this? For once again we have abandoned your commands! [11]Your servants the prophets warned us when they said, 'The land you are entering to possess is totally defiled by the detestable practices of the people living there. From one end to the other, the land is filled with corruption. [12]Don't let your daughters marry their sons! Don't take their daughters as wives for your sons. Don't ever promote the peace and prosperity of those nations. If you follow these instructions, you will be strong and will enjoy the good things the land produces, and you will leave this prosperity to your children forever.'

[13]"Now we are being punished because of our wickedness and our great guilt. But we have actually been punished far less than we deserve, for you, our God, have allowed some of us to survive as a remnant. [14]But even so, we are again breaking your commands and intermarrying with people who do these detestable things. Won't your anger be enough to destroy us, so that even this little remnant no longer survives? [15]O LORD, God of Israel, you are just. We come before you in our guilt as nothing but an escaped remnant, though in such a condition none of us can stand in your presence."

CHAPTER 10

The People Confess Their Sin

While Ezra prayed and made this confession, weeping and lying face down on the ground in front of the Temple of God, a very large crowd of people from Israel—men, women, and children—gathered and wept bitterly with him. [2]Then Shecaniah son of Jehiel, a descendant of Elam, said to Ezra, "We have been unfaithful to our God, for we have married these pagan women of the land. But in spite of this there is hope for Israel. [3]Let us now make a covenant with our God to divorce our pagan wives and to send them away with their children. We will follow the advice given by you and by the others who respect the commands of our God. Let it be done according to the Law of God. [4]Get up, for it is your duty to tell us how to proceed in setting things straight. We are behind you, so be strong and take action."

[5]So Ezra stood up and demanded that the leaders of the priests and the Levites and all the people of Israel swear that they would do as Shecaniah had said. And they all swore a solemn oath. [6]Then Ezra left the front of the Temple of God and went to the room of Jehohanan son of Eliashib. He spent the night there without eating or drinking anything. He was still in mourning because of the unfaithfulness of the returned exiles.

[7]Then a proclamation was made throughout Judah and Jerusalem that all the exiles should come to Jerusalem. [8]Those who failed to come within three days would, if the leaders and elders so decided, forfeit all their property and be expelled from the assembly of the exiles.

[9]Within three days, all the people of Judah and Benjamin had gathered in Jerusalem. This took place on December 19, and all the people were sitting in the square before the Temple of God. They were trembling both because of the seriousness of the matter and because it was raining. [10]Then Ezra the priest stood and said to them: "You have committed a terrible sin. By marrying pagan women, you have increased Israel's guilt. [11]So now confess your sin to the LORD, the God of your ancestors, and do what he demands. Separate yourselves from the people of the land and from these pagan women."

[12]Then the whole assembly raised their voices and answered, "Yes, you are right; we must do as you say!" [13]Then they added, "This isn't something that can be done in a day or two, for many of us are involved in this extremely sinful affair. And this is the rainy season, so we cannot stay out here much longer. [14]Let our leaders act on behalf of us all. Let everyone who has a pagan wife come at a scheduled time, accompanied by the leaders and judges of his city, so that the fierce anger of our God concerning this affair may be turned away from us."

[15]Only Jonathan son of Asahel and Jahzeiah son of Tikvah opposed this course of action, and they were supported by Meshullam and Shabbethai the Levite.

[16]So this was the plan they followed. Ezra selected leaders to represent their families, designating each of the representatives by name. On December 29, the leaders sat down to investigate the matter. [17]By March 27, the first day of the new year, they had finished dealing with all the men who had married pagan wives.

Those Guilty of Intermarriage

[18]These are the priests who had married pagan wives:

From the family of Jeshua son of Jehozadak and his brothers: Maaseiah, Eliezer, Jarib, and Gedaliah. [19]They vowed to divorce their

wives, and they each acknowledged their guilt by offering a ram as a guilt offering.
20 From the family of Immer: Hanani and Zebadiah.
21 From the family of Harim: Maaseiah, Elijah, Shemaiah, Jehiel, and Uzziah.
22 From the family of Pashhur: Elioenai, Maaseiah, Ishmael, Nethanel, Jozabad, and Elasah.

23 These are the Levites who were guilty: Jozabad, Shimei, Kelaiah (also called Kelita), Pethahiah, Judah, and Eliezer.

24 This is the singer who was guilty: Eliashib.

These are the gatekeepers who were guilty: Shallum, Telem, and Uri.

25 These are the other people of Israel who were guilty:
From the family of Parosh: Ramiah, Izziah, Malkijah, Mijamin, Eleazar, Hashabiah, and Benaiah.
26 From the family of Elam: Mattaniah, Zechariah, Jehiel, Abdi, Jeremoth, and Elijah.
27 From the family of Zattu: Elioenai, Eliashib, Mattaniah, Jeremoth, Zabad, and Aziza.
28 From the family of Bebai: Jehohanan, Hananiah, Zabbai, and Athlai.
29 From the family of Bani: Meshullam, Malluch, Adaiah, Jashub, Sheal, and Jeremoth.
30 From the family of Pahath-moab: Adna, Kelal, Benaiah, Maaseiah, Mattaniah, Bezalel, Binnui, and Manasseh.
31 From the family of Harim: Eliezer, Ishijah,
Malkijah, Shemaiah, Shimeon, 32 Benjamin,
Malluch, and Shemariah.
33 From the family of Hashum: Mattenai, Mattattah, Zabad, Eliphelet, Jeremai, Manasseh, and Shimei.
34 From the family of Bani: Maadai, Amram,
Uel, 35 Benaiah, Bedeiah, Keluhi, 36 Vaniah,
Meremoth, Eliashib, 37 Mattaniah, Mattenai,
and Jaasu.
38 From the family of Binnui: Shimei, 39 Shelemiah, Nathan, Adaiah, 40 Macnadebai,
Shashai, Sharai, 41 Azarel, Shelemiah, Shemariah, 42 Shallum, Amariah, and Joseph.
43 From the family of Nebo: Jeiel, Mattithiah, Zabad, Zebina, Jaddai, Joel, and Benaiah.

44 Each of these men had a pagan wife, and some even had children by these wives.

NEHEMIAH Rebuilding the Wall

Look for 5 hidden messages in Nehemiah!

The book of Nehemiah tells how the Israelites rebuilt the wall around Jerusalem. Read about

- **A GREAT LEADER WHO FOUND POWER IN PRAYER**
- **TWO TROUBLEMAKERS**
- **BUILDING A BIG WALL**
- **PEOPLE TURNING BACK TO GOD**

No... really... I'm just... fine.

Nehemiah just couldn't hold it in. He had to do *something*! **Read Nehemiah 1:1–2:8 to see what Nehemiah did.**

Lend a Hand

The rich Israelites were getting richer and the poor were getting poorer—until Nehemiah stepped in. **Read Nehemiah 5 to see how Nehemiah lent a helping hand.**

Neener, Neener, Neener

"Oh, yeah? Do you think those stones can come back to life?" shouted Sanballat. "A fox could smush your stones!" added Tobiah.

The Israelites kept working on the wall while Sanballat and Tobiah kept shouting really lame put-downs. **See how Nehemiah reacted as you read Nehemiah 4:1-6.**

A Change of Heart

The Israelites changed the city of Jerusalem by building the Temple and finishing the wall. God changed their hearts as Ezra read God's law to the people. **See how the people reacted in Nehemiah 8:1-11.**

Timeline

539 B.C. Babylon overthrown
586 B.C. Jerusalem destroyed
Around 500 B.C. Confucius forms his teachings in China
515 B.C. Temple rebuilt
445 B.C. Nehemiah comes to Jerusalem; wall completed
Jesus is born!

The JESUS CONNECTION

After Ezra read the Law to the people of Israel, all sorts of great things happened in their hearts. They worshiped God, they said they were sorry for their sins, and they changed the way they lived.

The Bible is God's Word, and it has the power to change your life too! Learn about freedom from sin and death by reading Romans 8:1-3. **Then learn how to find that freedom by reading ROMANS 10:9 and JOHN 3:16.**

CHAPTER 1

1These are the memoirs of Nehemiah son of Hacaliah.

Nehemiah's Concern for Jerusalem

In late autumn, in the month of Kislev, in the
twentieth year of King Artaxerxes' reign, I was at
the fortress of Susa. 2Hanani, one of my brothers,
came to visit me with some other men who had
just arrived from Judah. I asked them about the
Jews who had returned there from captivity and
about how things were going in Jerusalem.
3They said to me, "Things are not going well
for those who returned to the province of Judah.
They are in great trouble and disgrace. The wall
of Jerusalem has been torn down, and the gates
have been destroyed by fire."
4When I heard this, I sat down and wept. In
fact, for days I mourned, fasted, and prayed to the
God of heaven. 5Then I said,

"O LORD, God of heaven, the great and
awesome God who keeps his covenant of
unfailing love with those who love him and
obey his commands, 6listen to my prayer!
Look down and see me praying night and day
for your people Israel. I confess that we have
sinned against you. Yes, even my own family
and I have sinned! 7We have sinned terribly
by not obeying the commands, decrees, and
regulations that you gave us through your
servant Moses.
8"Please remember what you told your
servant Moses: 'If you are unfaithful to me,
I will scatter you among the nations. 9But if
you return to me and obey my commands
and live by them, then even if you are exiled
to the ends of the earth, I will bring you back
to the place I have chosen for my name to be
honored.'
10"The people you rescued by your great
power and strong hand are your servants.
11O Lord, please hear my prayer! Listen to
the prayers of those of us who delight in
honoring you. Please grant me success today
by making the king favorable to me. Put it
into his heart to be kind to me."

In those days I was the king's cup-bearer.

CHAPTER 2

Nehemiah Goes to Jerusalem

1Early the following spring, in the month of Nisan,
during the twentieth year of King Artaxerxes'
reign, I was serving the king his wine. I had never

Keep Praying!

Nehemiah was so upset that he didn't eat and he bawled and bawled! **Check out NEHEMIAH 1 to find out what troubled him and what he did about it.**

YOU CAN TALK TO GOD ABOUT ANYTHING.

But try a prayer like Nehemiah's. What is one thing that's bothering you more than anything else? Are you having a tough time at school? Are your parents fighting too much?

1 **Write down your big Nehemiah-like problem right here. If you can't think of one, ask God to show you what's going on in your heart.**

2 **The Bible says in PHILIPPIANS 4, "Don't worry... pray!" Find a place to be alone. Spend some time praying. Don't be afraid to tell God how you really feel.**

Share your prayer with a parent or teacher, and pray it together.

God answers your prayers! God gives you something else when you pray too. Find out what by reading Philippians 4:6-7.

3 **Read NEHEMIAH 2:1-8 to see how God answered Nehemiah's prayer. Put a bookmark or sticky note on this page in your Bible. When God answers your prayer, come back to this page and thank God!**

before appeared sad in his presence. 2So the king asked me, "Why are you looking so sad? You don't look sick to me. You must be deeply troubled."

Then I was terrified, 3but I replied, "Long live the king! How can I not be sad? For the city where my ancestors are buried is in ruins, and the gates have been destroyed by fire."

4The king asked, "Well, how can I help you?"

With a prayer to the God of heaven, 5I replied, "If it please the king, and if you are pleased with me, your servant, send me to Judah to rebuild the city where my ancestors are buried."

6The king, with the queen sitting beside him, asked, "How long will you be gone? When will you return?" After I told him how long I would be gone, the king agreed to my request.

7I also said to the king, "If it please the king, let me have letters addressed to the governors of the province west of the Euphrates River, instructing them to let me travel safely through their territories on my way to Judah. 8And please give me a letter addressed to Asaph, the manager of the king's forest, instructing him to give me timber. I will need it to make beams for the gates of the Temple fortress, for the city walls, and for a house for myself." And the king granted these requests, because the gracious hand of God was on me.

9When I came to the governors of the province west of the Euphrates River, I delivered the king's letters to them. The king, I should add, had sent along army officers and horsemen to protect me. 10But when Sanballat the Horonite and Tobiah the Ammonite official heard of my arrival, they were very displeased that someone had come to help the people of Israel.

Nehemiah Inspects Jerusalem's Wall

11So I arrived in Jerusalem. Three days later, 12I slipped out during the night, taking only a few others with me. I had not told anyone about the plans God had put in my heart for Jerusalem. We took no pack animals with us except the donkey I was riding. 13After dark I went out through the Valley Gate, past the Jackal's Well, and over to the Dung Gate to inspect the broken walls and burned gates. 14Then I went to the Fountain Gate and to the King's Pool, but my donkey couldn't get through the rubble. 15So, though it was still dark, I went up the Kidron Valley instead, inspecting the wall before I turned back and entered again at the Valley Gate.

16The city officials did not know I had been out there or what I was doing, for I had not yet said anything to anyone about my plans. I had not yet spoken to the Jewish leaders—the priests, the nobles, the officials, or anyone else in the administration. 17But now I said to them, "You know very well what trouble we are in. Jerusalem lies in ruins, and its gates have been destroyed by fire. Let us rebuild the wall of Jerusalem and end this disgrace!" 18Then I told them about how the gracious hand of God had been on me, and about my conversation with the king.

They replied at once, "Yes, let's rebuild the wall!" So they began the good work.

19But when Sanballat, Tobiah, and Geshem the Arab heard of our plan, they scoffed contemptuously. "What are you doing? Are you rebelling against the king?" they asked.

20I replied, "The God of heaven will help us succeed. We, his servants, will start rebuilding this wall. But you have no share, legal right, or historic claim in Jerusalem."

CHAPTER 3

Rebuilding the Wall of Jerusalem

Then Eliashib the high priest and the other priests started to rebuild at the Sheep Gate. They dedicated it and set up its doors, building the wall as far as the Tower of the Hundred, which they dedicated, and the Tower of Hananel. 2People from the town of Jericho worked next to them, and beyond them was Zaccur son of Imri.

3The Fish Gate was built by the sons of Hassenaah. They laid the beams, set up its doors, and installed its bolts and bars. 4Meremoth son of Uriah and grandson of Hakkoz repaired the next section of wall. Beside him were Meshullam son of Berekiah and grandson of Meshezabel, and then Zadok son of Baana. 5Next were the people from Tekoa, though their leaders refused to work with the construction supervisors.

6The Old City Gate was repaired by Joiada son of Paseah and Meshullam son of Besodeiah. They laid the beams, set up its doors, and installed its bolts and bars. 7Next to them were Melatiah from Gibeon, Jadon from Meronoth, people from Gibeon, and people from Mizpah, the headquarters of the governor of the province west of the Euphrates River. 8Next was Uzziel son of Harhaiah, a goldsmith by trade, who also worked on the wall. Beyond him was Hananiah, a manufacturer of perfumes. They left out a section of Jerusalem as they built the Broad Wall.

9Rephaiah son of Hur, the leader of half the district of Jerusalem, was next to them on the

wall. 10Next Jedaiah son of Harumaph repaired
the wall across from his own house, and next to
him was Hattush son of Hashabneiah. 11Then
came Malkijah son of Harim and Hasshub son of
Pahath-moab, who repaired another section of
the wall and the Tower of the Ovens. 12Shallum
son of Hallohesh and his daughters repaired the
next section. He was the leader of the other half
of the district of Jerusalem.

13The Valley Gate was repaired by the people
from Zanoah, led by Hanun. They set up its doors
and installed its bolts and bars. They also repaired the 1,500 feet of wall to the Dung Gate.

14The Dung Gate was repaired by Malkijah son
of Recab, the leader of the Beth-hakkerem district. He rebuilt it, set up its doors, and installed
its bolts and bars.

15The Fountain Gate was repaired by Shallum
son of Col-hozeh, the leader of the Mizpah district. He rebuilt it, roofed it, set up its doors, and
installed its bolts and bars. Then he repaired the
wall of the pool of Siloam near the king's garden,
and he rebuilt the wall as far as the stairs that descend from the City of David. 16Next to him was
Nehemiah son of Azbuk, the leader of half the
district of Beth-zur. He rebuilt the wall from a
place across from the tombs of David's family as
far as the water reservoir and the House of the
Warriors.

17Next to him, repairs were made by a group
of Levites working under the supervision of
Rehum son of Bani. Then came Hashabiah,
the leader of half the district of Keilah, who supervised the building of the wall on behalf of
his own district. 18Next down the line were his
countrymen led by Binnui son of Henadad, the
leader of the other half of the district of Keilah.

19Next to them, Ezer son of Jeshua, the leader
of Mizpah, repaired another section of wall
across from the ascent to the armory near the angle in the wall. 20Next to him was Baruch son of
Zabbai, who zealously repaired an additional
section from the angle to the door of the house
of Eliashib the high priest. 21Meremoth son of
Uriah and grandson of Hakkoz rebuilt another
section of the wall extending from the door of
Eliashib's house to the end of the house.

22The next repairs were made by the priests
from the surrounding region. 23After them,
Benjamin and Hasshub repaired the section
across from their house, and Azariah son of Maaseiah and grandson of Ananiah repaired the
section across from his house. 24Next was Binnui son of Henadad, who rebuilt another section
of the wall from Azariah's house to the angle and
the corner. 25Palal son of Uzai carried on the
work from a point opposite the angle and the
tower that projects up from the king's upper
house beside the court of the guard. Next to him
were Pedaiah son of Parosh, 26with the Temple
servants living on the hill of Ophel, who repaired
the wall as far as a point across from the Water
Gate to the east and the projecting tower.
27Then came the people of Tekoa, who repaired
another section across from the great projecting
tower and over to the wall of Ophel.

28Above the Horse Gate, the priests repaired
the wall. Each one repaired the section immediately across from his own house. 29Next Zadok
son of Immer also rebuilt the wall across from
his own house, and beyond him was Shemaiah
son of Shecaniah, the gatekeeper of the East
Gate. 30Next Hananiah son of Shelemiah and
Hanun, the sixth son of Zalaph, repaired another
section, while Meshullam son of Berekiah rebuilt the wall across from where he lived. 31Mal-
kijah, one of the goldsmiths, repaired the wall as
far as the housing for the Temple servants and
merchants, across from the Inspection Gate.
Then he continued as far as the upper room at
the corner. 32The other goldsmiths and merchants repaired the wall from that corner to the
Sheep Gate.

CHAPTER 4

Enemies Oppose the Rebuilding

Sanballat was very angry when he learned that
we were rebuilding the wall. He flew into a rage
and mocked the Jews, 2saying in front of his
friends and the Samarian army officers, "What
does this bunch of poor, feeble Jews think they're
doing? Do they think they can build the wall in a
single day by just offering a few sacrifices? Do
they actually think they can make something of
stones from a rubbish heap—and charred ones
at that?"

3Tobiah the Ammonite, who was standing beside him, remarked, "That stone wall would collapse if even a fox walked along the top of it!"

4Then I prayed, "Hear us, our God, for we are
being mocked. May their scoffing fall back on
their own heads, and may they themselves become captives in a foreign land! 5Do not ignore
their guilt. Do not blot out their sins, for they
have provoked you to anger here in front of the
builders."

6At last the wall was completed to half its
height around the entire city, for the people had
worked with enthusiasm.

7But when Sanballat and Tobiah and the

Against a Wall

Nehemiah and the Israelites worked so hard to build a new wall around Jerusalem. But Sanballat and Tobiah didn't just sit by and let it happen. **Check out NEHEMIAH 4 to see how they tried to put a stop to the construction.**

Ever feel tired of doing the right thing? Check out Galatians 6:9!

Try this to experience what the Israelites went through.

1. **Find a partner and a bunch of paper or plastic cups.**

2. **Use the paper cups to build a wall.**

3. **Have your friend stand about seven feet away from you. Every 10 seconds, your friend can try to knock down your wall by throwing a paper cup at it as you build.**

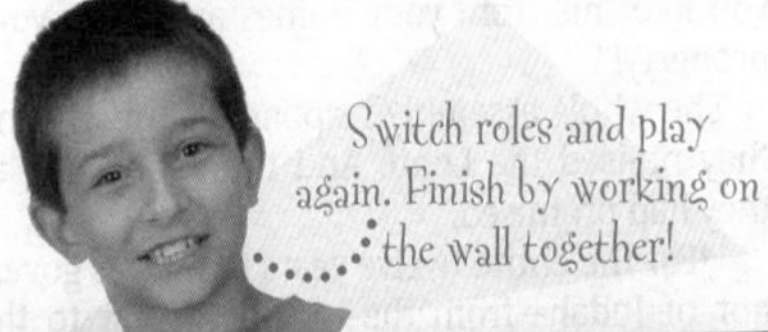

Switch roles and play again. Finish by working on the wall together!

TALK IT OVER

- How did the cup-thrower affect your progress on your wall?
- How do you think the Israelites felt as Sanballat and Tobiah kept making problems for them?
- Why do you think the Israelites kept building anyway?

Arabs, Ammonites, and Ashdodites heard that
the work was going ahead and that the gaps in
the wall of Jerusalem were being repaired, they
were furious. 8 They all made plans to come and
fight against Jerusalem and throw us into confusion. 9 But we prayed to our God and guarded the
city day and night to protect ourselves.

10 Then the people of Judah began to complain, "The workers are getting tired, and there is
so much rubble to be moved. We will never be
able to build the wall by ourselves."

11 Meanwhile, our enemies were saying, "Before they know what's happening, we will swoop
down on them and kill them and end their work."

12 The Jews who lived near the enemy came and
told us again and again, "They will come from all
directions and attack us!" 13 So I placed armed
guards behind the lowest parts of the wall in the
exposed areas. I stationed the people to stand
guard by families, armed with swords, spears, and
bows.

14 Then as I looked over the situation, I called
together the nobles and the rest of the people and
said to them, "Don't be afraid of the enemy! Remember the Lord, who is great and glorious, and
fight for your brothers, your sons, your daughters,
your wives, and your homes!"

15 When our enemies heard that we knew of
their plans and that God had frustrated them, we
all returned to our work on the wall. 16 But from
then on, only half my men worked while the
other half stood guard with spears, shields, bows,
and coats of mail. The leaders stationed themselves behind the people of Judah 17 who were
building the wall. The laborers carried on their
work with one hand supporting their load and
one hand holding a weapon. 18 All the builders
had a sword belted to their side. The trumpeter
stayed with me to sound the alarm.

19 Then I explained to the nobles and officials
and all the people, "The work is very spread out,
and we are widely separated from each other
along the wall. 20 When you hear the blast of the
trumpet, rush to wherever it is sounding. Then
our God will fight for us!"

21 We worked early and late, from sunrise to
sunset. And half the men were always on guard.
22 I also told everyone living outside the walls to
stay in Jerusalem. That way they and their servants could help with guard duty at night and
work during the day. 23 During this time, none of
us—not I, nor my relatives, nor my servants, nor
the guards who were with me—ever took off our
clothes. We carried our weapons with us at all
times, even when we went for water.

Nehemiah 5 . . . page 474

HELP...

The poor in Israel were in deep trouble. Nehemiah could have just stood by and watched, but he didn't! **Check out NEHEMIAH 5:1-13 to see what he did.**

There are lots of ways you can help! Here's one:

1. **WORK...** with an adult to find an organization that helps the poor.
2. **CALL...** the organization to see what kind of stuff you have that it needs.
3. **LOOK...** in your room for stuff to give away.

4. **LOAD...** up a box (or two or three).
5. **DROP...** the box off at the organization you called.

CHAPTER 5
Nehemiah Defends the Oppressed

About this time some of the men and their wives
raised a cry of protest against their fellow Jews.
2They were saying, "We have such large families.
We need more food to survive."
3Others said, "We have mortgaged our fields,
vineyards, and homes to get food during the
famine."
4And others said, "We have had to borrow
money on our fields and vineyards to pay our
taxes. 5We belong to the same family as those
who are wealthy, and our children are just like
theirs. Yet we must sell our children into slavery
just to get enough money to live. We have already
sold some of our daughters, and we are helpless
to do anything about it, for our fields and vineyards are already mortgaged to others."
6When I heard their complaints, I was very
angry. 7After thinking it over, I spoke out against
these nobles and officials. I told them, "You are
hurting your own relatives by charging interest
when they borrow money!" Then I called a public
meeting to deal with the problem.
8At the meeting I said to them, "We are doing
all we can to redeem our Jewish relatives who
have had to sell themselves to pagan foreigners,
but you are selling them back into slavery again.
How often must we redeem them?" And they had
nothing to say in their defense.
9Then I pressed further, "What you are doing
is not right! Should you not walk in the fear of
our God in order to avoid being mocked by enemy nations? 10I myself, as well as my brothers
and my workers, have been lending the people
money and grain, but now let us stop this business of charging interest. 11You must restore
their fields, vineyards, olive groves, and homes to
them this very day. And repay the interest you
charged when you lent them money, grain, new
wine, and olive oil."
12They replied, "We will give back everything
and demand nothing more from the people. We
will do as you say." Then I called the priests and
made the nobles and officials swear to do what
they had promised.
13I shook out the folds of my robe and said, "If
you fail to keep your promise, may God shake
you like this from your homes and from your
property!"
The whole assembly responded, "Amen," and
they praised the LORD. And the people did as
they had promised.
14For the entire twelve years that I was governor of Judah—from the twentieth year to the
thirty-second year of the reign of King Artaxerxes—neither I nor my officials drew on our official food allowance. 15The former governors, in
contrast, had laid heavy burdens on the people,
demanding a daily ration of food and wine, besides forty pieces of silver. Even their assistants
took advantage of the people. But because I
feared God, I did not act that way.
16I also devoted myself to working on the wall
and refused to acquire any land. And I required
all my servants to spend time working on the
wall. 17I asked for nothing, even though I regu-

larly fed 150 Jewish officials at my table, besides all the visitors from other lands! 18 The provisions I paid for each day included one ox, six choice sheep or goats, and a large number of poultry. And every ten days we needed a large supply of all kinds of wine. Yet I refused to claim the governor's food allowance because the people already carried a heavy burden.

19 Remember, O my God, all that I have done
for these people, and bless me for it.

CHAPTER 6

Continued Opposition to Rebuilding

Sanballat, Tobiah, Geshem the Arab, and the rest of our enemies found out that I had finished rebuilding the wall and that no gaps remained—though we had not yet set up the doors in the gates. 2 So Sanballat and Geshem sent a message asking me to meet them at one of the villages in the plain of Ono.

But I realized they were plotting to harm me, 3 so I replied by sending this message to them: "I am engaged in a great work, so I can't come. Why should I stop working to come and meet with you?"

4 Four times they sent the same message, and each time I gave the same reply. 5 The fifth time, Sanballat's servant came with an open letter in his hand, 6 and this is what it said:

"There is a rumor among the surrounding nations, and Geshem tells me it is true, that you and the Jews are planning to rebel and that is why you are building the wall. According to his reports, you plan to be their king. 7 He also reports that you have appointed prophets in Jerusalem to proclaim about you, 'Look! There is a king in Judah!'

"You can be very sure that this report will get back to the king, so I suggest that you come and talk it over with me."

8 I replied, "There is no truth in any part of your story. You are making up the whole thing."

9 They were just trying to intimidate us, imagining that they could discourage us and stop the work. So I continued the work with even greater determination.

10 Later I went to visit Shemaiah son of Delaiah and grandson of Mehetabel, who was confined to his home. He said, "Let us meet together inside the Temple of God and bolt the doors shut. Your enemies are coming to kill you tonight."

11 But I replied, "Should someone in my position run from danger? Should someone in my position enter the Temple to save his life? No, I won't do it!" 12 I realized that God had not spoken to him, but that he had uttered this prophecy against me because Tobiah and Sanballat had hired him. 13 They were hoping to intimidate me and make me sin. Then they would be able to accuse and discredit me.

14 Remember, O my God, all the evil things
that Tobiah and Sanballat have done. And
remember Noadiah the prophet and all
the prophets like her who have tried to
intimidate me.

The Builders Complete the Wall

15 So on October 2 the wall was finished—just fifty-two days after we had begun. 16 When our enemies and the surrounding nations heard about it, they were frightened and humiliated. They realized this work had been done with the help of our God.

17 During those fifty-two days, many letters went back and forth between Tobiah and the nobles of Judah. 18 For many in Judah had sworn allegiance to him because his father-in-law was Shecaniah son of Arah, and his son Jehohanan was married to the daughter of Meshullam son of Berekiah. 19 They kept telling me about Tobiah's good deeds, and then they told him everything I said. And Tobiah kept sending threatening letters to intimidate me.

CHAPTER 7

After the wall was finished and I had set up the doors in the gates, the gatekeepers, singers, and Levites were appointed. 2 I gave the responsibility of governing Jerusalem to my brother Hanani, along with Hananiah, the commander of the fortress, for he was a faithful man who feared God more than most. 3 I said to them, "Do not leave the gates open during the hottest part of the day. And even while the gatekeepers are on duty, have them shut and bar the doors. Appoint the residents of Jerusalem to act as guards, everyone on a regular watch. Some will serve at sentry posts and some in front of their own homes."

Nehemiah Registers the People

4 At that time the city was large and spacious, but the population was small, and none of the houses had been rebuilt. 5 So my God gave me the idea to call together all the nobles and leaders of the city, along with the ordinary citizens,

for registration. I had found the genealogical
record of those who had first returned to Judah.
This is what was written there:

6 Here is the list of the Jewish exiles of the
provinces who returned from their captivity.
King Nebuchadnezzar had deported them to
Babylon, but now they returned to Jerusalem
and the other towns in Judah where they
originally lived. 7 Their leaders were Zerubbabel, Jeshua, Nehemiah, Seraiah, Reelaiah,
Nahamani, Mordecai, Bilshan, Mispar, Bigvai,
Rehum, and Baanah.

This is the number of the men of Israel who
returned from exile:

8 The family of Parosh 2,172
9 The family of Shephatiah 372
10 The family of Arah 652
11 The family of Pahath-moab (descendants
of Jeshua and Joab) 2,818
12 The family of Elam 1,254
13 The family of Zattu 845
14 The family of Zaccai 760
15 The family of Bani 648
16 The family of Bebai 628
17 The family of Azgad 2,322
18 The family of Adonikam 667
19 The family of Bigvai 2,067
20 The family of Adin 655
21 The family of Ater (descendants
of Hezekiah) 98
22 The family of Hashum 328
23 The family of Bezai 324
24 The family of Jorah 112
25 The family of Gibbar 95
26 The people of Bethlehem and
Netophah 188
27 The people of Anathoth 128
28 The people of Beth-azmaveth 42
29 The people of Kiriath-jearim,
Kephirah, and Beeroth 743
30 The people of Ramah and Geba 621
31 The people of Micmash 122
32 The people of Bethel and Ai 123
33 The people of West Nebo 52
34 The citizens of West Elam 1,254
35 The citizens of Harim 320
36 The citizens of Jericho 345
37 The citizens of Lod, Hadid, and Ono . . 721
38 The citizens of Senaah 3,930

39 These are the priests who returned from
exile:
The family of Jedaiah (through the
line of Jeshua) 973
40 The family of Immer 1,052
41 The family of Pashhur 1,247
42 The family of Harim 1,017

43 These are the Levites who returned from
exile:
The families of Jeshua and Kadmiel
(descendants of Hodaviah) 74
44 The singers of the family of Asaph 148
45 The gatekeepers of the families of
Shallum, Ater, Talmon, Akkub,
Hatita, and Shobai 138

46 The descendants of the following Temple
servants returned from exile:
Ziha, Hasupha, Tabbaoth,
47 Keros, Siaha, Padon,
48 Lebanah, Hagabah, Shalmai,
49 Hanan, Giddel, Gahar,
50 Reaiah, Rezin, Nekoda,
51 Gazzam, Uzza, Paseah,
52 Besai, Meunim, Nephusim,
53 Bakbuk, Hakupha, Harhur,
54 Bazluth, Mehida, Harsha,
55 Barkos, Sisera, Temah,
56 Neziah, and Hatipha.

57 The descendants of these servants of King
Solomon returned from exile:
Sotai, Hassophereth, Peruda,
58 Jaalah, Darkon, Giddel,
59 Shephatiah, Hattil, Pokereth-hazzebaim,
and Ami.

60 In all, the Temple servants and the
descendants of Solomon's servants
numbered 392.

61 Another group returned at this time
from the towns of Tel-melah, Tel-harsha,
Kerub, Addan, and Immer. However, they
could not prove that they or their families
were descendants of Israel. 62 This group
included the families of Delaiah, Tobiah,
and Nekoda—a total of 642 people.

63 Three families of priests—Hobaiah,
Hakkoz, and Barzillai—also returned. (This
Barzillai had married a woman who was a
descendant of Barzillai of Gilead, and he had
taken her family name.) 64 They searched
for their names in the genealogical records,
but they were not found, so they were
disqualified from serving as priests. 65 The
governor told them not to eat the priests'
share of food from the sacrifices until a
priest could consult the LORD about the
matter by using the Urim and Thummim—
the sacred lots.

In Bible times, people built huge walls around their cities to protect them from other armies. The walls were as wide as 25 feet and 40 feet high! The wall in Jericho was so big that Rahab's house was built right into it (**see JOSHUA 2**). King Solomon built a wall around Jerusalem, but the armies of Babylon destroyed it. Nehemiah helped rebuild that wall (**see NEHEMIAH 3**).

Grab a map of your city (or any city). Make sure it's OK to draw on the map, then create a wall around the city. How many bricks do you think it would take? Good news! You don't have to build a wall for protection. **Check out JEREMIAH 15:19-21 and PROVERBS 18:10!**

66 So a total of 42,360 people returned to
Judah, 67 in addition to 7,337 servants and
245 singers, both men and women. 68 They
took with them 736 horses, 245 mules,
69 435 camels, and 6,720 donkeys.
70 Some of the family leaders gave gifts for
the work. The governor gave to the treasury
1,000 gold coins, 50 gold basins, and 530
robes for the priests. 71 The other leaders
gave to the treasury a total of 20,000 gold
coins and some 2,750 pounds of silver for
the work. 72 The rest of the people gave
20,000 gold coins, about 2,500 pounds
of silver, and 67 robes for the priests.
73 So the priests, the Levites, the gatekeepers, the singers, the Temple servants,
and some of the common people settled near
Jerusalem. The rest of the people returned
to their own towns throughout Israel.

CHAPTER 8

Ezra Reads the Law

In October, when the Israelites had settled in
their towns, 8:1 all the people assembled with a
unified purpose at the square just inside the Water Gate. They asked Ezra the scribe to bring out
the Book of the Law of Moses, which the LORD
had given for Israel to obey.
2 So on October 8 Ezra the priest brought the
Book of the Law before the assembly, which included the men and women and all the children
old enough to understand. 3 He faced the square
just inside the Water Gate from early morning
until noon and read aloud to everyone who could
understand. All the people listened closely to the
Book of the Law.
4 Ezra the scribe stood on a high wooden platform that had been made for the occasion.
To his right stood Mattithiah, Shema, Anaiah,
Uriah, Hilkiah, and Maaseiah. To his left stood
Pedaiah, Mishael, Malkijah, Hashum, Hashbad-
danah, Zechariah, and Meshullam. 5 Ezra stood
on the platform in full view of all the people.
When they saw him open the book, they all rose
to their feet.
6 Then Ezra praised the LORD, the great God,
and all the people chanted, "Amen! Amen!" as
they lifted their hands. Then they bowed down
and worshiped the LORD with their faces to the
ground.
7 The Levites—Jeshua, Bani, Sherebiah, Jamin,
Akkub, Shabbethai, Hodiah, Maaseiah, Kelita,
Azariah, Jozabad, Hanan, and Pelaiah—then instructed the people in the Law while everyone remained in their places. 8 They read from the
Book of the Law of God and clearly explained
the meaning of what was being read, helping the
people understand each passage.
9 Then Nehemiah the governor, Ezra the priest
and scribe, and the Levites who were interpreting for the people said to them, "Don't mourn or
weep on such a day as this! For today is a sacred
day before the LORD your God." For the people
had all been weeping as they listened to the
words of the Law.
10 And Nehemiah continued, "Go and celebrate with a feast of rich foods and sweet drinks,

and share gifts of food with people who have
nothing prepared. This is a sacred day before our
Lord. Don't be dejected and sad, for the joy of the
LORD is your strength!"
11And the Levites, too, quieted the people, telling them, "Hush! Don't weep! For this is a sacred
day." 12So the people went away to eat and drink
at a festive meal, to share gifts of food, and to celebrate with great joy because they had heard
God's words and understood them.

The Festival of Shelters

13On October 9 the family leaders of all the people, together with the priests and Levites, met
with Ezra the scribe to go over the Law in greater
detail. 14As they studied the Law, they discovered
that the LORD had commanded through Moses
that the Israelites should live in shelters during
the festival to be held that month. 15He had said
that a proclamation should be made throughout
their towns and in Jerusalem, telling the people
to go to the hills to get branches from olive, wild
olive, myrtle, palm, and other leafy trees. They
were to use these branches to make shelters in
which they would live during the festival, as prescribed in the Law.
16So the people went out and cut branches
and used them to build shelters on the roofs of
their houses, in their courtyards, in the courtyards of God's Temple, or in the squares just inside the Water Gate and the Ephraim Gate. 17So
everyone who had returned from captivity lived
in these shelters during the festival, and they
were all filled with great joy! The Israelites had
not celebrated like this since the days of Joshua
son of Nun.
18Ezra read from the Book of the Law of God
on each of the seven days of the festival. Then on
the eighth day they held a solemn assembly, as
was required by law.

CHAPTER 9

The People Confess Their Sins

On October 31 the people assembled again, and
this time they fasted and dressed in burlap and
sprinkled dust on their heads. 2Those of Israelite descent separated themselves from all foreigners as they confessed their own sins and the
sins of their ancestors. 3They remained standing in place for three hours while the Book of the
Law of the LORD their God was read aloud to
them. Then for three more hours they confessed
their sins and worshiped the LORD their God.
4The Levites—Jeshua, Bani, Kadmiel, Shebaniah,
Bunni, Sherebiah, Bani, and Kenani—stood on

Key Verse "But you are a God of forgiveness, gracious and merciful, slow to become angry, and rich in unfailing love and mercy."—NEHEMIAH 9:17b

Are We There Yet?

The Israelites kept a little pattern going that went like this: **1. Everything was OK. 2. They'd start worshiping false gods. 3. Things would go bad. 4. They'd ask God for help. 5. Everything was OK.** This little pattern had been going on for more than 1,000 years. (If you were sitting in the car for 1,000 years, you could drive across the United States more than 90,000 times.) But God never stopped loving, forgiving, and waiting for the Israelites. **Read Nehemiah 9:17b to see just how patient God is!**

Let's see how patient you are!
Want to see why God is so much better at patience? Check out 2 Peter 3:8-9.
1 Fill a plastic cup with potting soil, and drop in a few seeds.
2 Cover the seeds with soil, and add water.
3 Watch the cup until you see the seeds start to grow.
When a plant comes up, remember that God always watches over, forgives, and waits for you!

the stairway of the Levites and cried out to the
LORD their God with loud voices.
5 Then the leaders of the Levites—Jeshua, Kadmiel, Bani, Hashabneiah, Sherebiah, Hodiah,
Shebaniah, and Pethahiah—called out to the
people: "Stand up and praise the LORD your God,
for he lives from everlasting to everlasting!"
Then they prayed:

"May your glorious name be praised! May
it be exalted above all blessing and praise!
6 "You alone are the LORD. You made the
skies and the heavens and all the stars. You
made the earth and the seas and everything
in them. You preserve them all, and the
angels of heaven worship you.
7 "You are the LORD God, who chose Abram
and brought him from Ur of the Chaldeans
and renamed him Abraham. 8 When he had
proved himself faithful, you made a covenant
with him to give him and his descendants the
land of the Canaanites, Hittites, Amorites,
Perizzites, Jebusites, and Girgashites. And you
have done what you promised, for you are
always true to your word.
9 "You saw the misery of our ancestors in
Egypt, and you heard their cries from beside
the Red Sea. 10 You displayed miraculous
signs and wonders against Pharaoh, his
officials, and all his people, for you knew how
arrogantly they were treating our ancestors.
You have a glorious reputation that has never
been forgotten. 11 You divided the sea for
your people so they could walk through on
dry land! And then you hurled their enemies
into the depths of the sea. They sank like
stones beneath the mighty waters. 12 You led
our ancestors by a pillar of cloud during the
day and a pillar of fire at night so that they
could find their way.
13 "You came down at Mount Sinai and
spoke to them from heaven. You gave them
regulations and instructions that were just,
and decrees and commands that were good.
14 You instructed them concerning your
holy Sabbath. And you commanded them,
through Moses your servant, to obey all your
commands, decrees, and instructions.
15 "You gave them bread from heaven when
they were hungry and water from the rock
when they were thirsty. You commanded
them to go and take possession of the land
you had sworn to give them.
16 "But our ancestors were proud and
stubborn, and they paid no attention to your
commands. 17 They refused to obey and did
not remember the miracles you had done
for them. Instead, they became stubborn
and appointed a leader to take them back
to their slavery in Egypt. **But you are a
God of forgiveness, gracious and
merciful, slow to become angry,
and rich in unfailing love.** You did
not abandon them, 18 even when they made
an idol shaped like a calf and said, 'This is
your god who brought you out of Egypt!'
They committed terrible blasphemies.
19 "But in your great mercy you did not
abandon them to die in the wilderness. The
pillar of cloud still led them forward by day,
and the pillar of fire showed them the way
through the night. 20 You sent your good
Spirit to instruct them, and you did not stop
giving them manna from heaven or water for
their thirst. 21 For forty years you sustained
them in the wilderness, and they lacked
nothing. Their clothes did not wear out,
and their feet did not swell!
22 "Then you helped our ancestors
conquer kingdoms and nations, and you
placed your people in every corner of the
land. They took over the land of King Sihon
of Heshbon and the land of King Og of
Bashan. 23 You made their descendants as
numerous as the stars in the sky and brought
them into the land you had promised to their
ancestors.
24 "They went in and took possession of
the land. You subdued whole nations before
them. Even the Canaanites, who inhabited
the land, were powerless! Your people could
deal with these nations and their kings as
they pleased. 25 Our ancestors captured
fortified cities and fertile land. They took
over houses full of good things, with cisterns
already dug and vineyards and olive groves
and fruit trees in abundance. So they ate
until they were full and grew fat and enjoyed
themselves in all your blessings.
26 "But despite all this, they were
disobedient and rebelled against you.
They turned their backs on your Law, they
killed your prophets who warned them to
return to you, and they committed terrible
blasphemies. 27 So you handed them over to
their enemies, who made them suffer. But in
their time of trouble they cried to you, and
you heard them from heaven. In your great
mercy, you sent them liberators who rescued
them from their enemies.

[28]"But as soon as they were at peace, your
people again committed evil in your sight,
and once more you let their enemies
conquer them. Yet whenever your people
turned and cried to you again for help, you
listened once more from heaven. In your
wonderful mercy, you rescued them many
times!

[29]"You warned them to return to your Law,
but they became proud and obstinate and
disobeyed your commands. They did not
follow your regulations, by which people will
find life if only they obey. They stubbornly
turned their backs on you and refused to
listen. [30]In your love, you were patient with
them for many years. You sent your Spirit,
who warned them through the prophets. But
still they wouldn't listen! So once again you
allowed the peoples of the land to conquer
them. [31]But in your great mercy, you did not
destroy them completely or abandon them
forever. What a gracious and merciful God
you are!

[32]"And now, our God, the great and mighty
and awesome God, who keeps his covenant
of unfailing love, do not let all the hardships
we have suffered seem insignificant to you.
Great trouble has come upon us and upon
our kings and leaders and priests and
prophets and ancestors—all of your people—
from the days when the kings of Assyria first
triumphed over us until now. [33]Every time
you punished us you were being just. We
have sinned greatly, and you gave us only
what we deserved. [34]Our kings, leaders,
priests, and ancestors did not obey your Law
or listen to the warnings in your commands
and laws. [35]Even while they had their own
kingdom, they did not serve you, though you
showered your goodness on them. You gave
them a large, fertile land, but they refused to
turn from their wickedness.

[36]"So now today we are slaves in the land
of plenty that you gave our ancestors for their
enjoyment! We are slaves here in this good
land. [37]The lush produce of this land piles up
in the hands of the kings whom you have set
over us because of our sins. They have power
over us and our livestock. We serve them at
their pleasure, and we are in great misery."

The People Agree to Obey

[38]The people responded, "In view of all this, we
are making a solemn promise and putting it in
writing. On this sealed document are the names
of our leaders and Levites and priests."

CHAPTER 10

The document was ratified and sealed with the
following names:

The governor:
Nehemiah son of Hacaliah, and also
Zedekiah.

[2]The following priests:
Seraiah, Azariah, Jeremiah, [3]Pashhur,
Amariah, Malkijah, [4]Hattush, Shebaniah,
Malluch, [5]Harim, Meremoth, Obadiah,
[6]Daniel, Ginnethon, Baruch, [7]Meshullam,
Abijah, Mijamin, [8]Maaziah, Bilgai, and
Shemaiah. These were the priests.

[9]The following Levites:
Jeshua son of Azaniah, Binnui from the
family of Henadad, Kadmiel, [10]and their
fellow Levites: Shebaniah, Hodiah, Kelita,
Pelaiah, Hanan, [11]Mica, Rehob, Hashabiah,
[12]Zaccur, Sherebiah, Shebaniah, [13]Hodiah,
Bani, and Beninu.

[14]The following leaders:
Parosh, Pahath-moab, Elam, Zattu, Bani,
[15]Bunni, Azgad, Bebai, [16]Adonijah, Bigvai,
Adin, [17]Ater, Hezekiah, Azzur, [18]Hodiah,
Hashum, Bezai, [19]Hariph, Anathoth, Nebai,
[20]Magpiash, Meshullam, Hezir, [21]Meshezabel,
Zadok, Jaddua, [22]Pelatiah, Hanan, Anaiah,
[23]Hoshea, Hananiah, Hasshub,
[24]Hallohesh, Pilha, Shobek, [25]Rehum,
Hashabnah, Maaseiah, [26]Ahiah, Hanan,
Anan, [27]Malluch, Harim, and Baanah.

The Vow of the People

[28]Then the rest of the people—the priests,
Levites, gatekeepers, singers, Temple servants,
and all who had separated themselves from the
pagan people of the land in order to obey the
Law of God, together with their wives, sons,
daughters, and all who were old enough to
understand—[29]joined their leaders and bound
themselves with an oath. They swore a curse on
themselves if they failed to obey the Law of God
as issued by his servant Moses. They solemnly
promised to carefully follow all the commands,
regulations, and decrees of the LORD our Lord:

[30]"We promise not to let our daughters
marry the pagan people of the land, and
not to let our sons marry their daughters.

[31]"We also promise that if the people of
the land should bring any merchandise or
grain to be sold on the Sabbath or on any

other holy day, we will refuse to buy it. Every
seventh year we will let our land rest, and we
will cancel all debts owed to us.

32“In addition, we promise to obey the
command to pay the annual Temple tax of
one-eighth of an ounce of silver for the care
of the Temple of our God. 33This will provide
for the Bread of the Presence; for the regular
grain offerings and burnt offerings; for the
offerings on the Sabbaths, the new moon
celebrations, and the annual festivals; for
the holy offerings; and for the sin offerings to
make atonement for Israel. It will provide for
everything necessary for the work of the
Temple of our God.

34“We have cast sacred lots to determine
when—at regular times each year—the
families of the priests, Levites, and the
common people should bring wood to God's
Temple to be burned on the altar of the LORD
our God, as is written in the Law.

35“We promise to bring the first part of
every harvest to the LORD's Temple year after
year—whether it be a crop from the soil or
from our fruit trees. 36We agree to give God
our oldest sons and the firstborn of all our
herds and flocks, as prescribed in the Law.
We will present them to the priests who
minister in the Temple of our God. 37We
will store the produce in the storerooms of
the Temple of our God. We will bring the
best of our flour and other grain offerings,
the best of our fruit, and the best of our new
wine and olive oil. And we promise to bring
to the Levites a tenth of everything our land
produces, for it is the Levites who collect the
tithes in all our rural towns.

38“A priest—a descendant of Aaron—
will be with the Levites as they receive these
tithes. And a tenth of all that is collected
as tithes will be delivered by the Levites to
the Temple of our God and placed in the
storerooms. 39The people and the Levites
must bring these offerings of grain, new
wine, and olive oil to the storerooms and
place them in the sacred containers near
the ministering priests, the gatekeepers, and
the singers.

“We promise together not to neglect the
Temple of our God.”

CHAPTER 11
The People Occupy Jerusalem

The leaders of the people were living in Jerusalem, the holy city. A tenth of the people from the
other towns of Judah and Benjamin were chosen
by sacred lots to live there, too, while the rest
stayed where they were. 2And the people com-
mended everyone who volunteered to resettle in
Jerusalem.

3Here is a list of the names of the provincial
officials who came to live in Jerusalem. (Most of
the people, priests, Levites, Temple servants, and
descendants of Solomon's servants continued to
live in their own homes in the various towns of
Judah, 4but some of the people from Judah and
Benjamin resettled in Jerusalem.)

From the tribe of Judah:
Athaiah son of Uzziah, son of Zechariah,
son of Amariah, son of Shephatiah, son of
Mahalalel, of the family of Perez. 5Also
Maaseiah son of Baruch, son of Col-hozeh,
son of Hazaiah, son of Adaiah, son of Joiarib,
son of Zechariah, of the family of Shelah.
6There were 468 descendants of Perez who
lived in Jerusalem—all outstanding men.

7From the tribe of Benjamin:
Sallu son of Meshullam, son of Joed, son of
Pedaiah, son of Kolaiah, son of Maaseiah, son
of Ithiel, son of Jeshaiah. 8After him were
Gabbai and Sallai and a total of 928 relatives.
9Their chief officer was Joel son of Zicri, who
was assisted by Judah son of Hassenuah,
second-in-command over the city.

10From the priests:
Jedaiah son of Joiarib; Jakin; 11and Seraiah
son of Hilkiah, son of Meshullam, son of
Zadok, son of Meraioth, son of Ahitub, the
supervisor of the Temple of God. 12Also
822 of their associates, who worked at the
Temple. Also Adaiah son of Jeroham, son of
Pelaliah, son of Amzi, son of Zechariah, son
of Pashhur, son of Malkijah, 13along with
242 of his associates, who were heads of
their families. Also Amashsai son of Azarel,
son of Ahzai, son of Meshillemoth, son of
Immer, 14and 128 of his outstanding
associates. Their chief officer was Zabdiel
son of Haggedolim.

15From the Levites:
Shemaiah son of Hasshub, son of Azrikam,
son of Hashabiah, son of Bunni. 16Also
Shabbethai and Jozabad, who were in charge
of the work outside the Temple of God.
17Also Mattaniah son of Mica, son of Zabdi,
a descendant of Asaph, who led in thanksgiving and prayer. Also Bakbukiah, who
was Mattaniah's assistant, and Abda son of
Shammua, son of Galal, son of Jeduthun.

18 In all, there were 284 Levites in the holy
city.
19 From the gatekeepers:
Akkub, Talmon, and 172 of their associates,
who guarded the gates.

20 The other priests, Levites, and the rest of
the Israelites lived wherever their family inheritance was located in any of the towns of Judah.
21 The Temple servants, however, whose leaders
were Ziha and Gishpa, all lived on the hill of
Ophel.

22 The chief officer of the Levites in Jerusalem
was Uzzi son of Bani, son of Hashabiah, son of
Mattaniah, son of Mica, a descendant of Asaph,
whose family served as singers at God's Temple.
23 Their daily responsibilities were carried out
according to the terms of a royal command.
24 Pethahiah son of Meshezabel, a descendant
of Zerah son of Judah, was the royal adviser in all
matters of public administration.

25 As for the surrounding villages with their
open fields, some of the people of Judah lived in
Kiriath-arba with its settlements, Dibon with its
settlements, and Jekabzeel with its villages.
26 They also lived in Jeshua, Moladah, Beth-pelet,
27 Hazar-shual, Beersheba with its settlements,
28 Ziklag, and Meconah with its settlements.
29 They also lived in En-rimmon, Zorah, Jarmuth,
30 Zanoah, and Adullam with their surrounding
villages. They also lived in Lachish with its
nearby fields and Azekah with its surrounding
villages. So the people of Judah were living all the
way from Beersheba in the south to the valley of
Hinnom.

31 Some of the people of Benjamin lived at
Geba, Micmash, Aija, and Bethel with its settlements. 32 They also lived in Anathoth, Nob, Ananiah, 33 Hazor, Ramah, Gittaim, 34 Hadid, Zeboim,
Neballat, 35 Lod, Ono, and the Valley of Craftsmen. 36 Some of the Levites who lived in Judah
were sent to live with the tribe of Benjamin.

CHAPTER 12

A History of the Priests and Levites

Here is the list of the priests and Levites who returned with Zerubbabel son of Shealtiel and
Jeshua the high priest:

Seraiah, Jeremiah, Ezra,
2 Amariah, Malluch, Hattush,
3 Shecaniah, Harim, Meremoth,
4 Iddo, Ginnethon, Abijah,
5 Miniamin, Moadiah, Bilgah,
6 Shemaiah, Joiarib, Jedaiah,
7 Sallu, Amok, Hilkiah, and Jedaiah.

These were the leaders of the priests and their
associates in the days of Jeshua.

8 The Levites who returned with them were
Jeshua, Binnui, Kadmiel, Sherebiah, Judah, and
Mattaniah, who with his associates was in charge
of the songs of thanksgiving. 9 Their associates,
Bakbukiah and Unni, stood opposite them dur-
ing the service.

10 Jeshua the high priest was the father
of Joiakim.
Joiakim was the father of Eliashib.
Eliashib was the father of Joiada.
11 Joiada was the father of Johanan.
Johanan was the father of Jaddua.

12 Now when Joiakim was high priest, the family
leaders of the priests were as follows:

Meraiah was leader of the family of Seraiah.
Hananiah was leader of the family of
Jeremiah.
13 Meshullam was leader of the family of Ezra.
Jehohanan was leader of the family of
Amariah.
14 Jonathan was leader of the family of Malluch.
Joseph was leader of the family of Shecaniah.
15 Adna was leader of the family of Harim.
Helkai was leader of the family of Meremoth.
16 Zechariah was leader of the family of Iddo.
Meshullam was leader of the family of
Ginnethon.
17 Zicri was leader of the family of Abijah.
There was also a leader of the family of
Miniamin.
Piltai was leader of the family of Moadiah.
18 Shammua was leader of the family of Bilgah.
Jehonathan was leader of the family of
Shemaiah.
19 Mattenai was leader of the family of Joiarib.
Uzzi was leader of the family of Jedaiah.
20 Kallai was leader of the family of Sallu.
Eber was leader of the family of Amok.
21 Hashabiah was leader of the family of
Hilkiah.
Nethanel was leader of the family of Jedaiah.

22 A record of the Levite families was kept during the years when Eliashib, Joiada, Johanan, and
Jaddua served as high priest. Another record of
the priests was kept during the reign of Darius
the Persian. 23 A record of the heads of the Levite
families was kept in *The Book of History* down to
the days of Johanan, the grandson of Eliashib.
24 These were the family leaders of the Levites:

Hashabiah, Sherebiah, Jeshua, Binnui, Kadmiel,
and other associates, who stood opposite them
during the ceremonies of praise and thanksgiving, one section responding to the other, as
commanded by David, the man of God. 25 This
included Mattaniah, Bakbukiah, and Obadiah.
Meshullam, Talmon, and Akkub were the gatekeepers in charge of the storerooms at the gates.
26 These all served in the days of Joiakim son of
Jeshua, son of Jehozadak, and in the days of Nehemiah the governor and of Ezra the priest and
scribe.

Dedication of Jerusalem's Wall

27 For the dedication of the new wall of Jerusalem, the Levites throughout the land were asked
to come to Jerusalem to assist in the ceremonies.
They were to take part in the joyous occasion
with their songs of thanksgiving and with the
music of cymbals, harps, and lyres. 28 The singers
were brought together from the region around
Jerusalem and from the villages of the Netophathites. 29 They also came from Beth-gilgal and
the rural areas near Geba and Azmaveth, for the
singers had built their own settlements around
Jerusalem. 30 The priests and Levites first purified themselves; then they purified the people,
the gates, and the wall.
31 I led the leaders of Judah to the top of the
wall and organized two large choirs to give
thanks. One of the choirs proceeded southward
along the top of the wall to the Dung Gate. 32 Hoshaiah and half the leaders of Judah followed
them, 33 along with Azariah, Ezra, Meshullam,
34 Judah, Benjamin, Shemaiah, and Jeremiah.
35 Then came some priests who played trumpets, including Zechariah son of Jonathan, son
of Shemaiah, son of Mattaniah, son of Micaiah,
son of Zaccur, a descendant of Asaph. 36 And
Zechariah's colleagues were Shemaiah, Azarel,
Milalai, Gilalai, Maai, Nethanel, Judah, and Hanani. They used the musical instruments prescribed by David, the man of God. Ezra the
scribe led this procession. 37 At the Fountain
Gate they went straight up the steps on the ascent of the city wall toward the City of David.
They passed the house of David and then proceeded to the Water Gate on the east.
38 The second choir giving thanks went northward around the other way to meet them. I followed them, together with the other half of the
people, along the top of the wall past the Tower
of the Ovens to the Broad Wall, 39 then past the
Ephraim Gate to the Old City Gate, past the Fish
Gate and the Tower of Hananel, and on to the

Woozy

The Israelite people promised to obey God's laws, but they made some bad choices and got all mixed up. Good thing Nehemiah came back and straightened 'em out.

Read about it in NEHEMIAH 13.

BREAKING GOD'S LAW IS KIND OF LIKE THIS:

Read Zechariah 1:3 to find out what happens when we turn back to God.

1. **Grab a friend, and put a baseball bat in the middle of the room. Clear out anything that would hurt to fall into. (Better yet, go outside to a safe, open space.)**

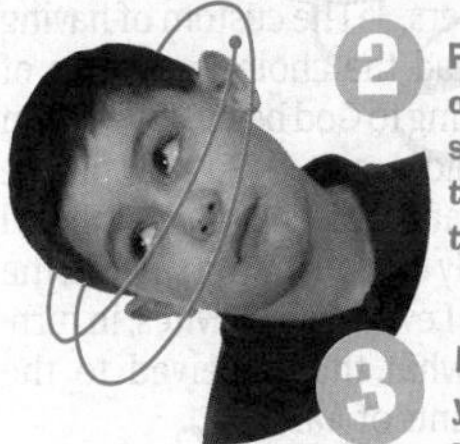

2. **Put your forehead on the bat, and spin around the bat five times.**
3. **Have your friend help you walk to the other side of the lawn.**

Could you walk straight?

How is that like what happens when we don't do what God says? God gives us rules for our protection. When we disobey those rules, we get confused, turned around, and sometimes we fall down.

When we tell God we're sorry and stop doing wrong things, he straightens us out. COOL!

Tower of the Hundred. Then we continued on to the Sheep Gate and stopped at the Guard Gate.

40 The two choirs that were giving thanks then proceeded to the Temple of God, where they took their places. So did I, together with the group of leaders who were with me. 41 We went together with the trumpet-playing priests—Eliakim, Maaseiah, Miniamin, Micaiah, Elioenai, Zechariah, and Hananiah—42 and the singers—Maaseiah, Shemaiah, Eleazar, Uzzi, Jehohanan, Malkijah, Elam, and Ezer. They played and sang loudly under the direction of Jezrahiah the choir director.

43 Many sacrifices were offered on that joyous day, for God had given the people cause for great joy. The women and children also participated in the celebration, and the joy of the people of Jerusalem could be heard far away.

Provisions for Temple Worship

44 On that day men were appointed to be in charge of the storerooms for the offerings, the first part of the harvest, and the tithes. They were responsible to collect from the fields outside the towns the portions required by the Law for the priests and Levites. For all the people of Judah took joy in the priests and Levites and their work. 45 They performed the service of their God and the service of purification, as commanded by David and his son Solomon, and so did the singers and the gatekeepers. 46 The custom of having choir directors to lead the choirs in hymns of praise and thanksgiving to God began long ago in the days of David and Asaph. 47 So now, in the days of Zerubbabel and of Nehemiah, all Israel brought a daily supply of food for the singers, the gatekeepers, and the Levites. The Levites, in turn, gave a portion of what they received to the priests, the descendants of Aaron.

CHAPTER 13

Nehemiah's Various Reforms

On that same day, as the Book of Moses was being read to the people, the passage was found that said no Ammonite or Moabite should ever be permitted to enter the assembly of God. 2 For they had not provided the Israelites with food and water in the wilderness. Instead, they hired Balaam to curse them, though our God turned the curse into a blessing. 3 When this passage of the Law was read, all those of foreign descent were immediately excluded from the assembly.

4 Before this had happened, Eliashib the priest, who had been appointed as supervisor of the storerooms of the Temple of our God and who was also a relative of Tobiah, 5 had converted a large storage room and placed it at Tobiah's disposal. The room had previously been used for storing the grain offerings, the frankincense, various articles for the Temple, and the tithes of grain, new wine, and olive oil (which were prescribed for the Levites, the singers, and the gatekeepers), as well as the offerings for the priests.

6 I was not in Jerusalem at that time, for I had returned to King Artaxerxes of Babylon in the thirty-second year of his reign, though I later asked his permission to return. 7 When I arrived back in Jerusalem, I learned about Eliashib's evil deed in providing Tobiah with a room in the courtyards of the Temple of God. 8 I became very upset and threw all of Tobiah's belongings out of the room. 9 Then I demanded that the rooms be purified, and I brought back the articles for God's Temple, the grain offerings, and the frankincense.

10 I also discovered that the Levites had not been given their prescribed portions of food, so they and the singers who were to conduct the worship services had all returned to work their fields. 11 I immediately confronted the leaders and demanded, "Why has the Temple of God been neglected?" Then I called all the Levites back again and restored them to their proper duties. 12 And once more all the people of Judah began bringing their tithes of grain, new wine, and olive oil to the Temple storerooms.

13 I assigned supervisors for the storerooms: Shelemiah the priest, Zadok the scribe, and Pedaiah, one of the Levites. And I appointed Hanan son of Zaccur and grandson of Mattaniah as their assistant. These men had an excellent reputation, and it was their job to make honest distributions to their fellow Levites.

14 Remember this good deed, O my God, and
do not forget all that I have faithfully done
for the Temple of my God and its services.

15 In those days I saw men of Judah treading out their winepresses on the Sabbath. They were also bringing in grain, loading it on donkeys, and bringing their wine, grapes, figs, and all sorts of produce to Jerusalem to sell on the Sabbath. So I rebuked them for selling their produce on that day. 16 Some men from Tyre, who lived in Jerusalem, were bringing in fish and all kinds of merchandise. They were selling it on the Sabbath to the people of Judah—and in Jerusalem at that!

17 So I confronted the nobles of Judah. "Why are you profaning the Sabbath in this evil way?" I asked. 18 "Wasn't it just this sort of thing that

your ancestors did that caused our God to bring
all this trouble upon us and our city? Now you are
bringing even more wrath upon Israel by permitting the Sabbath to be desecrated in this way!"
19Then I commanded that the gates of Jerusalem should be shut as darkness fell every Friday
evening, not to be opened until the Sabbath
ended. I sent some of my own servants to guard
the gates so that no merchandise could be
brought in on the Sabbath day. 20The merchants
and tradesmen with a variety of wares camped
outside Jerusalem once or twice. 21But I spoke
sharply to them and said, "What are you doing
out here, camping around the wall? If you do this
again, I will arrest you!" And that was the last
time they came on the Sabbath. 22Then I commanded the Levites to purify themselves and to
guard the gates in order to preserve the holiness
of the Sabbath.

Remember this good deed also, O my God!
Have compassion on me according to your
great and unfailing love.

23About the same time I realized that some of
the men of Judah had married women from Ashdod, Ammon, and Moab. 24Furthermore, half
their children spoke the language of Ashdod or
of some other people and could not speak the
language of Judah at all. 25So I confronted them
and called down curses on them. I beat some of
them and pulled out their hair. I made them
swear in the name of God that they would not let
their children intermarry with the pagan people
of the land.
26"Wasn't this exactly what led King Solomon
of Israel into sin?" I demanded. "There was no
king from any nation who could compare to him,
and God loved him and made him king over all
Israel. But even he was led into sin by his foreign
wives. 27How could you even think of committing this sinful deed and acting unfaithfully toward God by marrying foreign women?"
28One of the sons of Joiada son of Eliashib
the high priest had married a daughter of Sanballat the Horonite, so I banished him from my
presence.

29Remember them, O my God, for they have
defiled the priesthood and the solemn vows
of the priests and Levites.

30So I purged out everything foreign and assigned tasks to the priests and Levites, making
certain that each knew his work. 31I also made
sure that the supply of wood for the altar and the
first portions of the harvest were brought at the
proper times.

Remember this in my favor, O my God.

ESTHER More Than Just a Pretty Face

Look for 1 hidden message in Esther!

The book of Esther tells the story of a *really* courageous woman. Find out how she

- **USED HER BEAUTY *AND* HER BRAINS**
- **BECAME QUEEN**
- **TRICKED AN EVIL GUY**
- **RISKED EVERYTHING TO SAVE HER PEOPLE**
- **HELPED START A CELEBRATION**

Casting Call

When the king of Persia wanted a new queen, he sent out a decree to bring all the beautiful women in the kingdom to his palace. **Guess who won the job? Find out in Esther 2:16-17.**

Family Affairs

Queen Esther had a good advisor in her older cousin, Mordecai. **Read Esther 2:20 to find out what advice he gave her.**

The Secret's Out!

Mordecai, who had become a palace official, discovered a secret plot. **Check out Esther 2:21-23 to find out who the plot was against and what happened.**

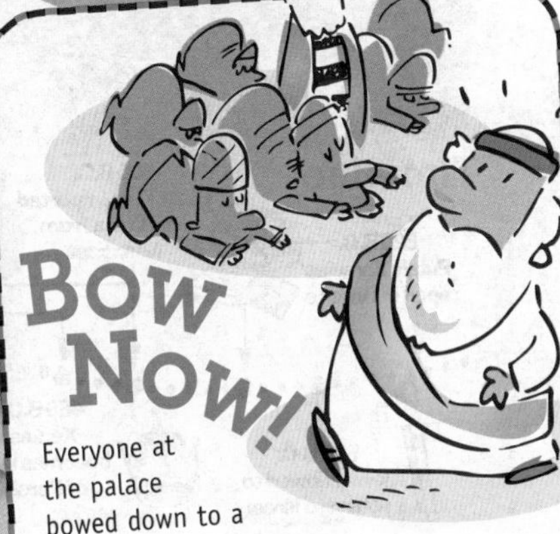

Bow Now!

Everyone at the palace bowed down to a guy named Haman, second in command to the king. Everyone, that is, except Mordecai. **Read Esther 3:5-6 to find out what Haman decided to do about the situation.**

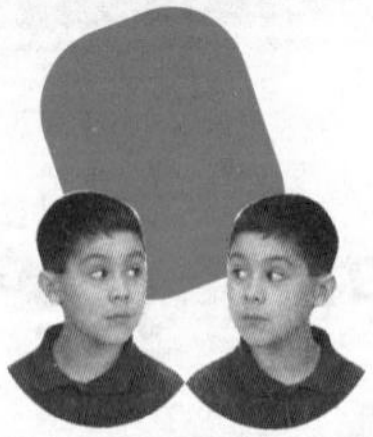

Mistaken Identity

OK, one guy deserved to be honored by the king. The king asked another guy how to honor the mystery guy. The other guy thought he was the mystery guy. But was he? **Read Esther 6:6-12 to find out who got honored and who was in for a big surprise!**

Esther to the Rescue

Mordecai told Esther about a plot to kill all the Jews. Esther knew she couldn't stand by and let her people be destroyed. But the only way she could help might get her killed. **Find out if she had the courage to act in Esther 4:16.**

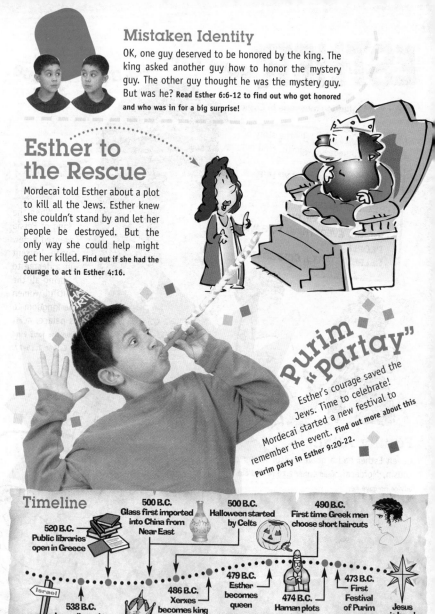

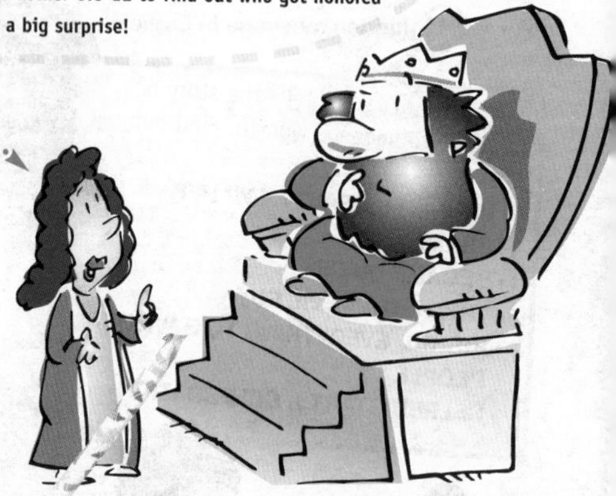

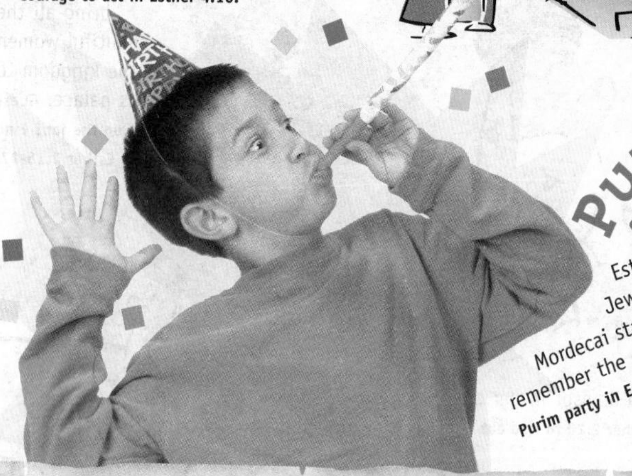

Purim "Partay"

Esther's courage saved the Jews. Time to celebrate! Mordecai started a new festival to remember the event. **Find out more about this Purim party in Esther 9:20-22.**

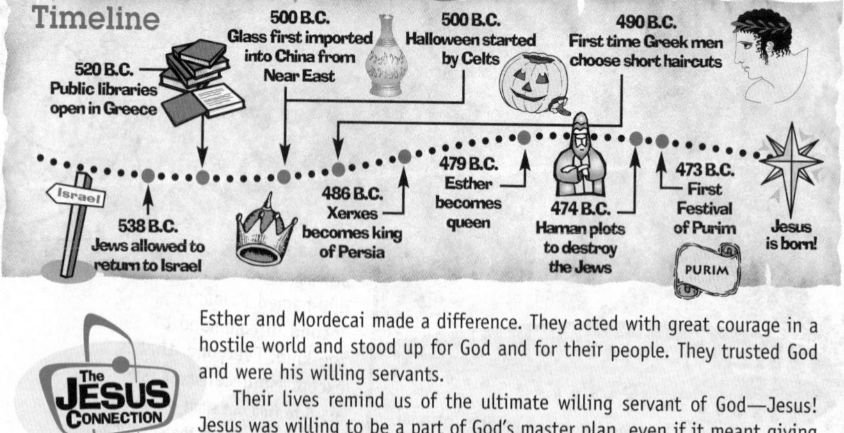

Timeline

- 538 B.C. Jews allowed to return to Israel
- 520 B.C. Public libraries open in Greece
- 500 B.C. Glass first imported into China from Near East
- 500 B.C. Halloween started by Celts
- 490 B.C. First time Greek men choose short haircuts
- 486 B.C. Xerxes becomes king of Persia
- 479 B.C. Esther becomes queen
- 474 B.C. Haman plots to destroy the Jews
- 473 B.C. First Festival of Purim
- Jesus is born!

Esther and Mordecai made a difference. They acted with great courage in a hostile world and stood up for God and for their people. They trusted God and were his willing servants.

Their lives remind us of the ultimate willing servant of God—Jesus! Jesus was willing to be a part of God's master plan, even if it meant giving up his life for us. While Esther and Mordecai made a difference for the Jews of their time, Jesus made the difference for *all* people for *all* time. **Jesus makes the eternal difference!**

CHAPTER 1
The King's Banquet
These events happened in the days of King
Xerxes, who reigned over 127 provinces
stretching from India to Ethiopia. 2At that time
Xerxes ruled his empire from his royal throne at
the fortress of Susa. 3In the third year of his
reign, he gave a banquet for all his nobles and officials. He invited all the military officers of Persia and Media as well as the princes and nobles
of the provinces. 4The celebration lasted
180 days—a tremendous display of the opulent
wealth of his empire and the pomp and splendor
of his majesty.
5When it was all over, the king gave a banquet
for all the people, from the greatest to the least,
who were in the fortress of Susa. It lasted for
seven days and was held in the courtyard of the
palace garden. 6The courtyard was beautifully
decorated with white cotton curtains and blue
hangings, which were fastened with white linen
cords and purple ribbons to silver rings embed-
ded in marble pillars. Gold and silver couches
stood on a mosaic pavement of porphyry, marble, mother-of-pearl, and other costly stones.
7Drinks were served in gold goblets of many
designs, and there was an abundance of royal
wine, reflecting the king's generosity. 8By edict
of the king, no limits were placed on the drinking, for the king had instructed all his palace officials to serve each man as much as he wanted.
9At the same time, Queen Vashti gave a banquet for the women in the royal palace of King
Xerxes.

Queen Vashti Deposed
10On the seventh day of the feast, when King
Xerxes was in high spirits because of the wine, he
told the seven eunuchs who attended him—Me-
human, Biztha, Harbona, Bigtha, Abagtha, Zethar,
and Carcas—11to bring Queen Vashti to him with
the royal crown on her head. He wanted the nobles and all the other men to gaze on her beauty,
for she was a very beautiful woman. 12But when
they conveyed the king's order to Queen Vashti,
she refused to come. This made the king furious,
and he burned with anger.
13He immediately consulted with his wise advisers, who knew all the Persian laws and customs, for he always asked their advice. 14The
names of these men were Carshena, Shethar, Ad-
matha, Tarshish, Meres, Marsena, and Memucan—seven nobles of Persia and Media. They
met with the king regularly and held the highest
positions in the empire.
15"What must be done to Queen Vashti?" the
king demanded. "What penalty does the law
provide for a queen who refuses to obey the
king's orders, properly sent through his eunuchs?"
16Memucan answered the king and his nobles, "Queen Vashti has wronged not only the
king but also every noble and citizen throughout
your empire. 17Women everywhere will begin to
despise their husbands when they learn that
Queen Vashti has refused to appear before the
king. 18Before this day is out, the wives of all the
king's nobles throughout Persia and Media will
hear what the queen did and will start treating
their husbands the same way. There will be no
end to their contempt and anger.
19"So if it please the king, we suggest that you
issue a written decree, a law of the Persians and
Medes that cannot be revoked. It should order
that Queen Vashti be forever banished from the
presence of King Xerxes, and that the king
should choose another queen more worthy than
she. 20When this decree is published throughout the king's vast empire, husbands everywhere,
whatever their rank, will receive proper respect
from their wives!"
21The king and his nobles thought this made
good sense, so he followed Memucan's counsel.
22He sent letters to all parts of the empire, to
each province in its own script and language,
proclaiming that every man should be the ruler
of his own home and should say whatever he
pleases.

CHAPTER 2
Esther Becomes Queen
But after Xerxes' anger had subsided, he began
thinking about Vashti and what she had done
and the decree he had made. 2So his personal attendants suggested, "Let us search the empire to
find beautiful young virgins for the king. 3Let the
king appoint agents in each province to bring
these beautiful young women into the royal
harem at the fortress of Susa. Hegai, the king's
eunuch in charge of the harem, will see that they
are all given beauty treatments. 4After that, the
young woman who most pleases the king will be
made queen instead of Vashti." This advice was
very appealing to the king, so he put the plan into
effect.
5At that time there was a Jewish man in the
fortress of Susa whose name was Mordecai son
of Jair. He was from the tribe of Benjamin and
was a descendant of Kish and Shimei. 6His
family had been among those who, with King

Jehoiachin of Judah, had been exiled from Jerusalem to Babylon by King Nebuchadnezzar. 7This man had a very beautiful and lovely young cousin, Hadassah, who was also called Esther. When her father and mother died, Mordecai adopted her into his family and raised her as his own daughter.

8As a result of the king's decree, Esther, along with many other young women, was brought to the king's harem at the fortress of Susa and placed in Hegai's care. 9Hegai was very impressed with Esther and treated her kindly. He quickly ordered a special menu for her and provided her with beauty treatments. He also assigned her seven maids specially chosen from the king's palace, and he moved her and her maids into the best place in the harem.

10Esther had not told anyone of her nationality and family background, because Mordecai had directed her not to do so. 11Every day Mordecai would take a walk near the courtyard of the harem to find out about Esther and what was happening to her.

12Before each young woman was taken to the king's bed, she was given the prescribed twelve months of beauty treatments—six months with oil of myrrh, followed by six months with special perfumes and ointments. 13When it was time for her to go to the king's palace, she was given her choice of whatever clothing or jewelry she wanted to take from the harem. 14That evening she was taken to the king's private rooms, and the next morning she was brought to the second harem, where the king's wives lived. There she would be under the care of Shaashgaz, the king's eunuch in charge of the concubines. She would never go to the king again unless he had especially enjoyed her and requested her by name.

15Esther was the daughter of Abihail, who was Mordecai's uncle. (Mordecai had adopted his younger cousin Esther.) When it was Esther's turn to go to the king, she accepted the advice of Hegai, the eunuch in charge of the harem. She asked for nothing except what he suggested, and she was admired by everyone who saw her.

16Esther was taken to King Xerxes at the royal palace in early winter of the seventh year of his reign. 17And the king loved Esther more than any of the other young women. He was so delighted with her that he set the royal crown on her head and declared her queen instead of Vashti. 18To celebrate the occasion, he gave a great banquet in Esther's honor for all his nobles and officials, declaring a public holiday for the provinces and giving generous gifts to everyone.

19Even after all the young women had been transferred to the second harem and Mordecai had become a palace official, 20Esther continued to keep her family background and nationality a secret. She was still following Mordecai's directions, just as she did when she lived in his home.

Mordecai's Loyalty to the King

21One day as Mordecai was on duty at the king's gate, two of the king's eunuchs, Bigthana and Teresh—who were guards at the door of the king's private quarters—became angry at King Xerxes and plotted to assassinate him. 22But Mordecai heard about the plot and gave the information to Queen Esther. She then told the king about it and gave Mordecai credit for the report. 23When an investigation was made and Mordecai's story was found to be true, the two men were impaled on a sharpened pole. This was all recorded in *The Book of the History of King Xerxes' Reign*.

CHAPTER 3

Haman's Plot against the Jews

Some time later King Xerxes promoted Haman son of Hammedatha the Agagite over all the other nobles, making him the most powerful official in the empire. 2All the king's officials would bow down before Haman to show him respect whenever he passed by, for so the king had commanded. But Mordecai refused to bow down or show him respect.

3Then the palace officials at the king's gate asked Mordecai, "Why are you disobeying the king's command?" 4They spoke to him day after day, but still he refused to comply with the order. So they spoke to Haman about this to see if he would tolerate Mordecai's conduct, since Mordecai had told them he was a Jew.

5When Haman saw that Mordecai would not bow down or show him respect, he was filled with rage. 6He had learned of Mordecai's nationality, so he decided it was not enough to lay hands on Mordecai alone. Instead, he looked for a way to destroy all the Jews throughout the entire empire of Xerxes.

7So in the month of April, during the twelfth year of King Xerxes' reign, lots were cast in Haman's presence (the lots were called *purim*) to determine the best day and month to take action. And the day selected was March 7, nearly a year later.

8Then Haman approached King Xerxes and said, "There is a certain race of people scattered through all the provinces of your empire who

Courageous Comebacks

Check out the story of Esther in ESTHER 4. Wow! Talk about courageous! Esther spoke up for her people even though she could have been *killed*. Yikes!

Have you ever had to speak up for your faith? Was it hard to get the words out? Next time try one of these Courageous Comebacks!

All that God stuff. It's not true.

That's what I used to think!

Now write your own Courageous Comebacks.

Reading the Bible is for nerds!

When you need help standing up for your faith, read 1 Corinthians 16:13-14.

Going to church is boring!

It takes courage to stand up for your faith. Think of Esther the next time you speak up for God.

keep themselves separate from everyone else.
Their laws are different from those of any other
people, and they refuse to obey the laws of the
king. So it is not in the king's interest to let them
live. 9If it please the king, issue a decree that they
be destroyed, and I will give 10,000 large sacks
of silver to the government administrators to be
deposited in the royal treasury."

10The king agreed, confirming his decision
by removing his signet ring from his finger and
giving it to Haman son of Hammedatha the Agagite, the enemy of the Jews. 11The king said,
"The money and the people are both yours to do
with as you see fit."

12So on April 17 the king's secretaries were
summoned, and a decree was written exactly as
Haman dictated. It was sent to the king's highest
officers, the governors of the respective provinces, and the nobles of each province in their
own scripts and languages. The decree was written in the name of King Xerxes and sealed with
the king's signet ring. 13Dispatches were sent by
swift messengers into all the provinces of the
empire, giving the order that all Jews—young and
old, including women and children—must be
killed, slaughtered, and annihilated on a single
day. This was scheduled to happen on March 7 of
the next year. The property of the Jews would be
given to those who killed them.

14A copy of this decree was to be issued as law
in every province and proclaimed to all peoples,
so that they would be ready to do their duty on
the appointed day. 15At the king's command, the
decree went out by swift messengers, and it was
also proclaimed in the fortress of Susa. Then the
king and Haman sat down to drink, but the city
of Susa fell into confusion.

CHAPTER 4

Mordecai Requests Esther's Help

When Mordecai learned about all that had been
done, he tore his clothes, put on burlap and
ashes, and went out into the city, crying with a
loud and bitter wail. 2He went as far as the gate
of the palace, for no one was allowed to enter the
palace gate while wearing clothes of mourning.
3And as news of the king's decree reached all the
provinces, there was great mourning among the
Jews. They fasted, wept, and wailed, and many
people lay in burlap and ashes.

4When Queen Esther's maids and eunuchs
came and told her about Mordecai, she was
deeply distressed. She sent clothing to him to replace the burlap, but he refused it. 5Then Esther
sent for Hathach, one of the king's eunuchs who
had been appointed as her attendant. She ordered him to go to Mordecai and find out what
was troubling him and why he was in mourning.
6So Hathach went out to Mordecai in the square
in front of the palace gate.

7Mordecai told him the whole story, including the exact amount of money Haman had

promised to pay into the royal treasury for the destruction of the Jews. 8 Mordecai gave Hathach a copy of the decree issued in Susa that called for the death of all Jews. He asked Hathach to show it to Esther and explain the situation to her. He also asked Hathach to direct her to go to the king to beg for mercy and plead for her people. 9 So Hathach returned to Esther with Mordecai's message.

10 Then Esther told Hathach to go back and relay this message to Mordecai: 11 "All the king's officials and even the people in the provinces know that anyone who appears before the king in his inner court without being invited is doomed to die unless the king holds out his gold scepter. And the king has not called for me to come to him for thirty days." 12 So Hathach gave Esther's message to Mordecai.

13 Mordecai sent this reply to Esther: "Don't think for a moment that because you're in the palace you will escape when all other Jews are killed. 14 If you keep quiet at a time like this, deliverance and relief for the Jews will arise from some other place, but you and your relatives will die. Who knows if perhaps you were made queen for just such a time as this?"

15 Then Esther sent this reply to Mordecai: 16 "Go and gather together all the Jews of Susa and fast for me. Do not eat or drink for three days, night or day. My maids and I will do the same. And then, though it is against the law, I will go in to see the king. If I must die, I must die." 17 So Mordecai went away and did everything as Esther had ordered him.

CHAPTER 5

Esther's Request to the King

On the third day of the fast, Esther put on her royal robes and entered the inner court of the palace, just across from the king's hall. The king was sitting on his royal throne, facing the entrance. 2 When he saw Queen Esther standing there in the inner court, he welcomed her and held out the gold scepter to her. So Esther approached and touched the end of the scepter.

3 Then the king asked her, "What do you want, Queen Esther? What is your request? I will give it to you, even if it is half the kingdom!"

4 And Esther replied, "If it please the king, let the king and Haman come today to a banquet I have prepared for the king."

5 The king turned to his attendants and said, "Tell Haman to come quickly to a banquet, as Esther has requested." So the king and Haman went to Esther's banquet.

6 And while they were drinking wine, the king said to Esther, "Now tell me what you really want. What is your request? I will give it to you, even if it is half the kingdom!"

7 Esther replied, "This is my request and deepest wish. 8 If I have found favor with the king, and

FUN fact
Courage for Girls?

In Bible times, men were usually expected to be strong and courageous. But some of the most courageous people in the Bible were women! Whether you're a boy or girl, try this experiment about courage.

Grab a strong magnet, a long nail, and some paper clips. Try to pick up the paper clips with the nail. Now put the magnet on the head of the nail and try it again. What do you know? It works!

When we try to be courageous without God, we're like the nail without the magnet. We can't do much. But God is like the magnet, helping us be strong and courageous!

Check out these courageous women in the Bible!
MARK 5:25-34
LUKE 21:1-4
1 SAMUEL 25:23-35
ESTHER 7:1-8

if it pleases the king to grant my request and do
what I ask, please come with Haman tomorrow
to the banquet I will prepare for you. Then I will
explain what this is all about."

Haman's Plan to Kill Mordecai

9Haman was a happy man as he left the banquet!
But when he saw Mordecai sitting at the palace
gate, not standing up or trembling nervously before him, Haman became furious. 10However, he
restrained himself and went on home.

Then Haman gathered together his friends
and Zeresh, his wife, 11and boasted to them
about his great wealth and his many children. He
bragged about the honors the king had given
him and how he had been promoted over all the
other nobles and officials.

12Then Haman added, "And that's not all!
Queen Esther invited only me and the king himself to the banquet she prepared for us. And she
has invited me to dine with her and the king
again tomorrow!" 13Then he added, "But this is
all worth nothing as long as I see Mordecai the
Jew just sitting there at the palace gate."

14So Haman's wife, Zeresh, and all his friends
suggested, "Set up a sharpened pole that stands
seventy-five feet tall, and in the morning ask the
king to impale Mordecai on it. When this is
done, you can go on your merry way to the banquet with the king." This pleased Haman, and he
ordered the pole set up.

CHAPTER 6
The King Honors Mordecai

That night the king had trouble sleeping, so he
ordered an attendant to bring the book of the
history of his reign so it could be read to him. 2In
those records he discovered an account of how
Mordecai had exposed the plot of Bigthana and
Teresh, two of the eunuchs who guarded the
door to the king's private quarters. They had
plotted to assassinate King Xerxes.

3"What reward or recognition did we ever
give Mordecai for this?" the king asked.

His attendants replied, "Nothing has been
done for him."

4"Who is that in the outer court?" the king in-
quired. As it happened, Haman had just arrived
in the outer court of the palace to ask the king to
impale Mordecai on the pole he had prepared.

5So the attendants replied to the king,
"Haman is out in the court."

"Bring him in," the king ordered. 6So Haman
came in, and the king said, "What should I do to
honor a man who truly pleases me?"

Haman thought to himself, "Whom would the
king wish to honor more than me?" 7So he replied, "If the king wishes to honor someone, 8he
should bring out one of the king's own royal
robes, as well as a horse that the king himself has
ridden—one with a royal emblem on its head.
9Let the robes and the horse be handed over to
one of the king's most noble officials. And let
him see that the man whom the king wishes to
honor is dressed in the king's robes and led
through the city square on the king's horse. Have
the official shout as they go, 'This is what the
king does for someone he wishes to honor!' "

10"Excellent!" the king said to Haman. "Quick!
Take the robes and my horse, and do just as you
have said for Mordecai the Jew, who sits at the
gate of the palace. Leave out nothing you have
suggested!"

11So Haman took the robes and put them on
Mordecai, placed him on the king's own horse,
and led him through the city square, shouting,
"This is what the king does for someone he
wishes to honor!" 12Afterward Mordecai returned to the palace gate, but Haman hurried
home dejected and completely humiliated.

13When Haman told his wife, Zeresh, and all
his friends what had happened, his wise advisers
and his wife said, "Since Mordecai—this man
who has humiliated you—is of Jewish birth, you
will never succeed in your plans against him. It
will be fatal to continue opposing him."

14While they were still talking, the king's eunuchs arrived and quickly took Haman to the
banquet Esther had prepared.

CHAPTER 7
The King Executes Haman

So the king and Haman went to Queen Esther's
banquet. 2On this second occasion, while they
were drinking wine, the king again said to Esther,
"Tell me what you want, Queen Esther. What is
your request? I will give it to you, even if it is half
the kingdom!"

3Queen Esther replied, "If I have found favor
with the king, and if it pleases the king to grant
my request, I ask that my life and the lives of my
people will be spared. 4For my people and I have
been sold to those who would kill, slaughter, and
annihilate us. If we had merely been sold as
slaves, I could remain quiet, for that would be
too trivial a matter to warrant disturbing the
king."

5"Who would do such a thing?" King Xerxes
demanded. "Who would be so presumptuous as
to touch you?"

6 Esther replied, "This wicked Haman is our adversary and our enemy." Haman grew pale with fright before the king and queen. 7 Then the king jumped to his feet in a rage and went out into the palace garden.

Haman, however, stayed behind to plead for his life with Queen Esther, for he knew that the king intended to kill him. 8 In despair he fell on the couch where Queen Esther was reclining, just as the king was returning from the palace garden.

The king exclaimed, "Will he even assault the queen right here in the palace, before my very eyes?" And as soon as the king spoke, his attendants covered Haman's face, signaling his doom.

9 Then Harbona, one of the king's eunuchs, said, "Haman has set up a sharpened pole that stands seventy-five feet tall in his own courtyard. He intended to use it to impale Mordecai, the man who saved the king from assassination."

"Then impale Haman on it!" the king ordered. 10 So they impaled Haman on the pole he had set up for Mordecai, and the king's anger subsided.

CHAPTER 8

A Decree to Help the Jews

On that same day King Xerxes gave the property of Haman, the enemy of the Jews, to Queen Esther. Then Mordecai was brought before the king, for Esther had told the king how they were related. 2 The king took off his signet ring—which he had taken back from Haman—and gave it to Mordecai. And Esther appointed Mordecai to be in charge of Haman's property.

3 Then Esther went again before the king, falling down at his feet and begging him with tears to stop the evil plot devised by Haman the Agagite against the Jews. 4 Again the king held out the gold scepter to Esther. So she rose and stood before him.

5 Esther said, "If it please the king, and if I have found favor with him, and if he thinks it is right, and if I am pleasing to him, let there be a decree that reverses the orders of Haman son of Hammedatha the Agagite, who ordered that Jews throughout all the king's provinces should be destroyed. 6 For how can I endure to see my people and my family slaughtered and destroyed?"

7 Then King Xerxes said to Queen Esther and Mordecai the Jew, "I have given Esther the property of Haman, and he has been impaled on a pole because he tried to destroy the Jews. 8 Now go ahead and send a message to the Jews in the king's name, telling them whatever you want, and seal it with the king's signet ring. But remember that whatever has already been written in the king's name and sealed with his signet ring can never be revoked."

9 So on June 25 the king's secretaries were summoned, and a decree was written exactly as Mordecai dictated. It was sent to the Jews and to the highest officers, the governors, and the nobles of all the 127 provinces stretching from India to Ethiopia. The decree was written in the scripts and languages of all the peoples of the empire, including that of the Jews. 10 The decree was written in the name of King Xerxes and sealed with the king's signet ring. Mordecai sent the dispatches by swift messengers, who rode fast horses especially bred for the king's service.

11 The king's decree gave the Jews in every city authority to unite to defend their lives. They were allowed to kill, slaughter, and annihilate anyone of any nationality or province who might attack them or their children and wives, and to take the property of their enemies. 12 The day chosen for this event throughout all the provinces of King Xerxes was March 7 of the next year.

13 A copy of this decree was to be issued as law in every province and proclaimed to all peoples, so that the Jews would be ready to take revenge on their enemies on the appointed day. 14 So urged on by the king's command, the messengers rode out swiftly on fast horses bred for the king's service. The same decree was also proclaimed in the fortress of Susa.

15 Then Mordecai left the king's presence, wearing the royal robe of blue and white, the great crown of gold, and an outer cloak of fine linen and purple. And the people of Susa celebrated the new decree. 16 The Jews were filled with joy and gladness and were honored everywhere. 17 In every province and city, wherever the king's decree arrived, the Jews rejoiced and had a great celebration and declared a public festival and holiday. And many of the people of the land became Jews themselves, for they feared what the Jews might do to them.

CHAPTER 9

The Victory of the Jews

So on March 7 the two decrees of the king were put into effect. On that day, the enemies of the Jews had hoped to overpower them, but quite the opposite happened. It was the Jews who overpowered their enemies. 2 The Jews gathered in their cities throughout all the king's provinces to attack anyone who tried to harm them. But no one could make a stand against them, for everyone was afraid of them. 3 And all the nobles of the provinces, the highest officers, the governors,

and the royal officials helped the Jews for fear of
Mordecai. 4For Mordecai had been promoted in
the king's palace, and his fame spread throughout
all the provinces as he became more and more
powerful.
5So the Jews went ahead on the appointed day
and struck down their enemies with the sword.
They killed and annihilated their enemies and
did as they pleased with those who hated them.
6In the fortress of Susa itself, the Jews killed
500 men. 7They also killed Parshandatha, Dal-
phon, Aspatha, 8Poratha, Adalia, Aridatha, 9Par-
mashta, Arisai, Aridai, and Vaizatha—10the ten
sons of Haman son of Hammedatha, the enemy
of the Jews. But they did not take any plunder.
11That very day, when the king was informed
of the number of people killed in the fortress of
Susa, 12he called for Queen Esther. He said, "The
Jews have killed 500 men in the fortress of Susa
alone, as well as Haman's ten sons. If they have
done that here, what has happened in the rest of
the provinces? But now, what more do you want?
It will be granted to you; tell me and I will do it."
13Esther responded, "If it please the king, give
the Jews in Susa permission to do again tomorrow as they have done today, and let the bodies of
Haman's ten sons be impaled on a pole."
14So the king agreed, and the decree was announced in Susa. And they impaled the bodies of
Haman's ten sons. 15Then the Jews at Susa gathered together on March 8 and killed 300 more
men, and again they took no plunder.
16Meanwhile, the other Jews throughout the
king's provinces had gathered together to defend their lives. They gained relief from all their
enemies, killing 75,000 of those who hated
them. But they did not take any plunder. 17This
was done throughout the provinces on March 7,
and on March 8 they rested, celebrating their
victory with a day of feasting and gladness.
18(The Jews at Susa killed their enemies on
March 7 and again on March 8, then rested on
March 9, making that their day of feasting and
gladness.) 19So to this day, rural Jews living in remote villages celebrate an annual festival and
holiday on the appointed day in late winter,
when they rejoice and send gifts of food to each
other.

The Festival of Purim

20Mordecai recorded these events and sent letters to the Jews near and far, throughout all the
provinces of King Xerxes, 21calling on them to
celebrate an annual festival on these two days.
22He told them to celebrate these days with
feasting and gladness and by giving gifts of food
to each other and presents to the poor. This
would commemorate a time when the Jews
gained relief from their enemies, when their sorrow was turned into gladness and their mourning into joy.
23So the Jews accepted Mordecai's proposal
and adopted this annual custom. 24Haman son
of Hammedatha the Agagite, the enemy of the
Jews, had plotted to crush and destroy them on
the date determined by casting lots (the lots were
called *purim*). 25But when Esther came before
the king, he issued a decree causing Haman's evil
plot to backfire, and Haman and his sons were
impaled on a sharpened pole. 26That is why this
celebration is called Purim, because it is the ancient word for casting lots.

So because of Mordecai's letter and because
of what they had experienced, 27the Jews
throughout the realm agreed to inaugurate this
tradition and to pass it on to their descendants
and to all who became Jews. They declared they
would never fail to celebrate these two prescribed days at the appointed time each year.
28These days would be remembered and kept
from generation to generation and celebrated by
every family throughout the provinces and cities
of the empire. This Festival of Purim would never
cease to be celebrated among the Jews, nor
would the memory of what happened ever die
out among their descendants.
29Then Queen Esther, the daughter of Abihail,
along with Mordecai the Jew, wrote another letter putting the queen's full authority behind
Mordecai's letter to establish the Festival of Purim. 30Letters wishing peace and security were
sent to the Jews throughout the 127 provinces
of the empire of Xerxes. 31These letters established the Festival of Purim—an annual celebration of these days at the appointed time, decreed
by both Mordecai the Jew and Queen Esther.
(The people decided to observe this festival, just
as they had decided for themselves and their descendants to establish the times of fasting and
mourning.) 32So the command of Esther confirmed the practices of Purim, and it was all
written down in the records.

CHAPTER 10

The Greatness of Xerxes and Mordecai

King Xerxes imposed a tribute throughout his
empire, even to the distant coastlands. 2His
great achievements and the full account of the
greatness of Mordecai, whom the king had

promoted, are recorded in *The Book of the His-*
tory of the Kings of Media and Persia. 3 Mordecai the Jew became the prime minister, with
authority next to that of King Xerxes himself. He
was very great among the Jews, who held him in
high esteem, because he continued to work for
the good of his people and to speak up for the
welfare of all their descendants.

JOB Talk About a Bad Day!

Look for 2 hidden messages in Job!

The book of Job (it's pronounced jobe) could be called "Job and the Terrible, Rotten, Miserable, Very-Bad-for-a-While Life." Discover how Job

- WAS ATTACKED BY SATAN
- LOST ALL HIS KIDS AND ALL HIS STUFF
- WAS COVERED WITH SORES
- GOT SICK OF HIS FRIENDS
- HAD QUITE A CONVERSATION WITH GOD
- STILL HAD A HAPPY ENDING

Is There a Doctor in the House?

Next, Satan struck Job with a horrible case of sores all over his body. Gross! Satan was still trying to make Job turn against God. **Find out what happened in Job 2:7-10.**

The Bad Day Begins

Rich. Great family. Good man. That's what people would have said about Job. But then the bad day started. **Read Job 1:13-22 to see how Job's life changed**

***big* time.**

Words From a Whirlwind

God answered Job's questions, and he did it in an unusual way! And what God said was even more amazing! Want to get a glimpse of God's power and majesty? **Just read Job 38–41!**

All's Well That Ends Well

Job's troubles didn't last forever. Things got better and better. **Check out the details in Job 42:7-17.**

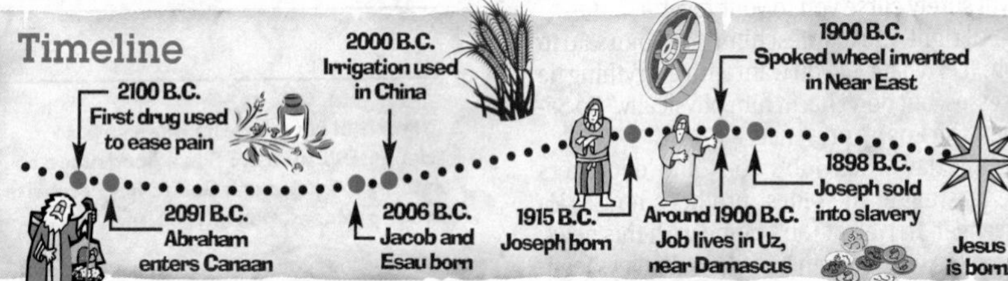

Timeline

- 2100 B.C. First drug used to ease pain
- 2091 B.C. Abraham enters Canaan
- 2006 B.C. Jacob and Esau born
- 2000 B.C. Irrigation used in China
- 1915 B.C. Joseph born
- Around 1900 B.C. Job lives in Uz, near Damascus
- 1900 B.C. Spoked wheel invented in Near East
- 1898 B.C. Joseph sold into slavery
- Jesus is born!

Job questioned God—a lot. Job asked how he could approach God. (Jesus provides the way.) Job asked about life after death. (Jesus makes eternal life with God possible.) Job asked what was important in life. (Jesus tells us that believing in him is the most important thing.)

Still, sometimes we all feel like Job—lots of problems and we don't know why. Job teaches us that God is in control even when difficult things happen to us or those we love. **We can be sure he's always working behind the scenes for our good (see ROMANS 8:28)!**

Job 1 . . . page 498

CHAPTER 1

Prologue

There once was a man named Job who lived in the land of Uz. He was blameless—a man of complete integrity. He feared God and stayed away from evil. 2He had seven sons and three daughters. 3He owned 7,000 sheep, 3,000 camels, 500 teams of oxen, and 500 female donkeys. He also had many servants. He was, in fact, the richest person in that entire area.

4Job's sons would take turns preparing feasts in their homes, and they would also invite their three sisters to celebrate with them. 5When these celebrations ended—sometimes after several days—Job would purify his children. He would get up early in the morning and offer a burnt offering for each of them. For Job said to himself, "Perhaps my children have sinned and have cursed God in their hearts." This was Job's regular practice.

Job's First Test

6One day the members of the heavenly court came to present themselves before the LORD, and the Accuser, Satan, came with them. 7"Where have you come from?" the LORD asked Satan.

Satan answered the LORD, "I have been patrolling the earth, watching everything that's going on."

8Then the LORD asked Satan, "Have you noticed my servant Job? He is the finest man in all the earth. He is blameless—a man of complete integrity. He fears God and stays away from evil."

9Satan replied to the LORD, "Yes, but Job has good reason to fear God. 10You have always put a wall of protection around him and his home and his property. You have made him prosper in everything he does. Look how rich he is! 11But reach out and take away everything he has, and he will surely curse you to your face!"

12"All right, you may test him," the LORD said to Satan. "Do whatever you want with everything he possesses, but don't harm him physically." So Satan left the LORD's presence.

13One day when Job's sons and daughters were feasting at the oldest brother's house, 14a messenger arrived at Job's home with this news: "Your oxen were plowing, with the donkeys feeding beside them, 15when the Sabeans raided us. They stole all the animals and killed all the farmhands. I am the only one who escaped to tell you."

16While he was still speaking, another messenger arrived with this news: "The fire of God has fallen from heaven and burned up your

Good Advice

Have you ever felt like your life was a mess?

Well, just read Job 1 and 2! Job's life got pretty rough! And Job's friends told him it was all his fault. Sometimes friends give good advice, and sometimes they don't. But you can *always* trust your best friend, God!

1. **Here's a good way to handle a tough problem. First, write the problem here.**

   ____

   ____

2. **Next, ask several people what to do about your problem. Parents, teachers, friends, and pastors are all good choices. Write the names of who you talked to here.**

   ____

   ____

   ____

3. **Then find out what the Bible says to do. (PROVERBS 3:5-6 is a good place to start.) Pray and ask God to help you with your problem. He will, you know!**

4. **After God helps you, write what he did!**

   ____

   ____

   ____

sheep and all the shepherds. I am the only one
who escaped to tell you."
17While he was still speaking, a third messenger arrived with this news: "Three bands of Chaldean raiders have stolen your camels and killed
your servants. I am the only one who escaped to
tell you."
18While he was still speaking, another messenger arrived with this news: "Your sons and
daughters were feasting in their oldest brother's
home. 19Suddenly, a powerful wind swept in
from the wilderness and hit the house on all
sides. The house collapsed, and all your children
are dead. I am the only one who escaped to tell
you."
20Job stood up and tore his robe in grief. Then
he shaved his head and fell to the ground to worship. 21He said,

"I came naked from my mother's womb,
and I will be naked when I leave.
The LORD gave me what I had,
and the LORD has taken it away.
Praise the name of the LORD!"

22In all of this, Job did not sin by blaming God.

CHAPTER 2
Job's Second Test

One day the members of the heavenly court
came again to present themselves before the
LORD, and the Accuser, Satan, came with them.
2"Where have you come from?" the LORD asked
Satan.
Satan answered the LORD, "I have been patrolling the earth, watching everything that's
going on."
3Then the LORD asked Satan, "Have you noticed my servant Job? He is the finest man in all
the earth. He is blameless—a man of complete
integrity. He fears God and stays away from evil.
And he has maintained his integrity, even
though you urged me to harm him without
cause."
4Satan replied to the LORD, "Skin for skin! A
man will give up everything he has to save his
life. 5But reach out and take away his health, and
he will surely curse you to your face!"
6"All right, do with him as you please," the
LORD said to Satan. "But spare his life." 7So Satan
left the LORD's presence, and he struck Job with
terrible boils from head to foot.
8Job scraped his skin with a piece of broken
pottery as he sat among the ashes. 9His wife said
to him, "Are you still trying to maintain your integrity? Curse God and die."
10But Job replied, "You talk like a foolish
woman. Should we accept only good things from
the hand of God and never anything bad?" So in
all this, Job said nothing wrong.

Job's Three Friends Share His Anguish

11When three of Job's friends heard of the tragedy he had suffered, they got together and traveled from their homes to comfort and console
him. Their names were Eliphaz the Temanite,
Bildad the Shuhite, and Zophar the Naamathite.
12When they saw Job from a distance, they
scarcely recognized him. Wailing loudly, they
tore their robes and threw dust into the air over
their heads to show their grief. 13Then they sat
on the ground with him for seven days and
nights. No one said a word to Job, for they saw
that his suffering was too great for words.

CHAPTER 3
Job's First Speech

At last Job spoke, and he cursed the day of his
birth. 2He said:

3 "Let the day of my birth be erased,
and the night I was conceived.
4 Let that day be turned to darkness.
Let it be lost even to God on high,
and let no light shine on it.
5 Let the darkness and utter gloom claim that
day for its own.
Let a black cloud overshadow it,
and let the darkness terrify it.
6 Let that night be blotted off the calendar,
never again to be counted among the days
of the year,
never again to appear among the months.
7 Let that night be childless.
Let it have no joy.
8 Let those who are experts at cursing—
whose cursing could rouse Leviathan—
curse that day.
9 Let its morning stars remain dark.
Let it hope for light, but in vain;
may it never see the morning light.
10 Curse that day for failing to shut my
mother's womb,
for letting me be born to see all this
trouble.

11 "Why wasn't I born dead?
Why didn't I die as I came from the
womb?
12 Why was I laid on my mother's lap?
Why did she nurse me at her breasts?

13 Had I died at birth, I would now be at peace.
I would be asleep and at rest.
14 I would rest with the world's kings and prime ministers,
whose great buildings now lie in ruins.
15 I would rest with princes, rich in gold,
whose palaces were filled with silver.
16 Why wasn't I buried like a stillborn child,
like a baby who never lives to see the light?
17 For in death the wicked cause no trouble,
and the weary are at rest.
18 Even captives are at ease in death,
with no guards to curse them.
19 Rich and poor are both there,
and the slave is free from his master.

20 "Oh, why give light to those in misery,
and life to those who are bitter?
21 They long for death, and it won't come.
They search for death more eagerly than for hidden treasure.
22 They're filled with joy when they finally die,
and rejoice when they find the grave.
23 Why is life given to those with no future,
those God has surrounded with difficulties?
24 I cannot eat for sighing;
my groans pour out like water.
25 What I always feared has happened to me.
What I dreaded has come true.
26 I have no peace, no quietness.
I have no rest; only trouble comes."

CHAPTER 4
Eliphaz's First Response to Job

Then Eliphaz the Temanite replied to Job:

2 "Will you be patient and let me say a word?
For who could keep from speaking out?

3 "In the past you have encouraged many people;
you have strengthened those who were weak.
4 Your words have supported those who were falling;
you encouraged those with shaky knees.
5 But now when trouble strikes, you lose heart.
You are terrified when it touches you.
6 Doesn't your reverence for God give you confidence?
Doesn't your life of integrity give you hope?

7 "Stop and think! Do the innocent die?
When have the upright been destroyed?
8 My experience shows that those who plant trouble
and cultivate evil will harvest the same.
9 A breath from God destroys them.
They vanish in a blast of his anger.
10 The lion roars and the wildcat snarls,
but the teeth of strong lions will be broken.
11 The fierce lion will starve for lack of prey,
and the cubs of the lioness will be scattered.

12 "This truth was given to me in secret,
as though whispered in my ear.
13 It came to me in a disturbing vision at night,
when people are in a deep sleep.
14 Fear gripped me,
and my bones trembled.
15 A spirit swept past my face,
and my hair stood on end.
16 The spirit stopped, but I couldn't see its shape.
There was a form before my eyes.
In the silence I heard a voice say,
17 'Can a mortal be innocent before God?
Can anyone be pure before the Creator?'

18 "If God does not trust his own angels
and has charged his messengers with foolishness,
19 how much less will he trust people made of clay!
They are made of dust, crushed as easily as a moth.
20 They are alive in the morning but dead by evening,
gone forever without a trace.
21 Their tent-cords are pulled and the tent collapses,
and they die in ignorance.

CHAPTER 5
Eliphaz's Response Continues

1 "Cry for help, but will anyone answer you?
Which of the angels will help you?
2 Surely resentment destroys the fool,
and jealousy kills the simple.
3 I have seen that fools may be successful for the moment,
but then comes sudden disaster.
4 Their children are abandoned far from help;
they are crushed in court with no one to defend them.
5 The hungry devour their harvest,
even when it is guarded by brambles.
The thirsty pant after their wealth.

6 But evil does not spring from the soil,
and trouble does not sprout from the earth.
7 People are born for trouble
as readily as sparks fly up from a fire.

8 "If I were you, I would go to God
and present my case to him.
9 He does great things too marvelous to understand.
He performs countless miracles.
10 He gives rain for the earth
and water for the fields.
11 He gives prosperity to the poor
and protects those who suffer.
12 He frustrates the plans of schemers
so the work of their hands will not succeed.
13 He traps the wise in their own cleverness
so their cunning schemes are thwarted.
14 They find it is dark in the daytime,
and they grope at noon as if it were night.
15 He rescues the poor from the cutting words of the strong,
and rescues them from the clutches of the powerful.
16 And so at last the poor have hope,
and the snapping jaws of the wicked are shut.

17 "But consider the joy of those corrected by God!
Do not despise the discipline of the Almighty when you sin.
18 For though he wounds, he also bandages.
He strikes, but his hands also heal.
19 From six disasters he will rescue you;
even in the seventh, he will keep you from evil.
20 He will save you from death in time of famine,
from the power of the sword in time of war.
21 You will be safe from slander
and have no fear when destruction comes.
22 You will laugh at destruction and famine;
wild animals will not terrify you.
23 You will be at peace with the stones of the field,
and its wild animals will be at peace with you.
24 You will know that your home is safe.
When you survey your possessions,
nothing will be missing.
25 You will have many children;
your descendants will be as plentiful as grass!
26 You will go to the grave at a ripe old age,
like a sheaf of grain harvested at the proper time!

27 "We have studied life and found all this to be true.
Listen to my counsel, and apply it to yourself."

CHAPTER 6

Job's Second Speech: A Response to Eliphaz

Then Job spoke again:

2 "If my misery could be weighed
and my troubles be put on the scales,
3 they would outweigh all the sands of the sea.
That is why I spoke impulsively.
4 For the Almighty has struck me down with his arrows.
Their poison infects my spirit.
God's terrors are lined up against me.
5 Don't I have a right to complain?
Don't wild donkeys bray when they find no grass,
and oxen bellow when they have no food?
6 Don't people complain about unsalted food?
Does anyone want the tasteless white of an egg?
7 My appetite disappears when I look at it;
I gag at the thought of eating it!

8 "Oh, that I might have my request,
that God would grant my desire.
9 I wish he would crush me.
I wish he would reach out his hand and kill me.
10 At least I can take comfort in this:
Despite the pain,
I have not denied the words of the Holy One.
11 But I don't have the strength to endure.
I have nothing to live for.
12 Do I have the strength of a stone?
Is my body made of bronze?
13 No, I am utterly helpless,
without any chance of success.

14 "One should be kind to a fainting friend,
but you accuse me without any fear of the Almighty.
15 My brothers, you have proved as unreliable as a seasonal brook
that overflows its banks in the spring

16 when it is swollen with ice and melting
snow.
17 But when the hot weather arrives, the water
disappears.
The brook vanishes in the heat.
18 The caravans turn aside to be refreshed,
but there is nothing to drink, so they die.
19 The caravans from Tema search for this
water;
the travelers from Sheba hope to find it.
20 They count on it but are disappointed.
When they arrive, their hopes are dashed.
21 You, too, have given no help.
You have seen my calamity, and you are
afraid.
22 But why? Have I ever asked you for a gift?
Have I begged for anything of yours for
myself?
23 Have I asked you to rescue me from my
enemies,
or to save me from ruthless people?
24 Teach me, and I will keep quiet.
Show me what I have done wrong.
25 Honest words can be painful,
but what do your criticisms amount to?
26 Do you think your words are convincing
when you disregard my cry of
desperation?
27 You would even send an orphan into slavery
or sell a friend.
28 Look at me!
Would I lie to your face?
29 Stop assuming my guilt,
for I have done no wrong.
30 Do you think I am lying?
Don't I know the difference between right
and wrong?

CHAPTER 7

1 "Is not all human life a struggle?
Our lives are like that of a hired hand,
2 like a worker who longs for the shade,
like a servant waiting to be paid.
3 I, too, have been assigned months of futility,
long and weary nights of misery.
4 Lying in bed, I think, 'When will it be
morning?'
But the night drags on, and I toss till dawn.
5 My body is covered with maggots and scabs.
My skin breaks open, oozing with pus.

Job Cries Out to God

6 "My days fly faster than a weaver's shuttle.
They end without hope.
7 O God, remember that my life is but a breath,
and I will never again feel happiness.
8 You see me now, but not for long.
You will look for me, but I will be gone.
9 Just as a cloud dissipates and vanishes,
those who die will not come back.
10 They are gone forever from their home—
never to be seen again.

11 "I cannot keep from speaking.
I must express my anguish.
My bitter soul must complain.
12 Am I a sea monster or a dragon
that you must place me under guard?
13 I think, 'My bed will comfort me,
and sleep will ease my misery,'
14 but then you shatter me with dreams
and terrify me with visions.
15 I would rather be strangled—
rather die than suffer like this.
16 I hate my life and don't want to go on living.
Oh, leave me alone for my few remaining
days.

17 "What are people, that you should make
so much of us,
that you should think of us so often?
18 For you examine us every morning
and test us every moment.
19 Why won't you leave me alone,
at least long enough for me to swallow!
20 If I have sinned, what have I done to you,
O watcher of all humanity?
Why make me your target?
Am I a burden to you?
21 Why not just forgive my sin
and take away my guilt?
For soon I will lie down in the dust and die.
When you look for me, I will be gone."

CHAPTER 8

Bildad's First Response to Job

Then Bildad the Shuhite replied to Job:
2 "How long will you go on like this?
You sound like a blustering wind.
3 Does God twist justice?
Does the Almighty twist what is right?
4 Your children must have sinned against him,
so their punishment was well deserved.
5 But if you pray to God
and seek the favor of the Almighty,
6 and if you are pure and live with integrity,
he will surely rise up and restore your
happy home.
7 And though you started with little,
you will end with much.

8 "Just ask the previous generation.
Pay attention to the experience of our ancestors.
9 For we were born but yesterday and know nothing.
Our days on earth are as fleeting as a shadow.
10 But those who came before us will teach you.
They will teach you the wisdom of old.

11 "Can papyrus reeds grow tall without a marsh?
Can marsh grass flourish without water?
12 While they are still flowering, not ready to be cut,
they begin to wither more quickly than grass.
13 The same happens to all who forget God.
The hopes of the godless evaporate.
14 Their confidence hangs by a thread.
They are leaning on a spider's web.
15 They cling to their home for security, but it won't last.
They try to hold it tight, but it will not endure.
16 The godless seem like a lush plant growing in the sunshine,
its branches spreading across the garden.
17 Its roots grow down through a pile of stones;
it takes hold on a bed of rocks.
18 But when it is uprooted,
it's as though it never existed!
19 That's the end of its life,
and others spring up from the earth to replace it.

20 "But look, God will not reject a person of integrity,
nor will he lend a hand to the wicked.
21 He will once again fill your mouth with laughter
and your lips with shouts of joy.
22 Those who hate you will be clothed with shame,
and the home of the wicked will be destroyed."

CHAPTER 9
Job's Third Speech: A Response to Bildad

Then Job spoke again:

2 "Yes, I know all this is true in principle.
But how can a person be declared innocent in God's sight?
3 If someone wanted to take God to court,
would it be possible to answer him even once in a thousand times?
4 For God is so wise and so mighty.
Who has ever challenged him successfully?

5 "Without warning, he moves the mountains,
overturning them in his anger.
6 He shakes the earth from its place,
and its foundations tremble.
7 If he commands it, the sun won't rise
and the stars won't shine.
8 He alone has spread out the heavens
and marches on the waves of the sea.
9 He made all the stars—the Bear and Orion,
the Pleiades and the constellations of the southern sky.
10 He does great things too marvelous to understand.
He performs countless miracles.

11 "Yet when he comes near, I cannot see him.
When he moves by, I do not see him go.
12 If he snatches someone in death, who can stop him?
Who dares to ask, 'What are you doing?'
13 And God does not restrain his anger.
Even the monsters of the sea are crushed beneath his feet.

14 "So who am I, that I should try to answer God
or even reason with him?
15 Even if I were right, I would have no defense.
I could only plead for mercy.
16 And even if I summoned him and he responded,
I'm not sure he would listen to me.
17 For he attacks me with a storm
and repeatedly wounds me without cause.
18 He will not let me catch my breath,
but fills me instead with bitter sorrows.
19 If it's a question of strength, he's the strong one.
If it's a matter of justice, who dares to summon him to court?
20 Though I am innocent, my own mouth would pronounce me guilty.
Though I am blameless, it would prove me wicked.

21 "I am innocent,
but it makes no difference to me—
I despise my life.
22 Innocent or wicked, it is all the same to God.
That's why I say, 'He destroys both the blameless and the wicked.'

23 When a plague sweeps through,
he laughs at the death of the innocent.
24 The whole earth is in the hands of the wicked,
and God blinds the eyes of the judges.
If he's not the one who does it, who is?

25 "My life passes more swiftly than a runner.
It flees away without a glimpse of happiness.
26 It disappears like a swift papyrus boat,
like an eagle swooping down on its prey.
27 If I decided to forget my complaints,
to put away my sad face and be cheerful,
28 I would still dread all the pain,
for I know you will not find me innocent, O God.
29 Whatever happens, I will be found guilty.
So what's the use of trying?
30 Even if I were to wash myself with soap
and clean my hands with lye,
31 you would plunge me into a muddy ditch,
and my own filthy clothing would hate me.
32 "God is not a mortal like me,
so I cannot argue with him or take him to trial.
33 If only there were a mediator between us,
someone who could bring us together.
34 The mediator could make God stop beating me,
and I would no longer live in terror of his punishment.
35 Then I could speak to him without fear,
but I cannot do that in my own strength.

CHAPTER 10
Job Frames His Plea to God

1 "I am disgusted with my life.
Let me complain freely.
My bitter soul must complain.
2 I will say to God, 'Don't simply condemn me—
tell me the charge you are bringing against me.
3 What do you gain by oppressing me?
Why do you reject me, the work of your own hands,
while smiling on the schemes of the wicked?
4 Are your eyes like those of a human?
Do you see things only as people see them?
5 Is your lifetime only as long as ours?
Is your life so short
6 that you must quickly probe for my guilt
and search for my sin?
7 Although you know I am not guilty,
no one can rescue me from your hands.

8 "'You formed me with your hands; you made me,
yet now you completely destroy me.
9 Remember that you made me from dust—
will you turn me back to dust so soon?
10 You guided my conception
and formed me in the womb.
11 You clothed me with skin and flesh,
and you knit my bones and sinews together.
12 You gave me life and showed me your unfailing love.
My life was preserved by your care.

13 "'Yet your real motive—
your true intent—
14 was to watch me, and if I sinned,
you would not forgive my guilt.
15 If I am guilty, too bad for me;
and even if I'm innocent, I can't hold my head high,
because I am filled with shame and misery.
16 And if I hold my head high, you hunt me like a lion
and display your awesome power against me.
17 Again and again you witness against me.
You pour out your growing anger on me
and bring fresh armies against me.

18 "'Why, then, did you deliver me from my mother's womb?
Why didn't you let me die at birth?
19 It would be as though I had never existed,
going directly from the womb to the grave.
20 I have only a few days left, so leave me alone,
that I may have a moment of comfort
21 before I leave—never to return—
for the land of darkness and utter gloom.
22 It is a land as dark as midnight,
a land of gloom and confusion,
where even the light is dark as midnight.'"

CHAPTER 11
Zophar's First Response to Job

Then Zophar the Naamathite replied to Job:
2 "Shouldn't someone answer this torrent of words?
Is a person proved innocent just by a lot of talking?
3 Should I remain silent while you babble on?

When you mock God, shouldn't someone
make you ashamed?
4 You claim, 'My beliefs are pure,'
and 'I am clean in the sight of God.'
5 If only God would speak;
if only he would tell you what he thinks!
6 If only he would tell you the secrets of
wisdom,
for true wisdom is not a simple matter.
Listen! God is doubtless punishing you
far less than you deserve!
7 "Can you solve the mysteries of God?
Can you discover everything about the
Almighty?
8 Such knowledge is higher than the heavens—
and who are you?
It is deeper than the underworld—
what do you know?
9 It is broader than the earth
and wider than the sea.
10 If God comes and puts a person in prison
or calls the court to order, who can stop
him?
11 For he knows those who are false,
and he takes note of all their sins.
12 An empty-headed person won't become wise
any more than a wild donkey can bear a
human child.

13 "If only you would prepare your heart
and lift up your hands to him in prayer!
14 Get rid of your sins,
and leave all iniquity behind you.
15 Then your face will brighten with innocence.
You will be strong and free of fear.
16 You will forget your misery;
it will be like water flowing away.
17 Your life will be brighter than the noonday.
Even darkness will be as bright as
morning.
18 Having hope will give you courage.
You will be protected and will rest
in safety.
19 You will lie down unafraid,
and many will look to you for help.
20 But the wicked will be blinded.
They will have no escape.
Their only hope is death."

Think of something sad that happened to you. How did you react?

Look at these passages to see how Bible-times people reacted to sadness and grief.

- **Jacob lost his son Joseph —GENESIS 37:34.**
- **King Saul and David's best friend, Jonathan, died —2 SAMUEL 1:11-12.**
- **Job lost everything he had —JOB 1:20.**

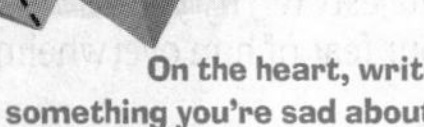

1 Cut a heart from construction paper.

2 On the heart, write something you're sad about.

3 Tear the heart in half from top to bottom.

Everyone feels a broken heart sometimes. In the Bible, people tore their clothes to show sadness. We tore our hearts. Either way, God wants us to talk to him. Tape your heart back together to remind you that God cares how you feel!

CHAPTER 12

Job's Fourth Speech: A Response to Zophar

Then Job spoke again:

2 "You people really know everything,
don't you?
And when you die, wisdom will die
with you!
3 Well, I know a few things myself—
and you're no better than I am.
Who doesn't know these things you've
been saying?
4 Yet my friends laugh at me,
for I call on God and expect an answer.

I am a just and blameless man,
yet they laugh at me.
5 People who are at ease mock those in trouble.
They give a push to people who are stumbling.
6 But robbers are left in peace,
and those who provoke God live in safety—
though God keeps them in his power.

7 "Just ask the animals, and they will teach you.
Ask the birds of the sky, and they will tell you.
8 Speak to the earth, and it will instruct you.
Let the fish in the sea speak to you.
9 For they all know
that my disaster has come from the hand of the LORD.
10 For the life of every living thing is in his hand,
and the breath of every human being.
11 The ear tests the words it hears
just as the mouth distinguishes between foods.
12 Wisdom belongs to the aged,
and understanding to the old.

13 "But true wisdom and power are found in God;
counsel and understanding are his.
14 What he destroys cannot be rebuilt.
When he puts someone in prison, there is no escape.
15 If he holds back the rain, the earth becomes a desert.
If he releases the waters, they flood the earth.
16 Yes, strength and wisdom are his;
deceivers and deceived are both in his power.
17 He leads counselors away, stripped of good judgment;
wise judges become fools.
18 He removes the royal robe of kings.
They are led away with ropes around their waist.
19 He leads priests away, stripped of status;
he overthrows those with long years in power.
20 He silences the trusted adviser
and removes the insight of the elders.
21 He pours disgrace upon princes
and disarms the strong.

22 "He uncovers mysteries hidden in darkness;
he brings light to the deepest gloom.
23 He builds up nations, and he destroys them.
He expands nations, and he abandons them.
24 He strips kings of understanding
and leaves them wandering in a pathless wasteland.
25 They grope in the darkness without a light.
He makes them stagger like drunkards.

CHAPTER 13

Job Wants to Argue His Case with God

1 "Look, I have seen all this with my own eyes
and heard it with my own ears, and now I understand.
2 I know as much as you do.
You are no better than I am.
3 As for me, I would speak directly to the Almighty.
I want to argue my case with God himself.
4 As for you, you smear me with lies.
As physicians, you are worthless quacks.
5 If only you could be silent!
That's the wisest thing you could do.
6 Listen to my charge;
pay attention to my arguments.

7 "Are you defending God with lies?
Do you make your dishonest arguments for his sake?
8 Will you slant your testimony in his favor?
Will you argue God's case for him?
9 What will happen when he finds out what you are doing?
Can you fool him as easily as you fool people?
10 No, you will be in trouble with him
if you secretly slant your testimony in his favor.
11 Doesn't his majesty terrify you?
Doesn't your fear of him overwhelm you?
12 Your platitudes are as valuable as ashes.
Your defense is as fragile as a clay pot.

13 "Be silent now and leave me alone.
Let me speak, and I will face the consequences.
14 Why should I put myself in mortal danger
and take my life in my own hands?
15 God might kill me, but I have no other hope.
I am going to argue my case with him.
16 But this is what will save me—I am not godless.
If I were, I could not stand before him.

17 "Listen closely to what I am about to say.
Hear me out.
18 I have prepared my case;
I will be proved innocent.
19 Who can argue with me over this?
And if you prove me wrong, I will remain silent and die.

Job Asks How He Has Sinned

20 "O God, grant me these two things,
and then I will be able to face you.
21 Remove your heavy hand from me,
and don't terrify me with your awesome presence.
22 Now summon me, and I will answer!
Or let me speak to you, and you reply.
23 Tell me, what have I done wrong?
Show me my rebellion and my sin.
24 Why do you turn away from me?
Why do you treat me as your enemy?
25 Would you terrify a leaf blown by the wind?
Would you chase dry straw?

26 "You write bitter accusations against me
and bring up all the sins of my youth.
27 You put my feet in stocks.
You examine all my paths.
You trace all my footprints.
28 I waste away like rotting wood,
like a moth-eaten coat.

CHAPTER 14

1 "How frail is humanity!
How short is life, how full of trouble!
2 We blossom like a flower and then wither.
Like a passing shadow, we quickly disappear.
3 Must you keep an eye on such a frail creature
and demand an accounting from me?
4 Who can bring purity out of an impure person?
No one!
5 You have decided the length of our lives.
You know how many months we will live,
and we are not given a minute longer.
6 So leave us alone and let us rest!
We are like hired hands, so let us finish our work in peace.

7 "Even a tree has more hope!
If it is cut down, it will sprout again
and grow new branches.
8 Though its roots have grown old in the earth
and its stump decays,
9 at the scent of water it will bud
and sprout again like a new seedling.
10 "But when people die, their strength is gone.
They breathe their last, and then where are they?
11 As water evaporates from a lake
and a river disappears in drought,
12 people are laid to rest and do not rise again.
Until the heavens are no more, they will not wake up
nor be roused from their sleep.

13 "I wish you would hide me in the grave
and forget me there until your anger has passed.
But mark your calendar to think of me again!
14 Can the dead live again?
If so, this would give me hope through all my years of struggle,
and I would eagerly await the release of death.
15 You would call and I would answer,
and you would yearn for me, your handiwork.
16 For then you would guard my steps,
instead of watching for my sins.
17 My sins would be sealed in a pouch,
and you would cover my guilt.

18 "But instead, as mountains fall and crumble
and as rocks fall from a cliff,
19 as water wears away the stones
and floods wash away the soil,
so you destroy people's hope.
20 You always overpower them, and they pass from the scene.
You disfigure them in death and send them away.
21 They never know if their children grow up in honor
or sink to insignificance.
22 They suffer painfully;
their life is full of trouble."

CHAPTER 15

Eliphaz's Second Response to Job

Then Eliphaz the Temanite replied:

2 "A wise man wouldn't answer with such empty talk!
You are nothing but a windbag.
3 The wise don't engage in empty chatter.
What good are such words?
4 Have you no fear of God,
no reverence for him?

5 Your sins are telling your mouth what to say.
Your words are based on clever deception.
6 Your own mouth condemns you, not I.
Your own lips testify against you.

7 "Were you the first person ever born?
Were you born before the hills were made?
8 Were you listening at God's secret council?
Do you have a monopoly on wisdom?
9 What do you know that we don't?
What do you understand that we do not?
10 On our side are aged, gray-haired men
much older than your father!

11 "Is God's comfort too little for you?
Is his gentle word not enough?
12 What has taken away your reason?
What has weakened your vision,
13 that you turn against God
and say all these evil things?
14 Can any mortal be pure?
Can anyone born of a woman be just?
15 Look, God does not even trust the angels.
Even the heavens are not absolutely pure in his sight.
16 How much less pure is a corrupt and sinful person
with a thirst for wickedness!

17 "If you will listen, I will show you.
I will answer you from my own experience.
18 And it is confirmed by the reports of wise men
who have heard the same thing from their fathers—
19 from those to whom the land was given
long before any foreigners arrived.

20 "The wicked writhe in pain throughout their lives.
Years of trouble are stored up for the ruthless.
21 The sound of terror rings in their ears,
and even on good days they fear the attack of the destroyer.
22 They dare not go out into the darkness
for fear they will be murdered.
23 They wander around, saying, 'Where can I find bread?'
They know their day of destruction is near.
24 That dark day terrifies them.
They live in distress and anguish,
like a king preparing for battle.
25 For they shake their fists at God,
defying the Almighty.
26 Holding their strong shields,
they defiantly charge against him.

27 "These wicked people are heavy and prosperous;
their waists bulge with fat.
28 But their cities will be ruined.
They will live in abandoned houses
that are ready to tumble down.
29 Their riches will not last,
and their wealth will not endure.
Their possessions will no longer spread across the horizon.

30 "They will not escape the darkness.
The burning sun will wither their shoots,
and the breath of God will destroy them.
31 Let them no longer fool themselves by trusting in empty riches,
for emptiness will be their only reward.
32 They will be cut down in the prime of life;
their branches will never again be green.
33 They will be like a vine whose grapes are harvested too early,
like an olive tree that loses its blossoms before the fruit can form.
34 For the godless are barren.
Their homes, enriched through bribery, will burn.
35 They conceive trouble and give birth to evil.
Their womb produces deceit."

CHAPTER 16

Job's Fifth Speech: A Response to Eliphaz

Then Job spoke again:

2 "I have heard all this before.
What miserable comforters you are!
3 Won't you ever stop blowing hot air?
What makes you keep on talking?
4 I could say the same things if you were in my place.
I could spout off criticism and shake my head at you.
5 But if it were me, I would encourage you.
I would try to take away your grief.
6 Instead, I suffer if I defend myself,
and I suffer no less if I refuse to speak.

7 "O God, you have ground me down
and devastated my family.

8 As if to prove I have sinned, you've reduced
me to skin and bones.
My gaunt flesh testifies against me.
9 God hates me and angrily tears me apart.
He snaps his teeth at me
and pierces me with his eyes.
10 People jeer and laugh at me.
They slap my cheek in contempt.
A mob gathers against me.
11 God has handed me over to sinners.
He has tossed me into the hands of the
wicked.

12 "I was living quietly until he shattered me.
He took me by the neck and broke me
in pieces.
Then he set me up as his target,
13 and now his archers surround me.
His arrows pierce me without mercy.
The ground is wet with my blood.
14 Again and again he smashes against me,
charging at me like a warrior.
15 I wear burlap to show my grief.
My pride lies in the dust.
16 My eyes are red with weeping;
dark shadows circle my eyes.
17 Yet I have done no wrong,
and my prayer is pure.

18 "O earth, do not conceal my blood.
Let it cry out on my behalf.
19 Even now my witness is in heaven.
My advocate is there on high.
20 My friends scorn me,
but I pour out my tears to God.
21 I need someone to mediate between God
and me,
as a person mediates between friends.
22 For soon I must go down that road
from which I will never return.

CHAPTER 17
Job Continues to Defend His Innocence

1 "My spirit is crushed,
and my life is nearly snuffed out.
The grave is ready to receive me.
2 I am surrounded by mockers.
I watch how bitterly they taunt me.

3 "You must defend my innocence, O God,
since no one else will stand up for me.
4 You have closed their minds to understanding,
but do not let them triumph.
5 They betray their friends for their own
advantage,
so let their children faint with hunger.

6 "God has made a mockery of me among the
people;
they spit in my face.
7 My eyes are swollen with weeping,
and I am but a shadow of my former self.
8 The virtuous are horrified when they see me.
The innocent rise up against the ungodly.
9 The righteous keep moving forward,
and those with clean hands become
stronger and stronger.

10 "As for all of you, come back with a better
argument,
though I still won't find a wise man
among you.
11 My days are over.
My hopes have disappeared.
My heart's desires are broken.
12 These men say that night is day;
they claim that the darkness is light.
13 What if I go to the grave
and make my bed in darkness?
14 What if I call the grave my father,
and the maggot my mother or my sister?
15 Where then is my hope?
Can anyone find it?
16 No, my hope will go down with me to the
grave.
We will rest together in the dust!"

CHAPTER 18
Bildad's Second Response to Job

Then Bildad the Shuhite replied:

2 "How long before you stop talking?
Speak sense if you want us to answer!
3 Do you think we are mere animals?
Do you think we are stupid?
4 You may tear out your hair in anger,
but will that destroy the earth?
Will it make the rocks tremble?

5 "Surely the light of the wicked will be
snuffed out.
The sparks of their fire will not glow.
6 The light in their tent will grow dark.
The lamp hanging above them will be
quenched.
7 The confident stride of the wicked will be
shortened.
Their own schemes will be their downfall.
8 The wicked walk into a net.
They fall into a pit.
9 A trap grabs them by the heel.
A snare holds them tight.

Job 19 . . . page 510

10 A noose lies hidden on the ground.
A rope is stretched across their path.

11 "Terrors surround the wicked
and trouble them at every step.
12 Hunger depletes their strength,
and calamity waits for them to stumble.
13 Disease eats their skin;
death devours their limbs.
14 They are torn from the security of their homes
and are brought down to the king of terrors.
15 The homes of the wicked will burn down;
burning sulfur rains on their houses.
16 Their roots will dry up,
and their branches will wither.
17 All memory of their existence will fade from the earth;
no one will remember their names.
18 They will be thrust from light into darkness,
driven from the world.
19 They will have neither children nor grandchildren,
nor any survivor in the place where they lived.
20 People in the west are appalled at their fate;
people in the east are horrified.
21 They will say, 'This was the home of a wicked person,
the place of one who rejected God.'"

CHAPTER 19
Job's Sixth Speech: A Response to Bildad

Then Job spoke again:

2 "How long will you torture me?
How long will you try to crush me with your words?
3 You have already insulted me ten times.
You should be ashamed of treating me so badly.
4 Even if I have sinned,
that is my concern, not yours.
5 You think you're better than I am,
using my humiliation as evidence of my sin.
6 But it is God who has wronged me,
capturing me in his net.

7 "I cry out, 'Help!' but no one answers me.
I protest, but there is no justice.
8 God has blocked my way so I cannot move.
He has plunged my path into darkness.
9 He has stripped me of my honor
and removed the crown from my head.
10 He has demolished me on every side, and I am finished.
He has uprooted my hope like a fallen tree.
11 His fury burns against me;
he counts me as an enemy.
12 His troops advance.
They build up roads to attack me.
They camp all around my tent.

13 "My relatives stay far away,
and my friends have turned against me.
14 My family is gone,
and my close friends have forgotten me.
15 My servants and maids consider me a stranger.
I am like a foreigner to them.
16 When I call my servant, he doesn't come;
I have to plead with him!
17 My breath is repulsive to my wife.
I am rejected by my own family.
18 Even young children despise me.
When I stand to speak, they turn their backs on me.
19 My close friends detest me.
Those I loved have turned against me.
20 I have been reduced to skin and bones
and have escaped death by the skin of my teeth.

21 "Have mercy on me, my friends, have mercy,
for the hand of God has struck me.
22 Must you also persecute me, like God does?
Haven't you chewed me up enough?

23 "Oh, that my words could be recorded.
Oh, that they could be inscribed on a monument,
24 carved with an iron chisel and filled with lead,
engraved forever in the rock.

25 "But as for me, I know that my Redeemer lives,
and he will stand upon the earth at last.
26 And after my body has decayed,
yet in my body I will see God!
27 I will see him for myself.
Yes, I will see him with my own eyes.
I am overwhelmed at the thought!

28 "How dare you go on persecuting me,
saying, 'It's his own fault'?
29 You should fear punishment yourselves,
for your attitude deserves punishment.
Then you will know that there is indeed a judgment."

BIBLE BIOS

Hear From the Heroes

Hi, my name is

NAAMAN *(military commander)*

I'm a military commander for a country that took over parts of Israel. There was a Hebrew girl in my household who helped save my life. You see, I came down with leprosy. Leprosy is a disease that causes spots all over you and sometimes even eats away at your body. Things didn't look good for me. But this Hebrew slave girl insisted that Elisha, a prophet from her country, could cure me.

Leprosy was one of the most feared diseases of its day. Some lepers were forced out of the cities and had to live in camps by themselves. No wonder Naaman wanted to be cured!

So I decided to give it a try. But when I arrived, a messenger came out and told me to go wash myself seven times in the Jordan River. The prophet didn't even bother to speak to me himself!

I was mad! I was an important commander, and this guy couldn't even come out to see me? And the Jordan River? It wasn't even a *nice* river! I was ready to turn around and go home.

The Jordan River was small and dirty compared to some of the greater rivers. Naaman thought he was too big a hero to wash in a piddly little river like the Jordan.

But the men I was with said, "Look, you've come all this way. You might as well try what he says." I felt stupid, but I did it anyway. When I came out of the water the seventh time, I was healed!

So if you want to know the biggest lesson I learned in my life, it's that God is real. And powerful. And good. I thought I was a big deal being a commander. I thought I was too important for Elisha and his dirty river. But I learned that I needed to humble myself and trust God.

Seeing Spots

WOW!

1. **Cut the corners off an index card.**
2. **On one side, draw Naaman with spots all over him. On the other side, draw a river.**
3. **Poke a hole in the top and bottom of the card, and tie a foot of string to each hole.**
4. **Have a friend gently twist the card around and around, winding it tight, as you hold the ends of the string. Then have your friend let go! As the picture spins, it will look like Naaman is in the water.**

Use your craft to tell someone the story of how Naaman was healed. Say that Naaman was cured of his pride, too! He was humbled by Elisha and healed by God.

DO YOU NEED HUMBLING? ASK GOD TO HELP!

BIBLE BIOS

Hear From the Heroes

Hi, my name is

NEHEMIAH *(cupbearer to the king)*

I had a really cool job—cupbearer to the king of Persia!

That means I tasted all the drinks before the king to make sure they weren't poisoned. I was ready to take a hit for the king! I quess you could say I was the most trusted person the king had. But the situation wasn't perfect. Hundreds of years ago, the Hebrew people had been conquered, and many of them had been taken as slaves to Persia. I was a Hebrew, which is how I wound up as the king's servant.

Anyway, one day some people arrived from Jerusalem. What terrible news they brought! The walls and gates of the city—*God's* city—were in ruins. I was so upset that I sat down and cried. But then I prayed. I asked God to forgive my sins and the sins of my people. And I asked him to be with me because I had come up with a *big* idea!

The walls aroun Jerusalem wer there for more than show. The walls on each si of the gates we taller and thick so soldiers coul stand guard to defend the gate against attack

I decided to ask the king if I could leave and go to Jerusalem. I wanted to rebuild the wall around the city—it's all I could think about! Believe it or not, the king said OK.

When I got to Jerusalem, I saw that we had a giant job ahead of us! Not only that, but some of the people in the area didn't even *want* the city wall rebuilt.

Anyway, I organized the whole community to help get the wall around the city rebuilt. We stood up to the people who were against us, and we worked and prayed, day and night. And you know what? We completed that wall in just 52 days!

The people cried when they heard Ezra read the Law. They realized how far they had strayed from God, and they were sorry for their sins. Ezra and Nehemiah told the people to rejoice because they had heard God's Word and understood it.

After the wall was built, Ezra the priest and I got out the Book of the Law and began teaching from it. It was great to see the people turn back to God. And then I realized that I wasn't sad anymore because God was once again being honored in Jerusalem!

Construction Zone

Worship God
Respect God
Don't steal
Don't lie
No Adultery
honor parents
Don't Kill
Don't cheat
Don't covet
Love God

BE A BUILDER, JUST LIKE NEHEMIAH!

First you'll need some bricks. **Stuff paper lunch bags with newspaper, and then tape them shut or slide each one into another paper bag.** Write one of God's laws on each brick. (You can say it in your own words, like "Don't lie.") Tape your bricks together to make a wall. You can think of God's laws as you admire your wall, just like the people in Jerusalem did.

CHAPTER 20
Zophar's Second Response to Job

Then Zophar the Naamathite replied:

2 "I must reply
because I am greatly disturbed.
3 I've had to endure your insults,
but now my spirit prompts me to reply.

4 "Don't you realize that from the beginning of time,
ever since people were first placed on the earth,
5 the triumph of the wicked has been short lived
and the joy of the godless has been only temporary?
6 Though the pride of the godless reaches to the heavens
and their heads touch the clouds,
7 yet they will vanish forever,
thrown away like their own dung.
Those who knew them will ask,
'Where are they?'
8 They will fade like a dream and not be found.
They will vanish like a vision in the night.
9 Those who once saw them will see them no more.
Their families will never see them again.
10 Their children will beg from the poor,
for they must give back their stolen riches.
11 Though they are young,
their bones will lie in the dust.

12 "They enjoyed the sweet taste of wickedness,
letting it melt under their tongue.
13 They savored it,
holding it long in their mouths.
14 But suddenly the food in their bellies turns sour,
a poisonous venom in their stomach.
15 They will vomit the wealth they swallowed.
God won't let them keep it down.
16 They will suck the poison of cobras.
The viper will kill them.
17 They will never again enjoy streams of olive oil
or rivers of milk and honey.
18 They will give back everything they worked for.
Their wealth will bring them no joy.
19 For they oppressed the poor and left them destitute.
They foreclosed on their homes.
20 They were always greedy and never satisfied.
Nothing remains of all the things they dreamed about.
21 Nothing is left after they finish gorging themselves.
Therefore, their prosperity will not endure.

22 "In the midst of plenty, they will run into trouble
and be overcome by misery.
23 May God give them a bellyful of trouble.
May God rain down his anger upon them.
24 When they try to escape an iron weapon,
a bronze-tipped arrow will pierce them.
25 The arrow is pulled from their back,
and the arrowhead glistens with blood.
The terrors of death are upon them.
26 Their treasures will be thrown into deepest darkness.
A wildfire will devour their goods,
consuming all they have left.
27 The heavens will reveal their guilt,
and the earth will testify against them.
28 A flood will sweep away their house.
God's anger will descend on them in torrents.
29 This is the reward that God gives the wicked.
It is the inheritance decreed by God."

CHAPTER 21
Job's Seventh Speech: A Response to Zophar

Then Job spoke again:

2 "Listen closely to what I am saying.
That's one consolation you can give me.
3 Bear with me, and let me speak.
After I have spoken, you may resume mocking me.

4 "My complaint is with God, not with people.
I have good reason to be so impatient.
5 Look at me and be stunned.
Put your hand over your mouth in shock.
6 When I think about what I am saying, I shudder.
My body trembles.

7 "Why do the wicked prosper,
growing old and powerful?
8 They live to see their children grow up and settle down,
and they enjoy their grandchildren.
9 Their homes are safe from every fear,
and God does not punish them.

10 Their bulls never fail to breed.
Their cows bear calves and never miscarry.
11 They let their children frisk about like lambs.
Their little ones skip and dance.
12 They sing with tambourine and harp.
They celebrate to the sound of the flute.
13 They spend their days in prosperity,
then go down to the grave in peace.
14 And yet they say to God, 'Go away.
We want no part of you and your ways.
15 Who is the Almighty, and why should we obey him?
What good will it do us to pray?'
16 (They think their prosperity is of their own doing,
but I will have nothing to do with that kind of thinking.)

17 "Yet the light of the wicked never seems to be extinguished.
Do they ever have trouble?
Does God distribute sorrows to them in anger?
18 Are they driven before the wind like straw?
Are they carried away by the storm like chaff?
Not at all!

19 "'Well,' you say, 'at least God will punish their children!'
But I say he should punish the ones who sin,
so that they understand his judgment.
20 Let them see their destruction with their own eyes.
Let them drink deeply of the anger of the Almighty.
21 For they will not care what happens to their family
after they are dead.

22 "But who can teach a lesson to God,
since he judges even the most powerful?
23 One person dies in prosperity,
completely comfortable and secure,
24 the picture of good health,
vigorous and fit.
25 Another person dies in bitter poverty,
never having tasted the good life.
26 But both are buried in the same dust,
both eaten by the same maggots.

27 "Look, I know what you're thinking.
I know the schemes you plot against me.
28 You will tell me of rich and wicked people
whose houses have vanished because of their sins.
29 But ask those who have been around,
and they will tell you the truth.
30 Evil people are spared in times of calamity
and are allowed to escape disaster.
31 No one criticizes them openly
or pays them back for what they have done.
32 When they are carried to the grave,
an honor guard keeps watch at their tomb.
33 A great funeral procession goes to the cemetery.
Many pay their respects as the body is laid to rest,
and the earth gives sweet repose.

34 "How can your empty clichés comfort me?
All your explanations are lies!"

CHAPTER 22
Eliphaz's Third Response to Job

Then Eliphaz the Temanite replied:

2 "Can a person do anything to help God?
Can even a wise person be helpful to him?
3 Is it any advantage to the Almighty if you are righteous?
Would it be any gain to him if you were perfect?
4 Is it because you're so pious that he accuses you
and brings judgment against you?
5 No, it's because of your wickedness!
There's no limit to your sins.

6 "For example, you must have lent money to your friend
and demanded clothing as security.
Yes, you stripped him to the bone.
7 You must have refused water for the thirsty
and food for the hungry.
8 You probably think the land belongs to the powerful
and only the privileged have a right to it!
9 You must have sent widows away empty-handed
and crushed the hopes of orphans.
10 That is why you are surrounded by traps
and tremble from sudden fears.
11 That is why you cannot see in the darkness,
and waves of water cover you.

12 "God is so great—higher than the heavens,
higher than the farthest stars.
13 But you reply, 'That's why God can't see what I am doing!
How can he judge through the thick darkness?

14 For thick clouds swirl about him, and he
cannot see us.
He is way up there, walking on the vault
of heaven.'
15 "Will you continue on the old paths
where evil people have walked?
16 They were snatched away in the prime of life,
the foundations of their lives washed away.
17 For they said to God, 'Leave us alone!
What can the Almighty do to us?'
18 Yet he was the one who filled their homes
with good things,
so I will have nothing to do with that kind
of thinking.

19 "The righteous will be happy to see the
wicked destroyed,
and the innocent will laugh in contempt.
20 They will say, 'See how our enemies have
been destroyed.
The last of them have been consumed
in the fire.'

21 "Submit to God, and you will have peace;
then things will go well for you.
22 Listen to his instructions,
and store them in your heart.
23 If you return to the Almighty, you will be
restored—
so clean up your life.
24 If you give up your lust for money
and throw your precious gold into the
river,
25 the Almighty himself will be your treasure.
He will be your precious silver!

26 "Then you will take delight in the Almighty
and look up to God.
27 You will pray to him, and he will hear you,
and you will fulfill your vows to him.
28 You will succeed in whatever you choose to do,
and light will shine on the road ahead of
you.
29 If people are in trouble and you say, 'Help
them,'
God will save them.
30 Even sinners will be rescued;
they will be rescued because your hands
are pure."

CHAPTER 23
Job's Eighth Speech: A Response to Eliphaz

Then Job spoke again:

2 "My complaint today is still a bitter one,
and I try hard not to groan aloud.
3 If only I knew where to find God,
I would go to his court.
4 I would lay out my case
and present my arguments.
5 Then I would listen to his reply
and understand what he says to me.
6 Would he use his great power to argue
with me?
No, he would give me a fair hearing.
7 Honest people can reason with him,
so I would be forever acquitted by my
judge.
8 I go east, but he is not there.
I go west, but I cannot find him.
9 I do not see him in the north, for he is
hidden.
I look to the south, but he is concealed.

10 "But he knows where I am going.
And when he tests me, I will come out
as pure as gold.
11 For I have stayed on God's paths;
I have followed his ways and not turned
aside.
12 I have not departed from his commands,
but have treasured his words more than
daily food.
13 But once he has made his decision, who can
change his mind?
Whatever he wants to do, he does.
14 So he will do to me whatever he has planned.
He controls my destiny.
15 No wonder I am so terrified in his presence.
When I think of it, terror grips me.
16 God has made me sick at heart;
the Almighty has terrified me.
17 Darkness is all around me;
thick, impenetrable darkness is
everywhere.

CHAPTER 24
Job Asks Why the Wicked Are Not Punished

1 "Why doesn't the Almighty bring the wicked
to judgment?
Why must the godly wait for him in vain?
2 Evil people steal land by moving the
boundary markers.
They steal livestock and put them in their
own pastures.
3 They take the orphan's donkey
and demand the widow's ox as security
for a loan.
4 The poor are pushed off the path;
the needy must hide together for safety.

5 Like wild donkeys in the wilderness,
the poor must spend all their time looking for food,
searching even in the desert for food for their children.
6 They harvest a field they do not own,
and they glean in the vineyards of the wicked.
7 All night they lie naked in the cold,
without clothing or covering.
8 They are soaked by mountain showers,
and they huddle against the rocks for want of a home.

9 "The wicked snatch a widow's child from her breast,
taking the baby as security for a loan.
10 The poor must go about naked, without any clothing.
They harvest food for others while they themselves are starving.
11 They press out olive oil without being allowed to taste it,
and they tread in the winepress as they suffer from thirst.
12 The groans of the dying rise from the city,
and the wounded cry for help,
yet God ignores their moaning.

13 "Wicked people rebel against the light.
They refuse to acknowledge its ways
or stay in its paths.
14 The murderer rises in the early dawn
to kill the poor and needy;
at night he is a thief.
15 The adulterer waits for the twilight,
saying, 'No one will see me then.'
He hides his face so no one will know him.
16 Thieves break into houses at night
and sleep in the daytime.
They are not acquainted with the light.
17 The black night is their morning.
They ally themselves with the terrors of the darkness.

18 "But they disappear like foam down a river.
Everything they own is cursed,
and they are afraid to enter their own vineyards.
19 The grave consumes sinners
just as drought and heat consume snow.
20 Their own mothers will forget them.
Maggots will find them sweet to eat.
No one will remember them.
Wicked people are broken like a tree in the storm.
21 They cheat the woman who has no son to help her.
They refuse to help the needy widow.

22 "God, in his power, drags away the rich.
They may rise high, but they have no assurance of life.
23 They may be allowed to live in security,
but God is always watching them.
24 And though they are great now,
in a moment they will be gone like all others,
cut off like heads of grain.
25 Can anyone claim otherwise?
Who can prove me wrong?"

CHAPTER 25
Bildad's Third Response to Job

Then Bildad the Shuhite replied:

2 "God is powerful and dreadful.
He enforces peace in the heavens.
3 Who is able to count his heavenly army?
Doesn't his light shine on all the earth?
4 How can a mortal be innocent before God?
Can anyone born of a woman be pure?
5 God is more glorious than the moon;
he shines brighter than the stars.
6 In comparison, people are maggots;
we mortals are mere worms."

CHAPTER 26
Job's Ninth Speech: A Response to Bildad

Then Job spoke again:

2 "How you have helped the powerless!
How you have saved the weak!
3 How you have enlightened my stupidity!
What wise advice you have offered!
4 Where have you gotten all these wise sayings?
Whose spirit speaks through you?

5 "The dead tremble—
those who live beneath the waters.
6 The underworld is naked in God's presence.
The place of destruction is uncovered.
7 God stretches the northern sky over empty space
and hangs the earth on nothing.
8 He wraps the rain in his thick clouds,
and the clouds don't burst with the weight.
9 He covers the face of the moon,
shrouding it with his clouds.

[10] They cut tunnels in the rocks
and uncover precious stones.
[11] They dam up the trickling streams
and bring to light the hidden treasures.

[12] "But do people know where to find wisdom?
Where can they find understanding?
[13] No one knows where to find it,
for it is not found among the living.
[14] 'It is not here,' says the ocean.
'Nor is it here,' says the sea.
[15] It cannot be bought with gold.
It cannot be purchased with silver.
[16] It's worth more than all the gold of Ophir,
greater than precious onyx or lapis lazuli.
[17] Wisdom is more valuable than gold and
crystal.
It cannot be purchased with jewels
mounted in fine gold.
[18] Coral and jasper are worthless in trying
to get it.
The price of wisdom is far above rubies.
[19] Precious peridot from Ethiopia cannot be
exchanged for it.
It's worth more than the purest gold.

[20] "But do people know where to find wisdom?
Where can they find understanding?
[21] It is hidden from the eyes of all humanity.
Even the sharp-eyed birds in the sky
cannot discover it.
[22] Destruction and Death say,
'We've heard only rumors of where
wisdom can be found.'

[23] "God alone understands the way to wisdom;
he knows where it can be found,
[24] for he looks throughout the whole earth
and sees everything under the heavens.
[25] He decided how hard the winds should blow
and how much rain should fall.
[26] He made the laws for the rain
and laid out a path for the lightning.
[27] Then he saw wisdom and evaluated it.
He set it in place and examined it
thoroughly.
[28] And this is what he says to all humanity:
'The fear of the Lord is true wisdom;
to forsake evil is real understanding.'"

CHAPTER 29
Job Speaks of His Former Blessings

Job continued speaking:

[2] "I long for the years gone by
when God took care of me,
[3] when he lit up the way before me
and I walked safely through the darkness.
[4] When I was in my prime,
God's friendship was felt in my home.
[5] The Almighty was still with me,
and my children were around me.
[6] My steps were awash in cream,
and the rocks gushed olive oil for me.

[7] "Those were the days when I went to the
city gate
and took my place among the honored
leaders.
[8] The young stepped aside when they saw me,
and even the aged rose in respect at my
coming.
[9] The princes stood in silence
and put their hands over their mouths.
[10] The highest officials of the city stood
quietly,
holding their tongues in respect.

[11] "All who heard me praised me.
All who saw me spoke well of me.
[12] For I assisted the poor in their need
and the orphans who required help.

What if your family decided to write a book and each person got a chapter? Would you write about your friends? school? What would your family write about? It would be an interesting book, but it wouldn't fit together like a story. The Bible was written by more than 40 people over 1,500 years in three different languages, and *it* fits together perfectly!

Give your family this assignment: Have each person write a description of one movie they've all seen. Then compare what they wrote. How close are their descriptions? How different? Now read an example of how different Bible writers presented the same story. **Read • MATTHEW 3:13-17 • MARK 1:9-11 • LUKE 3:21-22.**

10 He created the horizon when he separated
the waters;
he set the boundary between day and
night.
11 The foundations of heaven tremble;
they shudder at his rebuke.
12 By his power the sea grew calm.
By his skill he crushed the great sea
monster.
13 His Spirit made the heavens beautiful,
and his power pierced the gliding
serpent.
14 These are just the beginning of all that
he does,
merely a whisper of his power.
Who, then, can comprehend the thunder
of his power?"

CHAPTER 27
Job's Final Speech

Job continued speaking:

2 "I vow by the living God, who has taken away
my rights,
by the Almighty who has embittered my
soul—
3 As long as I live,
while I have breath from God,
4 my lips will speak no evil,
and my tongue will speak no lies.
5 I will never concede that you are right;
I will defend my integrity until I die.
6 I will maintain my innocence without
wavering.
My conscience is clear for as long as I live.

7 "May my enemy be punished like the
wicked,
my adversary like those who do evil.
8 For what hope do the godless have when
God cuts them off
and takes away their life?
9 Will God listen to their cry
when trouble comes upon them?
10 Can they take delight in the Almighty?
Can they call to God at any time?
11 I will teach you about God's power.
I will not conceal anything concerning the
Almighty.
12 But you have seen all this,
yet you say all these useless things to me.

13 "This is what the wicked will receive from
God;
this is their inheritance from the
Almighty.
14 They may have many children,
but the children will die in war or starve
to death.
15 Those who survive will die of a plague,
and not even their widows will mourn
them.

16 "Evil people may have piles of money
and may store away mounds of clothing.
17 But the righteous will wear that clothing,
and the innocent will divide that money.
18 The wicked build houses as fragile as a
spider's web,
as flimsy as a shelter made of branches.
19 The wicked go to bed rich
but wake to find that all their wealth is
gone.
20 Terror overwhelms them like a flood,
and they are blown away in the storms
of the night.
21 The east wind carries them away, and they
are gone.
It sweeps them away.
22 It whirls down on them without mercy.
They struggle to flee from its power.
23 But everyone jeers at them
and mocks them.

CHAPTER 28
Job Speaks of Wisdom and Understanding

1 "People know where to mine silver
and how to refine gold.
2 They know where to dig iron from the earth
and how to smelt copper from rock.
3 They know how to shine light in the darkness
and explore the farthest regions of the
earth
as they search in the dark for ore.
4 They sink a mine shaft into the earth
far from where anyone lives.
They descend on ropes, swinging back
and forth.
5 Food is grown on the earth above,
but down below, the earth is melted as
by fire.
6 Here the rocks contain precious lapis lazuli,
and the dust contains gold.
7 These are treasures no bird of prey can see,
no falcon's eye observe.
8 No wild animal has walked upon these
treasures;
no lion has ever set his paw there.
9 People know how to tear apart flinty rocks
and overturn the roots of mountains.

13 I helped those without hope, and they
blessed me.
And I caused the widows' hearts to sing for
joy.
14 Everything I did was honest.
Righteousness covered me like a robe,
and I wore justice like a turban.
15 I served as eyes for the blind
and feet for the lame.
16 I was a father to the poor
and assisted strangers who needed help.
17 I broke the jaws of godless oppressors
and plucked their victims from their
teeth.
18 "I thought, 'Surely I will die surrounded by
my family
after a long, good life.
19 For I am like a tree whose roots reach the
water,
whose branches are refreshed with the
dew.
20 New honors are constantly bestowed on me,
and my strength is continually renewed.'

21 "Everyone listened to my advice.
They were silent as they waited for me
to speak.
22 And after I spoke, they had nothing to add,
for my counsel satisfied them.
23 They longed for me to speak as people long
for rain.
They drank my words like a refreshing
spring rain.
24 When they were discouraged, I smiled at
them.
My look of approval was precious to them.
25 Like a chief, I told them what to do.
I lived like a king among his troops
and comforted those who mourned.

CHAPTER 30
Job Speaks of His Anguish

1 "But now I am mocked by people younger
than I,
by young men whose fathers are not
worthy to run with my sheepdogs.
2 A lot of good they are to me—
those worn-out wretches!
3 They are gaunt from poverty and hunger.
They claw the dry ground in desolate
wastelands,
to desolate and gloomy wastelands.
4 They pluck wild greens from among the
bushes
and eat from the roots of broom trees.
5 They are driven from human society,
and people shout at them as if they were
thieves.
6 So now they live in frightening ravines,
in caves and among the rocks.
7 They sound like animals howling among the
bushes,
huddled together beneath the nettles.
8 They are nameless fools,
outcasts from society.

9 "And now they mock me with vulgar songs!
They taunt me!
10 They despise me and won't come near me,
except to spit in my face.
11 For God has cut my bowstring.
He has humbled me,
so they have thrown off all restraint.
12 These outcasts oppose me to my face.
They send me sprawling
and lay traps in my path.
13 They block my road
and do everything they can to destroy me.
They know I have no one to help me.
14 They come at me from all directions.
They jump on me when I am down.
15 I live in terror now.
My honor has blown away in the wind,
and my prosperity has vanished like a
cloud.

16 "And now my life seeps away.
Depression haunts my days.
17 At night my bones are filled with pain,
which gnaws at me relentlessly.
18 With a strong hand, God grabs my shirt.
He grips me by the collar of my coat.
19 He has thrown me into the mud.
I'm nothing more than dust and ashes.

20 "I cry to you, O God, but you don't answer.
I stand before you, but you don't even
look.
21 You have become cruel toward me.
You use your power to persecute me.
22 You throw me into the whirlwind
and destroy me in the storm.
23 And I know you are sending me to my
death—
the destination of all who live.

24 "Surely no one would turn against the needy
when they cry for help in their trouble.
25 Did I not weep for those in trouble?
Was I not deeply grieved for the needy?
26 So I looked for good, but evil came instead.
I waited for the light, but darkness fell.

27 My heart is troubled and restless.
Days of suffering torment me.
28 I walk in gloom, without sunlight.
I stand in the public square and cry for help.
29 Instead, I am considered a brother to jackals
and a companion to owls.
30 My skin has turned dark,
and my bones burn with fever.
31 My harp plays sad music,
and my flute accompanies those who weep.

CHAPTER 31
Job's Final Protest of Innocence

1 "I made a covenant with my eyes
not to look with lust at a young woman.
2 For what has God above chosen for us?
What is our inheritance from the Almighty on high?
3 Isn't it calamity for the wicked
and misfortune for those who do evil?
4 Doesn't he see everything I do
and every step I take?

5 "Have I lied to anyone
or deceived anyone?
6 Let God weigh me on the scales of justice,
for he knows my integrity.
7 If I have strayed from his pathway,
or if my heart has lusted for what my eyes have seen,
or if I am guilty of any other sin,
8 then let someone else eat the crops I have planted.
Let all that I have planted be uprooted.

9 "If my heart has been seduced by a woman,
or if I have lusted for my neighbor's wife,
10 then let my wife serve another man;
let other men sleep with her.
11 For lust is a shameful sin,
a crime that should be punished.
12 It is a fire that burns all the way to hell.
It would wipe out everything I own.

13 "If I have been unfair to my male or female servants
when they brought their complaints to me,
14 how could I face God?
What could I say when he questioned me?
15 For God created both me and my servants.
He created us both in the womb.

16 "Have I refused to help the poor,
or crushed the hopes of widows?
17 Have I been stingy with my food
and refused to share it with orphans?
18 No, from childhood I have cared for orphans like a father,
and all my life I have cared for widows.
19 Whenever I saw the homeless without clothes
and the needy with nothing to wear,
20 did they not praise me
for providing wool clothing to keep them warm?

21 "If I raised my hand against an orphan,
knowing the judges would take my side,
22 then let my shoulder be wrenched out of place!
Let my arm be torn from its socket!
23 That would be better than facing God's judgment.
For if the majesty of God opposes me, what hope is there?

24 "Have I put my trust in money
or felt secure because of my gold?
25 Have I gloated about my wealth
and all that I own?

26 "Have I looked at the sun shining in the skies,
or the moon walking down its silver pathway,
27 and been secretly enticed in my heart
to throw kisses at them in worship?
28 If so, I should be punished by the judges,
for it would mean I had denied the God of heaven.

29 "Have I ever rejoiced when disaster struck my enemies,
or become excited when harm came their way?
30 No, I have never sinned by cursing anyone
or by asking for revenge.

31 "My servants have never said,
'He let others go hungry.'
32 I have never turned away a stranger
but have opened my doors to everyone.

33 "Have I tried to hide my sins like other people do,
concealing my guilt in my heart?
34 Have I feared the crowd
or the contempt of the masses,
so that I kept quiet and stayed indoors?

35 "If only someone would listen to me!
Look, I will sign my name to my defense.

Let the Almighty answer me.
Let my accuser write out the charges against me.
36 I would face the accusation proudly.
I would wear it like a crown.
37 For I would tell him exactly what I have done.
I would come before him like a prince.

38 "If my land accuses me
and all its furrows cry out together,
39 or if I have stolen its crops
or murdered its owners,
40 then let thistles grow on that land instead of wheat,
and weeds instead of barley."

Job's words are ended.

CHAPTER 32
Elihu Responds to Job's Friends

Job's three friends refused to reply further to
him because he kept insisting on his innocence.
2 Then Elihu son of Barakel the Buzite, of the
clan of Ram, became angry. He was angry because Job refused to admit that he had sinned
and that God was right in punishing him. 3 He
was also angry with Job's three friends, for they
made God appear to be wrong by their inability
to answer Job's arguments. 4 Elihu had waited for
the others to speak to Job because they were
older than he. 5 But when he saw that they had no
further reply, he spoke out angrily. 6 Elihu son of
Barakel the Buzite said,

"I am young and you are old,
so I held back from telling you what I think.
7 I thought, 'Those who are older should speak,
for wisdom comes with age.'
8 But there is a spirit within people,
the breath of the Almighty within them,
that makes them intelligent.
9 Sometimes the elders are not wise.
Sometimes the aged do not understand justice.
10 So listen to me,
and let me tell you what I think.

11 "I have waited all this time,
listening very carefully to your arguments,
listening to you grope for words.
12 I have listened,
but not one of you has refuted Job
or answered his arguments.
13 And don't tell me, 'He is too wise for us.
Only God can convince him.'
14 If Job had been arguing with me,
I would not answer with your kind of logic!
15 You sit there baffled,
with nothing more to say.
16 Should I continue to wait, now that you are silent?
Must I also remain silent?
17 No, I will say my piece.
I will speak my mind.
18 For I am full of pent-up words,
and the spirit within me urges me on.
19 I am like a cask of wine without a vent,
like a new wineskin ready to burst!
20 I must speak to find relief,
so let me give my answers.
21 I won't play favorites
or try to flatter anyone.
22 For if I tried flattery,
my Creator would soon destroy me.

CHAPTER 33
Elihu Presents His Case against Job

1 "Listen to my words, Job;
pay attention to what I have to say.
2 Now that I have begun to speak,
let me continue.
3 I speak with all sincerity;
I speak the truth.
4 For the Spirit of God has made me,
and the breath of the Almighty gives me life.
5 Answer me, if you can;
make your case and take your stand.
6 Look, you and I both belong to God.
I, too, was formed from clay.
7 So you don't need to be afraid of me.
I won't come down hard on you.

8 "You have spoken in my hearing,
and I have heard your very words.
9 You said, 'I am pure; I am without sin;
I am innocent; I have no guilt.
10 God is picking a quarrel with me,
and he considers me his enemy.
11 He puts my feet in the stocks
and watches my every move.'

12 "But you are wrong, and I will show you why.
For God is greater than any human being.
13 So why are you bringing a charge against him?
Why say he does not respond to people's complaints?
14 For God speaks again and again,
though people do not recognize it.

15 He speaks in dreams, in visions of the night,
when deep sleep falls on people
as they lie in their beds.
16 He whispers in their ears
and terrifies them with warnings.
17 He makes them turn from doing wrong;
he keeps them from pride.
18 He protects them from the grave,
from crossing over the river of death.

19 "Or God disciplines people with pain on
their sickbeds,
with ceaseless aching in their bones.
20 They lose their appetite
for even the most delicious food.
21 Their flesh wastes away,
and their bones stick out.
22 They are at death's door;
the angels of death wait for them.

23 "But if an angel from heaven appears—
a special messenger to intercede for
a person
and declare that he is upright—
24 he will be gracious and say,
'Rescue him from the grave,
for I have found a ransom for his life.'
25 Then his body will become as healthy as
a child's,
firm and youthful again.
26 When he prays to God,
he will be accepted.
And God will receive him with joy
and restore him to good standing.
27 He will declare to his friends,
'I sinned and twisted the truth,
but it was not worth it.
28 God rescued me from the grave,
and now my life is filled with light.'

29 "Yes, God does these things
again and again for people.
30 He rescues them from the grave
so they may enjoy the light of life.
31 Mark this well, Job. Listen to me,
for I have more to say.
32 But if you have anything to say, go ahead.
Speak, for I am anxious to see you justified.
33 But if not, then listen to me.
Keep silent and I will teach you wisdom!"

CHAPTER 34
Elihu Accuses Job of Arrogance

Then Elihu said:

2 "Listen to me, you wise men.
Pay attention, you who have knowledge.
3 Job said, 'The ear tests the words it hears
just as the mouth distinguishes between
foods.'
4 So let us discern for ourselves what is right;
let us learn together what is good.
5 For Job also said, 'I am innocent,
but God has taken away my rights.
6 I am innocent, but they call me a liar.
My suffering is incurable, though I have
not sinned.'

7 "Tell me, has there ever been a man
like Job,
with his thirst for irreverent talk?
8 He chooses evil people as companions.
He spends his time with wicked men.
9 He has even said, 'Why waste time
trying to please God?'

10 "Listen to me, you who have understanding.
Everyone knows that God doesn't sin!
The Almighty can do no wrong.
11 He repays people according to their deeds.
He treats people as they deserve.
12 Truly, God will not do wrong.
The Almighty will not twist justice.
13 Did someone else put the world in his care?
Who set the whole world in place?
14 If God were to take back his spirit
and withdraw his breath,
15 all life would cease,
and humanity would turn again to dust.

16 "Now listen to me if you are wise.
Pay attention to what I say.
17 Could God govern if he hated justice?
Are you going to condemn the almighty
judge?
18 For he says to kings, 'You are wicked,'
and to nobles, 'You are unjust.'
19 He doesn't care how great a person may be,
and he pays no more attention to the rich
than to the poor.
He made them all.
20 In a moment they die.
In the middle of the night they pass
away;
the mighty are removed without human
hand.

21 "For God watches how people live;
he sees everything they do.
22 No darkness is thick enough
to hide the wicked from his eyes.
23 We don't set the time
when we will come before God in
judgment.

24 He brings the mighty to ruin without asking anyone,
and he sets up others in their place.
25 He knows what they do,
and in the night he overturns and destroys them.
26 He strikes them down because they are wicked,
doing it openly for all to see.
27 For they turned away from following him.
They have no respect for any of his ways.
28 They cause the poor to cry out, catching God's attention.
He hears the cries of the needy.
29 But if he chooses to remain quiet,
who can criticize him?
When he hides his face, no one can find him,
whether an individual or a nation.
30 He prevents the godless from ruling
so they cannot be a snare to the people.

31 "Why don't people say to God, 'I have sinned,
but I will sin no more'?
32 Or 'I don't know what evil I have done—tell me.
If I have done wrong, I will stop at once'?

33 "Must God tailor his justice to your demands?
But you have rejected him!
The choice is yours, not mine.
Go ahead, share your wisdom with us.
34 After all, bright people will tell me,
and wise people will hear me say,
35 'Job speaks out of ignorance;
his words lack insight.'
36 Job, you deserve the maximum penalty
for the wicked way you have talked.
37 For you have added rebellion to your sin;
you show no respect,
and you speak many angry words against God."

CHAPTER 35

Elihu Reminds Job of God's Justice

Then Elihu said:

2 "Do you think it is right for you to claim,
'I am righteous before God'?
3 For you also ask, 'What's in it for me?
What's the use of living a righteous life?'

4 "I will answer you
and all your friends, too.
5 Look up into the sky,
and see the clouds high above you.
6 If you sin, how does that affect God?
Even if you sin again and again,
what effect will it have on him?
7 If you are good, is this some great gift to him?
What could you possibly give him?
8 No, your sins affect only people like yourself,
and your good deeds also affect only humans.

9 "People cry out when they are oppressed.
They groan beneath the power of the mighty.
10 Yet they don't ask, 'Where is God my Creator,
the one who gives songs in the night?
11 Where is the one who makes us smarter than the animals
and wiser than the birds of the sky?'
12 And when they cry out, God does not answer
because of their pride.
13 But it is wrong to say God doesn't listen,
to say the Almighty isn't concerned.
14 You say you can't see him,
but he will bring justice if you will only wait.
15 You say he does not respond to sinners with anger
and is not greatly concerned about wickedness.
16 But you are talking nonsense, Job.
You have spoken like a fool."

CHAPTER 36

Elihu continued speaking:

2 "Let me go on, and I will show you the truth.
For I have not finished defending God!
3 I will present profound arguments
for the righteousness of my Creator.
4 I am telling you nothing but the truth,
for I am a man of great knowledge.

5 "God is mighty, but he does not despise anyone!
He is mighty in both power and understanding.
6 He does not let the wicked live
but gives justice to the afflicted.
7 He never takes his eyes off the innocent,
but he sets them on thrones with kings
and exalts them forever.
8 If they are bound in chains
and caught up in a web of trouble,
9 he shows them the reason.
He shows them their sins of pride.
10 He gets their attention
and commands that they turn from evil.

11 "If they listen and obey God,
they will be blessed with prosperity
throughout their lives.
All their years will be pleasant.
12 But if they refuse to listen to him,
they will cross over the river of death,
dying from lack of understanding.
13 For the godless are full of resentment.
Even when he punishes them,
they refuse to cry out to him for help.
14 They die when they are young,
after wasting their lives in immoral living.
15 But by means of their suffering, he rescues
those who suffer.
For he gets their attention through
adversity.

16 "God is leading you away from danger, Job,
to a place free from distress.
He is setting your table with the best food.
17 But you are obsessed with whether the
godless will be judged.
Don't worry, judgment and justice will be
upheld.
18 But watch out, or you may be seduced by
wealth.
Don't let yourself be bribed into sin.
19 Could all your wealth
or all your mighty efforts
keep you from distress?
20 Do not long for the cover of night,
for that is when people will be destroyed.
21 Be on guard! Turn back from evil,
for God sent this suffering
to keep you from a life of evil.

Elihu Reminds Job of God's Power

22 "Look, God is all-powerful.
Who is a teacher like him?
23 No one can tell him what to do,
or say to him, 'You have done wrong.'
24 Instead, glorify his mighty works,
singing songs of praise.
25 Everyone has seen these things,
though only from a distance.

26 "Look, God is greater than we can
understand.
His years cannot be counted.
27 He draws up the water vapor
and then distills it into rain.
28 The rain pours down from the clouds,
and everyone benefits.
29 Who can understand the spreading of the
clouds
and the thunder that rolls forth from
heaven?
30 See how he spreads the lightning around him
and how it lights up the depths of the sea.
31 By these mighty acts he nourishes the people,
giving them food in abundance.
32 He fills his hands with lightning bolts
and hurls each at its target.
33 The thunder announces his presence;
the storm announces his indignant anger.

CHAPTER 37

1 "My heart pounds as I think of this.
It trembles within me.
2 Listen carefully to the thunder of God's voice
as it rolls from his mouth.
3 It rolls across the heavens,
and his lightning flashes in every
direction.
4 Then comes the roaring of the thunder—
the tremendous voice of his majesty.
He does not restrain it when he speaks.
5 God's voice is glorious in the thunder.
We can't even imagine the greatness of his
power.

6 "He directs the snow to fall on the earth
and tells the rain to pour down.
7 Then everyone stops working
so they can watch his power.
8 The wild animals take cover
and stay inside their dens.
9 The stormy wind comes from its chamber,
and the driving winds bring the cold.
10 God's breath sends the ice,
freezing wide expanses of water.
11 He loads the clouds with moisture,
and they flash with his lightning.
12 The clouds churn about at his direction.
They do whatever he commands
throughout the earth.
13 He makes these things happen either
to punish people
or to show his unfailing love.

14 "Pay attention to this, Job.
Stop and consider the wonderful miracles
of God!
15 Do you know how God controls the storm
and causes the lightning to flash from his
clouds?
16 Do you understand how he moves the clouds
with wonderful perfection and skill?
17 When you are sweltering in your clothes
and the south wind dies down and
everything is still,

18 he makes the skies reflect the heat like
a bronze mirror.
Can you do that?
19 "So teach the rest of us what to say to God.
We are too ignorant to make our own
arguments.
20 Should God be notified that I want to
speak?

Father Knows Best

Have you ever felt that your life was unfair?

Have you ever questioned God?

Check out Romans 8:28 the next time you question God.

After all the terrible things that happened, Job questioned God too. And guess what! God answered with a few questions of his own!

Read them in JOB 38-41.

GO AHEAD, I DARE YOU!

Finished reading? Tough questions, huh? **Choose your favorite verse or two from the passage, and draw a picture of what you read.**

Hang your picture in your room to remind you that God knows everything and can do everything.

No matter what happens, we don't need to question God—whatever he has planned for his people is for the best!

Want to find out what finally happened to Job? Read Job 42.

Can people even speak when they are
confused?
21 We cannot look at the sun,
for it shines brightly in the sky
when the wind clears away the clouds.
22 So also, golden splendor comes from the
mountain of God.
He is clothed in dazzling splendor.
23 We cannot imagine the power of the
Almighty;
but even though he is just and righteous,
he does not destroy us.
24 No wonder people everywhere fear him.
All who are wise show him reverence."

CHAPTER 38
The LORD Challenges Job

Then the LORD answered Job from the whirlwind:

2 "Who is this that questions my wisdom
with such ignorant words?
3 Brace yourself like a man,
because I have some questions for you,
and you must answer them.

4 "Where were you when I laid the foundations
of the earth?
Tell me, if you know so much.
5 Who determined its dimensions
and stretched out the surveying line?
6 What supports its foundations,
and who laid its cornerstone
7 as the morning stars sang together
and all the angels shouted for joy?

8 "Who kept the sea inside its boundaries
as it burst from the womb,
9 and as I clothed it with clouds
and wrapped it in thick darkness?
10 For I locked it behind barred gates,
limiting its shores.
11 I said, 'This far and no farther will you come.
Here your proud waves must stop!'

12 "Have you ever commanded the morning
to appear
and caused the dawn to rise in the east?
13 Have you made daylight spread to the ends
of the earth,
to bring an end to the night's wickedness?
14 As the light approaches,
the earth takes shape like clay pressed
beneath a seal;
it is robed in brilliant colors.
15 The light disturbs the wicked
and stops the arm that is raised in
violence.

16 "Have you explored the springs from which the seas come?
Have you explored their depths?
17 Do you know where the gates of death are located?
Have you seen the gates of utter gloom?
18 Do you realize the extent of the earth?
Tell me about it if you know!

19 "Where does light come from,
and where does darkness go?
20 Can you take each to its home?
Do you know how to get there?
21 But of course you know all this!
For you were born before it was all created,
and you are so very experienced!

22 "Have you visited the storehouses of the snow
or seen the storehouses of hail?
23 (I have reserved them as weapons for the time of trouble,
for the day of battle and war.)
24 Where is the path to the source of light?
Where is the home of the east wind?

25 "Who created a channel for the torrents of rain?
Who laid out the path for the lightning?
26 Who makes the rain fall on barren land,
in a desert where no one lives?
27 Who sends rain to satisfy the parched ground
and make the tender grass spring up?

28 "Does the rain have a father?
Who gives birth to the dew?
29 Who is the mother of the ice?
Who gives birth to the frost from the heavens?
30 For the water turns to ice as hard as rock,
and the surface of the water freezes.

31 "Can you direct the movement of the stars—
binding the cluster of the Pleiades
or loosening the cords of Orion?
32 Can you direct the constellations through the seasons
or guide the Bear with her cubs across the heavens?
33 Do you know the laws of the universe?
Can you use them to regulate the earth?

34 "Can you shout to the clouds
and make it rain?
35 Can you make lightning appear
and cause it to strike as you direct?
36 Who gives intuition to the heart
and instinct to the mind?
37 Who is wise enough to count all the clouds?
Who can tilt the water jars of heaven
38 when the parched ground is dry
and the soil has hardened into clods?

39 "Can you stalk prey for a lioness
and satisfy the young lions' appetites
40 as they lie in their dens
or crouch in the thicket?
41 Who provides food for the ravens
when their young cry out to God
and wander about in hunger?

CHAPTER 39
The LORD's Challenge Continues

1 "Do you know when the wild goats give birth?
Have you watched as deer are born in the wild?
2 Do you know how many months they carry their young?
Are you aware of the time of their delivery?
3 They crouch down to give birth to their young
and deliver their offspring.
4 Their young grow up in the open fields,
then leave home and never return.

5 "Who gives the wild donkey its freedom?
Who untied its ropes?
6 I have placed it in the wilderness;
its home is the wasteland.
7 It hates the noise of the city
and has no driver to shout at it.
8 The mountains are its pastureland,
where it searches for every blade of grass.

9 "Will the wild ox consent to being tamed?
Will it spend the night in your stall?
10 Can you hitch a wild ox to a plow?
Will it plow a field for you?
11 Given its strength, can you trust it?
Can you leave and trust the ox to do your work?
12 Can you rely on it to bring home your grain
and deliver it to your threshing floor?

13 "The ostrich flaps her wings grandly,
but they are no match for the feathers of the stork.
14 She lays her eggs on top of the earth,
letting them be warmed in the dust.
15 She doesn't worry that a foot might crush them
or a wild animal might destroy them.

16 She is harsh toward her young,
as if they were not her own.
She doesn't care if they die.
17 For God has deprived her of wisdom.
He has given her no understanding.
18 But whenever she jumps up to run,
she passes the swiftest horse with its rider.

19 "Have you given the horse its strength
or clothed its neck with a flowing mane?
20 Did you give it the ability to leap like a locust?
Its majestic snorting is terrifying!
21 It paws the earth and rejoices in its strength
when it charges out to battle.
22 It laughs at fear and is unafraid.
It does not run from the sword.
23 The arrows rattle against it,
and the spear and javelin flash.
24 It paws the ground fiercely
and rushes forward into battle when the ram's horn blows.
25 It snorts at the sound of the horn.
It senses the battle in the distance.
It quivers at the captain's commands
and the noise of battle.

26 "Is it your wisdom that makes the hawk soar
and spread its wings toward the south?
27 Is it at your command that the eagle rises
to the heights to make its nest?
28 It lives on the cliffs,
making its home on a distant, rocky crag.
29 From there it hunts its prey,
keeping watch with piercing eyes.
30 Its young gulp down blood.
Where there's a carcass, there you'll find it."

CHAPTER 40

Then the LORD said to Job,

2 "Do you still want to argue with the Almighty?
You are God's critic, but do you have the answers?"

Job Responds to the LORD

3 Then Job replied to the LORD,

4 "I am nothing—how could I ever find the answers?
I will cover my mouth with my hand.
5 I have said too much already.
I have nothing more to say."

The LORD Challenges Job Again

6 Then the LORD answered Job from the whirlwind:

7 "Brace yourself like a man,
because I have some questions for you,
and you must answer them.

8 "Will you discredit my justice
and condemn me just to prove you are right?
9 Are you as strong as God?
Can you thunder with a voice like his?
10 All right, put on your glory and splendor,
your honor and majesty.
11 Give vent to your anger.
Let it overflow against the proud.
12 Humiliate the proud with a glance;
walk on the wicked where they stand.
13 Bury them in the dust.
Imprison them in the world of the dead.
14 Then even I would praise you,
for your own strength would save you.

15 "Take a look at Behemoth,
which I made, just as I made you.
It eats grass like an ox.
16 See its powerful loins
and the muscles of its belly.
17 Its tail is as strong as a cedar.
The sinews of its thighs are knit tightly together.
18 Its bones are tubes of bronze.
Its limbs are bars of iron.
19 It is a prime example of God's handiwork,
and only its Creator can threaten it.
20 The mountains offer it their best food,
where all the wild animals play.
21 It lies under the lotus plants,
hidden by the reeds in the marsh.
22 The lotus plants give it shade
among the willows beside the stream.
23 It is not disturbed by the raging river,
not concerned when the swelling Jordan rushes around it.
24 No one can catch it off guard
or put a ring in its nose and lead it away.

CHAPTER 41

The LORD's Challenge Continues

1 "Can you catch Leviathan with a hook
or put a noose around its jaw?
2 Can you tie it with a rope through the nose
or pierce its jaw with a spike?
3 Will it beg you for mercy
or implore you for pity?

4 Will it agree to work for you,
to be your slave for life?
5 Can you make it a pet like a bird,
or give it to your little girls to play with?
6 Will merchants try to buy it
to sell it in their shops?
7 Will its hide be hurt by spears
or its head by a harpoon?
8 If you lay a hand on it,
you will certainly remember the battle
that follows.
You won't try that again!
9 No, it is useless to try to capture it.
The hunter who attempts it will be
knocked down.
10 And since no one dares to disturb it,
who then can stand up to me?
11 Who has given me anything that I need
to pay back?
Everything under heaven is mine.

12 "I want to emphasize Leviathan's limbs
and its enormous strength and graceful
form.
13 Who can strip off its hide,
and who can penetrate its double layer
of armor?
14 Who could pry open its jaws?
For its teeth are terrible!
15 The scales on its back are like rows of shields
tightly sealed together.
16 They are so close together
that no air can get between them.
17 Each scale sticks tight to the next.
They interlock and cannot be
penetrated.

18 "When it sneezes, it flashes light!
Its eyes are like the red of dawn.
19 Lightning leaps from its mouth;
flames of fire flash out.
20 Smoke streams from its nostrils
like steam from a pot heated over
burning rushes.
21 Its breath would kindle coals,
for flames shoot from its mouth.

22 "The tremendous strength in Leviathan's
neck
strikes terror wherever it goes.
23 Its flesh is hard and firm
and cannot be penetrated.
24 Its heart is hard as rock,
hard as a millstone.
25 When it rises, the mighty are afraid,
gripped by terror.
26 No sword can stop it,
no spear, dart, or javelin.
27 Iron is nothing but straw to that creature,
and bronze is like rotten wood.
28 Arrows cannot make it flee.
Stones shot from a sling are like bits of
grass.
29 Clubs are like a blade of grass,
and it laughs at the swish of javelins.
30 Its belly is covered with scales as sharp as
glass.
It plows up the ground as it drags through
the mud.

31 "Leviathan makes the water boil with its
commotion.
It stirs the depths like a pot of ointment.
32 The water glistens in its wake,
making the sea look white.
33 Nothing on earth is its equal,
no other creature so fearless.
34 Of all the creatures, it is the proudest.
It is the king of beasts."

CHAPTER 42
Job Responds to the LORD

Then Job replied to the LORD:

2 "I know that you can do anything,
and no one can stop you.
3 You asked, 'Who is this that questions my
wisdom with such ignorance?'
It is I—and I was talking about things
I knew nothing about,
things far too wonderful for me.
4 You said, 'Listen and I will speak!
I have some questions for you,
and you must answer them.'
5 I had only heard about you before,
but now I have seen you with my own eyes.
6 I take back everything I said,
and I sit in dust and ashes to show my
repentance."

Conclusion: The LORD Blesses Job

7 After the LORD had finished speaking to Job, he
said to Eliphaz the Temanite: "I am angry with
you and your two friends, for you have not spoken accurately about me, as my servant Job has.
8 So take seven bulls and seven rams and go to
my servant Job and offer a burnt offering for
yourselves. My servant Job will pray for you, and
I will accept his prayer on your behalf. I will not
treat you as you deserve, for you have not spoken accurately about me, as my servant Job has."

9 So Eliphaz the Temanite, Bildad the Shuhite,
and Zophar the Naamathite did as the LORD
commanded them, and the LORD accepted Job's
prayer.

10 When Job prayed for his friends, the LORD
restored his fortunes. In fact, the LORD gave him
twice as much as before! 11 Then all his brothers,
sisters, and former friends came and feasted with
him in his home. And they consoled him and
comforted him because of all the trials the LORD
had brought against him. And each of them
brought him a gift of money and a gold ring.

12 So the LORD blessed Job in the second half
of his life even more than in the beginning. For
now he had 14,000 sheep, 6,000 camels, 1,000
teams of oxen, and 1,000 female donkeys. 13 He
also gave Job seven more sons and three more
daughters. 14 He named his first daughter Jemi-
mah, the second Keziah, and the third Keren-
happuch. 15 In all the land no women were as
lovely as the daughters of Job. And their father
put them into his will along with their brothers.

16 Job lived 140 years after that, living to see
four generations of his children and grandchildren. 17 Then he died, an old man who had
lived a long, full life.

PSALMS Praises & Prayers

Look for 5 hidden messages in Psalms!

The book of Psalms contains songs of praise and prayers of all sorts. The psalms were written by people who

- **PRAISED GOD**
- **PLEADED WITH GOD**
- **PRAYED TO GOD**
- **PASSIONATELY LOVED GOD**

Name That Tune

David wrote most of the psalms in the Bible, and the rest were written by a few other people. Besides being a shepherd, king, and giant slayer, David could also carry a tune! Remember how he played music for King Saul? (If not, better go back and read 1 Samuel 16:14-23.) **Check out some of David's songs in Psalm 8 and Psalm 18.**

Hey, Little Lamb!

Why do you suppose there's so much talk about sheep and shepherds in the Bible? Maybe it's because sheep are such helpless animals. They need a shepherd to watch over them and protect them from wolves and other scary problems. Find out how *we're* like sheep, and see who's our shepherd. **Read Psalm 23 all the way through. (P.S. It's a great psalm to know when you're scared. It was written by David, who knew a little something about sheep, shepherds, and scary situations!)**

What a Chatterbox

Boy, David sure could talk—to God, that is. He talked to God when he was happy. He talked to God when he was sad. Then when he was scared, what did he do? You got it—he talked to God some more! **Look at Psalm 18:1-3 to see why David liked to talk so much (to God, that is).**

How Low Can You Go?

You didn't have to be happy to write one of the psalms. Some of the psalm writers were really sad and upset. But they knew that God likes to hear from us no matter *how* we're feeling! **Read how one person cried out to God in Psalm 130. (Then the next time you're upset, don't be afraid to go to God!)**

Help!

Where can you find help when you're in trouble? **Read Psalm 121 to find out!**

HELP!!

Shhhhh!

Soccer practice. Homework. Dishes. Friends. TV. Math test. Computer games. When's the last time you sat perfectly still for a few minutes? Why would you want to do that? **Check out a perfectly good reason in Psalm 46:10a.**

STOP

In God We Trust

Did you know that people who trust in God have extra protection? No way, you say? It's true! **Check out Psalm 91:11 to see who's protecting *you*! (In fact, read all of Psalm 91. It'll make you feel good!)**

Timeline

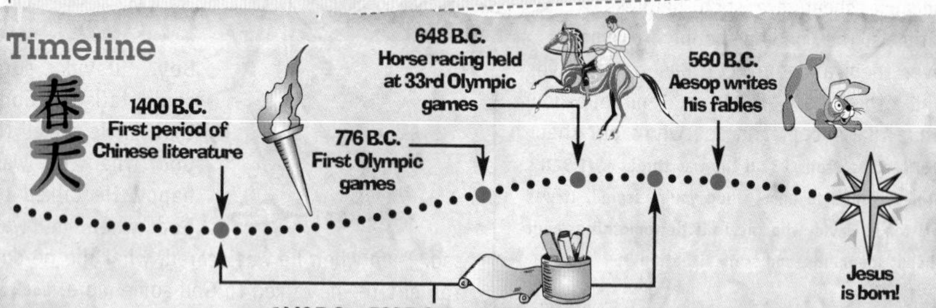

春天

1400 B.C. First period of Chinese literature

776 B.C. First Olympic games

648 B.C. Horse racing held at 33rd Olympic games

560 B.C. Aesop writes his fables

Jesus is born!

1440 B.C. – 586 B.C. Psalms are written

Jesus came from the same family as David. So it's not surprising that many of David's psalms told about things that would happen to Jesus. For example, Psalm 22:16-18 describes Jesus' crucifixion. And, believe it or not, Jesus quoted from Psalm 22 when he was on the cross! There's no such thing as coincidence in the Bible. **God's Word is real and true, and the whole thing points to one person: Jesus!**

Book One (Psalms 1–41)

Psalm 1

1 Oh, the joys of those who do not
follow the advice of the wicked,
or stand around with sinners,
or join in with mockers.
2 But they delight in the law of the Lord,
meditating on it day and night.
3 They are like trees planted along the
riverbank,
bearing fruit each season.
Their leaves never wither,
and they prosper in all they do.

4 But not the wicked!
They are like worthless chaff, scattered
by the wind.
5 They will be condemned at the time
of judgment.
Sinners will have no place among
the godly.
6 For the Lord watches over the path
of the godly,
but the path of the wicked leads
to destruction.

Psalm 2

1 Why are the nations so angry?
Why do they waste their time with futile
plans?
2 The kings of the earth prepare for battle;
the rulers plot together
against the Lord
and against his anointed one.
3 "Let us break their chains," they cry,
"and free ourselves from slavery to God."

4 But the one who rules in heaven laughs.
The Lord scoffs at them.
5 Then in anger he rebukes them,
terrifying them with his fierce fury.
6 For the Lord declares, "I have placed my
chosen king on the throne
in Jerusalem, on my holy mountain."

7 The king proclaims the Lord's decree:
"The Lord said to me, 'You are my son.
Today I have become your Father.
8 Only ask, and I will give you the nations
as your inheritance,
the whole earth as your possession.
9 You will break them with an iron rod
and smash them like clay pots.'"

10 Now then, you kings, act wisely!
Be warned, you rulers of the earth!
11 Serve the Lord with reverent fear,
and rejoice with trembling.
12 Submit to God's royal son, or he will become
angry,
and you will be destroyed in the midst
of all your activities—
for his anger flares up in an instant.
But what joy for all who take refuge in him!

Psalm 3

A psalm of David, regarding the time David fled from his son Absalom.

1 O Lord, I have so many enemies;
so many are against me.
2 So many are saying,
"God will never rescue him!" *Interlude*

3 But you, O Lord, are a shield around me;
you are my glory, the one who holds my
head high.
4 I cried out to the Lord,
and he answered me from his holy
mountain. *Interlude*

5 I lay down and slept,
yet I woke up in safety,
for the Lord was watching over me.
6 I am not afraid of ten thousand enemies
who surround me on every side.

7 Arise, O Lord!
Rescue me, my God!
Slap all my enemies in the face!
Shatter the teeth of the wicked!
8 Victory comes from you, O Lord.
May you bless your people. *Interlude*

Psalm 4

For the choir director: A psalm of David, to be accompanied by stringed instruments.

1 Answer me when I call to you,
O God who declares me innocent.
Free me from my troubles.
Have mercy on me and hear my prayer.

2 How long will you people ruin my
reputation?
How long will you make groundless
accusations?
How long will you continue your lies?
Interlude

3 You can be sure of this:
The Lord set apart the godly for himself.
The Lord will answer when I call to him.

4 Don't sin by letting anger control you.
Think about it overnight and remain silent. *Interlude*
5 Offer sacrifices in the right spirit,
and trust the LORD.

6 Many people say, "Who will show us better times?"
Let your face smile on us, LORD.
7 You have given me greater joy
than those who have abundant harvests of grain and new wine.
8 In peace I will lie down and sleep,
for you alone, O LORD, will keep me safe.

PSALM 5

For the choir director: A psalm of David, to be accompanied by the flute.

1 O LORD, hear me as I pray;
pay attention to my groaning.
2 Listen to my cry for help, my King and my God,
for I pray to no one but you.
3 Listen to my voice in the morning, LORD.
Each morning I bring my requests to you and wait expectantly.

4 O God, you take no pleasure in wickedness;
you cannot tolerate the sins of the wicked.
5 Therefore, the proud may not stand in your presence,
for you hate all who do evil.
6 You will destroy those who tell lies.
The LORD detests murderers and deceivers.

7 Because of your unfailing love, I can enter your house;
I will worship at your Temple with deepest awe.
8 Lead me in the right path, O LORD,
or my enemies will conquer me.
Make your way plain for me to follow.

9 My enemies cannot speak a truthful word.
Their deepest desire is to destroy others.
Their talk is foul, like the stench from an open grave.
Their tongues are filled with flattery.
10 O God, declare them guilty.
Let them be caught in their own traps.
Drive them away because of their many sins,
for they have rebelled against you.

11 But let all who take refuge in you rejoice;
let them sing joyful praises forever.
Spread your protection over them,
that all who love your name may be filled with joy.
12 For you bless the godly, O LORD;
you surround them with your shield of love.

PSALM 6

For the choir director: A psalm of David, to be accompanied by an eight-stringed instrument.

1 O LORD, don't rebuke me in your anger
or discipline me in your rage.
2 Have compassion on me, LORD, for I am weak.
Heal me, LORD, for my bones are in agony.
3 I am sick at heart.
How long, O LORD, until you restore me?

4 Return, O LORD, and rescue me.
Save me because of your unfailing love.
5 For the dead do not remember you.
Who can praise you from the grave?

6 I am worn out from sobbing.
All night I flood my bed with weeping,
drenching it with my tears.
7 My vision is blurred by grief;
my eyes are worn out because of all my enemies.

8 Go away, all you who do evil,
for the LORD has heard my weeping.
9 The LORD has heard my plea;
the LORD will answer my prayer.
10 May all my enemies be disgraced and terrified.
May they suddenly turn back in shame.

PSALM 7

A psalm of David, which he sang to the LORD concerning Cush of the tribe of Benjamin.

1 I come to you for protection, O LORD my God.
Save me from my persecutors—rescue me!
2 If you don't, they will maul me like a lion,
tearing me to pieces with no one to rescue me.

3 O LORD my God, if I have done wrong
or am guilty of injustice,
4 if I have betrayed a friend
or plundered my enemy without cause,
5 then let my enemies capture me.
Let them trample me into the ground
and drag my honor in the dust. *Interlude*

6 Arise, O LORD, in anger!
Stand up against the fury of my enemies!
Wake up, my God, and bring justice!

7 Gather the nations before you.
Rule over them from on high.
8 The LORD judges the nations.
Declare me righteous, O LORD,
for I am innocent, O Most High!
9 End the evil of those who are wicked,
and defend the righteous.
For you look deep within the mind and heart,
O righteous God.

10 God is my shield,
saving those whose hearts are true
and right.
11 God is an honest judge.
He is angry with the wicked every day.

12 If a person does not repent,
God will sharpen his sword;
he will bend and string his bow.
13 He will prepare his deadly weapons
and shoot his flaming arrows.

14 The wicked conceive evil;
they are pregnant with trouble
and give birth to lies.
15 They dig a deep pit to trap others,
then fall into it themselves.
16 The trouble they make for others backfires
on them.
The violence they plan falls on their
own heads.

17 I will thank the LORD because he is just;
I will sing praise to the name of the LORD
Most High.

PSALM 8

For the choir director: A psalm of David, to be accompanied by a stringed instrument.

1 O LORD, our Lord, your majestic name fills
the earth!
Your glory is higher than the heavens.
2 You have taught children and infants
to tell of your strength,
silencing your enemies
and all who oppose you.

3 When I look at the night sky and see the
work of your fingers—
the moon and the stars you set in place—
4 what are mere mortals that you should think
about them,
human beings that you should care
for them?
5 Yet you made them only a little lower
than God
and crowned them with glory and honor.
6 You gave them charge of everything you
made,
putting all things under their authority—
7 the flocks and the herds
and all the wild animals,
8 the birds in the sky, the fish in the sea,
and everything that swims the ocean
currents.

9 O LORD, our Lord, your majestic name fills
the earth!

PSALM 9

For the choir director: A psalm of David, to be sung to the tune "Death of the Son."

1 I will praise you, LORD, with all my heart;
I will tell of all the marvelous things you
have done.
2 I will be filled with joy because of you.
I will sing praises to your name, O Most
High.

3 My enemies retreated;
they staggered and died when you
appeared.
4 For you have judged in my favor;
from your throne you have judged with
fairness.
5 You have rebuked the nations and destroyed
the wicked;
you have erased their names forever.
6 The enemy is finished, in endless ruins;
the cities you uprooted are now
forgotten.

7 But the LORD reigns forever,
executing judgment from his throne.
8 He will judge the world with justice
and rule the nations with fairness.
9 The LORD is a shelter for the oppressed,
a refuge in times of trouble.
10 Those who know your name trust in you,
for you, O LORD, do not abandon those who
search for you.

11 Sing praises to the LORD who reigns in
Jerusalem.
Tell the world about his unforgettable
deeds.
12 For he who avenges murder cares for the
helpless.
He does not ignore the cries of those
who suffer.

13 LORD, have mercy on me.
See how my enemies torment me.
Snatch me back from the jaws of death.

14 Save me so I can praise you publicly at
Jerusalem's gates,
so I can rejoice that you have rescued me.

15 The nations have fallen into the pit they dug
for others.
Their own feet have been caught in the
trap they set.
16 The LORD is known for his justice.
The wicked are trapped by their own
deeds. *Quiet Interlude*

17 The wicked will go down to the grave.
This is the fate of all the nations who
ignore God.
18 But the needy will not be ignored forever;
the hopes of the poor will not always
be crushed.

19 Arise, O LORD!
Do not let mere mortals defy you!
Judge the nations!
20 Make them tremble in fear, O LORD.
Let the nations know they are merely
human. *Interlude*

PSALM 10

1 O LORD, why do you stand so far away?
Why do you hide when I am in trouble?
2 The wicked arrogantly hunt down the poor.
Let them be caught in the evil they plan
for others.
3 For they brag about their evil desires;
they praise the greedy and curse the LORD.

4 The wicked are too proud to seek God.
They seem to think that God is dead.
5 Yet they succeed in everything they do.
They do not see your punishment
awaiting them.
They sneer at all their enemies.
6 They think, "Nothing bad will ever happen
to us!
We will be free of trouble forever!"

7 Their mouths are full of cursing, lies, and
threats.
Trouble and evil are on the tips of their
tongues.
8 They lurk in ambush in the villages,
waiting to murder innocent people.
They are always searching for helpless
victims.
9 Like lions crouched in hiding,
they wait to pounce on the helpless.
Like hunters they capture the helpless
and drag them away in nets.

10 Their helpless victims are crushed;
they fall beneath the strength of the
wicked.
11 The wicked think, "God isn't watching us!
He has closed his eyes and won't even see
what we do!"

12 Arise, O LORD!
Punish the wicked, O God!
Do not ignore the helpless!
13 Why do the wicked get away with despising
God?
They think, "God will never call us to
account."
14 But you see the trouble and grief they cause.
You take note of it and punish them.
The helpless put their trust in you.
You defend the orphans.

15 Break the arms of these wicked, evil people!
Go after them until the last one is
destroyed.
16 The LORD is king forever and ever!
The godless nations will vanish from
the land.
17 LORD, you know the hopes of the helpless.
Surely you will hear their cries and
comfort them.
18 You will bring justice to the orphans and
the oppressed,
so mere people can no longer terrify them.

PSALM 11

For the choir director: A psalm of David.

1 I trust in the LORD for protection.
So why do you say to me,
"Fly like a bird to the mountains for
safety!
2 The wicked are stringing their bows
and fitting their arrows on the bowstrings.
They shoot from the shadows
at those whose hearts are right.
3 The foundations of law and order have
collapsed.
What can the righteous do?"

4 But the LORD is in his holy Temple;
the LORD still rules from heaven.
He watches everyone closely,
examining every person on earth.
5 The LORD examines both the righteous and
the wicked.
He hates those who love violence.
6 He will rain down blazing coals and burning
sulfur on the wicked,
punishing them with scorching winds.

7 For the righteous LORD loves justice.
The virtuous will see his face.

PSALM 12

For the choir director: A psalm of David, to be accompanied by an eight-stringed instrument.

1 Help, O LORD, for the godly are fast
disappearing!
The faithful have vanished from the earth!
2 Neighbors lie to each other,
speaking with flattering lips and deceitful
hearts.
3 May the LORD cut off their flattering lips
and silence their boastful tongues.
4 They say, "We will lie to our hearts' content.
Our lips are our own—who can stop us?"

5 The LORD replies, "I have seen violence done
to the helpless,
and I have heard the groans of the poor.
Now I will rise up to rescue them,
as they have longed for me to do."
6 The LORD's promises are pure,
like silver refined in a furnace,
purified seven times over.
7 Therefore, LORD, we know you will protect
the oppressed,
preserving them forever from this lying
generation,
8 even though the wicked strut about,
and evil is praised throughout the land.

PSALM 13

For the choir director: A psalm of David.

1 O LORD, how long will you forget me?
Forever?
How long will you look the other way?
2 How long must I struggle with anguish in
my soul,
with sorrow in my heart every day?
How long will my enemy have the upper
hand?

3 Turn and answer me, O LORD my God!
Restore the sparkle to my eyes, or
I will die.
4 Don't let my enemies gloat, saying, "We
have defeated him!"
Don't let them rejoice at my downfall.

5 But I trust in your unfailing love.
I will rejoice because you have
rescued me.
6 I will sing to the LORD
because he is good to me.

PSALM 14

For the choir director: A psalm of David.

1 Only fools say in their hearts,
"There is no God."
They are corrupt, and their actions are
evil;
not one of them does good!

2 The LORD looks down from heaven
on the entire human race;
he looks to see if anyone is truly wise,
if anyone seeks God.
3 But no, all have turned away;
all have become corrupt.
No one does good,
not a single one!

4 Will those who do evil never learn?
They eat up my people like bread
and wouldn't think of praying to the LORD.
5 Terror will grip them,
for God is with those who obey him.
6 The wicked frustrate the plans of the
oppressed,
but the LORD will protect his people.

7 Who will come from Mount Zion to rescue
Israel?
When the LORD restores his people,
Jacob will shout with joy, and Israel will
rejoice.

PSALM 15

A psalm of David.

1 Who may worship in your sanctuary,
LORD?
Who may enter your presence on your
holy hill?
2 Those who lead blameless lives and do what
is right,
speaking the truth from sincere hearts.
3 Those who refuse to gossip
or harm their neighbors
or speak evil of their friends.
4 Those who despise flagrant sinners,
and honor the faithful followers of
the LORD,
and keep their promises even when
it hurts.
5 Those who lend money without charging
interest,
and who cannot be bribed to lie about
the innocent.
Such people will stand firm forever.

Psalm 16 . . . page 538

PSALM 16
A psalm of David.

1 Keep me safe, O God,
for I have come to you for refuge.

2 I said to the LORD, "You are my Master!
Every good thing I have comes from you."
3 The godly people in the land
are my true heroes!
I take pleasure in them!
4 Troubles multiply for those who chase after
other gods.
I will not take part in their sacrifices
of blood
or even speak the names of their gods.

5 LORD, you alone are my inheritance, my cup
of blessing.
You guard all that is mine.
6 The land you have given me is a pleasant
land.
What a wonderful inheritance!

7 I will bless the LORD who guides me;
even at night my heart instructs me.
8 I know the LORD is always with me.
I will not be shaken, for he is right
beside me.

9 No wonder my heart is glad, and I rejoice.
My body rests in safety.
10 For you will not leave my soul among
the dead
or allow your holy one to rot in the grave.
11 You will show me the way of life,
granting me the joy of your presence
and the pleasures of living with you
forever.

PSALM 17
A prayer of David.

1 O LORD, hear my plea for justice.
Listen to my cry for help.
Pay attention to my prayer,
for it comes from honest lips.
2 Declare me innocent,
for you see those who do right.

3 You have tested my thoughts and examined
my heart in the night.
You have scrutinized me and found
nothing wrong.
I am determined not to sin in what I say.
4 I have followed your commands,
which keep me from following cruel and
evil people.
5 My steps have stayed on your path;
I have not wavered from following you.

6 I am praying to you because I know you will
answer, O God.
Bend down and listen as I pray.
7 Show me your unfailing love in wonderful
ways.
By your mighty power you rescue
those who seek refuge from their
enemies.
8 Guard me as you would guard your own eyes.
Hide me in the shadow of your wings.
9 Protect me from wicked people who
attack me,
from murderous enemies who
surround me.
10 They are without pity.
Listen to their boasting!
11 They track me down and surround me,
watching for the chance to throw me
to the ground.
12 They are like hungry lions, eager to tear
me apart—
like young lions hiding in ambush.

13 Arise, O LORD!
Stand against them, and bring them
to their knees!
Rescue me from the wicked with your
sword!
14 By the power of your hand, O LORD,
destroy those who look to this world for
their reward.
But satisfy the hunger of your treasured
ones.
May their children have plenty,
leaving an inheritance for their
descendants.
15 Because I am righteous, I will see you.
When I awake, I will see you face to face
and be satisfied.

PSALM 18
For the choir director: A psalm of David, the servant of the LORD. He sang this song to the LORD on the day the LORD rescued him from all his enemies and from Saul. He sang:

1 I love you, LORD;
you are my strength.
2 The LORD is my rock, my fortress, and
my savior;
my God is my rock, in whom I find
protection.
He is my shield, the power that saves me,
and my place of safety.

ROCK SOLID!

Remember the three little pigs? Sticks and straw just couldn't stand against the wolf's bad breath. If they had tried solid rock, things would've gone a little better.

It's Like This

1 Get a set of cards, and stand two of them up about three inches apart. (You can bend them a little to get going.)

2 Set a card on top of the two cards.

3 Keep building around and on top of the cards until you've built a house (or until it falls down)!

4 Now build a house using blocks. See the difference?

TRYING TO LIVE WITHOUT GOD IS LIKE TRYING TO BUILD A HOUSE OF CARDS TO KEEP YOU SAFE. But building a house out of blocks was a lot easier, right? Living with God is like living in a solid rock house.

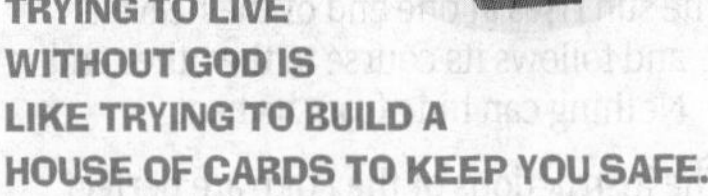

Read PSALM 18:1-36 to learn about God's rock-solid protection.

3 I called on the LORD, who is worthy of praise,
and he saved me from my enemies.

4 The ropes of death entangled me;
floods of destruction swept over me.
5 The grave wrapped its ropes around me;
death laid a trap in my path.
6 But in my distress I cried out to the LORD;
yes, I prayed to my God for help.
He heard me from his sanctuary;
my cry to him reached his ears.

7 Then the earth quaked and trembled.
The foundations of the mountains shook;
they quaked because of his anger.
8 Smoke poured from his nostrils;
fierce flames leaped from his mouth.
Glowing coals blazed forth from him.
9 He opened the heavens and came down;
dark storm clouds were beneath his feet.
10 Mounted on a mighty angelic being, he flew,
soaring on the wings of the wind.
11 He shrouded himself in darkness,
veiling his approach with dark rain clouds.
12 Thick clouds shielded the brightness
around him
and rained down hail and burning coals.
13 The LORD thundered from heaven;
the voice of the Most High resounded
amid the hail and burning coals.
14 He shot his arrows and scattered his
enemies;
great bolts of lightning flashed, and they
were confused.
15 Then at your command, O LORD,
at the blast of your breath,
the bottom of the sea could be seen,
and the foundations of the earth were
laid bare.

16 He reached down from heaven and
rescued me;
he drew me out of deep waters.
17 He rescued me from my powerful enemies,
from those who hated me and were too
strong for me.
18 They attacked me at a moment when I was
in distress,
but the LORD supported me.
19 He led me to a place of safety;
he rescued me because he delights in me.
20 The LORD rewarded me for doing right;
he restored me because of my innocence.
21 For I have kept the ways of the LORD;
I have not turned from my God to follow
evil.

22 I have followed all his regulations;
I have never abandoned his decrees.
23 I am blameless before God;
I have kept myself from sin.
24 The LORD rewarded me for doing right.
He has seen my innocence.

25 To the faithful you show yourself faithful;
to those with integrity you show integrity.
26 To the pure you show yourself pure,
but to the crooked you show yourself shrewd.
27 You rescue the humble,
but you humiliate the proud.
28 You light a lamp for me.
The LORD, my God, lights up my darkness.
29 In your strength I can crush an army;
with my God I can scale any wall.

30 God's way is perfect.
All the LORD's promises prove true.
He is a shield for all who look to him for protection.
31 For who is God except the LORD?
Who but our God is a solid rock?
32 God arms me with strength,
and he makes my way perfect.
33 He makes me as surefooted as a deer,
enabling me to stand on mountain heights.
34 He trains my hands for battle;
he strengthens my arm to draw a bronze bow.
35 You have given me your shield of victory.
Your right hand supports me;
your help has made me great.
36 You have made a wide path for my feet
to keep them from slipping.

37 I chased my enemies and caught them;
I did not stop until they were conquered.
38 I struck them down so they could not get up;
they fell beneath my feet.
39 You have armed me with strength for the battle;
you have subdued my enemies under my feet.
40 You placed my foot on their necks.
I have destroyed all who hated me.
41 They called for help, but no one came to their rescue.
They even cried to the LORD, but he refused to answer.
42 I ground them as fine as dust in the wind.
I swept them into the gutter like dirt.
43 You gave me victory over my accusers.
You appointed me ruler over nations;
people I don't even know now serve me.
44 As soon as they hear of me, they submit;
foreign nations cringe before me.
45 They all lose their courage
and come trembling from their strongholds.

46 The LORD lives! Praise to my Rock!
May the God of my salvation be exalted!
47 He is the God who pays back those who harm me;
he subdues the nations under me
48 and rescues me from my enemies.
You hold me safe beyond the reach of my enemies;
you save me from violent opponents.
49 For this, O LORD, I will praise you among the nations;
I will sing praises to your name.
50 You give great victories to your king;
you show unfailing love to your anointed,
to David and all his descendants forever.

PSALM 19

For the choir director: A psalm of David.

1 The heavens proclaim the glory of God.
The skies display his craftsmanship.
2 Day after day they continue to speak;
night after night they make him known.
3 They speak without a sound or word;
their voice is never heard.
4 Yet their message has gone throughout the earth,
and their words to all the world.

God has made a home in the heavens for the sun.
5 It bursts forth like a radiant bridegroom after his wedding.
It rejoices like a great athlete eager to run the race.
6 The sun rises at one end of the heavens
and follows its course to the other end.
Nothing can hide from its heat.

7 The instructions of the LORD are perfect,
reviving the soul.
The decrees of the LORD are trustworthy,
making wise the simple.
8 The commandments of the LORD are right,
bringing joy to the heart.
The commands of the LORD are clear,
giving insight for living.

9 Reverence for the LORD is pure,
lasting forever.
The laws of the LORD are true;
each one is fair.
10 They are more desirable than gold,
even the finest gold.
They are sweeter than honey,
even honey dripping from the comb.
11 They are a warning to your servant,
a great reward for those who obey them.

12 How can I know all the sins lurking in
my heart?
Cleanse me from these hidden faults.
13 Keep your servant from deliberate sins!
Don't let them control me.
Then I will be free of guilt
and innocent of great sin.

14 May the words of my mouth
and the meditation of my heart
be pleasing to you,
O LORD, my rock and my redeemer.

PSALM 20

For the choir director: A psalm of David.

1 In times of trouble, may the LORD answer
your cry.
May the name of the God of Jacob keep
you safe from all harm.
2 May he send you help from his sanctuary
and strengthen you from Jerusalem.
3 May he remember all your gifts
and look favorably on your burnt
offerings. *Interlude*

4 May he grant your heart's desires
and make all your plans succeed.
5 May we shout for joy when we hear of your
victory
and raise a victory banner in the name
of our God.
May the LORD answer all your prayers.

6 Now I know that the LORD rescues his
anointed king.
He will answer him from his holy heaven
and rescue him by his great power.
7 Some nations boast of their chariots and
horses,
but we boast in the name of the LORD
our God.
8 Those nations will fall down and collapse,
but we will rise up and stand firm.

9 Give victory to our king, O LORD!
Answer our cry for help.

PSALM 21

For the choir director: A psalm of David.

1 How the king rejoices in your strength,
O LORD!
He shouts with joy because you give him
victory.
2 For you have given him his heart's desire;
you have withheld nothing he requested.
Interlude

3 You welcomed him back with success and
prosperity.
You placed a crown of finest gold on
his head.
4 He asked you to preserve his life,
and you granted his request.
The days of his life stretch on forever.
5 Your victory brings him great honor,
and you have clothed him with splendor
and majesty.
6 You have endowed him with eternal
blessings
and given him the joy of your presence.
7 For the king trusts in the LORD.
The unfailing love of the Most High will
keep him from stumbling.

8 You will capture all your enemies.
Your strong right hand will seize all who
hate you.
9 You will throw them in a flaming furnace
when you appear.
The LORD will consume them in his anger;
fire will devour them.
10 You will wipe their children from the face
of the earth;
they will never have descendants.
11 Although they plot against you,
their evil schemes will never succeed.
12 For they will turn and run
when they see your arrows aimed
at them.
13 Rise up, O LORD, in all your power.
With music and singing we celebrate
your mighty acts.

PSALM 22

For the choir director: A psalm of David, to be sung to the tune "Doe of the Dawn."

1 My God, my God, why have you
abandoned me?
Why are you so far away when I groan
for help?
2 Every day I call to you, my God, but you do
not answer.

Every night I lift my voice, but I find no
relief.

3 Yet you are holy,
enthroned on the praises of Israel.
4 Our ancestors trusted in you,
and you rescued them.
5 They cried out to you and were saved.
They trusted in you and were never
disgraced.

6 But I am a worm and not a man.
I am scorned and despised by all!
7 Everyone who sees me mocks me.
They sneer and shake their heads, saying,
8 "Is this the one who relies on the LORD?
Then let the LORD save him!
If the LORD loves him so much,
let the LORD rescue him!"

9 Yet you brought me safely from my mother's
womb
and led me to trust you at my mother's
breast.
10 I was thrust into your arms at my birth.
You have been my God from the moment
I was born.

11 Do not stay so far from me,
for trouble is near,
and no one else can help me.
12 My enemies surround me like a herd of bulls;
fierce bulls of Bashan have hemmed me in!
13 Like lions they open their jaws against me,
roaring and tearing into their prey.
14 My life is poured out like water,
and all my bones are out of joint.
My heart is like wax,
melting within me.
15 My strength has dried up like sunbaked clay.
My tongue sticks to the roof of my mouth.
You have laid me in the dust and left me
for dead.
16 My enemies surround me like a pack of dogs;
an evil gang closes in on me.
They have pierced my hands and feet.
17 I can count all my bones.
My enemies stare at me and gloat.
18 They divide my garments among themselves
and throw dice for my clothing.

19 O LORD, do not stay far away!
You are my strength; come quickly
to my aid!
20 Save me from the sword;
spare my precious life from these dogs.
21 Snatch me from the lion's jaws
and from the horns of these wild oxen.

22 I will proclaim your name to my brothers and
sisters.
I will praise you among your assembled
people.
23 Praise the LORD, all you who fear him!
Honor him, all you descendants of Jacob!
Show him reverence, all you descendants
of Israel!
24 For he has not ignored or belittled the
suffering of the needy.
He has not turned his back on them,
but has listened to their cries for help.

25 I will praise you in the great assembly.
I will fulfill my vows in the presence of
those who worship you.
26 The poor will eat and be satisfied.
All who seek the LORD will praise him.
Their hearts will rejoice with everlasting
joy.
27 The whole earth will acknowledge the LORD
and return to him.
All the families of the nations will bow
down before him.
28 For royal power belongs to the LORD.
He rules all the nations.

29 Let the rich of the earth feast and worship.
Bow before him, all who are mortal,
all whose lives will end as dust.
30 Our children will also serve him.
Future generations will hear about the
wonders of the Lord.
31 His righteous acts will be told to those not
yet born.
They will hear about everything he
has done.

PSALM 23

A psalm of David.

1 The LORD is my shepherd;
I have all that I need.
2 He lets me rest in green
meadows;
he leads me beside peaceful
streams.
3 He renews my strength.
He guides me along right paths,
bringing honor to his name.
4 Even when I walk
through the darkest valley,
I will not be afraid,
for you are close beside me.
Your rod and your staff
protect and comfort me.

5 You prepare a feast for me
in the presence of my enemies.
You honor me by anointing my head
with oil.
My cup overflows with blessings.
6 Surely your goodness and unfailing love will
pursue me
all the days of my life,
and I will live in the house of the LORD
forever.

PSALM 24

A psalm of David.

1 The earth is the LORD's, and everything in it.
The world and all its people belong
to him.
2 For he laid the earth's foundation on the seas
and built it on the ocean depths.

3 Who may climb the mountain of the
LORD?
Who may stand in his holy place?
4 Only those whose hands and hearts
are pure,
who do not worship idols
and never tell lies.
5 They will receive the LORD's blessing
and have a right relationship with God
their savior.
6 Such people may seek you
and worship in your presence, O God
of Jacob. *Interlude*
7 Open up, ancient gates!
Open up, ancient doors,
and let the King of glory enter.
8 Who is the King of glory?
The LORD, strong and mighty;
the LORD, invincible in battle.
9 Open up, ancient gates!
Open up, ancient doors,
and let the King of glory enter.
10 Who is the King of glory?
The LORD of Heaven's Armies—
he is the King of glory. *Interlude*

PSALM 25

A psalm of David.

1 O LORD, I give my life to you.
2 I trust in you, my God!
Do not let me be disgraced,
or let my enemies rejoice in my defeat.
3 No one who trusts in you will ever be
disgraced,
but disgrace comes to those who try
to deceive others.

4 Show me the right path, O LORD;
point out the road for me to follow.
5 Lead me by your truth and teach me,
for you are the God who saves me.
All day long I put my hope in you.
6 Remember, O LORD, your compassion and
unfailing love,
which you have shown from long ages
past.
7 Do not remember the rebellious sins of
my youth.
Remember me in the light of your
unfailing love,
for you are merciful, O LORD.

8 The LORD is good and does what is right;
he shows the proper path to those who
go astray.
9 He leads the humble in doing right,
teaching them his way.
10 The LORD leads with unfailing love and
faithfulness
all who keep his covenant and obey
his demands.

11 For the honor of your name, O LORD,
forgive my many, many sins.
12 Who are those who fear the LORD?
He will show them the path they should
choose.
13 They will live in prosperity,
and their children will inherit the land.
14 The LORD is a friend to those who fear him.
He teaches them his covenant.
15 My eyes are always on the LORD,
for he rescues me from the traps of
my enemies.

16 Turn to me and have mercy,
for I am alone and in deep distress.
17 My problems go from bad to worse.
Oh, save me from them all!
18 Feel my pain and see my trouble.
Forgive all my sins.
19 See how many enemies I have
and how viciously they hate me!
20 Protect me! Rescue my life from them!
Do not let me be disgraced, for in you
I take refuge.
21 May integrity and honesty protect me,
for I put my hope in you.

22 O God, ransom Israel
from all its troubles.

Psalm 26 . . . page 544

PSALM 26
A psalm of David.

1 Declare me innocent, O LORD,
for I have acted with integrity;
I have trusted in the LORD without wavering.
2 Put me on trial, LORD, and cross-examine me.
Test my motives and my heart.
3 For I am always aware of your unfailing love,
and I have lived according to your truth.
4 I do not spend time with liars
or go along with hypocrites.
5 I hate the gatherings of those who do evil,
and I refuse to join in with the wicked.
6 I wash my hands to declare my innocence.
I come to your altar, O LORD,
7 singing a song of thanksgiving
and telling of all your wonders.
8 I love your sanctuary, LORD,
the place where your glorious presence dwells.
9 Don't let me suffer the fate of sinners.
Don't condemn me along with murderers.
10 Their hands are dirty with evil schemes,
and they constantly take bribes.
11 But I am not like that; I live with integrity.
So redeem me and show me mercy.
12 Now I stand on solid ground,
and I will publicly praise the LORD.

PSALM 27
A psalm of David.

1 The LORD is my light and my salvation—
so why should I be afraid?
The LORD is my fortress, protecting me from danger,
so why should I tremble?
2 When evil people come to devour me,
when my enemies and foes attack me,
they will stumble and fall.
3 Though a mighty army surrounds me,
my heart will not be afraid.
Even if I am attacked,
I will remain confident.
4 The one thing I ask of the LORD—
the thing I seek most—
is to live in the house of the LORD all the days of my life,
delighting in the LORD's perfections
and meditating in his Temple.
5 For he will conceal me there when troubles come;
he will hide me in his sanctuary.

Clues to the Savior

Faithful people searched the Scriptures to learn more about the promised Messiah. Clues pointing to the promised Savior could be found in every book of the Old Testament. When Jesus began his public ministry, the Holy Spirit used these clues to help people realize that Jesus was the Messiah!

Check out these pairs of clues from the Old and New Testament, and see how they lead to Jesus:

PSALM 16:8-10 and LUKE 24:5-7; PSALM 22:1-21 and MATTHEW 27:46.

YOU CAN LEAVE CLUES THAT WILL POINT OTHERS TO JESUS TOO!

Cut four strips of paper. On each one, draw or write something about Jesus' life. Fold the papers and hide them in the room. Invite a friend to search the room for clues to your mystery person. **See if your friend discovers that all the clues point to Jesus!**

He will place me out of reach on a high rock.
6 Then I will hold my head high
above my enemies who surround me.
At his sanctuary I will offer sacrifices with shouts of joy,
singing and praising the LORD with music.
7 Hear me as I pray, O LORD.
Be merciful and answer me!

8 My heart has heard you say, "Come and talk
with me."
And my heart responds, "Lord, I am
coming."
9 Do not turn your back on me.
Do not reject your servant in anger.
You have always been my helper.
Don't leave me now; don't abandon me,
O God of my salvation!
10 Even if my father and mother abandon me,
the Lord will hold me close.

11 Teach me how to live, O Lord.
Lead me along the right path,
for my enemies are waiting for me.
12 Do not let me fall into their hands.
For they accuse me of things I've
never done;
with every breath they threaten me
with violence.
13 Yet I am confident I will see the Lord's
goodness
while I am here in the land of the living.

14 Wait patiently for the Lord.
Be brave and courageous.
Yes, wait patiently for the Lord.

PSALM 28

A psalm of David.

1 I pray to you, O Lord, my rock.
Do not turn a deaf ear to me.
For if you are silent,
I might as well give up and die.
2 Listen to my prayer for mercy
as I cry out to you for help,
as I lift my hands toward your holy
sanctuary.

3 Do not drag me away with the wicked—
with those who do evil—
those who speak friendly words to their
neighbors
while planning evil in their hearts.
4 Give them the punishment they so richly
deserve!
Measure it out in proportion to their
wickedness.
Pay them back for all their evil deeds!
Give them a taste of what they have
done to others.
5 They care nothing for what the Lord
has done
or for what his hands have made.
So he will tear them down,
and they will never be rebuilt!

6 Praise the Lord!
For he has heard my cry for mercy.
7 The Lord is my strength and shield.
I trust him with all my heart.
He helps me, and my heart is filled with joy.
I burst out in songs of thanksgiving.
8 The Lord gives his people strength.
He is a safe fortress for his anointed
king.
9 Save your people!
Bless Israel, your special possession.
Lead them like a shepherd,
and carry them in your arms forever.

PSALM 29

A psalm of David.

1 Honor the Lord, you heavenly beings;
honor the Lord for his glory and strength.
2 Honor the Lord for the glory of his name.
Worship the Lord in the splendor of his
holiness.

3 The voice of the Lord echoes above the sea.
The God of glory thunders.
The Lord thunders over the mighty sea.
4 The voice of the Lord is powerful;
the voice of the Lord is majestic.
5 The voice of the Lord splits the mighty
cedars;
the Lord shatters the cedars of Lebanon.
6 He makes Lebanon's mountains skip like
a calf;
he makes Mount Hermon leap like
a young wild ox.
7 The voice of the Lord strikes
with bolts of lightning.
8 The voice of the Lord makes the barren
wilderness quake;
the Lord shakes the wilderness
of Kadesh.
9 The voice of the Lord twists mighty oaks
and strips the forests bare.
In his Temple everyone shouts, "Glory!"

10 The Lord rules over the floodwaters.
The Lord reigns as king forever.
11 The Lord gives his people strength.
The Lord blesses them with peace.

PSALM 30

A psalm of David. A song for the dedication of the Temple.

1 I will exalt you, Lord, for you rescued me.
You refused to let my enemies triumph
over me.

Psalm 31 • • • page 546

2 O LORD my God, I cried to you for help,
and you restored my health.
3 You brought me up from the grave, O LORD.
You kept me from falling into the pit
of death.

4 Sing to the LORD, all you godly ones!
Praise his holy name.
5 For his anger lasts only a moment,
but his favor lasts a lifetime!
Weeping may last through the night,
but joy comes with the morning.

6 When I was prosperous, I said,
"Nothing can stop me now!"
7 Your favor, O LORD, made me as secure
as a mountain.
Then you turned away from me, and
I was shattered.

8 I cried out to you, O LORD.
I begged the Lord for mercy, saying,
9 "What will you gain if I die,
if I sink into the grave?
Can my dust praise you?
Can it tell of your faithfulness?
10 Hear me, LORD, and have mercy on me.
Help me, O LORD."

11 You have turned my mourning into joyful
dancing.
You have taken away my clothes of
mourning and clothed me with joy,
12 that I might sing praises to you and not
be silent.
O LORD my God, I will give you thanks
forever!

PSALM 31

For the choir director: A psalm of David.

1 O LORD, I have come to you for protection;
don't let me be disgraced.
Save me, for you do what is right.
2 Turn your ear to listen to me;
rescue me quickly.
Be my rock of protection,
a fortress where I will be safe.
3 You are my rock and my fortress.
For the honor of your name, lead me out
of this danger.
4 Pull me from the trap my enemies set for me,
for I find protection in you alone.
5 I entrust my spirit into your hand.
Rescue me, LORD, for you are a faithful
God.

6 I hate those who worship worthless idols.
I trust in the LORD.
7 I will be glad and rejoice in your unfailing
love,
for you have seen my troubles,
and you care about the anguish of
my soul.
8 You have not handed me over to my enemies
but have set me in a safe place.

9 Have mercy on me, LORD, for I am in distress.
Tears blur my eyes.
My body and soul are withering away.
10 I am dying from grief;
my years are shortened by sadness.
Sin has drained my strength;
I am wasting away from within.
11 I am scorned by all my enemies
and despised by my neighbors—
even my friends are afraid to come
near me.
When they see me on the street,
they run the other way.
12 I am ignored as if I were dead,
as if I were a broken pot.
13 I have heard the many rumors about me,
and I am surrounded by terror.
My enemies conspire against me,
plotting to take my life.

14 But I am trusting you, O LORD,
saying, "You are my God!"
15 My future is in your hands.
Rescue me from those who hunt me
down relentlessly.
16 Let your favor shine on your servant.
In your unfailing love, rescue me.
17 Don't let me be disgraced, O LORD,
for I call out to you for help.
Let the wicked be disgraced;
let them lie silent in the grave.
18 Silence their lying lips—
those proud and arrogant lips that accuse
the godly.

19 How great is the goodness
you have stored up for those who fear you.
You lavish it on those who come to you for
protection,
blessing them before the watching world.
20 You hide them in the shelter of your
presence,
safe from those who conspire against
them.
You shelter them in your presence,
far from accusing tongues.

21 Praise the LORD,
for he has shown me the wonders of his unfailing love.
He kept me safe when my city was under attack.
22 In panic I cried out,
"I am cut off from the LORD!"
But you heard my cry for mercy
and answered my call for help.
23 Love the LORD, all you godly ones!
For the LORD protects those who are loyal to him,
but he harshly punishes the arrogant.
24 So be strong and courageous,
all you who put your hope in the LORD!

PSALM 32

A psalm of David.

1 Oh, what joy for those
whose disobedience is forgiven,
whose sin is put out of sight!
2 Yes, what joy for those
whose record the LORD has cleared of guilt,
whose lives are lived in complete honesty!
3 When I refused to confess my sin,
my body wasted away,
and I groaned all day long.
4 Day and night your hand of discipline was heavy on me.
My strength evaporated like water in the summer heat. *Interlude*
5 Finally, I confessed all my sins to you
and stopped trying to hide my guilt.
I said to myself, "I will confess my rebellion to the LORD."
And you forgave me! All my guilt is gone. *Interlude*
6 Therefore, let all the godly pray to you while there is still time,
that they may not drown in the floodwaters of judgment.
7 For you are my hiding place;
you protect me from trouble.
You surround me with songs of victory. *Interlude*
8 The LORD says, "I will guide you along the best pathway for your life.
I will advise you and watch over you.
9 Do not be like a senseless horse or mule
that needs a bit and bridle to keep it under control."
10 Many sorrows come to the wicked,
but unfailing love surrounds those who trust the LORD.
11 So rejoice in the LORD and be glad, all you who obey him!
Shout for joy, all you whose hearts are pure!

PSALM 33

1 Let the godly sing for joy to the LORD;
it is fitting for the pure to praise him.
2 Praise the LORD with melodies on the lyre;
make music for him on the ten-stringed harp.
3 Sing a new song of praise to him;
play skillfully on the harp, and sing with joy.
4 For the word of the LORD holds true,
and we can trust everything he does.
5 He loves whatever is just and good;
the unfailing love of the LORD fills the earth.
6 The LORD merely spoke,
and the heavens were created.
He breathed the word,
and all the stars were born.
7 He assigned the sea its boundaries
and locked the oceans in vast reservoirs.
8 Let the whole world fear the LORD,
and let everyone stand in awe of him.
9 For when he spoke, the world began!
It appeared at his command.
10 The LORD frustrates the plans of the nations
and thwarts all their schemes.
11 But the LORD's plans stand firm forever;
his intentions can never be shaken.
12 What joy for the nation whose God is the LORD,
whose people he has chosen as his inheritance.
13 The LORD looks down from heaven
and sees the whole human race.
14 From his throne he observes
all who live on the earth.
15 He made their hearts,
so he understands everything they do.
16 The best-equipped army cannot save a king,
nor is great strength enough to save a warrior.
17 Don't count on your warhorse to give you victory—
for all its strength, it cannot save you.

18 But the LORD watches over those who
fear him,
those who rely on his unfailing love.
19 He rescues them from death
and keeps them alive in times of famine.

20 We put our hope in the LORD.
He is our help and our shield.
21 In him our hearts rejoice,
for we trust in his holy name.
22 Let your unfailing love surround us, LORD,
for our hope is in you alone.

PSALM 34

A psalm of David, regarding the time he pretended to be insane in front of Abimelech, who sent him away.

1 I will praise the LORD at all times.
I will constantly speak his praises.
2 I will boast only in the LORD;
let all who are helpless take heart.
3 Come, let us tell of the LORD's greatness;
let us exalt his name together.

4 I prayed to the LORD, and he answered me.
He freed me from all my fears.
5 Those who look to him for help will be
radiant with joy;
no shadow of shame will darken
their faces.
6 In my desperation I prayed, and the LORD
listened;
he saved me from all my troubles.
7 For the angel of the LORD is a guard;
he surrounds and defends all who
fear him.

8 Taste and see that the LORD is good.
Oh, the joys of those who take refuge
in him!
9 Fear the LORD, you his godly people,
for those who fear him will have all
they need.
10 Even strong young lions sometimes
go hungry,
but those who trust in the LORD will lack
no good thing.

11 Come, my children, and listen to me,
and I will teach you to fear the LORD.
12 Does anyone want to live a life
that is long and prosperous?
13 Then keep your tongue from speaking evil
and your lips from telling lies!
14 Turn away from evil and do good.
Search for peace, and work to maintain it.

15 The eyes of the LORD watch over those who
do right;
his ears are open to their cries for help.
16 But the LORD turns his face against those who
do evil;
he will erase their memory from the earth.
17 The LORD hears his people when they call
to him for help.
He rescues them from all their troubles.
18 The LORD is close to the brokenhearted;
he rescues those whose spirits are
crushed.

19 The righteous person faces many troubles,
but the LORD comes to the rescue each
time.
20 For the LORD protects the bones of the
righteous;
not one of them is broken!

21 Calamity will surely destroy the wicked,
and those who hate the righteous will
be punished.
22 But the LORD will redeem those who serve
him.
No one who takes refuge in him will
be condemned.

PSALM 35

A psalm of David.

1 O LORD, oppose those who oppose me.
Fight those who fight against me.
2 Put on your armor, and take up your shield.
Prepare for battle, and come to my aid.
3 Lift up your spear and javelin
against those who pursue me.
Let me hear you say,
"I will give you victory!"
4 Bring shame and disgrace on those trying
to kill me;
turn them back and humiliate those who
want to harm me.
5 Blow them away like chaff in the wind—
a wind sent by the angel of the LORD.
6 Make their path dark and slippery,
with the angel of the LORD pursuing them.
7 I did them no wrong, but they laid a trap
for me.
I did them no wrong, but they dug a pit
to catch me.
8 So let sudden ruin come upon them!
Let them be caught in the trap they set
for me!
Let them be destroyed in the pit they dug
for me.

9 Then I will rejoice in the LORD.
I will be glad because he rescues me.
10 With every bone in my body I will praise him:
"LORD, who can compare with you?
Who else rescues the helpless from the strong?
Who else protects the helpless and poor from those who rob them?"

11 Malicious witnesses testify against me.
They accuse me of crimes I know nothing about.
12 They repay me evil for good.
I am sick with despair.
13 Yet when they were ill, I grieved for them.
I denied myself by fasting for them,
but my prayers returned unanswered.
14 I was sad, as though they were my friends or family,
as if I were grieving for my own mother.
15 But they are glad now that I am in trouble;
they gleefully join together against me.
I am attacked by people I don't even know;
they slander me constantly.
16 They mock me and call me names;
they snarl at me.

17 How long, O Lord, will you look on and do nothing?
Rescue me from their fierce attacks.
Protect my life from these lions!
18 Then I will thank you in front of the great assembly.
I will praise you before all the people.
19 Don't let my treacherous enemies rejoice over my defeat.
Don't let those who hate me without cause gloat over my sorrow.
20 They don't talk of peace;
they plot against innocent people who mind their own business.
21 They shout, "Aha! Aha!
With our own eyes we saw him do it!"

22 O LORD, you know all about this.
Do not stay silent.
Do not abandon me now, O Lord.
23 Wake up! Rise to my defense!
Take up my case, my God and my Lord.
24 Declare me not guilty, O LORD my God, for you give justice.
Don't let my enemies laugh about me in my troubles.
25 Don't let them say, "Look, we got what we wanted!
Now we will eat him alive!"

FUN-fact

Talk It Over

One of the best things about having really good friends is being able to tell them anything—

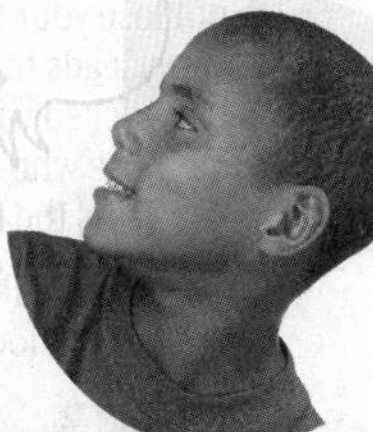

not just the great things about your life but the tough things too. God is that kind of friend. People in the Bible knew that God was their friend, and they talked to God whether they were happy, sad, scared, or confused. (Remember David? He was a *big* talker to God!)

PRAYER DOESN'T HAVE TO BE JUST TALK. TRY PRAYING ON PAPER!

Use a blank notebook to make a prayer journal. Use the left-hand pages to draw or write about the worst things that happened. On the right-hand pages, draw or write about the best things that happened. Talk to God about each situation. After a while, look back over your journal and see how God has listened to and helped you.

26 May those who rejoice at my troubles
be humiliated and disgraced.
May those who triumph over me
be covered with shame and dishonor.
27 But give great joy to those who came to
my defense.
Let them continually say, "Great is
the LORD,
who delights in blessing his servant
with peace!"
28 Then I will proclaim your justice,
and I will praise you all day long.

PSALM 36

For the choir director: A psalm of David, the servant of the LORD.

1 Sin whispers to the wicked, deep within their
hearts.
They have no fear of God at all.
2 In their blind conceit,
they cannot see how wicked they
really are.
3 Everything they say is crooked and deceitful.
They refuse to act wisely or do good.
4 They lie awake at night, hatching sinful plots.
Their actions are never good.
They make no attempt to turn from evil.

5 Your unfailing love, O LORD, is as vast as
the heavens;
your faithfulness reaches beyond the
clouds.
6 Your righteousness is like the mighty
mountains,
your justice like the ocean depths.
You care for people and animals alike,
O LORD.
7 How precious is your unfailing love,
O God!
All humanity finds shelter
in the shadow of your wings.
8 You feed them from the abundance of your
own house,
letting them drink from your river
of delights.
9 For you are the fountain of life,
the light by which we see.

10 Pour out your unfailing love on those who
love you;
give justice to those with honest hearts.
11 Don't let the proud trample me
or the wicked push me around.
12 Look! Those who do evil have fallen!
They are thrown down, never to rise again.

PSALM 37

A psalm of David.

1 Don't worry about the wicked
or envy those who do wrong.
2 For like grass, they soon fade away.
Like spring flowers, they soon wither.

3 Trust in the LORD and do good.
Then you will live safely in the land and
prosper.
4 Take delight in the LORD,
and he will give you your heart's desires.

5 Commit everything you do to the LORD.
Trust him, and he will help you.
6 He will make your innocence radiate like
the dawn,
and the justice of your cause will shine
like the noonday sun.

7 Be still in the presence of the LORD,
and wait patiently for him to act.
Don't worry about evil people who prosper
or fret about their wicked schemes.
8 Stop being angry!
Turn from your rage!
Do not lose your temper—
it only leads to harm.
9 For the wicked will be destroyed,
but those who trust in the LORD will
possess the land.
10 Soon the wicked will disappear.
Though you look for them, they will
be gone.
11 The lowly will possess the land
and will live in peace and prosperity.

12 The wicked plot against the godly;
they snarl at them in defiance.
13 But the Lord just laughs,
for he sees their day of judgment coming.
14 The wicked draw their swords
and string their bows
to kill the poor and the oppressed,
to slaughter those who do right.
15 But their swords will stab their own hearts,
and their bows will be broken.

16 It is better to be godly and have little
than to be evil and rich.
17 For the strength of the wicked will be
shattered,
but the LORD takes care of the godly.

18 Day by day the LORD takes care of the
innocent,

and they will receive an inheritance that
lasts forever.
19 They will not be disgraced in hard times;
even in famine they will have more than
enough.

20 But the wicked will die.
The LORD's enemies are like flowers
in a field—
they will disappear like smoke.
21 The wicked borrow and never repay,
but the godly are generous givers.
22 Those the LORD blesses will possess
the land,
but those he curses will die.
23 The LORD directs the steps of the godly.
He delights in every detail of their lives.
24 Though they stumble, they will never fall,
for the LORD holds them by the hand.

25 Once I was young, and now I am old.
Yet I have never seen the godly abandoned
or their children begging for bread.
26 The godly always give generous loans
to others,
and their children are a blessing.

27 Turn from evil and do good,
and you will live in the land forever.
28 For the LORD loves justice,
and he will never abandon the godly.

He will keep them safe forever,
but the children of the wicked will die.
29 The godly will possess the land
and will live there forever.

30 The godly offer good counsel;
they teach right from wrong.
31 They have made God's law their own,
so they will never slip from his path.

32 The wicked wait in ambush for the godly,
looking for an excuse to kill them.
33 But the LORD will not let the wicked succeed
or let the godly be condemned when they
are put on trial.

34 Put your hope in the LORD.
Travel steadily along his path.
He will honor you by giving you the land.
You will see the wicked destroyed.

35 I have seen wicked and ruthless people
flourishing like a tree in its native soil.
36 But when I looked again, they were gone!
Though I searched for them, I could not
find them!

37 Look at those who are honest and good,
for a wonderful future awaits those who
love peace.
38 But the rebellious will be destroyed;
they have no future.

39 The LORD rescues the godly;
he is their fortress in times of trouble.
40 The LORD helps them,
rescuing them from the wicked.
He saves them,
and they find shelter in him.

PSALM 38

A psalm of David, asking God to remember him.

1 O LORD, don't rebuke me in your anger
or discipline me in your rage!
2 Your arrows have struck deep,
and your blows are crushing me.
3 Because of your anger, my whole body is sick;
my health is broken because of my sins.
4 My guilt overwhelms me—
it is a burden too heavy to bear.
5 My wounds fester and stink
because of my foolish sins.
6 I am bent over and racked with pain.
All day long I walk around filled with grief.
7 A raging fever burns within me,
and my health is broken.
8 I am exhausted and completely crushed.
My groans come from an anguished heart.

9 You know what I long for, Lord;
you hear my every sigh.
10 My heart beats wildly, my strength fails,
and I am going blind.
11 My loved ones and friends stay away, fearing
my disease.
Even my own family stands at a distance.
12 Meanwhile, my enemies lay traps to kill me.
Those who wish me harm make plans to
ruin me.
All day long they plan their treachery.

13 But I am deaf to all their threats.
I am silent before them as one who cannot
speak.
14 I choose to hear nothing,
and I make no reply.
15 For I am waiting for you, O LORD.
You must answer for me, O Lord my God.
16 I prayed, "Don't let my enemies gloat over me
or rejoice at my downfall."

17 I am on the verge of collapse,
facing constant pain.

18 But I confess my sins;
I am deeply sorry for what I have done.
19 I have many aggressive enemies;
they hate me without reason.
20 They repay me evil for good
and oppose me for pursuing good.
21 Do not abandon me, O LORD.
Do not stand at a distance, my God.
22 Come quickly to help me,
O Lord my savior.

PSALM 39

For Jeduthun, the choir director: A psalm of David.

1 I said to myself, "I will watch what I do
and not sin in what I say.
I will hold my tongue
when the ungodly are around me."
2 But as I stood there in silence—
not even speaking of good things—
the turmoil within me grew worse.
3 The more I thought about it,
the hotter I got,
igniting a fire of words:
4 "LORD, remind me how brief my time on
earth will be.
Remind me that my days are numbered—
how fleeting my life is.
5 You have made my life no longer than the
width of my hand.
My entire lifetime is just a moment
to you;
at best, each of us is but a breath."
Interlude

6 We are merely moving shadows,
and all our busy rushing ends in nothing.
We heap up wealth,
not knowing who will spend it.
7 And so, Lord, where do I put my hope?
My only hope is in you.
8 Rescue me from my rebellion.
Do not let fools mock me.
9 I am silent before you; I won't say a word,
for my punishment is from you.
10 But please stop striking me!
I am exhausted by the blows from your
hand.
11 When you discipline us for our sins,
you consume like a moth what is precious
to us.
Each of us is but a breath. *Interlude*

12 Hear my prayer, O LORD!
Listen to my cries for help!
Don't ignore my tears.
For I am your guest—
a traveler passing through,
as my ancestors were before me.
13 Leave me alone so I can smile again
before I am gone and exist no more.

PSALM 40

For the choir director: A psalm of David.

1 I waited patiently for the LORD to help me,
and he turned to me and heard my cry.
2 He lifted me out of the pit of despair,
out of the mud and the mire.
He set my feet on solid ground
and steadied me as I walked along.
3 He has given me a new song to sing,
a hymn of praise to our God.
Many will see what he has done and be
amazed.
They will put their trust in the LORD.

4 Oh, the joys of those who trust the LORD,
who have no confidence in the proud
or in those who worship idols.
5 O LORD my God, you have performed many
wonders for us.
Your plans for us are too numerous to list.
You have no equal.
If I tried to recite all your wonderful deeds,
I would never come to the end of them.

6 You take no delight in sacrifices or
offerings.
Now that you have made me listen,
I finally understand—
you don't require burnt offerings or sin
offerings.
7 Then I said, "Look, I have come.
As is written about me in the Scriptures:
8 I take joy in doing your will, my God,
for your instructions are written on
my heart."

9 I have told all your people about your justice.
I have not been afraid to speak out,
as you, O LORD, well know.
10 I have not kept the good news of your justice
hidden in my heart;
I have talked about your faithfulness and
saving power.
I have told everyone in the great assembly
of your unfailing love and faithfulness.

11 LORD, don't hold back your tender mercies
from me.
Let your unfailing love and faithfulness
always protect me.

12 For troubles surround me—
too many to count!
My sins pile up so high
I can't see my way out.
They outnumber the hairs on my head.
I have lost all courage.

13 Please, LORD, rescue me!
Come quickly, LORD, and help me.
14 May those who try to destroy me
be humiliated and put to shame.
May those who take delight in my trouble
be turned back in disgrace.
15 Let them be horrified by their shame,
for they said, "Aha! We've got him now!"
16 But may all who search for you
be filled with joy and gladness in you.
May those who love your salvation
repeatedly shout, "The LORD is great!"
17 As for me, since I am poor and needy,
let the Lord keep me in his thoughts.
You are my helper and my savior.
O my God, do not delay.

PSALM 41

For the choir director: A psalm of David.

1 Oh, the joys of those who are kind
to the poor!
The LORD rescues them when they
are in trouble.
2 The LORD protects them
and keeps them alive.
He gives them prosperity in the land
and rescues them from their enemies.
3 The LORD nurses them when they are sick
and restores them to health.

4 "O LORD," I prayed, "have mercy on me.
Heal me, for I have sinned against you."
5 But my enemies say nothing but evil
about me.
"How soon will he die and be forgotten?"
they ask.
6 They visit me as if they were my friends,
but all the while they gather gossip,
and when they leave, they spread it
everywhere.
7 All who hate me whisper about me,
imagining the worst.
8 "He has some fatal disease," they say.
"He will never get out of that bed!"
9 Even my best friend, the one I trusted
completely,
the one who shared my food, has turned
against me.

Waaaatttteeeerrrr

What do you think that guy would do for a nice big glass of ice water? **PSALM 42 talks all about thirst... for God, that is.** We need to be with God, to know God, and to learn from God even more than we need water. **Check it out as you read PSALM 42:1-8.**

Rain on Me

Try this experiment as a reminder of how God gives us the things we need.

1 Cover a table with newspaper or an old towel. Tape a two-foot piece of yarn to the inside of a clear bowl.

2 Wet the yarn.

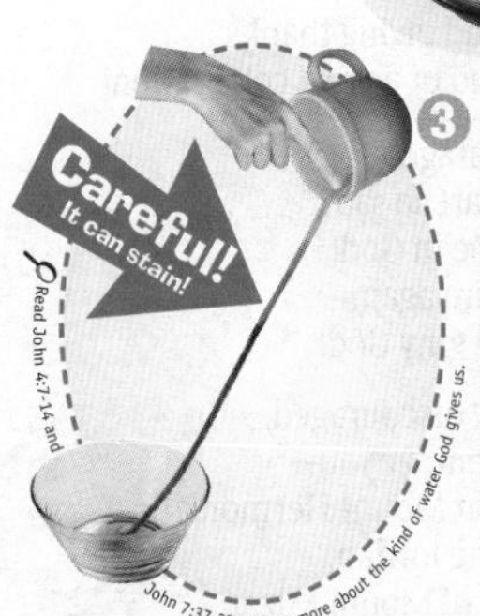
Careful! It can stain!
Read John 4:7-14 and John 7:37-38 to learn more about the kind of water God gives us.

3 Add food coloring to a cup of water. Hold the yarn up and out from the bowl, and pour the colored water down the top of the string. See how far down and away from the bowl you can go.

Just as the bowl filled up with water, God fills us with everything we need. He pours out his love for us in so many ways! **We should thirst after God so we can get closer and closer to him.**

Psalm 42 . . . page 554

10 LORD, have mercy on me.
Make me well again, so I can pay them back!
11 I know you are pleased with me,
for you have not let my enemies triumph over me.
12 You have preserved my life because I am innocent;
you have brought me into your presence forever.

13 Praise the LORD, the God of Israel,
who lives from everlasting to everlasting.
Amen and amen!

Book Two (Psalms 42–72)

PSALM 42

For the choir director: A psalm of the descendants of Korah.

1 **As the deer longs for streams of water,**
so I long for you, O God.
2 I thirst for God, the living God.
When can I go and stand before him?
3 Day and night I have only tears for food,
while my enemies continually taunt me, saying,
"Where is this God of yours?"

4 My heart is breaking
as I remember how it used to be:
I walked among the crowds of worshipers,
leading a great procession to the house of God,
singing for joy and giving thanks
amid the sound of a great celebration!

5 Why am I discouraged?
Why is my heart so sad?
I will put my hope in God!
I will praise him again—
my Savior and 6 my God!
Now I am deeply discouraged,
but I will remember you—
even from distant Mount Hermon, the source of the Jordan,
from the land of Mount Mizar.
7 I hear the tumult of the raging seas
as your waves and surging tides sweep over me.
8 But each day the LORD pours his unfailing love upon me,
and through each night I sing his songs,
praying to God who gives me life.

9 "O God my rock," I cry,
"Why have you forgotten me?
Why must I wander around in grief,
oppressed by my enemies?"
10 Their taunts break my bones.
They scoff, "Where is this God of yours?"

11 Why am I discouraged?
Why is my heart so sad?
I will put my hope in God!
I will praise him again—
my Savior and my God!

PSALM 43

1 Declare me innocent, O God!
Defend me against these ungodly people.
Rescue me from these unjust liars.
2 For you are God, my only safe haven.
Why have you tossed me aside?
Why must I wander around in grief,
oppressed by my enemies?
3 Send out your light and your truth;
let them guide me.
Let them lead me to your holy mountain,
to the place where you live.
4 There I will go to the altar of God,
to God—the source of all my joy.
I will praise you with my harp,
O God, my God!

5 Why am I discouraged?
Why is my heart so sad?
I will put my hope in God!
I will praise him again—
my Savior and my God!

PSALM 44

For the choir director: A psalm of the descendants of Korah.

1 O God, we have heard it with our own ears—
our ancestors have told us
of all you did in their day,
in days long ago:
2 You drove out the pagan nations by your power
and gave all the land to our ancestors.
You crushed their enemies
and set our ancestors free.
3 They did not conquer the land with their swords;
it was not their own strong arm that gave them victory.
It was your right hand and strong arm
and the blinding light from your face that helped them,
for you loved them.

4 You are my King and my God.
You command victories for Israel.
5 Only by your power can we push back
our enemies;
only in your name can we trample
our foes.
6 I do not trust in my bow;
I do not count on my sword to save me.
7 You are the one who gives us victory over
our enemies;
you disgrace those who hate us.
8 O God, we give glory to you all day long
and constantly praise your name.
Interlude

9 But now you have tossed us aside in
dishonor.
You no longer lead our armies to battle.
10 You make us retreat from our enemies
and allow those who hate us to plunder
our land.
11 You have butchered us like sheep
and scattered us among the nations.
12 You sold your precious people for a
pittance,
making nothing on the sale.
13 You let our neighbors mock us.
We are an object of scorn and derision
to those around us.
14 You have made us the butt of their jokes;
they shake their heads at us in scorn.
15 We can't escape the constant humiliation;
shame is written across our faces.
16 All we hear are the taunts of our mockers.
All we see are our vengeful enemies.

17 All this has happened though we have not
forgotten you.
We have not violated your covenant.
18 Our hearts have not deserted you.
We have not strayed from your path.
19 Yet you have crushed us in the jackal's
desert home.
You have covered us with darkness
and death.
20 If we had forgotten the name of our God
or spread our hands in prayer to foreign
gods,
21 God would surely have known it,
for he knows the secrets of every heart.
22 But for your sake we are killed every day;
we are being slaughtered like sheep.

23 Wake up, O Lord! Why do you sleep?
Get up! Do not reject us forever.
24 Why do you look the other way?
Why do you ignore our suffering and
oppression?
25 We collapse in the dust,
lying face down in the dirt.
26 Rise up! Help us!
Ransom us because of your unfailing love.

PSALM 45

For the choir director: A love song to be sung to the tune "Lilies." A psalm of the descendants of Korah.

1 Beautiful words stir my heart.
I will recite a lovely poem about the king,
for my tongue is like the pen of a skillful
poet.

2 You are the most handsome of all.
Gracious words stream from your lips.
God himself has blessed you forever.
3 Put on your sword, O mighty warrior!
You are so glorious, so majestic!
4 In your majesty, ride out to victory,
defending truth, humility, and justice.
Go forth to perform awe-inspiring deeds!
5 Your arrows are sharp, piercing your
enemies' hearts.
The nations fall beneath your feet.

6 Your throne, O God, endures forever
and ever.
You rule with a scepter of justice.
7 You love justice and hate evil.
Therefore God, your God, has anointed
you,
pouring out the oil of joy on you more
than on anyone else.
8 Myrrh, aloes, and cassia perfume your
robes.
In ivory palaces the music of strings
entertains you.
9 Kings' daughters are among your noble
women.
At your right side stands the queen,
wearing jewelry of finest gold from Ophir!

10 Listen to me, O royal daughter; take to heart
what I say.
Forget your people and your family
far away.
11 For your royal husband delights in your
beauty;
honor him, for he is your lord.
12 The princess of Tyre will shower you
with gifts.
The wealthy will beg your favor.
13 The bride, a princess, looks glorious
in her golden gown.

14 In her beautiful robes, she is led to
the king,
accompanied by her bridesmaids.
15 What a joyful and enthusiastic procession
as they enter the king's palace!
16 Your sons will become kings like their
father.
You will make them rulers over many
lands.
17 I will bring honor to your name in every
generation.
Therefore, the nations will praise you
forever and ever.

PSALM 46

For the choir director: A song of the descendants of Korah, to be sung by soprano voices.

1 God is our refuge and strength,
always ready to help in times of trouble.
2 So we will not fear when earthquakes come
and the mountains crumble into the sea.
3 Let the oceans roar and foam.
Let the mountains tremble as the waters
surge! *Interlude*
4 A river brings joy to the city of our God,
the sacred home of the Most High.
5 God dwells in that city; it cannot be
destroyed.
From the very break of day, God will
protect it.
6 The nations are in chaos,
and their kingdoms crumble!
God's voice thunders,
and the earth melts!
7 The LORD of Heaven's Armies is here
among us;
the God of Israel is our fortress.
Interlude
8 Come, see the glorious works of the LORD:
See how he brings destruction upon
the world.
9 He causes wars to end throughout the earth.
He breaks the bow and snaps the spear;
he burns the shields with fire.
10 **"Be still, and know that
I am God!**
I will be honored by every nation.
I will be honored throughout the world."
11 The LORD of Heaven's Armies is here
among us;
the God of Israel is our fortress.
Interlude

PSALM 47

For the choir director: A psalm of the descendants of Korah.

1 Come, everyone! Clap your hands!
Shout to God with joyful praise!
2 For the LORD Most High is awesome.
He is the great King of all the earth.
3 He subdues the nations before us,
putting our enemies beneath our feet.
4 He chose the Promised Land as our
inheritance,
the proud possession of Jacob's
descendants, whom he loves.
Interlude
5 God has ascended with a mighty shout.
The LORD has ascended with trumpets
blaring.
6 Sing praises to God, sing praises;
sing praises to our King, sing praises!
7 For God is the King over all the earth.
Praise him with a psalm.
8 God reigns above the nations,
sitting on his holy throne.
9 The rulers of the world have gathered
together
with the people of the God of
Abraham.
For all the kings of the earth belong
to God.
He is highly honored everywhere.

PSALM 48

A song. A psalm of the descendants of Korah.

1 How great is the LORD,
how deserving of praise,
in the city of our God,
which sits on his holy mountain!
2 It is high and magnificent;
the whole earth rejoices to see it!
Mount Zion, the holy mountain,
is the city of the great King!
3 God himself is in Jerusalem's towers,
revealing himself as its defender.
4 The kings of the earth joined forces
and advanced against the city.
5 But when they saw it, they were stunned;
they were terrified and ran away.
6 They were gripped with terror
and writhed in pain like a woman
in labor.
7 You destroyed them like the mighty ships
of Tarshish
shattered by a powerful east wind.

Key Verse **"Be still, and know that I am God!" —PSALM 46:10a**

There's a lot of noise out there—TVs, radios, video games. They're all making noise. There's a lot of noise inside our hearts, too—worries, fears, hurts. They're all making it hard to hear and trust God. Sometimes it's good to just turn the noise off for a little while.

1. **Sit still and just listen. What do you hear right now?**
2. **Listen a little more. Close your eyes and be really quiet. Wait for about a minute. What did you hear that time that you didn't hear before?**
3. **Read PSALM 46:10, pray for 30 seconds, just be still for the next 30 seconds, then pray some more.**

Check out Isaiah 30:15 to learn more about being still before God.

How did being still help your hearing? your praying?
- What else happened while you were sitting quietly?
- What does it mean to be still before God?

8 We had heard of the city's glory,
but now we have seen it ourselves—
the city of the LORD of Heaven's Armies.
It is the city of our God;
he will make it safe forever. *Interlude*
9 O God, we meditate on your unfailing love
as we worship in your Temple.
10 As your name deserves, O God,
you will be praised to the ends of the
earth.
Your strong right hand is filled with
victory.
11 Let the people on Mount Zion rejoice.
Let all the towns of Judah be glad
because of your justice.

12 Go, inspect the city of Jerusalem.
Walk around and count the many towers.
13 Take note of the fortified walls,
and tour all the citadels,
that you may describe them
to future generations.
14 For that is what God is like.
He is our God forever and ever,
and he will guide us until we die.

PSALM 49

For the choir director: A psalm of the descendants of Korah.

1 Listen to this, all you people!
Pay attention, everyone in the world!
2 High and low,
rich and poor—listen!
3 For my words are wise,
and my thoughts are filled with
insight.
4 I listen carefully to many proverbs
and solve riddles with inspiration from
a harp.

5 Why should I fear when trouble comes,
when enemies surround me?
6 They trust in their wealth
and boast of great riches.
7 Yet they cannot redeem themselves from
death
by paying a ransom to God.
8 Redemption does not come so easily,
for no one can ever pay enough
9 to live forever
and never see the grave.

10 Those who are wise must finally die,
just like the foolish and senseless,
leaving all their wealth behind.
11 The grave is their eternal home,
where they will stay forever.
They may name their estates after
themselves,
12 but their fame will not last.
They will die, just like animals.
13 This is the fate of fools,
though they are remembered
as being wise. *Interlude*

14 Like sheep, they are led to the grave,
where death will be their shepherd.
In the morning the godly will rule over
them.
Their bodies will rot in the grave,
far from their grand estates.
15 But as for me, God will redeem my life.
He will snatch me from the power
of the grave. *Interlude*

16 So don't be dismayed when the wicked
grow rich
and their homes become ever more
splendid.
17 For when they die, they take nothing with
them.
Their wealth will not follow them into
the grave.
18 In this life they consider themselves
fortunate
and are applauded for their success.
19 But they will die like all before them
and never again see the light of day.
20 People who boast of their wealth don't
understand;
they will die, just like animals.

PSALM 50

A psalm of Asaph.

1 The LORD, the Mighty One, is God,
and he has spoken;
he has summoned all humanity
from where the sun rises to where it sets.
2 From Mount Zion, the perfection of beauty,
God shines in glorious radiance.
3 Our God approaches,
and he is not silent.
Fire devours everything in his way,
and a great storm rages around him.
4 He calls on the heavens above and earth
below
to witness the judgment of his people.
5 "Bring my faithful people to me—
those who made a covenant with me
by giving sacrifices."
6 Then let the heavens proclaim his justice,
for God himself will be the judge.
Interlude

7 "O my people, listen as I speak.
Here are my charges against you,
O Israel:
I am God, your God!
8 I have no complaint about your sacrifices
or the burnt offerings you constantly
offer.
9 But I do not need the bulls from your barns
or the goats from your pens.
10 For all the animals of the forest are mine,
and I own the cattle on a thousand hills.
11 I know every bird on the mountains,
and all the animals of the field are mine.
12 If I were hungry, I would not tell you,
for all the world is mine and everything
in it.

Key Verse **"Create in me a clean heart, O God. Renew a loyal spirit within me." —PSALM 51:10**

Even great Bible heroes like David sinned. When we sin, we can either run away from God and get mad or turn around and repent. Repenting means we admit our mistake, say we're sorry, and ask God to help us change. When we repent, God forgives us and makes us clean.

It's Kinda Like This

1 Find about five old, dirty pennies.

2 Pour hot sauce on one side of each penny.

Let it sit for about three minutes. (Louisiana Hot Sauce works great!)

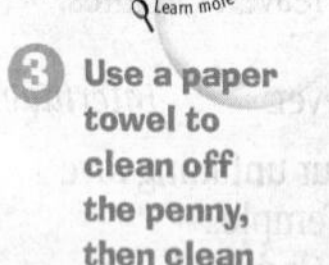

Learn more about forgiveness in 1 John 1:8-9.

3 Use a paper towel to clean off the penny, then clean off the other side.

Your penny may be a little cleaner, but it's not anywhere near as clean as we are when we repent. God *completely* cleans us and completely forgives us when we repent. **Learn all about it in PSALM 51:1-17. Next time you sin, you know what to do!**

13 Do I eat the meat of bulls?
Do I drink the blood of goats?
14 Make thankfulness your sacrifice to God,
and keep the vows you made to the Most High.
15 Then call on me when you are in trouble,
and I will rescue you,
and you will give me glory."

16 But God says to the wicked:
"Why bother reciting my decrees
and pretending to obey my covenant?
17 For you refuse my discipline
and treat my words like trash.
18 When you see thieves, you approve of them,
and you spend your time with adulterers.
19 Your mouth is filled with wickedness,
and your tongue is full of lies.
20 You sit around and slander your brother—
your own mother's son.
21 While you did all this, I remained silent,
and you thought I didn't care.
But now I will rebuke you,
listing all my charges against you.
22 Repent, all of you who forget me,
or I will tear you apart,
and no one will help you.
23 But giving thanks is a sacrifice that truly honors me.
If you keep to my path,
I will reveal to you the salvation of God."

PSALM 51

For the choir director: A psalm of David, regarding the time Nathan the prophet came to him after David had committed adultery with Bathsheba.

1 Have mercy on me, O God,
because of your unfailing love.
Because of your great compassion,
blot out the stain of my sins.
2 Wash me clean from my guilt.
Purify me from my sin.
3 For I recognize my rebellion;
it haunts me day and night.
4 Against you, and you alone, have I sinned;
I have done what is evil in your sight.
You will be proved right in what you say,
and your judgment against me is just.
5 For I was born a sinner—
yes, from the moment my mother conceived me.
6 But you desire honesty from the womb,
teaching me wisdom even there.
7 Purify me from my sins, and I will be clean;
wash me, and I will be whiter than snow.
8 Oh, give me back my joy again;
you have broken me—
now let me rejoice.
9 Don't keep looking at my sins.
Remove the stain of my guilt.
10 Create in me a clean heart, O God.
Renew a loyal spirit within me.
11 Do not banish me from your presence,
and don't take your Holy Spirit from me.

12 Restore to me the joy of your salvation,
and make me willing to obey you.
13 Then I will teach your ways to rebels,
and they will return to you.
14 Forgive me for shedding blood, O God who saves;
then I will joyfully sing of your forgiveness.
15 Unseal my lips, O Lord,
that my mouth may praise you.

16 You do not desire a sacrifice, or I would offer one.
You do not want a burnt offering.
17 The sacrifice you desire is a broken spirit.
You will not reject a broken and repentant heart, O God.
18 Look with favor on Zion and help her;
rebuild the walls of Jerusalem.
19 Then you will be pleased with sacrifices offered in the right spirit—
with burnt offerings and whole burnt offerings.
Then bulls will again be sacrificed on your altar.

PSALM 52

For the choir director: A psalm of David, regarding the time Doeg the Edomite said to Saul, "David has gone to see Ahimelech."

1 Why do you boast about your crimes, great warrior?
Don't you realize God's justice continues forever?
2 All day long you plot destruction.
Your tongue cuts like a sharp razor;
you're an expert at telling lies.
3 You love evil more than good
and lies more than truth. *Interlude*

4 You love to destroy others with your words,
you liar!

5 But God will strike you down once and for all.
He will pull you from your home
and uproot you from the land of
the living.
Interlude

6 The righteous will see it and be amazed.
They will laugh and say,
7 "Look what happens to mighty warriors
who do not trust in God.
They trust their wealth instead
and grow more and more bold in their
wickedness."

8 But I am like an olive tree, thriving in the
house of God.
I will always trust in God's unfailing love.
9 I will praise you forever, O God,
for what you have done.
I will trust in your good name
in the presence of your faithful people.

PSALM 53

For the choir director: A meditation; a psalm of David.

1 Only fools say in their hearts,
"There is no God."
They are corrupt, and their actions
are evil;
not one of them does good!
2 God looks down from heaven
on the entire human race;
he looks to see if anyone is truly wise,
if anyone seeks God.
3 But no, all have turned away;
all have become corrupt.
No one does good,
not a single one!

4 Will those who do evil never learn?
They eat up my people like bread
and wouldn't think of praying to God.
5 Terror will grip them,
terror like they have never known
before.
God will scatter the bones of your
enemies.
You will put them to shame, for God has
rejected them.

6 Who will come from Mount Zion to rescue
Israel?
When God restores his people,
Jacob will shout with joy, and Israel will
rejoice.

PSALM 54

For the choir director: A psalm of David, regarding the time the Ziphites came and said to Saul, "We know where David is hiding." To be accompanied by stringed instruments.

1 Come with great power, O God, and
rescue me!
Defend me with your might.
2 Listen to my prayer, O God.
Pay attention to my plea.
3 For strangers are attacking me;
violent people are trying to kill me.
They care nothing for God. *Interlude*

4 But God is my helper.
The Lord keeps me alive!
5 May the evil plans of my enemies be turned
against them.
Do as you promised and put an end
to them.

6 I will sacrifice a voluntary offering to you;
I will praise your name, O LORD,
for it is good.
7 For you have rescued me from my troubles
and helped me to triumph over my
enemies.

PSALM 55

For the choir director: A psalm of David, to be accompanied by stringed instruments.

1 Listen to my prayer, O God.
Do not ignore my cry for help!
2 Please listen and answer me,
for I am overwhelmed by my troubles.
3 My enemies shout at me,
making loud and wicked threats.
They bring trouble on me
and angrily hunt me down.

4 My heart pounds in my chest.
The terror of death assaults me.
5 Fear and trembling overwhelm me,
and I can't stop shaking.
6 Oh, that I had wings like a dove;
then I would fly away and rest!
7 I would fly far away
to the quiet of the wilderness. *Interlude*
8 How quickly I would escape—
far from this wild storm of hatred.

9 Confuse them, Lord, and frustrate their
plans,
for I see violence and conflict in the city.
10 Its walls are patrolled day and night against
invaders,

but the real danger is wickedness within
the city.
11 Everything is falling apart;
threats and cheating are rampant
in the streets.

12 It is not an enemy who taunts me—
I could bear that.
It is not my foes who so arrogantly
insult me—
I could have hidden from them.
13 Instead, it is you—my equal,
my companion and close friend.
14 What good fellowship we once enjoyed
as we walked together to the house of God.

15 Let death stalk my enemies;
let the grave swallow them alive,
for evil makes its home within them.

16 But I will call on God,
and the LORD will rescue me.
17 Morning, noon, and night
I cry out in my distress,
and the LORD hears my voice.
18 He ransoms me and keeps me safe
from the battle waged against me,
though many still oppose me.
19 God, who has ruled forever,
will hear me and humble them.
Interlude
For my enemies refuse to change their ways;
they do not fear God.

20 As for my companion, he betrayed his
friends;
he broke his promises.
21 His words are as smooth as butter,
but in his heart is war.
His words are as soothing as lotion,
but underneath are daggers!

22 Give your burdens to the LORD,
and he will take care of you.
He will not permit the godly to slip
and fall.

23 But you, O God, will send the wicked
down to the pit of destruction.
Murderers and liars will die young,
but I am trusting you to save me.

PSALM 56

For the choir director: A psalm of David, regarding the time the Philistines seized him in Gath. To be sung to the tune "Dove on Distant Oaks."

1 O God, have mercy on me,
for people are hounding me.
My foes attack me all day long.
2 I am constantly hounded by those who
slander me,
and many are boldly attacking me.
3 But when I am afraid,
I will put my trust in you.
4 I praise God for what he has promised.
I trust in God, so why should I be afraid?
What can mere mortals do to me?

5 They are always twisting what I say;
they spend their days plotting to
harm me.
6 They come together to spy on me—
watching my every step, eager to kill me.
7 Don't let them get away with their
wickedness;
in your anger, O God, bring them down.

8 You keep track of all my sorrows.
You have collected all my tears in your
bottle.
You have recorded each one in your book.

9 My enemies will retreat when I call to you for
help.
This I know: God is on my side!
10 I praise God for what he has promised;
yes, I praise the LORD for what he has
promised.
11 I trust in God, so why should I be afraid?
What can mere mortals do to me?

12 I will fulfill my vows to you, O God,
and will offer a sacrifice of thanks for your
help.
13 For you have rescued me from death;
you have kept my feet from slipping.
So now I can walk in your presence, O God,
in your life-giving light.

PSALM 57

For the choir director: A psalm of David, regarding the time he fled from Saul and went into the cave. To be sung to the tune "Do Not Destroy!"

1 Have mercy on me, O God, have mercy!
I look to you for protection.
I will hide beneath the shadow of your wings
until the danger passes by.
2 I cry out to God Most High,
to God who will fulfill his purpose
for me.
3 He will send help from heaven to rescue me,
disgracing those who hound me.
Interlude
My God will send forth his unfailing love and
faithfulness.

[4] I am surrounded by fierce lions
who greedily devour human prey—
whose teeth pierce like spears and arrows,
and whose tongues cut like swords.

[5] Be exalted, O God, above the highest
heavens!
May your glory shine over all the earth.

[6] My enemies have set a trap for me.
I am weary from distress.
They have dug a deep pit in my path,
but they themselves have fallen into it.
Interlude

[7] My heart is confident in you, O God;
my heart is confident.
No wonder I can sing your praises!

[8] Wake up, my heart!
Wake up, O lyre and harp!
I will wake the dawn with my song.

[9] I will thank you, Lord, among all the people.
I will sing your praises among the nations.

[10] For your unfailing love is as high as the
heavens.
Your faithfulness reaches to the clouds.

[11] Be exalted, O God, above the highest
heavens.
May your glory shine over all the earth.

PSALM 58

For the choir director: A psalm of David, to be sung to the tune "Do Not Destroy!"

[1] Justice—do you rulers know the meaning
of the word?
Do you judge the people fairly?

[2] No! You plot injustice in your hearts.
You spread violence throughout the land.

[3] These wicked people are born sinners;
even from birth they have lied and gone
their own way.

[4] They spit venom like deadly snakes;
they are like cobras that refuse to listen,

[5] ignoring the tunes of the snake charmers,
no matter how skillfully they play.

[6] Break off their fangs, O God!
Smash the jaws of these lions, O LORD!

[7] May they disappear like water into thirsty
ground.
Make their weapons useless in their
hands.

[8] May they be like snails that dissolve into
slime,
like a stillborn child who will never see
the sun.

[9] God will sweep them away, both young
and old,
faster than a pot heats over burning thorns.

[10] The godly will rejoice when they see
injustice avenged.
They will wash their feet in the blood
of the wicked.

[11] Then at last everyone will say,
"There truly is a reward for those who
live for God;
surely there is a God who judges justly here
on earth."

PSALM 59

For the choir director: A psalm of David, regarding the time Saul sent soldiers to watch David's house in order to kill him. To be sung to the tune "Do Not Destroy!"

[1] Rescue me from my enemies, O God.
Protect me from those who have come
to destroy me.

[2] Rescue me from these criminals;
save me from these murderers.

[3] They have set an ambush for me.
Fierce enemies are out there waiting, LORD,
though I have not sinned or offended
them.

[4] I have done nothing wrong,
yet they prepare to attack me.
Wake up! See what is happening and
help me!

[5] O LORD God of Heaven's Armies, the God
of Israel,
wake up and punish those hostile
nations.
Show no mercy to wicked traitors.
Interlude

[6] They come out at night,
snarling like vicious dogs
as they prowl the streets.

[7] Listen to the filth that comes from their
mouths;
their words cut like swords.
"After all, who can hear us?" they sneer.

[8] But LORD, you laugh at them.
You scoff at all the hostile nations.

[9] You are my strength; I wait for you to
rescue me,
for you, O God, are my fortress.

[10] In his unfailing love, my God will stand
with me.
He will let me look down in triumph on
all my enemies.

11 Don't kill them, for my people soon forget
such lessons;
stagger them with your power, and bring
them to their knees,
O Lord our shield.
12 Because of the sinful things they say,
because of the evil that is on their lips,
let them be captured by their pride,
their curses, and their lies.
13 Destroy them in your anger!
Wipe them out completely!
Then the whole world will know
that God reigns in Israel. *Interlude*

14 My enemies come out at night,
snarling like vicious dogs
as they prowl the streets.
15 They scavenge for food
but go to sleep unsatisfied.

16 But as for me, I will sing about your power.
Each morning I will sing with joy about
your unfailing love.
For you have been my refuge,
a place of safety when I am in distress.
17 O my Strength, to you I sing praises,
for you, O God, are my refuge,
the God who shows me unfailing love.

PSALM 60

For the choir director: A psalm of David useful for teaching, regarding the time David fought Aram-naharaim and Aram-zobah, and Joab returned and killed 12,000 Edomites in the Valley of Salt. To be sung to the tune "Lily of the Testimony."

1 You have rejected us, O God, and broken
our defenses.
You have been angry with us; now restore
us to your favor.
2 You have shaken our land and split it open.
Seal the cracks, for the land trembles.
3 You have been very hard on us,
making us drink wine that sent us
reeling.
4 But you have raised a banner for those who
fear you—
a rallying point in the face of attack.
Interlude

5 Now rescue your beloved people.
Answer and save us by your power.
6 God has promised this by his holiness:
"I will divide up Shechem with joy.
I will measure out the valley of Succoth.
7 Gilead is mine,
and Manasseh, too.
Ephraim, my helmet, will produce my
warriors,
and Judah, my scepter, will produce
my kings.
8 But Moab, my washbasin, will become
my servant,
and I will wipe my feet on Edom
and shout in triumph over Philistia."
9 Who will bring me into the fortified city?
Who will bring me victory over Edom?
10 Have you rejected us, O God?
Will you no longer march with our
armies?
11 Oh, please help us against our enemies,
for all human help is useless.
12 With God's help we will do mighty things,
for he will trample down our foes.

PSALM 61

For the choir director: A psalm of David, to be accompanied by stringed instruments.

1 O God, listen to my cry!
Hear my prayer!
2 From the ends of the earth,
I cry to you for help
when my heart is overwhelmed.
Lead me to the towering rock of safety,
3 for you are my safe refuge,
a fortress where my enemies cannot
reach me.
4 Let me live forever in your sanctuary,
safe beneath the shelter of your wings!
Interlude

5 For you have heard my vows, O God.
You have given me an inheritance
reserved for those who fear your name.
6 Add many years to the life of the king!
May his years span the generations!
7 May he reign under God's protection
forever.
May your unfailing love and faithfulness
watch over him.
8 Then I will sing praises to your name forever
as I fulfill my vows each day.

PSALM 62

For Jeduthun, the choir director: A psalm of David.

1 I wait quietly before God,
for my victory comes from him.
2 He alone is my rock and my salvation,
my fortress where I will never be shaken.

3 So many enemies against one man—
all of them trying to kill me.

To them I'm just a broken-down wall
or a tottering fence.
4 They plan to topple me from my high position.
They delight in telling lies about me.
They praise me to my face
but curse me in their hearts. *Interlude*

5 Let all that I am wait quietly before God,
for my hope is in him.
6 He alone is my rock and my salvation,
my fortress where I will not be shaken.
7 My victory and honor come from God alone.
He is my refuge, a rock where no enemy can reach me.
8 O my people, trust in him at all times.
Pour out your heart to him,
for God is our refuge. *Interlude*

9 Common people are as worthless as a puff of wind,
and the powerful are not what they appear to be.
If you weigh them on the scales,
together they are lighter than a breath of air.

10 Don't make your living by extortion
or put your hope in stealing.
And if your wealth increases,
don't make it the center of your life.

11 God has spoken plainly,
and I have heard it many times:
Power, O God, belongs to you;
12 unfailing love, O Lord, is yours.
Surely you repay all people
according to what they have done.

PSALM 63

A psalm of David, regarding a time when David was in the wilderness of Judah.

1 O God, you are my God;
I earnestly search for you.
My soul thirsts for you;
my whole body longs for you
in this parched and weary land
where there is no water.
2 I have seen you in your sanctuary
and gazed upon your power and glory.
3 Your unfailing love is better than life itself;
how I praise you!
4 I will praise you as long as I live,
lifting up my hands to you in prayer.
5 You satisfy me more than the richest feast.
I will praise you with songs of joy.
6 I lie awake thinking of you,
meditating on you through the night.
7 Because you are my helper,
I sing for joy in the shadow of your wings.
8 I cling to you;
your strong right hand holds me securely.
9 But those plotting to destroy me will come to ruin.
They will go down into the depths of the earth.
10 They will die by the sword
and become the food of jackals.
11 But the king will rejoice in God.
All who swear to tell the truth will praise him,
while liars will be silenced.

PSALM 64

For the choir director: A psalm of David.

1 O God, listen to my complaint.
Protect my life from my enemies' threats.
2 Hide me from the plots of this evil mob,
from this gang of wrongdoers.
3 They sharpen their tongues like swords
and aim their bitter words like arrows.
4 They shoot from ambush at the innocent,
attacking suddenly and fearlessly.
5 They encourage each other to do evil
and plan how to set their traps in secret.
"Who will ever notice?" they ask.
6 As they plot their crimes, they say,
"We have devised the perfect plan!"
Yes, the human heart and mind are cunning.

7 But God himself will shoot them with his arrows,
suddenly striking them down.
8 Their own tongues will ruin them,
and all who see them will shake their heads in scorn.
9 Then everyone will be afraid;
they will proclaim the mighty acts of God
and realize all the amazing things he does.
10 The godly will rejoice in the LORD
and find shelter in him.
And those who do what is right
will praise him.

PSALM 65

For the choir director: A song. A psalm of David.

1 What mighty praise, O God,
belongs to you in Zion.
We will fulfill our vows to you,
2 for you answer our prayers.

All of us must come to you.
3 Though we are overwhelmed by our sins,
you forgive them all.
4 What joy for those you choose to bring near,
those who live in your holy courts.
What festivities await us
inside your holy Temple.

5 You faithfully answer our prayers with
awesome deeds,
O God our savior.
You are the hope of everyone on earth,
even those who sail on distant seas.
6 You formed the mountains by your power
and armed yourself with mighty strength.
7 You quieted the raging oceans
with their pounding waves
and silenced the shouting of the nations.
8 Those who live at the ends of the earth
stand in awe of your wonders.
From where the sun rises to where it sets,
you inspire shouts of joy.

9 You take care of the earth and water it,
making it rich and fertile.
The river of God has plenty of water;
it provides a bountiful harvest of grain,
for you have ordered it so.
10 You drench the plowed ground with rain,
melting the clods and leveling the ridges.
You soften the earth with showers
and bless its abundant crops.
11 You crown the year with a bountiful harvest;
even the hard pathways overflow with
abundance.
12 The grasslands of the wilderness become
a lush pasture,
and the hillsides blossom with joy.
13 The meadows are clothed with flocks
of sheep,
and the valleys are carpeted with grain.
They all shout and sing for joy!

PSALM 66

For the choir director: A song. A psalm.

1 Shout joyful praises to God, all the earth!
2 Sing about the glory of his name!
Tell the world how glorious he is.
3 Say to God, "How awesome are your deeds!
Your enemies cringe before your mighty
power.
4 Everything on earth will worship you;
they will sing your praises,
shouting your name in glorious songs."
Interlude

**5 Come and see what our God
has done,
what awesome miracles he
performs for people!**
6 He made a dry path through the Red Sea,
and his people went across on foot.
There we rejoiced in him.
7 For by his great power he rules forever.
He watches every movement of the
nations;
let no rebel rise in defiance. *Interlude*

8 Let the whole world bless our God
and loudly sing his praises.
9 Our lives are in his hands,
and he keeps our feet from stumbling.
10 You have tested us, O God;
you have purified us like silver.
11 You captured us in your net
and laid the burden of slavery on our backs.
12 Then you put a leader over us.
We went through fire and flood,
but you brought us to a place of great
abundance.

13 Now I come to your Temple with burnt
offerings
to fulfill the vows I made to you—
14 yes, the sacred vows that I made
when I was in deep trouble.
15 That is why I am sacrificing burnt offerings
to you—
the best of my rams as a pleasing aroma,
and a sacrifice of bulls and male goats.
Interlude

16 Come and listen, all you who fear God,
and I will tell you what he did for me.
17 For I cried out to him for help,
praising him as I spoke.
18 If I had not confessed the sin in my heart,
the Lord would not have listened.
19 But God did listen!
He paid attention to my prayer.
20 Praise God, who did not ignore my prayer
or withdraw his unfailing love from me.

PSALM 67

For the choir director: A song. A psalm, to be accompanied by stringed instruments.

1 May God be merciful and bless us.
May his face smile with favor on us.
Interlude

2 May your ways be known throughout the
earth,

your saving power among people
everywhere.
3 May the nations praise you, O God.
Yes, may all the nations praise you.
4 Let the whole world sing for joy,
because you govern the nations with
justice
and guide the people of the whole world.
Interlude
5 May the nations praise you, O God.
Yes, may all the nations praise you.
6 Then the earth will yield its harvests,
and God, our God, will richly bless us.
7 Yes, God will bless us,
and people all over the world will fear him.

PSALM 68

For the choir director: A song. A psalm of David.

1 Rise up, O God, and scatter your enemies.
Let those who hate God run for their lives.
2 Blow them away like smoke.
Melt them like wax in a fire.
Let the wicked perish in the presence
of God.
3 But let the godly rejoice.
Let them be glad in God's presence.
Let them be filled with joy.
4 Sing praises to God and to his name!
Sing loud praises to him who rides
the clouds.
His name is the LORD—
rejoice in his presence!
5 Father to the fatherless, defender of
widows—
this is God, whose dwelling is holy.
6 God places the lonely in families;
he sets the prisoners free and gives
them joy.
But he makes the rebellious live in a sun-
scorched land.
7 O God, when you led your people out
from Egypt,
when you marched through the dry
wasteland, *Interlude*
8 the earth trembled, and the heavens poured
down rain
before you, the God of Sinai,
before God, the God of Israel.
9 You sent abundant rain, O God,
to refresh the weary land.
10 There your people finally settled,
and with a bountiful harvest, O God,
you provided for your needy people.

11 The Lord gives the word,
and a great army brings the good news.
12 Enemy kings and their armies flee,
while the women of Israel divide the
plunder.
13 Even those who lived among the sheepfolds
found treasures—
doves with wings of silver
and feathers of gold.
14 The Almighty scattered the enemy kings
like a blowing snowstorm on Mount
Zalmon.
15 The mountains of Bashan are majestic,
with many peaks stretching high into
the sky.
16 Why do you look with envy, O rugged
mountains,
at Mount Zion, where God has chosen
to live,
where the LORD himself will live forever?
17 Surrounded by unnumbered thousands
of chariots,
the Lord came from Mount Sinai into his
sanctuary.
18 When you ascended to the heights,
you led a crowd of captives.
You received gifts from the people,
even from those who rebelled against you.
Now the LORD God will live among us
there.
19 Praise the Lord; praise God our savior!
For each day he carries us in his arms.
Interlude
20 Our God is a God who saves!
The Sovereign LORD rescues us from
death.
21 But God will smash the heads of his enemies,
crushing the skulls of those who love their
guilty ways.
22 The Lord says, "I will bring my enemies down
from Bashan;
I will bring them up from the depths of the
sea.
23 You, my people, will wash your feet in their
blood,
and even your dogs will get their share!"
24 Your procession has come into view, O God—
the procession of my God and King as he
goes into the sanctuary.
25 Singers are in front, musicians behind;
between them are young women playing
tambourines.

26 Praise God, all you people of Israel;
praise the LORD, the source of Israel's life.
27 Look, the little tribe of Benjamin leads
the way.
Then comes a great throng of rulers
from Judah
and all the rulers of Zebulun and Naphtali.

28 Summon your might, O God.
Display your power, O God, as you have
in the past.
29 The kings of the earth are bringing tribute
to your Temple in Jerusalem.
30 Rebuke these enemy nations—
these wild animals lurking in the reeds,
this herd of bulls among the weaker calves.
Make them bring bars of silver in humble
tribute.
Scatter the nations that delight in war.
31 Let Egypt come with gifts of precious metals;
let Ethiopia bring tribute to God.
32 Sing to God, you kingdoms of the earth.
Sing praises to the Lord. *Interlude*
33 Sing to the one who rides across the ancient
heavens,
his mighty voice thundering from the sky.
34 Tell everyone about God's power.
His majesty shines down on Israel;
his strength is mighty in the heavens.
35 God is awesome in his sanctuary.
The God of Israel gives power and strength
to his people.

Praise be to God!

PSALM 69

For the choir director: A psalm of David, to be sung to the tune "Lilies."

1 Save me, O God,
for the floodwaters are up to my neck.
2 Deeper and deeper I sink into the mire;
I can't find a foothold.
I am in deep water,
and the floods overwhelm me.
3 I am exhausted from crying for help;
my throat is parched.
My eyes are swollen with weeping,
waiting for my God to help me.
4 Those who hate me without cause
outnumber the hairs on my head.
Many enemies try to destroy me with lies,
demanding that I give back what I didn't
steal.

5 O God, you know how foolish I am;
my sins cannot be hidden from you.
6 Don't let those who trust in you be ashamed
because of me,
O Sovereign LORD of Heaven's Armies.
Don't let me cause them to be humiliated,
O God of Israel.
7 For I endure insults for your sake;
humiliation is written all over my face.
8 Even my own brothers pretend they don't
know me;
they treat me like a stranger.

9 Passion for your house has consumed me,
and the insults of those who insult you
have fallen on me.
10 When I weep and fast,
they scoff at me.
11 When I dress in burlap to show sorrow,
they make fun of me.
12 I am the favorite topic of town gossip,
and all the drunks sing about me.

13 But I keep praying to you, LORD,
hoping this time you will show me favor.
In your unfailing love, O God,
answer my prayer with your sure salvation.
14 Rescue me from the mud;
don't let me sink any deeper!
Save me from those who hate me,
and pull me from these deep waters.
15 Don't let the floods overwhelm me,
or the deep waters swallow me,
or the pit of death devour me.

16 Answer my prayers, O LORD,
for your unfailing love is wonderful.
Take care of me,
for your mercy is so plentiful.
17 Don't hide from your servant;
answer me quickly, for I am in deep
trouble!
18 Come and redeem me;
free me from my enemies.

19 You know of my shame, scorn, and disgrace.
You see all that my enemies are doing.
20 Their insults have broken my heart,
and I am in despair.
If only one person would show some pity;
if only one would turn and comfort me.
21 But instead, they give me poison for food;
they offer me sour wine for my thirst.

22 Let the bountiful table set before them
become a snare
and their prosperity become a trap.
23 Let their eyes go blind so they cannot see,
and make their bodies shake continually.

24 Pour out your fury on them;
consume them with your burning anger.
25 Let their homes become desolate
and their tents be deserted.
26 To the one you have punished, they add
insult to injury;
they add to the pain of those you have
hurt.
27 Pile their sins up high,
and don't let them go free.
28 Erase their names from the Book of Life;
don't let them be counted among the
righteous.

29 I am suffering and in pain.
Rescue me, O God, by your saving power.
30 Then I will praise God's name with singing,
and I will honor him with thanksgiving.
31 For this will please the LORD more than
sacrificing cattle,
more than presenting a bull with its horns
and hooves.
32 The humble will see their God at work and
be glad.
Let all who seek God's help be encouraged.
33 For the LORD hears the cries of the needy;
he does not despise his imprisoned
people.

34 Praise him, O heaven and earth,
the seas and all that move in them.
35 For God will save Jerusalem
and rebuild the towns of Judah.
His people will live there
and settle in their own land.
36 The descendants of those who obey him
will inherit the land,
and those who love him will live there
in safety.

PSALM 70

For the choir director: A psalm of David, asking God to remember him.

1 Please, God, rescue me!
Come quickly, LORD, and help me.
2 May those who try to kill me
be humiliated and put to shame.
May those who take delight in my trouble
be turned back in disgrace.
3 Let them be horrified by their shame,
for they said, "Aha! We've got him now!"
4 But may all who search for you
be filled with joy and gladness in you.
May those who love your salvation
repeatedly shout, "God is great!"
5 But as for me, I am poor and needy;
please hurry to my aid, O God.
You are my helper and my savior;
O LORD, do not delay.

PSALM 71

1 O LORD, I have come to you for protection;
don't let me be disgraced.
2 Save me and rescue me,
for you do what is right.
Turn your ear to listen to me,
and set me free.
3 Be my rock of safety
where I can always hide.
Give the order to save me,
for you are my rock and my fortress.
4 My God, rescue me from the power of
the wicked,
from the clutches of cruel oppressors.
5 O Lord, you alone are my hope.
I've trusted you, O LORD, from childhood.
6 Yes, you have been with me from birth;
from my mother's womb you have cared
for me.
No wonder I am always praising you!

7 My life is an example to many,
because you have been my strength and
protection.
8 That is why I can never stop praising you;
I declare your glory all day long.
9 And now, in my old age, don't set me aside.
Don't abandon me when my strength
is failing.
10 For my enemies are whispering against me.
They are plotting together to kill me.
11 They say, "God has abandoned him.
Let's go and get him,
for no one will help him now."

12 O God, don't stay away.
My God, please hurry to help me.
13 Bring disgrace and destruction on my
accusers.
Humiliate and shame those who want
to harm me.
14 But I will keep on hoping for your help;
I will praise you more and more.
15 I will tell everyone about your righteousness.
All day long I will proclaim your saving
power,
though I am not skilled with words.
16 I will praise your mighty deeds, O Sovereign
LORD.
I will tell everyone that you alone
are just.

FUN-fact

Hey! It's a Poem!

Hebrew poetry was fancy stuff! **One cool type of poem was an acrostic poem.**

The first line began with the first letter of the Hebrew alphabet. The second line started with the second letter, and so on.

One acrostic poem is PSALM 119, the longest chapter in the Bible! It doesn't look like it's in alphabetical order to us because the Hebrew words have been translated into English!

CREATE AN ACROSTIC POEM WITH YOUR NAME. Write your name from top to bottom along the left side of a piece of lined paper, one letter per line.

Think of words describing God that begin with each of the letters. Write a word next to each letter of your name.

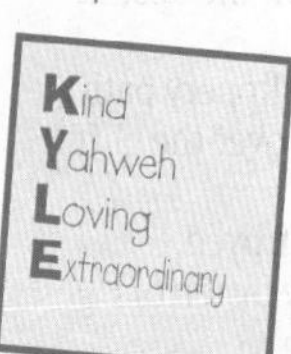

Read your acrostic poem to God, and praise him for how wonderful he is!

17 O God, you have taught me from my earliest
childhood,
and I constantly tell others about the
wonderful things you do.
18 Now that I am old and gray,
do not abandon me, O God.
Let me proclaim your power to this new
generation,
your mighty miracles to all who come
after me.
19 Your righteousness, O God, reaches to the
highest heavens.
You have done such wonderful things.
Who can compare with you, O God?
20 You have allowed me to suffer much
hardship,
but you will restore me to life again
and lift me up from the depths of the
earth.
21 You will restore me to even greater honor
and comfort me once again.
22 Then I will praise you with music on the
harp,
because you are faithful to your promises,
O my God.
I will sing praises to you with a lyre,
O Holy One of Israel.
23 I will shout for joy and sing your praises,
for you have ransomed me.
24 I will tell about your righteous deeds
all day long,
for everyone who tried to hurt me
has been shamed and humiliated.

PSALM 72

A psalm of Solomon.

1 Give your love of justice to the king, O God,
and righteousness to the king's son.
2 Help him judge your people in the right
way;
let the poor always be treated fairly.
3 May the mountains yield prosperity for all,
and may the hills be fruitful.
4 Help him to defend the poor,
to rescue the children of the needy,
and to crush their oppressors.
5 May they fear you as long as the sun shines,
as long as the moon remains in the sky.
Yes, forever!
6 May the king's rule be refreshing like spring
rain on freshly cut grass,
like the showers that water the earth.
7 May all the godly flourish during his reign.

May there be abundant prosperity until
the moon is no more.
8 May he reign from sea to sea,
and from the Euphrates River to the ends
of the earth.
9 Desert nomads will bow before him;
his enemies will fall before him in the dust.
10 The western kings of Tarshish and other
distant lands
will bring him tribute.
The eastern kings of Sheba and Seba
will bring him gifts.
11 All kings will bow before him,
and all nations will serve him.

12 He will rescue the poor when they cry to him;
he will help the oppressed, who have no
one to defend them.
13 He feels pity for the weak and the needy,
and he will rescue them.
14 He will redeem them from oppression
and violence,
for their lives are precious to him.

15 Long live the king!
May the gold of Sheba be given to him.
May the people always pray for him
and bless him all day long.
16 May there be abundant grain throughout
the land,
flourishing even on the hilltops.
May the fruit trees flourish like the trees
of Lebanon,
and may the people thrive like grass
in a field.
17 May the king's name endure forever;
may it continue as long as the sun shines.
May all nations be blessed through him
and bring him praise.

18 Praise the Lord God, the God of Israel,
who alone does such wonderful things.
19 Praise his glorious name forever!
Let the whole earth be filled with his glory.
Amen and amen!

20 (This ends the prayers of David son of Jesse.)

Book Three (Psalms 73–89)

PSALM 73

A psalm of Asaph.

1 Truly God is good to Israel,
to those whose hearts are pure.
2 But as for me, I almost lost my footing.
My feet were slipping, and I was
almost gone.
3 For I envied the proud
when I saw them prosper despite their
wickedness.
4 They seem to live such painless lives;
their bodies are so healthy and strong.
5 They don't have troubles like other people;
they're not plagued with problems like
everyone else.
6 They wear pride like a jeweled necklace
and clothe themselves with cruelty.
7 These fat cats have everything
their hearts could ever wish for!
8 They scoff and speak only evil;
in their pride they seek to crush others.
9 They boast against the very heavens,
and their words strut throughout the
earth.
10 And so the people are dismayed and
confused,
drinking in all their words.
11 "What does God know?" they ask.
"Does the Most High even know what's
happening?"
12 Look at these wicked people—
enjoying a life of ease while their riches
multiply.

13 Did I keep my heart pure for nothing?
Did I keep myself innocent for no reason?
14 I get nothing but trouble all day long;
every morning brings me pain.

15 If I had really spoken this way to others,
I would have been a traitor to your
people.
16 So I tried to understand why the wicked
prosper.
But what a difficult task it is!
17 Then I went into your sanctuary, O God,
and I finally understood the destiny
of the wicked.
18 Truly, you put them on a slippery path
and send them sliding over the cliff
to destruction.
19 In an instant they are destroyed,
completely swept away by terrors.
20 When you arise, O Lord,
you will laugh at their silly ideas
as a person laughs at dreams in the
morning.

21 Then I realized that my heart was bitter,
and I was all torn up inside.
22 I was so foolish and ignorant—
I must have seemed like a senseless
animal to you.

23 Yet I still belong to you;
you hold my right hand.
24 You guide me with your counsel,
leading me to a glorious destiny.
25 Whom have I in heaven but you?
I desire you more than anything on earth.
26 My health may fail, and my spirit may grow weak,
but God remains the strength of my heart;
he is mine forever.

27 Those who desert him will perish,
for you destroy those who abandon you.
28 But as for me, how good it is to be near God!
I have made the Sovereign LORD my shelter,
and I will tell everyone about the wonderful things you do.

PSALM 74

A psalm of Asaph.

1 O God, why have you rejected us so long?
Why is your anger so intense against the sheep of your own pasture?
2 Remember that we are the people you chose long ago,
the tribe you redeemed as your own special possession!
And remember Jerusalem, your home here on earth.
3 Walk through the awful ruins of the city;
see how the enemy has destroyed your sanctuary.
4 There your enemies shouted their victorious battle cries;
there they set up their battle standards.
5 They swung their axes
like woodcutters in a forest.
6 With axes and picks,
they smashed the carved paneling.
7 They burned your sanctuary to the ground.
They defiled the place that bears your name.
8 Then they thought, "Let's destroy everything!"
So they burned down all the places where God was worshiped.
9 We no longer see your miraculous signs.
All the prophets are gone,
and no one can tell us when it will end.
10 How long, O God, will you allow our enemies to insult you?
Will you let them dishonor your name forever?
11 Why do you hold back your strong right hand?
Unleash your powerful fist and destroy them.

12 You, O God, are my king from ages past,
bringing salvation to the earth.
13 You split the sea by your strength
and smashed the heads of the sea monsters.
14 You crushed the heads of Leviathan
and let the desert animals eat him.
15 You caused the springs and streams to gush forth,
and you dried up rivers that never run dry.
16 Both day and night belong to you;
you made the starlight and the sun.
17 You set the boundaries of the earth,
and you made both summer and winter.

18 See how these enemies insult you, LORD.
A foolish nation has dishonored your name.
19 Don't let these wild beasts destroy your turtledoves.
Don't forget your suffering people forever.

20 Remember your covenant promises,
for the land is full of darkness and violence!
21 Don't let the downtrodden be humiliated again.
Instead, let the poor and needy praise your name.

22 Arise, O God, and defend your cause.
Remember how these fools insult you all day long.
23 Don't overlook what your enemies have said
or their growing uproar.

PSALM 75

For the choir director: A psalm of Asaph. A song to be sung to the tune "Do Not Destroy!"

1 We thank you, O God!
We give thanks because you are near.
People everywhere tell of your wonderful deeds.

2 God says, "At the time I have planned,
I will bring justice against the wicked.
3 When the earth quakes and its people live in turmoil,
I am the one who keeps its foundations firm. *Interlude*

4 "I warned the proud, 'Stop your boasting!'
I told the wicked, 'Don't raise your fists!
5 Don't raise your fists in defiance at the heavens
or speak with such arrogance.'"
6 For no one on earth—from east or west,
or even from the wilderness—
should raise a defiant fist.
7 It is God alone who judges;
he decides who will rise and who will fall.
8 For the LORD holds a cup in his hand
that is full of foaming wine mixed with spices.
He pours out the wine in judgment,
and all the wicked must drink it,
draining it to the dregs.

9 But as for me, I will always proclaim what God has done;
I will sing praises to the God of Jacob.
10 For God says, "I will break the strength of the wicked,
but I will increase the power of the godly."

PSALM 76

For the choir director: A psalm of Asaph. A song to be accompanied by stringed instruments.

1 God is honored in Judah;
his name is great in Israel.
2 Jerusalem is where he lives;
Mount Zion is his home.
3 There he has broken the fiery arrows of the enemy,
the shields and swords and weapons of war. *Interlude*

4 You are glorious and more majestic
than the everlasting mountains.
5 Our boldest enemies have been plundered.
They lie before us in the sleep of death.
No warrior could lift a hand against us.
6 At the blast of your breath, O God of Jacob,
their horses and chariots lay still.

7 No wonder you are greatly feared!
Who can stand before you when your anger explodes?
8 From heaven you sentenced your enemies;
the earth trembled and stood silent before you.
9 You stand up to judge those who do evil, O God,
and to rescue the oppressed of the earth. *Interlude*

10 Human defiance only enhances your glory,
for you use it as a weapon.
11 Make vows to the LORD your God, and keep them.
Let everyone bring tribute to the Awesome One.
12 For he breaks the pride of princes,
and the kings of the earth fear him.

PSALM 77

For Jeduthun, the choir director: A psalm of Asaph.

1 I cry out to God; yes, I shout.
Oh, that God would listen to me!
2 When I was in deep trouble,
I searched for the Lord.
All night long I prayed, with hands lifted toward heaven,
but my soul was not comforted.
3 I think of God, and I moan,
overwhelmed with longing for his help. *Interlude*

4 You don't let me sleep.
I am too distressed even to pray!
5 I think of the good old days,
long since ended,
6 when my nights were filled with joyful songs.
I search my soul and ponder the difference now.
7 Has the Lord rejected me forever?
Will he never again be kind to me?
8 Is his unfailing love gone forever?
Have his promises permanently failed?
9 Has God forgotten to be gracious?
Has he slammed the door on his compassion? *Interlude*

10 And I said, "This is my fate;
the Most High has turned his hand against me."
11 But then I recall all you have done, O LORD;
I remember your wonderful deeds of long ago.
12 They are constantly in my thoughts.
I cannot stop thinking about your mighty works.

13 O God, your ways are holy.
Is there any god as mighty as you?
14 You are the God of great wonders!
You demonstrate your awesome power among the nations.
15 By your strong arm, you redeemed your people,
the descendants of Jacob and Joseph. *Interlude*

16 When the Red Sea saw you, O God,
its waters looked and trembled!
The sea quaked to its very depths.
17 The clouds poured down rain;
the thunder rumbled in the sky.
Your arrows of lightning flashed.
18 Your thunder roared from the whirlwind;
the lightning lit up the world!
The earth trembled and shook.
19 Your road led through the sea,
your pathway through the mighty
waters—
a pathway no one knew was there!
20 You led your people along that road like
a flock of sheep,
with Moses and Aaron as their shepherds.

PSALM 78

A psalm of Asaph.

1 O my people, listen to my instructions.
Open your ears to what I am saying,
2 for I will speak to you in a parable.
I will teach you hidden lessons from
our past—
3 stories we have heard and known,
stories our ancestors handed down to us.
4 We will not hide these truths from our
children;
we will tell the next generation
about the glorious deeds of the LORD,
about his power and his mighty wonders.
5 For he issued his laws to Jacob;
he gave his instructions to Israel.
He commanded our ancestors
to teach them to their children,
6 so the next generation might know them—
even the children not yet born—
and they in turn will teach their own
children.
7 So each generation should set its hope anew
on God,
not forgetting his glorious miracles
and obeying his commands.
8 Then they will not be like their ancestors—
stubborn, rebellious, and unfaithful,
refusing to give their hearts to God.

9 The warriors of Ephraim, though armed with
bows,
turned their backs and fled on the day
of battle.
10 They did not keep God's covenant
and refused to live by his instructions.
11 They forgot what he had done—
the great wonders he had shown them,
12 the miracles he did for their ancestors
on the plain of Zoan in the land of Egypt.
13 For he divided the sea and led them through,
making the water stand up like walls!
14 In the daytime he led them by a cloud,
and all night by a pillar of fire.
15 He split open the rocks in the wilderness
to give them water, as from a gushing
spring.
16 He made streams pour from the rock,
making the waters flow down like a river!

17 Yet they kept on sinning against him,
rebelling against the Most High in the
desert.
18 They stubbornly tested God in their hearts,
demanding the foods they craved.
19 They even spoke against God himself,
saying,
"God can't give us food in the wilderness.
20 Yes, he can strike a rock so water gushes out,
but he can't give his people bread and
meat."
21 When the LORD heard them, he was furious.
The fire of his wrath burned against Jacob.
Yes, his anger rose against Israel,
22 for they did not believe God
or trust him to care for them.
23 But he commanded the skies to open;
he opened the doors of heaven.
24 He rained down manna for them to eat;
he gave them bread from heaven.
25 They ate the food of angels!
God gave them all they could hold.
26 He released the east wind in the heavens
and guided the south wind by his mighty
power.
27 He rained down meat as thick as dust—
birds as plentiful as the sand on the
seashore!
28 He caused the birds to fall within their camp
and all around their tents.
29 The people ate their fill.
He gave them what they craved.
30 But before they satisfied their craving,
while the meat was yet in their mouths,
31 the anger of God rose against them,
and he killed their strongest men.
He struck down the finest of Israel's
young men.
32 But in spite of this, the people kept sinning.
Despite his wonders, they refused to
trust him.
33 So he ended their lives in failure,
their years in terror.

34 When God began killing them,
they finally sought him.
They repented and took God seriously.
35 Then they remembered that God was
their rock,
that God Most High was their redeemer.
36 But all they gave him was lip service;
they lied to him with their tongues.
37 Their hearts were not loyal to him.
They did not keep his covenant.
38 Yet he was merciful and forgave their sins
and did not destroy them all.
Many times he held back his anger
and did not unleash his fury!
39 For he remembered that they were merely
mortal,
gone like a breath of wind that never
returns.

40 Oh, how often they rebelled against him
in the wilderness
and grieved his heart in that dry
wasteland.
41 Again and again they tested God's
patience
and provoked the Holy One of Israel.
42 They did not remember his power
and how he rescued them from their
enemies.
43 They did not remember his miraculous
signs in Egypt,
his wonders on the plain of Zoan.
44 For he turned their rivers into blood,
so no one could drink from the streams.
45 He sent vast swarms of flies to consume
them
and hordes of frogs to ruin them.
46 He gave their crops to caterpillars;
their harvest was consumed by locusts.
47 He destroyed their grapevines with hail
and shattered their sycamore-figs
with sleet.
48 He abandoned their cattle to the hail,
their livestock to bolts of lightning.
49 He loosed on them his fierce anger—
all his fury, rage, and hostility.
He dispatched against them
a band of destroying angels.
50 He turned his anger against them;
he did not spare the Egyptians' lives
but ravaged them with the plague.
51 He killed the oldest son in each Egyptian
family,
the flower of youth throughout the land of
Egypt.
52 But he led his own people like a flock
of sheep,
guiding them safely through the
wilderness.
53 He kept them safe so they were not afraid;
but the sea covered their enemies.
54 He brought them to the border of his
holy land,
to this land of hills he had won for them.
55 He drove out the nations before them;
he gave them their inheritance by lot.
He settled the tribes of Israel into their
homes.

56 But they kept testing and rebelling against
God Most High.
They did not obey his laws.
57 They turned back and were as faithless
as their parents.
They were as undependable as a crooked
bow.
58 They angered God by building shrines
to other gods;
they made him jealous with their idols.
59 When God heard them, he was very angry,
and he completely rejected Israel.
60 Then he abandoned his dwelling at Shiloh,
the Tabernacle where he had lived among
the people.
61 He allowed the Ark of his might to be
captured;
he surrendered his glory into enemy hands.
62 He gave his people over to be butchered by
the sword,
because he was so angry with his own
people—his special possession.
63 Their young men were killed by fire;
their young women died before singing
their wedding songs.
64 Their priests were slaughtered,
and their widows could not mourn their
deaths.

65 Then the Lord rose up as though waking
from sleep,
like a warrior aroused from a drunken
stupor.
66 He routed his enemies
and sent them to eternal shame.
67 But he rejected Joseph's descendants;
he did not choose the tribe of Ephraim.
68 He chose instead the tribe of Judah,
and Mount Zion, which he loved.
69 There he built his sanctuary as high as
the heavens,
as solid and enduring as the earth.

Hi, my name is

ESTHER *(queen)*

Who would have thought that an orphan girl would one day become queen of the most powerful country in the world? I certainly wouldn't have—but that's exactly what happened to me. After my parents died, my older cousin, Mordecai, took me in and raised me like his own daughter. Mordecai taught me to love God and live for God no matter how good or bad things got.

Mordecai worked in the king's palace. Check out how he saved the king's life as you read ESTHER 2:21-23.

We lived in Susa, where the great King Xerxes had his palace. The king had a bad temper, and he really didn't do things God's way. Once he got mad at his wife and just decided to get a new one. Guess how the king decided to find his new wife. He held a kind of beauty pageant. They took me to the king's palace and gave me a huge makeover! Of all the women, the king chose *me* to be his queen—I couldn't believe it.

But Mordecai reminded me that God made me queen for a reason. It didn't take long to see why. A wicked man named Haman got permission from the king to kill all of my people, the Jews. I had to do something, but I knew that if I went to the king without being asked, he'd probably have me killed. I know that sounds weird since I was the queen. But that was the law, and like I said, the king had a temper.

Haman especially didn't like Mordecai. Read ESTHER 3:1-6 to find out why.

Esther didn't tell the king right away. Check out ESTHER 5:1-8 and 7:1-7 to find out how she made her request.

When I went to the king, I was so afraid that I could barely stand up. But the king held out his scepter (a gold rod) to me, which meant he would hear my request. I was given a chance to tell the king what the wicked Haman planned to do, and the king protected my people. Wherever you are and wherever you go, remember that God put you there. While you're there, find out what God wants you to do.

Who Is God Gonna Use?

For your safety: You probably should get permission from an adult before doing this one!

1. **Find a few *DRY-ERASE* markers—*not* permanent ones. A *DRY-ERASE* marker should have the words *DRY-ERASE* on it. Did we mention that the markers should be *DRY-ERASE*?**

BOLD COLOR DRY ERASE

2. **Draw a little line in the corner of an old mirror. Test it to make sure it completely wipes off.**

3. **Write, "Who will God use?" at the top of the mirror. Decorate the mirror. If you know who will use the mirror next, write little notes of encouragement to that person.**

who will God use?
i love you

WARNING! The longer you keep the marker on the mirror, the harder it is to get off. Use window cleaner if the marker won't erase. Don't leave it on too long or it might not completely erase!

BIBLE BIOS

Hear From the Heroes

Hi, my name is

JOB *(wealthy farmer)*

This may sound strange, but the only thing I'm famous for is having a rough life. Here's what happened. One day, I was minding my own business, taking care of my herds and flocks, enjoying all my children (seven sons and three daughters!), and trying to please God. And then it all started. In the blink of an eye, my animals were stolen and killed and all my children died. On top of that, I got a terrible disease and had sores all over my body! Talk about sad and miserable!

Why had such bad things happened? All I ever wanted to do was to lead a good life for God. What had I done to deserve all this misery? My three good friends told me it was *my* fault—that I'd sinned and this was my punishment. Even my wife told me to curse God and die. But I didn't believe any of them. I still trusted God, even though it was hard. Finally, God explained to me that he is the one in charge. He's the King of the universe. Only God is wise enough to understand why things happen. After I told God I believed him, he healed me and restored my herds and flocks and gave me more children. You can read my story in the Bible in the book of Job—yep, the whole book's about me!

Puzzle Pieces

Job was sure puzzled when his life seemed to be falling apart! But God knows all of the pieces to your life. He knows how all the pieces of your life will fit together!

On a piece of poster board, draw a scene from your life. Now cut the picture into puzzle pieces. Mix the pieces up, and ask a friend to put them together, but keep a few pieces out. Your friend can't see the whole picture because only you have all the pieces to the puzzle.

The next time you're puzzled about what's happening in your life, remember that God has control of all the pieces and knows what the whole picture will look like. So trust him, just like Job did!

70 He chose his servant David,
calling him from the sheep pens.
71 He took David from tending the ewes and lambs
and made him the shepherd of Jacob's descendants—
God's own people, Israel.
72 He cared for them with a true heart
and led them with skillful hands.

PSALM 79

A psalm of Asaph.

1 O God, pagan nations have conquered your land,
your special possession.
They have defiled your holy Temple
and made Jerusalem a heap of ruins.
2 They have left the bodies of your servants
as food for the birds of heaven.
The flesh of your godly ones
has become food for the wild animals.
3 Blood has flowed like water all around Jerusalem;
no one is left to bury the dead.
4 We are mocked by our neighbors,
an object of scorn and derision to those around us.

5 O LORD, how long will you be angry with us? Forever?
How long will your jealousy burn like fire?
6 Pour out your wrath on the nations that refuse to acknowledge you—
on kingdoms that do not call upon your name.
7 For they have devoured your people Israel,
making the land a desolate wilderness.
8 Do not hold us guilty for the sins of our ancestors!
Let your compassion quickly meet our needs,
for we are on the brink of despair.

9 Help us, O God of our salvation!
Help us for the glory of your name.
Save us and forgive our sins
for the honor of your name.
10 Why should pagan nations be allowed to scoff,
asking, "Where is their God?"
Show us your vengeance against the nations,
for they have spilled the blood of your servants.
11 Listen to the moaning of the prisoners.
Demonstrate your great power by saving those condemned to die.

12 O Lord, pay back our neighbors seven times
for the scorn they have hurled at you.
13 Then we your people, the sheep of your pasture,
will thank you forever and ever,
praising your greatness from generation to generation.

PSALM 80

For the choir director: A psalm of Asaph, to be sung to the tune "Lilies of the Covenant."

1 Please listen, O Shepherd of Israel,
you who lead Joseph's descendants like a flock.
O God, enthroned above the cherubim,
display your radiant glory
2 to Ephraim, Benjamin, and Manasseh.
Show us your mighty power.
Come to rescue us!

3 Turn us again to yourself, O God.
Make your face shine down upon us.
Only then will we be saved.
4 O LORD God of Heaven's Armies,
how long will you be angry with our prayers?
5 You have fed us with sorrow
and made us drink tears by the bucketful.
6 You have made us the scorn of neighboring nations.
Our enemies treat us as a joke.

7 Turn us again to yourself, O God of Heaven's Armies.
Make your face shine down upon us.
Only then will we be saved.
8 You brought us from Egypt like a grapevine;
you drove away the pagan nations and transplanted us into your land.
9 You cleared the ground for us,
and we took root and filled the land.
10 Our shade covered the mountains;
our branches covered the mighty cedars.
11 We spread our branches west to the Mediterranean Sea;
our shoots spread east to the Euphrates River.
12 But now, why have you broken down our walls
so that all who pass by may steal our fruit?
13 The wild boar from the forest devours it,
and the wild animals feed on it.

Psalm 81 . . . page 578

14 Come back, we beg you, O God of Heaven's Armies.
Look down from heaven and see our plight.
Take care of this grapevine
15 that you yourself have planted,
this son you have raised for yourself.
16 For we are chopped up and burned by our enemies.
May they perish at the sight of your frown.
17 Strengthen the man you love,
the son of your choice.
18 Then we will never abandon you again.
Revive us so we can call on your name once more.

19 Turn us again to yourself, O LORD God of Heaven's Armies.
Make your face shine down upon us.
Only then will we be saved.

PSALM 81

For the choir director: A psalm of Asaph, to be accompanied by a stringed instrument.

1 Sing praises to God, our strength.
Sing to the God of Jacob.
2 Sing! Beat the tambourine.
Play the sweet lyre and the harp.
3 Blow the ram's horn at new moon,
and again at full moon to call a festival!
4 For this is required by the decrees of Israel;
it is a regulation of the God of Jacob.
5 He made it a law for Israel
when he attacked Egypt to set us free.

I heard an unknown voice say,
6 "Now I will take the load from your shoulders;
I will free your hands from their heavy tasks.
7 You cried to me in trouble, and I saved you;
I answered out of the thundercloud
and tested your faith when there was no water at Meribah. *Interlude*

8 "Listen to me, O my people, while I give you stern warnings.
O Israel, if you would only listen to me!
9 You must never have a foreign god;
you must not bow down before a false god.
10 For it was I, the LORD your God,
who rescued you from the land of Egypt.
Open your mouth wide, and I will fill it with good things.

11 "But no, my people wouldn't listen.
Israel did not want me around.
12 So I let them follow their own stubborn desires,
living according to their own ideas.
13 Oh, that my people would listen to me!
Oh, that Israel would follow me, walking in my paths!
14 How quickly I would then subdue their enemies!
How soon my hands would be upon their foes!
15 Those who hate the LORD would cringe before him;
they would be doomed forever.
16 But I would feed you with the finest wheat.
I would satisfy you with wild honey from the rock."

PSALM 82

A psalm of Asaph.

1 God presides over heaven's court;
he pronounces judgment on the heavenly beings:
2 "How long will you hand down unjust decisions
by favoring the wicked? *Interlude*

3 "Give justice to the poor and the orphan;
uphold the rights of the oppressed and the destitute.
4 Rescue the poor and helpless;
deliver them from the grasp of evil people.
5 But these oppressors know nothing;
they are so ignorant!
They wander about in darkness,
while the whole world is shaken to the core.
6 I say, 'You are gods;
you are all children of the Most High.
7 But you will die like mere mortals
and fall like every other ruler.'"

8 Rise up, O God, and judge the earth,
for all the nations belong to you.

PSALM 83

A song. A psalm of Asaph.

1 O God, do not be silent!
Do not be deaf.
Do not be quiet, O God.
2 Don't you hear the uproar of your enemies?
Don't you see that your arrogant enemies are rising up?
3 They devise crafty schemes against your people;
they conspire against your precious ones.

4 "Come," they say, "let us wipe out Israel
as a nation.
We will destroy the very memory
of its existence."
5 Yes, this was their unanimous decision.
They signed a treaty as allies against
you—
6 these Edomites and Ishmaelites;
Moabites and Hagrites;
7 Gebalites, Ammonites, and Amalekites;
and people from Philistia and Tyre.
8 Assyria has joined them, too,
and is allied with the descendants of Lot.
Interlude

9 Do to them as you did to the Midianites
and as you did to Sisera and Jabin at the
Kishon River.
10 They were destroyed at Endor,
and their decaying corpses fertilized
the soil.
11 Let their mighty nobles die as Oreb and
Zeeb did.
Let all their princes die like Zebah and
Zalmunna,
12 for they said, "Let us seize for our own use
these pasturelands of God!"
13 O my God, scatter them like tumbleweed,
like chaff before the wind!
14 As a fire burns a forest
and as a flame sets mountains ablaze,
15 chase them with your fierce storm;
terrify them with your tempest.
16 Utterly disgrace them
until they submit to your name, O LORD.
17 Let them be ashamed and terrified
forever.
Let them die in disgrace.
18 Then they will learn that you alone are called
the LORD,
that you alone are the Most High,
supreme over all the earth.

PSALM 84

For the choir director: A psalm of the descendants of Korah, to be accompanied by a stringed instrument.

1 How lovely is your dwelling place,
O LORD of Heaven's Armies.
2 I long, yes, I faint with longing
to enter the courts of the LORD.
With my whole being, body and soul,
I will shout joyfully to the living God.
3 Even the sparrow finds a home,
and the swallow builds her nest and raises
her young
at a place near your altar,
O LORD of Heaven's Armies, my King and
my God!
4 What joy for those who can live in your
house,
always singing your praises. *Interlude*

5 What joy for those whose strength comes
from the LORD,
who have set their minds on a pilgrimage
to Jerusalem.
6 When they walk through the Valley of
Weeping,
it will become a place of refreshing
springs.
The autumn rains will clothe it with
blessings.
7 They will continue to grow stronger,
and each of them will appear before God
in Jerusalem.

8 O LORD God of Heaven's Armies, hear my
prayer.
Listen, O God of Jacob. *Interlude*
9 O God, look with favor upon the king, our
shield!
Show favor to the one you have anointed.

10 A single day in your courts
is better than a thousand anywhere else!
I would rather be a gatekeeper in the house
of my God
than live the good life in the homes of the
wicked.
11 For the LORD God is our sun and our shield.
He gives us grace and glory.
The LORD will withhold no good thing
from those who do what is right.
12 O LORD of Heaven's Armies,
what joy for those who trust in you.

PSALM 85

For the choir director: A psalm of the descendants of Korah.

1 LORD, you poured out blessings on your
land!
You restored the fortunes of Israel.
2 You forgave the guilt of your people—
yes, you covered all their sins. *Interlude*
3 You held back your fury.
You kept back your blazing anger.

4 Now restore us again, O God of our
salvation.
Put aside your anger against us once
more.

5 Will you be angry with us always?
Will you prolong your wrath to all generations?
6 Won't you revive us again,
so your people can rejoice in you?
7 Show us your unfailing love, O LORD,
and grant us your salvation.

8 I listen carefully to what God the LORD is saying,
for he speaks peace to his faithful people.
But let them not return to their foolish ways.
9 Surely his salvation is near to those who fear him,
so our land will be filled with his glory.

10 Unfailing love and truth have met together.
Righteousness and peace have kissed!
11 Truth springs up from the earth,
and righteousness smiles down from heaven.
12 Yes, the LORD pours down his blessings.
Our land will yield its bountiful harvest.
13 Righteousness goes as a herald before him,
preparing the way for his steps.

PSALM 86

A prayer of David.

1 Bend down, O LORD, and hear my prayer;
answer me, for I need your help.
2 Protect me, for I am devoted to you.
Save me, for I serve you and trust you.
You are my God.
3 Be merciful to me, O Lord,
for I am calling on you constantly.
4 Give me happiness, O Lord,
for I give myself to you.
5 O Lord, you are so good, so ready to forgive,
so full of unfailing love for all who ask for your help.
6 Listen closely to my prayer, O LORD;
hear my urgent cry.
7 I will call to you whenever I'm in trouble,
and you will answer me.

8 No pagan god is like you, O Lord.
None can do what you do!
9 All the nations you made
will come and bow before you, Lord;
they will praise your holy name.
10 For you are great and perform wonderful deeds.
You alone are God.

11 Teach me your ways, O LORD,
that I may live according to your truth!
Grant me purity of heart,
so that I may honor you.
12 With all my heart I will praise you, O Lord my God.
I will give glory to your name forever,
13 for your love for me is very great.
You have rescued me from the depths of death.

14 O God, insolent people rise up against me;
a violent gang is trying to kill me.
You mean nothing to them.
15 But you, O Lord,
are a God of compassion and mercy,
slow to get angry
and filled with unfailing love and faithfulness.
16 Look down and have mercy on me.
Give your strength to your servant;
save me, the son of your servant.
17 Send me a sign of your favor.
Then those who hate me will be put to shame,
for you, O LORD, help and comfort me.

PSALM 87

A song. A psalm of the descendants of Korah.

1 On the holy mountain
stands the city founded by the LORD.
2 He loves the city of Jerusalem
more than any other city in Israel.
3 O city of God,
what glorious things are said of you!
Interlude

4 I will count Egypt and Babylon among those who know me—
also Philistia and Tyre, and even distant Ethiopia.
They have all become citizens of Jerusalem!
5 Regarding Jerusalem it will be said,
"Everyone enjoys the rights of citizenship there."
And the Most High will personally bless this city.
6 When the LORD registers the nations,
he will say,
"They have all become citizens of Jerusalem." *Interlude*
7 The people will play flutes and sing,
"The source of my life springs from Jerusalem!"

PSALM 88

For the choir director: A psalm of the descendants of Korah. A song to be sung to the tune "The Suffering of Affliction." A psalm of Heman the Ezrahite.

1 O LORD, God of my salvation,
I cry out to you by day.
I come to you at night.
2 Now hear my prayer;
listen to my cry.
3 For my life is full of troubles,
and death draws near.
4 I am as good as dead,
like a strong man with no strength left.
5 They have left me among the dead,
and I lie like a corpse in a grave.
I am forgotten,
cut off from your care.
6 You have thrown me into the lowest pit,
into the darkest depths.
7 Your anger weighs me down;
with wave after wave you have engulfed me.
Interlude

8 You have driven my friends away
by making me repulsive to them.
I am in a trap with no way of escape.
9 My eyes are blinded by my tears.
Each day I beg for your help, O LORD;
I lift my hands to you for mercy.
10 Are your wonderful deeds of any use
to the dead?
Do the dead rise up and praise you?
Interlude

11 Can those in the grave declare your unfailing
love?
Can they proclaim your faithfulness in the
place of destruction?
12 Can the darkness speak of your wonderful
deeds?
Can anyone in the land of forgetfulness
talk about your righteousness?
13 O LORD, I cry out to you.
I will keep on pleading day by day.
14 O LORD, why do you reject me?
Why do you turn your face from me?

15 I have been sick and close to death since
my youth.
I stand helpless and desperate before
your terrors.
16 Your fierce anger has overwhelmed me.
Your terrors have paralyzed me.
17 They swirl around me like floodwaters all day
long.
They have engulfed me completely.
18 You have taken away my companions and
loved ones.
Darkness is my closest friend.

PSALM 89

A psalm of Ethan the Ezrahite.

1 I will sing of the LORD's unfailing love forever!
Young and old will hear of your
faithfulness.
2 Your unfailing love will last forever.
Your faithfulness is as enduring as the
heavens.

3 The LORD said, "I have made a covenant with
David, my chosen servant.
I have sworn this oath to him:
4 'I will establish your descendants as kings
forever;
they will sit on your throne from now until
eternity.'" *Interlude*
5 All heaven will praise your great wonders,
LORD;
myriads of angels will praise you for your
faithfulness.
6 For who in all of heaven can compare with
the LORD?
What mightiest angel is anything like
the LORD?
7 The highest angelic powers stand in awe
of God.
He is far more awesome than all who
surround his throne.
8 O LORD God of Heaven's Armies!
Where is there anyone as mighty as you,
O LORD?
You are entirely faithful.

9 You rule the oceans.
You subdue their storm-tossed waves.
10 You crushed the great sea monster.
You scattered your enemies with your
mighty arm.
11 The heavens are yours, and the earth is yours;
everything in the world is yours—you
created it all.
12 You created north and south.
Mount Tabor and Mount Hermon praise
your name.
13 Powerful is your arm!
Strong is your hand!
Your right hand is lifted high in glorious
strength.
14 Righteousness and justice are the foundation
of your throne.

Unfailing love and truth walk before you
as attendants.
15 Happy are those who hear the joyful call
to worship,
for they will walk in the light of your
presence, LORD.
16 They rejoice all day long in your wonderful
reputation.
They exult in your righteousness.
17 You are their glorious strength.
It pleases you to make us strong.
18 Yes, our protection comes from the LORD,
and he, the Holy One of Israel, has given
us our king.

19 Long ago you spoke in a vision to your
faithful people.
You said, "I have raised up a warrior.
I have selected him from the common
people to be king.
20 I have found my servant David.
I have anointed him with my holy oil.
21 I will steady him with my hand;
with my powerful arm I will make
him strong.
22 His enemies will not defeat him,
nor will the wicked overpower him.
23 I will beat down his adversaries before him
and destroy those who hate him.
24 My faithfulness and unfailing love will be
with him,
and by my authority he will grow in power.
25 I will extend his rule over the sea,
his dominion over the rivers.
26 And he will call out to me, 'You are my
Father,
my God, and the Rock of my salvation.'
27 I will make him my firstborn son,
the mightiest king on earth.
28 I will love him and be kind to him forever;
my covenant with him will never end.
29 I will preserve an heir for him;
his throne will be as endless as the days
of heaven.
30 But if his descendants forsake my
instructions
and fail to obey my regulations,
31 if they do not obey my decrees
and fail to keep my commands,
32 then I will punish their sin with the rod,
and their disobedience with beating.
33 But I will never stop loving him
nor fail to keep my promise to him.
34 No, I will not break my covenant;
I will not take back a single word I said.

Key Verse **"For he will order his angels to protect you wherever you go."—PSALM 91:11**

Protecting the Egg

Read PSALM 91:11 out loud. How do God's angels protect us? Maybe like this!

1. **Grab two large plastic or paper cups, some newspaper, a raw egg, and some tape.**
2. **Stuff the cups with newspaper to act as padding, leaving room for the egg.**
3. **Put the egg inside the newspaper padding, and tape the two cups together with lots of tape!**
4. **Drop the cups from the height of your shoulders!**

If you used plenty of padding and taped the cups well, your egg should be safe and sound! God has ways to keep us safe and sound too.

Read PSALM 91:11 again. Because God loves you so much, he sends his angels to protect you! The next time you're scared or worried, remember that God sends his angels to protect you, just like you protected the egg. (Know what else? God's protecting you even when you're *not* scared and worried! **God's awesome!**)

35 I have sworn an oath to David,
and in my holiness I cannot lie:
36 His dynasty will go on forever;
his kingdom will endure as the sun.
37 It will be as eternal as the moon,
my faithful witness in the sky!" *Interlude*

38 But now you have rejected him and cast
him off.
You are angry with your anointed king.

39 You have renounced your covenant with him;
you have thrown his crown in the dust.
40 You have broken down the walls protecting him
and ruined every fort defending him.
41 Everyone who comes along has robbed him,
and he has become a joke to his neighbors.
42 You have strengthened his enemies
and made them all rejoice.
43 You have made his sword useless
and refused to help him in battle.
44 You have ended his splendor
and overturned his throne.
45 You have made him old before his time
and publicly disgraced him. *Interlude*

46 O Lord, how long will this go on?
Will you hide yourself forever?
How long will your anger burn like fire?
47 Remember how short my life is,
how empty and futile this human existence!
48 No one can live forever; all will die.
No one can escape the power of the grave. *Interlude*

49 Lord, where is your unfailing love?
You promised it to David with a faithful pledge.
50 Consider, Lord, how your servants are disgraced!
I carry in my heart the insults of so many people.
51 Your enemies have mocked me, O Lord;
they mock your anointed king wherever he goes.

52 Praise the Lord forever!
Amen and amen!

Book Four (Psalms 90–106)

PSALM 90

A prayer of Moses, the man of God.

1 Lord, through all the generations
you have been our home!
2 Before the mountains were born,
before you gave birth to the earth and the world,
from beginning to end, you are God.

3 You turn people back to dust, saying,
"Return to dust, you mortals!"
4 For you, a thousand years are as a passing day,
as brief as a few night hours.
5 You sweep people away like dreams that disappear.
They are like grass that springs up in the morning.
6 In the morning it blooms and flourishes,
but by evening it is dry and withered.
7 We wither beneath your anger;
we are overwhelmed by your fury.
8 You spread out our sins before you—
our secret sins—and you see them all.
9 We live our lives beneath your wrath,
ending our years with a groan.

10 Seventy years are given to us!
Some even live to eighty.
But even the best years are filled with pain and trouble;
soon they disappear, and we fly away.
11 Who can comprehend the power of your anger?
Your wrath is as awesome as the fear you deserve.
12 Teach us to realize the brevity of life,
so that we may grow in wisdom.

13 O Lord, come back to us!
How long will you delay?
Take pity on your servants!
14 Satisfy us each morning with your unfailing love,
so we may sing for joy to the end of our lives.
15 Give us gladness in proportion to our former misery!
Replace the evil years with good.
16 Let us, your servants, see you work again;
let our children see your glory.
17 And may the Lord our God show us his approval
and make our efforts successful.
Yes, make our efforts successful!

PSALM 91

1 Those who live in the shelter of the Most High
will find rest in the shadow of the Almighty.
2 This I declare about the Lord:
He alone is my refuge, my place of safety;
he is my God, and I trust him.
3 For he will rescue you from every trap
and protect you from deadly disease.
4 He will cover you with his feathers.
He will shelter you with his wings.
His faithful promises are your armor and protection.
5 Do not be afraid of the terrors of the night,
nor the arrow that flies in the day.

Psalm 92 . . . page 584

6 Do not dread the disease that stalks in darkness,
nor the disaster that strikes at midday.
7 Though a thousand fall at your side,
though ten thousand are dying around you,
these evils will not touch you.
8 Just open your eyes,
and see how the wicked are punished.

9 If you make the LORD your refuge,
if you make the Most High your shelter,
10 no evil will conquer you;
no plague will come near your home.
11 For he will order his angels
to protect you wherever you go.
12 They will hold you up with their hands
so you won't even hurt your foot on a stone.
13 You will trample upon lions and cobras;
you will crush fierce lions and serpents under your feet!

14 The LORD says, "I will rescue those who love me.
I will protect those who trust in my name.
15 When they call on me, I will answer;
I will be with them in trouble.
I will rescue and honor them.
16 I will reward them with a long life
and give them my salvation."

PSALM 92

A psalm. A song to be sung on the Sabbath Day.

1 It is good to give thanks to the LORD,
to sing praises to the Most High.
2 It is good to proclaim your unfailing love in the morning,
your faithfulness in the evening,
3 accompanied by a ten-stringed instrument, a harp,
and the melody of a lyre.

4 You thrill me, LORD, with all you have done for me!
I sing for joy because of what you have done.
5 O LORD, what great works you do!
And how deep are your thoughts.
6 Only a simpleton would not know,
and only a fool would not understand this:
7 Though the wicked sprout like weeds
and evildoers flourish,
they will be destroyed forever.

8 But you, O LORD, will be exalted forever.
9 Your enemies, LORD, will surely perish;
all evildoers will be scattered.
10 But you have made me as strong as a wild ox.
You have anointed me with the finest oil.
11 My eyes have seen the downfall of my enemies;
my ears have heard the defeat of my wicked opponents.
12 But the godly will flourish like palm trees
and grow strong like the cedars of Lebanon.
13 For they are transplanted to the LORD's own house.
They flourish in the courts of our God.
14 Even in old age they will still produce fruit;
they will remain vital and green.
15 They will declare, "The LORD is just!
He is my rock!
There is no evil in him!"

PSALM 93

1 The LORD is king! He is robed in majesty.
Indeed, the LORD is robed in majesty and armed with strength.
The world stands firm
and cannot be shaken.

2 Your throne, O LORD, has stood from time immemorial.
You yourself are from the everlasting past.
3 The floods have risen up, O LORD.
The floods have roared like thunder;
the floods have lifted their pounding waves.
4 But mightier than the violent raging of the seas,
mightier than the breakers on the shore—
the LORD above is mightier than these!
5 Your royal laws cannot be changed.
Your reign, O LORD, is holy forever and ever.

PSALM 94

1 O LORD, the God of vengeance,
O God of vengeance, let your glorious justice shine forth!
2 Arise, O Judge of the earth.
Give the proud what they deserve.
3 How long, O LORD?
How long will the wicked be allowed to gloat?
4 How long will they speak with arrogance?
How long will these evil people boast?
5 They crush your people, LORD,
hurting those you claim as your own.
6 They kill widows and foreigners
and murder orphans.

Key Verse **"Come, let us worship and bow down. Let us kneel before the LORD our maker, for he is our God. We are the people he watches over, the flock under his care."—PSALM 95:6-7**

Why Worship?

Have you heard of sheep? Of course, everyone's *herd* of sheep! (That was a *baaaah-d joke!*) What's a herd of sheep have to do with why we should worship God? Let's see.

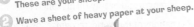

1. **Place a handful of cotton balls on a table. These are your sheep.**

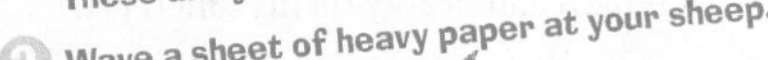

2. **Wave a sheet of heavy paper at your sheep.**

What happened to your sheep? Maybe they needed a shepherd to take care of them! God is our shepherd, and he always takes care of his sheep—which means us! What a great reason to worship God!

Read PSALM 95:6-7 out loud. Then kneel and pray, thanking God for always taking care of you.

Read John 10:11-15 to see just how much Jesus, the Good Shepherd, loves you!

7 "The LORD isn't looking," they say,
"and besides, the God of Israel doesn't care."

8 Think again, you fools!
When will you finally catch on?
9 Is he deaf—the one who made your ears?
Is he blind—the one who formed your eyes?
10 He punishes the nations—won't he also punish you?
He knows everything—doesn't he also know what you are doing?
11 The LORD knows people's thoughts;
he knows they are worthless!

12 Joyful are those you discipline, LORD,
those you teach with your instructions.
13 You give them relief from troubled times
until a pit is dug to capture the wicked.
14 The LORD will not reject his people;
he will not abandon his special possession.
15 Judgment will again be founded on justice,
and those with virtuous hearts will pursue it.

16 Who will protect me from the wicked?
Who will stand up for me against evildoers?
17 Unless the LORD had helped me,
I would soon have settled in the silence of the grave.
18 I cried out, "I am slipping!"
but your unfailing love, O LORD, supported me.
19 When doubts filled my mind,
your comfort gave me renewed hope and cheer.

20 Can unjust leaders claim that God is on their side—
leaders whose decrees permit injustice?
21 They gang up against the righteous
and condemn the innocent to death.
22 But the LORD is my fortress;
my God is the mighty rock where I hide.
23 God will turn the sins of evil people back on them.
He will destroy them for their sins.
The LORD our God will destroy them.

PSALM 95

1 Come, let us sing to the LORD!
Let us shout joyfully to the Rock of our salvation.
2 Let us come to him with thanksgiving.
Let us sing psalms of praise to him.
3 For the LORD is a great God,
a great King above all gods.
4 He holds in his hands the depths of the earth
and the mightiest mountains.
5 The sea belongs to him, for he made it.
His hands formed the dry land, too.

6 Come, let us worship and bow down.
Let us kneel before the LORD our maker,
7 for he is our God.
We are the people he watches over,
the flock under his care.

If only you would listen to his voice today!

Psalm 96 . . . page 586

Shout to the Lord!

There are so many ways to worship the Lord. One way is to shout your praise. Here's something to help!

1. **Cut a semicircle from a horizontal sheet of construction paper.**
2. **Starting at one corner, roll the paper into a funnel shape and tape it in place to make a megaphone.**

Read more about joy in Philippians 4:4-5.

3. **Have an adult help you cut about an inch or two from an empty paper towel roll. Put the small end of your megaphone into the tube piece, and tape them together.**
4. **Decorate your megaphone with reasons to praise God. NOW SHOUT!**

The Bible tells us to shout with joy to the Lord. Read Psalm 100 to see!

Make up a cheer to praise God. Then use your megaphone to perform your cheer for as many people as you can today!

8 The LORD says, "Don't harden your hearts
as Israel did at Meribah,
as they did at Massah in the wilderness.
9 For there your ancestors tested and tried
my patience,
even though they saw everything
I did.
10 For forty years I was angry with them,
and I said,
'They are a people whose hearts turn away
from me.
They refuse to do what I tell them.'
11 So in my anger I took an oath:
'They will never enter my place
of rest.'"

PSALM 96

1 Sing a new song to the LORD!
Let the whole earth sing to the LORD!
2 Sing to the LORD; praise his name.
Each day proclaim the good news that
he saves.
3 Publish his glorious deeds among the
nations.
Tell everyone about the amazing things
he does.
4 Great is the LORD! He is most worthy of praise!
He is to be feared above all gods.
5 The gods of other nations are mere idols,
but the LORD made the heavens!
6 Honor and majesty surround him;
strength and beauty fill his sanctuary.

7 O nations of the world, recognize the LORD;
recognize that the LORD is glorious and
strong.
8 Give to the LORD the glory he deserves!
Bring your offering and come into his
courts.
9 Worship the LORD in all his holy splendor.
Let all the earth tremble before him.
10 Tell all the nations, "The LORD reigns!"
The world stands firm and cannot
be shaken.
He will judge all peoples fairly.

11 Let the heavens be glad, and the earth rejoice!
Let the sea and everything in it shout his
praise!
12 Let the fields and their crops burst out
with joy!
Let the trees of the forest sing for joy
13 before the LORD, for he is coming!
He is coming to judge the earth.
He will judge the world with justice,
and the nations with his truth.

PSALM 97

1 The LORD is king!
Let the earth rejoice!
Let the farthest coastlands be glad.
2 Dark clouds surround him.
Righteousness and justice are the
foundation of his throne.
3 Fire spreads ahead of him
and burns up all his foes.
4 His lightning flashes out across the world.
The earth sees and trembles.
5 The mountains melt like wax before the
LORD,
before the Lord of all the earth.

6 The heavens proclaim his righteousness;
every nation sees his glory.
7 Those who worship idols are disgraced—
all who brag about their worthless gods—
for every god must bow to him.
8 Jerusalem has heard and rejoiced,
and all the towns of Judah are glad
because of your justice, O LORD!
9 For you, O LORD, are supreme over all the earth;
you are exalted far above all gods.
10 You who love the LORD, hate evil!
He protects the lives of his godly people
and rescues them from the power of the wicked.
11 Light shines on the godly,
and joy on those whose hearts are right.
12 May all who are godly rejoice in the LORD
and praise his holy name!

PSALM 98

A psalm.

1 Sing a new song to the LORD,
for he has done wonderful deeds.
His right hand has won a mighty victory;
his holy arm has shown his saving power!
2 The LORD has announced his victory
and has revealed his righteousness to every nation!
3 He has remembered his promise to love and be faithful to Israel.
The ends of the earth have seen the victory of our God.

4 Shout to the LORD, all the earth;
break out in praise and sing for joy!
5 Sing your praise to the LORD with the harp,
with the harp and melodious song,
6 with trumpets and the sound of the ram's horn.
Make a joyful symphony before the LORD, the King!

7 Let the sea and everything in it shout his praise!
Let the earth and all living things join in.
8 Let the rivers clap their hands in glee!
Let the hills sing out their songs of joy
9 before the LORD,
for he is coming to judge the earth.
He will judge the world with justice,
and the nations with fairness.

PSALM 99

1 The LORD is king!
Let the nations tremble!
He sits on his throne between the cherubim.
Let the whole earth quake!
2 The LORD sits in majesty in Jerusalem,
exalted above all the nations.
3 Let them praise your great and awesome name.
Your name is holy!
4 Mighty King, lover of justice,
you have established fairness.
You have acted with justice
and righteousness throughout Israel.
5 Exalt the LORD our God!
Bow low before his feet, for he is holy!

6 Moses and Aaron were among his priests;
Samuel also called on his name.
They cried to the LORD for help,
and he answered them.
7 He spoke to Israel from the pillar of cloud,
and they followed the laws and decrees he gave them.
8 O LORD our God, you answered them.
You were a forgiving God to them,
but you punished them when they went wrong.

9 Exalt the LORD our God,
and worship at his holy mountain in Jerusalem,
for the LORD our God is holy!

PSALM 100

A psalm of thanksgiving.

1 Shout with joy to the LORD, all the earth!
2 Worship the LORD with gladness.
Come before him, singing with joy.
3 Acknowledge that the LORD is God!
He made us, and we are his.
We are his people, the sheep of his pasture.
4 Enter his gates with thanksgiving;
go into his courts with praise.
Give thanks to him and praise his name.
5 For the LORD is good.
His unfailing love continues forever,
and his faithfulness continues to each generation.

PSALM 101

A psalm of David.

1 I will sing of your love and justice, LORD.
I will praise you with songs.
2 I will be careful to live a blameless life—
when will you come to help me?

I will lead a life of integrity
in my own home.
3 I will refuse to look at
anything vile and vulgar.
I hate all who deal crookedly;
I will have nothing to do with them.
4 I will reject perverse ideas
and stay away from every evil.
5 I will not tolerate people who slander their
neighbors.
I will not endure conceit and pride.

6 I will search for faithful people
to be my companions.
Only those who are above reproach
will be allowed to serve me.
7 I will not allow deceivers to serve in my
house,
and liars will not stay in my presence.
8 My daily task will be to ferret out the wicked
and free the city of the LORD from their
grip.

PSALM 102

A prayer of one overwhelmed with trouble, pouring out problems before the LORD.

1 LORD, hear my prayer!
Listen to my plea!
2 Don't turn away from me
in my time of distress.
Bend down to listen,
and answer me quickly when I call to you.
3 For my days disappear like smoke,
and my bones burn like red-hot coals.
4 My heart is sick, withered like grass,
and I have lost my appetite.
5 Because of my groaning,
I am reduced to skin and bones.
6 I am like an owl in the desert,
like a little owl in a far-off wilderness.
7 I lie awake,
lonely as a solitary bird on the roof.
8 My enemies taunt me day after day.
They mock and curse me.
9 I eat ashes for food.
My tears run down into my drink
10 because of your anger and wrath.
For you have picked me up and thrown me
out.
11 My life passes as swiftly as the evening
shadows.
I am withering away like grass.

12 But you, O LORD, will sit on your throne
forever.

Key Verse

"The LORD is compassionate and merciful, slow to get angry and filled with unfailing love."—PSALM 103:8

SLOW TO BOIL

Ever hear someone say, "He's boiling mad"? That means someone's so mad that angry words and actions bubble out. **God's not like that. PSALM 103:8 says so!** Read the verse out loud. **THEN TRY THIS EXPERIMENT.**

1 Place a small cup of water and a large pot of water on a towel. **Use a straw to blow air into the cup.** Look at those bubbles!

2 **Now use your straw to try to make all the water in the big pot boil.** Not too easy, is it? God is like the big pot of water—he's slow to boil or get angry. The Bible says he's full of love and forgives those who are sorry for their sins. That's great news!

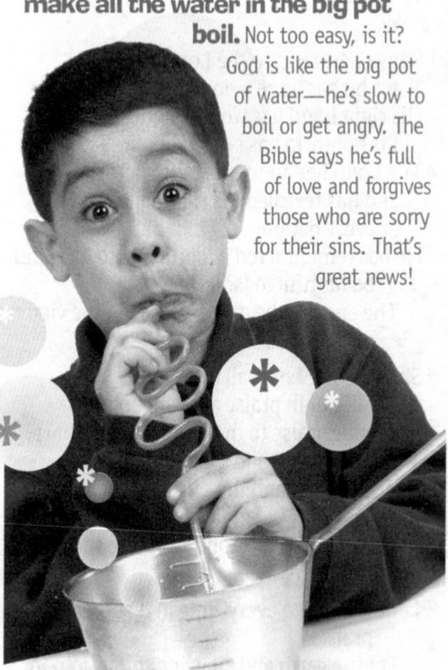

Your fame will endure to every generation.
13 You will arise and have mercy on Jerusalem—
and now is the time to pity her,
now is the time you promised to help.
14 For your people love every stone in her walls
and cherish even the dust in her streets.
15 Then the nations will tremble before the
LORD.

The kings of the earth will tremble before his glory.
16 For the LORD will rebuild Jerusalem.
He will appear in his glory.
17 He will listen to the prayers of the destitute.
He will not reject their pleas.

18 Let this be recorded for future generations,
so that a people not yet born will praise the LORD.
19 Tell them the LORD looked down
from his heavenly sanctuary.
He looked down to earth from heaven
20 to hear the groans of the prisoners,
to release those condemned to die.
21 And so the LORD's fame will be celebrated in Zion,
his praises in Jerusalem,
22 when multitudes gather together
and kingdoms come to worship the LORD.

23 He broke my strength in midlife,
cutting short my days.
24 But I cried to him, "O my God, who lives forever,
don't take my life while I am so young!
25 Long ago you laid the foundation of the earth
and made the heavens with your hands.
26 They will perish, but you remain forever;
they will wear out like old clothing.
You will change them like a garment
and discard them.
27 But you are always the same;
you will live forever.
28 The children of your people
will live in security.
Their children's children
will thrive in your presence."

PSALM 103

A psalm of David.

1 Let all that I am praise the LORD;
with my whole heart, I will praise his holy name.
2 Let all that I am praise the LORD;
may I never forget the good things he does for me.
3 He forgives all my sins
and heals all my diseases.
4 He redeems me from death
and crowns me with love and tender mercies.
5 He fills my life with good things.
My youth is renewed like the eagle's!
6 The LORD gives righteousness
and justice to all who are treated unfairly.
7 He revealed his character to Moses
and his deeds to the people of Israel.
8 The LORD is compassionate and merciful,
slow to get angry and filled with unfailing love.
9 He will not constantly accuse us,
nor remain angry forever.
10 He does not punish us for all our sins;
he does not deal harshly with us, as we deserve.
11 For his unfailing love toward those who fear him
is as great as the height of the heavens above the earth.
12 He has removed our sins as far from us
as the east is from the west.
13 The LORD is like a father to his children,
tender and compassionate to those who fear him.
14 For he knows how weak we are;
he remembers we are only dust.
15 Our days on earth are like grass;
like wildflowers, we bloom and die.
16 The wind blows, and we are gone—
as though we had never been here.
17 But the love of the LORD remains forever
with those who fear him.
His salvation extends to the children's children
18 of those who are faithful to his covenant,
of those who obey his commandments!

19 The LORD has made the heavens his throne;
from there he rules over everything.

20 Praise the LORD, you angels,
you mighty ones who carry out his plans,
listening for each of his commands.
21 Yes, praise the LORD, you armies of angels
who serve him and do his will!
22 Praise the LORD, everything he has created,
everything in all his kingdom.

Let all that I am praise the LORD.

PSALM 104

1 Let all that I am praise the LORD.

O LORD my God, how great you are!
You are robed with honor and majesty.
2 You are dressed in a robe of light.
You stretch out the starry curtain of the heavens;

3 you lay out the rafters of your home in the
rain clouds.
You make the clouds your chariot;
you ride upon the wings of the wind.
4 The winds are your messengers;
flames of fire are your servants.
5 You placed the world on its foundation
so it would never be moved.
6 You clothed the earth with floods of water,
water that covered even the mountains.
7 At your command, the water fled;
at the sound of your thunder, it hurried
away.
8 Mountains rose and valleys sank
to the levels you decreed.
9 Then you set a firm boundary for the seas,
so they would never again cover the earth.
10 You make springs pour water into the
ravines,
so streams gush down from the
mountains.
11 They provide water for all the animals,
and the wild donkeys quench their thirst.
12 The birds nest beside the streams
and sing among the branches of the trees.
13 You send rain on the mountains from your
heavenly home,
and you fill the earth with the fruit
of your labor.
14 You cause grass to grow for the livestock
and plants for people to use.
You allow them to produce food from
the earth—
15 wine to make them glad,
olive oil to soothe their skin,
and bread to give them strength.
16 The trees of the LORD are well cared for—
the cedars of Lebanon that he planted.
17 There the birds make their nests,
and the storks make their homes in the
cypresses.
18 High in the mountains live the wild goats,
and the rocks form a refuge for the
hyraxes.
19 You made the moon to mark the seasons,
and the sun knows when to set.
20 You send the darkness, and it becomes
night,
when all the forest animals prowl about.
21 Then the young lions roar for their prey,
stalking the food provided by God.
22 At dawn they slink back
into their dens to rest.
23 Then people go off to their work,
where they labor until evening.
24 O LORD, what a variety of things you have
made!
In wisdom you have made them all.
The earth is full of your creatures.
25 Here is the ocean, vast and wide,
teeming with life of every kind,
both large and small.
26 See the ships sailing along,
and Leviathan, which you made to play
in the sea.

27 They all depend on you
to give them food as they need it.
28 When you supply it, they gather it.
You open your hand to feed them,
and they are richly satisfied.
29 But if you turn away from them, they panic.
When you take away their breath,
they die and turn again to dust.
30 When you give them your breath, life is
created,
and you renew the face of the earth.

31 May the glory of the LORD continue
forever!
The LORD takes pleasure in all he
has made!
32 The earth trembles at his glance;
the mountains smoke at his touch.

33 I will sing to the LORD as long as I live.
I will praise my God to my last breath!
34 May all my thoughts be pleasing to him,
for I rejoice in the LORD.
35 Let all sinners vanish from the face
of the earth;
let the wicked disappear forever.

Let all that I am praise the LORD.

Praise the LORD!

PSALM 105

1 Give thanks to the LORD and proclaim
his greatness.
Let the whole world know what he
has done.
2 Sing to him; yes, sing his praises.
Tell everyone about his wonderful deeds.
3 Exult in his holy name;
rejoice, you who worship the LORD.
4 Search for the LORD and for his strength;
continually seek him.
5 Remember the wonders he has performed,
his miracles, and the rulings he has given,

6 you children of his servant Abraham,
you descendants of Jacob, his chosen ones.

7 He is the LORD our God.
His justice is seen throughout the land.
8 He always stands by his covenant—
the commitment he made to a thousand generations.
9 This is the covenant he made with Abraham
and the oath he swore to Isaac.
10 He confirmed it to Jacob as a decree,
and to the people of Israel as a never-ending covenant:
11 "I will give you the land of Canaan
as your special possession."

12 He said this when they were few in number,
a tiny group of strangers in Canaan.
13 They wandered from nation to nation,
from one kingdom to another.
14 Yet he did not let anyone oppress them.
He warned kings on their behalf:
15 "Do not touch my chosen people,
and do not hurt my prophets."

16 He called for a famine on the land of Canaan,
cutting off its food supply.
17 Then he sent someone to Egypt ahead of them—
Joseph, who was sold as a slave.
18 They bruised his feet with fetters
and placed his neck in an iron collar.
19 Until the time came to fulfill his dreams,
the LORD tested Joseph's character.
20 Then Pharaoh sent for him and set him free;
the ruler of the nation opened his prison door.
21 Joseph was put in charge of all the king's household;
he became ruler over all the king's possessions.
22 He could instruct the king's aides as he pleased
and teach the king's advisers.

23 Then Israel arrived in Egypt;
Jacob lived as a foreigner in the land of Ham.
24 And the LORD multiplied the people of Israel
until they became too mighty for their enemies.
25 Then he turned the Egyptians against the Israelites,
and they plotted against the LORD's servants.

26 But the LORD sent his servant Moses,
along with Aaron, whom he had chosen.
27 They performed miraculous signs among the Egyptians,
and wonders in the land of Ham.
28 The LORD blanketed Egypt in darkness,
for they had defied his commands to let his people go.
29 He turned their water into blood,
poisoning all the fish.
30 Then frogs overran the land
and even invaded the king's bedrooms.
31 When the LORD spoke, flies descended on the Egyptians,
and gnats swarmed across Egypt.
32 He sent them hail instead of rain,
and lightning flashed over the land.
33 He ruined their grapevines and fig trees
and shattered all the trees.
34 He spoke, and hordes of locusts came—
young locusts beyond number.
35 They ate up everything green in the land,
destroying all the crops in their fields.
36 Then he killed the oldest son in each Egyptian home,
the pride and joy of each family.

37 The LORD brought his people out of Egypt,
loaded with silver and gold;
and not one among the tribes of Israel even stumbled.
38 Egypt was glad when they were gone,
for they feared them greatly.
39 The LORD spread a cloud above them as a covering
and gave them a great fire to light the darkness.
40 They asked for meat, and he sent them quail;
he satisfied their hunger with manna—bread from heaven.
41 He split open a rock, and water gushed out
to form a river through the dry wasteland.
42 For he remembered his sacred promise
to his servant Abraham.
43 So he brought his people out of Egypt with joy,
his chosen ones with rejoicing.
44 He gave his people the lands of pagan nations,
and they harvested crops that others had planted.
45 All this happened so they would follow his decrees
and obey his instructions.

Praise the LORD!

Psalm 106 . . .

PSALM 106

1 Praise the LORD!

Give thanks to the LORD, for he is good!
His faithful love endures forever.
2 Who can list the glorious miracles of the LORD?
Who can ever praise him enough?
3 There is joy for those who deal justly with others
and always do what is right.

4 Remember me, LORD, when you show favor to your people;
come near and rescue me.
5 Let me share in the prosperity of your chosen ones.
Let me rejoice in the joy of your people;
let me praise you with those who are your heritage.

6 Like our ancestors, we have sinned.
We have done wrong! We have acted wickedly!
7 Our ancestors in Egypt
were not impressed by the LORD's miraculous deeds.
They soon forgot his many acts of kindness to them.
Instead, they rebelled against him at the Red Sea.
8 Even so, he saved them—
to defend the honor of his name
and to demonstrate his mighty power.
9 He commanded the Red Sea to dry up.
He led Israel across the sea as if it were a desert.
10 So he rescued them from their enemies
and redeemed them from their foes.
11 Then the water returned and covered their enemies;
not one of them survived.
12 Then his people believed his promises.
Then they sang his praise.

13 Yet how quickly they forgot what he had done!
They wouldn't wait for his counsel!
14 In the wilderness their desires ran wild,
testing God's patience in that dry wasteland.
15 So he gave them what they asked for,
but he sent a plague along with it.
16 The people in the camp were jealous of Moses
and envious of Aaron, the LORD's holy priest.
17 Because of this, the earth opened up;
it swallowed Dathan
and buried Abiram and the other rebels.
18 Fire fell upon their followers;
a flame consumed the wicked.

19 The people made a calf at Mount Sinai;
they bowed before an image made of gold.
20 They traded their glorious God
for a statue of a grass-eating bull.
21 They forgot God, their savior,
who had done such great things in Egypt—
22 such wonderful things in the land of Ham,
such awesome deeds at the Red Sea.
23 So he declared he would destroy them.
But Moses, his chosen one, stepped between the LORD and the people.
He begged him to turn from his anger and not destroy them.

24 The people refused to enter the pleasant land,
for they wouldn't believe his promise to care for them.
25 Instead, they grumbled in their tents
and refused to obey the LORD.
26 Therefore, he solemnly swore
that he would kill them in the wilderness,
27 that he would scatter their descendants among the nations,
exiling them to distant lands.

28 Then our ancestors joined in the worship of Baal at Peor;
they even ate sacrifices offered to the dead!
29 They angered the LORD with all these things,
so a plague broke out among them.
30 But Phinehas had the courage to intervene,
and the plague was stopped.
31 So he has been regarded as a righteous man
ever since that time.

32 At Meribah, too, they angered the LORD,
causing Moses serious trouble.
33 They made Moses angry,
and he spoke foolishly.

34 Israel failed to destroy the nations in the land,
as the LORD had commanded them.
35 Instead, they mingled among the pagans
and adopted their evil customs.
36 They worshiped their idols,
which led to their downfall.
37 They even sacrificed their sons
and their daughters to the demons.

38 They shed innocent blood,
the blood of their sons and daughters.
By sacrificing them to the idols of Canaan,
they polluted the land with murder.
39 They defiled themselves by their evil deeds,
and their love of idols was adultery in the LORD's sight.

40 That is why the LORD's anger burned against his people,
and he abhorred his own special possession.
41 He handed them over to pagan nations,
and they were ruled by those who hated them.
42 Their enemies crushed them
and brought them under their cruel power.
43 Again and again he rescued them,
but they chose to rebel against him,
and they were finally destroyed by their sin.
44 Even so, he pitied them in their distress
and listened to their cries.
45 He remembered his covenant with them
and relented because of his unfailing love.
46 He even caused their captors
to treat them with kindness.

47 Save us, O LORD our God!
Gather us back from among the nations,
so we can thank your holy name
and rejoice and praise you.

48 Praise the LORD, the God of Israel,
who lives from everlasting to everlasting!
Let all the people say, "Amen!"
Praise the LORD!

BOOK FIVE (Psalms 107–150)

PSALM 107

1 Give thanks to the LORD, for he is good!
His faithful love endures forever.
2 Has the LORD redeemed you? Then speak out!
Tell others he has redeemed you from your enemies.
3 For he has gathered the exiles from many lands,
from east and west,
from north and south.

4 Some wandered in the wilderness,
lost and homeless.
5 Hungry and thirsty,
they nearly died.
6 "LORD, help!" they cried in their trouble,
and he rescued them from their distress.
7 He led them straight to safety,
to a city where they could live.
8 Let them praise the LORD for his great love
and for the wonderful things he has done for them.
9 For he satisfies the thirsty
and fills the hungry with good things.

10 Some sat in darkness and deepest gloom,
imprisoned in iron chains of misery.
11 They rebelled against the words of God,
scorning the counsel of the Most High.
12 That is why he broke them with hard labor;
they fell, and no one was there to help them.
13 "LORD, help!" they cried in their trouble,
and he saved them from their distress.
14 He led them from the darkness and deepest gloom;
he snapped their chains.
15 Let them praise the LORD for his great love
and for the wonderful things he has done for them.
16 For he broke down their prison gates of bronze;
he cut apart their bars of iron.

17 Some were fools; they rebelled
and suffered for their sins.
18 They couldn't stand the thought of food,
and they were knocking on death's door.
19 "LORD, help!" they cried in their trouble,
and he saved them from their distress.
20 He sent out his word and healed them,
snatching them from the door of death.
21 Let them praise the LORD for his great love
and for the wonderful things he has done for them.
22 Let them offer sacrifices of thanksgiving
and sing joyfully about his glorious acts.

23 Some went off to sea in ships,
plying the trade routes of the world.
24 They, too, observed the LORD's power in action,
his impressive works on the deepest seas.
25 He spoke, and the winds rose,
stirring up the waves.
26 Their ships were tossed to the heavens
and plunged again to the depths;
the sailors cringed in terror.
27 They reeled and staggered like drunkards
and were at their wits' end.

28 "LORD, help!" they cried in their trouble,
and he saved them from their distress.
29 He calmed the storm to a whisper
and stilled the waves.
30 What a blessing was that stillness
as he brought them safely into harbor!
31 Let them praise the LORD for his great love
and for the wonderful things he has done for them.
32 Let them exalt him publicly before the congregation
and before the leaders of the nation.

33 He changes rivers into deserts,
and springs of water into dry, thirsty land.
34 He turns the fruitful land into salty wastelands,
because of the wickedness of those who live there.
35 But he also turns deserts into pools of water,
the dry land into springs of water.
36 He brings the hungry to settle there
and to build their cities.
37 They sow their fields, plant their vineyards,
and harvest their bumper crops.
38 How he blesses them!
They raise large families there,
and their herds of livestock increase.

39 When they decrease in number and become impoverished
through oppression, trouble, and sorrow,
40 the LORD pours contempt on their princes,
causing them to wander in trackless wastelands.
41 But he rescues the poor from trouble
and increases their families like flocks of sheep.
42 The godly will see these things and be glad,
while the wicked are struck silent.
43 Those who are wise will take all this to heart;
they will see in our history the faithful love of the LORD.

PSALM 108

A song. A psalm of David.

1 My heart is confident in you, O God;
no wonder I can sing your praises with all my heart!
2 Wake up, lyre and harp!
I will wake the dawn with my song.
3 I will thank you, LORD, among all the people.
I will sing your praises among the nations.
4 For your unfailing love is higher than the heavens.
Your faithfulness reaches to the clouds.
5 Be exalted, O God, above the highest heavens.
May your glory shine over all the earth.
6 Now rescue your beloved people.
Answer and save us by your power.
7 God has promised this by his holiness:
"I will divide up Shechem with joy.
I will measure out the valley of Succoth.
8 Gilead is mine,
and Manasseh, too.
Ephraim, my helmet, will produce my warriors,
and Judah, my scepter, will produce my kings.
9 But Moab, my washbasin, will become my servant,
and I will wipe my feet on Edom
and shout in triumph over Philistia."

10 Who will bring me into the fortified city?
Who will bring me victory over Edom?
11 Have you rejected us, O God?
Will you no longer march with our armies?
12 Oh, please help us against our enemies,
for all human help is useless.
13 With God's help we will do mighty things,
for he will trample down our foes.

PSALM 109

For the choir director: A psalm of David.

1 O God, whom I praise,
don't stand silent and aloof
2 while the wicked slander me
and tell lies about me.
3 They surround me with hateful words
and fight against me for no reason.
4 I love them, but they try to destroy me with accusations
even as I am praying for them!
5 They repay evil for good,
and hatred for my love.

6 They say, "Get an evil person to turn against him.
Send an accuser to bring him to trial.
7 When his case comes up for judgment,
let him be pronounced guilty.
Count his prayers as sins.
8 Let his years be few;
let someone else take his position.
9 May his children become fatherless,
and his wife a widow.
10 May his children wander as beggars
and be driven from their ruined homes.
11 May creditors seize his entire estate,
and strangers take all he has earned.

People in Bible times played instruments to worship God. Their instruments had names like ***Timbrel*** (a flat hand drum), ***Kinnor*** (a stringed instrument like a small harp), and ***Halil*** (a pipe played by blowing).

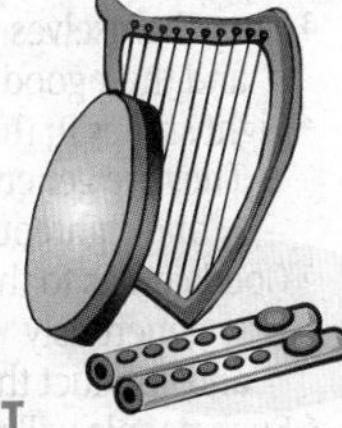

MAKE YOUR OWN MUSICAL INSTRUMENT TO PRAISE GOD.

Cut a four-inch square of wax paper. Fold the wax paper in half around the teeth of a new pocket comb. Hold the comb, teeth up, and place one side lightly against your lips. Part your lips slightly and sing "whoo." **YOUR INSTRUMENT WILL SOUND LIKE A KAZOO.**

Ask a friend to read words of praise from the Bible, pausing between each verse for you to play. **PSALM 98 is a great place to start!**

12 Let no one be kind to him;
let no one pity his fatherless children.
13 May all his offspring die.
May his family name be blotted out in the next generation.
14 May the LORD never forget the sins of his fathers;
may his mother's sins never be erased from the record.
15 May the LORD always remember these sins,
and may his name disappear from human memory.
16 For he refused all kindness to others;
he persecuted the poor and needy,
and he hounded the brokenhearted to death.
17 He loved to curse others;
now you curse him.
He never blessed others;
now don't you bless him.
18 Cursing is as natural to him as his clothing,
or the water he drinks,
or the rich food he eats.
19 Now may his curses return and cling to him like clothing;
may they be tied around him like a belt."

20 May those curses become the LORD's punishment
for my accusers who speak evil of me.
21 But deal well with me, O Sovereign LORD,
for the sake of your own reputation!
Rescue me
because you are so faithful and good.
22 For I am poor and needy,
and my heart is full of pain.
23 I am fading like a shadow at dusk;
I am brushed off like a locust.
24 My knees are weak from fasting,
and I am skin and bones.
25 I am a joke to people everywhere;
when they see me, they shake their heads in scorn.

26 Help me, O LORD my God!
Save me because of your unfailing love.
27 Let them see that this is your doing,
that you yourself have done it, LORD.
28 Then let them curse me if they like,
but you will bless me!
When they attack me, they will be disgraced!
But I, your servant, will go right on rejoicing!
29 May my accusers be clothed with disgrace;
may their humiliation cover them like a cloak.
30 But I will give repeated thanks to the LORD,
praising him to everyone.
31 For he stands beside the needy,
ready to save them from those who condemn them.

PSALM 110

A psalm of David.

1 The LORD said to my Lord,
"Sit in the place of honor at my right hand

until I humble your enemies,
making them a footstool under your feet."

2 The LORD will extend your powerful
kingdom from Jerusalem;
you will rule over your enemies.
3 When you go to war,
your people will serve you willingly.
You are arrayed in holy garments,
and your strength will be renewed each
day like the morning dew.

4 The LORD has taken an oath and will not
break his vow:
"You are a priest forever in the order
of Melchizedek."

5 The Lord stands at your right hand to
protect you.
He will strike down many kings when his
anger erupts.
6 He will punish the nations
and fill their lands with corpses;
he will shatter heads over the whole
earth.
7 But he himself will be refreshed from brooks
along the way.
He will be victorious.

PSALM 111

1 Praise the LORD!

I will thank the LORD with all my heart
as I meet with his godly people.
2 How amazing are the deeds of the LORD!
All who delight in him should ponder
them.
3 Everything he does reveals his glory and
majesty.
His righteousness never fails.
4 He causes us to remember his wonderful
works.
How gracious and merciful is our LORD!
5 He gives food to those who fear him;
he always remembers his covenant.
6 He has shown his great power to his people
by giving them the lands of other nations.
7 All he does is just and good,
and all his commandments are
trustworthy.
8 They are forever true,
to be obeyed faithfully and with
integrity.
9 He has paid a full ransom for his people.
He has guaranteed his covenant with
them forever.
What a holy, awe-inspiring name he has!
10 Fear of the LORD is the foundation of true
wisdom.
All who obey his commandments will
grow in wisdom.

Praise him forever!

PSALM 112

1 Praise the LORD!

How joyful are those who fear the LORD
and delight in obeying his commands.
2 Their children will be successful everywhere;
an entire generation of godly people will
be blessed.
3 They themselves will be wealthy,
and their good deeds will last forever.
4 Light shines in the darkness for the godly.
They are generous, compassionate,
and righteous.
5 Good comes to those who lend money
generously
and conduct their business fairly.
6 Such people will not be overcome by evil.
Those who are righteous will be long
remembered.
7 They do not fear bad news;
they confidently trust the LORD to care
for them.
8 They are confident and fearless
and can face their foes triumphantly.
9 They share freely and give generously to
those in need.
Their good deeds will be remembered
forever.
They will have influence and honor.
10 The wicked will see this and be infuriated.
They will grind their teeth in anger;
they will slink away, their hopes thwarted.

PSALM 113

1 Praise the LORD!

Yes, give praise, O servants of the LORD.
Praise the name of the LORD!
2 Blessed be the name of the LORD
now and forever.
3 Everywhere—from east to west—
praise the name of the LORD.
4 For the LORD is high above the nations;
his glory is higher than the heavens.

5 Who can be compared with the LORD
our God,
who is enthroned on high?
6 He stoops to look down
on heaven and on earth.

7 He lifts the poor from the dust
and the needy from the garbage dump.
8 He sets them among princes,
even the princes of his own people!
9 He gives the childless woman a family,
making her a happy mother.

Praise the LORD!

PSALM 114

1 When the Israelites escaped from Egypt—
when the family of Jacob left that foreign
land—
2 the land of Judah became God's sanctuary,
and Israel became his kingdom.

3 The Red Sea saw them coming and hurried
out of their way!
The water of the Jordan River turned away.
4 The mountains skipped like rams,
the hills like lambs!
5 What's wrong, Red Sea, that made you hurry
out of their way?
What happened, Jordan River, that you
turned away?
6 Why, mountains, did you skip like rams?
Why, hills, like lambs?

7 Tremble, O earth, at the presence of the Lord,
at the presence of the God of Jacob.
8 He turned the rock into a pool of water;
yes, a spring of water flowed from solid
rock.

PSALM 115

1 Not to us, O LORD, not to us,
but to your name goes all the glory
for your unfailing love and faithfulness.
2 Why let the nations say,
"Where is their God?"
3 Our God is in the heavens,
and he does as he wishes.
4 Their idols are merely things of silver
and gold,
shaped by human hands.
5 They have mouths but cannot speak,
and eyes but cannot see.
6 They have ears but cannot hear,
and noses but cannot smell.
7 They have hands but cannot feel,
and feet but cannot walk,
and throats but cannot make a sound.
8 And those who make idols are just like them,
as are all who trust in them.

9 O Israel, trust the LORD!
He is your helper and your shield.
10 O priests, descendants of Aaron, trust
the LORD!
He is your helper and your shield.
11 All you who fear the LORD, trust the LORD!
He is your helper and your shield.

12 The LORD remembers us and will bless us.
He will bless the people of Israel
and bless the priests, the descendants
of Aaron.
13 He will bless those who fear the LORD,
both great and lowly.

14 May the LORD richly bless
both you and your children.
15 May you be blessed by the LORD,
who made heaven and earth.
16 The heavens belong to the LORD,
but he has given the earth to all humanity.
17 The dead cannot sing praises to the LORD,
for they have gone into the silence of
the grave.
18 But we can praise the LORD
both now and forever!

Praise the LORD!

PSALM 116

1 I love the LORD because he hears my voice
and my prayer for mercy.
2 Because he bends down to listen,
I will pray as long as I have breath!
3 Death wrapped its ropes around me;
the terrors of the grave overtook me.
I saw only trouble and sorrow.
4 Then I called on the name of the LORD:
"Please, LORD, save me!"
5 How kind the LORD is! How good he is!
So merciful, this God of ours!
6 The LORD protects those of childlike faith;
I was facing death, and he saved me.
7 Let my soul be at rest again,
for the LORD has been good to me.
8 He has saved me from death,
my eyes from tears,
my feet from stumbling.
9 And so I walk in the LORD's presence
as I live here on earth!
10 I believed in you, so I said,
"I am deeply troubled, LORD."
11 In my anxiety I cried out to you,
"These people are all liars!"
12 What can I offer the LORD
for all he has done for me?
13 I will lift up the cup of salvation
and praise the LORD's name for saving me.

"This is the day the LORD has made. We will rejoice and be glad in it." —PSALM 118:24

DAY BY DAY

READ PSALM 118:24 OUT LOUD A FEW TIMES. When you think about it, this is kind of a tough verse. Some days are happy "sunny" days. Other days are hard "stormy" days. But *whatever* kind of day we have, we should remember that God made it and we can find reasons to be glad in it.

What are some of the happiest days you've had? Write or draw something to describe two of your happiest days.

1

2

NOW PRAY AND THANK GOD FOR GIVING YOU THOSE GREAT DAYS!

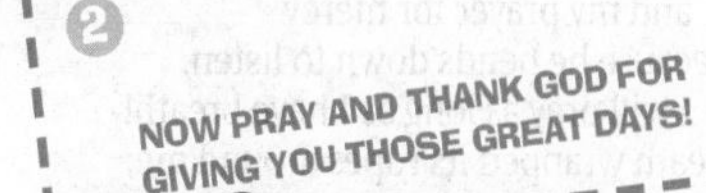

Now remember some of the stormiest days you've had. How did God help you through those hard times? Write or draw something about those stormy days.

1

2

NOW TAKE A MINUTE AND THANK GOD FOR HELPING YOU THROUGH STORMY TIMES.

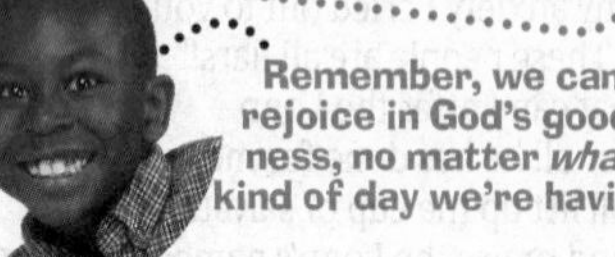

Remember, we can rejoice in God's goodness, no matter *what* kind of day we're having!

14 I will keep my promises to the LORD
in the presence of all his people.
15 The LORD cares deeply
when his loved ones die.
16 O LORD, I am your servant;
yes, I am your servant, born into your household;
you have freed me from my chains.
17 I will offer you a sacrifice of thanksgiving
and call on the name of the LORD.
18 I will fulfill my vows to the LORD
in the presence of all his people—
19 in the house of the LORD
in the heart of Jerusalem.

Praise the LORD!

PSALM 117

1 Praise the LORD, all you nations.
Praise him, all you people of the earth.
2 For his unfailing love for us is powerful;
the LORD's faithfulness endures forever.

Praise the LORD!

PSALM 118

1 Give thanks to the LORD, for he is good!
His faithful love endures forever.

2 Let all Israel repeat:
"His faithful love endures forever."
3 Let Aaron's descendants, the priests, repeat:
"His faithful love endures forever."
4 Let all who fear the LORD repeat:
"His faithful love endures forever."

5 In my distress I prayed to the LORD,
and the LORD answered me and set me free.
6 The LORD is for me, so I will have no fear.
What can mere people do to me?
7 Yes, the LORD is for me; he will help me.
I will look in triumph at those who hate me.
8 It is better to take refuge in the LORD
than to trust in people.
9 It is better to take refuge in the LORD
than to trust in princes.

10 Though hostile nations surrounded me,
I destroyed them all with the authority of the LORD.
11 Yes, they surrounded and attacked me,
but I destroyed them all with the authority of the LORD.
12 They swarmed around me like bees;
they blazed against me like a crackling fire.

But I destroyed them all with the authority
of the LORD.
13 My enemies did their best to kill me,
but the LORD rescued me.
14 The LORD is my strength and my song;
he has given me victory.
15 Songs of joy and victory are sung in the camp
of the godly.
The strong right arm of the LORD has done
glorious things!
16 The strong right arm of the LORD is raised
in triumph.
The strong right arm of the LORD has done
glorious things!
17 I will not die; instead, I will live
to tell what the LORD has done.
18 The LORD has punished me severely,
but he did not let me die.

19 Open for me the gates where the righteous
enter,
and I will go in and thank the LORD.
20 These gates lead to the presence of the LORD,
and the godly enter there.
21 I thank you for answering my prayer
and giving me victory!

22 The stone that the builders rejected
has now become the cornerstone.
23 This is the LORD's doing,
and it is wonderful to see.
24 This is the day the LORD has
made.
We will rejoice and be glad
in it.
25 Please, LORD, please save us.
Please, LORD, please give us success.
26 Bless the one who comes in the name
of the LORD.
We bless you from the house of the
LORD.
27 The LORD is God, shining upon us.
Take the sacrifice and bind it with cords
on the altar.
28 You are my God, and I will praise you!
You are my God, and I will exalt you!

29 Give thanks to the LORD, for he is good!
His faithful love endures forever.

PSALM 119

Aleph

1 Joyful are people of integrity,
who follow the instructions of the LORD.
2 Joyful are those who obey his laws
and search for him with all their hearts.
3 They do not compromise with evil,
and they walk only in his paths.
4 You have charged us
to keep your commandments carefully.
5 Oh, that my actions would consistently
reflect your decrees!
6 Then I will not be ashamed
when I compare my life with your
commands.
7 As I learn your righteous regulations,
I will thank you by living as I should!
8 I will obey your decrees.
Please don't give up on me!

Beth

9 How can a young person stay pure?
By obeying your word.
10 I have tried hard to find you—
don't let me wander from your commands.
11 I have hidden your word in my heart,
that I might not sin against you.
12 I praise you, O LORD;
teach me your decrees.
13 I have recited aloud
all the regulations you have given us.
14 I have rejoiced in your laws
as much as in riches.
15 I will study your commandments
and reflect on your ways.
16 I will delight in your decrees
and not forget your word.

Gimel

17 Be good to your servant,
that I may live and obey your word.
18 Open my eyes to see
the wonderful truths in your instructions.
19 I am only a foreigner in the land.
Don't hide your commands from me!
20 I am always overwhelmed
with a desire for your regulations.
21 You rebuke the arrogant;
those who wander from your commands
are cursed.
22 Don't let them scorn and insult me,
for I have obeyed your laws.
23 Even princes sit and speak against me,
but I will meditate on your decrees.
24 Your laws please me;
they give me wise advice.

Daleth

25 I lie in the dust;
revive me by your word.
26 I told you my plans, and you answered.
Now teach me your decrees.

27 Help me understand the meaning of your
commandments,
and I will meditate on your wonderful
deeds.
28 I weep with sorrow;
encourage me by your word.
29 Keep me from lying to myself;
give me the privilege of knowing your
instructions.
30 I have chosen to be faithful;
I have determined to live by your
regulations.
31 I cling to your laws.
LORD, don't let me be put to shame!
32 I will pursue your commands,
for you expand my understanding.

He

33 Teach me your decrees, O LORD;
I will keep them to the end.
34 Give me understanding and I will obey your
instructions;
I will put them into practice with all
my heart.
35 Make me walk along the path of your
commands,
for that is where my happiness is found.
36 Give me an eagerness for your laws
rather than a love for money!
37 Turn my eyes from worthless things,
and give me life through your word.
38 Reassure me of your promise,
made to those who fear you.
39 Help me abandon my shameful ways;
for your regulations are good.
40 I long to obey your commandments!
Renew my life with your goodness.

Waw

41 LORD, give me your unfailing love,
the salvation that you promised me.
42 Then I can answer those who taunt me,
for I trust in your word.
43 Do not snatch your word of truth from me,
for your regulations are my only hope.
44 I will keep on obeying your instructions
forever and ever.
45 I will walk in freedom,
for I have devoted myself to your
commandments.
46 I will speak to kings about your laws,
and I will not be ashamed.
47 How I delight in your commands!
How I love them!
48 I honor and love your commands.
I meditate on your decrees.

Zayin

49 Remember your promise to me;
it is my only hope.
50 Your promise revives me;
it comforts me in all my troubles.
51 The proud hold me in utter contempt,
but I do not turn away from your
instructions.
52 I meditate on your age-old regulations;
O LORD, they comfort me.
53 I become furious with the wicked,
because they reject your instructions.
54 Your decrees have been the theme of
my songs
wherever I have lived.
55 I reflect at night on who you are, O LORD;
therefore, I obey your instructions.
56 This is how I spend my life:
obeying your commandments.

Heth

57 LORD, you are mine!
I promise to obey your words!
58 With all my heart I want your blessings.
Be merciful as you promised.
59 I pondered the direction of my life,
and I turned to follow your laws.
60 I will hurry, without delay,
to obey your commands.
61 Evil people try to drag me into sin,
but I am firmly anchored to your
instructions.
62 I rise at midnight to thank you
for your just regulations.
63 I am a friend to anyone who fears you—
anyone who obeys your commandments.
64 O LORD, your unfailing love fills the earth;
teach me your decrees.

Teth

65 You have done many good things for me,
LORD,
just as you promised.
66 I believe in your commands;
now teach me good judgment and
knowledge.
67 I used to wander off until you
disciplined me;
but now I closely follow your word.
68 You are good and do only good;
teach me your decrees.
69 Arrogant people smear me with lies,
but in truth I obey your commandments
with all my heart.
70 Their hearts are dull and stupid,
but I delight in your instructions.

110 The wicked have set their traps for me,
but I will not turn from your
commandments.
111 Your laws are my treasure;
they are my heart's delight.
112 I am determined to keep your decrees
to the very end.

Samekh

113 I hate those with divided loyalties,
but I love your instructions.
114 You are my refuge and my shield;
your word is my source of hope.
115 Get out of my life, you evil-minded people,
for I intend to obey the commands of
my God.
116 LORD, sustain me as you promised, that
I may live!
Do not let my hope be crushed.
117 Sustain me, and I will be rescued;
then I will meditate continually on your
decrees.
118 But you have rejected all who stray from your
decrees.
They are only fooling themselves.
119 You skim off the wicked of the earth like
scum;
no wonder I love to obey your laws!
120 I tremble in fear of you;
I stand in awe of your regulations.

Ayin

121 Don't leave me to the mercy of my enemies,
for I have done what is just and right.
122 Please guarantee a blessing for me.
Don't let the arrogant oppress me!
123 My eyes strain to see your rescue,
to see the truth of your promise fulfilled.
124 I am your servant; deal with me in unfailing
love,
and teach me your decrees.
125 Give discernment to me, your servant;
then I will understand your laws.
126 LORD, it is time for you to act,
for these evil people have violated your
instructions.
127 Truly, I love your commands
more than gold, even the finest gold.
128 Each of your commandments is right.
That is why I hate every false way.

Pe

129 Your laws are wonderful.
No wonder I obey them!
130 The teaching of your word gives light,
so even the simple can understand.
131 I pant with expectation,
longing for your commands.
132 Come and show me your mercy,
as you do for all who love your name.
133 Guide my steps by your word,
so I will not be overcome by evil.
134 Ransom me from the oppression of evil
people;
then I can obey your commandments.
135 Look upon me with love;
teach me your decrees.
136 Rivers of tears gush from my eyes
because people disobey your instructions.

Tsadhe

137 O LORD, you are righteous,
and your regulations are fair.
138 Your laws are perfect
and completely trustworthy.
139 I am overwhelmed with indignation,
for my enemies have disregarded your
words.
140 Your promises have been thoroughly tested;
that is why I love them so much.
141 I am insignificant and despised,
but I don't forget your commandments.
142 Your justice is eternal,
and your instructions are perfectly true.
143 As pressure and stress bear down on me,
I find joy in your commands.
144 Your laws are always right;
help me to understand them so I may live.

Qoph

145 I pray with all my heart; answer me, LORD!
I will obey your decrees.
146 I cry out to you; rescue me,
that I may obey your laws.
147 I rise early, before the sun is up;
I cry out for help and put my hope
in your words.
148 I stay awake through the night,
thinking about your promise.
149 In your faithful love, O LORD, hear my cry;
let me be revived by following your
regulations.
150 Lawless people are coming to attack me;
they live far from your instructions.
151 But you are near, O LORD,
and all your commands are true.
152 I have known from my earliest days
that your laws will last forever.

Resh

153 Look upon my suffering and rescue me,
for I have not forgotten your instructions.

71 My suffering was good for me,
for it taught me to pay attention to your decrees.
72 Your instructions are more valuable to me
than millions in gold and silver.

Yodh

73 You made me; you created me.
Now give me the sense to follow your commands.
74 May all who fear you find in me a cause for joy,
for I have put my hope in your word.
75 I know, O LORD, that your regulations are fair;
you disciplined me because I needed it.
76 Now let your unfailing love comfort me,
just as you promised me, your servant.
77 Surround me with your tender mercies so I may live,
for your instructions are my delight.
78 Bring disgrace upon the arrogant people who lied about me;
meanwhile, I will concentrate on your commandments.
79 Let me be united with all who fear you,
with those who know your laws.
80 May I be blameless in keeping your decrees;
then I will never be ashamed.

Kaph

81 I am worn out waiting for your rescue,
but I have put my hope in your word.
82 My eyes are straining to see your promises come true.
When will you comfort me?
83 I am shriveled like a wineskin in the smoke,
but I have not forgotten to obey your decrees.
84 How long must I wait?
When will you punish those who persecute me?
85 These arrogant people who hate your instructions
have dug deep pits to trap me.
86 All your commands are trustworthy.
Protect me from those who hunt me down without cause.
87 They almost finished me off,
but I refused to abandon your commandments.
88 In your unfailing love, spare my life;
then I can continue to obey your laws.

Lamedh

89 Your eternal word, O LORD,
stands firm in heaven.
90 Your faithfulness extends to every generation,
as enduring as the earth you created.
91 Your regulations remain true to this day,
for everything serves your plans.
92 If your instructions hadn't sustained me with joy,
I would have died in my misery.
93 I will never forget your commandments,
for by them you give me life.
94 I am yours; rescue me!
For I have worked hard at obeying your commandments.
95 Though the wicked hide along the way to kill me,
I will quietly keep my mind on your laws.
96 Even perfection has its limits,
but your commands have no limit.

Mem

97 Oh, how I love your instructions!
I think about them all day long.
98 Your commands make me wiser than my enemies,
for they are my constant guide.
99 Yes, I have more insight than my teachers,
for I am always thinking of your laws.
100 I am even wiser than my elders,
for I have kept your commandments.
101 I have refused to walk on any evil path,
so that I may remain obedient to your word.
102 I haven't turned away from your regulations,
for you have taught me well.
103 How sweet your words taste to me;
they are sweeter than honey.
104 Your commandments give me understanding;
no wonder I hate every false way of life.

Nun

**105 Your word is a lamp to guide my feet
and a light for my path.**
106 I've promised it once, and I'll promise it again:
I will obey your righteous regulations.
107 I have suffered much, O LORD;
restore my life again as you promised.
108 LORD, accept my offering of praise,
and teach me your regulations.
109 My life constantly hangs in the balance,
but I will not stop obeying your instructions.

154 Argue my case; take my side!
Protect my life as you promised.
155 The wicked are far from rescue,
for they do not bother with your decrees.
156 LORD, how great is your mercy;
let me be revived by following your
regulations.
157 Many persecute and trouble me,
yet I have not swerved from your laws.
158 Seeing these traitors makes me sick at heart,
because they care nothing for your word.
159 See how I love your commandments, LORD.
Give back my life because of your
unfailing love.
160 The very essence of your words is truth;
all your just regulations will stand forever.

Shin

161 Powerful people harass me without cause,
but my heart trembles only at your word.
162 I rejoice in your word
like one who discovers a great treasure.
163 I hate and abhor all falsehood,
but I love your instructions.
164 I will praise you seven times a day
because all your regulations are just.
165 Those who love your instructions have
great peace
and do not stumble.
166 I long for your rescue, LORD,
so I have obeyed your commands.
167 I have obeyed your laws,
for I love them very much.
168 Yes, I obey your commandments and laws
because you know everything I do.

Taw

169 O LORD, listen to my cry;
give me the discerning mind you
promised.
170 Listen to my prayer;
rescue me as you promised.
171 Let praise flow from my lips,
for you have taught me your decrees.
172 Let my tongue sing about your word,
for all your commands are right.
173 Give me a helping hand,
for I have chosen to follow your
commandments.
174 O LORD, I have longed for your rescue,
and your instructions are my delight.
175 Let me live so I can praise you,
and may your regulations help me.
176 I have wandered away like a lost sheep;
come and find me,
for I have not forgotten your commands.

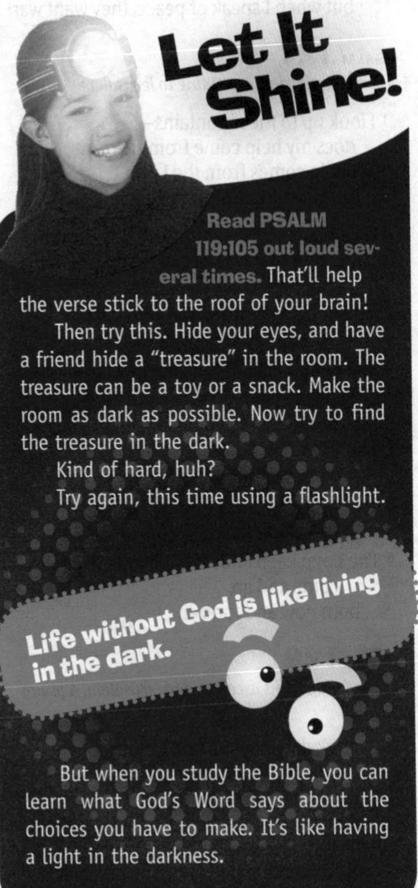

Key Verse
"Your word is a lamp to guide my feet and a light for my path."
—PSALM 119:105
Let It Shine!
Read PSALM 119:105 out loud several times. That'll help the verse stick to the roof of your brain!
Then try this. Hide your eyes, and have a friend hide a "treasure" in the room. The treasure can be a toy or a snack. Make the room as dark as possible. Now try to find the treasure in the dark.
Kind of hard, huh?
Try again, this time using a flashlight.
Life without God is like living in the dark.
But when you study the Bible, you can learn what God's Word says about the choices you have to make. It's like having a light in the darkness.

PSALM 120

A song for pilgrims ascending to Jerusalem.

1 I took my troubles to the LORD;
I cried out to him, and he answered
my prayer.
2 Rescue me, O LORD, from liars
and from all deceitful people.
3 O deceptive tongue, what will God do to you?
How will he increase your punishment?
4 You will be pierced with sharp arrows
and burned with glowing coals.

5 How I suffer in far-off Meshech.
It pains me to live in distant Kedar.
6 I am tired of living
among people who hate peace.
7 I search for peace;
but when I speak of peace, they want war!

PSALM 121

A song for pilgrims ascending to Jerusalem.

1 I look up to the mountains—
does my help come from there?
2 My help comes from the LORD,
who made heaven and earth!

3 He will not let you stumble;
the one who watches over you will not slumber.
4 Indeed, he who watches over Israel
never slumbers or sleeps.

5 The LORD himself watches over you!
The LORD stands beside you as your protective shade.
6 The sun will not harm you by day,
nor the moon at night.

7 The LORD keeps you from all harm
and watches over your life.
8 The LORD keeps watch over you as you come and go,
both now and forever.

PSALM 122

A song for pilgrims ascending to Jerusalem. A psalm of David.

1 I was glad when they said to me,
"Let us go to the house of the LORD."
2 And now here we are,
standing inside your gates, O Jerusalem.
3 Jerusalem is a well-built city;
its seamless walls cannot be breached.
4 All the tribes of Israel—the LORD's people—
make their pilgrimage here.
They come to give thanks to the name of the LORD,
as the law requires of Israel.
5 Here stand the thrones where judgment is given,
the thrones of the dynasty of David.

6 Pray for peace in Jerusalem.
May all who love this city prosper.
7 O Jerusalem, may there be peace within your walls
and prosperity in your palaces.

GOING TO CHURCH ROCKS!

At least King David thought so. **Read PSALM 122.** King David *loved* to go to the house of the Lord to worship God. Ever wonder what people like about going to your church? Find out!

1 Go to church, and ask at least 10 different people this question:

"WHAT'S YOUR FAVORITE PART OF GOING TO OUR CHURCH?"

Write their answers on a sheet of paper.

2 Gather some friends, and read your top 10 list of why going to your church is awesome.

3 Now work together to make a poster that shows why your church rocks! Ask your pastor or teacher if you can hang the poster somewhere in your church for every-one to see.

8 For the sake of my family and friends,
I will say,
"May you have peace."
9 For the sake of the house of the LORD our God,
I will seek what is best for you,
O Jerusalem.

PSALM 123

A song for pilgrims ascending to Jerusalem.

1 I lift my eyes to you,
O God, enthroned in heaven.
2 We keep looking to the LORD our God for his mercy,
just as servants keep their eyes on their master,
as a slave girl watches her mistress for the slightest signal.
3 Have mercy on us, LORD, have mercy,
for we have had our fill of contempt.

4 We have had more than our fill of the
scoffing of the proud
and the contempt of the arrogant.

PSALM 124

A song for pilgrims ascending to Jerusalem. A psalm of David.

1 What if the LORD had not been on our side?
Let all Israel repeat:
2 What if the LORD had not been on our side
when people attacked us?
3 They would have swallowed us alive
in their burning anger.
4 The waters would have engulfed us;
a torrent would have overwhelmed us.
5 Yes, the raging waters of their fury
would have overwhelmed our very lives.

6 Praise the LORD,
who did not let their teeth tear us apart!
7 We escaped like a bird from a hunter's trap.
The trap is broken, and we are free!
8 Our help is from the LORD,
who made heaven and earth.

PSALM 125

A song for pilgrims ascending to Jerusalem.

1 Those who trust in the LORD are as secure
as Mount Zion;
they will not be defeated but will endure
forever.
2 Just as the mountains surround Jerusalem,
so the LORD surrounds his people, both
now and forever.
3 The wicked will not rule the land of the godly,
for then the godly might be tempted
to do wrong.
4 O LORD, do good to those who are good,
whose hearts are in tune with you.
5 But banish those who turn to crooked ways,
O LORD.
Take them away with those who do evil.

May Israel have peace!

PSALM 126

A song for pilgrims ascending to Jerusalem.

1 When the LORD brought back his exiles
to Jerusalem,
it was like a dream!
2 We were filled with laughter,
and we sang for joy.
And the other nations said,
"What amazing things the LORD has done
for them."
3 Yes, the LORD has done amazing things
for us!
What joy!

4 Restore our fortunes, LORD,
as streams renew the desert.
5 Those who plant in tears
will harvest with shouts of joy.
6 They weep as they go to plant their seed,
but they sing as they return with the
harvest.

PSALM 127

A song for pilgrims ascending to Jerusalem. A psalm of Solomon.

1 Unless the LORD builds a house,
the work of the builders is wasted.
Unless the LORD protects a city,
guarding it with sentries will do no good.
2 It is useless for you to work so hard
from early morning until late at night,
anxiously working for food to eat;
for God gives rest to his loved ones.

3 Children are a gift from the LORD;
they are a reward from him.
4 Children born to a young man
are like arrows in a warrior's hands.
5 How joyful is the man whose quiver is full
of them!
He will not be put to shame when he
confronts his accusers at the city gates.

PSALM 128

A song for pilgrims ascending to Jerusalem.

1 How joyful are those who fear the LORD—
all who follow his ways!
2 You will enjoy the fruit of your labor.
How joyful and prosperous you will be!
3 Your wife will be like a fruitful grapevine,
flourishing within your home.
Your children will be like vigorous young
olive trees
as they sit around your table.
4 That is the LORD's blessing
for those who fear him.

5 May the LORD continually bless you from
Zion.
May you see Jerusalem prosper as long
as you live.
6 May you live to enjoy your grandchildren.
May Israel have peace!

PSALM 129

A song for pilgrims ascending to Jerusalem.

1 From my earliest youth my enemies have
persecuted me.
Let all Israel repeat this:
2 From my earliest youth my enemies have
persecuted me,
but they have never defeated me.
3 My back is covered with cuts,
as if a farmer had plowed long furrows.
4 But the LORD is good;
he has cut me free from the ropes of the
ungodly.

5 May all who hate Jerusalem
be turned back in shameful defeat.
6 May they be as useless as grass on a rooftop,
turning yellow when only half grown,
7 ignored by the harvester,
despised by the binder.
8 And may those who pass by
refuse to give them this blessing:
"The LORD bless you;
we bless you in the LORD's name."

PSALM 130

A song for pilgrims ascending to Jerusalem.

1 From the depths of despair, O LORD,
I call for your help.
2 Hear my cry, O Lord.
Pay attention to my prayer.

3 LORD, if you kept a record of our sins,
who, O Lord, could ever survive?
4 But you offer forgiveness,
that we might learn to fear you.

5 I am counting on the LORD;
yes, I am counting on him.
I have put my hope in his word.
6 I long for the Lord
more than sentries long for the dawn,
yes, more than sentries long for the dawn.

7 O Israel, hope in the LORD;
for with the LORD there is unfailing love.
His redemption overflows.
8 He himself will redeem Israel
from every kind of sin.

PSALM 131

A song for pilgrims ascending to Jerusalem. A psalm of David.

1 LORD, my heart is not proud;
my eyes are not haughty.
I don't concern myself with matters
too great
or too awesome for me to grasp.
2 Instead, I have calmed and quieted myself,
like a weaned child who no longer cries for
its mother's milk.
Yes, like a weaned child is my soul
within me.

3 O Israel, put your hope in the LORD—
now and always.

PSALM 132

A song for pilgrims ascending to Jerusalem.

1 LORD, remember David
and all that he suffered.
2 He made a solemn promise to the LORD.
He vowed to the Mighty One of Israel,
3 "I will not go home;
I will not let myself rest.
4 I will not let my eyes sleep
nor close my eyelids in slumber
5 until I find a place to build a house for
the LORD,
a sanctuary for the Mighty One of Israel."

6 We heard that the Ark was in Ephrathah;
then we found it in the distant countryside
of Jaar.
7 Let us go to the sanctuary of the LORD;
let us worship at the footstool of his
throne.
8 Arise, O LORD, and enter your resting place,
along with the Ark, the symbol of your
power.
9 May your priests be clothed in godliness;
may your loyal servants sing for joy.
10 For the sake of your servant David,
do not reject the king you have anointed.
11 The LORD swore an oath to David
with a promise he will never take back:
"I will place one of your descendants
on your throne.
12 If your descendants obey the terms
of my covenant
and the laws that I teach them,
then your royal line
will continue forever and ever."

13 For the LORD has chosen Jerusalem;
he has desired it for his home.
14 "This is my resting place forever," he said.
"I will live here, for this is the home
I desired.
15 I will bless this city and make it prosperous;
I will satisfy its poor with food.

16 I will clothe its priests with godliness;
its faithful servants will sing for joy.
17 Here I will increase the power of David;
my anointed one will be a light for
my people.
18 I will clothe his enemies with shame,
but he will be a glorious king."

PSALM 133

A song for pilgrims ascending to Jerusalem. A psalm of David.

1 How wonderful and pleasant it is
when brothers live together in harmony!
2 For harmony is as precious as the anointing
oil
that was poured over Aaron's head,
that ran down his beard
and onto the border of his robe.
3 Harmony is as refreshing as the dew from
Mount Hermon
that falls on the mountains of Zion.
And there the LORD has pronounced his
blessing,
even life everlasting.

PSALM 134

A song for pilgrims ascending to Jerusalem.

1 Oh, praise the LORD, all you servants
of the LORD,
you who serve at night in the house
of the LORD.
2 Lift your hands toward the sanctuary,
and praise the LORD.

3 May the LORD, who made heaven and earth,
bless you from Jerusalem.

PSALM 135

1 Praise the LORD!

Praise the name of the LORD!
Praise him, you who serve the LORD,
2 you who serve in the house of the LORD,
in the courts of the house of our God.

3 Praise the LORD, for the LORD is good;
celebrate his lovely name with music.
4 For the LORD has chosen Jacob for himself,
Israel for his own special treasure.

5 I know the greatness of the LORD—
that our Lord is greater than any
other god.
6 The LORD does whatever pleases him
throughout all heaven and earth,
and on the seas and in their depths.
7 He causes the clouds to rise over the whole
earth.
He sends the lightning with the rain
and releases the wind from his
storehouses.

8 He destroyed the firstborn in each Egyptian
home,
both people and animals.
9 He performed miraculous signs and
wonders in Egypt
against Pharaoh and all his people.
10 He struck down great nations
and slaughtered mighty kings—
11 Sihon king of the Amorites,
Og king of Bashan,
and all the kings of Canaan.
12 He gave their land as an inheritance,
a special possession to his people Israel.

13 Your name, O LORD, endures forever;
your fame, O LORD, is known to every
generation.
14 For the LORD will give justice to his people
and have compassion on his servants.

15 The idols of the nations are merely things
of silver and gold,
shaped by human hands.
16 They have mouths but cannot speak,
and eyes but cannot see.
17 They have ears but cannot hear,
and mouths but cannot breathe.
18 And those who make idols are just like them,
as are all who trust in them.

19 O Israel, praise the LORD!
O priests—descendants of Aaron—praise
the LORD!
20 O Levites, praise the LORD!
All you who fear the LORD, praise
the LORD!
21 The LORD be praised from Zion,
for he lives here in Jerusalem.

Praise the LORD!

PSALM 136

1 Give thanks to the LORD, for he is good!
His faithful love endures forever.
2 Give thanks to the God of gods.
His faithful love endures forever.
3 Give thanks to the Lord of lords.
His faithful love endures forever.

4 Give thanks to him who alone does
mighty miracles.
His faithful love endures forever.

Psalm 136 . . . page 608

Key Verse **"O Lord, you have examined my heart and know everything about me. You know when I sit down or stand up. You know my thoughts even when I'm far away. You see me when I travel and when I rest at home. You know everything I do."**
—PSALM 139:1-3

God Knows

Read PSALM 139:1-3 to learn who knows you best. Then find a map of your town.

Mark your map, using the key below.

Use a highlighter to trace the roads your family uses, then read PSALM 139:1-3 out loud.
God always knows where you are, what you're doing, and what you're thinking and feeling. Wherever you go, whatever you think or feel, God understands and loves you!

Use a red marker to draw a large heart that surrounds all the places you've highlighted on your map. Then hang your map in your room to help you remember the verse you just learned!

5 Give thanks to him who made the heavens
so skillfully.
His faithful love endures forever.
6 Give thanks to him who placed the earth
among the waters.
His faithful love endures forever.
7 Give thanks to him who made the heavenly
lights—
His faithful love endures forever.
8 the sun to rule the day,
His faithful love endures forever.
9 and the moon and stars to rule the night.
His faithful love endures forever.

10 Give thanks to him who killed the firstborn
of Egypt.
His faithful love endures forever.
11 He brought Israel out of Egypt.
His faithful love endures forever.
12 He acted with a strong hand and
powerful arm.
His faithful love endures forever.
13 Give thanks to him who parted the Red Sea.
His faithful love endures forever.
14 He led Israel safely through,
His faithful love endures forever.
15 but he hurled Pharaoh and his army into
the Red Sea.
His faithful love endures forever.
16 Give thanks to him who led his people
through the wilderness.
His faithful love endures forever.

17 Give thanks to him who struck down
mighty kings.
His faithful love endures forever.
18 He killed powerful kings—
His faithful love endures forever.
19 Sihon king of the Amorites,
His faithful love endures forever.
20 and Og king of Bashan.
His faithful love endures forever.
21 God gave the land of these kings as an
inheritance—
His faithful love endures forever.
22 a special possession to his servant Israel.
His faithful love endures forever.

23 He remembered us in our weakness.
His faithful love endures forever.
24 He saved us from our enemies.
His faithful love endures forever.
25 He gives food to every living thing.
His faithful love endures forever.
26 Give thanks to the God of heaven.
His faithful love endures forever.

PSALM 137

1 Beside the rivers of Babylon, we sat and wept
as we thought of Jerusalem.
2 We put away our harps,
hanging them on the branches of poplar
trees.
3 For our captors demanded a song from us.
Our tormentors insisted on a joyful hymn:
"Sing us one of those songs of Jerusalem!"
4 But how can we sing the songs of the LORD
while in a pagan land?

5 If I forget you, O Jerusalem,
let my right hand forget how to play
the harp.
6 May my tongue stick to the roof of my mouth
if I fail to remember you,
if I don't make Jerusalem my greatest joy.

7 O LORD, remember what the Edomites did
on the day the armies of Babylon captured
Jerusalem.
"Destroy it!" they yelled.
"Level it to the ground!"
8 O Babylon, you will be destroyed.
Happy is the one who pays you back
for what you have done to us.
9 Happy is the one who takes your babies
and smashes them against the rocks!

PSALM 138

A psalm of David.

1 I give you thanks, O LORD, with all my heart;
I will sing your praises before the gods.
2 I bow before your holy Temple as I worship.
I praise your name for your unfailing love
and faithfulness;
for your promises are backed
by all the honor of your name.
3 As soon as I pray, you answer me;
you encourage me by giving me strength.

4 Every king in all the earth will thank you,
LORD,
for all of them will hear your words.
5 Yes, they will sing about the LORD's ways,
for the glory of the LORD is very great.
6 Though the LORD is great, he cares for the
humble,
but he keeps his distance from the proud.

7 Though I am surrounded by troubles,
you will protect me from the anger of my
enemies.
You reach out your hand,
and the power of your right hand saves me.
8 The LORD will work out his plans for my
life—
for your faithful love, O LORD, endures
forever.
Don't abandon me, for you made me.

PSALM 139

For the choir director: A psalm of David.

**1 O LORD, you have examined
my heart
and know everything about me.
2 You know when I sit down or
stand up.
You know my thoughts even
when I'm far away.
3 You see me when I travel
and when I rest at home.
You know everything I do.**
4 You know what I am going to say
even before I say it, LORD.
5 You go before me and follow me.
You place your hand of blessing on
my head.
6 Such knowledge is too wonderful for me,
too great for me to understand!

7 I can never escape from your Spirit!
I can never get away from your
presence!
8 If I go up to heaven, you are there;
if I go down to the grave, you are there.
9 If I ride the wings of the morning,
if I dwell by the farthest oceans,
10 even there your hand will guide me,
and your strength will support me.
11 I could ask the darkness to hide me
and the light around me to become
night—
12 but even in darkness I cannot hide
from you.
To you the night shines as bright as day.
Darkness and light are the same to you.

13 You made all the delicate, inner parts of
my body
and knit me together in my mother's
womb.
14 Thank you for making me so wonderfully
complex!
Your workmanship is marvelous—how
well I know it.
15 You watched me as I was being formed
in utter seclusion,
as I was woven together in the dark
of the womb.

Psalm 140 . . . page 610

16 You saw me before I was born.
Every day of my life was recorded
in your book.
Every moment was laid out
before a single day had passed.

17 How precious are your thoughts about me,
O God.
They cannot be numbered!
18 I can't even count them;
they outnumber the grains of sand!
And when I wake up,
you are still with me!

19 O God, if only you would destroy the wicked!
Get out of my life, you murderers!
20 They blaspheme you;
your enemies misuse your name.
21 O LORD, shouldn't I hate those who hate you?
Shouldn't I despise those who oppose
you?
22 Yes, I hate them with total hatred,
for your enemies are my enemies.
23 Search me, O God, and know my heart;
test me and know my anxious thoughts.
24 Point out anything in me that offends you,
and lead me along the path of everlasting
life.

PSALM 140

For the choir director: A psalm of David.

1 O LORD, rescue me from evil people.
Protect me from those who are violent,
2 those who plot evil in their hearts
and stir up trouble all day long.
3 Their tongues sting like a snake;
the venom of a viper drips from their lips.
Interlude

4 O LORD, keep me out of the hands of the
wicked.
Protect me from those who are violent,
for they are plotting against me.
5 The proud have set a trap to catch me;
they have stretched out a net;
they have placed traps all along the way.
Interlude

6 I said to the LORD, "You are my God!"
Listen, O LORD, to my cries for mercy!
7 O Sovereign LORD, the strong one who
rescued me,
you protected me on the day of battle.
8 LORD, do not let evil people have their way.
Do not let their evil schemes succeed,
or they will become proud. *Interlude*

9 Let my enemies be destroyed
by the very evil they have planned for me.
10 Let burning coals fall down on their heads.
Let them be thrown into the fire
or into watery pits from which they
can't escape.
11 Don't let liars prosper here in our land.
Cause great disasters to fall on the violent.

12 But I know the LORD will help those they
persecute;
he will give justice to the poor.
13 Surely righteous people are praising your name;
the godly will live in your presence.

PSALM 141

A psalm of David.

1 O LORD, I am calling to you. Please hurry!
Listen when I cry to you for help!
2 Accept my prayer as incense offered to you,
and my upraised hands as an evening
offering.

3 Take control of what I say, O LORD,
and guard my lips.
4 Don't let me drift toward evil
or take part in acts of wickedness.
Don't let me share in the delicacies
of those who do wrong.

5 Let the godly strike me!
It will be a kindness!
If they correct me, it is soothing medicine.
Don't let me refuse it.

But I pray constantly
against the wicked and their deeds.
6 When their leaders are thrown down
from a cliff,
the wicked will listen to my words and
find them true.
7 Like rocks brought up by a plow,
the bones of the wicked will lie scattered
without burial.

8 I look to you for help, O Sovereign LORD.
You are my refuge; don't let them kill me.
9 Keep me from the traps they have set for me,
from the snares of those who do wrong.
10 Let the wicked fall into their own nets,
but let me escape.

PSALM 142

A psalm of David, regarding his experience in the cave. A prayer.

1 I cry out to the LORD;
I plead for the LORD's mercy.

2 I pour out my complaints before him
and tell him all my troubles.
3 When I am overwhelmed,
you alone know the way I should turn.
Wherever I go,
my enemies have set traps for me.
4 I look for someone to come and help me,
but no one gives me a passing thought!
No one will help me;
no one cares a bit what happens to me.
5 Then I pray to you, O LORD.
I say, "You are my place of refuge.
You are all I really want in life.
6 Hear my cry,
for I am very low.
Rescue me from my persecutors,
for they are too strong for me.
7 Bring me out of prison
so I can thank you.
The godly will crowd around me,
for you are good to me."

PSALM 143

A psalm of David.

1 Hear my prayer, O LORD;
listen to my plea!
Answer me because you are faithful and righteous.
2 Don't put your servant on trial,
for no one is innocent before you.
3 My enemy has chased me.
He has knocked me to the ground
and forces me to live in darkness like those in the grave.
4 I am losing all hope;
I am paralyzed with fear.
5 I remember the days of old.
I ponder all your great works
and think about what you have done.
6 I lift my hands to you in prayer.
I thirst for you as parched land thirsts for rain. *Interlude*
7 Come quickly, LORD, and answer me,
for my depression deepens.
Don't turn away from me,
or I will die.
8 Let me hear of your unfailing love each morning,
for I am trusting you.
Show me where to walk,
for I give myself to you.
9 Rescue me from my enemies, LORD;
I run to you to hide me.
10 Teach me to do your will,
for you are my God.
May your gracious Spirit lead me forward
on a firm footing.
11 For the glory of your name, O LORD, preserve my life.
Because of your faithfulness, bring me out of this distress.
12 In your unfailing love, silence all my enemies
and destroy all my foes,
for I am your servant.

PSALM 144

A psalm of David.

1 Praise the LORD, who is my rock.
He trains my hands for war
and gives my fingers skill for battle.
2 He is my loving ally and my fortress,
my tower of safety, my rescuer.
He is my shield, and I take refuge in him.
He makes the nations submit to me.
3 O LORD, what are human beings that you should notice them,
mere mortals that you should think about them?
4 For they are like a breath of air;
their days are like a passing shadow.
5 Open the heavens, LORD, and come down.
Touch the mountains so they billow smoke.
6 Hurl your lightning bolts and scatter your enemies!
Shoot your arrows and confuse them!
7 Reach down from heaven and rescue me;
rescue me from deep waters,
from the power of my enemies.
8 Their mouths are full of lies;
they swear to tell the truth, but they lie instead.
9 I will sing a new song to you, O God!
I will sing your praises with a ten-stringed harp.
10 For you grant victory to kings!
You rescued your servant David from the fatal sword.
11 Save me!
Rescue me from the power of my enemies.
Their mouths are full of lies;
they swear to tell the truth, but they lie instead.
12 May our sons flourish in their youth
like well-nurtured plants.
May our daughters be like graceful pillars,
carved to beautify a palace.

13 May our barns be filled
with crops of every kind.
May the flocks in our fields multiply
by the thousands,
even tens of thousands,
14 and may our oxen be loaded down with
produce.
May there be no enemy breaking through
our walls,
no going into captivity,
no cries of alarm in our town squares.
15 Yes, joyful are those who live like this!
Joyful indeed are those whose God
is the LORD.

PSALM 145

A psalm of praise of David.

1 I will exalt you, my God and King,
and praise your name forever and ever.
2 I will praise you every day;
yes, I will praise you forever.
3 Great is the LORD! He is most worthy
of praise!
No one can measure his greatness.

4 Let each generation tell its children of your
mighty acts;
let them proclaim your power.
5 I will meditate on your majestic, glorious
splendor
and your wonderful miracles.
6 Your awe-inspiring deeds will be on every
tongue;
I will proclaim your greatness.
7 Everyone will share the story of your
wonderful goodness;
they will sing with joy about your
righteousness.

8 The LORD is merciful and compassionate,
slow to get angry and filled with
unfailing love.
9 The LORD is good to everyone.
He showers compassion on all his
creation.
10 All of your works will thank you, LORD,
and your faithful followers will
praise you.
11 They will speak of the glory of your
kingdom;
they will give examples of your
power.
12 They will tell about your mighty deeds
and about the majesty and glory of
your reign.

**13 For your kingdom is an
everlasting kingdom.
You rule throughout all
generations.**

**The LORD always keeps his
promises;
he is gracious in all he does.**
14 The LORD helps the fallen
and lifts those bent beneath their loads.
15 The eyes of all look to you in hope;
you give them their food as they need it.
16 When you open your hand,
you satisfy the hunger and thirst of every
living thing.
17 The LORD is righteous in everything he does;
he is filled with kindness.
18 The LORD is close to all who call on him,
yes, to all who call on him in truth.
19 He grants the desires of those who fear him;
he hears their cries for help and rescues
them.
20 The LORD protects all those who love him,
but he destroys the wicked.

21 I will praise the LORD,
and may everyone on earth bless his
holy name
forever and ever.

PSALM 146

1 Praise the LORD!

Let all that I am praise the LORD.
2 I will praise the LORD as long as I live.
I will sing praises to my God with my
dying breath.

3 Don't put your confidence in powerful
people;
there is no help for you there.
4 When they breathe their last, they return
to the earth,
and all their plans die with them.
5 But joyful are those who have the God of
Israel as their helper,
whose hope is in the LORD their God.
6 He made heaven and earth,
the sea, and everything in them.
He keeps every promise forever.
7 He gives justice to the oppressed
and food to the hungry.
The LORD frees the prisoners.
8 The LORD opens the eyes of the blind.
The LORD lifts up those who are weighed
down.
The LORD loves the godly.

9 The LORD protects the foreigners among us.
He cares for the orphans and widows,
but he frustrates the plans of the wicked.

10 The LORD will reign forever.
He will be your God, O Jerusalem,
throughout the generations.

Praise the LORD!

PSALM 147

1 Praise the LORD!

How good to sing praises to our God!
How delightful and how fitting!
2 The LORD is rebuilding Jerusalem
and bringing the exiles back to Israel.
3 He heals the brokenhearted
and bandages their wounds.
4 He counts the stars
and calls them all by name.
5 How great is our Lord! His power
is absolute!
His understanding is beyond
comprehension!
6 The LORD supports the humble,
but he brings the wicked down into
the dust.

7 Sing out your thanks to the LORD;
sing praises to our God with a harp.
8 He covers the heavens with clouds,
provides rain for the earth,
and makes the grass grow in mountain
pastures.
9 He gives food to the wild animals
and feeds the young ravens when
they cry.
10 He takes no pleasure in the strength
of a horse
or in human might.
11 No, the LORD's delight is in those who
fear him,
those who put their hope in his
unfailing love.

12 Glorify the LORD, O Jerusalem!
Praise your God, O Zion!
13 For he has strengthened the bars of your
gates
and blessed your children within your
walls.
14 He sends peace across your nation
and satisfies your hunger with the
finest wheat.
15 He sends his orders to the world—
how swiftly his word flies!
16 He sends the snow like white wool;
he scatters frost upon the ground like
ashes.
17 He hurls the hail like stones.
Who can stand against his freezing
cold?
18 Then, at his command, it all melts.
He sends his winds, and the ice thaws.
19 He has revealed his words to Jacob,
his decrees and regulations to Israel.
20 He has not done this for any other nation;
they do not know his regulations.

Praise the LORD!

PSALM 148

1 Praise the LORD!

Praise the LORD from the heavens!
Praise him from the skies!
2 Praise him, all his angels!
Praise him, all the armies of heaven!
3 Praise him, sun and moon!
Praise him, all you twinkling stars!
4 Praise him, skies above!
Praise him, vapors high above the
clouds!
5 Let every created thing give praise
to the LORD,
for he issued his command, and they
came into being.
6 He set them in place forever and ever.
His decree will never be revoked.

7 Praise the LORD from the earth,
you creatures of the ocean depths,
8 fire and hail, snow and clouds,
wind and weather that obey him,
9 mountains and all hills,
fruit trees and all cedars,
10 wild animals and all livestock,
small scurrying animals and birds,
11 kings of the earth and all people,
rulers and judges of the earth,
12 young men and young women,
old men and children.

13 Let them all praise the name of the LORD.
For his name is very great;
his glory towers over the earth and
heaven!
14 He has made his people strong,
honoring his faithful ones—
the people of Israel who are close
to him.

Praise the LORD!

PSALM 149

1 Praise the LORD!

Sing to the LORD a new song.
Sing his praises in the assembly of the faithful.

2 O Israel, rejoice in your Maker.
O people of Jerusalem, exult in your King.
3 Praise his name with dancing,
accompanied by tambourine and harp.
4 For the LORD delights in his people;
he crowns the humble with victory.
5 Let the faithful rejoice that he honors them.
Let them sing for joy as they lie on their beds.

6 Let the praises of God be in their mouths,
and a sharp sword in their hands—
7 to execute vengeance on the nations
and punishment on the peoples,
8 to bind their kings with shackles
and their leaders with iron chains,
9 to execute the judgment written against them.
This is the glorious privilege of his faithful ones.

Praise the LORD!

PSALM 150

1 Praise the LORD!

Praise God in his sanctuary;
praise him in his mighty heaven!
2 Praise him for his mighty works;
praise his unequaled greatness!
3 Praise him with a blast of the ram's horn;
praise him with the lyre and harp!
4 Praise him with the tambourine and dancing;
praise him with strings and flutes!
5 Praise him with a clash of cymbals;
praise him with loud clanging cymbals.
6 Let everything that breathes sing praises to the LORD!

Praise the LORD!

PROVERBS Words for the Wise

Look for 3 hidden messages in Proverbs!

The book of Proverbs gives a ton of advice. But it's not the boring, long-lecture kind of advice. It's cool advice about

- **HOW TO KEEP YOUR FOOT OUT OF YOUR MOUTH**
- **HOW TO KEEP YOUR FRIENDS**
- **HOW TO KEEP YOUR MONEY**
- **HOW TO KEEP OUT OF TROUBLE**
- **(AND BEST OF ALL) HOW TO KEEP PLEASING GOD**

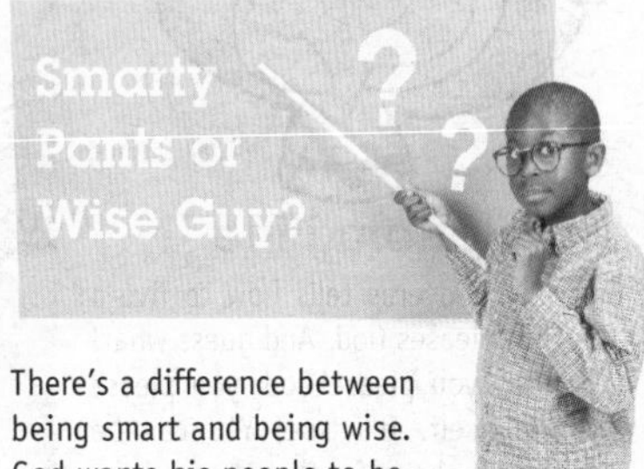

There's a difference between being smart and being wise. God wants his people to be wise. King Solomon told how to start being wise. **Read what Solomon wrote about wisdom in Proverbs 1:7.**

Listen Up!

Ever get tired of listening to your parents? Well, get over it! That's the advice Solomon gave. **Read more about parents in Proverbs 4:1-7.**

The Perfect Path

Have you ever faced a decision and you just didn't know what to do? **Well, Proverbs 3:5-6 has a simple but powerful solution for every decision you face. Check it out!**

No Foolin'!

Solomon compared foolish and wise people a lot. He said foolish people

- think they're smarter than everyone else (Proverbs 12:15),
- get angry a lot (Proverbs 12:16), and
- act without thinking (Proverbs 13:16).

Find out how *wise* people act by reading Proverbs 14:16; 15:2; and 17:27.

Watch Those Words!

There's power in the words you speak every day. At least that's what the wisest guy who ever lived said! Find out what Solomon said about words in Proverbs 16:23-24. (Want to know more about your words? Check out Proverbs 15:1 and 20:15.)

There's power not only in your words, but also in your silence! **Read Proverbs 21:23 (silently, of course).**

Love
Happiness
Riches
Safety
Children
Long Life

The Bottom Line

Basically, Proverbs tells how to live a life that pleases God. And guess what! When you please God, you please yourself. It's true! You can be truly happy only when you're doing things God's way. **Read Proverbs 19:23 and 22:4 for proof.**

DONT EVEN THINK ABOUT IT!!
COOKIES

Proud? Wicked? Watch Out!

Don't think you can fool God. He knows everything about us. And there are certain qualities he *really* doesn't like. **Read what God says about some of them in Proverbs 11:1; 15:9; and 16:5.**

Get Outta That Bed!

Hey, Lazybones! That's not the way to live. Listen to what happens to lazy people:

- They want a lot but get little (Proverbs 13:4).
- They have trouble all their lives (Proverbs 15:19).
- They go hungry (Proverbs 19:15).
- They're always greedy for more (Proverbs 21:26).

Then read Proverbs 12:11 and 14:23 to see what hard work will do for you!

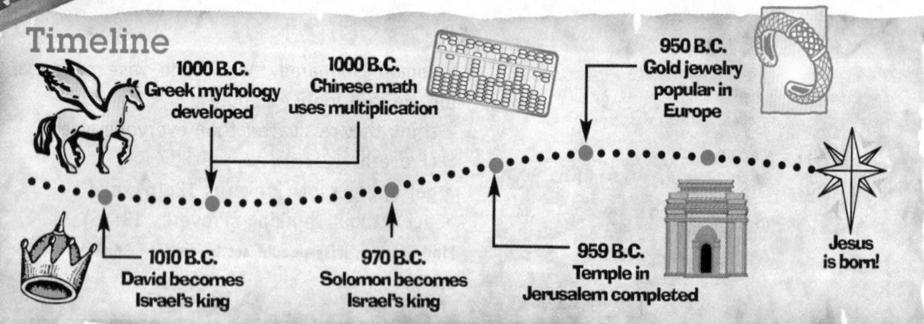
Timeline
1000 B.C. Greek mythology developed
1000 B.C. Chinese math uses multiplication
950 B.C. Gold jewelry popular in Europe
1010 B.C. David becomes Israel's king
970 B.C. Solomon becomes Israel's king
959 B.C. Temple in Jerusalem completed
Jesus is born!

The JESUS CONNECTION

In the book of Proverbs, we get practical advice for daily living. When Jesus lived on earth, his *whole life* was an example of how to live. He never lied, never cheated, always helped the poor, never gossiped, never stole, and always, always trusted God. **If we keep Jesus and his life in front of our eyes, we'll always know how to live a life that pleases God.**

CHAPTER 1

The Purpose of Proverbs

These are the proverbs of Solomon, David's son, king of Israel.

2 Their purpose is to teach people wisdom
and discipline,
to help them understand the insights
of the wise.
3 Their purpose is to teach people to live
disciplined and successful lives,
to help them do what is right, just, and fair.
4 These proverbs will give insight to the
simple,
knowledge and discernment to the young.

5 Let the wise listen to these proverbs and
become even wiser.
Let those with understanding receive
guidance
6 by exploring the meaning in these proverbs
and parables,
the words of the wise and their riddles.

7 Fear of the LORD is the foundation of true
knowledge,
but fools despise wisdom and discipline.

A Father's Exhortation: Acquire Wisdom

8 My child, listen when your father corrects
you.
Don't neglect your mother's instruction.
9 What you learn from them will crown you
with grace
and be a chain of honor around your neck.

10 My child, if sinners entice you,
turn your back on them!
11 They may say, "Come and join us.
Let's hide and kill someone!
Just for fun, let's ambush the innocent!
12 Let's swallow them alive, like the grave;
let's swallow them whole, like those who
go down to the pit of death.
13 Think of the great things we'll get!
We'll fill our houses with all the stuff
we take.
14 Come, throw in your lot with us;
we'll all share the loot."
15 My child, don't go along with them!
Stay far away from their paths.
16 They rush to commit evil deeds.
They hurry to commit murder.
17 If a bird sees a trap being set,
it knows to stay away.
18 But these people set an ambush for
themselves;
they are trying to get themselves killed.
19 Such is the fate of all who are greedy for
money;
it robs them of life.

Wisdom Shouts in the Streets

20 Wisdom shouts in the streets.
She cries out in the public square.
21 She calls to the crowds along the main street,
to those gathered in front of the city gate:
22 "How long, you simpletons,
will you insist on being simpleminded?
How long will you mockers relish your
mocking?
How long will you fools hate knowledge?
23 Come and listen to my counsel.
I'll share my heart with you
and make you wise.

24 "I called you so often, but you wouldn't
come.
I reached out to you, but you paid no
attention.
25 You ignored my advice
and rejected the correction I offered.
26 So I will laugh when you are in trouble!
I will mock you when disaster overtakes
you—
27 when calamity overtakes you like a storm,
when disaster engulfs you like a cyclone,
and anguish and distress overwhelm you.

28 "When they cry for help, I will not answer.
Though they anxiously search for me, they
will not find me.
29 For they hated knowledge
and chose not to fear the LORD.
30 They rejected my advice
and paid no attention when I corrected
them.
31 Therefore, they must eat the bitter fruit
of living their own way,
choking on their own schemes.
32 For simpletons turn away from me—
to death.
Fools are destroyed by their own
complacency.
33 But all who listen to me will live in peace,
untroubled by fear of harm."

CHAPTER 2

The Benefits of Wisdom

1 My child, listen to what I say,
and treasure my commands.

WHAT DOES IT MEAN TO TRUST GOD?

It's kind of like choosing to live in God's nest. Find a spot outside, or cover an inside surface with newspaper. This could get messy!

1
Collect a few handfuls of mud and a small ball. Then find string, straw, grass, leaves, and sticks.
2
Mix the string and other ingredients with the mud.
3
Put your ball in the center of the mixture. Form the mixture around the lower half of the ball to create a nest. Let your nest dry (takes about a day).
4
Pull the nest off the ball. Line the nest with cotton balls.
To learn more about how we—and birds—should trust God, see Matthew 6:25-27.

HEY, COOL NEST!

Put your nest outside. Watch to see if birds make a home in it.

God wants to provide for us the way you provided a nest for the birds. **Read PROVERBS 3:5-6 to see what God promises. Then decide if you want to live in God's nest! (If you do, just tell him so. Then let God take care of you!)**

2 Tune your ears to wisdom,
and concentrate on understanding.
3 Cry out for insight,
and ask for understanding.
4 Search for them as you would for silver;
seek them like hidden treasures.
5 Then you will understand what it means
to fear the LORD,
and you will gain knowledge of God.
6 For the LORD grants wisdom!
From his mouth come knowledge and
understanding.
7 He grants a treasure of common sense to the
honest.
He is a shield to those who walk with
integrity.
8 He guards the paths of the just
and protects those who are faithful
to him.

9 Then you will understand what is right,
just, and fair,
and you will find the right way to go.
10 For wisdom will enter your heart,
and knowledge will fill you with joy.
11 Wise choices will watch over you.
Understanding will keep you safe.

12 Wisdom will save you from evil people,
from those whose words are twisted.
13 These men turn from the right way
to walk down dark paths.
14 They take pleasure in doing wrong,
and they enjoy the twisted ways of evil.
15 Their actions are crooked,
and their ways are wrong.

16 Wisdom will save you from the immoral
woman,
from the seductive words of the
promiscuous woman.
17 She has abandoned her husband
and ignores the covenant she made before
God.
18 Entering her house leads to death;
it is the road to the grave.
19 The man who visits her is doomed.
He will never reach the paths of life.

20 Follow the steps of good men instead,
and stay on the paths of the righteous.
21 For only the godly will live in the land,
and those with integrity will remain
in it.
22 But the wicked will be removed from the
land,
and the treacherous will be uprooted.

CHAPTER 3
Trusting in the LORD

1 My child, never forget the things I have
taught you.
Store my commands in your heart.
2 If you do this, you will live many years,
and your life will be satisfying.
3 Never let loyalty and kindness leave you!
Tie them around your neck as a reminder.
Write them deep within your heart.
4 Then you will find favor with both God and
people,
and you will earn a good reputation.

**5 Trust in the LORD with all your
heart;
do not depend on your own
understanding.
6 Seek his will in all you do,
and he will show you which
path to take.**

7 Don't be impressed with your own wisdom.
Instead, fear the LORD and turn away
from evil.
8 Then you will have healing for your body
and strength for your bones.

9 Honor the LORD with your wealth
and with the best part of everything
you produce.
10 Then he will fill your barns with grain,
and your vats will overflow with good
wine.

11 My child, don't reject the LORD's discipline,
and don't be upset when he corrects you.
12 For the LORD corrects those he loves,
just as a father corrects a child in whom
he delights.

13 Joyful is the person who finds wisdom,
the one who gains understanding.
14 For wisdom is more profitable than silver,
and her wages are better than gold.
15 Wisdom is more precious than rubies;
nothing you desire can compare with her.
16 She offers you long life in her right hand,
and riches and honor in her left.
17 She will guide you down delightful paths;
all her ways are satisfying.
18 Wisdom is a tree of life to those who
embrace her;
happy are those who hold her tightly.

19 By wisdom the LORD founded the earth;
by understanding he created the
heavens.
20 By his knowledge the deep fountains of the
earth burst forth,
and the dew settles beneath the night
sky.

21 My child, don't lose sight of common sense
and discernment.
Hang on to them,
22 for they will refresh your soul.
They are like jewels on a necklace.
23 They keep you safe on your way,
and your feet will not stumble.
24 You can go to bed without fear;
you will lie down and sleep soundly.
25 You need not be afraid of sudden disaster
or the destruction that comes upon the
wicked,
26 for the LORD is your security.
He will keep your foot from being caught
in a trap.

27 Do not withhold good from those who
deserve it
when it's in your power to help them.
28 If you can help your neighbor now,
don't say,
"Come back tomorrow, and then I'll
help you."

29 Don't plot harm against your neighbor,
for those who live nearby trust you.
30 Don't pick a fight without reason,
when no one has done you harm.

31 Don't envy violent people
or copy their ways.
32 Such wicked people are detestable
to the LORD,
but he offers his friendship to the godly.

33 The LORD curses the house of the wicked,
but he blesses the home of the upright.
34 The LORD mocks the mockers
but is gracious to the humble.

35 The wise inherit honor,
but fools are put to shame!

CHAPTER 4
A Father's Wise Advice

1 My children, listen when your father
corrects you.
Pay attention and learn good judgment,
2 for I am giving you good guidance.
Don't turn away from my instructions.
3 For I, too, was once my father's son,
tenderly loved as my mother's only child.

4 My father taught me,
"Take my words to heart.
Follow my commands, and you will live.
5 Get wisdom; develop good judgment.
Don't forget my words or turn away from them.
6 Don't turn your back on wisdom, for she will protect you.
Love her, and she will guard you.
7 Getting wisdom is the wisest thing you can do!
And whatever else you do, develop good judgment.
8 If you prize wisdom, she will make you great.
Embrace her, and she will honor you.
9 She will place a lovely wreath on your head;
she will present you with a beautiful crown."

10 My child, listen to me and do as I say,
and you will have a long, good life.
11 I will teach you wisdom's ways
and lead you in straight paths.
12 When you walk, you won't be held back;
when you run, you won't stumble.
13 Take hold of my instructions; don't let them go.
Guard them, for they are the key to life.

14 Don't do as the wicked do,
and don't follow the path of evildoers.
15 Don't even think about it; don't go that way.
Turn away and keep moving.
16 For evil people can't sleep until they've done their evil deed for the day.
They can't rest until they've caused someone to stumble.
17 They eat the food of wickedness
and drink the wine of violence!

18 The way of the righteous is like the first gleam of dawn,
which shines ever brighter until the full light of day.
19 But the way of the wicked is like total darkness.
They have no idea what they are stumbling over.

20 My child, pay attention to what I say.
Listen carefully to my words.
21 Don't lose sight of them.
Let them penetrate deep into your heart,
22 for they bring life to those who find them,
and healing to their whole body.

23 Guard your heart above all else,
for it determines the course of your life.
24 Avoid all perverse talk;
stay away from corrupt speech.
25 Look straight ahead,
and fix your eyes on what lies before you.
26 Mark out a straight path for your feet;
stay on the safe path.
27 Don't get sidetracked;
keep your feet from following evil.

CHAPTER 5
Avoid Immoral Women

1 My son, pay attention to my wisdom;
listen carefully to my wise counsel.
2 Then you will show discernment,
and your lips will express what you've learned.
3 For the lips of an immoral woman are as sweet as honey,
and her mouth is smoother than oil.
4 But in the end she is as bitter as poison,
as dangerous as a double-edged sword.
5 Her feet go down to death;
her steps lead straight to the grave.
6 For she cares nothing about the path to life.
She staggers down a crooked trail and doesn't realize it.

7 So now, my sons, listen to me.
Never stray from what I am about to say:
8 Stay away from her!
Don't go near the door of her house!
9 If you do, you will lose your honor
and will lose to merciless people all you have achieved.
10 Strangers will consume your wealth,
and someone else will enjoy the fruit of your labor.
11 In the end you will groan in anguish
when disease consumes your body.
12 You will say, "How I hated discipline!
If only I had not ignored all the warnings!
13 Oh, why didn't I listen to my teachers?
Why didn't I pay attention to my instructors?
14 I have come to the brink of utter ruin,
and now I must face public disgrace."

15 Drink water from your own well—
share your love only with your wife.
16 Why spill the water of your springs in the streets,
having sex with just anyone?
17 You should reserve it for yourselves.
Never share it with strangers.

18 Let your wife be a fountain of blessing
for you.
Rejoice in the wife of your youth.
19 She is a loving deer, a graceful doe.
Let her breasts satisfy you always.
May you always be captivated by her love.
20 Why be captivated, my son, by an immoral
woman,
or fondle the breasts of a promiscuous
woman?

21 For the LORD sees clearly what a man does,
examining every path he takes.
22 An evil man is held captive by his own sins;
they are ropes that catch and hold him.
23 He will die for lack of self-control;
he will be lost because of his great
foolishness.

CHAPTER 6

Lessons for Daily Life

1 My child, if you have put up security for
a friend's debt
or agreed to guarantee the debt of
a stranger—
2 if you have trapped yourself by your
agreement
and are caught by what you said—
3 follow my advice and save yourself,
for you have placed yourself at your
friend's mercy.
Now swallow your pride;
go and beg to have your name erased.
4 Don't put it off; do it now!
Don't rest until you do.
5 Save yourself like a gazelle escaping from
a hunter,
like a bird fleeing from a net.

6 Take a lesson from the ants, you lazybones.
Learn from their ways and become wise!
7 Though they have no prince
or governor or ruler to make them work,
8 they labor hard all summer,
gathering food for the winter.
9 But you, lazybones, how long will you sleep?
When will you wake up?
10 A little extra sleep, a little more slumber,
a little folding of the hands to rest—
11 then poverty will pounce on you like a
bandit;
scarcity will attack you like an armed
robber.

12 What are worthless and wicked people like?
They are constant liars,
13 signaling their deceit with a wink of
the eye,
a nudge of the foot, or the wiggle
of fingers.
14 Their perverted hearts plot evil,
and they constantly stir up trouble.
15 But they will be destroyed suddenly,
broken in an instant beyond all hope
of healing.

16 There are six things the LORD hates—
no, seven things he detests:
17 haughty eyes,
a lying tongue,
hands that kill the innocent,
18 a heart that plots evil,
feet that race to do wrong,
19 a false witness who pours out lies,
a person who sows discord in a family.

20 My son, obey your father's commands,
and don't neglect your mother's
instruction.
21 Keep their words always in your heart.
Tie them around your neck.
22 When you walk, their counsel will
lead you.
When you sleep, they will protect you.
When you wake up, they will advise you.
23 For their command is a lamp
and their instruction a light;
their corrective discipline
is the way to life.
24 It will keep you from the immoral woman,
from the smooth tongue of a promiscuous
woman.
25 Don't lust for her beauty.
Don't let her coy glances seduce you.
26 For a prostitute will bring you to poverty,
but sleeping with another man's wife will
cost you your life.
27 Can a man scoop a flame into his lap
and not have his clothes catch on fire?
28 Can he walk on hot coals
and not blister his feet?
29 So it is with the man who sleeps with
another man's wife.
He who embraces her will not go
unpunished.

30 Excuses might be found for a thief
who steals because he is starving.
31 But if he is caught, he must pay back seven
times what he stole,
even if he has to sell everything in his
house.

32 But the man who commits adultery is an
utter fool,
for he destroys himself.
33 He will be wounded and disgraced.
His shame will never be erased.
34 For the woman's jealous husband will
be furious,
and he will show no mercy when he
takes revenge.
35 He will accept no compensation,
nor be satisfied with a payoff of any size.

CHAPTER 7
Another Warning about Immoral Women

1 Follow my advice, my son;
always treasure my commands.
2 Obey my commands and live!
Guard my instructions as you guard your
own eyes.
3 Tie them on your fingers as a reminder.
Write them deep within your heart.

4 Love wisdom like a sister;
make insight a beloved member
of your family.
5 Let them protect you from an affair with
an immoral woman,
from listening to the flattery of a
promiscuous woman.

6 While I was at the window of my house,
looking through the curtain,
7 I saw some naive young men,
and one in particular who lacked
common sense.
8 He was crossing the street near the house
of an immoral woman,
strolling down the path by her house.
9 It was at twilight, in the evening,
as deep darkness fell.
10 The woman approached him,
seductively dressed and sly of heart.
11 She was the brash, rebellious type,
never content to stay at home.
12 She is often in the streets and markets,
soliciting at every corner.
13 She threw her arms around him and
kissed him,
and with a brazen look she said,
14 "I've just made my peace offerings
and fulfilled my vows.
15 You're the one I was looking for!
I came out to find you, and here you are!
16 My bed is spread with beautiful blankets,
with colored sheets of Egyptian linen.
17 I've perfumed my bed
with myrrh, aloes, and cinnamon.
18 Come, let's drink our fill of love until
morning.
Let's enjoy each other's caresses,
19 for my husband is not home.
He's away on a long trip.
20 He has taken a wallet full of money
with him
and won't return until later this month."

21 So she seduced him with her pretty speech
and enticed him with her flattery.
22 He followed her at once,
like an ox going to the slaughter.
He was like a stag caught in a trap,
23 awaiting the arrow that would pierce
its heart.
He was like a bird flying into a snare,
little knowing it would cost him his life.

24 So listen to me, my sons,
and pay attention to my words.
25 Don't let your hearts stray away toward her.
Don't wander down her wayward path.
26 For she has been the ruin of many;
many men have been her victims.
27 Her house is the road to the grave.
Her bedroom is the den of death.

CHAPTER 8
Wisdom Calls for a Hearing

1 Listen as Wisdom calls out!
Hear as understanding raises her voice!
2 On the hilltop along the road,
she takes her stand at the crossroads.
3 By the gates at the entrance to the town,
on the road leading in, she cries aloud,
4 "I call to you, to all of you!
I raise my voice to all people.
5 You simple people, use good judgment.
You foolish people, show some
understanding.
6 Listen to me! For I have important things
to tell you.
Everything I say is right,
7 for I speak the truth
and detest every kind of deception.
8 My advice is wholesome.
There is nothing devious or crooked
in it.
9 My words are plain to anyone with
understanding,
clear to those with knowledge.
10 Choose my instruction rather than silver,
and knowledge rather than pure gold.

11 For wisdom is far more valuable than
rubies.
Nothing you desire can compare with it.

12 "I, Wisdom, live together with good
judgment.
I know where to discover knowledge and
discernment.
13 All who fear the LORD will hate evil.
Therefore, I hate pride and arrogance,
corruption and perverse speech.
14 Common sense and success belong to me.
Insight and strength are mine.
15 Because of me, kings reign,
and rulers make just decrees.
16 Rulers lead with my help,
and nobles make righteous judgments.
17 "I love all who love me.
Those who search will surely find me.
18 I have riches and honor,
as well as enduring wealth and justice.
19 My gifts are better than gold, even the purest
gold,
my wages better than sterling silver!
20 I walk in righteousness,
in paths of justice.
21 Those who love me inherit wealth.
I will fill their treasuries.

22 "The LORD formed me from the beginning,
before he created anything else.
23 I was appointed in ages past,
at the very first, before the earth began.
24 I was born before the oceans were created,
before the springs bubbled forth their
waters.
25 Before the mountains were formed,
before the hills, I was born—
26 before he had made the earth and fields
and the first handfuls of soil.
27 I was there when he established the
heavens,
when he drew the horizon on the oceans.
28 I was there when he set the clouds above,
when he established springs deep in
the earth.
29 I was there when he set the limits
of the seas,
so they would not spread beyond their
boundaries.
And when he marked off the earth's
foundations,
30 I was the architect at his side.
I was his constant delight,
rejoicing always in his presence.
31 And how happy I was with the world
he created;
how I rejoiced with the human family!

32 "And so, my children, listen to me,
for all who follow my ways are joyful.
33 Listen to my instruction and be wise.
Don't ignore it.
34 Joyful are those who listen to me,
watching for me daily at my gates,
waiting for me outside my home!
35 For whoever finds me finds life
and receives favor from the LORD.
36 But those who miss me injure themselves.
All who hate me love death."

CHAPTER 9

1 Wisdom has built her house;
she has carved its seven columns.
2 She has prepared a great banquet,
mixed the wines, and set the table.
3 She has sent her servants to invite everyone
to come.
She calls out from the heights overlooking
the city.
4 "Come in with me," she urges the simple.
To those who lack good judgment,
she says,
5 "Come, eat my food,
and drink the wine I have mixed.
6 Leave your simple ways behind, and begin
to live;
learn to use good judgment."

7 Anyone who rebukes a mocker will get an
insult in return.
Anyone who corrects the wicked will
get hurt.
8 So don't bother correcting mockers;
they will only hate you.
But correct the wise,
and they will love you.
9 Instruct the wise,
and they will be even wiser.
Teach the righteous,
and they will learn even more.

**10 Fear of the LORD is the foundation
of wisdom.
Knowledge of the Holy One
results in good judgment.**

11 Wisdom will multiply your days
and add years to your life.
12 If you become wise, you will be the one
to benefit.

If you scorn wisdom, you will be the one
to suffer.

Folly Calls for a Hearing

13 The woman named Folly is brash.
She is ignorant and doesn't know it.
14 She sits in her doorway
on the heights overlooking the city.
15 She calls out to men going by
who are minding their own business.
16 "Come in with me," she urges the simple.
To those who lack good judgment,
she says,
17 "Stolen water is refreshing;
food eaten in secret tastes the best!"
18 But little do they know that the dead are
there.
Her guests are in the depths of the grave.

CHAPTER 10

The Proverbs of Solomon

The proverbs of Solomon:

A wise child brings joy to a father;
a foolish child brings grief to a mother.

2 Tainted wealth has no lasting value,
but right living can save your life.

3 The LORD will not let the godly go hungry,
but he refuses to satisfy the craving
of the wicked.

4 Lazy people are soon poor;
hard workers get rich.
5 A wise youth harvests in the summer,
but one who sleeps during harvest is
a disgrace.

6 The godly are showered with blessings;
the words of the wicked conceal violent
intentions.

7 We have happy memories of the godly,
but the name of a wicked person rots away.

8 The wise are glad to be instructed,
but babbling fools fall flat on their faces.

9 People with integrity walk safely,
but those who follow crooked paths
will be exposed.

10 People who wink at wrong cause trouble,
but a bold reproof promotes peace.

11 The words of the godly are a life-giving
fountain;

Key Verse "Fear of the LORD is the foundation of wisdom. Knowledge of the Holy One results in good judgment." —PROVERBS 9:10

Got Wisdom?

Grab about 10 to 12 paper cups. **Can you stand on these cups without crushing them?**

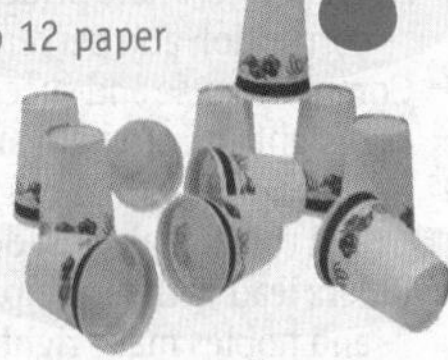

1 Arrange the paper cups upside down on top of a piece of cardboard. Place more cardboard on top.

2 Now try to stand on the structure you just built. Does it support your weight? Experiment with different numbers of cups to see how many cups it takes to support you.

Read all about the benefits of wisdom in Proverbs 9:1-12.

3 Now stand on your paper-cup foundation again, and say PROVERBS 9:10 **out loud.**

Just as the paper cups provided support—a foundation—when you stood on them, the fear of the Lord will provide a foundation as you grow in wisdom and understanding.

WANT WISDOM? START BY LEARNING MORE ABOUT GOD AND HIS WORD!

the words of the wicked conceal violent
intentions.

12 Hatred stirs up quarrels,
but love makes up for all offenses.

13 Wise words come from the lips of people
with understanding,
but those lacking sense will be beaten
with a rod.

14 Wise people treasure knowledge,
but the babbling of a fool invites disaster.

15 The wealth of the rich is their fortress;
the poverty of the poor is their
destruction.

16 The earnings of the godly enhance
their lives,
but evil people squander their money
on sin.

17 People who accept discipline are on the
pathway to life,
but those who ignore correction will
go astray.

18 Hiding hatred makes you a liar;
slandering others makes you a fool.

19 Too much talk leads to sin.
Be sensible and keep your mouth shut.

20 The words of the godly are like sterling
silver;
the heart of a fool is worthless.

21 The words of the godly encourage many,
but fools are destroyed by their lack of
common sense.

22 The blessing of the LORD makes a person
rich,
and he adds no sorrow with it.

23 Doing wrong is fun for a fool,
but living wisely brings pleasure
to the sensible.

24 The fears of the wicked will be fulfilled;
the hopes of the godly will be granted.

25 When the storms of life come, the wicked are
whirled away,
but the godly have a lasting foundation.

26 Lazy people irritate their employers,
like vinegar to the teeth or smoke
in the eyes.

27 Fear of the LORD lengthens one's life,
but the years of the wicked are cut short.

28 The hopes of the godly result in happiness,
but the expectations of the wicked come
to nothing.

29 The way of the LORD is a stronghold to those
with integrity,
but it destroys the wicked.

30 The godly will never be disturbed,
but the wicked will be removed from
the land.

31 The mouth of the godly person gives wise
advice,
but the tongue that deceives will be
cut off.

32 The lips of the godly speak helpful words,
but the mouth of the wicked speaks
perverse words.

CHAPTER 11

1 The LORD detests the use of dishonest scales,
but he delights in accurate weights.

2 Pride leads to disgrace,
but with humility comes wisdom.

3 Honesty guides good people;
dishonesty destroys treacherous people.

4 Riches won't help on the day of judgment,
but right living can save you from death.

5 The godly are directed by honesty;
the wicked fall beneath their load of sin.

6 The godliness of good people rescues them;
the ambition of treacherous people
traps them.

7 When the wicked die, their hopes die
with them,
for they rely on their own feeble strength.

8 The godly are rescued from trouble,
and it falls on the wicked instead.

9 With their words, the godless destroy their
friends,
but knowledge will rescue the righteous.

10 The whole city celebrates when the godly
succeed;
they shout for joy when the wicked die.

11 Upright citizens are good for a city and make
it prosper,
but the talk of the wicked tears it apart.

12 It is foolish to belittle one's neighbor;
a sensible person keeps quiet.

13 A gossip goes around telling secrets,
but those who are trustworthy can keep
a confidence.

14 Without wise leadership, a nation falls;
there is safety in having many advisers.

15 There's danger in putting up security for a
stranger's debt;
it's safer not to guarantee another person's
debt.

16 A gracious woman gains respect,
but ruthless men gain only wealth.

17 Your kindness will reward you,
but your cruelty will destroy you.

18 Evil people get rich for the moment,
but the reward of the godly will last.

19 Godly people find life;
evil people find death.

20 The LORD detests people with crooked
hearts,
but he delights in those with integrity.

21 Evil people will surely be punished,
but the children of the godly will go free.

22 A beautiful woman who lacks discretion
is like a gold ring in a pig's snout.

23 The godly can look forward to a reward,
while the wicked can expect only
judgment.

24 Give freely and become more wealthy;
be stingy and lose everything.

25 The generous will prosper;
those who refresh others will themselves
be refreshed.

26 People curse those who hoard their grain,
but they bless the one who sells in time
of need.

27 If you search for good, you will find favor;
but if you search for evil, it will find you!

28 Trust in your money and down you go!
But the godly flourish like leaves in spring.

29 Those who bring trouble on their families
inherit the wind.
The fool will be a servant to the wise.

30 The seeds of good deeds become a tree
of life;
a wise person wins friends.

31 If the righteous are rewarded here on earth,
what will happen to wicked sinners?

CHAPTER 12

1 To learn, you must love discipline;
it is stupid to hate correction.

2 The LORD approves of those who are good,
but he condemns those who plan
wickedness.

3 Wickedness never brings stability,
but the godly have deep roots.

4 A worthy wife is a crown for her husband,
but a disgraceful woman is like cancer
in his bones.

5 The plans of the godly are just;
the advice of the wicked is treacherous.

6 The words of the wicked are like a
murderous ambush,
but the words of the godly save lives.

7 The wicked die and disappear,
but the family of the godly stands firm.

8 A sensible person wins admiration,
but a warped mind is despised.

9 Better to be an ordinary person with
a servant
than to be self-important but have
no food.

10 The godly care for their animals,
but the wicked are always cruel.

11 A hard worker has plenty of food,
but a person who chases fantasies has
no sense.

12 Thieves are jealous of each other's loot,
but the godly are well rooted and bear
their own fruit.

13 The wicked are trapped by their own words,
but the godly escape such trouble.

14 Wise words bring many benefits,
and hard work brings rewards.

15 Fools think their own way is right,
but the wise listen to others.

16 A fool is quick-tempered,
but a wise person stays calm when
insulted.

17 An honest witness tells the truth;
a false witness tells lies.

18 Some people make cutting remarks,
but the words of the wise bring healing.

19 Truthful words stand the test of time,
but lies are soon exposed.

20 Deceit fills hearts that are plotting evil;
joy fills hearts that are planning peace!

21 No harm comes to the godly,
but the wicked have their fill of trouble.

22 The LORD detests lying lips,
but he delights in those who tell the truth.

23 The wise don't make a show of their knowledge,
but fools broadcast their foolishness.

24 Work hard and become a leader;
be lazy and become a slave.

25 Worry weighs a person down;
an encouraging word cheers a person up.

26 The godly give good advice to their friends;
the wicked lead them astray.

27 Lazy people don't even cook the game they catch,
but the diligent make use of everything they find.

28 The way of the godly leads to life;
that path does not lead to death.

CHAPTER 13

1 A wise child accepts a parent's discipline;
a mocker refuses to listen to correction.

2 Wise words will win you a good meal,
but treacherous people have an appetite for violence.

3 Those who control their tongue will have a long life;
opening your mouth can ruin everything.

4 Lazy people want much but get little,
but those who work hard will prosper.

5 The godly hate lies;
the wicked cause shame and disgrace.

6 Godliness guards the path of the blameless,
but the evil are misled by sin.

7 Some who are poor pretend to be rich;
others who are rich pretend to be poor.

8 The rich can pay a ransom for their lives,
but the poor won't even get threatened.

9 The life of the godly is full of light and joy,
but the light of the wicked will be snuffed out.

10 Pride leads to conflict;
those who take advice are wise.

11 Wealth from get-rich-quick schemes quickly disappears;
wealth from hard work grows over time.

12 Hope deferred makes the heart sick,
but a dream fulfilled is a tree of life.

13 People who despise advice are asking for trouble;
those who respect a command will succeed.

14 The instruction of the wise is like a life-giving fountain;
those who accept it avoid the snares of death.

15 A person with good sense is respected;
a treacherous person is headed for destruction.

16 Wise people think before they act;
fools don't—and even brag about their foolishness.

17 An unreliable messenger stumbles into trouble,
but a reliable messenger brings healing.

18 If you ignore criticism, you will end in poverty and disgrace;
if you accept correction, you will be honored.

19 It is pleasant to see dreams come true,
but fools refuse to turn from evil to attain them.

20 Walk with the wise and become wise;
associate with fools and get in trouble.

21 Trouble chases sinners,
while blessings reward the righteous.

22 Good people leave an inheritance to their grandchildren,
but the sinner's wealth passes to the godly.

23 A poor person's farm may produce much food,
but injustice sweeps it all away.

24 Those who spare the rod of discipline hate their children.
Those who love their children care enough to discipline them.

25 The godly eat to their hearts' content,
but the belly of the wicked goes hungry.

CHAPTER 14

1 A wise woman builds her home,
but a foolish woman tears it down with her own hands.

2 Those who follow the right path fear
the LORD;
those who take the wrong path
despise him.

3 A fool's proud talk becomes a rod that
beats him,
but the words of the wise keep them safe.

4 Without oxen a stable stays clean,
but you need a strong ox for a large
harvest.

5 An honest witness does not lie;
a false witness breathes lies.

6 A mocker seeks wisdom and never finds it,
but knowledge comes easily to those with
understanding.

7 Stay away from fools,
for you won't find knowledge on their lips.

8 The prudent understand where they
are going,
but fools deceive themselves.

9 Fools make fun of guilt,
but the godly acknowledge it and seek
reconciliation.

10 Each heart knows its own bitterness,
and no one else can fully share its joy.

11 The house of the wicked will be destroyed,
but the tent of the godly will flourish.

12 There is a path before each person that
seems right,
but it ends in death.

13 Laughter can conceal a heavy heart,
but when the laughter ends, the grief
remains.

14 Backsliders get what they deserve;
good people receive their reward.

15 Only simpletons believe everything
they're told!
The prudent carefully consider
their steps.

16 The wise are cautious and avoid danger;
fools plunge ahead with reckless
confidence.

17 Short-tempered people do foolish things,
and schemers are hated.

18 Simpletons are clothed with foolishness,
but the prudent are crowned with
knowledge.

19 Evil people will bow before good people;
the wicked will bow at the gates of
the godly.

20 The poor are despised even by their
neighbors,
while the rich have many "friends."

21 It is a sin to belittle one's neighbor;
blessed are those who help the poor.

22 If you plan to do evil, you will be lost;
if you plan to do good, you will receive
unfailing love and faithfulness.

23 Work brings profit,
but mere talk leads to poverty!

24 Wealth is a crown for the wise;
the effort of fools yields only
foolishness.

25 A truthful witness saves lives,
but a false witness is a traitor.

26 Those who fear the LORD are secure;
he will be a refuge for their children.

27 Fear of the LORD is a life-giving fountain;
it offers escape from the snares
of death.

28 A growing population is a king's glory;
a prince without subjects has nothing.

29 People with understanding control their
anger;
a hot temper shows great foolishness.

30 A peaceful heart leads to a healthy body;
jealousy is like cancer in the bones.

31 Those who oppress the poor insult their
Maker,
but helping the poor honors him.

32 The wicked are crushed by disaster,
but the godly have a refuge when
they die.

33 Wisdom is enshrined in an understanding
heart;
wisdom is not found among fools.

34 Godliness makes a nation great,
but sin is a disgrace to any people.

35 A king rejoices in wise servants
but is angry with those who disgrace him.

CHAPTER 15

1 A gentle answer deflects anger,
but harsh words make tempers flare.

2 The tongue of the wise makes knowledge appealing,
but the mouth of a fool belches out foolishness.

3 The LORD is watching everywhere,
keeping his eye on both the evil and the good.

4 Gentle words are a tree of life;
a deceitful tongue crushes the spirit.

5 Only a fool despises a parent's discipline;
whoever learns from correction is wise.

6 There is treasure in the house of the godly,
but the earnings of the wicked bring trouble.

7 The lips of the wise give good advice;
the heart of a fool has none to give.

8 The LORD detests the sacrifice of the wicked,
but he delights in the prayers of the upright.

9 The LORD detests the way of the wicked,
but he loves those who pursue godliness.

10 Whoever abandons the right path will be severely disciplined;
whoever hates correction will die.

11 Even Death and Destruction hold no secrets from the LORD.
How much more does he know the human heart!

12 Mockers hate to be corrected,
so they stay away from the wise.

13 A glad heart makes a happy face;
a broken heart crushes the spirit.

14 A wise person is hungry for knowledge,
while the fool feeds on trash.

15 For the despondent, every day brings trouble;
for the happy heart, life is a continual feast.

16 Better to have little, with fear for the LORD,
than to have great treasure and inner turmoil.

17 A bowl of vegetables with someone you love
is better than steak with someone you hate.

18 A hot-tempered person starts fights;
a cool-tempered person stops them.

19 A lazy person's way is blocked with briers,
but the path of the upright is an open highway.

20 Sensible children bring joy to their father;
foolish children despise their mother.

21 Foolishness brings joy to those with no sense;
a sensible person stays on the right path.

22 Plans go wrong for lack of advice;
many advisers bring success.

23 Everyone enjoys a fitting reply;
it is wonderful to say the right thing at the right time!

24 The path of life leads upward for the wise;
they leave the grave behind.

25 The LORD tears down the house of the proud,
but he protects the property of widows.

26 The LORD detests evil plans,
but he delights in pure words.

27 Greed brings grief to the whole family,
but those who hate bribes will live.

28 The heart of the godly thinks carefully before speaking;
the mouth of the wicked overflows with evil words.

29 The LORD is far from the wicked,
but he hears the prayers of the righteous.

30 A cheerful look brings joy to the heart;
good news makes for good health.

31 If you listen to constructive criticism,
you will be at home among the wise.

32 If you reject discipline, you only harm yourself;
but if you listen to correction, you grow in understanding.

33 Fear of the LORD teaches wisdom;
humility precedes honor.

CHAPTER 16

1 We can make our own plans,
but the LORD gives the right answer.

2 People may be pure in their own eyes,
but the LORD examines their motives.

3 Commit your actions to the LORD,
and your plans will succeed.

4 The LORD has made everything for his own purposes,
even the wicked for a day of disaster.

5 The LORD detests the proud;
they will surely be punished.

6 Unfailing love and faithfulness make
atonement for sin.
By fearing the LORD, people avoid evil.

7 When people's lives please the LORD,
even their enemies are at peace with them.

8 Better to have little, with godliness,
than to be rich and dishonest.

9 We can make our plans,
but the LORD determines our steps.

10 The king speaks with divine wisdom;
he must never judge unfairly.

11 The LORD demands accurate scales and
balances;
he sets the standards for fairness.

12 A king detests wrongdoing,
for his rule is built on justice.

13 The king is pleased with words from
righteous lips;
he loves those who speak honestly.

14 The anger of the king is a deadly threat;
the wise will try to appease it.

15 When the king smiles, there is life;
his favor refreshes like a spring rain.

16 How much better to get wisdom than gold,
and good judgment than silver!

17 The path of the virtuous leads away
from evil;
whoever follows that path is safe.

18 Pride goes before destruction,
and haughtiness before a fall.

19 Better to live humbly with the poor
than to share plunder with the proud.

20 Those who listen to instruction will prosper;
those who trust the LORD will be joyful.

21 The wise are known for their understanding,
and pleasant words are persuasive.

22 Discretion is a life-giving fountain to those
who possess it,
but discipline is wasted on fools.

23 From a wise mind comes wise speech;
the words of the wise are persuasive.

24 Kind words are like honey—
sweet to the soul and healthy for the body.

25 There is a path before each person that
seems right,
but it ends in death.

26 It is good for workers to have an appetite;
an empty stomach drives them on.

27 Scoundrels create trouble;
their words are a destructive blaze.

28 A troublemaker plants seeds of strife;
gossip separates the best of friends.

29 Violent people mislead their companions,
leading them down a harmful path.

30 With narrowed eyes, people plot evil;
with a smirk, they plan their mischief.

31 Gray hair is a crown of glory;
it is gained by living a godly life.

32 Better to be patient than powerful;
better to have self-control than to conquer
a city.

33 We may throw the dice,
but the LORD determines how they fall.

CHAPTER 17

1 Better a dry crust eaten in peace
than a house filled with feasting—and
conflict.

2 A wise servant will rule over the master's
disgraceful son
and will share the inheritance of the
master's children.

3 Fire tests the purity of silver and gold,
but the LORD tests the heart.

4 Wrongdoers eagerly listen to gossip;
liars pay close attention to slander.

5 Those who mock the poor insult their
Maker;
those who rejoice at the misfortune
of others will be punished.

6 Grandchildren are the crowning glory
of the aged;
parents are the pride of their children.

7 Eloquent words are not fitting for a fool;
even less are lies fitting for a ruler.

8 A bribe is like a lucky charm;
whoever gives one will prosper!

9 Love prospers when a fault is forgiven,
but dwelling on it separates close friends.

10 A single rebuke does more for a person
of understanding
than a hundred lashes on the back of
a fool.

11 Evil people are eager for rebellion,
but they will be severely punished.

12 It is safer to meet a bear robbed of her cubs
than to confront a fool caught in
foolishness.

13 If you repay good with evil,
evil will never leave your house.

14 Starting a quarrel is like opening a floodgate,
so stop before a dispute breaks out.

15 Acquitting the guilty and condemning the
innocent—
both are detestable to the LORD.

16 It is senseless to pay to educate a fool,
since he has no heart for learning.

**17 A friend is always loyal,
and a brother is born to help
in time of need.**

18 It's poor judgment to guarantee another
person's debt
or put up security for a friend.

19 Anyone who loves to quarrel loves sin;
anyone who trusts in high walls invites
disaster.

20 The crooked heart will not prosper;
the lying tongue tumbles into trouble.

21 It is painful to be the parent of a fool;
there is no joy for the father of a rebel.

22 A cheerful heart is good medicine,
but a broken spirit saps a person's strength.

23 The wicked take secret bribes
to pervert the course of justice.

24 Sensible people keep their eyes glued
on wisdom,
but a fool's eyes wander to the ends
of the earth.

25 Foolish children bring grief to their father
and bitterness to the one who gave them
birth.

26 It is wrong to punish the godly for being good
or to flog leaders for being honest.

27 A truly wise person uses few words;
a person with understanding is even-
tempered.

28 Even fools are thought wise when they
keep silent;
with their mouths shut, they seem
intelligent.

CHAPTER 18

1 Unfriendly people care only about
themselves;
they lash out at common sense.

2 Fools have no interest in understanding;
they only want to air their own opinions.

3 Doing wrong leads to disgrace,
and scandalous behavior brings contempt.

4 Wise words are like deep waters;
wisdom flows from the wise like a
bubbling brook.

5 It is not right to acquit the guilty
or deny justice to the innocent.

6 Fools' words get them into constant quarrels;
they are asking for a beating.

7 The mouths of fools are their ruin;
they trap themselves with their lips.

8 Rumors are dainty morsels
that sink deep into one's heart.

9 A lazy person is as bad as
someone who destroys things.

10 The name of the LORD is a strong fortress;
the godly run to him and are safe.

11 The rich think of their wealth as a strong
defense;
they imagine it to be a high wall of safety.

12 Haughtiness goes before destruction;
humility precedes honor.

13 Spouting off before listening to the facts
is both shameful and foolish.

14 The human spirit can endure a sick body,
but who can bear a crushed spirit?

15 Intelligent people are always ready to learn.
Their ears are open for knowledge.

16 Giving a gift can open doors;
it gives access to important people!

17 The first to speak in court sounds right—
until the cross-examination begins.

18 Flipping a coin can end arguments;
it settles disputes between powerful
opponents.

19 An offended friend is harder to win back
than a fortified city.
Arguments separate friends like a gate
locked with bars.

20 Wise words satisfy like a good meal;
the right words bring satisfaction.

21 The tongue can bring death or life;
those who love to talk will reap the consequences.

22 The man who finds a wife finds a treasure,
and he receives favor from the LORD.

23 The poor plead for mercy;
the rich answer with insults.

24 There are "friends" who destroy each other,
but a real friend sticks closer than a brother.

CHAPTER 19

1 Better to be poor and honest
than to be dishonest and a fool.

2 Enthusiasm without knowledge is no good;
haste makes mistakes.

3 People ruin their lives by their own foolishness
and then are angry at the LORD.

4 Wealth makes many "friends";
poverty drives them all away.

5 A false witness will not go unpunished,
nor will a liar escape.

6 Many seek favors from a ruler;
everyone is the friend of a person who gives gifts!

7 The relatives of the poor despise them;
how much more will their friends avoid them!
Though the poor plead with them,
their friends are gone.

8 To acquire wisdom is to love yourself;
people who cherish understanding will prosper.

9 A false witness will not go unpunished,
and a liar will be destroyed.

10 It isn't right for a fool to live in luxury
or for a slave to rule over princes!

11 Sensible people control their temper;
they earn respect by overlooking wrongs.

12 The king's anger is like a lion's roar,
but his favor is like dew on the grass.

13 A foolish child is a calamity to a father;
a quarrelsome wife is as annoying as constant dripping.

14 Fathers can give their sons an inheritance of houses and wealth,
but only the LORD can give an understanding wife.

15 Lazy people sleep soundly,
but idleness leaves them hungry.

16 Keep the commandments and keep your life;
despising them leads to death.

17 If you help the poor, you are lending to the LORD—
and he will repay you!

18 Discipline your children while there is hope.
Otherwise you will ruin their lives.

19 Hot-tempered people must pay the penalty.
If you rescue them once, you will have to do it again.

20 Get all the advice and instruction you can,
so you will be wise the rest of your life.

21 You can make many plans,
but the LORD's purpose will prevail.

22 Loyalty makes a person attractive.
It is better to be poor than dishonest.

23 Fear of the LORD leads to life,
bringing security and protection from harm.

24 Lazy people take food in their hand
but don't even lift it to their mouth.

25 If you punish a mocker, the simpleminded will learn a lesson;
if you correct the wise, they will be all the wiser.

26 Children who mistreat their father or chase away their mother
are an embarrassment and a public disgrace.

27 If you stop listening to instruction, my child,
you will turn your back on knowledge.

28 A corrupt witness makes a mockery of justice;
the mouth of the wicked gulps down evil.

29 Punishment is made for mockers,
and the backs of fools are made to be beaten.

CHAPTER 20

1 Wine produces mockers; alcohol leads to brawls.
Those led astray by drink cannot be wise.

STICK TOGETHER

Read what **PROVERBS 18:24** says about true friendship. Want to be a true friend? Get yourself into a sticky situation!

1 **Pour a half cup of fat-free milk (the fat-free is important) into a small bowl, and add two tablespoons of vinegar.**

2 **Stir the mixture, then let it sit for two minutes. Your milk will look a little chunky—YUM!**

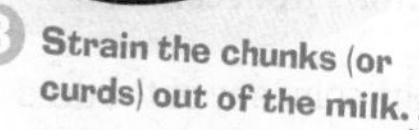

3 **Strain the chunks (or curds) out of the milk.**

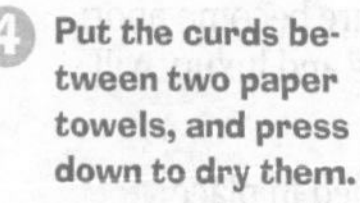

4 **Put the curds between two paper towels, and press down to dry them.**

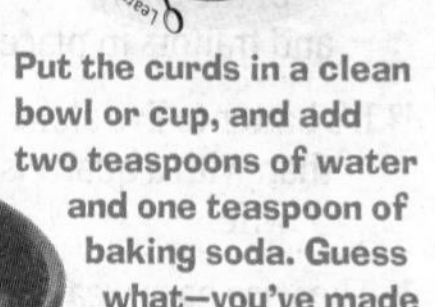

Learn more about stick-with-it friends in 1 Samuel 20; Ruth 1:1-18; and Philippians 1:1-11; 2:25-30.

5 **Put the curds in a clean bowl or cup, and add two teaspoons of water and one teaspoon of baking soda. Guess what—you've made your own glue!**

Now try your glue on various objects and surfaces. Can you find anything that sticks together so well you can't pull it apart?

THAT'S WHAT IT MEANS TO BE A TRUE FRIEND. YOU'LL STICK WITH YOUR FRIEND NO MATTER WHAT.

2 The king's fury is like a lion's roar;
to rouse his anger is to risk your life.

3 Avoiding a fight is a mark of honor;
only fools insist on quarreling.

4 Those too lazy to plow in the right season
will have no food at the harvest.

5 Though good advice lies deep within the heart,
a person with understanding will draw it out.

6 Many will say they are loyal friends,
but who can find one who is truly reliable?

7 The godly walk with integrity;
blessed are their children who follow them.

8 When a king sits in judgment, he weighs all the evidence,
distinguishing the bad from the good.

9 Who can say, "I have cleansed my heart;
I am pure and free from sin"?

10 False weights and unequal measures—
the LORD detests double standards of every kind.

11 Even children are known by the way they act,
whether their conduct is pure, and whether it is right.

12 Ears to hear and eyes to see—
both are gifts from the LORD.

13 If you love sleep, you will end in poverty.
Keep your eyes open, and there will be plenty to eat!

14 The buyer haggles over the price, saying, "It's worthless,"
then brags about getting a bargain!

15 Wise words are more valuable
than much gold and many rubies.

16 Get security from someone who guarantees a stranger's debt.
Get a deposit if he does it for foreigners.

17 Stolen bread tastes sweet,
but it turns to gravel in the mouth.

18 Plans succeed through good counsel;
don't go to war without wise advice.

19 A gossip goes around telling secrets,
so don't hang around with chatterers.

20 If you insult your father or mother,
your light will be snuffed out in total darkness.

21 An inheritance obtained too early in life
is not a blessing in the end.

22 Don't say, "I will get even for this wrong."
Wait for the LORD to handle the matter.

23 The LORD detests double standards;
he is not pleased by dishonest scales.

24 The LORD directs our steps,
so why try to understand everything along the way?

25 Don't trap yourself by making a rash promise to God
and only later counting the cost.

26 A wise king scatters the wicked like wheat,
then runs his threshing wheel over them.

27 The LORD's light penetrates the human spirit,
exposing every hidden motive.

28 Unfailing love and faithfulness protect the king;
his throne is made secure through love.

29 The glory of the young is their strength;
the gray hair of experience is the splendor of the old.

30 Physical punishment cleanses away evil;
such discipline purifies the heart.

CHAPTER 21

1 The king's heart is like a stream of water directed by the LORD;
he guides it wherever he pleases.

2 People may be right in their own eyes,
but the LORD examines their heart.

3 The LORD is more pleased when we do what is right and just
than when we offer him sacrifices.

4 Haughty eyes, a proud heart,
and evil actions are all sin.

5 Good planning and hard work lead to prosperity,
but hasty shortcuts lead to poverty.

6 Wealth created by a lying tongue
is a vanishing mist and a deadly trap.

7 The violence of the wicked sweeps them away,
because they refuse to do what is just.

8 The guilty walk a crooked path;
the innocent travel a straight road.

9 It's better to live alone in the corner of an attic
than with a quarrelsome wife in a lovely home.

10 Evil people desire evil;
their neighbors get no mercy from them.

11 If you punish a mocker, the simpleminded become wise;
if you instruct the wise, they will be all the wiser.

12 The Righteous One knows what is going on in the homes of the wicked;
he will bring disaster on them.

13 Those who shut their ears to the cries of the poor
will be ignored in their own time of need.

14 A secret gift calms anger;
a bribe under the table pacifies fury.

15 Justice is a joy to the godly,
but it terrifies evildoers.

16 The person who strays from common sense
will end up in the company of the dead.

17 Those who love pleasure become poor;
those who love wine and luxury will never be rich.

18 The wicked are punished in place of the godly,
and traitors in place of the honest.

19 It's better to live alone in the desert
than with a quarrelsome, complaining wife.

20 The wise have wealth and luxury,
but fools spend whatever they get.

21 Whoever pursues righteousness and unfailing love
will find life, righteousness, and honor.

22 The wise conquer the city of the strong
and level the fortress in which they trust.

23 Watch your tongue and keep your mouth shut,
and you will stay out of trouble.

24 Mockers are proud and haughty;
they act with boundless arrogance.

25 Despite their desires, the lazy will come to ruin,
for their hands refuse to work.

26 Some people are always greedy for more,
but the godly love to give!

27 The sacrifice of an evil person is detestable,
especially when it is offered with wrong motives.

28 A false witness will be cut off,
but a credible witness will be allowed to speak.

29 The wicked bluff their way through,
but the virtuous think before they act.

30 No human wisdom or understanding or plan
can stand against the LORD.

31 The horse is prepared for the day of battle,
but the victory belongs to the LORD.

CHAPTER 22

1 Choose a good reputation over great riches;
being held in high esteem is better than silver or gold.

2 The rich and poor have this in common:
The LORD made them both.

3 A prudent person foresees danger and takes precautions.
The simpleton goes blindly on and suffers the consequences.

4 True humility and fear of the LORD
lead to riches, honor, and long life.

5 Corrupt people walk a thorny, treacherous road;
whoever values life will avoid it.

6 Direct your children onto the right path,
and when they are older, they will not leave it.

7 Just as the rich rule the poor,
so the borrower is servant to the lender.

8 Those who plant injustice will harvest disaster,
and their reign of terror will come to an end.

9 Blessed are those who are generous,
because they feed the poor.

10 Throw out the mocker, and fighting goes, too.
Quarrels and insults will disappear.

11 Whoever loves a pure heart and gracious speech
will have the king as a friend.

12 The LORD preserves those with knowledge,
but he ruins the plans of the treacherous.

13 The lazy person claims, "There's a lion out there!
If I go outside, I might be killed!"

14 The mouth of an immoral woman is a dangerous trap;
those who make the LORD angry will fall into it.

15 A youngster's heart is filled with foolishness,
but physical discipline will drive it far away.

16 A person who gets ahead by oppressing the poor
or by showering gifts on the rich will end in poverty.

Sayings of the Wise

17 Listen to the words of the wise;
apply your heart to my instruction.
18 For it is good to keep these sayings in your heart
and always ready on your lips.
19 I am teaching you today—yes, you—
so you will trust in the LORD.
20 I have written thirty sayings for you,
filled with advice and knowledge.
21 In this way, you may know the truth
and take an accurate report to those who sent you.

22 Don't rob the poor just because you can,
or exploit the needy in court.
23 For the LORD is their defender.
He will ruin anyone who ruins them.

24 Don't befriend angry people
or associate with hot-tempered people,
25 or you will learn to be like them
and endanger your soul.

26 Don't agree to guarantee another person's debt
or put up security for someone else.
27 If you can't pay it,
even your bed will be snatched from under you.

28 Don't cheat your neighbor by moving the ancient boundary markers
set up by previous generations.

29 Do you see any truly competent workers?
They will serve kings
rather than working for ordinary people.

CHAPTER 23

1 While dining with a ruler,
pay attention to what is put before you.
2 If you are a big eater,
put a knife to your throat;
3 don't desire all the delicacies,
for he might be trying to trick you.

4 Don't wear yourself out trying to get rich.
Be wise enough to know when to quit.
5 In the blink of an eye wealth disappears,
for it will sprout wings
and fly away like an eagle.

6 Don't eat with people who are stingy;
don't desire their delicacies.
7 They are always thinking about how much
it costs.
"Eat and drink," they say, but they don't
mean it.
8 You will throw up what little you've eaten,
and your compliments will be wasted.

9 Don't waste your breath on fools,
for they will despise the wisest advice.

10 Don't cheat your neighbor by moving the
ancient boundary markers;
don't take the land of defenseless
orphans.
11 For their Redeemer is strong;
he himself will bring their charges
against you.

12 Commit yourself to instruction;
listen carefully to words of knowledge.

13 Don't fail to discipline your children.
The rod of punishment won't kill them.
14 Physical discipline
may well save them from death.

15 My child, if your heart is wise,
my own heart will rejoice!
16 Everything in me will celebrate
when you speak what is right.

17 Don't envy sinners,
but always continue to fear the LORD.
18 You will be rewarded for this;
your hope will not be disappointed.

19 My child, listen and be wise:
Keep your heart on the right course.
20 Do not carouse with drunkards
or feast with gluttons,
21 for they are on their way to poverty,
and too much sleep clothes them in rags.

22 Listen to your father, who gave you life,
and don't despise your mother when she
is old.
23 Get the truth and never sell it;
also get wisdom, discipline, and good
judgment.
24 The father of godly children has cause
for joy.
What a pleasure to have children who
are wise.
25 So give your father and mother joy!
May she who gave you birth be happy.

26 O my son, give me your heart.
May your eyes take delight in following
my ways.
27 A prostitute is a dangerous trap;
a promiscuous woman is as dangerous as
falling into a narrow well.
28 She hides and waits like a robber,
eager to make more men unfaithful.

29 Who has anguish? Who has sorrow?
Who is always fighting? Who is always
complaining?
Who has unnecessary bruises? Who has
bloodshot eyes?
30 It is the one who spends long hours in the
taverns,
trying out new drinks.
31 Don't gaze at the wine, seeing how red it is,
how it sparkles in the cup, how smoothly
it goes down.
32 For in the end it bites like a poisonous snake;
it stings like a viper.
33 You will see hallucinations,
and you will say crazy things.
34 You will stagger like a sailor tossed at sea,
clinging to a swaying mast.
35 And you will say, "They hit me, but I didn't
feel it.
I didn't even know it when they beat
me up.
When will I wake up
so I can look for another drink?"

CHAPTER 24

1 Don't envy evil people
or desire their company.
2 For their hearts plot violence,
and their words always stir up trouble.

3 A house is built by wisdom
and becomes strong through good sense.

4 Through knowledge its rooms are filled
with all sorts of precious riches and
valuables.

5 The wise are mightier than the strong,
and those with knowledge grow stronger
and stronger.
6 So don't go to war without wise guidance;
victory depends on having many advisers.

7 Wisdom is too lofty for fools.
Among leaders at the city gate, they have
nothing to say.

8 A person who plans evil
will get a reputation as a troublemaker.
9 The schemes of a fool are sinful;
everyone detests a mocker.

10 If you fail under pressure,
your strength is too small.

11 Rescue those who are unjustly sentenced
to die;
save them as they stagger to their death.
12 Don't excuse yourself by saying, "Look, we
didn't know."
For God understands all hearts, and he
sees you.
He who guards your soul knows you knew.
He will repay all people as their actions
deserve.

13 My child, eat honey, for it is good,
and the honeycomb is sweet to the taste.
14 In the same way, wisdom is sweet to your
soul.
If you find it, you will have a bright
future,
and your hopes will not be cut short.

15 Don't wait in ambush at the home of
the godly,
and don't raid the house where the
godly live.
16 The godly may trip seven times, but they
will get up again.
But one disaster is enough to overthrow
the wicked.

17 Don't rejoice when your enemies fall;
don't be happy when they stumble.
18 For the LORD will be displeased with you
and will turn his anger away from them.

19 Don't fret because of evildoers;
don't envy the wicked.
20 For evil people have no future;
the light of the wicked will be snuffed out.

21 My child, fear the LORD and the king.
Don't associate with rebels,
22 for disaster will hit them suddenly.
Who knows what punishment will come
from the LORD and the king?

More Sayings of the Wise
23 Here are some further sayings of the wise:

It is wrong to show favoritism when passing
judgment.
24 A judge who says to the wicked, "You are
innocent,"
will be cursed by many people and
denounced by the nations.
25 But it will go well for those who convict
the guilty;
rich blessings will be showered on them.

26 An honest answer
is like a kiss of friendship.

27 Do your planning and prepare your fields
before building your house.

28 Don't testify against your neighbors without
cause;
don't lie about them.
29 And don't say, "Now I can pay them back
for what they've done to me!
I'll get even with them!"

30 I walked by the field of a lazy person,
the vineyard of one with no common
sense.
31 I saw that it was overgrown with nettles.
It was covered with weeds,
and its walls were broken down.
32 Then, as I looked and thought about it,
I learned this lesson:
33 A little extra sleep, a little more slumber,
a little folding of the hands to rest—
34 then poverty will pounce on you like
a bandit;
scarcity will attack you like an armed
robber.

CHAPTER 25
More Proverbs of Solomon
These are more proverbs of Solomon, collected by the advisers of King Hezekiah of Judah.

2 It is God's privilege to conceal things
and the king's privilege to discover them.

3 No one can comprehend the height of
heaven, the depth of the earth,
or all that goes on in the king's mind!

4 Remove the impurities from silver,
and the sterling will be ready for the silversmith.
5 Remove the wicked from the king's court,
and his reign will be made secure by justice.
6 Don't demand an audience with the king
or push for a place among the great.
7 It's better to wait for an invitation to the head table
than to be sent away in public disgrace.

Just because you've seen something,
8 don't be in a hurry to go to court.
For what will you do in the end
if your neighbor deals you a shameful defeat?
9 When arguing with your neighbor,
don't betray another person's secret.
10 Others may accuse you of gossip,
and you will never regain your good reputation.

11 Timely advice is lovely,
like golden apples in a silver basket.

12 To one who listens, valid criticism
is like a gold earring or other gold jewelry.

13 Trustworthy messengers refresh like snow in summer.
They revive the spirit of their employer.

14 A person who promises a gift but doesn't give it
is like clouds and wind that bring no rain.

15 Patience can persuade a prince,
and soft speech can break bones.

16 Do you like honey?
Don't eat too much, or it will make you sick!

17 Don't visit your neighbors too often,
or you will wear out your welcome.

18 Telling lies about others
is as harmful as hitting them with an ax,
wounding them with a sword,
or shooting them with a sharp arrow.

19 Putting confidence in an unreliable person in times of trouble
is like chewing with a broken tooth or walking on a lame foot.

20 Singing cheerful songs to a person with a heavy heart
is like taking someone's coat in cold weather
or pouring vinegar in a wound.

21 If your enemies are hungry, give them food to eat.
If they are thirsty, give them water to drink.

FUN-fact: Short but Sweet

Advice doesn't have to be long and drawn out. Some of the Bible's writers shared their advice in power-packed messages—like the advice in the book of Proverbs.

Try giving some short-but-sweet advice of your own! Get together with a few friends and take turns writing pieces of advice. The advice has to be short, like in Proverbs. Collect everyone's advice into a small booklet or a box. In the future when you need advice, look through your collection and surprise your family!

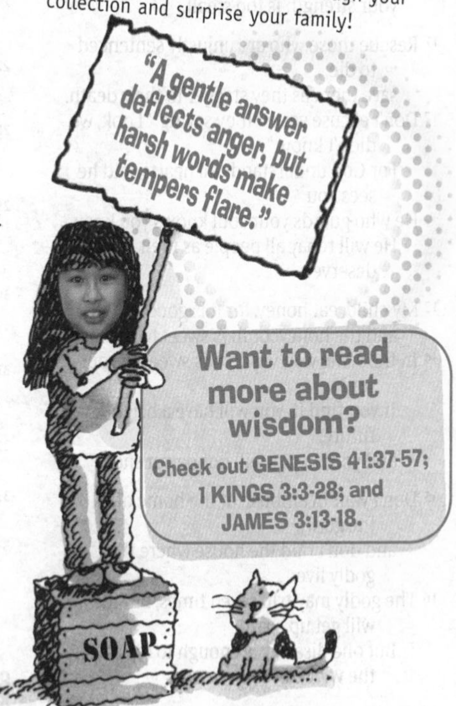

"A gentle answer deflects anger, but harsh words make tempers flare."
SOAP

Want to read more about wisdom?

Check out GENESIS 41:37-57; 1 KINGS 3:3-28; and JAMES 3:13-18.

22 You will heap burning coals of shame on
their heads,
and the LORD will reward you.

23 As surely as a north wind brings rain,
so a gossiping tongue causes anger!

24 It's better to live alone in the corner of
an attic
than with a quarrelsome wife in a lovely
home.

25 Good news from far away
is like cold water to the thirsty.

26 If the godly give in to the wicked,
it's like polluting a fountain or muddying
a spring.

27 It's not good to eat too much honey,
and it's not good to seek honors for
yourself.

28 A person without self-control
is like a city with broken-down walls.

CHAPTER 26

1 Honor is no more associated with fools
than snow with summer or rain with
harvest.

2 Like a fluttering sparrow or a darting
swallow,
an undeserved curse will not land on its
intended victim.

3 Guide a horse with a whip, a donkey with
a bridle,
and a fool with a rod to his back!

4 Don't answer the foolish arguments
of fools,
or you will become as foolish as they are.

5 Be sure to answer the foolish arguments
of fools,
or they will become wise in their own
estimation.

6 Trusting a fool to convey a message
is like cutting off one's feet or drinking
poison!

7 A proverb in the mouth of a fool
is as useless as a paralyzed leg.

8 Honoring a fool
is as foolish as tying a stone to a slingshot.

9 A proverb in the mouth of a fool
is like a thorny branch brandished by
a drunk.

10 An employer who hires a fool or a bystander
is like an archer who shoots at random.

11 As a dog returns to its vomit,
so a fool repeats his foolishness.

12 There is more hope for fools
than for people who think they are wise.

13 The lazy person claims, "There's a lion on
the road!
Yes, I'm sure there's a lion out there!"

14 As a door swings back and forth on its
hinges,
so the lazy person turns over in bed.

15 Lazy people take food in their hand
but don't even lift it to their mouth.

16 Lazy people consider themselves smarter
than seven wise counselors.

17 Interfering in someone else's argument
is as foolish as yanking a dog's ears.

18 Just as damaging
as a madman shooting a deadly weapon
19 is someone who lies to a friend
and then says, "I was only joking."

20 Fire goes out without wood,
and quarrels disappear when gossip stops.

21 A quarrelsome person starts fights
as easily as hot embers light charcoal or
fire lights wood.

22 Rumors are dainty morsels
that sink deep into one's heart.

23 Smooth words may hide a wicked heart,
just as a pretty glaze covers a clay pot.

24 People may cover their hatred with pleasant
words,
but they're deceiving you.
25 They pretend to be kind, but don't believe
them.
Their hearts are full of many evils.
26 While their hatred may be concealed
by trickery,
their wrongdoing will be exposed
in public.

27 If you set a trap for others,
you will get caught in it yourself.
If you roll a boulder down on others,
it will crush you instead.

28 A lying tongue hates its victims,
and flattering words cause ruin.

CHAPTER 27

1 Don't brag about tomorrow,
since you don't know what the day will bring.

2 Let someone else praise you, not your own mouth—
a stranger, not your own lips.

3 A stone is heavy and sand is weighty,
but the resentment caused by a fool is even heavier.

4 Anger is cruel, and wrath is like a flood,
but jealousy is even more dangerous.

5 An open rebuke
is better than hidden love!

6 Wounds from a sincere friend
are better than many kisses from an enemy.

7 A person who is full refuses honey,
but even bitter food tastes sweet to the hungry.

8 A person who strays from home
is like a bird that strays from its nest.

9 The heartfelt counsel of a friend
is as sweet as perfume and incense.

10 Never abandon a friend—
either yours or your father's.
When disaster strikes, you won't have to ask your brother for assistance.
It's better to go to a neighbor than to a brother who lives far away.

11 Be wise, my child, and make my heart glad.
Then I will be able to answer my critics.

12 A prudent person foresees danger and takes precautions.
The simpleton goes blindly on and suffers the consequences.

13 Get security from someone who guarantees a stranger's debt.
Get a deposit if he does it for foreigners.

14 A loud and cheerful greeting early in the morning
will be taken as a curse!

15 A quarrelsome wife is as annoying
as constant dripping on a rainy day.
16 Stopping her complaints is like trying to stop the wind
or trying to hold something with greased hands.

17 As iron sharpens iron,
so a friend sharpens a friend.

18 As workers who tend a fig tree are allowed to eat the fruit,
so workers who protect their employer's interests will be rewarded.

19 As a face is reflected in water,
so the heart reflects the real person.

20 Just as Death and Destruction are never satisfied,
so human desire is never satisfied.

21 Fire tests the purity of silver and gold,
but a person is tested by being praised.

22 You cannot separate fools from their foolishness,
even though you grind them like grain with mortar and pestle.

23 Know the state of your flocks,
and put your heart into caring for your herds,
24 for riches don't last forever,
and the crown might not be passed to the next generation.
25 After the hay is harvested and the new crop appears
and the mountain grasses are gathered in,
26 your sheep will provide wool for clothing,
and your goats will provide the price of a field.
27 And you will have enough goats' milk for yourself,
your family, and your servant girls.

CHAPTER 28

1 The wicked run away when no one is chasing them,
but the godly are as bold as lions.

2 When there is moral rot within a nation,
its government topples easily.
But wise and knowledgeable leaders bring stability.

3 A poor person who oppresses the poor
is like a pounding rain that destroys the crops.

4 To reject the law is to praise the wicked;
to obey the law is to fight them.

5 Evil people don't understand justice,
but those who follow the LORD understand completely.

6 Better to be poor and honest
than to be dishonest and rich.

7 Young people who obey the law are wise;
those with wild friends bring shame to
their parents.

8 Income from charging high interest rates
will end up in the pocket of someone who
is kind to the poor.

9 God detests the prayers
of a person who ignores the law.

10 Those who lead good people along an
evil path
will fall into their own trap,
but the honest will inherit good things.

11 Rich people may think they are wise,
but a poor person with discernment can
see right through them.

12 When the godly succeed, everyone is glad.
When the wicked take charge, people
go into hiding.

13 People who conceal their sins will not
prosper,
but if they confess and turn from them,
they will receive mercy.

14 Blessed are those who fear to do wrong,
but the stubborn are headed for serious
trouble.

15 A wicked ruler is as dangerous to the poor
as a roaring lion or an attacking bear.

16 A ruler with no understanding will oppress
his people,
but one who hates corruption will have
a long life.

17 A murderer's tormented conscience will
drive him into the grave.
Don't protect him!

18 The blameless will be rescued from harm,
but the crooked will be suddenly
destroyed.

19 A hard worker has plenty of food,
but a person who chases fantasies ends
up in poverty.

20 The trustworthy person will get a rich reward,
but a person who wants quick riches will
get into trouble.

21 Showing partiality is never good,
yet some will do wrong for a mere piece
of bread.

22 Greedy people try to get rich quick
but don't realize they're headed for
poverty.

23 In the end, people appreciate honest criticism
far more than flattery.

24 Anyone who steals from his father and
mother
and says, "What's wrong with that?"
is no better than a murderer.

25 Greed causes fighting;
trusting the LORD leads to prosperity.

26 Those who trust their own insight are foolish,
but anyone who walks in wisdom is safe.

27 Whoever gives to the poor will lack nothing,
but those who close their eyes to poverty
will be cursed.

28 When the wicked take charge, people go
into hiding.
When the wicked meet disaster, the
godly flourish.

CHAPTER 29

1 Whoever stubbornly refuses to accept
criticism
will suddenly be destroyed beyond
recovery.

2 When the godly are in authority, the
people rejoice.
But when the wicked are in power,
they groan.

3 The man who loves wisdom brings joy
to his father,
but if he hangs around with prostitutes,
his wealth is wasted.

4 A just king gives stability to his nation,
but one who demands bribes destroys it.

5 To flatter friends
is to lay a trap for their feet.

6 Evil people are trapped by sin,
but the righteous escape, shouting for joy.

7 The godly care about the rights of the poor;
the wicked don't care at all.

8 Mockers can get a whole town agitated,
but the wise will calm anger.

9 If a wise person takes a fool to court,
there will be ranting and ridicule but no
satisfaction.

10 The bloodthirsty hate blameless people,
but the upright seek to help them.

11 Fools vent their anger,
but the wise quietly hold it back.

12 If a ruler pays attention to liars,
all his advisers will be wicked.

13 The poor and the oppressor have this in common—
the LORD gives sight to the eyes of both.

14 If a king judges the poor fairly,
his throne will last forever.

15 To discipline a child produces wisdom,
but a mother is disgraced by an undisciplined child.

16 When the wicked are in authority, sin flourishes,
but the godly will live to see their downfall.

17 Discipline your children, and they will give you peace of mind
and will make your heart glad.

18 When people do not accept divine guidance, they run wild.
But whoever obeys the law is joyful.

19 Words alone will not discipline a servant;
the words may be understood, but they are not heeded.

20 There is more hope for a fool
than for someone who speaks without thinking.

21 A servant pampered from childhood
will become a rebel.

22 An angry person starts fights;
a hot-tempered person commits all kinds of sin.

23 Pride ends in humiliation,
while humility brings honor.

24 If you assist a thief, you only hurt yourself.
You are sworn to tell the truth, but you dare not testify.

25 Fearing people is a dangerous trap,
but trusting the LORD means safety.

26 Many seek the ruler's favor,
but justice comes from the LORD.

27 The righteous despise the unjust;
the wicked despise the godly.

CHAPTER 30
The Sayings of Agur

The sayings of Agur son of Jakeh contain this message.

I am weary, O God;
I am weary and worn out, O God.
2 I am too stupid to be human,
and I lack common sense.
3 I have not mastered human wisdom,
nor do I know the Holy One.

4 Who but God goes up to heaven and comes back down?
Who holds the wind in his fists?
Who wraps up the oceans in his cloak?
Who has created the whole wide world?
What is his name—and his son's name?
Tell me if you know!

5 Every word of God proves true.
He is a shield to all who come to him for protection.
6 Do not add to his words,
or he may rebuke you and expose you as a liar.

7 O God, I beg two favors from you;
let me have them before I die.
8 First, help me never to tell a lie.
Second, give me neither poverty nor riches!
Give me just enough to satisfy my needs.
9 For if I grow rich, I may deny you and say,
"Who is the LORD?"
And if I am too poor, I may steal and thus insult God's holy name.

10 Never slander a worker to the employer,
or the person will curse you, and you will pay for it.

11 Some people curse their father
and do not thank their mother.
12 They are pure in their own eyes,
but they are filthy and unwashed.
13 They look proudly around,
casting disdainful glances.
14 They have teeth like swords
and fangs like knives.
They devour the poor from the earth
and the needy from among humanity.

15 The leech has two suckers
that cry out, "More, more!"

There are three things that are never satisfied—
no, four that never say, "Enough!":

16 the grave,
the barren womb,
the thirsty desert,
the blazing fire.

17 The eye that mocks a father
and despises a mother's instructions
will be plucked out by ravens of the valley
and eaten by vultures.

18 There are three things that amaze me—
no, four things that I don't understand:
19 how an eagle glides through the sky,
how a snake slithers on a rock,
how a ship navigates the ocean,
how a man loves a woman.

20 An adulterous woman consumes a man,
then wipes her mouth and says, "What's
wrong with that?"

21 There are three things that make the earth
tremble—
no, four it cannot endure:
22 a slave who becomes a king,
an overbearing fool who prospers,
23 a bitter woman who finally gets a
husband,
a servant girl who supplants her mistress.

24 There are four things on earth that are small
but unusually wise:
25 Ants—they aren't strong,
but they store up food all summer.
26 Hyraxes—they aren't powerful,
but they make their homes among the
rocks.
27 Locusts—they have no king,
but they march in formation.
28 Lizards—they are easy to catch,
but they are found even in kings'
palaces.

29 There are three things that walk with
stately stride—
no, four that strut about:
30 the lion, king of animals, who won't turn
aside for anything,
31 the strutting rooster,
the male goat,
a king as he leads his army.

32 If you have been a fool by being proud or
plotting evil,
cover your mouth in shame.

33 As the beating of cream yields butter
and striking the nose causes bleeding,
so stirring up anger causes quarrels.

CHAPTER 31

The Sayings of King Lemuel

The sayings of King Lemuel contain this message, which his mother taught him.

2 O my son, O son of my womb,
O son of my vows,
3 do not waste your strength on women,
on those who ruin kings.

4 It is not for kings, O Lemuel, to guzzle wine.
Rulers should not crave alcohol.
5 For if they drink, they may forget the law
and not give justice to the oppressed.
6 Alcohol is for the dying,
and wine for those in bitter distress.
7 Let them drink to forget their poverty
and remember their troubles no more.

8 Speak up for those who cannot speak for
themselves;
ensure justice for those being crushed.
9 Yes, speak up for the poor and helpless,
and see that they get justice.

A Wife of Noble Character

10 Who can find a virtuous and capable wife?
She is more precious than rubies.
11 Her husband can trust her,
and she will greatly enrich his life.
12 She brings him good, not harm,
all the days of her life.

13 She finds wool and flax
and busily spins it.
14 She is like a merchant's ship,
bringing her food from afar.
15 She gets up before dawn to prepare breakfast
for her household
and plan the day's work for her
servant girls.

16 She goes to inspect a field and buys it;
with her earnings she plants a vineyard.
17 She is energetic and strong,
a hard worker.
18 She makes sure her dealings are profitable;
her lamp burns late into the night.

19 Her hands are busy spinning thread,
her fingers twisting fiber.
20 She extends a helping hand to the poor
and opens her arms to the needy.
21 She has no fear of winter for her household,
for everyone has warm clothes.

22 She makes her own bedspreads.
She dresses in fine linen and purple
gowns.

Proverbs 31 . . . page 644

23 Her husband is well known at the city gates,
where he sits with the other civic leaders.
24 She makes belted linen garments
and sashes to sell to the merchants.

25 She is clothed with strength and dignity,
and she laughs without fear of the future.
26 When she speaks, her words are wise,
and she gives instructions with kindness.
27 She carefully watches everything in her household
and suffers nothing from laziness.

28 Her children stand and bless her.
Her husband praises her:
29 "There are many virtuous and capable women in the world,
but you surpass them all!"

30 Charm is deceptive, and beauty does not last;
but a woman who fears the LORD will be greatly praised.
31 Reward her for all she has done.
Let her deeds publicly declare her praise.

ECCLESiASTES

What's the
Meaning of It All?

Solomon tried hard to find the meaning of life. He looked everywhere and found what it's *not*. In Ecclesiastes, you'll find that the true meaning of life is not found in

- **MONEY**
- **POWER**
- **FAME**
- **YOUTH**
- **FUN**

(But keep reading. Solomon finally figured it out!)

Here It Is! No Wait, It's Over There!

Ever tried to chase a bubble? What happens? Usually it disappears. If you do manage to catch it, it pops. That's what Solomon says it's like trying to find happiness without God. Well, actually he didn't say it was like chasing a bubble. He said it was like chasing something else. **Find out what in Ecclesiastes 2:11; 4:4; 4:16; 6:9...You get the picture.**

Only One Thing Matters!

Solomon was the wisest guy who ever lived (except for Jesus!). He was *super* rich. He had tons of gold and land and horses. But when he got old, he realized that none of that stuff mattered. Only God matters because without God *nothing* matters. **Read exactly how Solomon said it in Ecclesiastes 12:13.**

Hey, What Time Is It?

Did you know there's a time for everything? And I don't mean just soccer practice or school! **See what Solomon said about timing in Ecclesiastes 3:1-8.**

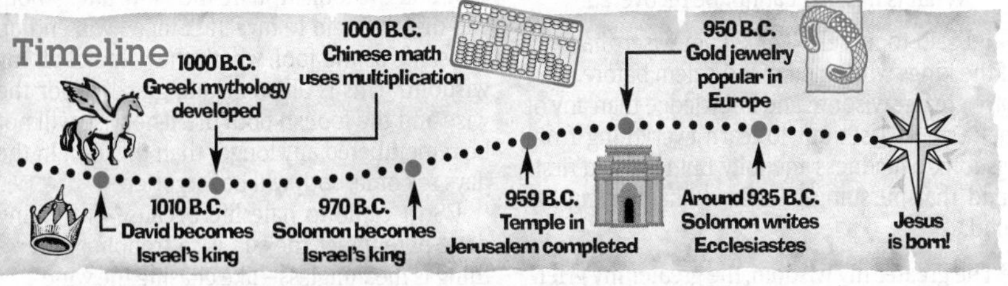
Timeline
1000 B.C. Greek mythology developed
1000 B.C. Chinese math uses multiplication
950 B.C. Gold jewelry popular in Europe
1010 B.C. David becomes Israel's king
970 B.C. Solomon becomes Israel's king
959 B.C. Temple in Jerusalem completed
Around 935 B.C. Solomon writes Ecclesiastes
Jesus is born!

The JESUS CONNECTION

Solomon wrote that all people will have to stand before God to be judged for what they have done. How can we make up for every bad thing we've done—every mean word and thought, every sin? It's impossible! But when we believe in Jesus, we can be forgiven for those bad things we've done. We can stand before God as his forgiven children because Jesus took our punishment on the cross. Jesus provides a way for us to live forever with him in heaven. **All we have to do is believe in Jesus!**

Ecclesiastes 1 . . . page 646

CHAPTER 1

These are the words of the Teacher, King David's son, who ruled in Jerusalem.

Everything Is Meaningless

2"Everything is meaningless," says the Teacher, "completely meaningless!"

3What do people get for all their hard work under the sun? 4Generations come and generations go, but the earth never changes. 5The sun rises and the sun sets, then hurries around to rise again. 6The wind blows south, and then turns north. Around and around it goes, blowing in circles. 7Rivers run into the sea, but the sea is never full. Then the water returns again to the rivers and flows out again to the sea. 8Everything is wearisome beyond description. No matter how much we see, we are never satisfied. No matter how much we hear, we are not content.

9History merely repeats itself. It has all been done before. Nothing under the sun is truly new. 10Sometimes people say, "Here is something new!" But actually it is old; nothing is ever truly new. 11We don't remember what happened in the past, and in future generations, no one will remember what we are doing now.

The Teacher Speaks: The Futility of Wisdom

12I, the Teacher, was king of Israel, and I lived in Jerusalem. 13I devoted myself to search for understanding and to explore by wisdom everything being done under heaven. I soon discovered that God has dealt a tragic existence to the human race. 14I observed everything going on under the sun, and really, it is all meaningless—like chasing the wind.

15 What is wrong cannot be made right.
What is missing cannot be recovered.

16I said to myself, "Look, I am wiser than any of the kings who ruled in Jerusalem before me. I have greater wisdom and knowledge than any of them." 17So I set out to learn everything from wisdom to madness and folly. But I learned firsthand that pursuing all this is like chasing the wind.

18 The greater my wisdom, the greater my grief.
To increase knowledge only increases sorrow.

CHAPTER 2

The Futility of Pleasure

I said to myself, "Come on, let's try pleasure. Let's look for the 'good things' in life." But I found that this, too, was meaningless. 2So I said, "Laughter is silly. What good does it do to seek pleasure?" 3After much thought, I decided to cheer myself with wine. And while still seeking wisdom, I clutched at foolishness. In this way, I tried to experience the only happiness most people find during their brief life in this world.

4I also tried to find meaning by building huge homes for myself and by planting beautiful vineyards. 5I made gardens and parks, filling them with all kinds of fruit trees. 6I built reservoirs to collect the water to irrigate my many flourishing groves. 7I bought slaves, both men and women, and others were born into my household. I also owned large herds and flocks, more than any of the kings who had lived in Jerusalem before me. 8I collected great sums of silver and gold, the treasure of many kings and provinces. I hired wonderful singers, both men and women, and had many beautiful concubines. I had everything a man could desire!

9So I became greater than all who had lived in Jerusalem before me, and my wisdom never failed me. 10Anything I wanted, I would take. I denied myself no pleasure. I even found great pleasure in hard work, a reward for all my labors. 11But as I looked at everything I had worked so hard to accomplish, it was all so meaningless—like chasing the wind. There was nothing really worthwhile anywhere.

The Wise and the Foolish

12So I decided to compare wisdom with foolishness and madness (for who can do this better than I, the king?). 13I thought, "Wisdom is better than foolishness, just as light is better than darkness. 14For the wise can see where they are going, but fools walk in the dark." Yet I saw that the wise and the foolish share the same fate. 15Both will die. So I said to myself, "Since I will end up the same as the fool, what's the value of all my wisdom? This is all so meaningless!" 16For the wise and the foolish both die. The wise will not be remembered any longer than the fool. In the days to come, both will be forgotten.

17So I came to hate life because everything done here under the sun is so troubling. Everything is meaningless—like chasing the wind.

The Futility of Work

18I came to hate all my hard work here on earth, for I must leave to others everything I have earned. 19And who can tell whether my successors will be wise or foolish? Yet they will control everything I have gained by my skill and hard work under the sun. How meaningless! [20]So I gave up in despair, questioning the value of all my hard work in this world.

[21]Some people work wisely with knowledge and skill, then must leave the fruit of their efforts to someone who hasn't worked for it. This, too, is meaningless, a great tragedy. [22]So what do people get in this life for all their hard work and anxiety? [23]Their days of labor are filled with pain and grief; even at night their minds cannot rest. It is all meaningless.

[24]So I decided there is nothing better than to enjoy food and drink and to find satisfaction in work. Then I realized that these pleasures are from the hand of God. [25]For who can eat or enjoy anything apart from him? [26]God gives wisdom, knowledge, and joy to those who please him. But if a sinner becomes wealthy, God takes the wealth away and gives it to those who please him. This, too, is meaningless—like chasing the wind.

CHAPTER 3

A Time for Everything

[1]For everything there is a season,
a time for every activity under heaven.

[2]A time to be born and a time to die.
A time to plant and a time to harvest.
[3]A time to kill and a time to heal.
A time to tear down and a time to build up.
[4]A time to cry and a time to laugh.
A time to grieve and a time to dance.
[5]A time to scatter stones and a time to gather stones.
A time to embrace and a time to turn away.
[6]A time to search and a time to quit searching.
A time to keep and a time to throw away.
[7]A time to tear and a time to mend.
A time to be quiet and a time to speak.
[8]A time to love and a time to hate.
A time for war and a time for peace.

[9]What do people really get for all their hard work? [10]I have seen the burden God has placed on us all. [11]Yet God has made everything beautiful for its own time. He has planted eternity in the human heart, but even so, people cannot see the whole scope of God's work from beginning to end. [12]So I concluded there is nothing better than to be happy and enjoy ourselves as long as we can. [13]And people should eat and drink and enjoy the fruits of their labor, for these are gifts from God.

[14]And I know that whatever God does is final. Nothing can be added to it or taken from it. God's purpose is that people should fear him. [15]What is happening now has happened before, and what will happen in the future has happened before, because God makes the same things happen over and over again.

The Injustices of Life

[16]I also noticed that under the sun there is evil in the courtroom. Yes, even the courts of law are corrupt! [17]I said to myself, "In due season God will judge everyone, both good and bad, for all their deeds."

[18]I also thought about the human condition—how God proves to people that they are like animals. [19]For people and animals share the same fate—both breathe and both must die. So people have no real advantage over the animals. How meaningless! [20]Both go to the same place—they came from dust and they return to dust. [21]For who can prove that the human spirit goes up and the spirit of animals goes down into the earth? [22]So I saw that there is nothing better for people than to be happy in their work. That is our lot in life. And no one can bring us back to see what happens after we die.

CHAPTER 4

Again, I observed all the oppression that takes place under the sun. I saw the tears of the oppressed, with no one to comfort them. The oppressors have great power, and their victims are helpless. [2]So I concluded that the dead are better off than the living. [3]But most fortunate of all are those who are not yet born. For they have not seen all the evil that is done under the sun.

[4]Then I observed that most people are motivated to success because they envy their neighbors. But this, too, is meaningless—like chasing the wind.

[5]"Fools fold their idle hands,
leading them to ruin."

[6]And yet,

"Better to have one handful with quietness
than two handfuls with hard work
and chasing the wind."

The Advantages of Companionship

[7]I observed yet another example of something meaningless under the sun. [8]This is the case of a

man who is all alone, without a child or a brother, yet who works hard to gain as much wealth as he can. But then he asks himself, "Who am I working for? Why am I giving up so much pleasure now?" It is all so meaningless and depressing.

9 Two people are better off than one, for they can help each other succeed. 10 If one person falls, the other can reach out and help. But someone who falls alone is in real trouble. 11 Likewise, two people lying close together can keep each other warm. But how can one be warm alone? **12 A person standing alone can be attacked and defeated, but two can stand back-to-back and conquer. Three are even better, for a triple-braided cord is not easily broken.**

The Futility of Political Power

13 It is better to be a poor but wise youth than an old and foolish king who refuses all advice. 14 Such a youth could rise from poverty and succeed. He might even become king, though he has been in prison. 15 But then everyone rushes to the side of yet another youth who replaces him. 16 Endless crowds stand around him, but then another generation grows up and rejects him, too. So it is all meaningless—like chasing the wind.

CHAPTER 5

Approaching God with Care

As you enter the house of God, keep your ears open and your mouth shut. It is evil to make mindless offerings to God. 2 Don't make rash promises, and don't be hasty in bringing matters before God. After all, God is in heaven, and you are here on earth. So let your words be few.

3 Too much activity gives you restless dreams; too many words make you a fool.

4 When you make a promise to God, don't delay in following through, for God takes no pleasure in fools. Keep all the promises you make to him. 5 It is better to say nothing than to make a promise and not keep it. 6 Don't let your mouth make you sin. And don't defend yourself by telling the Temple messenger that the promise you made was a mistake. That would make God angry, and he might wipe out everything you have achieved.

7 Talk is cheap, like daydreams and other useless activities. Fear God instead.

The Futility of Wealth

8 Don't be surprised if you see a poor person being oppressed by the powerful and if justice is being miscarried throughout the land. For every official is under orders from higher up, and matters of justice get lost in red tape and bureaucracy. 9 Even the king milks the land for his own profit!

10 Those who love money will never have enough. How meaningless to think that wealth brings true happiness! 11 The more you have, the more people come to help you spend it. So what good is wealth—except perhaps to watch it slip through your fingers!

12 People who work hard sleep well, whether they eat little or much. But the rich seldom get a good night's sleep.

13 There is another serious problem I have seen under the sun. Hoarding riches harms the saver. 14 Money is put into risky investments that turn sour, and everything is lost. In the end, there is nothing left to pass on to one's children. 15 We all come to the end of our lives as naked and empty-handed as on the day we were born. We can't take our riches with us.

16 And this, too, is a very serious problem. People leave this world no better off than when they came. All their hard work is for nothing—like working for the wind. 17 Throughout their lives, they live under a cloud—frustrated, discouraged, and angry.

18 Even so, I have noticed one thing, at least, that is good. It is good for people to eat, drink, and enjoy their work under the sun during the short life God has given them, and to accept their lot in life. 19 And it is a good thing to receive wealth from God and the good health to enjoy it. To enjoy your work and accept your lot in life—this is indeed a gift from God. 20 God keeps such people so busy enjoying life that they take no time to brood over the past.

CHAPTER 6

There is another serious tragedy I have seen under the sun, and it weighs heavily on humanity. 2 God gives some people great wealth and honor and everything they could ever want, but then he doesn't give them the chance to enjoy these things. They die, and someone else, even a stranger, ends up enjoying their wealth! This is meaningless—a sickening tragedy.

3 A man might have a hundred children and live to be very old. But if he finds no satisfaction in life and doesn't even get a decent burial, it would have been better for him to be born dead. 4 His birth would have been meaningless, and he would have ended in darkness. He wouldn't even have had a name, 5 and he would never have seen

the sun or known of its existence. Yet he would
have had more peace than in growing up to be
an unhappy man. 6 He might live a thousand
years twice over but still not find contentment.
And since he must die like everyone else—well,
what's the use?
7 All people spend their lives scratching for
food, but they never seem to have enough. 8 So
are wise people really better off than fools? Do
poor people gain anything by being wise and
knowing how to act in front of others?
9 Enjoy what you have rather than desiring
what you don't have. Just dreaming about nice
things is meaningless—like chasing the wind.

The Future—Determined and Unknown

10 Everything has already been decided. It was
known long ago what each person would be.
So there's no use arguing with God about your
destiny.
11 The more words you speak, the less they
mean. So what good are they?
12 In the few days of our meaningless lives,
who knows how our days can best be spent? Our
lives are like a shadow. Who can tell what will
happen on this earth after we are gone?

CHAPTER 7

Wisdom for Life

1 A good reputation is more valuable than
costly perfume.
And the day you die is better than the day
you are born.
2 Better to spend your time at funerals than
at parties.
After all, everyone dies—
so the living should take this to heart.
3 Sorrow is better than laughter,
for sadness has a refining influence
on us.
4 A wise person thinks a lot about death,
while a fool thinks only about having
a good time.

5 Better to be criticized by a wise person
than to be praised by a fool.
6 A fool's laughter is quickly gone,
like thorns crackling in a fire.
This also is meaningless.

7 Extortion turns wise people into fools,
and bribes corrupt the heart.

8 Finishing is better than starting.
Patience is better than pride.

9 Control your temper,
for anger labels you a fool.

10 Don't long for "the good old days."
This is not wise.

11 Wisdom is even better when you have
money.
Both are a benefit as you go through
life.
12 Wisdom and money can get you almost
anything,
but only wisdom can save your life.

13 Accept the way God does things,
for who can straighten what he has made
crooked?
14 Enjoy prosperity while you can,
but when hard times strike, realize that
both come from God.
Remember that nothing is certain in
this life.

The Limits of Human Wisdom

15 I have seen everything in this meaningless life,
including the death of good young people and
the long life of wicked people. 16 So don't be too
good or too wise! Why destroy yourself? 17 On
the other hand, don't be too wicked either. Don't
be a fool! Why die before your time? 18 Pay attention to these instructions, for anyone who fears
God will avoid both extremes.
19 One wise person is stronger than ten leading
citizens of a town!
20 Not a single person on earth is always good
and never sins.
21 Don't eavesdrop on others—you may hear
your servant curse you. 22 For you know how
often you yourself have cursed others.
23 I have always tried my best to let wisdom
guide my thoughts and actions. I said to myself,
"I am determined to be wise." But it didn't work.
24 Wisdom is always distant and difficult to find.
25 I searched everywhere, determined to find
wisdom and to understand the reason for
things. I was determined to prove to myself that
wickedness is stupid and that foolishness is
madness.
26 I discovered that a seductive woman is a trap
more bitter than death. Her passion is a snare,
and her soft hands are chains. Those who are
pleasing to God will escape her, but sinners will
be caught in her snare.
27 "This is my conclusion," says the Teacher.
"I discovered this after looking at the matter
from every possible angle. 28 Though I have

searched repeatedly, I have not found what I was
looking for. Only one out of a thousand men is
virtuous, but not one woman! 29But I did find
this: God created people to be virtuous, but they
have each turned to follow their own downward
path."

CHAPTER 8

1 How wonderful to be wise,
to analyze and interpret things.
Wisdom lights up a person's face,
softening its harshness.

Obedience to the King

2Obey the king since you vowed to God that you
would. 3Don't try to avoid doing your duty, and
don't stand with those who plot evil, for the king
can do whatever he wants. 4His command is
backed by great power. No one can resist or
question it. 5Those who obey him will not be
punished. Those who are wise will find a time
and a way to do what is right, 6for there is a time
and a way for everything, even when a person is
in trouble.

7Indeed, how can people avoid what they
don't know is going to happen? 8None of us can
hold back our spirit from departing. None of us
has the power to prevent the day of our death.
There is no escaping that obligation, that dark
battle. And in the face of death, wickedness will
certainly not rescue the wicked.

The Wicked and the Righteous

9I have thought deeply about all that goes on
here under the sun, where people have the power
to hurt each other. 10I have seen wicked people
buried with honor. Yet they were the very ones
who frequented the Temple and are now praised
in the same city where they committed their
crimes! This, too, is meaningless. 11When a
crime is not punished quickly, people feel it is
safe to do wrong. 12But even though a person
sins a hundred times and still lives a long time, I
know that those who fear God will be better off.
13The wicked will not prosper, for they do not
fear God. Their days will never grow long like the
evening shadows.

14And this is not all that is meaningless in our
world. In this life, good people are often treated
as though they were wicked, and wicked people
are often treated as though they were good. This
is so meaningless!

15So I recommend having fun, because there
is nothing better for people in this world than to
eat, drink, and enjoy life. That way they will experience some happiness along with all the hard
work God gives them under the sun.

16In my search for wisdom and in my observation of people's burdens here on earth, I discovered that there is ceaseless activity, day and night.
17I realized that no one can discover everything
God is doing under the sun. Not even the wisest
people discover everything, no matter what they
claim.

CHAPTER 9

Death Comes to All

This, too, I carefully explored: Even though the
actions of godly and wise people are in God's
hands, no one knows whether God will show
them favor. 2The same destiny ultimately awaits
everyone, whether righteous or wicked, good or
bad, ceremonially clean or unclean, religious or
irreligious. Good people receive the same treatment as sinners, and people who make promises
to God are treated like people who don't.

3It seems so wrong that everyone under the
sun suffers the same fate. Already twisted by
evil, people choose their own mad course, for
they have no hope. There is nothing ahead but
death anyway. 4There is hope only for the living.
As they say, "It's better to be a live dog than a
dead lion!"

5The living at least know they will die, but the
dead know nothing. They have no further reward, nor are they remembered. 6Whatever they
did in their lifetime—loving, hating, envying—is
all long gone. They no longer play a part in anything here on earth. 7So go ahead. Eat your food
with joy, and drink your wine with a happy heart,
for God approves of this! 8Wear fine clothes,
with a splash of cologne!

9Live happily with the woman you love
through all the meaningless days of life that God
has given you under the sun. The wife God gives
you is your reward for all your earthly toil.
10Whatever you do, do well. For when you go to
the grave, there will be no work or planning or
knowledge or wisdom.

11I have observed something else under the
sun. The fastest runner doesn't always win the
race, and the strongest warrior doesn't always
win the battle. The wise sometimes go hungry,
and the skillful are not necessarily wealthy. And
those who are educated don't always lead successful lives. It is all decided by chance, by being
in the right place at the right time.

12People can never predict when hard times
might come. Like fish in a net or birds in a trap,
people are caught by sudden tragedy.

FUN-fact

Books of Wisdom

There are five books in the Bible called wisdom books

1. JOB
2. PSALMS
3. PROVERBS
4. ECCLESIASTES
5. SONG OF SONGS

Each one of the books talks about a different part of being wise. **JOB** reminds us that we don't know the reasons for everything but we can always trust God. The book of **PSALMS** teaches us how to praise and worship God. **PROVERBS** tells us to respect God and to pay attention to his rules. **ECCLESIASTES** teaches us that we can't ever really be happy without God. The **SONG OF SONGS** teaches us how to be wise about marriage.

Think of one thing *you* think is important for everyone to know about God. Now write a song about that fact to the tune of "Three Blind Mice."

GOT IT? Now gather a group of friends or family members, and teach them your song. You'll be passing on a little bit of wisdom yourself!

Thoughts on Wisdom and Folly

13 Here is another bit of wisdom that has impressed me as I have watched the way our world
works. 14 There was a small town with only a few
people, and a great king came with his army and
besieged it. 15 A poor, wise man knew how to save
the town, and so it was rescued. But afterward no
one thought to thank him. 16 So even though wisdom is better than strength, those who are wise
will be despised if they are poor. What they say
will not be appreciated for long.

17 Better to hear the quiet words of a wise person
than the shouts of a foolish king.

18 Better to have wisdom than weapons of war,
but one sinner can destroy much that is good.

CHAPTER 10

1 As dead flies cause even a bottle of perfume to stink,
so a little foolishness spoils great wisdom and honor.

2 A wise person chooses the right road;
a fool takes the wrong one.

3 You can identify fools
just by the way they walk down the street!

4 If your boss is angry at you, don't quit!
A quiet spirit can overcome even great mistakes.

The Ironies of Life

5 There is another evil I have seen under the sun.
Kings and rulers make a grave mistake 6 when
they give great authority to foolish people and
low positions to people of proven worth. 7 I have
even seen servants riding horseback like
princes—and princes walking like servants!

8 When you dig a well,
you might fall in.
When you demolish an old wall,
you could be bitten by a snake.

9 When you work in a quarry,
stones might fall and crush you.
When you chop wood,
there is danger with each stroke of your ax.

10 Using a dull ax requires great strength,
so sharpen the blade.
That's the value of wisdom;
it helps you succeed.

11 If a snake bites before you charm it,
what's the use of being a snake charmer?

12 Wise words bring approval,
but fools are destroyed by their own words.

13 Fools base their thoughts on foolish assumptions,
so their conclusions will be wicked madness;
14 they chatter on and on.

No one really knows what is going to happen;
no one can predict the future.

15 Fools are so exhausted by a little work
that they can't even find their way home.

16 What sorrow for the land ruled by a servant,
the land whose leaders feast in the morning.

17 Happy is the land whose king is a noble leader
and whose leaders feast at the proper time
to gain strength for their work, not to get drunk.

18 Laziness leads to a sagging roof;
idleness leads to a leaky house.

19 A party gives laughter,
wine gives happiness,
and money gives everything!

20 Never make light of the king, even in your thoughts.
And don't make fun of the powerful, even in your own bedroom.
For a little bird might deliver your message
and tell them what you said.

CHAPTER 11

The Uncertainties of Life

1 Send your grain across the seas,
and in time, profits will flow back to you.
2 But divide your investments among many places,
for you do not know what risks might lie ahead.

3 When clouds are heavy, the rains come down.
Whether a tree falls north or south,
it stays where it falls.

4 Farmers who wait for perfect weather never plant.
If they watch every cloud, they never harvest.

5 Just as you cannot understand the path of the
wind or the mystery of a tiny baby growing in its
mother's womb, so you cannot understand the
activity of God, who does all things.
6 Plant your seed in the morning and keep
busy all afternoon, for you don't know if profit
will come from one activity or another—or
maybe both.

Advice for Young and Old

7 Light is sweet; how pleasant to see a new day
dawning.
8 When people live to be very old, let them
rejoice in every day of life. But let them also remember there will be many dark days. Everything still to come is meaningless.
9 Young people, it's wonderful to be young! Enjoy every minute of it. Do everything you want to
do; take it all in. But remember that you must
give an account to God for everything you do.
10 So refuse to worry, and keep your body healthy.
But remember that youth, with a whole life before you, is meaningless.

CHAPTER 12

Don't let the excitement of youth cause you to
forget your Creator. Honor him in your youth before you grow old and say, "Life is not pleasant
anymore." 2 Remember him before the light of
the sun, moon, and stars is dim to your old eyes,
and rain clouds continually darken your sky. 3 Remember him before your legs—the guards of
your house—start to tremble; and before your
shoulders—the strong men—stoop. Remember
him before your teeth—your few remaining servants—stop grinding; and before your eyes—the
women looking through the windows—see
dimly.
4 Remember him before the door to life's
opportunities is closed and the sound of work
fades. Now you rise at the first chirping of
the birds, but then all their sounds will grow
faint.
5 Remember him before you become fearful
of falling and worry about danger in the streets;
before your hair turns white like an almond tree
in bloom, and you drag along without energy
like a dying grasshopper, and the caperberry no
longer inspires sexual desire. Remember him
before you near the grave, your everlasting
home, when the mourners will weep at your
funeral.
6 Yes, remember your Creator now while you
are young, before the silver cord of life snaps

and the golden bowl is broken. Don't wait until
the water jar is smashed at the spring and the
pulley is broken at the well. 7For then the dust
will return to the earth, and the spirit will return
to God who gave it.

Concluding Thoughts about the Teacher

8"Everything is meaningless," says the Teacher,
"completely meaningless."

9Keep this in mind: The Teacher was considered wise, and he taught the people everything
he knew. He listened carefully to many proverbs,
studying and classifying them. 10The Teacher
sought to find just the right words to express
truths clearly.

11The words of the wise are like cattle prods—
painful but helpful. Their collected sayings are
like a nail-studded stick with which a shepherd
drives the sheep.

12But, my child, let me give you some further
advice: Be careful, for writing books is endless,
and much study wears you out.

13That's the whole story. Here now is my final
conclusion: Fear God and obey his commands,
for this is everyone's duty. 14God will judge us for
everything we do, including every secret thing,
whether good or bad.

SONG OF SONGS A Love Story

Song of Songs is a book about love and marriage. It was written by King Solomon and tells about

- **THE POWER OF LOVE**
- **A BEAUTIFUL BRIDE**
- **A HAPPY MARRIAGE**
- **SOME WEIRD WORDS OF PRAISE**

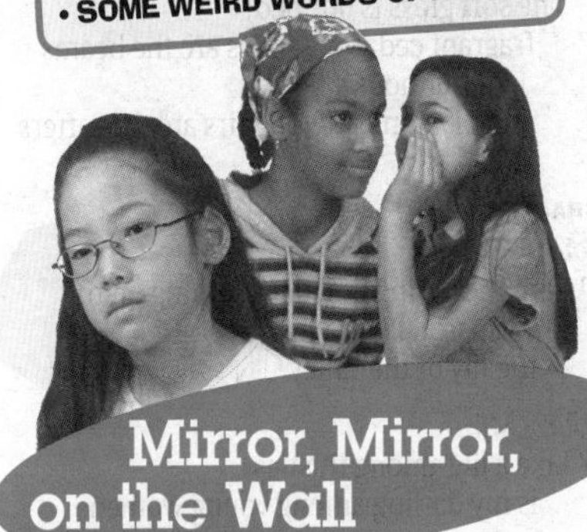

Mirror, Mirror, on the Wall

Have you ever felt funny or worried about the way you look? Well, you're not alone! The woman Solomon courted and later married was worried about the way she looked. Read what she said about herself in Song of Songs 1:6. But guess what? Solomon loved her just the way she was.

So the next time you look in the mirror, don't worry about how you look on the outside. Think about what you're like on the inside!

Just Married!

Love and Marriage

Man...were those two ever in love! Solomon and his wife, that is.

God intends the love between a husband and wife to be special. Do you know two people who have been married for a long time? Ask them about the time they first met!

My Teeth Are What?!

OK, things were a little bit different back when Solomon was living. Read a few of the compliments he gave to his bride. Check out Song of Songs 6:4-6. Her teeth were like newly washed sheep? Yikes! Sounds kind of silly!

Think of some words to describe people we think are beautiful today. Our words would probably sound silly to Solomon, don't you think?

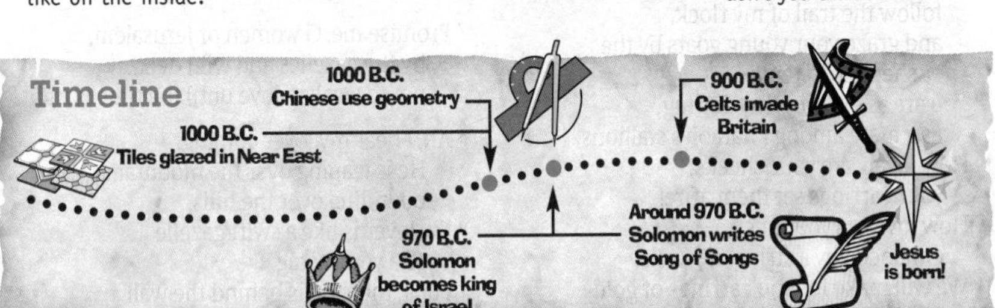
Timeline
1000 B.C. Chinese use geometry
1000 B.C. Tiles glazed in Near East
900 B.C. Celts invade Britain
970 B.C. Solomon becomes king of Israel
Around 970 B.C. Solomon writes Song of Songs
Jesus is born!

The JESUS CONNECTION

In the New Testament, Paul shows how marriage represents the relationship between Jesus and the church. Many people have thought that Song of Songs is actually more about Jesus' love for the church than it is about Solomon's love for his bride. **Whichever way you look at it, this book is all about love, and love describes Jesus perfectly!**

Song of Songs 1 . . . page 656

CHAPTER 1

This is Solomon's song of songs, more wonderful than any other.

Young Woman

2 Kiss me and kiss me again,
for your love is sweeter than wine.
3 How fragrant your cologne;
your name is like its spreading fragrance.
No wonder all the young women love you!
4 Take me with you; come, let's run!
The king has brought me into his bedroom.

Young Women of Jerusalem

How happy we are for you, O king.
We praise your love even more than wine.

Young Woman

How right they are to adore you.

5 I am dark but beautiful,
O women of Jerusalem—
dark as the tents of Kedar,
dark as the curtains of Solomon's tents.
6 Don't stare at me because I am dark—
the sun has darkened my skin.
My brothers were angry with me;
they forced me to care for their vineyards,
so I couldn't care for myself—my own vineyard.

7 Tell me, my love, where are you leading your flock today?
Where will you rest your sheep at noon?
For why should I wander like a prostitute
among your friends and their flocks?

Young Man

8 If you don't know, O most beautiful woman,
follow the trail of my flock,
and graze your young goats by the shepherds' tents.
9 You are as exciting, my darling,
as a mare among Pharaoh's stallions.
10 How lovely are your cheeks;
your earrings set them afire!
How lovely is your neck,
enhanced by a string of jewels.
11 We will make for you earrings of gold
and beads of silver.

Young Woman

12 The king is lying on his couch,
enchanted by the fragrance of my perfume.
13 My lover is like a sachet of myrrh
lying between my breasts.
14 He is like a bouquet of sweet henna blossoms
from the vineyards of En-gedi.

Young Man

15 How beautiful you are, my darling,
how beautiful!
Your eyes are like doves.

Young Woman

16 You are so handsome, my love,
pleasing beyond words!
The soft grass is our bed;
17 fragrant cedar branches are the beams of our house,
and pleasant smelling firs are the rafters.

CHAPTER 2

Young Woman

1 I am the spring crocus blooming on the Sharon Plain,
the lily of the valley.

Young Man

2 Like a lily among thistles
is my darling among young women.

Young Woman

3 Like the finest apple tree in the orchard
is my lover among other young men.
I sit in his delightful shade
and taste his delicious fruit.
4 He escorts me to the banquet hall;
it's obvious how much he loves me.
5 Strengthen me with raisin cakes,
refresh me with apples,
for I am weak with love.
6 His left arm is under my head,
and his right arm embraces me.

7 Promise me, O women of Jerusalem,
by the gazelles and wild deer,
not to awaken love until the time is right.

8 Ah, I hear my lover coming!
He is leaping over the mountains,
bounding over the hills.
9 My lover is like a swift gazelle
or a young stag.
Look, there he is behind the wall,
looking through the window,
peering into the room.

10 My lover said to me,
"Rise up, my darling!
Come away with me, my fair one!
11 Look, the winter is past,
and the rains are over and gone.

12 The flowers are springing up,
the season of singing birds has come,
and the cooing of turtledoves fills the air.
13 The fig trees are forming young fruit,
and the fragrant grapevines are blossoming.
Rise up, my darling!
Come away with me, my fair one!"

Young Man

14 My dove is hiding behind the rocks,
behind an outcrop on the cliff.
Let me see your face;
let me hear your voice.
For your voice is pleasant,
and your face is lovely.

Young Women of Jerusalem

15 Catch all the foxes,
those little foxes,
before they ruin the vineyard of love,
for the grapevines are blossoming!

Young Woman

16 My lover is mine, and I am his.
He browses among the lilies.
17 Before the dawn breezes blow
and the night shadows flee,
return to me, my love, like a gazelle
or a young stag on the rugged mountains.

CHAPTER 3

Young Woman

1 One night as I lay in bed, I yearned for my lover.
I yearned for him, but he did not come.
2 So I said to myself, "I will get up and roam the city,
searching in all its streets and squares.
I will search for the one I love."
So I searched everywhere but did not find him.
3 The watchmen stopped me as they made their rounds,
and I asked, "Have you seen the one I love?"
4 Then scarcely had I left them
when I found my love!
I caught and held him tightly,
then I brought him to my mother's house,
into my mother's bed, where I had been conceived.
5 Promise me, O women of Jerusalem,
by the gazelles and wild deer,
not to awaken love until the time is right.

Young Women of Jerusalem

6 Who is this sweeping in from the wilderness
like a cloud of smoke?
Who is it, fragrant with myrrh and frankincense
and every kind of spice?
7 Look, it is Solomon's carriage,
surrounded by sixty heroic men,
the best of Israel's soldiers.
8 They are all skilled swordsmen,
experienced warriors.
Each wears a sword on his thigh,
ready to defend the king against an attack in the night.
9 King Solomon's carriage is built
of wood imported from Lebanon.
10 Its posts are silver,
its canopy gold;
its cushions are purple.
It was decorated with love
by the young women of Jerusalem.

Young Woman

11 Come out to see King Solomon,
young women of Jerusalem.
He wears the crown his mother gave him
on his wedding day,
his most joyous day.

CHAPTER 4

Young Man

1 You are beautiful, my darling,
beautiful beyond words.
Your eyes are like doves
behind your veil.
Your hair falls in waves,
like a flock of goats winding down the slopes of Gilead.
2 Your teeth are as white as sheep,
recently shorn and freshly washed.
Your smile is flawless,
each tooth matched with its twin.
3 Your lips are like scarlet ribbon;
your mouth is inviting.
Your cheeks are like rosy pomegranates
behind your veil.
4 Your neck is as beautiful as the tower of David,
jeweled with the shields of a thousand heroes.
5 Your breasts are like two fawns,
twin fawns of a gazelle grazing among the lilies.
6 Before the dawn breezes blow
and the night shadows flee,

I will hurry to the mountain of myrrh
and to the hill of frankincense.
7 You are altogether beautiful, my darling,
beautiful in every way.

8 Come with me from Lebanon, my bride,
come with me from Lebanon.
Come down from Mount Amana,
from the peaks of Senir and Hermon,
where the lions have their dens
and leopards live among the hills.

9 You have captured my heart,
my treasure, my bride.
You hold it hostage with one glance
of your eyes,
with a single jewel of your necklace.
10 Your love delights me,
my treasure, my bride.
Your love is better than wine,
your perfume more fragrant than
spices.
11 Your lips are as sweet as nectar, my bride.
Honey and milk are under your tongue.
Your clothes are scented
like the cedars of Lebanon.

12 You are my private garden, my treasure,
my bride,
a secluded spring, a hidden fountain.
13 Your thighs shelter a paradise of
pomegranates
with rare spices—
henna with nard,
14 nard and saffron,
fragrant calamus and cinnamon,
with all the trees of frankincense, myrrh, and
fragrant aloes,
and every other lovely spice.
15 You are a garden fountain,
a well of fresh water
streaming down from Lebanon's
mountains.

Young Woman

16 Awake, north wind!
Rise up, south wind!
Blow on my garden
and spread its fragrance all around.
Come into your garden, my love;
taste its finest fruits.

CHAPTER 5

Young Man

1 I have entered my garden, my treasure,
my bride!
I gather myrrh with my spices
and eat honeycomb with my honey.
I drink wine with my milk.

Young Women of Jerusalem

Oh, lover and beloved, eat and drink!
Yes, drink deeply of your love!

Young Woman

2 I slept, but my heart was awake,
when I heard my lover knocking and
calling:
"Open to me, my treasure, my darling,
my dove, my perfect one.
My head is drenched with dew,
my hair with the dampness of the night."

3 But I responded,
"I have taken off my robe.
Should I get dressed again?
I have washed my feet.
Should I get them soiled?"

4 My lover tried to unlatch the door,
and my heart thrilled within me.
5 I jumped up to open the door for my love,
and my hands dripped with perfume.
My fingers dripped with lovely myrrh
as I pulled back the bolt.
6 I opened to my lover,
but he was gone!
My heart sank.
I searched for him
but could not find him anywhere.
I called to him,
but there was no reply.
7 The night watchmen found me
as they made their rounds.
They beat and bruised me
and stripped off my veil,
those watchmen on the walls.

8 Make this promise, O women of Jerusalem—
If you find my lover,
tell him I am weak with love.

Young Women of Jerusalem

9 Why is your lover better than all others,
O woman of rare beauty?
What makes your lover so special
that we must promise this?

Young Woman

10 My lover is dark and dazzling,
better than ten thousand others!
11 His head is finest gold,
his wavy hair is black as a raven.
12 His eyes sparkle like doves
beside springs of water;

they are set like jewels
washed in milk.
13 His cheeks are like gardens of spices
giving off fragrance.
His lips are like lilies,
perfumed with myrrh.
14 His arms are like rounded bars of gold,
set with beryl.
His body is like bright ivory,
glowing with lapis lazuli.
15 His legs are like marble pillars
set in sockets of finest gold.
His posture is stately,
like the noble cedars of Lebanon.
16 His mouth is sweetness itself;
he is desirable in every way.
Such, O women of Jerusalem,
is my lover, my friend.

CHAPTER 6

Young Women of Jerusalem

1 Where has your lover gone,
O woman of rare beauty?
Which way did he turn
so we can help you find him?

Young Woman

2 My lover has gone down to his garden,
to his spice beds,
to browse in the gardens
and gather the lilies.
3 I am my lover's, and my lover is mine.
He browses among the lilies.

Young Man

4 You are beautiful, my darling,
like the lovely city of Tirzah.
Yes, as beautiful as Jerusalem,
as majestic as an army with billowing
banners.
5 Turn your eyes away,
for they overpower me.
Your hair falls in waves,
like a flock of goats winding down the
slopes of Gilead.
6 Your teeth are as white as sheep
that are freshly washed.
Your smile is flawless,
each tooth matched with its twin.
7 Your cheeks are like rosy pomegranates
behind your veil.
8 Even among sixty queens
and eighty concubines
and countless young women,
9 I would still choose my dove, my perfect one—
the favorite of her mother,
dearly loved by the one who bore her.
The young women see her and praise her;
even queens and royal concubines sing
her praises:
10 "Who is this, arising like the dawn,
as fair as the moon,
as bright as the sun,
as majestic as an army with billowing
banners?"

Young Woman

11 I went down to the grove of walnut trees
and out to the valley to see the new spring
growth,
to see whether the grapevines had budded
or the pomegranates were in bloom.
12 Before I realized it,
my strong desires had taken me to the
chariot of a noble man.

Young Women of Jerusalem

13 Return, return to us, O maid of Shulam.
Come back, come back, that we may see
you again.

Young Man

Why do you stare at this young woman
of Shulam,
as she moves so gracefully between two
lines of dancers?

CHAPTER 7

1 How beautiful are your sandaled feet,
O queenly maiden.
Your rounded thighs are like jewels,
the work of a skilled craftsman.
2 Your navel is perfectly formed
like a goblet filled with mixed wine.
Between your thighs lies a mound of
wheat
bordered with lilies.
3 Your breasts are like two fawns,
twin fawns of a gazelle.
4 Your neck is as beautiful as an ivory tower.
Your eyes are like the sparkling pools in
Heshbon
by the gate of Bath-rabbim.
Your nose is as fine as the tower of Lebanon
overlooking Damascus.
5 Your head is as majestic as Mount Carmel,
and the sheen of your hair radiates royalty.
The king is held captive by its tresses.
6 Oh, how beautiful you are!
How pleasing, my love, how full of
delights!

7 You are slender like a palm tree,
and your breasts are like its clusters of fruit.
8 I said, "I will climb the palm tree
and take hold of its fruit."
May your breasts be like grape clusters,
and the fragrance of your breath like apples.
9 May your kisses be as exciting as the best wine—

Young Woman

Yes, wine that goes down smoothly for my lover,
flowing gently over lips and teeth.
10 I am my lover's,
and he claims me as his own.
11 Come, my love, let us go out to the fields
and spend the night among the wildflowers.
12 Let us get up early and go to the vineyards
to see if the grapevines have budded,
if the blossoms have opened,
and if the pomegranates have bloomed.
There I will give you my love.
13 There the mandrakes give off their fragrance,
and the finest fruits are at our door,
new delights as well as old,
which I have saved for you, my lover.

CHAPTER 8

Young Woman

1 Oh, I wish you were my brother,
who nursed at my mother's breasts.
Then I could kiss you no matter who was watching,
and no one would criticize me.
2 I would bring you to my childhood home,
and there you would teach me.
I would give you spiced wine to drink,
my sweet pomegranate wine.
3 Your left arm would be under my head,
and your right arm would embrace me.

4 Promise me, O women of Jerusalem,
not to awaken love until the time is right.

Young Women of Jerusalem

5 Who is this sweeping in from the desert,
leaning on her lover?

Young Woman

I aroused you under the apple tree,
where your mother gave you birth,
where in great pain she delivered you.
6 Place me like a seal over your heart,
like a seal on your arm.
For love is as strong as death,
its jealousy as enduring as the grave.
Love flashes like fire,
the brightest kind of flame.
7 Many waters cannot quench love,
nor can rivers drown it.
If a man tried to buy love
with all his wealth,
his offer would be utterly scorned.

The Young Woman's Brothers

8 We have a little sister
too young to have breasts.
What will we do for our sister
if someone asks to marry her?
9 If she is a virgin, like a wall,
we will protect her with a silver tower.
But if she is promiscuous, like a swinging door,
we will block her door with a cedar bar.

Young Woman

10 I was a virgin, like a wall;
now my breasts are like towers.
When my lover looks at me,
he is delighted with what he sees.

11 Solomon has a vineyard at Baal-hamon,
which he leases out to tenant farmers.
Each of them pays a thousand pieces of silver
for harvesting its fruit.
12 But my vineyard is mine to give,
and Solomon need not pay a thousand pieces of silver.
But I will give two hundred pieces
to those who care for its vines.

Young Man

13 O my darling, lingering in the gardens,
your companions are fortunate to hear your voice.
Let me hear it, too!

Young Woman

14 Come away, my love! Be like a gazelle
or a young stag on the mountains of spices.

ISAIAH The Greatest Prophet

Look for 3 hidden messages in Isaiah!

The book of Isaiah is full of words of wisdom. It tells of

- **WARNINGS TO THE WICKED**
- **WASHING AWAY OF SINS**
- **WONDERS TO COME**
- **A WONDERFUL COUNSELOR**

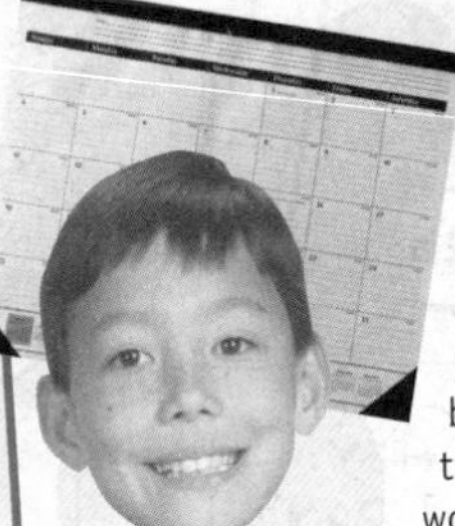

A Sign for the Times

Over seven hundred years before Jesus was born, Isaiah told what the sign of his birth would be.

Discover the sign for yourself in Isaiah 7:14.

Snow White

OK, not the movie! Isaiah was talking about a promise God made. **That promise applies to you, too, so read Isaiah 1:18-19 for the details!**

Fit for a King

Jesus had special names even before he was born! **Find out what they were in Isaiah 9:6.**

Boot Camp Blues?

Thinking of joining the military?

Well, that won't be necessary in the future. **Find out why in Isaiah 2:2-4.**

A New Zoo

Put a wolf and a lamb together, and what do you think will happen? How about cattle and bears? calves and lions? (It's not what you think!) **Read Isaiah 11:1-9 to see what really will happen someday.**

BEFORE

Flying High

Feeling tired? discouraged? like you just can't make it? Just wait awhile. Why? **Turn to Isaiah 40:27-31 to find out!**

AFTER!

HEY! I DON'T NEED YOU!

MY SINS

No Foolin'!

The people in Jerusalem thought they could fool God. No way! God set them straight with some straight talk. **See what he said in Isaiah 29:13-16!**

Suffering Servant

How could Isaiah possibly describe *exactly* what would happen to Jesus hundreds and hundreds of years before it happened? It's just the coolest thing! **Don't believe it? Better read Isaiah 53!**

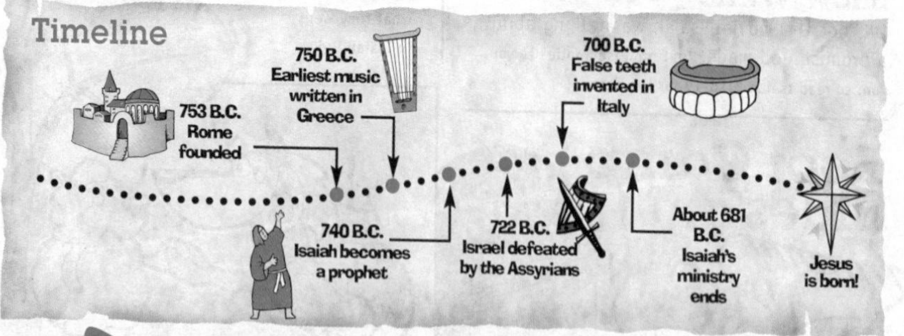

Timeline
753 B.C. Rome founded
750 B.C. Earliest music written in Greece
740 B.C. Isaiah becomes a prophet
722 B.C. Israel defeated by the Assyrians
700 B.C. False teeth invented in Italy
About 681 B.C. Isaiah's ministry ends
Jesus is born!

The JESUS CONNECTION

Isaiah's prophecies about Jesus are amazing! He described Jesus' birth, his name, his ministry, his death on the cross, his resurrection, and how he'll come again to rule forever. God spoke through Isaiah to give people hope and comfort because Jesus, the Messiah, was coming.

We have hope and comfort because we know that Jesus came once and that he's coming again!

CHAPTER 1
These are the visions that Isaiah son of Amoz saw concerning Judah and Jerusalem. He saw these visions during the years when Uzziah, Jotham, Ahaz, and Hezekiah were kings of Judah.

A Message for Rebellious Judah

2 Listen, O heavens! Pay attention, earth!
This is what the LORD says:
"The children I raised and cared for
have rebelled against me.
3 Even an ox knows its owner,
and a donkey recognizes its master's care—
but Israel doesn't know its master.
My people don't recognize my care for them."
4 Oh, what a sinful nation they are—
loaded down with a burden of guilt.
They are evil people,
corrupt children who have rejected the LORD.
They have despised the Holy One of Israel
and turned their backs on him.

5 Why do you continue to invite punishment?
Must you rebel forever?
Your head is injured,
and your heart is sick.
6 You are battered from head to foot—
covered with bruises, welts, and infected wounds—
without any soothing ointments or bandages.
7 Your country lies in ruins,
and your towns are burned.
Foreigners plunder your fields before your eyes
and destroy everything they see.
8 Beautiful Jerusalem stands abandoned
like a watchman's shelter in a vineyard,
like a lean-to in a cucumber field after the harvest,
like a helpless city under siege.
9 If the LORD of Heaven's Armies
had not spared a few of us,
we would have been wiped out like Sodom,
destroyed like Gomorrah.

10 Listen to the LORD, you leaders of "Sodom."
Listen to the law of our God, people of "Gomorrah."
11 "What makes you think I want all your sacrifices?"
says the LORD.
"I am sick of your burnt offerings of rams
and the fat of fattened cattle.
I get no pleasure from the blood
of bulls and lambs and goats.
12 When you come to worship me,
who asked you to parade through my courts with all your ceremony?
13 Stop bringing me your meaningless gifts;
the incense of your offerings disgusts me!
As for your celebrations of the new moon and the Sabbath
and your special days for fasting—
they are all sinful and false.
I want no more of your pious meetings.
14 I hate your new moon celebrations and your annual festivals.
They are a burden to me. I cannot stand them!
15 When you lift up your hands in prayer,
I will not look.
Though you offer many prayers, I will not listen,
for your hands are covered with the blood of innocent victims.
16 Wash yourselves and be clean!
Get your sins out of my sight.
Give up your evil ways.
17 Learn to do good.
Seek justice.
Help the oppressed.
Defend the cause of orphans.
Fight for the rights of widows.

18 "Come now, let's settle this,"
says the LORD.
"Though your sins are like scarlet,
I will make them as white as snow.
Though they are red like crimson,
I will make them as white as wool.
19 If you will only obey me,
you will have plenty to eat.
20 But if you turn away and refuse to listen,
you will be devoured by the sword of your enemies.
I, the LORD, have spoken!"

Unfaithful Jerusalem

21 See how Jerusalem, once so faithful,
has become a prostitute.
Once the home of justice and righteousness,
she is now filled with murderers.
22 Once like pure silver,
you have become like worthless slag.
Once so pure,
you are now like watered-down wine.

23 Your leaders are rebels,
the companions of thieves.
All of them love bribes
and demand payoffs,
but they refuse to defend the cause
of orphans
or fight for the rights of widows.

24 Therefore, the Lord, the LORD of Heaven's
Armies,
the Mighty One of Israel, says,
"I will take revenge on my enemies
and pay back my foes!
25 I will raise my fist against you.
I will melt you down and skim off
your slag.
I will remove all your impurities.
26 Then I will give you good judges again
and wise counselors like you used
to have.
Then Jerusalem will again be called the
Home of Justice
and the Faithful City."
27 Zion will be restored by justice;
those who repent will be revived by
righteousness.
28 But rebels and sinners will be completely
destroyed,
and those who desert the LORD will
be consumed.

29 You will be ashamed of your idol worship
in groves of sacred oaks.
You will blush because you worshiped
in gardens dedicated to idols.
30 You will be like a great tree with withered
leaves,
like a garden without water.
31 The strongest among you will disappear
like straw;
their evil deeds will be the spark that sets
it on fire.
They and their evil works will burn up
together,
and no one will be able to put out the fire.

CHAPTER 2

The LORD's Future Reign

This is a vision that Isaiah son of Amoz saw concerning Judah and Jerusalem:

2 In the last days, the mountain of the LORD's
house
will be the highest of all—
the most important place on earth.
It will be raised above the other hills,
and people from all over the world will
stream there to worship.
3 People from many nations will come and say,
"Come, let us go up to the mountain of the
LORD,
to the house of Jacob's God.
There he will teach us his ways,
and we will walk in his paths."
For the LORD's teaching will go out from
Zion;
his word will go out from Jerusalem.
4 The LORD will mediate between nations
and will settle international disputes.
They will hammer their swords into
plowshares
and their spears into pruning hooks.
Nation will no longer fight against nation,
nor train for war anymore.

A Warning of Judgment

5 Come, descendants of Jacob,
let us walk in the light of the LORD!
6 For the LORD has rejected his people,
the descendants of Jacob,
because they have filled their land with
practices from the East
and with sorcerers, as the Philistines do.
They have made alliances with pagans.
7 Israel is full of silver and gold;
there is no end to its treasures.
Their land is full of warhorses;
there is no end to its chariots.
8 Their land is full of idols;
the people worship things they have made
with their own hands.
9 So now they will be humbled,
and all will be brought low—
do not forgive them.
10 Crawl into caves in the rocks.
Hide in the dust
from the terror of the LORD
and the glory of his majesty.
11 Human pride will be brought down,
and human arrogance will be humbled.
Only the LORD will be exalted
on that day of judgment.

12 For the LORD of Heaven's Armies
has a day of reckoning.
He will punish the proud and mighty
and bring down everything that is exalted.
13 He will cut down the tall cedars of Lebanon
and all the mighty oaks of Bashan.
14 He will level all the high mountains
and all the lofty hills.

15 He will break down every high tower
and every fortified wall.
16 He will destroy all the great trading ships
and every magnificent vessel.
17 Human pride will be humbled,
and human arrogance will be
brought down.
Only the LORD will be exalted
on that day of judgment.

18 Idols will completely disappear.
19 When the LORD rises to shake the earth,
his enemies will crawl into holes in
the ground.
They will hide in caves in the rocks
from the terror of the LORD
and the glory of his majesty.
20 On that day of judgment they will abandon
the gold and silver idols
they made for themselves to worship.
They will leave their gods to the rodents
and bats,
21 while they crawl away into caverns
and hide among the jagged rocks
in the cliffs.
They will try to escape the terror
of the LORD
and the glory of his majesty
as he rises to shake the earth.
22 Don't put your trust in mere humans.
They are as frail as breath.
What good are they?

CHAPTER 3
Judgment against Judah

1 The Lord, the LORD of Heaven's Armies,
will take away from Jerusalem
and Judah
everything they depend on:
every bit of bread
and every drop of water,
2 all their heroes and soldiers,
judges and prophets,
fortune-tellers and elders,
3 army officers and high officials,
advisers, skilled sorcerers, and
astrologers.

4 I will make boys their leaders,
and toddlers their rulers.
5 People will oppress each other—
man against man,
neighbor against neighbor.
Young people will insult their elders,
and vulgar people will sneer at the
honorable.

6 In those days a man will say to his brother,
"Since you have a coat, you be our leader!
Take charge of this heap of ruins!"
7 But he will reply,
"No! I can't help.
I don't have any extra food or clothes.
Don't put me in charge!"

8 For Jerusalem will stumble,
and Judah will fall,
because they speak out against the LORD
and refuse to obey him.
They provoke him to his face.
9 The very look on their faces gives them away.
They display their sin like the people
of Sodom
and don't even try to hide it.
They are doomed!
They have brought destruction upon
themselves.

10 Tell the godly that all will be well for them.
They will enjoy the rich reward they have
earned!
11 But the wicked are doomed,
for they will get exactly what they
deserve.

12 Childish leaders oppress my people,
and women rule over them.
O my people, your leaders mislead you;
they send you down the wrong road.

13 The LORD takes his place in court
and presents his case against his people.
14 The LORD comes forward to pronounce
judgment
on the elders and rulers of his people:
"You have ruined Israel, my vineyard.
Your houses are filled with things stolen
from the poor.
15 How dare you crush my people,
grinding the faces of the poor into
the dust?"
demands the Lord, the LORD of
Heaven's Armies.

A Warning to Jerusalem

16 The LORD says, "Beautiful Zion is haughty:
craning her elegant neck,
flirting with her eyes,
walking with dainty steps,
tinkling her ankle bracelets.
17 So the Lord will send scabs on her head;
the LORD will make beautiful Zion bald."

[18] On that day of judgment
the Lord will strip away everything that
makes her beautiful:
ornaments, headbands, crescent necklaces,
[19] earrings, bracelets, and veils;
[20] scarves, ankle bracelets, sashes,
perfumes, and charms;
[21] rings, jewels,
[22] party clothes, gowns, capes, and purses;
[23] mirrors, fine linen garments,
head ornaments, and shawls.

[24] Instead of smelling of sweet perfume,
she will stink.
She will wear a rope for a sash,
and her elegant hair will fall out.
She will wear rough burlap instead
of rich robes.
Shame will replace her beauty.
[25] The men of the city will be killed with the
sword,
and her warriors will die in battle.
[26] The gates of Zion will weep and mourn.
The city will be like a ravaged woman,
huddled on the ground.

CHAPTER 4

In that day so few men will be left that seven
women will fight for each man, saying, "Let us all
marry you! We will provide our own food and
clothing. Only let us take your name so we won't
be mocked as old maids."

A Promise of Restoration

[2] But in that day, the branch of the LORD
will be beautiful and glorious;
the fruit of the land will be the pride and
glory
of all who survive in Israel.
[3] All who remain in Zion
will be a holy people—
those who survive the destruction
of Jerusalem
and are recorded among the living.
[4] The Lord will wash the filth from
beautiful Zion
and cleanse Jerusalem of its bloodstains
with the hot breath of fiery judgment.
[5] Then the LORD will provide shade for
Mount Zion
and all who assemble there.
He will provide a canopy of cloud during
the day
and smoke and flaming fire at night,
covering the glorious land.
[6] It will be a shelter from daytime heat
and a hiding place from storms and rain.

CHAPTER 5

A Song about the LORD's Vineyard

[1] Now I will sing for the one I love
a song about his vineyard:
My beloved had a vineyard
on a rich and fertile hill.
[2] He plowed the land, cleared its stones,
and planted it with the best vines.
In the middle he built a watchtower
and carved a winepress in the
nearby rocks.
Then he waited for a harvest of sweet grapes,
but the grapes that grew were bitter.

[3] Now, you people of Jerusalem and Judah,
you judge between me and my vineyard.
[4] What more could I have done for my
vineyard
that I have not already done?
When I expected sweet grapes,
why did my vineyard give me bitter grapes?

[5] Now let me tell you
what I will do to my vineyard:
I will tear down its hedges
and let it be destroyed.
I will break down its walls
and let the animals trample it.
[6] I will make it a wild place
where the vines are not pruned and
the ground is not hoed,
a place overgrown with briers and thorns.
I will command the clouds
to drop no rain on it.

[7] The nation of Israel is the vineyard of the
LORD of Heaven's Armies.
The people of Judah are his pleasant
garden.
He expected a crop of justice,
but instead he found oppression.
He expected to find righteousness,
but instead he heard cries of violence.

Judah's Guilt and Judgment

[8] What sorrow for you who buy up house
after house and field after field,
until everyone is evicted and you live
alone in the land.
[9] But I have heard the LORD of Heaven's
Armies
swear a solemn oath:

"Many houses will stand deserted;
even beautiful mansions will be empty.
10 Ten acres of vineyard will not produce
even six gallons of wine.
Ten baskets of seed will yield only one
basket of grain."

11 What sorrow for those who get up early
in the morning
looking for a drink of alcohol
and spend long evenings drinking wine
to make themselves flaming drunk.
12 They furnish wine and lovely music at their
grand parties—
lyre and harp, tambourine and flute—
but they never think about the LORD
or notice what he is doing.
13 So my people will go into exile far away
because they do not know me.
Those who are great and honored
will starve,
and the common people will die
of thirst.
14 The grave is licking its lips in anticipation,
opening its mouth wide.
The great and the lowly
and all the drunken mob will be
swallowed up.
15 Humanity will be destroyed, and people
brought down;
even the arrogant will lower their eyes
in humiliation.
16 But the LORD of Heaven's Armies will be
exalted by his justice.
The holiness of God will be displayed
by his righteousness.
17 In that day lambs will find good pastures,
and fattened sheep and young goats will
feed among the ruins.

18 What sorrow for those who drag their sins
behind them
with ropes made of lies,
who drag wickedness behind them
like a cart!
19 They even mock God and say,
"Hurry up and do something!
We want to see what you can do.
Let the Holy One of Israel carry out
his plan,
for we want to know what it is."

20 What sorrow for those who say
that evil is good and good is evil,
that dark is light and light is dark,
that bitter is sweet and sweet is bitter.
21 What sorrow for those who are wise in their
own eyes
and think themselves so clever.
22 What sorrow for those who are heroes at
drinking wine
and boast about all the alcohol they
can hold.
23 They take bribes to let the wicked
go free,
and they punish the innocent.

24 Therefore, just as fire licks up stubble
and dry grass shrivels in the flame,
so their roots will rot
and their flowers wither.
For they have rejected the law of the LORD
of Heaven's Armies;
they have despised the word of the Holy
One of Israel.
25 That is why the LORD's anger burns against
his people,
and why he has raised his fist to crush
them.
The mountains tremble,
and the corpses of his people litter the
streets like garbage.
But even then the LORD's anger is not
satisfied.
His fist is still poised to strike!

26 He will send a signal to distant nations
far away
and whistle to those at the ends
of the earth.
They will come racing toward Jerusalem.
27 They will not get tired or stumble.
They will not stop for rest or sleep.
Not a belt will be loose,
not a sandal strap broken.
28 Their arrows will be sharp
and their bows ready for battle.
Sparks will fly from their horses' hooves,
and the wheels of their chariots will spin
like a whirlwind.
29 They will roar like lions,
like the strongest of lions.
Growling, they will pounce on their victims
and carry them off,
and no one will be there to rescue them.
30 They will roar over their victims on that day
of destruction
like the roaring of the sea.
If someone looks across the land,
only darkness and distress will be seen;
even the light will be darkened
by clouds.

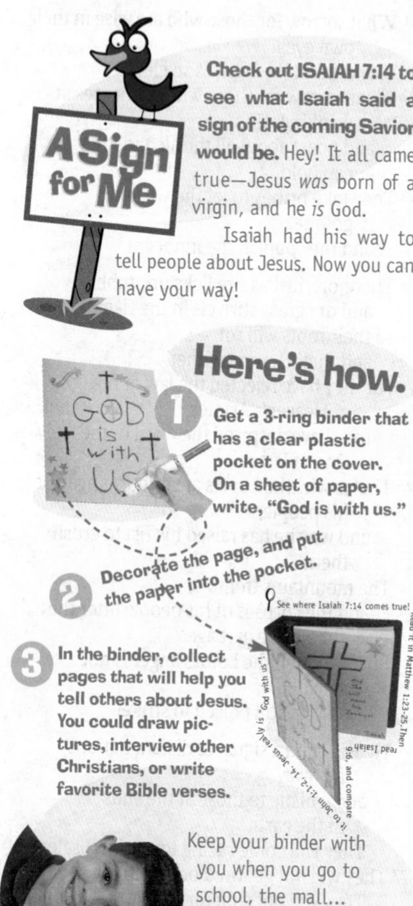

A Sign for Me
Check out ISAIAH 7:14 to see what Isaiah said a sign of the coming Savior would be. Hey! It all came true—Jesus *was* born of a virgin, and he *is* God.
Isaiah had his way to tell people about Jesus. Now you can have your way!
Here's how.
GOD is with US
1 Get a 3-ring binder that has a clear plastic pocket on the cover. On a sheet of paper, write, "God is with us."
2 Decorate the page, and put the paper into the pocket.
See where Isaiah 7:14 comes true!
Read it in Matthew 1:23-25. Then read Isaiah 9:6, and compare it to John 1:1-2, 14. Jesus really is "God with us."
3 In the binder, collect pages that will help you tell others about Jesus. You could draw pictures, interview other Christians, or write favorite Bible verses.

Keep your binder with you when you go to school, the mall... wherever! If your friends ask you about your binder, tell them about Jesus, just like Isaiah told the people he knew!

CHAPTER 6
Isaiah's Cleansing and Call

It was in the year King Uzziah died that I saw the
Lord. He was sitting on a lofty throne, and the
train of his robe filled the Temple. 2Attending
him were mighty seraphim, each having six
wings. With two wings they covered their faces,
with two they covered their feet, and with two
they flew. 3They were calling out to each other,

"Holy, holy, holy is the LORD of Heaven's
Armies!
The whole earth is filled with his glory!"

4Their voices shook the Temple to its foundations, and the entire building was filled with smoke.

5Then I said, "It's all over! I am doomed, for I am a sinful man. I have filthy lips, and I live among a people with filthy lips. Yet I have seen the King, the LORD of Heaven's Armies."

6Then one of the seraphim flew to me with a
burning coal he had taken from the altar with a
pair of tongs. 7He touched my lips with it and
said, "See, this coal has touched your lips. Now
your guilt is removed, and your sins are forgiven."

8Then I heard the Lord asking, "Whom should I send as a messenger to this people? Who will go for us?"

I said, "Here I am. Send me."

9And he said, "Yes, go, and say to this people,

'Listen carefully, but do not understand.
Watch closely, but learn nothing.'
10 Harden the hearts of these people.
Plug their ears and shut their eyes.
That way, they will not see with their eyes,
nor hear with their ears,
nor understand with their hearts
and turn to me for healing."

11Then I said, "Lord, how long will this go on?"
And he replied,

"Until their towns are empty,
their houses are deserted,
and the whole country is a wasteland;
12 until the LORD has sent everyone away,
and the entire land of Israel lies deserted.
13 If even a tenth—a remnant—survive,
it will be invaded again and burned.
But as a terebinth or oak tree leaves a stump
when it is cut down,
so Israel's stump will be a holy seed."

CHAPTER 7
A Message for Ahaz

When Ahaz, son of Jotham and grandson of Uzziah, was king of Judah, King Rezin of Syria and Pekah son of Remaliah, the king of Israel, set out to attack Jerusalem. However, they were unable to carry out their plan.

2The news had come to the royal court of Judah: "Syria is allied with Israel against us!" So the hearts of the king and his people trembled with fear, like trees shaking in a storm.

3Then the LORD said to Isaiah, "Take your son
Shear-jashub and go out to meet King Ahaz. You
will find him at the end of the aqueduct that
feeds water into the upper pool, near the road

leading to the field where cloth is washed. 4Tell
him to stop worrying. Tell him he doesn't need to
fear the fierce anger of those two burned-out
embers, King Rezin of Syria and Pekah son of
Remaliah. 5Yes, the kings of Syria and Israel are
plotting against him, saying, 6'We will attack Judah and capture it for ourselves. Then we will install the son of Tabeel as Judah's king.' 7But this
is what the Sovereign LORD says:

"This invasion will never happen;
it will never take place;
8 for Syria is no stronger than its capital,
Damascus,
and Damascus is no stronger than
its king, Rezin.
As for Israel, within sixty-five years
it will be crushed and completely
destroyed.
9 Israel is no stronger than its capital, Samaria,
and Samaria is no stronger than its king,
Pekah son of Remaliah.
Unless your faith is firm,
I cannot make you stand firm."

The Sign of Immanuel

10Later, the LORD sent this message to King Ahaz:
11"Ask the LORD your God for a sign of confirma-
tion, Ahaz. Make it as difficult as you want—as
high as heaven or as deep as the place of the
dead."

12But the king refused. "No," he said, "I will
not test the LORD like that."

13Then Isaiah said, "Listen well, you royal family of David! Isn't it enough to exhaust human patience? Must you exhaust the patience of my God
as well? 14All right then, the Lord himself will
give you the sign. **Look! The virgin will**
conceive a child! She will give birth
to a son and will call him Immanuel
(which means 'God is with us'). 15By the
time this child is old enough to choose what is
right and reject what is wrong, he will be eating
yogurt and honey. 16For before the child is that
old, the lands of the two kings you fear so much
will both be deserted.

17"Then the LORD will bring things on you,
your nation, and your family unlike anything
since Israel broke away from Judah. He will bring
the king of Assyria upon you!"

18In that day the LORD will whistle for the army
of southern Egypt and for the army of Assyria.
They will swarm around you like flies and bees.
19They will come in vast hordes and settle in the
fertile areas and also in the desolate valleys, caves,
and thorny places. 20In that day the Lord will hire
a "razor" from beyond the Euphrates River—the
king of Assyria—and use it to shave off everything:
your land, your crops, and your people.

21In that day a farmer will be fortunate to have
a cow and two sheep or goats left. 22Neverthe-
less, there will be enough milk for everyone because so few people will be left in the land. They
will eat their fill of yogurt and honey. 23In that
day the lush vineyards, now worth 1,000 pieces
of silver, will become patches of briers and
thorns. 24The entire land will become a vast ex-
panse of briers and thorns, a hunting ground
overrun by wildlife. 25No one will go to the fertile
hillsides where the gardens once grew, for briers
and thorns will cover them. Cattle, sheep, and
goats will graze there.

CHAPTER 8

The Coming Assyrian Invasion

Then the LORD said to me, "Make a large sign-
board and clearly write this name on it: Maher-
shalal-hash-baz." 2I asked Uriah the priest and
Zechariah son of Jeberekiah, both known as honest men, to witness my doing this.

3Then I slept with my wife, and she became
pregnant and gave birth to a son. And the LORD
said, "Call him Maher-shalal-hash-baz. 4For before this child is old enough to say 'Papa' or
'Mama,' the king of Assyria will carry away both
the abundance of Damascus and the riches of
Samaria."

5Then the LORD spoke to me again and said,
6"My care for the people of Judah is like the gently
flowing waters of Shiloah, but they have rejected
it. They are rejoicing over what will happen to
King Rezin and King Pekah. 7Therefore, the Lord
will overwhelm them with a mighty flood from
the Euphrates River—the king of Assyria and all
his glory. This flood will overflow all its channels
8and sweep into Judah until it is chin deep. It will
spread its wings, submerging your land from one
end to the other, O Immanuel.

9 "Huddle together, you nations, and be
terrified.
Listen, all you distant lands.
Prepare for battle, but you will be crushed!
Yes, prepare for battle, but you will be
crushed!
10 Call your councils of war, but they will be
worthless.
Develop your strategies, but they will not
succeed.
For God is with us!"

A Call to Trust the LORD

[11]The LORD has given me a strong warning not to think like everyone else does. He said,

[12] "Don't call everything a conspiracy,
like they do,
and don't live in dread of what
frightens them.
[13] Make the LORD of Heaven's Armies holy
in your life.
He is the one you should fear.
He is the one who should make you tremble.
[14] He will keep you safe.
But to Israel and Judah
he will be a stone that makes people
stumble,
a rock that makes them fall.
And for the people of Jerusalem
he will be a trap and a snare.
[15] Many will stumble and fall,
never to rise again.
They will be snared and captured."
[16] Preserve the teaching of God;
entrust his instructions to those who
follow me.
[17] I will wait for the LORD,
who has turned away from the
descendants of Jacob.
I will put my hope in him.

[18]I and the children the LORD has given me
serve as signs and warnings to Israel from the
LORD of Heaven's Armies who dwells in his Temple on Mount Zion.
[19]Someone may say to you, "Let's ask the mediums and those who consult the spirits of the
dead. With their whisperings and mutterings,
they will tell us what to do." But shouldn't people
ask God for guidance? Should the living seek
guidance from the dead?
[20]Look to God's instructions and teachings!
People who contradict his word are completely
in the dark. [21]They will go from one place to another, weary and hungry. And because they are
hungry, they will rage and curse their king and
their God. They will look up to heaven [22]and
down at the earth, but wherever they look, there
will be trouble and anguish and dark despair.
They will be thrown out into the darkness.

CHAPTER **9**

Hope in the Messiah

Nevertheless, that time of darkness and despair will not go on forever. The land of Zebulun and Naphtali will be humbled, but there will be a time in the future when Galilee of the Gentiles, which lies along the road that runs between the Jordan and the sea, will be filled with glory.

[2] The people who walk in darkness
will see a great light.
For those who live in a land of deep darkness,
a light will shine.
[3] You will enlarge the nation of Israel,
and its people will rejoice.
They will rejoice before you
as people rejoice at the harvest
and like warriors dividing the plunder.
[4] For you will break the yoke of their slavery
and lift the heavy burden from their
shoulders.
You will break the oppressor's rod,
just as you did when you destroyed the
army of Midian.
[5] The boots of the warrior
and the uniforms bloodstained by war
will all be burned.
They will be fuel for the fire.

**[6]For a child is born to us,
a son is given to us.
The government will rest
on his shoulders.
And he will be called:
Wonderful Counselor,
Mighty God,
Everlasting Father, Prince
of Peace.**

[7] His government and its peace
will never end.
He will rule with fairness and justice from
the throne of his ancestor David
for all eternity.
The passionate commitment of the LORD of
Heaven's Armies
will make this happen!

The LORD's Anger against Israel

[8] The Lord has spoken out against Jacob;
his judgment has fallen upon Israel.
[9] And the people of Israel and Samaria,
who spoke with such pride and arrogance,
will soon know it.
[10] They said, "We will replace the broken bricks
of our ruins with finished stone,
and replant the felled sycamore-fig trees
with cedars."
[11] But the LORD will bring Rezin's enemies
against Israel
and stir up all their foes.

12 The Syrians from the east and the Philistines
from the west
will bare their fangs and devour Israel.
But even then the LORD's anger will not
be satisfied.
His fist is still poised to strike.

13 For after all this punishment, the people
will still not repent.
They will not seek the LORD of Heaven's
Armies.
14 Therefore, in a single day the LORD will
destroy both the head and the tail,
the noble palm branch and the lowly reed.
15 The leaders of Israel are the head,
and the lying prophets are the tail.
16 For the leaders of the people have
misled them.
They have led them down the path
of destruction.
17 That is why the Lord takes no pleasure
in the young men
and shows no mercy even to the widows
and orphans.
For they are all wicked hypocrites,
and they all speak foolishness.
But even then the LORD's anger will not
be satisfied.
His fist is still poised to strike.

18 This wickedness is like a brushfire.
It burns not only briers and thorns
but also sets the forests ablaze.
Its burning sends up clouds of smoke.
19 The land will be blackened
by the fury of the LORD of Heaven's
Armies.
The people will be fuel for the fire,
and no one will spare even his own
brother.
20 They will attack their neighbor on the right
but will still be hungry.
They will devour their neighbor on the left
but will not be satisfied.
In the end they will even eat their own
children.
21 Manasseh will feed on Ephraim,
Ephraim will feed on Manasseh,
and both will devour Judah.
But even then the LORD's anger will not
be satisfied.
His fist is still poised to strike.

CHAPTER 10

1 What sorrow awaits the unjust judges
and those who issue unfair laws.

Key Verse **"For a child is born to us, a son is given to us. The government will rest on his shoulders. And he will be called: Wonderful Counselor, Mighty God, Everlasting Father, Prince of Peace." —ISAIAH 9:6**

ROYaL MOBiLe

Did you ever wonder who Jesus really is? **Read ISAIAH 9:6 to find out!** Then make this Mighty Mobile to remind you of Jesus' royal names.

1. **Cut a paper plate in half. Write "Jesus" on both sides of one of the halves and cut triangles around the curved edge so it looks like a crown.**
2. **Punch four holes along the straight edge and one hole at the top.**
3. **Write each of the royal titles on an index card. On the back of each card, write what the title means to you.**
4. **Hang the cards from the paper plate with yarn or ribbon.**

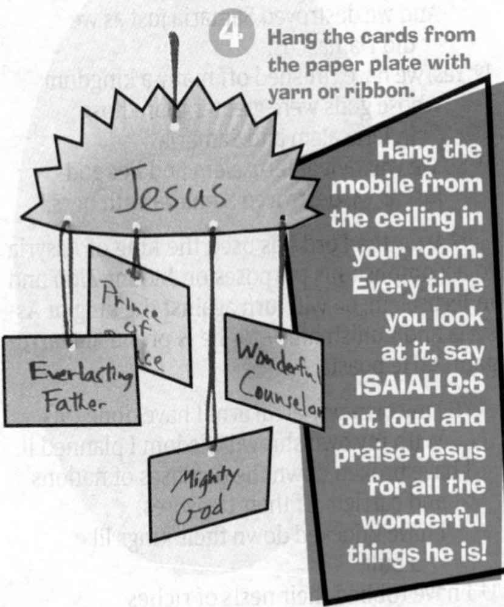

Hang the mobile from the ceiling in your room. Every time you look at it, say ISAIAH 9:6 out loud and praise Jesus for all the wonderful things he is!

2 They deprive the poor of justice
and deny the rights of the needy among my people.
They prey on widows
and take advantage of orphans.
3 What will you do when I punish you,
when I send disaster upon you from a distant land?
To whom will you turn for help?
Where will your treasures be safe?
4 You will stumble along as prisoners
or lie among the dead.
But even then the LORD's anger will not be satisfied.
His fist is still poised to strike.

Judgment against Assyria

5 "What sorrow awaits Assyria, the rod of my anger.
I use it as a club to express my anger.
6 I am sending Assyria against a godless nation,
against a people with whom I am angry.
Assyria will plunder them,
trampling them like dirt beneath its feet.
7 But the king of Assyria will not understand that he is my tool;
his mind does not work that way.
His plan is simply to destroy,
to cut down nation after nation.
8 He will say,
'Each of my princes will soon be a king.
9 We destroyed Calno just as we did Carchemish.
Hamath fell before us as Arpad did.
And we destroyed Samaria just as we did Damascus.
10 Yes, we have finished off many a kingdom
whose gods were greater than those in Jerusalem and Samaria.
11 So we will defeat Jerusalem and her gods,
just as we destroyed Samaria with hers.'"

12 After the Lord has used the king of Assyria
to accomplish his purposes on Mount Zion and
in Jerusalem, he will turn against the king of Assyria and punish him—for he is proud and arrogant. 13 He boasts,

"By my own powerful arm I have done this.
With my own shrewd wisdom I planned it.
I have broken down the defenses of nations
and carried off their treasures.
I have knocked down their kings like a bull.
14 I have robbed their nests of riches
and gathered up kingdoms as a farmer gathers eggs.
No one can even flap a wing against me
or utter a peep of protest."
15 But can the ax boast greater power than the person who uses it?
Is the saw greater than the person who saws?
Can a rod strike unless a hand moves it?
Can a wooden cane walk by itself?
16 Therefore, the Lord, the LORD of Heaven's Armies,
will send a plague among Assyria's proud troops,
and a flaming fire will consume its glory.
17 The LORD, the Light of Israel, will be a fire;
the Holy One will be a flame.
He will devour the thorns and briers with fire,
burning up the enemy in a single night.
18 The LORD will consume Assyria's glory
like a fire consumes a forest in a fruitful land;
it will waste away like sick people in a plague.
19 Of all that glorious forest, only a few trees will survive—
so few that a child could count them!

Hope for the LORD's People

20 In that day the remnant left in Israel,
the survivors in the house of Jacob,
will no longer depend on allies
who seek to destroy them.
But they will faithfully trust the LORD,
the Holy One of Israel.
21 A remnant will return;
yes, the remnant of Jacob will return
to the Mighty God.
22 But though the people of Israel are as numerous
as the sand of the seashore,
only a remnant of them will return.
The LORD has rightly decided to destroy his people.
23 Yes, the Lord, the LORD of Heaven's Armies,
has already decided to destroy the entire land.

24 So this is what the Lord, the LORD of
Heaven's Armies, says: "O my people in Zion, do
not be afraid of the Assyrians when they oppress
you with rod and club as the Egyptians did long
ago. 25 In a little while my anger against you will
end, and then my anger will rise up to destroy

them." 26The LORD of Heaven's Armies will lash
them with his whip, as he did when Gideon triumphed over the Midianites at the rock of Oreb,
or when the LORD's staff was raised to drown the
Egyptian army in the sea.

27 In that day the LORD will end the bondage
of his people.
He will break the yoke of slavery
and lift it from their shoulders.

28 Look, the Assyrians are now at Aiath.
They are passing through Migron
and are storing their equipment
at Micmash.
29 They are crossing the pass
and are camping at Geba.
Fear strikes the town of Ramah.
All the people of Gibeah, the hometown
of Saul,
are running for their lives.
30 Scream in terror,
you people of Gallim!
Shout out a warning to Laishah.
Oh, poor Anathoth!
31 There go the people of Madmenah,
all fleeing.
The citizens of Gebim are trying to hide.
32 The enemy stops at Nob for the rest of
that day.
He shakes his fist at beautiful Mount Zion,
the mountain of Jerusalem.

33 But look! The Lord, the LORD of Heaven's
Armies,
will chop down the mighty tree of Assyria
with great power!
He will cut down the proud.
That lofty tree will be brought down.
34 He will cut down the forest trees with an ax.
Lebanon will fall to the Mighty One.

CHAPTER 11

A Branch from David's Line

1 Out of the stump of David's family will grow a
shoot—
yes, a new Branch bearing fruit from the
old root.
2 And the Spirit of the LORD will rest on him—
the Spirit of wisdom and understanding,
the Spirit of counsel and might,
the Spirit of knowledge and the fear
of the LORD.
3 He will delight in obeying the LORD.
He will not judge by appearance
nor make a decision based on hearsay.
4 He will give justice to the poor
and make fair decisions for the exploited.
The earth will shake at the force of his word,
and one breath from his mouth will
destroy the wicked.
5 He will wear righteousness like a belt
and truth like an undergarment.

6 In that day the wolf and the lamb will live
together;
the leopard will lie down with the
baby goat.
The calf and the yearling will be safe
with the lion,
and a little child will lead them all.
7 The cow will graze near the bear.
The cub and the calf will lie down
together.
The lion will eat hay like a cow.
8 The baby will play safely near the hole
of a cobra.
Yes, a little child will put its hand
in a nest of deadly snakes without harm.
9 Nothing will hurt or destroy in all my
holy mountain,
for as the waters fill the sea,
so the earth will be filled with people
who know the LORD.

10 In that day the heir to David's throne
will be a banner of salvation to all
the world.
The nations will rally to him,
and the land where he lives will be
a glorious place.
11 In that day the Lord will reach out his
hand a second time
to bring back the remnant of
his people—
those who remain in Assyria and northern
Egypt;
in southern Egypt, Ethiopia, and Elam;
in Babylonia, Hamath, and all the distant
coastlands.
12 He will raise a flag among the nations
and assemble the exiles of Israel.
He will gather the scattered people of Judah
from the ends of the earth.

13 Then at last the jealousy between Israel
and Judah will end.
They will not be rivals anymore.
14 They will join forces to swoop down on
Philistia to the west.
Together they will attack and plunder
the nations to the east.

They will occupy the lands of Edom
and Moab,
and Ammon will obey them.
15 The Lord will make a dry path through the
gulf of the Red Sea.
He will wave his hand over the Euphrates
River,
sending a mighty wind to divide it into
seven streams
so it can easily be crossed on foot.
16 He will make a highway for the remnant
of his people,
the remnant coming from Assyria,
just as he did for Israel long ago
when they returned from Egypt.

CHAPTER 12

Songs of Praise for Salvation

1 In that day you will sing:
"I will praise you, O Lord!
You were angry with me, but not any more.
Now you comfort me.
2 See, God has come to save me.
I will trust in him and not be afraid.
The Lord God is my strength and my song;
he has given me victory."
3 With joy you will drink deeply
from the fountain of salvation!
4 In that wonderful day you will sing:
"Thank the Lord! Praise his name!
Tell the nations what he has done.
Let them know how mighty he is!
5 Sing to the Lord, for he has done
wonderful things.
Make known his praise around the world.
6 Let all the people of Jerusalem shout his
praise with joy!
For great is the Holy One of Israel who
lives among you."

CHAPTER 13

A Message about Babylon

Isaiah son of Amoz received this message concerning the destruction of Babylon:

2 "Raise a signal flag on a bare hilltop.
Call up an army against Babylon.
Wave your hand to encourage them
as they march into the palaces of the
high and mighty.
3 I, the Lord, have dedicated these soldiers
for this task.
Yes, I have called mighty warriors to
express my anger,
and they will rejoice when I am exalted."

4 Hear the noise on the mountains!
Listen, as the vast armies march!
It is the noise and shouting of many nations.
The Lord of Heaven's Armies has called
this army together.
5 They come from distant countries,
from beyond the farthest horizons.
They are the Lord's weapons to carry out
his anger.
With them he will destroy the
whole land.

6 Scream in terror, for the day of the Lord
has arrived—
the time for the Almighty to destroy.
7 Every arm is paralyzed with fear.
Every heart melts,
8 and people are terrified.
Pangs of anguish grip them,
like those of a woman in labor.
They look helplessly at one another,
their faces aflame with fear.
9 For see, the day of the Lord is coming—
the terrible day of his fury and fierce
anger.
The land will be made desolate,
and all the sinners destroyed with it.
10 The heavens will be black above them;
the stars will give no light.
The sun will be dark when it rises,
and the moon will provide no light.

11 "I, the Lord, will punish the world for
its evil
and the wicked for their sin.
I will crush the arrogance of the proud
and humble the pride of the mighty.
12 I will make people scarcer than gold—
more rare than the fine gold of Ophir.
13 For I will shake the heavens.
The earth will move from its place
when the Lord of Heaven's Armies displays
his wrath
in the day of his fierce anger."
14 Everyone in Babylon will run about like
a hunted gazelle,
like sheep without a shepherd.
They will try to find their own people
and flee to their own land.
15 Anyone who is captured will be cut down—
run through with a sword.
16 Their little children will be dashed to death
before their eyes.
Their homes will be sacked, and their
wives will be raped.

17 "Look, I will stir up the Medes against
Babylon.
They cannot be tempted by silver
or bribed with gold.
18 The attacking armies will shoot down the
young men with arrows.
They will have no mercy on helpless babies
and will show no compassion for children."

19 Babylon, the most glorious of kingdoms,
the flower of Chaldean pride,
will be devastated like Sodom and Gomorrah
when God destroyed them.
20 Babylon will never be inhabited again.
It will remain empty for generation
after generation.
Nomads will refuse to camp there,
and shepherds will not bed down
their sheep.
21 Desert animals will move into the ruined city,
and the houses will be haunted by howling
creatures.
Owls will live among the ruins,
and wild goats will go there to dance.
22 Hyenas will howl in its fortresses,
and jackals will make dens in its luxurious
palaces.
Babylon's days are numbered;
its time of destruction will soon arrive.

CHAPTER 14

A Taunt for Babylon's King

But the LORD will have mercy on the descendants
of Jacob. He will choose Israel as his special people once again. He will bring them back to settle
once again in their own land. And people from
many different nations will come and join them
there and unite with the people of Israel. 2 The
nations of the world will help the people of Israel
to return, and those who come to live in the
LORD's land will serve them. Those who captured
Israel will themselves be captured, and Israel will
rule over its enemies.

3 In that wonderful day when the LORD gives
his people rest from sorrow and fear, from slavery and chains, 4 you will taunt the king of Babylon. You will say,

"The mighty man has been destroyed.
Yes, your insolence is ended.
5 For the LORD has crushed your wicked power
and broken your evil rule.
6 You struck the people with endless blows
of rage
and held the nations in your angry grip
with unrelenting tyranny.
7 But finally the earth is at rest and quiet.
Now it can sing again!
8 Even the trees of the forest—
the cypress trees and the cedars
of Lebanon—
sing out this joyous song:
'Since you have been cut down,
no one will come now to cut us down!'

9 "In the place of the dead there is excitement
over your arrival.
The spirits of world leaders and mighty
kings long dead
stand up to see you.
10 With one voice they all cry out,
'Now you are as weak as we are!
11 Your might and power were buried
with you.
The sound of the harp in your palace
has ceased.
Now maggots are your sheet,
and worms your blanket.'

12 "How you are fallen from heaven,
O shining star, son of the morning!
You have been thrown down to the earth,
you who destroyed the nations of
the world.
13 For you said to yourself,
'I will ascend to heaven and set my throne
above God's stars.
I will preside on the mountain of the gods
far away in the north.
14 I will climb to the highest heavens
and be like the Most High.'
15 Instead, you will be brought down to the
place of the dead,
down to its lowest depths.
16 Everyone there will stare at you and ask,
'Can this be the one who shook the earth
and made the kingdoms of the world
tremble?
17 Is this the one who destroyed the world
and made it into a wasteland?
Is this the king who demolished the world's
greatest cities
and had no mercy on his prisoners?'

18 "The kings of the nations lie in stately glory,
each in his own tomb,
19 but you will be thrown out of your grave
like a worthless branch.
Like a corpse trampled underfoot,
you will be dumped into a mass grave
with those killed in battle.
You will descend to the pit.

20 You will not be given a proper burial,
for you have destroyed your nation
and slaughtered your people.
The descendants of such an evil person
will never again receive honor.
21 Kill this man's children!
Let them die because of their father's sins!
They must not rise and conquer the earth,
filling the world with their cities."
22 This is what the LORD of Heaven's
Armies says:
"I, myself, have risen against Babylon!
I will destroy its children and its children's
children,"
says the LORD.
23 "I will make Babylon a desolate place of owls,
filled with swamps and marshes.
I will sweep the land with the broom
of destruction.
I, the LORD of Heaven's Armies, have
spoken!"

A Message about Assyria

24 The LORD of Heaven's Armies has sworn this
oath:

"It will all happen as I have planned.
It will be as I have decided.
25 I will break the Assyrians when they are
in Israel;
I will trample them on my mountains.
My people will no longer be their slaves
nor bow down under their heavy loads.
26 I have a plan for the whole earth,
a hand of judgment upon all the nations.
27 The LORD of Heaven's Armies has spoken—
who can change his plans?
When his hand is raised,
who can stop him?"

A Message about Philistia

28 This message came to me the year King Ahaz
died:

29 Do not rejoice, you Philistines,
that the rod that struck you is broken—
that the king who attacked you is dead.
For from that snake a more poisonous snake
will be born,
a fiery serpent to destroy you!
30 I will feed the poor in my pasture;
the needy will lie down in peace.
But as for you, I will wipe you out with
famine
and destroy the few who remain.
31 Wail at the gates! Weep in the cities!
Melt with fear, you Philistines!
A powerful army comes like smoke from
the north.
Each soldier rushes forward eager to fight.

32 What should we tell the Philistine messengers? Tell them,

"The LORD has built Jerusalem;
its walls will give refuge to his oppressed
people."

CHAPTER 15

A Message about Moab

This message came to me concerning Moab:

In one night the town of Ar will be leveled,
and the city of Kir will be destroyed.
2 Your people will go to their temple in Dibon
to mourn.
They will go to their sacred shrines to weep.
They will wail for the fate of Nebo and
Medeba,
shaving their heads in sorrow and cutting
off their beards.
3 They will wear burlap as they wander
the streets.
From every home and public square will
come the sound of wailing.
4 The people of Heshbon and Elealeh will
cry out;
their voices will be heard as far away as
Jahaz!
The bravest warriors of Moab will cry out
in utter terror.
They will be helpless with fear.
5 My heart weeps for Moab.
Its people flee to Zoar and Eglath-
shelishiyah.
Weeping, they climb the road to Luhith.
Their cries of distress can be heard all
along the road to Horonaim.
6 Even the waters of Nimrim are dried up!
The grassy banks are scorched.
The tender plants are gone;
nothing green remains.
7 The people grab their possessions
and carry them across the Ravine of
Willows.
8 A cry of distress echoes through the land
of Moab
from one end to the other—
from Eglaim to Beer-elim.
9 The stream near Dibon runs red with blood,
but I am still not finished with Dibon!

Lions will hunt down the survivors—
both those who try to escape
and those who remain behind.

CHAPTER 16

1 Send lambs from Sela as tribute
to the ruler of the land.
Send them through the desert
to the mountain of beautiful Zion.
2 The women of Moab are left like
homeless birds
at the shallow crossings of the Arnon River.
3 "Help us," they cry.
"Defend us against our enemies.
Protect us from their relentless attack.
Do not betray us now that we have
escaped.
4 Let our refugees stay among you.
Hide them from our enemies until the
terror is past."

When oppression and destruction
have ended
and enemy raiders have disappeared,
5 then God will establish one of David's
descendants as king.
He will rule with mercy and truth.
He will always do what is just
and be eager to do what is right.

6 We have heard about proud Moab—
about its pride and arrogance and rage.
But all that boasting has disappeared.
7 The entire land of Moab weeps.
Yes, everyone in Moab mourns
for the cakes of raisins from Kir-hareseth.
They are all gone now.
8 The farms of Heshbon are abandoned;
the vineyards at Sibmah are deserted.
The rulers of the nations have broken
down Moab—
that beautiful grapevine.
Its tendrils spread north as far as the town
of Jazer
and trailed eastward into the wilderness.
Its shoots reached so far west
that they crossed over the Dead Sea.

9 So now I weep for Jazer and the vineyards
of Sibmah;
my tears will flow for Heshbon and
Elealeh.
There are no more shouts of joy
over your summer fruits and harvest.
10 Gone now is the gladness,
gone the joy of harvest.
There will be no singing in the vineyards,
no more happy shouts,
no treading of grapes in the winepresses.
I have ended all their harvest joys.
11 My heart's cry for Moab is like a lament
on a harp.
I am filled with anguish for Kir-hareseth.
12 The people of Moab will worship at their
pagan shrines,
but it will do them no good.
They will cry to the gods in their temples,
but no one will be able to save them.

13 The LORD has already said these things
about Moab in the past. 14 But now the LORD says,
"Within three years, counting each day, the
glory of Moab will be ended. From its great population, only a feeble few will be left alive."

CHAPTER 17

A Message about Damascus and Israel

This message came to me concerning Damascus:

"Look, the city of Damascus will disappear!
It will become a heap of ruins.
2 The towns of Aroer will be deserted.
Flocks will graze in the streets and lie
down undisturbed,
with no one to chase them away.
3 The fortified towns of Israel will also be
destroyed,
and the royal power of Damascus will end.
All that remains of Syria
will share the fate of Israel's departed
glory,"
declares the LORD of Heaven's Armies.

4 "In that day Israel's glory will grow dim;
its robust body will waste away.
5 The whole land will look like a grainfield
after the harvesters have gathered
the grain.
It will be desolate,
like the fields in the valley of Rephaim
after the harvest.
6 Only a few of its people will be left,
like stray olives left on a tree after
the harvest.
Only two or three remain in the highest
branches,
four or five scattered here and there on the
limbs,"
declares the LORD, the God of Israel.

7 Then at last the people will look to their
Creator

and turn their eyes to the Holy One
of Israel.
8 They will no longer look to their idols
for help
or worship what their own hands
have made.
They will never again bow down to their
Asherah poles
or worship at the pagan shrines they
have built.
9 Their largest cities will be like a deserted
forest,
like the land the Hivites and Amorites
abandoned
when the Israelites came here so long ago.
It will be utterly desolate.
10 Why? Because you have turned from the God
who can save you.
You have forgotten the Rock who can
hide you.
So you may plant the finest grapevines
and import the most expensive seedlings.
11 They may sprout on the day you set them out;
yes, they may blossom on the very
morning you plant them,

FUN-fact **How Did He Do That?**

Seven hundred years before Jesus was born, Isaiah wrote about what Jesus would be like. **Here are some things Isaiah wrote about**

Jesus'

birth—Isaiah 7:14; 9:6
character—Isaiah 11:1-5
looks—Isaiah 53:2
death—Isaiah 53:7-9
resurrection—Isaiah 53:10-12

How did Isaiah know what to tell people about Jesus? God told him what to say, of course! What can you tell people about Jesus?
Look in the Bible for five things you can tell others about Jesus. THEN START TALKING!

but you will never pick any grapes
from them.
Your only harvest will be a load of grief
and unrelieved pain.
12 Listen! The armies of many nations
roar like the roaring of the sea.
Hear the thunder of the mighty forces
as they rush forward like thundering
waves.
13 But though they thunder like breakers
on a beach,
God will silence them, and they will
run away.
They will flee like chaff scattered by
the wind,
like a tumbleweed whirling before
a storm.
14 In the evening Israel waits in terror,
but by dawn its enemies are dead.
This is the just reward of those who
plunder us,
a fitting end for those who destroy us.

CHAPTER 18

A Message about Ethiopia

1 Listen, Ethiopia—land of fluttering sails
that lies at the headwaters of the Nile,
2 that sends ambassadors
in swift boats down the river.

Go, swift messengers!
Take a message to a tall, smooth-skinned
people,
who are feared far and wide
for their conquests and destruction,
and whose land is divided by rivers.

3 All you people of the world,
everyone who lives on the earth—
when I raise my battle flag on the
mountain, look!
When I blow the ram's horn, listen!
4 For the LORD has told me this:
"I will watch quietly from my dwelling
place—
as quietly as the heat rises on a
summer day,
or as the morning dew forms during
the harvest."
5 Even before you begin your attack,
while your plans are ripening like grapes,
the LORD will cut off your new growth with
pruning shears.
He will snip off and discard your
spreading branches.

6 Your mighty army will be left dead
in the fields
for the mountain vultures and
wild animals.
The vultures will tear at the corpses
all summer.
The wild animals will gnaw at the bones
all winter.

7 At that time the LORD of Heaven's Armies
will receive gifts
from this land divided by rivers,
from this tall, smooth-skinned people,
who are feared far and wide for their
conquests and destruction.
They will bring the gifts to Jerusalem,
where the LORD of Heaven's Armies dwells.

CHAPTER 19

A Message about Egypt

This message came to me concerning Egypt:

Look! The LORD is advancing against Egypt,
riding on a swift cloud.
The idols of Egypt tremble.
The hearts of the Egyptians melt with fear.

2 "I will make Egyptian fight against
Egyptian—
brother against brother,
neighbor against neighbor,
city against city,
province against province.
3 The Egyptians will lose heart,
and I will confuse their plans.
They will plead with their idols for wisdom
and call on spirits, mediums, and those
who consult the spirits of the dead.
4 I will hand Egypt over
to a hard, cruel master.
A fierce king will rule them,"
says the Lord, the LORD of Heaven's
Armies.

5 The waters of the Nile will fail to rise and
flood the fields.
The riverbed will be parched and dry.
6 The canals of the Nile will dry up,
and the streams of Egypt will stink
with rotting reeds and rushes.
7 All the greenery along the riverbank
and all the crops along the river
will dry up and blow away.
8 The fishermen will lament for lack of work.
Those who cast hooks into the Nile
will groan,
and those who use nets will lose heart.
9 There will be no flax for the harvesters,
no thread for the weavers.
10 They will be in despair,
and all the workers will be sick at heart.

11 What fools are the officials of Zoan!
Their best counsel to the king of Egypt
is stupid and wrong.
Will they still boast to Pharaoh of their
wisdom?
Will they dare brag about all their wise
ancestors?
12 Where are your wise counselors, Pharaoh?
Let them tell you what God plans,
what the LORD of Heaven's Armies is going
to do to Egypt.
13 The officials of Zoan are fools,
and the officials of Memphis are deluded.
The leaders of the people
have led Egypt astray.
14 The LORD has sent a spirit of foolishness
on them,
so all their suggestions are wrong.
They cause Egypt to stagger
like a drunk in his vomit.
15 There is nothing Egypt can do.
All are helpless—
the head and the tail,
the noble palm branch and the lowly reed.

16 In that day the Egyptians will be as weak as
women. They will cower in fear beneath the upraised fist of the LORD of Heaven's Armies. 17 Just
to speak the name of Israel will terrorize them,
for the LORD of Heaven's Armies has laid out his
plans against them.

18 In that day five of Egypt's cities will follow
the LORD of Heaven's Armies. They will even begin to speak Hebrew, the language of Canaan.
One of these cities will be Heliopolis, the City of
the Sun.

19 In that day there will be an altar to the LORD
in the heart of Egypt, and there will be a monument to the LORD at its border. 20 It will be a sign
and a witness that the LORD of Heaven's Armies is
worshiped in the land of Egypt. When the people
cry to the LORD for help against those who oppress them, he will send them a savior who will
rescue them. 21 The LORD will make himself
known to the Egyptians. Yes, they will know the
LORD and will give their sacrifices and offerings
to him. They will make a vow to the LORD and will
keep it. 22 The LORD will strike Egypt, and then he
will bring healing. For the Egyptians will turn to
the LORD, and he will listen to their pleas and
heal them.

[23]In that day Egypt and Assyria will be connected by a highway. The Egyptians and Assyrians
will move freely between their lands, and they will
both worship God. [24]In that day Israel will be the
third, along with Egypt and Assyria, a blessing in
the midst of the earth. [25]For the LORD of Heaven's
Armies will say, "Blessed be Egypt, my people.
Blessed be Assyria, the land I have made. Blessed
be Israel, my special possession!"

CHAPTER 20

A Message about Egypt and Ethiopia

In the year when King Sargon of Assyria sent his
commander in chief to capture the Philistine
city of Ashdod, [2]the LORD told Isaiah son of
Amoz, "Take off the burlap you have been wearing, and remove your sandals." Isaiah did as he
was told and walked around naked and barefoot.

[3]Then the LORD said, "My servant Isaiah has
been walking around naked and barefoot for
the last three years. This is a sign—a symbol of
the terrible troubles I will bring upon Egypt and
Ethiopia. [4]For the king of Assyria will take away
the Egyptians and Ethiopians as prisoners. He
will make them walk naked and barefoot, both
young and old, their buttocks bared, to the
shame of Egypt. [5]Then the Philistines will be
thrown into panic, for they counted on the
power of Ethiopia and boasted of their allies in
Egypt! [6]They will say, 'If this can happen to
Egypt, what chance do we have? We were counting on Egypt to protect us from the king of Assyria.'"

CHAPTER 21

A Message about Babylon

This message came to me concerning Babylon—
the desert by the sea:

Disaster is roaring down on you from
the desert,
like a whirlwind sweeping in from
the Negev.
[2] I see a terrifying vision:
I see the betrayer betraying,
the destroyer destroying.
Go ahead, you Elamites and Medes,
attack and lay siege.
I will make an end
to all the groaning Babylon caused.
[3] My stomach aches and burns with pain.
Sharp pangs of anguish are upon me,
like those of a woman in labor.
I grow faint when I hear what God is
planning;
I am too afraid to look.
[4] My mind reels and my heart races.
I longed for evening to come,
but now I am terrified of the dark.
[5] Look! They are preparing a great feast.
They are spreading rugs for people
to sit on.
Everyone is eating and drinking.
But quick! Grab your shields and prepare
for battle.
You are being attacked!

[6] Meanwhile, the Lord said to me,
"Put a watchman on the city wall.
Let him shout out what he sees.
[7] He should look for chariots
drawn by pairs of horses,
and for riders on donkeys and camels.
Let the watchman be fully alert."

[8] Then the watchman called out,
"Day after day I have stood on the
watchtower, my lord.
Night after night I have remained
at my post.
[9] Now at last—look!
Here comes a man in a chariot
with a pair of horses!"
Then the watchman said,
"Babylon is fallen, fallen!
All the idols of Babylon
lie broken on the ground!"
[10] O my people, threshed and winnowed,
I have told you everything the LORD
of Heaven's Armies has said,
everything the God of Israel has told me.

A Message about Edom

[11]This message came to me concerning Edom:

Someone from Edom keeps calling to me,
"Watchman, how much longer until
morning?
When will the night be over?"
[12] The watchman replies,
"Morning is coming, but night will
soon return.
If you wish to ask again, then come
back and ask."

A Message about Arabia

[13]This message came to me concerning Arabia:

O caravans from Dedan,
hide in the deserts of Arabia.

14 O people of Tema,
bring water to these thirsty people,
food to these weary refugees.
15 They have fled from the sword,
from the drawn sword,
from the bent bow
and the terrors of battle.

16The Lord said to me, "Within a year, counting each day, all the glory of Kedar will come to
an end. 17Only a few of its courageous archers
will survive. I, the LORD, the God of Israel, have
spoken!"

CHAPTER 22

A Message about Jerusalem

This message came to me concerning Jerusalem—the Valley of Vision:

What is happening?
Why is everyone running to the rooftops?
2 The whole city is in a terrible uproar.
What do I see in this reveling city?
Bodies are lying everywhere,
killed not in battle but by famine
and disease.
3 All your leaders have fled.
They surrendered without resistance.
The people tried to slip away,
but they were captured, too.
4 That's why I said, "Leave me alone
to weep;
do not try to comfort me.
Let me cry for my people
as I watch them being destroyed."

5 Oh, what a day of crushing defeat!
What a day of confusion and terror
brought by the Lord, the LORD of Heaven's
Armies,
upon the Valley of Vision!
The walls of Jerusalem have been broken,
and cries of death echo from the
mountainsides.
6 Elamites are the archers,
with their chariots and charioteers.
The men of Kir hold up the shields.
7 Chariots fill your beautiful valleys,
and charioteers storm your gates.
8 Judah's defenses have been stripped away.
You run to the armory for your weapons.
9 You inspect the breaks in the walls of
Jerusalem.
You store up water in the lower pool.
10 You survey the houses and tear some down
for stone to strengthen the walls.
11 Between the city walls, you build a reservoir
for water from the old pool.
But you never ask for help from the One
who did all this.
You never considered the One who
planned this long ago.
12 At that time the Lord, the LORD of Heaven's
Armies,
called you to weep and mourn.
He told you to shave your heads in sorrow
for your sins
and to wear clothes of burlap to show
your remorse.
13 But instead, you dance and play;
you slaughter cattle and kill sheep.
You feast on meat and drink wine.
You say, "Let's feast and drink,
for tomorrow we die!"

14The LORD of Heaven's Armies has revealed this
to me: "Till the day you die, you will never be forgiven for this sin." That is the judgment of the
Lord, the LORD of Heaven's Armies.

A Message for Shebna

15This is what the Lord, the LORD of Heaven's
Armies, said to me: "Confront Shebna, the palace
administrator, and give him this message:

16 "Who do you think you are,
and what are you doing here,
building a beautiful tomb for yourself—
a monument high up in the rock?
17 For the LORD is about to hurl you away,
mighty man.
He is going to grab you,
18 crumple you into a ball,
and toss you away into a distant,
barren land.
There you will die,
and your glorious chariots will be broken
and useless.
You are a disgrace to your master!

19"Yes, I will drive you out of office," says the
LORD. "I will pull you down from your high position. 20And then I will call my servant Eliakim
son of Hilkiah to replace you. 21I will dress him in
your royal robes and will give him your title and
your authority. And he will be a father to the people of Jerusalem and Judah. 22I will give him the
key to the house of David—the highest position
in the royal court. When he opens doors, no one
will be able to close them; when he closes doors,
no one will be able to open them. 23He will
bring honor to his family name, for I will drive

him firmly in place like a nail in the wall. 24They
will give him great responsibility, and he will
bring honor to even the lowliest members of his
family."

25But the LORD of Heaven's Armies also says:
"The time will come when I will pull out the nail
that seemed so firm. It will come out and fall to
the ground. Everything it supports will fall with
it. I, the LORD, have spoken!"

CHAPTER 23

A Message about Tyre

This message came to me concerning Tyre:

Wail, you trading ships of Tarshish,
for the harbor and houses of Tyre
are gone!
The rumors you heard in Cyprus
are all true.
2 Mourn in silence, you people of the coast
and you merchants of Sidon.
Your traders crossed the sea,
3 sailing over deep waters.
They brought you grain from Egypt
and harvests from along the Nile.
You were the marketplace of the world.
4 But now you are put to shame, city
of Sidon,
for Tyre, the fortress of the sea, says,
"Now I am childless;
I have no sons or daughters."
5 When Egypt hears the news about Tyre,
there will be great sorrow.
6 Send word now to Tarshish!
Wail, you people who live in distant lands!
7 Is this silent ruin all that is left of your
once joyous city?
What a long history was yours!
Think of all the colonists you sent
to distant places.

8 Who has brought this disaster on Tyre,
that great creator of kingdoms?
Her traders were all princes,
her merchants were nobles.
9 The LORD of Heaven's Armies has done it
to destroy your pride
and bring low all earth's nobility.
10 Come, people of Tarshish,
sweep over the land like the flooding Nile,
for Tyre is defenseless.
11 The LORD held out his hand over the sea
and shook the kingdoms of the earth.
He has spoken out against Phoenicia,
ordering that her fortresses be destroyed.

12 He says, "Never again will you rejoice,
O daughter of Sidon, for you have
been crushed.
Even if you flee to Cyprus,
you will find no rest."

13 Look at the land of Babylonia—
the people of that land are gone!
The Assyrians have handed Babylon over
to the wild animals of the desert.
They have built siege ramps against its walls,
torn down its palaces,
and turned it to a heap of rubble.

14 Wail, you ships of Tarshish,
for your harbor is destroyed!

15For seventy years, the length of a king's life,
Tyre will be forgotten. But then the city will come
back to life as in the song about the prostitute:

16 Take a harp and walk the streets,
you forgotten harlot.
Make sweet melody and sing your songs
so you will be remembered again.

17Yes, after seventy years the LORD will revive
Tyre. But she will be no different than she was
before. She will again be a prostitute to all kingdoms around the world. 18But in the end her
profits will be given to the LORD. Her wealth will
not be hoarded but will provide good food and
fine clothing for the LORD's priests.

CHAPTER 24

Destruction of the Earth

1 Look! The LORD is about to destroy the earth
and make it a vast wasteland.
He devastates the surface of the earth
and scatters the people.
2 Priests and laypeople,
servants and masters,
maids and mistresses,
buyers and sellers,
lenders and borrowers,
bankers and debtors—none will be spared.
3 The earth will be completely emptied
and looted.
The LORD has spoken!

4 The earth mourns and dries up,
and the land wastes away and withers.
Even the greatest people on earth
waste away.
5 The earth suffers for the sins of its people,
for they have twisted God's instructions,
violated his laws,
and broken his everlasting covenant.

6 Therefore, a curse consumes the earth.
Its people must pay the price for their sin.
They are destroyed by fire,
and only a few are left alive.
7 The grapevines waste away,
and there is no new wine.
All the merrymakers sigh and mourn.
8 The cheerful sound of tambourines is stilled;
the happy cries of celebration are heard no more.
The melodious chords of the harp
are silent.
9 Gone are the joys of wine and song;
alcoholic drink turns bitter in the mouth.
10 The city writhes in chaos;
every home is locked to keep out
intruders.
11 Mobs gather in the streets, crying out
for wine.
Joy has turned to gloom.
Gladness has been banished from the land.
12 The city is left in ruins,
its gates battered down.
13 Throughout the earth the story is the same—
only a remnant is left,
like the stray olives left on the tree
or the few grapes left on the vine
after harvest.
14 But all who are left shout and sing for joy.
Those in the west praise the LORD's
majesty.
15 In eastern lands, give glory to the LORD.
In the lands beyond the sea, praise the
name of the LORD, the God of Israel.
16 We hear songs of praise from the ends
of the earth,
songs that give glory to the Righteous One!

But my heart is heavy with grief.
Weep for me, for I wither away.
Deceit still prevails,
and treachery is everywhere.
17 Terror and traps and snares will be your lot,
you people of the earth.
18 Those who flee in terror will fall into a trap,
and those who escape the trap will be
caught in a snare.
Destruction falls like rain from the heavens;
the foundations of the earth shake.
19 The earth has broken up.
It has utterly collapsed;
it is violently shaken.
20 The earth staggers like a drunk.
It trembles like a tent in a storm.
It falls and will not rise again,
for the guilt of its rebellion is very heavy.
21 In that day the LORD will punish the gods
in the heavens
and the proud rulers of the nations
on earth.
22 They will be rounded up and put in prison.
They will be shut up in prison
and will finally be punished.
23 Then the glory of the moon will wane,
and the brightness of the sun will fade,
for the LORD of Heaven's Armies will rule
on Mount Zion.
He will rule in great glory in Jerusalem,
in the sight of all the leaders of
his people.

CHAPTER 25

Praise for Judgment and Salvation

1 O LORD, I will honor and praise your name,
for you are my God.
You do such wonderful things!
You planned them long ago,
and now you have accomplished them.
2 You turn mighty cities into heaps of ruins.
Cities with strong walls are turned
to rubble.
Beautiful palaces in distant lands disappear
and will never be rebuilt.
3 Therefore, strong nations will declare
your glory;
ruthless nations will fear you.

4 But you are a tower of refuge to the poor,
O LORD,
a tower of refuge to the needy
in distress.
You are a refuge from the storm
and a shelter from the heat.
For the oppressive acts of ruthless people
are like a storm beating against a wall,
5 or like the relentless heat of the desert.
But you silence the roar of foreign nations.
As the shade of a cloud cools
relentless heat,
so the boastful songs of ruthless people
are stilled.

6 In Jerusalem, the LORD of Heaven's Armies
will spread a wonderful feast
for all the people of the world.
It will be a delicious banquet
with clear, well-aged wine and
choice meat.

[7] There he will remove the cloud of gloom,
the shadow of death that hangs over
the earth.
[8] He will swallow up death forever!
The Sovereign LORD will wipe away all tears.
He will remove forever all insults
and mockery
against his land and people.
The LORD has spoken!

[9] In that day the people will proclaim,
"This is our God!
We trusted in him, and he saved us!
This is the LORD, in whom we trusted.
Let us rejoice in the salvation he brings!"
[10] For the LORD's hand of blessing will rest
on Jerusalem.
But Moab will be crushed.
It will be like straw trampled down and left
to rot.
[11] God will push down Moab's people
as a swimmer pushes down water with
his hands.
He will end their pride
and all their evil works.
[12] The high walls of Moab will be demolished.
They will be brought down to the ground,
down into the dust.

CHAPTER 26

A Song of Praise to the LORD

In that day, everyone in the land of Judah will sing this song:

Our city is strong!
We are surrounded by the walls
of God's salvation.
[2] Open the gates to all who are righteous;
allow the faithful to enter.
[3] You will keep in perfect peace
all who trust in you,
all whose thoughts are fixed on you!
[4] Trust in the LORD always,
for the LORD GOD is the eternal Rock.
[5] He humbles the proud
and brings down the arrogant city.
He brings it down to the dust.
[6] The poor and oppressed trample it
underfoot,
and the needy walk all over it.

[7] But for those who are righteous,
the way is not steep and rough.
You are a God who does what is right,
and you smooth out the path ahead
of them.
[8] LORD, we show our trust in you by obeying
your laws;
our heart's desire is to glorify your name.
[9] In the night I search for you;
in the morning I earnestly seek you.
For only when you come to judge the earth
will people learn what is right.
[10] Your kindness to the wicked
does not make them do good.
Although others do right, the wicked keep
doing wrong
and take no notice of the LORD's majesty.
[11] O LORD, they pay no attention to your
upraised fist.
Show them your eagerness to defend
your people.
Then they will be ashamed.
Let your fire consume your enemies.

[12] LORD, you will grant us peace;
all we have accomplished is really
from you.
[13] O LORD our God, others have ruled us,
but you alone are the one we worship.
[14] Those we served before are dead and gone.
Their departed spirits will never return!
You attacked them and destroyed them,
and they are long forgotten.
[15] O LORD, you have made our nation great;
yes, you have made us great.
You have extended our borders,
and we give you the glory!

[16] LORD, in distress we searched for you.
We prayed beneath the burden of your
discipline.
[17] Just as a pregnant woman
writhes and cries out in pain as she
gives birth,
so were we in your presence, LORD.
[18] We, too, writhe in agony,
but nothing comes of our suffering.
We have not given salvation to the earth,
nor brought life into the world.
[19] But those who die in the LORD will live;
their bodies will rise again!
Those who sleep in the earth
will rise up and sing for joy!
For your life-giving light will fall like dew
on your people in the place of the dead!

Restoration for Israel

[20] Go home, my people,
and lock your doors!
Hide yourselves for a little while
until the LORD's anger has passed.

21 Look! The LORD is coming from heaven
to punish the people of the earth for
their sins.
The earth will no longer hide those who have
been killed.
They will be brought out for all to see.

CHAPTER 27

In that day the LORD will take his terrible, swift
sword and punish Leviathan, the swiftly moving
serpent, the coiling, writhing serpent. He will kill
the dragon of the sea.

2 "In that day,
sing about the fruitful vineyard.
3 I, the LORD, will watch over it,
watering it carefully.
Day and night I will watch so no one can
harm it.
4 My anger will be gone.
If I find briers and thorns growing,
I will attack them;
I will burn them up—
5 unless they turn to me for help.
Let them make peace with me;
yes, let them make peace with me."
6 The time is coming when Jacob's
descendants will take root.
Israel will bud and blossom
and fill the whole earth with fruit!

7 Has the LORD struck Israel
as he struck her enemies?
Has he punished her
as he punished them?
8 No, but he exiled Israel to call her
to account.
She was exiled from her land
as though blown away in a storm from
the east.
9 The LORD did this to purge Israel's
wickedness,
to take away all her sin.
As a result, all the pagan altars will be
crushed to dust.
No Asherah pole or pagan shrine will be
left standing.
10 The fortified towns will be silent and empty,
the houses abandoned, the streets
overgrown with weeds.
Calves will graze there,
chewing on twigs and branches.
11 The people are like the dead branches
of a tree,
broken off and used for kindling beneath
the cooking pots.
Israel is a foolish and stupid nation,
for its people have turned away from God.
Therefore, the one who made them
will show them no pity or mercy.

12 Yet the time will come when the LORD will
gather them together like handpicked grain. One
by one he will gather them—from the Euphrates
River in the east to the Brook of Egypt in the west.
13 In that day the great trumpet will sound. Many
who were dying in exile in Assyria and Egypt will
return to Jerusalem to worship the LORD on his
holy mountain.

CHAPTER 28

A Message about Samaria

1 What sorrow awaits the proud city of
Samaria—
the glorious crown of the drunks
of Israel.
It sits at the head of a fertile valley,
but its glorious beauty will fade like
a flower.
It is the pride of a people
brought down by wine.
2 For the Lord will send a mighty army
against it.
Like a mighty hailstorm and a torrential
rain,
they will burst upon it like a surging flood
and smash it to the ground.
3 The proud city of Samaria—
the glorious crown of the drunks of
Israel—
will be trampled beneath its enemies' feet.
4 It sits at the head of a fertile valley,
but its glorious beauty will fade like
a flower.
Whoever sees it will snatch it up,
as an early fig is quickly picked and eaten.

5 Then at last the LORD of Heaven's Armies
will himself be Israel's glorious crown.
He will be the pride and joy
of the remnant of his people.
6 He will give a longing for justice
to their judges.
He will give great courage
to their warriors who stand at the gates.

7 Now, however, Israel is led by drunks
who reel with wine and stagger with
alcohol.
The priests and prophets stagger with
alcohol
and lose themselves in wine.

They reel when they see visions
and stagger as they render decisions.
8 Their tables are covered with vomit;
filth is everywhere.
9 "Who does the LORD think we are?" they ask.
"Why does he speak to us like this?
Are we little children,
just recently weaned?
10 He tells us everything over and over—
one line at a time,
one line at a time,
a little here,
and a little there!"

11 So now God will have to speak to his people
through foreign oppressors who speak
a strange language!
12 God has told his people,
"Here is a place of rest;
let the weary rest here.
This is a place of quiet rest."
But they would not listen.
13 So the LORD will spell out his message
for them again,
one line at a time,
one line at a time,
a little here,
and a little there,
so that they will stumble and fall.
They will be injured, trapped, and captured.

14 Therefore, listen to this message from
the LORD,
you scoffing rulers in Jerusalem.
15 You boast, "We have struck a bargain to cheat
death
and have made a deal to dodge the grave.
The coming destruction can never touch us,
for we have built a strong refuge made
of lies and deception."
16 Therefore, this is what the Sovereign
LORD says:
"Look! I am placing a foundation stone
in Jerusalem,
a firm and tested stone.
It is a precious cornerstone that is safe
to build on.
Whoever believes need never be shaken.
17 I will test you with the measuring line of
justice
and the plumb line of righteousness.
Since your refuge is made of lies,
a hailstorm will knock it down.
Since it is made of deception,
a flood will sweep it away.
18 I will cancel the bargain you made to
cheat death,
and I will overturn your deal to dodge
the grave.
When the terrible enemy sweeps through,
you will be trampled into the ground.
19 Again and again that flood will come,
morning after morning,
day and night,
until you are carried away."

This message will bring terror to your
people.
20 The bed you have made is too short to lie on.
The blankets are too narrow to cover you.
21 The LORD will come as he did against the
Philistines at Mount Perazim
and against the Amorites at Gibeon.
He will come to do a strange thing;
he will come to do an unusual deed:
22 For the Lord, the LORD of Heaven's Armies,
has plainly said that he is determined
to crush the whole land.
So scoff no more,
or your punishment will be even greater.

23 Listen to me;
listen, and pay close attention.
24 Does a farmer always plow and never sow?
Is he forever cultivating the soil and
never planting?
25 Does he not finally plant his seeds—
black cumin, cumin, wheat, barley, and
emmer wheat—
each in its proper way,
and each in its proper place?
26 The farmer knows just what to do,
for God has given him understanding.
27 A heavy sledge is never used to thresh
black cumin;
rather, it is beaten with a light stick.
A threshing wheel is never rolled on cumin;
instead, it is beaten lightly with a flail.
28 Grain for bread is easily crushed,
so he doesn't keep on pounding it.
He threshes it under the wheels of a cart,
but he doesn't pulverize it.
29 The LORD of Heaven's Armies is a wonderful
teacher,
and he gives the farmer great wisdom.

CHAPTER 29

A Message about Jerusalem

1 "What sorrow awaits Ariel, the City
of David.
Year after year you celebrate your feasts.

FUN-fact

My name means "Eagle"!

What's in a NAME?

What's your last name?

Do you know what Jesus' last name was? You might think it's "Christ." Not so! "Christ" is a Hebrew title that means "anointed one."

A second name usually told who the person's father was, described the person, or told where a person lived. That's why Jesus was sometimes called **Jesus of Nazareth.**

Check out these second names that told

what someone did—**JOHN 1:19-26**

where someone was from—**MATTHEW 27:57-60**

what illness someone had—**MATTHEW 26:6**

Try this for fun.

Think of a talent or ability God has given you. Now make up a last name for yourself about that talent. Make up names to describe the talents of your friends and family members, too!

JUST CALL ME SETH THE SKATEBOARDER

2 Yet I will bring disaster upon you,
and there will be much weeping and sorrow.
For Jerusalem will become what her name Ariel means—
an altar covered with blood.
3 I will be your enemy,
surrounding Jerusalem and attacking its walls.
I will build siege towers
and destroy it.
4 Then deep from the earth you will speak;
from low in the dust your words will come.
Your voice will whisper from the ground
like a ghost conjured up from the grave.

5 "But suddenly, your ruthless enemies will be crushed
like the finest of dust.
Your many attackers will be driven away
like chaff before the wind.
Suddenly, in an instant,
6 I, the LORD of Heaven's Armies, will act for you
with thunder and earthquake and great noise,
with whirlwind and storm and consuming fire.
7 All the nations fighting against Jerusalem
will vanish like a dream!
Those who are attacking her walls
will vanish like a vision in the night.
8 A hungry person dreams of eating
but wakes up still hungry.
A thirsty person dreams of drinking
but is still faint from thirst when morning comes.
So it will be with your enemies,
with those who attack Mount Zion."

9 Are you amazed and incredulous?
Don't you believe it?
Then go ahead and be blind.
You are stupid, but not from wine!
You stagger, but not from liquor!
10 For the LORD has poured out on you a spirit of deep sleep.
He has closed the eyes of your prophets
and visionaries.

11 All the future events in this vision are like a
sealed book to them. When you give it to those
who can read, they will say, "We can't read it because it is sealed." 12 When you give it to those
who cannot read, they will say, "We don't know
how to read."

13 And so the Lord says,
"These people say they are mine.
They honor me with their lips,
but their hearts are far from me.
And their worship of me
is nothing but man-made rules learned by rote.

14 Because of this, I will once again astound
these hypocrites
with amazing wonders.
The wisdom of the wise will pass away,
and the intelligence of the intelligent
will disappear."

15 What sorrow awaits those who try to hide
their plans from the LORD,
who do their evil deeds in the dark!
"The LORD can't see us," they say.
"He doesn't know what's going on!"
16 How foolish can you be?
He is the Potter, and he is certainly
greater than you, the clay!
Should the created thing say of the one
who made it,
"He didn't make me"?
Does a jar ever say,
"The potter who made me is stupid"?

17 Soon—and it will not be very long—
the forests of Lebanon will become
a fertile field,
and the fertile field will yield bountiful
crops.
18 In that day the deaf will hear words read
from a book,
and the blind will see through the gloom
and darkness.
19 The humble will be filled with fresh joy
from the LORD.
The poor will rejoice in the Holy One
of Israel.
20 The scoffer will be gone,
the arrogant will disappear,
and those who plot evil will be killed.
21 Those who convict the innocent
by their false testimony will disappear.
A similar fate awaits those who use trickery
to pervert justice
and who tell lies to destroy the innocent.

22 That is why the LORD, who redeemed Abraham,
says to the people of Israel,

"My people will no longer be ashamed
or turn pale with fear.
23 For when they see their many children
and all the blessings I have given them,
they will recognize the holiness of the Holy
One of Jacob.
They will stand in awe of the God
of Israel.
24 Then the wayward will gain understanding,
and complainers will accept
instruction.

CHAPTER 30

Judah's Worthless Treaty with Egypt

1 "What sorrow awaits my rebellious children,"
says the LORD.
"You make plans that are contrary to mine.
You make alliances not directed by my
Spirit,
thus piling up your sins.
2 For without consulting me,
you have gone down to Egypt for help.
You have put your trust in Pharaoh's
protection.
You have tried to hide in his shade.
3 But by trusting Pharaoh, you will be
humiliated,
and by depending on him, you will be
disgraced.
4 For though his power extends to Zoan
and his officials have arrived in Hanes,
5 all who trust in him will be ashamed.
He will not help you.
Instead, he will disgrace you."

6 This message came to me concerning the animals in the Negev:

The caravan moves slowly
across the terrible desert to Egypt—
donkeys weighed down with riches
and camels loaded with treasure—
all to pay for Egypt's protection.
They travel through the wilderness,
a place of lionesses and lions,
a place where vipers and poisonous
snakes live.
All this, and Egypt will give you nothing
in return.
7 Egypt's promises are worthless!
Therefore, I call her Rahab—
the Harmless Dragon.

A Warning for Rebellious Judah

8 Now go and write down these words.
Write them in a book.
They will stand until the end of time
as a witness
9 that these people are stubborn rebels
who refuse to pay attention to the LORD's
instructions.
10 They tell the seers,
"Stop seeing visions!"
They tell the prophets,
"Don't tell us what is right.
Tell us nice things.
Tell us lies.

11 Forget all this gloom.
Get off your narrow path.
Stop telling us about your
'Holy One of Israel.'"

12 This is the reply of the Holy One of Israel:

"Because you despise what I tell you
and trust instead in oppression and lies,
13 calamity will come upon you suddenly—
like a bulging wall that bursts and falls.
In an instant it will collapse
and come crashing down.
14 You will be smashed like a piece of pottery—
shattered so completely that
there won't be a piece big enough
to carry coals from a fireplace
or a little water from the well."

15 This is what the Sovereign LORD,
the Holy One of Israel, says:
"Only in returning to me
and resting in me will you be saved.
In quietness and confidence is your strength.
But you would have none of it.
16 You said, 'No, we will get our help from
Egypt.
They will give us swift horses for riding
into battle.'
But the only swiftness you are going to see
is the swiftness of your enemies
chasing you!
17 One of them will chase a thousand of you.
Five of them will make all of you flee.
You will be left like a lonely flagpole on a hill
or a tattered banner on a distant
mountaintop."

Blessings for the LORD's People

18 So the LORD must wait for you to come to him
so he can show you his love and
compassion.
For the LORD is a faithful God.
Blessed are those who wait for his help.

19 O people of Zion, who live in Jerusalem,
you will weep no more.
He will be gracious if you ask for help.
He will surely respond to the sound
of your cries.
20 Though the Lord gave you adversity for food
and suffering for drink,
he will still be with you to teach you.
You will see your teacher with your
own eyes.
21 Your own ears will hear him.
Right behind you a voice will say,
"This is the way you should go,"
whether to the right or to the left.
22 Then you will destroy all your silver idols
and your precious gold images.
You will throw them out like filthy rags,
saying to them, "Good riddance!"

23 Then the LORD will bless you with rain at
planting time. There will be wonderful harvests
and plenty of pastureland for your livestock.
24 The oxen and donkeys that till the ground will
eat good grain, its chaff blown away by the wind.
25 In that day, when your enemies are slaughtered
and the towers fall, there will be streams of water
flowing down every mountain and hill. 26 The
moon will be as bright as the sun, and the sun
will be seven times brighter—like the light of
seven days in one! So it will be when the LORD begins to heal his people and cure the wounds he
gave them.

27 Look! The LORD is coming from far away,
burning with anger,
surrounded by thick, rising smoke.
His lips are filled with fury;
his words consume like fire.
28 His hot breath pours out like a flood
up to the neck of his enemies.
He will sift out the proud nations for
destruction.
He will bridle them and lead them away
to ruin.

29 But the people of God will sing a song of joy,
like the songs at the holy festivals.
You will be filled with joy,
as when a flutist leads a group of pilgrims
to Jerusalem, the mountain of the LORD—
to the Rock of Israel.
30 And the LORD will make his majestic voice
heard.
He will display the strength of his
mighty arm.
It will descend with devouring flames,
with cloudbursts, thunderstorms, and
huge hailstones.
31 At the LORD's command, the Assyrians will
be shattered.
He will strike them down with his royal
scepter.
32 And as the LORD strikes them with his rod
of punishment,
his people will celebrate with tambourines
and harps.
Lifting his mighty arm, he will fight the
Assyrians.

33 Topheth—the place of burning—
has long been ready for the Assyrian king;
the pyre is piled high with wood.
The breath of the LORD, like fire from
a volcano,
will set it ablaze.

CHAPTER 31
The Futility of Relying on Egypt

1 What sorrow awaits those who look to Egypt
for help,
trusting their horses, chariots,
and charioteers
and depending on the strength
of human armies
instead of looking to the LORD,
the Holy One of Israel.
2 In his wisdom, the LORD will send
great disaster;
he will not change his mind.
He will rise against the wicked
and against their helpers.
3 For these Egyptians are mere humans,
not God!
Their horses are puny flesh, not
mighty spirits!
When the LORD raises his fist against them,
those who help will stumble,
and those being helped will fall.
They will all fall down and die together.

4 But this is what the LORD has told me:

"When a strong young lion
stands growling over a sheep it has killed,
it is not frightened by the shouts and noise
of a whole crowd of shepherds.
In the same way, the LORD of Heaven's
Armies
will come down and fight on Mount Zion.
5 The LORD of Heaven's Armies will hover over
Jerusalem
and protect it like a bird protecting
its nest.
He will defend and save the city;
he will pass over it and rescue it."

6 Though you are such wicked rebels, my people, come and return to the LORD. 7 I know the
glorious day will come when each of you will
throw away the gold idols and silver images your
sinful hands have made.

8 "The Assyrians will be destroyed,
but not by the swords of men.
The sword of God will strike them,
and they will panic and flee.
The strong young Assyrians
will be taken away as captives.
9 Even the strongest will quake with terror,
and princes will flee when they see your
battle flags,"
says the LORD, whose fire burns in Zion,
whose flame blazes from Jerusalem.

CHAPTER 32
Israel's Ultimate Deliverance

1 Look, a righteous king is coming!
And honest princes will rule under him.
2 Each one will be like a shelter from the wind
and a refuge from the storm,
like streams of water in the desert
and the shadow of a great rock in a
parched land.

3 Then everyone who has eyes will be able
to see the truth,
and everyone who has ears will be able
to hear it.
4 Even the hotheads will be full of sense and
understanding.
Those who stammer will speak out plainly.
5 In that day ungodly fools will not be heroes.
Scoundrels will not be respected.
6 For fools speak foolishness
and make evil plans.
They practice ungodliness
and spread false teachings about the LORD.
They deprive the hungry of food
and give no water to the thirsty.
7 The smooth tricks of scoundrels are evil.
They plot crooked schemes.
They lie to convict the poor,
even when the cause of the poor is just.
8 But generous people plan to do what is
generous,
and they stand firm in their generosity.

9 Listen, you women who lie around in ease.
Listen to me, you who are so smug.
10 In a short time—just a little more than
a year—
you careless ones will suddenly begin
to care.
For your fruit crops will fail,
and the harvest will never take place.
11 Tremble, you women of ease;
throw off your complacency.
Strip off your pretty clothes,
and put on burlap to show your grief.
12 Beat your breasts in sorrow for your
bountiful farms
and your fruitful grapevines.

13 For your land will be overgrown with thorns
and briers.
Your joyful homes and happy towns will be
gone.
14 The palace and the city will be deserted,
and busy towns will be empty.
Wild donkeys will frolic and flocks will graze
in the empty forts and watchtowers
15 until at last the Spirit is poured out
on us from heaven.
Then the wilderness will become a
fertile field,
and the fertile field will yield
bountiful crops.

16 Justice will rule in the wilderness
and righteousness in the fertile field.
17 And this righteousness will bring peace.
Yes, it will bring quietness and confidence
forever.
18 My people will live in safety, quietly at home.
They will be at rest.
19 Even if the forest should be destroyed
and the city torn down,
20 the LORD will greatly bless his people.
Wherever they plant seed, bountiful
crops will spring up.
Their cattle and donkeys will graze freely.

CHAPTER 33
A Message about Assyria

1 What sorrow awaits you Assyrians, who have
destroyed others
but have never been destroyed yourselves.
You betray others,
but you have never been betrayed.
When you are done destroying,
you will be destroyed.
When you are done betraying,
you will be betrayed.
2 But LORD, be merciful to us,
for we have waited for you.
Be our strong arm each day
and our salvation in times of trouble.
3 The enemy runs at the sound of your voice.
When you stand up, the nations flee!
4 Just as caterpillars and locusts strip the
fields and vines,
so the fallen army of Assyria will be
stripped!

5 Though the LORD is very great and lives
in heaven,
he will make Jerusalem his home of justice
and righteousness.
6 In that day he will be your sure foundation,
providing a rich store of salvation, wisdom,
and knowledge.
The fear of the LORD will be your treasure.

7 But now your brave warriors weep in public.
Your ambassadors of peace cry in bitter
disappointment.
8 Your roads are deserted;
no one travels them anymore.
The Assyrians have broken their peace treaty
and care nothing for the promises they
made before witnesses.
They have no respect for anyone.
9 The land of Israel wilts in mourning.
Lebanon withers with shame.
The plain of Sharon is now a wilderness.
Bashan and Carmel have been plundered.

10 But the LORD says: "Now I will stand up.
Now I will show my power and might.
11 You Assyrians produce nothing but dry grass
and stubble.
Your own breath will turn to fire and
consume you.
12 Your people will be burned up completely,
like thornbushes cut down and tossed
in a fire.
13 Listen to what I have done, you nations
far away!
And you that are near, acknowledge
my might!"

14 The sinners in Jerusalem shake with fear.
Terror seizes the godless.
"Who can live with this devouring fire?"
they cry.
"Who can survive this all-consuming fire?"
15 Those who are honest and fair,
who refuse to profit by fraud,
who stay far away from bribes,
who refuse to listen to those who plot
murder,
who shut their eyes to all enticement
to do wrong—
16 these are the ones who will dwell on high.
The rocks of the mountains will be their
fortress.
Food will be supplied to them,
and they will have water in abundance.

17 Your eyes will see the king in all his splendor,
and you will see a land that stretches into
the distance.
18 You will think back to this time of terror,
asking,
"Where are the Assyrian officers
who counted our towers?

Where are the bookkeepers
who recorded the plunder taken from
our fallen city?"
19 You will no longer see these fierce,
violent people
with their strange, unknown language.
20 Instead, you will see Zion as a place
of holy festivals.
You will see Jerusalem, a city quiet
and secure.
It will be like a tent whose ropes are taut
and whose stakes are firmly fixed.
21 The LORD will be our Mighty One.
He will be like a wide river of protection
that no enemy can cross,
that no enemy ship can sail upon.
22 For the LORD is our judge,
our lawgiver, and our king.
He will care for us and save us.
23 The enemies' sails hang loose
on broken masts with useless tackle.
Their treasure will be divided by the people
of God.
Even the lame will take their share!
24 The people of Israel will no longer say,
"We are sick and helpless,"
for the LORD will forgive their sins.

CHAPTER 34

A Message for the Nations

1 Come here and listen, O nations of
the earth.
Let the world and everything in it hear
my words.
2 For the LORD is enraged against the nations.
His fury is against all their armies.
He will completely destroy them,
dooming them to slaughter.
3 Their dead will be left unburied,
and the stench of rotting bodies will fill
the land.
The mountains will flow with their blood.
4 The heavens above will melt away
and disappear like a rolled-up scroll.
The stars will fall from the sky
like withered leaves from a grapevine,
or shriveled figs from a fig tree.

5 And when my sword has finished its work
in the heavens,
it will fall upon Edom,
the nation I have marked for destruction.
6 The sword of the LORD is drenched
with blood
and covered with fat—
with the blood of lambs and goats,
with the fat of rams prepared for
sacrifice.
Yes, the LORD will offer a sacrifice in the
city of Bozrah.
He will make a mighty slaughter
in Edom.
7 Even men as strong as wild oxen will die—
the young men alongside the veterans.
The land will be soaked with blood
and the soil enriched with fat.
8 For it is the day of the LORD's revenge,
the year when Edom will be paid back
for all it did to Israel.
9 The streams of Edom will be filled with
burning pitch,
and the ground will be covered with fire.
10 This judgment on Edom will never end;
the smoke of its burning will rise forever.
The land will lie deserted from generation
to generation.
No one will live there anymore.
11 It will be haunted by the desert owl and the
screech owl,
the great owl and the raven.
For God will measure that land carefully;
he will measure it for chaos and
destruction.
12 It will be called the Land of Nothing,
and all its nobles will soon be gone.
13 Thorns will overrun its palaces;
nettles and thistles will grow in its forts.
The ruins will become a haunt for jackals
and a home for owls.
14 Desert animals will mingle there with
hyenas,
their howls filling the night.
Wild goats will bleat at one another among
the ruins,
and night creatures will come there
to rest.
15 There the owl will make her nest and lay
her eggs.
She will hatch her young and cover them
with her wings.
And the buzzards will come,
each one with its mate.

16 Search the book of the LORD,
and see what he will do.
Not one of these birds and animals will
be missing,
and none will lack a mate,
for the LORD has promised this.
His Spirit will make it all come true.

FUN-fact

You've Got Mail!

Have you ever had a pen pal? Reading the Bible is like having lots of pen pals! God used fishermen, shepherds, kings, prophets, and pastors to write the Bible. They wrote from three different continents (Asia, Africa, and Europe) in three different languages (Hebrew, Aramaic, and Greek.) They wrote from lots of different places, like prisons, palaces, the wilderness, and even islands. When we read the Bible, it's like having lots of pen pals to tell us God's messages for us!

Ask an adult to help you find an organization that matches kids with pen pals. As you get to know your pen pal, be sure to share your faith in Jesus. God can use *you* to spread his message too!

17 He has surveyed and divided the land
and deeded it over to those creatures.
They will possess it forever,
from generation to generation.

CHAPTER 35
Hope for Restoration

1 Even the wilderness and desert will be glad
in those days.
The wasteland will rejoice and blossom
with spring crocuses.
2 Yes, there will be an abundance of flowers
and singing and joy!
The deserts will become as green as the
mountains of Lebanon,
as lovely as Mount Carmel or the plain
of Sharon.
There the LORD will display his glory,
the splendor of our God.
3 With this news, strengthen those who have
tired hands,
and encourage those who have
weak knees.
4 Say to those with fearful hearts,
"Be strong, and do not fear,
for your God is coming to destroy
your enemies.
He is coming to save you."
5 And when he comes, he will open the eyes
of the blind
and unplug the ears of the deaf.
6 The lame will leap like a deer,
and those who cannot speak will sing
for joy!
Springs will gush forth in the wilderness,
and streams will water the wasteland.
7 The parched ground will become a pool,
and springs of water will satisfy the
thirsty land.
Marsh grass and reeds and rushes will flourish
where desert jackals once lived.

8 And a great road will go through that once
deserted land.
It will be named the Highway of Holiness.
Evil-minded people will never travel on it.
It will be only for those who walk
in God's ways;
fools will never walk there.
9 Lions will not lurk along its course,
nor any other ferocious beasts.
There will be no other dangers.
Only the redeemed will walk on it.
10 Those who have been ransomed by the LORD
will return.
They will enter Jerusalem singing,
crowned with everlasting joy.
Sorrow and mourning will disappear,
and they will be filled with joy and gladness.

CHAPTER 36
Assyria Invades Judah

In the fourteenth year of King Hezekiah's reign,
King Sennacherib of Assyria came to attack the
fortified towns of Judah and conquered them.
2 Then the king of Assyria sent his chief of staff
from Lachish with a huge army to confront King
Hezekiah in Jerusalem. The Assyrians took up a
position beside the aqueduct that feeds water
into the upper pool, near the road leading to the
field where cloth is washed.
3 These are the officials who went out to meet
with them: Eliakim son of Hilkiah, the palace administrator; Shebna the court secretary; and
Joah son of Asaph, the royal historian.

Sennacherib Threatens Jerusalem

4 Then the Assyrian king's chief of staff told them
to give this message to Hezekiah:

"This is what the great king of Assyria says:
What are you trusting in that makes you so
confident? 5 Do you think that mere words

can substitute for military skill and strength?
Who are you counting on, that you have
rebelled against me? 6On Egypt? If you lean
on Egypt, it will be like a reed that splinters
beneath your weight and pierces your hand.
Pharaoh, the king of Egypt, is completely
unreliable!

7"But perhaps you will say to me, 'We are
trusting in the LORD our God!' But isn't he the
one who was insulted by Hezekiah? Didn't
Hezekiah tear down his shrines and altars
and make everyone in Judah and Jerusalem
worship only at the altar here in Jerusalem?

8"I'll tell you what! Strike a bargain with
my master, the king of Assyria. I will give
you 2,000 horses if you can find that many
men to ride on them! 9With your tiny army,
how can you think of challenging even the
weakest contingent of my master's troops,
even with the help of Egypt's chariots and
charioteers? 10What's more, do you think
we have invaded your land without the
LORD's direction? The LORD himself told
us, 'Attack this land and destroy it!'"

11Then Eliakim, Shebna, and Joah said to the
Assyrian chief of staff, "Please speak to us in Ara-
maic, for we understand it well. Don't speak in
Hebrew, for the people on the wall will hear."

12But Sennacherib's chief of staff replied, "Do
you think my master sent this message only to
you and your master? He wants all the people to
hear it, for when we put this city under siege,
they will suffer along with you. They will be so
hungry and thirsty that they will eat their own
dung and drink their own urine."

13Then the chief of staff stood and shouted in
Hebrew to the people on the wall, "Listen to this
message from the great king of Assyria! 14This is
what the king says: Don't let Hezekiah deceive
you. He will never be able to rescue you. 15Don't
let him fool you into trusting in the LORD by saying, 'The LORD will surely rescue us. This city will
never fall into the hands of the Assyrian king!'

16"Don't listen to Hezekiah! These are the
terms the king of Assyria is offering: Make peace
with me—open the gates and come out. Then
each of you can continue eating from your own
grapevine and fig tree and drinking from your
own well. 17Then I will arrange to take you to another land like this one—a land of grain and new
wine, bread and vineyards.

18"Don't let Hezekiah mislead you by saying,
'The LORD will rescue us!' Have the gods of any
other nations ever saved their people from the
king of Assyria? 19What happened to the gods of
Hamath and Arpad? And what about the gods of
Sepharvaim? Did any god rescue Samaria from
my power? 20What god of any nation has ever
been able to save its people from my power? So
what makes you think that the LORD can rescue
Jerusalem from me?"

21But the people were silent and did not utter
a word because Hezekiah had commanded
them, "Do not answer him."

22Then Eliakim son of Hilkiah, the palace administrator; Shebna the court secretary; and
Joah son of Asaph, the royal historian, went back
to Hezekiah. They tore their clothes in despair,
and they went in to see the king and told him
what the Assyrian chief of staff had said.

CHAPTER 37

Hezekiah Seeks the LORD's Help

When King Hezekiah heard their report, he tore
his clothes and put on burlap and went into the
Temple of the LORD. 2And he sent Eliakim the
palace administrator, Shebna the court secretary,
and the leading priests, all dressed in burlap, to
the prophet Isaiah son of Amoz. 3They told him,
"This is what King Hezekiah says: Today is a day
of trouble, insults, and disgrace. It is like when a
child is ready to be born, but the mother has no
strength to deliver the baby. 4But perhaps the
LORD your God has heard the Assyrian chief of
staff, sent by the king to defy the living God, and
will punish him for his words. Oh, pray for those
of us who are left!"

5After King Hezekiah's officials delivered the
king's message to Isaiah, 6the prophet replied,
"Say to your master, 'This is what the LORD says:
Do not be disturbed by this blasphemous speech
against me from the Assyrian king's messengers.
7Listen! I myself will move against him, and the
king will receive a message that he is needed at
home. So he will return to his land, where I will
have him killed with a sword.'"

8Meanwhile, the Assyrian chief of staff left Jerusalem and went to consult the king of Assyria,
who had left Lachish and was attacking Libnah.

9Soon afterward King Sennacherib received
word that King Tirhakah of Ethiopia was leading
an army to fight against him. Before leaving to
meet the attack, he sent messengers back to
Hezekiah in Jerusalem with this message:

10"This message is for King Hezekiah of
Judah. Don't let your God, in whom you trust,
deceive you with promises that Jerusalem will
not be captured by the king of Assyria. 11You

know perfectly well what the kings of Assyria
have done wherever they have gone. They
have completely destroyed everyone who
stood in their way! Why should you be any
different? 12 Have the gods of other nations
rescued them—such nations as Gozan, Haran,
Rezeph, and the people of Eden who were in
Tel-assar? My predecessors destroyed them
all! 13 What happened to the king of Hamath
and the king of Arpad? What happened to the
kings of Sepharvaim, Hena, and Ivvah?"

14 After Hezekiah received the letter from
the messengers and read it, he went up to the
LORD's Temple and spread it out before the
LORD. 15 And Hezekiah prayed this prayer before
the LORD: 16 "O LORD of Heaven's Armies, God of
Israel, you are enthroned between the mighty
cherubim! You alone are God of all the kingdoms of the earth. You alone created the heavens and the earth. 17 Bend down, O LORD, and
listen! Open your eyes, O LORD, and see! Listen
to Sennacherib's words of defiance against the
living God.
18 "It is true, LORD, that the kings of Assyria
have destroyed all these nations. 19 And they have
thrown the gods of these nations into the fire and
burned them. But of course the Assyrians could
destroy them! They were not gods at all—only
idols of wood and stone shaped by human hands.
20 Now, O LORD our God, rescue us from his
power; then all the kingdoms of the earth will
know that you alone, O LORD, are God."

Isaiah Predicts Judah's Deliverance

21 Then Isaiah son of Amoz sent this message to
Hezekiah: "This is what the LORD, the God of Israel, says: Because you prayed about King
Sennacherib of Assyria, 22 the LORD has spoken
this word against him:

"The virgin daughter of Zion
despises you and laughs at you.
The daughter of Jerusalem
shakes her head in derision as you flee.

23 "Whom have you been defying and
ridiculing?
Against whom did you raise your voice?
At whom did you look with such
haughty eyes?
It was the Holy One of Israel!
24 By your messengers you have defied
the Lord.
You have said, 'With my many chariots
I have conquered the highest mountains—
yes, the remotest peaks of Lebanon.
I have cut down its tallest cedars
and its finest cypress trees.
I have reached its farthest heights
and explored its deepest forests.
25 I have dug wells in many foreign lands
and refreshed myself with their water.
With the sole of my foot,
I stopped up all the rivers of Egypt!'

26 "But have you not heard?
I decided this long ago.
Long ago I planned it,
and now I am making it happen.
I planned for you to crush fortified cities
into heaps of rubble.
27 That is why their people have so little power
and are so frightened and confused.
They are as weak as grass,
as easily trampled as tender green
shoots.
They are like grass sprouting on a housetop,
scorched before it can grow lush and tall.

28 "But I know you well—
where you stay
and when you come and go.
I know the way you have raged against me.
29 And because of your raging against me
and your arrogance, which I have heard for
myself,
I will put my hook in your nose
and my bit in your mouth.
I will make you return
by the same road on which you came."

30 Then Isaiah said to Hezekiah, "Here is the
proof that what I say is true:

"This year you will eat only what grows
up by itself,
and next year you will eat what springs
up from that.
But in the third year you will plant crops and
harvest them;
you will tend vineyards and eat their fruit.
31 And you who are left in Judah,
who have escaped the ravages of the siege,
will put roots down in your own soil
and grow up and flourish.
32 For a remnant of my people will spread out
from Jerusalem,
a group of survivors from Mount Zion.
The passionate commitment of the LORD
of Heaven's Armies
will make this happen!

[33]"And this is what the LORD says about the king
of Assyria:

" 'His armies will not enter Jerusalem.
They will not even shoot an arrow at it.
They will not march outside its gates with
their shields
nor build banks of earth against its walls.
[34] The king will return to his own country
by the same road on which he came.
He will not enter this city,'
says the LORD.
[35] 'For my own honor and for the sake of my
servant David,
I will defend this city and protect it.' "

[36]That night the angel of the LORD went out to
the Assyrian camp and killed 185,000 Assyrian
soldiers. When the surviving Assyrians woke up
the next morning, they found corpses everywhere. [37]Then King Sennacherib of Assyria
broke camp and returned to his own land. He
went home to his capital of Nineveh and stayed
there.

[38]One day while he was worshiping in the
temple of his god Nisroch, his sons Adram-
melech and Sharezer killed him with their
swords. They then escaped to the land of Ararat,
and another son, Esarhaddon, became the next
king of Assyria.

CHAPTER 38

Hezekiah's Sickness and Recovery

About that time Hezekiah became deathly ill,
and the prophet Isaiah son of Amoz went to visit
him. He gave the king this message: "This is
what the LORD says: 'Set your affairs in order, for
you are going to die. You will not recover from
this illness.'"

[2]When Hezekiah heard this, he turned his
face to the wall and prayed to the LORD, [3]"Remember, O LORD, how I have always been faithful
to you and have served you single-mindedly, always doing what pleases you." Then he broke
down and wept bitterly.

[4]Then this message came to Isaiah from the
LORD: [5]"Go back to Hezekiah and tell him, 'This
is what the LORD, the God of your ancestor David,
says: I have heard your prayer and seen your
tears. I will add fifteen years to your life, [6]and I
will rescue you and this city from the king of Assyria. Yes, I will defend this city.

[7]"'And this is the sign from the LORD to prove
that he will do as he promised: [8]I will cause the
sun's shadow to move ten steps backward on the
sundial of Ahaz!'" So the shadow on the sundial
moved backward ten steps.

Hezekiah's Poem of Praise

[9]When King Hezekiah was well again, he wrote
this poem:

[10] I said, "In the prime of my life,
must I now enter the place of the dead?
Am I to be robbed of the rest of my years?"
[11] I said, "Never again will I see the LORD GOD
while still in the land of the living.
Never again will I see my friends
or be with those who live in this world.
[12] My life has been blown away
like a shepherd's tent in a storm.
It has been cut short,
as when a weaver cuts cloth from a loom.
Suddenly, my life was over.
[13] I waited patiently all night,
but I was torn apart as though by lions.
Suddenly, my life was over.
[14] Delirious, I chattered like a swallow or a crane,
and then I moaned like a mourning dove.
My eyes grew tired of looking to heaven for
help.
I am in trouble, Lord. Help me!"
[15] But what could I say?
For he himself sent this sickness.
Now I will walk humbly throughout my years
because of this anguish I have felt.
[16] Lord, your discipline is good,
for it leads to life and health.
You restore my health
and allow me to live!
[17] Yes, this anguish was good for me,
for you have rescued me from death
and forgiven all my sins.
[18] For the dead cannot praise you;
they cannot raise their voices in praise.
Those who go down to the grave
can no longer hope in your faithfulness.
[19] Only the living can praise you as I do today.
Each generation tells of your faithfulness
to the next.
[20] Think of it—the LORD is ready to heal me!
I will sing his praises with instruments
every day of my life
in the Temple of the LORD.

[21]Isaiah had said to Hezekiah's servants,
"Make an ointment from figs and spread it over
the boil, and Hezekiah will recover."

[22]And Hezekiah had asked, "What sign will
prove that I will go to the Temple of the LORD?"

David

1 Samuel 16—2 Samuel 24

DON'T BE DISCOURAGED

Little guys can make a *big* difference.
One of the greatest men in the Bible almost got skipped over because he was small and young. **Read about it in 1 Samuel 16:1-13.** David didn't let the fact that he was small and young stop him from making a big difference. **Learn about a few of the things David did by reading 1 Samuel 17:1-50; 1 Samuel 30:1-20; and 2 Samuel 5:1-5.**

Stronger Than Strong

1. Have two helpers hold broom handles about 20 inches apart. Tie a nine-foot rope to one broom handle.

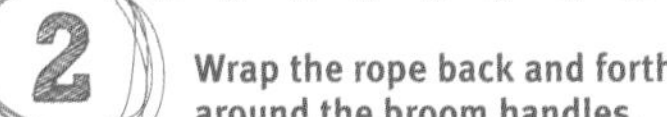

2. Wrap the rope back and forth around the broom handles.

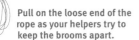

3. Pull on the loose end of the rope as your helpers try to keep the brooms apart.

Hey, you were stronger than your helpers. So was David. He never could have done everything he did alone. But he had God on his side!

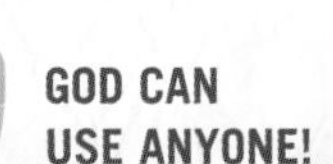

The JESUS CONNECTION

GOD CAN USE ANYONE!

God used David—the smallest member of an unimportant family—to do big things. Jesus came to save all people—whether they're beautiful, ugly, rich, poor, smart, or slow. God can use anyone! Don't believe it?
READ ROMANS 2:11 AND ACTS 10:34.

Elijah
1 Kings 18

NOW THAT'S POWER!

One bolt of lightning can deliver 100 million volts and can be as hot as 50,000 degrees Fahrenheit. The power in nature is amazing, but it's nothing compared to God's power. When the people of Israel worshiped false gods, Elijah held a contest to show who had the real power. **Read all about it in 1 Kings 18:16-39.**

Electrifying!

1. Pour some paper confetti on a table.

2. Rub a balloon on your head or a wool sweater for about 30 seconds. (Wool works better!)

3. Slowly move the balloon down to the confetti.

The confetti leaped up to the balloon because you gave it a charge with your hair or sweater. The charge pulled up the confetti. Keep your eyes open for God's power—it will definitely surprise you!

Did you know?

- **Tornado** winds can blow at 300 miles per hour.
- **Volcano flows can reach** nearly 1,300 degrees Fahrenheit.
- **Tsunamis (often caused by underwater earthquakes)** can make ocean waves that are more than 100 feet high and travel at more than 450 miles per hour.

God is more powerful than all these things!

The JESUS CONNECTION

JESUS IS GOD. Elijah set up a contest with the prophets of the false god Baal. The prophets lost, and the whole nation of Israel saw, through God's electrifying power, who was the one true God. Over 800 years later, Elijah (along with Moses) appeared to Jesus' disciples to help them see that Jesus was God. **YOU CAN READ ALL ABOUT IT IN LUKE 9:28-36.** Jesus was more than a good teacher or a great man; Jesus was also God on earth who came to save the world from sin.

Daniel

Daniel 6

WATCH OUT!

Don't get in her way. She's taking care of her little ones. You have people in your life who care for you. Guess what! God put them there! And God is watching over you, too.

You may face troubles and hard times, but God will help you through. Just look at what God did for Daniel. Read Daniel 6:1-23. God takes care of his children!

Balloon Bop

1. Grab two sheets and a bunch of friends. Make a bunch of water balloons, and go outside.
2. Form two teams. Gather one team around a sheet, put a water balloon in the middle, and launch it by pulling the sheet tight.
3. Have the other team catch the water balloon with its sheet. See how many times you can pass the balloon back and forth without breaking it.

TALK IT OVER WITH YOUR FRIENDS:

What was it like to pass the water balloon back and forth?

How is the balloon like us? different from us?

How is the sheet like God? different from God?

GOD TAKES CARE OF HIS CHILDREN.

Daniel obeyed God, and God protected him from getting chomped by lions. Your life won't always be easy, and sometimes doing the right thing will be difficult. But once you decide to follow Jesus, he will always be with you. Check it out in **ROMANS 8:38-39 AND JOHN 10:2-30.**

Psalm 23

HEY, YOU! CALM DOWN

Quit worrying! God is always with you. He's taking care of you like a shepherd takes care of his sheep. Shepherds make sure their sheep stay safe and have what they need. God is *your* **shepherd. Read all about it in Psalm 23.**

Good Shepherds

1. Create a safe, simple obstacle course in the center of a room.
2. Blindfold a friend, and use only your voice to guide the friend through the course.
3. Switch roles and play again. Then talk this over:

- How was leading your friend through the obstacle course like being a shepherd?
- Why do sheep need shepherds? What do shepherds do for their sheep?
- Read Psalm 23. What does it mean that God is your shepherd?
- How does God take care of you?

NEVER ALONE! We are never alone, and we are never forgotten! Jesus s[aid] he is a good shepherd who takes care of his sheep. In fact, he laid down his own life to save us! When you feel afraid or discourage[d], remember God's promises in **PSALM 23**. And read **JOHN 10:1-18** to learn more about how Jesus shepherds his people.

CHAPTER 39
Envoys from Babylon

Soon after this, Merodach-baladan son of
Baladan, king of Babylon, sent Hezekiah his best
wishes and a gift. He had heard that Hezekiah
had been very sick and that he had recovered.
2 Hezekiah was delighted with the Babylonian
envoys and showed them everything in his
treasure-houses—the silver, the gold, the spices,
and the aromatic oils. He also took them to see
his armory and showed them everything in his
royal treasuries! There was nothing in his palace
or kingdom that Hezekiah did not show them.
3 Then Isaiah the prophet went to King Hezekiah and asked him, "What did those men want?
Where were they from?"

Hezekiah replied, "They came from the distant land of Babylon."
4 "What did they see in your palace?" asked
Isaiah.

"They saw everything," Hezekiah replied. "I
showed them everything I own—all my royal
treasuries."
5 Then Isaiah said to Hezekiah, "Listen to this
message from the LORD of Heaven's Armies:
6 'The time is coming when everything in your
palace—all the treasures stored up by your ancestors until now—will be carried off to Babylon.
Nothing will be left,' says the LORD. 7 'Some of
your very own sons will be taken away into exile.
They will become eunuchs who will serve in the
palace of Babylon's king.'"
8 Then Hezekiah said to Isaiah, "This message
you have given me from the LORD is good." For
the king was thinking, "At least there will be
peace and security during my lifetime."

CHAPTER 40
Comfort for God's People

1 "Comfort, comfort my people,"
says your God.
2 "Speak tenderly to Jerusalem.
Tell her that her sad days are gone
and her sins are pardoned.
Yes, the LORD has punished her twice over
for all her sins."

3 Listen! It's the voice of someone shouting,
"Clear the way through the wilderness
for the LORD!
Make a straight highway through the
wasteland
for our God!
4 Fill in the valleys,
and level the mountains and hills.
Straighten the curves,
and smooth out the rough places.
5 Then the glory of the LORD will be revealed,
and all people will see it together.
The LORD has spoken!"

6 A voice said, "Shout!"
I asked, "What should I shout?"

"Shout that people are like the grass.
Their beauty fades as quickly
as the flowers in a field.
7 The grass withers and the flowers fade
beneath the breath of the LORD.
And so it is with people.
8 The grass withers and the flowers fade,
but the word of our God stands forever."

9 O Zion, messenger of good news,
shout from the mountaintops!
Shout it louder, O Jerusalem.
Shout, and do not be afraid.
Tell the towns of Judah,
"Your God is coming!"
10 Yes, the Sovereign LORD is coming
in power.
He will rule with a powerful arm.
See, he brings his reward with him
as he comes.
11 He will feed his flock like a shepherd.
He will carry the lambs in his arms,
holding them close to his heart.
He will gently lead the mother sheep
with their young.

The LORD Has No Equal

12 Who else has held the oceans in his hand?
Who has measured off the heavens with
his fingers?
Who else knows the weight of the earth
or has weighed the mountains and hills
on a scale?
13 Who is able to advise the Spirit of the LORD?
Who knows enough to give him advice
or teach him?
14 Has the LORD ever needed anyone's advice?
Does he need instruction about what
is good?
Did someone teach him what is right
or show him the path of justice?

15 No, for all the nations of the world
are but a drop in the bucket.
They are nothing more
than dust on the scales.
He picks up the whole earth
as though it were a grain of sand.

16 All the wood in Lebanon's forests
and all Lebanon's animals would not be enough
to make a burnt offering worthy of our God.
17 The nations of the world are worth nothing to him.
In his eyes they count for less than nothing—
mere emptiness and froth.

18 To whom can you compare God?
What image can you find to resemble him?
19 Can he be compared to an idol formed in a mold,
overlaid with gold, and decorated with silver chains?
20 Or if people are too poor for that,
they might at least choose wood that won't decay
and a skilled craftsman
to carve an image that won't fall down!

21 Haven't you heard? Don't you understand?
Are you deaf to the words of God—
the words he gave before the world began?
Are you so ignorant?
22 God sits above the circle of the earth.
The people below seem like grasshoppers to him!
He spreads out the heavens like a curtain
and makes his tent from them.
23 He judges the great people of the world
and brings them all to nothing.
24 They hardly get started, barely taking root,
when he blows on them and they wither.
The wind carries them off like chaff.

25 "To whom will you compare me?
Who is my equal?" asks the Holy One.

26 Look up into the heavens.
Who created all the stars?
He brings them out like an army, one after another,
calling each by its name.
Because of his great power and incomparable strength,
not a single one is missing.
27 O Jacob, how can you say the LORD does not see your troubles?
O Israel, how can you say God ignores your rights?
28 Have you never heard?
Have you never understood?
The LORD is the everlasting God,
the Creator of all the earth.
He never grows weak or weary.
No one can measure the depths of his understanding.
29 He gives power to the weak
and strength to the powerless.
30 Even youths will become weak and tired,
and young men will fall in exhaustion.
31 But those who trust in the LORD will find new strength.
They will soar high on wings like eagles.
They will run and not grow weary.
They will walk and not faint.

CHAPTER 41
God's Help for Israel

1 "Listen in silence before me, you lands beyond the sea.
Bring your strongest arguments.
Come now and speak.
The court is ready for your case.

2 "Who has stirred up this king from the east,
rightly calling him to God's service?
Who gives this man victory over many nations
and permits him to trample their kings underfoot?
With his sword, he reduces armies to dust.
With his bow, he scatters them like chaff before the wind.
3 He chases them away and goes on safely,
though he is walking over unfamiliar ground.
4 Who has done such mighty deeds,
summoning each new generation from the beginning of time?
It is I, the LORD, the First and the Last.
I alone am he."

5 The lands beyond the sea watch in fear.
Remote lands tremble and mobilize for war.
6 The idol makers encourage one another,
saying to each other, "Be strong!"
7 The carver encourages the goldsmith,
and the molder helps at the anvil.
"Good," they say. "It's coming along fine."
Carefully they join the parts together,
then fasten the thing in place so it won't fall over.

8 "But as for you, Israel my servant,
Jacob my chosen one,
descended from Abraham my friend,

9 I have called you back from the ends
of the earth,
saying, 'You are my servant.'
For I have chosen you
and will not throw you away.
10 **Don't be afraid, for I am with you.**
Don't be discouraged,
for I am your God.
I will strengthen you and
help you.
I will hold you up with my
victorious right hand.

11 "See, all your angry enemies lie there,
confused and humiliated.
Anyone who opposes you will die
and come to nothing.
12 You will look in vain
for those who tried to conquer you.
Those who attack you
will come to nothing.
13 For I hold you by your right hand—
I, the LORD your God.
And I say to you,
'Don't be afraid. I am here to help you.
14 Though you are a lowly worm, O Jacob,
don't be afraid, people of Israel, for I will
help you.
I am the LORD, your Redeemer.
I am the Holy One of Israel.'
15 You will be a new threshing instrument
with many sharp teeth.
You will tear your enemies apart,
making chaff of mountains.
16 You will toss them into the air,
and the wind will blow them all away;
a whirlwind will scatter them.
Then you will rejoice in the LORD.
You will glory in the Holy One of Israel.

17 "When the poor and needy search for water
and there is none,
and their tongues are parched from thirst,
then I, the LORD, will answer them.
I, the God of Israel, will never abandon
them.
18 I will open up rivers for them on the high
plateaus.
I will give them fountains of water in the
valleys.
I will fill the desert with pools of water.
Rivers fed by springs will flow across the
parched ground.
19 I will plant trees in the barren desert—
cedar, acacia, myrtle, olive, cypress, fir,
and pine.
20 I am doing this so all who see this miracle
will understand what it means—
that it is the LORD who has done this,
the Holy One of Israel who created it.

21 "Present the case for your idols,"
says the LORD.
"Let them show what they can do,"
says the King of Israel.
22 "Let them try to tell us what happened
long ago
so that we may consider the evidence.
Or let them tell us what the future holds,
so we can know what's going to happen.
23 Yes, tell us what will occur in the days ahead.
Then we will know you are gods.
In fact, do anything—good or bad!
Do something that will amaze and
frighten us.
24 But no! You are less than nothing and can
do nothing at all.
Those who choose you pollute themselves.

25 "But I have stirred up a leader who will
approach from the north.
From the east he will call on my name.
I will give him victory over kings and princes.
He will trample them as a potter treads
on clay.

26 "Who told you from the beginning that this
would happen?
Who predicted this,
making you admit that he was right?
No one said a word!
27 I was the first to tell Zion,
'Look! Help is on the way!'
I will send Jerusalem a messenger with
good news.
28 Not one of your idols told you this.
Not one gave any answer when I asked.
29 See, they are all foolish, worthless things.
All your idols are as empty as the wind.

CHAPTER 42
The LORD's Chosen Servant

1 "Look at my servant, whom I strengthen.
He is my chosen one, who pleases me.
I have put my Spirit upon him.
He will bring justice to the nations.
2 He will not shout
or raise his voice in public.
3 He will not crush the weakest reed
or put out a flickering candle.
He will bring justice to all who have been
wronged.

4 He will not falter or lose heart
until justice prevails throughout the earth.
Even distant lands beyond the sea will wait
for his instruction."

5 God, the LORD, created the heavens and
stretched them out.
He created the earth and everything in it.
He gives breath to everyone,
life to everyone who walks the earth.
And it is he who says,
6 "I, the LORD, have called you to demonstrate
my righteousness.
I will take you by the hand and guard you,
and I will give you to my people, Israel,
as a symbol of my covenant with them.
And you will be a light to guide the nations.
7 You will open the eyes of the blind.
You will free the captives from prison,
releasing those who sit in dark dungeons.

8 "I am the LORD; that is my name!
I will not give my glory to anyone else,
nor share my praise with carved idols.
9 Everything I prophesied has come true,
and now I will prophesy again.
I will tell you the future before it happens."

A Song of Praise to the LORD

10 Sing a new song to the LORD!
Sing his praises from the ends
of the earth!
Sing, all you who sail the seas,
all you who live in distant coastlands.
11 Join in the chorus, you desert towns;
let the villages of Kedar rejoice!
Let the people of Sela sing for joy;
shout praises from the mountaintops!
12 Let the whole world glorify the LORD;
let it sing his praise.
13 The LORD will march forth like
a mighty hero;
he will come out like a warrior, full of fury.
He will shout his battle cry
and crush all his enemies.

14 He will say, "I have long been silent;
yes, I have restrained myself.
But now, like a woman in labor,
I will cry and groan and pant.
15 I will level the mountains and hills
and blight all their greenery.
I will turn the rivers into dry land
and will dry up all the pools.
16 I will lead blind Israel down a new path,
guiding them along an unfamiliar way.

Key Verse **"But those who trust in the LORD will find new strength. They will soar high on wings like eagles. They will run and not grow weary. They will walk and not faint."—ISAIAH 40:31**

Strength to Fly

Ever wish you could fly? Read ISAIAH 40:31 out loud.

No, that verse isn't talking about people flying. It's a promise that if we just trust God, he'll give us new strength!

Try this trick to remind yourself to trust God!

Want to know more about God's strength? Check out Psalm 46:1!

1. **Stand in a doorway. Press the backs of your hands against the door frame as hard as you can.**
2. **Count to 25.**
3. **Move away from the doorway and relax your arms. What happens?**

YOU FOUND NEW STRENGTH!

When you stopped pressing so hard, your arms wanted to fly up. God promises to renew our strength when we trust him, even when we're tired and troubled. **Next time things get tough, remember that God promises to give you new strength!**

I will brighten the darkness before them
and smooth out the road ahead of them.
Yes, I will indeed do these things;
I will not forsake them.
17 But those who trust in idols,
who say, 'You are our gods,'
will be turned away in shame.

Israel's Failure to Listen and See

18 "Listen, you who are deaf!
Look and see, you blind!
19 Who is as blind as my own people,
my servant?
Who is as deaf as my messenger?
Who is as blind as my chosen people,
the servant of the LORD?
20 You see and recognize what is right
but refuse to act on it.
You hear with your ears,
but you don't really listen."

21 Because he is righteous,
the LORD has exalted his glorious law.
22 But his own people have been robbed and plundered,
enslaved, imprisoned, and trapped.
They are fair game for anyone
and have no one to protect them,
no one to take them back home.

23 Who will hear these lessons from the past
and see the ruin that awaits you in the future?
24 Who allowed Israel to be robbed and hurt?
It was the LORD, against whom we sinned,
for the people would not walk in his path,
nor would they obey his law.
25 Therefore, he poured out his fury on them
and destroyed them in battle.
They were enveloped in flames,
but they still refused to understand.
They were consumed by fire,
but they did not learn their lesson.

CHAPTER 43

The Savior of Israel

1 But now, O Jacob, listen to the LORD who created you.
O Israel, the one who formed you says,
"Do not be afraid, for I have ransomed you.
I have called you by name; you are mine.
2 When you go through deep waters,
I will be with you.
When you go through rivers of difficulty,
you will not drown.
When you walk through the fire
of oppression,
you will not be burned up;
the flames will not consume you.
3 For I am the LORD, your God,
the Holy One of Israel, your Savior.
I gave Egypt as a ransom for your freedom;
I gave Ethiopia and Seba in your place.
4 Others were given in exchange for you.
I traded their lives for yours
because you are precious to me.
You are honored, and I love you.

5 "Do not be afraid, for I am with you.
I will gather you and your children from east and west.
6 I will say to the north and south,
'Bring my sons and daughters back to Israel
from the distant corners of the earth.
7 Bring all who claim me as their God,
for I have made them for my glory.
It was I who created them.'"

8 Bring out the people who have eyes but are blind,
who have ears but are deaf.
9 Gather the nations together!
Assemble the peoples of the world!
Which of their idols has ever foretold such things?
Which can predict what will happen tomorrow?
Where are the witnesses of such predictions?
Who can verify that they spoke the truth?

10 "But you are my witnesses, O Israel!" says the LORD.
"You are my servant.
You have been chosen to know me, believe in me,
and understand that I alone am God.
There is no other God—
there never has been, and there never will be.
11 I, yes I, am the LORD,
and there is no other Savior.
12 First I predicted your rescue,
then I saved you and proclaimed it to the world.
No foreign god has ever done this.
You are witnesses that I am the only God,"
says the LORD.
13 "From eternity to eternity I am God.
No one can snatch anyone out of my hand.
No one can undo what I have done."

Isaiah 44 . . . page 702

The LORD's Promise of Victory

14This is what the LORD says—your Redeemer,
the Holy One of Israel:

"For your sakes I will send an army against
Babylon,
forcing the Babylonians to flee in those
ships they are so proud of.
15 I am the LORD, your Holy One,
Israel's Creator and King.
16 I am the LORD, who opened a way through the
waters,
making a dry path through the sea.
17 I called forth the mighty army of Egypt
with all its chariots and horses.
I drew them beneath the waves, and they
drowned,
their lives snuffed out like a smoldering
candlewick.

18 "But forget all that—
it is nothing compared to what I am going
to do.
19 For I am about to do something new.
See, I have already begun! Do you not see it?
I will make a pathway through the
wilderness.
I will create rivers in the dry wasteland.
20 The wild animals in the fields will thank me,
the jackals and owls, too,
for giving them water in the desert.
Yes, I will make rivers in the dry wasteland
so my chosen people can be refreshed.
21 I have made Israel for myself,
and they will someday honor me before
the whole world.

22 "But, dear family of Jacob, you refuse to ask
for my help.
You have grown tired of me, O Israel!
23 You have not brought me sheep or goats for
burnt offerings.
You have not honored me with sacrifices,
though I have not burdened and wearied you
with requests for grain offerings and
frankincense.
24 You have not brought me fragrant calamus
or pleased me with the fat from sacrifices.
Instead, you have burdened me with your sins
and wearied me with your faults.

25 "I—yes, I alone—will blot out your sins for my
own sake
and will never think of them again.
26 Let us review the situation together,
and you can present your case to prove
your innocence.
27 From the very beginning, your first ancestor
sinned against me;
all your leaders broke my laws.
28 That is why I have disgraced your priests;
I have decreed complete destruction
for Jacob
and shame for Israel.

CHAPTER 44

1 "But now, listen to me, Jacob my servant,
Israel my chosen one.
2 The LORD who made you and helps you says:
Do not be afraid, O Jacob, my servant,
O dear Israel, my chosen one.
3 For I will pour out water to quench your
thirst
and to irrigate your parched fields.
And I will pour out my Spirit on your
descendants,
and my blessing on your children.
4 They will thrive like watered grass,
like willows on a riverbank.
5 Some will proudly claim, 'I belong
to the LORD.'
Others will say, 'I am a descendant
of Jacob.'
Some will write the LORD's name on
their hands
and will take the name of Israel as
their own."

The Foolishness of Idols

6This is what the LORD says—Israel's King and
Redeemer, the LORD of Heaven's Armies:

"I am the First and the Last;
there is no other God.
7 Who is like me?
Let him step forward and prove to you
his power.
Let him do as I have done since ancient
times
when I established a people and
explained its future.
8 Do not tremble; do not be afraid.
Did I not proclaim my purposes for you
long ago?
You are my witnesses—is there any
other God?
No! There is no other Rock—not one!"

9 How foolish are those who manufacture idols.
These prized objects are really worthless.
The people who worship idols don't
know this,
so they are all put to shame.

10 Who but a fool would make his own god—
an idol that cannot help him one bit?
11 All who worship idols will be disgraced
along with all these craftsmen—
mere humans—
who claim they can make a god.
They may all stand together,
but they will stand in terror and shame.

12 The blacksmith stands at his forge to make
a sharp tool,
pounding and shaping it with all his
might.
His work makes him hungry and weak.
It makes him thirsty and faint.
13 Then the wood-carver measures a block
of wood
and draws a pattern on it.
He works with chisel and plane
and carves it into a human figure.
He gives it human beauty
and puts it in a little shrine.
14 He cuts down cedars;
he selects the cypress and the oak;
he plants the pine in the forest
to be nourished by the rain.
15 Then he uses part of the wood to make a fire.
With it he warms himself and bakes
his bread.
Then—yes, it's true—he takes the rest of it
and makes himself a god to worship!
He makes an idol
and bows down in front of it!
16 He burns part of the tree to roast his meat
and to keep himself warm.
He says, "Ah, that fire feels good."
17 Then he takes what's left
and makes his god: a carved idol!
He falls down in front of it,
worshiping and praying to it.
"Rescue me!" he says.
"You are my god!"
18 Such stupidity and ignorance!
Their eyes are closed, and they cannot see.
Their minds are shut, and they cannot
think.
19 The person who made the idol never stops
to reflect,
"Why, it's just a block of wood!
I burned half of it for heat
and used it to bake my bread and roast
my meat.
How can the rest of it be a god?
Should I bow down to worship a piece
of wood?"
20 The poor, deluded fool feeds on ashes.
He trusts something that can't help him
at all.
Yet he cannot bring himself to ask,
"Is this idol that I'm holding in my hand
a lie?"

Restoration for Jerusalem

21 "Pay attention, O Jacob,
for you are my servant, O Israel.
I, the LORD, made you,
and I will not forget you.
22 I have swept away your sins like a cloud.
I have scattered your offenses like the
morning mist.
Oh, return to me,
for I have paid the price to set you free."
23 Sing, O heavens, for the LORD has done this
wondrous thing.
Shout for joy, O depths of the earth!
Break into song,
O mountains and forests and every tree!
For the LORD has redeemed Jacob
and is glorified in Israel.

24 This is what the LORD says—
your Redeemer and Creator:
"I am the LORD, who made all things.
I alone stretched out the heavens.
Who was with me
when I made the earth?
25 I expose the false prophets as liars
and make fools of fortune-tellers.
I cause the wise to give bad advice,
thus proving them to be fools.
26 But I carry out the predictions of my
prophets!
By them I say to Jerusalem, 'People will
live here again,'
and to the towns of Judah, 'You will be
rebuilt;
I will restore all your ruins!'
27 When I speak to the rivers and say,
'Dry up!'
they will be dry.
28 When I say of Cyrus, 'He is my shepherd,'
he will certainly do as I say.
He will command, 'Rebuild Jerusalem';
he will say, 'Restore the Temple.'"

CHAPTER 45

Cyrus, the LORD's Chosen One

1 This is what the LORD says to Cyrus, his
anointed one,
whose right hand he will empower.

Before him, mighty kings will be paralyzed
with fear.
Their fortress gates will be opened,
never to shut again.
2 This is what the LORD says:
"I will go before you, Cyrus,
and level the mountains.
I will smash down gates of bronze
and cut through bars of iron.
3 And I will give you treasures hidden in the
darkness—
secret riches.
I will do this so you may know that I am
the LORD,
the God of Israel, the one who calls you
by name.

4 "And why have I called you for this work?
Why did I call you by name when you did
not know me?
It is for the sake of Jacob my servant,
Israel my chosen one.
5 I am the LORD;
there is no other God.
I have equipped you for battle,
though you don't even know me,
6 so all the world from east to west
will know there is no other God.
I am the LORD, and there is no other.
7 I create the light and make the darkness.
I send good times and bad times.
I, the LORD, am the one who does these
things.

8 "Open up, O heavens,
and pour out your righteousness.
Let the earth open wide
so salvation and righteousness can sprout
up together.
I, the LORD, created them.

9 "What sorrow awaits those who argue with
their Creator.
Does a clay pot argue with its maker?
Does the clay dispute with the one who
shapes it, saying,
'Stop, you're doing it wrong!'
Does the pot exclaim,
'How clumsy can you be?'
10 How terrible it would be if a newborn baby
said to its father,
'Why was I born?'
or if it said to its mother,
'Why did you make me this way?'"

11 This is what the LORD says—
the Holy One of Israel and your Creator:
"Do you question what I do for my children?
Do you give me orders about the work of
my hands?
12 I am the one who made the earth
and created people to live on it.
With my hands I stretched out the heavens.
All the stars are at my command.
13 I will raise up Cyrus to fulfill my righteous
purpose,
and I will guide his actions.
He will restore my city and free my captive
people—
without seeking a reward!
I, the LORD of Heaven's Armies, have
spoken!"

Future Conversion of Gentiles

14 This is what the LORD says:

"You will rule the Egyptians,
the Ethiopians, and the Sabeans.
They will come to you with all their
merchandise,
and it will all be yours.
They will follow you as prisoners in chains.
They will fall to their knees in front
of you and say,
'God is with you, and he is the only God.
There is no other.'"

15 Truly, O God of Israel, our Savior,
you work in mysterious ways.
16 All craftsmen who make idols will be
humiliated.
They will all be disgraced together.
17 But the LORD will save the people of Israel
with eternal salvation.
Throughout everlasting ages,
they will never again be humiliated
and disgraced.

18 For the LORD is God,
and he created the heavens and earth
and put everything in place.
He made the world to be lived in,
not to be a place of empty chaos.
"I am the LORD," he says,
"and there is no other.
19 I publicly proclaim bold promises.
I do not whisper obscurities in some dark
corner.
I would not have told the people of Israel
to seek me
if I could not be found.
I, the LORD, speak only what is true
and declare only what is right.

20 "Gather together and come,
you fugitives from surrounding nations.
What fools they are who carry around their
wooden idols
and pray to gods that cannot save!
21 Consult together, argue your case.
Get together and decide what to say.
Who made these things known so long ago?
What idol ever told you they would
happen?
Was it not I, the LORD?
For there is no other God but me,
a righteous God and Savior.
There is none but me.
22 Let all the world look to me for salvation!
For I am God; there is no other.
23 I have sworn by my own name;
I have spoken the truth,
and I will never go back on my word:
Every knee will bend to me,
and every tongue will declare allegiance
to me."
24 The people will declare,
"The LORD is the source of all my
righteousness and strength."
And all who were angry with him
will come to him and be ashamed.
25 In the LORD all the generations of Israel will
be justified,
and in him they will boast.

CHAPTER 46
Babylon's False Gods

1 Bel and Nebo, the gods of Babylon,
bow as they are lowered to the ground.
They are being hauled away on ox carts.
The poor beasts stagger under the weight.
2 Both the idols and their owners are
bowed down.
The gods cannot protect the people,
and the people cannot protect the gods.
They go off into captivity together.
3 "Listen to me, descendants of Jacob,
all you who remain in Israel.
I have cared for you since you were born.
Yes, I carried you before you were born.
4 I will be your God throughout your lifetime—
until your hair is white with age.
I made you, and I will care for you.
I will carry you along and save you.
5 "To whom will you compare me?
Who is my equal?
6 Some people pour out their silver and gold
and hire a craftsman to make a god from it.
Then they bow down and worship it!
7 They carry it around on their shoulders,
and when they set it down, it stays there.
It can't even move!
And when someone prays to it, there is
no answer.
It can't rescue anyone from trouble.
8 "Do not forget this! Keep it in mind!
Remember this, you guilty ones.
9 Remember the things I have done in the past.
For I alone am God!
I am God, and there is none like me.
10 Only I can tell you the future
before it even happens.
Everything I plan will come to pass,
for I do whatever I wish.
11 I will call a swift bird of prey from the east—
a leader from a distant land to come and
do my bidding.
I have said what I would do,
and I will do it.
12 "Listen to me, you stubborn people
who are so far from doing right.
13 For I am ready to set things right,
not in the distant future, but right now!
I am ready to save Jerusalem
and show my glory to Israel.

CHAPTER 47
Prediction of Babylon's Fall

1 "Come down, virgin daughter of Babylon,
and sit in the dust.
For your days of sitting on a throne
have ended.
O daughter of Babylonia, never again will
you be
the lovely princess, tender and delicate.
2 Take heavy millstones and grind flour.
Remove your veil, and strip off your robe.
Expose yourself to public view.
3 You will be naked and burdened with shame.
I will take vengeance against you
without pity."
4 Our Redeemer, whose name is the LORD of
Heaven's Armies,
is the Holy One of Israel.
5 "O beautiful Babylon, sit now in darkness and
silence.
Never again will you be known as the
queen of kingdoms.
6 For I was angry with my chosen people
and punished them by letting them fall
into your hands.

But you, Babylon, showed them no mercy.
You oppressed even the elderly.
7 You said, 'I will reign forever as queen of the world!'
You did not reflect on your actions
or think about their consequences.

8 "Listen to this, you pleasure-loving kingdom,
living at ease and feeling secure.
You say, 'I am the only one, and there is no other.
I will never be a widow or lose my children.'
9 Well, both these things will come upon you in a moment:
widowhood and the loss of your children.
Yes, these calamities will come upon you,
despite all your witchcraft and magic.

10 "You felt secure in your wickedness.
'No one sees me,' you said.
But your 'wisdom' and 'knowledge' have led you astray,
and you said, 'I am the only one, and there is no other.'
11 So disaster will overtake you,
and you won't be able to charm it away.
Calamity will fall upon you,
and you won't be able to buy your way out.
A catastrophe will strike you suddenly,
one for which you are not prepared.

12 "Now use your magical charms!
Use the spells you have worked at all these years!
Maybe they will do you some good.
Maybe they can make someone afraid of you.
13 All the advice you receive has made you tired.
Where are all your astrologers,
those stargazers who make predictions each month?
Let them stand up and save you from what the future holds.
14 But they are like straw burning in a fire;
they cannot save themselves from the flame.
You will get no help from them at all;
their hearth is no place to sit for warmth.
15 And all your friends,
those with whom you've done business since childhood,
will go their own ways,
turning a deaf ear to your cries.

CHAPTER 48

God's Stubborn People

1 "Listen to me, O family of Jacob,
you who are called by the name of Israel
and born into the family of Judah.
Listen, you who take oaths in the name of the LORD
and call on the God of Israel.
You don't keep your promises,
2 even though you call yourself the holy city
and talk about depending on the God of Israel,
whose name is the LORD of Heaven's Armies.
3 Long ago I told you what was going to happen.
Then suddenly I took action,
and all my predictions came true.
4 For I know how stubborn and obstinate you are.
Your necks are as unbending as iron.
Your heads are as hard as bronze.
5 That is why I told you what would happen;
I told you beforehand what I was going to do.
Then you could never say, 'My idols did it.
My wooden image and metal god commanded it to happen!'
6 You have heard my predictions and seen them fulfilled,
but you refuse to admit it.
Now I will tell you new things,
secrets you have not yet heard.
7 They are brand new, not things from the past.
So you cannot say, 'We knew that all the time!'

8 "Yes, I will tell you of things that are entirely new,
things you never heard of before.
For I know so well what traitors you are.
You have been rebels from birth.
9 Yet for my own sake and for the honor of my name,
I will hold back my anger and not wipe you out.
10 I have refined you, but not as silver is refined.
Rather, I have refined you in the furnace of suffering.
11 I will rescue you for my sake—
yes, for my own sake!
I will not let my reputation be tarnished,
and I will not share my glory with idols!

A Power-Packed Book

You're reading the Bible—that's great! If you want to grow closer to Jesus, reading God's Word is important. Why? Because the Bible is a very powerful book. But the power isn't in the pages made of paper. It's in understanding and believing what God says on those pages. **Read 2 TIMOTHY 3:16-17.** It says the Bible teaches us what is true and corrects us when we're wrong. That's a lot of power!

Make yourself a Bible bookmark, and on it write these four things the Bible can show you: what's true, what's wrong in my life, how to correct it, and the right thing to do.

Every time you read your Bible, look over your list. Welcome the power of God's power-packed book!

Freedom from Babylon

12 "Listen to me, O family of Jacob,
Israel my chosen one!
I alone am God,
the First and the Last.
13 It was my hand that laid the foundations
of the earth,
my right hand that spread out the
heavens above.
When I call out the stars,
they all appear in order."

14 Have any of your idols ever told you this?
Come, all of you, and listen:
The LORD has chosen Cyrus as his ally.
He will use him to put an end to the
empire of Babylon
and to destroy the Babylonian armies.

15 "I have said it: I am calling Cyrus!
I will send him on this errand and will
help him succeed.
16 Come closer, and listen to this.
From the beginning I have told you plainly
what would happen."
And now the Sovereign LORD and his Spirit
have sent me with this message.

17 This is what the LORD says—
your Redeemer, the Holy One of Israel:
"I am the LORD your God,
who teaches you what is good for you
and leads you along the paths you
should follow.
18 Oh, that you had listened to my commands!
Then you would have had peace flowing
like a gentle river
and righteousness rolling over you like
waves in the sea.
19 Your descendants would have been like the
sands along the seashore—
too many to count!
There would have been no need for your
destruction,
or for cutting off your family name."

20 Yet even now, be free from your captivity!
Leave Babylon and the Babylonians.
Sing out this message!
Shout it to the ends of the earth!
The LORD has redeemed his servants,
the people of Israel.
21 They were not thirsty
when he led them through the desert.
He divided the rock,
and water gushed out for them to drink.
22 "But there is no peace for the wicked,"
says the LORD.

CHAPTER 49

The LORD's Servant Commissioned

1 Listen to me, all you in distant lands!
Pay attention, you who are far away!
The LORD called me before my birth;
from within the womb he called me
by name.
2 He made my words of judgment as sharp
as a sword.
He has hidden me in the shadow of
his hand.
I am like a sharp arrow in his quiver.
3 He said to me, "You are my servant, Israel,
and you will bring me glory."
4 I replied, "But my work seems so useless!
I have spent my strength for nothing and
to no purpose.
Yet I leave it all in the LORD's hand;
I will trust God for my reward."
5 And now the LORD speaks—
the one who formed me in my mother's
womb to be his servant,

who commissioned me to bring Israel
back to him.
The LORD has honored me,
and my God has given me strength.
6 He says, "You will do more than restore the
people of Israel to me.
I will make you a light to the Gentiles,
and you will bring my salvation to the ends
of the earth."
7 The LORD, the Redeemer
and Holy One of Israel,
says to the one who is despised and rejected
by the nations,
to the one who is the servant of rulers:
"Kings will stand at attention when you
pass by.
Princes will also bow low
because of the LORD, the faithful one,
the Holy One of Israel, who has
chosen you."

Promises of Israel's Restoration

8 This is what the LORD says:

"At just the right time, I will respond to you.
On the day of salvation I will help you.
I will protect you and give you to the people
as my covenant with them.
Through you I will reestablish the land
of Israel
and assign it to its own people again.
9 I will say to the prisoners, 'Come out in
freedom,'
and to those in darkness, 'Come into
the light.'
They will be my sheep, grazing in green
pastures
and on hills that were previously bare.
10 They will neither hunger nor thirst.
The searing sun will not reach them
anymore.
For the LORD in his mercy will lead them;
he will lead them beside cool waters.
11 And I will make my mountains into level
paths for them.
The highways will be raised above the
valleys.
12 See, my people will return from far away,
from lands to the north and west,
and from as far south as Egypt."

13 Sing for joy, O heavens!
Rejoice, O earth!
Burst into song, O mountains!
For the LORD has comforted his people
and will have compassion on them in their
suffering.
14 Yet Jerusalem says, "The LORD has deserted us;
the Lord has forgotten us."
15 "Never! Can a mother forget her nursing
child?
Can she feel no love for the child she
has borne?
But even if that were possible,
I would not forget you!
16 See, I have written your name on the palms of
my hands.
Always in my mind is a picture of
Jerusalem's walls in ruins.
17 Soon your descendants will come back,
and all who are trying to destroy you will
go away.
18 Look around you and see,
for all your children will come back to you.
As surely as I live," says the LORD,
"they will be like jewels or bridal
ornaments for you to display.
19 "Even the most desolate parts of your
abandoned land
will soon be crowded with your people.
Your enemies who enslaved you
will be far away.
20 The generations born in exile will return
and say,
'We need more room! It's crowded here!'
21 Then you will think to yourself,
'Who has given me all these descendants?
For most of my children were killed,
and the rest were carried away into exile.
I was left here all alone.
Where did all these people come from?
Who bore these children?
Who raised them for me?'"
22 This is what the Sovereign LORD says:
"See, I will give a signal to the godless
nations.
They will carry your little sons back to you
in their arms;
they will bring your daughters on their
shoulders.
23 Kings and queens will serve you
and care for all your needs.
They will bow to the earth before you
and lick the dust from your feet.
Then you will know that I am the LORD.
Those who trust in me will never be put
to shame."

6 Look up to the skies above,
and gaze down on the earth below.
For the skies will disappear like smoke,
and the earth will wear out like a piece of clothing.
The people of the earth will die like flies,
but my salvation lasts forever.
My righteous rule will never end!

7 "Listen to me, you who know right from wrong,
you who cherish my law in your hearts.
Do not be afraid of people's scorn,
nor fear their insults.
8 For the moth will devour them as it devours clothing.
The worm will eat at them as it eats wool.
But my righteousness will last forever.
My salvation will continue from generation to generation."

9 Wake up, wake up, O LORD! Clothe yourself with strength!
Flex your mighty right arm!
Rouse yourself as in the days of old
when you slew Egypt, the dragon of the Nile.
10 Are you not the same today,
the one who dried up the sea,
making a path of escape through the depths
so that your people could cross over?
11 Those who have been ransomed by the LORD will return.
They will enter Jerusalem singing,
crowned with everlasting joy.
Sorrow and mourning will disappear,
and they will be filled with joy and gladness.

12 "I, yes I, am the one who comforts you.
So why are you afraid of mere humans,
who wither like the grass and disappear?
13 Yet you have forgotten the LORD, your Creator,
the one who stretched out the sky like a canopy
and laid the foundations of the earth.
Will you remain in constant dread
of human oppressors?
Will you continue to fear the anger
of your enemies?
Where is their fury and anger now?
It is gone!
14 Soon all you captives will be released!
Imprisonment, starvation, and death
will not be your fate!
15 For I am the LORD your God,
who stirs up the sea, causing its waves to roar.
My name is the LORD of Heaven's Armies.
16 And I have put my words in your mouth
and hidden you safely in my hand.
I stretched out the sky like a canopy
and laid the foundations of the earth.
I am the one who says to Israel,
'You are my people!'"

17 Wake up, wake up, O Jerusalem!
You have drunk the cup of the LORD's fury.
You have drunk the cup of terror,
tipping out its last drops.
18 Not one of your children is left alive
to take your hand and guide you.
19 These two calamities have fallen on you:
desolation and destruction, famine and war.
And who is left to sympathize with you?
Who is left to comfort you?
20 For your children have fainted and lie in the streets,
helpless as antelopes caught in a net.
The LORD has poured out his fury;
God has rebuked them.

21 But now listen to this, you afflicted ones
who sit in a drunken stupor,
though not from drinking wine.
22 This is what the Sovereign LORD,
your God and Defender, says:
"See, I have taken the terrible cup from your hands.
You will drink no more of my fury.
23 Instead, I will hand that cup to your tormentors,
those who said, 'We will trample you into the dust
and walk on your backs.'"

CHAPTER 52
Deliverance for Jerusalem

1 Wake up, wake up, O Zion!
Clothe yourself with strength.
Put on your beautiful clothes, O holy city of Jerusalem,
for unclean and godless people will enter
your gates no longer.
2 Rise from the dust, O Jerusalem.
Sit in a place of honor.
Remove the chains of slavery from your neck,
O captive daughter of Zion.

24 Who can snatch the plunder of war from the
hands of a warrior?
Who can demand that a tyrant let his
captives go?
25 But the LORD says,
"The captives of warriors will be released,
and the plunder of tyrants will be
retrieved.
For I will fight those who fight you,
and I will save your children.
26 I will feed your enemies with their own flesh.
They will be drunk with rivers of their
own blood.
All the world will know that I, the LORD,
am your Savior and your Redeemer,
the Mighty One of Israel."

CHAPTER 50

This is what the LORD says:

"Was your mother sent away because
I divorced her?
Did I sell you as slaves to my creditors?
No, you were sold because of your sins.
And your mother, too, was taken because
of your sins.
2 Why was no one there when I came?
Why didn't anyone answer when I called?
Is it because I have no power to rescue?
No, that is not the reason!
For I can speak to the sea and make
it dry up!
I can turn rivers into deserts covered with
dying fish.
3 I dress the skies in darkness,
covering them with clothes of mourning."

The LORD's Obedient Servant

4 The Sovereign LORD has given me his words
of wisdom,
so that I know how to comfort the weary.
Morning by morning he wakens me
and opens my understanding to his will.
5 The Sovereign LORD has spoken to me,
and I have listened.
I have not rebelled or turned away.
6 I offered my back to those who beat me
and my cheeks to those who pulled out
my beard.
I did not hide my face
from mockery and spitting.

7 Because the Sovereign LORD helps me,
I will not be disgraced.
Therefore, I have set my face like a stone,
determined to do his will.
And I know that I will not be put to shame.
8 He who gives me justice is near.
Who will dare to bring charges against
me now?
Where are my accusers?
Let them appear!
9 See, the Sovereign LORD is on my side!
Who will declare me guilty?
All my enemies will be destroyed
like old clothes that have been eaten
by moths!

10 Who among you fears the LORD
and obeys his servant?
If you are walking in darkness,
without a ray of light,
trust in the LORD
and rely on your God.
11 But watch out, you who live in your
own light
and warm yourselves by your own fires.
This is the reward you will receive from me:
You will soon fall down in great torment.

CHAPTER 51

A Call to Trust the LORD

1 "Listen to me, all who hope for deliverance—
all who seek the LORD!
Consider the rock from which you were cut,
the quarry from which you were mined.
2 Yes, think about Abraham, your ancestor,
and Sarah, who gave birth to your nation.
Abraham was only one man when
I called him.
But when I blessed him, he became
a great nation."

3 The LORD will comfort Israel again
and have pity on her ruins.
Her desert will blossom like Eden,
her barren wilderness like the garden
of the LORD.
Joy and gladness will be found there.
Songs of thanksgiving will fill the air.

4 "Listen to me, my people.
Hear me, Israel,
for my law will be proclaimed,
and my justice will become a light
to the nations.
5 My mercy and justice are coming soon.
My salvation is on the way.
My strong arm will bring justice to the
nations.
All distant lands will look to me
and wait in hope for my powerful arm.

3 For this is what the LORD says:
"When I sold you into exile,
I received no payment.
Now I can redeem you
without having to pay for you."

4This is what the Sovereign LORD says: "Long
ago my people chose to live in Egypt. Now they
are oppressed by Assyria. 5What is this?" asks
the LORD. "Why are my people enslaved again?
Those who rule them shout in exultation. My
name is blasphemed all day long. 6But I will reveal my name to my people, and they will come to
know its power. Then at last they will recognize
that I am the one who speaks to them."

7 How beautiful on the mountains
are the feet of the messenger who brings
good news,
the good news of peace and salvation,
the news that the God of Israel reigns!
8 The watchmen shout and sing with joy,
for before their very eyes
they see the LORD returning
to Jerusalem.
9 Let the ruins of Jerusalem break into
joyful song,
for the LORD has comforted his people.
He has redeemed Jerusalem.
10 The LORD has demonstrated his holy power
before the eyes of all the nations.
All the ends of the earth will see
the victory of our God.

11 Get out! Get out and leave your captivity,
where everything you touch is unclean.
Get out of there and purify yourselves,
you who carry home the sacred objects
of the LORD.
12 You will not leave in a hurry,
running for your lives.
For the LORD will go ahead of you;
yes, the God of Israel will protect you
from behind.

The LORD's Suffering Servant

13 See, my servant will prosper;
he will be highly exalted.
14 But many were amazed when they saw him.
His face was so disfigured he seemed
hardly human,
and from his appearance, one would
scarcely know he was a man.
15 And he will startle many nations.
Kings will stand speechless in his
presence.
For they will see what they had not been told;
they will understand what they had not
heard about.

CHAPTER 53

1 Who has believed our message?
To whom has the LORD revealed his
powerful arm?
2 My servant grew up in the LORD's presence
like a tender green shoot,
like a root in dry ground.
There was nothing beautiful or majestic
about his appearance,
nothing to attract us to him.
3 He was despised and rejected—
a man of sorrows, acquainted with
deepest grief.
We turned our backs on him and looked
the other way.
He was despised, and we did not care.

4 Yet it was our weaknesses he carried;
it was our sorrows that weighed him down.
And we thought his troubles were a
punishment from God,
a punishment for his own sins!
5 But he was pierced for our rebellion,
crushed for our sins.
He was beaten so we could be whole.
He was whipped so we could be healed.
6 All of us, like sheep, have strayed away.
We have left God's paths to follow our own.
Yet the LORD laid on him
the sins of us all.

**7 He was oppressed and treated
harshly,
yet he never said a word.
He was led like a lamb to the
slaughter.
And as a sheep is silent before
the shearers,
he did not open his mouth.
8 Unjustly condemned,
he was led away.
No one cared that he died
without descendants,
that his life was cut short
in midstream.
But he was struck down
for the rebellion of my people.**
9 He had done no wrong
and had never deceived anyone.
But he was buried like a criminal;
he was put in a rich man's grave.

10 But it was the LORD's good plan to crush him
and cause him grief.
Yet when his life is made an offering for sin,
he will have many descendants.
He will enjoy a long life,
and the LORD's good plan will prosper
in his hands.
11 When he sees all that is accomplished
by his anguish,
he will be satisfied.
And because of his experience,
my righteous servant will make it possible
for many to be counted righteous,
for he will bear all their sins.
12 I will give him the honors of a victorious
soldier,
because he exposed himself to death.
He was counted among the rebels.
He bore the sins of many and interceded
for rebels.

CHAPTER 54
Future Glory for Jerusalem

1 "Sing, O childless woman,
you who have never given birth!
Break into loud and joyful song,
O Jerusalem,
you who have never been in labor.
For the desolate woman now has
more children
than the woman who lives with
her husband,"
says the LORD.
2 "Enlarge your house; build an addition.
Spread out your home, and spare
no expense!
3 For you will soon be bursting at the seams.
Your descendants will occupy other nations
and resettle the ruined cities.

4 "Fear not; you will no longer live in shame.
Don't be afraid; there is no more disgrace
for you.
You will no longer remember the shame
of your youth
and the sorrows of widowhood.
5 For your Creator will be your husband;
the LORD of Heaven's Armies is his name!
He is your Redeemer, the Holy One of Israel,
the God of all the earth.
6 For the LORD has called you back from
your grief—
as though you were a young wife
abandoned by her husband,"
says your God.

NEVER a Loser

Have you ever been called a loser—or at least felt like one? Jesus knows how it feels!

Jesus is God, but he wasn't very popular here on earth! **Read all of ISAIAH 53.** This passage tells how he would suffer for you and me. He was wounded, beaten, and hung on a cross to die so that *we* can be forgiven for our sins! God looks at people who believe in Jesus and sees them as forgiven and righteous.

No one is ever a loser with Jesus!

1. **Find a clean, solid-color T-shirt, and place a piece of cardboard inside it.**
2. **Spread some fabric paint on a thick paper plate or plastic lid.**
3. **Dip the outside of your hand (from just above the wrist up to the tip of your pinky) into the paint, then on the shirt. Do it again with your other hand, and make a heart shape by overlapping at the bottom. Let it dry. *It may take until tomorrow.***
4. **Use permanent marker to draw a cross in the center of the heart. Write "Jesus" above the heart and your name underneath.**

Check out 1 John 1:9 to find more about being a winner in God's eyes!

Now make a shirt for a friend as a way to say that Jesus died for him or her, too!

7 "For a brief moment I abandoned you,
but with great compassion I will take you back.
8 In a burst of anger I turned my face away
for a little while.
But with everlasting love I will have compassion on you,"
says the LORD, your Redeemer.

9 "Just as I swore in the time of Noah
that I would never again let a flood cover the earth,
so now I swear
that I will never again be angry and punish you.
10 For the mountains may move
and the hills disappear,
but even then my faithful love for you will remain.
My covenant of blessing will never be broken,"
says the LORD, who has mercy on you.

11 "O storm-battered city,
troubled and desolate!
I will rebuild you with precious jewels
and make your foundations from lapis lazuli.
12 I will make your towers of sparkling rubies,
your gates of shining gems,
and your walls of precious stones.
13 I will teach all your children,
and they will enjoy great peace.
14 You will be secure under a government
that is just and fair.
Your enemies will stay far away.
You will live in peace,
and terror will not come near.
15 If any nation comes to fight you,
it is not because I sent them.
Whoever attacks you will go down in defeat.

16 "I have created the blacksmith
who fans the coals beneath the forge
and makes the weapons of destruction.
And I have created the armies that destroy.
17 But in that coming day
no weapon turned against you will succeed.
You will silence every voice
raised up to accuse you.
These benefits are enjoyed by the servants of the LORD;
their vindication will come from me.
I, the LORD, have spoken!

CHAPTER 55
Invitation to the LORD's Salvation

1 "Is anyone thirsty?
Come and drink—
even if you have no money!
Come, take your choice of wine or milk—
it's all free!
2 Why spend your money on food that does not give you strength?
Why pay for food that does you no good?
Listen to me, and you will eat what is good.
You will enjoy the finest food.

3 "Come to me with your ears wide open.
Listen, and you will find life.
I will make an everlasting covenant with you.
I will give you all the unfailing love I promised to David.
4 See how I used him to display my power among the peoples.
I made him a leader among the nations.
5 You also will command nations you do not know,
and peoples unknown to you will come running to obey,
because I, the LORD your God,
the Holy One of Israel, have made you glorious."

6 Seek the LORD while you can find him.
Call on him now while he is near.
7 Let the wicked change their ways
and banish the very thought of doing wrong.
Let them turn to the LORD that he may have mercy on them.
Yes, turn to our God, for he will forgive generously.

8 "My thoughts are nothing like your thoughts," says the LORD.
"And my ways are far beyond anything you could imagine.
9 For just as the heavens are higher than the earth,
so my ways are higher than your ways
and my thoughts higher than your thoughts.

10 "The rain and snow come down from the heavens
and stay on the ground to water the earth.
They cause the grain to grow,
producing seed for the farmer
and bread for the hungry.

11 It is the same with my word.
I send it out, and it always produces fruit.
It will accomplish all I want it to,
and it will prosper everywhere I send it.
12 You will live in joy and peace.
The mountains and hills will burst
into song,
and the trees of the field will clap
their hands!
13 Where once there were thorns, cypress trees
will grow.
Where nettles grew, myrtles will sprout up.
These events will bring great honor to the
LORD's name;
they will be an everlasting sign of his
power and love."

CHAPTER 56
Blessings for All Nations

This is what the LORD says:

"Be just and fair to all.
Do what is right and good,
for I am coming soon to rescue you
and to display my righteousness
among you.
2 Blessed are all those
who are careful to do this.
Blessed are those who honor my Sabbath
days of rest
and keep themselves from doing wrong.

3 "Don't let foreigners who commit
themselves to the LORD say,
'The LORD will never let me be part
of his people.'
And don't let the eunuchs say,
'I'm a dried-up tree with no children
and no future.'
4 For this is what the LORD says:
I will bless those eunuchs
who keep my Sabbath days holy
and who choose to do what pleases me
and commit their lives to me.
5 I will give them—within the walls
of my house—
a memorial and a name
far greater than sons and daughters
could give.
For the name I give them is an
everlasting one.
It will never disappear!
6 "I will also bless the foreigners who commit
themselves to the LORD,
who serve him and love his name,
who worship him and do not desecrate the
Sabbath day of rest,
and who hold fast to my covenant.
7 I will bring them to my holy mountain
of Jerusalem
and will fill them with joy in my house
of prayer.
I will accept their burnt offerings and
sacrifices,
because my Temple will be called a house
of prayer for all nations.
8 For the Sovereign LORD,
who brings back the outcasts
of Israel, says:
I will bring others, too,
besides my people Israel."

Sinful Leaders Condemned

9 Come, wild animals of the field!
Come, wild animals of the forest!
Come and devour my people!
10 For the leaders of my people—
the LORD's watchmen, his shepherds—
are blind and ignorant.
They are like silent watchdogs
that give no warning when danger comes.
They love to lie around, sleeping and
dreaming.
11 Like greedy dogs, they are never satisfied.
They are ignorant shepherds,
all following their own path
and intent on personal gain.
12 "Come," they say, "let's get some wine and
have a party.
Let's all get drunk.
Then tomorrow we'll do it again
and have an even bigger party!"

CHAPTER 57

1 Good people pass away;
the godly often die before their time.
But no one seems to care or wonder why.
No one seems to understand
that God is protecting them from the evil
to come.
2 For those who follow godly paths
will rest in peace when they die.

Idolatrous Worship Condemned

3 "But you—come here, you witches' children,
you offspring of adulterers and
prostitutes!
4 Whom do you mock,
making faces and sticking out your
tongues?

You children of sinners and liars!
5 You worship your idols with great passion
beneath the oaks and under every
green tree.
You sacrifice your children down in the
valleys,
among the jagged rocks in the cliffs.
6 Your gods are the smooth stones
in the valleys.
You worship them with liquid offerings
and grain offerings.
They, not I, are your inheritance.
Do you think all this makes me happy?
7 You have committed adultery on every
high mountain.
There you have worshiped idols
and have been unfaithful to me.
8 You have put pagan symbols
on your doorposts and behind
your doors.
You have left me
and climbed into bed with these
detestable gods.
You have committed yourselves to them.
You love to look at their naked bodies.
9 You have gone to Molech
with olive oil and many perfumes,
sending your agents far and wide,
even to the world of the dead.
10 You grew weary in your search,
but you never gave up.
Desire gave you renewed strength,
and you did not grow weary.

11 "Are you afraid of these idols?
Do they terrify you?
Is that why you have lied to me
and forgotten me and my words?
Is it because of my long silence
that you no longer fear me?
12 Now I will expose your so-called
good deeds.
None of them will help you.
13 Let's see if your idols can save you
when you cry to them for help.
Why, a puff of wind can knock them down!
If you just breathe on them, they fall over!
But whoever trusts in me will inherit
the land
and possess my holy mountain."

God Forgives the Repentant

14 God says, "Rebuild the road!
Clear away the rocks and stones
so my people can return from captivity."
15 The high and lofty one who lives in eternity,
the Holy One, says this:
"I live in the high and holy place
with those whose spirits are contrite
and humble.
I restore the crushed spirit of the humble
and revive the courage of those with
repentant hearts.
16 For I will not fight against you forever;
I will not always be angry.
If I were, all people would pass away—
all the souls I have made.
17 I was angry,
so I punished these greedy people.
I withdrew from them,
but they kept going on their own
stubborn way.
18 I have seen what they do,
but I will heal them anyway!
I will lead them.
I will comfort those who mourn,
19 bringing words of praise to their lips.
May they have abundant peace, both near
and far,"
says the LORD, who heals them.
20 "But those who still reject me are like the
restless sea,
which is never still
but continually churns up mud and dirt.
21 There is no peace for the wicked,"
says my God.

CHAPTER 58

True and False Worship

1 "Shout with the voice of a trumpet blast.
Shout aloud! Don't be timid.
Tell my people Israel of their sins!
2 Yet they act so pious!
They come to the Temple every day
and seem delighted to learn all about me.
They act like a righteous nation
that would never abandon the laws
of its God.
They ask me to take action on their behalf,
pretending they want to be near me.
3 'We have fasted before you!' they say.
'Why aren't you impressed?
We have been very hard on ourselves,
and you don't even notice it!'

"I will tell you why!" I respond.
"It's because you are fasting to please
yourselves.
Even while you fast,
you keep oppressing your workers.

4 What good is fasting
when you keep on fighting and
quarreling?
This kind of fasting
will never get you anywhere with me.
5 You humble yourselves
by going through the motions of penance,
bowing your heads
like reeds bending in the wind.
You dress in burlap
and cover yourselves with ashes.
Is this what you call fasting?
Do you really think this will please
the LORD?

6 "No, this is the kind of fasting I want:
Free those who are wrongly imprisoned;
lighten the burden of those who work
for you.
Let the oppressed go free,
and remove the chains that bind people.
7 Share your food with the hungry,
and give shelter to the homeless.
Give clothes to those who need them,
and do not hide from relatives who need
your help.

8 "Then your salvation will come like the dawn,
and your wounds will quickly heal.
Your godliness will lead you forward,
and the glory of the LORD will protect you
from behind.
9 Then when you call, the LORD will answer.
'Yes, I am here,' he will quickly reply.

"Remove the heavy yoke of oppression.
Stop pointing your finger and spreading
vicious rumors!
10 Feed the hungry,
and help those in trouble.
Then your light will shine out from the
darkness,
and the darkness around you will be as
bright as noon.
11 The LORD will guide you continually,
giving you water when you are dry
and restoring your strength.
You will be like a well-watered garden,
like an ever-flowing spring.
12 Some of you will rebuild the deserted
ruins of your cities.
Then you will be known as a rebuilder
of walls
and a restorer of homes.

13 "Keep the Sabbath day holy.
Don't pursue your own interests on that day,
but enjoy the Sabbath
and speak of it with delight as the LORD's
holy day.
Honor the Sabbath in everything you do on
that day,
and don't follow your own desires or
talk idly.
14 Then the LORD will be your delight.
I will give you great honor
and satisfy you with the inheritance
I promised to your ancestor Jacob.
I, the LORD, have spoken!"

CHAPTER 59

Warnings against Sin

1 Listen! The LORD's arm is not too weak
to save you,
nor is his ear too deaf to hear you call.
2 It's your sins that have cut you off from God.
Because of your sins, he has turned away
and will not listen anymore.
3 Your hands are the hands of murderers,
and your fingers are filthy with sin.
Your lips are full of lies,
and your mouth spews corruption.

4 No one cares about being fair and honest.
The people's lawsuits are based on lies.
They conceive evil deeds
and then give birth to sin.
5 They hatch deadly snakes
and weave spiders' webs.
Whoever eats their eggs will die;
whoever cracks them will hatch a viper.
6 Their webs can't be made into clothing,
and nothing they do is productive.
All their activity is filled with sin,
and violence is their trademark.
7 Their feet run to do evil,
and they rush to commit murder.
They think only about sinning.
Misery and destruction always
follow them.
8 They don't know where to find peace
or what it means to be just and good.
They have mapped out crooked roads,
and no one who follows them knows
a moment's peace.

9 So there is no justice among us,
and we know nothing about right living.
We look for light but find only darkness.
We look for bright skies but walk in gloom.
10 We grope like the blind along a wall,
feeling our way like people without eyes.

Even at brightest noontime,
we stumble as though it were dark.
Among the living,
we are like the dead.
11 We growl like hungry bears;
we moan like mournful doves.
We look for justice, but it never comes.
We look for rescue, but it is far away
from us.
12 For our sins are piled up before God
and testify against us.
Yes, we know what sinners we are.
13 We know we have rebelled and have denied
the LORD.
We have turned our backs on our God.
We know how unfair and oppressive we have
been,
carefully planning our deceitful lies.
14 Our courts oppose the righteous,
and justice is nowhere to be found.
Truth stumbles in the streets,
and honesty has been outlawed.
15 Yes, truth is gone,
and anyone who renounces evil is attacked.

The LORD looked and was displeased
to find there was no justice.
16 He was amazed to see that no one
intervened
to help the oppressed.
So he himself stepped in to save them with
his strong arm,
and his justice sustained him.
17 He put on righteousness as his body armor
and placed the helmet of salvation on his
head.
He clothed himself with a robe of vengeance
and wrapped himself in a cloak of divine
passion.
18 He will repay his enemies for their evil deeds.
His fury will fall on his foes.
He will pay them back even to the ends of
the earth.
19 In the west, people will respect the name of
the LORD;
in the east, they will glorify him.
For he will come like a raging flood tide
driven by the breath of the LORD.
20 "The Redeemer will come to Jerusalem
to buy back those in Israel
who have turned from their sins,"
says the LORD.

21 "And this is my covenant with them," says
the LORD. "My Spirit will not leave them, and neither will these words I have given you. They will
be on your lips and on the lips of your children
and your children's children forever. I, the LORD,
have spoken!

CHAPTER 60

Future Glory for Jerusalem

1 "Arise, Jerusalem! Let your light shine for
all to see.
For the glory of the LORD rises to shine
on you.
2 Darkness as black as night covers all the
nations of the earth,
but the glory of the LORD rises and appears
over you.
3 All nations will come to your light;
mighty kings will come to see your
radiance.

4 "Look and see, for everyone is coming home!
Your sons are coming from distant lands;
your little daughters will be carried home.
5 Your eyes will shine,
and your heart will thrill with joy,
for merchants from around the world will
come to you.
They will bring you the wealth of many
lands.
6 Vast caravans of camels will converge on you,
the camels of Midian and Ephah.
The people of Sheba will bring gold and
frankincense
and will come worshiping the LORD.
7 The flocks of Kedar will be given to you,
and the rams of Nebaioth will be brought
for my altars.
I will accept their offerings,
and I will make my Temple glorious.

8 "And what do I see flying like clouds to Israel,
like doves to their nests?
9 They are ships from the ends of the earth,
from lands that trust in me,
led by the great ships of Tarshish.
They are bringing the people of Israel home
from far away,
carrying their silver and gold.
They will honor the LORD your God,
the Holy One of Israel,
for he has filled you with splendor.

10 "Foreigners will come to rebuild your towns,
and their kings will serve you.
For though I have destroyed you in my anger,
I will now have mercy on you through
my grace.

11 Your gates will stay open day and night
to receive the wealth of many lands.
The kings of the world will be led as captives
in a victory procession.
12 For the nations that refuse to serve you
will be destroyed.

13 "The glory of Lebanon will be yours—
the forests of cypress, fir, and pine—
to beautify my sanctuary.
My Temple will be glorious!
14 The descendants of your tormentors
will come and bow before you.
Those who despised you
will kiss your feet.
They will call you the City of the LORD,
and Zion of the Holy One of Israel.

15 "Though you were once despised and hated,
with no one traveling through you,
I will make you beautiful forever,
a joy to all generations.
16 Powerful kings and mighty nations
will satisfy your every need,
as though you were a child
nursing at the breast of a queen.
You will know at last that I, the LORD,
am your Savior and your Redeemer,
the Mighty One of Israel.
17 I will exchange your bronze for gold,
your iron for silver,
your wood for bronze,
and your stones for iron.
I will make peace your leader
and righteousness your ruler.
18 Violence will disappear from your land;
the desolation and destruction of war
will end.
Salvation will surround you like city walls,
and praise will be on the lips of all who
enter there.

19 "No longer will you need the sun to shine
by day,
nor the moon to give its light by night,
for the LORD your God will be your
everlasting light,
and your God will be your glory.
20 Your sun will never set;
your moon will not go down.
For the LORD will be your everlasting light.
Your days of mourning will come to an end.
21 All your people will be righteous.
They will possess their land forever,
for I will plant them there with my own hands
in order to bring myself glory.
22 The smallest family will become a thousand
people,
and the tiniest group will become
a mighty nation.
At the right time, I, the LORD, will make
it happen."

CHAPTER 61
Good News for the Oppressed

1 The Spirit of the Sovereign LORD is upon me,
for the LORD has anointed me
to bring good news to the poor.
He has sent me to comfort the
brokenhearted
and to proclaim that captives will be
released
and prisoners will be freed.
2 He has sent me to tell those who mourn
that the time of the LORD's favor
has come,
and with it, the day of God's anger against
their enemies.
3 To all who mourn in Israel,
he will give a crown of beauty for ashes,
a joyous blessing instead of mourning,
festive praise instead of despair.
In their righteousness, they will be like
great oaks
that the LORD has planted for his
own glory.
4 They will rebuild the ancient ruins,
repairing cities destroyed long ago.
They will revive them,
though they have been deserted for many
generations.
5 Foreigners will be your servants.
They will feed your flocks
and plow your fields
and tend your vineyards.
6 You will be called priests of the LORD,
ministers of our God.
You will feed on the treasures of the nations
and boast in their riches.
7 Instead of shame and dishonor,
you will enjoy a double share of honor.
You will possess a double portion of
prosperity in your land,
and everlasting joy will be yours.

8 "For I, the LORD, love justice.
I hate robbery and wrongdoing.
I will faithfully reward my people for their
suffering
and make an everlasting covenant
with them.

9 Their descendants will be recognized
and honored among the nations.
Everyone will realize that they are a people
the LORD has blessed."
10 I am overwhelmed with joy in the LORD
my God!
For he has dressed me with the clothing
of salvation
and draped me in a robe of righteousness.
I am like a bridegroom dressed for his
wedding
or a bride with her jewels.
11 The Sovereign LORD will show his justice
to the nations of the world.
Everyone will praise him!
His righteousness will be like a garden
in early spring,
with plants springing up everywhere.

CHAPTER **62**

Isaiah's Prayer for Jerusalem

1 Because I love Zion,
I will not keep still.
Because my heart yearns for Jerusalem,
I cannot remain silent.
I will not stop praying for her
until her righteousness shines like
the dawn,
and her salvation blazes like a burning
torch.
2 The nations will see your righteousness.
World leaders will be blinded by your
glory.
And you will be given a new name
by the LORD's own mouth.
3 The LORD will hold you in his hand for all
to see—
a splendid crown in the hand of God.
4 Never again will you be called "The
Forsaken City"
or "The Desolate Land."
Your new name will be "The City of
God's Delight"
and "The Bride of God,"
for the LORD delights in you
and will claim you as his bride.
5 Your children will commit themselves
to you, O Jerusalem,
just as a young man commits himself
to his bride.
Then God will rejoice over you
as a bridegroom rejoices over his bride.
6 O Jerusalem, I have posted watchmen
on your walls;
they will pray day and night, continually.
Take no rest, all you who pray to the LORD.
7 Give the LORD no rest until he completes
his work,
until he makes Jerusalem the pride
of the earth.
8 The LORD has sworn to Jerusalem by his
own strength:
"I will never again hand you over to your
enemies.
Never again will foreign warriors come
and take away your grain and new wine.
9 You raised the grain, and you will eat it,
praising the LORD.
Within the courtyards of the Temple,
you yourselves will drink the wine you
have pressed."
10 Go out through the gates!
Prepare the highway for my people
to return!
Smooth out the road; pull out the boulders;
raise a flag for all the nations to see.
11 The LORD has sent this message to every land:
"Tell the people of Israel,
'Look, your Savior is coming.
See, he brings his reward with him as he
comes.'"

FUN-fact

How Did the Bible Become a Book?

Through canonization! No, not the kind of cannon an army uses. *Canonization* comes from the Greek word *Kanon*, which means "measuring rod."

After the books of the Bible were looked at by religious leaders to make sure they were inspired by God and written with his authority, they were all put together into one book. That's how the Bible became the "measuring rod" of our faith!

Get a ruler and on the back write, "The Bible is my measuring rod." Every time you use the ruler, thank God for the Bible!

12 They will be called "The Holy People"
and "The People Redeemed by the LORD."
And Jerusalem will be known as "The Desirable Place"
and "The City No Longer Forsaken."

CHAPTER 63

Judgment against the LORD's Enemies

1 Who is this who comes from Edom,
from the city of Bozrah,
with his clothing stained red?
Who is this in royal robes,
marching in his great strength?

"It is I, the LORD, announcing your salvation!
It is I, the LORD, who has the power to save!"

2 Why are your clothes so red,
as if you have been treading out grapes?

3 "I have been treading the winepress alone;
no one was there to help me.
In my anger I have trampled my enemies
as if they were grapes.
In my fury I have trampled my foes.
Their blood has stained my clothes.
4 For the time has come for me to avenge my people,
to ransom them from their oppressors.
5 I was amazed to see that no one intervened
to help the oppressed.
So I myself stepped in to save them with my strong arm,
and my wrath sustained me.
6 I crushed the nations in my anger
and made them stagger and fall to the ground,
spilling their blood upon the earth."

Praise for Deliverance

7 I will tell of the LORD's unfailing love.
I will praise the LORD for all he has done.
I will rejoice in his great goodness to Israel,
which he has granted according to his mercy and love.
8 He said, "They are my very own people.
Surely they will not betray me again."
And he became their Savior.
9 In all their suffering he also suffered,
and he personally rescued them.
In his love and mercy he redeemed them.
He lifted them up and carried them
through all the years.
10 But they rebelled against him
and grieved his Holy Spirit.
So he became their enemy
and fought against them.

11 Then they remembered those days of old
when Moses led his people out of Egypt.
They cried out, "Where is the one who
brought Israel through the sea,
with Moses as their shepherd?
Where is the one who sent his Holy Spirit
to be among his people?
12 Where is the one whose power was displayed
when Moses lifted up his hand—
the one who divided the sea before them,
making himself famous forever?
13 Where is the one who led them through the bottom of the sea?
They were like fine stallions
racing through the desert, never stumbling.
14 As with cattle going down into a peaceful valley,
the Spirit of the LORD gave them rest.
You led your people, LORD,
and gained a magnificent reputation."

Prayer for Mercy and Pardon

15 LORD, look down from heaven;
look from your holy, glorious home,
and see us.
Where is the passion and the might
you used to show on our behalf?
Where are your mercy and
compassion now?
16 Surely you are still our Father!
Even if Abraham and Jacob would
disown us,
LORD, you would still be our Father.
You are our Redeemer from ages past.
17 LORD, why have you allowed us to turn from your path?
Why have you given us stubborn hearts
so we no longer fear you?
Return and help us, for we are your servants,
the tribes that are your special possession.
18 How briefly your holy people possessed your holy place,
and now our enemies have destroyed it.
19 Sometimes it seems as though we never
belonged to you,
as though we had never been known
as your people.

CHAPTER 64

1 Oh, that you would burst from the heavens
and come down!

How the mountains would quake in your
presence!
2 As fire causes wood to burn
and water to boil,
your coming would make the nations tremble.
Then your enemies would learn the reason
for your fame!
3 When you came down long ago,
you did awesome deeds beyond our
highest expectations.
And oh, how the mountains quaked!
4 For since the world began,
no ear has heard
and no eye has seen a God like you,
who works for those who wait for him!
5 You welcome those who gladly do good,
who follow godly ways.
But you have been very angry with us,
for we are not godly.
We are constant sinners;
how can people like us be saved?
6 We are all infected and impure with sin.
When we display our righteous deeds,
they are nothing but filthy rags.
Like autumn leaves, we wither and fall,
and our sins sweep us away like the wind.
7 Yet no one calls on your name
or pleads with you for mercy.
Therefore, you have turned away from us
and turned us over to our sins.

8 And yet, O Lord, you are our Father.
We are the clay, and you are the potter.
We all are formed by your hand.
9 Don't be so angry with us, Lord.
Please don't remember our sins forever.
Look at us, we pray,
and see that we are all your people.
10 Your holy cities are destroyed.
Zion is a wilderness;
yes, Jerusalem is a desolate ruin.
11 The holy and beautiful Temple
where our ancestors praised you
has been burned down,
and all the things of beauty are destroyed.
12 After all this, Lord, must you still refuse
to help us?
Will you continue to be silent and
punish us?

CHAPTER 65
Judgment and Final Salvation

The Lord says,

"I was ready to respond, but no one asked
for help.
I was ready to be found, but no one was
looking for me.
I said, 'Here I am, here I am!'
to a nation that did not call on my name.
2 All day long I opened my arms to a rebellious
people.
But they follow their own evil paths
and their own crooked schemes.
3 All day long they insult me to my face
by worshiping idols in their sacred
gardens.
They burn incense on pagan altars.
4 At night they go out among the graves,
worshiping the dead.
They eat the flesh of pigs
and make stews with other forbidden
foods.
5 Yet they say to each other,
'Don't come too close or you will defile me!
I am holier than you!'
These people are a stench in my nostrils,
an acrid smell that never goes away.

6 "Look, my decree is written out in front
of me:
I will not stand silent;
I will repay them in full!
Yes, I will repay them—
7 both for their own sins
and for those of their ancestors,"
says the Lord.
"For they also burned incense on the
mountains
and insulted me on the hills.
I will pay them back in full!

8 "But I will not destroy them all,"
says the Lord.
"For just as good grapes are found among
a cluster of bad ones
(and someone will say, 'Don't throw
them all away—
some of those grapes are good!'),
so I will not destroy all Israel.
For I still have true servants there.
9 I will preserve a remnant of the people
of Israel
and of Judah to possess my land.
Those I choose will inherit it,
and my servants will live there.
10 The plain of Sharon will again be filled
with flocks
for my people who have searched for me,
and the valley of Achor will be a place
to pasture herds.

11 "But because the rest of you have forsaken
the LORD
and have forgotten his Temple,
and because you have prepared feasts
to honor the god of Fate
and have offered mixed wine to the god
of Destiny,
12 now I will 'destine' you for the sword.
All of you will bow down before the
executioner.
For when I called, you did not answer.
When I spoke, you did not listen.
You deliberately sinned—before my
very eyes—
and chose to do what you know I despise."

13 Therefore, this is what the Sovereign
LORD says:
"My servants will eat,
but you will starve.
My servants will drink,
but you will be thirsty.
My servants will rejoice,
but you will be sad and ashamed.
14 My servants will sing for joy,
but you will cry in sorrow and despair.
15 Your name will be a curse word among
my people,
for the Sovereign LORD will destroy you
and will call his true servants by another
name.
16 All who invoke a blessing or take an oath
will do so by the God of truth.
For I will put aside my anger
and forget the evil of earlier days.

17 "Look! I am creating new heavens and
a new earth,
and no one will even think about the old
ones anymore.
18 Be glad; rejoice forever in my creation!
And look! I will create Jerusalem as a place
of happiness.
Her people will be a source of joy.
19 I will rejoice over Jerusalem
and delight in my people.
And the sound of weeping and crying
will be heard in it no more.

20 "No longer will babies die when only a few
days old.
No longer will adults die before they have
lived a full life.
No longer will people be considered old at
one hundred!
Only the cursed will die that young!
21 In those days people will live in the houses
they build
and eat the fruit of their own vineyards.
22 Unlike the past, invaders will not take their
houses
and confiscate their vineyards.
For my people will live as long as trees,
and my chosen ones will have time to
enjoy their hard-won gains.
23 They will not work in vain,
and their children will not be doomed
to misfortune.
For they are people blessed by the LORD,
and their children, too, will be blessed.
24 I will answer them before they even call
to me.
While they are still talking about their
needs,
I will go ahead and answer their prayers!
25 The wolf and the lamb will feed together.
The lion will eat hay like a cow.
But the snakes will eat dust.
In those days no one will be hurt or
destroyed on my holy mountain.
I, the LORD, have spoken!"

CHAPTER 66

This is what the LORD says:

"Heaven is my throne,
and the earth is my footstool.
Could you build me a temple as good as that?
Could you build me such a resting place?
2 My hands have made both heaven and earth;
they and everything in them are mine.
I, the LORD, have spoken!

"I will bless those who have humble and
contrite hearts,
who tremble at my word.
3 But those who choose their own ways—
delighting in their detestable sins—
will not have their offerings accepted.
When such people sacrifice a bull,
it is no more acceptable than a human
sacrifice.
When they sacrifice a lamb,
it's as though they had sacrificed a dog!
When they bring an offering of grain,
they might as well offer the blood of a pig.
When they burn frankincense,
it's as if they had blessed an idol.
4 I will send them great trouble—
all the things they feared.
For when I called, they did not answer.
When I spoke, they did not listen.

They deliberately sinned before my
very eyes
and chose to do what they know I despise."

5 Hear this message from the LORD,
all you who tremble at his words:
"Your own people hate you
and throw you out for being loyal
to my name.
'Let the LORD be honored!' they scoff.
'Be joyful in him!'
But they will be put to shame.
6 What is all the commotion in the city?
What is that terrible noise from the
Temple?
It is the voice of the LORD
taking vengeance against his enemies.

7 "Before the birth pains even begin,
Jerusalem gives birth to a son.
8 Who has ever seen anything as strange
as this?
Who ever heard of such a thing?
Has a nation ever been born in a single day?
Has a country ever come forth in a mere
moment?
But by the time Jerusalem's birth
pains begin,
her children will be born.
9 Would I ever bring this nation to the point
of birth
and then not deliver it?" asks the LORD.
"No! I would never keep this nation from
being born,"
says your God.

10 "Rejoice with Jerusalem!
Be glad with her, all you who love her
and all you who mourn for her.
11 Drink deeply of her glory
even as an infant drinks at its mother's
comforting breasts."

12 This is what the LORD says:
"I will give Jerusalem a river of peace and
prosperity.
The wealth of the nations will flow
to her.
Her children will be nursed at her breasts,
carried in her arms, and held on her lap.
13 I will comfort you there in Jerusalem
as a mother comforts her child."

14 When you see these things, your heart will
rejoice.
You will flourish like the grass!
Everyone will see the LORD's hand of blessing
on his servants—
and his anger against his enemies.
15 See, the LORD is coming with fire,
and his swift chariots roar like a
whirlwind.
He will bring punishment with the fury
of his anger
and the flaming fire of his hot rebuke.
16 The LORD will punish the world by fire
and by his sword.
He will judge the earth,
and many will be killed by him.

17"Those who 'consecrate' and 'purify' themselves in a sacred garden with its idol in the center—feasting on pork and rats and other
detestable meats—will come to a terrible end,"
says the LORD.
18"I can see what they are doing, and I know
what they are thinking. So I will gather all nations and peoples together, and they will see my
glory. 19I will perform a sign among them. And I
will send those who survive to be messengers to
the nations—to Tarshish, to the Libyans and
Lydians (who are famous as archers), to Tubal
and Greece, and to all the lands beyond the sea
that have not heard of my fame or seen my glory.
There they will declare my glory to the nations.
20They will bring the remnant of your people
back from every nation. They will bring them to
my holy mountain in Jerusalem as an offering to
the LORD. They will ride on horses, in chariots
and wagons, and on mules and camels," says the
LORD. 21"And I will appoint some of them to be
my priests and Levites. I, the LORD, have spoken!

22 "As surely as my new heavens and earth
will remain,
so will you always be my people,
with a name that will never disappear,"
says the LORD.
23 "All humanity will come to worship me
from week to week
and from month to month.
24 And as they go out, they will see
the dead bodies of those who have
rebelled against me.
For the worms that devour them will
never die,
and the fire that burns them will never
go out.
All who pass by
will view them with utter horror."

They deliberately sinned before my very eyes
and chose to do what they know I despise."

5 Hear this message from the LORD,
all you who tremble at his words:
"Your own people hate you
and throw you out for being loyal
to my name.
'Let the LORD be honored!' they scoff.
'Be joyful in him!'
But they will be put to shame.
6 What is all the commotion in the city?
What is that terrible noise from the
Temple?
It is the voice of the LORD
taking vengeance against his enemies.

7 "Before the birth pains even begin,
Jerusalem gives birth to a son.
8 Who has ever seen anything as strange
as this?
Who ever heard of such a thing?
Has a nation ever been born in a single day?
Has a country ever come forth in a mere
moment?
But by the time Jerusalem's birth
pains begin,
her children will be born.
9 Would I ever bring this nation to the point
of birth
and then not deliver it?" asks the LORD.
"No! I would never keep this nation from
being born,"
says your God.

10 "Rejoice with Jerusalem!
Be glad with her, all you who love her
and all you who mourn for her.
11 Drink deeply of her glory
even as an infant drinks at its mother's
comforting breasts."

12 This is what the LORD says:
"I will give Jerusalem a river of peace and
prosperity.
The wealth of the nations will flow
to her.
Her children will be nursed at her breasts,
carried in her arms, and held on her lap.
13 I will comfort you there in Jerusalem
as a mother comforts her child."

14 When you see these things, your heart will
rejoice.
You will flourish like the grass!
Everyone will see the LORD's hand of blessing
on his servants—
and his anger against his enemies.
15 See, the LORD is coming with fire,
and his swift chariots roar like a
whirlwind.
He will bring punishment with the fury
of his anger
and the flaming fire of his hot rebuke.
16 The LORD will punish the world by fire
and by his sword.
He will judge the earth,
and many will be killed by him.

17 "Those who 'consecrate' and 'purify' themselves in a sacred garden with its idol in the center—feasting on pork and rats and other
detestable meats—will come to a terrible end,"
says the LORD.
18 "I can see what they are doing, and I know
what they are thinking. So I will gather all nations and peoples together, and they will see my
glory. 19 I will perform a sign among them. And I
will send those who survive to be messengers to
the nations—to Tarshish, to the Libyans and
Lydians (who are famous as archers), to Tubal
and Greece, and to all the lands beyond the sea
that have not heard of my fame or seen my glory.
There they will declare my glory to the nations.
20 They will bring the remnant of your people
back from every nation. They will bring them to
my holy mountain in Jerusalem as an offering to
the LORD. They will ride on horses, in chariots
and wagons, and on mules and camels," says the
LORD. 21 "And I will appoint some of them to be
my priests and Levites. I, the LORD, have spoken!

22 "As surely as my new heavens and earth
will remain,
so will you always be my people,
with a name that will never disappear,"
says the LORD.
23 "All humanity will come to worship me
from week to week
and from month to month.
24 And as they go out, they will see
the dead bodies of those who have
rebelled against me.
For the worms that devour them will
never die,
and the fire that burns them will never
go out.
All who pass by
will view them with utter horror."

JEREMIAH

Is Anybody Listening?

Look for 1 hidden message in Jeremiah!

The book of Jeremiah tells how the prophet Jeremiah

- **WARNED ABOUT THE FALL OF JERUSALEM**
- **EXPLAINED HOW TO AVOID IT**
- **WARNED SOME MORE**
- **THEN WATCHED AS THE GREAT CITY FELL**

Nice Clothes!

God told Jeremiah to bury a piece of clothing for a while and then dig it up when it was all mildewed and gross. A new fashion fad? Nope! **Find out the real reason in Jeremiah 13:1-11.**

Doctor?
Musician?
Pilot
?
Doctor

Ever wonder if God really has a plan for your life? What do you think God plans for you to do? **Read what God said about plans in Jeremiah 1:5.**

Uh...Where Do You Shop?

God told Jeremiah to wear another weird piece of clothing. Actually, it wasn't really *clothing*…it was more of a thing, sort of…Well, you'll just have to read it for yourself. **It's in Jeremiah 27:1-8.**

Judgment on Jerusalem

Just as God had warned, the day came when God judged the people of Jerusalem. Read Jeremiah 39:8-10 to find out what happened to them. **(Then go to Jeremiah 40:2-6 to see what became of Jeremiah!)**

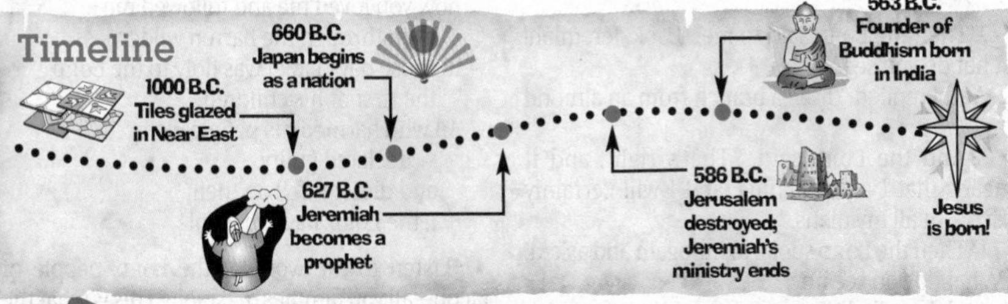

Timeline
1000 B.C. Tiles glazed in Near East
660 B.C. Japan begins as a nation
627 B.C. Jeremiah becomes a prophet
586 B.C. Jerusalem destroyed; Jeremiah's ministry ends
563 B.C. Founder of Buddhism born in India
Jesus is born!

The JESUS CONNECTION

Jeremiah told the people over and over to stop sinning and turn back to God. Or else! That was a common message that all of the prophets preached. But just like the other prophets, Jeremiah also told of a Messiah who would come to save his people. That Messiah was Jesus. It doesn't matter whether you're reading about the founders of the faith, the prophets of the Old Testament, or the disciples in the New Testament—

everything points to Jesus!

Jeremiah 1 . . . page 726

CHAPTER 1

These are the words of Jeremiah son of Hilkiah,
one of the priests from the town of Anathoth in
the land of Benjamin. 2 The LORD first gave messages to Jeremiah during the thirteenth year of
the reign of Josiah son of Amon, king of Judah.
3 The LORD's messages continued throughout
the reign of King Jehoiakim, Josiah's son, until
the eleventh year of the reign of King Zedekiah,
another of Josiah's sons. In August of that eleventh year the people of Jerusalem were taken
away as captives.

Jeremiah's Call and First Visions

4 The LORD gave me this message:

5 "I knew you before I formed you in your
mother's womb.
Before you were born I set you apart
and appointed you as my prophet
to the nations."

6 "O Sovereign LORD," I said, "I can't speak for
you! I'm too young!"
7 The LORD replied, "Don't say, 'I'm too young,'
for you must go wherever I send you and say
whatever I tell you. 8 And don't be afraid of the
people, for I will be with you and will protect
you. I, the LORD, have spoken!" 9 Then the LORD
reached out and touched my mouth and said,

"Look, I have put my words in
your mouth!
10 Today I appoint you to stand up
against nations and kingdoms.
Some you must uproot and tear down,
destroy and overthrow.
Others you must build up
and plant."

11 Then the LORD said to me, "Look, Jeremiah!
What do you see?"
And I replied, "I see a branch from an almond
tree."
12 And the LORD said, "That's right, and it
means that I am watching, and I will certainly
carry out all my plans."
13 Then the LORD spoke to me again and asked,
"What do you see now?"
And I replied, "I see a pot of boiling water,
spilling from the north."
14 "Yes," the LORD said, "for terror from the
north will boil out on the people of this land.
15 Listen! I am calling the armies of the kingdoms of the north to come to Jerusalem. I, the
LORD, have spoken!

"They will set their thrones
at the gates of the city.
They will attack its walls
and all the other towns of Judah.
16 I will pronounce judgment
on my people for all their evil—
for deserting me and burning incense
to other gods.
Yes, they worship idols made with their
own hands!

17 "Get up and prepare for action.
Go out and tell them everything I tell
you to say.
Do not be afraid of them,
or I will make you look foolish in front
of them.
18 For see, today I have made you strong
like a fortified city that cannot be
captured,
like an iron pillar or a bronze wall.
You will stand against the whole land—
the kings, officials, priests, and people
of Judah.
19 They will fight you, but they will fail.
For I am with you, and I will take care
of you.
I, the LORD, have spoken!"

CHAPTER 2

The LORD's Case against His People

The LORD gave me another message. He said,
2 "Go and shout this message to Jerusalem. This
is what the LORD says:

"I remember how eager you were
to please me
as a young bride long ago,
how you loved me and followed me
even through the barren wilderness.
3 In those days Israel was holy to the LORD,
the first of his children.
All who harmed his people were
declared guilty,
and disaster fell on them.
I, the LORD, have spoken!"

4 Listen to the word of the LORD, people of
Jacob—all you families of Israel! 5 This is what the
LORD says:

"What did your ancestors find wrong
with me
that led them to stray so far from me?
They worshiped worthless idols,
only to become worthless themselves.

6 They did not ask, 'Where is the LORD
who brought us safely out of Egypt
and led us through the barren wilderness—
a land of deserts and pits,
a land of drought and death,
where no one lives or even travels?'

7 "And when I brought you into a fruitful land
to enjoy its bounty and goodness,
you defiled my land and
corrupted the possession I had
promised you.
8 The priests did not ask,
'Where is the LORD?'
Those who taught my word ignored me,
the rulers turned against me,
and the prophets spoke in the name of Baal,
wasting their time on worthless idols.
9 Therefore, I will bring my case against you,"
says the LORD.
"I will even bring charges against your
children's children
in the years to come.

10 "Go west and look in the land of Cyprus;
go east and search through the land
of Kedar.
Has anyone ever heard of anything
as strange as this?
11 Has any nation ever traded its gods for
new ones,
even though they are not gods at all?
Yet my people have exchanged their
glorious God
for worthless idols!
12 The heavens are shocked at such a thing
and shrink back in horror and dismay,"
says the LORD.
13 "For my people have done two evil things:
They have abandoned me—
the fountain of living water.
And they have dug for themselves
cracked cisterns
that can hold no water at all!

The Results of Israel's Sin

14 "Why has Israel become a slave?
Why has he been carried away
as plunder?
15 Strong lions have roared against him,
and the land has been destroyed.
The towns are now in ruins,
and no one lives in them anymore.
16 Egyptians, marching from their cities
of Memphis and Tahpanhes,
have destroyed Israel's glory and power.
17 And you have brought this upon yourselves
by rebelling against the LORD your God,
even though he was leading you on
the way!

18 "What have you gained by your alliances
with Egypt
and your covenants with Assyria?
What good to you are the streams of the Nile
or the waters of the Euphrates River?
19 Your wickedness will bring its own
punishment.
Your turning from me will shame you.
You will see what an evil, bitter thing it is
to abandon the LORD your God and not
to fear him.
I, the Lord, the LORD of Heaven's Armies,
have spoken!

20 "Long ago I broke the yoke that
oppressed you
and tore away the chains of your slavery,
but still you said,
'I will not serve you.'
On every hill and under every green tree,
you have prostituted yourselves by bowing
down to idols.
21 But I was the one who planted you,
choosing a vine of the purest stock—
the very best.
How did you grow into this corrupt
wild vine?
22 No amount of soap or lye can make
you clean.
I still see the stain of your guilt.
I, the Sovereign LORD, have spoken!

Israel, an Unfaithful Wife

23 "You say, 'That's not true!
I haven't worshiped the images of Baal!'
But how can you say that?
Go and look in any valley in the land!
Face the awful sins you have done.
You are like a restless female camel
desperately searching for a mate.
24 You are like a wild donkey,
sniffing the wind at mating time.
Who can restrain her lust?
Those who desire her don't need to search,
for she goes running to them!
25 When will you stop running?
When will you stop panting after
other gods?
But you say, 'Save your breath.
I'm in love with these foreign gods,
and I can't stop loving them now!'

26 "Israel is like a thief
who feels shame only when he gets caught.
They, their kings, officials, priests, and
prophets—
all are alike in this.
27 To an image carved from a piece of wood
they say,
'You are my father.'
To an idol chiseled from a block of stone they
say,
'You are my mother.'
They turn their backs on me,
but in times of trouble they cry out to me,
'Come and save us!'
28 But why not call on these gods you
have made?
When trouble comes, let them save you
if they can!
For you have as many gods
as there are towns in Judah.
29 Why do you accuse me of doing wrong?
You are the ones who have rebelled,"
says the LORD.
30 "I have punished your children,
but they did not respond to my discipline.
You yourselves have killed your prophets
as a lion kills its prey.

31 "O my people, listen to the words
of the LORD!
Have I been like a desert to Israel?
Have I been to them a land of darkness?
Why then do my people say, 'At last we are
free from God!
We don't need him anymore!'
32 Does a young woman forget her jewelry,
or a bride her wedding dress?
Yet for years on end
my people have forgotten me.

33 "How you plot and scheme to win
your lovers.
Even an experienced prostitute could
learn from you!
34 Your clothing is stained with the blood
of the innocent and the poor,
though you didn't catch them breaking
into your houses!
35 And yet you say,
'I have done nothing wrong.
Surely God isn't angry with me!'
But now I will punish you severely
because you claim you have not sinned.
36 First here, then there—
you flit from one ally to another asking
for help.
But your new friends in Egypt will let
you down,
just as Assyria did before.
37 In despair, you will be led into exile
with your hands on your heads,
for the LORD has rejected the nations
you trust.
They will not help you at all.

CHAPTER 3

1 "If a man divorces a woman
and she goes and marries someone else,
he will not take her back again,
for that would surely corrupt the land.
But you have prostituted yourself with
many lovers,
so why are you trying to come back to me?"
says the LORD.
2 "Look at the shrines on every hilltop.
Is there any place you have not been defiled
by your adultery with other gods?
You sit like a prostitute beside the road
waiting for a customer
You sit alone like a nomad in the desert.
You have polluted the land with your
prostitution
and your wickedness.
3 That's why even the spring rains have failed.
For you are a brazen prostitute and
completely shameless.
4 Yet you say to me,
'Father, you have been my guide since
my youth.
5 Surely you won't be angry forever!
Surely you can forget about it!'
So you talk,
but you keep on doing all the evil
you can."

Judah Follows Israel's Example

6 During the reign of King Josiah, the LORD said
to me, "Have you seen what fickle Israel has
done? Like a wife who commits adultery, Israel
has worshiped other gods on every hill and
under every green tree. 7 I thought, 'After she has
done all this, she will return to me.' But she did
not return, and her faithless sister Judah saw
this. 8 She saw that I divorced faithless Israel because of her adultery. But that treacherous sister
Judah had no fear, and now she, too, has left me
and given herself to prostitution. 9 Israel treated
it all so lightly—she thought nothing of committing adultery by worshiping idols made of wood
and stone. So now the land has been polluted.
10 But despite all this, her faithless sister Judah

has never sincerely returned to me. She has only
pretended to be sorry. I, the LORD, have spoken!"

Hope for Wayward Israel

11 Then the LORD said to me, "Even faithless Israel
is less guilty than treacherous Judah! 12 Therefore, go and give this message to Israel. This is
what the LORD says:

"O Israel, my faithless people,
come home to me again,
for I am merciful.
I will not be angry with you forever.
13 Only acknowledge your guilt.
Admit that you rebelled against the LORD
your God
and committed adultery against him
by worshiping idols under every
green tree.
Confess that you refused to listen
to my voice.
I, the LORD, have spoken!
14 "Return home, you wayward children,"
says the LORD,
"for I am your master.
I will bring you back to the land of Israel—
one from this town and two from
that family—
from wherever you are scattered.
15 And I will give you shepherds after my
own heart,
who will guide you with knowledge and
understanding.

16 "And when your land is once more filled
with people," says the LORD, "you will no longer
wish for 'the good old days' when you possessed
the Ark of the LORD's Covenant. You will not miss
those days or even remember them, and there
will be no need to rebuild the Ark. 17 In that day
Jerusalem will be known as 'The Throne of the
LORD.' All nations will come there to honor the
LORD. They will no longer stubbornly follow
their own evil desires. 18 In those days the people
of Judah and Israel will return together from exile in the north. They will return to the land I gave
your ancestors as an inheritance forever.

19 "I thought to myself,
'I would love to treat you as my
own children!'
I wanted nothing more than to give you
this beautiful land—
the finest possession in the world.
I looked forward to your calling me 'Father,'
and I wanted you never to turn from me.
20 But you have been unfaithful to me, you
people of Israel!
You have been like a faithless wife who
leaves her husband.
I, the LORD, have spoken."

21 Voices are heard high on the windswept
mountains,
the weeping and pleading of Israel's
people.
For they have chosen crooked paths
and have forgotten the LORD their God.

22 "My wayward children," says the LORD,
"come back to me, and I will heal your
wayward hearts."

"Yes, we're coming," the people reply,
"for you are the LORD our God.
23 Our worship of idols on the hills
and our religious orgies on the mountains
are a delusion.
Only in the LORD our God
will Israel ever find salvation.
24 From childhood we have watched
as everything our ancestors worked for—
their flocks and herds, their sons and
daughters—
was squandered on a delusion.
25 Let us now lie down in shame
and cover ourselves with dishonor,
for we and our ancestors have sinned
against the LORD our God.
From our childhood to this day
we have never obeyed him."

CHAPTER 4

1 "O Israel," says the LORD,
"if you wanted to return to me, you could.
You could throw away your detestable idols
and stray away no more.
2 Then when you swear by my name, saying,
'As surely as the LORD lives,'
you could do so
with truth, justice, and righteousness.
Then you would be a blessing to the nations
of the world,
and all people would come and praise
my name."

Coming Judgment against Judah

3 This is what the LORD says to the people of Judah and Jerusalem:

"Plow up the hard ground of your hearts!
Do not waste your good seed among thorns.

4 O people of Judah and Jerusalem,
surrender your pride and power.
Change your hearts before the LORD,
or my anger will burn like an
unquenchable fire
because of all your sins.

5 "Shout to Judah, and broadcast to Jerusalem!
Tell them to sound the alarm throughout
the land:
'Run for your lives!
Flee to the fortified cities!'
6 Raise a signal flag as a warning for
Jerusalem:
'Flee now! Do not delay!'
For I am bringing terrible destruction
upon you
from the north."

7 A lion stalks from its den,
a destroyer of nations.
It has left its lair and is headed your way.
It's going to devastate your land!
Your towns will lie in ruins,
with no one living in them anymore.
8 So put on clothes of mourning
and weep with broken hearts,
for the fierce anger of the LORD
is still upon us.
9 "In that day," says the LORD,
"the king and the officials will tremble
in fear.
The priests will be struck with horror,
and the prophets will be appalled."

10 Then I said, "O Sovereign LORD,
the people have been deceived by what
you said,
for you promised peace for Jerusalem.
But the sword is held at their throats!"

11 The time is coming when the LORD will say
to the people of Jerusalem,
"My dear people, a burning wind is blowing
in from the desert,
and it's not a gentle breeze useful for
winnowing grain.
12 It is a roaring blast sent by me!
Now I will pronounce your destruction!"

13 Our enemy rushes down on us like
storm clouds!
His chariots are like whirlwinds.
His horses are swifter than eagles.
How terrible it will be, for we are doomed!
14 O Jerusalem, cleanse your heart
that you may be saved.
How long will you harbor
your evil thoughts?
15 Your destruction has been announced
from Dan and the hill country of Ephraim.
16 "Warn the surrounding nations
and announce this to Jerusalem:
The enemy is coming from a distant land,
raising a battle cry against the towns
of Judah.
17 They surround Jerusalem like watchmen
around a field,
for my people have rebelled against me,"
says the LORD.
18 "Your own actions have brought this upon you.
This punishment is bitter, piercing you
to the heart!"

Jeremiah Weeps for His People

19 My heart, my heart—I writhe in pain!
My heart pounds within me! I cannot
be still.
For I have heard the blast of enemy trumpets
and the roar of their battle cries.
20 Waves of destruction roll over the land,
until it lies in complete desolation.
Suddenly my tents are destroyed;
in a moment my shelters are crushed.
21 How long must I see the battle flags
and hear the trumpets of war?

22 "My people are foolish
and do not know me," says the LORD.
"They are stupid children
who have no understanding.
They are clever enough at doing wrong,
but they have no idea how to do right!"

Jeremiah's Vision of Coming Disaster

23 I looked at the earth, and it was empty
and formless.
I looked at the heavens, and there was
no light.
24 I looked at the mountains and hills,
and they trembled and shook.
25 I looked, and all the people were gone.
All the birds of the sky had flown away.
26 I looked, and the fertile fields had become
a wilderness.
The towns lay in ruins,
crushed by the LORD's fierce anger.

27 This is what the LORD says:
"The whole land will be ruined,
but I will not destroy it completely.

28 The earth will mourn
and the heavens will be draped in black
because of my decree against my people.
I have made up my mind and will not
change it."

29 At the noise of charioteers and archers,
the people flee in terror.
They hide in the bushes
and run for the mountains.
All the towns have been abandoned—
not a person remains!

30 What are you doing,
you who have been plundered?
Why do you dress up in beautiful clothing
and put on gold jewelry?
Why do you brighten your eyes with
mascara?
Your primping will do you no good!
The allies who were your lovers
despise you and seek to kill you.

31 I hear a cry, like that of a woman in labor,
the groans of a woman giving birth
to her first child.
It is beautiful Jerusalem
gasping for breath and crying out,
"Help! I'm being murdered!"

CHAPTER 5

The Sins of Judah

1 "Run up and down every street in Jerusalem,"
says the LORD.
"Look high and low; search throughout
the city!
If you can find even one just and honest
person,
I will not destroy the city.
2 But even when they are under oath,
saying, 'As surely as the LORD lives,'
they are still telling lies!"
3 LORD, you are searching for honesty.
You struck your people,
but they paid no attention.
You crushed them,
but they refused to be corrected.
They are determined, with faces set
like stone;
they have refused to repent.
4 Then I said, "But what can we expect from
the poor?
They are ignorant.
They don't know the ways of the LORD.
They don't understand God's laws.
5 So I will go and speak to their leaders.
Surely they know the ways of the LORD
and understand God's laws."
But the leaders, too, as one man,
had thrown off God's yoke
and broken his chains.
6 So now a lion from the forest will
attack them;
a wolf from the desert will pounce on them.
A leopard will lurk near their towns,
tearing apart any who dare to venture out.
For their rebellion is great,
and their sins are many.
7 "How can I pardon you?
For even your children have turned
from me.
They have sworn by gods that are not
gods at all!
I fed my people until they were full.
But they thanked me by committing adultery
and lining up at the brothels.
8 They are well-fed, lusty stallions,
each neighing for his neighbor's wife.
9 Should I not punish them for this?" says
the LORD.
"Should I not avenge myself against such
a nation?

10 "Go down the rows of the vineyards and
destroy the grapevines,
leaving a scattered few alive.
Strip the branches from the vines,
for these people do not belong to
the LORD.
11 The people of Israel and Judah
are full of treachery against me,"
says the LORD.
12 "They have lied about the LORD
and said, 'He won't bother us!
No disasters will come upon us.
There will be no war or famine.
13 God's prophets are all windbags
who don't really speak for him.
Let their predictions of disaster fall
on themselves!'"

14 Therefore, this is what the LORD God of Heaven's
Armies says:

"Because the people are talking like this,
my messages will flame out of your mouth
and burn the people like kindling wood.
15 O Israel, I will bring a distant nation
against you,"
says the LORD.
"It is a mighty nation,
an ancient nation,

a people whose language you do not know,
whose speech you cannot understand.
16 Their weapons are deadly;
their warriors are mighty.
17 They will devour the food of your harvest;
they will devour your sons and daughters.
They will devour your flocks and herds;
they will devour your grapes and figs.
And they will destroy your fortified towns,
which you think are so safe.

18 "Yet even in those days I will not blot you out
completely," says the LORD. 19 "And when your
people ask, 'Why did the LORD our God do all this
to us?' you must reply, 'You rejected him and gave
yourselves to foreign gods in your own land. Now
you will serve foreigners in a land that is not your
own.'

A Warning for God's People

20 "Make this announcement to Israel,
and say this to Judah:
21 Listen, you foolish and senseless people,
with eyes that do not see
and ears that do not hear.
22 Have you no respect for me?
Why don't you tremble in my presence?
I, the LORD, define the ocean's sandy
shoreline
as an everlasting boundary that the waters
cannot cross.
The waves may toss and roar,
but they can never pass the boundaries
I set.
23 But my people have stubborn and
rebellious hearts.
They have turned away and
abandoned me.
24 They do not say from the heart,
'Let us live in awe of the LORD our God,
for he gives us rain each spring and fall,
assuring us of a harvest when the time
is right.'
25 Your wickedness has deprived you of these
wonderful blessings.
Your sin has robbed you of all these
good things.

26 "Among my people are wicked men
who lie in wait for victims like a hunter
hiding in a blind.
They continually set traps
to catch people.
27 Like a cage filled with birds,
their homes are filled with evil plots.
And now they are great and rich.
28 They are fat and sleek,
and there is no limit to their
wicked deeds.
They refuse to provide justice to orphans
and deny the rights of the poor.
29 Should I not punish them for this?" says
the LORD.
"Should I not avenge myself against such
a nation?
30 A horrible and shocking thing
has happened in this land—
31 the prophets give false prophecies,
and the priests rule with an iron hand.
Worse yet, my people like it that way!
But what will you do when the end comes?

CHAPTER 6

Jerusalem's Last Warning

1 "Run for your lives, you people of Benjamin!
Get out of Jerusalem!
Sound the alarm in Tekoa!
Send up a signal at Beth-hakkerem!
A powerful army is coming from the north,
coming with disaster and destruction.
2 O Jerusalem, you are my beautiful and
delicate daughter—
but I will destroy you!
3 Enemies will surround you, like shepherds
camped around the city.
Each chooses a place for his troops
to devour.
4 They shout, 'Prepare for battle!
Attack at noon!'
'No, it's too late; the day is fading,
and the evening shadows are falling.'
5 'Well then, let's attack at night
and destroy her palaces!'"
6 This is what the LORD of Heaven's
Armies says:
"Cut down the trees for battering rams.
Build siege ramps against the walls of
Jerusalem.
This is the city to be punished,
for she is wicked through and through.
7 She spouts evil like a fountain.
Her streets echo with the sounds of
violence and destruction.
I always see her sickness and sores.
8 Listen to this warning, Jerusalem,
or I will turn from you in disgust.
Listen, or I will turn you into a heap of ruins,
a land where no one lives."
9 This is what the LORD of Heaven's
Armies says:

BIBLE BIOS

Hear From the Heroes

Hi, my name is

ISAIAH *(prophet)*

Did you know that my name, Isaiah, means "God is salvation"? That sure turned out to be the right name for me! God gave me the job of prophet and told me to tell people about his justice and mercy. I also wrote about Jesus' birth, death, resurrection, and return—700 years before he was even born! But I'm getting ahead of myself. Let me go back a little.

Just about the coolest thing that ever happened to me was on the day God called me to be a prophet. I actually saw the Lord! He was sitting on a throne, and he was surrounded by these angelic beings called seraphim, who were praising God and singing. Each of the seraphim had six wings. It was so amazing! I saw how completely holy God is, and I felt so sinful and unworthy to be there. But God cleansed me of my sins. Then he began to tell me his message for the people.

The seraphim used two wings to cover their faces, two to cover their feet, and two to fly. This is the only mention in the Bible of this type of angel.

One of the seraphim flew over to the altar and picked up a burning coal with a pair of tongs. He touched Isaiah's lips with the coal, then told Isaiah that his sins were forgiven.

And I spent the rest of my life delivering that message. I tried to get the people to realize how holy God is and how they should obey him. I warned them that God would punish them if they kept doing evil things. I tried to get them to turn back to God. Most of the time, they didn't want to listen. They ignored me, but I kept trying.

But not all of the messages God told me to give were warnings of punishment. God also told me to give the people a message of forgiveness and comfort and hope. God promised to send a Messiah to save his people. This Messiah would be Jesus, who would sacrifice himself for our sins. Not only that, Jesus will come again and rule forever!

Read what Isaiah said about Jesus in ISAIAH 7:14, then check out MATTHEW 1:20-23 and see how it came true!

God chose *me* to tell about Jesus! That was the biggest, best honor of my life. I only wish the people had listened. Are the people in your town listening? Are *you* listening?

People Chain

Cut paper into six-inch strips. On each strip, write the name of someone you've told about Jesus. Loop and tape the strips together to make a paper chain. Then hang the chain in your room, and add to it each time you tell someone else about Jesus!

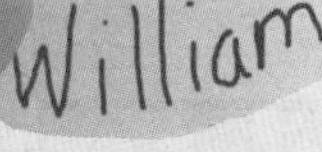

Isaiah told how Jesus would come to save us from our sins. How many people have you told about Jesus?

BIBLE BIOS

Hear From the Heroes

Hi, my name is

JEREMIAH *(prophet)*

OK, so I'm emotional. People even call me the Weeping Prophet. But I don't care. It was so sad to see what was happening to my people. I couldn't help crying!

When God called me to be a prophet, I thought I was too young. But God promised to take care of me, and he did. So I gave the people God's message to turn away from their sin and obey him, but no one listened. I talked and warned and cried and talked some more. But the people didn't pay any attention.

At times, God told me to get their attention in some pretty strange ways. One time he told me to use a moldy belt and say that he would rot the pride of the people. Another time he told me to smash a clay pot and say that God would shatter the people and the whole country if they didn't obey. God told me to use good and rotten figs as examples, and once I even had to wear a harness-like thing used for animals.

What do figs have to do with God? Find out in JEREMIAH 24!

But nothing worked. The people wouldn't listen, even though God gave them so many chances to come back to him. Finally, God had to punish the people. That made me cry even more!

I have to admit, being a prophet wasn't easy. Some people made fun of me, some hated me, and others even wanted to kill me. They put me in prison and even got so mad that they put me down into a muddy well. I was lonely and poor and so, so sad. But if I had it to do over again, I'd obey God just like I did back then. Because you know what? *Nothing's* more important than God!

Read JEREMIA[H] 37:11–38:13 to f[ind] out all about Jeremiah's pris[on] stay and his tim[e] in the well.

You Choose!

People may have seen Jeremiah as a failure. But in God's eyes, he was a big success. What do *you* think makes someone a success or a failure?

Make a chart with two columns. At the top of one column write, "The World." At the top of the other, write, "God." Then list the qualities that the world and God value. Which qualities do you have more of? Keep your chart handy to remind you of what's *really* important!

The world	God
nice clothes	obeying
money	praying
cool toys	being nice

"Even the few who remain in Israel
will be picked over again,
as when a harvester checks each vine
a second time
to pick the grapes that were missed."

Judah's Constant Rebellion

10 To whom can I give warning?
Who will listen when I speak?
Their ears are closed,
and they cannot hear.
They scorn the word of the LORD.
They don't want to listen at all.
11 So now I am filled with the LORD's fury.
Yes, I am tired of holding it in!
"I will pour out my fury on children playing
in the streets
and on gatherings of young men,
on husbands and wives
and on those who are old and gray.
12 Their homes will be turned over to their
enemies,
as will their fields and their wives.
For I will raise my powerful fist
against the people of this land,"
says the LORD.
13 "From the least to the greatest,
their lives are ruled by greed.
From prophets to priests,
they are all frauds.
14 They offer superficial treatments
for my people's mortal wound.
They give assurances of peace
when there is no peace.
15 Are they ashamed of their disgusting
actions?
Not at all—they don't even know how
to blush!
Therefore, they will lie among the
slaughtered.
They will be brought down when
I punish them,"
says the LORD.

Judah Rejects the LORD's Way

16 This is what the LORD says:
"Stop at the crossroads and look around.
Ask for the old, godly way, and walk in it.
Travel its path, and you will find rest for
your souls.
But you reply, 'No, that's not the road
we want!'
17 I posted watchmen over you who said,
'Listen for the sound of the alarm.'
But you replied,
'No! We won't pay attention!'
18 "Therefore, listen to this, all you nations.
Take note of my people's situation.
19 Listen, all the earth!
I will bring disaster on my people.
It is the fruit of their own schemes,
because they refuse to listen to me.
They have rejected my word.
20 There's no use offering me sweet
frankincense from Sheba.
Keep your fragrant calamus imported
from distant lands!
I will not accept your burnt offerings.
Your sacrifices have no pleasing aroma for
me."
21 Therefore, this is what the LORD says:
"I will put obstacles in my people's path.
Fathers and sons will both fall over them.
Neighbors and friends will die together."

An Invasion from the North

22 This is what the LORD says:
"Look! A great army coming from the north!
A great nation is rising against you from
far-off lands.
23 They are armed with bows and spears.
They are cruel and show no mercy.
They sound like a roaring sea
as they ride forward on horses.
They are coming in battle formation,
planning to destroy you, beautiful
Jerusalem."
24 We have heard reports about the enemy,
and we wring our hands in fright.
Pangs of anguish have gripped us,
like those of a woman in labor.
25 Don't go out to the fields!
Don't travel on the roads!
The enemy's sword is everywhere
and terrorizes us at every turn!
26 Oh, my people, dress yourselves in burlap
and sit among the ashes.
Mourn and weep bitterly, as for the loss of an
only son.
For suddenly the destroying armies will be
upon you!
27 "Jeremiah, I have made you a tester
of metals,
that you may determine the quality
of my people.
28 They are the worst kind of rebel,
full of slander.

They are as hard as bronze and iron,
and they lead others into corruption.
29 The bellows fiercely fan the flames
to burn out the corruption.
But it does not purify them,
for the wickedness remains.
30 I will label them 'Rejected Silver,'
for I, the LORD, am discarding them."

CHAPTER 7

Jeremiah Speaks at the Temple

The LORD gave another message to Jeremiah. He said, 2"Go to the entrance of the LORD's Temple, and give this message to the people: 'O Judah, listen to this message from the LORD! Listen to it, all of you who worship here! 3This is what the LORD of Heaven's Armies, the God of Israel, says:

"'Even now, if you quit your evil ways, I will let you stay in your own land. 4But don't be fooled by those who promise you safety simply because the LORD's Temple is here. They chant, "The LORD's Temple is here! The LORD's Temple is here!" 5But I will be merciful only if you stop your evil thoughts and deeds and start treating each other with justice; 6only if you stop exploiting foreigners, orphans, and widows; only if you stop your murdering; and only if you stop harming yourselves by worshiping idols. 7Then I will let you stay in this land that I gave to your ancestors to keep forever.

8"'Don't be fooled into thinking that you will never suffer because the Temple is here. It's a lie! 9Do you really think you can steal, murder, commit adultery, lie, and burn incense to Baal and all those other new gods of yours, 10and then come here and stand before me in my Temple and chant, "We are safe!"—only to go right back to all those evils again? 11Don't you yourselves admit that this Temple, which bears my name, has become a den of thieves? Surely I see all the evil going on there. I, the LORD, have spoken!

12"'Go now to the place at Shiloh where I once put the Tabernacle that bore my name. See what I did there because of all the wickedness of my people, the Israelites. 13While you were doing these wicked things, says the LORD, I spoke to you about it repeatedly, but you would not listen. I called out to you, but you refused to answer. 14So just as I destroyed Shiloh, I will now destroy this Temple that bears my name, this Temple that you trust in for help, this place that I gave to you and your ancestors. 15And I will send you out of my sight into exile, just as I did your relatives, the people of Israel.'

Judah's Persistent Idolatry

16"Pray no more for these people, Jeremiah. Do not weep or pray for them, and don't beg me to help them, for I will not listen to you. 17Don't you see what they are doing throughout the towns of Judah and in the streets of Jerusalem? 18No wonder I am so angry! Watch how the children gather wood and the fathers build sacrificial fires. See how the women knead dough and make cakes to offer to the Queen of Heaven. And they pour out liquid offerings to their other idol gods! 19Am I the one they are hurting?" asks the LORD. "Most of all, they hurt themselves, to their own shame."

20So this is what the Sovereign LORD says: "I will pour out my terrible fury on this place. Its people, animals, trees, and crops will be consumed by the unquenchable fire of my anger."

21This is what the LORD of Heaven's Armies, the God of Israel, says: "Take your burnt offerings and your other sacrifices and eat them yourselves! 22When I led your ancestors out of Egypt, it was not burnt offerings and sacrifices I wanted from them. 23This is what I told them: 'Obey me, and I will be your God, and you will be my people. Do everything as I say, and all will be well!'

24"But my people would not listen to me. They kept doing whatever they wanted, following the stubborn desires of their evil hearts. They went backward instead of forward. 25From the day your ancestors left Egypt until now, I have continued to send my servants, the prophets—day in and day out. 26But my people have not listened to me or even tried to hear. They have been stubborn and sinful—even worse than their ancestors.

27"Tell them all this, but do not expect them to listen. Shout out your warnings, but do not expect them to respond. 28Say to them, 'This is the nation whose people will not obey the LORD their God and who refuse to be taught. Truth has vanished from among them; it is no longer heard on their lips. 29Shave your head in mourning, and weep alone on the mountains. For the LORD has rejected and forsaken this generation that has provoked his fury.'

The Valley of Slaughter

30"The people of Judah have sinned before my very eyes," says the LORD. "They have set up their abominable idols right in the Temple that bears my name, defiling it. 31They have built pagan shrines at Topheth, the garbage dump in the valley of Ben-Hinnom, and there they burn their sons and daughters in the fire. I have never commanded such a horrible deed; it never even

crossed my mind to command such a thing! 32So
beware, for the time is coming," says the LORD,
"when that garbage dump will no longer be
called Topheth or the valley of Ben-Hinnom, but
the Valley of Slaughter. They will bury the bodies
in Topheth until there is no more room for them.
33The bodies of my people will be food for the
vultures and wild animals, and no one will be left
to scare them away. 34I will put an end to the
happy singing and laughter in the streets of Jerusalem. The joyful voices of bridegrooms and
brides will no longer be heard in the towns of Judah. The land will lie in complete desolation.

CHAPTER 8

"In that day," says the LORD, "the enemy will
break open the graves of the kings and officials
of Judah, and the graves of the priests, prophets,
and common people of Jerusalem. 2They will
spread out their bones on the ground before the
sun, moon, and stars—the gods my people have
loved, served, and worshiped. Their bones will
not be gathered up again or buried but will be
scattered on the ground like manure. 3And the
people of this evil nation who survive will wish to
die rather than live where I will send them. I, the
LORD of Heaven's Armies, have spoken!

Deception by False Prophets

4"Jeremiah, say to the people, 'This is what the
LORD says:

"'When people fall down, don't they get up again?
When they discover they're on the wrong road, don't they turn back?
5 Then why do these people stay on their self-destructive path?
Why do the people of Jerusalem refuse to turn back?
They cling tightly to their lies
and will not turn around.
6 I listen to their conversations
and don't hear a word of truth.
Is anyone sorry for doing wrong?
Does anyone say, "What a terrible thing I have done"?
No! All are running down the path of sin
as swiftly as a horse galloping into battle!
7 Even the stork that flies across the sky
knows the time of her migration,
as do the turtledove, the swallow, and the crane.
They all return at the proper time each year.
But not my people!
They do not know the LORD's laws.

8 "'How can you say, "We are wise because we have the word of the LORD,"
when your teachers have twisted it by writing lies?
9 These wise teachers will fall
into the trap of their own foolishness,
for they have rejected the word of the LORD.
Are they so wise after all?
10 I will give their wives to others
and their farms to strangers.
From the least to the greatest,
their lives are ruled by greed.
Yes, even my prophets and priests are like that.
They are all frauds.
11 They offer superficial treatments
for my people's mortal wound.
They give assurances of peace
when there is no peace.
12 Are they ashamed of these disgusting actions?
Not at all—they don't even know how to blush!
Therefore, they will lie among the slaughtered.
They will be brought down when I punish them,
says the LORD.
13 I will surely consume them.
There will be no more harvests of figs and grapes.
Their fruit trees will all die.
Whatever I gave them will soon be gone.
I, the LORD, have spoken!'

14 "Then the people will say,
'Why should we wait here to die?
Come, let's go to the fortified towns and die there.
For the LORD our God has decreed our destruction
and has given us a cup of poison to drink
because we sinned against the LORD.
15 We hoped for peace, but no peace came.
We hoped for a time of healing, but found only terror.'

16 "The snorting of the enemies' warhorses can be heard
all the way from the land of Dan in the north!
The neighing of their stallions makes the whole land tremble.

They are coming to devour the land and
everything in it—
cities and people alike.
17 I will send these enemy troops among you
like poisonous snakes you cannot charm.
They will bite you, and you will die.
I, the LORD, have spoken!"

Jeremiah Weeps for Sinful Judah

18 My grief is beyond healing;
my heart is broken.
19 Listen to the weeping of my people;
it can be heard all across the land.
"Has the LORD abandoned Jerusalem?"
the people ask.
"Is her King no longer there?"
"Oh, why have they provoked my anger
with their carved idols
and their worthless foreign gods?"
says the LORD.

20 "The harvest is finished,
and the summer is gone," the people cry,
"yet we are not saved!"

21 I hurt with the hurt of my people.
I mourn and am overcome with grief.
22 Is there no medicine in Gilead?
Is there no physician there?
Why is there no healing
for the wounds of my people?

CHAPTER 9

1 If only my head were a pool of water,
and my eyes a fountain of tears,
I would weep day and night
for all my people who have been
slaughtered.
2 Oh, that I could go away and forget my people
and live in a travelers' shack in the desert.
For they are all adulterers—
a pack of treacherous liars.

Judgment for Disobedience

3 "My people bend their tongues like bows
to shoot out lies.
They refuse to stand up for the truth.
They only go from bad to worse.
They do not know me,"
says the LORD.

4 "Beware of your neighbor!
Don't even trust your brother!
For brother takes advantage of brother,
and friend slanders friend.
5 They all fool and defraud each other;
no one tells the truth.
With practiced tongues they tell lies;
they wear themselves out with all their
sinning.
6 They pile lie upon lie
and utterly refuse to acknowledge me,"
says the LORD.

7 Therefore, this is what the LORD of Heaven's
Armies says:
"See, I will melt them down in a crucible
and test them like metal.
What else can I do with my people?
8 For their tongues shoot lies like
poisoned arrows.
They speak friendly words to their neighbors
while scheming in their heart to kill them.
9 Should I not punish them for this?" says
the LORD.
"Should I not avenge myself against such
a nation?"

10 I will weep for the mountains
and wail for the wilderness pastures.
For they are desolate and empty of life;
the lowing of cattle is heard no more;
the birds and wild animals have all fled.

11 "I will make Jerusalem into a heap of ruins,"
says the LORD.
"It will be a place haunted by jackals.
The towns of Judah will be ghost towns,
with no one living in them."

12 Who is wise enough to understand all this?
Who has been instructed by the LORD and can
explain it to others? Why has the land been so
ruined that no one dares to travel through it?
13 The LORD replies, "This has happened because my people have abandoned my instructions; they have refused to obey what I said.
14 Instead, they have stubbornly followed their
own desires and worshiped the images of Baal, as
their ancestors taught them. 15 So now, this is
what the LORD of Heaven's Armies, the God of Israel, says: Look! I will feed them with bitterness
and give them poison to drink. 16 I will scatter
them around the world, in places they and their
ancestors never heard of, and even there I will
chase them with the sword until I have destroyed
them completely."

Weeping in Jerusalem

17 This is what the LORD of Heaven's
Armies says:
"Consider all this, and call for the mourners.

Send for the women who mourn
at funerals.
18 Quick! Begin your weeping!
Let the tears flow from your eyes.
19 Hear the people of Jerusalem crying
in despair,
'We are ruined! We are completely
humiliated!
We must leave our land,
because our homes have been torn down.'"
20 Listen, you women, to the words of the LORD;
open your ears to what he has to say.
Teach your daughters to wail;
teach one another how to lament.
21 For death has crept in through our windows
and has entered our mansions.
It has killed off the flower of our youth:
Children no longer play in the streets,
and young men no longer gather in the
squares.
22 This is what the LORD says:
"Bodies will be scattered across the fields like
clumps of manure,
like bundles of grain after the harvest.
No one will be left to bury them."
23 This is what the LORD says:
"Don't let the wise boast in their wisdom,
or the powerful boast in their power,
or the rich boast in their riches.
24 But those who wish to boast
should boast in this alone:
that they truly know me and understand
that I am the LORD
who demonstrates unfailing love
and who brings justice and righteousness
to the earth,
and that I delight in these things.
I, the LORD, have spoken!

25 "A time is coming," says the LORD, "when I
will punish all those who are circumcised in body
but not in spirit—26 the Egyptians, Edomites,
Ammonites, Moabites, the people who live in the
desert in remote places, and yes, even the people
of Judah. And like all these pagan nations, the
people of Israel also have uncircumcised hearts."

CHAPTER 10

Idolatry Brings Destruction

Hear the word that the LORD speaks to you,
O Israel! 2 This is what the LORD says:

"Do not act like the other nations,
who try to read their future in the stars.
Do not be afraid of their predictions,
even though other nations are terrified
by them.
3 Their ways are futile and foolish.
They cut down a tree, and a craftsman
carves an idol.
4 They decorate it with gold and silver
and then fasten it securely with hammer
and nails
so it won't fall over.
5 Their gods are like
helpless scarecrows in a cucumber field!
They cannot speak,
and they need to be carried because they
cannot walk.
Do not be afraid of such gods,
for they can neither harm you nor do you
any good."

6 LORD, there is no one like you!
For you are great, and your name is full
of power.
7 Who would not fear you, O King of nations?
That title belongs to you alone!
Among all the wise people of the earth
and in all the kingdoms of the world,
there is no one like you.

8 People who worship idols are stupid
and foolish.
The things they worship are made of wood!
9 They bring beaten sheets of silver from
Tarshish
and gold from Uphaz,
and they give these materials to skillful
craftsmen
who make their idols.
Then they dress these gods in royal blue
and purple robes
made by expert tailors.
10 But the LORD is the only true God.
He is the living God and the everlasting
King!
The whole earth trembles at his anger.
The nations cannot stand up to his wrath.

11 Say this to those who worship other gods:
"Your so-called gods, who did not make the
heavens and earth, will vanish from the earth and
from under the heavens."

12 But the LORD made the earth by his power,
and he preserves it by his wisdom.
With his own understanding
he stretched out the heavens.
13 When he speaks in the thunder,
the heavens roar with rain.

He causes the clouds to rise over the earth.
He sends the lightning with the rain
and releases the wind from his
storehouses.
14 The whole human race is foolish and has
no knowledge!
The craftsmen are disgraced by the idols
they make,
for their carefully shaped works are
a fraud.
These idols have no breath or power.
15 Idols are worthless; they are ridiculous lies!
On the day of reckoning they will all
be destroyed.
16 But the God of Israel is no idol!
He is the Creator of everything that exists,
including Israel, his own special possession.
The LORD of Heaven's Armies is his name!

The Coming Destruction

17 Pack your bags and prepare to leave;
the siege is about to begin.
18 For this is what the LORD says:
"Suddenly, I will fling out
all you who live in this land.
I will pour great troubles upon you,
and at last you will feel my anger."

19 My wound is severe,
and my grief is great.
My sickness is incurable,
but I must bear it.
20 My home is gone,
and no one is left to help me rebuild it.
My children have been taken away,
and I will never see them again.
21 The shepherds of my people have lost
their senses.
They no longer seek wisdom from
the LORD.
Therefore, they fail completely,
and their flocks are scattered.
22 Listen! Hear the terrifying roar of great
armies
as they roll down from the north.
The towns of Judah will be destroyed
and become a haunt for jackals.

Jeremiah's Prayer

23 I know, LORD, that our lives are not our own.
We are not able to plan our own course.
24 So correct me, LORD, but please be gentle.
Do not correct me in anger, for I would die.
25 Pour out your wrath on the nations that
refuse to acknowledge you—
on the peoples that do not call upon
your name.
For they have devoured your people
Israel;
they have devoured and consumed
them,
making the land a desolate wilderness.

CHAPTER 11

Judah's Broken Covenant

The LORD gave another message to Jeremiah. He
said, 2"Remind the people of Judah and Jerusalem about the terms of my covenant with them.
3 Say to them, 'This is what the LORD, the God of
Israel, says: Cursed is anyone who does not obey
the terms of my covenant! 4 For I said to your ancestors when I brought them out of the iron-
smelting furnace of Egypt, "If you obey me and
do whatever I command you, then you will be my
people, and I will be your God." 5 I said this so I
could keep my promise to your ancestors to give
you a land flowing with milk and honey—the
land you live in today.'"

Then I replied, "Amen, LORD! May it be so."

6 Then the LORD said, "Broadcast this message
in the streets of Jerusalem. Go from town to
town throughout the land and say, 'Remember
the ancient covenant, and do everything it requires. 7 For I solemnly warned your ancestors
when I brought them out of Egypt, "Obey me!" I
have repeated this warning over and over to this
day, 8 but your ancestors did not listen or even
pay attention. Instead, they stubbornly followed
their own evil desires. And because they refused
to obey, I brought upon them all the curses described in this covenant.'"

9 Again the LORD spoke to me and said, "I have
discovered a conspiracy against me among the
people of Judah and Jerusalem. 10 They have returned to the sins of their ancestors. They have
refused to listen to me and are worshiping other
gods. Israel and Judah have both broken the covenant I made with their ancestors. 11 Therefore,
this is what the LORD says: I am going to bring calamity upon them, and they will not escape.
Though they beg for mercy, I will not listen to
their cries. 12 Then the people of Judah and Jerusalem will pray to their idols and burn incense
before them. But the idols will not save them
when disaster strikes! 13 Look now, people of Judah; you have as many gods as you have towns.
You have as many altars of shame—altars for
burning incense to your god Baal—as there are
streets in Jerusalem.

14"Pray no more for these people, Jeremiah.

Do not weep or pray for them, for I will not listen
to them when they cry out to me in distress.

15 "What right do my beloved people have
to come to my Temple,
when they have done so many
immoral things?
Can their vows and sacrifices prevent
their destruction?
They actually rejoice in doing evil!
16 I, the LORD, once called them a thriving
olive tree,
beautiful to see and full of good fruit.
But now I have sent the fury of their
enemies
to burn them with fire,
leaving them charred and broken.

17"I, the LORD of Heaven's Armies, who planted
this olive tree, have ordered it destroyed. For the
people of Israel and Judah have done evil, arousing my anger by burning incense to Baal."

A Plot against Jeremiah

18Then the LORD told me about the plots my enemies were making against me. 19I was like a lamb
being led to the slaughter. I had no idea that they
were planning to kill me! "Let's destroy this man
and all his words," they said. "Let's cut him down,
so his name will be forgotten forever."

20 O LORD of Heaven's Armies,
you make righteous judgments,
and you examine the deepest thoughts
and secrets.
Let me see your vengeance against them,
for I have committed my cause to you.

21This is what the LORD says about the men of
Anathoth who wanted me dead. They had said,
"We will kill you if you do not stop prophesying
in the LORD's name." 22So this is what the LORD of
Heaven's Armies says about them: "I will punish
them! Their young men will die in battle, and
their boys and girls will starve to death. 23Not
one of these plotters from Anathoth will survive,
for I will bring disaster upon them when their
time of punishment comes."

CHAPTER 12

Jeremiah Questions the LORD's Justice

1 LORD, you always give me justice
when I bring a case before you.
So let me bring you this complaint:
Why are the wicked so prosperous?
Why are evil people so happy?
2 You have planted them,
and they have taken root and prospered.
Your name is on their lips,
but you are far from their hearts.
3 But as for me, LORD, you know my heart.
You see me and test my thoughts.
Drag these people away like sheep to be
butchered!
Set them aside to be slaughtered!

4 How long must this land mourn?
Even the grass in the fields has withered.
The wild animals and birds have
disappeared
because of the evil in the land.
For the people have said,
"The LORD doesn't see what's ahead
for us!"

The LORD's Reply to Jeremiah

5 "If racing against mere men makes
you tired,
how will you race against horses?
If you stumble and fall on open ground,
what will you do in the thickets near
the Jordan?
6 Even your brothers, members of your
own family,
have turned against you.
They plot and raise complaints against you.
Do not trust them,
no matter how pleasantly they speak.

7 "I have abandoned my people, my special
possession.
I have surrendered my dearest ones
to their enemies.
8 My chosen people have roared at me like
a lion of the forest,
so I have treated them with contempt.
9 My chosen people act like speckled vultures,
but they themselves are surrounded
by vultures.
Bring on the wild animals to pick their
corpses clean!
10 "Many rulers have ravaged my vineyard,
trampling down the vines
and turning all its beauty into a barren
wilderness.
11 They have made it an empty wasteland;
I hear its mournful cry.
The whole land is desolate,
and no one even cares.
12 On all the bare hilltops,
destroying armies can be seen.

Jeremiah 13 . . . page 742

FUN-fact **Object Lessons**

Could you use a belt to tell someone about God? How about fruit? God told the prophet Jeremiah to use everyday objects to tell people about God.

How could *you* use an everyday object to tell others about God? Just look around, find an object, and think!

HERE'S ONE IDEA:

You could use a backpack to help someone see that God wants to carry our load when we feel worried or tired.

NOW THINK of YOUR OWN!

The sword of the LORD devours people
from one end of the nation to the other.
No one will escape!
13 My people have planted wheat
but are harvesting thorns.
They have worn themselves out,
but it has done them no good.
They will harvest a crop of shame
because of the fierce anger of the LORD."

A Message for Israel's Neighbors

14Now this is what the LORD says: "I will uproot
from their land all the evil nations reaching out
for the possession I gave my people Israel. And I
will uproot Judah from among them. 15But afterward I will return and have compassion on all of
them. I will bring them home to their own lands
again, each nation to its own possession. 16And if
these nations truly learn the ways of my people,
and if they learn to swear by my name, saying, 'As
surely as the LORD lives' (just as they taught my
people to swear by the name of Baal), then they
will be given a place among my people. 17But any
nation who refuses to obey me will be uprooted
and destroyed. I, the LORD, have spoken!"

CHAPTER 13

Jeremiah's Linen Loincloth

This is what the LORD said to me: "Go and buy a
linen loincloth and put it on, but do not wash it."
2So I bought the loincloth as the LORD directed
me, and I put it on.

3Then the LORD gave me another message:
4"Take the linen loincloth you are wearing, and
go to the Euphrates River. Hide it there in a hole
in the rocks." 5So I went and hid it by the Euphrates as the LORD had instructed me.

6A long time afterward the LORD said to me,
"Go back to the Euphrates and get the loincloth I
told you to hide there." 7So I went to the Euphrates and dug it out of the hole where I had hidden
it. But now it was rotting and falling apart. The
loincloth was good for nothing.

8Then I received this message from the LORD:
9"This is what the LORD says: This shows how I
will rot away the pride of Judah and Jerusalem.
10These wicked people refuse to listen to me.
They stubbornly follow their own desires and
worship other gods. Therefore, they will become
like this loincloth—good for nothing! 11As a loincloth clings to a man's waist, so I created Judah
and Israel to cling to me, says the LORD. They were
to be my people, my pride, my glory—an honor to
my name. But they would not listen to me.

12"So tell them, 'This is what the LORD, the God
of Israel, says: May all your jars be filled with
wine.' And they will reply, 'Of course! Jars are
made to be filled with wine!'

13"Then tell them, 'No, this is what the LORD
means: I will fill everyone in this land with drunkenness—from the king sitting on David's throne
to the priests and the prophets, right down to the
common people of Jerusalem. 14I will smash
them against each other, even parents against
children, says the LORD. I will not let my pity or
mercy or compassion keep me from destroying
them.'"

A Warning against Pride

15 Listen and pay attention!
Do not be arrogant, for the LORD
has spoken.
16 Give glory to the LORD your God
before it is too late.
Acknowledge him before he brings
darkness upon you,
causing you to stumble and fall on the
darkening mountains.
For then, when you look for light,
you will find only terrible darkness
and gloom.

17 And if you still refuse to listen,
I will weep alone because of your pride.
My eyes will overflow with tears,
because the LORD's flock will be led away
into exile.

18 Say to the king and his mother,
"Come down from your thrones
and sit in the dust,
for your glorious crowns
will soon be snatched from your heads."
19 The towns of the Negev will close their gates,
and no one will be able to open them.
The people of Judah will be taken away
as captives.
All will be carried into exile.

20 Open up your eyes and see
the armies marching down from the north!
Where is your flock—
your beautiful flock—
that he gave you to care for?
21 What will you say when the LORD takes the
allies you have cultivated
and appoints them as your rulers?
Pangs of anguish will grip you,
like those of a woman in labor!
22 You may ask yourself,
"Why is all this happening to me?"
It is because of your many sins!
That is why you have been stripped
and raped by invading armies.
23 Can an Ethiopian change the color of his skin?
Can a leopard take away its spots?
Neither can you start doing good,
for you have always done evil.

24 "I will scatter you like chaff
that is blown away by the desert winds.
25 This is your allotment,
the portion I have assigned to you,"
says the LORD,
"for you have forgotten me,
putting your trust in false gods.
26 I myself will strip you
and expose you to shame.
27 I have seen your adultery and lust,
and your disgusting idol worship out in
the fields and on the hills.
What sorrow awaits you, Jerusalem!
How long before you are pure?"

CHAPTER 14

Judah's Terrible Drought

This message came to Jeremiah from the LORD,
explaining why he was holding back the rain:

2 "Judah wilts;
commerce at the city gates grinds to a halt.
All the people sit on the ground in mourning,
and a great cry rises from Jerusalem.
3 The nobles send servants to get water,
but all the wells are dry.
The servants return with empty pitchers,
confused and desperate,
covering their heads in grief.
4 The ground is parched
and cracked for lack of rain.
The farmers are deeply troubled;
they, too, cover their heads.
5 Even the doe abandons her newborn fawn
because there is no grass in the field.
6 The wild donkeys stand on the bare hills
panting like thirsty jackals.
They strain their eyes looking for grass,
but there is none to be found."

7 The people say, "Our wickedness has caught
up with us, LORD,
but help us for the sake of your own
reputation.
We have turned away from you
and sinned against you again and again.
8 O Hope of Israel, our Savior in times
of trouble,
why are you like a stranger to us?
Why are you like a traveler passing through
the land,
stopping only for the night?
9 Are you also confused?
Is our champion helpless to save us?
You are right here among us, LORD.
We are known as your people.
Please don't abandon us now!"

10 So this is what the LORD says to his people:
"You love to wander far from me
and do not restrain yourselves.
Therefore, I will no longer accept you
as my people.
Now I will remember all your wickedness
and will punish you for your sins."

The LORD Forbids Jeremiah to Intercede

11 Then the LORD said to me, "Do not pray for
these people anymore. 12 When they fast, I will
pay no attention. When they present their burnt
offerings and grain offerings to me, I will not accept them. Instead, I will devour them with war,
famine, and disease."
13 Then I said, "O Sovereign LORD, their
prophets are telling them, 'All is well—no war or

famine will come. The LORD will surely send you
peace.'"
14Then the LORD said, "These prophets are
telling lies in my name. I did not send them or
tell them to speak. I did not give them any messages. They prophesy of visions and revelations
they have never seen or heard. They speak foolishness made up in their own lying hearts.
15Therefore, this is what the LORD says: I will punish these lying prophets, for they have spoken in
my name even though I never sent them. They
say that no war or famine will come, but they
themselves will die by war and famine! 16As for
the people to whom they prophesy—their bodies
will be thrown out into the streets of Jerusalem,
victims of famine and war. There will be no one
left to bury them. Husbands, wives, sons, and
daughters—all will be gone. For I will pour out
their own wickedness on them. 17Now, Jeremiah,
say this to them:

"Night and day my eyes overflow with tears.
I cannot stop weeping,
for my virgin daughter—my precious
people—
has been struck down
and lies mortally wounded.
18 If I go out into the fields,
I see the bodies of people slaughtered
by the enemy.
If I walk the city streets,
I see people who have died of starvation.
The prophets and priests continue with
their work,
but they don't know what they're doing."

A Prayer for Healing

19 LORD, have you completely rejected Judah?
Do you really hate Jerusalem?
Why have you wounded us past all hope
of healing?
We hoped for peace, but no peace came.
We hoped for a time of healing, but found
only terror.
20 LORD, we confess our wickedness
and that of our ancestors, too.
We all have sinned against you.
21 For the sake of your reputation, LORD, do not
abandon us.
Do not disgrace your own glorious throne.
Please remember us,
and do not break your covenant with us.
22 Can any of the worthless foreign gods send
us rain?
Does it fall from the sky by itself?
No, you are the one, O LORD our God!
Only you can do such things.
So we will wait for you to help us.

CHAPTER 15

Judah's Inevitable Doom

Then the LORD said to me, "Even if Moses and
Samuel stood before me pleading for these people, I wouldn't help them. Away with them! Get
them out of my sight! 2And if they say to you, 'But
where can we go?' tell them, 'This is what the
LORD says:

"'Those who are destined for death, to death;
those who are destined for war, to war;
those who are destined for famine, to famine;
those who are destined for captivity,
to captivity.'

3"I will send four kinds of destroyers against
them," says the LORD. "I will send the sword to
kill, the dogs to drag away, the vultures to devour,
and the wild animals to finish up what is left.
4Because of the wicked things Manasseh son of
Hezekiah, king of Judah, did in Jerusalem, I will
make my people an object of horror to all the
kingdoms of the earth.

5 "Who will feel sorry for you, Jerusalem?
Who will weep for you?
Who will even bother to ask how you are?
6 You have abandoned me
and turned your back on me,"
says the LORD.
"Therefore, I will raise my fist to destroy you.
I am tired of always giving you another
chance.
7 I will winnow you like grain at the gates
of your cities
and take away the children you hold dear.
I will destroy my own people,
because they refuse to change their evil ways.
8 There will be more widows
than the grains of sand on the seashore.
At noontime I will bring a destroyer
against the mothers of young men.
I will cause anguish and terror
to come upon them suddenly.
9 The mother of seven grows faint and gasps
for breath;
her sun has gone down while it is still day.
She sits childless now,
disgraced and humiliated.
And I will hand over those who are left
to be killed by the enemy.
I, the LORD, have spoken!"

Jeremiah's Complaint

10Then I said,

"What sorrow is mine, my mother.
Oh, that I had died at birth!
I am hated everywhere I go.
I am neither a lender who threatens
to foreclose
nor a borrower who refuses to pay—
yet they all curse me."

11The LORD replied,

"I will take care of you, Jeremiah.
Your enemies will ask you to plead on their
behalf
in times of trouble and distress.
12 Can a man break a bar of iron from
the north,
or a bar of bronze?
13 At no cost to them,
I will hand over your wealth and treasures
as plunder to your enemies,
for sin runs rampant in your land.
14 I will tell your enemies to take you
as captives to a foreign land.
For my anger blazes like a fire
that will burn forever."

15Then I said,

"LORD, you know what's happening to me.
Please step in and help me. Punish my
persecutors!
Please give me time; don't let me die young.
It's for your sake that I am suffering.
16 When I discovered your words, I
devoured them.
They are my joy and my heart's delight,
for I bear your name,
O LORD God of Heaven's Armies.
17 I never joined the people in their
merry feasts.
I sat alone because your hand was on me.
I was filled with indignation at their sins.
18 Why then does my suffering continue?
Why is my wound so incurable?
Your help seems as uncertain as
a seasonal brook,
like a spring that has gone dry."

19This is how the LORD responds:

"If you return to me, I will restore you
so you can continue to serve me.
If you speak good words rather than
worthless ones,
you will be my spokesman.
You must influence them;
do not let them influence you!
20 They will fight against you like an
attacking army,
but I will make you as secure as a
fortified wall of bronze.
They will not conquer you,
for I am with you to protect and
rescue you.
I, the LORD, have spoken!
21 Yes, I will certainly keep you safe from these
wicked men.
I will rescue you from their cruel hands."

CHAPTER 16

Jeremiah Forbidden to Marry

The LORD gave me another message. He said,
2"Do not get married or have children in this
place. 3For this is what the LORD says about the
children born here in this city and about their
mothers and fathers: 4They will die from terrible
diseases. No one will mourn for them or bury
them, and they will lie scattered on the ground
like manure. They will die from war and famine,
and their bodies will be food for the vultures and
wild animals."

Judah's Coming Punishment

5This is what the LORD says: "Do not go to funerals to mourn and show sympathy for these people, for I have removed my protection and peace
from them. I have taken away my unfailing love
and my mercy. 6Both the great and the lowly will
die in this land. No one will bury them or mourn
for them. Their friends will not cut themselves in
sorrow or shave their heads in sadness. 7No one
will offer a meal to comfort those who mourn for
the dead—not even at the death of a mother or
father. No one will send a cup of wine to console
them.

8"And do not go to their feasts and parties. Do
not eat and drink with them at all. 9For this is
what the LORD of Heaven's Armies, the God of Israel, says: In your own lifetime, before your very
eyes, I will put an end to the happy singing and
laughter in this land. The joyful voices of bridegrooms and brides will no longer be heard.

10"When you tell the people all these things,
they will ask, 'Why has the LORD decreed such
terrible things against us? What have we done to
deserve such treatment? What is our sin against
the LORD our God?'

11"Then you will give them the LORD's reply: 'It
is because your ancestors were unfaithful to me.
They worshiped other gods and served them.

They abandoned me and did not obey my word.
12And you are even worse than your ancestors!
You stubbornly follow your own evil desires and
refuse to listen to me. 13So I will throw you out of
this land and send you into a foreign land where
you and your ancestors have never been. There
you can worship idols day and night—and I will
grant you no favors!'

Hope despite the Disaster

14"But the time is coming," says the LORD, "when
people who are taking an oath will no longer say,
'As surely as the LORD lives, who rescued the people of Israel from the land of Egypt.' 15Instead,
they will say, 'As surely as the LORD lives, who
brought the people of Israel back to their own
land from the land of the north and from all the
countries to which he had exiled them.' For I will
bring them back to this land that I gave their ancestors.

16"But now I am sending for many fishermen
who will catch them," says the LORD. "I am sending for hunters who will hunt them down in the
mountains, hills, and caves. 17I am watching
them closely, and I see every sin. They cannot
hope to hide from me. 18I will double their punishment for all their sins, because they have defiled my land with lifeless images of their
detestable gods and have filled my territory with
their evil deeds."

Jeremiah's Prayer of Confidence

19 LORD, you are my strength and fortress,
my refuge in the day of trouble!
Nations from around the world
will come to you and say,
"Our ancestors left us a foolish heritage,
for they worshiped worthless idols.
20 Can people make their own gods?
These are not real gods at all!"
21 The LORD says,
"Now I will show them my power;
now I will show them my might.
At last they will know and understand
that I am the LORD.

CHAPTER 17

Judah's Sin and Punishment

1 "The sin of Judah
is inscribed with an iron chisel—
engraved with a diamond point on their
stony hearts
and on the corners of their altars.
2 Even their children go to worship
at their pagan altars and Asherah poles,
beneath every green tree
and on every high hill.
3 So I will hand over my holy mountain—
along with all your wealth and treasures
and your pagan shrines—
as plunder to your enemies,
for sin runs rampant in your land.
4 The wonderful possession I have reserved for
you
will slip from your hands.
I will tell your enemies to take you
as captives to a foreign land.
For my anger blazes like a fire
that will burn forever."

Wisdom from the LORD

5 This is what the LORD says:
"Cursed are those who put their trust
in mere humans,
who rely on human strength
and turn their hearts away from
the LORD.
6 They are like stunted shrubs in the desert,
with no hope for the future.
They will live in the barren wilderness,
in an uninhabited salty land.

7 "But blessed are those who trust in the LORD
and have made the LORD their hope and
confidence.
8 They are like trees planted along a riverbank,
with roots that reach deep into the water.
Such trees are not bothered by the heat
or worried by long months of drought.
Their leaves stay green,
and they never stop producing fruit.

9 "The human heart is the most deceitful
of all things,
and desperately wicked.
Who really knows how bad it is?
10 But I, the LORD, search all hearts
and examine secret motives.
I give all people their due rewards,
according to what their actions deserve."

Jeremiah's Trust in the LORD

11 Like a partridge that hatches eggs she
has not laid,
so are those who get their wealth
by unjust means.
At midlife they will lose their riches;
in the end, they will become poor
old fools.

12 But we worship at your throne—
eternal, high, and glorious!
13 O LORD, the hope of Israel,
all who turn away from you will
be disgraced.
They will be buried in the dust of the earth,
for they have abandoned the LORD, the
fountain of living water.

14 O LORD, if you heal me, I will be truly healed;
if you save me, I will be truly saved.
My praises are for you alone!
15 People scoff at me and say,
"What is this 'message from the LORD'
you talk about?
Why don't your predictions come true?"
16 LORD, I have not abandoned my job
as a shepherd for your people.
I have not urged you to send disaster.
You have heard everything I've said.
17 LORD, don't terrorize me!
You alone are my hope in the day of
disaster.
18 Bring shame and dismay on all who
persecute me,
but don't let me experience shame
and dismay.
Bring a day of terror on them.
Yes, bring double destruction upon them!

Observing the Sabbath

19 This is what the LORD said to me: "Go and
stand in the gates of Jerusalem, first in the gate
where the king goes in and out, and then in each
of the other gates. 20 Say to all the people, 'Listen
to this message from the LORD, you kings of Judah and all you people of Judah and everyone
living in Jerusalem. 21 This is what the LORD says:
Listen to my warning! Stop carrying on your
trade at Jerusalem's gates on the Sabbath day.
22 Do not do your work on the Sabbath, but make
it a holy day. I gave this command to your ancestors, 23 but they did not listen or obey. They stubbornly refused to pay attention or accept my
discipline.

24 "'But if you obey me, says the LORD, and do
not carry on your trade at the gates or work on
the Sabbath day, and if you keep it holy, 25 then
kings and their officials will go in and out of
these gates forever. There will always be a descendant of David sitting on the throne here in
Jerusalem. Kings and their officials will always
ride in and out among the people of Judah in
chariots and on horses, and this city will remain
forever. 26 And from all around Jerusalem, from
the towns of Judah and Benjamin, from the western foothills and the hill country and the Negev,
the people will come with their burnt offerings
and sacrifices. They will bring their grain offerings, frankincense, and thanksgiving offerings to
the LORD's Temple.

27 "'But if you do not listen to me and refuse to
keep the Sabbath holy, and if on the Sabbath day
you bring loads of merchandise through the
gates of Jerusalem just as on other days, then I
will set fire to these gates. The fire will spread to
the palaces, and no one will be able to put out the
roaring flames.'"

CHAPTER 18

The Potter and the Clay

The LORD gave another message to Jeremiah. He
said, 2 "Go down to the potter's shop, and I will
speak to you there." 3 So I did as he told me and
found the potter working at his wheel. 4 But the
jar he was making did not turn out as he had
hoped, so he crushed it into a lump of clay again
and started over.

5 Then the LORD gave me this message: 6 "O Israel, can I not do to you as this potter has done to
his clay? As the clay is in the potter's hand, so are
you in my hand. 7 If I announce that a certain nation or kingdom is to be uprooted, torn down,
and destroyed, 8 but then that nation renounces
its evil ways, I will not destroy it as I had planned.
9 And if I announce that I will plant and build up a
certain nation or kingdom, 10 but then that nation turns to evil and refuses to obey me, I will
not bless it as I said I would.

11 "Therefore, Jeremiah, go and warn all Judah
and Jerusalem. Say to them, 'This is what the
LORD says: I am planning disaster for you instead
of good. So turn from your evil ways, each of you,
and do what is right.'"

12 But the people replied, "Don't waste your
breath. We will continue to live as we want to,
stubbornly following our own evil desires."

13 So this is what the LORD says:

"Has anyone ever heard of such a thing,
even among the pagan nations?
My virgin daughter Israel
has done something terrible!
14 Does the snow ever disappear from the
mountaintops of Lebanon?
Do the cold streams flowing from those
distant mountains ever run dry?
15 But my people are not so reliable, for they
have deserted me;
they burn incense to worthless idols.

They have stumbled off the ancient highways
and walk in muddy paths.
16 Therefore, their land will become desolate,
a monument to their stupidity.
All who pass by will be astonished
and will shake their heads in amazement.
17 I will scatter my people before their enemies
as the east wind scatters dust.
And in all their trouble I will turn my back
on them
and refuse to notice their distress."

A Plot against Jeremiah

18 Then the people said, "Come on, let's plot a way
to stop Jeremiah. We have plenty of priests and
wise men and prophets. We don't need him to
teach the word and give us advice and prophecies. Let's spread rumors about him and ignore
what he says."

19 LORD, hear me and help me!
Listen to what my enemies are saying.
20 Should they repay evil for good?
They have dug a pit to kill me,
though I pleaded for them
and tried to protect them from your anger.
21 So let their children starve!
Let them die by the sword!
Let their wives become childless widows.
Let their old men die in a plague,
and let their young men be killed in battle!
22 Let screaming be heard from their homes
as warriors come suddenly upon them.
For they have dug a pit for me
and have hidden traps along my path.
23 LORD, you know all about their murderous
plots against me.
Don't forgive their crimes and blot out
their sins.
Let them die before you.
Deal with them in your anger.

CHAPTER 19
Jeremiah's Shattered Jar

This is what the LORD said to me: "Go and buy a
clay jar. Then ask some of the leaders of the people and of the priests to follow you. 2 Go out
through the Gate of Broken Pots to the garbage
dump in the valley of Ben-Hinnom, and give
them this message. 3 Say to them, 'Listen to this
message from the LORD, you kings of Judah and
citizens of Jerusalem! This is what the LORD of
Heaven's Armies, the God of Israel, says: I will
bring a terrible disaster on this place, and the
ears of those who hear about it will ring!

4 "'For Israel has forsaken me and turned this
valley into a place of wickedness. The people
burn incense to foreign gods—idols never before acknowledged by this generation, by their
ancestors, or by the kings of Judah. And they
have filled this place with the blood of innocent children. 5 They have built pagan shrines
to Baal, and there they burn their sons as sacrifices to Baal. I have never commanded such a
horrible deed; it never even crossed my mind to
command such a thing! 6 So beware, for the
time is coming, says the LORD, when this garbage dump will no longer be called Topheth or
the valley of Ben-Hinnom, but the Valley of
Slaughter.

7 "'For I will upset the careful plans of Judah
and Jerusalem. I will allow the people to be
slaughtered by invading armies, and I will leave
their dead bodies as food for the vultures and
wild animals. 8 I will reduce Jerusalem to ruins,
making it a monument to their stupidity. All who
pass by will be astonished and will gasp at the destruction they see there. 9 I will see to it that your
enemies lay siege to the city until all the food is
gone. Then those trapped inside will eat their
own sons and daughters and friends. They will
be driven to utter despair.'

10 "As these men watch you, Jeremiah, smash
the jar you brought. 11 Then say to them, 'This is
what the LORD of Heaven's Armies says: As this
jar lies shattered, so I will shatter the people of
Judah and Jerusalem beyond all hope of repair.
They will bury the bodies here in Topheth, the
garbage dump, until there is no more room for
them. 12 This is what I will do to this place and its
people, says the LORD. I will cause this city to become defiled like Topheth. 13 Yes, all the houses
in Jerusalem, including the palace of Judah's
kings, will become like Topheth—all the houses
where you burned incense on the rooftops to
your star gods, and where liquid offerings were
poured out to your idols.'"

14 Then Jeremiah returned from Topheth, the
garbage dump where he had delivered this message, and he stopped in front of the Temple of
the LORD. He said to the people there, 15 "This is
what the LORD of Heaven's Armies, the God of Israel, says: 'I will bring disaster upon this city and
its surrounding towns as I promised, because
you have stubbornly refused to listen to me.'"

CHAPTER 20
Jeremiah and Pashhur

Now Pashhur son of Immer, the priest in charge
of the Temple of the LORD, heard what Jeremiah

was prophesying. 2So he arrested Jeremiah the
prophet and had him whipped and put in stocks
at the Benjamin Gate of the LORD's Temple.
3The next day, when Pashhur finally released
him, Jeremiah said, "Pashhur, the LORD has
changed your name. From now on you are to be
called 'The Man Who Lives in Terror.' 4For this is
what the LORD says: 'I will send terror upon you
and all your friends, and you will watch as they
are slaughtered by the swords of the enemy. I will
hand the people of Judah over to the king of Babylon. He will take them captive to Babylon or run
them through with the sword. 5And I will let your
enemies plunder Jerusalem. All the famed treasures of the city—the precious jewels and gold
and silver of your kings—will be carried off to
Babylon. 6As for you, Pashhur, you and all your
household will go as captives to Babylon. There
you will die and be buried, you and all your
friends to whom you prophesied that everything
would be all right.'"

Jeremiah's Complaint

7 O LORD, you misled me,
and I allowed myself to be misled.
You are stronger than I am,
and you overpowered me.
Now I am mocked every day;
everyone laughs at me.
8 When I speak, the words burst out.
"Violence and destruction!" I shout.
So these messages from the LORD
have made me a household joke.
9 But if I say I'll never mention the LORD
or speak in his name,
his word burns in my heart like a fire.
It's like a fire in my bones!
I am worn out trying to hold it in!
I can't do it!
10 I have heard the many rumors about me.
They call me "The Man Who Lives
in Terror."
They threaten, "If you say anything, we will
report it."
Even my old friends are watching me,
waiting for a fatal slip.
"He will trap himself," they say,
"and then we will get our revenge on him."

11 But the LORD stands beside me like a great
warrior.
Before him my persecutors will stumble.
They cannot defeat me.
They will fail and be thoroughly humiliated.
Their dishonor will never be forgotten.
12 O LORD of Heaven's Armies,
you test those who are righteous,
and you examine the deepest thoughts
and secrets.
Let me see your vengeance against them,
for I have committed my cause to you.
13 Sing to the LORD!
Praise the LORD!
For though I was poor and needy,
he rescued me from my oppressors.

14 Yet I curse the day I was born!
May no one celebrate the day of
my birth.
15 I curse the messenger who told my father,
"Good news—you have a son!"
16 Let him be destroyed like the cities of old
that the LORD overthrew without mercy.
Terrify him all day long with battle shouts,
17 because he did not kill me at birth.
Oh, that I had died in my mother's womb,
that her body had been my grave!
18 Why was I ever born?
My entire life has been filled
with trouble, sorrow, and shame.

CHAPTER 21

No Deliverance from Babylon

The LORD spoke through Jeremiah when King
Zedekiah sent Pashhur son of Malkijah and
Zephaniah son of Maaseiah, the priest, to speak
with him. They begged Jeremiah, 2"Please speak
to the LORD for us and ask him to help us. King
Nebuchadnezzar of Babylon is attacking Judah.
Perhaps the LORD will be gracious and do a
mighty miracle as he has done in the past. Perhaps he will force Nebuchadnezzar to withdraw
his armies."
3Jeremiah replied, "Go back to King Zedekiah
and tell him, 4'This is what the LORD, the God of
Israel, says: I will make your weapons useless
against the king of Babylon and the Babylonians
who are outside your walls attacking you. In fact,
I will bring your enemies right into the heart of
this city. 5I myself will fight against you with a
strong hand and a powerful arm, for I am very angry. You have made me furious! 6I will send a terrible plague upon this city, and both people and
animals will die. 7And after all that, says the
LORD, I will hand over King Zedekiah, his staff,
and everyone else in the city who survives the
disease, war, and famine. I will hand them over to
King Nebuchadnezzar of Babylon and to their
other enemies. He will slaughter them and show
them no mercy, pity, or compassion.'

Jeremiah 22 . . . page 750

8"Tell all the people, 'This is what the LORD
says: Take your choice of life or death! 9Everyone
who stays in Jerusalem will die from war, famine,
or disease, but those who go out and surrender to
the Babylonians will live. Their reward will be
life! 10For I have decided to bring disaster and
not good upon this city, says the LORD. It will be
handed over to the king of Babylon, and he will
reduce it to ashes.'

Judgment on Judah's Kings

11"Say to the royal family of Judah, 'Listen to this
message from the LORD! 12This is what the LORD
says to the dynasty of David:

"'Give justice each morning to the people
you judge!
Help those who have been robbed;
rescue them from their oppressors.
Otherwise, my anger will burn like an
unquenchable fire
because of all your sins.
13 I will personally fight against the people
in Jerusalem,
that mighty fortress—
the people who boast, "No one can touch
us here.
No one can break in here."
14 And I myself will punish you for your
sinfulness,
says the LORD.
I will light a fire in your forests
that will burn up everything
around you.'"

CHAPTER 22

A Message for Judah's Kings

This is what the LORD said to me: "Go over and
speak directly to the king of Judah. Say to him,
2'Listen to this message from the LORD, you king
of Judah, sitting on David's throne. Let your attendants and your people listen, too. 3This is
what the LORD says: Be fair-minded and just. Do
what is right! Help those who have been robbed;
rescue them from their oppressors. Quit your
evil deeds! Do not mistreat foreigners, orphans,
and widows. Stop murdering the innocent! 4If
you obey me, there will always be a descendant
of David sitting on the throne here in Jerusalem.
The king will ride through the palace gates in
chariots and on horses, with his parade of attendants and subjects. 5But if you refuse to pay attention to this warning, I swear by my own
name, says the LORD, that this palace will become a pile of rubble.'"

A Message about the Palace

6Now this is what the LORD says concerning
Judah's royal palace:

"I love you as much as fruitful Gilead
and the green forests of Lebanon.
But I will turn you into a desert,
with no one living within your walls.
7 I will call for wreckers,
who will bring out their tools to
dismantle you.
They will tear out all your fine cedar beams
and throw them on the fire.

8"People from many nations will pass by the
ruins of this city and say to one another, 'Why did
the LORD destroy such a great city?' 9And the answer will be, 'Because they violated their covenant with the LORD their God by worshiping
other gods.'"

A Message about Jehoahaz

10 Do not weep for the dead king or mourn
his loss.
Instead, weep for the captive king
being led away!
For he will never return to see his native
land again.

11For this is what the LORD says about Jehoahaz,
who succeeded his father, King Josiah, and was
taken away as a captive: "He will never return.
12He will die in a distant land and will never
again see his own country."

A Message about Jehoiakim

13 And the LORD says, "What sorrow awaits
Jehoiakim,
who builds his palace with forced labor.
He builds injustice into its walls,
for he makes his neighbors work
for nothing.
He does not pay them for their labor.
14 He says, 'I will build a magnificent palace
with huge rooms and many windows.
I will panel it throughout with fragrant
cedar and paint it a lovely red.'
15 But a beautiful cedar palace does not make
a great king!
Your father, Josiah, also had plenty to eat
and drink.
But he was just and right in all his dealings.
That is why God blessed him.
16 He gave justice and help to the poor
and needy,
and everything went well for him.

FUN-fact
Pack your sheep; it's
Moving Day
Can you imagine moving in Bible times?

You couldn't exactly pack your sheep into boxes and load them on a truck! Sometimes people had to move because there wasn't enough food in the land. Sometimes a conquering army took over and forced the people to move. That's what happened to the Israelites during Jeremiah's time.

DO YOU KNOW SOMEONE WHO MOVED AWAY?

Write that person a letter or postcard. Say that God will take care of us wherever we go!

Isn't that what it means to know me?"
says the LORD.
17 "But you! You have eyes only for greed
and dishonesty!
You murder the innocent,
oppress the poor, and reign ruthlessly."

18 Therefore, this is what the LORD says about
Jehoiakim, son of King Josiah:

"The people will not mourn for him, crying
to one another,
'Alas, my brother! Alas, my sister!'
His subjects will not mourn for him, crying,
'Alas, our master is dead! Alas, his splendor
is gone!'
19 He will be buried like a dead donkey—
dragged out of Jerusalem and dumped
outside the gates!
20 Weep for your allies in Lebanon.
Shout for them in Bashan.
Search for them in the regions east
of the river.
See, they are all destroyed.
Not one is left to help you.
21 I warned you when you were prosperous,
but you replied, 'Don't bother me.'
You have been that way since childhood—
you simply will not obey me!
22 And now the wind will blow away your allies.
All your friends will be taken away
as captives.
Surely then you will see your wickedness
and be ashamed.
23 It may be nice to live in a beautiful palace
paneled with wood from the cedars
of Lebanon,
but soon you will groan with pangs
of anguish—
anguish like that of a woman in labor.

A Message for Jehoiachin

24 "As surely as I live," says the LORD, "I will abandon you, Jehoiachin son of Jehoiakim, king of Judah. Even if you were the signet ring on my right
hand, I would pull you off. 25 I will hand you over
to those who seek to kill you, those you so desperately fear—to King Nebuchadnezzar of Babylon and the mighty Babylonian army. 26 I will
expel you and your mother from this land, and
you will die in a foreign country, not in your native land. 27 You will never again return to the
land you yearn for.

28 "Why is this man Jehoiachin like a discarded,
broken jar?
Why are he and his children to be exiled to
a foreign land?
29 O earth, earth, earth!
Listen to this message from the LORD!
30 This is what the LORD says:
'Let the record show that this man
Jehoiachin was childless.
He is a failure,
for none of his children will succeed him
on the throne of David
to rule over Judah.'

CHAPTER 23

The Righteous Descendant

"What sorrow awaits the leaders of my people—
the shepherds of my sheep—for they have destroyed and scattered the very ones they were
expected to care for," says the LORD.

Jeremiah 23 . . . page 752

2Therefore, this is what the LORD, the God of Israel, says to these shepherds: "Instead of caring
for my flock and leading them to safety, you have
deserted them and driven them to destruction.
Now I will pour out judgment on you for the evil
you have done to them. 3But I will gather together
the remnant of my flock from the countries
where I have driven them. I will bring them back
to their own sheepfold, and they will be fruitful
and increase in number. 4Then I will appoint responsible shepherds who will care for them, and
they will never be afraid again. Not a single one
will be lost or missing. I, the LORD, have spoken!

5 "For the time is coming,"
says the LORD,
"when I will raise up a righteous descendant
from King David's line.
He will be a King who rules with wisdom.
He will do what is just and right
throughout the land.
6 And this will be his name:
'The LORD Is Our Righteousness.'
In that day Judah will be saved,
and Israel will live in safety.

7"In that day," says the LORD, "when people are
taking an oath, they will no longer say, 'As surely
as the LORD lives, who rescued the people of Israel from the land of Egypt.' 8Instead, they will
say, 'As surely as the LORD lives, who brought the
people of Israel back to their own land from the
land of the north and from all the countries to
which he had exiled them.' Then they will live in
their own land."

Judgment on False Prophets

9 My heart is broken because of the false
prophets,
and my bones tremble.
I stagger like a drunkard,
like someone overcome by wine,
because of the holy words
the LORD has spoken against them.
10 For the land is full of adultery,
and it lies under a curse.
The land itself is in mourning—
its wilderness pastures are dried up.
For they all do evil
and abuse what power they have.

11 "Even the priests and prophets
are ungodly, wicked men.
I have seen their despicable acts
right here in my own Temple,"
says the LORD.
12 "Therefore, the paths they take
will become slippery.
They will be chased through the dark,
and there they will fall.
For I will bring disaster upon them
at the time fixed for their punishment.
I, the LORD, have spoken!

13 "I saw that the prophets of Samaria were
terribly evil,
for they prophesied in the name of Baal
and led my people of Israel into sin.
14 But now I see that the prophets of Jerusalem
are even worse!
They commit adultery and love dishonesty.
They encourage those who are doing evil
so that no one turns away from their sins.
These prophets are as wicked
as the people of Sodom and Gomorrah
once were."

15Therefore, this is what the LORD of Heaven's
Armies says concerning the prophets:

"I will feed them with bitterness
and give them poison to drink.
For it is because of Jerusalem's prophets
that wickedness has filled this land."

16This is what the LORD of Heaven's Armies says
to his people:

"Do not listen to these prophets when they
prophesy to you,
filling you with futile hopes.
They are making up everything they say.
They do not speak for the LORD!
17 They keep saying to those who despise
my word,
'Don't worry! The LORD says you will
have peace!'
And to those who stubbornly follow their
own desires,
they say, 'No harm will come your way!'

18 "Have any of these prophets been in the
LORD's presence
to hear what he is really saying?
Has even one of them cared enough
to listen?
19 Look! The LORD's anger bursts out like
a storm,
a whirlwind that swirls down on the
heads of the wicked.
20 The anger of the LORD will not diminish
until it has finished all he has planned.
In the days to come
you will understand all this very clearly.

21 "I have not sent these prophets,
yet they run around claiming to speak
for me.
I have given them no message,
yet they go on prophesying.
22 If they had stood before me and listened to me,
they would have spoken my words,
and they would have turned my people
from their evil ways and deeds.
23 Am I a God who is only close at hand?"
says the LORD.
"No, I am far away at the same time.
24 Can anyone hide from me in a secret place?
Am I not everywhere in all the heavens
and earth?"
says the LORD.

25 "I have heard these prophets say, 'Listen to
the dream I had from God last night.' And then
they proceed to tell lies in my name. 26 How long
will this go on? If they are prophets, they are
prophets of deceit, inventing everything they say.
27 By telling these false dreams, they are trying to
get my people to forget me, just as their ancestors did by worshiping the idols of Baal.

28 "Let these false prophets tell their dreams,
but let my true messengers faithfully
proclaim my every word.
There is a difference between straw
and grain!
29 Does not my word burn like fire?"
says the LORD.
"Is it not like a mighty hammer
that smashes a rock to pieces?

30 "Therefore," says the LORD, "I am against
these prophets who steal messages from each
other and claim they are from me. 31 I am against
these smooth-tongued prophets who say, 'This
prophecy is from the LORD!' 32 I am against these
false prophets. Their imaginary dreams are flagrant lies that lead my people into sin. I did not
send or appoint them, and they have no message
at all for my people. I, the LORD, have spoken!

False Prophecies and False Prophets

33 "Suppose one of the people or one of the
prophets or priests asks you, 'What prophecy
has the LORD burdened you with now?' You must
reply, 'You are the burden! The LORD says he will
abandon you!'

34 "If any prophet, priest, or anyone else says, 'I
have a prophecy from the LORD,' I will punish that
person along with his entire family. 35 You should
keep asking each other, 'What is the LORD's answer?' or 'What is the LORD saying?' 36 But stop
using this phrase, 'prophecy from the LORD.' For
people are using it to give authority to their own
ideas, turning upside down the words of our God,
the living God, the LORD of Heaven's Armies.

37 "This is what you should say to the prophets: 'What is the LORD's answer?' or 'What is the
LORD saying?' 38 But suppose they respond, 'This
is a prophecy from the LORD!' Then you should
say, 'This is what the LORD says: Because you have
used this phrase, "prophecy from the LORD," even
though I warned you not to use it, 39 I will forget
you completely. I will expel you from my presence, along with this city that I gave to you and
your ancestors. 40 And I will make you an object
of ridicule, and your name will be infamous
throughout the ages.'"

CHAPTER 24

Good and Bad Figs

After King Nebuchadnezzar of Babylon exiled
Jehoiachin son of Jehoiakim, king of Judah, to
Babylon along with the officials of Judah and all
the craftsmen and artisans, the LORD gave me
this vision. I saw two baskets of figs placed in
front of the LORD's Temple in Jerusalem. 2 One
basket was filled with fresh, ripe figs, while the
other was filled with bad figs that were too rotten to eat.

3 Then the LORD said to me, "What do you see,
Jeremiah?"

I replied, "Figs, some very good and some very
bad, too rotten to eat."

4 Then the LORD gave me this message: 5 "This
is what the LORD, the God of Israel, says: The good
figs represent the exiles I sent from Judah to the
land of the Babylonians. 6 I will watch over and
care for them, and I will bring them back here
again. I will build them up and not tear them
down. I will plant them and not uproot them. 7 I
will give them hearts that recognize me as the
LORD. They will be my people, and I will be their
God, for they will return to me wholeheartedly.

8 "But the bad figs," the LORD said, "represent
King Zedekiah of Judah, his officials, all the people left in Jerusalem, and those who live in Egypt.
I will treat them like bad figs, too rotten to eat.
9 I will make them an object of horror and a symbol of evil to every nation on earth. They will be
disgraced and mocked, taunted and cursed,
wherever I scatter them. 10 And I will send war,
famine, and disease until they have vanished
from the land of Israel, which I gave to them and
their ancestors."

CHAPTER 25

Seventy Years of Captivity

This message for all the people of Judah came to
Jeremiah from the LORD during the fourth year
of Jehoiakim's reign over Judah. This was the
year when King Nebuchadnezzar of Babylon began his reign.
2Jeremiah the prophet said to all the people in
Judah and Jerusalem, 3"For the past twenty-three
years—from the thirteenth year of the reign of
Josiah son of Amon, king of Judah, until now—
the LORD has been giving me his messages. I have
faithfully passed them on to you, but you have
not listened.
4"Again and again the LORD has sent you his
servants, the prophets, but you have not listened or even paid attention. 5Each time the
message was this: 'Turn from the evil road you
are traveling and from the evil things you are
doing. Only then will I let you live in this land
that the LORD gave to you and your ancestors
forever. 6Do not provoke my anger by worshiping idols you made with your own hands. Then I
will not harm you.'
7"But you would not listen to me," says the
LORD. "You made me furious by worshiping idols
you made with your own hands, bringing on
yourselves all the disasters you now suffer. 8And
now the LORD of Heaven's Armies says: Because
you have not listened to me, 9I will gather together all the armies of the north under King
Nebuchadnezzar of Babylon, whom I have appointed as my deputy. I will bring them all
against this land and its people and against the
surrounding nations. I will completely destroy
you and make you an object of horror and contempt and a ruin forever. 10I will take away your
happy singing and laughter. The joyful voices of
bridegrooms and brides will no longer be heard.
Your millstones will fall silent, and the lights in
your homes will go out. 11This entire land will
become a desolate wasteland. Israel and her
neighboring lands will serve the king of Babylon
for seventy years.
12"Then, after the seventy years of captivity are
over, I will punish the king of Babylon and his
people for their sins," says the LORD. "I will make
the country of the Babylonians a wasteland forever. 13I will bring upon them all the terrors I
have promised in this book—all the penalties announced by Jeremiah against the nations. 14Many
nations and great kings will enslave the Babylonians, just as they enslaved my people. I will punish them in proportion to the suffering they
cause my people."

The Cup of the LORD's Anger

15This is what the LORD, the God of Israel, said to
me: "Take from my hand this cup filled to the
brim with my anger, and make all the nations to
whom I send you drink from it. 16When they
drink from it, they will stagger, crazed by the
warfare I will send against them."
17So I took the cup of anger from the LORD and
made all the nations drink from it—every nation
to which the LORD sent me. 18I went to Jerusalem
and the other towns of Judah, and their kings and
officials drank from the cup. From that day until
this, they have been a desolate ruin, an object of
horror, contempt, and cursing. 19I gave the cup to
Pharaoh, king of Egypt, his attendants, his officials, and all his people, 20along with all the foreigners living in that land. I also gave it to all the
kings of the land of Uz and the kings of the
Philistine cities of Ashkelon, Gaza, Ekron, and
what remains of Ashdod. 21Then I gave the cup to
the nations of Edom, Moab, and Ammon, 22and
the kings of Tyre and Sidon, and the kings of the
regions across the sea. 23I gave it to Dedan, Tema,
and Buz, and to the people who live in distant
places. 24I gave it to the kings of Arabia, the kings
of the nomadic tribes of the desert, 25and to the
kings of Zimri, Elam, and Media. 26And I gave it
to the kings of the northern countries, far and
near, one after the other—all the kingdoms of the
world. And finally, the king of Babylon himself
drank from the cup of the LORD's anger.
27Then the LORD said to me, "Now tell them,
'This is what the LORD of Heaven's Armies, the
God of Israel, says: Drink from this cup of my anger. Get drunk and vomit; fall to rise no more, for
I am sending terrible wars against you.' 28And if
they refuse to accept the cup, tell them, 'The
LORD of Heaven's Armies says: You have no
choice but to drink from it. 29I have begun to
punish Jerusalem, the city that bears my name.
Now should I let you go unpunished? No, you will
not escape disaster. I will call for war against all
the nations of the earth. I, the LORD of Heaven's
Armies, have spoken!'
30"Now prophesy all these things, and say to
them,

"'The LORD will roar against his own land
    from his holy dwelling in heaven.
He will shout like those who tread grapes;
    he will shout against everyone on earth.
31 His cry of judgment will reach the ends of the
        earth,
    for the LORD will bring his case against all
        the nations.

He will judge all the people of the earth,
slaughtering the wicked with the sword.
I, the LORD, have spoken!'"

32 This is what the LORD of Heaven's
Armies says:
"Look! Disaster will fall upon nation
after nation!
A great whirlwind of fury is rising
from the most distant corners of
the earth!"

33 In that day those the LORD has slaughtered
will fill the earth from one end to the other. No
one will mourn for them or gather up their bodies to bury them. They will be scattered on the
ground like manure.

34 Weep and moan, you evil shepherds!
Roll in the dust, you leaders of the flock!
The time of your slaughter has arrived;
you will fall and shatter like a fragile
vase.
35 You will find no place to hide;
there will be no way to escape.
36 Listen to the frantic cries of the shepherds.
The leaders of the flock are wailing
in despair,
for the LORD is ruining their pastures.
37 Peaceful meadows will be turned into
a wasteland
by the LORD's fierce anger.
38 He has left his den like a strong lion
seeking its prey,
and their land will be made desolate
by the sword of the enemy
and the LORD's fierce anger.

CHAPTER 26

Jeremiah's Escape from Death

This message came to Jeremiah from the LORD
early in the reign of Jehoiakim son of Josiah, king
of Judah. 2"This is what the LORD says: Stand in
the courtyard in front of the Temple of the LORD,
and make an announcement to the people who
have come there to worship from all over Judah.
Give them my entire message; include every
word. 3Perhaps they will listen and turn from
their evil ways. Then I will change my mind
about the disaster I am ready to pour out on
them because of their sins.

4"Say to them, 'This is what the LORD says: If
you will not listen to me and obey my word I have
given you, 5and if you will not listen to my servants, the prophets—for I sent them again and
again to warn you, but you would not listen to
them—6then I will destroy this Temple as I destroyed Shiloh, the place where the Tabernacle
was located. And I will make Jerusalem an object
of cursing in every nation on earth.'"

7The priests, the prophets, and all the people
listened to Jeremiah as he spoke in front of the
LORD's Temple. 8But when Jeremiah had finished his message, saying everything the LORD
had told him to say, the priests and prophets
and all the people at the Temple mobbed him.
"Kill him!" they shouted. 9"What right do you
have to prophesy in the LORD's name that this
Temple will be destroyed like Shiloh? What do
you mean, saying that Jerusalem will be destroyed and left with no inhabitants?" And all
the people threatened him as he stood in front
of the Temple.

10When the officials of Judah heard what was
happening, they rushed over from the palace
and sat down at the New Gate of the Temple to
hold court. 11The priests and prophets presented their accusations to the officials and the
people. "This man should die!" they said. "You
have heard with your own ears what a traitor he
is, for he has prophesied against this city."

12Then Jeremiah spoke to the officials and the
people in his own defense. "The LORD sent me to
prophesy against this Temple and this city," he
said. "The LORD gave me every word that I have
spoken. 13But if you stop your sinning and begin
to obey the LORD your God, he will change his
mind about this disaster that he has announced
against you. 14As for me, I am in your hands—do
with me as you think best. 15But if you kill me,
rest assured that you will be killing an innocent
man! The responsibility for such a deed will lie
on you, on this city, and on every person living in
it. For it is absolutely true that the LORD sent me
to speak every word you have heard."

16Then the officials and the people said to the
priests and prophets, "This man does not deserve the death sentence, for he has spoken to us
in the name of the LORD our God."

17Then some of the wise old men stood and
spoke to all the people assembled there. 18They
said, "Remember when Micah of Moresheth
prophesied during the reign of King Hezekiah of
Judah. He told the people of Judah,

'This is what the LORD of Heaven's Armies
says:
Mount Zion will be plowed like an open field;
Jerusalem will be reduced to ruins!
A thicket will grow on the heights
where the Temple now stands.'

19But did King Hezekiah and the people kill him
for saying this? No, they turned from their sins
and worshiped the LORD. They begged him for
mercy. Then the LORD changed his mind about
the terrible disaster he had pronounced against
them. So we are about to do ourselves great
harm."

20At this time Uriah son of Shemaiah from
Kiriath-jearim was also prophesying for the
LORD. And he predicted the same terrible disaster against the city and nation as Jeremiah did.
21When King Jehoiakim and the army officers
and officials heard what he was saying, the king
sent someone to kill him. But Uriah heard about
the plan and escaped in fear to Egypt. 22Then
King Jehoiakim sent Elnathan son of Acbor to
Egypt along with several other men to capture
Uriah. 23They took him prisoner and brought
him back to King Jehoiakim. The king then
killed Uriah with a sword and had him buried in
an unmarked grave.

24Nevertheless, Ahikam son of Shaphan
stood up for Jeremiah and persuaded the court
not to turn him over to the mob to be killed.

CHAPTER 27
Jeremiah Wears an Ox Yoke

This message came to Jeremiah from the LORD
early in the reign of Zedekiah son of Josiah, king
of Judah.

2This is what the LORD said to me: "Make a
yoke, and fasten it on your neck with leather
straps. 3Then send messages to the kings of
Edom, Moab, Ammon, Tyre, and Sidon through
their ambassadors who have come to see King
Zedekiah in Jerusalem. 4Give them this message for their masters: 'This is what the LORD of
Heaven's Armies, the God of Israel, says: 5With
my great strength and powerful arm I made the
earth and all its people and every animal. I can
give these things of mine to anyone I choose.
6Now I will give your countries to King Nebuchadnezzar of Babylon, who is my servant. I
have put everything, even the wild animals,
under his control. 7All the nations will serve
him, his son, and his grandson until his time is
up. Then many nations and great kings will conquer and rule over Babylon. 8So you must submit to Babylon's king and serve him; put your
neck under Babylon's yoke! I will punish any nation that refuses to be his slave, says the LORD. I
will send war, famine, and disease upon that nation until Babylon has conquered it.

9"'Do not listen to your false prophets, fortune-
tellers, interpreters of dreams, mediums, and
sorcerers who say, "The king of Babylon will not
conquer you." 10They are all liars, and their lies
will lead to your being driven out of your land.
I will drive you out and send you far away to die.
11But the people of any nation that submits to
the king of Babylon will be allowed to stay in
their own country to farm the land as usual.
I the LORD, have spoken!'"

12Then I repeated this same message to King
Zedekiah of Judah. "If you want to live, submit
to the yoke of the king of Babylon and his people. 13Why do you insist on dying—you and
your people? Why should you choose war, famine, and disease, which the LORD will bring
against every nation that refuses to submit to
Babylon's king? 14Do not listen to the false
prophets who keep telling you, 'The king of
Babylon will not conquer you.' They are liars.
15This is what the LORD says: 'I have not sent
these prophets! They are telling you lies in my
name, so I will drive you from this land. You will
all die—you and all these prophets, too.'"

16Then I spoke to the priests and the people
and said, "This is what the LORD says: 'Do not listen to your prophets who claim that soon the
gold articles taken from my Temple will be returned from Babylon. It is all a lie! 17Do not listen to them. Surrender to the king of Babylon,
and you will live. Why should this whole city be
destroyed? 18If they really are prophets and
speak the LORD's messages, let them pray to the
LORD of Heaven's Armies. Let them pray that the
articles remaining in the LORD's Temple and in
the king's palace and in the palaces of Jerusalem
will not be carried away to Babylon!'

19"For the LORD of Heaven's Armies has spoken about the pillars in front of the Temple,
the great bronze basin called the Sea, the water carts, and all the other ceremonial articles.
20King Nebuchadnezzar of Babylon left them
here when he exiled Jehoiachin son of Jehoiakim, king of Judah, to Babylon, along with all the
other nobles of Judah and Jerusalem. 21Yes, this
is what the LORD of Heaven's Armies, the God of
Israel, says about the precious things still in the
Temple, in the palace of Judah's king, and in
Jerusalem: 22'They will all be carried away to
Babylon and will stay there until I send for
them,' says the LORD. 'Then I will bring them
back to Jerusalem again.'"

CHAPTER 28
Jeremiah Condemns Hananiah

One day in late summer of that same year—the
fourth year of the reign of Zedekiah, king of

Judah—Hananiah son of Azzur, a prophet from
Gibeon, addressed me publicly in the Temple
while all the priests and people listened. He
said, 2“This is what the LORD of Heaven's
Armies, the God of Israel, says: ‘I will remove the
yoke of the king of Babylon from your necks.
3Within two years I will bring back all the Temple treasures that King Nebuchadnezzar carried
off to Babylon. 4And I will bring back Jehoiachin
son of Jehoiakim, king of Judah, and all the other
captives that were taken to Babylon. I will surely
break the yoke that the king of Babylon has put
on your necks. I, the LORD, have spoken!’”

5Jeremiah responded to Hananiah as they
stood in front of all the priests and people at the
Temple. 6He said, “Amen! May your prophecies
come true! I hope the LORD does everything you
say. I hope he does bring back from Babylon the
treasures of this Temple and all the captives.
7But listen now to the solemn words I speak to
you in the presence of all these people. 8The ancient prophets who preceded you and me spoke
against many nations, always warning of war, disaster, and disease. 9So a prophet who predicts
peace must show he is right. Only when his predictions come true can we know that he is really
from the LORD.”

10Then Hananiah the prophet took the yoke
off Jeremiah's neck and broke it in pieces.
11And Hananiah said again to the crowd that
had gathered, “This is what the LORD says: ‘Just
as this yoke has been broken, within two years I
will break the yoke of oppression from all the
nations now subject to King Nebuchadnezzar
of Babylon.’” With that, Jeremiah left the Temple area.

12Soon after this confrontation with Hananiah, the LORD gave this message to Jeremiah:
13“Go and tell Hananiah, ‘This is what the LORD
says: You have broken a wooden yoke, but
you have replaced it with a yoke of iron. 14The
LORD of Heaven's Armies, the God of Israel,
says: I have put a yoke of iron on the necks of all
these nations, forcing them into slavery under
King Nebuchadnezzar of Babylon. I have put
everything, even the wild animals, under his
control.’”

15Then Jeremiah the prophet said to Hananiah, “Listen, Hananiah! The LORD has not sent
you, but the people believe your lies. 16There-
fore, this is what the LORD says: ‘You must die.
Your life will end this very year because you
have rebelled against the LORD.’”

17Two months later the prophet Hananiah
died.

Key Verse **“For I know the plans I have for you,” says the LORD. “They are plans for good and not for disaster, to give you a future and a hope.” —JEREMIAH 29:11**

Pick a Day, Any Day

Here's something to help when you're worried.

Read **JEREMIAH 29:11** out loud.

God knows *everything* that's going to happen. And he has good plans for us. Here's a way to remember that!

“For I know the plans I have for you,” says the Lord. “They are plans for good and not for disaster, to give you a future and a hope.” —Jeremiah 29:11

APRIL

1 **Make a calendar that includes this month and next. Write the words of JEREMIAH 29:11 at the top.**

2 **Draw a star on one day in each week. (It doesn't matter which day—just pick one in each week.)**

3 **Write what you already know will happen on your star days. (You might write, “go to school” or “soccer game.”)**

4 **At the end of your star days, write what God already knew was going to happen on those days. (You might write, “won the soccer game” or “got an A on my test.”)**

Here's another great passage to read when you're worried about the future: Matthew 6:25-33.

No matter which days you pick, God knows what will happen, and he has good plans for those days. **When your star days arrive, read JEREMIAH 29:11 again, and thank God for making good plans for you.**

Jeremiah 29 . . . page 758

CHAPTER 29

A Letter to the Exiles

Jeremiah wrote a letter from Jerusalem to the elders, priests, prophets, and all the people who had been exiled to Babylon by King Nebuchadnezzar. 2 This was after King Jehoiachin, the queen mother, the court officials, the other officials of Judah, and all the craftsmen and artisans had been deported from Jerusalem. 3 He sent the letter with Elasah son of Shaphan and Gemariah son of Hilkiah when they went to Babylon as King Zedekiah's ambassadors to Nebuchadnezzar. This is what Jeremiah's letter said:

4 This is what the LORD of Heaven's Armies, the God of Israel, says to all the captives he has exiled to Babylon from Jerusalem: 5 "Build homes, and plan to stay. Plant gardens, and eat the food they produce. 6 Marry and have children. Then find spouses for them so that you may have many grandchildren. Multiply! Do not dwindle away! 7 And work for the peace and prosperity of the city where I sent you into exile. Pray to the LORD for it, for its welfare will determine your welfare."

8 This is what the LORD of Heaven's Armies, the God of Israel, says: "Do not let your prophets and fortune-tellers who are with you in the land of Babylon trick you. Do not listen to their dreams, 9 because they are telling you lies in my name. I have not sent them," says the LORD.

10 This is what the LORD says: "You will be in Babylon for seventy years. But then I will come and do for you all the good things I have promised, and I will bring you home again. **11 For I know the plans I have for you," says the LORD. "They are plans for good and not for disaster, to give you a future and a hope.** 12 In those days when you pray, I will listen. 13 If you look for me wholeheartedly, you will find me. 14 I will be found by you," says the LORD. "I will end your captivity and restore your fortunes. I will gather you out of the nations where I sent you and will bring you home again to your own land."

15 You claim that the LORD has raised up prophets for you in Babylon. 16 But this is what the LORD says about the king who sits on David's throne and all those still living here in Jerusalem—your relatives who were not exiled to Babylon. 17 This is what the LORD of Heaven's Armies says: "I will send war, famine, and disease upon them and make them like bad figs, too rotten to eat. 18 Yes, I will pursue them with war, famine, and disease, and I will scatter them around the world. In every nation where I send them, I will make them an object of damnation, horror, contempt, and mockery. 19 For they refuse to listen to me, though I have spoken to them repeatedly through the prophets I sent. And you who are in exile have not listened either," says the LORD.

20 Therefore, listen to this message from the LORD, all you captives there in Babylon. 21 This is what the LORD of Heaven's Armies, the God of Israel, says about your prophets—Ahab son of Kolaiah and Zedekiah son of Maaseiah—who are telling you lies in my name: "I will turn them over to Nebuchadnezzar for execution before your eyes. 22 Their terrible fate will become proverbial, so that the Judean exiles will curse someone by saying, 'May the LORD make you like Zedekiah and Ahab, whom the king of Babylon burned alive!' 23 For these men have done terrible things among my people. They have committed adultery with their neighbors' wives and have lied in my name, saying things I did not command. I am a witness to this. I, the LORD, have spoken."

A Message for Shemaiah

24 The LORD sent this message to Shemaiah the Nehelamite in Babylon: 25 "This is what the LORD of Heaven's Armies, the God of Israel, says: You wrote a letter on your own authority to Zephaniah son of Maaseiah, the priest, and you sent copies to the other priests and people in Jerusalem. You wrote to Zephaniah,

26 "The LORD has appointed you to replace Jehoiada as the priest in charge of the house of the LORD. You are responsible to put into stocks and neck irons any crazy man who claims to be a prophet. 27 So why have you done nothing to stop Jeremiah from Anathoth, who pretends to be a prophet among you? 28 Jeremiah sent a letter here to Babylon, predicting that our captivity will be a long one. He said, 'Build homes, and plan to stay. Plant gardens, and eat the food they produce.'"

29 But when Zephaniah the priest received Shemaiah's letter, he took it to Jeremiah and read it to him. 30 Then the LORD gave this message to Jeremiah: 31 "Send an open letter to all

the exiles in Babylon. Tell them, 'This is what the
LORD says concerning Shemaiah the Nehelamite: Since he has prophesied to you when I did
not send him and has tricked you into believing
his lies, 32 I will punish him and his family. None
of his descendants will see the good things I will
do for my people, for he has incited you to rebel
against me. I, the LORD, have spoken!'"

CHAPTER 30

Promises of Deliverance

The LORD gave another message to Jeremiah. He
said, 2 "This is what the LORD, the God of Israel,
says: Write down for the record everything I have
said to you, Jeremiah. 3 For the time is coming
when I will restore the fortunes of my people of
Israel and Judah. I will bring them home to this
land that I gave to their ancestors, and they will
possess it again. I, the LORD, have spoken!"

4 This is the message the LORD gave concerning Israel and Judah. 5 This is what the LORD says:

"I hear cries of fear;
there is terror and no peace.
6 Now let me ask you a question:
Do men give birth to babies?
Then why do they stand there, ashen-faced,
hands pressed against their sides
like a woman in labor?
7 In all history there has never been such
a time of terror.
It will be a time of trouble for my
people Israel.
Yet in the end they will be saved!
8 For in that day,"
says the LORD of Heaven's Armies,
"I will break the yoke from their necks
and snap their chains.
Foreigners will no longer be their masters.
9 For my people will serve the LORD
their God
and their king descended from David—
the king I will raise up for them.

10 "So do not be afraid, Jacob, my servant;
do not be dismayed, Israel,"
says the LORD.
"For I will bring you home again from
distant lands,
and your children will return from
their exile.
Israel will return to a life of peace and quiet,
and no one will terrorize them.
11 For I am with you and will save you,"
says the LORD.
"I will completely destroy the nations where
I have scattered you,
but I will not completely destroy you.
I will discipline you, but with justice;
I cannot let you go unpunished."

12 This is what the LORD says:
"Your injury is incurable—
a terrible wound.
13 There is no one to help you
or to bind up your injury.
No medicine can heal you.
14 All your lovers—your allies—have left you
and do not care about you anymore.
I have wounded you cruelly,
as though I were your enemy.
For your sins are many,
and your guilt is great.
15 Why do you protest your punishment—
this wound that has no cure?
I have had to punish you
because your sins are many
and your guilt is great.

16 "But all who devour you will be devoured,
and all your enemies will be sent
into exile.
All who plunder you will be plundered,
and all who attack you will be attacked.
17 I will give you back your health
and heal your wounds," says the LORD.
"For you are called an outcast—
'Jerusalem for whom no one cares.'"

18 This is what the LORD says:
"When I bring Israel home again
from captivity
and restore their fortunes,
Jerusalem will be rebuilt on its ruins,
and the palace reconstructed as before.
19 There will be joy and songs of thanksgiving,
and I will multiply my people, not
diminish them;
I will honor them, not despise them.
20 Their children will prosper as they did
long ago.
I will establish them as a nation before me,
and I will punish anyone who hurts them.
21 They will have their own ruler again,
and he will come from their own people.
I will invite him to approach me," says
the LORD,
"for who would dare to come
unless invited?
22 You will be my people,
and I will be your God."

23 Look! The LORD's anger bursts out
like a storm,
a driving wind that swirls down
on the heads of the wicked.
24 The fierce anger of the LORD will
not diminish
until it has finished all he has planned.
In the days to come
you will understand all this.

CHAPTER **31**

Hope for Restoration

"In that day," says the LORD, "I will be the God of
all the families of Israel, and they will be my people. 2 This is what the LORD says:

"Those who survive the coming destruction
will find blessings even in the barren land,
for I will give rest to the people of Israel."

3 Long ago the LORD said to Israel:
"I have loved you, my people, with an
everlasting love.
With unfailing love I have drawn you
to myself.
4 I will rebuild you, my virgin Israel.
You will again be happy
and dance merrily with your tambourines.
5 Again you will plant your vineyards on the
mountains of Samaria
and eat from your own gardens there.
6 The day will come when watchmen
will shout
from the hill country of Ephraim,
'Come, let us go up to Jerusalem
to worship the LORD our God.'"

7 Now this is what the LORD says:
"Sing with joy for Israel.
Shout for the greatest of nations!
Shout out with praise and joy:
'Save your people, O LORD,
the remnant of Israel!'
8 For I will bring them from the north
and from the distant corners of the earth.
I will not forget the blind and lame,
the expectant mothers and women
in labor.
A great company will return!
9 Tears of joy will stream down their faces,
and I will lead them home with great care.
They will walk beside quiet streams
and on smooth paths where they will
not stumble.
For I am Israel's father,
and Ephraim is my oldest child.

10 "Listen to this message from the LORD,
you nations of the world;
proclaim it in distant coastlands:
The LORD, who scattered his people,
will gather them and watch over them
as a shepherd does his flock.
11 For the LORD has redeemed Israel
from those too strong for them.
12 They will come home and sing songs of joy
on the heights of Jerusalem.
They will be radiant because of the
LORD's good gifts—
the abundant crops of grain, new wine,
and olive oil,
and the healthy flocks and herds.
Their life will be like a watered garden,
and all their sorrows will be gone.
13 The young women will dance for joy,
and the men—old and young—will join
in the celebration.
I will turn their mourning into joy.
I will comfort them and exchange their
sorrow for rejoicing.
14 The priests will enjoy abundance,
and my people will feast on my
good gifts.
I, the LORD, have spoken!"

Rachel's Sadness Turns to Joy

15 This is what the LORD says:

"A cry is heard in Ramah—
deep anguish and bitter weeping.
Rachel weeps for her children,
refusing to be comforted—
for her children are gone."

16 But now this is what the LORD says:
"Do not weep any longer,
for I will reward you," says the LORD.
"Your children will come back to you
from the distant land of the enemy.
17 There is hope for your future," says the LORD.
"Your children will come again to their
own land.
18 I have heard Israel saying,
'You disciplined me severely,
like a calf that needs training for
the yoke.
Turn me again to you and restore me,
for you alone are the LORD my God.
19 I turned away from God,
but then I was sorry.
I kicked myself for my stupidity!
I was thoroughly ashamed of all I did
in my younger days.'

20 "Is not Israel still my son,
my darling child?" says the LORD.
"I often have to punish him,
but I still love him.
That's why I long for him
and surely will have mercy on him.
21 Set up road signs;
put up guideposts.
Mark well the path
by which you came.
Come back again, my virgin Israel;
return to your towns here.
22 How long will you wander,
my wayward daughter?
For the LORD will cause something new to
happen—
Israel will embrace her God."

23 This is what the LORD of Heaven's Armies,
the God of Israel, says: "When I bring them back
from captivity, the people of Judah and its towns
will again say, 'The LORD bless you, O righteous
home, O holy mountain!' 24 Townspeople and
farmers and shepherds alike will live together in
peace and happiness. 25 For I have given rest to
the weary and joy to the sorrowing."
26 At this, I woke up and looked around. My
sleep had been very sweet.
27 "The day is coming," says the LORD, "when I
will greatly increase the human population and
the number of animals here in Israel and Judah.
28 In the past I deliberately uprooted and tore
down this nation. I overthrew it, destroyed it, and
brought disaster upon it. But in the future I will
just as deliberately plant it and build it up. I, the
LORD, have spoken!
29 "The people will no longer quote this
proverb:

'The parents have eaten sour grapes,
but their children's mouths pucker
at the taste.'

30 All people will die for their own sins—those
who eat the sour grapes will be the ones whose
mouths will pucker.
31 "The day is coming," says the LORD, "when I
will make a new covenant with the people of Israel and Judah. 32 This covenant will not be like
the one I made with their ancestors when I took
them by the hand and brought them out of the
land of Egypt. They broke that covenant, though I
loved them as a husband loves his wife," says the
LORD.
33 "But this is the new covenant I will make
with the people of Israel after those days," says
the LORD. "I will put my instructions deep within
them, and I will write them on their hearts. I will
be their God, and they will be my people. 34 And
they will not need to teach their neighbors, nor
will they need to teach their relatives, saying,
'You should know the LORD.' For everyone, from
the least to the greatest, will know me already,"
says the LORD. "And I will forgive their wickedness, and I will never again remember their sins."

35 It is the LORD who provides the sun to light
the day
and the moon and stars to light the night,
and who stirs the sea into roaring waves.
His name is the LORD of Heaven's Armies,
and this is what he says:
36 "I am as likely to reject my people Israel
as I am to abolish the laws of nature!"
37 This is what the LORD says:
"Just as the heavens cannot be measured
and the foundations of the earth cannot be
explored,
so I will not consider casting them away
for the evil they have done.
I, the LORD, have spoken!

38 "The day is coming," says the LORD, "when
all Jerusalem will be rebuilt for me, from the
Tower of Hananel to the Corner Gate. 39 A measuring line will be stretched out over the hill of
Gareb and across to Goah. 40 And the entire
area—including the graveyard and ash dump in
the valley, and all the fields out to the Kidron Valley on the east as far as the Horse Gate—will be
holy to the LORD. The city will never again be captured or destroyed."

CHAPTER 32

Jeremiah's Land Purchase

The following message came to Jeremiah from
the LORD in the tenth year of the reign of
Zedekiah, king of Judah. This was also the eighteenth year of the reign of King Nebuchadnezzar. 2 Jerusalem was then under siege from
the Babylonian army, and Jeremiah was imprisoned in the courtyard of the guard in the royal
palace. 3 King Zedekiah had put him there, asking why he kept giving this prophecy: "This is
what the LORD says: 'I am about to hand this city
over to the king of Babylon, and he will take it.
4 King Zedekiah will be captured by the Babylonians and taken to meet the king of Babylon face
to face. 5 He will take Zedekiah to Babylon, and I
will deal with him there,' says the LORD. 'If you
fight against the Babylonians, you will never
succeed.'"

Jeremiah 32 . . . page 762

6 At that time the LORD sent me a message. He said, 7 "Your cousin Hanamel son of Shallum will come and say to you, 'Buy my field at Anathoth. By law you have the right to buy it before it is offered to anyone else.'"

8 Then, just as the LORD had said he would, my cousin Hanamel came and visited me in the prison. He said, "Please buy my field at Anathoth in the land of Benjamin. By law you have the right to buy it before it is offered to anyone else, so buy it for yourself." Then I knew that the message I had heard was from the LORD.

9 So I bought the field at Anathoth, paying Hanamel seventeen pieces of silver for it. 10 I signed and sealed the deed of purchase before witnesses, weighed out the silver, and paid him. 11 Then I took the sealed deed and an unsealed copy of the deed, which contained the terms and conditions of the purchase, 12 and I handed them to Baruch son of Neriah and grandson of Mahseiah. I did all this in the presence of my cousin Hanamel, the witnesses who had signed the deed, and all the men of Judah who were there in the courtyard of the guardhouse.

13 Then I said to Baruch as they all listened, 14 "This is what the LORD of Heaven's Armies, the God of Israel, says: 'Take both this sealed deed and the unsealed copy, and put them into a pottery jar to preserve them for a long time.' 15 For this is what the LORD of Heaven's Armies, the God of Israel, says: 'Someday people will again own property here in this land and will buy and sell houses and vineyards and fields.'"

Jeremiah's Prayer

16 Then after I had given the papers to Baruch, I prayed to the LORD:

> 17 "O Sovereign LORD! You made the heavens and earth by your strong hand and powerful arm. Nothing is too hard for you! 18 You show unfailing love to thousands, but you also bring the consequences of one generation's sin upon the next. You are the great and powerful God, the LORD of Heaven's Armies. 19 You have all wisdom and do great and mighty miracles. You see the conduct of all people, and you give them what they deserve. 20 You performed miraculous signs and wonders in the land of Egypt—things still remembered to this day! And you have continued to do great miracles in Israel and all around the world. You have made your name famous to this day.
>
> 21 "You brought Israel out of Egypt with mighty signs and wonders, with a strong hand and powerful arm, and with overwhelming terror. 22 You gave the people of Israel this land that you had promised their ancestors long before—a land flowing with milk and honey. 23 Our ancestors came and conquered it and lived in it, but they refused to obey you or follow your word. They have not done anything you commanded. That is why you have sent this terrible disaster upon them.
>
> 24 "See how the siege ramps have been built against the city walls! Through war, famine, and disease, the city will be handed over to the Babylonians, who will conquer it. Everything has happened just as you said. 25 And yet, O Sovereign LORD, you have told me to buy the field—paying good money for it before these witnesses—even though the city will soon be handed over to the Babylonians."

A Prediction of Jerusalem's Fall

26 Then this message came to Jeremiah from the LORD: 27 "I am the LORD, the God of all the peoples of the world. Is anything too hard for me? 28 Therefore, this is what the LORD says: I will hand this city over to the Babylonians and to Nebuchadnezzar, king of Babylon, and he will capture it. 29 The Babylonians outside the walls will come in and set fire to the city. They will burn down all these houses where the people provoked my anger by burning incense to Baal on the rooftops and by pouring out liquid offerings to other gods. 30 Israel and Judah have done nothing but wrong since their earliest days. They have infuriated me with all their evil deeds," says the LORD. 31 "From the time this city was built until now, it has done nothing but anger me, so I am determined to get rid of it.

32 "The sins of Israel and Judah—the sins of the people of Jerusalem, the kings, the officials, the priests, and the prophets—have stirred up my anger. 33 My people have turned their backs on me and have refused to return. Even though I diligently taught them, they would not receive instruction or obey. 34 They have set up their abominable idols right in my own Temple, defiling it. 35 They have built pagan shrines to Baal in the valley of Ben-Hinnom, and there they sacrifice their sons and daughters to Molech. I have never commanded such a horrible deed; it never even crossed my mind to command such a thing. What an incredible evil, causing Judah to sin so greatly!

A Promise of Restoration

36“Now I want to say something more about this
city. You have been saying, ‘It will fall to the king
of Babylon through war, famine, and disease.’ But
this is what the LORD, the God of Israel, says: 37I
will certainly bring my people back again from
all the countries where I will scatter them in my
fury. I will bring them back to this very city and
let them live in peace and safety. 38They will be
my people, and I will be their God. 39And I will
give them one heart and one purpose: to worship
me forever, for their own good and for the good
of all their descendants. 40And I will make an
everlasting covenant with them: I will never stop
doing good for them. I will put a desire in their
hearts to worship me, and they will never leave
me. 41I will find joy doing good for them and will
faithfully and wholeheartedly replant them in
this land.

42“This is what the LORD says: Just as I have
brought all these calamities on them, so I will do
all the good I have promised them. 43Fields will
again be bought and sold in this land about which
you now say, ‘It has been ravaged by the Babylonians, a desolate land where people and animals
have all disappeared.’ 44Yes, fields will once again
be bought and sold—deeds signed and sealed
and witnessed—in the land of Benjamin and here
in Jerusalem, in the towns of Judah and in the hill
country, in the foothills of Judah and in the Negev,
too. For someday I will restore prosperity to them.
I, the LORD, have spoken!”

CHAPTER 33
Promises of Peace and Prosperity

While Jeremiah was still confined in the courtyard of the guard, the LORD gave him this second
message: 2“This is what the LORD says—the
LORD who made the earth, who formed and established it, whose name is the LORD: 3Ask me
and I will tell you remarkable secrets you do not
know about things to come. 4For this is what the
LORD, the God of Israel, says: You have torn down
the houses of this city and even the king’s palace
to get materials to strengthen the walls against
the siege ramps and swords of the enemy. 5You
expect to fight the Babylonians, but the men of
this city are already as good as dead, for I have
determined to destroy them in my terrible anger. I have abandoned them because of all their
wickedness.

6“Nevertheless, the time will come when I will
heal Jerusalem’s wounds and give it prosperity
and true peace. 7I will restore the fortunes of Judah and Israel and rebuild their towns. 8I will
cleanse them of their sins against me and forgive
all their sins of rebellion. 9Then this city will
bring me joy, glory, and honor before all the nations of the earth! The people of the world will
see all the good I do for my people, and they will
tremble with awe at the peace and prosperity I
provide for them.

10“This is what the LORD says: You have said,
‘This is a desolate land where people and animals
have all disappeared.’ Yet in the empty streets of
Jerusalem and Judah’s other towns, there will be
heard once more 11the sounds of joy and laughter. The joyful voices of bridegrooms and brides
will be heard again, along with the joyous songs
of people bringing thanksgiving offerings to the
LORD. They will sing,

‘Give thanks to the LORD of Heaven’s Armies,
for the LORD is good.
His faithful love endures forever!’

For I will restore the prosperity of this land to
what it was in the past, says the LORD.

12“This is what the LORD of Heaven’s Armies
says: This land—though it is now desolate and
has no people and animals—will once more have
pastures where shepherds can lead their flocks.
13Once again shepherds will count their flocks
in the towns of the hill country, the foothills of
Judah, the Negev, the land of Benjamin, the vicinity of Jerusalem, and all the towns of Judah. I, the
LORD, have spoken!

14“The day will come, says the LORD, when I
will do for Israel and Judah all the good things
I have promised them.

15 “In those days and at that time
I will raise up a righteous descendant
from King David’s line.
He will do what is just and right
throughout the land.
16 In that day Judah will be saved,
and Jerusalem will live in safety.
And this will be its name:
‘The LORD Is Our Righteousness.’

17For this is what the LORD says: David will have a
descendant sitting on the throne of Israel forever. 18And there will always be Levitical priests
to offer burnt offerings and grain offerings and
sacrifices to me.”

19Then this message came to Jeremiah from
the LORD: 20“This is what the LORD says: If you
can break my covenant with the day and the night
so that one does not follow the other, 21only then
will my covenant with my servant David be

broken. Only then will he no longer have a descendant to reign on his throne. The same is true
for my covenant with the Levitical priests who
minister before me. 22 And as the stars of the sky
cannot be counted and the sand on the seashore
cannot be measured, so I will multiply the descendants of my servant David and the Levites
who minister before me."

23 The LORD gave another message to Jeremiah. He said, 24 "Have you noticed what people
are saying?—'The LORD chose Judah and Israel
and then abandoned them!' They are sneering
and saying that Israel is not worthy to be counted
as a nation. 25 But this is what the LORD says: I
would no more reject my people than I would
change my laws that govern night and day, earth
and sky. 26 I will never abandon the descendants
of Jacob or David, my servant, or change the plan
that David's descendants will rule the descendants of Abraham, Isaac, and Jacob. Instead, I will
restore them to their land and have mercy on
them."

CHAPTER 34
A Warning for Zedekiah
King Nebuchadnezzar of Babylon came with all
the armies from the kingdoms he ruled, and he
fought against Jerusalem and the towns of Judah.
At that time this message came to Jeremiah from
the LORD: 2 "Go to King Zedekiah of Judah, and
tell him, 'This is what the LORD, the God of Israel,
says: I am about to hand this city over to the king
of Babylon, and he will burn it down. 3 You will
not escape his grasp but will be captured and
taken to meet the king of Babylon face to face.
Then you will be exiled to Babylon.

4 "But listen to this promise from the LORD,
O Zedekiah, king of Judah. This is what the LORD
says: You will not be killed in war 5 but will die
peacefully. People will burn incense in your
memory, just as they did for your ancestors, the
kings who preceded you. They will mourn for
you, crying, "Alas, our master is dead!" This I have
decreed, says the LORD.'"

6 So Jeremiah the prophet delivered the mes-
sage to King Zedekiah of Judah. 7 At this time the
Babylonian army was besieging Jerusalem,
Lachish, and Azekah—the only fortified cities of
Judah not yet captured.

Freedom for Hebrew Slaves
8 This message came to Jeremiah from the LORD
after King Zedekiah made a covenant with the
people, proclaiming freedom for the slaves. 9 He
had ordered all the people to free their Hebrew
slaves—both men and women. No one was to
keep a fellow Judean in bondage. 10 The officials
and all the people had obeyed the king's command, 11 but later they changed their minds.
They took back the men and women they had
freed, forcing them to be slaves again.

12 So the LORD gave them this message
through Jeremiah: 13 "This is what the LORD, the
God of Israel, says: I made a covenant with your
ancestors long ago when I rescued them from
their slavery in Egypt. 14 I told them that every
Hebrew slave must be freed after serving six
years. But your ancestors paid no attention to
me. 15 Recently you repented and did what was
right, following my command. You freed your
slaves and made a solemn covenant with me in
the Temple that bears my name. 16 But now you
have shrugged off your oath and defiled my
name by taking back the men and women you
had freed, forcing them to be slaves once again.

17 "Therefore, this is what the LORD says: Since
you have not obeyed me by setting your countrymen free, I will set you free to be destroyed by
war, disease, and famine. You will be an object of
horror to all the nations of the earth. 18 Because
you have broken the terms of our covenant, I will
cut you apart just as you cut apart the calf when
you walked between its halves to solemnize your
vows. 19 Yes, I will cut you apart, whether you are
officials of Judah or Jerusalem, court officials,
priests, or common people—for you have broken
your oath. 20 I will give you to your enemies, and
they will kill you. Your bodies will be food for the
vultures and wild animals.

21 "I will hand over King Zedekiah of Judah and
his officials to the army of the king of Babylon.
And although they have left Jerusalem for a
while, 22 I will call the Babylonian armies back
again. They will fight against this city and will
capture it and burn it down. I will see to it that all
the towns of Judah are destroyed, with no one living there."

CHAPTER 35
The Faithful Recabites
This is the message the LORD gave Jeremiah
when Jehoiakim son of Josiah was king of Judah:
2 "Go to the settlement where the families of the
Recabites live, and invite them to the LORD's
Temple. Take them into one of the inner rooms,
and offer them some wine."

3 So I went to see Jaazaniah son of Jeremiah
and grandson of Habazziniah and all his brothers and sons—representing all the Recabite families. 4 I took them to the Temple, and we went

into the room assigned to the sons of Hanan son
of Igdaliah, a man of God. This room was located
next to the one used by the Temple officials, directly above the room of Maaseiah son of
Shallum, the Temple gatekeeper.
5I set cups and jugs of wine before them and
invited them to have a drink, 6but they refused.
"No," they said, "we don't drink wine, because
our ancestor Jehonadab son of Recab gave us
this command: 'You and your descendants
must never drink wine. 7And do not build
houses or plant crops or vineyards, but always
live in tents. If you follow these commands, you
will live long, good lives in the land.' 8So we
have obeyed him in all these things. We have
never had a drink of wine to this day, nor have
our wives, our sons, or our daughters. 9We
haven't built houses or owned vineyards or
farms or planted crops. 10We have lived in tents
and have fully obeyed all the commands of
Jehonadab, our ancestor. 11But when King
Nebuchadnezzar of Babylon attacked this
country, we were afraid of the Babylonian and
Syrian armies. So we decided to move to Jerusalem. That is why we are here."
12Then the LORD gave this message to Jeremiah: 13"This is what the LORD of Heaven's
Armies, the God of Israel, says: Go and say to the
people in Judah and Jerusalem, 'Come and learn
a lesson about how to obey me. 14The Recabites
do not drink wine to this day because their ancestor Jehonadab told them not to. But I have
spoken to you again and again, and you refuse to
obey me. 15Time after time I sent you prophets,
who told you, "Turn from your wicked ways, and
start doing things right. Stop worshiping other
gods so that you might live in peace here in the
land I have given to you and your ancestors." But
you would not listen to me or obey me. 16The
descendants of Jehonadab son of Recab have
obeyed their ancestor completely, but you have
refused to listen to me.'
17"Therefore, this is what the LORD God of
Heaven's Armies, the God of Israel, says: 'Because you refuse to listen or answer when I call, I
will send upon Judah and Jerusalem all the disasters I have threatened.'"
18Then Jeremiah turned to the Recabites and
said, "This is what the LORD of Heaven's Armies,
the God of Israel, says: 'You have obeyed your ancestor Jehonadab in every respect, following all
his instructions.' 19Therefore, this is what the
LORD of Heaven's Armies, the God of Israel, says:
'Jehonadab son of Recab will always have descendants who serve me.'"

CHAPTER 36
Baruch Reads the LORD's Messages

During the fourth year that Jehoiakim son of
Josiah was king in Judah, the LORD gave this message to Jeremiah: 2"Get a scroll, and write down
all my messages against Israel, Judah, and the
other nations. Begin with the first message back
in the days of Josiah, and write down every message, right up to the present time. 3Perhaps the
people of Judah will repent when they hear again
all the terrible things I have planned for them.
Then I will be able to forgive their sins and
wrongdoings."
4So Jeremiah sent for Baruch son of Neriah,
and as Jeremiah dictated all the prophecies that
the LORD had given him, Baruch wrote them on a
scroll. 5Then Jeremiah said to Baruch, "I am a
prisoner here and unable to go to the Temple.
6So you go to the Temple on the next day of fasting, and read the messages from the LORD that I
have had you write on this scroll. Read them so
the people who are there from all over Judah will
hear them. 7Perhaps even yet they will turn from
their evil ways and ask the LORD's forgiveness before it is too late. For the LORD has threatened
them with his terrible anger."
8Baruch did as Jeremiah told him and read
these messages from the LORD to the people at
the Temple. 9He did this on a day of sacred fasting held in late autumn, during the fifth year of
the reign of Jehoiakim son of Josiah. People from
all over Judah had come to Jerusalem to attend
the services at the Temple on that day. 10Baruch
read Jeremiah's words on the scroll to all the people. He stood in front of the Temple room of
Gemariah, son of Shaphan the secretary. This
room was just off the upper courtyard of the
Temple, near the New Gate entrance.
11When Micaiah son of Gemariah and grandson of Shaphan heard the messages from the
LORD, 12he went down to the secretary's room in
the palace where the administrative officials
were meeting. Elishama the secretary was there,
along with Delaiah son of Shemaiah, Elnathan
son of Acbor, Gemariah son of Shaphan,
Zedekiah son of Hananiah, and all the other officials. 13When Micaiah told them about the messages Baruch was reading to the people, 14the
officials sent Jehudi son of Nethaniah, grandson
of Shelemiah and great-grandson of Cushi, to ask
Baruch to come and read the messages to them,
too. So Baruch took the scroll and went to them.
15"Sit down and read the scroll to us," the officials
said, and Baruch did as they requested.

Jeremiah 37 . . . page 766

16When they heard all the messages, they looked at one another in alarm. "We must tell the king what we have heard," they said to Baruch. 17"But first, tell us how you got these messages. Did they come directly from Jeremiah?"

18So Baruch explained, "Jeremiah dictated them, and I wrote them down in ink, word for word, on this scroll."

19"You and Jeremiah should both hide," the officials told Baruch. "Don't tell anyone where you are!" 20Then the officials left the scroll for safekeeping in the room of Elishama the secretary and went to tell the king what had happened.

King Jehoiakim Burns the Scroll

21The king sent Jehudi to get the scroll. Jehudi brought it from Elishama's room and read it to the king as all his officials stood by. 22It was late autumn, and the king was in a winterized part of the palace, sitting in front of a fire to keep warm. 23Each time Jehudi finished reading three or four columns, the king took a knife and cut off that section of the scroll. He then threw it into the fire, section by section, until the whole scroll was burned up. 24Neither the king nor his attendants showed any signs of fear or repentance at what they heard. 25Even when Elnathan, Delaiah, and Gemariah begged the king not to burn the scroll, he wouldn't listen.

26Then the king commanded his son Jerahmeel, Seraiah son of Azriel, and Shelemiah son of Abdeel to arrest Baruch and Jeremiah. But the LORD had hidden them.

Jeremiah Rewrites the Scroll

27After the king had burned the scroll on which Baruch had written Jeremiah's words, the LORD gave Jeremiah another message. He said, 28"Get another scroll, and write everything again just as you did on the scroll King Jehoiakim burned. 29Then say to the king, 'This is what the LORD says: You burned the scroll because it said the king of Babylon would destroy this land and empty it of people and animals. 30Now this is what the LORD says about King Jehoiakim of Judah: He will have no heirs to sit on the throne of David. His dead body will be thrown out to lie unburied—exposed to the heat of the day and the frost of the night. 31I will punish him and his family and his attendants for their sins. I will pour out on them and on all the people of Jerusalem and Judah all the disasters I promised, for they would not listen to my warnings.'"

32So Jeremiah took another scroll and dictated again to his secretary, Baruch. He wrote everything that had been on the scroll King Jehoiakim had burned in the fire. Only this time he added much more!

CHAPTER 37

Zedekiah Calls for Jeremiah

Zedekiah son of Josiah succeeded Jehoiachin son of Jehoiakim as the king of Judah. He was appointed by King Nebuchadnezzar of Babylon. 2But neither King Zedekiah nor his attendants nor the people who were left in the land listened to what the LORD said through Jeremiah.

3Nevertheless, King Zedekiah sent Jehucal son of Shelemiah, and Zephaniah the priest, son of Maaseiah, to ask Jeremiah, "Please pray to the LORD our God for us." 4Jeremiah had not yet been imprisoned, so he could come and go among the people as he pleased.

5At this time the army of Pharaoh Hophra of Egypt appeared at the southern border of Judah. When the Babylonian army heard about it, they withdrew from their siege of Jerusalem.

6Then the LORD gave this message to Jeremiah: 7"This is what the LORD, the God of Israel, says: The king of Judah sent you to ask me what is going to happen. Tell him, 'Pharaoh's army is about to return to Egypt, though he came here to help you. 8Then the Babylonians will come back and capture this city and burn it to the ground.'

9"This is what the LORD says: Do not fool yourselves into thinking that the Babylonians are gone for good. They aren't! 10Even if you were to destroy the entire Babylonian army, leaving only a handful of wounded survivors, they would still stagger from their tents and burn this city to the ground!"

Jeremiah Is Imprisoned

11When the Babylonian army left Jerusalem because of Pharaoh's approaching army, 12Jeremiah started to leave the city on his way to the territory of Benjamin, to claim his share of the property among his relatives there. 13But as he was walking through the Benjamin Gate, a sentry arrested him and said, "You are defecting to the Babylonians!" The sentry making the arrest was Irijah son of Shelemiah, grandson of Hananiah.

14"That's not true!" Jeremiah protested. "I had no intention of doing any such thing." But Irijah wouldn't listen, and he took Jeremiah before the officials. 15They were furious with Jeremiah and had him flogged and imprisoned in the house of Jonathan the secretary. Jonathan's house had been converted into a prison. 16Jeremiah was

BIBLE BIOS

Hear From the Heroes

Hi, my name is

JONAH *(prophet)*

"No way! Not a chance! I'm outta here!"

I'm not proud to tell you, but that's pretty much what I said to God when he gave me a job to do. Not only that, I thought I could run away and hide from God. Duh! How could I have been so silly? Here's what happened.

God told me to go to the evil city of Nineveh and tell the people there to stop sinning. But the people there were *really* mean. Plus, they were our enemies. No way did I want to go there! So I got on a boat going in the opposite direction, hid down below, and thought I was safe. But then there was this huge storm, and I finally had to tell the sailors that I thought it was my fault because I was hiding from God. They threw me overboard, and I thought I was a goner!

It wasn't the sailors' idea to throw Jonah into the sea. They didn't want to do it. But Jonah told them to! Read all about the storm in JONAH 1:4-17.

But God sent this big fish to swallow me so I wouldn't drown. 'Course then God let me *stay* inside that fish for three days! Let me tell ya, there's nothing like living in a smelly fish belly to help you see your evil ways. I realized how wrong I had been to disobey God, so I prayed and told God I was ready to obey. Then that fish swam over to the shore and spit me out!

Needless to say, I went straight to Nineveh and told the people to stop sinning or God would destroy them. They listened, and God didn't hurt their city. But I have to admit, that made me mad. I guess you could say I didn't remember my smelly-belly lesson in the fish very well. I thought it was great that God had saved *me* when I disobeyed, but I was mad that he saved the people of Nineveh. God set me straight again, but that's another story.

No, God didn't put Jonah inside another big fish. But he did send a worm! Find out all the details in JONAH 4.

God Is Tops!

Here's a fun way to thank God.

God turned Jonah around in the right direction. **How many times have you disobeyed God, just to have him gently turn you around again?**

Get a toy top, and set it in front of you on a bare floor. Spin the top once, and before it stops spinning, tell God some things you're sorry for. Spin the top again, and ask God to forgive you. Spin the top a third time, and while it's spinning, thank God for forgiving you. **Remember that God is always willing to turn us in the right direction!**

BIBLE BIOS

Hear From the Heroes

Hi, we're the

MINOR PROPHETS *(prophets, what a surprise, huh?)*

My name is Hosea, and these guys with me are the rest of the minor prophets. We're a group of regular guys—there's me (Hosea), and Joel, Amos, Obadiah, Jonah, Micah, Nahum, Habakkuk, Zephaniah, Haggai, Zechariah, and Malachi. Now let me make one thing clear—we're called the "minor" prophets because our writings are much shorter than the other prophets writings, not because we're less important!

Amos was a shepherd when he was called to be a prophet. But we don't even know that much about most of the other minor prophets. All we know is their names and where they lived!

In our day, most of us weren't important people in the world's eyes, but we loved and obeyed God. He told us to give messages to his people and we did. Basically, we all had pretty much the same message. Repent! Stop sinning! Turn back to God! Worship only God! But it wasn't as if all we said was doom and gloom. We also talked about God's mercy and love.

MICAH 6:8 sums up what the prophets tried to tell the people. Read it and see how you measure up!

But few listened. Many of the people had become wealthy and content, and they seemed to forget all about God. Sure, some of them *pretended* to worship God, but it was fake worship. You know what I mean? They just went through the motions. They didn't really love and honor God. We kept warning them that if they didn't turn back to God, he would punish them. (God didn't want to punish them, you understand. In fact, he gave them *tons* of chances to stop sinning and turn back to him.)

Sometimes it was so frustrating to be a prophet! No one listened. No one changed. It was sad. We knew what was going to happen, and there was nothing we could do but keep trying to get the people to turn back to God. Oh well, we did the best we could. We obeyed God and tried our hardest. I guess sometimes that's all you can do.

Pray Today!

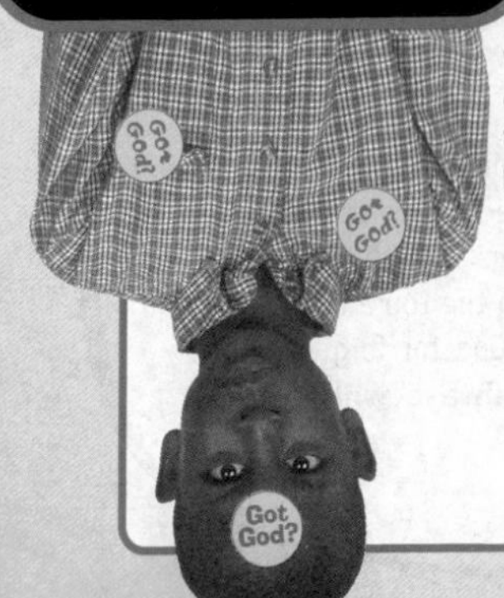

When is it hard for you to keep obeying God? One of the ways the prophets kept going was by praying to God—a lot!

Get some plain round stickers, and write this in the center of each

Got God?

Then put the stickers in places where they will remind you to pray when it's hard to obey God. Maybe you'll put a sticker on your math notebook because you get frustrated with the kid who sits next to you. Or maybe you'll put a sticker on the phone to remind you not to gossip. **Remember: If you've got God, you've got it all!**

put into a dungeon cell, where he remained for
many days.
17 Later King Zedekiah secretly requested that
Jeremiah come to the palace, where the king
asked him, "Do you have any messages from the
LORD?"
"Yes, I do!" said Jeremiah. "You will be defeated by the king of Babylon."
18 Then Jeremiah asked the king, "What crime
have I committed? What have I done against you,
your attendants, or the people that I should be
imprisoned like this? 19 Where are your prophets
now who told you the king of Babylon would not
attack you or this land? 20 Listen, my lord the
king, I beg you. Don't send me back to the dungeon in the house of Jonathan the secretary, for I
will die there."
21 So King Zedekiah commanded that Jeremiah not be returned to the dungeon. Instead, he
was imprisoned in the courtyard of the guard in
the royal palace. The king also commanded that
Jeremiah be given a loaf of fresh bread every day
as long as there was any left in the city. So Jeremiah was put in the palace prison.

CHAPTER 38

Jeremiah in a Cistern

Now Shephatiah son of Mattan, Gedaliah son of
Pashhur, Jehucal son of Shelemiah, and Pashhur
son of Malkijah heard what Jeremiah had been
telling the people. He had been saying, 2 "This is
what the LORD says: 'Everyone who stays in Jerusalem will die from war, famine, or disease, but
those who surrender to the Babylonians will live.
Their reward will be life. They will live!' 3 The
LORD also says: 'The city of Jerusalem will certainly be handed over to the army of the king of
Babylon, who will capture it.'"
4 So these officials went to the king and said,
"Sir, this man must die! That kind of talk will
undermine the morale of the few fighting men
we have left, as well as that of all the people. This
man is a traitor!"
5 King Zedekiah agreed. "All right," he said.
"Do as you like. I can't stop you."
6 So the officials took Jeremiah from his cell
and lowered him by ropes into an empty cistern
in the prison yard. It belonged to Malkijah, a
member of the royal family. There was no water
in the cistern, but there was a thick layer of mud
at the bottom, and Jeremiah sank down into it.
7 But Ebed-melech the Ethiopian, an important court official, heard that Jeremiah was in the
cistern. At that time the king was holding court
at the Benjamin Gate, 8 so Ebed-melech rushed
from the palace to speak with him. 9 "My lord the
king," he said, "these men have done a very evil
thing in putting Jeremiah the prophet into the
cistern. He will soon die of hunger, for almost all
the bread in the city is gone."
10 So the king told Ebed-melech, "Take thirty
of my men with you, and pull Jeremiah out of the
cistern before he dies."
11 So Ebed-melech took the men with him and
went to a room in the palace beneath the treasury,
where he found some old rags and discarded
clothing. He carried these to the cistern and lowered them to Jeremiah on a rope. 12 Ebed-melech
called down to Jeremiah, "Put these rags under
your armpits to protect you from the ropes."
Then when Jeremiah was ready, 13 they pulled
him out. So Jeremiah was returned to the courtyard of the guard—the palace prison—where he
remained.

Zedekiah Questions Jeremiah

14 One day King Zedekiah sent for Jeremiah and
had him brought to the third entrance of the
LORD's Temple. "I want to ask you something,"
the king said. "And don't try to hide the truth."
15 Jeremiah said, "If I tell you the truth, you will
kill me. And if I give you advice, you won't listen
to me anyway."
16 So King Zedekiah secretly promised him,
"As surely as the LORD our Creator lives, I will not
kill you or hand you over to the men who want
you dead."
17 Then Jeremiah said to Zedekiah, "This is
what the LORD God of Heaven's Armies, the God
of Israel, says: 'If you surrender to the Babylonian
officers, you and your family will live, and the city
will not be burned down. 18 But if you refuse to
surrender, you will not escape! This city will be
handed over to the Babylonians, and they will
burn it to the ground.'"
19 "But I am afraid to surrender," the king said,
"for the Babylonians may hand me over to the
Judeans who have defected to them. And who
knows what they will do to me!"
20 Jeremiah replied, "You won't be handed over
to them if you choose to obey the LORD. Your life
will be spared, and all will go well for you. 21 But if
you refuse to surrender, this is what the LORD has
revealed to me: 22 All the women left in your palace will be brought out and given to the officers
of the Babylonian army. Then the women will
taunt you, saying,

'What fine friends you have!
They have betrayed and misled you.

When your feet sank in the mud,
they left you to your fate!'

23All your wives and children will be led out to
the Babylonians, and you will not escape. You
will be seized by the king of Babylon, and this
city will be burned down."

24Then Zedekiah said to Jeremiah, "Don't tell
anyone you told me this, or you will die! 25My officials may hear that I spoke to you, and they may
say, 'Tell us what you and the king were talking
about. If you don't tell us, we will kill you.' 26If
this happens, just tell them you begged me not to
send you back to Jonathan's dungeon, for fear
you would die there."

27Sure enough, it wasn't long before the king's
officials came to Jeremiah and asked him why the
king had called for him. But Jeremiah followed the
king's instructions, and they left without finding
out the truth. No one had overheard the conversation between Jeremiah and the king. 28And Jeremiah remained a prisoner in the courtyard of the
guard until the day Jerusalem was captured.

CHAPTER 39

The Fall of Jerusalem

In January of the ninth year of King Zedekiah's
reign, King Nebuchadnezzar of Babylon came
with his entire army to besiege Jerusalem. 2Two
and a half years later, on July 18 in the eleventh
year of Zedekiah's reign, a section of the city wall
was broken down. 3All the officers of the Babylonian army came in and sat in triumph at the
Middle Gate: Nergal-sharezer of Samgar, and
Nebo-sarsekim, a chief officer, and Nergal-
sharezer, the king's adviser, and all the other
officers of the king of Babylon.

4When King Zedekiah of Judah and all the soldiers saw that the Babylonians had broken into
the city, they fled. They waited for nightfall and
then slipped through the gate between the two
walls behind the king's garden and headed toward the Jordan Valley.

5But the Babylonian troops chased them and
overtook Zedekiah on the plains of Jericho. They
captured him and took him to King Nebuchadnezzar of Babylon, who was at Riblah in the land
of Hamath. There the king of Babylon pronounced judgment upon Zedekiah. 6The king of
Babylon made Zedekiah watch as he slaughtered
his sons at Riblah. The king of Babylon also
slaughtered all the nobles of Judah. 7Then he
gouged out Zedekiah's eyes and bound him in
bronze chains to lead him away to Babylon.

8Meanwhile, the Babylonians burned Jerusalem, including the royal palace and the houses
of the people, and they tore down the walls of
the city. 9Then Nebuzaradan, the captain of the
guard, took as exiles to Babylon the rest of the
people who remained in the city, those who had
defected to him, and everyone else who remained.
10But Nebuzaradan allowed some of the poorest
people to stay behind in the land of Judah, and he
assigned them to care for the vineyards and fields.

Jeremiah Remains in Judah

11King Nebuchadnezzar had told Nebuzaradan,
the captain of the guard, to find Jeremiah. 12"See
that he isn't hurt," he said. "Look after him well,
and give him anything he wants." 13So Nebuzaradan, the captain of the guard; Nebushazban, a
chief officer; Nergal-sharezer, the king's adviser;
and the other officers of Babylon's king 14sent
messengers to bring Jeremiah out of the prison.
They put him under the care of Gedaliah son of
Ahikam and grandson of Shaphan, who took him
back to his home. So Jeremiah stayed in Judah
among his own people.

15The LORD had given the following message to
Jeremiah while he was still in prison: 16"Say to
Ebed-melech the Ethiopian, 'This is what the
LORD of Heaven's Armies, the God of Israel, says: I
will do to this city everything I have threatened. I
will send disaster, not prosperity. You will see its
destruction, 17but I will rescue you from those
you fear so much. 18Because you trusted me, I will
give you your life as a reward. I will rescue you
and keep you safe. I, the LORD, have spoken!'"

CHAPTER 40

The LORD gave a message to Jeremiah after
Nebuzaradan, the captain of the guard, had released him at Ramah. He had found Jeremiah
bound in chains among all the other captives of
Jerusalem and Judah who were being sent to exile in Babylon.

2The captain of the guard called for Jeremiah
and said, "The LORD your God has brought this disaster on this land, 3just as he said he would. For
these people have sinned against the LORD and
disobeyed him. That is why it happened. 4But I
am going to take off your chains and let you go. If
you want to come with me to Babylon, you are
welcome. I will see that you are well cared for. But
if you don't want to come, you may stay here. The
whole land is before you—go wherever you like.
5If you decide to stay, then return to Gedaliah son
of Ahikam and grandson of Shaphan. He has
been appointed governor of Judah by the king of

Babylon. Stay there with the people he rules. But
it's up to you; go wherever you like."
Then Nebuzaradan, the captain of the guard,
gave Jeremiah some food and money and let him
go. 6So Jeremiah returned to Gedaliah son of
Ahikam at Mizpah, and he lived in Judah with the
few who were still left in the land.

Gedaliah Governs in Judah

7The leaders of the Judean guerrilla bands in the
countryside heard that the king of Babylon had
appointed Gedaliah son of Ahikam as governor
over the poor people who were left behind in Judah—the men, women, and children who hadn't
been exiled to Babylon. 8So they went to see
Gedaliah at Mizpah. These included: Ishmael
son of Nethaniah, Johanan and Jonathan sons of
Kareah, Seraiah son of Tanhumeth, the sons of
Ephai the Netophathite, Jezaniah son of the
Maacathite, and all their men.
9Gedaliah vowed to them that the Babylonians
meant them no harm. "Don't be afraid to serve
them. Live in the land and serve the king of Babylon, and all will go well for you," he promised.
10"As for me, I will stay at Mizpah to represent
you before the Babylonians who come to meet
with us. Settle in the towns you have taken, and
live off the land. Harvest the grapes and summer
fruits and olives, and store them away."
11When the Judeans in Moab, Ammon, Edom,
and the other nearby countries heard that the
king of Babylon had left a few people in Judah
and that Gedaliah was the governor, 12they began to return to Judah from the places to which
they had fled. They stopped at Mizpah to meet
with Gedaliah and then went into the Judean
countryside to gather a great harvest of grapes
and other crops.

A Plot against Gedaliah

13Soon after this, Johanan son of Kareah and the
other guerrilla leaders came to Gedaliah at
Mizpah. 14They said to him, "Did you know that
Baalis, king of Ammon, has sent Ishmael son of
Nethaniah to assassinate you?" But Gedaliah refused to believe them.
15Later Johanan had a private conference with
Gedaliah and volunteered to kill Ishmael secretly. "Why should we let him come and murder
you?" Johanan asked. "What will happen then to
the Judeans who have returned? Why should the
few of us who are still left be scattered and lost?"
16But Gedaliah said to Johanan, "I forbid you
to do any such thing, for you are lying about
Ishmael."

CHAPTER **41**

The Murder of Gedaliah

But in midautumn of that year, Ishmael son of
Nethaniah and grandson of Elishama, who was a
member of the royal family and had been one of
the king's high officials, went to Mizpah with ten
men to meet Gedaliah. While they were eating
together, 2Ishmael and his ten men suddenly
jumped up, drew their swords, and killed
Gedaliah, whom the king of Babylon had appointed governor. 3Ishmael also killed all the
Judeans and the Babylonian soldiers who were
with Gedaliah at Mizpah.
4The next day, before anyone had heard about
Gedaliah's murder, 5eighty men arrived from
Shechem, Shiloh, and Samaria to worship at the
Temple of the LORD. They had shaved off their
beards, torn their clothes, and cut themselves,
and had brought along grain offerings and
frankincense. 6Ishmael left Mizpah to meet
them, weeping as he went. When he reached
them, he said, "Oh, come and see what has happened to Gedaliah!"
7But as soon as they were all inside the town,
Ishmael and his men killed all but ten of them
and threw their bodies into a cistern. 8The other
ten had talked Ishmael into letting them go by
promising to bring him their stores of wheat,
barley, olive oil, and honey that they had hidden
away. 9The cistern where Ishmael dumped the
bodies of the men he murdered was the large
one dug by King Asa when he fortified Mizpah to
protect himself against King Baasha of Israel.
Ishmael son of Nethaniah filled it with corpses.
10Then Ishmael made captives of the king's
daughters and the other people who had been
left under Gedaliah's care in Mizpah by Nebuzaradan, the captain of the guard. Taking them
with him, he started back toward the land of
Ammon.
11But when Johanan son of Kareah and the
other guerrilla leaders heard about Ishmael's
crimes, 12they took all their men and set out to
stop him. They caught up with him at the large
pool near Gibeon. 13The people Ishmael had captured shouted for joy when they saw Johanan and
the other guerrilla leaders. 14And all the captives
from Mizpah escaped and began to help Johanan.
15Meanwhile, Ishmael and eight of his men escaped from Johanan into the land of Ammon.
16Then Johanan son of Kareah and the other
guerrilla leaders took all the people they had rescued in Gibeon—the soldiers, women, children,
and court officials whom Ishmael had captured
after he killed Gedaliah. 17They took them all to

the village of Geruth-kimham near Bethlehem,
where they prepared to leave for Egypt. 18They
were afraid of what the Babylonians would do
when they heard that Ishmael had killed
Gedaliah, the governor appointed by the Babylonian king.

CHAPTER **42**

Warning to Stay in Judah

Then all the guerrilla leaders, including Johanan
son of Kareah and Jezaniah son of Hoshaiah, and
all the people, from the least to the greatest, approached 2Jeremiah the prophet. They said,
"Please pray to the LORD your God for us. As you
can see, we are only a tiny remnant compared to
what we were before. 3Pray that the LORD your
God will show us what to do and where to go."

4"All right," Jeremiah replied. "I will pray to the
LORD your God, as you have asked, and I will tell
you everything he says. I will hide nothing from
you."

5Then they said to Jeremiah, "May the LORD
your God be a faithful witness against us if we refuse to obey whatever he tells us to do! 6Whether
we like it or not, we will obey the LORD our God to
whom we are sending you with our plea. For if we
obey him, everything will turn out well for us."

7Ten days later the LORD gave his reply to Jeremiah. 8So he called for Johanan son of Kareah
and the other guerrilla leaders, and for all the
people, from the least to the greatest. 9He said to
them, "You sent me to the LORD, the God of Israel,
with your request, and this is his reply: 10'Stay
here in this land. If you do, I will build you up and
not tear you down; I will plant you and not uproot
you. For I am sorry about all the punishment I
have had to bring upon you. 11Do not fear the
king of Babylon anymore,' says the LORD. 'For I am
with you and will save you and rescue you from
his power. 12I will be merciful to you by making
him kind, so he will let you stay here in your land.'

13"But if you refuse to obey the LORD your God,
and if you say, 'We will not stay here; 14instead, we
will go to Egypt where we will be free from war,
the call to arms, and hunger,' 15then hear the
LORD's message to the remnant of Judah. This is
what the LORD of Heaven's Armies, the God of Israel, says: 'If you are determined to go to Egypt
and live there, 16the very war and famine you fear
will catch up to you, and you will die there. 17That
is the fate awaiting every one of you who insists
on going to live in Egypt. Yes, you will die from
war, famine, and disease. None of you will escape
the disaster I will bring upon you there.'

18"This is what the LORD of Heaven's Armies,
the God of Israel, says: 'Just as my anger and fury
have been poured out on the people of Jerusalem, so they will be poured out on you when you
enter Egypt. You will be an object of damnation,
horror, cursing, and mockery. And you will never
see your homeland again.'

19"Listen, you remnant of Judah. The LORD has
told you: 'Do not go to Egypt!' Don't forget this
warning I have given you today. 20For you were
not being honest when you sent me to pray to the
LORD your God for you. You said, 'Just tell us what
the LORD our God says, and we will do it!' 21And
today I have told you exactly what he said, but
you will not obey the LORD your God any better
now than you have in the past. 22So you can be
sure that you will die from war, famine, and disease in Egypt, where you insist on going."

CHAPTER **43**

Jeremiah Taken to Egypt

When Jeremiah had finished giving this message
from the LORD their God to all the people,
2Azariah son of Hoshaiah and Johanan son of
Kareah and all the other proud men said to Jeremiah, "You lie! The LORD our God hasn't forbidden us to go to Egypt! 3Baruch son of Neriah has
convinced you to say this, because he wants us to
stay here and be killed by the Babylonians or be
carried off into exile."

4So Johanan and the other guerrilla leaders
and all the people refused to obey the LORD's
command to stay in Judah. 5Johanan and the
other leaders took with them all the people who
had returned from the nearby countries to which
they had fled. 6In the crowd were men, women,
and children, the king's daughters, and all those
whom Nebuzaradan, the captain of the guard,
had left with Gedaliah. The prophet Jeremiah and
Baruch were also included. 7The people refused
to obey the voice of the LORD and went to Egypt,
going as far as the city of Tahpanhes.

8Then at Tahpanhes, the LORD gave another
message to Jeremiah. He said, 9"While the people of Judah are watching, take some large rocks
and bury them under the pavement stones at the
entrance of Pharaoh's palace here in Tahpanhes.
10Then say to the people of Judah, 'This is what
the LORD of Heaven's Armies, the God of Israel,
says: I will certainly bring my servant Nebuchadnezzar, king of Babylon, here to Egypt. I will set
his throne over these stones that I have hidden.
He will spread his royal canopy over them. 11And
when he comes, he will destroy the land of Egypt.
He will bring death to those destined for death,
captivity to those destined for captivity, and war

to those destined for war. 12He will set fire to the
temples of Egypt's gods; he will burn the temples
and carry the idols away as plunder. He will pick
clean the land of Egypt as a shepherd picks fleas
from his cloak. And he himself will leave unharmed. 13He will break down the sacred pillars
standing in the temple of the sun in Egypt, and he
will burn down the temples of Egypt's gods.'"

CHAPTER 44

Judgment for Idolatry

This is the message Jeremiah received concerning the Judeans living in northern Egypt in the
cities of Migdol, Tahpanhes, and Memphis, and
in southern Egypt as well: 2"This is what the
LORD of Heaven's Armies, the God of Israel, says:
You saw the calamity I brought on Jerusalem and
all the towns of Judah. They now lie deserted and
in ruins. 3They provoked my anger with all their
wickedness. They burned incense and worshiped other gods—gods that neither they nor
you nor any of your ancestors had ever even
known.

4"Again and again I sent my servants, the
prophets, to plead with them, 'Don't do these
horrible things that I hate so much.' 5But my
people would not listen or turn back from their
wicked ways. They kept on burning incense to
these gods. 6And so my fury boiled over and fell
like fire on the towns of Judah and into the
streets of Jerusalem, and they are still a desolate
ruin today.

7"And now the LORD God of Heaven's Armies,
the God of Israel, asks you: Why are you destroying yourselves? For not one of you will survive—
not a man, woman, or child among you who has
come here from Judah, not even the babies in
your arms. 8Why provoke my anger by burning
incense to the idols you have made here in
Egypt? You will only destroy yourselves and
make yourselves an object of cursing and mockery for all the nations of the earth. 9Have you forgotten the sins of your ancestors, the sins of the
kings and queens of Judah, and the sins you and
your wives committed in Judah and Jerusalem?
10To this very hour you have shown no remorse
or reverence. No one has chosen to follow my
word and the decrees I gave to you and your ancestors before you.

11"Therefore, this is what the LORD of Heaven's
Armies, the God of Israel, says: I am determined
to destroy every one of you! 12I will take this
remnant of Judah—those who were determined
to come here and live in Egypt—and I will consume them. They will fall here in Egypt, killed
by war and famine. All will die, from the least
to the greatest. They will be an object of damnation, horror, cursing, and mockery. 13I will punish them in Egypt just as I punished them in
Jerusalem, by war, famine, and disease. 14Of that
remnant who fled to Egypt, hoping someday to return to Judah, there will be no survivors. Even
though they long to return home, only a handful
will do so."

15Then all the women present and all the men
who knew that their wives had burned incense to
idols—a great crowd of all the Judeans living in
northern Egypt and southern Egypt—answered
Jeremiah, 16"We will not listen to your messages
from the LORD! 17We will do whatever we want.
We will burn incense and pour out liquid offerings to the Queen of Heaven just as much as we
like—just as we, and our ancestors, and our kings
and officials have always done in the towns of Judah and in the streets of Jerusalem. For in those
days we had plenty to eat, and we were well off
and had no troubles! 18But ever since we quit
burning incense to the Queen of Heaven and
stopped worshiping her with liquid offerings, we
have been in great trouble and have been dying
from war and famine."

19"Besides," the women added, "do you suppose that we were burning incense and pouring
out liquid offerings to the Queen of Heaven, and
making cakes marked with her image, without
our husbands knowing it and helping us? Of
course not!"

20Then Jeremiah said to all of them, men and
women alike, who had given him that answer,
21"Do you think the LORD did not know that you
and your ancestors, your kings and officials, and
all the people were burning incense to idols in
the towns of Judah and in the streets of Jerusalem? 22It was because the LORD could no longer
bear all the disgusting things you were doing that
he made your land an object of cursing—a desolate ruin without inhabitants—as it is today. 23All
these terrible things happened to you because
you have burned incense to idols and sinned
against the LORD. You have refused to obey him
and have not followed his instructions, his decrees, and his laws."

24Then Jeremiah said to them all, including
the women, "Listen to this message from the
LORD, all you citizens of Judah who live in Egypt.
25This is what the LORD of Heaven's Armies, the
God of Israel, says: 'You and your wives have said,
"We will keep our promises to burn incense
and pour out liquid offerings to the Queen of
Heaven," and you have proved by your actions

that you meant it. So go ahead and carry out your
promises and vows to her!'

26 "But listen to this message from the LORD, all
you Judeans now living in Egypt: 'I have sworn by
my great name,' says the LORD, 'that my name will
no longer be spoken by any of the Judeans in the
land of Egypt. None of you may invoke my name
or use this oath: "As surely as the Sovereign LORD
lives." 27 For I will watch over you to bring you disaster and not good. Everyone from Judah who is
now living in Egypt will suffer war and famine
until all of you are dead. 28 Only a small number
will escape death and return to Judah from
Egypt. Then all those who came to Egypt will find
out whose words are true—mine or theirs!

29 "'And this is the proof I give you,' says the
LORD, 'that all I have threatened will happen to
you and that I will punish you here.' 30 This is
what the LORD says: 'I will turn Pharaoh Hophra,
king of Egypt, over to his enemies who want to
kill him, just as I turned King Zedekiah of Judah
over to King Nebuchadnezzar of Babylon.'"

CHAPTER 45
A Message for Baruch

The prophet Jeremiah gave a message to Baruch
son of Neriah in the fourth year of the reign of
Jehoiakim son of Josiah, after Baruch had written down everything Jeremiah had dictated to
him. He said, 2 "This is what the LORD, the God
of Israel, says to you, Baruch: 3 You have said, 'I
am overwhelmed with trouble! Haven't I had
enough pain already? And now the LORD has
added more! I am worn out from sighing and
can find no rest.'

4 "Baruch, this is what the LORD says: 'I will destroy this nation that I built. I will uproot what I
planted. 5 Are you seeking great things for yourself? Don't do it! I will bring great disaster upon all
these people; but I will give you your life as a reward wherever you go. I, the LORD, have spoken!'"

CHAPTER 46
Messages for the Nations

The following messages were given to Jeremiah
the prophet from the LORD concerning foreign
nations.

Messages about Egypt

2 This message concerning Egypt was given in
the fourth year of the reign of Jehoiakim son of
Josiah, the king of Judah, on the occasion of the
battle of Carchemish when Pharaoh Neco, king
of Egypt, and his army were defeated beside the
Euphrates River by King Nebuchadnezzar of
Babylon.

3 "Prepare your shields,
 and advance into battle!
4 Harness the horses,
 and mount the stallions.
Take your positions.
 Put on your helmets.
Sharpen your spears,
 and prepare your armor.
5 But what do I see?
 The Egyptian army flees in terror.
The bravest of its fighting men run
 without a backward glance.
They are terrorized at every turn,"
 says the LORD.
6 "The swiftest runners cannot flee;
 the mightiest warriors cannot escape.
By the Euphrates River to the north,
 they stumble and fall.
7 "Who is this, rising like the Nile at floodtime,
 overflowing all the land?
8 It is the Egyptian army,
 overflowing all the land,
boasting that it will cover the earth
 like a flood,
 destroying cities and their people.
9 Charge, you horses and chariots;
 attack, you mighty warriors of Egypt!
Come, all you allies from Ethiopia, Libya,
 and Lydia
 who are skilled with the shield and bow!
10 For this is the day of the Lord, the LORD of
 Heaven's Armies,
 a day of vengeance on his enemies.
The sword will devour until it is satisfied,
 yes, until it is drunk with your blood!
The Lord, the LORD of Heaven's Armies, will
 receive a sacrifice today
 in the north country beside the
 Euphrates River.

11 "Go up to Gilead to get medicine,
 O virgin daughter of Egypt!
But your many treatments
 will bring you no healing.
12 The nations have heard of your shame.
 The earth is filled with your cries of despair.
Your mightiest warriors will run into
 each other
 and fall down together."

13 Then the LORD gave the prophet Jeremiah
this message about King Nebuchadnezzar's
plans to attack Egypt.

14 "Shout it out in Egypt!
Publish it in the cities of Migdol,
Memphis, and Tahpanhes!
Mobilize for battle,
for the sword will devour everyone around you.
15 Why have your warriors fallen?
They cannot stand, for the LORD
has knocked them down.
16 They stumble and fall over each other
and say among themselves,
'Come, let's go back to our people,
to the land of our birth.
Let's get away from the sword of the enemy!'
17 There they will say,
'Pharaoh, the king of Egypt, is a loudmouth
who missed his opportunity!'

18 "As surely as I live," says the King,
whose name is the LORD of Heaven's Armies,
"one is coming against Egypt
who is as tall as Mount Tabor,
or as Mount Carmel by the sea!
19 Pack up! Get ready to leave for exile,
you citizens of Egypt!
The city of Memphis will be destroyed,
without a single inhabitant.
20 Egypt is as sleek as a beautiful heifer,
but a horsefly from the north is on its way!
21 Egypt's mercenaries have become like
fattened calves.
They, too, will turn and run,
for it is a day of great disaster for Egypt,
a time of great punishment.
22 Egypt flees, silent as a serpent gliding away.
The invading army marches in;
they come against her with axes like
woodsmen.
23 They will cut down her people like trees,"
says the LORD,
"for they are more numerous than locusts.
24 Egypt will be humiliated;
she will be handed over to people from
the north."

25 The LORD of Heaven's Armies, the God of Israel, says: "I will punish Amon, the god of
Thebes, and all the other gods of Egypt. I will
punish its rulers and Pharaoh, too, and all who
trust in him. 26 I will hand them over to those
who want them killed—to King Nebuchadnezzar of Babylon and his army. But afterward the
land will recover from the ravages of war. I, the
LORD, have spoken!

27 "But do not be afraid, Jacob, my servant;
do not be dismayed, Israel.
For I will bring you home again from
distant lands,
and your children will return from their
exile.
Israel will return to a life of peace and quiet,
and no one will terrorize them.
28 Do not be afraid, Jacob, my servant,
for I am with you," says the LORD.
"I will completely destroy the nations to
which I have exiled you,
but I will not completely destroy you.
I will discipline you, but with justice;
I cannot let you go unpunished."

CHAPTER 47
A Message about Philistia

This is the LORD's message to the prophet Jeremiah concerning the Philistines of Gaza, before
it was captured by the Egyptian army. 2 This is
what the LORD says:

"A flood is coming from the north
to overflow the land.
It will destroy the land and everything in it—
cities and people alike.
People will scream in terror,
and everyone in the land will wail.
3 Hear the clatter of stallions' hooves
and the rumble of wheels as the chariots
rush by.
Terrified fathers run madly,
without a backward glance at their
helpless children.

4 "The time has come for the Philistines
to be destroyed,
along with their allies from Tyre and Sidon.
Yes, the LORD is destroying the remnant
of the Philistines,
those colonists from the island of Crete.
5 Gaza will be humiliated, its head shaved bald;
Ashkelon will lie silent.
You remnant from the Mediterranean coast,
how long will you cut yourselves in mourning?

6 "Now, O sword of the LORD,
when will you be at rest again?
Go back into your sheath;
rest and be still.

7 "But how can it be still
when the LORD has sent it on a mission?
For the city of Ashkelon
and the people living along the sea
must be destroyed."

CHAPTER **48**

A Message about Moab

This message was given concerning Moab. This is what the LORD of Heaven's Armies, the God of Israel, says:

"What sorrow awaits the city of Nebo;
it will soon lie in ruins.
The city of Kiriathaim will be humiliated
and captured;
the fortress will be humiliated and
broken down.
2 No one will ever brag about Moab again,
for in Heshbon there is a plot to
destroy her.
'Come,' they say, 'we will cut her off from
being a nation.'
The town of Madmen, too, will be silenced;
the sword will follow you there.
3 Listen to the cries from Horonaim,
cries of devastation and great destruction.
4 All Moab is destroyed.
Her little ones will cry out.
5 Her refugees weep bitterly,
climbing the slope to Luhith.
They cry out in terror,
descending the slope to Horonaim.
6 Flee for your lives!
Hide in the wilderness!
7 Because you have trusted in your wealth
and skill,
you will be taken captive.
Your god Chemosh, with his priests
and officials,
will be hauled off to distant lands!

8 "All the towns will be destroyed,
and no one will escape—
either on the plateaus or in the valleys,
for the LORD has spoken.
9 Oh, that Moab had wings
so she could fly away,
for her towns will be left empty,
with no one living in them.
10 Cursed are those who refuse to do the LORD's
work,
who hold back their swords from
shedding blood!

11 "From his earliest history, Moab has lived
in peace,
never going into exile.
He is like wine that has been allowed to settle.
He has not been poured from flask
to flask,
and he is now fragrant and smooth.

It's as if the people were driving the wrong way down God's one-way street!

God told people to worship only him. Instead, they worshiped other gods. God told them to take care of others. Instead, they mistreated others. Wrong way! So God sent prophets to tell the people the right way to live.

Which direction are you traveling? Are you being selfish? hurting others? lying? Turn around and go God's way!

Make a street sign to help you remember which way to go.

Cut a big arrow out of poster board. On it, write, "One Way—God's Way!" Think of ways you've been heading in the wrong direction. Then tell God you want to turn around and go his way. Hang the sign where it will remind you to go God's way!

12 But the time is coming soon," says the LORD,
"when I will send men to pour him
from his jar.
They will pour him out,
then shatter the jar!
13 At last Moab will be ashamed of his
idol Chemosh,
as the people of Israel were ashamed
of their gold calf at Bethel.
14 "You used to boast, 'We are heroes,
mighty men of war.'

15 But now Moab and his towns will be
destroyed.
His most promising youth are doomed
to slaughter,"
says the King, whose name is the LORD
of Heaven's Armies.
16 "Destruction is coming fast for Moab;
calamity threatens ominously.
17 You friends of Moab,
weep for him and cry!
See how the strong scepter is broken,
how the beautiful staff is shattered!

18 "Come down from your glory
and sit in the dust, you people of Dibon,
for those who destroy Moab will shatter
Dibon, too.
They will tear down all your towers.
19 You people of Aroer,
stand beside the road and watch.
Shout to those who flee from Moab,
'What has happened there?'

20 "And the reply comes back,
'Moab lies in ruins, disgraced;
weep and wail!
Tell it by the banks of the Arnon River:
Moab has been destroyed!'
21 Judgment has been poured out on the
towns of the plateau—
on Holon and Jahaz and Mephaath,
22 on Dibon and Nebo and Beth-diblathaim,
23 on Kiriathaim and Beth-gamul and
Beth-meon,
24 on Kerioth and Bozrah—
all the towns of Moab, far and near.

25 "The strength of Moab has ended.
His arm has been broken," says the LORD.
26 "Let him stagger and fall like a drunkard,
for he has rebelled against the LORD.
Moab will wallow in his own vomit,
ridiculed by all.
27 Did you not ridicule the people of Israel?
Were they caught in the company
of thieves
that you should despise them as you do?

28 "You people of Moab,
flee from your towns and live
in the caves.
Hide like doves that nest
in the clefts of the rocks.
29 We have all heard of the pride of Moab,
for his pride is very great.
We know of his lofty pride,
his arrogance, and his haughty heart.
30 I know about his insolence,"
says the LORD,
"but his boasts are empty—
as empty as his deeds.
31 So now I wail for Moab;
yes, I will mourn for Moab.
My heart is broken for the men
of Kir-hareseth.

32 "You people of Sibmah, rich in vineyards,
I will weep for you even more than I did
for Jazer.
Your spreading vines once reached as far
as the Dead Sea,
but the destroyer has stripped you bare!
He has harvested your grapes and
summer fruits.
33 Joy and gladness are gone from fruitful
Moab.
The presses yield no wine.
No one treads the grapes with shouts of joy.
There is shouting, yes, but not of joy.

34 "Instead, their awful cries of terror can be
heard from Heshbon clear across to Elealeh and
Jahaz; from Zoar all the way to Horonaim and
Eglath-shelishiyah. Even the waters of Nimrim
are dried up now.
35 "I will put an end to Moab," says the LORD,
"for the people offer sacrifices at the pagan
shrines and burn incense to their false gods.
36 My heart moans like a flute for Moab and Kir-
hareseth, for all their wealth has disappeared.
37 The people shave their heads and beards in
mourning. They slash their hands and put on
clothes made of burlap. 38 There is crying and
sorrow in every Moabite home and on every
street. For I have smashed Moab like an old, unwanted jar. 39 How it is shattered! Hear the wailing! See the shame of Moab! It has become an
object of ridicule, an example of ruin to all its
neighbors."
40 This is what the LORD says:

"Look! The enemy swoops down like
an eagle,
spreading his wings over Moab.
41 Its cities will fall,
and its strongholds will be seized.
Even the mightiest warriors will be
in anguish
like a woman in labor.
42 Moab will no longer be a nation,
for it has boasted against the LORD.
43 "Terror and traps and snares will be your lot,
O Moab," says the LORD.

44 "Those who flee in terror will fall into a trap,
and those who escape the trap will step
into a snare.
I will see to it that you do not get away,
for the time of your judgment has come,"
says the LORD.
45 "The people flee as far as Heshbon
but are unable to go on.
For a fire comes from Heshbon,
King Sihon's ancient home,
to devour the entire land
with all its rebellious people.
46 "What sorrow awaits you, O people of Moab!
The people of the god Chemosh are
destroyed!
Your sons and your daughters
have been taken away as captives.
47 But I will restore the fortunes of Moab
in days to come.
I, the LORD, have spoken!"

This is the end of Jeremiah's prophecy concerning Moab.

CHAPTER 49

A Message about Ammon

This message was given concerning the Ammonites. This is what the LORD says:

"Are there no descendants of Israel
to inherit the land of Gad?
Why are you, who worship Molech,
living in its towns?
2 In the days to come," says the LORD,
"I will sound the battle cry against your
city of Rabbah.
It will become a desolate heap of ruins,
and the neighboring towns will be burned.
Then Israel will take back the land
you took from her," says the LORD.
3 "Cry out, O Heshbon,
for the town of Ai is destroyed.
Weep, O people of Rabbah!
Put on your clothes of mourning.
Weep and wail, hiding in the hedges,
for your god Molech, with his priests and
officials,
will be hauled off to distant lands.
4 You are proud of your fertile valleys,
but they will soon be ruined.
You trusted in your wealth,
you rebellious daughter,
and thought no one could ever harm you.
5 But look! I will bring terror upon you,"
says the Lord, the LORD of Heaven's Armies.
"Your neighbors will chase you from your land,
and no one will help your exiles as they flee.
6 But I will restore the fortunes of the
Ammonites
in days to come.
I, the LORD, have spoken."

Messages about Edom

7 This message was given concerning Edom. This is what the LORD of Heaven's Armies says:

"Is there no wisdom in Teman?
Is no one left to give wise counsel?
8 Turn and flee!
Hide in deep caves, you people of Dedan!
For when I bring disaster on Edom,
I will punish you, too!
9 Those who harvest grapes
always leave a few for the poor.
If thieves came at night,
they would not take everything.
10 But I will strip bare the land of Edom,
and there will be no place left to hide.
Its children, its brothers, and its neighbors
will all be destroyed,
and Edom itself will be no more.
11 But I will protect the orphans who remain
among you.
Your widows, too, can depend on me
for help."

12 And this is what the LORD says: "If the innocent must suffer, how much more must you! You
will not go unpunished! You must drink this cup
of judgment! 13 For I have sworn by my own
name," says the LORD, "that Bozrah will become
an object of horror and a heap of ruins; it will be
mocked and cursed. All its towns and villages
will be desolate forever."

14 I have heard a message from the LORD
that an ambassador was sent to the
nations to say,
"Form a coalition against Edom,
and prepare for battle!"
15 The LORD says to Edom,
"I will cut you down to size among
the nations.
You will be despised by all.
16 You have been deceived
by the fear you inspire in others
and by your own pride.
You live in a rock fortress
and control the mountain heights.
But even if you make your nest among the
peaks with the eagles,

I will bring you crashing down,"
says the LORD.

17 "Edom will be an object of horror.
All who pass by will be appalled
and will gasp at the destruction they
see there.
18 It will be like the destruction of Sodom
and Gomorrah
and their neighboring towns,"
says the LORD.
"No one will live there;
no one will inhabit it.
19 I will come like a lion from the thickets of the
Jordan,
leaping on the sheep in the pasture.
I will chase Edom from its land,
and I will appoint the leader of my choice.
For who is like me, and who can
challenge me?
What ruler can oppose my will?"
20 Listen to the LORD's plans against Edom
and the people of Teman.
Even the little children will be dragged off
like sheep,
and their homes will be destroyed.
21 The earth will shake with the noise of
Edom's fall,
and its cry of despair will be heard all the
way to the Red Sea.
22 Look! The enemy swoops down like an eagle,
spreading his wings over Bozrah.
Even the mightiest warriors will be in
anguish
like a woman in labor.

A Message about Damascus

23 This message was given concerning Damascus. This is what the LORD says:

"The towns of Hamath and Arpad are
struck with fear,
for they have heard the news of their
destruction.
Their hearts are troubled
like a wild sea in a raging storm.
24 Damascus has become feeble,
and all her people turn to flee.
Fear, anguish, and pain have gripped her
as they grip a woman in labor.
25 That famous city, a city of joy,
will be forsaken!
26 Her young men will fall in the streets and die.
Her soldiers will all be killed,"
says the LORD of Heaven's Armies.
27 "And I will set fire to the walls of Damascus
that will burn up the palaces of Ben-hadad."

A Message about Kedar and Hazor

28 This message was given concerning Kedar and
the kingdoms of Hazor, which were attacked by
King Nebuchadnezzar of Babylon. This is what
the LORD says:

"Advance against Kedar!
Destroy the warriors from the East!
29 Their flocks and tents will be captured,
and their household goods and camels
will be taken away.
Everywhere shouts of panic will be heard:
'We are terrorized at every turn!'
30 Run for your lives," says the LORD.
"Hide yourselves in deep caves, you people
of Hazor,
for King Nebuchadnezzar of Babylon has
plotted against you
and is preparing to destroy you.

31 "Go up and attack that complacent nation,"
says the LORD.
"Its people live alone in the desert
without walls or gates.
32 Their camels and other livestock will
all be yours.
I will scatter to the winds these people
who live in remote places.
I will bring calamity upon them
from every direction," says the LORD.
33 "Hazor will be inhabited by jackals,
and it will be desolate forever.
No one will live there;
no one will inhabit it."

A Message about Elam

34 This message concerning Elam came to the
prophet Jeremiah from the LORD at the beginning of the reign of King Zedekiah of Judah.
35 This is what the LORD of Heaven's Armies says:

"I will destroy the archers of Elam—
the best of their forces.
36 I will bring enemies from all directions,
and I will scatter the people of Elam
to the four winds.
They will be exiled to countries around
the world.
37 I myself will go with Elam's enemies
to shatter it.
In my fierce anger, I will bring great disaster
upon the people of Elam," says the LORD.

"Their enemies will chase them with
the sword
until I have destroyed them completely.
38 I will set my throne in Elam," says the LORD,
"and I will destroy its king and officials.
39 But I will restore the fortunes of Elam
in days to come.
I, the LORD, have spoken!"

CHAPTER 50

A Message about Babylon

The LORD gave Jeremiah the prophet this message concerning Babylon and the land of the
Babylonians. 2 This is what the LORD says:

"Tell the whole world,
and keep nothing back.
Raise a signal flag
to tell everyone that Babylon will fall!
Her images and idols will be shattered.
Her gods Bel and Marduk will be utterly
disgraced.
3 For a nation will attack her from the north
and bring such destruction that no one
will live there again.
Everything will be gone;
both people and animals will flee.

Hope for Israel and Judah

4 "In those coming days,"
says the LORD,
"the people of Israel will return home
together with the people of Judah.
They will come weeping
and seeking the LORD their God.
5 They will ask the way to Jerusalem
and will start back home again.
They will bind themselves to the LORD
with an eternal covenant that will never
be forgotten.

6 "My people have been lost sheep.
Their shepherds have led them astray
and turned them loose in the mountains.
They have lost their way
and can't remember how to get back
to the sheepfold.
7 All who found them devoured them.
Their enemies said,
'We did nothing wrong in attacking them,
for they sinned against the LORD,
their true place of rest,
and the hope of their ancestors.'

8 "But now, flee from Babylon!
Leave the land of the Babylonians.
Like male goats at the head of the flock,
lead my people home again.
9 For I am raising up an army
of great nations from the north.
They will join forces to attack Babylon,
and she will be captured.
The enemies' arrows will go straight
to the mark;
they will not miss!
10 Babylonia will be looted
until the attackers are glutted with loot.
I, the LORD, have spoken!

Babylon's Sure Fall

11 "You rejoice and are glad,
you who plundered my chosen people.
You frisk about like a calf in a meadow
and neigh like a stallion.
12 But your homeland will be overwhelmed
with shame and disgrace.
You will become the least of nations—
a wilderness, a dry and desolate land.
13 Because of the LORD's anger,
Babylon will become a deserted wasteland.
All who pass by will be horrified
and will gasp at the destruction they
see there.

14 "Yes, prepare to attack Babylon,
all you surrounding nations.
Let your archers shoot at her; spare
no arrows.
For she has sinned against the LORD.
15 Shout war cries against her from every side.
Look! She surrenders!
Her walls have fallen.
It is the LORD's vengeance,
so take vengeance on her.
Do to her as she has done to others!
16 Take from Babylon all those who plant crops;
send all the harvesters away.
Because of the sword of the enemy,
everyone will run away and rush back
to their own lands.

Hope for God's People

17 "The Israelites are like sheep
that have been scattered by lions.
First the king of Assyria ate them up.
Then King Nebuchadnezzar of Babylon
cracked their bones."
18 Therefore, this is what the LORD of
Heaven's Armies,
the God of Israel, says:

"Now I will punish the king of Babylon and
his land,
just as I punished the king of Assyria.
19 And I will bring Israel home again
to its own land,
to feed in the fields of Carmel and Bashan,
and to be satisfied once more
in the hill country of Ephraim and Gilead.
20 In those days," says the LORD,
"no sin will be found in Israel or in Judah,
for I will forgive the remnant I preserve.

The LORD's Judgment on Babylon

21 "Go up, my warriors, against the land
of Merathaim
and against the people of Pekod.
Pursue, kill, and completely destroy them,
as I have commanded you," says the LORD.
22 "Let the battle cry be heard in the land,
a shout of great destruction.
23 Babylon, the mightiest hammer in all
the earth,
lies broken and shattered.
Babylon is desolate among the nations!
24 Listen, Babylon, for I have set a trap for you.
You are caught, for you have fought against
the LORD.
25 The LORD has opened his armory
and brought out weapons to vent his fury.
The terror that falls upon the Babylonians
will be the work of the Sovereign LORD
of Heaven's Armies.
26 Yes, come against her from distant lands.
Break open her granaries.
Crush her walls and houses into heaps
of rubble.
Destroy her completely, and leave
nothing!
27 Destroy even her young bulls—
it will be terrible for them, too!
Slaughter them all!
For Babylon's day of reckoning has come.
28 Listen to the people who have escaped
from Babylon,
as they tell in Jerusalem
how the LORD our God has taken vengeance
against those who destroyed his Temple.

29 "Send out a call for archers to come
to Babylon.
Surround the city so none can escape.
Do to her as she has done to others,
for she has defied the LORD, the Holy One
of Israel.
30 Her young men will fall in the streets and die.
Her soldiers will all be killed,"
says the LORD.

31 "See, I am your enemy, you arrogant people,"
says the Lord, the LORD of Heaven's Armies.
"Your day of reckoning has arrived—
the day when I will punish you.
32 O land of arrogance, you will stumble
and fall,
and no one will raise you up.
For I will light a fire in the cities of Babylon
that will burn up everything around them."

33 This is what the LORD of Heaven's
Armies says:
"The people of Israel and Judah have
been wronged.
Their captors hold them and refuse
to let them go.
34 But the one who redeems them is strong.
His name is the LORD of Heaven's Armies.
He will defend them
and give them rest again in Israel.
But for the people of Babylon
there will be no rest!

35 "The sword of destruction will strike the
Babylonians,"
says the LORD.
"It will strike the people of Babylon—
her officials and wise men, too.
36 The sword will strike her wise counselors,
and they will become fools.
The sword will strike her mightiest warriors,
and panic will seize them.
37 The sword will strike her horses and chariots
and her allies from other lands,
and they will all become like women.
The sword will strike her treasures,
and they all will be plundered.
38 A drought will strike her water supply,
causing it to dry up.
And why? Because the whole land is filled
with idols,
and the people are madly in love
with them.

39 "Soon Babylon will be inhabited by desert
animals and hyenas.
It will be a home for owls.
Never again will people live there;
it will lie desolate forever.
40 I will destroy it as I destroyed Sodom
and Gomorrah
and their neighboring towns," says
the LORD.

"No one will live there;
no one will inhabit it.
41 "Look! A great army is coming from
the north.
A great nation and many kings
are rising against you from far-off lands.
42 They are armed with bows and spears.
They are cruel and show no mercy.
As they ride forward on horses,
they sound like a roaring sea.
They are coming in battle formation,
planning to destroy you, Babylon.
43 The king of Babylon has heard reports
about the enemy,
and he is weak with fright.
Pangs of anguish have gripped him,
like those of a woman in labor.

44 "I will come like a lion from the thickets
of the Jordan,
leaping on the sheep in the pasture.
I will chase Babylon from its land,
and I will appoint the leader of my
choice.
For who is like me, and who can
challenge me?
What ruler can oppose my will?"

45 Listen to the LORD's plans against Babylon
and the land of the Babylonians.
Even the little children will be dragged off
like sheep,
and their homes will be destroyed.
46 The earth will shake with the shout,
"Babylon has been taken!"
and its cry of despair will be heard
around the world.

CHAPTER 51

1 This is what the LORD says:
"I will stir up a destroyer against Babylon
and the people of Babylonia.
2 Foreigners will come and winnow her,
blowing her away as chaff.
They will come from every side
to rise against her in her day of trouble.
3 Don't let the archers put on their armor
or draw their bows.
Don't spare even her best soldiers!
Let her army be completely destroyed.
4 They will fall dead in the land of the
Babylonians,
slashed to death in her streets.
5 For the LORD of Heaven's Armies
has not abandoned Israel and Judah.
He is still their God,
even though their land was filled with sin
against the Holy One of Israel."
6 Flee from Babylon! Save yourselves!
Don't get trapped in her punishment!
It is the LORD's time for vengeance;
he will repay her in full.
7 Babylon has been a gold cup in the
LORD's hands,
a cup that made the whole earth drunk.
The nations drank Babylon's wine,
and it drove them all mad.
8 But suddenly Babylon, too, has fallen.
Weep for her.
Give her medicine.
Perhaps she can yet be healed.
9 We would have helped her if we could,
but nothing can save her now.
Let her go; abandon her.
Return now to your own land.
For her punishment reaches to the heavens;
it is so great it cannot be measured.
10 The LORD has vindicated us.
Come, let us announce in Jerusalem
everything the LORD our God has done.
11 Sharpen the arrows!
Lift up the shields!

FUN-fact God's Address Book

How do letters find their way to your house? Because of the address! The Bible has addresses too.

Here's how it works. Like our country is divided into states, the Bible is divided into two main sections: the Old and New Testaments. Each testament is divided into books (like cities). Each book is broken into chapters (like streets), and each chapter is broken into verses (like house numbers).

Want to know more about the different books of the Bible? Check out the introduction to each book in *this* Bible!

So if you wanted to find ROMANS 12:4, you would turn to the New Testament, the book of ROMANS, chapter 12, and verse 4.

Take turns with a friend calling out different Bible addresses to find. Keep practicing, and eventually you'll know exactly where to find any Bible verse!

For the LORD has inspired the kings
of the Medes
to march against Babylon and
destroy her.
This is his vengeance against those
who desecrated his Temple.
12 Raise the battle flag against Babylon!
Reinforce the guard and station the
watchmen.
Prepare an ambush,
for the LORD will fulfill all his plans
against Babylon.
13 You are a city by a great river,
a great center of commerce,
but your end has come.
The thread of your life is cut.
14 The LORD of Heaven's Armies has taken
this vow
and has sworn to it by his own name:
"Your cities will be filled with enemies,
like fields swarming with locusts,
and they will shout in triumph over you."

A Hymn of Praise to the LORD

15 The LORD made the earth by his power,
and he preserves it by his wisdom.
With his own understanding
he stretched out the heavens.
16 When he speaks in the thunder,
the heavens roar with rain.
He causes the clouds to rise over the earth.
He sends the lightning with the rain
and releases the wind from his
storehouses.
17 The whole human race is foolish and has
no knowledge!
The craftsmen are disgraced by the idols
they make,
for their carefully shaped works are a fraud.
These idols have no breath or power.
18 Idols are worthless; they are ridiculous lies!
On the day of reckoning they will all
be destroyed.
19 But the God of Israel is no idol!
He is the Creator of everything that exists,
including his people, his own special
possession.
The LORD of Heaven's Armies is his name!

Babylon's Great Punishment

20 "You are my battle-ax and sword,"
says the LORD.
"With you I will shatter nations
and destroy many kingdoms.
21 With you I will shatter armies—
destroying the horse and rider,
the chariot and charioteer.
22 With you I will shatter men and women,
old people and children,
young men and young women.
23 With you I will shatter shepherds
and flocks,
farmers and oxen,
captains and officers.

24 "I will repay Babylon
and the people of Babylonia
for all the wrong they have done
to my people in Jerusalem," says the LORD.

25 "Look, O mighty mountain, destroyer
of the earth!
I am your enemy," says the LORD.
"I will raise my fist against you,
to knock you down from the heights.
When I am finished,
you will be nothing but a heap
of burnt rubble.
26 You will be desolate forever.
Even your stones will never again
be used for building.
You will be completely wiped out,"
says the LORD.

27 Raise a signal flag to the nations.
Sound the battle cry!
Mobilize them all against Babylon.
Prepare them to fight against her!
Bring out the armies of Ararat, Minni,
and Ashkenaz.
Appoint a commander,
and bring a multitude of horses like
swarming locusts!
28 Bring against her the armies of the
nations—
led by the kings of the Medes
and all their captains and officers.
29 The earth trembles and writhes in pain,
for everything the LORD has planned
against Babylon stands unchanged.
Babylon will be left desolate without
a single inhabitant.
30 Her mightiest warriors no longer fight.
They stay in their barracks, their courage
gone.
They have become like women.
The invaders have burned the houses
and broken down the city gates.
31 The news is passed from one runner
to the next

as the messengers hurry to tell the king
that his city has been captured.
32 All the escape routes are blocked.
The marshes have been set aflame,
and the army is in a panic.

33 This is what the LORD of Heaven's Armies,
the God of Israel, says:
"Babylon is like wheat on a threshing floor,
about to be trampled.
In just a little while
her harvest will begin."

34 "King Nebuchadnezzar of Babylon has eaten
and crushed us
and drained us of strength.
He has swallowed us like a great monster
and filled his belly with our riches.
He has thrown us out of our own country.
35 Make Babylon suffer as she made us suffer,"
say the people of Zion.
"Make the people of Babylonia pay for
spilling our blood,"
says Jerusalem.

The LORD's Vengeance on Babylon

36 This is what the LORD says to Jerusalem:

"I will be your lawyer to plead your case,
and I will avenge you.
I will dry up her river,
as well as her springs,
37 and Babylon will become a heap of ruins,
haunted by jackals.
She will be an object of horror and
contempt,
a place where no one lives.
38 Her people will roar together like strong
lions.
They will growl like lion cubs.
39 And while they lie inflamed with all
their wine,
I will prepare a different kind of feast
for them.
I will make them drink until they fall asleep,
and they will never wake up again,"
says the LORD.
40 "I will bring them down
like lambs to the slaughter,
like rams and goats to be sacrificed.

41 "How Babylon is fallen—
great Babylon, praised throughout
the earth!
Now she has become an object of horror
among the nations.
42 The sea has risen over Babylon;
she is covered by its crashing waves.
43 Her cities now lie in ruins;
she is a dry wasteland
where no one lives or even passes by.
44 And I will punish Bel, the god of Babylon,
and make him vomit up all he has eaten.
The nations will no longer come and
worship him.
The wall of Babylon has fallen!

A Message for the Exiles

45 "Come out, my people, flee from Babylon.
Save yourselves! Run from the LORD's
fierce anger.
46 But do not panic; don't be afraid
when you hear the first rumor of
approaching forces.
For rumors will keep coming year
by year.
Violence will erupt in the land
as the leaders fight against each other.
47 For the time is surely coming
when I will punish this great city and all
her idols.
Her whole land will be disgraced,
and her dead will lie in the streets.
48 Then the heavens and earth will rejoice,
for out of the north will come destroying
armies
against Babylon," says the LORD.
49 "Just as Babylon killed the people of Israel
and others throughout the world,
so must her people be killed.
50 Get out, all you who have escaped the sword!
Do not stand and watch—flee while
you can!
Remember the LORD, though you are
in a far-off land,
and think about your home in Jerusalem."

51 "We are ashamed," the people say.
"We are insulted and disgraced
because the LORD's Temple
has been defiled by foreigners."

52 "Yes," says the LORD, "but the time is coming
when I will destroy Babylon's idols.
The groans of her wounded people
will be heard throughout the land.
53 Though Babylon reaches as high as the
heavens
and makes her fortifications incredibly
strong,
I will still send enemies to plunder her.
I, the LORD, have spoken!

Babylon's Complete Destruction

54 "Listen! Hear the cry of Babylon,
the sound of great destruction from the
land of the Babylonians.
55 For the LORD is destroying Babylon.
He will silence her loud voice.
Waves of enemies pound against her;
the noise of battle rings through
the city.
56 Destroying armies come against Babylon.
Her mighty men are captured,
and their weapons break in their hands.
For the LORD is a God who gives just
punishment;
he always repays in full.
57 I will make her officials and wise men
drunk,
along with her captains, officers,
and warriors.
They will fall asleep
and never wake up again!"
says the King, whose name is
the LORD of Heaven's Armies.
58 This is what the LORD of Heaven's
Armies says:
"The thick walls of Babylon will be leveled
to the ground,
and her massive gates will be burned.
The builders from many lands have worked
in vain,
for their work will be destroyed by fire!"

Jeremiah's Message Sent to Babylon

59 The prophet Jeremiah gave this message to
Seraiah son of Neriah and grandson of Mahseiah,
a staff officer, when Seraiah went to Babylon
with King Zedekiah of Judah. This was during the
fourth year of Zedekiah's reign. 60 Jeremiah had
recorded on a scroll all the terrible disasters that
would soon come upon Babylon—all the words
written here. 61 He said to Seraiah, "When you get
to Babylon, read aloud everything on this scroll.
62 Then say, 'LORD, you have said that you will
destroy Babylon so that neither people nor animals will remain here. She will lie empty and
abandoned forever.' 63 When you have finished
reading the scroll, tie it to a stone and throw it
into the Euphrates River. 64 Then say, 'In this
same way Babylon and her people will sink, never
again to rise, because of the disasters I will bring
upon her.'"

This is the end of Jeremiah's messages.

CHAPTER 52

The Fall of Jerusalem

Zedekiah was twenty-one years old when he became king, and he reigned in Jerusalem eleven
years. His mother was Hamutal, the daughter of
Jeremiah from Libnah. 2 But Zedekiah did what
was evil in the LORD's sight, just as Jehoiakim had
done. 3 These things happened because of the
LORD's anger against the people of Jerusalem and
Judah, until he finally banished them from his
presence and sent them into exile.

Zedekiah rebelled against the king of Babylon.
4 So on January 15, during the ninth year of
Zedekiah's reign, King Nebuchadnezzar of Babylon led his entire army against Jerusalem. They
surrounded the city and built siege ramps against
its walls. 5 Jerusalem was kept under siege until
the eleventh year of King Zedekiah's reign.

6 By July 18 in the eleventh year of Zedekiah's
reign, the famine in the city had become very severe, and the last of the food was entirely gone.
7 Then a section of the city wall was broken
down, and all the soldiers fled. Since the city was
surrounded by the Babylonians, they waited for
nightfall. Then they slipped through the gate between the two walls behind the king's garden and
headed toward the Jordan Valley.

8 But the Babylonian troops chased King
Zedekiah and overtook him on the plains of Jericho, for his men had all deserted him and scattered. 9 They captured the king and took him to
the king of Babylon at Riblah in the land of
Hamath. There the king of Babylon pronounced
judgment upon Zedekiah. 10 The king of Babylon
made Zedekiah watch as he slaughtered his sons.
He also slaughtered all the officials of Judah at
Riblah. 11 Then he gouged out Zedekiah's eyes
and bound him in bronze chains, and the king of
Babylon led him away to Babylon. Zedekiah remained there in prison until the day of his death.

The Temple Destroyed

12 On August 17 of that year, which was the nineteenth year of King Nebuchadnezzar's reign,
Nebuzaradan, the captain of the guard and an official of the Babylonian king, arrived in Jerusalem. 13 He burned down the Temple of the LORD,
the royal palace, and all the houses of Jerusalem.
He destroyed all the important buildings in the
city. 14 Then he supervised the entire Babylonian
army as they tore down the walls of Jerusalem on
every side. 15 Then Nebuzaradan, the captain of
the guard, took as exiles some of the poorest of
the people, the rest of the people who remained
in the city, the defectors who had declared their

allegiance to the king of Babylon, and the rest of
the craftsmen. 16But Nebuzaradan allowed
some of the poorest people to stay behind to care
for the vineyards and fields.
17The Babylonians broke up the bronze pillars
in front of the LORD's Temple, the bronze water
carts, and the great bronze basin called the Sea,
and they carried all the bronze away to Babylon.
18They also took all the ash buckets, shovels,
lamp snuffers, basins, dishes, and all the other
bronze articles used for making sacrifices at the
Temple. 19The captain of the guard also took the
small bowls, incense burners, basins, pots,
lampstands, ladles, bowls used for liquid offerings, and all the other articles made of pure gold
or silver.
20The weight of the bronze from the two pillars, the Sea with the twelve bronze oxen beneath it, and the water carts was too great to be
measured. These things had been made for the
LORD's Temple in the days of King Solomon.
21Each of the pillars was 27 feet tall and 18 feet
in circumference. They were hollow, with walls
3 inches thick. 22The bronze capital on top of
each pillar was 7½ feet high and was decorated
with a network of bronze pomegranates all the
way around. 23There were 96 pomegranates on
the sides, and a total of 100 pomegranates on the
network around the top.
24Nebuzaradan, the captain of the guard, took
with him as prisoners Seraiah the high priest,
Zephaniah the priest of the second rank, and the
three chief gatekeepers. 25And from among the
people still hiding in the city, he took an officer
who had been in charge of the Judean army;
seven of the king's personal advisers; the army
commander's chief secretary, who was in charge
of recruitment; and sixty other citizens. 26Nebu-
zaradan, the captain of the guard, took them all
to the king of Babylon at Riblah. 27And there at
Riblah, in the land of Hamath, the king of Babylon had them all put to death. So the people of
Judah were sent into exile from their land.
28The number of captives taken to Babylon in
the seventh year of Nebuchadnezzar's reign was
3,023. 29Then in Nebuchadnezzar's eighteenth
year he took 832 more. 30In Nebuchadnezzar's
twenty-third year he sent Nebuzaradan, the captain of the guard, who took 745 more—a total of
4,600 captives in all.

Hope for Israel's Royal Line

31In the thirty-seventh year of the exile of King
Jehoiachin of Judah, Evil-merodach ascended to
the Babylonian throne. He was kind to Jehoiachin
and released him from prison on March 31 of
that year. 32He spoke kindly to Jehoiachin and
gave him a higher place than all the other exiled
kings in Babylon. 33He supplied Jehoiachin with
new clothes to replace his prison garb and allowed him to dine in the king's presence for the
rest of his life. 34So the Babylonian king gave him
a regular food allowance as long as he lived. This
continued until the day of his death.

LAMENTATIONS
The Book of Tears

The book of Lamentations looks back at a sad day. It describes how
- **JERUSALEM WAS DEFEATED BY HER ENEMY**
- **THE TEMPLE WAS TORN DOWN**
- **GOD'S PEOPLE BECAME SLAVES**
- **THE SILENT CITY SUFFERED**

Hand Me a Tissue, Please

Jeremiah is known as the Weeping Prophet. Why did Jeremiah weep so much? **Read Lamentations 1:1-4 to find out what all the tears were about.**

They Had Their Chance

God gave the people of Judah lots of chances to repent and obey him. But they didn't listen. *After* they were punished, they finally got the message. **Listen to Jerusalem's sad statement in Lamentations 1:11-20.**

Forever Faithful

Could it be? Could Jeremiah dare to hope for better days? **Find out why in Lamentations 3:19-33.**

Time for a U-Turn

Jeremiah knew what the people needed to do to get back to God. **Discover the answer yourself in Lamentations 3:40.**

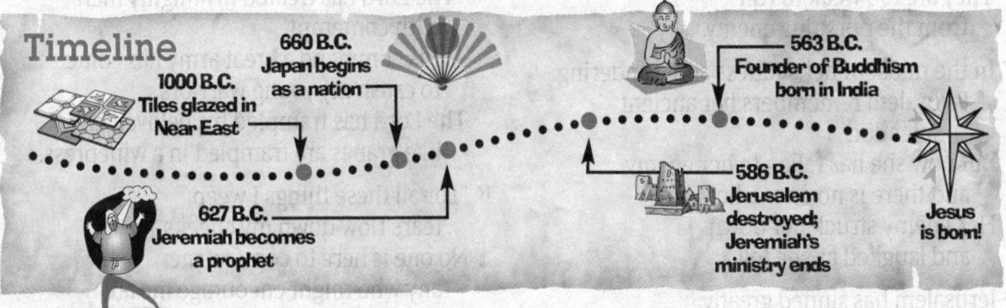

Timeline
1000 B.C. Tiles glazed in Near East
660 B.C. Japan begins as a nation
627 B.C. Jeremiah becomes a prophet
586 B.C. Jerusalem destroyed; Jeremiah's ministry ends
563 B.C. Founder of Buddhism born in India
Jesus is born!

The JESUS CONNECTION

Jeremiah knew that God is loving and faithful and that God is always willing to forgive. God sure proved that when he sent Jesus! God's Son, Jesus, was punished for our sins so we could stand before God as his forgiven children. What a gift! **All you have to do is accept Jesus, and you will have God's gift of forgiveness.**

Lamentations 1 . . . page 788

CHAPTER 1

Sorrow in Jerusalem

1 Jerusalem, once so full of people,
is now deserted.
She who was once great among the nations
now sits alone like a widow.
Once the queen of all the earth,
she is now a slave.

2 She sobs through the night;
tears stream down her cheeks.
Among all her lovers,
there is no one left to comfort her.
All her friends have betrayed her
and become her enemies.

3 Judah has been led away into captivity,
oppressed with cruel slavery.
She lives among foreign nations
and has no place of rest.
Her enemies have chased her down,
and she has nowhere to turn.

4 The roads to Jerusalem are in mourning,
for crowds no longer come to celebrate
the festivals.
The city gates are silent,
her priests groan,
her young women are crying—
how bitter is her fate!

5 Her oppressors have become her masters,
and her enemies prosper,
for the LORD has punished Jerusalem
for her many sins.
Her children have been captured
and taken away to distant lands.

6 All the majesty of beautiful Jerusalem
has been stripped away.
Her princes are like starving deer
searching for pasture.
They are too weak to run
from the pursuing enemy.

7 In the midst of her sadness and wandering,
Jerusalem remembers her ancient
splendor.
But now she has fallen to her enemy,
and there is no one to help her.
Her enemy struck her down
and laughed as she fell.

8 Jerusalem has sinned greatly,
so she has been tossed away like
a filthy rag.
All who once honored her now despise her,
for they have seen her stripped naked
and humiliated.
All she can do is groan
and hide her face.

9 She defiled herself with immorality
and gave no thought to her future.
Now she lies in the gutter
with no one to lift her out.
"LORD, see my misery," she cries.
"The enemy has triumphed."

10 The enemy has plundered her completely,
taking every precious thing she owns.
She has seen foreigners violate her
sacred Temple,
the place the LORD had forbidden them
to enter.

11 Her people groan as they search for bread.
They have sold their treasures for food
to stay alive.
"O LORD, look," she mourns,
"and see how I am despised.

12 "Does it mean nothing to you, all you who
pass by?
Look around and see if there is any
suffering like mine,
which the LORD brought on me
when he erupted in fierce anger.

13 "He has sent fire from heaven that burns
in my bones.
He has placed a trap in my path and
turned me back.
He has left me devastated,
racked with sickness all day long.

14 "He wove my sins into ropes
to hitch me to a yoke of captivity.
The Lord sapped my strength and turned
me over to my enemies;
I am helpless in their hands.

15 "The Lord has treated my mighty men
with contempt.
At his command a great army has come
to crush my young warriors.
The Lord has trampled his beloved city
like grapes are trampled in a winepress.

16 "For all these things I weep;
tears flow down my cheeks.
No one is here to comfort me;
any who might encourage me are
far away.
My children have no future,
for the enemy has conquered us."

17 Jerusalem reaches out for help,
but no one comforts her.

Regarding his people Israel,
  the LORD has said,
"Let their neighbors be their enemies!
  Let them be thrown away like a filthy rag!"

18 "The LORD is right," Jerusalem says,
  "for I rebelled against him.
Listen, people everywhere;
  look upon my anguish and despair,
for my sons and daughters
  have been taken captive to distant lands.

19 "I begged my allies for help,
  but they betrayed me.
My priests and leaders
  starved to death in the city,
even as they searched for food
  to save their lives.

20 "LORD, see my anguish!
  My heart is broken
and my soul despairs,
  for I have rebelled against you.
In the streets the sword kills,
  and at home there is only death.

21 "Others heard my groans,
  but no one turned to comfort me.
When my enemies heard about my troubles,
  they were happy to see what you
    had done.
Oh, bring the day you promised,
  when they will suffer as I have suffered.

22 "Look at all their evil deeds, LORD.
  Punish them,
as you have punished me
  for all my sins.
My groans are many,
  and I am sick at heart."

CHAPTER 2

God's Anger at Sin

1 The Lord in his anger
  has cast a dark shadow over beautiful
    Jerusalem.
The fairest of Israel's cities lies in the dust,
  thrown down from the heights of heaven.
In his day of great anger,
  the Lord has shown no mercy even
    to his Temple.

2 Without mercy the Lord has destroyed
  every home in Israel.
In his anger he has broken down
  the fortress walls of beautiful Jerusalem.
He has brought them to the ground,
  dishonoring the kingdom and its rulers.

3 All the strength of Israel
  vanishes beneath his fierce anger.
The Lord has withdrawn his protection
  as the enemy attacks.
He consumes the whole land of Israel
  like a raging fire.

4 He bends his bow against his people,
  as though he were their enemy.
His strength is used against them
  to kill their finest youth.
His fury is poured out like fire
  on beautiful Jerusalem.

5 Yes, the Lord has vanquished Israel
  like an enemy.
He has destroyed her palaces
  and demolished her fortresses.
He has brought unending sorrow and tears
  upon beautiful Jerusalem.

6 He has broken down his Temple
  as though it were merely a garden shelter.
The LORD has blotted out all memory
  of the holy festivals and Sabbath days.
Kings and priests fall together
  before his fierce anger.

7 The Lord has rejected his own altar;
  he despises his own sanctuary.
He has given Jerusalem's palaces
  to her enemies.
They shout in the LORD's Temple
  as though it were a day of celebration.

8 The LORD was determined
  to destroy the walls of beautiful Jerusalem.
He made careful plans for their destruction,
  then did what he had planned.
Therefore, the ramparts and walls
  have fallen down before him.

9 Jerusalem's gates have sunk into the ground.
  He has smashed their locks and bars.
Her kings and princes have been exiled
    to distant lands;
  her law has ceased to exist.
Her prophets receive
  no more visions from the LORD.

10 The leaders of beautiful Jerusalem
  sit on the ground in silence.
They are clothed in burlap
  and throw dust on their heads.
The young women of Jerusalem
  hang their heads in shame.

11 I have cried until the tears no longer come;
  my heart is broken.

My spirit is poured out in agony
as I see the desperate plight of my people.
Little children and tiny babies
are fainting and dying in the streets.

12 They cry out to their mothers,
"We need food and drink!"
Their lives ebb away in the streets
like the life of a warrior wounded in battle.
They gasp for life
as they collapse in their mothers' arms.

13 What can I say about you?
Who has ever seen such sorrow?
O daughter of Jerusalem,
to what can I compare your anguish?
O virgin daughter of Zion,
how can I comfort you?
For your wound is as deep as the sea.
Who can heal you?

14 Your prophets have said
so many foolish things, false to the core.
They did not save you from exile
by pointing out your sins.
Instead, they painted false pictures,
filling you with false hope.

15 All who pass by jeer at you.
They scoff and insult beautiful Jerusalem,
saying,
"Is this the city called 'Most Beautiful
in All the World'
and 'Joy of All the Earth'?"

16 All your enemies mock you.
They scoff and snarl and say,
"We have destroyed her at last!
We have long waited for this day,
and it is finally here!"

17 But it is the LORD who did just as he planned.
He has fulfilled the promises of disaster
he made long ago.
He has destroyed Jerusalem without mercy.
He has caused her enemies to gloat
over her
and has given them power over her.

18 Cry aloud before the Lord,
O walls of beautiful Jerusalem!
Let your tears flow like a river
day and night.
Give yourselves no rest;
give your eyes no relief.

19 Rise during the night and cry out.
Pour out your hearts like water
to the Lord.
Lift up your hands to him in prayer,
pleading for your children,
for in every street
they are faint with hunger.

20 "O LORD, think about this!
Should you treat your own people
this way?
Should mothers eat their own children,
those they once bounced on their knees?
Should priests and prophets be killed
within the Lord's Temple?

21 "See them lying in the streets—
young and old,
boys and girls,
killed by the swords of the enemy.
You have killed them in your anger,
slaughtering them without mercy.

22 "You have invited terrors from all around,
as though you were calling them to a day
of feasting.
In the day of the LORD's anger,
no one has escaped or survived.
The enemy has killed all the children
whom I carried and raised."

CHAPTER 3

Hope in the LORD's Faithfulness

1 I am the one who has seen the afflictions
that come from the rod of the
LORD's anger.
2 He has led me into darkness,
shutting out all light.
3 He has turned his hand against me
again and again, all day long.

4 He has made my skin and flesh grow old.
He has broken my bones.
5 He has besieged and surrounded me
with anguish and distress.
6 He has buried me in a dark place,
like those long dead.

7 He has walled me in, and I cannot escape.
He has bound me in heavy chains.
8 And though I cry and shout,
he has shut out my prayers.
9 He has blocked my way with a high
stone wall;
he has made my road crooked.

10 He has hidden like a bear or a lion,
waiting to attack me.
11 He has dragged me off the path and torn
me in pieces,
leaving me helpless and devastated.

BIBLE BIOS
Hear From the Heroes

Hi, my name is
DANIEL *(prophet)*

See if you can guess what I *haven't* been: prophet, servant, hostage, dream interpreter, sign interpreter, visionary, government official, pizza delivery guy, lion tamer. (OK, so maybe I don't know a lot about pizza.)

I worked hard all my life trying to live right for God. And I had a lot of chances to stand up for him! For one thing, three buddies and I ended up living in the king's court. God even helped me interpret the kings' dreams. Later in my life, I had dreams and visions of my own that God interpreted for me. They were visions about things that would happen in the future. (You can read about them in my book of the Bible.)

Daniel interpreted several dreams for King Nebuchadnezzar. Read DANIEL 4 to find out about one of the strangest dreams and interpretations. Here's a hint: The king ends up eating like a cow!

Daniel had visions not only of the future, but of the very end of time. Gabriel, the same angel who announced the birth of John the Baptist and Jesus, came to Daniel to explain his vision. Check it out in DANIEL 8:15-27.

Yep, it was an interesting life. But I'll tell ya...there were days when it was tough. Like the day they threw my buddies into the fiery furnace. Or how about that day with the lions? The king had made a law that no one could pray to anyone but him. If they did, they'd be thrown to the lions! Well, lions or no lions, I wasn't about to pray to any old king. And I sure wasn't about to stop praying to the one true God. So it was into the lions' den for me! But God sent an angel to shut the lions' mouths, and I wasn't hurt at all.

Read what my buddies had to say about the fiery furnace in their own biography. Their names were Shadrach, Meshach, and Abednego.

Looking back, I'd have to say that the best part of my life was being close to God. He's the only thing that really matters, you know. He gave me wisdom. He kept me safe. And he loved and cared for me. And I loved to obey him. God was my very best friend! Is he yours?

You Can Trust God—No Lyin'!

Even when it meant being thrown into the lions' den, Daniel refused to stop praying to God. When are you tempted to follow the world's rules instead of God's?

Make a lion's face out of two paper plates. Cut one plate in half, and staple it to the other plate. Draw a lion's face on the plates, making the half plate the mouth. Glue yarn around the plate for the lion's mane. When you're tempted to turn away from God's rules, write the situation on a slip of paper and put it in the lion's mouth.

Then pray!

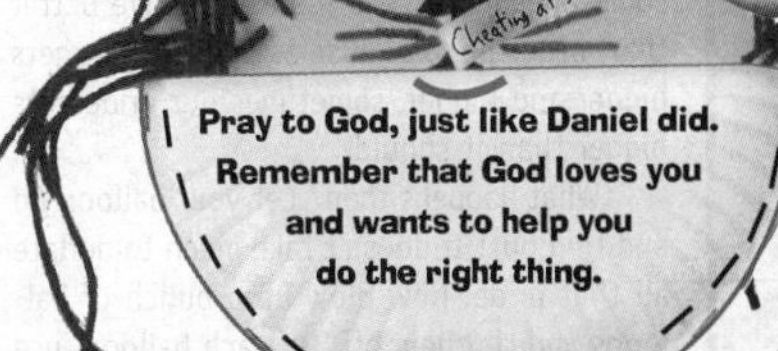

Pray to God, just like Daniel did. Remember that God loves you and wants to help you do the right thing.

Hi, my name is

NEBUCHADNEZZAR *(king of Babylon)*

Yeah, it's me. The one whose name always shows up in a paragraph when it's your turn to read out loud in Sunday school. My name is Aramaic for "the one whose name cannot be pronounced." Just kidding! It's pronounced, NEH-boo-kad-NEZZ-ur. It means "O Nebo, protect the crown." Nebo was one of the many gods that I worshiped for a while, instead of the one true God I should have!

Anyway, I was the king of Babylon for quite a while. I'm the king who conquered Judah, captured Jerusalem, and took some of the people captive to Babylon. But what you really should know about me is how God worked in my life. I wasn't following God, you know. It took heroes like Daniel and his friends to make me see the truth. Did you know Daniel interpreted my dreams? (Go to Daniel's biography for more details!) And then there's Shadrach, Meshach, and Abednego. I see them every year at the "Bible Characters With Unpronounceable Names" convention. (Kidding again.) I learned a lot about God through their experience in the furnace.

Daniel interpreted dreams for other kings too. He explained some mysterious writing on the wall to King Belshazzar. Read about it in DANIEL 5.

There's another story about me that's not so easy to tell. It happened at a time when I was really full of myself. Very proud, you know? I even had this big gold statue of myself made for people to bow down to. But God brought me to my knees—in more ways than one. You can read about it in **DANIEL 4** if you want to.

Ever hear of a king eating like a cow? That's what happened to King Nebuchadnezzar when he became too proud. He lived in the fields and ate like an animal for seven years! Read DANIEL 4:28-33 for details.

Take some time to read about me, and you'll learn about a guy who wasn't always faithful to God. Even so, God made things happen through me and to me. I can't explain it. I guess God has a bigger plan than we realize sometimes. God's awesome!

When King Nebuchadnezzar became puffed up with pride, God deflated him. Don't let pride puff *you* up!

Puffed Up With Pride

GET A BALLOON AND BEGIN TO BLOW IT UP. Before each breath, think of something that sometimes makes you feel that you're better than other people. Just as the balloon gets bigger and bigger, sometimes our pride gets bigger than it should.

What happens then? Let your balloon go and find out! It doesn't take much to deflate all that pride. Now blow up a bunch of balloons and tie them off. On each balloon, use a marker to thank God for one talent he's given you. Tie strings to the balloons, and you'll have a bouquet of praise instead of pride!

DRAWING
writing
Dancing

12 He has drawn his bow
and made me the target for his arrows.

13 He shot his arrows
deep into my heart.
14 My own people laugh at me.
All day long they sing their
mocking songs.
15 He has filled me with bitterness
and given me a bitter cup of sorrow
to drink.

16 He has made me chew on gravel.
He has rolled me in the dust.
17 Peace has been stripped away,
and I have forgotten what prosperity is.
18 I cry out, "My splendor is gone!
Everything I had hoped for from the
LORD is lost!"

19 The thought of my suffering and
homelessness
is bitter beyond words.
20 I will never forget this awful time,
as I grieve over my loss.
21 Yet I still dare to hope
when I remember this:

22 The faithful love of the LORD never ends!
His mercies never cease.
23 Great is his faithfulness;
his mercies begin afresh each morning.
24 I say to myself, "The LORD is my inheritance;
therefore, I will hope in him!"

25 The LORD is good to those who depend
on him,
to those who search for him.
26 So it is good to wait quietly
for salvation from the LORD.
27 And it is good for people to submit
at an early age
to the yoke of his discipline:

28 Let them sit alone in silence
beneath the LORD's demands.
29 Let them lie face down in the dust,
for there may be hope at last.
30 Let them turn the other cheek to those
who strike them
and accept the insults of their enemies.

31 For no one is abandoned
by the Lord forever.
32 Though he brings grief, he also shows
compassion
because of the greatness of his
unfailing love.
33 For he does not enjoy hurting people
or causing them sorrow.

34 If people crush underfoot
all the prisoners of the land,
35 if they deprive others of their rights
in defiance of the Most High,
36 if they twist justice in the courts—
doesn't the Lord see all these things?

37 Who can command things to happen
without the Lord's permission?
38 Does not the Most High
send both calamity and good?
39 Then why should we, mere humans,
complain
when we are punished for our sins?

40 Instead, let us test and examine our ways.
Let us turn back to the LORD.
41 Let us lift our hearts and hands
to God in heaven and say,
42 "We have sinned and rebelled,
and you have not forgiven us.

43 "You have engulfed us with your anger,
chased us down,
and slaughtered us without mercy.
44 You have hidden yourself in a cloud
so our prayers cannot reach you.
45 You have discarded us as refuse
and garbage
among the nations.

46 "All our enemies
have spoken out against us.
47 We are filled with fear,
for we are trapped, devastated,
and ruined."
48 Tears stream from my eyes
because of the destruction of my people!

49 My tears flow endlessly;
they will not stop
50 until the LORD looks down
from heaven and sees.
51 My heart is breaking
over the fate of all the women
of Jerusalem.

52 My enemies, whom I have never harmed,
hunted me down like a bird.
53 They threw me into a pit
and dropped stones on me.
54 The water rose over my head,
and I cried out, "This is the end!"

55 But I called on your name, LORD,
from deep within the pit.

56 You heard me when I cried, "Listen
to my pleading!
Hear my cry for help!"
57 Yes, you came when I called;
you told me, "Do not fear."
58 Lord, you are my lawyer! Plead my case!
For you have redeemed my life.
59 You have seen the wrong they have done
to me, LORD.
Be my judge, and prove me right.
60 You have seen the vengeful plots
my enemies have laid against me.
61 LORD, you have heard the vile names they
call me.
You know all about the plans they
have made.
62 My enemies whisper and mutter
as they plot against me all day long.
63 Look at them! Whether they sit or stand,
I am the object of their mocking songs.
64 Pay them back, LORD,
for all the evil they have done.
65 Give them hard and stubborn hearts,
and then let your curse fall on them!
66 Chase them down in your anger,
destroying them beneath the LORD's
heavens.

CHAPTER 4
God's Anger Satisfied

1 How the gold has lost its luster!
Even the finest gold has become dull.
The sacred gemstones
lie scattered in the streets!
2 See how the precious children of Jerusalem,
worth their weight in fine gold,
are now treated like pots of clay
made by a common potter.
3 Even the jackals feed their young,
but not my people Israel.
They ignore their children's cries,
like ostriches in the desert.
4 The parched tongues of their little ones
stick to the roofs of their mouths
in thirst.
The children cry for bread,
but no one has any to give them.
5 The people who once ate the richest foods
now beg in the streets for anything
they can get.
Those who once wore the finest clothes
now search the garbage dumps for food.

FUN-fact

A lamentation is a song about being sad.

Jeremiah wrote *his* lamentation because Jerusalem had been destroyed and the people killed or captured. He filled a whole book of the Bible with sad songs asking God for help. Maybe that's why some people call Jeremiah the Weeping Prophet.

What makes you sad?

What's bothering you right now? Tell God about it. **Write your lamentation to God in a few sentences.**

____

____

God heard Jeremiah's lament, and he hears yours, too. **Write a quick prayer to thank God for listening!**

____

____

6 The guilt of my people
is greater than that of Sodom,
where utter disaster struck in a moment
and no hand offered help.
7 Our princes once glowed with health—
brighter than snow, whiter than milk.
Their faces were as ruddy as rubies,
their appearance like fine jewels.
8 But now their faces are blacker than soot.
No one recognizes them in the streets.
Their skin sticks to their bones;
it is as dry and hard as wood.
9 Those killed by the sword are better off
than those who die of hunger.
Starving, they waste away
for lack of food from the fields.
10 Tenderhearted women
have cooked their own children.
They have eaten them
to survive the siege.

11 But now the anger of the LORD is satisfied.
His fierce anger has been poured out.
He started a fire in Jerusalem
that burned the city to its foundations.

12 Not a king in all the earth—
no one in all the world—
would have believed that an enemy
could march through the gates
of Jerusalem.

13 Yet it happened because of the sins
of her prophets
and the sins of her priests,
who defiled the city
by shedding innocent blood.

14 They wandered blindly
through the streets,
so defiled by blood
that no one dared touch them.

15 "Get away!" the people shouted at them.
"You're defiled! Don't touch us!"
So they fled to distant lands
and wandered among foreign nations,
but none would let them stay.

16 The LORD himself has scattered them,
and he no longer helps them.
People show no respect for the priests
and no longer honor the leaders.

17 We looked in vain for our allies
to come and save us,
but we were looking to nations
that could not help us.

18 We couldn't go into the streets
without danger to our lives.
Our end was near; our days were numbered.
We were doomed!

19 Our enemies were swifter than eagles
in flight.
If we fled to the mountains, they found us.
If we hid in the wilderness,
they were waiting for us there.

20 Our king—the LORD's anointed, the very life
of our nation—
was caught in their snares.
We had thought that his shadow
would protect us against any nation
on earth!

21 Are you rejoicing in the land of Uz,
O people of Edom?
But you, too, must drink from the cup of the
LORD's anger.
You, too, will be stripped naked in your
drunkenness.

22 O beautiful Jerusalem, your punishment
will end;
you will soon return from exile.
But Edom, your punishment is just
beginning;
soon your many sins will be exposed.

CHAPTER 5

Prayer for Restoration

1 LORD, remember what has happened to us.
See how we have been disgraced!
2 Our inheritance has been turned over
to strangers,
our homes to foreigners.
3 We are orphaned and fatherless.
Our mothers are widowed.
4 We have to pay for water to drink,
and even firewood is expensive.
5 Those who pursue us are at our heels;
we are exhausted but are given no rest.
6 We submitted to Egypt and Assyria
to get enough food to survive.
7 Our ancestors sinned, but they have died—
and we are suffering the punishment
they deserved!

8 Slaves have now become our masters;
there is no one left to rescue us.
9 We hunt for food at the risk of our lives,
for violence rules the countryside.
10 The famine has blackened our skin
as though baked in an oven.
11 Our enemies rape the women in Jerusalem
and the young girls in all the towns
of Judah.
12 Our princes are being hanged by their
thumbs,
and our elders are treated with
contempt.
13 Young men are led away to work at
millstones,
and boys stagger under heavy loads
of wood.
14 The elders no longer sit in the city gates;
the young men no longer dance and sing.
15 Joy has left our hearts;
our dancing has turned to mourning.
16 The garlands have fallen from our heads.
Weep for us because we have sinned.
17 Our hearts are sick and weary,
and our eyes grow dim with tears.
18 For Jerusalem is empty and desolate,
a place haunted by jackals.

Lamentations 5 . . . page 796

19 But LORD, you remain the same forever!
Your throne continues from generation
to generation.
20 Why do you continue to forget us?
Why have you abandoned us for so long?
21 Restore us, O LORD, and bring us back
to you again!
Give us back the joys we once had!
22 Or have you utterly rejected us?
Are you angry with us still?

EZEKIEL More Words of Warning

The book of Ezekiel offers the same warnings that the other books of the prophets gave. But Ezekiel used a few unusual methods to get God's point across, like

- **STAYING HOME**
- **STAYING STILL**
- **LEARNING TO COOK (SORT OF)**
- **SHAVING HIS HAIR OFF**

You Want Me to Eat What?!?

While Ezekiel was lying on his side all that time, God told him exactly what to eat and how to cook it. **It's kind of gross, but you can read all about it in Ezekiel 4:9-17.**

When will they learn?

Same Story

The people of Jerusalem didn't listen when Jeremiah said God would destroy their city if they didn't repent.

Meanwhile, the same thing happened when Ezekiel told the Israelites that Jerusalem would be destroyed. How did God react? **Read his words to Ezekiel in Ezekiel 3:7-11.**

MODIAL HOTEL
PARIS

Don't Turn Over!...

God gave Ezekiel some pretty weird ways to get his message across. One time he told Ezekiel to lie on his left side for 390 days and his right side for 40 days. **Find out why in Ezekiel 4:4-6.**

Moving Day

Who wants to live in exile? God told Ezekiel to put on a little demonstration for the Israelites. **Find out what it was in Ezekiel 12:1-11.**

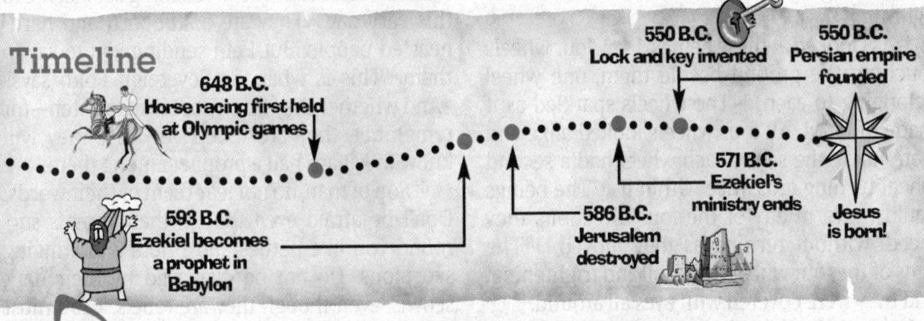
Timeline
648 B.C. Horse racing first held at Olympic games
593 B.C. Ezekiel becomes a prophet in Babylon
586 B.C. Jerusalem destroyed
571 B.C. Ezekiel's ministry ends
550 B.C. Lock and key invented
550 B.C. Persian empire founded
Jesus is born!

The JESUS CONNECTION

In the book of Ezekiel, God compares himself to a shepherd who lovingly cares for his flock. In the New Testament, Jesus says he's the good shepherd. God sent Jesus to be our shepherd, to love us and lead us and save us from our sins. **With a shepherd like Jesus, we have nothing to fear!**

Ezekiel 1 . . . page 798

CHAPTER 1

A Vision of Living Beings

On July 31 of my thirtieth year, while I was with
the Judean exiles beside the Kebar River in Babylon, the heavens were opened and I saw visions
of God. 2This happened during the fifth year of
King Jehoiachin's captivity. 3(The LORD gave this
message to Ezekiel son of Buzi, a priest, beside the
Kebar River in the land of the Babylonians, and he
felt the hand of the LORD take hold of him.)

4As I looked, I saw a great storm coming from
the north, driving before it a huge cloud that
flashed with lightning and shone with brilliant
light. There was fire inside the cloud, and in the
middle of the fire glowed something like gleaming amber. 5From the center of the cloud came
four living beings that looked human, 6except
that each had four faces and four wings. 7Their
legs were straight, and their feet had hooves like
those of a calf and shone like burnished bronze.
8Under each of their four wings I could see human hands. So each of the four beings had four
faces and four wings. 9The wings of each living
being touched the wings of the beings beside it.
Each one moved straight forward in any direction
without turning around.

10Each had a human face in the front, the face
of a lion on the right side, the face of an ox on the
left side, and the face of an eagle at the back.
11Each had two pairs of outstretched wings—one
pair stretched out to touch the wings of the living
beings on either side of it, and the other pair covered its body. 12They went in whatever direction
the spirit chose, and they moved straight forward
in any direction without turning around.

13The living beings looked like bright coals of
fire or brilliant torches, and lightning seemed
to flash back and forth among them. 14And the
living beings darted to and fro like flashes of
lightning.

15As I looked at these beings, I saw four wheels
touching the ground beside them, one wheel
belonging to each. 16The wheels sparkled as if
made of beryl. All four wheels looked alike and
were made the same; each wheel had a second
wheel turning crosswise within it. 17The beings
could move in any of the four directions they
faced, without turning as they moved. 18The
rims of the four wheels were tall and frightening,
and they were covered with eyes all around.

19When the living beings moved, the wheels
moved with them. When they flew upward,
the wheels went up, too. 20The spirit of the living beings was in the wheels. So wherever the
spirit went, the wheels and the living beings
also went. 21When the beings moved, the
wheels moved. When the beings stopped, the
wheels stopped. When the beings flew upward,
the wheels rose up, for the spirit of the living
beings was in the wheels.

22Spread out above them was a surface like the
sky, glittering like crystal. 23Beneath this surface
the wings of each living being stretched out to
touch the others' wings, and each had two wings
covering its body. 24As they flew, their wings
sounded to me like waves crashing against the
shore or like the voice of the Almighty or like the
shouting of a mighty army. When they stopped,
they let down their wings. 25As they stood with
wings lowered, a voice spoke from beyond the
crystal surface above them.

26Above this surface was something that
looked like a throne made of blue lapis lazuli.
And on this throne high above was a figure
whose appearance resembled a man. 27From
what appeared to be his waist up, he looked like
gleaming amber, flickering like a fire. And from
his waist down, he looked like a burning flame,
shining with splendor. 28All around him was a
glowing halo, like a rainbow shining in the clouds
on a rainy day. This is what the glory of the LORD
looked like to me. When I saw it, I fell face down
on the ground, and I heard someone's voice
speaking to me.

CHAPTER 2

Ezekiel's Call and Commission

"Stand up, son of man," said the voice. "I want to
speak with you." 2The Spirit came into me as he
spoke, and he set me on my feet. I listened carefully to his words. 3"Son of man," he said, "I am
sending you to the nation of Israel, a rebellious
nation that has rebelled against me. They and
their ancestors have been rebelling against me to
this very day. 4They are a stubborn and hard-
hearted people. But I am sending you to say to
them, 'This is what the Sovereign LORD says!'
5And whether they listen or refuse to listen—for
remember, they are rebels—at least they will
know they have had a prophet among them.

6"Son of man, do not fear them or their words.
Don't be afraid even though their threats surround you like nettles and briers and stinging
scorpions. Do not be dismayed by their dark
scowls, even though they are rebels. 7You must
give them my messages whether they listen or
not. But they won't listen, for they are completely
rebellious! 8Son of man, listen to what I say to
you. Do not join them in their rebellion. Open
your mouth, and eat what I give you."

9 Then I looked and saw a hand reaching out to me. It held a scroll, 10 which he unrolled. And I saw that both sides were covered with funeral songs, words of sorrow, and pronouncements of doom.

CHAPTER 3

The voice said to me, "Son of man, eat what I am giving you—eat this scroll! Then go and give its message to the people of Israel." 2 So I opened my mouth, and he fed me the scroll. 3 "Fill your stomach with this," he said. And when I ate it, it tasted as sweet as honey in my mouth.

4 Then he said, "Son of man, go to the people of Israel and give them my messages. 5 I am not sending you to a foreign people whose language you cannot understand. 6 No, I am not sending you to people with strange and difficult speech. If I did, they would listen! 7 But the people of Israel won't listen to you any more than they listen to me! For the whole lot of them are hard-hearted and stubborn. 8 But look, I have made you as obstinate and hard-hearted as they are. 9 I have made your forehead as hard as the hardest rock! So don't be afraid of them or fear their angry looks, even though they are rebels."

10 Then he added, "Son of man, let all my words sink deep into your own heart first. Listen to them carefully for yourself. 11 Then go to your people in exile and say to them, 'This is what the Sovereign LORD says!' Do this whether they listen to you or not."

12 Then the Spirit lifted me up, and I heard a loud rumbling sound behind me. (May the glory of the LORD be praised in his place!) 13 It was the sound of the wings of the living beings as they brushed against each other and the rumbling of their wheels beneath them.

14 The Spirit lifted me up and took me away. I went in bitterness and turmoil, but the LORD's hold on me was strong. 15 Then I came to the colony of Judean exiles in Tel-abib, beside the Kebar River. I was overwhelmed and sat among them for seven days.

A Watchman for Israel

16 After seven days the LORD gave me a message. He said, 17 "Son of man, I have appointed you as a watchman for Israel. Whenever you receive a message from me, warn people immediately. 18 If I warn the wicked, saying, 'You are under the penalty of death,' but you fail to deliver the warning, they will die in their sins. And I will hold you responsible for their deaths. 19 If you warn them and they refuse to repent and keep on sinning, they will die in their sins. But you will have saved yourself because you obeyed me.

20 "If righteous people turn away from their righteous behavior and ignore the obstacles I put in their way, they will die. And if you do not warn them, they will die in their sins. None of their righteous acts will be remembered, and I will hold you responsible for their deaths. 21 But if you warn righteous people not to sin and they listen to you and do not sin, they will live, and you will have saved yourself, too."

22 Then the LORD took hold of me and said, "Get up and go out into the valley, and I will speak to you there." 23 So I got up and went, and there I saw the glory of the LORD, just as I had seen in my first vision by the Kebar River. And I fell face down on the ground.

24 Then the Spirit came into me and set me on my feet. He spoke to me and said, "Go to your house and shut yourself in. 25 There, son of man, you will be tied with ropes so you cannot go out among the people. 26 And I will make your tongue stick to the roof of your mouth so that you will be speechless and unable to rebuke them, for they are rebels. 27 But when I give you a message, I will loosen your tongue and let you speak. Then you will say to them, 'This is what the Sovereign LORD says!' Those who choose to listen will listen, but those who refuse will refuse, for they are rebels.

CHAPTER 4

A Sign of the Coming Siege

"And now, son of man, take a large clay brick and set it down in front of you. Then draw a map of the city of Jerusalem on it. 2 Show the city under siege. Build a wall around it so no one can escape. Set up the enemy camp, and surround the city with siege ramps and battering rams. 3 Then take an iron griddle and place it between you and the city. Turn toward the city and demonstrate how harsh the siege will be against Jerusalem. This will be a warning to the people of Israel.

4 "Now lie on your left side and place the sins of Israel on yourself. You are to bear their sins for the number of days you lie there on your side. 5 I am requiring you to bear Israel's sins for 390 days—one day for each year of their sin. 6 After that, turn over and lie on your right side for 40 days—one day for each year of Judah's sin.

7 "Meanwhile, keep staring at the siege of Jerusalem. Lie there with your arm bared and prophesy her destruction. 8 I will tie you up with ropes so you won't be able to turn from side to

side until the days of your siege have been completed.
9"Now go and get some wheat, barley, beans,
lentils, millet, and emmer wheat, and mix them
together in a storage jar. Use them to make bread
for yourself during the 390 days you will be lying
on your side. 10Ration this out to yourself, eight
ounces of food for each day, and eat it at set
times. 11Then measure out a jar of water for each
day, and drink it at set times. 12Prepare and eat
this food as you would barley cakes. While all the
people are watching, bake it over a fire using
dried human dung as fuel and then eat the
bread." 13Then the LORD said, "This is how Israel
will eat defiled bread in the Gentile lands to
which I will banish them!"

14Then I said, "O Sovereign LORD, must I be
defiled by using human dung? For I have never
been defiled before. From the time I was a child
until now I have never eaten any animal that died
of sickness or was killed by other animals. I have
never eaten any meat forbidden by the law."

15"All right," the LORD said. "You may bake
your bread with cow dung instead of human
dung." 16Then he told me, "Son of man, I will
make food very scarce in Jerusalem. It will be
weighed out with great care and eaten fearfully.
The water will be rationed out drop by drop, and
the people will drink it with dismay. 17Lacking
food and water, people will look at one another
in terror, and they will waste away under their
punishment.

CHAPTER 5
A Sign of the Coming Judgment

"Son of man, take a sharp sword and use it as a
razor to shave your head and beard. Use a scale
to weigh the hair into three equal parts. 2Place a
third of it at the center of your map of Jerusalem. After acting out the siege, burn it there.
Scatter another third across your map and chop
it with a sword. Scatter the last third to the
wind, for I will scatter my people with the
sword. 3Keep just a bit of the hair and tie it up in
your robe. 4Then take some of these hairs out
and throw them into the fire, burning them up. A
fire will then spread from this remnant and
destroy all of Israel.

5"This is what the Sovereign LORD says: This is
an illustration of what will happen to Jerusalem.
I placed her at the center of the nations, 6but she
has rebelled against my regulations and decrees
and has been even more wicked than the surrounding nations. She has refused to obey the
regulations and decrees I gave her to follow.

7"Therefore, this is what the Sovereign LORD
says: You people have behaved worse than your
neighbors and have refused to obey my decrees
and regulations. You have not even lived up to
the standards of the nations around you. 8There-
fore, I myself, the Sovereign LORD, am now your
enemy. I will punish you publicly while all the
nations watch. 9Because of your detestable idols,
I will punish you like I have never punished anyone before or ever will again. 10Parents will eat
their own children, and children will eat their
parents. I will punish you and scatter to the
winds the few who survive.

11"As surely as I live, says the Sovereign LORD, I
will cut you off completely. I will show you no
pity at all because you have defiled my Temple
with your vile images and detestable sins. 12A
third of your people will die in the city from disease and famine. A third of them will be slaughtered by the enemy outside the city walls. And I
will scatter a third to the winds, chasing them
with my sword. 13Then at last my anger will be
spent, and I will be satisfied. And when my fury
against them has subsided, all Israel will know
that I, the LORD, have spoken to them in my jealous anger.

14"So I will turn you into a ruin, a mockery in
the eyes of the surrounding nations and to all
who pass by. 15You will become an object of
mockery and taunting and horror. You will be a
warning to all the nations around you. They will
see what happens when the LORD punishes a nation in anger and rebukes it, says the LORD.

16"I will shower you with the deadly arrows of
famine to destroy you. The famine will become
more and more severe until every crumb of food
is gone. 17And along with the famine, wild animals will attack you and rob you of your children.
Disease and war will stalk your land, and I will
bring the sword of the enemy against you. I, the
LORD, have spoken!"

CHAPTER 6
Judgment against Israel's Mountains

Again a message came to me from the LORD:
2"Son of man, turn and face the mountains of Israel and prophesy against them. 3Proclaim this
message from the Sovereign LORD against the
mountains of Israel. This is what the Sovereign
LORD says to the mountains and hills and to the
ravines and valleys: I am about to bring war upon
you, and I will smash your pagan shrines. 4All
your altars will be demolished, and your places
of worship will be destroyed. I will kill your peo-

ple in front of your idols. 5 I will lay your corpses
in front of your idols and scatter your bones
around your altars. 6 Wherever you live there will
be desolation, and I will destroy your pagan
shrines. Your altars will be demolished, your
idols will be smashed, your places of worship will
be torn down, and all the religious objects you
have made will be destroyed. 7 The place will be
littered with corpses, and you will know that I
alone am the LORD.

8 "But I will let a few of my people escape destruction, and they will be scattered among the
nations of the world. 9 Then when they are exiled
among the nations, they will remember me. They
will recognize how hurt I am by their unfaithful
hearts and lustful eyes that long for their idols.
Then at last they will hate themselves for all their
detestable sins. 10 They will know that I alone
am the LORD and that I was serious when I said
I would bring this calamity on them.

11 "This is what the Sovereign LORD says: Clap
your hands in horror, and stamp your feet. Cry out
because of all the detestable sins the people of
Israel have committed. Now they are going to die
from war and famine and disease. 12 Disease will
strike down those who are far away in exile. War
will destroy those who are nearby. And anyone
who survives will be killed by famine. So at last I
will spend my fury on them. 13 They will know that
I am the LORD when their dead lie scattered
among their idols and altars on every hill and
mountain and under every green tree and every
great shade tree—the places where they offered
sacrifices to their idols. 14 I will crush them and
make their cities desolate from the wilderness in
the south to Riblah in the north. Then they will
know that I am the LORD."

CHAPTER 7

The Coming of the End

Then this message came to me from the LORD:
2 "Son of man, this is what the Sovereign LORD
says to Israel:

"The end is here!
  Wherever you look—
east, west, north, or south—
  your land is finished.
3 No hope remains,
  for I will unleash my anger against you.
I will call you to account
  for all your detestable sins.
4 I will turn my eyes away and show no pity.
  I will repay you for all your detestable sins.
Then you will know that I am the LORD.

5 "This is what the Sovereign LORD says:
Disaster after disaster
  is coming your way!
6 The end has come.
  It has finally arrived.
  Your final doom is waiting!
7 O people of Israel, the day of your
    destruction is dawning.
  The time has come; the day of trouble
    is near.
Shouts of anguish will be heard on the
    mountains,
  not shouts of joy.
8 Soon I will pour out my fury on you
  and unleash my anger against you.
I will call you to account
  for all your detestable sins.
9 I will turn my eyes away and show no pity.
  I will repay you for all your detestable sins.
Then you will know that it is I, the LORD,
  who is striking the blow.

10 "The day of judgment is here;
  your destruction awaits!
The people's wickedness and pride
  have blossomed to full flower.
11 Their violence has grown into a rod
  that will beat them for their wickedness.
None of these proud and wicked people
    will survive.
  All their wealth and prestige will be
    swept away.
12 Yes, the time has come;
  the day is here!
Buyers should not rejoice over bargains,
  nor sellers grieve over losses,
for all of them will fall
  under my terrible anger.
13 Even if the merchants survive,
  they will never return to their business.
For what God has said applies to everyone—
  it will not be changed!
Not one person whose life is twisted by sin
  will ever recover.

The Desolation of Israel

14 "The trumpet calls Israel's army to mobilize,
  but no one listens,
  for my fury is against them all.
15 There is war outside the city
  and disease and famine within.
Those outside the city walls
  will be killed by enemy swords.
Those inside the city
  will die of famine and disease.

16 The survivors who escape to the mountains
will moan like doves, weeping for
their sins.
17 Their hands will hang limp,
their knees will be weak as water.
18 They will dress themselves in burlap;
horror and shame will cover them.
They will shave their heads
in sorrow and remorse.

19 "They will throw their money in the streets,
tossing it out like worthless trash.
Their silver and gold won't save them
on that day of the LORD's anger.
It will neither satisfy nor feed them,
for their greed can only trip them up.
20 They were proud of their beautiful jewelry
and used it to make detestable idols
and vile images.
Therefore, I will make all their wealth
disgusting to them.
21 I will give it as plunder to foreigners,
to the most wicked of nations,
and they will defile it.
22 I will turn my eyes from them
as these robbers invade and defile my
treasured land.

23 "Prepare chains for my people,
for the land is bloodied by terrible
crimes.
Jerusalem is filled with violence.
24 I will bring the most ruthless of nations
to occupy their homes.
I will break down their proud fortresses
and defile their sanctuaries.
25 Terror and trembling will overcome
my people.
They will look for peace but not find it.
26 Calamity will follow calamity;
rumor will follow rumor.
They will look in vain
for a vision from the prophets.
They will receive no teaching from the
priests
and no counsel from the leaders.
27 The king and the prince will stand
helpless,
weeping in despair,
and the people's hands
will tremble with fear.
I will bring on them
the evil they have done to others,
and they will receive the punishment
they so richly deserve.
Then they will know that I am the LORD."

CHAPTER 8

Idolatry in the Temple

Then on September 17, during the sixth year of
King Jehoiachin's captivity, while the leaders of
Judah were in my home, the Sovereign LORD took
hold of me. 2 I saw a figure that appeared to be a
man. From what appeared to be his waist down,
he looked like a burning flame. From the waist
up he looked like gleaming amber. 3 He reached
out what seemed to be a hand and took me by the
hair. Then the Spirit lifted me up into the sky and
transported me to Jerusalem in a vision from
God. I was taken to the north gate of the inner
courtyard of the Temple, where there is a large
idol that has made the LORD very jealous. 4 Suddenly, the glory of the God of Israel was there, just
as I had seen it before in the valley.

5 Then the LORD said to me, "Son of man, look
toward the north." So I looked, and there to the
north, beside the entrance to the gate near the
altar, stood the idol that had made the LORD so
jealous.

6 "Son of man," he said, "do you see what they
are doing? Do you see the detestable sins the
people of Israel are committing to drive me from
my Temple? But come, and you will see even
more detestable sins than these!" 7 Then he
brought me to the door of the Temple courtyard,
where I could see a hole in the wall. 8 He said to
me, "Now, son of man, dig into the wall." So I dug
into the wall and found a hidden doorway.

9 "Go in," he said, "and see the wicked and detestable sins they are committing in there!" 10 So
I went in and saw the walls covered with engrav-
ings of all kinds of crawling animals and detestable creatures. I also saw the various idols
worshiped by the people of Israel. 11 Seventy
leaders of Israel were standing there with Jaazaniah son of Shaphan in the center. Each of them
held an incense burner, from which a cloud of incense rose above their heads.

12 Then the LORD said to me, "Son of man, have
you seen what the leaders of Israel are doing with
their idols in dark rooms? They are saying, 'The
LORD doesn't see us; he has deserted our land!'"
13 Then the LORD added, "Come, and I will show
you even more detestable sins than these!"

14 He brought me to the north gate of the
LORD's Temple, and some women were sitting
there, weeping for the god Tammuz. 15 "Have you
seen this?" he asked. "But I will show you even
more detestable sins than these!"

16 Then he brought me into the inner courtyard of the LORD's Temple. At the entrance to the
sanctuary, between the entry room and the

bronze altar, there were about twenty-five men
with their backs to the sanctuary of the LORD.
They were facing east, bowing low to the ground,
worshiping the sun!
17"Have you seen this, son of man?" he asked.
"Is it nothing to the people of Judah that they
commit these detestable sins, leading the whole
nation into violence, thumbing their noses at me,
and provoking my anger? 18Therefore, I will respond in fury. I will neither pity nor spare them.
And though they cry for mercy, I will not listen."

CHAPTER 9
The Slaughter of Idolaters

Then the LORD thundered, "Bring on the men
appointed to punish the city! Tell them to bring
their weapons with them!" 2Six men soon appeared from the upper gate that faces north,
each carrying a deadly weapon in his hand. With
them was a man dressed in linen, who carried a
writer's case at his side. They all went into the
Temple courtyard and stood beside the bronze
altar.
3Then the glory of the God of Israel rose up
from between the cherubim, where it had rested,
and moved to the entrance of the Temple. And
the LORD called to the man dressed in linen who
was carrying the writer's case. 4He said to him,
"Walk through the streets of Jerusalem and put a
mark on the foreheads of all who weep and sigh
because of the detestable sins being committed
in their city."
5Then I heard the LORD say to the other men,
"Follow him through the city and kill everyone
whose forehead is not marked. Show no mercy;
have no pity! 6Kill them all—old and young, girls
and women and little children. But do not touch
anyone with the mark. Begin right here at the
Temple." So they began by killing the seventy
leaders.
7"Defile the Temple!" the LORD commanded.
"Fill its courtyards with corpses. Go!" So they
went and began killing throughout the city.
8While they were out killing, I was all alone. I
fell face down on the ground and cried out,
"O Sovereign LORD! Will your fury against Jerusalem wipe out everyone left in Israel?"
9Then he said to me, "The sins of the people of
Israel and Judah are very, very great. The entire
land is full of murder; the city is filled with injustice. They are saying, 'The LORD doesn't see it!
The LORD has abandoned the land!' 10So I will
not spare them or have any pity on them. I will
fully repay them for all they have done."
11Then the man in linen clothing, who carried
the writer's case, reported back and said, "I have
done as you commanded."

CHAPTER 10
The LORD's Glory Leaves the Temple

In my vision I saw what appeared to be a throne
of blue lapis lazuli above the crystal surface over
the heads of the cherubim. 2Then the LORD
spoke to the man in linen clothing and said, "Go
between the whirling wheels beneath the cherubim, and take a handful of burning coals and
scatter them over the city." He did this as I
watched.
3The cherubim were standing at the south
end of the Temple when the man went in, and the
cloud of glory filled the inner courtyard. 4Then
the glory of the LORD rose up from above the
cherubim and went over to the entrance of the
Temple. The Temple was filled with this cloud of
glory, and the courtyard glowed brightly with
the glory of the LORD. 5The moving wings of
the cherubim sounded like the voice of God
Almighty and could be heard even in the outer
courtyard.
6The LORD said to the man in linen clothing,
"Go between the cherubim and take some burning coals from between the wheels." So the man
went in and stood beside one of the wheels.
7Then one of the cherubim reached out his hand
and took some live coals from the fire burning
among them. He put the coals into the hands of
the man in linen clothing, and the man took
them and went out. 8(All the cherubim had what
looked like human hands under their wings.)
9I looked, and each of the four cherubim had a
wheel beside him, and the wheels sparkled like
beryl. 10All four wheels looked alike and were
made the same; each wheel had a second wheel
turning crosswise within it. 11The cherubim
could move in any of the four directions they
faced, without turning as they moved. They went
straight in the direction they faced, never turning
aside. 12Both the cherubim and the wheels were
covered with eyes. The cherubim had eyes all over
their bodies, including their hands, their backs,
and their wings. 13I heard someone refer to
the wheels as "the whirling wheels." 14Each of the
four cherubim had four faces: the first was the
face of an ox, the second was a human face,
the third was the face of a lion, and the fourth was
the face of an eagle.
15Then the cherubim rose upward. These
were the same living beings I had seen beside the
Kebar River. 16When the cherubim moved, the

wheels moved with them. When they lifted their wings to fly, the wheels stayed beside them. 17When the cherubim stopped, the wheels stopped. When they flew upward, the wheels rose up, for the spirit of the living beings was in the wheels.

18Then the glory of the LORD moved out from the entrance of the Temple and hovered above the cherubim. 19And as I watched, the cherubim flew with their wheels to the east gate of the LORD's Temple. And the glory of the God of Israel hovered above them.

20These were the same living beings I had seen beneath the God of Israel when I was by the Kebar River. I knew they were cherubim, 21for each had four faces and four wings and what looked like human hands under their wings. 22And their faces were just like the faces of the beings I had seen at the Kebar, and they traveled straight ahead, just as the others had.

CHAPTER 11

Judgment on Israel's Leaders

Then the Spirit lifted me and brought me to the east gateway of the LORD's Temple, where I saw twenty-five prominent men of the city. Among them were Jaazaniah son of Azzur and Pelatiah son of Benaiah, who were leaders among the people.

2The Spirit said to me, "Son of man, these are the men who are planning evil and giving wicked counsel in this city. 3They say to the people, 'Is it not a good time to build houses? This city is like an iron pot. We are safe inside it like meat in a pot.' 4Therefore, son of man, prophesy against them loudly and clearly."

5Then the Spirit of the LORD came upon me, and he told me to say, "This is what the LORD says to the people of Israel: I know what you are saying, for I know every thought that comes into your minds. 6You have murdered many in this city and filled its streets with the dead.

7"Therefore, this is what the Sovereign LORD says: This city is an iron pot all right, but the pieces of meat are the victims of your injustice. As for you, I will soon drag you from this pot. 8I will bring on you the sword of war you so greatly fear, says the Sovereign LORD. 9I will drive you out of Jerusalem and hand you over to foreigners, who will carry out my judgments against you. 10You will be slaughtered all the way to the borders of Israel. I will execute judgment on you, and you will know that I am the LORD. 11No, this city will not be an iron pot for you, and you will not be like meat safe inside it. I will judge you even to the borders of Israel, 12and you will know that I am the LORD. For you have refused to obey my decrees and regulations; instead, you have copied the standards of the nations around you."

13While I was still prophesying, Pelatiah son of Benaiah suddenly died. Then I fell face down on the ground and cried out, "O Sovereign LORD, are you going to kill everyone in Israel?"

Hope for Exiled Israel

14Then this message came to me from the LORD: 15"Son of man, the people still left in Jerusalem are talking about you and your relatives and all the people of Israel who are in exile. They are saying, 'Those people are far away from the LORD, so now he has given their land to us!'

16"Therefore, tell the exiles, 'This is what the Sovereign LORD says: Although I have scattered you in the countries of the world, I will be a sanctuary to you during your time in exile. 17I, the Sovereign LORD, will gather you back from the nations where you have been scattered, and I will give you the land of Israel once again.'

18"When the people return to their homeland, they will remove every trace of their vile images and detestable idols. 19And I will give them singleness of heart and put a new spirit within them. I will take away their stony, stubborn heart and give them a tender, responsive heart, 20so they will obey my decrees and regulations. Then they will truly be my people, and I will be their God. 21But as for those who long for vile images and detestable idols, I will repay them fully for their sins. I, the Sovereign LORD, have spoken!"

The LORD's Glory Leaves Jerusalem

22Then the cherubim lifted their wings and rose into the air with their wheels beside them, and the glory of the God of Israel hovered above them. 23Then the glory of the LORD went up from the city and stopped above the mountain to the east.

24Afterward the Spirit of God carried me back again to Babylonia, to the people in exile there. And so ended the vision of my visit to Jerusalem. 25And I told the exiles everything the LORD had shown me.

CHAPTER 12

Signs of the Coming Exile

Again a message came to me from the LORD: 2"Son of man, you live among rebels who have

eyes but refuse to see. They have ears but refuse
to hear. For they are a rebellious people.
3"So now, son of man, pretend you are being
sent into exile. Pack the few items an exile could
carry, and leave your home to go somewhere else.
Do this right in front of the people so they can
see you. For perhaps they will pay attention to
this, even though they are such rebels. 4Bring
your baggage outside during the day so they can
watch you. Then in the evening, as they are
watching, leave your house as captives do when
they begin a long march to distant lands. 5Dig a
hole through the wall while they are watching
and go out through it. 6As they watch, lift your
pack to your shoulders and walk away into the
night. Cover your face so you cannot see the land
you are leaving. For I have made you a sign for the
people of Israel."
7So I did as I was told. In broad daylight I
brought my pack outside, filled with the things I
might carry into exile. Then in the evening while
the people looked on, I dug through the wall with
my hands and went out into the night with my
pack on my shoulder.
8The next morning this message came to me
from the LORD: 9"Son of man, these rebels, the
people of Israel, have asked you what all this
means. 10Say to them, 'This is what the Sovereign LORD says: These actions contain a message
for King Zedekiah in Jerusalem and for all the
people of Israel.' 11Explain that your actions are a
sign to show what will soon happen to them, for
they will be driven into exile as captives.
12"Even Zedekiah will leave Jerusalem at night
through a hole in the wall, taking only what he
can carry with him. He will cover his face, and his
eyes will not see the land he is leaving. 13Then I
will throw my net over him and capture him in
my snare. I will bring him to Babylon, the land of
the Babylonians, though he will never see it, and
he will die there. 14I will scatter his servants and
warriors to the four winds and send the sword
after them. 15And when I scatter them among
the nations, they will know that I am the LORD.
16But I will spare a few of them from death by
war, famine, or disease, so they can confess all
their detestable sins to their captors. Then they
will know that I am the LORD."
17Then this message came to me from the
LORD: 18"Son of man, tremble as you eat your
food. Shake with fear as you drink your water.
19Tell the people, 'This is what the Sovereign
LORD says concerning those living in Israel and
Jerusalem: They will eat their food with trembling and sip their water in despair, for their land
will be stripped bare because of their violence.
20The cities will be destroyed and the farmland
made desolate. Then you will know that I am the
LORD.'"

A New Proverb for Israel

21Again a message came to me from the LORD:
22"Son of man, you've heard that proverb they
quote in Israel: 'Time passes, and prophecies
come to nothing.' 23Tell the people, 'This is what
the Sovereign LORD says: I will put an end to this
proverb, and you will soon stop quoting it.' Now
give them this new proverb to replace the old
one: 'The time has come for every prophecy to be
fulfilled!'
24"There will be no more false visions and
flattering predictions in Israel. 25For I am the
LORD! If I say it, it will happen. There will be no
more delays, you rebels of Israel. I will fulfill my

threat of destruction in your own lifetime. I, the
Sovereign LORD, have spoken!"
26 Then this message came to me from the
LORD: 27 "Son of man, the people of Israel are saying, 'He's talking about the distant future. His
visions won't come true for a long, long time.'
28 Therefore, tell them, 'This is what the Sovereign LORD says: No more delay! I will now do
everything I have threatened. I, the Sovereign
LORD, have spoken!'"

CHAPTER 13

Judgment against False Prophets

Then this message came to me from the LORD:
2 "Son of man, prophesy against the false prophets of Israel who are inventing their own prophecies. Say to them, 'Listen to the word of the
LORD. 3 This is what the Sovereign LORD says:
What sorrow awaits the false prophets who are
following their own imaginations and have seen
nothing at all!'
4 "O people of Israel, these prophets of yours
are like jackals digging in the ruins. 5 They have
done nothing to repair the breaks in the walls
around the nation. They have not helped it to
stand firm in battle on the day of the LORD. 6 Instead, they have told lies and made false predictions. They say, 'This message is from the LORD,'
even though the LORD never sent them. And yet
they expect him to fulfill their prophecies! 7 Can
your visions be anything but false if you claim,
'This message is from the LORD,' when I have not
even spoken to you?
8 "Therefore, this is what the Sovereign LORD
says: Because what you say is false and your visions are a lie, I will stand against you, says the
Sovereign LORD. 9 I will raise my fist against all
the prophets who see false visions and make lying predictions, and they will be banished from
the community of Israel. I will blot their names
from Israel's record books, and they will never
again set foot in their own land. Then you will
know that I am the Sovereign LORD.
10 "This will happen because these evil prophets deceive my people by saying, 'All is peaceful'
when there is no peace at all! It's as if the people
have built a flimsy wall, and these prophets are
trying to reinforce it by covering it with whitewash! 11 Tell these whitewashers that their wall
will soon fall down. A heavy rainstorm will
undermine it; great hailstones and mighty winds
will knock it down. 12 And when the wall falls, the
people will cry out, 'What happened to your
whitewash?'
13 "Therefore, this is what the Sovereign LORD
says: I will sweep away your whitewashed wall
with a storm of indignation, with a great flood of
anger, and with hailstones of fury. 14 I will break
down your wall right to its foundation, and when
it falls, it will crush you. Then you will know that I
am the LORD. 15 At last my anger against the wall
and those who covered it with whitewash will be
satisfied. Then I will say to you: 'The wall and
those who whitewashed it are both gone. 16 They
were lying prophets who claimed peace would
come to Jerusalem when there was no peace. I,
the Sovereign LORD, have spoken!'

Judgment against False Women Prophets

17 "Now, son of man, speak out against the
women who prophesy from their own imaginations. 18 This is what the Sovereign LORD says:
What sorrow awaits you women who are ensnar-
ing the souls of my people, young and old alike.
You tie magic charms on their wrists and furnish
them with magic veils. Do you think you can trap
others without bringing destruction on yourselves? 19 You bring shame on me among my
people for a few handfuls of barley or a piece of
bread. By lying to my people who love to listen to
lies, you kill those who should not die, and you
promise life to those who should not live.
20 "This is what the Sovereign LORD says: I am
against all your magic charms, which you use to
ensnare my people like birds. I will tear them
from your arms, setting my people free like birds
set free from a cage. 21 I will tear off the magic
veils and save my people from your grasp. They
will no longer be your victims. Then you will
know that I am the LORD. 22 You have discouraged the righteous with your lies, but I didn't
want them to be sad. And you have encouraged
the wicked by promising them life, even though
they continue in their sins. 23 Because of all this,
you will no longer talk of seeing visions that you
never saw, nor will you make predictions. For I
will rescue my people from your grasp. Then you
will know that I am the LORD."

CHAPTER 14

The Idolatry of Israel's Leaders

Then some of the leaders of Israel visited me, and
while they were sitting with me, 2 this message
came to me from the LORD: 3 "Son of man, these
leaders have set up idols in their hearts. They
have embraced things that will make them fall
into sin. Why should I listen to their requests?
4 Tell them, 'This is what the Sovereign LORD says:

The people of Israel have set up idols in their hearts and fallen into sin, and then they go to a prophet asking for a message. So I, the LORD, will give them the kind of answer their great idolatry deserves. 5 I will do this to capture the minds and hearts of all my people who have turned from me to worship their detestable idols.'

6 "Therefore, tell the people of Israel, 'This is what the Sovereign LORD says: Repent and turn away from your idols, and stop all your detestable sins. 7 I, the LORD, will answer all those, both Israelites and foreigners, who reject me and set up idols in their hearts and so fall into sin, and who then come to a prophet asking for my advice. 8 I will turn against such people and make a terrible example of them, eliminating them from among my people. Then you will know that I am the LORD.

9 "'And if a prophet is deceived into giving a message, it is because I, the LORD, have deceived that prophet. I will lift my fist against such prophets and cut them off from the community of Israel. 10 False prophets and those who seek their guidance will all be punished for their sins. 11 In this way, the people of Israel will learn not to stray from me, polluting themselves with sin. They will be my people, and I will be their God. I, the Sovereign LORD, have spoken!'"

The Certainty of the LORD's Judgment

12 Then this message came to me from the LORD: 13 "Son of man, suppose the people of a country were to sin against me, and I lifted my fist to crush them, cutting off their food supply and sending a famine to destroy both people and animals. 14 Even if Noah, Daniel, and Job were there, their righteousness would save no one but themselves, says the Sovereign LORD.

15 "Or suppose I were to send wild animals to invade the country, kill the people, and make the land too desolate and dangerous to pass through. 16 As surely as I live, says the Sovereign LORD, even if those three men were there, they wouldn't be able to save their own sons or daughters. They alone would be saved, but the land would be made desolate.

17 "Or suppose I were to bring war against the land, and I sent enemy armies to destroy both people and animals. 18 As surely as I live, says the Sovereign LORD, even if those three men were there, they wouldn't be able to save their own sons or daughters. They alone would be saved.

19 "Or suppose I were to pour out my fury by sending an epidemic into the land, and the disease killed people and animals alike. 20 As surely as I live, says the Sovereign LORD, even if Noah, Daniel, and Job were there, they wouldn't be able to save their own sons or daughters. They alone would be saved by their righteousness.

21 "Now this is what the Sovereign LORD says: How terrible it will be when all four of these dreadful punishments fall upon Jerusalem—war, famine, wild animals, and disease—destroying all her people and animals. 22 Yet there will be survivors, and they will come here to join you as exiles in Babylon. You will see with your own eyes how wicked they are, and then you will feel better about what I have done to Jerusalem. 23 When you meet them and see their behavior, you will understand that these things are not being done to Israel without cause. I, the Sovereign LORD, have spoken!"

CHAPTER 15

Jerusalem—a Useless Vine

Then this message came to me from the LORD: 2 "Son of man, how does a grapevine compare to a tree? Is a vine's wood as useful as the wood of a tree? 3 Can its wood be used for making things, like pegs to hang up pots and pans? 4 No, it can only be used for fuel, and even as fuel, it burns too quickly. 5 Vines are useless both before and after being put into the fire!

6 "And this is what the Sovereign LORD says: The people of Jerusalem are like grapevines growing among the trees of the forest. Since they are useless, I have thrown them on the fire to be burned. 7 And I will see to it that if they escape from one fire, they will fall into another. When I turn against them, you will know that I am the LORD. 8 And I will make the land desolate because my people have been unfaithful to me. I, the Sovereign LORD, have spoken!"

CHAPTER 16

Jerusalem—an Unfaithful Wife

Then another message came to me from the LORD: 2 "Son of man, confront Jerusalem with her detestable sins. 3 Give her this message from the Sovereign LORD: You are nothing but a Canaanite! Your father was an Amorite and your mother a Hittite. 4 On the day you were born, no one cared about you. Your umbilical cord was not cut, and you were never washed, rubbed with salt, and wrapped in cloth. 5 No one had the slightest interest in you; no one pitied you or cared for you. On the day you were born, you were unwanted, dumped in a field and left to die.

6 "But I came by and saw you there, helplessly

kicking about in your own blood. As you lay there, I said, 'Live!' 7And I helped you to thrive like a plant in the field. You grew up and became a beautiful jewel. Your breasts became full, and your body hair grew, but you were still naked. 8And when I passed by again, I saw that you were old enough for love. So I wrapped my cloak around you to cover your nakedness and declared my marriage vows. I made a covenant with you, says the Sovereign LORD, and you became mine.

9"Then I bathed you and washed off your blood, and I rubbed fragrant oils into your skin. 10I gave you expensive clothing of fine linen and silk, beautifully embroidered, and sandals made of fine goatskin leather. 11I gave you lovely jewelry, bracelets, beautiful necklaces, 12a ring for your nose, earrings for your ears, and a lovely crown for your head. 13And so you were adorned with gold and silver. Your clothes were made of fine linen and costly fabric and were beautifully embroidered. You ate the finest foods—choice flour, honey, and olive oil—and became more beautiful than ever. You looked like a queen, and so you were! 14Your fame soon spread throughout the world because of your beauty. I dressed you in my splendor and perfected your beauty, says the Sovereign LORD.

15"But you thought your fame and beauty were your own. So you gave yourself as a prostitute to every man who came along. Your beauty was theirs for the asking. 16You used the lovely things I gave you to make shrines for idols, where you played the prostitute. Unbelievable! How could such a thing ever happen? 17You took the very jewels and gold and silver ornaments I had given you and made statues of men and worshiped them. This is adultery against me! 18You used the beautifully embroidered clothes I gave you to dress your idols. Then you used my special oil and my incense to worship them. 19Imagine it! You set before them as a sacrifice the choice flour, olive oil, and honey I had given you, says the Sovereign LORD.

20"Then you took your sons and daughters—the children you had borne to me—and sacrificed them to your gods. Was your prostitution not enough? 21Must you also slaughter my children by sacrificing them to idols? 22In all your years of adultery and detestable sin, you have not once remembered the days long ago when you lay naked in a field, kicking about in your own blood.

23"What sorrow awaits you, says the Sovereign LORD. In addition to all your other wickedness, 24you built a pagan shrine and put altars to idols in every town square. 25On every street corner you defiled your beauty, offering your body to every passerby in an endless stream of prostitution. 26Then you added lustful Egypt to your lovers, provoking my anger with your increasing promiscuity. 27That is why I struck you with my fist and reduced your boundaries. I handed you over to your enemies, the Philistines, and even they were shocked by your lewd conduct. 28You have prostituted yourself with the Assyrians, too. It seems you can never find enough new lovers! And after your prostitution there, you still were not satisfied. 29You added to your lovers by embracing Babylonia, the land of merchants, but you still weren't satisfied.

30"What a sick heart you have, says the Sovereign LORD, to do such things as these, acting like a shameless prostitute. 31You build your pagan shrines on every street corner and your altars to idols in every square. In fact, you have been worse than a prostitute, so eager for sin that you have not even demanded payment. 32Yes, you are an adulterous wife who takes in strangers instead of her own husband. 33Prostitutes charge for their services—but not you! You give gifts to your lovers, bribing them to come and have sex with you. 34So you are the opposite of other prostitutes. You pay your lovers instead of their paying you!

Judgment on Jerusalem's Prostitution

35"Therefore, you prostitute, listen to this message from the LORD! 36This is what the Sovereign LORD says: Because you have poured out your lust and exposed yourself in prostitution to all your lovers, and because you have worshiped detestable idols, and because you have slaughtered your children as sacrifices to your gods, 37this is what I am going to do. I will gather together all your allies—the lovers with whom you have sinned, both those you loved and those you hated—and I will strip you naked in front of them so they can stare at you. 38I will punish you for your murder and adultery. I will cover you with blood in my jealous fury. 39Then I will give you to these many nations who are your lovers, and they will destroy you. They will knock down your pagan shrines and the altars to your idols. They will strip you and take your beautiful jewels, leaving you stark naked. 40They will band together in a mob to stone you and cut you up with swords. 41They will burn your homes and punish you in front of many women. I will stop your prostitution and end your payments to your many lovers.

42"Then at last my fury against you will be

spent, and my jealous anger will subside. I will
be calm and will not be angry with you anymore.
43 But first, because you have not remembered
your youth but have angered me by doing all
these evil things, I will fully repay you for all of
your sins, says the Sovereign LORD. For you
have added lewd acts to all your detestable sins.
44 Everyone who makes up proverbs will say of
you, 'Like mother, like daughter.' 45 For your
mother loathed her husband and her children,
and so do you. And you are exactly like your sisters, for they despised their husbands and their
children. Truly your mother was a Hittite and
your father an Amorite.

46 "Your older sister was Samaria, who lived
with her daughters in the north. Your younger
sister was Sodom, who lived with her daughters
in the south. 47 But you have not merely sinned
as they did. You quickly surpassed them in corruption. 48 As surely as I live, says the Sovereign
LORD, Sodom and her daughters were never as
wicked as you and your daughters. 49 Sodom's
sins were pride, gluttony, and laziness, while the
poor and needy suffered outside her door.
50 She was proud and committed detestable
sins, so I wiped her out, as you have seen.

51 "Even Samaria did not commit half your
sins. You have done far more detestable things
than your sisters ever did. They seem righteous
compared to you. 52 Shame on you! Your sins are
so terrible that you make your sisters seem righteous, even virtuous.

53 "But someday I will restore the fortunes of
Sodom and Samaria, and I will restore you, too.
54 Then you will be truly ashamed of everything
you have done, for your sins make them feel good
in comparison. 55 Yes, your sisters, Sodom and
Samaria, and all their people will be restored,
and at that time you also will be restored. 56 In
your proud days you held Sodom in contempt.
57 But now your greater wickedness has been exposed to all the world, and you are the one who is
scorned—by Edom and all her neighbors and by
Philistia. 58 This is your punishment for all your
lewdness and detestable sins, says the LORD.

59 "Now this is what the Sovereign LORD says: I
will give you what you deserve, for you have
taken your solemn vows lightly by breaking your
covenant. 60 Yet I will remember the covenant I
made with you when you were young, and I will
establish an everlasting covenant with you.
61 Then you will remember with shame all the
evil you have done. I will make your sisters,
Samaria and Sodom, to be your daughters, even
though they are not part of our covenant. 62 And
I will reaffirm my covenant with you, and you
will know that I am the LORD. 63 You will remember your sins and cover your mouth in silent
shame when I forgive you of all that you have
done. I, the Sovereign LORD, have spoken!"

CHAPTER 17

A Story of Two Eagles

Then this message came to me from the LORD:
2 "Son of man, give this riddle, and tell this story
to the people of Israel. 3 Give them this message
from the Sovereign LORD:

"A great eagle with broad wings and
long feathers,
covered with many-colored plumage,
came to Lebanon.
He seized the top of a cedar tree
4 and plucked off its highest branch.
He carried it away to a city filled with
merchants.
He planted it in a city of traders.
5 He also took a seedling from the land
and planted it in fertile soil.
He placed it beside a broad river,
where it could grow like a willow tree.
6 It took root there and
grew into a low, spreading vine.
Its branches turned up toward the eagle,
and its roots grew down into the ground.
It produced strong branches
and put out shoots.
7 But then another great eagle came
with broad wings and full plumage.
So the vine now sent its roots and branches
toward him for water,
8 even though it was already planted
in good soil
and had plenty of water
so it could grow into a splendid vine
and produce rich leaves and luscious fruit.

9 "So now the Sovereign LORD asks:
Will this vine grow and prosper?
No! I will pull it up, roots and all!
I will cut off its fruit
and let its leaves wither and die.
I will pull it up easily
without a strong arm or a large army.
10 But when the vine is transplanted,
will it thrive?
No, it will wither away
when the east wind blows against it.
It will die in the same good soil
where it had grown so well."

Ezekiel 18 . . . page 810

The Riddle Explained

11 Then this message came to me from the LORD:
12 "Say to these rebels of Israel: Don't you understand the meaning of this riddle of the eagles?
The king of Babylon came to Jerusalem, took
away her king and princes, and brought them to
Babylon. 13 He made a treaty with a member of
the royal family and forced him to take an oath of
loyalty. He also exiled Israel's most influential
leaders, 14 so Israel would not become strong
again and revolt. Only by keeping her treaty with
Babylon could Israel survive.

15 "Nevertheless, this man of Israel's royal family rebelled against Babylon, sending ambassadors to Egypt to request a great army and many
horses. Can Israel break her sworn treaties like
that and get away with it? 16 No! For as surely as I
live, says the Sovereign LORD, the king of Israel
will die in Babylon, the land of the king who put
him in power and whose treaty he disregarded
and broke. 17 Pharaoh and all his mighty army
will fail to help Israel when the king of Babylon
lays siege to Jerusalem again and destroys many
lives. 18 For the king of Israel disregarded his
treaty and broke it after swearing to obey; therefore, he will not escape.

19 "So this is what the Sovereign LORD says: As
surely as I live, I will punish him for breaking my
covenant and disregarding the solemn oath he
made in my name. 20 I will throw my net over him
and capture him in my snare. I will bring him to
Babylon and put him on trial for this treason
against me. 21 And all his best warriors will be
killed in battle, and those who survive will be
scattered to the four winds. Then you will know
that I, the LORD, have spoken.

22 "This is what the Sovereign LORD says: I will
take a branch from the top of a tall cedar, and I
will plant it on the top of Israel's highest mountain. 23 It will become a majestic cedar, sending
forth its branches and producing seed. Birds of
every sort will nest in it, finding shelter in the
shade of its branches. 24 And all the trees will
know that it is I, the LORD, who cuts the tall tree
down and makes the short tree grow tall. It is I
who makes the green tree wither and gives the
dead tree new life. I, the LORD, have spoken, and I
will do what I said!"

CHAPTER 18

The Justice of a Righteous God

Then another message came to me from the
LORD: 2 "Why do you quote this proverb concerning the land of Israel: 'The parents have eaten sour
grapes, but their children's mouths pucker at the
taste'? 3 As surely as I live, says the Sovereign LORD,
you will not quote this proverb anymore in Israel.
4 For all people are mine to judge—both parents
and children alike. And this is my rule: The person
who sins is the one who will die.

5 "Suppose a certain man is righteous and does
what is just and right. 6 He does not feast in the
mountains before Israel's idols or worship them.
He does not commit adultery or have intercourse
with a woman during her menstrual period. 7 He
is a merciful creditor, not keeping the items given
as security by poor debtors. He does not rob the
poor but instead gives food to the hungry and
provides clothes for the needy. 8 He grants loans
without interest, stays away from injustice, is
honest and fair when judging others, 9 and faithfully obeys my decrees and regulations. Anyone
who does these things is just and will surely live,
says the Sovereign LORD.

10 "But suppose that man has a son who grows
up to be a robber or murderer and refuses to
do what is right. 11 And that son does all the evil
things his father would never do—he worships
idols on the mountains, commits adultery, 12 oppresses the poor and helpless, steals from debtors by refusing to let them redeem their security,
worships idols, commits detestable sins, 13 and
lends money at excessive interest. Should such a
sinful person live? No! He must die and must
take full blame.

14 "But suppose that sinful son, in turn, has a
son who sees his father's wickedness and decides
against that kind of life. 15 This son refuses to
worship idols on the mountains and does not
commit adultery. 16 He does not exploit the poor,
but instead is fair to debtors and does not rob
them. He gives food to the hungry and provides
clothes for the needy. 17 He helps the poor, does
not lend money at interest, and obeys all my regulations and decrees. Such a person will not die
because of his father's sins; he will surely live.
18 But the father will die for his many sins—for
being cruel, robbing people, and doing what was
clearly wrong among his people.

19 "'What?' you ask. 'Doesn't the child pay for
the parent's sins?' No! For if the child does what
is just and right and keeps my decrees, that child
will surely live. 20 The person who sins is the one
who will die. The child will not be punished for
the parent's sins, and the parent will not be punished for the child's sins. Righteous people will
be rewarded for their own righteous behavior,
and wicked people will be punished for their
own wickedness. 21 But if wicked people turn
away from all their sins and begin to obey my

decrees and do what is just and right, they will
surely live and not die. 22All their past sins will be
forgotten, and they will live because of the righteous things they have done.

23"Do you think that I like to see wicked people
die? says the Sovereign LORD. Of course not! I
want them to turn from their wicked ways and
live. 24However, if righteous people turn from
their righteous behavior and start doing sinful
things and act like other sinners, should they be
allowed to live? No, of course not! All their righteous acts will be forgotten, and they will die for
their sins.

25"Yet you say, 'The Lord isn't doing what's
right!' Listen to me, O people of Israel. Am I the
one not doing what's right, or is it you? 26When
righteous people turn from their righteous behavior and start doing sinful things, they will die
for it. Yes, they will die because of their sinful
deeds. 27And if wicked people turn from their
wickedness, obey the law, and do what is just and
right, they will save their lives. 28They will live
because they thought it over and decided to turn
from their sins. Such people will not die. 29And
yet the people of Israel keep saying, 'The Lord
isn't doing what's right!' O people of Israel, it is
you who are not doing what's right, not I.

30"Therefore, I will judge each of you, O people of Israel, according to your actions, says the
Sovereign LORD. Repent, and turn from your
sins. Don't let them destroy you! 31Put all your
rebellion behind you, and find yourselves a new
heart and a new spirit. For why should you die,
O people of Israel? 32I don't want you to die, says
the Sovereign LORD. Turn back and live!

CHAPTER 19

A Funeral Song for Israel's Kings

"Sing this funeral song for the princes of Israel:

2 "What is your mother?
A lioness among lions!
She lay down among the young lions
and reared her cubs.
3 She raised one of her cubs
to become a strong young lion.
He learned to hunt and devour prey,
and he became a man-eater.
4 Then the nations heard about him,
and he was trapped in their pit.
They led him away with hooks
to the land of Egypt.

5 "When the lioness saw
that her hopes for him were gone,
she took another of her cubs
and taught him to be a strong young lion.
6 He prowled among the other lions
and stood out among them in his strength.
He learned to hunt and devour prey,
and he, too, became a man-eater.
7 He demolished fortresses
and destroyed their towns and cities.
Their farms were desolated,
and their crops were destroyed.
The land and its people trembled in fear
when they heard him roar.
8 Then the armies of the nations attacked him,
surrounding him from every direction.
They threw a net over him
and captured him in their pit.
9 With hooks, they dragged him into a cage
and brought him before the king of
Babylon.
They held him in captivity,
so his voice could never again be heard
on the mountains of Israel.

10 "Your mother was like a vine
planted by the water's edge.
It had lush, green foliage
because of the abundant water.
11 Its branches became strong—
strong enough to be a ruler's scepter.
It grew very tall,
towering above all others.
It stood out because of its height
and its many lush branches.
12 But the vine was uprooted in fury
and thrown down to the ground.
The desert wind dried up its fruit
and tore off its strong branches,
so that it withered
and was destroyed by fire.
13 Now the vine is transplanted to the
wilderness,
where the ground is hard and dry.
14 A fire has burst out from its branches
and devoured its fruit.
Its remaining limbs are not
strong enough to be a ruler's scepter.

"This is a funeral song, and it will be used in a
funeral."

CHAPTER 20

The Rebellion of Israel

On August 14, during the seventh year of King
Jehoiachin's captivity, some of the leaders of Isra-
el came to request a message from the LORD.
They sat down in front of me to wait for his reply.

FUN-fact A Tough Job

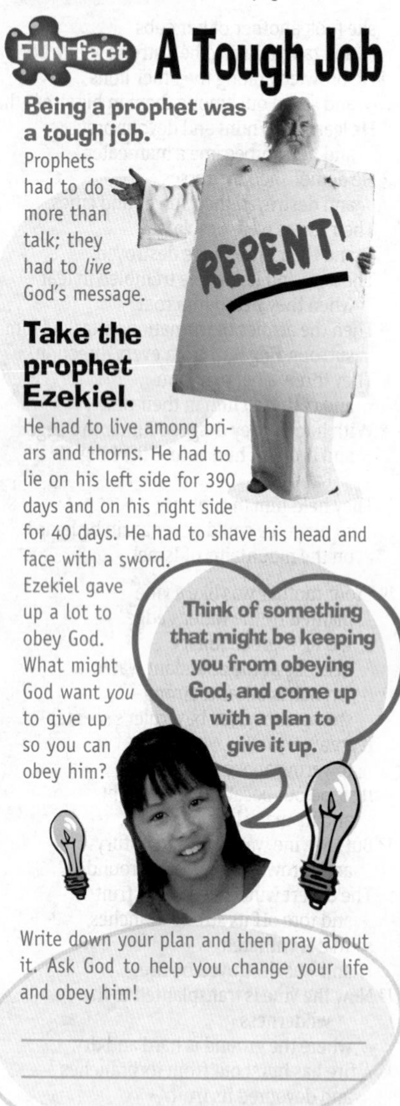

REPENT!
Think of something that might be keeping you from obeying God, and come up with a plan to give it up.

Being a prophet was a tough job. Prophets had to do more than talk; they had to *live* God's message.

Take the prophet Ezekiel. He had to live among briars and thorns. He had to lie on his left side for 390 days and on his right side for 40 days. He had to shave his head and face with a sword. Ezekiel gave up a lot to obey God. What might God want *you* to give up so you can obey him?

Write down your plan and then pray about it. Ask God to help you change your life and obey him!

____

____

____

2Then this message came to me from the LORD:
3"Son of man, tell the leaders of Israel, 'This is
what the Sovereign LORD says: How dare you
come to ask me for a message? As surely as I live,
says the Sovereign LORD, I will tell you nothing!'
4"Son of man, bring charges against them and
condemn them. Make them realize how detestable the sins of their ancestors really were. 5Give
them this message from the Sovereign LORD:
When I chose Israel—when I revealed myself to
the descendants of Jacob in Egypt—I took a solemn oath that I, the LORD, would be their God. 6I
took a solemn oath that day that I would bring
them out of Egypt to a land I had discovered and
explored for them—a good land, a land flowing
with milk and honey, the best of all lands anywhere. 7Then I said to them, 'Each of you, get rid
of the vile images you are so obsessed with. Do
not defile yourselves with the idols of Egypt, for I
am the LORD your God.'
8"But they rebelled against me and would not
listen. They did not get rid of the vile images they
were obsessed with, or forsake the idols of Egypt.
Then I threatened to pour out my fury on them to
satisfy my anger while they were still in Egypt.
9But I didn't do it, for I acted to protect the honor
of my name. I would not allow shame to be
brought on my name among the surrounding
nations who saw me reveal myself by bringing
the Israelites out of Egypt. 10So I brought them
out of Egypt and led them into the wilderness.
11There I gave them my decrees and regulations
so they could find life by keeping them. 12And I
gave them my Sabbath days of rest as a sign between them and me. It was to remind them that I
am the LORD, who had set them apart to be holy.
13"But the people of Israel rebelled against
me, and they refused to obey my decrees there in
the wilderness. They wouldn't obey my regulations even though obedience would have given
them life. They also violated my Sabbath days. So
I threatened to pour out my fury on them, and I
made plans to utterly consume them in the wilderness. 14But again I held back in order to protect the honor of my name before the nations
who had seen my power in bringing Israel out of
Egypt. 15But I took a solemn oath against them in
the wilderness. I swore I would not bring them
into the land I had given them, a land flowing
with milk and honey, the most beautiful place on
earth. 16For they had rejected my regulations, refused to follow my decrees, and violated my Sabbath days. Their hearts were given to their idols.
17Nevertheless, I took pity on them and held
back from destroying them in the wilderness.
18"Then I warned their children not to follow
in their parents' footsteps, defiling themselves
with their idols. 19'I am the LORD your God,' I told
them. 'Follow my decrees, pay attention to my
regulations, 20and keep my Sabbath days holy,
for they are a sign to remind you that I am the
LORD your God.'
21"But their children, too, rebelled against me.
They refused to keep my decrees and follow my

regulations, even though obedience would have
given them life. And they also violated my Sabbath days. So again I threatened to pour out my
fury on them in the wilderness. 22 Nevertheless, I
withdrew my judgment against them to protect
the honor of my name before the nations that had
seen my power in bringing them out of Egypt.
23 But I took a solemn oath against them in the
wilderness. I swore I would scatter them among
all the nations 24 because they did not obey my
regulations. They scorned my decrees by violating my Sabbath days and longing for the idols of
their ancestors. 25 I gave them over to worthless
decrees and regulations that would not lead to
life. 26 I let them pollute themselves with the very
gifts I had given them, and I allowed them to give
their firstborn children as offerings to their
gods—so I might devastate them and remind
them that I alone am the LORD.

Judgment and Restoration

27 "Therefore, son of man, give the people of Israel this message from the Sovereign LORD: Your
ancestors continued to blaspheme and betray
me, 28 for when I brought them into the land I
had promised them, they offered sacrifices on
every high hill and under every green tree they
saw! They roused my fury as they offered up sacrifices to their gods. They brought their perfumes and incense and poured out their liquid
offerings to them. 29 I said to them, 'What is this
high place where you are going?' (This kind of
pagan shrine has been called Bamah—'high
place'—ever since.)

30 "Therefore, give the people of Israel this
message from the Sovereign LORD: Do you plan
to pollute yourselves just as your ancestors did?
Do you intend to keep prostituting yourselves by
worshiping vile images? 31 For when you offer
gifts to them and give your little children to be
burned as sacrifices, you continue to pollute
yourselves with idols to this day. Should I allow
you to ask for a message from me, O people of
Israel? As surely as I live, says the Sovereign LORD,
I will tell you nothing.

32 "You say, 'We want to be like the nations all
around us, who serve idols of wood and stone.'
But what you have in mind will never happen.
33 As surely as I live, says the Sovereign LORD, I
will rule over you with an iron fist in great anger
and with awesome power. 34 And in anger I will
reach out with my strong hand and powerful
arm, and I will bring you back from the lands
where you are scattered. 35 I will bring you into
the wilderness of the nations, and there I will
judge you face to face. 36 I will judge you there
just as I did your ancestors in the wilderness
after bringing them out of Egypt, says the Sovereign LORD. 37 I will examine you carefully and
hold you to the terms of the covenant. 38 I will
purge you of all those who rebel and revolt
against me. I will bring them out of the countries
where they are in exile, but they will never enter
the land of Israel. Then you will know that I am
the LORD.

39 "As for you, O people of Israel, this is what the
Sovereign LORD says: Go right ahead and worship
your idols, but sooner or later you will obey me
and will stop bringing shame on my holy name by
worshiping idols. 40 For on my holy mountain, the
great mountain of Israel, says the Sovereign LORD,
the people of Israel will someday worship me,
and I will accept them. There I will require that
you bring me all your offerings and choice gifts
and sacrifices. 41 When I bring you home from
exile, you will be like a pleasing sacrifice to me.
And I will display my holiness through you as all
the nations watch. 42 Then when I have brought
you home to the land I promised with a solemn
oath to give to your ancestors, you will know that I
am the LORD. 43 You will look back on all the ways
you defiled yourselves and will hate yourselves
because of the evil you have done. 44 You will
know that I am the LORD, O people of Israel, when
I have honored my name by treating you mercifully in spite of your wickedness. I, the Sovereign
LORD, have spoken!"

Judgment against the Negev

45 Then this message came to me from the
LORD: 46 "Son of man, turn and face the south
and speak out against it; prophesy against the
brushlands of the Negev. 47 Tell the southern
wilderness, 'This is what the Sovereign LORD
says: Hear the word of the LORD! I will set you
on fire, and every tree, both green and dry, will
be burned. The terrible flames will not be
quenched and will scorch everything from
south to north. 48 And everyone in the world will
see that I, the LORD, have set this fire. It will not
be put out.'"

49 Then I said, "O Sovereign LORD, they are saying of me, 'He only talks in riddles!'"

CHAPTER 21

The LORD's Sword of Judgment

1 Then this message came to me from the LORD:
2 "Son of man, turn and face Jerusalem and
prophesy against Israel and her sanctuaries.
3 Tell her, 'This is what the LORD says: I am your

enemy, O Israel, and I am about to unsheath my
sword to destroy your people—the righteous and
the wicked alike. 4 Yes, I will cut off both the righteous and the wicked! I will draw my sword
against everyone in the land from south to north.
5 Everyone in the world will know that I am the
LORD. My sword is in my hand, and it will not return to its sheath until its work is finished.'
6 "Son of man, groan before the people! Groan
before them with bitter anguish and a broken
heart. 7 When they ask why you are groaning, tell
them, 'I groan because of the terrifying news I
have heard. When it comes true, the boldest
heart will melt with fear; all strength will disappear. Every spirit will faint; strong knees will
become as weak as water. And the Sovereign
LORD says: It is coming! It's on its way!'"
8 Then the LORD said to me, 9 "Son of man, give
the people this message from the Lord:

"A sword, a sword
is being sharpened and polished.
10 It is sharpened for terrible slaughter
and polished to flash like lightning!
Now will you laugh?
Those far stronger than you have fallen
beneath its power!
11 Yes, the sword is now being sharpened
and polished;
it is being prepared for the executioner.
12 "Son of man, cry out and wail;
pound your thighs in anguish,
for that sword will slaughter my people and
their leaders—
everyone will die!
13 It will put them all to the test.
What chance do they have?
says the Sovereign LORD.
14 "Son of man, prophesy to them
and clap your hands.
Then take the sword and brandish
it twice,
even three times,
to symbolize the great massacre,
the great massacre facing them
on every side.
15 Let their hearts melt with terror,
for the sword glitters at every gate.
It flashes like lightning
and is polished for slaughter!
16 O sword, slash to the right,
then slash to the left,
wherever you will,
wherever you want.
17 I, too, will clap my hands,
and I will satisfy my fury.
I, the LORD, have spoken!"

Omens for Babylon's King

18 Then this message came to me from the LORD:
19 "Son of man, make a map and trace two routes
on it for the sword of Babylon's king to follow.
Put a signpost on the road that comes out of Babylon where the road forks into two—20 one road
going to Ammon and its capital, Rabbah, and the
other to Judah and fortified Jerusalem. 21 The
king of Babylon now stands at the fork, uncertain whether to attack Jerusalem or Rabbah. He
calls his magicians to look for omens. They cast
lots by shaking arrows from the quiver. They inspect the livers of animal sacrifices. 22 The omen
in his right hand says, 'Jerusalem!' With battering rams his soldiers will go against the gates,
shouting for the kill. They will put up siege towers and build ramps against the walls. 23 The
people of Jerusalem will think it is a false omen,
because of their treaty with the Babylonians. But
the king of Babylon will remind the people of
their rebellion. Then he will attack and capture
them.
24 "Therefore, this is what the Sovereign LORD
says: Again and again you remind me of your sin
and your guilt. You don't even try to hide it! In
everything you do, your sins are obvious for all to
see. So now the time of your punishment has
come!
25 "O you corrupt and wicked prince of Israel,
your final day of reckoning is here! 26 This is what
the Sovereign LORD says:

"Take off your jeweled crown,
for the old order changes.
Now the lowly will be exalted,
and the mighty will be brought down.
27 Destruction! Destruction!
I will surely destroy the kingdom.
And it will not be restored until the one
appears
who has the right to judge it.
Then I will hand it over to him.

A Message for the Ammonites

28 "And now, son of man, prophesy concerning
the Ammonites and their mockery. Give them
this message from the Sovereign LORD:

"A sword, a sword
is drawn for your slaughter.
It is polished to destroy,
flashing like lightning!

29 Your prophets have given false visions,
and your fortune-tellers have told lies.
The sword will fall on the necks of the
wicked
for whom the day of final reckoning
has come.

30 "Now return the sword to its sheath,
for in your own country,
the land of your birth,
I will pass judgment upon you.
31 I will pour out my fury on you
and blow on you with the fire
of my anger.
I will hand you over to cruel men
who are skilled in destruction.
32 You will be fuel for the fire,
and your blood will be spilled in your
own land.
You will be utterly wiped out,
your memory lost to history,
for I, the LORD, have spoken!"

CHAPTER 22

The Sins of Jerusalem

Now this message came to me from the LORD:
2"Son of man, are you ready to judge Jerusalem?
Are you ready to judge this city of murderers?
Publicly denounce her detestable sins, 3and give
her this message from the Sovereign LORD: O city
of murderers, doomed and damned—city of
idols, filthy and foul—4you are guilty because of
the blood you have shed. You are defiled because
of the idols you have made. Your day of destruction has come! You have reached the end of your
years. I will make you an object of mockery
throughout the world. 5O infamous city, filled
with confusion, you will be mocked by people far
and near.
6"Every leader in Israel who lives within your
walls is bent on murder. 7Fathers and mothers
are treated with contempt. Foreigners are forced
to pay for protection. Orphans and widows are
wronged and oppressed among you. 8You despise my holy things and violate my Sabbath days
of rest. 9People accuse others falsely and send
them to their death. You are filled with idol worshipers and people who do obscene things.
10Men sleep with their fathers' wives and force
themselves on women who are menstruating.
11Within your walls live men who commit adultery with their neighbors' wives, who defile their
daughters-in-law, or who rape their own sisters.
12There are hired murderers, loan racketeers,
and extortioners everywhere. They never even
think of me and my commands, says the Sovereign LORD.
13"But now I clap my hands in indignation over
your dishonest gain and bloodshed. 14How
strong and courageous will you be in my day of
reckoning? I, the LORD, have spoken, and I will do
what I said. 15I will scatter you among the nations
and purge you of your wickedness. 16And when I
have been dishonored among the nations because of you, you will know that I am the LORD."

The LORD's Refining Furnace

17Then this message came to me from the LORD:
18"Son of man, the people of Israel are the worthless slag that remains after silver is smelted.
They are the dross that is left over—a useless
mixture of copper, tin, iron, and lead. 19So tell
them, 'This is what the Sovereign LORD says: Because you are all worthless slag, I will bring you
to my crucible in Jerusalem. 20Just as silver,
copper, iron, lead, and tin are melted down in a
furnace, I will melt you down in the heat of my
fury. 21I will gather you together and blow the
fire of my anger upon you, 22and you will melt
like silver in fierce heat. Then you will know that
I, the LORD, have poured out my fury on you.'"

The Sins of Israel's Leaders

23Again a message came to me from the LORD:
24"Son of man, give the people of Israel this message: In the day of my indignation, you will be
like a polluted land, a land without rain. 25Your
princes plot conspiracies just as lions stalk their
prey. They devour innocent people, seizing treasures and extorting wealth. They make many
widows in the land. 26Your priests have violated
my instructions and defiled my holy things. They
make no distinction between what is holy and
what is not. And they do not teach my people the
difference between what is ceremonially clean
and unclean. They disregard my Sabbath days so
that I am dishonored among them. 27Your leaders are like wolves who tear apart their victims.
They actually destroy people's lives for money!
28And your prophets cover up for them by announcing false visions and making lying predictions. They say, 'My message is from the
Sovereign LORD,' when the LORD hasn't spoken
a single word to them. 29Even common people
oppress the poor, rob the needy, and deprive foreigners of justice.
30"I looked for someone who might rebuild
the wall of righteousness that guards the land. I
searched for someone to stand in the gap in the
wall so I wouldn't have to destroy the land, but I

found no one. 31So now I will pour out my fury on them, consuming them with the fire of my anger. I will heap on their heads the full penalty for all their sins. I, the Sovereign LORD, have spoken!"

CHAPTER 23

The Adultery of Two Sisters

This message came to me from the LORD: 2"Son of man, once there were two sisters who were daughters of the same mother. 3They became prostitutes in Egypt. Even as young girls, they allowed men to fondle their breasts. 4The older girl was named Oholah, and her sister was Oholibah. I married them, and they bore me sons and daughters. I am speaking of Samaria and Jerusalem, for Oholah is Samaria and Oholibah is Jerusalem.

5"Then Oholah lusted after other lovers instead of me, and she gave her love to the Assyrian officers. 6They were all attractive young men, captains and commanders dressed in handsome blue, charioteers driving their horses. 7And so she prostituted herself with the most desirable men of Assyria, worshiping their idols and defiling herself. 8For when she left Egypt, she did not leave her spirit of prostitution behind. She was still as lewd as in her youth, when the Egyptians slept with her, fondled her breasts, and used her as a prostitute.

9"And so I handed her over to her Assyrian lovers, whom she desired so much. 10They stripped her, took away her children as their slaves, and then killed her. After she received her punishment, her reputation was known to every woman in the land.

11"Yet even though Oholibah saw what had happened to Oholah, her sister, she followed right in her footsteps. And she was even more depraved, abandoning herself to her lust and prostitution. 12She fawned over all the Assyrian officers—those captains and commanders in handsome uniforms, those charioteers driving their horses—all of them attractive young men. 13I saw the way she was going, defiling herself just like her older sister.

14"Then she carried her prostitution even further. She fell in love with pictures that were painted on a wall—pictures of Babylonian military officers, outfitted in striking red uniforms. 15Handsome belts encircled their waists, and flowing turbans crowned their heads. They were dressed like chariot officers from the land of Babylonia. 16When she saw these paintings, she longed to give herself to them, so she sent messengers to Babylonia to invite them to come to her. 17So they came and committed adultery with her, defiling her in the bed of love. After being defiled, however, she rejected them in disgust.

18"In the same way, I became disgusted with Oholibah and rejected her, just as I had rejected her sister, because she flaunted herself before them and gave herself to satisfy their lusts. 19Yet she turned to even greater prostitution, remembering her youth when she was a prostitute in Egypt. 20She lusted after lovers with genitals as large as a donkey's and emissions like those of a horse. 21And so, Oholibah, you relived your former days as a young girl in Egypt, when you first allowed your breasts to be fondled.

The LORD's Judgment of Oholibah

22"Therefore, Oholibah, this is what the Sovereign LORD says: I will send your lovers against you from every direction—those very nations from which you turned away in disgust. 23For the Babylonians will come with all the Chaldeans from Pekod and Shoa and Koa. And all the Assyrians will come with them—handsome young captains, commanders, chariot officers, and other high-ranking officers, all riding their horses. 24They will all come against you from the north with chariots, wagons, and a great army prepared for attack. They will take up positions on every side, surrounding you with men armed with shields and helmets. And I will hand you over to them for punishment so they can do with you as they please. 25I will turn my jealous anger against you, and they will deal harshly with you. They will cut off your nose and ears, and any survivors will then be slaughtered by the sword. Your children will be taken away as captives, and everything that is left will be burned. 26They will strip you of your beautiful clothes and jewels. 27In this way, I will put a stop to the lewdness and prostitution you brought from Egypt. You will never again cast longing eyes on those things or fondly remember your time in Egypt.

28"For this is what the Sovereign LORD says: I will surely hand you over to your enemies, to those you loathe, those you rejected. 29They will treat you with hatred and rob you of all you own, leaving you stark naked. The shame of your prostitution will be exposed to all the world. 30You brought all this on yourself by prostituting yourself to other nations, defiling yourself with all their idols. 31Because you have followed in your sister's footsteps, I will force you to drink the same cup of terror she drank.

32"Yes, this is what the Sovereign LORD says:

"You will drink from your sister's cup of
terror,
a cup that is large and deep.
It is filled to the brim
with scorn and derision.
33 Drunkenness and anguish will fill you,
for your cup is filled to the brim with
distress and desolation,
the same cup your sister Samaria drank.
34 You will drain that cup of terror
to the very bottom.
Then you will smash it to pieces
and beat your breast in anguish.
I, the Sovereign LORD, have spoken!

35"And because you have forgotten me and
turned your back on me, this is what the Sovereign LORD says: You must bear the consequences
of all your lewdness and prostitution."

The LORD's Judgment on Both Sisters

36The LORD said to me, "Son of man, you must
accuse Oholah and Oholibah of all their detestable sins. 37They have committed both adultery
and murder—adultery by worshiping idols and
murder by burning as sacrifices the children
they bore to me. 38Furthermore, they have defiled my Temple and violated my Sabbath day!
39On the very day that they sacrificed their children to their idols, they boldly came into my
Temple to worship! They came in and defiled my
house.

40"You sisters sent messengers to distant
lands to get men. Then when they arrived, you
bathed yourselves, painted your eyelids, and put
on your finest jewels for them. 41You sat with
them on a beautifully embroidered couch and
put my incense and my special oil on a table that
was spread before you. 42From your room came
the sound of many men carousing. They were
lustful men and drunkards from the wilderness,
who put bracelets on your wrists and beautiful
crowns on your heads. 43Then I said, 'If they
really want to have sex with old worn-out prostitutes like these, let them!' 44And that is what they
did. They had sex with Oholah and Oholibah,
these shameless prostitutes. 45But righteous
people will judge these sister cities for what they
really are—adulterers and murderers.

46"Now this is what the Sovereign LORD says:
Bring an army against them and hand them over
to be terrorized and plundered. 47For their enemies will stone them and kill them with swords.
They will butcher their sons and daughters and
burn their homes. 48In this way, I will put an end
to lewdness and idolatry in the land, and my
judgment will be a warning to all women not to
follow your wicked example. 49You will be fully
repaid for all your prostitution—your worship of
idols. Yes, you will suffer the full penalty. Then
you will know that I am the Sovereign LORD."

CHAPTER 24

The Sign of the Cooking Pot

On January 15, during the ninth year of King
Jehoiachin's captivity, this message came to me
from the LORD: 2"Son of man, write down today's
date, because on this very day the king of Babylon is beginning his attack against Jerusalem.
3Then give these rebels an illustration with this
message from the Sovereign LORD:

"Put a pot on the fire,
and pour in some water.
4 Fill it with choice pieces of meat—
the rump and the shoulder
and all the most tender cuts.
5 Use only the best sheep from the flock,
and heap fuel on the fire beneath the pot.
Bring the pot to a boil,
and cook the bones along with the meat.

6 "Now this is what the Sovereign LORD says:
What sorrow awaits Jerusalem,
the city of murderers!
She is a cooking pot
whose corruption can't be cleaned out.
Take the meat out in random order,
for no piece is better than another.
7 For the blood of her murders
is splashed on the rocks.
It isn't even spilled on the ground,
where the dust could cover it!
8 So I will splash her blood on a rock
for all to see,
an expression of my anger
and vengeance against her.

9 "This is what the Sovereign LORD says:
What sorrow awaits Jerusalem,
the city of murderers!
I myself will pile up the fuel beneath her.
10 Yes, heap on the wood!
Let the fire roar to make the pot boil.
Cook the meat with many spices,
and afterward burn the bones.
11 Now set the empty pot on the coals.
Heat it red hot!
Burn away the filth and corruption.

12 But it's hopeless;
the corruption can't be cleaned out.
So throw it into the fire.
13 Your impurity is your lewdness
and the corruption of your idolatry.
I tried to cleanse you,
but you refused.
So now you will remain in your filth
until my fury against you has been
satisfied.

14 "I, the LORD, have spoken! The time has
come, and I won't hold back. I will not change my
mind, and I will have no pity on you. You will be
judged on the basis of all your wicked actions,
says the Sovereign LORD."

The Death of Ezekiel's Wife

15 Then this message came to me from the LORD:
16 "Son of man, with one blow I will take away
your dearest treasure. Yet you must not show any
sorrow at her death. Do not weep; let there be no
tears. 17 Groan silently, but let there be no wailing
at her grave. Do not uncover your head or take
off your sandals. Do not perform the usual rituals of mourning or accept any food brought to
you by consoling friends."

18 So I proclaimed this to the people the next
morning, and in the evening my wife died. The
next morning I did everything I had been told to
do. 19 Then the people asked, "What does all this
mean? What are you trying to tell us?"

20 So I said to them, "A message came to me
from the LORD, 21 and I was told to give this
message to the people of Israel. This is what
the Sovereign LORD says: I will defile my Temple,
the source of your security and pride, the place
your heart delights in. Your sons and daughters
whom you left behind in Judah will be slaughtered by the sword. 22 Then you will do as Ezekiel
has done. You will not mourn in public or console yourselves by eating the food brought by
friends. 23 Your heads will remain covered, and
your sandals will not be taken off. You will not
mourn or weep, but you will waste away because
of your sins. You will groan among yourselves
for all the evil you have done. 24 Ezekiel is an example for you; you will do just as he has done.
And when that time comes, you will know that I
am the Sovereign LORD."

25 Then the LORD said to me, "Son of man, on
the day I take away their stronghold—their joy
and glory, their heart's desire, their dearest treasure—I will also take away their sons and daughters. 26 And on that day a survivor from Jerusalem
will come to you in Babylon and tell you what has
happened. 27 And when he arrives, your voice will
suddenly return so you can talk to him, and you
will be a symbol for these people. Then they will
know that I am the LORD."

CHAPTER 25

A Message for Ammon

Then this message came to me from the LORD:
2 "Son of man, turn and face the land of Ammon
and prophesy against its people. 3 Give the Ammonites this message from the Sovereign LORD:
Hear the word of the Sovereign LORD! Because
you cheered when my Temple was defiled,
mocked Israel in her desolation, and laughed at
Judah as she went away into exile, 4 I will allow nomads from the eastern deserts to overrun your
country. They will set up their camps among you
and pitch their tents on your land. They will harvest all your fruit and drink the milk from your
livestock. 5 And I will turn the city of Rabbah into
a pasture for camels, and all the land of the
Ammonites into a resting place for sheep and
goats. Then you will know that I am the LORD.

6 "This is what the Sovereign LORD says: Because you clapped and danced and cheered with
glee at the destruction of my people, 7 I will raise
my fist of judgment against you. I will give you as
plunder to many nations. I will cut you off from
being a nation and destroy you completely. Then
you will know that I am the LORD.

A Message for Moab

8 "This is what the Sovereign LORD says: Because
the people of Moab have said that Judah is just
like all the other nations, 9 I will open up their
eastern flank and wipe out their glorious frontier towns—Beth-jeshimoth, Baal-meon, and
Kiriathaim. 10 And I will hand Moab over to nomads from the eastern deserts, just as I handed
over Ammon. Yes, the Ammonites will no longer
be counted among the nations. 11 In the same
way, I will bring my judgment down on the Moabites. Then they will know that I am the LORD.

A Message for Edom

12 "This is what the Sovereign LORD says: The
people of Edom have sinned greatly by aveng-
ing themselves against the people of Judah.
13 Therefore, says the Sovereign LORD, I will raise
my fist of judgment against Edom. I will wipe out
its people and animals with the sword. I will
make a wasteland of everything from Teman to
Dedan. 14 I will accomplish this by the hand of my
people of Israel. They will carry out my vengeance

with anger, and Edom will know that this vengeance is from me. I, the Sovereign LORD, have
spoken!

A Message for Philistia

15"This is what the Sovereign LORD says: The
people of Philistia have acted against Judah out
of bitter revenge and long-standing contempt.
16Therefore, this is what the Sovereign LORD
says: I will raise my fist of judgment against the
land of the Philistines. I will wipe out the Kerethites and utterly destroy the people who live by
the sea. 17I will execute terrible vengeance
against them to punish them for what they have
done. And when I have inflicted my revenge, they
will know that I am the LORD."

CHAPTER 26

A Message for Tyre

On February 3, during the twelfth year of King
Jehoiachin's captivity, this message came to me
from the LORD: 2"Son of man, Tyre has rejoiced
over the fall of Jerusalem, saying, 'Ha! She who
was the gateway to the rich trade routes to the
east has been broken, and I am the heir! Because
she has been made desolate, I will become
wealthy!'

3"Therefore, this is what the Sovereign LORD
says: I am your enemy, O Tyre, and I will bring
many nations against you, like the waves of the
sea crashing against your shoreline. 4They will
destroy the walls of Tyre and tear down its towers. I will scrape away its soil and make it a bare
rock! 5It will be just a rock in the sea, a place for
fishermen to spread their nets, for I have spoken,
says the Sovereign LORD. Tyre will become the
prey of many nations, 6and its mainland villages
will be destroyed by the sword. Then they will
know that I am the LORD.

7"This is what the Sovereign LORD says: From
the north I will bring King Nebuchadnezzar of
Babylon against Tyre. He is king of kings and
brings his horses, chariots, charioteers, and great
army. 8First he will destroy your mainland villages. Then he will attack you by building a siege
wall, constructing a ramp, and raising a roof of
shields against you. 9He will pound your walls
with battering rams and demolish your towers
with sledgehammers. 10The hooves of his horses
will choke the city with dust, and the noise of the
charioteers and chariot wheels will shake your
walls as they storm through your broken gates.
11His horsemen will trample through every
street in the city. They will butcher your people,
and your strong pillars will topple.

12"They will plunder all your riches and merchandise and break down your walls. They will
destroy your lovely homes and dump your stones
and timbers and even your dust into the sea. 13I
will stop the music of your songs. No more will
the sound of harps be heard among your people.
14I will make your island a bare rock, a place for
fishermen to spread their nets. You will never be
rebuilt, for I, the LORD, have spoken. Yes, the Sovereign LORD has spoken!

The Effect of Tyre's Destruction

15"This is what the Sovereign LORD says to Tyre:
The whole coastline will tremble at the sound of
your fall, as the screams of the wounded echo in
the continuing slaughter. 16All the seaport rulers
will step down from their thrones and take off
their royal robes and beautiful clothing. They
will sit on the ground trembling with horror at
your destruction. 17Then they will wail for you,
singing this funeral song:

"O famous island city,
  once ruler of the sea,
  how you have been destroyed!
Your people, with their naval power,
  once spread fear around the world.
18 Now the coastlands tremble at your fall.
  The islands are dismayed as you
    disappear.

19"This is what the Sovereign LORD says: I will
make Tyre an uninhabited ruin, like many others. I will bury you beneath the terrible waves of
enemy attack. Great seas will swallow you. 20I
will send you to the pit to join those who descended there long ago. Your city will lie in ruins,
buried beneath the earth, like those in the pit
who have entered the world of the dead. You will
have no place of respect here in the land of the
living. 21I will bring you to a terrible end, and you
will exist no more. You will be looked for, but you
will never again be found. I, the Sovereign LORD,
have spoken!"

CHAPTER 27

The End of Tyre's Glory

Then this message came to me from the LORD:
2"Son of man, sing a funeral song for Tyre, 3that
mighty gateway to the sea, the trading center of
the world. Give Tyre this message from the Sovereign LORD:

"You boasted, O Tyre,
  'My beauty is perfect!'

4 You extended your boundaries into the sea.
Your builders made your beauty perfect.
5 You were like a great ship
built of the finest cypress from Senir.
They took a cedar from Lebanon
to make a mast for you.
6 They carved your oars
from the oaks of Bashan.
Your deck of pine from the coasts of Cyprus
was inlaid with ivory.
7 Your sails were made of Egypt's finest linen,
and they flew as a banner above you.
You stood beneath blue and purple awnings
made bright with dyes from the coasts
of Elishah.
8 Your oarsmen came from Sidon and Arvad;
your helmsmen were skilled men from
Tyre itself.
9 Wise old craftsmen from Gebal did
the caulking.
Ships from every land came with goods
to barter for your trade.

10"Men from distant Persia, Lydia, and Libya
served in your great army. They hung their
shields and helmets on your walls, giving you
great honor. 11Men from Arvad and Helech stood
on your walls. Your towers were manned by men
from Gammad. Their shields hung on your walls,
completing your beauty.

12"Tarshish sent merchants to buy your
wares in exchange for silver, iron, tin, and lead.
13Merchants from Greece, Tubal, and Meshech
brought slaves and articles of bronze to trade
with you.

14"From Beth-togarmah came riding horses,
chariot horses, and mules, all in exchange for
your goods. 15Merchants came to you from
Dedan. Numerous coastlands were your captive
markets; they brought payment in ivory tusks
and ebony wood.

16"Syria sent merchants to buy your rich variety of goods. They traded turquoise, purple dyes,
embroidery, fine linen, and jewelry of coral and
rubies. 17Judah and Israel traded for your wares,
offering wheat from Minnith, figs, honey, olive
oil, and balm.

18"Damascus sent merchants to buy your rich
variety of goods, bringing wine from Helbon and
white wool from Zahar. 19Greeks from Uzal came
to trade for your merchandise. Wrought iron,
cassia, and fragrant calamus were bartered for
your wares.

20"Dedan sent merchants to trade their expensive saddle blankets with you. 21The Ara-
bians and the princes of Kedar sent merchants to
trade lambs and rams and male goats in exchange for your goods. 22The merchants of Sheba and Raamah came with all kinds of spices,
jewels, and gold in exchange for your wares.

23"Haran, Canneh, Eden, Sheba, Asshur, and
Kilmad came with their merchandise, too.
24They brought choice fabrics to trade—blue
cloth, embroidery, and multicolored carpets
rolled up and bound with cords. 25The ships of
Tarshish were your ocean caravans. Your island
warehouse was filled to the brim!

The Destruction of Tyre

26 "But look! Your oarsmen
have taken you into stormy seas!
A mighty eastern gale
has wrecked you in the heart of the sea!
27 Everything is lost—
your riches and wares,
your sailors and pilots,
your ship builders, merchants,
and warriors.
On the day of your ruin,
everyone on board sinks into the
depths of the sea.
28 Your cities by the sea tremble
as your pilots cry out in terror.
29 All the oarsmen abandon their ships;
the sailors and pilots stand on the
shore.
30 They cry aloud over you
and weep bitterly.
They throw dust on their heads
and roll in ashes.
31 They shave their heads in grief for you
and dress themselves in burlap.
They weep for you with bitter anguish
and deep mourning.
32 As they wail and mourn over you,
they sing this sad funeral song:
'Was there ever such a city as Tyre,
now silent at the bottom of the sea?
33 The merchandise you traded
satisfied the desires of many nations.
Kings at the ends of the earth
were enriched by your trade.
34 Now you are a wrecked ship,
broken at the bottom of the sea.
All your merchandise and crew
have gone down with you.
35 All who live along the coastlands
are appalled at your terrible fate.
Their kings are filled with horror
and look on with twisted faces.

36 The merchants among the nations
shake their heads at the sight of you,
for you have come to a horrible end
and will exist no more.'"

CHAPTER 28

A Message for Tyre's King

Then this message came to me from the LORD:
2"Son of man, give the prince of Tyre this message from the Sovereign LORD:

"In your great pride you claim, 'I am a god!
I sit on a divine throne in the heart
of the sea.'
But you are only a man and not a god,
though you boast that you are a god.
3 You regard yourself as wiser than Daniel
and think no secret is hidden from you.
4 With your wisdom and understanding you
have amassed great wealth—
gold and silver for your treasuries.
5 Yes, your wisdom has made you very rich,
and your riches have made you very proud.

6 "Therefore, this is what the Sovereign
LORD says:
Because you think you are as wise as a god,
7 I will now bring against you a
foreign army,
the terror of the nations.
They will draw their swords against your
marvelous wisdom
and defile your splendor!
8 They will bring you down to the pit,
and you will die in the heart of the sea,
pierced with many wounds.
9 Will you then boast, 'I am a god!'
to those who kill you?
To them you will be no god
but merely a man!
10 You will die like an outcast
at the hands of foreigners.
I, the Sovereign LORD, have spoken!"

11Then this further message came to me from
the LORD: 12"Son of man, sing this funeral song
for the king of Tyre. Give him this message from
the Sovereign LORD:

"You were the model of perfection,
full of wisdom and exquisite in beauty.
13 You were in Eden,
the garden of God.
Your clothing was adorned with every
precious stone—
red carnelian, pale-green peridot,
white moonstone,
blue-green beryl, onyx, green jasper,
blue lapis lazuli, turquoise, and
emerald—
all beautifully crafted for you
and set in the finest gold.
They were given to you
on the day you were created.
14 I ordained and anointed you
as the mighty angelic guardian.
You had access to the holy mountain of God
and walked among the stones of fire.

15 "You were blameless in all you did
from the day you were created
until the day evil was found in you.
16 Your rich commerce led you to violence,
and you sinned.
So I banished you in disgrace
from the mountain of God.
I expelled you, O mighty guardian,
from your place among the stones of fire.
17 Your heart was filled with pride
because of all your beauty.
Your wisdom was corrupted
by your love of splendor.

PERSONAL SERVANTS

Imagine that you have a personal servant. What would you ask that person to do? Make you a snack after school? Do your homework? In Bible times it was common for wealthy families to have slaves. And some of those slaves were assigned to boys—like their own personal servants.

But those slaves were like bosses! They walked the boys to and from school and kept them from hanging out with the wrong crowd.

For a few hours, pretend someone is watching your every move, making sure you behave. Or find a friend and "shadow" each other for an afternoon.

THEN THINK ABOUT THIS: Other people are watching you to see how you behave. They want to know if your faith makes a difference in your life. See if that helps you live the way God wants you to.

So I threw you to the ground
and exposed you to the curious gaze
of kings.
18 You defiled your sanctuaries
with your many sins and your
dishonest trade.
So I brought fire out from within you,
and it consumed you.
I reduced you to ashes on the ground
in the sight of all who were watching.
19 All who knew you are appalled at your fate.
You have come to a terrible end,
and you will exist no more."

A Message for Sidon

20Then another message came to me from the
LORD: 21"Son of man, turn and face the city of
Sidon and prophesy against it. 22Give the people
of Sidon this message from the Sovereign LORD:

"I am your enemy, O Sidon,
and I will reveal my glory by what
I do to you.
When I bring judgment against you
and reveal my holiness among you,
everyone watching will know
that I am the LORD.
23 I will send a plague against you,
and blood will be spilled in your streets.
The attack will come from every direction,
and your people will lie slaughtered
within your walls.
Then everyone will know
that I am the LORD.
24 No longer will Israel's scornful neighbors
prick and tear at her like briers and thorns.
For then they will know
that I am the Sovereign LORD.

Restoration for Israel

25"This is what the Sovereign LORD says: The
people of Israel will again live in their own land,
the land I gave my servant Jacob. For I will gather
them from the distant lands where I have scattered them. I will reveal to the nations of the
world my holiness among my people. 26They will
live safely in Israel and build homes and plant
vineyards. And when I punish the neighboring
nations that treated them with contempt, they
will know that I am the LORD their God."

CHAPTER 29

A Message for Egypt

On January 7, during the tenth year of King Jehoiachin's captivity, this message came to me from
the LORD: 2"Son of man, turn and face Egypt and
prophesy against Pharaoh the king and all the
people of Egypt. 3Give them this message from
the Sovereign LORD:

"I am your enemy, O Pharaoh,
king of Egypt—
you great monster, lurking in the
streams of the Nile.
For you have said, 'The Nile River
is mine;
I made it for myself.'
4 I will put hooks in your jaws
and drag you out on the land
with fish sticking to your scales.
5 I will leave you and all your fish
stranded in the wilderness to die.
You will lie unburied on the open ground,
for I have given you as food to the wild
animals and birds.
6 All the people of Egypt will know that
I am the LORD,
for to Israel you were just a staff made
of reeds.
7 When Israel leaned on you,
you splintered and broke
and stabbed her in the armpit.
When she put her weight on you,
you collapsed, and her legs gave way.

8"Therefore, this is what the Sovereign LORD
says: I will bring an army against you, O Egypt,
and destroy both people and animals. 9The land
of Egypt will become a desolate wasteland, and
the Egyptians will know that I am the LORD.

"Because you said, 'The Nile River is mine; I
made it,' 10I am now the enemy of both you and
your river. I will make the land of Egypt a totally
desolate wasteland, from Migdol to Aswan, as
far south as the border of Ethiopia. 11For forty
years not a soul will pass that way, neither people
nor animals. It will be completely uninhabited.
12I will make Egypt desolate, and it will be surrounded by other desolate nations. Its cities will
be empty and desolate for forty years, surrounded by other ruined cities. I will scatter the
Egyptians to distant lands.

13"But this is what the Sovereign LORD also
says: At the end of the forty years I will bring the
Egyptians home again from the nations to which
they have been scattered. 14I will restore the
prosperity of Egypt and bring its people back to
the land of Pathros in southern Egypt from
which they came. But Egypt will remain an unimportant, minor kingdom. 15It will be the low-

liest of all the nations, never again great enough
to rise above its neighbors.
16"Then Israel will no longer be tempted to
trust in Egypt for help. Egypt's shattered condition will remind Israel of how sinful she was to
trust Egypt in earlier days. Then Israel will know
that I am the Sovereign LORD."

Nebuchadnezzar to Conquer Egypt

17On April 26, the first day of the new year, during
the twenty-seventh year of King Jehoiachin's captivity, this message came to me from the LORD:
18"Son of man, the army of King Nebuchadnezzar
of Babylon fought so hard against Tyre that the
warriors' heads were rubbed bare and their shoulders were raw and blistered. Yet Nebuchadnezzar
and his army won no plunder to compensate
them for all their work. 19Therefore, this is what
the Sovereign LORD says: I will give the land of
Egypt to Nebuchadnezzar, king of Babylon. He
will carry off its wealth, plundering everything it
has so he can pay his army. 20Yes, I have given him
the land of Egypt as a reward for his work, says the
Sovereign LORD, because he was working for me
when he destroyed Tyre.
21"And the day will come when I will cause the
ancient glory of Israel to revive, and then, Ezekiel,
your words will be respected. Then they will
know that I am the LORD."

CHAPTER 30

A Sad Day for Egypt

This is another message that came to me from
the LORD: 2"Son of man, prophesy and give this
message from the Sovereign LORD:

"Weep and wail
for that day,
3 for the terrible day is almost here—
the day of the LORD!
It is a day of clouds and gloom,
a day of despair for the nations.
4 A sword will come against Egypt,
and those who are slaughtered will cover
the ground.
Its wealth will be carried away
and its foundations destroyed.
The land of Ethiopia will be ravished.
5 Ethiopia, Libya, Lydia, all Arabia,
and all their other allies
will be destroyed in that war.

6 "For this is what the LORD says:
All of Egypt's allies will fall,
and the pride of her power will end.
From Migdol to Aswan
they will be slaughtered by the sword,
says the Sovereign LORD.
7 Egypt will be desolate,
surrounded by desolate nations,
and its cities will be in ruins,
surrounded by other ruined cities.
8 And the people of Egypt will know that
I am the LORD
when I have set Egypt on fire
and destroyed all their allies.
9 At that time I will send swift messengers
in ships
to terrify the complacent Ethiopians.
Great panic will come upon them
on that day of Egypt's certain destruction.
Watch for it!
It is sure to come!

10 "For this is what the Sovereign LORD says:
By the power of King Nebuchadnezzar
of Babylon,
I will destroy the hordes of Egypt.
11 He and his armies—the most ruthless
of all—
will be sent to demolish the land.
They will make war against Egypt
until slaughtered Egyptians cover
the ground.
12 I will dry up the Nile River
and sell the land to wicked men.
I will destroy the land of Egypt and
everything in it
by the hands of foreigners.
I, the LORD, have spoken!

13 "This is what the Sovereign LORD says:
I will smash the idols of Egypt
and the images at Memphis.
There will be no rulers left in Egypt;
terror will sweep the land.
14 I will destroy southern Egypt,
set fire to Zoan,
and bring judgment against Thebes.
15 I will pour out my fury on Pelusium,
the strongest fortress of Egypt,
and I will stamp out
the hordes of Thebes.
16 Yes, I will set fire to all Egypt!
Pelusium will be racked with pain;
Thebes will be torn apart;
Memphis will live in constant terror.
17 The young men of Heliopolis and Bubastis
will die in battle,
and the women will be taken away
as slaves.

18 When I come to break the proud strength
of Egypt,
it will be a dark day for Tahpanhes, too.
A dark cloud will cover Tahpanhes,
and its daughters will be led away
as captives.
19 And so I will greatly punish Egypt,
and they will know that I am the LORD."

The Broken Arms of Pharaoh

20 On April 29, during the eleventh year of King
Jehoiachin's captivity, this message came to me
from the LORD: 21 "Son of man, I have broken the
arm of Pharaoh, the king of Egypt. His arm has
not been put in a cast so that it may heal. Neither
has it been bound up with a splint to make it
strong enough to hold a sword. 22 Therefore, this
is what the Sovereign LORD says: I am the enemy
of Pharaoh, the king of Egypt! I will break both of
his arms—the good arm along with the broken
one—and I will make his sword clatter to the
ground. 23 I will scatter the Egyptians to many
lands throughout the world. 24 I will strengthen
the arms of Babylon's king and put my sword in
his hand. But I will break the arms of Pharaoh,
king of Egypt, and he will lie there mortally
wounded, groaning in pain. 25 I will strengthen
the arms of the king of Babylon, while the arms
of Pharaoh fall useless to his sides. And when I
put my sword in the hand of Babylon's king and
he brings it against the land of Egypt, Egypt will
know that I am the LORD. 26 I will scatter the
Egyptians among the nations, dispersing them
throughout the earth. Then they will know that I
am the LORD."

CHAPTER 31

Egypt Compared to Fallen Assyria

On June 21, during the eleventh year of King
Jehoiachin's captivity, this message came to me
from the LORD: 2 "Son of man, give this message
to Pharaoh, king of Egypt, and all his hordes:

"To whom would you compare your
greatness?
3 You are like mighty Assyria,
which was once like a cedar of Lebanon,
with beautiful branches that cast deep
forest shade
and with its top high among the clouds.
4 Deep springs watered it
and helped it to grow tall and luxuriant.
The water flowed around it like a river,
streaming to all the trees nearby.
5 This great tree towered high,
higher than all the other trees around it.
It prospered and grew long thick branches
because of all the water at its roots.
6 The birds nested in its branches,
and in its shade all the wild animals
gave birth.
All the great nations of the world
lived in its shadow.
7 It was strong and beautiful,
with wide-spreading branches,
for its roots went deep
into abundant water.
8 No other cedar in the garden of God
could rival it.
No cypress had branches to equal it;
no plane tree had boughs to compare.
No tree in the garden of God
came close to it in beauty.
9 Because I made this tree so beautiful,
and gave it such magnificent foliage,
it was the envy of all the other trees of Eden,
the garden of God.

10 "Therefore, this is what the Sovereign LORD
says: Because Egypt became proud and arrogant,
and because it set itself so high above the others,
with its top reaching to the clouds, 11 I will hand it
over to a mighty nation that will destroy it as its
wickedness deserves. I have already discarded it.
12 A foreign army—the terror of the nations—has
cut it down and left it fallen on the ground. Its
branches are scattered across the mountains and
valleys and ravines of the land. All those who
lived in its shadow have gone away and left it
lying there.

13 "The birds roost on its fallen trunk,
and the wild animals lie among
its branches.
14 Let the tree of no other nation
proudly exult in its own prosperity,
though it be higher than the clouds
and it be watered from the depths.
For all are doomed to die,
to go down to the depths of the earth.
They will land in the pit
along with everyone else on earth.

15 "This is what the Sovereign LORD says:
When Assyria went down to the grave, I made the
deep springs mourn. I stopped its rivers and
dried up its abundant water. I clothed Lebanon
in black and caused the trees of the field to wilt.
16 I made the nations shake with fear at the
sound of its fall, for I sent it down to the grave

with all the others who descend to the pit. And
all the other proud trees of Eden, the most beautiful and the best of Lebanon, the ones whose
roots went deep into the water, took comfort to
find it there with them in the depths of the earth.
17 Its allies, too, were all destroyed and had
passed away. They had gone down to the grave—
all those nations that had lived in its shade.
18 "O Egypt, to which of the trees of Eden will
you compare your strength and glory? You, too,
will be brought down to the depths with all these
other nations. You will lie there among the outcasts who have died by the sword. This will be
the fate of Pharaoh and all his hordes. I, the
Sovereign LORD, have spoken!"

CHAPTER 32

A Warning for Pharaoh

On March 3, during the twelfth year of King
Jehoiachin's captivity, this message came to me
from the LORD: 2 "Son of man, mourn for Pharaoh, king of Egypt, and give him this message:

"You think of yourself as a strong young lion
among the nations,
but you are really just a sea monster,
heaving around in your own rivers,
stirring up mud with your feet.
3 Therefore, this is what the Sovereign
LORD says:
I will send many people
to catch you in my net
and haul you out of the water.
4 I will leave you stranded on the land to die.
All the birds of the heavens will land
on you,
and the wild animals of the whole earth
will gorge themselves on you.
5 I will scatter your flesh on the hills
and fill the valleys with your bones.
6 I will drench the earth with your
gushing blood
all the way to the mountains,
filling the ravines to the brim.
7 When I blot you out,
I will veil the heavens and darken
the stars.
I will cover the sun with a cloud,
and the moon will not give you its light.
8 I will darken the bright stars overhead
and cover your land in darkness.
I, the Sovereign LORD, have spoken!

9 "I will disturb many hearts when I bring news
of your downfall to distant nations you have
never seen. 10 Yes, I will shock many lands, and
their kings will be terrified at your fate. They will
shudder in fear for their lives as I brandish my
sword before them on the day of your fall. 11 For
this is what the Sovereign LORD says:

"The sword of the king of Babylon
will come against you.
12 I will destroy your hordes with the swords
of mighty warriors—
the terror of the nations.
They will shatter the pride of Egypt,
and all its hordes will be destroyed.
13 I will destroy all your flocks and herds
that graze beside the streams.
Never again will people or animals
muddy those waters with their feet.
14 Then I will let the waters of Egypt become
calm again,
and they will flow as smoothly as olive oil,
says the Sovereign LORD.
15 And when I destroy Egypt
and strip you of everything you own
and strike down all your people,
then you will know that I am the LORD.
16 Yes, this is the funeral song
they will sing for Egypt.
Let all the nations mourn.
Let them mourn for Egypt and its hordes.
I, the Sovereign LORD, have spoken!"

Egypt Falls into the Pit

17 On March 17, during the twelfth year, another
message came to me from the LORD: 18 "Son of
man, weep for the hordes of Egypt and for the
other mighty nations. For I will send them down
to the world below in company with those who
descend to the pit. 19 Say to them,

'O Egypt, are you lovelier than the other
nations?
No! So go down to the pit and lie there
among the outcasts.'

20 The Egyptians will fall with the many who
have died by the sword, for the sword is drawn
against them. Egypt and its hordes will be
dragged away to their judgment. 21 Down in the
grave mighty leaders will mockingly welcome
Egypt and its allies, saying, 'They have come
down; they lie among the outcasts, hordes
slaughtered by the sword.'
22 "Assyria lies there surrounded by the graves
of its army, those who were slaughtered by the
sword. 23 Their graves are in the depths of the pit,
and they are surrounded by their allies. They
struck terror in the hearts of people everywhere,

but now they have been slaughtered by the sword.

24"Elam lies there surrounded by the graves of all its hordes, those who were slaughtered by the sword. They struck terror in the hearts of people everywhere, but now they have descended as outcasts to the world below. Now they lie in the pit and share the shame of those who have gone before them. 25They have a resting place among the slaughtered, surrounded by the graves of all their hordes. Yes, they terrorized the nations while they lived, but now they lie in shame with others in the pit, all of them outcasts, slaughtered by the sword.

26"Meshech and Tubal are there, surrounded by the graves of all their hordes. They once struck terror in the hearts of people everywhere. But now they are outcasts, all slaughtered by the sword. 27They are not buried in honor like their fallen heroes, who went down to the grave with their weapons—their shields covering their bodies and their swords beneath their heads. Their guilt rests upon them because they brought terror to everyone while they were still alive.

28"You too, Egypt, will lie crushed and broken among the outcasts, all slaughtered by the sword.

29"Edom is there with its kings and princes. Mighty as they were, they also lie among those slaughtered by the sword, with the outcasts who have gone down to the pit.

30"All the princes of the north and the Sidonians are there with others who have died. Once a terror, they have been put to shame. They lie there as outcasts with others who were slaughtered by the sword. They share the shame of all who have descended to the pit.

31"When Pharaoh and his entire army arrive, he will take comfort that he is not alone in having his hordes killed, says the Sovereign LORD. 32Although I have caused his terror to fall upon all the living, Pharaoh and his hordes will lie there among the outcasts who were slaughtered by the sword. I, the Sovereign LORD, have spoken!"

CHAPTER 33

Ezekiel as Israel's Watchman

Once again a message came to me from the LORD: 2"Son of man, give your people this message: 'When I bring an army against a country, the people of that land choose one of their own to be a watchman. 3When the watchman sees the enemy coming, he sounds the alarm to warn the people. 4Then if those who hear the alarm refuse to take action, it is their own fault if they die. 5They heard the alarm but ignored it, so the responsibility is theirs. If they had listened to the warning, they could have saved their lives. 6But if the watchman sees the enemy coming and doesn't sound the alarm to warn the people, he is responsible for their captivity. They will die in their sins, but I will hold the watchman responsible for their deaths.'

7"Now, son of man, I am making you a watchman for the people of Israel. Therefore, listen to what I say and warn them for me. 8If I announce that some wicked people are sure to die and you fail to tell them to change their ways, then they will die in their sins, and I will hold you responsible for their deaths. 9But if you warn them to repent and they don't repent, they will die in their sins, but you will have saved yourself.

The Watchman's Message

10"Son of man, give the people of Israel this message: You are saying, 'Our sins are heavy upon us; we are wasting away! How can we survive?' 11As surely as I live, says the Sovereign LORD, I take no pleasure in the death of wicked people. I only want them to turn from their wicked ways so they can live. Turn! Turn from your wickedness, O people of Israel! Why should you die?

12"Son of man, give your people this message: The righteous behavior of righteous people will not save them if they turn to sin, nor will the wicked behavior of wicked people destroy them if they repent and turn from their sins. 13When I tell righteous people that they will live, but then they sin, expecting their past righteousness to save them, then none of their righteous acts will be remembered. I will destroy them for their sins. 14And suppose I tell some wicked people that they will surely die, but then they turn from their sins and do what is just and right. 15For instance, they might give back a debtor's security, return what they have stolen, and obey my life-giving laws, no longer doing what is evil. If they do this, then they will surely live and not die. 16None of their past sins will be brought up again, for they have done what is just and right, and they will surely live.

17"Your people are saying, 'The Lord isn't doing what's right,' but it is they who are not doing what's right. 18For again I say, when righteous people turn away from their righteous behavior and turn to evil, they will die. 19But if wicked people turn from their wickedness and do what is just and right, they will live. 20O people of Israel, you are saying, 'The Lord isn't doing what's right.' But I judge each of you according to your deeds."

BIBLE BIOS

Hear From the Heroes

Hi, our names are

SHADRACH, MESHACH, AND ABEDNEGO *(advisers, leaders)*

The heat from the flames was so hot it could soften metal. Fire blasted outside of the furnace—we could feel it from the other side of the courtyard. And we were about to be thrown into the middle of that blaze!

After King Nebuchadnezzar defeated our armies in Judah, he took most of us away from our homeland to Babylon. The king made Daniel ruler of a big part of Babylon, and we were Daniel's assistants.

Things were going great until King Nebuchadnezzar made that big golden statue. It was *huge!* If you put a ladder next to it, you would have to climb up about 100 steps to get to the top. The king got the crazy idea that everyone should go outside, bow down, and worship that statue. We just couldn't do it. God says that we are to worship only him. So when everyone else bowed down, we refused.

When the king found out, he was furious! He gave us a choice. We could either worship the statue or get thrown into the furnace. For us, there was no choice. We wouldn't go against God no matter what we had to face. We were ready to die for what we knew was right. But we didn't die! After we were thrown in, God sent a heavenly visitor to keep us safe. We didn't even get burned! The king called us out of the furnace and gave us higher positions than we had before.

Sometimes it's tough to stand up for God, but we've got to do it. The tough times last just a little while, and our time with God lasts forever.

Shadrach, Meshach, and Abednego were names the Babylonian rulers gave these men to make them more loyal to Babylon. Check out DANIEL 1:6-7 to find out their real names.

Daniel stood up for God with his friends Shadrach, Meshach, and Abednego during this time, too. Check out DANIEL 1:3-17 to learn how.

Read DANIEL 3:16-18 to learn their brave response to the king.

Takin' the Heat

Make sure you get help from an adult to make these heat-holdin' potholders.

Hang your potholder somewhere in your house to remind you that God will help you take the heat for your faith in him!

1. **Cut some cotton material into two 8x8-inch squares. Cut cotton batting into four 6x6-inch squares. (Don't use polyester, because it can't take the heat.)**
2. **Sandwich the batting between the two material squares. Use an embroidery needle and thread to go through all six layers of material and to tie a knot in each corner.**
3. **Tie a knot in one end of the thread. Sew the edges of the material together. (Don't sew the cotton batting except in the corners as in step 2.) Tie a knot in the end of the thread when you're done.**
4. **Read DANIEL 3:1-18. Use fabric paint or puffy paint to decorate the potholder so it reminds you of Shadrach, Meshach, and Abednego's faith.**

BIBLE BIOS

Hear From the Heroes

THE ISRAELITE CAPTIVITY

An Israelite in Babylon Speaks Out: Have you heard the news? We're going back! After 70 years in Babylon, we're finally going back home to Judah!

In the book of Ezra, you can read all about how the Israelites rebuilt the Temple.

Maybe you don't know the story of how we, God's chosen people, ended up as prisoners in a foreign land. When David ruled over Israel, the people followed God and our nation grew strong. But David's son, Solomon, began to worship false gods. His sons followed his example, and the kingdom split into two countries. They called the northern country Israel and the southern kingdom Judah, but we were all still called Israelites or Jewish people. Sadly, most of the kings from both kingdoms followed worthless idols. God sent prophets, including Jeremiah and Hosea, to warn the people and the kings, but the kings ignored them.

God sent other prophets to warn the Jews. They include Isaiah, Micah, Habakkuk, Zephaniah, Amos, and Joel.

So Assyria conquered Israel and took the people away. Judah hung on for a little while longer—more than 130 years. But my people were finally carried off to Babylon by the mighty armies of King Nebuchadnezzar. He took the treasure from the Temple of God, then burned the Temple down. God sent prophets like Ezekiel and Daniel while we were in Babylon to encourage us and to remind us to turn back to God. And now we're going back to Judah. Just as God promised through the prophet Jeremiah, we're going back 70 years after the Babylonians took us away!

Jeremiah told the people this before they had even been taken into captivity. Check it out in JEREMIAH 25:7-14.

I need to get going now. We have a long journey ahead. But remember, no matter how bad your sin, God can pick you back up as long as you turn to him.

Get Back Up Again

Make this little wobbling character to remind you that whenever you fall down or sin you should turn to God and get right back up.

1 **Pack the bottom half of a plastic egg with clay or modeling dough.**

2 **Close the egg. Make a little character that looks like you by coloring the egg with markers and gluing felt features on it.**

3 **Set the little character on a table and push it over. It'll tip over, but it won't stay down.**

Explanation of Jerusalem's Fall

21 On January 8, during the twelfth year of our captivity, a survivor from Jerusalem came to me and said, "The city has fallen!" 22 The previous evening the LORD had taken hold of me and given me back my voice. So I was able to speak when this man arrived the next morning.

23 Then this message came to me from the LORD: 24 "Son of man, the scattered remnants of Israel living among the ruined cities keep saying, 'Abraham was only one man, yet he gained possession of the entire land. We are many; surely the land has been given to us as a possession.' 25 So tell these people, 'This is what the Sovereign LORD says: You eat meat with blood in it, you worship idols, and you murder the innocent. Do you really think the land should be yours? 26 Murderers! Idolaters! Adulterers! Should the land belong to you?'

27 "Say to them, 'This is what the Sovereign LORD says: As surely as I live, those living in the ruins will die by the sword. And I will send wild animals to eat those living in the open fields. Those hiding in the forts and caves will die of disease. 28 I will completely destroy the land and demolish her pride. Her arrogant power will come to an end. The mountains of Israel will be so desolate that no one will even travel through them. 29 When I have completely destroyed the land because of their detestable sins, then they will know that I am the LORD.'

30 "Son of man, your people talk about you in their houses and whisper about you at the doors. They say to each other, 'Come on, let's go hear the prophet tell us what the LORD is saying!' 31 So my people come pretending to be sincere and sit before you. They listen to your words, but they have no intention of doing what you say. Their mouths are full of lustful words, and their hearts seek only after money. 32 You are very entertaining to them, like someone who sings love songs with a beautiful voice or plays fine music on an instrument. They hear what you say, but they don't act on it! 33 But when all these terrible things happen to them—as they certainly will—then they will know a prophet has been among them."

CHAPTER 34

The Shepherds of Israel

Then this message came to me from the LORD: 2 "Son of man, prophesy against the shepherds, the leaders of Israel. Give them this message from the Sovereign LORD: What sorrow awaits you shepherds who feed yourselves instead of your flocks. Shouldn't shepherds feed their sheep? 3 You drink the milk, wear the wool, and butcher the best animals, but you let your flocks starve. 4 You have not taken care of the weak. You have not tended the sick or bound up the injured. You have not gone looking for those who have wandered away and are lost. Instead, you have ruled them with harshness and cruelty. 5 So my sheep have been scattered without a shepherd, and they are easy prey for any wild animal. 6 They have wandered through all the mountains and all the hills, across the face of the earth, yet no one has gone to search for them.

7 "Therefore, you shepherds, hear the word of the LORD: 8 As surely as I live, says the Sovereign LORD, you abandoned my flock and left them to be attacked by every wild animal. And though you were my shepherds, you didn't search for my sheep when they were lost. You took care of yourselves and left the sheep to starve. 9 Therefore, you shepherds, hear the word of the LORD. 10 This is what the Sovereign LORD says: I now consider these shepherds my enemies, and I will hold them responsible for what has happened to my flock. I will take away their right to feed the flock, and I will stop them from feeding themselves. I will rescue my flock from their mouths; the sheep will no longer be their prey.

The Good Shepherd

11 "For this is what the Sovereign LORD says: I myself will search and find my sheep. 12 I will be like a shepherd looking for his scattered flock. I will find my sheep and rescue them from all the places where they were scattered on that dark and cloudy day. 13 I will bring them back home to their own land of Israel from among the peoples and nations. I will feed them on the mountains of Israel and by the rivers and in all the places where people live. 14 Yes, I will give them good pastureland on the high hills of Israel. There they will lie down in pleasant places and feed in the lush pastures of the hills. 15 I myself will tend my sheep and give them a place to lie down in peace, says the Sovereign LORD. 16 I will search for my lost ones who strayed away, and I will bring them safely home again. I will bandage the injured and strengthen the weak. But I will destroy those who are fat and powerful. I will feed them, yes—feed them justice!

17 "And as for you, my flock, this is what the Sovereign LORD says to his people: I will judge between one animal of the flock and another,

separating the sheep from the goats. 18Isn't it enough for you to keep the best of the pastures for yourselves? Must you also trample down the rest? Isn't it enough for you to drink clear water for yourselves? Must you also muddy the rest with your feet? 19Why must my flock eat what you have trampled down and drink water you have fouled?

20"Therefore, this is what the Sovereign LORD says: I will surely judge between the fat sheep and the scrawny sheep. 21For you fat sheep pushed and butted and crowded my sick and hungry flock until you scattered them to distant lands. 22So I will rescue my flock, and they will no longer be abused. I will judge between one animal of the flock and another. 23And I will set over them one shepherd, my servant David. He will feed them and be a shepherd to them. 24And I, the LORD, will be their God, and my servant David will be a prince among my people. I, the LORD, have spoken!

The LORD's Covenant of Peace

25"I will make a covenant of peace with my people and drive away the dangerous animals from the land. Then they will be able to camp safely in the wildest places and sleep in the woods without fear. 26I will bless my people and their homes around my holy hill. And in the proper season I will send the showers they need. There will be showers of blessing. 27The orchards and fields of my people will yield bumper crops, and everyone will live in safety. When I have broken their chains of slavery and rescued them from those who enslaved them, then they will know that I am the LORD. 28They will no longer be prey for other nations, and wild animals will no longer devour them. They will live in safety, and no one will frighten them.

29"And I will make their land famous for its crops, so my people will never again suffer from famines or the insults of foreign nations. 30In this way, they will know that I, the LORD their God, am with them. And they will know that they, the people of Israel, are my people, says the Sovereign LORD. 31You are my flock, the sheep of my pasture. You are my people, and I am your God. I, the Sovereign LORD, have spoken!"

CHAPTER 35

A Message for Edom

Again a message came to me from the LORD: 2"Son of man, turn and face Mount Seir, and prophesy against its people. 3Give them this message from the Sovereign LORD:

"I am your enemy, O Mount Seir,
and I will raise my fist against you
to destroy you completely.
4I will demolish your cities
and make you desolate.
Then you will know that I am the LORD.

5"Your eternal hatred for the people of Israel led you to butcher them when they were helpless, when I had already punished them for all their sins. 6As surely as I live, says the Sovereign LORD, since you show no distaste for blood, I will give you a bloodbath of your own. Your turn has come! 7I will make Mount Seir utterly desolate, killing off all who try to escape and any who return. 8I will fill your mountains with the dead. Your hills, your valleys, and your ravines will be filled with people slaughtered by the sword. 9I will make you desolate forever. Your cities will never be rebuilt. Then you will know that I am the LORD.

10"For you said, 'The lands of Israel and Judah will be ours. We will take possession of them. What do we care that the LORD is there!' 11Therefore, as surely as I live, says the Sovereign LORD, I will pay back your angry deeds with my own. I will punish you for all your acts of anger, envy, and hatred. And I will make myself known to Israel by what I do to you. 12Then you will know that I, the LORD, have heard every contemptuous word you spoke against the mountains of Israel. For you said, 'They are desolate; they have been given to us as food to eat!' 13In saying that, you boasted proudly against me, and I have heard it all!

14"This is what the Sovereign LORD says: The whole world will rejoice when I make you desolate. 15You rejoiced at the desolation of Israel's territory. Now I will rejoice at yours! You will be wiped out, you people of Mount Seir and all who live in Edom! Then you will know that I am the LORD.

CHAPTER 36

Restoration for Israel

"Son of man, prophesy to Israel's mountains. Give them this message: O mountains of Israel, hear the word of the LORD! 2This is what the Sovereign LORD says: Your enemies have taunted you, saying, 'Aha! Now the ancient heights belong to us!' 3Therefore, son of man, give the mountains of Israel this message from the Sovereign LORD: Your enemies have attacked you from all directions, making you the property of many nations and the object of much mocking and slander. 4Therefore, O mountains of Israel, hear the word of the Sovereign LORD. He speaks to the hills and mountains, ravines and valleys, and to ruined wastes and long-deserted cities that have been destroyed and mocked by the surrounding nations. 5This is what the Sovereign LORD says: My jealous anger burns against these nations, especially Edom, because they have shown utter contempt for me by gleefully taking my land for themselves as plunder.

6"Therefore, prophesy to the hills and mountains, the ravines and valleys of Israel. This is what the Sovereign LORD says: I am furious that you have suffered shame before the surrounding nations. 7Therefore, this is what the Sovereign LORD says: I have taken a solemn oath that those nations will soon have their own shame to endure.

8"But the mountains of Israel will produce heavy crops of fruit for my people—for they will be coming home again soon! 9See, I care about you, and I will pay attention to you. Your ground will be plowed and your crops planted. 10I will greatly increase the population of Israel, and the ruined cities will be rebuilt and filled with people. 11I will increase not only the people, but also your animals. O mountains of Israel, I will bring people to live on you once again. I will make you even more prosperous than you were before. Then you will know that I am the LORD. 12I will cause my people to walk on you once again, and you will be their territory. You will never again rob them of their children.

13"This is what the Sovereign LORD says: The other nations taunt you, saying, 'Israel is a land that devours its own people and robs them of their children!' 14But you will never again devour your people or rob them of their children, says the Sovereign LORD. 15I will not let you hear those other nations insult you, and you will no longer be mocked by them. You will not be a land that causes its nation to fall, says the Sovereign LORD."

16Then this further message came to me from the LORD: 17"Son of man, when the people of Israel were living in their own land, they defiled it by the evil way they lived. To me their conduct was as unclean as a woman's menstrual cloth. 18They polluted the land with murder and the worship of idols, so I poured out my fury on them. 19I scattered them to many lands to punish them for the evil way they had lived. 20But when they were scattered among the nations, they brought shame on my holy name. For the nations said, 'These are the people of the LORD, but he couldn't keep them safe in his own land!' 21Then I was concerned for my holy name, on which my people brought shame among the nations.

22"Therefore, give the people of Israel this message from the Sovereign LORD: I am bringing you back, but not because you deserve it. I am doing it to protect my holy name, on which you brought shame while you were scattered among the nations. 23I will show how holy my great name is—the name on which you brought shame among the nations. And when I reveal my holiness through you before their very eyes, says the Sovereign LORD, then the nations will know that I am the LORD. 24For I will gather you up from all the nations and bring you home again to your land.

25"Then I will sprinkle clean water on you, and you will be clean. Your filth will be washed away, and you will no longer worship idols. 26And I will give you a new heart, and I will put a new spirit in you. I will take out your stony, stubborn heart and give you a tender, responsive heart. 27And I will put my Spirit in you so that you will follow my decrees and be careful to obey my regulations.

28"And you will live in Israel, the land I gave your ancestors long ago. You will be my people, and I will be your God. 29I will cleanse you of your filthy behavior. I will give you good crops of grain, and I will send no more famines on the land. 30I will give you great harvests from your fruit trees and fields, and never again will the surrounding nations be able to scoff at your land for its famines. 31Then you will remember your past sins and despise yourselves for all the detestable things you did. 32But remember, says the Sovereign LORD, I am not doing this because you deserve it. O my people of Israel, you should be utterly ashamed of all you have done!

33"This is what the Sovereign LORD says: When I cleanse you from your sins, I will repopulate your cities, and the ruins will be rebuilt. 34The fields that used to lie empty and desolate in plain view of everyone will again be farmed. 35And when I bring you back, people will say, 'This former wasteland is now like the Garden of Eden! The abandoned and ruined cities now have strong walls and are filled with people!' 36Then the surrounding nations that survive will know that I, the LORD, have rebuilt the ruins and replanted the wasteland. For I, the LORD, have spoken, and I will do what I say.

37"This is what the Sovereign LORD says: I am ready to hear Israel's prayers and to increase their numbers like a flock. 38They will be as numerous as the sacred flocks that fill Jerusalem's streets at the time of her festivals. The ruined

cities will be crowded with people once more,
and everyone will know that I am the LORD."

CHAPTER 37

A Valley of Dry Bones

The LORD took hold of me, and I was carried away
by the Spirit of the LORD to a valley filled with
bones. 2He led me all around among the bones
that covered the valley floor. They were scattered
everywhere across the ground and were completely dried out. 3Then he asked me, "Son of
man, can these bones become living people
again?"

"O Sovereign LORD," I replied, "you alone know
the answer to that."

4Then he said to me, "Speak a prophetic message to these bones and say, 'Dry bones, listen to
the word of the LORD! 5This is what the Sovereign LORD says: Look! I am going to put breath
into you and make you live again! 6I will put flesh
and muscles on you and cover you with skin. I
will put breath into you, and you will come to life.
Then you will know that I am the LORD.'"

7So I spoke this message, just as he told me.
Suddenly as I spoke, there was a rattling noise all
across the valley. The bones of each body came
together and attached themselves as complete
skeletons. 8Then as I watched, muscles and flesh
formed over the bones. Then skin formed to
cover their bodies, but they still had no breath in
them.

9Then he said to me, "Speak a prophetic message to the winds, son of man. Speak a prophetic
message and say, 'This is what the Sovereign
LORD says: Come, O breath, from the four winds!
Breathe into these dead bodies so they may live
again.'"

10So I spoke the message as he commanded
me, and breath came into their bodies. They all
came to life and stood up on their feet—a great
army.

11Then he said to me, "Son of man, these
bones represent the people of Israel. They are
saying, 'We have become old, dry bones—all
hope is gone. Our nation is finished.' 12There-
fore, prophesy to them and say, 'This is what the
Sovereign LORD says: O my people, I will open
your graves of exile and cause you to rise again.
Then I will bring you back to the land of Israel.
13When this happens, O my people, you will
know that I am the LORD. 14I will put my Spirit in
you, and you will live again and return home to
your own land. Then you will know that I, the
LORD, have spoken, and I have done what I said.
Yes, the LORD has spoken!'"

Reunion of Israel and Judah

15Again a message came to me from the LORD:
16"Son of man, take a piece of wood and carve on
it these words: 'This represents Judah and its allied tribes.' Then take another piece and carve
these words on it: 'This represents Ephraim and
the northern tribes of Israel.' 17Now hold them
together in your hand as if they were one piece of
wood. 18When your people ask you what your
actions mean, 19say to them, 'This is what the
Sovereign LORD says: I will take Ephraim and the
northern tribes and join them to Judah. I will
make them one piece of wood in my hand.'

20"Then hold out the pieces of wood you have
inscribed, so the people can see them. 21And give
them this message from the Sovereign LORD: I
will gather the people of Israel from among the
nations. I will bring them home to their own land
from the places where they have been scattered.
22I will unify them into one nation on the mountains of Israel. One king will rule them all; no longer will they be divided into two nations or into
two kingdoms. 23They will never again pollute
themselves with their idols and vile images and
rebellion, for I will save them from their sinful
apostasy. I will cleanse them. Then they will truly
be my people, and I will be their God.

24"My servant David will be their king, and
they will have only one shepherd. They will obey
my regulations and be careful to keep my decrees. 25They will live in the land I gave my servant Jacob, the land where their ancestors lived.
They and their children and their grandchildren
after them will live there forever, generation
after generation. And my servant David will
be their prince forever. 26And I will make a covenant of peace with them, an everlasting covenant. I will give them their land and increase
their numbers, and I will put my Temple among
them forever. 27I will make my home among
them. I will be their God, and they will be my
people. 28And when my Temple is among them
forever, the nations will know that I am the LORD,
who makes Israel holy."

CHAPTER 38

A Message for Gog

This is another message that came to me from
the LORD: 2"Son of man, turn and face Gog of the
land of Magog, the prince who rules over the
nations of Meshech and Tubal, and prophesy
against him. 3Give him this message from the
Sovereign LORD: Gog, I am your enemy! 4I will
turn you around and put hooks in your jaws to
lead you out with your whole army—your horses

and charioteers in full armor and a great horde
armed with shields and swords. 5Persia, Ethiopia, and Libya will join you, too, with all their
weapons. 6Gomer and all its armies will also join
you, along with the armies of Beth-togarmah
from the distant north, and many others.
7"Get ready; be prepared! Keep all the armies
around you mobilized, and take command of
them. 8A long time from now you will be called
into action. In the distant future you will swoop
down on the land of Israel, which will be enjoying peace after recovering from war and after its
people have returned from many lands to the
mountains of Israel. 9You and all your allies—a
vast and awesome army—will roll down on them
like a storm and cover the land like a cloud.
10"This is what the Sovereign LORD says: At
that time evil thoughts will come to your mind,
and you will devise a wicked scheme. 11You will
say, 'Israel is an unprotected land filled with
unwalled villages! I will march against her and
destroy these people who live in such confidence! 12I will go to those formerly desolate
cities that are now filled with people who have
returned from exile in many nations. I will capture vast amounts of plunder, for the people are
rich with livestock and other possessions now.
They think the whole world revolves around
them!' 13But Sheba and Dedan and the merchants of Tarshish will ask, 'Do you really think
the armies you have gathered can rob them of
silver and gold? Do you think you can drive away
their livestock and seize their goods and carry
off plunder?'
14"Therefore, son of man, prophesy against
Gog. Give him this message from the Sovereign
LORD: When my people are living in peace in
their land, then you will rouse yourself. 15You will
come from your homeland in the distant north
with your vast cavalry and your mighty army,
16and you will attack my people Israel, covering
their land like a cloud. At that time in the distant
future, I will bring you against my land as everyone watches, and my holiness will be displayed
by what happens to you, Gog. Then all the nations will know that I am the LORD.
17"This is what the Sovereign LORD asks: Are
you the one I was talking about long ago, when I
announced through Israel's prophets that in the
future I would bring you against my people?
18But this is what the Sovereign LORD says:
When Gog invades the land of Israel, my fury will
boil over! 19In my jealousy and blazing anger, I
promise a mighty shaking in the land of Israel on
that day. 20All living things—the fish in the sea,
the birds of the sky, the animals of the field, the
small animals that scurry along the ground, and
all the people on earth—will quake in terror at
my presence. Mountains will be thrown down;
cliffs will crumble; walls will fall to the earth. 21I
will summon the sword against you on all the
hills of Israel, says the Sovereign LORD. Your men
will turn their swords against each other. 22I will
punish you and your armies with disease and
bloodshed; I will send torrential rain, hailstones,
fire, and burning sulfur! 23In this way, I will show
my greatness and holiness, and I will make myself known to all the nations of the world. Then
they will know that I am the LORD.

CHAPTER 39

The Slaughter of Gog's Hordes

"Son of man, prophesy against Gog. Give him this
message from the Sovereign LORD: I am your enemy, O Gog, ruler of the nations of Meshech and
Tubal. 2I will turn you around and drive you toward the mountains of Israel, bringing you from
the distant north. 3I will knock the bow from
your left hand and the arrows from your right
hand, and I will leave you helpless. 4You and your
army and your allies will all die on the mountains. I will feed you to the vultures and wild animals. 5You will fall in the open fields, for I have
spoken, says the Sovereign LORD. 6And I will rain
down fire on Magog and on all your allies who
live safely on the coasts. Then they will know that
I am the LORD.
7"In this way, I will make known my holy name
among my people of Israel. I will not let anyone
bring shame on it. And the nations, too, will
know that I am the LORD, the Holy One of Israel.
8That day of judgment will come, says the Sovereign LORD. Everything will happen just as I have
declared it.
9"Then the people in the towns of Israel will
go out and pick up your small and large shields,
bows and arrows, javelins and spears, and they
will use them for fuel. There will be enough to
last them seven years! 10They won't need to cut
wood from the fields or forests, for these weapons will give them all the fuel they need. They
will plunder those who planned to plunder
them, and they will rob those who planned to rob
them, says the Sovereign LORD.
11"And I will make a vast graveyard for Gog
and his hordes in the Valley of the Travelers, east
of the Dead Sea. It will block the way of those
who travel there, and they will change the name
of the place to the Valley of Gog's Hordes. 12It
will take seven months for the people of Israel to

bury the bodies and cleanse the land. 13 Everyone in Israel will help, for it will be a glorious victory for Israel when I demonstrate my glory on that day, says the Sovereign LORD.

14 "After seven months, teams of men will be appointed to search the land for skeletons to bury, so the land will be made clean again. 15 Whenever bones are found, a marker will be set up so the burial crews will take them to be buried in the Valley of Gog's Hordes. 16 (There will be a town there named Hamonah, which means 'horde.') And so the land will finally be cleansed.

17 "And now, son of man, this is what the Sovereign LORD says: Call all the birds and wild animals. Say to them: Gather together for my great sacrificial feast. Come from far and near to the mountains of Israel, and there eat flesh and drink blood! 18 Eat the flesh of mighty men and drink the blood of princes as though they were rams, lambs, goats, and bulls—all fattened animals from Bashan! 19 Gorge yourselves with flesh until you are glutted; drink blood until you are drunk. This is the sacrificial feast I have prepared for you. 20 Feast at my banquet table—feast on horses and charioteers, on mighty men and all kinds of valiant warriors, says the Sovereign LORD.

21 "In this way, I will demonstrate my glory to the nations. Everyone will see the punishment I have inflicted on them and the power of my fist when I strike. 22 And from that time on the people of Israel will know that I am the LORD their God. 23 The nations will then know why Israel was sent away to exile—it was punishment for sin, for they were unfaithful to their God. Therefore, I turned away from them and let their enemies destroy them. 24 I turned my face away and punished them because of their defilement and their sins.

Restoration for God's People

25 "So now, this is what the Sovereign LORD says: I will end the captivity of my people; I will have mercy on all Israel, for I jealously guard my holy reputation! 26 They will accept responsibility for their past shame and unfaithfulness after they come home to live in peace in their own land, with no one to bother them. 27 When I bring them home from the lands of their enemies, I will display my holiness among them for all the nations to see. 28 Then my people will know that I am the LORD their God, because I sent them away to exile and brought them home again. I will leave none of my people behind. 29 And I will never again turn my face from them, for I will pour out my Spirit upon the people of Israel. I, the Sovereign LORD, have spoken!"

CHAPTER 40

The New Temple Area

On April 28, during the twenty-fifth year of our captivity—fourteen years after the fall of Jerusalem—the LORD took hold of me. 2 In a vision from God he took me to the land of Israel and set me down on a very high mountain. From there I could see toward the south what appeared to be a city. 3 As he brought me nearer, I saw a man whose face shone like bronze standing beside a gateway entrance. He was holding in his hand a linen measuring cord and a measuring rod.

4 He said to me, "Son of man, watch and listen. Pay close attention to everything I show you. You have been brought here so I can show you many things. Then you will return to the people of Israel and tell them everything you have seen."

The East Gateway

5 I could see a wall completely surrounding the Temple area. The man took a measuring rod that was 10½ feet long and measured the wall, and the wall was 10½ feet thick and 10½ feet high.

6 Then he went over to the eastern gateway. He climbed the steps and measured the threshold of the gateway; it was 10½ feet front to back. 7 There were guard alcoves on each side built into the gateway passage. Each of these alcoves was 10½ feet square, with a distance between them of 8¾ feet along the passage wall. The gateway's inner threshold, which led to the entry room at the inner end of the gateway passage, was 10½ feet front to back. 8 He also measured the entry room of the gateway. 9 It was 14 feet across, with supporting columns 3½ feet thick. This entry room was at the inner end of the gateway structure, facing toward the Temple.

10 There were three guard alcoves on each side of the gateway passage. Each had the same measurements, and the dividing walls separating them were also identical. 11 The man measured the gateway entrance, which was 17½ feet wide at the opening and 22¾ feet wide in the gateway passage. 12 In front of each of the guard alcoves was a 21-inch curb. The alcoves themselves were 10½ feet on each side.

13 Then he measured the entire width of the gateway, measuring the distance between the back walls of facing guard alcoves; this distance was 43¾ feet. 14 He measured the dividing walls all along the inside of the gateway up to the entry

room of the gateway; this distance was 105 feet.
15 The full length of the gateway passage was
87½ feet from one end to the other. 16 There
were recessed windows that narrowed inward
through the walls of the guard alcoves and their
dividing walls. There were also windows in the
entry room. The surfaces of the dividing walls
were decorated with carved palm trees.

The Outer Courtyard

17 Then the man brought me through the gateway
into the outer courtyard of the Temple. A stone
pavement ran along the walls of the courtyard,
and thirty rooms were built against the walls,
opening onto the pavement. 18 This pavement
flanked the gates and extended out from the
walls into the courtyard the same distance as the
gateway entrance. This was the lower pavement.
19 Then the man measured across the Temple's
outer courtyard between the outer and inner
gateways; the distance was 175 feet.

The North Gateway

20 The man measured the gateway on the north
just like the one on the east. 21 Here, too, there
were three guard alcoves on each side, with dividing walls and an entry room. All the measurements matched those of the east gateway. The
gateway passage was 87½ feet long and 43¾ feet
wide between the back walls of facing guard
alcoves. 22 The windows, the entry room, and the
palm tree decorations were identical to those in
the east gateway. There were seven steps leading
up to the gateway entrance, and the entry room
was at the inner end of the gateway passage.
23 Here on the north side, just as on the east, there
was another gateway leading to the Temple's inner courtyard directly opposite this outer gateway. The distance between the two gateways was
175 feet.

The South Gateway

24 Then the man took me around to the south
gateway and measured its various parts, and they
were exactly the same as in the others. 25 It had
windows along the walls as the others did, and
there was an entry room where the gateway passage opened into the outer courtyard. And like
the others, the gateway passage was 87½ feet
long and 43¾ feet wide between the back walls
of facing guard alcoves. 26 This gateway also had
a stairway of seven steps leading up to it, and an
entry room at the inner end, and palm tree decorations along the dividing walls. 27 And here
again, directly opposite the outer gateway, was
another gateway that led into the inner courtyard. The distance between the two gateways
was 175 feet.

Gateways to the Inner Courtyard

28 Then the man took me to the south gateway
leading into the inner courtyard. He measured it,
and it had the same measurements as the other
gateways. 29 Its guard alcoves, dividing walls, and
entry room were the same size as those in the
others. It also had windows along its walls and in
the entry room. And like the others, the gateway
passage was 87½ feet long and 43¾ feet wide.
30 (The entry rooms of the gateways leading into
the inner courtyard were 14 feet across and 43¾
feet wide.) 31 The entry room to the south gateway faced into the outer courtyard. It had palm
tree decorations on its columns, and there were
eight steps leading to its entrance.

32 Then he took me to the east gateway leading
to the inner courtyard. He measured it, and it had
the same measurements as the other gateways.
33 Its guard alcoves, dividing walls, and entry
room were the same size as those of the others,
and there were windows along the walls and in
the entry room. The gateway passage measured
87½ feet long and 43¾ feet wide. 34 Its entry
room faced into the outer courtyard. It had palm
tree decorations on its columns, and there were
eight steps leading to its entrance.

35 Then he took me around to the north gateway leading to the inner courtyard. He measured
it, and it had the same measurements as the
other gateways. 36 The guard alcoves, dividing
walls, and entry room of this gateway had the
same measurements as in the others and the
same window arrangements. The gateway passage measured 87½ feet long and 43¾ feet wide.
37 Its entry room faced into the outer courtyard,
and it had palm tree decorations on the columns.
There were eight steps leading to its entrance.

Rooms for Preparing Sacrifices

38 A door led from the entry room of one of the
inner gateways into a side room, where the meat
for sacrifices was washed. 39 On each side of this
entry room were two tables, where the sacrificial
animals were slaughtered for the burnt offerings, sin offerings, and guilt offerings. 40 Outside
the entry room, on each side of the stairs going
up to the north entrance, were two more tables.
41 So there were eight tables in all—four inside
and four outside—where the sacrifices were cut

up and prepared. 42There were also four tables
of finished stone for preparation of the burnt offerings, each 31½ inches square and 21 inches
high. On these tables were placed the butchering
knives and other implements for slaughtering
the sacrificial animals. 43There were hooks, each
3 inches long, fastened all around the foyer
walls. The sacrificial meat was laid on the tables.

Rooms for the Priests

44Inside the inner courtyard were two rooms,
one beside the north gateway, facing south, and
the other beside the south gateway, facing
north. 45And the man said to me, "The room beside the north inner gate is for the priests who
supervise the Temple maintenance. 46The room
beside the south inner gate is for the priests in
charge of the altar—the descendants of Zadok—
for they alone of all the Levites may approach
the LORD to minister to him."

The Inner Courtyard and Temple

47Then the man measured the inner courtyard,
and it was a square, 175 feet wide and 175 feet
across. The altar stood in the courtyard in front
of the Temple. 48Then he brought me to the entry room of the Temple. He measured the walls
on either side of the opening to the entry room,
and they were 8¾ feet thick. The entrance itself
was 24½ feet wide, and the walls on each side of
the entrance were an additional 5¼ feet long.
49The entry room was 35 feet wide and 21 feet
deep. There were ten steps leading up to it, with a
column on each side.

CHAPTER 41

After that, the man brought me into the sanctuary
of the Temple. He measured the walls on either
side of its doorway, and they were 10½ feet thick.
2The doorway was 17½ feet wide, and the walls
on each side of it were 8¾ feet long. The sanctuary
itself was 70 feet long and 35 feet wide.

3Then he went beyond the sanctuary into the
inner room. He measured the walls on either side
of its entrance, and they were 3½ feet thick. The
entrance was 10½ feet wide, and the walls on
each side of the entrance were 12¼ feet long.
4The inner room of the sanctuary was 35 feet
long and 35 feet wide. "This," he told me, "is the
Most Holy Place."

5Then he measured the wall of the Temple,
and it was 10½ feet thick. There was a row of
rooms along the outside wall; each room was
7 feet wide. 6These side rooms were built in three
levels, one above the other, with thirty rooms on
each level. The supports for these side rooms
rested on exterior ledges on the Temple wall; they
did not extend into the wall. 7Each level was
wider than the one below it, corresponding to the
narrowing of the Temple wall as it rose higher. A
stairway led up from the bottom level through
the middle level to the top level.

8I saw that the Temple was built on a terrace,
which provided a foundation for the side rooms.
This terrace was 10½ feet high. 9The outer wall
of the Temple's side rooms was 8¾ feet thick.
This left an open area between these side rooms
10and the row of rooms along the outer wall of
the inner courtyard. This open area was 35 feet
wide, and it went all the way around the Temple.
11Two doors opened from the side rooms into the
terrace yard, which was 8¾ feet wide. One door
faced north and the other south.

12A large building stood on the west, facing the
Temple courtyard. It was 122½ feet wide and
157½ feet long, and its walls were 8¾ feet thick.
13Then the man measured the Temple, and it was
175 feet long. The courtyard around the building, including its walls, was an additional
175 feet in length. 14The inner courtyard to the

FUN-fact **Parents & Kids**

Things were sure different for kids back in Bible times. There were no cars, no malls, no video games, and no fast food restaurants. But one thing *hasn't* changed! God still desires that kids honor, obey, and love their parents.

TRY COMING UP WITH SOME FUN AND UNUSUAL WAYS TO HONOR, OBEY, AND LOVE YOUR PARENTS.

You might give your mom a neck massage at the end of the day. Or rent your dad's favorite movie and share a bowl of popcorn with him. Write all your ideas on slips of paper. Put the paper slips in a bowl or box in your room. (Keep it a secret from your parents.) **Once a week, choose a paper slip, and do whatever you wrote on it. Your parents won't know what to make of it!**

east of the Temple was also 175 feet wide. 15The
building to the west, including its two walls, was
also 175 feet wide.

The sanctuary, the inner room, and the entry
room of the Temple 16were all paneled with
wood, as were the frames of the recessed windows. The inner walls of the Temple were paneled with wood above and below the windows.
17The space above the door leading into the inner room, and its walls inside and out, were also
paneled. 18All the walls were decorated with
carvings of cherubim, each with two faces, and
there was a carving of a palm tree between each
of the cherubim. 19One face—that of a man—
looked toward the palm tree on one side. The
other face—that of a young lion—looked toward
the palm tree on the other side. The figures were
carved all along the inside of the Temple, 20from
the floor to the top of the walls, including the
outer wall of the sanctuary.

21There were square columns at the entrance
to the sanctuary, and the ones at the entrance of
the Most Holy Place were similar. 22There was an
altar made of wood, 5¼ feet high and 3½ feet
across. Its corners, base, and sides were all made
of wood. "This," the man told me, "is the table
that stands in the LORD's presence."

23Both the sanctuary and the Most Holy Place
had double doorways, 24each with two swinging
doors. 25The doors leading into the sanctuary
were decorated with carved cherubim and palm
trees, just as on the walls. And there was a
wooden roof at the front of the entry room to the
Temple. 26On both sides of the entry room were
recessed windows decorated with carved palm
trees. The side rooms along the outside wall also
had roofs.

CHAPTER 42
Rooms for the Priests

Then the man led me out of the Temple courtyard by way of the north gateway. We entered the
outer courtyard and came to a group of rooms
against the north wall of the inner courtyard.
2This structure, whose entrance opened toward
the north, was 175 feet long and 87½ feet wide.
3One block of rooms overlooked the 35-foot
width of the inner courtyard. Another block of
rooms looked out onto the pavement of the outer
courtyard. The two blocks were built three levels
high and stood across from each other. 4Between
the two blocks of rooms ran a walkway 17½ feet
wide. It extended the entire 175 feet of the complex, and all the doors faced north. 5Each of the
two upper levels of rooms was narrower than the
one beneath it because the upper levels had to allow space for walkways in front of them. 6Since
there were three levels and they did not have supporting columns as in the courtyards, each of the
upper levels was set back from the level beneath
it. 7There was an outer wall that separated the
rooms from the outer courtyard; it was 87½ feet
long. 8This wall added length to the outer block
of rooms, which extended for only 87½ feet,
while the inner block—the rooms toward the
Temple—extended for 175 feet. 9There was an
eastern entrance from the outer courtyard to
these rooms.

10On the south side of the Temple there were
two blocks of rooms just south of the inner
courtyard between the Temple and the outer
courtyard. These rooms were arranged just like
the rooms on the north. 11There was a walkway
between the two blocks of rooms just like the
complex on the north side of the Temple. This
complex of rooms was the same length and
width as the other one, and it had the same entrances and doors. The dimensions of each were
identical. 12So there was an entrance in the wall
facing the doors of the inner block of rooms, and
another on the east at the end of the interior
walkway.

13Then the man told me, "These rooms that
overlook the Temple from the north and south
are holy. Here the priests who offer sacrifices to
the LORD will eat the most holy offerings. And because these rooms are holy, they will be used to
store the sacred offerings—the grain offerings,
sin offerings, and guilt offerings. 14When the
priests leave the sanctuary, they must not go directly to the outer courtyard. They must first take
off the clothes they wore while ministering, because these clothes are holy. They must put on
other clothes before entering the parts of the
building complex open to the public."

15When the man had finished measuring the
inside of the Temple area, he led me out through
the east gateway to measure the entire perimeter.
16He measured the east side with his measuring
rod, and it was 875 feet long. 17Then he measured the north side, and it was also 875 feet.
18The south side was also 875 feet, 19and the
west side was also 875 feet. 20So the area was
875 feet on each side with a wall all around it to
separate what was holy from what was common.

CHAPTER 43
The LORD's Glory Returns

After this, the man brought me back around to
the east gateway. 2Suddenly, the glory of the God

of Israel appeared from the east. The sound of
his coming was like the roar of rushing waters,
and the whole landscape shone with his glory.
3This vision was just like the others I had seen,
first by the Kebar River and then when he came
to destroy Jerusalem. I fell face down on the
ground. 4And the glory of the LORD came into the
Temple through the east gateway.

5Then the Spirit took me up and brought me
into the inner courtyard, and the glory of the
LORD filled the Temple. 6And I heard someone
speaking to me from within the Temple, while
the man who had been measuring stood beside
me. 7The LORD said to me, "Son of man, this is the
place of my throne and the place where I will rest
my feet. I will live here forever among the people
of Israel. They and their kings will not defile my
holy name any longer by their adulterous worship of other gods or by honoring the relics of
their kings who have died. 8They put their idol
altars right next to mine with only a wall between
them and me. They defiled my holy name by
such detestable sin, so I consumed them in my
anger. 9Now let them stop worshiping other
gods and honoring the relics of their kings, and I
will live among them forever.

10"Son of man, describe to the people of Israel
the Temple I have shown you, so they will be
ashamed of all their sins. Let them study its plan,
11and they will be ashamed of what they have
done. Describe to them all the specifications of
the Temple—including its entrances and exits—
and everything else about it. Tell them about its
decrees and laws. Write down all these specifications and decrees as they watch so they will be
sure to remember and follow them. 12And this is
the basic law of the Temple: absolute holiness!
The entire top of the mountain where the Temple is built is holy. Yes, this is the basic law of the
Temple.

The Altar

13"These are the measurements of the altar:
There is a gutter all around the altar 21 inches
deep and 21 inches wide, with a curb 9 inches
wide around its edge. And this is the height of
the altar: 14From the gutter the altar rises 3½ feet
to a lower ledge that surrounds the altar and is
21 inches wide. From the lower ledge the altar
rises 7 feet to the upper ledge that is also
21 inches wide. 15The top of the altar, the hearth,
rises another 7 feet higher, with a horn rising up
from each of the four corners. 16The top of the
altar is square, measuring 21 feet by 21 feet.
17The upper ledge also forms a square, measuring 24½ feet by 24½ feet, with a 21-inch gutter
and a 10½-inch curb all around the edge. There
are steps going up the east side of the altar."

18Then he said to me, "Son of man, this is what
the Sovereign LORD says: These will be the regulations for the burning of offerings and the
sprinkling of blood when the altar is built. 19At
that time, the Levitical priests of the family of
Zadok, who minister before me, are to be given a
young bull for a sin offering, says the Sovereign
LORD. 20You will take some of its blood and
smear it on the four horns of the altar, the four
corners of the upper ledge, and the curb that
runs around that ledge. This will cleanse and
make atonement for the altar. 21Then take the
young bull for the sin offering and burn it at the
appointed place outside the Temple area.

22"On the second day, sacrifice as a sin offering a young male goat that has no physical defects. Then cleanse and make atonement for the
altar again, just as you did with the young bull.
23When you have finished the cleansing ceremony, offer another young bull that has no defects and a perfect ram from the flock. 24You are
to present them to the LORD, and the priests are
to sprinkle salt on them and offer them as a
burnt offering to the LORD.

25"Every day for seven days a male goat, a
young bull, and a ram from the flock will be sacrificed as a sin offering. None of these animals
may have physical defects of any kind. 26Do this
each day for seven days to cleanse and make
atonement for the altar, thus setting it apart for
holy use. 27On the eighth day, and on each day
afterward, the priests will sacrifice on the altar
the burnt offerings and peace offerings of the
people. Then I will accept you. I, the Sovereign
LORD, have spoken!"

CHAPTER 44

The Prince, Levites, and Priests

Then the man brought me back to the east gateway in the outer wall of the Temple area, but it
was closed. 2And the LORD said to me, "This gate
must remain closed; it will never again be
opened. No one will ever open it and pass
through, for the LORD, the God of Israel, has entered here. Therefore, it must always remain
shut. 3Only the prince himself may sit inside this
gateway to feast in the LORD's presence. But he
may come and go only through the entry room of
the gateway."

4Then the man brought me through the north
gateway to the front of the Temple. I looked and

saw that the glory of the LORD filled the Temple of the LORD, and I fell face down on the ground.

5 And the LORD said to me, "Son of man, take careful notice. Use your eyes and ears, and listen to everything I tell you about the regulations concerning the LORD's Temple. Take careful note of the procedures for using the Temple's entrances and exits. 6 And give these rebels, the people of Israel, this message from the Sovereign LORD: O people of Israel, enough of your detestable sins! 7 You have brought uncircumcised foreigners into my sanctuary—people who have no heart for God. In this way, you defiled my Temple even as you offered me my food, the fat and blood of sacrifices. In addition to all your other detestable sins, you have broken my covenant. 8 Instead of safeguarding my sacred rituals, you have hired foreigners to take charge of my sanctuary.

9 "So this is what the Sovereign LORD says: No foreigners, including those who live among the people of Israel, will enter my sanctuary if they have not been circumcised and have not surrendered themselves to the LORD. 10 And the men of the tribe of Levi who abandoned me when Israel strayed away from me to worship idols must bear the consequences of their unfaithfulness. 11 They may still be Temple guards and gatekeepers, and they may slaughter the animals brought for burnt offerings and be present to help the people. 12 But they encouraged my people to worship idols, causing Israel to fall into deep sin. So I have taken a solemn oath that they must bear the consequences for their sins, says the Sovereign LORD. 13 They may not approach me to minister as priests. They may not touch any of my holy things or the holy offerings, for they must bear the shame of all the detestable sins they have committed. 14 They are to serve as the Temple caretakers, taking charge of the maintenance work and performing general duties.

15 "However, the Levitical priests of the family of Zadok continued to minister faithfully in the Temple when Israel abandoned me for idols. These men will serve as my ministers. They will stand in my presence and offer the fat and blood of the sacrifices, says the Sovereign LORD. 16 They alone will enter my sanctuary and approach my table to serve me. They will fulfill all my requirements.

17 "When they enter the gateway to the inner courtyard, they must wear only linen clothing. They must wear no wool while on duty in the inner courtyard or in the Temple itself. 18 They must wear linen turbans and linen undergarments. They must not wear anything that would cause them to perspire. 19 When they return to the outer courtyard where the people are, they must take off the clothes they wear while ministering to me. They must leave them in the sacred rooms and put on other clothes so they do not endanger anyone by transmitting holiness to them through this clothing.

20 "They must neither shave their heads nor let their hair grow too long. Instead, they must trim it regularly. 21 The priests must not drink wine before entering the inner courtyard. 22 They may choose their wives only from among the virgins of Israel or the widows of the priests. They may not marry other widows or divorced women. 23 They will teach my people the difference between what is holy and what is common, what is ceremonially clean and unclean.

24 "They will serve as judges to resolve any disagreements among my people. Their decisions must be based on my regulations. And the priests themselves must obey my instructions and decrees at all the sacred festivals, and see to it that the Sabbaths are set apart as holy days.

25 "A priest must not defile himself by being in the presence of a dead person unless it is his father, mother, child, brother, or unmarried sister. In such cases it is permitted. 26 Even then, he can return to his Temple duties only after being ceremonially cleansed and then waiting for seven days. 27 The first day he returns to work and enters the inner courtyard and the sanctuary, he must offer a sin offering for himself, says the Sovereign LORD.

28 "The priests will not have any property or possession of land, for I alone am their special possession. 29 Their food will come from the gifts and sacrifices brought to the Temple by the people—the grain offerings, the sin offerings, and the guilt offerings. Whatever anyone sets apart for the LORD will belong to the priests. 30 The first of the ripe fruits and all the gifts brought to the LORD will go to the priests. The first batch of dough must also be given to the priests so the LORD will bless your homes. 31 The priests may not eat meat from any bird or animal that dies a natural death or that dies after being attacked by another animal.

CHAPTER 45

Division of the Land

"When you divide the land among the tribes of Israel, you must set aside a section for the LORD as his holy portion. This piece of land will be 8⅓ miles long and 6⅔ miles wide. The entire area will be holy. 2 A section of this land, measuring 875 feet by 875 feet, will be set aside for the Temple. An additional strip of land 87½ feet wide is to be left empty all around it. 3 Within the larger sacred area, measure out a portion of land 8⅓ miles long and 3⅓ miles wide. Within it the sanctuary of the Most Holy Place will be located. 4 This area will be holy, set aside for the priests who minister to the LORD in the sanctuary. They will use it for their homes, and my Temple will be located within it. 5 The strip of sacred land next to it, also 8⅓ miles long and 3⅓ miles wide, will be a living area for the Levites who work at the Temple. It will be their possession and a place for their towns.

6 "Adjacent to the larger sacred area will be a section of land 8⅓ miles long and 1⅔ miles wide. This will be set aside for a city where anyone in Israel can live.

7 "Two special sections of land will be set apart for the prince. One section will share a border with the east side of the sacred lands and city, and the second section will share a border on the west side. Then the far eastern and western borders of the prince's lands will line up with the eastern and western boundaries of the tribal areas. 8 These sections of land will be the prince's allotment. Then my princes will no longer oppress and rob my people; they will assign the rest of the land to the people, giving an allotment to each tribe.

Rules for the Princes

9 "For this is what the Sovereign LORD says: Enough, you princes of Israel! Stop your violence and oppression and do what is just and right. Quit robbing and cheating my people out of their land. Stop expelling them from their homes, says the Sovereign LORD. 10 Use only honest weights and scales and honest measures, both dry and liquid. 11 The homer will be your standard unit for measuring volume. The ephah and the bath will each measure one-tenth of a homer. 12 The standard unit for weight will be the silver shekel. One shekel will consist of twenty gerahs, and sixty shekels will be equal to one mina.

Special Offerings and Celebrations

13 "You must give this tax to the prince: one bushel of wheat or barley for every 60 you harvest, 14 one percent of your olive oil, 15 and one sheep or goat for every 200 in your flocks in Israel. These will be the grain offerings, burnt offerings, and peace offerings that will make atonement for the people who bring them, says the Sovereign LORD. 16 All the people of Israel must join in bringing these offerings to the prince. 17 The prince will be required to provide offerings that are given at the religious festivals, the new moon celebrations, the Sabbath days, and all other similar occasions. He will provide the sin offerings, burnt offerings, grain offerings, liquid offerings, and peace offerings to purify the people of Israel, making them right with the LORD.

18 "This is what the Sovereign LORD says: In early spring, on the first day of each new year, sacrifice a young bull with no defects to purify the Temple. 19 The priest will take blood from this sin offering and put it on the doorposts of the Temple, the four corners of the upper ledge of the altar, and the gateposts at the entrance to the inner courtyard. 20 Do this also on the seventh day of the new year for anyone who has sinned through error or ignorance. In this way, you will purify the Temple.

21 "On the fourteenth day of the first month, you must celebrate the Passover. This festival will last for seven days. The bread you eat during that time must be made without yeast. 22 On the day of Passover the prince will provide a young bull as a sin offering for himself and the people of Israel. 23 On each of the seven days of the feast he will prepare a burnt offering to the LORD, consisting of seven young bulls and seven rams without defects. A male goat will also be given each day for a sin offering. 24 The prince will provide a basket of flour as a grain offering and a gallon of olive oil with each young bull and ram.

25 "During the seven days of the Festival of Shelters, which occurs every year in early autumn, the prince will provide these same sacrifices for the sin offering, the burnt offering, and the grain offering, along with the required olive oil.

CHAPTER 46

"This is what the Sovereign LORD says: The east gateway of the inner courtyard will be closed during the six workdays each week, but it will be open on Sabbath days and the days of new moon celebrations. 2 The prince will enter the entry room of the gateway from the outside. Then he will stand by the gatepost while the priest offers his burnt offering and peace offering. He will bow down in worship inside the gateway passage and then go back out the way he came. The gateway will not be closed until evening. 3The common people will bow down and worship the LORD in front of this gateway on Sabbath days and the days of new moon celebrations.

4"Each Sabbath day the prince will present to the LORD a burnt offering of six lambs and one ram, all with no defects. 5He will present a grain offering of a basket of choice flour to go with the ram and whatever amount of flour he chooses to go with each lamb, and he is to offer one gallon of olive oil for each basket of flour. 6At the new moon celebrations, he will bring one young bull, six lambs, and one ram, all with no defects. 7With the young bull he must bring a basket of choice flour for a grain offering. With the ram he must bring another basket of flour. And with each lamb he is to bring whatever amount of flour he chooses to give. With each basket of flour he must offer one gallon of olive oil.

8"The prince must enter the gateway through the entry room, and he must leave the same way. 9But when the people come in through the north gateway to worship the LORD during the religious festivals, they must leave by the south gateway. And those who entered through the south gateway must leave by the north gateway. They must never leave by the same gateway they came in, but must always use the opposite gateway. 10The prince will enter and leave with the people on these occasions.

11"So at the special feasts and sacred festivals, the grain offering will be a basket of choice flour with each young bull, another basket of flour with each ram, and as much flour as the worshiper chooses to give with each lamb. Give one gallon of olive oil with each basket of flour. 12When the prince offers a voluntary burnt offering or peace offering to the LORD, the east gateway to the inner courtyard will be opened for him, and he will offer his sacrifices as he does on Sabbath days. Then he will leave, and the gateway will be shut behind him.

13"Each morning you must sacrifice a one-year-old lamb with no defects as a burnt offering to the LORD. 14With the lamb, a grain offering must also be given to the LORD—about three quarts of flour with a third of a gallon of olive oil to moisten the choice flour. This will be a permanent law for you. 15The lamb, the grain offering, and the olive oil must be given as a daily sacrifice every morning without fail.

16"This is what the Sovereign LORD says: If the prince gives a gift of land to one of his sons as his inheritance, it will belong to him and his descendants forever. 17But if the prince gives a gift of land from his inheritance to one of his servants, the servant may keep it only until the Year of Jubilee, which comes every fiftieth year. At that time the land will return to the prince. But when the prince gives gifts to his sons, those gifts will be permanent. 18And the prince may never take anyone's property by force. If he gives property to his sons, it must be from his own land, for I do not want any of my people unjustly evicted from their property."

The Temple Kitchens

19In my vision, the man brought me through the entrance beside the gateway and led me to the sacred rooms assigned to the priests, which faced toward the north. He showed me a place at the extreme west end of these rooms. 20He explained, "This is where the priests will cook the meat from the guilt offerings and sin offerings and bake the flour from the grain offerings into bread. They will do it here to avoid carrying the sacrifices through the outer courtyard and endangering the people by transmitting holiness to them."

21Then he brought me back to the outer courtyard and led me to each of its four corners. In each corner I saw an enclosure. 22Each of these enclosures was 70 feet long and 52½ feet wide, surrounded by walls. 23Along the inside of these walls was a ledge of stone with fireplaces under the ledge all the way around. 24The man said to me, "These are the kitchens to be used by the Temple assistants to boil the sacrifices offered by the people."

CHAPTER 47

The River of Healing

In my vision, the man brought me back to the entrance of the Temple. There I saw a stream flowing east from beneath the door of the Temple and passing to the right of the altar on its south side. 2The man brought me outside the wall through the north gateway and led me around to the eastern entrance. There I could see the water flowing out through the south side of the east gateway.

3Measuring as he went, he took me along the stream for 1,750 feet and then led me across. The water was up to my ankles. 4He measured off another 1,750 feet and led me across again. This time the water was up to my knees. After another 1,750 feet, it was up to my waist. 5Then he measured another 1,750 feet, and the river was too deep to walk across. It was deep enough to swim in, but too deep to walk through.

6He asked me, "Have you been watching, son
of man?" Then he led me back along the riverbank. 7When I returned, I was surprised by the
sight of many trees growing on both sides of the
river. 8Then he said to me, "This river flows east
through the desert into the valley of the Dead
Sea. The waters of this stream will make the
salty waters of the Dead Sea fresh and pure.
9There will be swarms of living things wherever
the water of this river flows. Fish will abound in
the Dead Sea, for its waters will become fresh.
Life will flourish wherever this water flows.
10Fishermen will stand along the shores of
the Dead Sea. All the way from En-gedi to En-
eglaim, the shores will be covered with nets drying in the sun. Fish of every kind will fill the
Dead Sea, just as they fill the Mediterranean.
11But the marshes and swamps will not be purified; they will still be salty. 12Fruit trees of all
kinds will grow along both sides of the river.
The leaves of these trees will never turn brown
and fall, and there will always be fruit on their
branches. There will be a new crop every
month, for they are watered by the river flowing
from the Temple. The fruit will be for food and
the leaves for healing."

Boundaries for the Land

13This is what the Sovereign LORD says: "Divide
the land in this way for the twelve tribes of Israel:
The descendants of Joseph will be given two
shares of land. 14Otherwise each tribe will receive
an equal share. I took a solemn oath and swore
that I would give this land to your ancestors, and
it will now come to you as your possession.

15"These are the boundaries of the land:
The northern border will run from the
Mediterranean toward Hethlon, then on
through Lebo-hamath to Zedad; 16then it
will run to Berothah and Sibraim, which
are on the border between Damascus and
Hamath, and finally to Hazer-hatticon, on
the border of Hauran. 17So the northern
border will run from the Mediterranean to
Hazar-enan, on the border between Hamath
to the north and Damascus to the south.

18"The eastern border starts at a point
between Hauran and Damascus and runs
south along the Jordan River between Israel
and Gilead, past the Dead Sea and as far
south as Tamar. This will be the eastern
border.

19"The southern border will go west from
Tamar to the waters of Meribah at Kadesh
and then follow the course of the Brook of
Egypt to the Mediterranean. This will be the
southern border.

20"On the west side, the Mediterranean
itself will be your border from the southern
border to the point where the northern
border begins, opposite Lebo-hamath.

21"Divide the land within these boundaries
among the tribes of Israel. 22Distribute the land
as an allotment for yourselves and for the foreigners who have joined you and are raising their
families among you. They will be like native-
born Israelites to you and will receive an allotment among the tribes. 23These foreigners are to
be given land within the territory of the tribe
with whom they now live. I, the Sovereign LORD,
have spoken!

CHAPTER **48**

Division of the Land

"Here is the list of the tribes of Israel and the territory each is to receive. The territory of Dan is in
the extreme north. Its boundary line follows the
Hethlon road to Lebo-hamath and then runs on
to Hazar-enan on the border of Damascus, with
Hamath to the north. Dan's territory extends all
the way across the land of Israel from east to
west.

2"Asher's territory lies south of Dan's and also
extends from east to west. 3Naphtali's land lies
south of Asher's, also extending from east to
west. 4Then comes Manasseh south of Naphtali,
and its territory also extends from east to west.
5South of Manasseh is Ephraim, 6and then Reuben, 7and then Judah, all of whose boundaries
extend from east to west.

8"South of Judah is the land set aside for a special purpose. It will be 8⅓ miles wide and will extend as far east and west as the tribal territories,
with the Temple at the center.

9"The area set aside for the LORD's Temple will
be 8⅓ miles long and 6⅔ miles wide. 10For the
priests there will be a strip of land measuring 8⅓
miles long by 3⅓ miles wide, with the LORD's
Temple at the center. 11This area is set aside for
the ordained priests, the descendants of Zadok
who served me faithfully and did not go astray
with the people of Israel and the rest of the
Levites. 12It will be their special portion when
the land is distributed, the most sacred land of
all. Next to the priests' territory will lie the land
where the other Levites will live.

13"The land allotted to the Levites will be the
same size and shape as that belonging to the

priests—8⅓ miles long and 3⅓ miles wide. Together these portions of land will measure 8⅓
miles long by 6⅔ miles wide. 14 None of this special land may ever be sold or traded or used by
others, for it belongs to the LORD; it is set apart
as holy.
15 "An additional strip of land 8⅓ miles long by
1⅔ miles wide, south of the sacred Temple area,
will be allotted for public use—homes, pasturelands, and common lands, with a city at the center. 16 The city will measure 1½ miles on each
side—north, south, east, and west. 17 Open lands
will surround the city for 150 yards in every direction. 18 Outside the city there will be a farming area that stretches 3⅓ miles to the east and
3⅓ miles to the west along the border of the
sacred area. This farmland will produce food for
the people working in the city. 19 Those who
come from the various tribes to work in the city
may farm it. 20 This entire area—including the sacred lands and the city—is a square that measures 8⅓ miles on each side.
21 "The areas that remain, to the east and to the
west of the sacred lands and the city, will belong
to the prince. Each of these areas will be 8⅓
miles wide, extending in opposite directions to
the eastern and western borders of Israel, with
the sacred lands and the sanctuary of the Temple
in the center. 22 So the prince's land will include
everything between the territories allotted to Judah and Benjamin, except for the areas set aside
for the sacred lands and the city.
23 "These are the territories allotted to the rest
of the tribes. Benjamin's territory lies just south
of the prince's lands, and it extends across the
entire land of Israel from east to west. 24 South of
Benjamin's territory lies that of Simeon, also extending across the land from east to west. 25 Next
is the territory of Issachar with the same eastern
and western boundaries.
26 "Then comes the territory of Zebulun,
which also extends across the land from east to
west. 27 The territory of Gad is just south of Zebulun with the same borders to the east and west.
28 The southern border of Gad runs from Tamar
to the waters of Meribah at Kadesh and then follows the Brook of Egypt to the Mediterranean.
29 "These are the allotments that will be set
aside for each tribe's exclusive possession. I, the
Sovereign LORD, have spoken!

The Gates of the City

30 "These will be the exits to the city: On the
north wall, which is 1½ miles long, 31 there will
be three gates, each one named after a tribe of Israel. The first will be named for Reuben, the second for Judah, and the third for Levi. 32 On the
east wall, also 1½ miles long, the gates will be
named for Joseph, Benjamin, and Dan. 33 The
south wall, also 1½ miles long, will have gates
named for Simeon, Issachar, and Zebulun. 34 And
on the west wall, also 1½ miles long, the gates
will be named for Gad, Asher, and Naphtali.
35 "The distance around the entire city will be
6 miles. And from that day the name of the city
will be 'The LORD Is There.'"

DANiEL A Dedicated Life

Look for 1 hidden message in Daniel!

In the book of Daniel, you'll see a man who stayed true to God through some pretty tough times. Look for

- **A CAPTIVE'S TALE**
- **A LION'S TAIL**
- **TALL TALES BY SOME JEALOUS GUYS**
- **FRIENDS STANDING TALL**
- **A TON OF PRAYER**
- **SOME TERRIBLE DREAMS**
- **A TASTE OF THE FUTURE**

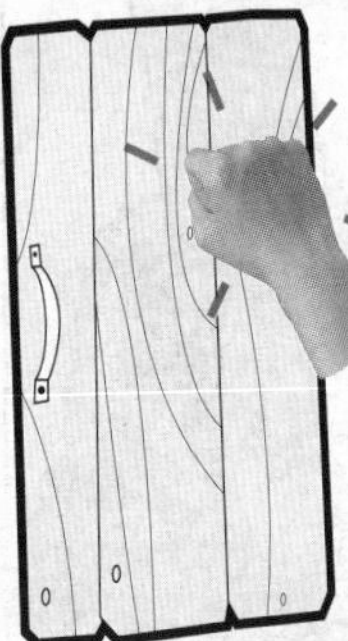

Anyone Home?

Knock, knock. Who's there? The commander of the king's guard, sent to kill you.

Wow! That was no joke for Daniel and his friends. You'd better read it for yourself. **It's in Daniel 2:1-23.**

The Name Game

After Daniel and his three buddies were taken as captives to Babylon, the king changed their names. He wanted to turn them into Babylonians. (It didn't work!) **Read Daniel 1:6-7 to see what their new names were.**

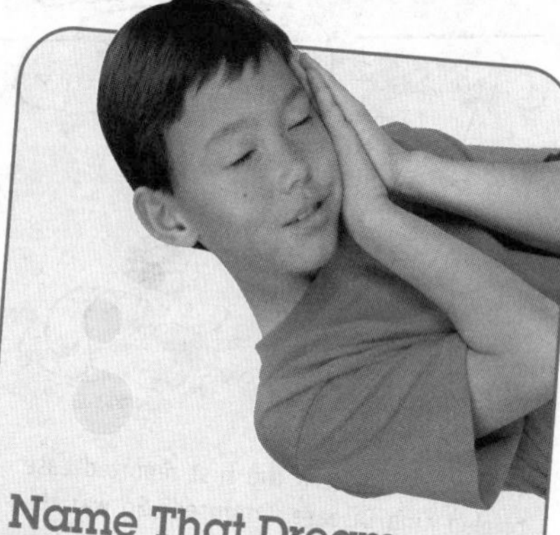

Name That Dream

It sure wasn't about counting sheep! King Nebuchadnezzar's dream was *way* weirder than that! What *was* the weird dream, anyway? **Daniel 2:24-45 tells about it!**

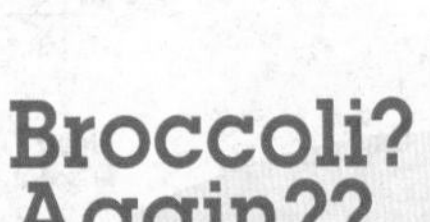

Broccoli? Again??

Vegetables and water—that's all they ate. Sound terrible? Not so! That's all Daniel and his friends *wanted* to eat. **Find out why in Daniel 1:8-16.**

Bow Now!

Bow! Bow now!
Really! I mean it.
You'd better bow...or else!
Or else what? **Find out in Daniel 3:1-6.**

Taking the Hot Seat

Daniel's three friends (Shadrach, Meshach, and Abednego) really got themselves into some hot water. Well, not water actually, but it *was* really hot! **See what happened and if they could take the heat. Read Daniel 3:8-30.**

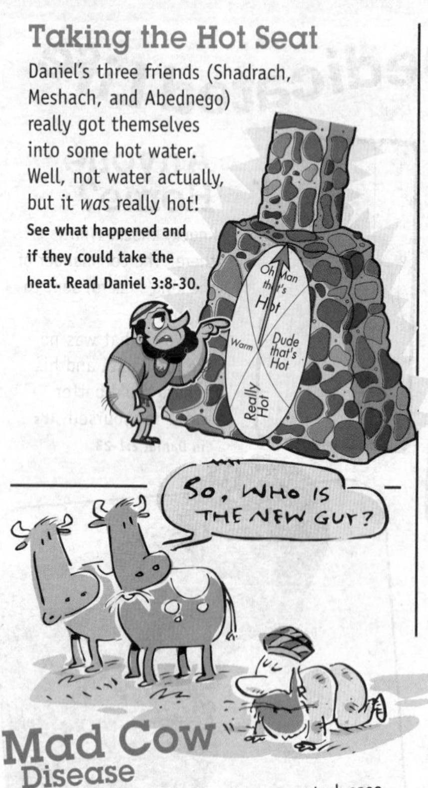

Oh Man that's Hot
Dude that's Hot
Really Hot
Warm
SO, WHO IS THE NEW GUY?

Writing on the Wall

Did you ever write on the wall when you were little? Did you get in trouble? Well, the writing on the wall in *this* story sure got someone in trouble, but it wasn't the writer. **Find out who it was in Daniel 5!**

Mad Cow Disease

This may have been the first reported case of Mad King Disease. Confused? So was the king! (For seven years!) **Find out why the king was put out to pasture in Daniel 4.**

No Lyin'!

Pray? Every day? "No way!" they say. Who were *they,* and why did they say that? Find out what the upROAR was all about in this amazing TAIL. **(It's a joke. You'll get it when you read Daniel 6!)**

Timeline

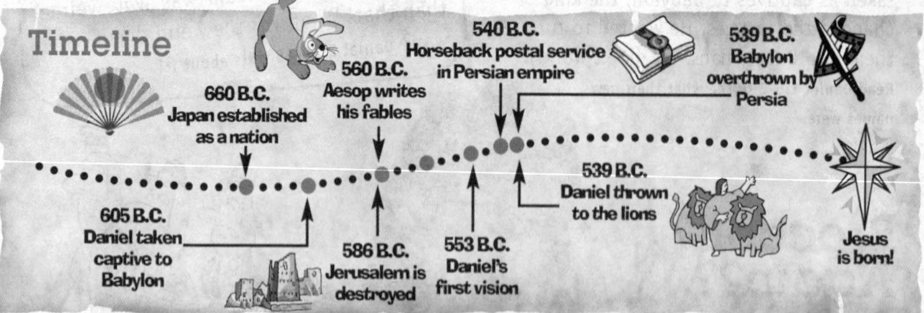

660 B.C. Japan established as a nation
605 B.C. Daniel taken captive to Babylon
586 B.C. Jerusalem is destroyed
560 B.C. Aesop writes his fables
553 B.C. Daniel's first vision
540 B.C. Horseback postal service in Persian empire
539 B.C. Babylon overthrown by Persia
539 B.C. Daniel thrown to the lions
Jesus is born!

The JESUS CONNECTION

When Gabriel told Daniel what his visions meant, he talked about the Anointed One, who was Jesus. He said that the Anointed One would be killed (that's just what happened to Jesus). But he told Daniel not to worry because God was in control and would make things right in the end. We know from other parts of the Bible that the way God will make things right is that Jesus will come again. When he does, the people who believe in him (both the living and those who have already died) will live with him forever! **You can too if you decide to follow Jesus!**

CHAPTER 1

Daniel in Nebuchadnezzar's Court

During the third year of King Jehoiakim's reign in
Judah, King Nebuchadnezzar of Babylon came to
Jerusalem and besieged it. 2The Lord gave him
victory over King Jehoiakim of Judah and permitted him to take some of the sacred objects from
the Temple of God. So Nebuchadnezzar took
them back to the land of Babylonia and placed
them in the treasure-house of his god.
3Then the king ordered Ashpenaz, his chief
of staff, to bring to the palace some of the young
men of Judah's royal family and other noble
families, who had been brought to Babylon
as captives. 4"Select only strong, healthy, and
good-looking young men," he said. "Make sure
they are well versed in every branch of learning,
are gifted with knowledge and good judgment,
and are suited to serve in the royal palace. Train
these young men in the language and literature
of Babylon." 5The king assigned them a daily
ration of food and wine from his own kitchens.
They were to be trained for three years, and then
they would enter the royal service.
6Daniel, Hananiah, Mishael, and Azariah were
four of the young men chosen, all from the tribe
of Judah. 7The chief of staff renamed them with
these Babylonian names:

Daniel was called Belteshazzar.
Hananiah was called Shadrach.
Mishael was called Meshach.
Azariah was called Abednego.

8But Daniel was determined not to defile himself by eating the food and wine given to them by
the king. He asked the chief of staff for permission not to eat these unacceptable foods. 9Now
God had given the chief of staff both respect and
affection for Daniel. 10But he responded, "I am
afraid of my lord the king, who has ordered that
you eat this food and wine. If you become pale
and thin compared to the other youths your age, I
am afraid the king will have me beheaded."
11Daniel spoke with the attendant who had
been appointed by the chief of staff to look after
Daniel, Hananiah, Mishael, and Azariah. 12"Please
test us for ten days on a diet of vegetables and
water," Daniel said. 13"At the end of the ten days,
see how we look compared to the other young
men who are eating the king's food. Then make
your decision in light of what you see." 14The attendant agreed to Daniel's suggestion and tested
them for ten days.
15At the end of the ten days, Daniel and his

Hate eating your spinach? Daniel didn't! He loved vegetables so much that that's about all he *would* eat! (OK, Daniel loved something else even more!)

Get all the juicy details in DANIEL 1:1-16.

FINISHED DIGESTING THAT STORY?

Good! Daniel loved God more than anything. Daniel could have tried to fit in with his surroundings. Instead, he obeyed God.

Are there times you're tempted to fit in rather than obey God?

TRY THIS! Get your favorite dip, raw vegetables, and a friend. Each time you dip a vegetable, say a time you might want to fit in, even if it would mean disobeying God. Talk about how to resist those temptations. Soon you'll be full of vitamins *and* good ideas!

three friends looked healthier and better nourished than the young men who had been eating
the food assigned by the king. 16 So after that,
the attendant fed them only vegetables instead
of the food and wine provided for the others.

17 God gave these four young men an unusual
aptitude for understanding every aspect of literature and wisdom. And God gave Daniel the special ability to interpret the meanings of visions
and dreams.

18 When the training period ordered by the
king was completed, the chief of staff brought all
the young men to King Nebuchadnezzar. 19 The
king talked with them, and no one impressed him
as much as Daniel, Hananiah, Mishael, and Azariah. So they entered the royal service. 20 Whenever
the king consulted them in any matter requiring
wisdom and balanced judgment, he found them
ten times more capable than any of the magicians
and enchanters in his entire kingdom.

21 Daniel remained in the royal service until the
first year of the reign of King Cyrus.

CHAPTER 2

Nebuchadnezzar's Dream

One night during the second year of his reign,
Nebuchadnezzar had such disturbing dreams
that he couldn't sleep. 2 He called in his magicians, enchanters, sorcerers, and astrologers, and
he demanded that they tell him what he had
dreamed. As they stood before the king, 3 he said,
"I have had a dream that deeply troubles me, and
I must know what it means."

4 Then the astrologers answered the king in
Aramaic, "Long live the king! Tell us the dream,
and we will tell you what it means."

5 But the king said to the astrologers, "I am serious about this. If you don't tell me what my
dream was and what it means, you will be torn
limb from limb, and your houses will be turned
into heaps of rubble! 6 But if you tell me what I
dreamed and what the dream means, I will give
you many wonderful gifts and honors. Just tell
me the dream and what it means!"

7 They said again, "Please, Your Majesty. Tell us
the dream, and we will tell you what it means."

8 The king replied, "I know what you are doing!
You're stalling for time because you know I am
serious when I say, 9 'If you don't tell me the
dream, you are doomed.' So you have conspired
to tell me lies, hoping I will change my mind. But
tell me the dream, and then I'll know that you can
tell me what it means."

10 The astrologers replied to the king, "No one
on earth can tell the king his dream! And no king,
however great and powerful, has ever asked such
a thing of any magician, enchanter, or astrologer!
11 The king's demand is impossible. No one except the gods can tell you your dream, and they
do not live here among people."

12 The king was furious when he heard this, and
he ordered that all the wise men of Babylon be executed. 13 And because of the king's decree, men
were sent to find and kill Daniel and his friends.

14 When Arioch, the commander of the king's
guard, came to kill them, Daniel handled the situation with wisdom and discretion. 15 He asked
Arioch, "Why has the king issued such a harsh
decree?" So Arioch told him all that had happened. 16 Daniel went at once to see the king and
requested more time to tell the king what the
dream meant.

17 Then Daniel went home and told his friends
Hananiah, Mishael, and Azariah what had happened. 18 He urged them to ask the God of heaven
to show them his mercy by telling them the secret, so they would not be executed along with
the other wise men of Babylon. 19 That night the
secret was revealed to Daniel in a vision. Then
Daniel praised the God of heaven. **20 He said,**

"Praise the name of God
forever and ever,
for he has all wisdom
and power.
21 He controls the course of world
events;
he removes kings and sets
up other kings.
He gives wisdom to the wise
and knowledge to the scholars.
22 He reveals deep and mysterious
things
and knows what lies hidden
in darkness,
though he is surrounded
by light.
23 I thank and praise you, God of my ancestors,
for you have given me wisdom and
strength.
You have told me what we asked of you
and revealed to us what the king
demanded."

Daniel Interprets the Dream

24 Then Daniel went in to see Arioch, whom the
king had ordered to execute the wise men of
Babylon. Daniel said to him, "Don't kill the wise
men. Take me to the king, and I will tell him the
meaning of his dream."

25 Arioch quickly took Daniel to the king and
said, "I have found one of the captives from Judah
who will tell the king the meaning of his dream!"
26 The king said to Daniel (also known as Belteshazzar), "Is this true? Can you tell me what my
dream was and what it means?"
27 Daniel replied, "There are no wise men, enchanters, magicians, or fortune-tellers who can
reveal the king's secret. 28 But there is a God in
heaven who reveals secrets, and he has shown
King Nebuchadnezzar what will happen in the
future. Now I will tell you your dream and the
visions you saw as you lay on your bed.
29 "While Your Majesty was sleeping, you
dreamed about coming events. He who reveals
secrets has shown you what is going to happen.
30 And it is not because I am wiser than anyone
else that I know the secret of your dream, but because God wants you to understand what was in
your heart.
31 "In your vision, Your Majesty, you saw standing before you a huge, shining statue of a man. It
was a frightening sight. 32 The head of the statue
was made of fine gold. Its chest and arms were
silver, its belly and thighs were bronze, 33 its legs
were iron, and its feet were a combination of iron
and baked clay. 34 As you watched, a rock was cut
from a mountain, but not by human hands. It
struck the feet of iron and clay, smashing them to
bits. 35 The whole statue was crushed into small
pieces of iron, clay, bronze, silver, and gold. Then
the wind blew them away without a trace, like
chaff on a threshing floor. But the rock that
knocked the statue down became a great mountain that covered the whole earth.
36 "That was the dream. Now we will tell the
king what it means. 37 Your Majesty, you are the
greatest of kings. The God of heaven has given you
sovereignty, power, strength, and honor. 38 He has
made you the ruler over all the inhabited world
and has put even the wild animals and birds
under your control. You are the head of gold.
39 "But after your kingdom comes to an end,
another kingdom, inferior to yours, will rise to
take your place. After that kingdom has fallen,
yet a third kingdom, represented by bronze, will
rise to rule the world. 40 Following that kingdom,
there will be a fourth one, as strong as iron. That
kingdom will smash and crush all previous
empires, just as iron smashes and crushes everything it strikes. 41 The feet and toes you saw were
a combination of iron and baked clay, showing
that this kingdom will be divided. Like iron
mixed with clay, it will have some of the strength
of iron. 42 But while some parts of it will be as
strong as iron, other parts will be as weak as clay.
43 This mixture of iron and clay also shows that
these kingdoms will try to strengthen themselves by forming alliances with each other
through intermarriage. But they will not hold
together, just as iron and clay do not mix.
44 "During the reigns of those kings, the God of
heaven will set up a kingdom that will never be
destroyed or conquered. It will crush all these
kingdoms into nothingness, and it will stand
forever. 45 That is the meaning of the rock cut
from the mountain, though not by human hands,
that crushed to pieces the statue of iron, bronze,
clay, silver, and gold. The great God was showing
the king what will happen in the future. The
dream is true, and its meaning is certain."

Nebuchadnezzar Rewards Daniel

46 Then King Nebuchadnezzar threw himself
down before Daniel and worshiped him, and he
commanded his people to offer sacrifices and
burn sweet incense before him. 47 The king said
to Daniel, "Truly, your God is the greatest of gods,
the Lord over kings, a revealer of mysteries, for
you have been able to reveal this secret."
48 Then the king appointed Daniel to a high
position and gave him many valuable gifts. He
made Daniel ruler over the whole province of
Babylon, as well as chief over all his wise men.
49 At Daniel's request, the king appointed Shadrach, Meshach, and Abednego to be in charge of
all the affairs of the province of Babylon, while
Daniel remained in the king's court.

CHAPTER 3

Nebuchadnezzar's Gold Statue

King Nebuchadnezzar made a gold statue ninety
feet tall and nine feet wide and set it up on the
plain of Dura in the province of Babylon. 2 Then
he sent messages to the high officers, officials,
governors, advisers, treasurers, judges, magis-
trates, and all the provincial officials to come to
the dedication of the statue he had set up. 3 So all
these officials came and stood before the statue
King Nebuchadnezzar had set up.
4 Then a herald shouted out, "People of all
races and nations and languages, listen to the
king's command! 5 When you hear the sound of
the horn, flute, zither, lyre, harp, pipes, and other
musical instruments, bow to the ground to worship King Nebuchadnezzar's gold statue. 6 Anyone who refuses to obey will immediately be
thrown into a blazing furnace."
7 So at the sound of the musical instruments,

all the people, whatever their race or nation or
language, bowed to the ground and worshiped
the gold statue that King Nebuchadnezzar had
set up.
8But some of the astrologers went to the king
and informed on the Jews. 9They said to King
Nebuchadnezzar, "Long live the king! 10You issued a decree requiring all the people to bow
down and worship the gold statue when they
hear the sound of the horn, flute, zither, lyre,
harp, pipes, and other musical instruments.
11That decree also states that those who refuse
to obey must be thrown into a blazing furnace.
12But there are some Jews—Shadrach, Meshach,
and Abednego—whom you have put in charge of
the province of Babylon. They pay no attention
to you, Your Majesty. They refuse to serve your
gods and do not worship the gold statue you
have set up."
13Then Nebuchadnezzar flew into a rage and
ordered that Shadrach, Meshach, and Abednego
be brought before him. When they were brought
in, 14Nebuchadnezzar said to them, "Is it true,
Shadrach, Meshach, and Abednego, that you refuse to serve my gods or to worship the gold
statue I have set up? 15I will give you one more
chance to bow down and worship the statue I
have made when you hear the sound of the musical instruments. But if you refuse, you will be
thrown immediately into the blazing furnace.
And then what god will be able to rescue you
from my power?"
16Shadrach, Meshach, and Abednego replied,
"O Nebuchadnezzar, we do not need to defend
ourselves before you. 17If we are thrown into the
blazing furnace, the God whom we serve is able
to save us. He will rescue us from your power,
Your Majesty. 18But even if he doesn't, we want to
make it clear to you, Your Majesty, that we will
never serve your gods or worship the gold statue
you have set up."

The Blazing Furnace

19Nebuchadnezzar was so furious with Shadrach, Meshach, and Abednego that his face became distorted with rage. He commanded that
the furnace be heated seven times hotter than
usual. 20Then he ordered some of the strongest
men of his army to bind Shadrach, Meshach, and
Abednego and throw them into the blazing furnace. 21So they tied them up and threw them into
the furnace, fully dressed in their pants, turbans,
robes, and other garments. 22And because the
king, in his anger, had demanded such a hot fire
in the furnace, the flames killed the soldiers as
they threw the three men in. 23So Shadrach, Meshach, and Abednego, securely tied, fell into the
roaring flames.
24But suddenly, Nebuchadnezzar jumped up
in amazement and exclaimed to his advisers,
"Didn't we tie up three men and throw them into
the furnace?"
"Yes, Your Majesty, we certainly did," they replied.
25"Look!" Nebuchadnezzar shouted. "I see
four men, unbound, walking around in the fire
unharmed! And the fourth looks like a god!"
26Then Nebuchadnezzar came as close as he
could to the door of the flaming furnace and
shouted: "Shadrach, Meshach, and Abednego,
servants of the Most High God, come out! Come
here!"
So Shadrach, Meshach, and Abednego stepped
out of the fire. 27Then the high officers, officials,
governors, and advisers crowded around them
and saw that the fire had not touched them. Not a
hair on their heads was singed, and their clothing
was not scorched. They didn't even smell of
smoke!
28Then Nebuchadnezzar said, "Praise to the
God of Shadrach, Meshach, and Abednego! He
sent his angel to rescue his servants who trusted
in him. They defied the king's command and
were willing to die rather than serve or worship
any god except their own God. 29Therefore, I
make this decree: If any people, whatever their
race or nation or language, speak a word against
the God of Shadrach, Meshach, and Abednego,
they will be torn limb from limb, and their
houses will be turned into heaps of rubble.
There is no other god who can rescue like this!"
30Then the king promoted Shadrach, Meshach, and Abednego to even higher positions in
the province of Babylon.

CHAPTER 4
Nebuchadnezzar's Dream about a Tree

King Nebuchadnezzar sent this message to the
people of every race and nation and language
throughout the world:

"Peace and prosperity to you!
2"I want you all to know about the
miraculous signs and wonders the Most
High God has performed for me.

3 How great are his signs,
how powerful his wonders!
His kingdom will last forever,
his rule through all generations.

4 “I, Nebuchadnezzar, was living in my
palace in comfort and prosperity. 5 But one
night I had a dream that frightened me; I saw
visions that terrified me as I lay in my bed.
6 So I issued an order calling in all the wise
men of Babylon, so they could tell me what
my dream meant. 7 When all the magicians,
enchanters, astrologers, and fortune-tellers
came in, I told them the dream, but they
could not tell me what it meant. 8 At last
Daniel came in before me, and I told him the
dream. (He was named Belteshazzar after my
god, and the spirit of the holy gods is in him.)

9 “I said to him, ‘Belteshazzar, chief of the
magicians, I know that the spirit of the holy
gods is in you and that no mystery is too
great for you to solve. Now tell me what my
dream means.

10 “‘While I was lying in my bed, this is
what I dreamed. I saw a large tree in the
middle of the earth. 11 The tree grew very tall
and strong, reaching high into the heavens
for all the world to see. 12 It had fresh green
leaves, and it was loaded with fruit for all to
eat. Wild animals lived in its shade, and birds
nested in its branches. All the world was fed
from this tree.

13 “‘Then as I lay there dreaming, I saw a
messenger, a holy one, coming down from
heaven. 14 The messenger shouted,

“Cut down the tree and lop off its
branches!
Shake off its leaves and scatter its fruit!
Chase the wild animals from its shade
and the birds from its branches.
15 But leave the stump and the roots
in the ground,
bound with a band of iron and bronze
and surrounded by tender grass.
Now let him be drenched with the dew
of heaven,
and let him live with the wild animals
among the plants of the field.
16 For seven periods of time,
let him have the mind of a wild animal
instead of the mind of a human.
17 For this has been decreed by the
messengers;
it is commanded by the holy ones,
so that everyone may know
that the Most High rules over the
kingdoms of the world.
He gives them to anyone he chooses—
even to the lowliest of people.”

18 “‘Belteshazzar, that was the dream
that I, King Nebuchadnezzar, had. Now tell
me what it means, for none of the wise men
of my kingdom can do so. But you can tell
me because the spirit of the holy gods is
in you.’

Daniel Explains the Dream

19 “Upon hearing this, Daniel (also known
as Belteshazzar) was overcome for a time,
frightened by the meaning of the dream.
Then the king said to him, ‘Belteshazzar,
don’t be alarmed by the dream and what
it means.’

“Belteshazzar replied, ‘I wish the events
foreshadowed in this dream would happen to
your enemies, my lord, and not to you! 20 The
tree you saw was growing very tall and strong,
reaching high into the heavens for all the
world to see. 21 It had fresh green leaves and
was loaded with fruit for all to eat. Wild
animals lived in its shade, and birds nested
in its branches. 22 That tree, Your Majesty,
is you. For you have grown strong and great;
your greatness reaches up to heaven, and
your rule to the ends of the earth.

23 “‘Then you saw a messenger, a holy
one, coming down from heaven and saying,
“Cut down the tree and destroy it. But leave
the stump and the roots in the ground,
bound with a band of iron and bronze and
surrounded by tender grass. Let him be
drenched with the dew of heaven. Let him
live with the animals of the field for seven
periods of time.”

24 “‘This is what the dream means, Your
Majesty, and what the Most High has
declared will happen to my lord the king.
25 You will be driven from human society, and
you will live in the fields with the wild
animals. You will eat grass like a cow, and you
will be drenched with the dew of heaven.
Seven periods of time will pass while you live
this way, until you learn that the Most High
rules over the kingdoms of the world and
gives them to anyone he chooses. 26 But the
stump and roots of the tree were left in the
ground. This means that you will receive your
kingdom back again when you have learned
that heaven rules.

27 “‘King Nebuchadnezzar, please accept
my advice. Stop sinning and do what is right.
Break from your wicked past and be merciful
to the poor. Perhaps then you will continue to
prosper.’

Daniel 4 . . . page 852

The Dream's Fulfillment

28"But all these things did happen to
King Nebuchadnezzar. 29Twelve months
later he was taking a walk on the flat roof
of the royal palace in Babylon. 30As he
looked out across the city, he said, 'Look
at this great city of Babylon! By my own
mighty power, I have built this beautiful
city as my royal residence to display my
majestic splendor.'

31"While these words were still in his
mouth, a voice called down from heaven,
'O King Nebuchadnezzar, this message is
for you! You are no longer ruler of this
kingdom. 32You will be driven from
human society. You will live in the fields
with the wild animals, and you will eat grass
like a cow. Seven periods of time will pass
while you live this way, until you learn that
the Most High rules over the kingdoms of
the world and gives them to anyone he
chooses.'

33"That same hour the judgment was
fulfilled, and Nebuchadnezzar was driven
from human society. He ate grass like a
cow, and he was drenched with the dew of
heaven. He lived this way until his hair was
as long as eagles' feathers and his nails were
like birds' claws.

Nebuchadnezzar Praises God

34"After this time had passed, I, Nebuchadnezzar, looked up to heaven. My sanity
returned, and I praised and worshiped the
Most High and honored the one who lives
forever.

His rule is everlasting,
  and his kingdom is eternal.
35 All the people of the earth
  are nothing compared to him.
He does as he pleases
  among the angels of heaven
  and among the people of
    the earth.
No one can stop him or say to him,
  'What do you mean by doing
    these things?'

36"When my sanity returned to me,
so did my honor and glory and kingdom.
My advisers and nobles sought me out,
and I was restored as head of my kingdom,
with even greater honor than before.

37"Now I, Nebuchadnezzar, praise and
glorify and honor the King of heaven. All

Magnetic Tree

Think *you* have strange dreams? **Read DANIEL 4 to find out about King Nebuchadnezzar's weird dream!** Daniel told the king that the great tree that was chopped down in the dream was the king because the king had forgotten that it was God who had made him great. Feel like doing a little tree chopping? Read on!

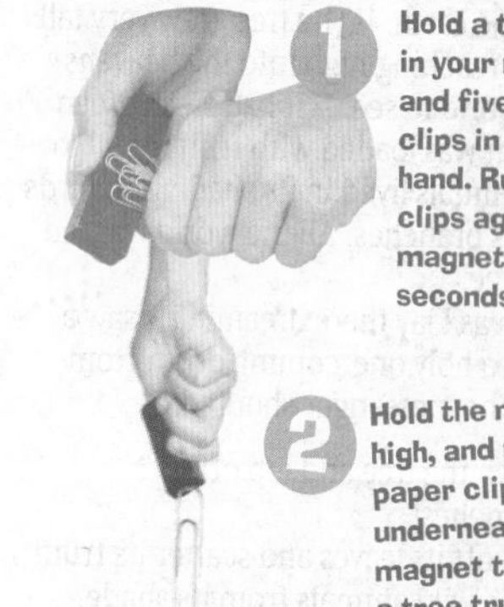

1 Hold a thick magnet in your right hand and five or six paper clips in your left hand. Rub the paper clips against the magnet for 30 seconds.

2 Hold the magnet up high, and place the paper clips in a line underneath the magnet to resemble a tree trunk.

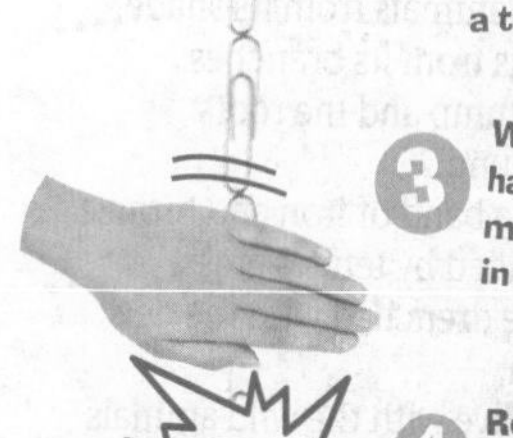

3 With your other hand, chop that magnetic tree in half!

4 Repeat step 2 without the magnet, and see how many paper clips will still stick together.

Think About It!

Just like paper clips without a magnet, Nebuchadnezzar was nothing without God. Nebuchadnezzar finally learned that his power and greatness came from God. That's a great lesson to learn!

his acts are just and true, and he is able
to humble the proud."

CHAPTER 5

The Writing on the Wall

Many years later King Belshazzar gave a great
feast for 1,000 of his nobles, and he drank wine
with them. 2 While Belshazzar was drinking the
wine, he gave orders to bring in the gold and silver cups that his predecessor, Nebuchadnezzar,
had taken from the Temple in Jerusalem. He
wanted to drink from them with his nobles, his
wives, and his concubines. 3 So they brought
these gold cups taken from the Temple, the
house of God in Jerusalem, and the king and his
nobles, his wives, and his concubines drank from
them. 4 While they drank from them they
praised their idols made of gold, silver, bronze,
iron, wood, and stone.

5 Suddenly, they saw the fingers of a human
hand writing on the plaster wall of the king's palace, near the lampstand. The king himself saw
the hand as it wrote, 6 and his face turned pale
with fright. His knees knocked together in fear
and his legs gave way beneath him.

7 The king shouted for the enchanters, astrologers, and fortune-tellers to be brought before
him. He said to these wise men of Babylon,
"Whoever can read this writing and tell me what
it means will be dressed in purple robes of royal
honor and will have a gold chain placed around
his neck. He will become the third highest ruler
in the kingdom!"

8 But when all the king's wise men had come
in, none of them could read the writing or tell
him what it meant. 9 So the king grew even more
alarmed, and his face turned pale. His nobles,
too, were shaken.

10 But when the queen mother heard what was
happening, she hurried to the banquet hall. She
said to Belshazzar, "Long live the king! Don't be
so pale and frightened. 11 There is a man in your
kingdom who has within him the spirit of the
holy gods. During Nebuchadnezzar's reign, this
man was found to have insight, understanding,
and wisdom like that of the gods. Your predecessor, the king—your predecessor King Nebuchadnezzar—made him chief over all the magicians,
enchanters, astrologers, and fortune-tellers of
Babylon. 12 This man Daniel, whom the king
named Belteshazzar, has exceptional ability and
is filled with divine knowledge and understanding. He can interpret dreams, explain riddles, and solve difficult problems. Call for Daniel,
and he will tell you what the writing means."

Daniel Explains the Writing

13 So Daniel was brought in before the king. The
king asked him, "Are you Daniel, one of the exiles
brought from Judah by my predecessor, King
Nebuchadnezzar? 14 I have heard that you have
the spirit of the gods within you and that you are
filled with insight, understanding, and wisdom.
15 My wise men and enchanters have tried to read
the words on the wall and tell me their meaning,
but they cannot do it. 16 I am told that you can
give interpretations and solve difficult problems. If you can read these words and tell me
their meaning, you will be clothed in purple
robes of royal honor, and you will have a gold
chain placed around your neck. You will become
the third highest ruler in the kingdom."

17 Daniel answered the king, "Keep your gifts or
give them to someone else, but I will tell you what
the writing means. 18 Your Majesty, the Most High
God gave sovereignty, majesty, glory, and honor to
your predecessor, Nebuchadnezzar. 19 He made
him so great that people of all races and nations
and languages trembled before him in fear. He
killed those he wanted to kill and spared those
he wanted to spare. He honored those he wanted
to honor and disgraced those he wanted to disgrace. 20 But when his heart and mind were
puffed up with arrogance, he was brought down
from his royal throne and stripped of his glory.
21 He was driven from human society. He was
given the mind of a wild animal, and he lived
among the wild donkeys. He ate grass like a cow,
and he was drenched with the dew of heaven,
until he learned that the Most High God rules
over the kingdoms of the world and appoints
anyone he desires to rule over them.

22 "You are his successor, O Belshazzar, and you
knew all this, yet you have not humbled yourself.
23 For you have proudly defied the Lord of heaven
and have had these cups from his Temple
brought before you. You and your nobles and
your wives and concubines have been drinking
wine from them while praising gods of silver,
gold, bronze, iron, wood, and stone—gods that
neither see nor hear nor know anything at all. But
you have not honored the God who gives you the
breath of life and controls your destiny! 24 So God
has sent this hand to write this message.

25 "This is the message that was written: MENE,
MENE, TEKEL, and PARSIN. 26 This is what these
words mean:

Mene means 'numbered'—God has
numbered the days of your reign
and has brought it to an end.

Daniel 6 . . . page 854

27 *Tekel* means 'weighed'—you have been
weighed on the balances and have not
measured up.
28 *Parsin* means 'divided'—your kingdom has
been divided and given to the Medes
and Persians."

29 Then at Belshazzar's command, Daniel was
dressed in purple robes, a gold chain was hung
around his neck, and he was proclaimed the
third highest ruler in the kingdom.
30 That very night Belshazzar, the Babylonian
king, was killed.
31 And Darius the Mede took over the kingdom
at the age of sixty-two.

CHAPTER **6**

Daniel in the Lions' Den

Darius the Mede decided to divide the kingdom
into 120 provinces, and he appointed a high officer to rule over each province. 2 The king also
chose Daniel and two others as administrators to
supervise the high officers and protect the king's
interests. 3 Daniel soon proved himself more capable than all the other administrators and high
officers. Because of Daniel's great ability, the king
made plans to place him over the entire empire.
4 Then the other administrators and high officers began searching for some fault in the way
Daniel was handling government affairs, but
they couldn't find anything to criticize or condemn. He was faithful, always responsible, and
completely trustworthy. 5 So they concluded,
"Our only chance of finding grounds for accusing Daniel will be in connection with the rules of
his religion."
6 So the administrators and high officers went
to the king and said, "Long live King Darius! 7 We
are all in agreement—we administrators, officials, high officers, advisers, and governors—
that the king should make a law that will be
strictly enforced. Give orders that for the next
thirty days any person who prays to anyone, divine or human—except to you, Your Majesty—
will be thrown into the den of lions. 8 And now,
Your Majesty, issue and sign this law so it cannot
be changed, an official law of the Medes and Persians that cannot be revoked." 9 So King Darius
signed the law.
10 But when Daniel learned that the law had
been signed, he went home and knelt down as
usual in his upstairs room, with its windows
open toward Jerusalem. He prayed three times a
day, just as he had always done, giving thanks to
his God. 11 Then the officials went together to
Daniel's house and found him praying and asking for God's help. 12 So they went straight to the
king and reminded him about his law. "Did you
not sign a law that for the next thirty days any
person who prays to anyone, divine or human—
except to you, Your Majesty—will be thrown into
the den of lions?"
"Yes," the king replied, "that decision stands; it
is an official law of the Medes and Persians that
cannot be revoked."
13 Then they told the king, "That man Daniel,
one of the captives from Judah, is ignoring you
and your law. He still prays to his God three times
a day."
14 Hearing this, the king was deeply troubled,
and he tried to think of a way to save Daniel. He
spent the rest of the day looking for a way to get
Daniel out of this predicament.
15 In the evening the men went together to the
king and said, "Your Majesty, you know that according to the law of the Medes and the Persians,
no law that the king signs can be changed."
16 So at last the king gave orders for Daniel to
be arrested and thrown into the den of lions. The
king said to him, "May your God, whom you serve
so faithfully, rescue you."
17 A stone was brought and placed over the
mouth of the den. The king sealed the stone with
his own royal seal and the seals of his nobles, so
that no one could rescue Daniel. 18 Then the king
returned to his palace and spent the night fasting. He refused his usual entertainment and
couldn't sleep at all that night.
19 Very early the next morning, the king got up
and hurried out to the lions' den. 20 When he got
there, he called out in anguish, "Daniel, servant of
the living God! Was your God, whom you serve so
faithfully, able to rescue you from the lions?"
21 Daniel answered, "Long live the king! 22 My
God sent his angel to shut the lions' mouths so
that they would not hurt me, for I have been
found innocent in his sight. And I have not
wronged you, Your Majesty."
23 The king was overjoyed and ordered that
Daniel be lifted from the den. Not a scratch was
found on him, for he had trusted in his God.
24 Then the king gave orders to arrest the men
who had maliciously accused Daniel. He had
them thrown into the lions' den, along with their
wives and children. The lions leaped on them
and tore them apart before they even hit the
floor of the den.
25 Then King Darius sent this message to the
people of every race and nation and language
throughout the world:

"Peace and prosperity to you!
26"I decree that everyone throughout my
kingdom should tremble with fear before the
God of Daniel.

For he is the living God,
and he will endure forever.
His kingdom will never be destroyed,
and his rule will never end.
27 He rescues and saves his people;
he performs miraculous signs
and wonders
in the heavens and on earth.
He has rescued Daniel
from the power of the lions."

28So Daniel prospered during the reign of
Darius and the reign of Cyrus the Persian.

CHAPTER 7

Daniel's Vision of Four Beasts

Earlier, during the first year of King Belshazzar's
reign in Babylon, Daniel had a dream and saw visions as he lay in his bed. He wrote down the
dream, and this is what he saw.
2In my vision that night, I, Daniel, saw a great
storm churning the surface of a great sea, with
strong winds blowing from every direction.
3Then four huge beasts came up out of the water,
each different from the others.
4The first beast was like a lion with eagles'
wings. As I watched, its wings were pulled off,
and it was left standing with its two hind feet on
the ground, like a human being. And it was given
a human mind.
5Then I saw a second beast, and it looked like a
bear. It was rearing up on one side, and it had
three ribs in its mouth between its teeth. And I
heard a voice saying to it, "Get up! Devour the
flesh of many people!"
6Then the third of these strange beasts appeared, and it looked like a leopard. It had four
bird's wings on its back, and it had four heads.
Great authority was given to this beast.
7Then in my vision that night, I saw a fourth
beast—terrifying, dreadful, and very strong. It
devoured and crushed its victims with huge iron
teeth and trampled their remains beneath its
feet. It was different from any of the other beasts,
and it had ten horns.
8As I was looking at the horns, suddenly another small horn appeared among them. Three
of the first horns were torn out by the roots to
make room for it. This little horn had eyes like
human eyes and a mouth that was boasting
arrogantly.

9 I watched as thrones were put in place
and the Ancient One sat down to judge.
His clothing was as white as snow,
his hair like purest wool.
He sat on a fiery throne
with wheels of blazing fire,
10 and a river of fire was pouring out,
flowing from his presence.
Millions of angels ministered to him;
many millions stood to attend him.
Then the court began its session,
and the books were opened.

11I continued to watch because I could hear
the little horn's boastful speech. I kept watching
until the fourth beast was killed and its body was
destroyed by fire. 12The other three beasts had
their authority taken from them, but they were
allowed to live a while longer.
13As my vision continued that night, I saw
someone like a son of man coming with the
clouds of heaven. He approached the Ancient
One and was led into his presence. 14He was
given authority, honor, and sovereignty over all
the nations of the world, so that people of every
race and nation and language would obey him.
His rule is eternal—it will never end. His kingdom will never be destroyed.

The Vision Is Explained

15I, Daniel, was troubled by all I had seen, and my
visions terrified me. 16So I approached one of
those standing beside the throne and asked him
what it all meant. He explained it to me like this:
17"These four huge beasts represent four kingdoms that will arise from the earth. 18But in the
end, the holy people of the Most High will be
given the kingdom, and they will rule forever
and ever."
19Then I wanted to know the true meaning of
the fourth beast, the one so different from the
others and so terrifying. It had devoured and
crushed its victims with iron teeth and bronze
claws, trampling their remains beneath its feet.
20I also asked about the ten horns on the fourth
beast's head and the little horn that came up
afterward and destroyed three of the other
horns. This horn had seemed greater than the
others, and it had human eyes and a mouth that
was boasting arrogantly. 21As I watched, this
horn was waging war against God's holy people
and was defeating them, 22until the Ancient
One—the Most High—came and judged in favor
of his holy people. Then the time arrived for the
holy people to take over the kingdom.

23 Then he said to me, "This fourth beast is the
fourth world power that will rule the earth. It will
be different from all the others. It will devour the
whole world, trampling and crushing everything
in its path. 24 Its ten horns are ten kings who will
rule that empire. Then another king will arise,
different from the other ten, who will subdue
three of them. 25 He will defy the Most High and
oppress the holy people of the Most High. He will
try to change their sacred festivals and laws, and
they will be placed under his control for a time,
times, and half a time.

26 "But then the court will pass judgment, and
all his power will be taken away and completely
destroyed. 27 Then the sovereignty, power, and
greatness of all the kingdoms under heaven will
be given to the holy people of the Most High. His
kingdom will last forever, and all rulers will serve
and obey him."

28 That was the end of the vision. I, Daniel, was
terrified by my thoughts and my face was pale
with fear, but I kept these things to myself.

CHAPTER 8

Daniel's Vision of a Ram and Goat

During the third year of King Belshazzar's reign,
I, Daniel, saw another vision, following the one
that had already appeared to me. 2 In this vision I
was at the fortress of Susa, in the province of
Elam, standing beside the Ulai River.

3 As I looked up, I saw a ram with two long
horns standing beside the river. One of the horns
was longer than the other, even though it had
grown later than the other one. 4 The ram butted
everything out of his way to the west, to the
north, and to the south, and no one could stand
against him or help his victims. He did as he
pleased and became very great.

5 While I was watching, suddenly a male goat
appeared from the west, crossing the land so
swiftly that he didn't even touch the ground.
This goat, which had one very large horn between its eyes, 6 headed toward the two-horned
ram that I had seen standing beside the river,
rushing at him in a rage. 7 The goat charged furi-
ously at the ram and struck him, breaking off
both his horns. Now the ram was helpless, and
the goat knocked him down and trampled him.
No one could rescue the ram from the goat's
power.

8 The goat became very powerful. But at the
height of his power, his large horn was broken
off. In the large horn's place grew four prominent horns pointing in the four directions of the
earth. 9 Then from one of the prominent horns
came a small horn whose power grew very great.
It extended toward the south and the east and toward the glorious land of Israel. 10 Its power
reached to the heavens, where it attacked the
heavenly army, throwing some of the heavenly
beings and some of the stars to the ground and
trampling them. 11 It even challenged the Commander of heaven's army by canceling the daily
sacrifices offered to him and by destroying his
Temple. 12 The army of heaven was restrained
from responding to this rebellion. So the daily
sacrifice was halted, and truth was overthrown.
The horn succeeded in everything it did.

13 Then I heard two holy ones talking to each
other. One of them asked, "How long will the
events of this vision last? How long will the rebellion that causes desecration stop the daily sacrifices? How long will the Temple and heaven's
army be trampled on?"

14 The other replied, "It will take 2,300 evenings and mornings; then the Temple will be
made right again."

Gabriel Explains the Vision

15 As I, Daniel, was trying to understand the
meaning of this vision, someone who looked like
a man stood in front of me. 16 And I heard a
human voice calling out from the Ulai River,
"Gabriel, tell this man the meaning of his vision."

17 As Gabriel approached the place where I
was standing, I became so terrified that I fell
with my face to the ground. "Son of man," he
said, "you must understand that the events you
have seen in your vision relate to the time of the
end."

18 While he was speaking, I fainted and lay
there with my face to the ground. But Gabriel
roused me with a touch and helped me to my
feet.

19 Then he said, "I am here to tell you what will
happen later in the time of wrath. What you have
seen pertains to the very end of time. 20 The two-
horned ram represents the kings of Media and
Persia. 21 The shaggy male goat represents the
king of Greece, and the large horn between his
eyes represents the first king of the Greek Empire. 22 The four prominent horns that replaced
the one large horn show that the Greek Empire
will break into four kingdoms, but none as great
as the first.

23 "At the end of their rule, when their sin is at
its height, a fierce king, a master of intrigue, will
rise to power. 24 He will become very strong, but
not by his own power. He will cause a shocking

amount of destruction and succeed in everything he does. He will destroy powerful leaders
and devastate the holy people. 25 He will be a
master of deception and will become arrogant;
he will destroy many without warning. He will
even take on the Prince of princes in battle, but
he will be broken, though not by human power.
26 "This vision about the 2,300 evenings and
mornings is true. But none of these things will
happen for a long time, so keep this vision a
secret."
27 Then I, Daniel, was overcome and lay sick
for several days. Afterward I got up and performed my duties for the king, but I was greatly
troubled by the vision and could not understand it.

CHAPTER 9

Daniel's Prayer for His People

It was the first year of the reign of Darius the
Mede, the son of Ahasuerus, who became king of
the Babylonians. 2 During the first year of his
reign, I, Daniel, learned from reading the word of
the LORD, as revealed to Jeremiah the prophet,
that Jerusalem must lie desolate for seventy
years. 3 So I turned to the Lord God and pleaded
with him in prayer and fasting. I also wore rough
burlap and sprinkled myself with ashes.
4 I prayed to the LORD my God and confessed:

"O Lord, you are a great and awesome God!
You always fulfill your covenant and keep
your promises of unfailing love to those
who love you and obey your commands.
5 But we have sinned and done wrong.
We have rebelled against you and scorned
your commands and regulations. 6 We
have refused to listen to your servants the
prophets, who spoke on your authority to
our kings and princes and ancestors and
to all the people of the land.
7 "Lord, you are in the right; but as you
see, our faces are covered with shame. This
is true of all of us, including the people of
Judah and Jerusalem and all Israel, scattered
near and far, wherever you have driven us
because of our disloyalty to you. 8 O LORD,
we and our kings, princes, and ancestors
are covered with shame because we have
sinned against you. 9 But the Lord our God
is merciful and forgiving, even though we
have rebelled against him. 10 We have not
obeyed the LORD our God, for we have not
followed the instructions he gave us through
his servants the prophets. 11 All Israel has

Bad to Good

WAIT! Don't throw away that dryer lint!

Think of dryer lint as shame. When you sin, your shame can build up like dryer lint. Daniel showed us that we can admit our sins to God in prayer.

Read DANIEL 9:1-19.

Daniel asked God for forgiveness. When God forgives us, our shame can turn to joy. Here's how to turn dryer lint into something good!

1. **Collect dryer lint, and place it in a bag. Collect two cups of lint.**

2. **Tear the lint into tiny bits and place it in a bowl. As you do, say a prayer like Daniel's in DANIEL 9: Ask for forgiveness for you and your family.**
3. **Add 1/3 cup of warm water, 6 tablespoons of white glue, and 1 tablespoon of clear dishwashing liquid.**
4. **Mix well. Add a little food coloring if you want. When it's all mixed together, you've made clay! You can mold it and let it dry for a couple of days and paint it.**

Thanks, God!
Sometimes it's unbelievable that God could forgive us for the things we've done. But he does! Just read 1 John 1:9.

Shape your clay into something that shows how you feel after God forgives you. Remember that we can always pray for forgiveness.

disobeyed your instruction and turned away,
refusing to listen to your voice.
"So now the solemn curses and judgments
written in the Law of Moses, the servant of
God, have been poured down on us because
of our sin. 12You have kept your word and
done to us and our rulers exactly as you
warned. Never has there been such a
disaster as happened in Jerusalem. 13Every
curse written against us in the Law of Moses
has come true. Yet we have refused to seek
mercy from the LORD our God by turning
from our sins and recognizing his truth.
14Therefore, the LORD has brought upon us
the disaster he prepared. The LORD our God
was right to do all of these things, for we did
not obey him.
15"O Lord our God, you brought lasting
honor to your name by rescuing your people
from Egypt in a great display of power. But
we have sinned and are full of wickedness.
16In view of all your faithful mercies, Lord,
please turn your furious anger away from
your city Jerusalem, your holy mountain. All
the neighboring nations mock Jerusalem and
your people because of our sins and the sins
of our ancestors.
17"O our God, hear your servant's prayer!
Listen as I plead. For your own sake, Lord,
smile again on your desolate sanctuary.
18"O my God, lean down and listen to me.
Open your eyes and see our despair. See how
your city—the city that bears your name—lies
in ruins. We make this plea, not because we
deserve help, but because of your mercy.
19"O Lord, hear. O Lord, forgive. O Lord,
listen and act! For your own sake, do not
delay, O my God, for your people and your
city bear your name."

Gabriel's Message about the Anointed One

20I went on praying and confessing my sin and
the sin of my people, pleading with the LORD my
God for Jerusalem, his holy mountain. 21As I was
praying, Gabriel, whom I had seen in the earlier
vision, came swiftly to me at the time of the evening sacrifice. 22He explained to me, "Daniel, I
have come here to give you insight and understanding. 23The moment you began praying, a
command was given. And now I am here to tell
you what it was, for you are very precious to God.
Listen carefully so that you can understand the
meaning of your vision.
24"A period of seventy sets of seven has been
decreed for your people and your holy city to finish their rebellion, to put an end to their sin, to
atone for their guilt, to bring in everlasting righteousness, to confirm the prophetic vision, and
to anoint the Most Holy Place. 25Now listen and
understand! Seven sets of seven plus sixty-two
sets of seven will pass from the time the command is given to rebuild Jerusalem until a ruler—
the Anointed One—comes. Jerusalem will be rebuilt with streets and strong defenses, despite
the perilous times.
26"After this period of sixty-two sets of seven,
the Anointed One will be killed, appearing to
have accomplished nothing, and a ruler will arise
whose armies will destroy the city and the Temple. The end will come with a flood, and war and
its miseries are decreed from that time to the
very end. 27The ruler will make a treaty with the
people for a period of one set of seven, but after
half this time, he will put an end to the sacrifices
and offerings. And as a climax to all his terrible
deeds, he will set up a sacrilegious object that
causes desecration, until the fate decreed for this
defiler is finally poured out on him."

CHAPTER 10

Daniel's Vision of a Messenger

In the third year of the reign of King Cyrus of Persia, Daniel (also known as Belteshazzar) had another vision. He understood that the vision
concerned events certain to happen in the future—times of war and great hardship.
2When this vision came to me, I, Daniel, had
been in mourning for three whole weeks. 3All
that time I had eaten no rich food. No meat or
wine crossed my lips, and I used no fragrant lotions until those three weeks had passed.
4On April 23, as I was standing on the bank of
the great Tigris River, 5I looked up and saw a man
dressed in linen clothing, with a belt of pure gold
around his waist. 6His body looked like a precious gem. His face flashed like lightning, and
his eyes flamed like torches. His arms and feet
shone like polished bronze, and his voice roared
like a vast multitude of people.
7Only I, Daniel, saw this vision. The men with
me saw nothing, but they were suddenly terrified and ran away to hide. 8So I was left there all
alone to see this amazing vision. My strength left
me, my face grew deathly pale, and I felt very
weak. 9Then I heard the man speak, and when I
heard the sound of his voice, I fainted and lay
there with my face to the ground.
10Just then a hand touched me and lifted me,
still trembling, to my hands and knees. 11And the

man said to me, "Daniel, you are very precious to
God, so listen carefully to what I have to say to
you. Stand up, for I have been sent to you." When
he said this to me, I stood up, still trembling.
12Then he said, "Don't be afraid, Daniel. Since
the first day you began to pray for understanding
and to humble yourself before your God, your
request has been heard in heaven. I have come
in answer to your prayer. 13But for twenty-one
days the spirit prince of the kingdom of Persia
blocked my way. Then Michael, one of the arch-
angels, came to help me, and I left him there with
the spirit prince of the kingdom of Persia. 14Now
I am here to explain what will happen to your
people in the future, for this vision concerns a
time yet to come."
15While he was speaking to me, I looked down
at the ground, unable to say a word. 16Then the
one who looked like a man touched my lips, and I
opened my mouth and began to speak. I said to
the one standing in front of me, "I am filled with
anguish because of the vision I have seen, my
lord, and I am very weak. 17How can someone
like me, your servant, talk to you, my lord? My
strength is gone, and I can hardly breathe."
18Then the one who looked like a man touched
me again, and I felt my strength returning.
19"Don't be afraid," he said, "for you are very precious to God. Peace! Be encouraged! Be strong!"
As he spoke these words to me, I suddenly felt
stronger and said to him, "Please speak to me, my
lord, for you have strengthened me."
20He replied, "Do you know why I have come?
Soon I must return to fight against the spirit
prince of the kingdom of Persia, and after that
the spirit prince of the kingdom of Greece will
come. 21Meanwhile, I will tell you what is written
in the Book of Truth. (No one helps me against
these spirit princes except Michael, your spirit
prince. 11:1I have been standing beside Michael
to support and strengthen him since the first
year of the reign of Darius the Mede.)

CHAPTER 11

Kings of the South and North

2"Now then, I will reveal the truth to you. Three
more Persian kings will reign, to be succeeded by
a fourth, far richer than the others. He will use
his wealth to stir up everyone to fight against the
kingdom of Greece.
3"Then a mighty king will rise to power who
will rule with great authority and accomplish
everything he sets out to do. 4But at the height of
his power, his kingdom will be broken apart and
divided into four parts. It will not be ruled by the
king's descendants, nor will the kingdom hold
the authority it once had. For his empire will be
uprooted and given to others.
5"The king of the south will increase in power,
but one of his own officials will become more
powerful than he and will rule his kingdom with
great strength.
6"Some years later an alliance will be formed
between the king of the north and the king of the
south. The daughter of the king of the south will
be given in marriage to the king of the north to
secure the alliance, but she will lose her influence over him, and so will her father. She will be
abandoned along with her supporters. 7But
when one of her relatives becomes king of the
south, he will raise an army and enter the fortress
of the king of the north and defeat him. 8When
he returns to Egypt, he will carry back their idols
with him, along with priceless articles of gold
and silver. For some years afterward he will leave
the king of the north alone.
9"Later the king of the north will invade the
realm of the king of the south but will soon return to his own land. 10However, the sons of the
king of the north will assemble a mighty army
that will advance like a flood and carry the battle
as far as the enemy's fortress.
11"Then, in a rage, the king of the south will
rally against the vast forces assembled by the
king of the north and will defeat them. 12After
the enemy army is swept away, the king of the
south will be filled with pride and will execute
many thousands of his enemies. But his success
will be short lived.
13"A few years later the king of the north will
return with a fully equipped army far greater
than before. 14At that time there will be a general
uprising against the king of the south. Violent
men among your own people will join them in
fulfillment of this vision, but they will not succeed. 15Then the king of the north will come and
lay siege to a fortified city and capture it. The
best troops of the south will not be able to stand
in the face of the onslaught.
16"The king of the north will march onward
unopposed; none will be able to stop him. He will
pause in the glorious land of Israel, intent on destroying it. 17He will make plans to come with the
might of his entire kingdom and will form an
alliance with the king of the south. He will give
him a daughter in marriage in order to overthrow the kingdom from within, but his plan
will fail.
18"After this, he will turn his attention to
the coastland and conquer many cities. But a

Slavery was an accepted part of life in Bible times. Want to learn more about slavery and how God helped the slaves? **Read GENESIS 37-47; EXODUS 1-14; and DANIEL 1-2.**

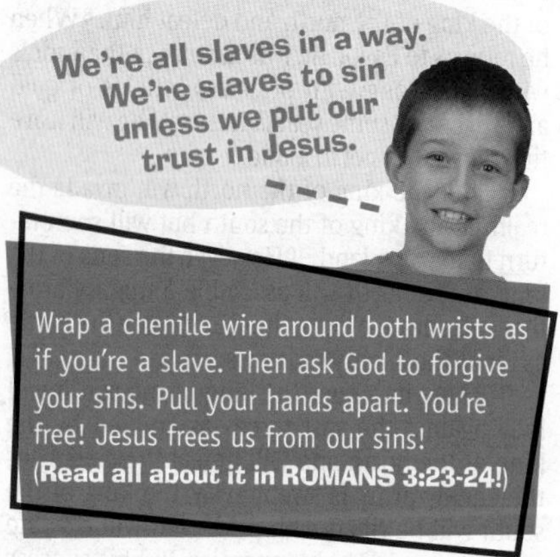

We're all slaves in a way. We're slaves to sin unless we put our trust in Jesus.

Wrap a chenille wire around both wrists as if you're a slave. Then ask God to forgive your sins. Pull your hands apart. You're free! Jesus frees us from our sins! **(Read all about it in ROMANS 3:23-24!)**

commander from another land will put an end to
his insolence and cause him to retreat in shame.
19He will take refuge in his own fortresses but
will stumble and fall and be seen no more.
20"His successor will send out a tax collector
to maintain the royal splendor. But after a very
brief reign, he will die, though not from anger or
in battle.
21"The next to come to power will be a despicable man who is not in line for royal succession.
He will slip in when least expected and take over
the kingdom by flattery and intrigue. 22Before
him great armies will be swept away, including a
covenant prince. 23With deceitful promises, he
will make various alliances. He will become
strong despite having only a handful of followers. 24Without warning he will enter the richest
areas of the land. Then he will distribute among
his followers the plunder and wealth of the
rich—something his predecessors had never
done. He will plot the overthrow of strongholds,
but this will last for only a short while.

25"Then he will stir up his courage and raise a
great army against the king of the south. The
king of the south will go to battle with a mighty
army, but to no avail, for there will be plots
against him. 26His own household will cause his
downfall. His army will be swept away, and many
will be killed. 27Seeking nothing but each other's
harm, these kings will plot against each other at
the conference table, attempting to deceive each
other. But it will make no difference, for the end
will come at the appointed time.
28"The king of the north will then return
home with great riches. On the way he will set
himself against the people of the holy covenant,
doing much damage before continuing his
journey.
29"Then at the appointed time he will once
again invade the south, but this time the result
will be different. 30For warships from western
coastlands will scare him off, and he will withdraw and return home. But he will vent his anger
against the people of the holy covenant and reward those who forsake the covenant.
31"His army will take over the Temple fortress,
pollute the sanctuary, put a stop to the daily sacrifices, and set up the sacrilegious object that
causes desecration. 32He will flatter and win
over those who have violated the covenant. But
the people who know their God will be strong
and will resist him.
33"Wise leaders will give instruction to many,
but these teachers will die by fire and sword, or
they will be jailed and robbed. 34During these
persecutions, little help will arrive, and many
who join them will not be sincere. 35And some of
the wise will fall victim to persecution. In this
way, they will be refined and cleansed and made
pure until the time of the end, for the appointed
time is still to come.
36"The king will do as he pleases, exalting
himself and claiming to be greater than every
god, even blaspheming the God of gods. He will
succeed, but only until the time of wrath is completed. For what has been determined will surely
take place. 37He will have no respect for the gods
of his ancestors, or for the god loved by women,
or for any other god, for he will boast that he is
greater than them all. 38Instead of these, he will
worship the god of fortresses—a god his ancestors never knew—and lavish on him gold, silver,
precious stones, and expensive gifts. 39Claiming
this foreign god's help, he will attack the strongest fortresses. He will honor those who submit
to him, appointing them to positions of authority

and dividing the land among them as their
reward.
40"Then at the time of the end, the king of the
south will attack the king of the north. The king
of the north will storm out with chariots, charioteers, and a vast navy. He will invade various
lands and sweep through them like a flood. 41He
will enter the glorious land of Israel, and many
nations will fall, but Moab, Edom, and the best
part of Ammon will escape. 42He will conquer
many countries, and even Egypt will not escape.
43He will gain control over the gold, silver, and
treasures of Egypt, and the Libyans and Ethiopians will be his servants.
44"But then news from the east and the north
will alarm him, and he will set out in great anger
to destroy and obliterate many. 45He will stop between the glorious holy mountain and the sea
and will pitch his royal tents. But while he is
there, his time will suddenly run out, and no one
will help him.

CHAPTER 12

The Time of the End

"At that time Michael, the archangel who stands
guard over your nation, will arise. Then there
will be a time of anguish greater than any since
nations first came into existence. But at that
time every one of your people whose name is
written in the book will be rescued. 2Many of
those whose bodies lie dead and buried will rise
up, some to everlasting life and some to shame
and everlasting disgrace. 3Those who are wise
will shine as bright as the sky, and those who
lead many to righteousness will shine like the
stars forever. 4But you, Daniel, keep this prophecy a secret; seal up the book until the time of
the end, when many will rush here and there,
and knowledge will increase."
5Then I, Daniel, looked and saw two others
standing on opposite banks of the river. 6One of
them asked the man dressed in linen, who was
now standing above the river, "How long will it
be until these shocking events are over?"
7The man dressed in linen, who was standing
above the river, raised both his hands toward
heaven and took a solemn oath by the One who
lives forever, saying, "It will go on for a time,
times, and half a time. When the shattering of
the holy people has finally come to an end, all
these things will have happened."
8I heard what he said, but I did not understand what he meant. So I asked, "How will all
this finally end, my lord?"
9But he said, "Go now, Daniel, for what I have
said is kept secret and sealed until the time of the
end. 10Many will be purified, cleansed, and refined by these trials. But the wicked will continue in their wickedness, and none of them will
understand. Only those who are wise will know
what it means.
11"From the time the daily sacrifice is stopped
and the sacrilegious object that causes desecration is set up to be worshiped, there will be 1,290
days. 12And blessed are those who wait and remain until the end of the 1,335 days!
13"As for you, go your way until the end. You
will rest, and then at the end of the days, you will
rise again to receive the inheritance set aside
for you."

HOSEA A Living Example

Look for 1 hidden message in Hosea!

In Hosea, we see a man who obeyed God without question. He let God turn his whole life into an example for the people of Israel and Judah. Look for

- **AN UNTRUE WIFE**
- **A CALL TO REPENT**
- **A WARNING OF WOE**
- **A LETTER OF LOVE**

PROPHETS NEEDED
LINE STARTS HERE

It's a Tough Job, but Somebody...

Yup, that's right. Somebody had to do it. Be a prophet, that is. Think the prophets had it easy? Think again! **Just read Hosea 9:7-8 to see what the prophets faced.**

Wedding Bell Blues

God told his prophet Hosea to marry a woman who would be untrue to him. (Hosea obeyed, by the way.) Then God compared an untrue wife to the people of Israel who had turned away from God.

But God wanted to forgive the people. **Read Hosea 6:1-3 to see what they needed to do to be forgiven.**

Crime and Punishment

God told Hosea to warn the people about what would happen to them if they didn't stop worshiping false gods and turn back to the one true God. **Read Hosea 5:10-12 to see what God said would happen.**

Thanks, Dad

Think God's a big meanie? His people had turned to false gods. God was angry, sure; but he was something else, too. **Find out what God was feeling by reading Hosea 11. (Read it whenever you sin and wonder if God will forgive you. He will!)**

Timeline

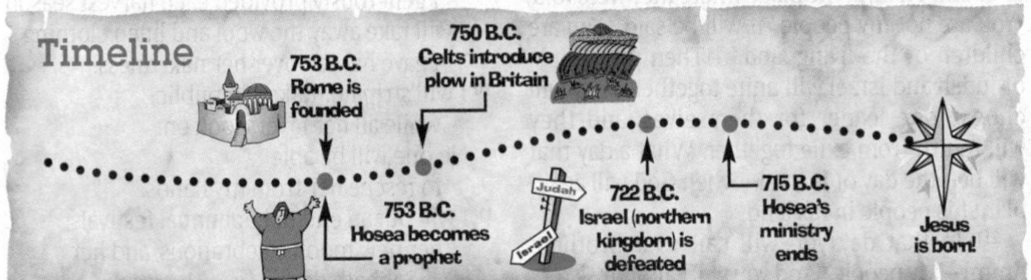
753 B.C. Rome is founded
750 B.C. Celts introduce plow in Britain
753 B.C. Hosea becomes a prophet
Judah
Israel
722 B.C. Israel (northern kingdom) is defeated
715 B.C. Hosea's ministry ends
Jesus is born!

The JESUS CONNECTION

In the book of Hosea, we see how much God wanted to forgive his people. God even said his heart was torn within him, and his compassion overflowed. That's what God is like—a loving father who wants nothing more than to forgive his children when they're sorry for their sins. That's why he sent Jesus—because he loves us and wants to forgive us. All we have to do to get that forgiveness is believe in Jesus. **It's simple. It's love. It's God.**

It's simple. It's God.

Hosea 1 . . . page 864

CHAPTER 1

The LORD gave this message to Hosea son of
Beeri during the years when Uzziah, Jotham,
Ahaz, and Hezekiah were kings of Judah, and
Jeroboam son of Jehoash was king of Israel.

Hosea's Wife and Children

2When the LORD first began speaking to Israel
through Hosea, he said to him, "Go and marry a
prostitute, so that some of her children will be
conceived in prostitution. This will illustrate how
Israel has acted like a prostitute by turning
against the LORD and worshiping other gods."

3So Hosea married Gomer, the daughter of
Diblaim, and she became pregnant and gave
Hosea a son. 4And the LORD said, "Name the
child Jezreel, for I am about to punish King
Jehu's dynasty to avenge the murders he com-
mitted at Jezreel. In fact, I will bring an end to
Israel's independence. 5I will break its military
power in the Jezreel Valley."

6Soon Gomer became pregnant again and
gave birth to a daughter. And the LORD said to
Hosea, "Name your daughter Lo-ruhamah—'Not
loved'—for I will no longer show love to the people of Israel or forgive them. 7But I will show love
to the people of Judah. I will free them from their
enemies—not with weapons and armies or horses
and charioteers, but by my power as the LORD
their God."

8After Gomer had weaned Lo-ruhamah, she
again became pregnant and gave birth to a second
son. 9And the LORD said, "Name him Lo-ammi—
'Not my people'—for Israel is not my people, and I
am not their God.

10"Yet the time will come when Israel's people
will be like the sands of the seashore—too many
to count! Then, at the place where they were told,
'You are not my people,' it will be said, 'You are
children of the living God.' 11Then the people
of Judah and Israel will unite together. They will
choose one leader for themselves, and they
will return from exile together. What a day that
will be—the day of Jezreel—when God will again
plant his people in his land.

2:1"In that day you will call your brothers
Ammi—'My people.' And you will call your sisters
Ruhamah—'The ones I love.'

CHAPTER 2

Charges against an Unfaithful Wife

2 "But now bring charges against Israel—
your mother—
for she is no longer my wife,
and I am no longer her husband.
Tell her to remove the prostitute's makeup
from her face
and the clothing that exposes her breasts.
3 Otherwise, I will strip her as naked
as she was on the day she was born.
I will leave her to die of thirst,
as in a dry and barren wilderness.
4 And I will not love her children,
for they were conceived in prostitution.
5 Their mother is a shameless prostitute
and became pregnant in a shameful way.
She said, 'I'll run after other lovers
and sell myself to them for food
and water,
for clothing of wool and linen,
and for olive oil and drinks.'

6 "For this reason I will fence her in with
thornbushes.
I will block her path with a wall
to make her lose her way.
7 When she runs after her lovers,
she won't be able to catch them.
She will search for them
but not find them.
Then she will think,
'I might as well return to my husband,
for I was better off with him than
I am now.'
8 She doesn't realize it was I who gave her
everything she has—
the grain, the new wine, the olive oil;
I even gave her silver and gold.
But she gave all my gifts to Baal.

9 "But now I will take back the ripened grain
and new wine
I generously provided each harvest season.
I will take away the wool and linen clothing
I gave her to cover her nakedness.
10 I will strip her naked in public,
while all her lovers look on.
No one will be able
to rescue her from my hands.
11 I will put an end to her annual festivals,
her new moon celebrations, and her
Sabbath days—
all her appointed festivals.
12 I will destroy her grapevines and fig trees,
things she claims her lovers gave her.
I will let them grow into tangled thickets,
where only wild animals will eat the fruit.
13 I will punish her for all those times
when she burned incense to her images
of Baal,

when she put on her earrings and jewels
and went out to look for her lovers
but forgot all about me,"
says the LORD.

The LORD's Love for Unfaithful Israel

14 "But then I will win her back once again.
I will lead her into the desert
and speak tenderly to her there.
15 I will return her vineyards to her
and transform the Valley of Trouble
into a gateway of hope.
She will give herself to me there,
as she did long ago when she was young,
when I freed her from her captivity
in Egypt.
16 When that day comes," says the LORD,
"you will call me 'my husband'
instead of 'my master.'
17 O Israel, I will wipe the many names of Baal
from your lips,
and you will never mention them again.
18 On that day I will make a covenant
with all the wild animals and the birds
of the sky
and the animals that scurry along the ground
so they will not harm you.
I will remove all weapons of war from
the land,
all swords and bows,
so you can live unafraid
in peace and safety.
19 I will make you my wife forever,
showing you righteousness and justice,
unfailing love and compassion.
20 I will be faithful to you and make you mine,
and you will finally know me as the LORD.

21 "In that day, I will answer,"
says the LORD.
"I will answer the sky as it pleads for clouds.
And the sky will answer the earth with rain.
22 Then the earth will answer the thirsty cries
of the grain, the grapevines, and the
olive trees.
And they in turn will answer,
'Jezreel'—'God plants!'
23 At that time I will plant a crop
of Israelites
and raise them for myself.
I will show love
to those I called 'Not loved.'
And to those I called 'Not my
people,'
I will say, 'Now you are
my people.'
And they will reply, 'You are
our God!'"

CHAPTER 3
Hosea's Wife Is Redeemed

Then the LORD said to me, "Go and love your wife
again, even though she commits adultery with
another lover. This will illustrate that the LORD
still loves Israel, even though the people have
turned to other gods and love to worship them."
2 So I bought her back for fifteen pieces of silver and five bushels of barley and a measure of
wine. 3 Then I said to her, "You must live in my
house for many days and stop your prostitution.
During this time, you will not have sexual relations with anyone, not even with me."
4 This shows that Israel will go a long time
without a king or prince, and without sacrifices,
sacred pillars, priests, or even idols! 5 But afterward the people will return and devote themselves to the LORD their God and to David's
descendant, their king. In the last days, they will
tremble in awe of the LORD and of his goodness.

CHAPTER 4
The LORD's Case against Israel

1 Hear the word of the LORD, O people
of Israel!
The LORD has brought charges against
you, saying:
"There is no faithfulness, no kindness,
no knowledge of God in your land.
2 You make vows and break them;
you kill and steal and commit adultery.
There is violence everywhere—
one murder after another.
3 That is why your land is in mourning,
and everyone is wasting away.
Even the wild animals, the birds of the sky,
and the fish of the sea are disappearing.

4 "Don't point your finger at someone else
and try to pass the blame!
My complaint, you priests,
is with you.
5 So you will stumble in broad daylight,
and your false prophets will fall with you
in the night.
And I will destroy Israel, your mother.
6 My people are being destroyed
because they don't know me.
Since you priests refuse to know me,
I refuse to recognize you as my priests.

Since you have forgotten the laws
of your God,
I will forget to bless your children.
7 The more priests there are,
the more they sin against me.
They have exchanged the glory of God
for the shame of idols.

8 "When the people bring their sin offerings,
the priests get fed.
So the priests are glad when the people sin!
9 'And what the priests do, the people also do.'
So now I will punish both priests and
people
for their wicked deeds.
10 They will eat and still be hungry.
They will play the prostitute and gain
nothing from it,
for they have deserted the LORD
11 to worship other gods.

"Wine has robbed my people
of their understanding.
12 They ask a piece of wood for advice!
They think a stick can tell them the future!
Longing after idols
has made them foolish.
They have played the prostitute,
serving other gods and deserting their God.
13 They offer sacrifices to idols on the
mountaintops.
They go up into the hills to burn incense
in the pleasant shade of oaks, poplars,
and terebinth trees.

"That is why your daughters turn
to prostitution,
and your daughters-in-law commit
adultery.
14 But why should I punish them
for their prostitution and adultery?
For your men are doing the same thing,
sinning with whores and shrine
prostitutes.
O foolish people! You refuse to understand,
so you will be destroyed.

15 "Though you, Israel, are a prostitute,
may Judah not be guilty of such things.
Do not join the false worship at Gilgal
or Beth-aven,
and do not take oaths there
in the LORD's name.
16 Israel is stubborn,
like a stubborn heifer.
So should the LORD feed her
like a lamb in a lush pasture?
17 Leave Israel alone,
because she is married to idolatry.
18 When the rulers of Israel finish their
drinking,
off they go to find some prostitutes.
They love shame more than honor.
19 So a mighty wind will sweep them away.
Their sacrifices to idols will bring
them shame.

CHAPTER 5
The Failure of Israel's Leaders

1 "Hear this, you priests.
Pay attention, you leaders of Israel.
Listen, you members of the royal family.
Judgment has been handed down
against you.
For you have led the people into a snare
by worshiping the idols at Mizpah
and Tabor.
2 You have dug a deep pit to trap them
at Acacia Grove.
But I will settle with you for what you
have done.
3 I know what you are like, O Ephraim.
You cannot hide yourself from me,
O Israel.
You have left me as a prostitute leaves
her husband;
you are utterly defiled.
4 Your deeds won't let you return to your God.
You are a prostitute through and through,
and you do not know the LORD.

5 "The arrogance of Israel testifies against her;
Israel and Ephraim will stumble under
their load of guilt.
Judah, too, will fall with them.
6 When they come with their flocks and herds
to offer sacrifices to the LORD,
they will not find him,
because he has withdrawn from them.
7 They have betrayed the honor of the LORD,
bearing children that are not his.
Now their false religion will devour them
along with their wealth.

8 "Sound the alarm in Gibeah!
Blow the trumpet in Ramah!
Raise the battle cry in Beth-aven!
Lead on into battle, O warriors
of Benjamin!
9 One thing is certain, Israel:
On your day of punishment,
you will become a heap of rubble.

10 "The leaders of Judah have become
like thieves.
So I will pour my anger on them like
a waterfall.
11 The people of Israel will be crushed
and broken by my judgment
because they are determined
to worship idols.
12 I will destroy Israel as a moth
consumes wool.
I will make Judah as weak as rotten wood.

13 "When Israel and Judah saw how sick
they were,
Israel turned to Assyria—
to the great king there—
but he could neither help nor cure them.
14 I will be like a lion to Israel,
like a strong young lion to Judah.
I will tear them to pieces!
I will carry them off,
and no one will be left to rescue them.
15 Then I will return to my place
until they admit their guilt and turn to me.
For as soon as trouble comes,
they will earnestly search for me."

CHAPTER 6
A Call to Repentance

1 "Come, let us return to the LORD.
He has torn us to pieces;
now he will heal us.
He has injured us;
now he will bandage our wounds.
2 In just a short time he will restore us,
so that we may live in his presence.
3 Oh, that we might know the LORD!
Let us press on to know him.
He will respond to us as surely as the
arrival of dawn
or the coming of rains in early spring."

4 "O Israel and Judah,
what should I do with you?" asks the LORD.
"For your love vanishes like the
morning mist
and disappears like dew in the sunlight.
5 I sent my prophets to cut you to pieces—
to slaughter you with my words,
with judgments as inescapable as light.
6 I want you to show love,
not offer sacrifices.
I want you to know me
more than I want burnt offerings.
7 But like Adam, you broke my covenant
and betrayed my trust.
8 "Gilead is a city of sinners,
tracked with footprints of blood.
9 Priests form bands of robbers,
waiting in ambush for their victims.
They murder travelers along the road
to Shechem
and practice every kind of sin.
10 Yes, I have seen something horrible
in Ephraim and Israel:
My people are defiled by prostituting
themselves with other gods!

11 "O Judah, a harvest of punishment is also
waiting for you,
though I wanted to restore the fortunes
of my people.

CHAPTER 7
Israel's Love for Wickedness

1 "I want to heal Israel, but its sins are too
great.
Samaria is filled with liars.
Thieves are on the inside
and bandits on the outside!
2 Its people don't realize
that I am watching them.
Their sinful deeds are all around them,
and I see them all.

3 "The people entertain the king with their
wickedness,
and the princes laugh at their lies.
4 They are all adulterers,
always aflame with lust.
They are like an oven that is kept hot
while the baker is kneading the dough.
5 On royal holidays, the princes get drunk
with wine,
carousing with those who mock them.
6 Their hearts are like an oven
blazing with intrigue.
Their plot smolders through the night,
and in the morning it breaks out like
a raging fire.
7 Burning like an oven,
they consume their leaders.
They kill their kings one after another,
and no one cries to me for help.

8 "The people of Israel mingle with godless
foreigners,
making themselves as worthless as
a half-baked cake!
9 Worshiping foreign gods has sapped their
strength,
but they don't even know it.

Their hair is gray,
but they don't realize they're old
and weak.
10 Their arrogance testifies against them,
yet they don't return to the LORD their God
or even try to find him.

11 "The people of Israel have become like silly,
witless doves,
first calling to Egypt, then flying to Assyria
for help.
12 But as they fly about,
I will throw my net over them
and bring them down like a bird from
the sky.
I will punish them for all the evil they do.

13 "What sorrow awaits those who have
deserted me!
Let them die, for they have rebelled
against me.
I wanted to redeem them,
but they have told lies about me.
14 They do not cry out to me with sincere
hearts.
Instead, they sit on their couches and wail.
They cut themselves, begging foreign gods
for grain and new wine,
and they turn away from me.
15 I trained them and made them strong,
yet now they plot evil against me.
16 They look everywhere except to the
Most High.
They are as useless as a crooked bow.
Their leaders will be killed by their enemies
because of their insolence toward me.
Then the people of Egypt
will laugh at them.

CHAPTER 8

Israel Harvests the Whirlwind

1 "Sound the alarm!
The enemy descends like an eagle
on the people of the LORD,
for they have broken my covenant
and revolted against my law.
2 Now Israel pleads with me,
'Help us, for you are our God!'
3 But it is too late.
The people of Israel have rejected what
is good,
and now their enemies will chase
after them.
4 The people have appointed kings without
my consent,
and princes without my approval.
By making idols for themselves from their
silver and gold,
they have brought about their own
destruction.

5 "O Samaria, I reject this calf—
this idol you have made.
My fury burns against you.
How long will you be incapable
of innocence?
6 This calf you worship in Samaria
was crafted by your own hands!
It is not God!
Therefore, it must be smashed to bits.

7 "They have planted the wind
and will harvest the whirlwind.
The stalks of grain wither
and produce nothing to eat.
And even if there is any grain,
foreigners will eat it.
8 The people of Israel have been
swallowed up;
they lie among the nations like an old
discarded pot.
9 Like a wild donkey looking for a mate,
they have gone up to Assyria.
The people of Israel have sold themselves—
sold themselves to many lovers.
10 But though they have sold themselves
to many allies,
I will now gather them together for
judgment.
Then they will writhe
under the burden of the great king.

11 "Israel has built many altars to take
away sin,
but these very altars became places
for sinning!
12 Even though I gave them all my laws,
they act as if those laws don't apply
to them.
13 The people love to offer sacrifices to me,
feasting on the meat,
but I do not accept their sacrifices.
I will hold my people accountable
for their sins,
and I will punish them.
They will return to Egypt.
14 Israel has forgotten its Maker and built
great palaces,
and Judah has fortified its cities.
Therefore, I will send down fire on
their cities
and will burn up their fortresses."

CHAPTER 9

Hosea Announces Israel's Punishment

1 O people of Israel,
do not rejoice as other nations do.
For you have been unfaithful to your God,
hiring yourselves out like prostitutes,
worshiping other gods on every
threshing floor.
2 So now your harvests will be too small
to feed you.
There will be no grapes for making
new wine.
3 You may no longer stay here in the
LORD's land.
Instead, you will return to Egypt,
and in Assyria you will eat food
that is ceremonially unclean.
4 There you will make no offerings of wine
to the LORD.
None of your sacrifices there will
please him.
They will be unclean, like food touched
by a person in mourning.
All who present such sacrifices will
be defiled.
They may eat this food themselves,
but they may not offer it to the LORD.
5 What then will you do on festival days?
How will you observe the LORD's festivals?
6 Even if you escape destruction from Assyria,
Egypt will conquer you, and Memphis
will bury you.
Nettles will take over your treasures of silver;
thistles will invade your ruined homes.

7 The time of Israel's punishment has come;
the day of payment is here.
Soon Israel will know this all too well.
Because of your great sin and hostility,
you say, "The prophets are crazy
and the inspired men are fools!"
8 The prophet is a watchman over Israel
for my God,
yet traps are laid for him wherever
he goes.
He faces hostility even in the house of God.
9 The things my people do are as depraved
as what they did in Gibeah long ago.
God will not forget.
He will surely punish them for their sins.

10 The LORD says, "O Israel, when I first
found you,
it was like finding fresh grapes
in the desert.
When I saw your ancestors,
it was like seeing the first ripe figs
of the season.
But then they deserted me for Baal-peor,
giving themselves to that shameful idol.
Soon they became vile,
as vile as the god they worshiped.
11 The glory of Israel will fly away like a bird,
for your children will not be born
or grow in the womb
or even be conceived.
12 Even if you do have children who grow up,
I will take them from you.
It will be a terrible day when I turn away
and leave you alone.
13 I have watched Israel become as beautiful
as Tyre.
But now Israel will bring out her children
for slaughter."

14 O LORD, what should I request for your
people?
I will ask for wombs that don't give birth
and breasts that give no milk.

15 The LORD says, "All their wickedness
began at Gilgal;
there I began to hate them.
I will drive them from my land
because of their evil actions.
I will love them no more
because all their leaders are rebels.
16 The people of Israel are struck down.
Their roots are dried up,
and they will bear no more fruit.
And if they give birth,
I will slaughter their beloved children."

17 My God will reject the people of Israel
because they will not listen or obey.
They will be wanderers,
homeless among the nations.

CHAPTER 10

The LORD's Judgment against Israel

1 How prosperous Israel is—
a luxuriant vine loaded with fruit.
But the richer the people get,
the more pagan altars they build.
The more bountiful their harvests,
the more beautiful their sacred pillars.
2 The hearts of the people are fickle;
they are guilty and must be punished.
The LORD will break down their altars
and smash their sacred pillars.

3 Then they will say, "We have no king
because we didn't fear the LORD.
But even if we had a king,
what could he do for us anyway?"
4 They spout empty words
and make covenants they don't intend
to keep.
So injustice springs up among them
like poisonous weeds in a farmer's field.

5 The people of Samaria tremble in fear
for their calf idol at Beth-aven,
and they mourn for it.
Though its priests rejoice over it,
its glory will be stripped away.
6 This idol will be carted away to Assyria,
a gift to the great king there.
Ephraim will be ridiculed and Israel will
be shamed,
because its people have trusted
in this idol.
7 Samaria and its king will be cut off;
they will float away like driftwood
on an ocean wave.
8 And the pagan shrines of Aven, the place
of Israel's sin, will crumble.
Thorns and thistles will grow up around
their altars.
They will beg the mountains, "Bury us!"
and plead with the hills, "Fall on us!"

9 The LORD says, "O Israel, ever since Gibeah,
there has been only sin and more sin!
You have made no progress whatsoever.
Was it not right that the wicked men
of Gibeah were attacked?
10 Now whenever it fits my plan,
I will attack you, too.
I will call out the armies of the nations
to punish you for your multiplied sins.

11 "Israel is like a trained heifer treading
out the grain—
an easy job she loves.
But I will put a heavy yoke on her
tender neck.
I will force Judah to pull the plow
and Israel to break up the hard ground.
12 I said, 'Plant the good seeds of righteousness,
and you will harvest a crop of love.
Plow up the hard ground of your hearts,
for now is the time to seek the LORD,
that he may come
and shower righteousness upon you.'

13 "But you have cultivated wickedness
and harvested a thriving crop of sins.
You have eaten the fruit of lies—
trusting in your military might,
believing that great armies
could make your nation safe.
14 Now the terrors of war
will rise among your people.
All your fortifications will fall,
just as when Shalman destroyed
Beth-arbel.
Even mothers and children
were dashed to death there.
15 You will share that fate, Bethel,
because of your great wickedness.
When the day of judgment dawns,
the king of Israel will be completely
destroyed.

CHAPTER 11

The LORD's Love for Israel

1 "When Israel was a child, I loved him,
and I called my son out of Egypt.
2 But the more I called to him,
the farther he moved from me,
offering sacrifices to the images of Baal
and burning incense to idols.
3 I myself taught Israel how to walk,
leading him along by the hand.
But he doesn't know or even care
that it was I who took care of him.
4 I led Israel along
with my ropes of kindness and love.
I lifted the yoke from his neck,
and I myself stooped to feed him.

5 "But since my people refuse to return
to me,
they will return to Egypt
and will be forced to serve Assyria.
6 War will swirl through their cities;
their enemies will crash through
their gates.
They will destroy them,
trapping them in their own evil plans.
7 For my people are determined to desert me.
They call me the Most High,
but they don't truly honor me.

8 "Oh, how can I give you up, Israel?
How can I let you go?
How can I destroy you like Admah
or demolish you like Zeboiim?
My heart is torn within me,
and my compassion overflows.
9 No, I will not unleash my fierce anger.
I will not completely destroy Israel,
for I am God and not a mere mortal.

God's Children

The people of Israel were God's children, but they had turned away from him. Did God turn away from *them*? No! **Read HOSEA 11 to see how God describes himself as a parent. Cool, huh?**

Here's a doll to make that will remind you that God wants *you* to be his child!

1 **Take a 3x5-inch cardboard, and wrap yarn around it lengthwise 50 times. Thread a piece of yarn through the top of your wrapped yarn and tie it off. Slide the yarn off the cardboard.**

2 **Then wrap yarn around the cardboard widthwise 25 times. Tie it off, and slide your yarn off the cardboard.**

3 **To make a doll, take your first bundle of yarn, and tie off a head about 1 1/2 inches from the top. Take the second bundle, and thread it through the middle of the first bundle to make arms. Tie off your doll at the waist.**

Glue eyes and a mouth on your doll if you want!

4 **Separate the loops into two legs, and tie off the foot on each leg.**

Read HOSEA 11 again.
Your "child of God" doll can help you remember that God loves you.

I am the Holy One living among you,
and I will not come to destroy.
10 For someday the people will follow me.
I, the LORD, will roar like a lion.
And when I roar,
my people will return trembling from the west.
11 Like a flock of birds, they will come from Egypt.
Trembling like doves, they will return from Assyria.
And I will bring them home again,"
says the LORD.

Charges against Israel and Judah

12 Israel surrounds me with lies and deceit,
but Judah still obeys God
and is faithful to the Holy One.

CHAPTER 12

1 The people of Israel feed on the wind;
they chase after the east wind all day long.
They pile up lies and violence;
they are making an alliance with Assyria
while sending olive oil to buy support from Egypt.

2 Now the LORD is bringing charges against Judah.
He is about to punish Jacob for all his deceitful ways,
and pay him back for all he has done.
3 Even in the womb,
Jacob struggled with his brother;
when he became a man,
he even fought with God.
4 Yes, he wrestled with the angel and won.
He wept and pleaded for a blessing from him.
There at Bethel he met God face to face,
and God spoke to him—
5 the LORD God of Heaven's Armies,
the LORD is his name!
6 So now, come back to your God.
Act with love and justice,
and always depend on him.

7 But no, the people are like crafty merchants
selling from dishonest scales—
they love to cheat.
8 Israel boasts, "I am rich!
I've made a fortune all by myself!
No one has caught me cheating!
My record is spotless!"

9 "But I am the LORD your God,
who rescued you from slavery
in Egypt.
And I will make you live in tents again,
as you do each year at the Festival
of Shelters.
10 I sent my prophets to warn you
with many visions and parables."

11 But the people of Gilead are worthless
because of their idol worship.
And in Gilgal, too, they sacrifice bulls;
their altars are lined up like the heaps
of stone
along the edges of a plowed field.
12 Jacob fled to the land of Aram,
and there he earned a wife by
tending sheep.
13 Then by a prophet
the LORD brought Jacob's descendants
out of Egypt;
and by that prophet
they were protected.
14 But the people of Israel
have bitterly provoked the LORD,
so their Lord will now sentence them
to death
in payment for their sins.

CHAPTER 13
The LORD's Anger against Israel

1 When the tribe of Ephraim spoke,
the people shook with fear,
for that tribe was important in Israel.
But the people of Ephraim sinned by
worshiping Baal
and thus sealed their destruction.
2 Now they continue to sin by making
silver idols,
images shaped skillfully with
human hands.
"Sacrifice to these," they cry,
"and kiss the calf idols!"
3 Therefore, they will disappear like the
morning mist,
like dew in the morning sun,
like chaff blown by the wind,
like smoke from a chimney.

4 "I have been the LORD your God
ever since I brought you out of Egypt.
You must acknowledge no God but me,
for there is no other savior.
5 I took care of you in the wilderness,
in that dry and thirsty land.
6 But when you had eaten and were
satisfied,
you became proud and forgot me.
7 So now I will attack you like a lion,
like a leopard that lurks along the road.
8 Like a bear whose cubs have been
taken away,
I will tear out your heart.
I will devour you like a hungry lioness
and mangle you like a wild animal.

9 "You are about to be destroyed,
O Israel—
yes, by me, your only helper.
10 Now where is your king?
Let him save you!
Where are all the leaders of the land,
the king and the officials you
demanded of me?
11 In my anger I gave you kings,
and in my fury I took them away.

12 "Ephraim's guilt has been collected,
and his sin has been stored up
for punishment.
13 Pain has come to the people
like the pain of childbirth,
but they are like a child
who resists being born.
The moment of birth has arrived,
but they stay in the womb!

14 "Should I ransom them from the grave?
Should I redeem them from death?
O death, bring on your terrors!
O grave, bring on your plagues!
For I will not take pity on them.
15 Ephraim was the most fruitful of all
his brothers,
but the east wind—a blast from
the LORD—
will arise in the desert.
All their flowing springs will run dry,
and all their wells will disappear.
Every precious thing they own
will be plundered and carried away.
16 The people of Samaria
must bear the consequences
of their guilt
because they rebelled against
their God.
They will be killed by an invading army,
their little ones dashed to death
against the ground,
their pregnant women ripped open
by swords."

CHAPTER 14

Healing for the Repentant

1 Return, O Israel, to the LORD
your God,
for your sins have brought
you down.
2 Bring your confessions, and return
to the LORD.
Say to him,
"Forgive all our sins and graciously
receive us,
so that we may offer you our praises.
3 Assyria cannot save us,
nor can our warhorses.
Never again will we say to the idols
we have made,
'You are our gods.'
No, in you alone
do the orphans find mercy."

4 The LORD says,
"Then I will heal you of your faithlessness;
my love will know no bounds,
for my anger will be gone forever.
5 I will be to Israel
like a refreshing dew from heaven.
Israel will blossom like the lily;
it will send roots deep into the soil
like the cedars in Lebanon.
6 Its branches will spread out like beautiful
olive trees,
as fragrant as the cedars of Lebanon.
7 My people will again live under my shade.
They will flourish like grain and blossom
like grapevines.
They will be as fragrant as the wines
of Lebanon.

8 "O Israel, stay away from idols!
I am the one who answers your prayers
and cares for you.
I am like a tree that is always green;
all your fruit comes from me."

9 Let those who are wise understand
these things.
Let those with discernment listen
carefully.
The paths of the LORD are true and right,
and righteous people live by walking
in them.
But in those paths sinners stumble and fall.

JOEL The Day of the Lord Is Coming

The book of Joel is short, but it packs a punch. You'll find
- **MUNCHING BUGS**
- **A CALL TO REPENT**
- **A PRETTY PICTURE OF THE FUTURE**
- **A LOT OF TALK ABOUT TIME**

Time's Up!

The Day of the Lord

OK, time's up! That's what God's going to say one day, and then it'll be judgment time for everyone. **Find out what that day will be like in Joel 2:28-32.**

Hand Me That Bug Spray

Um ... maybe bug spray wasn't such a great idea. (Unless they had about a gazillion cans of it!) **Read Joel 1:1-7 to see what was bugging the people in Jerusalem.**

Bunches of Blessings

After the day of judgment, things are going to be great for the people who trusted in God. How great? **Just read Joel 3:18-21 to find out!**

Wake-Up Call

Joel wasn't kidding when he told the people that God had seen about enough of their rebellion. But he said there was still time for the people to turn back to God. **Find out how he knew by reading Joel 2:12-14.**

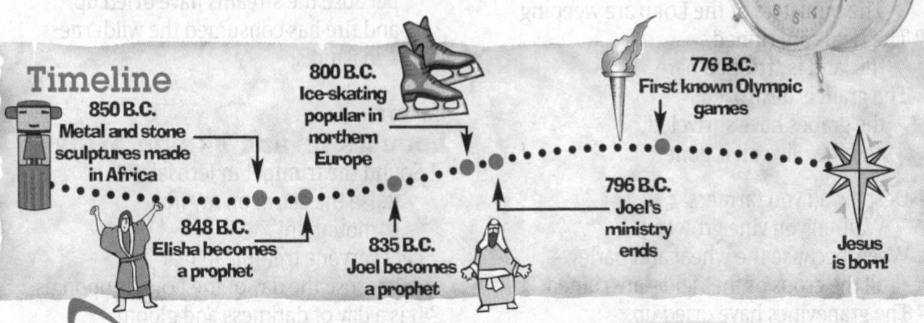
Timeline
850 B.C. Metal and stone sculptures made in Africa
848 B.C. Elisha becomes a prophet
835 B.C. Joel becomes a prophet
800 B.C. Ice-skating popular in northern Europe
796 B.C. Joel's ministry ends
776 B.C. First known Olympic games
Jesus is born!

The JESUS CONNECTION

Joel said that God would pour out his Spirit on all people. In the New Testament, Peter quoted Joel using the same words. Cool, huh? (You can read about it in Acts 2:16-21.) God *did* pour out his Spirit on the day of Pentecost. Since then, God's Holy Spirit has been available to everyone who believes in Jesus. **And that means he's available to you!**

Joel 1 . . . page 876

CHAPTER 1

The LORD gave this message to Joel son of Pethuel.

Mourning over the Locust Plague

2 Hear this, you leaders of the people.
Listen, all who live in the land.
In all your history,
has anything like this happened before?
3 Tell your children about it in the years
to come,
and let your children tell their children.
Pass the story down from generation
to generation.
4 After the cutting locusts finished eating
the crops,
the swarming locusts took what was left!
After them came the hopping locusts,
and then the stripping locusts, too!

5 Wake up, you drunkards, and weep!
Wail, all you wine-drinkers!
All the grapes are ruined,
and all your sweet wine is gone.
6 A vast army of locusts has invaded my land,
a terrible army too numerous to count.
Its teeth are like lions' teeth,
its fangs like those of a lioness.
7 It has destroyed my grapevines
and ruined my fig trees,
stripping their bark and destroying it,
leaving the branches white and bare.

8 Weep like a bride dressed in black,
mourning the death of her husband.
9 For there is no grain or wine
to offer at the Temple of the LORD.
So the priests are in mourning.
The ministers of the LORD are weeping.
10 The fields are ruined,
the land is stripped bare.
The grain is destroyed,
the grapes have shriveled,
and the olive oil is gone.

11 Despair, all you farmers!
Wail, all you vine growers!
Weep, because the wheat and barley—
all the crops of the field—are ruined.
12 The grapevines have dried up,
and the fig trees have withered.
The pomegranate trees, palm trees, and apple
trees—
all the fruit trees—have dried up.
And the people's joy has dried up
with them.

13 Dress yourselves in burlap and weep,
you priests!
Wail, you who serve before the altar!
Come, spend the night in burlap,
you ministers of my God.
For there is no grain or wine
to offer at the Temple of your God.
14 Announce a time of fasting;
call the people together for a solemn
meeting.
Bring the leaders
and all the people of the land
into the Temple of the LORD your God,
and cry out to him there.
15 The day of the LORD is near,
the day when destruction comes
from the Almighty.
How terrible that day will be!

16 Our food disappears before our very eyes.
No joyful celebrations are held in the
house of our God.
17 The seeds die in the parched ground,
and the grain crops fail.
The barns stand empty,
and granaries are abandoned.
18 How the animals moan with hunger!
The herds of cattle wander about
confused,
because they have no pasture.
The flocks of sheep and goats bleat
in misery.

19 LORD, help us!
The fire has consumed the wilderness
pastures,
and flames have burned up all the trees.
20 Even the wild animals cry out to you
because the streams have dried up,
and fire has consumed the wilderness
pastures.

CHAPTER 2

Locusts Invade like an Army

1 Sound the trumpet in Jerusalem!
Raise the alarm on my holy
mountain!
Let everyone tremble in fear
because the day of the LORD is upon us.
2 It is a day of darkness and gloom,
a day of thick clouds and deep blackness.
Suddenly, like dawn spreading across the
mountains,
a great and mighty army appears.
Nothing like it has been seen before
or will ever be seen again.

3 Fire burns in front of them,
and flames follow after them.
Ahead of them the land lies
as beautiful as the Garden of Eden.
Behind them is nothing but desolation;
not one thing escapes.
4 They look like horses;
they charge forward like warhorses.
5 Look at them as they leap along the
mountaintops.
Listen to the noise they make—like
the rumbling of chariots,
like the roar of fire sweeping across a field
of stubble,
or like a mighty army moving into battle.
6 Fear grips all the people;
every face grows pale with terror.
7 The attackers march like warriors
and scale city walls like soldiers.
Straight forward they march,
never breaking rank.
8 They never jostle each other;
each moves in exactly the right position.
They break through defenses
without missing a step.
9 They swarm over the city
and run along its walls.
They enter all the houses,
climbing like thieves through the
windows.
10 The earth quakes as they advance,
and the heavens tremble.
The sun and moon grow dark,
and the stars no longer shine.
11 The LORD is at the head of the column.
He leads them with a shout.
This is his mighty army,
and they follow his orders.
The day of the LORD is an awesome,
terrible thing.
Who can possibly survive?

A Call to Repentance

12 That is why the LORD says,
"Turn to me now, while there is time.
Give me your hearts.
Come with fasting, weeping, and
mourning.
**13 Don't tear your clothing
in your grief,
but tear your hearts instead."
Return to the LORD your God,
for he is merciful and
compassionate,
slow to get angry and filled
with unfailing love.
He is eager to relent and
not punish.**
14 Who knows? Perhaps he will give you
a reprieve,
sending you a blessing instead
of this curse.
Perhaps you will be able to offer grain
and wine
to the LORD your God as before.

15 Blow the ram's horn in Jerusalem!
Announce a time of fasting;
call the people together
for a solemn meeting.
16 Gather all the people—
the elders, the children, and even the
babies.
Call the bridegroom from his quarters
and the bride from her private room.
17 Let the priests, who minister in the
LORD's presence,
stand and weep between the entry room
to the Temple and the altar.
Let them pray, "Spare your people, LORD!
Don't let your special possession become
an object of mockery.
Don't let them become a joke for unbelieving
foreigners who say,
'Has the God of Israel left them?'"

The LORD's Promise of Restoration

18 Then the LORD will pity his people
and jealously guard the honor of his land.
19 The LORD will reply,
"Look! I am sending you grain and new wine
and olive oil,
enough to satisfy your needs.
You will no longer be an object of mockery
among the surrounding nations.
20 I will drive away these armies from the north.
I will send them into the parched
wastelands.
Those in the front will be driven into the
Dead Sea,
and those at the rear into the
Mediterranean.
The stench of their rotting bodies will rise
over the land."

Surely the LORD has done great things!
21 Don't be afraid, O land.
Be glad now and rejoice,
for the LORD has done great things.

22 Don't be afraid, you animals of the field,
for the wilderness pastures will soon be green.
The trees will again be filled with fruit;
fig trees and grapevines will be loaded down once more.
23 Rejoice, you people of Jerusalem!
Rejoice in the LORD your God!
For the rain he sends demonstrates his faithfulness.
Once more the autumn rains will come,
as well as the rains of spring.
24 The threshing floors will again be piled high with grain,
and the presses will overflow with new wine and olive oil.

25 The LORD says, "I will give you back what you lost
to the swarming locusts, the hopping locusts,
the stripping locusts, and the cutting locusts.
It was I who sent this great destroying army against you.
26 Once again you will have all the food you want,
and you will praise the LORD your God,
who does these miracles for you.
Never again will my people be disgraced.
27 Then you will know that I am among my people Israel,
that I am the LORD your God, and there is no other.
Never again will my people be disgraced.

The LORD's Promise of His Spirit

28 "Then, after doing all those things,
I will pour out my Spirit upon all people.
Your sons and daughters will prophesy.
Your old men will dream dreams,
and your young men will see visions.
29 In those days I will pour out my Spirit
even on servants—men and women alike.
30 And I will cause wonders in the heavens
and on the earth—
blood and fire and columns of smoke.
31 The sun will become dark,
and the moon will turn blood red
before that great and terrible day
of the LORD arrives.
32 But everyone who calls on the name
of the LORD
will be saved,
for some on Mount Zion in Jerusalem
will escape,
just as the LORD has said.
These will be among the survivors
whom the LORD has called.

CHAPTER 3

Judgment against Enemy Nations

1 "At the time of those events," says the LORD,
"when I restore the prosperity of Judah and Jerusalem,
2 I will gather the armies of the world
into the valley of Jehoshaphat.
There I will judge them
for harming my people, my special possession,
for scattering my people among the nations,
and for dividing up my land.
3 They threw dice to decide which of my people
would be their slaves.
They traded boys to obtain prostitutes
and sold girls for enough wine to get drunk.

4 "What do you have against me, Tyre and Sidon and you cities of Philistia? Are you trying to
take revenge on me? If you are, then watch out! I
will strike swiftly and pay you back for everything you have done. 5 You have taken my silver
and gold and all my precious treasures, and have
carried them off to your pagan temples. 6 You
have sold the people of Judah and Jerusalem to
the Greeks, so they could take them far from
their homeland.

7 "But I will bring them back from all the
places to which you sold them, and I will pay you
back for everything you have done. 8 I will sell
your sons and daughters to the people of Judah,
and they will sell them to the people of Arabia, a
nation far away. I, the LORD, have spoken!"

9 Say to the nations far and wide:
"Get ready for war!
Call out your best warriors.
Let all your fighting men advance
for the attack.
10 Hammer your plowshares into swords
and your pruning hooks into spears.
Train even your weaklings to be warriors.
11 Come quickly, all you nations everywhere.
Gather together in the valley."

And now, O LORD, call out your warriors!
12 "Let the nations be called to arms.
Let them march to the valley of
Jehoshaphat.
There I, the LORD, will sit
to pronounce judgment on them all.
13 Swing the sickle,
for the harvest is ripe.
Come, tread the grapes,
for the winepress is full.
The storage vats are overflowing
with the wickedness of these people."

14 Thousands upon thousands are waiting
in the valley of decision.
There the day of the LORD will
soon arrive.
15 The sun and moon will grow dark,
and the stars will no longer shine.
16 The LORD's voice will roar from Zion
and thunder from Jerusalem,
and the heavens and the earth
will shake.
But the LORD will be a refuge for
his people,
a strong fortress for the people of Israel.

Blessings for God's People

17 "Then you will know that I, the LORD
your God,
live in Zion, my holy mountain.
Jerusalem will be holy forever,
and foreign armies will never conquer
her again.
18 In that day the mountains will drip with
sweet wine,
and the hills will flow with milk.
Water will fill the streambeds of Judah,
and a fountain will burst forth from the
LORD's Temple,
watering the arid valley of acacias.
19 But Egypt will become a wasteland
and Edom will become a wilderness,
because they attacked the people of Judah
and killed innocent people in their land.

20 "But Judah will be filled with people forever,
and Jerusalem will endure through all
generations.
21 I will pardon my people's crimes,
which I have not yet pardoned;
and I, the LORD, will make my home
in Jerusalem with my people."

AMOS A Shepherd's Warning

Amos was just a shepherd who also took care of trees. But God used him to spread a mighty message. Look for

- **A REGULAR GUY TURNED PROPHET**
- **A BUNCH OF "FAT COW" RICH PEOPLE**
- **A BUNCH OF POORLY TREATED POOR PEOPLE**
- **A BUNCH OF PUNISHMENT (AND HOPE!) ON THE WAY**

WHO...?
ME?!

Uh...You Talkin' to Me?

The people of Israel and Judah thought God was going to punish only *other* nations. But they were wrong. **Find out how in Amos 2:4-6.**

#1
GOD
GOD
D

Go Get 'Em, God!

God had a plan for all the nations that had hurt Israel. Those nations were in big trouble! **Read what God said he would do in Amos 1:3–2:3.**

The Poor Poor

God had just about had it with the way the Israelites treated poor people. **Find out what God told the rich people in Amos 4:1-3.**

Ready to Rebuild

COMING SOON
KINGDOM OF DAVID
NEW & IMPROVED

Even though God knew he had to punish the Israelites, he gave them hope, too. Find out what (and who!) that hope was in Amos 9:11-15. **(Not sure about the "who" part? Read the Jesus Connection at the bottom of this page!)**

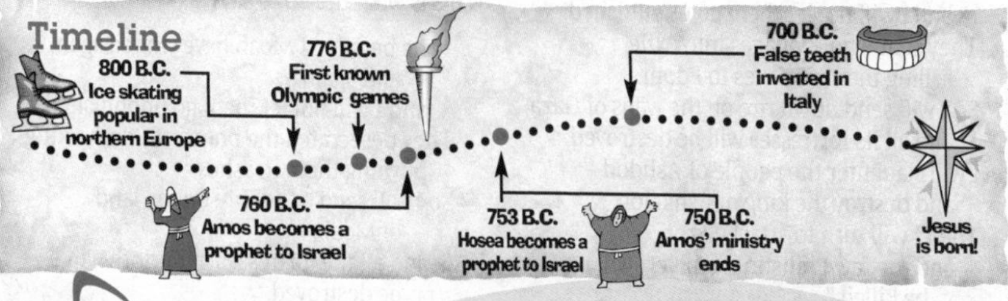

Timeline
800 B.C. Ice skating popular in northern Europe
776 B.C. First known Olympic games
760 B.C. Amos becomes a prophet to Israel
753 B.C. Hosea becomes a prophet to Israel
750 B.C. Amos' ministry ends
700 B.C. False teeth invented in Italy
Jesus is born!

The JESUS CONNECTION

Because God is holy, he couldn't put up with the people's sins forever. God sent prophet after prophet to warn the people. But God also gave them hope for the future. And that hope in the end was Jesus! God let the people know that one day he would send a Messiah to save people from their sins and restore David's kingdom forever.

What a good God we have!

CHAPTER 1

This message was given to Amos, a shepherd from the town of Tekoa in Judah. He received this message in visions two years before the earthquake, when Uzziah was king of Judah and Jeroboam II, the son of Jehoash, was king of Israel.
2 This is what he saw and heard:

"The LORD's voice will roar from Zion
and thunder from Jerusalem!
The lush pastures of the shepherds will dry up;
the grass on Mount Carmel will wither and die."

God's Judgment on Israel's Neighbors

3 This is what the LORD says:

"The people of Damascus have sinned again and again,
and I will not let them go unpunished!
They beat down my people in Gilead
as grain is threshed with iron sledges.
4 So I will send down fire on King Hazael's palace,
and the fortresses of King Ben-hadad will be destroyed.
5 I will break down the gates of Damascus
and slaughter the people in the valley of Aven.
I will destroy the ruler in Beth-eden,
and the people of Aram will go as captives to Kir,"
says the LORD.

6 This is what the LORD says:

"The people of Gaza have sinned again and again,
and I will not let them go unpunished!
They sent whole villages into exile,
selling them as slaves to Edom.
7 So I will send down fire on the walls of Gaza,
and all its fortresses will be destroyed.
8 I will slaughter the people of Ashdod
and destroy the king of Ashkelon.
Then I will turn to attack Ekron,
and the few Philistines still left will be killed,"
says the Sovereign LORD.

9 This is what the LORD says:

"The people of Tyre have sinned again and again,
and I will not let them go unpunished!
They broke their treaty of brotherhood with Israel,
selling whole villages as slaves to Edom.
10 So I will send down fire on the walls of Tyre,
and all its fortresses will be destroyed."

11 This is what the LORD says:

"The people of Edom have sinned again and again,
and I will not let them go unpunished!
They chased down their relatives, the Israelites, with swords,
showing them no mercy.
In their rage, they slashed them continually
and were unrelenting in their anger.
12 So I will send down fire on Teman,
and the fortresses of Bozrah will be destroyed."

13 This is what the LORD says:

"The people of Ammon have sinned again and again,
and I will not let them go unpunished!
When they attacked Gilead to extend their borders,
they ripped open pregnant women with their swords.
14 So I will send down fire on the walls of Rabbah,
and all its fortresses will be destroyed.
The battle will come upon them with shouts,
like a whirlwind in a mighty storm.
15 And their king and his princes will go into exile together,"
says the LORD.

CHAPTER 2

This is what the LORD says:

"The people of Moab have sinned again and again,
and I will not let them go unpunished!
They desecrated the bones of Edom's king,
burning them to ashes.
2 So I will send down fire on the land of Moab,
and all the fortresses in Kerioth will be destroyed.
The people will fall in the noise of battle,
as the warriors shout and the ram's horn sounds.
3 And I will destroy their king
and slaughter all their princes,"
says the LORD.

God's Judgment on Judah and Israel

4 This is what the LORD says:

"The people of Judah have sinned again
and again,
and I will not let them go unpunished!
They have rejected the instruction
of the LORD,
refusing to obey his decrees.
They have been led astray by the same lies
that deceived their ancestors.
5 So I will send down fire on Judah,
and all the fortresses of Jerusalem will
be destroyed."

6 This is what the LORD says:

"The people of Israel have sinned again
and again,
and I will not let them go unpunished!
They sell honorable people for silver
and poor people for a pair of sandals.
7 They trample helpless people in the dust
and shove the oppressed out of the way.
Both father and son sleep with the same
woman,
corrupting my holy name.
8 At their religious festivals,
they lounge in clothing their debtors
put up as security.
In the house of their gods,
they drink wine bought with unjust fines.

9 "But as my people watched,
I destroyed the Amorites,
though they were as tall as cedars
and as strong as oaks.
I destroyed the fruit on their branches
and dug out their roots.
10 It was I who rescued you from Egypt
and led you through the desert for
forty years,
so you could possess the land of the
Amorites.
11 I chose some of your sons to be prophets
and others to be Nazirites.
Can you deny this, my people of Israel?"
asks the LORD.
12 "But you caused the Nazirites to sin by
making them drink wine,
and you commanded the prophets,
'Shut up!'
13 "So I will make you groan
like a wagon loaded down with sheaves
of grain.
14 Your fastest runners will not get away.
The strongest among you will become weak.
Even mighty warriors will be unable to save
themselves.
15 The archers will not stand their ground.
The swiftest runners won't be fast enough
to escape.
Even those riding horses won't be able
to save themselves.
16 On that day the most courageous of your
fighting men
will drop their weapons and run for
their lives,"
says the LORD.

CHAPTER 3

Listen to this message that the LORD has spoken
against you, O people of Israel—against the entire family I rescued from Egypt:

2 "From among all the families on the earth,
I have been intimate with you alone.
That is why I must punish you
for all your sins."

Witnesses against Guilty Israel

3 Can two people walk together
without agreeing on the direction?
4 Does a lion ever roar in a thicket
without first finding a victim?
Does a young lion growl in its den
without first catching its prey?
5 Does a bird ever get caught in a trap
that has no bait?
Does a trap spring shut
when there's nothing to catch?
6 When the ram's horn blows a warning,
shouldn't the people be alarmed?
Does disaster come to a city
unless the LORD has planned it?
7 Indeed, the Sovereign LORD never does
anything
until he reveals his plans to his servants
the prophets.
8 The lion has roared—
so who isn't frightened?
The Sovereign LORD has spoken—
so who can refuse to proclaim his message?
9 Announce this to the leaders of Philistia
and to the great ones of Egypt:
"Take your seats now on the hills around
Samaria,
and witness the chaos and oppression
in Israel."

10 "My people have forgotten how to do right,"
says the LORD.
"Their fortresses are filled with wealth
taken by theft and violence.
11 Therefore," says the Sovereign LORD,
"an enemy is coming!
He will surround them and shatter their
defenses.
Then he will plunder all their fortresses."

12 This is what the LORD says:

"A shepherd who tries to rescue a sheep from
a lion's mouth
will recover only two legs or a piece
of an ear.
So it will be for the Israelites in Samaria
lying on luxurious beds,
and for the people of Damascus reclining
on couches.

13 "Now listen to this, and announce it throughout all Israel," says the Lord, the LORD God of
Heaven's Armies.

14 "On the very day I punish Israel for its sins,
I will destroy the pagan altars at Bethel.
The horns of the altar will be cut off
and fall to the ground.
15 And I will destroy the beautiful homes of the
wealthy—
their winter mansions and their summer
houses, too—
all their palaces filled with ivory,"
says the LORD.

CHAPTER 4

Israel's Failure to Learn

1 Listen to me, you fat cows
living in Samaria,
you women who oppress the poor
and crush the needy,
and who are always calling to your husbands,
"Bring us another drink!"
2 The Sovereign LORD has sworn this by his
holiness:
"The time will come when you will be led away
with hooks in your noses.
Every last one of you will be dragged away
like a fish on a hook!
3 You will be led out through the ruins of the
wall;
you will be thrown from your fortresses,"
says the LORD.

4 "Go ahead and offer sacrifices to the idols
at Bethel.
Keep on disobeying at Gilgal.
Offer sacrifices each morning,
and bring your tithes every three days.
5 Present your bread made with yeast
as an offering of thanksgiving.
Then give your extra voluntary offerings
so you can brag about it everywhere!
This is the kind of thing you Israelites love
to do,"
says the Sovereign LORD.

6 "I brought hunger to every city
and famine to every town.
But still you would not return to me,"
says the LORD.

7 "I kept the rain from falling
when your crops needed it the most.
I sent rain on one town
but withheld it from another.
Rain fell on one field,
while another field withered away.
8 People staggered from town to town
looking for water,
but there was never enough.
But still you would not return to me,"
says the LORD.

9 "I struck your farms and vineyards
with blight and mildew.
Locusts devoured all your fig and
olive trees.
But still you would not return to me,"
says the LORD.

10 "I sent plagues on you
like the plagues I sent on Egypt long ago.
I killed your young men in war
and led all your horses away.
The stench of death filled the air!
But still you would not return to me,"
says the LORD.

11 "I destroyed some of your cities,
as I destroyed Sodom and Gomorrah.
Those of you who survived
were like charred sticks pulled from a fire.
But still you would not return to me,"
says the LORD.

12 "Therefore, I will bring upon you all the
disasters I have announced.
Prepare to meet your God in judgment,
you people of Israel!"

13 For the LORD is the one who shaped the
mountains,
stirs up the winds, and reveals his
thoughts to mankind.

He turns the light of dawn into darkness
and treads on the heights of the earth.
The LORD God of Heaven's Armies is
his name!

CHAPTER 5

A Call to Repentance

Listen, you people of Israel! Listen to this funeral
song I am singing:

2 "The virgin Israel has fallen,
never to rise again!
She lies abandoned on the ground,
with no one to help her up."

3 The Sovereign LORD says:

"When a city sends a thousand men to battle,
only a hundred will return.
When a town sends a hundred,
only ten will come back alive."

4 Now this is what the LORD says to the family of
Israel:

"Come back to me and live!
5 Don't worship at the pagan altars at Bethel;
don't go to the shrines at Gilgal or
Beersheba.
For the people of Gilgal will be dragged off
into exile,
and the people of Bethel will be reduced
to nothing."
6 Come back to the LORD and live!
Otherwise, he will roar through Israel like
a fire,
devouring you completely.
Your gods in Bethel
won't be able to quench the flames.
7 You twist justice, making it a bitter pill for
the oppressed.
You treat the righteous like dirt.

8 It is the LORD who created the stars,
the Pleiades and Orion.
He turns darkness into morning
and day into night.
He draws up water from the oceans
and pours it down as rain on the land.
The LORD is his name!
9 With blinding speed and power he destroys
the strong,
crushing all their defenses.

10 How you hate honest judges!
How you despise people who tell the truth!
11 You trample the poor,
stealing their grain through taxes and
unfair rent.
Therefore, though you build beautiful stone
houses,
you will never live in them.
Though you plant lush vineyards,
you will never drink wine from them.
12 For I know the vast number of your sins
and the depth of your rebellions.
You oppress good people by taking bribes
and deprive the poor of justice in the
courts.

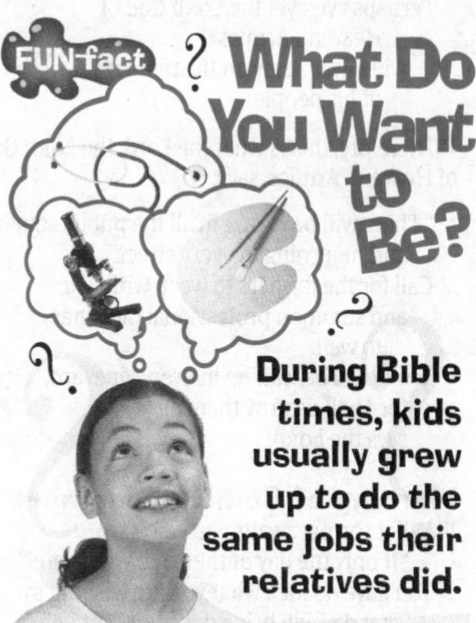

What Do You Want to Be?

During Bible times, kids usually grew up to do the same jobs their relatives did.

But sometimes God had different job plans for his people.

God called Gideon, David, and Amos to new jobs that no one else in their families had. They hadn't been trained, but God helped them. Imagine if God suddenly told you to teach a class at your school. Do you think your friends and the teachers would listen to you? **How do you think God's people got others to believe that God had given them new jobs?**

Draw a "WHAT DO YOU WANT TO BE?" family job tree that lists the jobs your parents and grandparents have had. Then write what job you think God has planned for you!

13 So those who are smart keep their
mouths shut,
for it is an evil time.

14 Do what is good and run from evil
so that you may live!
Then the LORD God of Heaven's Armies
will be your helper,
just as you have claimed.
15 Hate evil and love what is good;
turn your courts into true halls of justice.
Perhaps even yet the LORD God of
Heaven's Armies
will have mercy on the remnant
of his people.

16 Therefore, this is what the Lord, the LORD God
of Heaven's Armies, says:

"There will be crying in all the public squares
and mourning in every street.
Call for the farmers to weep with you,
and summon professional mourners
to wail.
17 There will be wailing in every vineyard,
for I will destroy them all,"
says the LORD.

Warning of Coming Judgment

18 What sorrow awaits you who say,
"If only the day of the LORD were here!"
You have no idea what you are wishing for.
That day will bring darkness, not light.
19 In that day you will be like a man who runs
from a lion—
only to meet a bear.
Escaping from the bear, he leans his hand
against a wall in his house—
and he's bitten by a snake.
20 Yes, the day of the LORD will be dark and
hopeless,
without a ray of joy or hope.

21 "I hate all your show and pretense—
the hypocrisy of your religious festivals
and solemn assemblies.
22 I will not accept your burnt offerings and
grain offerings.
I won't even notice all your choice peace
offerings.
23 Away with your noisy hymns of praise!
I will not listen to the music of your
harps.
24 Instead, I want to see a mighty flood
of justice,
an endless river of righteous living.

25 "Was it to me you were bringing sacrifices
and offerings during the forty years in the wilderness, Israel? 26 No, you served your pagan
gods—Sakkuth your king god and Kaiwan your
star god—the images you made for yourselves.
27 So I will send you into exile, to a land east of
Damascus," says the LORD, whose name is the
God of Heaven's Armies.

CHAPTER 6

1 What sorrow awaits you who lounge
in luxury in Jerusalem,
and you who feel secure in Samaria!
You are famous and popular in Israel,
and people go to you for help.
2 But go over to Calneh
and see what happened there.
Then go to the great city of Hamath
and down to the Philistine city of Gath.
You are no better than they were,
and look at how they were destroyed.
3 You push away every thought of coming
disaster,
but your actions only bring the day
of judgment closer.
4 How terrible for you who sprawl on
ivory beds
and lounge on your couches,
eating the meat of tender lambs from the
flock
and of choice calves fattened in the stall.
5 You sing trivial songs to the sound of
the harp
and fancy yourselves to be great
musicians like David.
6 You drink wine by the bowlful
and perfume yourselves with fragrant
lotions.
You care nothing about the ruin of
your nation.
7 Therefore, you will be the first to be led away
as captives.
Suddenly, all your parties will end.

8 The Sovereign LORD has sworn by his own name,
and this is what he, the LORD God of Heaven's
Armies, says:

"I despise the arrogance of Israel,
and I hate their fortresses.
I will give this city
and everything in it to their enemies."

9 (If there are ten men left in one house, they will
all die. 10 And when a relative who is responsible
to dispose of the dead goes into the house to

carry out the bodies, he will ask the last survivor, "Is anyone else with you?" When the person begins to swear, "No, by . . . ," he will interrupt and say, "Stop! Don't even mention the name of the LORD.")

11 When the LORD gives the command,
homes both great and small will be
smashed to pieces.

12 Can horses gallop over boulders?
Can oxen be used to plow them?
But that's how foolish you are when you
turn justice into poison
and the sweet fruit of righteousness
into bitterness.
13 And you brag about your conquest of
Lo-debar.
You boast, "Didn't we take Karnaim
by our own strength?"

14 "O people of Israel, I am about to bring
an enemy nation against you,"
says the LORD God of Heaven's Armies.
"They will oppress you throughout
your land—
from Lebo-hamath in the north
to the Arabah Valley in the south."

CHAPTER 7

A Vision of Locusts

The Sovereign LORD showed me a vision. I saw him preparing to send a vast swarm of locusts over the land. This was after the king's share had been harvested from the fields and as the main
crop was coming up. 2In my vision the locusts
ate every green plant in sight. Then I said, "O Sovereign LORD, please forgive us or we will not survive, for Israel is so small."
3So the LORD relented from this plan. "I will not do it," he said.

A Vision of Fire

4Then the Sovereign LORD showed me another vision. I saw him preparing to punish his people with a great fire. The fire had burned up the depths of the sea and was devouring the entire
land. 5Then I said, "O Sovereign LORD, please stop or we will not survive, for Israel is so small."
6Then the LORD relented from this plan, too. "I will not do that either," said the Sovereign LORD.

A Vision of a Plumb Line

7Then he showed me another vision. I saw the Lord standing beside a wall that had been built using a plumb line. He was using a plumb line to see if it was still straight. 8And the LORD said to me, "Amos, what do you see?"

I answered, "A plumb line."

And the Lord replied, "I will test my people with this plumb line. I will no longer ignore all
their sins. 9The pagan shrines of your ancestors will be ruined, and the temples of Israel will be destroyed; I will bring the dynasty of King Jeroboam to a sudden end."

Amos and Amaziah

10Then Amaziah, the priest of Bethel, sent a message to Jeroboam, king of Israel: "Amos is hatching a plot against you right here on your very
doorstep! What he is saying is intolerable. 11He
is saying, 'Jeroboam will soon be killed, and the people of Israel will be sent away into exile.'"
12Then Amaziah sent orders to Amos: "Get out of here, you prophet! Go on back to the land of Judah, and earn your living by prophesying there!
13Don't bother us with your prophecies here in Bethel. This is the king's sanctuary and the national place of worship!"
14But Amos replied, "I'm not a professional prophet, and I was never trained to be one. I'm just a shepherd, and I take care of sycamore-fig
trees. 15But the LORD called me away from my flock and told me, 'Go and prophesy to my people
in Israel.' 16Now then, listen to this message
from the LORD:

"You say,
'Don't prophesy against Israel.
Stop preaching against my people.'
17 But this is what the LORD says:
'Your wife will become a prostitute
in this city,
and your sons and daughters will be killed.
Your land will be divided up,
and you yourself will die in a foreign land.
And the people of Israel will certainly
become captives in exile,
far from their homeland.'"

CHAPTER 8

A Vision of Ripe Fruit

Then the Sovereign LORD showed me another vision. In it I saw a basket filled with ripe fruit.
2"What do you see, Amos?" he asked.

I replied, "A basket full of ripe fruit."

Then the LORD said, "Like this fruit, Israel is ripe for punishment! I will not delay their punishment again. 3In that day the singing in the
Temple will turn to wailing. Dead bodies will be scattered everywhere. They will be carried out of

the city in silence. I, the Sovereign LORD, have spoken!"

4 Listen to this, you who rob the poor
and trample down the needy!
5 You can't wait for the Sabbath day to be over
and the religious festivals to end
so you can get back to cheating the helpless.
You measure out grain with dishonest measures
and cheat the buyer with dishonest scales.
6 And you mix the grain you sell
with chaff swept from the floor.
Then you enslave poor people
for one piece of silver or a pair of sandals.

7 Now the LORD has sworn this oath
by his own name, the Pride of Israel:
"I will never forget
the wicked things you have done!
8 The earth will tremble for your deeds,
and everyone will mourn.
The ground will rise like the Nile River at floodtime;
it will heave up, then sink again.

9 "In that day," says the Sovereign LORD,
"I will make the sun go down at noon
and darken the earth while it is still day.
10 I will turn your celebrations into times of mourning
and your singing into weeping.
You will wear funeral clothes
and shave your heads to show your sorrow—
as if your only son had died.
How very bitter that day will be!

11 "The time is surely coming," says the Sovereign LORD,
"when I will send a famine on the land—
not a famine of bread or water
but of hearing the words of the LORD.
12 People will stagger from sea to sea
and wander from border to border
searching for the word of the LORD,
but they will not find it.
13 Beautiful girls and strong young men
will grow faint in that day,
thirsting for the LORD's word.
14 And those who swear by the shameful idols of Samaria—
who take oaths in the name of the god of Dan
and make vows in the name of the god of Beersheba—
they will all fall down,
never to rise again."

CHAPTER 9

A Vision of God at the Altar

Then I saw a vision of the Lord standing beside the altar. He said,

"Strike the tops of the Temple columns,
so that the foundation will shake.
Bring down the roof
on the heads of the people below.
I will kill with the sword those who survive.
No one will escape!

2 "Even if they dig down to the place of the dead,
I will reach down and pull them up.
Even if they climb up into the heavens,
I will bring them down.
3 Even if they hide at the very top of Mount Carmel,
I will search them out and capture them.
Even if they hide at the bottom of the ocean,
I will send the sea serpent after them to bite them.
4 Even if their enemies drive them into exile,
I will command the sword to kill them there.
I am determined to bring disaster upon them
and not to help them."

5 The Lord, the LORD of Heaven's Armies,
touches the land and it melts,
and all its people mourn.
The ground rises like the Nile River at floodtime,
and then it sinks again.
6 The LORD's home reaches up to the heavens,
while its foundation is on the earth.
He draws up water from the oceans
and pours it down as rain on the land.
The LORD is his name!

7 "Are you Israelites more important to me
than the Ethiopians?" asks the LORD.
"I brought Israel out of Egypt,
but I also brought the Philistines from Crete
and led the Arameans out of Kir.

8 "I, the Sovereign LORD,
am watching this sinful nation of Israel.
I will destroy it
from the face of the earth.

But I will never completely destroy the
family of Israel,"
says the LORD.
9 "For I will give the command
and will shake Israel along with the
other nations
as grain is shaken in a sieve,
yet not one true kernel will be lost.
10 But all the sinners will die by the sword—
all those who say, 'Nothing bad will
happen to us.'

A Promise of Restoration

11 "In that day I will restore the fallen house
of David.
I will repair its damaged walls.
From the ruins I will rebuild it
and restore its former glory.
12 And Israel will possess what is left
of Edom
and all the nations I have called
to be mine."
The LORD has spoken,
and he will do these things.

13 "The time will come," says the LORD,
"when the grain and grapes will grow
faster
than they can be harvested.
Then the terraced vineyards on the hills
of Israel
will drip with sweet wine!
14 I will bring my exiled people of Israel
back from distant lands,
and they will rebuild their ruined cities
and live in them again.
They will plant vineyards and gardens;
they will eat their crops and drink
their wine.
15 I will firmly plant them there
in their own land.
They will never again be uprooted
from the land I have given them,"
says the LORD your God.

OBADIAH A Little Book With a Lot to Say

Obadiah is the shortest book in the Old Testament, but don't let that fool you. It's full of big ideas. Look for

- **A NATION THAT THOUGHT IT WAS TOPS**
- **A NATION OF LOUSY NEIGHBORS**
- **A NATION THAT HEARD FROM A PROPHET**
- **A NATION ABOUT TO BE BROUGHT LOW**

OPEN WIDE!

King of the Hill

Did you ever play King of the Hill, where you stand on top of a hill and try to keep everyone else away? Well, the people who lived in Edom played a great game of King of the Hill. But it backfired on them. **Find out why in Obadiah 1:2-4.**

Time to Take Your Medicine

Had you ever heard of a nation taking medicine? No? Well, this one did. **Find out more in Obadiah 1:15-16.**

THANKS A LOT!

You're Our Neighbors?

What a neighborhood! The Edomites were the Israelites' neighbors, but they sure didn't act like it. And God was angry! **Find out why in Obadiah 1:10-11.**

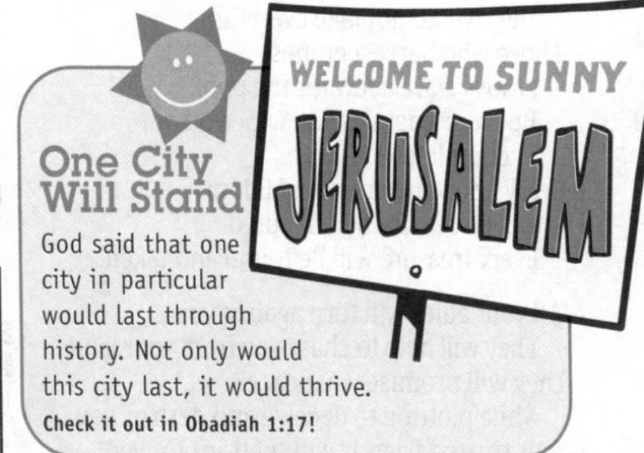

WELCOME TO SUNNY
JERUSALEM

One City Will Stand

God said that one city in particular would last through history. Not only would this city last, it would thrive. **Check it out in Obadiah 1:17!**

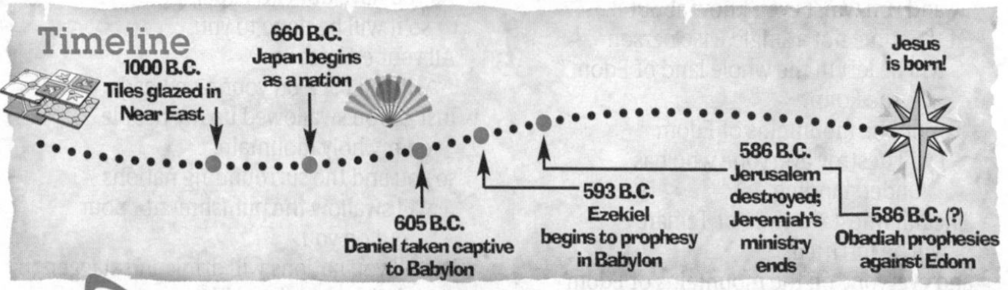

Timeline
1000 B.C. Tiles glazed in Near East
660 B.C. Japan begins as a nation
605 B.C. Daniel taken captive to Babylon
593 B.C. Ezekiel begins to prophesy in Babylon
586 B.C. Jerusalem destroyed; Jeremiah's ministry ends
586 B.C. (?) Obadiah prophesies against Edom
Jesus is born!

The JESUS CONNECTION

What God says goes. Period. End of story. Even though Edom was strong, its citizens treated the people of Judah badly. So God said that Edom would end and Judah would survive. Guess what? Edom's gone and Judah (Israel) is still there. When God says that anyone who believes in Jesus will last and everyone else will be gone, you can believe it! Believe in Jesus, and you will live with him forever in heaven.

What God says goes.

Obadiah . . . page 892

This is the vision that the Sovereign LORD revealed to Obadiah concerning the land of Edom.

Edom's Judgment Announced

We have heard a message from the LORD
that an ambassador was sent to the nations to say,
"Get ready, everyone!
Let's assemble our armies and attack Edom!"

2 The LORD says to Edom,
"I will cut you down to size among the nations;
you will be greatly despised.
3 You have been deceived by your own pride
because you live in a rock fortress
and make your home high in the mountains.
'Who can ever reach us way up here?'
you ask boastfully.
4 But even if you soar as high as eagles
and build your nest among the stars,
I will bring you crashing down,"
says the LORD.

5 "If thieves came at night and robbed you
(what a disaster awaits you!),
they would not take everything.
Those who harvest grapes
always leave a few for the poor.
But your enemies will wipe you out completely!
6 Every nook and cranny of Edom
will be searched and looted.
Every treasure will be found and taken.

7 "All your allies will turn against you.
They will help to chase you from your land.
They will promise you peace
while plotting to deceive and destroy you.
Your trusted friends will set traps for you,
and you won't even know about it.
8 At that time not a single wise person
will be left in the whole land of Edom,"
says the LORD.
"For on the mountains of Edom
I will destroy everyone who has understanding.
9 The mightiest warriors of Teman
will be terrified,
and everyone on the mountains of Edom
will be cut down in the slaughter.

Reasons for Edom's Punishment

10 "Because of the violence you did
to your close relatives in Israel,
you will be filled with shame
and destroyed forever.
11 When they were invaded,
you stood aloof, refusing to help them.
Foreign invaders carried off their wealth
and cast lots to divide up Jerusalem,
but you acted like one of Israel's enemies.

12 "You should not have gloated
when they exiled your relatives
to distant lands.
You should not have rejoiced
when the people of Judah suffered
such misfortune.
You should not have spoken arrogantly
in that terrible time of trouble.
13 You should not have plundered the land of Israel
when they were suffering such calamity.
You should not have gloated over their destruction
when they were suffering such calamity.
You should not have seized their wealth
when they were suffering such calamity.
14 You should not have stood at the crossroads,
killing those who tried to escape.
You should not have captured the survivors
and handed them over in their terrible time of trouble.

Edom Destroyed, Israel Restored

15 "The day is near when I, the LORD,
will judge all godless nations!
As you have done to Israel,
so it will be done to you.
All your evil deeds
will fall back on your own heads.
16 Just as you swallowed up my people
on my holy mountain,
so you and the surrounding nations
will swallow the punishment I pour out on you.
Yes, all you nations will drink and stagger
and disappear from history.

17 "But Jerusalem will become a refuge
for those who escape;
it will be a holy place.
And the people of Israel will come back
to reclaim their inheritance.

18 The people of Israel will be a raging fire,
and Edom a field of dry stubble.
The descendants of Joseph will be a flame
roaring across the field, devouring
everything.
There will be no survivors in Edom.
I, the LORD, have spoken!

19 "Then my people living in the Negev
will occupy the mountains of Edom.
Those living in the foothills of Judah
will possess the Philistine plains
and take over the fields of Ephraim
and Samaria.
And the people of Benjamin
will occupy the land of Gilead.
20 The exiles of Israel will return to their land
and occupy the Phoenician coast as far
north as Zarephath.
The captives from Jerusalem exiled in the
north
will return home and resettle the towns
of the Negev.
21 Those who have been rescued will go up
to Mount Zion in Jerusalem
to rule over the mountains of Edom.
And the LORD himself will be king!"

jONAH The Runaway Prophet

Look for 1 hidden message in Jonah!

Jonah was a prophet who took quite a "vacation." As you read, look for

- A BIG MISTAKE
- A BIG STORM
- A BIG FISH
- A BIG GULP
- A BIG BURP
- A BIG JOB

Gone Fishin'

It's amazing that Jonah tried to run from God and that he almost slept through the big storm. But what happened next is even *more* amazing! **Dive in, and read Jonah 1:15-17.**

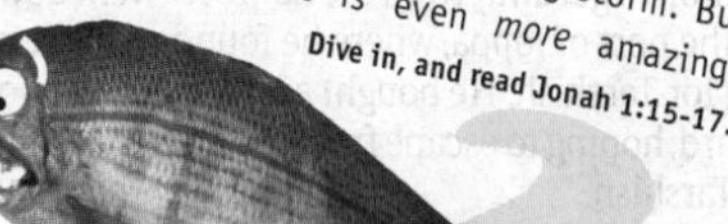

Hey, Where Ya Goin'?

God told Jonah to go preach to the people in the big bad city of Nineveh. So guess what Jonah did? (It might surprise you!) **Check it out in Jonah 1:3.**

A Major Timeout!

Jonah sat inside the fish for three days. (Bet *that* smelled great!) Would he ever get out? **Find out in Jonah 2:1-10.**

All Hands on Deck!

Jonah hopped on a boat to try to hide from God. (Duh!) God saw him, of course, and sent a big storm. The sailors were terrified, but Jonah... well, you won't believe it. **Read it yourself in Jonah 1:4-12.**

Let's Try This Again

After the fish spit Jonah onto the beach (gross!), Jonah was right back where he started. God *still* wanted him to go preach in Nineveh. Would he do it this time? **Find the answer in Jonah 3!**

Timeline

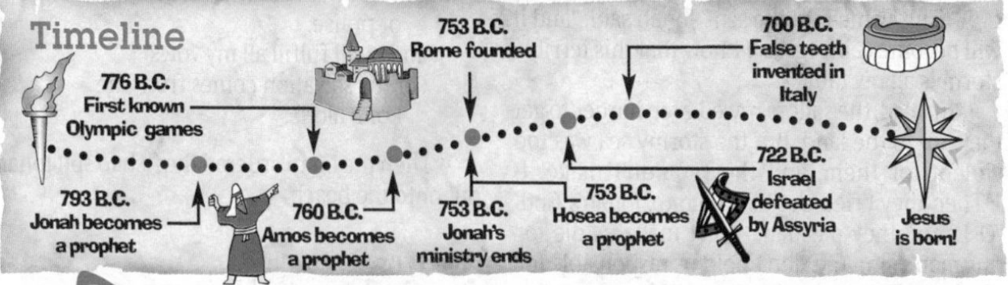
776 B.C. First known Olympic games
753 B.C. Rome founded
700 B.C. False teeth invented in Italy
793 B.C. Jonah becomes a prophet
760 B.C. Amos becomes a prophet
753 B.C. Jonah's ministry ends
753 B.C. Hosea becomes a prophet
722 B.C. Israel defeated by Assyria
Jesus is born!

The JESUS CONNECTION

After God didn't destroy Nineveh, Jonah said, "I knew that you are a merciful and compassionate God, slow to get angry and filled with unfailing love." That's God: loving, forgiving, full of second chances. He gave Jonah and Nineveh second chances. And he gives us *tons* of chances! When those who believe in Jesus ask God to forgive their sins, he does. Every time. That's why Jesus went to the cross, so we can have that kind of relationship with God!

Jonah 1 . . . page 896

CHAPTER 1
Jonah Runs from the LORD

The LORD gave this message to Jonah son of Amittai: 2 "Get up and go to the great city of Nineveh. Announce my judgment against it because I have seen how wicked its people are."

3 But Jonah got up and went in the opposite direction to get away from the LORD. He went down to the port of Joppa, where he found a ship leaving for Tarshish. He bought a ticket and went on board, hoping to escape from the LORD by sailing to Tarshish.

4 But the LORD hurled a powerful wind over the sea, causing a violent storm that threatened to break the ship apart. 5 Fearing for their lives, the desperate sailors shouted to their gods for help and threw the cargo overboard to lighten the ship.

But all this time Jonah was sound asleep down in the hold. 6 So the captain went down after him. "How can you sleep at a time like this?" he shouted. "Get up and pray to your god! Maybe he will pay attention to us and spare our lives."

7 Then the crew cast lots to see which of them had offended the gods and caused the terrible storm. When they did this, the lots identified Jonah as the culprit. 8 "Why has this awful storm come down on us?" they demanded. "Who are you? What is your line of work? What country are you from? What is your nationality?"

9 Jonah answered, "I am a Hebrew, and I worship the LORD, the God of heaven, who made the sea and the land."

10 The sailors were terrified when they heard this, for he had already told them he was running away from the LORD. "Oh, why did you do it?" they groaned. 11 And since the storm was getting worse all the time, they asked him, "What should we do to you to stop this storm?"

12 "Throw me into the sea," Jonah said, "and it will become calm again. I know that this terrible storm is all my fault."

13 Instead, the sailors rowed even harder to get the ship to the land. But the stormy sea was too violent for them, and they couldn't make it. 14 Then they cried out to the LORD, Jonah's God. "O LORD," they pleaded, "don't make us die for this man's sin. And don't hold us responsible for his death. O LORD, you have sent this storm upon him for your own good reasons."

15 Then the sailors picked Jonah up and threw him into the raging sea, and the storm stopped at once! 16 The sailors were awestruck by the LORD's great power, and they offered him a sacrifice and vowed to serve him.

17 Now the LORD had arranged for a great fish to swallow Jonah. And Jonah was inside the fish for three days and three nights.

CHAPTER 2
Jonah's Prayer

Then Jonah prayed to the LORD his God from inside the fish. 2 He said,

"I cried out to the LORD in my great trouble,
 and he answered me.
I called to you from the land of the dead,
 and LORD, you heard me!
3 You threw me into the ocean depths,
 and I sank down to the heart of the sea.
The mighty waters engulfed me;
 I was buried beneath your wild and
  stormy waves.
4 Then I said, 'O LORD, you have driven me
  from your presence.
 Yet I will look once more toward your
  holy Temple.'

5 "I sank beneath the waves,
 and the waters closed over me.
 Seaweed wrapped itself around
  my head.
6 I sank down to the very roots of the
  mountains.
 I was imprisoned in the earth,
 whose gates lock shut forever.
But you, O LORD my God,
 snatched me from the jaws of death!
7 As my life was slipping away,
 I remembered the LORD.
And my earnest prayer went out to you
 in your holy Temple.
8 Those who worship false gods
 turn their backs on all God's mercies.
9 But I will offer sacrifices to you with songs
  of praise,
 and I will fulfill all my vows.
 For my salvation comes from the
  LORD alone."

10 Then the LORD ordered the fish to spit Jonah out onto the beach.

CHAPTER 3
Jonah Goes to Nineveh

Then the LORD spoke to Jonah a second time: 2 "Get up and go to the great city of Nineveh, and deliver the message I have given you."

3 This time Jonah obeyed the LORD's command and went to Nineveh, a city so large that it took three days to see it all. 4 On the day Jonah

entered the city, he shouted to the crowds: "Forty
days from now Nineveh will be destroyed!" 5 The
people of Nineveh believed God's message, and
from the greatest to the least, they declared a fast
and put on burlap to show their sorrow.
6 When the king of Nineveh heard what Jonah
was saying, he stepped down from his throne
and took off his royal robes. He dressed himself
in burlap and sat on a heap of ashes. 7 Then the
king and his nobles sent this decree throughout
the city:

"No one, not even the animals from your
herds and flocks, may eat or drink anything
at all. 8 People and animals alike must wear
garments of mourning, and everyone must
pray earnestly to God. They must turn from
their evil ways and stop all their violence.
9 Who can tell? Perhaps even yet God will
change his mind and hold back his fierce
anger from destroying us."

10 When God saw what they had done and how
they had put a stop to their evil ways, he changed
his mind and did not carry out the destruction he
had threatened.

CHAPTER 4
Jonah's Anger at the LORD's Mercy
This change of plans greatly upset Jonah, and he
became very angry. 2 So he complained to the
LORD about it: "Didn't I say before I left home that
you would do this, LORD? That is why I ran away
to Tarshish! I knew that you are a merciful and
compassionate God, slow to get angry and filled
with unfailing love. You are eager to turn back
from destroying people. 3 Just kill me now, LORD!
I'd rather be dead than alive if what I predicted
will not happen."
4 The LORD replied, "Is it right for you to be
angry about this?"
5 Then Jonah went out to the east side of the
city and made a shelter to sit under as he waited
to see what would happen to the city. 6 And the
LORD God arranged for a leafy plant to grow
there, and soon it spread its broad leaves over
Jonah's head, shading him from the sun. This
eased his discomfort, and Jonah was very grateful for the plant.
7 But God also arranged for a worm! The next
morning at dawn the worm ate through the stem
of the plant so that it withered away. 8 And as the
sun grew hot, God arranged for a scorching east
wind to blow on Jonah. The sun beat down on his
head until he grew faint and wished to die.

Want to read a cool story? Go read JONAH 1. Then come back to make something fishy!

1 **Cut a piece of paper to look like a special diamond gemstone. Draw Jonah on this diamond shape to remind you that Jonah was a special prophet of God.**

2 **Fold the paper in half to remind you that Jonah hopped on a boat to try to hide from God.**

Check out some more second chance people in Exodus 32, Jonah 3, and Acts 3.

3 **Fold the long end down to remind you that Jonah went overboard. Then flip the paper upside down to see the fish that swallowed Jonah.**

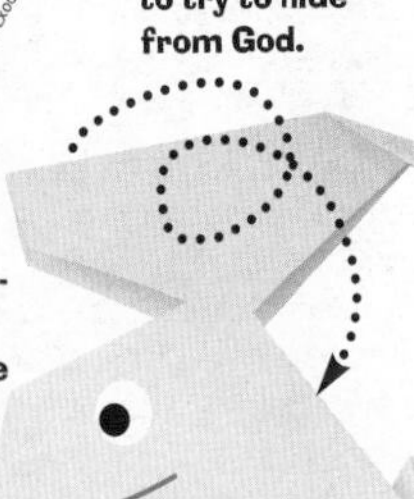

PRAY TODAY!
Now you have your very own Jonah storyteller! But that's not the end of this tale. **Read JONAH 2 to see what happened next.**

Jonah prayed to thank God for another chance to follow him.

Think about all the second chances God gives *you* to obey him. Then write a note to God on the fish's belly, thanking him for fishing you out of your troubles.

"Death is certainly better than living like this!" he
exclaimed.
9Then God said to Jonah, "Is it right for you to
be angry because the plant died?"

"Yes," Jonah retorted, "even angry enough to
die!"

10Then the LORD said, "You feel sorry about
the plant, though you did nothing to put it there.
It came quickly and died quickly. 11But Nineveh
has more than 120,000 people living in spiritual
darkness, not to mention all the animals.
Shouldn't I feel sorry for such a great city?"

MiCAH A Man of Visions

Look for 2 hidden messages in Micah!

Micah was another prophet who told the people to turn back to God. He also told about

- **HOW BAD IT WOULD BE IF THEY DIDN'T**
- **HOW SOMETHING GOOD WOULD COME OUT OF BETHLEHEM**
- **HOW GREAT JESUS WOULD BE**
- **HOW AWESOME IT WILL BE WHEN HE RETURNS**

The Future Looks Good!

Micah told the people what it will be like when God reigns over his perfect kingdom. **Get a glimpse of what's still to come by reading Micah 4:1-4. Sounds pretty good, huh?**

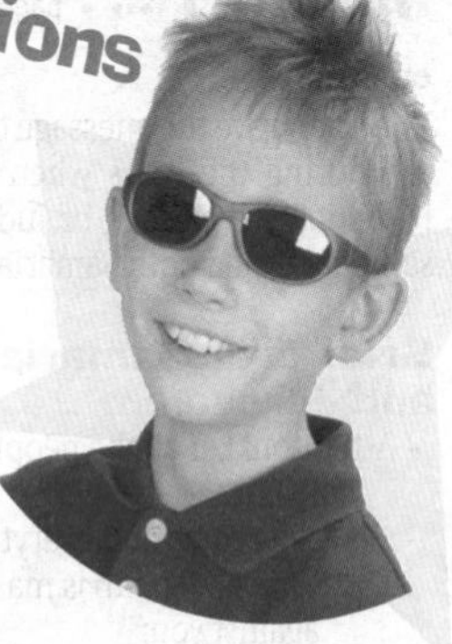

It's Time!

God told Micah through a vision that the time had come for action. What kind of action? Where was the action going to be? **Find out in Micah 1:1-5.**

Reap What You Sow

God said that the rich people who had treated others badly were in for a bad time themselves. **Find out how bad in Micah 2:1-5.**

A Big Deal From Bethlehem

Micah predicted that the tiny village of Bethlehem in Judah would become a big center of attention in the future. Find out why in Micah 5:2-5. **(Not sure who Micah's talking about? Find out more in the Jesus Connection below!)**

Coming Soon!
Bethlehem As Birthplace

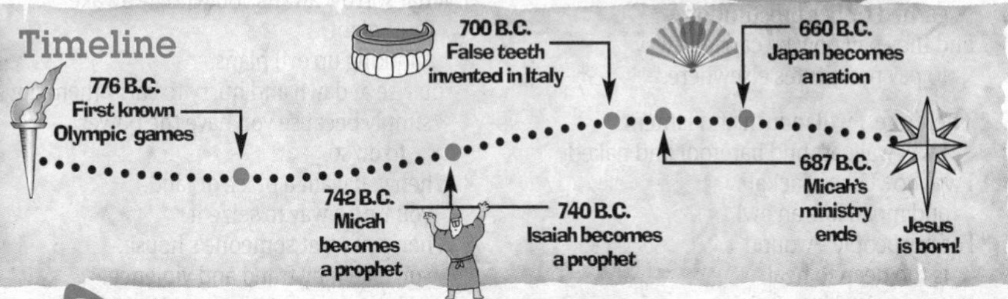
Timeline
776 B.C. First known Olympic games
742 B.C. Micah becomes a prophet
740 B.C. Isaiah becomes a prophet
700 B.C. False teeth invented in Italy
687 B.C. Micah's ministry ends
660 B.C. Japan becomes a nation
Jesus is born!

The JESUS CONNECTION

Through Micah, God told about some powerful events long before they happened. Micah prophesied that Jesus would be born in Bethlehem. (He was!) He said that Jesus would be the source of our peace (He is! Check out what Jesus said in John 14:27.) And he said that Jesus would come back to rule in the last days in a perfect, peaceful kingdom. (**He will! You can count on it!**)

Micah 1 . . . page 900

CHAPTER 1

The LORD gave this message to Micah of Moresheth during the years when Jotham, Ahaz, and Hezekiah were kings of Judah. The visions he saw concerned both Samaria and Jerusalem.

Grief over Samaria and Jerusalem

2 Attention! Let all the people of the world
listen!
Let the earth and everything in it hear.
The Sovereign LORD is making accusations
against you;
the Lord speaks from his holy Temple.
3 Look! The LORD is coming!
He leaves his throne in heaven
and tramples the heights of the earth.
4 The mountains melt beneath his feet
and flow into the valleys
like wax in a fire,
like water pouring down a hill.
5 And why is this happening?
Because of the rebellion of Israel—
yes, the sins of the whole nation.
Who is to blame for Israel's rebellion?
Samaria, its capital city!
Where is the center of idolatry in Judah?
In Jerusalem, its capital!

6 "So I, the LORD, will make the city of Samaria
a heap of ruins.
Her streets will be plowed up
for planting vineyards.
I will roll the stones of her walls into the
valley below,
exposing her foundations.
7 All her carved images will be smashed.
All her sacred treasures will be burned.
These things were bought with the money
earned by her prostitution,
and they will now be carried away
to pay prostitutes elsewhere."

8 Therefore, I will mourn and lament.
I will walk around barefoot and naked.
I will howl like a jackal
and moan like an owl.
9 For my people's wound
is too deep to heal.
It has reached into Judah,
even to the gates of Jerusalem.

10 Don't tell our enemies in Gath;
don't weep at all.
You people in Beth-leaphrah,
roll in the dust to show your despair.
11 You people in Shaphir,
go as captives into exile—naked and
ashamed.
The people of Zaanan
dare not come outside their walls.
The people of Beth-ezel mourn,
for their house has no support.
12 The people of Maroth anxiously wait for
relief,
but only bitterness awaits them
as the LORD's judgment reaches
even to the gates of Jerusalem.

13 Harness your chariot horses and flee,
you people of Lachish.
You were the first city in Judah
to follow Israel in her rebellion,
and you led Jerusalem into sin.
14 Send farewell gifts to Moresheth-gath;
there is no hope of saving it.
The town of Aczib
has deceived the kings of Israel.
15 O people of Mareshah,
I will bring a conqueror to capture
your town.
And the leaders of Israel
will go to Adullam.

16 Oh, people of Judah, shave your heads
in sorrow,
for the children you love will be snatched
away.
Make yourselves as bald as a vulture,
for your little ones will be exiled to distant
lands.

CHAPTER 2

Judgment against Wealthy Oppressors

1 What sorrow awaits you who lie awake
at night,
thinking up evil plans.
You rise at dawn and hurry to carry them out,
simply because you have the power
to do so.
2 When you want a piece of land,
you find a way to seize it.
When you want someone's house,
you take it by fraud and violence.
You cheat a man of his property,
stealing his family's inheritance.

3 But this is what the LORD says:
"I will reward your evil with evil;
you won't be able to pull your neck out
of the noose.

You will no longer walk around proudly,
for it will be a terrible time."

4 In that day your enemies will make fun
of you
by singing this song of despair about you:
"We are finished,
completely ruined!
God has confiscated our land,
taking it from us.
He has given our fields
to those who betrayed us."
5 Others will set your boundaries then,
and the LORD's people will have no say
in how the land is divided.

True and False Prophets

6 "Don't say such things,"
the people respond.
"Don't prophesy like that.
Such disasters will never come our way!"

7 Should you talk that way, O family of Israel?
Will the LORD's Spirit have patience with
such behavior?
If you would do what is right,
you would find my words comforting.
8 Yet to this very hour
my people rise against me like an enemy!
You steal the shirts right off the backs
of those who trusted you,
making them as ragged as men
returning from battle.
9 You have evicted women from their pleasant
homes
and forever stripped their children of all
that God would give them.
10 Up! Begone!
This is no longer your land and home,
for you have filled it with sin
and ruined it completely.
11 Suppose a prophet full of lies would say
to you,
"I'll preach to you the joys of wine and
alcohol!"
That's just the kind of prophet you would
like!

Hope for Restoration

12 "Someday, O Israel, I will gather you;
I will gather the remnant who are left.
I will bring you together again like sheep
in a pen,
like a flock in its pasture.
Yes, your land will again
be filled with noisy crowds!
13 Your leader will break out
and lead you out of exile,
out through the gates of the enemy cities,
back to your own land.
Your king will lead you;
the LORD himself will guide you."

CHAPTER 3

Judgment against Israel's Leaders

1 I said, "Listen, you leaders of Israel!
You are supposed to know right from
wrong,
2 but you are the very ones
who hate good and love evil.
You skin my people alive
and tear the flesh from their bones.
3 Yes, you eat my people's flesh,
strip off their skin,
and break their bones.
You chop them up
like meat for the cooking pot.
4 Then you beg the LORD for help in times
of trouble!
Do you really expect him to answer?
After all the evil you have done,
he won't even look at you!"

5 This is what the LORD says:
"You false prophets are leading my people
astray!
You promise peace for those who give you
food,
but you declare war on those who refuse
to feed you.
6 Now the night will close around you,
cutting off all your visions.
Darkness will cover you,
putting an end to your predictions.
The sun will set for you prophets,
and your day will come to an end.
7 Then you seers will be put to shame,
and you fortune-tellers will be disgraced.
And you will cover your faces
because there is no answer from God."

8 But as for me, I am filled with power—
with the Spirit of the LORD.
I am filled with justice and strength
to boldly declare Israel's sin and rebellion.
9 Listen to me, you leaders of Israel!
You hate justice and twist all that is right.
10 You are building Jerusalem
on a foundation of murder and
corruption.

Micah 4 . . . page 902

Who's President?

OK, here's a challenge.

Make a prediction. Who will be the president of the United States 400 years from now? Don't know?

What about *this* amazing prediction? God told the prophet Micah that Jesus, the Messiah, was coming. Not only that, God even told him *where* Jesus would be born. **You can read it in MICAH 5:2.**

Next time you wonder if God knows your future, read Jeremiah 29:11!

God's in control of your future too.

1. **Make 10 predictions about your future for the next six months.** How do you think your soccer team will do this season? What teachers will you have at school?
2. **Hide your list.** After six months, take out your list to see if your predictions were right.

Were you right? wrong? You were just guessing what would happen in the future. But God *knows*! He never has to guess.

Take a minute and pray, thanking God for being in charge of all of your tomorrows.

11 You rulers make decisions based on bribes;
you priests teach God's laws only
for a price;
you prophets won't prophesy unless you
are paid.
Yet all of you claim to depend on the LORD.
"No harm can come to us," you say,
"for the LORD is here among us."
12 Because of you, Mount Zion will be plowed
like an open field;
Jerusalem will be reduced to ruins!
A thicket will grow on the heights
where the Temple now stands.

CHAPTER 4

The LORD's Future Reign

1 In the last days, the mountain of the
LORD's house
will be the highest of all—
the most important place on earth.
It will be raised above the other hills,
and people from all over the world will
stream there to worship.
2 People from many nations will come and say,
"Come, let us go up to the mountain of
the LORD,
to the house of Jacob's God.
There he will teach us his ways,
and we will walk in his paths."
For the LORD's teaching will go out from Zion;
his word will go out from Jerusalem.
3 The LORD will mediate between peoples
and will settle disputes between strong
nations far away.
They will hammer their swords into
plowshares
and their spears into pruning hooks.
Nation will no longer fight against nation,
nor train for war anymore.
4 Everyone will live in peace and prosperity,
enjoying their own grapevines and
fig trees,
for there will be nothing to fear.
The LORD of Heaven's Armies
has made this promise!
5 Though the nations around us follow
their idols,
we will follow the LORD our God forever
and ever.

Israel's Return from Exile

6 "In that coming day," says the LORD,
"I will gather together those who are lame,
those who have been exiles,
and those whom I have filled with grief.

7 Those who are weak will survive as
a remnant;
those who were exiles will become
a strong nation.
Then I, the LORD, will rule from Jerusalem
as their king forever."
8 As for you, Jerusalem,
the citadel of God's people,
your royal might and power
will come back to you again.
The kingship will be restored
to my precious Jerusalem.

9 But why are you now screaming in terror?
Have you no king to lead you?
Have your wise people all died?
Pain has gripped you like a woman
in childbirth.
10 Writhe and groan like a woman in labor,
you people of Jerusalem,
for now you must leave this city
to live in the open country.
You will soon be sent in exile
to distant Babylon.
But the LORD will rescue you there;
he will redeem you from the grip
of your enemies.

11 Now many nations have gathered against you.
"Let her be desecrated," they say.
"Let us see the destruction of Jerusalem."
12 But they do not know the LORD's thoughts
or understand his plan.
These nations don't know
that he is gathering them together
to be beaten and trampled
like sheaves of grain on a threshing floor.
13 "Rise up and crush the nations, O Jerusalem!"
says the LORD.
"For I will give you iron horns and bronze
hooves,
so you can trample many nations to pieces.
You will present their stolen riches to
the LORD,
their wealth to the Lord of all the earth."

CHAPTER 5

1 Mobilize! Marshal your troops!
The enemy is laying siege to Jerusalem.
They will strike Israel's leader
in the face with a rod.

A Ruler from Bethlehem

2 But you, O Bethlehem Ephrathah,
are only a small village among all the
people of Judah.
Yet a ruler of Israel,
whose origins are in the distant past,
will come from you on my behalf.
3 The people of Israel will be abandoned
to their enemies
until the woman in labor gives birth.
Then at last his fellow countrymen
will return from exile to their own land.
4 And he will stand to lead his flock with the
LORD's strength,
in the majesty of the name of the LORD
his God.
Then his people will live there undisturbed,
for he will be highly honored around
the world.
5 And he will be the source of peace.

When the Assyrians invade our land
and break through our defenses,
we will appoint seven rulers to watch over us,
eight princes to lead us.
6 They will rule Assyria with drawn swords
and enter the gates of the land of Nimrod.
He will rescue us from the Assyrians
when they pour over the borders to invade
our land.

The Remnant Purified

7 Then the remnant left in Israel
will take their place among the nations.
They will be like dew sent by the LORD
or like rain falling on the grass,
which no one can hold back
and no one can restrain.
8 The remnant left in Israel
will take their place among the nations.
They will be like a lion among the animals
of the forest,
like a strong young lion among flocks
of sheep and goats,
pouncing and tearing as they go
with no rescuer in sight.
9 The people of Israel will stand up to
their foes,
and all their enemies will be wiped out.

10 "In that day," says the LORD,
"I will slaughter your horses
and destroy your chariots.
11 I will tear down your walls
and demolish your defenses.
12 I will put an end to all witchcraft,
and there will be no more fortune-tellers.
13 I will destroy all your idols and sacred pillars,
so you will never again worship the work
of your own hands.

14 I will abolish your idol shrines with their
Asherah poles
and destroy your pagan cities.
15 I will pour out my vengeance
on all the nations that refuse to obey me."

CHAPTER 6

The LORD's Case against Israel

Listen to what the LORD is saying:

"Stand up and state your case against me.
Let the mountains and hills be called to
witness your complaints.
2 And now, O mountains,
listen to the LORD's complaint!
He has a case against his people.
He will bring charges against Israel.

3 "O my people, what have I done to you?
What have I done to make you tired
of me?
Answer me!
4 For I brought you out of Egypt
and redeemed you from slavery.
I sent Moses, Aaron, and Miriam
to help you.
5 Don't you remember, my people,
how King Balak of Moab tried to have
you cursed
and how Balaam son of Beor blessed
you instead?
And remember your journey from Acacia
Grove to Gilgal,
when I, the LORD, did everything I could
to teach you about my faithfulness."

6 What can we bring to the LORD?
Should we bring him burnt offerings?
Should we bow before God Most High
with offerings of yearling calves?
7 Should we offer him thousands of rams
and ten thousand rivers of olive oil?
Should we sacrifice our firstborn children
to pay for our sins?

8 No, O people, the LORD has told you what
is good,
and **this is what he requires
of you:
to do what is right, to love
mercy,
and to walk humbly with
your God.**

Israel's Guilt and Punishment

9 Fear the LORD if you are wise!
His voice calls to everyone in Jerusalem:
"The armies of destruction are coming;
the LORD is sending them.
10 What shall I say about the homes of
the wicked
filled with treasures gained by cheating?
What about the disgusting practice
of measuring out grain with dishonest
measures?
11 How can I tolerate your merchants
who use dishonest scales and weights?
12 The rich among you have become wealthy
through extortion and violence.
Your citizens are so used to lying
that their tongues can no longer tell
the truth.

13 "Therefore, I will wound you!
I will bring you to ruin for all your sins.
14 You will eat but never have enough.
Your hunger pangs and emptiness
will remain.
And though you try to save your money,
it will come to nothing in the end.
You will save a little,
but I will give it to those who conquer you.
15 You will plant crops
but not harvest them.
You will press your olives
but not get enough oil to anoint
yourselves.
You will trample the grapes
but get no juice to make your wine.
16 You keep only the laws of evil King Omri;
you follow only the example of wicked
King Ahab!
Therefore, I will make an example of you,
bringing you to complete ruin.
You will be treated with contempt,
mocked by all who see you."

CHAPTER 7

Misery Turned to Hope

1 How miserable I am!
I feel like the fruit picker after the harvest
who can find nothing to eat.
Not a cluster of grapes or a single early fig
can be found to satisfy my hunger.
2 The godly people have all disappeared;
not one honest person is left on the earth.
They are all murderers,
setting traps even for their own brothers.
3 Both their hands are equally skilled at
doing evil!
Officials and judges alike demand bribes.

"This is what he requires of you: to do what is right, to love mercy, and to walk humbly with your God."—MICAH 6:8b

It All Adds Up
Do Right
+ Love Mercy
+ Walk Humbly With God

What God Wants

Read MICAH 6:8b out loud.

The prophet Micah wanted to let people know three things that make God happy. Use this verse as *your* guide for making God happy.

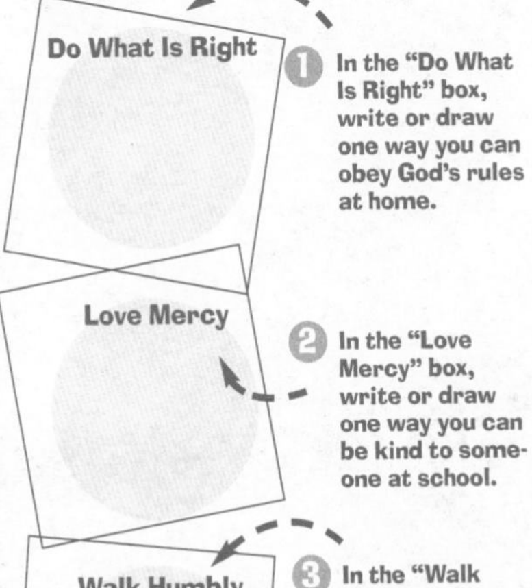

1 In the "Do What Is Right" box, write or draw one way you can obey God's rules at home.

2 In the "Love Mercy" box, write or draw one way you can be kind to someone at school.

3 In the "Walk Humbly With Your God" box, write or draw one way that you can get to know God better.

Read Mark 12:29-31 for more about how to please God.

Ask God to help you follow through on these three goals this week. God loves it when we try to make him happy. And God wants you to succeed!

The people with influence get what
they want,
and together they scheme to twist justice.
4 Even the best of them is like a brier;
the most honest is as dangerous as
a hedge of thorns.
But your judgment day is coming swiftly now.
Your time of punishment is here, a time
of confusion.
5 Don't trust anyone—
not your best friend or even your wife!
6 For the son despises his father.
The daughter defies her mother.
The daughter-in-law defies her mother-
in-law.
Your enemies are right in your own
household!

7 As for me, I look to the LORD for help.
I wait confidently for God to save me,
and my God will certainly hear me.
8 Do not gloat over me, my enemies!
For though I fall, I will rise again.
Though I sit in darkness,
the LORD will be my light.
9 I will be patient as the LORD punishes me,
for I have sinned against him.
But after that, he will take up my case
and give me justice for all I have suffered
from my enemies.
The LORD will bring me into the light,
and I will see his righteousness.
10 Then my enemies will see that the LORD
is on my side.
They will be ashamed that they taunted
me, saying,
"So where is the LORD—
that God of yours?"
With my own eyes I will see their downfall;
they will be trampled like mud in the
streets.

11 In that day, Israel, your cities will be rebuilt,
and your borders will be extended.
12 People from many lands will come and honor
you—
from Assyria all the way to the towns
of Egypt,
from Egypt all the way to the Euphrates River,
and from distant seas and mountains.
13 But the land will become empty and
desolate
because of the wickedness of those
who live there.

Micah 7 . . . page 906

The Lord's Compassion on Israel

14 O Lord, protect your people with your
shepherd's staff;
lead your flock, your special possession.
Though they live alone in a thicket
on the heights of Mount Carmel,
let them graze in the fertile pastures
of Bashan and Gilead
as they did long ago.

15 "Yes," says the Lord,
"I will do mighty miracles for you,
like those I did when I rescued you
from slavery in Egypt."

16 All the nations of the world will stand amazed
at what the Lord will do for you.
They will be embarrassed
at their feeble power.
They will cover their mouths in silent awe,
deaf to everything around them.
17 Like snakes crawling from their holes,
they will come out to meet the Lord
our God.
They will fear him greatly,
trembling in terror at his presence.

18 Where is another God like you,
who pardons the guilt of the remnant,
overlooking the sins of his special
people?
You will not stay angry with your people
forever,
because you delight in showing
unfailing love.
19 Once again you will have compassion on us.
You will trample our sins under your feet
and throw them into the depths of
the ocean!
20 You will show us your faithfulness and
unfailing love
as you promised to our ancestors
Abraham and Jacob long ago.

NAHUM

Look for 1 hidden message in Nahum!

God sent the prophet Nahum to preach against the city of Nineveh. In Nahum, look for

- **NASTY NINEVEH**
- **BAD NEWS FROM NAHUM**
- **A NIGHTMARE PREDICTED**
- **GOOD NEWS FOR JUDAH**

Welcome to Nineveh
Idols for sale

Nineveh's Time Is Up!

NINEVEH

On the Run

Nahum told the people of Nineveh that God was getting ready to punish them—big time! **Find out more in Nahum 2:3-6.**

No Lyin', Lion!

Nineveh was once proud and powerful, like a mighty lion. But all that was about to change. **See what Nahum predicted in Nahum 2:11-13.**

That Didn't Last Long...

About a hundred years before the prophet Nahum, the prophet Jonah preached in Nineveh. After the people heard Jonah, they repented. So why did God tell Nahum to preach in Nineveh *again*? **Find out in Nahum 1:9-14.**

GOOD NEWS

Justice for Judah

Assyria, the most powerful country on earth, had already conquered the northern kingdom of Israel. Now they were causing a lot of trouble in Judah, the southern kingdom. But Nahum brought good news. **Discover what it was in Nahum 1:15.**

Timeline

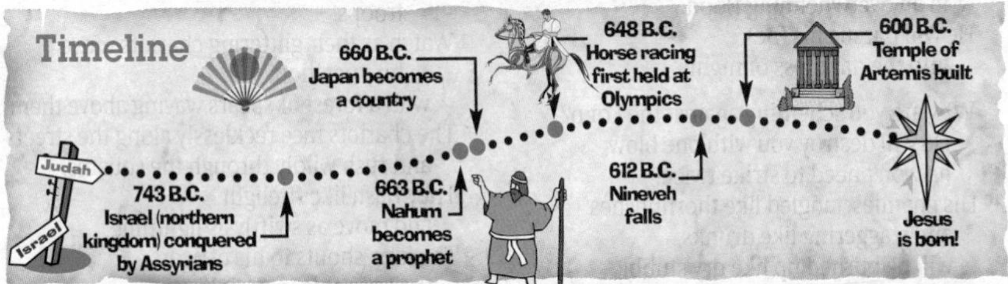

Judah
Israel
743 B.C. Israel (northern kingdom) conquered by Assyrians
660 B.C. Japan becomes a country
663 B.C. Nahum becomes a prophet
648 B.C. Horse racing first held at Olympics
612 B.C. Nineveh falls
600 B.C. Temple of Artemis built
Jesus is born!

The JESUS CONNECTION

Ever wonder what the world would be like if God hadn't sent his Son, Jesus? The book of Nahum shows how God is angry toward sin. But Jesus came to take the punishment for our sins upon himself. If we believe in Jesus, our sins are forgiven and we experience God's love all through our lives. Jesus can be our best friend! **And then, we can live with him forever in heaven.**

Nahum 1 . . . page 908

CHAPTER 1

This message concerning Nineveh came as a vision to Nahum, who lived in Elkosh.

The LORD's Anger against Nineveh

2 The LORD is a jealous God,
filled with vengeance and rage.
He takes revenge on all who oppose him
and continues to rage against his enemies!
3 The LORD is slow to get angry, but his power
is great,
and he never lets the guilty go
unpunished.
He displays his power in the whirlwind
and the storm.
The billowing clouds are the dust beneath
his feet.
4 At his command the oceans dry up,
and the rivers disappear.
The lush pastures of Bashan and
Carmel fade,
and the green forests of Lebanon wither.
5 In his presence the mountains quake,
and the hills melt away;
the earth trembles,
and its people are destroyed.
6 Who can stand before his fierce anger?
Who can survive his burning fury?
His rage blazes forth like fire,
and the mountains crumble to dust
in his presence.

7 The LORD is good,
a strong refuge when trouble
comes.
He is close to those who trust
in him.
8 But he will sweep away his enemies
in an overwhelming flood.
He will pursue his foes
into the darkness of night.

9 Why are you scheming against the LORD?
He will destroy you with one blow;
he won't need to strike twice!
10 His enemies, tangled like thornbushes
and staggering like drunks,
will be burned up like dry stubble
in a field.
11 Who is this wicked counselor of yours
who plots evil against the LORD?

12 This is what the LORD says:
"Though the Assyrians have many allies,
they will be destroyed and disappear.
O my people, I have punished you before,
but I will not punish you again.
13 Now I will break the yoke of bondage
from your neck
and tear off the chains of Assyrian
oppression."

14 And this is what the LORD says concerning
the Assyrians in Nineveh:
"You will have no more children to carry
on your name.
I will destroy all the idols in the temples
of your gods.
I am preparing a grave for you
because you are despicable!"

15 Look! A messenger is coming over the
mountains with good news!
He is bringing a message of peace.
Celebrate your festivals, O people of Judah,
and fulfill all your vows,
for your wicked enemies will never invade
your land again.
They will be completely destroyed!

CHAPTER 2

The Fall of Nineveh

1 Your enemy is coming to crush you,
Nineveh.
Man the ramparts! Watch the roads!
Prepare your defenses! Call out your
forces!

2 Even though the destroyer has destroyed
Judah,
the LORD will restore its honor.
Israel's vine has been stripped of branches,
but he will restore its splendor.
3 Shields flash red in the sunlight!
See the scarlet uniforms of the valiant
troops!
Watch as their glittering chariots move
into position,
with a forest of spears waving above them.
4 The chariots race recklessly along the streets
and rush wildly through the squares.
They flash like firelight
and move as swiftly as lightning.
5 The king shouts to his officers;
they stumble in their haste,
rushing to the walls to set up their
defenses.
6 The river gates have been torn open!
The palace is about to collapse!
7 Nineveh's exile has been decreed,
and all the servant girls mourn its capture.

They moan like doves
and beat their breasts in sorrow.
8 Nineveh is like a leaking water reservoir!
The people are slipping away.
"Stop, stop!" someone shouts,
but no one even looks back.
9 Loot the silver!
Plunder the gold!
There's no end to Nineveh's treasures—
its vast, uncounted wealth.
10 Soon the city is plundered, empty,
and ruined.
Hearts melt and knees shake.
The people stand aghast,
their faces pale and trembling.

11 Where now is that great Nineveh,
that den filled with young lions?
It was a place where people—like lions
and their cubs—
walked freely and without fear.
12 The lion tore up meat for his cubs
and strangled prey for his mate.
He filled his den with prey,
his caverns with his plunder.

13 "I am your enemy!"
says the LORD of Heaven's Armies.
"Your chariots will soon go up in smoke.
Your young men will be killed in battle.
Never again will you plunder conquered
nations.
The voices of your proud messengers
will be heard no more."

CHAPTER 3
The LORD's Judgment against Nineveh

1 What sorrow awaits Nineveh,
the city of murder and lies!
She is crammed with wealth
and is never without victims.
2 Hear the crack of whips,
the rumble of wheels!
Horses' hooves pound,
and chariots clatter wildly.
3 See the flashing swords and glittering spears
as the charioteers charge past!
There are countless casualties,
heaps of bodies—
so many bodies that
people stumble over them.
4 All this because Nineveh,
the beautiful and faithless city,
mistress of deadly charms,
enticed the nations with her beauty.

Key Verse **"The LORD is good, a strong refuge when trouble comes. He is close to those who trust in him."—NAHUM 1:7**

God's My Home Base

You know how when you play Hide and Seek, there's one place where you're safe? Home base is your safe place, your refuge. (See? You learned a new word—a *refuge* is a safe place!)

A refuge can be wherever you feel safe, kind of like a home base. And the safest "place" of all is with God! **Read NAHUM 1:7 out loud so you remember where your home base should be!**

GOD WANTS TO BE OUR HOME BASE!

1. **Write, "God Is My Home Base" in the center of a sheet of poster board.**

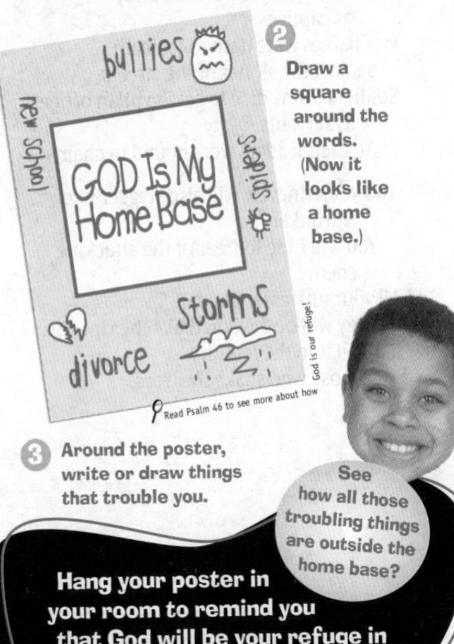

2. **Draw a square around the words. (Now it looks like a home base.)**
3. **Around the poster, write or draw things that trouble you.**

See how all those troubling things are outside the home base?

Hang your poster in your room to remind you that God will be your refuge in times of trouble!

She taught them all her magic,
enchanting people everywhere.
5 "I am your enemy!"
says the LORD of Heaven's Armies.
"And now I will lift your skirts
and show all the earth your nakedness
and shame.
6 I will cover you with filth
and show the world how vile you
really are.
7 All who see you will shrink back and say,
'Nineveh lies in ruins.
Where are the mourners?'
Does anyone regret your destruction?"

8 Are you any better than the city of Thebes,
situated on the Nile River, surrounded
by water?
She was protected by the river
on all sides,
walled in by water.
9 Ethiopia and the land of Egypt
gave unlimited assistance.
The nations of Put and Libya
were among her allies.
10 Yet Thebes fell,
and her people were led away
as captives.
Her babies were dashed to death
against the stones of the streets.
Soldiers threw dice to get Egyptian officers
as servants.
All their leaders were bound in chains.

11 And you, Nineveh, will also stagger like
a drunkard.
You will hide for fear of the attacking
enemy.
12 All your fortresses will fall.
They will be devoured like the ripe figs
that fall into the mouths
of those who shake the trees.
13 Your troops will be as weak
and helpless as women.
The gates of your land will be opened
wide to the enemy
and set on fire and burned.
14 Get ready for the siege!
Store up water!
Strengthen the defenses!
Go into the pits to trample clay,
and pack it into molds,
making bricks to repair the walls.

15 But the fire will devour you;
the sword will cut you down.
The enemy will consume you like locusts,
devouring everything they see.
There will be no escape,
even if you multiply like swarming locusts.
16 Your merchants have multiplied
until they outnumber the stars.
But like a swarm of locusts,
they strip the land and fly away.
17 Your guards and officials are also like
swarming locusts
that crowd together in the hedges
on a cold day.
But like locusts that fly away when the
sun comes up,
all of them will fly away and disappear.

18 Your shepherds are asleep,
O Assyrian king;
your princes lie dead in the dust.
Your people are scattered across the
mountains
with no one to gather them together.
19 There is no healing for your wound;
your injury is fatal.
All who hear of your destruction
will clap their hands for joy.
Where can anyone be found
who has not suffered from your
continual cruelty?

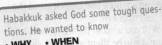

HABAKKUK Tough Questions, Tough Answers

Habakkuk asked God some tough questions. He wanted to know
- WHY
- WHEN
- WHO
- HOW

AND YES, GOD ANSWERED!

Ahem... Are You Listening?

Have you ever felt like maybe God wasn't paying attention to you? That's OK—the prophet Habakkuk felt the same way once. **Read what he said to God in Habakkuk 1:1-4.**

You're Gonna What?!?

Habakkuk couldn't believe what God said he was going to do. So he had to ask God just one question. Well, actually it was *more* than one. **Read all of Habakkuk's questions in Habakkuk 1:12-17.**

TIME OUT!

God's Game Plan

Habakkuk asked God why there was so much sin and misery in the world. God's answer must have surprised him. **Read what God said in Habakkuk 1:5-11.**

The Game's Not Over

Habakkuk was worried that the Babylonians would get away with all their evil deeds. "Not to worry!" God said, although not in those exact words. **Read God's *real* words in Habakkuk 2:4-14.**

What a Wonderful God!

After Habakkuk's vision from God, the prophet was struck with God's glory. **Read his amazing words of worship in Habakkuk 3!**

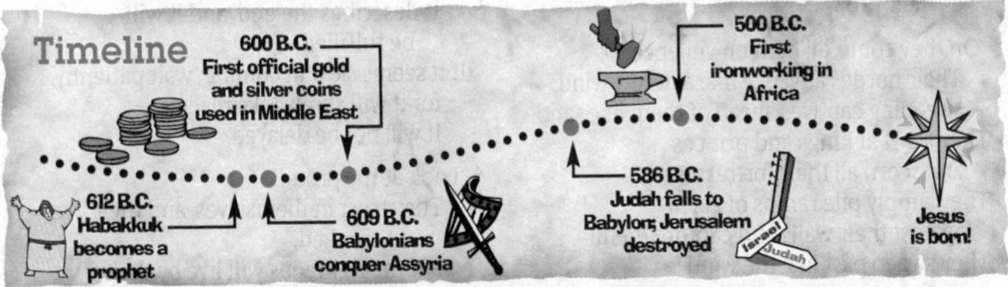
Timeline
612 B.C. Habakkuk becomes a prophet
609 B.C. Babylonians conquer Assyria
600 B.C. First official gold and silver coins used in Middle East
586 B.C. Judah falls to Babylon; Jerusalem destroyed
Israel
Judah
500 B.C. First ironworking in Africa
Jesus is born!

The JESUS CONNECTION

Habakkuk's conversation with God is unusual. Often, the prophets simply told the people what God said. But here we actually witness Habakkuk's conversation with God. Habakkuk gives us a great example of how to talk to God.

Like Habakkuk, Jesus carries the great message and lesson of prayer. Jesus says how important it is to keep connected with God the Father, and Jesus himself did that through prayer. In fact, **Jesus taught his disciples to pray in Matthew 6:9-13! Take a look for yourself!**

Habakkuk 1 . . . page 912

CHAPTER 1

This is the message that the prophet Habakkuk received in a vision.

Habakkuk's Complaint

2 How long, O LORD, must I call for help?
But you do not listen!
"Violence is everywhere!" I cry,
but you do not come to save.
3 Must I forever see these evil deeds?
Why must I watch all this misery?
Wherever I look,
I see destruction and violence.
I am surrounded by people
who love to argue and fight.
4 The law has become paralyzed,
and there is no justice in the courts.
The wicked far outnumber the righteous,
so that justice has become perverted.

The LORD's Reply

5 The LORD replied,

"Look around at the nations;
look and be amazed!
For I am doing something in your own day,
something you wouldn't believe
even if someone told you about it.
6 I am raising up the Babylonians,
a cruel and violent people.
They will march across the world
and conquer other lands.
7 They are notorious for their cruelty
and do whatever they like.
8 Their horses are swifter than cheetahs
and fiercer than wolves at dusk.
Their charioteers charge from far away.
Like eagles, they swoop down to devour
their prey.

9 "On they come, all bent on violence.
Their hordes advance like a desert wind,
sweeping captives ahead of them like sand.
10 They scoff at kings and princes
and scorn all their fortresses.
They simply pile ramps of earth
against their walls and capture them!
11 They sweep past like the wind
and are gone.
But they are deeply guilty,
for their own strength is their god."

Habakkuk's Second Complaint

12 O LORD my God, my Holy One, you who
are eternal—
surely you do not plan to wipe us out?
O LORD, our Rock, you have sent these
Babylonians to correct us,
to punish us for our many sins.
13 But you are pure and cannot stand the
sight of evil.
Will you wink at their treachery?
Should you be silent while the wicked
swallow up people more righteous
than they?

14 Are we only fish to be caught and killed?
Are we only sea creatures that have
no leader?
15 Must we be strung up on their hooks
and caught in their nets while they rejoice
and celebrate?
16 Then they will worship their nets
and burn incense in front of them.
"These nets are the gods who have made
us rich!"
they will claim.
17 Will you let them get away with
this forever?
Will they succeed forever in their
heartless conquests?

CHAPTER 2

1 I will climb up to my watchtower
and stand at my guardpost.
There I will wait to see what the LORD says
and how he will answer my complaint.

The LORD's Second Reply

2 Then the LORD said to me,

"Write my answer plainly on tablets,
so that a runner can carry the correct
message to others.
3 This vision is for a future time.
It describes the end, and it will
be fulfilled.
If it seems slow in coming, wait patiently,
for it will surely take place.
It will not be delayed.

4 "Look at the proud!
They trust in themselves, and their lives
are crooked.
But the righteous will live by their
faithfulness to God.
5 Wealth is treacherous,
and the arrogant are never at rest.
They open their mouths as wide as the grave,
and like death, they are never satisfied.
In their greed they have gathered up
many nations
and swallowed many peoples.

20 But the LORD is in his holy Temple.
Let all the earth be silent before him."

CHAPTER 3

Habakkuk's Prayer

This prayer was sung by the prophet Habakkuk:

2 I have heard all about you, LORD.
I am filled with awe by your amazing works.
In this time of our deep need,
help us again as you did in years gone by.
And in your anger,
remember your mercy.

3 I see God moving across the deserts
from Edom,
the Holy One coming from Mount Paran.
His brilliant splendor fills the heavens,
and the earth is filled with his praise.
4 His coming is as brilliant as the sunrise.
Rays of light flash from his hands,
where his awesome power is hidden.
5 Pestilence marches before him;
plague follows close behind.
6 When he stops, the earth shakes.
When he looks, the nations tremble.
He shatters the everlasting mountains
and levels the eternal hills.
He is the Eternal One!
7 I see the people of Cushan in distress,
and the nation of Midian trembling
in terror.

8 Was it in anger, LORD, that you struck
the rivers
and parted the sea?
Were you displeased with them?
No, you were sending your chariots
of salvation!
9 You brandished your bow
and your quiver of arrows.
You split open the earth with
flowing rivers.
10 The mountains watched and trembled.
Onward swept the raging waters.
The mighty deep cried out,
lifting its hands in submission.
11 The sun and moon stood still in the sky
as your brilliant arrows flew
and your glittering spear flashed.

12 You marched across the land in anger
and trampled the nations in your fury.
13 You went out to rescue your chosen people,
to save your anointed ones.
You crushed the heads of the wicked
and stripped their bones from head
to toe.
14 With his own weapons,
you destroyed the chief of those
who rushed out like a whirlwind,
thinking Israel would be easy prey.
15 You trampled the sea with your horses,
and the mighty waters piled high.

16 I trembled inside when I heard this;
my lips quivered with fear.
My legs gave way beneath me,
and I shook in terror.
I will wait quietly for the coming day
when disaster will strike the people
who invade us.
17 Even though the fig trees have no blossoms,
and there are no grapes on the vines;
even though the olive crop fails,
and the fields lie empty and barren;
even though the flocks die in the fields,
and the cattle barns are empty,
18 yet I will rejoice in the LORD!
I will be joyful in the God of my salvation!
19 The Sovereign LORD is my strength!
He makes me as surefooted as a deer,
able to tread upon the heights.

(For the choir director: This prayer is to be accompanied by stringed instruments.)

FUN-fact

Etched in Stone

God sometimes asked his followers to etch his words in stone, clay, or metal so they would last for future generations. In **HABAKKUK 2:2,** God told the prophet Habakkuk to write God's prophecy in big letters on a stone tablet. In **EXODUS 24:12,** God himself wrote his words on stone tablets.

Find a large, flat rock or brick and a permanent marker. Pick a favorite Bible verse, and write it on your rock. Read the verse out loud after you've written it, then place the rock in your garden.

Wait a week, and see if you can remember the verse. If you can't, go check out your rock! Spend the next couple of weeks testing your family members to see if they can remember your verse that's "etched in stone."

6 "But soon their captives will taunt them.
They will mock them, saying,
'What sorrow awaits you thieves!
Now you will get what you deserve!
You've become rich by extortion,
but how much longer can this go on?'
7 Suddenly, your debtors will take action.
They will turn on you and take all you have,
while you stand trembling and helpless.
8 Because you have plundered many nations,
now all the survivors will plunder you.
You committed murder throughout the
countryside
and filled the towns with violence.

9 "What sorrow awaits you who build
big houses
with money gained dishonestly!
You believe your wealth will buy security,
putting your family's nest beyond the
reach of danger.
10 But by the murders you committed,
you have shamed your name and
forfeited your lives.
11 The very stones in the walls cry out
against you,
and the beams in the ceilings echo the
complaint.

12 "What sorrow awaits you who build cities
with money gained through murder
and corruption!
13 Has not the LORD of Heaven's Armies
promised
that the wealth of nations will turn
to ashes?
They work so hard,
but all in vain!
14 For as the waters fill the sea,
the earth will be filled with an awareness
of the glory of the LORD.

15 "What sorrow awaits you who make your
neighbors drunk!
You force your cup on them
so you can gloat over their shameful
nakedness.
16 But soon it will be your turn to be disgraced.
Come, drink and be exposed!
Drink from the cup of the LORD's judgment,
and all your glory will be turned to shame.
17 You cut down the forests of Lebanon.
Now you will be cut down.
You destroyed the wild animals,
so now their terror will be yours.
You committed murder throughout
the countryside
and filled the towns with violence.

18 "What good is an idol carved by man,
or a cast image that deceives you?
How foolish to trust in your own creation—
a god that can't even talk!
19 What sorrow awaits you who say
to wooden idols,
'Wake up and save us!'
To speechless stone images you say,
'Rise up and teach us!'
Can an idol tell you what to do?
They may be overlaid with gold and silver,
but they are lifeless inside.

ZEPHANIAH There's Still Time

Zephaniah called the people to repent and pray for the Lord to save them. Look for

- **A WORD TO THE WISE**
- **A WARNING TO THE WICKED**
- **A WAY TO TURN BACK**
- **A WONDERFUL WORLD TO COME**

Rags to Riches and Back Again

God promised to destroy all the proud nations that refused to worship him. Remember Nineveh, the capital of the great nation of Assyria? **Read Zephaniah 2:13-15 to see what God had in store for that city!**

NINEVEH

Sing and Shout!

Zephaniah didn't just preach about the bad things that would happen if the people didn't turn back to God. He preached about some really great things too! **Discover what they were in Zephaniah 3:9-20.**

IT'S NOT TOO LATE!

There's Still Time

Zephaniah tried to convince the people in Judah that there was still time—that it wasn't too late. Too late for what? **Find out in Zephaniah 2:1-3.**

What a Zoo!

Boy, Jerusalem was so full of animals that it must have been a zoo! **See what kind of animals roamed the streets by reading Zephaniah 3:3-5.**

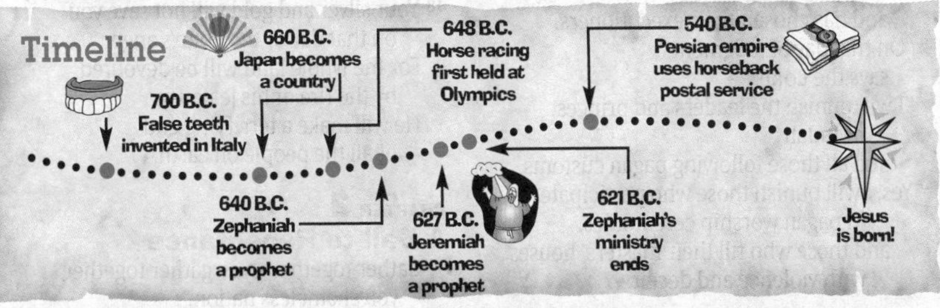
Timeline
700 B.C. False teeth invented in Italy
660 B.C. Japan becomes a country
648 B.C. Horse racing first held at Olympics
640 B.C. Zephaniah becomes a prophet
627 B.C. Jeremiah becomes a prophet
621 B.C. Zephaniah's ministry ends
540 B.C. Persian empire uses horseback postal service
Jesus is born!

The JESUS CONNECTION

Like the other minor prophets, Zephaniah gave the people God's message of hope that he would send a Messiah to save them. And God did! He sent his Son, Jesus! But there's more—Jesus is coming back. And when he does, he'll rule forever over a perfect kingdom filled with all the people who believed in him. If you believe in Jesus, you can be a part of that wonderful crowd! **(And you can have Jesus as your very best friend all through your life too!)**

Zephaniah 1 . . . page 916

CHAPTER 1

The LORD gave this message to Zephaniah when Josiah son of Amon was king of Judah. Zephaniah was the son of Cushi, son of Gedaliah, son of Amariah, son of Hezekiah.

Coming Judgment against Judah

2 "I will sweep away everything
from the face of the earth," says the LORD.
3 "I will sweep away people and animals alike.
I will sweep away the birds of the sky and
the fish in the sea.
I will reduce the wicked to heaps of rubble,
and I will wipe humanity from the face
of the earth," says the LORD.
4 "I will crush Judah and Jerusalem with my fist
and destroy every last trace of their
Baal worship.
I will put an end to all the idolatrous priests,
so that even the memory of them will
disappear.
5 For they go up to their roofs
and bow down to the sun, moon, and stars.
They claim to follow the LORD,
but then they worship Molech, too.
6 And I will destroy those who used
to worship me
but now no longer do.
They no longer ask for the LORD's guidance
or seek my blessings."

7 Stand in silence in the presence of the
Sovereign LORD,
for the awesome day of the LORD's
judgment is near.
The LORD has prepared his people for
a great slaughter
and has chosen their executioners.
8 "On that day of judgment,"
says the LORD,
"I will punish the leaders and princes
of Judah
and all those following pagan customs.
9 Yes, I will punish those who participate
in pagan worship ceremonies,
and those who fill their masters' houses
with violence and deceit.

10 "On that day," says the LORD,
"a cry of alarm will come from the
Fish Gate
and echo throughout the New Quarter
of the city.
And a great crash will sound from
the hills.
11 Wail in sorrow, all you who live in the
market area,
for all the merchants and traders will be
destroyed.

12 "I will search with lanterns in Jerusalem's
darkest corners
to punish those who sit complacent
in their sins.
They think the LORD will do nothing to them,
either good or bad.
13 So their property will be plundered,
their homes will be ransacked.
They will build new homes
but never live in them.
They will plant vineyards
but never drink wine from them.

14 "That terrible day of the LORD is near.
Swiftly it comes—
a day of bitter tears,
a day when even strong men will cry out.
15 It will be a day when the LORD's anger is
poured out—
a day of terrible distress and anguish,
a day of ruin and desolation,
a day of darkness and gloom,
a day of clouds and blackness,
16 a day of trumpet calls and battle cries.
Down go the walled cities
and the strongest battlements!

17 "Because you have sinned against the LORD,
I will make you grope around like
the blind.
Your blood will be poured into the dust,
and your bodies will lie rotting on
the ground."

18 Your silver and gold will not save you
on that day of the LORD's anger.
For the whole land will be devoured
by the fire of his jealousy.
He will make a terrifying end
of all the people on earth.

CHAPTER 2

A Call to Repentance

1 Gather together—yes, gather together,
you shameless nation.
2 Gather before judgment begins,
before your time to repent is blown
away like chaff.
Act now, before the fierce fury of the
LORD falls
and the terrible day of the LORD's
anger begins.

3 Seek the LORD, all who are humble,
and follow his commands.
Seek to do what is right
and to live humbly.
Perhaps even yet the LORD will
protect you—
protect you from his anger on that
day of destruction.

Judgment against Philistia

4 Gaza and Ashkelon will be abandoned,
Ashdod and Ekron torn down.
5 And what sorrow awaits you Philistines
who live along the coast and in the land
of Canaan,
for this judgment is against you, too!
The LORD will destroy you
until not one of you is left.
6 The Philistine coast will become a
wilderness pasture,
a place of shepherd camps
and enclosures for sheep and goats.
7 The remnant of the tribe of Judah will
pasture there.
They will rest at night in the abandoned
houses in Ashkelon.
For the LORD their God will visit his people
in kindness
and restore their prosperity again.

Judgment against Moab and Ammon

8 "I have heard the taunts of the Moabites
and the insults of the Ammonites,
mocking my people
and invading their borders.
9 Now, as surely as I live,"
says the LORD of Heaven's Armies,
the God of Israel,
"Moab and Ammon will be destroyed—
destroyed as completely as Sodom
and Gomorrah.
Their land will become a place of
stinging nettles,
salt pits, and eternal desolation.
The remnant of my people will
plunder them
and take their land."

10 They will receive the wages of their
pride,
for they have scoffed at the people of the
LORD of Heaven's Armies.
11 The LORD will terrify them
as he destroys all the gods in the land.
Then nations around the world will worship
the LORD,
each in their own land.

Judgment against Ethiopia and Assyria

12 "You Ethiopians will also be slaughtered
by my sword," says the LORD.

13 And the LORD will strike the lands of the
north with his fist,
destroying the land of Assyria.
He will make its great capital, Nineveh,
a desolate wasteland,
parched like a desert.
14 The proud city will become a pasture
for flocks and herds,
and all sorts of wild animals will
settle there.
The desert owl and screech owl will roost
on its ruined columns,
their calls echoing through the gaping
windows.
Rubble will block all the doorways,
and the cedar paneling will be exposed
to the weather.
15 This is the boisterous city,
once so secure.
"I am the greatest!" it boasted.
"No other city can compare with me!"
But now, look how it has become an utter ruin,
a haven for wild animals.
Everyone passing by will laugh in derision
and shake a defiant fist.

CHAPTER 3

Jerusalem's Rebellion and Redemption

1 What sorrow awaits rebellious, polluted
Jerusalem,
the city of violence and crime!
2 No one can tell it anything;
it refuses all correction.
It does not trust in the LORD
or draw near to its God.
3 Its leaders are like roaring lions
hunting for their victims.
Its judges are like ravenous wolves at
evening time,
who by dawn have left no trace of
their prey.
4 Its prophets are arrogant liars seeking their
own gain.
Its priests defile the Temple by disobeying
God's instructions.

5 But the LORD is still there in the city,
and he does no wrong.
Day by day he hands down justice,
and he does not fail.
But the wicked know no shame.

6 "I have wiped out many nations,
devastating their fortress walls
and towers.
Their streets are now deserted;
their cities lie in silent ruin.
There are no survivors—
none at all.
7 I thought, 'Surely they will have reverence
for me now!
Surely they will listen to my warnings.
Then I won't need to strike again,
destroying their homes.'
But no, they get up early
to continue their evil deeds.
8 Therefore, be patient," says the LORD.
"Soon I will stand and accuse these
evil nations.
For I have decided to gather the kingdoms
of the earth
and pour out my fiercest anger and fury on
them.
All the earth will be devoured
by the fire of my jealousy.

9 "Then I will purify the speech of all people,
so that everyone can worship the LORD
together.
10 My scattered people who live beyond the
rivers of Ethiopia
will come to present their offerings.
11 On that day you will no longer need to be
ashamed,
for you will no longer be rebels against me.
I will remove all proud and arrogant people
from among you.
There will be no more haughtiness
on my holy mountain.
12 Those who are left will be the lowly
and humble,
for it is they who trust in the name
of the LORD.
13 The remnant of Israel will do no wrong;
they will never tell lies or deceive
one another.
They will eat and sleep in safety,
and no one will make them afraid."

14 Sing, O daughter of Zion;
shout aloud, O Israel!
Be glad and rejoice with all your heart,
O daughter of Jerusalem!
15 For the LORD will remove his hand
of judgment
and will disperse the armies of your
enemy.
And the LORD himself, the King of Israel,
will live among you!
At last your troubles will be over,
and you will never again fear disaster.
16 On that day the announcement to Jerusalem
will be,
"Cheer up, Zion! Don't be afraid!
17 For the LORD your God is living among you.
He is a mighty savior.
He will take delight in you with gladness.
With his love, he will calm all your fears.
He will rejoice over you with joyful songs."

18 "I will gather you who mourn for the
appointed festivals;
you will be disgraced no more.
19 And I will deal severely with all who have
oppressed you.
I will save the weak and helpless ones;
I will bring together
those who were chased away.
I will give glory and fame to my former
exiles,
wherever they have been mocked
and shamed.
20 On that day I will gather you together
and bring you home again.
I will give you a good name, a name of
distinction,
among all the nations of the earth,
as I restore your fortunes before their
very eyes.
I, the LORD, have spoken!"

HAGGAI The Temple Is the Topic

Haggai describes God's call for the Israelites to rebuild God's Temple. Look for

- A SPECIAL MESSAGE
- A SPECIAL BUILDING
- A SPECIAL JOB
- A SPECIAL PROMISE
- SPECIAL BLESSINGS

Get Movin'!

God told his people to finish building his Temple. Fifteen years later, they still hadn't finished. So Haggai delivered a message from God, and God's people got moving. **See which way they moved by reading Haggai 1:12-15.**

BLESSINGS
CHANNEL SEVEN WEATHER

And the Forecast Is...

When the people started rebuilding the Temple, God didn't waste any time reacting. What did God say and do? **Find out for yourself in Haggai 2:18-19.**

Dear Blabby

Times Are Tough

Q: Everything seems to be going wrong. We don't have enough food, we're cold, prices keep going up, and it hasn't rained. What's going on? **A. Find the answer in Haggai 1:1-11.**

A Special Promise

RESERVED FOR OUR FUTURE SAVIOR

Haggai delivered another message from God—a really special one about something that would happen in the future. **Read all about it in Haggai 2:6-9.**

Timeline

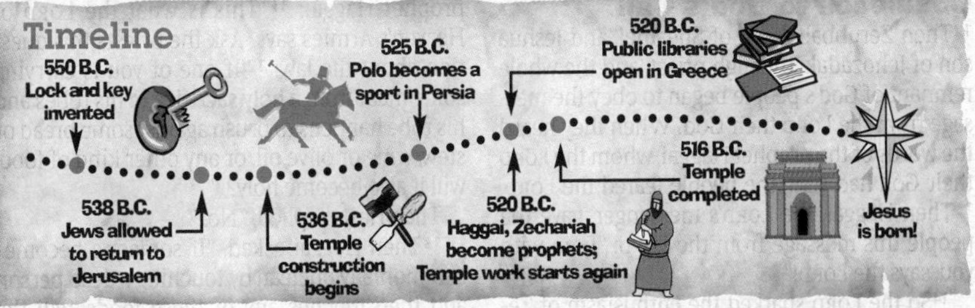

550 B.C. Lock and key invented
538 B.C. Jews allowed to return to Jerusalem
536 B.C. Temple construction begins
525 B.C. Polo becomes a sport in Persia
520 B.C. Haggai, Zechariah become prophets; Temple work starts again
520 B.C. Public libraries open in Greece
516 B.C. Temple completed
Jesus is born!

The JESUS CONNECTION

Through Haggai, God promised to "shake the heavens and earth" and send a Messiah who would bring peace and change everything. About 500 years later, that's just what God did! God sent his Son, Jesus, to earth. He was the Messiah everyone was waiting for, and he really did "shake the heavens and the earth!" Nothing would ever be the same again because Jesus died on the cross for *our* sins and rose from the grave to prove his victory over death. When we believe in Jesus, we can live with him forever in heaven. **Jesus turned everything upside down!**

Haggai 1 . . . page 920

CHAPTER 1

A Call to Rebuild the Temple

On August 29 of the second year of King Darius's reign, the LORD gave a message through the prophet Haggai to Zerubbabel son of Shealtiel, governor of Judah, and to Jeshua son of Jehozadak, the high priest.

2"This is what the LORD of Heaven's Armies says: The people are saying, 'The time has not yet come to rebuild the house of the LORD.'"

3Then the LORD sent this message through the prophet Haggai: 4"Why are you living in luxurious houses while my house lies in ruins? 5This is what the LORD of Heaven's Armies says: Look at what's happening to you! 6You have planted much but harvest little. You eat but are not satisfied. You drink but are still thirsty. You put on clothes but cannot keep warm. Your wages disappear as though you were putting them in pockets filled with holes!

7"This is what the LORD of Heaven's Armies says: Look at what's happening to you! 8Now go up into the hills, bring down timber, and rebuild my house. Then I will take pleasure in it and be honored, says the LORD. 9You hoped for rich harvests, but they were poor. And when you brought your harvest home, I blew it away. Why? Because my house lies in ruins, says the LORD of Heaven's Armies, while all of you are busy building your own fine houses. 10It's because of you that the heavens withhold the dew and the earth produces no crops. 11I have called for a drought on your fields and hills—a drought to wither the grain and grapes and olive trees and all your other crops, a drought to starve you and your livestock and to ruin everything you have worked so hard to get."

Obedience to God's Call

12Then Zerubbabel son of Shealtiel, and Jeshua son of Jehozadak, the high priest, and the whole remnant of God's people began to obey the message from the LORD their God. When they heard the words of the prophet Haggai, whom the LORD their God had sent, the people feared the LORD. 13Then Haggai, the LORD's messenger, gave the people this message from the LORD: "I am with you, says the LORD!"

14So the LORD sparked the enthusiasm of Zerubbabel son of Shealtiel, governor of Judah, and the enthusiasm of Jeshua son of Jehozadak, the high priest, and the enthusiasm of the whole remnant of God's people. They began to work on the house of their God, the LORD of Heaven's Armies, 15on September 21 of the second year of King Darius's reign.

CHAPTER 2

The New Temple's Diminished Splendor

Then on October 17 of that same year, the LORD sent another message through the prophet Haggai. 2"Say this to Zerubbabel son of Shealtiel, governor of Judah, and to Jeshua son of Jehozadak, the high priest, and to the remnant of God's people there in the land: 3'Does anyone remember this house—this Temple—in its former splendor? How, in comparison, does it look to you now? It must seem like nothing at all! 4But now the LORD says: Be strong, Zerubbabel. Be strong, Jeshua son of Jehozadak, the high priest. Be strong, all you people still left in the land. And now get to work, for I am with you, says the LORD of Heaven's Armies. 5My Spirit remains among you, just as I promised when you came out of Egypt. So do not be afraid.'

6"For this is what the LORD of Heaven's Armies says: In just a little while I will again shake the heavens and the earth, the oceans and the dry land. 7I will shake all the nations, and the treasures of all the nations will be brought to this Temple. I will fill this place with glory, says the LORD of Heaven's Armies. 8The silver is mine, and the gold is mine, says the LORD of Heaven's Armies. 9The future glory of this Temple will be greater than its past glory, says the LORD of Heaven's Armies. And in this place I will bring peace. I, the LORD of Heaven's Armies, have spoken!"

Blessings Promised for Obedience

10On December 18 of the second year of King Darius's reign, the LORD sent this message to the prophet Haggai: 11"This is what the LORD of Heaven's Armies says. Ask the priests this question about the law: 12'If one of you is carrying some meat from a holy sacrifice in his robes and his robe happens to brush against some bread or stew, wine or olive oil, or any other kind of food, will it also become holy?'"

The priests replied, "No."

13Then Haggai asked, "If someone becomes ceremonially unclean by touching a dead person and then touches any of these foods, will the food be defiled?"

And the priests answered, "Yes."

14Then Haggai responded, "That is how it is with this people and this nation, says the LORD. Everything they do and everything they offer is defiled by their sin. 15Look at what was happening to you before you began to lay the foundation

of the LORD's Temple. [16]When you hoped for a
twenty-bushel crop, you harvested only ten.
When you expected to draw fifty gallons from
the winepress, you found only twenty. [17]I sent
blight and mildew and hail to destroy everything
you worked so hard to produce. Even so, you
refused to return to me, says the LORD.

[18]"Think about this eighteenth day of December, the day when the foundation of the LORD's
Temple was laid. Think carefully. [19]I am giving
you a promise now while the seed is still in the
barn. You have not yet harvested your grain, and
your grapevines, fig trees, pomegranates, and
olive trees have not yet produced their crops. But
from this day onward I will bless you."

Promises for Zerubbabel

[20]On that same day, December 18, the LORD sent
this second message to Haggai: [21]"Tell Zerubbabel, the governor of Judah, that I am about to
shake the heavens and the earth. [22]I will overthrow royal thrones and destroy the power of
foreign kingdoms. I will overturn their chariots
and riders. The horses will fall, and their riders
will kill each other.

[23]"But when this happens, says the LORD of
Heaven's Armies, I will honor you, Zerubbabel
son of Shealtiel, my servant. I will make you like a
signet ring on my finger, says the LORD, for I have
chosen you. I, the LORD of Heaven's Armies, have
spoken!"

ZECHARiAH

Your King Is Coming!

Through Zechariah, God encouraged the people to finish rebuilding the Temple. But God said a whole lot more! Look for

- **VISIONS AT NIGHT**
- **DAYS OF BUILDING**
- **A TIME OF HOPE**
- **A FUTURE KING**

The Cornerstone

A cornerstone is the most important part of the foundation of a building. Zechariah predicted that Jesus would be *the* cornerstone. **It's an amazing prophecy—read it in Zechariah 10:3b-6!**

Time to Come Home

God's people were taken away to other countries after they disobeyed God. But now God was calling them home. **Read how God called them back to Jerusalem in Zechariah 2:6-13.**

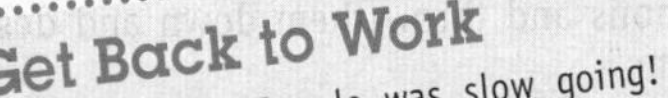
Get Back to Work

Rebuilding the Temple was slow going! But God encouraged the people to keep at it. Why? **Read Zechariah 8:9-13.**

Hand Me the Soap!

Zechariah told how one day, people would be completely cleansed. But not with soap—with the blood of Jesus! **Read all about it in Zechariah 13:1.**

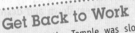

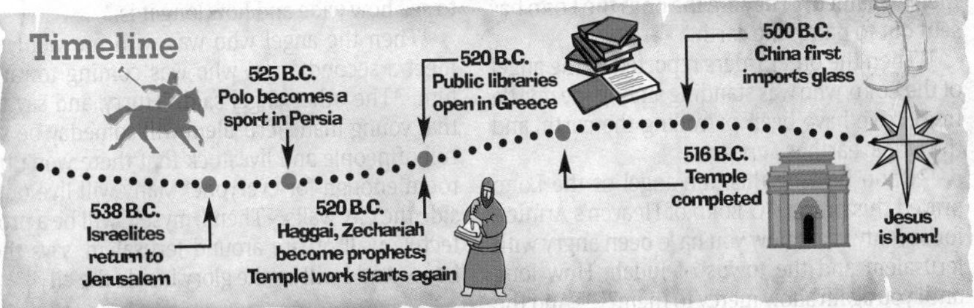
Timeline
525 B.C.
Polo becomes a sport in Persia
520 B.C.
Public libraries open in Greece
500 B.C.
China first imports glass
538 B.C.
Israelites return to Jerusalem
520 B.C.
Haggai, Zechariah become prophets; Temple work starts again
516 B.C.
Temple completed
Jesus is born!

The JESUS CONNECTION

Like other prophets, Zechariah talked about the promise that Jesus would come. Read Zechariah 9, then read Matthew 21:1-11 to see how the promise was fulfilled. (Remember how Jesus rode into Jerusalem on Palm Sunday?)

We have the promise that Jesus will come back one day to rule forever. **Believe in Jesus, and you'll be able to live with him forever in his kingdom. (And have the very best friend here on earth as you wait for his return.)**

Zechariah 1 . . . page 924

CHAPTER 1

A Call to Return to the LORD

In November of the second year of King Darius's reign, the LORD gave this message to the prophet Zechariah son of Berekiah and grandson of Iddo:

2"I, the LORD, was very angry with your ancestors. 3Therefore, say to the people, 'This is what the LORD of Heaven's Armies says: Return to me, and I will return to you, says the LORD of Heaven's Armies.' 4Don't be like your ancestors who would not listen or pay attention when the earlier prophets said to them, 'This is what the LORD of Heaven's Armies says: Turn from your evil ways, and stop all your evil practices.'

5"Where are your ancestors now? They and the prophets are long dead. 6But everything I said through my servants the prophets happened to your ancestors, just as I said. As a result, they repented and said, 'We have received what we deserved from the LORD of Heaven's Armies. He has done what he said he would do.'"

A Man among the Myrtle Trees

7Three months later, on February 15, the LORD sent another message to the prophet Zechariah son of Berekiah and grandson of Iddo.

8In a vision during the night, I saw a man sitting on a red horse that was standing among some myrtle trees in a small valley. Behind him were riders on red, brown, and white horses. 9I asked the angel who was talking with me, "My lord, what do these horses mean?"

"I will show you," the angel replied.

10The rider standing among the myrtle trees then explained, "They are the ones the LORD has sent out to patrol the earth."

11Then the other riders reported to the angel of the LORD, who was standing among the myrtle trees, "We have been patrolling the earth, and the whole earth is at peace."

12Upon hearing this, the angel of the LORD prayed this prayer: "O LORD of Heaven's Armies, for seventy years now you have been angry with Jerusalem and the towns of Judah. How long until you again show mercy to them?" 13And the LORD spoke kind and comforting words to the angel who talked with me.

14Then the angel said to me, "Shout this message for all to hear: 'This is what the LORD of Heaven's Armies says: My love for Jerusalem and Mount Zion is passionate and strong. 15But I am very angry with the other nations that are now enjoying peace and security. I was only a little angry with my people, but the nations inflicted harm on them far beyond my intentions.

16"'Therefore, this is what the LORD says: I have returned to show mercy to Jerusalem. My Temple will be rebuilt, says the LORD of Heaven's Armies, and measurements will be taken for the reconstruction of Jerusalem.'

17"Say this also: 'This is what the LORD of Heaven's Armies says: The towns of Israel will again overflow with prosperity, and the LORD will again comfort Zion and choose Jerusalem as his own.'"

Four Horns and Four Blacksmiths

18Then I looked up and saw four animal horns. 19"What are these?" I asked the angel who was talking with me.

He replied, "These horns represent the nations that scattered Judah, Israel, and Jerusalem."

20Then the LORD showed me four blacksmiths. 21"What are these men coming to do?" I asked.

The angel replied, "These four horns—these nations—scattered and humbled Judah. Now these blacksmiths have come to terrify those nations and throw them down and destroy them."

CHAPTER 2

Future Prosperity of Jerusalem

When I looked again, I saw a man with a measuring line in his hand. 2"Where are you going?" I asked.

He replied, "I am going to measure Jerusalem, to see how wide and how long it is."

3Then the angel who was with me went to meet a second angel who was coming toward him. 4The other angel said, "Hurry, and say to that young man, 'Jerusalem will someday be so full of people and livestock that there won't be room enough for everyone! Many will live outside the city walls. 5Then I, myself, will be a protective wall of fire around Jerusalem, says the LORD. And I will be the glory inside the city!'"

The Exiles Are Called Home

6The LORD says, "Come away! Flee from Babylon in the land of the north, for I have scattered you to the four winds. 7Come away, people of Zion, you who are exiled in Babylon!"

8After a period of glory, the LORD of Heaven's Armies sent me against the nations who plundered you. For he said, "Anyone who harms you harms my most precious possession. 9 I will raise my fist to crush them, and their own slaves will plunder them." Then you will know that the LORD of Heaven's Armies has sent me.

10 The LORD says, "Shout and rejoice, O beautiful Jerusalem, for I am coming to live among you. 11 Many nations will join themselves to the LORD on that day, and they, too, will be my people. I will live among you, and you will know that the LORD of Heaven's Armies sent me to you. 12 The land of Judah will be the LORD's special possession in the holy land, and he will once again choose Jerusalem to be his own city. 13 Be silent before the LORD, all humanity, for he is springing into action from his holy dwelling."

CHAPTER 3
Cleansing for the High Priest

Then the angel showed me Jeshua the high priest standing before the angel of the LORD. The Accuser, Satan, was there at the angel's right hand, making accusations against Jeshua. 2 And the LORD said to Satan, "I, the LORD, reject your accusations, Satan. Yes, the LORD, who has chosen Jerusalem, rebukes you. This man is like a burning stick that has been snatched from the fire."

3 Jeshua's clothing was filthy as he stood there before the angel. 4 So the angel said to the others standing there, "Take off his filthy clothes." And turning to Jeshua he said, "See, I have taken away your sins, and now I am giving you these fine new clothes."

5 Then I said, "They should also place a clean turban on his head." So they put a clean priestly turban on his head and dressed him in new clothes while the angel of the LORD stood by.

6 Then the angel of the LORD spoke very solemnly to Jeshua and said, 7 "This is what the LORD of Heaven's Armies says: If you follow my ways and carefully serve me, then you will be given authority over my Temple and its courtyards. I will let you walk among these others standing here.

8 "Listen to me, O Jeshua the high priest, and all you other priests. You are symbols of things to come. Soon I am going to bring my servant, the Branch. 9 Now look at the jewel I have set before Jeshua, a single stone with seven facets. I will engrave an inscription on it, says the LORD of Heaven's Armies, and I will remove the sins of this land in a single day.

10 "And on that day, says the LORD of Heaven's Armies, each of you will invite your neighbor to sit with you peacefully under your own grapevine and fig tree."

CHAPTER 4
A Lampstand and Two Olive Trees

Then the angel who had been talking with me returned and woke me, as though I had been asleep. 2 "What do you see now?" he asked.

I answered, "I see a solid gold lampstand with a bowl of oil on top of it. Around the bowl are seven lamps, each having seven spouts with wicks. 3 And I see two olive trees, one on each side of the bowl." 4 Then I asked the angel, "What are these, my lord? What do they mean?"

5 "Don't you know?" the angel asked.

"No, my lord," I replied.

6 Then he said to me, "This is what the LORD says to Zerubbabel: It is not by force nor by strength, but by my Spirit, says the LORD of Heaven's Armies. 7 Nothing, not even a mighty mountain, will stand in Zerubbabel's way; it will become a level plain before him! And when Zerubbabel sets the final stone of the Temple in place, the people will shout: 'May God bless it! May God bless it!'"

8 Then another message came to me from the LORD: 9 "Zerubbabel is the one who laid the foundation of this Temple, and he will complete it. Then you will know that the LORD of Heaven's Armies has sent me. 10 Do not despise these small beginnings, for the LORD rejoices to see the work begin, to see the plumb line in Zerubbabel's hand."

(The seven lamps represent the eyes of the LORD that search all around the world.)

11 Then I asked the angel, "What are these two olive trees on each side of the lampstand, 12 and what are the two olive branches that pour out golden oil through two gold tubes?"

13 "Don't you know?" he asked.

"No, my lord," I replied.

14 Then he said to me, "They represent the two anointed ones who stand in the court of the Lord of all the earth."

CHAPTER 5
A Flying Scroll

I looked up again and saw a scroll flying through the air.

2 "What do you see?" the angel asked.

"I see a flying scroll," I replied. "It appears to be about 30 feet long and 15 feet wide."

3 Then he said to me, "This scroll contains the curse that is going out over the entire land. One side of the scroll says that those who steal will be banished from the land; the other side says that those who swear falsely will be banished

from the land. 4And this is what the LORD of
Heaven's Armies says: I am sending this curse
into the house of every thief and into the house
of everyone who swears falsely using my name.
And my curse will remain in that house and
completely destroy it—even its timbers and
stones."

A Woman in a Basket

5Then the angel who was talking with me
came forward and said, "Look up and see what's
coming."
6"What is it?" I asked.
He replied, "It is a basket for measuring grain,
and it's filled with the sins of everyone throughout the land."
7Then the heavy lead cover was lifted off the
basket, and there was a woman sitting inside it.
8The angel said, "The woman's name is Wickedness," and he pushed her back into the basket
and closed the heavy lid again.
9Then I looked up and saw two women flying
toward us, gliding on the wind. They had wings
like a stork, and they picked up the basket and
flew into the sky.
10"Where are they taking the basket?" I asked
the angel.
11He replied, "To the land of Babylonia, where
they will build a temple for the basket. And when
the temple is ready, they will set the basket there
on its pedestal."

CHAPTER 6

Four Chariots

Then I looked up again and saw four chariots
coming from between two bronze mountains.
2The first chariot was pulled by red horses, the
second by black horses, 3the third by white
horses, and the fourth by powerful dappled-gray
horses. 4"And what are these, my lord?" I asked
the angel who was talking with me.
5The angel replied, "These are the four spirits of heaven who stand before the Lord of all
the earth. They are going out to do his work.
6The chariot with black horses is going north,
the chariot with white horses is going west,
and the chariot with dappled-gray horses is
going south."
7The powerful horses were eager to set out
to patrol the earth. And the LORD said, "Go and
patrol the earth!" So they left at once on their
patrol.
8Then the LORD summoned me and said,
"Look, those who went north have vented the anger of my Spirit there in the land of the north."

The Crowning of Jeshua

9Then I received another message from the
LORD: 10"Heldai, Tobijah, and Jedaiah will bring
gifts of silver and gold from the Jews exiled in
Babylon. As soon as they arrive, meet them at the
home of Josiah son of Zephaniah. 11Accept their
gifts, and make a crown from the silver and gold.
Then put the crown on the head of Jeshua son of
Jehozadak, the high priest. 12Tell him, 'This is
what the LORD of Heaven's Armies says: Here is

All of the prophets said that God was going to send a Messiah, or Savior, to save the people and give them hope.

The prophets wanted the people to get ready for the Messiah by turning away from their sins.

We know that the prophets were talking about Jesus. And *we* know that Jesus is coming back again! But we don't know exactly when. **But we can get ready for Jesus' coming by turning away from our sins.**

Think of three sins that you need to turn away from.

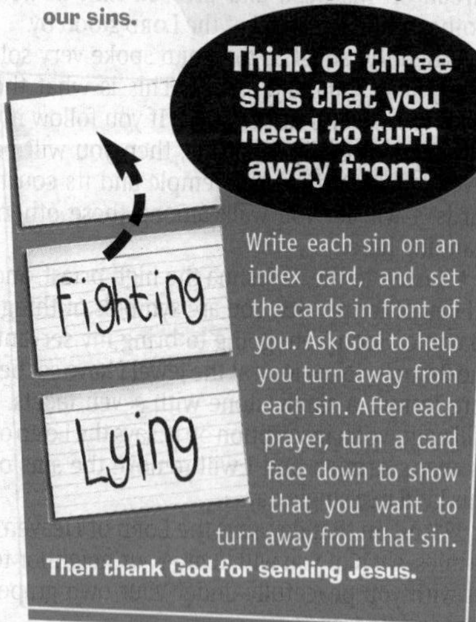

Write each sin on an index card, and set the cards in front of you. Ask God to help you turn away from each sin. After each prayer, turn a card face down to show that you want to turn away from that sin. **Then thank God for sending Jesus.**

the man called the Branch. He will branch out
from where he is and build the Temple of the
LORD. 13 Yes, he will build the Temple of the LORD.
Then he will receive royal honor and will rule as
king from his throne. He will also serve as priest
from his throne, and there will be perfect harmony between his two roles.'

14 "The crown will be a memorial in the Tem-
ple of the LORD to honor those who gave it—
Heldai, Tobijah, Jedaiah, and Josiah son of
Zephaniah."

15 People will come from distant lands to rebuild the Temple of the LORD. And when this happens, you will know that my messages have been
from the LORD of Heaven's Armies. All this will
happen if you carefully obey what the LORD your
God says.

CHAPTER 7
A Call to Justice and Mercy

On December 7 of the fourth year of King Darius's reign, another message came to Zechariah
from the LORD. 2 The people of Bethel had sent
Sharezer and Regemmelech, along with their attendants, to seek the LORD's favor. 3 They were to
ask this question of the prophets and the priests
at the Temple of the LORD of Heaven's Armies:
"Should we continue to mourn and fast each
summer on the anniversary of the Temple's destruction, as we have done for so many years?"

4 The LORD of Heaven's Armies sent me this
message in reply: 5 "Say to all your people and
your priests, 'During these seventy years of exile,
when you fasted and mourned in the summer
and in early autumn, was it really for me that you
were fasting? 6 And even now in your holy festivals, aren't you eating and drinking just to please
yourselves? 7 Isn't this the same message the
LORD proclaimed through the prophets in years
past when Jerusalem and the towns of Judah
were bustling with people, and the Negev and the
foothills of Judah were well populated?'"

8 Then this message came to Zechariah from
the LORD: 9 "This is what the LORD of Heaven's Armies says: Judge fairly, and show mercy and kindness to one another. 10 Do not oppress widows,
orphans, foreigners, and the poor. And do not
scheme against each other.

11 "Your ancestors refused to listen to this
message. They stubbornly turned away and put
their fingers in their ears to keep from hearing.
12 They made their hearts as hard as stone, so
they could not hear the instructions or the messages that the LORD of Heaven's Armies had sent
them by his Spirit through the earlier prophets.
That is why the LORD of Heaven's Armies was so
angry with them.

13 "Since they refused to listen when I called to
them, I would not listen when they called to me,
says the LORD of Heaven's Armies. 14 As with a
whirlwind, I scattered them among the distant
nations, where they lived as strangers. Their land
became so desolate that no one even traveled
through it. They turned their pleasant land into
a desert."

CHAPTER 8
Promised Blessings for Jerusalem

Then another message came to me from the
LORD of Heaven's Armies: 2 "This is what the
LORD of Heaven's Armies says: My love for
Mount Zion is passionate and strong; I am con-
sumed with passion for Jerusalem!

3 "And now the LORD says: I am returning to
Mount Zion, and I will live in Jerusalem. Then Jerusalem will be called the Faithful City; the
mountain of the LORD of Heaven's Armies will be
called the Holy Mountain.

4 "This is what the LORD of Heaven's Armies
says: Once again old men and women will walk
Jerusalem's streets with their canes and will sit
together in the city squares. 5 And the streets of
the city will be filled with boys and girls at play.

6 "This is what the LORD of Heaven's Armies
says: All this may seem impossible to you now, a
small remnant of God's people. But is it impossible for me? says the LORD of Heaven's Armies.

7 "This is what the LORD of Heaven's Armies
says: You can be sure that I will rescue my people
from the east and from the west. 8 I will bring
them home again to live safely in Jerusalem.
They will be my people, and I will be faithful and
just toward them as their God.

9 "This is what the LORD of Heaven's Armies
says: Be strong and finish the task! Ever since the
laying of the foundation of the Temple of the
LORD of Heaven's Armies, you have heard what
the prophets have been saying about completing
the building. 10 Before the work on the Temple
began, there were no jobs and no money to hire
people or animals. No traveler was safe from the
enemy, for there were enemies on all sides. I had
turned everyone against each other.

11 "But now I will not treat the remnant of my
people as I treated them before, says the LORD of
Heaven's Armies. 12 For I am planting seeds of
peace and prosperity among you. The grapevines
will be heavy with fruit. The earth will produce its
crops, and the heavens will release the dew. Once

more I will cause the remnant in Judah and Israel
to inherit these blessings. 13 Among the other
nations, Judah and Israel became symbols of a
cursed nation. But no longer! Now I will rescue
you and make you both a symbol and a source of
blessing. So don't be afraid. Be strong, and get on
with rebuilding the Temple!

14 "For this is what the LORD of Heaven's Armies
says: I was determined to punish you when your
ancestors angered me, and I did not change my
mind, says the LORD of Heaven's Armies. 15 But
now I am determined to bless Jerusalem and the
people of Judah. So don't be afraid. 16 But this is
what you must do: Tell the truth to each other.
Render verdicts in your courts that are just and
that lead to peace. 17 Don't scheme against each
other. Stop your love of telling lies that you swear
are the truth. I hate all these things, says the
LORD."

18 Here is another message that came to me
from the LORD of Heaven's Armies. 19 "This is
what the LORD of Heaven's Armies says: The tra-
ditional fasts and times of mourning you have
kept in early summer, midsummer, autumn, and
winter are now ended. They will become festivals of joy and celebration for the people of
Judah. So love truth and peace.

20 "This is what the LORD of Heaven's Armies
says: People from nations and cities around the
world will travel to Jerusalem. 21 The people of
one city will say to the people of another, 'Come
with us to Jerusalem to ask the LORD to bless us.
Let's worship the LORD of Heaven's Armies. I'm
determined to go.' 22 Many peoples and powerful
nations will come to Jerusalem to seek the LORD
of Heaven's Armies and to ask for his blessing.

23 "This is what the LORD of Heaven's Armies
says: In those days ten men from different nations and languages of the world will clutch at
the sleeve of one Jew. And they will say, 'Please let
us walk with you, for we have heard that God is
with you.'"

CHAPTER **9**

Judgment against Israel's Enemies

This is the message from the LORD against the
land of Aram and the city of Damascus, for the
eyes of humanity, including all the tribes of Israel, are on the LORD.

2 Doom is certain for Hamath,
near Damascus,
and for the cities of Tyre and Sidon,
though they are so clever.
3 Tyre has built a strong fortress
and has made silver and gold
as plentiful as dust in the streets!
4 But now the Lord will strip away Tyre's
possessions
and hurl its fortifications into the sea,
and it will be burned to the ground.
5 The city of Ashkelon will see Tyre fall
and will be filled with fear.
Gaza will shake with terror,
as will Ekron, for their hopes will be
dashed.
Gaza's king will be killed,
and Ashkelon will be deserted.
6 Foreigners will occupy the city of Ashdod.
I will destroy the pride of the Philistines.
7 I will grab the bloody meat from their
mouths
and snatch the detestable sacrifices
from their teeth.
Then the surviving Philistines will worship
our God
and become like a clan in Judah.
The Philistines of Ekron will join
my people,
as the ancient Jebusites once did.
8 I will guard my Temple
and protect it from invading armies.
I am watching closely to ensure
that no more foreign oppressors overrun
my people's land.

Zion's Coming King

9 Rejoice, O people of Zion!
Shout in triumph, O people
of Jerusalem!
Look, your king is coming to you.
He is righteous and victorious,
yet he is humble, riding on a
donkey—
riding on a donkey's colt.
10 I will remove the battle chariots from Israel
and the warhorses from Jerusalem.
I will destroy all the weapons used in battle,
and your king will bring peace to the
nations.
His realm will stretch from sea to sea
and from the Euphrates River to the ends
of the earth.
11 Because of the covenant I made with you,
sealed with blood,
I will free your prisoners
from death in a waterless dungeon.
12 Come back to the place of safety,
all you prisoners who still have hope!

I promise this very day
that I will repay two blessings for each
of your troubles.
13 Judah is my bow,
and Israel is my arrow.
Jerusalem is my sword,
and like a warrior, I will brandish
it against the Greeks.

14 The LORD will appear above his people;
his arrows will fly like lightning!
The Sovereign LORD will sound the
ram's horn
and attack like a whirlwind from the
southern desert.
15 The LORD of Heaven's Armies will protect his
people,
and they will defeat their enemies by
hurling great stones.
They will shout in battle as though drunk
with wine.
They will be filled with blood like a bowl,
drenched with blood like the corners
of the altar.
16 On that day the LORD their God will rescue
his people,
just as a shepherd rescues his sheep.
They will sparkle in his land
like jewels in a crown.
17 How wonderful and beautiful they will be!
The young men will thrive on abundant
grain,
and the young women will flourish
on new wine.

CHAPTER 10
The LORD Will Restore His People

1 Ask the LORD for rain in the spring,
for he makes the storm clouds.
And he will send showers of rain
so every field becomes a lush pasture.
2 Household gods give worthless advice,
fortune-tellers predict only lies,
and interpreters of dreams pronounce
falsehoods that give no comfort.
So my people are wandering like lost sheep;
they are attacked because they have no
shepherd.

3 "My anger burns against your shepherds,
and I will punish these leaders.
For the LORD of Heaven's Armies has arrived
to look after Judah, his flock.
He will make them strong and glorious,
like a proud warhorse in battle.
4 From Judah will come the cornerstone,
the tent peg,
the bow for battle,
and all the rulers.
5 They will be like mighty warriors in battle,
trampling their enemies in the mud
under their feet.
Since the LORD is with them as they fight,
they will overthrow even the enemy's
horsemen.

6 "I will strengthen Judah and save Israel;
I will restore them because of my
compassion.
It will be as though I had never rejected them,
for I am the LORD their God, who will
hear their cries.
7 The people of Israel will become like
mighty warriors,
and their hearts will be made happy
as if by wine.
Their children, too, will see it and be glad;
their hearts will rejoice in the LORD.
8 When I whistle to them, they will come
running,
for I have redeemed them.
From the few who are left,
they will grow as numerous as they
were before.
9 Though I have scattered them like seeds
among the nations,
they will still remember me in distant lands.
They and their children will survive
and return again to Israel.
10 I will bring them back from Egypt
and gather them from Assyria.
I will resettle them in Gilead and Lebanon
until there is no more room for them all.
11 They will pass safely through the sea
of distress,
for the waves of the sea will be held back,
and the waters of the Nile will dry up.
The pride of Assyria will be crushed,
and the rule of Egypt will end.
12 By my power I will make my people strong,
and by my authority they will go wherever
they wish.
I, the LORD, have spoken!"

CHAPTER 11

1 Open your doors, Lebanon,
so that fire may devour your cedar forests.
2 Weep, you cypress trees, for all the ruined
cedars;
the most majestic ones have fallen.

Zechariah 12 . . . page 930

Weep, you oaks of Bashan,
for the thick forests have been cut down.
3 Listen to the wailing of the shepherds,
for their rich pastures are destroyed.
Hear the young lions roaring,
for their thickets in the Jordan Valley
are ruined.

The Good and Evil Shepherds

4 This is what the LORD my God says: "Go and
care for the flock that is intended for slaughter.
5 The buyers slaughter their sheep without remorse. The sellers say, 'Praise the LORD! Now I'm
rich!' Even the shepherds have no compassion
for them. 6 Likewise, I will no longer have pity on
the people of the land," says the LORD. "I will let
them fall into each other's hands and into the
hands of their king. They will turn the land into
a wilderness, and I will not rescue them."

7 So I cared for the flock intended for slaughter—the flock that was oppressed. Then I took
two shepherd's staffs and named one Favor and
the other Union. 8 I got rid of their three evil
shepherds in a single month.

But I became impatient with these sheep, and
they hated me, too. 9 So I told them, "I won't be
your shepherd any longer. If you die, you die. If
you are killed, you are killed. And let those who
remain devour each other!"

10 Then I took my staff called Favor and cut it
in two, showing that I had revoked the covenant
I had made with all the nations. 11 That was the
end of my covenant with them. The suffering
flock was watching me, and they knew that the
LORD was speaking through my actions.

12 And I said to them, "If you like, give me my
wages, whatever I am worth; but only if you
want to." So they counted out for my wages
thirty pieces of silver.

13 And the LORD said to me, "Throw it to the
potter"—this magnificent sum at which they
valued me! So I took the thirty coins and threw
them to the potter in the Temple of the LORD.

14 Then I took my other staff, Union, and cut it
in two, showing that the bond of unity between
Judah and Israel was broken.

15 Then the LORD said to me, "Go again and
play the part of a worthless shepherd. 16 This
illustrates how I will give this nation a shepherd
who will not care for those who are dying, nor
look after the young, nor heal the injured, nor
feed the healthy. Instead, this shepherd will eat
the meat of the fattest sheep and tear off their
hooves.

17 "What sorrow awaits this worthless
shepherd
who abandons the flock!
The sword will cut his arm
and pierce his right eye.
His arm will become useless,
and his right eye completely blind."

CHAPTER **12**

Future Deliverance for Jerusalem

This message concerning the fate of Israel came
from the LORD: "This message is from the LORD,
who stretched out the heavens, laid the foundations of the earth, and formed the human spirit.
2 I will make Jerusalem like an intoxicating drink
that makes the nearby nations stagger when
they send their armies to besiege Jerusalem and
Judah. 3 On that day I will make Jerusalem an immovable rock. All the nations will gather against
it to try to move it, but they will only hurt themselves.

4 "On that day," says the LORD, "I will cause
every horse to panic and every rider to lose his
nerve. I will watch over the people of Judah, but I
will blind all the horses of their enemies. 5 And
the clans of Judah will say to themselves, 'The
people of Jerusalem have found strength in the
LORD of Heaven's Armies, their God.'

6 "On that day I will make the clans of Judah
like a flame that sets a woodpile ablaze or like a
burning torch among sheaves of grain. They will
burn up all the neighboring nations right and
left, while the people living in Jerusalem remain
secure.

7 "The LORD will give victory to the rest of
Judah first, before Jerusalem, so that the people
of Jerusalem and the royal line of David will not
have greater honor than the rest of Judah. 8 On
that day the LORD will defend the people of Jerusalem; the weakest among them will be as
mighty as King David! And the royal descendants will be like God, like the angel of the LORD
who goes before them! 9 For on that day I will begin to destroy all the nations that come against
Jerusalem.

10 "Then I will pour out a spirit of grace and
prayer on the family of David and on the people
of Jerusalem. They will look on me whom they
have pierced and mourn for him as for an only
son. They will grieve bitterly for him as for a
firstborn son who has died. 11 The sorrow and
mourning in Jerusalem on that day will be like
the great mourning for Hadad-rimmon in the
valley of Megiddo.

12 "All Israel will mourn, each clan by itself, and
with the husbands separate from their wives. The
clan of David will mourn alone, as will the clan
of Nathan, 13 the clan of Levi, and the clan of Shimei.
14 Each of the surviving clans from Judah will
mourn separately, and with the husbands separate from their wives.

CHAPTER 13

A Fountain of Cleansing

"On that day a fountain will be opened for the dynasty of David and for the people of Jerusalem, a
fountain to cleanse them from all their sins and
impurity.

2 "And on that day," says the LORD of Heaven's
Armies, "I will erase idol worship throughout the
land, so that even the names of the idols will be
forgotten. I will remove from the land both the
false prophets and the spirit of impurity that
came with them. 3 If anyone continues to prophesy, his own father and mother will tell him, 'You
must die, for you have prophesied lies in the
name of the LORD.' And as he prophesies, his own
father and mother will stab him.

4 "On that day people will be ashamed to claim
the prophetic gift. No one will pretend to be a
prophet by wearing prophet's clothes. 5 He will
say, 'I'm no prophet; I'm a farmer. I began working for a farmer as a boy.' 6 And if someone asks,
'Then what about those wounds on your chest?'
he will say, 'I was wounded at my friends' house!'

The Scattering of the Sheep

7 "Awake, O sword, against my shepherd,
the man who is my partner,"
says the LORD of Heaven's Armies.
"Strike down the shepherd,
and the sheep will be scattered,
and I will turn against the lambs.
8 Two-thirds of the people in the land
will be cut off and die," says the LORD.
"But one-third will be left in the land.
9 I will bring that group through the fire
and make them pure.
I will refine them like silver
and purify them like gold.
They will call on my name,
and I will answer them.
I will say, 'These are my people,'
and they will say, 'The LORD is our God.'"

CHAPTER 14

The LORD Will Rule the Earth

Watch, for the day of the LORD is coming when
your possessions will be plundered right in front
of you! 2 I will gather all the nations to fight
against Jerusalem. The city will be taken, the
houses looted, and the women raped. Half the
population will be taken into captivity, and
the rest will be left among the ruins of the city.

3 Then the LORD will go out to fight against
those nations, as he has fought in times past.
4 On that day his feet will stand on the Mount of
Olives, east of Jerusalem. And the Mount of
Olives will split apart, making a wide valley running from east to west. Half the mountain will
move toward the north and half toward the
south. 5 You will flee through this valley, for it
will reach across to Azal. Yes, you will flee as you
did from the earthquake in the days of King
Uzziah of Judah. Then the LORD my God will
come, and all his holy ones with him.

6 On that day the sources of light will no longer
shine, 7 yet there will be continuous day! Only the
LORD knows how this could happen. There will
be no normal day and night, for at evening time it
will still be light.

8 On that day life-giving waters will flow out
from Jerusalem, half toward the Dead Sea and
half toward the Mediterranean, flowing continuously in both summer and winter.

9 And the LORD will be king over all the earth.
On that day there will be one LORD—his name
alone will be worshiped.

10 All the land from Geba, north of Judah, to
Rimmon, south of Jerusalem, will become one
vast plain. But Jerusalem will be raised up in its
original place and will be inhabited all the way
from the Benjamin Gate over to the site of the old
gate, then to the Corner Gate, and from the Tower
of Hananel to the king's winepresses. 11 And Jerusalem will be filled, safe at last, never again to be
cursed and destroyed.

12 And the LORD will send a plague on all the
nations that fought against Jerusalem. Their people will become like walking corpses, their flesh
rotting away. Their eyes will rot in their sockets,
and their tongues will rot in their mouths. 13 On
that day they will be terrified, stricken by the
LORD with great panic. They will fight their
neighbors hand to hand. 14 Judah, too, will be
fighting at Jerusalem. The wealth of all the neighboring nations will be captured—great quantities
of gold and silver and fine clothing. 15 This same
plague will strike the horses, mules, camels, donkeys, and all the other animals in the enemy
camps.

16 In the end, the enemies of Jerusalem who
survive the plague will go up to Jerusalem each
year to worship the King, the LORD of Heaven's

Armies, and to celebrate the Festival of Shelters.
17Any nation in the world that refuses to come to
Jerusalem to worship the King, the LORD of
Heaven's Armies, will have no rain. 18If the people of Egypt refuse to attend the festival, the
LORD will punish them with the same plague that
he sends on the other nations who refuse to go.
19Egypt and the other nations will all be punished if they don't go to celebrate the Festival of
Shelters.

20On that day even the harness bells of the
horses will be inscribed with these words: HOLY
TO THE LORD. And the cooking pots in the Temple
of the LORD will be as sacred as the basins used beside the altar. 21In fact, every cooking pot in Jerusalem and Judah will be holy to the LORD of
Heaven's Armies. All who come to worship will be
free to use any of these pots to boil their sacrifices. And on that day there will no longer be traders in the Temple of the LORD of Heaven's Armies.

MALACHI

God's Friendly Reminder

Malachi, the last Old Testament prophet, warned the people to turn back to God. He also told of the coming of the Messiah. Look for

- **LOTS OF QUESTIONS AND ANSWERS**
- **LOTS OF WARNINGS**
- **LOTS OF PROMISES**
- **LOTS OF GOD'S LOVE AND MERCY**

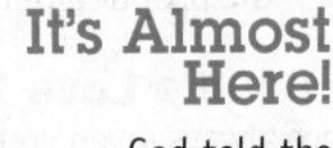

It's Almost Here!

God told the people that something *incredible* was on its way. Want to know more? **Check out Malachi 3:1-4!**

You Call That a Sacrifice?

The people were offering their sacrifices to God, so why was God unhappy? **Just take a look at Malachi 1:6-14 to find out!**

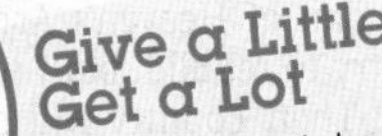

Give a Little, Get a Lot

The people had been cheating God. But instead of punishing them, God offered a way for them to get amazing blessings. Sound odd? **Find out more in Malachi 3:8-12.**

A Bad Report Card

PROPHETIC TIMES
BAD REPORT CARD

The priests of Israel got a really bad report card from God for their performance. God was *not* happy! **Read all about it in Malachi 2:1-9.**

A Happy Day

God said that on the day of judgment, the people who obeyed him would be like baby cows. Huh? (Don't worry—it's a *good* thing!) **See what God said in Malachi 4:1-3.**

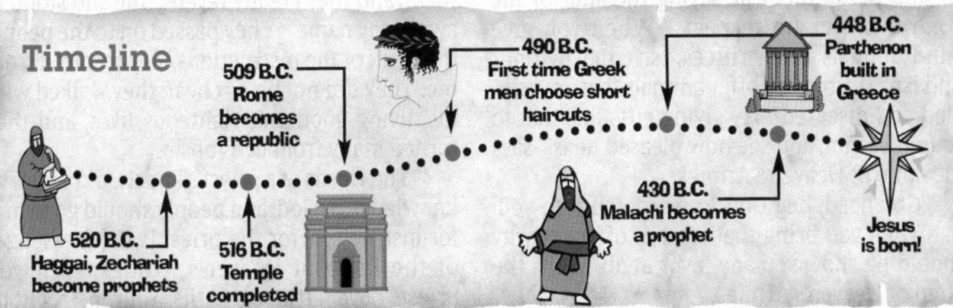
Timeline
520 B.C. Haggai, Zechariah become prophets
516 B.C. Temple completed
509 B.C. Rome becomes a republic
490 B.C. First time Greek men choose short haircuts
448 B.C. Parthenon built in Greece
430 B.C. Malachi becomes a prophet
Jesus is born!

The JESUS CONNECTION

Through Malachi, God promised blessings for the people of Israel if they would obey him. But he also made a great promise for the future—someday the Messiah, Jesus, would come to earth and make it possible for *everyone* to have a relationship with God. When Jesus did come, he opened the door of heaven for everyone who believes in him. **Not only that, he'll be with you during your life here on earth. Now that's a promise!**

CHAPTER 1

This is the message that the LORD gave to Israel
through the prophet Malachi.

The LORD's Love for Israel

2"I have always loved you," says the LORD.
But you retort, "Really? How have you loved us?"
And the LORD replies, "This is how I showed
my love for you: I loved your ancestor Jacob, 3but
I rejected his brother, Esau, and devastated his
hill country. I turned Esau's inheritance into a
desert for jackals."
4Esau's descendants in Edom may say, "We
have been shattered, but we will rebuild the
ruins."
But the LORD of Heaven's Armies replies,
"They may try to rebuild, but I will demolish
them again. Their country will be known as
'The Land of Wickedness,' and their people
will be called 'The People with Whom the
LORD Is Forever Angry.' 5When you see the destruction for yourselves, you will say, 'Truly, the
LORD's greatness reaches far beyond Israel's
borders!'"

Unworthy Sacrifices

6The LORD of Heaven's Armies says to the
priests: "A son honors his father, and a servant
respects his master. If I am your father and master, where are the honor and respect I deserve?
You have shown contempt for my name!
"But you ask, 'How have we ever shown contempt for your name?'
7"You have shown contempt by offering defiled sacrifices on my altar.
"Then you ask, 'How have we defiled the sacrifices?'
"You defile them by saying the altar of the
LORD deserves no respect. 8When you give
blind animals as sacrifices, isn't that wrong?
And isn't it wrong to offer animals that are crippled and diseased? Try giving gifts like that to
your governor, and see how pleased he is!" says
the LORD of Heaven's Armies.
9"Go ahead, beg God to be merciful to you!
But when you bring that kind of offering, why
should he show you any favor at all?" asks the
LORD of Heaven's Armies.
10"How I wish one of you would shut the
Temple doors so that these worthless sacrifices
could not be offered! I am not pleased with
you," says the LORD of Heaven's Armies, "and I
will not accept your offerings. 11But my name is
honored by people of other nations from morning till night. All around the world they offer
sweet incense and pure offerings in honor of
my name. For my name is great among the
nations," says the LORD of Heaven's Armies.
12"But you dishonor my name with your actions. By bringing contemptible food, you are
saying it's all right to defile the Lord's table.
13You say, 'It's too hard to serve the LORD,' and
you turn up your noses at my commands," says
the LORD of Heaven's Armies. "Think of it! Animals that are stolen and crippled and sick are
being presented as offerings! Should I accept
from you such offerings as these?" asks the
LORD.
14"Cursed is the cheat who promises to give a
fine ram from his flock but then sacrifices a defective one to the Lord. For I am a great king,"
says the LORD of Heaven's Armies, "and my
name is feared among the nations!

CHAPTER 2

A Warning to the Priests

"Listen, you priests—this command is for you!
2Listen to me and make up your minds to honor
my name," says the LORD of Heaven's Armies, "or
I will bring a terrible curse against you. I will
curse even the blessings you receive. Indeed, I
have already cursed them, because you have not
taken my warning to heart. 3I will punish your
descendants and splatter your faces with the
manure from your festival sacrifices, and I will
throw you on the manure pile. 4Then at last you
will know it was I who sent you this warning so
that my covenant with the Levites can continue," says the LORD of Heaven's Armies.
5"The purpose of my covenant with the Levites was to bring life and peace, and that is
what I gave them. This required reverence from
them, and they greatly revered me and stood in
awe of my name. 6They passed on to the people
the truth of the instructions they received from
me. They did not lie or cheat; they walked with
me, living good and righteous lives, and they
turned many from lives of sin.
7"The words of a priest's lips should preserve
knowledge of God, and people should go to him
for instruction, for the priest is the messenger
of the LORD of Heaven's Armies. 8But you
priests have left God's paths. Your instructions
have caused many to stumble into sin. You have
corrupted the covenant I made with the Levites," says the LORD of Heaven's Armies. 9"So I
have made you despised and humiliated in the
eyes of all the people. For you have not obeyed
me but have shown favoritism in the way you
carry out my instructions."

A Call to Faithfulness

10 Are we not all children of the same Father? Are
we not all created by the same God? Then why do
we betray each other, violating the covenant of
our ancestors?
11 Judah has been unfaithful, and a detestable
thing has been done in Israel and in Jerusalem.
The men of Judah have defiled the LORD's beloved
sanctuary by marrying women who worship idols.
12 May the LORD cut off from the nation of Israel
every last man who has done this and yet brings
an offering to the LORD of Heaven's Armies.
13 Here is another thing you do. You cover the
LORD's altar with tears, weeping and groaning because he pays no attention to your offerings and
doesn't accept them with pleasure. 14 You cry out,
"Why doesn't the LORD accept my worship?" I'll
tell you why! Because the LORD witnessed the
vows you and your wife made when you were
young. But you have been unfaithful to her,
though she remained your faithful partner, the
wife of your marriage vows.
15 Didn't the LORD make you one with your
wife? In body and spirit you are his. And what
does he want? Godly children from your union.
So guard your heart; remain loyal to the wife of
your youth. 16 "For I hate divorce!" says the LORD,
the God of Israel. "To divorce your wife is to
overwhelm her with cruelty," says the LORD of
Heaven's Armies. "So guard your heart; do not
be unfaithful to your wife."
17 You have wearied the LORD with your words.
"How have we wearied him?" you ask.
You have wearied him by saying that all who
do evil are good in the LORD's sight, and he is
pleased with them. You have wearied him by
asking, "Where is the God of justice?"

CHAPTER 3

The Coming Day of Judgment

"Look! I am sending my messenger, and he will
prepare the way before me. Then the Lord you
are seeking will suddenly come to his Temple.
The messenger of the covenant, whom you look
for so eagerly, is surely coming," says the LORD of
Heaven's Armies.
2 "But who will be able to endure it when he
comes? Who will be able to stand and face him
when he appears? For he will be like a blazing
fire that refines metal, or like a strong soap that
bleaches clothes. 3 He will sit like a refiner of silver, burning away the dross. He will purify the
Levites, refining them like gold and silver, so that
they may once again offer acceptable sacrifices
to the LORD. 4 Then once more the LORD will accept the offerings brought to him by the people
of Judah and Jerusalem, as he did in the past.
5 "At that time I will put you on trial. I am eager
to witness against all sorcerers and adulterers
and liars. I will speak against those who cheat
employees of their wages, who oppress widows
and orphans, or who deprive the foreigners living among you of justice, for these people do not
fear me," says the LORD of Heaven's Armies.

A Call to Repentance

6 "I am the LORD, and I do not change. That is why
you descendants of Jacob are not already destroyed. 7 Ever since the days of your ancestors,
you have scorned my decrees and failed to obey
them. Now return to me, and I will return to you,"
says the LORD of Heaven's Armies.
"But you ask, 'How can we return when we
have never gone away?'
8 "Should people cheat God? Yet you have
cheated me!
"But you ask, 'What do you mean? When did
we ever cheat you?'
"You have cheated me of the tithes and offerings due to me. 9 You are under a curse, for your
whole nation has been cheating me. 10 Bring all
the tithes into the storehouse so there will be
enough food in my Temple. If you do," says the
LORD of Heaven's Armies, "I will open the windows of heaven for you. I will pour out a blessing
so great you won't have enough room to take it in!
Try it! Put me to the test! 11 Your crops will be
abundant, for I will guard them from insects and
disease. Your grapes will not fall from the vine
before they are ripe," says the LORD of Heaven's
Armies. 12 "Then all nations will call you blessed,
for your land will be such a delight," says the
LORD of Heaven's Armies.
13 "You have said terrible things about me,"
says the LORD.
"But you say, 'What do you mean? What have
we said against you?'
14 "You have said, 'What's the use of serving
God? What have we gained by obeying his commands or by trying to show the LORD of Heaven's
Armies that we are sorry for our sins? 15 From
now on we will call the arrogant blessed. For
those who do evil get rich, and those who dare
God to punish them suffer no harm.'"

The LORD's Promise of Mercy

16 Then those who feared the LORD spoke with
each other, and the LORD listened to what they
said. In his presence, a scroll of remembrance
was written to record the names of those who

feared him and always thought about the honor
of his name.
[17]"They will be my people," says the LORD of
Heaven's Armies. "On the day when I act in judgment, they will be my own special treasure. I will
spare them as a father spares an obedient child.
[18]Then you will again see the difference between
the righteous and the wicked, between those
who serve God and those who do not."

CHAPTER **4**

The Coming Day of Judgment

The LORD of Heaven's Armies says, "The day of
judgment is coming, burning like a furnace. On
that day the arrogant and the wicked will be
burned up like straw. They will be consumed—
roots, branches, and all.

[2]**"But for you who fear my name,
the Sun of Righteousness will rise
with healing in his wings. And you will
go free, leaping with joy like calves
let out to pasture.** [3]On the day when I act,
you will tread upon the wicked as if they were
dust under your feet," says the LORD of Heaven's
Armies.

[4]"Remember to obey the Law of Moses, my
servant—all the decrees and regulations that I
gave him on Mount Sinai for all Israel.

[5]"Look, I am sending you the prophet Elijah
before the great and dreadful day of the LORD
arrives. [6]His preaching will turn the hearts of
fathers to their children, and the hearts of children to their fathers. Otherwise I will come and
strike the land with a curse."

NEW
TESTAMENT

MATTHEW The Messiah Is Here!

Look for  hidden messages in Matthew!

Matthew wrote his book of the Bible to prove that Jesus is the Messiah. Look for these events in Jesus' life:

- **BIRTH AS A BABY**
- **MANHOOD MIRACLES**
- **POWERFUL PARABLES**
- **SUFFERING SERVANTHOOD**
- **CRUCIFIXION ON THE CROSS**
- **RESURRECTION AS THE RISEN SAVIOR!**

Messiah Makes Waves—and Calms Them Too!

Jesus made lots of waves with his words and actions. Not only did he make waves, he *talked* to waves. Want to know more? **Read the stormy story in Matthew 8:23-27.**

Sports Report—Getting Warmed Up

Jesus put himself through some pretty rough workouts as he "warmed up" for his ministry. **Read more about Jesus' warm-up for the big job ahead in Matthew 3:1–4:11.**

Show Us the King!

A group of wise men came all the way to Jerusalem to see the new king. That was quite a surprise to Herod, who thought *he* was the only king around. **Read all about it in Matthew 2:1-12.**

HEY! Have You Heard?

Everyone was talking about him! Some said good things, some said bad. But *everyone* had an opinion. Who were they talking about, and what did they say? **Read Matthew 4:23-25 (for some good reactions) and Matthew 12:9-14 (for some bad ones).**

Jesus Shocks Religious Community
Pharisees Up In Arms
Who is Jesus
And Why Is He Saying Those Things?

Tell Us More!

Jesus had a way of talking about God so that everyone could understand. **Read a few of his stories (actually they're called parables) in Matthew 13:1-52!**

A Verrry Long Week

It may have seemed like the longest week in history. It started with a parade, but went downhill fast from there. **Read about the high and low points in Matthew 21:1-11 and Matthew 27:26-50.**

Sneak Preview

Storms were on the horizon and growing closer. Jesus knew exactly what was going to happen, and he gave his disciples a shocking sneak preview. **Read what he said in Matthew 20:17-19.**

WANTED
FOR LOVING EVERYONE

Oh Happy Day!

Jesus had died. He had been crucified. His body had been placed in a guarded tomb. So why were his followers so happy? **Find out the amazing reason for yourself in Matthew 28:1-10!**

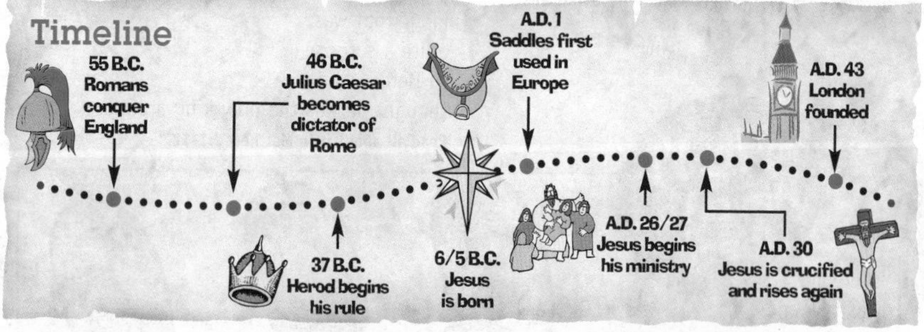
Timeline
55 B.C. Romans conquer England
46 B.C. Julius Caesar becomes dictator of Rome
37 B.C. Herod begins his rule
6/5 B.C. Jesus is born
A.D. 1 Saddles first used in Europe
A.D. 26/27 Jesus begins his ministry
A.D. 30 Jesus is crucified and rises again
A.D. 43 London founded

The JESUS CONNECTION

The book of Matthew is *all* about Jesus. It's one of the four Gospels, the books that tell us about Jesus' life. We get to follow Jesus from birth to death, to his resurrection, and into the clouds as he ascended to heaven. **Thanks to the Gospel writers, we understand who Jesus is—God's Son!—and what his life on earth was all about—reaching out to people with God's gift of love.**

CHAPTER 1

The Ancestors of Jesus the Messiah

This is a record of the ancestors of Jesus the Messiah, a descendant of David and of Abraham:

2 Abraham was the father of Isaac.
Isaac was the father of Jacob.
Jacob was the father of Judah and
his brothers.
3 Judah was the father of Perez and Zerah
(whose mother was Tamar).
Perez was the father of Hezron.
Hezron was the father of Ram.
4 Ram was the father of Amminadab.
Amminadab was the father of Nahshon.
Nahshon was the father of Salmon.
5 Salmon was the father of Boaz (whose
mother was Rahab).
Boaz was the father of Obed (whose
mother was Ruth).
Obed was the father of Jesse.
6 Jesse was the father of King David.
David was the father of Solomon (whose
mother was Bathsheba, the widow
of Uriah).
7 Solomon was the father of Rehoboam.
Rehoboam was the father of Abijah.
Abijah was the father of Asa.
8 Asa was the father of Jehoshaphat.
Jehoshaphat was the father of Jehoram.
Jehoram was the father of Uzziah.
9 Uzziah was the father of Jotham.
Jotham was the father of Ahaz.
Ahaz was the father of Hezekiah.
10 Hezekiah was the father of Manasseh.
Manasseh was the father of Amon.
Amon was the father of Josiah.
11 Josiah was the father of Jehoiachin and
his brothers (born at the time of the
exile to Babylon).
12 After the Babylonian exile:
Jehoiachin was the father of Shealtiel.
Shealtiel was the father of Zerubbabel.
13 Zerubbabel was the father of Abiud.
Abiud was the father of Eliakim.
Eliakim was the father of Azor.
14 Azor was the father of Zadok.
Zadok was the father of Akim.
Akim was the father of Eliud.
15 Eliud was the father of Eleazar.
Eleazar was the father of Matthan.
Matthan was the father of Jacob.
16 Jacob was the father of Joseph, the
husband of Mary.
Mary gave birth to Jesus, who is called
the Messiah.

17 All those listed above include fourteen generations from Abraham to David, fourteen from
David to the Babylonian exile, and fourteen from
the Babylonian exile to the Messiah.

The Birth of Jesus the Messiah

18 This is how Jesus the Messiah was born. His
mother, Mary, was engaged to be married to Joseph. But before the marriage took place, while
she was still a virgin, she became pregnant
through the power of the Holy Spirit. 19 Joseph,
her fiancé, was a good man and did not want to
disgrace her publicly, so he decided to break the
engagement quietly.

20 As he considered this, an angel of the Lord
appeared to him in a dream. "Joseph, son of
David," the angel said, "do not be afraid to take
Mary as your wife. For the child within her was
conceived by the Holy Spirit. 21 And she will have
a son, and you are to name him Jesus, for he will
save his people from their sins."

22 All of this occurred to fulfill the Lord's message through his prophet:

23 "Look! The virgin will conceive a child!
She will give birth to a son,
and they will call him Immanuel,
which means 'God is with us.'"

24 When Joseph woke up, he did as the angel of
the Lord commanded and took Mary as his wife.
25 But he did not have sexual relations with her
until her son was born. And Joseph named him
Jesus.

CHAPTER 2

Visitors from the East

Jesus was born in Bethlehem in Judea, during the
reign of King Herod. About that time some wise
men from eastern lands arrived in Jerusalem,
asking, 2 "Where is the newborn king of the Jews?
We saw his star as it rose, and we have come to
worship him."

3 King Herod was deeply disturbed when he
heard this, as was everyone in Jerusalem. 4 He
called a meeting of the leading priests and teachers of religious law and asked, "Where is the
Messiah supposed to be born?"

5 "In Bethlehem in Judea," they said, "for this is
what the prophet wrote:

6 'And you, O Bethlehem in the land of Judah,
are not least among the ruling cities
of Judah,

for a ruler will come from you
  who will be the shepherd for my
    people Israel.'"

7 Then Herod called for a private meeting with
the wise men, and he learned from them the time
when the star first appeared. 8 Then he told them,
"Go to Bethlehem and search carefully for the
child. And when you find him, come back and tell
me so that I can go and worship him, too!"

9 After this interview the wise men went their
way. And the star they had seen in the east guided
them to Bethlehem. It went ahead of them and
stopped over the place where the child was.
10 When they saw the star, they were filled with
joy! 11 They entered the house and saw the child
with his mother, Mary, and they bowed down and
worshiped him. Then they opened their treasure
chests and gave him gifts of gold, frankincense,
and myrrh.

12 When it was time to leave, they returned to
their own country by another route, for God had
warned them in a dream not to return to Herod.

The Escape to Egypt

13 After the wise men were gone, an angel of the
Lord appeared to Joseph in a dream. "Get up!
Flee to Egypt with the child and his mother," the
angel said. "Stay there until I tell you to return,
because Herod is going to search for the child to
kill him."

14 That night Joseph left for Egypt with the
child and Mary, his mother, 15 and they stayed
there until Herod's death. This fulfilled what the
Lord had spoken through the prophet: "I called
my Son out of Egypt."

16 Herod was furious when he realized that the
wise men had outwitted him. He sent soldiers to
kill all the boys in and around Bethlehem who
were two years old and under, based on the wise
men's report of the star's first appearance. 17 Herod's brutal action fulfilled what God had spoken
through the prophet Jeremiah:

18 "A cry was heard in Ramah—
  weeping and great mourning.
Rachel weeps for her children,
  refusing to be comforted,
  for they are dead."

The Return to Nazareth

19 When Herod died, an angel of the Lord appeared in a dream to Joseph in Egypt. 20 "Get up!"
the angel said. "Take the child and his mother
back to the land of Israel, because those who
were trying to kill the child are dead."

21 So Joseph got up and returned to the land of
Israel with Jesus and his mother. 22 But when he
learned that the new ruler of Judea was Herod's
son Archelaus, he was afraid to go there. Then, after being warned in a dream, he left for the region
of Galilee. 23 So the family went and lived in a
town called Nazareth. This fulfilled what the
prophets had said: "He will be called a Nazarene."

CHAPTER 3

John the Baptist Prepares the Way

In those days John the Baptist came to the Judean
wilderness and began preaching. His message
was, 2 "Repent of your sins and turn to God, for
the Kingdom of Heaven is near." 3 The prophet
Isaiah was speaking about John when he said,

"He is a voice shouting in the wilderness,
'Prepare the way for the LORD's coming!
  Clear the road for him!'"

4 John's clothes were woven from coarse
camel hair, and he wore a leather belt around his
waist. For food he ate locusts and wild honey.
5 People from Jerusalem and from all of Judea
and all over the Jordan Valley went out to see and
hear John. 6 And when they confessed their sins,
he baptized them in the Jordan River.

7 But when he saw many Pharisees and Sadducees coming to watch him baptize, he denounced
them. "You brood of snakes!" he exclaimed.
"Who warned you to flee God's coming wrath?
8 Prove by the way you live that you have repented
of your sins and turned to God. 9 Don't just say to
each other, 'We're safe, for we are descendants of
Abraham.' That means nothing, for I tell you, God
can create children of Abraham from these very
stones. 10 Even now the ax of God's judgment is
poised, ready to sever the roots of the trees. Yes,
every tree that does not produce good fruit will
be chopped down and thrown into the fire.

11 "I baptize with water those who repent of
their sins and turn to God. But someone is coming soon who is greater than I am—so much
greater that I'm not worthy even to be his slave
and carry his sandals. He will baptize you with
the Holy Spirit and with fire. 12 He is ready to separate the chaff from the wheat with his winnowing fork. Then he will clean up the threshing area,
gathering the wheat into his barn but burning
the chaff with never-ending fire."

The Baptism of Jesus

13 Then Jesus went from Galilee to the Jordan
River to be baptized by John. 14 But John tried to

Disappearing Act

MATTHEW 2:13-15 tells how Jesus and his family "disappeared."
Read it! Make something disappear yourself!

Read Psalm 121 for more about God's protection!

1. **Sit at a table. Place a quarter on top of a saltshaker.**
2. **Cover the coin and saltshaker with a handkerchief, and place your hand over the top. Wave the saltshaker and quarter back and forth.**
3. **Secretly drop the saltshaker into your lap while still holding the coin so it looks like you're still holding the saltshaker.**
4. **Smash the handkerchief down on the table.**

handkerchief

quarter

saltshaker

POOF

YOU MADE THE SALTSHAKER DISAPPEAR!
(Not really, but it was a pretty good trick.)
God helped Jesus and his family "disappear" when Jesus was in danger, and that was *no* trick!

talk him out of it. "I am the one who needs to be
baptized by you," he said, "so why are you coming
to me?"
15But Jesus said, "It should be done, for we
must carry out all that God requires." So John
agreed to baptize him.
16After his baptism, as Jesus came up out of the
water, the heavens were opened and he saw the
Spirit of God descending like a dove and settling
on him. 17And a voice from heaven said, "This is
my dearly loved Son, who brings me great joy."

CHAPTER 4

The Temptation of Jesus

Then Jesus was led by the Spirit into the wilderness to be tempted there by the devil. 2For forty
days and forty nights he fasted and became very
hungry.
3During that time the devil came and said to
him, "If you are the Son of God, tell these stones
to become loaves of bread."
4But Jesus told him, "No! The Scriptures say,

'People do not live by bread alone,
but by every word that comes from the
mouth of God.'"

5Then the devil took him to the holy city, Jerusalem, to the highest point of the Temple, 6and
said, "If you are the Son of God, jump off! For the
Scriptures say,

'He will order his angels to protect you.
And they will hold you up with their hands
so you won't even hurt your foot
on a stone.'"

7Jesus responded, "The Scriptures also say,
'You must not test the LORD your God.'"
8Next the devil took him to the peak of a very
high mountain and showed him all the kingdoms of the world and their glory. 9"I will give it
all to you," he said, "if you will kneel down and
worship me."
10"Get out of here, Satan," Jesus told him. "For
the Scriptures say,

'You must worship the LORD your God
and serve only him.'"

11Then the devil went away, and angels came
and took care of Jesus.

The Ministry of Jesus Begins

12When Jesus heard that John had been arrested, he left Judea and returned to Galilee.
13He went first to Nazareth, then left there and
moved to Capernaum, beside the Sea of Galilee,
in the region of Zebulun and Naphtali. 14This
fulfilled what God said through the prophet
Isaiah:

15 "In the land of Zebulun and of Naphtali,
beside the sea, beyond the Jordan River,
in Galilee where so many Gentiles live,
16 the people who sat in darkness
have seen a great light.
And for those who lived in the land where
death casts its shadow,
a light has shined."

17From then on Jesus began to preach, "Repent
of your sins and turn to God, for the Kingdom of
Heaven is near."

Matthew 5 . . . page 944

The First Disciples

18One day as Jesus was walking along the shore
of the Sea of Galilee, he saw two brothers—
Simon, also called Peter, and Andrew—throwing
a net into the water, for they fished for a living.
19Jesus called out to them, "Come, follow me,
and I will show you how to fish for people!"
20And they left their nets at once and followed
him.
21A little farther up the shore he saw two
other brothers, James and John, sitting in a boat
with their father, Zebedee, repairing their nets.
And he called them to come, too. 22They immediately followed him, leaving the boat and their
father behind.

Crowds Follow Jesus

23Jesus traveled throughout the region of Galilee, teaching in the synagogues and announcing the Good News about the Kingdom. And
he healed every kind of disease and illness.
24News about him spread as far as Syria, and
people soon began bringing to him all who were
sick. And whatever their sickness or disease,
or if they were demon possessed or epileptic or
paralyzed—he healed them all. 25Large crowds
followed him wherever he went—people from
Galilee, the Ten Towns, Jerusalem, from all over
Judea, and from east of the Jordan River.

CHAPTER 5

The Sermon on the Mount

One day as he saw the crowds gathering, Jesus
went up on the mountainside and sat down. His
disciples gathered around him, 2and he began to
teach them.

The Beatitudes

3 "God blesses those who are poor and
realize their need for him,
for the Kingdom of Heaven is theirs.
4 God blesses those who mourn,
for they will be comforted.
5 God blesses those who are humble,
for they will inherit the whole earth.
6 God blesses those who hunger and thirst
for justice,
for they will be satisfied.
7 God blesses those who are merciful,
for they will be shown mercy.
8 God blesses those whose hearts
are pure,
for they will see God.
9 God blesses those who work for peace,
for they will be called the children
of God.
10 God blesses those who are persecuted
for doing right,
for the Kingdom of Heaven
is theirs.

11"God blesses you when people mock you
and persecute you and lie about you and say all
sorts of evil things against you because you are
my followers. 12Be happy about it! Be very glad!

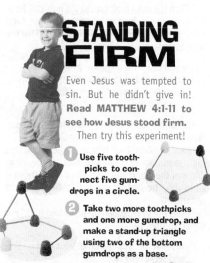

STANDING FIRM

Even Jesus was tempted to sin. But he didn't give in! **Read MATTHEW 4:1-11 to see how Jesus stood firm.** Then try this experiment!

1. **Use five toothpicks to connect five gumdrops in a circle.**

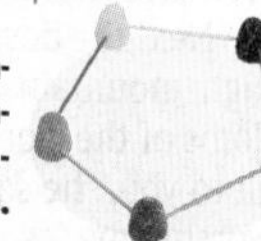

2. **Take two more toothpicks and one more gumdrop, and make a stand-up triangle using two of the bottom gumdrops as a base.**
3. **Keep making triangles until you have five triangles sticking up from the base.**

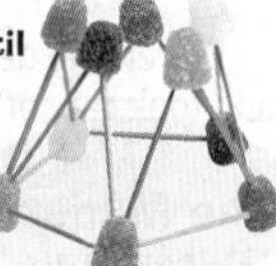

Make as many structures as you want, and let them dry overnight. Then see how many books you can stack on top!

As the gumdrops got harder, they became stronger.

SCRIPTURE HELPS US STAND STRONG.

Cut three small paper flags. On each flag write a Scripture verse that will help you stand firm against temptation. Attach the flags to toothpicks, and stick each flag in a gumdrop. Keep them by your bed to remind you that Jesus taught us how to resist temptation!

For a great reward awaits you in heaven. And
remember, the ancient prophets were persecuted in the same way.

Teaching about Salt and Light

13"You are the salt of the earth. But what good is
salt if it has lost its flavor? Can you make it salty
again? It will be thrown out and trampled
underfoot as worthless.
14"You are the light of the world—like a city
on a hilltop that cannot be hidden. 15No one
lights a lamp and then puts it under a basket.
Instead, a lamp is placed on a stand, where it
gives light to everyone in the house. 16In the
same way, let your good deeds shine out for all to
see, so that everyone will praise your heavenly
Father.

Teaching about the Law

17"Don't misunderstand why I have come. I did
not come to abolish the law of Moses or the writings of the prophets. No, I came to accomplish
their purpose. 18I tell you the truth, until heaven
and earth disappear, not even the smallest detail
of God's law will disappear until its purpose is
achieved. 19So if you ignore the least commandment and teach others to do the same, you will
be called the least in the Kingdom of Heaven.
But anyone who obeys God's laws and teaches
them will be called great in the Kingdom of
Heaven.
20"But I warn you—unless your righteousness
is better than the righteousness of the teachers
of religious law and the Pharisees, you will never
enter the Kingdom of Heaven!

Teaching about Anger

21"You have heard that our ancestors were told,
'You must not murder. If you commit murder,
you are subject to judgment.' 22But I say, if you
are even angry with someone, you are subject to
judgment! If you call someone an idiot, you are
in danger of being brought before the court.
And if you curse someone, you are in danger of
the fires of hell.
23"So if you are presenting a sacrifice at the
altar in the Temple and you suddenly remember
that someone has something against you,
24leave your sacrifice there at the altar. Go and
be reconciled to that person. Then come and offer your sacrifice to God.
25"When you are on the way to court with
your adversary, settle your differences quickly.
Otherwise, your accuser may hand you over to
the judge, who will hand you over to an officer,
and you will be thrown into prison. 26And if that
happens, you surely won't be free again until you
have paid the last penny.

Teaching about Adultery

27"You have heard the commandment that
says, 'You must not commit adultery.' 28But I
say, anyone who even looks at a woman with
lust has already committed adultery with her in
his heart. 29So if your eye—even your good
eye—causes you to lust, gouge it out and throw
it away. It is better for you to lose one part of
your body than for your whole body to be
thrown into hell. 30And if your hand—even
your stronger hand—causes you to sin, cut it off
and throw it away. It is better for you to lose one
part of your body than for your whole body to
be thrown into hell.

Teaching about Divorce

31"You have heard the law that says, 'A man can
divorce his wife by merely giving her a written
notice of divorce.' 32But I say that a man who
divorces his wife, unless she has been unfaithful, causes her to commit adultery. And anyone
who marries a divorced woman also commits
adultery.

Teaching about Vows

33"You have also heard that our ancestors were
told, 'You must not break your vows; you must
carry out the vows you make to the LORD.' 34But
I say, do not make any vows! Do not say, 'By
heaven!' because heaven is God's throne. 35And
do not say, 'By the earth!' because the earth is his
footstool. And do not say, 'By Jerusalem!' for
Jerusalem is the city of the great King. 36Do not
even say, 'By my head!' for you can't turn one
hair white or black. 37Just say a simple, 'Yes, I
will,' or 'No, I won't.' Anything beyond this is
from the evil one.

Teaching about Revenge

38"You have heard the law that says the punishment must match the injury: 'An eye for an eye,
and a tooth for a tooth.' 39But I say, do not resist
an evil person! If someone slaps you on the right
cheek, offer the other cheek also. 40If you are
sued in court and your shirt is taken from you,
give your coat, too. 41If a soldier demands that
you carry his gear for a mile, carry it two miles.
42Give to those who ask, and don't turn away
from those who want to borrow.

Matthew 6 . . . page 946

Teaching about Love for Enemies

43"You have heard the law that says, 'Love your
neighbor' and hate your enemy. **44But I say,
love your enemies!* Pray for those
who persecute you!** 45In that way, you will
be acting as true children of your Father in
heaven. For he gives his sunlight to both the evil
and the good, and he sends rain on the just and
the unjust alike. 46If you love only those who
love you, what reward is there for that? Even
corrupt tax collectors do that much. 47If you are
kind only to your friends, how are you different
from anyone else? Even pagans do that. 48But
you are to be perfect, even as your Father in
heaven is perfect.

CHAPTER **6**

Teaching about Giving to the Needy

"Watch out! Don't do your good deeds publicly,
to be admired by others, for you will lose the reward from your Father in heaven. 2When you
give to someone in need, don't do as the hypocrites do—blowing trumpets in the synagogues
and streets to call attention to their acts of char-
ity! I tell you the truth, they have received all the
reward they will ever get. 3But when you give to
someone in need, don't let your left hand know
what your right hand is doing. 4Give your gifts
in private, and your Father, who sees everything,
will reward you.

Teaching about Prayer and Fasting

5"When you pray, don't be like the hypocrites
who love to pray publicly on street corners and
in the synagogues where everyone can see
them. I tell you the truth, that is all the reward
they will ever get. 6But when you pray, go away
by yourself, shut the door behind you, and pray
to your Father in private. Then your Father, who
sees everything, will reward you.

7"When you pray, don't babble on and on as
people of other religions do. They think their
prayers are answered merely by repeating their
words again and again. 8Don't be like them, for
your Father knows exactly what you need even
before you ask him! 9Pray like this:

Our Father in heaven,
  may your name be kept holy.
10 May your Kingdom come soon.
  May your will be done on earth,
  as it is in heaven.
11 Give us today the food we need,
12 and forgive us our sins,
  as we have forgiven those who sin
  against us.
13 And don't let us yield to temptation,
  but rescue us from the evil one.*

14"If you forgive those who sin against you,
your heavenly Father will forgive you. 15But if you
refuse to forgive others, your Father will not forgive your sins.

16"And when you fast, don't make it obvious, as
the hypocrites do, for they try to look miserable
and disheveled so people will admire them for
their fasting. I tell you the truth, that is the only
reward they will ever get. 17But when you fast,
comb your hair and wash your face. 18Then no
one will notice that you are fasting, except your
Father, who knows what you do in private. And
your Father, who sees everything, will reward
you.

Teaching about Money and Possessions

19"Don't store up treasures here on earth, where
moths eat them and rust destroys them, and
where thieves break in and steal. 20Store your
treasures in heaven, where moths and rust cannot destroy, and thieves do not break in and steal.
21Wherever your treasure is, there the desires of
your heart will also be.

22"Your eye is a lamp that provides light for
your body. When your eye is good, your whole
body is filled with light. 23But when your eye is
bad, your whole body is filled with darkness. And
if the light you think you have is actually darkness, how deep that darkness is!

24"No one can serve two masters. For you will
hate one and love the other; you will be devoted
to one and despise the other. You cannot serve
both God and money.

25"That is why I tell you not to worry about
everyday life—whether you have enough food
and drink, or enough clothes to wear. Isn't life
more than food, and your body more than clothing? 26Look at the birds. They don't plant or harvest or store food in barns, for your heavenly
Father feeds them. And aren't you far more valuable to him than they are? 27Can all your worries
add a single moment to your life?

28"And why worry about your clothing? Look at
the lilies of the field and how they grow. They

5:44 Some manuscripts add *Bless those who curse you. Do good to those who hate you.* Compare Luke 6:27-28. 6:13 Some manuscripts add *For yours is the kingdom and the power and the glory forever. Amen.*

don't work or make their clothing, 29 yet Solomon
in all his glory was not dressed as beautifully as
they are. 30 And if God cares so wonderfully for
wildflowers that are here today and thrown into
the fire tomorrow, he will certainly care for you.
Why do you have so little faith?
31 "So don't worry about these things, saying,
'What will we eat? What will we drink? What will
we wear?' 32 These things dominate the thoughts
of unbelievers, but your heavenly Father already
knows all your needs. 33 Seek the Kingdom of
God above all else, and live righteously, and he
will give you everything you need.
34 "So don't worry about tomorrow, for tomorrow will bring its own worries. Today's trouble is
enough for today.

CHAPTER 7

Do Not Judge Others

"Do not judge others, and you will not be judged.
2 For you will be treated as you treat others. The
standard you use in judging is the standard by
which you will be judged.
3 "And why worry about a speck in your
friend's eye when you have a log in your own?
4 How can you think of saying to your friend, 'Let
me help you get rid of that speck in your eye,'
when you can't see past the log in your own eye?
5 Hypocrite! First get rid of the log in your own
eye; then you will see well enough to deal with
the speck in your friend's eye.
6 "Don't waste what is holy on people who are
unholy. Don't throw your pearls to pigs! They
will trample the pearls, then turn and attack you.

Effective Prayer

7 "Keep on asking, and you will receive what you
ask for. Keep on seeking, and you will find. Keep
on knocking, and the door will be opened to you.
8 For everyone who asks, receives. Everyone who
seeks, finds. And to everyone who knocks, the
door will be opened.
9 "You parents—if your children ask for a loaf
of bread, do you give them a stone instead? 10 Or
if they ask for a fish, do you give them a snake?
Of course not! 11 So if you sinful people know
how to give good gifts to your children, how
much more will your heavenly Father give good
gifts to those who ask him.

The Golden Rule

**12 "Do to others whatever you would
like them to do to you. This is the essence of all that is taught in the law
and the prophets.**

The Way to Pray

Jesus taught us the best way to pray.
Read his recipe for prayer in MATTHEW 6:9-13.

THEN MAKE YOUR OWN RECIPE.

1 **Gather five trail mix ingredients in separate bowls.**

2 **Put a small handful of each ingredient in a small plastic bag. Then zip the bag shut. Keep making bags.**

3 **Use a fine-tipped permanent marker to write, "MATTHEW 6:9-13: The Recipe for Prayer" on each bag.**

The **five ingredients** in your trail mix can remind you of **five ingredients** in the Lord's Prayer:

- **Praise** *(honoring God)*
- **Purpose** *(wanting God's will, not our own)*
- **Provision** *(trusting God to take care of us)*
- **Pardon** *(forgiveness from God and for others)*
- **Protection** *(from temptation and evil)*

GIVE YOUR BAGS AWAY TO FAMILY MEMBERS AND FRIENDS. TELL THEM TO READ THE LORD'S PRAYER TO LEARN THE WAY TO PRAY!

The Narrow Gate

13 "You can enter God's Kingdom only through
the narrow gate. The highway to hell is broad,
and its gate is wide for the many who choose that
way. 14 But the gateway to life is very narrow and
the road is difficult, and only a few ever find it.

The Tree and Its Fruit

15 "Beware of false prophets who come disguised
as harmless sheep but are really vicious wolves.
16 You can identify them by their fruit, that is,
by the way they act. Can you pick grapes from
thornbushes, or figs from thistles? 17 A good tree
produces good fruit, and a bad tree produces
bad fruit. 18 A good tree can't produce bad fruit,
and a bad tree can't produce good fruit. 19 So
every tree that does not produce good fruit is

chopped down and thrown into the fire. 20 Yes,
just as you can identify a tree by its fruit, so you
can identify people by their actions.

True Disciples

21 "Not everyone who calls out to me, 'Lord! Lord!'
will enter the Kingdom of Heaven. Only those
who actually do the will of my Father in heaven
will enter. 22 On judgment day many will say to
me, 'Lord! Lord! We prophesied in your name
and cast out demons in your name and performed many miracles in your name.' 23 But I will
reply, 'I never knew you. Get away from me, you
who break God's laws.'

Building on a Solid Foundation

24 "Anyone who listens to my teaching and follows
it is wise, like a person who builds a house on
solid rock. 25 Though the rain comes in torrents
and the floodwaters rise and the winds beat
against that house, it won't collapse because it is
built on bedrock. 26 But anyone who hears my
teaching and doesn't obey it is foolish, like a person who builds a house on sand. 27 When the
rains and floods come and the winds beat against
that house, it will collapse with a mighty crash."
28 When Jesus had finished saying these
things, the crowds were amazed at his teaching,
29 for he taught with real authority—quite unlike
their teachers of religious law.

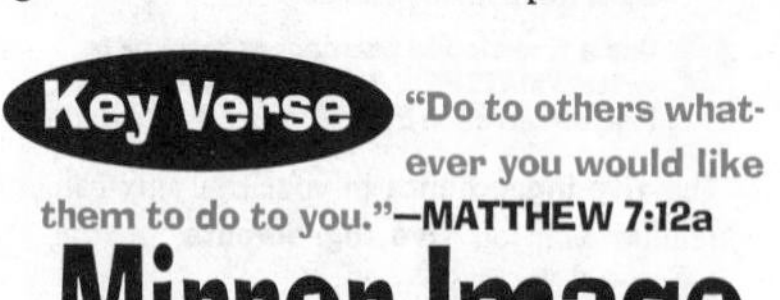

Key Verse **"Do to others whatever you would like them to do to you."—MATTHEW 7:12a**

Mirror Image

Read MATTHEW 7:12a out loud with a friend. Say it together a few times.

Place your palms near your friend's palms, about an inch apart. Slowly move your hands while your friend tries to follow your motions. Then switch roles.

You tried to mirror your friend's motions.

Jesus wants us to treat other people exactly how we'd like to be treated—to be a mirror image of how we'd like to be treated! Write this verse on a sticky note on your bathroom mirror to remind you to be a mirror image!

CHAPTER 8

Jesus Heals a Man with Leprosy

Large crowds followed Jesus as he came down
the mountainside. 2 Suddenly, a man with leprosy approached him and knelt before him.
"Lord," the man said, "if you are willing, you can
heal me and make me clean."
3 Jesus reached out and touched him. "I am
willing," he said. "Be healed!" And instantly the
leprosy disappeared. 4 Then Jesus said to him,
"Don't tell anyone about this. Instead, go to the
priest and let him examine you. Take along the
offering required in the law of Moses for those
who have been healed of leprosy. This will be a
public testimony that you have been cleansed."

The Faith of a Roman Officer

5 When Jesus returned to Capernaum, a Roman
officer came and pleaded with him, 6 "Lord, my
young servant lies in bed, paralyzed and in terrible pain."
7 Jesus said, "I will come and heal him."
8 But the officer said, "Lord, I am not worthy to
have you come into my home. Just say the word
from where you are, and my servant will
be healed. 9 I know this because I am under the
authority of my superior officers, and I have
authority over my soldiers. I only need to say,
'Go,' and they go, or 'Come,' and they come. And
if I say to my slaves, 'Do this,' they do it."
10 When Jesus heard this, he was amazed.
Turning to those who were following him, he
said, "I tell you the truth, I haven't seen faith like
this in all Israel! 11 And I tell you this, that many
Gentiles will come from all over the world—from
east and west—and sit down with Abraham,
Isaac, and Jacob at the feast in the Kingdom of
Heaven. 12 But many Israelites—those for whom
the Kingdom was prepared—will be thrown into
outer darkness, where there will be weeping and
gnashing of teeth."
13 Then Jesus said to the Roman officer, "Go
back home. Because you believed, it has happened." And the young servant was healed that
same hour.

the pigs, and the whole herd plunged down the
steep hillside into the lake and drowned in the
water.
33 The herdsmen fled to the nearby town, telling everyone what happened to the demon-
possessed men. 34 Then the entire town came
out to meet Jesus, but they begged him to go
away and leave them alone.

CHAPTER 9

Jesus Heals a Paralyzed Man

Jesus climbed into a boat and went back across
the lake to his own town. 2 Some people brought
to him a paralyzed man on a mat. Seeing their
faith, Jesus said to the paralyzed man, "Be encouraged, my child! Your sins are forgiven."
3 But some of the teachers of religious law said
to themselves, "That's blasphemy! Does he think
he's God?"
4 Jesus knew what they were thinking, so he
asked them, "Why do you have such evil thoughts
in your hearts? 5 Is it easier to say 'Your sins are
forgiven,' or 'Stand up and walk'? 6 So I will prove
to you that the Son of Man has the authority on
earth to forgive sins." Then Jesus turned to the
paralyzed man and said, "Stand up, pick up your
mat, and go home!"
7 And the man jumped up and went home!
8 Fear swept through the crowd as they saw this
happen. And they praised God for sending a man
with such great authority.

Jesus Calls Matthew

9 As Jesus was walking along, he saw a man
named Matthew sitting at his tax collector's
booth. "Follow me and be my disciple," Jesus said
to him. So Matthew got up and followed him.
10 Later, Matthew invited Jesus and his disciples to his home as dinner guests, along with
many tax collectors and other disreputable sinners. 11 But when the Pharisees saw this, they
asked his disciples, "Why does your teacher eat
with such scum?"
12 When Jesus heard this, he said, "Healthy
people don't need a doctor—sick people do."
13 Then he added, "Now go and learn the meaning of this Scripture: 'I want you to show mercy,
not offer sacrifices.' For I have come to call not
those who think they are righteous, but those
who know they are sinners."

A Discussion about Fasting

14 One day the disciples of John the Baptist came
to Jesus and asked him, "Why don't your disciples fast like we do and the Pharisees do?"
15 Jesus replied, "Do wedding guests mourn
while celebrating with the groom? Of course
not. But someday the groom will be taken away
from them, and then they will fast.
16 "Besides, who would patch old clothing with
new cloth? For the new patch would shrink and
rip away from the old cloth, leaving an even bigger tear than before.
17 "And no one puts new wine into old wineskins. For the old skins would burst from the
pressure, spilling the wine and ruining the skins.
New wine is stored in new wineskins so that both
are preserved."

Jesus Heals in Response to Faith

18 As Jesus was saying this, the leader of a synagogue came and knelt before him. "My daughter
has just died," he said, "but you can bring her
back to life again if you just come and lay your
hand on her."
19 So Jesus and his disciples got up and went
with him. 20 Just then a woman who had suffered
for twelve years with constant bleeding came up
behind him. She touched the fringe of his robe,
21 for she thought, "If I can just touch his robe, I
will be healed."
22 Jesus turned around, and when he saw her
he said, "Daughter, be encouraged! Your faith has
made you well." And the woman was healed at
that moment.
23 When Jesus arrived at the official's home,
he saw the noisy crowd and heard the funeral
music. 24 "Get out!" he told them. "The girl isn't
dead; she's only asleep." But the crowd laughed
at him. 25 After the crowd was put outside, however, Jesus went in and took the girl by the hand,
and she stood up! 26 The report of this miracle
swept through the entire countryside.

Jesus Heals the Blind

27 After Jesus left the girl's home, two blind men
followed along behind him, shouting, "Son of
David, have mercy on us!"
28 They went right into the house where he
was staying, and Jesus asked them, "Do you
believe I can make you see?"
"Yes, Lord," they told him, "we do."
29 Then he touched their eyes and said, "Because of your faith, it will happen." 30 Then their
eyes were opened, and they could see! Jesus
sternly warned them, "Don't tell anyone about
this." 31 But instead, they went out and spread his
fame all over the region.
32 When they left, a demon-possessed man

Jesus Heals Many People
14When Jesus arrived at Peter's house, Peter's
mother-in-law was sick in bed with a high fever.
15But when Jesus touched her hand, the fever left
her. Then she got up and prepared a meal for him.
16That evening many demon-possessed people were brought to Jesus. He cast out the evil
spirits with a simple command, and he healed all
the sick. 17This fulfilled the word of the Lord
through the prophet Isaiah, who said,

"He took our sicknesses
and removed our diseases."

The Cost of Following Jesus
18When Jesus saw the crowd around him, he instructed his disciples to cross to the other side of
the lake.
19Then one of the teachers of religious law
said to him, "Teacher, I will follow you wherever
you go."
20But Jesus replied, "Foxes have dens to live in,
and birds have nests, but the Son of Man has no
place even to lay his head."
21Another of his disciples said, "Lord, first let
me return home and bury my father."
22But Jesus told him, "Follow me now. Let the
spiritually dead bury their own dead."

Jesus Calms the Storm
23Then Jesus got into the boat and started across
the lake with his disciples. 24Suddenly, a fierce
storm struck the lake, with waves breaking into
the boat. But Jesus was sleeping. 25The disciples
went and woke him up, shouting, "Lord, save us!
We're going to drown!"
26Jesus responded, "Why are you afraid? You
have so little faith!" Then he got up and rebuked
the wind and waves, and suddenly there was a
great calm.
27The disciples were amazed. "Who is this
man?" they asked. "Even the winds and waves
obey him!"

Jesus Heals Two Demon-Possessed Men
28When Jesus arrived on the other side of the
lake, in the region of the Gadarenes, two men
who were possessed by demons met him. They
lived in a cemetery and were so violent that no
one could go through that area.
29They began screaming at him, "Why are
you interfering with us, Son of God? Have you
come here to torture us before God's appointed
time?"
30There happened to be a large herd of pigs
feeding in the distance. 31So the demons begged,
"If you cast us out, send us into that herd of pigs."
32"All right, go!" Jesus commanded them. So
the demons came out of the men and entered

COMPLETE Control

Do *you* get scared in storms? **Read about a stormy situation in MATTHEW 8:23-27.** The next time you're scared, remember that Jesus is in complete control. **HERE'S A REMINDER.**

1 Draw the outline of a cross on a plastic lid. Use fine-tipped markers to decorate your cross everywhere but in the center.

2 Add food coloring to a little water. Use an eye dropper to put a drop of the colored water in the center of the cross.

3 Cover the cross and drop of water with clear packing tape, pressing around, but not on top of, the droplet.

4 Trim around the cross. Poke a hole in the top of the cross, and add yarn to make a necklace.

The drop of water in the center of your necklace can remind you that Jesus was in control in the center of the storm.

REMEMBER THAT JESUS IS IN CONTROL OF EVERYTHING IN YOUR LIFE TOO!

who couldn't speak was brought to Jesus. 33 So
Jesus cast out the demon, and then the man began
to speak. The crowds were amazed. "Nothing like
this has ever happened in Israel!" they exclaimed.
34 But the Pharisees said, "He can cast out demons because he is empowered by the prince of
demons."

The Need for Workers

35 Jesus traveled through all the towns and villages of that area, teaching in the synagogues and
announcing the Good News about the Kingdom.
And he healed every kind of disease and illness.
36 When he saw the crowds, he had compassion
on them because they were confused and helpless, like sheep without a shepherd. 37 He said to
his disciples, "The harvest is great, but the workers are few. 38 So pray to the Lord who is in charge
of the harvest; ask him to send more workers into
his fields."

CHAPTER 10

Jesus Sends Out the Twelve Apostles

Jesus called his twelve disciples together and
gave them authority to cast out evil spirits and to
heal every kind of disease and illness. 2 Here are
the names of the twelve apostles:

first, Simon (also called Peter),
then Andrew (Peter's brother),
James (son of Zebedee),
John (James's brother),
3 Philip,
Bartholomew,
Thomas,
Matthew (the tax collector),
James (son of Alphaeus),
Thaddaeus,
4 Simon (the zealot),
Judas Iscariot (who later betrayed him).

5 Jesus sent out the twelve apostles with these
instructions: "Don't go to the Gentiles or the
Samaritans, 6 but only to the people of Israel—
God's lost sheep. 7 Go and announce to them that
the Kingdom of Heaven is near. 8 Heal the sick,
raise the dead, cure those with leprosy, and cast
out demons. Give as freely as you have received!
9 "Don't take any money in your money belts—
no gold, silver, or even copper coins. 10 Don't
carry a traveler's bag with a change of clothes
and sandals or even a walking stick. Don't hesitate to accept hospitality, because those who
work deserve to be fed.
11 "Whenever you enter a city or village, search
for a worthy person and stay in his home until
you leave town. 12 When you enter the home, give
it your blessing. 13 If it turns out to be a worthy
home, let your blessing stand; if it is not, take
back the blessing. 14 If any household or town refuses to welcome you or listen to your message,
shake its dust from your feet as you leave. 15 I tell
you the truth, the wicked cities of Sodom and
Gomorrah will be better off than such a town on
the judgment day.
16 "Look, I am sending you out as sheep among
wolves. So be as shrewd as snakes and harmless
as doves. 17 But beware! For you will be handed
over to the courts and will be flogged with whips
in the synagogues. 18 You will stand trial before
governors and kings because you are my followers. But this will be your opportunity to tell the
rulers and other unbelievers about me. 19 When
you are arrested, don't worry about how to respond or what to say. God will give you the right
words at the right time. 20 For it is not you who
will be speaking—it will be the Spirit of your
Father speaking through you.
21 "A brother will betray his brother to death, a
father will betray his own child, and children will
rebel against their parents and cause them to be
killed. 22 And all nations will hate you because
you are my followers. But everyone who endures
to the end will be saved. 23 When you are persecuted in one town, flee to the next. I tell you the
truth, the Son of Man will return before you have
reached all the towns of Israel.
24 "Students are not greater than their teacher,
and slaves are not greater than their master.
25 Students are to be like their teacher, and slaves
are to be like their master. And since I, the master
of the household, have been called the prince of
demons, the members of my household will be
called by even worse names!
26 "But don't be afraid of those who threaten
you. For the time is coming when everything that
is covered will be revealed, and all that is secret
will be made known to all. 27 What I tell you now
in the darkness, shout abroad when daybreak
comes. What I whisper in your ear, shout from
the housetops for all to hear!
28 "Don't be afraid of those who want to kill
your body; they cannot touch your soul. Fear only
God, who can destroy both soul and body in hell.
29 What is the price of two sparrows—one copper coin? But not a single sparrow can fall to the
ground without your Father knowing it. 30 And
the very hairs on your head are all numbered.
31 So don't be afraid; you are more valuable to
God than a whole flock of sparrows.

Matthew 11 . . . page 952

32"Everyone who acknowledges me publicly
here on earth, I will also acknowledge before my
Father in heaven. 33But everyone who denies me
here on earth, I will also deny before my Father in
heaven.
34"Don't imagine that I came to bring peace to
the earth! I came not to bring peace, but a sword.

35 'I have come to set a man against his father,
  a daughter against her mother,
 and a daughter-in-law against her mother-in-law.
36 Your enemies will be right in your own
  household!'

37"If you love your father or mother more than
you love me, you are not worthy of being mine; or
if you love your son or daughter more than me,
you are not worthy of being mine. 38If you refuse
to take up your cross and follow me, you are not
worthy of being mine. 39If you cling to your life,
you will lose it; but if you give up your life for me,
you will find it.
40"Anyone who receives you receives me, and
anyone who receives me receives the Father who
sent me. 41If you receive a prophet as one who
speaks for God, you will be given the same reward as a prophet. And if you receive righteous
people because of their righteousness, you will
be given a reward like theirs. 42And if you give
even a cup of cold water to one of the least of my
followers, you will surely be rewarded."

CHAPTER **11**
Jesus and John the Baptist
When Jesus had finished giving these instructions to his twelve disciples, he went out to teach
and preach in towns throughout the region.
2John the Baptist, who was in prison, heard
about all the things the Messiah was doing. So he
sent his disciples to ask Jesus, 3"Are you the Messiah we've been expecting, or should we keep
looking for someone else?"
4Jesus told them, "Go back to John and tell
him what you have heard and seen—5the blind
see, the lame walk, the lepers are cured, the deaf
hear, the dead are raised to life, and the Good
News is being preached to the poor. 6And tell
him, 'God blesses those who do not turn away
because of me.'"
7As John's disciples were leaving, Jesus began
talking about him to the crowds. "What kind of
man did you go into the wilderness to see? Was
he a weak reed, swayed by every breath of wind?
8Or were you expecting to see a man dressed in
expensive clothes? No, people with expensive
clothes live in palaces. 9Were you looking for a
prophet? Yes, and he is more than a prophet.
10John is the man to whom the Scriptures refer
when they say,

'Look, I am sending my messenger ahead
  of you,
 and he will prepare your way before you.'

11"I tell you the truth, of all who have ever lived,
none is greater than John the Baptist. Yet even the
least person in the Kingdom of Heaven is greater
than he is! 12And from the time John the Baptist

Key Verse **"Come to me, all of you who are weary and carry heavy burdens, and I will give you rest."—MATTHEW 11:28**

Jesus Attraction

Read MATTHEW 11:28 out loud until you can say it by yourself. Jesus wants us to come to him. Here's an experiment to show what that's like.

1. **Tie several O-shaped cereal pieces to the end of a piece of string.**
2. **Rub a plastic comb on a wool sweater or your hair so the comb's full of static electricity.**

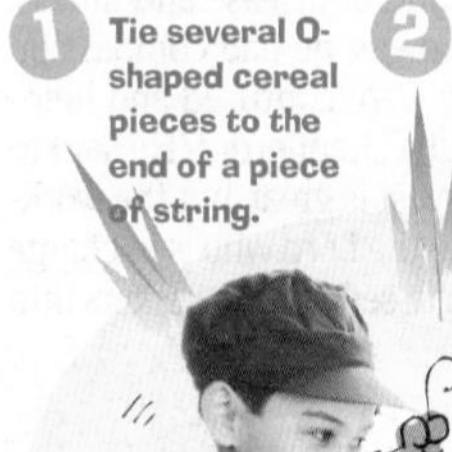

3. **Carefully move the comb toward the cereal.**

What happens? The cereal comes toward the comb, just like Jesus wants us to come to him!

Glue pieces of cereal to a sheet of construction paper so they spell a reminder of this verse. (You might write, "Jesus" or "Come to me.") Spray the sheet with hair spray, and hang it in your kitchen to remind you that Jesus wants you to come to him!

began preaching until now, the Kingdom of
Heaven has been forcefully advancing, and violent people are attacking it. 13For before John
came, all the prophets and the law of Moses
looked forward to this present time. 14And if you
are willing to accept what I say, he is Elijah, the
one the prophets said would come. 15Anyone
with ears to hear should listen and understand!

16"To what can I compare this generation? It is
like children playing a game in the public square.
They complain to their friends,

17 'We played wedding songs,
and you didn't dance,
so we played funeral songs,
and you didn't mourn.'

18For John didn't spend his time eating and
drinking, and you say, 'He's possessed by a
demon.' 19The Son of Man, on the other hand,
feasts and drinks, and you say, 'He's a glutton and
a drunkard, and a friend of tax collectors and
other sinners!' But wisdom is shown to be right
by its results."

Judgment for the Unbelievers

20Then Jesus began to denounce the towns
where he had done so many of his miracles, because they hadn't repented of their sins and
turned to God. 21"What sorrow awaits you, Korazin and Bethsaida! For if the miracles I did in you
had been done in wicked Tyre and Sidon, their
people would have repented of their sins long
ago, clothing themselves in burlap and throwing
ashes on their heads to show their remorse. 22I
tell you, Tyre and Sidon will be better off on judgment day than you.

23"And you people of Capernaum, will you be
honored in heaven? No, you will go down to the
place of the dead. For if the miracles I did for you
had been done in wicked Sodom, it would still
be here today. 24I tell you, even Sodom will be
better off on judgment day than you."

Jesus' Prayer of Thanksgiving

25At that time Jesus prayed this prayer: "O Father, Lord of heaven and earth, thank you for
hiding these things from those who think themselves wise and clever, and for revealing them to
the childlike. 26Yes, Father, it pleased you to do it
this way!

27"My Father has entrusted everything to me.
No one truly knows the Son except the Father,
and no one truly knows the Father except the
Son and those to whom the Son chooses to reveal him."

28Then Jesus said, "Come to me,
all of you who are weary and carry
heavy burdens, and I will give you
rest. 29Take my yoke upon you. Let me teach
you, because I am humble and gentle at heart,
and you will find rest for your souls. 30For my
yoke is easy to bear, and the burden I give you is
light."

CHAPTER 12

A Discussion about the Sabbath

At about that time Jesus was walking through
some grainfields on the Sabbath. His disciples
were hungry, so they began breaking off some
heads of grain and eating them. 2But some Pharisees saw them do it and protested, "Look, your
disciples are breaking the law by harvesting
grain on the Sabbath."

3Jesus said to them, "Haven't you read in the
Scriptures what David did when he and his companions were hungry? 4He went into the house
of God, and he and his companions broke the
law by eating the sacred loaves of bread that only
the priests are allowed to eat. 5And haven't you
read in the law of Moses that the priests on duty
in the Temple may work on the Sabbath? 6I tell
you, there is one here who is even greater than
the Temple! 7But you would not have condemned my innocent disciples if you knew the
meaning of this Scripture: 'I want you to show
mercy, not offer sacrifices.' 8For the Son of Man
is Lord, even over the Sabbath!"

Jesus Heals on the Sabbath

9Then Jesus went over to their synagogue,
10where he noticed a man with a deformed
hand. The Pharisees asked Jesus, "Does the law
permit a person to work by healing on the Sabbath?" (They were hoping he would say yes, so
they could bring charges against him.)

11And he answered, "If you had a sheep that
fell into a well on the Sabbath, wouldn't you work
to pull it out? Of course you would. 12And how
much more valuable is a person than a sheep!
Yes, the law permits a person to do good on the
Sabbath."

13Then he said to the man, "Hold out your
hand." So the man held out his hand, and it was
restored, just like the other one! 14Then the Pharisees called a meeting to plot how to kill Jesus.

Jesus, God's Chosen Servant

15But Jesus knew what they were planning. So he
left that area, and many people followed him. He
healed all the sick among them, 16but he warned

them not to reveal who he was. 17This fulfilled
the prophecy of Isaiah concerning him:

18 "Look at my Servant, whom I have chosen.
He is my Beloved, who pleases me.
I will put my Spirit upon him,
and he will proclaim justice to the nations.
19 He will not fight or shout
or raise his voice in public.
20 He will not crush the weakest reed
or put out a flickering candle.
Finally he will cause justice to be
victorious.
21 And his name will be the hope
of all the world."

Jesus and the Prince of Demons

22Then a demon-possessed man, who was blind
and couldn't speak, was brought to Jesus. He
healed the man so that he could both speak
and see. 23The crowd was amazed and asked,
"Could it be that Jesus is the Son of David, the
Messiah?"

24But when the Pharisees heard about the
miracle, they said, "No wonder he can cast out
demons. He gets his power from Satan, the
prince of demons."

25Jesus knew their thoughts and replied, "Any
kingdom divided by civil war is doomed. A town
or family splintered by feuding will fall apart.
26And if Satan is casting out Satan, he is divided
and fighting against himself. His own kingdom
will not survive. 27And if I am empowered by
Satan, what about your own exorcists? They cast
out demons, too, so they will condemn you for
what you have said. 28But if I am casting out demons by the Spirit of God, then the Kingdom of
God has arrived among you. 29For who is powerful enough to enter the house of a strong man
like Satan and plunder his goods? Only someone
even stronger—someone who could tie him up
and then plunder his house.

30"Anyone who isn't with me opposes me, and
anyone who isn't working with me is actually
working against me.

31"So I tell you, every sin and blasphemy can
be forgiven—except blasphemy against the Holy
Spirit, which will never be forgiven. 32Anyone
who speaks against the Son of Man can be forgiven, but anyone who speaks against the Holy
Spirit will never be forgiven, either in this world
or in the world to come.

33"A tree is identified by its fruit. If a tree is
good, its fruit will be good. If a tree is bad, its
fruit will be bad. 34You brood of snakes! How
could evil men like you speak what is good and
right? For whatever is in your heart determines
what you say. 35A good person produces good
things from the treasury of a good heart, and an
evil person produces evil things from the treasury of an evil heart. 36And I tell you this, you
must give an account on judgment day for every
idle word you speak. 37The words you say will
either acquit you or condemn you."

The Sign of Jonah

38One day some teachers of religious law and
Pharisees came to Jesus and said, "Teacher, we
want you to show us a miraculous sign to prove
your authority."

39But Jesus replied, "Only an evil, adulterous
generation would demand a miraculous sign; but
the only sign I will give them is the sign of the
prophet Jonah. 40For as Jonah was in the belly of
the great fish for three days and three nights, so
will the Son of Man be in the heart of the earth
for three days and three nights.

41"The people of Nineveh will stand up
against this generation on judgment day and
condemn it, for they repented of their sins at
the preaching of Jonah. Now someone greater than Jonah is here—but you refuse to repent.
42The queen of Sheba will also stand up
against this generation on judgment day and
condemn it, for she came from a distant land
to hear the wisdom of Solomon. Now someone
greater than Solomon is here—but you refuse to
listen.

43"When an evil spirit leaves a person, it goes
into the desert, seeking rest but finding none.
44Then it says, 'I will return to the person I came
from.' So it returns and finds its former home
empty, swept, and in order. 45Then the spirit
finds seven other spirits more evil than itself,
and they all enter the person and live there. And
so that person is worse off than before. That will
be the experience of this evil generation."

The True Family of Jesus

46As Jesus was speaking to the crowd, his mother
and brothers stood outside, asking to speak to
him. 47Someone told Jesus, "Your mother and
your brothers are standing outside, and they
want to speak to you."

48Jesus asked, "Who is my mother? Who are
my brothers?" 49Then he pointed to his disciples
and said, "Look, these are my mother and brothers. 50Anyone who does the will of my Father in
heaven is my brother and sister and mother!"

CHAPTER 13

Parable of the Farmer Scattering Seed

Later that same day Jesus left the house and sat
beside the lake. 2A large crowd soon gathered
around him, so he got into a boat. Then he sat
there and taught as the people stood on the
shore. 3He told many stories in the form of parables, such as this one:

"Listen! A farmer went out to plant some
seeds. 4As he scattered them across his field,
some seeds fell on a footpath, and the birds came
and ate them. 5Other seeds fell on shallow soil
with underlying rock. The seeds sprouted
quickly because the soil was shallow. 6But the
plants soon wilted under the hot sun, and since
they didn't have deep roots, they died. 7Other
seeds fell among thorns that grew up and choked
out the tender plants. 8Still other seeds fell on
fertile soil, and they produced a crop that was
thirty, sixty, and even a hundred times as much as
had been planted! 9Anyone with ears to hear
should listen and understand."

10His disciples came and asked him, "Why do
you use parables when you talk to the people?"

11He replied, "You are permitted to understand the secrets of the Kingdom of Heaven, but
others are not. 12To those who listen to my
teaching, more understanding will be given, and
they will have an abundance of knowledge. But
for those who are not listening, even what little
understanding they have will be taken away from
them. 13That is why I use these parables,

For they look, but they don't really see.
They hear, but they don't really listen
or understand.

14This fulfills the prophecy of Isaiah that says,

'When you hear what I say,
you will not understand.
When you see what I do,
you will not comprehend.
15 For the hearts of these people are hardened,
and their ears cannot hear,
and they have closed their eyes—
so their eyes cannot see,
and their ears cannot hear,
and their hearts cannot understand,
and they cannot turn to me
and let me heal them.'

16"But blessed are your eyes, because they see;
and your ears, because they hear. 17I tell you the
truth, many prophets and righteous people
longed to see what you see, but they didn't see it.
And they longed to hear what you hear, but they
didn't hear it.

18"Now listen to the explanation of the parable
about the farmer planting seeds: 19The seed that
fell on the footpath represents those who hear
the message about the Kingdom and don't
understand it. Then the evil one comes and
snatches away the seed that was planted in their
hearts. 20The seed on the rocky soil represents
those who hear the message and immediately receive it with joy. 21But since they don't have deep
roots, they don't last long. They fall away as soon
as they have problems or are persecuted for believing God's word. 22The seed that fell among
the thorns represents those who hear God's word,
but all too quickly the message is crowded out by
the worries of this life and the lure of wealth, so
no fruit is produced. 23The seed that fell on good
soil represents those who truly hear and understand God's word and produce a harvest of thirty,
sixty, or even a hundred times as much as had
been planted!"

Parable of the Wheat and Weeds

24Here is another story Jesus told: "The Kingdom of Heaven is like a farmer who planted
good seed in his field. 25But that night as the
workers slept, his enemy came and planted
weeds among the wheat, then slipped away.
26When the crop began to grow and produce
grain, the weeds also grew.

27"The farmer's workers went to him and said,
'Sir, the field where you planted that good seed is
full of weeds! Where did they come from?'

28"'An enemy has done this!' the farmer exclaimed.

"'Should we pull out the weeds?' they asked.

29"'No,' he replied, 'you'll uproot the wheat if
you do. 30Let both grow together until the harvest. Then I will tell the harvesters to sort out the
weeds, tie them into bundles, and burn them,
and to put the wheat in the barn.'"

Parable of the Mustard Seed

31Here is another illustration Jesus used: "The
Kingdom of Heaven is like a mustard seed
planted in a field. 32It is the smallest of all seeds,
but it becomes the largest of garden plants; it
grows into a tree, and birds come and make nests
in its branches."

Parable of the Yeast

33Jesus also used this illustration: "The Kingdom of Heaven is like the yeast a woman used in

making bread. Even though she put only a little
yeast in three measures of flour, it permeated
every part of the dough."
34 Jesus always used stories and illustrations
like these when speaking to the crowds. In fact,
he never spoke to them without using such parables. 35 This fulfilled what God had spoken
through the prophet:

"I will speak to you in parables.
I will explain things hidden since the
creation of the world."

Parable of the Wheat and Weeds Explained

36 Then, leaving the crowds outside, Jesus went
into the house. His disciples said, "Please explain
to us the story of the weeds in the field."
37 Jesus replied, "The Son of Man is the farmer
who plants the good seed. 38 The field is the
world, and the good seed represents the people
of the Kingdom. The weeds are the people who
belong to the evil one. 39 The enemy who planted
the weeds among the wheat is the devil. The harvest is the end of the world, and the harvesters
are the angels.
40 "Just as the weeds are sorted out and burned
in the fire, so it will be at the end of the world.
41 The Son of Man will send his angels, and they
will remove from his Kingdom everything that
causes sin and all who do evil. 42 And the angels
will throw them into the fiery furnace, where
there will be weeping and gnashing of teeth.
43 Then the righteous will shine like the sun in
their Father's Kingdom. Anyone with ears to hear
should listen and understand!

Parables of the Hidden Treasure and the Pearl

44 "The Kingdom of Heaven is like a treasure that
a man discovered hidden in a field. In his excitement, he hid it again and sold everything he
owned to get enough money to buy the field.
45 "Again, the Kingdom of Heaven is like a merchant on the lookout for choice pearls. 46 When
he discovered a pearl of great value, he sold
everything he owned and bought it!

Parable of the Fishing Net

47 "Again, the Kingdom of Heaven is like a fishing
net that was thrown into the water and caught
fish of every kind. 48 When the net was full, they
dragged it up onto the shore, sat down, and
sorted the good fish into crates, but threw the
bad ones away. 49 That is the way it will be at the
end of the world. The angels will come and separate the wicked people from the righteous,
50 throwing the wicked into the fiery furnace,
where there will be weeping and gnashing of
teeth. 51 Do you understand all these things?"
"Yes," they said, "we do."
52 Then he added, "Every teacher of religious
law who becomes a disciple in the Kingdom of
Heaven is like a homeowner who brings from his
storeroom new gems of truth as well as old."

Jesus Rejected at Nazareth

53 When Jesus had finished telling these stories
and illustrations, he left that part of the country.
54 He returned to Nazareth, his hometown.
When he taught there in the synagogue, everyone was amazed and said, "Where does he get
this wisdom and the power to do miracles?"
55 Then they scoffed, "He's just the carpenter's
son, and we know Mary, his mother, and his
brothers—James, Joseph, Simon, and Judas. 56 All
his sisters live right here among us. Where did
he learn all these things?" 57 And they were
deeply offended and refused to believe in him.
Then Jesus told them, "A prophet is honored
everywhere except in his own hometown and
among his own family." 58 And so he did only a
few miracles there because of their unbelief.

CHAPTER 14

The Death of John the Baptist

When Herod Antipas, the ruler of Galilee, heard
about Jesus, 2 he said to his advisers, "This must
be John the Baptist raised from the dead! That is
why he can do such miracles."
3 For Herod had arrested and imprisoned John
as a favor to his wife Herodias (the former wife of
Herod's brother Philip). 4 John had been telling
Herod, "It is against God's law for you to marry
her." 5 Herod wanted to kill John, but he was
afraid of a riot, because all the people believed
John was a prophet.
6 But at a birthday party for Herod, Herodias's
daughter performed a dance that greatly pleased
him, 7 so he promised with a vow to give her anything she wanted. 8 At her mother's urging, the
girl said, "I want the head of John the Baptist on a
tray!" 9 Then the king regretted what he had said;
but because of the vow he had made in front of
his guests, he issued the necessary orders. 10 So
John was beheaded in the prison, 11 and his head
was brought on a tray and given to the girl, who
took it to her mother. 12 Later, John's disciples
came for his body and buried it. Then they went
and told Jesus what had happened.

Jesus Feeds Five Thousand

13 As soon as Jesus heard the news, he left in a
boat to a remote area to be alone. But the crowds
heard where he was headed and followed on foot
from many towns. 14 Jesus saw the huge crowd as
he stepped from the boat, and he had compassion on them and healed their sick.

15 That evening the disciples came to him and
said, "This is a remote place, and it's already getting late. Send the crowds away so they can go to
the villages and buy food for themselves."

16 But Jesus said, "That isn't necessary—you
feed them."

17 "But we have only five loaves of bread and
two fish!" they answered.

18 "Bring them here," he said. 19 Then he told
the people to sit down on the grass. Jesus took
the five loaves and two fish, looked up toward
heaven, and blessed them. Then, breaking the
loaves into pieces, he gave the bread to the disciples, who distributed it to the people. 20 They all
ate as much as they wanted, and afterward, the
disciples picked up twelve baskets of leftovers.
21 About 5,000 men were fed that day, in addition
to all the women and children!

Jesus Walks on Water

22 Immediately after this, Jesus insisted that his
disciples get back into the boat and cross to the
other side of the lake, while he sent the people
home. 23 After sending them home, he went up
into the hills by himself to pray. Night fell while
he was there alone.

24 Meanwhile, the disciples were in trouble far
away from land, for a strong wind had risen, and
they were fighting heavy waves. 25 About three
o'clock in the morning Jesus came toward them,
walking on the water. 26 When the disciples saw
him walking on the water, they were terrified. In
their fear, they cried out, "It's a ghost!"

27 But Jesus spoke to them at once. "Don't be
afraid," he said. "Take courage. I am here!"

28 Then Peter called to him, "Lord, if it's really
you, tell me to come to you, walking on the
water."

29 "Yes, come," Jesus said.

So Peter went over the side of the boat and
walked on the water toward Jesus. 30 But when he
saw the strong wind and the waves, he was terrified and began to sink. "Save me, Lord!" he
shouted.

31 Jesus immediately reached out and grabbed
him. "You have so little faith," Jesus said. "Why
did you doubt me?"

32 When they climbed back into the boat, the
wind stopped. 33 Then the disciples worshiped
him. "You really are the Son of God!" they exclaimed.

34 After they had crossed the lake, they landed
at Gennesaret. 35 When the people recognized
Jesus, the news of his arrival spread quickly
throughout the whole area, and soon people
were bringing all their sick to be healed. 36 They
begged him to let the sick touch at least the
fringe of his robe, and all who touched him were
healed.

CHAPTER 15

Jesus Teaches about Inner Purity

Some Pharisees and teachers of religious law
now arrived from Jerusalem to see Jesus. They
asked him, 2 "Why do your disciples disobey our
age-old tradition? For they ignore our tradition
of ceremonial hand washing before they eat."

3 Jesus replied, "And why do you, by your traditions, violate the direct commandments of God?
4 For instance, God says, 'Honor your father and
mother,' and 'Anyone who speaks disrespectfully
of father or mother must be put to death.' 5 But
you say it is all right for people to say to their parents, 'Sorry, I can't help you. For I have vowed to
give to God what I would have given to you.' 6 In
this way, you say they don't need to honor their
parents. And so you cancel the word of God for
the sake of your own tradition. 7 You hypocrites!
Isaiah was right when he prophesied about you,
for he wrote,

8 'These people honor me with their lips,
but their hearts are far from me.
9 Their worship is a farce,
for they teach man-made ideas as
commands from God.'"

10 Then Jesus called to the crowd to come and
hear. "Listen," he said, "and try to understand.
11 It's not what goes into your mouth that defiles
you; you are defiled by the words that come out
of your mouth."

12 Then the disciples came to him and asked,
"Do you realize you offended the Pharisees by
what you just said?"

13 Jesus replied, "Every plant not planted by my
heavenly Father will be uprooted, 14 so ignore
them. They are blind guides leading the blind,
and if one blind person guides another, they will
both fall into a ditch."

15 Then Peter said to Jesus, "Explain to us the
parable that says people aren't defiled by what
they eat."

16"Don't you understand yet?" Jesus asked.
17"Anything you eat passes through the stomach
and then goes into the sewer. 18But the words
you speak come from the heart—that's what
defiles you. 19For from the heart come evil
thoughts, murder, adultery, all sexual immorality,
theft, lying, and slander. 20These are what defile
you. Eating with unwashed hands will never defile you."

The Faith of a Gentile Woman

21Then Jesus left Galilee and went north to the
region of Tyre and Sidon. 22A Gentile woman
who lived there came to him, pleading, "Have
mercy on me, O Lord, Son of David! For my
daughter is possessed by a demon that torments
her severely."

23But Jesus gave her no reply, not even a word.
Then his disciples urged him to send her away.
"Tell her to go away," they said. "She is bothering
us with all her begging."

24Then Jesus said to the woman, "I was sent only
to help God's lost sheep—the people of Israel."

25But she came and worshiped him, pleading
again, "Lord, help me!"

26Jesus responded, "It isn't right to take food
from the children and throw it to the dogs."

27She replied, "That's true, Lord, but even
dogs are allowed to eat the scraps that fall beneath their masters' table."

28"Dear woman," Jesus said to her, "your faith
is great. Your request is granted." And her daughter was instantly healed.

Jesus Heals Many People

29Jesus returned to the Sea of Galilee and
climbed a hill and sat down. 30A vast crowd
brought to him people who were lame, blind,
crippled, those who couldn't speak, and many
others. They laid them before Jesus, and he
healed them all. 31The crowd was amazed! Those
who hadn't been able to speak were talking, the
crippled were made well, the lame were walking,
and the blind could see again! And they praised
the God of Israel.

Jesus Feeds Four Thousand

32Then Jesus called his disciples and told them,
"I feel sorry for these people. They have been
here with me for three days, and they have nothing left to eat. I don't want to send them away
hungry, or they will faint along the way."

33The disciples replied, "Where would we get
enough food here in the wilderness for such a
huge crowd?"

34Jesus asked, "How much bread do you
have?"

They replied, "Seven loaves, and a few small
fish."

35So Jesus told all the people to sit down on
the ground. 36Then he took the seven loaves and
the fish, thanked God for them, and broke them
into pieces. He gave them to the disciples, who
distributed the food to the crowd.

37They all ate as much as they wanted. Afterward, the disciples picked up seven large baskets
of leftover food. 38There were 4,000 men who
were fed that day, in addition to all the women
and children. 39Then Jesus sent the people
home, and he got into a boat and crossed over to
the region of Magadan.

CHAPTER 16

Leaders Demand a Miraculous Sign

One day the Pharisees and Sadducees came to
test Jesus, demanding that he show them a
miraculous sign from heaven to prove his
authority.

2He replied, "You know the saying, 'Red sky at
night means fair weather tomorrow; 3red sky in
the morning means foul weather all day.' You
know how to interpret the weather signs in the
sky, but you don't know how to interpret the
signs of the times! 4Only an evil, adulterous generation would demand a miraculous sign, but
the only sign I will give them is the sign of the
prophet Jonah." Then Jesus left them and went
away.

Yeast of the Pharisees and Sadducees

5Later, after they crossed to the other side of the
lake, the disciples discovered they had forgotten
to bring any bread. 6"Watch out!" Jesus warned
them. "Beware of the yeast of the Pharisees and
Sadducees."

7At this they began to argue with each other
because they hadn't brought any bread. 8Jesus
knew what they were saying, so he said, "You
have so little faith! Why are you arguing with
each other about having no bread? 9Don't you
understand even yet? Don't you remember the
5,000 I fed with five loaves, and the baskets of
leftovers you picked up? 10Or the 4,000 I fed
with seven loaves, and the large baskets of leftovers you picked up? 11Why can't you understand that I'm not talking about bread? So again
I say, 'Beware of the yeast of the Pharisees and
Sadducees.'"

12 Then at last they understood that he wasn't
speaking about the yeast in bread, but about
the deceptive teaching of the Pharisees and
Sadducees.

Peter's Declaration about Jesus

13 When Jesus came to the region of Caesarea
Philippi, he asked his disciples, "Who do people
say that the Son of Man is?"

14 "Well," they replied, "some say John the
Baptist, some say Elijah, and others say Jeremiah
or one of the other prophets."

15 Then he asked them, "But who do you say
I am?"

16 Simon Peter answered, "You are the Messiah, the Son of the living God."

17 Jesus replied, "You are blessed, Simon son of
John, because my Father in heaven has revealed
this to you. You did not learn this from any human being. 18 Now I say to you that you are Peter
(which means 'rock'), and upon this rock I will
build my church, and all the powers of hell will
not conquer it. 19 And I will give you the keys of
the Kingdom of Heaven. Whatever you forbid on
earth will be forbidden in heaven, and whatever
you permit on earth will be permitted in
heaven."

20 Then he sternly warned the disciples not to
tell anyone that he was the Messiah.

Jesus Predicts His Death

21 From then on Jesus began to tell his disciples
plainly that it was necessary for him to go to Jerusalem, and that he would suffer many terrible
things at the hands of the elders, the leading
priests, and the teachers of religious law. He
would be killed, but on the third day he would be
raised from the dead.

22 But Peter took him aside and began to reprimand him for saying such things. "Heaven forbid, Lord," he said. "This will never happen to
you!"

23 Jesus turned to Peter and said, "Get away
from me, Satan! You are a dangerous trap to me.
You are seeing things merely from a human
point of view, not from God's."

24 Then Jesus said to his disciples, "If any of
you wants to be my follower, you must turn from
your selfish ways, take up your cross, and follow
me. 25 If you try to hang on to your life, you will
lose it. But if you give up your life for my sake, you
will save it. 26 And what do you benefit if you gain
the whole world but lose your own soul? Is anything worth more than your soul? 27 For the Son
of Man will come with his angels in the glory of
his Father and will judge all people according to
their deeds. 28 And I tell you the truth, some
standing here right now will not die before they
see the Son of Man coming in his Kingdom."

CHAPTER 17

The Transfiguration

Six days later Jesus took Peter and the two brothers, James and John, and led them up a high
mountain to be alone. 2 As the men watched,
Jesus' appearance was transformed so that his
face shone like the sun, and his clothes became
as white as light. 3 Suddenly, Moses and Elijah
appeared and began talking with Jesus.

4 Peter exclaimed, "Lord, it's wonderful for us
to be here! If you want, I'll make three shelters as
memorials—one for you, one for Moses, and one
for Elijah."

5 But even as he spoke, a bright cloud overshadowed them, and a voice from the cloud said,
"This is my dearly loved Son, who brings me
great joy. Listen to him." 6 The disciples were terrified and fell face down on the ground.

7 Then Jesus came over and touched them.
"Get up," he said. "Don't be afraid." 8 And when
they looked up, Moses and Elijah were gone, and
they saw only Jesus.

9 As they went back down the mountain, Jesus
commanded them, "Don't tell anyone what you
have seen until the Son of Man has been raised
from the dead."

10 Then his disciples asked him, "Why do the
teachers of religious law insist that Elijah must
return before the Messiah comes?"

11 Jesus replied, "Elijah is indeed coming first
to get everything ready. 12 But I tell you, Elijah has
already come, but he wasn't recognized, and they
chose to abuse him. And in the same way they
will also make the Son of Man suffer." 13 Then the
disciples realized he was talking about John the
Baptist.

Jesus Heals a Demon-Possessed Boy

14 At the foot of the mountain, a large crowd was
waiting for them. A man came and knelt before
Jesus and said, 15 "Lord, have mercy on my son. He
has seizures and suffers terribly. He often falls
into the fire or into the water. 16 So I brought him
to your disciples, but they couldn't heal him."

17 Jesus said, "You faithless and corrupt people! How long must I be with you? How long must
I put up with you? Bring the boy here to me."
18 Then Jesus rebuked the demon in the boy, and
it left him. From that moment the boy was well.

19Afterward the disciples asked Jesus privately, "Why couldn't we cast out that demon?"
20"You don't have enough faith," Jesus told
them. "I tell you the truth, if you had faith even as
small as a mustard seed, you could say to this
mountain, 'Move from here to there,' and it
would move. Nothing would be impossible.*"

Jesus Again Predicts His Death

22After they gathered again in Galilee, Jesus told
them, "The Son of Man is going to be betrayed
into the hands of his enemies. 23He will be killed,
but on the third day he will be raised from the
dead." And the disciples were filled with grief.

Payment of the Temple Tax

24On their arrival in Capernaum, the collectors
of the Temple tax came to Peter and asked him,
"Doesn't your teacher pay the Temple tax?"
25"Yes, he does," Peter replied. Then he went
into the house.

But before he had a chance to speak, Jesus
asked him, "What do you think, Peter? Do kings
tax their own people or the people they have
conquered?"

26"They tax the people they have conquered,"
Peter replied.

"Well, then," Jesus said, "the citizens are free!
27However, we don't want to offend them, so go
down to the lake and throw in a line. Open the
mouth of the first fish you catch, and you will
find a large silver coin. Take it and pay the tax for
both of us."

CHAPTER **18**

The Greatest in the Kingdom

About that time the disciples came to Jesus and
asked, "Who is greatest in the Kingdom of
Heaven?"

2Jesus called a little child to him and put the
child among them. 3Then he said, "I tell you the
truth, unless you turn from your sins and become like little children, you will never get into
the Kingdom of Heaven. 4So anyone who becomes as humble as this little child is the greatest in the Kingdom of Heaven.

5"And anyone who welcomes a little child like
this on my behalf is welcoming me. 6But if you
cause one of these little ones who trusts in me to
fall into sin, it would be better for you to have a
large millstone tied around your neck and be
drowned in the depths of the sea.

7"What sorrow awaits the world, because it
tempts people to sin. Temptations are inevitable,
but what sorrow awaits the person who does the
tempting. 8So if your hand or foot causes you to
sin, cut it off and throw it away. It's better to enter
eternal life with only one hand or one foot than
to be thrown into eternal fire with both of your
hands and feet. 9And if your eye causes you to
sin, gouge it out and throw it away. It's better to
enter eternal life with only one eye than to have
two eyes and be thrown into the fire of hell.

10"Beware that you don't look down on any of
these little ones. For I tell you that in heaven their
angels are always in the presence of my heavenly
Father.*

Parable of the Lost Sheep

12"If a man has a hundred sheep and one of them
wanders away, what will he do? Won't he leave
the ninety-nine others on the hills and go out to
search for the one that is lost? 13And if he finds
it, I tell you the truth, he will rejoice over it more
than over the ninety-nine that didn't wander
away! 14In the same way, it is not my heavenly
Father's will that even one of these little ones
should perish.

Correcting Another Believer

15"If another believer sins against you, go privately and point out the offense. If the other person listens and confesses it, you have won that
person back. 16But if you are unsuccessful, take
one or two others with you and go back again, so
that everything you say may be confirmed by two
or three witnesses. 17If the person still refuses to
listen, take your case to the church. Then if he or
she won't accept the church's decision, treat that
person as a pagan or a corrupt tax collector.

18"I tell you the truth, whatever you forbid on
earth will be forbidden in heaven, and whatever
you permit on earth will be permitted in heaven.

19"I also tell you this: If two of you agree here
on earth concerning anything you ask, my Father
in heaven will do it for you. **20For where two
or three gather together as my followers, I am there among them."**

Parable of the Unforgiving Debtor

21Then Peter came to him and asked, "Lord, how
often should I forgive someone who sins against
me? Seven times?"

22"No, not seven times," Jesus replied, "but
seventy times seven!

17:20 Some manuscripts add verse 21, *But this kind of demon won't leave except by prayer and fasting.* Compare Mark 9:29.
18:10 Some manuscripts add verse 11, *And the Son of Man came to save those who are lost.* Compare Luke 19:10.

23"Therefore, the Kingdom of Heaven can be
compared to a king who decided to bring his
accounts up to date with servants who had borrowed money from him. 24In the process, one of
his debtors was brought in who owed him millions of dollars. 25He couldn't pay, so his master
ordered that he be sold—along with his wife, his
children, and everything he owned—to pay the
debt.
26"But the man fell down before his master
and begged him, 'Please, be patient with me, and
I will pay it all.' 27Then his master was filled with
pity for him, and he released him and forgave
his debt.
28"But when the man left the king, he went to
a fellow servant who owed him a few thousand
dollars. He grabbed him by the throat and demanded instant payment.
29"His fellow servant fell down before him
and begged for a little more time. 'Be patient
with me, and I will pay it,' he pleaded. 30But his
creditor wouldn't wait. He had the man arrested
and put in prison until the debt could be paid
in full.
31"When some of the other servants saw this,
they were very upset. They went to the king
and told him everything that had happened.
32Then the king called in the man he had forgiven and said, 'You evil servant! I forgave you
that tremendous debt because you pleaded
with me. 33Shouldn't you have mercy on your
fellow servant, just as I had mercy on you?'
34Then the angry king sent the man to prison to
be tortured until he had paid his entire debt.
35"That's what my heavenly Father will do to
you if you refuse to forgive your brothers and sisters from your heart."

CHAPTER 19

Discussion about Divorce and Marriage

When Jesus had finished saying these things,
he left Galilee and went down to the region
of Judea east of the Jordan River. 2Large
crowds followed him there, and he healed their
sick.
3Some Pharisees came and tried to trap him
with this question: "Should a man be allowed to
divorce his wife for just any reason?"
4"Haven't you read the Scriptures?" Jesus replied. "They record that from the beginning
'God made them male and female.'" 5And he
said, "'This explains why a man leaves his father
and mother and is joined to his wife, and the two
are united into one.' 6Since they are no longer
two but one, let no one split apart what God has
joined together."
7"Then why did Moses say in the law that a
man could give his wife a written notice of divorce and send her away?" they asked.
8Jesus replied, "Moses permitted divorce
only as a concession to your hard hearts, but it
was not what God had originally intended.
9And I tell you this, whoever divorces his wife

Key Verse **"For where two or three gather together as my followers, I am there among them."—MATTHEW 18:20**

A Real Reaction!

Find a friend or two, and read MATTHEW 18:20 out loud. Then think about this.

In science, a chemical reaction can happen when you put two things together. When two or more Christians gather together, a spiritual reaction happens!

TRY THIS!

Read about a cool spiritual reaction in Acts 2:1-4!

1. **Pour cranberry juice into several clear plastic cups.**
2. **Add a teaspoon of baking soda to each cup.**
3. **Add other liquids, like lemon juice or cola, to the cups. See if you can make the juice turn back to its original color.**

Adding two or three ingredients together caused chemical reactions in this experiment. **How can you and your friends cause a spiritual reaction?** Pray and ask God the best way to serve him this week!

and marries someone else commits adultery—
unless his wife has been unfaithful.*"
10Jesus' disciples then said to him, "If this is
the case, it is better not to marry!"
11"Not everyone can accept this statement,"
Jesus said. "Only those whom God helps. 12Some
are born as eunuchs, some have been made eunuchs by others, and some choose not to marry
for the sake of the Kingdom of Heaven. Let anyone accept this who can."

Jesus Blesses the Children

13One day some parents brought their children
to Jesus so he could lay his hands on them and
pray for them. But the disciples scolded the parents for bothering him.
14But Jesus said, "Let the children come to me.
Don't stop them! For the Kingdom of Heaven
belongs to those who are like these children."
15And he placed his hands on their heads and
blessed them before he left.

The Rich Man

16Someone came to Jesus with this question:
"Teacher, what good deed must I do to have eternal life?"
17"Why ask me about what is good?" Jesus
replied. "There is only One who is good. But to
answer your question—if you want to receive
eternal life, keep the commandments."
18"Which ones?" the man asked.
And Jesus replied: "'You must not murder. You
must not commit adultery. You must not steal.
You must not testify falsely. 19Honor your father
and mother. Love your neighbor as yourself.'"
20"I've obeyed all these commandments," the
young man replied. "What else must I do?"
21Jesus told him, "If you want to be perfect, go
and sell all your possessions and give the money
to the poor, and you will have treasure in heaven.
Then come, follow me."
22But when the young man heard this, he went
away sad, for he had many possessions.
23Then Jesus said to his disciples, "I tell you
the truth, it is very hard for a rich person to enter
the Kingdom of Heaven. 24I'll say it again—it is
easier for a camel to go through the eye of a needle than for a rich person to enter the Kingdom
of God!"
25The disciples were astounded. "Then who
in the world can be saved?" they asked.
26Jesus looked at them intently and said, "Humanly speaking, it is impossible. But with God
everything is possible."
27Then Peter said to him, "We've given up
everything to follow you. What will we get?"
28Jesus replied, "I assure you that when the
world is made new and the Son of Man sits upon
his glorious throne, you who have been my followers will also sit on twelve thrones, judging the
twelve tribes of Israel. 29And everyone who has
given up houses or brothers or sisters or father
or mother or children or property, for my sake,
will receive a hundred times as much in return
and will inherit eternal life. 30But many who are
the greatest now will be least important then,
and those who seem least important now will be
the greatest then.

CHAPTER 20

Parable of the Vineyard Workers

"For the Kingdom of Heaven is like the landowner who went out early one morning to hire
workers for his vineyard. 2He agreed to pay the
normal daily wage and sent them out to work.
3"At nine o'clock in the morning he was passing through the marketplace and saw some people standing around doing nothing. 4So he hired
them, telling them he would pay them whatever
was right at the end of the day. 5So they went to
work in the vineyard. At noon and again at three
o'clock he did the same thing.
6"At five o'clock that afternoon he was in town
again and saw some more people standing
around. He asked them, 'Why haven't you been
working today?'
7"They replied, 'Because no one hired us.'
"The landowner told them, 'Then go out and
join the others in my vineyard.'
8"That evening he told the foreman to call
the workers in and pay them, beginning with
the last workers first. 9When those hired at
five o'clock were paid, each received a full day's
wage. 10When those hired first came to get
their pay, they assumed they would receive
more. But they, too, were paid a day's wage.
11When they received their pay, they protested
to the owner, 12'Those people worked only one
hour, and yet you've paid them just as much as
you paid us who worked all day in the scorching
heat.'
13"He answered one of them, 'Friend, I
haven't been unfair! Didn't you agree to work all
day for the usual wage? 14Take your money and
go. I wanted to pay this last worker the same as
you. 15Is it against the law for me to do what
I want with my money? Should you be jealous
because I am kind to others?'

19:9 Some manuscripts add *And anyone who marries a divorced woman commits adultery.* Compare Matt 5:32.

16"So those who are last now will be first then,
and those who are first will be last."

Jesus Again Predicts His Death

17As Jesus was going up to Jerusalem, he took the
twelve disciples aside privately and told them
what was going to happen to him. 18"Listen," he
said, "we're going up to Jerusalem, where the Son
of Man will be betrayed to the leading priests and
the teachers of religious law. They will sentence
him to die. 19Then they will hand him over to the
Romans to be mocked, flogged with a whip, and
crucified. But on the third day he will be raised
from the dead."

Jesus Teaches about Serving Others

20Then the mother of James and John, the sons
of Zebedee, came to Jesus with her sons. She
knelt respectfully to ask a favor. 21"What is your
request?" he asked.

She replied, "In your Kingdom, please let my
two sons sit in places of honor next to you, one
on your right and the other on your left."

22But Jesus answered by saying to them, "You
don't know what you are asking! Are you able to
drink from the bitter cup of suffering I am about
to drink?"

"Oh yes," they replied, "we are able!"

23Jesus told them, "You will indeed drink
from my bitter cup. But I have no right to say who
will sit on my right or my left. My Father has prepared those places for the ones he has chosen."

24When the ten other disciples heard what
James and John had asked, they were indignant.
25But Jesus called them together and said, "You
know that the rulers in this world lord it over
their people, and officials flaunt their authority
over those under them. 26But among you it will
be different. Whoever wants to be a leader
among you must be your servant, 27and whoever
wants to be first among you must become your
slave. 28For even the Son of Man came not to be
served but to serve others and to give his life as a
ransom for many."

Jesus Heals Two Blind Men

29As Jesus and the disciples left the town of Jericho, a large crowd followed behind. 30Two blind
men were sitting beside the road. When they
heard that Jesus was coming that way, they began shouting, "Lord, Son of David, have mercy
on us!"

31"Be quiet!" the crowd yelled at them.

But they only shouted louder, "Lord, Son of
David, have mercy on us!"

32When Jesus heard them, he stopped and
called, "What do you want me to do for you?"

33"Lord," they said, "we want to see!" 34Jesus
felt sorry for them and touched their eyes. Instantly they could see! Then they followed him.

CHAPTER 21

Jesus' Triumphant Entry

As Jesus and the disciples approached Jerusalem, they came to the town of Bethphage on the
Mount of Olives. Jesus sent two of them on
ahead. 2"Go into the village over there," he said.
"As soon as you enter it, you will see a donkey tied
there, with its colt beside it. Untie them and
bring them to me. 3If anyone asks what you are
doing, just say, 'The Lord needs them,' and he will
immediately let you take them."

4This took place to fulfill the prophecy that
said,

5 "Tell the people of Jerusalem,
'Look, your King is coming to you.
He is humble, riding on a donkey—
riding on a donkey's colt.'"

6The two disciples did as Jesus commanded.
7They brought the donkey and the colt to him
and threw their garments over the colt, and he
sat on it.

8Most of the crowd spread their garments on
the road ahead of him, and others cut branches
from the trees and spread them on the road.
9Jesus was in the center of the procession, and
the people all around him were shouting,

"Praise God for the Son of David!
Blessings on the one who comes in the
name of the LORD!
Praise God in highest heaven!"

10The entire city of Jerusalem was in an uproar as he entered. "Who is this?" they asked.

11And the crowds replied, "It's Jesus, the
prophet from Nazareth in Galilee."

Jesus Clears the Temple

12Jesus entered the Temple and began to drive out
all the people buying and selling animals for sacrifice. He knocked over the tables of the money
changers and the chairs of those selling doves.
13He said to them, "The Scriptures declare, 'My
Temple will be called a house of prayer,' but you
have turned it into a den of thieves!"

14The blind and the lame came to him in the
Temple, and he healed them. 15The leading

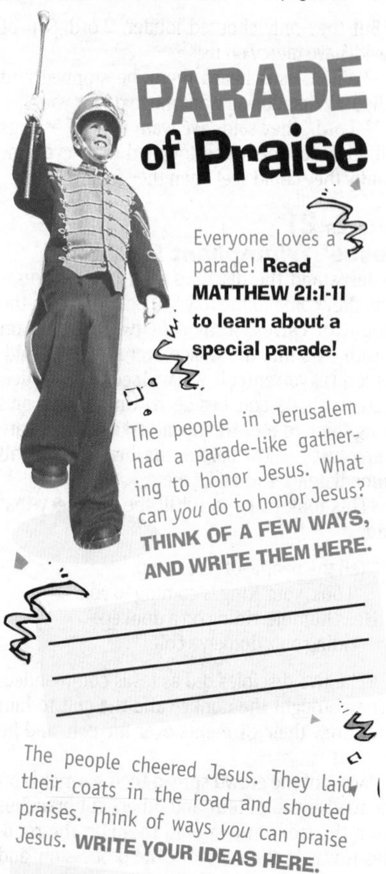

PARADE of Praise
Everyone loves a parade! **Read MATTHEW 21:1-11 to learn about a special parade!**
The people in Jerusalem had a parade-like gathering to honor Jesus. What can *you* do to honor Jesus? **THINK OF A FEW WAYS, AND WRITE THEM HERE.**
The people cheered Jesus. They laid their coats in the road and shouted praises. Think of ways *you* can praise Jesus. **WRITE YOUR IDEAS HERE.**

NOW THAT YOU'VE MADE A PLAN, GET GOING! Show Jesus that he's more important than anything else in your life.

priests and the teachers of religious law saw
these wonderful miracles and heard even the
children in the Temple shouting, "Praise God for
the Son of David."

But the leaders were indignant. 16 They asked
Jesus, "Do you hear what these children are
saying?"

"Yes," Jesus replied. "Haven't you ever read the
Scriptures? For they say, 'You have taught children
and infants to give you praise.'" 17 Then he returned to Bethany, where he stayed overnight.

Jesus Curses the Fig Tree

18 In the morning, as Jesus was returning to Jerusalem, he was hungry, 19 and he noticed a fig tree
beside the road. He went over to see if there were
any figs, but there were only leaves. Then he said
to it, "May you never bear fruit again!" And immediately the fig tree withered up.

20 The disciples were amazed when they saw
this and asked, "How did the fig tree wither so
quickly?"

21 Then Jesus told them, "I tell you the truth, if
you have faith and don't doubt, you can do
things like this and much more. You can even
say to this mountain, 'May you be lifted up and
thrown into the sea,' and it will happen. 22 You
can pray for anything, and if you have faith, you
will receive it."

The Authority of Jesus Challenged

23 When Jesus returned to the Temple and began
teaching, the leading priests and elders came up
to him. They demanded, "By what authority are
you doing all these things? Who gave you the
right?"

24 "I'll tell you by what authority I do these
things if you answer one question," Jesus replied.
25 "Did John's authority to baptize come from
heaven, or was it merely human?"

They talked it over among themselves. "If we
say it was from heaven, he will ask us why we
didn't believe John. 26 But if we say it was merely
human, we'll be mobbed because the people
believe John was a prophet." 27 So they finally
replied, "We don't know."

And Jesus responded, "Then I won't tell you by
what authority I do these things.

Parable of the Two Sons

28 "But what do you think about this? A man with
two sons told the older boy, 'Son, go out and work
in the vineyard today.' 29 The son answered, 'No, I
won't go,' but later he changed his mind and

went anyway. 30 Then the father told the other
son, 'You go,' and he said, 'Yes, sir, I will.' But he
didn't go.

31 "Which of the two obeyed his father?"

They replied, "The first."

Then Jesus explained his meaning: "I tell you
the truth, corrupt tax collectors and prostitutes
will get into the Kingdom of God before you do.
32 For John the Baptist came and showed you the
right way to live, but you didn't believe him,
while tax collectors and prostitutes did. And
even when you saw this happening, you refused
to believe him and repent of your sins.

Parable of the Evil Farmers

33 "Now listen to another story. A certain landowner planted a vineyard, built a wall around it,
dug a pit for pressing out the grape juice, and
built a lookout tower. Then he leased the vineyard to tenant farmers and moved to another
country. 34 At the time of the grape harvest, he
sent his servants to collect his share of the crop.
35 But the farmers grabbed his servants, beat
one, killed one, and stoned another. 36 So the
landowner sent a larger group of his servants to
collect for him, but the results were the same.

37 "Finally, the owner sent his son, thinking,
'Surely they will respect my son.'

38 "But when the tenant farmers saw his son
coming, they said to one another, 'Here comes
the heir to this estate. Come on, let's kill him and
get the estate for ourselves!' 39 So they grabbed
him, dragged him out of the vineyard, and murdered him.

40 "When the owner of the vineyard returns,"
Jesus asked, "what do you think he will do to
those farmers?"

41 The religious leaders replied, "He will put
the wicked men to a horrible death and lease the
vineyard to others who will give him his share of
the crop after each harvest."

42 Then Jesus asked them, "Didn't you ever
read this in the Scriptures?

'The stone that the builders rejected
has now become the cornerstone.
This is the LORD's doing,
and it is wonderful to see.'

43 I tell you, the Kingdom of God will be taken
away from you and given to a nation that will produce the proper fruit. 44 Anyone who stumbles
over that stone will be broken to pieces, and it
will crush anyone it falls on."

45 When the leading priests and Pharisees
heard this parable, they realized he was telling
the story against them—they were the wicked
farmers. 46 They wanted to arrest him, but they
were afraid of the crowds, who considered Jesus
to be a prophet.

CHAPTER 22

Parable of the Great Feast

Jesus also told them other parables. He said,
2 "The Kingdom of Heaven can be illustrated by
the story of a king who prepared a great wedding
feast for his son. 3 When the banquet was ready,
he sent his servants to notify those who were invited. But they all refused to come!

4 "So he sent other servants to tell them, 'The
feast has been prepared. The bulls and fattened
cattle have been killed, and everything is ready.
Come to the banquet!' 5 But the guests he had invited ignored them and went their own way, one
to his farm, another to his business. 6 Others
seized his messengers and insulted them and
killed them.

7 "The king was furious, and he sent out his
army to destroy the murderers and burn their
town. 8 And he said to his servants, 'The wedding
feast is ready, and the guests I invited aren't worthy of the honor. 9 Now go out to the street corners and invite everyone you see.' 10 So the
servants brought in everyone they could find,
good and bad alike, and the banquet hall was
filled with guests.

11 "But when the king came in to meet the
guests, he noticed a man who wasn't wearing the
proper clothes for a wedding. 12 'Friend,' he
asked, 'how is it that you are here without wedding clothes?' But the man had no reply. 13 Then
the king said to his aides, 'Bind his hands and feet
and throw him into the outer darkness, where
there will be weeping and gnashing of teeth.'

14 "For many are called, but few are chosen."

Taxes for Caesar

15 Then the Pharisees met together to plot how
to trap Jesus into saying something for which he
could be arrested. 16 They sent some of their
disciples, along with the supporters of Herod, to
meet with him. "Teacher," they said, "we know
how honest you are. You teach the way of God
truthfully. You are impartial and don't play favorites. 17 Now tell us what you think about this:
Is it right to pay taxes to Caesar or not?"

18 But Jesus knew their evil motives. "You hypocrites!" he said. "Why are you trying to trap
me? 19 Here, show me the coin used for the tax."
When they handed him a Roman coin, 20 he asked,
"Whose picture and title are stamped on it?"

21"Caesar's," they replied.
"Well, then," he said, "give to Caesar what
belongs to Caesar, and give to God what belongs
to God."
22His reply amazed them, and they went away.

Discussion about Resurrection

23That same day Jesus was approached by some
Sadducees—religious leaders who say there is
no resurrection from the dead. They posed this
question: 24"Teacher, Moses said, 'If a man dies
without children, his brother should marry the
widow and have a child who will carry on the
brother's name.' 25Well, suppose there were
seven brothers. The oldest one married and
then died without children, so his brother married the widow. 26But the second brother also
died, and the third brother married her. This
continued with all seven of them. 27Last of all,
the woman also died. 28So tell us, whose wife
will she be in the resurrection? For all seven
were married to her."
29Jesus replied, "Your mistake is that you don't
know the Scriptures, and you don't know the
power of God. 30For when the dead rise, they will
neither marry nor be given in marriage. In this
respect they will be like the angels in heaven.
31"But now, as to whether there will be a resurrection of the dead—haven't you ever read about
this in the Scriptures? Long after Abraham, Isaac,
and Jacob had died, God said, 32'I am the God of
Abraham, the God of Isaac, and the God of Jacob.'
So he is the God of the living, not the dead."
33When the crowds heard him, they were astounded at his teaching.

The Most Important Commandment

34But when the Pharisees heard that he had silenced the Sadducees with his reply, they met together to question him again. 35One of them, an
expert in religious law, tried to trap him with this
question: 36"Teacher, which is the most important commandment in the law of Moses?"
37Jesus replied, "'You must love
the LORD your God with all your heart,
all your soul, and all your mind.' 38This
is the first and greatest commandment. 39A
second is equally important: 'Love your neighbor as yourself.' 40The entire law and all the demands of the prophets are based on these two
commandments."

Whose Son Is the Messiah?

41Then, surrounded by the Pharisees, Jesus
asked them a question: 42"What do you think
about the Messiah? Whose son is he?"
They replied, "He is the son of David."
43Jesus responded, "Then why does David,
speaking under the inspiration of the Spirit, call
the Messiah 'my Lord'? For David said,

44 'The LORD said to my Lord,
Sit in the place of honor at my right hand
until I humble your enemies beneath
your feet.'

45Since David called the Messiah 'my Lord,' how
can the Messiah be his son?"
46No one could answer him. And after that, no
one dared to ask him any more questions.

CHAPTER 23
Jesus Criticizes the Religious Leaders

Then Jesus said to the crowds and to his disciples, 2"The teachers of religious law and the
Pharisees are the official interpreters of the law
of Moses. 3So practice and obey whatever they
tell you, but don't follow their example. For they
don't practice what they teach. 4They crush people with unbearable religious demands and
never lift a finger to ease the burden.
5"Everything they do is for show. On their
arms they wear extra wide prayer boxes with
Scripture verses inside, and they wear robes with
extra long tassels. 6And they love to sit at the
head table at banquets and in the seats of honor
in the synagogues. 7They love to receive respectful greetings as they walk in the marketplaces,
and to be called 'Rabbi.'
8"Don't let anyone call you 'Rabbi,' for you
have only one teacher, and all of you are equal as
brothers and sisters. 9And don't address anyone
here on earth as 'Father,' for only God in heaven is
your spiritual Father. 10And don't let anyone call
you 'Teacher,' for you have only one teacher, the
Messiah. 11The greatest among you must be a
servant. 12But those who exalt themselves will be
humbled, and those who humble themselves will
be exalted.
13"What sorrow awaits you teachers of religious law and you Pharisees. Hypocrites! For you
shut the door of the Kingdom of Heaven in people's faces. You won't go in yourselves, and you
don't let others enter either.*
15"What sorrow awaits you teachers of reli-

23:13 Some manuscripts add verse 14, *What sorrow awaits you teachers of religious law and you Pharisees. Hypocrites! You shamelessly cheat widows out of their property and then pretend to be pious by making long prayers in public. Because of this, you will be severely punished.* Compare Mark 12:40 and Luke 20:47.

gious law and you Pharisees. Hypocrites! For you
cross land and sea to make one convert, and then
you turn that person into twice the child of hell
you yourselves are!
16"Blind guides! What sorrow awaits you! For
you say that it means nothing to swear 'by God's
Temple,' but that it is binding to swear 'by the
gold in the Temple.' 17Blind fools! Which is more
important—the gold or the Temple that makes
the gold sacred? 18And you say that to swear 'by
the altar' is not binding, but to swear 'by the gifts
on the altar' is binding. 19How blind! For which is
more important—the gift on the altar or the altar
that makes the gift sacred? 20When you swear
'by the altar,' you are swearing by it and by everything on it. 21And when you swear 'by the Temple,' you are swearing by it and by God, who lives
in it. 22And when you swear 'by heaven,' you are
swearing by the throne of God and by God, who
sits on the throne.
23"What sorrow awaits you teachers of religious law and you Pharisees. Hypocrites! For you
are careful to tithe even the tiniest income from
your herb gardens, but you ignore the more important aspects of the law—justice, mercy, and
faith. You should tithe, yes, but do not neglect the
more important things. 24Blind guides! You
strain your water so you won't accidentally swallow a gnat, but you swallow a camel!
25"What sorrow awaits you teachers of religious law and you Pharisees. Hypocrites! For you
are so careful to clean the outside of the cup and
the dish, but inside you are filthy—full of greed
and self-indulgence! 26You blind Pharisee! First
wash the inside of the cup and the dish, and then
the outside will become clean, too.
27"What sorrow awaits you teachers of religious law and you Pharisees. Hypocrites! For you
are like whitewashed tombs—beautiful on the
outside but filled on the inside with dead
people's bones and all sorts of impurity. 28Out-
wardly you look like righteous people, but in-
wardly your hearts are filled with hypocrisy and
lawlessness.
29"What sorrow awaits you teachers of religious law and you Pharisees. Hypocrites! For you
build tombs for the prophets your ancestors
killed, and you decorate the monuments of the
godly people your ancestors destroyed. 30Then
you say, 'If we had lived in the days of our ancestors, we would never have joined them in killing
the prophets.'
31"But in saying that, you testify against yourselves that you are indeed the descendants of
those who murdered the prophets. 32Go ahead
and finish what your ancestors started. 33Snakes!
Sons of vipers! How will you escape the judgment
of hell?
34"Therefore, I am sending you prophets and
wise men and teachers of religious law. But you
will kill some by crucifixion, and you will flog
others with whips in your synagogues, chasing
them from city to city. 35As a result, you will be
held responsible for the murder of all godly
people of all time—from the murder of righteous
Abel to the murder of Zechariah son of Berekiah,
whom you killed in the Temple between the
sanctuary and the altar. 36I tell you the truth, this
judgment will fall on this very generation.

Jesus Grieves over Jerusalem

37"O Jerusalem, Jerusalem, the city that kills the
prophets and stones God's messengers! How
often I have wanted to gather your children together as a hen protects her chicks beneath her
wings, but you wouldn't let me. 38And now, look,
your house is abandoned and desolate. 39For I
tell you this, you will never see me again until you
say, 'Blessings on the one who comes in the name
of the LORD!'"

CHAPTER 24

Jesus Foretells the Future

As Jesus was leaving the Temple grounds, his disciples pointed out to him the various Temple
buildings. 2But he responded, "Do you see all
these buildings? I tell you the truth, they will be
completely demolished. Not one stone will be
left on top of another!"
3Later, Jesus sat on the Mount of Olives. His
disciples came to him privately and said, "Tell us,
when will all this happen? What sign will signal
your return and the end of the world?"
4Jesus told them, "Don't let anyone mislead
you, 5for many will come in my name, claiming, 'I
am the Messiah.' They will deceive many. 6And
you will hear of wars and threats of wars, but
don't panic. Yes, these things must take place,
but the end won't follow immediately. 7Nation
will go to war against nation, and kingdom
against kingdom. There will be famines and
earthquakes in many parts of the world. 8But all
this is only the first of the birth pains, with more
to come.
9"Then you will be arrested, persecuted, and
killed. You will be hated all over the world because you are my followers. 10And many will
turn away from me and betray and hate each
other. 11And many false prophets will appear
and will deceive many people. 12Sin will be

rampant everywhere, and the love of many will
grow cold. 13 But the one who endures to the end
will be saved. 14 And the Good News about the
Kingdom will be preached throughout the
whole world, so that all nations will hear it; and
then the end will come.

15 "The day is coming when you will see what
Daniel the prophet spoke about—the sacrilegious object that causes desecration standing in
the Holy Place." (Reader, pay attention!) 16 "Then
those in Judea must flee to the hills. 17 A person
out on the deck of a roof must not go down into
the house to pack. 18 A person out in the field
must not return even to get a coat. 19 How terrible
it will be for pregnant women and for nursing
mothers in those days. 20 And pray that your
flight will not be in winter or on the Sabbath.
21 For there will be greater anguish than at any
time since the world began. And it will never
be so great again. 22 In fact, unless that time of
calamity is shortened, not a single person will
survive. But it will be shortened for the sake of
God's chosen ones.

23 "Then if anyone tells you, 'Look, here is the
Messiah,' or 'There he is,' don't believe it. 24 For
false messiahs and false prophets will rise up
and perform great signs and wonders so as to deceive, if possible, even God's chosen ones. 25 See,
I have warned you about this ahead of time.

26 "So if someone tells you, 'Look, the Messiah
is out in the desert,' don't bother to go and look.
Or, 'Look, he is hiding here,' don't believe it! 27 For
as the lightning flashes in the east and shines to
the west, so it will be when the Son of Man
comes. 28 Just as the gathering of vultures shows
there is a carcass nearby, so these signs indicate
that the end is near.

29 "Immediately after the anguish of those
days,

the sun will be darkened,
  the moon will give no light,
the stars will fall from the sky,
  and the powers in the heavens will be
    shaken.

30 And then at last, the sign that the Son of Man is
coming will appear in the heavens, and there will
be deep mourning among all the peoples of the
earth. And they will see the Son of Man coming
on the clouds of heaven with power and great
glory. 31 And he will send out his angels with the
mighty blast of a trumpet, and they will gather
his chosen ones from all over the world—from
the farthest ends of the earth and heaven.

32 "Now learn a lesson from the fig tree. When
its branches bud and its leaves begin to sprout,
you know that summer is near. 33 In the same
way, when you see all these things, you can know
his return is very near, right at the door. 34 I tell
you the truth, this generation will not pass from
the scene until all these things take place.
35 Heaven and earth will disappear, but my words
will never disappear.

36 "However, no one knows the day or hour
when these things will happen, not even the angels in heaven or the Son himself. Only the Father knows.

37 "When the Son of Man returns, it will be like
it was in Noah's day. 38 In those days before the
flood, the people were enjoying banquets and
parties and weddings right up to the time Noah
entered his boat. 39 People didn't realize what
was going to happen until the flood came and
swept them all away. That is the way it will be
when the Son of Man comes.

40 "Two men will be working together in the
field; one will be taken, the other left. 41 Two
women will be grinding flour at the mill; one will
be taken, the other left.

42 "So you, too, must keep watch! For you don't
know what day your Lord is coming. 43 Understand this: If a homeowner knew exactly when a
burglar was coming, he would keep watch and
not permit his house to be broken into. 44 You
also must be ready all the time, for the Son of
Man will come when least expected.

45 "A faithful, sensible servant is one to whom
the master can give the responsibility of managing his other household servants and feeding
them. 46 If the master returns and finds that the
servant has done a good job, there will be a reward. 47 I tell you the truth, the master will put
that servant in charge of all he owns. 48 But what
if the servant is evil and thinks, 'My master won't
be back for a while,' 49 and he begins beating the
other servants, partying, and getting drunk?
50 The master will return unannounced and unexpected, 51 and he will cut the servant to pieces
and assign him a place with the hypocrites. In
that place there will be weeping and gnashing of
teeth.

CHAPTER 25

Parable of the Ten Bridesmaids

"Then the Kingdom of Heaven will be like ten
bridesmaids who took their lamps and went to
meet the bridegroom. 2 Five of them were foolish, and five were wise. 3 The five who were
foolish didn't take enough olive oil for their
lamps, 4 but the other five were wise enough to

take along extra oil. 5When the bridegroom
was delayed, they all became drowsy and fell
asleep.
6"At midnight they were roused by the shout,
'Look, the bridegroom is coming! Come out and
meet him!'
7"All the bridesmaids got up and prepared
their lamps. 8Then the five foolish ones asked
the others, 'Please give us some of your oil because our lamps are going out.'
9"But the others replied, 'We don't have
enough for all of us. Go to a shop and buy some
for yourselves.'
10"But while they were gone to buy oil, the
bridegroom came. Then those who were ready
went in with him to the marriage feast, and the
door was locked. 11Later, when the other five
bridesmaids returned, they stood outside, calling, 'Lord! Lord! Open the door for us!'
12"But he called back, 'Believe me, I don't
know you!'
13"So you, too, must keep watch! For you do
not know the day or hour of my return.

Parable of the Three Servants

14"Again, the Kingdom of Heaven can be illustrated by the story of a man going on a long trip.
He called together his servants and entrusted
his money to them while he was gone. 15He gave
five bags of silver to one, two bags of silver to another, and one bag of silver to the last—dividing
it in proportion to their abilities. He then left on
his trip.
16"The servant who received the five bags of
silver began to invest the money and earned five
more. 17The servant with two bags of silver also
went to work and earned two more. 18But the
servant who received the one bag of silver dug a
hole in the ground and hid the master's money.
19"After a long time their master returned
from his trip and called them to give an account
of how they had used his money. 20The servant to
whom he had entrusted the five bags of silver
came forward with five more and said, 'Master,
you gave me five bags of silver to invest, and I
have earned five more.'
21"The master was full of praise. 'Well done,
my good and faithful servant. You have been
faithful in handling this small amount, so now I
will give you many more responsibilities. Let's
celebrate together!'
22"The servant who had received the two bags
of silver came forward and said, 'Master, you gave
me two bags of silver to invest, and I have earned
two more.'
23"The master said, 'Well done, my good and
faithful servant. You have been faithful in handling this small amount, so now I will give you
many more responsibilities. Let's celebrate together!'
24"Then the servant with the one bag of silver
came and said, 'Master, I knew you were a harsh
man, harvesting crops you didn't plant and gathering crops you didn't cultivate. 25I was afraid I
would lose your money, so I hid it in the earth.
Look, here is your money back.'
26"But the master replied, 'You wicked and
lazy servant! If you knew I harvested crops I
didn't plant and gathered crops I didn't cultivate,
27why didn't you deposit my money in the bank?
At least I could have gotten some interest on it.'
28"Then he ordered, 'Take the money from
this servant, and give it to the one with the ten
bags of silver. 29To those who use well what they
are given, even more will be given, and they will
have an abundance. But from those who do
nothing, even what little they have will be taken
away. 30Now throw this useless servant into
outer darkness, where there will be weeping and
gnashing of teeth.'

The Final Judgment

31"But when the Son of Man comes in his glory,
and all the angels with him, then he will sit upon
his glorious throne. 32All the nations will be
gathered in his presence, and he will separate the
people as a shepherd separates the sheep from
the goats. 33He will place the sheep at his right
hand and the goats at his left.
34"Then the King will say to those on his right,
'Come, you who are blessed by my Father, inherit
the Kingdom prepared for you from the creation
of the world. 35For I was hungry, and you fed me.
I was thirsty, and you gave me a drink. I was a
stranger, and you invited me into your home. 36I
was naked, and you gave me clothing. I was sick,
and you cared for me. I was in prison, and you
visited me.'
37"Then these righteous ones will reply, 'Lord,
when did we ever see you hungry and feed you?
Or thirsty and give you something to drink? 38Or
a stranger and show you hospitality? Or naked
and give you clothing? 39When did we ever see
you sick or in prison and visit you?'
40"And the King will say, 'I tell you the truth,
when you did it to one of the least of these my
brothers and sisters, you were doing it to me!'
41"Then the King will turn to those on the left
and say, 'Away with you, you cursed ones, into the
eternal fire prepared for the devil and his

demons. 42For I was hungry, and you didn't feed
me. I was thirsty, and you didn't give me a drink.
43I was a stranger, and you didn't invite me into
your home. I was naked, and you didn't give me
clothing. I was sick and in prison, and you didn't
visit me.'

44"Then they will reply, 'Lord, when did we
ever see you hungry or thirsty or a stranger or
naked or sick or in prison, and not help you?'

45"And he will answer, 'I tell you the truth, when
you refused to help the least of these my brothers
and sisters, you were refusing to help me.'

46"And they will go away into eternal punishment, but the righteous will go into eternal life."

CHAPTER 26

The Plot to Kill Jesus

When Jesus had finished saying all these things,
he said to his disciples, 2"As you know, Passover
begins in two days, and the Son of Man will be
handed over to be crucified."

3At that same time the leading priests and elders were meeting at the residence of Caiaphas,
the high priest, 4plotting how to capture Jesus
secretly and kill him. 5"But not during the Passover celebration," they agreed, "or the people
may riot."

Jesus Anointed at Bethany

6Meanwhile, Jesus was in Bethany at the home of
Simon, a man who had previously had leprosy.
7While he was eating, a woman came in with a
beautiful alabaster jar of expensive perfume and
poured it over his head.

8The disciples were indignant when they saw
this. "What a waste!" they said. 9"It could have
been sold for a high price and the money given to
the poor."

10But Jesus, aware of this, replied, "Why criticize this woman for doing such a good thing
to me? 11You will always have the poor among
you, but you will not always have me. 12She
has poured this perfume on me to prepare my
body for burial. 13I tell you the truth, wherever
the Good News is preached throughout the
world, this woman's deed will be remembered
and discussed."

Judas Agrees to Betray Jesus

14Then Judas Iscariot, one of the twelve disciples,
went to the leading priests 15and asked, "How
much will you pay me to betray Jesus to you?"
And they gave him thirty pieces of silver. 16From
that time on, Judas began looking for an opportunity to betray Jesus.

The Last Supper

17On the first day of the Festival of Unleavened
Bread, the disciples came to Jesus and asked,
"Where do you want us to prepare the Passover
meal for you?"

18"As you go into the city," he told them, "you
will see a certain man. Tell him, 'The Teacher
says: My time has come, and I will eat the Passover meal with my disciples at your house.'" 19So
the disciples did as Jesus told them and prepared
the Passover meal there.

20When it was evening, Jesus sat down at the
table with the Twelve. 21While they were eating,
he said, "I tell you the truth, one of you will betray
me."

22Greatly distressed, each one asked in turn,
"Am I the one, Lord?"

23He replied, "One of you who has just eaten
from this bowl with me will betray me. 24For the
Son of Man must die, as the Scriptures declared
long ago. But how terrible it will be for the one
who betrays him. It would be far better for that
man if he had never been born!"

25Judas, the one who would betray him, also
asked, "Rabbi, am I the one?"

And Jesus told him, "You have said it."

26As they were eating, Jesus took some bread
and blessed it. Then he broke it in pieces and
gave it to the disciples, saying, "Take this and eat
it, for this is my body."

27And he took a cup of wine and gave thanks
to God for it. He gave it to them and said, "Each of
you drink from it, 28for this is my blood, which
confirms the covenant between God and his
people. It is poured out as a sacrifice to forgive
the sins of many. 29Mark my words—I will not
drink wine again until the day I drink it new with
you in my Father's Kingdom."

30Then they sang a hymn and went out to the
Mount of Olives.

Jesus Predicts Peter's Denial

31On the way, Jesus told them, "Tonight all of you
will desert me. For the Scriptures say,

'God will strike the Shepherd,
and the sheep of the flock will be
scattered.'

32But after I have been raised from the dead, I
will go ahead of you to Galilee and meet you
there."

33Peter declared, "Even if everyone else
deserts you, I will never desert you."

34Jesus replied, "I tell you the truth, Peter—

this very night, before the rooster crows, you will
deny three times that you even know me."
35"No!" Peter insisted. "Even if I have to die
with you, I will never deny you!" And all the other
disciples vowed the same.

Jesus Prays in Gethsemane

36Then Jesus went with them to the olive grove
called Gethsemane, and he said, "Sit here while I
go over there to pray." 37He took Peter and Zebedee's two sons, James and John, and he became
anguished and distressed. 38He told them, "My
soul is crushed with grief to the point of death.
Stay here and keep watch with me."
39He went on a little farther and bowed with
his face to the ground, praying, "My Father! If it is
possible, let this cup of suffering be taken away
from me. Yet I want your will to be done, not
mine."
40Then he returned to the disciples and found
them asleep. He said to Peter, "Couldn't you watch
with me even one hour? 41Keep watch and pray,
so that you will not give in to temptation. For the
spirit is willing, but the body is weak!"
42Then Jesus left them a second time and
prayed, "My Father! If this cup cannot be taken
away unless I drink it, your will be done." 43When
he returned to them again, he found them sleeping, for they couldn't keep their eyes open.
44So he went to pray a third time, saying the
same things again. 45Then he came to the disciples and said, "Go ahead and sleep. Have your
rest. But look—the time has come. The Son of
Man is betrayed into the hands of sinners. 46Up,
let's be going. Look, my betrayer is here!"

Jesus Is Betrayed and Arrested

47And even as Jesus said this, Judas, one of the
twelve disciples, arrived with a crowd of men
armed with swords and clubs. They had been
sent by the leading priests and elders of the
people. 48The traitor, Judas, had given them a
prearranged signal: "You will know which one to
arrest when I greet him with a kiss." 49So Judas
came straight to Jesus. "Greetings, Rabbi!" he
exclaimed and gave him the kiss.
50Jesus said, "My friend, go ahead and do what
you have come for."
Then the others grabbed Jesus and arrested
him. 51But one of the men with Jesus pulled out
his sword and struck the high priest's slave,
slashing off his ear.
52"Put away your sword," Jesus told him.
"Those who use the sword will die by the sword.
53Don't you realize that I could ask my Father for
thousands of angels to protect us, and he would
send them instantly? 54But if I did, how would
the Scriptures be fulfilled that describe what
must happen now?"
55Then Jesus said to the crowd, "Am I some
dangerous revolutionary, that you come with
swords and clubs to arrest me? Why didn't you
arrest me in the Temple? I was there teaching
every day. 56But this is all happening to fulfill the
words of the prophets as recorded in the Scriptures." At that point, all the disciples deserted
him and fled.

Jesus before the Council

57Then the people who had arrested Jesus led
him to the home of Caiaphas, the high priest,
where the teachers of religious law and the elders had gathered. 58Meanwhile, Peter followed
him at a distance and came to the high priest's
courtyard. He went in and sat with the guards
and waited to see how it would all end.
59Inside, the leading priests and the entire high
council were trying to find witnesses who would
lie about Jesus, so they could put him to death.
60But even though they found many who agreed
to give false witness, they could not use anyone's
testimony. Finally, two men came forward 61who
declared, "This man said, 'I am able to destroy the
Temple of God and rebuild it in three days.'"
62Then the high priest stood up and said to
Jesus, "Well, aren't you going to answer these
charges? What do you have to say for yourself?"
63But Jesus remained silent. Then the high priest
said to him, "I demand in the name of the living
God—tell us if you are the Messiah, the Son
of God."
64Jesus replied, "You have said it. And in the
future you will see the Son of Man seated in the
place of power at God's right hand and coming
on the clouds of heaven."
65Then the high priest tore his clothing to
show his horror and said, "Blasphemy! Why do
we need other witnesses? You have all heard his
blasphemy. 66What is your verdict?"
"Guilty!" they shouted. "He deserves to die!"
67Then they began to spit in Jesus' face and
beat him with their fists. And some slapped him,
68jeering, "Prophesy to us, you Messiah! Who hit
you that time?"

Peter Denies Jesus

69Meanwhile, Peter was sitting outside in the
courtyard. A servant girl came over and said
to him, "You were one of those with Jesus the
Galilean."

70But Peter denied it in front of everyone. "I
don't know what you're talking about," he said.
71Later, out by the gate, another servant girl
noticed him and said to those standing around,
"This man was with Jesus of Nazareth."
72Again Peter denied it, this time with an oath.
"I don't even know the man," he said.
73A little later some of the other bystanders
came over to Peter and said, "You must be one of
them; we can tell by your Galilean accent."
74Peter swore, "A curse on me if I'm lying—
I don't know the man!" And immediately the
rooster crowed.
75Suddenly, Jesus' words flashed through
Peter's mind: "Before the rooster crows, you will
deny three times that you even know me." And he
went away, weeping bitterly.

CHAPTER 27

Judas Hangs Himself

Very early in the morning the leading priests
and the elders of the people met again to lay
plans for putting Jesus to death. 2Then they
bound him, led him away, and took him to Pilate,
the Roman governor.
3When Judas, who had betrayed him, realized
that Jesus had been condemned to die, he was
filled with remorse. So he took the thirty pieces
of silver back to the leading priests and the elders. 4"I have sinned," he declared, "for I have
betrayed an innocent man."
"What do we care?" they retorted. "That's
your problem."
5Then Judas threw the silver coins down in
the Temple and went out and hanged himself.
6The leading priests picked up the coins. "It
wouldn't be right to put this money in the Temple treasury," they said, "since it was payment for
murder." 7After some discussion they finally decided to buy the potter's field, and they made it
into a cemetery for foreigners. 8That is why the
field is still called the Field of Blood. 9This fulfilled the prophecy of Jeremiah that says,

"They took the thirty pieces of silver—
the price at which he was valued by the
people of Israel,
10 and purchased the potter's field,
as the LORD directed."

Jesus' Trial before Pilate

11Now Jesus was standing before Pilate, the
Roman governor. "Are you the king of the Jews?"
the governor asked him.
Jesus replied, "You have said it."
12But when the leading priests and the elders
made their accusations against him, Jesus
remained silent. 13"Don't you hear all these
charges they are bringing against you?" Pilate demanded. 14But Jesus made no response to any of
the charges, much to the governor's surprise.
15Now it was the governor's custom each year
during the Passover celebration to release one
prisoner to the crowd—anyone they wanted.
16This year there was a notorious prisoner, a man
named Barabbas. 17As the crowds gathered before Pilate's house that morning, he asked them,
"Which one do you want me to release to you—
Barabbas, or Jesus who is called the Messiah?"
18(He knew very well that the religious leaders
had arrested Jesus out of envy.)
19Just then, as Pilate was sitting on the judgment seat, his wife sent him this message:
"Leave that innocent man alone. I suffered
through a terrible nightmare about him last
night."
20Meanwhile, the leading priests and the elders persuaded the crowd to ask for Barabbas to
be released and for Jesus to be put to death. 21So
the governor asked again, "Which of these two
do you want me to release to you?"
The crowd shouted back, "Barabbas!"
22Pilate responded, "Then what should I do
with Jesus who is called the Messiah?"
They shouted back, "Crucify him!"
23"Why?" Pilate demanded. "What crime has
he committed?"
But the mob roared even louder, "Crucify
him!"
24Pilate saw that he wasn't getting anywhere
and that a riot was developing. So he sent for a
bowl of water and washed his hands before the
crowd, saying, "I am innocent of this man's
blood. The responsibility is yours!"
25And all the people yelled back, "We will
take responsibility for his death—we and our
children!"
26So Pilate released Barabbas to them. He
ordered Jesus flogged with a lead-tipped whip,
then turned him over to the Roman soldiers to
be crucified.

The Soldiers Mock Jesus

27Some of the governor's soldiers took Jesus into
their headquarters and called out the entire regiment. 28They stripped him and put a scarlet robe
on him. 29They wove thorn branches into a
crown and put it on his head, and they placed a
reed stick in his right hand as a scepter. Then
they knelt before him in mockery and taunted,
"Hail! King of the Jews!" 30And they spit on him

and grabbed the stick and struck him on the
head with it. 31When they were finally tired of
mocking him, they took off the robe and put his
own clothes on him again. Then they led him
away to be crucified.

The Crucifixion

32Along the way, they came across a man named
Simon, who was from Cyrene, and the soldiers
forced him to carry Jesus' cross. 33And they went
out to a place called Golgotha (which means
"Place of the Skull"). 34The soldiers gave Jesus
wine mixed with bitter gall, but when he had
tasted it, he refused to drink it.

35After they had nailed him to the cross, the
soldiers gambled for his clothes by throwing
dice.* 36Then they sat around and kept guard
as he hung there. 37A sign was fastened above
Jesus' head, announcing the charge against
him. It read: "This is Jesus, the King of the Jews."
38Two revolutionaries were crucified with him,
one on his right and one on his left.

39The people passing by shouted abuse, shaking their heads in mockery. 40"Look at you now!"
they yelled at him. "You said you were going to
destroy the Temple and rebuild it in three days.
Well then, if you are the Son of God, save yourself and come down from the cross!"

41The leading priests, the teachers of religious law, and the elders also mocked Jesus.
42"He saved others," they scoffed, "but he can't
save himself! So he is the King of Israel, is he? Let
him come down from the cross right now, and
we will believe in him! 43He trusted God, so let
God rescue him now if he wants him! For he said,
'I am the Son of God.'" 44Even the revolutionaries who were crucified with him ridiculed him
in the same way.

The Death of Jesus

45At noon, darkness fell across the whole land
until three o'clock. 46At about three o'clock,
Jesus called out with a loud voice, *"Eli, Eli, lema
sabachthani?"* which means "My God, my God,
why have you abandoned me?"

47Some of the bystanders misunderstood
and thought he was calling for the prophet Elijah. 48One of them ran and filled a sponge with
sour wine, holding it up to him on a reed stick so
he could drink. 49But the rest said, "Wait! Let's
see whether Elijah comes to save him."*

50Then Jesus shouted out again, and he released his spirit. 51At that moment the curtain in
the sanctuary of the Temple was torn in two,
from top to bottom. The earth shook, rocks split
apart, 52and tombs opened. The bodies of many
godly men and women who had died were
raised from the dead. 53They left the cemetery
after Jesus' resurrection, went into the holy city
of Jerusalem, and appeared to many people.

54The Roman officer and the other soldiers at
the crucifixion were terrified by the earthquake
and all that had happened. They said, "This man
truly was the Son of God!"

55And many women who had come from

Worth the Effort

It's not always easy to tell others about Jesus. Sometimes it's kind of like this!

1. **Find a friend, two wrapped pieces of gum, and four socks.**
2. **Put the socks over your hands.**
3. **See who can unwrap the gum first!**

What was it like to unwrap the gum wearing socks on your hands?

Sometimes we may feel like we're "all thumbs" when we share our faith. **Read MATTHEW 28:18-20 with your friend.** Jesus promises to be with us as we tell others about him. We don't have to feel nervous because he'll help us say the right thing. Say a quick prayer with your friend, asking for opportunities to share your faith in Jesus!

27:35 Greek *by casting lots.* A few late manuscripts add *This fulfilled the word of the prophet: "They divided my garments among themselves and cast lots for my robe."* See Ps 22:18. 27:49 Some manuscripts add *And another took a spear and pierced his side, and out flowed water and blood.* Compare John 19:34.

Galilee with Jesus to care for him were watching
from a distance. 56 Among them were Mary Magdalene, Mary (the mother of James and Joseph),
and the mother of James and John, the sons of
Zebedee.

The Burial of Jesus

57 As evening approached, Joseph, a rich man
from Arimathea who had become a follower of
Jesus, 58 went to Pilate and asked for Jesus' body.
And Pilate issued an order to release it to him.
59 Joseph took the body and wrapped it in a long
sheet of clean linen cloth. 60 He placed it in his
own new tomb, which had been carved out of
the rock. Then he rolled a great stone across the
entrance and left. 61 Both Mary Magdalene and
the other Mary were sitting across from the
tomb and watching.

The Guard at the Tomb

62 The next day, on the Sabbath, the leading
priests and Pharisees went to see Pilate. 63 They
told him, "Sir, we remember what that deceiver
once said while he was still alive: 'After three days
I will rise from the dead.' 64 So we request that
you seal the tomb until the third day. This will
prevent his disciples from coming and stealing
his body and then telling everyone he was raised
from the dead! If that happens, we'll be worse off
than we were at first."

65 Pilate replied, "Take guards and secure it the
best you can." 66 So they sealed the tomb and
posted guards to protect it.

CHAPTER 28

The Resurrection

Early on Sunday morning, as the new day was
dawning, Mary Magdalene and the other Mary
went out to visit the tomb.

2 Suddenly there was a great earthquake! For an
angel of the Lord came down from heaven, rolled
aside the stone, and sat on it. 3 His face shone like
lightning, and his clothing was as white as snow.
4 The guards shook with fear when they saw him,
and they fell into a dead faint.

5 Then the angel spoke to the women. "Don't
be afraid!" he said. "I know you are looking for
Jesus, who was crucified. 6 He isn't here! He is
risen from the dead, just as he said would happen. Come, see where his body was lying. 7 And
now, go quickly and tell his disciples that he has
risen from the dead, and he is going ahead of you
to Galilee. You will see him there. Remember
what I have told you."

8 The women ran quickly from the tomb. They
were very frightened but also filled with great joy,
and they rushed to give the disciples the angel's
message. 9 And as they went, Jesus met them
and greeted them. And they ran to him, grasped
his feet, and worshiped him. 10 Then Jesus said
to them, "Don't be afraid! Go tell my brothers to
leave for Galilee, and they will see me there."

The Report of the Guard

11 As the women were on their way, some of the
guards went into the city and told the leading
priests what had happened. 12 A meeting with
the elders was called, and they decided to give
the soldiers a large bribe. 13 They told the soldiers, "You must say, 'Jesus' disciples came during the night while we were sleeping, and they
stole his body.' 14 If the governor hears about it,
we'll stand up for you so you won't get in trouble." 15 So the guards accepted the bribe and said
what they were told to say. Their story spread
widely among the Jews, and they still tell it today.

The Great Commission

16 Then the eleven disciples left for Galilee, going
to the mountain where Jesus had told them to go.
17 When they saw him, they worshiped him—but
some of them doubted!

18 Jesus came and told his disciples, "I have
been given all authority in heaven and on earth.
**19 Therefore, go and make disciples
of all the nations, baptizing them in
the name of the Father and the Son
and the Holy Spirit. 20 Teach these
new disciples to obey all the commands I have given you. And be sure
of this: I am with you always, even to
the end of the age."**

MARK The Messiah in Motion

Look for 2 hidden messages in Mark!

Mark gives us pictures of what Jesus did during his ministry—one right after another. Look for the Messiah (that's Jesus!)

- TEACHING
- HEALING
- SERVING
- SAVING
- PREACHING
- FEEDING
- SACRIFICING

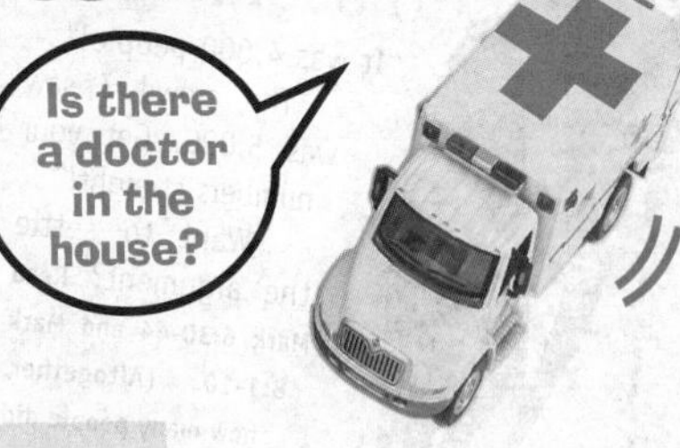

ER

He wasn't a doctor, but he performed heart surgery. He never used medicine, but he healed tons of people. **Read about one of his famous patients in Mark 2:1-12.**

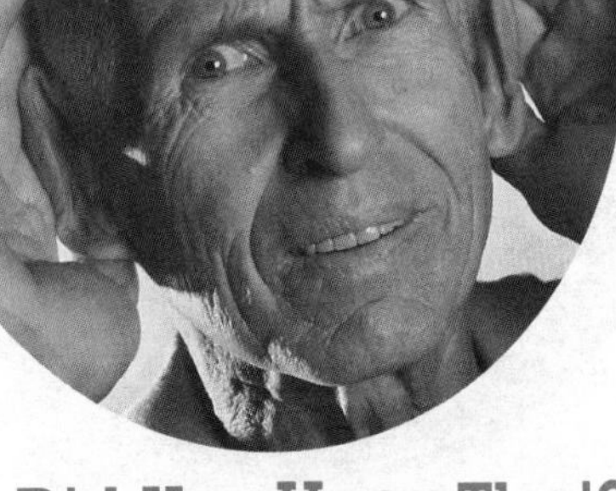

Did You Hear That?

John the Baptist hung out in the wilderness, telling people to confess their sins and be baptized. When John baptized Jesus, even though he had never sinned, something *incredible* happened. **Discover what it was in Mark 1:9-11!**

Digging Deeper

Boy, you'd think Jesus was a farmer, the way he talked about seeds and soil so much. He *wasn't* a farmer, but he knew a lot about planting seeds. **Dig into Mark 4:1-34 to hear from the Master Gardener himself!**

"Put down your fishing gear. You won't need it anymore."

"Huh? But I thought we were goin' fishin'!"

Hmm...this story sounds a little fishy.

Better read it for yourself in Mark 1:16-20!

How'd He Do That?

Inflatable shoes? Water wings? An invisible raft? How *else* could Jesus walk on water? Guess what—Jesus didn't need any of those things! **Get the details in Mark 6:45-52!**

Food for Thought

"It was 4,000 people!"

"The crowd *I* saw was 5,000. Get your numbers straight!"

Want to settle the argument? **Read Mark 6:30-44 and Mark 8:1-10. (Altogether, how many people did Jesus really feed?)**

A Dark Day—for Real!

Darkness at noon? *Staying* dark for three hours?

You could say it was truly the world's darkest day. **Find out why in Mark 15:33-41.**

Everyone Loves a Parade

This may have been the most important parade in history! There weren't floats or giant cartoon balloons, but there was plenty of celebrating. **Read Mark 11:1-11 to see where—and why—this amazing parade took place.**

Sonrise!

An amazing thing happened at *Sonrise* three days after Jesus was crucified. **Read Mark 16:1-6 to see if you can guess what this strange spelling means!**

Timeline

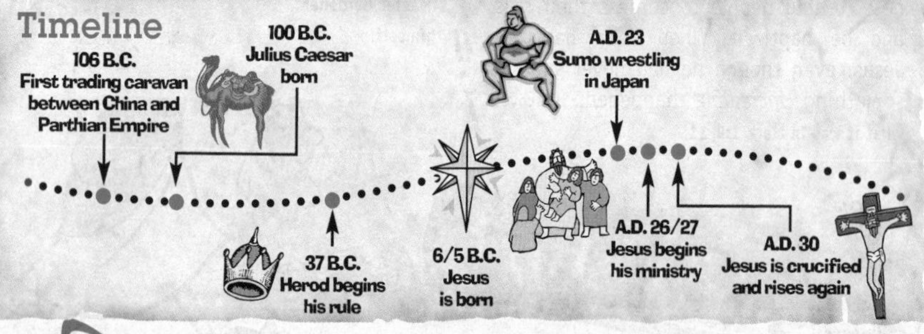
106 B.C.
First trading caravan between China and Parthian Empire
100 B.C.
Julius Caesar born
37 B.C.
Herod begins his rule
6/5 B.C.
Jesus is born
A.D. 23
Sumo wrestling in Japan
A.D. 26/27
Jesus begins his ministry
A.D. 30
Jesus is crucified and rises again

The
JESUS
CONNECTION

Mark's focus for this Gospel is simple: to show Jesus in action. Think about it! The Son of God, the King of the universe, came to serve others! How? Tons of ways! But the most important was when he died on the cross for our sins. Three days later, he rose from the dead and lives forever! If you believe in Jesus, your sins are forgiven. **He'll live in your heart here on earth, and later you can live with him forever in heaven.**

CHAPTER 1

John the Baptist Prepares the Way

This is the Good News about Jesus the Messiah,
the Son of God. It began 2 just as the prophet
Isaiah had written:

"Look, I am sending my messenger ahead
of you,
and he will prepare your way.
3 He is a voice shouting in the wilderness,
'Prepare the way for the LORD's coming!
Clear the road for him!'"

4 This messenger was John the Baptist. He was in
the wilderness and preached that people should
be baptized to show that they had repented of
their sins and turned to God to be forgiven. 5 All
of Judea, including all the people of Jerusalem,
went out to see and hear John. And when they
confessed their sins, he baptized them in the
Jordan River. 6 His clothes were woven from
coarse camel hair, and he wore a leather belt
around his waist. For food he ate locusts and
wild honey.

7 John announced: "Someone is coming soon
who is greater than I am—so much greater that
I'm not even worthy to stoop down like a slave
and untie the straps of his sandals. 8 I baptize you
with water, but he will baptize you with the Holy
Spirit!"

The Baptism and Temptation of Jesus

9 One day Jesus came from Nazareth in Galilee,
and John baptized him in the Jordan River. 10 As
Jesus came up out of the water, he saw the heavens splitting apart and the Holy Spirit descending on him like a dove. 11 And a voice from heaven
said, "You are my dearly loved Son, and you bring
me great joy."

12 The Spirit then compelled Jesus to go into
the wilderness, 13 where he was tempted by
Satan for forty days. He was out among the wild
animals, and angels took care of him.

14 Later on, after John was arrested, Jesus went
into Galilee, where he preached God's Good
News. 15 "The time promised by God has come at
last!" he announced. "The Kingdom of God is
near! Repent of your sins and believe the Good
News!"

The First Disciples

16 One day as Jesus was walking along the shore of
the Sea of Galilee, he saw Simon and his brother
Andrew throwing a net into the water, for they
fished for a living. **17 Jesus called out to
them, "Come, follow me, and I will
show you how to fish for people!"**
18 And they left their nets at once and followed
him.

19 A little farther up the shore Jesus saw Zebedee's sons, James and John, in a boat repairing
their nets. 20 He called them at once, and they
also followed him, leaving their father, Zebedee,
in the boat with the hired men.

Jesus Casts Out an Evil Spirit

21 Jesus and his companions went to the town
of Capernaum. When the Sabbath day came, he
went into the synagogue and began to teach.
22 The people were amazed at his teaching, for he
taught with real authority—quite unlike the
teachers of religious law.

23 Suddenly, a man in the synagogue who was
possessed by an evil spirit began shouting,
24 "Why are you interfering with us, Jesus of
Nazareth? Have you come to destroy us? I know
who you are—the Holy One of God!"

25 Jesus cut him short. "Be quiet! Come out of
the man," he ordered. 26 At that, the evil spirit
screamed, threw the man into a convulsion, and
then came out of him.

27 Amazement gripped the audience, and
they began to discuss what had happened.
"What sort of new teaching is this?" they asked
excitedly. "It has such authority! Even evil spirits obey his orders!" 28 The news about Jesus
spread quickly throughout the entire region of
Galilee.

Jesus Heals Many People

29 After Jesus left the synagogue with James and
John, they went to Simon and Andrew's home.
30 Now Simon's mother-in-law was sick in bed
with a high fever. They told Jesus about her right
away. 31 So he went to her bedside, took her by
the hand, and helped her sit up. Then the fever
left her, and she prepared a meal for them.

32 That evening after sunset, many sick and
demon-possessed people were brought to Jesus.
33 The whole town gathered at the door to watch.
34 So Jesus healed many people who were sick
with various diseases, and he cast out many
demons. But because the demons knew who he
was, he did not allow them to speak.

Jesus Preaches in Galilee

35 Before daybreak the next morning, Jesus got
up and went out to an isolated place to pray.
36 Later Simon and the others went out to find

him. 37When they found him, they said, "Everyone is looking for you."

38But Jesus replied, "We must go on to other towns as well, and I will preach to them, too. That is why I came." 39So he traveled throughout the region of Galilee, preaching in the synagogues and casting out demons.

Jesus Heals a Man with Leprosy

40A man with leprosy came and knelt in front of Jesus, begging to be healed. "If you are willing, you can heal me and make me clean," he said.

41Moved with compassion, Jesus reached out and touched him. "I am willing," he said. "Be healed!" 42Instantly the leprosy disappeared, and the man was healed. 43Then Jesus sent him on his way with a stern warning: 44"Don't tell anyone about this. Instead, go to the priest and let him examine you. Take along the offering required in the law of Moses for those who have been healed of leprosy. This will be a public testimony that you have been cleansed."

45But the man went and spread the word, proclaiming to everyone what had happened. As a result, large crowds soon surrounded Jesus, and he couldn't publicly enter a town anywhere. He had to stay out in the secluded places, but people from everywhere kept coming to him.

CHAPTER 2

Jesus Heals a Paralyzed Man

When Jesus returned to Capernaum several days later, the news spread quickly that he was back home. 2Soon the house where he was staying was so packed with visitors that there was no more room, even outside the door. While he was preaching God's word to them, 3four men arrived carrying a paralyzed man on a mat. 4They couldn't bring him to Jesus because of the crowd, so they dug a hole through the roof above his head. Then they lowered the man on his mat, right down in front of Jesus. 5Seeing their faith, Jesus said to the paralyzed man, "My child, your sins are forgiven."

6But some of the teachers of religious law who were sitting there thought to themselves, 7"What is he saying? This is blasphemy! Only God can forgive sins!"

8Jesus knew immediately what they were thinking, so he asked them, "Why do you question this in your hearts? 9Is it easier to say to the paralyzed man 'Your sins are forgiven,' or 'Stand up, pick up your mat, and walk'? 10So I will prove to you that the Son of Man has the authority on earth to forgive sins." Then Jesus turned to the paralyzed man and said, 11"Stand up, pick up your mat, and go home!"

12And the man jumped up, grabbed his mat, and walked out through the stunned onlookers. They were all amazed and praised God, exclaiming, "We've never seen anything like this before!"

Jesus Calls Levi (Matthew)

13Then Jesus went out to the lakeshore again and taught the crowds that were coming to him. 14As he walked along, he saw Levi son of Alphaeus sitting at his tax collector's booth. "Follow me and be my disciple," Jesus said to him. So Levi got up and followed him.

15Later, Levi invited Jesus and his disciples to his home as dinner guests, along with many tax collectors and other disreputable sinners. (There were many people of this kind among Jesus' followers.) 16But when the teachers of religious law who were Pharisees saw him eating with tax collectors and other sinners, they asked his disciples, "Why does he eat with such scum?"

17When Jesus heard this, he told them, "Healthy people don't need a doctor—sick people do. I have come to call not those who think they are righteous, but those who know they are sinners."

A Discussion about Fasting

18Once when John's disciples and the Pharisees were fasting, some people came to Jesus and asked, "Why don't your disciples fast like John's disciples and the Pharisees do?"

19Jesus replied, "Do wedding guests fast while celebrating with the groom? Of course not. They can't fast while the groom is with them. 20But someday the groom will be taken away from them, and then they will fast.

21"Besides, who would patch old clothing with new cloth? For the new patch would shrink and rip away from the old cloth, leaving an even bigger tear than before.

22"And no one puts new wine into old wineskins. For the wine would burst the wineskins, and the wine and the skins would both be lost. New wine calls for new wineskins."

A Discussion about the Sabbath

23One Sabbath day as Jesus was walking through some grainfields, his disciples began breaking off heads of grain to eat. 24But the Pharisees said to Jesus, "Look, why are they breaking the law by harvesting grain on the Sabbath?"

25Jesus said to them, "Haven't you ever read in

the Scriptures what David did when he and his
companions were hungry? 26He went into the
house of God (during the days when Abiathar
was high priest) and broke the law by eating
the sacred loaves of bread that only the priests
are allowed to eat. He also gave some to his
companions."
27Then Jesus said to them, "The Sabbath was
made to meet the needs of people, and not
people to meet the requirements of the Sabbath. 28So the Son of Man is Lord, even over the
Sabbath!"

CHAPTER 3

Jesus Heals on the Sabbath

Jesus went into the synagogue again and noticed
a man with a deformed hand. 2Since it was the
Sabbath, Jesus' enemies watched him closely. If
he healed the man's hand, they planned to accuse him of working on the Sabbath.
3Jesus said to the man with the deformed
hand, "Come and stand in front of everyone."
4Then he turned to his critics and asked, "Does
the law permit good deeds on the Sabbath, or is it
a day for doing evil? Is this a day to save life or to
destroy it?" But they wouldn't answer him.
5He looked around at them angrily and was
deeply saddened by their hard hearts. Then he
said to the man, "Hold out your hand." So the
man held out his hand, and it was restored! 6At
once the Pharisees went away and met with the
supporters of Herod to plot how to kill Jesus.

Crowds Follow Jesus

7Jesus went out to the lake with his disciples, and
a large crowd followed him. They came from all
over Galilee, Judea, 8Jerusalem, Idumea, from
east of the Jordan River, and even from as far
north as Tyre and Sidon. The news about his miracles had spread far and wide, and vast numbers
of people came to see him.
9Jesus instructed his disciples to have a boat
ready so the crowd would not crush him. 10He
had healed many people that day, so all the sick
people eagerly pushed forward to touch him.
11And whenever those possessed by evil spirits
caught sight of him, the spirits would throw
them to the ground in front of him shrieking,
"You are the Son of God!" 12But Jesus sternly
commanded the spirits not to reveal who he was.

Jesus Chooses the Twelve Apostles

13Afterward Jesus went up on a mountain and
called out the ones he wanted to go with him.
And they came to him. 14Then he appointed
twelve of them and called them his apostles. They
were to accompany him, and he would send them
out to preach, 15giving them authority to cast out
demons. 16These are the twelve he chose:

Simon (whom he named Peter),
17 James and John (the sons of Zebedee, but
Jesus nicknamed them "Sons of
Thunder"),
18 Andrew,
Philip,
Bartholomew,
Matthew,
Thomas,
James (son of Alphaeus),
Thaddaeus,
Simon (the zealot),
19 Judas Iscariot (who later betrayed him).

Jesus and the Prince of Demons

20One time Jesus entered a house, and the
crowds began to gather again. Soon he and his
disciples couldn't even find time to eat. 21When
his family heard what was happening, they tried
to take him away. "He's out of his mind," they
said.
22But the teachers of religious law who had
arrived from Jerusalem said, "He's possessed by
Satan, the prince of demons. That's where he
gets the power to cast out demons."
23Jesus called them over and responded with
an illustration. "How can Satan cast out Satan?"
he asked. 24"A kingdom divided by civil war will
collapse. 25Similarly, a family splintered by feuding will fall apart. 26And if Satan is divided and
fights against himself, how can he stand? He
would never survive. 27Let me illustrate this further. Who is powerful enough to enter the house
of a strong man like Satan and plunder his
goods? Only someone even stronger—someone
who could tie him up and then plunder his
house.
28"I tell you the truth, all sin and blasphemy
can be forgiven, 29but anyone who blasphemes
the Holy Spirit will never be forgiven. This is a sin
with eternal consequences." 30He told them this
because they were saying, "He's possessed by an
evil spirit."

The True Family of Jesus

31Then Jesus' mother and brothers came to see
him. They stood outside and sent word for him
to come out and talk with them. 32There was a

crowd sitting around Jesus, and someone said,
"Your mother and your brothers are outside
asking for you."
33Jesus replied, "Who is my mother? Who are
my brothers?" 34Then he looked at those around
him and said, "Look, these are my mother and
brothers. 35Anyone who does God's will is my
brother and sister and mother."

CHAPTER **4**

Parable of the Farmer Scattering Seed

Once again Jesus began teaching by the lakeshore. A very large crowd soon gathered around
him, so he got into a boat. Then he sat in the boat
while all the people remained on the shore. 2He
taught them by telling many stories in the form
of parables, such as this one:
3"Listen! A farmer went out to plant some
seed. 4As he scattered it across his field, some of
the seed fell on a footpath, and the birds came
and ate it. 5Other seed fell on shallow soil with
underlying rock. The seed sprouted quickly because the soil was shallow. 6But the plant soon
wilted under the hot sun, and since it didn't have
deep roots, it died. 7Other seed fell among
thorns that grew up and choked out the tender
plants so they produced no grain. 8Still other
seeds fell on fertile soil, and they sprouted, grew,
and produced a crop that was thirty, sixty, and
even a hundred times as much as had been
planted!" 9Then he said, "Anyone with ears to
hear should listen and understand."
10Later, when Jesus was alone with the twelve
disciples and with the others who were gathered
around, they asked him what the parables
meant.
11He replied, "You are permitted to understand the secret of the Kingdom of God. But I use
parables for everything I say to outsiders, 12so
that the Scriptures might be fulfilled:

'When they see what I do,
they will learn nothing.
When they hear what I say,
they will not understand.
Otherwise, they will turn to me
and be forgiven.'"

13Then Jesus said to them, "If you can't understand the meaning of this parable, how will you
understand all the other parables? 14The farmer
plants seed by taking God's word to others. 15The
seed that fell on the footpath represents those
who hear the message, only to have Satan come
at once and take it away. 16The seed on the rocky

Do you have a green thumb? To find out collect four small flower pots and a packet of seeds. **Read Jesus' parable of the four soils in MARK 4:1-20.**

1 **Fill your first pot with flat stones, and plant a few seeds in it. Read MARK 4:15 again.**

2 **Fill your second pot with pebbles, and plant a few seeds in it. Read MARK 4:16-17 again.**

3 **Fill your third pot with sticks, and plant a few seeds in it. Read MARK 4:18-19.**

4 **Fill your fourth pot with good potting soil, and plant a few seeds in it. Keep it lightly watered. Read MARK 4:20 again.**

WHICH SOIL WILL BE BEST?

Paint, **"What kind of soil am I?"** on the fourth pot. Every time you water your seedling, ask God to help you be good soil.

Read Mark 4:30-34 to see what else Jesus said about seeds!

soil represents those who hear the message and immediately receive it with joy. 17But since they don't have deep roots, they don't last long. They fall away as soon as they have problems or are persecuted for believing God's word. 18The seed that fell among the thorns represents others who hear God's word, 19but all too quickly the message is crowded out by the worries of this life, the lure of wealth, and the desire for other things, so no fruit is produced. 20And the seed that fell on good soil represents those who hear and accept God's word and produce a harvest of thirty, sixty, or even a hundred times as much as had been planted!"

Parable of the Lamp

21Then Jesus asked them, "Would anyone light a lamp and then put it under a basket or under a bed? Of course not! A lamp is placed on a stand, where its light will shine. 22For everything that is hidden will eventually be brought into the open, and every secret will be brought to light. 23Anyone with ears to hear should listen and understand."

24Then he added, "Pay close attention to what you hear. The closer you listen, the more understanding you will be given—and you will receive even more. 25To those who listen to my teaching, more understanding will be given. But for those who are not listening, even what little understanding they have will be taken away from them."

Parable of the Growing Seed

26Jesus also said, "The Kingdom of God is like a farmer who scatters seed on the ground. 27Night and day, while he's asleep or awake, the seed sprouts and grows, but he does not understand how it happens. 28The earth produces the crops on its own. First a leaf blade pushes through, then the heads of wheat are formed, and finally the grain ripens. 29And as soon as the grain is ready, the farmer comes and harvests it with a sickle, for the harvest time has come."

Parable of the Mustard Seed

30Jesus said, "How can I describe the Kingdom of God? What story should I use to illustrate it? 31It is like a mustard seed planted in the ground. It is the smallest of all seeds, 32but it becomes the largest of all garden plants; it grows long branches, and birds can make nests in its shade."

33Jesus used many similar stories and illustrations to teach the people as much as they could understand. 34In fact, in his public ministry he never taught without using parables; but afterward, when he was alone with his disciples, he explained everything to them.

Jesus Calms the Storm

35As evening came, Jesus said to his disciples, "Let's cross to the other side of the lake." 36So they took Jesus in the boat and started out, leaving the crowds behind (although other boats followed). 37But soon a fierce storm came up. High waves were breaking into the boat, and it began to fill with water.

38Jesus was sleeping at the back of the boat with his head on a cushion. The disciples woke him up, shouting, "Teacher, don't you care that we're going to drown?"

39When Jesus woke up, he rebuked the wind and said to the waves, "Silence! Be still!" Suddenly the wind stopped, and there was a great calm. 40Then he asked them, "Why are you afraid? Do you still have no faith?"

41The disciples were absolutely terrified. "Who is this man?" they asked each other. "Even the wind and waves obey him!"

CHAPTER 5

Jesus Heals a Demon-Possessed Man

So they arrived at the other side of the lake, in the region of the Gerasenes. 2When Jesus climbed out of the boat, a man possessed by an evil spirit came out from a cemetery to meet him. 3This man lived among the burial caves and could no longer be restrained, even with a chain. 4Whenever he was put into chains and shackles—as he often was—he snapped the chains from his wrists and smashed the shackles. No one was strong enough to subdue him. 5Day and night he wandered among the burial caves and in the hills, howling and cutting himself with sharp stones.

6When Jesus was still some distance away, the man saw him, ran to meet him, and bowed low before him. 7With a shriek, he screamed, "Why are you interfering with me, Jesus, Son of the Most High God? In the name of God, I beg you, don't torture me!" 8For Jesus had already said to the spirit, "Come out of the man, you evil spirit."

9Then Jesus demanded, "What is your name?"

And he replied, "My name is Legion, because there are many of us inside this man." 10Then the evil spirits begged him again and again not to send them to some distant place.

11There happened to be a large herd of pigs

feeding on the hillside nearby. 12"Send us into those pigs," the spirits begged. "Let us enter them."

13So Jesus gave them permission. The evil spirits came out of the man and entered the pigs, and the entire herd of about 2,000 pigs plunged down the steep hillside into the lake and drowned in the water.

14The herdsmen fled to the nearby town and the surrounding countryside, spreading the news as they ran. People rushed out to see what had happened. 15A crowd soon gathered around Jesus, and they saw the man who had been possessed by the legion of demons. He was sitting there fully clothed and perfectly sane, and they were all afraid. 16Then those who had seen what happened told the others about the demon-possessed man and the pigs. 17And the crowd began pleading with Jesus to go away and leave them alone.

18As Jesus was getting into the boat, the man who had been demon possessed begged to go with him. 19But Jesus said, "No, go home to your family, and tell them everything the Lord has done for you and how merciful he has been." 20So the man started off to visit the Ten Towns of that region and began to proclaim the great things Jesus had done for him; and everyone was amazed at what he told them.

Jesus Heals in Response to Faith

21Jesus got into the boat again and went back to the other side of the lake, where a large crowd gathered around him on the shore. 22Then a leader of the local synagogue, whose name was Jairus, arrived. When he saw Jesus, he fell at his feet, 23pleading fervently with him. "My little daughter is dying," he said. "Please come and lay your hands on her; heal her so she can live."

24Jesus went with him, and all the people followed, crowding around him. 25A woman in the crowd had suffered for twelve years with constant bleeding. 26She had suffered a great deal from many doctors, and over the years she had spent everything she had to pay them, but she had gotten no better. In fact, she had gotten worse. 27She had heard about Jesus, so she came up behind him through the crowd and touched his robe. 28For she thought to herself, "If I can just touch his robe, I will be healed." 29Immediately the bleeding stopped, and she could feel in her body that she had been healed of her terrible condition.

30Jesus realized at once that healing power had gone out from him, so he turned around in the crowd and asked, "Who touched my robe?"

31His disciples said to him, "Look at this crowd pressing around you. How can you ask, 'Who touched me?'"

32But he kept on looking around to see who had done it. 33Then the frightened woman, trembling at the realization of what had happened to her, came and fell to her knees in front of him and told him what she had done. 34And he said to her, "Daughter, your faith has made you well. Go in peace. Your suffering is over."

35While he was still speaking to her, messengers arrived from the home of Jairus, the leader of the synagogue. They told him, "Your daughter is dead. There's no use troubling the Teacher now."

36But Jesus overheard them and said to Jairus, "Don't be afraid. Just have faith."

37Then Jesus stopped the crowd and wouldn't let anyone go with him except Peter, James, and John (the brother of James). 38When they came to the home of the synagogue leader, Jesus saw much commotion and weeping and wailing. 39He went inside and asked, "Why all this commotion and weeping? The child isn't dead; she's only asleep."

40The crowd laughed at him. But he made them all leave, and he took the girl's father and mother and his three disciples into the room where the girl was lying. 41Holding her hand, he said to her, *"Talitha koum,"* which means "Little girl, get up!" 42And the girl, who was twelve years old, immediately stood up and walked around! They were overwhelmed and totally amazed. 43Jesus gave them strict orders not to tell anyone what had happened, and then he told them to give her something to eat.

CHAPTER 6

Jesus Rejected at Nazareth

Jesus left that part of the country and returned with his disciples to Nazareth, his hometown. 2The next Sabbath he began teaching in the synagogue, and many who heard him were amazed. They asked, "Where did he get all this wisdom and the power to perform such miracles?" 3Then they scoffed, "He's just a carpenter, the son of Mary and the brother of James, Joseph, Judas, and Simon. And his sisters live right here among us." They were deeply offended and refused to believe in him.

4Then Jesus told them, "A prophet is honored everywhere except in his own hometown and among his relatives and his own family." 5And

because of their unbelief, he couldn't do any
miracles among them except to place his hands
on a few sick people and heal them. 6And he was
amazed at their unbelief.

Jesus Sends Out the Twelve Disciples

Then Jesus went from village to village, teaching
the people. 7And he called his twelve disciples
together and began sending them out two by
two, giving them authority to cast out evil spirits.
8He told them to take nothing for their journey
except a walking stick—no food, no traveler's
bag, no money. 9He allowed them to wear sandals but not to take a change of clothes.

10"Wherever you go," he said, "stay in the
same house until you leave town. 11But if any
place refuses to welcome you or listen to you,
shake its dust from your feet as you leave to show
that you have abandoned those people to their
fate."

12So the disciples went out, telling everyone
they met to repent of their sins and turn to God.
13And they cast out many demons and healed
many sick people, anointing them with olive oil.

The Death of John the Baptist

14Herod Antipas, the king, soon heard about
Jesus, because everyone was talking about him.
Some were saying, "This must be John the Baptist raised from the dead. That is why he can do
such miracles." 15Others said, "He's the prophet
Elijah." Still others said, "He's a prophet like the
other great prophets of the past."

16When Herod heard about Jesus, he said,
"John, the man I beheaded, has come back from
the dead."

17For Herod had sent soldiers to arrest and imprison John as a favor to Herodias. She had been
his brother Philip's wife, but Herod had married
her. 18John had been telling Herod, "It is against
God's law for you to marry your brother's wife."
19So Herodias bore a grudge against John and
wanted to kill him. But without Herod's approval
she was powerless, 20for Herod respected John;
and knowing that he was a good and holy man,
he protected him. Herod was greatly disturbed
whenever he talked with John, but even so, he
liked to listen to him.

21Herodias's chance finally came on Herod's
birthday. He gave a party for his high government officials, army officers, and the leading
citizens of Galilee. 22Then his daughter, also
named Herodias, came in and performed a
dance that greatly pleased Herod and his guests.
"Ask me for anything you like," the king said to
the girl, "and I will give it to you." 23He even
vowed, "I will give you whatever you ask, up to
half my kingdom!"

24She went out and asked her mother, "What
should I ask for?"

Her mother told her, "Ask for the head of John
the Baptist!"

25So the girl hurried back to the king and told
him, "I want the head of John the Baptist, right
now, on a tray!"

26Then the king deeply regretted what he had
said; but because of the vows he had made in
front of his guests, he couldn't refuse her. 27So

Walk on water? Can't be done, right? **WRONG! Read MARK 6:45-52 for the world's first—and only—account of a man able to walk on water!** Then try this experiment.

1. **Grab two pieces of clay of equal size. Roll one into a ball. Pat the other into a flat "raft" shape. Fill a cup with water.**
2. **Place the ball of clay on the water. Then try the flat piece. What happened?**

The flat piece floated and the ball sank. Why? The flat piece had more surface for the water to push against.

There's no way, according to science, that a man should be able to walk on water. Unless the man is Jesus! Make a list of Jesus' other miracles. Keep the list by your bed. Remember—**Jesus isn't limited by the laws of science—he can do anything.**

Trust him whenever you get a "sinking"

feeling, and let him keep you afloat!

he immediately sent an executioner to the
prison to cut off John's head and bring it to
him. The soldier beheaded John in the prison,
28brought his head on a tray, and gave it to the
girl, who took it to her mother. 29When John's
disciples heard what had happened, they came
to get his body and buried it in a tomb.

Jesus Feeds Five Thousand

30The apostles returned to Jesus from their ministry tour and told him all they had done and
taught. 31Then Jesus said, "Let's go off by ourselves to a quiet place and rest awhile." He said
this because there were so many people coming
and going that Jesus and his apostles didn't even
have time to eat.

32So they left by boat for a quiet place, where
they could be alone. 33But many people recognized them and saw them leaving, and people
from many towns ran ahead along the shore and
got there ahead of them. 34Jesus saw the huge
crowd as he stepped from the boat, and he had
compassion on them because they were like
sheep without a shepherd. So he began teaching
them many things.

35Late in the afternoon his disciples came to
him and said, "This is a remote place, and it's
already getting late. 36Send the crowds away so
they can go to the nearby farms and villages and
buy something to eat."

37But Jesus said, "You feed them."

"With what?" they asked. "We'd have to work
for months to earn enough money to buy food
for all these people!"

38"How much bread do you have?" he asked.
"Go and find out."

They came back and reported, "We have five
loaves of bread and two fish."

39Then Jesus told the disciples to have the people sit down in groups on the green grass. 40So
they sat down in groups of fifty or a hundred.

41Jesus took the five loaves and two fish,
looked up toward heaven, and blessed them.
Then, breaking the loaves into pieces, he kept
giving the bread to the disciples so they could
distribute it to the people. He also divided the
fish for everyone to share. 42They all ate as much
as they wanted, 43and afterward, the disciples
picked up twelve baskets of leftover bread and
fish. 44A total of 5,000 men and their families
were fed.

Jesus Walks on Water

45Immediately after this, Jesus insisted that his
disciples get back into the boat and head across
the lake to Bethsaida, while he sent the people
home. 46After telling everyone good-bye, he
went up into the hills by himself to pray.

47Late that night, the disciples were in their
boat in the middle of the lake, and Jesus was alone
on land. 48He saw that they were in serious trouble, rowing hard and struggling against the wind
and waves. About three o'clock in the morning
Jesus came toward them, walking on the water.
He intended to go past them, 49but when they
saw him walking on the water, they cried out in
terror, thinking he was a ghost. 50They were all
terrified when they saw him.

But Jesus spoke to them at once. "Don't be
afraid," he said. "Take courage! I am here!"
51Then he climbed into the boat, and the wind
stopped. They were totally amazed, 52for they
still didn't understand the significance of the
miracle of the loaves. Their hearts were too hard
to take it in.

53After they had crossed the lake, they landed
at Gennesaret. They brought the boat to shore
54and climbed out. The people recognized Jesus
at once, 55and they ran throughout the whole
area, carrying sick people on mats to wherever
they heard he was. 56Wherever he went—in
villages, cities, or the countryside—they brought
the sick out to the marketplaces. They begged
him to let the sick touch at least the fringe of his
robe, and all who touched him were healed.

CHAPTER **7**

Jesus Teaches about Inner Purity

One day some Pharisees and teachers of religious law arrived from Jerusalem to see Jesus.
2They noticed that some of his disciples failed
to follow the Jewish ritual of hand washing before eating. 3(The Jews, especially the Pharisees,
do not eat until they have poured water over
their cupped hands, as required by their ancient
traditions. 4Similarly, they don't eat anything
from the market until they immerse their hands
in water. This is but one of many traditions they
have clung to—such as their ceremonial washing of cups, pitchers, and kettles.)

5So the Pharisees and teachers of religious
law asked him, "Why don't your disciples follow
our age-old tradition? They eat without first
performing the hand-washing ceremony."

6Jesus replied, "You hypocrites! Isaiah was
right when he prophesied about you, for he wrote,

'These people honor me with their lips,
  but their hearts are far from me.

[7] Their worship is a farce,
for they teach man-made ideas as
commands from God.'

[8]For you ignore God's law and substitute your
own tradition."

[9]Then he said, "You skillfully sidestep God's
law in order to hold on to your own tradition.
[10]For instance, Moses gave you this law from
God: 'Honor your father and mother,' and 'Anyone who speaks disrespectfully of father or
mother must be put to death.' [11]But you say it is
all right for people to say to their parents, 'Sorry, I
can't help you. For I have vowed to give to God
what I would have given to you.' [12]In this way, you
let them disregard their needy parents. [13]And so
you cancel the word of God in order to hand
down your own tradition. And this is only one example among many others."

[14]Then Jesus called to the crowd to come and
hear. "All of you listen," he said, "and try to understand. [15]It's not what goes into your body that
defiles you; you are defiled by what comes from
your heart.*"

[17]Then Jesus went into a house to get away
from the crowd, and his disciples asked him
what he meant by the parable he had just used.
[18]"Don't you understand either?" he asked.
"Can't you see that the food you put into your
body cannot defile you? [19]Food doesn't go into
your heart, but only passes through the stomach
and then goes into the sewer." (By saying this, he
declared that every kind of food is acceptable in
God's eyes.)

[20]And then he added, "It is what comes from
inside that defiles you. [21]For from within, out of a
person's heart, come evil thoughts, sexual immorality, theft, murder, [22]adultery, greed, wickedness, deceit, lustful desires, envy, slander, pride,
and foolishness. [23]All these vile things come
from within; they are what defile you."

The Faith of a Gentile Woman

[24]Then Jesus left Galilee and went north to the
region of Tyre. He didn't want anyone to know
which house he was staying in, but he couldn't
keep it a secret. [25]Right away a woman who had
heard about him came and fell at his feet. Her
little girl was possessed by an evil spirit, [26]and
she begged him to cast out the demon from her
daughter.

Since she was a Gentile, born in Syrian Phoenicia, [27]Jesus told her, "First I should feed the
children—my own family, the Jews. It isn't right
to take food from the children and throw it to the
dogs."

[28]She replied, "That's true, Lord, but even the
dogs under the table are allowed to eat the scraps
from the children's plates."

[29]"Good answer!" he said. "Now go home, for
the demon has left your daughter." [30]And when
she arrived home, she found her little girl lying
quietly in bed, and the demon was gone.

Jesus Heals a Deaf Man

[31]Jesus left Tyre and went up to Sidon before
going back to the Sea of Galilee and the region of
the Ten Towns. [32]A deaf man with a speech im-
pediment was brought to him, and the people
begged Jesus to lay his hands on the man to heal
him.

[33]Jesus led him away from the crowd so they
could be alone. He put his fingers into the man's
ears. Then, spitting on his own fingers, he
touched the man's tongue. [34]Looking up to
heaven, he sighed and said, *"Ephphatha,"* which
means, "Be opened!" [35]Instantly the man could
hear perfectly, and his tongue was freed so he
could speak plainly!

[36]Jesus told the crowd not to tell anyone, but
the more he told them not to, the more they
spread the news. [37]They were completely amazed
and said again and again, "Everything he does is
wonderful. He even makes the deaf to hear and
gives speech to those who cannot speak."

CHAPTER 8

Jesus Feeds Four Thousand

About this time another large crowd had gathered, and the people ran out of food again. Jesus
called his disciples and told them, [2]"I feel sorry
for these people. They have been here with me
for three days, and they have nothing left to eat.
[3]If I send them home hungry, they will faint
along the way. For some of them have come a
long distance."

[4]His disciples replied, "How are we supposed
to find enough food to feed them out here in the
wilderness?"

[5]Jesus asked, "How much bread do you have?"
"Seven loaves," they replied.

[6]So Jesus told all the people to sit down on the
ground. Then he took the seven loaves, thanked
God for them, and broke them into pieces. He
gave them to his disciples, who distributed the
bread to the crowd. [7]A few small fish were found,
too, so Jesus also blessed these and told the disciples to distribute them.

7:15 Some manuscripts add verse 16, *Anyone with ears to hear should listen and understand.* Compare 4:9, 23.

8They ate as much as they wanted. Afterward, the disciples picked up seven large baskets of leftover food. 9There were about 4,000 people in the crowd that day, and Jesus sent them home after they had eaten. 10Immediately after this, he got into a boat with his disciples and crossed over to the region of Dalmanutha.

Pharisees Demand a Miraculous Sign

11When the Pharisees heard that Jesus had arrived, they came and started to argue with him. Testing him, they demanded that he show them a miraculous sign from heaven to prove his authority.

12When he heard this, he sighed deeply in his spirit and said, "Why do these people keep demanding a miraculous sign? I tell you the truth, I will not give this generation any such sign." 13So he got back into the boat and left them, and he crossed to the other side of the lake.

Yeast of the Pharisees and Herod

14But the disciples had forgotten to bring any food. They had only one loaf of bread with them in the boat. 15As they were crossing the lake, Jesus warned them, "Watch out! Beware of the yeast of the Pharisees and of Herod."

16At this they began to argue with each other because they hadn't brought any bread. 17Jesus knew what they were saying, so he said, "Why are you arguing about having no bread? Don't you know or understand even yet? Are your hearts too hard to take it in? 18'You have eyes—can't you see? You have ears—can't you hear?' Don't you remember anything at all? 19When I fed the 5,000 with five loaves of bread, how many baskets of leftovers did you pick up afterward?"

"Twelve," they said.

20"And when I fed the 4,000 with seven loaves, how many large baskets of leftovers did you pick up?"

"Seven," they said.

21"Don't you understand yet?" he asked them.

Jesus Heals a Blind Man

22When they arrived at Bethsaida, some people brought a blind man to Jesus, and they begged him to touch the man and heal him. 23Jesus took the blind man by the hand and led him out of the village. Then, spitting on the man's eyes, he laid his hands on him and asked, "Can you see anything now?"

24The man looked around. "Yes," he said, "I see people, but I can't see them very clearly. They look like trees walking around."

25Then Jesus placed his hands on the man's eyes again, and his eyes were opened. His sight was completely restored, and he could see everything clearly. 26Jesus sent him away, saying, "Don't go back into the village on your way home."

Peter's Declaration about Jesus

27Jesus and his disciples left Galilee and went up to the villages near Caesarea Philippi. As they were walking along, he asked them, "Who do people say I am?"

28"Well," they replied, "some say John the Baptist, some say Elijah, and others say you are one of the other prophets."

29Then he asked them, "But who do you say I am?"

Peter replied, "You are the Messiah."

30But Jesus warned them not to tell anyone about him.

Jesus Predicts His Death

31Then Jesus began to tell them that the Son of Man must suffer many terrible things and be rejected by the elders, the leading priests, and the teachers of religious law. He would be killed, but three days later he would rise from the dead. 32As he talked about this openly with his disciples, Peter took him aside and began to reprimand him for saying such things.

33Jesus turned around and looked at his disciples, then reprimanded Peter. "Get away from me, Satan!" he said. "You are seeing things merely from a human point of view, not from God's."

34Then, calling the crowd to join his disciples, he said, "If any of you wants to be my follower, you must turn from your selfish ways, take up your cross, and follow me. 35If you try to hang on to your life, you will lose it. But if you give up your life for my sake and for the sake of the Good News, you will save it. 36And what do you benefit if you gain the whole world but lose your own soul? 37Is anything worth more than your soul? 38If anyone is ashamed of me and my message in these adulterous and sinful days, the Son of Man will be ashamed of that person when he returns in the glory of his Father with the holy angels."

CHAPTER 9

Jesus went on to say, "I tell you the truth, some standing here right now will not die before they see the Kingdom of God arrive in great power!"

The Transfiguration

2Six days later Jesus took Peter, James, and John,
and led them up a high mountain to be alone. As
the men watched, Jesus' appearance was transformed, 3and his clothes became dazzling white,
far whiter than any earthly bleach could ever
make them. 4Then Elijah and Moses appeared
and began talking with Jesus.
5Peter exclaimed, "Rabbi, it's wonderful for us
to be here! Let's make three shelters as memorials—one for you, one for Moses, and one for
Elijah." 6He said this because he didn't really
know what else to say, for they were all terrified.
7Then a cloud overshadowed them, and a
voice from the cloud said, "This is my dearly
loved Son. Listen to him." 8Suddenly, when they
looked around, Moses and Elijah were gone, and
they saw only Jesus with them.
9As they went back down the mountain, he
told them not to tell anyone what they had seen
until the Son of Man had risen from the dead.
10So they kept it to themselves, but they often
asked each other what he meant by "rising from
the dead."
11Then they asked him, "Why do the teachers
of religious law insist that Elijah must return
before the Messiah comes?"
12Jesus responded, "Elijah is indeed coming
first to get everything ready. Yet why do the
Scriptures say that the Son of Man must suffer
greatly and be treated with utter contempt?
13But I tell you, Elijah has already come, and
they chose to abuse him, just as the Scriptures
predicted."

Jesus Heals a Demon-Possessed Boy

14When they returned to the other disciples, they
saw a large crowd surrounding them, and some
teachers of religious law were arguing with them.
15When the crowd saw Jesus, they were overwhelmed with awe, and they ran to greet him.
16"What is all this arguing about?" Jesus
asked.
17One of the men in the crowd spoke up and
said, "Teacher, I brought my son so you could heal
him. He is possessed by an evil spirit that won't
let him talk. 18And whenever this spirit seizes
him, it throws him violently to the ground. Then
he foams at the mouth and grinds his teeth and
becomes rigid. So I asked your disciples to cast
out the evil spirit, but they couldn't do it."
19Jesus said to them, "You faithless people!
How long must I be with you? How long must I
put up with you? Bring the boy to me."

"Whoever wants to be first must take last place and be the servant of everyone else."—MARK 9:35b

Read MARK 9:35b out loud a few times so it sticks. Then try this challenge. For one whole day, do what this verse says—put others first. How? Here are a few ideas:

After You!
Let everyone go in front of you in line!
Let others be the first to be served food or drinks.
Let others choose what movie to watch or game to play.
Open doors for others.
AT THE END OF THE DAY, write in this space what it was like to be last at things and to put others first.

It may have felt a little weird at first, but putting others first is what Jesus wants us to do. AFTER ALL, THAT'S WHAT HE DID FOR US!

Mark 10 . . . page 988

20So they brought the boy. But when the evil
spirit saw Jesus, it threw the child into a violent
convulsion, and he fell to the ground, writhing
and foaming at the mouth.
21"How long has this been happening?" Jesus
asked the boy's father.
He replied, "Since he was a little boy. 22The
spirit often throws him into the fire or into water,
trying to kill him. Have mercy on us and help us,
if you can."
23"What do you mean, 'If I can'?" Jesus asked.
"Anything is possible if a person believes."
24The father instantly cried out, "I do believe,
but help me overcome my unbelief!"
25When Jesus saw that the crowd of onlookers
was growing, he rebuked the evil spirit. "Listen,
you spirit that makes this boy unable to hear and
speak," he said. "I command you to come out of
this child and never enter him again!"
26Then the spirit screamed and threw the boy
into another violent convulsion and left him. The
boy appeared to be dead. A murmur ran through
the crowd as people said, "He's dead." 27But Jesus
took him by the hand and helped him to his feet,
and he stood up.
28Afterward, when Jesus was alone in the
house with his disciples, they asked him, "Why
couldn't we cast out that evil spirit?"
29Jesus replied, "This kind can be cast out only
by prayer."

Jesus Again Predicts His Death

30Leaving that region, they traveled through
Galilee. Jesus didn't want anyone to know he
was there, 31for he wanted to spend more time
with his disciples and teach them. He said to
them, "The Son of Man is going to be betrayed
into the hands of his enemies. He will be killed,
but three days later he will rise from the dead."
32They didn't understand what he was saying,
however, and they were afraid to ask him what
he meant.

The Greatest in the Kingdom

33After they arrived at Capernaum and settled in a
house, Jesus asked his disciples, "What were you
discussing out on the road?" 34But they didn't answer, because they had been arguing about which
of them was the greatest. **35He sat down,
called the twelve disciples over to
him, and said, "Whoever wants to be
first must take last place and be the
servant of everyone else."**
36Then he put a little child among them.
Taking the child in his arms, he said to them,
37"Anyone who welcomes a little child like this
on my behalf welcomes me, and anyone who
welcomes me welcomes not only me but also my
Father who sent me."

Using the Name of Jesus

38John said to Jesus, "Teacher, we saw someone
using your name to cast out demons, but we told
him to stop because he wasn't in our group."
39"Don't stop him!" Jesus said. "No one who
performs a miracle in my name will soon be able
to speak evil of me. 40Anyone who is not against
us is for us. 41If anyone gives you even a cup of water because you belong to the Messiah, I tell you
the truth, that person will surely be rewarded.
42"But if you cause one of these little ones
who trusts in me to fall into sin, it would be
better for you to be thrown into the sea with a
large millstone hung around your neck. 43If
your hand causes you to sin, cut it off. It's better
to enter eternal life with only one hand than to
go into the unquenchable fires of hell with two
hands.* 45If your foot causes you to sin, cut it
off. It's better to enter eternal life with only one
foot than to be thrown into hell with two feet.*
47And if your eye causes you to sin, gouge it out.
It's better to enter the Kingdom of God with only
one eye than to have two eyes and be thrown into
hell, 48'where the maggots never die and the fire
never goes out.'
49"For everyone will be tested with fire. 50Salt
is good for seasoning. But if it loses its flavor, how
do you make it salty again? You must have the
qualities of salt among yourselves and live in
peace with each other."

CHAPTER 10

Discussion about Divorce and Marriage

Then Jesus left Capernaum and went down to
the region of Judea and into the area east of the
Jordan River. Once again crowds gathered
around him, and as usual he was teaching them.
2Some Pharisees came and tried to trap him
with this question: "Should a man be allowed to
divorce his wife?"
3Jesus answered them with a question: "What
did Moses say in the law about divorce?"
4"Well, he permitted it," they replied. "He said
a man can give his wife a written notice of divorce and send her away."

9:43 Some manuscripts add verse 44, *'where the maggots never die and the fire never goes out.'* See 9:48. 9:45 Some manuscripts add verse 46, *'where the maggots never die and the fire never goes out.'* See 9:48.

5But Jesus responded, "He wrote this commandment only as a concession to your hard
hearts. 6But 'God made them male and female'
from the beginning of creation. 7'This explains
why a man leaves his father and mother and is
joined to his wife, 8and the two are united into
one.' Since they are no longer two but one,
9let no one split apart what God has joined
together."
10Later, when he was alone with his disciples
in the house, they brought up the subject again.
11He told them, "Whoever divorces his wife
and marries someone else commits adultery
against her. 12And if a woman divorces her husband and marries someone else, she commits
adultery."

Jesus Blesses the Children

13One day some parents brought their children
to Jesus so he could touch and bless them. But
the disciples scolded the parents for bothering
him.
**14When Jesus saw what was hap-
pening, he was angry with his disciples. He said to them, "Let the
children come to me. Don't stop
them! For the Kingdom of God belongs to those who are like these
children. 15I tell you the truth, anyone who doesn't receive the Kingdom of God like a child will never
enter it."** 16Then he took the children in his
arms and placed his hands on their heads and
blessed them.

The Rich Man

17As Jesus was starting out on his way to Jerusalem, a man came running up to him, knelt down,
and asked, "Good Teacher, what must I do to inherit eternal life?"
18"Why do you call me good?" Jesus asked.
"Only God is truly good. 19But to answer your
question, you know the commandments: 'You
must not murder. You must not commit adultery.
You must not steal. You must not testify falsely.
You must not cheat anyone. Honor your father
and mother.'"
20"Teacher," the man replied, "I've obeyed all
these commandments since I was young."
21Looking at the man, Jesus felt genuine love
for him. "There is still one thing you haven't
done," he told him. "Go and sell all your possessions and give the money to the poor, and
you will have treasure in heaven. Then come,
follow me."
22At this the man's face fell, and he went away
sad, for he had many possessions.
23Jesus looked around and said to his disciples, "How hard it is for the rich to enter the
Kingdom of God!" 24This amazed them. But
Jesus said again, "Dear children, it is very hard to
enter the Kingdom of God. 25In fact, it is easier
for a camel to go through the eye of a needle than
for a rich person to enter the Kingdom of God!"
26The disciples were astounded. "Then who
in the world can be saved?" they asked.
27Jesus looked at them intently and said, "Humanly speaking, it is impossible. But not with
God. Everything is possible with God."
28Then Peter began to speak up. "We've given
up everything to follow you," he said.
29"Yes," Jesus replied, "and I assure you that
everyone who has given up house or brothers or
sisters or mother or father or children or property, for my sake and for the Good News, 30will
receive now in return a hundred times as many
houses, brothers, sisters, mothers, children, and
property—along with persecution. And in the
world to come that person will have eternal life.
31But many who are the greatest now will be least
important then, and those who seem least important now will be the greatest then."

Jesus Again Predicts His Death

32They were now on the way up to Jerusalem,
and Jesus was walking ahead of them. The disciples were filled with awe, and the people following behind were overwhelmed with fear.
Taking the twelve disciples aside, Jesus once
more began to describe everything that was
about to happen to him. 33"Listen," he said,
"we're going up to Jerusalem, where the Son of
Man will be betrayed to the leading priests and
the teachers of religious law. They will sentence him to die and hand him over to the Romans. 34They will mock him, spit on him, flog
him with a whip, and kill him, but after three
days he will rise again."

Jesus Teaches about Serving Others

35Then James and John, the sons of Zebedee,
came over and spoke to him. "Teacher," they
said, "we want you to do us a favor."
36"What is your request?" he asked.
37They replied, "When you sit on your glorious throne, we want to sit in places of honor
next to you, one on your right and the other on
your left."
38But Jesus said to them, "You don't know

what you are asking! Are you able to drink from
the bitter cup of suffering I am about to drink?
Are you able to be baptized with the baptism of
suffering I must be baptized with?"
39"Oh yes," they replied, "we are able!"
Then Jesus told them, "You will indeed drink
from my bitter cup and be baptized with my
baptism of suffering. 40But I have no right to
say who will sit on my right or my left. God
has prepared those places for the ones he has
chosen."
41When the ten other disciples heard what
James and John had asked, they were indignant.
42So Jesus called them together and said, "You
know that the rulers in this world lord it over
their people, and officials flaunt their authority
over those under them. 43But among you it will
be different. Whoever wants to be a leader
among you must be your servant, 44and whoever
wants to be first among you must be the slave of
everyone else. 45For even the Son of Man came
not to be served but to serve others and to give
his life as a ransom for many."

Jesus Heals Blind Bartimaeus

46Then they reached Jericho, and as Jesus and
his disciples left town, a large crowd followed
him. A blind beggar named Bartimaeus (son of
Timaeus) was sitting beside the road. 47When
Bartimaeus heard that Jesus of Nazareth was
nearby, he began to shout, "Jesus, Son of David,
have mercy on me!"
48"Be quiet!" many of the people yelled at him.
But he only shouted louder, "Son of David,
have mercy on me!"
49When Jesus heard him, he stopped and said,
"Tell him to come here."
So they called the blind man. "Cheer up," they
said. "Come on, he's calling you!" 50Bartimaeus
threw aside his coat, jumped up, and came to
Jesus.
51"What do you want me to do for you?" Jesus
asked.
"My Rabbi," the blind man said, "I want to see!"
52And Jesus said to him, "Go, for your faith has
healed you." Instantly the man could see, and he
followed Jesus down the road.

CHAPTER **11**

Jesus' Triumphant Entry

As Jesus and his disciples approached Jerusalem, they came to the towns of Bethphage and
Bethany on the Mount of Olives. Jesus sent two
of them on ahead. 2"Go into that village over
there," he told them. "As soon as you enter it, you
will see a young donkey tied there that no one
has ever ridden. Untie it and bring it here. 3If
anyone asks, 'What are you doing?' just say, 'The
Lord needs it and will return it soon.'"
4The two disciples left and found the colt
standing in the street, tied outside the front door.
5As they were untying it, some bystanders demanded, "What are you doing, untying that
colt?" 6They said what Jesus had told them to say,
and they were permitted to take it. 7Then they
brought the colt to Jesus and threw their garments over it, and he sat on it.

Hey! Who turned out the lights?
Head and Shoulders, Knees and Toes

Find a friend and a Bible. **Read MARK 10:46-52 together.** Then try this activity.

Try to do these tasks wearing a blindfold: Tie your shoes, write your name, and do your math homework. Then switch roles.

Discuss these questions together.

What was it like trying to do things while you were blindfolded?

What do you think it would have been like to be blind in Bible times? (How would it be different from today?)

Read about another blind man Jesus healed in Mark 8:22-26.

The blind man must have been thankful. **Be thankful yourself!**

Write today's date here

From this day on, try to be aware of your amazing senses and abilities.

Thank God for blessing you so richly when you use your hands, feet, eyes, ears, nose, mouth, arms, or legs!

8Many in the crowd spread their garments on
the road ahead of him, and others spread leafy
branches they had cut in the fields. 9Jesus was in
the center of the procession, and the people all
around him were shouting,

"Praise God!
Blessings on the one who comes in the
name of the LORD!
10 Blessings on the coming Kingdom of our
ancestor David!
Praise God in highest heaven!"

11So Jesus came to Jerusalem and went into
the Temple. After looking around carefully at
everything, he left because it was late in the
afternoon. Then he returned to Bethany with the
twelve disciples.

Jesus Curses the Fig Tree

12The next morning as they were leaving Bethany, Jesus was hungry. 13He noticed a fig tree in
full leaf a little way off, so he went over to see if
he could find any figs. But there were only leaves
because it was too early in the season for fruit.
14Then Jesus said to the tree, "May no one ever
eat your fruit again!" And the disciples heard him
say it.

Jesus Clears the Temple

15When they arrived back in Jerusalem, Jesus entered the Temple and began to drive out the people buying and selling animals for sacrifices. He
knocked over the tables of the money changers
and the chairs of those selling doves, 16and he
stopped everyone from using the Temple as a
marketplace. 17He said to them, "The Scriptures
declare, 'My Temple will be called a house of
prayer for all nations,' but you have turned it into
a den of thieves."

18When the leading priests and teachers of religious law heard what Jesus had done, they
began planning how to kill him. But they were
afraid of him because the people were so amazed
at his teaching.

19That evening Jesus and the disciples left the
city.

20The next morning as they passed by the fig
tree he had cursed, the disciples noticed it had
withered from the roots up. 21Peter remembered
what Jesus had said to the tree on the previous
day and exclaimed, "Look, Rabbi! The fig tree you
cursed has withered and died!"

22Then Jesus said to the disciples, "Have
faith in God. 23I tell you the truth, you can say to
this mountain, 'May you be lifted up and
thrown into the sea,' and it will happen. But you
must really believe it will happen and have no
doubt in your heart. 24I tell you, you can pray
for anything, and if you believe that you've received it, it will be yours. 25But when you are
praying, first forgive anyone you are holding a
grudge against, so that your Father in heaven
will forgive your sins, too.*"

The Authority of Jesus Challenged

27Again they entered Jerusalem. As Jesus was
walking through the Temple area, the leading
priests, the teachers of religious law, and the
elders came up to him. 28They demanded, "By
what authority are you doing all these things?
Who gave you the right to do them?"

29"I'll tell you by what authority I do these
things if you answer one question," Jesus replied.
30"Did John's authority to baptize come from
heaven, or was it merely human? Answer me!"

31They talked it over among themselves. "If we
say it was from heaven, he will ask why we didn't
believe John. 32But do we dare say it was merely
human?" For they were afraid of what the people
would do, because everyone believed that John
was a prophet. 33So they finally replied, "We
don't know."

And Jesus responded, "Then I won't tell you by
what authority I do these things."

CHAPTER 12

Parable of the Evil Farmers

Then Jesus began teaching them with stories: "A
man planted a vineyard. He built a wall around it,
dug a pit for pressing out the grape juice, and
built a lookout tower. Then he leased the vineyard to tenant farmers and moved to another
country. 2At the time of the grape harvest, he
sent one of his servants to collect his share of the
crop. 3But the farmers grabbed the servant, beat
him up, and sent him back empty-handed. 4The
owner then sent another servant, but they insulted him and beat him over the head. 5The
next servant he sent was killed. Others he sent
were either beaten or killed, 6until there was
only one left—his son whom he loved dearly. The
owner finally sent him, thinking, 'Surely they will
respect my son.'

7"But the tenant farmers said to one another,
'Here comes the heir to this estate. Let's kill him
and get the estate for ourselves!' 8So they

11:25 Some manuscripts add verse 26, *But if you refuse to forgive, your Father in heaven will not forgive your sins.* Compare Matt 6:15.

grabbed him and murdered him and threw his body out of the vineyard.

9 "What do you suppose the owner of the vineyard will do?" Jesus asked. "I'll tell you—he will come and kill those farmers and lease the vineyard to others. 10 Didn't you ever read this in the Scriptures?

'The stone that the builders rejected
has now become the cornerstone.
11 This is the LORD's doing,
and it is wonderful to see.'"

12 The religious leaders wanted to arrest Jesus because they realized he was telling the story against them—they were the wicked farmers. But they were afraid of the crowd, so they left him and went away.

Taxes for Caesar

13 Later the leaders sent some Pharisees and supporters of Herod to trap Jesus into saying something for which he could be arrested. 14 "Teacher," they said, "we know how honest you are. You are impartial and don't play favorites. You teach the way of God truthfully. Now tell us—is it right to pay taxes to Caesar or not? 15 Should we pay them, or shouldn't we?"

Jesus saw through their hypocrisy and said, "Why are you trying to trap me? Show me a Roman coin, and I'll tell you." 16 When they handed it to him, he asked, "Whose picture and title are stamped on it?"

"Caesar's," they replied.

17 "Well, then," Jesus said, "give to Caesar what belongs to Caesar, and give to God what belongs to God."

His reply completely amazed them.

Discussion about Resurrection

18 Then Jesus was approached by some Sadducees—religious leaders who say there is no resurrection from the dead. They posed this question: 19 "Teacher, Moses gave us a law that if a man dies, leaving a wife without children, his brother should marry the widow and have a child who will carry on the brother's name. 20 Well, suppose there were seven brothers. The oldest one married and then died without children. 21 So the second brother married the widow, but he also died without children. Then the third brother married her. 22 This continued with all seven of them, and still there were no children. Last of all, the woman also died. 23 So tell us, whose wife will she be in the resurrection? For all seven were married to her."

24 Jesus replied, "Your mistake is that you don't know the Scriptures, and you don't know the power of God. 25 For when the dead rise, they will neither marry nor be given in marriage. In this respect they will be like the angels in heaven.

26 "But now, as to whether the dead will be raised—haven't you ever read about this in the writings of Moses, in the story of the burning bush? Long after Abraham, Isaac, and Jacob had died, God said to Moses, 'I am the God of Abraham, the God of Isaac, and the God of Jacob.' 27 So he is the God of the living, not the dead. You have made a serious error."

The Most Important Commandment

28 One of the teachers of religious law was standing there listening to the debate. He realized that Jesus had answered well, so he asked, "Of all the commandments, which is the most important?"

29 Jesus replied, "The most important commandment is this: 'Listen, O Israel! The LORD our God is the one and only LORD. 30 And you must love the LORD your God with all your heart, all your soul, all your mind, and all your strength.' 31 The second is equally important: 'Love your neighbor as yourself.' No other commandment is greater than these."

32 The teacher of religious law replied, "Well said, Teacher. You have spoken the truth by saying that there is only one God and no other. 33 And I know it is important to love him with all my heart and all my understanding and all my strength, and to love my neighbor as myself. This is more important than to offer all of the burnt offerings and sacrifices required in the law."

34 Realizing how much the man understood, Jesus said to him, "You are not far from the Kingdom of God." And after that, no one dared to ask him any more questions.

Whose Son Is the Messiah?

35 Later, as Jesus was teaching the people in the Temple, he asked, "Why do the teachers of religious law claim that the Messiah is the son of David? 36 For David himself, speaking under the inspiration of the Holy Spirit, said,

'The LORD said to my Lord,
Sit in the place of honor at my right hand
until I humble your enemies beneath
your feet.'

37 Since David himself called the Messiah 'my Lord,' how can the Messiah be his son?" The large crowd listened to him with great delight.

38Jesus also taught: "Beware of these teachers
of religious law! For they like to parade around in
flowing robes and receive respectful greetings
as they walk in the marketplaces. 39And how
they love the seats of honor in the synagogues
and the head table at banquets. 40Yet they
shamelessly cheat widows out of their property
and then pretend to be pious by making long
prayers in public. Because of this, they will be
more severely punished."

The #1 COMMAND
Grab a friend, a pencil, some markers, and two big sheets of newsprint.
GET ARTISTIC!
1 Lie on your back on a sheet of newsprint.
If you don't have newsprint, just draw pictures of each other on regular paper.
2 Have your friend use the pencil to trace around your body outline. Do the same for your friend with the other paper.
3 Use markers to fill in facial features, hair, and clothing.
Then read MARK 12:28-31 together.
Around your shape outline, write ways you can love God with all your heart, soul, mind, and strength.

On the bottom, write three ways you can love your friend as yourself.
(Stuck? Think how you'd like to be treated!)

The Widow's Offering

41Jesus sat down near the collection box in the
Temple and watched as the crowds dropped in
their money. Many rich people put in large
amounts. 42Then a poor widow came and
dropped in two small coins.
43Jesus called his disciples to him and said, "I
tell you the truth, this poor widow has given
more than all the others who are making contributions. 44For they gave a tiny part of their surplus, but she, poor as she is, has given everything
she had to live on."

CHAPTER 13

Jesus Foretells the Future

As Jesus was leaving the Temple that day, one of
his disciples said, "Teacher, look at these magnificent buildings! Look at the impressive
stones in the walls."
2Jesus replied, "Yes, look at these great buildings. But they will be completely demolished.
Not one stone will be left on top of another!"
3Later, Jesus sat on the Mount of Olives across
the valley from the Temple. Peter, James, John,
and Andrew came to him privately and asked
him, 4"Tell us, when will all this happen? What
sign will show us that these things are about to
be fulfilled?"
5Jesus replied, "Don't let anyone mislead you,
6for many will come in my name, claiming, 'I am
the Messiah.' They will deceive many. 7And you
will hear of wars and threats of wars, but don't
panic. Yes, these things must take place, but the
end won't follow immediately. 8Nation will go to
war against nation, and kingdom against kingdom. There will be earthquakes in many parts of
the world, as well as famines. But this is only the
first of the birth pains, with more to come.
9"When these things begin to happen, watch
out! You will be handed over to the local councils
and beaten in the synagogues. You will stand
trial before governors and kings because you are
my followers. But this will be your opportunity to
tell them about me. 10For the Good News must
first be preached to all nations. 11But when you
are arrested and stand trial, don't worry in advance about what to say. Just say what God tells

you at that time, for it is not you who will be
speaking, but the Holy Spirit.
12"A brother will betray his brother to death, a
father will betray his own child, and children will
rebel against their parents and cause them to be
killed. 13 And everyone will hate you because you
are my followers. But the one who endures to the
end will be saved.

14"The day is coming when you will see the
sacrilegious object that causes desecration
standing where he should not be." (Reader, pay
attention!) "Then those in Judea must flee to the
hills. 15 A person out on the deck of a roof must
not go down into the house to pack. 16 A person
out in the field must not return even to get a coat.
17 How terrible it will be for pregnant women and
for nursing mothers in those days. 18 And pray
that your flight will not be in winter. 19 For there
will be greater anguish in those days than at any
time since God created the world. And it will
never be so great again. 20 In fact, unless the Lord
shortens that time of calamity, not a single person will survive. But for the sake of his chosen
ones he has shortened those days.

21"Then if anyone tells you, 'Look, here is the
Messiah,' or 'There he is,' don't believe it. 22 For
false messiahs and false prophets will rise up
and perform signs and wonders so as to deceive,
if possible, even God's chosen ones. 23 Watch out!
I have warned you about this ahead of time!

24"At that time, after the anguish of those days,

the sun will be darkened,
  the moon will give no light,
25 the stars will fall from the sky,
  and the powers in the heavens will be
    shaken.

26 Then everyone will see the Son of Man coming
on the clouds with great power and glory. 27 And
he will send out his angels to gather his chosen
ones from all over the world—from the farthest
ends of the earth and heaven.

28"Now learn a lesson from the fig tree. When
its branches bud and its leaves begin to sprout,
you know that summer is near. 29 In the same
way, when you see all these things taking place,
you can know that his return is very near, right at
the door. 30 I tell you the truth, this generation
will not pass from the scene before all these
things take place. 31 Heaven and earth will disappear, but my words will never disappear.

32"However, no one knows the day or hour
when these things will happen, not even the
angels in heaven or the Son himself. Only the
Father knows. 33 And since you don't know when
that time will come, be on guard! Stay alert!

34"The coming of the Son of Man can be illustrated by the story of a man going on a long trip.
When he left home, he gave each of his slaves
instructions about the work they were to do, and
he told the gatekeeper to watch for his return.
35 You, too, must keep watch! For you don't know
when the master of the household will return—
in the evening, at midnight, before dawn, or at
daybreak. 36 Don't let him find you sleeping
when he arrives without warning. 37 I say to you
what I say to everyone: Watch for him!"

CHAPTER 14

Jesus Anointed at Bethany

It was now two days before Passover and the Festival of Unleavened Bread. The leading priests
and the teachers of religious law were still looking for an opportunity to capture Jesus secretly
and kill him. 2"But not during the Passover celebration," they agreed, "or the people may riot."

3 Meanwhile, Jesus was in Bethany at the home
of Simon, a man who had previously had leprosy.
While he was eating, a woman came in with a
beautiful alabaster jar of expensive perfume
made from essence of nard. She broke open the
jar and poured the perfume over his head.

4 Some of those at the table were indignant.
"Why waste such expensive perfume?" they
asked. 5"It could have been sold for a year's
wages and the money given to the poor!" So they
scolded her harshly.

6 But Jesus replied, "Leave her alone. Why criticize her for doing such a good thing to me?
7 You will always have the poor among you, and
you can help them whenever you want to. But
you will not always have me. 8 She has done what
she could and has anointed my body for burial
ahead of time. 9 I tell you the truth, wherever the
Good News is preached throughout the world,
this woman's deed will be remembered and
discussed."

Judas Agrees to Betray Jesus

10 Then Judas Iscariot, one of the twelve disciples, went to the leading priests to arrange to betray Jesus to them. 11 They were delighted when
they heard why he had come, and they promised
to give him money. So he began looking for an
opportunity to betray Jesus.

The Last Supper

12 On the first day of the Festival of Unleavened
Bread, when the Passover lamb is sacrificed,

Jesus' disciples asked him, "Where do you want
us to go to prepare the Passover meal for you?"
13 So Jesus sent two of them into Jerusalem
with these instructions: "As you go into the city, a
man carrying a pitcher of water will meet you.
Follow him. 14 At the house he enters, say to the
owner, 'The Teacher asks: Where is the guest
room where I can eat the Passover meal with my
disciples?' 15 He will take you upstairs to a large
room that is already set up. That is where you
should prepare our meal." 16 So the two disciples
went into the city and found everything just as
Jesus had said, and they prepared the Passover
meal there.
17 In the evening Jesus arrived with the Twelve.
18 As they were at the table eating, Jesus said, "I
tell you the truth, one of you eating with me here
will betray me."
19 Greatly distressed, each one asked in turn,
"Am I the one?"
20 He replied, "It is one of you twelve who is
eating from this bowl with me. 21 For the Son of
Man must die, as the Scriptures declared long
ago. But how terrible it will be for the one who
betrays him. It would be far better for that man if
he had never been born!"
22 As they were eating, Jesus took some bread
and blessed it. Then he broke it in pieces and
gave it to the disciples, saying, "Take it, for this is
my body."
23 And he took a cup of wine and gave thanks
to God for it. He gave it to them, and they all
drank from it. 24 And he said to them, "This is my
blood, which confirms the covenant between
God and his people. It is poured out as a sacrifice
for many. 25 I tell you the truth, I will not drink
wine again until the day I drink it new in the
Kingdom of God."
26 Then they sang a hymn and went out to the
Mount of Olives.

Jesus Predicts Peter's Denial

27 On the way, Jesus told them, "All of you will
desert me. For the Scriptures say,

'God will strike the Shepherd,
and the sheep will be scattered.'

28 But after I am raised from the dead, I will go
ahead of you to Galilee and meet you there."
29 Peter said to him, "Even if everyone else
deserts you, I never will."
30 Jesus replied, "I tell you the truth, Peter—this
very night, before the rooster crows twice, you
will deny three times that you even know me."
31 "No!" Peter declared emphatically. "Even if I
have to die with you, I will never deny you!" And
all the others vowed the same.

Jesus Prays in Gethsemane

32 They went to the olive grove called Gethsemane, and Jesus said, "Sit here while I go and pray."
33 He took Peter, James, and John with him, and
he became deeply troubled and distressed.
34 He told them, "My soul is crushed with grief
to the point of death. Stay here and keep watch
with me."
35 He went on a little farther and fell to the
ground. He prayed that, if it were possible, the
awful hour awaiting him might pass him by.
36 "Abba, Father," he cried out, "everything is possible for you. Please take this cup of suffering
away from me. Yet I want your will to be done, not
mine."
37 Then he returned and found the disciples
asleep. He said to Peter, "Simon, are you asleep?
Couldn't you watch with me even one hour?
38 Keep watch and pray, so that you will not give
in to temptation. For the spirit is willing, but the
body is weak."
39 Then Jesus left them again and prayed the
same prayer as before. 40 When he returned to
them again, he found them sleeping, for they
couldn't keep their eyes open. And they didn't
know what to say.
41 When he returned to them the third time, he
said, "Go ahead and sleep. Have your rest. But
no—the time has come. The Son of Man is
betrayed into the hands of sinners. 42 Up, let's be
going. Look, my betrayer is here!"

Jesus Is Betrayed and Arrested

43 And immediately, even as Jesus said this, Judas,
one of the twelve disciples, arrived with a crowd
of men armed with swords and clubs. They had
been sent by the leading priests, the teachers of
religious law, and the elders. 44 The traitor, Judas,
had given them a prearranged signal: "You will
know which one to arrest when I greet him with a
kiss. Then you can take him away under guard."
45 As soon as they arrived, Judas walked up to
Jesus. "Rabbi!" he exclaimed, and gave him the
kiss.
46 Then the others grabbed Jesus and arrested
him. 47 But one of the men with Jesus pulled out
his sword and struck the high priest's slave, slashing off his ear.
48 Jesus asked them, "Am I some dangerous
revolutionary, that you come with swords and
clubs to arrest me? 49 Why didn't you arrest me in
the Temple? I was there among you teaching

every day. But these things are happening to fulfill what the Scriptures say about me."

50 Then all his disciples deserted him and ran away. 51 One young man following behind was clothed only in a long linen shirt. When the mob tried to grab him, 52 he slipped out of his shirt and ran away naked.

Jesus before the Council

53 They took Jesus to the high priest's home where the leading priests, the elders, and the teachers of religious law had gathered. 54 Meanwhile, Peter followed him at a distance and went right into the high priest's courtyard. There he sat with the guards, warming himself by the fire.

55 Inside, the leading priests and the entire high council were trying to find evidence against Jesus, so they could put him to death. But they couldn't find any. 56 Many false witnesses spoke against him, but they contradicted each other. 57 Finally, some men stood up and gave this false testimony: 58 "We heard him say, 'I will destroy this Temple made with human hands, and in three days I will build another, made without human hands.'" 59 But even then they didn't get their stories straight!

60 Then the high priest stood up before the others and asked Jesus, "Well, aren't you going to answer these charges? What do you have to say for yourself?" 61 But Jesus was silent and made no reply. Then the high priest asked him, "Are you the Messiah, the Son of the Blessed One?"

62 Jesus said, "I AM. And you will see the Son of Man seated in the place of power at God's right hand and coming on the clouds of heaven."

63 Then the high priest tore his clothing to show his horror and said, "Why do we need other witnesses? 64 You have all heard his blasphemy. What is your verdict?"

"Guilty!" they all cried. "He deserves to die!"

65 Then some of them began to spit at him, and they blindfolded him and beat him with their fists. "Prophesy to us," they jeered. And the guards slapped him as they took him away.

Peter Denies Jesus

66 Meanwhile, Peter was in the courtyard below. One of the servant girls who worked for the high priest came by 67 and noticed Peter warming himself at the fire. She looked at him closely and said, "You were one of those with Jesus of Nazareth."

68 But Peter denied it. "I don't know what you're talking about," he said, and he went out into the entryway. Just then, a rooster crowed.

69 When the servant girl saw him standing there, she began telling the others, "This man is definitely one of them!" 70 But Peter denied it again.

A little later some of the other bystanders confronted Peter and said, "You must be one of them, because you are a Galilean."

71 Peter swore, "A curse on me if I'm lying—I don't know this man you're talking about!" 72 And immediately the rooster crowed the second time.

Suddenly, Jesus' words flashed through Peter's mind: "Before the rooster crows twice, you will deny three times that you even know me." And he broke down and wept.

CHAPTER 15

Jesus' Trial before Pilate

Very early in the morning the leading priests, the elders, and the teachers of religious law—the entire high council—met to discuss their next step. They bound Jesus, led him away, and took him to Pilate, the Roman governor.

FUN fact
I Know I'm Fast, but Is That Fasting?

You may be really fast when you run in soccer, but is that what the Bible means when it talks about fasting? Nah! In the Bible, fasting means going without food for a certain length of time so you can pray and focus on God. **Jesus himself fasted for forty days when Satan was tempting him (MATTHEW 4:1-2).**

Try fasting through one meal (ask your parents for permission first, and don't pick the night you're having liver and onions!).

While others are eating, spend time praying, reading your Bible, and focusing on God.

2 Pilate asked Jesus, "Are you the king of the
Jews?"
Jesus replied, "You have said it."
3 Then the leading priests kept accusing him
of many crimes, 4 and Pilate asked him, "Aren't
you going to answer them? What about all these
charges they are bringing against you?" 5 But
Jesus said nothing, much to Pilate's surprise.
6 Now it was the governor's custom each year
during the Passover celebration to release one
prisoner—anyone the people requested. 7 One
of the prisoners at that time was Barabbas, a
revolutionary who had committed murder in an
uprising. 8 The crowd went to Pilate and asked
him to release a prisoner as usual.
9 "Would you like me to release to you this
'King of the Jews'?" Pilate asked. 10 (For he realized by now that the leading priests had arrested
Jesus out of envy.) 11 But at this point the leading
priests stirred up the crowd to demand the release of Barabbas instead of Jesus. 12 Pilate asked
them, "Then what should I do with this man you
call the king of the Jews?"
13 They shouted back, "Crucify him!"
14 "Why?" Pilate demanded. "What crime has
he committed?"
But the mob roared even louder, "Crucify
him!"
15 So to pacify the crowd, Pilate released Barabbas to them. He ordered Jesus flogged with a
lead-tipped whip, then turned him over to the
Roman soldiers to be crucified.

The Soldiers Mock Jesus

16 The soldiers took Jesus into the courtyard of
the governor's headquarters (called the Praetori-
um) and called out the entire regiment. 17 They
dressed him in a purple robe, and they wove
thorn branches into a crown and put it on his
head. 18 Then they saluted him and taunted,
"Hail! King of the Jews!" 19 And they struck him
on the head with a reed stick, spit on him, and
dropped to their knees in mock worship.
20 When they were finally tired of mocking him,
they took off the purple robe and put his own
clothes on him again. Then they led him away to
be crucified.

The Crucifixion

21 A passerby named Simon, who was from Cyrene, was coming in from the countryside just
then, and the soldiers forced him to carry Jesus'
cross. (Simon was the father of Alexander and
Rufus.) 22 And they brought Jesus to a place
called Golgotha (which means "Place of the
Skull"). 23 They offered him wine drugged with
myrrh, but he refused it.
24 Then the soldiers nailed him to the cross.
They divided his clothes and threw dice to decide who would get each piece. 25 It was nine
o'clock in the morning when they crucified him.
26 A sign announced the charge against him. It
read, "The King of the Jews." 27 Two revolutionaries were crucified with him, one on his right
and one on his left.*
29 The people passing by shouted abuse, shaking their heads in mockery. "Ha! Look at you
now!" they yelled at him. "You said you were going to destroy the Temple and rebuild it in three
days. 30 Well then, save yourself and come down
from the cross!"
31 The leading priests and teachers of religious law also mocked Jesus. "He saved others,"
they scoffed, "but he can't save himself! 32 Let
this Messiah, this King of Israel, come down
from the cross so we can see it and believe him!"
Even the men who were crucified with Jesus ridiculed him.

The Death of Jesus

33 At noon, darkness fell across the whole land
until three o'clock. 34 Then at three o'clock Jesus
called out with a loud voice, *"Eloi, Eloi, lema
sabachthani?"* which means "My God, my God,
why have you abandoned me?"
35 Some of the bystanders misunderstood and
thought he was calling for the prophet Elijah.
36 One of them ran and filled a sponge with sour
wine, holding it up to him on a reed stick so he
could drink. "Wait!" he said. "Let's see whether
Elijah comes to take him down!"
37 Then Jesus uttered another loud cry and
breathed his last. 38 And the curtain in the sanctuary of the Temple was torn in two, from top to
bottom.
39 When the Roman officer who stood facing
him saw how he had died, he exclaimed, "This
man truly was the Son of God!"
40 Some women were there, watching from a
distance, including Mary Magdalene, Mary (the
mother of James the younger and of Joseph), and
Salome. 41 They had been followers of Jesus and
had cared for him while he was in Galilee. Many
other women who had come with him to Jerusalem were also there.

15:27 Some manuscripts add verse 28, *And the Scripture was fulfilled that said, "He was counted among those who were rebels."* See Isa 53:12; also compare Luke 22:37.

Mark 16 . . . page 998

The Burial of Jesus

42 This all happened on Friday, the day of preparation, the day before the Sabbath. As evening
approached, 43 Joseph of Arimathea took a risk
and went to Pilate and asked for Jesus' body.
(Joseph was an honored member of the high
council, and he was waiting for the Kingdom of
God to come.) 44 Pilate couldn't believe that
Jesus was already dead, so he called for the
Roman officer and asked if he had died yet.
45 The officer confirmed that Jesus was dead,
so Pilate told Joseph he could have the body.
46 Joseph bought a long sheet of linen cloth.
Then he took Jesus' body down from the cross,
wrapped it in the cloth, and laid it in a tomb that
had been carved out of the rock. Then he rolled
a stone in front of the entrance. 47 Mary Magdalene and Mary the mother of Joseph saw where
Jesus' body was laid.

CHAPTER 16

The Resurrection

Saturday evening, when the Sabbath ended,
Mary Magdalene, Mary the mother of James,
and Salome went out and purchased burial
spices so they could anoint Jesus' body. 2 Very
early on Sunday morning, just at sunrise, they
went to the tomb. 3 On the way they were asking
each other, "Who will roll away the stone for us
from the entrance to the tomb?" 4 But as they arrived, they looked up and saw that the stone,
which was very large, had already been rolled
aside.

5 When they entered the tomb, they saw a
young man clothed in a white robe sitting on the
right side. The women were shocked, 6 but the
angel said, "Don't be alarmed. You are looking
for Jesus of Nazareth, who was crucified. He isn't
here! He is risen from the dead! Look, this is
where they laid his body. 7 Now go and tell his
disciples, including Peter, that Jesus is going
ahead of you to Galilee. You will see him there,
just as he told you before he died."

8 The women fled from the tomb, trembling
and bewildered, and they said nothing to anyone
because they were too frightened.

[The most ancient manuscripts of Mark conclude with verse 16:8. Later manuscripts add one or both of the following endings.]

[Shorter Ending of Mark]

Then they briefly reported all this to Peter and
his companions. Afterward Jesus himself sent
them out from east to west with the sacred and
unfailing message of salvation that gives eternal
life. Amen.

[Longer Ending of Mark]

9 After Jesus rose from the dead early on Sunday
morning, the first person who saw him was Mary
Magdalene, the woman from whom he had cast
out seven demons. 10 She went to the disciples,
who were grieving and weeping, and told them
what had happened. 11 But when she told them
that Jesus was alive and she had seen him, they
didn't believe her.

12 Afterward he appeared in a different form
to two of his followers who were walking from
Jerusalem into the country. 13 They rushed back
to tell the others, but no one believed them.

14 Still later he appeared to the eleven disciples
as they were eating together. He rebuked them
for their stubborn unbelief because they refused
to believe those who had seen him after he had
been raised from the dead.

15 And then he told them, "Go into all the world
and preach the Good News to everyone. 16 Anyone who believes and is baptized will be saved.
But anyone who refuses to believe will be condemned. 17 These miraculous signs will accompany those who believe: They will cast out
demons in my name, and they will speak in new
languages. 18 They will be able to handle snakes
with safety, and if they drink anything poisonous,
it won't hurt them. They will be able to place
their hands on the sick, and they will be healed."

19 When the Lord Jesus had finished talking with
them, he was taken up into heaven and sat down
in the place of honor at God's right hand. 20 And
the disciples went everywhere and preached, and
the Lord worked through them, confirming what
they said by many miraculous signs.

LUKE A Look at Jesus' Life

Look for 7 hidden messages in Luke!

Luke, a Greek doctor, gives a detailed account of Jesus' life. Look for

- A SPECIAL BIRTHDAY
- PRAYERS AND PREACHING
- A CLIMB TO THE CROSS
- OUR RISEN SAVIOR

Did you at least catch his name?

What's in a Name?

Did you know that there are only two angels mentioned by name in the whole Bible? **Meet one of them in Luke 1:11-25.**

He's Back

Did you find out the name of that messenger who appeared to Zechariah?

Well, he came back with an even more amazing message. **Find out in Luke 1:26-38 what it was and who it was he gave it to.**

"KNOCK, KNOCK."
"WHO'S THERE?"
"MARY AND JOSEPH."
GO AWAY. THERE'S NO ROOM.

Is Anybody Home?

OK, so it isn't a very good joke. It was no joke for Mary and Joseph either. **Read Luke 2:1-7 to find out all about a special night and special birthday.**

A Night to Remember

What's that in the sky? A bird? A plane? It's... **Read Luke 2:8-20 to find out what some shepherds saw in a long-ago sky.**

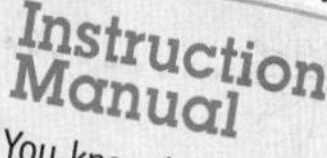

Instruction Manual

You know it's good to pray. But do you always know what to say? (Hey, a poem!) **Read Luke 11:1-13 for complete instructions!**

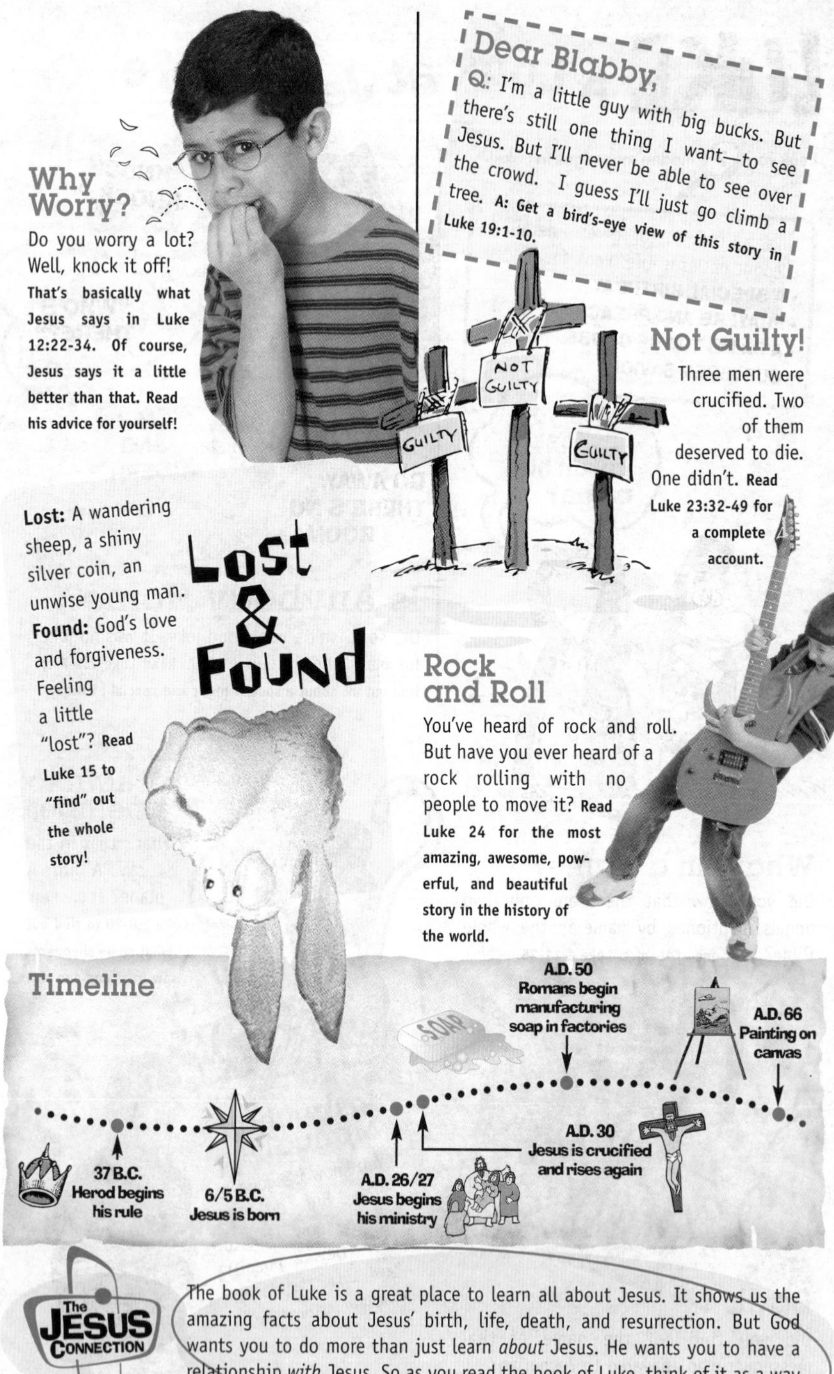

Dear Blabby,

Q: I'm a little guy with big bucks. But there's still one thing I want—to see Jesus. But I'll never be able to see over the crowd. I guess I'll just go climb a tree. **A: Get a bird's-eye view of this story in Luke 19:1-10.**

Why Worry?

Do you worry a lot? Well, knock it off! **That's basically what Jesus says in Luke 12:22-34. Of course, Jesus says it a little better than that. Read his advice for yourself!**

Not Guilty!

Three men were crucified. Two of them deserved to die. One didn't. **Read Luke 23:32-49 for a complete account.**

Lost & Found

Lost: A wandering sheep, a shiny silver coin, an unwise young man. **Found:** God's love and forgiveness. Feeling a little "lost"? **Read Luke 15 to "find" out the whole story!**

Rock and Roll

You've heard of rock and roll. But have you ever heard of a rock rolling with no people to move it? **Read Luke 24 for the most amazing, awesome, powerful, and beautiful story in the history of the world.**

Timeline

- **37 B.C.** Herod begins his rule
- **6/5 B.C.** Jesus is born
- **A.D. 26/27** Jesus begins his ministry
- **A.D. 30** Jesus is crucified and rises again
- **A.D. 50** Romans begin manufacturing soap in factories
- **A.D. 66** Painting on canvas

The JESUS Connection

The book of Luke is a great place to learn all about Jesus. It shows us the amazing facts about Jesus' birth, life, death, and resurrection. But God wants you to do more than just learn *about* Jesus. He wants you to have a relationship *with* Jesus. So as you read the book of Luke, think of it as a way to get to know a friend—**the best friend you'll ever have!**

CHAPTER 1

Introduction

Many people have set out to write accounts
about the events that have been fulfilled among
us. 2They used the eyewitness reports circulat-
ing among us from the early disciples. 3Having
carefully investigated everything from the beginning, I also have decided to write a careful
account for you, most honorable Theophilus, 4so
you can be certain of the truth of everything you
were taught.

The Birth of John the Baptist Foretold

5When Herod was king of Judea, there was a Jewish priest named Zechariah. He was a member of
the priestly order of Abijah, and his wife, Elizabeth, was also from the priestly line of Aaron.
6Zechariah and Elizabeth were righteous in
God's eyes, careful to obey all of the Lord's commandments and regulations. 7They had no children because Elizabeth was unable to conceive,
and they were both very old.

8One day Zechariah was serving God in the
Temple, for his order was on duty that week. 9As
was the custom of the priests, he was chosen by
lot to enter the sanctuary of the Lord and burn
incense. 10While the incense was being burned,
a great crowd stood outside, praying.

11While Zechariah was in the sanctuary, an angel of the Lord appeared to him, standing to the
right of the incense altar. 12Zechariah was
shaken and overwhelmed with fear when he saw
him. 13But the angel said, "Don't be afraid, Zechariah! God has heard your prayer. Your wife, Elizabeth, will give you a son, and you are to name
him John. 14You will have great joy and gladness,
and many will rejoice at his birth, 15for he will be
great in the eyes of the Lord. He must never
touch wine or other alcoholic drinks. He will be
filled with the Holy Spirit, even before his birth.
16And he will turn many Israelites to the Lord
their God. 17He will be a man with the spirit and
power of Elijah. He will prepare the people for
the coming of the Lord. He will turn the hearts of
the fathers to their children, and he will cause
those who are rebellious to accept the wisdom
of the godly."

18Zechariah said to the angel, "How can I be
sure this will happen? I'm an old man now, and
my wife is also well along in years."

19Then the angel said, "I am Gabriel! I stand in
the very presence of God. It was he who sent me
to bring you this good news! 20But now, since you
didn't believe what I said, you will be silent and
unable to speak until the child is born. For my
words will certainly be fulfilled at the proper
time."

21Meanwhile, the people were waiting for
Zechariah to come out of the sanctuary, wondering why he was taking so long. 22When he finally
did come out, he couldn't speak to them. Then
they realized from his gestures and his silence
that he must have seen a vision in the sanctuary.

23When Zechariah's week of service in the
Temple was over, he returned home. 24Soon
afterward his wife, Elizabeth, became pregnant
and went into seclusion for five months. 25"How
kind the Lord is!" she exclaimed. "He has taken
away my disgrace of having no children."

The Birth of Jesus Foretold

26In the sixth month of Elizabeth's pregnancy,
God sent the angel Gabriel to Nazareth, a village
in Galilee, 27to a virgin named Mary. She was
engaged to be married to a man named Joseph,
a descendant of King David. 28Gabriel appeared
to her and said, "Greetings, favored woman! The
Lord is with you!*"

29Confused and disturbed, Mary tried to think
what the angel could mean. 30"Don't be afraid,
Mary," the angel told her, "for you have found favor with God! 31You will conceive and give birth
to a son, and you will name him Jesus. 32He will
be very great and will be called the Son of the
Most High. The Lord God will give him the
throne of his ancestor David. 33And he will reign
over Israel forever; his Kingdom will never end!"

34Mary asked the angel, "But how can this
happen? I am a virgin."

35The angel replied, "The Holy Spirit will come
upon you, and the power of the Most High will
overshadow you. So the baby to be born will
be holy, and he will be called the Son of God.
36What's more, your relative Elizabeth has
become pregnant in her old age! People used
to say she was barren, but she has conceived a son
and is now in her sixth month. **37For the
word of God will never fail."**

38Mary responded, "I am the Lord's servant.
May everything you have said about me come
true." And then the angel left her.

Mary Visits Elizabeth

39A few days later Mary hurried to the hill country of Judea, to the town 40where Zechariah lived.
She entered the house and greeted Elizabeth.
41At the sound of Mary's greeting, Elizabeth's

1:28 Some manuscripts add *Blessed are you among women.*

God sent an angel to give an amazing message to a young woman named Mary. **Read LUKE 1:26-38 to see for yourself.** The message must have seemed impossible!

Try this "impossible" activity!

1. **Fill a drinking glass *almost* to the top with water.**
2. **Drop a small cork into the glass, and make the cork float in the center of the water without touching the glass.**

WHAT HAPPENS?

The cork keeps floating off to the side. It seems impossible to keep it in the center!

Slowly pour water from another glass until the water rises just above the rim without spilling. The cork will move to where the water is the highest—the center. It wasn't impossible when you knew what to do.

With God, truly *nothing* is impossible!

child leaped within her, and Elizabeth was filled
with the Holy Spirit.
42Elizabeth gave a glad cry and exclaimed to
Mary, "God has blessed you above all women, and
your child is blessed. 43Why am I so honored,
that the mother of my Lord should visit me?
44When I heard your greeting, the baby in my
womb jumped for joy. 45You are blessed because
you believed that the Lord would do what he
said."

The Magnificat: Mary's Song of Praise

46Mary responded,

"Oh, how my soul praises the Lord.
47 How my spirit rejoices in God my Savior!
48 For he took notice of his lowly servant girl,
and from now on all generations will
call me blessed.
49 For the Mighty One is holy,
and he has done great things for me.
50 He shows mercy from generation to
generation
to all who fear him.
51 His mighty arm has done tremendous things!
He has scattered the proud and
haughty ones.
52 He has brought down princes from their
thrones
and exalted the humble.
53 He has filled the hungry with good things
and sent the rich away with empty hands.
54 He has helped his servant Israel
and remembered to be merciful.
55 For he made this promise to our ancestors,
to Abraham and his children forever."

56Mary stayed with Elizabeth about three
months and then went back to her own home.

The Birth of John the Baptist

57When it was time for Elizabeth's baby to be
born, she gave birth to a son. 58And when her
neighbors and relatives heard that the Lord had
been very merciful to her, everyone rejoiced with
her.

59When the baby was eight days old, they all
came for the circumcision ceremony. They
wanted to name him Zechariah, after his father.
60But Elizabeth said, "No! His name is John!"

61"What?" they exclaimed. "There is no one in
all your family by that name." 62So they used gestures to ask the baby's father what he wanted to
name him. 63He motioned for a writing tablet,
and to everyone's surprise he wrote, "His name is

John." 64Instantly Zechariah could speak again,
and he began praising God.

65Awe fell upon the whole neighborhood, and
the news of what had happened spread throughout the Judean hills. 66Everyone who heard about
it reflected on these events and asked, "What will
this child turn out to be?" For the hand of the
Lord was surely upon him in a special way.

Zechariah's Prophecy

67Then his father, Zechariah, was filled with the
Holy Spirit and gave this prophecy:

68 "Praise the Lord, the God of Israel,
because he has visited and redeemed
his people.
69 He has sent us a mighty Savior
from the royal line of his servant David,
70 just as he promised
through his holy prophets long ago.
71 Now we will be saved from our enemies
and from all who hate us.
72 He has been merciful to our ancestors
by remembering his sacred covenant—
73 the covenant he swore with an oath
to our ancestor Abraham.
74 We have been rescued from our enemies
so we can serve God without fear,
75 in holiness and righteousness
for as long as we live.

76 "And you, my little son,
will be called the prophet of the
Most High,
because you will prepare the way for
the Lord.
77 You will tell his people how to find salvation
through forgiveness of their sins.
78 Because of God's tender mercy,
the morning light from heaven is about
to break upon us,
79 to give light to those who sit in darkness
and in the shadow of death,
and to guide us to the path of peace."

80John grew up and became strong in spirit.
And he lived in the wilderness until he began his
public ministry to Israel.

CHAPTER 2

The Birth of Jesus

At that time the Roman emperor, Augustus, decreed that a census should be taken throughout
the Roman Empire. 2(This was the first census
taken when Quirinius was governor of Syria.) 3All
returned to their own ancestral towns to register
for this census. 4And because Joseph was a
descendant of King David, he had to go to Bethlehem in Judea, David's ancient home. He traveled
there from the village of Nazareth in Galilee. 5He
took with him Mary, his fiancée, who was now
obviously pregnant.

6And while they were there, the time came for
her baby to be born. 7She gave birth to her first
child, a son. She wrapped him snugly in strips of
cloth and laid him in a manger, because there
was no lodging available for them.

The Shepherds and Angels

8That night there were shepherds staying in the
fields nearby, guarding their flocks of sheep.
9Suddenly, an angel of the Lord appeared among
them, and the radiance of the Lord's glory surrounded them. They were terrified, 10but the angel reassured them. "Don't be afraid!" he said.
"I bring you good news that will bring great joy
to all people. 11The Savior—yes, the Messiah, the
Lord—has been born today in Bethlehem, the
city of David! 12And you will recognize him by
this sign: You will find a baby wrapped snugly in
strips of cloth, lying in a manger."

13Suddenly, the angel was joined by a vast host
of others—the armies of heaven—praising God
and saying,

14 "Glory to God in highest heaven,
and peace on earth to those with whom
God is pleased."

15When the angels had returned to heaven,
the shepherds said to each other, "Let's go to
Bethlehem! Let's see this thing that has happened, which the Lord has told us about."

16They hurried to the village and found Mary
and Joseph. And there was the baby, lying in the
manger. 17After seeing him, the shepherds told
everyone what had happened and what the angel
had said to them about this child. 18All who
heard the shepherds' story were astonished,
19but Mary kept all these things in her heart and
thought about them often. 20The shepherds
went back to their flocks, glorifying and praising
God for all they had heard and seen. It was just as
the angel had told them.

Jesus Is Presented in the Temple

21Eight days later, when the baby was circumcised, he was named Jesus, the name given him
by the angel even before he was conceived.

22Then it was time for their purification offering, as required by the law of Moses after the birth

of a child; so his parents took him to Jerusalem to
present him to the Lord. 23The law of the Lord
says, "If a woman's first child is a boy, he must be
dedicated to the LORD." 24So they offered the sacrifice required in the law of the Lord—"either a
pair of turtledoves or two young pigeons."

The Prophecy of Simeon

25At that time there was a man in Jerusalem
named Simeon. He was righteous and devout
and was eagerly waiting for the Messiah to come
and rescue Israel. The Holy Spirit was upon him
26and had revealed to him that he would not die
until he had seen the Lord's Messiah. 27That day
the Spirit led him to the Temple. So when Mary
and Joseph came to present the baby Jesus to the
Lord as the law required, 28Simeon was there.
He took the child in his arms and praised God,
saying,

29 "Sovereign Lord, now let your servant die in
        peace,
    as you have promised.
30 I have seen your salvation,
31   which you have prepared for all people.
32 He is a light to reveal God to the nations,
    and he is the glory of your people Israel!"

33Jesus' parents were amazed at what was
being said about him. 34Then Simeon blessed
them, and he said to Mary, the baby's mother,
"This child is destined to cause many in Israel to
fall, but he will be a joy to many others. He has
been sent as a sign from God, but many will oppose him. 35As a result, the deepest thoughts of
many hearts will be revealed. And a sword will
pierce your very soul."

The Prophecy of Anna

36Anna, a prophet, was also there in the Temple.
She was the daughter of Phanuel from the tribe
of Asher, and she was very old. Her husband died
when they had been married only seven years.
37Then she lived as a widow to the age of eighty-
four. She never left the Temple but stayed there
day and night, worshiping God with fasting and
prayer. 38She came along just as Simeon was
talking with Mary and Joseph, and she began
praising God. She talked about the child to everyone who had been waiting expectantly for God to
rescue Jerusalem.

39When Jesus' parents had fulfilled all the requirements of the law of the Lord, they returned
home to Nazareth in Galilee. 40There the child
grew up healthy and strong. He was filled with
wisdom, and God's favor was on him.

Armies of Heaven

HAVE YOU EVER SEEN AN ANGEL?

READ LUKE 2:13 to find out about the "armies of heaven," a whole bunch of angels who came to tell the shepherds about the birth of the Messiah. **Whoa! Angels everywhere!**

Use this idea to create an army of angels.

1. **With a permanent marker, draw a face on the back of a plastic spoon.**
2. **Fold a piece of gold or silver foil back and forth like an accordion.**

Read more about angels in Psalm 91:11.

3. **Tape the foil to the handle of the spoon behind the angel's spoon face to remind you of the angel's radiance.**

Make a bunch of these angels, and stick them in the ground outside your house. Or poke them in a flat piece of craft foam, and put them in your house. When visitors ask what they are, be sure to tell them the story from **LUKE 2:8-15**!

Jesus Speaks with the Teachers

41Every year Jesus' parents went to Jerusalem for
the Passover festival. 42When Jesus was twelve
years old, they attended the festival as usual.
43After the celebration was over, they started
home to Nazareth, but Jesus stayed behind in Jerusalem. His parents didn't miss him at first,
44because they assumed he was among the
other travelers. But when he didn't show up that

evening, they started looking for him among their relatives and friends.
45When they couldn't find him, they went back to Jerusalem to search for him there.
46Three days later they finally discovered him in the Temple, sitting among the religious teachers, listening to them and asking questions. 47All who heard him were amazed at his understanding and his answers.
48His parents didn't know what to think. "Son," his mother said to him, "why have you done this to us? Your father and I have been frantic, searching for you everywhere."
49"But why did you need to search?" he asked. "Didn't you know that I must be in my Father's house?" 50But they didn't understand what he meant.
51Then he returned to Nazareth with them and was obedient to them. And his mother stored all these things in her heart.
52Jesus grew in wisdom and in stature and in favor with God and all the people.

CHAPTER 3

John the Baptist Prepares the Way

It was now the fifteenth year of the reign of Tiberius, the Roman emperor. Pontius Pilate was governor over Judea; Herod Antipas was ruler over Galilee; his brother Philip was ruler over Iturea and Traconitis; Lysanias was ruler over Abilene.
2Annas and Caiaphas were the high priests. At this time a message from God came to John son of Zechariah, who was living in the wilderness.
3Then John went from place to place on both sides of the Jordan River, preaching that people should be baptized to show that they had repented of their sins and turned to God to be forgiven. 4Isaiah had spoken of John when he said,

"He is a voice shouting in the wilderness,
'Prepare the way for the LORD's coming!
Clear the road for him!
5 The valleys will be filled,
and the mountains and hills made level.
The curves will be straightened,
and the rough places made smooth.
6 And then all people will see
the salvation sent from God.'"

7When the crowds came to John for baptism, he said, "You brood of snakes! Who warned you to flee God's coming wrath? 8Prove by the way you live that you have repented of your sins and turned to God. Don't just say to each other, 'We're safe, for we are descendants of Abraham.' That means nothing, for I tell you, God can create children of Abraham from these very stones.
9Even now the ax of God's judgment is poised, ready to sever the roots of the trees. Yes, every tree that does not produce good fruit will be chopped down and thrown into the fire."
10The crowds asked, "What should we do?"
11John replied, "If you have two shirts, give one to the poor. If you have food, share it with those who are hungry."
12Even corrupt tax collectors came to be baptized and asked, "Teacher, what should we do?"
13He replied, "Collect no more taxes than the government requires."
14"What should we do?" asked some soldiers.
John replied, "Don't extort money or make false accusations. And be content with your pay."
15Everyone was expecting the Messiah to come soon, and they were eager to know whether John
might be the Messiah. 16John answered their

When Jesus was twelve, he had quite a discussion about God with a group of adults. **Read what happened in LUKE 2:41-47.**

Read 1 Timothy 4:12 for advice about being young!

You can talk to adults about God too! Find two adults (or more!) to talk to about God—maybe parents, grandparents, teachers, or pastors. Talk together about your favorite Bible stories and how God answered your prayers.

Remember your talk by having the adults sign and date your Bible on the lines below. Then you sign too!

WE SHARED OUR FAITH TOGETHER...

____

____

____

questions by saying, "I baptize you with water; but
someone is coming soon who is greater than I
am—so much greater that I'm not even worthy to
be his slave and untie the straps of his sandals. He
will baptize you with the Holy Spirit and with fire.
17He is ready to separate the chaff from the wheat
with his winnowing fork. Then he will clean up
the threshing area, gathering the wheat into his
barn but burning the chaff with never-ending
fire." 18John used many such warnings as he announced the Good News to the people.

19John also publicly criticized Herod Antipas,
the ruler of Galilee, for marrying Herodias, his
brother's wife, and for many other wrongs he had
done. 20So Herod put John in prison, adding this
sin to his many others.

The Baptism of Jesus

21One day when the crowds were being baptized,
Jesus himself was baptized. As he was praying,
the heavens opened, 22and the Holy Spirit, in
bodily form, descended on him like a dove. And a
voice from heaven said, "You are my dearly loved
Son, and you bring me great joy."

The Ancestors of Jesus

23Jesus was about thirty years old when he began
his public ministry.

Jesus was known as the son of Joseph.
Joseph was the son of Heli.
24 Heli was the son of Matthat.
Matthat was the son of Levi.
Levi was the son of Melki.
Melki was the son of Jannai.
Jannai was the son of Joseph.
25 Joseph was the son of Mattathias.
Mattathias was the son of Amos.
Amos was the son of Nahum.
Nahum was the son of Esli.
Esli was the son of Naggai.
26 Naggai was the son of Maath.
Maath was the son of Mattathias.
Mattathias was the son of Semein.
Semein was the son of Josech.
Josech was the son of Joda.
27 Joda was the son of Joanan.
Joanan was the son of Rhesa.
Rhesa was the son of Zerubbabel.
Zerubbabel was the son of Shealtiel.
Shealtiel was the son of Neri.
28 Neri was the son of Melki.
Melki was the son of Addi.
Addi was the son of Cosam.
Cosam was the son of Elmadam.
Elmadam was the son of Er.
29 Er was the son of Joshua.
Joshua was the son of Eliezer.
Eliezer was the son of Jorim.
Jorim was the son of Matthat.
Matthat was the son of Levi.
30 Levi was the son of Simeon.
Simeon was the son of Judah.
Judah was the son of Joseph.
Joseph was the son of Jonam.
Jonam was the son of Eliakim.
31 Eliakim was the son of Melea.
Melea was the son of Menna.
Menna was the son of Mattatha.
Mattatha was the son of Nathan.
Nathan was the son of David.
32 David was the son of Jesse.
Jesse was the son of Obed.
Obed was the son of Boaz.
Boaz was the son of Salmon.
Salmon was the son of Nahshon.
33 Nahshon was the son of Amminadab.
Amminadab was the son of Admin.
Admin was the son of Arni.
Arni was the son of Hezron.
Hezron was the son of Perez.
Perez was the son of Judah.
34 Judah was the son of Jacob.
Jacob was the son of Isaac.
Isaac was the son of Abraham.
Abraham was the son of Terah.
Terah was the son of Nahor.
35 Nahor was the son of Serug.
Serug was the son of Reu.
Reu was the son of Peleg.
Peleg was the son of Eber.
Eber was the son of Shelah.
36 Shelah was the son of Cainan.
Cainan was the son of Arphaxad.
Arphaxad was the son of Shem.
Shem was the son of Noah.
Noah was the son of Lamech.
37 Lamech was the son of Methuselah.
Methuselah was the son of Enoch.
Enoch was the son of Jared.
Jared was the son of Mahalalel.
Mahalalel was the son of Kenan.
38 Kenan was the son of Enosh.
Enosh was the son of Seth.
Seth was the son of Adam.
Adam was the son of God.

CHAPTER 4

The Temptation of Jesus

Then Jesus, full of the Holy Spirit, returned from
the Jordan River. He was led by the Spirit in the

wilderness, 2where he was tempted by the devil
for forty days. Jesus ate nothing all that time and
became very hungry.
3Then the devil said to him, "If you are the Son
of God, tell this stone to become a loaf of bread."
4But Jesus told him, "No! The Scriptures say,
'People do not live by bread alone.'"
5Then the devil took him up and revealed
to him all the kingdoms of the world in a
moment of time. 6"I will give you the glory of
these kingdoms and authority over them,"
the devil said, "because they are mine to give to
anyone I please. 7I will give it all to you if you
will worship me."
8Jesus replied, "The Scriptures say,

'You must worship the LORD your God
and serve only him.'"

9Then the devil took him to Jerusalem, to the
highest point of the Temple, and said, "If you
are the Son of God, jump off! 10For the Scriptures say,

'He will order his angels to protect and
guard you.
11 And they will hold you up with their hands
so you won't even hurt your foot on
a stone.'"

12Jesus responded, "The Scriptures also say,
'You must not test the LORD your God.'"
13When the devil had finished tempting
Jesus, he left him until the next opportunity
came.

Jesus Rejected at Nazareth

14Then Jesus returned to Galilee, filled with the
Holy Spirit's power. Reports about him spread
quickly through the whole region. 15He taught
regularly in their synagogues and was praised by
everyone.
16When he came to the village of Nazareth, his
boyhood home, he went as usual to the synagogue on the Sabbath and stood up to read the
Scriptures. 17The scroll of Isaiah the prophet was
handed to him. He unrolled the scroll and found
the place where this was written:

18 "The Spirit of the LORD is upon me,
for he has anointed me to bring Good
News to the poor.
He has sent me to proclaim that captives
will be released,
that the blind will see,
that the oppressed will be set free,
19 and that the time of the LORD's favor
has come."

20He rolled up the scroll, handed it back to the
attendant, and sat down. All eyes in the synagogue looked at him intently. 21Then he began to
speak to them. "The Scripture you've just heard
has been fulfilled this very day!"
22Everyone spoke well of him and was amazed
by the gracious words that came from his lips.
"How can this be?" they asked. "Isn't this Joseph's
son?"
23Then he said, "You will undoubtedly quote
me this proverb: 'Physician, heal yourself'—
meaning, 'Do miracles here in your hometown
like those you did in Capernaum.' 24But I tell you
the truth, no prophet is accepted in his own
hometown.
25"Certainly there were many needy widows in
Israel in Elijah's time, when the heavens were
closed for three and a half years, and a severe
famine devastated the land. 26Yet Elijah was not
sent to any of them. He was sent instead to a
foreigner—a widow of Zarephath in the land of
Sidon. 27And there were many lepers in Israel in
the time of the prophet Elisha, but the only one
healed was Naaman, a Syrian."
28When they heard this, the people in the
synagogue were furious. 29Jumping up, they
mobbed him and forced him to the edge of the
hill on which the town was built. They intended
to push him over the cliff, 30but he passed right
through the crowd and went on his way.

Jesus Casts Out a Demon

31Then Jesus went to Capernaum, a town in Galilee, and taught there in the synagogue every Sabbath day. 32There, too, the people were amazed at
his teaching, for he spoke with authority.
33Once when he was in the synagogue, a man
possessed by a demon—an evil spirit—began
shouting at Jesus, 34"Go away! Why are you interfering with us, Jesus of Nazareth? Have you come
to destroy us? I know who you are—the Holy One
of God!"
35Jesus cut him short. "Be quiet! Come out of
the man," he ordered. At that, the demon threw
the man to the floor as the crowd watched; then
it came out of him without hurting him further.
36Amazed, the people exclaimed, "What authority and power this man's words possess!
Even evil spirits obey him, and they flee at his
command!" 37The news about Jesus spread
through every village in the entire region.

Jesus Heals Many People

38After leaving the synagogue that day, Jesus went
to Simon's home, where he found Simon's

mother-in-law very sick with a high fever. "Please heal her," everyone begged. 39Standing at her bedside, he rebuked the fever, and it left her. And she got up at once and prepared a meal for them.

40As the sun went down that evening, people throughout the village brought sick family members to Jesus. No matter what their diseases were, the touch of his hand healed every one. 41Many were possessed by demons; and the demons came out at his command, shouting, "You are the Son of God!" But because they knew he was the Messiah, he rebuked them and refused to let them speak.

Jesus Continues to Preach

42Early the next morning Jesus went out to an isolated place. The crowds searched everywhere for him, and when they finally found him, they begged him not to leave them. 43But he replied, "I must preach the Good News of the Kingdom of God in other towns, too, because that is why I was sent." 44So he continued to travel around, preaching in synagogues throughout Judea.

CHAPTER 5

The First Disciples

One day as Jesus was preaching on the shore of the Sea of Galilee, great crowds pressed in on him to listen to the word of God. 2He noticed two empty boats at the water's edge, for the fishermen had left them and were washing their nets. 3Stepping into one of the boats, Jesus asked Simon, its owner, to push it out into the water. So he sat in the boat and taught the crowds from there.

4When he had finished speaking, he said to Simon, "Now go out where it is deeper, and let down your nets to catch some fish."

5"Master," Simon replied, "we worked hard all last night and didn't catch a thing. But if you say so, I'll let the nets down again." 6And this time their nets were so full of fish they began to tear! 7A shout for help brought their partners in the other boat, and soon both boats were filled with fish and on the verge of sinking.

8When Simon Peter realized what had happened, he fell to his knees before Jesus and said, "Oh, Lord, please leave me—I'm too much of a sinner to be around you." 9For he was awestruck by the number of fish they had caught, as were the others with him. 10His partners, James and John, the sons of Zebedee, were also amazed.

Jesus replied to Simon, "Don't be afraid! From now on you'll be fishing for people!" 11And as soon as they landed, they left everything and followed Jesus.

Jesus Heals a Man with Leprosy

12In one of the villages, Jesus met a man with an advanced case of leprosy. When the man saw Jesus, he bowed with his face to the ground, begging to be healed. "Lord," he said, "if you are willing, you can heal me and make me clean."

13Jesus reached out and touched him. "I am willing," he said. "Be healed!" And instantly the leprosy disappeared. 14Then Jesus instructed him not to tell anyone what had happened. He said, "Go to the priest and let him examine you. Take along the offering required in the law of Moses for those who have been healed of leprosy. This will be a public testimony that you have been cleansed."

15But despite Jesus' instructions, the report of his power spread even faster, and vast crowds came to hear him preach and to be healed of their diseases. 16But Jesus often withdrew to the wilderness for prayer.

Jesus Heals a Paralyzed Man

17One day while Jesus was teaching, some Pharisees and teachers of religious law were sitting nearby. (It seemed that these men showed up from every village in all Galilee and Judea, as well as from Jerusalem.) And the Lord's healing power was strongly with Jesus.

18Some men came carrying a paralyzed man on a sleeping mat. They tried to take him inside to Jesus, 19but they couldn't reach him because of the crowd. So they went up to the roof and took off some tiles. Then they lowered the sick man on his mat down into the crowd, right in front of Jesus. 20Seeing their faith, Jesus said to the man, "Young man, your sins are forgiven."

21But the Pharisees and teachers of religious law said to themselves, "Who does he think he is? That's blasphemy! Only God can forgive sins!"

22Jesus knew what they were thinking, so he asked them, "Why do you question this in your hearts? 23Is it easier to say 'Your sins are forgiven,' or 'Stand up and walk'? 24So I will prove to you that the Son of Man has the authority on earth to forgive sins." Then Jesus turned to the paralyzed man and said, "Stand up, pick up your mat, and go home!"

25And immediately, as everyone watched, the man jumped up, picked up his mat, and went home praising God. 26Everyone was gripped with great wonder and awe, and they praised God, exclaiming, "We have seen amazing things today!"

Gone Fishin'

Have you ever caught a fish? **Read LUKE 5:1-11 to learn about an amazing fishing trip!**

Huh? Fishing for people? Yup! Think who you could tell about Jesus as you do this fishy experiment.

1. **Tape a bar magnet to a table edge. The magnet should stick out over the edge.**
2. **Bend some paper clips open.**
3. **Touch the unbent end of a paper clip to the underside of the magnet, and let the other end hang down like a fish hook.**
4. **See how many other paper clips you can hang on the hook before the hook falls.**

FISHING'S FUN! Especially when you fish for people, like Jesus said to do.

So start fishing!

God, these are people I want to "catch" for you:

____

____

____

Write those named on slips of paper, and "hook" them with a paper clip. Add more names as you tell more people about Jesus!

Jesus Calls Levi (Matthew)

27Later, as Jesus left the town, he saw a tax collector named Levi sitting at his tax collector's
booth. "Follow me and be my disciple," Jesus
said to him. 28So Levi got up, left everything, and
followed him.

29Later, Levi held a banquet in his home with
Jesus as the guest of honor. Many of Levi's fellow
tax collectors and other guests also ate with
them. 30But the Pharisees and their teachers
of religious law complained bitterly to Jesus'
disciples, "Why do you eat and drink with such
scum?"

31Jesus answered them, "Healthy people
don't need a doctor—sick people do. 32I have
come to call not those who think they are righteous, but those who know they are sinners and
need to repent."

A Discussion about Fasting

33One day some people said to Jesus, "John the
Baptist's disciples fast and pray regularly, and so
do the disciples of the Pharisees. Why are your
disciples always eating and drinking?"

34Jesus responded, "Do wedding guests fast
while celebrating with the groom? Of course
not. 35But someday the groom will be taken
away from them, and then they will fast."

36Then Jesus gave them this illustration: "No
one tears a piece of cloth from a new garment
and uses it to patch an old garment. For then the
new garment would be ruined, and the new
patch wouldn't even match the old garment.

37"And no one puts new wine into old wineskins. For the new wine would burst the wineskins, spilling the wine and ruining the skins.
38New wine must be stored in new wineskins.
39But no one who drinks the old wine seems to
want the new wine. 'The old is just fine,' they say."

CHAPTER 6

A Discussion about the Sabbath

One Sabbath day as Jesus was walking through
some grainfields, his disciples broke off heads of
grain, rubbed off the husks in their hands, and
ate the grain. 2But some Pharisees said, "Why
are you breaking the law by harvesting grain on
the Sabbath?"

3Jesus replied, "Haven't you read in the Scriptures what David did when he and his companions were hungry? 4He went into the house of
God and broke the law by eating the sacred loaves
of bread that only the priests can eat. He also gave
some to his companions." 5And Jesus added,
"The Son of Man is Lord, even over the Sabbath."

Anything Is Possible

Want to read about something that sounds impossible to do? Try LUKE 6:27-36!

Love your enemies? Sounds impossible. But as sure as there's a hole in your hand, you can do it!

What? There's no hole in your hand?

TRY THIS:

Turn to John 13:34-35 to read more about love.

1. **Stand by a white wall, and roll up a piece of paper. Look through it toward the wall with your left eye.**
2. **Hold your right hand up, close to the rolled paper. Keep both eyes open! Can you see the hole in your hand?**

Actually, that hole is an optical illusion. But Jesus telling us to love our enemies is for real!

But don't worry—you don't have to do it by yourself! Ask God to help you love your enemies, and it won't be impossible at all!

Jesus Heals on the Sabbath

6On another Sabbath day, a man with a deformed right hand was in the synagogue while
Jesus was teaching. 7The teachers of religious
law and the Pharisees watched Jesus closely. If he
healed the man's hand, they planned to accuse
him of working on the Sabbath.

8But Jesus knew their thoughts. He said to the
man with the deformed hand, "Come and stand
in front of everyone." So the man came forward.
9Then Jesus said to his critics, "I have a question
for you. Does the law permit good deeds on the
Sabbath, or is it a day for doing evil? Is this a day
to save life or to destroy it?"

10He looked around at them one by one and
then said to the man, "Hold out your hand." So
the man held out his hand, and it was restored!
11At this, the enemies of Jesus were wild with
rage and began to discuss what to do with him.

Jesus Chooses the Twelve Apostles

12One day soon afterward Jesus went up on a
mountain to pray, and he prayed to God all night.
13At daybreak he called together all of his disciples and chose twelve of them to be apostles.
Here are their names:

14 Simon (whom he named Peter),
Andrew (Peter's brother),
James,
John,
Philip,
Bartholomew,
15 Matthew,
Thomas,
James (son of Alphaeus),
Simon (who was called the zealot),
16 Judas (son of James),
Judas Iscariot (who later betrayed him).

Crowds Follow Jesus

17When they came down from the mountain, the
disciples stood with Jesus on a large, level area,
surrounded by many of his followers and by the
crowds. There were people from all over Judea
and from Jerusalem and from as far north as the
seacoasts of Tyre and Sidon. 18They had come
to hear him and to be healed of their diseases;
and those troubled by evil spirits were healed.
19Everyone tried to touch him, because healing
power went out from him, and he healed everyone.

The Beatitudes

20Then Jesus turned to his disciples and said,

"God blesses you who are poor,
for the Kingdom of God is yours.
21 God blesses you who are hungry now,
for you will be satisfied.
God blesses you who weep now,
for in due time you will laugh.

22What blessings await you when people hate
you and exclude you and mock you and curse you
as evil because you follow the Son of Man.
23When that happens, be happy! Yes, leap for joy!
For a great reward awaits you in heaven. And
remember, their ancestors treated the ancient
prophets that same way.

Sorrows Foretold

24 "What sorrow awaits you who are rich,
for you have your only happiness now.
25 What sorrow awaits you who are fat and
prosperous now,
for a time of awful hunger awaits you.
What sorrow awaits you who laugh now,
for your laughing will turn to mourning
and sorrow.
26 What sorrow awaits you who are praised
by the crowds,
for their ancestors also praised false
prophets.

Love for Enemies

27"But to you who are willing to listen, I say, love
your enemies! Do good to those who hate you.
28Bless those who curse you. Pray for those who
hurt you. 29If someone slaps you on one cheek,
offer the other cheek also. If someone demands
your coat, offer your shirt also. 30Give to anyone
who asks; and when things are taken away from
you, don't try to get them back. **31Do to others
as you would like them to do to you.**
32"If you love only those who love you, why
should you get credit for that? Even sinners love
those who love them! 33And if you do good only
to those who do good to you, why should you get
credit? Even sinners do that much! 34And if you
lend money only to those who can repay you, why
should you get credit? Even sinners will lend to
other sinners for a full return.
35"Love your enemies! Do good to them. Lend
to them without expecting to be repaid. Then
your reward from heaven will be very great, and
you will truly be acting as children of the Most
High, for he is kind to those who are unthankful
and wicked. 36You must be compassionate, just
as your Father is compassionate.

Do Not Judge Others

37"Do not judge others, and you will not be
judged. Do not condemn others, or it will all
come back against you. Forgive others, and you
will be forgiven. 38Give, and you will receive.
Your gift will return to you in full—pressed
down, shaken together to make room for more,
running over, and poured into your lap. The
amount you give will determine the amount you
get back."
39Then Jesus gave the following illustration:
"Can one blind person lead another? Won't they
both fall into a ditch? 40Students are not greater
than their teacher. But the student who is fully
trained will become like the teacher.
41"And why worry about a speck in your
friend's eye when you have a log in your own?
42How can you think of saying, 'Friend, let me
help you get rid of that speck in your eye,' when
you can't see past the log in your own eye? Hypocrite! First get rid of the log in your own eye; then
you will see well enough to deal with the speck in
your friend's eye.

The Tree and Its Fruit

43"A good tree can't produce bad fruit, and a bad
tree can't produce good fruit. 44A tree is identified by its fruit. Figs are never gathered from
thornbushes, and grapes are not picked from
bramble bushes. 45A good person produces
good things from the treasury of a good heart,
and an evil person produces evil things from the
treasury of an evil heart. What you say flows
from what is in your heart.

Building on a Solid Foundation

46"So why do you keep calling me 'Lord, Lord!'
when you don't do what I say? 47I will show you
what it's like when someone comes to me, listens
to my teaching, and then follows it. 48It is like a
person building a house who digs deep and lays
the foundation on solid rock. When the floodwaters rise and break against that house, it
stands firm because it is well built. 49But anyone
who hears and doesn't obey is like a person who
builds a house without a foundation. When the
floods sweep down against that house, it will collapse into a heap of ruins."

CHAPTER 7

The Faith of a Roman Officer

When Jesus had finished saying all this to the
people, he returned to Capernaum. 2At that time
the highly valued slave of a Roman officer was
sick and near death. 3When the officer heard
about Jesus, he sent some respected Jewish elders to ask him to come and heal his slave. 4So
they earnestly begged Jesus to help the man. "If
anyone deserves your help, he does," they said,
5"for he loves the Jewish people and even built
a synagogue for us."
6So Jesus went with them. But just before they
arrived at the house, the officer sent some friends
to say, "Lord, don't trouble yourself by coming to
my home, for I am not worthy of such an honor. 7I
am not even worthy to come and meet you. Just
say the word from where you are, and my servant
will be healed. 8I know this because I am under
the authority of my superior officers, and I have
authority over my soldiers. I only need to say, 'Go,'

and they go, or 'Come,' and they come. And if I say
to my slaves, 'Do this,' they do it."
9 When Jesus heard this, he was amazed. Turning to the crowd that was following him, he said,
"I tell you, I haven't seen faith like this in all Israel!" 10 And when the officer's friends returned to
his house, they found the slave completely
healed.

Jesus Raises a Widow's Son

11 Soon afterward Jesus went with his disciples to
the village of Nain, and a large crowd followed
him. 12 A funeral procession was coming out as
he approached the village gate. The young man
who had died was a widow's only son, and a large
crowd from the village was with her. 13 When
the Lord saw her, his heart overflowed with compassion. "Don't cry!" he said. 14 Then he walked
over to the coffin and touched it, and the bearers
stopped. "Young man," he said, "I tell you, get
up." 15 Then the dead boy sat up and began to
talk! And Jesus gave him back to his mother.
16 Great fear swept the crowd, and they
praised God, saying, "A mighty prophet has
risen among us," and "God has visited his people today." 17 And the news about Jesus spread
throughout Judea and the surrounding countryside.

Jesus and John the Baptist

18 The disciples of John the Baptist told John
about everything Jesus was doing. So John called
for two of his disciples, 19 and he sent them to the
Lord to ask him, "Are you the Messiah we've been
expecting, or should we keep looking for someone else?"
20 John's two disciples found Jesus and said to
him, "John the Baptist sent us to ask, 'Are you the
Messiah we've been expecting, or should we
keep looking for someone else?'"
21 At that very time, Jesus cured many people of
their diseases, illnesses, and evil spirits, and he
restored sight to many who were blind. 22 Then
he told John's disciples, "Go back to John and tell
him what you have seen and heard—the blind
see, the lame walk, the lepers are cured, the deaf
hear, the dead are raised to life, and the Good
News is being preached to the poor. 23 And tell
him, 'God blesses those who do not turn away because of me.'"
24 After John's disciples left, Jesus began talking about him to the crowds. "What kind of man
did you go into the wilderness to see? Was he a
weak reed, swayed by every breath of wind? 25 Or
were you expecting to see a man dressed in expensive clothes? No, people who wear beautiful
clothes and live in luxury are found in palaces.
26 Were you looking for a prophet? Yes, and he is
more than a prophet. 27 John is the man to whom
the Scriptures refer when they say,

'Look, I am sending my messenger ahead
of you,
and he will prepare your way before you.'

28 I tell you, of all who have ever lived, none is
greater than John. Yet even the least person in
the Kingdom of God is greater than he is!"
29 When they heard this, all the people—even
the tax collectors—agreed that God's way was
right, for they had been baptized by John. 30 But
the Pharisees and experts in religious law rejected
God's plan for them, for they had refused John's
baptism.
31 "To what can I compare the people of this
generation?" Jesus asked. "How can I describe
them? 32 They are like children playing a game in
the public square. They complain to their
friends,

'We played wedding songs,
and you didn't dance,
so we played funeral songs,
and you didn't weep.'

33 For John the Baptist didn't spend his time eating bread or drinking wine, and you say, 'He's
possessed by a demon.' 34 The Son of Man, on
the other hand, feasts and drinks, and you say,
'He's a glutton and a drunkard, and a friend
of tax collectors and other sinners!' 35 But wisdom is shown to be right by the lives of those
who follow it."

Jesus Anointed by a Sinful Woman

36 One of the Pharisees asked Jesus to have dinner with him, so Jesus went to his home and sat
down to eat. 37 When a certain immoral woman
from that city heard he was eating there, she
brought a beautiful alabaster jar filled with expensive perfume. 38 Then she knelt behind him
at his feet, weeping. Her tears fell on his feet, and
she wiped them off with her hair. Then she kept
kissing his feet and putting perfume on them.
39 When the Pharisee who had invited him
saw this, he said to himself, "If this man were a
prophet, he would know what kind of woman is
touching him. She's a sinner!"
40 Then Jesus answered his thoughts. "Simon,"
he said to the Pharisee, "I have something to say
to you."

"Go ahead, Teacher," Simon replied.
41Then Jesus told him this story: "A man
loaned money to two people—500 pieces of
silver to one and 50 pieces to the other. 42But
neither of them could repay him, so he kindly
forgave them both, canceling their debts. Who
do you suppose loved him more after that?"
43Simon answered, "I suppose the one for
whom he canceled the larger debt."
"That's right," Jesus said. 44Then he turned to
the woman and said to Simon, "Look at this
woman kneeling here. When I entered your
home, you didn't offer me water to wash the dust
from my feet, but she has washed them with her
tears and wiped them with her hair. 45You didn't
greet me with a kiss, but from the time I first
came in, she has not stopped kissing my feet.
46You neglected the courtesy of olive oil to
anoint my head, but she has anointed my feet
with rare perfume.
47"I tell you, her sins—and they are many—
have been forgiven, so she has shown me much
love. But a person who is forgiven little shows
only little love." 48Then Jesus said to the woman,
"Your sins are forgiven."
49The men at the table said among themselves,
"Who is this man, that he goes around forgiving
sins?"
50And Jesus said to the woman, "Your faith has
saved you; go in peace."

CHAPTER 8

Women Who Followed Jesus

Soon afterward Jesus began a tour of the nearby
towns and villages, preaching and announcing
the Good News about the Kingdom of God. He
took his twelve disciples with him, 2along with
some women who had been cured of evil spirits
and diseases. Among them were Mary Magdalene, from whom he had cast out seven demons;
3Joanna, the wife of Chuza, Herod's business
manager; Susanna; and many others who were
contributing from their own resources to support Jesus and his disciples.

Parable of the Farmer Scattering Seed

4One day Jesus told a story in the form of a parable
to a large crowd that had gathered from many
towns to hear him: 5"A farmer went out to plant
his seed. As he scattered it across his field, some
seed fell on a footpath, where it was stepped on,
and the birds ate it. 6Other seed fell among rocks.
It began to grow, but the plant soon wilted and
died for lack of moisture. 7Other seed fell among
thorns that grew up with it and choked out the
tender plants. 8Still other seed fell on fertile soil.
This seed grew and produced a crop that was a
hundred times as much as had been planted!"
When he had said this, he called out, "Anyone with
ears to hear should listen and understand."
9His disciples asked him what this parable
meant. 10He replied, "You are permitted to
understand the secrets of the Kingdom of God.
But I use parables to teach the others so that the
Scriptures might be fulfilled:

'When they look, they won't really see.
When they hear, they won't understand.'

11"This is the meaning of the parable: The
seed is God's word. 12The seeds that fell on the
footpath represent those who hear the message,
only to have the devil come and take it away from
their hearts and prevent them from believing
and being saved. 13The seeds on the rocky soil
represent those who hear the message and receive it with joy. But since they don't have deep
roots, they believe for a while, then they fall away
when they face temptation. 14The seeds that fell
among the thorns represent those who hear the
message, but all too quickly the message is
crowded out by the cares and riches and pleasures of this life. And so they never grow into
maturity. 15And the seeds that fell on the good
soil represent honest, good-hearted people who
hear God's word, cling to it, and patiently produce a huge harvest.

Parable of the Lamp

16"No one lights a lamp and then covers it with a
bowl or hides it under a bed. A lamp is placed on
a stand, where its light can be seen by all who enter the house. 17For all that is secret will eventually be brought into the open, and everything
that is concealed will be brought to light and
made known to all.
18"So pay attention to how you hear. To those
who listen to my teaching, more understanding
will be given. But for those who are not listening,
even what they think they understand will be
taken away from them."

The True Family of Jesus

19Then Jesus' mother and brothers came to see
him, but they couldn't get to him because of the
crowd. 20Someone told Jesus, "Your mother
and your brothers are standing outside, and
they want to see you."
21Jesus replied, "My mother and my brothers
are all those who hear God's word and obey it."

Luke 8 . . . page 1014

Jesus Calms the Storm

22 One day Jesus said to his disciples, "Let's cross to the other side of the lake." So they got into a boat and started out. 23 As they sailed across, Jesus settled down for a nap. But soon a fierce storm came down on the lake. The boat was filling with water, and they were in real danger.

24 The disciples went and woke him up, shouting, "Master, Master, we're going to drown!"

When Jesus woke up, he rebuked the wind and the raging waves. Suddenly the storm stopped and all was calm. 25 Then he asked them, "Where is your faith?"

The disciples were terrified and amazed. "Who is this man?" they asked each other. "When he gives a command, even the wind and waves obey him!"

Jesus Heals a Demon-Possessed Man

26 So they arrived in the region of the Gerasenes, across the lake from Galilee. 27 As Jesus was climbing out of the boat, a man who was possessed by demons came out to meet him. For a long time he had been homeless and naked, living in a cemetery outside the town.

28 As soon as he saw Jesus, he shrieked and fell down in front of him. Then he screamed, "Why are you interfering with me, Jesus, Son of the Most High God? Please, I beg you, don't torture me!" 29 For Jesus had already commanded the evil spirit to come out of him. This spirit had often taken control of the man. Even when he was placed under guard and put in chains and shackles, he simply broke them and rushed out into the wilderness, completely under the demon's power.

30 Jesus demanded, "What is your name?"

"Legion," he replied, for he was filled with many demons. 31 The demons kept begging Jesus not to send them into the bottomless pit.

32 There happened to be a large herd of pigs feeding on the hillside nearby, and the demons begged him to let them enter into the pigs.

So Jesus gave them permission. 33 Then the demons came out of the man and entered the pigs, and the entire herd plunged down the steep hillside into the lake and drowned.

34 When the herdsmen saw it, they fled to the nearby town and the surrounding countryside, spreading the news as they ran. 35 People rushed out to see what had happened. A crowd soon gathered around Jesus, and they saw the man who had been freed from the demons. He was sitting at Jesus' feet, fully clothed and perfectly sane, and they were all afraid. 36 Then those who had seen what happened told the others how the demon-possessed man had been healed. 37 And all the people in the region of the Gerasenes begged Jesus to go away and leave them alone, for a great wave of fear swept over them.

So Jesus returned to the boat and left, crossing back to the other side of the lake. 38 The man who had been freed from the demons begged to go with him. But Jesus sent him home, saying, 39 "No, go back to your family, and tell them everything God has done for you." So he went all through the town proclaiming the great things Jesus had done for him.

Jesus Heals in Response to Faith

40 On the other side of the lake the crowds welcomed Jesus, because they had been waiting for him. 41 Then a man named Jairus, a leader of the local synagogue, came and fell at Jesus' feet, pleading with him to come home with him. 42 His only daughter, who was about twelve years old, was dying.

As Jesus went with him, he was surrounded by the crowds. 43 A woman in the crowd had suffered for twelve years with constant bleeding, and she could find no cure. 44 Coming up behind Jesus, she touched the fringe of his robe. Immediately, the bleeding stopped.

45 "Who touched me?" Jesus asked.

Everyone denied it, and Peter said, "Master, this whole crowd is pressing up against you."

46 But Jesus said, "Someone deliberately touched me, for I felt healing power go out from me." 47 When the woman realized that she could not stay hidden, she began to tremble and fell to her knees in front of him. The whole crowd heard her explain why she had touched him and that she had been immediately healed. 48 "Daughter," he said to her, "your faith has made you well. Go in peace."

49 While he was still speaking to her, a messenger arrived from the home of Jairus, the leader of the synagogue. He told him, "Your daughter is dead. There's no use troubling the Teacher now."

50 But when Jesus heard what had happened, he said to Jairus, "Don't be afraid. Just have faith, and she will be healed."

51 When they arrived at the house, Jesus wouldn't let anyone go in with him except Peter, John, James, and the little girl's father and mother. 52 The house was filled with people

weeping and wailing, but he said, "Stop the
weeping! She isn't dead; she's only asleep."
53 But the crowd laughed at him because they
all knew she had died. 54 Then Jesus took her by
the hand and said in a loud voice, "My child, get
up!" 55 And at that moment her life returned, and
she immediately stood up! Then Jesus told them
to give her something to eat. 56 Her parents were
overwhelmed, but Jesus insisted that they not
tell anyone what had happened.

CHAPTER 9

Jesus Sends Out the Twelve Disciples

One day Jesus called together his twelve disciples
and gave them power and authority to cast out all
demons and to heal all diseases. 2 Then he sent
them out to tell everyone about the Kingdom of
God and to heal the sick. 3 "Take nothing for your
journey," he instructed them. "Don't take a walking stick, a traveler's bag, food, money, or even a
change of clothes. 4 Wherever you go, stay in the
same house until you leave town. 5 And if a town
refuses to welcome you, shake its dust from your
feet as you leave to show that you have abandoned those people to their fate."
6 So they began their circuit of the villages,
preaching the Good News and healing the sick.

Herod's Confusion

7 When Herod Antipas, the ruler of Galilee, heard
about everything Jesus was doing, he was puzzled. Some were saying that John the Baptist had
been raised from the dead. 8 Others thought
Jesus was Elijah or one of the other prophets
risen from the dead.
9 "I beheaded John," Herod said, "so who is this
man about whom I hear such stories?" And he
kept trying to see him.

Jesus Feeds Five Thousand

10 When the apostles returned, they told Jesus
everything they had done. Then he slipped quietly away with them toward the town of Bethsaida. 11 But the crowds found out where he was
going, and they followed him. He welcomed
them and taught them about the Kingdom of
God, and he healed those who were sick.
12 Late in the afternoon the twelve disciples
came to him and said, "Send the crowds away to
the nearby villages and farms, so they can find
food and lodging for the night. There is nothing
to eat here in this remote place."
13 But Jesus said, "You feed them."
"But we have only five loaves of bread and two
fish," they answered. "Or are you expecting us to
go and buy enough food for this whole crowd?"
14 For there were about 5,000 men there.
Jesus replied, "Tell them to sit down in groups
of about fifty each." 15 So the people all sat down.
16 Jesus took the five loaves and two fish, looked
up toward heaven, and blessed them. Then,
breaking the loaves into pieces, he kept giving
the bread and fish to the disciples so they could
distribute it to the people. 17 They all ate as much
as they wanted, and afterward, the disciples
picked up twelve baskets of leftovers!

Peter's Declaration about Jesus

18 One day Jesus left the crowds to pray alone.
Only his disciples were with him, and he asked
them, "Who do people say I am?"
19 "Well," they replied, "some say John the Baptist, some say Elijah, and others say you are one of
the other ancient prophets risen from the dead."
20 Then he asked them, "But who do you say
I am?"
Peter replied, "You are the Messiah sent from
God!"

Jesus Predicts His Death

21 Jesus warned his disciples not to tell anyone
who he was. 22 "The Son of Man must suffer
many terrible things," he said. "He will be rejected by the elders, the leading priests, and the
teachers of religious law. He will be killed, but on
the third day he will be raised from the dead."
23 Then he said to the crowd, "If any of you
wants to be my follower, you must turn from your
selfish ways, take up your cross daily, and follow
me. 24 If you try to hang on to your life, you will
lose it. But if you give up your life for my sake, you
will save it. 25 And what do you benefit if you gain
the whole world but are yourself lost or destroyed? 26 If anyone is ashamed of me and my
message, the Son of Man will be ashamed of that
person when he returns in his glory and in the
glory of the Father and the holy angels. 27 I tell you
the truth, some standing here right now will not
die before they see the Kingdom of God."

The Transfiguration

28 About eight days later Jesus took Peter, John,
and James up on a mountain to pray. 29 And as he
was praying, the appearance of his face was
transformed, and his clothes became dazzling
white. 30 Suddenly, two men, Moses and Elijah,
appeared and began talking with Jesus. 31 They
were glorious to see. And they were speaking

about his exodus from this world, which was about to be fulfilled in Jerusalem.

32 Peter and the others had fallen asleep. When they woke up, they saw Jesus' glory and the two men standing with him.
33 As Moses and Elijah were starting to leave, Peter, not even knowing what he was saying, blurted out, "Master, it's wonderful for us to be here! Let's make three shelters as memorials—one for you, one for Moses, and one for Elijah."
34 But even as he was saying this, a cloud overshadowed them, and terror gripped them as the cloud covered them.

35 Then a voice from the cloud said, "This is my Son, my Chosen One. Listen to him."
36 When the voice finished, Jesus was there alone. They didn't tell anyone at that time what they had seen.

Jesus Heals a Demon-Possessed Boy

37 The next day, after they had come down the mountain, a large crowd met Jesus.
38 A man in the crowd called out to him, "Teacher, I beg you to look at my son, my only child.
39 An evil spirit keeps seizing him, making him scream. It throws him into convulsions so that he foams at the mouth. It batters him and hardly ever leaves him alone.
40 I begged your disciples to cast out the spirit, but they couldn't do it."

41 Jesus said, "You faithless and corrupt people! How long must I be with you and put up with you?" Then he said to the man, "Bring your son here."

42 As the boy came forward, the demon knocked him to the ground and threw him into a violent convulsion. But Jesus rebuked the evil spirit and healed the boy. Then he gave him back to his father.
43 Awe gripped the people as they saw this majestic display of God's power.

Jesus Again Predicts His Death

While everyone was marveling at everything he was doing, Jesus said to his disciples,
44 "Listen to me and remember what I say. The Son of Man is going to be betrayed into the hands of his enemies."
45 But they didn't know what he meant. Its significance was hidden from them, so they couldn't understand it, and they were afraid to ask him about it.

The Greatest in the Kingdom

46 Then his disciples began arguing about which of them was the greatest.
47 But Jesus knew their thoughts, so he brought a little child to his side.
48 Then he said to them, "Anyone who welcomes a little child like this on my behalf welcomes me, and anyone who welcomes me also welcomes my Father who sent me. Whoever is the least among you is the greatest."

Using the Name of Jesus

49 John said to Jesus, "Master, we saw someone using your name to cast out demons, but we told him to stop because he isn't in our group."

50 But Jesus said, "Don't stop him! Anyone who is not against you is for you."

Opposition from Samaritans

51 As the time drew near for him to ascend to heaven, Jesus resolutely set out for Jerusalem.
52 He sent messengers ahead to a Samaritan village to prepare for his arrival.
53 But the people of the village did not welcome Jesus because he was on his way to Jerusalem.
54 When James and John saw this, they said to Jesus, "Lord, should we call down fire from heaven to burn them up?"
55 But Jesus turned and rebuked them.*
56 So they went on to another village.

The Cost of Following Jesus

57 As they were walking along, someone said to Jesus, "I will follow you wherever you go."

58 But Jesus replied, "Foxes have dens to live in, and birds have nests, but the Son of Man has no place even to lay his head."

59 He said to another person, "Come, follow me."

The man agreed, but he said, "Lord, first let me return home and bury my father."

60 But Jesus told him, "Let the spiritually dead bury their own dead! Your duty is to go and preach about the Kingdom of God."

61 Another said, "Yes, Lord, I will follow you, but first let me say good-bye to my family."

62 But Jesus told him, "Anyone who puts a hand to the plow and then looks back is not fit for the Kingdom of God."

CHAPTER 10

Jesus Sends Out His Disciples

The Lord now chose seventy-two other disciples and sent them ahead in pairs to all the towns and places he planned to visit.
2 These were his instructions to them: "The harvest is great, but the workers are few. So pray to the Lord who is in charge of the harvest; ask him to send more workers into his fields.
3 Now go, and remember

9:55 Some manuscripts add an expanded conclusion to verse 55 and an additional sentence in verse 56: *And he said, "You don't realize what your hearts are like. [56] For the Son of Man has not come to destroy people's lives, but to save them."*

Jesus' Birth
Luke 2:1-20

HAPPY BIRTHDAY

God gave the best present of all time when he sent his Son, Jesus, to earth. Jesus' birthday was the most important birthday ever because he came to save the whole world from sin. Even though Jesus is God, he didn't come to earth with a huge parade or with a giant palace to live in. Read **Luke 2:1-7** to see how Jesus made his entrance.

Give Back!

Read **Matthew 25:37-40**. Then make a plan to give back to Jesus by giving to others.

1. Think of three people you'd like to give gifts to.
2. For each person, make a gift certificate of one thing you can do for that person. (Like clean his or her room or make breakfast.)
3. Put the notes in boxes, and wrap the boxes. Let the three people open their presents.

COUPON
FOR ONE BEDROOM CLEANING!
You are getting this gift to remind you that Jesus is the greatest gift of all.

Follow through with your gifts by doing the work.

GOD LOVES YOU AND WANTS TO BE WITH YOU. That's why God sent his Son, Jesus, to earth. If you put your faith in Jesus, your sins will be forgiven and you can have a friendship with God! Best of all, you'll get to be with God forever in heaven. That's the best gift of all time! **READ JOHN 3:1-21** to learn more about this awesome gift.

Jesus' Miracles

Matthew 14:13-33

WHICH CENTER CIRCLE IS BIGGER?

Neither! They're the same size. The circle on the left looks bigger because it's an optical illusion.

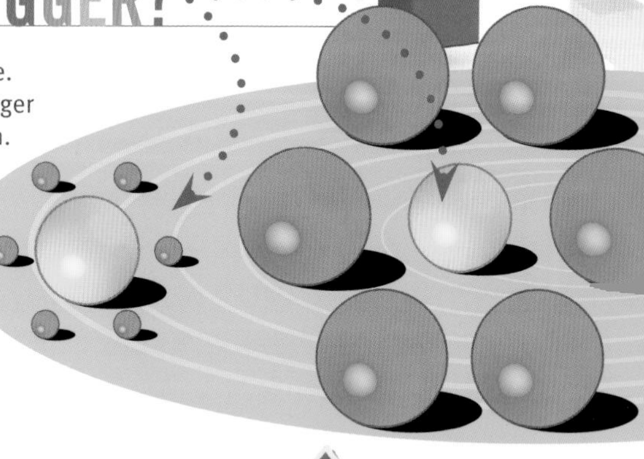

Now try your own optical illusion.

1. Cut two arch shapes from a sheet of colored paper. Make sure the shapes are the same size.

2. Hold both arches out in front of you, one above the other. Then switch their positions a few times. Which arch looks bigger?

The bottom arch always looks bigger! But you know you cut them the same size. Hmm...it's just an optical illusion. But Jesus' miracles were no illusions! They were real and powerful.

What's the difference between your optical illusion and the miracles Jesus did?

What exactly is a miracle?

Has anyone else in history ever been able to do the things Jesus did? Explain.

JESUS' AMAZING MIRACLES

JOHN 20:30-31 explains why Jesus performed the miracle he did. Jesus wants everyone to believe in him because b believing in Jesus we can have life. And not just life here on earth; when we believe in Jesus we can live with him i heaven forever! That's a pretty good deal, don't you think? Read about some o Jesus' amazing miracles in **MATTHEW 8:23-27; MATTHEW 14:15-21; MATTHEW 14:22-33; AND JOHN 2:1-11.**

Jesus' Resurrection

Luke 23:32–24:7

HE DID IT!!

Jesus caught the biggest bike jump? NOT!
He did something way cooler. He died on the cross and then three days later came back to life. (Read **Luke 23:32–24:7** for the amazing story.) Jesus had Resurrection Power! He broke the chains of death and sin, and because he did, *we* can be forgiven for our sins.

DEATH COULDN'T HOLD JESUS. HIS RESURRECTION POWER RULES!

Build this rocket...

Build this rocket to remind you that Jesus broke the bonds of death.

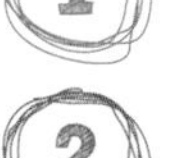

1. Go outside. Pour half an inch of lemon juice into a clean, empty 16-ounce plastic bottle. Then fill the bottle with water until it's not quite half full.

2. **Put a teaspoon of baking soda into a square of bathroom tissue, and fold it like a packet.**

3. Cut two strips of paper towel, and tape them to the top of a cork.

4. **Drop the packet into the bottle, put the cork in place, and tape the paper towel strips to either side of the bottle. Shake the bottle, and stand back!**

BE CAREFUL! You'll need safety glasses and an adult to help you.

The cork blasts into the air because of the reaction between the lemon juice and baking soda. Jesus' Resurrection Power came from the fact that JESUS IS GOD'S SON!

JESUS' RESURRECTION RULES!

Jesus was willing to die on the cross and take the punishment for all of our sins. But he didn't just die—he rose again and defeated death forever. When we believe in Jesus, we know that we can live forever with him in heaven. And while we're here on earth, he'll live in our hearts and be our best friend. **WHAT A GIFT!**

WANNA BE HERE?

What's the very coolest place to be? Did you say "heaven"? According to the Bible, heaven will be the most awesome place ever. Look at **Revelation 21:1–22:5** for just a glimpse!

Then Picture This!

Grab magazines, newspapers, and catalogs. Cut out things you'd like to see in heaven.

Make a collage on the top of a sheet of poster board.

On the bottom, make a collage of the things you'll be glad to leave behind when you go to heaven.

Make your poster 3-D by using fabric, yarn, straws, chenille wires, buttons, sponges, and more!

HEAVEN'S GOING TO BE GREAT!

There's no doubt about it. But do you have doubts about whether *you'll* get to go there? There's a way to be sure. Jesus says *he's* the way. Jesus took the punishment for our sins when he died on the cross, and he rose again to make eternal life with him possible. Where? You got it—heaven! Read **ROMANS 10:9-10** for exactly how to get to heaven!

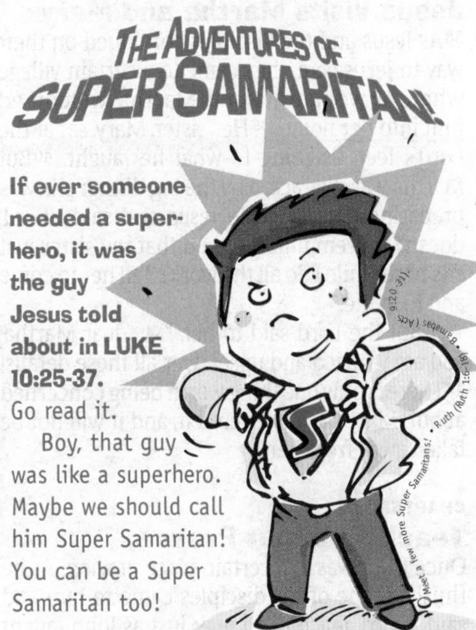

If ever someone needed a superhero, it was the guy Jesus told about in LUKE 10:25-37. Go read it.

Boy, that guy was like a superhero. Maybe we should call him Super Samaritan! You can be a Super Samaritan too!

1. **Draw a large S on a stick-on name tag.**
2. **Decorate the rest of the sticker to look like your very own superhero logo.**
3. **Stick the tag to the inside of your shirt where no one else can see it.**

Now ask God to help you be on the lookout for people to help. **Maybe you can even help someone you don't usually get along with!**

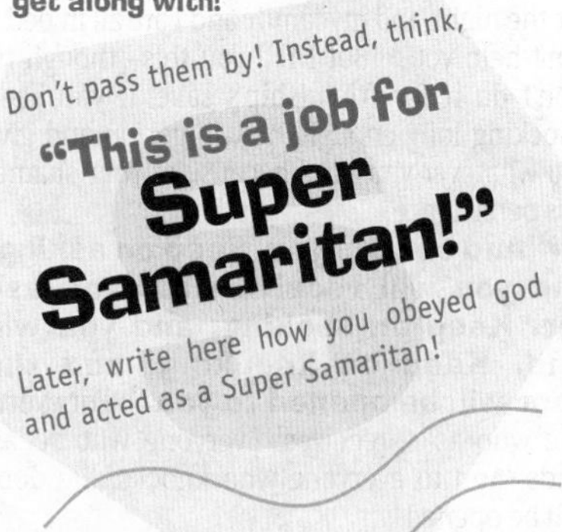

that I am sending you out as lambs among
wolves. 4Don't take any money with you, nor a
traveler's bag, nor an extra pair of sandals. And
don't stop to greet anyone on the road.

Don't pass them by! Instead, think,
"This is a job for Super Samaritan!"
Later, write here how you obeyed God and acted as a Super Samaritan!

5"Whenever you enter someone's home, first
say, 'May God's peace be on this house.' 6If those
who live there are peaceful, the blessing will
stand; if they are not, the blessing will return to
you. 7Don't move around from home to home.
Stay in one place, eating and drinking what they
provide. Don't hesitate to accept hospitality,
because those who work deserve their pay.

8"If you enter a town and it welcomes you, eat
whatever is set before you. 9Heal the sick, and
tell them, 'The Kingdom of God is near you now.'
10But if a town refuses to welcome you, go out
into its streets and say, 11'We wipe even the dust
of your town from our feet to show that we have
abandoned you to your fate. And know this—the
Kingdom of God is near!' 12I assure you, even
wicked Sodom will be better off than such a
town on judgment day.

13"What sorrow awaits you, Korazin and Bethsaida! For if the miracles I did in you had been
done in wicked Tyre and Sidon, their people
would have repented of their sins long ago, clothing themselves in burlap and throwing ashes on
their heads to show their remorse. 14Yes, Tyre
and Sidon will be better off on judgment day
than you. 15And you people of Capernaum, will
you be honored in heaven? No, you will go down
to the place of the dead."

16Then he said to the disciples, "Anyone
who accepts your message is also accepting me.
And anyone who rejects you is rejecting me.
And anyone who rejects me is rejecting God,
who sent me."

17When the seventy-two disciples returned,
they joyfully reported to him, "Lord, even the
demons obey us when we use your name!"

18"Yes," he told them, "I saw Satan fall from
heaven like lightning! 19Look, I have given you
authority over all the power of the enemy, and
you can walk among snakes and scorpions and
crush them. Nothing will injure you. 20But don't
rejoice because evil spirits obey you; rejoice because your names are registered in heaven."

Jesus' Prayer of Thanksgiving

21At that same time Jesus was filled with the joy
of the Holy Spirit, and he said, "O Father, Lord of
heaven and earth, thank you for hiding these
things from those who think themselves wise
and clever, and for revealing them to the childlike. Yes, Father, it pleased you to do it this way.

22"My Father has entrusted everything to me.
No one truly knows the Son except the Father, and
no one truly knows the Father except the Son and
those to whom the Son chooses to reveal him."
23Then when they were alone, he turned to the
disciples and said, "Blessed are the eyes that see
what you have seen. 24I tell you, many prophets
and kings longed to see what you see, but they
didn't see it. And they longed to hear what you
hear, but they didn't hear it."

The Most Important Commandment

25One day an expert in religious law stood up to
test Jesus by asking him this question: "Teacher,
what should I do to inherit eternal life?"
26Jesus replied, "What does the law of Moses
say? How do you read it?"
27The man answered, "'You must love the
LORD your God with all your heart, all your soul,
all your strength, and all your mind.' And, 'Love
your neighbor as yourself.'"
28"Right!" Jesus told him. "Do this and you will
live!"
29The man wanted to justify his actions, so he
asked Jesus, "And who is my neighbor?"

Parable of the Good Samaritan

30Jesus replied with a story: "A Jewish man was
traveling from Jerusalem down to Jericho, and he
was attacked by bandits. They stripped him of
his clothes, beat him up, and left him half dead
beside the road.
31"By chance a priest came along. But when he
saw the man lying there, he crossed to the other
side of the road and passed him by. 32A Temple
assistant walked over and looked at him lying
there, but he also passed by on the other side.
33"Then a despised Samaritan came along,
and when he saw the man, he felt compassion for
him. 34Going over to him, the Samaritan soothed
his wounds with olive oil and wine and bandaged
them. Then he put the man on his own donkey
and took him to an inn, where he took care of
him. 35The next day he handed the innkeeper
two silver coins, telling him, 'Take care of this
man. If his bill runs higher than this, I'll pay you
the next time I'm here.'
36"Now which of these three would you say
was a neighbor to the man who was attacked by
bandits?" Jesus asked.
37The man replied, "The one who showed him
mercy."
Then Jesus said, "Yes, now go and do the
same."

Jesus Visits Martha and Mary

38As Jesus and the disciples continued on their
way to Jerusalem, they came to a certain village
where a woman named Martha welcomed
him into her home. 39Her sister, Mary, sat at the
Lord's feet, listening to what he taught. 40But
Martha was distracted by the big dinner she was
preparing. She came to Jesus and said, "Lord,
doesn't it seem unfair to you that my sister just
sits here while I do all the work? Tell her to come
and help me."
41But the Lord said to her, "My dear Martha,
you are worried and upset over all these details!
42There is only one thing worth being concerned
about. Mary has discovered it, and it will not be
taken away from her."

CHAPTER 11

Teaching about Prayer

Once Jesus was in a certain place praying. As he
finished, one of his disciples came to him and
said, "Lord, teach us to pray, just as John taught
his disciples."
2Jesus said, "This is how you should pray:

"Father, may your name be kept holy.
May your Kingdom come soon.
3 Give us each day the food we need,
4 and forgive us our sins,
as we forgive those who sin against us.
And don't let us yield to temptation."

5Then, teaching them more about prayer, he
used this story: "Suppose you went to a friend's
house at midnight, wanting to borrow three
loaves of bread. You say to him, 6'A friend of mine
has just arrived for a visit, and I have nothing for
him to eat.' 7And suppose he calls out from his
bedroom, 'Don't bother me. The door is locked
for the night, and my family and I are all in bed. I
can't help you.' 8But I tell you this—though he
won't do it for friendship's sake, if you keep
knocking long enough, he will get up and give
you whatever you need because of your shameless persistence.
9"And so I tell you, keep on asking,
and you will receive what you ask
for. Keep on seeking, and you will
find. Keep on knocking, and the
door will be opened to you. 10For everyone who asks, receives. Everyone who seeks,
finds. And to everyone who knocks, the door
will be opened.
11"You fathers—if your children ask for a fish,
do you give them a snake instead? 12Or if they
ask for an egg, do you give them a scorpion? Of

course not! 13 So if you sinful people know how
to give good gifts to your children, how much
more will your heavenly Father give the Holy
Spirit to those who ask him."

Jesus and the Prince of Demons

14 One day Jesus cast out a demon from a man
who couldn't speak, and when the demon was
gone, the man began to speak. The crowds were
amazed, 15 but some of them said, "No wonder he
can cast out demons. He gets his power from
Satan, the prince of demons." 16 Others, trying to
test Jesus, demanded that he show them a miraculous sign from heaven to prove his authority.

17 He knew their thoughts, so he said, "Any
kingdom divided by civil war is doomed. A family splintered by feuding will fall apart. 18 You
say I am empowered by Satan. But if Satan is
divided and fighting against himself, how can
his kingdom survive? 19 And if I am empowered
by Satan, what about your own exorcists? They
cast out demons, too, so they will condemn you
for what you have said. 20 But if I am casting out
demons by the power of God, then the Kingdom
of God has arrived among you. 21 For when a
strong man like Satan is fully armed and guards
his palace, his possessions are safe—22 until
someone even stronger attacks and overpowers
him, strips him of his weapons, and carries off
his belongings.

23 "Anyone who isn't with me opposes me, and
anyone who isn't working with me is actually
working against me.

24 "When an evil spirit leaves a person, it goes
into the desert, searching for rest. But when it
finds none, it says, 'I will return to the person I
came from.' 25 So it returns and finds that its former home is all swept and in order. 26 Then the
spirit finds seven other spirits more evil than itself, and they all enter the person and live there.
And so that person is worse off than before."

27 As he was speaking, a woman in the crowd
called out, "God bless your mother—the womb
from which you came, and the breasts that
nursed you!"

28 Jesus replied, "But even more blessed are
all who hear the word of God and put it into
practice."

The Sign of Jonah

29 As the crowd pressed in on Jesus, he said, "This
evil generation keeps asking me to show them a
miraculous sign. But the only sign I will give
them is the sign of Jonah. 30 What happened to

Key Verse **"And so I tell you, keep on asking, and you will receive what you ask for. Keep on seeking, and you will find. Keep on knocking, and the door will be opened to you."—LUKE 11:9**

ASK, SEEK, KNOCK

God doesn't want you to close your eyes and make a wish. He wants you to pray. **Read LUKE 11:9 to find out why!**

And when you think you've prayed enough, pray some more! Use these ways to ask, seek, and knock:

- Pray every 60 minutes for a whole day.
- Write your prayers in a journal every day.
- Ask a friend to pray for you or with you.

KEEP ON SEEKING

- How many verses in the Bible can you find about prayer?
- Look at something God made. Then say thanks to him!
- Seek people you can pray for.

- Knock on the door of someone who really loves God. Ask how and when that person likes to pray.
- Knock a rhythm on your door as you sing a praise song.
- Knock on your parents' door. Ask them to pray with you.

him was a sign to the people of Nineveh that God had sent him. What happens to the Son of Man will be a sign to these people that he was sent by God.

31 "The queen of Sheba will stand up against this generation on judgment day and condemn it, for she came from a distant land to hear the wisdom of Solomon. Now someone greater than Solomon is here—but you refuse to listen. 32 The people of Nineveh will also stand up against this generation on judgment day and condemn it, for they repented of their sins at the preaching of Jonah. Now someone greater than Jonah is here—but you refuse to repent.

Receiving the Light

33 "No one lights a lamp and then hides it or puts it under a basket. Instead, a lamp is placed on a stand, where its light can be seen by all who enter the house.

34 "Your eye is a lamp that provides light for your body. When your eye is good, your whole body is filled with light. But when it is bad, your body is filled with darkness. 35 Make sure that the light you think you have is not actually darkness. 36 If you are filled with light, with no dark corners, then your whole life will be radiant, as though a floodlight were filling you with light."

Jesus Criticizes the Religious Leaders

37 As Jesus was speaking, one of the Pharisees invited him home for a meal. So he went in and took his place at the table. 38 His host was amazed to see that he sat down to eat without first performing the hand-washing ceremony required by Jewish custom. 39 Then the Lord said to him, "You Pharisees are so careful to clean the outside of the cup and the dish, but inside you are filthy—full of greed and wickedness! 40 Fools! Didn't God make the inside as well as the outside? 41 So clean the inside by giving gifts to the poor, and you will be clean all over.

42 "What sorrow awaits you Pharisees! For you are careful to tithe even the tiniest income from your herb gardens, but you ignore justice and the love of God. You should tithe, yes, but do not neglect the more important things.

43 "What sorrow awaits you Pharisees! For you love to sit in the seats of honor in the synagogues and receive respectful greetings as you walk in the marketplaces. 44 Yes, what sorrow awaits you! For you are like hidden graves in a field. People walk over them without knowing the corruption they are stepping on."

45 "Teacher," said an expert in religious law, "you have insulted us, too, in what you just said."

46 "Yes," said Jesus, "what sorrow also awaits you experts in religious law! For you crush people with unbearable religious demands, and you never lift a finger to ease the burden. 47 What sorrow awaits you! For you build monuments for the prophets your own ancestors killed long ago. 48 But in fact, you stand as witnesses who agree with what your ancestors did. They killed the prophets, and you join in their crime by building the monuments! 49 This is what God in his wisdom said about you: 'I will send prophets and apostles to them, but they will kill some and persecute the others.'

50 "As a result, this generation will be held responsible for the murder of all God's prophets from the creation of the world— 51 from the murder of Abel to the murder of Zechariah, who was killed between the altar and the sanctuary. Yes, it will certainly be charged against this generation.

52 "What sorrow awaits you experts in religious law! For you remove the key to knowledge from the people. You don't enter the Kingdom yourselves, and you prevent others from entering."

53 As Jesus was leaving, the teachers of religious law and the Pharisees became hostile and tried to provoke him with many questions. 54 They wanted to trap him into saying something they could use against him.

CHAPTER 12

A Warning against Hypocrisy

Meanwhile, the crowds grew until thousands were milling about and stepping on each other. Jesus turned first to his disciples and warned them, "Beware of the yeast of the Pharisees—their hypocrisy. 2 The time is coming when everything that is covered up will be revealed, and all that is secret will be made known to all. 3 Whatever you have said in the dark will be heard in the light, and what you have whispered behind closed doors will be shouted from the housetops for all to hear!

4 "Dear friends, don't be afraid of those who want to kill your body; they cannot do any more to you after that. 5 But I'll tell you whom to fear. Fear God, who has the power to kill you and then throw you into hell. Yes, he's the one to fear.

6 "What is the price of five sparrows—two copper coins? Yet God does not forget a single one of them. 7 And the very hairs on your head are all numbered. So don't be afraid; you are more valuable to God than a whole flock of sparrows.

8"I tell you the truth, everyone who acknowledges me publicly here on earth, the Son of Man
will also acknowledge in the presence of God's
angels. 9But anyone who denies me here on
earth will be denied before God's angels. 10Any-
one who speaks against the Son of Man can be
forgiven, but anyone who blasphemes the Holy
Spirit will not be forgiven.

11"And when you are brought to trial in the
synagogues and before rulers and authorities,
don't worry about how to defend yourself or
what to say, 12for the Holy Spirit will teach you at
that time what needs to be said."

Parable of the Rich Fool

13Then someone called from the crowd, "Teacher, please tell my brother to divide our father's
estate with me."

14Jesus replied, "Friend, who made me a
judge over you to decide such things as that?"
15Then he said, "Beware! Guard against every
kind of greed. Life is not measured by how
much you own."

16Then he told them a story: "A rich man had a
fertile farm that produced fine crops. 17He said
to himself, 'What should I do? I don't have room
for all my crops.' 18Then he said, 'I know! I'll tear
down my barns and build bigger ones. Then I'll
have room enough to store all my wheat and
other goods. 19And I'll sit back and say to myself,
"My friend, you have enough stored away for
years to come. Now take it easy! Eat, drink, and be
merry!"'

20"But God said to him, 'You fool! You will die
this very night. Then who will get everything you
worked for?'

21"Yes, a person is a fool to store up earthly
wealth but not have a rich relationship with God."

Teaching about Money and Possessions

22Then, turning to his disciples, Jesus said, "That
is why I tell you not to worry about everyday
life—whether you have enough food to eat or
enough clothes to wear. 23For life is more than
food, and your body more than clothing. 24Look
at the ravens. They don't plant or harvest or store
food in barns, for God feeds them. And you are
far more valuable to him than any birds! 25Can
all your worries add a single moment to your life?
26And if worry can't accomplish a little thing like
that, what's the use of worrying over bigger
things?

27"Look at the lilies and how they grow. They
don't work or make their clothing, yet Solomon
in all his glory was not dressed as beautifully as
they are. 28And if God cares so wonderfully for
flowers that are here today and thrown into the
fire tomorrow, he will certainly care for you. Why
do you have so little faith?

29"And don't be concerned about what to eat
and what to drink. Don't worry about such
things. 30These things dominate the thoughts of
unbelievers all over the world, but your Father
already knows your needs. 31Seek the Kingdom
of God above all else, and he will give you everything you need.

32"So don't be afraid, little flock. For it gives
your Father great happiness to give you the
Kingdom.

33"Sell your possessions and give to those in
need. This will store up treasure for you in
heaven! And the purses of heaven never get old
or develop holes. Your treasure will be safe; no
thief can steal it and no moth can destroy it.
34Wherever your treasure is, there the desires of
your heart will also be.

Be Ready for the Lord's Coming

35"Be dressed for service and keep your lamps
burning, 36as though you were waiting for your
master to return from the wedding feast. Then
you will be ready to open the door and let him
in the moment he arrives and knocks. 37The servants who are ready and waiting for his return
will be rewarded. I tell you the truth, he himself
will seat them, put on an apron, and serve them
as they sit and eat! 38He may come in the middle
of the night or just before dawn. But whenever he
comes, he will reward the servants who are ready.

39"Understand this: If a homeowner knew
exactly when a burglar was coming, he would not
permit his house to be broken into. 40You also
must be ready all the time, for the Son of Man will
come when least expected."

41Peter asked, "Lord, is that illustration just for
us or for everyone?"

42And the Lord replied, "A faithful, sensible
servant is one to whom the master can give the
responsibility of managing his other household
servants and feeding them. 43If the master returns and finds that the servant has done a good
job, there will be a reward. 44I tell you the truth,
the master will put that servant in charge of all he
owns. 45But what if the servant thinks, 'My master won't be back for a while,' and he begins beating the other servants, partying, and getting
drunk? 46The master will return unannounced
and unexpected, and he will cut the servant in
pieces and banish him with the unfaithful.

47"And a servant who knows what the master
wants, but isn't prepared and doesn't carry out
those instructions, will be severely punished.
48But someone who does not know, and then
does something wrong, will be punished only
lightly. When someone has been given much,
much will be required in return; and when someone has been entrusted with much, even more
will be required.

Jesus Causes Division

49"I have come to set the world on fire, and I wish
it were already burning! 50I have a terrible baptism of suffering ahead of me, and I am under a
heavy burden until it is accomplished. 51Do you
think I have come to bring peace to the earth?
No, I have come to divide people against each
other! 52From now on families will be split apart,
three in favor of me, and two against—or two in
favor and three against.

53 'Father will be divided against son
and son against father;
mother against daughter
and daughter against mother;
and mother-in-law against daughter-in-law
and daughter-in-law against
mother-in-law.'"

54Then Jesus turned to the crowd and said,
"When you see clouds beginning to form in the
west, you say, 'Here comes a shower.' And you are
right. 55When the south wind blows, you say,
'Today will be a scorcher.' And it is. 56You fools!
You know how to interpret the weather signs of
the earth and sky, but you don't know how to
interpret the present times.

57"Why can't you decide for yourselves what
is right? 58When you are on the way to court with
your accuser, try to settle the matter before you
get there. Otherwise, your accuser may drag you
before the judge, who will hand you over to an
officer, who will throw you into prison. 59And if
that happens, you won't be free again until you
have paid the very last penny."

CHAPTER 13

A Call to Repentance

About this time Jesus was informed that Pilate
had murdered some people from Galilee as they
were offering sacrifices at the Temple. 2"Do you
think those Galileans were worse sinners than all
the other people from Galilee?" Jesus asked. "Is
that why they suffered? 3Not at all! And you will
perish, too, unless you repent of your sins and
turn to God. 4And what about the eighteen people who died when the tower in Siloam fell on
them? Were they the worst sinners in Jerusalem?
5No, and I tell you again that unless you repent,
you will perish, too."

Parable of the Barren Fig Tree

6Then Jesus told this story: "A man planted a fig
tree in his garden and came again and again to
see if there was any fruit on it, but he was always
disappointed. 7Finally, he said to his gardener,
'I've waited three years, and there hasn't been a
single fig! Cut it down. It's just taking up space in
the garden.'

8"The gardener answered, 'Sir, give it one more
chance. Leave it another year, and I'll give it special attention and plenty of fertilizer. 9If we get
figs next year, fine. If not, then you can cut it
down.'"

Jesus Heals on the Sabbath

10One Sabbath day as Jesus was teaching in a
synagogue, 11he saw a woman who had been

Everyone loves a winner, right? But in the Bible, the *losers* seem to end up winning. **Remember Zacchaeus?** *Loser.* Everyone hated that cheat! (Everyone but Jesus, that is.) **Who did Jesus spend all his time with?** Poor people. Sick people. Lonely people. The people who everyone thought were losers. But it was the people who thought they knew it all and didn't need Jesus who were the *real* losers.

So who in your school gets called a loser? Make friends with that person. Be kind to that person. Help that person. TRY TO BE LIKE JESUS.

crippled by an evil spirit. She had been bent
double for eighteen years and was unable to
stand up straight. 12When Jesus saw her, he
called her over and said, "Dear woman, you are
healed of your sickness!" 13Then he touched her,
and instantly she could stand straight. How she
praised God!

14But the leader in charge of the synagogue
was indignant that Jesus had healed her on the
Sabbath day. "There are six days of the week for
working," he said to the crowd. "Come on those
days to be healed, not on the Sabbath."

15But the Lord replied, "You hypocrites! Each
of you works on the Sabbath day! Don't you untie your ox or your donkey from its stall on the
Sabbath and lead it out for water? 16This dear
woman, a daughter of Abraham, has been held in
bondage by Satan for eighteen years. Isn't it right
that she be released, even on the Sabbath?"

17This shamed his enemies, but all the people
rejoiced at the wonderful things he did.

Parable of the Mustard Seed

18Then Jesus said, "What is the Kingdom of God
like? How can I illustrate it? 19It is like a tiny mustard seed that a man planted in a garden; it grows
and becomes a tree, and the birds make nests in
its branches."

Parable of the Yeast

20He also asked, "What else is the Kingdom of
God like? 21It is like the yeast a woman used in
making bread. Even though she put only a little
yeast in three measures of flour, it permeated
every part of the dough."

The Narrow Door

22Jesus went through the towns and villages,
teaching as he went, always pressing on toward
Jerusalem. 23Someone asked him, "Lord, will
only a few be saved?"

He replied, 24"Work hard to enter the narrow
door to God's Kingdom, for many will try to enter
but will fail. 25When the master of the house has
locked the door, it will be too late. You will stand
outside knocking and pleading, 'Lord, open the
door for us!' But he will reply, 'I don't know you or
where you come from.' 26Then you will say, 'But
we ate and drank with you, and you taught in our
streets.' 27And he will reply, 'I tell you, I don't
know you or where you come from. Get away
from me, all you who do evil.'

28"There will be weeping and gnashing of
teeth, for you will see Abraham, Isaac, Jacob, and
all the prophets in the Kingdom of God, but you
will be thrown out. 29And people will come from
all over the world—from east and west, north and
south—to take their places in the Kingdom of
God. 30And note this: Some who seem least important now will be the greatest then, and some
who are the greatest now will be least important
then."

Jesus Grieves over Jerusalem

31At that time some Pharisees said to him, "Get
away from here if you want to live! Herod Antipas
wants to kill you!"

32Jesus replied, "Go tell that fox that I will keep
on casting out demons and healing people today
and tomorrow; and the third day I will accomplish my purpose. 33Yes, today, tomorrow, and
the next day I must proceed on my way. For it
wouldn't do for a prophet of God to be killed except in Jerusalem!

34"O Jerusalem, Jerusalem, the city that kills
the prophets and stones God's messengers! How
often I have wanted to gather your children together as a hen protects her chicks beneath her
wings, but you wouldn't let me. 35And now, look,
your house is abandoned. And you will never see
me again until you say, 'Blessings on the one who
comes in the name of the LORD!'"

CHAPTER 14

Jesus Heals on the Sabbath

One Sabbath day Jesus went to eat dinner in the
home of a leader of the Pharisees, and the people
were watching him closely. 2There was a man
there whose arms and legs were swollen. 3Jesus
asked the Pharisees and experts in religious law,
"Is it permitted in the law to heal people on the
Sabbath day, or not?" 4When they refused to answer, Jesus touched the sick man and healed him
and sent him away. 5Then he turned to them and
said, "Which of you doesn't work on the Sabbath? If your son or your cow falls into a pit, don't
you rush to get him out?" 6Again they could not
answer.

Jesus Teaches about Humility

7When Jesus noticed that all who had come to
the dinner were trying to sit in the seats of honor
near the head of the table, he gave them this advice: 8"When you are invited to a wedding feast,
don't sit in the seat of honor. What if someone
who is more distinguished than you has also
been invited? 9The host will come and say, 'Give
this person your seat.' Then you will be embarrassed, and you will have to take whatever seat is
left at the foot of the table!

10"Instead, take the lowest place at the foot of
the table. Then when your host sees you, he will
come and say, 'Friend, we have a better place for
you!' Then you will be honored in front of all the
other guests. 11For those who exalt themselves
will be humbled, and those who humble themselves will be exalted."

12Then he turned to his host. "When you put
on a luncheon or a banquet," he said, "don't invite your friends, brothers, relatives, and rich
neighbors. For they will invite you back, and that
will be your only reward. 13Instead, invite the
poor, the crippled, the lame, and the blind.
14Then at the resurrection of the righteous, God
will reward you for inviting those who could not
repay you."

Parable of the Great Feast

15Hearing this, a man sitting at the table with
Jesus exclaimed, "What a blessing it will be to
attend a banquet in the Kingdom of God!"

16Jesus replied with this story: "A man prepared a great feast and sent out many invitations.
17When the banquet was ready, he sent his servant to tell the guests, 'Come, the banquet is
ready.' 18But they all began making excuses. One
said, 'I have just bought a field and must inspect
it. Please excuse me.' 19Another said, 'I have just
bought five pairs of oxen, and I want to try them
out. Please excuse me.' 20Another said, 'I now
have a wife, so I can't come.'

21"The servant returned and told his master
what they had said. His master was furious and
said, 'Go quickly into the streets and alleys of the
town and invite the poor, the crippled, the blind,
and the lame.' 22After the servant had done this,
he reported, 'There is still room for more.' 23So
his master said, 'Go out into the country lanes
and behind the hedges and urge anyone you find
to come, so that the house will be full. 24For none
of those I first invited will get even the smallest
taste of my banquet.'"

The Cost of Being a Disciple

25A large crowd was following Jesus. He turned
around and said to them, 26"If you want to be my
disciple, you must hate everyone else by comparison—your father and mother, wife and children,
brothers and sisters—yes, even your own life.
Otherwise, you cannot be my disciple. 27And if
you do not carry your own cross and follow me,
you cannot be my disciple.

28"But don't begin until you count the cost.
For who would begin construction of a building
without first calculating the cost to see if there is
enough money to finish it? 29Otherwise, you
might complete only the foundation before running out of money, and then everyone would
laugh at you. 30They would say, 'There's the person who started that building and couldn't
afford to finish it!'

31"Or what king would go to war against
another king without first sitting down with his
counselors to discuss whether his army of
10,000 could defeat the 20,000 soldiers marching against him? 32And if he can't, he will send a
delegation to discuss terms of peace while the
enemy is still far away. 33So you cannot become
my disciple without giving up everything you
own.

34"Salt is good for seasoning. But if it loses its
flavor, how do you make it salty again? 35Flavor-
less salt is good neither for the soil nor for the
manure pile. It is thrown away. Anyone with ears
to hear should listen and understand!"

CHAPTER 15

Parable of the Lost Sheep

Tax collectors and other notorious sinners often
came to listen to Jesus teach. 2This made the
Pharisees and teachers of religious law complain
that he was associating with such sinful people—
even eating with them!

3So Jesus told them this story: 4"If a man has a
hundred sheep and one of them gets lost, what
will he do? Won't he leave the ninety-nine others
in the wilderness and go to search for the one
that is lost until he finds it? 5And when he has
found it, he will joyfully carry it home on his
shoulders. 6When he arrives, he will call together his friends and neighbors, saying, 'Rejoice with me because I have found my lost
sheep.' 7In the same way, there is more joy in
heaven over one lost sinner who repents and
returns to God than over ninety-nine others who
are righteous and haven't strayed away!

Parable of the Lost Coin

8"Or suppose a woman has ten silver coins and
loses one. Won't she light a lamp and sweep the
entire house and search carefully until she finds
it? 9And when she finds it, she will call in her
friends and neighbors and say, 'Rejoice with me
because I have found my lost coin.' 10In the same
way, there is joy in the presence of God's angels
when even one sinner repents."

Parable of the Lost Son

11To illustrate the point further, Jesus told them
this story: "A man had two sons. 12The younger

son told his father, 'I want my share of your estate
now before you die.' So his father agreed to
divide his wealth between his sons.
13"A few days later this younger son packed all
his belongings and moved to a distant land, and
there he wasted all his money in wild living.
14About the time his money ran out, a great famine swept over the land, and he began to starve.
15He persuaded a local farmer to hire him, and
the man sent him into his fields to feed the pigs.
16The young man became so hungry that even
the pods he was feeding the pigs looked good to
him. But no one gave him anything.
17"When he finally came to his senses, he said
to himself, 'At home even the hired servants have
food enough to spare, and here I am dying of
hunger! 18I will go home to my father and say,
"Father, I have sinned against both heaven and
you, 19and I am no longer worthy of being called
your son. Please take me on as a hired servant." '
20"So he returned home to his father. And
while he was still a long way off, his father saw
him coming. Filled with love and compassion, he
ran to his son, embraced him, and kissed him.
21His son said to him, 'Father, I have sinned
against both heaven and you, and I am no longer
worthy of being called your son.'
22"But his father said to the servants, 'Quick!
Bring the finest robe in the house and put it on
him. Get a ring for his finger and sandals for his
feet. 23And kill the calf we have been fattening.
We must celebrate with a feast, 24for this son of
mine was dead and has now returned to life. He
was lost, but now he is found.' So the party began.
25"Meanwhile, the older son was in the fields
working. When he returned home, he heard
music and dancing in the house, 26and he asked
one of the servants what was going on. 27'Your
brother is back,' he was told, 'and your father has
killed the fattened calf. We are celebrating because of his safe return.'
28"The older brother was angry and wouldn't
go in. His father came out and begged him, 29but
he replied, 'All these years I've slaved for you and
never once refused to do a single thing you told
me to. And in all that time you never gave me
even one young goat for a feast with my friends.
30Yet when this son of yours comes back after
squandering your money on prostitutes, you celebrate by killing the fattened calf!'
31"His father said to him, 'Look, dear son, you
have always stayed by me, and everything I have
is yours. 32We had to celebrate this happy day.
For your brother was dead and has come back to
life! He was lost, but now he is found!' "

CHAPTER 16

Parable of the Shrewd Manager

Jesus told this story to his disciples: "There was a
certain rich man who had a manager handling
his affairs. One day a report came that the manager was wasting his employer's money. 2So the
employer called him in and said, 'What's this I
hear about you? Get your report in order, because you are going to be fired.'
3"The manager thought to himself, 'Now
what? My boss has fired me. I don't have the
strength to dig ditches, and I'm too proud to beg.
4Ah, I know how to ensure that I'll have plenty of
friends who will give me a home when I am fired.'
5"So he invited each person who owed money
to his employer to come and discuss the situation. He asked the first one, 'How much do you
owe him?' 6The man replied, 'I owe him 800 gallons of olive oil.' So the manager told him, 'Take
the bill and quickly change it to 400 gallons.'
7" 'And how much do you owe my employer?'
he asked the next man. 'I owe him 1,000 bushels
of wheat,' was the reply. 'Here,' the manager said,
'take the bill and change it to 800 bushels.'
8"The rich man had to admire the dishonest
rascal for being so shrewd. And it is true that the
children of this world are more shrewd in dealing with the world around them than are the children of the light. 9Here's the lesson: Use your
worldly resources to benefit others and make
friends. Then, when your earthly possessions are
gone, they will welcome you to an eternal home.
10"If you are faithful in little things, you will be
faithful in large ones. But if you are dishonest in
little things, you won't be honest with greater responsibilities. 11And if you are untrustworthy
about worldly wealth, who will trust you with the
true riches of heaven? 12And if you are not faithful with other people's things, why should you be
trusted with things of your own?
13"No one can serve two masters. For you will
hate one and love the other; you will be devoted
to one and despise the other. You cannot serve
both God and money."
14The Pharisees, who dearly loved their
money, heard all this and scoffed at him. 15Then
he said to them, "You like to appear righteous in
public, but God knows your hearts. What this
world honors is detestable in the sight of God.
16"Until John the Baptist, the law of Moses and
the messages of the prophets were your guides.
But now the Good News of the Kingdom of God
is preached, and everyone is eager to get in. 17But
that doesn't mean that the law has lost its force.
It is easier for heaven and earth to disappear

than for the smallest point of God's law to be
overturned.

18"For example, a man who divorces his wife
and marries someone else commits adultery.
And anyone who marries a woman divorced
from her husband commits adultery."

Parable of the Rich Man and Lazarus

19Jesus said, "There was a certain rich man who
was splendidly clothed in purple and fine linen
and who lived each day in luxury. 20At his gate lay
a poor man named Lazarus who was covered
with sores. 21As Lazarus lay there longing for
scraps from the rich man's table, the dogs would
come and lick his open sores.

22"Finally, the poor man died and was carried by the angels to be with Abraham. The rich
man also died and was buried, 23and his soul
went to the place of the dead. There, in torment, he saw Abraham in the far distance with
Lazarus at his side.

24"The rich man shouted, 'Father Abraham,
have some pity! Send Lazarus over here to dip
the tip of his finger in water and cool my tongue.
I am in anguish in these flames.'

25"But Abraham said to him, 'Son, remember
that during your lifetime you had everything you
wanted, and Lazarus had nothing. So now he is
here being comforted, and you are in anguish.
26And besides, there is a great chasm separating
us. No one can cross over to you from here, and
no one can cross over to us from there.'

27"Then the rich man said, 'Please, Father
Abraham, at least send him to my father's home.
28For I have five brothers, and I want him to
warn them so they don't end up in this place of
torment.'

29"But Abraham said, 'Moses and the prophets
have warned them. Your brothers can read what
they wrote.'

30"The rich man replied, 'No, Father Abraham!
But if someone is sent to them from the dead,
then they will repent of their sins and turn to
God.'

31"But Abraham said, 'If they won't listen to
Moses and the prophets, they won't be persuaded even if someone rises from the dead.'"

CHAPTER 17

Teachings about Forgiveness and Faith

One day Jesus said to his disciples, "There will
always be temptations to sin, but what sorrow
awaits the person who does the tempting! 2It
would be better to be thrown into the sea with a
millstone hung around your neck than to cause
one of these little ones to fall into sin. 3So watch
yourselves!

"If another believer sins, rebuke that person;
then if there is repentance, forgive. 4Even if that
person wrongs you seven times a day and each
time turns again and asks forgiveness, you must
forgive."

5The apostles said to the Lord, "Show us how
to increase our faith."

6The Lord answered, "If you had faith even as
small as a mustard seed, you could say to this
mulberry tree, 'May you be uprooted and thrown
into the sea,' and it would obey you!

7"When a servant comes in from plowing or
taking care of sheep, does his master say, 'Come
in and eat with me'? 8No, he says, 'Prepare my
meal, put on your apron, and serve me while I eat.
Then you can eat later.' 9And does the master
thank the servant for doing what he was told to
do? Of course not. 10In the same way, when you
obey me you should say, 'We are unworthy servants who have simply done our duty.'"

Ten Healed of Leprosy

11As Jesus continued on toward Jerusalem, he
reached the border between Galilee and Samaria. 12As he entered a village there, ten lepers
stood at a distance, 13crying out, "Jesus, Master,
have mercy on us!"

14He looked at them and said, "Go show yourselves to the priests." And as they went, they were
cleansed of their leprosy.

15One of them, when he saw that he was
healed, came back to Jesus, shouting, "Praise
God!" 16He fell to the ground at Jesus' feet,
thanking him for what he had done. This man
was a Samaritan.

17Jesus asked, "Didn't I heal ten men? Where
are the other nine? 18Has no one returned to give
glory to God except this foreigner?" 19And Jesus
said to the man, "Stand up and go. Your faith has
healed you."

The Coming of the Kingdom

20One day the Pharisees asked Jesus, "When will
the Kingdom of God come?"

Jesus replied, "The Kingdom of God can't be
detected by visible signs. 21You won't be able to
say, 'Here it is!' or 'It's over there!' For the Kingdom of God is already among you."

22Then he said to his disciples, "The time is
coming when you will long to see the day when
the Son of Man returns, but you won't see it.

23People will tell you, 'Look, there is the Son of
Man,' or 'Here he is,' but don't go out and follow
them. 24For as the lightning flashes and lights
up the sky from one end to the other, so it will be
on the day when the Son of Man comes. 25But
first the Son of Man must suffer terribly and be
rejected by this generation.
26"When the Son of Man returns, it will be like
it was in Noah's day. 27In those days, the people
enjoyed banquets and parties and weddings
right up to the time Noah entered his boat and
the flood came and destroyed them all.
28"And the world will be as it was in the days of
Lot. People went about their daily business—eating and drinking, buying and selling, farming
and building—29until the morning Lot left Sodom. Then fire and burning sulfur rained down
from heaven and destroyed them all. 30Yes, it will
be 'business as usual' right up to the day when
the Son of Man is revealed. 31On that day
a person out on the deck of a roof must not go
down into the house to pack. A person out in the
field must not return home. 32Remember what
happened to Lot's wife! 33If you cling to your life,
you will lose it, and if you let your life go, you will
save it. 34That night two people will be asleep in
one bed; one will be taken, the other left. 35Two
women will be grinding flour together at the
mill; one will be taken, the other left.*"
37"Where will this happen, Lord?" the disciples asked.

Jesus replied, "Just as the gathering of vultures shows there is a carcass nearby, so these signs indicate that the end is near."

CHAPTER 18

Parable of the Persistent Widow

One day Jesus told his disciples a story to show
that they should always pray and never give up.
2"There was a judge in a certain city," he said,
"who neither feared God nor cared about people.
3A widow of that city came to him repeatedly,
saying, 'Give me justice in this dispute with my
enemy.' 4The judge ignored her for a while, but
finally he said to himself, 'I don't fear God or care
about people, 5but this woman is driving me
crazy. I'm going to see that she gets justice, because she is wearing me out with her constant requests!'"
6Then the Lord said, "Learn a lesson from this
unjust judge. 7Even he rendered a just decision

17:35 Some manuscripts add verse 36, *Two men will be working in the field; one will be taken, the other left.* Compare Matt 24:40.

When you were a little kid, did you ever take your parent's hand to cross the street? Little kids trust their parents. So what's that got to do with the Bible? **Read LUKE 18:15-17 to find out.** Jesus wants everyone (even grown-ups!) to have faith like little kids. We *all* need Jesus, *all* the time! Here's something to remind you that Jesus wants you to trust him the same way little kids trust their parents.

1. **Write "JESUS" in the middle of a sheet of construction paper. Draw a heart around his name.**
2. **Get a picture of yourself when you were little. Tape it to the left side of the paper.**
3. **Now get a recent picture of yourself. Tape it to the right side of the paper.**
4. **Decorate your paper any way you want.**

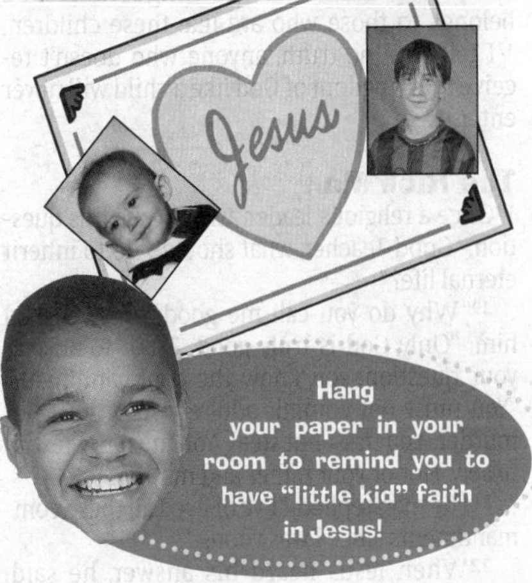

Hang your paper in your room to remind you to have "little kid" faith in Jesus!

in the end. So don't you think God will surely give
justice to his chosen people who cry out to him
day and night? Will he keep putting them off? 8I
tell you, he will grant justice to them quickly! But
when the Son of Man returns, how many will he
find on the earth who have faith?"

Parable of the Pharisee and Tax Collector

9Then Jesus told this story to some who had
great confidence in their own righteousness and
scorned everyone else: 10"Two men went to the
Temple to pray. One was a Pharisee, and the other
was a despised tax collector. 11The Pharisee
stood by himself and prayed this prayer: 'I thank
you, God, that I am not a sinner like everyone
else. For I don't cheat, I don't sin, and I don't commit adultery. I'm certainly not like that tax collector! 12I fast twice a week, and I give you a tenth of
my income.'

13"But the tax collector stood at a distance and
dared not even lift his eyes to heaven as he
prayed. Instead, he beat his chest in sorrow, saying, 'O God, be merciful to me, for I am a sinner.'
14I tell you, this sinner, not the Pharisee, returned
home justified before God. For those who exalt
themselves will be humbled, and those who
humble themselves will be exalted."

Jesus Blesses the Children

15One day some parents brought their little children to Jesus so he could touch and bless them.
But when the disciples saw this, they scolded the
parents for bothering him.

16Then Jesus called for the children and said
to the disciples, "Let the children come to me.
Don't stop them! For the Kingdom of God
belongs to those who are like these children.
17I tell you the truth, anyone who doesn't receive the Kingdom of God like a child will never
enter it."

The Rich Man

18Once a religious leader asked Jesus this question: "Good Teacher, what should I do to inherit
eternal life?"

19"Why do you call me good?" Jesus asked
him. "Only God is truly good. 20But to answer
your question, you know the commandments:
'You must not commit adultery. You must not
murder. You must not steal. You must not testify
falsely. Honor your father and mother.'"

21The man replied, "I've obeyed all these commandments since I was young."

22When Jesus heard his answer, he said,
"There is still one thing you haven't done. Sell all
your possessions and give the money to the poor,
and you will have treasure in heaven. Then come,
follow me."

23But when the man heard this he became
very sad, for he was very rich.

24When Jesus saw this, he said, "How hard it is
for the rich to enter the Kingdom of God! 25In
fact, it is easier for a camel to go through the eye
of a needle than for a rich person to enter the
Kingdom of God!"

26Those who heard this said, "Then who in
the world can be saved?"

27He replied, "What is impossible for people
is possible with God."

28Peter said, "We've left our homes to follow
you."

29"Yes," Jesus replied, "and I assure you that
everyone who has given up house or wife or
brothers or parents or children, for the sake of
the Kingdom of God, 30will be repaid many times
over in this life, and will have eternal life in the
world to come."

Jesus Again Predicts His Death

31Taking the twelve disciples aside, Jesus said,
"Listen, we're going up to Jerusalem, where all
the predictions of the prophets concerning the
Son of Man will come true. 32He will be handed
over to the Romans, and he will be mocked,
treated shamefully, and spit upon. 33They will
flog him with a whip and kill him, but on the
third day he will rise again."

34But they didn't understand any of this. The
significance of his words was hidden from them,
and they failed to grasp what he was talking
about.

Jesus Heals a Blind Beggar

35As Jesus approached Jericho, a blind beggar
was sitting beside the road. 36When he heard
the noise of a crowd going past, he asked what
was happening. 37They told him that Jesus the
Nazarene was going by. 38So he began shouting,
"Jesus, Son of David, have mercy on me!"

39"Be quiet!" the people in front yelled at him.

But he only shouted louder, "Son of David,
have mercy on me!"

40When Jesus heard him, he stopped and ordered that the man be brought to him. As the
man came near, Jesus asked him, 41"What do you
want me to do for you?"

"Lord," he said, "I want to see!"

42And Jesus said, "All right, receive your sight!
Your faith has healed you." 43Instantly the man

could see, and he followed Jesus, praising God. And all who saw it praised God, too.

CHAPTER 19

Jesus and Zacchaeus

Jesus entered Jericho and made his way through the town. 2 There was a man there named Zacchaeus. He was the chief tax collector in the region, and he had become very rich. 3 He tried to get a look at Jesus, but he was too short to see over the crowd. 4 So he ran ahead and climbed a sycamore-fig tree beside the road, for Jesus was going to pass that way.

5 When Jesus came by, he looked up at Zacchaeus and called him by name. "Zacchaeus!" he said. "Quick, come down! I must be a guest in your home today."

6 Zacchaeus quickly climbed down and took Jesus to his house in great excitement and joy. 7 But the people were displeased. "He has gone to be the guest of a notorious sinner," they grumbled.

8 Meanwhile, Zacchaeus stood before the Lord and said, "I will give half my wealth to the poor, Lord, and if I have cheated people on their taxes, I will give them back four times as much!"

9 Jesus responded, "Salvation has come to this home today, for this man has shown himself to be a true son of Abraham. **10 For the Son of Man came to seek and save those who are lost."**

Parable of the Ten Servants

11 The crowd was listening to everything Jesus said. And because he was nearing Jerusalem, he told them a story to correct the impression that the Kingdom of God would begin right away. 12 He said, "A nobleman was called away to a distant empire to be crowned king and then return. 13 Before he left, he called together ten of his servants and divided among them ten pounds of silver, saying, 'Invest this for me while I am gone.' 14 But his people hated him and sent a delegation after him to say, 'We do not want him to be our king.'

15 "After he was crowned king, he returned and called in the servants to whom he had given the money. He wanted to find out what their profits were. 16 The first servant reported, 'Master, I invested your money and made ten times the original amount!'

17 "'Well done!' the king exclaimed. 'You are a good servant. You have been faithful with the little I entrusted to you, so you will be governor of ten cities as your reward.'

18 "The next servant reported, 'Master, I invested your money and made five times the original amount.'

19 "'Well done!' the king said. 'You will be governor over five cities.'

20 "But the third servant brought back only the original amount of money and said, 'Master, I hid your money and kept it safe. 21 I was afraid because you are a hard man to deal with, taking what isn't yours and harvesting crops you didn't plant.'

22 "'You wicked servant!' the king roared. 'Your own words condemn you. If you knew that I'm a hard man who takes what isn't mine and harvests crops I didn't plant, 23 why didn't you deposit my money in the bank? At least I could have gotten some interest on it.'

24 "Then, turning to the others standing nearby, the king ordered, 'Take the money from this servant, and give it to the one who has ten pounds.'

25 "'But, master,' they said, 'he already has ten pounds!'

26 "'Yes,' the king replied, 'and to those who use well what they are given, even more will be given. But from those who do nothing, even what little they have will be taken away. 27 And as for these enemies of mine who didn't want me to be their king—bring them in and execute them right here in front of me.'"

Jesus' Triumphant Entry

28 After telling this story, Jesus went on toward Jerusalem, walking ahead of his disciples. 29 As he came to the towns of Bethphage and Bethany on the Mount of Olives, he sent two disciples ahead. 30 "Go into that village over there," he told them. "As you enter it, you will see a young donkey tied there that no one has ever ridden. Untie it and bring it here. 31 If anyone asks, 'Why are you untying that colt?' just say, 'The Lord needs it.'"

32 So they went and found the colt, just as Jesus had said. 33 And sure enough, as they were untying it, the owners asked them, "Why are you untying that colt?"

34 And the disciples simply replied, "The Lord needs it." 35 So they brought the colt to Jesus and threw their garments over it for him to ride on.

36 As he rode along, the crowds spread out their garments on the road ahead of him. 37 When he reached the place where the road started down the Mount of Olives, all of his followers began to shout and sing as they walked along, praising God for all the wonderful miracles they had seen.

38 "Blessings on the King who comes in the
name of the LORD!
Peace in heaven, and glory in highest
heaven!"

39 But some of the Pharisees among the crowd
said, "Teacher, rebuke your followers for saying
things like that!"
40 He replied, "If they kept quiet, the stones
along the road would burst into cheers!"

Jesus Weeps over Jerusalem

41 But as he came closer to Jerusalem and saw the
city ahead, he began to weep. 42 "How I wish today
that you of all people would understand the way
to peace. But now it is too late, and peace is hidden from your eyes. 43 Before long your enemies
will build ramparts against your walls and encir-
cle you and close in on you from every side.
44 They will crush you into the ground, and your
children with you. Your enemies will not leave a
single stone in place, because you did not recognize it when God visited you."

Jesus Clears the Temple

45 Then Jesus entered the Temple and began to
drive out the people selling animals for sacrifices. 46 He said to them, "The Scriptures declare,
'My Temple will be a house of prayer,' but you
have turned it into a den of thieves."
47 After that, he taught daily in the Temple, but
the leading priests, the teachers of religious law,
and the other leaders of the people began planning how to kill him. 48 But they could think of
nothing, because all the people hung on every
word he said.

CHAPTER 20

The Authority of Jesus Challenged

One day as Jesus was teaching the people and
preaching the Good News in the Temple, the
leading priests, the teachers of religious law, and
the elders came up to him. 2 They demanded, "By
what authority are you doing all these things?
Who gave you the right?"
3 "Let me ask you a question first," he replied.
4 "Did John's authority to baptize come from
heaven, or was it merely human?"
5 They talked it over among themselves. "If we
say it was from heaven, he will ask why we didn't
believe John. 6 But if we say it was merely human,
the people will stone us because they are convinced John was a prophet." 7 So they finally
replied that they didn't know.

CLEAN UP Your Act

Have you ever done something wrong? A guy named Zacchaeus had done a *lot* wrong. **Read LUKE 19:1-9 for details.**

Jesus didn't wait for Zacchaeus to stop sinning before he called to him. It's the same with us. We don't have to clean up our lives before we get to know Jesus.

JESUS CALLS TO US JUST THE WAY WE ARE.

1. **Pour a cup of water into a glass. Add a few drops of red food coloring. This red water represents your sinful life.**
2. **Now use food coloring to make a glass of blue water. The blue water can represent Jesus.**
3. **Pour the blue water into the red water.**

LOOK— A BIG CHANGE!

When we follow Jesus, he makes big changes in our lives.

Jesus changed Zacchaeus, and he can change you, too!

8 And Jesus responded, "Then I won't tell you
by what authority I do these things."

Parable of the Evil Farmers

9 Now Jesus turned to the people again and told
them this story: "A man planted a vineyard,
leased it to tenant farmers, and moved to another country to live for several years. 10 At the
time of the grape harvest, he sent one of his servants to collect his share of the crop. But the
farmers attacked the servant, beat him up, and
sent him back empty-handed. 11 So the owner
sent another servant, but they also insulted him,
beat him up, and sent him away empty-handed.
12 A third man was sent, and they wounded him
and chased him away.
13 "'What will I do?' the owner asked himself.

'I know! I'll send my cherished son. Surely they
will respect him.'

14"But when the tenant farmers saw his son,
they said to each other, 'Here comes the heir to
this estate. Let's kill him and get the estate for
ourselves!' 15So they dragged him out of the vineyard and murdered him.

"What do you suppose the owner of the vineyard will do to them?" Jesus asked. 16"I'll tell
you—he will come and kill those farmers and
lease the vineyard to others."

"How terrible that such a thing should ever
happen," his listeners protested.

17Jesus looked at them and said, "Then what
does this Scripture mean?

'The stone that the builders rejected
has now become the cornerstone.'

18Everyone who stumbles over that stone will
be broken to pieces, and it will crush anyone it
falls on."

19The teachers of religious law and the leading priests wanted to arrest Jesus immediately
because they realized he was telling the story
against them—they were the wicked farmers.
But they were afraid of the people's reaction.

Taxes for Caesar

20Watching for their opportunity, the leaders
sent spies pretending to be honest men. They
tried to get Jesus to say something that could
be reported to the Roman governor so he would
arrest Jesus. 21"Teacher," they said, "we know
that you speak and teach what is right and are
not influenced by what others think. You teach
the way of God truthfully. 22Now tell us—is it
right for us to pay taxes to Caesar or not?"

23He saw through their trickery and said,
24"Show me a Roman coin. Whose picture and
title are stamped on it?"

"Caesar's," they replied.

25"Well then," he said, "give to Caesar what belongs to Caesar, and give to God what belongs to
God."

26So they failed to trap him by what he said in
front of the people. Instead, they were amazed
by his answer, and they became silent.

Discussion about Resurrection

27Then Jesus was approached by some Sadducees—religious leaders who say there is no resurrection from the dead. 28They posed this
question: "Teacher, Moses gave us a law that if a
man dies, leaving a wife but no children, his
brother should marry the widow and have a
child who will carry on the brother's name.
29Well, suppose there were seven brothers. The
oldest one married and then died without children. 30So the second brother married the
widow, but he also died. 31Then the third
brother married her. This continued with all
seven of them, who died without children.
32Finally, the woman also died. 33So tell us,
whose wife will she be in the resurrection? For
all seven were married to her!"

34Jesus replied, "Marriage is for people here
on earth. 35But in the age to come, those worthy
of being raised from the dead will neither marry
nor be given in marriage. 36And they will never
die again. In this respect they will be like angels.
They are children of God and children of the
resurrection.

37"But now, as to whether the dead will be
raised—even Moses proved this when he wrote
about the burning bush. Long after Abraham,
Isaac, and Jacob had died, he referred to the
Lord as 'the God of Abraham, the God of
Isaac, and the God of Jacob.' 38So he is the God
of the living, not the dead, for they are all alive to
him."

39"Well said, Teacher!" remarked some of the
teachers of religious law who were standing
there. 40And then no one dared to ask him any
more questions.

Whose Son Is the Messiah?

41Then Jesus presented them with a question.
"Why is it," he asked, "that the Messiah is said to
be the son of David? 42For David himself wrote in
the book of Psalms:

'The LORD said to my Lord,
Sit in the place of honor at my
right hand
43 until I humble your enemies,
making them a footstool under
your feet.'

44Since David called the Messiah 'Lord,' how can
the Messiah be his son?"

45Then, with the crowds listening, he turned
to his disciples and said, 46"Beware of these
teachers of religious law! For they like to parade
around in flowing robes and love to receive
respectful greetings as they walk in the marketplaces. And how they love the seats of honor in
the synagogues and the head table at banquets.
47Yet they shamelessly cheat widows out of
their property and then pretend to be pious by
making long prayers in public. Because of this,
they will be severely punished."

Luke 21 . . . page 1032

CHAPTER 21

The Widow's Offering

While Jesus was in the Temple, he watched the rich people dropping their gifts in the collection box. 2 Then a poor widow came by and dropped in two small coins.

3 "I tell you the truth," Jesus said, "this poor widow has given more than all the rest of them. 4 For they have given a tiny part of their surplus, but she, poor as she is, has given everything she has."

Jesus Foretells the Future

5 Some of his disciples began talking about the majestic stonework of the Temple and the memorial decorations on the walls. But Jesus said, 6 "The time is coming when all these things will be completely demolished. Not one stone will be left on top of another!"

7 "Teacher," they asked, "when will all this happen? What sign will show us that these things are about to take place?"

8 He replied, "Don't let anyone mislead you, for many will come in my name, claiming, 'I am the Messiah,' and saying, 'The time has come!' But don't believe them. 9 And when you hear of wars and insurrections, don't panic. Yes, these things must take place first, but the end won't follow immediately." 10 Then he added, "Nation will go to war against nation, and kingdom against kingdom. 11 There will be great earthquakes, and there will be famines and plagues in many lands, and there will be terrifying things and great miraculous signs from heaven.

12 "But before all this occurs, there will be a time of great persecution. You will be dragged into synagogues and prisons, and you will stand trial before kings and governors because you are my followers. 13 But this will be your opportunity to tell them about me. 14 So don't worry in advance about how to answer the charges against you, 15 for I will give you the right words and such wisdom that none of your opponents will be able to reply or refute you! 16 Even those closest to you—your parents, brothers, relatives, and friends—will betray you. They will even kill some of you. 17 And everyone will hate you because you are my followers. 18 But not a hair of your head will perish! 19 By standing firm, you will win your souls.

20 "And when you see Jerusalem surrounded by armies, then you will know that the time of its destruction has arrived. 21 Then those in Judea must flee to the hills. Those in Jerusalem must get out, and those out in the country should not return to the city. 22 For those will be days of God's vengeance, and the prophetic words of the Scriptures will be fulfilled. 23 How terrible it will be for pregnant women and for nursing mothers in those days. For there will be disaster in the land and great anger against this people. 24 They will be killed by the sword or sent away as captives to all the nations of the world. And Jerusalem will be trampled down by the Gentiles until the period of the Gentiles comes to an end.

25 "And there will be strange signs in the sun, moon, and stars. And here on earth the nations will be in turmoil, perplexed by the roaring seas and strange tides. 26 People will be terrified at what they see coming upon the earth, for the powers in the heavens will be shaken. 27 Then everyone will see the Son of Man coming on a cloud with power and great glory. 28 So when all these things begin to happen, stand and look up, for your salvation is near!"

29 Then he gave them this illustration: "Notice the fig tree, or any other tree. 30 When the leaves come out, you know without being told that summer is near. 31 In the same way, when you see all these things taking place, you can know that the Kingdom of God is near. 32 I tell you the truth, this generation will not pass from the scene until all these things have taken place. 33 Heaven and earth will disappear, but my words will never disappear.

34 "Watch out! Don't let your hearts be dulled by carousing and drunkenness, and by the worries of this life. Don't let that day catch you unaware, 35 like a trap. For that day will come upon everyone living on the earth. 36 Keep alert at all times. And pray that you might be strong enough to escape these coming horrors and stand before the Son of Man."

37 Every day Jesus went to the Temple to teach, and each evening he returned to spend the night on the Mount of Olives. 38 The crowds gathered at the Temple early each morning to hear him.

CHAPTER 22

Judas Agrees to Betray Jesus

The Festival of Unleavened Bread, which is also called Passover, was approaching. 2 The leading priests and teachers of religious law were plotting how to kill Jesus, but they were afraid of the people's reaction.

3 Then Satan entered into Judas Iscariot, who was one of the twelve disciples, 4 and he went to the leading priests and captains of the Temple guard to discuss the best way to betray Jesus to them. 5 They were delighted, and they promised

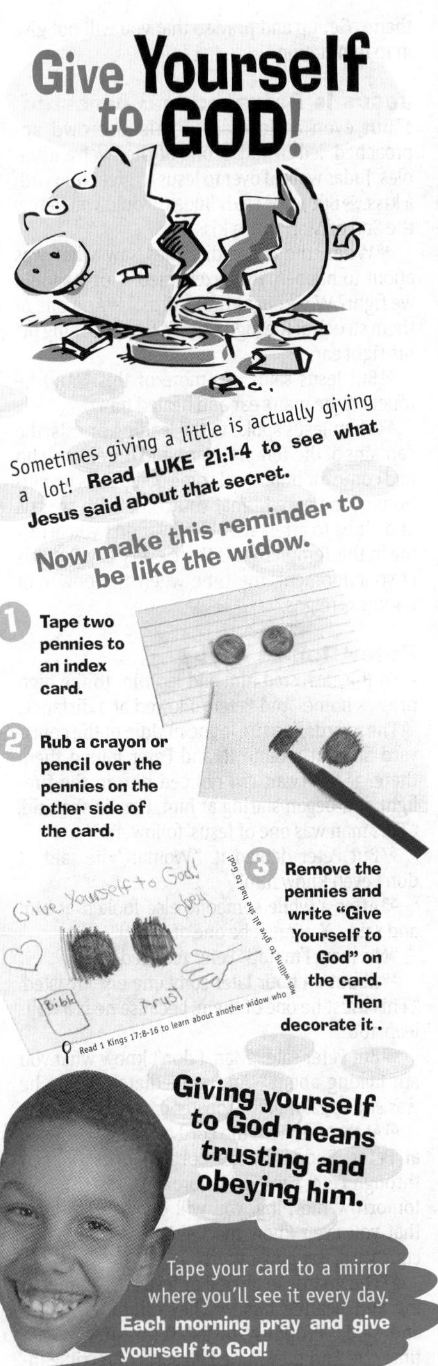

to give him money. 6So he agreed and began
looking for an opportunity to betray Jesus so
they could arrest him when the crowds weren't
around.

Give Yourself to GOD!
Sometimes giving a little is actually giving a lot! Read LUKE 21:1-4 to see what Jesus said about that secret.
Now make this reminder to be like the widow.
1 Tape two pennies to an index card.
2 Rub a crayon or pencil over the pennies on the other side of the card.
3 Remove the pennies and write "Give Yourself to God" on the card. Then decorate it .
Give Yourself to God!
obey
Bible
trust
Read 1 Kings 17:8-16 to learn about another widow who was willing to give all she had to God!
Giving yourself to God means trusting and obeying him.
Tape your card to a mirror where you'll see it every day.
Each morning pray and give yourself to God!

The Last Supper

7Now the Festival of Unleavened Bread arrived,
when the Passover lamb is sacrificed. 8Jesus sent
Peter and John ahead and said, "Go and prepare
the Passover meal, so we can eat it together."

9"Where do you want us to prepare it?" they
asked him.

10He replied, "As soon as you enter Jerusalem,
a man carrying a pitcher of water will meet you.
Follow him. At the house he enters, 11say to the
owner, 'The Teacher asks: Where is the guest
room where I can eat the Passover meal with my
disciples?' 12He will take you upstairs to a large
room that is already set up. That is where you
should prepare our meal." 13They went off to the
city and found everything just as Jesus had said,
and they prepared the Passover meal there.

14When the time came, Jesus and the apostles
sat down together at the table. 15Jesus said, "I
have been very eager to eat this Passover meal
with you before my suffering begins. 16For I tell
you now that I won't eat this meal again until its
meaning is fulfilled in the Kingdom of God."

17Then he took a cup of wine and gave thanks
to God for it. Then he said, "Take this and share it
among yourselves. 18For I will not drink wine
again until the Kingdom of God has come."

19He took some bread and gave thanks to God
for it. Then he broke it in pieces and gave it to
the disciples, saying, "This is my body, which is
given for you. Do this to remember me."

20After supper he took another cup of wine
and said, "This cup is the new covenant between
God and his people—an agreement confirmed
with my blood, which is poured out as a sacrifice
for you.

21"But here at this table, sitting among us as a
friend, is the man who will betray me. 22For it has
been determined that the Son of Man must die.
But what sorrow awaits the one who betrays
him." 23The disciples began to ask each other
which of them would ever do such a thing.

24Then they began to argue among themselves about who would be the greatest among
them. 25Jesus told them, "In this world the kings
and great men lord it over their people, yet they
are called 'friends of the people.' 26But among
you it will be different. Those who are the greatest among you should take the lowest rank, and
the leader should be like a servant. 27Who is

more important, the one who sits at the table
or the one who serves? The one who sits at the
table, of course. But not here! For I am among you
as one who serves.
28"You have stayed with me in my time of trial.
29And just as my Father has granted me a Kingdom, I now grant you the right 30to eat and drink
at my table in my Kingdom. And you will sit on
thrones, judging the twelve tribes of Israel.

Jesus Predicts Peter's Denial

31"Simon, Simon, Satan has asked to sift each of
you like wheat. 32But I have pleaded in prayer for
you, Simon, that your faith should not fail. So
when you have repented and turned to me again,
strengthen your brothers."
33Peter said, "Lord, I am ready to go to prison
with you, and even to die with you."
34But Jesus said, "Peter, let me tell you something. Before the rooster crows tomorrow morning, you will deny three times that you even
know me."
35Then Jesus asked them, "When I sent you
out to preach the Good News and you did not
have money, a traveler's bag, or an extra pair of
sandals, did you need anything?"
"No," they replied.
36"But now," he said, "take your money and a
traveler's bag. And if you don't have a sword, sell
your cloak and buy one! 37For the time has come
for this prophecy about me to be fulfilled: 'He
was counted among the rebels.' Yes, everything
written about me by the prophets will come
true."
38"Look, Lord," they replied, "we have two
swords among us."
"That's enough," he said.

Jesus Prays on the Mount of Olives

39Then, accompanied by the disciples, Jesus left
the upstairs room and went as usual to the
Mount of Olives. 40There he told them, "Pray that
you will not give in to temptation."
41He walked away, about a stone's throw, and
knelt down and prayed, 42"Father, if you are willing, please take this cup of suffering away from
me. Yet I want your will to be done, not mine."
43Then an angel from heaven appeared and
strengthened him. 44He prayed more fervently,
and he was in such agony of spirit that his sweat
fell to the ground like great drops of blood.
45At last he stood up again and returned to the
disciples, only to find them asleep, exhausted
from grief. 46"Why are you sleeping?" he asked
them. "Get up and pray, so that you will not give
in to temptation."

Jesus Is Betrayed and Arrested

47But even as Jesus said this, a crowd approached, led by Judas, one of the twelve disciples. Judas walked over to Jesus to greet him with
a kiss. 48But Jesus said, "Judas, would you betray
the Son of Man with a kiss?"
49When the other disciples saw what was
about to happen, they exclaimed, "Lord, should
we fight? We brought the swords!" 50And one of
them struck at the high priest's slave, slashing off
his right ear.
51But Jesus said, "No more of this." And he
touched the man's ear and healed him.
52Then Jesus spoke to the leading priests, the
captains of the Temple guard, and the elders who
had come for him. "Am I some dangerous revolutionary," he asked, "that you come with swords
and clubs to arrest me? 53Why didn't you arrest
me in the Temple? I was there every day. But this
is your moment, the time when the power of
darkness reigns."

Peter Denies Jesus

54So they arrested him and led him to the high
priest's home. And Peter followed at a distance.
55The guards lit a fire in the middle of the courtyard and sat around it, and Peter joined them
there. 56A servant girl noticed him in the firelight and began staring at him. Finally she said,
"This man was one of Jesus' followers!"
57But Peter denied it. "Woman," he said, "I
don't even know him!"
58After a while someone else looked at him
and said, "You must be one of them!"
"No, man, I'm not!" Peter retorted.
59About an hour later someone else insisted,
"This must be one of them, because he is a Galilean, too."
60But Peter said, "Man, I don't know what you
are talking about." And immediately, while he
was still speaking, the rooster crowed.
61At that moment the Lord turned and looked
at Peter. Suddenly, the Lord's words flashed
through Peter's mind: "Before the rooster crows
tomorrow morning, you will deny three times
that you even know me." 62And Peter left the
courtyard, weeping bitterly.
63The guards in charge of Jesus began mocking and beating him. 64They blindfolded him
and said, "Prophesy to us! Who hit you that
time?" 65And they hurled all sorts of terrible insults at him.

Jesus before the Council

66 At daybreak all the elders of the people assembled, including the leading priests and the teachers of religious law. Jesus was led before this high
council, 67 and they said, "Tell us, are you the
Messiah?"

But he replied, "If I tell you, you won't believe
me. 68 And if I ask you a question, you won't answer. 69 But from now on the Son of Man will be
seated in the place of power at God's right hand."
70 They all shouted, "So, are you claiming to be
the Son of God?"

And he replied, "You say that I am."
71 "Why do we need other witnesses?" they
said. "We ourselves heard him say it."

CHAPTER **23**

Jesus' Trial before Pilate

Then the entire council took Jesus to Pilate, the
Roman governor. 2 They began to state their case:
"This man has been leading our people astray by
telling them not to pay their taxes to the Roman
government and by claiming he is the Messiah,
a king."
3 So Pilate asked him, "Are you the king of the
Jews?"

Jesus replied, "You have said it."
4 Pilate turned to the leading priests and to the
crowd and said, "I find nothing wrong with this
man!"
5 Then they became insistent. "But he is causing riots by his teaching wherever he goes—all
over Judea, from Galilee to Jerusalem!"
6 "Oh, is he a Galilean?" Pilate asked. 7 When
they said that he was, Pilate sent him to Herod
Antipas, because Galilee was under Herod's ju-
risdiction, and Herod happened to be in Jerusalem at the time.
8 Herod was delighted at the opportunity to see
Jesus, because he had heard about him and had
been hoping for a long time to see him perform a
miracle. 9 He asked Jesus question after question,
but Jesus refused to answer. 10 Meanwhile, the
leading priests and the teachers of religious law
stood there shouting their accusations. 11 Then
Herod and his soldiers began mocking and ridiculing Jesus. Finally, they put a royal robe on him
and sent him back to Pilate. 12 (Herod and Pilate,
who had been enemies before, became friends
that day.)
13 Then Pilate called together the leading
priests and other religious leaders, along with the
people, 14 and he announced his verdict. "You
brought this man to me, accusing him of leading
a revolt. I have examined him thoroughly on
this point in your presence and find him innocent. 15 Herod came to the same conclusion and
sent him back to us. Nothing this man has done
calls for the death penalty. 16 So I will have him
flogged, and then I will release him."*
18 Then a mighty roar rose from the crowd,
and with one voice they shouted, "Kill him, and
release Barabbas to us!" 19 (Barabbas was in
prison for taking part in an insurrection in Jerusalem against the government, and for murder.)
20 Pilate argued with them, because he wanted to
release Jesus. 21 But they kept shouting, "Crucify
him! Crucify him!"
22 For the third time he demanded, "Why?
What crime has he committed? I have found no
reason to sentence him to death. So I will have
him flogged, and then I will release him."
23 But the mob shouted louder and louder,
demanding that Jesus be crucified, and their
voices prevailed. 24 So Pilate sentenced Jesus to
die as they demanded. 25 As they had requested,
he released Barabbas, the man in prison for insurrection and murder. But he turned Jesus over
to them to do as they wished.

The Crucifixion

26 As they led Jesus away, a man named Simon,
who was from Cyrene, happened to be coming in
from the countryside. The soldiers seized him
and put the cross on him and made him carry it
behind Jesus. 27 A large crowd trailed behind, including many grief-stricken women. 28 But Jesus
turned and said to them, "Daughters of Jerusalem, don't weep for me, but weep for yourselves
and for your children. 29 For the days are coming
when they will say, 'Fortunate indeed are the
women who are childless, the wombs that have
not borne a child and the breasts that have never
nursed.' 30 People will beg the mountains, 'Fall on
us,' and plead with the hills, 'Bury us.' 31 For if
these things are done when the tree is green,
what will happen when it is dry?"
32 Two others, both criminals, were led out to
be executed with him. 33 When they came to a
place called The Skull, they nailed him to the
cross. And the criminals were also crucified—
one on his right and one on his left.
34 Jesus said, "Father, forgive them, for they
don't know what they are doing." And the soldiers gambled for his clothes by throwing dice.
35 The crowd watched and the leaders scoffed.

23:16 Some manuscripts add verse 17, *Now it was necessary for him to release one prisoner to them during the Passover celebration*. Compare Matt 27:15; Mark 15:6; John 18:39.

"He saved others," they said, "let him save himself
if he is really God's Messiah, the Chosen One."
36The soldiers mocked him, too, by offering him a
drink of sour wine. 37They called out to him, "If
you are the King of the Jews, save yourself!" 38A
sign was fastened above him with these words:
"This is the King of the Jews."

39One of the criminals hanging beside him
scoffed, "So you're the Messiah, are you? Prove
it by saving yourself—and us, too, while you're
at it!"

40But the other criminal protested, "Don't you
fear God even when you have been sentenced to
die? 41We deserve to die for our crimes, but this
man hasn't done anything wrong." 42Then he
said, "Jesus, remember me when you come into
your Kingdom."

43And Jesus replied, "I assure you, today you
will be with me in paradise."

The Death of Jesus

44By this time it was about noon, and darkness
fell across the whole land until three o'clock.
45The light from the sun was gone. And suddenly,
the curtain in the sanctuary of the Temple was
torn down the middle. 46Then Jesus shouted,
"Father, I entrust my spirit into your hands!" And
with those words he breathed his last.

47When the Roman officer overseeing the execution saw what had happened, he worshiped
God and said, "Surely this man was innocent."
48And when all the crowd that came to see the
crucifixion saw what had happened, they went
home in deep sorrow. 49But Jesus' friends, including the women who had followed him from
Galilee, stood at a distance watching.

The Burial of Jesus

50Now there was a good and righteous man
named Joseph. He was a member of the Jewish
high council, 51but he had not agreed with the
decision and actions of the other religious leaders. He was from the town of Arimathea in
Judea, and he was waiting for the Kingdom of
God to come. 52He went to Pilate and asked for
Jesus' body. 53Then he took the body down from
the cross and wrapped it in a long sheet of linen
cloth and laid it in a new tomb that had been
carved out of rock. 54This was done late on
Friday afternoon, the day of preparation, as the
Sabbath was about to begin.

55As his body was taken away, the women
from Galilee followed and saw the tomb where
his body was placed. 56Then they went home
and prepared spices and ointments to anoint his
body. But by the time they were finished the
Sabbath had begun, so they rested as required
by the law.

CHAPTER 24

The Resurrection

But very early on Sunday morning the women
went to the tomb, taking the spices they had prepared. 2They found that the stone had been
rolled away from the entrance. 3So they went in,
but they didn't find the body of the Lord Jesus.
4As they stood there puzzled, two men suddenly
appeared to them, clothed in dazzling robes.

5The women were terrified and bowed with
their faces to the ground. Then the men asked,
"Why are you looking among the dead for
someone who is alive? 6He isn't here! He is risen
from the dead! Remember what he told you
back in Galilee, 7that the Son of Man must be
betrayed into the hands of sinful men and be
crucified, and that he would rise again on the
third day."

8Then they remembered that he had said this.
9So they rushed back from the tomb to tell his
eleven disciples—and everyone else—what had
happened. 10It was Mary Magdalene, Joanna,
Mary the mother of James, and several other
women who told the apostles what had happened. 11But the story sounded like nonsense to
the men, so they didn't believe it. 12However,
Peter jumped up and ran to the tomb to look.
Stooping, he peered in and saw the empty linen
wrappings; then he went home again, wondering what had happened.

The Walk to Emmaus

13That same day two of Jesus' followers were
walking to the village of Emmaus, seven miles
from Jerusalem. 14As they walked along they
were talking about everything that had happened. 15As they talked and discussed these
things, Jesus himself suddenly came and began
walking with them. 16But God kept them from
recognizing him.

17He asked them, "What are you discussing so
intently as you walk along?"

They stopped short, sadness written across
their faces. 18Then one of them, Cleopas, replied,
"You must be the only person in Jerusalem who
hasn't heard about all the things that have happened there the last few days."

19"What things?" Jesus asked.

"The things that happened to Jesus, the man
from Nazareth," they said. "He was a prophet
who did powerful miracles, and he was a mighty

teacher in the eyes of God and all the people. 20 But our leading priests and other religious leaders handed him over to be condemned to death, and they crucified him. 21 We had hoped he was the Messiah who had come to rescue Israel. This all happened three days ago.

22 "Then some women from our group of his followers were at his tomb early this morning, and they came back with an amazing report. 23 They said his body was missing, and they had seen angels who told them Jesus is alive! 24 Some of our men ran out to see, and sure enough, his body was gone, just as the women had said."

25 Then Jesus said to them, "You foolish people! You find it so hard to believe all that the prophets wrote in the Scriptures. 26 Wasn't it clearly predicted that the Messiah would have to suffer all these things before entering his glory?" 27 Then Jesus took them through the writings of Moses and all the prophets, explaining from all the Scriptures the things concerning himself.

28 By this time they were nearing Emmaus and the end of their journey. Jesus acted as if he were going on, 29 but they begged him, "Stay the night with us, since it is getting late." So he went home with them. 30 As they sat down to eat, he took the bread and blessed it. Then he broke it and gave it to them. 31 Suddenly, their eyes were opened, and they recognized him. And at that moment he disappeared!

32 They said to each other, "Didn't our hearts burn within us as he talked with us on the road and explained the Scriptures to us?" 33 And within the hour they were on their way back to Jerusalem. There they found the eleven disciples and the others who had gathered with them, 34 who said, "The Lord has really risen! He appeared to Peter."

Jesus Appears to the Disciples

35 Then the two from Emmaus told their story of how Jesus had appeared to them as they were walking along the road, and how they had recognized him as he was breaking the bread. 36 And just as they were telling about it, Jesus himself was suddenly standing there among them. "Peace be with you," he said. 37 But the whole group was startled and frightened, thinking they were seeing a ghost!

38 "Why are you frightened?" he asked. "Why are your hearts filled with doubt? 39 Look at my hands. Look at my feet. You can see that it's really me. Touch me and make sure that I am not a ghost, because ghosts don't have bodies, as you see that I do." 40 As he spoke, he showed them his hands and his feet.

41 Still they stood there in disbelief, filled with joy and wonder. Then he asked them, "Do you have anything here to eat?" 42 They gave him a piece of broiled fish, 43 and he ate it as they watched.

44 Then he said, "When I was with you before, I told you that everything written about me in the law of Moses and the prophets and in the Psalms must be fulfilled." 45 Then he opened their minds to understand the Scriptures. 46 And he said, "Yes, it was written long ago that the Messiah would suffer and die and rise from the dead on the third day. 47 It was also written that this message would be proclaimed in the authority of his name to all the nations, beginning in Jerusalem: 'There is forgiveness of sins for all who repent.' 48 You are witnesses of all these things.

49 "And now I will send the Holy Spirit, just as my Father promised. But stay here in the city until the Holy Spirit comes and fills you with power from heaven."

The Ascension

50 Then Jesus led them to Bethany, and lifting his hands to heaven, he blessed them. 51 While he was blessing them, he left them and was taken up to heaven. 52 So they worshiped him and then returned to Jerusalem filled with great joy. 53 And they spent all of their time in the Temple, praising God.

JOHN Jesus Is the Son of God!

Look for 3 hidden messages in John!

All of the Gospels reveal that Jesus is the Son of God. But the book of John really focuses on that fact. John also tells about some miracles Jesus did that the other Gospels don't mention. Look for

- **WATER TO WINE**
- **MUD IN YOUR EYE**
- **A SUPER SUPPER**
- **A FISHING FRENZY**
- **EMPTY TOMBS**

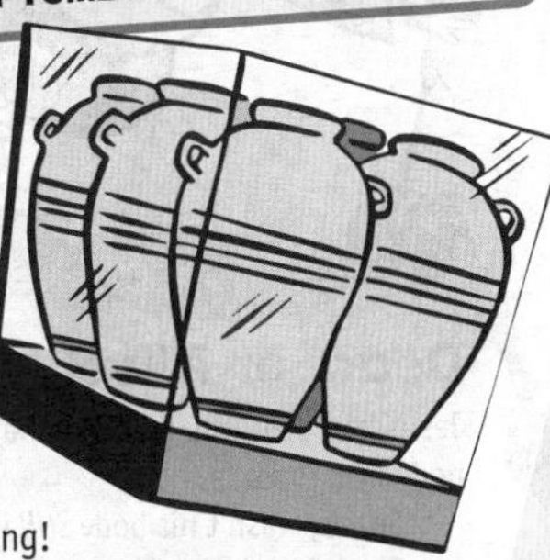

It's Not the Pots!

What's so special about these stone pots? Nothing!

But something special happened *in* the pots. **Find out what it was by reading John 2:1-11.**

Here's Mud in Your Eye

Take one blind man. Add one part dirt, two parts spit, and, oh yeah, the one and only Son of God, and what do you get? **Find out in John 9:1-12! (For the whole story, read the whole chapter.)**

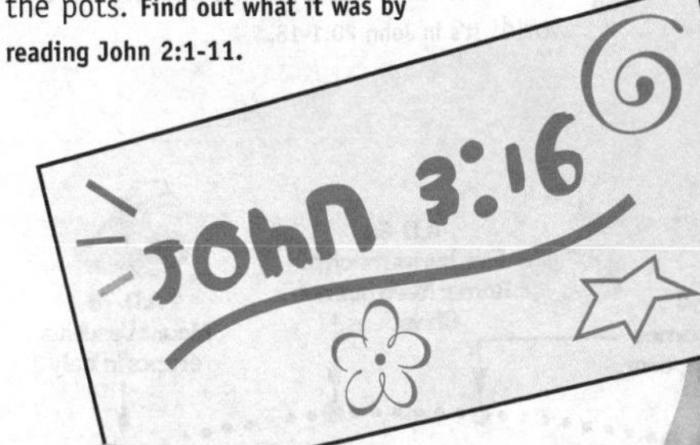

This Says It All

Did you ever wish for a Bible verse that sums it all up for you?

Have you ever wanted to tell someone about your faith but didn't know quite what to say?

Does God have a verse for you! **Check it out in John 3:16!**

HEY, Wasn't This Guy Dead?

The obituary that said "Lazarus Dies" was wrong. Well, it was right for a while, because he *did* die. But he didn't *stay* dead. Confused? **You won't be after you read John 11:38-44!**

A Special Supper

It was a special supper because it was the Passover meal. It was even more special because it was the last supper they would share together. And it was even *more* special because of what Jesus did at this supper. **Get all the details in John 13:1-20!**

Which room is Mine?!

Go to Your Room

In heaven, going to your room will be a good thing! **Read all about it in John 14:1-3.**

Dead...or Alive!

Jesus had died. His followers had placed his body in a tomb.

So why wasn't his body *still* in the tomb?

Read John's eyewitness account of the most amazing event in the history of the world! **It's in John 20:1-18.**

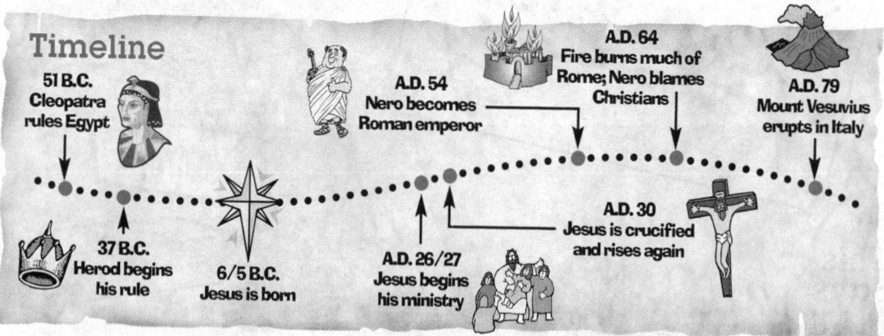
Timeline
51 B.C. Cleopatra rules Egypt
37 B.C. Herod begins his rule
6/5 B.C. Jesus is born
A.D. 26/27 Jesus begins his ministry
A.D. 30 Jesus is crucified and rises again
A.D. 54 Nero becomes Roman emperor
A.D. 64 Fire burns much of Rome; Nero blames Christians
A.D. 79 Mount Vesuvius erupts in Italy

The JESUS CONNECTION

The book of John shows without question who Jesus really is—the Son of God, the living Savior! As you read this book, remember that the powerful Savior who once walked on earth and did many miracles is still with us today. He is powerful and loving enough to help you through tough times. And more than anything, he wants to have a relationship with you. **Ask God to help you get to know and love his Son more and more.**

CHAPTER 1

Prologue: Christ, the Eternal Word

1In the beginning the Word
already existed.
The Word was with God,
and the Word was God.
2He existed in the beginning
with God.
3God created everything through him,
and nothing was created except
through him.
4The Word gave life to everything that
was created,
and his life brought light to everyone.
5The light shines in the darkness,
and the darkness can never extinguish it.

6God sent a man, John the Baptist, 7to tell
about the light so that everyone might believe
because of his testimony. 8John himself was not
the light; he was simply a witness to tell about the
light. 9The one who is the true light, who gives
light to everyone, was coming into the world.

10He came into the very world he created, but
the world didn't recognize him. 11He came to his
own people, and even they rejected him. 12But to
all who believed him and accepted him, he gave
the right to become children of God. 13They are
reborn—not with a physical birth resulting from
human passion or plan, but a birth that comes
from God.

14So the Word became human and
made his home among us. He was
full of unfailing love and faithful-
ness. And we have seen his glory,
the glory of the Father's one and
only Son.

15John testified about him when he shouted
to the crowds, "This is the one I was talking
about when I said, 'Someone is coming after me
who is far greater than I am, for he existed long
before me.'"

16From his abundance we have all received
one gracious blessing after another. 17For the
law was given through Moses, but God's unfailing love and faithfulness came through Jesus
Christ. 18No one has ever seen God. But the
unique One, who is himself God, is near to the
Father's heart. He has revealed God to us.

The Testimony of John the Baptist

19This was John's testimony when the Jewish
leaders sent priests and Temple assistants from
Jerusalem to ask John, "Who are you?" 20He
came right out and said, "I am not the Messiah."

21"Well then, who are you?" they asked. "Are
you Elijah?"

"No," he replied.

"Are you the Prophet we are expecting?"

"No."

22"Then who are you? We need an answer for
those who sent us. What do you have to say about
yourself?"

23John replied in the words of the prophet Isaiah:

"I am a voice shouting in the wilderness,
'Clear the way for the LORD's coming!'"

24Then the Pharisees who had been sent
25asked him, "If you aren't the Messiah or Elijah
or the Prophet, what right do you have to baptize?"

26John told them, "I baptize with water, but
right here in the crowd is someone you do not
recognize. 27Though his ministry follows mine,
I'm not even worthy to be his slave and untie the
straps of his sandal."

28This encounter took place in Bethany, an
area east of the Jordan River, where John was
baptizing.

Jesus, the Lamb of God

29The next day John saw Jesus coming toward
him and said, "Look! The Lamb of God who
takes away the sin of the world! 30He is the one I
was talking about when I said, 'A man is coming
after me who is far greater than I am, for he existed long before me.' 31I did not recognize him
as the Messiah, but I have been baptizing with
water so that he might be revealed to Israel."

32Then John testified, "I saw the Holy Spirit
descending like a dove from heaven and resting
upon him. 33I didn't know he was the one,
but when God sent me to baptize with water, he
told me, 'The one on whom you see the Spirit
descend and rest is the one who will baptize
with the Holy Spirit.' 34I saw this happen to
Jesus, so I testify that he is the Chosen One of
God."

The First Disciples

35The following day John was again standing
with two of his disciples. 36As Jesus walked by,
John looked at him and declared, "Look! There is
the Lamb of God!" 37When John's two disciples
heard this, they followed Jesus.

38Jesus looked around and saw them following. "What do you want?" he asked them.

"In the beginning the Word already existed. The Word was with God, and the Word was God."—JOHN 1:1

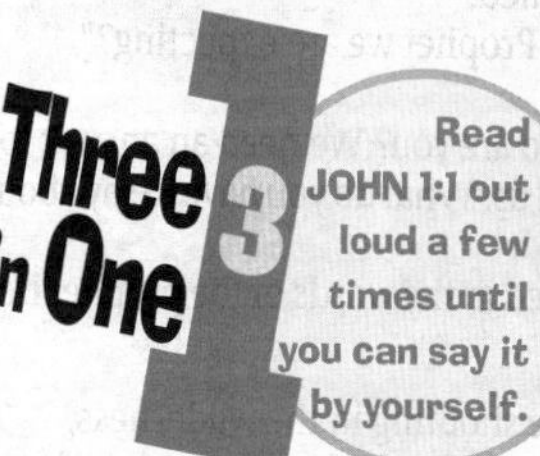

Read JOHN 1:1 out loud a few times until you can say it by yourself.

What do you think this verse means? Well, first of all, "the Word" means Jesus. Read the verse again, substituting "Jesus" for "the Word."

Then do this experiment to help you understand the meaning of the verse.

1. **Have an adult help you to carefully fill a clean, empty plastic bottle about one-third full with hot water.**
2. **Place an ice cube over the opening of the bottle.**

Read Revelation 19:13 for more on Jesus as the Word of God.

Fog begins to develop. That's three different forms of water—fog, ice, and water—but they're all still water. It's sort of the same with God, Jesus, and the Holy Spirit. All three are God, but each is a distinct person. **Now read JOHN 1:1 again, and then read JOHN 1:14.** Below, write the verses in your own words.

____

____

____

They replied, "Rabbi" (which means "Teacher"),
"where are you staying?"
39"Come and see," he said. It was about four
o'clock in the afternoon when they went with
him to the place where he was staying, and they
remained with him the rest of the day.
40Andrew, Simon Peter's brother, was one of
these men who heard what John said and then
followed Jesus. 41Andrew went to find his
brother, Simon, and told him, "We have found
the Messiah" (which means "Christ").
42Then Andrew brought Simon to meet Jesus.
Looking intently at Simon, Jesus said, "Your
name is Simon, son of John—but you will be
called Cephas" (which means "Peter").
43The next day Jesus decided to go to Galilee.
He found Philip and said to him, "Come, follow
me." 44Philip was from Bethsaida, Andrew and
Peter's hometown.
45Philip went to look for Nathanael and told
him, "We have found the very person Moses and
the prophets wrote about! His name is Jesus, the
son of Joseph from Nazareth."
46"Nazareth!" exclaimed Nathanael. "Can anything good come from Nazareth?"
"Come and see for yourself," Philip replied.
47As they approached, Jesus said, "Now here
is a genuine son of Israel—a man of complete
integrity."
48"How do you know about me?" Nathanael
asked.
Jesus replied, "I could see you under the fig
tree before Philip found you."
49Then Nathanael exclaimed, "Rabbi, you are
the Son of God—the King of Israel!"
50Jesus asked him, "Do you believe this just
because I told you I had seen you under the fig
tree? You will see greater things than this."
51Then he said, "I tell you the truth, you will all
see heaven open and the angels of God going up
and down on the Son of Man, the one who is the
stairway between heaven and earth."

CHAPTER **2**

The Wedding at Cana

The next day there was a wedding celebration in
the village of Cana in Galilee. Jesus' mother was
there, 2and Jesus and his disciples were also invited to the celebration. 3The wine supply ran
out during the festivities, so Jesus' mother told
him, "They have no more wine."
4"Dear woman, that's not our problem," Jesus
replied. "My time has not yet come."
5But his mother told the servants, "Do whatever he tells you."

[6]Standing nearby were six stone water jars,
used for Jewish ceremonial washing. Each could
hold twenty to thirty gallons. [7]Jesus told the servants, "Fill the jars with water." When the jars
had been filled, [8]he said, "Now dip some out, and
take it to the master of ceremonies." So the servants followed his instructions.
[9]When the master of ceremonies tasted the
water that was now wine, not knowing where it
had come from (though, of course, the servants
knew), he called the bridegroom over. [10]"A host
always serves the best wine first," he said. "Then,
when everyone has had a lot to drink, he brings
out the less expensive wine. But you have kept
the best until now!"
[11]This miraculous sign at Cana in Galilee was
the first time Jesus revealed his glory. And his
disciples believed in him.
[12]After the wedding he went to Capernaum
for a few days with his mother, his brothers, and
his disciples.

Jesus Clears the Temple

[13]It was nearly time for the Jewish Passover celebration, so Jesus went to Jerusalem. [14]In the
Temple area he saw merchants selling cattle,
sheep, and doves for sacrifices; he also saw deal-
ers at tables exchanging foreign money. [15]Jesus
made a whip from some ropes and chased them
all out of the Temple. He drove out the sheep and
cattle, scattered the money changers' coins over
the floor, and turned over their tables. [16]Then,
going over to the people who sold doves, he told
them, "Get these things out of here. Stop turning
my Father's house into a marketplace!"
[17]Then his disciples remembered this prophecy from the Scriptures: "Passion for God's house
will consume me."
[18]But the Jewish leaders demanded, "What
are you doing? If God gave you authority to do
this, show us a miraculous sign to prove it."
[19]"All right," Jesus replied. "Destroy this temple, and in three days I will raise it up."
[20]"What!" they exclaimed. "It has taken forty-
six years to build this Temple, and you can rebuild it in three days?" [21]But when Jesus said
"this temple," he meant his own body. [22]After he
was raised from the dead, his disciples remembered he had said this, and they believed both
the Scriptures and what Jesus had said.

Jesus and Nicodemus

[23]Because of the miraculous signs Jesus did in
Jerusalem at the Passover celebration, many
began to trust in him. [24]But Jesus didn't trust

A Wonderful Wedding

Find JOHN 2:1-12, and read about Jesus' very first miracle!

Jesus turned water into wine. You can't do that, but you *can* turn something red. Here's how!

Have an adult help gather these supplies:

- **shallow pan**
- **small bowl**
- **1/4 cup liquid dish soap**
- **1/2 cup vinegar**
- **1 tablespoon baking soda**
- **1 cup water**
- **1 packet of red powdered drink mix**

Cover a table with newspaper.

1. **Pour the dish soap and vinegar into the bowl, and set it inside the shallow pan.**
2. **In a separate container, add the baking soda to the water and stir. Sprinkle some of the powdered drink mix into the water and baking soda until it turns dark red like wine.**
3. **Slowly pour the water mixture into the soap and vinegar mixture, and watch as it erupts into a foaming red volcano!**

SURPRISED?

The chemical reaction that made your cool red volcano was *nothing* compared to Jesus turning water into wine!

Use the red foam and a paintbrush to paint the words, **"Jesus can do anything!"** on a sheet of paper. Hang the paper in your room to remind you of Jesus' first miracle!

them, because he knew all about people. 25No
one needed to tell him about human nature, for
he knew what was in each person's heart.

CHAPTER 3

There was a man named Nicodemus, a Jewish religious leader who was a Pharisee. 2After dark
one evening, he came to speak with Jesus. "Rabbi," he said, "we all know that God has sent you to
teach us. Your miraculous signs are evidence that
God is with you."

3Jesus replied, "I tell you the truth, unless you
are born again, you cannot see the Kingdom of
God."

4"What do you mean?" exclaimed Nicodemus. "How can an old man go back into his
mother's womb and be born again?"

5Jesus replied, "I assure you, no one can enter
the Kingdom of God without being born of water
and the Spirit. 6Humans can reproduce only human life, but the Holy Spirit gives birth to spiritual
life. 7So don't be surprised when I say, 'You must
be born again.' 8The wind blows wherever it
wants. Just as you can hear the wind but can't tell
where it comes from or where it is going, so you
can't explain how people are born of the Spirit."

9"How are these things possible?" Nicodemus
asked.

10Jesus replied, "You are a respected Jewish
teacher, and yet you don't understand these
things? 11I assure you, we tell you what we know
and have seen, and yet you won't believe our testimony. 12But if you don't believe me when I tell
you about earthly things, how can you possibly
believe if I tell you about heavenly things? 13No
one has ever gone to heaven and returned. But
the Son of Man has come down from heaven.
14And as Moses lifted up the bronze snake on a
pole in the wilderness, so the Son of Man must
be lifted up, 15so that everyone who believes in
him will have eternal life.

16**"For this is how God loved the
world: He gave his one and only Son,
so that everyone who believes in him
will not perish but have eternal life.**
17God sent his Son into the world not to judge the
world, but to save the world through him.

18"There is no judgment against anyone who
believes in him. But anyone who does not believe
in him has already been judged for not believing
in God's one and only Son. 19And the judgment is
based on this fact: God's light came into the
world, but people loved the darkness more than
the light, for their actions were evil. 20All who do
evil hate the light and refuse to go near it for fear

Key Verse **"For God loved the world so much that he gave his one and only Son, so that everyone who believes in him will not perish but have eternal life."—JOHN 3:16**

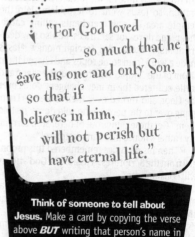

Read JOHN 3:16 a bunch of times. Practice saying it out loud too.

God loves us, he sent his Son to save us, and if we believe in Jesus we'll have eternal life with him.

Just so you *really* understand this verse, fill in your name in the blanks below.

"For God loved
_______ so much that he
gave his one and only Son,
so that if _______
believes in him, _______
will not perish but
have eternal life."

Think of someone to tell about Jesus. Make a card by copying the verse above ***BUT*** writing that person's name in the blanks. Mail your card, or deliver it in person!

their sins will be exposed. 21But those who do
what is right come to the light so others can see
that they are doing what God wants."

John the Baptist Exalts Jesus

22Then Jesus and his disciples left Jerusalem and
went into the Judean countryside. Jesus spent
some time with them there, baptizing people.

23At this time John the Baptist was baptizing
at Aenon, near Salim, because there was plenty of
water there; and people kept coming to him for
baptism. 24(This was before John was thrown
into prison.) 25A debate broke out between
John's disciples and a certain Jew over ceremonial cleansing. 26So John's disciples came to him
and said, "Rabbi, the man you met on the other
side of the Jordan River, the one you identified as
the Messiah, is also baptizing people. And everybody is going to him instead of coming to us."

27John replied, "No one can receive anything
unless God gives it from heaven. 28You yourselves know how plainly I told you, 'I am not the
Messiah. I am only here to prepare the way for
him.' 29It is the bridegroom who marries the
bride, and the best man is simply glad to stand
with him and hear his vows. Therefore, I am
filled with joy at his success. 30He must become greater and greater, and I must become
less and less.

31"He has come from above and is greater
than anyone else. We are of the earth, and we
speak of earthly things, but he has come from
heaven and is greater than anyone else. 32He
testifies about what he has seen and heard, but
how few believe what he tells them! 33Anyone
who accepts his testimony can affirm that God
is true. 34For he is sent by God. He speaks God's
words, for God gives him the Spirit without
limit. 35The Father loves his Son and has put
everything into his hands. 36And anyone who
believes in God's Son has eternal life. Anyone
who doesn't obey the Son will never experience
eternal life but remains under God's angry
judgment."

CHAPTER 4

Jesus and the Samaritan Woman

Jesus knew the Pharisees had heard that he was
baptizing and making more disciples than John
2(though Jesus himself didn't baptize them—his
disciples did). 3So he left Judea and returned to
Galilee.

4He had to go through Samaria on the way.
5Eventually he came to the Samaritan village of
Sychar, near the field that Jacob gave to his son
Joseph. 6Jacob's well was there; and Jesus, tired
from the long walk, sat wearily beside the well
about noontime. 7Soon a Samaritan woman
came to draw water, and Jesus said to her, "Please
give me a drink." 8He was alone at the time because his disciples had gone into the village to
buy some food.

9The woman was surprised, for Jews refuse to
have anything to do with Samaritans. She said
to Jesus, "You are a Jew, and I am a Samaritan
woman. Why are you asking me for a drink?"

10Jesus replied, "If you only knew the gift God
has for you and who you are speaking to, you
would ask me, and I would give you living water."

11"But sir, you don't have a rope or a bucket,"
she said, "and this well is very deep. Where
would you get this living water? 12And besides,
do you think you're greater than our ancestor
Jacob, who gave us this well? How can you offer
better water than he and his sons and his animals enjoyed?"

13Jesus replied, "Anyone who drinks this water
will soon become thirsty again. 14But those who
drink the water I give will never be thirsty again.
It becomes a fresh, bubbling spring within them,
giving them eternal life."

15"Please, sir," the woman said, "give me this
water! Then I'll never be thirsty again, and I won't
have to come here to get water."

16"Go and get your husband," Jesus told her.

17"I don't have a husband," the woman
replied.

Jesus said, "You're right! You don't have a husband—18for you have had five husbands, and you
aren't even married to the man you're living with
now. You certainly spoke the truth!"

19"Sir," the woman said, "you must be a
prophet. 20So tell me, why is it that you Jews insist that Jerusalem is the only place of worship,
while we Samaritans claim it is here at Mount
Gerizim, where our ancestors worshiped?"

21Jesus replied, "Believe me, dear woman, the
time is coming when it will no longer matter
whether you worship the Father on this mountain or in Jerusalem. 22You Samaritans know
very little about the one you worship, while we
Jews know all about him, for salvation comes
through the Jews. 23But the time is coming—indeed it's here now—when true worshipers will
worship the Father in spirit and in truth. The
Father is looking for those who will worship
him that way. 24For God is Spirit, so those who
worship him must worship in spirit and in
truth."

25The woman said, "I know the Messiah is
coming—the one who is called Christ. When he
comes, he will explain everything to us."

26Then Jesus told her, "I Am the Messiah!"

27Just then his disciples came back. They
were shocked to find him talking to a woman,
but none of them had the nerve to ask, "What do
you want with her?" or "Why are you talking to

her?" 28The woman left her water jar beside the
well and ran back to the village, telling everyone,
29"Come and see a man who told me everything I
ever did! Could he possibly be the Messiah?"
30So the people came streaming from the village
to see him.

31Meanwhile, the disciples were urging Jesus,
"Rabbi, eat something."

32But Jesus replied, "I have a kind of food you
know nothing about."

33"Did someone bring him food while we
were gone?" the disciples asked each other.

34Then Jesus explained: "My nourishment
comes from doing the will of God, who sent me,
and from finishing his work. 35You know the saying, 'Four months between planting and harvest.'
But I say, wake up and look around. The fields are
already ripe for harvest. 36The harvesters are
paid good wages, and the fruit they harvest is
people brought to eternal life. What joy awaits
both the planter and the harvester alike! 37You
know the saying, 'One plants and another harvests.' And it's true. 38I sent you to harvest where
you didn't plant; others had already done the
work, and now you will get to gather the harvest."

Many Samaritans Believe

39Many Samaritans from the village believed in
Jesus because the woman had said, "He told me
everything I ever did!" 40When they came out to
see him, they begged him to stay in their village.
So he stayed for two days, 41long enough for
many more to hear his message and believe.
42Then they said to the woman, "Now we believe,
not just because of what you told us, but because
we have heard him ourselves. Now we know that
he is indeed the Savior of the world."

Jesus Heals an Official's Son

43At the end of the two days, Jesus went on to
Galilee. 44He himself had said that a prophet is
not honored in his own hometown. 45Yet the
Galileans welcomed him, for they had been in
Jerusalem at the Passover celebration and had
seen everything he did there.

46As he traveled through Galilee, he came to
Cana, where he had turned the water into wine.
There was a government official in nearby Capernaum whose son was very sick. 47When he
heard that Jesus had come from Judea to Galilee,
he went and begged Jesus to come to Capernaum
to heal his son, who was about to die.

48Jesus asked, "Will you never believe in me
unless you see miraculous signs and wonders?"

49The official pleaded, "Lord, please come
now before my little boy dies."

50Then Jesus told him, "Go back home. Your
son will live!" And the man believed what Jesus
said and started home.

51While the man was on his way, some of his
servants met him with the news that his son was
alive and well. 52He asked them when the boy had
begun to get better, and they replied, "Yesterday
afternoon at one o'clock his fever suddenly disappeared!" 53Then the father realized that that
was the very time Jesus had told him, "Your son
will live." And he and his entire household believed in Jesus. 54This was the second miraculous
sign Jesus did in Galilee after coming from Judea.

CHAPTER 5

Jesus Heals a Lame Man

Afterward Jesus returned to Jerusalem for one of
the Jewish holy days. 2Inside the city, near the
Sheep Gate, was the pool of Bethesda, with five
covered porches. 3Crowds of sick people—blind,
lame, or paralyzed—lay on the porches.* 5One of
the men lying there had been sick for thirty-
eight years. 6When Jesus saw him and knew he
had been ill for a long time, he asked him,
"Would you like to get well?"

7"I can't, sir," the sick man said, "for I have
no one to put me into the pool when the water
bubbles up. Someone else always gets there
ahead of me."

8Jesus told him, "Stand up, pick up your mat,
and walk!"

9Instantly, the man was healed! He rolled up
his sleeping mat and began walking! But this
miracle happened on the Sabbath, 10so the Jewish leaders objected. They said to the man who
was cured, "You can't work on the Sabbath! The
law doesn't allow you to carry that sleeping mat!"

11But he replied, "The man who healed me
told me, 'Pick up your mat and walk.'"

12"Who said such a thing as that?" they demanded.

13The man didn't know, for Jesus had disappeared into the crowd. 14But afterward Jesus
found him in the Temple and told him, "Now you
are well; so stop sinning, or something even
worse may happen to you." 15Then the man went
and told the Jewish leaders that it was Jesus who
had healed him.

5:3 Some manuscripts add an expanded conclusion to verse 3 and all of verse 4: *waiting for a certain movement of the water,*
4for an angel of the Lord came from time to time and stirred up the water. And the first person to step in after the water was
stirred was healed of whatever disease he had.

Jesus Claims to Be the Son of God

16So the Jewish leaders began harassing Jesus for
breaking the Sabbath rules. 17But Jesus replied,
"My Father is always working, and so am I." 18So
the Jewish leaders tried all the harder to find a
way to kill him. For he not only broke the Sabbath, he called God his Father, thereby making
himself equal with God.

19So Jesus explained, "I tell you the truth, the
Son can do nothing by himself. He does only
what he sees the Father doing. Whatever the
Father does, the Son also does. 20For the Father
loves the Son and shows him everything he is
doing. In fact, the Father will show him how to do
even greater works than healing this man. Then
you will truly be astonished. 21For just as the
Father gives life to those he raises from the dead,
so the Son gives life to anyone he wants. 22In
addition, the Father judges no one. Instead, he
has given the Son absolute authority to judge,
23so that everyone will honor the Son, just as
they honor the Father. Anyone who does not
honor the Son is certainly not honoring the
Father who sent him.

24"I tell you the truth, those who listen to my
message and believe in God who sent me have
eternal life. They will never be condemned for
their sins, but they have already passed from
death into life.

25"And I assure you that the time is coming, indeed it's here now, when the dead will hear my
voice—the voice of the Son of God. And those
who listen will live. 26The Father has life in himself, and he has granted that same life-giving
power to his Son. 27And he has given him authority to judge everyone because he is the Son
of Man. 28Don't be so surprised! Indeed, the time
is coming when all the dead in their graves will
hear the voice of God's Son, 29and they will rise
again. Those who have done good will rise to experience eternal life, and those who have continued in evil will rise to experience judgment. 30I
can do nothing on my own. I judge as God tells
me. Therefore, my judgment is just, because I
carry out the will of the one who sent me, not my
own will.

Witnesses to Jesus

31"If I were to testify on my own behalf, my testimony would not be valid. 32But someone else is
also testifying about me, and I assure you that
everything he says about me is true. 33In fact, you
sent investigators to listen to John the Baptist,
and his testimony about me was true. 34Of

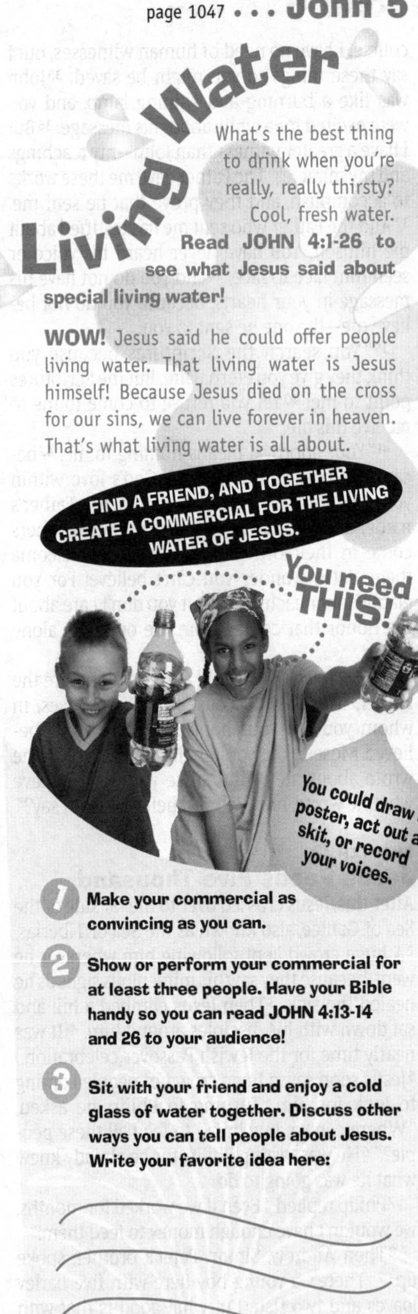

Living Water
What's the best thing to drink when you're really, really thirsty? Cool, fresh water.
Read JOHN 4:1-26 to see what Jesus said about special living water!
WOW! Jesus said he could offer people living water. That living water is Jesus himself! Because Jesus died on the cross for our sins, we can live forever in heaven. That's what living water is all about.
FIND A FRIEND, AND TOGETHER CREATE A COMMERCIAL FOR THE LIVING WATER OF JESUS.
You need THIS!
You could draw a poster, act out a skit, or record your voices.
1 Make your commercial as convincing as you can.
2 Show or perform your commercial for at least three people. Have your Bible handy so you can read JOHN 4:13-14 and 26 to your audience!
3 Sit with your friend and enjoy a cold glass of water together. Discuss other ways you can tell people about Jesus. Write your favorite idea here:
NOW COMMIT WITH YOUR FRIEND TO FOLLOW THROUGH!

course, I have no need of human witnesses, but I say these things so you might be saved. 35 John was like a burning and shining lamp, and you were excited for a while about his message. 36 But I have a greater witness than John—my teachings and my miracles. The Father gave me these works to accomplish, and they prove that he sent me. 37 And the Father who sent me has testified about me himself. You have never heard his voice or seen him face to face, 38 and you do not have his message in your hearts, because you do not believe me—the one he sent to you.

39 "You search the Scriptures because you think they give you eternal life. But the Scriptures point to me! 40 Yet you refuse to come to me to receive this life.

41 "Your approval means nothing to me, 42 because I know you don't have God's love within you. 43 For I have come to you in my Father's name, and you have rejected me. Yet if others come in their own name, you gladly welcome them. 44 No wonder you can't believe! For you gladly honor each other, but you don't care about the honor that comes from the one who alone is God.

45 "Yet it isn't I who will accuse you before the Father. Moses will accuse you! Yes, Moses, in whom you put your hopes. 46 If you really believed Moses, you would believe me, because he wrote about me. 47 But since you don't believe what he wrote, how will you believe what I say?"

CHAPTER 6

Jesus Feeds Five Thousand

After this, Jesus crossed over to the far side of the Sea of Galilee, also known as the Sea of Tiberias. 2 A huge crowd kept following him wherever he went, because they saw his miraculous signs as he healed the sick. 3 Then Jesus climbed a hill and sat down with his disciples around him. 4 (It was nearly time for the Jewish Passover celebration.) 5 Jesus soon saw a huge crowd of people coming to look for him. Turning to Philip, he asked, "Where can we buy bread to feed all these people?" 6 He was testing Philip, for he already knew what he was going to do.

7 Philip replied, "Even if we worked for months, we wouldn't have enough money to feed them!"

8 Then Andrew, Simon Peter's brother, spoke up. 9 "There's a young boy here with five barley loaves and two fish. But what good is that with this huge crowd?"

10 "Tell everyone to sit down," Jesus said. So they all sat down on the grassy slopes. (The men alone numbered about 5,000.) 11 Then Jesus took the loaves, gave thanks to God, and distributed them to the people. Afterward he did the same with the fish. And they all ate as much as they wanted. 12 After everyone was full, Jesus told his disciples, "Now gather the leftovers, so that nothing is wasted." 13 So they picked up the pieces and filled twelve baskets with scraps left by the people who had eaten from the five barley loaves.

14 When the people saw him do this miraculous sign, they exclaimed, "Surely, he is the Prophet we have been expecting!" 15 When Jesus saw that they were ready to force him to be their king, he slipped away into the hills by himself.

Jesus Walks on Water

16 That evening Jesus' disciples went down to the shore to wait for him. 17 But as darkness fell and Jesus still hadn't come back, they got into the boat and headed across the lake toward Capernaum. 18 Soon a gale swept down upon them, and the sea grew very rough. 19 They had rowed three or four miles when suddenly they saw Jesus walking on the water toward the boat. They were terrified, 20 but he called out to them, "Don't be afraid. I am here!" 21 Then they were eager to let him in the boat, and immediately they arrived at their destination!

Jesus, the Bread of Life

22 The next day the crowd that had stayed on the far shore saw that the disciples had taken the only boat, and they realized Jesus had not gone with them. 23 Several boats from Tiberias landed near the place where the Lord had blessed the bread and the people had eaten. 24 So when the crowd saw that neither Jesus nor his disciples were there, they got into the boats and went across to Capernaum to look for him. 25 They found him on the other side of the lake and asked, "Rabbi, when did you get here?"

26 Jesus replied, "I tell you the truth, you want to be with me because I fed you, not because you understood the miraculous signs. 27 But don't be so concerned about perishable things like food. Spend your energy seeking the eternal life that the Son of Man can give you. For God the Father has given me the seal of his approval."

28 They replied, "We want to perform God's works, too. What should we do?"

29 Jesus told them, "This is the only work God wants from you: Believe in the one he has sent."

30 They answered, "Show us a miraculous sign if you want us to believe in you. What can you do? 31 After all, our ancestors ate manna while they journeyed through the wilderness! The

Scriptures say, 'Moses gave them bread from
heaven to eat.'"
32 Jesus said, "I tell you the truth, Moses didn't
give you bread from heaven. My Father did. And
now he offers you the true bread from heaven.
33 The true bread of God is the one who comes
down from heaven and gives life to the world."
34 "Sir," they said, "give us that bread every day."
35 Jesus replied, "I am the bread of life. Whoever comes to me will never be hungry again.
Whoever believes in me will never be thirsty.
36 But you haven't believed in me even though
you have seen me. 37 However, those the Father
has given me will come to me, and I will never reject them. 38 For I have come down from heaven
to do the will of God who sent me, not to do my
own will. 39 And this is the will of God, that I
should not lose even one of all those he has given
me, but that I should raise them up at the last day.
40 For it is my Father's will that all who see his Son
and believe in him should have eternal life. I will
raise them up at the last day."
41 Then the people began to murmur in disagreement because he had said, "I am the bread
that came down from heaven." 42 They said, "Isn't
this Jesus, the son of Joseph? We know his father
and mother. How can he say, 'I came down from
heaven'?"
43 But Jesus replied, "Stop complaining about
what I said. 44 For no one can come to me unless
the Father who sent me draws them to me, and at
the last day I will raise them up. 45 As it is written
in the Scriptures, 'They will all be taught by God.'
Everyone who listens to the Father and learns
from him comes to me. 46 (Not that anyone has
ever seen the Father; only I, who was sent from
God, have seen him.)
47 "I tell you the truth, anyone who believes has
eternal life. 48 Yes, I am the bread of life! 49 Your
ancestors ate manna in the wilderness, but they
all died. 50 Anyone who eats the bread from
heaven, however, will never die. 51 I am the living
bread that came down from heaven. Anyone who
eats this bread will live forever; and this bread,
which I will offer so the world may live, is my
flesh."
52 Then the people began arguing with each
other about what he meant. "How can this man
give us his flesh to eat?" they asked.
53 So Jesus said again, "I tell you the truth, unless you eat the flesh of the Son of Man and drink
his blood, you cannot have eternal life within you.
54 But anyone who eats my flesh and drinks my
blood has eternal life, and I will raise that person
at the last day. 55 For my flesh is true food, and my
blood is true drink. 56 Anyone who eats my flesh
and drinks my blood remains in me, and I in him.
57 I live because of the living Father who sent me;
in the same way, anyone who feeds on me will live
because of me. 58 I am the true bread that came
down from heaven. Anyone who eats this bread
will not die as your ancestors did (even though
they ate the manna) but will live forever."
59 He said these things while he was teaching
in the synagogue in Capernaum.

Many Disciples Desert Jesus

60 Many of his disciples said, "This is very hard to
understand. How can anyone accept it?"
61 Jesus was aware that his disciples were complaining, so he said to them, "Does this offend
you? 62 Then what will you think if you see the
Son of Man ascend to heaven again? 63 The Spirit
alone gives eternal life. Human effort accom-
plishes nothing. And the very words I have spoken to you are spirit and life. 64 But some of you
do not believe me." (For Jesus knew from the beginning which ones didn't believe, and he knew
who would betray him.) 65 Then he said, "That is
why I said that people can't come to me unless
the Father gives them to me."
66 At this point many of his disciples turned
away and deserted him. 67 Then Jesus turned to
the Twelve and asked, "Are you also going to
leave?"
68 Simon Peter replied, "Lord, to whom would
we go? You have the words that give eternal life.
69 We believe, and we know you are the Holy One
of God."
70 Then Jesus said, "I chose the twelve of you,
but one is a devil." 71 He was speaking of Judas,
son of Simon Iscariot, one of the Twelve, who
would later betray him.

CHAPTER 7

Jesus and His Brothers

After this, Jesus traveled around Galilee. He
wanted to stay out of Judea, where the Jewish
leaders were plotting his death. 2 But soon it was
time for the Jewish Festival of Shelters, 3 and
Jesus' brothers said to him, "Leave here and go
to Judea, where your followers can see your miracles! 4 You can't become famous if you hide like
this! If you can do such wonderful things, show
yourself to the world!" 5 For even his brothers
didn't believe in him.
6 Jesus replied, "Now is not the right time for
me to go, but you can go anytime. 7 The world
can't hate you, but it does hate me because I
accuse it of doing evil. 8 You go on. I'm not going

Several stories in the New Testament mention some bad feelings that Jews had toward Samaritans.

It goes way back! When Assyria and Babylon took the Jews captive, some Jews stayed in the land. They married people who weren't Jews. Their children from those marriages grew up and had their own children, and that whole race of people became known as Samaritans. The Jews looked down on them because they came from marriages outside the Jewish faith. But Jesus showed that God loves all people the same.

Think of one action you can take this week to work against discrimination or racism.

Maybe you'll stand up for someone who's being made fun of because of his or her family background.

Write below what you plan to do.

THEN DO IT!

(Add the date that you did it!)

to this festival, because my time has not yet
come." 9After saying these things, Jesus remained in Galilee.

Jesus Teaches Openly at the Temple

10But after his brothers left for the festival, Jesus
also went, though secretly, staying out of public
view. 11The Jewish leaders tried to find him at
the festival and kept asking if anyone had seen
him. 12There was a lot of grumbling about him
among the crowds. Some argued, "He's a good
man," but others said, "He's nothing but a fraud
who deceives the people." 13But no one had the
courage to speak favorably about him in public,
for they were afraid of getting in trouble with the
Jewish leaders.

14Then, midway through the festival, Jesus
went up to the Temple and began to teach. 15The
people were surprised when they heard him.
"How does he know so much when he hasn't
been trained?" they asked.

16So Jesus told them, "My message is not my
own; it comes from God who sent me. 17Anyone
who wants to do the will of God will know
whether my teaching is from God or is merely my
own. 18Those who speak for themselves want
glory only for themselves, but a person who seeks
to honor the one who sent him speaks truth, not
lies. 19Moses gave you the law, but none of you
obeys it! In fact, you are trying to kill me."

20The crowd replied, "You're demon possessed! Who's trying to kill you?"

21Jesus replied, "I did one miracle on the Sabbath, and you were amazed. 22But you work on
the Sabbath, too, when you obey Moses' law of
circumcision. (Actually, this tradition of circumcision began with the patriarchs, long before the
law of Moses.) 23For if the correct time for cir-
cumcising your son falls on the Sabbath, you go
ahead and do it so as not to break the law of
Moses. So why should you be angry with me for
healing a man on the Sabbath? 24Look beneath
the surface so you can judge correctly."

Is Jesus the Messiah?

25Some of the people who lived in Jerusalem
started to ask each other, "Isn't this the man they
are trying to kill? 26But here he is, speaking in
public, and they say nothing to him. Could our
leaders possibly believe that he is the Messiah?
27But how could he be? For we know where this
man comes from. When the Messiah comes, he
will simply appear; no one will know where he
comes from."

28While Jesus was teaching in the Temple, he
called out, "Yes, you know me, and you know
where I come from. But I'm not here on my own.
The one who sent me is true, and you don't know
him. 29But I know him because I come from him,
and he sent me to you." 30Then the leaders tried
to arrest him; but no one laid a hand on him,
because his time had not yet come.

31Many among the crowds at the Temple
believed in him. "After all," they said, "would you
expect the Messiah to do more miraculous signs
than this man has done?"

32When the Pharisees heard that the crowds
were whispering such things, they and the leading priests sent Temple guards to arrest Jesus.
33But Jesus told them, "I will be with you only a
little longer. Then I will return to the one who
sent me. 34You will search for me but not find
me. And you cannot go where I am going."

35The Jewish leaders were puzzled by this
statement. "Where is he planning to go?" they
asked. "Is he thinking of leaving the country and
going to the Jews in other lands? Maybe he will
even teach the Greeks! 36What does he mean
when he says, 'You will search for me but not find
me,' and 'You cannot go where I am going'?"

Jesus Promises Living Water

37On the last day, the climax of the festival, Jesus
stood and shouted to the crowds, "Anyone who is
thirsty may come to me! 38Anyone who believes
in me may come and drink! For the Scriptures
declare, 'Rivers of living water will flow from his
heart.'" 39(When he said "living water," he was
speaking of the Spirit, who would be given to
everyone believing in him. But the Spirit had not
yet been given, because Jesus had not yet entered
into his glory.)

Division and Unbelief

40When the crowds heard him say this, some of
them declared, "Surely this man is the Prophet
we've been expecting." 41Others said, "He is the
Messiah." Still others said, "But he can't be! Will
the Messiah come from Galilee? 42For the
Scriptures clearly state that the Messiah will be
born of the royal line of David, in Bethlehem,
the village where King David was born." 43So
the crowd was divided about him. 44Some even
wanted him arrested, but no one laid a hand on
him.

45When the Temple guards returned without
having arrested Jesus, the leading priests and
Pharisees demanded, "Why didn't you bring
him in?"

46"We have never heard anyone speak like
this!" the guards responded.

47"Have you been led astray, too?" the Pharisees mocked. 48"Is there a single one of us rulers
or Pharisees who believes in him? 49This foolish
crowd follows him, but they are ignorant of the
law. God's curse is on them!"

50Then Nicodemus, the leader who had met
with Jesus earlier, spoke up. 51"Is it legal to convict a man before he is given a hearing?" he
asked.

52They replied, "Are you from Galilee, too?
Search the Scriptures and see for yourself—no
prophet ever comes from Galilee!"

[*The most ancient Greek manuscripts do not include John 7:53–8:11.*]

53Then the meeting broke up, and everybody
went home.

CHAPTER 8

A Woman Caught in Adultery

Jesus returned to the Mount of Olives, 2but early
the next morning he was back again at the Temple. A crowd soon gathered, and he sat down and
taught them. 3As he was speaking, the teachers
of religious law and the Pharisees brought a
woman who had been caught in the act of adultery. They put her in front of the crowd.

4"Teacher," they said to Jesus, "this woman
was caught in the act of adultery. 5The law of
Moses says to stone her. What do you say?"

6They were trying to trap him into saying
something they could use against him, but Jesus
stooped down and wrote in the dust with his finger. 7They kept demanding an answer, so he
stood up again and said, "All right, but let the one
who has never sinned throw the first stone!"
8Then he stooped down again and wrote in the
dust.

9When the accusers heard this, they slipped
away one by one, beginning with the oldest, until
only Jesus was left in the middle of the crowd
with the woman. 10Then Jesus stood up again
and said to the woman, "Where are your accusers? Didn't even one of them condemn you?"

11"No, Lord," she said.

And Jesus said, "Neither do I. Go and sin no
more."

Jesus, the Light of the World

12Jesus spoke to the people once more and said,
"I am the light of the world. If you follow me, you

won't have to walk in darkness, because you will
have the light that leads to life."
13The Pharisees replied, "You are making
those claims about yourself! Such testimony is
not valid."
14Jesus told them, "These claims are valid even
though I make them about myself. For I know
where I came from and where I am going, but you
don't know this about me. 15You judge me by human standards, but I do not judge anyone. 16And
if I did, my judgment would be correct in every
respect because I am not alone. The Father who
sent me is with me. 17Your own law says that if
two people agree about something, their witness
is accepted as fact. 18I am one witness, and my
Father who sent me is the other."
19"Where is your father?" they asked.
Jesus answered, "Since you don't know who I
am, you don't know who my Father is. If you knew
me, you would also know my Father." 20Jesus
made these statements while he was teaching in
the section of the Temple known as the Treasury.
But he was not arrested, because his time had not
yet come.

The Unbelieving People Warned

21Later Jesus said to them again, "I am going
away. You will search for me but will die in your
sin. You cannot come where I am going."
22The people asked, "Is he planning to commit suicide? What does he mean, 'You cannot
come where I am going'?"
23Jesus continued, "You are from below; I am
from above. You belong to this world; I do not.
24That is why I said that you will die in your sins;
for unless you believe that I AM who I claim to be,
you will die in your sins."
25"Who are you?" they demanded.
Jesus replied, "The one I have always claimed
to be. 26I have much to say about you and much
to condemn, but I won't. For I say only what I
have heard from the one who sent me, and he is
completely truthful." 27But they still didn't
understand that he was talking about his Father.
28So Jesus said, "When you have lifted up the
Son of Man on the cross, then you will understand
that I AM he. I do nothing on my own but say only
what the Father taught me. 29And the one who
sent me is with me—he has not deserted me. For I
always do what pleases him." 30Then many who
heard him say these things believed in him.

Jesus and Abraham

31Jesus said to the people who believed in him,
"You are truly my disciples if you remain faithful
to my teachings. 32And you will know the truth,
and the truth will set you free."
33"But we are descendants of Abraham," they
said. "We have never been slaves to anyone.
What do you mean, 'You will be set free'?"
34Jesus replied, "I tell you the truth, everyone
who sins is a slave of sin. 35A slave is not a permanent member of the family, but a son is part
of the family forever. **36So if the Son sets
you free, you are truly free.** 37Yes, I realize that you are descendants of Abraham. And
yet some of you are trying to kill me because
there's no room in your hearts for my message.
38I am telling you what I saw when I was with
my Father. But you are following the advice of
your father."
39"Our father is Abraham!" they declared.
"No," Jesus replied, "for if you were really the
children of Abraham, you would follow his
example. 40Instead, you are trying to kill me
because I told you the truth, which I heard from
God. Abraham never did such a thing. 41No, you
are imitating your real father."
They replied, "We aren't illegitimate children!
God himself is our true Father."
42Jesus told them, "If God were your Father,
you would love me, because I have come to you
from God. I am not here on my own, but he sent
me. 43Why can't you understand what I am saying? It's because you can't even hear me! 44For
you are the children of your father the devil, and
you love to do the evil things he does. He was a
murderer from the beginning. He has always
hated the truth, because there is no truth in
him. When he lies, it is consistent with his character; for he is a liar and the father of lies. 45So
when I tell the truth, you just naturally don't believe me! 46Which of you can truthfully accuse
me of sin? And since I am telling you the truth,
why don't you believe me? 47Anyone who belongs to God listens gladly to the words of God.
But you don't listen because you don't belong to
God."
48The people retorted, "You Samaritan devil!
Didn't we say all along that you were possessed
by a demon?"
49"No," Jesus said, "I have no demon in me. For
I honor my Father—and you dishonor me. 50And
though I have no wish to glorify myself, God is
going to glorify me. He is the true judge. 51I tell
you the truth, anyone who obeys my teaching
will never die!"
52The people said, "Now we know you are possessed by a demon. Even Abraham and the
prophets died, but you say, 'Anyone who obeys

my teaching will never die!' 53 Are you greater
than our father Abraham? He died, and so did
the prophets. Who do you think you are?"
54 Jesus answered, "If I want glory for myself, it
doesn't count. But it is my Father who will glorify
me. You say, 'He is our God,' 55 but you don't even
know him. I know him. If I said otherwise, I
would be as great a liar as you! But I do know him
and obey him. 56 Your father Abraham rejoiced
as he looked forward to my coming. He saw it
and was glad."
57 The people said, "You aren't even fifty years
old. How can you say you have seen Abraham?"
58 Jesus answered, "I tell you the truth, before
Abraham was even born, I AM!" 59 At that point
they picked up stones to throw at him. But Jesus
was hidden from them and left the Temple.

CHAPTER 9

Jesus Heals a Man Born Blind

As Jesus was walking along, he saw a man who
had been blind from birth. 2 "Rabbi," his disciples asked him, "why was this man born blind?
Was it because of his own sins or his parents'
sins?"
3 "It was not because of his sins or his parents'
sins," Jesus answered. "This happened so the
power of God could be seen in him. 4 We must
quickly carry out the tasks assigned us by the one
who sent us. The night is coming, and then no
one can work. 5 But while I am here in the world, I
am the light of the world."
6 Then he spit on the ground, made mud with
the saliva, and spread the mud over the blind
man's eyes. 7 He told him, "Go wash yourself in
the pool of Siloam" (Siloam means "sent"). So the
man went and washed and came back seeing!
8 His neighbors and others who knew him as a
blind beggar asked each other, "Isn't this the man
who used to sit and beg?" 9 Some said he was, and
others said, "No, he just looks like him!"
But the beggar kept saying, "Yes, I am the same
one!"
10 They asked, "Who healed you? What happened?"
11 He told them, "The man they call Jesus made
mud and spread it over my eyes and told me, 'Go
to the pool of Siloam and wash yourself.' So I
went and washed, and now I can see!"
12 "Where is he now?" they asked.
"I don't know," he replied.
13 Then they took the man who had been blind
to the Pharisees, 14 because it was on the Sabbath
that Jesus had made the mud and healed him.
15 The Pharisees asked the man all about it. So he
told them, "He put the mud over my eyes, and
when I washed it away, I could see!"
16 Some of the Pharisees said, "This man Jesus
is not from God, for he is working on the Sabbath." Others said, "But how could an ordinary
sinner do such miraculous signs?" So there was a
deep division of opinion among them.
17 Then the Pharisees again questioned the
man who had been blind and demanded,
"What's your opinion about this man who
healed you?"
The man replied, "I think he must be a
prophet."
18 The Jewish leaders still refused to believe
the man had been blind and could now see, so
they called in his parents. 19 They asked them, "Is
this your son? Was he born blind? If so, how can
he now see?"
20 His parents replied, "We know this is our
son and that he was born blind, 21 but we don't
know how he can see or who healed him. Ask
him. He is old enough to speak for himself."
22 His parents said this because they were afraid
of the Jewish leaders, who had announced that
anyone saying Jesus was the Messiah would be
expelled from the synagogue. 23 That's why they
said, "He is old enough. Ask him."
24 So for the second time they called in the
man who had been blind and told him, "God
should get the glory for this, because we know
this man Jesus is a sinner."
25 "I don't know whether he is a sinner," the
man replied. "But I know this: I was blind, and
now I can see!"
26 "But what did he do?" they asked. "How did
he heal you?"
27 "Look!" the man exclaimed. "I told you once.
Didn't you listen? Why do you want to hear it
again? Do you want to become his disciples, too?"
28 Then they cursed him and said, "You are his
disciple, but we are disciples of Moses! 29 We
know God spoke to Moses, but we don't even
know where this man comes from."
30 "Why, that's very strange!" the man replied.
"He healed my eyes, and yet you don't know
where he comes from? 31 We know that God
doesn't listen to sinners, but he is ready to hear
those who worship him and do his will. 32 Ever
since the world began, no one has been able
to open the eyes of someone born blind. 33 If
this man were not from God, he couldn't have
done it."
34 "You were born a total sinner!" they answered. "Are you trying to teach us?" And they
threw him out of the synagogue.

Spiritual Blindness

35When Jesus heard what had happened, he
found the man and asked, "Do you believe in the
Son of Man?"

36The man answered, "Who is he, sir? I want
to believe in him."

37"You have seen him," Jesus said, "and he is
speaking to you!"

38"Yes, Lord, I believe!" the man said. And he
worshiped Jesus.

39Then Jesus told him, "I entered this world to
render judgment—to give sight to the blind and
to show those who think they see that they are
blind."

40Some Pharisees who were standing nearby
heard him and asked, "Are you saying we're
blind?"

41"If you were blind, you wouldn't be guilty,"
Jesus replied. "But you remain guilty because you
claim you can see.

CHAPTER 10

The Good Shepherd and His Sheep

"I tell you the truth, anyone who sneaks over the
wall of a sheepfold, rather than going through
the gate, must surely be a thief and a robber! 2But
the one who enters through the gate is the shepherd of the sheep. 3The gatekeeper opens the
gate for him, and the sheep recognize his voice
and come to him. He calls his own sheep by name
and leads them out. 4After he has gathered his
own flock, he walks ahead of them, and they follow him because they know his voice. 5They
won't follow a stranger; they will run from him
because they don't know his voice."

6Those who heard Jesus use this illustration
didn't understand what he meant, 7so he explained it to them: "I tell you the truth, I am the
gate for the sheep. 8All who came before me were
thieves and robbers. But the true sheep did not
listen to them. 9Yes, I am the gate. Those who
come in through me will be saved. They will come
and go freely and will find good pastures. 10The
thief's purpose is to steal and kill and destroy. My
purpose is to give them a rich and satisfying life.

11"I am the good shepherd. The good shepherd sacrifices his life for the sheep. 12A hired
hand will run when he sees a wolf coming. He
will abandon the sheep because they don't belong to him and he isn't their shepherd. And so
the wolf attacks them and scatters the flock.
13The hired hand runs away because he's working only for the money and doesn't really care
about the sheep.

14"I am the good shepherd; I know my own
sheep, and they know me, 15just as my Father
knows me and I know the Father. So I sacrifice
my life for the sheep. 16I have other sheep, too,
that are not in this sheepfold. I must bring them
also. They will listen to my voice, and there will
be one flock with one shepherd.

17"The Father loves me because I sacrifice my
life so I may take it back again. 18No one can take
my life from me. I sacrifice it voluntarily. For I
have the authority to lay it down when I want to
and also to take it up again. For this is what my
Father has commanded."

19When he said these things, the people were
again divided in their opinions about him.
20Some said, "He's demon possessed and out of
his mind. Why listen to a man like that?" 21Oth-
ers said, "This doesn't sound like a man possessed by a demon! Can a demon open the eyes
of the blind?"

Jesus Claims to Be the Son of God

22It was now winter, and Jesus was in Jerusalem
at the time of Hanukkah, the Festival of Dedication. 23He was in the Temple, walking through
the section known as Solomon's Colonnade.
24The people surrounded him and asked, "How
long are you going to keep us in suspense? If you
are the Messiah, tell us plainly."

25Jesus replied, "I have already told you, and
you don't believe me. The proof is the work I do
in my Father's name. 26But you don't believe me
because you are not my sheep. 27My sheep listen
to my voice; I know them, and they follow me. 28I
give them eternal life, and they will never perish.
No one can snatch them away from me, 29for my
Father has given them to me, and he is more powerful than anyone else. No one can snatch them
from the Father's hand. 30The Father and I are
one."

31Once again the people picked up stones to
kill him. 32Jesus said, "At my Father's direction I
have done many good works. For which one are
you going to stone me?"

33They replied, "We're stoning you not for any
good work, but for blasphemy! You, a mere man,
claim to be God."

34Jesus replied, "It is written in your own
Scriptures that God said to certain leaders of the
people, 'I say, you are gods!' 35And you know that
the Scriptures cannot be altered. So if those people who received God's message were called
'gods,' 36why do you call it blasphemy when I say,
'I am the Son of God'? After all, the Father set me

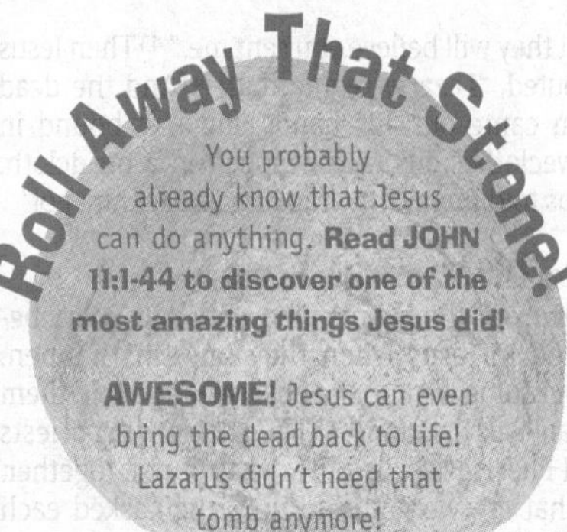

Roll Away That Stone!

You probably already know that Jesus can do anything. **Read JOHN 11:1-44 to discover one of the most amazing things Jesus did!**

AWESOME! Jesus can even bring the dead back to life! Lazarus didn't need that tomb anymore!

MAKE THIS COOL CRAFT TO REMIND YOU OF THIS STORY.

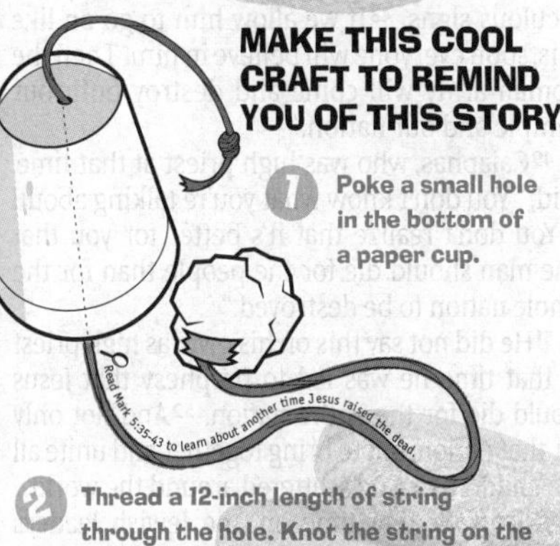

Read Mark 5:35-43 to learn about another time Jesus raised the dead.

1. **Poke a small hole in the bottom of a paper cup.**
2. **Thread a 12-inch length of string through the hole. Knot the string on the outside of the bottom of the cup.**
3. **Crumple a piece of paper into a ball that's just big enough to sit inside the rim of the cup. Tape the free end of the string to the paper ball.**

Think of the cup as the empty tomb of Lazarus and the paper ball as the stone they rolled away. See how many times you can catch the paper ball "stone" in the paper cup "tomb."

Use your "tomb" and "stone" as you tell a friend the Bible story!

apart and sent me into the world. 37Don't believe
me unless I carry out my Father's work. 38But if I
do his work, believe in the evidence of the miraculous works I have done, even if you don't believe
me. Then you will know and understand that the
Father is in me, and I am in the Father."
39Once again they tried to arrest him, but he
got away and left them. 40He went beyond the
Jordan River near the place where John was first
baptizing and stayed there awhile. 41And many
followed him. "John didn't perform miraculous
signs," they remarked to one another, "but everything he said about this man has come true."
42And many who were there believed in Jesus.

CHAPTER 11

The Raising of Lazarus

A man named Lazarus was sick. He lived in Bethany with his sisters, Mary and Martha. 2This is
the Mary who later poured the expensive perfume on the Lord's feet and wiped them with her
hair. Her brother, Lazarus, was sick. 3So the two
sisters sent a message to Jesus telling him, "Lord,
your dear friend is very sick."
4But when Jesus heard about it he said, "Lazarus's sickness will not end in death. No, it happened for the glory of God so that the Son of God
will receive glory from this." 5So although Jesus
loved Martha, Mary, and Lazarus, 6he stayed
where he was for the next two days. 7Finally, he
said to his disciples, "Let's go back to Judea."
8But his disciples objected. "Rabbi," they said,
"only a few days ago the people in Judea were trying to stone you. Are you going there again?"
9Jesus replied, "There are twelve hours of daylight every day. During the day people can walk
safely. They can see because they have the light
of this world. 10But at night there is danger of
stumbling because they have no light." 11Then
he said, "Our friend Lazarus has fallen asleep, but
now I will go and wake him up."
12The disciples said, "Lord, if he is sleeping, he
will soon get better!" 13They thought Jesus
meant Lazarus was simply sleeping, but Jesus
meant Lazarus had died.
14So he told them plainly, "Lazarus is dead.
15And for your sakes, I'm glad I wasn't there, for
now you will really believe. Come, let's go see
him."
16Thomas, nicknamed the Twin, said to his
fellow disciples, "Let's go, too—and die with
Jesus."
17When Jesus arrived at Bethany, he was told
that Lazarus had already been in his grave for
four days. 18Bethany was only a few miles down

John 12 . . . page 1056

the road from Jerusalem, 19and many of the people had come to console Martha and Mary in
their loss. 20When Martha got word that Jesus
was coming, she went to meet him. But Mary
stayed in the house. 21Martha said to Jesus,
"Lord, if only you had been here, my brother
would not have died. 22But even now I know that
God will give you whatever you ask."

23Jesus told her, "Your brother will rise
again."

24"Yes," Martha said, "he will rise when everyone else rises, at the last day."

**25Jesus told her, "I am the resur-
rection and the life. Anyone who believes in me will live, even after
dying.** 26Everyone who lives in me and believes in me will never ever die. Do you believe
this, Martha?"

27"Yes, Lord," she told him. "I have always believed you are the Messiah, the Son of God, the
one who has come into the world from God."
28Then she returned to Mary. She called Mary
aside from the mourners and told her, "The
Teacher is here and wants to see you." 29So Mary
immediately went to him.

30Jesus had stayed outside the village, at the
place where Martha met him. 31When the people who were at the house consoling Mary saw
her leave so hastily, they assumed she was going
to Lazarus's grave to weep. So they followed her
there. 32When Mary arrived and saw Jesus, she
fell at his feet and said, "Lord, if only you had
been here, my brother would not have died."

33When Jesus saw her weeping and saw the
other people wailing with her, a deep anger
welled up within him, and he was deeply troubled. 34"Where have you put him?" he asked
them.

They told him, "Lord, come and see." 35Then
Jesus wept. 36The people who were standing
nearby said, "See how much he loved him!"
37But some said, "This man healed a blind man.
Couldn't he have kept Lazarus from dying?"

38Jesus was still angry as he arrived at the
tomb, a cave with a stone rolled across its entrance. 39"Roll the stone aside," Jesus told them.

But Martha, the dead man's sister, protested,
"Lord, he has been dead for four days. The smell
will be terrible."

40Jesus responded, "Didn't I tell you that you
would see God's glory if you believe?" 41So they
rolled the stone aside. Then Jesus looked up to
heaven and said, "Father, thank you for hearing
me. 42You always hear me, but I said it out loud
for the sake of all these people standing here, so
that they will believe you sent me." 43Then Jesus
shouted, "Lazarus, come out!" 44And the dead
man came out, his hands and feet bound in
graveclothes, his face wrapped in a headcloth.
Jesus told them, "Unwrap him and let him go!"

The Plot to Kill Jesus

45Many of the people who were with Mary believed in Jesus when they saw this happen.
46But some went to the Pharisees and told them
what Jesus had done. 47Then the leading priests
and Pharisees called the high council together.
"What are we going to do?" they asked each
other. "This man certainly performs many miraculous signs. 48If we allow him to go on like
this, soon everyone will believe in him. Then the
Roman army will come and destroy both our
Temple and our nation."

49Caiaphas, who was high priest at that time,
said, "You don't know what you're talking about!
50You don't realize that it's better for you that
one man should die for the people than for the
whole nation to be destroyed."

51He did not say this on his own; as high priest
at that time he was led to prophesy that Jesus
would die for the entire nation. 52And not only
for that nation, but to bring together and unite all
the children of God scattered around the world.

53So from that time on, the Jewish leaders
began to plot Jesus' death. 54As a result, Jesus
stopped his public ministry among the people
and left Jerusalem. He went to a place near the
wilderness, to the village of Ephraim, and stayed
there with his disciples.

55It was now almost time for the Jewish Passover celebration, and many people from all over
the country arrived in Jerusalem several days
early so they could go through the purification
ceremony before Passover began. 56They kept
looking for Jesus, but as they stood around in the
Temple, they said to each other, "What do you
think? He won't come for Passover, will he?"
57Meanwhile, the leading priests and Pharisees
had publicly ordered that anyone seeing Jesus
must report it immediately so they could arrest
him.

CHAPTER 12

Jesus Anointed at Bethany

Six days before the Passover celebration began,
Jesus arrived in Bethany, the home of Lazarus—
the man he had raised from the dead. 2A dinner
was prepared in Jesus' honor. Martha served, and
Lazarus was among those who ate with him.
3Then Mary took a twelve-ounce jar of expensive

perfume made from essence of nard, and she
anointed Jesus' feet with it, wiping his feet with
her hair. The house was filled with the fragrance.
4But Judas Iscariot, the disciple who would
soon betray him, said, 5"That perfume was
worth a year's wages. It should have been sold
and the money given to the poor." 6Not that he
cared for the poor—he was a thief, and since he
was in charge of the disciples' money, he often
stole some for himself.
7Jesus replied, "Leave her alone. She did this
in preparation for my burial. 8You will always
have the poor among you, but you will not always
have me."
9When all the people heard of Jesus' arrival,
they flocked to see him and also to see Lazarus,
the man Jesus had raised from the dead. 10Then
the leading priests decided to kill Lazarus, too,
11for it was because of him that many of the people had deserted them and believed in Jesus.

Jesus' Triumphant Entry

12The next day, the news that Jesus was on the
way to Jerusalem swept through the city. A large
crowd of Passover visitors 13took palm branches
and went down the road to meet him. They
shouted,

"Praise God!
Blessings on the one who comes
in the name of the LORD!
Hail to the King of Israel!"

14Jesus found a young donkey and rode on it,
fulfilling the prophecy that said:

15 "Don't be afraid, people of Jerusalem.
Look, your King is coming,
riding on a donkey's colt."

16His disciples didn't understand at the time
that this was a fulfillment of prophecy. But after
Jesus entered into his glory, they remembered
what had happened and realized that these
things had been written about him.
17Many in the crowd had seen Jesus call Lazarus from the tomb, raising him from the dead,
and they were telling others about it. 18That was
the reason so many went out to meet him—because they had heard about this miraculous sign.
19Then the Pharisees said to each other, "There's
nothing we can do. Look, everyone has gone after
him!"

Jesus Predicts His Death

20Some Greeks who had come to Jerusalem for
the Passover celebration 21paid a visit to Philip,
who was from Bethsaida in Galilee. They said, "Sir,
we want to meet Jesus." 22Philip told Andrew
about it, and they went together to ask Jesus.
23Jesus replied, "Now the time has come for
the Son of Man to enter into his glory. 24I tell you
the truth, unless a kernel of wheat is planted
in the soil and dies, it remains alone. But its death
will produce many new kernels—a plentiful harvest of new lives. 25Those who love their life in
this world will lose it. Those who care nothing for
their life in this world will keep it for eternity.
26Anyone who wants to serve me must follow me,
because my servants must be where I am. And the
Father will honor anyone who serves me.
27"Now my soul is deeply troubled. Should I
pray, 'Father, save me from this hour'? But this is
the very reason I came! 28Father, bring glory to
your name."
Then a voice spoke from heaven, saying, "I
have already brought glory to my name, and I will
do so again." 29When the crowd heard the voice,
some thought it was thunder, while others declared an angel had spoken to him.
30Then Jesus told them, "The voice was for
your benefit, not mine. 31The time for judging this
world has come, when Satan, the ruler of this
world, will be cast out. 32And when I am lifted up
from the earth, I will draw everyone to myself."
33He said this to indicate how he was going to die.
34The crowd responded, "We understood
from Scripture that the Messiah would live forever. How can you say the Son of Man will die?
Just who is this Son of Man, anyway?"
35Jesus replied, "My light will shine for you just
a little longer. Walk in the light while you can, so
the darkness will not overtake you. Those who
walk in the darkness cannot see where they are
going. 36Put your trust in the light while there is
still time; then you will become children of the
light."
After saying these things, Jesus went away and
was hidden from them.

The Unbelief of the People

37But despite all the miraculous signs Jesus had
done, most of the people still did not believe in
him. 38This is exactly what Isaiah the prophet
had predicted:

"LORD, who has believed our message?
To whom has the LORD revealed his
powerful arm?"

39But the people couldn't believe, for as Isaiah
also said,

40 "The Lord has blinded their eyes
and hardened their hearts—
so that their eyes cannot see,
and their hearts cannot understand,
and they cannot turn to me
and have me heal them."

41 Isaiah was referring to Jesus when he said this,
because he saw the future and spoke of the Messiah's glory. 42 Many people did believe in him,
however, including some of the Jewish leaders.
But they wouldn't admit it for fear that the Pharisees would expel them from the synagogue.
43 For they loved human praise more than the
praise of God.

44 Jesus shouted to the crowds, "If you trust
me, you are trusting not only me, but also God
who sent me. 45 For when you see me, you are
seeing the one who sent me. 46 I have come as a
light to shine in this dark world, so that all who
put their trust in me will no longer remain in the
dark. 47 I will not judge those who hear me but
don't obey me, for I have come to save the world
and not to judge it. 48 But all who reject me and
my message will be judged on the day of judgment by the truth I have spoken. 49 I don't speak
on my own authority. The Father who sent me
has commanded me what to say and how to say
it. 50 And I know his commands lead to eternal
life; so I say whatever the Father tells me to say."

CHAPTER 13

Jesus Washes His Disciples' Feet

Before the Passover celebration, Jesus knew that
his hour had come to leave this world and return
to his Father. He had loved his disciples during
his ministry on earth, and now he loved them to
the very end. 2 It was time for supper, and the
devil had already prompted Judas, son of Simon
Iscariot, to betray Jesus. 3 Jesus knew that the
Father had given him authority over everything
and that he had come from God and would return to God. 4 So he got up from the table, took
off his robe, wrapped a towel around his waist,
5 and poured water into a basin. Then he began
to wash the disciples' feet, drying them with the
towel he had around him.

6 When Jesus came to Simon Peter, Peter said
to him, "Lord, are you going to wash my feet?"

7 Jesus replied, "You don't understand now
what I am doing, but someday you will."

8 "No," Peter protested, "you will never ever
wash my feet!"

Jesus replied, "Unless I wash you, you won't
belong to me."

Jesus, the Son of God, served his disciples in an incredible way. **Read all about it in JOHN 13:1-17!** Imagine having no paved roads or sidewalks. And wearing sandals all the time. In Jesus' time, servants would wash the feet of guests. It was a lowly job. But Jesus washed the disciples' feet himself! He showed that we should serve others.

How can you serve others this week? Write your ideas below.

Date

________________ ______

________________ ______

________________ ______

When you accomplish each service idea, write the date you did it.

9 Simon Peter exclaimed, "Then wash my
hands and head as well, Lord, not just my feet!"

10 Jesus replied, "A person who has bathed all
over does not need to wash, except for the feet, to
be entirely clean. And you disciples are clean, but
not all of you." 11 For Jesus knew who would
betray him. That is what he meant when he said,
"Not all of you are clean."

12 After washing their feet, he put on his robe
again and sat down and asked, "Do you understand what I was doing? 13 You call me 'Teacher'
and 'Lord,' and you are right, because that's what I

am. 14 And since I, your Lord and Teacher, have
washed your feet, you ought to wash each other's
feet. 15 I have given you an example to follow. Do
as I have done to you. 16 I tell you the truth, slaves
are not greater than their master. Nor is the messenger more important than the one who sends
the message. 17 Now that you know these things,
God will bless you for doing them.

Jesus Predicts His Betrayal

18 "I am not saying these things to all of you; I
know the ones I have chosen. But this fulfills the
Scripture that says, 'The one who eats my food
has turned against me.' 19 I tell you this beforehand, so that when it happens you will believe
that I AM the Messiah. 20 I tell you the truth, anyone who welcomes my messenger is welcoming
me, and anyone who welcomes me is welcoming
the Father who sent me."

21 Now Jesus was deeply troubled, and he
exclaimed, "I tell you the truth, one of you will
betray me!"

22 The disciples looked at each other, wondering whom he could mean. 23 The disciple Jesus
loved was sitting next to Jesus at the table.
24 Simon Peter motioned to him to ask, "Who's he
talking about?" 25 So that disciple leaned over to
Jesus and asked, "Lord, who is it?"

26 Jesus responded, "It is the one to whom I give
the bread I dip in the bowl." And when he had
dipped it, he gave it to Judas, son of Simon Iscariot. 27 When Judas had eaten the bread, Satan entered into him. Then Jesus told him, "Hurry and
do what you're going to do." 28 None of the others
at the table knew what Jesus meant. 29 Since
Judas was their treasurer, some thought Jesus was
telling him to go and pay for the food or to give
some money to the poor. 30 So Judas left at once,
going out into the night.

Jesus Predicts Peter's Denial

31 As soon as Judas left the room, Jesus said, "The
time has come for the Son of Man to enter into
his glory, and God will be glorified because of
him. 32 And since God receives glory because of
the Son, he will give his own glory to the Son, and
he will do so at once. 33 Dear children, I will be
with you only a little longer. And as I told the Jewish leaders, you will search for me, but you can't
come where I am going. **34 So now I am giving you a new commandment: Love
each other. Just as I have loved you,
you should love each other. 35 Your
love for one another will prove to the
world that you are my disciples."**

36 Simon Peter asked, "Lord, where are you going?"

And Jesus replied, "You can't go with me now,
but you will follow me later."

37 "But why can't I come now, Lord?" he asked.
"I'm ready to die for you."

38 Jesus answered, "Die for me? I tell you the
truth, Peter—before the rooster crows tomorrow
morning, you will deny three times that you even
know me.

CHAPTER 14

Jesus, the Way to the Father

"Don't let your hearts be troubled. Trust in God,
and trust also in me. 2 There is more than enough
room in my Father's home. If this were not so,
would I have told you that I am going to prepare a
place for you? 3 When everything is ready, I will
come and get you, so that you will always be with
me where I am. 4 And you know the way to where
I am going."

5 "No, we don't know, Lord," Thomas said. "We
have no idea where you are going, so how can we
know the way?"

**6 Jesus told him, "I am the way, the
truth, and the life. No one can come
to the Father except through me.** 7 If
you had really known me, you would know who
my Father is. From now on, you do know him and
have seen him!"

8 Philip said, "Lord, show us the Father, and we
will be satisfied."

9 Jesus replied, "Have I been with you all this
time, Philip, and yet you still don't know who I
am? Anyone who has seen me has seen the
Father! So why are you asking me to show him to
you? 10 Don't you believe that I am in the Father
and the Father is in me? The words I speak are
not my own, but my Father who lives in me does
his work through me. 11 Just believe that I am in
the Father and the Father is in me. Or at least believe because of the work you have seen me do.

12 "I tell you the truth, anyone who believes in
me will do the same works I have done, and even
greater works, because I am going to be with the
Father. 13 You can ask for anything in my name,
and I will do it, so that the Son can bring glory to
the Father. 14 Yes, ask me for anything in my
name, and I will do it!

Jesus Promises the Holy Spirit

15 "If you love me, obey my commandments.
16 And I will ask the Father, and he will give you
another Advocate, who will never leave you. 17 He
is the Holy Spirit, who leads into all truth. The

John 15 . . . page 1060

Key Verse **"I am the way, the truth, and the life. No one can come to the Father except through me." —JOHN 14:6**

The Only Way

Ever want to be an artist? Now's your chance. **But first, read JOHN 14:6 a couple of times.**

Jesus says he's the only way to the Father. Think of it this way: You and God are separated because of your sin. When you believe in Jesus, he acts as the bridge so you can get close to God and be forgiven.

DRAW A PICTURE OF YOUR OWN IDEA TO EXPLAIN THE VERSE.

Maybe you'll draw yourself in one city and God in another, and Jesus is the only bus that runs between the cities.

Now read JOHN 14:6 to someone else, and explain your picture.

Ask that person to draw a picture and explain the verse to someone. Who knows how many people will learn this verse because of you!

world cannot receive him, because it isn't looking for him and doesn't recognize him. But you know him, because he lives with you now and
later will be in you. [18]No, I will not abandon you
as orphans—I will come to you. [19]Soon the world
will no longer see me, but you will see me. Since I
live, you also will live. [20]When I am raised to life
again, you will know that I am in my Father, and
you are in me, and I am in you. [21]Those who accept my commandments and obey them are the ones who love me. And because they love me, my Father will love them. And I will love them and reveal myself to each of them."
[22]Judas (not Judas Iscariot, but the other disciple with that name) said to him, "Lord, why are you going to reveal yourself only to us and not to the world at large?"
[23]Jesus replied, "All who love me will do what I say. My Father will love them, and we will come
and make our home with each of them. [24]Anyone who doesn't love me will not obey me. And remember, my words are not my own. What I am telling you is from the Father who sent me.
[25]I am telling you these things now while I am
still with you. [26]But when the Father sends the Advocate as my representative—that is, the Holy Spirit—he will teach you everything and will remind you of everything I have told you.
[27]"I am leaving you with a gift—peace of mind and heart. And the peace I give is a gift the world cannot give. So don't be troubled or
afraid. [28]Remember what I told you: I am going away, but I will come back to you again. If you really loved me, you would be happy that I am
going to the Father, who is greater than I am. [29]I
have told you these things before they happen so that when they do happen, you will believe.
[30]"I don't have much more time to talk to you, because the ruler of this world approaches. He
has no power over me, [31]but I will do what the Father requires of me, so that the world will know that I love the Father. Come, let's be going.

CHAPTER 15
Jesus, the True Vine

"I am the true grapevine, and my Father is the
gardener. [2]He cuts off every branch of mine that doesn't produce fruit, and he prunes the branches that do bear fruit so they will produce
even more. [3]You have already been pruned and
purified by the message I have given you. [4]Remain in me, and I will remain in you. For a branch cannot produce fruit if it is severed from the vine, and you cannot be fruitful unless you remain in me.
[5]**"Yes, I am the vine; you are the branches. Those who remain in me, and I in them, will produce much fruit. For apart from me you can do
nothing.** [6]Anyone who does not remain in me is thrown away like a useless branch and withers. Such branches are gathered into a pile to be
burned. [7]But if you remain in me and my words remain in you, you may ask for anything you
want, and it will be granted! [8]When you produce

much fruit, you are my true disciples. This brings great glory to my Father.

9"I have loved you even as the Father has loved me. Remain in my love. 10When you obey my commandments, you remain in my love, just as I obey my Father's commandments and remain in his love. 11I have told you these things so that you will be filled with my joy. Yes, your joy will overflow! 12This is my commandment: Love each other in the same way I have loved you. 13There is no greater love than to lay down one's life for one's friends. 14You are my friends if you do what I command. 15I no longer call you slaves, because a master doesn't confide in his slaves. Now you are my friends, since I have told you everything the Father told me. 16You didn't choose me. I chose you. I appointed you to go and produce lasting fruit, so that the Father will give you whatever you ask for, using my name. 17This is my command: Love each other.

The World's Hatred

18"If the world hates you, remember that it hated me first. 19The world would love you as one of its own if you belonged to it, but you are no longer part of the world. I chose you to come out of the world, so it hates you. 20Do you remember what I told you? 'A slave is not greater than the master.' Since they persecuted me, naturally they will persecute you. And if they had listened to me, they would listen to you. 21They will do all this to you because of me, for they have rejected the one who sent me. 22They would not be guilty if I had not come and spoken to them. But now they have no excuse for their sin. 23Anyone who hates me also hates my Father. 24If I hadn't done such miraculous signs among them that no one else could do, they would not be guilty. But as it is, they have seen everything I did, yet they still hate me and my Father. 25This fulfills what is written in their Scriptures: 'They hated me without cause.'

26"But I will send you the Advocate—the Spirit of truth. He will come to you from the Father and will testify all about me. 27And you must also testify about me because you have been with me from the beginning of my ministry.

CHAPTER 16

"I have told you these things so that you won't abandon your faith. 2For you will be expelled from the synagogues, and the time is coming when those who kill you will think they are doing a holy service for God. 3This is because they have never known the Father or me. 4Yes, I'm telling you these things now, so that when they happen, you will remember my warning. I didn't tell you earlier because I was going to be with you for a while longer.

The Work of the Holy Spirit

5"But now I am going away to the one who sent me, and not one of you is asking where I am going. 6Instead, you grieve because of what I've told you. 7But in fact, it is best for you that I go away, because if I don't, the Advocate won't come. If I do go away, then I will send him to you. 8And when he comes, he will convict the world of its sin, and of God's righteousness, and of the coming judgment. 9The world's sin is that it refuses to believe in me. 10Righteousness is available because I go to the Father, and you will see me no more. 11Judgment will come because the ruler of this world has already been judged.

12"There is so much more I want to tell you, but you can't bear it now. 13When the Spirit of truth comes, he will guide you into all truth. He will not speak on his own but will tell you what he has heard. He will tell you about the future. 14He will bring me glory by telling you whatever he receives from me. 15All that belongs to the Father is mine; this is why I said, 'The Spirit will tell you whatever he receives from me.'

Sadness Will Be Turned to Joy

16"In a little while you won't see me anymore. But a little while after that, you will see me again."

17Some of the disciples asked each other, "What does he mean when he says, 'In a little while you won't see me, but then you will see me,' and 'I am going to the Father'? 18And what does he mean by 'a little while'? We don't understand."

19Jesus realized they wanted to ask him about it, so he said, "Are you asking yourselves what I meant? I said in a little while you won't see me, but a little while after that you will see me again. 20I tell you the truth, you will weep and mourn over what is going to happen to me, but the world will rejoice. You will grieve, but your grief will suddenly turn to wonderful joy. 21It will be like a woman suffering the pains of labor. When her child is born, her anguish gives way to joy because she has brought a new baby into the world. 22So you have sorrow now, but I will see you again; then you will rejoice, and no one can rob you of that joy. 23At that time you won't need to ask me for anything. I tell you the truth, you will ask the Father directly, and he will grant your

request because you use my name. 24You haven't
done this before. Ask, using my name, and you
will receive, and you will have abundant joy.
25"I have spoken of these matters in figures of
speech, but soon I will stop speaking figuratively
and will tell you plainly all about the Father.
26Then you will ask in my name. I'm not saying
I will ask the Father on your behalf, 27for the
Father himself loves you dearly because you love
me and believe that I came from God. 28Yes, I
came from the Father into the world, and now
I will leave the world and return to the Father."
29Then his disciples said, "At last you are
speaking plainly and not figuratively. 30Now we
understand that you know everything, and
there's no need to question you. From this we
believe that you came from God."
31Jesus asked, "Do you finally believe? 32But
the time is coming—indeed it's here now—when
you will be scattered, each one going his own
way, leaving me alone. Yet I am not alone because
the Father is with me. 33I have told you all this so
that you may have peace in me. Here on earth you
will have many trials and sorrows. But take heart,
because I have overcome the world."

CHAPTER 17

The Prayer of Jesus

After saying all these things, Jesus looked up to
heaven and said, "Father, the hour has come. Glorify your Son so he can give glory back to you.
2For you have given him authority over everyone.
He gives eternal life to each one you have given
him. 3And this is the way to have eternal life—to
know you, the only true God, and Jesus Christ, the
one you sent to earth. 4I brought glory to you
here on earth by completing the work you gave
me to do. 5Now, Father, bring me into the glory
we shared before the world began.
6"I have revealed you to the ones you gave me
from this world. They were always yours. You
gave them to me, and they have kept your word.
7Now they know that everything I have is a gift
from you, 8for I have passed on to them the
message you gave me. They accepted it and
know that I came from you, and they believe you
sent me.
9"My prayer is not for the world, but for those
you have given me, because they belong to you.
10All who are mine belong to you, and you have
given them to me, so they bring me glory. 11Now I
am departing from the world; they are staying in
this world, but I am coming to you. Holy Father,
you have given me your name; now protect them
by the power of your name so that they will be

Key Verse **"Yes, I am the vine; you are the branches. Those who remain in me, and I in them, will produce much fruit. For apart from me you can do nothing."—JOHN 15:5**

Chain Reaction

Find a friend, and read JOHN 15:5 a few times until you can say it to each other without reading it. Discuss these questions with your friend:

- **Why can't a branch survive if it's not connected to the main vine?**
- **Why is it so important for us to be connected to Jesus?**
- **What are some ways to stay connected to Jesus?**

Brainstorm with your friend ways to stay connected to Jesus. (You might say reading the Bible.) Then think of fruit you can produce by staying connected to Jesus. (You might say being loving.)

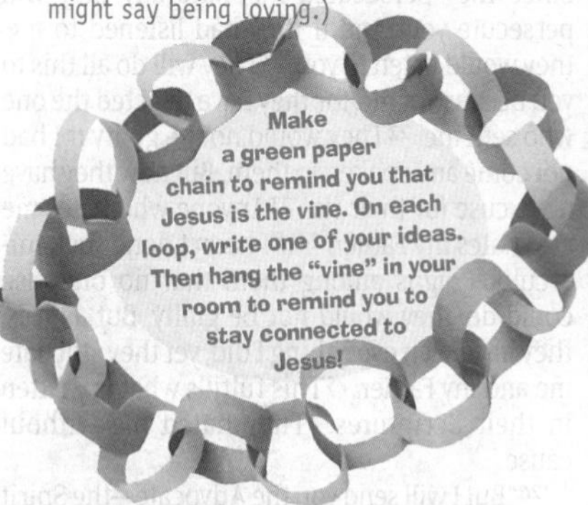
Make
a green paper
chain to remind you that
Jesus is the vine. On each
loop, write one of your ideas.
Then hang the "vine" in your
room to remind you to
stay connected to
Jesus!

united just as we are. 12During my time here, I
protected them by the power of the name you
gave me. I guarded them so that not one was lost,
except the one headed for destruction, as the
Scriptures foretold.
13"Now I am coming to you. I told them many
things while I was with them in this world so they
would be filled with my joy. 14I have given them
your word. And the world hates them because
they do not belong to the world, just as I do not
belong to the world. 15I'm not asking you to take

them out of the world, but to keep them safe
from the evil one. 16They do not belong to this
world any more than I do. 17Make them holy by
your truth; teach them your word, which is truth.
18Just as you sent me into the world, I am sending them into the world. 19And I give myself as a
holy sacrifice for them so they can be made holy
by your truth.

20"I am praying not only for these disciples
but also for all who will ever believe in me
through their message. 21I pray that they will all
be one, just as you and I are one—as you are in
me, Father, and I am in you. And may they be in us
so that the world will believe you sent me.

22"I have given them the glory you gave me, so
they may be one as we are one. 23I am in them
and you are in me. May they experience such
perfect unity that the world will know that you
sent me and that you love them as much as you
love me. 24Father, I want these whom you have
given me to be with me where I am. Then they
can see all the glory you gave me because you
loved me even before the world began!

25"O righteous Father, the world doesn't know
you, but I do; and these disciples know you sent
me. 26I have revealed you to them, and I will continue to do so. Then your love for me will be in
them, and I will be in them."

CHAPTER 18

Jesus Is Betrayed and Arrested

After saying these things, Jesus crossed the Kidron Valley with his disciples and entered a grove
of olive trees. 2Judas, the betrayer, knew this
place, because Jesus had often gone there with
his disciples. 3The leading priests and Pharisees
had given Judas a contingent of Roman soldiers
and Temple guards to accompany him. Now
with blazing torches, lanterns, and weapons,
they arrived at the olive grove.

4Jesus fully realized all that was going to happen to him, so he stepped forward to meet them.
"Who are you looking for?" he asked.

5"Jesus the Nazarene," they replied.

"I Am he," Jesus said. (Judas, who betrayed him,
was standing with them.) 6As Jesus said "I Am
he," they all drew back and fell to the ground!
7Once more he asked them, "Who are you looking for?"

And again they replied, "Jesus the Nazarene."

8"I told you that I Am he," Jesus said. "And
since I am the one you want, let these others go."
9He did this to fulfill his own statement: "I did
not lose a single one of those you have given me."

10Then Simon Peter drew a sword and slashed
off the right ear of Malchus, the high priest's
slave. 11But Jesus said to Peter, "Put your sword
back into its sheath. Shall I not drink from the
cup of suffering the Father has given me?"

Jesus at the High Priest's House

12So the soldiers, their commanding officer,
and the Temple guards arrested Jesus and tied
him up. 13First they took him to Annas, since he
was the father-in-law of Caiaphas, the high
priest at that time. 14Caiaphas was the one who
had told the other Jewish leaders, "It's better
that one man should die for the people."

Peter's First Denial

15Simon Peter followed Jesus, as did another of
the disciples. That other disciple was acquainted
with the high priest, so he was allowed to enter
the high priest's courtyard with Jesus. 16Peter
had to stay outside the gate. Then the disciple
who knew the high priest spoke to the woman
watching at the gate, and she let Peter in. 17The
woman asked Peter, "You're not one of that man's
disciples, are you?"

"No," he said, "I am not."

18Because it was cold, the household servants
and the guards had made a charcoal fire. They
stood around it, warming themselves, and Peter
stood with them, warming himself.

The High Priest Questions Jesus

19Inside, the high priest began asking Jesus
about his followers and what he had been teaching them. 20Jesus replied, "Everyone knows what
I teach. I have preached regularly in the synagogues and the Temple, where the people gather.
I have not spoken in secret. 21Why are you asking
me this question? Ask those who heard me. They
know what I said."

22Then one of the Temple guards standing
nearby slapped Jesus across the face. "Is that the
way to answer the high priest?" he demanded.

23Jesus replied, "If I said anything wrong, you
must prove it. But if I'm speaking the truth, why
are you beating me?"

24Then Annas bound Jesus and sent him to
Caiaphas, the high priest.

Peter's Second and Third Denials

25Meanwhile, as Simon Peter was standing by
the fire warming himself, they asked him again,
"You're not one of his disciples, are you?"

He denied it, saying, "No, I am not."

26 But one of the household slaves of the high priest, a relative of the man whose ear Peter had cut off, asked, "Didn't I see you out there in the olive grove with Jesus?" 27 Again Peter denied it. And immediately a rooster crowed.

Jesus' Trial before Pilate

28 Jesus' trial before Caiaphas ended in the early hours of the morning. Then he was taken to the headquarters of the Roman governor. His accusers didn't go inside because it would defile them, and they wouldn't be allowed to celebrate the Passover. 29 So Pilate, the governor, went out to them and asked, "What is your charge against this man?"

30 "We wouldn't have handed him over to you if he weren't a criminal!" they retorted.

31 "Then take him away and judge him by your own law," Pilate told them.

"Only the Romans are permitted to execute someone," the Jewish leaders replied. 32 (This fulfilled Jesus' prediction about the way he would die.)

33 Then Pilate went back into his headquarters and called for Jesus to be brought to him. "Are you the king of the Jews?" he asked him.

34 Jesus replied, "Is this your own question, or did others tell you about me?"

35 "Am I a Jew?" Pilate retorted. "Your own people and their leading priests brought you to me for trial. Why? What have you done?"

36 Jesus answered, "My Kingdom is not an earthly kingdom. If it were, my followers would fight to keep me from being handed over to the Jewish leaders. But my Kingdom is not of this world."

37 Pilate said, "So you are a king?"

Jesus responded, "You say I am a king. Actually, I was born and came into the world to testify to the truth. All who love the truth recognize that what I say is true."

38 "What is truth?" Pilate asked. Then he went out again to the people and told them, "He is not guilty of any crime. 39 But you have a custom of asking me to release one prisoner each year at Passover. Would you like me to release this 'King of the Jews'?"

40 But they shouted back, "No! Not this man. We want Barabbas!" (Barabbas was a revolutionary.)

CHAPTER 19

Jesus Sentenced to Death

Then Pilate had Jesus flogged with a lead-tipped whip. 2 The soldiers wove a crown of thorns and put it on his head, and they put a purple robe on him. 3 "Hail! King of the Jews!" they mocked, as they slapped him across the face.

4 Pilate went outside again and said to the people, "I am going to bring him out to you now, but understand clearly that I find him not guilty." 5 Then Jesus came out wearing the crown of thorns and the purple robe. And Pilate said, "Look, here is the man!"

6 When they saw him, the leading priests and Temple guards began shouting, "Crucify him! Crucify him!"

"Take him yourselves and crucify him," Pilate said. "I find him not guilty."

7 The Jewish leaders replied, "By our law he ought to die because he called himself the Son of God."

8 When Pilate heard this, he was more frightened than ever. 9 He took Jesus back into the headquarters again and asked him, "Where are you from?" But Jesus gave no answer. 10 "Why don't you talk to me?" Pilate demanded. "Don't you realize that I have the power to release you or crucify you?"

11 Then Jesus said, "You would have no power over me at all unless it were given to you from above. So the one who handed me over to you has the greater sin."

12 Then Pilate tried to release him, but the Jewish leaders shouted, "If you release this man, you are no 'friend of Caesar.' Anyone who declares himself a king is a rebel against Caesar."

13 When they said this, Pilate brought Jesus out to them again. Then Pilate sat down on the judgment seat on the platform that is called the Stone Pavement (in Hebrew, *Gabbatha*). 14 It was now about noon on the day of preparation for the Passover. And Pilate said to the people, "Look, here is your king!"

15 "Away with him," they yelled. "Away with him! Crucify him!"

"What? Crucify your king?" Pilate asked.

"We have no king but Caesar," the leading priests shouted back.

16 Then Pilate turned Jesus over to them to be crucified.

The Crucifixion

So they took Jesus away. 17 Carrying the cross by himself, he went to the place called Place of the Skull (in Hebrew, *Golgotha*). 18 There they nailed him to the cross. Two others were crucified with him, one on either side, with Jesus between them. 19 And Pilate posted a sign on the cross that read, "Jesus of Nazareth, the King of the Jews." 20 The

place where Jesus was crucified was near the city,
and the sign was written in Hebrew, Latin, and
Greek, so that many people could read it.
21 Then the leading priests objected and said
to Pilate, "Change it from 'The King of the Jews'
to 'He said, I am King of the Jews.'"
22 Pilate replied, "No, what I have written, I
have written."
23 When the soldiers had crucified Jesus, they
divided his clothes among the four of them. They
also took his robe, but it was seamless, woven in
one piece from top to bottom. 24 So they said,
"Rather than tearing it apart, let's throw dice for
it." This fulfilled the Scripture that says, "They divided my garments among themselves and threw
dice for my clothing." So that is what they did.
25 Standing near the cross were Jesus' mother,
and his mother's sister, Mary (the wife of Clopas),
and Mary Magdalene. 26 When Jesus saw his
mother standing there beside the disciple he
loved, he said to her, "Dear woman, here is your
son." 27 And he said to this disciple, "Here is your
mother." And from then on this disciple took her
into his home.

The Death of Jesus

28 Jesus knew that his mission was now finished,
and to fulfill Scripture he said, "I am thirsty." 29 A
jar of sour wine was sitting there, so they soaked
a sponge in it, put it on a hyssop branch, and held
it up to his lips. 30 When Jesus had tasted it, he
said, "It is finished!" Then he bowed his head and
released his spirit.
31 It was the day of preparation, and the Jewish
leaders didn't want the bodies hanging there the
next day, which was the Sabbath (and a very special Sabbath, because it was the Passover). So they
asked Pilate to hasten their deaths by ordering
that their legs be broken. Then their bodies could
be taken down. 32 So the soldiers came and broke
the legs of the two men crucified with Jesus.
33 But when they came to Jesus, they saw that he
was already dead, so they didn't break his legs.
34 One of the soldiers, however, pierced his side
with a spear, and immediately blood and water
flowed out. 35 (This report is from an eyewitness
giving an accurate account. He speaks the truth
so that you also may continue to believe.) 36 These
things happened in fulfillment of the Scriptures
that say, "Not one of his bones will be broken,"
37 and "They will look on the one they pierced."

The Burial of Jesus

38 Afterward Joseph of Arimathea, who had been
a secret disciple of Jesus (because he feared the
Jewish leaders), asked Pilate for permission to
take down Jesus' body. When Pilate gave permission, Joseph came and took the body away.
39 With him came Nicodemus, the man who
had come to Jesus at night. He brought about
seventy-five pounds of perfumed ointment
made from myrrh and aloes. 40 Following Jewish
burial custom, they wrapped Jesus' body with the
spices in long sheets of linen cloth. 41 The place
of crucifixion was near a garden, where there
was a new tomb, never used before. 42 And so, because it was the day of preparation for the Jewish
Passover and since the tomb was close at hand,
they laid Jesus there.

FUN-fact

Pack It Up

If you were a Bible-times traveler, you might have carried a **hollowed-out gourd** weighted with a stone for drawing water from wells. You might also have carried a **stick** and a **money belt.** You may not have to travel to tell others about Jesus but you can still be prepared just the same!

What three items can you carry with you to tell others about Jesus?

Maybe you can keep a pocket Bible in your backpack. Or maybe you can write invitations to your church and keep them with you. Write your ideas below.

1. ________________
2. ________________
3. ________________

Then start telling others about Jesus!

Have you ever doubted God? Guess what: You're not alone. **Read JOHN 20:24-31 to meet a doubting disciple.**

One good thing to do when you have doubts is to separate what you *know* from what you *feel*. **Here's an example:** You may doubt that God loves you because you didn't make the soccer team. You *feel* alone and unloved.

But the Bible says that God loves you, and that he'll take care of you. Because the Bible says it, you *know* it's true, even if it doesn't *feel* that way right now.

Fill in this chart with what you feel and what you know from the Bible.

What I Feel
What I Know
Lonely
God is with me.
—MATTHEW 28:20

Turn to John 13:34-35 to read more about love.

The index in this Bible can help you know where to look in the Bible!

CHAPTER **20**

The Resurrection

Early on Sunday morning, while it was still dark,
Mary Magdalene came to the tomb and found
that the stone had been rolled away from the
entrance. 2She ran and found Simon Peter and
the other disciple, the one whom Jesus loved.
She said, "They have taken the Lord's body out
of the tomb, and we don't know where they have
put him!"

3Peter and the other disciple started out for
the tomb. 4They were both running, but the
other disciple outran Peter and reached the
tomb first. 5He stooped and looked in and saw
the linen wrappings lying there, but he didn't
go in. 6Then Simon Peter arrived and went inside. He also noticed the linen wrappings lying
there, 7while the cloth that had covered Jesus'
head was folded up and lying apart from the
other wrappings. 8Then the disciple who had
reached the tomb first also went in, and he saw
and believed—9for until then they still hadn't
understood the Scriptures that said Jesus must
rise from the dead. 10Then they went home.

Jesus Appears to Mary Magdalene

11Mary was standing outside the tomb crying,
and as she wept, she stooped and looked in.
12She saw two white-robed angels, one sitting
at the head and the other at the foot of the place
where the body of Jesus had been lying. 13"Dear
woman, why are you crying?" the angels asked
her.

"Because they have taken away my Lord," she
replied, "and I don't know where they have put
him."

14She turned to leave and saw someone standing there. It was Jesus, but she didn't recognize
him. 15"Dear woman, why are you crying?" Jesus
asked her. "Who are you looking for?"

She thought he was the gardener. "Sir," she
said, "if you have taken him away, tell me where
you have put him, and I will go and get him."

16"Mary!" Jesus said.

She turned to him and cried out, "Rabboni!"
(which is Hebrew for "Teacher").

17"Don't cling to me," Jesus said, "for I haven't
yet ascended to the Father. But go find my
brothers and tell them, 'I am ascending to my
Father and your Father, to my God and your
God.' "

18Mary Magdalene found the disciples and
told them, "I have seen the Lord!" Then she gave
them his message.

Jesus Appears to His Disciples

19 That Sunday evening the disciples were meeting behind locked doors because they were
afraid of the Jewish leaders. Suddenly, Jesus
was standing there among them! "Peace be with
you," he said. 20 As he spoke, he showed them the
wounds in his hands and his side. They were
filled with joy when they saw the Lord! 21 Again he
said, "Peace be with you. As the Father has sent
me, so I am sending you." 22 Then he breathed on
them and said, "Receive the Holy Spirit. 23 If you
forgive anyone's sins, they are forgiven. If you do
not forgive them, they are not forgiven."

Jesus Appears to Thomas

24 One of the twelve disciples, Thomas (nick-
named the Twin), was not with the others when
Jesus came. 25 They told him, "We have seen the
Lord!"

But he replied, "I won't believe it unless I see
the nail wounds in his hands, put my fingers into
them, and place my hand into the wound in his
side."

26 Eight days later the disciples were together
again, and this time Thomas was with them. The
doors were locked; but suddenly, as before, Jesus
was standing among them. "Peace be with you,"
he said. 27 Then he said to Thomas, "Put your
finger here, and look at my hands. Put your hand
into the wound in my side. Don't be faithless any
longer. Believe!"

28 "My Lord and my God!" Thomas exclaimed.

29 Then Jesus told him, "You believe because
you have seen me. Blessed are those who believe
without seeing me."

Purpose of the Book

30 The disciples saw Jesus do many other miraculous signs in addition to the ones recorded in
this book. 31 But these are written so that you
may continue to believe that Jesus is the Messiah, the Son of God, and that by believing in him
you will have life by the power of his name.

CHAPTER 21

Epilogue: Jesus Appears to Seven Disciples

Later, Jesus appeared again to the disciples beside the Sea of Galilee. This is how it happened.
2 Several of the disciples were there—Simon
Peter, Thomas (nicknamed the Twin), Nathanael
from Cana in Galilee, the sons of Zebedee, and
two other disciples.

3 Simon Peter said, "I'm going fishing."

"We'll come, too," they all said. So they went
out in the boat, but they caught nothing all night.

4 At dawn Jesus was standing on the beach, but
the disciples couldn't see who he was. 5 He called
out, "Fellows, have you caught any fish?"

"No," they replied.

6 Then he said, "Throw out your net on the
right-hand side of the boat, and you'll get some!"
So they did, and they couldn't haul in the net because there were so many fish in it.

7 Then the disciple Jesus loved said to Peter,
"It's the Lord!" When Simon Peter heard that it
was the Lord, he put on his tunic (for he had
stripped for work), jumped into the water, and
headed to shore. 8 The others stayed with the
boat and pulled the loaded net to the shore, for
they were only about a hundred yards from
shore. 9 When they got there, they found breakfast waiting for them—fish cooking over a charcoal fire, and some bread.

10 "Bring some of the fish you've just caught,"
Jesus said. 11 So Simon Peter went aboard and
dragged the net to the shore. There were
153 large fish, and yet the net hadn't torn.

12 "Now come and have some breakfast!" Jesus
said. None of the disciples dared to ask him,
"Who are you?" They knew it was the Lord.
13 Then Jesus served them the bread and the fish.
14 This was the third time Jesus had appeared to
his disciples since he had been raised from the
dead.

15 After breakfast Jesus asked Simon Peter,
"Simon son of John, do you love me more than
these?"

"Yes, Lord," Peter replied, "you know I love
you."

"Then feed my lambs," Jesus told him.

16 Jesus repeated the question: "Simon son of
John, do you love me?"

"Yes, Lord," Peter said, "you know I love you."

"Then take care of my sheep," Jesus said.

17 A third time he asked him, "Simon son of
John, do you love me?"

Peter was hurt that Jesus asked the question a
third time. He said, "Lord, you know everything.
You know that I love you."

Jesus said, "Then feed my sheep.

18 "I tell you the truth, when you were young,
you were able to do as you liked; you dressed
yourself and went wherever you wanted to go.
But when you are old, you will stretch out your
hands, and others will dress you and take you
where you don't want to go." 19 Jesus said this to
let him know by what kind of death he would
glorify God. Then Jesus told him, "Follow me."

20Peter turned around and saw behind them
the disciple Jesus loved—the one who had
leaned over to Jesus during supper and asked,
"Lord, who will betray you?" 21Peter asked Jesus,
"What about him, Lord?"

22Jesus replied, "If I want him to remain alive
until I return, what is that to you? As for you, follow me." 23So the rumor spread among the community of believers that this disciple wouldn't
die. But that isn't what Jesus said at all. He only
said, "If I want him to remain alive until I return,
what is that to you?"

24This disciple is the one who testifies to these
events and has recorded them here. And we know
that his account of these things is accurate.

25Jesus also did many other things. If they were
all written down, I suppose the whole world could
not contain the books that would be written.

ACTS A Book of Amazing Adventures!

Look for 4 hidden messages in Acts!

Acts is about an exciting time that completely changed the world. It tells about

- **TONGUES ON FIRE**
- **MANY, MANY MIRACLES BY MANY DISCIPLES**
- **A BLINDING CHANGE OF HEART**
- **THOUSANDS TURNING TO JESUS**

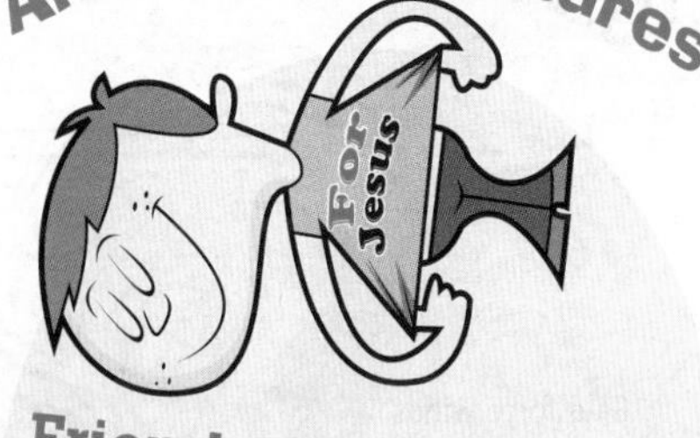

Friend or Foe?

Saul thought he was on the right side. One day, though, something happened that changed his mind, and he switched sides pretty quickly! **Find out what happened in Acts 9:1-31!**

Tongues of Fire and Tongues on Fire

Call the fire department! Burning to know more? **Read Acts 2.**

Up, Up, and Away

One day Jesus was standing on the ground talking to his disciples, and the next minute he was in the air. **Read the whole uplifting story for yourself in Acts 1:1-11!**

Workin' on a Chain Gang

The disciples couldn't seem to stay out of jail. But God always came to their rescue. **Read about their troubles with the authorities in the book of Acts. Here are just a few of the stories: Acts 4:1-31; Acts 5:12-42; Acts 12:1-19; and Acts 16:16-40.**

Smooth Sailin'

Smooth Sailin'

Gale force winds. Smashing waves. Driving rain. Why wasn't Paul worried? **Find out in Acts 27:13-44.**

Hit the Beach

Paul spent part of one winter on an island, but it was no vacation! **Read Acts 28:1-14 to find out what he was doing there!**

Keepin' On Keepin' On

Paul walked lots of miles and started lots of churches, and he kept in touch with them by writing lots of letters. (Those letters make up a lot of the New Testament!) **See Acts 13:1-3 to read about a big missionary send-off.**

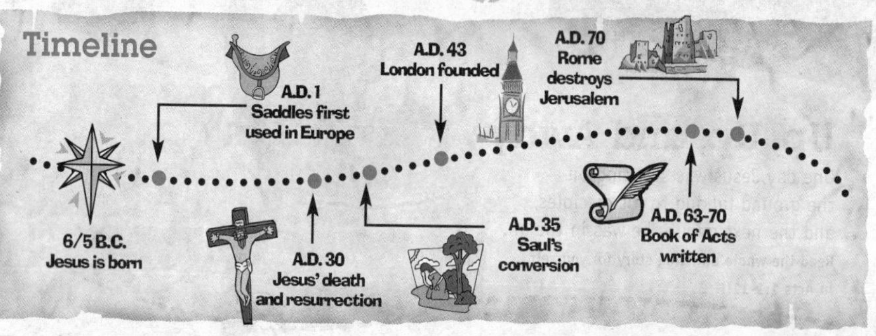
Timeline
6/5 B.C. Jesus is born
A.D. 1 Saddles first used in Europe
A.D. 30 Jesus' death and resurrection
A.D. 35 Saul's conversion
A.D. 43 London founded
A.D. 63-70 Book of Acts written
A.D. 70 Rome destroys Jerusalem

The JESUS CONNECTION

The whole Bible centers around Jesus. From the time Adam and Eve first sinned, God had been working on a plan to forgive people's sin. In Acts, the first part of God's plan had been completed. Jesus took the punishment for our sins when he died on the cross. After he rose from the dead, there was only one thing left to do—people had to find out about what Jesus did. That's why Jesus told his followers to go around the world with the good news about him. (Who can *you* tell about Jesus?)

The second part of God's plan will be completed when Jesus comes back to redeem his believers and establish a new heaven and earth.

What an amazing plan!

CHAPTER 1

The Promise of the Holy Spirit

In my first book I told you, Theophilus, about
everything Jesus began to do and teach 2until the
day he was taken up to heaven after giving his
chosen apostles further instructions through
the Holy Spirit. 3During the forty days after he
suffered and died, he appeared to the apostles
from time to time, and he proved to them in
many ways that he was actually alive. And he
talked to them about the Kingdom of God.

4Once when he was eating with them, he commanded them, "Do not leave Jerusalem until the
Father sends you the gift he promised, as I told
you before. 5John baptized with water, but in just
a few days you will be baptized with the Holy
Spirit."

The Ascension of Jesus

6So when the apostles were with Jesus, they kept
asking him, "Lord, has the time come for you to
free Israel and restore our kingdom?"

7He replied, "The Father alone has the authority to set those dates and times, and they are not
for you to know. 8But you will receive power
when the Holy Spirit comes upon you. And you
will be my witnesses, telling people about me
everywhere—in Jerusalem, throughout Judea, in
Samaria, and to the ends of the earth."

9After saying this, he was taken up into a cloud
while they were watching, and they could no longer see him. 10As they strained to see him rising
into heaven, two white-robed men suddenly
stood among them. 11"Men of Galilee," they said,
"why are you standing here staring into heaven?
Jesus has been taken from you into heaven, but
someday he will return from heaven in the same
way you saw him go!"

Matthias Replaces Judas

12Then the apostles returned to Jerusalem from
the Mount of Olives, a distance of half a mile.
13When they arrived, they went to the upstairs
room of the house where they were staying.

Here are the names of those who were present:
Peter, John, James, Andrew, Philip, Thomas, Bartholomew, Matthew, James (son of Alphaeus), Simon (the Zealot), and Judas (son of James). 14They
all met together and were constantly united in
prayer, along with Mary the mother of Jesus, several other women, and the brothers of Jesus.

15During this time, when about 120 believers
were together in one place, Peter stood up and
addressed them. 16"Brothers," he said, "the
Scriptures had to be fulfilled concerning Judas,
who guided those who arrested Jesus. This was
predicted long ago by the Holy Spirit, speaking
through King David. 17Judas was one of us and
shared in the ministry with us."

18(Judas had bought a field with the money he
received for his treachery. Falling headfirst
there, his body split open, spilling out all his
intestines. 19The news of his death spread to all
the people of Jerusalem, and they gave the place
the Aramaic name *Akeldama,* which means
"Field of Blood.")

20Peter continued, "This was written in the
book of Psalms, where it says, 'Let his home become desolate, with no one living in it.' It also
says, 'Let someone else take his position.'

21"So now we must choose a replacement for
Judas from among the men who were with us
the entire time we were traveling with the Lord
Jesus—22from the time he was baptized by
John until the day he was taken from us. Whoever is chosen will join us as a witness of Jesus'
resurrection."

23So they nominated two men: Joseph called
Barsabbas (also known as Justus) and Matthias.
24Then they all prayed, "O Lord, you know every
heart. Show us which of these men you have chosen 25as an apostle to replace Judas in this ministry, for he has deserted us and gone where he
belongs." 26Then they cast lots, and Matthias
was selected to become an apostle with the other
eleven.

CHAPTER 2

The Holy Spirit Comes

On the day of Pentecost all the believers were
meeting together in one place. 2Suddenly, there
was a sound from heaven like the roaring of a
mighty windstorm, and it filled the house where
they were sitting. 3Then, what looked like flames
or tongues of fire appeared and settled on each
of them. 4And everyone present was filled with
the Holy Spirit and began speaking in other languages, as the Holy Spirit gave them this ability.

5At that time there were devout Jews from
every nation living in Jerusalem. 6When they
heard the loud noise, everyone came running,
and they were bewildered to hear their own languages being spoken by the believers.

7They were completely amazed. "How can
this be?" they exclaimed. "These people are all
from Galilee, 8and yet we hear them speaking
in our own native languages! 9Here we are—
Parthians, Medes, Elamites, people from Mesopotamia, Judea, Cappadocia, Pontus, the province of Asia, 10Phrygia, Pamphylia, Egypt, and

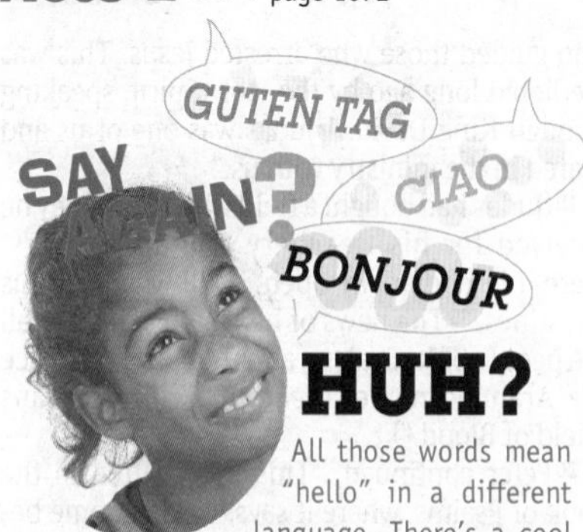

All those words mean "hello" in a different language. There's a cool story in the Bible about people speaking different languages. But they were speaking in languages they didn't even know! **Read the whole amazing story in ACTS 2:1-42.**

GRAB A FRIEND AND TRY THIS.

Together, make up your own foreign language. In your new language, what words represent these pictures?

Now, with your friend, go talk to three people using only your new language. They didn't understand you, did they? So how come on the day of Pentecost the people were able to speak in new languages and others were able to understand them? Because of God! God poured out his Holy Spirit on the people!

Think of three things you can tell about Jesus, and tell them to three people this week.

SPREAD THE NEWS, JUST LIKE THE DISCIPLES DID!

the areas of Libya around Cyrene, visitors from
Rome [11](both Jews and converts to Judaism),
Cretans, and Arabs. And we all hear these
people speaking in our own languages about
the wonderful things God has done!" [12]They
stood there amazed and perplexed. "What can
this mean?" they asked each other.

[13]But others in the crowd ridiculed them, saying, "They're just drunk, that's all!"

Peter Preaches to the Crowd

[14]Then Peter stepped forward with the eleven
other apostles and shouted to the crowd, "Listen
carefully, all of you, fellow Jews and residents of
Jerusalem! Make no mistake about this. [15]These
people are not drunk, as some of you are assuming. Nine o'clock in the morning is much too
early for that. [16]No, what you see was predicted
long ago by the prophet Joel:

[17] 'In the last days,' God says,
'I will pour out my Spirit upon all people.
Your sons and daughters will prophesy.
Your young men will see visions,
and your old men will dream dreams.
[18] In those days I will pour out my Spirit
even on my servants—men and women alike—
and they will prophesy.
[19] And I will cause wonders in the heavens above
and signs on the earth below—
blood and fire and clouds of smoke.
[20] The sun will become dark,
and the moon will turn blood red
before that great and glorious day
of the LORD arrives.
[21] But everyone who calls on the name
of the LORD
will be saved.'

[22]"People of Israel, listen! God publicly endorsed Jesus the Nazarene by doing powerful
miracles, wonders, and signs through him, as you
well know. [23]But God knew what would happen,
and his prearranged plan was carried out when
Jesus was betrayed. With the help of lawless
Gentiles, you nailed him to a cross and killed
him. [24]But God released him from the horrors of
death and raised him back to life, for death could
not keep him in its grip. [25]King David said this
about him:

'I see that the LORD is always with me.
I will not be shaken, for he is right beside me.

26 No wonder my heart is glad,
and my tongue shouts his praises!
My body rests in hope.
27 For you will not leave my soul among
the dead
or allow your Holy One to rot
in the grave.
28 You have shown me the way of life,
and you will fill me with the joy
of your presence.'

29 "Dear brothers, think about this! You can be
sure that the patriarch David wasn't referring to
himself, for he died and was buried, and his
tomb is still here among us. 30 But he was a
prophet, and he knew God had promised with an
oath that one of David's own descendants would
sit on his throne. 31 David was looking into the future and speaking of the Messiah's resurrection.
He was saying that God would not leave him
among the dead or allow his body to rot in the
grave.

32 "God raised Jesus from the dead, and we are
all witnesses of this. 33 Now he is exalted to the
place of highest honor in heaven, at God's right
hand. And the Father, as he had promised, gave
him the Holy Spirit to pour out upon us, just as
you see and hear today. 34 For David himself
never ascended into heaven, yet he said,

'The LORD said to my Lord,
"Sit in the place of honor at my
right hand
35 until I humble your enemies,
making them a footstool under
your feet."'

36 "So let everyone in Israel know for certain
that God has made this Jesus, whom you crucified, to be both Lord and Messiah!"

37 Peter's words pierced their hearts, and they
said to him and to the other apostles, "Brothers,
what should we do?"

38 Peter replied, "Each of you must repent of
your sins and turn to God, and be baptized in the
name of Jesus Christ for the forgiveness of your
sins. Then you will receive the gift of the Holy
Spirit. 39 This promise is to you, to your children,
and to those far away—all who have been called
by the Lord our God." 40 Then Peter continued
preaching for a long time, strongly urging all his
listeners, "Save yourselves from this crooked
generation!"

41 Those who believed what Peter said were
baptized and added to the church that day—
about 3,000 in all.

The Believers Form a Community

42 All the believers devoted themselves to the
apostles' teaching, and to fellowship, and to
sharing in meals (including the Lord's Supper),
and to prayer.

43 A deep sense of awe came over them all, and
the apostles performed many miraculous signs
and wonders. 44 And all the believers met together in one place and shared everything they
had. 45 They sold their property and possessions
and shared the money with those in need.
46 They worshiped together at the Temple each
day, met in homes for the Lord's Supper, and
shared their meals with great joy and generosity—47 all the while praising God and enjoying
the goodwill of all the people. And each day the
Lord added to their fellowship those who were
being saved.

CHAPTER 3

Peter Heals a Crippled Beggar

Peter and John went to the Temple one afternoon to take part in the three o'clock prayer service. 2 As they approached the Temple, a man
lame from birth was being carried in. Each day
he was put beside the Temple gate, the one called
the Beautiful Gate, so he could beg from the people going into the Temple. 3 When he saw Peter
and John about to enter, he asked them for some
money.

4 Peter and John looked at him intently, and
Peter said, "Look at us!" 5 The lame man looked at
them eagerly, expecting some money. 6 But Peter
said, "I don't have any silver or gold for you. But
I'll give you what I have. In the name of Jesus
Christ the Nazarene, get up and walk!"

7 Then Peter took the lame man by the right
hand and helped him up. And as he did, the man's
feet and ankles were instantly healed and
strengthened. 8 He jumped up, stood on his feet,
and began to walk! Then, walking, leaping, and
praising God, he went into the Temple with them.

9 All the people saw him walking and heard
him praising God. 10 When they realized he was
the lame beggar they had seen so often at the
Beautiful Gate, they were absolutely astounded!
11 They all rushed out in amazement to Solomon's Colonnade, where the man was holding
tightly to Peter and John.

Peter Preaches in the Temple

12 Peter saw his opportunity and addressed the
crowd. "People of Israel," he said, "what is so surprising about this? And why stare at us as though

we had made this man walk by our own power or
godliness? 13For it is the God of Abraham, Isaac,
and Jacob—the God of all our ancestors—who
has brought glory to his servant Jesus by doing
this. This is the same Jesus whom you handed
over and rejected before Pilate, despite Pilate's
decision to release him. 14You rejected this holy,
righteous one and instead demanded the release
of a murderer. 15You killed the author of life, but
God raised him from the dead. And we are witnesses of this fact!

16"Through faith in the name of Jesus, this
man was healed—and you know how crippled he
was before. Faith in Jesus' name has healed him
before your very eyes.

17"Friends, I realize that what you and your
leaders did to Jesus was done in ignorance.
18But God was fulfilling what all the prophets
had foretold about the Messiah—that he must
suffer these things. 19Now repent of your sins
and turn to God, so that your sins may be wiped
away. 20Then times of refreshment will come
from the presence of the Lord, and he will again
send you Jesus, your appointed Messiah. 21For
he must remain in heaven until the time for the
final restoration of all things, as God promised
long ago through his holy prophets. 22Moses
said, 'The LORD your God will raise up for you a
Prophet like me from among your own people.
Listen carefully to everything he tells you.'
23Then Moses said, 'Anyone who will not listen
to that Prophet will be completely cut off from
God's people.'

24"Starting with Samuel, every prophet spoke
about what is happening today. 25You are the
children of those prophets, and you are included
in the covenant God promised to your ancestors.
For God said to Abraham, 'Through your descendants all the families on earth will be
blessed.' 26When God raised up his servant,
Jesus, he sent him first to you people of Israel, to
bless you by turning each of you back from your
sinful ways."

CHAPTER 4

Peter and John before the Council

While Peter and John were speaking to the people, they were confronted by the priests, the captain of the Temple guard, and some of the
Sadducees. 2These leaders were very disturbed
that Peter and John were teaching the people
that through Jesus there is a resurrection of the
dead. 3They arrested them and, since it was already evening, put them in jail until morning.
4But many of the people who heard their message believed it, so the number of believers now
totaled about 5,000 men, not counting women
and children.

5The next day the council of all the rulers and
elders and teachers of religious law met in Jerusalem. 6Annas the high priest was there, along
with Caiaphas, John, Alexander, and other relatives of the high priest. 7They brought in the two
disciples and demanded, "By what power, or in
whose name, have you done this?"

8Then Peter, filled with the Holy Spirit, said to
them, "Rulers and elders of our people, 9are we
being questioned today because we've done a
good deed for a crippled man? Do you want to
know how he was healed? 10Let me clearly state
to all of you and to all the people of Israel that he
was healed by the powerful name of Jesus Christ
the Nazarene, the man you crucified but whom
God raised from the dead. 11For Jesus is the one
referred to in the Scriptures, where it says,

'The stone that you builders rejected
has now become the cornerstone.'

12There is salvation in no one else! God has given
no other name under heaven by which we must
be saved."

13The members of the council were amazed
when they saw the boldness of Peter and John,
for they could see that they were ordinary men
with no special training in the Scriptures. They
also recognized them as men who had been with
Jesus. 14But since they could see the man who
had been healed standing right there among
them, there was nothing the council could say.
15So they ordered Peter and John out of the
council chamber and conferred among themselves.

16"What should we do with these men?" they
asked each other. "We can't deny that they have
performed a miraculous sign, and everybody in
Jerusalem knows about it. 17But to keep them
from spreading their propaganda any further, we
must warn them not to speak to anyone in Jesus'
name again." 18So they called the apostles back
in and commanded them never again to speak or
teach in the name of Jesus.

19But Peter and John replied, "Do you think
God wants us to obey you rather than him? 20We
cannot stop telling about everything we have
seen and heard."

21The council then threatened them further,
but they finally let them go because they didn't
know how to punish them without starting a riot.
For everyone was praising God 22for this miracu-

lous sign—the healing of a man who had been
lame for more than forty years.

The Believers Pray for Courage

23 As soon as they were freed, Peter and John
returned to the other believers and told them
what the leading priests and elders had said.
24 When they heard the report, all the believers
lifted their voices together in prayer to God:
"O Sovereign Lord, Creator of heaven and earth,
the sea, and everything in them—25 you spoke
long ago by the Holy Spirit through our ancestor
David, your servant, saying,

'Why were the nations so angry?
Why did they waste their time
with futile plans?
26 The kings of the earth prepared for battle;
the rulers gathered together
against the LORD
and against his Messiah.'

27 "In fact, this has happened here in this very
city! For Herod Antipas, Pontius Pilate the governor, the Gentiles, and the people of Israel were all
united against Jesus, your holy servant, whom
you anointed. 28 But everything they did was
determined beforehand according to your will.
29 And now, O Lord, hear their threats, and give
us, your servants, great boldness in preaching
your word. 30 Stretch out your hand with healing
power; may miraculous signs and wonders be
done through the name of your holy servant
Jesus."

31 After this prayer, the meeting place shook,
and they were all filled with the Holy Spirit. Then
they preached the word of God with boldness.

The Believers Share Their Possessions

32 All the believers were united in heart and
mind. And they felt that what they owned was
not their own, so they shared everything they
had. 33 The apostles testified powerfully to the
resurrection of the Lord Jesus, and God's great
blessing was upon them all. 34 There were no
needy people among them, because those who
owned land or houses would sell them 35 and
bring the money to the apostles to give to those
in need.

36 For instance, there was Joseph, the one the
apostles nicknamed Barnabas (which means
"Son of Encouragement"). He was from the tribe
of Levi and came from the island of Cyprus. 37 He
sold a field he owned and brought the money to
the apostles.

CHAPTER 5

Ananias and Sapphira

But there was a certain man named Ananias who,
with his wife, Sapphira, sold some property. 2 He
brought part of the money to the apostles, claiming it was the full amount. With his wife's consent, he kept the rest.

3 Then Peter said, "Ananias, why have you let
Satan fill your heart? You lied to the Holy Spirit,
and you kept some of the money for yourself.
4 The property was yours to sell or not sell, as you
wished. And after selling it, the money was also
yours to give away. How could you do a thing like
this? You weren't lying to us but to God!"

5 As soon as Ananias heard these words, he fell
to the floor and died. Everyone who heard about it
was terrified. 6 Then some young men got up,
wrapped him in a sheet, and took him out and
buried him.

7 About three hours later his wife came in, not
knowing what had happened. 8 Peter asked her,
"Was this the price you and your husband received for your land?"

"Yes," she replied, "that was the price."

9 And Peter said, "How could the two of you
even think of conspiring to test the Spirit of the
Lord like this? The young men who buried your
husband are just outside the door, and they will
carry you out, too."

10 Instantly, she fell to the floor and died. When
the young men came in and saw that she was dead,
they carried her out and buried her beside her
husband. 11 Great fear gripped the entire church
and everyone else who heard what had happened.

The Apostles Heal Many

12 The apostles were performing many miraculous signs and wonders among the people. And
all the believers were meeting regularly at the
Temple in the area known as Solomon's Colonnade. 13 But no one else dared to join them, even
though all the people had high regard for them.
14 Yet more and more people believed and were
brought to the Lord—crowds of both men and
women. 15 As a result of the apostles' work, sick
people were brought out into the streets on beds
and mats so that Peter's shadow might fall across
some of them as he went by. 16 Crowds came from
the villages around Jerusalem, bringing their sick
and those possessed by evil spirits, and they were
all healed.

The Apostles Meet Opposition

17 The high priest and his officials, who were Sadducees, were filled with jealousy. 18 They arrested

the apostles and put them in the public jail. 19But an angel of the Lord came at night, opened the gates of the jail, and brought them out. Then he told them, 20"Go to the Temple and give the people this message of life!"

21So at daybreak the apostles entered the Temple, as they were told, and immediately began teaching.

When the high priest and his officials arrived, they convened the high council—the full assembly of the elders of Israel. Then they sent for the apostles to be brought from the jail for trial. 22But when the Temple guards went to the jail, the men were gone. So they returned to the council and reported, 23"The jail was securely locked, with the guards standing outside, but when we opened the gates, no one was there!"

24When the captain of the Temple guard and the leading priests heard this, they were perplexed, wondering where it would all end. 25Then someone arrived with startling news: "The men you put in jail are standing in the Temple, teaching the people!"

26The captain went with his Temple guards and arrested the apostles, but without violence, for they were afraid the people would stone them. 27Then they brought the apostles before the high council, where the high priest confronted them. 28"We gave you strict orders never again to teach in this man's name!" he said. "Instead, you have filled all Jerusalem with your teaching about him, and you want to make us responsible for his death!"

29But Peter and the apostles replied, "We must obey God rather than any human authority. 30The God of our ancestors raised Jesus from the dead after you killed him by hanging him on a cross. 31Then God put him in the place of honor at his right hand as Prince and Savior. He did this so the people of Israel would repent of their sins and be forgiven. 32We are witnesses of these things and so is the Holy Spirit, who is given by God to those who obey him."

33When they heard this, the high council was furious and decided to kill them. 34But one member, a Pharisee named Gamaliel, who was an expert in religious law and respected by all the people, stood up and ordered that the men be sent outside the council chamber for a while. 35Then he said to his colleagues, "Men of Israel, take care what you are planning to do to these men! 36Some time ago there was that fellow Theudas, who pretended to be someone great. About 400 others joined him, but he was killed, and all his followers went their various ways. The whole movement came to nothing. 37After him, at the time of the census, there was Judas of Galilee. He got people to follow him, but he was killed, too, and all his followers were scattered.

38"So my advice is, leave these men alone. Let them go. If they are planning and doing these things merely on their own, it will soon be overthrown. 39But if it is from God, you will not be able to overthrow them. You may even find yourselves fighting against God!"

40The others accepted his advice. They called in the apostles and had them flogged. Then they ordered them never again to speak in the name of Jesus, and they let them go.

41The apostles left the high council rejoicing that God had counted them worthy to suffer disgrace for the name of Jesus. 42And every day, in the Temple and from house to house, they continued to teach and preach this message: "Jesus is the Messiah."

CHAPTER 6

Seven Men Chosen to Serve

But as the believers rapidly multiplied, there were rumblings of discontent. The Greek-speaking believers complained about the Hebrew-speaking believers, saying that their widows were being discriminated against in the daily distribution of food.

2So the Twelve called a meeting of all the believers. They said, "We apostles should spend our time teaching the word of God, not running a food program. 3And so, brothers, select seven men who are well respected and are full of the Spirit and wisdom. We will give them this responsibility. 4Then we apostles can spend our time in prayer and teaching the word."

5Everyone liked this idea, and they chose the following: Stephen (a man full of faith and the Holy Spirit), Philip, Procorus, Nicanor, Timon, Parmenas, and Nicolas of Antioch (an earlier convert to the Jewish faith). 6These seven were presented to the apostles, who prayed for them as they laid their hands on them.

7So God's message continued to spread. The number of believers greatly increased in Jerusalem, and many of the Jewish priests were converted, too.

Stephen Is Arrested

8Stephen, a man full of God's grace and power, performed amazing miracles and signs among the people. 9But one day some men from the Synagogue of Freed Slaves, as it was called, started to debate with him. They were Jews from Cyrene, Alexandria, Cilicia, and the province of Asia. 10None of them could stand against the wisdom and the Spirit with which Stephen spoke.

11So they persuaded some men to lie about Stephen, saying, "We heard him blaspheme Moses, and even God." 12This roused the people, the elders, and the teachers of religious law. So they arrested Stephen and brought him before the high council.

13The lying witnesses said, "This man is always speaking against the holy Temple and against the law of Moses. 14We have heard him say that this Jesus of Nazareth will destroy the Temple and change the customs Moses handed down to us."

15At this point everyone in the high council stared at Stephen, because his face became as bright as an angel's.

CHAPTER 7

Stephen Addresses the Council

Then the high priest asked Stephen, "Are these accusations true?"

Want to learn about a *real* superhero? **Read ACTS 6:8-15 and ACTS 7:54-60.**

Stephen died for his faith. But all around us are heroes who live their lives for Jesus. Think about someone you know who's a hero of the faith.

Write your hero's name below.

....

Now write that person a note, to thank him or her for being an example of faith for you.

WRITE NOTES TO EVERY HERO OF THE FAITH YOU KNOW!

2This was Stephen's reply: "Brothers and fathers, listen to me. Our glorious God appeared to our ancestor Abraham in Mesopotamia before he settled in Haran. 3God told him, 'Leave your native land and your relatives, and come into the land that I will show you.' 4So Abraham left the land of the Chaldeans and lived in Haran until his father died. Then God brought him here to the land where you now live.

5"But God gave him no inheritance here, not even one square foot of land. God did promise, however, that eventually the whole land would belong to Abraham and his descendants—even though he had no children yet. 6God also told him that his descendants would live in a foreign land, where they would be oppressed as slaves for 400 years. 7'But I will punish the nation that enslaves them,' God said, 'and in the end they will come out and worship me here in this place.'

8"God also gave Abraham the covenant of circumcision at that time. So when Abraham became the father of Isaac, he circumcised him on the eighth day. And the practice was continued when Isaac became the father of Jacob, and when Jacob became the father of the twelve patriarchs of the Israelite nation.

9"These patriarchs were jealous of their brother Joseph, and they sold him to be a slave in Egypt. But God was with him 10and rescued him from all his troubles. And God gave him favor before Pharaoh, king of Egypt. God also gave Joseph unusual wisdom, so that Pharaoh appointed him governor over all of Egypt and put him in charge of the palace.

11"But a famine came upon Egypt and Canaan. There was great misery, and our ancestors ran out of food. 12Jacob heard that there was still grain in Egypt, so he sent his sons—our ancestors—to buy some. 13The second time they went, Joseph revealed his identity to his brothers, and they were introduced to Pharaoh. 14Then Joseph sent for his father, Jacob, and all his relatives to come to Egypt, seventy-five persons in all. 15So Jacob went to Egypt. He died there, as did our ancestors. 16Their bodies were taken to Shechem and buried in the tomb Abraham had bought for a certain price from Hamor's sons in Shechem.

17"As the time drew near when God would fulfill his promise to Abraham, the number of our people in Egypt greatly increased. 18But then a new king came to the throne of Egypt who knew nothing about Joseph. 19This king exploited our people and oppressed them, forcing parents to abandon their newborn babies so they would die.

20 “At that time Moses was born—a beautiful
child in God’s eyes. His parents cared for him at
home for three months. 21 When they had to
abandon him, Pharaoh’s daughter adopted him
and raised him as her own son. 22 Moses was
taught all the wisdom of the Egyptians, and he
was powerful in both speech and action.

23 “One day when Moses was forty years old, he
decided to visit his relatives, the people of Israel.
24 He saw an Egyptian mistreating an Israelite. So
Moses came to the man’s defense and avenged
him, killing the Egyptian. 25 Moses assumed his
fellow Israelites would realize that God had sent
him to rescue them, but they didn’t.

26 “The next day he visited them again and saw
two men of Israel fighting. He tried to be a peacemaker. ‘Men,’ he said, ‘you are brothers. Why are
you fighting each other?’

27 “But the man in the wrong pushed Moses
aside. ‘Who made you a ruler and judge over us?’
he asked. 28 ‘Are you going to kill me as you killed
that Egyptian yesterday?’ 29 When Moses heard
that, he fled the country and lived as a foreigner
in the land of Midian. There his two sons were
born.

30 “Forty years later, in the desert near Mount
Sinai, an angel appeared to Moses in the flame of
a burning bush. 31 When Moses saw it, he was
amazed at the sight. As he went to take a closer
look, the voice of the LORD called out to him, 32 ‘I
am the God of your ancestors—the God of Abraham, Isaac, and Jacob.’ Moses shook with terror
and did not dare to look.

33 “Then the LORD said to him, ‘Take off your
sandals, for you are standing on holy ground. 34 I
have certainly seen the oppression of my people
in Egypt. I have heard their groans and have
come down to rescue them. Now go, for I am
sending you back to Egypt.’

35 “So God sent back the same man his people
had previously rejected when they demanded,
‘Who made you a ruler and judge over us?’
Through the angel who appeared to him in the
burning bush, God sent Moses to be their ruler
and savior. 36 And by means of many wonders
and miraculous signs, he led them out of Egypt,
through the Red Sea, and through the wilderness
for forty years.

37 “Moses himself told the people of Israel,
‘God will raise up for you a Prophet like me from
among your own people.’ 38 Moses was with our
ancestors, the assembly of God’s people in the
wilderness, when the angel spoke to him at
Mount Sinai. And there Moses received life-
giving words to pass on to us.

39 “But our ancestors refused to listen to
Moses. They rejected him and wanted to return
to Egypt. 40 They told Aaron, ‘Make us some gods
who can lead us, for we don’t know what has
become of this Moses, who brought us out of
Egypt.’ 41 So they made an idol shaped like a calf,
and they sacrificed to it and celebrated over this
thing they had made. 42 Then God turned away
from them and abandoned them to serve the
stars of heaven as their gods! In the book of the
prophets it is written,

‘Was it to me you were bringing sacrifices
and offerings
during those forty years in the
wilderness, Israel?
43 No, you carried your pagan gods—
the shrine of Molech,
the star of your god Rephan,
and the images you made to
worship them.
So I will send you into exile
as far away as Babylon.’

44 “Our ancestors carried the Tabernacle with
them through the wilderness. It was constructed
according to the plan God had shown to Moses.
45 Years later, when Joshua led our ancestors in
battle against the nations that God drove out of
this land, the Tabernacle was taken with them
into their new territory. And it stayed there until
the time of King David.

46 “David found favor with God and asked for
the privilege of building a permanent Temple for
the God of Jacob. 47 But it was Solomon who actually built it. 48 However, the Most High doesn’t
live in temples made by human hands. As the
prophet says,

49 ‘Heaven is my throne,
and the earth is my footstool.
Could you build me a temple as good as that?’
asks the LORD.
‘Could you build me such a resting place?
50 Didn’t my hands make both heaven
and earth?’

51 “You stubborn people! You are heathen at
heart and deaf to the truth. Must you forever resist the Holy Spirit? That’s what your ancestors
did, and so do you! 52 Name one prophet your ancestors didn’t persecute! They even killed the
ones who predicted the coming of the Righteous
One—the Messiah whom you betrayed and
murdered. 53 You deliberately disobeyed God’s
law, even though you received it from the hands
of angels.”

54The Jewish leaders were infuriated by Stephen's accusation, and they shook their fists at
him in rage. 55But Stephen, full of the Holy Spirit,
gazed steadily into heaven and saw the glory of
God, and he saw Jesus standing in the place of
honor at God's right hand. 56And he told them,
"Look, I see the heavens opened and the Son of
Man standing in the place of honor at God's right
hand!"
57Then they put their hands over their ears
and began shouting. They rushed at him 58and
dragged him out of the city and began to stone
him. His accusers took off their coats and laid
them at the feet of a young man named Saul.
59As they stoned him, Stephen prayed, "Lord
Jesus, receive my spirit." 60He fell to his knees,
shouting, "Lord, don't charge them with this sin!"
And with that, he died.

CHAPTER 8

Saul was one of the witnesses, and he agreed
completely with the killing of Stephen.

Persecution Scatters the Believers

A great wave of persecution began that day,
sweeping over the church in Jerusalem; and all
the believers except the apostles were scattered
through the regions of Judea and Samaria.
2(Some devout men came and buried Stephen
with great mourning.) 3But Saul was going everywhere to destroy the church. He went from
house to house, dragging out both men and
women to throw them into prison.

Philip Preaches in Samaria

4But the believers who were scattered preached
the Good News about Jesus wherever they went.
5Philip, for example, went to the city of Samaria
and told the people there about the Messiah.
6Crowds listened intently to Philip because they
were eager to hear his message and see the miraculous signs he did. 7Many evil spirits were
cast out, screaming as they left their victims. And
many who had been paralyzed or lame were
healed. 8So there was great joy in that city.
9A man named Simon had been a sorcerer
there for many years, amazing the people of
Samaria and claiming to be someone great.
10Everyone, from the least to the greatest, often
spoke of him as "the Great One—the Power of
God." 11They listened closely to him because for
a long time he had astounded them with his
magic.
12But now the people believed Philip's

Look in the mirror and what do you see? Yup—you see a reflection. **Read ACTS 8:26-40 to meet a man who reflected the love of Jesus!**

THEN TRY THIS!
Gather two empty paper towel tubes, a mirror, a flashlight—and a friend!

Read what Jesus had to say about sharing your faith in him. Check out Matthew 28:19-20.

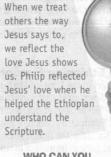

1 **Set the paper towel tubes on a table in front of a mirror. Place them in a V-shape pointing toward the mirror.**

2 **Use a flashlight to shine light through one tube toward the mirror. Angle the second tube until you see the light reflected back through the second tube.**

THAT'S ENLIGHTENING!

When we treat others the way Jesus says to, we reflect the love Jesus shows us. Philip reflected Jesus' love when he helped the Ethiopian understand the Scripture.

WHO CAN YOU REFLECT THE LOVE OF JESUS TO THIS WEEK?

Write that person's name below.

message of Good News concerning the Kingdom of God and the name of Jesus Christ. As a
result, many men and women were baptized.
13 Then Simon himself believed and was baptized. He began following Philip wherever he
went, and he was amazed by the signs and great
miracles Philip performed.
14 When the apostles in Jerusalem heard that
the people of Samaria had accepted God's message, they sent Peter and John there. 15 As soon as
they arrived, they prayed for these new believers
to receive the Holy Spirit. 16 The Holy Spirit had
not yet come upon any of them, for they had only
been baptized in the name of the Lord Jesus.
17 Then Peter and John laid their hands upon
these believers, and they received the Holy
Spirit.
18 When Simon saw that the Spirit was given
when the apostles laid their hands on people, he
offered them money to buy this power. 19 "Let me
have this power, too," he exclaimed, "so that
when I lay my hands on people, they will receive
the Holy Spirit!"
20 But Peter replied, "May your money be destroyed with you for thinking God's gift can be
bought! 21 You can have no part in this, for your
heart is not right with God. 22 Repent of your
wickedness and pray to the Lord. Perhaps he will
forgive your evil thoughts, 23 for I can see that you
are full of bitter jealousy and are held captive by
sin."
24 "Pray to the Lord for me," Simon exclaimed,
"that these terrible things you've said won't happen to me!"
25 After testifying and preaching the word of
the Lord in Samaria, Peter and John returned to
Jerusalem. And they stopped in many Samaritan villages along the way to preach the Good
News.

Philip and the Ethiopian Eunuch

26 As for Philip, an angel of the Lord said to him,
"Go south down the desert road that runs from
Jerusalem to Gaza." 27 So he started out, and he
met the treasurer of Ethiopia, a eunuch of great
authority under the Kandake, the queen of Ethiopia. The eunuch had gone to Jerusalem to worship, 28 and he was now returning. Seated in his
carriage, he was reading aloud from the book of
the prophet Isaiah.
29 The Holy Spirit said to Philip, "Go over and
walk along beside the carriage."
30 Philip ran over and heard the man reading
from the prophet Isaiah. Philip asked, "Do you
understand what you are reading?"

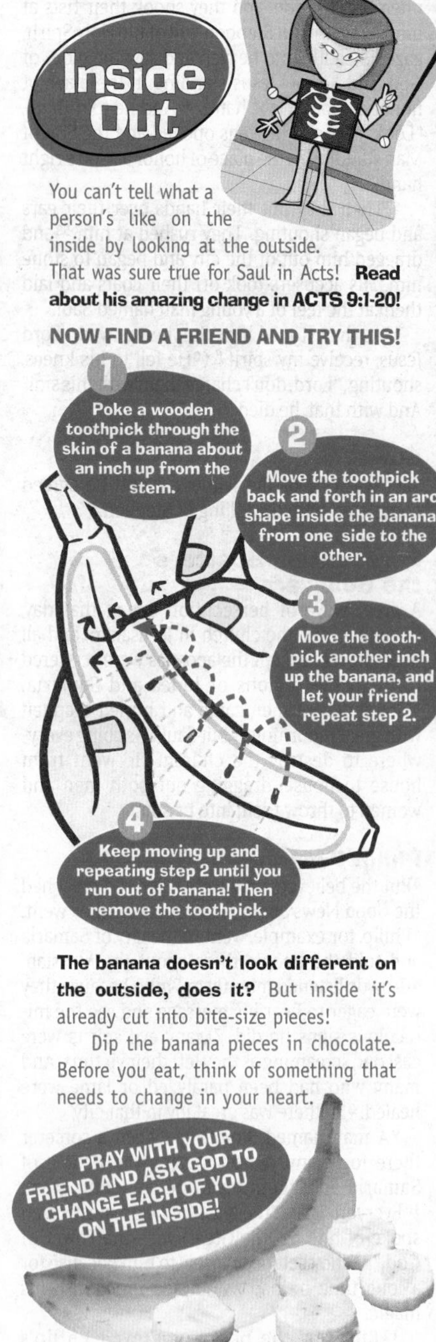

Inside Out
You can't tell what a person's like on the inside by looking at the outside. That was sure true for Saul in Acts! **Read about his amazing change in ACTS 9:1-20!**
NOW FIND A FRIEND AND TRY THIS!
1 Poke a wooden toothpick through the skin of a banana about an inch up from the stem.
2 Move the toothpick back and forth in an arc shape inside the banana, from one side to the other.
3 Move the toothpick another inch up the banana, and let your friend repeat step 2.
4 Keep moving up and repeating step 2 until you run out of banana! Then remove the toothpick.
The banana doesn't look different on the outside, does it? But inside it's already cut into bite-size pieces!
Dip the banana pieces in chocolate. Before you eat, think of something that needs to change in your heart.
PRAY WITH YOUR FRIEND AND ASK GOD TO CHANGE EACH OF YOU ON THE INSIDE!

31The man replied, "How can I, unless someone instructs me?" And he urged Philip to come
up into the carriage and sit with him.
32The passage of Scripture he had been reading was this:

"He was led like a sheep to the slaughter.
And as a lamb is silent before the shearers,
he did not open his mouth.
33 He was humiliated and received no justice.
Who can speak of his descendants?
For his life was taken from the earth."

34The eunuch asked Philip, "Tell me, was the
prophet talking about himself or someone else?"
35So beginning with this same Scripture, Philip
told him the Good News about Jesus.
36As they rode along, they came to some water, and the eunuch said, "Look! There's some
water! Why can't I be baptized? "* 38He ordered
the carriage to stop, and they went down into the
water, and Philip baptized him.
39When they came up out of the water, the
Spirit of the Lord snatched Philip away. The eunuch never saw him again but went on his way
rejoicing. 40Meanwhile, Philip found himself
farther north at the town of Azotus. He preached
the Good News there and in every town along the
way until he came to Caesarea.

CHAPTER 9
Saul's Conversion

Meanwhile, Saul was uttering threats with every
breath and was eager to kill the Lord's followers.
So he went to the high priest. 2He requested letters addressed to the synagogues in Damascus,
asking for their cooperation in the arrest of any
followers of the Way he found there. He wanted
to bring them—both men and women—back to
Jerusalem in chains.
3As he was approaching Damascus on this
mission, a light from heaven suddenly shone
down around him. 4He fell to the ground and
heard a voice saying to him, "Saul! Saul! Why are
you persecuting me?"
5"Who are you, lord?" Saul asked.
And the voice replied, "I am Jesus, the one you
are persecuting! 6Now get up and go into the city,
and you will be told what you must do."
7The men with Saul stood speechless, for they
heard the sound of someone's voice but saw no
one! 8Saul picked himself up off the ground, but
when he opened his eyes he was blind. So his
companions led him by the hand to Damascus.
9He remained there blind for three days and did
not eat or drink.
10Now there was a believer in Damascus
named Ananias. The Lord spoke to him in a vision,
calling, "Ananias!"
"Yes, Lord!" he replied.
11The Lord said, "Go over to Straight Street, to
the house of Judas. When you get there, ask for a
man from Tarsus named Saul. He is praying to
me right now. 12I have shown him a vision of a
man named Ananias coming in and laying hands
on him so he can see again."
13"But Lord," exclaimed Ananias, "I've heard
many people talk about the terrible things this
man has done to the believers in Jerusalem!
14And he is authorized by the leading priests to
arrest everyone who calls upon your name."
15But the Lord said, "Go, for Saul is my chosen
instrument to take my message to the Gentiles
and to kings, as well as to the people of Israel.
16And I will show him how much he must suffer
for my name's sake."
17So Ananias went and found Saul. He laid
his hands on him and said, "Brother Saul, the
Lord Jesus, who appeared to you on the road,
has sent me so that you might regain your sight
and be filled with the Holy Spirit." 18Instantly
something like scales fell from Saul's eyes, and
he regained his sight. Then he got up and was
baptized. 19Afterward he ate some food and
regained his strength.

Saul in Damascus and Jerusalem

Saul stayed with the believers in Damascus for a
few days. 20And immediately he began preaching about Jesus in the synagogues, saying, "He is
indeed the Son of God!"
21All who heard him were amazed. "Isn't this
the same man who caused such devastation
among Jesus' followers in Jerusalem?" they
asked. "And didn't he come here to arrest them
and take them in chains to the leading priests?"
22Saul's preaching became more and more
powerful, and the Jews in Damascus couldn't refute his proofs that Jesus was indeed the Messiah. 23After a while some of the Jews plotted
together to kill him. 24They were watching for
him day and night at the city gate so they could
murder him, but Saul was told about their plot.
25So during the night, some of the other believers lowered him in a large basket through an
opening in the city wall.

8:36 Some manuscripts add verse 37, *"You can," Philip answered, "if you believe with all your heart." And the eunuch replied, "I believe that Jesus Christ is the Son of God."*

26When Saul arrived in Jerusalem, he tried to
meet with the believers, but they were all afraid
of him. They did not believe he had truly become
a believer! 27Then Barnabas brought him to the
apostles and told them how Saul had seen the
Lord on the way to Damascus and how the Lord
had spoken to Saul. He also told them that Saul
had preached boldly in the name of Jesus in
Damascus.

28So Saul stayed with the apostles and went all
around Jerusalem with them, preaching boldly in
the name of the Lord. 29He debated with some
Greek-speaking Jews, but they tried to murder
him. 30When the believers heard about this, they
took him down to Caesarea and sent him away to
Tarsus, his hometown.

31The church then had peace throughout Judea, Galilee, and Samaria, and it became stronger
as the believers lived in the fear of the Lord. And
with the encouragement of the Holy Spirit, it also
grew in numbers.

Peter Heals Aeneas and Raises Dorcas

32Meanwhile, Peter traveled from place to place,
and he came down to visit the believers in the
town of Lydda. 33There he met a man named
Aeneas, who had been paralyzed and bedridden
for eight years. 34Peter said to him, "Aeneas,
Jesus Christ heals you! Get up, and roll up your
sleeping mat!" And he was healed instantly.
35Then the whole population of Lydda and
Sharon saw Aeneas walking around, and they
turned to the Lord.

36There was a believer in Joppa named Tabitha
(which in Greek is Dorcas). She was always doing
kind things for others and helping the poor.
37About this time she became ill and died. Her
body was washed for burial and laid in an upstairs room. 38But the believers had heard that
Peter was nearby at Lydda, so they sent two men
to beg him, "Please come as soon as possible!"

39So Peter returned with them; and as soon as
he arrived, they took him to the upstairs room.
The room was filled with widows who were
weeping and showing him the coats and other
clothes Dorcas had made for them. 40But Peter
asked them all to leave the room; then he knelt
and prayed. Turning to the body he said, "Get up,
Tabitha." And she opened her eyes! When she
saw Peter, she sat up! 41He gave her his hand and
helped her up. Then he called in the widows and
all the believers, and he presented her to them
alive.

42The news spread through the whole town,
and many believed in the Lord. 43And Peter
stayed a long time in Joppa, living with Simon, a
tanner of hides.

CHAPTER 10

Cornelius Calls for Peter

In Caesarea there lived a Roman army officer
named Cornelius, who was a captain of the Ital-
ian Regiment. 2He was a devout, God-fearing
man, as was everyone in his household. He gave
generously to the poor and prayed regularly to
God. 3One afternoon about three o'clock, he had
a vision in which he saw an angel of God coming
toward him. "Cornelius!" the angel said.

4Cornelius stared at him in terror. "What is it,
sir?" he asked the angel.

And the angel replied, "Your prayers and gifts
to the poor have been received by God as an offering! 5Now send some men to Joppa, and summon a man named Simon Peter. 6He is staying
with Simon, a tanner who lives near the seashore."

7As soon as the angel was gone, Cornelius
called two of his household servants and a devout soldier, one of his personal attendants. 8He
told them what had happened and sent them off
to Joppa.

Peter Visits Cornelius

9The next day as Cornelius's messengers were
nearing the town, Peter went up on the flat roof
to pray. It was about noon, 10and he was hungry.
But while a meal was being prepared, he fell into
a trance. 11He saw the sky open, and something
like a large sheet was let down by its four corners.
12In the sheet were all sorts of animals, reptiles,
and birds. 13Then a voice said to him, "Get up,
Peter; kill and eat them."

14"No, Lord," Peter declared. "I have never
eaten anything that our Jewish laws have
declared impure and unclean."

15But the voice spoke again: "Do not call something unclean if God has made it clean." 16The
same vision was repeated three times. Then the
sheet was suddenly pulled up to heaven.

17Peter was very perplexed. What could the vision mean? Just then the men sent by Cornelius
found Simon's house. Standing outside the gate,
18they asked if a man named Simon Peter was
staying there.

19Meanwhile, as Peter was puzzling over the
vision, the Holy Spirit said to him, "Three men
have come looking for you. 20Get up, go downstairs, and go with them without hesitation.
Don't worry, for I have sent them."

21So Peter went down and said, "I'm the man you are looking for. Why have you come?"

22They said, "We were sent by Cornelius, a Roman officer. He is a devout and God-fearing man, well respected by all the Jews. A holy angel instructed him to summon you to his house so that he can hear your message." 23So Peter invited the men to stay for the night. The next day he went with them, accompanied by some of the brothers from Joppa.

24They arrived in Caesarea the following day. Cornelius was waiting for them and had called together his relatives and close friends. 25As Peter entered his home, Cornelius fell at his feet and worshiped him. 26But Peter pulled him up and said, "Stand up! I'm a human being just like you!" 27So they talked together and went inside, where many others were assembled.

28Peter told them, "You know it is against our laws for a Jewish man to enter a Gentile home like this or to associate with you. But God has shown me that I should no longer think of anyone as impure or unclean. 29So I came without objection as soon as I was sent for. Now tell me why you sent for me."

30Cornelius replied, "Four days ago I was praying in my house about this same time, three o'clock in the afternoon. Suddenly, a man in dazzling clothes was standing in front of me. 31He told me, 'Cornelius, your prayer has been heard, and your gifts to the poor have been noticed by God! 32Now send messengers to Joppa, and summon a man named Simon Peter. He is staying in the home of Simon, a tanner who lives near the seashore.' 33So I sent for you at once, and it was good of you to come. Now we are all here, waiting before God to hear the message the Lord has given you."

The Gentiles Hear the Good News

34Then Peter replied, "I see very clearly that God shows no favoritism. 35In every nation he accepts those who fear him and do what is right. 36This is the message of Good News for the people of Israel—that there is peace with God through Jesus Christ, who is Lord of all. 37You know what happened throughout Judea, beginning in Galilee, after John began preaching his message of baptism. 38And you know that God anointed Jesus of Nazareth with the Holy Spirit and with power. Then Jesus went around doing good and healing all who were oppressed by the devil, for God was with him.

39"And we apostles are witnesses of all he did throughout Judea and in Jerusalem. They put him to death by hanging him on a cross, 40but God raised him to life on the third day. Then God allowed him to appear, 41not to the general public, but to us whom God had chosen in advance to be his witnesses. We were those who ate and drank with him after he rose from the dead. 42And he ordered us to preach everywhere and to testify that Jesus is the one appointed by God to be the judge of all—the living and the dead. 43He is the one all the prophets testified about, saying that everyone who believes in him will have their sins forgiven through his name."

The Gentiles Receive the Holy Spirit

44Even as Peter was saying these things, the Holy Spirit fell upon all who were listening to the message. 45The Jewish believers who came with Peter were amazed that the gift of the Holy Spirit had been poured out on the Gentiles, too. 46For they heard them speaking in other tongues and praising God.

Then Peter asked, 47"Can anyone object to their being baptized, now that they have received the Holy Spirit just as we did?" 48So he gave orders for them to be baptized in the name of Jesus Christ. Afterward Cornelius asked him to stay with them for several days.

CHAPTER 11

Peter Explains His Actions

Soon the news reached the apostles and other believers in Judea that the Gentiles had received the word of God. 2But when Peter arrived back in Jerusalem, the Jewish believers criticized him. 3"You entered the home of Gentiles and even ate with them!" they said.

4Then Peter told them exactly what had happened. 5"I was in the town of Joppa," he said, "and while I was praying, I went into a trance and saw a vision. Something like a large sheet was let down by its four corners from the sky. And it came right down to me. 6When I looked inside the sheet, I saw all sorts of tame and wild animals, reptiles, and birds. 7And I heard a voice say, 'Get up, Peter; kill and eat them.'

8"'No, Lord,' I replied. 'I have never eaten anything that our Jewish laws have declared impure or unclean.'

9"But the voice from heaven spoke again: 'Do not call something unclean if God has made it clean.' 10This happened three times before the sheet and all it contained was pulled back up to heaven.

11"Just then three men who had been sent
from Caesarea arrived at the house where we
were staying. 12The Holy Spirit told me to go
with them and not to worry that they were
Gentiles. These six brothers here accompanied
me, and we soon entered the home of the man
who had sent for us. 13He told us how an angel
had appeared to him in his home and had told
him, 'Send messengers to Joppa, and summon a
man named Simon Peter. 14He will tell you how
you and everyone in your household can be
saved!'

15"As I began to speak," Peter continued, "the
Holy Spirit fell on them, just as he fell on us at the
beginning. 16Then I thought of the Lord's words
when he said, 'John baptized with water, but you
will be baptized with the Holy Spirit.' 17And
since God gave these Gentiles the same gift he
gave us when we believed in the Lord Jesus
Christ, who was I to stand in God's way?"

18When the others heard this, they stopped
objecting and began praising God. They said,
"We can see that God has also given the Gentiles
the privilege of repenting of their sins and receiving eternal life."

The Church in Antioch of Syria

19Meanwhile, the believers who had been scattered during the persecution after Stephen's
death traveled as far as Phoenicia, Cyprus, and
Antioch of Syria. They preached the word of God,
but only to Jews. 20However, some of the believers who went to Antioch from Cyprus and Cyrene began preaching to the Gentiles about the
Lord Jesus. 21The power of the Lord was with
them, and a large number of these Gentiles believed and turned to the Lord.

22When the church at Jerusalem heard what
had happened, they sent Barnabas to Antioch.
23When he arrived and saw this evidence of
God's blessing, he was filled with joy, and he encouraged the believers to stay true to the Lord.
24Barnabas was a good man, full of the Holy
Spirit and strong in faith. And many people were
brought to the Lord.

25Then Barnabas went on to Tarsus to look for
Saul. 26When he found him, he brought him
back to Antioch. Both of them stayed there with
the church for a full year, teaching large crowds
of people. (It was at Antioch that the believers
were first called Christians.)

27During this time some prophets traveled
from Jerusalem to Antioch. 28One of them
named Agabus stood up in one of the meetings
and predicted by the Spirit that a great famine
was coming upon the entire Roman world. (This
was fulfilled during the reign of Claudius.) 29So
the believers in Antioch decided to send relief to
the brothers and sisters in Judea, everyone giving
as much as they could. 30This they did, entrust-
ing their gifts to Barnabas and Saul to take to the
elders of the church in Jerusalem.

CHAPTER 12

James Is Killed and Peter Is Imprisoned

About that time King Herod Agrippa began to
persecute some believers in the church. 2He
had the apostle James (John's brother) killed
with a sword. 3When Herod saw how much this
pleased the Jewish people, he also arrested Peter. (This took place during the Passover celebration.) 4Then he imprisoned him, placing him
under the guard of four squads of four soldiers
each. Herod intended to bring Peter out for
public trial after the Passover. 5But while Peter
was in prison, the church prayed very earnestly
for him.

Peter's Miraculous Escape from Prison

6The night before Peter was to be placed on trial,
he was asleep, fastened with two chains between
two soldiers. Others stood guard at the prison
gate. 7Suddenly, there was a bright light in the
cell, and an angel of the Lord stood before Peter.
The angel struck him on the side to awaken him
and said, "Quick! Get up!" And the chains fell off
his wrists. 8Then the angel told him, "Get
dressed and put on your sandals." And he did.
"Now put on your coat and follow me," the angel
ordered.

9So Peter left the cell, following the angel. But
all the time he thought it was a vision. He didn't
realize it was actually happening. 10They passed
the first and second guard posts and came to the
iron gate leading to the city, and this opened for
them all by itself. So they passed through and
started walking down the street, and then the angel suddenly left him.

11Peter finally came to his senses. "It's really
true!" he said. "The Lord has sent his angel and
saved me from Herod and from what the Jewish
leaders had planned to do to me!"

12When he realized this, he went to the home
of Mary, the mother of John Mark, where many
were gathered for prayer. 13He knocked at the
door in the gate, and a servant girl named Rhoda
came to open it. 14When she recognized Peter's
voice, she was so overjoyed that, instead of open-

WHO'S THERE?

PETER.

NO WAY, PETER'S IN PRISON!

Hey, it was an honest mistake.

Peter *was* in jail. But not for long. **Read ACTS 12:6-19 for an account of a most amazing jailbreak!**

NOW TRY THIS!

1 **Hold a large book in one hand and a sheet of paper in the other.**

2 **Drop them both at the same time.**

Read about another prison adventure in Acts 16:16-34.

WHICH HITS THE FLOOR FIRST? YOU'RE RIGHT! THE BOOK.

NOW TRY IT AGAIN, WITH THIS CHANGE.

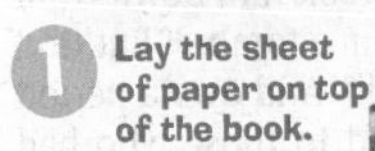

1 **Lay the sheet of paper on top of the book.**

2 **Drop them together.**

SEE?

The paper followed the book right down to the floor, just like Peter followed the angel out of jail!

On your paper, draw a picture of this Bible story. Then use your picture to tell the Bible story to two people this week. Write on your paper the names of the people you tell and the dates you talked to them.

ing the door, she ran back inside and told everyone, "Peter is standing at the door!"
15"You're out of your mind!" they said. When
she insisted, they decided, "It must be his angel."
16Meanwhile, Peter continued knocking.
When they finally opened the door and saw him,
they were amazed. 17He motioned for them to
quiet down and told them how the Lord had led
him out of prison. "Tell James and the other
brothers what happened," he said. And then he
went to another place.
18At dawn there was a great commotion
among the soldiers about what had happened to
Peter. 19Herod Agrippa ordered a thorough
search for him. When he couldn't be found, Herod interrogated the guards and sentenced them
to death. Afterward Herod left Judea to stay in
Caesarea for a while.

The Death of Herod Agrippa

20Now Herod was very angry with the people of
Tyre and Sidon. So they sent a delegation to
make peace with him because their cities were
dependent upon Herod's country for food. The
delegates won the support of Blastus, Herod's
personal assistant, 21and an appointment with
Herod was granted. When the day arrived, Herod
put on his royal robes, sat on his throne, and
made a speech to them. 22The people gave him a
great ovation, shouting, "It's the voice of a god,
not of a man!"
23Instantly, an angel of the Lord struck Herod
with a sickness, because he accepted the people's worship instead of giving the glory to God.
So he was consumed with worms and died.
24Meanwhile, the word of God continued to
spread, and there were many new believers.
25When Barnabas and Saul had finished their
mission to Jerusalem, they returned, taking John
Mark with them.

CHAPTER 13

Barnabas and Saul Are Commissioned

Among the prophets and teachers of the church
at Antioch of Syria were Barnabas, Simeon
(called "the black man"), Lucius (from Cyrene),
Manaen (the childhood companion of King
Herod Antipas), and Saul. 2One day as these
men were worshiping the Lord and fasting, the
Holy Spirit said, "Dedicate Barnabas and Saul
for the special work to which I have called
them." 3So after more fasting and prayer, the
men laid their hands on them and sent them on
their way.

Acts 13 . . . page 1086

Paul's First Missionary Journey

4So Barnabas and Saul were sent out by the
Holy Spirit. They went down to the seaport of
Seleucia and then sailed for the island of Cyprus. 5There, in the town of Salamis, they went
to the Jewish synagogues and preached the
word of God. John Mark went with them as their
assistant.

6Afterward they traveled from town to town
across the entire island until finally they
reached Paphos, where they met a Jewish sorcerer, a false prophet named Bar-Jesus. 7He had
attached himself to the governor, Sergius
Paulus, who was an intelligent man. The governor invited Barnabas and Saul to visit him, for
he wanted to hear the word of God. 8But Ely-
mas, the sorcerer (as his name means in Greek),
interfered and urged the governor to pay no attention to what Barnabas and Saul said. He was
trying to keep the governor from believing.

9Saul, also known as Paul, was filled with the
Holy Spirit, and he looked the sorcerer in the
eye. 10Then he said, "You son of the devil, full of
every sort of deceit and fraud, and enemy of all
that is good! Will you never stop perverting the
true ways of the Lord? 11Watch now, for the
Lord has laid his hand of punishment upon you,
and you will be struck blind. You will not see the
sunlight for some time." Instantly mist and
darkness came over the man's eyes, and he began groping around begging for someone to
take his hand and lead him.

12When the governor saw what had happened, he became a believer, for he was astonished at the teaching about the Lord.

Paul Preaches in Antioch of Pisidia

13Paul and his companions then left Paphos by
ship for Pamphylia, landing at the port town of
Perga. There John Mark left them and returned
to Jerusalem. 14But Paul and Barnabas traveled
inland to Antioch of Pisidia.

On the Sabbath they went to the synagogue
for the services. 15After the usual readings from
the books of Moses and the prophets, those in
charge of the service sent them this message:
"Brothers, if you have any word of encouragement for the people, come and give it."

16So Paul stood, lifted his hand to quiet them,
and started speaking. "Men of Israel," he said,
"and you God-fearing Gentiles, listen to me.

17"The God of this nation of Israel chose our
ancestors and made them multiply and grow
strong during their stay in Egypt. Then with a
powerful arm he led them out of their slavery.
18He put up with them through forty years of
wandering in the wilderness. 19Then he destroyed seven nations in Canaan and gave their
land to Israel as an inheritance. 20All this took
about 450 years.

"After that, God gave them judges to rule until
the time of Samuel the prophet. 21Then the
people begged for a king, and God gave them
Saul son of Kish, a man of the tribe of Benjamin,
who reigned for forty years. 22But God removed
Saul and replaced him with David, a man about
whom God said, 'I have found David son of Jesse,
a man after my own heart. He will do everything
I want him to do.'

23"And it is one of King David's descendants,
Jesus, who is God's promised Savior of Israel!
24Before he came, John the Baptist preached
that all the people of Israel needed to repent of
their sins and turn to God and be baptized. 25As
John was finishing his ministry he asked, 'Do
you think I am the Messiah? No, I am not! But he
is coming soon—and I'm not even worthy to be
his slave and untie the sandals on his feet.'

26"Brothers—you sons of Abraham, and also
you God-fearing Gentiles—this message of salvation has been sent to us! 27The people in Jerusalem and their leaders did not recognize Jesus
as the one the prophets had spoken about. Instead, they condemned him, and in doing this
they fulfilled the prophets' words that are read
every Sabbath. 28They found no legal reason to
execute him, but they asked Pilate to have him
killed anyway.

29"When they had done all that the prophecies said about him, they took him down from
the cross and placed him in a tomb. 30But God
raised him from the dead! 31And over a period
of many days he appeared to those who had
gone with him from Galilee to Jerusalem. They
are now his witnesses to the people of Israel.

32"And now we are here to bring you this
Good News. The promise was made to our ancestors, 33and God has now fulfilled it for us,
their descendants, by raising Jesus. This is what
the second psalm says about Jesus:

'You are my Son.
Today I have become your Father.'

34For God had promised to raise him from the
dead, not leaving him to rot in the grave. He said,
'I will give you the sacred blessings I promised to
David.' 35Another psalm explains it more fully:
'You will not allow your Holy One to rot in the
grave.' 36This is not a reference to David, for

after David had done the will of God in his own
generation, he died and was buried with his ancestors, and his body decayed. 37No, it was a reference to someone else—someone whom God
raised and whose body did not decay.

38"Brothers, listen! We are here to proclaim
that through this man Jesus there is forgiveness
for your sins. 39Everyone who believes in him is
declared right with God—something the law of
Moses could never do. 40Be careful! Don't let the
prophets' words apply to you. For they said,

41 'Look, you mockers,
be amazed and die!
For I am doing something in your
own day,
something you wouldn't believe
even if someone told you about it.'"

42As Paul and Barnabas left the synagogue
that day, the people begged them to speak about
these things again the next week. 43Many Jews
and devout converts to Judaism followed Paul
and Barnabas, and the two men urged them to
continue to rely on the grace of God.

Paul Turns to the Gentiles

44The following week almost the entire city
turned out to hear them preach the word of the
Lord. 45But when some of the Jews saw the
crowds, they were jealous; so they slandered
Paul and argued against whatever he said.

46Then Paul and Barnabas spoke out boldly
and declared, "It was necessary that we first
preach the word of God to you Jews. But since
you have rejected it and judged yourselves unworthy of eternal life, we will offer it to the
Gentiles. 47For the Lord gave us this command
when he said,

'I have made you a light to the Gentiles,
to bring salvation to the farthest corners of
the earth.'"

48When the Gentiles heard this, they were
very glad and thanked the Lord for his message;
and all who were chosen for eternal life became
believers. 49So the Lord's message spread
throughout that region.

50Then the Jews stirred up the influential
religious women and the leaders of the city,
and they incited a mob against Paul and Barnabas and ran them out of town. 51So they shook
the dust from their feet as a sign of rejection
and went to the town of Iconium. 52And the believers were filled with joy and with the Holy
Spirit.

CHAPTER 14

Paul and Barnabas in Iconium

The same thing happened in Iconium. Paul and
Barnabas went to the Jewish synagogue and
preached with such power that a great number
of both Jews and Greeks became believers.
2Some of the Jews, however, spurned God's message and poisoned the minds of the Gentiles
against Paul and Barnabas. 3But the apostles
stayed there a long time, preaching boldly about
the grace of the Lord. And the Lord proved their
message was true by giving them power to do
miraculous signs and wonders. 4But the people
of the town were divided in their opinion about
them. Some sided with the Jews, and some with
the apostles.

5Then a mob of Gentiles and Jews, along with
their leaders, decided to attack and stone them.
6When the apostles learned of it, they fled to the
region of Lycaonia—to the towns of Lystra and
Derbe and the surrounding area. 7And there they
preached the Good News.

Paul and Barnabas in Lystra and Derbe

8While they were at Lystra, Paul and Barnabas
came upon a man with crippled feet. He had
been that way from birth, so he had never
walked. He was sitting 9and listening as Paul
preached. Looking straight at him, Paul realized
he had faith to be healed. 10So Paul called to him
in a loud voice, "Stand up!" And the man jumped
to his feet and started walking.

11When the crowd saw what Paul had done,
they shouted in their local dialect, "These men
are gods in human form!" 12They decided that
Barnabas was the Greek god Zeus and that Paul
was Hermes, since he was the chief speaker.
13Now the temple of Zeus was located just outside the town. So the priest of the temple and the
crowd brought bulls and wreaths of flowers to
the town gates, and they prepared to offer sacrifices to the apostles.

14But when the apostles Barnabas and Paul
heard what was happening, they tore their clothing in dismay and ran out among the people,
shouting, 15"Friends, why are you doing this? We
are merely human beings—just like you! We have
come to bring you the Good News that you
should turn from these worthless things and
turn to the living God, who made heaven and
earth, the sea, and everything in them. 16In the
past he permitted all the nations to go their own
ways, 17but he never left them without evidence
of himself and his goodness. For instance, he

sends you rain and good crops and gives you
food and joyful hearts." 18But even with these
words, Paul and Barnabas could scarcely restrain
the people from sacrificing to them.
19Then some Jews arrived from Antioch and
Iconium and won the crowds to their side. They
stoned Paul and dragged him out of town,
thinking he was dead. 20But as the believers
gathered around him, he got up and went back
into the town. The next day he left with Barnabas for Derbe.

Paul and Barnabas Return to Antioch of Syria

21After preaching the Good News in Derbe and
making many disciples, Paul and Barnabas returned to Lystra, Iconium, and Antioch of Pisidia, 22where they strengthened the believers.
They encouraged them to continue in the faith,
reminding them that we must suffer many
hardships to enter the Kingdom of God. 23Paul
and Barnabas also appointed elders in every
church. With prayer and fasting, they turned
the elders over to the care of the Lord, in whom
they had put their trust. 24Then they traveled
back through Pisidia to Pamphylia. 25They
preached the word in Perga, then went down to
Attalia.
26Finally, they returned by ship to Antioch of
Syria, where their journey had begun. The believers there had entrusted them to the grace
of God to do the work they had now completed.
27Upon arriving in Antioch, they called the
church together and reported everything God
had done through them and how he had
opened the door of faith to the Gentiles, too.
28And they stayed there with the believers for a
long time.

CHAPTER 15

The Council at Jerusalem

While Paul and Barnabas were at Antioch of
Syria, some men from Judea arrived and began
to teach the believers: "Unless you are circumcised as required by the law of Moses, you cannot be saved." 2Paul and Barnabas disagreed
with them, arguing vehemently. Finally, the
church decided to send Paul and Barnabas to Jerusalem, accompanied by some local believers,
to talk to the apostles and elders about this
question. 3The church sent the delegates to
Jerusalem, and they stopped along the way in
Phoenicia and Samaria to visit the believers.
They told them—much to everyone's joy—that
the Gentiles, too, were being converted.
4When they arrived in Jerusalem, Barnabas
and Paul were welcomed by the whole church,
including the apostles and elders. They reported
everything God had done through them. 5But
then some of the believers who belonged to the
sect of the Pharisees stood up and insisted, "The
Gentile converts must be circumcised and
required to follow the law of Moses."
6So the apostles and elders met together to
resolve this issue. 7At the meeting, after a long
discussion, Peter stood and addressed them as
follows: "Brothers, you all know that God chose
me from among you some time ago to preach to
the Gentiles so that they could hear the Good
News and believe. 8God knows people's hearts,
and he confirmed that he accepts Gentiles by
giving them the Holy Spirit, just as he did to us.
9He made no distinction between us and them,
for he cleansed their hearts through faith. 10So
why are you now challenging God by burdening
the Gentile believers with a yoke that neither
we nor our ancestors were able to bear? 11We believe that we are all saved the same way, by the
undeserved grace of the Lord Jesus."
12Everyone listened quietly as Barnabas and
Paul told about the miraculous signs and wonders God had done through them among the
Gentiles.
13When they had finished, James stood and
said, "Brothers, listen to me. 14Peter has told you
about the time God first visited the Gentiles to
take from them a people for himself. 15And this
conversion of Gentiles is exactly what the prophets predicted. As it is written:

16 'Afterward I will return
and restore the fallen house of David.
I will rebuild its ruins
and restore it,
17 so that the rest of humanity might seek
the LORD,
including the Gentiles—
all those I have called to be mine.
The LORD has spoken—
18 he who made these things known
so long ago.'

19"And so my judgment is that we should not
make it difficult for the Gentiles who are turning
to God. 20Instead, we should write and tell them
to abstain from eating food offered to idols, from
sexual immorality, from eating the meat of strangled animals, and from consuming blood. 21For
these laws of Moses have been preached in Jewish synagogues in every city on every Sabbath for
many generations."

The Letter for Gentile Believers

22Then the apostles and elders together with
the whole church in Jerusalem chose delegates,
and they sent them to Antioch of Syria with Paul
and Barnabas to report on this decision. The
men chosen were two of the church leaders—
Judas (also called Barsabbas) and Silas. 23This is
the letter they took with them:

"This letter is from the apostles and elders,
your brothers in Jerusalem. It is written to
the Gentile believers in Antioch, Syria, and
Cilicia. Greetings!

24"We understand that some men from
here have troubled you and upset you
with their teaching, but we did not send
them! 25So we decided, having come to
complete agreement, to send you official
representatives, along with our beloved
Barnabas and Paul, 26who have risked their
lives for the name of our Lord Jesus Christ.
27We are sending Judas and Silas to confirm
what we have decided concerning your
question.

28"For it seemed good to the Holy Spirit
and to us to lay no greater burden on
you than these few requirements: 29You
must abstain from eating food offered to
idols, from consuming blood or the meat
of strangled animals, and from sexual
immorality. If you do this, you will do well.
Farewell."

30The messengers went at once to Antioch,
where they called a general meeting of the believers and delivered the letter. 31And there was
great joy throughout the church that day as they
read this encouraging message.

32Then Judas and Silas, both being prophets,
spoke at length to the believers, encouraging
and strengthening their faith. 33They stayed for
a while, and then the believers sent them back
to the church in Jerusalem with a blessing of
peace.* 35Paul and Barnabas stayed in Antioch.
They and many others taught and preached the
word of the Lord there.

Paul and Barnabas Separate

36After some time Paul said to Barnabas, "Let's
go back and visit each city where we previously preached the word of the Lord, to see how the
new believers are doing." 37Barnabas agreed
and wanted to take along John Mark. 38But
Paul disagreed strongly, since John Mark had
deserted them in Pamphylia and had not continued with them in their work. 39Their disagreement was so sharp that they separated.
Barnabas took John Mark with him and sailed
for Cyprus. 40Paul chose Silas, and as he left, the
believers entrusted him to the Lord's gracious
care. 41Then he traveled throughout Syria and
Cilicia, strengthening the churches there.

15:33 Some manuscripts add verse 34, *But Silas decided to stay there.*

Stayin' Put

IF YOU WERE IN A TIGHT SPOT AND HAD THE CHANCE TO GET OUT OF IT, WOULD YOU?

Read ACTS 16:16-40 to see what two guys in the Bible did! Would you have stayed put like Paul and Silas did? Here's an experiment all about staying put!

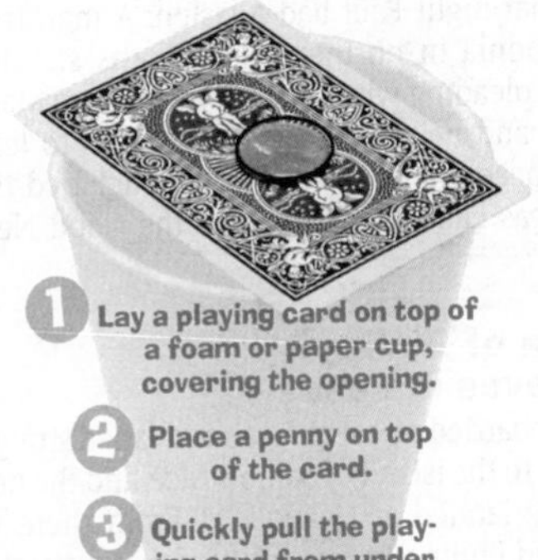

1. **Lay a playing card on top of a foam or paper cup, covering the opening.**
2. **Place a penny on top of the card.**
3. **Quickly pull the playing card from under the penny.**

What happened? The penny didn't follow the card—it stayed put and dropped in the cup!

DO YOUR TRICK FOR A FRIEND.
Then tell your friend how Paul and Silas stayed put. Who knows—maybe the friend you tell will believe in Jesus too!

CHAPTER 16

Paul's Second Missionary Journey

Paul went first to Derbe and then to Lystra,
where there was a young disciple named Timothy. His mother was a Jewish believer, but his
father was a Greek. 2Timothy was well thought
of by the believers in Lystra and Iconium, 3so
Paul wanted him to join them on their journey.
In deference to the Jews of the area, he arranged
for Timothy to be circumcised before they left,
for everyone knew that his father was a Greek.
4Then they went from town to town, instructing
the believers to follow the decisions made by
the apostles and elders in Jerusalem. 5So the
churches were strengthened in their faith and
grew larger everyday.

A Call from Macedonia

6Next Paul and Silas traveled through the area
of Phrygia and Galatia, because the Holy Spirit
had prevented them from preaching the word
in the province of Asia at that time. 7Then coming to the borders of Mysia, they headed north
for the province of Bithynia, but again the Spirit
of Jesus did not allow them to go there. 8So instead, they went on through Mysia to the seaport of Troas.

9That night Paul had a vision: A man from
Macedonia in northern Greece was standing
there, pleading with him, "Come over to Macedonia and help us!" 10So we decided to leave
for Macedonia at once, having concluded that
God was calling us to preach the Good News
there.

Lydia of Philippi Believes in Jesus

11We boarded a boat at Troas and sailed straight
across to the island of Samothrace, and the next
day we landed at Neapolis. 12From there we
reached Philippi, a major city of that district of
Macedonia and a Roman colony. And we stayed
there several days.

13On the Sabbath we went a little way outside the city to a riverbank, where we thought
people would be meeting for prayer, and we
sat down to speak with some women who had
gathered there. 14One of them was Lydia from
Thyatira, a merchant of expensive purple cloth,
who worshiped God. As she listened to us, the
Lord opened her heart, and she accepted what
Paul was saying. 15She and her household were
baptized, and she asked us to be her guests. "If
you agree that I am a true believer in the Lord,"
she said, "come and stay at my home." And she
urged us until we agreed.

Paul and Silas in Prison

16One day as we were going down to the place of
prayer, we met a slave girl who had a spirit that
enabled her to tell the future. She earned a lot of
money for her masters by telling fortunes.
17She followed Paul and the rest of us, shouting,
"These men are servants of the Most High God,
and they have come to tell you how to be saved."

18This went on day after day until Paul got so
exasperated that he turned and said to the
demon within her, "I command you in the name
of Jesus Christ to come out of her." And instantly
it left her.

19Her masters' hopes of wealth were now
shattered, so they grabbed Paul and Silas and
dragged them before the authorities at the
marketplace. 20"The whole city is in an uproar
because of these Jews!" they shouted to the city
officials. 21"They are teaching customs that are
illegal for us Romans to practice."

22A mob quickly formed against Paul and
Silas, and the city officials ordered them stripped
and beaten with wooden rods. 23They were severely beaten, and then they were thrown into
prison. The jailer was ordered to make sure they
didn't escape. 24So the jailer put them into the
inner dungeon and clamped their feet in the
stocks.

25Around midnight Paul and Silas were praying and singing hymns to God, and the other
prisoners were listening. 26Suddenly, there was
a massive earthquake, and the prison was
shaken to its foundations. All the doors immediately flew open, and the chains of every prisoner fell off! 27The jailer woke up to see the
prison doors wide open. He assumed the prisoners had escaped, so he drew his sword to kill
himself. 28But Paul shouted to him, "Stop! Don't
kill yourself! We are all here!"

29The jailer called for lights and ran to the
dungeon and fell down trembling before Paul
and Silas. **30Then he brought them out
and asked, "Sirs, what must I do to
be saved?"**

**31They replied, "Believe in the Lord
Jesus and you will be saved, along
with everyone in your household."**
32And they shared the word of the Lord with him
and with all who lived in his household. 33Even
at that hour of the night, the jailer cared for them
and washed their wounds. Then he and everyone

in his household were immediately baptized.
34He brought them into his house and set a meal
before them, and he and his entire household
rejoiced because they all believed in God.
35The next morning the city officials sent the
police to tell the jailer, "Let those men go!" 36So
the jailer told Paul, "The city officials have said
you and Silas are free to leave. Go in peace."
37But Paul replied, "They have publicly beaten
us without a trial and put us in prison—and we
are Roman citizens. So now they want us to leave
secretly? Certainly not! Let them come themselves to release us!"
38When the police reported this, the city officials were alarmed to learn that Paul and Silas
were Roman citizens. 39So they came to the jail
and apologized to them. Then they brought
them out and begged them to leave the city.
40When Paul and Silas left the prison, they returned to the home of Lydia. There they met with
the believers and encouraged them once more.
Then they left town.

CHAPTER 17

Paul Preaches in Thessalonica

Paul and Silas then traveled through the towns
of Amphipolis and Apollonia and came to Thessalonica, where there was a Jewish synagogue.
2As was Paul's custom, he went to the synagogue
service, and for three Sabbaths in a row he used
the Scriptures to reason with the people. 3He
explained the prophecies and proved that the
Messiah must suffer and rise from the dead. He
said, "This Jesus I'm telling you about is the Messiah." 4Some of the Jews who listened were persuaded and joined Paul and Silas, along with
many God-fearing Greek men and quite a few
prominent women.
5But some of the Jews were jealous, so they
gathered some troublemakers from the marketplace to form a mob and start a riot. They attacked the home of Jason, searching for Paul and
Silas so they could drag them out to the crowd.
6Not finding them there, they dragged out Jason
and some of the other believers instead and
took them before the city council. "Paul and
Silas have caused trouble all over the world,"
they shouted, "and now they are here disturbing
our city, too. 7And Jason has welcomed them
into his home. They are all guilty of treason
against Caesar, for they profess allegiance to another king, named Jesus."
8The people of the city, as well as the city
council, were thrown into turmoil by these
reports. 9So the officials forced Jason and the
other believers to post bond, and then they released them.

Paul and Silas in Berea

10That very night the believers sent Paul and
Silas to Berea. When they arrived there, they
went to the Jewish synagogue. 11And the people
of Berea were more open-minded than those
in Thessalonica, and they listened eagerly to
Paul's message. They searched the Scriptures
day after day to see if Paul and Silas were teaching the truth. 12As a result, many Jews believed,
as did many of the prominent Greek women
and men.
13But when some Jews in Thessalonica
learned that Paul was preaching the word of God
in Berea, they went there and stirred up trouble.
14The believers acted at once, sending Paul on to
the coast, while Silas and Timothy remained behind. 15Those escorting Paul went with him all
the way to Athens; then they returned to Berea
with instructions for Silas and Timothy to hurry
and join him.

Paul Preaches in Athens

16While Paul was waiting for them in Athens, he
was deeply troubled by all the idols he saw everywhere in the city. 17He went to the synagogue to
reason with the Jews and the God-fearing Gentiles, and he spoke daily in the public square to
all who happened to be there.
18He also had a debate with some of the Epi-
curean and Stoic philosophers. When he told
them about Jesus and his resurrection, they
said, "What's this babbler trying to say with
these strange ideas he's picked up?" Others
said, "He seems to be preaching about some foreign gods."
19Then they took him to the high council of
the city. "Come and tell us about this new teaching," they said. 20"You are saying some rather
strange things, and we want to know what it's all
about." 21(It should be explained that all the
Athenians as well as the foreigners in Athens
seemed to spend all their time discussing the
latest ideas.)
22So Paul, standing before the council, addressed them as follows: "Men of Athens, I
notice that you are very religious in every way,
23for as I was walking along I saw your many
shrines. And one of your altars had this inscription on it: 'To an Unknown God.' This God,
whom you worship without knowing, is the one
I'm telling you about.
24"He is the God who made the world and

everything in it. Since he is Lord of heaven and earth, he doesn't live in man-made temples, 25and human hands can't serve his needs—for he has no needs. He himself gives life and breath to everything, and he satisfies every need. 26From one man he created all the nations throughout the whole earth. He decided beforehand when they should rise and fall, and he determined their boundaries.

27"His purpose was for the nations to seek after God and perhaps feel their way toward him and find him—though he is not far from any one of us. 28For in him we live and move and exist. As some of your own poets have said, 'We are his offspring.' 29And since this is true, we shouldn't think of God as an idol designed by craftsmen from gold or silver or stone.

30"God overlooked people's ignorance about these things in earlier times, but now he commands everyone everywhere to repent of their sins and turn to him. 31For he has set a day for judging the world with justice by the man he has appointed, and he proved to everyone who this is by raising him from the dead."

32When they heard Paul speak about the resurrection of the dead, some laughed in contempt, but others said, "We want to hear more about this later." 33That ended Paul's discussion with them, 34but some joined him and became believers. Among them were Dionysius, a member of the council, a woman named Damaris, and others with them.

CHAPTER 18

Paul Meets Priscilla and Aquila in Corinth

Then Paul left Athens and went to Corinth. 2There he became acquainted with a Jew named Aquila, born in Pontus, who had recently arrived from Italy with his wife, Priscilla. They had left Italy when Claudius Caesar deported all Jews from Rome. 3Paul lived and worked with them, for they were tentmakers just as he was.

4Each Sabbath found Paul at the synagogue, trying to convince the Jews and Greeks alike. 5And after Silas and Timothy came down from Macedonia, Paul spent all his time preaching the word. He testified to the Jews that Jesus was the Messiah. 6But when they opposed and insulted him, Paul shook the dust from his clothes and said, "Your blood is upon your own heads—I am innocent. From now on I will go preach to the Gentiles."

7Then he left and went to the home of Titius Justus, a Gentile who worshiped God and lived next door to the synagogue. 8Crispus, the leader of the synagogue, and everyone in his household believed in the Lord. Many others in Corinth also heard Paul, became believers, and were baptized.

9One night the Lord spoke to Paul in a vision and told him, "Don't be afraid! Speak out! Don't be silent! 10For I am with you, and no one will attack and harm you, for many people in this city belong to me." 11So Paul stayed there for the next year and a half, teaching the word of God.

12But when Gallio became governor of Achaia, some Jews rose up together against Paul and brought him before the governor for judgment. 13They accused Paul of "persuading people to worship God in ways that are contrary to our law."

14But just as Paul started to make his defense, Gallio turned to Paul's accusers and said, "Listen, you Jews, if this were a case involving some wrongdoing or a serious crime, I would have a reason to accept your case. 15But since it is merely a question of words and names and your Jewish law, take care of it yourselves. I refuse to judge such matters." 16And he threw them out of the courtroom.

17The crowd then grabbed Sosthenes, the leader of the synagogue, and beat him right there in the courtroom. But Gallio paid no attention.

Paul Returns to Antioch of Syria

18Paul stayed in Corinth for some time after that, then said good-bye to the brothers and sisters and went to nearby Cenchrea. There he shaved his head according to Jewish custom, marking the end of a vow. Then he set sail for Syria, taking Priscilla and Aquila with him.

19They stopped first at the port of Ephesus, where Paul left the others behind. While he was there, he went to the synagogue to reason with the Jews. 20They asked him to stay longer, but he declined. 21As he left, however, he said, "I will come back later, God willing." Then he set sail from Ephesus. 22The next stop was at the port of Caesarea. From there he went up and visited the church at Jerusalem and then went back to Antioch.

23After spending some time in Antioch, Paul went back through Galatia and Phrygia, visiting and strengthening all the believers.

Apollos Instructed at Ephesus

24Meanwhile, a Jew named Apollos, an eloquent speaker who knew the Scriptures well, had arrived in Ephesus from Alexandria in Egypt. 25He

had been taught the way of the Lord, and he
taught others about Jesus with an enthusiastic
spirit and with accuracy. However, he knew only
about John's baptism. 26 When Priscilla and
Aquila heard him preaching boldly in the synagogue, they took him aside and explained the
way of God even more accurately.
27 Apollos had been thinking about going to
Achaia, and the brothers and sisters in Ephesus
encouraged him to go. They wrote to the believers in Achaia, asking them to welcome him.
When he arrived there, he proved to be of great
benefit to those who, by God's grace, had believed. 28 He refuted the Jews with powerful arguments in public debate. Using the Scriptures,
he explained to them that Jesus was the Messiah.

CHAPTER **19**

Paul's Third Missionary Journey

While Apollos was in Corinth, Paul traveled
through the interior regions until he reached
Ephesus, on the coast, where he found several
believers. 2 "Did you receive the Holy Spirit when
you believed?" he asked them.

"No," they replied, "we haven't even heard that
there is a Holy Spirit."

3 "Then what baptism did you experience?" he
asked.

And they replied, "The baptism of John."

4 Paul said, "John's baptism called for repentance from sin. But John himself told the people
to believe in the one who would come later,
meaning Jesus."

5 As soon as they heard this, they were baptized in the name of the Lord Jesus. 6 Then when
Paul laid his hands on them, the Holy Spirit
came on them, and they spoke in other tongues
and prophesied. 7 There were about twelve men
in all.

Paul Ministers in Ephesus

8 Then Paul went to the synagogue and preached
boldly for the next three months, arguing per-
suasively about the Kingdom of God. 9 But some
became stubborn, rejecting his message and
publicly speaking against the Way. So Paul left
the synagogue and took the believers with him.
Then he held daily discussions at the lecture hall
of Tyrannus. 10 This went on for the next two
years, so that people throughout the province of
Asia—both Jews and Greeks—heard the word of
the Lord.

11 God gave Paul the power to perform unusual
miracles. 12 When handkerchiefs or aprons that
had merely touched his skin were placed on sick
people, they were healed of their diseases, and
evil spirits were expelled.

13 A group of Jews was traveling from town to
town casting out evil spirits. They tried to use the
name of the Lord Jesus in their incantation, saying, "I command you in the name of Jesus, whom
Paul preaches, to come out!" 14 Seven sons of
Sceva, a leading priest, were doing this. 15 But one
time when they tried it, the evil spirit replied, "I
know Jesus, and I know Paul, but who are you?"
16 Then the man with the evil spirit leaped on
them, overpowered them, and attacked them
with such violence that they fled from the house,
naked and battered.

17 The story of what happened spread quickly
all through Ephesus, to Jews and Greeks alike. A
solemn fear descended on the city, and the name
of the Lord Jesus was greatly honored. 18 Many
who became believers confessed their sinful
practices. 19 A number of them who had been
practicing sorcery brought their incantation
books and burned them at a public bonfire. The
value of the books was several million dollars.
20 So the message about the Lord spread widely
and had a powerful effect.

21 Afterward Paul felt compelled by the Spirit
to go over to Macedonia and Achaia before going
to Jerusalem. "And after that," he said, "I must go
on to Rome!" 22 He sent his two assistants, Timothy and Erastus, ahead to Macedonia while he
stayed awhile longer in the province of Asia.

The Riot in Ephesus

23 About that time, serious trouble developed in
Ephesus concerning the Way. 24 It began with
Demetrius, a silversmith who had a large business manufacturing silver shrines of the Greek
goddess Artemis. He kept many craftsmen busy.
25 He called them together, along with others
employed in similar trades, and addressed them
as follows:

"Gentlemen, you know that our wealth comes
from this business. 26 But as you have seen and
heard, this man Paul has persuaded many people
that handmade gods aren't really gods at all. And
he's done this not only here in Ephesus but
throughout the entire province! 27 Of course, I'm
not just talking about the loss of public respect
for our business. I'm also concerned that the
temple of the great goddess Artemis will lose its
influence and that Artemis—this magnificent
goddess worshiped throughout the province of
Asia and all around the world—will be robbed of
her great prestige!"

28 At this their anger boiled, and they began

shouting, "Great is Artemis of the Ephesians!" 29Soon the whole city was filled with confusion. Everyone rushed to the amphitheater, dragging along Gaius and Aristarchus, who were Paul's traveling companions from Macedonia. 30Paul wanted to go in, too, but the believers wouldn't let him. 31Some of the officials of the province, friends of Paul, also sent a message to him, begging him not to risk his life by entering the amphitheater.

32Inside, the people were all shouting, some one thing and some another. Everything was in confusion. In fact, most of them didn't even know why they were there. 33The Jews in the crowd pushed Alexander forward and told him to explain the situation. He motioned for silence and tried to speak. 34But when the crowd realized he was a Jew, they started shouting again and kept it up for about two hours: "Great is Artemis of the Ephesians! Great is Artemis of the Ephesians!"

35At last the mayor was able to quiet them down enough to speak. "Citizens of Ephesus," he said. "Everyone knows that Ephesus is the official guardian of the temple of the great Artemis, whose image fell down to us from heaven. 36Since this is an undeniable fact, you should stay calm and not do anything rash. 37You have brought these men here, but they have stolen nothing from the temple and have not spoken against our goddess.

38"If Demetrius and the craftsmen have a case against them, the courts are in session and the officials can hear the case at once. Let them make formal charges. 39And if there are complaints about other matters, they can be settled in a legal assembly. 40I am afraid we are in danger of being charged with rioting by the Roman government, since there is no cause for all this commotion. And if Rome demands an explanation, we won't know what to say." 41Then he dismissed them, and they dispersed.

CHAPTER 20

Paul Goes to Macedonia and Greece

When the uproar was over, Paul sent for the believers and encouraged them. Then he said good-bye and left for Macedonia. 2While there, he encouraged the believers in all the towns he passed through. Then he traveled down to Greece, 3where he stayed for three months. He was preparing to sail back to Syria when he discovered a plot by some Jews against his life, so he decided to return through Macedonia.

4Several men were traveling with him. They were Sopater son of Pyrrhus from Berea; Aristarchus and Secundus from Thessalonica; Gaius from Derbe; Timothy; and Tychicus and Trophimus from the province of Asia. 5They went on ahead and waited for us at Troas. 6After the Passover ended, we boarded a ship at Philippi in Macedonia and five days later joined them in Troas, where we stayed a week.

Paul's Final Visit to Troas

7On the first day of the week, we gathered with the local believers to share in the Lord's Supper. Paul was preaching to them, and since he was leaving the next day, he kept talking until midnight. 8The upstairs room where we met was lighted with many flickering lamps. 9As Paul spoke on and on, a young man named Eutychus, sitting on the windowsill, became very drowsy. Finally, he fell sound asleep and dropped three stories to his death below. 10Paul went down, bent over him, and took him into his arms. "Don't worry," he said, "he's alive!" 11Then they all went back upstairs, shared in the Lord's Supper, and ate together. Paul continued talking to them until dawn, and then he left. 12Meanwhile, the young man was taken home alive and well, and everyone was greatly relieved.

Paul Meets the Ephesian Elders

13Paul went by land to Assos, where he had arranged for us to join him, while we traveled by ship. 14He joined us there, and we sailed together to Mitylene. 15The next day we sailed past the island of Kios. The following day we crossed to the island of Samos, and a day later we arrived at Miletus.

16Paul had decided to sail on past Ephesus, for he didn't want to spend any more time in the province of Asia. He was hurrying to get to Jerusalem, if possible, in time for the Festival of Pentecost. 17But when we landed at Miletus, he sent a message to the elders of the church at Ephesus, asking them to come and meet him.

18When they arrived he declared, "You know that from the day I set foot in the province of Asia until now 19I have done the Lord's work humbly and with many tears. I have endured the trials that came to me from the plots of the Jews. 20I never shrank back from telling you what you needed to hear, either publicly or in your homes. 21I have had one message for Jews and Greeks alike—the necessity of repenting from sin and turning to God, and of having faith in our Lord Jesus.

22"And now I am bound by the Spirit to go to

FUN-fact
Sentenced to DEATH
More than once, the Bible tells about someone being killed by having stones thrown at him or her. Several crimes were punishable by stoning, one of which was blasphemy—saying something about God that isn't true. Those who had witnessed the crime were supposed to throw the first stones.
Have you ever not spoken up for God when your friends said something untrue about him? Write a prayer to God, asking him to help you stand up for him, just as Stephen did!

Jerusalem. I don't know what awaits me, 23except that the Holy Spirit tells me in city after city that jail and suffering lie ahead. 24But my life is worth nothing to me unless I use it for finishing the work assigned me by the Lord Jesus—the work of telling others the Good News about the wonderful grace of God.

25"And now I know that none of you to whom I have preached the Kingdom will ever see me again. 26I declare today that I have been faithful. If anyone suffers eternal death, it's not my fault, 27for I didn't shrink from declaring all that God wants you to know.

28"So guard yourselves and God's people. Feed and shepherd God's flock—his church, purchased with his own blood—over which the Holy Spirit has appointed you as elders. 29I know that false teachers, like vicious wolves, will come in among you after I leave, not sparing the flock. 30Even some men from your own group will rise up and distort the truth in order to draw a following. 31Watch out! Remember the three years I was with you—my constant watch and care over you night and day, and my many tears for you.

32"And now I entrust you to God and the message of his grace that is able to build you up and give you an inheritance with all those he has set apart for himself.

33"I have never coveted anyone's silver or gold or fine clothes. 34You know that these hands of mine have worked to supply my own needs and even the needs of those who were with me. 35And I have been a constant example of how you can help those in need by working hard. You should remember the words of the Lord Jesus: 'It is more blessed to give than to receive.'"

36When he had finished speaking, he knelt and prayed with them. 37They all cried as they embraced and kissed him good-bye. 38They were sad most of all because he had said that they would never see him again. Then they escorted him down to the ship.

CHAPTER 21

Paul's Journey to Jerusalem

After saying farewell to the Ephesian elders, we sailed straight to the island of Cos. The next day we reached Rhodes and then went to Patara. 2There we boarded a ship sailing for Phoenicia. 3We sighted the island of Cyprus, passed it on our left, and landed at the harbor of Tyre, in Syria, where the ship was to unload its cargo.

4We went ashore, found the local believers, and stayed with them a week. These believers prophesied through the Holy Spirit that Paul should not go on to Jerusalem. 5When we returned to the ship at the end of the week, the entire congregation, including women and children, left the city and came down to the shore with us. There we knelt, prayed, 6and said our farewells. Then we went aboard, and they returned home.

7The next stop after leaving Tyre was Ptolemais, where we greeted the brothers and sisters and stayed for one day. 8The next day we went on to Caesarea and stayed at the home of Philip the Evangelist, one of the seven men who had been chosen to distribute food. 9He had four unmarried daughters who had the gift of prophecy.

10Several days later a man named Agabus, who also had the gift of prophecy, arrived from Judea. 11He came over, took Paul's belt, and bound his own feet and hands with it. Then he said, "The Holy Spirit declares, 'So shall the owner of this belt be bound by the Jewish leaders in Jerusalem and turned over to the Gentiles.'" 12When we heard this, we and the local believers all begged Paul not to go on to Jerusalem.

13But he said, "Why all this weeping? You are breaking my heart! I am ready not only to be jailed at Jerusalem but even to die for the sake of the Lord Jesus." 14When it was clear that we couldn't persuade him, we gave up and said, "The Lord's will be done."

Paul Arrives at Jerusalem

15After this we packed our things and left for Jerusalem. 16Some believers from Caesarea accompanied us, and they took us to the home of Mnason, a man originally from Cyprus and one of the early believers. 17When we arrived, the brothers and sisters in Jerusalem welcomed us warmly.

18The next day Paul went with us to meet with James, and all the elders of the Jerusalem church were present. 19After greeting them, Paul gave a detailed account of the things God had accomplished among the Gentiles through his ministry.

20After hearing this, they praised God. And then they said, "You know, dear brother, how many thousands of Jews have also believed, and they all follow the law of Moses very seriously. 21But the Jewish believers here in Jerusalem have been told that you are teaching all the Jews who live among the Gentiles to turn their backs on the laws of Moses. They've heard that you teach them not to circumcise their children or follow other Jewish customs. 22What should we do? They will certainly hear that you have come.

23"Here's what we want you to do. We have four men here who have completed their vow. 24Go with them to the Temple and join them in the purification ceremony, paying for them to have their heads ritually shaved. Then everyone will know that the rumors are all false and that you yourself observe the Jewish laws.

25"As for the Gentile believers, they should do what we already told them in a letter: They should abstain from eating food offered to idols, from consuming blood or the meat of strangled animals, and from sexual immorality."

Paul Is Arrested

26So Paul went to the Temple the next day with the other men. They had already started the purification ritual, so he publicly announced the date when their vows would end and sacrifices would be offered for each of them.

27The seven days were almost ended when some Jews from the province of Asia saw Paul in the Temple and roused a mob against him. They grabbed him, 28yelling, "Men of Israel, help us! This is the man who preaches against our people everywhere and tells everybody to disobey the Jewish laws. He speaks against the Temple—and even defiles this holy place by bringing in Gentiles." 29(For earlier that day they had seen him in the city with Trophimus, a Gentile from Ephesus, and they assumed Paul had taken him into the Temple.)

30The whole city was rocked by these accusations, and a great riot followed. Paul was grabbed and dragged out of the Temple, and immediately the gates were closed behind him. 31As they were trying to kill him, word reached the commander of the Roman regiment that all Jerusalem was in an uproar. 32He immediately called out his soldiers and officers and ran down among the crowd. When the mob saw the commander and the troops coming, they stopped beating Paul.

33Then the commander arrested him and ordered him bound with two chains. He asked the crowd who he was and what he had done. 34Some shouted one thing and some another. Since he couldn't find out the truth in all the uproar and confusion, he ordered that Paul be taken to the fortress. 35As Paul reached the stairs, the mob grew so violent the soldiers had to lift him to their shoulders to protect him. 36And the crowd followed behind, shouting, "Kill him, kill him!"

Paul Speaks to the Crowd

37As Paul was about to be taken inside, he said to the commander, "May I have a word with you?"

"Do you know Greek?" the commander asked, surprised. 38"Aren't you the Egyptian who led a rebellion some time ago and took 4,000 members of the Assassins out into the desert?"

39"No," Paul replied, "I am a Jew and a citizen of Tarsus in Cilicia, which is an important city. Please, let me talk to these people." 40The commander agreed, so Paul stood on the stairs and motioned to the people to be quiet. Soon a deep silence enveloped the crowd, and he addressed them in their own language, Aramaic.

CHAPTER 22

"Brothers and esteemed fathers," Paul said, "listen to me as I offer my defense." 2When they heard him speaking in their own language, the silence was even greater.

3Then Paul said, "I am a Jew, born in Tarsus, a

city in Cilicia, and I was brought up and educated
here in Jerusalem under Gamaliel. As his student, I was carefully trained in our Jewish laws
and customs. I became very zealous to honor
God in everything I did, just like all of you today.
4And I persecuted the followers of the Way,
hounding some to death, arresting both men and
women and throwing them in prison. 5The high
priest and the whole council of elders can testify
that this is so. For I received letters from them to
our Jewish brothers in Damascus, authorizing
me to bring the followers of the Way from there
to Jerusalem, in chains, to be punished.

6"As I was on the road, approaching Damascus
about noon, a very bright light from heaven
suddenly shone down around me. 7I fell to the
ground and heard a voice saying to me, 'Saul,
Saul, why are you persecuting me?'

8"'Who are you, lord?' I asked.

"And the voice replied, 'I am Jesus the Nazarene, the one you are persecuting.' 9The people
with me saw the light but didn't understand the
voice speaking to me.

10"I asked, 'What should I do, Lord?'

"And the Lord told me, 'Get up and go into
Damascus, and there you will be told everything
you are to do.'

11"I was blinded by the intense light and had
to be led by the hand to Damascus by my companions. 12A man named Ananias lived there. He
was a godly man, deeply devoted to the law, and
well regarded by all the Jews of Damascus. 13He
came and stood beside me and said, 'Brother
Saul, regain your sight.' And that very moment I
could see him!

14"Then he told me, 'The God of our ancestors
has chosen you to know his will and to see the
Righteous One and hear him speak. 15For you are
to be his witness, telling everyone what you have
seen and heard. 16What are you waiting for? Get
up and be baptized. Have your sins washed away
by calling on the name of the Lord.'

17"After I returned to Jerusalem, I was praying
in the Temple and fell into a trance. 18I saw a vision of Jesus saying to me, 'Hurry! Leave Jerusalem, for the people here won't accept your
testimony about me.'

19"'But Lord,' I argued, 'they certainly know
that in every synagogue I imprisoned and beat
those who believed in you. 20And I was in complete agreement when your witness Stephen was
killed. I stood by and kept the coats they took off
when they stoned him.'

21"But the Lord said to me, 'Go, for I will send
you far away to the Gentiles!'"

22The crowd listened until Paul said that
word. Then they all began to shout, "Away with
such a fellow! He isn't fit to live!" 23They yelled,
threw off their coats, and tossed handfuls of dust
into the air.

Paul Reveals His Roman Citizenship

24The commander brought Paul inside and
ordered him lashed with whips to make him
confess his crime. He wanted to find out why the
crowd had become so furious. 25When they tied
Paul down to lash him, Paul said to the officer
standing there, "Is it legal for you to whip a
Roman citizen who hasn't even been tried?"

26When the officer heard this, he went to the
commander and asked, "What are you doing?
This man is a Roman citizen!"

27So the commander went over and asked
Paul, "Tell me, are you a Roman citizen?"

"Yes, I certainly am," Paul replied.

28"I am, too," the commander muttered, "and
it cost me plenty!"

Paul answered, "But I am a citizen by birth!"

29The soldiers who were about to interrogate
Paul quickly withdrew when they heard he was a
Roman citizen, and the commander was frightened because he had ordered him bound and
whipped.

Paul before the High Council

30The next day the commander ordered the
leading priests into session with the Jewish high
council. He wanted to find out what the trouble
was all about, so he released Paul to have him
stand before them.

CHAPTER 23

Gazing intently at the high council, Paul began:
"Brothers, I have always lived before God with a
clear conscience!"

2Instantly Ananias the high priest commanded those close to Paul to slap him on the
mouth. 3But Paul said to him, "God will slap you,
you corrupt hypocrite! What kind of judge are
you to break the law yourself by ordering me
struck like that?"

4Those standing near Paul said to him, "Do
you dare to insult God's high priest?"

5"I'm sorry, brothers. I didn't realize he was
the high priest," Paul replied, "for the Scriptures say, 'You must not speak evil of any of
your rulers.'"

6Paul realized that some members of the
high council were Sadducees and some were

Pharisees, so he shouted, "Brothers, I am a Pharisee, as were my ancestors! And I am on trial
because my hope is in the resurrection of the
dead!"
7This divided the council—the Pharisees
against the Sadducees—8for the Sadducees say
there is no resurrection or angels or spirits, but
the Pharisees believe in all of these. 9So there
was a great uproar. Some of the teachers of religious law who were Pharisees jumped up and
began to argue forcefully. "We see nothing
wrong with him," they shouted. "Perhaps a spirit
or an angel spoke to him." 10As the conflict grew
more violent, the commander was afraid they
would tear Paul apart. So he ordered his soldiers
to go and rescue him by force and take him back
to the fortress.
11That night the Lord appeared to Paul and
said, "Be encouraged, Paul. Just as you have been
a witness to me here in Jerusalem, you must
preach the Good News in Rome as well."

In Bible times, Jewish people would often shake the dust off their feet when leaving a Gentile town. This was a symbolic way of cleansing themselves. But the tables turned!

Sometimes the Jewish people and leaders didn't want to hear about Jesus. One time, Paul and Barnabas were run out of town for talking about Jesus. But as they left, they shook the dust off their feet!

Even today, missionaries face opposition. **SO WRITE A LETTER TO ENCOURAGE THE MISSIONARIES YOUR CHURCH SUPPORTS!**

The Plan to Kill Paul

12The next morning a group of Jews got together
and bound themselves with an oath not to eat or
drink until they had killed Paul. 13There were
more than forty of them in the conspiracy.
14They went to the leading priests and elders and
told them, "We have bound ourselves with an
oath to eat nothing until we have killed Paul. 15So
you and the high council should ask the commander to bring Paul back to the council again.
Pretend you want to examine his case more fully.
We will kill him on the way."
16But Paul's nephew—his sister's son—heard
of their plan and went to the fortress and told
Paul. 17Paul called for one of the Roman officers
and said, "Take this young man to the commander. He has something important to tell
him."
18So the officer did, explaining, "Paul, the
prisoner, called me over and asked me to bring
this young man to you because he has something
to tell you."
19The commander took his hand, led him
aside, and asked, "What is it you want to tell me?"
20Paul's nephew told him, "Some Jews are going to ask you to bring Paul before the high council tomorrow, pretending they want to get some
more information. 21But don't do it! There are
more than forty men hiding along the way ready
to ambush him. They have vowed not to eat or
drink anything until they have killed him. They
are ready now, just waiting for your consent."
22"Don't let anyone know you told me this,"
the commander warned the young man.

Paul Is Sent to Caesarea

23Then the commander called two of his officers
and ordered, "Get 200 soldiers ready to leave for
Caesarea at nine o'clock tonight. Also take
200 spearmen and 70 mounted troops. 24Pro-
vide horses for Paul to ride, and get him safely to
Governor Felix." 25Then he wrote this letter to
the governor:

26"From Claudius Lysias, to his Excellency,
Governor Felix: Greetings!
27"This man was seized by some Jews, and
they were about to kill him when I arrived
with the troops. When I learned that he was
a Roman citizen, I removed him to safety.
28Then I took him to their high council to try
to learn the basis of the accusations against
him. 29I soon discovered the charge was
something regarding their religious law—
certainly nothing worthy of imprisonment

or death. 30But when I was informed of a plot
to kill him, I immediately sent him on to you.
I have told his accusers to bring their charges
before you."

31So that night, as ordered, the soldiers took
Paul as far as Antipatris. 32They returned to the
fortress the next morning, while the mounted
troops took him on to Caesarea. 33When they
arrived in Caesarea, they presented Paul and the
letter to Governor Felix. 34He read it and then
asked Paul what province he was from. "Cilicia,"
Paul answered.

35"I will hear your case myself when your accusers arrive," the governor told him. Then the
governor ordered him kept in the prison at
Herod's headquarters.

CHAPTER 24

Paul Appears before Felix

Five days later Ananias, the high priest, arrived
with some of the Jewish elders and the lawyer
Tertullus, to present their case against Paul to the
governor. 2When Paul was called in, Tertullus
presented the charges against Paul in the following address to the governor:

"You have provided a long period of peace for
us Jews and with foresight have enacted reforms
for us. 3For all of this, Your Excellency, we are
very grateful to you. 4But I don't want to bore you,
so please give me your attention for only a moment. 5We have found this man to be a troublemaker who is constantly stirring up riots among
the Jews all over the world. He is a ringleader of
the cult known as the Nazarenes. 6Furthermore,
he was trying to desecrate the Temple when we
arrested him.* 8You can find out the truth of our
accusations by examining him yourself." 9Then
the other Jews chimed in, declaring that everything Tertullus said was true.

10The governor then motioned for Paul to
speak. Paul said, "I know, sir, that you have been a
judge of Jewish affairs for many years, so I gladly
present my defense before you. 11You can quickly
discover that I arrived in Jerusalem no more than
twelve days ago to worship at the Temple. 12My
accusers never found me arguing with anyone in
the Temple, nor stirring up a riot in any synagogue
or on the streets of the city. 13These men cannot
prove the things they accuse me of doing.

14"But I admit that I follow the Way, which
they call a cult. I worship the God of our ancestors, and I firmly believe the Jewish law and
everything written in the prophets. 15I have the
same hope in God that these men have, that he
will raise both the righteous and the unrigh-
teous. 16Because of this, I always try to maintain
a clear conscience before God and all people.

17"After several years away, I returned to Jerusalem with money to aid my people and to offer
sacrifices to God. 18My accusers saw me in the
Temple as I was completing a purification ceremony. There was no crowd around me and no
rioting. 19But some Jews from the province of Asia
were there—and they ought to be here to bring
charges if they have anything against me! 20Ask
these men here what crime the Jewish high council found me guilty of, 21except for the one time I
shouted out, 'I am on trial before you today because I believe in the resurrection of the dead!'"

22At that point Felix, who was quite familiar
with the Way, adjourned the hearing and said,
"Wait until Lysias, the garrison commander, arrives. Then I will decide the case." 23He ordered
an officer to keep Paul in custody but to give him
some freedom and allow his friends to visit him
and take care of his needs.

24A few days later Felix came back with his
wife, Drusilla, who was Jewish. Sending for Paul,
they listened as he told them about faith in Christ
Jesus. 25As he reasoned with them about righteousness and self-control and the coming day of
judgment, Felix became frightened. "Go away for
now," he replied. "When it is more convenient, I'll
call for you again." 26He also hoped that Paul
would bribe him, so he sent for him quite often
and talked with him.

27After two years went by in this way, Felix was
succeeded by Porcius Festus. And because Felix
wanted to gain favor with the Jewish people, he
left Paul in prison.

CHAPTER 25

Paul Appears before Festus

Three days after Festus arrived in Caesarea to take
over his new responsibilities, he left for Jerusalem, 2where the leading priests and other Jewish
leaders met with him and made their accusations
against Paul. 3They asked Festus as a favor to
transfer Paul to Jerusalem (planning to ambush
and kill him on the way). 4But Festus replied that
Paul was at Caesarea and he himself would be returning there soon. 5So he said, "Those of you in
authority can return with me. If Paul has done
anything wrong, you can make your accusations."

24:6 Some manuscripts add an expanded conclusion to verse 6, all of verse 7, and an additional phrase in verse 8: *We would have judged him by our law, 7but Lysias, the commander of the garrison, came and violently took him away from us, 8commanding his accusers to come before you.*

6About eight or ten days later Festus returned
to Caesarea, and on the following day he took his
seat in court and ordered that Paul be brought in.
7When Paul arrived, the Jewish leaders from
Jerusalem gathered around and made many serious accusations they couldn't prove.

8Paul denied the charges. "I am not guilty of
any crime against the Jewish laws or the Temple
or the Roman government," he said.

9Then Festus, wanting to please the Jews,
asked him, "Are you willing to go to Jerusalem
and stand trial before me there?"

10But Paul replied, "No! This is the official
Roman court, so I ought to be tried right here.
You know very well I am not guilty of harming
the Jews. 11If I have done something worthy of
death, I don't refuse to die. But if I am innocent,
no one has a right to turn me over to these men
to kill me. I appeal to Caesar!"

12Festus conferred with his advisers and then
replied, "Very well! You have appealed to Caesar,
and to Caesar you will go!"

13A few days later King Agrippa arrived with
his sister, Bernice, to pay their respects to Festus.
14During their stay of several days, Festus discussed Paul's case with the king. "There is a prisoner here," he told him, "whose case was left for
me by Felix. 15When I was in Jerusalem, the leading priests and Jewish elders pressed charges
against him and asked me to condemn him. 16I
pointed out to them that Roman law does not
convict people without a trial. They must be
given an opportunity to confront their accusers
and defend themselves.

17"When his accusers came here for the trial, I
didn't delay. I called the case the very next day
and ordered Paul brought in. 18But the accusations made against him weren't any of the crimes
I expected. 19Instead, it was something about
their religion and a dead man named Jesus, who
Paul insists is alive. 20I was at a loss to know how
to investigate these things, so I asked him
whether he would be willing to stand trial on
these charges in Jerusalem. 21But Paul appealed
to have his case decided by the emperor. So I ordered that he be held in custody until I could arrange to send him to Caesar."

22"I'd like to hear the man myself," Agrippa
said.

And Festus replied, "You will—tomorrow!"

Paul Speaks to Agrippa

23So the next day Agrippa and Bernice arrived
at the auditorium with great pomp, accompanied by military officers and prominent men of
the city. Festus ordered that Paul be brought in.
24Then Festus said, "King Agrippa and all who
are here, this is the man whose death is demanded by all the Jews, both here and in Jerusalem. 25But in my opinion he has done nothing
deserving death. However, since he appealed
his case to the emperor, I have decided to send
him to Rome.

26"But what shall I write the emperor? For
there is no clear charge against him. So I have
brought him before all of you, and especially you,
King Agrippa, so that after we examine him, I
might have something to write. 27For it makes no
sense to send a prisoner to the emperor without
specifying the charges against him!"

CHAPTER 26

Then Agrippa said to Paul, "You may speak in
your defense."

So Paul, gesturing with his hand, started his
defense: 2"I am fortunate, King Agrippa, that you
are the one hearing my defense today against all
these accusations made by the Jewish leaders,
3for I know you are an expert on all Jewish customs and controversies. Now please listen to me
patiently!

4"As the Jewish leaders are well aware, I was
given a thorough Jewish training from my earliest childhood among my own people and in
Jerusalem. 5If they would admit it, they know
that I have been a member of the Pharisees, the
strictest sect of our religion. 6Now I am on trial
because of my hope in the fulfillment of God's
promise made to our ancestors. 7In fact, that is
why the twelve tribes of Israel zealously worship
God night and day, and they share the same hope
I have. Yet, Your Majesty, they accuse me for
having this hope! 8Why does it seem incredible
to any of you that God can raise the dead?

9"I used to believe that I ought to do everything I could to oppose the very name of Jesus
the Nazarene. 10Indeed, I did just that in Jerusalem. Authorized by the leading priests, I caused
many believers there to be sent to prison. And I
cast my vote against them when they were condemned to death. 11Many times I had them punished in the synagogues to get them to curse
Jesus. I was so violently opposed to them that I
even chased them down in foreign cities.

12"One day I was on such a mission to Damascus, armed with the authority and commission
of the leading priests. 13About noon, Your Majesty, as I was on the road, a light from heaven
brighter than the sun shone down on me and my
companions. 14We all fell down, and I heard a

voice saying to me in Aramaic, 'Saul, Saul, why
are you persecuting me? It is useless for you to
fight against my will.'
15"'Who are you, lord?' I asked.
"And the Lord replied, 'I am Jesus, the one you
are persecuting. 16Now get to your feet! For I
have appeared to you to appoint you as my servant and witness. Tell people that you have seen
me, and tell them what I will show you in the
future. 17And I will rescue you from both your
own people and the Gentiles. Yes, I am sending
you to the Gentiles 18to open their eyes, so they
may turn from darkness to light and from the
power of Satan to God. Then they will receive
forgiveness for their sins and be given a place
among God's people, who are set apart by faith
in me.'
19"And so, King Agrippa, I obeyed that vision
from heaven. 20I preached first to those in
Damascus, then in Jerusalem and throughout
all Judea, and also to the Gentiles, that all must
repent of their sins and turn to God—and prove
they have changed by the good things they do.
21Some Jews arrested me in the Temple for
preaching this, and they tried to kill me. 22But
God has protected me right up to this present
time so I can testify to everyone, from the least
to the greatest. I teach nothing except what the
prophets and Moses said would happen—23that
the Messiah would suffer and be the first to rise
from the dead, and in this way announce God's
light to Jews and Gentiles alike."
24Suddenly, Festus shouted, "Paul, you are
insane. Too much study has made you crazy!"
25But Paul replied, "I am not insane, Most
Excellent Festus. What I am saying is the sober
truth. 26And King Agrippa knows about these
things. I speak boldly, for I am sure these events
are all familiar to him, for they were not done in
a corner! 27King Agrippa, do you believe the
prophets? I know you do—"
28Agrippa interrupted him. "Do you think
you can persuade me to become a Christian so
quickly?"
29Paul replied, "Whether quickly or not, I pray
to God that both you and everyone here in this
audience might become the same as I am, except
for these chains."
30Then the king, the governor, Bernice, and all
the others stood and left. 31As they went out,
they talked it over and agreed, "This man hasn't
done anything to deserve death or imprisonment."
32And Agrippa said to Festus, "He could have
been set free if he hadn't appealed to Caesar."

CHAPTER 27

Paul Sails for Rome

When the time came, we set sail for Italy. Paul
and several other prisoners were placed in the
custody of a Roman officer named Julius, a captain of the Imperial Regiment. 2Aristarchus, a
Macedonian from Thessalonica, was also with
us. We left on a ship whose home port was Adra-
myttium on the northwest coast of the province
of Asia; it was scheduled to make several stops at
ports along the coast of the province.
3The next day when we docked at Sidon, Julius
was very kind to Paul and let him go ashore to
visit with friends so they could provide for his
needs. 4Putting out to sea from there, we encountered strong headwinds that made it difficult to
keep the ship on course, so we sailed north of
Cyprus between the island and the mainland.
5Keeping to the open sea, we passed along the
coast of Cilicia and Pamphylia, landing at Myra, in
the province of Lycia. 6There the commanding
officer found an Egyptian ship from Alexandria
that was bound for Italy, and he put us on board.
7We had several days of slow sailing, and after
great difficulty we finally neared Cnidus. But the
wind was against us, so we sailed across to Crete
and along the sheltered coast of the island, past
the cape of Salmone. 8We struggled along the
coast with great difficulty and finally arrived at
Fair Havens, near the town of Lasea. 9We had lost
a lot of time. The weather was becoming dangerous for sea travel because it was so late in the fall,
and Paul spoke to the ship's officers about it.
10"Men," he said, "I believe there is trouble
ahead if we go on—shipwreck, loss of cargo, and
danger to our lives as well." 11But the officer in
charge of the prisoners listened more to the
ship's captain and the owner than to Paul. 12And
since Fair Havens was an exposed harbor—a
poor place to spend the winter—most of the
crew wanted to go on to Phoenix, farther up the
coast of Crete, and spend the winter there. Phoenix was a good harbor with only a southwest and
northwest exposure.

The Storm at Sea

13When a light wind began blowing from the
south, the sailors thought they could make it. So
they pulled up anchor and sailed close to the
shore of Crete. 14But the weather changed
abruptly, and a wind of typhoon strength (called a
"northeaster") burst across the island and blew us
out to sea. 15The sailors couldn't turn the ship
into the wind, so they gave up and let it run before
the gale.

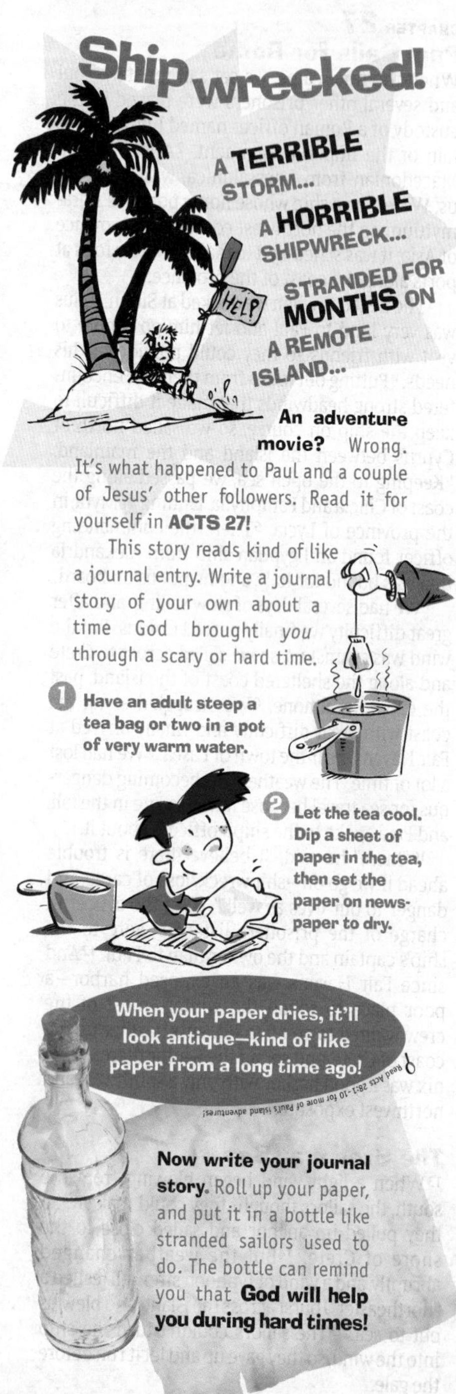

Ship wrecked!
A TERRIBLE STORM...
A HORRIBLE SHIPWRECK...
STRANDED FOR MONTHS ON A REMOTE ISLAND...
HELP
An adventure movie? Wrong. It's what happened to Paul and a couple of Jesus' other followers. Read it for yourself in ACTS 27!
This story reads kind of like a journal entry. Write a journal story of your own about a time God brought you through a scary or hard time.
1 Have an adult steep a tea bag or two in a pot of very warm water.
2 Let the tea cool. Dip a sheet of paper in the tea, then set the paper on newspaper to dry.
When your paper dries, it'll look antique—kind of like paper from a long time ago!
Read Acts 28:1-10 for more of Paul's island adventures!
Now write your journal story. Roll up your paper, and put it in a bottle like stranded sailors used to do. The bottle can remind you that God will help you during hard times!

16 We sailed along the sheltered side of a small
island named Cauda, where with great difficulty
we hoisted aboard the lifeboat being towed behind us. 17 Then the sailors bound ropes around
the hull of the ship to strengthen it. They were
afraid of being driven across to the sandbars of
Syrtis off the African coast, so they lowered the
sea anchor to slow the ship and were driven
before the wind.

18 The next day, as gale-force winds continued
to batter the ship, the crew began throwing the
cargo overboard. 19 The following day they even
took some of the ship's gear and threw it overboard. 20 The terrible storm raged for many days,
blotting out the sun and the stars, until at last all
hope was gone.

21 No one had eaten for a long time. Finally,
Paul called the crew together and said, "Men,
you should have listened to me in the first place
and not left Crete. You would have avoided all
this damage and loss. 22 But take courage! None
of you will lose your lives, even though the
ship will go down. 23 For last night an angel of
the God to whom I belong and whom I serve
stood beside me, 24 and he said, 'Don't be afraid,
Paul, for you will surely stand trial before Caesar! What's more, God in his goodness has
granted safety to everyone sailing with you.'
25 So take courage! For I believe God. It will be
just as he said. 26 But we will be shipwrecked on
an island."

The Shipwreck

27 About midnight on the fourteenth night of the
storm, as we were being driven across the Sea of
Adria, the sailors sensed land was near. 28 They
dropped a weighted line and found that the water was 120 feet deep. But a little later they measured again and found it was only 90 feet deep.
29 At this rate they were afraid we would soon be
driven against the rocks along the shore, so they
threw out four anchors from the back of the ship
and prayed for daylight.

30 Then the sailors tried to abandon the ship;
they lowered the lifeboat as though they were
going to put out anchors from the front of the
ship. 31 But Paul said to the commanding officer
and the soldiers, "You will all die unless the sailors stay aboard." 32 So the soldiers cut the ropes
to the lifeboat and let it drift away.

33 Just as day was dawning, Paul urged everyone to eat. "You have been so worried that you
haven't touched food for two weeks," he said.
34 "Please eat something now for your own
good. For not a hair of your heads will perish."

35Then he took some bread, gave thanks to God
before them all, and broke off a piece and ate it.
36Then everyone was encouraged and began to
eat—37all 276 of us who were on board. 38After
eating, the crew lightened the ship further by
throwing the cargo of wheat overboard.
39When morning dawned, they didn't recognize the coastline, but they saw a bay with a
beach and wondered if they could get to shore by
running the ship aground. 40So they cut off the
anchors and left them in the sea. Then they lowered the rudders, raised the foresail, and headed
toward shore. 41But they hit a shoal and ran the
ship aground too soon. The bow of the ship
stuck fast, while the stern was repeatedly
smashed by the force of the waves and began to
break apart.
42The soldiers wanted to kill the prisoners to
make sure they didn't swim ashore and escape.
43But the commanding officer wanted to spare
Paul, so he didn't let them carry out their plan.
Then he ordered all who could swim to jump
overboard first and make for land. 44The others
held on to planks or debris from the broken ship.
So everyone escaped safely to shore.

CHAPTER 28

Paul on the Island of Malta

Once we were safe on shore, we learned that we
were on the island of Malta. 2The people of the
island were very kind to us. It was cold and rainy,
so they built a fire on the shore to welcome us.
3As Paul gathered an armful of sticks and was
laying them on the fire, a poisonous snake,
driven out by the heat, bit him on the hand. 4The
people of the island saw it hanging from his hand
and said to each other, "A murderer, no doubt!
Though he escaped the sea, justice will not permit him to live." 5But Paul shook off the snake
into the fire and was unharmed. 6The people
waited for him to swell up or suddenly drop
dead. But when they had waited a long time and
saw that he wasn't harmed, they changed their
minds and decided he was a god.
7Near the shore where we landed was an
estate belonging to Publius, the chief official of
the island. He welcomed us and treated us
kindly for three days. 8As it happened, Publius's
father was ill with fever and dysentery. Paul went
in and prayed for him, and laying his hands on
him, he healed him. 9Then all the other sick
people on the island came and were healed. 10As
a result we were showered with honors, and
when the time came to sail, people supplied us
with everything we would need for the trip.

Paul Arrives at Rome

11It was three months after the shipwreck that
we set sail on another ship that had wintered
at the island—an Alexandrian ship with the
twin gods as its figurehead. 12Our first stop was
Syracuse, where we stayed three days. 13From
there we sailed across to Rhegium. A day later a
south wind began blowing, so the following day
we sailed up the coast to Puteoli. 14There we
found some believers, who invited us to spend a
week with them. And so we came to Rome.
15The brothers and sisters in Rome had
heard we were coming, and they came to meet
us at the Forum on the Appian Way. Others
joined us at The Three Taverns. When Paul saw
them, he was encouraged and thanked God.
16When we arrived in Rome, Paul was permitted to have his own private lodging, though
he was guarded by a soldier.

Paul Preaches at Rome under Guard

17Three days after Paul's arrival, he called together the local Jewish leaders. He said to them,
"Brothers, I was arrested in Jerusalem and
handed over to the Roman government, even
though I had done nothing against our people
or the customs of our ancestors. 18The Romans
tried me and wanted to release me, because
they found no cause for the death sentence.
19But when the Jewish leaders protested the
decision, I felt it necessary to appeal to Caesar,
even though I had no desire to press charges
against my own people. 20I asked you to come
here today so we could get acquainted and so I
could explain to you that I am bound with this
chain because I believe that the hope of Israel—
the Messiah—has already come."
21They replied, "We have had no letters from
Judea or reports against you from anyone who
has come here. 22But we want to hear what
you believe, for the only thing we know about
this movement is that it is denounced everywhere."
23So a time was set, and on that day a large
number of people came to Paul's lodging. He
explained and testified about the Kingdom of
God and tried to persuade them about Jesus
from the Scriptures. Using the law of Moses and
the books of the prophets, he spoke to them
from morning until evening. 24Some were persuaded by the things he said, but others did not
believe. 25And after they had argued back and
forth among themselves, they left with this final
word from Paul: "The Holy Spirit was right

when he said to your ancestors through Isaiah
the prophet,

26 'Go and say to this people:
When you hear what I say,
you will not understand.
When you see what I do,
you will not comprehend.
27 For the hearts of these people are
hardened,
and their ears cannot hear,
and they have closed their eyes—
so their eyes cannot see,
and their ears cannot hear,
and their hearts cannot understand,
and they cannot turn to me
and let me heal them.'

28 So I want you to know that this salvation from
God has also been offered to the Gentiles, and
they will accept it."*

30 For the next two years, Paul lived in Rome at
his own expense. He welcomed all who visited
him, 31 boldly proclaiming the Kingdom of God
and teaching about the Lord Jesus Christ. And no
one tried to stop him.

28:28 Some manuscripts add verse 29, *And when he had said these words, the Jews departed, greatly disagreeing with each other.*

ROMANS A State of Grace

Look for 2 hidden messages in Romans!

Paul wrote to the believers living in Rome to explain the basics of the Christian faith. He talked about

- **LAW VS. GRACE**
- **FAITH VS. DEEDS**
- **DEAD VS. ALIVE**
- **WEAK VS. STRONG**

Feeling Bad!

Having a hard time? Feeling a little down? Things aren't going all that well? **Take heart! Find out why in Romans 5:3-5.**

A Good Example

In his letter to the Romans, Paul talked about a hero from the past. **Find out who, and why he remembered him. Read Romans 4:1-25.**

Perfect Timing

God doesn't wear a watch, but his timing is perfect. **Read Romans 5:6-8 to see what God timed so perfectly!**

We're All the Same

Think you're different from other people? Think again! **Read Romans 3:22-23 to find out how and why we're all the same.**

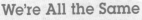

We're All the Same —Again!

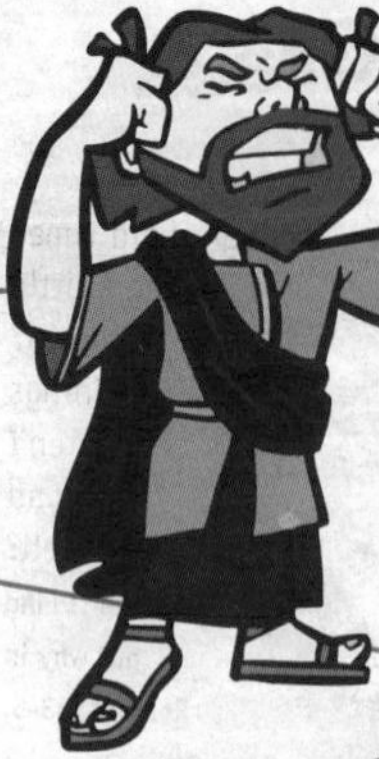

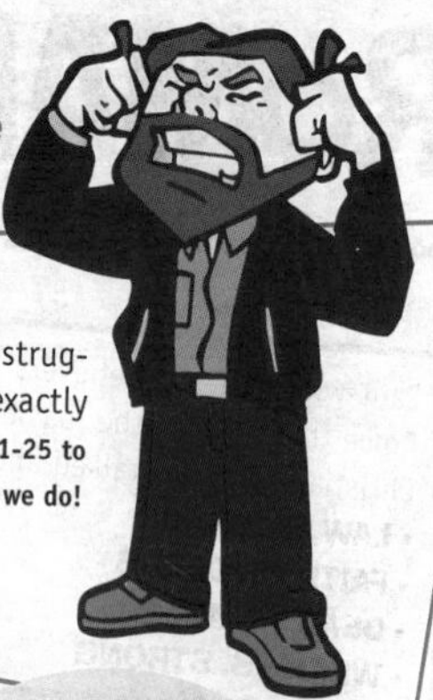

I'm OK. You're OK. *Not!*

Think you're the only one who struggles to do right? Well, Paul had exactly the same problems. **Read Romans 7:21-25 to see how Paul struggled with sin, just like we do!**

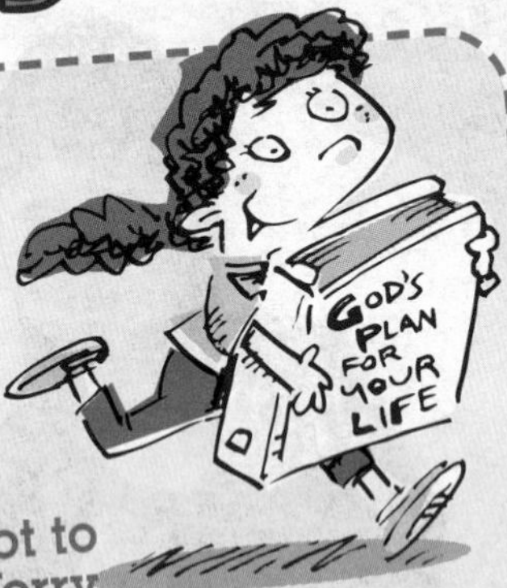

Not to Worry

Ever worry about why things happen the way they do? Well, stop worrying! God has a perfect plan for those who believe in him. **Read Romans 8:28 for proof of that perfect plan!**

And the Winner Is...

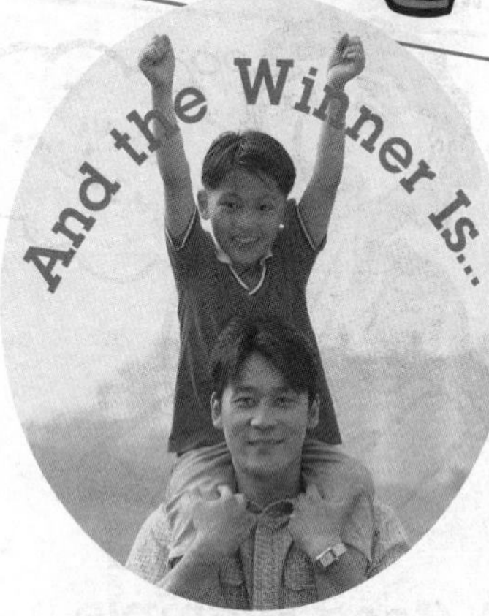

I'm the greatest! No, I'm the greatest! No, no, no—*I'm* the greatest! Which of God's commandments is the greatest? **Read Romans 13:8-10 to find the winner!**

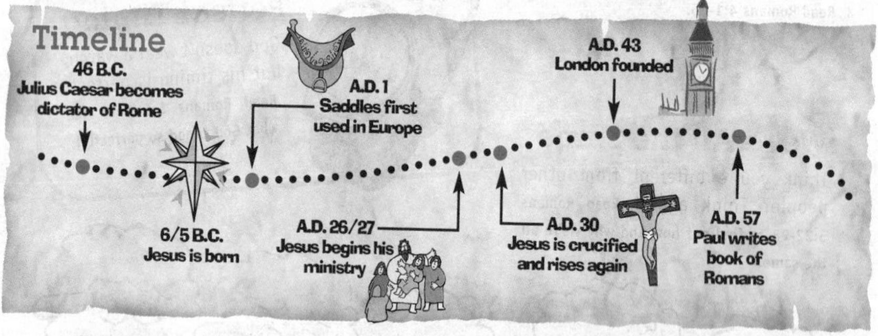

Timeline

- 46 B.C. Julius Caesar becomes dictator of Rome
- 6/5 B.C. Jesus is born
- A.D. 1 Saddles first used in Europe
- A.D. 26/27 Jesus begins his ministry
- A.D. 30 Jesus is crucified and rises again
- A.D. 43 London founded
- A.D. 57 Paul writes book of Romans

The book of Romans is a great guideline for what it means to be a follower of Jesus. In his letter to the Roman believers, Paul laid it all out—ask God to forgive your sins and believe in Jesus to be saved. He made it clear that you can't be saved by doing good deeds. You can be saved only by believing that Jesus died to save you. Paul's words were true back then, and they're true today. **Just believe—it's that simple.**

CHAPTER 1
Greetings from Paul
This letter is from Paul, a slave of Christ Jesus,
chosen by God to be an apostle and sent out to
preach his Good News. 2 God promised this
Good News long ago through his prophets in the
holy Scriptures. 3 The Good News is about his
Son. In his earthly life he was born into King
David's family line, 4 and he was shown to be the
Son of God when he was raised from the dead by
the power of the Holy Spirit. He is Jesus Christ
our Lord. 5 Through Christ, God has given us the
privilege and authority as apostles to tell
Gentiles everywhere what God has done for
them, so that they will believe and obey him,
bringing glory to his name.

6 And you are included among those Gentiles who have been called to belong to Jesus
Christ. 7 I am writing to all of you in Rome who
are loved by God and are called to be his own
holy people.

May God our Father and the Lord Jesus Christ
give you grace and peace.

God's Good News
8 Let me say first that I thank my God through
Jesus Christ for all of you, because your faith in
him is being talked about all over the world.
9 God knows how often I pray for you. Day and
night I bring you and your needs in prayer to
God, whom I serve with all my heart by spreading
the Good News about his Son.

10 One of the things I always pray for is the opportunity, God willing, to come at last to see you.
11 For I long to visit you so I can bring you some
spiritual gift that will help you grow strong in
the Lord. 12 When we get together, I want to encourage you in your faith, but I also want to be
encouraged by yours.

13 I want you to know, dear brothers and sisters, that I planned many times to visit you, but I
was prevented until now. I want to work among
you and see spiritual fruit, just as I have seen
among other Gentiles. 14 For I have a great sense
of obligation to people in both the civilized
world and the rest of the world, to the educated
and uneducated alike. 15 So I am eager to come to
you in Rome, too, to preach the Good News.

**16 For I am not ashamed of this
Good News about Christ. It is the
power of God at work, saving everyone who believes—the Jew first and
also the Gentile.** 17 This Good News tells us
how God makes us right in his sight. This is accomplished from start to finish by faith. As the
Scriptures say, "It is through faith that a righteous person has life."

God's Anger at Sin
18 But God shows his anger from heaven against
all sinful, wicked people who suppress the truth
by their wickedness. 19 They know the truth
about God because he has made it obvious to
them. 20 For ever since the world was created,
people have seen the earth and sky. Through
everything God made, they can clearly see his
invisible qualities—his eternal power and divine nature. So they have no excuse for not
knowing God.

21 Yes, they knew God, but they wouldn't worship him as God or even give him thanks. And
they began to think up foolish ideas of what
God was like. As a result, their minds became
dark and confused. 22 Claiming to be wise, they
instead became utter fools. 23 And instead of
worshiping the glorious, ever-living God, they
worshiped idols made to look like mere people
and birds and animals and reptiles.

24 So God abandoned them to do whatever
shameful things their hearts desired. As a result, they did vile and degrading things with
each other's bodies. 25 They traded the truth
about God for a lie. So they worshiped and
served the things God created instead of the
Creator himself, who is worthy of eternal
praise! Amen. 26 That is why God abandoned
them to their shameful desires. Even the
women turned against the natural way to have
sex and instead indulged in sex with each
other. 27 And the men, instead of having normal
sexual relations with women, burned with lust
for each other. Men did shameful things
with other men, and as a result of this sin, they
suffered within themselves the penalty they
deserved.

28 Since they thought it foolish to acknowledge God, he abandoned them to their foolish
thinking and let them do things that should
never be done. 29 Their lives became full of every
kind of wickedness, sin, greed, hate, envy, murder, quarreling, deception, malicious behavior,
and gossip. 30 They are backstabbers, haters of
God, insolent, proud, and boastful. They invent
new ways of sinning, and they disobey their parents. 31 They refuse to understand, break their
promises, are heartless, and have no mercy.
32 They know God's justice requires that those
who do these things deserve to die, yet they do
them anyway. Worse yet, they encourage others
to do them, too.

Romans 2 . . . page 1108

"For I am not ashamed of this Good News about Christ. It is the power of God at work, saving everyone who believes—the Jew first and also the Gentile."—ROMANS 1:16

Read ROMANS 1:16 out loud a few times until you know it by heart.

Whoever believes in Jesus will be saved and live with him forever in heaven. Now *that's* power!

Believing in Jesus has the awesome power to save you, change your life, and let you live in heaven forever.

Here's an experiment about SIMPLE POWER!

1. **Zip a resealable gallon-size plastic bag closed.**
2. **Poke a hole in the side of the bag with a drinking straw. Tape around the straw where it's poked inside the bag.**

3. **Place a heavy book on the bag. Now blow through the straw, and watch what happens.**

AMAZING! You may not have thought the bag was powerful at first, but it turned out to be very powerful!

You may not think at first that believing in Jesus is powerful, but it is. It's the only thing that can get you into heaven!

Show this experiment to a friend, then explain the power of believing in Jesus!

CHAPTER **2**

God's Judgment of Sin

You may think you can condemn such people,
but you are just as bad, and you have no excuse!
When you say they are wicked and should be
punished, you are condemning yourself, for you
who judge others do these very same things.
2And we know that God, in his justice, will punish
anyone who does such things. 3Since you judge
others for doing these things, why do you think
you can avoid God's judgment when you do the
same things? 4Don't you see how wonderfully
kind, tolerant, and patient God is with you? Does
this mean nothing to you? Can't you see that his
kindness is intended to turn you from your sin?
5But because you are stubborn and refuse to
turn from your sin, you are storing up terrible
punishment for yourself. For a day of anger is
coming, when God's righteous judgment will be
revealed. 6He will judge everyone according to
what they have done. 7He will give eternal life to
those who keep on doing good, seeking after the
glory and honor and immortality that God offers.
8But he will pour out his anger and wrath on
those who live for themselves, who refuse to
obey the truth and instead live lives of wickedness. 9There will be trouble and calamity for
everyone who keeps on doing what is evil—for
the Jew first and also for the Gentile. 10But there
will be glory and honor and peace from God for
all who do good—for the Jew first and also for the
Gentile. 11For God does not show favoritism.
12When the Gentiles sin, they will be destroyed, even though they never had God's written law. And the Jews, who do have God's law, will
be judged by that law when they fail to obey it.
13For merely listening to the law doesn't make
us right with God. It is obeying the law that
makes us right in his sight. 14Even Gentiles, who
do not have God's written law, show that they
know his law when they instinctively obey it,
even without having heard it. 15They demonstrate that God's law is written in their hearts, for
their own conscience and thoughts either accuse them or tell them they are doing right.
16And this is the message I proclaim—that the
day is coming when God, through Christ Jesus,
will judge everyone's secret life.

The Jews and the Law

17You who call yourselves Jews are relying on
God's law, and you boast about your special relationship with him. 18You know what he wants;
you know what is right because you have been
taught his law. 19You are convinced that you are

a guide for the blind and a light for people who
are lost in darkness. 20 You think you can instruct
the ignorant and teach children the ways of God.
For you are certain that God's law gives you complete knowledge and truth.
21 Well then, if you teach others, why don't you
teach yourself? You tell others not to steal, but do
you steal? 22 You say it is wrong to commit adultery, but do you commit adultery? You condemn
idolatry, but do you use items stolen from pagan
temples? 23 You are so proud of knowing the law,
but you dishonor God by breaking it. 24 No wonder the Scriptures say, "The Gentiles blaspheme
the name of God because of you."
25 The Jewish ceremony of circumcision has
value only if you obey God's law. But if you don't
obey God's law, you are no better off than an
uncircumcised Gentile. 26 And if the Gentiles
obey God's law, won't God declare them to be his
own people? 27 In fact, uncircumcised Gentiles
who keep God's law will condemn you Jews who
are circumcised and possess God's law but don't
obey it.
28 For you are not a true Jew just because you
were born of Jewish parents or because you have
gone through the ceremony of circumcision.
29 No, a true Jew is one whose heart is right with
God. And true circumcision is not merely obeying the letter of the law; rather, it is a change of
heart produced by the Spirit. And a person with a
changed heart seeks praise from God, not from
people.

CHAPTER 3
God Remains Faithful
Then what's the advantage of being a Jew? Is
there any value in the ceremony of circumcision? 2 Yes, there are great benefits! First of all,
the Jews were entrusted with the whole revelation of God.
3 True, some of them were unfaithful; but just
because they were unfaithful, does that mean
God will be unfaithful? 4 Of course not! Even if
everyone else is a liar, God is true. As the Scriptures say about him,

"You will be proved right in what you say,
and you will win your case in court."

5 "But," some might say, "our sinfulness serves
a good purpose, for it helps people see how righteous God is. Isn't it unfair, then, for him to punish us?" (This is merely a human point of view.)
6 Of course not! If God were not entirely fair, how
would he be qualified to judge the world?
7 "But," someone might still argue, "how can God
condemn me as a sinner if my dishonesty highlights his truthfulness and brings him more
glory?" 8 And some people even slander us by
claiming that we say, "The more we sin, the
better it is!" Those who say such things deserve
to be condemned.

All People Are Sinners
9 Well then, should we conclude that we Jews are
better than others? No, not at all, for we have
already shown that all people, whether Jews or
Gentiles, are under the power of sin. 10 As the
Scriptures say,

"No one is righteous—
not even one.
11 No one is truly wise;
no one is seeking God.
12 All have turned away;
all have become useless.
No one does good,
not a single one."
13 "Their talk is foul, like the stench from
an open grave.
Their tongues are filled with lies."
"Snake venom drips from their lips."
14 "Their mouths are full of cursing
and bitterness."
15 "They rush to commit murder.
16 Destruction and misery always
follow them.
17 They don't know where to find peace."
18 "They have no fear of God at all."

19 Obviously, the law applies to those to whom
it was given, for its purpose is to keep people
from having excuses, and to show that the entire
world is guilty before God. 20 For no one can ever
be made right with God by doing what the law
commands. The law simply shows us how sinful
we are.

Christ Took Our Punishment
21 But now God has shown us a way to be made
right with him without keeping the requirements of the law, as was promised in the writings
of Moses and the prophets long ago. 22 We are
made right with God by placing our faith in
Jesus Christ. And this is true for everyone who
believes, no matter who we are.
**23 For everyone has sinned; we all
fall short of God's glorious stan-
dard.** 24 Yet God freely and graciously declares
that we are righteous. He did this through Christ
Jesus when he freed us from the penalty for our
sins. 25 For God presented Jesus as the sacrifice

for sin. People are made right with God when
they believe that Jesus sacrificed his life, shedding his blood. This sacrifice shows that God was
being fair when he held back and did not punish
those who sinned in times past, 26 for he was
looking ahead and including them in what he
would do in this present time. God did this to
demonstrate his righteousness, for he himself is
fair and just, and he declares sinners to be right
in his sight when they believe in Jesus.

27 Can we boast, then, that we have done anything to be accepted by God? No, because our
acquittal is not based on obeying the law. It is
based on faith. 28 So we are made right with God
through faith and not by obeying the law.

29 After all, is God the God of the Jews only?
Isn't he also the God of the Gentiles? Of course
he is. 30 There is only one God, and he makes
people right with himself only by faith, whether
they are Jews or Gentiles. 31 Well then, if we emphasize faith, does this mean that we can forget
about the law? Of course not! In fact, only when
we have faith do we truly fulfill the law.

CHAPTER 4

The Faith of Abraham

Abraham was, humanly speaking, the founder of
our Jewish nation. What did he discover about
being made right with God? 2 If his good deeds
had made him acceptable to God, he would have
had something to boast about. But that was not
God's way. 3 For the Scriptures tell us, "Abraham
believed God, and God counted him as righteous
because of his faith."

4 When people work, their wages are not a gift,
but something they have earned. 5 But people are
counted as righteous, not because of their work,
but because of their faith in God who forgives
sinners. 6 David also spoke of this when he described the happiness of those who are declared
righteous without working for it:

7 "Oh, what joy for those
whose disobedience is forgiven,
whose sins are put out of sight.
8 Yes, what joy for those
whose record the LORD has cleared of sin."

9 Now, is this blessing only for the Jews, or is it
also for uncircumcised Gentiles? Well, we have
been saying that Abraham was counted as righteous by God because of his faith. 10 But how did
this happen? Was he counted as righteous only
after he was circumcised, or was it before he was
circumcised? Clearly, God accepted Abraham
before he was circumcised!

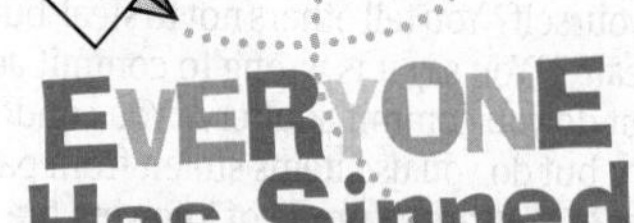

"For everyone has sinned; we all fall short of God's glorious standard." —ROMANS 3:23

EVERYONE Has Sinned

Read ROMANS 3:23 out loud a few times until you have it stuck in your brain.

No matter how much we try, we just can't be as good as God.

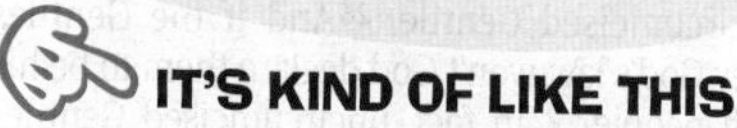

IT'S KIND OF LIKE THIS!

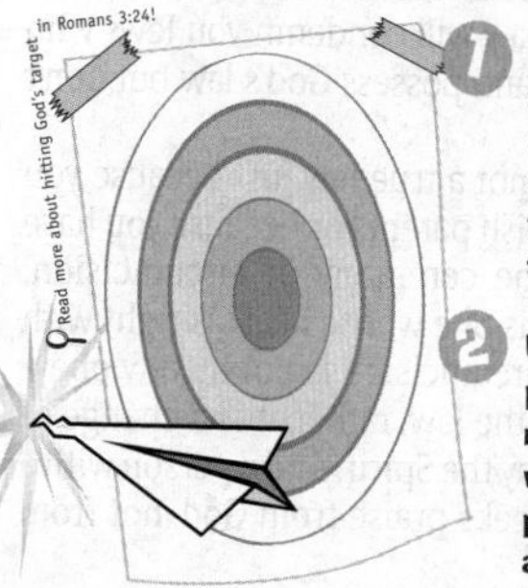

Read more about hitting God's target in Romans 3:24!

1 Draw a bull's-eye target on a sheet of paper. Tape the paper to a wall.

2 Use more paper to make paper wads or paper airplanes.

3 Step as far away from the target as the room allows, and try to hit the center of the target with your paper wads or airplanes. Play several rounds.

If you think of God as the center of the target, we just can't hit the target every time.

But that's OK. Do you know why? BECAUSE OF JESUS!

Jesus took the punishment for our sins when he died on the cross. After we believe in Jesus, God helps us choose to follow Jesus so we can be on target.

THAT'S THE ONLY WAY TO HIT GOD'S TARGET—TO BELIEVE IN JESUS!

11 Circumcision was a sign that Abraham already had faith and that God had already accepted him and declared him to be righteous—even before he was circumcised. So Abraham is the spiritual father of those who have faith but have not been circumcised. They are counted as righteous because of their faith. 12 And Abraham is also the spiritual father of those who have been circumcised, but only if they have the same kind of faith Abraham had before he was circumcised.

13 Clearly, God's promise to give the whole earth to Abraham and his descendants was based not on his obedience to God's law, but on a right relationship with God that comes by faith. 14 If God's promise is only for those who obey the law, then faith is not necessary and the promise is pointless. 15 For the law always brings punishment on those who try to obey it. (The only way to avoid breaking the law is to have no law to break!)

16 So the promise is received by faith. It is given as a free gift. And we are all certain to receive it, whether or not we live according to the law of Moses, if we have faith like Abraham's. For Abraham is the father of all who believe. 17 That is what the Scriptures mean when God told him, "I have made you the father of many nations." This happened because Abraham believed in the God who brings the dead back to life and who creates new things out of nothing.

18 Even when there was no reason for hope, Abraham kept hoping—believing that he would become the father of many nations. For God had said to him, "That's how many descendants you will have!" 19 And Abraham's faith did not weaken, even though, at about 100 years of age, he figured his body was as good as dead—and so was Sarah's womb.

20 Abraham never wavered in believing God's promise. In fact, his faith grew stronger, and in this he brought glory to God. 21 He was fully convinced that God is able to do whatever he promises. 22 And because of Abraham's faith, God counted him as righteous. 23 And when God counted him as righteous, it wasn't just for Abraham's benefit. It was recorded 24 for our benefit, too, assuring us that God will also count us as righteous if we believe in him, the one who raised Jesus our Lord from the dead. 25 He was handed over to die because of our sins, and he was raised to life to make us right with God.

CHAPTER 5

Faith Brings Joy

Therefore, since we have been made right in God's sight by faith, we have peace with God because of what Jesus Christ our Lord has done for us. 2 Because of our faith, Christ has brought us into this place of undeserved privilege where we now stand, and we confidently and joyfully look forward to sharing God's glory.

3 We can rejoice, too, when we run into problems and trials, for we know that they help us develop endurance. 4 And endurance develops strength of character, and character strengthens our confident hope of salvation. 5 And this hope will not lead to disappointment. For we know how dearly God loves us, because he has given us the Holy Spirit to fill our hearts with his love.

6 When we were utterly helpless, Christ came at just the right time and died for us sinners. 7 Now, most people would not be willing to die for an upright person, though someone might perhaps be willing to die for a person who is especially good. **8 But God showed his great love for us by sending Christ to die for us while we were still sinners.** 9 And since we have been made right in God's sight by the blood of Christ, he will certainly save us from God's condemnation. 10 For since our friendship with God was restored by the death of his Son while we were still his enemies, we will certainly be saved through the life of his Son. 11 So now we can rejoice in our wonderful new relationship with God because our Lord Jesus Christ has made us friends of God.

Adam and Christ Contrasted

12 When Adam sinned, sin entered the world. Adam's sin brought death, so death spread to everyone, for everyone sinned. 13 Yes, people sinned even before the law was given. But it was not counted as sin because there was not yet any law to break. 14 Still, everyone died—from the time of Adam to the time of Moses—even those who did not disobey an explicit commandment of God, as Adam did. Now Adam is a symbol, a representation of Christ, who was yet to come. 15 But there is a great difference between Adam's sin and God's gracious gift. For the sin of this one man, Adam, brought death to many. But even greater is God's wonderful grace and his gift of forgiveness to many through this other man, Jesus Christ. 16 And the result of God's gracious gift is very different from the result of that one man's sin. For Adam's sin led to condemnation, but God's free gift leads to our being made right with God, even though we are guilty of many sins. 17 For

the sin of this one man, Adam, caused death
to rule over many. But even greater is God's
wonderful grace and his gift of righteousness, for all who receive it will live in triumph
over sin and death through this one man, Jesus
Christ.
18Yes, Adam's one sin brings condemnation
for everyone, but Christ's one act of righteousness brings a right relationship with God and
new life for everyone. 19Because one person disobeyed God, many became sinners. But because
one other person obeyed God, many will be
made righteous.
20God's law was given so that all people could
see how sinful they were. But as people sinned
more and more, God's wonderful grace became
more abundant. 21So just as sin ruled over all
people and brought them to death, now God's
wonderful grace rules instead, giving us right
standing with God and resulting in eternal life
through Jesus Christ our Lord.

CHAPTER 6

Sin's Power Is Broken

Well then, should we keep on sinning so that God
can show us more and more of his wonderful
grace? 2Of course not! Since we have died to sin,
how can we continue to live in it? 3Or have you
forgotten that when we were joined with Christ
Jesus in baptism, we joined him in his death?
4For we died and were buried with Christ by baptism. And just as Christ was raised from the dead
by the glorious power of the Father, now we also
may live new lives.
5Since we have been united with him in his
death, we will also be raised to life as he was.
6We know that our old sinful selves were crucified with Christ so that sin might lose its power
in our lives. We are no longer slaves to sin. 7For
when we died with Christ we were set free from
the power of sin. 8And since we died with
Christ, we know we will also live with him. 9We
are sure of this because Christ was raised from
the dead, and he will never die again. Death no
longer has any power over him. 10When he
died, he died once to break the power of sin. But
now that he lives, he lives for the glory of God.
11So you also should consider yourselves to be
dead to the power of sin and alive to God
through Christ Jesus.
12Do not let sin control the way you live; do
not give in to sinful desires. 13Do not let any part
of your body become an instrument of evil to
serve sin. Instead, give yourselves completely to
God, for you were dead, but now you have new
life. So use your whole body as an instrument to
do what is right for the glory of God. 14Sin is no
longer your master, for you no longer live under
the requirements of the law. Instead, you live
under the freedom of God's grace.
15Well then, since God's grace has set us free
from the law, does that mean we can go on sinning? Of course not! 16Don't you realize that you
become the slave of whatever you choose to
obey? You can be a slave to sin, which leads to
death, or you can choose to obey God, which
leads to righteous living. 17Thank God! Once you
were slaves of sin, but now you wholeheartedly
obey this teaching we have given you. 18Now you
are free from your slavery to sin, and you have
become slaves to righteous living.
19Because of the weakness of your human nature, I am using the illustration of slavery to help
you understand all this. Previously, you let yourselves be slaves to impurity and lawlessness,
which led ever deeper into sin. Now you must
give yourselves to be slaves to righteous living so
that you will become holy.
20When you were slaves to sin, you were free
from the obligation to do right. 21And what was
the result? You are now ashamed of the things
you used to do, things that end in eternal doom.
22But now you are free from the power of sin
and have become slaves of God. Now you do
those things that lead to holiness and result in
eternal life. **23For the wages of sin is
death, but the free gift of God is
eternal life through Christ Jesus
our Lord.**

CHAPTER 7

No Longer Bound to the Law

Now, dear brothers and sisters—you who are familiar with the law—don't you know that the law
applies only while a person is living? 2For example, when a woman marries, the law binds her to
her husband as long as he is alive. But if he dies,
the laws of marriage no longer apply to her. 3So
while her husband is alive, she would be committing adultery if she married another man. But
if her husband dies, she is free from that law and
does not commit adultery when she remarries.
4So, my dear brothers and sisters, this is the
point: You died to the power of the law when you
died with Christ. And now you are united with the
one who was raised from the dead. As a result, we
can produce a harvest of good deeds for God.
5When we were controlled by our old nature,
sinful desires were at work within us, and the law
aroused these evil desires that produced a har-

vest of sinful deeds, resulting in death. 6But now
we have been released from the law, for we died to
it and are no longer captive to its power. Now we
can serve God, not in the old way of obeying the
letter of the law, but in the new way of living in the
Spirit.

God's Law Reveals Our Sin

7Well then, am I suggesting that the law of God is
sinful? Of course not! In fact, it was the law that
showed me my sin. I would never have known
that coveting is wrong if the law had not said,
"You must not covet." 8But sin used this command to arouse all kinds of covetous desires
within me! If there were no law, sin would not
have that power. 9At one time I lived without
understanding the law. But when I learned the
command not to covet, for instance, the power of
sin came to life, 10and I died. So I discovered that
the law's commands, which were supposed to
bring life, brought spiritual death instead. 11Sin
took advantage of those commands and deceived me; it used the commands to kill me.
12But still, the law itself is holy, and its commands are holy and right and good.
13But how can that be? Did the law, which is
good, cause my death? Of course not! Sin used
what was good to bring about my condemnation
to death. So we can see how terrible sin really is.
It uses God's good commands for its own evil
purposes.

Struggling with Sin

14So the trouble is not with the law, for it is spiritual and good. The trouble is with me, for I am
all too human, a slave to sin. 15I don't really
understand myself, for I want to do what is
right, but I don't do it. Instead, I do what I hate.
16But if I know that what I am doing is wrong,
this shows that I agree that the law is good. 17So
I am not the one doing wrong; it is sin living in
me that does it.
18And I know that nothing good lives in me,
that is, in my sinful nature. I want to do what is
right, but I can't. 19I want to do what is good, but I
don't. I don't want to do what is wrong, but I do it
anyway. 20But if I do what I don't want to do, I am
not really the one doing wrong; it is sin living in
me that does it.
21I have discovered this principle of life—
that when I want to do what is right, I inevitably
do what is wrong. 22I love God's law with all my
heart. 23But there is another power within me
that is at war with my mind. This power makes
me a slave to the sin that is still within me. 24Oh,

Key Verse **"But God showed his great love for us by sending Christ to die for us while we were still sinners."—ROMANS 5:8**

GOD
LOVES
YOU!

Read ROMANS 5:8 out loud. Then read it again. And again.

God loves you so much that he sent his Son to die for you, just as you are. He didn't wait until you cleaned up your act. *That's* how much he loves you!

THINK OF SOMEONE IN YOUR LIFE WHO LOVES YOU.

1. **Write that person's name in the sentence on the left of the chart below. Then write a few ways that person shows love for you.**
2. **On the right, write ways that God shows love for you. (The most important way is already written there!)**

THIS IS HOW ______ SHOWS LOVE FOR ME:	THIS IS HOW GOD SHOWS LOVE FOR ME:
	He sent Jesus to die for me.

Read more about love in 1 Corinthians 13:4-7.

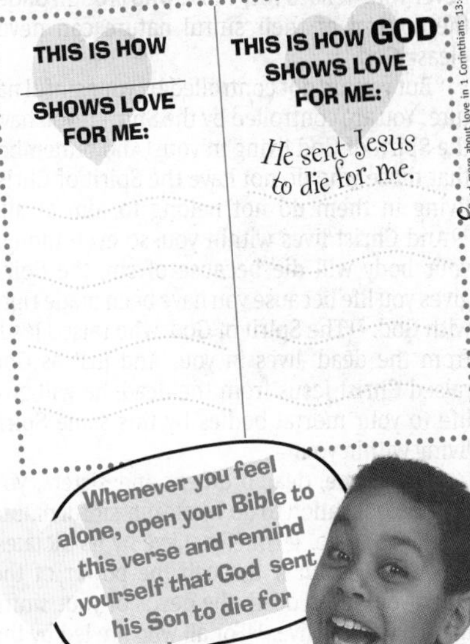
Whenever you feel alone, open your Bible to this verse and remind yourself that God sent his Son to die for you!

what a miserable person I am! Who will free me
from this life that is dominated by sin and
death? 25 Thank God! The answer is in Jesus
Christ our Lord. So you see how it is: In my mind
I really want to obey God's law, but because of
my sinful nature I am a slave to sin.

CHAPTER 8
Life in the Spirit

So now there is no condemnation for those who
belong to Christ Jesus. 2 And because you belong
to him, the power of the life-giving Spirit has
freed you from the power of sin that leads to
death. 3 The law of Moses was unable to save us
because of the weakness of our sinful nature. So
God did what the law could not do. He sent his
own Son in a body like the bodies we sinners
have. And in that body God declared an end to
sin's control over us by giving his Son as a sacrifice for our sins. 4 He did this so that the just
requirement of the law would be fully satisfied
for us, who no longer follow our sinful nature but
instead follow the Spirit.

5 Those who are dominated by the sinful nature think about sinful things, but those who are
controlled by the Holy Spirit think about things
that please the Spirit. 6 So letting your sinful
nature control your mind leads to death. But letting the Spirit control your mind leads to life
and peace. 7 For the sinful nature is always hostile to God. It never did obey God's laws, and it
never will. 8 That's why those who are still under
the control of their sinful nature can never
please God.

9 But you are not controlled by your sinful nature. You are controlled by the Spirit if you have
the Spirit of God living in you. (And remember
that those who do not have the Spirit of Christ
living in them do not belong to him at all.)
10 And Christ lives within you, so even though
your body will die because of sin, the Spirit
gives you life because you have been made right
with God. 11 The Spirit of God, who raised Jesus
from the dead, lives in you. And just as God
raised Christ Jesus from the dead, he will give
life to your mortal bodies by this same Spirit
living within you.

12 Therefore, dear brothers and sisters, you
have no obligation to do what your sinful nature
urges you to do. 13 For if you live by its dictates,
you will die. But if through the power of the
Spirit you put to death the deeds of your sinful
nature, you will live. 14 For all who are led by the
Spirit of God are children of God.

15 So you have not received a spirit that makes
you fearful slaves. Instead, you received God's
Spirit when he adopted you as his own children.
Now we call him, "Abba, Father." 16 For his Spirit
joins with our spirit to affirm that we are God's
children. 17 And since we are his children, we are
his heirs. In fact, together with Christ we are
heirs of God's glory. But if we are to share his
glory, we must also share his suffering.

Key Verse **"For the wages of sin is death, but the free gift of God is eternal life through Christ Jesus our Lord." —ROMANS 6:23**

Read ROMANS 6:23 out loud to a friend or family member.

HEY, WHO DOESN'T LIKE A FREE GIFT? God gives us the free gift of eternal life through Jesus. That's a gift worth sharing, don't you think?

HERE'S HOW!

1. **Write the words of the verse on a sheet of paper. Decorate the paper any way you choose.**
2. **Put the paper in a box and gift-wrap the box.**
3. **Make a gift tag that says, "Here's the greatest gift of all!"**

GIVE THE GIFT TO SOMEONE WHO NEEDS TO KNOW ABOUT JESUS. Then make another gift box, and another. *Everyone* needs to know about Jesus!

The Future Glory

18 Yet what we suffer now is nothing compared
to the glory he will reveal to us later. 19 For all
creation is waiting eagerly for that future day
when God will reveal who his children really
are. 20 Against its will, all creation was sub-
jected to God's curse. But with eager hope,
21 the creation looks forward to the day when it
will join God's children in glorious freedom
from death and decay. 22 For we know that all
creation has been groaning as in the pains of
childbirth right up to the present time. 23 And
we believers also groan, even though we have
the Holy Spirit within us as a foretaste of future
glory, for we long for our bodies to be released
from sin and suffering. We, too, wait with eager
hope for the day when God will give us our full
rights as his adopted children, including the
new bodies he has promised us. 24 We were
given this hope when we were saved. (If we already have something, we don't need to hope
for it. 25 But if we look forward to something we
don't yet have, we must wait patiently and confidently.)

26 And the Holy Spirit helps us in our weakness. For example, we don't know what God
wants us to pray for. But the Holy Spirit prays for
us with groanings that cannot be expressed in
words. 27 And the Father who knows all hearts
knows what the Spirit is saying, for the Spirit
pleads for us believers in harmony with God's
own will. **28 And we know that God
causes everything to work together
for the good of those who love God
and are called according to his purpose for them.** 29 For God knew his people
in advance, and he chose them to become like
his Son, so that his Son would be the firstborn
among many brothers and sisters. 30 And having
chosen them, he called them to come to him.
And having called them, he gave them right
standing with himself. And having given them
right standing, he gave them his glory.

Nothing Can Separate Us from God's Love

31 What shall we say about such wonderful
things as these? If God is for us, who can ever be
against us? 32 Since he did not spare even his
own Son but gave him up for us all, won't he also
give us everything else? 33 Who dares accuse us
whom God has chosen for his own? No one—for
God himself has given us right standing with
himself. 34 Who then will condemn us? No
one—for Christ Jesus died for us and was raised
to life for us, and he is sitting in the place of
honor at God's right hand, pleading for us.

35 Can anything ever separate us from Christ's
love? Does it mean he no longer loves us if we
have trouble or calamity, or are persecuted, or
hungry, or destitute, or in danger, or threatened
with death? 36 (As the Scriptures say, "For your
sake we are killed every day; we are being slaughtered like sheep.") 37 No, despite all these things,
overwhelming victory is ours through Christ,
who loved us.

38 And I am convinced that nothing can ever
separate us from God's love. Neither death nor
life, neither angels nor demons, neither our fears
for today nor our worries about tomorrow—not
even the powers of hell can separate us from
God's love. 39 No power in the sky above or in the
earth below—indeed, nothing in all creation will
ever be able to separate us from the love of God
that is revealed in Christ Jesus our Lord.

CHAPTER 9

God's Selection of Israel

With Christ as my witness, I speak with utter
truthfulness. My conscience and the Holy Spirit
confirm it. 2 My heart is filled with bitter sorrow
and unending grief 3 for my people, my Jewish
brothers and sisters. I would be willing to be forever cursed—cut off from Christ!—if that would
save them. 4 They are the people of Israel, chosen
to be God's adopted children. God revealed his
glory to them. He made covenants with them
and gave them his law. He gave them the privilege of worshiping him and receiving his wonderful promises. 5 Abraham, Isaac, and Jacob are
their ancestors, and Christ himself was an Israelite as far as his human nature is concerned. And
he is God, the one who rules over everything and
is worthy of eternal praise! Amen.

6 Well then, has God failed to fulfill his promise
to Israel? No, for not all who are born into
the nation of Israel are truly members of God's
people! 7 Being descendants of Abraham doesn't
make them truly Abraham's children. For the Scriptures say, "Isaac is the son through whom your descendants will be counted," though Abraham had
other children, too. 8 This means that Abraham's
physical descendants are not necessarily children of God. Only the children of the promise are
considered to be Abraham's children. 9 For God
had promised, "I will return about this time next
year, and Sarah will have a son."

10 This son was our ancestor Isaac. When he
married Rebekah, she gave birth to twins. 11 But
before they were born, before they had done

Key Verse **"And we know that God causes everything to work together for the good of those who love God and are called according to his purpose for them." —ROMANS 8:28**

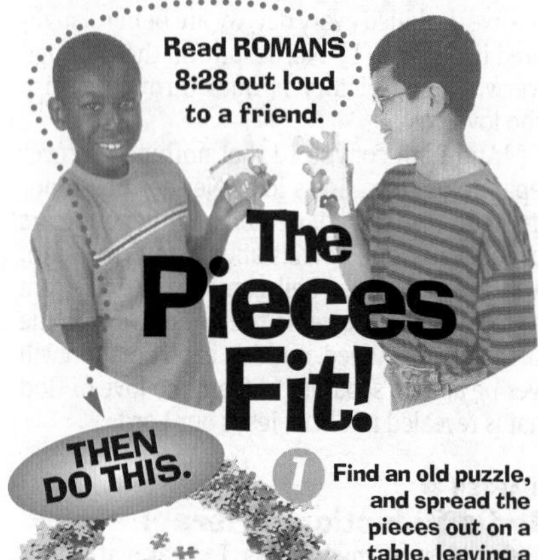

Read ROMANS 8:28 out loud to a friend.
The Pieces Fit!

THEN DO THIS.

1 **Find an old puzzle, and spread the pieces out on a table, leaving a clear space in the center.**

2 **Take turns with your friend picking up a puzzle piece and laying it in the clear space. For each piece you pick up, tell your friend about a time you were confused or troubled.**

The picture on the puzzle box is a complete picture, made up of little pieces that all fit together like the pieces of your life. Glue some puzzle pieces to a square of colored poster board. Write the words of **ROMANS 8:28** around the border.

DO THIS! **Keep your puzzle in your room to remind you that God sees the big picture of your life!**

anything good or bad, she received a message
from God. (This message shows that God
chooses people according to his own purposes;
12he calls people, but not according to their good
or bad works.) She was told, "Your older son will
serve your younger son." 13In the words of the
Scriptures, "I loved Jacob, but I rejected Esau."

14Are we saying, then, that God was unfair?
Of course not! 15For God said to Moses,

"I will show mercy to anyone I choose,
and I will show compassion to anyone
I choose."

16So it is God who decides to show mercy. We
can neither choose it nor work for it.

17For the Scriptures say that God told Pharaoh,
"I have appointed you for the very purpose of displaying my power in you and to spread my fame
throughout the earth." 18So you see, God chooses
to show mercy to some, and he chooses to harden
the hearts of others so they refuse to listen.

19Well then, you might say, "Why does God
blame people for not responding? Haven't they
simply done what he makes them do?"

20No, don't say that. Who are you, a mere human being, to argue with God? Should the thing
that was created say to the one who created it,
"Why have you made me like this?" 21When a potter makes jars out of clay, doesn't he have a right to
use the same lump of clay to make one jar for dec-
oration and another to throw garbage into? 22In
the same way, even though God has the right to
show his anger and his power, he is very patient
with those on whom his anger falls, who are destined for destruction. 23He does this to make the
riches of his glory shine even brighter on those
to whom he shows mercy, who were prepared in
advance for glory. 24And we are among those
whom he selected, both from the Jews and from
the Gentiles.

25Concerning the Gentiles, God says in the
prophecy of Hosea,

"Those who were not my people,
I will now call my people.
And I will love those
whom I did not love before."

26And,

"Then, at the place where they were told,
'You are not my people,'
there they will be called
'children of the living God.'"

27And concerning Israel, Isaiah the prophet
cried out,

"Though the people of Israel are as
numerous as the sand of the seashore,
only a remnant will be saved.
28 For the LORD will carry out his sentence
upon the earth
quickly and with finality."

29 And Isaiah said the same thing in another
place:

"If the LORD of Heaven's Armies
had not spared a few of our children,
we would have been wiped out like Sodom,
destroyed like Gomorrah."

Israel's Unbelief

30 What does all this mean? Even though the
Gentiles were not trying to follow God's standards, they were made right with God. And it was
by faith that this took place. 31 But the people of
Israel, who tried so hard to get right with God by
keeping the law, never succeeded. 32 Why not?
Because they were trying to get right with God by
keeping the law instead of by trusting in him.
They stumbled over the great rock in their path.
33 God warned them of this in the Scriptures
when he said,

"I am placing a stone in Jerusalem
that makes people stumble,
a rock that makes them fall.
But anyone who trusts in him
will never be disgraced."

CHAPTER 10

Dear brothers and sisters, the longing of my
heart and my prayer to God is for the people of
Israel to be saved. 2 I know what enthusiasm they
have for God, but it is misdirected zeal. 3 For they
don't understand God's way of making people
right with himself. Refusing to accept God's way,
they cling to their own way of getting right with
God by trying to keep the law. 4 For Christ has
already accomplished the purpose for which the
law was given. As a result, all who believe in him
are made right with God.

Salvation Is for Everyone

5 For Moses writes that the law's way of making a
person right with God requires obedience to all
of its commands. 6 But faith's way of getting right
with God says, "Don't say in your heart, 'Who will
go up to heaven?' (to bring Christ down to earth).
7 And don't say, 'Who will go down to the place of
the dead?' (to bring Christ back to life again)."
8 In fact, it says,

"The message is very close at hand;
it is on your lips and in your heart."

And that message is the very message about faith
that we preach: **9 If you openly declare
that Jesus is Lord and believe in your
heart that God raised him from the
dead, you will be saved.** 10 For it is by believing in your heart that you are made right with
God, and it is by openly declaring your faith that
you are saved. 11 As the Scriptures tell us, "Anyone
who trusts in him will never be disgraced." 12 Jew
and Gentile are the same in this respect. They
have the same Lord, who gives generously to all
who call on him. 13 For "Everyone who calls on the
name of the LORD will be saved."

14 But how can they call on him to save them
unless they believe in him? And how can they believe in him if they have never heard about him?
And how can they hear about him unless someone tells them? 15 And how will anyone go and tell
them without being sent? That is why the Scriptures say, "How beautiful are the feet of messengers who bring good news!"

16 But not everyone welcomes the Good News,
for Isaiah the prophet said, "LORD, who has believed our message?" 17 So faith comes from hearing, that is, hearing the Good News about Christ.
18 But I ask, have the people of Israel actually
heard the message? Yes, they have:

"The message has gone throughout the earth,
and the words to all the world."

19 But I ask, did the people of Israel really understand? Yes, they did, for even in the time of
Moses, God said,

"I will rouse your jealousy through people
who are not even a nation.
I will provoke your anger through the
foolish Gentiles."

20 And later Isaiah spoke boldly for God, saying,

"I was found by people who were not
looking for me.
I showed myself to those who were
not asking for me."

21 But regarding Israel, God said,

"All day long I opened my arms to them,
but they were disobedient and rebellious."

CHAPTER 11

God's Mercy on Israel

I ask, then, has God rejected his own people, the
nation of Israel? Of course not! I myself am an

Israelite, a descendant of Abraham and a member of the tribe of Benjamin.
2No, God has not rejected his own people,
whom he chose from the very beginning. Do you
realize what the Scriptures say about this? Elijah
the prophet complained to God about the people
of Israel and said, 3"LORD, they have killed your
prophets and torn down your altars. I am the only
one left, and now they are trying to kill me, too."
4And do you remember God's reply? He said,
"No, I have 7,000 others who have never bowed
down to Baal!"
5It is the same today, for a few of the people of
Israel have remained faithful because of God's
grace—his undeserved kindness in choosing
them. 6And since it is through God's kindness,
then it is not by their good works. For in that
case, God's grace would not be what it really is—
free and undeserved.
7So this is the situation: Most of the people of
Israel have not found the favor of God they are
looking for so earnestly. A few have—the ones
God has chosen—but the hearts of the rest were
hardened. 8As the Scriptures say,

"God has put them into a deep sleep.
To this day he has shut their eyes so they
do not see,
and closed their ears so they do not hear."

9Likewise, David said,

"Let their bountiful table become a snare,
a trap that makes them think all is well.
Let their blessings cause them to stumble,
and let them get what they deserve.
10 Let their eyes go blind so they cannot see,
and let their backs be bent forever."

11Did God's people stumble and fall beyond
recovery? Of course not! They were disobedient,
so God made salvation available to the Gentiles.
But he wanted his own people to become jealous
and claim it for themselves. 12Now if the Gentiles were enriched because the people of Israel
turned down God's offer of salvation, think how
much greater a blessing the world will share
when they finally accept it.
13I am saying all this especially for you Gentiles. God has appointed me as the apostle to the
Gentiles. I stress this, 14for I want somehow to
make the people of Israel jealous of what you
Gentiles have, so I might save some of them.
15For since their rejection meant that God offered salvation to the rest of the world, their ac-
ceptance will be even more wonderful. It will be
life for those who were dead! 16And since Abraham and the other patriarchs were holy, their descendants will also be holy—just as the entire
batch of dough is holy because the portion given
as an offering is holy. For if the roots of the tree
are holy, the branches will be, too.
17But some of these branches from Abraham's tree—some of the people of Israel—have
been broken off. And you Gentiles, who were
branches from a wild olive tree, have been
grafted in. So now you also receive the blessing
God has promised Abraham and his children,
sharing in the rich nourishment from the root of
God's special olive tree. 18But you must not brag
about being grafted in to replace the branches
that were broken off. You are just a branch, not
the root.
19"Well," you may say, "those branches were
broken off to make room for me." 20Yes, but remember—those branches were broken off because they didn't believe in Christ, and you are
there because you do believe. So don't think
highly of yourself, but fear what could happen.
21For if God did not spare the original branches,
he won't spare you either.
22Notice how God is both kind and severe. He
is severe toward those who disobeyed, but kind
to you if you continue to trust in his kindness.
But if you stop trusting, you also will be cut off.
23And if the people of Israel turn from their unbelief, they will be grafted in again, for God has
the power to graft them back into the tree.
24You, by nature, were a branch cut from a wild
olive tree. So if God was willing to do something
contrary to nature by grafting you into his cultivated tree, he will be far more eager to graft the
original branches back into the tree where they
belong.

God's Mercy Is for Everyone

25I want you to understand this mystery, dear
brothers and sisters, so that you will not feel
proud about yourselves. Some of the people of
Israel have hard hearts, but this will last only
until the full number of Gentiles comes to
Christ. 26And so all Israel will be saved. As the
Scriptures say,

"The one who rescues will come from
Jerusalem,
and he will turn Israel away from
ungodliness.
27 And this is my covenant with them,
that I will take away their sins."

28Many of the people of Israel are now enemies of the Good News, and this benefits you

Gentiles. Yet they are still the people he loves because he chose their ancestors Abraham, Isaac,
and Jacob. 29For God's gifts and his call can never
be withdrawn. 30Once, you Gentiles were rebels
against God, but when the people of Israel rebelled against him, God was merciful to you instead. 31Now they are the rebels, and God's mercy
has come to you so that they, too, will share in
God's mercy. 32For God has imprisoned everyone in disobedience so he could have mercy on
everyone.
33Oh, how great are God's riches and wisdom
and knowledge! How impossible it is for us to
understand his decisions and his ways!

34 For who can know the LORD's thoughts?
Who knows enough to give him advice?
35 And who has given him so much
that he needs to pay it back?

36For everything comes from him and exists
by his power and is intended for his glory. All
glory to him forever! Amen.

CHAPTER 12
A Living Sacrifice to God

And so, dear brothers and sisters, I plead with
you to give your bodies to God because of all he
has done for you. Let them be a living and holy
sacrifice—the kind he will find acceptable. This
is truly the way to worship him. 2Don't copy the
behavior and customs of this world, but let God
transform you into a new person by changing
the way you think. Then you will learn to know
God's will for you, which is good and pleasing
and perfect.
3Because of the privilege and authority God
has given me, I give each of you this warning:
Don't think you are better than you really are. Be
honest in your evaluation of yourselves, measuring yourselves by the faith God has given us.
4Just as our bodies have many parts and each
part has a special function, 5so it is with Christ's
body. We are many parts of one body, and we all
belong to each other.
6In his grace, God has given us different gifts
for doing certain things well. So if God has given
you the ability to prophesy, speak out with as
much faith as God has given you. 7If your gift is
serving others, serve them well. If you are a
teacher, teach well. 8If your gift is to encourage
others, be encouraging. If it is giving, give generously. If God has given you leadership ability,
take the responsibility seriously. And if you have
a gift for showing kindness to others, do it
gladly.
9Don't just pretend to love others. Really love
them. Hate what is wrong. Hold tightly to what is
good. **10Love each other with genuine
affection, and take delight in honoring each other.** 11Never be lazy, but work
hard and serve the Lord enthusiastically. 12Re-
joice in our confident hope. Be patient in trouble, and keep on praying. 13When God's people
are in need, be ready to help them. Always be
eager to practice hospitality.
14Bless those who persecute you. Don't curse
them; pray that God will bless them. 15Be happy
with those who are happy, and weep with those
who weep. 16Live in harmony with each other.
Don't be too proud to enjoy the company of ordinary people. And don't think you know it all!
17Never pay back evil with more evil. Do
things in such a way that everyone can see you
are honorable. 18Do all that you can to live in
peace with everyone.
19Dear friends, never take revenge. Leave that
to the righteous anger of God. For the Scriptures
say,

"I will take revenge;
I will pay them back,"
says the LORD.

20Instead,

"If your enemies are hungry, feed them.
If they are thirsty, give them something
to drink.
In doing this, you will heap
burning coals of shame on their heads."

21Don't let evil conquer you, but conquer evil by
doing good.

CHAPTER 13
Respect for Authority

Everyone must submit to governing authorities.
For all authority comes from God, and those in
positions of authority have been placed there
by God. 2So anyone who rebels against authority is rebelling against what God has instituted,
and they will be punished. 3For the authorities
do not strike fear in people who are doing right,
but in those who are doing wrong. Would you
like to live without fear of the authorities? Do
what is right, and they will honor you. 4The authorities are God's servants, sent for your good.
But if you are doing wrong, of course you
should be afraid, for they have the power to
punish you. They are God's servants, sent for
the very purpose of punishing those who do
what is wrong. 5So you must submit to them,

not only to avoid punishment, but also to keep a
clear conscience.
6Pay your taxes, too, for these same reasons.
For government workers need to be paid. They
are serving God in what they do. 7Give to everyone what you owe them: Pay your taxes and government fees to those who collect them, and give
respect and honor to those who are in authority.

Love Fulfills God's Requirements

8Owe nothing to anyone—except for your obligation to love one another. If you love your
neighbor, you will fulfill the requirements of
God's law. 9For the commandments say, "You
must not commit adultery. You must not murder. You must not steal. You must not covet."
These—and other such commandments—are
summed up in this one commandment: "Love
your neighbor as yourself." 10Love does no
wrong to others, so love fulfills the requirements of God's law.
11This is all the more urgent, for you know how
late it is; time is running out. Wake up, for our
salvation is nearer now than when we first believed. 12The night is almost gone; the day of salvation will soon be here. So remove your dark
deeds like dirty clothes, and put on the shining
armor of right living. 13Because we belong to the
day, we must live decent lives for all to see. Don't
participate in the darkness of wild parties and
drunkenness, or in sexual promiscuity and immoral living, or in quarreling and jealousy. 14In-
stead, clothe yourself with the presence of the
Lord Jesus Christ. And don't let yourself think
about ways to indulge your evil desires.

CHAPTER 14

The Danger of Criticism

Accept other believers who are weak in faith,
and don't argue with them about what they
think is right or wrong. 2For instance, one person believes it's all right to eat anything. But
another believer with a sensitive conscience
will eat only vegetables. 3Those who feel free
to eat anything must not look down on those
who don't. And those who don't eat certain
foods must not condemn those who do, for God
has accepted them. 4Who are you to condemn
someone else's servants? Their own master
will judge whether they stand or fall. And with
the Lord's help, they will stand and receive his
approval.
5In the same way, some think one day is more
holy than another day, while others think every
day is alike. You should each be fully convinced
that whichever day you choose is acceptable.
6Those who worship the Lord on a special day
do it to honor him. Those who eat any kind of
food do so to honor the Lord, since they give
thanks to God before eating. And those who refuse to eat certain foods also want to please the
Lord and give thanks to God. 7For we don't live
for ourselves or die for ourselves. 8If we live, it's
to honor the Lord. And if we die, it's to honor the
Lord. So whether we live or die, we belong to the
Lord. 9Christ died and rose again for this very

You've Got Mail!

The Apostle Paul wrote letters to tell others about Jesus. Some of those letters became books of the Bible! **For instance, Paul wrote a letter to the Christians in Rome, and that letter became the book of ROMANS!** Paul wanted to go to Rome to teach the people there about Jesus, but he also had to return to Jerusalem (which was in the opposite direction). So Paul wrote a letter instead!

GRAB A PENCIL!

Write a letter to someone who doesn't know Jesus. Maybe you'll write to a stranger in another country like Paul wrote to the Romans. In your letter, tell what you know about Jesus and what he means to you just like Paul did!

purpose—to be Lord both of the living and of the
dead.
10So why do you condemn another believer?
Why do you look down on another believer? Remember, we will all stand before the judgment
seat of God. 11For the Scriptures say,

"'As surely as I live,' says the LORD,
'every knee will bend to me,
and every tongue will declare allegiance
to God.'"

12Yes, each of us will give a personal account to
God. 13So let's stop condemning each other. Decide instead to live in such a way that you will not
cause another believer to stumble and fall.
14I know and am convinced on the authority
of the Lord Jesus that no food, in and of itself, is
wrong to eat. But if someone believes it is
wrong, then for that person it is wrong. 15And if
another believer is distressed by what you eat,
you are not acting in love if you eat it. Don't let
your eating ruin someone for whom Christ
died. 16Then you will not be criticized for doing
something you believe is good. 17For the Kingdom of God is not a matter of what we eat or
drink, but of living a life of goodness and peace
and joy in the Holy Spirit. 18If you serve Christ
with this attitude, you will please God, and others will approve of you, too. 19So then, let us aim
for harmony in the church and try to build each
other up.
20Don't tear apart the work of God over what
you eat. Remember, all foods are acceptable, but
it is wrong to eat something if it makes another
person stumble. 21It is better not to eat meat or
drink wine or do anything else if it might cause
another believer to stumble. 22You may believe
there's nothing wrong with what you are doing,
but keep it between yourself and God. Blessed
are those who don't feel guilty for doing something they have decided is right. 23But if you
have doubts about whether or not you should
eat something, you are sinning if you go ahead
and do it. For you are not following your convic-
tions. If you do anything you believe is not right,
you are sinning.

CHAPTER 15

Living to Please Others

We who are strong must be considerate of those
who are sensitive about things like this. We must
not just please ourselves. 2We should help others do what is right and build them up in the
Lord. 3For even Christ didn't live to please himself. As the Scriptures say, "The insults of those
who insult you, O God, have fallen on me." 4Such
things were written in the Scriptures long ago to
teach us. And the Scriptures give us hope and
encouragement as we wait patiently for God's
promises to be fulfilled.
5May God, who gives this patience and encouragement, help you live in complete harmony
with each other, as is fitting for followers of
Christ Jesus. 6Then all of you can join together
with one voice, giving praise and glory to God,
the Father of our Lord Jesus Christ.
7Therefore, accept each other just as Christ
has accepted you so that God will be given glory.
8Remember that Christ came as a servant to the
Jews to show that God is true to the promises he
made to their ancestors. 9He also came so that
the Gentiles might give glory to God for his mercies to them. That is what the psalmist meant
when he wrote:

"For this, I will praise you among
the Gentiles;
I will sing praises to your name."

10And in another place it is written,

"Rejoice with his people,
you Gentiles."

11And yet again,

"Praise the LORD, all you Gentiles.
Praise him, all you people of the earth."

12And in another place Isaiah said,

"The heir to David's throne will come,
and he will rule over the Gentiles.
They will place their hope on him."

13I pray that God, the source of hope, will fill
you completely with joy and peace because you
trust in him. Then you will overflow with confident hope through the power of the Holy Spirit.

Paul's Reason for Writing

14I am fully convinced, my dear brothers and sisters, that you are full of goodness. You know
these things so well you can teach each other all
about them. 15Even so, I have been bold enough
to write about some of these points, knowing
that all you need is this reminder. For by God's
grace, 16I am a special messenger from Christ
Jesus to you Gentiles. I bring you the Good News
so that I might present you as an acceptable offering to God, made holy by the Holy Spirit. 17So I
have reason to be enthusiastic about all Christ
Jesus has done through me in my service to God.
18Yet I dare not boast about anything except

what Christ has done through me, bringing the
Gentiles to God by my message and by the way I
worked among them. 19They were convinced by
the power of miraculous signs and wonders and
by the power of God's Spirit. In this way, I have
fully presented the Good News of Christ from
Jerusalem all the way to Illyricum.

20My ambition has always been to preach the
Good News where the name of Christ has never
been heard, rather than where a church has already been started by someone else. 21I have
been following the plan spoken of in the Scriptures, where it says,

"Those who have never been told about
him will see,
and those who have never heard of him
will understand."

22In fact, my visit to you has been delayed so long
because I have been preaching in these places.

Paul's Travel Plans

23But now I have finished my work in these regions, and after all these long years of waiting, I
am eager to visit you. 24I am planning to go to
Spain, and when I do, I will stop off in Rome. And
after I have enjoyed your fellowship for a little
while, you can provide for my journey.

25But before I come, I must go to Jerusalem to
take a gift to the believers there. 26For you see,
the believers in Macedonia and Achaia have eagerly taken up an offering for the poor among
the believers in Jerusalem. 27They were glad to
do this because they feel they owe a real debt to
them. Since the Gentiles received the spiritual
blessings of the Good News from the believers in
Jerusalem, they feel the least they can do in return is to help them financially. 28As soon as I
have delivered this money and completed this
good deed of theirs, I will come to see you on my
way to Spain. 29And I am sure that when I come,
Christ will richly bless our time together.

30Dear brothers and sisters, I urge you in the
name of our Lord Jesus Christ to join in my
struggle by praying to God for me. Do this because of your love for me, given to you by the
Holy Spirit. 31Pray that I will be rescued from
those in Judea who refuse to obey God. Pray also
that the believers there will be willing to accept
the donation I am taking to Jerusalem. 32Then,
by the will of God, I will be able to come to you
with a joyful heart, and we will be an encouragement to each other.

33And now may God, who gives us his peace,
be with you all. Amen.

CHAPTER 16

Paul Greets His Friends

I commend to you our sister Phoebe, who is a
deacon in the church in Cenchrea. 2Welcome
her in the Lord as one who is worthy of honor
among God's people. Help her in whatever she
needs, for she has been helpful to many, and
especially to me.

3Give my greetings to Priscilla and Aquila, my
co-workers in the ministry of Christ Jesus. 4In
fact, they once risked their lives for me. I am
thankful to them, and so are all the Gentile
churches. 5Also give my greetings to the church
that meets in their home.

Greet my dear friend Epenetus. He was the
first person from the province of Asia to become a follower of Christ. 6Give my greetings to
Mary, who has worked so hard for your benefit.
7Greet Andronicus and Junia, my fellow Jews,
who were in prison with me. They are highly respected among the apostles and became followers of Christ before I did. 8Greet Ampliatus,
my dear friend in the Lord. 9Greet Urbanus,
our co-worker in Christ, and my dear friend
Stachys.

10Greet Apelles, a good man whom Christ approves. And give my greetings to the believers
from the household of Aristobulus. 11Greet He-
rodion, my fellow Jew. Greet the Lord's people
from the household of Narcissus. 12Give my
greetings to Tryphena and Tryphosa, the Lord's
workers, and to dear Persis, who has worked so
hard for the Lord. 13Greet Rufus, whom the
Lord picked out to be his very own; and also his
dear mother, who has been a mother to me.

14Give my greetings to Asyncritus, Phlegon,
Hermes, Patrobas, Hermas, and the brothers
and sisters who meet with them. 15Give my
greetings to Philologus, Julia, Nereus and his
sister, and to Olympas and all the believers who
meet with them. 16Greet each other with a sacred kiss. All the churches of Christ send you
their greetings.

Paul's Final Instructions

17And now I make one more appeal, my dear
brothers and sisters. Watch out for people who
cause divisions and upset people's faith by
teaching things contrary to what you have been
taught. Stay away from them. 18Such people are
not serving Christ our Lord; they are serving
their own personal interests. By smooth talk
and glowing words they deceive innocent people. 19But everyone knows that you are obedient
to the Lord. This makes me very happy. I want

you to be wise in doing right and to stay innocent of any wrong. 20 The God of peace will soon
crush Satan under your feet. May the grace of
our Lord Jesus be with you.

21 Timothy, my fellow worker, sends you his
greetings, as do Lucius, Jason, and Sosipater, my
fellow Jews.

22 I, Tertius, the one writing this letter for
Paul, send my greetings, too, as one of the Lord's
followers.

23 Gaius says hello to you. He is my host and
also serves as host to the whole church. Erastus,
the city treasurer, sends you his greetings, and so
does our brother Quartus.*

25 Now all glory to God, who is able to make
you strong, just as my Good News says. This message about Jesus Christ has revealed his plan for
you Gentiles, a plan kept secret from the beginning of time. 26 But now as the prophets foretold
and as the eternal God has commanded, this
message is made known to all Gentiles everywhere, so that they too might believe and obey
him. 27 All glory to the only wise God, through
Jesus Christ, forever. Amen.

16:23 Some manuscripts add verse 24, *May the grace of our Lord Jesus Christ be with you all. Amen.* Still others add this sentence after verse 27.

1 CORINTHIANS Hot Topics

Look for 1 hidden message in 1 Corinthians!

Paul heard disturbing rumors that the Christians in the city of Corinth were having disagreements that could hurt the church. Look for

- **WISDOM AND WARNINGS**
- **MATTERS OF MARRIAGE**
- **SOME SPECIAL GIFTS**
- **LOTS AND LOTS ABOUT LOVE**

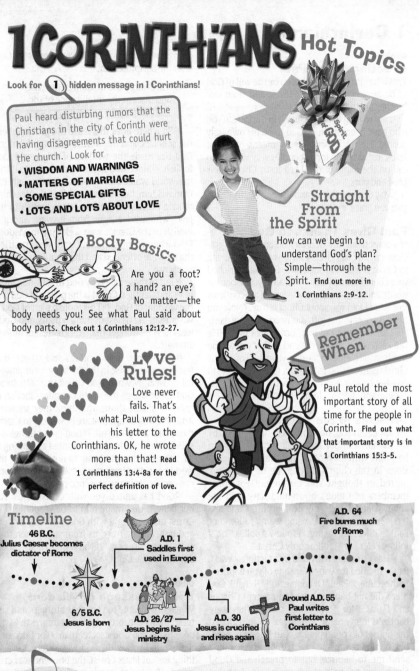

Straight From the Spirit

How can we begin to understand God's plan? Simple—through the Spirit. **Find out more in 1 Corinthians 2:9-12.**

Body Basics

Are you a foot? a hand? an eye? No matter—the body needs you! See what Paul said about body parts. **Check out 1 Corinthians 12:12-27.**

Remember When

Paul retold the most important story of all time for the people in Corinth. **Find out what that important story is in 1 Corinthians 15:3-5.**

Love Rules!

Love never fails. That's what Paul wrote in his letter to the Corinthians. OK, he wrote more than that! **Read 1 Corinthians 13:4-8a for the perfect definition of love.**

Timeline

- 46 B.C. Julius Caesar becomes dictator of Rome
- 6/5 B.C. Jesus is born
- A.D. 1 Saddles first used in Europe
- A.D. 26/27 Jesus begins his ministry
- A.D. 30 Jesus is crucified and rises again
- Around A.D. 55 Paul writes first letter to Corinthians
- A.D. 64 Fire burns much of Rome

In his first letter to the Christians in Corinth, Paul addressed the tough problems the early church had. And he offered solutions. Those solutions still work today when we have problems. Trust God, believe in Jesus, recognize that Jesus died for *you*. **The answers that worked back then still work today.**

1 Corinthians 1 . . . page 1126

CHAPTER 1

Greetings from Paul

This letter is from Paul, chosen by the will of God to be an apostle of Christ Jesus, and from our brother Sosthenes.

2 I am writing to God's church in Corinth, to you who have been called by God to be his own holy people. He made you holy by means of Christ Jesus, just as he did for all people everywhere who call on the name of our Lord Jesus Christ, their Lord and ours.

3 May God our Father and the Lord Jesus Christ give you grace and peace.

Paul Gives Thanks to God

4 I always thank my God for you and for the gracious gifts he has given you, now that you belong to Christ Jesus. 5 Through him, God has enriched your church in every way—with all of your eloquent words and all of your knowledge. 6 This confirms that what I told you about Christ is true. 7 Now you have every spiritual gift you need as you eagerly wait for the return of our Lord Jesus Christ. 8 He will keep you strong to the end so that you will be free from all blame on the day when our Lord Jesus Christ returns. 9 God will do this, for he is faithful to do what he says, and he has invited you into partnership with his Son, Jesus Christ our Lord.

Divisions in the Church

10 I appeal to you, dear brothers and sisters, by the authority of our Lord Jesus Christ, to live in harmony with each other. Let there be no divisions in the church. Rather, be of one mind, united in thought and purpose. 11 For some members of Chloe's household have told me about your quarrels, my dear brothers and sisters. 12 Some of you are saying, "I am a follower of Paul." Others are saying, "I follow Apollos," or "I follow Peter," or "I follow only Christ."

13 Has Christ been divided into factions? Was I, Paul, crucified for you? Were any of you baptized in the name of Paul? Of course not! 14 I thank God that I did not baptize any of you except Crispus and Gaius, 15 for now no one can say they were baptized in my name. 16 (Oh yes, I also baptized the household of Stephanas, but I don't remember baptizing anyone else.) 17 For Christ didn't send me to baptize, but to preach the Good News—and not with clever speech, for fear that the cross of Christ would lose its power.

The Wisdom of God

18 The message of the cross is foolish to those who are headed for destruction! But we who are being saved know it is the very power of God. 19 As the Scriptures say,

> "I will destroy the wisdom of the wise
> and discard the intelligence of the
> intelligent."

20 So where does this leave the philosophers, the scholars, and the world's brilliant debaters? God has made the wisdom of this world look foolish. 21 Since God in his wisdom saw to it that the world would never know him through human wisdom, he has used our foolish preaching to save those who believe. 22 It is foolish to the Jews, who ask for signs from heaven. And it is foolish to the Greeks, who seek human wisdom. 23 So when we preach that Christ was crucified, the Jews are offended and the Gentiles say it's all nonsense.

24 But to those called by God to salvation, both Jews and Gentiles, Christ is the power of God and the wisdom of God. 25 This foolish plan of God is wiser than the wisest of human plans, and God's weakness is stronger than the greatest of human strength.

26 Remember, dear brothers and sisters, that few of you were wise in the world's eyes or powerful or wealthy when God called you. 27 Instead, God chose things the world considers foolish in order to shame those who think they are wise. And he chose things that are powerless to shame those who are powerful. 28 God chose things despised by the world, things counted as nothing at all, and used them to bring to nothing what the world considers important. 29 As a result, no one can ever boast in the presence of God.

30 God has united you with Christ Jesus. For our benefit God made him to be wisdom itself. Christ made us right with God; he made us pure and holy, and he freed us from sin. 31 Therefore, as the Scriptures say, "If you want to boast, boast only about the LORD."

CHAPTER 2

Paul's Message of Wisdom

When I first came to you, dear brothers and sisters, I didn't use lofty words and impressive wisdom to tell you God's secret plan. 2 For I decided that while I was with you I would forget everything except Jesus Christ, the one who was crucified. 3 I came to you in weakness—timid and trembling. 4 And my message and my preaching were very plain. Rather than using clever and persuasive speeches, I relied only on the power of the Holy Spirit. 5 I did this so you would trust not in human wisdom but in the power of God.

The Apostle Paul wrote lots of letters during his ministry. Sometimes he tried to help people solve problems and resolve conflicts. For example, in the city of Corinth, people worshiped a lot of different gods.

So Paul wrote to the church to guide the church toward what a church *should* be.

THINK OF A CONFLICT YOU HAVE WITH SOMEONE. Pray about how God might want you to resolve that conflict. Then go do what God says!

6Yet when I am among mature believers, I do
speak with words of wisdom, but not the kind of
wisdom that belongs to this world or to the rulers of this world, who are soon forgotten. 7No,
the wisdom we speak of is the mystery of God—
his plan that was previously hidden, even though
he made it for our ultimate glory before the
world began. 8But the rulers of this world have
not understood it; if they had, they would not
have crucified our glorious Lord. 9That is what
the Scriptures mean when they say,

"No eye has seen, no ear has heard,
and no mind has imagined
what God has prepared
for those who love him."

10But it was to us that God revealed these
things by his Spirit. For his Spirit searches out
everything and shows us God's deep secrets.
11No one can know a person's thoughts except
that person's own spirit, and no one can know
God's thoughts except God's own Spirit. 12And
we have received God's Spirit (not the world's
spirit), so we can know the wonderful things God
has freely given us.
13When we tell you these things, we do not
use words that come from human wisdom. Instead, we speak words given to us by the Spirit,
using the Spirit's words to explain spiritual
truths. 14But people who aren't spiritual can't receive these truths from God's Spirit. It all sounds
foolish to them and they can't understand it, for
only those who are spiritual can understand
what the Spirit means. 15Those who are spiritual
can evaluate all things, but they themselves cannot be evaluated by others. 16For,

"Who can know the LORD's thoughts?
Who knows enough to teach him?"

But we understand these things, for we have the mind of Christ.

CHAPTER 3

Paul and Apollos, Servants of Christ

Dear brothers and sisters, when I was with you I
couldn't talk to you as I would to spiritual people. I
had to talk as though you belonged to this world
or as though you were infants in Christ. 2I had to
feed you with milk, not with solid food, because
you weren't ready for anything stronger. And you
still aren't ready, 3for you are still controlled by
your sinful nature. You are jealous of one another
and quarrel with each other. Doesn't that prove
you are controlled by your sinful nature? Aren't
you living like people of the world? 4When one of
you says, "I am a follower of Paul," and another
says, "I follow Apollos," aren't you acting just like
people of the world?
5After all, who is Apollos? Who is Paul? We are
only God's servants through whom you believed
the Good News. Each of us did the work the Lord
gave us. 6I planted the seed in your hearts, and
Apollos watered it, but it was God who made it
grow. 7It's not important who does the planting,
or who does the watering. What's important is
that God makes the seed grow. 8The one who
plants and the one who waters work together
with the same purpose. And both will be rewarded for their own hard work. 9For we are
both God's workers. And you are God's field. You
are God's building.
10Because of God's grace to me, I have laid the
foundation like an expert builder. Now others
are building on it. But whoever is building on this
foundation must be very careful. 11For no one
can lay any foundation other than the one we already have—Jesus Christ.

12Anyone who builds on that foundation may
use a variety of materials—gold, silver, jewels,
wood, hay, or straw. 13But on the judgment day,
fire will reveal what kind of work each builder
has done. The fire will show if a person's work
has any value. 14If the work survives, that builder
will receive a reward. 15But if the work is burned
up, the builder will suffer great loss. The builder
will be saved, but like someone barely escaping
through a wall of flames.

16Don't you realize that all of you together are
the temple of God and that the Spirit of God lives
in you? 17God will destroy anyone who destroys
this temple. For God's temple is holy, and you are
that temple.

18Stop deceiving yourselves. If you think you
are wise by this world's standards, you need to
become a fool to be truly wise. 19For the wisdom
of this world is foolishness to God. As the Scriptures say,

"He traps the wise
in the snare of their own cleverness."

20And again,

"The Lord knows the thoughts of the wise;
he knows they are worthless."

21So don't boast about following a particular
human leader. For everything belongs to you:
22whether Paul or Apollos or Peter, or the world,
or life and death, or the present and the future.
Everything belongs to you, 23and you belong to
Christ, and Christ belongs to God.

CHAPTER 4
Paul's Relationship with the Corinthians

So look at Apollos and me as mere servants of
Christ who have been put in charge of explaining
God's mysteries. 2Now, a person who is put in
charge as a manager must be faithful. 3As for me,
it matters very little how I might be evaluated by
you or by any human authority. I don't even trust
my own judgment on this point. 4My conscience
is clear, but that doesn't prove I'm right. It is the
Lord himself who will examine me and decide.

5So don't make judgments about anyone
ahead of time—before the Lord returns. For he
will bring our darkest secrets to light and will reveal our private motives. Then God will give to
each one whatever praise is due.

6Dear brothers and sisters, I have used Apollos and myself to illustrate what I've been saying.
If you pay attention to what I have quoted from
the Scriptures, you won't be proud of one of your
leaders at the expense of another. 7For what
gives you the right to make such a judgment?
What do you have that God hasn't given you? And
if everything you have is from God, why boast as
though it were not a gift?

8You think you already have everything you
need. You think you are already rich. You have
begun to reign in God's kingdom without us! I
wish you really were reigning already, for then we
would be reigning with you. 9Instead, I sometimes think God has put us apostles on display,
like prisoners of war at the end of a victor's parade, condemned to die. We have become a spec-
tacle to the entire world—to people and angels
alike.

10Our dedication to Christ makes us look like
fools, but you claim to be so wise in Christ! We
are weak, but you are so powerful! You are honored, but we are ridiculed. 11Even now we go
hungry and thirsty, and we don't have enough
clothes to keep warm. We are often beaten and
have no home. 12We work wearily with our own
hands to earn our living. We bless those who
curse us. We are patient with those who abuse
us. 13We appeal gently when evil things are said
about us. Yet we are treated like the world's
garbage, like everybody's trash—right up to the
present moment.

14I am not writing these things to shame you,
but to warn you as my beloved children. 15For
even if you had ten thousand others to teach you
about Christ, you have only one spiritual father.
For I became your father in Christ Jesus when I
preached the Good News to you. 16So I urge you
to imitate me.

17That's why I have sent Timothy, my beloved
and faithful child in the Lord. He will remind you
of how I follow Christ Jesus, just as I teach in all
the churches wherever I go.

18Some of you have become arrogant, thinking I will not visit you again. 19But I will come—
and soon—if the Lord lets me, and then I'll find
out whether these arrogant people just give pretentious speeches or whether they really have
God's power. 20For the Kingdom of God is not
just a lot of talk; it is living by God's power.
21Which do you choose? Should I come with a
rod to punish you, or should I come with love
and a gentle spirit?

CHAPTER 5
Paul Condemns Spiritual Pride

I can hardly believe the report about the sexual
immorality going on among you—something
that even pagans don't do. I am told that a man in

BIBLE BIOS

Hear From the Heroes

Hi, my name is

JOHN the BAPTIST *(prophet, baptizer, advance man for Jesus)*

My greatest claim to fame is being the one who prepared the way for Jesus' coming. That doesn't mean that I rolled out a red carpet or anything like that, but I did try to prepare peoples' hearts for Jesus by encouraging them to repent of their sins.

I lived out in the country, away from the distractions of the city. I preached repentance, and people came to me to be baptized. That's where I got my nickname, the Baptist. I baptized people in water, which symbolized washing away the sins. You might think my lifestyle was strange because I just lived out in the desert, eating whatever I could find—mostly locusts and wild honey. And I wore clothing made out of camel skins. But hey, it worked for me!

My strange dress and eating habits didn't keep people from coming out to hear me preach though. In fact, I became so popular that some people actually thought that I might be the Messiah. But I was careful to set them straight! I was not even worthy to untie the sandals of the real Messiah, Jesus.

Want to know more about John's attitude toward Jesus? Read JOHN 3:27-30.

One of the finest moments of my life was when Jesus came to me to be baptized. There was no way I felt worthy—I would rather he baptized me! But Jesus insisted, so I baptized him. And God spoke from heaven when I did! Wow, what an experience!

Read all about John's baptism of Jesus in MATTHEW 3:13-17.

I guess I'd have to say that the thing I look back on most fondly is what Jesus said about me. He once told a crowd of people that "of all who have ever lived, none is greater than John the Baptist." I've never thought of myself as being better than any other prophet, but it sure felt good to know that the Savior of the world thought that about me!

How can you follow Jesus?

Jot down on a note card one way you could serve Jesus more faithfully. Keep that note card with you so you can see it every day as a reminder. Really work on the action you wrote down. Then next month, read the Bible and make a new note card with another way you could follow Jesus more faithfully. Keep your note cards in a special "Follow Jesus" box. Pretty soon you'll be a much better follower of Jesus than you are right now!

help others

be thankful

pray more

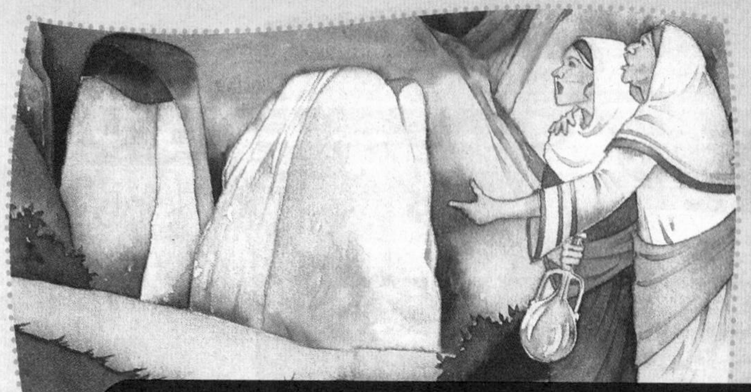

BIBLE BIOS

Hear From the Heroes

THE MARYS *(mother of Jesus; friend of Jesus)*

"Hi! I'm Mary, the mother of Jesus!"

"Hi from me, too! I'm Mary Magdalene. Jesus' mother and I have the same name, so sometimes people get us confused. But we're two very different women. I'll let the other Mary, Jesus' mother, tell her story first."

"Thanks, Mary. My story begins when I was a young woman. I was engaged to marry Joseph. An angel appeared to me, and wow, was I shocked. God had chosen *me* to be the mother of his own Son, Jesus! Then an angel appeared to Joseph, too, and told him the same thing.

Want to know more about Mary and the birth of Jesus? Read LUKE 2:1-21.

I got to watch Jesus grow up. He went out on his own, preaching and healing. About three years later I had to watch him die. That was the darkest day of my life. But then came Sunday! I'll let Mary Magdalene tell the rest of that story!"

"Thanks, Mary. What an incredible morning that was! On that Sunday morning after Jesus died, Mary and I and a couple other women went to Jesus' tomb, where we were met by angels. Jesus wasn't there! The angels said that Jesus had risen. After we ran and told the disciples, I went back and hung around the tomb, confused about what was really happening. When I realized someone was standing near me, I thought it was the gardener, and I asked him if he knew where Jesus was. But then he said my name, and it had never sounded so good! I knew it was Jesus. He really *was* alive!

For the whole story of Mary's encounter with Jesus at the tomb, read LUKE 24:1-10.

Chronicle of Change

How has Jesus changed your life or the lives of people you know? Create a booklet that tells all about it. Interview as many Christians as you can, asking them to tell you how Jesus has changed their lives. Decorate the cover of your booklet with pictures that remind you of Jesus. Show your booklet to at least two other people, so they can get to know Jesus too!

"I always have a friend in Jesus."
Aunt Pat

"Because of Jesus, I know I'm going to heaven."
Dad

your church is living in sin with his stepmother.
2You are so proud of yourselves, but you should
be mourning in sorrow and shame. And you
should remove this man from your fellowship.

3Even though I am not with you in person, I
am with you in the Spirit. And as though I were
there, I have already passed judgment on this
man 4in the name of the Lord Jesus. You must
call a meeting of the church. I will be present
with you in spirit, and so will the power of our
Lord Jesus. 5Then you must throw this man out
and hand him over to Satan so that his sinful
nature will be destroyed and he himself will be
saved on the day the Lord returns.

6Your boasting about this is terrible. Don't
you realize that this sin is like a little yeast that
spreads through the whole batch of dough? 7Get
rid of the old "yeast" by removing this wicked
person from among you. Then you will be like a
fresh batch of dough made without yeast, which
is what you really are. Christ, our Passover Lamb,
has been sacrificed for us. 8So let us celebrate
the festival, not with the old bread of wickedness
and evil, but with the new bread of sincerity and
truth.

9When I wrote to you before, I told you not to
associate with people who indulge in sexual sin.
10But I wasn't talking about unbelievers who indulge in sexual sin, or are greedy, or cheat people,
or worship idols. You would have to leave this
world to avoid people like that. 11I meant that
you are not to associate with anyone who claims
to be a believer yet indulges in sexual sin, or is
greedy, or worships idols, or is abusive, or is a
drunkard, or cheats people. Don't even eat with
such people.

12It isn't my responsibility to judge outsiders,
but it certainly is your responsibility to judge
those inside the church who are sinning. 13God
will judge those on the outside; but as the Scriptures say, "You must remove the evil person from
among you."

CHAPTER 6

Avoiding Lawsuits with Christians

When one of you has a dispute with another believer, how dare you file a lawsuit and ask a secu-
lar court to decide the matter instead of taking it
to other believers! 2Don't you realize that someday we believers will judge the world? And since
you are going to judge the world, can't you decide
even these little things among yourselves?
3Don't you realize that we will judge angels? So
you should surely be able to resolve ordinary disputes in this life. 4If you have legal disputes
about such matters, why go to outside judges
who are not respected by the church? 5I am saying this to shame you. Isn't there anyone in all the
church who is wise enough to decide these issues? 6But instead, one believer sues another—
right in front of unbelievers!

7Even to have such lawsuits with one another
is a defeat for you. Why not just accept the injustice and leave it at that? Why not let yourselves
be cheated? 8Instead, you yourselves are the
ones who do wrong and cheat even your fellow
believers.

9Don't you realize that those who do wrong
will not inherit the Kingdom of God? Don't fool
yourselves. Those who indulge in sexual sin, or
who worship idols, or commit adultery, or are
male prostitutes, or practice homosexuality, 10or
are thieves, or greedy people, or drunkards, or
are abusive, or cheat people—none of these will
inherit the Kingdom of God. 11Some of you were
once like that. But you were cleansed; you were
made holy; you were made right with God by
calling on the name of the Lord Jesus Christ and
by the Spirit of our God.

Avoiding Sexual Sin

12You say, "I am allowed to do anything"—but
not everything is good for you. And even though
"I am allowed to do anything," I must not become a slave to anything. 13You say, "Food was
made for the stomach, and the stomach for
food." (This is true, though someday God will do
away with both of them.) But you can't say that
our bodies were made for sexual immorality.
They were made for the Lord, and the Lord cares
about our bodies. 14And God will raise us from
the dead by his power, just as he raised our Lord
from the dead.

15Don't you realize that your bodies are actually parts of Christ? Should a man take his body,
which is part of Christ, and join it to a prostitute?
Never! 16And don't you realize that if a man joins
himself to a prostitute, he becomes one body
with her? For the Scriptures say, "The two are
united into one." 17But the person who is joined
to the Lord is one spirit with him.

18Run from sexual sin! No other sin so clearly
affects the body as this one does. For sexual immorality is a sin against your own body. 19Don't
you realize that your body is the temple of the
Holy Spirit, who lives in you and was given to you
by God? You do not belong to yourself, 20for God
bought you with a high price. So you must honor
God with your body.

1 Corinthians 7 . . . page 1132

CHAPTER 7
Instruction on Marriage

Now regarding the questions you asked in your letter. Yes, it is good to abstain from sexual relations. 2But because there is so much sexual immorality, each man should have his own wife, and each woman should have her own husband.

3The husband should fulfill his wife's sexual needs, and the wife should fulfill her husband's needs. 4The wife gives authority over her body to her husband, and the husband gives authority over his body to his wife.

5Do not deprive each other of sexual relations, unless you both agree to refrain from sexual intimacy for a limited time so you can give yourselves more completely to prayer. Afterward, you should come together again so that Satan won't be able to tempt you because of your lack of self-control. 6I say this as a concession, not as a command. 7But I wish everyone were single, just as I am. Yet each person has a special gift from God, of one kind or another.

8So I say to those who aren't married and to widows—it's better to stay unmarried, just as I am. 9But if they can't control themselves, they should go ahead and marry. It's better to marry than to burn with lust.

10But for those who are married, I have a command that comes not from me, but from the Lord. A wife must not leave her husband. 11But if she does leave him, let her remain single or else be reconciled to him. And the husband must not leave his wife.

12Now, I will speak to the rest of you, though I do not have a direct command from the Lord. If a fellow believer has a wife who is not a believer and she is willing to continue living with him, he must not leave her. 13And if a believing woman has a husband who is not a believer and he is willing to continue living with her, she must not leave him. 14For the believing wife brings holiness to her marriage, and the believing husband brings holiness to his marriage. Otherwise, your children would not be holy, but now they are holy. 15(But if the husband or wife who isn't a believer insists on leaving, let them go. In such cases the believing husband or wife is no longer bound to the other, for God has called you to live in peace.) 16Don't you wives realize that your husbands might be saved because of you? And don't you husbands realize that your wives might be saved because of you?

17Each of you should continue to live in whatever situation the Lord has placed you, and remain as you were when God first called you. This is my rule for all the churches. 18For instance, a man who was circumcised before he became a believer should not try to reverse it. And the man who was uncircumcised when he became a believer should not be circumcised now. 19For it makes no difference whether or not a man has been circumcised. The important thing is to keep God's commandments.

20Yes, each of you should remain as you were when God called you. 21Are you a slave? Don't let that worry you—but if you get a chance to be free, take it. 22And remember, if you were a slave when the Lord called you, you are now free in the Lord. And if you were free when the Lord called you, you are now a slave of Christ. 23God paid a high price for you, so don't be enslaved by the world. 24Each of you, dear brothers and sisters, should remain as you were when God first called you.

25Now regarding your question about the young women who are not yet married. I do not have a command from the Lord for them. But the Lord in his mercy has given me wisdom that can be trusted, and I will share it with you. 26Because of the present crisis, I think it is best to remain as you are. 27If you have a wife, do not seek to end the marriage. If you do not have a wife, do not seek to get married. 28But if you do get married, it is not a sin. And if a young woman gets married, it is not a sin. However, those who get married at this time will have troubles, and I am trying to spare you those problems.

29But let me say this, dear brothers and sisters: The time that remains is very short. So from now on, those with wives should not focus only on their marriage. 30Those who weep or who rejoice or who buy things should not be absorbed by their weeping or their joy or their possessions. 31Those who use the things of the world should not become attached to them. For this world as we know it will soon pass away.

32I want you to be free from the concerns of this life. An unmarried man can spend his time doing the Lord's work and thinking how to please him. 33But a married man has to think about his earthly responsibilities and how to please his wife. 34His interests are divided. In the same way, a woman who is no longer married or has never been married can be devoted to the Lord and holy in body and in spirit. But a married woman has to think about her earthly responsibilities and how to please her husband. 35I am saying this for your benefit, not to place restrictions on you. I want you to do whatever will help you serve the Lord best, with as few distractions as possible.

36But if a man thinks that he's treating his
fiancée improperly and will inevitably give in to
his passion, let him marry her as he wishes. It is
not a sin. 37But if he has decided firmly not to
marry and there is no urgency and he can control
his passion, he does well not to marry. 38So the
person who marries his fiancée does well, and
the person who doesn't marry does even better.
39A wife is bound to her husband as long as he
lives. If her husband dies, she is free to marry
anyone she wishes, but only if he loves the Lord.
40But in my opinion it would be better for her to
stay single, and I think I am giving you counsel
from God's Spirit when I say this.

CHAPTER 8
Food Sacrificed to Idols

Now regarding your question about food that
has been offered to idols. Yes, we know that "we
all have knowledge" about this issue. But while
knowledge makes us feel important, it is love
that strengthens the church. 2Anyone who
claims to know all the answers doesn't really
know very much. 3But the person who loves God
is the one whom God recognizes.
4So, what about eating meat that has been
offered to idols? Well, we all know that an idol is
not really a god and that there is only one God.
5There may be so-called gods both in heaven and
on earth, and some people actually worship
many gods and many lords. 6But for us,

There is one God, the Father,
by whom all things were created,
and for whom we live.
And there is one Lord, Jesus Christ,
through whom all things were created,
and through whom we live.

7However, not all believers know this. Some
are accustomed to thinking of idols as being real,
so when they eat food that has been offered to
idols, they think of it as the worship of real gods,
and their weak consciences are violated. 8It's
true that we can't win God's approval by what we
eat. We don't lose anything if we don't eat it, and
we don't gain anything if we do.
9But you must be careful so that your freedom
does not cause others with a weaker conscience
to stumble. 10For if others see you—with your "superior knowledge"—eating in the temple of an
idol, won't they be encouraged to violate their
conscience by eating food that has been offered
to an idol? 11So because of your superior knowledge, a weak believer for whom Christ died will be
destroyed. 12And when you sin against other believers by encouraging them to do something they
believe is wrong, you are sinning against Christ.
13So if what I eat causes another believer to sin, I
will never eat meat again as long as I live—for I
don't want to cause another believer to stumble.

CHAPTER 9
Paul Gives Up His Rights

Am I not as free as anyone else? Am I not an
apostle? Haven't I seen Jesus our Lord with my
own eyes? Isn't it because of my work that you
belong to the Lord? 2Even if others think I am
not an apostle, I certainly am to you. You yourselves are proof that I am the Lord's apostle.
3This is my answer to those who question my
authority. 4Don't we have the right to live in your
homes and share your meals? 5Don't we have the
right to bring a believing wife with us as the
other apostles and the Lord's brothers do, and
as Peter does? 6Or is it only Barnabas and I who
have to work to support ourselves?
7What soldier has to pay his own expenses?
What farmer plants a vineyard and doesn't have
the right to eat some of its fruit? What shepherd
cares for a flock of sheep and isn't allowed to
drink some of the milk? 8Am I expressing merely
a human opinion, or does the law say the same
thing? 9For the law of Moses says, "You must not
muzzle an ox to keep it from eating as it treads
out the grain." Was God thinking only about oxen
when he said this? 10Wasn't he actually speaking
to us? Yes, it was written for us, so that the one
who plows and the one who threshes the grain
might both expect a share of the harvest.
11Since we have planted spiritual seed among
you, aren't we entitled to a harvest of physical food
and drink? 12If you support others who preach to
you, shouldn't we have an even greater right to be
supported? But we have never used this right. We
would rather put up with anything than be an obstacle to the Good News about Christ.
13Don't you realize that those who work in the
temple get their meals from the offerings
brought to the temple? And those who serve at
the altar get a share of the sacrificial offerings.
14In the same way, the Lord ordered that those
who preach the Good News should be supported
by those who benefit from it. 15Yet I have never
used any of these rights. And I am not writing
this to suggest that I want to start now. In fact, I
would rather die than lose my right to boast
about preaching without charge. 16Yet preaching the Good News is not something I can boast
about. I am compelled by God to do it. How terrible for me if I didn't preach the Good News!

17If I were doing this on my own initiative, I
would deserve payment. But I have no choice, for
God has given me this sacred trust. 18What then
is my pay? It is the opportunity to preach the
Good News without charging anyone. That's why
I never demand my rights when I preach the
Good News.

19Even though I am a free man with no master,
I have become a slave to all people to bring many
to Christ. 20When I was with the Jews, I lived like
a Jew to bring the Jews to Christ. When I was
with those who follow the Jewish law, I too lived
under that law. Even though I am not subject to
the law, I did this so I could bring to Christ those
who are under the law. 21When I am with the
Gentiles who do not follow the Jewish law, I too
live apart from that law so I can bring them to
Christ. But I do not ignore the law of God; I obey
the law of Christ.

22When I am with those who are weak, I share
their weakness, for I want to bring the weak to
Christ. Yes, I try to find common ground with
everyone, doing everything I can to save some.
23I do everything to spread the Good News and
share in its blessings.

24Don't you realize that in a race everyone
runs, but only one person gets the prize? So run
to win! 25All athletes are disciplined in their
training. They do it to win a prize that will fade
away, but we do it for an eternal prize. 26So I run
with purpose in every step. I am not just shadow-
boxing. 27I discipline my body like an athlete,
training it to do what it should. Otherwise, I fear
that after preaching to others I myself might be
disqualified.

CHAPTER 10

Lessons from Israel's Idolatry

I don't want you to forget, dear brothers and sisters, about our ancestors in the wilderness long
ago. All of them were guided by a cloud that
moved ahead of them, and all of them walked
through the sea on dry ground. 2In the cloud
and in the sea, all of them were baptized as followers of Moses. 3All of them ate the same spiritual food, 4and all of them drank the same
spiritual water. For they drank from the spiritual rock that traveled with them, and that rock
was Christ. 5Yet God was not pleased with most
of them, and their bodies were scattered in the
wilderness.

6These things happened as a warning to us, so
that we would not crave evil things as they did,
7or worship idols as some of them did. As the
Scriptures say, "The people celebrated with
feasting and drinking, and they indulged in pagan revelry." 8And we must not engage in sexual
immorality as some of them did, causing 23,000
of them to die in one day.

9Nor should we put Christ to the test, as some
of them did and then died from snakebites.
10And don't grumble as some of them did, and
then were destroyed by the angel of death.
11These things happened to them as examples
for us. They were written down to warn us who
live at the end of the age.

12If you think you are standing strong, be careful not to fall. 13The temptations in your life are
no different from what others experience. And
God is faithful. He will not allow the temptation
to be more than you can stand. When you are
tempted, he will show you a way out so that you
can endure.

14So, my dear friends, flee from the worship of
idols. 15You are reasonable people. Decide for
yourselves if what I am saying is true. 16When
we bless the cup at the Lord's Table, aren't we
sharing in the blood of Christ? And when we
break the bread, aren't we sharing in the body
of Christ? 17And though we are many, we all eat
from one loaf of bread, showing that we are
one body. 18Think about the people of Israel.
Weren't they united by eating the sacrifices at
the altar?

19What am I trying to say? Am I saying that
food offered to idols has some significance, or
that idols are real gods? 20No, not at all. I am saying that these sacrifices are offered to demons,
not to God. And I don't want you to participate
with demons. 21You cannot drink from the cup
of the Lord and from the cup of demons, too. You
cannot eat at the Lord's Table and at the table of
demons, too. 22What? Do we dare to rouse the
Lord's jealousy? Do you think we are stronger
than he is?

23You say, "I am allowed to do anything"—but
not everything is good for you. You say, "I am
allowed to do anything"—but not everything is
beneficial. 24Don't be concerned for your own
good but for the good of others.

25So you may eat any meat that is sold in the
marketplace without raising questions of conscience. 26For "the earth is the LORD's, and everything in it."

27If someone who isn't a believer asks you
home for dinner, accept the invitation if you
want to. Eat whatever is offered to you without
raising questions of conscience. 28(But suppose
someone tells you, "This meat was offered to an
idol." Don't eat it, out of consideration for the

conscience of the one who told you. 29It might
not be a matter of conscience for you, but it is for
the other person.) For why should my freedom
be limited by what someone else thinks? 30If I
can thank God for the food and enjoy it, why
should I be condemned for eating it?

**31So whether you eat or drink, or
whatever you do, do it all for the
glory of God.** 32Don't give offense to Jews or
Gentiles or the church of God. 33I, too, try to
please everyone in everything I do. I don't just do
what is best for me; I do what is best for others so
that many may be saved. 11:1And you should imitate me, just as I imitate Christ.

CHAPTER 11

Instructions for Public Worship

2I am so glad that you always keep me in your
thoughts, and that you are following the teachings I passed on to you. 3But there is one thing I
want you to know: The head of every man is
Christ, the head of woman is man, and the head
of Christ is God. 4A man dishonors his head if he
covers his head while praying or prophesying.
5But a woman dishonors her head if she prays or
prophesies without a covering on her head, for
this is the same as shaving her head. 6Yes, if she
refuses to wear a head covering, she should cut
off all her hair! But since it is shameful for a
woman to have her hair cut or her head shaved,
she should wear a covering.

7A man should not wear anything on his head
when worshiping, for man is made in God's image and reflects God's glory. And woman reflects
man's glory. 8For the first man didn't come from
woman, but the first woman came from man.
9And man was not made for woman, but woman
was made for man. 10For this reason, and because the angels are watching, a woman should
wear a covering on her head to show she is under
authority.

11But among the Lord's people, women are not
independent of men, and men are not independent of women. 12For although the first woman
came from man, every other man was born from
a woman, and everything comes from God.

13Judge for yourselves. Is it right for a woman
to pray to God in public without covering her
head? 14Isn't it obvious that it's disgraceful for a
man to have long hair? 15And isn't long hair a
woman's pride and joy? For it has been given to
her as a covering. 16But if anyone wants to argue
about this, I simply say that we have no other custom than this, and neither do God's other
churches.

Order at the Lord's Supper

17But in the following instructions, I cannot
praise you. For it sounds as if more harm than
good is done when you meet together. 18First, I
hear that there are divisions among you when
you meet as a church, and to some extent I believe it. 19But, of course, there must be divisions
among you so that you who have God's approval
will be recognized!

20When you meet together, you are not really
interested in the Lord's Supper. 21For some of
you hurry to eat your own meal without sharing
with others. As a result, some go hungry while
others get drunk. 22What? Don't you have your
own homes for eating and drinking? Or do you
really want to disgrace God's church and shame
the poor? What am I supposed to say? Do you

Key Verse **"So whether you eat or drink, or whatever you do, do it all for the glory of God." —1 CORINTHIANS 10:31**

Give God Your Best

Read 1 CORINTHIANS 10:31 out loud to your family. Ask each person to say what he or she thinks this verse means. Whatever we do, we should do it so we honor and glorify God—even if all we're doing is eating and drinking.

Have a "GIVE GOD YOUR BEST" dinner with your family.

Use your **best tablecloth**, wear your **best clothes**, make your **favorite food**, and serve your **best dessert. Ask each person to name one way to honor God this week with words or actions.**

want me to praise you? Well, I certainly will not
praise you for this!
[23]For I pass on to you what I received from the
Lord himself. On the night when he was betrayed,
the Lord Jesus took some bread [24]and gave
thanks to God for it. Then he broke it in pieces
and said, "This is my body, which is given for you.
Do this to remember me." [25]In the same way, he
took the cup of wine after supper, saying, "This
cup is the new covenant between God and his
people—an agreement confirmed with my blood.
Do this to remember me as often as you drink it."
[26]For every time you eat this bread and drink this
cup, you are announcing the Lord's death until he
comes again.
[27]So anyone who eats this bread or drinks
this cup of the Lord unworthily is guilty of sinning against the body and blood of the Lord.
[28]That is why you should examine yourself
before eating the bread and drinking the cup.
[29]For if you eat the bread or drink the cup without honoring the body of Christ, you are eating
and drinking God's judgment upon yourself.
[30]That is why many of you are weak and sick and
some have even died.
[31]But if we would examine ourselves, we
would not be judged by God in this way. [32]Yet
when we are judged by the Lord, we are being
disciplined so that we will not be condemned
along with the world.
[33]So, my dear brothers and sisters, when you
gather for the Lord's Supper, wait for each other.
[34]If you are really hungry, eat at home so you
won't bring judgment upon yourselves when you
meet together. I'll give you instructions about the
other matters after I arrive.

CHAPTER 12
Spiritual Gifts

Now, dear brothers and sisters, regarding your
question about the special abilities the Spirit
gives us. I don't want you to misunderstand this.
[2]You know that when you were still pagans, you
were led astray and swept along in worshiping
speechless idols. [3]So I want you to know that no
one speaking by the Spirit of God will curse
Jesus, and no one can say Jesus is Lord, except by
the Holy Spirit.
[4]There are different kinds of spiritual gifts,
but the same Spirit is the source of them all.
[5]There are different kinds of service, but we
serve the same Lord. [6]God works in different
ways, but it is the same God who does the work in
all of us.
[7]A spiritual gift is given to each of us so we

Love All Around

YOU KNOW WHAT A DICTIONARY'S FOR, RIGHT?

IT GIVES YOU DEFINITIONS OF WORDS.

Well, there's a cool definition in the Bible, too! **Read 1 CORINTHIANS 13:4-7.**

To help you remember everything that love is, make this rolling reminder.

FIRST GATHER

- glue
- cup
- water
- paintbrush
- magazines
- permanent markers
- inexpensive ball (the bigger the better, like a soccer ball).

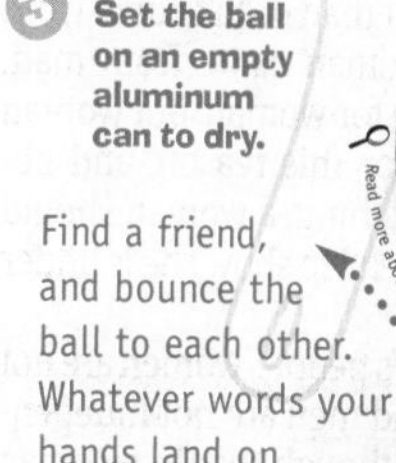

1. **In a cup, add a little water to some white glue.**
2. **Look through old magazines, and tear out words that remind you of what the Bible says love is. Use the paintbrush and glue mixture to attach the words to the ball, and paint a little of the mixture over the words so they're smooth.**
3. **Set the ball on an empty aluminum can to dry.**

Find a friend, and bounce the ball to each other. Whatever words your hands land on when you catch the ball, ask yourselves, **"Is this how I treat others?"**

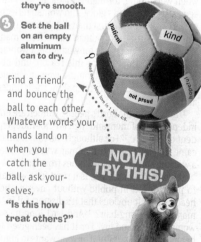

can help each other. 8To one person the Spirit
gives the ability to give wise advice; to another
the same Spirit gives a message of special
knowledge. 9The same Spirit gives great faith to
another, and to someone else the one Spirit
gives the gift of healing. 10He gives one person
the power to perform miracles, and another the
ability to prophesy. He gives someone else the
ability to discern whether a message is from
the Spirit of God or from another spirit. Still
another person is given the ability to speak in
unknown languages, while another is given the
ability to interpret what is being said. 11It is the
one and only Spirit who distributes all these
gifts. He alone decides which gift each person
should have.

One Body with Many Parts

12The human body has many parts, but the many
parts make up one whole body. So it is with the
body of Christ. 13Some of us are Jews, some are
Gentiles, some are slaves, and some are free. But
we have all been baptized into one body by one
Spirit, and we all share the same Spirit.

14Yes, the body has many different parts, not
just one part. 15If the foot says, "I am not a part of
the body because I am not a hand," that does not
make it any less a part of the body. 16And if the
ear says, "I am not part of the body because I am
not an eye," would that make it any less a part of
the body? 17If the whole body were an eye, how
would you hear? Or if your whole body were an
ear, how would you smell anything?

18But our bodies have many parts, and God
has put each part just where he wants it. 19How
strange a body would be if it had only one part!
20Yes, there are many parts, but only one body.
21The eye can never say to the hand, "I don't
need you." The head can't say to the feet, "I don't
need you."

22In fact, some parts of the body that seem
weakest and least important are actually the
most necessary. 23And the parts we regard as less
honorable are those we clothe with the greatest
care. So we carefully protect those parts that
should not be seen, 24while the more honorable
parts do not require this special care. So God has
put the body together such that extra honor and
care are given to those parts that have less dignity. 25This makes for harmony among the members, so that all the members care for each other.
26If one part suffers, all the parts suffer with it,
and if one part is honored, all the parts are glad.

27All of you together are Christ's body, and
each of you is a part of it. 28Here are some of the
parts God has appointed for the church:

first are apostles,
second are prophets,
third are teachers,
then those who do miracles,
those who have the gift of healing,
those who can help others,
those who have the gift of leadership,
those who speak in unknown languages.

29Are we all apostles? Are we all prophets? Are
we all teachers? Do we all have the power to do
miracles? 30Do we all have the gift of healing?
Do we all have the ability to speak in unknown
languages? Do we all have the ability to interpret
unknown languages? Of course not! 31So you
should earnestly desire the most helpful gifts.

But now let me show you a way of life that is
best of all.

CHAPTER 13

Love Is the Greatest

If I could speak all the languages of earth and of
angels, but didn't love others, I would only be a
noisy gong or a clanging cymbal. 2If I had the gift
of prophecy, and if I understood all of God's secret plans and possessed all knowledge, and if I
had such faith that I could move mountains, but
didn't love others, I would be nothing. 3If I gave
everything I have to the poor and even sacrificed
my body, I could boast about it; but if I didn't love
others, I would have gained nothing.

**4Love is patient and kind. Love is
not jealous or boastful or proud 5or
rude. It does not demand its own
way. It is not irritable, and it keeps
no record of being wronged. 6It does
not rejoice about injustice but rejoices whenever the truth wins out.
7Love never gives up, never loses
faith, is always hopeful, and endures
through every circumstance.**

8Prophecy and speaking in unknown languages and special knowledge will become
useless. But love will last forever! 9Now our
knowledge is partial and incomplete, and even
the gift of prophecy reveals only part of the
whole picture! 10But when the time of perfection
comes, these partial things will become useless.

11When I was a child, I spoke and thought and
reasoned as a child. But when I grew up, I put
away childish things. 12Now we see things im-
perfectly, like puzzling reflections in a mirror,
but then we will see everything with perfect

clarity. All that I know now is partial and incomplete, but then I will know everything completely,
just as God now knows me completely.
13 Three things will last forever—faith, hope,
and love—and the greatest of these is love.

CHAPTER 14

Tongues and Prophecy

Let love be your highest goal! But you should also
desire the special abilities the Spirit gives—especially the ability to prophesy. 2 For if you have the
ability to speak in tongues, you will be talking
only to God, since people won't be able to understand you. You will be speaking by the power of
the Spirit, but it will all be mysterious. 3 But one
who prophesies strengthens others, encourages
them, and comforts them. 4 A person who speaks
in tongues is strengthened personally, but one
who speaks a word of prophecy strengthens the
entire church.
5 I wish you could all speak in tongues, but
even more I wish you could all prophesy. For
prophecy is greater than speaking in tongues,
unless someone interprets what you are saying
so that the whole church will be strengthened.
6 Dear brothers and sisters, if I should come to
you speaking in an unknown language, how
would that help you? But if I bring you a revelation or some special knowledge or prophecy or
teaching, that will be helpful. 7 Even lifeless instruments like the flute or the harp must play the
notes clearly, or no one will recognize the melody. 8 And if the bugler doesn't sound a clear call,
how will the soldiers know they are being called
to battle?
9 It's the same for you. If you speak to people in
words they don't understand, how will they know
what you are saying? You might as well be talking
into empty space.
10 There are many different languages in the
world, and every language has meaning. 11 But if I
don't understand a language, I will be a foreigner
to someone who speaks it, and the one who
speaks it will be a foreigner to me. 12 And the
same is true for you. Since you are so eager to
have the special abilities the Spirit gives, seek
those that will strengthen the whole church.
13 So anyone who speaks in tongues should
pray also for the ability to interpret what has
been said. 14 For if I pray in tongues, my spirit is
praying, but I don't understand what I am saying.
15 Well then, what shall I do? I will pray in the
spirit, and I will also pray in words I understand. I
will sing in the spirit, and I will also sing in words
I understand. 16 For if you praise God only in the
spirit, how can those who don't understand you
praise God along with you? How can they join
you in giving thanks when they don't understand
what you are saying? 17 You will be giving thanks
very well, but it won't strengthen the people who
hear you.
18 I thank God that I speak in tongues more
than any of you. 19 But in a church meeting I
would rather speak five understandable words
to help others than ten thousand words in an
unknown language.
20 Dear brothers and sisters, don't be childish
in your understanding of these things. Be innocent as babies when it comes to evil, but be
mature in understanding matters of this kind.
21 It is written in the Scriptures:

"I will speak to my own people
through strange languages
and through the lips of foreigners.
But even then, they will not listen to me,"
says the LORD.

22 So you see that speaking in tongues is a
sign, not for believers, but for unbelievers.
Prophecy, however, is for the benefit of believers, not unbelievers. 23 Even so, if unbelievers or
people who don't understand these things come
into your church meeting and hear everyone
speaking in an unknown language, they will
think you are crazy. 24 But if all of you are prophesying, and unbelievers or people who don't
understand these things come into your meeting, they will be convicted of sin and judged by
what you say. 25 As they listen, their secret
thoughts will be exposed, and they will fall to
their knees and worship God, declaring, "God is
truly here among you."

A Call to Orderly Worship

26 Well, my brothers and sisters, let's summarize.
When you meet together, one will sing, another
will teach, another will tell some special revelation God has given, one will speak in tongues,
and another will interpret what is said. But
everything that is done must strengthen all of
you.
27 No more than two or three should speak in
tongues. They must speak one at a time, and
someone must interpret what they say. 28 But if
no one is present who can interpret, they must be
silent in your church meeting and speak in
tongues to God privately.
29 Let two or three people prophesy, and let
the others evaluate what is said. 30 But if someone is prophesying and another person receives

a revelation from the Lord, the one who is speaking must stop. 31 In this way, all who prophesy
will have a turn to speak, one after the other, so
that everyone will learn and be encouraged.
32 Remember that people who prophesy are in
control of their spirit and can take turns. 33 For
God is not a God of disorder but of peace, as in
all the meetings of God's holy people.

34 Women should be silent during the church
meetings. It is not proper for them to speak.
They should be submissive, just as the law says.
35 If they have any questions, they should ask
their husbands at home, for it is improper for
women to speak in church meetings.

36 Or do you think God's word originated with
you Corinthians? Are you the only ones to whom
it was given? 37 If you claim to be a prophet or
think you are spiritual, you should recognize that
what I am saying is a command from the Lord
himself. 38 But if you do not recognize this, you
yourself will not be recognized.

39 So, my dear brothers and sisters, be eager to
prophesy, and don't forbid speaking in tongues.
40 But be sure that everything is done properly
and in order.

CHAPTER 15

The Resurrection of Christ

Let me now remind you, dear brothers and sisters, of the Good News I preached to you before.
You welcomed it then, and you still stand firm in
it. 2 It is this Good News that saves you if you continue to believe the message I told you—unless,
of course, you believed something that was never
true in the first place.

3 I passed on to you what was most important
and what had also been passed on to me. Christ
died for our sins, just as the Scriptures said. 4 He
was buried, and he was raised from the dead on
the third day, just as the Scriptures said. 5 He was
seen by Peter and then by the Twelve. 6 After that,
he was seen by more than 500 of his followers at
one time, most of whom are still alive, though
some have died. 7 Then he was seen by James and
later by all the apostles. 8 Last of all, as though I
had been born at the wrong time, I also saw him.
9 For I am the least of all the apostles. In fact, I'm
not even worthy to be called an apostle after the
way I persecuted God's church.

10 But whatever I am now, it is all because God
poured out his special favor on me—and not
without results. For I have worked harder than
any of the other apostles; yet it was not I but God
who was working through me by his grace. 11 So
it makes no difference whether I preach or they
preach, for we all preach the same message you
have already believed.

The Resurrection of the Dead

12 But tell me this—since we preach that Christ
rose from the dead, why are some of you saying
there will be no resurrection of the dead? 13 For
if there is no resurrection of the dead, then
Christ has not been raised either. 14 And if Christ
has not been raised, then all our preaching is
useless, and your faith is useless. 15 And we apostles would all be lying about God—for we have
said that God raised Christ from the grave. But
that can't be true if there is no resurrection of
the dead. 16 And if there is no resurrection of the
dead, then Christ has not been raised. 17 And if
Christ has not been raised, then your faith is useless and you are still guilty of your sins. 18 In that
case, all who have died believing in Christ are
lost! 19 And if our hope in Christ is only for this
life, we are more to be pitied than anyone in the
world.

20 But in fact, Christ has been raised from the
dead. He is the first of a great harvest of all who
have died.

21 So you see, just as death came into the world
through a man, now the resurrection from the
dead has begun through another man. 22 Just as
everyone dies because we all belong to Adam,
everyone who belongs to Christ will be given new
life. 23 But there is an order to this resurrection:
Christ was raised as the first of the harvest; then
all who belong to Christ will be raised when he
comes back.

24 After that the end will come, when he will
turn the Kingdom over to God the Father, having
destroyed every ruler and authority and power.
25 For Christ must reign until he humbles all his
enemies beneath his feet. 26 And the last enemy
to be destroyed is death. 27 For the Scriptures say,
"God has put all things under his authority." (Of
course, when it says "all things are under his
authority," that does not include God himself,
who gave Christ his authority.) 28 Then, when all
things are under his authority, the Son will put
himself under God's authority, so that God, who
gave his Son authority over all things, will be utterly supreme over everything everywhere.

29 If the dead will not be raised, what point is
there in people being baptized for those who are
dead? Why do it unless the dead will someday
rise again?

30 And why should we ourselves risk our lives
hour by hour? 31 For I swear, dear brothers and
sisters, that I face death daily. This is as certain as

my pride in what Christ Jesus our Lord has done in you. 32And what value was there in fighting wild beasts—those people of Ephesus—if there will be no resurrection from the dead? And if there is no resurrection, "Let's feast and drink, for tomorrow we die!" 33Don't be fooled by those who say such things, for "bad company corrupts good character." 34Think carefully about what is right, and stop sinning. For to your shame I say that some of you don't know God at all.

The Resurrection Body

35But someone may ask, "How will the dead be raised? What kind of bodies will they have?" 36What a foolish question! When you put a seed into the ground, it doesn't grow into a plant unless it dies first. 37And what you put in the ground is not the plant that will grow, but only a bare seed of wheat or whatever you are planting. 38Then God gives it the new body he wants it to have. A different plant grows from each kind of seed. 39Similarly there are different kinds of flesh—one kind for humans, another for animals, another for birds, and another for fish.

40There are also bodies in the heavens and bodies on the earth. The glory of the heavenly bodies is different from the glory of the earthly bodies. 41The sun has one kind of glory, while the moon and stars each have another kind. And even the stars differ from each other in their glory.

42It is the same way with the resurrection of the dead. Our earthly bodies are planted in the ground when we die, but they will be raised to live forever. 43Our bodies are buried in brokenness, but they will be raised in glory. They are buried in weakness, but they will be raised in strength. 44They are buried as natural human bodies, but they will be raised as spiritual bodies. For just as there are natural bodies, there are also spiritual bodies.

45The Scriptures tell us, "The first man, Adam, became a living person." But the last Adam—that is, Christ—is a life-giving Spirit. 46What comes first is the natural body, then the spiritual body comes later. 47Adam, the first man, was made from the dust of the earth, while Christ, the second man, came from heaven. 48Earthly people are like the earthly man, and heavenly people are like the heavenly man. 49Just as we are now like the earthly man, we will someday be like the heavenly man.

50What I am saying, dear brothers and sisters, is that our physical bodies cannot inherit the Kingdom of God. These dying bodies cannot inherit what will last forever.

51But let me reveal to you a wonderful secret. We will not all die, but we will all be transformed! 52It will happen in a moment, in the blink of an eye, when the last trumpet is blown. For when the trumpet sounds, those who have died will be raised to live forever. And we who are living will also be transformed. 53For our dying bodies must be transformed into bodies that will never die; our mortal bodies must be transformed into immortal bodies.

54Then, when our dying bodies have been transformed into bodies that will never die, this Scripture will be fulfilled:

"Death is swallowed up in victory.
55 O death, where is your victory?
O death, where is your sting?"

56For sin is the sting that results in death, and the law gives sin its power. 57But thank God! He gives us victory over sin and death through our Lord Jesus Christ.

58So, my dear brothers and sisters, be strong and immovable. Always work enthusiastically for the Lord, for you know that nothing you do for the Lord is ever useless.

CHAPTER **16**

The Collection for Jerusalem

Now regarding your question about the money being collected for God's people in Jerusalem. You should follow the same procedure I gave to the churches in Galatia. 2On the first day of each week, you should each put aside a portion of the money you have earned. Don't wait until I get there and then try to collect it all at once. 3When I come, I will write letters of recommendation for the messengers you choose to deliver your gift to Jerusalem. 4And if it seems appropriate for me to go along, they can travel with me.

Paul's Final Instructions

5I am coming to visit you after I have been to Macedonia, for I am planning to travel through Macedonia. 6Perhaps I will stay awhile with you, possibly all winter, and then you can send me on my way to my next destination. 7This time I don't want to make just a short visit and then go right on. I want to come and stay awhile, if the Lord will let me. 8In the meantime, I will be staying here at Ephesus until the Festival of Pentecost. 9There is a wide-open door for a great work here, although many oppose me.

10When Timothy comes, don't intimidate
him. He is doing the Lord's work, just as I am.
11Don't let anyone treat him with contempt.
Send him on his way with your blessing when he
returns to me. I expect him to come with the
other believers.
12Now about our brother Apollos—I urged
him to visit you with the other believers, but he
was not willing to go right now. He will see you
later when he has the opportunity.
13Be on guard. Stand firm in the faith. Be courageous. Be strong. 14And do everything with love.
15You know that Stephanas and his household were the first of the harvest of believers in
Greece, and they are spending their lives in service to God's people. I urge you, dear brothers
and sisters, 16to submit to them and others like
them who serve with such devotion. 17I am very
glad that Stephanas, Fortunatus, and Achaicus
have come here. They have been providing the
help you weren't here to give me. 18They have
been a wonderful encouragement to me, as they
have been to you. You must show your apprecia-
tion to all who serve so well.

Paul's Final Greetings

19The churches here in the province of Asia send
greetings in the Lord, as do Aquila and Priscilla
and all the others who gather in their home for
church meetings. 20All the brothers and sisters
here send greetings to you. Greet each other with
a sacred kiss.
21HERE IS MY GREETING IN MY OWN HAND-
WRITING—PAUL.
22If anyone does not love the Lord, that person
is cursed. Our Lord, come!
23May the grace of the Lord Jesus be with you.
24My love to all of you in Christ Jesus.

2 CORINTHIANS A Calm Voice

Look for 1 hidden message in 2 Corinthians!

Paul wrote another letter to the troubled church in Corinth, trying to help the people there resolve their problems. Look for

- **COMFORTING WORDS**
- **JARS OF CLAY**
- **NEW CREATIONS**
- **CARE AND CONCERN**

Comfort and Care

You know, there just may be a reason you're going through something hard right now. **Find out what that reason could be in 2 Corinthians 1:3-4!**

Jars of Clay

If you had a special treasure, where would you put it?

Where God put his special treasure—the Good News about Jesus—might just surprise you. **Read 2 Corinthians 4:6-7 for the answer.**

Cheerful Giving

God wants our gifts, but not if we don't really want to give them. **Get it? You can, by reading 2 Corinthians 9:7-12!**

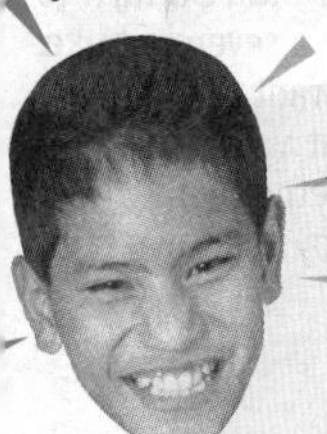

Brand-New

Ready for a make-over? Well, God can do one for you! **Find out how in 2 Corinthians 5:17.**

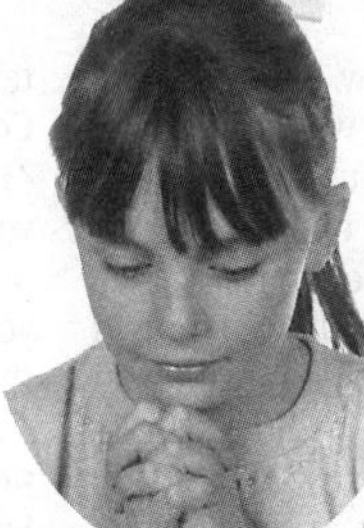

It's Enough!

Sometimes we ask God to take away our problems, but he doesn't. The same thing happened to Paul. But Paul was happy about it! **Read 2 Corinthians 12:6-10 to find out why.**

Timeline

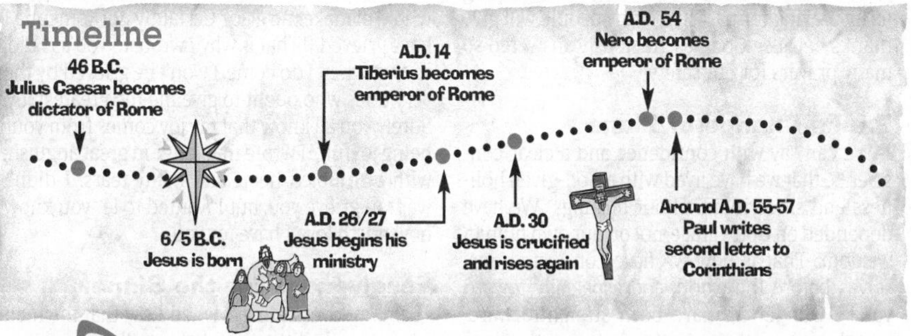

46 B.C. Julius Caesar becomes dictator of Rome
6/5 B.C. Jesus is born
A.D. 14 Tiberius becomes emperor of Rome
A.D. 26/27 Jesus begins his ministry
A.D. 30 Jesus is crucified and rises again
A.D. 54 Nero becomes emperor of Rome
Around A.D. 55-57 Paul writes second letter to Corinthians

The JESUS CONNECTION

In 2 Corinthians, Paul's emotions come through loud and clear—his joy in spreading the gospel, his pain in suffering for his faith, and his love and concern for the believers in Corinth. Paul put everything on the line to share the Good News about Jesus. He didn't care what he had to do to get the word out about Jesus. He knew that **Jesus is the most important thing in the world!**

2 Corinthians 1 . . . page 1144

CHAPTER 1

Greetings from Paul

This letter is from Paul, chosen by the will of God
to be an apostle of Christ Jesus, and from our
brother Timothy.

I am writing to God's church in Corinth and to
all of his holy people throughout Greece.

2 May God our Father and the Lord Jesus Christ
give you grace and peace.

God Offers Comfort to All

3 All praise to God, the Father of our Lord Jesus
Christ. God is our merciful Father and the source
of all comfort. 4 He comforts us in all our troubles
so that we can comfort others. When they are
troubled, we will be able to give them the same
comfort God has given us. 5 For the more we suffer for Christ, the more God will shower us with
his comfort through Christ. 6 Even when we are
weighed down with troubles, it is for your comfort and salvation! For when we ourselves are
comforted, we will certainly comfort you. Then
you can patiently endure the same things we suffer. 7 We are confident that as you share in our
sufferings, you will also share in the comfort God
gives us.

8 We think you ought to know, dear brothers
and sisters, about the trouble we went through in
the province of Asia. We were crushed and overwhelmed beyond our ability to endure, and we
thought we would never live through it. 9 In fact,
we expected to die. But as a result, we stopped
relying on ourselves and learned to rely only on
God, who raises the dead. 10 And he did rescue us
from mortal danger, and he will rescue us again.
We have placed our confidence in him, and he
will continue to rescue us. 11 And you are helping
us by praying for us. Then many people will give
thanks because God has graciously answered so
many prayers for our safety.

Paul's Change of Plans

12 We can say with confidence and a clear conscience that we have lived with a God-given holiness and sincerity in all our dealings. We have
depended on God's grace, not on our own human
wisdom. That is how we have conducted ourselves before the world, and especially toward
you. 13 Our letters have been straightforward,
and there is nothing written between the lines
and nothing you can't understand. I hope someday you will fully understand us, 14 even if you
don't understand us now. Then on the day when
the Lord Jesus returns, you will be proud of us in
the same way we are proud of you.

15 Since I was so sure of your understanding
and trust, I wanted to give you a double blessing
by visiting you twice—16 first on my way to Macedonia and again when I returned from Macedonia. Then you could send me on my way to Judea.

17 You may be asking why I changed my plan.
Do you think I make my plans carelessly? Do
you think I am like people of the world who say
"Yes" when they really mean "No"? 18 As surely
as God is faithful, our word to you does not waver between "Yes" and "No." 19 For Jesus Christ,
the Son of God, does not waver between "Yes"
and "No." He is the one whom Silas, Timothy,
and I preached to you, and as God's ultimate
"Yes," he always does what he says. 20 For all of
God's promises have been fulfilled in Christ
with a resounding "Yes!" And through Christ,
our "Amen" (which means "Yes") ascends to God
for his glory.

21 It is God who enables us, along with you, to
stand firm for Christ. He has commissioned us,
22 and he has identified us as his own by placing
the Holy Spirit in our hearts as the first install-
ment that guarantees everything he has promised us.

23 Now I call upon God as my witness that I am
telling the truth. The reason I didn't return to
Corinth was to spare you from a severe rebuke.
24 But that does not mean we want to dominate
you by telling you how to put your faith into
practice. We want to work together with you so
you will be full of joy, for it is by your own faith
that you stand firm.

CHAPTER 2

So I decided that I would not bring you grief with
another painful visit. 2 For if I cause you grief,
who will make me glad? Certainly not someone I
have grieved. 3 That is why I wrote to you as I did,
so that when I do come, I won't be grieved by the
very ones who ought to give me the greatest joy.
Surely you all know that my joy comes from your
being joyful. 4 I wrote that letter in great anguish,
with a troubled heart and many tears. I didn't
want to grieve you, but I wanted to let you know
how much love I have for you.

Forgiveness for the Sinner

5 I am not overstating it when I say that the man
who caused all the trouble hurt all of you more
than he hurt me. 6 Most of you opposed him, and
that was punishment enough. 7 Now, however, it
is time to forgive and comfort him. Otherwise he
may be overcome by discouragement. 8 So I urge
you now to reaffirm your love for him.

9I wrote to you as I did to test you and see if you would fully comply with my instructions. 10When you forgive this man, I forgive him, too. And when I forgive whatever needs to be forgiven, I do so with Christ's authority for your benefit, 11so that Satan will not outsmart us. For we are familiar with his evil schemes.

12When I came to the city of Troas to preach the Good News of Christ, the Lord opened a door of opportunity for me. 13But I had no peace of mind because my dear brother Titus hadn't yet arrived with a report from you. So I said good-bye and went on to Macedonia to find him.

Ministers of the New Covenant

14But thank God! He has made us his captives and continues to lead us along in Christ's triumphal procession. Now he uses us to spread the knowledge of Christ everywhere, like a sweet perfume. 15Our lives are a Christ-like fragrance rising up to God. But this fragrance is perceived differently by those who are being saved and by those who are perishing. 16To those who are perishing, we are a dreadful smell of death and doom. But to those who are being saved, we are a life-giving perfume. And who is adequate for such a task as this?

17You see, we are not like the many hucksters who preach for personal profit. We preach the word of God with sincerity and with Christ's authority, knowing that God is watching us.

CHAPTER 3

Are we beginning to praise ourselves again? Are we like others, who need to bring you letters of recommendation, or who ask you to write such letters on their behalf? Surely not! 2The only letter of recommendation we need is you yourselves. Your lives are a letter written in our hearts; everyone can read it and recognize our good work among you. 3Clearly, you are a letter from Christ showing the result of our ministry among you. This "letter" is written not with pen and ink, but with the Spirit of the living God. It is carved not on tablets of stone, but on human hearts.

4We are confident of all this because of our great trust in God through Christ. 5It is not that we think we are qualified to do anything on our own. Our qualification comes from God. 6He has enabled us to be ministers of his new covenant. This is a covenant not of written laws, but of the Spirit. The old written covenant ends in death; but under the new covenant, the Spirit gives life.

The Glory of the New Covenant

7The old way, with laws etched in stone, led to death, though it began with such glory that the people of Israel could not bear to look at Moses' face. For his face shone with the glory of God, even though the brightness was already fading away. 8Shouldn't we expect far greater glory under the new way, now that the Holy Spirit is giving life? 9If the old way, which brings condemnation, was glorious, how much more glorious is the new way, which makes us right with God! 10In fact, that first glory was not glorious at all compared with the overwhelming glory of the new way. 11So if the old way, which has been replaced, was glorious, how much more glorious is the new, which remains forever!

12Since this new way gives us such confidence, we can be very bold. 13We are not like Moses, who put a veil over his face so the people of Israel would not see the glory, even though it was destined to fade away. 14But the people's minds were hardened, and to this day whenever the old covenant is being read, the same veil covers their minds so they cannot understand the truth. And this veil can be removed only by believing in Christ. 15Yes, even today when they read Moses' writings, their hearts are covered with that veil, and they do not understand.

16But whenever someone turns to the Lord, the veil is taken away. 17For the Lord is the Spirit, and wherever the Spirit of the Lord is, there is freedom. 18So all of us who have had that veil removed can see and reflect the glory of the Lord. And the Lord—who is the Spirit—makes us more and more like him as we are changed into his glorious image.

CHAPTER 4

Treasure in Fragile Clay Jars

Therefore, since God in his mercy has given us this new way, we never give up. 2We reject all shameful deeds and underhanded methods. We don't try to trick anyone or distort the word of God. We tell the truth before God, and all who are honest know this.

3If the Good News we preach is hidden behind a veil, it is hidden only from people who are perishing. 4Satan, who is the god of this world, has blinded the minds of those who don't believe. They are unable to see the glorious light of the Good News. They don't understand this message about the glory of Christ, who is the exact likeness of God.

5You see, we don't go around preaching about ourselves. We preach that Jesus Christ is Lord,

and we ourselves are your servants for Jesus'
sake. 6For God, who said, "Let there be light in
the darkness," has made this light shine in our
hearts so we could know the glory of God that is
seen in the face of Jesus Christ.
7We now have this light shining in our hearts,
but we ourselves are like fragile clay jars containing this great treasure. This makes it clear that
our great power is from God, not from ourselves.
8We are pressed on every side by troubles, but
we are not crushed. We are perplexed, but not
driven to despair. 9We are hunted down, but
never abandoned by God. We get knocked down,
but we are not destroyed. 10Through suffering,
our bodies continue to share in the death of
Jesus so that the life of Jesus may also be seen in
our bodies.
11Yes, we live under constant danger of death
because we serve Jesus, so that the life of Jesus
will be evident in our dying bodies. 12So we live
in the face of death, but this has resulted in eternal life for you.
13But we continue to preach because we have
the same kind of faith the psalmist had when he
said, "I believed in God, so I spoke." 14We know
that God, who raised the Lord Jesus, will also
raise us with Jesus and present us to himself together with you. 15All of this is for your benefit.
And as God's grace reaches more and more people, there will be great thanksgiving, and God will
receive more and more glory.
16That is why we never give up. Though our
bodies are dying, our spirits are being renewed
every day. 17For our present troubles are small
and won't last very long. Yet they produce for us a
glory that vastly outweighs them and will last forever! 18So we don't look at the troubles we can
see now; rather, we fix our gaze on things that
cannot be seen. For the things we see now will
soon be gone, but the things we cannot see will
last forever.

CHAPTER 5

New Bodies

For we know that when this earthly tent we live in
is taken down (that is, when we die and leave this
earthly body), we will have a house in heaven, an
eternal body made for us by God himself and not
by human hands. 2We grow weary in our present
bodies, and we long to put on our heavenly bodies like new clothing. 3For we will put on heavenly bodies; we will not be spirits without
bodies. 4While we live in these earthly bodies,
we groan and sigh, but it's not that we want to die
and get rid of these bodies that clothe us. Rather,

Key Verse **"This means that anyone who belongs to Christ has become a new person. The old life is gone; a new life has begun!"—2 CORINTHIANS 5:17**

Presto Chango!
News

Read 2 CORINTHIANS 5:17 out loud a few times.

When we believe in Jesus, the Holy Spirit lives in us and begins teaching and guiding us.

THE CHANGE IS KIND OF LIKE THIS!

GATHER:

- old colored comic section from a newspaper
- container
- white glue
- liquid starch
- spoon

1. **Mix two parts glue with one part liquid starch. Stir well.**
2. **Continue adding starch one spoonful at a time, using your fingers to work the mixture into a smooth putty.**
3. **Press the putty onto a colored comic picture, then pull it off.**

The putty was plain. But after you pressed it onto the colored picture, it became colorful itself! That's kind of how it is when you believe in Jesus. Just like the putty changed when it came in contact with the picture, you change when you believe in Jesus. Then the Holy Spirit helps you become more and more like Jesus each day.

Do this experiment with a friend. Read this verse to your friend, and explain how your friend can become new by believing in Jesus!

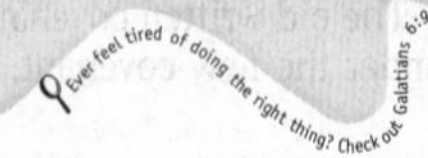
Ever feel tired of doing the right thing? Check out Galatians 6:9.

we want to put on our new bodies so that these dying bodies will be swallowed up by life. 5God himself has prepared us for this, and as a guarantee he has given us his Holy Spirit.

6So we are always confident, even though we know that as long as we live in these bodies we are not at home with the Lord. 7For we live by believing and not by seeing. 8Yes, we are fully confident, and we would rather be away from these earthly bodies, for then we will be at home with the Lord. 9So whether we are here in this body or away from this body, our goal is to please him. 10For we must all stand before Christ to be judged. We will each receive whatever we deserve for the good or evil we have done in this earthly body.

We Are God's Ambassadors

11Because we understand our fearful responsibility to the Lord, we work hard to persuade others. God knows we are sincere, and I hope you know this, too. 12Are we commending ourselves to you again? No, we are giving you a reason to be proud of us, so you can answer those who brag about having a spectacular ministry rather than having a sincere heart. 13If it seems we are crazy, it is to bring glory to God. And if we are in our right minds, it is for your benefit. 14Either way, Christ's love controls us. Since we believe that Christ died for all, we also believe that we have all died to our old life. 15He died for everyone so that those who receive his new life will no longer live for themselves. Instead, they will live for Christ, who died and was raised for them.

16So we have stopped evaluating others from a human point of view. At one time we thought of Christ merely from a human point of view. How differently we know him now! **17This means that anyone who belongs to Christ has become a new person. The old life is gone; a new life has begun!**

18And all of this is a gift from God, who brought us back to himself through Christ. And God has given us this task of reconciling people to him. 19For God was in Christ, reconciling the world to himself, no longer counting people's sins against them. And he gave us this wonderful message of reconciliation. 20So we are Christ's ambassadors; God is making his appeal through us. We speak for Christ when we plead, "Come back to God!" 21For God made Christ, who never sinned, to be the offering for our sin, so that we could be made right with God through Christ.

CHAPTER 6

As God's partners, we beg you not to accept this marvelous gift of God's kindness and then ignore it. 2For God says,

> "At just the right time, I heard you.
> On the day of salvation, I helped you."

Indeed, the "right time" is now. Today is the day of salvation.

Paul's Hardships

3We live in such a way that no one will stumble because of us, and no one will find fault with our ministry. 4In everything we do, we show that we are true ministers of God. We patiently endure troubles and hardships and calamities of every kind. 5We have been beaten, been put in prison, faced angry mobs, worked to exhaustion, endured sleepless nights, and gone without food. 6We prove ourselves by our purity, our understanding, our patience, our kindness, by the Holy Spirit within us, and by our sincere love. 7We faithfully preach the truth. God's power is working in us. We use the weapons of righteousness in the right hand for attack and the left hand for defense. 8We serve God whether people honor us or despise us, whether they slander us or praise us. We are honest, but they call us impostors. 9We are ignored, even though we are well known. We live close to death, but we are still alive. We have been beaten, but we have not been killed. 10Our hearts ache, but we always have joy. We are poor, but we give spiritual riches to others. We own nothing, and yet we have everything.

11Oh, dear Corinthian friends! We have spoken honestly with you, and our hearts are open to you. 12There is no lack of love on our part, but you have withheld your love from us. 13I am asking you to respond as if you were my own children. Open your hearts to us!

The Temple of the Living God

14Don't team up with those who are unbelievers. How can righteousness be a partner with wickedness? How can light live with darkness? 15What harmony can there be between Christ and the devil? How can a believer be a partner with an unbeliever? 16And what union can there be between God's temple and idols? For we are the temple of the living God. As God said:

> "I will live in them
> and walk among them.
> I will be their God,
> and they will be my people.

17 Therefore, come out from among
unbelievers,
and separate yourselves from them,
says the LORD.
Don't touch their filthy things,
and I will welcome you.
18 And I will be your Father,
and you will be my sons and daughters,
says the LORD Almighty."

CHAPTER 7

Because we have these promises, dear friends, let
us cleanse ourselves from everything that can
defile our body or spirit. And let us work toward
complete holiness because we fear God.

2 Please open your hearts to us. We have not
done wrong to anyone, nor led anyone astray, nor
taken advantage of anyone. 3 I'm not saying this
to condemn you. I said before that you are in our
hearts, and we live or die together with you. 4 I
have the highest confidence in you, and I take
great pride in you. You have greatly encouraged
me and made me happy despite all our troubles.

Paul's Joy at the Church's Repentance

5 When we arrived in Macedonia, there was no
rest for us. We faced conflict from every direction,
with battles on the outside and fear on the inside.
6 But God, who encourages those who are discouraged, encouraged us by the arrival of Titus. 7 His
presence was a joy, but so was the news he
brought of the encouragement he received from
you. When he told us how much you long to see
me, and how sorry you are for what happened, and
how loyal you are to me, I was filled with joy!

8 I am not sorry that I sent that severe letter to
you, though I was sorry at first, for I know it was
painful to you for a little while. 9 Now I am glad I
sent it, not because it hurt you, but because the
pain caused you to repent and change your ways.
It was the kind of sorrow God wants his people to
have, so you were not harmed by us in any way.
10 For the kind of sorrow God wants us to experience leads us away from sin and results in salvation. There's no regret for that kind of sorrow.
But worldly sorrow, which lacks repentance, results in spiritual death.

11 Just see what this godly sorrow produced in
you! Such earnestness, such concern to clear
yourselves, such indignation, such alarm, such
longing to see me, such zeal, and such a readi-
ness to punish wrong. You showed that you have
done everything necessary to make things right.
12 My purpose, then, was not to write about who
did the wrong or who was wronged. I wrote to
you so that in the sight of God you could see for
yourselves how loyal you are to us. 13 We have
been greatly encouraged by this.

In addition to our own encouragement, we
were especially delighted to see how happy Titus
was about the way all of you welcomed him and
set his mind at ease. 14 I had told him how proud I
was of you—and you didn't disappoint me. I have
always told you the truth, and now my boasting
to Titus has also proved true! 15 Now he cares for
you more than ever when he remembers the way
all of you obeyed him and welcomed him with
such fear and deep respect. 16 I am very happy
now because I have complete confidence in you.

CHAPTER 8

A Call to Generous Giving

Now I want you to know, dear brothers and sisters, what God in his kindness has done through
the churches in Macedonia. 2 They are being
tested by many troubles, and they are very poor.
But they are also filled with abundant joy, which
has overflowed in rich generosity.

3 For I can testify that they gave not only what
they could afford, but far more. And they did it of
their own free will. 4 They begged us again and
again for the privilege of sharing in the gift for
the believers in Jerusalem. 5 They even did more
than we had hoped, for their first action was to
give themselves to the Lord and to us, just as God
wanted them to do.

6 So we have urged Titus, who encouraged
your giving in the first place, to return to you and
encourage you to finish this ministry of giving.
7 Since you excel in so many ways—in your faith,
your gifted speakers, your knowledge, your enthusiasm, and your love from us—I want you to
excel also in this gracious act of giving.

8 I am not commanding you to do this. But I am
testing how genuine your love is by comparing it
with the eagerness of the other churches.

9 You know the generous grace of our Lord
Jesus Christ. Though he was rich, yet for your
sakes he became poor, so that by his poverty he
could make you rich.

10 Here is my advice: It would be good for you
to finish what you started a year ago. Last year
you were the first who wanted to give, and you
were the first to begin doing it. 11 Now you should
finish what you started. Let the eagerness you
showed in the beginning be matched now by
your giving. Give in proportion to what you have.
12 Whatever you give is acceptable if you give it
eagerly. And give according to what you have,

not what you don't have. 13Of course, I don't
mean your giving should make life easy for
others and hard for yourselves. I only mean that
there should be some equality. 14Right now you
have plenty and can help those who are in need.
Later, they will have plenty and can share with
you when you need it. In this way, things will be
equal. 15As the Scriptures say,

"Those who gathered a lot had nothing
left over,
and those who gathered only a little
had enough."

Titus and His Companions

16But thank God! He has given Titus the same enthusiasm for you that I have. 17Titus welcomed
our request that he visit you again. In fact, he himself was very eager to go and see you. 18We are
also sending another brother with Titus. All the
churches praise him as a preacher of the Good
News. 19He was appointed by the churches to accompany us as we take the offering to Jerusalem—a service that glorifies the Lord and shows
our eagerness to help.

20We are traveling together to guard against
any criticism for the way we are handling this
generous gift. 21We are careful to be honorable
before the Lord, but we also want everyone else
to see that we are honorable.

22We are also sending with them another of
our brothers who has proven himself many
times and has shown on many occasions how
eager he is. He is now even more enthusiastic because of his great confidence in you. 23If anyone
asks about Titus, say that he is my partner who
works with me to help you. And the brothers
with him have been sent by the churches, and
they bring honor to Christ. 24So show them your
love, and prove to all the churches that our boasting about you is justified.

CHAPTER **9**

The Collection for Christians in Jerusalem

I really don't need to write to you about this ministry of giving for the believers in Jerusalem. 2For
I know how eager you are to help, and I have been
boasting to the churches in Macedonia that you
in Greece were ready to send an offering a year
ago. In fact, it was your enthusiasm that stirred
up many of the Macedonian believers to begin
giving.

3But I am sending these brothers to be sure
you really are ready, as I have been telling them,
and that your money is all collected. I don't want
to be wrong in my boasting about you. 4We
would be embarrassed—not to mention your
own embarrassment—if some Macedonian believers came with me and found that you weren't
ready after all I had told them! 5So I thought I
should send these brothers ahead of me to make
sure the gift you promised is ready. But I want it
to be a willing gift, not one given grudgingly.

6Remember this—a farmer who plants only a
few seeds will get a small crop. But the one who
plants generously will get a generous crop. **7You**
must each decide in your heart how
much to give. And don't give re-
luctantly or in response to pressure.
"For God loves a person who gives
cheerfully." 8And God will generously provide all you need. Then you will always have everything you need and plenty left over to share with
others. 9As the Scriptures say,

"They share freely and give generously
to the poor.
Their good deeds will be remembered
forever."

10For God is the one who provides seed for the
farmer and then bread to eat. In the same way, he
will provide and increase your resources and
then produce a great harvest of generosity in you.

11Yes, you will be enriched in every way so that
you can always be generous. And when we take
your gifts to those who need them, they will
thank God. 12So two good things will result from
this ministry of giving—the needs of the believers in Jerusalem will be met, and they will joyfully express their thanks to God.

13As a result of your ministry, they will give
glory to God. For your generosity to them and to
all believers will prove that you are obedient to
the Good News of Christ. 14And they will pray for
you with deep affection because of the overflowing grace God has given to you. 15Thank God for
this gift too wonderful for words!

CHAPTER **10**

Paul Defends His Authority

Now I, Paul, appeal to you with the gentleness and
kindness of Christ—though I realize you think I
am timid in person and bold only when I write
from far away. 2Well, I am begging you now so
that when I come I won't have to be bold with
those who think we act from human motives.

3We are human, but we don't wage war as
humans do. 4We use God's mighty weapons, not
worldly weapons, to knock down the strongholds

of human reasoning and to destroy false arguments. 5We destroy every proud obstacle that
keeps people from knowing God. We capture
their rebellious thoughts and teach them to obey
Christ. 6And after you have become fully obedient, we will punish everyone who remains disobedient.

7Look at the obvious facts. Those who say they
belong to Christ must recognize that we belong
to Christ as much as they do. 8I may seem to be
boasting too much about the authority given to
us by the Lord. But our authority builds you up; it
doesn't tear you down. So I will not be ashamed
of using my authority.

9I'm not trying to frighten you by my letters.
10For some say, "Paul's letters are demanding
and forceful, but in person he is weak, and his
speeches are worthless!" 11Those people should
realize that our actions when we arrive in person
will be as forceful as what we say in our letters
from far away.

12Oh, don't worry; we wouldn't dare say that
we are as wonderful as these other men who tell
you how important they are! But they are only
comparing themselves with each other, using
themselves as the standard of measurement.
How ignorant!

13We will not boast about things done outside
our area of authority. We will boast only about
what has happened within the boundaries of the
work God has given us, which includes our working with you. 14We are not reaching beyond these
boundaries when we claim authority over you, as
if we had never visited you. For we were the first
to travel all the way to Corinth with the Good
News of Christ.

15Nor do we boast and claim credit for the
work someone else has done. Instead, we hope
that your faith will grow so that the boundaries of
our work among you will be extended. 16Then we
will be able to go and preach the Good News in
other places far beyond you, where no one else is
working. Then there will be no question of our
boasting about work done in someone else's
territory. 17As the Scriptures say, "If you want to
boast, boast only about the LORD."

18When people commend themselves, it
doesn't count for much. The important thing is
for the Lord to commend them.

CHAPTER 11

Paul and the False Apostles

I hope you will put up with a little more of my
foolishness. Please bear with me. 2For I am jealous for you with the jealousy of God himself. I
promised you as a pure bride to one husband—
Christ. 3But I fear that somehow your pure and
undivided devotion to Christ will be corrupted,
just as Eve was deceived by the cunning ways of
the serpent. 4You happily put up with whatever
anyone tells you, even if they preach a different
Jesus than the one we preach, or a different kind
of Spirit than the one you received, or a different
kind of gospel than the one you believed.

5But I don't consider myself inferior in any
way to these "super apostles" who teach such
things. 6I may be unskilled as a speaker, but I'm
not lacking in knowledge. We have made this
clear to you in every possible way.

7Was I wrong when I humbled myself and
honored you by preaching God's Good News to
you without expecting anything in return? 8I
"robbed" other churches by accepting their contributions so I could serve you at no cost. 9And
when I was with you and didn't have enough to
live on, I did not become a financial burden to
anyone. For the brothers who came from Macedonia brought me all that I needed. I have never
been a burden to you, and I never will be. 10As
surely as the truth of Christ is in me, no one in all
of Greece will ever stop me from boasting about
this. 11Why? Because I don't love you? God knows
that I do.

12But I will continue doing what I have always
done. This will undercut those who are looking
for an opportunity to boast that their work is just
like ours. 13These people are false apostles. They
are deceitful workers who disguise themselves
as apostles of Christ. 14But I am not surprised!
Even Satan disguises himself as an angel of light.
15So it is no wonder that his servants also disguise themselves as servants of righteousness. In
the end they will get the punishment their
wicked deeds deserve.

Paul's Many Trials

16Again I say, don't think that I am a fool to talk
like this. But even if you do, listen to me, as you
would to a foolish person, while I also boast a little. 17Such boasting is not from the Lord, but I am
acting like a fool. 18And since others boast about
their human achievements, I will, too. 19After all,
you think you are so wise, but you enjoy putting
up with fools! 20You put up with it when someone
enslaves you, takes everything you have, takes advantage of you, takes control of everything, and
slaps you in the face. 21I'm ashamed to say that
we've been too "weak" to do that!

But whatever they dare to boast about—I'm
talking like a fool again—I dare to boast about it,

too. 22Are they Hebrews? So am I. Are they Israelites? So am I. Are they descendants of Abraham?
So am I. 23Are they servants of Christ? I know I
sound like a madman, but I have served him far
more! I have worked harder, been put in prison
more often, been whipped times without number,
and faced death again and again. 24Five different times the Jewish leaders gave me thirty-nine
lashes. 25Three times I was beaten with rods.
Once I was stoned. Three times I was shipwrecked. Once I spent a whole night and a day
adrift at sea. 26I have traveled on many long journeys. I have faced danger from rivers and from
robbers. I have faced danger from my own people,
the Jews, as well as from the Gentiles. I have faced
danger in the cities, in the deserts, and on the
seas. And I have faced danger from men who
claim to be believers but are not. 27I have worked
hard and long, enduring many sleepless nights. I
have been hungry and thirsty and have often gone
without food. I have shivered in the cold, without
enough clothing to keep me warm.

28Then, besides all this, I have the daily burden of my concern for all the churches. 29Who is
weak without my feeling that weakness? Who is
led astray, and I do not burn with anger?

30If I must boast, I would rather boast about
the things that show how weak I am. 31God, the
Father of our Lord Jesus, who is worthy of eternal
praise, knows I am not lying. 32When I was in
Damascus, the governor under King Aretas kept
guards at the city gates to catch me. 33I had to be
lowered in a basket through a window in the city
wall to escape from him.

CHAPTER 12

Paul's Vision and His Thorn in the Flesh

This boasting will do no good, but I must go on. I
will reluctantly tell about visions and revelations
from the Lord. 2I was caught up to the third
heaven fourteen years ago. Whether I was in my
body or out of my body, I don't know—only God
knows. 3Yes, only God knows whether I was in
my body or outside my body. But I do know 4that
I was caught up to paradise and heard things so
astounding that they cannot be expressed in
words, things no human is allowed to tell.

5That experience is worth boasting about, but
I'm not going to do it. I will boast only about my
weaknesses. 6If I wanted to boast, I would be no
fool in doing so, because I would be telling the
truth. But I won't do it, because I don't want anyone to give me credit beyond what they can see
in my life or hear in my message, 7even though I
have received such wonderful revelations from
God. So to keep me from becoming proud, I was
given a thorn in my flesh, a messenger from
Satan to torment me and keep me from becoming proud.

8Three different times I begged the Lord to
take it away. 9Each time he said, "My grace is all
you need. My power works best in weakness." So
now I am glad to boast about my weaknesses, so
that the power of Christ can work through me.
10That's why I take pleasure in my weaknesses,
and in the insults, hardships, persecutions, and
troubles that I suffer for Christ. For when I am
weak, then I am strong.

Paul's Concern for the Corinthians

11You have made me act like a fool. You ought to
be writing commendations for me, for I am not at
all inferior to these "super apostles," even though
I am nothing at all. 12When I was with you, I certainly gave you proof that I am an apostle. For I
patiently did many signs and wonders and miracles among you. 13The only thing I failed to do,
which I do in the other churches, was to become a
financial burden to you. Please forgive me for this
wrong!

14Now I am coming to you for the third time,
and I will not be a burden to you. I don't want what
you have—I want you. After all, children don't provide for their parents. Rather, parents provide for
their children. 15I will gladly spend myself and all I
have for you, even though it seems that the more I
love you, the less you love me.

16Some of you admit I was not a burden to
you. But others still think I was sneaky and took
advantage of you by trickery. 17But how? Did any
of the men I sent to you take advantage of you?
18When I urged Titus to visit you and sent our
other brother with him, did Titus take advantage
of you? No! For we have the same spirit and walk
in each other's steps, doing things the same way.

19Perhaps you think we're saying these things
just to defend ourselves. No, we tell you this as
Christ's servants, and with God as our witness.
Everything we do, dear friends, is to strengthen
you. 20For I am afraid that when I come I won't
like what I find, and you won't like my response. I
am afraid that I will find quarreling, jealousy, anger, selfishness, slander, gossip, arrogance, and
disorderly behavior. 21Yes, I am afraid that when
I come again, God will humble me in your presence. And I will be grieved because many of you
have not given up your old sins. You have not

2 Corinthians 13 . . . page 1152

repented of your impurity, sexual immorality,
and eagerness for lustful pleasure.

CHAPTER 13

Paul's Final Advice

This is the third time I am coming to visit you
(and as the Scriptures say, "The facts of every
case must be established by the testimony of two
or three witnesses"). 2 I have already warned
those who had been sinning when I was there on
my second visit. Now I again warn them and all
others, just as I did before, that next time I will
not spare them.

3 I will give you all the proof you want that
Christ speaks through me. Christ is not weak
when he deals with you; he is powerful among
you. 4 Although he was crucified in weakness, he
now lives by the power of God. We, too, are weak,
just as Christ was, but when we deal with you we
will be alive with him and will have God's power.

5 Examine yourselves to see if your faith is genuine. Test yourselves. Surely you know that Jesus
Christ is among you; if not, you have failed the
test of genuine faith. 6 As you test yourselves, I
hope you will recognize that we have not failed
the test of apostolic authority.

7 We pray to God that you will not do what is
wrong by refusing our correction. I hope we
won't need to demonstrate our authority when
we arrive. Do the right thing before we come—
even if that makes it look like we have failed to
demonstrate our authority. 8 For we cannot oppose the truth, but must always stand for the
truth. 9 We are glad to seem weak if it helps show
that you are actually strong. We pray that you will
become mature.

10 I am writing this to you before I come, hoping that I won't need to deal severely with you
when I do come. For I want to use the authority
the Lord has given me to strengthen you, not to
tear you down.

Paul's Final Greetings

11 Dear brothers and sisters, I close my letter with
these last words: Be joyful. Grow to maturity. Encourage each other. Live in harmony and peace.
Then the God of love and peace will be with you.

12 Greet each other with a sacred kiss. 13 All of
God's people here send you their greetings.

14 May the grace of the Lord Jesus Christ, the
love of God, and the fellowship of the Holy Spirit
be with you all.

GALATiANS Back to Basics

Look for 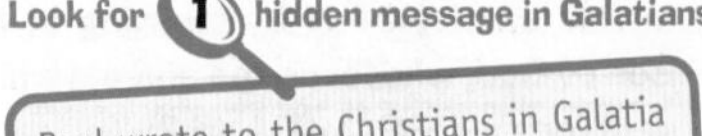 hidden message in Galatians!

Paul wrote to the Christians in Galatia to help them get rid of false teachings. Look for

- **THE ONE AND ONLY GOSPEL**
- **THE LETTER OF THE LAW**
- **FREEDOM FROM SIN**
- **SALVATION AND THE SPIRIT**

Obituaries

Paul of Tarsus is dead. At least that's what he says. Hey, wait a minute! How can he say it if he's dead? **Read Galatians 2:20 to find the answer to this mystery.**

Farmer's Market

Fruit with personality. Huh? A patient pineapple? A kind kiwi? A faithful fig? **To find out more about this attitude-changing produce, read Galatians 5:22.**

Healthy Harvest

If you plant a good seed, what do you think you'll harvest? **Dig up the whole story in Galatians 6:7-10.**

Reality Show

The Bible is the ultimate reality show! Paul didn't pull any punches when he talked about his past life. **Read Galatians 1:11-24 to find out all the details of Paul's call.**

Timeline

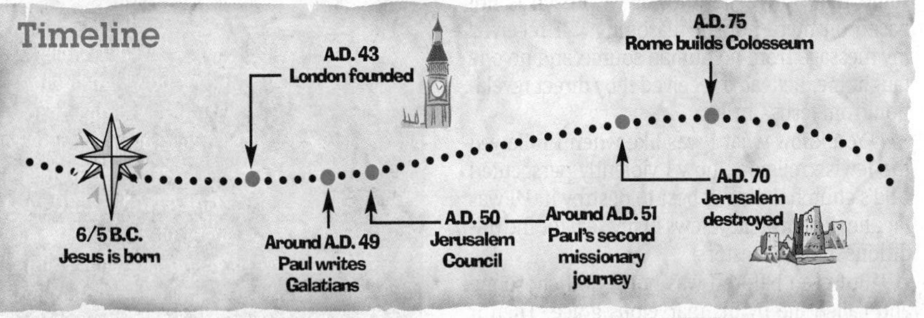

The book of Galatians shows us that our relationship with Jesus isn't about trying to be good—it's about the freedom from sin he gives us just because he loves us. When we put our faith in Jesus, he frees us from sin's enslaving power. The Holy Spirit helps us turn from temptation and do what is right. And even when we mess up, we're forgiven and free—because Jesus paid the price for our sins by dying on the cross. **Jesus really has set us free!**

CHAPTER 1

Greetings from Paul

This letter is from Paul, an apostle. I was not
appointed by any group of people or any human
authority, but by Jesus Christ himself and by God
the Father, who raised Jesus from the dead.
2All the brothers and sisters here join me in
sending this letter to the churches of Galatia.
3May God the Father and our Lord Jesus Christ
give you grace and peace. 4Jesus gave his life for
our sins, just as God our Father planned, in order
to rescue us from this evil world in which we live.
5All glory to God forever and ever! Amen.

There Is Only One Good News

6I am shocked that you are turning away so soon
from God, who called you to himself through the
loving mercy of Christ. You are following a different way that pretends to be the Good News 7but
is not the Good News at all. You are being fooled
by those who deliberately twist the truth concerning Christ.
8Let God's curse fall on anyone, including us
or even an angel from heaven, who preaches a
different kind of Good News than the one we
preached to you. 9I say again what we have said
before: If anyone preaches any other Good News
than the one you welcomed, let that person be
cursed.
10Obviously, I'm not trying to win the approval
of people, but of God. If pleasing people were my
goal, I would not be Christ's servant.

Paul's Message Comes from Christ

11Dear brothers and sisters, I want you to understand that the gospel message I preach is not
based on mere human reasoning. 12I received
my message from no human source, and no one
taught me. Instead, I received it by direct revelation from Jesus Christ.
13You know what I was like when I followed
the Jewish religion—how I violently persecuted
God's church. I did my best to destroy it. 14I was
far ahead of my fellow Jews in my zeal for the traditions of my ancestors.
15But even before I was born, God chose me
and called me by his marvelous grace. Then it
pleased him 16to reveal his Son to me so that I
would proclaim the Good News about Jesus to
the Gentiles.
When this happened, I did not rush out to consult with any human being. 17Nor did I go up to Jerusalem to consult with those who were apostles

"It is no longer I who live, but Christ lives in me. So I live in this earthly body by trusting in the Son of God, who loved me and gave himself for me."—GALATIANS 2:20

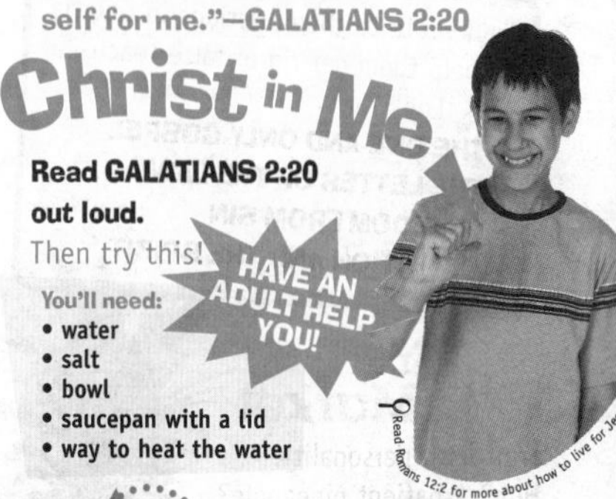

Christ in Me
HAVE AN ADULT HELP YOU!
12:2 for more about how to live for

Read GALATIANS 2:20 out loud.

Then try this!

You'll need:
- **water**
- **salt**
- **bowl**
- **saucepan with a lid**
- **way to heat the water**

1. **Add salt to the water. Take a taste. Pretty salty, huh?**
2. **Heat the water in a microwave or on the stove until the water boils.**
3. **HAVE THE ADULT remove the bowl or pan from the heat source, and put the lid on.**
4. **After 30 seconds, remove the lid. Wait until the water on the lid cools and then take a taste.**

THE SALTINESS IS GONE!

When we believe in Jesus, our sinful selves start to disappear, just like the salt disappeared.

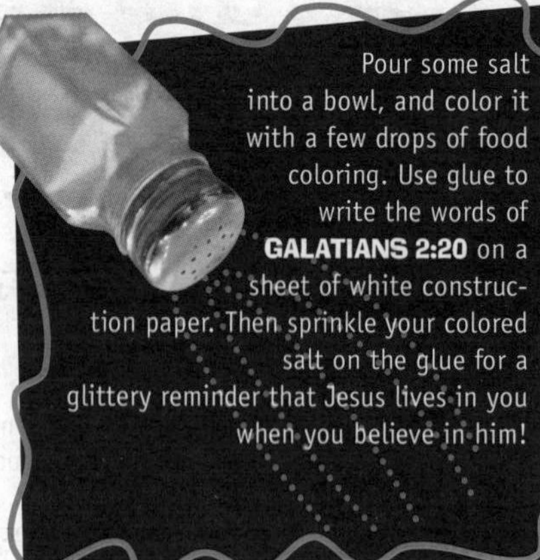

Pour some salt into a bowl, and color it with a few drops of food coloring. Use glue to write the words of **GALATIANS 2:20** on a sheet of white construction paper. Then sprinkle your colored salt on the glue for a glittery reminder that Jesus lives in you when you believe in him!

before I was. Instead, I went away into Arabia, and
later I returned to the city of Damascus.
18 Then three years later I went to Jerusalem to
get to know Peter, and I stayed with him for fifteen
days. 19 The only other apostle I met at that time
was James, the Lord's brother. 20 I declare before
God that what I am writing to you is not a lie.
21 After that visit I went north into the provinces of Syria and Cilicia. 22 And still the
churches in Christ that are in Judea didn't know
me personally. 23 All they knew was that people
were saying, "The one who used to persecute us
is now preaching the very faith he tried to destroy!" 24 And they praised God because of me.

CHAPTER 2

The Apostles Accept Paul

Then fourteen years later I went back to Jerusalem again, this time with Barnabas; and Titus
came along, too. 2 I went there because God revealed to me that I should go. While I was there I
met privately with those considered to be leaders of the church and shared with them the
message I had been preaching to the Gentiles. I
wanted to make sure that we were in agreement,
for fear that all my efforts had been wasted and I
was running the race for nothing. 3 And they supported me and did not even demand that my
companion Titus be circumcised, though he was
a Gentile.
4 Even that question came up only because of
some so-called believers there—false ones, really—who were secretly brought in. They sneaked
in to spy on us and take away the freedom we
have in Christ Jesus. They wanted to enslave us
and force us to follow their Jewish regulations.
5 But we refused to give in to them for a single
moment. We wanted to preserve the truth of the
gospel message for you.
6 And the leaders of the church had nothing to
add to what I was preaching. (By the way, their
reputation as great leaders made no difference to
me, for God has no favorites.) 7 Instead, they saw
that God had given me the responsibility of
preaching the gospel to the Gentiles, just as he
had given Peter the responsibility of preaching to
the Jews. 8 For the same God who worked through
Peter as the apostle to the Jews also worked
through me as the apostle to the Gentiles.
9 In fact, James, Peter, and John, who were
known as pillars of the church, recognized the
gift God had given me, and they accepted Barnabas and me as their co-workers. They encouraged us to keep preaching to the Gentiles, while
they continued their work with the Jews. 10 Their
only suggestion was that we keep on helping the
poor, which I have always been eager to do.

Paul Confronts Peter

11 But when Peter came to Antioch, I had to oppose him to his face, for what he did was very
wrong. 12 When he first arrived, he ate with the
Gentile believers, who were not circumcised. But
afterward, when some friends of James came,
Peter wouldn't eat with the Gentiles anymore. He
was afraid of criticism from these people who
insisted on the necessity of circumcision. 13 As a
result, other Jewish believers followed Peter's hypocrisy, and even Barnabas was led astray by their
hypocrisy.
14 When I saw that they were not following the
truth of the gospel message, I said to Peter in
front of all the others, "Since you, a Jew by birth,
have discarded the Jewish laws and are living like
a Gentile, why are you now trying to make these
Gentiles follow the Jewish traditions?
15 "You and I are Jews by birth, not 'sinners' like
the Gentiles. 16 Yet we know that a person is
made right with God by faith in Jesus Christ, not
by obeying the law. And we have believed in
Christ Jesus, so that we might be made right with
God because of our faith in Christ, not because
we have obeyed the law. For no one will ever be
made right with God by obeying the law."
17 But suppose we seek to be made right with
God through faith in Christ and then we are
found guilty because we have abandoned the
law. Would that mean Christ has led us into sin?
Absolutely not! 18 Rather, I am a sinner if I rebuild
the old system of law I already tore down. 19 For
when I tried to keep the law, it condemned me.
So I died to the law—I stopped trying to meet all
its requirements—so that I might live for God.
**20 My old self has been crucified with
Christ. It is no longer I who live, but
Christ lives in me. So I live in this
earthly body by trusting in the Son
of God, who loved me and gave him-
self for me.** 21 I do not treat the grace of God
as meaningless. For if keeping the law could
make us right with God, then there was no need
for Christ to die.

CHAPTER 3

The Law and Faith in Christ

Oh, foolish Galatians! Who has cast an evil spell
on you? For the meaning of Jesus Christ's death
was made as clear to you as if you had seen a picture of his death on the cross. 2 Let me ask you
this one question: Did you receive the Holy Spirit

by obeying the law of Moses? Of course not! You
received the Spirit because you believed the
message you heard about Christ. 3How foolish
can you be? After starting your new lives in the
Spirit, why are you now trying to become perfect
by your own human effort? 4Have you experienced so much for nothing? Surely it was not in
vain, was it?
5I ask you again, does God give you the Holy
Spirit and work miracles among you because you
obey the law? Of course not! It is because you believe the message you heard about Christ.
6In the same way, "Abraham believed God, and
God counted him as righteous because of his
faith." 7The real children of Abraham, then, are
those who put their faith in God.
8What's more, the Scriptures looked forward
to this time when God would declare the Gentiles
to be righteous because of their faith. God proclaimed this good news to Abraham long ago
when he said, "All nations will be blessed through
you." 9So all who put their faith in Christ share
the same blessing Abraham received because of
his faith.
10But those who depend on the law to make
them right with God are under his curse, for the
Scriptures say, "Cursed is everyone who does not
observe and obey all the commands that are
written in God's Book of the Law." 11So it is clear
that no one can be made right with God by trying
to keep the law. For the Scriptures say, "It is
through faith that a righteous person has life."
12This way of faith is very different from the way
of law, which says, "It is through obeying the law
that a person has life."
13But Christ has rescued us from the curse
pronounced by the law. When he was hung on
the cross, he took upon himself the curse for our
wrongdoing. For it is written in the Scriptures,
"Cursed is everyone who is hung on a tree."
14Through Christ Jesus, God has blessed the
Gentiles with the same blessing he promised to
Abraham, so that we who are believers might
receive the promised Holy Spirit through faith.

The Law and God's Promise

15Dear brothers and sisters, here's an example
from everyday life. Just as no one can set aside or
amend an irrevocable agreement, so it is in this
case. 16God gave the promises to Abraham and
his child. And notice that the Scripture doesn't
say "to his children," as if it meant many descendants. Rather, it says "to his child"—and that, of
course, means Christ. 17This is what I am trying
to say: The agreement God made with Abraham
could not be canceled 430 years later when God
gave the law to Moses. God would be breaking
his promise. 18For if the inheritance could be
received by keeping the law, then it would not be
the result of accepting God's promise. But God
graciously gave it to Abraham as a promise.
19Why, then, was the law given? It was given
alongside the promise to show people their sins.
But the law was designed to last only until the
coming of the child who was promised. God gave
his law through angels to Moses, who was the
mediator between God and the people. 20Now a
mediator is helpful if more than one party must
reach an agreement. But God, who is one, did not
use a mediator when he gave his promise to
Abraham.
21Is there a conflict, then, between God's law
and God's promises? Absolutely not! If the law
could give us new life, we could be made right
with God by obeying it. 22But the Scriptures declare that we are all prisoners of sin, so we receive
God's promise of freedom only by believing in
Jesus Christ.

God's Children through Faith

23Before the way of faith in Christ was available
to us, we were placed under guard by the law. We
were kept in protective custody, so to speak, until
the way of faith was revealed.
24Let me put it another way. The law was our
guardian until Christ came; it protected us until
we could be made right with God through faith.
25And now that the way of faith has come, we no
longer need the law as our guardian.
26For you are all children of God through faith
in Christ Jesus. 27And all who have been united
with Christ in baptism have put on Christ, like
putting on new clothes. 28There is no longer Jew
or Gentile, slave or free, male and female. For you
are all one in Christ Jesus. 29And now that you
belong to Christ, you are the true children of
Abraham. You are his heirs, and God's promise to
Abraham belongs to you.

CHAPTER 4

Think of it this way. If a father dies and leaves an
inheritance for his young children, those children are not much better off than slaves until
they grow up, even though they actually own
everything their father had. 2They have to obey
their guardians until they reach whatever age
their father set. 3And that's the way it was with us
before Christ came. We were like children; we
were slaves to the basic spiritual principles of
this world.

all MiXeD-UP

In the early church, some Jewish Christians were mixing their Jewish faith with their new Christian faith. Not only that, some of them required new Christians who weren't Jewish to follow some of the Jewish laws.

But Paul clearly pointed out (in his letter to Galatia and through other writings) **that faith in Jesus is all that is required to be a Christian**—not any rituals we can perform or traditions we can follow.

Do you ever fall into the trap of thinking that you can earn your way to heaven? **If so, read what Paul says in GALATIANS 2:16.** Then make a reminder that faith in Jesus is what really matters. You could make up a song, draw a poster, or write a poem.

4But when the right time came, God sent his
Son, born of a woman, subject to the law. 5God
sent him to buy freedom for us who were slaves
to the law, so that he could adopt us as his very
own children. 6And because we are his children,
God has sent the Spirit of his Son into our hearts,
prompting us to call out, "Abba, Father." 7Now
you are no longer a slave but God's own child.
And since you are his child, God has made you
his heir.

Paul's Concern for the Galatians

8Before you Gentiles knew God, you were slaves
to so-called gods that do not even exist. 9So now
that you know God (or should I say, now that God
knows you), why do you want to go back again
and become slaves once more to the weak and
useless spiritual principles of this world? 10You
are trying to earn favor with God by observing
certain days or months or seasons or years. 11I
fear for you. Perhaps all my hard work with you
was for nothing. 12Dear brothers and sisters, I
plead with you to live as I do in freedom from
these things, for I have become like you Gentiles—free from those laws.

You did not mistreat me when I first preached
to you. 13Surely you remember that I was sick
when I first brought you the Good News. 14But
even though my condition tempted you to reject
me, you did not despise me or turn me away. No,
you took me in and cared for me as though I were
an angel from God or even Christ Jesus himself.
15Where is that joyful and grateful spirit you felt
then? I am sure you would have taken out your
own eyes and given them to me if it had been possible.
16Have I now become your enemy because
I am telling you the truth?

17Those false teachers are so eager to win
your favor, but their intentions are not good.
They are trying to shut you off from me so that
you will pay attention only to them. 18If someone
is eager to do good things for you, that's all
right; but let them do it all the time, not just
when I'm with you.

19Oh, my dear children! I feel as if I'm going
through labor pains for you again, and they will
continue until Christ is fully developed in your
lives. 20I wish I were with you right now so I
could change my tone. But at this distance I don't
know how else to help you.

Abraham's Two Children

21Tell me, you who want to live under the law, do
you know what the law actually says? 22The
Scriptures say that Abraham had two sons, one
from his slave wife and one from his freeborn
wife. 23The son of the slave wife was born in a
human attempt to bring about the fulfillment
of God's promise. But the son of the freeborn
wife was born as God's own fulfillment of his
promise.

24These two women serve as an illustration of
God's two covenants. The first woman, Hagar,
represents Mount Sinai where people received
the law that enslaved them. 25And now Jerusalem
is just like Mount Sinai in Arabia, because
she and her children live in slavery to the law.
26But the other woman, Sarah, represents the
heavenly Jerusalem. She is the free woman, and
she is our mother. 27As Isaiah said,

"Rejoice, O childless woman,
you who have never given birth!
Break into a joyful shout,
you who have never been in labor!

For the desolate woman now has more
children
than the woman who lives with her
husband!"

28And you, dear brothers and sisters, are children of the promise, just like Isaac. 29But you are
now being persecuted by those who want you to
keep the law, just as Ishmael, the child born by
human effort, persecuted Isaac, the child born
by the power of the Spirit.
30But what do the Scriptures say about that?
"Get rid of the slave and her son, for the son of
the slave woman will not share the inheritance
with the free woman's son." 31So, dear brothers
and sisters, we are not children of the slave
woman; we are children of the free woman.

Key Verse **"But the Holy Spirit produces this kind of fruit in our lives: love, joy, peace, patience, kindness, goodness, faithfulness, gentleness, and self-control." —GALATIANS 5:22-23a**

Fruit of the Spirit

Read GALATIANS 5:22-23. Keep reading it until you can say all nine fruits of the Spirit without looking at the verse.

Find an adult, and make this Fruit of the Spirit reminder.

1. **Gather nine kinds of fruit. You could use red apples, green apples, bananas, strawberries, cantaloupe, red grapes, green grapes, pears, and pineapple.**
2. **Have an adult cut the fruit into bite-sized pieces.**
3. **Put nine different pieces of fruit on a wooden skewer to represent the fruit of the Spirit.**

Invite friends and family to a **Fruit of the Spirit Festival.** Ask God to help each of you grow more and more good fruit in your life!

CHAPTER 5
Freedom in Christ
So Christ has truly set us free. Now make sure
that you stay free, and don't get tied up again in
slavery to the law.
2Listen! I, Paul, tell you this: If you are counting
on circumcision to make you right with God,
then Christ will be of no benefit to you. 3I'll say it
again. If you are trying to find favor with God by
being circumcised, you must obey every regulation in the whole law of Moses. 4For if you are
trying to make yourselves right with God by
keeping the law, you have been cut off from
Christ! You have fallen away from God's grace.
5But we who live by the Spirit eagerly wait to
receive by faith the righteousness God has promised to us. 6For when we place our faith in Christ
Jesus, there is no benefit in being circumcised or
being uncircumcised. What is important is faith
expressing itself in love.
7You were running the race so well. Who has
held you back from following the truth? 8It certainly isn't God, for he is the one who called you to
freedom. 9This false teaching is like a little yeast
that spreads through the whole batch of dough!
10I am trusting the Lord to keep you from believing false teachings. God will judge that person,
whoever he is, who has been confusing you.
11Dear brothers and sisters, if I were still
preaching that you must be circumcised—as
some say I do—why am I still being persecuted?
If I were no longer preaching salvation through
the cross of Christ, no one would be offended. 12I
just wish that those troublemakers who want to
mutilate you by circumcision would mutilate
themselves.
13For you have been called to live in freedom,
my brothers and sisters. But don't use your freedom to satisfy your sinful nature. Instead, use
your freedom to serve one another in love. 14For
the whole law can be summed up in this one
command: "Love your neighbor as yourself."
15But if you are always biting and devouring one
another, watch out! Beware of destroying one another.

Living by the Spirit's Power
16So I say, let the Holy Spirit guide your lives.
Then you won't be doing what your sinful nature

craves. 17The sinful nature wants to do evil, which is just the opposite of what the Spirit wants. And the Spirit gives us desires that are the opposite of what the sinful nature desires. These two forces are constantly fighting each other, so you are not free to carry out your good intentions. 18But when you are directed by the Spirit, you are not under obligation to the law of Moses.

19When you follow the desires of your sinful nature, the results are very clear: sexual immorality, impurity, lustful pleasures, 20idolatry, sorcery, hostility, quarreling, jealousy, outbursts of anger, selfish ambition, dissension, division, 21envy, drunkenness, wild parties, and other sins like these. Let me tell you again, as I have before, that anyone living that sort of life will not inherit the Kingdom of God.

22But the Holy Spirit produces this kind of fruit in our lives: love, joy, peace, patience, kindness, goodness, faithfulness, 23gentleness, and self-control. There is no law against these things!

24Those who belong to Christ Jesus have nailed the passions and desires of their sinful nature to his cross and crucified them there. 25Since we are living by the Spirit, let us follow the Spirit's leading in every part of our lives. 26Let us not become conceited, or provoke one another, or be jealous of one another.

CHAPTER 6

We Harvest What We Plant

Dear brothers and sisters, if another believer is overcome by some sin, you who are godly should gently and humbly help that person back onto the right path. And be careful not to fall into the same temptation yourself. 2Share each other's burdens, and in this way obey the law of Christ. 3If you think you are too important to help someone, you are only fooling yourself. You are not that important.

4Pay careful attention to your own work, for then you will get the satisfaction of a job well done, and you won't need to compare yourself to anyone else. 5For we are each responsible for our own conduct.

6Those who are taught the word of God should provide for their teachers, sharing all good things with them.

7Don't be misled—you cannot mock the justice of God. You will always harvest what you plant. 8Those who live only to satisfy their own sinful nature will harvest decay and death from that sinful nature. But those who live to please the Spirit will harvest everlasting life from the Spirit. 9So let's not get tired of doing what is good. At just the right time we will reap a harvest of blessing if we don't give up. 10Therefore, whenever we have the opportunity, we should do good to everyone—especially to those in the family of faith.

Paul's Final Advice

11NOTICE WHAT LARGE LETTERS I USE AS I WRITE THESE CLOSING WORDS IN MY OWN HANDWRITING.

12Those who are trying to force you to be circumcised want to look good to others. They don't want to be persecuted for teaching that the cross of Christ alone can save. 13And even those who advocate circumcision don't keep the whole law themselves. They only want you to be circumcised so they can boast about it and claim you as their disciples.

14As for me, may I never boast about anything except the cross of our Lord Jesus Christ. Because of that cross, my interest in this world has been crucified, and the world's interest in me has also died. 15It doesn't matter whether we have been circumcised or not. What counts is whether we have been transformed into a new creation. 16May God's peace and mercy be upon all who live by this principle; they are the new people of God.

17From now on, don't let anyone trouble me with these things. For I bear on my body the scars that show I belong to Jesus.

18Dear brothers and sisters, may the grace of our Lord Jesus Christ be with your spirit. Amen.

EPHESIANS The Church Family

Look for 1 hidden message in Ephesians!

Ephesians is all about what it means to be part of the Christian church. It tells about

- **A NEW FAMILY**
- **NEW GIFTS**
- **NEW LIFE**
- **NEW RESPONSIBILITIES**

Gear Up, Dude!

Before you go boardin' you get geared up, right? I mean, you wouldn't ride fakie without protection! Well, God wants you to gear up too. **Go to Ephesians 6:10-17 to read about God's gear.**

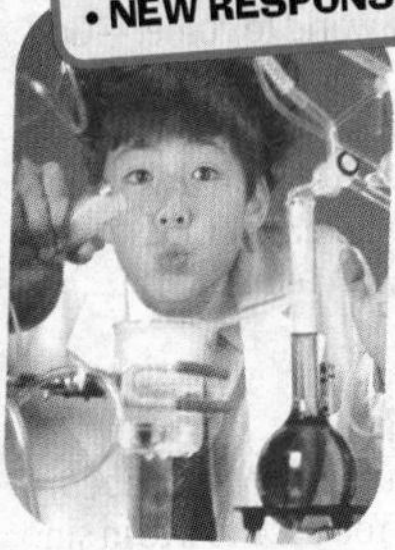

Enjoy Life—Here's How!

No, it's not a new super-vitamin. It's not a new sports drink or diet. But it *is* a proven formula to help you enjoy life. **Read Ephesians 6:1-3 to learn the secret!**

WOW! That's Deep!

Did you know that the deepest part of the ocean is 36,201 feet deep? Did you know that the highest mountain is 29,035 feet high?

And did you know that God's love for you is deeper and higher than anything? **Check out the depths of God's love in Ephesians 3:17-19!**

Best Seat in the House

Have you ever gone to a game and gotten really horrible seats? Well, good seats aren't a problem for God! He has the best seats in the house reserved for you.

Check out Ephesians 2:4-10 to find out about the seats in heaven!

Timeline

- 6/5 B.C. Jesus is born
- A.D. 50-52 Paul's second missionary trip
- About A.D. 60 Paul writes Ephesians
- A.D. 66 Painting on canvas
- A.D. 70 Jerusalem destroyed
- A.D. 74 China opens silk trade with the West

Becoming a Christian is the most important decision in your life, but it's only the first step in your relationship with God. Being a Christian means growing in Christ, following God in *everything* you do, and living for Jesus here on earth. If you've just begun your adventure with God, way to go! **But get ready, because God has so much more for you on your way to eternal life with him!**

CHAPTER 1

Greetings from Paul

This letter is from Paul, chosen by the will of God to be an apostle of Christ Jesus.

I am writing to God's holy people in Ephesus, who are faithful followers of Christ Jesus.

2May God our Father and the Lord Jesus Christ give you grace and peace.

Spiritual Blessings

3All praise to God, the Father of our Lord Jesus Christ, who has blessed us with every spiritual blessing in the heavenly realms because we are united with Christ. 4Even before he made the world, God loved us and chose us in Christ to be holy and without fault in his eyes. 5God decided in advance to adopt us into his own family by bringing us to himself through Jesus Christ. This is what he wanted to do, and it gave him great pleasure. 6So we praise God for the glorious grace he has poured out on us who belong to his dear Son. 7He is so rich in kindness and grace that he purchased our freedom with the blood of his Son and forgave our sins. 8He has showered his kindness on us, along with all wisdom and understanding.

9God has now revealed to us his mysterious plan regarding Christ, a plan to fulfill his own good pleasure. 10And this is the plan: At the right time he will bring everything together under the authority of Christ—everything in heaven and on earth. 11Furthermore, because we are united with Christ, we have received an inheritance from God, for he chose us in advance, and he makes everything work out according to his plan.

12God's purpose was that we Jews who were the first to trust in Christ would bring praise and glory to God. 13And now you Gentiles have also heard the truth, the Good News that God saves you. And when you believed in Christ, he identified you as his own by giving you the Holy Spirit, whom he promised long ago. 14The Spirit is God's guarantee that he will give us the inheritance he promised and that he has purchased us to be his own people. He did this so we would praise and glorify him.

Paul's Prayer for Spiritual Wisdom

15Ever since I first heard of your strong faith in the Lord Jesus and your love for God's people everywhere, 16I have not stopped thanking God for you. I pray for you constantly, 17asking God, the glorious Father of our Lord Jesus Christ, to give you spiritual wisdom and insight so that you might grow in your knowledge of God. 18I pray that your hearts will be flooded with light so that you can understand the confident hope he has given to those he called—his holy people who are his rich and glorious inheritance.

19I also pray that you will understand the incredible greatness of God's power for us who believe him. This is the same mighty power 20that raised Christ from the dead and seated him in the place of honor at God's right hand in the heavenly realms. 21Now he is far above any ruler or authority or power or leader or anything else—not only in this world but also in the world to come. 22God has put all things under the authority of Christ and has made him head over all things for the benefit of the church. 23And the church is his body; it is made full and complete by Christ, who fills all things everywhere with himself.

CHAPTER 2

Made Alive with Christ

Once you were dead because of your disobedience and your many sins. 2You used to live in sin, just like the rest of the world, obeying the devil—the commander of the powers in the unseen world. He is the spirit at work in the hearts of those who refuse to obey God. 3All of us used to live that way, following the passionate desires and inclinations of our sinful nature. By our very nature we were subject to God's anger, just like everyone else.

4But God is so rich in mercy, and he loved us so much, 5that even though we were dead because of our sins, he gave us life when he raised Christ from the dead. (It is only by God's grace that you have been saved!) 6For he raised us from the dead along with Christ and seated us with him in the heavenly realms because we are united with Christ Jesus. 7So God can point to us in all future ages as examples of the incredible wealth of his grace and kindness toward us, as shown in all he has done for us who are united with Christ Jesus.

8God saved you by his grace when you believed. And you can't take credit for this; it is a gift from God. 9Salvation is not a reward for the good things we have done, so none of us can boast about it. 10For we are God's masterpiece. He has created us anew in Christ Jesus, so we can do the good things he planned for us long ago.

Oneness and Peace in Christ

11Don't forget that you Gentiles used to be outsiders. You were called "uncircumcised heathens"

by the Jews, who were proud of their circumcision, even though it affected only their bodies and
not their hearts. 12In those days you were living
apart from Christ. You were excluded from citizenship among the people of Israel, and you did
not know the covenant promises God had made
to them. You lived in this world without God and
without hope. 13But now you have been united
with Christ Jesus. Once you were far away from
God, but now you have been brought near to him
through the blood of Christ.
14For Christ himself has brought peace to us.
He united Jews and Gentiles into one people
when, in his own body on the cross, he broke
down the wall of hostility that separated us. 15He
did this by ending the system of law with its commandments and regulations. He made peace between Jews and Gentiles by creating in himself
one new people from the two groups. 16Together
as one body, Christ reconciled both groups to
God by means of his death on the cross, and our
hostility toward each other was put to death.
17He brought this Good News of peace to you
Gentiles who were far away from him, and peace
to the Jews who were near. 18Now all of us can
come to the Father through the same Holy Spirit
because of what Christ has done for us.

A Temple for the Lord

19So now you Gentiles are no longer strangers
and foreigners. You are citizens along with all of
God's holy people. You are members of God's
family. 20Together, we are his house, built on the
foundation of the apostles and the prophets.
And the cornerstone is Christ Jesus himself.
21We are carefully joined together in him, becoming a holy temple for the Lord. 22Through
him you Gentiles are also being made part of this
dwelling where God lives by his Spirit.

CHAPTER 3

God's Mysterious Plan Revealed

When I think of all this, I, Paul, a prisoner of
Christ Jesus for the benefit of you Gentiles . . .
2assuming, by the way, that you know God gave
me the special responsibility of extending his
grace to you Gentiles. 3As I briefly wrote earlier,
God himself revealed his mysterious plan to me.
4As you read what I have written, you will understand my insight into this plan regarding Christ.
5God did not reveal it to previous generations,
but now by his Spirit he has revealed it to his holy
apostles and prophets.
6And this is God's plan: Both Gentiles and Jews
who believe the Good News share equally in the

Key Verse **"God saved you by his grace when you believed. And you can't take credit for this; it is a gift from God." —EPHESIANS 2:8**

It's FREE!

Read EPHESIANS 2:8 a few times until you really know it. Then write the verse in your own words below.

WOW! **Being saved is a free gift that God gives us when we believe in Jesus.** We can't earn it. We can't take credit for it. But we can *give* credit for it—to God, of course!

Write a thank you note to God, explaining how you feel about his free gift.

Now fill in your name in the verse below, so you remember that God has given this free gift to you!

"God saved ______ by his grace when ______ believed. And ______ can't take credit for this; it is a gift from God."

—EPHESIANS 2:8

riches inherited by God's children. Both are part of the same body, and both enjoy the promise of blessings because they belong to Christ Jesus. 7 By God's grace and mighty power, I have been given the privilege of serving him by spreading this Good News.

8 Though I am the least deserving of all God's people, he graciously gave me the privilege of telling the Gentiles about the endless treasures available to them in Christ. 9 I was chosen to explain to everyone this mysterious plan that God, the Creator of all things, had kept secret from the beginning.

10 God's purpose in all this was to use the church to display his wisdom in its rich variety to all the unseen rulers and authorities in the heavenly places. 11 This was his eternal plan, which he carried out through Christ Jesus our Lord.

12 Because of Christ and our faith in him, we can now come boldly and confidently into God's presence. 13 So please don't lose heart because of my trials here. I am suffering for you, so you should feel honored.

Paul's Prayer for Spiritual Growth

14 When I think of all this, I fall to my knees and pray to the Father, 15 the Creator of everything in heaven and on earth. 16 I pray that from his glorious, unlimited resources he will empower you with inner strength through his Spirit. 17 Then Christ will make his home in your hearts as you trust in him. Your roots will grow down into God's love and keep you strong. 18 And may you have the power to understand, as all God's people should, how wide, how long, how high, and how deep his love is. 19 May you experience the love of Christ, though it is too great to understand fully. Then you will be made complete with all the fullness of life and power that comes from God.

20 Now all glory to God, who is able, through his mighty power at work within us, to accomplish infinitely more than we might ask or think. 21 Glory to him in the church and in Christ Jesus through all generations forever and ever! Amen.

CHAPTER 4

Unity in the Body

Therefore I, a prisoner for serving the Lord, beg you to lead a life worthy of your calling, for you have been called by God. 2 Always be humble and gentle. Be patient with each other, making allowance for each other's faults because of your love. 3 Make every effort to keep yourselves united in the Spirit, binding yourselves together with peace. 4 For there is one body and one Spirit, just as you have been called to one glorious hope for the future.

5 There is one Lord, one faith, one baptism,
6 one God and Father of all,
who is over all, in all, and living through all.

7 However, he has given each one of us a special gift through the generosity of Christ. 8 That is why the Scriptures say,

"When he ascended to the heights,
he led a crowd of captives
and gave gifts to his people."

9 Notice that it says "he ascended." This clearly means that Christ also descended to our lowly world. 10 And the same one who descended is the one who ascended higher than all the heavens, so that he might fill the entire universe with himself.

11 Now these are the gifts Christ gave to the church: the apostles, the prophets, the evangelists, and the pastors and teachers. 12 Their responsibility is to equip God's people to do his work and build up the church, the body of Christ. 13 This will continue until we all come to such unity in our faith and knowledge of God's Son that we will be mature in the Lord, measuring up to the full and complete standard of Christ.

14 Then we will no longer be immature like children. We won't be tossed and blown about by every wind of new teaching. We will not be influenced when people try to trick us with lies so clever they sound like the truth. 15 Instead, we will speak the truth in love, growing in every way more and more like Christ, who is the head of his body, the church. 16 He makes the whole body fit together perfectly. As each part does its own special work, it helps the other parts grow, so that the whole body is healthy and growing and full of love.

Living as Children of Light

17 With the Lord's authority I say this: Live no longer as the Gentiles do, for they are hopelessly confused. 18 Their minds are full of darkness; they wander far from the life God gives because they have closed their minds and hardened their hearts against him. 19 They have no sense of shame. They live for lustful pleasure and eagerly practice every kind of impurity.

20 But that isn't what you learned about Christ. 21 Since you have heard about Jesus and have learned the truth that comes from him, 22 throw off your old sinful nature and your former way of life, which is corrupted by lust and deception.

23 Instead, let the Spirit renew your thoughts and
attitudes. 24 Put on your new nature, created to be
like God—truly righteous and holy.

25 So stop telling lies. Let us tell our neighbors
the truth, for we are all parts of the same body.
26 And "don't sin by letting anger control you."
Don't let the sun go down while you are still
angry, 27 for anger gives a foothold to the devil.

28 If you are a thief, quit stealing. Instead, use
your hands for good hard work, and then give
generously to others in need. 29 Don't use foul or
abusive language. Let everything you say be good
and helpful, so that your words will be an encouragement to those who hear them.

30 And do not bring sorrow to God's Holy Spirit
by the way you live. Remember, he has identified
you as his own, guaranteeing that you will be
saved on the day of redemption.

31 Get rid of all bitterness, rage,
anger, harsh words, and slander, as
well as all types of evil behavior. 32 In-
stead, be kind to each other,
tenderhearted, forgiving one an-
other, just as God through Christ
has forgiven you.

CHAPTER 5
Living in the Light

Imitate God, therefore, in everything you do, because you are his dear children. 2 Live a life filled
with love, following the example of Christ. He
loved us and offered himself as a sacrifice for us,
a pleasing aroma to God.

3 Let there be no sexual immorality, impurity,
or greed among you. Such sins have no place
among God's people. 4 Obscene stories, foolish
talk, and coarse jokes—these are not for you. Instead, let there be thankfulness to God. 5 You can
be sure that no immoral, impure, or greedy person will inherit the Kingdom of Christ and of
God. For a greedy person is an idolater, worshiping the things of this world.

6 Don't be fooled by those who try to excuse
these sins, for the anger of God will fall on all who
disobey him. 7 Don't participate in the things
these people do. 8 For once you were full of darkness, but now you have light from the Lord. So
live as people of light! 9 For this light within you
produces only what is good and right and true.

10 Carefully determine what pleases the Lord.
11 Take no part in the worthless deeds of evil and
darkness; instead, expose them. 12 It is shameful
even to talk about the things that ungodly people
do in secret. 13 But their evil intentions will be
exposed when the light shines on them, 14 for the
light makes everything visible. This is why it is
said,

"Awake, O sleeper,
rise up from the dead,
and Christ will give you light."

Living by the Spirit's Power

15 So be careful how you live. Don't live like fools,
but like those who are wise. 16 Make the most of
every opportunity in these evil days. 17 Don't act
thoughtlessly, but understand what the Lord
wants you to do. 18 Don't be drunk with wine,
because that will ruin your life. Instead, be filled
with the Holy Spirit, 19 singing psalms and hymns
and spiritual songs among yourselves, and making music to the Lord in your hearts. 20 And give
thanks for everything to God the Father in the
name of our Lord Jesus Christ.

Spirit-Guided Relationships: Wives and Husbands

21 And further, submit to one another out of
reverence for Christ.

22 For wives, this means submit to your husbands as to the Lord. 23 For a husband is the head
of his wife as Christ is the head of the church.
He is the Savior of his body, the church. 24 As the
church submits to Christ, so you wives should
submit to your husbands in everything.

25 For husbands, this means love your wives,
just as Christ loved the church. He gave up his
life for her 26 to make her holy and clean, washed
by the cleansing of God's word. 27 He did this to
present her to himself as a glorious church without a spot or wrinkle or any other blemish. Instead, she will be holy and without fault. 28 In the
same way, husbands ought to love their wives as
they love their own bodies. For a man who loves
his wife actually shows love for himself. 29 No
one hates his own body but feeds and cares for
it, just as Christ cares for the church. 30 And we
are members of his body.

31 As the Scriptures say, "A man leaves his father and mother and is joined to his wife, and the
two are united into one." 32 This is a great mystery, but it is an illustration of the way Christ and
the church are one. 33 So again I say, each man
must love his wife as he loves himself, and the
wife must respect her husband.

CHAPTER 6
Children and Parents

Children, obey your parents because you belong
to the Lord, for this is the right thing to do.

"Put on all of God's armor so that you will be able to stand firm against all strategies of the devil. For we are not fighting against flesh-and-blood enemies, but against evil rulers and authorities of the unseen world."— EPHESIANS 6:11-12a

Read EPHESIANS 6:11-12a out loud. Then read it again.
God gives us spiritual armor to protect us and make us stronger. Cool!

STAND Firm!

1. **Cut a big poster-board circle shield.**
2. **Cover the front of the shield with aluminum foil.**
3. **Use a permanent marker to write words from EPHESIANS 6:11-12a on your shield.**
4. **Cut a chenille wire in half, and tape it as a "handle" to the back.**

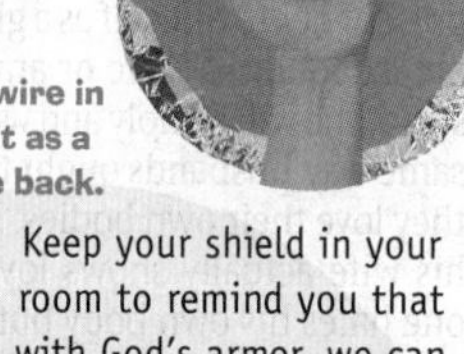

Keep your shield in your room to remind you that with God's armor, we can stand firm against the devil. **Read EPHESIANS 6:13-17 to learn more!**

SEE HOW MANY REMINDERS OF GOD'S ARMOR YOU CAN COME UP WITH.

Write **"peace"** on a pair of shoelaces to remind you that you can put on the shoes of peace.

Read Philippians 4:13 to learn more about strength from God!

2"Honor your father and mother." This is the
first commandment with a promise: 3If you
honor your father and mother, "things will go
well for you, and you will have a long life on the
earth."
4Fathers, do not provoke your children to
anger by the way you treat them. Rather, bring
them up with the discipline and instruction that
comes from the Lord.

Slaves and Masters

5Slaves, obey your earthly masters with deep respect and fear. Serve them sincerely as you
would serve Christ. 6Try to please them all the
time, not just when they are watching you. As
slaves of Christ, do the will of God with all your
heart. 7Work with enthusiasm, as though you
were working for the Lord rather than for people. 8Remember that the Lord will reward each
one of us for the good we do, whether we are
slaves or free.
9Masters, treat your slaves in the same way.
Don't threaten them; remember, you both have the
same Master in heaven, and he has no favorites.

The Whole Armor of God

10A final word: Be strong in the Lord and in his
mighty power. **11Put on all of God's armor so that you will be able to stand
firm against all strategies of the
devil. 12For we are not fighting
against flesh-and-blood enemies,
but against evil rulers and authorities of the unseen world, against
mighty powers in this dark world,
and against evil spirits in the heavenly places.**
13Therefore, put on every piece of God's armor
so you will be able to resist the enemy in the time
of evil. Then after the battle you will still be standing firm. 14Stand your ground, putting on the belt
of truth and the body armor of God's righteousness. 15For shoes, put on the peace that comes
from the Good News so that you will be fully prepared. 16In addition to all of these, hold up the
shield of faith to stop the fiery arrows of the devil.
17Put on salvation as your helmet, and take the
sword of the Spirit, which is the word of God.
18Pray in the Spirit at all times and on every
occasion. Stay alert and be persistent in your
prayers for all believers everywhere.
19And pray for me, too. Ask God to give me the
right words so I can boldly explain God's mysterious plan that the Good News is for Jews and
Gentiles alike. 20I am in chains now, still preach-

ing this message as God's ambassador. So pray that I will keep on speaking boldly for him, as I should.

Final Greetings

21 To bring you up to date, Tychicus will give you a full report about what I am doing and how I am getting along. He is a beloved brother and faithful helper in the Lord's work. 22 I have sent him to you for this very purpose—to let you know how we are doing and to encourage you.

23 Peace be with you, dear brothers and sisters, and may God the Father and the Lord Jesus Christ give you love with faithfulness. 24 May God's grace be eternally upon all who love our Lord Jesus Christ.

PHILIPPIANS A Joyful Letter

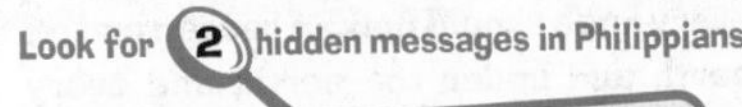
Look for 2 hidden messages in Philippians!

Philippians is the letter Paul wrote to the Christians in Philippi. It tells how to

- **GO FORWARD, EVEN WHEN YOU'RE TIRED**
- **HAVE PEACE, EVEN WHEN THINGS GO WRONG**
- **BE STRONG, EVEN WHEN YOU FEEL WEAK**
- **BE HAPPY, EVEN WHEN TIMES ARE TOUGH**

Dear Blabby

Q: I'm worried I may fail math. I'm worried about my new school. I'm worried about everything! Please help. **A: Find out how to handle worry in Philippians 4:6.**

MR. UNIVERSE
?

The *Real* Hero

He's smarter than Einstein and stronger than Mr. Universe. Yet he was born in a lowly stable, and he lived a humble life. He's the Lord of lords, yet he lived on the earth as a man. **Who is it? Find out in Philippians 2:5-11!**

Amazing Feats

According to the Guinness World Records Web site, the longest time spent on a tightrope was 205 days!

That's an amazing feat! But does it matter? *You* can do truly amazing things—things that matter and make a difference in people's lives. **Find out how by reading Philippians 4:13.**

On Your Mark, Get Set, Go...and Go, and Keep Going!

Marathon runners may win a prize, or they might not. You're in a race, and your prize is way cooler than any ribbon. **Check out this special race in Philippians 3:13-14!**

Timeline

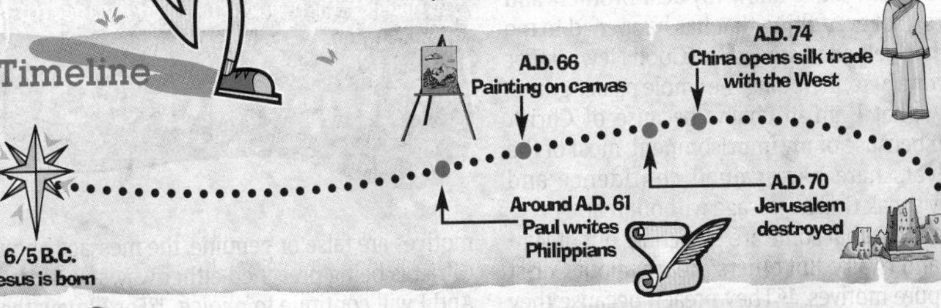
6/5 B.C.
Jesus is born
Around A.D. 61
Paul writes Philippians
A.D. 66
Painting on canvas
A.D. 70
Jerusalem destroyed
A.D. 74
China opens silk trade with the West

The JESUS CONNECTION

You may already know that becoming a Christian doesn't make all of your problems go away. In fact, following Jesus can cause problems that you otherwise wouldn't have (like standing up for what's right). But God has given us everything we need to live for him. Jesus died on the cross for our sins so that, when we believe in him, we have a friendship with God that no one can take away! **No matter what happens, we can rejoice and praise God!**

CHAPTER 1

Greetings from Paul

This letter is from Paul and Timothy, slaves of
Christ Jesus.
I am writing to all of God's holy people in Philippi who belong to Christ Jesus, including the
elders and deacons.
2May God our Father and the Lord Jesus Christ
give you grace and peace.

Paul's Thanksgiving and Prayer

3Every time I think of you, I give thanks to my God.
4Whenever I pray, I make my requests for all of
you with joy, 5for you have been my partners in
spreading the Good News about Christ from the
time you first heard it until now. 6And I am certain
that God, who began the good work within you,
will continue his work until it is finally finished on
the day when Christ Jesus returns.
7So it is right that I should feel as I do about all
of you, for you have a special place in my heart.
You share with me the special favor of God, both
in my imprisonment and in defending and confirming the truth of the Good News. 8God knows
how much I love you and long for you with the
tender compassion of Christ Jesus.
9I pray that your love will overflow more and
more, and that you will keep on growing in knowledge and understanding. 10For I want you to
understand what really matters, so that you may
live pure and blameless lives until the day of
Christ's return. 11May you always be filled with the
fruit of your salvation—the righteous character
produced in your life by Jesus Christ—for this will
bring much glory and praise to God.

Paul's Joy That Christ Is Preached

12And I want you to know, my dear brothers and
sisters, that everything that has happened to me
here has helped to spread the Good News. 13For
everyone here, including the whole palace guard,
knows that I am in chains because of Christ.
14And because of my imprisonment, most of the
believers here have gained confidence and
boldly speak God's message without fear.
15It's true that some are preaching out of jealousy and rivalry. But others preach about Christ
with pure motives. 16They preach because they
love me, for they know I have been appointed to
defend the Good News. 17Those others do not
have pure motives as they preach about Christ.
They preach with selfish ambition, not sincerely,
intending to make my chains more painful to
me. 18But that doesn't matter. Whether their
motives are false or genuine, the message about
Christ is being preached either way, so I rejoice.
And I will continue to rejoice. 19For I know that
as you pray for me and the Spirit of Jesus Christ
helps me, this will lead to my deliverance.

Paul's Life for Christ

20For I fully expect and hope that I will never be
ashamed, but that I will continue to be bold for

Key Verse "That at the name of Jesus every knee should bow, in heaven and on earth and under the earth, and every tongue confess that Jesus Christ is Lord, to the glory of God the Father." —PHILIPPIANS 2:10-11

Move It!

Find a friend, and take turns reading PHILIPPIANS 2:10-11 out loud. Then work together to make up motions to show the meaning of this verse.

HERE ARE A FEW IDEAS TO GET YOU STARTED.

Hug yourself when you say "Jesus" because Jesus loves us. **Drop to one knee** when you say "every knee should bow." **Wiggle your tongue** when you say "and every tongue confess."

Here's another verse about confessing who Jesus is—Romans 10:9.

ONCE YOU BOTH HAVE MADE UP MOTIONS, see if you can set this verse to music! Then put on a performance to teach the verse to someone else.

WAY TO GO!

Christ, as I have been in the past. And I trust that
my life will bring honor to Christ, whether I live
or die. 21For to me, living means living for Christ,
and dying is even better. 22But if I live, I can do
more fruitful work for Christ. So I really don't
know which is better. 23I'm torn between two
desires: I long to go and be with Christ, which
would be far better for me. 24But for your sakes,
it is better that I continue to live.

25Knowing this, I am convinced that I will remain alive so I can continue to help all of you
grow and experience the joy of your faith. 26And
when I come to you again, you will have even
more reason to take pride in Christ Jesus because
of what he is doing through me.

Live as Citizens of Heaven

27Above all, you must live as citizens of heaven,
conducting yourselves in a manner worthy of the
Good News about Christ. Then, whether I come
and see you again or only hear about you, I will
know that you are standing together with one
spirit and one purpose, fighting together for the
faith, which is the Good News. 28Don't be intimi-
dated in any way by your enemies. This will be a
sign to them that they are going to be destroyed,
but that you are going to be saved, even by God
himself. 29For you have been given not only the
privilege of trusting in Christ but also the privilege of suffering for him. 30We are in this struggle
together. You have seen my struggle in the past,
and you know that I am still in the midst of it.

CHAPTER 2

Have the Attitude of Christ

Is there any encouragement from belonging to
Christ? Any comfort from his love? Any fellowship together in the Spirit? Are your hearts tender and compassionate? 2Then make me truly
happy by agreeing wholeheartedly with each
other, loving one another, and working together
with one mind and purpose.

3Don't be selfish; don't try to impress others.
Be humble, thinking of others as better than
yourselves. 4Don't look out only for your own
interests, but take an interest in others, too.

5You must have the same attitude that Christ
Jesus had.

6 Though he was God,
he did not think of equality with God
as something to cling to.
7 Instead, he gave up his divine privileges;
he took the humble position of a slave
and was born as a human being.
When he appeared in human form,
8 he humbled himself in obedience to God
and died a criminal's death on a cross.
9 Therefore, God elevated him to the place
of highest honor
and gave him the name above all
other names,
**10 that at the name of Jesus every
knee should bow,
in heaven and on earth and
under the earth,
11 and every tongue declare that
Jesus Christ is Lord,
to the glory of God the Father.**

Shine Brightly for Christ

12Dear friends, you always followed my instructions when I was with you. And now that I am
away, it is even more important. Work hard to
show the results of your salvation, obeying God
with deep reverence and fear. 13For God is working in you, giving you the desire and the power to
do what pleases him.

14Do everything without complaining and arguing, 15so that no one can criticize you. Live
clean, innocent lives as children of God, shining
like bright lights in a world full of crooked and
perverse people. 16Hold firmly to the word of life;
then, on the day of Christ's return, I will be proud
that I did not run the race in vain and that my
work was not useless. 17But I will rejoice even if I
lose my life, pouring it out like a liquid offering to
God, just like your faithful service is an offering to
God. And I want all of you to share that joy. 18Yes,
you should rejoice, and I will share your joy.

Paul Commends Timothy

19If the Lord Jesus is willing, I hope to send Timothy to you soon for a visit. Then he can cheer me
up by telling me how you are getting along. 20I
have no one else like Timothy, who genuinely
cares about your welfare. 21All the others care
only for themselves and not for what matters to
Jesus Christ. 22But you know how Timothy has
proved himself. Like a son with his father, he has
served with me in preaching the Good News. 23I
hope to send him to you just as soon as I find out
what is going to happen to me here. 24And I have
confidence from the Lord that I myself will come
to see you soon.

Paul Commends Epaphroditus

25Meanwhile, I thought I should send Epaphroditus back to you. He is a true brother, co-worker,

and fellow soldier. And he was your messenger to help me in my need. 26I am sending him because he has been longing to see you, and he was very distressed that you heard he was ill. 27And he certainly was ill; in fact, he almost died. But God had mercy on him—and also on me, so that I would not have one sorrow after another.

28So I am all the more anxious to send him back to you, for I know you will be glad to see him, and then I will not be so worried about you. 29Welcome him in the Lord's love and with great joy, and give him the honor that people like him deserve. 30For he risked his life for the work of Christ, and he was at the point of death while doing for me what you couldn't do from far away.

CHAPTER 3

The Priceless Value of Knowing Christ

Whatever happens, my dear brothers and sisters, rejoice in the Lord. I never get tired of telling you these things, and I do it to safeguard your faith.

2Watch out for those dogs, those people who do evil, those mutilators who say you must be circumcised to be saved. 3For we who worship by the Spirit of God are the ones who are truly circumcised. We rely on what Christ Jesus has done for us. We put no confidence in human effort, 4though I could have confidence in my own effort if anyone could. Indeed, if others have reason for confidence in their own efforts, I have even more!

5I was circumcised when I was eight days old. I am a pure-blooded citizen of Israel and a member of the tribe of Benjamin—a real Hebrew if there ever was one! I was a member of the Pharisees, who demand the strictest obedience to the Jewish law. 6I was so zealous that I harshly persecuted the church. And as for righteousness, I obeyed the law without fault.

7I once thought these things were valuable, but now I consider them worthless because of what Christ has done. 8Yes, everything else is worthless when compared with the infinite value of knowing Christ Jesus my Lord. For his sake I have discarded everything else, counting it all as garbage, so that I could gain Christ 9and become one with him. I no longer count on my own righteousness through obeying the law; rather, I become righteous through faith in Christ. For God's way of making us right with himself depends on faith. 10I want to know Christ and experience the mighty power that raised him from the dead. I want to suffer with him, sharing in his death, 11so that one way or another I will experience the resurrection from the dead!

Pressing toward the Goal

12I don't mean to say that I have already achieved these things or that I have already reached perfection. But I press on to possess that perfection for which Christ Jesus first possessed me. 13No, dear brothers and sisters, I have not achieved it, but I focus on this one thing: Forgetting the past and looking forward to what lies ahead, 14I press on to reach the end of the race and receive the heavenly prize for which God, through Christ Jesus, is calling us.

15Let all who are spiritually mature agree on these things. If you disagree on some point, I believe God will make it plain to you. 16But we must hold on to the progress we have already made.

17Dear brothers and sisters, pattern your lives after mine, and learn from those who follow our example. 18For I have told you often before, and I say it again with tears in my eyes, that there are many whose conduct shows they are really enemies of the cross of Christ. 19They are headed for destruction. Their god is their appetite, they brag about shameful things, and they think only about this life here on earth. 20But we are citizens of heaven, where the Lord Jesus Christ lives. And we are eagerly waiting for him to return as our Savior. 21He will take our weak mortal bodies and change them into glorious bodies like his own, using the same power with which he will bring everything under his control.

CHAPTER 4

Therefore, my dear brothers and sisters, stay true to the Lord. I love you and long to see you, dear friends, for you are my joy and the crown I receive for my work.

Words of Encouragement

2Now I appeal to Euodia and Syntyche. Please, because you belong to the Lord, settle your disagreement. 3And I ask you, my true partner, to help these two women, for they worked hard with me in telling others the Good News. They worked along with Clement and the rest of my co-workers, whose names are written in the Book of Life.

4Always be full of joy in the Lord. I say it again—rejoice! 5Let everyone see that you are considerate in all you do. Remember, the Lord is coming soon.

6Don't worry about anything; instead, pray about everything. Tell God what you need, and thank him for all he has done. 7Then you will ex-

Don't Worry, Be Happy

Got life? Then you've got worries! **Read PHILIPPIANS 4:6-7** to find a way to get rid of those worries!

When you pray instead of worrying, your worries will start to melt away. It's kind of like this!

LOOK OUT! This is going to get messy!

You'll need:
- cornstarch
- water
- bowl
- spoon
- measuring spoons

1 **Mix one heaping tablespoon of cornstarch with two teaspoons of water. (Hint: You may want to do this in the sink or over a piece of newspaper.)**

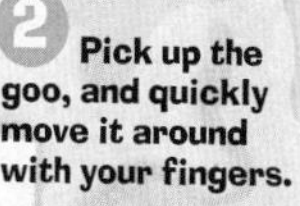

2 **Pick up the goo, and quickly move it around with your fingers.**

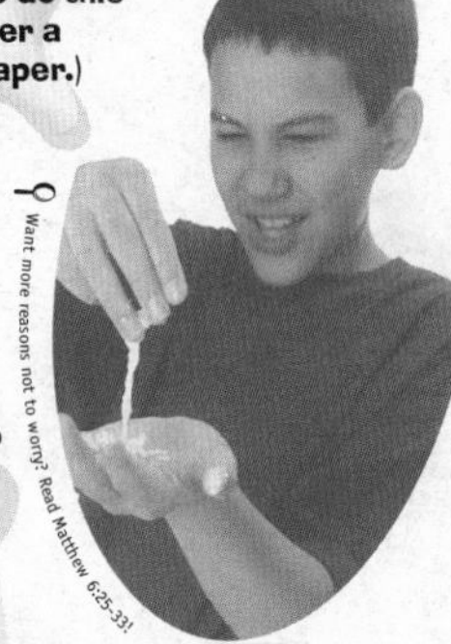

Want more reasons not to worry? Read Matthew 6:25-33!

3 **Then set the goo ball in the center of your hand.**

Imagine that this goo is something you're worried about. The more we keep trying to "handle" our fears on our own, the more anxious we become. Now stop!

See how quickly your "worries" melt when you stop trying to "handle" your problems on your own?

COOL, HUH?

Think of one thing you're worried about today. Now pray—and quit worrying!

perience God's peace, which exceeds anything
we can understand. His peace will guard your
hearts and minds as you live in Christ Jesus.
8And now, dear brothers and sisters, one final
thing. Fix your thoughts on what is true, and honorable, and right, and pure, and lovely, and admirable. Think about things that are excellent and
worthy of praise. 9Keep putting into practice all
you learned and received from me—everything
you heard from me and saw me doing. Then the
God of peace will be with you.

Paul's Thanks for Their Gifts

10How I praise the Lord that you are concerned
about me again. I know you have always been
concerned for me, but you didn't have the
chance to help me. 11Not that I was ever in need,
for I have learned how to be content with whatever I have. 12I know how to live on almost nothing or with everything. I have learned the secret
of living in every situation, whether it is with a
full stomach or empty, with plenty or little.
**13For I can do everything through
Christ, who gives me strength.** 14Even
so, you have done well to share with me in my
present difficulty.
15As you know, you Philippians were the only
ones who gave me financial help when I first
brought you the Good News and then traveled on
from Macedonia. No other church did this.
16Even when I was in Thessalonica you sent help
more than once. 17I don't say this because I want
a gift from you. Rather, I want you to receive a
reward for your kindness.
18At the moment I have all I need—and more! I
am generously supplied with the gifts you sent
me with Epaphroditus. They are a sweet-smelling
sacrifice that is acceptable and pleasing to God.
19And this same God who takes care of me will
supply all your needs from his glorious riches,
which have been given to us in Christ Jesus.
20Now all glory to God our Father forever and
ever! Amen.

Paul's Final Greetings

21Give my greetings to each of God's holy people—all who belong to Christ Jesus. The brothers
who are with me send you their greetings. 22And
all the rest of God's people send you greetings,
too, especially those in Caesar's household.
23May the grace of the Lord Jesus Christ be
with your spirit.

COLOSSIANS Doing It God's Way

Look for 1 hidden message in Colossians!

Colossians is all about being connected to Jesus. It tells about
- **WHO JESUS REALLY IS**
- **WHAT JESUS REALLY DID**
- **WHERE SIN REALLY LEADS**
- **WHAT FOLLOWING JESUS *REALLY* MEANS**

Hidden Treasure

How would it feel to find a real treasure chest, break open the lock, and lift the lid?

Guess what? There *is* a real treasure for you to find! **Read Colossians 2:2-3 to discover the treasure God has for you.**

Wanna Be a Star?

Wouldn't it be fun to be famous and sign autographs? As a Christian, you don't have to be in the spotlight. You're already being watched!

Find out who's watching in Colossians 4:5-6.

Clear the Record

Imagine that you've committed a crime but the judge offers to take the punishment himself in your place. Would you take the offer? **Find God's offer for you in Colossians 2:13-15!**

Get Dressed!

Have you ever had a dream that you go to school still wearing your pajamas? Yikes! Better get dressed. **Read Colossians 3:14 to find out what clothes God wants you to wear.**

Timeline

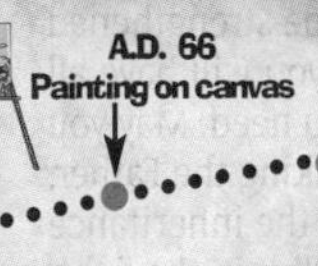

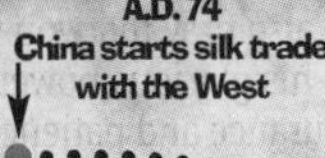

- 6/5 B.C. Jesus is born
- Around A.D. 60 Paul writes Colossians
- A.D. 66 Painting on canvas
- A.D. 70 Jerusalem destroyed
- A.D. 74 China starts silk trade with the West

Being a Christian is all about having a relationship with God through Jesus. The whole point of Jesus' death and resurrection was so sinners could come to know God and live with him forever. You can't earn your way to heaven. And as long as you believe in Jesus, your sins don't ruin your relationship with God. We need to always try to do the right thing. But remember that being a Christian means being forgiven and accepted by God. **It's a gift, not something you can earn.**

CHAPTER 1

Greetings from Paul

This letter is from Paul, chosen by the will of God
to be an apostle of Christ Jesus, and from our
brother Timothy.

2 We are writing to God's holy people in the
city of Colosse, who are faithful brothers and
sisters in Christ.

May God our Father give you grace and peace.

Paul's Thanksgiving and Prayer

3 We always pray for you, and we give thanks to
God, the Father of our Lord Jesus Christ. 4 For we
have heard of your faith in Christ Jesus and your
love for all of God's people, 5 which come from
your confident hope of what God has reserved
for you in heaven. You have had this expectation
ever since you first heard the truth of the Good
News.

6 This same Good News that came to you is
going out all over the world. It is bearing fruit
everywhere by changing lives, just as it changed
your lives from the day you first heard and
understood the truth about God's wonderful
grace.

7 You learned about the Good News from Epaphras, our beloved co-worker. He is Christ's
faithful servant, and he is helping us on your
behalf. 8 He has told us about the love for others
that the Holy Spirit has given you.

9 So we have not stopped praying for you
since we first heard about you. We ask God to
give you complete knowledge of his will and to
give you spiritual wisdom and understanding.
10 Then the way you live will always honor and
please the Lord, and your lives will produce
every kind of good fruit. All the while, you will
grow as you learn to know God better and
better.

11 We also pray that you will be strengthened
with all his glorious power so you will have all
the endurance and patience you need. May you
be filled with joy, 12 always thanking the Father.
He has enabled you to share in the inheritance
that belongs to his people, who live in the light.
13 For he has rescued us from the kingdom of
darkness and transferred us into the Kingdom
of his dear Son, 14 who purchased our freedom
and forgave our sins.

Christ Is Supreme

15 Christ is the visible image of the
invisible God.
He existed before anything was created
and is supreme over all creation,
16 for through him God created everything
in the heavenly realms and on earth.
He made the things we can see
and the things we can't see—
such as thrones, kingdoms, rulers, and
authorities in the unseen world.
Everything was created through him
and for him.
17 He existed before anything else,
and he holds all creation together.
18 Christ is also the head of the church,
which is his body.
He is the beginning,
supreme over all who rise from the dead.
So he is first in everything.
19 For God in all his fullness
was pleased to live in Christ,
20 and through him God reconciled
everything to himself.
He made peace with everything in heaven
and on earth
by means of Christ's blood on the cross.

21 This includes you who were once far away
from God. You were his enemies, separated from
him by your evil thoughts and actions. 22 Yet now
he has reconciled you to himself through the
death of Christ in his physical body. As a result,
he has brought you into his own presence, and
you are holy and blameless as you stand before
him without a single fault.

23 But you must continue to believe this truth
and stand firmly in it. Don't drift away from the
assurance you received when you heard the
Good News. The Good News has been preached
all over the world, and I, Paul, have been appointed as God's servant to proclaim it.

Paul's Work for the Church

24 I am glad when I suffer for you in my body, for
I am participating in the sufferings of Christ
that continue for his body, the church. 25 God
has given me the responsibility of serving his
church by proclaiming his entire message to
you. 26 This message was kept secret for centuries and generations past, but now it has been
revealed to God's people. 27 For God wanted
them to know that the riches and glory of Christ
are for you Gentiles, too. And this is the secret:
Christ lives in you. This gives you assurance of
sharing his glory.

28 So we tell others about Christ, warning
everyone and teaching everyone with all the wisdom God has given us. We want to present them
to God, perfect in their relationship to Christ.

29 That's why I work and struggle so hard, depending on Christ's mighty power that works
within me.

CHAPTER 2

I want you to know how much I have agonized
for you and for the church at Laodicea, and for
many other believers who have never met me
personally. 2 I want them to be encouraged and
knit together by strong ties of love. I want them
to have complete confidence that they understand God's mysterious plan, which is Christ
himself. 3 In him lie hidden all the treasures of
wisdom and knowledge.
4 I am telling you this so no one will deceive
you with well-crafted arguments. 5 For though I
am far away from you, my heart is with you. And I
rejoice that you are living as you should and that
your faith in Christ is strong.

Freedom from Rules and New Life in Christ

6 And now, just as you accepted Christ Jesus as
your Lord, you must continue to follow him. 7 Let
your roots grow down into him, and let your lives
be built on him. Then your faith will grow strong
in the truth you were taught, and you will overflow with thankfulness.
8 Don't let anyone capture you with empty phi-
losophies and high-sounding nonsense that
come from human thinking and from the spiritual powers of this world, rather than from
Christ. 9 For in Christ lives all the fullness of God
in a human body. 10 So you also are complete
through your union with Christ, who is the head
over every ruler and authority.
11 When you came to Christ, you were "circumcised," but not by a physical procedure. Christ
performed a spiritual circumcision—the cutting
away of your sinful nature. 12 For you were buried
with Christ when you were baptized. And with
him you were raised to new life because you
trusted the mighty power of God, who raised
Christ from the dead.
13 You were dead because of your sins and because your sinful nature was not yet cut away.
Then God made you alive with Christ, for he forgave all our sins. 14 He canceled the record of the
charges against us and took it away by nailing it
to the cross. 15 In this way, he disarmed
the spiritual rulers and authorities. He shamed
them publicly by his victory over them on the
cross.
16 So don't let anyone condemn you for what
you eat or drink, or for not celebrating certain

Key Verse **"And whatever you do or say, do it as a representative of the Lord Jesus, giving thanks through him to God the Father."—COLOSSIANS 3:17**

"Mirror, Mirror
on the wall, who represents Jesus to one and all?"

The answer? You!

When you believe in Jesus, you become his representative here on earth. **Read COLOSSIANS 3:17 for more on your mission!**

Whatever you do or say, you can represent Jesus.

Make this mirror to remind you that people will be looking at you, so give a good impression of Jesus!

1. **Get an inexpensive pocket or hand mirror.**
2. **Use colored permanent markers to write the words of COLOSSIANS 3:17 around the edge of the mirror.**

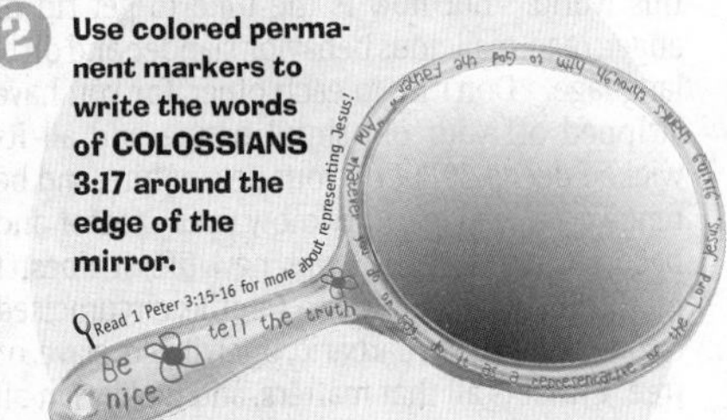

Read 1 Peter 3:15-16 for more about representing Jesus!
tell the truth
Be
nice

3. **Decorate the handle or back of the mirror with words or pictures to remind you to represent Jesus in what you say and do!**

holy days or new moon ceremonies or Sabbaths.
17 For these rules are only shadows of the reality
yet to come. And Christ himself is that reality.
18 Don't let anyone condemn you by insisting on
pious self-denial or the worship of angels, saying
they have had visions about these things. Their
sinful minds have made them proud, 19 and they
are not connected to Christ, the head of the
body. For he holds the whole body together with
its joints and ligaments, and it grows as God
nourishes it.

20You have died with Christ, and he has set
you free from the spiritual powers of this world.
So why do you keep on following the rules of
the world, such as, 21"Don't handle! Don't taste!
Don't touch!"? 22Such rules are mere human
teachings about things that deteriorate as we
use them. 23These rules may seem wise because
they require strong devotion, pious self-denial,
and severe bodily discipline. But they provide no
help in conquering a person's evil desires.

CHAPTER 3

Living the New Life

Since you have been raised to new life with
Christ, set your sights on the realities of heaven,
where Christ sits in the place of honor at God's
right hand. 2Think about the things of heaven,
not the things of earth. 3For you died to this
life, and your real life is hidden with Christ in
God. 4And when Christ, who is your life, is revealed to the whole world, you will share in all
his glory.

5So put to death the sinful, earthly things lurking within you. Have nothing to do with sexual
immorality, impurity, lust, and evil desires. Don't
be greedy, for a greedy person is an idolater,
worshiping the things of this world. 6Because of
these sins, the anger of God is coming. 7You used
to do these things when your life was still part of
this world. 8But now is the time to get rid of
anger, rage, malicious behavior, slander, and dirty
language. 9Don't lie to each other, for you have
stripped off your old sinful nature and all its
wicked deeds. 10Put on your new nature, and be
renewed as you learn to know your Creator and
become like him. 11In this new life, it doesn't
matter if you are a Jew or a Gentile, circumcised
or uncircumcised, barbaric, uncivilized, slave, or
free. Christ is all that matters, and he lives in all
of us.

12Since God chose you to be the holy people
he loves, you must clothe yourselves with tenderhearted mercy, kindness, humility, gentleness,
and patience. 13Make allowance for each other's
faults, and forgive anyone who offends you. Remember, the Lord forgave you, so you must forgive others. 14Above all, clothe yourselves with
love, which binds us all together in perfect harmony. 15And let the peace that comes from
Christ rule in your hearts. For as members of one
body you are called to live in peace. And always
be thankful.

16Let the message about Christ, in all its richness, fill your lives. Teach and counsel each other
with all the wisdom he gives. Sing psalms and
hymns and spiritual songs to God with thankful
hearts. **17And whatever you do or say,
do it as a representative of the Lord
Jesus, giving thanks through him to
God the Father.**

Instructions for Christian Households

18Wives, submit to your husbands, as is fitting
for those who belong to the Lord.

19Husbands, love your wives and never treat
them harshly.

20Children, always obey your parents, for this
pleases the Lord. 21Fathers, do not aggravate
your children, or they will become discouraged.

22Slaves, obey your earthly masters in everything you do. Try to please them all the time, not
just when they are watching you. Serve them sincerely because of your reverent fear of the Lord.
23Work willingly at whatever you do, as though
you were working for the Lord rather than for
people. 24Remember that the Lord will give you
an inheritance as your reward, and that the Master you are serving is Christ. 25But if you do what
is wrong, you will be paid back for the wrong you
have done. For God has no favorites.

CHAPTER 4

Masters, be just and fair to your slaves. Remember that you also have a Master—in heaven.

An Encouragement for Prayer

2Devote yourselves to prayer with an alert mind
and a thankful heart. 3Pray for us, too, that God
will give us many opportunities to speak about
his mysterious plan concerning Christ. That is
why I am here in chains. 4Pray that I will proclaim this message as clearly as I should.

5Live wisely among those who are not believers, and make the most of every opportunity.
6Let your conversation be gracious and attractive so that you will have the right response for
everyone.

Paul's Final Instructions and Greetings

7Tychicus will give you a full report about how I
am getting along. He is a beloved brother and
faithful helper who serves with me in the Lord's
work. 8I have sent him to you for this very purpose—to let you know how we are doing and to
encourage you. 9I am also sending Onesimus,
a faithful and beloved brother, one of your own
people. He and Tychicus will tell you everything
that's happening here.

10 Aristarchus, who is in prison with me, sends
you his greetings, and so does Mark, Barnabas's
cousin. As you were instructed before, make
Mark welcome if he comes your way. 11 Jesus (the
one we call Justus) also sends his greetings.
These are the only Jewish believers among my
co-workers; they are working with me here for
the Kingdom of God. And what a comfort they
have been!

12 Epaphras, a member of your own fellowship and a servant of Christ Jesus, sends you his
greetings. He always prays earnestly for you, asking God to make you strong and perfect, fully
confident that you are following the whole will
of God. 13 I can assure you that he prays hard for
you and also for the believers in Laodicea and
Hierapolis.

14 Luke, the beloved doctor, sends his greetings,
and so does Demas. 15 Please give my greetings to
our brothers and sisters at Laodicea, and to Nym-
pha and the church that meets in her house.

16 After you have read this letter, pass it on to
the church at Laodicea so they can read it, too.
And you should read the letter I wrote to them.

17 And say to Archippus, "Be sure to carry out
the ministry the Lord gave you."

18 HERE IS MY GREETING IN MY OWN HAND-
WRITING—PAUL.

Remember my chains.

May God's grace be with you.

1 THESSALONIANS Words of Comfort

Paul wrote a letter to the Christians in the young church he had founded in Thessalonica. That letter became this book in the Bible! Look for

- **A WARM WELCOME**
- **A REALLY GOOD REPORT**
- **A SURPRISE VISIT**
- **LESSONS FOR LIVING**

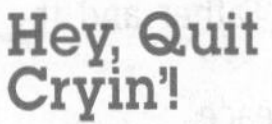

Hey, Quit Cryin'!

Funerals are sad in lots of ways. But there's something special about the funerals of believers. **Read all about it in 1 Thessalonians 4:13-18!**

Remember When...

Paul told some Christians to remember a cool thing that had happened to them. **Find out what it was in 1 Thessalonians 1:4-7.**

"KNOCK!"
"KNOCK!"
"KNOCK!"

A Surprise Visit

There's a big day coming, and it might surprise you if you're not careful. **Read all about it in 1 Thessalonians 5:1-11.**

Life Lessons

How does God want you to live? Find out! **Read Paul's advice in 1 Thessalonians 5:12-22.**

How to live your life

Timeline

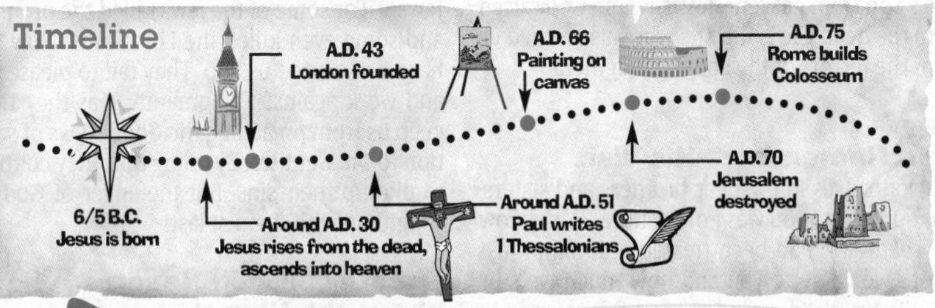
6/5 B.C. Jesus is born
Around A.D. 30 Jesus rises from the dead, ascends into heaven
A.D. 43 London founded
Around A.D. 51 Paul writes 1 Thessalonians
A.D. 66 Painting on canvas
A.D. 70 Jerusalem destroyed
A.D. 75 Rome builds Colosseum

The JESUS CONNECTION

Paul wrote to the Christians in Thessalonica to encourage them to remain strong in their faith in Jesus. He knew that it's not always easy to be a Christian—sometimes Christians are made fun of or even hurt for their beliefs. But Paul knew that believing in Jesus is the most important decision a person can ever make. **That fact was true for the Thessalonians, and it's still true for us today!**

1 Thessalonians 1 . . . page 1182

CHAPTER 1

Greetings from Paul

This letter is from Paul, Silas, and Timothy.
We are writing to the church in Thessalonica,
to you who belong to God the Father and the
Lord Jesus Christ.
May God give you grace and peace.

The Faith of the Thessalonian Believers

2We always thank God for all of you and pray
for you constantly. 3As we pray to our God and
Father about you, we think of your faithful work,
your loving deeds, and the enduring hope you
have because of our Lord Jesus Christ.
4We know, dear brothers and sisters, that God
loves you and has chosen you to be his own people. 5For when we brought you the Good News, it
was not only with words but also with power, for
the Holy Spirit gave you full assurance that what
we said was true. And you know of our concern
for you from the way we lived when we were with
you. 6So you received the message with joy from
the Holy Spirit in spite of the severe suffering it
brought you. In this way, you imitated both us
and the Lord. 7As a result, you have become an
example to all the believers in Greece—throughout both Macedonia and Achaia.
8And now the word of the Lord is ringing out
from you to people everywhere, even beyond
Macedonia and Achaia, for wherever we go we
find people telling us about your faith in God.
We don't need to tell them about it, 9for they
keep talking about the wonderful welcome you
gave us and how you turned away from idols to
serve the living and true God. 10And they speak
of how you are looking forward to the coming of
God's Son from heaven—Jesus, whom God raised
from the dead. He is the one who has rescued us
from the terrors of the coming judgment.

CHAPTER 2

Paul Remembers His Visit

You yourselves know, dear brothers and sisters,
that our visit to you was not a failure. 2You know
how badly we had been treated at Philippi just
before we came to you and how much we suffered there. Yet our God gave us the courage to
declare his Good News to you boldly, in spite of
great opposition. 3So you can see we were not
preaching with any deceit or impure motives or
trickery.
4For we speak as messengers approved by
God to be entrusted with the Good News. Our
purpose is to please God, not people. He alone
examines the motives of our hearts. 5Never once
did we try to win you with flattery, as you well
know. And God is our witness that we were not
pretending to be your friends just to get your
money! 6As for human praise, we have never
sought it from you or anyone else.
7As apostles of Christ we certainly had a right
to make some demands of you, but instead we
were like children among you. Or we were like a
mother feeding and caring for her own children. 8We loved you so much that we shared
with you not only God's Good News but our own
lives, too.
9Don't you remember, dear brothers and sisters, how hard we worked among you? Night and
day we toiled to earn a living so that we would not
be a burden to any of you as we preached God's
Good News to you. 10You yourselves are our witnesses—and so is God—that we were devout and
honest and faultless toward all of you believers.
11And you know that we treated each of you as
a father treats his own children. 12We pleaded
with you, encouraged you, and urged you to live
your lives in a way that God would consider worthy. For he called you to share in his Kingdom
and glory.
13Therefore, we never stop thanking God that
when you received his message from us, you
didn't think of our words as mere human ideas.
You accepted what we said as the very word of
God—which, of course, it is. And this word continues to work in you who believe.
14And then, dear brothers and sisters, you suffered persecution from your own countrymen.
In this way, you imitated the believers in God's
churches in Judea who, because of their belief in
Christ Jesus, suffered from their own people, the
Jews. 15For some of the Jews killed the prophets,
and some even killed the Lord Jesus. Now they
have persecuted us, too. They fail to please God
and work against all humanity 16as they try to
keep us from preaching the Good News of salvation to the Gentiles. By doing this, they continue
to pile up their sins. But the anger of God has
caught up with them at last.

Timothy's Good Report about the Church

17Dear brothers and sisters, after we were separated from you for a little while (though our
hearts never left you), we tried very hard to come
back because of our intense longing to see you
again. 18We wanted very much to come to you,
and I, Paul, tried again and again, but Satan prevented us. 19After all, what gives us hope and joy,

and what will be our proud reward and crown as
we stand before our Lord Jesus when he returns?
It is you! 20 Yes, you are our pride and joy.

CHAPTER 3

Finally, when we could stand it no longer, we decided to stay alone in Athens, 2 and we sent Timothy to visit you. He is our brother and God's coworker in proclaiming the Good News of Christ. We sent him to strengthen you, to encourage you in your faith, 3 and to keep you from being shaken by the troubles you were going through. But you know that we are destined for such troubles. 4 Even while we were with you, we warned you that troubles would soon come—and they did, as you well know. 5 That is why, when I could bear it no longer, I sent Timothy to find out whether your faith was still strong. I was afraid that the tempter had gotten the best of you and that our work had been useless.

6 But now Timothy has just returned, bringing us good news about your faith and love. He reports that you always remember our visit with joy and that you want to see us as much as we want to see you. 7 So we have been greatly encouraged in the midst of our troubles and suffering, dear brothers and sisters, because you have remained strong in your faith. 8 It gives us new life to know that you are standing firm in the Lord.

9 How we thank God for you! Because of you we have great joy as we enter God's presence. 10 Night and day we pray earnestly for you, asking God to let us see you again to fill the gaps in your faith.

11 May God our Father and our Lord Jesus bring us to you very soon. 12 And may the Lord make your love for one another and for all people grow and overflow, just as our love for you overflows. 13 May he, as a result, make your hearts strong, blameless, and holy as you stand before God our Father when our Lord Jesus comes again with all his holy people. Amen.

CHAPTER 4

Live to Please God

Finally, dear brothers and sisters, we urge you in the name of the Lord Jesus to live in a way that pleases God, as we have taught you. You live this way already, and we encourage you to do so even more. 2 For you remember what we taught you by the authority of the Lord Jesus.

3 God's will is for you to be holy, so stay away from all sexual sin. 4 Then each of you will control his own body and live in holiness and

FUN-fact

Are You Ready?

The term ***day of the Lord*** is used in both the Old and New Testaments. It means the day Jesus will come back to earth to judge sin and set up his eternal kingdom.

No one knows exactly when that day will be. But we should be ready every day for Jesus to return! Are *you* ready?

If Jesus were to come back today, what would he find in your life?

Make a list of areas in your life that need work. Every day this week, pray about those areas, asking God to help you live so that you'll be ready for Jesus' return.

Stop fighting

Don't lie

Update your list every month so your focus will stay on being ready!

honor—5 not in lustful passion like the pagans who do not know God and his ways. 6 Never harm or cheat a fellow believer in this matter by violating his wife, for the Lord avenges all such sins, as we have solemnly warned you before. 7 God has called us to live holy lives, not impure lives. 8 Therefore, anyone who refuses to live by these rules is not disobeying human teaching but is rejecting God, who gives his Holy Spirit to you.

9 But we don't need to write to you about the importance of loving each other, for God himself has taught you to love one another. 10 Indeed, you already show your love for all the believers throughout Macedonia. Even so, dear brothers and sisters, we urge you to love them even more.

11 Make it your goal to live a quiet life, minding your own business and working with your hands, just as we instructed you before. 12 Then people who are not believers will respect the way you live, and you will not need to depend on others.

1 Thessalonians 5 . . . page 1184

The Hope of the Resurrection

13 And now, dear brothers and sisters, we want
you to know what will happen to the believers
who have died so you will not grieve like people
who have no hope. 14 For since we believe that
Jesus died and was raised to life again, we also
believe that when Jesus returns, God will bring
back with him the believers who have died.

15 We tell you this directly from the Lord: We
who are still living when the Lord returns will not
meet him ahead of those who have died. 16 For
the Lord himself will come down from heaven
with a commanding shout, with the voice of the
archangel, and with the trumpet call of God.
First, the believers who have died will rise from
their graves. 17 Then, together with them, we who
are still alive and remain on the earth will be
caught up in the clouds to meet the Lord in the
air. Then we will be with the Lord forever. 18 So
encourage each other with these words.

CHAPTER 5

Now concerning how and when all this will happen, dear brothers and sisters, we don't really
need to write you. 2 For you know quite well that
the day of the Lord's return will come unexpectedly, like a thief in the night. 3 When people are
saying, "Everything is peaceful and secure," then
disaster will fall on them as suddenly as a pregnant woman's labor pains begin. And there will
be no escape.

4 But you aren't in the dark about these things,
dear brothers and sisters, and you won't be surprised when the day of the Lord comes like a
thief. 5 For you are all children of the light and of
the day; we don't belong to darkness and night.
6 So be on your guard, not asleep like the others.
Stay alert and be clearheaded. 7 Night is the time
when people sleep and drinkers get drunk. 8 But
let us who live in the light be clearheaded, protected by the armor of faith and love, and wearing
as our helmet the confidence of our salvation.

9 For God chose to save us through our Lord
Jesus Christ, not to pour out his anger on us.
10 Christ died for us so that, whether we are dead
or alive when he returns, we can live with him
forever. 11 So encourage each other and build
each other up, just as you are already doing.

Paul's Final Advice

12 Dear brothers and sisters, honor those who are
your leaders in the Lord's work. They work hard
among you and give you spiritual guidance.
13 Show them great respect and wholehearted
love because of their work. And live peacefully
with each other.

14 Brothers and sisters, we urge you to warn
those who are lazy. Encourage those who are
timid. Take tender care of those who are weak.
Be patient with everyone.

15 See that no one pays back evil for evil, but
always try to do good to each other and to all
people.

16 Always be joyful. 17 Never stop praying. 18 Be
thankful in all circumstances, for this is God's
will for you who belong to Christ Jesus.

19 Do not stifle the Holy Spirit. 20 Do not scoff
at prophecies, 21 but test everything that is said.
Hold on to what is good. 22 Stay away from every
kind of evil.

Paul's Final Greetings

23 Now may the God of peace make you holy in
every way, and may your whole spirit and soul
and body be kept blameless until our Lord Jesus
Christ comes again. 24 God will make this happen, for he who calls you is faithful.

25 Dear brothers and sisters, pray for us.

26 Greet all the brothers and sisters with a sacred kiss.

27 I command you in the name of the Lord to
read this letter to all the brothers and sisters.

28 May the grace of our Lord Jesus Christ be
with you.

2 THESSALONIANS A Call to Courage

Paul wrote a second letter to the Christians in Thessalonica. And *that* letter became *this* book in the Bible. Look for

- **A PERSECUTION PROMISE**
- **TOUGH TALK ABOUT TIME**
- **A PLEA FOR PRAYER**
- **THE WISDOM OF WORK**

It's About Time

This. Then that. And this.

Paul said that certain events would take place before Jesus would come back to earth. **Read 2 Thessalonians 2:3-12 for the clues Paul gave.**

Prayers, Please

Have you ever asked someone else to pray for you? Paul did. **Read his prayer requests in 2 Thessalonians 3:1-5, and compare them to your prayer requests!**

Get to Work!

Work? Me?

Some Christians had it all wrong when it came to work. **Find out why in 2 Thessalonians 3:6-15.**

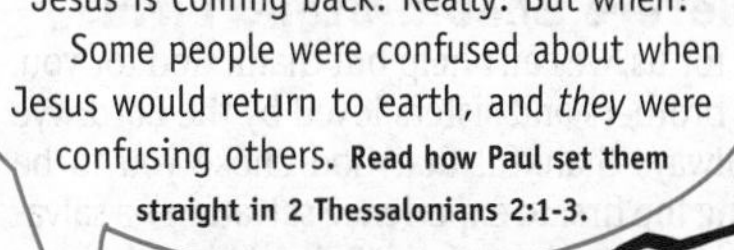

Don't Be Fooled

Jesus is coming back! Really! But when?

Some people were confused about when Jesus would return to earth, and *they* were confusing others. **Read how Paul set them straight in 2 Thessalonians 2:1-3.**

Timeline

6/5 B.C. Jesus is born
A.D. 43 London founded
Around A.D. 30 Jesus rises from the dead, ascends into heaven
Around A.D. 51 Paul writes 1 Thessalonians
Around A.D. 51 or 52 Paul writes 2 Thessalonians
A.D. 64 Fire burns much of Rome
A.D. 66 Painting on canvas
A.D. 75 Rome builds Colosseum

The JESUS CONNECTION

As Christians, we know that Jesus will come back to earth some day. But we don't know exactly when that great day will be. The Christians in Thessalonica didn't know when Jesus would come back, either. Paul's advice to those Christians is good advice for us, too. **Don't listen to rumors; stand firm in your faith; pray for strength; tell others about Jesus; and live in a way that's pleasing to God.**

2 Thessalonians 1 . . . page 1186

CHAPTER 1
Greetings from Paul
This letter is from Paul, Silas, and Timothy.
We are writing to the church in Thessalonica,
to you who belong to God our Father and the
Lord Jesus Christ.
2May God our Father and the Lord Jesus Christ
give you grace and peace.

Encouragement during Persecution
3Dear brothers and sisters, we can't help but
thank God for you, because your faith is flourishing and your love for one another is growing.
4We proudly tell God's other churches about
your endurance and faithfulness in all the persecutions and hardships you are suffering. 5And
God will use this persecution to show his justice
and to make you worthy of his Kingdom, for
which you are suffering. 6In his justice he will
pay back those who persecute you.
7And God will provide rest for you who are being persecuted and also for us when the Lord
Jesus appears from heaven. He will come with
his mighty angels, 8in flaming fire, bringing
judgment on those who don't know God and on
those who refuse to obey the Good News of our
Lord Jesus. 9They will be punished with eternal
destruction, forever separated from the Lord and
from his glorious power. 10When he comes on
that day, he will receive glory from his holy people—praise from all who believe. And this includes you, for you believed what we told you
about him.
11So we keep on praying for you, asking our
God to enable you to live a life worthy of his call.
May he give you the power to accomplish all the
good things your faith prompts you to do.
12Then the name of our Lord Jesus will be honored because of the way you live, and you will be
honored along with him. This is all made possible because of the grace of our God and Lord,
Jesus Christ.

CHAPTER 2
Events prior to the Lord's Second Coming
Now, dear brothers and sisters, let us clarify
some things about the coming of our Lord Jesus
Christ and how we will be gathered to meet him.
2Don't be so easily shaken or alarmed by those
who say that the day of the Lord has already begun. Don't believe them, even if they claim to
have had a spiritual vision, a revelation, or a letter supposedly from us. 3Don't be fooled by
what they say. For that day will not come until
there is a great rebellion against God and the
man of lawlessness is revealed—the one who
brings destruction. 4He will exalt himself and
defy everything that people call god and every
object of worship. He will even sit in the temple
of God, claiming that he himself is God.
5Don't you remember that I told you about all
this when I was with you? 6And you know what is
holding him back, for he can be revealed only
when his time comes. 7For this lawlessness is already at work secretly, and it will remain secret
until the one who is holding it back steps out of
the way. 8Then the man of lawlessness will be
revealed, but the Lord Jesus will kill him with the
breath of his mouth and destroy him by the
splendor of his coming.
9This man will come to do the work of Satan
with counterfeit power and signs and miracles.
10He will use every kind of evil deception to fool
those on their way to destruction, because they
refuse to love and accept the truth that would
save them. 11So God will cause them to be greatly
deceived, and they will believe these lies. 12Then
they will be condemned for enjoying evil rather
than believing the truth.

Believers Should Stand Firm
13As for us, we can't help but thank God for you,
dear brothers and sisters loved by the Lord. We
are always thankful that God chose you to be
among the first to experience salvation—a salvation that came through the Spirit who makes you
holy and through your belief in the truth. 14He
called you to salvation when we told you the
Good News; now you can share in the glory of our
Lord Jesus Christ.
15With all these things in mind, dear brothers
and sisters, stand firm and keep a strong grip on
the teaching we passed on to you both in person
and by letter.
16Now may our Lord Jesus Christ himself and
God our Father, who loved us and by his grace
gave us eternal comfort and a wonderful hope,
17comfort you and strengthen you in every good
thing you do and say.

CHAPTER 3
Paul's Request for Prayer
Finally, dear brothers and sisters, we ask you to
pray for us. Pray that the Lord's message will
spread rapidly and be honored wherever it goes,
just as when it came to you. 2Pray, too, that we
will be rescued from wicked and evil people, for
not everyone is a believer. 3But the Lord is faith-

ful; he will strengthen you and guard you from
the evil one. [4]And we are confident in the Lord
that you are doing and will continue to do the
things we commanded you. [5]May the Lord lead
your hearts into a full understanding and expression of the love of God and the patient
endurance that comes from Christ.

An Exhortation to Proper Living

[6]And now, dear brothers and sisters, we give you
this command in the name of our Lord Jesus
Christ: Stay away from all believers who live idle
lives and don't follow the tradition they received
from us. [7]For you know that you ought to imitate
us. We were not idle when we were with you. [8]We
never accepted food from anyone without paying
for it. We worked hard day and night so we would
not be a burden to any of you. [9]We certainly had
the right to ask you to feed us, but we wanted to
give you an example to follow. [10]Even while we
were with you, we gave you this command: "Those
unwilling to work will not get to eat."

[11]Yet we hear that some of you are living idle
lives, refusing to work and meddling in other
people's business. [12]We command such people
and urge them in the name of the Lord Jesus
Christ to settle down and work to earn their own
living. [13]As for the rest of you, dear brothers and
sisters, never get tired of doing good.

[14]Take note of those who refuse to obey what
we say in this letter. Stay away from them so they
will be ashamed. [15]Don't think of them as enemies, but warn them as you would a brother or
sister.

Paul's Final Greetings

[16]Now may the Lord of peace himself give you
his peace at all times and in every situation. The
Lord be with you all.

[17]HERE IS MY GREETING IN MY OWN HAND-
WRITING—PAUL. I DO THIS IN ALL MY LETTERS TO
PROVE THEY ARE FROM ME.

[18]May the grace of our Lord Jesus Christ be
with you all.

1 TiMoTHY A Letter to a Young Leader

Look for 1 hidden message in 1 Timothy!

Paul wrote a letter to his young friend Timothy, whom he had sent to lead the church in the city of Ephesus. Look for

- CANDID CONFESSIONS
- GETTING RIGHT WITH GOD
- LEARNING TO LEAD
- MINDING YOUR MONEY

Help Wanted

Think you have what it takes to be a leader? a church leader? Well, you'll have to meet certain standards. **Read 1 Timothy 3:1-13 to see what they are.**

True Confessions

BIBLE TIMES
I WAS WRONG!

Paul wasn't afraid to admit he had been wrong. In fact, the more he talked about it, the more thankful he was. Why? **Find out in 1 Timothy 1:12-17.**

True Riches?

News flash—money may be bad for your health! **Find out why in 1 Timothy 6:6-10.**

One Way, OK?

GO GOD

There's only one way to get right with God, and Paul knew what it was. **You can discover it in 1 Timothy 2:1-6!**

Timeline

- 6/5 B.C. Jesus is born
- Around A.D. 30 Jesus rises from the dead, ascends into heaven
- A.D. 43 London founded
- Around A.D. 51 Paul writes 1 Thessalonians
- Around A.D. 64 Paul writes 1 Timothy
- A.D. 66 Painting on canvas
- A.D. 79 Mount Vesuvius erupts in Italy

Paul told Timothy that, even though he was young, God could use Timothy in a big way. It doesn't matter how old you are or how long you've been a Christian—God has good works prepared for you to do. Take a lesson from Timothy. Listen to the advice of older, more experienced Christians; pray; and trust the Holy Spirit to help you. You can be an example and lead others to Jesus. **Who could ask for a better job?**

CHAPTER 1

Greetings from Paul

This letter is from Paul, an apostle of Christ Jesus,
appointed by the command of God our Savior
and Christ Jesus, who gives us hope.
2I am writing to Timothy, my true son in the
faith.

May God the Father and Christ Jesus our Lord
give you grace, mercy, and peace.

Warnings against False Teachings

3When I left for Macedonia, I urged you to stay
there in Ephesus and stop those whose teaching
is contrary to the truth. 4Don't let them waste
their time in endless discussion of myths and
spiritual pedigrees. These things only lead to
meaningless speculations, which don't help people live a life of faith in God.
5The purpose of my instruction is that all believers would be filled with love that comes from
a pure heart, a clear conscience, and genuine
faith. 6But some people have missed this whole
point. They have turned away from these things
and spend their time in meaningless discussions.
7They want to be known as teachers of the law of
Moses, but they don't know what they are talking
about, even though they speak so confidently.
8We know that the law is good when used
correctly. 9For the law was not intended for
people who do what is right. It is for people who
are lawless and rebellious, who are ungodly and
sinful, who consider nothing sacred and defile
what is holy, who kill their father or mother or
commit other murders. 10The law is for people
who are sexually immoral, or who practice
homosexuality, or are slave traders, liars, promise breakers, or who do anything else that con-
tradicts the wholesome teaching 11that comes
from the glorious Good News entrusted to me
by our blessed God.

Paul's Gratitude for God's Mercy

12I thank Christ Jesus our Lord, who has given
me strength to do his work. He considered me
trustworthy and appointed me to serve him,
13even though I used to blaspheme the name of
Christ. In my insolence, I persecuted his people.
But God had mercy on me because I did it in
ignorance and unbelief. 14Oh, how generous
and gracious our Lord was! He filled me with the
faith and love that come from Christ Jesus.
15This is a trustworthy saying, and everyone
should accept it: "Christ Jesus came into the world
to save sinners"—and I am the worst of them all.
16But God had mercy on me so that Christ Jesus
could use me as a prime example of his great patience with even the worst sinners. Then others
will realize that they, too, can believe in him and
receive eternal life. 17All honor and glory to God
forever and ever! He is the eternal King, the unseen one who never dies; he alone is God. Amen.

Timothy's Responsibility

18Timothy, my son, here are my instructions for
you, based on the prophetic words spoken about
you earlier. May they help you fight well in the
Lord's battles. 19Cling to your faith in Christ, and
keep your conscience clear. For some people
have deliberately violated their consciences; as a
result, their faith has been shipwrecked. 20Hy-
menaeus and Alexander are two examples. I
threw them out and handed them over to Satan
so they might learn not to blaspheme God.

CHAPTER 2

Instructions about Worship

I urge you, first of all, to pray for all people. Ask
God to help them; intercede on their behalf, and
give thanks for them. 2Pray this way for kings
and all who are in authority so that we can live
peaceful and quiet lives marked by godliness
and dignity. 3This is good and pleases God our
Savior, 4who wants everyone to be saved and to
understand the truth. **5For,**

> **There is one God and one**
> **Mediator who can reconcile**
> **God and humanity—the man**
> **Christ Jesus.** 6He gave his life to
> purchase freedom for everyone.

This is the message God gave to the world at just
the right time. 7And I have been chosen as a
preacher and apostle to teach the Gentiles this
message about faith and truth. I'm not exagger-
ating—just telling the truth.
8In every place of worship, I want men to pray
with holy hands lifted up to God, free from anger
and controversy.
9And I want women to be modest in their appearance. They should wear decent and appropriate clothing and not draw attention to
themselves by the way they fix their hair or by
wearing gold or pearls or expensive clothes.
10For women who claim to be devoted to God
should make themselves attractive by the good
things they do.
11Women should learn quietly and submis-
sively. 12I do not let women teach men or have

Key Verse "For there is only one God and one Mediator who can reconcile God and humanity—the man Christ Jesus." —1 TIMOTHY 2:5

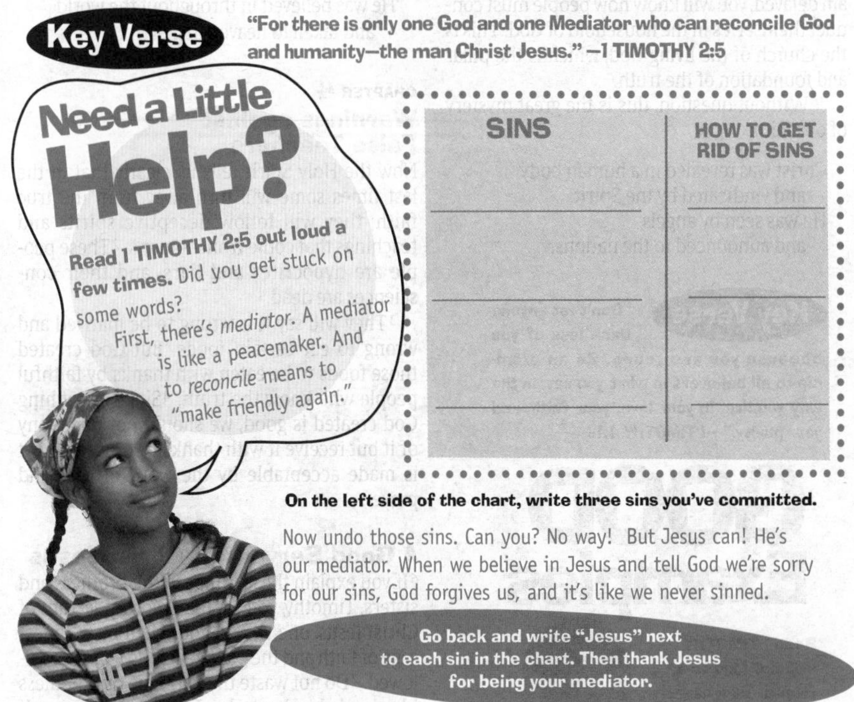

Need a Little Help?
Read 1 TIMOTHY 2:5 out loud a few times. Did you get stuck on some words?
First, there's *mediator*. A mediator is like a peacemaker. And to *reconcile* means to "make friendly again."
SINS
HOW TO GET RID OF SINS

On the left side of the chart, write three sins you've committed.

Now undo those sins. Can you? No way! But Jesus can! He's our mediator. When we believe in Jesus and tell God we're sorry for our sins, God forgives us, and it's like we never sinned.

Go back and write "Jesus" next to each sin in the chart. Then thank Jesus for being your mediator.

authority over them. Let them listen quietly.
13For God made Adam first, and afterward he
made Eve. 14And it was not Adam who was deceived by Satan. The woman was deceived, and
sin was the result. 15But women will be saved
through childbearing, assuming they continue
to live in faith, love, holiness, and modesty.

CHAPTER 3
Leaders in the Church

This is a trustworthy saying: "If someone aspires
to be an elder, he desires an honorable position."
2So an elder must be a man whose life is above
reproach. He must be faithful to his wife. He
must exercise self-control, live wisely, and have a
good reputation. He must enjoy having guests in
his home, and he must be able to teach. 3He must
not be a heavy drinker or be violent. He must
be gentle, not quarrelsome, and not love money.
4He must manage his own family well, having
children who respect and obey him. 5For if a
man cannot manage his own household, how
can he take care of God's church?

6An elder must not be a new believer, because
he might become proud, and the devil would
cause him to fall. 7Also, people outside the
church must speak well of him so that he will not
be disgraced and fall into the devil's trap.

8In the same way, deacons must be well respected and have integrity. They must not be
heavy drinkers or dishonest with money. 9They
must be committed to the mystery of the faith
now revealed and must live with a clear conscience. 10Before they are appointed as deacons,
let them be closely examined. If they pass the
test, then let them serve as deacons.

11In the same way, their wives must be respected and must not slander others. They must
exercise self-control and be faithful in everything they do.

12A deacon must be faithful to his wife, and
he must manage his children and household
well. 13Those who do well as deacons will be rewarded with respect from others and will have
increased confidence in their faith in Christ
Jesus.

The Truths of Our Faith

14I am writing these things to you now, even
though I hope to be with you soon, 15so that if I

am delayed, you will know how people must conduct themselves in the household of God. This is
the church of the living God, which is the pillar
and foundation of the truth.
16Without question, this is the great mystery
of our faith:

Christ was revealed in a human body
and vindicated by the Spirit.
He was seen by angels
and announced to the nations.
He was believed in throughout the world
and taken to heaven in glory.

Key Verse **"Don't let anyone think less of you because you are young. Be an example to all believers in what you say, in the way you live, in your love, your faith, and your purity." —1 TIMOTHY 4:12**

GOOD Examples

Read 1 TIMOTHY 4:12 out loud to a friend. Then have your friend read it to you. Then read it together!

Read more about being a good example in 1 Peter 4:10-11.

WOW! YOU CAN BE GREAT EXAMPLES!

Here's a way to get started.

Faith

Love

life

Write **"speech," "life," "love," "faith,"** and **"purity"** on cards. Put the cards in a bag. With your friend, take turns picking a card and acting out a situation where you can be a good example of what's on the card.

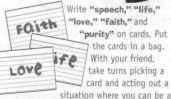

During the coming weeks, keep track of the ways you've been an example to others. **ASK GOD TO HELP YOU BE A GOOD EXAMPLE EVERY DAY!**

CHAPTER 4
Warnings against False Teachers

Now the Holy Spirit tells us clearly that in the
last times some will turn away from the true
faith; they will follow deceptive spirits and
teachings that come from demons. 2These people are hypocrites and liars, and their consciences are dead.
3They will say it is wrong to be married and
wrong to eat certain foods. But God created
those foods to be eaten with thanks by faithful
people who know the truth. 4Since everything
God created is good, we should not reject any
of it but receive it with thanks. 5For we know it
is made acceptable by the word of God and
prayer.

A Good Servant of Christ Jesus

6If you explain these things to the brothers and
sisters, Timothy, you will be a worthy servant of
Christ Jesus, one who is nourished by the message of faith and the good teaching you have followed. 7Do not waste time arguing over godless
ideas and old wives' tales. Instead, train yourself
to be godly. 8"Physical training is good, but
training for godliness is much better, promising
benefits in this life and in the life to come."
9This is a trustworthy saying, and everyone
should accept it. 10This is why we work hard and
continue to struggle, for our hope is in the living
God, who is the Savior of all people and particu-
larly of all believers.
11Teach these things and insist that everyone
learn them. **12Don't let anyone think less
of you because you are young. Be an
example to all believers in what you
say, in the way you live, in your love,
your faith, and your purity.** 13Until I get
there, focus on reading the Scriptures to the
church, encouraging the believers, and teaching
them.
14Do not neglect the spiritual gift you received
through the prophecy spoken over you when the
elders of the church laid their hands on you.
15Give your complete attention to these matters.
Throw yourself into your tasks so that everyone
will see your progress. 16Keep a close watch on
how you live and on your teaching. Stay true to
what is right for the sake of your own salvation
and the salvation of those who hear you.

THE DISCIPLES' INNER CIRCLE *(former fishermen)*

Hi! Our names are Simon Peter, James, and John. Just so you don't get confused, I'm James. I'm writing this on behalf of the three of us. We're just simple fishermen. Well, that's what we were before we met Jesus! Since then we've been fishers-for-men. Jesus came by the lake where we were cleaning our fishing nets one day, and we dropped everything and followed him.

Want to know more about Jesus' calling of Peter, James, and John? Read the whole story in LUKE 5:1-11.

Peter was the most outspoken one among us and really became the leader of the whole batch. Peter made some bold statements, but he did his share of wrong things, just like the rest of us.

For one of Peter's bold and accurate statements, read MATTHEW 16:13-20. For one of his slightly misdirected bold statements, read MATTHEW 16:21-23.

Speaking of mistakes, the one that John and I are most known for is based on our misunderstanding of how Jesus' kingdom was going to work. We thought he had come to earth to set up a new kingdom where he would rule right then and there, getting rid of all our enemies. Unfortunately, we acted on that mistaken notion and asked Jesus if we could be his right- and left-hand men! Not only was Jesus unhappy with us about that request, but so were the other disciples! Jesus made it clear that his kingdom was not going to be like that at all. He said if we wanted to be great, we had to be servants. Boy, that sure wasn't what we had in mind!

Peter's biggest blunder was denying that he knew Jesus—not once, but three times—on the night Jesus was arrested. Jesus had predicted that Peter would deny him, but Peter never believed it would happen. When he realized what he had done, Peter was so sad and upset. But Jesus forgave him.

BLUNDERS OF YOUR OWN?

TURN THE PAGE TO FIND OUT MORE ABOUT THE REST OF THE DISCIPLES!

Do you know how to be forgiven?

Just believe in Jesus, admit the wrong things you've done, and ask for forgiveness.

Write on a slip of paper any sins you haven't asked forgiveness for. Then ask God to forgive you and to help you avoid those sins in the future. Then throw those sins in the wastebasket! **Why? Because you're forgiven! That's why.**

BIBLE BIOS

Hear From the Heroes

THE TWELVE *(fishermen, tax collectors, regular guys)*

We're "the Twelve," better known as Jesus' disciples or apostles.

Our lives were very different before Jesus called us to follow him. Some of us were commercial fishermen, and Matthew was a tax collector. We weren't a high-class bunch. Even Peter and John, who were kind of the leaders among us, were considered to be uneducated, ordinary men.

You can find our names by reading MATTHEW 10:2-4; MARK 3:14-19; LUKE 6:13-16. (The lists are a little different. That's because some of us were known by two different names.)

One of our best-known but most-ashamed-of "feats" was how we deserted Jesus the night he was arrested. We had pretty much lived with Jesus for three years. We had heard him teach. We had seen him live a perfect, sinless life. We had seen him perform miracles. We had even heard him predict that he would die and then rise from the dead. But we still didn't get it.

And then Jesus rose from the dead. Even when we saw the empty tomb, we were confused; we *still* didn't get it. But Jesus didn't give up on us, even after that! He let us see that he was really alive, and then he forgave us. We were so excited about what had happened that we couldn't stop telling people about Jesus! And when the Holy Spirit came to us at Pentecost, God empowered us to spread the news about Jesus to many nations!

What happened at Pentecost was really exciting! Read all about it in ACTS 2:1-47.

From that point on, we got it! So we spent the rest of our lives telling everyone we met about Jesus.

PRESSING ON

Do you ever find yourself embarrassed to be a Christian or afraid to speak up for your faith?

Read ACTS 4:1-31 and think about how you can stand up for Jesus in your life. Journal your thoughts and pray, asking God to help you be faithful to him. Then write a script of what you can tell others about Jesus. Practice your script with a friend, then commit to telling three other people about Jesus this week.

Then tell!

Oh, oh, me, me, me! Let me tell!!!

CHAPTER 5

Advice about Widows, Elders, and Slaves

Never speak harshly to an older man, but appeal to him respectfully as you would to your own father. Talk to younger men as you would to your own brothers. 2 Treat older women as you would your mother, and treat younger women with all purity as you would your own sisters.

3 Take care of any widow who has no one else to care for her. 4 But if she has children or grandchildren, their first responsibility is to show godliness at home and repay their parents by taking care of them. This is something that pleases God.

5 Now a true widow, a woman who is truly alone in this world, has placed her hope in God. She prays night and day, asking God for his help. 6 But the widow who lives only for pleasure is spiritually dead even while she lives. 7 Give these instructions to the church so that no one will be open to criticism.

8 But those who won't care for their relatives, especially those in their own household, have denied the true faith. Such people are worse than unbelievers.

9 A widow who is put on the list for support must be a woman who is at least sixty years old and was faithful to her husband. 10 She must be well respected by everyone because of the good she has done. Has she brought up her children well? Has she been kind to strangers and served other believers humbly? Has she helped those who are in trouble? Has she always been ready to do good?

11 The younger widows should not be on the list, because their physical desires will overpower their devotion to Christ and they will want to remarry. 12 Then they would be guilty of breaking their previous pledge. 13 And if they are on the list, they will learn to be lazy and will spend their time gossiping from house to house, meddling in other people's business and talking about things they shouldn't. 14 So I advise these younger widows to marry again, have children, and take care of their own homes. Then the enemy will not be able to say anything against them. 15 For I am afraid that some of them have already gone astray and now follow Satan.

16 If a woman who is a believer has relatives who are widows, she must take care of them and not put the responsibility on the church. Then the church can care for the widows who are truly alone.

17 Elders who do their work well should be respected and paid well, especially those who work hard at both preaching and teaching. 18 For the Scripture says, "You must not muzzle an ox to keep it from eating as it treads out the grain." And in another place, "Those who work deserve their pay!"

19 Do not listen to an accusation against an elder unless it is confirmed by two or three witnesses. 20 Those who sin should be reprimanded in front of the whole church; this will serve as a strong warning to others.

21 I solemnly command you in the presence of God and Christ Jesus and the highest angels to obey these instructions without taking sides or showing favoritism to anyone.

22 Never be in a hurry about appointing a church leader. Do not share in the sins of others. Keep yourself pure.

23 Don't drink only water. You ought to drink a little wine for the sake of your stomach because you are sick so often.

24 Remember, the sins of some people are obvious, leading them to certain judgment. But there are others whose sins will not be revealed until later. 25 In the same way, the good deeds of some people are obvious. And the good deeds done in secret will someday come to light.

CHAPTER 6

All slaves should show full respect for their masters so they will not bring shame on the name of God and his teaching. 2 If the masters are believers, that is no excuse for being disrespectful. Those slaves should work all the harder because their efforts are helping other believers who are well loved.

False Teaching and True Riches

Teach these things, Timothy, and encourage everyone to obey them. 3 Some people may contradict our teaching, but these are the wholesome teachings of the Lord Jesus Christ. These teachings promote a godly life. 4 Anyone who teaches something different is arrogant and lacks understanding. Such a person has an unhealthy desire to quibble over the meaning of words. This stirs up arguments ending in jealousy, division, slander, and evil suspicions. 5 These people always cause trouble. Their minds are corrupt, and they have turned their backs on the truth. To them, a show of godliness is just a way to become wealthy.

6 Yet true godliness with contentment is itself great wealth. 7 After all, we brought nothing with

us when we came into the world, and we can't
take anything with us when we leave it. 8So if we
have enough food and clothing, let us be content.
9But people who long to be rich fall into temptation and are trapped by many foolish and
harmful desires that plunge them into ruin and
destruction. 10For the love of money is the root
of all kinds of evil. And some people, craving
money, have wandered from the true faith and
pierced themselves with many sorrows.

Paul's Final Instructions

11But you, Timothy, are a man of God; so run
from all these evil things. Pursue righteousness
and a godly life, along with faith, love, persever-
ance, and gentleness. 12Fight the good fight for
the true faith. Hold tightly to the eternal life to
which God has called you, which you have declared so well before many witnesses. 13And I
charge you before God, who gives life to all, and
before Christ Jesus, who gave a good testimony
before Pontius Pilate, 14that you obey this command without wavering. Then no one can find
fault with you from now until our Lord Jesus
Christ comes again. 15For,

At just the right time Christ will be revealed
from heaven by the blessed and only
almighty God, the King of all kings and Lord
of all lords. 16He alone can never die, and he
lives in light so brilliant that no human can
approach him. No human eye has ever seen
him, nor ever will. All honor and power to
him forever! Amen.

17Teach those who are rich in this world not to
be proud and not to trust in their money, which is
so unreliable. Their trust should be in God, who
richly gives us all we need for our enjoyment.
18Tell them to use their money to do good. They
should be rich in good works and generous to
those in need, always being ready to share with
others. 19By doing this they will be storing up
their treasure as a good foundation for the future
so that they may experience true life.
20Timothy, guard what God has entrusted to
you. Avoid godless, foolish discussions with
those who oppose you with their so-called
knowledge. 21Some people have wandered from
the faith by following such foolishness.
May God's grace be with you all.

2 TiMoTHY

Famous Last Words

Look for 1 hidden message in 2 Timothy!

Paul wrote his second letter to Timothy not long before he was put to death for his faith in Jesus. Look for

- **FLAMES OF FAITH**
- **A PURPOSEFUL PLAN**
- **USEFUL UTENSILS**
- **STEADFAST SCRIPTURE**

Fan the Flames

Was there a fire? You bet there was! **Find out more in 2 Timothy 1:5-8.**

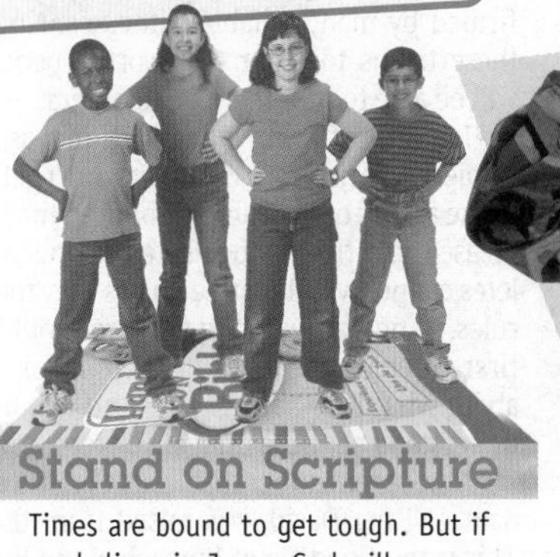

Stand on Scripture

Times are bound to get tough. But if you believe in Jesus, God will see you through. You can count on it. **Just read 2 Timothy 3:10-17!**

Atten-*tion!*

Timothy was supposed to act like a soldier, but he wasn't in the army. He was supposed to act like an athlete, but he wasn't on a sports team. Huh? **Read 2 Timothy 2:3-7 to clear things up!**

Useful Utensils

Paul told Timothy he could be a fork. OK, not really. But he did say Timothy could be a utensil for God to use. **Read all about it in 2 Timothy 2:20-21.**

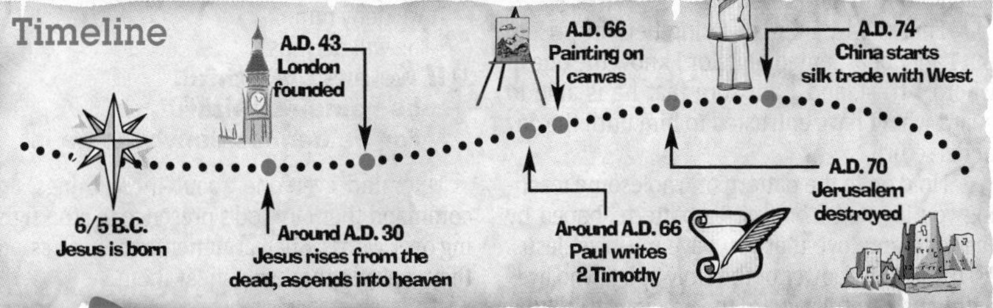
Timeline
6/5 B.C. Jesus is born
Around A.D. 30 Jesus rises from the dead, ascends into heaven
A.D. 43 London founded
Around A.D. 66 Paul writes 2 Timothy
A.D. 66 Painting on canvas
A.D. 70 Jerusalem destroyed
A.D. 74 China starts silk trade with West

The JESUS CONNECTION

The book of 2 Timothy was the last letter Paul wrote before his death. He was alone in prison, writing to his young friend Timothy, who was a pastor of a church Paul had founded. He gave Timothy advice about standing firm in his faith, trusting the Bible, and telling others about Jesus. **If you believe in Jesus, this letter is for you, too!**

2 Timothy 1 . . . page 1198

CHAPTER 1

Greetings from Paul

This letter is from Paul, chosen by the will of God
to be an apostle of Christ Jesus. I have been sent
out to tell others about the life he has promised
through faith in Christ Jesus.
2 I am writing to Timothy, my dear son.
May God the Father and Christ Jesus our Lord
give you grace, mercy, and peace.

Encouragement to Be Faithful

3 Timothy, I thank God for you—the God I serve
with a clear conscience, just as my ancestors did.
Night and day I constantly remember you in my
prayers. 4 I long to see you again, for I remember
your tears as we parted. And I will be filled with
joy when we are together again.
5 I remember your genuine faith, for you share
the faith that first filled your grandmother Lois
and your mother, Eunice. And I know that same
faith continues strong in you. 6 This is why I remind you to fan into flames the spiritual gift God
gave you when I laid my hands on you. 7 For God
has not given us a spirit of fear and timidity, but
of power, love, and self-discipline.
8 So never be ashamed to tell others about our
Lord. And don't be ashamed of me, either, even
though I'm in prison for him. With the strength
God gives you, be ready to suffer with me for the
sake of the Good News. 9 For God saved us and
called us to live a holy life. He did this, not because we deserved it, but because that was his
plan from before the beginning of time—to
show us his grace through Christ Jesus. 10 And
now he has made all of this plain to us by the appearing of Christ Jesus, our Savior. He broke the
power of death and illuminated the way to life
and immortality through the Good News. 11 And
God chose me to be a preacher, an apostle, and a
teacher of this Good News.
12 That is why I am suffering here in prison.
But I am not ashamed of it, for I know the one in
whom I trust, and I am sure that he is able to
guard what I have entrusted to him until the day
of his return.
13 Hold on to the pattern of wholesome teaching you learned from me—a pattern shaped by
the faith and love that you have in Christ Jesus.
14 Through the power of the Holy Spirit who lives
within us, carefully guard the precious truth that
has been entrusted to you.
15 As you know, everyone from the province
of Asia has deserted me—even Phygelus and
Hermogenes.
16 May the Lord show special kindness to
Onesiphorus and all his family because he often
visited and encouraged me. He was never
ashamed of me because I was in chains.
17 When he came to Rome, he searched everywhere until he found me. 18 May the Lord show
him special kindness on the day of Christ's return. And you know very well how helpful he
was in Ephesus.

CHAPTER 2

A Good Soldier of Christ Jesus

Timothy, my dear son, be strong through the
grace that God gives you in Christ Jesus. 2 You
have heard me teach things that have been confirmed by many reliable witnesses. Now teach
these truths to other trustworthy people who
will be able to pass them on to others.
3 Endure suffering along with me, as a good
soldier of Christ Jesus. 4 Soldiers don't get tied up
in the affairs of civilian life, for then they cannot
please the officer who enlisted them. 5 And athletes cannot win the prize unless they follow the
rules. 6 And hardworking farmers should be the
first to enjoy the fruit of their labor. 7 Think
about what I am saying. The Lord will help you
understand all these things.
8 Always remember that Jesus Christ, a descendant of King David, was raised from the dead.
This is the Good News I preach. 9 And because I
preach this Good News, I am suffering and have
been chained like a criminal. But the word of God
cannot be chained. 10 So I am willing to endure
anything if it will bring salvation and eternal
glory in Christ Jesus to those God has chosen.
11 This is a trustworthy saying:

If we die with him,
we will also live with him.
12 If we endure hardship,
we will reign with him.
If we deny him,
he will deny us.
13 **If we are unfaithful,**
he remains faithful,
for he cannot deny who he is.

14 Remind everyone about these things, and
command them in God's presence to stop fighting over words. Such arguments are useless, and
they can ruin those who hear them.

An Approved Worker

15 Work hard so you can present yourself to God
and receive his approval. Be a good worker, one
who does not need to be ashamed and who
correctly explains the word of truth. 16 Avoid

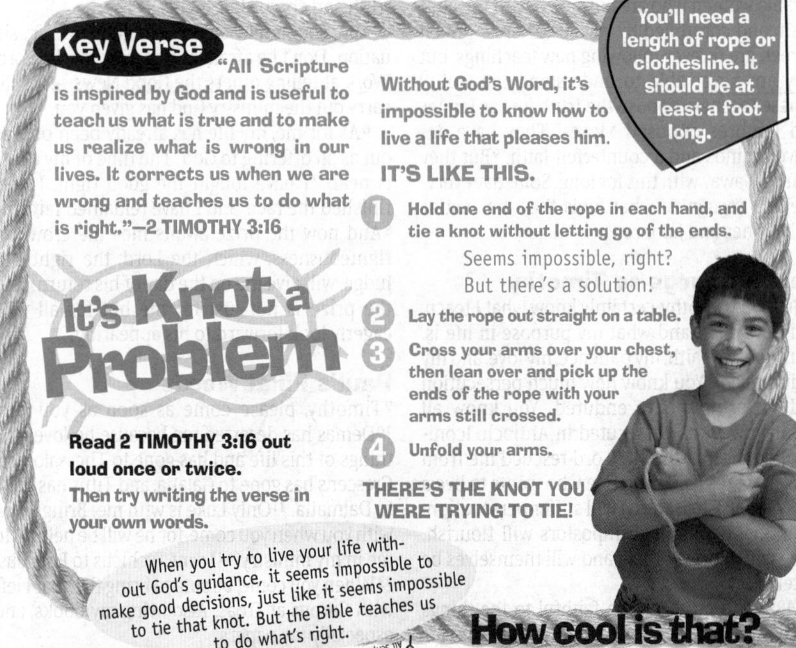
Key Verse
"All Scripture is inspired by God and is useful to teach us what is true and to make us realize what is wrong in our lives. It corrects us when we are wrong and teaches us to do what is right."—2 TIMOTHY 3:16
It's Knot a Problem
Read 2 TIMOTHY 3:16 out loud once or twice.
Then try writing the verse in your own words.
When you try to live your life without God's guidance, it seems impossible to make good decisions, just like it seems impossible to tie that knot. But the Bible teaches us to do what's right.
All Scripture points to one thing. Read what Jesus said in John 5:39!
Without God's Word, it's impossible to know how to live a life that pleases him.
You'll need a length of rope or clothesline. It should be at least a foot long.
IT'S LIKE THIS.
1 Hold one end of the rope in each hand, and tie a knot without letting go of the ends.
Seems impossible, right?
But there's a solution!
2 Lay the rope out straight on a table.
3 Cross your arms over your chest, then lean over and pick up the ends of the rope with your arms still crossed.
4 Unfold your arms.
THERE'S THE KNOT YOU WERE TRYING TO TIE!
How cool is that?

worthless, foolish talk that only leads to more
godless behavior. 17This kind of talk spreads
like cancer, as in the case of Hymenaeus and
Philetus. 18They have left the path of truth,
claiming that the resurrection of the dead has
already occurred; in this way, they have turned
some people away from the faith.
19But God's truth stands firm like a foundation
stone with this inscription: "The LORD knows
those who are his," and "All who belong to the
LORD must turn away from evil."
20In a wealthy home some utensils are made of
gold and silver, and some are made of wood and
clay. The expensive utensils are used for special
occasions, and the cheap ones are for everyday
use. 21If you keep yourself pure, you will be a special utensil for honorable use. Your life will be
clean, and you will be ready for the Master to use
you for every good work.
22Run from anything that stimulates youthful
lusts. Instead, pursue righteous living, faithfulness, love, and peace. Enjoy the companionship
of those who call on the Lord with pure hearts.
23Again I say, don't get involved in foolish,
ignorant arguments that only start fights. 24A
servant of the Lord must not quarrel but must
be kind to everyone, be able to teach, and be patient with difficult people. 25Gently instruct
those who oppose the truth. Perhaps God will
change those people's hearts, and they will
learn the truth. 26Then they will come to their
senses and escape from the devil's trap. For they
have been held captive by him to do whatever
he wants.

CHAPTER 3
The Dangers of the Last Days

You should know this, Timothy, that in the last
days there will be very difficult times. 2For people will love only themselves and their money.
They will be boastful and proud, scoffing at God,
disobedient to their parents, and ungrateful.
They will consider nothing sacred. 3They will be
unloving and unforgiving; they will slander others and have no self-control. They will be cruel
and hate what is good. 4They will betray their
friends, be reckless, be puffed up with pride, and
love pleasure rather than God. 5They will act religious, but they will reject the power that could
make them godly. Stay away from people like
that!
6They are the kind who work their way into

people's homes and win the confidence of vulnerable women who are burdened with the guilt
of sin and controlled by various desires. 7(Such
women are forever following new teachings, but
they are never able to understand the truth.)
8These teachers oppose the truth just as Jannes
and Jambres opposed Moses. They have depraved minds and a counterfeit faith. 9But they
won't get away with this for long. Someday everyone will recognize what fools they are, just as
with Jannes and Jambres.

Paul's Charge to Timothy

10But you, Timothy, certainly know what I teach,
and how I live, and what my purpose in life is.
You know my faith, my patience, my love, and my
endurance. 11You know how much persecution
and suffering I have endured. You know all
about how I was persecuted in Antioch, Iconium, and Lystra—but the Lord rescued me from
all of it. 12Yes, and everyone who wants to live a
godly life in Christ Jesus will suffer persecution.
13But evil people and impostors will flourish.
They will deceive others and will themselves be
deceived.

14But you must remain faithful to the things
you have been taught. You know they are true, for
you know you can trust those who taught you.
15You have been taught the holy Scriptures from
childhood, and they have given you the wisdom
to receive the salvation that comes by trusting in
Christ Jesus. **16All Scripture is inspired
by God and is useful to teach us what
is true and to make us realize what
is wrong in our lives. It corrects us
when we are wrong and teaches us
to do what is right. 17God uses it to
prepare and equip his people to do
every good work.**

CHAPTER 4

I solemnly urge you in the presence of God and
Christ Jesus, who will someday judge the living
and the dead when he comes to set up his Kingdom: 2Preach the word of God. Be prepared,
whether the time is favorable or not. Patiently
correct, rebuke, and encourage your people with
good teaching.

3For a time is coming when people will no longer listen to sound and wholesome teaching.
They will follow their own desires and will look
for teachers who will tell them whatever their
itching ears want to hear. 4They will reject the
truth and chase after myths.

5But you should keep a clear mind in every situation. Don't be afraid of suffering for the Lord.
Work at telling others the Good News, and fully
carry out the ministry God has given you.

6As for me, my life has already been poured
out as an offering to God. The time of my death
is near. 7I have fought the good fight, I have
finished the race, and I have remained faithful.
8And now the prize awaits me—the crown of
righteousness, which the Lord, the righteous
Judge, will give me on the day of his return. And
the prize is not just for me but for all who
eagerly look forward to his appearing.

Paul's Final Words

9Timothy, please come as soon as you can.
10Demas has deserted me because he loves the
things of this life and has gone to Thessalonica.
Crescens has gone to Galatia, and Titus has gone
to Dalmatia. 11Only Luke is with me. Bring Mark
with you when you come, for he will be helpful to
me in my ministry. 12I sent Tychicus to Ephesus.
13When you come, be sure to bring the coat I left
with Carpus at Troas. Also bring my books, and
especially my papers.

14Alexander the coppersmith did me much
harm, but the Lord will judge him for what he has
done. 15Be careful of him, for he fought against
everything we said.

16The first time I was brought before the
judge, no one came with me. Everyone abandoned me. May it not be counted against them.
17But the Lord stood with me and gave me
strength so that I might preach the Good News in
its entirety for all the Gentiles to hear. And he rescued me from certain death. 18Yes, and the Lord
will deliver me from every evil attack and will
bring me safely into his heavenly Kingdom. All
glory to God forever and ever! Amen.

Paul's Final Greetings

19Give my greetings to Priscilla and Aquila and
those living in the household of Onesiphorus.
20Erastus stayed at Corinth, and I left Trophimus
sick at Miletus.

21Do your best to get here before winter. Eubu-
lus sends you greetings, and so do Pudens, Linus,
Claudia, and all the brothers and sisters.

22May the Lord be with your spirit. And may
his grace be with all of you.

TiTUS How to Live Right

Look for (1) hidden message in Titus!

The book of Titus is a letter from Paul to a Gentile leader of the church named Titus. It tells about

- THE GOOD LIFE
- GOOD LEADERS
- GOOD TEACHING
- AND DOING GOOD

And the Winner Is...

The World Series. The Super Bowl. The Stanley Cup. Athletes who win those awards work hard to be the best.

But did you know there's an award you can receive that doesn't depend on you? **Check out Titus 3:5-6 to learn about God's amazing award!**

Instruction Manual
Instruction Manual
Instruction Manual
Instruction Manual
INSTRUCTION MANUAL

Instruction Manual

It really does matter how you live. **Find out why in Titus 2:1-8.**

CHURCH LEADER REQUIREMENTS

It's a Tough Job, But...

According to Paul, there are certain things a church leader should be—*and* shouldn't be. **Get the complete job description in Titus 1:5-9.**

It's a Jungle Out There

Have you ever been to camp? It can be hard to be away from home—in strange surroundings, with different people.

It's kind of like that for us as Christians. **Learn more in Titus 2:11-13.**

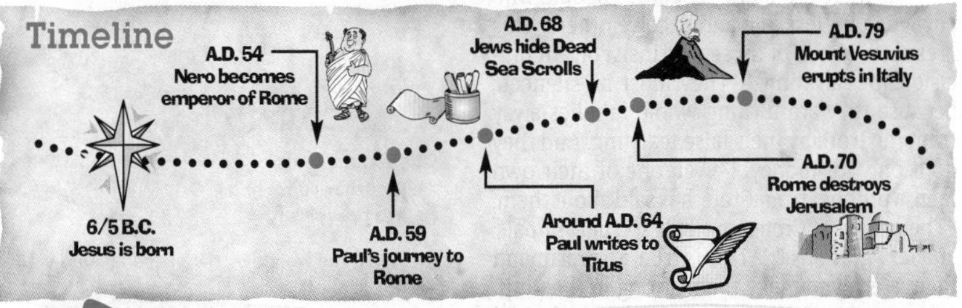

Timeline
A.D. 54
Nero becomes emperor of Rome
A.D. 68
Jews hide Dead Sea Scrolls
A.D. 79
Mount Vesuvius erupts in Italy
6/5 B.C.
Jesus is born
A.D. 59
Paul's journey to Rome
Around A.D. 64
Paul writes to Titus
A.D. 70
Rome destroys Jerusalem

The JESUS CONNECTION

The world needs Jesus. And the people out there are going to have a tough time finding Jesus if his church is a big mess. If you're a Christian, the way you live and act affects what people think about Christianity. The Bible never tells us to be fake or judgmental. It does tell us to do the right thing so our behavior won't get in the way of others who are seeking Jesus. God wants to save *all* people because of his mercy, and he doesn't want our bad behavior getting in the way.

Titus 1 . . . page 1202

CHAPTER 1

Greetings from Paul

This letter is from Paul, a slave of God and an
apostle of Jesus Christ. I have been sent to proclaim faith to those God has chosen and to
teach them to know the truth that shows them
how to live godly lives. 2 This truth gives them
confidence that they have eternal life, which
God—who does not lie—promised them before
the world began. 3 And now at just the right time
he has revealed this message, which we announce to everyone. It is by the command of
God our Savior that I have been entrusted with
this work for him.
4 I am writing to Titus, my true son in the faith
that we share.

May God the Father and Christ Jesus our
Savior give you grace and peace.

Titus's Work in Crete

5 I left you on the island of Crete so you could
complete our work there and appoint elders in
each town as I instructed you. 6 An elder must
live a blameless life. He must be faithful to his
wife, and his children must be believers who
don't have a reputation for being wild or rebellious. 7 An elder is a manager of God's household,
so he must live a blameless life. He must not be
arrogant or quick-tempered; he must not be a
heavy drinker, violent, or dishonest with money.
8 Rather, he must enjoy having guests in his
home, and he must love what is good. He must
live wisely and be just. He must live a devout
and disciplined life. 9 He must have a strong belief in the trustworthy message he was taught;
then he will be able to encourage others with
wholesome teaching and show those who oppose it where they are wrong.
10 For there are many rebellious people who
engage in useless talk and deceive others. This
is especially true of those who insist on circumcision for salvation. 11 They must be silenced,
because they are turning whole families away
from the truth by their false teaching. And they
do it only for money. 12 Even one of their own
men, a prophet from Crete, has said about them,
"The people of Crete are all liars, cruel animals,
and lazy gluttons." 13 This is true. So reprimand
them sternly to make them strong in the faith.
14 They must stop listening to Jewish myths and
the commands of people who have turned away
from the truth.
15 Everything is pure to those whose hearts
are pure. But nothing is pure to those who are
corrupt and unbelieving, because their minds

Key Verse "He saved us, not because of the righteous things we had done, but because of his mercy." —TITUS 3:5a

Life Preserver
JESUS SAVES US!
JESUS is like a life preserver because he saves us from drowning in sin.

Read Titus 3:5a out loud. (The "a" means the first sentence in the verse.)

AWESOME! God sent his Son, Jesus, to save us.

When someone is drowning, what does that person need? A life preserver!

Make this!

You'll need a rectangle of light-colored cloth (about 4x12 inches), a permanent marker, quilt batting or tissues, and colorful electrical tape.

1. **Lay your fabric on a table, good side down. Place batting or tissues all along the center of the rectangle.**
2. **Roll the fabric around the batting and tape it into a long "snake."**
3. **Tape the ends together to form a life preserver.**
4. **Write the words of the verse around your life preserver.**

He saved us, not because of the righteous things we had done, but because of his mercy." —TITUS 3:5a

Read John 3:16 for more about being saved!

Keep your life preserver to remind you that salvation is a free gift when you believe in Jesus!

Titus was leading the church on an island called Crete. It's a large island (3,190 square miles) in the Mediterranean Sea, and it was a Roman province at the time. Paul said that one of Crete's own prophets called the people there **"liars, cruel animals, and lazy gluttons."**

A fun place? **NOT!** But that's where God called Titus to tell others about Jesus.

God doesn't want you to be lazy.

Write the name of someone you can tell about Jesus. Commit to telling that person about your faith this week. After you do, write the date below.

WHO did you tell about Jesus?

WHEN did you tell this person?

and consciences are corrupted. [16]Such people claim they know God, but they deny him by the way they live. They are detestable and disobedient, worthless for doing anything good.

CHAPTER 2

Promote Right Teaching

As for you, Titus, promote the kind of living that
reflects wholesome teaching. [2]Teach the older
men to exercise self-control, to be worthy of respect, and to live wisely. They must have sound
faith and be filled with love and patience.
[3]Similarly, teach the older women to live in a
way that honors God. They must not slander
others or be heavy drinkers. Instead, they
should teach others what is good. [4]These older
women must train the younger women to love
their husbands and their children, [5]to live
wisely and be pure, to work in their homes, to
do good, and to be submissive to their husbands. Then they will not bring shame on the
word of God.
[6]In the same way, encourage the young men
to live wisely. [7]And you yourself must be an example to them by doing good works of every
kind. Let everything you do reflect the integrity
and seriousness of your teaching. [8]Teach the
truth so that your teaching can't be criticized.
Then those who oppose us will be ashamed and
have nothing bad to say about us.
[9]Slaves must always obey their masters and
do their best to please them. They must not talk
back [10]or steal, but must show themselves to be
entirely trustworthy and good. Then they will
make the teaching about God our Savior attractive in every way.
[11]For the grace of God has been revealed,
bringing salvation to all people. [12]And we are
instructed to turn from godless living and sinful
pleasures. We should live in this evil world with
wisdom, righteousness, and devotion to God,
[13]while we look forward with hope to that wonderful day when the glory of our great God and
Savior, Jesus Christ, will be revealed. [14]He gave
his life to free us from every kind of sin, to
cleanse us, and to make us his very own people,
totally committed to doing good deeds.
[15]You must teach these things and encourage
the believers to do them. You have the authority
to correct them when necessary, so don't let
anyone disregard what you say.

CHAPTER 3

Do What Is Good

Remind the believers to submit to the government and its officers. They should be obedient,
always ready to do what is good. [2]They must not
slander anyone and must avoid quarreling. Instead, they should be gentle and show true humility to everyone.
[3]Once we, too, were foolish and disobedient.
We were misled and became slaves to many
lusts and pleasures. Our lives were full of evil
and envy, and we hated each other. [4]But—

Titus 3 . . . page 1204

When God our Savior revealed his kindness
and love, **5he saved us, not because
of the righteous things we had
done, but because of his mercy.**
He washed away our sins, giving us a new
birth and new life through the Holy Spirit.
6He generously poured out the Spirit upon us
through Jesus Christ our Savior. 7Because of
his grace he declared us righteous and gave us
confidence that we will inherit eternal life.

8This is a trustworthy saying, and I want you to
insist on these teachings so that all who trust in
God will devote themselves to doing good. These
teachings are good and beneficial for everyone.
9Do not get involved in foolish discussions
about spiritual pedigrees or in quarrels and
fights about obedience to Jewish laws. These
things are useless and a waste of time. 10If
people are causing divisions among you, give a
first and second warning. After that, have nothing more to do with them. 11For people like that
have turned away from the truth, and their own
sins condemn them.

Paul's Final Remarks and Greetings

12I am planning to send either Artemas or
Tychicus to you. As soon as one of them arrives,
do your best to meet me at Nicopolis, for I have
decided to stay there for the winter. 13Do everything you can to help Zenas the lawyer and
Apollos with their trip. See that they are given
everything they need. 14Our people must learn
to do good by meeting the urgent needs of others; then they will not be unproductive.
15Everybody here sends greetings. Please give
my greetings to the believers—all who love us.
May God's grace be with you all.

PHILEMON

Faith and Forgiveness

The book of Philemon is a letter Paul wrote to his friend Philemon. Look for

- **SOME FRIENDLY ADVICE**
- **A FRIEND IN NEED**
- **FAITH AND FRIENDSHIP**
- **FRIENDLY FORGIVENESS**

Many Thanks

There are probably many people and things in your life that you could say thank you for. Have you? **Look at Philemon 1:4-6 to see Paul's own personal thank-you words to a friend.**

S-o-o-o Refreshing

There are all sorts of ways we refresh ourselves. But what if your heart needs refreshing? **Read Philemon 1:7 to find one thing that can refresh our hearts.**

Dear Blabby

Q: Onesimus was my slave. I think he stole some stuff from me, then ran away. Well, he's on his way back, and I'm not sure what to do. My friend Paul sent me a letter asking me to…well, read it yourself. **A: It's in Philemon 1:8-19.**

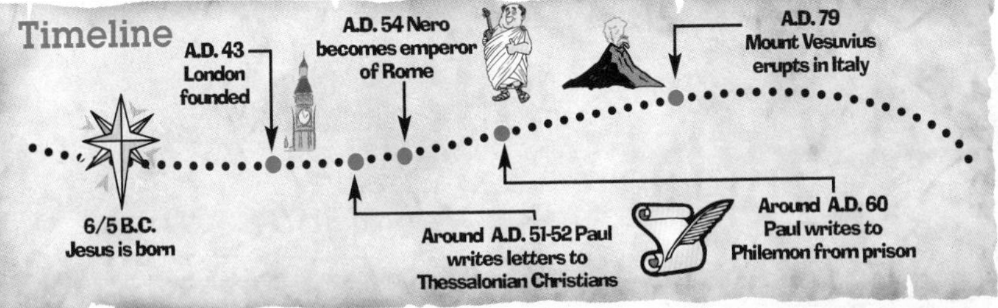

Timeline
6/5 B.C. Jesus is born
A.D. 43 London founded
Around A.D. 51-52 Paul writes letters to Thessalonian Christians
A.D. 54 Nero becomes emperor of Rome
Around A.D. 60 Paul writes to Philemon from prison
A.D. 79 Mount Vesuvius erupts in Italy

The JESUS CONNECTION

Onesimus was a slave who ran away from his owner, Philemon. The laws of that day said that Onesimus could be killed for running away. But Paul asked Philemon to show forgiveness to Onesimus and love him like a brother. We're all kind of like Onesimus. Without Jesus, we're slaves to our sin and we deserve death away from God. **But if we believe in Jesus, he sets us free from our sin and welcomes us into God's family!**

Philemon • • • page 1206

Greetings from Paul

This letter is from Paul, a prisoner for preaching
the Good News about Christ Jesus, and from our
brother Timothy.
I am writing to Philemon, our beloved co-
worker, 2and to our sister Apphia, and to our fellow soldier Archippus, and to the church that
meets in your house.
3May God our Father and the Lord Jesus Christ
give you grace and peace.

Paul's Thanksgiving and Prayer

4I always thank my God when I pray for you,
Philemon, 5because I keep hearing about your
faith in the Lord Jesus and your love for all of
God's people. 6And I am praying that you will put
into action the generosity that comes from your
faith as you understand and experience all the
good things we have in Christ. 7Your love has
given me much joy and comfort, my brother, for
your kindness has often refreshed the hearts of
God's people.

Paul's Appeal for Onesimus

8That is why I am boldly asking a favor of you.
I could demand it in the name of Christ because it is the right thing for you to do. 9But because of our love, I prefer simply to ask you.
Consider this as a request from me—Paul, an
old man and now also a prisoner for the sake of
Christ Jesus.
10I appeal to you to show kindness to my
child, Onesimus. I became his father in the faith
while here in prison. 11Onesimus hasn't been of
much use to you in the past, but now he is very
useful to both of us. 12I am sending him back to
you, and with him comes my own heart.
13I wanted to keep him here with me while I
am in these chains for preaching the Good
News, and he would have helped me on your behalf. 14But I didn't want to do anything without
your consent. I wanted you to help because you
were willing, not because you were forced. 15It
seems you lost Onesimus for a little while so that
you could have him back forever. 16He is no longer like a slave to you. He is more than a slave, for
he is a beloved brother, especially to me. Now he
will mean much more to you, both as a man and
as a brother in the Lord.
17So if you consider me your partner, welcome him as you would welcome me. 18If he has
wronged you in any way or owes you anything,
charge it to me. 19I, PAUL, WRITE THIS WITH MY
OWN HAND: I WILL REPAY IT. AND I WON'T MENTION
THAT YOU OWE ME YOUR VERY SOUL!
20Yes, my brother, please do me this favor for
the Lord's sake. Give me this encouragement in
Christ.
21I am confident as I write this letter that you
will do what I ask and even more! 22One more
thing—please prepare a guest room for me, for I
am hoping that God will answer your prayers
and let me return to you soon.

Paul's Final Greetings

23Epaphras, my fellow prisoner in Christ Jesus,
sends you his greetings. 24So do Mark, Aristarchus, Demas, and Luke, my co-workers.
25May the grace of the Lord Jesus Christ be
with your spirit.

HEBREWS

All About Jesus

Look for 1 hidden message in Hebrews!

Hebrews tells how Jesus fulfills the Old Testament. It tells about

- **JESUS THE MESSIAH**
- **JESUS THE SON OF GOD**
- **JESUS THE SACRIFICE**
- **JESUS THE GREAT PRIEST**

Guess Who's Coming to Dinner?

The people you meet aren't always what they seem. **Find out more about this mystery in Hebrews 13:2!**

Definite Definition

You can look up the word *faith* in the dictionary, but you'll never find *this* kind of definition! **Read God's definition of *faith* in Hebrews 11:1.**

Now That's Sharp!

It's finally here! The new Bible Blade, the sharpest knife in the drawer. It dices! It slices! It cuts to the heart of the matter—our relationship with God! **Learn more about this amazingly sharp blade in Hebrews 4:12.**

Anchors Away!

Some of the largest ships in the world are held by anchors that weigh more than four tons! Even in the roughest water, that anchor can keep a huge ship from drifting away. **Read Hebrews 6:16-19 to discover how God is our anchor!**

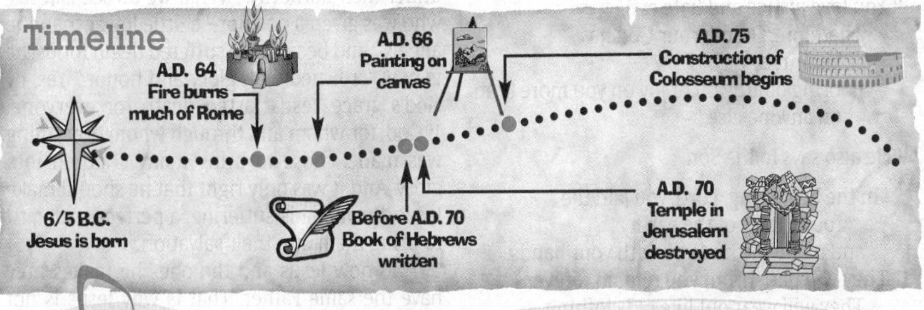
Timeline
6/5 B.C.
Jesus is born
A.D. 64
Fire burns much of Rome
A.D. 66
Painting on canvas
Before A.D. 70
Book of Hebrews written
A.D. 70
Temple in Jerusalem destroyed
A.D. 75
Construction of Colosseum begins

The JESUS CONNECTION

When Jesus came, he didn't throw out the Old Testament or the Jewish religion. Instead, he fulfilled it, or made it complete. Judaism (the religion of the Israelites) and all of the Old Testament point to Jesus. The book of Hebrews shows how Jesus is the promised Messiah who came to sacrifice himself for our sin. Jesus came to earth for you. **And you can live forever in heaven if you put your faith in Jesus.**

Hebrews 1
. . . page 1208

CHAPTER 1
Jesus Christ Is God's Son

Long ago God spoke many times and in many
ways to our ancestors through the prophets.
2 And now in these final days, he has spoken to us
through his Son. God promised everything to the
Son as an inheritance, and through the Son he
created the universe. 3 The Son radiates God's
own glory and expresses the very character of
God, and he sustains everything by the mighty
power of his command. When he had cleansed
us from our sins, he sat down in the place of
honor at the right hand of the majestic God in
heaven. 4 This shows that the Son is far greater
than the angels, just as the name God gave him is
greater than their names.

The Son Is Greater Than the Angels

5 For God never said to any angel what he said to
Jesus:

"You are my Son.
Today I have become your Father."

God also said,

"I will be his Father,
and he will be my Son."

6 And when he brought his supreme Son into the
world, God said,

"Let all of God's angels worship him."

7 Regarding the angels, he says,

"He sends his angels like the winds,
his servants like flames of fire."

8 But to the Son he says,

"Your throne, O God, endures forever and ever.
You rule with a scepter of justice.
9 You love justice and hate evil.
Therefore, O God, your God has
anointed you,
pouring out the oil of joy on you more than
on anyone else."

10 He also says to the Son,

"In the beginning, Lord, you laid the
foundation of the earth
and made the heavens with your hands.
11 They will perish, but you remain forever.
They will wear out like old clothing.
12 You will fold them up like a cloak
and discard them like old clothing.
But you are always the same;
you will live forever."

13 And God never said to any of the angels,

"Sit in the place of honor at my right hand
until I humble your enemies,
making them a footstool under your feet."

14 Therefore, angels are only servants—spirits
sent to care for people who will inherit salvation.

CHAPTER 2
A Warning against Drifting Away

So we must listen very carefully to the truth we
have heard, or we may drift away from it. 2 For the
message God delivered through angels has always stood firm, and every violation of the law
and every act of disobedience was punished. 3 So
what makes us think we can escape if we ignore
this great salvation that was first announced by
the Lord Jesus himself and then delivered to us
by those who heard him speak? 4 And God confirmed the message by giving signs and wonders
and various miracles and gifts of the Holy Spirit
whenever he chose.

Jesus, the Man

5 And furthermore, it is not angels who will control the future world we are talking about. 6 For in
one place the Scriptures say,

"What are mere mortals that you should
think about them,
or a son of man that you should care
for him?
7 Yet you made them only a little lower
than the angels
and crowned them with glory and honor.
8 You gave them authority over all things."

Now when it says "all things," it means nothing is
left out. But we have not yet seen all things put
under their authority. 9 What we do see is Jesus,
who was given a position "a little lower than the
angels"; and because he suffered death for us, he
is now "crowned with glory and honor." Yes, by
God's grace, Jesus tasted death for everyone.
10 God, for whom and through whom everything
was made, chose to bring many children into
glory. And it was only right that he should make
Jesus, through his suffering, a perfect leader, fit
to bring them into their salvation.

11 So now Jesus and the ones he makes holy
have the same Father. That is why Jesus is not
ashamed to call them his brothers and sisters.
12 For he said to God,

"I will proclaim your name to my brothers
and sisters.

BIBLE BIOS
Hear From the Heroes

Hi, my name is
SAUL *(religious leader)*

Oh, the stories I could tell! First, you need to know who I really am. (I'm not King Saul of the Old Testament.) I'm sometimes known as Saul of Tarsus, since Tarsus is where I came from. But after I became a follower of Jesus, I became known as Paul. Before I met Jesus, I thought Christians were trying to change our Jewish faith with wrong teachings. So I was all about trying to stop them.

But Jesus stopped me in my tracks—literally! I was on my way to Damascus to nab some more Christians, when Jesus stopped me. A light from heaven shone down on me, and I heard a man's voice but couldn't see anyone! The voice said, "I am Jesus, the one you are persecuting." He told me to go into the city and wait.

When I stood up, I was blind! My friends led me into town, and I stayed there blind for three days. Then God sent a man named Ananias, a believer in Jesus, to restore my sight and get me started on the right path of telling others about Jesus.

God is amazing! Even though I had once tried to stop Christians, God changed my life and used me to spread the truth about Jesus. During my life I went on three big missionary trips. At God's direction and with his inspiration, I wrote a whole bunch of letters to people and churches, many of which are in this very Bible you're reading. I realized that nothing was more important than believing in Jesus!

For the whole artling story of aul becoming a hristian, read ACTS 9:1-22.

CAN GOD USE YOU?

List the talents and abilities God has given you. Next to each talent, write a way you could use that talent to honor God. (Maybe you're a good listener, or maybe you encourage people. Those are talents too!) Every time you notice God using you, write the date on your paper. Let God use you in big—and little—ways!

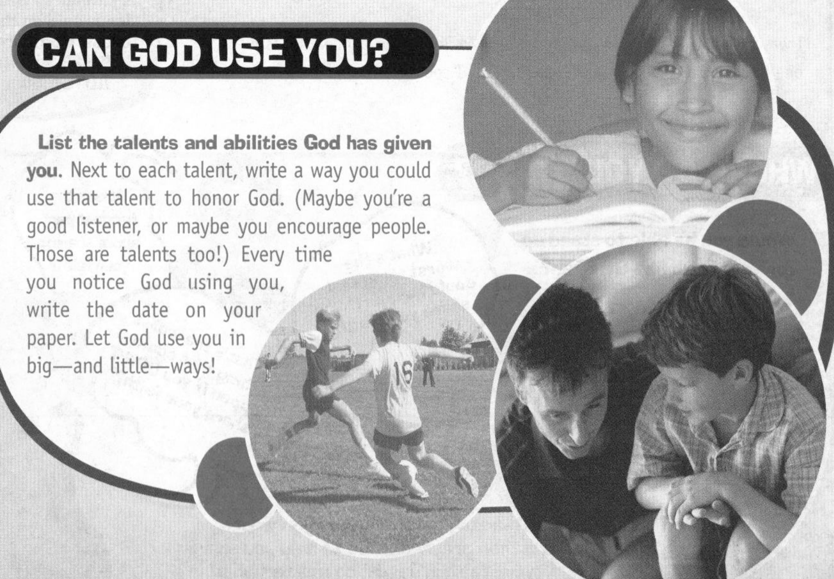

STEPHEN *(server of the poor)*

Not many people are known more for their death than for their life, but that's sure true for me! But hey, I'd like to talk a little bit about my life before I talk about my death!

I was a follower of Jesus from the early days of the church. More and more people were becoming Christians every day. At first, Jesus' disciples handled all the leadership. But soon they needed help.

Stephen gave quite a speech to the Jewish leaders! Read the whole thing in ACTS 7:1-53.

They chose seven of us to help out so they could spend more time preaching. With God's power, I performed miracles that attracted people to Jesus. Unfortunately, they also attracted the attention of the Jewish leaders.

What came next was definitely not fun. When the leaders confronted me, God was with me. People even said that my face glowed like an angel when I answered them! At the end of my speech, I looked up toward heaven and I could actually see the glory of God, along with Jesus standing right beside God! When I told the Jewish leaders what I saw, I guess that was all they could take.

They dragged me out of the city and started throwing stones at me—a form of execution at the time. The stones hurt, but with God's help I was able to keep my focus on Jesus. Even as I was being killed, I asked God not to hold the people responsible for what they were doing to me.

What Stephen said when he was dying is similar to what Jesus said on the cross. Compare LUKE 23:34 with ACTS 7:60.

I was the first Christian to die for his faith in Jesus, but my death was just one of many to come. I'm just thankful that I could stand up for Jesus!

WHERE DO YOU STAND?

Would you be able to stand up for your faith like Stephen?

ANSWER THESE QUESTIONS WITH A FRIEND:

What's the worst thing that could happen if you share your faith?

What's the hardest part about sharing your faith?

What's the worst thing that could happen if you DON'T share your faith?

Read over the answers you wrote, and then pray. Ask God to help you share your faith in Jesus, no matter what!

I will praise you among your
assembled people."

13He also said,

"I will put my trust in him,"
that is, "I and the children God has given me."

14Because God's children are human beings—
made of flesh and blood—the Son also became
flesh and blood. For only as a human being could
he die, and only by dying could he break the
power of the devil, who had the power of death.
15Only in this way could he set free all who have
lived their lives as slaves to the fear of dying.

16We also know that the Son did not come to
help angels; he came to help the descendants of
Abraham. 17Therefore, it was necessary for him
to be made in every respect like us, his brothers
and sisters, so that he could be our merciful and
faithful High Priest before God. Then he could
offer a sacrifice that would take away the sins of
the people. **18Since he himself has
gone through suffering and testing,
he is able to help us when we are being tested.**

CHAPTER 3

Jesus Is Greater Than Moses

And so, dear brothers and sisters who belong to
God and are partners with those called to heaven,
think carefully about this Jesus whom we declare
to be God's messenger and High Priest. 2For he
was faithful to God, who appointed him, just as
Moses served faithfully when he was entrusted
with God's entire house.

3But Jesus deserves far more glory than
Moses, just as a person who builds a house deserves more praise than the house itself. 4For
every house has a builder, but the one who built
everything is God.

5Moses was certainly faithful in God's house
as a servant. His work was an illustration of the
truths God would reveal later. 6But Christ, as the
Son, is in charge of God's entire house. And we
are God's house, if we keep our courage and remain confident in our hope in Christ.

7That is why the Holy Spirit says,

"Today when you hear his voice,
8 don't harden your hearts
as Israel did when they rebelled,
when they tested me in the wilderness.
9 There your ancestors tested and tried
my patience,
even though they saw my miracles
for forty years.
10 So I was angry with them, and I said,
'Their hearts always turn away from me.
They refuse to do what I tell them.'
11 So in my anger I took an oath:
'They will never enter my place of rest.'"

12Be careful then, dear brothers and sisters.
Make sure that your own hearts are not evil and
unbelieving, turning you away from the living
God. 13You must warn each other every day,
while it is still "today," so that none of you will
be deceived by sin and hardened against God.
14For if we are faithful to the end, trusting God
just as firmly as when we first believed, we will
share in all that belongs to Christ. 15Remember
what it says:

"Today when you hear his voice,
don't harden your hearts
as Israel did when they rebelled."

16And who was it who rebelled against God,
even though they heard his voice? Wasn't it the
people Moses led out of Egypt? 17And who made
God angry for forty years? Wasn't it the people
who sinned, whose corpses lay in the wilderness? 18And to whom was God speaking when he
took an oath that they would never enter his rest?
Wasn't it the people who disobeyed him? 19So we
see that because of their unbelief they were not
able to enter his rest.

CHAPTER 4

Promised Rest for God's People

God's promise of entering his rest still stands, so
we ought to tremble with fear that some of you
might fail to experience it. 2For this good
news—that God has prepared this rest—has
been announced to us just as it was to them. But
it did them no good because they didn't share
the faith of those who listened to God. 3For only
we who believe can enter his rest. As for the others, God said,

"In my anger I took an oath:
'They will never enter my place
of rest,'"

even though this rest has been ready since he
made the world. 4We know it is ready because
of the place in the Scriptures where it mentions
the seventh day: "On the seventh day God rested
from all his work." 5But in the other passage
God said, "They will never enter my place of
rest."

6So God's rest is there for people to enter, but
those who first heard this good news failed to
enter because they disobeyed God. 7So God set

another time for entering his rest, and that time
is today. God announced this through David
much later in the words already quoted:

"Today when you hear his voice,
don't harden your hearts."

8 Now if Joshua had succeeded in giving them
this rest, God would not have spoken about another day of rest still to come. 9 So there is a special rest still waiting for the people of God. 10 For
all who have entered into God's rest have rested
from their labors, just as God did after creating
the world. 11 So let us do our best to enter that
rest. But if we disobey God, as the people of Israel
did, we will fall.

12 For the word of God is alive and powerful.
It is sharper than the sharpest two-edged
sword, cutting between soul and spirit, between
joint and marrow. It exposes our innermost
thoughts and desires. 13 Nothing in all creation
is hidden from God. Everything is naked and
exposed before his eyes, and he is the one to
whom we are accountable.

Christ Is Our High Priest

14 So then, since we have a great High Priest who
has entered heaven, Jesus the Son of God, let us
hold firmly to what we believe. 15 This High
Priest of ours understands our weaknesses, for
he faced all of the same testings we do, yet he did
not sin. **16 So let us come boldly to the
throne of our gracious God. There
we will receive his mercy, and we
will find grace to help us when we
need it most.**

CHAPTER 5

Every high priest is a man chosen to represent
other people in their dealings with God. He
presents their gifts to God and offers sacrifices
for their sins. 2 And he is able to deal gently with
ignorant and wayward people because he himself is subject to the same weaknesses. 3 That is
why he must offer sacrifices for his own sins as
well as theirs.

4 And no one can become a high priest simply
because he wants such an honor. He must be
called by God for this work, just as Aaron was.
5 That is why Christ did not honor himself by
assuming he could become High Priest. No, he
was chosen by God, who said to him,

"You are my Son.
Today I have become your Father."

6 And in another passage God said to him,

"You are a priest forever in the order
of Melchizedek."

7 While Jesus was here on earth, he offered
prayers and pleadings, with a loud cry and tears,
to the one who could rescue him from death.
And God heard his prayers because of his deep
reverence for God. 8 Even though Jesus was God's
Son, he learned obedience from the things he
suffered. 9 In this way, God qualified him as a
perfect High Priest, and he became the source of
eternal salvation for all those who obey him.
10 And God designated him to be a High Priest in
the order of Melchizedek.

A Call to Spiritual Growth

11 There is much more we would like to say about
this, but it is difficult to explain, especially since
you are spiritually dull and don't seem to listen.
12 You have been believers so long now that you
ought to be teaching others. Instead, you need
someone to teach you again the basic things
about God's word. You are like babies who need
milk and cannot eat solid food. 13 For someone
who lives on milk is still an infant and doesn't
know how to do what is right. 14 Solid food is for
those who are mature, who through training have
the skill to recognize the difference between
right and wrong.

CHAPTER 6

So let us stop going over the basic teachings
about Christ again and again. Let us go on
instead and become mature in our understanding. Surely we don't need to start again
with the fundamental importance of repenting
from evil deeds and placing our faith in God.
2 You don't need further instruction about baptisms, the laying on of hands, the resurrection of
the dead, and eternal judgment. 3 And so, God
willing, we will move forward to further understanding.

4 For it is impossible to bring back to repentance those who were once enlightened—those
who have experienced the good things of heaven
and shared in the Holy Spirit, 5 who have tasted
the goodness of the word of God and the power
of the age to come—6 and who then turn away
from God. It is impossible to bring such people
back to repentance; by rejecting the Son of God,
they themselves are nailing him to the cross once
again and holding him up to public shame.

7 When the ground soaks up the falling rain
and bears a good crop for the farmer, it has God's
blessing. 8 But if a field bears thorns and thistles,

Key Verse **"So let us come boldly to the throne of our gracious God. There we will receive his mercy, and we will find grace to help us when we need it most."—HEBREWS 4:16**

Read HEBREWS 4:16. Then read it again until you can say it to someone else.

Coming boldly to God's throne means praying with complete confidence. Make this **Confidence Carryall** to remind you that you can pray boldly.

1. **Write the words of this verse on an empty container.**

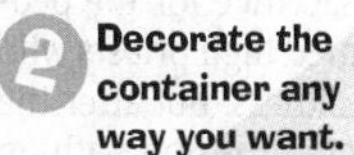

2. **Decorate the container any way you want.**
3. **Think of things you're confident about. Write those things on slips of paper. (Can you ride a bike? tie your shoes? multiply? Write it down!)**

Look at all your confidence slips! Put your slips in your Confidence Carryall. Any time you feel shy about talking to God, open your Confidence Carryall.

THEN REMEMBER WHAT IT FEELS LIKE TO BE BOLD AND CONFIDENT.

it is useless. The farmer will soon condemn that
field and burn it.
9 Dear friends, even though we are talking this
way, we really don't believe it applies to you. We
are confident that you are meant for better
things, things that come with salvation. 10 For
God is not unjust. He will not forget how hard
you have worked for him and how you have
shown your love to him by caring for other believers, as you still do. 11 Our great desire is that
you will keep on loving others as long as life lasts,
in order to make certain that what you hope for
will come true. 12 Then you will not become spiritually dull and indifferent. Instead, you will follow the example of those who are going to
inherit God's promises because of their faith and
endurance.

God's Promises Bring Hope

13 For example, there was God's promise to Abraham. Since there was no one greater to swear by,
God took an oath in his own name, saying:

14 "I will certainly bless you,
and I will multiply your descendants
beyond number."

15 Then Abraham waited patiently, and he received what God had promised.
16 Now when people take an oath, they call on
someone greater than themselves to hold them
to it. And without any question that oath is binding. 17 God also bound himself with an oath, so
that those who received the promise could be
perfectly sure that he would never change his
mind. 18 So God has given both his promise and
his oath. These two things are unchangeable because it is impossible for God to lie. Therefore, we
who have fled to him for refuge can have great
confidence as we hold to the hope that lies before
us. 19 This hope is a strong and trustworthy anchor for our souls. It leads us through the curtain
into God's inner sanctuary. 20 Jesus has already
gone in there for us. He has become our eternal
High Priest in the order of Melchizedek.

CHAPTER 7

Melchizedek Is Greater Than Abraham

This Melchizedek was king of the city of Salem
and also a priest of God Most High. When Abraham was returning home after winning a great
battle against the kings, Melchizedek met him
and blessed him. 2 Then Abraham took a tenth of
all he had captured in battle and gave it to Melchizedek. The name Melchizedek means "king

of justice," and king of Salem means "king of
peace." 3There is no record of his father or
mother or any of his ancestors—no beginning
or end to his life. He remains a priest forever,
resembling the Son of God.

4Consider then how great this Melchizedek
was. Even Abraham, the great patriarch of Israel,
recognized this by giving him a tenth of what he
had taken in battle. 5Now the law of Moses required that the priests, who are descendants of
Levi, must collect a tithe from the rest of the
people of Israel, who are also descendants of
Abraham. 6But Melchizedek, who was not a descendant of Levi, collected a tenth from Abraham. And Melchizedek placed a blessing upon
Abraham, the one who had already received the
promises of God. 7And without question, the
person who has the power to give a blessing is
greater than the one who is blessed.

8The priests who collect tithes are men who
die, so Melchizedek is greater than they are, because we are told that he lives on. 9In addition, we
might even say that these Levites—the ones who
collect the tithe—paid a tithe to Melchizedek
when their ancestor Abraham paid a tithe to him.
10For although Levi wasn't born yet, the seed
from which he came was in Abraham's body
when Melchizedek collected the tithe from him.

11So if the priesthood of Levi, on which the law
was based, could have achieved the perfection
God intended, why did God need to establish a
different priesthood, with a priest in the order of
Melchizedek instead of the order of Levi and
Aaron?

12And if the priesthood is changed, the law
must also be changed to permit it. 13For the
priest we are talking about belongs to a different
tribe, whose members have never served at the
altar as priests. 14What I mean is, our Lord came
from the tribe of Judah, and Moses never mentioned priests coming from that tribe.

Jesus Is like Melchizedek

15This change has been made very clear since a
different priest, who is like Melchizedek, has appeared. 16Jesus became a priest, not by meeting
the physical requirement of belonging to the
tribe of Levi, but by the power of a life that cannot be destroyed. 17And the psalmist pointed
this out when he prophesied,

> "You are a priest forever in the order of
> Melchizedek."

18Yes, the old requirement about the priesthood
was set aside because it was weak and useless.
19For the law never made anything perfect. But
now we have confidence in a better hope,
through which we draw near to God.

20This new system was established with a solemn oath. Aaron's descendants became priests
without such an oath, 21but there was an oath
regarding Jesus. For God said to him,

> "The Lord has taken an oath and will not
> break his vow:
> 'You are a priest forever.'"

22Because of this oath, Jesus is the one who guarantees this better covenant with God.

23There were many priests under the old system, for death prevented them from remaining
in office. 24But because Jesus lives forever, his
priesthood lasts forever. 25Therefore he is able,
once and forever, to save those who come to God
through him. He lives forever to intercede with
God on their behalf.

26He is the kind of high priest we need because he is holy and blameless, unstained by sin.
He has been set apart from sinners and has been
given the highest place of honor in heaven.
27Unlike those other high priests, he does not
need to offer sacrifices every day. They did this
for their own sins first and then for the sins of
the people. But Jesus did this once for all when
he offered himself as the sacrifice for the people's sins. 28The law appointed high priests who
were limited by human weakness. But after the
law was given, God appointed his Son with an
oath, and his Son has been made the perfect
High Priest forever.

CHAPTER 8

Christ Is Our High Priest

Here is the main point: We have a High Priest
who sat down in the place of honor beside the
throne of the majestic God in heaven. 2There he
ministers in the heavenly Tabernacle, the true
place of worship that was built by the Lord and
not by human hands.

3And since every high priest is required to offer gifts and sacrifices, our High Priest must
make an offering, too. 4If he were here on earth,
he would not even be a priest, since there already
are priests who offer the gifts required by the
law. 5They serve in a system of worship that is
only a copy, a shadow of the real one in heaven.
For when Moses was getting ready to build the
Tabernacle, God gave him this warning: "Be sure
that you make everything according to the pattern I have shown you here on the mountain."

6But now Jesus, our High Priest, has been

given a ministry that is far superior to the old
priesthood, for he is the one who mediates for us
a far better covenant with God, based on better
promises.
7 If the first covenant had been faultless, there
would have been no need for a second covenant
to replace it. 8 But when God found fault with the
people, he said:

"The day is coming, says the LORD,
  when I will make a new covenant
  with the people of Israel and Judah.
9 This covenant will not be like the one
  I made with their ancestors
when I took them by the hand
  and led them out of the land of Egypt.
They did not remain faithful to my
    covenant,
  so I turned my back on them, says
    the LORD.
10 But this is the new covenant I will make
  with the people of Israel on that day,
    says the LORD:
I will put my laws in their minds,
  and I will write them on their hearts.
I will be their God,
  and they will be my people.
11 And they will not need to teach their
    neighbors,
  nor will they need to teach their relatives,
  saying, 'You should know the LORD.'
For everyone, from the least to the greatest,
  will know me already.
12 And I will forgive their wickedness,
  and I will never again remember
    their sins."

13 When God speaks of a "new" covenant, it
means he has made the first one obsolete. It is
now out of date and will soon disappear.

CHAPTER 9

Old Rules about Worship

That first covenant between God and Israel had
regulations for worship and a place of worship
here on earth. 2 There were two rooms in that
Tabernacle. In the first room were a lampstand,
a table, and sacred loaves of bread on the table.
This room was called the Holy Place. 3 Then
there was a curtain, and behind the curtain was
the second room called the Most Holy Place. 4 In
that room were a gold incense altar and a
wooden chest called the Ark of the Covenant,
which was covered with gold on all sides. Inside
the Ark were a gold jar containing manna,
Aaron's staff that sprouted leaves, and the stone
tablets of the covenant. 5 Above the Ark were
the cherubim of divine glory, whose wings
stretched out over the Ark's cover, the place of
atonement. But we cannot explain these things
in detail now.
6 When these things were all in place, the
priests regularly entered the first room as they
performed their religious duties. 7 But only the
high priest ever entered the Most Holy Place, and
only once a year. And he always offered blood for
his own sins and for the sins the people had
committed in ignorance. 8 By these regulations
the Holy Spirit revealed that the entrance to the
Most Holy Place was not freely open as long as
the Tabernacle and the system it represented
were still in use.
9 This is an illustration pointing to the present
time. For the gifts and sacrifices that the priests
offer are not able to cleanse the consciences of
the people who bring them. 10 For that old system deals only with food and drink and various
cleansing ceremonies—physical regulations that
were in effect only until a better system could be
established.

Christ Is the Perfect Sacrifice

11 So Christ has now become the High Priest over
all the good things that have come. He has entered that greater, more perfect Tabernacle in
heaven, which was not made by human hands
and is not part of this created world. 12 With his
own blood—not the blood of goats and calves—
he entered the Most Holy Place once for all time
and secured our redemption forever.
13 Under the old system, the blood of goats
and bulls and the ashes of a heifer could cleanse
people's bodies from ceremonial impurity. 14 Just
think how much more the blood of Christ will
purify our consciences from sinful deeds so that
we can worship the living God. For by the power
of the eternal Spirit, Christ offered himself to
God as a perfect sacrifice for our sins. 15 That is
why he is the one who mediates a new covenant
between God and people, so that all who are
called can receive the eternal inheritance God
has promised them. For Christ died to set them
free from the penalty of the sins they had committed under that first covenant.
16 Now when someone leaves a will, it is necessary to prove that the person who made it is
dead. 17 The will goes into effect only after the
person's death. While the person who made it is
still alive, the will cannot be put into effect.
18 That is why even the first covenant was put
into effect with the blood of an animal. 19 For

after Moses had read each of God's commandments to all the people, he took the blood of
calves and goats, along with water, and sprinkled
both the book of God's law and all the people, using hyssop branches and scarlet wool. 20Then
he said, "This blood confirms the covenant God
has made with you." 21And in the same way, he
sprinkled blood on the Tabernacle and on
everything used for worship. 22In fact, according to the law of Moses, nearly everything was
purified with blood. For without the shedding of
blood, there is no forgiveness.

23That is why the Tabernacle and everything
in it, which were copies of things in heaven, had
to be purified by the blood of animals. But the
real things in heaven had to be purified with far
better sacrifices than the blood of animals.

24For Christ did not enter into a holy place
made with human hands, which was only a copy
of the true one in heaven. He entered into
heaven itself to appear now before God on our
behalf. 25And he did not enter heaven to offer
himself again and again, like the high priest here
on earth who enters the Most Holy Place year after year with the blood of an animal. 26If that
had been necessary, Christ would have had to
die again and again, ever since the world began.
But now, once for all time, he has appeared at the
end of the age to remove sin by his own death as
a sacrifice.

27And just as each person is destined to die
once and after that comes judgment, 28so also
Christ was offered once for all time as a sacrifice
to take away the sins of many people. He will
come again, not to deal with our sins, but to bring
salvation to all who are eagerly waiting for him.

CHAPTER 10

Christ's Sacrifice Once for All

The old system under the law of Moses was only
a shadow, a dim preview of the good things to
come, not the good things themselves. The sacrifices under that system were repeated again and
again, year after year, but they were never able to
provide perfect cleansing for those who came to
worship. 2If they could have provided perfect
cleansing, the sacrifices would have stopped, for
the worshipers would have been purified once
for all time, and their feelings of guilt would have
disappeared.

3But instead, those sacrifices actually reminded them of their sins year after year. 4For it
is not possible for the blood of bulls and goats to
take away sins. 5That is why, when Christ came
into the world, he said to God,

"You did not want animal sacrifices
or sin offerings.
But you have given me a body to offer.
6 You were not pleased with burnt offerings
or other offerings for sin.
7 Then I said, 'Look, I have come to do your
will, O God—
as is written about me in the Scriptures.'"

8First, Christ said, "You did not want animal sacrifices or sin offerings or burnt offerings or
other offerings for sin, nor were you pleased with
them" (though they are required by the law of
Moses). 9Then he said, "Look, I have come to do
your will." He cancels the first covenant in order
to put the second into effect. 10For God's will was
for us to be made holy by the sacrifice of the
body of Jesus Christ, once for all time.

11Under the old covenant, the priest stands
and ministers before the altar day after day,
offering the same sacrifices again and again,
which can never take away sins. 12But our High
Priest offered himself to God as a single sacrifice
for sins, good for all time. Then he sat down in
the place of honor at God's right hand. 13There
he waits until his enemies are humbled and
made a footstool under his feet. 14For by that one
offering he forever made perfect those who are
being made holy.

15And the Holy Spirit also testifies that this is
so. For he says,

16 "This is the new covenant I will make
with my people on that day, says the LORD:
I will put my laws in their hearts,
and I will write them on their minds."

17Then he says,

"I will never again remember
their sins and lawless deeds."

18And when sins have been forgiven, there is no
need to offer any more sacrifices.

A Call to Persevere

19And so, dear brothers and sisters, we can boldly
enter heaven's Most Holy Place because of the
blood of Jesus. 20By his death, Jesus opened a
new and life-giving way through the curtain into
the Most Holy Place. 21And since we have a great
High Priest who rules over God's house, 22let us
go right into the presence of God with sincere
hearts fully trusting him. For our guilty consciences have been sprinkled with Christ's blood
to make us clean, and our bodies have been
washed with pure water.

23 Let us hold tightly without wavering to the
hope we affirm, for God can be trusted to keep
his promise. **24 Let us think of ways to**
motivate one another to acts of love
and good works. 25 And let us not ne-
glect our meeting together, as some
people do, but encourage one an-
other, especially now that the day of
his return is drawing near.
26 Dear friends, if we deliberately continue
sinning after we have received knowledge of
the truth, there is no longer any sacrifice that
will cover these sins. 27 There is only the terrible
expectation of God's judgment and the raging
fire that will consume his enemies. 28 For anyone who refused to obey the law of Moses was
put to death without mercy on the testimony of
two or three witnesses. 29 Just think how much
worse the punishment will be for those who
have trampled on the Son of God, and have
treated the blood of the covenant, which made
us holy, as if it were common and unholy, and
have insulted and disdained the Holy Spirit who
brings God's mercy to us. 30 For we know the
one who said,

"I will take revenge.
I will pay them back."

He also said,

"The LORD will judge his own people."

31 It is a terrible thing to fall into the hands of the
living God.
32 Think back on those early days when you
first learned about Christ. Remember how you
remained faithful even though it meant terrible
suffering. 33 Sometimes you were exposed to
public ridicule and were beaten, and sometimes
you helped others who were suffering the same
things. 34 You suffered along with those who
were thrown into jail, and when all you owned
was taken from you, you accepted it with joy. You
knew there were better things waiting for you
that will last forever.
35 So do not throw away this confident trust in
the Lord. Remember the great reward it brings
you! 36 Patient endurance is what you need now,
so that you will continue to do God's will. Then
you will receive all that he has promised.

37 "For in just a little while,
the Coming One will come and not delay.
38 And my righteous ones will live by faith.
But I will take no pleasure in anyone
who turns away."

Key Verse **"Faith is the confidence that what we hope for will actually happen; it gives us assurance about things we cannot see."—HEBREWS 11:1**

Faith is . . .

Read HEBREWS 11:1 out loud. We can't see God, but we see evidence of him all around us. It's like the wind. We can't see the wind, but we can see evidence of it when we see leaves blow and when we feel a breeze.

Make this windsock reminder that God is REAL!

1. **Decorate one side of a sheet of construction paper to remind you of this verse.**
2. **Roll the paper into a cylinder, decorated side out. Tape the edges together.**
3. **Tape crepe paper strips to the inside of one end of the cylinder.**
4. **Punch two holes opposite each other at the other end of the cylinder. Thread yarn through the holes, and knot them to form a hanger.**

Read James 2:17-18 to find out how to show your faith!

HANG YOUR WINDSOCK OUTSIDE.
Every time you see it blowing in the wind, remember that even though we can't see God, we can know he's real!

39 But we are not like those who turn away from God to their own destruction. We are the faithful ones, whose souls will be saved.

CHAPTER 11

Great Examples of Faith

Faith is the confidence that what we hope for will actually happen; it gives us assurance about things we cannot see. 2 Through their faith, the people in days of old earned a good reputation.

3 By faith we understand that the entire universe was formed at God's command, that what we now see did not come from anything that can be seen.

4 It was by faith that Abel brought a more acceptable offering to God than Cain did. Abel's offering gave evidence that he was a righteous man, and God showed his approval of his gifts. Although Abel is long dead, he still speaks to us by his example of faith.

5 It was by faith that Enoch was taken up to heaven without dying—"he disappeared, because God took him." For before he was taken up, he was known as a person who pleased God. 6 And it is impossible to please God without faith. Anyone who wants to come to him must believe that God exists and that he rewards those who sincerely seek him.

7 It was by faith that Noah built a large boat to save his family from the flood. He obeyed God, who warned him about things that had never happened before. By his faith Noah condemned the rest of the world, and he received the righteousness that comes by faith.

8 It was by faith that Abraham obeyed when God called him to leave home and go to another land that God would give him as his inheritance. He went without knowing where he was going. 9 And even when he reached the land God promised him, he lived there by faith—for he was like a foreigner, living in tents. And so did Isaac and Jacob, who inherited the same promise. 10 Abraham was confidently looking forward to a city with eternal foundations, a city designed and built by God.

11 It was by faith that even Sarah was able to have a child, though she was barren and was too old. She believed that God would keep his promise. 12 And so a whole nation came from this one man who was as good as dead—a nation with so many people that, like the stars in the sky and the sand on the seashore, there is no way to count them.

13 All these people died still believing what God had promised them. They did not receive what was promised, but they saw it all from a distance and welcomed it. They agreed that they were foreigners and nomads here on earth. 14 Obviously people who say such things are looking forward to a country they can call their own. 15 If they had longed for the country they came from, they could have gone back. 16 But they were looking for a better place, a heavenly homeland. That is why God is not ashamed to be called their God, for he has prepared a city for them.

17 It was by faith that Abraham offered Isaac as a sacrifice when God was testing him. Abraham, who had received God's promises, was ready to sacrifice his only son, Isaac, 18 even though God had told him, "Isaac is the son through whom your descendants will be counted." 19 Abraham reasoned that if Isaac died, God was able to bring him back to life again. And in a sense, Abraham did receive his son back from the dead.

20 It was by faith that Isaac promised blessings for the future to his sons, Jacob and Esau.

21 It was by faith that Jacob, when he was old and dying, blessed each of Joseph's sons and bowed in worship as he leaned on his staff.

22 It was by faith that Joseph, when he was about to die, said confidently that the people of Israel would leave Egypt. He even commanded them to take his bones with them when they left.

23 It was by faith that Moses' parents hid him for three months when he was born. They saw that God had given them an unusual child, and they were not afraid to disobey the king's command.

24 It was by faith that Moses, when he grew up, refused to be called the son of Pharaoh's daughter. 25 He chose to share the oppression of God's people instead of enjoying the fleeting pleasures of sin. 26 He thought it was better to suffer for the sake of Christ than to own the treasures of Egypt, for he was looking ahead to his great reward. 27 It was by faith that Moses left the land of Egypt, not fearing the king's anger. He kept right on going because he kept his eyes on the one who is invisible. 28 It was by faith that Moses commanded the people of Israel to keep the Passover and to sprinkle blood on the doorposts so that the angel of death would not kill their firstborn sons.

29 It was by faith that the people of Israel went right through the Red Sea as though they were on dry ground. But when the Egyptians tried to follow, they were all drowned.

30 It was by faith that the people of Israel

marched around Jericho for seven days, and the walls came crashing down.
31It was by faith that Rahab the prostitute was not destroyed with the people in her city who refused to obey God. For she had given a friendly welcome to the spies.

32How much more do I need to say? It would take too long to recount the stories of the faith of Gideon, Barak, Samson, Jephthah, David, Samuel, and all the prophets. 33By faith these people overthrew kingdoms, ruled with justice, and received what God had promised them. They shut the mouths of lions, 34quenched the flames of fire, and escaped death by the edge of the sword. Their weakness was turned to strength. They became strong in battle and put whole armies to flight. 35Women received their loved ones back again from death.

But others were tortured, refusing to turn from God in order to be set free. They placed their hope in a better life after the resurrection. 36Some were jeered at, and their backs were cut open with whips. Others were chained in prisons. 37Some died by stoning, some were sawed in half, and others were killed with the sword. Some went about wearing skins of sheep and goats, destitute and oppressed and mistreated. 38They were too good for this world, wandering over deserts and mountains, hiding in caves and holes in the ground.

39All these people earned a good reputation because of their faith, yet none of them received all that God had promised. 40For God had something better in mind for us, so that they would not reach perfection without us.

CHAPTER 12

God's Discipline Proves His Love

Therefore, since we are surrounded by such a huge crowd of witnesses to the life of faith, let us strip off every weight that slows us down, especially the sin that so easily trips us up. And let us run with endurance the race God has set before us. 2We do this by keeping our eyes on Jesus, the champion who initiates and perfects our faith. Because of the joy awaiting him, he endured the cross, disregarding its shame. Now he is seated in the place of honor beside God's throne. 3Think of all the hostility he endured from sinful people; then you won't become weary and give up. 4After all, you have not yet given your lives in your struggle against sin.

5And have you forgotten the encouraging words God spoke to you as his children? He said,

"My child, don't make light of the LORD's
  discipline,
 and don't give up when he corrects you.
6 For the LORD disciplines those he loves,
 and he punishes each one he accepts as
  his child."

7As you endure this divine discipline, remember that God is treating you as his own children. Who ever heard of a child who is never disciplined by its father? 8If God doesn't discipline you as he does all of his children, it means that you are illegitimate and are not really his children at all. 9Since we respected our earthly fathers who disciplined us, shouldn't we submit even more to the discipline of the Father of our spirits, and live forever?

10For our earthly fathers disciplined us for a few years, doing the best they knew how. But God's discipline is always good for us, so that we might share in his holiness. 11No discipline is enjoyable while it is happening—it's painful! But afterward there will be a peaceful harvest of right living for those who are trained in this way.

12So take a new grip with your tired hands and strengthen your weak knees. 13Mark out a straight path for your feet so that those who are weak and lame will not fall but become strong.

A Call to Listen to God

14Work at living in peace with everyone, and work at living a holy life, for those who are not holy will not see the Lord. 15Look after each other so that none of you fails to receive the grace of God. Watch out that no poisonous root of bitterness grows up to trouble you, corrupting many. 16Make sure that no one is immoral or godless like Esau, who traded his birthright as the firstborn son for a single meal. 17You know that afterward, when he wanted his father's blessing, he was rejected. It was too late for repentance, even though he begged with bitter tears.

18You have not come to a physical mountain, to a place of flaming fire, darkness, gloom, and whirlwind, as the Israelites did at Mount Sinai. 19For they heard an awesome trumpet blast and a voice so terrible that they begged God to stop speaking. 20They staggered back under God's command: "If even an animal touches the mountain, it must be stoned to death." 21Moses himself was so frightened at the sight that he said, "I am terrified and trembling."

22No, you have come to Mount Zion, to the city of the living God, the heavenly Jerusalem, and to countless thousands of angels in a joyful gathering. 23You have come to the assembly of God's firstborn children, whose names are written in heaven. You have come to God himself, who is the judge over all things. You have come to the spirits of the righteous ones in heaven who have now been made perfect. 24You have come to Jesus, the one who mediates the new covenant between God and people, and to the sprinkled blood, which speaks of forgiveness instead of crying out for vengeance like the blood of Abel.

25Be careful that you do not refuse to listen to the One who is speaking. For if the people of Israel did not escape when they refused to listen to Moses, the earthly messenger, we will certainly not escape if we reject the One who speaks to us from heaven! 26When God spoke from Mount Sinai his voice shook the earth, but now he makes another promise: "Once again I will shake not only the earth but the heavens also." 27This means that all of creation will be shaken and removed, so that only unshakable things will remain.

28Since we are receiving a Kingdom that is unshakable, let us be thankful and please God by worshiping him with holy fear and awe. 29For our God is a devouring fire.

CHAPTER 13

Concluding Words

Keep on loving each other as brothers and sisters. 2Don't forget to show hospitality to strangers, for some who have done this have entertained angels without realizing it! 3Remember those in prison, as if you were there yourself. Remember also those being mistreated, as if you felt their pain in your own bodies.

4Give honor to marriage, and remain faithful to one another in marriage. God will surely judge people who are immoral and those who commit adultery.

5Don't love money; be satisfied with what you have. For God has said,

"I will never fail you.
 I will never abandon you."

6So we can say with confidence,

"The LORD is my helper,
 so I will have no fear.
 What can mere people do to me?"

7Remember your leaders who taught you the word of God. Think of all the good that has come from their lives, and follow the example of their faith.

8Jesus Christ is the same yesterday, today, and forever. 9So do not be attracted by strange, new ideas. Your strength comes from God's grace, not from rules about food, which don't help those who follow them.

10We have an altar from which the priests in the Tabernacle have no right to eat. 11Under the old system, the high priest brought the blood of animals into the Holy Place as a sacrifice for sin, and the bodies of the animals were burned outside the camp. 12So also Jesus suffered and died outside the city gates to make his people holy by means of his own blood. 13So let us go out to him, outside the camp, and bear the disgrace he bore. 14For this world is not our permanent home; we are looking forward to a home yet to come.

15Therefore, let us offer through Jesus a continual sacrifice of praise to God, proclaiming our allegiance to his name. 16And don't forget to do good and to share with those in need. These are the sacrifices that please God.

17Obey your spiritual leaders, and do what they say. Their work is to watch over your souls, and they are accountable to God. Give them reason to do this with joy and not with sorrow. That would certainly not be for your benefit.

18Pray for us, for our conscience is clear and we want to live honorably in everything we do. 19And especially pray that I will be able to come back to you soon.

20 Now may the God of peace—
 who brought up from the dead our
  Lord Jesus,
 the great Shepherd of the sheep,
  and ratified an eternal covenant
   with his blood—
21 may he equip you with all you need
  for doing his will.
 May he produce in you,
  through the power of Jesus Christ,
 every good thing that is pleasing to him.
  All glory to him forever and ever! Amen.

22I urge you, dear brothers and sisters, to pay attention to what I have written in this brief exhortation.

23I want you to know that our brother Timothy has been released from jail. If he comes here soon, I will bring him with me to see you.

24Greet all your leaders and all the believers there. The believers from Italy send you their greetings.

25May God's grace be with you all.

JAMES Encouraging Words

Look for 1 hidden message in James!

The book of James is all about putting our faith into action. It encourages us to

- **FURTHER OUR FAITH**
- **TURN FROM TEMPTATION**
- **TAME OUR TONGUES**
- **PATIENTLY PRAY**

Just Ask!

Want an A? Study! Want to become a good basketball player? Practice! But there's something that God will do *for* you, and all you have to do is ask! **Check it out in James 1:5.**

WiLd ThInG!

It's out of control! Even the most skilled animal tamers can't get this creature to behave. Don't let its small size fool you. Its power is huge! **If you dare, read James 3:2-10 to learn more about this beast.**

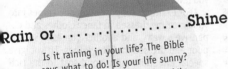

Rain or . . . . Shine

Is it raining in your life? The Bible says what to do! Is your life sunny? There's advice for that, too! **Read the Bible's advice for every kind of day in James 5:13!**

Hats for Sale!

Picture a hat store—big hats, little hats, cowboy hats, sun hats.

But there's a special hat that's *not* for sale. You'll have to ask God about that hat. There's a special way to get it. **Look in James 1:12 to find out how.**

Timeline

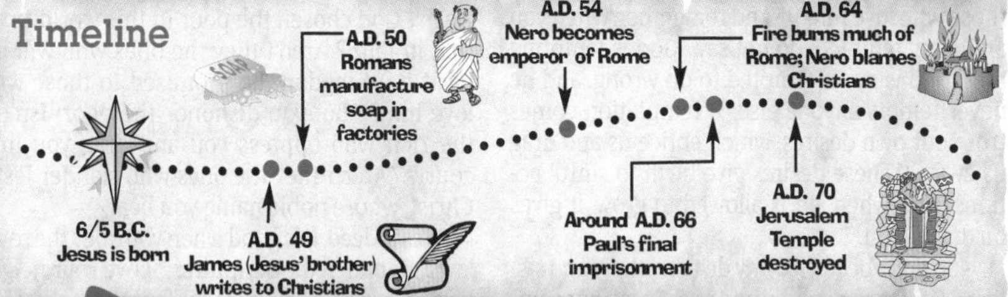

6/5 B.C. Jesus is born
A.D. 49 James (Jesus' brother) writes to Christians
A.D. 50 Romans manufacture soap in factories
A.D. 54 Nero becomes emperor of Rome
A.D. 64 Fire burns much of Rome; Nero blames Christians
Around A.D. 66 Paul's final imprisonment
A.D. 70 Jerusalem Temple destroyed

The JESUS CONNECTION

You can't get to heaven by doing good things. In fact, the only way to get to heaven is by having faith in Jesus. But if you believe in Jesus and he is Lord over your life, you're going to want to do things his way. The book of James encourages us to put our faith into practice. It's great to be saved. **It's even better to be saved and to spend our lives serving others!**

James 1 . . . page 1222

CHAPTER 1

Greetings from James

This letter is from James, a slave of God and of the Lord Jesus Christ.

I am writing to the "twelve tribes"—Jewish believers scattered abroad.

Greetings!

Faith and Endurance

2Dear brothers and sisters, when troubles of any kind come your way, consider it an opportunity for great joy. 3For you know that when your faith is tested, your endurance has a chance to grow. 4So let it grow, for when your endurance is fully developed, you will be perfect and complete, needing nothing.

5If you need wisdom, ask our generous God, and he will give it to you. He will not rebuke you for asking. 6But when you ask him, be sure that your faith is in God alone. Do not waver, for a person with divided loyalty is as unsettled as a wave of the sea that is blown and tossed by the wind. 7Such people should not expect to receive anything from the Lord. 8Their loyalty is divided between God and the world, and they are unstable in everything they do.

9Believers who are poor have something to boast about, for God has honored them. 10And those who are rich should boast that God has humbled them. They will fade away like a little flower in the field. 11The hot sun rises and the grass withers; the little flower droops and falls, and its beauty fades away. In the same way, the rich will fade away with all of their achievements.

12God blesses those who patiently endure testing and temptation. Afterward they will receive the crown of life that God has promised to those who love him. 13And remember, when you are being tempted, do not say, "God is tempting me." God is never tempted to do wrong, and he never tempts anyone else. 14Temptation comes from our own desires, which entice us and drag us away. 15These desires give birth to sinful actions. And when sin is allowed to grow, it gives birth to death.

16So don't be misled, my dear brothers and sisters. 17Whatever is good and perfect is a gift coming down to us from God our Father, who created all the lights in the heavens. He never changes or casts a shifting shadow. 18He chose to give birth to us by giving us his true word. And we, out of all creation, became his prized possession.

Listening and Doing

19Understand this, my dear brothers and sisters: You must all be quick to listen, slow to speak, and slow to get angry. 20Human anger does not produce the righteousness God desires. 21So get rid of all the filth and evil in your lives, and humbly accept the word God has planted in your hearts, for it has the power to save your souls.

22But don't just listen to God's word. You must do what it says. Otherwise, you are only fooling yourselves. 23For if you listen to the word and don't obey, it is like glancing at your face in a mirror. 24You see yourself, walk away, and forget what you look like. 25But if you look carefully into the perfect law that sets you free, and if you do what it says and don't forget what you heard, then God will bless you for doing it.

26If you claim to be religious but don't control your tongue, you are fooling yourself, and your religion is worthless. 27Pure and genuine religion in the sight of God the Father means caring for orphans and widows in their distress and refusing to let the world corrupt you.

CHAPTER 2

A Warning against Prejudice

My dear brothers and sisters, how can you claim to have faith in our glorious Lord Jesus Christ if you favor some people over others?

2For example, suppose someone comes into your meeting dressed in fancy clothes and expensive jewelry, and another comes in who is poor and dressed in dirty clothes. 3If you give special attention and a good seat to the rich person, but you say to the poor one, "You can stand over there, or else sit on the floor"—well, 4doesn't this discrimination show that your judgments are guided by evil motives?

5Listen to me, dear brothers and sisters. Hasn't God chosen the poor in this world to be rich in faith? Aren't they the ones who will inherit the Kingdom he promised to those who love him? 6But you dishonor the poor! Isn't it the rich who oppress you and drag you into court? 7Aren't they the ones who slander Jesus Christ, whose noble name you bear?

8Yes indeed, it is good when you obey the royal law as found in the Scriptures: "Love your neighbor as yourself." 9But if you favor some people over others, you are committing a sin. You are guilty of breaking the law.

10For the person who keeps all of the laws except one is as guilty as a person who has broken all of God's laws. 11For the same God who said,

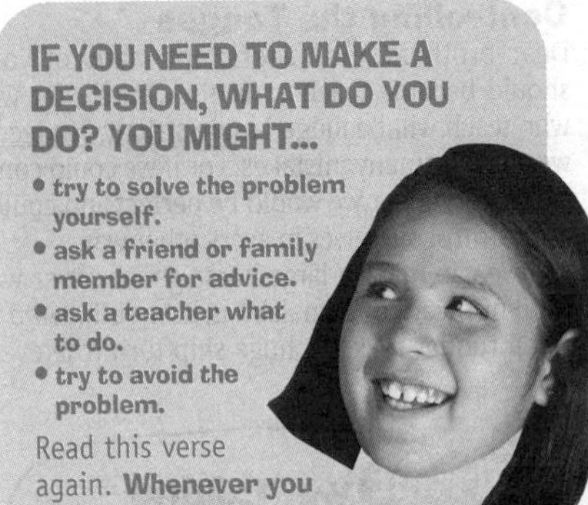

Make a bunch of fun stickers to remind you to go to God first!

1. Cut colored self-adhesive paper into fun shapes.
2. On each shape, write something to remind you of this verse.
3. Now peel off the backing, and stick those stickers all over the place.

Remember to go to God *first* whenever you need wisdom.

Got God? Need wisdom? Go to God first!

Read Proverbs 9:10 for more about wisdom!

"You must not commit adultery," also said, "You
must not murder." So if you murder someone
but do not commit adultery, you have still broken
the law.

12So whatever you say or whatever you do, remember that you will be judged by the law that
sets you free. 13There will be no mercy for those
who have not shown mercy to others. But if you
have been merciful, God will be merciful when
he judges you.

Faith without Good Deeds Is Dead

14What good is it, dear brothers and sisters, if
you say you have faith but don't show it by your
actions? Can that kind of faith save anyone?
15Suppose you see a brother or sister who has no
food or clothing, 16and you say, "Good-bye and
have a good day; stay warm and eat well"—but
then you don't give that person any food or clothing. What good does that do?

17So you see, faith by itself isn't enough. Unless
it produces good deeds, it is dead and useless.

18Now someone may argue, "Some people
have faith; others have good deeds." But I say,
"How can you show me your faith if you don't
have good deeds? I will show you my faith by my
good deeds."

19You say you have faith, for you believe that
there is one God. Good for you! Even the demons
believe this, and they tremble in terror. 20How
foolish! Can't you see that faith without good
deeds is useless?

21Don't you remember that our ancestor
Abraham was shown to be right with God by his
actions when he offered his son Isaac on the altar? 22You see, his faith and his actions worked
together. His actions made his faith complete.
23And so it happened just as the Scriptures say:
"Abraham believed God, and God counted him
as righteous because of his faith." He was even
called the friend of God. 24So you see, we are
shown to be right with God by what we do, not
by faith alone.

25Rahab the prostitute is another example.
She was shown to be right with God by her actions when she hid those messengers and sent
them safely away by a different road. 26Just as
the body is dead without breath, so also faith is
dead without good works.

CHAPTER 3
Controlling the Tongue

Dear brothers and sisters, not many of you
should become teachers in the church, for we
who teach will be judged more strictly. 2Indeed,
we all make many mistakes. For if we could control our tongues, we would be perfect and could
also control ourselves in every other way.
3We can make a large horse go wherever we
want by means of a small bit in its mouth. 4And a
small rudder makes a huge ship turn wherever

FUN-fact
You Talking to Me?
JAMES
JAMES
JAMES

Have you ever had two friends with the same name? It can get confusing!

That's how it is with the three guys named **James** in the New Testament. Two of the original twelve disciples were named James. But it was probably Jesus' half brother James who wrote the book of James.

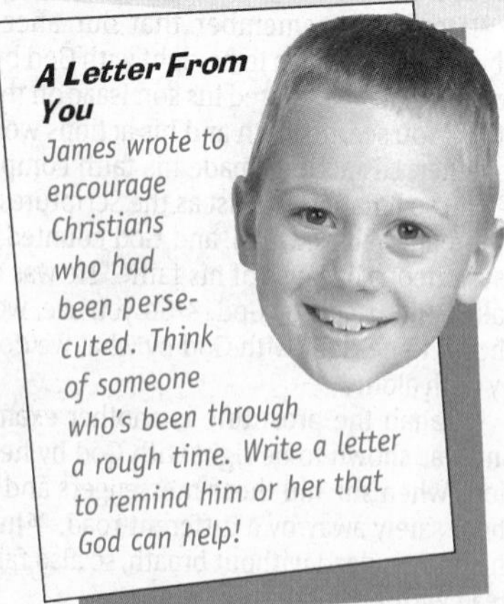
A Letter From You
James wrote to encourage Christians who had been persecuted. Think of someone who's been through a rough time. Write a letter to remind him or her that God can help!

the pilot chooses to go, even though the winds
are strong. 5In the same way, the tongue is a small
thing that makes grand speeches.
But a tiny spark can set a great forest on fire.
6And among all the parts of the body, the
tongue is a flame of fire. It is a whole world of
wickedness, corrupting your entire body. It can
set your whole life on fire, for it is set on fire by
hell itself.
7People can tame all kinds of animals, birds,
reptiles, and fish, 8but no one can tame the
tongue. It is restless and evil, full of deadly poison. 9Sometimes it praises our Lord and Father,
and sometimes it curses those who have been
made in the image of God. 10And so blessing and
cursing come pouring out of the same mouth.
Surely, my brothers and sisters, this is not right!
11Does a spring of water bubble out with both
fresh water and bitter water? 12Does a fig tree
produce olives, or a grapevine produce figs? No,
and you can't draw fresh water from a salty
spring.

True Wisdom Comes from God

13If you are wise and understand God's ways,
prove it by living an honorable life, doing good
works with the humility that comes from wisdom. 14But if you are bitterly jealous and there is
selfish ambition in your heart, don't cover up the
truth with boasting and lying. 15For jealousy and
selfishness are not God's kind of wisdom. Such
things are earthly, unspiritual, and demonic.
16For wherever there is jealousy and selfish
ambition, there you will find disorder and evil of
every kind.
17But the wisdom from above is first of all
pure. It is also peace loving, gentle at all times,
and willing to yield to others. It is full of mercy
and the fruit of good deeds. It shows no favoritism and is always sincere. 18And those who are
peacemakers will plant seeds of peace and reap a
harvest of righteousness.

CHAPTER 4
Drawing Close to God

What is causing the quarrels and fights among
you? Don't they come from the evil desires at war
within you? 2You want what you don't have, so
you scheme and kill to get it. You are jealous of
what others have, but you can't get it, so you fight
and wage war to take it away from them. Yet you
don't have what you want because you don't ask
God for it. 3And even when you ask, you don't get
it because your motives are all wrong—you want
only what will give you pleasure.

4You adulterers! Don't you realize that friendship with the world makes you an enemy of God?
I say it again: If you want to be a friend of the
world, you make yourself an enemy of God. 5Do
you think the Scriptures have no meaning? They
say that God is passionate that the spirit he has
placed within us should be faithful to him. 6And
he gives grace generously. As the Scriptures say,

> "God opposes the proud
> but gives grace to the humble."

7So humble yourselves before God. Resist the
devil, and he will flee from you. 8Come close to
God, and God will come close to you. Wash your
hands, you sinners; purify your hearts, for your
loyalty is divided between God and the world.
9Let there be tears for what you have done. Let
there be sorrow and deep grief. Let there be sadness instead of laughter, and gloom instead of
joy. 10Humble yourselves before the Lord, and he
will lift you up in honor.

Warning against Judging Others

11Don't speak evil against each other, dear brothers and sisters. If you criticize and judge each
other, then you are criticizing and judging God's
law. But your job is to obey the law, not to judge
whether it applies to you. 12God alone, who gave
the law, is the Judge. He alone has the power to
save or to destroy. So what right do you have to
judge your neighbor?

Warning about Self-Confidence

13Look here, you who say, "Today or tomorrow
we are going to a certain town and will stay there
a year. We will do business there and make a
profit." 14How do you know what your life will be
like tomorrow? Your life is like the morning fog—
it's here a little while, then it's gone. 15What you
ought to say is, "If the Lord wants us to, we will
live and do this or that." 16Otherwise you are
boasting about your own pretentious plans, and
all such boasting is evil.

17Remember, it is sin to know what you ought
to do and then not do it.

CHAPTER 5

Warning to the Rich

Look here, you rich people: Weep and groan with
anguish because of all the terrible troubles
ahead of you. 2Your wealth is rotting away, and
your fine clothes are moth-eaten rags. 3Your
gold and silver are corroded. The very wealth you
were counting on will eat away your flesh like
fire. This corroded treasure you have hoarded
will testify against you on the day of judgment.
4For listen! Hear the cries of the field workers
whom you have cheated of their pay. The cries of
those who harvest your fields have reached the
ears of the LORD of Heaven's Armies.

5You have spent your years on earth in luxury,
satisfying your every desire. You have fattened
yourselves for the day of slaughter. 6You have
condemned and killed innocent people, who do
not resist you.

Patience and Endurance

7Dear brothers and sisters, be patient as you wait
for the Lord's return. Consider the farmers who
patiently wait for the rains in the fall and in the
spring. They eagerly look for the valuable harvest
to ripen. 8You, too, must be patient. Take courage, for the coming of the Lord is near.

9Don't grumble about each other, brothers
and sisters, or you will be judged. For look—the
Judge is standing at the door!

10For examples of patience in suffering, dear
brothers and sisters, look at the prophets who
spoke in the name of the Lord. 11We give great
honor to those who endure under suffering. For
instance, you know about Job, a man of great endurance. You can see how the Lord was kind to
him at the end, for the Lord is full of tenderness
and mercy.

12But most of all, my brothers and sisters,
never take an oath, by heaven or earth or anything else. Just say a simple yes or no, so that you
will not sin and be condemned.

The Power of Prayer

13Are any of you suffering hardships? You
should pray. Are any of you happy? You should
sing praises. 14Are any of you sick? You should
call for the elders of the church to come and pray
over you, anointing you with oil in the name of
the Lord. 15Such a prayer offered in faith will
heal the sick, and the Lord will make you well.
And if you have committed any sins, you will be
forgiven.

**16Confess your sins to each other
and pray for each other so that you
may be healed. The earnest prayer
of a righteous person has great
power and produces wonderful re-
sults.** 17Elijah was as human as we are, and yet
when he prayed earnestly that no rain would fall,
none fell for three and a half years! 18Then, when
he prayed again, the sky sent down rain and the
earth began to yield its crops.

James 5 . . . page 1226

Restore Wandering Believers

[19]My dear brothers and sisters, if someone
among you wanders away from the truth and is
brought back, [20]you can be sure that whoever
brings the sinner back from wandering will save
that person from death and bring about the forgiveness of many sins.

1 PETER Words of Encouragement

Look for 2 hidden messages in 1 Peter!

Peter wrote this letter to Christians who were suffering for their faith. It tells about
- **FAITH AND FIRE**
- **PAIN AND PAYMENT**
- **CHRIST THE CORNERSTONE**
- **BEAUTIFUL BLESSINGS**

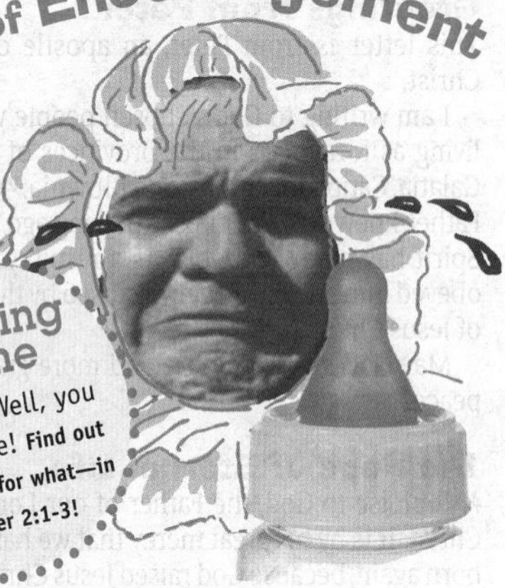

Feeding Time

Thirsty? Well, you should be! **Find out why—and for what—in 1 Peter 2:1-3!**

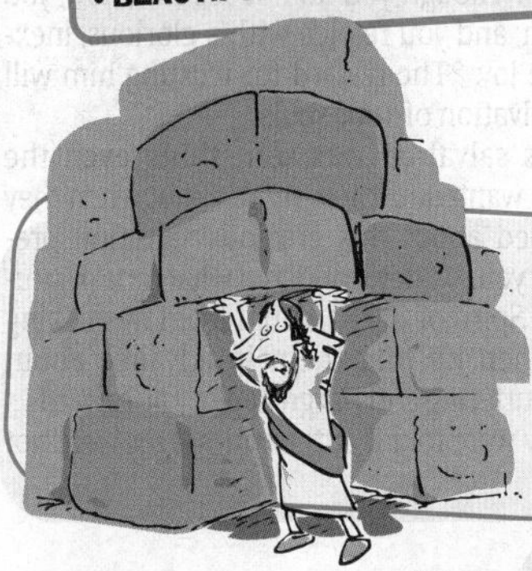

Construction Zone

God is a builder, but his construction project isn't like any other in the world. And you're part of it! **See for yourself in 1 Peter 2:4-6.**

You're Worth How Much?

Did you know that someone paid a price for you? A *huge* price? **Find out how much you're worth by reading 1 Peter 1:18-20.**

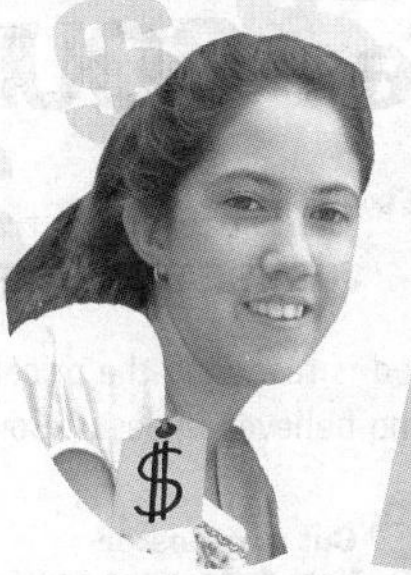

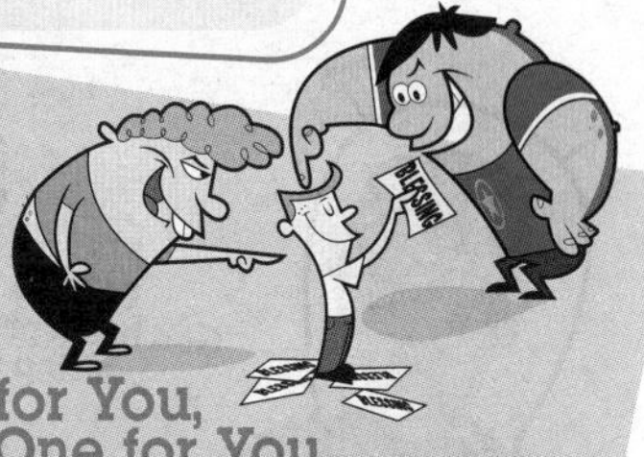

One for You, and One for You...

If someone insults you, what do you do? OK, let's rephrase that—what *should* you do? **The answer might surprise you. Check it out in 1 Peter 3:8-9!**

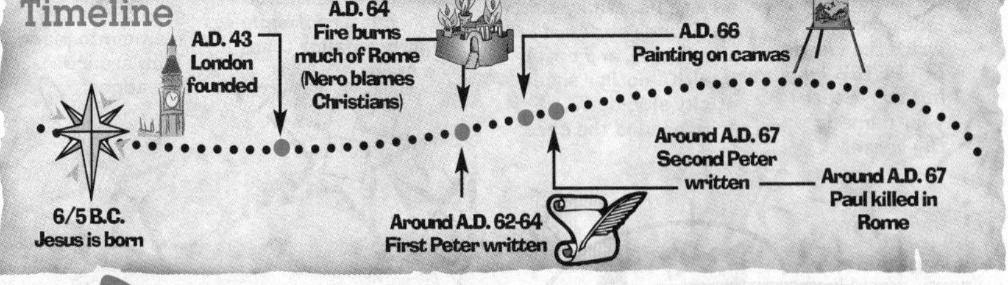

Timeline
6/5 B.C. Jesus is born
A.D. 43 London founded
A.D. 64 Fire burns much of Rome (Nero blames Christians)
Around A.D. 62-64 First Peter written
A.D. 66 Painting on canvas
Around A.D. 67 Second Peter written
Around A.D. 67 Paul killed in Rome

The JESUS CONNECTION

Peter knew what he was talking about when he encouraged other Christians. He himself had been beaten and jailed for being a Christian, and he was eventually killed for his faith. But Peter knew that faith in Jesus is the most important thing in life, and he had grown to the point that nothing could shake his faith in Jesus. **The next time you feel like it's hard to be a Christian, remember Peter and read this book again.**

CHAPTER 1

Greetings from Peter

This letter is from Peter, an apostle of Jesus
Christ.
I am writing to God's chosen people who are
living as foreigners in the provinces of Pontus,
Galatia, Cappadocia, Asia, and Bithynia. 2God the
Father knew you and chose you long ago, and his
Spirit has made you holy. As a result, you have
obeyed him and have been cleansed by the blood
of Jesus Christ.
May God give you more and more grace and
peace.

The Hope of Eternal Life

3All praise to God, the Father of our Lord Jesus
Christ. It is by his great mercy that we have been
born again, because God raised Jesus Christ from
the dead. Now we live with great expectation,
4and we have a priceless inheritance—an inheritance that is kept in heaven for you, pure and un-
defiled, beyond the reach of change and decay.
5And through your faith, God is protecting you
by his power until you receive this salvation,
which is ready to be revealed on the last day for
all to see.
6So be truly glad. There is wonderful joy
ahead, even though you must endure many trials
for a little while. 7These trials will show that your
faith is genuine. It is being tested as fire tests and
purifies gold—though your faith is far more precious than mere gold. So when your faith remains strong through many trials, it will bring
you much praise and glory and honor on the day
when Jesus Christ is revealed to the whole world.
8You love him even though you have never
seen him. Though you do not see him now, you
trust him; and you rejoice with a glorious, inex-
pressible joy. 9The reward for trusting him will
be the salvation of your souls.
10This salvation was something even the
prophets wanted to know more about when they
prophesied about this gracious salvation prepared for you. 11They wondered what time or situation the Spirit of Christ within them was talking
about when he told them in advance about
Christ's suffering and his great glory afterward.
12They were told that their messages were not

Safe and SOUND

GUESS WHAT!
God has a priceless gift waiting for you.

Want to find out what it is?
JUST READ 1 PETER 1:3-6!

WOW! God is reserving the priceless gift of salvation for everyone who believes in Jesus. So make this reminder!

1. On a colorful index card, write the words of 1 PETER 1:4, but substitute your name in the verse.
2. Lay one sheet of clear Con-Tact paper on a table, sticky side up. Place your card in the center, and cover it with another sheet, sticky side down. Trim around the card.
3. Cut two poster-board stars the same size. In the center of each, cut a rectangle slightly smaller than the card.
4. Sandwich the card between the two star shapes, and glue the starry frame into place. Trim around the edges.

Hang your star reminder in your room so you can see it every day.

See how your card is kept safe between the clear sheets? That's how your gift of salvation is being kept safe for you in heaven!

for themselves, but for you. And now this Good
News has been announced to you by those who
preached in the power of the Holy Spirit sent
from heaven. It is all so wonderful that even the
angels are eagerly watching these things happen.

A Call to Holy Living

13So prepare your minds for action and exercise
self-control. Put all your hope in the gracious salvation that will come to you when Jesus Christ is
revealed to the world. 14So you must live as God's
obedient children. Don't slip back into your old
ways of living to satisfy your own desires. You
didn't know any better then. 15But now you must
be holy in everything you do, just as God who
chose you is holy. 16For the Scriptures say, "You
must be holy because I am holy."

17And remember that the heavenly Father to
whom you pray has no favorites. He will judge or
reward you according to what you do. So you
must live in reverent fear of him during your time
here as "temporary residents." 18For you know
that God paid a ransom to save you from the
empty life you inherited from your ancestors.
And it was not paid with mere gold or silver,
which lose their value. 19It was the precious
blood of Christ, the sinless, spotless Lamb of God.
20God chose him as your ransom long before the
world began, but now in these last days he has
been revealed for your sake.

21Through Christ you have come to trust in
God. And you have placed your faith and hope in
God because he raised Christ from the dead and
gave him great glory.

22You were cleansed from your sins when you
obeyed the truth, so now you must show sincere
love to each other as brothers and sisters. Love
each other deeply with all your heart.

23For you have been born again, but not to a
life that will quickly end. Your new life will last
forever because it comes from the eternal, living
word of God. 24As the Scriptures say,

"People are like grass;
their beauty is like a flower in the field.
The grass withers and the flower fades.
25 But the word of the Lord remains forever."

And that word is the Good News that was
preached to you.

CHAPTER 2

So get rid of all evil behavior. Be done with all deceit, hypocrisy, jealousy, and all unkind speech.
2Like newborn babies, you must crave pure spiritual milk so that you will grow into a full experience of salvation. Cry out for this nourishment,
3now that you have had a taste of the Lord's
kindness.

Living Stones for God's House

4You are coming to Christ, who is the living
cornerstone of God's temple. He was rejected by
people, but he was chosen by God for great honor.

5And you are living stones that God is building
into his spiritual temple. What's more, you are
his holy priests. Through the mediation of Jesus
Christ, you offer spiritual sacrifices that please
God. 6As the Scriptures say,

"I am placing a cornerstone in Jerusalem,
chosen for great honor,
and anyone who trusts in him
will never be disgraced."

7Yes, you who trust him recognize the honor God
has given him. But for those who reject him,

"The stone that the builders rejected
has now become the cornerstone."

8And,

"He is the stone that makes people stumble,
the rock that makes them fall."

FUN-fact What's the Church?

Did you know the Bible never mentions "church buildings," but the word *church* is mentioned more than 100 times? That's because the church isn't a building! The church is people!

After Jesus went back to heaven, God sent the Holy Spirit to live inside Jesus' followers. That's when the church began.

Wow—think about it! God's Holy Spirit is working in you to make you more like Jesus. And that's true of every other Christian.

Think of Christians you know and how you've seen God's presence in them. Then write a short note to each one, describing what you've seen. Mail or hand out the notes as an encouragement to the church!

They stumble because they do not obey God's
word, and so they meet the fate that was planned
for them.
9But you are not like that, for you are a chosen
people. You are royal priests, a holy nation, God's
very own possession. As a result, you can show
others the goodness of God, for he called you out
of the darkness into his wonderful light.

10 "Once you had no identity as a people;
now you are God's people.
Once you received no mercy;
now you have received God's mercy."

11Dear friends, I warn you as "temporary residents and foreigners" to keep away from worldly
desires that wage war against your very souls.
12Be careful to live properly among your unbelieving neighbors. Then even if they accuse you
of doing wrong, they will see your honorable behavior, and they will give honor to God when he
judges the world.

Respecting People in Authority

13For the Lord's sake, submit to all human authority—whether the king as head of state, 14or
the officials he has appointed. For the king has
sent them to punish those who do wrong and to
honor those who do right.
15It is God's will that your honorable lives
should silence those ignorant people who make
foolish accusations against you. 16For you are
free, yet you are God's slaves, so don't use your
freedom as an excuse to do evil. 17Respect everyone, and love the family of believers. Fear God,
and respect the king.

Slaves

18You who are slaves must submit to your masters with all respect. Do what they tell you—not
only if they are kind and reasonable, but even if
they are cruel. 19For God is pleased when, conscious of his will, you patiently endure unjust
treatment. 20Of course, you get no credit for being patient if you are beaten for doing wrong. But
if you suffer for doing good and endure it patiently, God is pleased with you.
21For God called you to do good, even if it
means suffering, just as Christ suffered for you.
He is your example, and you must follow in his
steps.

22 He never sinned,
nor ever deceived anyone.
23 He did not retaliate when he was insulted,
nor threaten revenge when he suffered.

Key Verse **"Instead, you must worship Christ as Lord of your life. And if someone asks about your Christian hope, always be ready to explain it."—1 PETER 3:15**

Grab a friend and take turns reading 1 PETER 3:15 out loud to each other.

Now, talk with your friend about how you can explain your faith in Jesus to others.

BE READY AT SCHOOL!

- Draw pictures of your favorite Bible stories on a book cover. Be ready to tell the stories to anyone who asks.
- Wrap a chenille wire around a pencil up to the eraser. Cut a small strip of poster board and write your favorite verse on it. Attach the verse to the pencil topper. Be ready to explain why it's your favorite verse.

you must worship Christ as the Lord of your life.

BE READY WITH YOUR FRIENDS!

- Use fabric paint and markers to create a faith T-shirt. Be ready to explain what you wrote and drew.

- Make invitations to your church. Keep them with you so you can invite friends to learn about God.

Read what Jesus said about sharing your faith in Matthew 28:18-20!

He left his case in the hands of God,
who always judges fairly.
24 He personally carried our sins
in his body on the cross
so that we can be dead to sin
and live for what is right.
By his wounds
you are healed.
25 Once you were like sheep
who wandered away.
But now you have turned to your Shepherd,
the Guardian of your souls.

CHAPTER **3**

Wives

In the same way, you wives must accept the authority of your husbands. Then, even if some refuse to obey the Good News, your godly lives will
speak to them without any words. They will be
won over 2by observing your pure and reverent
lives.
3Don't be concerned about the outward
beauty of fancy hairstyles, expensive jewelry, or
beautiful clothes. 4You should clothe yourselves instead with the beauty that comes from
within, the unfading beauty of a gentle and
quiet spirit, which is so precious to God. 5This is
how the holy women of old made themselves
beautiful. They put their trust in God and accepted the authority of their husbands. 6For instance, Sarah obeyed her husband, Abraham,
and called him her master. You are her daughters when you do what is right without fear of
what your husbands might do.

Husbands

7In the same way, you husbands must give honor
to your wives. Treat your wife with understanding
as you live together. She may be weaker than you
are, but she is your equal partner in God's gift of
new life. Treat her as you should so your prayers
will not be hindered.

All Christians

8Finally, all of you should be of one mind. Sympathize with each other. Love each other as brothers and sisters. Be tenderhearted, and keep a
humble attitude. 9Don't repay evil for evil. Don't
retaliate with insults when people insult you. Instead, pay them back with a blessing. That is
what God has called you to do, and he will grant
you his blessing. 10For the Scriptures say,

"If you want to enjoy life
and see many happy days,
keep your tongue from speaking evil
and your lips from telling lies.
11 Turn away from evil and do good.
Search for peace, and work to maintain it.
12 The eyes of the LORD watch over those who
do right,
and his ears are open to their prayers.
But the LORD turns his face
against those who do evil."

Suffering for Doing Good

13Now, who will want to harm you if you are eager
to do good? 14But even if you suffer for doing what
is right, God will reward you for it. So don't worry
or be afraid of their threats. **15Instead, you
must worship Christ as Lord of your
life. And if someone asks about your
hope as a believer, always be ready
to explain it.** 16But do this in a gentle and respectful way. Keep your conscience clear. Then if
people speak against you, they will be ashamed
when they see what a good life you live because
you belong to Christ. 17Remember, it is better to
suffer for doing good, if that is what God wants,
than to suffer for doing wrong!
18Christ suffered for our sins once for all time.
He never sinned, but he died for sinners to bring
you safely home to God. He suffered physical
death, but he was raised to life in the Spirit.
19So he went and preached to the spirits in
prison—20those who disobeyed God long ago
when God waited patiently while Noah was
building his boat. Only eight people were saved
from drowning in that terrible flood. 21And that
water is a picture of baptism, which now saves
you, not by removing dirt from your body, but as a
response to God from a clean conscience. It is
effective because of the resurrection of Jesus
Christ.
22Now Christ has gone to heaven. He is seated
in the place of honor next to God, and all the
angels and authorities and powers accept his
authority.

CHAPTER **4**

Living for God

So then, since Christ suffered physical pain, you
must arm yourselves with the same attitude he
had, and be ready to suffer, too. For if you have
suffered physically for Christ, you have finished
with sin. 2You won't spend the rest of your lives
chasing your own desires, but you will be anxious
to do the will of God. 3You have had enough in the
past of the evil things that godless people enjoy—
their immorality and lust, their feasting and

1 Peter 4 . . . page 1232

"Give all your worries and cares to God, for he cares about you." —1 PETER 5:7

No Pressure!

Read 1 PETER 5:7 a few times.

Sounds simple, huh? But is it?

Read more about giving your cares to God in Luke 12:22-32.
1 Make a list of all the things that are worrying you right now.
2 Add all the things that worried you last week or last month.
3 Now go through the list, and see which worries you can solve on your own.
WHOA—look at all those worries!

Most of the things we worry about are out of our control. So it makes perfect sense to give them to God! If you don't, this could happen to you.

Take a lump of clay, and form it into a person shape.
For each worry on your list, press down on your clay person's head a little.
What happened?
ALL THOSE WORRIES PRESSED YOUR PERSON FLAT!

DON'T LET THAT HAPPEN TO YOU!
Give your worries to God!

drunkenness and wild parties, and their terrible
worship of idols.
4Of course, your former friends are surprised
when you no longer plunge into the flood of wild
and destructive things they do. So they slander
you. 5But remember that they will have to face
God, who stands ready to judge everyone, both
the living and the dead. 6That is why the Good
News was preached to those who are now dead—
so although they were destined to die like all people, they now live forever with God in the Spirit.
7The end of the world is coming soon. Therefore, be earnest and disciplined in your prayers.
8Most important of all, continue to show deep
love for each other, for love covers a multitude of
sins. 9Cheerfully share your home with those
who need a meal or a place to stay.
10God has given each of you a gift from his
great variety of spiritual gifts. Use them well to
serve one another. 11Do you have the gift of
speaking? Then speak as though God himself
were speaking through you. Do you have the gift
of helping others? Do it with all the strength and
energy that God supplies. Then everything you
do will bring glory to God through Jesus Christ.
All glory and power to him forever and ever!
Amen.

Suffering for Being a Christian

12Dear friends, don't be surprised at the fiery
trials you are going through, as if something
strange were happening to you. 13Instead, be
very glad—for these trials make you partners
with Christ in his suffering, so that you will have
the wonderful joy of seeing his glory when it is
revealed to all the world.
14If you are insulted because you bear the
name of Christ, you will be blessed, for the glorious Spirit of God rests upon you. 15If you suffer,
however, it must not be for murder, stealing,
making trouble, or prying into other people's
affairs. 16But it is no shame to suffer for being a
Christian. Praise God for the privilege of being
called by his name! 17For the time has come for
judgment, and it must begin with God's household. And if judgment begins with us, what terrible fate awaits those who have never obeyed
God's Good News? 18And also,

"If the righteous are barely saved,
what will happen to godless sinners?"

19So if you are suffering in a manner that pleases
God, keep on doing what is right, and trust your
lives to the God who created you, for he will
never fail you.

CHAPTER 5

Advice for Elders and Young Men

And now, a word to you who are elders in the
churches. I, too, am an elder and a witness to the
sufferings of Christ. And I, too, will share in his
glory when he is revealed to the whole world. As
a fellow elder, I appeal to you: 2Care for the flock
that God has entrusted to you. Watch over it
willingly, not grudgingly—not for what you will
get out of it, but because you are eager to serve
God. 3Don't lord it over the people assigned to
your care, but lead them by your own good example. 4And when the Great Shepherd appears,
you will receive a crown of never-ending glory
and honor.

5In the same way, you who are younger must
accept the authority of the elders. And all of
you, dress yourselves in humility as you relate to
one another, for

"God opposes the proud
but gives grace to the humble."

6So humble yourselves under the mighty power
of God, and at the right time he will lift you up
in honor. **7Give all your worries and**
cares to God, for he cares about
you.

8Stay alert! Watch out for your great enemy,
the devil. He prowls around like a roaring lion,
looking for someone to devour. 9Stand firm
against him, and be strong in your faith. Remember that your family of believers all over the
world is going through the same kind of suffering you are.

10In his kindness God called you to share in
his eternal glory by means of Christ Jesus. So
after you have suffered a little while, he will restore, support, and strengthen you, and he will
place you on a firm foundation. 11All power to
him forever! Amen.

Peter's Final Greetings

12I have written and sent this short letter to you
with the help of Silas, whom I commend to you
as a faithful brother. My purpose in writing is to
encourage you and assure you that what you are
experiencing is truly part of God's grace for you.
Stand firm in this grace.

13Your sister church here in Babylon sends
you greetings, and so does my son Mark. 14Greet
each other with a kiss of love.

Peace be with all of you who are in Christ.

2 PETER

Words of Warning

Peter wrote this second letter to the early Christians not long before he was killed. He talked about

- **KNOWING GOD**
- **KNOWING THE BIBLE**
- **KNOWING TRUE FROM FALSE**
- **KNOWING HOW TO LIVE**

LOVE
SELF CONTROL
FAITH

Growing Strong

Have you ever measured yourself on a growth chart to see how tall you were getting? Well, God gives you a growth chart in the Bible! **See how tall you are by reading 2 Peter 1:5-8.**

False Teachers bEwARe

Peter warned about people who would teach lies, instead of the truth, about Jesus. But watch out! Those false teachers are in for a nasty surprise.

Read more in 2 Peter 2:1-3.

Are You Ready?

Because Jesus is coming back, Peter tells us how we should be living our lives until that day. **Read his words for yourself in 2 Peter 3:11-15a.**

What's Taking Him So Long?

We know that Jesus will come back one day. But when? **Read 2 Peter 3:8-9 to see what Peter said about Jesus' return.**

Timeline

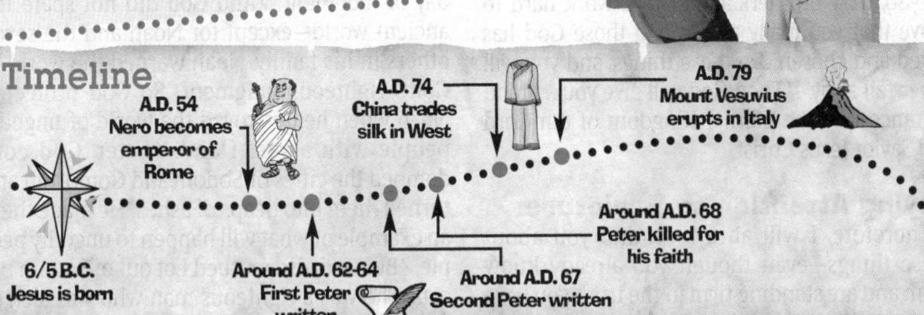

A.D. 54
Nero becomes emperor of Rome
A.D. 74
China trades silk in West
A.D. 79
Mount Vesuvius erupts in Italy
Around A.D. 68
Peter killed for his faith
6/5 B.C.
Jesus is born
Around A.D. 62-64
First Peter written
Around A.D. 67
Second Peter written

The JESUS CONNECTION

The book of Second Peter gives great advice about how to keep your faith, even when times are tough. Peter knew that Christians would face hard times and temptations, but he urged us to keep our eyes on Jesus. **Faith in Jesus is all you need to be happy in this life, and to enjoy eternal life later in heaven.**

2 Peter 1 . . . page 1236

CHAPTER 1

Greetings from Peter

This letter is from Simon Peter, a slave and apostle of Jesus Christ.

I am writing to you who share the same precious faith we have. This faith was given to you because of the justice and fairness of Jesus Christ, our God and Savior.

2May God give you more and more grace and peace as you grow in your knowledge of God and Jesus our Lord.

Growing in Faith

3By his divine power, God has given us everything we need for living a godly life. We have received all of this by coming to know him, the one who called us to himself by means of his marvelous glory and excellence. 4And because of his glory and excellence, he has given us great and precious promises. These are the promises that enable you to share his divine nature and escape the world's corruption caused by human desires.

5In view of all this, make every effort to respond to God's promises. Supplement your faith with a generous provision of moral excellence, and moral excellence with knowledge, 6and knowledge with self-control, and self-control with patient endurance, and patient endurance with godliness, 7and godliness with brotherly affection, and brotherly affection with love for everyone.

8The more you grow like this, the more productive and useful you will be in your knowledge of our Lord Jesus Christ. 9But those who fail to develop in this way are shortsighted or blind, forgetting that they have been cleansed from their old sins.

10So, dear brothers and sisters, work hard to prove that you really are among those God has called and chosen. Do these things, and you will never fall away. 11Then God will give you a grand entrance into the eternal Kingdom of our Lord and Savior Jesus Christ.

Paying Attention to Scripture

12Therefore, I will always remind you about these things—even though you already know them and are standing firm in the truth you have been taught. 13And it is only right that I should keep on reminding you as long as I live. 14For our Lord Jesus Christ has shown me that I must soon leave this earthly life, 15so I will work hard to make sure you always remember these things after I am gone.

16For we were not making up clever stories when we told you about the powerful coming of our Lord Jesus Christ. We saw his majestic splendor with our own eyes 17when he received honor and glory from God the Father. The voice from the majestic glory of God said to him, "This is my dearly loved Son, who brings me great joy." 18We ourselves heard that voice from heaven when we were with him on the holy mountain.

19Because of that experience, we have even greater confidence in the message proclaimed by the prophets. You must pay close attention to what they wrote, for their words are like a lamp shining in a dark place—until the Day dawns, and Christ the Morning Star shines in your hearts. 20Above all, you must realize that no prophecy in Scripture ever came from the prophet's own understanding, 21or from human initiative. No, those prophets were moved by the Holy Spirit, and they spoke from God.

CHAPTER 2

The Danger of False Teachers

But there were also false prophets in Israel, just as there will be false teachers among you. They will cleverly teach destructive heresies and even deny the Master who bought them. In this way, they will bring sudden destruction on themselves. 2Many will follow their evil teaching and shameful immorality. And because of these teachers, the way of truth will be slandered. 3In their greed they will make up clever lies to get hold of your money. But God condemned them long ago, and their destruction will not be delayed.

4For God did not spare even the angels who sinned. He threw them into hell, in gloomy pits of darkness, where they are being held until the day of judgment. 5And God did not spare the ancient world—except for Noah and the seven others in his family. Noah warned the world of God's righteous judgment. So God protected Noah when he destroyed the world of ungodly people with a vast flood. 6Later, God condemned the cities of Sodom and Gomorrah and turned them into heaps of ashes. He made them an example of what will happen to ungodly people. 7But God also rescued Lot out of Sodom because he was a righteous man who was sick of the shameful immorality of the wicked people around him. 8Yes, Lot was a righteous man who was tormented in his soul by the wickedness he saw and heard day after day. 9So you see, the Lord knows how to rescue godly people from their trials, even while keeping the wicked under punishment until the day of final judgment. 10 He is especially hard on those who follow their own twisted sexual desire, and who despise authority.

These people are proud and arrogant, daring even to scoff at supernatural beings without so much as trembling. 11 But the angels, who are far greater in power and strength, do not dare to bring from the Lord a charge of blasphemy against those supernatural beings.

12 These false teachers are like unthinking animals, creatures of instinct, born to be caught and destroyed. They scoff at things they do not understand, and like animals, they will be destroyed. 13 Their destruction is their reward for the harm they have done. They love to indulge in evil pleasures in broad daylight. They are a disgrace and a stain among you. They delight in deception even as they eat with you in your fellowship meals. 14 They commit adultery with their eyes, and their desire for sin is never satisfied. They lure unstable people into sin, and they are well trained in greed. They live under God's curse. 15 They have wandered off the right road and followed the footsteps of Balaam son of Beor, who loved to earn money by doing wrong. 16 But Balaam was stopped from his mad course when his donkey rebuked him with a human voice.

17 These people are as useless as dried-up springs or as mist blown away by the wind. They are doomed to blackest darkness. 18 They brag about themselves with empty, foolish boasting. With an appeal to twisted sexual desires, they lure back into sin those who have barely escaped from a lifestyle of deception. 19 They promise freedom, but they themselves are slaves of sin and corruption. For you are a slave to whatever controls you. 20 And when people escape from the wickedness of the world by knowing our Lord and Savior Jesus Christ and then get tangled up and enslaved by sin again, they are worse off than before. 21 It would be better if they had never known the way to righteousness than to know it and then reject the command they were given to live a holy life. 22 They prove the truth of this proverb: "A dog returns to its vomit." And another says, "A washed pig returns to the mud."

CHAPTER 3

The Day of the Lord Is Coming

This is my second letter to you, dear friends, and in both of them I have tried to stimulate your wholesome thinking and refresh your memory. 2 I want you to remember what the holy prophets said long ago and what our Lord and Savior commanded through your apostles.

3 Most importantly, I want to remind you that in the last days scoffers will come, mocking the truth and following their own desires. 4 They will say, "What happened to the promise that Jesus is coming again? From before the times of our ancestors, everything has remained the same since the world was first created."

5 They deliberately forget that God made the heavens long ago by the word of his command, and he brought the earth out from the water and surrounded it with water. 6 Then he used the water to destroy the ancient world with a mighty flood. 7 And by the same word, the present heavens and earth have been stored up for fire. They are being kept for the day of judgment, when ungodly people will be destroyed.

8 But you must not forget this one thing, dear friends: A day is like a thousand years to the Lord, and a thousand years is like a day. **9 The Lord isn't really being slow about his promise, as some people think. No, he is being patient for your sake. He does not want anyone to be destroyed, but wants everyone to repent.** 10 But the day of the Lord will come as unexpectedly as a thief. Then the heavens will pass away with a terrible noise, and the very elements themselves will disappear in fire, and the earth and everything on it will be found to deserve judgment.

11 Since everything around us is going to be destroyed like this, what holy and godly lives you should live, 12 looking forward to the day of God and hurrying it along. On that day, he will set the heavens on fire, and the elements will melt away in the flames. 13 But we are looking forward to the new heavens and new earth he has promised, a world filled with God's righteousness.

14 And so, dear friends, while you are waiting for these things to happen, make every effort to be found living peaceful lives that are pure and blameless in his sight.

15 And remember, our Lord's patience gives people time to be saved. This is what our beloved brother Paul also wrote to you with the wisdom God gave him—16 speaking of these things in all of his letters. Some of his comments are hard to understand, and those who are ignorant and unstable have twisted his letters to mean something quite different, just as they do with other parts of Scripture. And this will result in their destruction.

Peter's Final Words

17You already know these things, dear friends. So be on guard; then you will not be carried away by the errors of these wicked people and lose your own secure footing. 18Rather, you must grow in the grace and knowledge of our Lord and Savior Jesus Christ.

All glory to him, both now and forever! Amen.

1 JOHN A Love Letter

Look for 2 hidden messages in 1 John!

John wrote this letter to encourage Christians everywhere in their faith. It tells about

- **LIGHT AND DARK**
- **GOOD AND BAD**
- **TRUE AND FALSE**
- **LIFE AND DEATH**
- **LOVE AND MORE LOVE**

All Talk?

Blah, blah blah!

blah blah!

I ALWAYS help others. I'm good!

Yeah, right!

Maybe you've heard the expression, "Talk is cheap." Or how about, "Actions speak louder than words"? Well, the Bible says it best! **Check it out in 1 John 3:18. (Then follow that advice!)**

'Fess Up

Have you ever committed a sin and been afraid to admit it? Well, don't be afraid anymore! **Find out why in 1 John 1:8-9!**

True Love

What is love? *Real* love? Find out in 1 John 4:9-10!

Family Reunion

FAMILY REUNION

Welcome to the family! Whose family, you ask? **Find out in 1 John 3:1-2.**

Timeline

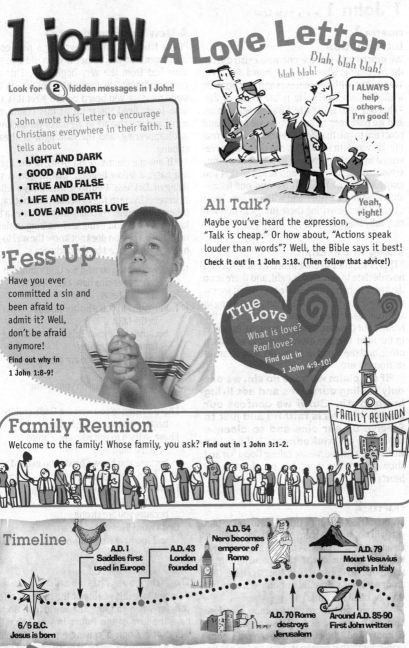

- 6/5 B.C. Jesus is born
- A.D. 1 Saddles first used in Europe
- A.D. 43 London founded
- A.D. 54 Nero becomes emperor of Rome
- A.D. 70 Rome destroys Jerusalem
- A.D. 79 Mount Vesuvius erupts in Italy
- Around A.D. 85-90 First John written

This letter of John's is a real love story. It tells how much God loves us and how much we should love others. And right in the middle of all that love is Jesus, who loves us so much that he was willing to die on the cross for our sins. If we believe in him and confess our sins, God's love and light will shine on us forever. **It doesn't get any better than that!**

CHAPTER 1

Introduction

We proclaim to you the one who existed from the beginning, whom we have heard and seen. We saw him with our own eyes and touched him with our own hands. He is the Word of life. 2This one who is life itself was revealed to us, and we have seen him. And now we testify and proclaim to you that he is the one who is eternal life. He was with the Father, and then he was revealed to us. 3We proclaim to you what we ourselves have actually seen and heard so that you may have fellowship with us. And our fellowship is with the Father and with his Son, Jesus Christ. 4We are writing these things so that you may fully share our joy.

Living in the Light

5This is the message we heard from Jesus and now declare to you: God is light, and there is no darkness in him at all. 6So we are lying if we say we have fellowship with God but go on living in spiritual darkness; we are not practicing the truth. 7But if we are living in the light, as God is in the light, then we have fellowship with each other, and the blood of Jesus, his Son, cleanses us from all sin.

8If we claim we have no sin, we are only fooling ourselves and not living in the truth. 9But if we confess our sins to him, he is faithful and just to forgive us our sins and to cleanse us from all wickedness. 10If we claim we have not sinned, we are calling God a liar and showing that his word has no place in our hearts.

CHAPTER 2

My dear children, I am writing this to you so that you will not sin. But if anyone does sin, we have an advocate who pleads our case before the Father. He is Jesus Christ, the one who is truly righteous. 2He himself is the sacrifice that atones for our sins—and not only our sins but the sins of all the world.

3And we can be sure that we know him if we obey his commandments. 4If someone claims, "I know God," but doesn't obey God's commandments, that person is a liar and is not living in the truth. 5But those who obey God's word truly show how completely they love him. That is how we know we are living in him. 6Those who say they live in God should live their lives as Jesus did.

A New Commandment

7Dear friends, I am not writing a new commandment for you; rather it is an old one you have had from the very beginning. This old commandment—to love one another—is the same message you heard before. 8Yet it is also new. Jesus lived the truth of this commandment, and you also are living it. For the darkness is disappearing, and the true light is already shining.

9If anyone claims, "I am living in the light," but hates a fellow believer, that person is still living in darkness. 10Anyone who loves a fellow believer is living in the light and does not cause others to stumble. 11But anyone who hates a fellow believer is still living and walking in darkness. Such a person does not know the way to go, having been blinded by the darkness.

12 I am writing to you who are God's children
because your sins have been forgiven
through Jesus.
13 I am writing to you who are mature
in the faith
because you know Christ, who existed
from the beginning.
I am writing to you who are young
in the faith
because you have won your battle
with the evil one.
14 I have written to you who are God's children
because you know the Father.
I have written to you who are mature
in the faith
because you know Christ, who existed
from the beginning.
I have written to you who are young
in the faith
because you are strong.
God's word lives in your hearts,
and you have won your battle with
the evil one.

Do Not Love This World

15Do not love this world nor the things it offers you, for when you love the world, you do not have the love of the Father in you. 16For the world offers only a craving for physical pleasure, a craving for everything we see, and pride in our achievements and possessions. These are not from the Father, but are from this world. 17And this world is fading away, along with everything that people crave. But anyone who does what pleases God will live forever.

Warning about Antichrists

18 Dear children, the last hour is here. You have
heard that the Antichrist is coming, and already
many such antichrists have appeared. From this
we know that the last hour has come. 19 These
people left our churches, but they never really
belonged with us; otherwise they would have
stayed with us. When they left, it proved that
they did not belong with us.

20 But you are not like that, for the Holy One
has given you his Spirit, and all of you know the
truth. 21 So I am writing to you not because you
don't know the truth but because you know the
difference between truth and lies. 22 And who is
a liar? Anyone who says that Jesus is not the
Christ. Anyone who denies the Father and the Son
is an antichrist. 23 Anyone who denies the Son
doesn't have the Father, either. But anyone who
acknowledges the Son has the Father also.

24 So you must remain faithful to what you
have been taught from the beginning. If you do,
you will remain in fellowship with the Son and
with the Father. 25 And in this fellowship we enjoy the eternal life he promised us.

26 I am writing these things to warn you about
those who want to lead you astray. 27 But you
have received the Holy Spirit, and he lives
within you, so you don't need anyone to teach
you what is true. For the Spirit teaches you
everything you need to know, and what he
teaches is true—it is not a lie. So just as he has
taught you, remain in fellowship with Christ.

Living as Children of God

28 And now, dear children, remain in fellowship
with Christ so that when he returns, you will be
full of courage and not shrink back from him in
shame.

29 Since we know that Christ is righteous, we
also know that all who do what is right are God's
children.

CHAPTER 3

See how very much our Father loves us, for he
calls us his children, and that is what we are! But
the people who belong to this world don't recognize that we are God's children because they
don't know him. 2 Dear friends, we are already
God's children, but he has not yet shown us
what we will be like when Christ appears. But
we do know that we will be like him, for we will
see him as he really is. 3 And all who have this eager expectation will keep themselves pure, just
as he is pure.

Think of a sin you've committed.

Got one?

OK, now undo it. Make it like it never happened.

Having trouble? Of course! We can't undo our sins. But God can! **Just read 1 JOHN 1:9.**

If we confess our sins to God and tell him we're sorry (and mean it!), he'll forgive us. We might have to deal with the consequences of our sins, but when God forgives a sin, it's gone!

THINK OF IT LIKE THIS:

1. **Use a highlighter to write on a coffee filter a sin you've committed.**

2. **Now confess that sin to God and ask him to forgive you. Next, put a few drops of lemon juice on the writing, and watch as your "sin" disappears!**

Read more about forgiveness in Romans 3:21

The lemon juice made the writing disappear. When we confess our sins to God, he forgives us. He makes our sins completely disappear from his sight!

COOL!

Key Verse **"Dear friends, let us continue to love one another, for love comes from God. Anyone who loves is a child of God and knows God. But anyone who does not love does not know God, for God is love." —1 JOHN 4:7-8**

GOD IS LOVE

Read 1 JOHN 4:7-8 out loud a few times. Notice anything? Two words keep popping up. **God** and **love.**

When we show love to others, like this passage says to do, we're spreading God's love.

TRY THIS!

1 Cut a heart out of white poster board. Mount it on a slightly bigger piece of colored poster board. Hang it on your wall.

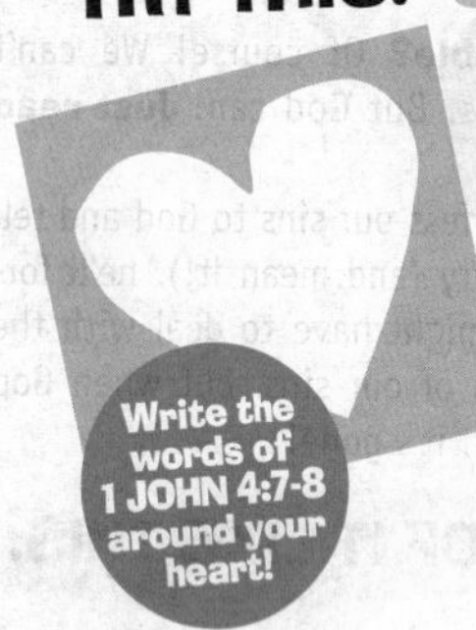

Write the words of 1 JOHN 4:7-8 around your heart!

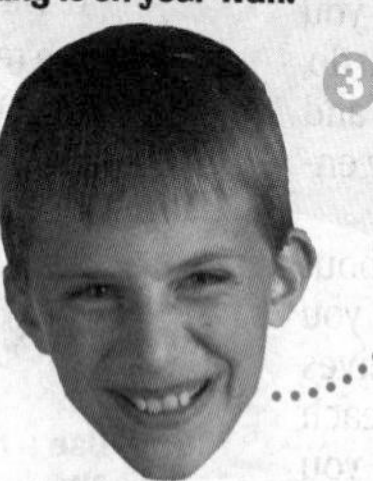

2 Tear red construction paper into small pieces big enough to write on. Put the pieces in a bag or bowl near your poster.

3 Every time you show love to someone, write what you did on one of the paper pieces. Glue or tape the piece to the heart.

See how long it takes you to fill up the heart with loving actions!

GO SHOW GOD'S LOVE!

For more about love, go to 1 Corinthians 13:4-7!

4Everyone who sins is breaking God's law, for
all sin is contrary to the law of God. 5And you
know that Jesus came to take away our sins, and
there is no sin in him. 6Anyone who continues to
live in him will not sin. But anyone who keeps on sinning does not know him or understand who he is.

7Dear children, don't let anyone deceive you about this: When people do what is right, it shows that they are righteous, even as Christ is righteous.
8But when people keep on sinning, it shows that they belong to the devil, who has been sinning since the beginning. But the Son of God came to
destroy the works of the devil. 9Those who have been born into God's family do not make a practice of sinning, because God's life is in them. So they can't keep on sinning, because they are children of God. 10So now we can tell who are children of God and who are children of the devil. Anyone who does not live righteously and does not love other believers does not belong to God.

Love One Another

11This is the message you have heard from the
beginning: We should love one another. 12We
must not be like Cain, who belonged to the evil one and killed his brother. And why did he kill him? Because Cain had been doing what was evil, and his brother had been doing what was righteous. 13So don't be surprised, dear brothers and sisters, if the world hates you.

14If we love our brothers and sisters who are believers, it proves that we have passed from death to life. But a person who has no love is still
dead. 15Anyone who hates another brother or sister is really a murderer at heart. And you know that murderers don't have eternal life within them.

16We know what real love is because Jesus gave up his life for us. So we also ought to give up
our lives for our brothers and sisters. 17If someone has enough money to live well and sees a brother or sister in need but shows no compassion—how can God's love be in that person?

18Dear children, let's not merely say that we love each other; let us show the truth by our actions. 19Our actions will show that we belong to the truth, so we will be confident when we stand
before God. 20Even if we feel guilty, God is greater than our feelings, and he knows everything.

21 Dear friends, if we don't feel guilty, we can
come to God with bold confidence. 22 And we
will receive from him whatever we ask because
we obey him and do the things that please him.
23 And this is his commandment: We must
believe in the name of his Son, Jesus Christ, and
love one another, just as he commanded us.
24 Those who obey God's commandments remain in fellowship with him, and he with them.
And we know he lives in us because the Spirit he
gave us lives in us.

CHAPTER 4

Discerning False Prophets

Dear friends, do not believe everyone who
claims to speak by the Spirit. You must test
them to see if the spirit they have comes from
God. For there are many false prophets in the
world. 2 This is how we know if they have the
Spirit of God: If a person claiming to be a
prophet acknowledges that Jesus Christ came
in a real body, that person has the Spirit of God.
3 But if someone claims to be a prophet and
does not acknowledge the truth about Jesus,
that person is not from God. Such a person has
the spirit of the Antichrist, which you heard is
coming into the world and indeed is already
here.

4 But you belong to God, my dear children.
You have already won a victory over those people, because the Spirit who lives in you is greater
than the spirit who lives in the world. 5 Those
people belong to this world, so they speak from
the world's viewpoint, and the world listens to
them. 6 But we belong to God, and those who
know God listen to us. If they do not belong to
God, they do not listen to us. That is how we
know if someone has the Spirit of truth or the
spirit of deception.

Loving One Another

**7 Dear friends, let us continue to love
one another, for love comes from
God. Anyone who loves is a child of
God and knows God.** 8 But anyone who
does not love does not know God, for God is love.
9 God showed how much he loved us by sending his one and only Son into the world so that
we might have eternal life through him. 10 This
is real love—not that we loved God, but that he
loved us and sent his Son as a sacrifice to take
away our sins.
11 Dear friends, since God loved us that much,
we surely ought to love each other. 12 No one has
ever seen God. But if we love each other, God
lives in us, and his love is brought to full expression in us.
13 And God has given us his Spirit as proof
that we live in him and he in us. 14 Furthermore,
we have seen with our own eyes and now testify
that the Father sent his Son to be the Savior of
the world. 15 All who declare that Jesus is the Son
of God have God living in them, and they live in
God. 16 We know how much God loves us, and
we have put our trust in his love.
God is love, and all who live in love live in God,
and God lives in them. 17 And as we live in God,
our love grows more perfect. So we will not be
afraid on the day of judgment, but we can face
him with confidence because we live like Jesus
here in this world.
18 Such love has no fear, because perfect love
expels all fear. If we are afraid, it is for fear of
punishment, and this shows that we have not
fully experienced his perfect love. 19 We love
each other because he loved us first.
20 If someone says, "I love God," but hates a
fellow believer, that person is a liar; for if we
don't love people we can see, how can we love
God, whom we cannot see? 21 And he has given
us this command: Those who love God must also
love their fellow believers.

CHAPTER 5

Faith in the Son of God

Everyone who believes that Jesus is the Christ
has become a child of God. And everyone who
loves the Father loves his children, too. 2 We
know we love God's children if we love God
and obey his commandments. 3 Loving God
means keeping his commandments, and his
commandments are not burdensome. 4 For
every child of God defeats this evil world,
and we achieve this victory through our faith.
5 And who can win this battle against the world?
Only those who believe that Jesus is the Son
of God.
6 And Jesus Christ was revealed as God's Son
by his baptism in water and by shedding his
blood on the cross—not by water only, but by
water and blood. And the Spirit, who is truth,
confirms it with his testimony. 7 So we have
these three witnesses—8 the Spirit, the water,
and the blood—and all three agree. 9 Since we
believe human testimony, surely we can believe
the greater testimony that comes from God.
And God has testified about his Son. 10 All who
believe in the Son of God know in their hearts
that this testimony is true. Those who don't
believe this are actually calling God a liar be-

cause they don't believe what God has testified
about his Son.
11 And this is what God has testified: He has
given us eternal life, and this life is in his Son.
12 Whoever has the Son has life; who-
ever does not have God's Son does
not have life.

Conclusion

13 I have written this to you who believe in the
name of the Son of God, so that you may know
you have eternal life. 14 And we are confident
that he hears us whenever we ask for anything
that pleases him. 15 And since we know he hears
us when we make our requests, we also know
that he will give us what we ask for.
16 If you see a fellow believer sinning in a way
that does not lead to death, you should pray, and
God will give that person life. But there is a sin
that leads to death, and I am not saying you
should pray for those who commit it. 17 All wicked
actions are sin, but not every sin leads to death.
18 We know that God's children do not make a
practice of sinning, for God's Son holds them
securely, and the evil one cannot touch them.
19 We know that we are children of God and that
the world around us is under the control of the
evil one.
20 And we know that the Son of God has come,
and he has given us understanding so that we
can know the true God. And now we live in
fellowship with the true God because we live in
fellowship with his Son, Jesus Christ. He is the
only true God, and he is eternal life.
21 Dear children, keep away from anything
that might take God's place in your hearts.

2 JOHN Words of Truth and Love

John wrote this letter to a friend and her family. Look for wisdom about
- **TRUTH AND LOVE**
- **WHY TO LOVE**
- **HOW TO LOVE**
- **WHO DOESN'T LOVE**

Don't Lose Your Way

If you stay on the path, one thing will happen. If you wander away, another thing will happen. What was John talking about? **Find out for yourself in 2 John 1:9!**

And Nothing But the Truth

John placed a lot of emphasis on truth. Not just on telling the truth, but on *the* truth. **What truth was so important to John? Read 2 John 1:1-3.**

LOVE

Old Advice, New Advice

Different letter, same advice. **Discover what John found worth repeating by reading 2 John 1:5-6.**

A Bad Crowd

You've probably been told to stay away from the bad crowd, right? Well, John said the same thing way back in Bible times. **Read 2 John 1:10-11 to find out who was in John's bad crowd.**

Don't Listen to Them!

John warned his friends about listening to a certain type of person. And guess what? His advice applies to you, too! **Find out who he was talking about in 2 John 1:7-8.**

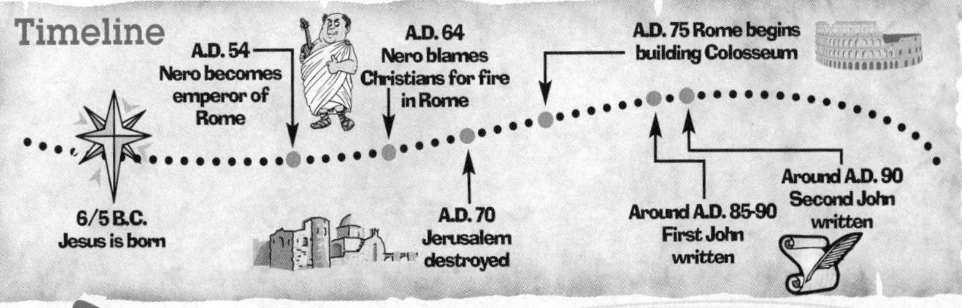
Timeline
6/5 B.C. Jesus is born
A.D. 54 Nero becomes emperor of Rome
A.D. 64 Nero blames Christians for fire in Rome
A.D. 70 Jerusalem destroyed
A.D. 75 Rome begins building Colosseum
Around A.D. 85-90 First John written
Around A.D. 90 Second John written

The JESUS CONNECTION

John talks a lot about love. The Gospel of John, the three letters, and even the book of Revelation (yup, he wrote all of them) talk about the importance of love. Maybe that's because he had known Jesus personally and experienced his love firsthand. If *we* believe in Jesus, we can have a personal friendship with him and experience his love forever. **What an awesome offer! Do you know him?**

2 John . . . page 1246

Greetings

This letter is from John, the elder.
I am writing to the chosen lady and to her children, whom I love in the truth—as does everyone
else who knows the truth—2because the truth
lives in us and will be with us forever.
3Grace, mercy, and peace, which come from
God the Father and from Jesus Christ—the Son
of the Father—will continue to be with us who
live in truth and love.

Live in the Truth

4How happy I was to meet some of your children
and find them living according to the truth, just
as the Father commanded.
5I am writing to remind you, dear friends, that
we should love one another. This is not a new
commandment, but one we have had from the
beginning. 6Love means doing what God has
commanded us, and he has commanded us to
love one another, just as you heard from the
beginning.
7I say this because many deceivers have gone
out into the world. They deny that Jesus Christ
came in a real body. Such a person is a deceiver
and an antichrist. 8Watch out that you do not
lose what we have worked so hard to achieve.
Be diligent so that you receive your full reward.
9Anyone who wanders away from this teaching
has no relationship with God. But anyone who
remains in the teaching of Christ has a relationship with both the Father and the Son.
10If anyone comes to your meeting and does
not teach the truth about Christ, don't invite
that person into your home or give any kind of
encouragement. 11Anyone who encourages
such people becomes a partner in their evil
work.

Conclusion

12I have much more to say to you, but I don't want
to do it with paper and ink. For I hope to visit you
soon and talk with you face to face. Then our joy
will be complete.
13Greetings from the children of your sister,
chosen by God.

3 JOHN More Thoughts on Love

This third letter of John's, written to a dear friend, contains familiar themes. Look for

- **LESSONS ON LOVE**
- **TRAVELING TEACHERS**
- **EVIL EXAMPLES**

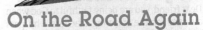

Report Card Gaius

Faithfulness	A
Truthfulness	A
Love	A
Worthiness	A

Happy News

Are you happy when your friends do well? Well, John was! **Read 3 John 1:3-4 to find what made him happy about his friends.**

On the Road Again

Back in Bible times, teachers traveled from town to town to spread the good news about Jesus. That was their job. But what would they eat, and where would they stay? **Go to 3 John 1:5-8 for the answer!**

Body and Soul

As an apostle of Jesus, John *might* have been concerned only with his friend's spiritual health. Not so! **Read 3 John 1:2 to see what John wrote to his friend.**

WE RECYCLE

A Good Example

What you do tells the world a lot about who you are, what you believe, and whether you know God or not. Don't believe it? **Read 3 John 1:11-12 to find out what John said about a friend of his.**

Timeline

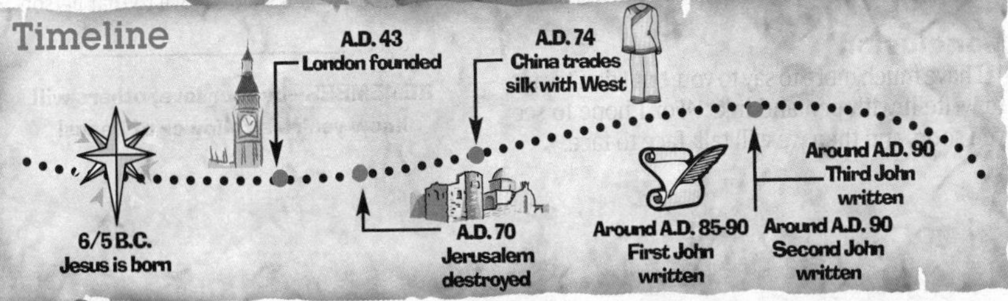

6/5 B.C. Jesus is born
A.D. 43 London founded
A.D. 70 Jerusalem destroyed
A.D. 74 China trades silk with West
Around A.D. 85-90 First John written
Around A.D. 90 Second John written
Around A.D. 90 Third John written

The JESUS CONNECTION

Love one another. Be kind to one another. Follow Jesus. Stay away from evil. John talks about these things over and over. Why? Because he learned them from the Master himself. John knew that to love and follow Jesus were the most important things he could do in his life, and he wrote accordingly. **His words were true thousands of years ago, and they are still true for us today!**

3 John . . . page 1248

Greetings
This letter is from John, the elder.
I am writing to Gaius, my dear friend, whom I
love in the truth.
2Dear friend, I hope all is well with you and that
you are as healthy in body as you are strong in
spirit. 3Some of the traveling teachers recently
returned and made me very happy by telling
me about your faithfulness and that you are living
according to the truth. 4I could have no greater
joy than to hear that my children are following
the truth.

Caring for the Lord's Workers
5Dear friend, you are being faithful to God when
you care for the traveling teachers who pass
through, even though they are strangers to you.
6They have told the church here of your loving
friendship. Please continue providing for such
teachers in a manner that pleases God. 7For they
are traveling for the Lord, and they accept nothing from people who are not believers. 8So we
ourselves should support them so that we can be
their partners as they teach the truth.
9I wrote to the church about this, but Diotre-
phes, who loves to be the leader, refuses to have
anything to do with us. 10When I come, I will report some of the things he is doing and the evil
accusations he is making against us. Not only
does he refuse to welcome the traveling teachers,
he also tells others not to help them. And when
they do help, he puts them out of the church.
11Dear friend, don't let this bad example influence you. Follow only what is good. Remember
that those who do good prove that they are God's
children, and those who do evil prove that they
do not know God.
12Everyone speaks highly of Demetrius, as
does the truth itself. We ourselves can say the
same for him, and you know we speak the truth.

Conclusion
13I have much more to say to you, but I don't want
to write it with pen and ink. 14For I hope to see
you soon, and then we will talk face to face.
15Peace be with you.
Your friends here send you their greetings.
Please give my personal greetings to each of our
friends there.

When people talk about love today, they don't always mean what the Bible means. Christian love is **a sacrificing and eternal love, a love that's modeled after God's love for us.**

WHO DO YOU LOVE?

Think of someone who isn't all that nice to you. God wants you to show his love to that person. Below, write at least two ways you could show love to that person.

Choose one of those ways, and do it! Ask God to help. Write how you think God felt when you showed love to that person.

date: ____________________

REMEMBER—by your love, others will know you're a follower of Jesus!

JUDE The Book of Unchanging Truth

Jude, the brother of Jesus and James, wrote this book to remind Christians to stay strong in their faith. It warns about

- **STINKING THINKING**
- **TERRIBLE TEACHERS**
- **FALSE FRIENDS**
- **OUR GREAT GOD**

Building Tips

You wouldn't want to build a house on a pile of wet noodles, would you? You have to start with a good foundation.

The same is true for you and your life. **Read Jude 1:17-20 to see what kind of foundation Jude recommends.**

Watch Out for Worms

You may think that what you're eating is good, but there could be worms hiding inside.

It's the same way with what you hear! Huh? Worms in words? **Read Jude 1:3-4 for the juicy report.**

Show Mercy

While You Wait

If you believe in Jesus, you're going to heaven! While you wait, there are some things you need to be doing. **Find out what they are in Jude 1:21-23!**

Bad NEWS Dudes

Stay away from them. They pretend to be nice and good, but they're sneaky, and they lie. **Who? Find out in Jude 1:12-13.**

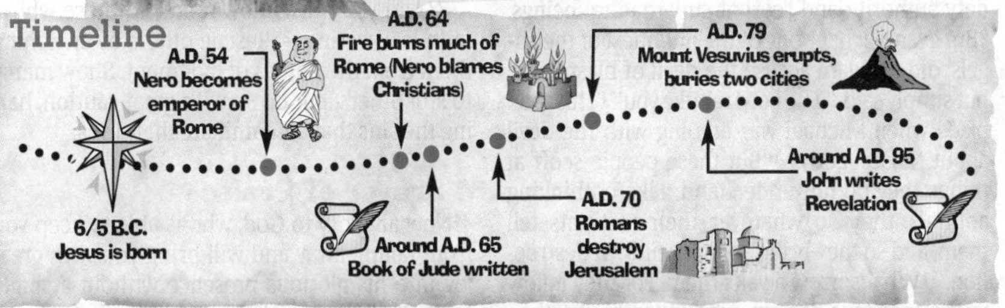
Timeline
A.D. 54 Nero becomes emperor of Rome
A.D. 64 Fire burns much of Rome (Nero blames Christians)
A.D. 79 Mount Vesuvius erupts, buries two cities
6/5 B.C. Jesus is born
Around A.D. 65 Book of Jude written
A.D. 70 Romans destroy Jerusalem
Around A.D. 95 John writes Revelation

The JESUS CONNECTION

Jesus said that he is "*the* way, *the* truth, and *the* life" and that he is the only way to God (John 14:6). The book of Jude warns us to watch out for false teachers who say otherwise. Ideas that take us away from Jesus are so incredibly dangerous because believing in Jesus is the only way we can be saved. It's OK to ask questions, and it's good to think things over, but guard your heart against any teaching that takes you away from Jesus. **Jesus made it clear that he is the only way to God!**

Jude • • • page 1250

Greetings from Jude

This letter is from Jude, a slave of Jesus Christ and a brother of James.

I am writing to all who have been called by God the Father, who loves you and keeps you safe in the care of Jesus Christ.

2May God give you more and more mercy, peace, and love.

The Danger of False Teachers

3Dear friends, I had been eagerly planning to write to you about the salvation we all share. But now I find that I must write about something else, urging you to defend the faith that God has entrusted once for all time to his holy people. 4I say this because some ungodly people have wormed their way into your churches, saying that God's marvelous grace allows us to live immoral lives. The condemnation of such people was recorded long ago, for they have denied our only Master and Lord, Jesus Christ.

5So I want to remind you, though you already know these things, that Jesus first rescued the nation of Israel from Egypt, but later he destroyed those who did not remain faithful. 6And I remind you of the angels who did not stay within the limits of authority God gave them but left the place where they belonged. God has kept them securely chained in prisons of darkness, waiting for the great day of judgment. 7And don't forget Sodom and Gomorrah and their neighboring towns, which were filled with immorality and every kind of sexual perversion. Those cities were destroyed by fire and serve as a warning of the eternal fire of God's judgment.

8In the same way, these people—who claim authority from their dreams—live immoral lives, defy authority, and scoff at supernatural beings. 9But even Michael, one of the mightiest of the angels, did not dare accuse the devil of blasphemy, but simply said, "The Lord rebuke you!" (This took place when Michael was arguing with the devil about Moses' body.) 10But these people scoff at things they do not understand. Like unthinking animals, they do whatever their instincts tell them, and so they bring about their own destruction. 11What sorrow awaits them! For they follow in the footsteps of Cain, who killed his brother. Like Balaam, they deceive people for money. And like Korah, they perish in their rebellion.

12When these people eat with you in your fellowship meals commemorating the Lord's love, they are like dangerous reefs that can shipwreck you. They are like shameless shepherds who care only for themselves. They are like clouds blowing over the land without giving any rain. They are like trees in autumn that are doubly dead, for they bear no fruit and have been pulled up by the roots. 13They are like wild waves of the sea, churning up the foam of their shameful deeds. They are like wandering stars, doomed forever to blackest darkness.

14Enoch, who lived in the seventh generation after Adam, prophesied about these people. He said, "Listen! The Lord is coming with countless thousands of his holy ones 15to execute judgment on the people of the world. He will convict every person of all the ungodly things they have done and for all the insults that ungodly sinners have spoken against him."

16These people are grumblers and complainers, living only to satisfy their desires. They brag loudly about themselves, and they flatter others to get what they want.

A Call to Remain Faithful

17But you, my dear friends, must remember what the apostles of our Lord Jesus Christ predicted. 18They told you that in the last times there would be scoffers whose purpose in life is to satisfy their ungodly desires. 19These people are the ones who are creating divisions among you. They follow their natural instincts because they do not have God's Spirit in them.

20But you, dear friends, must build each other up in your most holy faith, pray in the power of the Holy Spirit, 21and await the mercy of our Lord Jesus Christ, who will bring you eternal life. In this way, you will keep yourselves safe in God's love.

22And you must show mercy to those whose faith is wavering. 23Rescue others by snatching them from the flames of judgment. Show mercy to still others, but do so with great caution, hating the sins that contaminate their lives.

A Prayer of Praise

24Now all glory to God, who is able to keep you from falling away and will bring you with great joy into his glorious presence without a single fault. 25All glory to him who alone is God, our Savior through Jesus Christ our Lord. All glory, majesty, power, and authority are his before all time, and in the present, and beyond all time! Amen.

REVELATION

THE END

Look for 2 hidden messages in Revelation!

Revelation reveals what will happen when Jesus comes back. It tells about

- THE WAY CHURCHES SHOULD REALLY WORK
- THE POWER JESUS REALLY HAS
- THE HOME IN HEAVEN THAT'S REALLY WAITING FOR US
- THE VICTORY JESUS WILL REALLY HAVE

Always and Forever

Everything has a start and finish, right? Well, *almost* everything! **Check out Revelation 1:8.**

knock knock

Knock, knock!
Who's there?
Dwayne.
Dwayne who?
Dwayne the bathtub!
I'm dwowning!

Knock-knock jokes are just plain silly. **Read Revelation 3:20 to learn about a knock-knock that's no joke!**

Hot or Cold, but Not Lukewarm!

Maybe you've been helping your dad shovel the walk. Your mom calls you in for a nice steamy cup of hot cocoa. You take a sip. Yuck! Lukewarm. **Jesus doesn't like things lukewarm either. Find out more in Revelation 3:15-16.**

No Contest

What if the best NFL team came to play a game with your football team? No contest, right? You'd know who was going to win and who would get crushed. Well, it's a lot like that between God and Satan and his henchmen. **See who crushes whom in Revelation 19:11–20:10!**

Dear Blabby

Q: I've heard about heaven and how long our time there is going to be—like forever, right? Well, I'm a little worried about what I'll do for such a long time. I'm afraid I might get bored.

A: No way! Read Revelation 7:9-15 to find out what we'll be doing with the angels in heaven!

It's Gonna Be Great!

Heaven's going to be so amazing! How amazing? **Find out for yourself by reading Revelation 21:10-27.**

The End

The bad guy gets caught, the hero gets the girl, and they ride off into the sunset. That's a standard ending, but here's a story that has the best ending of all. And it's not just a story—it's real!

Read Revelation 21:1-7 for the end of one story and the beginning of another!

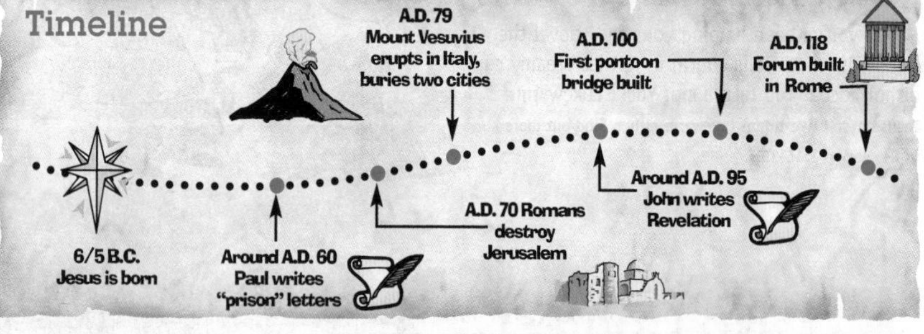

Timeline
6/5 B.C. Jesus is born
Around A.D. 60 Paul writes "prison" letters
A.D. 70 Romans destroy Jerusalem
A.D. 79 Mount Vesuvius erupts in Italy, buries two cities
Around A.D. 95 John writes Revelation
A.D. 100 First pontoon bridge built
A.D. 118 Forum built in Rome

The JESUS Connection

The book of Revelation shows who Jesus really is. The first time he came to earth, Jesus was humble and gave himself as a sacrifice for our sins. When Jesus comes back, he'll show all the world his full glory and power. Every knee will bow before Jesus. Either people will bow out of love and joy at seeing their King, or they'll bow out of fear and horror because they didn't follow Jesus when they had the chance. **The King of kings will return. And you can look forward to that day if you give your heart and life to Jesus today.**

CHAPTER **1**

Prologue

This is a revelation from Jesus Christ, which God
gave him to show his servants the events that
must soon take place. He sent an angel to present
this revelation to his servant John, 2who faithfully reported everything he saw. This is his report of the word of God and the testimony of
Jesus Christ.

3God blesses the one who reads the words of
this prophecy to the church, and he blesses all
who listen to its message and obey what it says,
for the time is near.

John's Greeting to the Seven Churches

4This letter is from John to the seven churches in
the province of Asia.

Grace and peace to you from the one who is,
who always was, and who is still to come; from
the sevenfold Spirit before his throne; 5and from
Jesus Christ. He is the faithful witness to these
things, the first to rise from the dead, and the
ruler of all the kings of the world.

All glory to him who loves us and has freed us
from our sins by shedding his blood for us. 6He
has made us a Kingdom of priests for God his Father. All glory and power to him forever and ever!
Amen.

7 Look! He comes with the clouds of heaven.
And everyone will see him—
even those who pierced him.
And all the nations of the world
will mourn for him.
Yes! Amen!

8"I am the Alpha and the Omega—
the beginning and the end," says the
Lord God. "I am the one who is, who
always was, and who is still to
come—the Almighty One."

Vision of the Son of Man

9I, John, am your brother and your partner in
suffering and in God's Kingdom and in the patient endurance to which Jesus calls us. I was
exiled to the island of Patmos for preaching the
word of God and for my testimony about Jesus.
10It was the Lord's Day, and I was worshiping in
the Spirit. Suddenly, I heard behind me a loud
voice like a trumpet blast. 11It said, "Write in a
book everything you see, and send it to the
seven churches in the cities of Ephesus, Smyrna, Pergamum, Thyatira, Sardis, Philadelphia,
and Laodicea."

12When I turned to see who was speaking to
me, I saw seven gold lampstands. 13And standing
in the middle of the lampstands was someone
like the Son of Man. He was wearing a long robe
with a gold sash across his chest. 14His head and
his hair were white like wool, as white as snow.
And his eyes were like flames of fire. 15His feet
were like polished bronze refined in a furnace,
and his voice thundered like mighty ocean
waves. 16He held seven stars in his right hand,
and a sharp two-edged sword came from his
mouth. And his face was like the sun in all its
brilliance.

17When I saw him, I fell at his feet as if I were
dead. But he laid his right hand on me and said,
"Don't be afraid! I am the First and the Last. 18I
am the living one. I died, but look—I am alive forever and ever! And I hold the keys of death and
the grave.

19"Write down what you have seen—both the
things that are now happening and the things
that will happen. 20This is the meaning of the
mystery of the seven stars you saw in my right
hand and the seven gold lampstands: The seven
stars are the angels of the seven churches, and
the seven lampstands are the seven churches.

CHAPTER **2**

The Message to the Church in Ephesus

"Write this letter to the angel of the church in
Ephesus. This is the message from the one who
holds the seven stars in his right hand, the one
who walks among the seven gold lampstands:

2"I know all the things you do. I have seen
your hard work and your patient endurance.
I know you don't tolerate evil people. You
have examined the claims of those who
say they are apostles but are not. You have
discovered they are liars. 3You have patiently
suffered for me without quitting.

4"But I have this complaint against you.
You don't love me or each other as you did
at first! 5Look how far you have fallen! Turn
back to me and do the works you did at first.
If you don't repent, I will come and remove
your lampstand from its place among the
churches. 6But this is in your favor: You hate
the evil deeds of the Nicolaitans, just as I do.

7"Anyone with ears to hear must listen
to the Spirit and understand what he is
saying to the churches. To everyone who
is victorious I will give fruit from the tree
of life in the paradise of God.

Revelation 3 . . . page 1254

The Message to the Church in Smyrna

8"Write this letter to the angel of the church in
Smyrna. This is the message from the one who
is the First and the Last, who was dead but is
now alive:

9"I know about your suffering and your
poverty—but you are rich! I know the
blasphemy of those opposing you. They
say they are Jews, but they are not, because
their synagogue belongs to Satan. 10Don't
be afraid of what you are about to suffer.
The devil will throw some of you into
prison to test you. You will suffer for ten
days. But if you remain faithful even when
facing death, I will give you the crown
of life.

11"Anyone with ears to hear must listen to
the Spirit and understand what he is saying
to the churches. Whoever is victorious will
not be harmed by the second death.

The Message to the Church in Pergamum

12"Write this letter to the angel of the church in
Pergamum. This is the message from the one
with the sharp two-edged sword:

13"I know that you live in the city where
Satan has his throne, yet you have remained
loyal to me. You refused to deny me even
when Antipas, my faithful witness, was
martyred among you there in Satan's city.

14"But I have a few complaints against
you. You tolerate some among you whose
teaching is like that of Balaam, who showed
Balak how to trip up the people of Israel.
He taught them to sin by eating food
offered to idols and by committing sexual
sin. 15In a similar way, you have some
Nicolaitans among you who follow the
same teaching. 16Repent of your sin, or
I will come to you suddenly and fight
against them with the sword of my mouth.

17"Anyone with ears to hear must listen to
the Spirit and understand what he is saying
to the churches. To everyone who
is victorious I will give some of the manna
that has been hidden away in heaven. And
I will give to each one a white stone, and on
the stone will be engraved a new name that
no one understands except the one who
receives it.

The Message to the Church in Thyatira

18"Write this letter to the angel of the church in
Thyatira. This is the message from the Son of
God, whose eyes are like flames of fire, whose
feet are like polished bronze:

19"I know all the things you do. I have seen
your love, your faith, your service, and your
patient endurance. And I can see your
constant improvement in all these things.

20"But I have this complaint against you.
You are permitting that woman—that Jezebel
who calls herself a prophet—to lead my
servants astray. She teaches them to commit
sexual sin and to eat food offered to idols.
21I gave her time to repent, but she does not
want to turn away from her immorality.

22"Therefore, I will throw her on a bed
of suffering, and those who commit adultery
with her will suffer greatly unless they
repent and turn away from their evil deeds.
23I will strike her children dead. Then all the
churches will know that I am the one who
searches out the thoughts and intentions of
every person. And I will give to each of you
whatever you deserve.

24"But I also have a message for the rest
of you in Thyatira who have not followed
this false teaching ('deeper truths,' as they
call them—depths of Satan, actually). I will
ask nothing more of you 25except that you
hold tightly to what you have until I come.
26To all who are victorious, who obey me
to the very end,

To them I will give authority over all
the nations.
27 They will rule the nations with an iron rod
and smash them like clay pots.

28They will have the same authority I
received from my Father, and I will also
give them the morning star!

29"Anyone with ears to hear must listen to
the Spirit and understand what he is saying
to the churches.

CHAPTER 3

The Message to the Church in Sardis

"Write this letter to the angel of the church in
Sardis. This is the message from the one who has
the sevenfold Spirit of God and the seven stars:

"I know all the things you do, and that you
have a reputation for being alive—but you

are dead. 2Wake up! Strengthen what little
remains, for even what is left is almost dead.
I find that your actions do not meet the
requirements of my God. 3Go back to what
you heard and believed at first; hold to it
firmly. Repent and turn to me again. If you
don't wake up, I will come to you suddenly,
as unexpected as a thief.

4"Yet there are some in the church in
Sardis who have not soiled their clothes
with evil. They will walk with me in white,
for they are worthy. 5All who are victorious
will be clothed in white. I will never erase
their names from the Book of Life, but I will
announce before my Father and his angels
that they are mine.

6"Anyone with ears to hear must listen to
the Spirit and understand what he is saying
to the churches.

The Message to the Church in Philadelphia

7"Write this letter to the angel of the church in
Philadelphia.

This is the message from the one who is holy
and true,
the one who has the key of David.
What he opens, no one can close;
and what he closes, no one can open:

8"I know all the things you do, and I have
opened a door for you that no one can close.
You have little strength, yet you obeyed my
word and did not deny me. 9Look, I will force
those who belong to Satan's synagogue—
those liars who say they are Jews but are not—
to come and bow down at your feet. They will
acknowledge that you are the ones I love.

10"Because you have obeyed my command
to persevere, I will protect you from the great
time of testing that will come upon the whole
world to test those who belong to this world.
11I am coming soon. Hold on to what you
have, so that no one will take away your
crown. 12All who are victorious will become
pillars in the Temple of my God, and they
will never have to leave it. And I will write
on them the name of my God, and they will
be citizens in the city of my God—the new
Jerusalem that comes down from heaven
from my God. And I will also write on them
my new name.

13"Anyone with ears to hear must listen to
the Spirit and understand what he is saying
to the churches.

Jesus is Knocking

Make this door hanger to remind you that Jesus is knocking at the door!

The Bible says that someone is knocking at the door. Just read **REVELATION 3:20-21** to find out who!

1. **Cut a 4x12-inch rectangle from poster board.**
2. **Cut two slits like a cross near one end of the rectangle. (But don't cut all the way to the edges.)**
3. **Now write the words of Revelation 3:20 on it to remind you that Jesus is knocking at the door!**

LOOK! I Stand at the door and knock. If you hear my voice and open the door, I will come in, and we will share a meal together as friends.

AND GUESS WHAT?

JESUS IS KNOCKING ON EVERYBODY'S DOOR!

Make a whole bunch of door hangers with the words of **REVELATION 3:20** on them. Then hang them on every door at church. Or ask an adult to help you make a batch of cookies, then together deliver door hangers and little bags of cookies to all your neighbors.

Revelation 4 . . . page 1256

The Message to the Church in Laodicea

14 "Write this letter to the angel of the church in
Laodicea. This is the message from the one who
is the Amen—the faithful and true witness, the
beginning of God's new creation:

15 "I know all the things you do, that you are
neither hot nor cold. I wish that you were
one or the other! 16 But since you are like
lukewarm water, neither hot nor cold, I will
spit you out of my mouth! 17 You say, 'I am
rich. I have everything I want. I don't need
a thing!' And you don't realize that you are
wretched and miserable and poor and blind
and naked. 18 So I advise you to buy gold
from me—gold that has been purified by
fire. Then you will be rich. Also buy white
garments from me so you will not be
shamed by your nakedness, and ointment
for your eyes so you will be able to see. 19 I
correct and discipline everyone I love. So
be diligent and turn from your indifference.

20 **"Look! I stand at the door and
knock. If you hear my voice and
open the door, I will come in, and
we will share a meal together as
friends.** 21 Those who are victorious will sit
with me on my throne, just as I was victorious
and sat with my Father on his throne.

22 "Anyone with ears to hear must listen to
the Spirit and understand what he is saying
to the churches."

CHAPTER 4

Worship in Heaven

Then as I looked, I saw a door standing open in
heaven, and the same voice I had heard before
spoke to me like a trumpet blast. The voice said,
"Come up here, and I will show you what must
happen after this." 2 And instantly I was in the
Spirit, and I saw a throne in heaven and someone
sitting on it. 3 The one sitting on the throne was as
brilliant as gemstones—like jasper and carnelian.
And the glow of an emerald circled his throne like
a rainbow. 4 Twenty-four thrones surrounded him,
and twenty-four elders sat on them. They were all
clothed in white and had gold crowns on their
heads. 5 From the throne came flashes of lightning and the rumble of thunder. And in front of
the throne were seven torches with burning
flames. This is the sevenfold Spirit of God. 6 In
front of the throne was a shiny sea of glass, sparkling like crystal.

In the center and around the throne were four
living beings, each covered with eyes, front and
back. 7 The first of these living beings was like a
lion; the second was like an ox; the third had a
human face; and the fourth was like an eagle in
flight. 8 Each of these living beings had six wings,
and their wings were covered all over with eyes,
inside and out. Day after day and night after
night they keep on saying,

"Holy, holy, holy is the Lord God, the
Almighty—
the one who always was, who is,
and who is still to come."

9 Whenever the living beings give glory and
honor and thanks to the one sitting on the
throne (the one who lives forever and ever),
10 the twenty-four elders fall down and worship
the one sitting on the throne (the one who lives
forever and ever). And they lay their crowns before the throne and say,

11 "You are worthy, O Lord our God,
to receive glory and honor and power.
For you created all things,
and they exist because you created
what you pleased."

CHAPTER 5

The Lamb Opens the Scroll

Then I saw a scroll in the right hand of the one
who was sitting on the throne. There was writing
on the inside and the outside of the scroll, and it
was sealed with seven seals. 2 And I saw a strong
angel, who shouted with a loud voice: "Who is
worthy to break the seals on this scroll and open
it?" 3 But no one in heaven or on earth or under
the earth was able to open the scroll and read it.

4 Then I began to weep bitterly because no one
was found worthy to open the scroll and read it.
5 But one of the twenty-four elders said to me,
"Stop weeping! Look, the Lion of the tribe of Judah, the heir to David's throne, has won the victory. He is worthy to open the scroll and its seven
seals."

6 Then I saw a Lamb that looked as if it had
been slaughtered, but it was now standing between the throne and the four living beings and
among the twenty-four elders. He had seven
horns and seven eyes, which represent the
sevenfold Spirit of God that is sent out into every
part of the earth. 7 He stepped forward and took
the scroll from the right hand of the one sitting
on the throne. 8 And when he took the scroll, the
four living beings and the twenty-four elders fell
down before the Lamb. Each one had a harp, and

they held gold bowls filled with incense, which
are the prayers of God's people. 9 And they sang a
new song with these words:

"You are worthy to take the scroll
and break its seals and open it.
For you were slaughtered, and your blood
has ransomed people for God
from every tribe and language and people
and nation.
10 And you have caused them to become
a Kingdom of priests for our God.
And they will reign on the earth."

11 Then I looked again, and I heard the voices
of thousands and millions of angels around the
throne and of the living beings and the elders.
12 And they sang in a mighty chorus:

"Worthy is the Lamb who was slaughtered—
to receive power and riches
and wisdom and strength
and honor and glory and blessing."

13 And then I heard every creature in heaven
and on earth and under the earth and in the sea.
They sang:

"Blessing and honor and glory and power
belong to the one sitting on the throne
and to the Lamb forever and ever."

14 And the four living beings said, "Amen!" And
the twenty-four elders fell down and worshiped
the Lamb.

CHAPTER 6
The Lamb Breaks the First Six Seals

As I watched, the Lamb broke the first of the
seven seals on the scroll. Then I heard one of the
four living beings say with a voice like thunder,
"Come!" 2 I looked up and saw a white horse
standing there. Its rider carried a bow, and a
crown was placed on his head. He rode out to win
many battles and gain the victory.
3 When the Lamb broke the second seal, I
heard the second living being say, "Come!" 4 Then
another horse appeared, a red one. Its rider was
given a mighty sword and the authority to take
peace from the earth. And there was war and
slaughter everywhere.
5 When the Lamb broke the third seal, I heard
the third living being say, "Come!" I looked up
and saw a black horse, and its rider was holding
a pair of scales in his hand. 6 And I heard a voice
from among the four living beings say, "A loaf of
wheat bread or three loaves of barley will cost a
day's pay. And don't waste the olive oil and
wine."
7 When the Lamb broke the fourth seal, I
heard the fourth living being say, "Come!" 8 I
looked up and saw a horse whose color was pale
green. Its rider was named Death, and his companion was the Grave. These two were given authority over one-fourth of the earth, to kill with
the sword and famine and disease and wild
animals.
9 When the Lamb broke the fifth seal, I saw
under the altar the souls of all who had been martyred for the word of God and for being faithful in
their testimony. 10 They shouted to the Lord and
said, "O Sovereign Lord, holy and true, how long
before you judge the people who belong to this
world and avenge our blood for what they have
done to us?" 11 Then a white robe was given to
each of them. And they were told to rest a little
longer until the full number of their brothers and
sisters—their fellow servants of Jesus who were to
be martyred—had joined them.
12 I watched as the Lamb broke the sixth seal,
and there was a great earthquake. The sun became as dark as black cloth, and the moon became as red as blood. 13 Then the stars of the sky
fell to the earth like green figs falling from a tree
shaken by a strong wind. 14 The sky was rolled up
like a scroll, and all of the mountains and islands
were moved from their places.
15 Then everyone—the kings of the earth, the
rulers, the generals, the wealthy, the powerful,
and every slave and free person—all hid themselves in the caves and among the rocks of the
mountains. 16 And they cried to the mountains
and the rocks, "Fall on us and hide us from the
face of the one who sits on the throne and from
the wrath of the Lamb. 17 For the great day of their
wrath has come, and who is able to survive?"

CHAPTER 7
God's People Will Be Preserved

Then I saw four angels standing at the four corners of the earth, holding back the four winds so
they did not blow on the earth or the sea, or even
on any tree. 2 And I saw another angel coming up
from the east, carrying the seal of the living God.
And he shouted to those four angels, who had
been given power to harm land and sea, 3 "Wait!
Don't harm the land or the sea or the trees until
we have placed the seal of God on the foreheads
of his servants."
4 And I heard how many were marked with the
seal of God—144,000 were sealed from all the
tribes of Israel:

5 from Judah 12,000
from Reuben. 12,000
from Gad 12,000
6 from Asher 12,000
from Naphtali. 12,000
from Manasseh 12,000
7 from Simeon. 12,000
from Levi 12,000
from Issachar. 12,000
8 from Zebulun 12,000

No More Tears

Things will really be different in heaven! Read **REVELATION 7:16-17** to see how great things will be.

Then make this reminder that you won't need tissues when you get there!

1. **Use fun wrapping paper to wrap an open box of tissues like a present.**
2. **Carefully cut the wrapping paper away from the opening for the tissues.**
3. **Write REVELATION 7:16-17 in your own words on a small card. Glue the card to the box.**

There will be NO tears in heaven!

Read what Isaiah said about heaven in Isaiah 65:17-19. Sound familiar?

Give the box to someone else. Remind that person that in heaven there will be no more tears or sadness!

Then wrap a box for your family. The next time you reach for a tissue, remember that heaven will be a happy place!

from Joseph. 12,000
from Benjamin 12,000

Praise from the Great Crowd

9 After this I saw a vast crowd, too great to count,
from every nation and tribe and people and language, standing in front of the throne and before
the Lamb. They were clothed in white robes and
held palm branches in their hands. 10 And they
were shouting with a great roar,

"Salvation comes from our God
who sits on the throne
and from the Lamb!"

11 And all the angels were standing around
the throne and around the elders and the four
living beings. And they fell before the throne
with their faces to the ground and worshiped
God. 12 They sang,

"Amen! Blessing and glory and wisdom
and thanksgiving and honor
and power and strength belong to our God
forever and ever! Amen."

13 Then one of the twenty-four elders asked
me, "Who are these who are clothed in white?
Where did they come from?"
14 And I said to him, "Sir, you are the one who
knows."

Then he said to me, "These are the ones who died in the great tribulation. They have washed their robes in the blood of the Lamb and made them white.

15 "That is why they stand in front
of God's throne
and serve him day and night
in his Temple.
And he who sits on the throne
will give them shelter.
16 They will never again be hungry or thirsty;
they will never be scorched by the heat
of the sun.
17 For the Lamb on the throne
will be their Shepherd.
He will lead them to springs of
life-giving water.
And God will wipe every tear
from their eyes."

CHAPTER 8
The Lamb Breaks the Seventh Seal

When the Lamb broke the seventh seal on the scroll, there was silence throughout heaven for

about half an hour. 2I saw the seven angels who
stand before God, and they were given seven
trumpets.
3Then another angel with a gold incense
burner came and stood at the altar. And a great
amount of incense was given to him to mix with
the prayers of God's people as an offering on the
gold altar before the throne. 4The smoke of the
incense, mixed with the prayers of God's holy
people, ascended up to God from the altar where
the angel had poured them out. 5Then the angel
filled the incense burner with fire from the altar
and threw it down upon the earth; and thunder
crashed, lightning flashed, and there was a terrible earthquake.

The First Four Trumpets

6Then the seven angels with the seven trumpets
prepared to blow their mighty blasts.
7The first angel blew his trumpet, and hail and
fire mixed with blood were thrown down on the
earth. One-third of the earth was set on fire, one-
third of the trees were burned, and all the green
grass was burned.
8Then the second angel blew his trumpet,
and a great mountain of fire was thrown into the
sea. One-third of the water in the sea became
blood, 9one-third of all things living in the sea
died, and one-third of all the ships on the sea
were destroyed.
10Then the third angel blew his trumpet, and
a great star fell from the sky, burning like a
torch. It fell on one-third of the rivers and on
the springs of water. 11The name of the star was
Bitterness. It made one-third of the water bitter,
and many people died from drinking the bitter
water.
12Then the fourth angel blew his trumpet, and
one-third of the sun was struck, and one-third of
the moon, and one-third of the stars, and they
became dark. And one-third of the day was dark,
and also one-third of the night.
13Then I looked, and I heard a single eagle
crying loudly as it flew through the air, "Terror,
terror, terror to all who belong to this world because of what will happen when the last three angels blow their trumpets."

CHAPTER 9

The Fifth Trumpet Brings the First Terror

Then the fifth angel blew his trumpet, and I saw a
star that had fallen to earth from the sky, and he
was given the key to the shaft of the bottomless
pit. 2When he opened it, smoke poured out as
though from a huge furnace, and the sunlight
and air turned dark from the smoke.
3Then locusts came from the smoke and descended on the earth, and they were given power
to sting like scorpions. 4They were told not to
harm the grass or plants or trees, but only the
people who did not have the seal of God on their
foreheads. 5They were told not to kill them but
to torture them for five months with pain like the
pain of a scorpion sting. 6In those days people
will seek death but will not find it. They will long
to die, but death will flee from them!
7The locusts looked like horses prepared for
battle. They had what looked like gold crowns on
their heads, and their faces looked like human
faces. 8They had hair like women's hair and teeth
like the teeth of a lion. 9They wore armor made
of iron, and their wings roared like an army of
chariots rushing into battle. 10They had tails that
stung like scorpions, and for five months they
had the power to torment people. 11Their king is
the angel from the bottomless pit; his name in
Hebrew is *Abaddon*, and in Greek, *Apollyon*—the
Destroyer.
12The first terror is past, but look, two more
terrors are coming!

The Sixth Trumpet Brings the Second Terror

13Then the sixth angel blew his trumpet, and I
heard a voice speaking from the four horns of
the gold altar that stands in the presence of God.
14And the voice said to the sixth angel who held
the trumpet, "Release the four angels who are
bound at the great Euphrates River." 15Then the
four angels who had been prepared for this hour
and day and month and year were turned loose
to kill one-third of all the people on earth. 16I
heard the size of their army, which was 200 million mounted troops.
17And in my vision, I saw the horses and the
riders sitting on them. The riders wore armor
that was fiery red and dark blue and yellow. The
horses had heads like lions, and fire and smoke
and burning sulfur billowed from their mouths.
18One-third of all the people on earth were killed
by these three plagues—by the fire and smoke
and burning sulfur that came from the mouths of
the horses. 19Their power was in their mouths
and in their tails. For their tails had heads like
snakes, with the power to injure people.
20But the people who did not die in these
plagues still refused to repent of their evil deeds
and turn to God. They continued to worship demons and idols made of gold, silver, bronze,

stone, and wood—idols that can neither see nor hear nor walk! 21 And they did not repent of their murders or their witchcraft or their sexual immorality or their thefts.

CHAPTER 10
The Angel and the Small Scroll

Then I saw another mighty angel coming down from heaven, surrounded by a cloud, with a rainbow over his head. His face shone like the sun, and his feet were like pillars of fire. 2 And in his hand was a small scroll that had been opened. He stood with his right foot on the sea and his left foot on the land. 3 And he gave a great shout like the roar of a lion. And when he shouted, the seven thunders answered.

4 When the seven thunders spoke, I was about to write. But I heard a voice from heaven saying, "Keep secret what the seven thunders said, and do not write it down."

5 Then the angel I saw standing on the sea and on the land raised his right hand toward heaven. 6 He swore an oath in the name of the one who lives forever and ever, who created the heavens and everything in them, the earth and everything in it, and the sea and everything in it. He said, "There will be no more delay. 7 When the seventh angel blows his trumpet, God's mysterious plan will be fulfilled. It will happen just as he announced it to his servants the prophets."

8 Then the voice from heaven spoke to me again: "Go and take the open scroll from the hand of the angel who is standing on the sea and on the land."

9 So I went to the angel and told him to give me the small scroll. "Yes, take it and eat it," he said. "It will be sweet as honey in your mouth, but it will turn sour in your stomach!" 10 So I took the small scroll from the hand of the angel, and I ate it! It was sweet in my mouth, but when I swallowed it, it turned sour in my stomach.

11 Then I was told, "You must prophesy again about many peoples, nations, languages, and kings."

CHAPTER 11
The Two Witnesses

Then I was given a measuring stick, and I was told, "Go and measure the Temple of God and the altar, and count the number of worshipers. 2 But do not measure the outer courtyard, for it has been turned over to the nations. They will trample the holy city for 42 months. 3 And I will give power to my two witnesses, and they will be clothed in burlap and will prophesy during those 1,260 days."

4 These two prophets are the two olive trees and the two lampstands that stand before the Lord of all the earth. 5 If anyone tries to harm them, fire flashes from their mouths and consumes their enemies. This is how anyone who tries to harm them must die. 6 They have power to shut the sky so that no rain will fall for as long as they prophesy. And they have the power to turn the rivers and oceans into blood, and to strike the earth with every kind of plague as often as they wish.

7 When they complete their testimony, the beast that comes up out of the bottomless pit will declare war against them, and he will conquer them and kill them. 8 And their bodies will lie in the main street of Jerusalem, the city that is figuratively called "Sodom" and "Egypt," the city where their Lord was crucified. 9 And for three and a half days, all peoples, tribes, languages, and nations will stare at their bodies. No one will be allowed to bury them. 10 All the people who belong to this world will gloat over them and give presents to each other to celebrate the death of the two prophets who had tormented them.

11 But after three and a half days, God breathed life into them, and they stood up! Terror struck all who were staring at them. 12 Then a loud voice from heaven called to the two prophets, "Come up here!" And they rose to heaven in a cloud as their enemies watched.

13 At the same time there was a terrible earthquake that destroyed a tenth of the city. Seven thousand people died in that earthquake, and everyone else was terrified and gave glory to the God of heaven.

14 The second terror is past, but look, the third terror is coming quickly.

The Seventh Trumpet Brings the Third Terror

15 Then the seventh angel blew his trumpet, and there were loud voices shouting in heaven:

"The world has now become the Kingdom
of our Lord and of his Christ,
and he will reign forever and ever."

16 The twenty-four elders sitting on their thrones before God fell with their faces to the ground and worshiped him. 17 And they said,

"We give thanks to you, Lord God, the
Almighty,
the one who is and who always was,
for now you have assumed your great power
and have begun to reign.

There's something special about numbers in the Bible. Take the number **12**, for instance. Why do you think this number might be so important?

Here's why:

- the **12** sons of Jacob,
- the **12** tribes of Israel,
- the **12** apostles,
- the **12** gates of the New Jerusalem, and
- the tree of life bears **12** crops of fruit.

Pretty cool, right? See if you can find other numbers in the Bible that are mentioned often. You could ask your teacher or parents for sources. Below, write three cool facts you find about numbers in the Bible. (Here's a hint: 40 and 7 appear a lot.)

1. ____________________
2. ____________________
3. ____________________

18 The nations were filled with wrath,
but now the time of your wrath has come.
It is time to judge the dead
and reward your servants the prophets,
as well as your holy people,
and all who fear your name,
from the least to the greatest.
It is time to destroy
all who have caused destruction on
the earth."

19Then, in heaven, the Temple of God was
opened and the Ark of his covenant could be
seen inside the Temple. Lightning flashed, thunder crashed and roared, and there was an earthquake and a terrible hailstorm.

CHAPTER **12**

The Woman and the Dragon

Then I witnessed in heaven an event of great significance. I saw a woman clothed with the sun,
with the moon beneath her feet, and a crown of
twelve stars on her head. 2She was pregnant, and
she cried out because of her labor pains and the
agony of giving birth.

3Then I witnessed in heaven another significant event. I saw a large red dragon with seven heads and ten horns, with seven crowns on his
heads. 4His tail swept away one-third of the stars
in the sky, and he threw them to the earth. He stood in front of the woman as she was about to give birth, ready to devour her baby as soon as it was born.

5She gave birth to a son who was to rule all
nations with an iron rod. And her child was snatched away from the dragon and was caught
up to God and to his throne. 6And the woman
fled into the wilderness, where God had prepared a place to care for her for 1,260 days.

7Then there was war in heaven. Michael and
his angels fought against the dragon and his angels. 8And the dragon lost the battle, and he and
his angels were forced out of heaven. 9This great
dragon—the ancient serpent called the devil, or Satan, the one deceiving the whole world—was thrown down to the earth with all his angels.

10Then I heard a loud voice shouting across
the heavens,

"It has come at last—
salvation and power
and the Kingdom of our God,
and the authority of his Christ.
For the accuser of our brothers and sisters
has been thrown down to earth—
the one who accuses them
before our God day and night.
11 And they have defeated him by the blood
of the Lamb
and by their testimony.
And they did not love their lives so much
that they were afraid to die.
12 Therefore, rejoice, O heavens!
And you who live in the heavens, rejoice!
But terror will come on the earth and
the sea,
for the devil has come down to you in
great anger,
knowing that he has little time."

13When the dragon realized that he had been
thrown down to the earth, he pursued the woman who had given birth to the male child.
14But she was given two wings like those of a
great eagle so she could fly to the place prepared for her in the wilderness. There she would be

cared for and protected from the dragon for a
time, times, and half a time.
15 Then the dragon tried to drown the woman
with a flood of water that flowed from his
mouth. 16 But the earth helped her by opening
its mouth and swallowing the river that gushed
out from the mouth of the dragon. 17 And the
dragon was angry at the woman and declared
war against the rest of her children—all who
keep God's commandments and maintain their
testimony for Jesus.
18 Then the dragon took his stand on the shore
beside the sea.

CHAPTER 13

The Beast out of the Sea

Then I saw a beast rising up out of the sea. It had
seven heads and ten horns, with ten crowns on
its horns. And written on each head were names
that blasphemed God. 2 This beast looked like a
leopard, but it had the feet of a bear and the
mouth of a lion! And the dragon gave the beast
his own power and throne and great authority.
3 I saw that one of the heads of the beast
seemed wounded beyond recovery—but the fatal wound was healed! The whole world mar-
veled at this miracle and gave allegiance to the
beast. 4 They worshiped the dragon for giving
the beast such power, and they also worshiped
the beast. "Who is as great as the beast?" they
exclaimed. "Who is able to fight against him?"
5 Then the beast was allowed to speak great
blasphemies against God. And he was given authority to do whatever he wanted for forty-two
months. 6 And he spoke terrible words of
blasphemy against God, slandering his name
and his dwelling—that is, those who dwell in
heaven. 7 And the beast was allowed to wage war
against God's holy people and to conquer them.
And he was given authority to rule over every
tribe and people and language and nation. 8 And
all the people who belong to this world worshiped the beast. They are the ones whose
names were not written in the Book of Life that
belongs to the Lamb who was slaughtered before the world was made.

9 Anyone with ears to hear
should listen and understand.
10 Anyone who is destined for prison
will be taken to prison.
Anyone destined to die by the sword
will die by the sword.

This means that God's holy people must endure
persecution patiently and remain faithful.

The Beast out of the Earth

11 Then I saw another beast come up out of the
earth. He had two horns like those of a lamb, but
he spoke with the voice of a dragon. 12 He exercised all the authority of the first beast. And he
required all the earth and its people to worship
the first beast, whose fatal wound had been
healed. 13 He did astounding miracles, even
making fire flash down to earth from the sky
while everyone was watching. 14 And with all the
miracles he was allowed to perform on behalf of
the first beast, he deceived all the people who
belong to this world. He ordered the people to
make a great statue of the first beast, who was fa-
tally wounded and then came back to life. 15 He
was then permitted to give life to this statue so
that it could speak. Then the statue of the beast
commanded that anyone refusing to worship it
must die.
16 He required everyone—small and great,
rich and poor, free and slave—to be given a mark
on the right hand or on the forehead. 17 And no
one could buy or sell anything without that
mark, which was either the name of the beast or
the number representing his name. 18 Wisdom
is needed here. Let the one with understanding
solve the meaning of the number of the beast,
for it is the number of a man. His number is
666.

CHAPTER 14

The Lamb and the 144,000

Then I saw the Lamb standing on Mount Zion,
and with him were 144,000 who had his name
and his Father's name written on their foreheads.
2 And I heard a sound from heaven like the roar
of mighty ocean waves or the rolling of loud
thunder. It was like the sound of many harpists
playing together.
3 This great choir sang a wonderful new song
in front of the throne of God and before the four
living beings and the twenty-four elders. No one
could learn this song except the 144,000 who
had been redeemed from the earth. 4 They have
kept themselves as pure as virgins, following the
Lamb wherever he goes. They have been purchased from among the people on the earth as a
special offering to God and to the Lamb. 5 They
have told no lies; they are without blame.

The Three Angels

6 And I saw another angel flying through the sky,
carrying the eternal Good News to proclaim to
the people who belong to this world—to every
nation, tribe, language, and people. 7 "Fear God,"

BIBLE BIOS

Hear From the Heroes

ANGELS *(full-time servants and worshipers of God)*

Hi! I'm Michael! I'm one of God's leading angels, and I'm going to be speaking for all of us today. First, I want to get one thing straight. We are not humans who have died and gone to heaven. Let me repeat that: We are not humans who have died and gone to heaven! No matter how many TV shows and movies try to make you think that, don't buy it. We're separate beings, created by God, and actually we're a little higher than humans in the whole scheme of things.

We also are not pretty females with white robes and wings. The white robe idea comes from times when we appeared as humans. Though we are spirit beings, we sometimes need to take human form. But the Bible never records an angel appearing as a woman. And the wings thing? I'm not sure where that came from.

Want to check that out? Look at ZECHARIAH 4:11-13; LUKE 1:18-19; 2:8-11; and MATTHEW 28:2-6, just to name a few!

We angels do lots of things: We worship God, we deliver God's messages to people, we follow God's direction to help people or watch over them. There are lots of us—no human really knows how many! But we all follow God's directions.

Well, I guess I should say all of us who are on God's side follow his directions. God created us all as good beings. But he didn't force us to follow him. So at one point, some of the angels decided to rebel and follow Satan's leadership. (Yes, he actually was one of us.) All of those angels rebelling against God were thrown out of heaven.

Do angels die, like humans do? Look at LUKE 20:34-36 for the answer!

When Jesus lived as a human on earth, we appeared a lot. Angels appeared to Mary and Joseph to let them know Jesus was going to be born. Then we announced Jesus' birth to the shepherds in the fields. One of us told Joseph to take Jesus and Mary to Egypt to escape Herod's evil plan. Then after Jesus was tempted by Satan, we went and ministered to him. And it was a great day when we got to announce Jesus' resurrection at the tomb!

Did you know that angels have broken people out of jail? Read ACTS 5:17-20 and 12:5-11.

It's a wonderful life, being an angel! And we look forward to joining humans in worshiping God for eternity!

WHERE'S MY ANGEL?

See what the Bible says about guardian angels in **PSALM 91:9-12**. Now, from what you've learned in this Bible Bio, draw a picture of a time you would like to have an angel watching over you. Then write a heading on the paper: "God sends angels to watch over me." Keep your drawing where it will remind you that God cares about you so much that he uses angels to look after you.

he shouted. "Give glory to him. For the time has
come when he will sit as judge. Worship him
who made the heavens, the earth, the sea, and all
the springs of water."
8Then another angel followed him through
the sky, shouting, "Babylon is fallen—that great
city is fallen—because she made all the nations
of the world drink the wine of her passionate immorality."
9Then a third angel followed them, shouting,
"Anyone who worships the beast and his statue
or who accepts his mark on the forehead or on
the hand 10must drink the wine of God's anger. It
has been poured full strength into God's cup of
wrath. And they will be tormented with fire and
burning sulfur in the presence of the holy angels
and the Lamb. 11The smoke of their torment will
rise forever and ever, and they will have no relief
day or night, for they have worshiped the beast
and his statue and have accepted the mark of his
name."
12This means that God's holy people must endure persecution patiently, obeying his commands and maintaining their faith in Jesus.
13And I heard a voice from heaven saying,
"Write this down: Blessed are those who die in
the Lord from now on. Yes, says the Spirit, they
are blessed indeed, for they will rest from their
hard work; for their good deeds follow them!"

The Harvest of the Earth

14Then I saw a white cloud, and seated on the
cloud was someone like the Son of Man. He had
a gold crown on his head and a sharp sickle in
his hand.
15Then another angel came from the Temple
and shouted to the one sitting on the cloud,
"Swing the sickle, for the time of harvest has
come; the crop on earth is ripe." 16So the one sitting on the cloud swung his sickle over the earth,
and the whole earth was harvested.
17After that, another angel came from the
Temple in heaven, and he also had a sharp
sickle. 18Then another angel, who had power to
destroy with fire, came from the altar. He
shouted to the angel with the sharp sickle,
"Swing your sickle now to gather the clusters of
grapes from the vines of the earth, for they are
ripe for judgment." 19So the angel swung his
sickle over the earth and loaded the grapes into
the great winepress of God's wrath. 20The
grapes were trampled in the winepress outside
the city, and blood flowed from the winepress in
a stream about 180 miles long and as high as a
horse's bridle.

CHAPTER 15

The Song of Moses and of the Lamb

Then I saw in heaven another marvelous event of
great significance. Seven angels were holding
the seven last plagues, which would bring God's
wrath to completion. 2I saw before me what
seemed to be a glass sea mixed with fire. And on
it stood all the people who had been victorious
over the beast and his statue and the number
representing his name. They were all holding
harps that God had given them. 3And they were
singing the song of Moses, the servant of God,
and the song of the Lamb:

"Great and marvelous are your works,
O Lord God, the Almighty.
Just and true are your ways,
O King of the nations.
4 Who will not fear you, Lord,
and glorify your name?
For you alone are holy.
All nations will come and worship
before you,
for your righteous deeds have
been revealed."

The Seven Bowls of the Seven Plagues

5Then I looked and saw that the Temple in
heaven, God's Tabernacle, was thrown wide
open. 6The seven angels who were holding the
seven plagues came out of the Temple. They
were clothed in spotless white linen with gold
sashes across their chests. 7Then one of the four
living beings handed each of the seven angels a
gold bowl filled with the wrath of God, who lives
forever and ever. 8The Temple was filled with
smoke from God's glory and power. No one could
enter the Temple until the seven angels had
completed pouring out the seven plagues.

CHAPTER 16

Then I heard a mighty voice from the Temple say
to the seven angels, "Go your ways and pour out
on the earth the seven bowls containing God's
wrath."
2So the first angel left the Temple and poured
out his bowl on the earth, and horrible, malig-
nant sores broke out on everyone who had the
mark of the beast and who worshiped his statue.
3Then the second angel poured out his bowl
on the sea, and it became like the blood of a
corpse. And everything in the sea died.
4Then the third angel poured out his bowl on

Alpha and Omega

The Bible says that God is the Alpha and Omega. (Alpha and omega are the first and last letters of the Greek alphabet.)

So it's natural that the first and last books of the Bible tell about the beginning and the end of the world. Look at this!

Genesis	Revelation
Sun created	Sun not needed
Satan gets his way	Satan defeated
Sin enters the world	Sin thrown out of the world
Tears shed because of sin	No more tears, no more sin

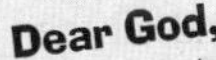

This prayer is already started. Fill in the endings for yourself!

Dear God,

Thanks for being the Alpha and Omega. Thanks for creating the world. A few of my favorite things you created are

____

____

____

I know that believing in Jesus is how I can get to heaven. This is how I feel about Jesus:

____

____

____

Thanks, God, for sending Jesus.

Love, ______________________

the rivers and springs, and they became blood.
5 And I heard the angel who had authority over all
water saying,

"You are just, O Holy One, who is and
who always was,
because you have sent these judgments.
6 Since they shed the blood
of your holy people and your prophets,
you have given them blood to drink.
It is their just reward."

7 And I heard a voice from the altar, saying,

"Yes, O Lord God, the Almighty,
your judgments are true and just."

8 Then the fourth angel poured out his bowl on
the sun, causing it to scorch everyone with its
fire. 9 Everyone was burned by this blast of heat,
and they cursed the name of God, who had control over all these plagues. They did not repent of
their sins and turn to God and give him glory.
10 Then the fifth angel poured out his bowl on
the throne of the beast, and his kingdom was
plunged into darkness. His subjects ground their
teeth in anguish, 11 and they cursed the God of
heaven for their pains and sores. But they did not
repent of their evil deeds and turn to God.
12 Then the sixth angel poured out his bowl on
the great Euphrates River, and it dried up so that
the kings from the east could march their armies
toward the west without hindrance. 13 And I saw
three evil spirits that looked like frogs leap from
the mouths of the dragon, the beast, and the false
prophet. 14 They are demonic spirits who work
miracles and go out to all the rulers of the world
to gather them for battle against the Lord on that
great judgment day of God the Almighty.

15 "Look, I will come as unexpectedly as a
thief! Blessed are all who are watching for
me, who keep their clothing ready so they
will not have to walk around naked and
ashamed."

16 And the demonic spirits gathered all the rulers and their armies to a place with the Hebrew
name *Armageddon*.
17 Then the seventh angel poured out his bowl
into the air. And a mighty shout came from the
throne in the Temple, saying, "It is finished!"
18 Then the thunder crashed and rolled, and

lightning flashed. And a great earthquake struck—
the worst since people were placed on the earth.
19The great city of Babylon split into three sections, and the cities of many nations fell into
heaps of rubble. So God remembered all of
Babylon's sins, and he made her drink the cup
that was filled with the wine of his fierce wrath.
20And every island disappeared, and all the
mountains were leveled. 21There was a terrible
hailstorm, and hailstones weighing as much as
seventy-five pounds fell from the sky onto the
people below. They cursed God because of the
terrible plague of the hailstorm.

CHAPTER 17
The Great Prostitute

One of the seven angels who had poured out the
seven bowls came over and spoke to me. "Come
with me," he said, "and I will show you the judgment that is going to come on the great prostitute, who rules over many waters. 2The kings of
the world have committed adultery with her, and
the people who belong to this world have been
made drunk by the wine of her immorality."
3So the angel took me in the Spirit into the
wilderness. There I saw a woman sitting on a
scarlet beast that had seven heads and ten horns,
and blasphemies against God were written all
over it. 4The woman wore purple and scarlet
clothing and beautiful jewelry made of gold and
precious gems and pearls. In her hand she held a
gold goblet full of obscenities and the impurities
of her immorality. 5A mysterious name was written on her forehead: "Babylon the Great, Mother
of All Prostitutes and Obscenities in the World."
6I could see that she was drunk—drunk with the
blood of God's holy people who were witnesses
for Jesus. I stared at her in complete amazement.
7"Why are you so amazed?" the angel asked. "I
will tell you the mystery of this woman and of the
beast with seven heads and ten horns on which
she sits. 8The beast you saw was once alive but
isn't now. And yet he will soon come up out of the
bottomless pit and go to eternal destruction.
And the people who belong to this world, whose
names were not written in the Book of Life before the world was made, will be amazed at the
reappearance of this beast who had died.
9"This calls for a mind with understanding:
The seven heads of the beast represent the seven
hills where the woman rules. They also represent
seven kings. 10Five kings have already fallen, the
sixth now reigns, and the seventh is yet to come,
but his reign will be brief.
11"The scarlet beast that was, but is no longer,
is the eighth king. He is like the other seven, and
he, too, is headed for destruction. 12The ten
horns of the beast are ten kings who have not yet
risen to power. They will be appointed to their
kingdoms for one brief moment to reign with the
beast. 13They will all agree to give him their
power and authority. 14Together they will go to
war against the Lamb, but the Lamb will defeat
them because he is Lord of all lords and King of
all kings. And his called and chosen and faithful
ones will be with him."
15Then the angel said to me, "The waters where
the prostitute is ruling represent masses of people
of every nation and language. 16The scarlet

FUN-fact
STAMP OF APPROVAL
APPROVED

Kings used to have a special way of sealing their letters. They'd roll them up and pour a small dab of wax on the edges to keep them rolled shut. Before the wax dried, they'd stamp it with a special seal. The seal looked kind of like a rubber stamp.

TRY THIS! **Write a letter to a friend. Roll it up, and have an adult pour a small amount of candle wax from a lit candle onto your letter to keep the edges together. Press a stamper or a coin into the wax as a seal. (Don't forget to deliver your letter!)**

STOP!! Before you read any further, go get an adult to help you light a candle!

Not that kind of seal!!!
This kind!

beast and his ten horns all hate the prostitute.
They will strip her naked, eat her flesh, and burn
her remains with fire. 17For God has put a plan
into their minds, a plan that will carry out his purposes. They will agree to give their authority to the
scarlet beast, and so the words of God will be fulfilled. 18And this woman you saw in your vision
represents the great city that rules over the kings
of the world."

CHAPTER 18

The Fall of Babylon

After all this I saw another angel come down
from heaven with great authority, and the earth
grew bright with his splendor. 2He gave a mighty
shout:

"Babylon is fallen—that great city is fallen!
She has become a home for demons.
She is a hideout for every foul spirit,
a hideout for every foul vulture
and every foul and dreadful animal.
3 For all the nations have fallen
because of the wine of her passionate
immorality.
The kings of the world
have committed adultery with her.
Because of her desires for extravagant luxury,
the merchants of the world have
grown rich."

4Then I heard another voice calling from heaven,
"Come away from her, my people.
Do not take part in her sins,
or you will be punished with her.
5 For her sins are piled as high as heaven,
and God remembers her evil deeds.
6 Do to her as she has done to others.
Double her penalty for all her evil deeds.
She brewed a cup of terror for others,
so brew twice as much for her.
7 She glorified herself and lived in luxury,
so match it now with torment and sorrow.
She boasted in her heart,
'I am queen on my throne.
I am no helpless widow,
and I have no reason to mourn.'
8 Therefore, these plagues will overtake
her in a single day—
death and mourning and famine.
She will be completely consumed by fire,
for the Lord God who judges her is
mighty."

9And the kings of the world who committed
adultery with her and enjoyed her great luxury
will mourn for her as they see the smoke rising
from her charred remains. 10They will stand at a
distance, terrified by her great torment. They
will cry out,

"How terrible, how terrible for you,
O Babylon, you great city!
In a single moment
God's judgment came on you."

11The merchants of the world will weep and
mourn for her, for there is no one left to buy their
goods. 12She bought great quantities of gold, silver, jewels, and pearls; fine linen, purple, silk, and
scarlet cloth; things made of fragrant thyine
wood, ivory goods, and objects made of expensive wood; and bronze, iron, and marble. 13She
also bought cinnamon, spice, incense, myrrh,
frankincense, wine, olive oil, fine flour, wheat,
cattle, sheep, horses, wagons, and bodies—that is,
human slaves.

14 "The fancy things you loved so much
are gone," they cry.
"All your luxuries and splendor
are gone forever,
never to be yours again."

15The merchants who became wealthy by selling her these things will stand at a distance, terrified by her great torment. They will weep and cry
out,

16 "How terrible, how terrible for that great city!
She was clothed in finest purple and
scarlet linens,
decked out with gold and precious
stones and pearls!
17 In a single moment
all the wealth of the city is gone!"

And all the captains of the merchant ships and
their passengers and sailors and crews will stand
at a distance. 18They will cry out as they watch
the smoke ascend, and they will say, "Where is
there another city as great as this?" 19And they
will weep and throw dust on their heads to show
their grief. And they will cry out,

"How terrible, how terrible for that
great city!
The shipowners became wealthy
by transporting her great wealth
on the seas.
In a single moment it is all gone."

20 Rejoice over her fate, O heaven
and people of God and apostles
and prophets!

For at last God has judged her
for your sakes.

21 Then a mighty angel picked up a boulder the
size of a huge millstone. He threw it into the
ocean and shouted,

"Just like this, the great city Babylon
will be thrown down with violence
and will never be found again.
22 The sound of harps, singers, flutes,
and trumpets
will never be heard in you again.
No craftsmen and no trades
will ever be found in you again.
The sound of the mill
will never be heard in you again.
23 The light of a lamp
will never shine in you again.
The happy voices of brides and grooms
will never be heard in you again.
For your merchants were the greatest
in the world,
and you deceived the nations with your
sorceries.
24 In your streets flowed the blood of the
prophets and of God's holy people
and the blood of people slaughtered all
over the world."

CHAPTER 19

Songs of Victory in Heaven

After this, I heard what sounded like a vast crowd
in heaven shouting,

"Praise the LORD!
Salvation and glory and power belong
to our God.
2 His judgments are true and just.
He has punished the great prostitute
who corrupted the earth with her
immorality.
He has avenged the murder of his
servants."

3 And again their voices rang out:

"Praise the LORD!
The smoke from that city ascends forever
and ever!"

4 Then the twenty-four elders and the four living beings fell down and worshiped God, who
was sitting on the throne. They cried out, "Amen!
Praise the LORD!"
5 And from the throne came a voice that said,

"Praise our God,
all his servants,
all who fear him,
from the least to the greatest."

6 Then I heard again what sounded like the
shout of a vast crowd or the roar of mighty ocean
waves or the crash of loud thunder:

"Praise the LORD!
For the Lord our God, the Almighty, reigns.
7 Let us be glad and rejoice,
and let us give honor to him.
For the time has come for the wedding feast
of the Lamb,
and his bride has prepared herself.
8 She has been given the finest of pure white
linen to wear."
For the fine linen represents the good
deeds of God's holy people.

9 And the angel said to me, "Write this: Blessed
are those who are invited to the wedding feast of
the Lamb." And he added, "These are true words
that come from God."
10 Then I fell down at his feet to worship him,
but he said, "No, don't worship me. I am a servant
of God, just like you and your brothers and sisters who testify about their faith in Jesus. Worship only God. For the essence of prophecy is to
give a clear witness for Jesus."

The Rider on the White Horse

11 Then I saw heaven opened, and a white horse
was standing there. Its rider was named Faithful
and True, for he judges fairly and wages a righteous war. 12 His eyes were like flames of fire, and
on his head were many crowns. A name was written on him that no one understood except himself. 13 He wore a robe dipped in blood, and his
title was the Word of God. 14 The armies of
heaven, dressed in the finest of pure white linen,
followed him on white horses. 15 From his mouth
came a sharp sword to strike down the nations.
He will rule them with an iron rod. He will release the fierce wrath of God, the Almighty, like
juice flowing from a winepress. 16 On his robe at
his thigh was written this title: King of all kings
and Lord of all lords.
17 Then I saw an angel standing in the sun,
shouting to the vultures flying high in the sky:
"Come! Gather together for the great banquet
God has prepared. 18 Come and eat the flesh of
kings, generals, and strong warriors; of horses
and their riders; and of all humanity, both free
and slave, small and great."
19 Then I saw the beast and the kings of the
world and their armies gathered together to

fight against the one sitting on the horse and his
army. 20 And the beast was captured, and with
him the false prophet who did mighty miracles on behalf of the beast—miracles that deceived all who had accepted the mark of the beast and who worshiped his statue. Both the beast and his false prophet were thrown alive into the fiery
lake of burning sulfur. 21 Their entire army was
killed by the sharp sword that came from the mouth of the one riding the white horse. And the vultures all gorged themselves on the dead bodies.

CHAPTER **20**

The Thousand Years

Then I saw an angel coming down from heaven with the key to the bottomless pit and a heavy
chain in his hand. 2 He seized the dragon—that old serpent, who is the devil, Satan—and bound
him in chains for a thousand years. 3 The angel
threw him into the bottomless pit, which he then shut and locked so Satan could not deceive the nations anymore until the thousand years were finished. Afterward he must be released for a little while.
4 Then I saw thrones, and the people sitting on them had been given the authority to judge. And I saw the souls of those who had been beheaded for their testimony about Jesus and for proclaiming the word of God. They had not worshiped the beast or his statue, nor accepted his mark on their foreheads or their hands. They all came to life again, and they reigned with Christ for a thousand years.
5 This is the first resurrection. (The rest of the dead did not come back to life until the thousand
years had ended.) 6 Blessed and holy are those who share in the first resurrection. For them the second death holds no power, but they will be priests of God and of Christ and will reign with him a thousand years.

The Defeat of Satan

7 When the thousand years come to an end, Satan will be let out of his prison. 8 He will go out to
deceive the nations—called Gog and Magog—in every corner of the earth. He will gather them together for battle—a mighty army, as numberless
as sand along the seashore. 9 And I saw them as
they went up on the broad plain of the earth and surrounded God's people and the beloved city. But fire from heaven came down on the attacking armies and consumed them.
10 Then the devil, who had deceived them,
was thrown into the fiery lake of burning sulfur,

We know that Jesus is coming back. And when he comes, boy, are things going to change!

Read **REVELATION 21:10-21** to get a glimpse of what the New Jerusalem will be like after Jesus has judged the world. Wow!

Have a New Jerusalem party to celebrate the beautiful place where Jesus will live with his followers forever!

1 Spread colored frosting on graham crackers, and use them to build a square city wall. Hold the walls together with more frosting.
2 Stick small candies to the walls as gems.
3 Serve apple juice to represent the streets of gold.
NOW CELEBRATE!
Before you eat, make sure everyone knows that the only way to live in the New Jerusalem is by believing in Jesus. Then celebrate because it's going to be a great day when Jesus comes back!

Did you ever get up so early in the morning you could still see a bright star in the sky? That's a morning star.

Jesus calls himself the bright morning star—read it for yourself in **REVELATION 22:16**!

Make a star of your own to remind you that Jesus is coming back. Write **"REVELATION 22:16"** somewhere on your creation. Here are a few ideas to get you started.

- **Cut a star from a white doily, and glue it to a sheet of black paper.**
- **Draw a star shape on dark paper. Glue bits of white paper or foil inside the star outline.**
- **Use paper reinforcements or glitter glue to make your star on dark paper.**
- **Make an edible morning star! Spread chocolate pudding on a small plate. Decorate a star-shaped cookie with sprinkles, then place it in your pudding "night sky."**

joining the beast and the false prophet. There
they will be tormented day and night forever
and ever.

USE YOUR MORNING STAR REMINDER TO TELL SOMEONE ELSE THAT JESUS IS COMING BACK.
Read Matthew 24:26-27 for more about Jesus' return.

The Final Judgment

11And I saw a great white throne and the one sitting on it. The earth and sky fled from his presence, but they found no place to hide. 12I saw the
dead, both great and small, standing before God's
throne. And the books were opened, including
the Book of Life. And the dead were judged according to what they had done, as recorded in
the books. 13The sea gave up its dead, and death
and the grave gave up their dead. And all were
judged according to their deeds. 14Then death
and the grave were thrown into the lake of fire.
This lake of fire is the second death. 15And anyone whose name was not found recorded in the
Book of Life was thrown into the lake of fire.

CHAPTER 21

The New Jerusalem

Then I saw a new heaven and a new earth, for the
old heaven and the old earth had disappeared.
And the sea was also gone. 2And I saw the holy
city, the new Jerusalem, coming down from God
out of heaven like a bride beautifully dressed for
her husband.

3I heard a loud shout from the throne, saying,
"Look, God's home is now among his people! He
will live with them, and they will be his people.
God himself will be with them. 4He will wipe
every tear from their eyes, and there will be no
more death or sorrow or crying or pain. All these
things are gone forever."

5And the one sitting on the throne said, "Look,
I am making everything new!" And then he said
to me, "Write this down, for what I tell you is
trustworthy and true." 6And he also said, "It is
finished! I am the Alpha and the Omega—the Beginning and the End. To all who are thirsty I will
give freely from the springs of the water of life.
7All who are victorious will inherit all these
blessings, and I will be their God, and they will be
my children.

8"But cowards, unbelievers, the corrupt, murderers, the immoral, those who practice witchcraft, idol worshipers, and all liars—their fate is
in the fiery lake of burning sulfur. This is the second death."

9Then one of the seven angels who held the
seven bowls containing the seven last plagues
came and said to me, "Come with me! I will show
you the bride, the wife of the Lamb."

10So he took me in the Spirit to a great, high

mountain, and he showed me the holy city, Jerusalem, descending out of heaven from God. 11It
shone with the glory of God and sparkled like a
precious stone—like jasper as clear as crystal.
12The city wall was broad and high, with twelve
gates guarded by twelve angels. And the names of
the twelve tribes of Israel were written on the
gates. 13There were three gates on each side—
east, north, south, and west. 14The wall of the city
had twelve foundation stones, and on them were
written the names of the twelve apostles of the
Lamb.

15The angel who talked to me held in his hand
a gold measuring stick to measure the city, its
gates, and its wall. 16When he measured it, he
found it was a square, as wide as it was long. In
fact, its length and width and height were each
1,400 miles. 17Then he measured the walls and
found them to be 216 feet thick (according to
the human standard used by the angel).

18The wall was made of jasper, and the city
was pure gold, as clear as glass. 19The wall of the
city was built on foundation stones inlaid with
twelve precious stones: the first was jasper, the
second sapphire, the third agate, the fourth
emerald, 20the fifth onyx, the sixth carnelian,
the seventh chrysolite, the eighth beryl, the
ninth topaz, the tenth chrysoprase, the eleventh
jacinth, the twelfth amethyst.

21The twelve gates were made of pearls—each
gate from a single pearl! And the main street was
pure gold, as clear as glass.

22I saw no temple in the city, for the Lord God
Almighty and the Lamb are its temple. 23And the
city has no need of sun or moon, for the glory of
God illuminates the city, and the Lamb is its light.
24The nations will walk in its light, and the kings
of the world will enter the city in all their glory.
25Its gates will never be closed at the end of day
because there is no night there. 26And all the nations will bring their glory and honor into the
city. 27Nothing evil will be allowed to enter, nor
anyone who practices shameful idolatry and dishonesty—but only those whose names are written in the Lamb's Book of Life.

CHAPTER 22

Then the angel showed me a river with the water
of life, clear as crystal, flowing from the throne of
God and of the Lamb. 2It flowed down the center
of the main street. On each side of the river grew
a tree of life, bearing twelve crops of fruit, with a
fresh crop each month. The leaves were used for
medicine to heal the nations.

3No longer will there be a curse upon anything. For the throne of God and of the Lamb will
be there, and his servants will worship him. 4And
they will see his face, and his name will be written on their foreheads. 5And there will be no
night there—no need for lamps or sun—for the
Lord God will shine on them. And they will reign
forever and ever.

6Then the angel said to me, "Everything you
have heard and seen is trustworthy and true. The
Lord God, who inspires his prophets, has sent his
angel to tell his servants what will happen soon."

Jesus Is Coming

7"Look, I am coming soon! Blessed are those
who obey the words of prophecy written in
this book."

8I, John, am the one who heard and saw all
these things. And when I heard and saw them, I
fell down to worship at the feet of the angel who
showed them to me. 9But he said, "No, don't worship me. I am a servant of God, just like you and
your brothers the prophets, as well as all who obey
what is written in this book. Worship only God!"

10Then he instructed me, "Do not seal up the
prophetic words in this book, for the time is near.
11Let the one who is doing harm continue to do
harm; let the one who is vile continue to be vile;
let the one who is righteous continue to live righteously; let the one who is holy continue to be
holy."

12"Look, I am coming soon, bringing my
reward with me to repay all people according
to their deeds. 13I am the Alpha and the
Omega, the First and the Last, the Beginning
and the End."

14Blessed are those who wash their robes.
They will be permitted to enter through the gates
of the city and eat the fruit from the tree of life.
15Outside the city are the dogs—the sorcerers,
the sexually immoral, the murderers, the idol
worshipers, and all who love to live a lie.

16"I, Jesus, have sent my angel to give you
this message for the churches. I am both the
source of David and the heir to his throne.
I am the bright morning star."

17The Spirit and the bride say, "Come." Let
anyone who hears this say, "Come." Let anyone
who is thirsty come. Let anyone who desires
drink freely from the water of life. 18And I solemnly declare to everyone who hears the words
of prophecy written in this book: If anyone adds
anything to what is written here, God will add to

that person the plagues described in this book.
19And if anyone removes any of the words from
this book of prophecy, God will remove that person's share in the tree of life and in the holy city
that are described in this book.

20He who is the faithful witness to all these
things says, "Yes, I am coming soon!"
Amen! Come, Lord Jesus!

21May the grace of the Lord Jesus be with
God's holy people.

Where to Turn in My Bible

No matter what's happening in your life, the Bible can help! The Bible gives great advice—because it's God's advice. And he knows everything. God made you. He knows you. So it's natural that he would know how to solve your problems.

The next time you're upset, scared, or confused, let God help you. Read his words. Follow his advice. You'll be glad you did!

Here are a few ideas to get you started. Add your own favorite verses whenever you want. Pretty soon, you'll have your very own handy advice guide. Then you can start helping others follow God's good advice!

Where to Turn in My Bible When I Feel...

ANGRY

PROVERBS 15:1 • "A gentle answer..."
19:11 • "Sensible people control..."
LUKE 6:27-30 • "But to you who are willing..."
6:31 • "Do to others..."
JOHN 13:34-35 • "So now I am giving you..."
EPHESIANS 4:26-27 • "And 'don't sin by...' "
4:31-32 • "Get rid of all bitterness..."
COLOSSIANS 3:8-10 • "But now is the time..."

JOSHUA 1:9 • "This is my command..."
PSALM 46:10 • "Be still, and know..."
91:11 • "For he will order his angels..."
118:6 • "The LORD is for me..."
ISAIAH 41:10 • "Don't be afraid, for..."
ROMANS 8:28 • "And we know that God..."
EPHESIANS 6:11-12 • "Put on all of God's armor..."
JAMES 1:2-3 • "Dear brothers and sisters, when troubles come..."

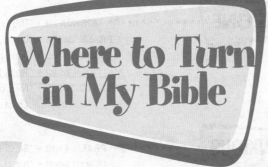

ALONE → JOSHUA 1:9 • "This is my command..."
PSALM 139:1-6 • "O LORD, you have examined..."
ISAIAH 41:10 • "Don't be afraid, for..."
MATTHEW 28:20 • "Teach these new disciples..."
PHILIPPIANS 4:13 • "For I can do everything through Christ..."

ANXIOUS → PSALM 46:10 • "Be still, and know..."
ISAIAH 40:31 • "But those who trust..."
MATTHEW 6:25-26 • "That is why I tell you..."
6:33-34 • "Seek the Kingdom of God..."
11:28 • "Then Jesus said, 'Come to me...' "
ROMANS 8:28 • "And we know that God..."
PHILIPPIANS 4:6-7 • "Don't worry about anything..."
1 PETER 5:7 • "Give all your worries and cares..."

ASHAMED → LUKE 15:10 • "In the same way..."
JOHN 1:12 • "But to all who believed him..."
3:17-18 • "God sent his Son..."
2 CORINTHIANS 5:17 • "This means that anyone..."
1 JOHN 1:9 • "But if we confess our sins..."

DEPRESSED → PSALM 34:19 • "The righteous person..."
46:10 • "Be still, and know..."
JOHN 14:27 • "I am leaving you with a gift..."
16:33 • "I have told you..."
PHILIPPIANS 4:6-7 • "Don't worry about anything..."

JEALOUS → PSALM 37:8 • "Stop being angry..."
PROVERBS 14:30 • "A peaceful heart..."
23:17-18 • "Don't envy sinners..."
MATTHEW 6:19-21 • "Don't store up treasures here..."
1 CORINTHIANS 13:4-5 • "Love is patient..."
JAMES 3:14-15 • "But if you are..."

TEMPTED → MATTHEW 26:41 • "Keep watch and pray..."
1 CORINTHIANS 10:13 • "The temptations in your life..."
GALATIANS 6:1 • "Dear brothers and sisters, if..."
EPHESIANS 6:11-12 • "Put on all of God's armor..."
HEBREWS 2:18 • "Since he himself has gone through..."

Where to Turn in My Bible When I Need...

CONFIDENCE

PSALM 139:14 • "Thank you for making me..."
MATTHEW 5:16 • "In the same way, let your..."
JOHN 15:5 • "Yes, I am the vine..."
2 CORINTHIANS 5:17 • "This means that anyone..."
EPHESIANS 6:11-12 • "Put on all of God's armor..."
PHILIPPIANS 4:13 • "For I can do everything through Christ..."
HEBREWS 4:16 • "So let us come boldly to the throne..."

ENCOURAGEMENT

MATTHEW 6:33-34 • "Seek the Kingdom of God..."
11:28 • "Then Jesus said, 'Come to me...' "
LUKE 11:9 • "And so I tell you, keep on asking..."
JOHN 1:12 • "But to all who believed him..."
ROMANS 8:28 • "And we know that God causes..."
PHILIPPIANS 4:6-7 • "Don't worry about anything..."
4:13 • "For I can do everything through Christ..."
1 THESSALONIANS 5:11 • "So encourage each other..."

FORGIVENESS

2 CHRONICLES 7:14 • "Then if my people who are called by my name..."
NEHEMIAH 9:17b • "But you are a God of forgiveness..."
LUKE 6:9-13 • "Then Jesus said to his critics..."
6:31 • "Do to others..."
15:10 • "In the same way..."
JOHN 3:17-18 • "God sent his Son..."
COLOSSIANS 3:13 • "Make allowance for each other's faults..."
1 JOHN 1:9 • "But if we confess our sins..."

LUKE 6:27-30 • "But to you who are willing..."
6:31 • "Do to others..."
1 CORINTHIANS 13:4-10 • "Love is patient and kind..."
EPHESIANS 4:32 • "Instead, be kind to each other..."
COLOSSIANS 3:13 • "Make allowance for each other's faults..."

HELP

PSALM 23 • "The Lord is my shepherd..."

121:1-2 • "I look up to the mountains..."

ISAIAH 40:31 • "But those who trust..."

41:10 • "Don't be afraid, for..."

LUKE 11:9 • "And so I tell you, keep on asking..."

JOHN 15:5 • "Yes, I am the vine..."

EPHESIANS 6:11-12 • "Put on all of God's armor..."

REVELATION 3:20 • "Look! I stand at the door and knock..."

TO OBEY

DEUTERONOMY 6:5-6 • "And you must love the Lord your God..."

MATTHEW 5:16 • "In the same way, let your..."

MARK 16:15 • "And then he told them, 'Go into all the world...' "

LUKE 6:31 • "Do to others..."

JOHN 13:34 • "So now I am giving you..."

14:15 • "If you love me, obey..."

ROMANS 12:1-2 • "And so, dear brothers and sisters..."

12:13 • "When God's people are in need..."

1 PETER 5:7 • "Give all your worries and cares..."

PATIENCE

PSALM 23 • "The Lord is my shepherd..."

37:7 • "Be still in the presence of the Lord..."

46:10 • "Be still, and know..."

MATTHEW 6:33-34 • "Seek the Kingdom of God..."

ROMANS 8:38-39 • "And I am convinced that nothing..."

GALATIANS 5:22 • "But the Holy Spirit produces this kind of fruit..."

WISDOM

PROVERBS 1:7 • "Fear of the Lord is the foundation..."

10:14 • "Wise people treasure knowledge..."

JEREMIAH 33:3 • "Ask me and I will tell you..."

MATTHEW 6:19-21 • "Don't store up treasures here..."

JOHN 14:26 • "But when the Father sends the Advocate..."

EPHESIANS 6:11-12 • "Put on all of God's armor..."

JAMES 1:5 • "If you need wisdom, ask..."

Where to Turn in My Bible When...

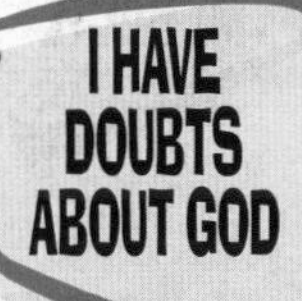
I HAVE
DOUBTS
ABOUT GOD

PSALM 19:1 • "The heavens proclaim the glory..."
46:10 • "Be still, and know..."
LUKE 21:33 • "Heaven and earth will disappear..."
JOHN 1:1 • "In the beginning the Word already..."
1:14 • "So the Word became human..."
3:16 • "For God loved the world so much..."
14:6 • "Jesus told him, 'I am the way...' "
20:31 • "But these are written so that you may continue to believe..."
HEBREWS 4:16 • "So let us come boldly to the throne..."
11:1 • "Faith is the confidence that what we hope for..."
1 JOHN 4:10 • "This is real love—not..."

I DON'T KNOW WHAT DECISION TO MAKE

DEUTERONOMY 6:5-6 • "And you must love the LORD your God..."
ISAIAH 40:8 • "The grass withers and the flowers..."
MATTHEW 19:19 • "Honor your father and mother..."
LUKE 6:31 • "Do to others..."
JOHN 14:26 • "But when the Father sends the Advocate..."
ROMANS 12:1-2 • "And so, dear brothers and sisters..."
GALATIANS 6:7 • "Don't be misled—you cannot mock..."
EPHESIANS 6:11-12 • "Put on all of God's armor..."
PHILIPPIANS 4:8 • "And now, dear brothers and sisters..."
JAMES 1:5 • "If you need wisdom, ask..."

I DON'T
KNOW HOW
TO PRAY

PSALM 100:4 • "Enter his gates with thanksgiving..."
118:1 • "Give thanks to the LORD, for..."
LUKE 6:27-30 • "But to you who are willing..."
11:9 • "And so I tell you, keep on asking..."
1 THESSALONIANS 5:16-18 • "Always be joyful..."

I'M WORRIED
ABOUT GOING
TO HEAVEN

JOHN 3:16 • "For God loved the world so much..."
3:17-18 • "God sent his Son..."
ROMANS 6:23 • "For the wages of sin is death..."
10:9 • "If you confess with your mouth..."
EPHESIANS 2:8-9 • "God saved you by his grace..."
1 JOHN 4:10 • "This is real love—not..."
5:12 • "Whoever has the Son has life..."

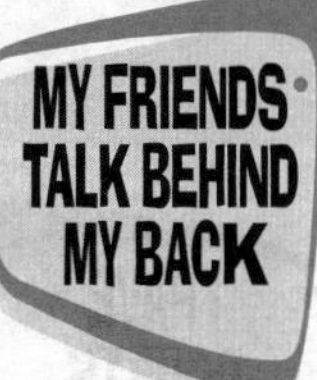
MY FRIENDS TALK BEHIND MY BACK

LUKE 6:31 • "Do to others..."

ROMANS 3:23 • "For everyone has sinned..."

EPHESIANS 4:32 • "Instead, be kind to each other..."

PHILIPPIANS 4:6-7 • "Don't worry about anything..."

COLOSSIANS 3:13 • "Make allowance for each other's faults..."

1 PETER 3:9 • "Don't repay evil for evil..."

I'M AFRAID TO SHARE MY FAITH

ISAIAH 55:10-11 • "The rain and snow..."

MATTHEW 5:15-16 • "No one lights a lamp and then puts it..."

28:19-20 • "Therefore, go and make disciples..."

ACTS 1:8 • "But you will receive power..."

ROMANS 1:16 • "For I am not ashamed of this Good News..."

2 CORINTHIANS 2:14-17 • "But thank God!..."

HEBREWS 11:6 • "And it is impossible to please God without..."

1 PETER 3:15 • "Instead, you must worship Christ..."

1 JOHN 3:18 • "Dear children, let's not merely say..."

MY PARENTS FIGHT

PSALM 23 • "The Lord is my shepherd..."

46:1 • "God is our refuge and strength..."

MATTHEW 6:33-34 • "Seek the Kingdom of God..."

11:28 • "Then Jesus said, 'Come to me...' "

PHILIPPIANS 4:6-7 • "Don't worry about anything..."

HEBREWS 4:16 • "So let us come boldly to the throne..."

Guess What!

There's a really cool tool you can use when you want to know more about any subject! It's called a concordance, and there's one at the back of this very Bible! It's like a dictionary of subjects and people, and it tells you where to look in the Bible for information.

Want to know more about angels? Prayer? David? Just look up the word or name!

It's a cool tool you'll use a lot!

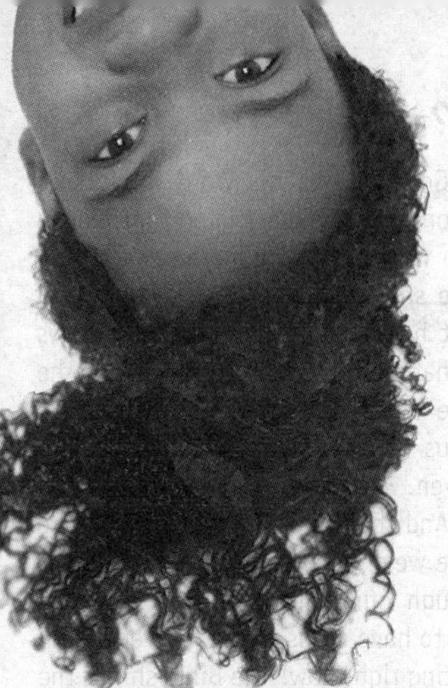

Did You Know?

Frequently Asked Questions About the Bible

Who wrote the Bible?

The Bible has more than forty different authors and only one author! Sound confusing? Not really!

God is the one true author of Scripture. From Genesis to Revelation, it all comes from him. That's why we call it God's Word. Now here's the tricky part: God chose to use more than forty different human authors to do the actual writing.

That's what it means when people say the Bible is "inspired by God." God inspired Moses, for example, to write the first five books of the Bible. That means he guided Moses along so that he wrote exactly what God wanted him to write. God did the same thing with prophets such as Isaiah, who wrote the book of Isaiah, and the Apostle Paul, who wrote 13 New Testament books. You get the idea.

Now take some time to look up these verses, which tell a little more about the Bible-writing process: **2 TIMOTHY 3:16** and **2 PETER 1:20-21**.

When was the Bible written?

How long do you think it would take you to read the whole Bible, cover to cover? Six months? A year? Two years? Well, that's nothing compared to how long it took to write the Bible.

It took more than 1,000 years to write the whole Bible! God inspired Moses to write the first five books of the Bible around 1400 B.C. (The book of Job might have been written even earlier than that!) The apostle John wrote Revelation, the last book of the Bible, in the late first century A.D. That's close to 1,500 years later!

Why did it take so long? Think about it—the Bible covers a ton of history, from the creation of the world to the days when Jesus' disciples founded the church. The Bible kept growing and growing until the New Testament was finished.

And there's something really amazing about the Bible: It still speaks to us today, even though it's been almost 2,000 years since John laid down his pen after writing Revelation. The Bible is the most important book you can ever read. It was written long ago, but it was written for you!

Why was the Bible written?

Let's let the Bible speak for itself. Here's what the Bible says about why it was written!

Your word is a lamp to guide my feet and a light for my path.

PSALM 119:105

All Scripture is inspired by God and is useful to teach us what is true and to make us realize what is wrong in our lives. It corrects us when we are wrong and teaches us to do what is right. God uses it to prepare and equip his people to do every good work.

2 TIMOTHY 3:16-17

For the word of God is alive and powerful. It is sharper than the sharpest two-edged sword, cutting between soul and spirit, between joint and marrow. It exposes our innermost thoughts and desires.

HEBREWS 4:12

God gave us his Word for lots of reasons, but the most important reason is so we can know him personally. The Bible shows us who God really is and what he's really like. The Bible shows us that God loves us so much that he made a way through his Son, Jesus, for us to spend forever with him in heaven.

And the Bible shows us how to live while we're here on earth. It guides us through our daily lives and shows us how to have Jesus as our forever friend, starting right now! The Bible shines the brightness of God's truth on our path.

What other book can do all those things? None! You got that right. The Bible's awesome!

Will God put new stories in the Bible?

Nope, that's all he wrote.

Christians believe that God won't add anything new to the 66 books of the Bible we already have. There's no need. God's already told us all we need to know. The Bible tells us how the world and the human race got started, how sin entered God's perfect creation, how God made a plan to save sinful people, how God put that plan into action through Jesus, and how God will complete his plan when Jesus returns. That's the whole story from start to finish.

Our job is to study and obey God's perfect Word as we wait for Jesus to return. That day will be the start of a whole new, wonderful story—the story of eternity! The Bible gives us only hints of what eternity will be like (look at **REVELATION 21:3-4** for starters). But it's clear from those hints that you won't want to miss out on it!

Is all of the Bible true?

Absolutely! The Bible is the very Word of God, and God can't lie. He can't make mistakes either. You and I might be tempted to lie sometimes, but God never is. You and I might make mistakes sometimes, but God never does.

God is perfect, which means he never does anything wrong. He's given us his Word because he wants us to know the truth about some very important stuff—like who he is, how much he loves us, and how to get to heaven!

So when you open the Bible, you can rely on every word because, after all, it's God's Word!

Why does the Bible have two parts?

The Bible covers a big chunk of history, from the creation of the world and everything we see in it (including human beings like you and me) to the time just after Jesus was on earth. That's a lot of years!

Part of that time, God dealt mainly with the nation called Israel. The Old Testament is all about his dealings with Israel. The New Testament tells of a big turning point in history, when the focus shifted from the nation of Israel to the entire world.

What caused the shift? Jesus came and died on the cross for the sins of everyone. After he rose from the dead, Jesus sent his disciples out into the world to tell everyone about the Good News of salvation through faith in him. That triggered a chain reaction that hasn't stopped yet! In fact, the very reason that you're reading this Bible is because you're a part of what started way back then.

Tell someone about Jesus today and keep the chain reaction going!

Do all the promises and commands God gave to the Israelites apply to my life?

Hey, you're asking some good questions here!

Before we answer this one, go back and read the answer to the last question again. Some things that God said to Israel in the Old Testament don't apply to us today. For example, Christians can eat pork if they want, but the Israelites couldn't because God wanted to set them apart from their neighbors. (Compare **DEUTERONOMY 14:8** with **MARK 7:19** and **ACTS 10:9-15**.)

On the other hand, there are lots of things that do still apply to us today. For example, Christians today shouldn't murder or steal or worship idols, just like the Ten Commandments and other parts of the Old Testament say.

How can you know what applies to you today? Ask yourself, Does the New Testament give Christians the same command or promise I'm finding in the Old Testament? (To find out, you'll need to do some detective work. Use the easy concordance that starts on page 1292, or ask your Sunday school teacher or another Christian for help.) If it does, then you know you need to obey that command or believe that promise.

For example, think about God's promise to create a new heaven and earth some day. Isaiah, an Old Testament book, says it (see **ISAIAH 65:17**), and so does 2 Peter, a New Testament book (see **2 PETER 3:13**). Since both the Old and New Testaments say it, you know that it's a promise that applies to you, just like it did to the Israelites.

There's a lot more to say on this subject, but you can start by practicing the kind of checking you just learned. (Hey, what are you waiting for?)

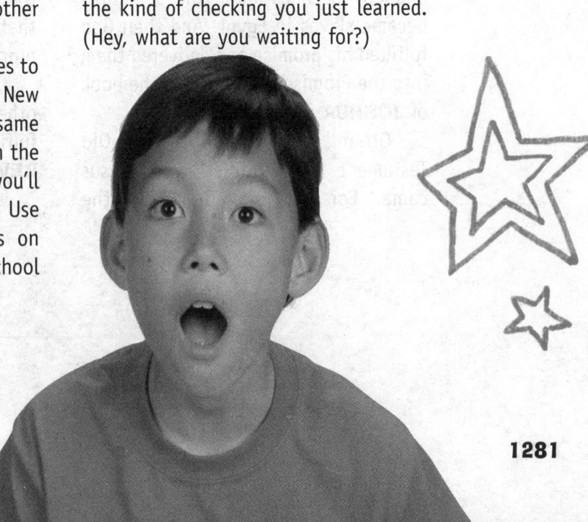

Does Jesus really want us to poke our eye out if it makes us sin?

Yikes! What Jesus said in **MATTHEW 5:29-30** is a shocker. That's because Jesus wanted to shock people with those words! Sin is seriously bad news. It can ruin your life, and for those who never turn to Jesus to save them from their sins, it will cause them to go to hell when they die.

The problem is, people can get comfortable with sin. Any one of us can trick ourselves into believing sin isn't really that big a deal, right? Well, Jesus blows that idea right out of the water in these verses! Jesus' point is this: Don't get comfortable with sin in your life. Take radical steps to get rid of the sin and its cause because sin causes problems that are way worse than anything that could happen to your body. Jesus made his point in a way that gets our attention. The question is, Will we pay attention?

There are other places in the Bible where shocking or colorful language is used in a way that makes us say, "Huh?" Our job then is to understand the point. It's not always easy, but there are tools to help you, including some of the notes in this Bible. So keep reading, and keep asking God to help you understand his Word!

Does the Bible talk about things that haven't happened yet?

The Bible is full of prophecies—statements God made ahead of time before the events actually happened. Many of those prophecies have already come to pass.

For example, way back in Abraham's day, God told Abraham that future members of his family would live as slaves in a foreign land for four hundred years before God rescued them and brought them into the Promised Land (see **GENESIS 15:13-16**). Sure enough, decades later the Israelites became slaves in Egypt. And then God fulfilled his promise and delivered them into the Promised Land. (Read the book of **JOSHUA** for details!)

Other prophecies in the Old Testament were fulfilled when Jesus came. For example, God told the prophet Isaiah that the Messiah would be born of a virgin (see **ISAIAH 7:14**). Hundreds of years later, Jesus was born to a virgin named Mary (see **MATTHEW 1:22-23**). Pretty cool, right?

The Bible also talks about things that haven't happened yet. The main one is that Jesus will one day return to set up his kingdom (see **MATTHEW 24:44**; **JOHN 14:2-4**). The fact that we can look back and see so many prophecies that God fulfilled in the past gives us complete confidence that God will fulfill this and other prophecies for the future.

Look up these verses for some other prophecies that have yet to be fulfilled: **2 THESSALONIANS 2:1-12**; **REVELATION 20:1-15**.

Why is it so important to read the Bible?

Imagine setting off on a journey in a foreign land. If you didn't have a map, you'd probably get lost; you might even die. Or imagine trying to build a house without a plan in mind. Trying to live life without regularly reading the Bible is kind of like setting off on a journey with no map or trying to build a house with no blueprint.

The Bible helps us make good decisions and helps us know what is right and wrong. Most important of all, it teaches us to know God and tells us what to do if we want to spend eternity with him in heaven. God's given us a real treasure chest in the Bible. We'd be silly not to read it—a lot!

Many people try to read a little bit every single day. That's a smart plan! Others read it more, some less. The important thing to remember is that the more you read, study, and obey God's Word, the more you'll benefit from it. Because the Bible is a collection of smaller books, you can begin your reading at a lot of different places.

The Gospel of John is a good place to start to learn about Jesus. The book of Genesis tells about the creation of the world. And there are lots of places in Psalms, Proverbs, and the New Testament letters where even reading a verse or chapter a day really pays off! You could also use a plan that helps you read all the way through the Bible in one or two years.

You've got tons of options. So start reading!

There's a reading plan you can look at online at MyHandsOnBible.com!

Some Other BIG Questions

Why can't I see God? How do we know God is real?

There are a number of things that we can't see, yet know they're real. We know the wind is real because we can feel it on our skin or because we can see it blow the leaves off a tree. Yet we can't technically see the wind.

Because God is a spirit, he's invisible unless he chooses to reveal himself in some way for some special occasion. (Look at these examples of God revealing himself in special ways: **EXODUS 3:4-6**; **1 KINGS 19:11-13**; **MATTHEW 3:16-17**.) Only a few people in history have met God in these ways. For the rest of us, there are other ways we can "know" God exists, even though we don't see him.

First, we know by faith that God exists. The Bible says he's real. So those who believe the Bible believe God is real. (Take a look at what **HEBREWS 11:6** says.) Second, we know God exists because of the impact he has on our lives. Just like we know the wind is real because we see what it does, we know God is real because he changes our lives. He lets us know when we do wrong. He comforts us when we're sad. He answers our prayers. And the list goes on and on. Those who have faith know that God is real because he really is active in their lives.

How old is God? What has God been doing for all that time?

Good luck trying to wrap your mind around this one! God has been around forever. It's impossible to say how old he is, because he had no beginning and will have no end. That means you can try to imagine the biggest number ever, and God would still be older than that. God is infinite. Everything else had a beginning.

The Bible doesn't tell us everything there is to know about God, including all that God has been doing for eternity. Even the biggest book in the world couldn't hold all there is to know about him. Many people spend their entire lives trying to learn all that the Bible has to teach about God, and even that is a tall order. Better get started!

Why does God let bad things happen?

People have wrestled with this question for a long, long time. In the Old Testament book of Job (possibly the oldest book in the Bible), the main character, Job, had a bunch of bad things happen to him one day. He wondered why God would allow such bad things to happen, but Job never lost trust in God. We don't always know why God allows hard things to happen.

Whatever happens, it's important to remember these truths: First, God is always in control. We never need to worry that bad things could happen without God allowing them to happen. And second, God always does what is right and good. Even when Christians suffer, we can know that God is using suffering for our benefit (see **ROMANS 8:28** and **2 CORINTHIANS 12:7-10**). Sometimes when we're suffering, we can feel like God has forgotten us. But that's impossible. God has promised never to leave us (see **HEBREWS 13:5**). And God keeps his promises!

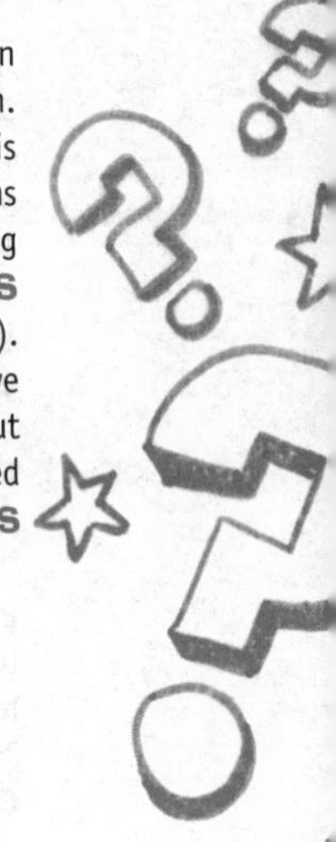

How is Jesus different from other teachers?

Good question. There have been many people throughout history who've claimed to be prophets and teachers sent from God. Some were real, like the true prophets of the Old Testament. Others were fakers, like the false prophets of the Old Testament and those who've started their own religions.

Jesus is special because he's much more than just a teacher. He's the Son of God! He is God in human form. The entire Bible is about Jesus in one way or another. That's why Christians should have nothing to do with the writings and teachings of other religions. The Bible is all we need, and it's all we can trust because it alone comes from God.

Human beings were designed to know God. But because of sin, humans don't want to come to God on his terms. They want to make up their own way to live. So it's easy to see why so many other religions have sprung up throughout history. But that displeases God greatly. God's Word is true, so stay focused right there!

Why did Jesus have to die?

The Bible says that the penalty for sin is death (see **ROMANS 6:23**). That's real bad news because it also says that all people have sinned, including you and me (see **ROMANS 3:23**).

But there's some real good news too. God loved us enough to make a way for us sinners to be holy in his sight. It was a way that cost God a lot, because it meant sending Jesus, his only Son, to the world to take our punishment for us.

Jesus never sinned, but he allowed himself to be treated like a criminal by taking our sin upon himself and dying in our place on the cross. Three days later God raised Jesus from the dead so that now whoever believes in Jesus is pure and holy in God's sight.

The penalty for sin has been paid, and we can go to heaven because of that payment. That's good news—no, that's great news! (Hey, did you know that the word *gospel* means "good news"? You better believe it!)

What does it mean to be a Christian?

First of all, to be a Christian means that you know Jesus Christ as your personal Savior. You've realized that you are a sinner and that the only way to heaven is through faith in Jesus, who died on the cross to take the punishment for your sins. Knowing Jesus as your personal Savior means you'll spend eternity with him in heaven and have him as your best friend here on earth. Way to go!

But there's more to it than that. Being a Christian also means that we live our lives each day in a way that honors Jesus. A true Christian has Jesus living inside his or her heart (see **COLOSSIANS 1:27**). So a Christian can't just go on living as he or she feels like. Christians are supposed to love Jesus and grow in faith and obedience to him with each new day (see **COLOSSIANS 3:1-17**).

Sure, sometimes we mess up, but Jesus is always there to help us get back on the right path again. Sometimes obeying Jesus is hard. But God gives every Christian a special gift to help—the Holy Spirit. When you believe in Jesus, the Holy Spirit comes and changes your heart so that living for God is something you want to do, not something you have to do. Cool, huh?

Who is the Holy Spirit?

Like God the Father and Jesus, the Holy Spirit is God. Wait, does that mean there are three Gods? Nope! At the heart of the Christian faith is a giant mystery. (No, not the kind a detective solves. This mystery is a truth that's not easy for us humans to understand.) Here it is: There is only one God, but he has always existed as three persons—the Father, the Son (that's Jesus), and the Holy Spirit. Just like Jesus came to earth with a special purpose—to save us—the Holy Spirit has a special role. Actually he has a few.

Here are some important roles: The Holy Spirit shows people their sin so they'll believe in Jesus and be saved (see **JOHN 16:8**). He lives inside Christians (see **ROMANS 8:9-11**) and helps them live in a way that honors Jesus (see **GALATIANS 5:22-24**). The Holy Spirit living in us is God's seal of ownership on us. And the Holy Spirit gives us spiritual gifts that we can use to serve God. (Check out these lists of spiritual gifts: **ROMANS 12:6-8; 1 CORINTHIANS 12:4-11; 1 PETER 4:10-11**.) The Holy Spirit helps us pray, too, and reminds us of God's Word. What a helper!

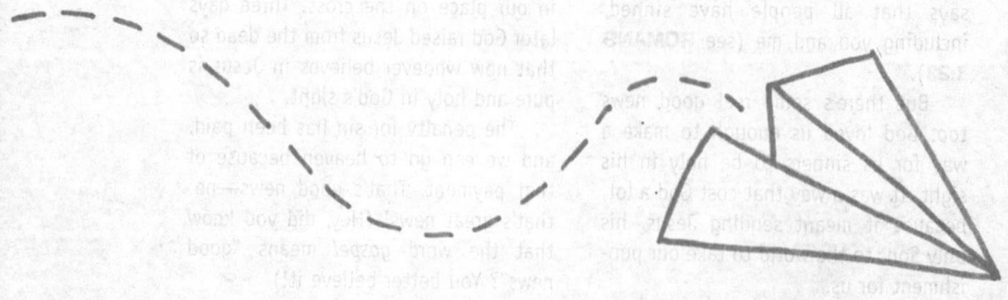

Should I be afraid of demons? What are they?

Demons are angels who rebelled against God at the same time the devil, the prince of demons, rebelled. God threw them out of heaven but has permitted some of them to be active in the world until the time he has planned to banish them to hell. Demons can sometimes trouble people through temptation or other forms of harassment such as illness. That's why the Bible tells Christians to be ready by putting on the spiritual armor that God provides (see **EPHESIANS 6:10-12**).

It's important to remember that although demons try to work against God's plans, they are totally powerless against him. When Jesus was on earth, he cast out many demons from people, and when he died and rose again, he won the final victory over the devil and all fallen angels.

So Christians can be sure that God will protect them from harm by demons (see **1 JOHN 5:18**). But we are called to be on guard against the temptations and suffering the devil and his helpers can trouble us with (see **1 PETER 5:8-9**). So put on that spiritual armor—and don't be afraid, because Jesus has already won the battle!

Does God talk to us? How can I hear him?

Throughout the Bible, there are times God spoke out loud to people. (Moses heard God speak to him lots of times.) For most of us, though, God speaks mostly through his Word, the Bible. The Bible is so full of truth that we can find answers there to all of life's big questions.

Sometimes, though, God uses other ways to talk to us. God might send a wise person to give you the advice you need (see **EXODUS 18:13-27**). Or he might show you what to do by making other options impossible (see **ACTS 16:6-10**). Sometimes the Holy Spirit might put the right decision in your heart (see **ROMANS 8:14, 16**).

The most important thing to remember is that no matter how God communicates, his message will never go against the Bible. So if you get advice from someone, but that advice goes against what the Bible teaches, you can be sure that the advice didn't come from God.

Does God answer all our prayers?

God does always answer our prayers, but he doesn't always give us the answer we want. Suppose you really wanted to go away to summer camp one year. You prayed and prayed, but Dad and Mom decided they needed you to be at home to help the family. Did God answer your prayer? Yes, even though it wasn't the answer you wanted.

We should always remember that God is a lot smarter than we are. He knows the future, and he knows what's best for you. Next time you pray for something and God says no or not right now, thank him for knowing what's best for you. (The apostle Paul did just that when God said no to him one time. See for yourself in **2 CORINTHIANS 12:7-9**.)

To Obey–Or Not

Here are a few examples of people in the Bible who didn't obey. Carefully read what each did about one of God's instructions and what happened as a result. Read it over, and then ask God to help you obey every day, every way! (And remember: If you believe in Jesus and really mean it when you tell God you're sorry for a sin, God forgives you and wipes that sin away!)

Who	God's Instruction	Disobedience	What Happened
ADAM AND EVE	Don't eat fruit from the tree of the knowledge of good and evil. **(GENESIS 2:16-17)**	Satan tempted them, and they ate. **(GENESIS 3:1-6)**	They were banished from the Garden of Eden; pain and death were inflicted on all humanity. **(GENESIS 3:24; ROMANS 5:12)**
NADAB AND ABIHU	Fire for the sacrifice must come from the proper source. **(LEVITICUS 6:12-13)**	They used a different kind of fire for their sacrifice. **(LEVITICUS 10:1)**	They were struck dead. **(LEVITICUS 10:2)**
MOSES	"Speak to the rock over there, and it will pour out its water." **(NUMBERS 20:8)**	He struck it with his staff. **(NUMBERS 20:11)**	He wasn't allowed to enter the Promised Land. **(NUMBERS 20:12)**
SAUL	Completely destroy the evil Amalekites. **(1 SAMUEL 15:3)**	He spared the king and kept some of the plunder. **(1 SAMUEL 15:8-9)**	God promised to end his reign. **(1 SAMUEL 15:16-26)**
UZZAH	Only a priest can touch the Tabernacle's furnishings and articles. **(NUMBERS 4:15)**	He touched the ark of the covenant. **(2 SAMUEL 6:6)**	He died instantly. **(2 SAMUEL 6:7)**
UZZIAH	Only the priests can offer incense in the Temple or Tabernacle sanctuary. **(NUMBERS 16:39-40; 18:7)**	He entered the sanctuary in the Temple, where only priests were allowed to go. **(2 CHRONICLES 26:16-18)**	He became a leper. **(2 CHRONICLES 26:19)**

The Beginning and the End

The Bible tells us about the beginning of the world and the end of the world. The story of the human race, from beginning to end—from our fall into sin to our redemption by Jesus and God's victory over evil—is all found in the Bible!

Look at this chart to see how the first and last books of the Bible compare.

Genesis	Revelation
THE SUN IS CREATED	THE SUN IS NOT NEEDED
SATAN IS VICTORIOUS	SATAN IS DEFEATED
SIN ENTERS THE HUMAN RACE	SIN IS BANISHED
PEOPLE RUN AND HIDE FROM GOD	PEOPLE ARE INVITED TO LIVE WITH GOD FOREVER
PEOPLE ARE CURSED	THE CURSE IS REMOVED
TEARS ARE SHED, WITH SORROW FOR SIN	NO MORE SIN, NO MORE TEARS OR SORROW
THE GARDEN AND EARTH ARE CURSED	GOD'S CITY IS GLORIFIED, THE EARTH IS MADE NEW
THE FRUIT FROM THE TREE OF LIFE IS NOT TO BE EATEN	GOD'S PEOPLE MAY EAT FROM THE TREE OF LIFE
PARADISE IS LOST	PARADISE IS REGAINED
PEOPLE ARE DOOMED TO DEATH	DEATH IS DEFEATED, BELIEVERS LIVE FOREVER WITH GOD

Jesus' Appearances After His Resurrection

The truth of Christianity rests on the Resurrection. Jesus died on the cross for our sins. Then he rose from the dead in a final victory over death and Satan.

The people who saw Jesus after he rose from the grave went on to turn the world upside down. (Most of them also died for being followers of Jesus.)

Here are people who saw Jesus after he rose from the grave.

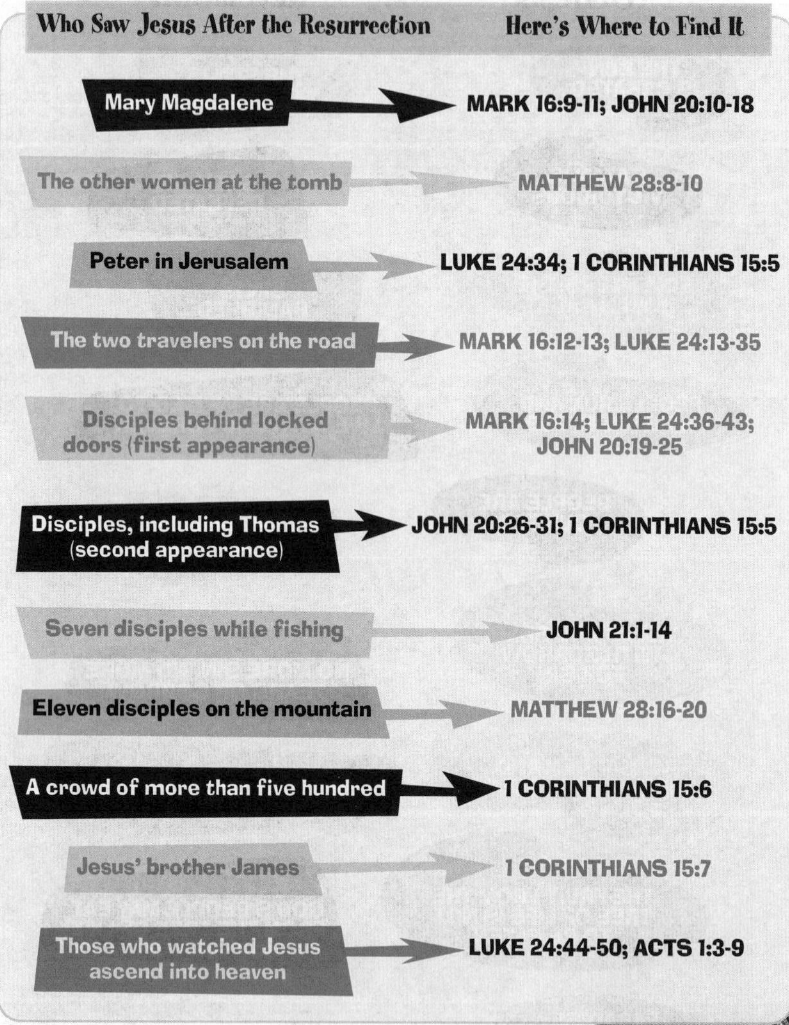

Who Saw Jesus After the Resurrection	Here's Where to Find It
Mary Magdalene	MARK 16:9-11; JOHN 20:10-18
The other women at the tomb	MATTHEW 28:8-10
Peter in Jerusalem	LUKE 24:34; 1 CORINTHIANS 15:5
The two travelers on the road	MARK 16:12-13; LUKE 24:13-35
Disciples behind locked doors (first appearance)	MARK 16:14; LUKE 24:36-43; JOHN 20:19-25
Disciples, including Thomas (second appearance)	JOHN 20:26-31; 1 CORINTHIANS 15:5
Seven disciples while fishing	JOHN 21:1-14
Eleven disciples on the mountain	MATTHEW 28:16-20
A crowd of more than five hundred	1 CORINTHIANS 15:6
Jesus' brother James	1 CORINTHIANS 15:7
Those who watched Jesus ascend into heaven	LUKE 24:44-50; ACTS 1:3-9

Unsung Heroes in Acts

When we think of the success of the early church, we often think of the work of the apostles. But the church might have died if it hadn't been for some unsung heroes, men and women who through some small act helped move the church forward.

So read about these unsung heroes from the book of Acts, and then think of a way you can help others find out more about Jesus!

Bible Hero	Reference	Heroic Action
LAME BEGGAR	ACTS 3:9-10	After his healing, he praised God. As crowds gathered to see what happened, Peter used that opportunity to tell many about Jesus.
FIVE DEACONS	ACTS 6:2-5	Everyone knows Stephen, and many people know Philip, but there were five other men chosen to be deacons. Not only did they set the standard for service in the church, but their hard work gave the apostles more time to preach the gospel.
ANANIAS	ACTS 9:10-19	He had the responsibility of bringing Christ's love to Saul (Paul) after his conversion.
CORNELIUS	ACTS 10:30-35	He showed Peter that the gospel was for all people, Jews and Gentiles.
RHODA	ACTS 12:13-16	Her persistence brought Peter inside Mary's home, where the people could "see" the answers to their prayers.
JAMES	ACTS 15:13-21	He took command of the Jerusalem council and had the courage to make a decision that would affect millions of Gentiles over many generations.
LYDIA	ACTS 16:13-15	She invited Paul to her home, from where he led many to Christ.
JASON	ACTS 17:5-9	He risked his life for the gospel by letting Paul stay in his home. He stood up for what was right, even though he faced persecution for it.
PAUL'S NEPHEW	ACTS 23:16-24	He saved Paul's life by telling officials of a plot to murder Paul.
JULIUS	ACTS 27:1, 43	He spared Paul's life when the other soldiers wanted to kill him.

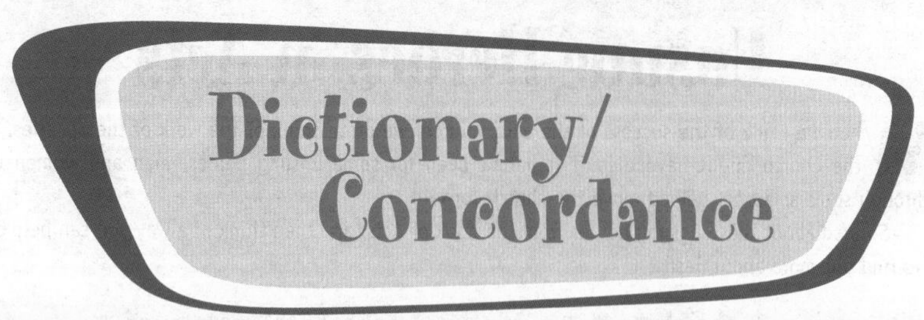

A

ABANDON, ABANDONED, ABANDONS (V) to desert or forsake
Josh 1:5 . . . will not fail you or ***a*** you.
Heb 13:5 . . . I will never ***a*** you.

ACCEPT, ACCEPTED, ACCEPTS (V) to receive willingly
Gen 4:4 . . . The LORD ***a-ed*** Abel
Luke 4:24 . . . no prophet is ***a-ed*** in his
John 1:12 . . . believed him and ***a-ed*** him,
John 17:8 . . . They ***a-ed*** it and know that
Gal 2:9 . . . they ***a-ed*** Barnabas and me
Col 2:6 . . . just as you ***a-ed*** Christ Jesus

ADOPT, ADOPTED (V) to take another's child into one's own family
Gal 4:5 . . . so that he could ***a*** us as
Eph 1:5 . . . decided in advance to ***a*** us

ADVICE (N) recommendation regarding a decision or course of conduct; counsel
Prov 12:26 . . . godly give good ***a*** to their
Prov 15:22 . . . Plans go wrong for lack of ***a;***
Isa 44:25 . . . I cause the wise to give bad ***a,***
Rom 11:34 . . . enough to give him ***a?***

ADVOCATE (N) one who pleads the cause of another; defender
see also COUNSELOR
John 14:16 . . . he will give you another ***A,***
John 14:26 . . . the Father sends the ***A***
John 15:26 . . . I will send you the ***A***—
1 Jn 2:1 . . . an ***a*** who pleads our case

ALMIGHTY (N) having absolute power over all; God
Gen 17:1 . . . I am El-Shaddai—'God ***A.***'
Exod 6:3 . . . as El-Shaddai—'God ***A***'—
Rev 4:8 . . . the ***A***—the one who always was,
Rev 15:3 . . . O Lord God, the ***A.***
Rev 19:6 . . . our God, the ***A,*** reigns.

ALTAR, ALTARS (N) high places of worship on which sacrifices are offered or incense is burned
Gen 12:7 . . . Abram built an ***a*** there
Gen 26:25 . . . Isaac built an ***a*** there
Exod 30:1 . . . make another ***a*** of acacia
Josh 8:30 . . . Joshua built an ***a*** to the LORD,
1 Sam 7:17 . . . Samuel built an ***a*** to the
2 Chr 4:19 . . . Temple of God: the gold ***a;***
2 Chr 33:16 . . . restored the ***a*** of the LORD
Ezra 3:2 . . . rebuilding the ***a*** of the God
Matt 5:23 . . . presenting a sacrifice at the ***a***
Rev 6:9 . . . I saw under the ***a*** the souls

ANGEL, ANGELS (N) human or superhuman agent or messenger of God
2 Sam 24:16 . . . and said to the death ***a,***
Ps 91:11 . . . will order his ***a-s*** to protect
Matt 4:6 . . . will order his ***a-s*** to protect
Matt 28:2 . . . an ***a*** of the Lord came down
Luke 2:9 . . . an ***a*** of the Lord appeared
2 Cor 11:14 . . . disguises himself as an ***a***
Gal 1:8 . . . or even an ***a*** from heaven,
Heb 2:7 . . . a little lower than the ***a-s***
Heb 13:2 . . . entertained ***a-s*** without

ANGER (N) a strong feeling of displeasure
Exod 34:6 . . . slow to ***a*** and filled with
Ps 30:5 . . . his ***a*** lasts only a moment,
Eph 4:26 . . . by letting ***a*** control you.
Jas 1:20 . . . Human ***a*** does not produce

ANTICHRIST, ANTICHRISTS (N) opponent of Christ; the personification of evil
1 Jn 2:18 . . . heard that the ***A*** is coming,
1 Jn 2:18 . . . many such ***a-s*** have appeared.
1 Jn 4:3 . . . has the spirit of the ***A,***
2 Jn 1:7 . . . deceiver and an ***a.***

APPEARED (V) to come out of hiding and show up in public view; to make one's presence known
Deut 33:16 . . . ***a*** in the burning bush.
Luke 2:9 . . . angel of the Lord ***a*** among
Phil 2:7 . . . When he ***a*** in human form,

ARGUE, ARGUING (V) to contend or disagree in words; to dispute
Job 40:2 . . . to ***a*** with the Almighty?
Prov 25:9 . . . ***a-ing*** with your neighbor,
Rom 14:1 . . . and don't ***a*** with them
1 Cor 11:16 . . . anyone wants to ***a***

ARMOR (N) weapons of war or self-defense; figurative of spiritual resources
Rom 13:12 . . . put on the shining ***a***
Eph 6:11 . . . Put on all of God's ***a***
Eph 6:13 . . . put on every piece of God's ***a***
1 Thes 5:8 . . . protected by the ***a*** of faith

ARMY, ARMIES (N) large band of men organized and armed for war; any large multitude devoted to a cause
Ps 33:16 . . . best-equipped ***a*** cannot save
Ps 84:12 . . . LORD of Heaven's ***A-ies,***
Isa 6:3 . . . LORD of Heaven's ***A-ies!***
Isa 45:13 . . . LORD of Heaven's ***A-ies,***
Isa 51:15 . . . the LORD of Heaven's ***A-ies.***
Hag 1:5 . . . LORD of Heaven's ***A-ies*** says:
Zech 8:6 . . . LORD of Heaven's ***A-ies*** says:
Rev 19:14 . . . The ***a-ies*** of heaven,
Rev 19:19 . . . the horse and his ***a.***

ASHAMED (ADJ) feeling shame, guilt, or disgrace
Mark 8:38 . . . If anyone is ***a*** of me
Rom 1:16 . . . I am not ***a*** of this Good News
2 Tim 1:8 . . . So never be ***a*** to tell others
2 Tim 2:15 . . . who does not need to be ***a***

ATHLETE, ATHLETES (N) a person who is trained or skilled in exercises, sports, or games requiring physical strength, agility, or stamina
Ps 19:5 . . . like a great ***a*** eager to run
1 Cor 9:25 . . . All ***a-s*** are disciplined
1 Cor 9:27 . . . body like an ***a,*** training it
2 Tim 2:5 . . . ***a-s*** cannot win the prize unless

ATTITUDE, ATTITUDES (N) a mental position with regard to a fact or state; a feeling or emotion toward a fact or state
Eph 4:23 . . . your thoughts and ***a-s.***

Phil 2:5 . . . have the same *a* that Christ
1 Pet 3:8 . . . keep a humble *a*.

AUTHORITY (N) the right to govern; the freedom or ability to act; one entrusted with the right to govern
Matt 28:18 . . . been given all *a* in heaven
John 5:22 . . . absolute *a* to judge,
Rom 13:1 . . . For all *a* comes from God,
1 Cor 15:24 . . . ruler and *a* and power.
Eph 1:22 . . . things under the *a* of Christ
1 Tim 2:2 . . . all who are in *a* so that
1 Pet 5:5 . . . accept the *a* of the elders.

AWE (N) an emotion variously combining dread, respect, and wonder that is inspired by authority or the sacred
see also FEAR, REVERENCE
Ps 119:120 . . . I stand in *a* of your
Acts 2:43 . . . sense of *a* came over them
Heb 12:28 . . . holy fear and *a*.

AWESOME (ADJ) characterized by reverential fear; expressive of or inspiring awe
see also WONDERFUL
Deut 7:21 . . . a great and *a* God.
Neh 1:5 . . . the great and *a* God
Ps 47:2 . . . Most High is *a*.
Ps 99:3 . . . your great and *a* name.
Ps 131:1 . . . too *a* for me to grasp.

B

BABY, BABIES (N) infant child; youngest of a group; figurative of new or immature Christians
Luke 1:44 . . . *b* in my womb jumped for
Luke 2:12 . . . find a *b* wrapped snugly
1 Cor 14:20 . . . Be innocent as *b-ies* when
1 Pet 2:2 . . . Like newborn *b-ies*, you must

BAPTISM, BAPTISMS (N) a Christian ordinance; a washing with water to demonstrate cleansing from sin, linked with repentance and admission into the community of faith; figurative of an ordeal or initiation
Matt 3:16 . . . After his *b*, as Jesus came up
Rom 6:3 . . . joined with Christ Jesus in *b*,
Eph 4:5 . . . one Lord, one faith, one *b*,
Heb 6:2 . . . further instruction about *b-s*,
1 Pet 3:21 . . . that water is a picture of *b*,

BELIEVE, BELIEVED (V) to trust in; to hold a firm conviction about; to accept as true, genuine, or real
see also FAITH, TRUST
Gen 15:6 . . . Abram *b-d* the LORD,
Isa 53:1 . . . Who has *b-d* our message?
Mark 9:24 . . . I do *b*, but help me
Luke 24:25 . . . You find it so hard to *b*
John 4:41 . . . hear his message and *b*.
John 9:35 . . . asked, "Do you *b* in the Son
John 11:40 . . . see God's glory if you *b?*
John 19:35 . . . so that you also can *b*.
Acts 16:31 . . . *B* in the Lord Jesus and
Acts 27:25 . . . For I *b* God. I will be just
Rom 3:25 . . . *b* that Jesus sacrificed his life,
Rom 10:9 . . . *b* in your heart that God
Rom 14:23 . . . anything you *b* is not right,
Rom 16:26 . . . they too might *b* and obey
1 Cor 1:21 . . . to save those who *b*.
Eph 2:8 . . . his grace when you *b-d*.
1 Thes 4:14 . . . For since we *b* that Jesus
Heb 11:6 . . . must *b* that God exists
1 Jn 5:10 . . . All who *b* in the Son

BIRTH (N) the emergence of a new individual from the body of its parent; beginning, start
John 3:6 . . . Spirit gives *b* to spiritual life.
Titus 3:5 . . . giving us a new *b* and new life

BLAMELESS (ADJ) characterized by being free from sin and fault
see also INTEGRITY, RIGHTEOUS
Gen 6:9 . . . only *b* person living on earth
Job 1:8 . . . *b*—a man of complete integrity.
Phil 1:10 . . . live pure and *b* lives
Titus 1:6 . . . must live a *b* life.
2 Pet 3:14 . . . pure and *b* in his sight.

BLESS, BLESSED, BLESSES (V) to confer prosperity or happiness upon; to honor in worship; to offer approval or encouragement; to bring pleasure or divine favor
Gen 12:3 . . . I will *b* those who *b* you
Ps 16:7 . . . I will *b* the LORD who guides
Prov 31:28 . . . Her children stand and *b*
Matt 5:3 . . . God *b-es* those who are poor
Matt 5:7 . . . *b-es* those who are merciful,
Jas 1:12 . . . God *b-es* those who patiently
Rev 22:7 . . . *B-ed* are those who obey
Rev 22:14 . . . *B-ed* are those who wash

BLOOD (N) fluid in the circulatory system; signifies human life; kinfolk; of animals, used in priestly sacrifices; of Christ, effective for the forgiveness of sins; on hands or head, symbolic of guilt
Exod 12:13 . . . When I see the *b*, I will pass
Mark 14:24 . . . my *b*, which confirms the
John 6:53 . . . and drink his *b*, you cannot
1 Pet 1:19 . . . the precious *b* of Christ,
1 Jn 1:7 . . . the *b* of Jesus, his Son, cleanses
Rev 1:5 . . . by shedding his *b* for us.

BOAST, BOASTED, BOASTING (V) to puff oneself up in speech, brag
Isa 20:5 . . . *b-ed* of their allies in Egypt!
Jer 9:23 . . . the wise *b* in their wisdom,
Rom 2:17 . . . *b* about your special
1 Cor 1:31 . . . *b*, *b* only about the Lord.
2 Cor 8:24 . . . our *b-ing* about you is justified.
2 Cor 10:13 . . . We will *b* only about
Gal 6:14 . . . *b* about anything except
Eph 2:9 . . . none of us can *b* about it.
Jas 1:9 . . . have something to *b* about,
Jas 4:16 . . . *b-ing* about your own pretentious plans,

BODY, BODIES (N) one's physical essence; a corpse; a group of people
Job 19:26 . . . in my *b* I will see God!
Ps 49:14 . . . Their *b-ies* will rot in the grave,
Isa 26:19 . . . their *b-ies* will rise again!
Matt 26:41 . . . willing, but the *b* is weak!
Mark 14:22 . . . Take it, for this is my *b*.
Rom 12:4 . . . our *b-ies* have many parts
1 Cor 6:15 . . . that your *b-ies* are actually
1 Cor 6:19 . . . that your *b* is the temple
1 Cor 6:20 . . . honor God with your *b*.
1 Cor 11:24 . . . my *b*, which is given for
1 Cor 12:13 . . . into one *b* by one Spirit,
1 Cor 15:44 . . . be raised as spiritual *b-ies*.
2 Cor 5:1 . . . eternal *b* made for us by God
2 Cor 5:2 . . . to put on our heavenly *b-ies*
2 Cor 5:4 . . . so that these dying *b-ies* will
Eph 1:23 . . . the church is his *b*;
Eph 3:6 . . . Both are part of the same *b*,
Eph 5:28 . . . love their own *b-ies*.
Eph 5:30 . . . are members of his *b*.
Col 1:24 . . . for his *b*, the church.

BOOK (N) a long written or printed literary composition; written records, register, or accounting
Josh 1:8 . . . Study this *B* of Instruction
Ps 69:28 . . . names from the *B* of Life;
Phil 4:3 . . . are written in the *B* of Life.
Rev 3:5 . . . names from the *B* of Life,
Rev 20:12 . . . including the *B* of Life.
Rev 21:27 . . . in the Lamb's *B* of Life.

BORN (V) to be given birth to or produced; to be productive; spiritually, to be renewed or confirm a commitment of faith
Ps 51:5 . . . For I was *b* a sinner—
John 3:3 . . . unless you are *b* again,
John 3:7 . . . You must be *b* again.
1 Pet 1:3 . . . we have been *b* again,
1 Pet 1:23 . . . you have been *b* again,

BRANCH, BRANCHES (N) limb of a (family) tree; part of a complex body (of knowledge); figurative of offspring and of disciples (of Christ and his disciples)
Isa 4:2 . . . the *b* of the LORD will be beautiful
John 15:2 . . . *b* of mine that doesn't
John 15:4 . . . a *b* cannot produce fruit if
John 15:5 . . . you are the *b-es.*

BREAD (N) basic staple in diet of ancient Israel, usually baked using flour or meal; signifies livelihood
Mark 14:22 . . . Jesus took some *b* and
John 6:48 . . . Yes, I am the *b* of life!
John 6:51 . . . I am the living *b*
1 Cor 10:16 . . . when we break the *b,*
1 Cor 11:23 . . . the Lord Jesus took some *b*

BURDEN, BURDENS (N) a (usually) heavy load to be borne—physically, emotionally, or spiritually
Matt 11:30 . . . the *b* I give you is light.
2 Cor 11:9 . . . a financial *b* to anyone.
2 Cor 12:14 . . . I will not be a *b* to you.
Gal 6:2 . . . Share each other's *b-s,*
2 Thes 3:8 . . . so we would not be a *b*

C

CALF (N) the young of a domestic cow
Exod 32:4 . . . it into the shape of a *c.*
Luke 15:23 . . . kill the *c* we have been
Acts 7:41 . . . made an idol shaped like a *c,*

CALL, CALLED (V) to make a request or demand; to designate or name
see also CHOSEN
1 Kgs 18:24 . . . *c* on the name of your god,
Mark 2:17 . . . I have come to *c* not those
Rom 8:28 . . . *c-ed* according to his purpose
Rom 10:12 . . . to all who *c* on him.
1 Cor 1:2 . . . who have been *c-ed* by God
1 Cor 1:2 . . . *c* on the name of our Lord
1 Thes 4:7 . . . God has *c-ed* us to live holy
1 Pet 3:9 . . . what God has *c-ed* you to do,

CARE (V) to feel interest or concern; to attend to or provide for the needs, operation, or treatment of
Ps 37:17 . . . LORD takes *c* of the godly.
Prov 12:10 . . . godly *c* for their animals,
John 10:13 . . . really *c* about the sheep.
John 21:16 . . . Then take *c* of my sheep,
1 Tim 5:14 . . . take *c* of their own homes.
1 Pet 5:2 . . . *C* for the flock that God

CELEBRATE (V) to perform (a sacrament or ceremony) publicly and with appropriate rites; to observe a notable occasion with festivities
Exod 12:47 . . . Israel must *c* this Passover
2 Sam 6:21 . . . so I *c* before the LORD.
2 Kgs 23:21 . . . *c* the Passover to the LORD
Luke 15:23 . . . We must *c* with a feast,
John 18:28 . . . to *c* the Passover.

CHARACTER (N) moral excellence and firmness; main or essential nature
Rom 5:4 . . . develops strength of *c,*
1 Cor 15:33 . . . corrupts good *c.*
Heb 1:3 . . . expresses the very *c* of God,

CHEAT, CHEATED (V) to deprive of something valuable by deceit or fraud; to practice fraud or trickery
1 Sam 12:3 . . . Have I ever *c-ed* any of you?
Mal 3:8 . . . You have *c-ed* me of the tithes
Mark 10:19 . . . You must not *c* anyone.
1 Cor 6:7 . . . not let yourselves be *c-ed?*
1 Cor 6:8 . . . who do wrong and *c* even
1 Cor 6:10 . . . abusive, or *c* people—

CHILD, CHILDREN (N) an unborn or recently born person; a young person between infancy and youth, not yet of age; offspring or descendants
Deut 32:43 . . . avenge the blood of his *c-ren;*
Ps 8:2 . . . have taught *c-ren* and infants
Isa 7:14 . . . The virgin will conceive a *c!*
Isa 9:6 . . . For a *c* is born to us,
Isa 54:13 . . . I will teach all your *c-ren,*
Matt 1:23 . . . The virgin will conceive a *c!*
Matt 5:9 . . . will be called the *c-ren* of God.
Mark 10:14 . . . Let the *c-ren* come to me.
Luke 18:15 . . . their little *c-ren* to Jesus
John 1:12 . . . to become *c-ren* of God.
Rom 9:26 . . . called '*c-ren* of the living God.'
1 Cor 13:11 . . . and reasoned as a *c.*
Gal 3:26 . . . you are all *c-ren* of God
Eph 3:6 . . . riches inherited by God's *c-ren.*
Eph 6:1 . . . *C-ren,* obey your parents
Col 3:21 . . . do not aggravate your *c-ren,*
1 Tim 3:4 . . . having *c-ren* who respect and
Heb 12:7 . . . treating you as his own *c-ren.*
1 Jn 4:7 . . . who loves is a *c* of God

CHILDLIKE (ADJ) resembling, suggesting, or appropriate to a child; marked by innocence, trust, and ingenuousness
Ps 116:6 . . . protects those of *c* faith;
Matt 11:25 . . . revealing them to the *c.*

CHOSEN (ADJ) selected or marked for special favor or privilege
see also CALL
1 Chr 16:22 . . . Do not touch my *c* people,
Isa 41:8 . . . my *c* one, descended from Abraham
Mark 13:20 . . . for the sake of his *c* ones
Luke 23:35 . . . God's Messiah, the *C* One.
John 1:34 . . . that he is the *C* One of God.
1 Pet 1:1 . . . writing to God's *c* people
1 Pet 2:9 . . . for you are a *c* people.

CHRISTIAN, CHRISTIANS (N) one who professes belief in and follows the teachings of Jesus Christ; believer
Acts 11:26 . . . believers were first called *C-s.*
Acts 26:28 . . . persuade me to become a *C*
Gal 2:4 . . . some so-called *C-s*
1 Thes 4:12 . . . people who are not *C-s*
1 Pet 4:14 . . . insulted for being a *C,*
1 Pet 4:16 . . . to suffer for being a *C.*
1 Pet 5:9 . . . your *C* brothers and sisters

CHURCH (N) "assembly" or "called ones"; the body of believers gathered to worship Jesus (not the building in which they meet)
Matt 16:18 . . . this rock I will build my *c,*
Matt 18:17 . . . take your case to the *c.*
Acts 20:28 . . . shepherd God's flock—his *c,*
1 Cor 15:9 . . . way I persecuted God's *c.*
Eph 5:23 . . . Christ is the head of the *c.*
Col 1:24 . . . continue for his body, the *c.*

COMFORT (N) consolation in time of trouble or worry; solace
Gen 24:67 . . . she was a special *c* to him
Job 10:20 . . . I may have a moment of *c*
Ps 94:19 . . . your *c* gave me renewed hope
Zech 10:2 . . . falsehoods that give no *c.*
2 Cor 1:5 . . . shower us with his *c*

2 Cor 1:7 . . . share in the *c* God gives us.
Col 4:11 . . . And what a *c* they have been!

COMFORT (V) to give strength and hope to; to console
Job 2:11 . . . traveled from their homes to *c*
Ps 69:20 . . . one would turn and *c* me.
Ps 86:17 . . . O LORD, help and *c* me.
Ps 119:52 . . . O LORD, they *c* me.
Isa 40:1 . . . *C, c* my people,
Isa 51:3 . . . The LORD will *c* Israel again
Isa 51:19 . . . Who is left to *c* you?
Isa 61:1 . . . to *c* the brokenhearted
Lam 1:2 . . . there is no one left to *c* her.
Zech 1:17 . . . the LORD will again *c* Zion
2 Cor 1:4 . . . so that we can *c* others.
2 Cor 1:6 . . . we will certainly *c* you.
2 Cor 2:7 . . . forgive and *c* him.

COMMAND (N) an order given; religious instruction
see also COMMANDMENT(S)
Josh 1:9 . . . my *c*—be strong and
Ps 33:9 . . . It appeared at his *c*.
John 15:17 . . . my *c:* Love each other.

COMMAND, COMMANDED (V) to issue a charge or directive
Gen 7:5 . . . everything as the LORD *c-ed*
Exod 7:6 . . . did just as the LORD had *c-ed*
Deut 6:1 . . . your God *c-ed* me to teach
Deut 6:24 . . . our God *c-ed* us to obey
John 15:14 . . . my friends if you do what I *c*.
1 Jn 3:23 . . . just as he *c-ed* us.
2 Jn 1:4 . . . just as the Father *c-ed*.

COMMANDMENT, COMMANDMENTS (N) a gracious provision of God's law or covenant, obeyed as an act of love and devotion
see also COMMAND
Exod 34:28 . . . Ten *C-s*—on the stone
Deut 4:13 . . . his covenant—the Ten *C-s*
Deut 10:4 . . . LORD wrote the Ten *C-s* on
Ps 103:18 . . . of those who obey his *c-s!*
Ps 111:7 . . . all his *c-s* are trustworthy.
Ps 111:10 . . . who obey his *c-s* will grow
Ps 119:93 . . . I will never forget your *c-s*,
Prov 19:16 . . . the *c-s* and keep your life;
Matt 5:19 . . . if you ignore the least *c*
Matt 19:17 . . . eternal life, keep the *c-s*.
Matt 22:36 . . . the most important *c*
Matt 22:38 . . . the first and greatest *c*.
Mark 10:19 . . . you know the *c-s:*
Mark 12:28 . . . *c-s*, which is the most
Luke 18:20 . . . you know the *c-s:*
John 13:34 . . . a new *c:* Love each other.
John 14:15 . . . If you love me, obey my *c-s*.
Rom 13:9 . . . in this one *c:* "Love your
1 Cor 7:19 . . . is to keep God's *c-s*.
Eph 2:15 . . . law with its *c-s* and regulations.
Eph 6:2 . . . the first *c* with a promise:
Heb 9:19 . . . had read each of God's *c-s*
1 Jn 2:3 . . . know him if we obey his *c-s*.
1 Jn 3:24 . . . Those who obey God's *c-s*
1 Jn 5:3 . . . God means keeping his *c-s*,
Rev 12:17 . . . who keep God's *c-s* and

COMPASSION (N) sympathy, usually granted because of unusual or distressing circumstances
Exod 34:6 . . . The God of *c* and mercy!
Ps 51:1 . . . Because of your great *c*,
Ps 145:9 . . . He showers *c* on all
Lam 3:32 . . . brings grief, he also shows *c*
Mark 6:34 . . . and he had *c* on them
Luke 15:20 . . . with love and *c*, he ran to

COMPLAINED, COMPLAINING (V) to express grief, pain, or discontent; to make a formal accusation or charge
Exod 15:24 . . . the people *c* and turned
Num 14:2 . . . in the wilderness!" they *c*.
Num 14:29 . . . Because you *c* against me,
John 6:43 . . . Jesus replied, "Stop *c-ing*
Phil 2:14 . . . Do everything without *c-ing*

CONFESS, CONFESSED (V) to admit or acknowledge (sin or faith)
Ps 32:3 . . . I refused to *c* my sin,
Ps 32:5 . . . Finally, I *c-ed* all my sins
Ps 38:18 . . . But I *c* my sins;
Mark 1:5 . . . And when they *c-ed* their sins,
Jas 5:16 . . . *C* your sins to each other
1 Jn 1:9 . . . But if we *c* our sins to him,

CONFIDENCE (N) faith or belief that one will act in a right, proper, or effective way; a feeling or consciousness of one's powers; a quality or state of being certain
Ps 146:3 . . . Don't put your *c* in powerful
2 Cor 8:22 . . . of his great *c* in you.
Phil 1:14 . . . believers here have gained *c*
Phil 2:24 . . . And I have *c* from the Lord
Phil 3:4 . . . I could have *c* in my own
Col 2:2 . . . want them to have complete *c*
Titus 1:2 . . . This truth gives them *c*
Heb 11:1 . . . Faith is the *c* that what we

CONFLICT (N) fight, battle, war
Prov 13:10 . . . Pride leads to *c;*
Prov 17:1 . . . filled with feasting—and *c*.
Gal 3:21 . . . Is there a *c*, then, between

CONSCIENCE, CONSCIENCES (N) one's moral sensitivity or scruples
Acts 24:16 . . . maintain a clear *c* before God
1 Cor 8:7 . . . their weak *c-s* are violated.
1 Tim 1:5 . . . a clear *c*, and genuine faith.
1 Tim 1:19 . . . and keep your *c* clear.
Titus 1:15 . . . minds and *c-s* are corrupted.
Heb 9:14 . . . will purify our *c-s* from sinful
1 Pet 3:16 . . . Keep your *c* clear.
1 Pet 3:21 . . . to God from a clean *c*.

CONTENT, CONTENTED (ADJ) feeling or showing satisfaction with one's possessions, status, or situation; pleased
Josh 7:7 . . . If only we had been *c*
1 Kgs 4:20 . . . They were very *c-ed*,
Prov 13:25 . . . godly eat to their hearts' *c*,
Phil 4:11 . . . I have learned how to be *c*
1 Tim 6:8 . . . food and clothing, let us be *c*.

CONTROL (V) to exercise restraining or directing influence over; to rule
Rom 6:12 . . . Do not let sin *c*
Rom 8:6 . . . letting the Spirit *c* your mind
Rom 8:8 . . . still under the *c* of
Jas 1:26 . . . but don't *c* your tongue,
Jas 3:2 . . . could also *c* ourselves

CONVICT, CONVICTED (V) to find or prove guilty of an offense
Prov 24:25 . . . for those who *c* the guilty;
John 7:51 . . . Is it legal to *c* a man
John 16:8 . . . he will *c* the world of
1 Cor 14:24 . . . they will be *c-ed* of sin
Jude 1:15 . . . He will *c* every person

CORNERSTONE (N) a stone forming a corner or angle in a wall; foundation
Ps 118:22 . . . now become the *c*.
Mark 12:10 . . . now become the *c*.
Acts 4:11 . . . now become the *c*.
Eph 2:20 . . . And the *c* is Christ
1 Pet 2:7 . . . now become the *c*.

CORRECT, CORRECTED, CORRECTING, CORRECTS (V) to set right with remedies, revisions, or reforms
Job 5:17 . . . joy of those *c-ed* by God!
Ps 141:5 . . . If they *c* me,
Prov 3:12 . . . For the LORD *c-s* those
Prov 9:8 . . . don't bother *c-ing* mockers;
Prov 19:25 . . . if you *c* the wise,
Jer 5:3 . . . refused to be *c-ed.*
Jer 10:24 . . . Do not *c* me in anger,
2 Tim 3:16 . . . It *c-s* us when we
2 Tim 4:2 . . . Patiently *c,* rebuke,
Titus 2:15 . . . the authority to *c* them
Heb 12:5 . . . give up when he *c-s* you.

CORRECTION (N) a rebuke or punishment; the action of making right
Prov 10:17 . . . those who ignore *c*
Prov 12:1 . . . it is stupid to hate *c.*
Prov 15:5 . . . learns from *c* is wise.
Prov 15:10 . . . whoever hates *c* will die.
Prov 15:32 . . . if you listen to *c,*
Zeph 3:2 . . . it refuses all *c.*

CORRUPT (ADJ) morally degenerate and perverted; depraved
Ps 14:1 . . . They are *c,*
Prov 19:28 . . . A *c* witness

CORRUPT, CORRUPTED, CORRUPTS (V) to change from good to bad, physically or morally
Eccl 7:7 . . . and bribes *c* the heart.
1 Cor 15:33 . . . bad company *c-s* good
Titus 1:15 . . . and consciences are *c-ed.*
Jas 1:27 . . . let the world *c* you.

COUNSEL (N) advice; policy, plan, or action
Prov 27:9 . . . The heartfelt *c* of a friend
1 Cor 7:40 . . . I am giving you *c*

COUNSEL (V) to advise
Col 3:16 . . . Teach and *c* each other

COUNSELOR (N) one who gives advice or wisdom
see also ADVOCATE, HOLY SPIRIT
Isa 9:6 . . . Wonderful *C,* Mighty God,

COURAGE (N) mental or moral strength
Mark 6:50 . . . Take *c!* I am here!
Acts 27:22 . . . But take *c!*
Heb 3:6 . . . if we keep our *c*
Jas 5:8 . . . Take *c,* for the coming
1 Jn 2:28 . . . be full of *c* and not shrink

COURAGEOUS (ADJ) having or characterized by courage; brave
Josh 1:6 . . . Be strong and *c,*
2 Chr 32:7 . . . Be strong and *c!*
Ps 31:24 . . . be strong and *c,*
1 Cor 16:13 . . . Be *c.* Be strong.

COVENANT, COVENANTS (N) a mutual agreement or contract (between persons, between nations, or between God and humanity) with conditions and consequences spelled out
see also PROMISE(S), VOW
Gen 17:2 . . . I will make a *c* with you,
Exod 19:5 . . . and keep my *c,*
Neh 1:5 . . . keeps his *c* of unfailing love
Ps 105:8 . . . stands by his *c*—
Prov 2:17 . . . and ignores the *c*
Isa 61:8 . . . an everlasting *c* with them.
Hos 10:4 . . . make *c-s* they don't intend
Luke 22:20 . . . new *c* between God and his
Rom 9:4 . . . He made *c-s* with them
2 Cor 3:6 . . . under the new *c,*
Heb 9:15 . . . mediates a new *c* between
Heb 12:24 . . . the new *c* between God and

COVET, COVETED, COVETING (V) to inordinately desire unjust gain or another's property
Exod 20:17 . . . not *c* your neighbor's wife,
Exod 34:24 . . . so no one will *c* and conquer
Deut 7:25 . . . must not *c* the silver or gold
Acts 20:33 . . . *c-ed* anyone's silver or gold
Rom 7:7 . . . known that *c-ing* is wrong
Rom 13:9 . . . You must not *c.*

CREATE, CREATED, CREATING (V) to bring into being; to form, make, or produce
Gen 1:1 . . . God *c-d* the heavens
Gen 1:27 . . . male and female he *c-d* them;
Gen 6:7 . . . human race I have *c-d* from
Ps 51:10 . . . *C* in me a clean heart
Ps 104:30 . . . life is *c-d,* and you renew
Prov 8:22 . . . before he *c-d* anything else.
Isa 43:1 . . . the LORD who *c-d* you.
Isa 43:7 . . . I who *c-d* them.
Isa 45:8 . . . I, the LORD, *c-d* them.
Isa 54:16 . . . I have *c-d* the blacksmith
Isa 65:17 . . . I am *c-ing* new heavens and
John 1:3 . . . *c-d* everything through him,
Rom 1:20 . . . since the world was *c-d,*
Rom 1:25 . . . served the things God *c-d*
Rom 9:20 . . . the thing that was *c-d* say
Eph 2:10 . . . He has *c-d* us anew
Eph 2:15 . . . by *c-ing* in himself
Eph 4:24 . . . *c-d* to be like God—
Col 1:16 . . . Everything was *c-d* through
1 Tim 4:3 . . . But God *c-d* those foods
Heb 1:2 . . . through the Son he *c-d*
1 Pet 4:19 . . . to the God who *c-d* you,
Rev 4:11 . . . For you *c-d* all things,
Rev 10:6 . . . who *c-d* the heavens

CREATION (N) something that is created; the world; the act of bringing the world into existence
Gen 2:3 . . . from all his work of *c.*
Mark 10:6 . . . from the beginning of *c.*
Rom 8:19 . . . For all *c* is waiting
Rom 8:39 . . . nothing in all *c* will ever
Gal 6:15 . . . into a new *c.*
Col 1:17 . . . holds all *c* together.
Heb 12:27 . . . all of *c* will be shaken
Jas 1:18 . . . we, out of all *c,*
Rev 3:14 . . . of God's new *c:*

CREATOR (N) maker; one who creates
Gen 14:19 . . . God Most High, *C* of heaven
Job 40:19 . . . only its *C* can threaten
Eccl 12:1 . . . to forget your *C.*
Isa 40:28 . . . the *C* of all the earth.
Isa 45:9 . . . argue with their *C.*
Isa 51:13 . . . the LORD, your *C,*
Jer 51:19 . . . He is the *C* of everything
Rom 1:25 . . . instead of the *C* himself,
Eph 3:9 . . . the *C* of all things,
Eph 3:15 . . . the *C* of everything

CRITICISM (N) a critical observation or remark; critique
Prov 15:31 . . . listen to constructive *c,*
Prov 25:12 . . . valid *c* is like a gold
Prov 29:1 . . . refuses to accept *c*
2 Cor 8:20 . . . guard against any *c*

CROSS (N) an upright post used as an instrument of death in ancient times; the means by which atonement was made between God and humanity
Mark 8:34 . . . take up your *c,*
Luke 9:23 . . . take up your *c* daily,
Acts 2:23 . . . you nailed him to a *c*
Acts 5:30 . . . hanging him on a *c.*
1 Cor 1:18 . . . message of the *c* is
Gal 3:1 . . . death on the *c.*

Gal 6:12 . . . that the *c* of Christ alone
Phil 2:8 . . . criminal's death on a *c*.
Col 1:20 . . . Christ's blood on the *c*.
Heb 12:2 . . . he endured the *c*,
1 Pet 2:24 . . . his body on the *c*

CROWN (N) top of the head; a cap or headdress worn by victors, priests, or royalty
Matt 27:29 . . . thorn branches into a *c*
Mark 15:17 . . . thorn branches into a *c*
John 19:2 . . . wove a *c* of thorns
John 19:5 . . . wearing the *c* of thorns
Phil 4:1 . . . and the *c* I receive
1 Thes 2:19 . . . our proud reward and *c*
Jas 1:12 . . . will receive the *c* of life
Rev 2:10 . . . will give you the *c* of life.
Rev 14:14 . . . He had a gold *c* on his head

CRUCIFY, CRUCIFIED (V) to execute or nail to the cross; to put to death
Mark 15:13 . . . "*C* him!"
Mark 15:32 . . . who were ***c-ied*** with Jesus
Mark 16:6 . . . who was ***c-ied***.
Luke 23:23 . . . that Jesus be ***c-ied***,
Luke 23:33 . . . criminals were also ***c-ied***—
Luke 24:20 . . . and they ***c-ied*** him.
John 19:6 . . . "*C* him! *C* him!"
John 19:10 . . . to release you or *c* you?
John 19:20 . . . where Jesus was ***c-ied***
John 19:32 . . . the two men ***c-ied*** with Jesus.
Rom 6:6 . . . were ***c-ied*** with Christ
1 Cor 1:23 . . . preach that Christ was ***c-ied***,
1 Cor 2:8 . . . would not have ***c-ied***
Gal 5:24 . . . and ***c-ied*** them there.
Rev 11:8 . . . where their Lord was ***c-ied***.

CURE (N) recovery or relief from a disease; a complete or permanent solution
Jer 30:15 . . . wound that has no *c*?
Luke 8:43 . . . she could find no *c*.

CURE, CURED (V) to restore to health, soundness, or normality
Isa 30:26 . . . and *c* the wounds
Matt 11:5 . . . the lepers are ***c-d***,
John 5:10 . . . said to the man who was ***c-d***,

D

DANGER (N) harm or damage
Ps 57:1 . . . until the *d* passes by.
Prov 22:3 . . . prudent person foresees *d*
Matt 5:22 . . . in *d* of being brought
Rom 8:35 . . . or in *d*, or threatened
2 Cor 1:10 . . . did rescue us from mortal *d*,
2 Cor 11:26 . . . I have faced *d* from rivers

DEAD (N) Those who have died (physically or spiritually)
Matt 8:22 . . . the spiritually *d* bury their
Luke 24:46 . . . rise from the *d* on the third
1 Cor 15:29 . . . If the *d* will not be raised
Rev 20:12 . . . I saw the *d*, both great and

DEAD (ADJ) without (physical or spiritual) life; fatal; useless; unresponsive
Rom 6:11 . . . be *d* to the power of sin
Eph 2:1 . . . Once you were *d* because of
Jas 2:17 . . . good deeds, it is *d* and useless.
1 Pet 2:24 . . . that we can be *d* to sin and
Rev 2:8 . . . Last, who was *d* but is now

DEATH (N) the cessation of (physical or spiritual) life; personification and consequence of evil
Prov 23:14 . . . save them from *d*.
Isa 38:17 . . . have rescued me from *d*
Acts 2:24 . . . for *d* could not keep him
Rom 5:12 . . . brought *d*, so *d* spread to
Rom 6:23 . . . the wages of sin is *d*,
1 Cor 15:21 . . . see, just as *d* came into the
1 Cor 15:26 . . . enemy to be destroyed is *d*.
Gal 3:1 . . . the meaning of Jesus Christ's *d*
Heb 2:14 . . . who had the power of *d*.

DECEIVE, DECEIVED, DECEIVES, DECEIVING (V) to lead astray; to cause to accept as true what is false
Gen 3:13 . . . "The serpent ***d-d*** me," she
Prov 10:31 . . . the tongue that ***d-s*** will be
Prov 14:8 . . . but fools *d* themselves.
Prov 26:24 . . . but they're ***d-ing*** you.
Matt 24:24 . . . so as to *d*, if possible, even
Mark 13:6 . . . They will *d* many.
Rom 7:11 . . . those commands and ***d-d*** me;
Rom 16:18 . . . they *d* innocent people.
1 Cor 3:18 . . . Stop ***d-ing*** yourselves.
2 Cor 11:3 . . . as Eve was ***d-d*** by the cunning
Col 2:4 . . . so no one will *d* you with
1 Tim 2:14 . . . The woman was ***d-d***, and sin
2 Tim 3:13 . . . They will *d* others and will
2 Tim 3:13 . . . will themselves be ***d-d***.
Heb 3:13 . . . you will be ***d-d*** by sin
Rev 20:3 . . . Satan could not *d* the nations
Rev 20:10 . . . devil, who had ***d-d*** them, was

DEFEND, DEFENDING, DEFENDS (V) to maintain or support in the face of argument or hostile criticism; to drive danger or attack away from
Deut 33:7 . . . strength to *d* their cause;
Ps 10:14 . . . You *d* the orphans.
Ps 34:7 . . . he surrounds and ***d-s*** all who
Ps 72:4 . . . Help him to *d* the poor,
Ps 106:8 . . . saved them—to *d* the honor of
Phil 1:7 . . . and in ***d-ing*** and confirming
Phil 1:16 . . . been appointed to *d* the Good
Jude 1:3 . . . urging you to *d* the faith

DELIGHT, DELIGHTS (N) source of great pleasure; joy
Ps 36:8 . . . your river of ***d-s***.
Ps 40:6 . . . You take no *d* in sacrifices
Ps 119:111 . . . they are my heart's *d*.
Prov 8:30 . . . I was his constant *d*,
Isa 58:13 . . . and speak of it with *d*
Jer 15:16 . . . my joy and my heart's *d*,
Mal 3:12 . . . your land will be such a *d*,
Mark 12:37 . . . to him with great *d*.

DELIGHT, DELIGHTED, DELIGHTING, DELIGHTS (V) to enjoy
Exod 4:14 . . . He will be ***d-ed*** to see you.
2 Sam 22:20 . . . because he ***d-s*** in me.
Ps 1:2 . . . But they *d* in the law of
Ps 18:19 . . . he rescued me because he ***d-s***
Ps 27:4 . . . ***d-ing*** in the LORD's
Ps 37:4 . . . Take *d* in the LORD,
Ps 119:70 . . . I *d* in your instructions.
Prov 3:12 . . . a child in whom he ***d-s***.
Prov 11:1 . . . he ***d-s*** in accurate weights.
Prov 11:20 . . . he ***d-s*** in those with integrity.
Song 8:10 . . . he is ***d-ed*** with what he sees.
Isa 11:3 . . . He will *d* in obeying
Isa 65:19 . . . and *d* in my people.
Isa 66:3 . . . ***d-ing*** in their detestable sins—
Jer 9:24 . . . I *d* in these things.

DENY, DENIED, DENIES (V) to disavow or refuse to accept as true; to refuse to grant
Exod 23:6 . . . you must not *d* justice to the
Deut 27:19 . . . is anyone who ***d-ies*** justice
Prov 30:9 . . . I may *d* you and say,
Matt 10:33 . . . everyone who ***d-ies*** me
Matt 26:35 . . . I will never *d* you!
Matt 26:70 . . . But Peter ***d-ied*** it
Luke 12:9 . . . anyone who ***d-ies*** me

Luke 22:34 . . . you will ***d*** three times
John 18:25 . . . He ***d-ied*** it, saying,
Acts 4:16 . . . We can't ***d*** that they
1 Tim 5:8 . . . have ***d-ied*** the true faith.
2 Tim 2:12 . . . ***d*** him, he will ***d*** us.
Titus 1:16 . . . ***d*** him by the way they live.
2 Pet 2:1 . . . and even ***d*** the Master who
1 Jn 2:22 . . . Anyone who ***d-ies*** the Father
1 Jn 2:23 . . . Anyone who ***d-ies*** the Son
Jude 1:4 . . . they have ***d-ied*** our only Master
Rev 3:8 . . . and did not ***d*** me.

DESTROY, DESTROYED (V) to kill; to cause devastation or ruin
see also PERISH
Gen 6:17 . . . that will ***d*** every living
Gen 9:11 . . . will a flood ***d*** the earth.
Josh 10:40 . . . He completely ***d-ed*** everyone
Prov 10:21 . . . fools are ***d-ed*** by their lack
Prov 11:9 . . . the godless ***d*** their friends,
Prov 18:24 . . . "friends" who ***d*** each other,
Prov 29:1 . . . will suddenly be ***d-ed*** beyond
Isa 11:4 . . . his mouth will ***d*** the wicked.
Dan 2:44 . . . never be ***d-ed*** or conquered.
Matt 10:28 . . . God, who can ***d*** both soul
Luke 9:25 . . . but are yourself lost or ***d-ed?***
John 10:10 . . . and kill and ***d.***
Rom 2:12 . . . they will be ***d-ed,*** even though
1 Cor 5:5 . . . nature will be ***d-ed*** and he
1 Cor 8:11 . . . died will be ***d-ed.***
1 Cor 15:24 . . . ***d-ed*** every ruler and
1 Cor 15:26 . . . enemy to be ***d-ed*** is death.
2 Cor 4:9 . . . are not ***d-ed.***
Heb 7:16 . . . that cannot be ***d-ed.***
2 Pet 2:12 . . . be caught and ***d-ed.***
2 Pet 3:7 . . . people will be ***d-ed.***
Jude 1:5 . . . but later he ***d-ed*** those who did
Rev 11:18 . . . It is time to ***d*** all who have

DETEST, DETESTS (V) to loathe; to denounce
Prov 8:7 . . . the truth and ***d*** every kind of
Prov 12:22 . . . The LORD ***d-s*** lying lips,
Prov 15:8 . . . The LORD ***d-s*** the sacrifice
Prov 15:26 . . . The LORD ***d-s*** evil plans,
Prov 16:5 . . . The LORD ***d-s*** the proud;
Prov 20:10 . . . the LORD ***d-s*** double
Prov 24:9 . . . everyone ***d-s*** a mocker.

DIE, DIED (V) to pass from physical life; to cease from existence
see also PERISH
Gen 2:17 . . . you are sure to ***d.***
Esth 4:16 . . . If I must ***d,*** I must ***d.***
Prov 5:23 . . . He will ***d*** for lack of
Prov 11:7 . . . When the wicked ***d,*** their
Prov 11:10 . . . when the wicked ***d.***
Jer 31:30 . . . All people will ***d*** for their
Luke 16:22 . . . The rich man also ***d-d*** and
John 13:37 . . . I'm ready to ***d*** for you.
Rom 4:25 . . . handed over to ***d*** because of
Rom 5:6 . . . the right time and ***d-d*** for us
Rom 5:8 . . . by sending Christ to ***d*** for us
Rom 6:7 . . . when we ***d-d*** with Christ we
Rom 6:10 . . . When he ***d-d,*** he ***d-d*** once
Rom 14:8 . . . whether we live or ***d,*** we
1 Cor 9:15 . . . I would rather ***d*** than lose
1 Cor 15:18 . . . all who have ***d-d*** believing in
1 Cor 15:32 . . . for tomorrow we ***d!***
1 Cor 15:36 . . . plant unless it ***d-s*** first.
1 Cor 15:42 . . . in the ground when we ***d,***
1 Cor 15:51 . . . will not all ***d,*** but we will
2 Cor 5:15 . . . for Christ, who ***d-d*** and was
1 Thes 4:16 . . . who have ***d-d*** will rise from
1 Thes 5:10 . . . Christ ***d-d*** for us so
2 Tim 2:11 . . . saying: If we ***d*** with him,
Heb 9:27 . . . is destined to ***d*** once and
1 Pet 3:18 . . . sinned, but he ***d-d*** for sinners

DISCIPLE, DISCIPLES (N) student or follower of some doctrine or teacher
Matt 28:19 . . . go and make ***d-s*** of all the
Mark 16:20 . . . the ***d-s*** went everywhere and
Luke 14:26 . . . you cannot be my ***d.***
Luke 14:33 . . . become my ***d*** without
John 8:31 . . . are truly my ***d-s*** if you remain
John 13:5 . . . to wash the ***d-s'*** feet, drying
John 13:23 . . . The ***d*** Jesus loved
John 15:8 . . . fruit, you are my true ***d-s.***
John 21:7 . . . Then the ***d*** Jesus loved
John 21:20 . . . the ***d*** Jesus loved—

DISCIPLINE (N) punishment; instruction
Prov 10:17 . . . People who accept ***d*** are on
Prov 13:1 . . . child accepts a parent's ***d;***
Prov 15:32 . . . If you reject ***d,*** you only
Heb 12:5 . . . of the LORD's ***d,*** and don't
Heb 12:11 . . . No ***d*** is enjoyable

DISCIPLINE, DISCIPLINES (V) to punish or correct with love; to exercise self-control
Deut 8:5 . . . as a parent ***d-s*** a child,
Deut 8:5 . . . your God ***d-s*** you for your
Ps 39:11 . . . When you ***d*** us for our
1 Cor 9:27 . . . I ***d*** my body like an athlete
Heb 12:6 . . . For the LORD ***d-s*** those he

DISCOURAGED (V) to dissuade or hinder; to deprive of courage or confidence
Deut 31:8 . . . be afraid or ***d,*** for the LORD
2 Sam 11:25 . . . not to be ***d,"*** David said.
1 Chr 28:20 . . . afraid or ***d,*** for the LORD
Isa 41:10 . . . Don't be ***d,*** for I am
2 Cor 7:6 . . . who are ***d,*** encouraged us by
Col 3:21 . . . will become ***d.***

DISHONEST (ADJ) characterized by lack of truth, honesty, or trustworthiness
Lev 19:35 . . . Do not use ***d*** standards when
Prov 20:23 . . . not pleased by ***d*** scales.
Luke 16:8 . . . to admire the ***d*** rascal for
Luke 16:10 . . . But if you are ***d*** in little

DISHONESTY (N) lack of honesty or integrity
Jer 22:17 . . . eyes only for greed and ***d!***
Jer 23:14 . . . commit adultery and love ***d.***
Rom 3:7 . . . sinner if my ***d*** highlights his
Rev 21:27 . . . idolatry and ***d***—but only

DISOBEY, DISOBEYED, DISOBEYING (V) to fail to obey
Judg 2:2 . . . But you ***d-ed*** my command.
1 Kgs 13:26 . . . man of God who ***d-ed*** the
2 Chr 24:20 . . . says: Why do you ***d*** the
Neh 9:29 . . . and obstinate and ***d-ed*** your
Esth 3:3 . . . Why are you ***d-ing*** the king's
Dan 9:11 . . . Israel has ***d-ed*** your instruction
Acts 7:53 . . . You deliberately ***d-ed*** God's
Rom 1:30 . . . and they ***d*** their parents.
Rom 5:19 . . . Because one person ***d-ed*** God,
Eph 5:6 . . . fall on all who ***d*** him.
Heb 3:18 . . . the people who ***d-ed*** him?
Heb 4:6 . . . enter because they ***d-ed*** God.
Heb 4:11 . . . But if we ***d*** God, as the
1 Pet 3:20 . . . those who ***d-ed*** God long ago

DIVORCE (N) the action or an instance of legally dissolving a marriage
Deut 24:1 . . . a letter of ***d,*** hands it to
Mal 2:16 . . . "For I hate ***d!"*** says the
Matt 19:8 . . . Moses permitted ***d*** only as a

DIVORCE, DIVORCED, DIVORCES (V) to dissolve a marriage; to end a relationship
Matt 5:31 . . . A man can *d* his wife by
Matt 5:32 . . . a man who *d-s* his wife, unless
Matt 5:32 . . . who marries a *d-d* woman also
Mark 10:2 . . . be allowed to *d* his wife?
Mark 10:11 . . . Whoever *d-s* his wife and
Mark 10:12 . . . if a woman *d-s* her husband
Luke 16:18 . . . a man who *d-s* his wife and
Luke 16:18 . . . marries a woman *d-d* from

DOUBT, DOUBTS (N) uncertainty of belief or opinion; lack of confidence; distrust
Mark 11:23 . . . have no *d* in your heart.
Luke 24:38 . . . hearts filled with *d?*
Rom 14:23 . . . if you have *d-s* about whether

DOUBT (V) to distrust; to be uncertain
Matt 14:31 . . . Why did you *d* me?
Matt 21:21 . . . faith and don't *d*, you

E

EAGLE, EAGLES (N) any of various large diurnal birds of prey noted for their strength, size, keenness of vision, and powers of flight
Deut 32:11 . . . Like an *e* that rouses her chicks
Isa 40:31 . . . soar high on wings like *e-s*.
Rev 4:7 . . . was like an *e* in flight.
Rev 12:14 . . . wings like those of a great *e*

EAT (V) to ingest, chew, and swallow in turn
Gen 2:16 . . . You may freely *e* the fruit
Matt 26:26 . . . Take this and *e* it,
1 Cor 11:26 . . . every time you *e* this bread

EDEN (N) the garden where Adam and Eve first lived
Gen 2:8 . . . a garden in *E* in the east,
Ezek 28:13 . . . in *E*, the garden of God.

ENCOURAGE, ENCOURAGED (V) to inspire with courage or hope; to spur on
Acts 11:23 . . . and he *e-d* the believers
Acts 20:1 . . . sent for the believers and *e-d*
Rom 1:12 . . . I also want to be *e-d* by yours.
Rom 12:8 . . . your gift is to *e* others,
2 Cor 7:6 . . . *e-d* us by the arrival of Titus.
2 Cor 7:13 . . . have been greatly *e-d* by this.
Eph 6:22 . . . how we are doing and to *e*
Col 4:8 . . . how we are doing and to *e* you.
1 Thes 2:12 . . . pleaded with you, *e-d* you,
1 Thes 3:2 . . . to strengthen you, to *e* you
1 Thes 3:7 . . . we have been greatly *e-d* in
1 Thes 5:11 . . . So *e* each other and build
Titus 1:9 . . . he will be able to *e* others
1 Pet 5:12 . . . purpose in writing is to *e* you

ENDURE (V) to withstand, suffer, or persevere
see also PERSEVERE
2 Cor 1:6 . . . Then you can patiently *e*
2 Cor 6:4 . . . patiently *e* troubles and
2 Tim 2:3 . . . *E* suffering along with me,
2 Tim 2:12 . . . If we *e* hardship,
Heb 12:7 . . . As you *e* this divine discipline,
Jas 1:12 . . . who patiently *e* testing and
Jas 5:11 . . . those who *e* under suffering.
1 Pet 2:19 . . . patiently *e* unjust treatment.
Rev 13:10 . . . must *e* persecution patiently

ENEMY, ENEMIES (N) foe—personal, national, or spiritual
Ps 23:5 . . . the presence of my *e-ies.*
Ps 62:7 . . . rock where no *e* can reach me.
Prov 16:7 . . . even their *e-ies* are at peace
Prov 25:21 . . . If your *e-ies* are hungry,
Matt 5:44 . . . love your *e-ies!* Pray for those
Luke 10:19 . . . over all the power of the *e*,
Rom 5:10 . . . while we were still his *e-ies,*
Rom 12:20 . . . If your *e-ies* are hungry,
1 Cor 15:26 . . . the last *e* to be destroyed
Phil 3:18 . . . they are really *e-ies* of the cross
Jas 4:4 . . . makes you an *e* of God?
1 Pet 5:8 . . . Watch out for your great *e*,

ENVY (N) discontent or resentment because of another's success, advantages, or superiority
see also JEALOUSY
Mark 7:22 . . . lustful desires, *e*, slander,
Rom 1:29 . . . sin, greed, hate, *e*, murder,
Gal 5:21 . . . *e*, drunkenness, wild parties,
Titus 3:3 . . . full of evil and *e*, and we hated

ENVY (V) to feel or show envy; to begrudge
Prov 3:31 . . . Don't *e* violent people
Prov 24:1 . . . Don't *e* evil people

ETERNAL (ADJ) having infinite duration; valid or existing at all times
see also FOREVER
Dan 4:34 . . . and his kingdom is *e*.
Luke 10:25 . . . should I do to inherit *e* life?
Luke 18:18 . . . should I do to inherit *e* life?
John 3:16 . . . not perish but have *e* life.
John 5:29 . . . will rise to experience *e* life,
John 6:68 . . . the words that give *e* life.
John 17:2 . . . He gives *e* life prepared for
Rom 5:21 . . . resulting in *e* life through
Rom 6:23 . . . free gift of God is *e* life
Rom 16:26 . . . the *e* God has commanded,
Eph 3:11 . . . This was his *e* plan,
Titus 3:7 . . . we will inherit *e* life.
Heb 5:9 . . . source of *e* salvation
Heb 9:15 . . . *e* inheritance God has
Heb 13:20 . . . an *e* covenant with his blood—
1 Pet 1:23 . . . from the *e*, living word
1 Pet 5:10 . . . to share in his *e* glory
1 Jn 2:25 . . . we enjoy the *e* life he
1 Jn 5:20 . . . and he is *e* life.
Jude 1:21 . . . who will bring you *e* life.

EVIL (ADJ) bad, sinful, or morally reprehensible; of the devil
Ps 51:4 . . . what is *e* in your sight.
Matt 6:13 . . . rescue us from the *e* one.
Matt 15:19 . . . from the heart come *e*
John 17:15 . . . them safe from the *e* one.
2 Thes 3:3 . . . guard you from the *e* one.
1 Jn 5:18 . . . the *e* one cannot touch

EVIL (N) something that brings sorrow, distress, or misfortune
Gen 2:9 . . . the knowledge of good and *e*.
Gen 3:5 . . . knowing both good and *e*.
Ps 37:27 . . . Turn from *e* and do good,
Ps 45:7 . . . You love justice and hate *e*.
Ps 101:4 . . . and stay away from every *e*.
Prov 20:30 . . . cleanses away *e;* such
Isa 5:20 . . . those who say that *e* is good
Hab 1:13 . . . cannot stand the sight of *e*.
John 3:20 . . . All who do *e* hate the light
Rom 12:21 . . . Don't let *e* conquer you,
1 Thes 5:15 . . . no one pays back *e* for *e*,
1 Thes 5:22 . . . away from every kind of *e*.
1 Tim 6:10 . . . the root of all kinds of *e*.
Heb 1:9 . . . You love justice and hate *e*.
Jas 1:21 . . . get rid of all the filth and *e*
1 Pet 3:9 . . . Don't repay *e* for *e*.
1 Pet 3:11 . . . Turn away from *e* and do

EXALT (V) to elevate; to glorify; to raise in rank or power
Exod 15:2 . . . and I will *e* him!
Ps 30:1 . . . I will *e* you, LORD,

Ps 107:32 . . . Let them *e* him publicly
Ps 145:1 . . . I will *e* you, my God and King,
Luke 14:11 . . . those who *e* themselves will
2 Thes 2:4 . . . He will *e* himself

EXAMINE (V) to test the condition of; to inspect closely
1 Chr 29:17 . . . you *e* our hearts
Jer 11:20 . . . you *e* the deepest thoughts
Jer 17:10 . . . and *e* secret motives.
Lam 3:40 . . . let us test and *e* our ways.
1 Cor 4:4 . . . Lord himself who will *e*
1 Cor 11:28 . . . you should *e* yourself
2 Cor 13:5 . . . *E* yourselves to see

EXCUSE (N) the apology or justification offered
Rom 1:20 . . . no *e* for not knowing God.
Rom 2:1 . . . and you have no *e!*
1 Pet 2:16 . . . your freedom as an *e*

EXCUSE (V) to overlook, justify, or make an apology for
Exod 34:7 . . . But I do not *e* the guilty.
Eph 5:6 . . . those who try to *e* these sins,

F

FAIL (V) to disappoint; to fall short; to weaken; to miss performing an expected service; to be unsuccessful
Deut 31:6 . . . He will neither *f* you
Luke 13:24 . . . try to enter but will *f*.
Luke 22:32 . . . faith should not *f*.
Heb 13:5 . . . I will never *f* you.
1 Pet 4:19 . . . he will never *f* you.

FAIR (ADJ) free from self-interest, prejudice, or favoritism; beautiful
Isa 11:4 . . . make *f* decisions for the
Rom 3:25 . . . God was being *f* when he
Rom 3:26 . . . he himself is *f* and just,
Col 4:1 . . . be just and *f* to your slaves.

FAITH (N) reliance, loyalty, or complete trust in God; a system of religious beliefs
see also BELIEVE, TRUST
Matt 9:29 . . . Because of your *f*, it will
Matt 17:20 . . . *f* even as small as a mustard
Luke 7:50 . . . Your *f* has saved you;
Luke 12:28 . . . Why do you have so little *f*?
Rom 3:28 . . . right with God through *f*
Rom 4:12 . . . same kind of *f* Abraham had
Rom 10:17 . . . So *f* comes from hearing,
1 Cor 13:13 . . . *f*, hope, and love—
Gal 3:24 . . . made right with God through *f*.
Eph 4:5 . . . one Lord, one *f*, one baptism,
Eph 6:16 . . . hold up the shield of *f*
Phil 3:9 . . . righteous through *f* in Christ.
Heb 10:38 . . . righteous ones will live by *f*.
Heb 12:2 . . . initiates and perfects our *f*.
Jas 2:14 . . . Can that kind of *f* save anyone?
Jas 2:26 . . . so also *f* is dead without good
Jas 5:15 . . . prayer offered in *f* will heal

FAITHFUL (ADJ) firm in adherence, utterly loyal
see also LOYAL, TRUSTWORTHY
Ps 18:25 . . . you show yourself *f*;
Ps 143:1 . . . you are *f* and righteous.
1 Thes 5:24 . . . for he who calls you is *f*.
2 Thes 3:3 . . . But the Lord is *f*; he will
2 Tim 4:7 . . . I have remained *f*.
Heb 2:17 . . . merciful and *f* High Priest
1 Jn 1:9 . . . to him, he is *f* and just to
Rev 17:14 . . . chosen and *f* ones will be

FAITHFULNESS (N) the quality of steadfast loyalty or firm adherence to promises
Exod 34:6 . . . unfailing love and *f*.
Ps 25:10 . . . with unfailing love and *f*
Ps 57:10 . . . Your *f* reaches to the clouds.
Ps 92:2 . . . your *f* in the evening,
Ps 100:5 . . . *f* continues to each
Lam 3:23 . . . Great is his *f*;
Gal 5:22 . . . kindness, goodness, *f*,
Eph 6:23 . . . give you love with *f*.
2 Thes 1:4 . . . your endurance and *f*
2 Tim 2:22 . . . pursue righteous living, *f*,

FALSE (ADJ) intentionally untrue; dishonest; misleading; unwise; faithless
Matt 24:11 . . . And many *f* prophets will
Mark 13:22 . . . For *f* messiahs and *f* prophets
1 Jn 4:1 . . . many *f* prophets in the world.
Rev 20:10 . . . the beast and the *f* prophet.

FAMILY (N) a household unit of related people, as in a clan
Josh 24:15 . . . my *f*, we will serve the LORD.
Mark 3:25 . . . a *f* splintered by feuding
Gal 6:10 . . . to those in the *f* of faith.
Eph 2:19 . . . members of God's *f*.
1 Tim 3:4 . . . manage his own *f* well,
1 Jn 3:9 . . . have been born into God's *f*

FASTING (V) the practice of abstaining, usually from food
Ps 35:13 . . . denied myself by *f* for
Joel 2:12 . . . Come with *f*, weeping,
Acts 13:2 . . . worshiping the Lord and *f*,
Acts 14:23 . . . prayer and *f*, they turned

FATHER, FATHERS (N) male parent; ancestor(s); characteristic of a mentor or provider relationship; name and role for God in relation to the children he fosters/adopts; originator or creator
see also PARENT(S)
Gen 2:24 . . . a man leaves his *f* and mother
Gen 17:4 . . . make you the *f* of a multitude
Exod 20:12 . . . Honor your *f* and mother.
Exod 21:15 . . . Anyone who strikes *f* or
2 Sam 7:14 . . . I will be his *f*, and he
Prov 10:1 . . . wise child brings joy to a *f*;
Prov 23:22 . . . Listen to your *f*, who gave you
Ezek 22:10 . . . sleep with their *f-s'* wives
Mal 4:6 . . . will turn the hearts of *f-s*
Matt 10:37 . . . If you love your *f* or mother
Matt 15:4 . . . Honor your *f* and mother,
Matt 19:5 . . . a man leaves his *f* and mother
Matt 19:29 . . . or *f* or mother or children
Luke 1:17 . . . hearts of the *f-s* to their
Rom 4:11 . . . Abraham is the spiritual *f*
Rom 4:16 . . . Abraham is the *f* of all who
Eph 5:31 . . . man leaves his *f* and mother
Eph 6:2 . . . Honor your *f* and mother.
Eph 6:4 . . . *F-s*, do not provoke
Col 3:21 . . . *F-s*, do not aggravate
Heb 12:7 . . . is never disciplined by its *f*?
Heb 12:9 . . . earthly *f-s* who disciplined

FEAR, FEARS (N) dread or alarm in facing danger; profound reverence and awe
Ps 2:11 . . . Serve the LORD with reverent *f*,
Prov 1:33 . . . untroubled by *f* of harm.
Heb 13:6 . . . will have no *f*.

FEAR (V) to have reverential awe of God; to be afraid or apphrehensive
Deut 13:4 . . . your God and *f* him alone.
Josh 4:24 . . . might *f* the LORD your God
Ps 34:7 . . . and defends all who *f* him.
Ps 46:2 . . . not *f* when earthquakes come
Ps 61:5 . . . for those who *f* your name.
Ps 103:17 . . . with those who *f* him.
Ps 128:1 . . . joyful are those who *f* the
Prov 8:13 . . . All who *f* the LORD will

Prov 28:14 . . . those who *f* to do wrong,
Isa 25:3 . . . nations will *f* you.
Mal 4:2 . . . for you who *f* my name,
2 Cor 7:1 . . . because we *f* God.
Rev 11:18 . . . and all who *f* your name,

FIGHT, FIGHTING, FIGHTS (V) to actively oppose or combat, as with weapons; to gain by struggle
Exod 14:14 . . . LORD himself will *f* for you.
Josh 23:10 . . . LORD your God *f-s* for you,
1 Sam 17:32 . . . I'll go *f* him!
1 Sam 25:28 . . . are *f-ing* the LORD's battles.
Neh 4:20 . . . our God will *f* for us!
Ps 35:1 . . . *F* those who *f* against me.
Prov 28:25 . . . Greed causes *f-ing;*
Isa 49:25 . . . I will *f* those who *f* you,
1 Cor 15:32 . . . value was there in *f-ing* wild
Phil 1:27 . . . one purpose, *f-ing* together for
1 Tim 6:12 . . . *F* the good fight
Jas 4:2 . . . so you *f* and wage war

FIND (V) to attain or reach (a goal or conclusion); to discover by searching or effort; to experience
Prov 11:27 . . . you will *f* favor;
Jer 6:16 . . . will *f* rest for your souls.
Matt 7:7 . . . seeking, and you will *f.*
Matt 10:39 . . . your life for me, you will *f* it.

FIRSTBORN (ADJ) eldest; the most prominent; the rightful heir
Exod 11:5 . . . All the *f* sons will die
Exod 34:20 . . . buy back every *f* son.
Ps 89:27 . . . I will make him my *f* son,
Mic 6:7 . . . sacrifice our *f* children to pay
Heb 12:23 . . . assembly of God's *f* children

FIRSTBORN (N) the eldest offspring; one possessing special rights of inheritance
Gen 25:34 . . . for his rights as the *f.*
Exod 13:2 . . . every *f* among the Israelites.
Exod 34:19 . . . The *f* of every animal

FISH (N) any of numerous cold-blooded aquatic vertebrates
Jonah 1:17 . . . had arranged for a great *f*
Matt 12:40 . . . in the belly of the great *f*
Luke 9:13 . . . loaves of bread and two *f,*
John 6:9 . . . five barley loaves and two *f.*

FISH, FISHED, FISHING (V) to attempt to catch fish
Mark 1:16 . . . for they *f-ed* for a living.
Mark 1:17 . . . how to *f* for people!
Luke 5:10 . . . you'll be *f-ing* for people!

FOLLOW (V) to pursue or run after; to imitate; to obey
Isa 57:2 . . . For those who *f* godly paths
Matt 8:19 . . . I will *f* you wherever you go.
Matt 8:22 . . . *F* me now. Let the
Matt 16:24 . . . take up your cross, and *f*
Matt 19:27 . . . given up everything to *f* you.
Mark 1:17 . . . Come, *f* me, and I will show
Luke 9:23 . . . your cross daily, and *f* me.
Luke 17:23 . . . go out and *f* them.
John 8:12 . . . If you *f* me, you won't have to
John 10:4 . . . they *f* him because they know
John 12:26 . . . wants to serve me must *f* me,
John 21:19 . . . Jesus told him, "*F* me."
Gal 5:25 . . . *f* the Spirit's leading
Phil 3:17 . . . those who *f* our example.
1 Pet 2:21 . . . must *f* in his steps.

FOOL, FOOLS (N) one deficient in intellectual, practical, or moral sense
Ps 14:1 . . . Only *f-s* say in their hearts,
Prov 6:32 . . . commits adultery is an utter *f,*
Prov 10:23 . . . wrong is fun for a *f,*
Prov 17:16 . . . senseless to pay to educate a *f,*
Prov 26:1 . . . associated with *f-s* than snow
Prov 29:20 . . . more hope for a *f* than for
Rom 1:22 . . . became utter *f-s.*
1 Cor 3:18 . . . need to become a *f* to be
Eph 5:15 . . . Don't live like *f-s,*
2 Tim 3:9 . . . recognize what *f-s* they are,

FOOLISH (ADJ) lacking in sense, judgment, or discretion; irreverent
Prov 26:4 . . . the *f* arguments of fools,
1 Cor 1:18 . . . the cross is *f* to those who
1 Cor 1:27 . . . world considers *f* in order to
1 Cor 2:14 . . . It all sounds *f* to them
Eph 5:4 . . . Obscene stories, *f* talk,
1 Tim 6:20 . . . Avoid godless, *f* discussions
Titus 3:9 . . . not get involved in *f* discussions

FOREVER (ADV) for a limitless time; continually
see also ETERNAL
Gen 3:22 . . . they will live *f!*
Gen 17:8 . . . be their possession *f,*
Ps 9:7 . . . the LORD reigns *f,*
Ps 100:5 . . . unfailing love continues *f,*
Isa 51:6 . . . but my salvation lasts *f.*
John 6:51 . . . eats this bread will live *f;*
1 Cor 13:13 . . . Three things will last *f*—
1 Thes 4:17 . . . will be with the Lord *f.*
Heb 7:24 . . . Jesus lives *f,*
Heb 13:8 . . . yesterday, today, and *f.*
1 Pet 1:25 . . . word of the Lord remains *f.*
1 Jn 2:17 . . . will live *f.*
Rev 22:5 . . . they will reign *f* and ever.

FORGAVE (V) to pardon or acquit of guilt
see also FORGIVE
Ps 78:38 . . . was merciful and *f* their sins
Luke 7:42 . . . so he kindly *f* them both,
Eph 1:7 . . . his Son and *f* our sins.
Col 1:14 . . . our freedom and *f* our sins.
Col 2:13 . . . with Christ, for he *f* all our

FORGIVE, FORGIVING (V) to pardon or acquit of sins
see also FORGAVE
Gen 50:17 . . . Please *f* your brothers
Ps 79:9 . . . Save us and *f* our sins
Ps 86:5 . . . so good, so ready to *f,*
Isa 55:7 . . . for he will *f* generously.
Jer 31:34 . . . I will *f* their wickedness,
Dan 9:19 . . . O Lord, hear. O Lord, *f.*
Hos 14:2 . . . *F* all our sins and
Matt 6:12 . . . and *f* us our sins,
Matt 6:15 . . . if you refuse to *f* others,
Matt 9:6 . . . authority on earth to *f* sins.
Matt 26:28 . . . to *f* the sins of many.
Mark 2:7 . . . Only God can *f* sins!
Mark 11:25 . . . first *f* anyone you are
Luke 6:37 . . . *F* others, and you will be
Luke 7:49 . . . he goes around *f-ing* sins?
Luke 17:4 . . . asks forgiveness, you must *f.*
Luke 23:34 . . . Father, *f* them,
1 Jn 1:9 . . . is faithful and just to *f* us

FORGIVENESS (N) aquittal or pardon of sins
see also MERCY
Neh 9:17 . . . you are a God of *f,*
Luke 24:47 . . . There is *f* of sins for all
Acts 13:38 . . . this man Jesus there is *f*
Rom 5:15 . . . his gift of *f* to many
Heb 9:22 . . . of blood, there is no *f.*
Jas 5:20 . . . bring about the *f* of many sins.

FORTRESS (N) a fortified place; a place of security or survival
see also REFUGE
2 Sam 22:2 . . . my *f,* and my savior;

Ps 27:1 . . . The LORD is my *f*,
Ps 71:3 . . . my rock and my *f*.
Ps 144:2 . . . and my *f*, my tower of safety,
Prov 18:10 . . . LORD is a strong *f*;
Zeph 3:6 . . . devastating their *f* walls and

FREEDOM (N) liberation from slavery, restraint, or the power of another
Ps 119:45 . . . I will walk in *f*, for I have
2 Cor 3:17 . . . the Lord is, there is *f*.
Gal 2:4 . . . the *f* we have in Christ
Gal 4:5 . . . sent him to buy *f* for us
Gal 5:13 . . . don't use your *f* to satisfy
Eph 1:7 . . . purchased our *f* with the blood
1 Pet 2:16 . . . don't use your *f* as an excuse

FRIEND, FRIENDS (N) intimate associate; a favored companion
Prov 16:28 . . . separates the best of *f-s*.
Prov 20:6 . . . will say they are loyal *f-s*,
Prov 27:6 . . . Wounds from a sincere *f* are
Prov 29:5 . . . To flatter *f-s* is to lay a trap
John 11:3 . . . Lord, your dear *f* is very sick.
John 15:13 . . . one's life for one's *f-s*.
John 15:14 . . . You are my *f-s* if you do
John 15:15 . . . Now you are my *f-s*,
Jas 2:23 . . . even called the *f* of God.
Jas 4:4 . . . want to be a *f* of the world,

FRIENDSHIP (N) association of familiarity and companionship
Prov 3:32 . . . he offers his *f* to the godly.
Rom 5:10 . . . since our *f* with God was
Jas 4:4 . . . you realize that *f* with the world

FRUIT (N) a product of plant growth; product or result
Matt 3:10 . . . not produce good *f* will be
Matt 7:20 . . . can identify a tree by its *f*,
Matt 12:33 . . . is bad, its *f* will be bad.
John 15:2 . . . that doesn't produce *f*,
Gal 5:22 . . . produces this kind of *f*

FUTURE (N) time that is to come; what is going to happen
Num 24:14 . . . do to your people in the *f*.
Ps 31:15 . . . My *f* is in your hands.
Ps 37:37 . . . a wonderful *f* awaits those
Isa 42:9 . . . tell you the *f* before it happens.
Isa 46:10 . . . can tell you the *f* before it
Jer 29:11 . . . to give you a *f* and a hope.
Jer 31:17 . . . There is hope for your *f*,

G

GENEROUS (ADJ) magnanimous, kindly; liberal in giving; abundant
Deut 15:8 . . . Instead, be *g* and lend
Ps 37:26 . . . godly always give *g* loans to
2 Cor 9:6 . . . will get a *g* crop.
1 Tim 6:18 . . . *g* to those in need,

GIFT (N) a present from people to people (often a bribe); a sacrifice from people to God; anything given voluntarily or at no cost; that which is given from God, enabling or empowering his people
Rom 4:16 . . . given as a free *g*.
Rom 5:15 . . . and God's gracious *g*.
Rom 6:23 . . . free *g* of God is eternal
1 Cor 12:7 . . . A spiritual *g* is given
2 Cor 9:5 . . . I want it to be a willing *g*,
Gal 2:9 . . . recognized the *g* God had
Eph 2:8 . . . it is a *g* from God.
2 Tim 1:6 . . . the spiritual *g* God gave you
1 Pet 3:7 . . . equal partner in God's *g*

GIVE, GIVEN (V) to grant, bestow, convey, offer, provide, or designate; to yield or produce; to suffer the loss of (life)
Exod 30:15 . . . poor must not *g* less.
Prov 21:26 . . . the godly love to *g*!
Prov 23:26 . . . O my son, *g* me your heart.
Isa 9:6 . . . a son is *g-n* to us.
Matt 7:11 . . . heavenly Father *g* good gifts
Matt 16:19 . . . And I will *g* you the keys
Luke 11:13 . . . know how to *g* good gifts to
Luke 22:19 . . . body, which is *g-n* for you.
John 14:27 . . . And the peace I *g* is a gift
Acts 5:32 . . . Spirit, who is *g-n* by God
Acts 20:35 . . . is more blessed to *g* than to
Rom 2:7 . . . He will *g* eternal life
Rom 5:5 . . . because he has *g-n* us the Holy
Rom 12:8 . . . is giving, *g* generously.
1 Cor 11:24 . . . body, which is *g-n* for you.
2 Cor 9:7 . . . how much to *g*.
Eph 4:7 . . . he has *g-n* each one of us
Eph 4:28 . . . and then *g* generously to
1 Jn 4:13 . . . And God has *g-n* us his Spirit

GLAD (ADJ) joyful or happy, often with shouts
Matt 5:12 . . . Be very *g*!
Acts 13:48 . . . they were very *g*
1 Cor 12:26 . . . the parts are *g*.
2 Cor 2:2 . . . will make me *g*?
Rev 19:7 . . . Let us be *g* and rejoice,

GLORY (N) honor bestowed; splendor or magnificence; a distinguishing quality, asset, or attribute
Exod 16:10 . . . awesome *g* of the LORD
Ps 29:1 . . . LORD for his *g* and strength.
Ps 44:8 . . . O God, we give *g* to you
Isa 6:3 . . . earth is filled with his *g*!
Isa 42:8 . . . not give my *g* to anyone else,
Matt 16:27 . . . angels in the *g* of his Father
Matt 25:31 . . . comes in his *g*, and all the
Mark 13:26 . . . great power and *g*.
Luke 2:14 . . . *G* to God in highest heaven,
Luke 9:32 . . . they saw Jesus' *g* and the two
Rom 8:18 . . . compared to the *g* he will
Rom 9:4 . . . God revealed his *g* to them.
Rom 15:6 . . . giving praise and *g* to God,
Rom 16:27 . . . All *g* to the only wise God
1 Cor 10:31 . . . all for the *g* of God.
Phil 4:20 . . . Now all *g* to God our
2 Tim 4:18 . . . All *g* to God forever
Heb 2:9 . . . crowned with *g* and honor.
1 Pet 5:4 . . . of never-ending *g* and honor.
Jude 1:25 . . . All *g*, majesty, power,
Rev 4:9 . . . beings give *g* and honor and
Rev 5:12 . . . honor and *g* and blessing.
Rev 21:11 . . . shone with the *g* of God and
Rev 21:23 . . . for the *g* of God
Rev 21:26 . . . will bring their *g* and honor

GOOD (N) something that is excellent, profitable, or morally right; advancement of prosperity or well-being; something useful or beneficial
Gen 2:9 . . . the knowledge of *g* and evil.
Gen 3:22 . . . knowing both *g* and evil.
Gen 50:20 . . . God intended it all for *g*.
Ps 14:1 . . . not one of them does *g*!
Ps 53:3 . . . No one does *g*, not a single
Prov 11:27 . . . If you search for *g*, you will
Matt 5:45 . . . evil and the *g*, and he sends
Rom 3:12 . . . No one does *g*, not a single
Rom 8:28 . . . together for the *g* of those

GOSSIP (N) rumor or report revealing personal or sensational facts about others
Prov 16:28 . . . of strife; *g* separates the

Prov 26:20 . . . disappear when *g* stops.
2 Cor 12:20 . . . slander, *g*, arrogance,

GOSSIP, GOSSIPING (V) to relate rumors or reports about others
Ps 15:3 . . . who refuse to *g* or harm their
1 Tim 5:13 . . . spend their time *g-ing*

GRACE (N) God's free and unmerited favor toward sinful humanity
Rom 11:5 . . . of God's *g*—his undeserved
1 Cor 3:10 . . . Because of God's *g* to me,
1 Cor 16:23 . . . May the *g* of the Lord
2 Cor 4:15 . . . And as God's *g* reaches more
2 Cor 9:14 . . . of the overflowing *g* God has
Gal 1:15 . . . by his marvelous *g*.
Gal 2:21 . . . do not treat the *g* of God as
Gal 5:4 . . . away from God's *g*.
Eph 1:7 . . . in kindness and *g* that he
Eph 2:8 . . . saved you by his *g* when you
Eph 3:2 . . . of extending his *g* to you
Eph 3:7 . . . By God's *g* and mighty
Phil 4:23 . . . May the *g* of the Lord
2 Thes 2:16 . . . and by his *g* gave us eternal
1 Tim 1:2 . . . Lord give you *g*, mercy,
2 Tim 1:9 . . . show us his *g* through Christ
2 Tim 2:1 . . . strong through the *g* that God
Titus 2:11 . . . For the *g* of God has
Titus 3:7 . . . Because of his *g* he declared
Heb 4:16 . . . and we will find *g* to help us
Heb 13:9 . . . comes from God's *g*, not from
Heb 13:25 . . . May God's *g* be with you all.
Jas 4:6 . . . And he gives *g* generously
2 Pet 3:18 . . . grow in the *g* and knowledge
Rev 22:21 . . . May the *g* of the Lord

GREED (N) a selfish and excessive desire for more of something (as money) than is needed
Prov 15:27 . . . *G* brings grief
Rom 1:29 . . . of wickedness, sin, *g*, hate,
2 Pet 2:3 . . . In their *g* they will make up

GRIEF (N) deep and poignant distress due to bereavement; a cause of suffering
Prov 10:1 . . . a foolish child brings *g* to a
John 16:20 . . . your *g* will suddenly turn

GRIEVE, GRIEVED (V) to feel, show, or cause distress, vexation, sorrow, or regret
Eccl 3:4 . . . A time to *g* and a time
Isa 63:10 . . . rebelled against him and *g-d*
Lam 3:20 . . . time, as I *g* over my loss.
1 Thes 4:13 . . . so you will not *g* like people

GROW, GROWING, GROWS (V) to become; to spring up and develop to maturity
Isa 40:31 . . . run and not *g* weary.
1 Cor 3:6 . . . God who made it *g*.
Eph 4:16 . . . is healthy and *g-ing* and full of
Phil 1:25 . . . all of you *g* and experience
Col 2:19 . . . it *g-s* as God nourishes it.
2 Thes 1:3 . . . one another is *g-ing*.
Jas 1:15 . . . when sin is allowed to *g*,
2 Pet 3:18 . . . Rather, you must *g* in the

GUARD, GUARDING, GUARDS (V) to protect by watchful attention; to watch over
see also KEEP
Prov 4:23 . . . *G* your heart
Prov 7:2 . . . as you *g* your own eyes.
Prov 24:12 . . . He who *g-s* your soul knows
Luke 2:8 . . . fields nearby, *g-ing* their flocks
Phil 4:7 . . . His peace will *g* your hearts
2 Thes 3:3 . . . and *g* you from

GUARDIAN (N) one caring for another person or the property of another
Gen 4:9 . . . Am I my brother's *g*?

Gal 3:25 . . . the law as our *g*.
1 Pet 2:25 . . . your Shepherd, the *G* of your

GUIDE (V) to direct, supervise, or influence usually to a particular end
Exod 15:13 . . . In your might, you *g* them
Ps 139:10 . . . your hand will *g* me,
John 16:13 . . . he will *g* you into all
Gal 5:16 . . . let the Holy Spirit *g* your lives.

GUILT (N) the state or feeling of one who has committed an offense
Job 6:29 . . . Stop assuming my *g*, for I
Ps 32:2 . . . the LORD has cleared of *g*,
Ps 38:4 . . . My *g* overwhelms me—
Ps 51:2 . . . Wash me clean from my *g*.
Isa 6:7 . . . Now your *g* is removed,
Dan 9:24 . . . atone for their *g*, to bring

GUILTY (ADJ) justly chargeable with wrongdoing
Lev 19:17 . . . not be held *g* for their sin.
Rom 3:19 . . . entire world is *g* before God.
1 Cor 11:27 . . . *g* of sinning against
1 Jn 3:20 . . . if we feel *g*, God is greater
1 Jn 3:21 . . . we don't feel *g*, we can come

H

HAPPY (ADJ) expressing, reflecting, or suggestive of happiness
Deut 16:14 . . . festival will be a *h* time
Ps 113:9 . . . making her a *h* mother.
Prov 15:15 . . . for the *h* heart, life is
Rom 12:15 . . . Be *h* with those who are *h*,
Phil 2:2 . . . make me truly *h* by agreeing
Jas 5:13 . . . Are any of you *h*?

HARMONY (N) tranquility; agreement; unity
Rom 12:16 . . . Live in *h* with each other.
Rom 14:19 . . . aim for *h* in the church
1 Cor 12:25 . . . This makes for *h*
2 Cor 6:15 . . . What *h* can there be
2 Cor 13:11 . . . Live in *h* and peace.
Col 3:14 . . . together in perfect *h*.

HARVEST (N) the time or fruit of reaping or gathering in a crop—physically or spiritually
Matt 9:37 . . . The *h* is great, but
John 4:35 . . . fields are already ripe for *h*.

HARVEST, HARVESTS (V) to gather in (a crop); to reap
Gen 8:22 . . . there will be planting and *h*,
Job 4:8 . . . and cultivate evil will *h*
Prov 10:5 . . . wise youth *h-s* in the summer,
Gal 6:8 . . . sinful nature will *h* decay and

HATE (V) to feel extreme enmity toward; to have a strong aversion to
Prov 1:22 . . . you fools *h* knowledge?
Mal 2:16 . . . "For I *h* divorce!"
Matt 5:43 . . . and *h* your enemy.
Luke 6:22 . . . when people *h* you
John 3:20 . . . All who do evil *h* the light
2 Tim 3:3 . . . be cruel and *h* what is good.
Heb 1:9 . . . You love justice and *h* evil.

HEAL, HEALED, HEALING, HEALS (V) to mend, cure, make whole; to restore to health
Num 12:13 . . . I beg you, please *h* her!
2 Chr 30:20 . . . prayer and *h-ed* the people.
Ps 6:2 . . . *H* me, LORD,
Isa 57:18 . . . but I will *h* them anyway!
Jer 17:14 . . . O LORD, if you *h* me, I will
Hos 6:1 . . . now he will *h* us.
Hos 14:4 . . . Then I will *h* you of your
Matt 4:23 . . . And he *h-ed* every kind
Matt 8:7 . . . will come and *h* him.
Matt 8:16 . . . and he *h-ed* all the sick.

Matt 9:35 . . . he ***h-ed*** every kind of disease
Matt 15:30 . . . Jesus, and he ***h-ed*** them all.
Mark 1:34 . . . So Jesus ***h-ed*** many people
Mark 3:2 . . . If he ***h-ed*** the man's
Mark 3:10 . . . He had ***h-ed*** many people
Mark 5:28 . . . touch his robe, I will be ***h-ed.***
Mark 6:56 . . . who touched him were ***h-ed.***
Luke 4:23 . . . Physician, ***h*** yourself
Luke 4:40 . . . his hand ***h-ed*** every one.
Luke 8:50 . . . faith, and she will be ***h-ed.***
Luke 14:3 . . . ***h*** people on the Sabbath
Luke 14:4 . . . the sick man and ***h-ed*** him
Luke 17:19 . . . Your faith has ***h-ed*** you.
Luke 18:42 . . . Your faith has ***h-ed*** you.
John 4:47 . . . to Capernaum to ***h*** his son,
John 12:40 . . . and have me ***h*** them.
Acts 3:16 . . . this man was ***h-ed***—
Acts 4:9 . . . to know how he was ***h-ed?***
Acts 4:14 . . . see the man who had been ***h-ed***
Acts 8:7 . . . or lame were ***h-ed.***
Acts 28:8 . . . his hands on him, he ***h-ed***
Acts 28:27 . . . turn to me and let me ***h***
Jas 5:16 . . . so that you may be ***h-ed.***
1 Pet 2:24 . . . By his wounds you are ***h-ed.***

HEAR (V) to perceive sound; to listen with attention; to be informed of; to take testimony from and make a legal decision
see also LISTEN
2 Chr 7:14 . . . I will ***h*** from heaven and will
Ps 5:1 . . . O LORD, ***h*** me as I pray;
Ps 89:1 . . . Young and old will ***h*** of your
Isa 30:21 . . . own ears will ***h*** him.
Matt 11:5 . . . cured, the deaf ***h,*** the dead
Matt 13:14 . . . When you ***h*** what I say,
Mark 4:12 . . . When they ***h*** what I say,
Luke 7:22 . . . cured, the deaf ***h,*** the dead
Acts 13:7 . . . he wanted to ***h*** the word of
Rom 10:14 . . . how can they ***h*** about him
1 Cor 12:17 . . . how would you ***h?***
Heb 3:7 . . . Today when you ***h*** his voice,
Rev 3:20 . . . If you ***h*** my voice and

HEART, HEARTS (N) figuratively, the seat of emotions, thoughts, and intentions; personality, disposition; courage; love, affection; central or most vital part of something
Gen 6:6 . . . It broke his ***h.***
Deut 6:5 . . . LORD your God with all your ***h,***
Josh 22:5 . . . with all your ***h*** and all your
1 Sam 12:20 . . . the LORD with all your ***h,***
1 Sam 13:14 . . . a man after his own ***h.***
1 Sam 16:7 . . . but the LORD looks at the ***h.***
Ps 9:1 . . . praise you, LORD, with all my ***h;***
Ps 19:14 . . . meditation of my ***h***
Ps 51:10 . . . Create in me a clean ***h,*** O God.
Ps 111:1 . . . thank the LORD with all my ***h***
Ps 139:23 . . . and know my ***h;*** test me and
Prov 3:3 . . . deep within your ***h.***
Prov 4:23 . . . Guard your ***h*** above all else,
Prov 15:13 . . . a broken ***h*** crushes the
Matt 12:34 . . . whatever is in your ***h***
Matt 15:19 . . . For from the ***h*** come evil
Matt 22:37 . . . God with all your ***h,*** all your
Mark 12:33 . . . love him with all my ***h*** and
Acts 1:24 . . . you know every ***h.*** Show us
Rom 2:29 . . . changed ***h*** seeks praise
Rom 10:9 . . . believe in your ***h*** that God
Eph 3:13 . . . don't lose ***h*** because of my

HEAVEN, HEAVENS (N) sky and stars above; God's dwelling place; abode of eternal bliss
Deut 30:12 . . . is not kept in ***h,*** so distant
Job 41:11 . . . Everything under ***h*** is mine.
Ps 18:16 . . . down from ***h*** and rescued me;
Ps 71:19 . . . to the highest ***h-s.*** You have
Ps 108:4 . . . than the ***h-s.*** Your faithfulness
Matt 11:25 . . . Father, Lord of ***h*** and earth,
Matt 24:30 . . . appear in the ***h-s,*** and there
Rom 10:6 . . . go up to ***h?'*** (to bring Christ
2 Cor 12:2 . . . to the third ***h*** fourteen years
Heb 9:24 . . . He entered into ***h*** itself to

HELL (N) abode of the dead; place of punishment; personification of evil; lowest place one can go
Matt 5:22 . . . of the fires of ***h.***
Matt 16:18 . . . all the powers of ***h*** will not
Matt 23:33 . . . judgment of ***h?***
Mark 9:43 . . . fires of ***h*** with two hands.
Luke 12:5 . . . throw you into ***h.***
Jas 3:6 . . . on fire by ***h*** itself.
2 Pet 2:4 . . . threw them into ***h,*** in gloomy

HELP, HELPED, HELPING, HELPS (V) to give assistance or support; to rescue or save
Exod 23:5 . . . Instead, stop and ***h.***
Deut 2:36 . . . our God also ***h-ed*** us conquer
1 Sam 7:12 . . . the LORD has ***h-ed*** us!
Ps 46:1 . . . always ready to ***h*** in times of
Ps 72:12 . . . he will ***h*** the oppressed,
Ps 145:14 . . . The LORD ***h-s*** the fallen
Prov 11:4 . . . Riches won't ***h*** on the
Prov 14:31 . . . their Maker, but ***h-ing*** the poor
Prov 19:17 . . . If you ***h*** the poor,
Isa 41:10 . . . strengthen you and ***h*** you.
Isa 44:10 . . . that cannot ***h*** him one bit?
Jer 51:9 . . . We would have ***h-ed*** her if we
Lam 4:16 . . . he no longer ***h-s*** them.
Mark 9:24 . . . but ***h*** me overcome
Acts 9:36 . . . for others and ***h-ing*** the poor.
Acts 16:9 . . . to Macedonia and ***h*** us!
Rom 12:13 . . . be ready to ***h*** them.
1 Cor 12:28 . . . those who can ***h*** others,
2 Cor 6:2 . . . salvation, I ***h-ed*** you.
Gal 6:1 . . . and humbly ***h*** that person back
1 Tim 5:10 . . . Has she ***h-ed*** those who
2 Tim 2:7 . . . Lord will ***h*** you understand
Heb 10:33 . . . you ***h-ed*** others who
1 Pet 4:11 . . . the gift of ***h-ing*** others?

HELPLESS (ADJ) without any aid, comfort, protection, or chance of success
Ps 9:12 . . . cares for the ***h.*** He does not
Ps 10:12 . . . not ignore the ***h!***
Ps 34:2 . . . let all who are ***h*** take heart.
Ps 35:10 . . . Who else protects the ***h***
Amos 2:7 . . . They trample ***h*** people in the
Matt 9:36 . . . confused and ***h,*** like sheep
Rom 5:6 . . . were utterly ***h,*** Christ came

HOLY (ADJ) consecrated or set aside for sacred use (as opposed to pagan or common use); standing apart from sin and evil; characteristic of God, especially the third person of the Trinity
Gen 2:3 . . . and declared it ***h,*** because it
Exod 26:33 . . . separate the ***H*** Place
Exod 31:13 . . . the LORD, who makes you ***h.***
Lev 11:45 . . . you must be ***h*** because I am
Lev 22:32 . . . the LORD who makes you ***h.***
Deut 5:12 . . . by keeping it ***h,*** as the LORD
Josh 5:15 . . . where you are standing is ***h.***
Isa 6:3 . . . to each other, "***H, h, h***
Mark 1:24 . . . you are—the ***H*** One of God
Luke 1:35 . . . baby to be born will be ***h,***
Rom 15:16 . . . made ***h*** by the ***H*** Spirit.
1 Cor 1:2 . . . be his own ***h*** people.
1 Cor 1:30 . . . made us pure and ***h,***
Eph 1:4 . . . in Christ to be ***h*** and without
Eph 2:21 . . . becoming a ***h*** temple for

Eph 4:24 . . . righteous and ***h.***
Col 1:22 . . . and you are ***h*** and blameless
1 Thes 4:7 . . . called us to live ***h*** lives,
1 Thes 5:23 . . . make you ***h*** in every
2 Tim 1:9 . . . called us to live a ***h*** life.
Heb 10:29 . . . which made us ***h,*** as if it
1 Pet 1:16 . . . You must be ***h*** because I am
Rev 3:7 . . . one who is ***h*** and true,
Rev 4:8 . . . on saying, "***H, h, h*** is

HOLY SPIRIT the third person of the Holy Trinity
see ADVOCATE, COUNSELOR
Luke 11:13 . . . give the ***H*** to those
2 Cor 5:5 . . . he has given us his ***H.***
Eph 1:13 . . . ***H,*** whom he promised
Eph 4:30 . . . sorrow to God's ***H***
1 Thes 4:8 . . . gives his ***H*** to you

HONEST (ADJ) truthful; genuine; reputable; marked by integrity
Exod 18:21 . . . some capable, ***h*** men
2 Kgs 12:15 . . . were ***h*** and trustworthy
Ps 37:37 . . . those who are ***h*** and good,
Prov 12:17 . . . An ***h*** witness tells
Prov 28:6 . . . Better to be poor and ***h*** than
Jer 5:1 . . . even one just and ***h*** person,
Matt 22:16 . . . we know how ***h*** you are.
1 Thes 2:10 . . . devout and ***h*** and faultless

HOPE, HOPES (N) confident trust with the expectation of fulfillment
1 Sam 9:20 . . . focus of all Israel's ***h-s.***
Job 31:16 . . . crushed the ***h-s*** of widows?
Ps 10:17 . . . LORD, you know the ***h-s*** of the
Ps 42:5 . . . I will put my ***h*** in God!
Ps 112:10 . . . slink away, their ***h-s*** thwarted.
Ps 119:49 . . . to me; it is my only ***h.***
Ps 119:74 . . . I have put my ***h*** in your word.
Prov 10:24 . . . the ***h-s*** of the godly will be
Prov 13:12 . . . ***H*** deferred makes the heart
Zech 9:12 . . . prisoners who still have ***h!***
Rom 5:4 . . . our confident ***h*** of salvation.
Rom 8:20 . . . curse. But with eager ***h,***
Rom 12:12 . . . Rejoice in our confident ***h.***
Rom 15:4 . . . give us ***h*** and encouragement
Rom 15:13 . . . God, the source of ***h,*** will
1 Cor 13:13 . . . faith, ***h,*** and love—
1 Cor 15:19 . . . And if our ***h*** in Christ is
Eph 2:12 . . . without God and without ***h.***
1 Thes 1:3 . . . and the enduring ***h*** you have
1 Tim 4:10 . . . struggle, for our ***h*** is in the
Heb 10:23 . . . wavering to the ***h*** we affirm,
1 Pet 3:15 . . . about your ***h*** as a believer,

HUMBLE (ADJ) not proud or haughty; can imply lower social or economic status; meek or gentle
Num 12:3 . . . Moses was very ***h***—
Ps 138:6 . . . cares for the ***h,*** but he keeps
Ps 149:4 . . . he crowns the ***h*** with victory.
Zech 9:9 . . . yet he is ***h,*** riding on a
Matt 5:5 . . . those who are ***h,***
Matt 11:29 . . . I am ***h*** and gentle at
Matt 21:5 . . . He is ***h,*** riding on a
Eph 4:2 . . . Always be ***h*** and gentle.
Phil 2:3 . . . Be ***h,*** thinking of
Jas 4:6 . . . but gives grace to the ***h.***
1 Pet 3:8 . . . and keep a ***h*** attitude.

HUMBLE (V) to not think too highly of oneself; to bring low or prostrate
Jas 4:10 . . . ***H*** yourselves before the Lord,
1 Pet 5:6 . . . So ***h*** yourselves under

HUMILITY (N) show of meekness; quality of being humble
Prov 11:2 . . . but with ***h*** comes wisdom.
Prov 15:33 . . . ***h*** precedes honor.
Prov 22:4 . . . True ***h*** and fear
Col 3:12 . . . kindness, ***h,*** gentleness,
Jas 3:13 . . . works with the ***h*** that comes
1 Pet 5:5 . . . dress yourselves in ***h*** as you

HYPOCRITE, HYPOCRITES (N) a person who portrays a false appearance of religion; a pretender
Matt 6:16 . . . make it obvious, as the ***h-s***
Matt 7:5 . . . ***H!*** First get rid of the log
Matt 23:13 . . . and you Pharisees. ***H-s!***
Luke 6:42 . . . the log in your own eye? ***H!***
Luke 13:15 . . . Lord replied, "You ***h-s!***
1 Tim 4:2 . . . These people are ***h-s*** and liars,

I

IDOL, IDOLS (N) a representation or symbol of a false god
Exod 20:4 . . . make for yourself an ***i***
Deut 27:15 . . . who carves or casts an ***i***
1 Sam 15:23 . . . as bad as worshiping ***i-s.***
Isa 40:19 . . . Can he be compared to an ***i***
Isa 44:9 . . . who worship ***i-s*** don't know
Isa 44:15 . . . makes an ***i*** and bows down
Isa 44:17 . . . and makes his god: a carved ***i!***
Isa 44:19 . . . who made the ***i*** never stops to
Hab 2:18 . . . What good is an ***i*** carved
Acts 15:20 . . . eating food offered to ***i-s,***
Rom 1:23 . . . worshiped ***i-s*** made to look
1 Cor 6:9 . . . or who worship ***i-s,*** or commit
1 Cor 8:1 . . . has been offered to ***i-s.***
1 Cor 8:4 . . . an ***i*** is not really a god
Rev 2:14 . . . sin by eating food offered to ***i-s***

IMAGE (N) a God-given likeness or reflection; a tangible or visible representation
Gen 1:26 . . . make human beings in our ***i,***
Gen 1:27 . . . human beings in his own ***i.***
Gen 9:6 . . . made human beings in his own ***i.***
Col 1:15 . . . Christ is the visible ***i*** of the
Jas 3:9 . . . made in the ***i*** of God.

IMPOSSIBLE (ADJ) incapable of being or occurring
Zech 8:6 . . . this may seem ***i*** to you now,
Heb 6:4 . . . it is ***i*** to bring back
Heb 11:6 . . . it is ***i*** to please God

INHERITANCE (N) the acquisition of a possession, condition, or trait from past generations; something that is or may be inherited
Gal 4:30 . . . will not share the ***i***
Eph 1:14 . . . give us the ***i*** he promised
Col 3:24 . . . give you an ***i*** as your reward,
Heb 9:15 . . . receive the eternal ***i*** God has

INNOCENT (ADJ) regarded as righteous; free from guilt or sin; unaware or ignorant
Ps 7:8 . . . for I am ***i,*** O Most High!
Matt 27:4 . . . I have betrayed an ***i*** man.
Matt 27:24 . . . I am ***i*** of this man's blood.
Rom 16:18 . . . they deceive ***i*** people.

INSTRUCT (V) to provide with authoritative information or advice; to teach, train, or direct
Exod 4:12 . . . I will ***i*** you in what to say.
Prov 9:9 . . . ***I*** the wise, and they will be
Prov 21:11 . . . if you ***i*** the wise,
2 Tim 2:25 . . . Gently ***i*** those who oppose

INSTRUCTION, INSTRUCTIONS (N) a command or principle intended especially as a general rule of action; an order; directions; the action, practice, or profession of teaching
see also COMMANDMENT(S), LAW
Exod 34:32 . . . Moses gave them all the ***i-s***

Deut 31:11 . . . you must read this Book of *I*
Josh 1:7 . . . Be careful to obey all the *i-s*
Josh 1:8 . . . Study this Book of *I*
Ps 40:8 . . . *i-s* are written on my heart.
Prov 4:13 . . . Take hold of my *i-s;*
Prov 7:2 . . . Guard my *i-s* as you guard
Prov 8:33 . . . Listen to my *i* and be wise.
Prov 23:12 . . . Commit yourself to *i;*
Isa 40:14 . . . need *i* about what is good?
Jer 31:33 . . . put my *i-s* deep within
Zech 7:12 . . . they could not hear the *i-s*
1 Tim 1:5 . . . purpose of my *i* is that all
1 Tim 1:18 . . . here are my *i-s* for you,

INTEGRITY (N) honesty; without compromise or corruption
Job 2:3 . . . a man of complete *i.*
Ps 111:8 . . . faithfully and with *i.*
Ps 119:1 . . . Joyful are people of *i,*
Prov 2:7 . . . shield to those who walk with *i.*
Prov 10:9 . . . People with *i* walk safely,
Titus 2:7 . . . you do reflect the *i*

ISRAEL 1. Another name for Jacob (Gen 32:28).
2. The united kingdom of Israel, including all twelve tribes, as ruled by Saul, David, and Solomon.
3. The northern kingdom of Israel, including the ten northern tribes, in contrast to Judah (southern kingdom) (*see* 2 Sam 19:41-43).

J

JEALOUSY (N) a jealous feeling, disposition, or attitude
Rom 13:13 . . . or in quarreling and *j.*
Gal 5:20 . . . *j,* outbursts of anger,
1 Tim 6:4 . . . arguments ending in *j,*
1 Pet 2:1 . . . with all deceit, hypocrisy, *j,*

JERUSALEM (N) sacred city and well-known capital of Palestine during Bible times
2 Chr 3:1 . . . the Temple of the LORD in *J*
2 Chr 36:19 . . . tore down the walls of *J,*
Ezra 2:1 . . . but now they returned to *J*
Neh 1:3 . . . The wall of *J* has been torn
Ps 51:18 . . . rebuild the walls of *J.*
Ps 122:6 . . . Pray for peace in *J.*
Dan 6:10 . . . windows open toward *J.*
Zech 14:8 . . . waters will flow out from *J,*
Matt 20:18 . . . going up to *J,* where the Son
Luke 2:22 . . . parents took him to *J*
Luke 4:9 . . . Then the devil took him to *J,*
Acts 1:8 . . . about me everywhere—in *J,*
Rev 21:10 . . . he showed me the holy city, *J,*

JOY (N) the emotion evoked by well-being, success, or good fortune
Deut 16:15 . . . be a time of great *j* for all.
Neh 8:10 . . . *j* of the LORD is your strength!
Ps 9:2 . . . filled with *j* because of you.
Ps 28:7 . . . my heart is filled with *j.*
Ps 32:2 . . . what *j* for those whose record
Ps 51:12 . . . to me the *j* of your salvation,
Ps 65:13 . . . They all shout and sing for *j!*
Ps 92:4 . . . I sing for *j* because of what
Ps 132:9 . . . loyal servants sing for *j.*
Prov 10:1 . . . A wise child brings *j*
Prov 15:20 . . . Sensible children bring *j* to
Prov 23:25 . . . your father and mother *j!*
Isa 35:10 . . . crowned with everlasting *j.*
Isa 51:11 . . . filled with *j* and gladness.
Isa 61:7 . . . everlasting *j* will be yours.
Matt 2:10 . . . they were filled with *j!*
John 15:11 . . . you will be filled with my *j.*
John 16:20 . . . turn to wonderful *j.*
Acts 2:28 . . . you will fill me with the *j*
Acts 2:46 . . . their meals with great *j*
Acts 11:23 . . . he was filled with *j,*
Acts 13:52 . . . believers were filled with *j*
Gal 5:22 . . . fruit in our lives: love, *j,* peace,
Phil 4:1 . . . you are my *j* and the crown
1 Thes 1:6 . . . received the message with *j*
1 Thes 2:19 . . . what gives us hope and *j,*
1 Thes 3:9 . . . we have great *j*
Jas 1:2 . . . it an opportunity for great *j.*
1 Jn 1:4 . . . you may fully share our *j.*

JUDEA (N) the Greco-Roman name for the land of Judah
Matt 2:1 . . . was born in Bethlehem in *J,*
Matt 24:16 . . . in *J* must flee to the hills.
Luke 3:1 . . . Pilate was governor over *J;*
Acts 1:8 . . . throughout *J,* in Samaria,
Acts 9:31 . . . had peace throughout *J,*
1 Thes 2:14 . . . in God's churches in *J*

JUDGE, JUDGES (N) a public official authorized to decide issues brought before a court; one of a cycle of charismatic deliverers of ancient Israel
Deut 17:12 . . . to reject the verdict of the *j*
Judg 2:16 . . . LORD raised up *j-s* to rescue
Judg 2:18 . . . the LORD raised up a *j*
1 Sam 7:6 . . . Samuel became Israel's *j.*)
1 Sam 7:15 . . . continued as Israel's *j*
Ps 50:6 . . . God himself will be the *j.*
Isa 33:22 . . . the LORD is our *j,* our lawgiver,
Acts 7:35 . . . you a ruler and *j* over us?
Acts 10:42 . . . *j* of all—the living and
Rev 14:7 . . . he will sit as *j.*

JUDGE, JUDGED, JUDGES, JUDGING (V) to form an evaluation of; to decide as a judge; to govern or rule; to punish or condemn; to form a negative opinion about
1 Sam 16:7 . . . Don't *j* by his appearance or
1 Sam 24:12 . . . the LORD *j* between us.
2 Chr 19:7 . . . *j* with integrity, for the LORD
Ps 7:8 . . . The LORD *j-s* the nations.
Ps 9:4 . . . For you have *j-d* in my favor;
Ps 9:8 . . . He will *j* the world
Ps 82:8 . . . Rise up, O God, and *j* the earth,
Ps 96:10 . . . He will *j* all peoples fairly.
Ps 96:13 . . . will *j* the world with justice,
Prov 16:10 . . . he must never *j* unfairly.
Prov 29:14 . . . If a king *j-s* the poor fairly,
Isa 11:3 . . . He will not *j* by appearance
Isa 66:16 . . . He will *j* the earth,
Matt 7:1 . . . Do not *j* others, and you
Matt 16:27 . . . will *j* all people according
Matt 19:28 . . . thrones, *j-ing* the twelve
John 3:18 . . . been *j-d* for not believing
John 5:22 . . . the Father *j-s* no one.
John 5:22 . . . absolute authority to *j,*
John 5:27 . . . authority to *j* everyone
John 5:30 . . . I *j* as God tells me.
John 12:31 . . . time for *j-ing* this world
John 12:47 . . . not *j* those who hear me
Acts 17:31 . . . he has set a day for *j-ing*
Rom 2:16 . . . Jesus, will *j* everyone's secret
Rom 3:6 . . . be qualified to *j* the world?
1 Cor 6:2 . . . we believers will *j* the world?
1 Cor 11:31 . . . we would not be *j-d*
2 Cor 5:10 . . . stand before Christ to be *j-d.*
2 Tim 4:1 . . . Jesus, who will someday *j*
Heb 10:30 . . . The LORD will *j* his own
Heb 13:4 . . . *j* people who are immoral
Jas 2:13 . . . will be merciful when he *j-s*
Jas 3:1 . . . we who teach will be *j-d* more
Jas 4:11 . . . criticizing and *j-ing* God's law.
Jas 4:12 . . . So what right do you have to *j*
1 Pet 1:17 . . . He will *j* or reward you
1 Pet 2:23 . . . God, who always *j-s* fairly.

Rev 19:11 . . . *j-s* fairly and wages a righteous
Rev 20:4 . . . given the authority to *j.*
Rev 20:12 . . . the dead were *j-d* according to

JUSTICE (N) the administration of law that determines what is right, based on principles of equity and correctness, and rewards accordingly; the quality of being just, impartial, or fair
see also RIGHTEOUSNESS
Exod 23:2 . . . by the crowd to twist *j.*
Lev 19:15 . . . Do not twist *j* in legal matters
Deut 32:36 . . . LORD will give *j* to his
Ps 9:8 . . . He will judge the world with *j*
Ps 45:7 . . . You love *j* and hate evil.
Ps 72:1 . . . Give your love of *j* to the king,
Ps 96:13 . . . He will judge the world with *j,*
Ps 98:9 . . . *j,* and the nations with fairness.
Ps 99:4 . . . You have acted with *j*
Ps 103:6 . . . *j* to all who are treated
Prov 16:12 . . . his rule is built on *j.*
Prov 19:28 . . . makes a mockery of *j;*
Prov 29:26 . . . but *j* comes from the LORD.
Prov 31:9 . . . and see that they get *j.*
Isa 10:2 . . . They deprive the poor of *j*
Isa 28:17 . . . with the measuring line of *j*
Isa 42:1 . . . He will bring *j* to the nations.
Isa 59:9 . . . there is no *j* among us,
Isa 61:8 . . . I, the LORD, love *j.*
Jer 4:2 . . . you could do so with truth, *j,*
Jer 21:12 . . . Give *j* each morning
Jer 30:11 . . . discipline you, but with *j;*
Lam 3:36 . . . if they twist *j* in the courts—
Amos 5:15 . . . courts into true halls of *j.*
Mic 3:8 . . . I am filled with *j* and strength
Hab 1:4 . . . there is no *j* in the courts.
Zeph 3:5 . . . Day by day he hands down *j,*
Mal 2:17 . . . Where is the God of *j?*
Matt 5:6 . . . who hunger and thirst for *j,*
Matt 12:18 . . . proclaim *j* to the nations.
Luke 11:42 . . . ignore *j* and the love of God.
Luke 18:3 . . . Give me *j* in this dispute
Acts 17:31 . . . *j* by the man he has appointed
Rom 2:2 . . . God, in his *j,* will punish
2 Thes 1:5 . . . persecution to show his *j*
2 Thes 1:6 . . . In his *j* he will pay back
Heb 1:8 . . . You rule with a scepter of *j.*
Heb 11:33 . . . ruled with *j,* and received

K

KEEP, KEPT (V) to be faithful to; to have in control; to refrain from granting, giving, or allowing; to cause to remain in a given place, situation, or condition; to refrain from revealing; to maintain or preserve
see also GUARD, OBEY, PROTECT
Exod 12:42 . . . the LORD *k-pt* his promise
Deut 7:12 . . . your God will *k* his covenant
Ps 15:4 . . . *k* their promises even when
Prov 10:19 . . . and *k* your mouth shut
Eccl 3:6 . . . A time to *k* and a time to
John 17:6 . . . and they have *k-pt* your word.
Acts 2:24 . . . death could not *k* him in its
Rom 10:3 . . . by trying to *k* the law.
Rom 14:22 . . . *k* it between yourself
1 Cor 1:8 . . . He will *k* you strong
1 Cor 13:5 . . . it *k-s* no record
Eph 4:3 . . . effort to *k* yourselves united
1 Tim 5:22 . . . *K* yourself pure.
2 Tim 4:5 . . . But you should *k* a clear mind
Heb 11:27 . . . going because he *k-pt* his eyes
1 Pet 1:4 . . . *k-pt* in heaven for you, pure
Jude 1:21 . . . *k* yourselves safe in God's love.
Rev 12:17 . . . *k* God's commandments

KILL (V) to take or deprive of life
Job 13:15 . . . God might *k* me, but I
Prov 6:17 . . . hands that *k* the innocent,
Prov 23:13 . . . punishment won't *k* them
Eccl 3:3 . . . A time to *k* and a time to
Matt 10:28 . . . who want to *k* your body;
Mark 10:34 . . . flog him with a whip, and *k*
1 Tim 1:9 . . . who *k* their father or mother

KINGDOM (N) rule or realm; dominion of a king
Ps 145:11 . . . glory of your *k;*
Matt 3:2 . . . for the *K* of Heaven is near.
Matt 5:10 . . . right, for the *K* of Heaven is
Matt 6:10 . . . May your *K* come soon.
Matt 7:21 . . . will enter the *K* of Heaven.
Matt 18:4 . . . greatest in the *K* of Heaven.
Matt 19:12 . . . sake of the *K* of Heaven.
Matt 19:23 . . . to enter the *K* of Heaven.
Matt 20:1 . . . For the *K* of Heaven is
Mark 9:1 . . . they see the *K* of God arrive
Luke 10:11 . . . know this—the *K* of God is
Luke 12:31 . . . Seek the *K* of God
Luke 13:18 . . . What is the *K* of God like?
Luke 17:20 . . . When will the *K* of God
Luke 23:42 . . . come into your *K.*
John 3:3 . . . you cannot see the *K* of God.
John 18:36 . . . But my *K* is not of
1 Cor 6:10 . . . will inherit the *K* of God.
1 Cor 15:24 . . . will turn the *K* over to God
Gal 5:21 . . . will not inherit the *K* of God.
Eph 5:5 . . . will inherit the *K* of Christ

KNEEL, KNELT (V) to bend the knee; to fall or rest on the knees; usually a gesture of submission, defeat, or reverence
2 Chr 6:13 . . . then he *k-lt* in front of
Ps 95:6 . . . Let us *k* before the LORD
Dan 6:10 . . . went home and *k-lt* down
Matt 8:2 . . . approached him and *k-lt*
Matt 9:18 . . . came and *k-lt* before him.
Matt 17:14 . . . came and *k-lt* before Jesus
Matt 27:29 . . . *k-lt* before him in mockery
Luke 22:41 . . . stone's throw, and *k-lt* down
Acts 20:36 . . . speaking, he *k-lt* and prayed
Acts 21:5 . . . There we *k-lt,* prayed,

KNOW (V) to be intimately familiar with; to discern, recognize, regard, acknowledge, pay heed to, approve, learn
Exod 6:7 . . . Then you will *k* that I am the
Ps 46:10 . . . Be still, and *k* that I am
Ps 139:2 . . . You *k* when I sit
Jer 31:34 . . . will *k* me already,
Matt 6:3 . . . don't let your left hand *k* what
Mark 12:24 . . . you don't *k* the Scriptures,
Luke 13:25 . . . will reply, 'I don't *k* you
Luke 23:34 . . . they don't *k* what they are
John 3:11 . . . you what we *k* and have seen,
John 6:69 . . . we *k* you are the Holy One
John 7:28 . . . Yes, you *k* me, and you
John 8:32 . . . And you will *k* the truth,
John 10:4 . . . because they *k* his voice.
John 10:27 . . . I *k* them, and they follow
Acts 1:24 . . . O Lord, you *k* every heart.
Rom 1:19 . . . They *k* the truth
Rom 12:16 . . . And don't think you *k* it all!
1 Cor 2:11 . . . no one can *k* God's thoughts
Phil 3:10 . . . I want to *k* Christ and
Col 1:10 . . . you learn to *k* God better and
Jas 4:17 . . . it is sin to *k* what you ought
1 Jn 2:3 . . . we can be sure that we *k* him
1 Jn 2:29 . . . Since we *k* that Christ
1 Jn 3:1 . . . they don't *k* him.
1 Jn 3:24 . . . And we *k* he lives in us

1 Jn 4:8 . . . does not ***k*** God, for God
1 Jn 5:15 . . . And since we ***k*** he hears us
Rev 3:15 . . . I ***k*** all the things you do,

KNOWLEDGE (N) the fact or condition of being aware of something, of having information, or of being learned; information, wisdom
Gen 2:9 . . . the tree of the ***k*** of good and
Gen 2:17 . . . the tree of the ***k*** of good and
Prov 2:6 . . . From his mouth come ***k*** and
Prov 8:10 . . . ***k*** rather than pure gold.
Prov 18:15 . . . Their ears are open for ***k***.
Luke 11:52 . . . remove the key to ***k*** from
Rom 2:20 . . . gives you complete ***k***
2 Cor 2:14 . . . to spread the ***k*** of Christ
Eph 1:17 . . . grow in your ***k*** of God.
Eph 4:13 . . . our faith and ***k*** of God's Son
Phil 1:9 . . . will keep on growing in ***k*** and
Col 1:9 . . . to give you complete ***k*** of his
Col 2:3 . . . treasures of wisdom and ***k***.
Heb 10:26 . . . we have received ***k*** of the
2 Pet 1:5 . . . and moral excellence with ***k***,
2 Pet 1:8 . . . ***k*** of our Lord Jesus Christ.
2 Pet 3:18 . . . the grace and ***k*** of our Lord

L

LAMB, LAMBS (N) a young sheep that is less than one year old
Exod 12:21 . . . pick out a ***l*** or young goat
Isa 53:7 . . . He was led like a ***l*** to the
Mark 14:12 . . . the Passover ***l*** is sacrificed,
Luke 10:3 . . . out as ***l-s*** among wolves.
John 1:29 . . . and said, "Look! The ***L*** of God
John 21:15 . . . "Then feed my ***l-s***," Jesus
Acts 8:32 . . . And as a ***l*** is silent before
1 Pet 1:19 . . . sinless, spotless ***L*** of God.
Rev 5:6 . . . Then I saw a ***L*** that looked as
Rev 5:12 . . . Worthy is the ***L*** who was
Rev 7:14 . . . robes in the blood of the ***L***
Rev 15:3 . . . the song of the ***L***:
Rev 17:14 . . . to war against the ***L***, but the
Rev 19:9 . . . to the wedding feast of the ***L***.
Rev 21:23 . . . and the ***L*** is its light.

LAMP, LAMPS (N) a source of intellectual or spiritual illumination; any of various devices for producing light
2 Sam 22:29 . . . O LORD, you are my ***l***.
Ps 18:28 . . . You light a ***l*** for me.
Ps 119:105 . . . Your word is a ***l*** to guide my
Prov 6:23 . . . For their command is a ***l***
Prov 31:18 . . . her ***l*** burns late
Matt 6:22 . . . Your eye is a ***l*** that
Matt 25:1 . . . who took their ***l-s***
Matt 25:7 . . . got up and prepared their ***l-s***.
Luke 8:16 . . . No one lights a ***l*** and then
Luke 12:35 . . . and keep your ***l-s*** burning,
Rev 22:5 . . . no need for ***l-s*** or sun—for the

LAMPSTAND, LAMPSTANDS (N) a support that holds a lamp
Exod 25:31 . . . Make the entire ***l*** and its
2 Chr 4:7 . . . cast ten gold ***l-s*** according to
Zech 4:2 . . . a solid gold ***l*** with a bowl of
Zech 4:11 . . . on each side of the ***l***,
Heb 9:2 . . . In the first room were a ***l***,
Rev 1:12 . . . I saw seven gold ***l-s***.
Rev 1:20 . . . the seven gold ***l-s***:
Rev 2:5 . . . and remove your ***l*** from its

LAST (ADJ) following all the rest; being the only remaining; belonging to the final stage; of or relating to being continuous in time; existing or continuing a long while
Acts 2:17 . . . 'In the ***l*** days,' God says,
1 Cor 15:52 . . . ***l*** trumpet is blown.
2 Tim 3:1 . . . that in the ***l*** days there will
2 Pet 3:3 . . . that in the ***l*** days scoffers
Jude 1:18 . . . you that in the ***l*** times there
Rev 1:17 . . . I am the First and the ***L***.
Rev 22:13 . . . the Omega, the First and the ***L***,

LAUGH, LAUGHED, LAUGHS (V) to show mirth or joy or to despise or mock something with a chuckle or explosive vocal sound
Gen 17:17 . . . ***l-ed*** to himself in disbelief.
Gen 18:12 . . . So she ***l-ed*** silently to herself
Ps 2:4 . . . one who rules in heaven ***l-s***.
Ps 37:13 . . . the LORD just ***l-s***, for he sees
Ps 59:8 . . . But LORD, you ***l*** at them.
Prov 31:25 . . . and she ***l-s*** without fear of
Eccl 3:4 . . . and a time to ***l***. A time to
Luke 6:21 . . . for in due time you will ***l***.
Luke 6:25 . . . awaits you who ***l*** now,

LAW (N) words of Moses; a binding decree; a universal principle; governing authority
see also COMMANDMENT(S), INSTRUCTION(S)
Ps 1:2 . . . delight in the ***l*** of the LORD,
Matt 5:17 . . . to abolish the ***l*** of Moses or
Matt 22:40 . . . The entire ***l*** and all the
Mark 7:8 . . . ignore God's ***l*** and substitute
John 1:17 . . . For the ***l*** was given
Rom 2:15 . . . that God's ***l*** is written in
Rom 7:22 . . . I love God's ***l*** with all my
Rom 7:25 . . . I really want to obey God's ***l***,
Rom 8:3 . . . did what the ***l*** could not do.
Rom 9:31 . . . with God by keeping the ***l***,
1 Cor 9:9 . . . For the ***l*** of Moses
1 Cor 9:21 . . . I obey the ***l*** of Christ.
Gal 5:14 . . . the whole ***l*** can be summed
Gal 6:2 . . . this way obey the ***l*** of Christ.
Eph 2:15 . . . the system of ***l*** with its
Phil 3:6 . . . I obeyed the ***l*** without fault.
1 Tim 1:8 . . . know that the ***l*** is good when
Jas 1:25 . . . into the perfect ***l*** that sets
Jas 2:8 . . . obey the royal ***l*** as found in

LEAD, LEADING, LEADS (V) to guide by direction or example; to go at the head of; to result in
see also LED
Deut 27:18 . . . anyone who ***l-s*** a blind
Deut 31:2 . . . no longer able to ***l*** you.
Josh 1:6 . . . one who will ***l*** these people
2 Chr 1:10 . . . knowledge to ***l*** them
Ps 25:9 . . . He ***l-s*** the humble in
Ps 73:24 . . . with your counsel, ***l-ing*** me to a
Prov 6:22 . . . counsel will ***l*** you.
Prov 14:30 . . . A peaceful heart ***l-s*** to a
Prov 19:23 . . . Fear of the LORD ***l-s*** to life,
Isa 11:6 . . . little child will ***l*** them all.
Matt 15:14 . . . blind guides ***l-ing*** the blind,
John 10:3 . . . by name and ***l-s*** them out.
Rom 6:16 . . . to sin, which ***l-s*** to death,
Rom 6:22 . . . things that ***l*** to holiness and
1 Tim 5:24 . . . ***l-ing*** them to certain judgment.
Rev 7:17 . . . He will ***l*** them to

LEADER (N) a person who has commanding authority or influence; chief among others
1 Sam 13:14 . . . to be the ***l*** of his people,
Mark 10:43 . . . a ***l*** among you must be
Luke 22:26 . . . ***l*** should be like a servant.
3 Jn 1:9 . . . to be the ***l***, refuses to have

LEARN, LEARNED, LEARNS (V) to come to know or realize; to acquire knowledge, skill, or behavioral tendency
Deut 4:10 . . . Then they will ***l*** to fear me
Deut 5:1 . . . so you may ***l*** them and obey
Prov 9:9 . . . and they will ***l*** even more.

Prov 18:15 . . . are always ready to *l.*
Isa 1:17 . . . *L* to do good.
Isa 26:9 . . . will people *l* what is right.
Isa 29:13 . . . man-made rules *l-ed* by rote.
Matt 2:7 . . . and he *l-ed* from them the time
John 6:45 . . . listens to the Father and *l-s*
Phil 4:9 . . . all you *l-ed* and received from
Phil 4:11 . . . have *l-ed* how to be content
Col 1:10 . . . grow as you *l* to know God
1 Tim 2:11 . . . Women should *l* quietly and
2 Tim 1:13 . . . teaching you *l-ed* from me—
Heb 5:8 . . . he *l-ed* obedience from the

LED (V) to guide by direction or example
see also LEAD
Ps 68:18 . . . the heights, you *l* a crowd of
Isa 53:7 . . . He was *l* like a lamb
Jer 11:19 . . . like a lamb being *l* to the
Luke 4:1 . . . He was *l* by the Spirit
Acts 8:32 . . . He was *l* like a sheep
Rom 8:14 . . . all who are *l* by the Spirit
Eph 4:8 . . . the heights, he *l* a crowd of

LEPROSY (N) a chronic infectious disease affecting the skin and peripheral nerves which causes loss of sensation, paralysis, and deformities
Num 12:10 . . . as white as snow from *l.*
2 Kgs 5:1 . . . he suffered from *l.*
2 Kgs 7:3 . . . four men with *l* sitting at
2 Chr 26:21 . . . King Uzziah had *l* until the

LIAR (N) a person who deceives by telling untruths or falsehoods
Rom 3:4 . . . else is a *l,* God is true.
1 Jn 1:10 . . . calling God a *l* and showing
1 Jn 2:4 . . . that person is a *l* and is not
1 Jn 5:10 . . . calling God a *l* because they

LIE, LIES (N) an untrue or inaccurate statement; something that misleads or deceives
Ps 34:13 . . . lips from telling *l-s!*
John 8:44 . . . the father of *l-s.*
Rom 1:25 . . . about God for a *l.*
Rom 3:13 . . . filled with *l-s.*
Eph 4:14 . . . to trick us with *l-s* so clever
Eph 4:25 . . . So stop telling *l-s.*
2 Thes 2:11 . . . they will believe these *l-s.*
1 Pet 3:10 . . . and your lips from telling *l-s.*
2 Pet 2:3 . . . make up clever *l-s* to get hold
Rev 14:5 . . . They have told no *l-s;*

LIE, LIES (V) to make an untrue statement with intent to deceive; to create a false or misleading impression
Prov 24:28 . . . don't *l* about them.
Prov 26:19 . . . who *l-s* to a friend
Matt 5:11 . . . persecute you and *l*
Col 3:9 . . . Don't *l* to each other,

LIFE (N) the quality that distinguishes a vital and functional being from a dead body; period from birth to death; a way or manner of living; spiritual existence transcending death; salvation
Gen 2:7 . . . He breathed the breath of *l*
Gen 2:9 . . . the tree of *l* and the tree of
Deut 30:19 . . . choice between *l* and death,
Ps 23:6 . . . the days of my *l,* and I will
Ps 139:24 . . . the path of everlasting *l.*
Prov 6:26 . . . will cost you your *l.*
Prov 15:4 . . . Gentle words are a tree of *l;*
Prov 28:16 . . . will have a long *l.*
Lam 3:58 . . . you have redeemed my *l.*
Matt 7:14 . . . But the gateway to *l* is very
Matt 18:8 . . . to enter eternal *l* with only
Matt 20:28 . . . and to give his *l* as a ransom
Mark 8:35 . . . to hang on to your *l,*
Luke 6:9 . . . a day to save *l* or to destroy
Luke 9:24 . . . give up your *l* for my sake,
Luke 12:25 . . . single moment to your *l?*
John 1:4 . . . The Word gave *l* to everything
John 3:15 . . . will have eternal *l.*
John 5:24 . . . passed from death into *l.*
John 6:35 . . . I am the bread of *l.*
John 6:68 . . . the words that give eternal *l.*
John 10:10 . . . a rich and satisfying *l.*
John 14:6 . . . the truth, and the *l.*
Rom 5:10 . . . be saved through the *l* of his
Rom 6:23 . . . is eternal *l* through Christ
Rom 8:38 . . . death nor *l,* neither angels
2 Cor 3:6 . . . the Spirit gives *l.*
Phil 4:3 . . . written in the Book of *L.*
1 Pet 3:7 . . . God's gift of new *l.*
Rev 22:2 . . . a tree of *l,* bearing twelve
Rev 22:17 . . . from the water of *l.*
Rev 22:19 . . . in the tree of *l* and in the

LIGHT (N) daylight; brightness; illumination; celestial body; spiritual enlightenment; exposure to the truth and justice
Gen 1:3 . . . "Let there be *l,*" and there
Exod 13:21 . . . and he provided *l* at night
Ps 27:1 . . . The LORD is my *l* and my
Ps 56:13 . . . in your life-giving *l.*
Ps 139:12 . . . Darkness and *l* are the
Isa 42:6 . . . you will be a *l* to guide the
Isa 45:7 . . . I create the *l* and make the
Isa 49:6 . . . make you a *l* to the Gentiles,
Matt 5:14 . . . You are the *l* of the world—
Luke 2:32 . . . He is a *l* to reveal God to
Luke 11:33 . . . its *l* can be seen by all
John 1:4 . . . life brought *l* to everyone.
John 1:9 . . . who is the true *l,* who gives
John 3:21 . . . come to the *l* so others can
John 9:5 . . . I am the *l* of the world.
2 Cor 4:6 . . . said, "Let there be *l* in the
2 Cor 6:14 . . . can *l* live with darkness?
2 Cor 11:14 . . . as an angel of *l.*
1 Pet 2:9 . . . into his wonderful *l.*
1 Jn 1:5 . . . God is *l,* and there is
1 Jn 1:7 . . . living in the *l,* as God is in
1 Jn 2:9 . . . I am living in the *l,*
Rev 21:23 . . . city, and the Lamb is its *l.*

LION, LIONS (N) a wild beast with a threatening roar; symbolic of a strong and fierce enemy
Isa 65:25 . . . The *l* will eat hay like a cow.
Dan 6:7 . . . thrown into the den of *l-s.*
Dan 7:4 . . . was like a *l* with eagles'
1 Pet 5:8 . . . like a roaring *l,* looking for
Rev 5:5 . . . Look, the *L* of the tribe of

LISTEN (V) to hear something with thoughtful attention
see also HEAR
Deut 6:4 . . . *L,* O Israel! The LORD
Deut 18:15 . . . You must *l* to him.
Prov 12:15 . . . but the wise *l* to others.
Isa 6:9 . . . to this people, '*L* carefully,
Mark 9:7 . . . dearly loved Son. *L* to him.
John 10:27 . . . My sheep *l* to my
1 Tim 2:12 . . . Let them *l* quietly.
Jas 1:19 . . . be quick to *l,* slow to speak,
1 Jn 4:6 . . . they do not *l* to us.
Rev 1:3 . . . he blesses all who *l* to its
Rev 2:7 . . . to hear must *l* to the Spirit

LOCUSTS (N) a short-horned grasshopper
Exod 10:4 . . . a swarm of *l* on your country.
Joel 2:25 . . . and the cutting *l.* It was I
Matt 3:4 . . . he ate *l* and wild honey.
Rev 9:3 . . . Then *l* came from

LOVE (N) the ultimate expression of God's loyalty, purity, and mercy extended toward his people—to be reflected in human relationships of brotherly concern, marital fidelity, and adoration of God; a beloved person
Gen 32:10 . . . unfailing *l* and faithfulness
Exod 20:6 . . . unfailing *l* for a thousand
1 Kgs 8:23 . . . and show unfailing *l* to all
Ps 6:4 . . . because of your unfailing *l*.
Ps 23:6 . . . and unfailing *l* will pursue
Ps 36:10 . . . Pour out your unfailing *l* on
Ps 103:17 . . . But the *l* of the LORD
Jer 33:11 . . . His faithful *l* endures
Hos 12:6 . . . Act with *l* and justice,
Mark 10:21 . . . Jesus felt genuine *l* for him.
John 5:42 . . . have God's *l* within you.
John 15:9 . . . Remain in my *l*.
John 15:13 . . . is no greater *l* than to lay
Rom 5:8 . . . showed his great *l* for us by
Rom 8:35 . . . us from Christ's *l*?
Rom 8:39 . . . us from the *l* of God that is
Rom 13:10 . . . *L* does no wrong
1 Cor 13:13 . . . the greatest of these is *l*.
Gal 5:22 . . . *l*, joy, peace, patience,
Eph 3:18 . . . how deep his *l* is.
Eph 4:15 . . . the truth in *l*, growing in
1 Tim 6:10 . . . For the *l* of money is the
1 Pet 4:8 . . . for *l* covers a multitude
1 Jn 4:7 . . . for *l* comes from God.
1 Jn 4:16 . . . God is *l*, and all who
1 Jn 4:18 . . . because perfect *l* expels all

LOVE, LOVED, LOVING (V) to hold dear; to feel a lover's passion, devotion, or tenderness for; to feel affection or experience desire; to like or desire actively
Deut 6:5 . . . And you must *l* the LORD your
Deut 30:20 . . . this choice by ***l-ing*** the LORD
Deut 30:20 . . . And if you *l* and obey the
Ps 119:119 . . . no wonder I *l* to obey your
Eccl 3:8 . . . A time to *l* and a time
Isa 61:8 . . . I, the LORD, *l* justice.
Mic 6:8 . . . is right, to *l* mercy, and to
Matt 5:46 . . . If you *l* only those
Matt 6:24 . . . hate one and *l* the other;
Matt 10:37 . . . If you *l* your father or
Matt 19:19 . . . *L* your neighbor
Matt 22:37 . . . You must *l* the LORD your
Luke 6:27 . . . I say, *l* your enemies!
John 13:34 . . . *L* each other. Just as I have
John 13:34 . . . as I have ***l-d*** you, you should
John 21:15 . . . do you *l* me more than
Rom 8:28 . . . of those who *l* God and are
Heb 13:5 . . . Don't *l* money;

LOYAL (ADJ) unswerving in allegiance; faithful
see also FAITHFUL, TRUSTWORTHY
1 Sam 26:23 . . . and for being *l*,
2 Sam 2:6 . . . May the LORD be *l* to you in
1 Chr 12:33 . . . and completely *l* to David.
Ps 31:23 . . . those who are *l* to him,
Ps 51:10 . . . Renew a *l* spirit within
Prov 17:17 . . . A friend is always *l*, and a
Prov 20:6 . . . say they are *l* friends,

M

MANGER (N) a trough or open box in a stable designed to hold feed for livestock
Luke 2:7 . . . cloth and laid him in a ***m***,
Luke 2:12 . . . strips of cloth, lying in a ***m***.

MANNA (N) miraculous supply of food given to Israel in the wilderness; symbolic of spiritual nourishment
Exod 16:31 . . . Israelites called the food ***m***.
Deut 8:16 . . . He fed you with ***m*** in the
John 6:49 . . . Your ancestors ate ***m*** in the
Rev 2:17 . . . some of the ***m*** that has been

MEDITATE, MEDITATING (V) to contemplate, reflect, or ponder
see also THINK
Gen 24:63 . . . ***m-ing*** in the fields,
Ps 1:2 . . . ***m-ing*** on it day and night.
Ps 48:9 . . . O God, we ***m*** on your unfailing
Ps 63:6 . . . ***m-ing*** on you through the night.
Ps 119:23 . . . but I will ***m*** on your decrees.
Ps 119:27 . . . ***m*** on your wonderful deeds.
Ps 119:48 . . . I ***m*** on your decrees.
Ps 145:5 . . . I will ***m*** on your majestic,

MEDITATION (N) the act or process of meditating
Ps 19:14 . . . words of my mouth and the ***m***

MERCIFUL (ADJ) compassionate; forgiving
Deut 4:31 . . . your God is a ***m*** God;
Ps 78:38 . . . Yet he was ***m*** and forgave
Dan 4:27 . . . and be ***m*** to the poor.
Dan 9:9 . . . our God is ***m*** and forgiving,
Matt 5:7 . . . God blesses those who are ***m***,
Luke 1:54 . . . and remembered to be ***m***.
Heb 2:17 . . . ***m*** and faithful High Priest
Jas 2:13 . . . God will be ***m*** when he judges

MERCY, MERCIES (N) a blessing that is an act of divine favor or compassion; withholding of the punishment or judgment our sins deserve
see also COMPASSION, FORGIVENESS
Ps 103:4 . . . me with love and tender ***m-ies***.
Ps 119:77 . . . with your tender ***m-ies*** so I
Ps 119:156 . . . how great is your ***m***;
Isa 49:10 . . . LORD in his ***m*** will lead
Mic 6:8 . . . do what is right, to love ***m***,
Matt 5:7 . . . for they will be shown ***m***.
Matt 9:13 . . . I want you to show ***m***,
Matt 18:33 . . . just as I had ***m*** on you?
Matt 23:23 . . . law—justice, ***m***, and faith.
Rom 11:32 . . . have ***m*** on everyone.
2 Cor 4:1 . . . God in his ***m*** has given us
Gal 1:6 . . . through the loving ***m*** of Christ.
Eph 2:4 . . . But God is so rich in ***m***, and
1 Tim 1:13 . . . But God had ***m*** on me
Titus 3:5 . . . but because of his ***m***.
Heb 4:16 . . . we will receive his ***m***,
Jas 3:17 . . . It is full of ***m*** and the fruit
1 Pet 1:3 . . . by his great ***m*** that we
Jude 1:22 . . . show ***m*** to those whose faith

MIGHTY, MIGHTIER, MIGHTIEST (ADJ) powerful; great or imposing in size or extent
Gen 49:24 . . . hands of the ***M*** One of Jacob,
Deut 10:17 . . . God, the ***m*** and awesome
Deut 34:12 . . . With ***m*** power, Moses
2 Sam 23:8 . . . David's ***m-iest*** warriors.
2 Chr 20:6 . . . You are powerful and ***m***;
Neh 9:32 . . . and ***m*** and awesome God,
Job 9:4 . . . For God is so wise and so ***m***.
Job 36:5 . . . He is ***m*** in both power and
Ps 24:8 . . . LORD, strong and ***m***;
Ps 47:5 . . . ascended with a ***m*** shout.
Ps 50:1 . . . LORD, the ***M*** One, is God,
Ps 71:16 . . . I will praise your ***m*** deeds,
Ps 77:12 . . . thinking about your ***m*** works.
Ps 89:27 . . . son, the ***m-iest*** king on earth.
Ps 93:4 . . . ***m-ier*** than the violent raging
Ps 93:4 . . . LORD above is ***m-ier*** than these!
Ps 95:4 . . . and the ***m-iest*** mountains.
Ps 145:4 . . . children of your ***m*** acts;
Ps 145:12 . . . will tell about your ***m*** deeds
Ps 150:2 . . . Praise him for his ***m*** works;
Prov 24:5 . . . wise are ***m-ier*** than the strong,

Isa 9:6 . . . Wonderful Counselor, *M* God,
Isa 60:16 . . . your Redeemer, the *M* One of
Zeph 3:17 . . . He is a ***m*** savior.
Eph 1:19 . . . This is the same ***m*** power
Eph 6:10 . . . in the Lord and in his ***m***
Heb 1:3 . . . sustains everything by the ***m***
1 Pet 5:6 . . . yourselves under the ***m***
Jude 1:9 . . . Michael, one of the ***m-iest*** of the angels,

MIND, MINDS (N) the part of humans that engages in conscious thinking, feeling, and decision making; in the Bible, mind is akin to the heart, not the brain
Num 23:19 . . . he does not change his ***m***.
1 Sam 15:29 . . . nor will he change his ***m***,
Mark 12:30 . . . all your soul, all your ***m***,
Luke 24:45 . . . opened their ***m-s***
Acts 4:32 . . . were united in heart and ***m***.
Rom 8:6 . . . Spirit control your ***m***
1 Cor 1:10 . . . be of one ***m***, united in
1 Cor 2:9 . . . heard, and no ***m*** has imagined
2 Cor 4:4 . . . has blinded the ***m-s*** of those
Col 2:18 . . . sinful ***m-s*** have made them
2 Tim 4:5 . . . clear ***m*** in every situation.
Heb 8:10 . . . I will put my laws in their ***m-s***,
Heb 10:16 . . . I will write them on their ***m-s***.

MIRACLE, MIRACLES (N) an extraordinary event manifesting divine intervention in human affairs
Exod 3:20 . . . performing all kinds of ***m-s***
Exod 7:9 . . . demand, 'Show me a ***m***.'
Deut 13:1 . . . they promise you signs or ***m-s***,
Job 9:10 . . . He performs countless ***m-s***.
Ps 105:5 . . . he has performed, his ***m-s***,
Ps 106:2 . . . the glorious ***m-s*** of the LORD?
Jer 32:19 . . . and do great and mighty ***m-s***.
Matt 7:22 . . . and performed many ***m-s***
Matt 13:54 . . . and the power to do ***m-s?***
Mark 6:2 . . . power to perform such ***m-s?***
Mark 9:39 . . . No one who performs a ***m***
Luke 19:37 . . . wonderful ***m-s*** they had
Luke 23:8 . . . to see him perform a ***m***.
John 7:21 . . . I did one ***m*** on the Sabbath,
Acts 2:22 . . . by doing powerful ***m-s***,
Acts 8:13 . . . ***m-s*** Philip performed.
Acts 19:11 . . . to perform unusual ***m-s***.
1 Cor 12:28 . . . those who do ***m-s***, those
2 Cor 12:12 . . . and ***m-s*** among you.
Gal 3:5 . . . and work ***m-s*** among you
Heb 2:4 . . . and various ***m-s*** and gifts of

MOTHER (N) a female parent; a woman in authority
see also PARENT(S)
Gen 2:24 . . . a man leaves his father and ***m***
Gen 3:20 . . . she would be the ***m*** of all who
Exod 20:12 . . . Honor your father and ***m***.
Prov 10:1 . . . brings grief to a ***m***.
Matt 10:37 . . . father or ***m*** more than you
Matt 12:48 . . . Who is my ***m?***
Mark 10:19 . . . Honor your father and ***m***.
John 19:27 . . . disciple, "Here is your ***m***."
Eph 5:31 . . . A man leaves his father and ***m***
Eph 6:2 . . . Honor your father and ***m***.

MOTIVES (N) something (as a need or desire) that causes a person to act
1 Chr 29:17 . . . all this with good ***m***,
Ps 26:2 . . . Test my ***m*** and my heart.
Prov 16:2 . . . LORD examines their ***m***.
Jer 17:10 . . . hearts and examine secret ***m***.
1 Cor 4:5 . . . will reveal our private ***m***.
Phil 1:18 . . . Whether their ***m*** are false or
1 Thes 2:3 . . . with any deceit or impure ***m***
1 Thes 2:4 . . . He alone examines the ***m*** of
Jas 4:3 . . . your ***m*** are all wrong—

MOUNTAIN, MOUNTAINS (N) a landmass that projects conspicuously above its surroundings and is higher than a hill
Exod 24:18 . . . on the ***m*** forty days
Deut 5:4 . . . At the ***m*** the LORD
Ps 36:6 . . . is like the mighty ***m-s***,
Ps 121:1 . . . I look up to the ***m-s***—
Isa 14:13 . . . preside on the ***m*** of the gods
Matt 17:20 . . . say to this ***m***, 'Move
Mark 9:2 . . . led them up a high ***m***
Mark 9:9 . . . went back down the ***m***,
Luke 23:30 . . . beg the ***m-s***, 'Fall on us,'
1 Cor 13:2 . . . faith that I could move ***m-s***,
2 Pet 1:18 . . . with him on the holy ***m***.
Rev 6:16 . . . they cried to the ***m-s*** and

MURDER, MURDERED, MURDERS (V) to kill (a human being) unlawfully and with premeditated malice
Gen 9:5 . . . ***m-s*** a fellow human must die.
Exod 20:13 . . . You must not ***m***.
Deut 5:17 . . . You must not ***m***.
Matt 23:31 . . . who ***m-ed*** the prophets.
Acts 7:52 . . . whom you betrayed and ***m-ed***.
Rom 13:9 . . . You must not ***m***.
Jas 2:11 . . . You must not ***m***.

MUSIC (N) vocal, instrumental, or mechanical sounds having rhythm, melody, or harmony
Judg 5:3 . . . I will make ***m*** to the LORD,
1 Chr 6:31 . . . lead the ***m*** at the house of
Neh 12:27 . . . and with the ***m*** of cymbals,
Ps 45:8 . . . the ***m*** of strings entertains
Amos 5:23 . . . to the ***m*** of your harps.
Eph 5:19 . . . and making ***m*** to the Lord

MYSTERY, MYSTERIES (N) something not understood or beyond understanding; a religious truth that one can know only by revelation and cannot fully understand
see also SECRET(S)
Dan 4:9 . . . and that no ***m*** is too great
Rom 11:25 . . . to understand this ***m***,
1 Cor 2:7 . . . speak of is the ***m*** of God—
1 Cor 4:1 . . . explaining God's ***m-ies***.
1 Tim 3:9 . . . to the ***m*** of the faith
1 Tim 3:16 . . . the great ***m*** of our faith:
Rev 1:20 . . . the ***m*** of the seven stars
Rev 17:7 . . . tell you the ***m*** of this woman

N

NAILED, NAILING (V) to fasten with or as if with a nail
Matt 27:35 . . . had ***n*** him to the cross,
Mark 15:24 . . . soldiers ***n*** him to the
Acts 2:23 . . . you ***n*** him to a cross
Col 2:14 . . . away by ***n-ing*** it to the cross.
Heb 6:6 . . . are ***n-ing*** him to the cross

NATION, NATIONS (N) group of people defined by geography or ethnicity
see also PEOPLE(S)
Gen 12:2 . . . I will make you into a great ***n***.
Gen 17:4 . . . father of a multitude of ***n-s!***
Gen 17:16 . . . the mother of many ***n-s***.
Ps 46:10 . . . I will be honored by every ***n***.
Isa 11:10 . . . The ***n-s*** will rally to him,
Isa 42:1 . . . He will bring justice to the ***n-s***.
Matt 12:18 . . . proclaim justice to the ***n-s***.
Matt 24:14 . . . so that all ***n-s*** will hear it;
Matt 28:19 . . . make disciples of all the ***n-s***,
Mark 11:17 . . . house of prayer for all ***n-s***,
Gal 3:8 . . . All ***n-s*** will be blessed through
1 Pet 2:9 . . . royal priests, a holy ***n***,
Rev 5:9 . . . language and people and ***n***.

Rev 21:24 . . . The **n-s** will walk in its light,
Rev 22:2 . . . for medicine to heal the **n-s**.

NEIGHBOR, NEIGHBORS (N) one living or located near another; fellow man
Lev 19:18 . . . but love your **n** as yourself.
Ps 15:3 . . . to gossip or harm their **n-s**
Prov 24:28 . . . your **n-s** without cause;
Prov 27:10 . . . better to go to a **n** than
Jer 31:34 . . . not need to teach their **n-s**,
Mark 12:31 . . . Love your **n** as yourself.
Luke 10:29 . . . And who is my **n**?
Rom 13:8 . . . If you love your **n**, you will
Gal 5:14 . . . Love your **n** as yourself.
Eph 4:25 . . . Let us tell our **n-s** the truth,
Heb 8:11 . . . not need to teach their **n-s**,
Jas 2:8 . . . Love your **n** as yourself.

NEW (ADJ) fresh; original; different than before; unfamiliar
Jer 31:31 . . . I will make a **n** covenant with
Mark 16:17 . . . will speak in **n** languages.
Luke 22:20 . . . cup is the **n** covenant
Rom 6:4 . . . we also may live **n** lives.
Rom 12:2 . . . you into a **n** person
1 Cor 11:25 . . . cup is the **n** covenant
2 Cor 3:6 . . . but under the **n** covenant,
2 Cor 5:17 . . . is gone; a **n** life has begun!
Gal 6:15 . . . into a **n** creation.
Eph 4:24 . . . Put on your **n** nature,
Heb 8:8 . . . when I will make a **n** covenant
Heb 9:15 . . . mediates a **n** covenant
Heb 12:24 . . . the **n** covenant
2 Pet 3:13 . . . **n** heavens and **n** earth he
Rev 2:17 . . . a **n** name that no one
Rev 21:1 . . . **n** heaven and a **n** earth,

NEWS (N) a report of recent events; "Good News": the Gospel of Jesus Christ
Isa 40:9 . . . of good **n**, shout from the
Mark 1:15 . . . sins and believe the Good **N**!
Acts 13:32 . . . to bring you this Good **N**.
Rom 1:16 . . . not ashamed of this Good **N**
Rom 10:17 . . . the Good **N** about Christ.
Rom 15:16 . . . I bring you the Good **N**
1 Cor 1:17 . . . to preach the Good **N**—
1 Cor 9:16 . . . preach the Good **N**!
1 Cor 9:23 . . . to spread the Good **N**
1 Cor 15:1 . . . the Good **N** I preached
2 Cor 4:4 . . . glorious light of the Good **N**.
2 Cor 11:7 . . . preaching God's Good **N**
Eph 6:15 . . . comes from the Good **N**
Col 1:5 . . . heard the truth of the Good **N**.
1 Thes 2:4 . . . entrusted with the Good **N**.
2 Thes 1:8 . . . obey the Good **N** of our Lord
2 Tim 1:10 . . . through the Good **N**.
2 Tim 4:5 . . . telling others the Good **N**,
Rev 14:6 . . . the eternal Good **N**

O

OBEY (V) to follow the commands or guidance of; to conform to or comply with
see also KEEP
Deut 13:4 . . . **O** his commands, listen to his
Deut 30:20 . . . love and **o** the LORD,
Ps 119:17 . . . I may live and **o** your word.
Eccl 12:13 . . . and **o** his commands,
Mic 5:15 . . . nations that refuse to **o** me.
Matt 28:20 . . . to **o** all the commands
Luke 8:21 . . . hear God's word and **o** it.
John 3:36 . . . who doesn't **o** the Son
John 14:15 . . . **o** my commandments.
Acts 4:19 . . . to **o** you rather than him?
Acts 5:29 . . . We must **o** God rather than
Rom 6:17 . . . wholeheartedly **o** this
Rom 15:31 . . . in Judea who refuse to **o** God.
2 Cor 10:5 . . . teach them to **o** Christ.
Gal 3:10 . . . and **o** all the commands
Eph 2:2 . . . who refuse to **o** God.
Eph 6:1 . . . Children, **o** your parents
Rev 22:7 . . . Blessed are those who **o** the

OFFERING, OFFERINGS (N) a sacrifice ceremonially offered as a part of worship; a contribution to the support of a church
Gen 22:8 . . . a sheep for the burnt **o**,
1 Sam 13:9 . . . Bring me the burnt **o**
1 Sam 15:22 . . . burnt **o-s** and sacrifices
Ps 40:6 . . . no delight in sacrifices or **o-s**.
Ps 141:2 . . . hands as an evening **o**.
Isa 53:10 . . . his life is made an **o** for sin,
Hos 6:6 . . . more than I want burnt **o-s**.
Mal 3:8 . . . of the tithes and **o-s**
Mark 12:33 . . . all of the burnt **o-s**
Rom 15:26 . . . taken up an **o** for the poor
Phil 2:17 . . . faithful service is an **o**
Heb 10:5 . . . animal sacrifices or sin **o-s**.
Heb 10:14 . . . that one **o** he forever made
Heb 11:4 . . . Abel's **o** gave evidence that he

OIL (N) liquid produced from olives used in biblical times for lamp fuel, anointing, and dressing wounds; often symbolic of the Holy Spirit
Exod 29:7 . . . anointing **o** over his head.
Exod 30:25 . . . to make a holy anointing **o**.
1 Sam 10:1 . . . **o** and poured it over Saul's
1 Sam 16:13 . . . **o** he had brought and
Ps 23:5 . . . anointing my head with **o**.
Ps 133:2 . . . as precious as the anointing **o**
Heb 1:9 . . . pouring out the **o** of joy

ORPHAN, ORPHANS (N) a child deprived by death of one or usually both parents
Exod 22:22 . . . not exploit a widow or an **o**.
Deut 10:18 . . . **o-s** and widows receive
Deut 24:17 . . . among you and to **o-s**,
Deut 24:19 . . . **o-s**, and widows.
Ps 10:14 . . . in you. You defend the **o-s**.
Ps 82:3 . . . justice to the poor and the **o**;
Prov 23:10 . . . the land of defenseless **o-s**.
John 14:18 . . . will not abandon you as **o-s**—
Jas 1:27 . . . caring for **o-s** and widows in

PAGAN, PAGANS (N) a follower of a false god or religion; one who delights in sensual pleasures and material goods
Ps 106:35 . . . they mingled among the **p-s**
Isa 2:6 . . . have made alliances with **p-s**.
Matt 5:47 . . . Even **p-s** do that.
Matt 18:17 . . . treat that person as a **p**
1 Cor 5:1 . . . something that even **p-s** don't
1 Cor 12:2 . . . when you were still **p-s**, you

PAIN, PAINS (N) physical, mental, or emotional suffering; the spasms of childbirth
Job 6:10 . . . Despite the **p**, I have not
Ps 73:14 . . . every morning brings me **p**.
Jer 4:19 . . . my heart—I writhe in **p**!
Matt 24:8 . . . only the first of the birth **p-s**,
John 16:21 . . . suffering the **p-s** of labor.
Rom 8:22 . . . in the **p-s** of childbirth
Gal 4:19 . . . going through labor **p-s** for
1 Thes 5:3 . . . woman's labor **p-s** begin.
Heb 13:3 . . . as if you felt their **p** in your
Rev 21:4 . . . death or sorrow or crying or **p**.

PARABLE, PARABLES (N) a brief narrative story told with earthly analogies to illustrate a spiritual truth
Ps 78:2 . . . I will speak to you in a ***p***.
Matt 13:35 . . . I will speak to you in ***p-s***.
Luke 8:10 . . . I use ***p-s*** to teach the

PARENT, PARENTS (N) one who produces and cares for offspring
see also FATHER, MOTHER
Exod 20:5 . . . I lay the sins of the ***p-s*** upon
Prov 13:1 . . . child accepts a ***p's*** discipline;
Jer 31:29 . . . ***p-s*** have eaten sour grapes,
Ezek 18:19 . . . child pay for the ***p's*** sins?
Matt 10:21 . . . will rebel against their ***p-s***
Rom 1:30 . . . and they disobey their ***p-s***.
Eph 6:1 . . . Children, obey your ***p-s***
Col 3:20 . . . always obey your ***p-s***,

PASSOVER (N) a festival that commemorated the Hebrew departure from Egypt in haste
Num 9:2 . . . celebrate the ***P***
Deut 16:1 . . . celebrate the ***P*** each year
Ezra 6:19 . . . returned exiles celebrated ***P***.
Mark 14:12 . . . ***P*** lamb is sacrificed,
Heb 11:28 . . . to keep the ***P*** and to sprinkle

PATH, PATHS (N) course, route; a way of life, conduct, or thought
1 Kgs 8:36 . . . follow the right ***p***,
Ps 23:3 . . . He guides me along right ***p-s***,
Ps 27:11 . . . Lead me along the right ***p***,
Prov 2:13 . . . to walk down dark ***p-s***.
Prov 3:6 . . . show you which ***p*** to take.
Prov 5:21 . . . examining every ***p*** he takes.
Prov 8:20 . . . in ***p-s*** of justice.
Prov 14:12 . . . a ***p*** before each person that
Isa 48:17 . . . leads you along the ***p-s***
Hos 14:9 . . . ***p-s*** of the LORD are true
2 Tim 2:18 . . . have left the ***p*** of truth,
Heb 12:13 . . . Mark out a straight ***p***

PATIENCE (N) the power or capacity to endure without complaint something difficult or disagreeable; forbearance, longsuffering
Rom 15:5 . . . May God, who gives this ***p***
Gal 5:22 . . . joy, peace, ***p***, kindness,
Col 1:11 . . . endurance and ***p*** you need.
Col 3:12 . . . humility, gentleness, and ***p***.
2 Tim 3:10 . . . my faith, my ***p***, my love,
Titus 2:2 . . . and be filled with love and ***p***.
Jas 5:10 . . . examples of ***p*** in suffering,
2 Pet 3:15 . . . Lord's ***p*** gives people time

PEACE (N) a state of tranquility or quiet; a pact or agreement to end hostilities between those who have been at war or in a state of enmity; harmony in personal relations, especially with God; a state of security or order within a community; freedom from disquieting or oppressive thoughts or emotions
Lev 26:6 . . . I will give you ***p*** in the land,
Num 6:26 . . . his favor and give you his ***p***.
Ps 34:14 . . . Search for ***p***, and work to
Ps 37:37 . . . awaits those who love ***p***.
Prov 12:20 . . . hearts that are planning ***p!***
Eccl 3:8 . . . for war and a time for ***p***.
Isa 9:6 . . . Everlasting Father, Prince of ***P***.
Matt 5:9 . . . blesses those who work for ***p***,
Mark 9:50 . . . live in ***p*** with each other.
Luke 1:79 . . . guide us to the path of ***p***.
John 16:33 . . . you may have ***p*** in me.
Rom 5:1 . . . by faith, we have ***p*** with God
Rom 8:6 . . . your mind leads to life and ***p***.
1 Cor 14:33 . . . God of disorder but of ***p***,
Gal 5:22 . . . love, joy, ***p***, patience,
Eph 2:14 . . . Christ himself has brought ***p***
Eph 6:15 . . . put on the ***p*** that comes from
Phil 4:7 . . . experience God's ***p***,
Heb 13:20 . . . the God of ***p***—who brought
Jas 3:17 . . . It is also ***p*** loving, gentle
1 Pet 3:11 . . . Search for ***p***, and work to

PENTECOST (N) a Jewish feast celebrated on the 50th day after the Feast of Unleavened Bread; the day God sent the Holy Spirit after Christ's resurrection
Acts 2:1 . . . the day of ***P*** all the believers
Acts 20:16 . . . in time for the Festival of ***P***.
1 Cor 16:8 . . . until the Festival of ***P***.

PEOPLE, PEOPLES (N) human beings making up a group or assembly or linked by a common interest; clan or nation; humanity
see also NATION(S)
Exod 5:1 . . . says: Let my ***p*** go
Lev 26:12 . . . and you will be my ***p***.
Deut 7:6 . . . you are a holy ***p***, who belong
Ruth 1:16 . . . Your ***p*** will be my ***p***,
Ps 94:14 . . . will not reject his ***p***;
Ps 96:10 . . . He will judge all ***p-s*** fairly.
Ps 135:14 . . . will give justice to his ***p***
Isa 2:2 . . . ***p*** from all over the world
Isa 40:1 . . . Comfort, comfort my ***p***,
Isa 49:13 . . . LORD has comforted his ***p***
Jer 2:32 . . . my ***p*** have forgotten me.
Jer 32:27 . . . of all the ***p-s*** of the world.
Mic 4:1 . . . ***p*** from all over the world
Matt 4:19 . . . show you how to fish for ***p!***
Mark 8:27 . . . Who do ***p*** say I am?
Eph 1:14 . . . purchased us to be his own ***p***.
2 Tim 3:17 . . . and equip his ***p*** to do every
Titus 2:11 . . . bringing salvation to all ***p***.
Titus 2:14 . . . make us his very own ***p***,
Heb 4:9 . . . waiting for the ***p*** of God.
1 Pet 2:9 . . . for you are a chosen ***p***.
1 Pet 2:10 . . . now you are God's ***p***.

PERFECT (ADJ) being entirely without fault or defect; corresponding to an ideal standard or abstract concept; mature, pure, complete
Deut 32:4 . . . the Rock; his deeds are ***p***.
Ps 19:7 . . . instructions of the LORD are ***p***,
Ps 119:138 . . . laws are ***p*** and completely
Matt 5:48 . . . you are to be ***p***, even as
John 17:23 . . . experience such ***p*** unity
Gal 3:3 . . . become ***p*** by your
Col 4:12 . . . God to make you strong and ***p***,
Heb 2:10 . . . suffering, a ***p*** leader,
Heb 5:9 . . . as a ***p*** High Priest,
Heb 7:19 . . . law never made anything ***p***.
Heb 9:11 . . . greater, more ***p*** Tabernacle
Heb 9:14 . . . as a ***p*** sacrifice for our sins.
Heb 10:14 . . . he forever made ***p*** those
Heb 12:23 . . . who have now been made ***p***.
Jas 1:25 . . . look carefully into the ***p*** law
1 Jn 4:18 . . . because ***p*** love expels all fear.

PERISH, PERISHING (V) to become destroyed or ruined physically or spiritually; to die
see also DESTROY, DIE
Ps 102:26 . . . They will ***p***, but you remain
John 3:16 . . . believes in him will not ***p*** but
John 10:28 . . . they will never ***p***.
2 Cor 2:15 . . . by those who are ***p-ing***.
2 Cor 4:3 . . . from people who are ***p-ing***.
Jude 1:11 . . . they ***p*** in their rebellion.

PERSECUTE, PERSECUTED, PERSECUTING (V) to harass or punish in a manner designed to injure, grieve, or afflict; to cause to suffer because of belief
Ps 140:12 . . . help those they ***p***;
Matt 5:10 . . . blesses those who are ***p-d***
Matt 5:11 . . . when people mock you and ***p***
Matt 5:12 . . . prophets were ***p-d***

Matt 5:44 . . . Pray for those who ***p*** you!
Matt 13:21 . . . ***p-d*** for believing God's
John 15:20 . . . they ***p-d*** me, naturally they will ***p*** you.
Acts 9:4 . . . Why are you ***p-ing*** me?
Rom 8:35 . . . or are ***p-d***, or hungry,
Rom 12:14 . . . Bless those who ***p*** you.
1 Cor 15:9 . . . the way I ***p-d*** God's church.
2 Thes 1:7 . . . for you who are being ***p-d***

PERSEVERE (V) to persist in a state, enterprise, or undertaking in spite of opposition or discouragement
see also ENDURE
Rev 3:10 . . . obeyed my command to ***p***,

PHYSICAL (ADJ) having material existence; of or relating to the body
John 1:13 . . . reborn—not with a ***p*** birth
Col 1:22 . . . of Christ in his ***p*** body.
1 Tim 4:8 . . . ***P*** training is good, but
1 Tim 5:11 . . . ***p*** desires will overpower
1 Jn 2:16 . . . a craving for ***p*** pleasure

PIERCE, PIERCED (V) to make a hole through; to stab
Exod 21:6 . . . and publicly ***p*** his ear
Ps 22:16 . . . have ***p-d*** my hands and feet.
Zech 12:10 . . . me whom they have ***p-d***
Luke 2:35 . . . sword will ***p*** your very soul.
John 19:37 . . . look on the one they ***p-d***.
Rev 1:7 . . . even those who ***p-d*** him.

PLAGUE, PLAGUES (N) a disastrous evil, affliction, or epidemic of infectious disease, issued by God in judgment
2 Chr 6:28 . . . or a ***p*** or crop disease
Luke 21:11 . . . will be famines and ***p-s***
Rev 21:9 . . . the seven last ***p-s*** came
Rev 22:18 . . . add to that person the ***p-s***

PLAN, PLANS (N) a detailed formulation of a program of action; goal, aim
see also PURPOSE(S)
Ps 2:1 . . . waste their time with futile ***p-s***?
Ps 33:10 . . . frustrates the ***p-s*** of the
Ps 40:5 . . . ***p-s*** for us are too numerous
Isa 30:1 . . . You make ***p-s*** that are contrary
Isa 32:6 . . . and make evil ***p-s***.
Jer 29:11 . . . I know the ***p-s*** I have for you
Acts 2:23 . . . his prearranged ***p*** was carried
Acts 4:25 . . . waste their time with futile ***p-s***?
Acts 7:44 . . . according to the ***p*** God had
Rom 16:25 . . . ***p*** kept secret from
Eph 3:9 . . . this mysterious ***p*** that God,
Eph 3:11 . . . This was his eternal ***p***,
2 Tim 1:9 . . . ***p*** from before the beginning

PLEASE, PLEASED, PLEASES (V) to make glad; to satisfy; to like or wish; to be the will or pleasure of
Deut 12:25 . . . doing what ***p-s*** the LORD.
Ps 135:6 . . . The LORD does whatever ***p-s***
Isa 42:1 . . . my chosen one, who ***p-s*** me.
Matt 12:18 . . . my Beloved, who ***p-s*** me.
Luke 2:14 . . . those with whom God is ***p-d***.
John 8:29 . . . I always do what ***p-s*** him.
Rom 8:8 . . . sinful nature can never ***p*** God.
2 Cor 5:9 . . . our goal is to ***p*** him.
Gal 6:8 . . . live to ***p*** the Spirit will harvest
Col 1:10 . . . always honor and ***p*** the Lord,
1 Thes 2:4 . . . Our purpose is to ***p*** God,
Heb 11:6 . . . to ***p*** God without faith.
Heb 13:16 . . . sacrifices that ***p*** God.
1 Pet 2:19 . . . God is ***p-d*** when, conscious of
1 Jn 2:17 . . . does what ***p-s*** God will live
Rev 4:11 . . . you created what you ***p-d***.

POOR (ADJ) characterized by poverty or insufficient resources; humble
Deut 15:4 . . . should be no ***p*** among you,
Deut 15:11 . . . some in the land who are ***p***.
Ps 35:10 . . . protects the helpless and ***p***
Prov 10:4 . . . Lazy people are soon ***p***;
Mark 12:42 . . . Then a ***p*** widow came and
2 Cor 8:9 . . . for your sakes he became ***p***,
Jas 2:2 . . . another comes in who is ***p***

POOR (N) those characterized by poverty or insufficient resources
Lev 19:10 . . . Leave them for the ***p***
Ps 41:1 . . . those who are kind to the ***p***!
Ps 82:3 . . . Give justice to the ***p*** and the
Prov 14:21 . . . those who help the ***p***.
Prov 21:13 . . . cries of the ***p*** will be ignored
Prov 31:20 . . . helping hand to the ***p***
Isa 61:1 . . . to bring good news to the ***p***.
Matt 11:5 . . . is being preached to the ***p***.
Matt 19:21 . . . and give the money to the ***p***,
Luke 4:18 . . . to bring Good News to the ***p***.
Luke 14:13 . . . Instead, invite the ***p***, the
Rom 15:26 . . . an offering for the ***p*** among
Jas 2:6 . . . you dishonor the ***p***!

POSSESSION, POSSESSIONS (N) something owned, occupied, or controlled
see also INHERITANCE, TREASURE(S)
Exod 6:8 . . . as your very own ***p***.
Deut 4:20 . . . and his special ***p***,
Deut 32:9 . . . is his special ***p***.
Zech 2:12 . . . the LORD's special ***p***
Matt 19:21 . . . sell all your ***p-s*** and
Mark 10:22 . . . for he had many ***p-s***.
1 Pet 2:9 . . . God's very own ***p***.

POWER, POWERS (N) ability to act or produce an effect; possession of control, authority, or influence over others; physical might; mental or moral efficacy; a controlling group
see also STRENGTH
Exod 15:6 . . . LORD, is glorious in ***p***.
Deut 8:18 . . . one who gives you ***p*** to be
Ps 89:7 . . . angelic ***p-s*** stand in awe
Isa 40:26 . . . great ***p*** and incomparable
Jer 9:23 . . . the powerful boast in their ***p***,
Mic 3:8 . . . I am filled with ***p***—
Matt 16:18 . . . all the ***p-s*** of hell will not
Matt 22:29 . . . don't know the ***p*** of God.
Luke 1:35 . . . the ***p*** of the Most High will
Luke 4:14 . . . the Holy Spirit's ***p***.
Luke 9:1 . . . gave them ***p*** and authority
Luke 10:19 . . . over all the ***p*** of the enemy,
Luke 11:20 . . . demons by the ***p*** of God,
Acts 1:8 . . . receive ***p*** when the Holy Spirit
Rom 1:16 . . . the ***p*** of God at work,
Rom 1:20 . . . his eternal ***p*** and divine
Rom 6:9 . . . Death no longer has any ***p*** over
Rom 7:23 . . . another ***p*** within me that is
Rom 8:38 . . . not even the ***p-s*** of hell can
Rom 15:13 . . . the ***p*** of the Holy Spirit.
1 Cor 1:18 . . . is the very ***p*** of God.
1 Cor 6:14 . . . from the dead by his ***p***,
1 Cor 15:24 . . . ruler and authority and ***p***.
2 Cor 4:7 . . . our great ***p*** is from God,
2 Cor 13:4 . . . now lives by the ***p*** of God.
Eph 6:10 . . . Lord and in his mighty ***p***.
Phil 3:10 . . . and experience the mighty ***p***
Col 1:11 . . . with all his glorious ***p***
Col 1:29 . . . on Christ's mighty ***p***
1 Thes 1:5 . . . words but also with ***p***,
2 Tim 1:7 . . . but of ***p***, love, and
2 Tim 3:5 . . . reject the ***p*** that could make
Heb 2:14 . . . break the ***p*** of the devil,
Jas 5:16 . . . righteous person has great ***p***
1 Pet 1:5 . . . is protecting you by his ***p***

1 Pet 3:22 . . . ***p-s*** accept his authority.
1 Pet 4:11 . . . All glory and ***p*** to him
2 Pet 1:3 . . . ***p***, God has given us everything
Jude 1:25 . . . ***p***, and authority are his
Rev 4:11 . . . receive glory and honor and ***p***.
Rev 5:12 . . . receive ***p*** and riches and
Rev 19:1 . . . glory and ***p*** belong to our God.
Rev 20:6 . . . the second death holds no ***p***,

PRAISE, PRAISES (N) worship; commendation; value, merit
Deut 26:19 . . . ***p***, honor, and renown.
2 Sam 22:4 . . . LORD, who is worthy of ***p***,
2 Chr 29:30 . . . So they offered joyous ***p***
Ps 7:17 . . . I will sing ***p*** to the name
Ps 18:49 . . . I will sing ***p-s*** to your name.
Ps 34:1 . . . will constantly speak his ***p-s***.
Ps 65:1 . . . What mighty ***p***, O God,
Ps 81:1 . . . Sing ***p-s*** to God,
Ps 100:4 . . . into his courts with ***p***.
Ps 108:1 . . . your ***p-s*** with all my heart!
Ps 145:3 . . . He is most worthy of ***p***!
Ps 149:6 . . . Let the ***p-s*** of God be in
John 12:43 . . . loved human ***p*** more than
Rom 2:29 . . . heart seeks ***p*** from God,
Rom 15:9 . . . will sing ***p-s*** to your name.
1 Thes 2:6 . . . As for human ***p***,
2 Thes 1:10 . . . his holy people—***p*** from all
Jas 5:13 . . . You should sing ***p-s***.

PRAISE, PRAISED, PRAISES, PRAISING (V) to worship, commend, or give honor to
Exod 15:2 . . . and I will ***p*** him—
1 Chr 16:35 . . . name and rejoice and ***p*** you.
2 Chr 5:13 . . . together in unison to ***p*** and
2 Chr 20:21 . . . ***p-ing*** him for his holy
Neh 9:5 . . . Stand up and ***p*** the LORD
Ps 9:1 . . . I will ***p*** you, LORD,
Ps 12:8 . . . evil is ***p-d*** throughout the land.
Ps 34:1 . . . I will ***p*** the LORD
Ps 42:5 . . . I will ***p*** him again—
Ps 45:17 . . . nations will ***p*** you forever
Ps 51:15 . . . my mouth may ***p*** you.
Ps 63:3 . . . how I ***p*** you!
Ps 71:8 . . . I can never stop ***p-ing*** you;
Ps 71:14 . . . I will ***p*** you more and
Ps 74:21 . . . and needy ***p*** your name.
Ps 89:5 . . . angels will ***p*** you for your
Ps 96:2 . . . LORD; ***p*** his name.
Ps 102:18 . . . not yet born will ***p*** the
Ps 104:1 . . . all that I am ***p*** the
Ps 115:18 . . . But we can ***p*** the LORD
Ps 135:20 . . . LORD, ***p*** the LORD!
Ps 144:1 . . . ***P*** the LORD, who is
Ps 148:13 . . . Let them all ***p*** the name
Ps 150:2 . . . ***p*** his unequaled greatness!
Prov 27:2 . . . Let someone else ***p*** you,
Prov 27:21 . . . person is tested by being ***p-d***.
Isa 63:7 . . . I will ***p*** the LORD
Dan 2:19 . . . Daniel ***p-d*** the God of heaven.
Dan 2:20 . . . He said, "***P*** the name
Dan 4:34 . . . ***p-d*** and worshiped the Most
Matt 5:16 . . . will ***p*** your heavenly Father.
Mark 11:9 . . . were shouting, "***P*** God!
Luke 1:46 . . . how my soul ***p-s*** the Lord.
Luke 2:13 . . . armies of heaven—***p-ing*** God
Luke 2:20 . . . glorifying and ***p-ing*** God for
Luke 18:43 . . . all who saw it ***p-d*** God, too.
Luke 19:37 . . . ***p-ing*** God for all the wonderful
Acts 2:47 . . . all the while ***p-ing*** God
Acts 10:46 . . . in other tongues and ***p-ing*** God
1 Cor 14:16 . . . if you ***p*** God only in
Gal 1:24 . . . they ***p-d*** God because of me.
Eph 1:6 . . . we ***p*** God for the glorious
Jas 3:9 . . . Sometimes it ***p-s*** our Lord
Rev 19:1 . . . heaven shouting, "***P*** the LORD!

PRAY, PRAYED, PRAYING, PRAYS (V) to address God with adoration, confession, supplication, or thanksgiving; to intercede
Gen 24:45 . . . I had finished ***p-ing*** in my
1 Sam 1:12 . . . she was ***p-ing*** to the LORD,
2 Chr 7:14 . . . humble themselves and ***p*** and
2 Chr 30:18 . . . King Hezekiah ***p-ed*** for
Neh 4:9 . . . we ***p-ed*** to our God and
Job 42:8 . . . servant Job will ***p*** for you,
Job 42:10 . . . When Job ***p-ed*** for his friends,
Ps 5:2 . . . I ***p*** to no one but you.
Ps 32:6 . . . all the godly ***p*** to you
Ps 34:6 . . . In my desperation I ***p-ed***,
Dan 6:10 . . . He ***p-ed*** three times a day,
Dan 9:4 . . . I ***p-ed*** to the LORD
Jonah 2:1 . . . Jonah ***p-ed*** to the LORD
Matt 6:5 . . . When you ***p***, don't be like
Matt 6:9 . . . ***P*** like this: Our Father in
Matt 26:39 . . . face to the ground, ***p-ing***,
Mark 11:24 . . . you can ***p*** for anything,
Mark 11:25 . . . when you are ***p-ing***, first
Luke 3:21 . . . ***p-ing***, the heavens opened,
Luke 9:29 . . . he was ***p-ing***, the appearance
Luke 11:1 . . . teach us to ***p***, just as John
Luke 22:41 . . . and knelt down and ***p-ed***,
John 17:20 . . . I am ***p-ing*** not only for these
Acts 6:6 . . . apostles, who ***p-ed*** for them
Acts 9:11 . . . He is ***p-ing*** to me right now.
Acts 16:25 . . . Paul and Silas were ***p-ing***
Rom 8:26 . . . the Holy Spirit ***p-s*** for us
Rom 12:12 . . . and keep on ***p-ing***.
Rom 15:30 . . . join in my struggle by ***p-ing***
1 Cor 14:14 . . . For if I ***p*** in tongues,
1 Cor 14:14 . . . my spirit is ***p-ing***,
2 Cor 13:9 . . . We ***p*** that you will become
Eph 1:18 . . . I ***p*** that your hearts will be
Eph 3:16 . . . I ***p*** that from his glorious,
Phil 4:6 . . . instead, ***p*** about everything.
1 Thes 1:3 . . . As we ***p*** to our God and
1 Thes 5:17 . . . Never stop ***p-ing***.
2 Thes 1:11 . . . we keep on ***p-ing*** for you,
1 Tim 2:8 . . . to ***p*** with holy hands
Jas 5:13 . . . You should ***p***.
Jas 5:16 . . . ***p*** for each other so that
Jude 1:20 . . . ***p*** in the power of the Holy

PRAYER, PRAYERS (N) conversation with God—in praise, thanksgiving, or intercession
2 Chr 30:27 . . . God heard their ***p*** from
Ps 4:1 . . . mercy on me and hear my ***p***.
Ps 17:1 . . . Pay attention to my ***p***,
Ps 20:5 . . . LORD answer all your ***p-s***.
Ps 86:6 . . . Listen closely to my ***p***,
Prov 15:8 . . . in the ***p-s*** of the upright.
Isa 1:15 . . . Though you offer many ***p-s***,
Isa 56:7 . . . will be called a house of ***p***
Matt 11:25 . . . Jesus prayed this ***p***:
John 17:9 . . . My ***p*** is not for the world,
Acts 1:14 . . . were constantly united in ***p***,
Acts 4:31 . . . After this ***p***, the meeting
Acts 6:4 . . . can spend our time in ***p***
Acts 10:31 . . . your ***p*** has been heard,
Acts 13:3 . . . So after more fasting and ***p***,
Eph 6:18 . . . persistent in your ***p-s*** for all
Col 4:2 . . . Devote yourselves to ***p*** with an
1 Pet 3:7 . . . your ***p-s*** will not be hindered.
1 Pet 3:12 . . . ears are open to their ***p-s***.
Rev 5:8 . . . are the ***p-s*** of God's people.

PRETEND, PRETENDED (V) to give a false appearance of being, possessing, or performing
1 Sam 21:13 . . . So he ***p-ed*** to be insane,

Zech 13:4 . . . No one will *p* to be a prophet
Rom 12:9 . . . Don't just *p* to love

PRIDE (N) inordinate self-esteem or conceit; disdainful behavior or treatment of others
Ps 101:5 . . . will not endure conceit and *p.*
Prov 6:3 . . . Now swallow your *p;*
Prov 8:13 . . . I hate *p* and arrogance,
Mark 7:22 . . . envy, slander, *p,* and
1 Jn 2:16 . . . *p* in our achievements and

PRIEST, PRIESTS (N) one authorized to perform the sacred rites of sacrifice and worship; a mediator between God and humans
Exod 19:6 . . . will be my kingdom of *p-s,*
Ps 110:4 . . . You are a *p* forever
Mal 1:6 . . . Armies says to the *p-s:*
Heb 4:14 . . . since we have a great High *P*
Heb 5:6 . . . You are a *p* forever
Heb 6:20 . . . our eternal High *P*
Heb 8:1 . . . a High *P* who sat down
1 Pet 2:5 . . . you are his holy *p-s.*
1 Pet 2:9 . . . You are royal *p-s,*
Rev 5:10 . . . Kingdom of *p-s* for our God.
Rev 20:6 . . . but they will be *p-s* of God

PRISON, PRISONS (N) a state of confinement or captivity; jail
Ps 142:7 . . . Bring me out of *p*
Isa 42:7 . . . will free the captives from *p,*
Matt 25:36 . . . I was in *p,* and you visited
2 Cor 11:23 . . . been put in *p* more often,
Heb 11:36 . . . were chained in *p-s.*
Heb 13:3 . . . Remember those in *p,*
1 Pet 3:19 . . . preached to the spirits in *p*—
Jude 1:6 . . . chained in *p-s* of darkness,
Rev 20:7 . . . Satan will be let out of his *p.*

PRIZE (N) something offered or striven for in competitions or in contests
1 Cor 9:24 . . . one person gets the *p?*
1 Cor 9:25 . . . we do it for an eternal *p.*
Phil 3:14 . . . heavenly *p* for which God,
2 Tim 2:5 . . . cannot win the *p* unless
2 Tim 4:8 . . . *p* awaits me—the crown

PROCLAIM, PROCLAIMING, PROCLAIMS (V) to declare publicly
Lev 25:10 . . . a time to *p* freedom
Deut 32:3 . . . I will *p* the name of
1 Chr 16:8 . . . and *p* his greatness.
Ps 2:7 . . . king *p-s* the LORD's decree:
Ps 50:6 . . . heavens *p* his justice,
Ps 97:6 . . . heavens *p* his righteousness;
Ps 145:4 . . . let them *p* your power.
Isa 61:1 . . . to *p* that captives will be
Acts 28:31 . . . *p-ing* the Kingdom of God
Col 1:25 . . . *p-ing* his entire message to you.
1 Thes 3:2 . . . in *p-ing* the Good News
Titus 1:1 . . . I have been sent to *p* faith
1 Jn 1:1 . . . *p* to you the one who existed

PROMISE, PROMISES (N) a declaration that one will do or refrain from doing something specified
see also COVENANT(S)
2 Sam 7:25 . . . a *p* that will last forever.
Neh 5:13 . . . If you fail to keep your *p,*
Ps 91:4 . . . faithful *p-s* are your armor
Ps 116:14 . . . keep my *p-s* to the LORD
Ps 145:13 . . . LORD always keeps his *p-s;*
Ps 146:6 . . . He keeps every *p* forever.
Rom 4:20 . . . in believing God's *p.*
Rom 9:4 . . . receiving his wonderful *p-s.*
Rom 15:4 . . . patiently for God's *p-s* to be
2 Cor 1:20 . . . *p-s* have been fulfilled
2 Cor 7:1 . . . Because we have these *p-s,*
Eph 2:12 . . . covenant *p-s* God had made
Heb 6:13 . . . God's *p* to Abraham.
Heb 8:6 . . . based on better *p-s.*
Heb 10:23 . . . be trusted to keep his *p.*
Heb 11:11 . . . that God would keep his *p.*
2 Pet 3:4 . . . *p* that Jesus is coming again?
2 Pet 3:9 . . . being slow about his *p,*

PROMISED, PROMISES, PROMISING (V) to pledge to do, bring about, or provide
Exod 3:17 . . . I have *p-d* to rescue you
Deut 15:6 . . . bless you as he has *p-d.*
Josh 23:15 . . . the good things he *p-d,*
Luke 24:49 . . . as my Father *p-d.*
Acts 1:4 . . . sends you the gift he *p-d,*
Rom 4:21 . . . able to do whatever he *p-s.*
Gal 3:14 . . . blessing he *p-d* to Abraham,
1 Tim 4:8 . . . *p-ing* benefits in this life
Titus 1:2 . . . God—who does not lie—*p-d*
Heb 10:36 . . . receive all that he has *p-d.*
Jas 1:12 . . . of life that God has *p-d*
Jas 2:5 . . . inherit the Kingdom he *p-d*
2 Pet 3:13 . . . new earth he has *p-d,*
1 Jn 2:25 . . . eternal life he *p-d* us.

PROPHET, PROPHETS (N) an interpreter of the times and people's hearts; one who issues divinely inspired revelations
Deut 13:1 . . . there are *p-s* among you
Deut 18:18 . . . I will raise up a *p* like you
1 Sam 9:9 . . . *p-s* used to be called seers.
1 Kgs 18:36 . . . Elijah the *p* walked up to
2 Kgs 5:8 . . . a true *p* here in Israel.
2 Kgs 6:12 . . . Elisha, the *p* in Israel,
Matt 5:17 . . . or the writings of the *p-s.*
Matt 7:12 . . . in the law and the *p-s.*
2 Pet 1:21 . . . those *p-s* were moved by
2 Pet 3:2 . . . what the holy *p-s* said long
Rev 11:10 . . . death of the two *p-s* who
Rev 18:20 . . . God and apostles and *p-s!*

PROSPER, PROSPERS (V) to achieve economic success; to become strong and flourishing
Deut 28:63 . . . pleasure in causing you to *p*
Ps 37:3 . . . safely in the land and *p.*
Ps 73:3 . . . *p* despite their wickedness.
Prov 16:20 . . . listen to instruction will *p;*
Prov 17:9 . . . Love *p-s* when a fault is forgiven,
Prov 19:8 . . . cherish understanding will *p.*
Isa 53:10 . . . LORD's good plan will *p*
Isa 55:11 . . . it will *p* everywhere I send it.
Dan 4:27 . . . then you will continue to *p.*

PROTECT, PROTECTED, PROTECTING, PROTECTS (V) to cover or shield from exposure, injury, damage, or destruction; to defend
see also KEEP
Gen 15:1 . . . for I will *p* you,
Num 6:24 . . . bless you and *p* you.
Josh 6:17 . . . for she *p-ed* our spies.
1 Sam 2:9 . . . He will *p* his faithful ones,
Ps 23:4 . . . your staff *p* and comfort me.
Ps 27:1 . . . fortress, *p-ing* me from danger,
Ps 41:2 . . . LORD *p-s* them and keeps
Ps 116:6 . . . LORD *p-s* those of childlike
Ps 127:1 . . . Unless the LORD *p-s* a city,
Ps 145:20 . . . LORD *p-s* all those who love
Ps 146:9 . . . LORD *p-s* the foreigners
Prov 2:8 . . . *p-s* those who are faithful
Isa 31:5 . . . like a bird *p-ing* its nest.
Isa 57:1 . . . God is *p-ing* them from the
John 17:11 . . . now *p* them by the power of
Acts 26:22 . . . But God has *p-ed* me
Gal 3:24 . . . *p-ed* us until we could be

1 Pet 1:5 . . . God is ***p-ing*** you by his power
Rev 3:10 . . . I will ***p*** you from the great

PROUD (ADJ) having or displaying excessive self-esteem
Ps 5:5 . . . ***p*** may not stand in your
Prov 21:4 . . . Haughty eyes, a ***p*** heart,
Rom 1:30 . . . haters of God, insolent, ***p***,
1 Cor 13:4 . . . not jealous or boastful or ***p***
1 Tim 3:6 . . . he might become ***p***,
1 Tim 6:17 . . . rich in this world not to be ***p***
2 Tim 3:2 . . . They will be boastful and ***p***,

PROUD (N) those having or displaying excessive self-esteem
Prov 16:5 . . . LORD detests the ***p***;
Dan 4:37 . . . he is able to humble the ***p***.
Jas 4:6 . . . God opposes the ***p*** but gives
1 Pet 5:5 . . . God opposes the ***p*** but gives

PROVIDE, PROVIDED, PROVIDES (V) to furnish or supply, implying foresight in making provision for the future
Gen 22:8 . . . God will ***p*** a sheep
Gen 22:14 . . . means "the LORD will ***p***"
Ps 68:10 . . . O God, you ***p-d*** for your needy
Isa 4:5 . . . the LORD will ***p*** shade
Jer 5:28 . . . refuse to ***p*** justice to orphans
Ezek 18:7 . . . and ***p-s*** clothes for the needy.
2 Cor 9:8 . . . God will generously ***p*** all you
2 Cor 9:10 . . . he will ***p*** and increase your

PUNISH, PUNISHED, PUNISHES, PUNISHING (V) to impose a penalty to fit the crime: from corrective measures (fines or scolding) and corporal punishment (spanking or whipping) to capital punishment and eternal damnation
Gen 15:14 . . . But I will ***p*** the nation
1 Kgs 8:32 . . . ***P*** the guilty as they deserve.
Prov 11:21 . . . people will surely be ***p-ed***,
Jer 25:14 . . . I will ***p*** them in proportion
Lam 3:39 . . . when we are ***p-ed*** for our sins?
Mark 12:40 . . . will be more severely ***p-ed***.
Acts 7:7 . . . But I will ***p*** the nation
Rom 2:2 . . . God, in his justice, will ***p***
Rom 13:4 . . . they have the power to ***p*** you.
Rom 13:4 . . . the very purpose of ***p-ing***
2 Thes 1:9 . . . ***p-ed*** with eternal destruction,
Heb 2:2 . . . act of disobedience was ***p-ed***.
Heb 12:6 . . . he ***p-es*** each one he accepts
1 Pet 2:14 . . . sent them to ***p*** those who
Rev 19:2 . . . has ***p-ed*** the great prostitute

PURPOSE, PURPOSES (N) something set up as an object or end to be attained; resolution, determination
see also PLAN(S)
Exod 9:16 . . . I have spared you for a ***p***—
Prov 19:21 . . . the LORD's ***p*** will prevail.
Rom 8:28 . . . according to his ***p*** for them.
Rom 9:11 . . . according to his own ***p-s***;
Rom 9:17 . . . for the very ***p*** of displaying
1 Cor 3:8 . . . with the same ***p***.
1 Cor 9:26 . . . I run with ***p*** in every step.
Phil 2:2 . . . together with one mind and ***p***.

Q

QUARREL, QUARRELS (N) a usually verbal conflict between antagonists
Prov 10:12 . . . Hatred stirs up ***q-s***,
Prov 17:14 . . . Starting a ***q*** is like opening
Prov 26:20 . . . ***q-s*** disappear when gossip
Prov 30:33 . . . anger causes ***q-s***.
Titus 3:9 . . . ***q-s*** and fights about
Jas 4:1 . . . causing the ***q-s*** and fights

QUARREL, QUARRELING (V) to find fault; to contend or dispute actively
Exod 21:18 . . . "Now suppose two men ***q***,
Prov 17:19 . . . Anyone who loves to ***q*** loves
Prov 20:3 . . . fools insist on ***q-ing***.
Isa 58:4 . . . keep on fighting and ***q-ing***?
Rom 13:13 . . . or in ***q-ing*** and jealousy.
1 Cor 3:3 . . . and ***q*** with each other.
2 Cor 12:20 . . . will find ***q-ing***, jealousy,

QUIET (ADJ) calm; gentle; peaceful, still; free from noise
Prov 11:12 . . . a sensible person keeps ***q***.
Eccl 3:7 . . . A time to be ***q*** and a time
Eccl 9:17 . . . to hear the ***q*** words of a wise
Luke 19:40 . . . If they kept ***q***, the stones
1 Thes 4:11 . . . to live a ***q*** life,
1 Tim 2:2 . . . peaceful and ***q*** lives marked

R

RACE (N) an athletic contest; an ethnic classification
Ps 19:5 . . . athlete eager to run the ***r***.
Eccl 9:11 . . . doesn't always win the ***r***,
Dan 7:14 . . . people of every ***r*** and nation
1 Cor 9:24 . . . that in a ***r*** everyone runs,
Gal 2:2 . . . running the ***r*** for nothing.
Gal 5:7 . . . were running the ***r*** so well.
2 Tim 4:7 . . . I have finished the ***r***,
Heb 12:1 . . . run with endurance the ***r*** God

RAISE, RAISED (V) to recall from death
see also RESURRECTION
Judg 2:16 . . . the Lord ***r-d*** up judges
Luke 7:22 . . . the dead are ***r-d*** to life,
John 6:39 . . . that I should ***r*** them up
Acts 2:32 . . . God ***r-d*** Jesus from the dead,
Acts 24:15 . . . that he will ***r*** both the
Rom 1:4 . . . he was ***r-d*** from the dead
Rom 6:5 . . . we will also be ***r-d*** to life
Rom 10:9 . . . God ***r-d*** him from the dead,
1 Cor 15:4 . . . he was ***r-d*** from the dead
Phil 3:10 . . . mighty power that ***r-d*** him
1 Thes 4:14 . . . died and was ***r-d*** to life
1 Pet 1:3 . . . because God ***r-d*** Jesus Christ

READ, READING, READS (V) to receive and interpret letters or symbols by sight
Deut 17:19 . . . with him and ***r*** it daily
Josh 8:34 . . . Joshua then ***r*** to them
2 Kgs 23:2 . . . There the king ***r*** to them
Acts 8:28 . . . carriage, he was ***r-ing*** aloud
2 Cor 3:2 . . . everyone can ***r*** it and
1 Tim 4:13 . . . focus on ***r-ing*** the Scriptures
Rev 1:3 . . . the one who ***r-s*** the words of

REBEL, REBELLED, REBELLING, REBELS (V) to oppose or disobey one in authority or control
Num 14:9 . . . Do not ***r*** against the
Num 27:14 . . . of Israel ***r-led***, you failed to
1 Sam 12:14 . . . if you do not ***r*** against the
Ps 78:56 . . . testing and ***r-ling*** against God
Isa 63:10 . . . But they ***r-led*** against him
Matt 10:21 . . . children will ***r*** against their
Rom 13:2 . . . So anyone who ***r-s*** against

REBELLION (N) opposition to one in authority or dominance; defiance
Exod 34:7 . . . forgive iniquity, ***r***, and sin.
Ps 32:5 . . . I will confess my ***r*** to the
Ps 39:8 . . . Rescue me from my ***r***.
Dan 9:24 . . . to finish their ***r***, to put an
2 Thes 2:3 . . . is a great ***r*** against God

RECEIVE, RECEIVED, RECEIVES (V) to acquire or take possession of; to welcome
Matt 7:8 . . . For everyone who asks, *r-s*.
Matt 19:17 . . . you want to *r* eternal life,
John 20:22 . . . said, "*R* the Holy Spirit.
Acts 1:8 . . . But you will *r* power when the
Acts 2:38 . . . Then you will *r* the gift of
Acts 8:17 . . . they *r-d* the Holy Spirit.
Acts 10:47 . . . they have *r-d* the Holy
Acts 19:2 . . . Did you *r* the Holy Spirit
Rom 8:15 . . . Instead, you *r-d* God's Spirit
1 Tim 1:16 . . . in him and *r* eternal life.
Rev 4:11 . . . our God, to *r* glory and honor

REDEEM, REDEEMED, REDEEMS (V) to buy back; to save by payment of a ransom; to free from the consequences of sin
see also RESCUE
Exod 6:6 . . . I will *r* you with a powerful
2 Sam 7:23 . . . have you *r-ed* from slavery
Ps 34:22 . . . the LORD will *r* those
Ps 49:15 . . . God will *r* my life.
Ps 74:2 . . . the tribe you *r-ed* as your own
Ps 103:4 . . . He *r-s* me from death and
Ps 107:2 . . . Has the LORD *r-ed* you?
Ps 130:8 . . . He himself will *r* Israel from
Isa 35:9 . . . Only the *r-ed* will walk
Isa 63:9 . . . love and mercy he *r-ed* them.
Hos 7:13 . . . I wanted to *r* them, but they

REFUGE (N) shelter or protection from danger or distress
see also FORTRESS, SHELTER
Deut 33:27 . . . eternal God is your *r*,
2 Sam 22:3 . . . He is my *r*, my savior,
Ps 2:12 . . . for all who take *r* in him!
Ps 5:11 . . . But let all who take *r* in you
Ps 17:7 . . . those who seek *r* from their
Ps 34:8 . . . those who take *r* in him!
Ps 46:1 . . . God is our *r* and strength,
Ps 91:2 . . . He alone is my *r*, my place

REIGN, REIGNED, REIGNING, REIGNS (V) to possess or exercise sovereign power; to rule
Exod 15:18 . . . The LORD will *r* forever
Ps 9:7 . . . But the LORD *r-s* forever,
Ps 29:10 . . . LORD *r-s* as king forever.
Ps 96:10 . . . The LORD *r-s!*
Ps 146:10 . . . The LORD will *r* forever.
Isa 52:7 . . . that the God of Israel *r-s!*
1 Cor 4:8 . . . we would be *r-ing* with you.
1 Cor 15:25 . . . For Christ must *r* until he
Rev 5:10 . . . And they will *r* on the earth.
Rev 11:15 . . . and he will *r* forever
Rev 19:6 . . . our God, the Almighty, *r-s*.
Rev 20:4 . . . and they *r-ed* with Christ
Rev 22:5 . . . And they will *r* forever

REJOICE, REJOICED, REJOICES, REJOICING (V) to feel joy or great delight; to gladden
1 Chr 16:31 . . . glad, and the earth *r!*
Esth 8:17 . . . decree arrived, the Jews *r-d*
Ps 5:11 . . . who take refuge in you *r;*
Ps 13:5 . . . I will *r* because you
Ps 35:9 . . . I will *r* in the LORD.
Ps 48:2 . . . the whole earth *r-s* to see it!
Ps 68:4 . . . LORD—*r* in his presence!
Lam 4:21 . . . Are you *r-ing* in the land
Zeph 3:17 . . . He will *r* over you
Zech 2:10 . . . Shout and *r*, O beautiful
Luke 1:14 . . . and many will *r* at his birth,
Luke 1:47 . . . How my spirit *r-s* in God my
Luke 1:58 . . . everyone *r-d* with her.
1 Cor 13:6 . . . *r* about injustice but *r-s*
Phil 2:18 . . . you should *r*, and I will
Phil 3:1 . . . and sisters, *r* in the Lord.
Phil 4:4 . . . I say it again—*r!*
Col 2:5 . . . I *r* that you are living as
Rev 19:7 . . . Let us be glad and *r*, and

REMEMBER, REMEMBERED, REMEMBERING, REMEMBERS (V) to bring to mind or think of again; to keep in mind for attention or consideration; to retain in the memory
Gen 9:15 . . . I will *r* my covenant with
Exod 2:24 . . . *r-ed* his covenant promise
1 Chr 16:12 . . . *R* the wonders he has
Ps 49:13 . . . though they are *r-ed* as being
Ps 103:14 . . . he *r-s* we are only dust.
Ps 106:45 . . . *r-ed* his covenant with them
Ps 111:5 . . . he always *r-s* his covenant.
Ps 136:23 . . . He *r-ed* us in our weakness.
Jer 31:34 . . . never again *r* their sins.
Jer 32:20 . . . things still *r-ed* to this day!
Hab 3:2 . . . in your anger, *r* your mercy.
Matt 26:13 . . . will be *r-ed* and discussed.
Luke 1:72 . . . *r-ing* his sacred covenant—
Luke 22:19 . . . Do this to *r* me.
1 Cor 11:24 . . . Do this to *r* me.
2 Tim 2:8 . . . Always *r* that Jesus
Heb 8:12 . . . never again *r* their sins.
2 Pet 1:15 . . . you always *r* these things

RENEW, RENEWED, RENEWS (V) to restore to freshness, vigor, or perfection; to make new spiritually
Ps 23:3 . . . He *r-s* my strength.
Ps 51:10 . . . *R* a loyal spirit within me.
Isa 57:10 . . . Desire gave you *r-ed* strength,
Eph 4:23 . . . let the Spirit *r* your thoughts
Col 3:10 . . . be *r-ed* as you learn to know

REPENT, REPENTED, REPENTING, REPENTS (V) to turn from sin and change one's heart and behavior; to feel regret and contrition
Matt 3:2 . . . *R* of your sins and turn
Matt 3:8 . . . that you have *r-ed* of your sins
Matt 4:17 . . . began to preach, "*R* of your
Matt 11:21 . . . people would have *r-ed* of
Luke 3:8 . . . that you have *r-ed* of your sins
Luke 15:7 . . . sinner who *r-s* and returns
Luke 15:10 . . . when even one sinner *r-s*.
Acts 2:38 . . . you must *r* of your sins
Acts 17:30 . . . everywhere to *r* of their sins
Acts 20:21 . . . necessity of *r-ing* from sin
Heb 6:1 . . . importance of *r-ing* from evil
2 Pet 3:9 . . . but wants everyone to *r*.
Rev 2:5 . . . If you don't *r*, I will come

REPUTATION (N) overall quality or character as seen or judged by people in general
Prov 3:4 . . . you will earn a good *r*.
1 Tim 3:2 . . . wisely, and have a good *r*.
Heb 11:39 . . . good *r* because of their

RESCUE, RESCUED, RESCUES, RESCUING (V) to save or deliver
see also REDEEM, SAVE
2 Kgs 13:5 . . . someone to *r* the Israelites
Ps 9:14 . . . rejoice that you have *r-d* me.
Ps 17:7 . . . mighty power you *r* those who
Ps 22:8 . . . let the LORD *r* him!
Ps 31:2 . . . listen to me; *r* me quickly.
Ps 37:39 . . . The LORD *r-s* the godly;
Ps 37:40 . . . LORD helps them, *r-ing* them
Ps 68:20 . . . The Sovereign LORD *r-s* us
Ps 72:12 . . . He will *r* the poor when
Ps 145:19 . . . cries for help and *r-s* them.
Prov 11:8 . . . godly are *r-d* from trouble,
Isa 56:1 . . . coming soon to *r* you and
Dan 6:27 . . . He *r-s* and saves his people;

Zech 8:7 . . . that I will *r* my people from
Matt 6:13 . . . but *r* us from the evil one.
Rom 11:26 . . . The one who *r-s* will come
2 Cor 1:10 . . . And he did *r* us from mortal
Gal 1:4 . . . in order to *r* us from this
Gal 3:13 . . . But Christ has *r-d* us from the
Col 1:13 . . . For he has *r-d* us from the
1 Thes 1:10 . . . the one who has *r-d* us
2 Pet 2:9 . . . knows how to *r* godly people

RESPECT (N) a high or special regard; esteem
see also AWE, REVERENCE
Prov 11:16 . . . A gracious woman gains *r*,
Mal 1:6 . . . the honor and *r* I deserve?
Titus 2:2 . . . be worthy of *r*, and to live

RESPONSIBLE (ADJ) marked by or involving responsibility or accountability; liable to be called to account as the primary cause, motive, or agent
Exod 32:34 . . . hold them *r* for their sins.
Num 1:53 . . . The Levites are *r* to stand
Ezek 33:6 . . . he is *r* for their captivity.
Jonah 1:14 . . . And don't hold us *r* for his
Gal 6:5 . . . For we are each *r* for our own

REST (N) freedom from activity or labor; peace of mind or spirit; repose, sleep
see also SABBATH
Exod 31:15 . . . day of complete *r*, a holy
Exod 33:14 . . . and I will give you *r*—
Ps 91:1 . . . Most High will find *r* in the
Ps 127:2 . . . for God gives *r* to his loved
Jer 6:16 . . . you will find *r* for your
Matt 11:28 . . . and I will give you *r*.
2 Thes 1:7 . . . God will provide *r* for you
Heb 4:3 . . . even though this *r* has been
Heb 4:9 . . . a special *r* still waiting
Heb 4:10 . . . who have entered into God's *r*

RESURRECTION (N) the state of one risen from the dead; the rising again to life of all the human dead before the final judgment
see also RAISE, RISE
Matt 27:53 . . . cemetery after Jesus' *r*,
Mark 12:23 . . . will she be in the *r*?
Luke 20:36 . . . children of the *r*.
John 11:25 . . . I am the *r* and the life.
Acts 1:22 . . . as a witness of Jesus' *r*.
Acts 2:31 . . . speaking of the Messiah's *r*.
Acts 4:2 . . . there is a *r* of the dead.
Acts 4:33 . . . powerfully to the *r* of
Acts 17:32 . . . Paul speak about the *r* of
1 Cor 15:13 . . . if there is no *r* of the
1 Cor 15:42 . . . way with the *r* of the dead.
Phil 3:11 . . . experience the *r* from the
2 Tim 2:18 . . . claiming that the *r* of the
Heb 6:2 . . . of hands, the *r* of the dead,
Heb 11:35 . . . a better life after the *r*.
1 Pet 3:21 . . . because of the *r* of Jesus
Rev 20:5 . . . This is the first *r*.

REVERENCE (N) profound, adoring, awed respect
see also AWE, FEAR, RESPECT
Lev 19:30 . . . of rest, and show *r* toward
Job 15:4 . . . fear of God, no *r* for him?
Job 37:24 . . . who are wise show him *r*.
Eph 5:21 . . . another out of *r* for Christ.
Heb 5:7 . . . of his deep *r* for God.

REWARD, REWARDS (N) something that is given in return for good or evil done or received or that is offered or given for some service or attainment
Gen 15:1 . . . and your *r* will be
1 Sam 26:23 . . . gives his own *r* for doing
Prov 12:14 . . . and hard work brings *r-s*.
Isa 49:4 . . . I will trust God for my *r*.
Matt 5:12 . . . For a great *r* awaits you
Matt 6:5 . . . all the *r* they will ever
Luke 6:23 . . . For a great *r* awaits you
Luke 6:35 . . . your *r* from heaven will
Phil 4:17 . . . you to receive a *r* for your
1 Thes 2:19 . . . be our proud *r* and crown
Heb 10:35 . . . the great *r* it brings you!
1 Pet 1:9 . . . The *r* for trusting him

RICH (ADJ) having abundant possessions and especially material wealth
Prov 10:4 . . . poor; hard workers get *r*.
Prov 28:6 . . . than to be dishonest and *r*.
Prov 28:22 . . . Greedy people try to get *r*
Eccl 5:12 . . . But the *r* seldom get a
Matt 19:23 . . . hard for a *r* person to enter
Luke 1:53 . . . and sent the *r* away with
Luke 6:24 . . . you who are *r*, for you have
Luke 21:1 . . . watched the *r* people
2 Cor 8:9 . . . Though he was *r*, yet for your
1 Tim 6:17 . . . who are *r* in this world
Jas 1:10 . . . those who are *r* should boast
Jas 2:3 . . . seat to the *r* person, but you

RIGHT (ADJ) being in accordance with what is good, just, or proper; being in a correct or proper state; located opposite of left; acting or judging in accordance with truth or fact
see also RIGHTEOUS
Exod 15:26 . . . do what is *r* in his sight,
Deut 6:18 . . . Do what is *r* and good
Judg 17:6 . . . whatever seemed *r* in their
Ps 84:11 . . . from those who do what is *r*.
Ps 106:3 . . . and always do what is *r*.
Ps 119:144 . . . laws are always *r*; help me
Prov 1:3 . . . do what is *r*, just, and fair.
Eccl 8:5 . . . and a way to do what is *r*,
Isa 16:5 . . . be eager to do what is *r*.
Jer 23:5 . . . is just and *r* throughout the
Mic 3:1 . . . to know *r* from wrong,
Mic 6:8 . . . do what is *r*, to love mercy,
Acts 13:39 . . . is declared *r* with God—
Rom 1:17 . . . God makes us *r* in his sight.
Rom 5:1 . . . we have been made *r* in God's
Gal 3:24 . . . could be made *r* with God
Phil 4:8 . . . honorable, and *r*, and pure,
2 Tim 3:16 . . . teaches us to do what is *r*.
1 Jn 2:29 . . . who do what is *r* are God's

RIGHTEOUS (ADJ) acting in accord with divine or moral law; free from guilt or sin; morally right or justifiable
see also RIGHT
Gen 15:6 . . . counted him as *r* because of
Rom 3:10 . . . No one is *r*—not even one.
Rom 4:3 . . . counted him as *r* because of
Titus 3:7 . . . he declared us *r* and gave us
Jas 5:16 . . . prayer of a *r* person has
1 Jn 2:1 . . . the one who is truly *r*.
1 Jn 3:7 . . . that they are *r*, even as

RIGHTEOUSNESS (N) the state or quality of being righteous
see also JUSTICE
Eph 6:14 . . . the body armor of God's *r*.
2 Tim 4:8 . . . the crown of *r*, which
Heb 11:7 . . . he received the *r* that comes
Jas 3:18 . . . and reap a harvest of *r*.
2 Pet 3:13 . . . filled with God's *r*.

RISE, RISEN, RISES (V) to ascend or extend above other objects; to return from death; to assume an upright position
see also RESURRECTION
Num 24:17 . . . A star will *r* from Jacob;
Isa 26:19 . . . bodies will *r* again!

Mal 4:2 . . . of Righteousness will *r* with
Matt 22:30 . . . when the dead *r*, they will
Matt 27:63 . . . I will *r* from the dead.
Matt 28:6 . . . He is *r-n* from the dead,
Mark 8:31 . . . later he would *r* from the
Mark 16:6 . . . He is *r-n* from the dead!
Luke 18:33 . . . day he will *r* again.
Luke 24:34 . . . The Lord has really *r-n!*
John 5:29 . . . and they will *r* again.
John 11:24 . . . when everyone else *r-s*, at
John 20:9 . . . said Jesus must *r* from the
Acts 17:3 . . . must suffer and *r* from the
1 Thes 4:16 . . . have died will *r* from

RUIN, RUINED, RUINING, RUINS (V) to damage irreparably; to subject to frustration, failure, or disaster
Prov 19:3 . . . People *r* their lives by
Prov 19:18 . . . you will *r* their lives.
Prov 22:23 . . . He will *r* anyone who *r-s*
Isa 3:14 . . . You have *r-ed* Israel,
Matt 9:17 . . . the wine and *r-ing* the skins.
2 Tim 2:14 . . . they can *r* those who hear

RULER, RULERS (N) person with authority; tribal chief; prince or king; city magistrate; powerful spiritual beings; God himself
Judg 8:22 . . . to Gideon, "Be our *r!*
1 Sam 10:1 . . . to be the *r* over Israel,
Prov 19:6 . . . favors from a *r;* everyone is
Prov 23:1 . . . with a *r*, pay attention to
Jer 30:21 . . . have their own *r* again,
Dan 7:27 . . . all *r-s* will serve and obey him.
Dan 9:25 . . . until a *r*—the Anointed One—
Mic 5:2 . . . a *r* of Israel, whose origins
Matt 2:6 . . . for a *r* will come from
Matt 20:25 . . . that the *r-s* in this world
John 12:31 . . . when Satan, the *r* of this
1 Cor 2:6 . . . or to the *r-s* of this world,
Eph 1:21 . . . far above any *r* or authority
Eph 3:10 . . . the unseen *r-s* and authorities
Eph 6:12 . . . but against evil *r-s* and
Col 1:16 . . . as thrones, kingdoms, *r-s*, and
Col 2:15 . . . disarmed the spiritual *r-s* and
Rev 1:5 . . . and the *r* of all the kings

RUN, RUNNING (V) to go faster than a walk; to flee
Ps 19:5 . . . athlete eager to *r* the race.
Prov 4:12 . . . when you *r*, you won't
Isa 40:31 . . . will *r* and not grow weary.
1 Cor 9:26 . . . So I *r* with purpose in
Gal 2:2 . . . and I was *r-ning* the race for
Gal 5:7 . . . You were *r-ning* the race so
Phil 2:16 . . . that I did not *r* the race in
1 Tim 6:11 . . . so *r* from all these evil
2 Tim 2:22 . . . *R* from anything that
Heb 12:1 . . . let us *r* with endurance

S

SABBATH, SABBATHS (N) cessation of activity; a holy day set aside to honor God through rest and worship
see also REST
Exod 20:8 . . . to observe the *S* day by
Exod 31:14 . . . must keep the *S* day, for it
Lev 25:2 . . . must observe a *S* rest before
Deut 5:12 . . . Observe the *S* day by
2 Chr 2:4 . . . and evening, on the *S-s*,
Isa 56:2 . . . who honor my *S* days of rest
Isa 56:6 . . . do not desecrate the *S* day
Isa 58:13 . . . Honor the *S* in everything
Matt 12:1 . . . some grainfields on the *S*.
Luke 13:10 . . . One *S* day as Jesus was
Col 2:16 . . . new moon ceremonies or *S-s*.

SACRIFICE, SACRIFICES (N) worship or atonement offering; something given up or lost
Exod 12:27 . . . It is the Passover *s* to the
1 Sam 15:22 . . . Obedience is better than *s*,
Ps 40:6 . . . no delight in *s-s* or offerings.
Ps 51:16 . . . do not desire a *s*, or I would
Ps 51:17 . . . The *s* you desire is
Ps 107:22 . . . offer *s-s* of thanksgiving
Prov 15:8 . . . LORD detests the *s* of
Hos 6:6 . . . to show love, not offer *s-s*.
Matt 9:13 . . . to show mercy, not offer *s-s*.
Rom 3:25 . . . Jesus as the *s* for sin.
Rom 8:3 . . . Son as a *s* for our sins.
Rom 12:1 . . . a living and holy *s*—the
Eph 5:2 . . . himself as a *s* for us,
Heb 5:3 . . . he must offer *s-s* for his own
Heb 7:27 . . . need to offer *s-s* every day.
Heb 9:28 . . . time as a *s* to take away
Heb 10:5 . . . did not want animal *s-s* or sin
Heb 10:10 . . . holy by the *s* of the body of
Heb 13:15 . . . Jesus a continual *s* of praise
Heb 13:16 . . . These are the *s-s* that please
1 Pet 2:5 . . . offer spiritual *s-s* that please
1 Jn 2:2 . . . himself is the *s* that atones
1 Jn 4:10 . . . his Son as a *s* to take away

SAFE (ADJ) free from harm or risk; secure from threat of danger, harm, or loss
Deut 29:19 . . . I am *s*, even though I am
1 Sam 30:23 . . . has kept us *s* and helped
Ps 4:8 . . . O LORD, will keep me *s*.
Ps 28:8 . . . He is a *s* fortress for his
Prov 2:11 . . . will keep you *s*.
Prov 4:26 . . . stay on the *s* path.
Prov 18:10 . . . run to him and are *s*.
Prov 28:26 . . . who walks in wisdom is *s*.
John 17:15 . . . keep them *s* from the evil

SALVATION (N) deliverance from the power and effects of sin, danger, or difficulty by God's intervention
see also SAVE
2 Sam 22:47 . . . Rock of my *s*, be exalted!
2 Chr 6:41 . . . be clothed with *s;* may your
Ps 18:46 . . . God of my *s* be exalted!
Ps 27:1 . . . light and my *s*—so why should
Ps 40:16 . . . love your *s* repeatedly shout,
Ps 51:12 . . . joy of your *s*, and make me
Ps 62:2 . . . rock and my *s*, my fortress
Ps 69:13 . . . my prayer with your sure *s*.
Ps 74:12 . . . ages past, bringing *s* to
Ps 85:4 . . . us again, O God of our *s*.
Ps 89:26 . . . and the Rock of my *s*.
Ps 91:16 . . . long life and give them my *s*.
Ps 95:1 . . . joyfully to the Rock of our *s*.
Isa 25:9 . . . rejoice in the *s* he brings!
Isa 26:18 . . . We have not given *s* to the
Isa 33:6 . . . rich store of *s*, wisdom,
Isa 45:8 . . . wide so *s* and righteousness
Isa 45:22 . . . the world look to me for *s!*
Isa 49:6 . . . will bring my *s* to the ends
Isa 51:6 . . . but my *s* lasts forever.
Isa 52:7 . . . of peace and *s*, the news that
Isa 59:17 . . . the helmet of *s* on his head.
Isa 62:1 . . . dawn, and her *s* blazes like
Lam 3:26 . . . wait quietly for *s* from the
Jonah 2:9 . . . For my *s* comes from the
Luke 1:77 . . . to find *s* through forgiveness
Luke 2:30 . . . I have seen your *s*,
Luke 3:6 . . . will see the *s* sent from
Luke 21:28 . . . up, for your *s* is near!
John 4:22 . . . him, for *s* comes through the
Acts 13:26 . . . this message of *s* has been
Acts 13:47 . . . Gentiles, to bring *s* to the
Acts 28:28 . . . know that this *s* from God

Rom 11:11 . . . so God made *s* available to
Rom 13:11 . . . for our *s* is nearer now
2 Cor 6:2 . . . the day of *s*, I helped you.
2 Cor 7:10 . . . from sin and results in *s*.
Eph 6:17 . . . Put on *s* as your helmet,
Phil 2:12 . . . show the results of your *s*,
2 Thes 2:13 . . . to experience *s*—a *s*
Titus 2:11 . . . bringing *s* to all people.
Heb 2:3 . . . if we ignore this great *s* that
Heb 5:9 . . . source of eternal *s* for all
Heb 9:28 . . . but to bring *s* to all who
1 Pet 1:9 . . . will be the *s* of your souls.
1 Pet 1:13 . . . in the gracious *s* that will
1 Pet 2:2 . . . into a full experience of *s*.
Rev 7:10 . . . a great roar, "*S* comes from

SANCTUARY (N) a holy place set apart for worship of God or refuge from danger
see also TABERNACLE, TEMPLE
Exod 25:8 . . . build me a holy *s* so I can
Lev 19:30 . . . show reverence toward my *s*.
Ps 27:5 . . . he will hide me in his *s*.
Ps 63:2 . . . you in your *s* and gazed upon
Ps 68:35 . . . God is awesome in his *s*.
Ps 150:1 . . . Praise God in his *s*; praise
Heb 6:19 . . . curtain into God's inner *s*.

SAVE, SAVED, SAVES, SAVING (V) to rescue or deliver from danger or harm; to deliver from sin; to preserve or guard from injury, destruction, or loss; to maintain or preserve
see also RESCUE, SALVATION
2 Sam 22:3 . . . the power that *s-s* me,
1 Chr 16:23 . . . good news that he *s-s*.
Ps 7:10 . . . is my shield, *s-ing* those whose
Ps 18:48 . . . you *s* me from violent
Ps 22:8 . . . let the LORD *s* him!
Ps 25:5 . . . you are the God who *s-s* me.
Ps 33:16 . . . army cannot *s* a king, nor
Ps 34:6 . . . LORD listened; he *s-d* me
Ps 44:6 . . . not count on my sword to *s*
Ps 68:20 . . . Our God is a God who *s-s!*
Ps 109:31 . . . the needy, ready to *s* them
Ps 116:6 . . . death, and he *s-d* me.
Prov 2:16 . . . Wisdom will *s* you from
Prov 10:2 . . . right living can *s* your
Isa 25:9 . . . trusted in him, and he *s-d* us!
Isa 30:15 . . . resting in me will you be *s-d*.
Isa 35:4 . . . He is coming to *s* you.
Isa 59:1 . . . arm is not too weak to *s*
Isa 63:1 . . . who has the power to *s!*
Jer 4:14 . . . your heart that you may be *s-d*.
Jer 17:14 . . . if you *s* me, I will
Jer 51:9 . . . nothing can *s* her now.
Dan 3:17 . . . we serve is able to *s* us.
Joel 2:32 . . . name of the LORD will be *s-d*,
Mic 7:7 . . . wait confidently for God to *s*
Zeph 1:18 . . . gold will not *s* you
Matt 1:21 . . . he will *s* his people
Matt 16:25 . . . my sake, you will *s* it.
Matt 24:13 . . . to the end will be *s-d*.
Luke 17:33 . . . life go, you will *s* it.
Luke 19:10 . . . seek and *s* those who are
John 10:9 . . . in through me will be *s-d*.
John 12:47 . . . I have come to *s* the world
Acts 2:21 . . . name of the LORD will be *s-d*.
Acts 4:12 . . . by which we must be *s-d*.
Acts 15:11 . . . we are all *s-d* the same way,
Acts 16:30 . . . what must I do to be *s-d?*
Rom 1:16 . . . God at work, *s-ing* everyone
Rom 5:9 . . . he will certainly *s* us from
Rom 10:9 . . . the dead, you will be *s-d*.
Rom 10:13 . . . of the LORD will be *s-d*.
1 Cor 1:18 . . . we who are being *s-d* know
1 Cor 5:5 . . . himself will be *s-d* on the
1 Cor 7:16 . . . wives might be *s-d* because
1 Cor 10:33 . . . so that many may be *s-d*.
1 Cor 15:2 . . . this Good News that *s-s*
Eph 1:13 . . . Good News that God *s-s* you.
1 Thes 5:9 . . . God chose to *s* us through
1 Tim 1:15 . . . the world to *s* sinners
1 Tim 2:4 . . . wants everyone to be *s-d* and
1 Tim 2:15 . . . women will be *s-d* through
2 Tim 1:9 . . . For God *s-d* us and called
Titus 3:5 . . . he *s-d* us, not because of the
Heb 7:25 . . . and forever, to *s* those who
Jas 5:20 . . . will *s* that person from death
2 Pet 3:15 . . . gives people time to be *s-d*.

SAVIOR (N) one who delivers from trouble, sin, or judgment
2 Sam 22:2 . . . my fortress, and my *s*;
Ps 38:22 . . . help me, O LORD my *s*.
Ps 40:17 . . . You are my helper and my *s*.
Ps 106:21 . . . They forgot God, their *s*,
Isa 43:11 . . . and there is no other *S*.
Isa 45:21 . . . a righteous God and *S*.
Isa 49:26 . . . the LORD, am your *S* and
Isa 62:11 . . . Look, your *S* is coming.
Jer 14:8 . . . Hope of Israel, our *S* in
Hos 13:4 . . . for there is no other *s*.
Zeph 3:17 . . . He is a mighty *s*.
Luke 1:47 . . . rejoices in God my *S!*
Luke 1:69 . . . He has sent us a mighty *S*
John 4:42 . . . he is indeed the *S* of the
Acts 5:31 . . . right hand as Prince and *S*.
Acts 13:23 . . . God's promised *S* of Israel!
Eph 5:23 . . . He is the *S* of his body,
1 Tim 2:3 . . . good and pleases God our *S*,
1 Tim 4:10 . . . who is the *S* of all people
Titus 2:10 . . . about God our *S* attractive
Titus 3:4 . . . When God our *S* revealed his
2 Pet 3:2 . . . Lord and *S* commanded
1 Jn 4:14 . . . Son to be the *S* of the world.

SCRIPTURE, SCRIPTURES (N) the law; the writings of Moses; the entire collection of sacred books
Matt 21:16 . . . you ever read the *S-s?*
Matt 22:29 . . . you don't know the *S-s*,
Luke 24:27 . . . from all the *S-s* the things
Luke 24:45 . . . to understand the *S-s*.
John 2:22 . . . believed both the *S-s* and
John 5:39 . . . You search the *S-s* because
John 7:42 . . . the *S-s* clearly state that
John 10:35 . . . know that the *S-s* cannot
Acts 8:32 . . . The passage of *S* he had
1 Cor 4:6 . . . quoted from the *S-s*, you won't
1 Tim 4:13 . . . focus on reading the *S-s* to
2 Tim 3:16 . . . All *S* is inspired by God
Heb 10:7 . . . written about me in the *S-s*.
2 Pet 1:20 . . . no prophecy in *S* ever came
2 Pet 3:16 . . . do with other parts of *S*.

SEA, SEAS (N) a great body of salt water that covers much of the earth; a large basin used in the Temple
Exod 14:16 . . . middle of the *s* on dry
Deut 30:13 . . . not kept beyond the *s*,
1 Kgs 7:23 . . . rim to rim, called the *S*.
Job 11:9 . . . and wider than the *s*.
Ps 93:4 . . . violent raging of the *s-s*,
Ps 95:5 . . . The *s* belongs to him,
Eccl 11:1 . . . your grain across the *s-s*,
Isa 57:20 . . . like the restless *s*, which
Jonah 1:4 . . . wind over the *s*, causing a
Hab 2:14 . . . waters fill the *s*, the earth
Matt 18:6 . . . in the depths of the *s*.
Jas 1:6 . . . wave of the *s* that is blown
Jude 1:13 . . . waves of the *s*, churning up

Rev 10:2 . . . right foot on the *s* and
Rev 13:1 . . . rising up out of the *s*.
Rev 20:13 . . . The *s* gave up its dead,
Rev 21:1 . . . And the *s* was also gone.

SEARCH, SEARCHES (V) to investigate or examine thoroughly in an effort to find or verify something
Ps 34:14 . . . *S* for peace, and work
Ps 139:23 . . . *S* me, O God, and know
Eccl 3:6 . . . A time to *s* and a time to
Jer 17:10 . . . I, the LORD, *s* all hearts
1 Cor 2:10 . . . Spirit *s-es* out everything
1 Pet 3:11 . . . *S* for peace, and work

SECRET (ADJ) kept from knowledge or view; hidden
Ps 90:8 . . . before you—our *s* sins—
Jer 23:24 . . . from me in a *s* place?
Matt 10:26 . . . all that is *s* will be
Rom 2:16 . . . judge everyone's *s* life.
Rom 16:25 . . . a plan kept *s* from the
1 Cor 13:2 . . . all of God's *s* plans
1 Cor 14:25 . . . their *s* thoughts will be
Col 1:26 . . . was kept *s* for centuries and

SECRET, SECRETS (N) something kept hidden or unexplained; something kept from the knowledge of others or shared only confidentially with a few
see also MYSTERY
Deut 29:29 . . . God has *s-s* known to no
Judg 16:15 . . . don't share your *s-s* with
Ps 44:21 . . . he knows the *s-s* of every
Prov 11:13 . . . goes around telling *s-s*.
Dan 2:28 . . . heaven who reveals *s-s*, and
Dan 2:29 . . . who reveals *s-s* has shown
Mark 4:11 . . . to understand the *s*
Mark 4:22 . . . and every *s* will be brought
Luke 8:10 . . . to understand the *s-s* of
1 Cor 15:51 . . . reveal to you a wonderful *s*.
Phil 4:12 . . . have learned the *s* of living
Col 1:27 . . . the *s*: Christ lives in you.

SEED, SEEDS (N) the grains of plants used for sowing
Gen 1:11 . . . These *s-s* will then produce
Prov 11:30 . . . The *s-s* of good deeds
Matt 13:3 . . . went out to plant some *s-s*.
Matt 13:31 . . . like a mustard *s* planted in
Matt 17:20 . . . as a mustard *s*, you could say
Mark 4:15 . . . The *s* that fell on
Luke 8:12 . . . The *s-s* that fell on
1 Cor 3:6 . . . I planted the *s* in your
2 Cor 9:6 . . . few *s-s* will get a small
2 Cor 9:10 . . . one who provides *s* for the

SEEK, SEEKING, SEEKS (V) to go in search of; to try to acquire or gain
2 Chr 7:14 . . . pray and *s* my face and
2 Chr 15:2 . . . Whenever you *s* him,
Prov 3:6 . . . *S* his will in all you do,
Prov 25:27 . . . not good to *s* honors
Prov 29:26 . . . Many *s* the ruler's favor,
Isa 55:6 . . . *S* the LORD while you can
Hos 10:12 . . . time to *s* the LORD,
Zeph 2:3 . . . *S* the LORD, all who are
Matt 6:33 . . . *S* the Kingdom of God above
Matt 7:7 . . . Keep on *s-ing*, and you
Matt 7:8 . . . Everyone who *s-s*, finds.
Luke 12:31 . . . *S* the Kingdom of God
Luke 19:10 . . . Son of Man came to *s* and
Rom 3:11 . . . no one is *s-ing* God.
1 Cor 7:27 . . . have a wife, do not *s* to get
Heb 11:6 . . . those who sincerely *s* him.

SELF-CONTROL (N) restraint exercised over one's own impulses, emotions, or desires
Prov 5:23 . . . He will die for lack of *s*;
Prov 16:32 . . . better to have *s* than to
Acts 24:25 . . . righteousness and *s* and the
Gal 5:23 . . . gentleness, and *s*. There is no
1 Tim 3:2 . . . must exercise *s*, live wisely,
1 Tim 3:11 . . . They must exercise *s* and be
Titus 2:2 . . . older men to exercise *s*,
1 Pet 1:13 . . . for action and exercise *s*.
2 Pet 1:6 . . . and knowledge with *s*, and

SELFISH (ADJ) seeking or concentrating on one's own advantage, pleasure, or well-being without regard for others
Matt 16:24 . . . turn from your *s* ways,
Luke 9:23 . . . turn from your *s* ways,
Gal 5:20 . . . of anger, *s* ambition,
Phil 1:17 . . . They preach with *s* ambition,
Jas 3:14 . . . and there is *s* ambition in
Jas 3:16 . . . is jealousy and *s* ambition,

SEND, SENDING (V) to direct, order, or request to go
see also SENT
Isa 6:8 . . . Here I am. *S* me.
Isa 55:11 . . . with my word. I *s* it out,
Mal 3:1 . . . I am *s-ing* my messenger,
Matt 9:38 . . . ask him to *s* more workers
Mark 1:2 . . . I am *s-ing* my messenger
1 Cor 1:17 . . . For Christ didn't *s* me to

SENT (V) to direct, order, or request to go
see also SEND
Exod 3:14 . . . I AM has *s* me
Matt 10:40 . . . the Father who *s* me.
Luke 10:16 . . . God, who *s* me.
John 3:17 . . . God *s* his Son into the
John 20:21 . . . As the Father has *s* me, so
Rom 8:3 . . . He *s* his own Son in a
Rom 10:15 . . . them without being *s*?
Gal 4:4 . . . time came, God *s* his Son,

SEPARATE, SEPARATED, SEPARATES (V) to set or keep apart; to sort
Prov 17:9 . . . on it *s-s* close friends.
Matt 25:32 . . . a shepherd *s-s* the sheep
Rom 8:35 . . . Can anything ever *s* us
Eph 2:14 . . . of hostility that *s-d* us.
Col 1:21 . . . his enemies, *s-d* from him

SERPENT (N) a snake or crawling reptile often associated with temptation, sin, and evil; Satan
Gen 3:1 . . . The *s* was the shrewdest of
Isa 27:1 . . . *s*, the coiling, writhing *s*.
2 Cor 11:3 . . . the cunning ways of the *s*.
Rev 12:9 . . . the ancient *s* called the devil,
Rev 20:2 . . . that old *s*, who is the devil,

SERVANT, SERVANTS (N) one who performs tasks under the direction of another
Exod 14:31 . . . LORD and in his *s* Moses.
Lev 25:55 . . . They are my *s-s*, whom I
1 Sam 3:10 . . . Speak, your *s* is listening.
2 Kgs 17:13 . . . my *s-s* the prophets.
Job 1:8 . . . Have you noticed my *s* Job?
Ps 19:13 . . . Keep your *s* from deliberate
Ps 31:16 . . . your favor shine on your *s*.
Ps 89:3 . . . with David, my chosen *s*.
Ps 104:4 . . . flames of fire are your *s-s*.
Prov 14:35 . . . king rejoices in wise *s-s*
Prov 17:2 . . . A wise *s* will rule
Prov 22:7 . . . so the borrower is *s* to the
Prov 31:15 . . . work for her *s* girls.
Eccl 7:21 . . . may hear your *s* curse you.
Eccl 10:7 . . . seen *s-s* riding horseback
Isa 53:11 . . . my righteous *s* will make it
Isa 65:8 . . . I still have true *s-s* there.
Zech 3:8 . . . to bring my *s*, the Branch.

Mal 1:6 . . . father, and a *s* respects his
Matt 20:26 . . . among you must be your *s*,
Matt 24:45 . . . faithful, sensible *s* is one
Luke 1:48 . . . of his lowly *s* girl, and
Luke 17:10 . . . We are unworthy *s-s* who
Luke 22:26 . . . leader should be like a *s*.
John 12:26 . . . because my *s-s* must be
Rom 13:4 . . . authorities are God's *s-s*,
1 Cor 3:5 . . . are only God's *s-s* through
Col 1:23 . . . God's *s* to proclaim it.
1 Tim 4:6 . . . be a worthy *s* of Christ
Heb 1:7 . . . his *s-s* like flames of fire.
Heb 1:14 . . . angels are only *s-s*—spirits

SERVE, SERVED, SERVES, SERVING (V) to meet the needs of and subject one's will to that of another
Deut 10:12 . . . love him and *s* him with
Deut 11:13 . . . your God and *s* him with
Deut 28:47 . . . If you do not *s* the LORD
Deut 30:17 . . . drawn away to *s* and
Josh 24:15 . . . family, we will *s* the LORD.
2 Chr 12:8 . . . between *s-ing* me and
Ps 34:22 . . . redeem those who *s* him.
Ps 101:6 . . . be allowed to *s* me.
Ps 103:21 . . . of angels who *s* him and do
Isa 38:3 . . . have *s-d* you single-mindedly
Dan 3:17 . . . the God whom we *s* is able to
Matt 4:10 . . . your God and *s* only him.
Matt 6:24 . . . No one can *s* two masters.
Matt 20:28 . . . not to be *s-d* but to *s*
Luke 22:27 . . . among you as one who *s-s*.
John 12:2 . . . Martha *s-d*, and Lazarus was
John 12:26 . . . honor anyone who *s-s* me.
Acts 17:25 . . . hands can't *s* his needs—
Rom 1:25 . . . worshiped and *s-d* the things
Rom 12:7 . . . your gift is *s-ing* others, *s*
Rom 12:11 . . . work hard and *s* the Lord
Rom 13:6 . . . They are *s-ing* God in what
Rom 14:18 . . . If you *s* Christ with
Rom 16:18 . . . people are not *s-ing* Christ
1 Cor 16:18 . . . to all who *s* so well.
Gal 5:13 . . . your freedom to *s* one another
Col 3:24 . . . Master you are *s-ing* is Christ.
1 Tim 5:10 . . . kind to strangers and *s-d* other

SHAME (N) a condition or feeling of humiliating disgrace or disrepute; something that brings censure and reproach
Lev 19:12 . . . Do not bring *s* on the name
Ps 34:5 . . . no shadow of *s* will darken
Prov 28:7 . . . wild friends bring *s* to
Dan 12:2 . . . some to *s* and everlasting
Titus 2:5 . . . not bring *s* on the word
Heb 6:6 . . . holding him up to public *s*.
1 Jn 2:28 . . . shrink back from him in *s*.

SHARE, SHARED, SHARING (V) to grant or give a share in; to partake of, use, experience, occupy, or enjoy with others; to have in common
Gen 21:10 . . . to *s* the inheritance
1 Sam 30:24 . . . We *s* and *s* alike—
Ps 41:9 . . . the one who *s-d* my food,
Luke 3:11 . . . If you have food, *s* it with
Acts 2:42 . . . fellowship, and to *s-ing* in
Acts 2:45 . . . possessions and *s-d* the
Rom 8:17 . . . we must also *s* his suffering.
Rom 11:31 . . . they, too, will *s* in God's
1 Cor 10:16 . . . aren't we *s-ing* in the blood
1 Cor 12:13 . . . we all *s* the same Spirit.
2 Cor 1:7 . . . as you *s* in our sufferings,
2 Cor 9:8 . . . left over to *s* with others.
Gal 4:30 . . . will not *s* the inheritance
Gal 6:6 . . . teachers, *s-ing* all good things
Phil 3:10 . . . suffer with him, *s-ing* in his
Col 1:12 . . . has enabled you to *s* in the
1 Thes 2:8 . . . much that we *s-d* with you
2 Thes 2:14 . . . you can *s* in the glory
1 Tim 6:18 . . . ready to *s* with others.
Heb 6:4 . . . and *s-d* in the Holy Spirit,
Heb 12:10 . . . we might *s* in his holiness.
Heb 13:16 . . . to *s* with those in need.
Rev 3:20 . . . and we will *s* a meal together

SHEEP (N) a small domesticated animal, representing wealth and livelihood for many Israelites; figurative of God's people
Gen 22:8 . . . God will provide a *s* for
Num 27:17 . . . not be like *s* without a
Deut 17:1 . . . defective cattle, *s*, or
1 Sam 15:14 . . . bleating of *s* and goats
Ps 44:22 . . . being slaughtered like *s*.
Ps 78:52 . . . people like a flock of *s*,
Ps 100:3 . . . We are his people, the *s*
Ps 119:176 . . . wandered away like a lost *s*;
Isa 53:7 . . . as a *s* is silent before
Jer 50:6 . . . people have been lost *s*.
Matt 7:15 . . . disguised as harmless *s* but
Matt 9:36 . . . like *s* without a shepherd.
Matt 10:16 . . . you out as *s* among wolves.
Matt 12:11 . . . a *s* that fell into a well
Matt 25:32 . . . separates the *s* from the
John 10:3 . . . calls his own *s* by name
John 10:7 . . . I am the gate for the *s*.
John 10:15 . . . sacrifice my life for the *s*.
John 21:17 . . . Then feed my *s*.
1 Pet 2:25 . . . were like *s* who wandered

SHELTER, SHELTERS (N) something that covers or affords protection
see also REFUGE
Lev 23:34 . . . the Festival of *S-s* on the
Deut 16:16 . . . the Festival of *S-s*.
Ps 9:9 . . . LORD is a *s* for the
Ps 31:20 . . . hide them in the *s* of your
Ps 36:7 . . . All humanity finds *s* in the
Ps 61:4 . . . safe beneath the *s* of your
Isa 4:6 . . . will be a *s* from daytime heat
Isa 32:2 . . . be like a *s* from the wind
Isa 58:7 . . . give *s* to the homeless.
Zech 14:16 . . . the Festival of *S-s*.

SHEPHERD, SHEPHERDS (N) a person who tends sheep; figurative of political and religious leaders, especially those who care for God's people
Gen 48:15 . . . has been my *s* all my life,
Gen 49:24 . . . by the *S*, the Rock of Israel.
Num 27:17 . . . be like sheep without a *s*.
2 Sam 7:7 . . . tribal leaders, the *s-s* of my
1 Kgs 22:17 . . . like sheep without a *s*.
Ps 23:1 . . . The LORD is my *s*;
Ps 28:9 . . . Lead them like a *s*, and
Isa 40:11 . . . feed his flock like a *s*.
Jer 23:1 . . . my people—the *s-s* of my
Jer 31:10 . . . as a *s* does his flock.
Ezek 34:5 . . . scattered without a *s*, and
Ezek 34:8 . . . you were my *s-s*, you didn't
Ezek 34:12 . . . like a *s* looking for his
Zech 11:9 . . . won't be your *s* any longer.
Zech 13:7 . . . Strike down the *s*, and
Matt 2:6 . . . will be the *s* for my people
Matt 9:36 . . . like sheep without a *s*.
Matt 26:31 . . . God will strike the *S*,
John 10:11 . . . I am the good *s*.
Acts 20:28 . . . Feed and *s* God's flock—
Heb 13:20 . . . Jesus, the great *S* of the
Jude 1:12 . . . are like shameless *s-s* who care
Rev 7:17 . . . on the throne will be their *S*.

SHIELD (N) a broad piece of defensive armor carried on the arm; one who protects or defends
2 Sam 22:3 . . . He is my *s,* the power that
2 Sam 22:36 . . . me your *s* of victory;
Ps 3:3 . . . LORD, are a *s* around me;
Ps 5:12 . . . them with your *s* of love.
Ps 7:10 . . . God is my *s,* saving those
Ps 18:2 . . . He is my *s,* the power that
Ps 28:7 . . . LORD is my strength and *s.*
Ps 33:20 . . . is our help and our *s.*
Ps 35:2 . . . armor, and take up your *s.*
Ps 84:11 . . . God is our sun and our *s.*
Ps 119:114 . . . are my refuge and my *s;*
Ps 144:2 . . . He is my *s,* and I take refuge
Prov 2:7 . . . He is a *s* to those who walk
Eph 6:16 . . . hold up the *s* of faith

SHOUT, SHOUTED, SHOUTING (V) to utter a loud cry or in a loud voice
Job 38:7 . . . all the angels ***s-ed*** for joy?
Ps 95:1 . . . Let us *s* joyfully to
Ps 100:1 . . . *S* with joy to the LORD,
Isa 12:6 . . . people of Jerusalem *s* his
Isa 40:3 . . . someone ***s-ing,*** "Clear the way
Isa 40:9 . . . *s* from the mountaintops!
Isa 42:2 . . . He will not *s* or raise his
Zech 9:9 . . . people of Zion! *S* in triumph,
Matt 3:3 . . . a voice ***s-ing*** in the wilderness,
Matt 10:27 . . . *s* from the housetops for

SICK (ADJ) affected with disease or ill health; lacking vigor
Ps 41:3 . . . when they are *s* and restores
Prov 13:12 . . . deferred makes the heart *s,*
Matt 9:12 . . . need a doctor—*s* people do.
Matt 10:8 . . . Heal the *s,* raise the dead,
Matt 25:36 . . . I was *s,* and you cared for
Mark 3:10 . . . all the *s* people eagerly
1 Cor 11:30 . . . many of you are weak and *s*
Jas 5:14 . . . Are any of you *s?*

SIGN, SIGNS (N) something indicating the presence or existence of something else; something material or external that stands for or signifies something spiritual
Gen 9:12 . . . you a *s* of my covenant
Gen 17:11 . . . your foreskin as a *s* of
Ps 105:27 . . . performed miraculous ***s-s***
Isa 55:13 . . . be an everlasting *s* of
Dan 6:27 . . . he performs miraculous ***s-s***
Matt 12:38 . . . a miraculous *s* to prove
Matt 24:3 . . . What *s* will signal your
Matt 24:30 . . . the *s* that the Son of Man
Mark 16:17 . . . These miraculous ***s-s*** will
Luke 11:29 . . . them is the *s* of Jonah.
John 3:2 . . . Your miraculous ***s-s*** are
John 20:30 . . . do many other miraculous ***s-s***
1 Cor 14:22 . . . in tongues is a *s,* not for
2 Cor 12:12 . . . did many ***s-s*** and wonders
2 Thes 2:9 . . . counterfeit power and ***s-s***

SILENT (ADJ) mute, speechless; still
Ps 30:12 . . . praises to you and not be *s.*
Isa 53:7 . . . as a sheep is *s* before the
Isa 62:1 . . . Jerusalem, I cannot remain *s.*
Hab 2:20 . . . the earth be *s* before him.
Acts 8:32 . . . And as a lamb is *s* before
Acts 18:9 . . . Speak out! Don't be *s!*
1 Cor 14:34 . . . Women should be *s* during

SIN, SINS (N) moral evil; transgression of or rebellion against God's laws
Gen 4:7 . . . *S* is crouching at the door,
Lev 5:5 . . . ways, you must confess your *s.*
Num 32:23 . . . be sure that your *s* will find
Deut 24:16 . . . to death for the ***s-s*** of their
Ps 19:13 . . . servant from deliberate ***s-s!***
Ps 32:1 . . . whose *s* is put out of sight!
Ps 38:18 . . . I confess my ***s-s;*** I am deeply
Ps 51:1 . . . blot out the stain of my ***s-s.***
Ps 51:2 . . . Purify me from my *s.*
Ps 65:3 . . . are overwhelmed by our ***s-s,***
Ps 79:9 . . . Save us and forgive our ***s-s***
Ps 103:12 . . . removed our ***s-s*** as far from
Prov 5:22 . . . held captive by his own ***s-s;***
Prov 10:19 . . . Too much talk leads to *s.*
Prov 14:21 . . . *s* to belittle one's neighbor;
Prov 17:19 . . . who loves to quarrel loves *s;*
Prov 28:13 . . . who conceal their ***s-s*** will
Prov 29:22 . . . commits all kinds of *s.*
Isa 1:18 . . . your ***s-s*** are like scarlet,
Isa 53:6 . . . laid on him the ***s-s*** of us all.
Isa 59:2 . . . Because of your ***s-s,*** he has
Jer 31:30 . . . die for their own ***s-s***—
Jer 31:34 . . . again remember their ***s-s.***
Ezek 18:19 . . . pay for the parent's ***s-s?***
Matt 1:21 . . . save his people from their ***s-s.***
Matt 6:12 . . . forgive us our ***s-s,*** as we
Matt 26:28 . . . to forgive the ***s-s*** of many.
Mark 3:29 . . . This is a *s* with eternal
Luke 5:24 . . . on earth to forgive ***s-s.***
John 1:29 . . . takes away the *s* of the world!
John 20:23 . . . forgive anyone's ***s-s,*** they
Acts 2:38 . . . repent of your ***s-s*** and turn
Rom 4:25 . . . because of our ***s-s,*** and he
Rom 6:2 . . . we have died to *s,* how can
Rom 6:11 . . . the power of *s* and alive to
Rom 6:23 . . . the wages of *s* is death,
Rom 7:7 . . . law that showed me my *s.*
Rom 7:25 . . . nature I am a slave to *s.*
1 Cor 6:18 . . . is a *s* against your own body.
1 Cor 15:3 . . . died for our ***s-s,*** just as
1 Cor 15:56 . . . the law gives *s* its power.
Gal 1:4 . . . gave his life for our ***s-s,*** just
Gal 6:1 . . . believer is overcome by some *s,*
Eph 2:5 . . . were dead because of our ***s-s,***
1 Tim 5:22 . . . share in the ***s-s*** of others.
Heb 2:17 . . . would take away the ***s-s*** of
Heb 9:28 . . . to take away the ***s-s*** of many
Heb 10:12 . . . sacrifice for ***s-s,*** good for
Heb 12:1 . . . the *s* that so easily trips
Jas 1:15 . . . when *s* is allowed to grow,
Jas 4:17 . . . is *s* to know what you ought
Jas 5:16 . . . Confess your ***s-s*** to each other
1 Pet 2:24 . . . carried our ***s-s*** in his body
1 Pet 3:18 . . . suffered for our ***s-s*** once for
1 Jn 1:8 . . . claim we have no *s,* we are
1 Jn 1:9 . . . to forgive us our ***s-s*** and to
1 Jn 2:1 . . . if anyone does *s,* we have
1 Jn 3:5 . . . take away our ***s-s,*** and
1 Jn 3:5 . . . there is no *s* in him.
1 Jn 5:16 . . . a *s* that leads to death,
Rev 1:5 . . . from our ***s-s*** by shedding his

SIN, SINNED, SINNING, SINS (V) to commit an offense or fault against God; to break God's law
Exod 20:20 . . . will keep you from ***s-ning!***
2 Sam 12:13 . . . I have ***s-ned*** against the
2 Chr 6:37 . . . We have ***s-ned,*** done evil,
Job 1:5 . . . my children have ***s-ned***
Ps 51:4 . . . and you alone, have I ***s-ned;***
Ps 119:11 . . . I might not *s* against you.
Jer 14:20 . . . all have ***s-ned*** against you.
Dan 9:5 . . . have ***s-ned*** and done wrong.
Mark 9:43 . . . causes you to *s,* cut it off.
Luke 15:18 . . . I have ***s-ned*** against both
Luke 17:3 . . . another believer ***s-s,*** rebuke
John 8:7 . . . who has never ***s-ned*** throw
John 8:11 . . . Go and *s* no more.

Rom 1:30 . . . invent new ways of ***s-ning,***
Rom 3:23 . . . everyone has ***s-ned;*** we all
Rom 5:12 . . . When Adam ***s-ned,*** sin entered
Rom 14:23 . . . is not right, you are ***s-ning.***
1 Cor 15:34 . . . is right, and stop ***s-ning.***
Heb 4:15 . . . we do, yet he did not *s.*
Heb 10:26 . . . deliberately continue ***s-ning***
1 Pet 2:22 . . . He never ***s-ned,*** nor ever
1 Jn 1:10 . . . we have not ***s-ned,*** we are
1 Jn 3:6 . . . who keeps on ***s-ning*** does not
1 Jn 5:18 . . . not make a practice of ***s-ning,***

SINNER, SINNERS (N) those guilty of sin
Ps 51:5 . . . I was born a *s*—yes,
Prov 1:10 . . . if *s-s* entice you, turn
Prov 23:17 . . . Don't envy *s-s,* but
Eccl 9:18 . . . one *s* can destroy much that
Isa 59:12 . . . we know what *s-s* we are.
Isa 64:5 . . . We are constant *s-s;* how
Matt 9:13 . . . who know they are *s-s.*
Luke 5:8 . . . I'm too much of a *s* to be
Luke 15:7 . . . over one lost *s* who repents
Luke 18:13 . . . to me, for I am a *s.*
Rom 4:5 . . . faith in God who forgives *s-s.*
Rom 5:6 . . . time and died for us *s-s.*
1 Tim 1:15 . . . into the world to save *s-s*
Jas 5:20 . . . whoever brings the *s* back
1 Pet 3:18 . . . he died for *s-s* to bring

SNAKE, SNAKES (N) any of numerous limbless scaled reptiles
Num 21:8 . . . replica of a poisonous *s* and
Prov 23:32 . . . it bites like a poisonous *s;*
Matt 10:16 . . . shrewd as *s-s* and harmless
Luke 3:7 . . . You brood of *s-s!* Who warned
John 3:14 . . . lifted up the bronze *s* on a
Rom 3:13 . . . *S* venom drips from their

SNOW (N) precipitation in the form of small white ice crystals
Prov 25:13 . . . refresh like *s* in summer.
Isa 1:18 . . . will make them as white as *s.*
Dan 7:9 . . . clothing was as white as *s,*

SORROW, SORROWS (N) deep distress, sadness, or regret
Ps 116:3 . . . I saw only trouble and *s.*
Isa 65:14 . . . will cry in *s* and despair.
Jer 31:12 . . . all their *s-s* will be gone.
Ezek 34:2 . . . What *s* awaits you
Amos 5:18 . . . What *s* awaits you
Matt 18:7 . . . What *s* awaits the
Matt 23:13 . . . What *s* awaits you
Luke 11:46 . . . what *s* also awaits
Rom 9:2 . . . with bitter *s* and unending
2 Cor 7:10 . . . the kind of *s* God wants
Eph 4:30 . . . do not bring *s* to God's Holy
1 Tim 6:10 . . . themselves with many *s-s.*
Heb 13:17 . . . with joy and not with *s.*
Jude 1:11 . . . What *s* awaits them!
Rev 21:4 . . . more death or *s* or crying

SOUL, SOULS (N) the inner life of a human being, the seat of emotions, and the center of human personality
Deut 6:5 . . . heart, all your *s,* and all
Deut 28:65 . . . fail, and your *s* to despair.
Deut 30:6 . . . your heart and *s* and so you
Josh 22:5 . . . all your heart and all your *s.*
2 Kgs 23:25 . . . heart and *s* and strength,
Prov 3:22 . . . for they will refresh your *s.*
Prov 16:24 . . . sweet to the *s* and healthy
Jer 6:16 . . . you will find rest for your *s-s.*
Matt 10:28 . . . can destroy both *s* and body
Matt 11:29 . . . you will find rest for your *s-s.*
Matt 22:37 . . . all your heart, all your *s,*
Mark 8:37 . . . worth more than your *s?*
Mark 12:30 . . . heart, all your *s,* all your
Luke 16:23 . . . his *s* went to the place of
Luke 21:19 . . . firm, you will win your *s-s.*
John 12:27 . . . my *s* is deeply troubled.
Heb 4:12 . . . cutting between *s* and spirit,

SPEAK, SPEAKING, SPEAKS (V) to express thoughts, opinions, or feelings orally; to talk
Deut 18:22 . . . If the prophet *s-s* in the
Ps 15:3 . . . or *s* evil of their friends.
Ps 78:2 . . . will *s* to you in a parable.
Isa 3:8 . . . because they *s* out against
Isa 32:4 . . . stammer will *s* out plainly.
Matt 12:34 . . . men like you *s* what is good
Matt 15:18 . . . the words you *s* come from
Acts 2:11 . . . hear these people ***s-ing*** in our
1 Cor 14:2 . . . ability to *s* in tongues,
1 Cor 14:19 . . . I would rather *s* five
1 Pet 3:16 . . . if people *s* against you,

SPIRIT, SPIRITS (N) "wind" or "breath"; a supernatural being; the third member of the Trinity, with God the Father and Jesus the Son; an attitude, mood, or disposition; an evil presence that can possess or influence a person; invisible, nonmaterial part of humans (as opposed to body or flesh)
Deut 34:9 . . . full of the *s* of wisdom,
1 Sam 16:14 . . . a tormenting *s* that filled
2 Kgs 2:9 . . . double share of your *s* and
Ps 31:5 . . . I entrust my *s* into your
Ps 34:18 . . . those whose *s-s* are crushed.
Ps 51:10 . . . Renew a loyal *s* within me.
Ps 51:17 . . . you desire is a broken *s.*
Ezek 11:19 . . . put a new *s* within them.
Mark 5:12 . . . pigs," the *s-s* begged.
2 Cor 5:3 . . . not be *s-s* without bodies.
Eph 6:12 . . . and against evil *s-s* in the
2 Tim 1:7 . . . not given us a *s* of fear
1 Pet 3:4 . . . gentle and quiet *s,* which

STAFF (N) a long stick used for walking or a weapon, often a symbol of authority and protection
Gen 49:10 . . . nor the ruler's *s* from his
Exod 7:12 . . . then Aaron's *s* swallowed up
Num 17:6 . . . Aaron, brought Moses a *s.*
2 Kgs 4:29 . . . travel; take my *s* and go!
Ps 23:4 . . . Your rod and your *s* protect

STAND, STANDING, STANDS (V) to remain stationary; to remain erect; to maintain one's position; to endure successfully
Exod 3:5 . . . you are ***s-ing*** on holy ground.
Josh 5:15 . . . where you are ***s-ing*** is holy.
Josh 10:12 . . . Let the sun *s* still
2 Chr 20:17 . . . then *s* still and
Ps 24:3 . . . Who may *s* in his holy
Ps 33:11 . . . LORD's plans *s* firm
Ps 76:7 . . . Who can *s* before you
Ps 119:89 . . . word, O LORD, *s-s* firm
Prov 12:7 . . . family of the godly *s-s* firm.
Isa 40:8 . . . word of our God *s-s* forever.
Mal 3:2 . . . be able to *s* and face him
Luke 6:48 . . . that house, it *s-s* firm because
Rom 14:10 . . . all *s* before the judgment
1 Cor 10:12 . . . think you are ***s-ing*** strong,
1 Cor 10:13 . . . to be more than you can *s.*
2 Cor 5:10 . . . we must all *s* before Christ
Eph 6:14 . . . *S* your ground, putting on the
Phil 1:27 . . . you are ***s-ing*** together with
2 Tim 2:19 . . . But God's truth *s-s* firm like
1 Pet 5:9 . . . *S* firm against him, and
Rev 3:20 . . . I *s* at the door and knock.

STAR, STARS (N) a natural luminous body visible in the sky especially at night; sometimes symbolic for angels
Gen 1:16 . . . He also made the *s-s.*

Num 24:17 . . . A *s* will rise from Jacob;
Job 38:7 . . . morning *s-s* sang together
Isa 14:12 . . . O shining *s*, son of the
Dan 12:3 . . . shine like the *s-s* forever.
Matt 2:2 . . . We saw his *s* as it rose,
2 Pet 1:19 . . . the Morning *S* shines in
Rev 2:28 . . . also give them the morning *s!*
Rev 22:16 . . . I am the bright morning *s*.

STEAL, STEALING, STEALS (V) to take the property of another wrongfully
Exod 20:15 . . . You must not *s*.
Lev 19:11 . . . Do not *s*.
Deut 5:19 . . . You must not *s*.
Prov 28:24 . . . who *s-s* from his father
Matt 19:18 . . . You must not *s*.
Matt 27:64 . . . coming and *s-ing* his body
Rom 13:9 . . . You must not *s*.
Eph 4:28 . . . If you are a thief, quit *s-ing*.
1 Pet 4:15 . . . not be for murder, *s-ing*,

STOP, STOPS (V) to cease activity or operation; to pause or hesitate; to restrain or prevent
Job 37:14 . . . *S* and consider the wonderful
Prov 15:18 . . . cool-tempered person *s-s*
Jer 7:5 . . . only if you *s* your evil
Jer 32:40 . . . I will never *s* doing good
Lam 3:49 . . . flow endlessly; they will not *s*
Dan 4:35 . . . No one can *s* him or say to
Matt 19:14 . . . come to me. Don't *s* them!
Eph 6:16 . . . shield of faith to *s* the

STORM (N) a heavy fall of rain, snow, or hail sometimes accompanied by thunder and lightning; a disturbed or agitated state
see also WHIRLWIND
Ps 50:3 . . . and a great *s* rages around
Ps 55:8 . . . from this wild *s* of hatred.
Ps 107:29 . . . He calmed the *s* to a whisper
Luke 8:24 . . . *s* stopped and all was calm.

STRANGER, STRANGERS (N) a person who is unknown or with whom one is unacquainted
see also FOREIGNER(S)
Job 31:32 . . . turned away a *s* but have
Matt 25:35 . . . I was a *s*, and you invited
John 10:5 . . . They won't follow a *s*;
1 Tim 5:10 . . . been kind to *s-s* and served
Heb 13:2 . . . to show hospitality to *s-s*, for

STRAYED (V) to wander
Isa 53:6 . . . like sheep, have *s* away.
Ezek 34:16 . . . lost ones who *s* away, and

STRENGTH (N) capacity for exertion or endurance; support; the power of a person or of God, measured variously in terms of wealth, wisdom, military might, orphysical prowess
Exod 15:2 . . . LORD is my *s* and my
Deut 6:5 . . . your soul, and all your *s*.
2 Kgs 23:25 . . . his heart and soul and *s*,
1 Chr 16:11 . . . LORD and for his *s*;
Neh 8:10 . . . of the LORD is your *s!*
Ps 23:3 . . . He renews my *s*. He guides me
Ps 28:7 . . . LORD is my *s* and shield.
Ps 33:16 . . . nor is great *s* enough to save
Ps 46:1 . . . God is our refuge and *s*,
Ps 59:17 . . . O my *S*, to you I sing
Ps 65:6 . . . armed yourself with mighty *s*.
Ps 84:5 . . . for those whose *s* comes from
Ps 139:10 . . . your *s* will support me.
Isa 31:1 . . . depending on the *s* of human
Isa 40:26 . . . power and incomparable *s*,
Jer 27:5 . . . With my great *s* and powerful
Mic 5:4 . . . with the LORD's *s*, in
Hab 3:19 . . . LORD is my *s!*
Zech 4:6 . . . nor by *s*, but by my Spirit,
Mark 12:30 . . . your mind, and all your *s*.
1 Cor 1:25 . . . the greatest of human *s*.
Phil 4:13 . . . Christ, who gives me *s*.
Heb 11:34 . . . weakness was turned to *s*.
Heb 13:9 . . . Your *s* comes from God's

STUBBORN (ADJ) unreasonably or perversely unyielding
Exod 33:5 . . . You are a *s* and rebellious
Exod 34:9 . . . this is a *s* and rebellious
Lev 26:41 . . . at last their *s* hearts will
Deut 10:16 . . . hearts and stop being *s*.
2 Chr 36:13 . . . a hard and *s* man, refusing
Ps 78:8 . . . ancestors—*s*, rebellious,
Prov 28:14 . . . the *s* are headed for serious
Ezek 36:26 . . . out your stony, *s* heart and
Rom 2:5 . . . because you are *s* and refuse

STUDY (V) to read in detail, especially with the intention of learning
Josh 1:8 . . . *S* this Book of Instruction
Ezra 7:10 . . . had determined to *s* and obey

STUMBLE, STUMBLES, STUMBLING (V) to trip or walk unsteadily; to fall into sin or waywardness
Lev 19:14 . . . or cause the blind to *s*.
Ps 37:24 . . . Though they *s*, they will
Ps 66:9 . . . he keeps our feet from *s-ing*.
Ps 119:165 . . . great peace and do not *s*.
Ps 121:3 . . . He will not let you *s*;
Prov 3:23 . . . and your feet will not *s*.
Prov 24:17 . . . don't be happy when they *s*.
Isa 8:14 . . . stone that makes people *s*,
Jer 13:16 . . . causing you to *s* and fall
Hos 14:9 . . . paths sinners *s* and fall.
Mal 2:8 . . . caused many to *s* into sin.
Matt 21:44 . . . Anyone who *s-s* over that
John 11:10 . . . is danger of *s-ing* because
Rom 9:33 . . . that makes people *s*,
Rom 14:13 . . . believer to *s* and fall.
Rom 14:20 . . . makes another person *s*.
1 Cor 8:9 . . . weaker conscience to *s*.
2 Cor 6:3 . . . no one will *s* because of us,
1 Jn 2:10 . . . does not cause others to *s*.

SUCCEED (V) to turn out well; to attain a desired end
Gen 39:23 . . . everything he did to *s*.
Josh 1:8 . . . prosper and *s* in all you
1 Sam 2:9 . . . No one will *s* by strength
1 Sam 18:14 . . . continued to *s* in
2 Chr 20:20 . . . prophets, and you will *s*.
Ps 20:4 . . . and make all your plans *s*.
Prov 11:10 . . . celebrates when the godly *s*;
Prov 13:13 . . . respect a command will *s*.
Prov 16:3 . . . and your plans will *s*.
Prov 20:18 . . . Plans *s* through good
Prov 28:12 . . . When the godly *s*, everyone
Eccl 10:10 . . . wisdom; it helps you *s*.

SUFFER, SUFFERED, SUFFERING, SUFFERS (V) to endure death, pain, distress, or loss
Job 36:15 . . . rescues those who *s*.
Mark 8:31 . . . Son of Man must *s* many
Luke 24:26 . . . would have to *s* all these
Luke 24:46 . . . Messiah would *s* and die
Rom 8:18 . . . Yet what we *s* now is nothing
1 Cor 12:26 . . . If one part *s-s*, all the parts
2 Cor 1:5 . . . the more we *s* for Christ,
2 Cor 12:10 . . . troubles that I *s* for Christ.
Phil 3:10 . . . I want to *s* with him, sharing
2 Thes 1:4 . . . and hardships you are *s-ing*.
Heb 11:26 . . . better to *s* for the sake
1 Pet 2:21 . . . just as Christ *s-ed* for you.

1 Pet 4:1 . . . since Christ *s-ed* physical pain,
1 Pet 4:16 . . . is no shame to *s* for being
1 Pet 5:10 . . . So after you have *s-ed* a little
Rev 2:3 . . . You have patiently *s-ed* for me

SUFFERING, SUFFERINGS (N) the state or experience of one that suffers; pain, distress
Deut 16:3 . . . the bread of *s*—so that
Job 36:15 . . . means of their *s*, he rescues
Ps 119:71 . . . My *s* was good for me,
Isa 48:10 . . . you in the furnace of *s*.
Isa 49:13 . . . on them in their *s*.
Lam 1:12 . . . if there is any *s* like mine,
Luke 22:15 . . . you before my *s* begins.
2 Cor 1:7 . . . as you share in our *s-s*, you
Phil 1:29 . . . the privilege of *s* for him.
Col 1:24 . . . participating in the *s-s* of
2 Tim 2:3 . . . Endure *s* along with me,
2 Tim 4:5 . . . afraid of *s* for the Lord.
Heb 2:10 . . . through his *s*, a perfect
Heb 2:18 . . . gone through *s* and testing,
1 Pet 1:11 . . . about Christ's *s* and his
1 Pet 4:13 . . . Christ in his *s*, so that

SWORD, SWORDS (N) a handheld weapon with a long blade; figurative of war or persecution by government, also of God's word in spiritual warfare
Gen 3:24 . . . a flaming *s* that flashed
Deut 32:41 . . . my flashing *s* and begin
1 Sam 17:45 . . . come to me with *s*, spear,
1 Sam 31:4 . . . Take your *s* and kill me
2 Sam 12:10 . . . live by the *s* because you
1 Kgs 20:11 . . . putting on his *s* for battle
Ps 44:6 . . . not count on my *s* to save me.
Ps 45:3 . . . Put on your *s*, O mighty
Ps 64:3 . . . their tongues like *s-s* and aim
Joel 3:10 . . . plowshares into *s-s* and your
Amos 9:4 . . . I will command the *s* to kill
Mic 4:3 . . . will hammer their *s-s* into
Matt 10:34 . . . not to bring peace, but a *s*.
Matt 26:52 . . . who use the *s* will die by
Luke 2:35 . . . a *s* will pierce your very
Eph 6:17 . . . take the *s* of the Spirit,
Heb 4:12 . . . sharpest two-edged *s*, cutting
Rev 1:16 . . . sharp two-edged *s* came
Rev 19:15 . . . came a sharp *s* to strike

SYNAGOGUE (N) the house of worship and communal center of a Jewish congregation
Luke 4:16 . . . to the *s* on the Sabbath
John 12:42 . . . expel them from the *s*.
Acts 17:2 . . . he went to the *s* service,
Rev 3:9 . . . who belong to Satan's *s*—

T

TABERNACLE (N) portable shrine or tent designated for the worship of God; metaphor for God dwelling among his people
see also SANCTUARY, TEMPLE
Exod 27:21 . . . stand in the *T*, in front of
Exod 40:2 . . . Set up the *T* on the first
Exod 40:34 . . . cloud covered the *T*, and
Exod 40:34 . . . of the LORD filled the *T*.
Num 3:29 . . . area south of the *T* for their
Heb 8:5 . . . to build the *T*, God gave him
Heb 9:11 . . . more perfect *T* in heaven,
Heb 9:21 . . . blood on the *T* and on
Rev 15:5 . . . heaven, God's *T*, was thrown

TABLETS (N) flat slabs or plaques suited for or bearing an inscription
Exod 31:18 . . . two stone *t* inscribed with
Deut 10:5 . . . and placed the *t* in the Ark
2 Cor 3:3 . . . carved not on *t* of stone,

TEACH, TEACHES, TEACHING (V) to cause to know something; to instruct by precept, example, or experience
see also INSTRUCT, TRAIN
Lev 10:11 . . . you must *t* the Israelites
Deut 6:1 . . . commanded me to *t* you.
2 Chr 17:9 . . . of Judah, *t-ing* the people.
Job 21:22 . . . who can *t* a lesson to God,
Ps 37:30 . . . they *t* right from wrong.
Ps 51:13 . . . Then I will *t* your ways
Prov 15:33 . . . the LORD *t-es* wisdom;
Isa 2:3 . . . he will *t* us his ways,
Matt 5:19 . . . obeys God's laws and *t-es*
Matt 11:29 . . . Let me *t* you, because
Matt 15:9 . . . they *t* man-made ideas
Matt 22:16 . . . You *t* the way of God
Matt 28:20 . . . *T* these new disciples to
Mark 10:1 . . . as usual he was *t-ing* them.
Luke 11:1 . . . Lord, *t* us to pray,
Luke 12:12 . . . Holy Spirit will *t* you
John 14:26 . . . he will *t* you everything
Acts 6:4 . . . in prayer and *t-ing* the word.
Rom 15:4 . . . Scriptures long ago to *t*
Rom 15:14 . . . you can *t* each other all
1 Cor 2:16 . . . knows enough to *t* him?
1 Cor 14:26 . . . another will *t*, another
1 Tim 2:12 . . . do not let women *t* men
1 Tim 3:2 . . . he must be able to *t*.
2 Tim 3:16 . . . is useful to *t* us what
2 Tim 3:16 . . . *t-es* us to do what is right.
Titus 2:15 . . . You must *t* these things
Heb 5:12 . . . you ought to be *t-ing* others.
1 Jn 2:27 . . . need anyone to *t* you what

TEACHER, TEACHERS (N) one who teaches
Job 36:22 . . . Who is a *t* like him?
Prov 5:13 . . . didn't I listen to my *t-s*?
Eccl 1:1 . . . words of the *T*, King David's
Matt 10:24 . . . not greater than their *t*,
Matt 23:10 . . . only one *t*, the Messiah.
Luke 6:40 . . . will become like the *t*.
Luke 20:46 . . . these *t-s* of religious law!
John 13:14 . . . Lord and *T*, have washed
Rom 12:7 . . . If you are a *t*, teach well.
1 Cor 12:28 . . . third are *t-s*, then those
Gal 6:6 . . . should provide for their *t-s*,
Eph 4:11 . . . and the pastors and *t-s*.
2 Tim 4:3 . . . look for *t-s* who will tell
Jas 3:1 . . . of you should become *t-s*
3 Jn 1:10 . . . the traveling *t-s*, he also

TEAR, TEARS (N) a drop of clear saline fluid secreted from the eye
Job 16:20 . . . I pour out my *t-s* to God.
Isa 25:8 . . . will wipe away all *t-s*.
Rev 7:17 . . . will wipe every *t* from their
Rev 21:4 . . . will wipe every *t* from their

TEMPER (N) disposition; characteristic state of mind or of emotion; proneness to anger
Ps 37:8 . . . Do not lose your *t*—it only
Prov 14:29 . . . *t* shows great foolishness.
Prov 19:11 . . . people control their *t*;
Eccl 7:9 . . . Control your *t*, for anger

TEMPLE, TEMPLES (N) first built in Solomon's reign as a permanent worship center, which was destroyed and then rebuilt under Herod's reign; figurative of the human body and of Christ
see also SANCTUARY, TABERNACLE
1 Kgs 6:1 . . . to construct the *T* of the
1 Kgs 8:10 . . . cloud filled the *T* of the
1 Chr 29:16 . . . to build a *T* to honor your
2 Chr 36:19 . . . his army burned the *T*
Ps 27:4 . . . meditating in his *T*.

Isa 6:1 . . . train of his robe filled the *T.*
Jer 7:8 . . . suffer because the *T* is here.
Joel 3:18 . . . forth from the LORD's *T,*
Hab 2:20 . . . LORD is in his holy *T.*
Hag 2:18 . . . of the LORD's *T* was laid.
Matt 12:6 . . . is even greater than the *T!*
Matt 26:61 . . . able to destroy the *T* of God
Matt 27:51 . . . sanctuary of the *T* was torn
Luke 21:5 . . . stonework of the *T* and the
John 2:14 . . . the *T* area he saw merchants
Acts 5:20 . . . Go to the *T* and give the
Acts 17:24 . . . live in man-made ***t-s,***
1 Cor 3:16 . . . together are the ***t*** of God
1 Cor 6:19 . . . body is the ***t*** of the Holy
Eph 2:21 . . . becoming a holy ***t*** for the
1 Pet 2:5 . . . building into his spiritual ***t.***
Rev 21:22 . . . and the Lamb are its ***t.***

TEMPTATION, TEMPTATIONS (N) a cause or occasion of enticement
Matt 6:13 . . . don't let us yield to ***t,***
Matt 18:7 . . . ***T-s*** are inevitable, but what
Matt 26:41 . . . will not give in to ***t.***
Luke 8:13 . . . fall away when they face ***t.***
1 Cor 10:13 . . . The ***t-s*** in your life are
1 Cor 10:13 . . . not allow the ***t*** to be
Gal 6:1 . . . fall into the same ***t*** yourself.
1 Tim 6:9 . . . to be rich fall into ***t*** and
Jas 1:12 . . . endure testing and ***t.***

TEST, TESTINGS, TESTS (N) a critical examination, observation, or evaluation
see also TRIAL(S), TROUBLE(S)
Deut 29:3 . . . all the great ***t-s*** of strength,
1 Cor 10:9 . . . should we put Christ to the ***t,***
1 Tim 3:10 . . . If they pass the ***t,*** then let
Heb 4:15 . . . of the same ***t-ings*** we do, yet

TEST, TESTED, TESTING, TESTS (V) to put to test or proof
Gen 22:1 . . . God ***t-ed*** Abraham's faith.
Deut 6:16 . . . You must not ***t*** the LORD your
Judg 3:1 . . . land to ***t*** those Israelites
1 Kgs 10:1 . . . she came to ***t*** him with hard
Job 23:10 . . . when he ***t-s*** me, I will come
Ps 17:3 . . . You have ***t-ed*** my thoughts
Ps 66:10 . . . You have ***t-ed*** us,
Ps 78:18 . . . They stubbornly ***t-ed*** God in
Ps 106:14 . . . ran wild, ***t-ing*** God's patience
Ps 139:23 . . . ***t*** me and know my anxious
Prov 17:3 . . . the LORD ***t-s*** the heart.
Luke 4:12 . . . You must not ***t*** the LORD your
Acts 5:9 . . . of conspiring to ***t*** the Spirit
1 Thes 5:21 . . . but ***t*** everything that is said.
Heb 2:18 . . . suffering and ***t-ing,*** he is able
Heb 2:18 . . . us when we are being ***t-ed.***
Heb 3:8 . . . they ***t-ed*** me in the wilderness.
Heb 11:17 . . . when God was ***t-ing*** him.
Jas 1:3 . . . when your faith is ***t-ed,*** your
Jas 1:12 . . . who patiently endure ***t-ing*** and
1 Pet 1:7 . . . It is being ***t-ed*** as fire tests
1 Jn 4:1 . . . You must ***t*** them to see if
Rev 2:10 . . . you into prison to ***t*** you.
Rev 3:10 . . . great time of ***t-ing*** that will

THANKFUL (ADJ) conscious of benefit received; expressive of thanks
Col 3:15 . . . And always be ***t.***
Col 3:16 . . . to God with ***t*** hearts.
1 Thes 5:18 . . . Be ***t*** in all circumstances,
Heb 12:28 . . . let us be ***t*** and please God by

THANKS (N) kindly or grateful thoughts; gratitude
1 Chr 16:4 . . . to give ***t,*** and to praise
Ps 30:12 . . . I will give you ***t*** forever!
Ps 107:1 . . . Give ***t*** to the LORD,
Rom 1:21 . . . as God or even give him ***t.***
1 Cor 11:24 . . . gave ***t*** to God for it.
Phil 1:3 . . . of you, I give ***t*** to my God.
1 Tim 2:1 . . . behalf, and give ***t*** for them.
1 Tim 4:3 . . . be eaten with ***t*** by faithful
Rev 4:9 . . . and honor and ***t*** to the one

THANKSGIVING (N) a prayer expressing gratitude; a public acknowledgment or celebration of God's goodness
Ps 26:7 . . . singing a song of ***t*** and telling
Ps 28:7 . . . I burst out in songs of ***t.***
Ps 100:4 . . . Enter his gates with ***t;*** go
Isa 51:3 . . . Songs of ***t*** will fill the air.

THIEF, THIEVES (N) one who steals, especially stealthily or secretly
Prov 6:30 . . . might be found for a ***t***
Prov 29:24 . . . If you assist a ***t,*** you only
Jer 7:11 . . . has become a den of ***t-ves?***
Matt 6:19 . . . where ***t-ves*** break in and steal.
Luke 19:46 . . . turned it into a den of ***t-ves.***
John 10:1 . . . surely be a ***t*** and a robber!
John 10:8 . . . me were ***t-ves*** and robbers.
1 Cor 6:10 . . . or are ***t-ves,*** or greedy people,
1 Thes 5:2 . . . unexpectedly, like a ***t*** in the
Rev 16:15 . . . as unexpectedly as a ***t!***

THINK, THINKING, THINKS (V) to reflect, ponder, or remember; to subject to the processes of logical thought; to have as an opinion; to conceive or reason
see also MEDITATE
1 Sam 12:24 . . . *T* of all the wonderful
2 Chr 19:6 . . . Always ***t*** carefully before
Ps 8:4 . . . you should ***t*** about them,
Ps 63:6 . . . I lie awake ***t-ing*** of you,
Ps 77:12 . . . I cannot stop ***t-ing*** about your
Ps 119:97 . . . I ***t*** about them all day long.
Ps 119:148 . . . the night, ***t-ing*** about your
Prov 13:16 . . . Wise people ***t*** before they
Prov 15:28 . . . godly ***t-s*** carefully before
Prov 21:29 . . . the virtuous ***t*** before they
Prov 23:7 . . . are always ***t-ing*** about how
Prov 29:20 . . . who speaks without ***t-ing.***
Isa 44:18 . . . are shut, and they cannot ***t.***
Matt 22:42 . . . What do you ***t*** about the
Rom 11:20 . . . So don't ***t*** highly of
Phil 1:3 . . . Every time I ***t*** of you, I give
Phil 2:3 . . . Be humble, ***t-ing*** of others as
Phil 3:19 . . . they ***t*** only about this life
Heb 10:24 . . . Let us ***t*** of ways to motivate

THIRSTY (ADJ) feeling a desire for liquids; having a strong desire
Ps 107:9 . . . he satisfies the ***t*** and fills
Prov 25:21 . . . If they are ***t,*** give them
Isa 55:1 . . . Is anyone ***t?*** Come and drink—
Matt 25:35 . . . I was ***t,*** and you gave
John 4:14 . . . will never be ***t*** again.
John 19:28 . . . Scripture he said, "I am ***t.***"
Rom 12:20 . . . If they are ***t,*** give them
2 Cor 11:27 . . . been hungry and ***t*** and
Rev 7:16 . . . never again be hungry or ***t;***
Rev 22:17 . . . Let anyone who is ***t*** come.

THORN, THORNS (N) a woody plant bearing sharp impeding prickles or spines; something that causes distress or irritation
Gen 3:18 . . . It will grow ***t-s*** and thistles
Num 33:55 . . . in your eyes and ***t-s*** in your
Matt 13:7 . . . seeds fell among ***t-s*** that
Matt 27:29 . . . wove ***t*** branches into a
2 Cor 12:7 . . . I was given a ***t*** in my flesh,
Heb 6:8 . . . a field bears ***t-s*** and thistles,

THOUGHT, THOUGHTS (N) the action or process of thinking; a developed intention or plan; recollection, remembrance
Ps 77:12 . . . They are constantly in my ***t-s***.
Ps 92:5 . . . And how deep are your ***t-s***.
Ps 94:11 . . . LORD knows people's ***t-s;***
Ps 104:34 . . . May all my ***t-s*** be pleasing
Ps 139:23 . . . and know my anxious ***t-s***.
Ps 142:4 . . . no one gives me a passing ***t!***
Isa 26:3 . . . whose ***t-s*** are fixed on you!
Isa 55:8 . . . My ***t-s*** are nothing like your
Matt 9:4 . . . you have such evil ***t-s*** in your
Matt 15:19 . . . heart come evil ***t-s***, murder,
1 Cor 14:25 . . . their secret ***t-s*** will be
Eph 4:23 . . . renew your ***t-s*** and attitudes.
Rev 2:23 . . . searches out the ***t-s*** and

THRONE, THRONES (N) seat of power for a king or deity; symbolic of royal authority and the king's role as a judge
Deut 17:18 . . . he sits on the ***t*** as king,
2 Sam 7:16 . . . and your ***t*** will be secure
1 Chr 17:12 . . . will secure his ***t*** forever.
Job 36:7 . . . sets them on ***t-s*** with kings
Ps 45:6 . . . Your ***t***, O God, endures
Ps 47:8 . . . nations, sitting on his holy ***t***.
Ps 89:14 . . . are the foundation of your ***t***.
Ps 99:1 . . . He sits on his ***t*** between the
Ps 102:12 . . . sit on your ***t*** forever.
Ps 103:19 . . . has made the heavens his ***t;***
Isa 6:1 . . . He was sitting on a lofty ***t***,
Isa 66:1 . . . Heaven is my ***t***, and the
Dan 7:9 . . . on a fiery ***t*** with wheels
Matt 19:28 . . . upon his glorious ***t***, you who
Matt 19:28 . . . sit on twelve ***t-s***, judging
Acts 7:49 . . . Heaven is my ***t***, and the
Rom 15:12 . . . heir to David's ***t*** will come,
Col 1:16 . . . such as ***t-s***, kingdoms, rulers,
Heb 12:2 . . . place of honor beside God's ***t***.
Rev 3:21 . . . sat with my Father on his ***t***.
Rev 4:2 . . . and I saw a ***t*** in heaven
Rev 4:4 . . . Twenty-four ***t-s*** surrounded
Rev 5:5 . . . heir to David's ***t***, has won
Rev 20:11 . . . a great white ***t*** and the
Rev 22:3 . . . the ***t*** of God and of the Lamb

TIRED (ADJ) drained of strength and energy
Exod 17:12 . . . became so ***t*** he could no
Isa 35:3 . . . those who have ***t*** hands,
Gal 6:9 . . . let's not get ***t*** of doing what
2 Thes 3:13 . . . never get ***t*** of doing good.
Heb 12:12 . . . new grip with your ***t*** hands

TITHE, TITHES (N) one-tenth of any property or produce
Num 18:21 . . . give them the ***t-s*** from the
Deut 12:17 . . . neither the ***t*** of your grain
2 Chr 31:12 . . . brought all the gifts, ***t-s***, and
Amos 4:4 . . . bring your ***t-s*** every three
Mal 3:8 . . . of the ***t-s*** and offerings due
Mal 3:10 . . . Bring all the ***t-s*** into the

TITHE (V) to pay or give a tenth of as an offering to God
Matt 23:23 . . . You should ***t***, yes,
Luke 11:42 . . . you are careful to ***t*** even the

TOUCH, TOUCHED, TOUCHES (V) to reach out or come in contact with; to lay hands upon; to have an influence upon
Gen 3:3 . . . must not eat it or even ***t*** it;
Exod 19:12 . . . or even ***t*** its boundaries.
Exod 19:12 . . . Anyone who ***t-es*** the mountain
Isa 6:7 . . . this coal has ***t-ed*** your lips.
Matt 9:21 . . . If I can just ***t*** his robe,
Matt 14:36 . . . who ***t-ed*** him were healed.
Luke 8:45 . . . "Who ***t-ed*** me?" Jesus asked.
Luke 18:15 . . . so he could ***t*** and bless
Luke 24:39 . . . ***T*** me and make sure that
2 Cor 6:17 . . . Don't ***t*** their filthy things,
Col 2:21 . . . Don't taste! Don't ***t!***"?
1 Jn 1:1 . . . ***t-ed*** him with our own hands.
1 Jn 5:18 . . . evil one cannot ***t*** them.

TRAIN, TRAINED (V) to form by or undergo instruction or discipline
see also TEACH
Isa 2:4 . . . against nation, nor ***t*** for war
Luke 6:40 . . . who is fully ***t-ed*** will become
John 7:15 . . . when he hasn't been ***t-ed?***
Acts 22:3 . . . I was carefully ***t-ed*** in our
1 Tim 4:7 . . . ***t*** yourself to be godly.
Titus 2:4 . . . women must ***t*** the younger
Heb 12:11 . . . those who are ***t-ed*** in this way.

TRANSFORM, TRANSFORMED (V) to change the outward appearance of; to change in character or condition
Matt 17:2 . . . appearance was ***t-ed*** so that
Rom 12:2 . . . let God ***t*** you into a new
1 Cor 15:51 . . . but we will all be ***t-ed!***

TRAP, TRAPS (N) something by which one is caught or stopped unawares; a position or situation from which it is difficult or impossible to escape; a device for taking game or other animals
Deut 7:25 . . . will become a ***t*** to you,
Deut 12:30 . . . fall into the ***t*** of following
Ps 91:3 . . . you from every ***t*** and protect
Prov 1:17 . . . a bird sees a ***t*** being set,
Prov 3:26 . . . foot from being caught in a ***t***.
Prov 28:10 . . . into their own ***t***, but the
Prov 29:5 . . . is to lay a ***t*** for their feet.
Prov 29:25 . . . a dangerous ***t***, but trusting
Isa 8:14 . . . he will be a ***t*** and a snare.
Isa 24:17 . . . Terror and ***t-s*** and snares will
Matt 16:23 . . . are a dangerous ***t*** to me.
Rom 11:9 . . . a snare, a ***t*** that makes them
1 Tim 3:7 . . . into the devil's ***t***.
2 Tim 2:26 . . . from the devil's ***t***.

TRAP, TRAPPED, TRAPS (V) to catch or take in or as if in a trap
Ps 7:15 . . . a deep pit to ***t*** others, then
Ps 9:16 . . . wicked are ***t-ped*** by their own
Prov 6:2 . . . if you have ***t-ped*** yourself by
Prov 12:13 . . . wicked are ***t-ped*** by their
Prov 18:7 . . . they ***t*** themselves with
Matt 22:15 . . . to plot how to ***t*** Jesus into
1 Cor 3:19 . . . He ***t-s*** the wise in the snare
1 Tim 6:9 . . . temptation and are ***t-ped*** by

TREASURE, TREASURES (N) wealth or a collection of precious things; something of great value
Exod 19:5 . . . my own special ***t*** from
Deut 7:6 . . . to be his own special ***t***.
1 Chr 29:3 . . . my own private ***t-s*** of gold
Ps 119:111 . . . Your laws are my ***t;*** they
Ps 135:4 . . . Israel for his own special ***t***.
Prov 2:4 . . . seek them like hidden ***t-s***.
Prov 18:22 . . . finds a wife finds a ***t***,
Song 4:10 . . . delights me, my ***t***, my bride.
Isa 10:3 . . . Where will your ***t-s*** be safe?
Hag 2:7 . . . the ***t-s*** of all the nations
Mal 3:17 . . . they will be my own special ***t***.
Matt 6:19 . . . Don't store up ***t-s*** here on
Matt 6:21 . . . Wherever your ***t*** is, there the
Matt 13:44 . . . Heaven is like a ***t*** that a man
Luke 12:33 . . . will store up ***t*** for you in
2 Cor 4:7 . . . jars containing this great ***t***.
Eph 3:8 . . . the endless ***t-s*** available to
Col 2:3 . . . hidden all the ***t-s*** of wisdom

1 Tim 6:19 . . . storing up their *t* as a good
Heb 11:26 . . . to own the *t-s* of Egypt, for

TREASURE, TREASURED (V) to hold or keep as precious
Job 23:12 . . . but have *t-d* his words more
Prov 2:1 . . . I say, and *t* my commands.
Prov 7:1 . . . always *t* my commands.
Prov 10:14 . . . Wise people *t* knowledge,

TREE, TREES (N) woody perennial plants, many of which produce crops; highly treasured natural resource; often linked with worship of pagan gods; symbolic of a growing believer
Gen 2:9 . . . he placed the *t* of life and
Deut 21:23 . . . from the *t* overnight.
Judg 9:8 . . . the *t-s* decided to choose
2 Sam 18:9 . . . got caught in the *t*.
1 Kgs 14:23 . . . and under every green *t*.
Ps 1:3 . . . They are like *t-s* planted along
Ps 52:8 . . . like an olive *t*, thriving in
Ps 92:12 . . . like palm *t-s* and grow
Ps 96:12 . . . Let the *t-s* of the forest
Prov 3:18 . . . Wisdom is a *t* of life to
Prov 11:30 . . . deeds become a *t* of life;
Isa 55:12 . . . and the *t-s* of the field
Isa 65:22 . . . people will live as long as *t-s*,
Jer 17:8 . . . They are like *t-s* planted along
Dan 4:10 . . . saw a large *t* in the middle
Mic 4:4 . . . and fig *t-s*, for there will be
Matt 3:10 . . . sever the roots of the *t-s*.
Matt 3:10 . . . every *t* that does not produce
Matt 12:33 . . . *t* is identified by its fruit.
Mark 8:24 . . . look like *t-s* walking
Luke 19:4 . . . a sycamore-fig *t* beside the
Rom 11:24 . . . cut from a wild olive *t*.
Gal 3:13 . . . everyone who is hung on a *t*.
Jas 3:12 . . . Does a fig *t* produce olives,
Jude 1:12 . . . They are like *t-s* in autumn
Rev 22:2 . . . the river grew a *t* of life,
Rev 22:14 . . . the fruit from the *t* of life.
Rev 22:19 . . . share in the *t* of life and

TRIAL, TRIALS (N) a legal proceeding based in court; a test of faith, patience, or stamina through subjection to suffering or temptation
see also TEMPTATION(S), TEST(S), TROUBLE(S)
Job 42:11 . . . all the *t-s* the LORD had
Ps 26:2 . . . Put me on *t*, LORD,
Ps 37:33 . . . when they are put on *t*.
Ps 143:2 . . . Don't put your servant on *t*,
Mark 13:11 . . . and stand *t*, don't worry in
Luke 22:28 . . . with me in my time of *t*.
John 16:33 . . . have many *t-s* and sorrows.
Rom 5:3 . . . into problems and *t-s*, for we
1 Pet 1:7 . . . through many *t-s*, it will
1 Pet 4:12 . . . the fiery *t-s* you are going
2 Pet 2:9 . . . from their *t-s*, even while

TROUBLE, TROUBLES (N) a state, condition, or cause of distress, annoyance, difficulty, or inconvenience
see also TEST(S), TRIAL(S)
Gen 41:51 . . . made me forget all my *t-s*
Josh 7:25 . . . have you brought *t* on us?
2 Chr 15:4 . . . they were in *t* and turned
Job 5:7 . . . are born for *t* as readily as
Ps 7:14 . . . they are pregnant with *t*
Ps 9:9 . . . a refuge in times of *t*.
Ps 10:14 . . . you see the *t* and grief
Ps 22:11 . . . from me, for *t* is near,
Ps 27:5 . . . me there when *t-s* come;
Ps 32:7 . . . you protect me from *t*.
Ps 34:17 . . . them from all their *t-s*.
Ps 37:39 . . . their fortress in times of *t*.
Ps 40:12 . . . For *t-s* surround me—
Ps 41:1 . . . them when they are in *t*.
Ps 46:1 . . . ready to help in times of *t*.
Ps 49:5 . . . I fear when *t* comes, when
Ps 50:15 . . . when you are in *t*, and I will
Ps 54:7 . . . have rescued me from my *t-s*
Ps 55:3 . . . They bring *t* on me
Ps 66:14 . . . I was in deep *t*.
Ps 81:7 . . . cried to me in *t*, and
Ps 86:7 . . . whenever I'm in *t*, and
Ps 91:15 . . . I will be with them in *t*.
Ps 107:6 . . . they cried in their *t*,
Ps 107:41 . . . rescues the poor from *t*
Ps 116:3 . . . I saw only *t* and sorrow.
Ps 120:1 . . . took my *t-s* to the LORD;
Ps 138:7 . . . I am surrounded by *t-s*, you
Prov 6:14 . . . they constantly stir up *t*.
Prov 10:10 . . . who wink at wrong cause *t*,
Prov 11:8 . . . godly are rescued from *t*,
Prov 11:29 . . . Those who bring *t* on their
Prov 12:13 . . . the godly escape such *t*.
Prov 12:21 . . . wicked have their fill of *t*.
Prov 13:20 . . . with fools and get in *t*.
Prov 25:19 . . . in times of *t* is like chewing
Eccl 4:10 . . . falls alone is in real *t*.
Isa 38:14 . . . I am in *t*, LORD. Help me!
Isa 53:4 . . . And we thought his *t-s* were
Isa 58:10 . . . and help those in *t*.
Hos 5:15 . . . as soon as *t* comes, they
Nah 1:7 . . . strong refuge when *t* comes.
Matt 6:34 . . . Today's *t* is enough
Rom 8:35 . . . if we have *t* or calamity,
1 Cor 7:28 . . . at this time will have *t-s*,
2 Cor 4:17 . . . our present *t-s* are small
2 Cor 6:4 . . . We patiently endure *t-s* and
2 Cor 7:4 . . . me happy despite all our *t-s*.
2 Cor 8:2 . . . being tested by many *t-s*,
1 Thes 3:3 . . . shaken by the *t-s* you were
1 Tim 6:5 . . . These people always cause *t*.
Jas 1:2 . . . when *t-s* of any kind come
Jas 5:1 . . . all the terrible *t-s* ahead

TRUE (ADJ) fully realized or fulfilled; accurate; properly so called; steadfast, loyal, honest, and just; ideal, essential; being in accordance with the actual state of affairs; legitimate, rightful
Num 11:23 . . . my word comes *t!*
Deut 18:22 . . . does not happen or come *t*,
Josh 23:14 . . . your God has come *t*.
1 Sam 9:6 . . . everything he says comes *t*.
1 Kgs 10:6 . . . and wisdom is *t!*
2 Chr 15:3 . . . without the *t* God,
Ps 7:10 . . . hearts are *t* and right.
Ps 19:9 . . . laws of the LORD are *t*;
Ps 119:142 . . . instructions are perfectly *t*.
Ps 119:151 . . . your commands are *t*.
Isa 45:19 . . . speak only what is *t* and
Jer 10:10 . . . is the only *t* God.
Jer 26:15 . . . it is absolutely *t* that
Jer 28:9 . . . when his predictions come *t*
Luke 16:11 . . . the *t* riches of heaven?
Luke 18:31 . . . Son of Man will come *t*.
John 1:9 . . . one who is the *t* light,
John 3:33 . . . can affirm that God is *t*.
John 4:23 . . . *t* worshipers will worship
John 6:32 . . . offers you the *t* bread
John 6:55 . . . my flesh is *t* food, and
John 7:28 . . . one who sent me is *t*,
John 15:1 . . . I am the *t* grapevine,
John 17:3 . . . know you, the only *t* God,
Rom 3:4 . . . else is a liar, God is *t*.
Rom 15:8 . . . God is *t* to the promises
Eph 5:9 . . . is good and right and *t*.
Phil 4:1 . . . stay *t* to the Lord.

Phil 4:8 . . . thoughts on what is *t*,
Jas 1:18 . . . giving us his *t* word.
1 Jn 2:8 . . . the *t* light is already
1 Jn 2:27 . . . to teach you what is *t*.
1 Jn 5:20 . . . He is the only *t* God,
Rev 19:9 . . . These are *t* words that come
Rev 22:6 . . . seen is trustworthy and *t*.

TRUMPET, TRUMPETS (N) a wind instrument made of metal or an animal horn used to rally troops on the battlefield or by priests during sacrifices
Isa 27:13 . . . the great *t* will sound.
Matt 24:31 . . . blast of a *t*, and they will
1 Cor 15:52 . . . when the last *t* is blown.
1 Thes 4:16 . . . with the *t* call of God.
Rev 8:2 . . . they were given seven *t-s*.
Rev 8:7 . . . angel blew his *t*, and hail
Rev 18:22 . . . flutes, and *t-s* will never

TRUST (N) assured reliance on the character, ability, strength, or truth of someone or something; hope
see also BELIEVE, FAITH
Job 31:24 . . . Have I put my *t* in money
Ps 40:3 . . . put their *t* in the LORD.
Ps 56:3 . . . I will put my *t* in you.
Isa 2:22 . . . Don't put your *t* in mere
Jer 13:25 . . . putting your *t* in false
Jer 17:5 . . . who put their *t* in mere
John 12:46 . . . who put their *t* in me
Heb 2:13 . . . will put my *t* in him,
1 Jn 4:16 . . . have put our *t* in his love.

TRUST, TRUSTED, TRUSTING, TRUSTS (V) to place confidence or depend; to commit or place in one's care or keeping; to rely on the truthfulness or accuracy of
see also BELIEVE, FAITH
Gen 39:8 . . . master *t-s* me with everything
Deut 1:32 . . . refused to *t* the LORD
Deut 28:52 . . . walls you *t-ed* to protect
2 Kgs 18:5 . . . Hezekiah *t-ed* in the
2 Kgs 18:19 . . . What are you *t-ing* in that
1 Chr 5:20 . . . because they *t-ed* in him.
2 Chr 13:18 . . . they *t-ed* in the LORD,
Job 4:18 . . . God does not *t* his own angels
Job 15:31 . . . fool themselves by *t-ing* in
Ps 13:5 . . . I *t* in your unfailing love.
Ps 21:7 . . . the king *t-s* in the LORD.
Ps 25:2 . . . I *t* in you, my God!
Ps 25:3 . . . No one who *t-s* in you will
Ps 31:14 . . . I am *t-ing* you, O LORD,
Ps 33:4 . . . we can *t* everything he
Ps 37:3 . . . *T* in the LORD and do
Ps 41:9 . . . the one I *t-ed* completely,
Ps 44:6 . . . I do not *t* in my bow;
Ps 55:23 . . . but I am *t-ing* you to save
Ps 62:8 . . . O my people, *t* in him at
Ps 71:5 . . . I've *t-ed* you, O LORD,
Ps 84:12 . . . for those who *t* in you.
Ps 86:2 . . . serve you and *t* you.
Ps 112:7 . . . confidently *t* the LORD
Ps 115:8 . . . as are all who *t* in them.
Ps 118:8 . . . LORD than to *t* in
Ps 119:42 . . . for I *t* in your word.
Prov 3:5 . . . *T* in the LORD with
Prov 21:22 . . . fortress in which they *t*.
Prov 28:25 . . . *t-ing* the LORD leads to
Prov 28:26 . . . who *t* their own insight
Prov 29:25 . . . *t-ing* the LORD means safety.
Prov 31:11 . . . Her husband can *t* her,
Isa 12:2 . . . I will *t* in him and
Isa 25:9 . . . We *t-ed* in him, and he saved
Isa 26:3 . . . peace all who *t* in you,
Isa 31:1 . . . for help, *t-ing* their horses,
Isa 40:31 . . . who *t* in the LORD
Jer 7:14 . . . this Temple that you *t* in
Jer 12:6 . . . Do not *t* them, no matter
Jer 48:7 . . . Because you have *t-ed* in your
Dan 3:28 . . . his servants who *t-ed* in him.
Dan 6:23 . . . for he had *t-ed* in his God.
Nah 1:7 . . . to those who *t* in him.
Hab 2:4 . . . They *t* in themselves,
Hab 2:18 . . . foolish to *t* in your own
Matt 18:6 . . . little ones who *t-s* in me to
John 2:24 . . . Jesus didn't *t* them,
John 12:44 . . . you are *t-ing* not only me,
John 14:1 . . . in God, and *t* also in me.
Rom 9:32 . . . instead of by *t-ing* in him.
Rom 9:33 . . . But anyone who *t-s* in him will
Rom 10:11 . . . Anyone who *t-s* in him will
Rom 15:13 . . . peace because you *t* in
1 Cor 2:5 . . . so you would *t* not in
1 Cor 7:25 . . . wisdom that can be *t-ed*,
Eph 3:17 . . . hearts as you *t* in him.
Phil 1:29 . . . the privilege of *t-ing* in Christ
Col 2:12 . . . because you *t-ed* the mighty
1 Tim 6:17 . . . not to *t* in their money,
2 Tim 1:12 . . . the one in whom I *t*,
2 Tim 3:15 . . . that comes by *t-ing* in Christ
Heb 10:22 . . . hearts fully *t-ing* him.
Heb 10:23 . . . God can be *t-ed* to keep his
1 Pet 1:9 . . . reward for *t-ing* him will be
1 Pet 2:6 . . . anyone who *t-s* in him will
1 Pet 2:7 . . . you who *t* him recognize

TRUSTWORTHY (ADJ) worthy of confidence; dependable
see also FAITHFUL, LOYAL
2 Kgs 22:7 . . . honest and *t* men.
Ps 19:7 . . . of the LORD are *t*,
Ps 119:86 . . . All your commands are *t*.
Ps 119:138 . . . perfect and completely *t*.
Prov 11:13 . . . those who are *t* can keep
Dan 6:4 . . . responsible, and completely *t*.
Titus 2:10 . . . to be entirely *t* and good.
Heb 6:19 . . . a strong and *t* anchor

TRUTH, TRUTHS (N) the property (as of a statement) of being in accord with fact or reality (natural and spiritual); sincerity in action, character, and utterance
Ps 15:2 . . . speaking the *t* from sincere
Ps 25:5 . . . Lead me by your *t* and teach
Ps 26:3 . . . lived according to your *t*.
Ps 43:3 . . . light and your *t*; let them
Ps 45:4 . . . defending *t*, humility, and
Ps 86:11 . . . live according to your *t*!
Ps 119:160 . . . essence of your words is *t*;
Prov 8:7 . . . for I speak the *t* and detest
Prov 12:17 . . . honest witness tells the *t*;
Prov 12:22 . . . in those who tell the *t*.
Prov 23:23 . . . Get the *t* and never sell
Isa 45:23 . . . I have spoken the *t*,
Isa 59:15 . . . Yes, *t* is gone,
Jer 4:2 . . . do so with *t*, justice,
Jer 9:3 . . . to stand up for the *t*.
Dan 10:21 . . . written in the Book of *T*.
Dan 11:2 . . . I will reveal the *t* to you.
Amos 5:10 . . . people who tell the *t*!
Zech 8:16 . . . Tell the *t* to each other.
Zech 8:19 . . . So love *t* and peace.
Luke 1:4 . . . can be certain of the *t*
John 4:23 . . . Father in spirit and in *t*.
John 7:18 . . . him speaks *t*, not lies.
John 8:32 . . . the *t* will set you free.
John 8:44 . . . there is no *t* in him.
John 14:6 . . . way, the *t*, and the life.
John 14:17 . . . who leads into all *t*.
John 15:26 . . . Advocate—the Spirit of *t*.

John 16:13 . . . the Spirit of *t* comes,
John 17:17 . . . your word, which is *t*.
John 18:37 . . . to testify to the *t*.
Acts 20:30 . . . distort the *t* in order
Acts 21:34 . . . find out the *t* in all
Acts 24:8 . . . can find out the *t* of our
Rom 1:18 . . . who suppress the *t* by their
Rom 1:25 . . . They traded the *t* about God
Rom 2:8 . . . to obey the *t* and instead
Rom 2:20 . . . complete knowledge and *t*.
1 Cor 2:13 . . . to explain spiritual *t-s*.
2 Cor 6:7 . . . We faithfully preach the *t*.
2 Cor 13:8 . . . always stand for the *t*.
Gal 2:5 . . . wanted to preserve the *t*
Gal 5:7 . . . back from following the *t*?
Eph 1:13 . . . also heard the *t*, the Good
Eph 4:15 . . . will speak the *t* in love,
Eph 6:14 . . . the belt of *t* and the body
2 Thes 2:10 . . . *t* that would save them.
2 Thes 2:12 . . . rather than believing the *t*.
1 Tim 2:4 . . . and to understand the *t*.
1 Tim 3:15 . . . and foundation of the *t*.
1 Tim 4:3 . . . people who know the *t*.
1 Tim 6:5 . . . their backs on the *t*.
2 Tim 2:15 . . . explains the word of *t*.
2 Tim 3:7 . . . able to understand the *t*.
Titus 1:14 . . . turned away from the *t*.
Heb 10:26 . . . received knowledge of the *t*,
Jas 3:14 . . . don't cover up the *t* with
Jas 5:19 . . . wanders away from the *t*
1 Pet 1:22 . . . you obeyed the *t*, so now
2 Pet 1:12 . . . standing firm in the *t*
2 Pet 2:2 . . . the way of *t* will be
1 Jn 1:8 . . . and not living in the *t*.
1 Jn 2:20 . . . all of you know the *t*.
1 Jn 3:19 . . . belong to the *t*, so we
1 Jn 4:6 . . . Spirit of *t* or the spirit
1 Jn 5:6 . . . Spirit, who is *t*, confirms
2 Jn 1:2 . . . because the *t* lives
2 Jn 1:3 . . . who live in *t* and love.
3 Jn 1:3 . . . living according to the *t*.
3 Jn 1:8 . . . partners as they teach the *t*.

TWELVE (ADJ) of or relating to the number 12
Gen 35:22 . . . names of the *t* sons of Jacob:
Gen 49:28 . . . These are the *t* tribes of
Matt 10:1 . . . Jesus called his *t* disciples
Luke 9:17 . . . picked up *t* baskets of
Rev 21:12 . . . names of the *t* tribes of
Rev 21:14 . . . names of the *t* apostles of
Rev 21:21 . . . The *t* gates were made of

U

UNBELIEF (N) incredulity or skepticism in matters of religious truth
Matt 13:58 . . . there because of their *u*.
Mark 6:6 . . . he was amazed at their *u*.
Mark 9:24 . . . help me overcome my *u*!
Mark 16:14 . . . them for their stubborn *u*
Rom 11:23 . . . Israel turn from their *u*,
1 Tim 1:13 . . . it in ignorance and *u*.
Heb 3:19 . . . because of their *u* they

UNDERSTAND (V) to grasp the meaning or reasonableness of; to be thoroughly familiar with
Job 5:9 . . . things too marvelous to *u*.
Job 36:26 . . . is greater than we can *u*.
Ps 73:16 . . . tried to *u* why the wicked
Ps 119:27 . . . Help me *u* the meaning of
Ps 119:125 . . . then I will *u* your laws.
Ps 119:130 . . . so even the simple can *u*.
Prov 2:5 . . . will *u* what it means to fear
Prov 2:9 . . . you will *u* what is right,
Prov 28:5 . . . the LORD *u* completely.
Prov 30:18 . . . things that I don't *u*:
Eccl 7:25 . . . and to *u* the reason
Isa 6:9 . . . carefully, but do not *u*.
Isa 40:21 . . . you heard? Don't you *u*?
Jer 9:24 . . . truly know me and *u* that
Hos 14:9 . . . who are wise *u* these things.
Matt 13:11 . . . permitted to *u* the secrets
Matt 13:23 . . . truly hear and *u* God's
Luke 19:42 . . . people would *u* the way
Luke 24:45 . . . minds to *u* the Scriptures.
Acts 8:30 . . . Do you *u* what you are
Rom 7:15 . . . I don't really *u* myself,
Rom 15:21 . . . never heard of him will *u*.
1 Cor 2:14 . . . and they can't *u* it,
1 Cor 14:14 . . . but I don't *u* what I am
2 Cor 3:14 . . . they cannot *u* the truth.
Gal 1:11 . . . you to *u* that the gospel
Eph 1:18 . . . you can *u* the confident
Eph 5:17 . . . thoughtlessly, but *u* what
Phil 1:10 . . . want you to *u* what really
Phil 4:7 . . . exceeds anything we can *u*.
Col 2:2 . . . that they *u* God's mysterious
1 Tim 2:4 . . . saved and to *u* the truth.
2 Tim 2:7 . . . will help you *u* all these
Heb 11:3 . . . By faith we *u* that the entire
2 Pet 3:16 . . . are hard to *u*, and those

V

VALUABLE (ADJ) having desirable or esteemed characteristics or qualities; of great use or service
Job 28:17 . . . Wisdom is more *v* than gold
Ps 119:72 . . . instructions are more *v*
Prov 8:11 . . . is far more *v* than rubies.
Prov 20:15 . . . words are more *v* than
Matt 10:31 . . . you are more *v* to God than
Luke 12:24 . . . are far more *v* to him than
Phil 3:7 . . . these things were *v*, but now

VICTORY, VICTORIES (N) the overcoming of an enemy, antagonist, or struggle
Exod 15:2 . . . he has given me *v*.
2 Sam 22:51 . . . You give great *v-ies* to your
Ps 18:50 . . . You give great *v-ies* to your
Ps 20:5 . . . we hear of your *v* and
Ps 21:1 . . . because you give him *v*.
Ps 35:3 . . . I will give you *v*!
Ps 44:4 . . . You command *v-ies* for Israel.
Ps 45:4 . . . majesty, ride out to *v*,
Ps 48:10 . . . right hand is filled with *v*.
Ps 62:1 . . . for my *v* comes from him.
Ps 98:3 . . . have seen the *v* of our God.
Ps 118:14 . . . he has given me *v*.
Ps 149:4 . . . crowns the humble with *v*.
Isa 12:2 . . . he has given me *v*.
Isa 52:10 . . . see the *v* of our God.
Rom 8:37 . . . overwhelming *v* is ours
1 Cor 15:54 . . . Death is swallowed up in *v*.
Col 2:15 . . . publicly by his *v* over them
Rev 5:5 . . . David's throne, has won the *v*.

VIOLENCE (N) exertion of physical force so as to injure or abuse
Gen 6:11 . . . and was filled with *v*.
Ps 12:5 . . . I have seen *v* done to the
Ps 72:14 . . . them from oppression and *v*,
Isa 60:18 . . . *V* will disappear from your
Jonah 3:8 . . . and stop all their *v*.
Mic 2:2 . . . take it by fraud and *v*.

VOICE (N) verbal communication by human and divine means
Isa 40:3 . . . the *v* of someone shouting,

Mark 1:3 . . . He is a *v* shouting in the
John 10:3 . . . sheep recognize his *v* and
John 12:28 . . . a *v* spoke from heaven,
Rev 3:20 . . . If you hear my *v* and open

W

WAGE, WAGES (N) payment for labor or services; compensation
Hag 1:6 . . . Your ***w-s*** disappear as though
Zech 11:12 . . . give me my ***w-s***, whatever
Mal 3:5 . . . cheat employees of their ***w-s***,
Matt 20:2 . . . the normal daily ***w*** and
Rom 4:4 . . . their ***w-s*** are not a gift,
Rom 6:23 . . . For the ***w-s*** of sin is death,

WAIT, WAITED, WAITING (V) to look forward expectantly; to stay in place in expectation of
Ps 40:1 . . . I ***w-ed*** patiently for the LORD
Ps 62:5 . . . all that I am ***w*** quietly before
Ps 69:3 . . . ***w-ing*** for my God to help me.
Isa 30:18 . . . Blessed are those who ***w*** for
Mic 7:7 . . . I ***w*** confidently for God to
Hab 3:16 . . . I will ***w*** quietly for the
Luke 12:37 . . . who are ready and ***w-ing***
Rom 8:19 . . . all creation is ***w-ing*** eagerly
Rom 8:23 . . . We, too, ***w*** with eager hope
Heb 9:28 . . . are eagerly ***w-ing*** for him.

WALK, WALKED, WALKING (V) to roam, traverse, or advance by steps; to pursue a course of action or way of life
Gen 3:8 . . . God ***w-ing*** about in the garden.
Lev 26:12 . . . I will ***w*** among you;
Deut 11:22 . . . God by ***w-ing*** in his ways
Deut 26:17 . . . promised to ***w*** in his ways,
Josh 22:5 . . . God, ***w*** in all his ways,
Ps 23:4 . . . when I ***w*** through the
Ps 89:15 . . . they will ***w*** in the light
Prov 4:12 . . . When you ***w***, you won't
Prov 6:22 . . . When you ***w***, their counsel
Isa 2:3 . . . we will ***w*** in his paths.
Isa 40:31 . . . They will ***w*** and not
Isa 43:2 . . . When you ***w*** through the
Jer 6:16 . . . godly way, and ***w*** in it.
Dan 3:25 . . . ***w-ing*** around in the fire
Amos 3:3 . . . two people ***w*** together
Mic 6:8 . . . to ***w*** humbly with your God.
Mal 2:6 . . . they ***w-ed*** with me, living good
Matt 14:29 . . . boat and ***w-ed*** on the water
Mark 2:9 . . . pick up your mat, and ***w***
John 8:12 . . . have to ***w*** in darkness,

WAR, WARS (N) armed conflict with an opposing military force; a state of hostility, conflict, or antagonism
Josh 11:23 . . . finally had rest from ***w***.
Ps 46:9 . . . He causes ***w-s*** to end
Ps 68:30 . . . nations that delight in ***w***.
Ps 120:7 . . . peace, they want ***w!***
Ps 144:1 . . . He trains my hands for ***w***
Isa 2:4 . . . nor train for ***w*** anymore.
2 Cor 10:3 . . . we don't wage ***w*** as humans
1 Pet 2:11 . . . that wage ***w*** against your
Rev 12:7 . . . Then there was ***w*** in heaven.
Rev 19:11 . . . and wages a righteous ***w***.

WARN, WARNED, WARNING (V) to give notice to beforehand especially of danger or evil; to counsel
Gen 2:16 . . . God ***w-ed*** him, "You may
Gen 31:24 . . . told him, "I'm ***w-ing*** you—
Gen 31:29 . . . to me last night and ***w-ed*** me,
Exod 19:21 . . . down and ***w*** the people
Num 16:40 . . . This would ***w*** the Israelites
1 Sam 8:9 . . . but solemnly ***w*** them about
1 Kgs 2:42 . . . LORD and ***w*** you not to
2 Kgs 17:13 . . . and seers to ***w*** both Israel
2 Chr 19:10 . . . must ***w*** them not to sin
Ezek 3:18 . . . If I ***w*** the wicked,
Ezek 33:3 . . . the alarm to ***w*** the people.
Matt 16:6 . . . "Watch out!" Jesus ***w-ed*** them.
Luke 16:28 . . . I want him to ***w*** them so
Acts 4:17 . . . must ***w*** them not to speak
1 Cor 4:14 . . . to ***w*** you as my beloved
1 Cor 10:11 . . . written down to ***w*** us who
Col 1:28 . . . ***w-ing*** everyone and teaching
1 Thes 4:6 . . . solemnly ***w-ed*** you before.
1 Thes 5:14 . . . urge you to ***w*** those who
2 Thes 3:15 . . . but ***w*** them as you would
Heb 3:13 . . . You must ***w*** each other

WASH, WASHED (V) to cleanse—of physical, ceremonial, or spiritual significance
Ps 51:7 . . . ***w*** me, and I will be whiter
John 13:5 . . . he began to ***w*** the disciples'
John 13:10 . . . does not need to ***w***, except
Acts 22:16 . . . Have your sins ***w-ed*** away
Eph 5:26 . . . holy and clean, ***w-ed*** by the
Titus 3:5 . . . He ***w-ed*** away our sins,
Heb 10:22 . . . bodies have been ***w-ed***
Jas 4:8 . . . ***W*** your hands, you sinners;
2 Pet 2:22 . . . ***w-ed*** pig returns to the mud.
Rev 7:14 . . . They have ***w-ed*** their robes in
Rev 22:14 . . . those who ***w*** their robes.

WATER, WATERS (N) precious resource for drink and irrigation, usually associated with blessing; a body of water
Exod 7:20 . . . struck the ***w*** of the Nile.
Exod 17:1 . . . there was no ***w*** there for
Num 20:2 . . . was no ***w*** for the people
2 Sam 23:15 . . . good ***w*** from the well
Ps 42:1 . . . streams of ***w***, so I long
Prov 25:21 . . . give them ***w*** to drink.
Song 8:7 . . . Many ***w-s*** cannot quench
Isa 11:9 . . . for as the ***w-s*** fill the sea,
Isa 32:2 . . . like streams of ***w*** in the
Isa 43:2 . . . through deep ***w-s***, I will be
Isa 49:10 . . . lead them beside cool ***w-s***.
Jer 17:8 . . . reach deep into the ***w***.
Jonah 2:3 . . . The mighty ***w-s*** engulfed me;
Hab 2:14 . . . For as the ***w-s*** fill the sea,
Zech 14:8 . . . life-giving ***w-s*** will flow
Matt 14:25 . . . them, walking on the ***w***.
John 3:5 . . . born of ***w*** and the Spirit.
John 4:10 . . . would give you living ***w***.
John 7:38 . . . Rivers of living ***w*** will
1 Jn 5:6 . . . his baptism in ***w*** and by
Rev 7:17 . . . springs of life-giving ***w***.
Rev 21:6 . . . springs of the ***w*** of life.

WEAK, WEAKER, WEAKEST (ADJ) lacking strength; not able to withstand temptation or persuasion
Ps 72:13 . . . pity for the ***w*** and the
Ps 103:14 . . . he knows how ***w*** we are;
Isa 59:1 . . . arm is not too ***w*** to save
Matt 12:20 . . . will not crush the ***w-est*** reed
Matt 26:41 . . . but the body is ***w!***
Rom 14:1 . . . who are ***w*** in faith,
1 Cor 8:9 . . . others with a ***w-er*** conscience
1 Cor 9:22 . . . bring the ***w*** to Christ.
1 Cor 11:30 . . . many of you are ***w*** and
1 Cor 12:22 . . . of the body that seem ***w-est***
2 Cor 12:10 . . . For when I am ***w***, then
1 Thes 5:14 . . . care of those who are ***w***.

WEARY (ADJ) exhausted in strength, endurance, or vigor
Isa 40:31 . . . They will run and not grow ***w***.
Isa 50:4 . . . know how to comfort the ***w***.
Matt 11:28 . . . you who are ***w*** and carry

2 Cor 5:2 . . . We grow *w* in our present
Heb 12:3 . . . won't become *w* and give up.

WEEP, WEEPING (V) to cry aloud, often linked with prayer and repentance
2 Sam 1:26 . . . How I *w* for you,
Ps 126:6 . . . They *w* as they go to
Jer 31:16 . . . Do not *w* any longer,
Jer 50:4 . . . will come *w-ing* and seeking
Matt 2:18 . . . heard in Ramah—*w-ing* and
Matt 8:12 . . . will be *w-ing* and gnashing
Luke 6:21 . . . blesses you who *w* now,
Luke 22:62 . . . the courtyard, *w-ing* bitterly.
Luke 23:28 . . . don't *w* for me, but *w*
Rom 12:15 . . . and *w* with those who *w*.

WHIRLWIND (N) a small rotating windstorm, sometimes violent and destructive
see also STORM
2 Kgs 2:1 . . . to heaven in a *w*,
Job 38:1 . . . answered Job from the *w*:
Hos 8:7 . . . and will harvest the *w*.
Nah 1:3 . . . in the *w* and the storm.

WHISPER (N) a minor or softer reflection of the original noise; hint, trace
1 Kgs 19:12 . . . sound of a gentle *w*.
Job 26:14 . . . merely a *w* of his power.
Ps 107:29 . . . calmed the storm to a *w*

WHITE, WHITER (ADJ) free from color; of the color white
Ps 51:7 . . . I will be *w-r* than snow.
Isa 1:18 . . . make them as *w* as snow.
Dan 7:9 . . . clothing was as *w* as snow,
Matt 28:3 . . . clothing was as *w* as snow.
Rev 1:14 . . . like wool, as *w* as snow.
Rev 6:2 . . . saw a *w* horse standing
Rev 19:11 . . . a *w* horse was standing
Rev 20:11 . . . saw a great *w* throne

WHITE (N) the absence of color; free from spot or blemish
Rev 3:4 . . . will walk with me in *w*,
Rev 7:13 . . . who are clothed in *w*?

WICKED (ADJ) morally very bad
Gen 13:13 . . . area were extremely *w* and
Ps 7:9 . . . those who are *w*, and defend
Prov 10:7 . . . name of a *w* person rots
Prov 26:23 . . . may hide a *w* heart, just
Jer 35:15 . . . Turn from your *w* ways,
Ezek 18:21 . . . But if *w* people turn away
Ezek 21:25 . . . you corrupt and *w* prince
Ezek 33:8 . . . that some *w* people are sure
Hos 10:9 . . . not right that the *w* men of
Jonah 1:2 . . . I have seen how *w* its people
Luke 6:35 . . . who are unthankful and *w*.
1 Jn 5:17 . . . All *w* actions are sin,

WICKED (N) those who practice evil
Ps 1:1 . . . the advice of the *w*, or stand
Ps 10:13 . . . Why do the *w* get away with
Ps 12:8 . . . though the *w* strut about,
Ps 14:6 . . . The *w* frustrate the plans
Ps 37:1 . . . worry about the *w* or envy
Ps 82:2 . . . by favoring the *w*?
Ps 101:8 . . . ferret out the *w* and free
Ps 139:19 . . . you would destroy the *w*!
Ps 146:9 . . . the plans of the *w*.
Prov 4:14 . . . Don't do as the *w* do,
Prov 9:7 . . . who corrects the *w* will
Prov 10:28 . . . expectations of the *w* come
Prov 12:5 . . . of the *w* is treacherous.
Prov 29:7 . . . the *w* don't care at all.
Isa 5:23 . . . to let the *w* go free,
Isa 11:4 . . . mouth will destroy the *w*.
Isa 26:10 . . . the *w* keep doing wrong
Isa 48:22 . . . no peace for the *w*,
Mal 4:1 . . . arrogant and the *w* will be

WILDERNESS (N) any desolate, barren, or unpopulated area, usually linked with danger
Num 16:13 . . . kill us here in this *w*,
Num 26:65 . . . all die in the *w*.
Num 32:13 . . . wander in the *w* for forty
Deut 8:16 . . . manna in the *w*, a food
Deut 29:5 . . . led you through the *w*,
Ps 78:19 . . . give us food in the *w*.
Ps 78:52 . . . safely through the *w*.
Isa 32:15 . . . *w* will become a fertile
Isa 35:6 . . . will gush forth in the *w*,
Matt 3:3 . . . the *w*, 'Prepare the way
Luke 5:16 . . . withdrew to the *w* for
Rev 12:6 . . . fled into the *w*, where God

WILL (N) desire, wish
Ps 40:8 . . . in doing your *w*, my God,
Ps 143:10 . . . me to do your *w*, for you
Prov 3:6 . . . Seek his *w* in all you do,
Matt 6:10 . . . May your *w* be done on
Matt 7:21 . . . who actually do the *w*
Matt 12:50 . . . does the *w* of my Father
Matt 18:14 . . . heavenly Father's *w* that
Matt 26:39 . . . want your *w* to be done,
Matt 26:42 . . . I drink it, your *w* be done.
John 5:30 . . . carry out the *w* of the one
John 6:38 . . . heaven to do the *w* of God
Rom 12:2 . . . learn to know God's *w*
1 Thes 5:18 . . . this is God's *w* for you
Heb 10:7 . . . come to do your *w*, O God—
Heb 13:21 . . . need for doing his *w*.
1 Pet 4:2 . . . to do the *w* of God.

WISDOM (N) knowledge, insight, judgment
Gen 3:6 . . . she wanted the *w* it would
1 Kgs 4:29 . . . gave Solomon very great *w*
1 Kgs 10:24 . . . to hear the *w* God had
2 Chr 1:10 . . . Give me the *w* and
Job 11:6 . . . *w*, for true *w* is not
Job 42:3 . . . that questions my *w* with such
Ps 51:6 . . . teaching me *w* even there.
Prov 2:6 . . . the LORD grants *w*!
Prov 3:13 . . . the person who finds *w*,
Prov 8:11 . . . *w* is far more valuable
Prov 11:2 . . . with humility comes *w*.
Prov 16:16 . . . better to get *w* than gold,
Prov 23:23 . . . also get *w*, discipline,
Prov 29:3 . . . man who loves *w* brings joy
Eccl 10:10 . . . the value of *w*; it helps
Isa 11:2 . . . on him—the Spirit of *w*
Isa 50:4 . . . me his words of *w*, so that
Luke 2:52 . . . Jesus grew in *w* and in
Acts 6:3 . . . full of the Spirit and *w*.
1 Cor 1:21 . . . him through human *w*, he
Eph 1:17 . . . you spiritual *w* and insight
Col 2:3 . . . treasures of *w* and knowledge.
Col 3:16 . . . with all the *w* he gives.
2 Tim 3:15 . . . given you the *w* to receive
Titus 2:12 . . . world with *w*, righteousness,
Jas 1:5 . . . If you need *w*, ask our
Rev 5:12 . . . riches and *w* and strength

WISE, WISER, WISEST (ADJ) marked by deep understanding, keen discernment, and a capacity for sound judgment
1 Kgs 3:12 . . . you a *w* and understanding
Job 9:4 . . . God is so *w* and so mighty.
Ps 14:2 . . . anyone is truly *w*, if anyone
Ps 19:7 . . . are trustworthy, making *w* the
Ps 119:100 . . . I am even *w-r* than my
Prov 4:7 . . . wisdom is the *w-st* thing

Prov 9:8 . . . correct the ***w***, and they
Prov 10:1 . . . A ***w*** child brings joy to
Prov 11:30 . . . a ***w*** person wins friends.
Prov 12:16 . . . a ***w*** person stays calm
Prov 12:18 . . . of the ***w*** bring healing.
Prov 13:1 . . . A ***w*** child accepts a parent's
Prov 13:10 . . . who take advice are ***w***.
Prov 13:20 . . . Walk with the ***w*** and
Prov 15:5 . . . learns from correction is ***w***.
Prov 16:23 . . . From a ***w*** mind comes ***w***
Prov 18:4 . . . wisdom flows from the ***w***
Prov 19:25 . . . they will be all the ***w-r***.
Prov 24:5 . . . ***w*** are mightier than the
Prov 28:7 . . . who obey the law are ***w***;
Eccl 8:5 . . . who are ***w*** will find a time
Eccl 9:17 . . . quiet words of a ***w*** person
Matt 2:1 . . . some ***w*** men from eastern
Matt 11:25 . . . who think themselves ***w***
Matt 25:2 . . . foolish, and five were ***w***.
Rom 3:11 . . . No one is truly ***w***; no one
1 Cor 1:19 . . . wisdom of the ***w*** and
1 Cor 1:25 . . . plan of God is ***w-r*** than
1 Cor 12:8 . . . ability to give ***w*** advice;
Jas 3:13 . . . If you are ***w*** and understand

WITCHCRAFT (N) the use of sorcery or magic
Lev 19:26 . . . practice fortune-telling or ***w***.
Deut 18:10 . . . omens, or engage in ***w***,
Rev 21:8 . . . those who practice ***w***, idol

WITNESS, WITNESSES (N) a person who gives testimony; one asked to be present at a transaction so as to be able to testify to its having taken place
Deut 19:15 . . . of two or three ***w-es***.
Prov 19:5 . . . A false ***w*** will not go
Prov 21:28 . . . but a credible ***w*** will be
Matt 18:16 . . . by two or three ***w-es***.
John 1:8 . . . simply a ***w*** to tell about
Acts 1:8 . . . will be my ***w-es***, telling people
1 Tim 5:19 . . . by two or three ***w-es***.
1 Jn 5:7 . . . we have these three ***w-es***—

WONDERFUL (ADJ) marked by a marvelous, amazing, or extraordinary quality
1 Chr 16:9 . . . about his ***w*** deeds.
Job 37:14 . . . consider the ***w*** miracles
Ps 16:6 . . . What a ***w*** inheritance!
Ps 17:7 . . . unfailing love in ***w*** ways.
Ps 71:17 . . . about the ***w*** things you
Ps 72:18 . . . does such ***w*** things.
Ps 75:1 . . . tell of your ***w*** deeds.
Ps 105:2 . . . about his ***w*** deeds.
Ps 118:23 . . . it is ***w*** to see.
Ps 119:18 . . . to see the ***w*** truths in
Ps 119:27 . . . meditate on your ***w*** deeds.
Ps 119:129 . . . Your laws are ***w***.
Ps 139:6 . . . knowledge is too ***w*** for
Ps 145:5 . . . and your ***w*** miracles.
Eccl 11:9 . . . Young people, it's ***w*** to be
Isa 9:6 . . . be called: ***W*** Counselor,
Isa 12:5 . . . he has done ***w*** things.
Isa 25:1 . . . You do such ***w*** things!
Matt 21:15 . . . saw these ***w*** miracles
Matt 21:42 . . . and it is ***w*** to see.
Luke 13:17 . . . rejoiced at the ***w*** things
Acts 2:11 . . . about the ***w*** things God has
Acts 20:24 . . . News about the ***w*** grace of
2 Cor 10:12 . . . we are as ***w*** as these
Titus 2:13 . . . hope to that ***w*** day when

WORD, WORDS (N) something that is said; special revelation from God; commands
Deut 8:3 . . . live by every ***w*** that comes
Deut 11:18 . . . to these ***w-s*** of mine. Tie
Job 38:2 . . . with such ignorant ***w-s***?
Ps 19:3 . . . speak without a sound or ***w***;
Ps 52:4 . . . others with your ***w-s***, you liar!
Ps 119:9 . . . pure? By obeying your ***w***.
Ps 119:11 . . . hidden your ***w*** in my heart,
Ps 119:103 . . . How sweet your ***w-s*** taste
Ps 119:160 . . . essence of your ***w-s*** is
Ps 119:162 . . . I rejoice in your ***w*** like
Prov 12:19 . . . Truthful ***w-s*** stand the test
Prov 12:25 . . . an encouraging ***w*** cheers
Prov 16:24 . . . Kind ***w-s*** are like honey—
Prov 17:27 . . . wise person uses few ***w-s***;
Prov 26:23 . . . Smooth ***w-s*** may hide a
Isa 40:21 . . . deaf to the ***w-s*** of God—
Jer 15:16 . . . your ***w-s***, I devoured
Jer 23:29 . . . Does not my ***w*** burn like
Amos 8:13 . . . for the LORD's ***w***.
Matt 4:4 . . . but by every ***w*** that comes
Matt 15:6 . . . you cancel the ***w*** of God
Matt 24:35 . . . ***w-s*** will never disappear.
John 1:1 . . . the beginning the ***W*** already
John 6:68 . . . the ***w-s*** that give eternal life.
John 15:7 . . . and my ***w-s*** remain in you,
John 17:17 . . . teach them your ***w***, which
Rom 10:18 . . . the ***w-s*** to all the world.
1 Cor 2:1 . . . use lofty ***w-s*** and impressive
1 Cor 2:13 . . . do not use ***w-s*** that come
1 Cor 14:9 . . . to people in ***w-s*** they don't
1 Cor 14:19 . . . than ten thousand ***w-s*** in
2 Cor 2:17 . . . We preach the ***w*** of God
2 Cor 4:2 . . . or distort the ***w*** of God.
Eph 6:17 . . . which is the ***w*** of God.
Phil 2:16 . . . firmly to the ***w*** of life;
2 Tim 2:15 . . . explains the ***w*** of truth.
Titus 2:5 . . . shame on the ***w*** of God.
Heb 4:12 . . . For the ***w*** of God is
Heb 5:12 . . . things about God's ***w***.
Jas 1:22 . . . listen to God's ***w***.
1 Pet 1:23 . . . eternal, living ***w*** of God.
1 Pet 2:8 . . . not obey God's ***w***, and so
1 Pet 3:1 . . . to them without any ***w-s***.
2 Pet 3:5 . . . long ago by the ***w*** of
Rev 19:13 . . . title was the ***W*** of God.
Rev 22:19 . . . of the ***w-s*** from this book

WORK, WORKS (N) one's occupation; physical or creative effort
Gen 2:2 . . . finished his ***w*** of creation,
Exod 20:9 . . . week for your ordinary ***w***,
Deut 5:13 . . . week for your ordinary ***w***,
Ps 77:12 . . . about your mighty ***w-s***.
Ps 107:24 . . . impressive ***w-s*** on the
Ps 127:1 . . . ***w*** of the builders is wasted.
Ps 150:2 . . . Praise him for his mighty ***w-s***;
Prov 21:5 . . . planning and hard ***w*** lead
Eccl 2:19 . . . my skill and hard ***w*** under
Eccl 5:19 . . . To enjoy your ***w*** and accept
John 4:34 . . . and from finishing his ***w***.
John 5:36 . . . Father gave me these ***w-s*** to
John 10:32 . . . have done many good ***w-s***.
Acts 13:2 . . . for the special ***w*** to which
Acts 20:24 . . . finishing the ***w*** assigned
Rom 4:5 . . . not because of their ***w***, but
1 Cor 3:5 . . . the ***w*** the Lord gave us.
Gal 6:4 . . . attention to your own ***w***, for
Eph 4:12 . . . people to do his ***w*** and build
Eph 4:16 . . . part does its own special ***w***,
Eph 4:28 . . . your hands for good hard ***w***,
Phil 1:6 . . . began the good ***w*** within you,
1 Tim 6:18 . . . rich in good ***w-s*** and
2 Tim 3:17 . . . people to do every good ***w***.
Heb 10:24 . . . acts of love and good ***w-s***.
Jas 2:26 . . . faith is dead without good ***w-s***.
Rev 15:3 . . . marvelous are your ***w-s***,

WORK, WORKED, WORKING (V) to exert oneself physically or mentally
Prov 13:4 . . . but those who *w* hard will
Eccl 5:12 . . . who *w* hard sleep well,
Matt 6:28 . . . They don't *w* or make their
Matt 12:30 . . . anyone who isn't ***w-ing*** with
Luke 10:7 . . . who *w* deserve their pay.
Luke 13:24 . . . *W* hard to enter the narrow
Rom 4:6 . . . righteous without ***w-ing*** for
Rom 8:28 . . . to *w* together for the good
Rom 12:11 . . . Never be lazy, but *w* hard
1 Cor 15:10 . . . I have ***w-ed*** harder than
1 Cor 15:58 . . . Always *w* enthusiastically
2 Cor 11:27 . . . I have ***w-ed*** hard and
Eph 6:7 . . . you were ***w-ing*** for the Lord
1 Thes 4:11 . . . and ***w-ing*** with your hands,
2 Thes 3:10 . . . unwilling to *w* will not
1 Tim 5:18 . . . Those who *w* deserve their
1 Tim 6:2 . . . slaves should *w* all the harder
Heb 6:10 . . . how hard you have ***w-ed*** for
2 Pet 1:10 . . . *w* hard to prove that you

WORLD (N) the earth and its inhabitants; the human race; the current age and its value system
Ps 33:9 . . . he spoke, the *w* began!
Ps 50:12 . . . for all the *w* is mine
Ps 96:13 . . . judge the *w* with justice,
Isa 13:11 . . . will punish the *w* for its
Matt 16:26 . . . you gain the whole *w* but
John 1:29 . . . away the sin of the *w!*
John 3:16 . . . this is how God loved the *w:*
John 8:12 . . . I am the light of the *w.*
John 13:35 . . . prove to the *w* that you
John 16:33 . . . I have overcome the *w.*
John 17:5 . . . shared before the *w* began.
John 17:14 . . . And the *w* hates them
John 18:36 . . . Kingdom is not of this *w.*
Rom 3:19 . . . the entire *w* is guilty
1 Cor 1:27 . . . things the *w* considers
1 Cor 2:7 . . . glory before the *w* began.
1 Cor 3:1 . . . you belonged to this *w* or
1 Cor 3:19 . . . of this *w* is foolishness
1 Cor 6:2 . . . to judge the *w*, can't you
2 Cor 5:19 . . . reconciling the *w* to himself,
Eph 2:12 . . . lived in this *w* without God
Eph 4:9 . . . also descended to our lowly *w.*
Phil 2:15 . . . lights in a *w* full of crooked
Titus 1:2 . . . them before the *w* began.
Heb 9:26 . . . ever since the *w* began.
Jas 2:5 . . . poor in this *w* to be rich
Jas 4:4 . . . a friend of the *w*, you make
1 Jn 2:2 . . . the sins of all the *w.*
1 Jn 2:15 . . . Do not love this *w* nor
1 Jn 5:4 . . . defeats this evil *w*, and

WORRY, WORRIES (N) mental distress or agitation resulting from concern; anxiety
Prov 12:25 . . . *W* weighs a person down;
Matt 6:27 . . . Can all your ***w-ies*** add a single
Luke 21:34 . . . and by the ***w-ies*** of this life.
1 Pet 5:7 . . . Give all your ***w-ies*** and cares

WORRY, WORRIED, WORRYING (V) to feel or experience concern or anxiety
Deut 20:8 . . . anyone here afraid or ***w-ied?***
Ps 37:1 . . . Don't *w* about the wicked
Isa 7:4 . . . Tell him to stop ***w-ing.***
Matt 6:25 . . . I tell you not to *w* about
Matt 10:19 . . . don't *w* about how to
Luke 6:41 . . . And why *w* about a speck in
Acts 27:33 . . . You have been so ***w-ied*** that
Phil 4:6 . . . Don't *w* about anything;

WORSHIP, WORSHIPED, WORSHIPING, WORSHIPS (V) to regard with great respect, honor, or devotion
Gen 12:8 . . . and he ***w-ed*** the LORD.
Gen 13:4 . . . and there he ***w-ed*** the LORD
Gen 21:33 . . . and there he ***w-ed*** the LORD,
Gen 26:25 . . . there and ***w-ed*** the LORD.
Deut 12:30 . . . and ***w-ing*** their gods.
2 Kgs 17:36 . . . But *w* only the LORD,
Ps 29:2 . . . *W* the LORD in the splendor
Ps 95:6 . . . Come, let us *w* and bow down.
Ps 105:3 . . . rejoice, you who *w* the LORD.
Isa 44:19 . . . bow down to *w* a piece of
Jer 16:11 . . . ***w-ed*** other gods and served
Dan 3:28 . . . die rather than serve or *w* any
Hos 9:1 . . . like prostitutes, ***w-ing*** other
Hos 9:10 . . . as vile as the god they ***w-ed.***
Hos 13:1 . . . Ephraim sinned by ***w-ing*** Baal
Zeph 3:9 . . . everyone can *w* the LORD
Zech 14:17 . . . to Jerusalem to *w* the King,
Matt 2:2 . . . we have come to *w* him.
Matt 4:9 . . . kneel down and *w* me.
Matt 15:25 . . . she came and ***w-ed*** him,
Matt 28:9 . . . grasped his feet, and ***w-ed***
Luke 23:47 . . . he ***w-ed*** God and said,
John 4:24 . . . *w* in spirit and in truth.
1 Cor 5:11 . . . is greedy, or ***w-s*** idols,
Heb 9:14 . . . we can *w* the living God.

WRONG (N) an injurious, unfair, or unjust act; something wrong, immoral, or unethical
Exod 23:2 . . . the crowd in doing *w.*
Deut 32:4 . . . faithful God who does no *w;*
Job 34:10 . . . The Almighty can do no *w.*
Ps 141:9 . . . snares of those who do *w.*
Isa 53:9 . . . done no *w* and had never
Rom 13:10 . . . Love does no *w* to others,
Rom 16:19 . . . to stay innocent of any *w.*
1 Cor 6:9 . . . those who do *w* will not
Jas 1:13 . . . God is never tempted to do *w*,
1 Pet 3:17 . . . to suffer for doing *w!*

Y

YOUNG, YOUNGER (ADJ) being in the first or an early stage of life, growth, or development
2 Chr 10:14 . . . counsel of his ***y-er*** advisers.
Ps 119:9 . . . How can a *y* person stay pure?
Prov 20:29 . . . The glory of the *y* is their
Joel 2:28 . . . your *y* men will see visions.
Acts 2:17 . . . Your *y* men will see visions,
Acts 7:58 . . . feet of a *y* man named Saul.
1 Tim 5:1 . . . Talk to ***y-er*** men as you
Titus 2:4 . . . must train the ***y-er*** women to
Titus 2:6 . . . encourage the *y* men to live
1 Pet 5:5 . . . same way, you who are ***y-er***
1 Jn 2:13 . . . you who are *y* in the faith

Z

ZEAL (N) eagerness and ardent interest in pursuit of something
Num 25:13 . . . in his *z* for me, his God,
Rom 10:2 . . . but it is misdirected *z.*
Gal 1:14 . . . *z* for the traditions of my ancestors

Living in a Bible-Time Village

Can you count the houses in this Bible-time village? How many people can you find? What else do you see? If you lived in this village, your life would be much different. Do you see any stoplights? Do you see any cars or trucks? Are there any buses or trains or planes? You won't find any policemen or firemen, either. You won't find a post office, bank, supermarket, or gas station. Streets are stone or dirt. Houses are made of stone with flat roofs. You won't find any blacktop or concrete. There are no sidewalks. The stores are not like ours, either. You'll see people selling things in little booths. Can you find the village well? People got water from it with a pot or bucket. They lowered the pot into the well and pulled the water out. You probably don't have many camels or donkeys in your town. But you'll find some here. Can you count them? What else do you see that is different from your town? Would you like to live in this Bible-time village?

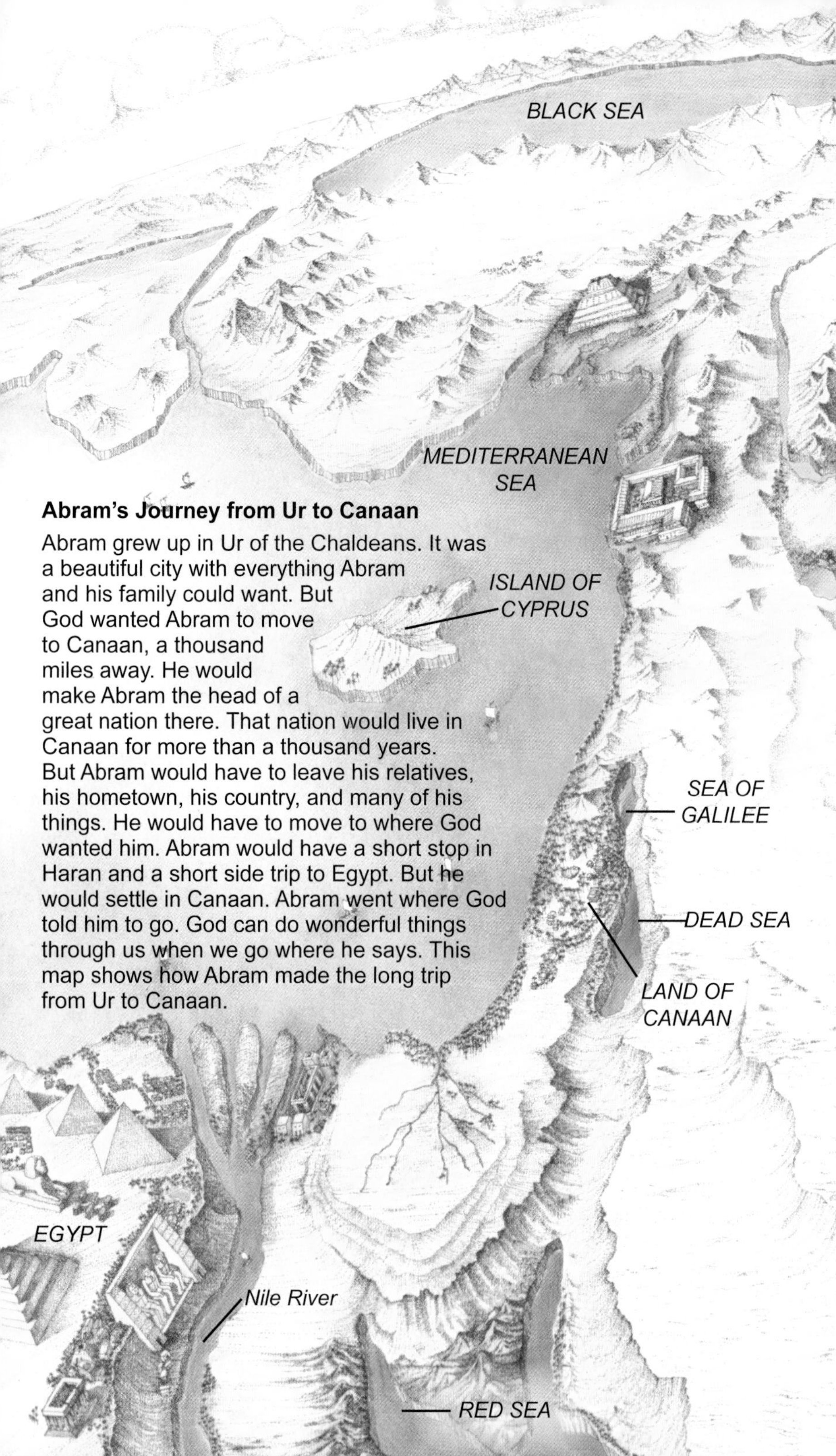

Abram's Journey from Ur to Canaan

Abram grew up in Ur of the Chaldeans. It was a beautiful city with everything Abram and his family could want. But God wanted Abram to move to Canaan, a thousand miles away. He would make Abram the head of a great nation there. That nation would live in Canaan for more than a thousand years. But Abram would have to leave his relatives, his hometown, his country, and many of his things. He would have to move to where God wanted him. Abram would have a short stop in Haran and a short side trip to Egypt. But he would settle in Canaan. Abram went where God told him to go. God can do wonderful things through us when we go where he says. This map shows how Abram made the long trip from Ur to Canaan.

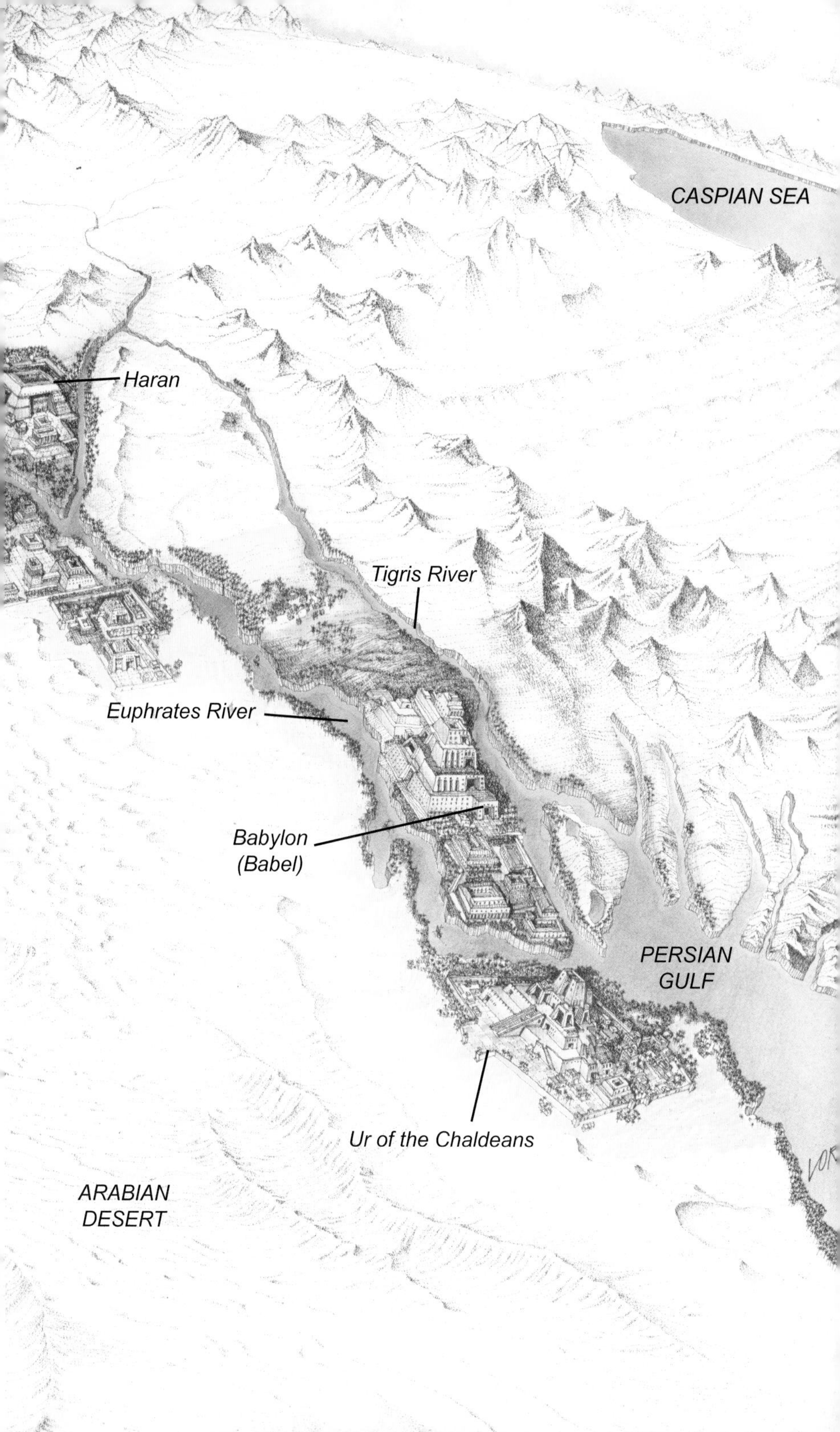
CASPIAN SEA
Haran
Tigris River
Euphrates River
Babylon
(Babel)
PERSIAN
GULF
Ur of the Chaldeans
ARABIAN
DESERT

The Exodus and 40 Years in the Wilderness

The people of Israel were slaves in Egypt. They had been there 400 years. It must have seemed that God had forgotten them. But he hadn't. God had plans for them in Canaan. He would lead them there and would make them a great nation.

Why didn't the people of Israel go straight from Egypt to Canaan? God knew they were not ready to fight the enemies along that route. For 40 years he would lead them through the wilderness where he would help them become an army. At Mount Sinai, God would give them his laws. There he would show them how to make his house, the Tabernacle. The Israelites could not become a great nation without God's laws and God's house.

Sometimes it may seem that the way we are going is the hard way. But if God is leading us, we are going the right way. God's way is always the right way!

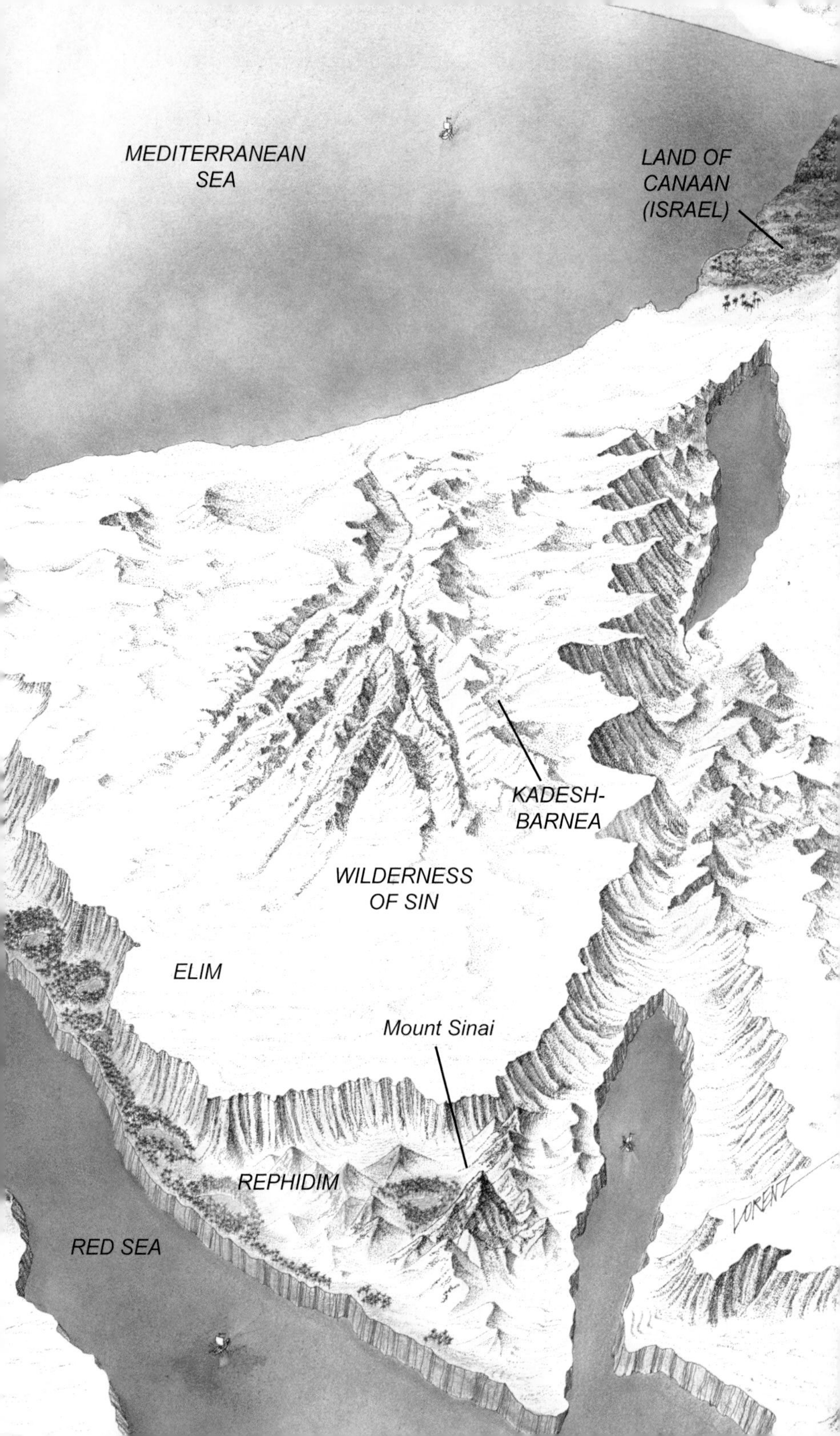
MEDITERRANEAN SEA
LAND OF CANAAN (ISRAEL)
KADESH-BARNEA
WILDERNESS OF SIN
ELIM
Mount Sinai
REPHIDIM
RED SEA
LORENZ

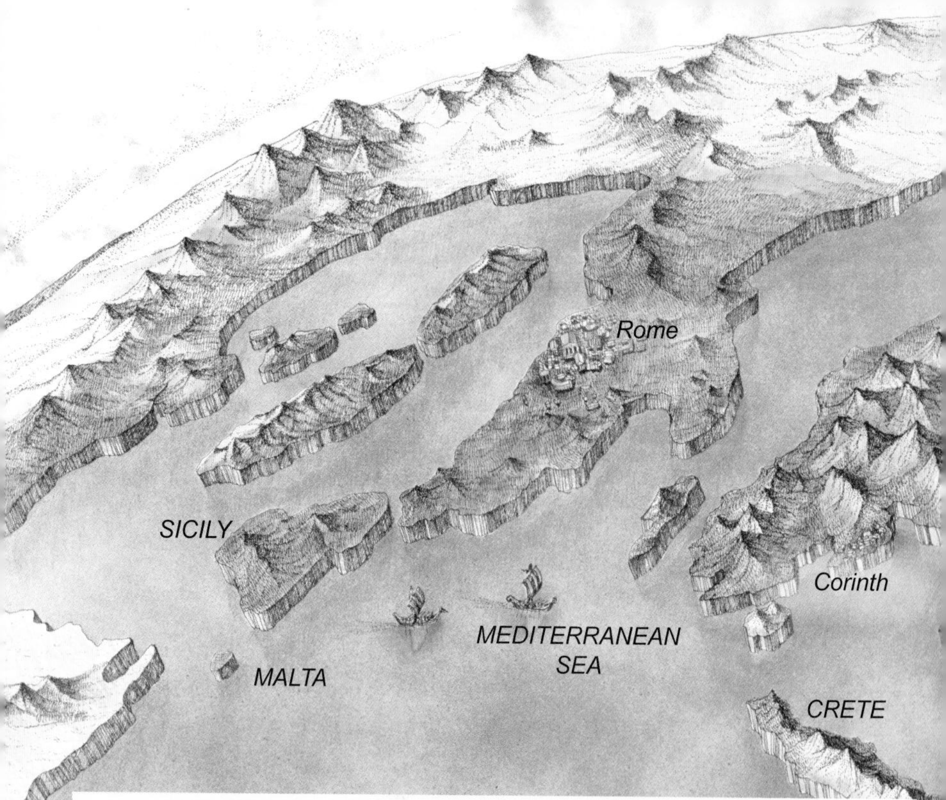

Paul's Journeys

Do you have a globe of the world? Is it about a foot wide? If so, Paul's journeys would fit on about one square inch of this globe. But it was the most important square inch on the globe in Paul's day because it was the Roman Empire.

Paul was a missionary in the Roman Empire. He started churches in many cities. Paul went on three missionary journeys. He usually started his journeys from Antioch in Syria. Paul also took one trip to Rome.

Travel was difficult in Paul's time. There were no planes, trains, cars, or buses. On land, Paul would have walked or ridden a donkey to cities like Iconium, Lystra, and Derbe. Travel was dangerous. Robbers often hid by a road to rob travelers. Storms made life on a ship very dangerous. Read about Paul's shipwreck and you'll see how dangerous it could be (Acts 27).

Paul also was beaten in Thessalonica, mocked in Athens and Corinth, and forced out of many towns. He was thrown into prison in Philippi.

But many people accepted Paul. They saw that what he said about Jesus was true.

We should be thankful for missionaries like Paul.

Philippi
Thessalonica
Troas
Ephesus
Iconium
Lystra
Antioch in
PISIDIA
Derbe
Perga
CYPRUS
Paphos
Salamis
Antioch
Ptolemais
Caesarea
ISRAEL

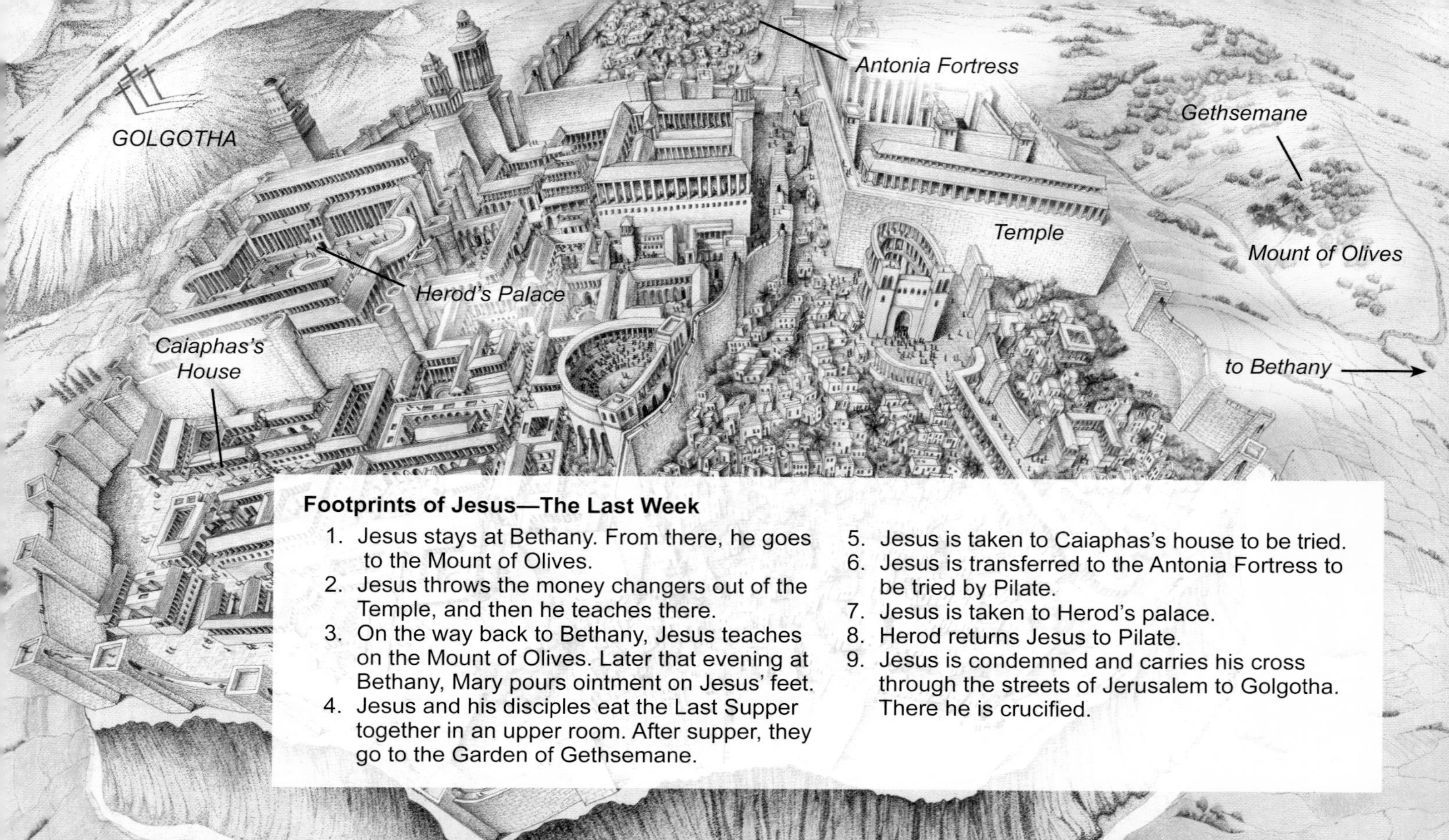
GOLGOTHA
Antonia Fortress
Gethsemane
Temple
Mount of Olives
Herod's Palace
Caiaphas's House
to Bethany
Footprints of Jesus—The Last Week
1. Jesus stays at Bethany. From there, he goes to the Mount of Olives.
2. Jesus throws the money changers out of the Temple, and then he teaches there.
3. On the way back to Bethany, Jesus teaches on the Mount of Olives. Later that evening at Bethany, Mary pours ointment on Jesus' feet.
4. Jesus and his disciples eat the Last Supper together in an upper room. After supper, they go to the Garden of Gethsemane.
5. Jesus is taken to Caiaphas's house to be tried.
6. Jesus is transferred to the Antonia Fortress to be tried by Pilate.
7. Jesus is taken to Herod's palace.
8. Herod returns Jesus to Pilate.
9. Jesus is condemned and carries his cross through the streets of Jerusalem to Golgotha. There he is crucified.